Peterson's
Two-Year
Colleges
2007

THOMSON

PETERSON'S

Australia • Canada • Mexico • Singapore • Spain • United Kingdom • United States

About Thomson Peterson's

Thomson Peterson's (www.petersons.com) is a leading provider of education information and advice, with books and online resources focusing on education search, test preparation, and financial aid. Its Web site offers searchable databases and interactive tools for contacting educational institutions, online practice tests and instruction, and planning tools for securing financial aid. Thomson Peterson's serves 110 million education consumers annually.

For more information, contact Thomson Peterson's, 2000 Lenox Drive, Lawrenceville, NJ 08648; 800-338-3282; or find us on the World Wide Web at www.petersons.com/about.

Editor: Fern A. Oram; Production Editor: Teresina Jonkoski; Copy Editors: Bret Bollmann, Michael Haines, Sally Ross, Jill C. Schwartz, Mark D. Snider, Pam Sullivan, and Valerie Bolus Vaughan; Research Project Manager: Daniel Margolin; Research Associates: Mary Meyer-Penniston and Amy L. Weber; Programmers: Phyllis Johnson and Alex Lin; Manufacturing Manager: Ivona Skibicki; Composition Manager: Linda M. Williams; Client Relations Representatives: Danielle Groncki, Mimi Kaufman, Karen Mount, and Eric Wallace; Contributing Editors: Kitty M. Villa and Richard Woodland.

ISSN 0894-9328
ISBN-13: 978-0-7689-2154-0
ISBN-10: 0-7689-2154-6

Printed in the United States of America

10 9 8 7 6 5 4 3 2 1   08 07 06

Thirty-seventh Edition

Contents

APPENDIX

INDEXES

A Note from the Peterson's Editors

For nearly 40 years, Thomson Peterson's has given students and parents the most comprehensive, up-to-date information on undergraduate institutions in the United States. Thomson Peterson's researches the data published in *Peterson's Two-Year Colleges* each year. The information is furnished by the colleges and is accurate at the time of publishing.

This guide also features advice and tips on the college search and selection process, such as how to decide if a two-year college is right for you, how to approach transferring between colleges, and what's in store for adults returning to college. If you seem to be getting more, not less, anxious about choosing and getting into the right college, *Peterson's Two-Year Colleges* provides just the right help, giving you the information you need to make important college decisions and ace the admission process.

Opportunities abound for students, and this guide can help you find what you want in a number of ways:

- In "What You Need to Know About Two-Year Colleges," David R. Pierce, former President of the American Association of Community Colleges, outlines the basic features and advantages of two-year colleges. "Surviving Standardized Tests" gives an overview of the common examinations students take prior to attending college. "Who's Paying for This? Financial Aid Basics" provides guidelines for financing your college education. "Frequently Asked Questions About Transferring" takes a look at the two-year college scene from the perspective of a student who is looking toward the day when he or she may pursue additional education at a four-year institution. "Returning to School: Advice for Adult Students" is an analysis of the pros and cons (mostly pros) of returning to college after already having begun a professional career. "What International Students Need to Know About Admission to U.S. Colleges and Universities" is an article written particularly for students overseas who are considering a U.S. college education. "Searching for Two-Year Colleges Online" outlines why you'll want to visit Petersons.com for even more college search and selection resources. Finally, "How to Use This Guide" gives details on the data in this guide: what terms mean and why they're here.
- If you already have specifics in mind, such as a particular institution or major, turn to the easy-to-use **Quick-Refer-ence Chart** or **Indexes.** You can look up a particular feature—location and programs offered—or use the alphabetical index and immediately find the colleges that meet your criteria.
- For information about particular colleges, turn to the **Profiles of Two-Year Colleges** section. Here, our comprehensive college descriptions are arranged alphabetically by state. They provide a complete picture of need-to-know information about every accredited two-year college—from admission to graduation, including expenses, financial aid, majors, and campus safety. All the information you need to apply is placed together at the conclusion of each college profile. In addition, for nearly 100 colleges, two-page narrative descriptions appear in the **College Close-Ups** section, in the back of the book. These descriptions are paid for and written by college officials and offer great detail about each college. They are edited to provide a consistent format across entries for your ease of comparison.

Thomson Peterson's publishes a full line of resources to help you and your family with any information you need to guide you through the admissions process. Peterson's publications can be found at your local bookstore, library, and high school guidance office—or visit us on the Web at www.petersons.com.

We welcome any comments or suggestions you may have about this publication and invite you to complete our online survey at **www.petersons.com/booksurvey.** Or you can fill out the survey at the back of this book, tear it out, and mail it to us at:

Publishing Department
Thomson Peterson's
2000 Lenox Drive
Lawrenceville, NJ 08648

Your feedback will help us to provide personalized solutions for your educational advancement.

Colleges will be pleased to know that Thomson Peterson's helped you in your selection. Admissions staff members are more than happy to answer questions, address specific problems and help in any way they can. The editors at Peterson's wish you great success in your college search.

The College Admissions Process:

AN OVERVIEW

What You Need to Know About Two-Year Colleges

David R. Pierce

Two-year colleges—better known as community colleges—are often called "the people's colleges." With their open-door policies (admission is open to individuals with a high school diploma or its equivalent), community colleges provide access to higher education for millions of Americans who might otherwise be excluded from higher education. Community college students are diverse and of all ages, races, and economic backgrounds. While many community college students enroll full-time, an equally large number attend on a part-time basis so they can fulfill employment and family commitments as they advance their education.

Community colleges can also be referred to as either technical or junior colleges, and they may either be under public or independent control. What unites these two-year colleges is that they are regionally accredited, postsecondary institutions, whose highest credential awarded is the associate degree. With few exceptions, community colleges offer a comprehensive curriculum, which includes transfer, technical, and continuing education programs.

IMPORTANT FACTORS IN A COMMUNITY COLLEGE EDUCATION

The student who attends a community college can count on receiving high-quality instruction in a supportive learning community. This setting frees the student to pursue his or her own goals, nurture special talents, explore new fields of learning, and develop the capacity for lifelong learning.

From the student's perspective, four characteristics capture the essence of community colleges:

- They are community-based institutions that work in close partnership with high schools, community groups, and employers in extending high-quality programs at convenient times and places.
- Community colleges are cost effective. Annual tuition and fees at public community colleges average approximately half those at public four-year colleges and less than 15 percent of private four-year institutions. In addition, since most community colleges are generally close to their students' homes, these students can also save a significant amount of money on the room, board, and transportation expenses traditionally associated with a college education.
- They provide a caring environment, with faculty members who are expert instructors, known for excellent teaching and for meeting students at the point of their individual needs, regardless of age, sex, race, current job status, or previous academic preparation. Community colleges join a strong curriculum with a broad range of counseling and career services that are intended to assist students in making the most of their educational opportunities.
- Many offer comprehensive programs, including transfer curricula in such liberal arts programs as chemistry, psychology, and business management, that lead directly to a baccalaureate degree and career programs that prepare students for employment or assist those already employed in upgrading their skills. For those students who need to strengthen their academic skills, community colleges also offer a wide range of developmental programs in mathematics, languages, and learning skills, designed to prepare the student for success in college studies.

GETTING TO KNOW YOUR TWO-YEAR COLLEGE

The first step in determining the quality of a community college is to check the status of its accreditation. Once you have established that a community college is appropriately accredited, find out as much as you can about the programs and services it has to offer. Much of that information can be found in materials the college provides. However, the best way to learn about a college is to visit in person.

During a campus visit, be prepared to ask a lot of questions. Talk to students, faculty members, administrators, and counselors about the college and its programs, particularly those in which you have a special interest. Ask about available certificates and associate degrees. Don't be shy. Do what you can to dig below the surface. Ask college officials about the transfer rate to four-year colleges. If a college emphasizes student services, find out what particular assistance is offered, such as educational or career guidance. Colleges are eager to provide you with the information you need to make informed decisions.

COMMUNITY COLLEGES CAN SAVE YOU MONEY

If you are able to live at home while you attend college, you will certainly save money on room and board, but it does cost something to commute. Many two-year colleges offer you instruction in your own home through cable television or public broadcast stations or through home study courses that can save both time and money. Look into all the options, and be sure to add up all the costs of attending various colleges before deciding which is best for you.

FINANCIAL AID

Many students who attend community colleges are eligible for a range of financial aid programs, including Federal Pell Grants, Perkins and Stafford Loans, state aid, and on-campus jobs. Your high school counselor or the financial aid officer at a community college will also be able to help you. It is in your interest to apply for financial aid months in advance of the date you intend to start your college program, so find out early what assistance is available to you. While many community colleges are able to help students who make a last-minute decision to attend college, either through short-term loans or emergency grants, if you are considering entering college and think you might need financial aid, it is best to find out as much as you can as early as you can.

WORKING AND GOING TO SCHOOL

Many two-year college students maintain full-time or part-time employment while they earn their degrees. Over the years, a steadily growing number of students have chosen to attend community colleges while they fulfill family and employment responsibilities. To enable these students to balance the demands of home, work, and school, most community colleges offer classes at night and on weekends.

For the full-time student, the usual length of time it takes to obtain an associate degree is two years. However, your length of study will depend on the course load you take: the fewer credits you earn each term, the longer it will take you to earn a degree. To assist you in moving more quickly to your degree, many community colleges now award credit through examination or for equivalent knowledge gained through relevant life experiences. Be certain to find out the credit options that are available to

you at the college in which you are interested. You may discover that it will take less time to earn a degree than you first thought.

PREPARATION FOR TRANSFER

Studies have repeatedly shown that students who first attend a community college and then transfer to a four-year college or university do at least as well academically as the students who entered the four-year institutions as freshmen. Most community colleges have agreements with nearby four-year institutions to make transfer of credits easier. If you are thinking of transferring, be sure to meet with a counselor or faculty adviser before choosing your courses. You will want to map out a course of study with transfer in mind. Make sure you also find out the credit-transfer requirements of the four-year institution you might want to attend.

ATTENDING A TWO-YEAR COLLEGE IN ANOTHER REGION

Although many community colleges serve a specific county or district, they are committed (to the extent of their ability) to the goal of equal educational opportunity without regard to economic status, race, creed, color, sex, or national origin. Independent two-year colleges recruit from a much broader geographical area—throughout the United States and, increasingly, around the world.

Although some community colleges do provide on-campus housing for their students, most do not. However, even if on-campus housing is not available, most colleges do have housing referral services.

NEW CAREER OPPORTUNITIES

Community colleges realize that many entering students are not sure about the field in which they want to focus their studies or the career they would like to pursue. Often, students discover fields and careers they never knew existed. Community colleges have the resources to help students identify areas of career interest and to set challenging occupational goals.

Once a career goal is set, you can be confident that a community college will provide job-relevant, technical education. About half of the students who take courses for credit at community colleges do so to prepare for employment or to acquire or upgrade skills for their current job. Especially helpful in charting a career path is the assistance of a counselor or a faculty adviser, who can discuss job opportunities in your chosen field and help you map out your course of study.

In addition, since community colleges have close ties to their communities, they are in constant contact with leaders in business, industry, organized labor, and public life. Community colleges work with these individuals and their organizations to prepare students for direct entry into the world of work. For example, some community colleges have established partnerships with local businesses and industries to provide specialized training programs. Some also provide the academic portion of apprenticeship training, while others offer extensive job-shadowing and cooperative education opportunities. Be sure to examine all of the career-preparation opportunities offered by the community colleges in which you are interested.

David R. Pierce is the former President of the American Association of Community Colleges.

Surviving Standardized Tests

WHAT ARE STANDARDIZED TESTS?

Colleges and universities in the United States use tests to help evaluate applicants' readiness for admission or to place them in appropriate courses. The tests that are most frequently used by colleges are the ACT Assessment of American College Testing, Inc., and the College Board's SAT. In addition, the Educational Testing Service (ETS) offers the TOEFL test, which evaluates the English-language proficiency of nonnative speakers. The tests are offered at designated testing centers located at high schools and colleges throughout the United States and U.S. territories and at testing centers in various countries throughout the world. The ACT Assessment test and the SAT tests are each taken by more than a million students each year. The TOEFL test is taken by more than 800,000 students each year.

Upon request, special accommodations for students with documented visual, hearing, physical, or learning disabilities are available. Examples of special accommodations include tests in Braille or large print and such aids as a reader, recorder, magnifying glass, or sign language interpreter. Additional testing time may be allowed in some instances. Contact the appropriate testing program or your guidance counselor for details on how to request special accommodations.

College Board SAT Program

Currently, the SAT Program consists of the SAT and the SAT Subject Tests. The SAT is a 3-hour 45-minute test made up of ten sections, primarily multiple-choice, that focuses on college success skills of writing, critical reading, and mathematics. The writing component measures grammar and usage and includes a short, student-written essay. The critical reading sections test verbal reasoning and critical reading skills. Emphasis is placed on reading passages, which are 400–850 words in length. Some reading passages are paired; the second opposes, supports, or in some way complements the point of view expressed in the first. The three mathematics sections test a student's ability to solve problems involving arithmetic, Algebra I and II, and geometry. They include questions that require students to produce their own responses, in addition to questions with four or five answer choices from which students can choose. Calculators may be used on the SAT mathematics sections.

The SAT Subject Tests are 1-hour tests, primarily multiple-choice, in specific subjects that measure students' knowledge of these subjects and their ability to apply that knowledge. Some colleges may require or recommend these tests for placement, or even admission. The Subject Tests measure a student's academic achievement in high school and may indicate readiness for certain college programs. Tests offered include Literature, U.S. History, World

History, Mathematics Level 1, Mathematics Level 2, Biology E/M (Ecological/Molecular), Chemistry, Physics, French, German, Modern Hebrew, Italian, Latin, and Spanish, as well as Foreign Language Tests with Listening in Chinese, French, German, Japanese, Korean, and Spanish. The Mathematics Level 1 and 2 tests require the use of a scientific calculator.

SAT scores are automatically sent to each student who has taken the test. On average, they are mailed about three weeks after the test. Students may request that the scores be reported to their high schools or to the colleges to which they are applying.

ACT Assessment Program

The ACT Assessment Program is a comprehensive data collection, processing, and reporting service designed to assist in educational and career planning. The ACT Assessment instrument consists of four academic tests, taken under timed conditions, and a Student Profile Section and Interest Inventory, completed when students register for the ACT Assessment.

The academic tests cover four areas—English, mathematics, reading, and science reasoning. The ACT Assessment consists of 215 multiple-choice questions and takes approximately 3 hours and 30 minutes to complete with breaks (testing time is actually 2 hours and 55 minutes). They are designed to assess the student's educational development and readiness to handle college-level work. The minimum standard score is 1, the maximum is 36, and the national average is 21. Students should note that an optional writing test is also offered.

The Student Profile Section requests information about each student's admission and enrollment plans, aca-

---

DON'T FORGET TO . . .

- Take the SAT or ACT Assessment before application deadlines.
- Note that test registration deadlines precede test dates by about six weeks.
- Register to take the TOEFL test if English is not your native language and you are planning on studying at a North American college.
- Practice your test-taking skills with **Peterson's Ultimate SAT Tool Kit, Peterson's Ultimate ACT Tool Kit, The Real ACT Prep Guide** (published by Peterson's), and **ARCO Master TOEFL Reading Skills, ARCO Master TOEFL Vocabulary Skills,** and **ARCO Master TOEFL Writing Skills.**
- Contact the College Board or American College Testing, Inc., in advance if you need special accommodations when taking tests.

demic and out-of-class high school achievements and aspirations, and high school course work. The student is also asked to supply biographical data and self-reported high school grades in the four subject-matter areas covered by the academic tests.

The ACT Assessment has a number of career planning services, including the ACT Assessment Interest Inventory, which is designed to measure six major dimensions of student interests–business contact, business operations, technical, science, arts, and social service. Results are used to compare the student's interests with those of college-bound students who later majored in each of a wide variety of areas. Inventory results are also used to help students compare their work-activity preferences with work activities that characterize twenty-three "job families."

Because the information resulting from the ACT Assessment Program is used in a variety of educational settings, American College Testing, Inc., prepares three reports for each student: the Student Report, the High School Report, and the College Report. The Student Report normally is sent to the student's high school, except after the June test date, when it is sent directly to the student's home address. The College Report is sent to the colleges the student designates.

Early in the school year, American College Testing, Inc., sends registration packets to high schools across the country that contain all the information a student needs to register for the ACT Assessment. High school guidance offices also receive a supply of *Preparing for the ACT Assessment,* a booklet that contains a complete practice test, an answer key, and general information about preparing for the test.

Test of English as a Foreign Language (TOEFL)

The TOEFL is used by various organizations, such as colleges and universities, to determine English proficiency. The test is offered in different formats depending on the test taker's location. The TOEFL iBT tests students in the areas of speaking, listening, reading, and writing in an Internet-based format.

The TOEFL CBT (computer-based test) and PBT (paper-based test) test students in the areas of listening, structure, reading comprehension, and writing. Score requirements are set by individual institutions. For more information on TOEFL, and to obtain a copy of the Information Bulletin, contact the Educational Testing Service.

Peterson's *TOEFL CBT Success* can help you prepare for the computer-based test. The CD version of the book includes a TOEFL practice test and adaptive English skill building exercise. An online CBT test can also be taken for a small fee at Petersons.com.

2006–07 ACT ASSESSMENT AND SAT TEST DATES

ACT Assessment
September 16, 2006*
October 28, 2006
December 9, 2006
February 10, 2007**
April 14, 2007
June 9, 2007

All test dates fall on a Saturday. Tests are also given on the Sundays following the Saturday test dates for students who cannot take the test on Saturday because of religious reasons. The basic ACT Assessment registration fee for 2005–06 was $29 ($47 outside of the U.S.). The optional writing test is $14 and is refundable for students who are absent on test day.

*The September test is available only in Arizona, California, Florida, Georgia, Illinois, Indiana, Maryland, Nevada, North Carolina, Pennsylvania, South Carolina, Texas, and Washington.

**The February test date is not available in New York.

SAT
October 14, 2006 (SAT and SAT Subject Tests)
November 4, 2006 (SAT, SAT Subject Tests, and Language Tests with Listening*)
December 2, 2006 (SAT and SAT Subject Tests)
January 27, 2007 (SAT and SAT Subject Tests)
March 10, 2007 (SAT only)**
May 5, 2007 (SAT and SAT Subject Tests)
June 2, 2007 (SAT and SAT Subject Tests)

For the 2005–06 academic year, the basic fee for the SAT was $41.50. The basic fee for the SAT Subject Tests was $18, $19 for the Language Tests with Listening, and $8 each for all other Subject Tests. Students can take up to three SAT Subject Tests on a single date, and an $18 basic registration and reporting fee should be added for each test date. Tests are also given on the Sundays following the Saturday test dates for students who cannot take the test on Saturday because of religious reasons. Fee waivers are available to juniors and seniors who cannot afford test fees.

*Language Tests with Listening are only offered on November 4. See the Registration Bulletin for details.

**The March 10 test date is only available in the U.S. and its territories.

Who's Paying for This?
Financial Aid Basics

A college education can be expensive—costing more than $150,000 for four years at some of the higher priced private colleges and universities. Even at the lower cost state colleges and universities, the cost of a four-year education can approach $50,000. Determining how you and your family will come up with the necessary funds to pay for your education requires planning, perseverance, and learning as much as you can about the options that are available to you.

Paying for college should not be looked at as a four-year financial commitment. For many families, paying the total cost of a student's college education out of current income and savings is usually not realistic. For families that have planned ahead and have financial savings established for higher education, the burden is a lot easier. But for most, meeting the cost of college requires the pooling of current income and assets and investing in longer-term loan options. These family resources, together with financial assistance from state, federal, and institutional sources, enable millions of students each year to attend the institution of their choice.

FINANCIAL AID PROGRAMS

There are three types of financial aid:

1. **Gift-aid**—Scholarships and grants are funds that do not have to be repaid.
2. **Loans**—Loans must be repaid, usually after graduation; the amount you have to pay back is the total you've borrowed plus any accrued interest. This is considered a source of self-help aid.
3. **Student employment**—Student employment is a job arranged for you by the financial aid office. This is another source of self-help aid.

The federal government has two major grant programs—the Federal Pell Grant and the Federal Supplemental Educational Opportunity Grant. These grants are targeted to low-to-moderate income families with significant financial need. The federal government also sponsors a student employment program called Federal Work-Study, which offers jobs both on and off campus; and several loan programs, including those for students and for parents of undergraduate students.

There are two types of student loan programs, subsidized and unsubsidized. The Subsidized Stafford Loan and the Federal Perkins Loan are need-based, government-subsidized loans. Students who borrow through these programs do not have to pay interest on the loan until after they graduate or leave school. The Unsubsidized Stafford Loan and the Parent Loan Program are not based on need, and borrowers are responsible for the interest while the student is in school. There are different methods on how these loans are administered. Once you choose your college, the financial aid office will guide you through this process.

After you've submitted your financial aid application and you've been accepted for admission, each college will send you a letter describing your financial aid award. Most award letters show estimated college costs, how much you and your family are expected to contribute, and the amount and types of aid you have been awarded. Most students are awarded aid from a combination of sources and programs. Hence, your award is often called a financial aid "package."

SOURCES OF FINANCIAL AID

More than 14 million people apply for financial aid each year. The largest single source of aid is the federal government, which awarded more than $90 billion during 2004–05.

The next largest source of financial aid is found in the college and university community. Institutions award an estimated $24 billion to students each year. Most of this aid is awarded to students who have a demonstrated need based on the Federal Methodology. Some institutions use a different formula, the Institutional Methodology (IM), to award their own funds in conjunction with other forms of aid. Institutional aid may be either need-based or non-need based. Aid that is not based on need is usually awarded for a student's academic performance (merit awards), specific talents or abilities, or to attract the type of students a college seeks to enroll.

Another source of financial aid is from state government, awarding more than $6 billion per year. All states offer grant and/or scholarship aid, most of which is need-based. However, more and more states are offering substantial merit-based aid programs. Most state programs award aid only to students attending college in their home state.

Other sources of financial aid include:

- Private agencies
- Foundations
- Corporations
- Clubs
- Fraternal and service organizations
- Civic associations
- Unions
- Religious groups that award grants, scholarships, and low-interest loans
- Employers that provide tuition reimbursement benefits for employees and their children

More information about these different sources of aid is available from high school guidance offices, public libraries, college financial aid offices, directly from the sponsoring organizations, and on the Web at www. petersons.com and www.finaid.org.

HOW NEED-BASED FINANCIAL AID IS AWARDED

When you apply for aid, your family's financial situation is analyzed using a government-approved formula called the Federal Methodology. This formula looks at five items:

1. Demographic information of the family
2. Income of the parents
3. Assets of the parents
4. Income of the student
5. Assets of the student

This analysis determines the amount you and your family are expected to contribute toward your college expenses, called your Expected Family Contribution or EFC. If the EFC is equal to or more than the cost of attendance at a particular college, then you do not demonstrate financial need. However, even if you don't have financial need, you may still qualify for aid, as there are grants, scholarships, and loan programs that are not need-based.

If the cost of your education is greater than your EFC, then you do demonstrate financial need and qualify for assistance. The amount of your financial need that can be met varies from school to school. Some are able to meet your full need, while others can only cover a certain percentage of need. Here's the formula:

> Cost of Attendance
> − Expected Family Contribution
> ⎯⎯⎯⎯⎯⎯⎯⎯⎯
> = Financial Need

The EFC remains constant, but your need will vary according to the costs of attendance at a particular college. In general, the higher the tuition and fees at a particular college, the higher the cost of attendance will be. Expenses for books and supplies, room and board, transportation, and other miscellaneous costs are included in the overall cost of attendance. It is important to remember that you do not have to be "needy" to qualify for financial aid. Many middle and upper-middle income families qualify for need-based financial aid.

APPLYING FOR FINANCIAL AID

Every student must complete the Free Application for Federal Student Aid (FAFSA) to be considered for financial aid. The FAFSA is available from your high school guidance office, many public libraries, colleges in your area, or directly from the U.S. Department of Education.

Students are encouraged to apply for federal student aid on the Web. The electronic version of the FAFSA can be accessed at http://www.fafsa.ed.gov. Both the student and at least one parent must apply for a federal pin number at http://www.pin.ed.gov. The pin number serves as your electronic signature when applying for aid on the Web.

To award their own funds, some colleges require an additional application, the Financial Aid PROFILE® form. The PROFILE asks supplemental questions that some colleges and awarding agencies feel provide a more accurate assessment of the family's ability to pay for college. It is up to the college to decide whether it will use only the FAFSA or both the FAFSA and the PROFILE. PROFILE applications are available from the high school guidance office and on the Web. Both the paper application and the Web site list those colleges and programs that require the PROFILE application.

If Every College You're Applying to for Fall 2007 Requires the FAFSA

. . . then it's pretty simple: Complete the FAFSA after January 1, 2007, being certain to send it in before any college-imposed deadlines. (You are not permitted to send in the 2007-08 FAFSA before January 1, 2007.) Most college FAFSA application deadlines are in February or early March. It is easier if you have all your financial records for the previous year available, but if that is not possible, you are strongly encouraged to use estimated figures.

After you send in your FAFSA, either with the paper application or electronically, you'll receive a Student Aid Report (SAR) that includes all of the information you reported and shows your EFC. If you provided an e-mail address, the SAR is sent to you electronically; otherwise, you will receive a paper copy in the mail. Be sure to review the SAR, checking to see if the information you reported is accurate. If you used estimated numbers to complete the FAFSA, you may have to resubmit the SAR with any corrections to the data. The college(s) you have designated on the FAFSA will receive the information you reported and will use that data to make their decision. In many instances, the colleges you've applied to will ask you to send copies of your and your parents' federal income tax returns for 2006, plus any other documents needed to verify the information you reported.

If a College Requires the PROFILE

Step 1: Register for the Financial Aid PROFILE in the fall of your senior year in high school.

You can apply for the PROFILE online at http://profileonline.collegeboard.com/index.jsp. Registration information with a list of the colleges that require the PROFILE are available in most high school guidance offices. There is a fee for using the Financial Aid PROFILE application ($23 for the first college and $18 for each additional college). You must pay for the service by credit card when you register. If you do not have a credit card, you will be billed.

Step 2: Fill out your customized Financial Aid PROFILE.

Once you register, your application will be immediately available online and will have questions which all students must complete, questions which must be completed by the student's parents (unless the student is independent and the colleges or programs selected do not require parental information), and *may* have supplemental questions needed by one or more of your schools or programs. If required, those will be found in Section Q of the application.

In addition to the PROFILE Application you complete online, you may also be required to complete a Business/Farm Supplement via traditional paper format. Completion of this form is not a part of the online process. If this form is required, instructions on how to download and print the supplemental form are provided. If your biological or adoptive parents are separated or divorced and your colleges and programs require it, your noncustodial parent may be asked to complete the Noncustodial POFILE.

Once you complete and submit your PROFILE Application, it will be processed and sent directly to your requested colleges and programs.

IF YOU DON'T QUALIFY FOR NEED-BASED AID

If you are not eligible for need-based aid, you can still find ways to lessen the burden on your parents.

Here are some suggestions:

- Search for merit scholarships. You can start at the initial stages of your application process. College merit awards are becoming increasingly important as more and more colleges award these grants to students they especially want to attract. As a result, applying to a college at which your qualifications put you at the top of the entering class may give you a larger merit award. Another source of aid to look for is private scholarships that are given for special skills and talents. Additional information can be found at Petersons.com and at www.finaid.org.

- Seek employment during the summer and the academic year. The student employment office at your college can help you locate a school-year job. Many colleges and local businesses have vacancies remaining after they have hired students who are receiving Federal Work-Study financial aid.

- Borrow through the Unsubsidized Stafford Loan programs. These are open to all students. The terms and conditions are similar to the subsidized loans. The biggest difference is that the borrower is responsible for the interest while still in college, although most lenders permit students to delay paying the interest right away and add the accrued interest to the total amount owed. You must file the FAFSA to be considered.

- After you've secured what you can through scholarships, working, and borrowing, your parents will be expected to meet their share of the college bill (the Expected Family Contribution). Many colleges offer monthly payment plans that spread the cost over the academic year. If the monthly payments are too high, parents can borrow through the Federal Parent Loan for Undergraduate Students (PLUS program), through one of the many private education loan programs available, or through home equity loans and lines of credit. Families seeking assistance in financing college expenses should inquire at the financial aid office about what programs are available at the college. Some families seek the advice of professional financial advisers and tax consultants.

HOW IS YOUR EXPECTED FAMILY CONTRIBUTION CALCULATED?

The chart on the next page makes the following assumptions:

- two-parent family where age of older parent is 45
- lower-income families (under $30,000) will file the 1040A or 1040EZ tax form
- student income is less than $2300
- there are no student assets
- there is only one family member attending college

All figures are estimates and may vary when the complete FAFSA or PROFILE application is submitted.

Approximate Expected Family Contribution

ASSETS	FAMILY SIZE	$20,000	30,000	40,000	50,000	60,000	70,000	80,000	90,000	100,000
$ 20,000										
	3	$ 0	900	2,500	4,400	7,000	10,400	13,800	16,700	19,900
	4	0	50	1,700	3,400	5,600	8,700	12,100	15,100	18,300
	5	0	0	850	2,500	4,400	7,000	10,400	13,600	16,800
	6	0	0	50	1,700	3,300	5,500	8,500	11,900	15,100
$ 30,000										
	3	$ 0	900	2,500	4,400	7,000	10,400	13,800	16,700	19,900
	4	0	50	1,700	3,400	5,600	8,700	12,100	15,100	18,300
	5	0	0	850	2,500	4,400	7,000	10,400	13,600	16,800
	6	0	0	50	1,700	3,300	5,500	8,500	11,900	15,100
$ 40,000										
	3	$ 0	900	2,500	4,400	7,000	10,400	13,800	16,700	19,900
	4	0	50	1,700	3,400	5,600	8,700	12,100	15,100	18,300
	5	0	0	850	2,500	4,400	7,000	10,400	13,600	16,800
	6	0	0	50	1,700	3,300	5,500	8,500	11,900	15,100
$ 50,000										
	3	$ 0	900	2,500	4,600	7,200	10,700	14,100	17,000	20,200
	4	0	50	1,700	3,600	5,800	9,000	12,400	15,400	18,600
	5	0	0	850	2,700	4,600	7,300	10,700	13,900	17,100
	6	0	0	50	1,800	3,500	5,800	8,800	12,200	15,400
$ 60,000										
	3	$ 0	900	2,500	5,000	7,600	11,100	14,500	17,500	20,800
	4	0	50	1,700	4,000	6,200	9,400	12,800	15,900	19,200
	5	0	0	850	3,100	5,000	7,700	11,100	14,400	17,700
	6	0	0	50	2,200	3,900	6,200	9,200	12,700	16,000
$ 80,000										
	3	$ 0	900	2,800	5,700	9,000	12,450	15,800	18,700	21,900
	4	0	50	2,000	4,700	7,300	10,700	14,100	17,100	20,300
	5	0	0	1,150	3,800	5,800	9,000	12,400	15,600	18,800
	6	0	0	350	2,900	4,500	7,200	10,600	13,900	17,100
$ 100,000										
	3	$ 0	900	3,100	6,800	10,200	13,600	16,900	19,850	23,100
	4	0	50	2,300	5,400	8,400	11,800	15,200	18,250	21,500
	5	0	0	1,450	4,250	6,800	10,150	13,500	16,700	20,000
	6	0	0	650	3,200	5,300	8,300	11,700	15,000	18,250
$ 120,000										
	3	$ 0	900	3,400	8,000	11,400	14,800	18,100	21,050	24,300
	4	0	50	2,600	7,900	11,300	14,700	18,000	20,950	24,200
	5	0	0	1,750	5,350	7,900	11,250	14,600	17,800	21,100
	6	0	0	950	3,800	6,200	9,400	12,800	16,100	19,400
$ 140,000										
	3	$ 0	900	3,700	9,200	12,600	16,000	19,300	22,250	25,500
	4	0	50	2,900	9,100	12,500	15,900	19,200	22,150	25,400
	5	0	0	2,050	6,450	9,000	12,350	15,700	18,900	22,200
	6	0	0	1,250	4,500	7,100	10,500	13,900	17,300	20,500

Frequently Asked Questions About Transferring

Muriel M. Shishkoff

Among the students attending two-year colleges are a large number who began their higher education knowing they would eventually transfer to a four-year school to obtain their bachelor's degree. There are many reasons why students are going this route. Upon graduating from high school, some simply do not have definite career goals. Although they don't want to put their education on hold, they prefer not to pay exorbitant amounts in tuition while trying to "find themselves." As the cost of a university education escalates—even in public institutions—the option of spending the freshman and sophomore years at a two-year college looks attractive to many students. Others attend a two-year college because they are unable to meet the initial entrance standards—a specified grade point average (GPA), standardized test scores, or knowledge of specific academic subjects—required by the four-year school of their choice. Many such students praise the community college system for giving them the chance to be, academically speaking, "born again." In addition, students from other countries often find that they can adapt more easily to language and cultural changes at a two-year school before transferring to a larger, more diverse four-year college.

If your plan is to attend a two-year college with the ultimate goal of transferring to a four-year school, you will be pleased to know that the increased importance of the community college route to a bachelor's degree is recognized by all segments of higher education. As a result, many two-year schools have revised their course outlines and established new courses in order to comply with the programs and curricular offerings of the universities. Institutional improvements to make transferring easier have also proliferated at both the two- and four-year levels. The generous transfer policies of the Pennsylvania, New York, and Florida state university systems, among others, reflect this attitude; these systems accept *all* credits from students who have graduated from accredited community colleges.

If you are interested in moving from a two-year college to a four-year school, the sooner you make up your mind that you are going to make the switch, the better position you will be in to transfer successfully (that is, without having wasted valuable time and credits). The ideal point at which to make such a decision is *before* you register for classes at your two-year school; a counselor can help you plan your course work with an eye toward fulfilling the requirements needed for your major course of study.

Naturally, it is not always possible to plan your transferring strategy that far in advance, but keep in mind that the key to a successful transfer is *preparation,* and preparation takes time—time to think through your objectives and time to plan the right classes to take at that school.

As students face the prospect of transferring from a two-year to a four-year school, many thoughts and concerns about this complicated and often frustrating process race through their minds. Here are answers to the questions that are most frequently asked by transferring students.

Q Does every college and university accept transfer students?

A Most four-year institutions accept transfer students, but some do so more enthusiastically than others. Graduating from a community college is an advantage at, for example, Arizona State University and the University of Massachusetts Boston; both accept more community college transfer students than traditional freshmen. At the State University of New York at Albany, graduates of two-year transfer programs within the State University of New York System are given priority for upper-division (i.e., junior- and senior-level) vacancies.

Schools offering undergraduate work at the upper division only, such as Metropolitan State University in St. Paul, Minnesota, are especially receptive to transfer applications. On the other hand, some schools accept only a few transfer students; others refuse entrance to sophomores or those in their final year. Princeton University requires an "excellent academic record and particularly compelling reasons to transfer." Check the catalogs of several colleges for their transfer requirements before you make your final choice.

Q Do students who go directly from high school to a four-year college do better academically than transfer students from community colleges?

A On the contrary: some institutions report that transfers from two-year schools who persevere until graduation do *better* than those who started as freshmen.

Q Why is it so important that my two-year college be accredited?

A Four-year colleges and universities accept transfer credits only from schools formally recognized by a regional, national, or professional educational agency. This accreditation signifies that an institution or program of study meets or exceeds a minimum level of educational quality necessary for meeting stated educational objectives.

Q After enrolling at a four-year school, may I still make up necessary courses at a community college?

A Some institutions restrict credit after transfer to their own facilities. Others allow students to take a limited number of transfer courses after matriculation, depending on the subject matter. A few provide opportunities for cross-registration or dual enrollment, which means taking classes on more than one campus.

Q What do I need to do to transfer?

A First, send for your high school and college transcripts. Having chosen the school you wish to transfer to, check its admission requirements against your transcripts. If you find that you are admissible, file an application as early as possible before the deadline. Part of the process will be asking your former schools to send *official transcripts* to the admission office, i.e., not the copies you used in determining your admissibility.

Plan your transfer program with the head of your new department as soon as you have decided to transfer. Determine the recommended general education pattern and necessary preparation for your major. At your present school, take the courses you will need to meet transfer requirements for the new one.

Q What qualifies me for admission as a transfer student?

A Admission requirements for most four-year institutions vary. Depending on the reputation or popularity of the school and program you wish to enter, requirements may be quite selective and competitive. Usually, you will need to show satisfactory test scores, an academic record up to a certain standard, and completion of specific subject matter.

Transfer students can be eligible to enter a four-year school in a number of ways: by having been eligible for admission directly upon graduation from high school, by making up shortcomings in grades (or in subject matter not covered in high school) at a community college, or by satisfactory completion of necessary courses or credit hours at another postsecondary institution. Ordinarily, students coming from a community college or from another four-year institution must meet or exceed the receiving institution's standards for freshmen and show appropriate college-level course work taken since high school. Students who did not graduate from high school can present proof of proficiency through results on the General Educational Development (GED) test.

Q Are exceptions ever made for students who don't meet all the requirements for transfer?

A Extenuating circumstances, such as disability, low family income, refugee or veteran status, or athletic talent, may permit the special enrollment of students who would not otherwise be eligible but who demonstrate the potential for academic success. Consult the appropriate office—the Educational Opportunity Program, the disabled students' office, the athletic department, or the academic dean—to see whether an exception can be made in your case.

Q How far in advance do I need to apply for transfer?

A Some schools have a rolling admission policy, which means that they process transfer applications as they are received, all year long. With other schools, you must apply during the priority filing period, which can be up to a year before you wish to enter. Check the date with the admission office at your prospective campus.

Q Is it possible to transfer courses from several different institutions?

A Institutions ordinarily accept the courses that they consider transferable, regardless of the number of accredited schools involved. However, there is the danger of exceeding the maximum number of credit hours that can be transferred from all other schools or earned through credit by examination, extension courses, or correspondence courses. The limit placed on transfer credits varies from school to school, so read the catalog carefully to avoid taking courses you won't be able to use. To avoid duplicating courses, keep attendance at different campuses to a minimum.

Q What is involved in transferring from a semester system to a quarter or trimester system?

A In the semester system, the academic calendar is divided into two equal parts. The quarter system is more aptly named trimester, since the academic calendar is divided into three equal terms (not counting a summer session). To convert semester units into quarter units or credit hours, simply multiply the semester units by one and a half. Conversely, multiply quarter units by two thirds to come up with semester units. If you are used to a semester system of fifteen- to sixteen-week courses, the ten-week courses of the quarter system may seem to fly by.

Q Why might a course be approved for transfer credit by one four-year school but not by another?

A The beauty of postsecondary education in the United States lies in its variety. Entrance policies and graduation requirements are designed to reflect and serve each institution's mission. Because institutional policies vary so widely, schools may interpret the subject matter of a course from quite different points of view. Given that the granting of transfer credit indicates that a course is viewed as being, in effect, parallel to one offered by the receiving institution, it is easy to see how this might be the case at one university and not another.

Q Must I take a foreign language to transfer?

A Foreign language proficiency is often required for admission to a four-year institution; such proficiency also often figures in certain majors or in the general education pattern. At Princeton University, for example, where foreign language proficiency is a

graduation requirement, all students must demonstrate it by the end of their junior year.

However, at the University of Southern California and other schools, the foreign language competence necessary for admission can be certified before entrance. Often, two or three years of a single language in high school will do the trick. Find out if scores received on Advanced Placement examinations, placement examinations given by the foreign language department, or SAT Subject Tests will be accepted in lieu of college course work.

Q Will the school to which I'm transferring accept pass/no pass, pass/fail, or credit/no credit grades in lieu of letter grades?

A Usually, a limit is placed on the number of these courses you can transfer, and there may be other restrictions as well. If you want to use other-than-letter grades for the fulfillment of general education requirements or lower-division (freshman and sophomore) preparation for the major, check with the receiving institution.

Q Which is more important for transfer—my grade point average or my course completion pattern?

A Some schools believe that your past grades indicate academic potential and overshadow prior preparation for a specific degree program. Others require completion of certain introductory courses before transfer to prepare you for upper-division work in your major. In any case, appropriate course selection will cut down the time to graduation and increase your chances of making a successful transfer.

Q What happens to my credits if I change majors?

A If you change majors after admission, your transferable course credit should remain fairly intact. However, because you may need extra or different preparation for your new major, some of the courses you've taken may now be useful only as electives. The need for additional lower-level preparation may mean you're staying longer at your new school than you originally planned. On the other hand, you may already have taken courses that count toward your new major as part of the university's general education pattern.

Excerpted from *Transferring Made Easy: A Guide to Changing Colleges Successfully,* by Muriel M. Shishkoff, © 1991 by Muriel M. Shishkoff (published by Peterson's).

Returning to School: Advice for Adult Students

Sandra Cook, Ph.D.
Director, University Advising Center, San Diego State University

Many adults think for a long time about returning to school without taking any action. One purpose of this article is to help the "thinkers" finally make some decisions by examining what is keeping them from action. Another purpose is to describe not only some of the difficulties and obstacles that adult students may face when returning to school but also tactics for coping with them.

If you have been thinking about going back to college, and believing that you are the only person your age contemplating college, you should know that approximately 7 million adult students are currently enrolled in higher education institutions. This number represents 50 percent of total higher education enrollments. The majority of adult students are enrolled at two-year colleges.

There are many reasons why adult students choose to attend a two-year college. Studies have shown that the three most important criteria that adult students consider when choosing a college are location, cost, and availability of the major or program desired. Most two-year colleges are public institutions that serve a geographic district, making them readily accessible to the community. Costs at most two-year colleges are far less than at other types of higher education institutions. For many students who plan to pursue a bachelor's degree, completing their first two years of college at a community college is an affordable means to that end. If you are interested in an academic program that will transfer to a four-year institution, most two-year colleges offer the "general education" courses that comprise most freshman and sophomore years. If you are interested in a vocational or technical program, two-year colleges excel in providing this type of training.

SETTING THE STAGE

There are three different "stages" in the process of adults returning to school. The first stage is uncertainty. Do I really want to go back to school? What will my friends or family think? Can I compete with those 18-year-old whiz kids? Am I too old? The second stage is choice. Once the decision to return has been made, you must choose where you will attend. There are many criteria to use in making this decision. The third stage is support. You have just added another role to your already-too-busy life. There are, however, strategies that will help you accomplish your goals—perhaps not without struggle, but with grace and humor nonetheless. Let's look at each of these stages.

UNCERTAINTY

Why are you thinking about returning to school? Is it to:

- fulfill a dream that had to be delayed?
- become more educationally well-rounded?
- fill an intellectual void in your life?

These reasons focus on *personal growth*.

If you are returning to school to:

- meet people and make friends
- attain and enjoy higher social status and prestige among friends, relatives, and associates
- understand/study a cultural heritage, or
- have a medium in which to exchange ideas,

you are interested in *social and cultural opportunities*.

If you are like most adult students, you want to:

- qualify for a new occupation
- enter or reenter the job market
- increase earnings potential, or
- qualify for a more challenging position in the same field of work.

You are seeking *career growth*.

Understanding the reasons why you want to go back to school is an important step in setting your educational goals and will help you to establish some criteria for selecting a college. However, don't delay your decision because you have not been able to clearly define your motives. Many times, these aren't clear until you have already begun the process, and they may change as you move through your college experience.

Assuming you agree that additional education will benefit you, what is it that keeps you from returning to school? You may have a litany of excuses running through your mind:

- I don't have time.
- I can't afford it.
- I'm too old to learn.
- My friends will think I'm crazy.
- The teachers will be younger than I.
- My family can't survive without me to take care of them every minute.
- I'll be X years old when I finish.
- I'm afraid.
- I don't know what to expect.

And that is just what these are—excuses. You can make school, like anything else in your life, a priority or not. If you really want to return, you can. The more you understand your motivation for returning to school and the more you understand what excuses are keeping you from taking action, the easier your task will be.

If you think you don't have time: The best way to decide how attending class and studying can fit into your schedule is to keep track of what you do with your time each day for several weeks. Completing a standard time-management grid (each day is plotted out by the half hour) is helpful for visualizing how your time is spent. For each 3-credit-hour class you take, you will need to find 3 hours for class plus 6 to 9 hours for reading-studying-library time. This study time should be spaced evenly throughout the week, not loaded up on one day. It is not possible to learn or retain the material that way. When you examine your grid, see where there are activities that could be replaced with school and study time. You may decide to give up your bowling league or some time in front of the TV. Try not to give up sleeping, and don't cut out every moment of free time. Here are some suggestions that have come from adults who have returned to school:

- Enroll in a time-management workshop. It helps you rethink how you use your time.
- Don't think you have to take more than one course at a time. You may eventually want to work up to taking more, but consider starting with one. (It is more than you are taking now!)
- If you have a family, start assigning to them those household chores that you usually do—and don't redo what they do.
- Use your lunch hour or commuting time for reading.

If you think you cannot afford it: As mentioned earlier, two-year colleges are extremely affordable. If you cannot afford the tuition, look into the various financial aid options. Most federal and state funds are available to full- and part-time students. Loans are also available. While many people prefer not to accumulate a debt for

school, these same people will think nothing of taking out a loan to buy a car. After five or six years, which is the better investment? Adult students who work should look into whether their company has a tuition-reimbursement policy. There are also private scholarships, available through foundations, service organizations, and clubs, that are focused on adult learners. Your public library, the Web, and a college financial aid adviser are three excellent sources for reference materials regarding financial aid.

If you think you are too old to learn: This is pure myth. A number of studies have shown that adult learners perform as well as or better than traditional-age students.

If you are afraid your friends will think you're crazy: Who cares? Maybe they will, maybe they won't. Usually, they will admire your courage and be just a little jealous of your ambition (although they'll never tell you that). Follow your dreams, not theirs.

If you are concerned because the teachers or students will be younger than you: Don't be. The age differences that may be apparent in other settings evaporate in the classroom. If anything, an adult in the classroom strikes fear into the hearts of some 18-year-olds because adults have been known to be prepared, ask questions, be truly motivated, and be there to learn!

If you think your family will have a difficult time surviving while you are in school: If you have done everything for them up to now, they might struggle. Consider this an opportunity to help them become independent and self-sufficient. Your family can only make you feel guilty if you let them. You are not abandoning them; you are becoming an educational role model. When you are happy and working toward your goals, everyone benefits. Admittedly, it sometimes takes time for them to realize this. For single parents, there are schools that offer support groups, child care, and cooperative babysitting.

If you're appalled at the thought of being X years old when you graduate in Y years: How old will you be in Y years if you don't go back to school?

If you are afraid or don't know what to expect: Know that these are natural feelings when one encounters any new situation. Adult students find that their fears usually dissipate once they begin classes. Fear of trying is usually the biggest roadblock to the reentry process.

No doubt you have dreamed up a few more reasons for not making the decision to return to school. Keep in mind that what you are doing is making up excuses, and you are using these excuses to release you from the obligation to make a decision about your life. The thought of returning to college can be scary. Anytime anyone ventures into unknown territory, there is a risk, but taking risks is a necessary component of personal and professional growth. It is your life, and you alone are responsible for making the decisions that determine its course. Education is an investment in your future.

CHOICE

Once you have decided to go back to school, your next task is to decide where to go. If your educational goals are well defined (e.g., you want to pursue a degree in order to change careers), then your task is a bit easier. But even if your educational goals are still evolving, do not defer your return. Many students who enter higher education with a specific major in mind change that major at least once.

Most students who attend a public two-year college choose the community college in the district in which they live. This is generally the closest and least expensive option if the school offers the programs you want. If you are planning to begin your education at a two-year college and then transfer to a four-year school, there are distinct advantages to choosing your four-year school early. Many community and four-year colleges have "articulation" agreements that designate what credits from the two-year school will transfer to the four-year college and how. Some four-year institutions accept an associate degree as equivalent to the freshman and sophomore years, regardless of the courses you have taken. Some four-year schools accept two-year college work only on a course-by-course basis. If you can identify which school you will transfer to, you can know in advance exactly how your two-year credits will apply, preventing an unexpected loss of credit or time.

Each institution of higher education is distinctive. Your goal in choosing a college is to come up with the best student-institution fit—matching your needs with the offerings and characteristics of the school. The first step in choosing a college is to determine what criteria are most important to you in attaining your educational goals. Location, cost, and program availability are the three main factors that influence an adult student's college choice. In considering location, don't forget that some colleges have conveniently located branch campuses. In considering cost, remember to explore your financial aid options before ruling out an institution because of its tuition. Program availability should include not only the major in which you are interested, but also whether or not classes in that major are available when you can take them.

Some additional considerations beyond location, cost, and programs are:

- Does the school have a commitment to adult students and offer appropriate services, such as child care, tutoring, and advising?
- Are classes offered at times when you can take them?
- Are there academic options for adults, such as credit for life or work experience, credit by examination (including CLEP and PEP), credit for military service, or accelerated programs?
- Is the faculty sensitive to the needs of adult learners?

Once you determine which criteria are vital in your choice of an institution, you can begin to narrow your choices. There are myriad ways for you to locate the information you desire. Many urban newspapers publish a "School Guide" several times a year in which colleges and universities advertise to an adult student market. In addition, schools themselves publish catalogs, class schedules, and promotional materials that contain much of the information you need, and they are yours for the asking. Many colleges sponsor information sessions and open houses that allow you to visit the campus and ask questions. An appointment with an adviser is a good way to assess the fit between you and the institution. Be sure to bring your questions with you to your interview.

SUPPORT

Once you have made the decision to return to school and have chosen the institution that best meets your needs, take some additional steps to ensure your success during your crucial first semester. Take advantage of institutional support and build some social support systems of your own. Here are some ways of doing just that:

- Plan to participate in any orientation programs. These serve the threefold purpose of providing you with a great deal of important information, familiarizing you with the campus and its facilities, and giving you the opportunity to meet and begin networking with other students.
- Take steps to deal with any academic weaknesses. Take mathematics and writing placement tests if you have reason to believe you may need some extra help in these areas. It is not uncommon for adult students to need a math refresher course or a program to help alleviate math anxiety. Ignoring a weakness won't make it go away.
- Look into adult reentry programs. Many institutions offer adults workshops focusing on ways to improve study skills, textbook reading, test-taking, and time-management skills.
- Build new support networks by joining an adult student organization, making a point of meeting other adult students through workshops, or actively seeking out a "study buddy" in each class—that invaluable friend who shares and understands your experience.
- You can incorporate your new status as "student" into your family life. Doing your homework with your children at a designated "homework time" is a valuable family activity and reinforces the importance of education.
- Make sure you take a reasonable course load in your first semester. It is far better to have some extra time on your hands and to succeed magnificently than to spend the entire semester on the brink of a breakdown. Also, whenever possible, try to focus your first courses not only on requirements, but also on areas of personal interest.

■ Faculty members, advisers, and student affairs personnel are there to help you during difficult times—let them assist you as often as necessary.

After completing your first semester, you will probably look back in wonder at why you thought going back to school was so imposing. Certainly, it's not without its occasional exasperations. But, as with life, keeping things in perspective and maintaining your sense of humor make the difference between just coping and succeeding brilliantly.

What International Students Need to Know About Admission to U.S. Colleges and Universities

Kitty M. Villa

Selecting an institution and securing admission require a significant investment of time and effort.

There are two principles to remember about admission to a university in the United States. First, applying is almost never a one-time request for admission but an ongoing process that may involve several exchanges of information between applicant and institution. "Admission process" or "application process" means that a "yes" or "no" is usually not immediate, and requests for additional information are to be expected. To successfully manage this process, you must be prepared to send additional information when requested and then wait for replies. You need a thoughtful balance of persistence to communicate regularly and effectively with your selected universities and patience to endure what can be a very long process.

The second principle involves a marketplace analogy. The most successful applicants are alert to opportunities to create a positive impression that sets them apart from other applicants. They are able to market themselves to their target institution. Institutions are also trying to attract the highest-quality student that they can. The admissions process presents you with the opportunity to analyze your strengths and weaknesses as a student and to look for ways to present yourself in the most marketable manner.

FIRST STEP—SELECTING INSTITUTIONS

With thousands of institutions of higher education in the U.S., how do you begin to narrow your choices down to the institutions that are best for you? There are many factors to consider, and you must ultimately decide which factors are most important to you.

Location

You may spend several years studying in the U.S. Do you prefer an urban or rural campus? Large or small metropolitan area? If you need to live on campus, will you be unhappy at a university where most students commute from off-campus housing? How do you feel about extremely hot summers or cold winters? Eliminating institutions that do not match your preferences in terms of location will narrow your choices.

Recommendations from Friends, Professors, or Others

There are valid academic reasons to consider the recommendations of people who know you well and have firsthand knowledge about particular institutions. Friends and contacts may be able to provide you with "inside information" about the campus or its academic programs to which published sources have no access. You should carefully balance anecdotal information with your own research and your own impressions. However, current and former students, professors, and others may provide excellent information during the application process.

Your Own Academic and Career Goals

Consideration of your academic goals is more complex than it may seem at first glance. All institutions do not offer the same academic programs. The application form usually provides a definitive listing of the academic programs offered by an institution. A course catalog describes the degree program and all the courses offered. In addition to printed sources, there is a tremendous amount of institutional information available on the Web. Program descriptions, even course descriptions and course syllabi, are often available to peruse via computer.

You may be interested in the rankings of either the university or of a program of study. Keep in mind, however, that rankings usually assume that quality is quantifiable. Rankings are usually based on presumptions about how data relate to quality that are likely to be unproven. It is important to carefully consider the source and the criteria of any ranking information before believing and acting upon it.

Your Own Educational Background

You may be concerned about the interpretation of your educational credentials, since your country's degree nomenclature and the grading scale may differ from those in the U.S. Universities use reference books about the educational systems of other countries to help them understand specific educational credentials. Generally, these credentials are interpreted by each institution; there is not a single interpretation that applies to every institution. The lack of uniformity is good news for most students, since it means that students from a wide variety of educational backgrounds can find a U.S. university that is appropriate to their needs.

To choose an appropriate institution, you can and should do an informal self-evaluation of your educational background. This self-analysis involves three important questions:

1. How Many Years of Study Have You Completed?

Completion of secondary school with at least twelve total years of education usually qualifies students to apply for undergraduate (bachelor's) degree programs. Completion of a university degree program that involves at least sixteen years of total education qualifies one to apply for admission to graduate (master's) degree programs in the U.S.

2. Does the Education That You Have Completed in Your Country Provide Access to Further Study in the U.S.?

Consider the kind of institution where you completed your previous studies. If educational opportunities in your country are limited, it may be necessary to investigate many U.S. institutions and programs in order to find a match.

3. Are Your Previous Marks or Grades Excellent, Average, or Poor?

Your educational record influences your choice of U.S. institutions. If your grades are average or poor, it may be advisable to apply to several institutions with minimally difficult or noncompetitive entrance levels.

YOU are one of the best sources of information about the level and quality of your previous studies. Awareness of your educational assets and liabilities will serve you well throughout the application process.

SECOND STEP—PLANNING AND ASSEMBLING THE APPLICATION

Planning and assembling a university application can be compared to the construction of a building. First, you must start with a solid foundation, which is the application form itself. The application, often available online as well as in paper form, usually contains a wealth of useful information, such as deadlines, fees, and degree programs available at that institution. To build a solid application, it is best to begin well in advance of the application deadline.

How to Obtain the Application Form

Application forms and links to institutional Web sites may also be available at a U.S. educational advising center associated with the American Embassy or Consulate in your country. These centers are excellent resources for international students and provide information about standardized test administration, scholarships, and other matters to students who are interested in studying in the U.S. Your local U.S. Embassy or Consulate can guide you to the nearest educational advising center.

What Are the Key Components of a Complete Application?

Institutional requirements vary, but the standard components of a complete application include:

- Transcript
- Required standardized examination scores
- Evidence of financial support
- Letters of recommendation
- Application fee

Transcript

A complete academic record or transcript includes all courses completed, grades earned, and degrees awarded. Most universities require an official transcript to be sent directly from the school or university. In many other countries, however, the practice is to issue official transcripts and degree certificates directly to the student. If you have only one official copy of your transcript, it may be a challenge to get additional certified copies that are acceptable to U.S. universities. Some institutions will issue additional official copies for application purposes.

If your institution does not provide this service, you may have to seek an alternate source of certification. As a last resort, you may send a photocopy of your official transcript, explain that you have only one original, and ask the university for advice on how to deal with this situation.

Required Standardized Examination Scores

Arranging to take standardized examinations and earning the required scores seem to cause the most anxiety for international students.

The university application form usually indicates which examinations are required. The standardized examination required most often for undergraduate admission is the Test of English as a Foreign Language (TOEFL). In most countries, TOEFL has changed from a paper-and-pencil test to a computer-based test. Institutions may also require the SAT of undergraduate applicants. Some institutions also require the Test of Spoken English (TSE). These standardized examinations are administered by the Educational Testing Service (ETS). Please note: Effective September 2005, the TOEFL CBT includes a speaking section.

These examinations are offered in almost every country of the world. It is advisable to begin planning for standardized examinations at least six months prior to the application deadline of your desired institutions. Test centers fill up quickly, so it is important to register as soon as possible. Information about the examinations is available at U.S. educational advising centers associated with embassies or consulates.

FOR MORE INFORMATION

Questions about test formats, locations, dates, and registration may be addressed to:

Educational Testing Service
Rosedale Road
Princeton, New Jersey 08541
Web sites: http://www.ets.org
http://www.toefl.org
Telephone: 609-921-9000
Fax: 609-734-5410

Most universities require that the original test scores, not a student copy, be sent directly by the testing service. When you register for the test, be sure to indicate that the testing service should send the test scores directly to the universities.

You should begin your application process before you receive your test scores. Delaying submission of your application until the test scores arrive may cause you to miss deadlines and negatively effect the outcome of your application. If you want to know your scores in order to assess your chances of admission to an institution with rigorous admission standards, you should take the tests early.

Many universities in the U.S. set minimum required scores on the TOEFL or on other standardized examinations. Test scores are an important factor, but most institutions also look at a number of other factors in their consideration of a candidate for admission.

Evidence of Financial Support

Evidence of financial support is required to issue immigration documents to admitted students. This is part of a complete application package but usually plays no role in determining admission. Most institutions make admissions decisions without regard to the source and amount of financial support.

Letters of Recommendation

Most institutions require one or more letters of recommendation. The best letters are written by former professors, employers, or others who can comment on your academic achievements or professional potential.

Some universities provide a special form for the letters of recommendation. If possible, use the forms provided. If you are applying to a large number of universities, however, or if your recommenders are not available to complete several forms, it may be necessary for you to duplicate a general recommendation letter.

Application Fee

Most universities also require an application fee, ranging from $25 to $100, which must be paid to initiate consideration of the application.

Completing the Application Form

Whether sent by mail or electronically, the application form must be neat and thoroughly filled out. Parts of the application may not seem to apply to you or your situation. Do your best to answer all the questions.

Remember that this is a process. You provide information, and your proposed university then requests clarification and further information. If you have questions, it is better to initiate the entire process by submitting the application form rather than asking questions before you apply. The university will be better able to respond to you after it has your application. Always complete as much as you can. Do not permit uncertainty about the completion of the application form to cause unnecessary delays.

THIRD STEP—DISTINGUISH YOUR APPLICATION

To distinguish your application—to market yourself successfully—is ultimately the most important part of the application process. As you select your prospective universities, you begin to analyze your strengths and weaknesses as a prospective student. As you complete your application, you should strive to create a positive impression and set yourself apart from other applicants, to highlight your assets and bring these qualities to the attention of the appropriate university administrators and professors. Applying early is a very easy way to distinguish your application.

Deadline or Guideline?

The application deadline is the last date that an application for a given semester will be accepted. Often, the application will specify that all required documents and information be submitted before the deadline date. To meet the deadlines, start the application process early. This also gives you more time to take—and perhaps retake and improve—the required standardized tests.

Admissions deliberations may take several weeks or months. In the meantime, most institutions accept additional information, including improved test scores, after the posted deadline.

Even if your application is initially rejected, you may be able to provide additional information to change the decision. You can request reconsideration based on additional information, such as improved test scores, strong letters of recommendation, or information about your class rank. Applying early allows more time to improve your application. Also, some students may decide not to accept their offers of admission, leaving room for offers to students on a waiting list. Reconsideration of the admission decisions can occur well beyond the application deadline.

Think of the deadline as a guideline rather than an impermeable barrier. Many factors—the strength of the application, your research interests, the number of spaces available at the proposed institution—can override the enforcement of an application deadline. So, if you lack a test score or transcript by the official deadline, you may still be able to apply and be accepted.

Statement of Purpose

The statement of purpose is your first and perhaps best opportunity to present yourself as an excellent candidate for admission. Whether or not a personal history essay or statement of purpose is required, always include a carefully written statement of purpose with your applications. A compelling statement of purpose does not have to be lengthy, but it should include some basic components:

- Part One—Introduce yourself and describe your previous educational background. This is your opportunity to describe any facet of your educational experience that you wish to emphasize. Perhaps you attended a highly ranked secondary school or university in your home country. Mention the name and any noteworthy characteristics of the secondary school or university from which you graduated. Explain the grading scale used at your university. Do not forget to mention your rank in your graduating class and any honors you may have received. This is not the time to be modest.
- Part Two—Describe your current academic and career interests and goals. Think about how these will fit into those of the institution to which you are applying, and mention the reasons why you have selected that institution.
- Part Three—Describe your long-term goals. When you finish your program of study, what do you plan to do next? If you already have a job offer or a career plan, describe it. Give some thought to how you'll demonstrate that studying in the U.S. will ultimately benefit others.

Use Personal Contacts When Possible

Appropriate and judicious use of your own network of contacts can be very helpful. Friends, former professors, former students of your selected institutions, and others may be willing to advise you during the application process and provide you with introductions to key administrators or professors. If suggested, you may wish to contact certain professors or administrators by mail, telephone, or e-mail. A personal visit to discuss your interest in the institution may be appropriate. Whatever your choice of communication, try to make the encounter pleasant and personal. Your goal is to make a positive impression, not to rush the admission decision.

There is no single right way to be admitted to U.S. universities. The same characteristics that make the educational choice in the U.S. so difficult—the number of institutions and the variety of programs of study—are the same attributes that allow so many international students to find the institution that's right for them.

Kitty M. Villa is the former Assistant Director, International Office, at the University of Texas at Austin.

Searching for Two-Year Colleges Online

The Internet can be a great tool for gathering information about four-year colleges and universities. There are many worthwhile sites that are ready to help guide you through the various aspects of the selection process, including Peterson's College Search at www.petersons.com.

HOW PETERSON'S COLLEGE SEARCH CAN HELP

Peterson's College Search is a comprehensive information resource that will help you make sense of the college admissions process and is a great place to start your college search-and-selection journey—it's as easy as:

1. Decide What's Important
2. Define Your Criteria
3. Get Results

Decide What's Important

There's no such thing as a best college—there's only the best college *for you*! Peterson's College Search site is organized into various sections and offers you enhanced search criteria—and it's easy to use! You can find colleges by name or keyword for starters, or do a detailed search based on the following:

- The Basics (location, setting, size, cost, type, religious and ethnic affiliation)
- Student Body (male-female ratio, diversity, in-state vs. out-of-state)
- Getting In (selectivity, SAT/ACT scores, GPA)
- Academics (degree type, majors, special programs)
- Campus Life (sports, clubs, fraternities and sororities)

Define Your Criteria

Now it's time to take to define your criteria by taking a closer look at some more specific details. Here you are able to answer questions about what is important to you, skip questions that aren't important, and click for instant results. You'll be prompted to think about criteria such as:

- Where do you want to study?
- What range of tuition are you willing to consider?
- What kind of degree are you looking to earn?
- What kinds of clubs and activities are you looking for?
- Should your school guarantee on-campus housing?

Get Results

Once you have gotten your results, simply click on any school to get information about the institution, including a *School Snapshot* (school type, setting, degrees offered, comprehensive cost, entrance difficulty, and application deadline), a *Student Snapshot* (undergraduate student population, minority breakdown, international population, and housing info) and *School Details* (freshman, faculty, majors, academic programs, student life, athletics, facilities/endowment, costs, financial aid, and applying). Keep reading but take a peek at all the great info you'll see on Petersons.com on the next page!

Get Free Info

If, after looking at the information provided on Peterson's College Search, you still have questions, you can send an e-mail directly to the admissions department of the school. Just click on the "Get Free Info" button and send your message!

Visit School Site

For institutions that have provided information about their Web sites, simply click on the "Visit School Site" button and you will be taken directly to that institution's Web page. Once you arrive at the school's Web site, look around and get a feel for the place. Often, schools offer virtual tours of the campus, complete with photos and commentary.

College Close-Up

If the schools you are interested in have provided Thomson Peterson's with a **College Close-Up,** you can do a keyword search on that description. Here, schools are given the opportunity to communicate unique features of their programs to prospective students.

Add to My Saved Schools/Add Notes/Apply

The "Add to My Saved Schools" features are designed to help you with your college planning with management tools to create notes about and track the school. The Apply link gives you the ability to directly apply to the school online.

WRITE ADMISSIONS ESSAYS

This year, 500,000 college applicants will write 500,000 different admissions essays. Half will be rejected by their first-choice school, while only 11 percent will gain admission to the nation's most selective colleges. With acceptance rates at all-time lows, setting yourself apart requires more than just blockbuster SAT scores and impeccable transcripts-it requires the perfect application essay. Named "the world's premier application essay editing service" by the *New York Times* Learning Network and "one of the best essay services on the Internet" by the *Washington Post*, EssayEdge (www.essayedge.com) has helped more applicants write successful personal statements than any other company in the world. Learn more about EssayEdge and how it can give you an edge over hundreds of applicants with comparable academic credentials.

PRACTICE FOR YOUR TEST

At Thomson Peterson's, we understand that the college admissions process can be very stressful. With the stakes so high and the competition getting tighter every year, it's easy to feel like the process is out of your control. Fortunately, preparing for college admissions tests, like the PSAT, SAT, and ACT Assessment, helps you exert some control over the options you will have available to you. You can visit Peterson's Prep Central to learn more about how Thomson Peterson's can help you maximize your scores—and your options.

USE THE TOOLS TO YOUR ADVANTAGE

Choosing a college is an involved and complicated process. The tools available to you on www.petersons.com can help you to be more productive in this process. So, what are you waiting for? Fire up your computer; your future alma mater may be just a click away!

MY PETERSON'S LOGIN

| COLLEGE HOME | GET STARTED | FIND A SCHOOL | PREPARE FOR TESTS | PAY FOR SCHOOL |

College Search | Nursing | Visual & Performing Arts | International Students | Online Learning
Culinary Program | Career Colleges | Go Abroad | Advice Center

Not registered? Register now

Enter Username

Forgot your Username or Password?

One-click access to the school's home page

Management tools allowing students to apply to, create notes about, and track the progress of the institution

Deep links providing one-click access to key areas of the school's Web site

Google— Free text Google search

School tabs— Quick access to top-level and detailed information about the institution

College Overview

Print | E-mail to a Friend | My Saved Schools | Post to del.icio.us

THE UNIVERSITY
Address
City, State Zip
Phone: 999-999-9999
Fax: 888-888-8888

GET FREE INFO

Easy way for students to e-mail the school for more information

VISIT SCHOOL SITE

Logo/Photo— Graphic presentation of the school's photo and logo

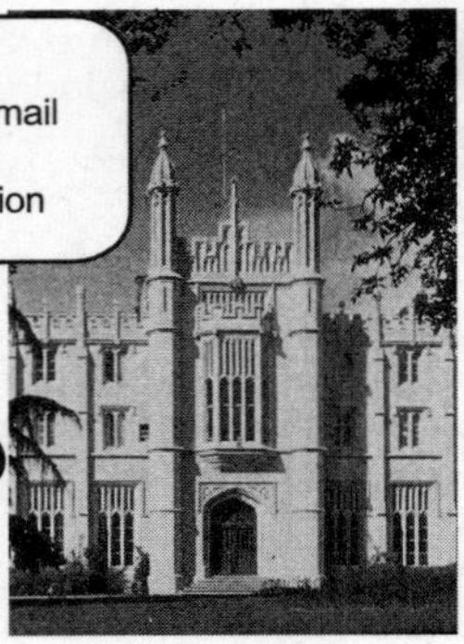

SCHOOL SPOTLIGHT

Targeted messaging highlighting key attributes of the school

The University

Add to My Saved Schools

Add Notes

Apply

Find Out More! ▼

Find out more— Cross-channel access to specialty program offerings

Online Tour

College Close Up

Chat

Student Perspective

Visitor Info

Admissions Process

College Newspaper

Sports Central

What's Hot Now— Dynamic presentation of the latest news and events on campus via RSS feed integration

Google   This school's site   (Go)

| **School Snapshot** | **Student Snapshot** | **School Details** | **What's Hot Now** |

School Type
Independent, Coed

Setting
Suburban 8500-acre campus

Degrees Offered
Bachelor's, Master's, Doctoral, First Professional, Post-Master's, and Postbachelor's Certificates

Comprehensive Cost
$43,115 includes full-time tuition ($32,845), mandatory fees ($1118), and room and board ($9152)
(Cost includes full-time tuition plus additional fees such as room and board, books, and mandatory fees)

Entrance Difficulty
Most difficult , 22% of applicants were admitted

Application Deadlines
1/2 (freshmen), 3/15 (transfers)

How to Use This Guide

*P*eterson's *Two-Year Colleges 2007* contains a wealth of information for anyone interested in colleges offering associate degrees. This section details the criteria that institutions must meet to be included in this guide and provides information about research procedures used by Thomson Peterson's.

QUICK-REFERENCE CHART

The **Two-Year Colleges At-a-Glance** chart is a geographically arranged table that lists colleges by name and city within the state, territory, or country in which they are located. Areas are listed in the following order: United States, U.S. territories, and other countries; the institutions in these countries are included because they are accredited by recognized U.S. accrediting bodies (see **Criteria for Inclusion** section).

The At-a-Glance chart contains basic information that enables you to compare institutions quickly according to broad characteristics such as enrollment, application requirements, types of financial aid available, and numbers of sports and majors offered. An asterisk (*) after an institution's name denotes that a **Special Message** is included in the college's profile, and a dagger (†) indicates that an institution has one or more entries in the **College Close-Ups** section.

Column 1: Degrees Awarded

C = *college transfer associate degree:* the degree awarded after a "university-parallel" program, equivalent to the first two years of a bachelor's degree.
T = *terminal associate degree:* the degree resulting from a one- to three-year program providing training for a specific occupation.
B = *bachelor's degree (baccalaureate):* the degree resulting from a liberal arts, science, professional, or preprofessional program normally lasting four years, although in some cases an accelerated program can be completed in three years.
M = *master's degree:* the first graduate (postbaccalaureate) degree in the liberal arts and sciences and certain professional fields, usually requiring one to two years of full-time study.
D = *doctoral degree (doctorate):* the highest degree awarded in research-oriented academic disciplines, usually requiring from three to six years of full-time study beyond

the baccalaureate and intended as preparation for university-level teaching and research.
F = *first professional degree:* the degree required to be academically qualified to practice in certain professions, such as law and medicine, having as a prerequisite at least two years of college credit and usually requiring a total of at least six years of study including prior college-level work.

Column 2: Institutional Control

Private institutions are designated as one of the following:
    Ind = *independent* (nonprofit)
    I-R = *independent-religious:* nonprofit; sponsored by or affiliated with a particular religious group or having a nondenominational or interdenominational religious orientation.
    Prop = *proprietary* (profit-making)
Public institutions are designated by the source of funding, as follows:
    Fed = *federal*
    St = *state*
    Comm = *commonwealth* (Puerto Rico)
    Terr = *territory* (U.S. territories)
    Cou = *county*
    Dist = *district:* an administrative unit of public education, often having boundaries different from units of local government.
    City = *city*
    St-L = *state and local:* "local" may refer to county, district, or city.
    St-R = *state-related:* funded primarily by the state but administratively autonomous.

Column 3: Student Body

M = *men only* (100% of student body)
PM = *coed, primarily men*
W = *women only* (100% of student body)
PW = *coed, primarily women*
M/W = *coeducational*

Column 4: Undergraduate Enrollment

The figure shown represents the number of full-time and part-time students enrolled in undergraduate degree programs as of fall 2005.

Columns 5–7: Enrollment Percentages

Figures are shown for the percentages of the fall 2005 undergraduate enrollment made up of students attending part-time (column 5) and students 25 years of age or older (column 6). Also listed is the percentage of students in the last graduating class who completed a college-transfer associate program and went directly on to four-year colleges (column 7).

For columns 8 through 15, the following letter codes are used: Y = yes; N = no; R = recommended; S = for some.

Columns 8–10: Admission Policies

The information in these columns shows whether the college has an open admission policy (column 8) whereby virtually all applicants are accepted without regard to standardized test scores, grade average, or class rank; whether a high school equivalency certificate is accepted in place of a high school diploma for admission consideration (column 9); and whether a high school transcript (column 10) is required as part of the application process. In column 10, the combination of the codes R and S indicates that a high school transcript is recommended for all applicants (R) and required for some (S).

Columns 11–12: Financial Aid

These columns show which colleges offer the following types of financial aid: need-based aid (column 11) and part-time jobs (column 12), including those offered through the federal government's Federal Work-Study program.

Columns 13–15: Services and Facilities

These columns show which colleges offer the following: career counseling (column 13) on either an individual or group basis, job placement services (column 14) for individual students, and college-owned or -operated housing facilities (column 16) for noncommuting students.

Column 16: Sports

This figure indicates the number of sports that a college offers at the intramural and/or intercollegiate levels.

Column 17: Majors

This figure indicates the number of major fields of study in which a college offers degree programs.

PROFILES OF TWO-YEAR COLLEGES AND SPECIAL MESSAGES

The **Profiles of Two-Year Colleges** contain basic data in capsule form for quick review and comparison. The following outline of the Profile format shows the section headings and the items that each section covers. Any item that does not apply to a particular college or for which no information was supplied is omitted from that college's Profile. **Special Messages,** which appear in the Profiles just below the bulleted highlights, have been written by those colleges that chose to supplement their Profile data with additional information.

Bulleted Highlights

The bulleted highlights section features important information, including the institution's Web site, for quick reference and comparison. The number of possible bulleted highlights that an ideal Profile would have if all questions were answered in a timely manner follow. However, not every institution provides all of the information necessary to fill out every bulleted line. In such instances, the line will not appear.

First bullet

Institutional control: Private institutions are designated as independent (nonprofit), proprietary (profit-making), or independent, with a specific religious denomination or affiliation. Nondenominational or interdenominational religious orientation is possible and would be indicated.

Public institutions are designated by the source of funding. Designations include federal, state, province, commonwealth (Puerto Rico), territory (U.S. territories), county, district (an educational administrative unit often having boundaries different from units of local government), city, state and local (local may refer to county, district, or city), or state-related (funded primarily by the state but administratively autonomous).

Religious affiliation is also noted here.

Institutional type: Each institution is classified as one of the following:

Primarily two-year college: Awards baccalaureate degrees, but the vast majority of students are enrolled in two-year programs.

Four-year college: Awards baccalaureate degrees; may also award associate degrees; does not award graduate (postbaccalaureate) degrees.

Five-year college: Awards a five-year baccalaureate in a professional field such as architecture or pharmacy; does not award graduate degrees.

Upper-level institution: Awards baccalaureate degrees, but entering students must have at least two years of previous college-level credit; may also offer graduate degrees.

Comprehensive institution: Awards baccalaureate degrees; may also award associate degrees; offers graduate degree programs, primarily at the master's, specialist's, or professional level, although one or two doctoral programs may be offered.

University: Offers four years of undergraduate work plus graduate degrees through the doctorate in more than two academic or professional fields.

Founding date: If the year an institution was chartered differs from the year when instruction actually began, the earlier date is given.

System or administrative affiliation: Any coordinate institutions or system affiliations are indicated. An institution that has separate colleges or campuses for men and women but shares facilities and courses is termed a coordinate institution. A formal administrative grouping of institutions, either private or public, of which the college is a part, or the name of a single institution with which the college is administratively affiliated, is a system.

Second bullet

Setting: Schools are designated as urban (located within a major city), suburban (a residential area within commuting distance of a major city), small-town (a small but compactly settled area not within commuting distance of a major city), or rural (a remote and sparsely populated area). The phrase easy access to . . . indicates that the campus is within an hour's drive of the nearest major metropolitan area that has a population greater than 500,000.

Third bullet

Endowment: The total dollar value of donations to the institution or the multicampus educational system of which the institution is a part.

Fourth bullet

Student body: An institution is coed (coeducational—admits men and women), primarily (80 percent or more) women, primarily men, women only, or men only.

Undergraduate students: Represents the number of full-time and part-time students enrolled in undergraduate degree programs as of fall 2005. The percentage of full-time undergraduates and the percentages of men and women are given.

Special Messages

These messages have been written by those colleges that chose to supplement the Profile data with additional, timely, important information.

Category Overviews

Undergraduates

For fall 2005, the number of full- and part-time undergraduate students is listed. This list provides the number of states and U.S. territories, including the District of Columbia and Puerto Rico (or, for Canadian institutions, provinces and territories), and other countries from which undergraduates come. Percentages are given of undergraduates who are from out of state; Native American, African American, and Asian American or Pacific Islander; international students; transfer students; and living on campus.

Retention: The percentage of 2004 freshmen (or, for upper-level institutions, entering students) who returned for the fall 2005 term.

Freshmen

Admission: Figures are given for the number of students who applied for fall 2005 admission, the number of those who were admitted, and the number who enrolled. Freshman statistics include the average high school GPA; the percentage of freshmen who took the SAT and received verbal and math scores above 500, above 600, and above 700; as well as the percentage of freshmen taking the ACT Assessment who received a composite score of 18 or higher.

Faculty

Total: The total number of faculty members; the percentage of full-time faculty members as of fall 2005; and the percentage of full-time faculty members who hold doctoral/first professional/terminal degrees.

Student-faculty ratio: The school's estimate of the ratio of matriculated undergraduate students to faculty members teaching undergraduate courses.

Majors

This section lists the major fields of study offered by the college.

Academics

Calendar: Most colleges indicate one of the following: 4-1-4, 4-4-1, or a similar arrangement (two terms of equal length plus an abbreviated winter or spring term, with the numbers referring to months); semesters; trimesters; quarters; 3-3 (three courses for each of three terms); modular (the academic year is divided into small blocks of time; courses of varying lengths are assembled according to individual programs); or standard year (for most Canadian institutions).

Degrees: This names the full range of levels of certificates, diplomas, and degrees, including prebaccalaureate, graduate, and professional, that are offered by this institution:

Associate degree: Normally requires at least two but fewer than four years of full-time college work or its equivalent.

Bachelor's degree (baccalaureate): Requires at least four years but not more than five years of full-time college-level work or its equivalent. This includes all bachelor's degrees in which the normal four years of work are completed in three years and bachelor's degrees conferred in a five-year cooperative (work-study plan) program. A cooperative plan provides for alternate class attendance and employment in business, industry, or government. This allows students to combine actual work experience with their college studies.

Master's degree: Requires the successful completion of a program of study of at least the full-time equivalent of one but not more than two years of work beyond the bachelor's degree.

Doctoral degree (doctorate): The highest degree in graduate study. The doctoral degree classification includes Doctor of Education, Doctor of Juridical Science, Doctor of Public Health, and the Doctor of Philosophy in any nonprofessional field.

First professional degree: The first postbaccalaureate degree in one of the following fields: chiropractic (DC, DCM), dentistry (DDS, DMD), medicine (MD), optometry (OD), osteopathic medicine (DO), rabbinical and Talmudic studies (MHL, Rav), pharmacy (BPharm, PharmD), podiatry (PodD, DP, DPM), veterinary medicine (DVM), law (JD), or divinity/ministry (BD, MDiv).

First professional certificate (postdegree): Requires completion of an organized program of study after completion of the first professional degree. Examples are refresher courses or additional units of study in a specialty or subspecialty.

Post-master's certificate: Requires completion of an organized program of study of 24 credit hours beyond the master's degree but does not meet the requirements of academic degrees at the doctoral level.

Special study options: Details are next given here on study options available at each college:

Accelerated degree program: Students may earn a bachelor's degree in three academic years.

Academic remediation for entering students: Instructional courses designed for students deficient in the general competencies necessary for a regular postsecondary curriculum and educational setting.

Adult/continuing education programs: Courses offered for nontraditional students who are currently working or are returning to formal education.

Advanced placement: Credit toward a degree awarded for acceptable scores on College Board Advanced Placement (AP) tests.

Cooperative (co-op) education programs: Formal arrangements with off-campus employers allowing students to combine work and study in order to gain degree-related experience, usually extending the time required to complete a degree.

Distance learning: For-credit courses that can be accessed off-campus via cable television, the Internet, satellite, videotape, correspondence course, or other media.

Double major: A program of study in which a student concurrently completes the requirements of two majors.

English as a second language (ESL): A course of study designed specifically for students whose native language is not English.

External degree programs: A program of study in which students earn credits toward a degree through a combination of independent study, college courses,

proficiency examinations, and personal experience. External degree programs require minimal or no classroom attendance.

Freshmen honors college: A separate academic program for talented freshmen.

Honors programs: Any special program for very able students offering the opportunity for educational enrichment, independent study, acceleration, or some combination of these.

Independent study: Academic work, usually undertaken outside the regular classroom structure, chosen or designed by the student with departmental approval and instructor supervision.

Internships: Any short-term, supervised work experience usually related to a student's major field, for which the student earns academic credit. The work can be full- or part-time, on or off-campus, paid or unpaid.

Off-campus study: A formal arrangement with one or more domestic institutions under which students may take courses at the other institution(s) for credit.

Part-time degree program: Students may earn a degree through part-time enrollment in regular session (daytime) classes or evening, weekend, or summer classes.

Self-designed major: Program of study based on individual interests, designed by the student with the assistance of an adviser.

Services for LD students: Special help for learning-disabled students with resolvable difficulties, such as dyslexia.

Study abroad: An arrangement by which a student completes part of the academic program studying in another country. A college may operate a campus abroad or it may have a cooperative agreement with other U.S. institutions or institutions in other countries.

Summer session for credit: Summer courses through which students may make up degree work or accelerate their program.

Tutorials: Undergraduates can arrange for special in-depth academic assignments (not for remediation) working with faculty members one-on-one or in small groups.

ROTC: Army, Naval, or Air Force Reserve Officers' Training Corps programs offered either on campus, at a branch campus [designated by a (b)], or at a cooperating host institution [designated by (c)].

Unusual degree programs: Nontraditional programs such as a 3-2 degree program, in which 3 years of liberal arts study is followed by 2 years of study in a professional field at another institution (or in a professional division of the same institution), resulting in two bachelor's degrees or a bachelor's and a master's degree.

Student Life

Housing options: The institution's policy about whether students are permitted to live off-campus or are required to live on campus for a specified period; whether freshmen-only, coed, single-sex, cooperative, and disabled student housing options are available; whether campus housing is leased by the school and/or provided by a third party; whether freshman applicants are given priority for college housing. The phrase college housing not available indicates that no college-owned or -operated housing facilities are provided for undergraduates and that noncommuting students must arrange for their own accommodations.

Activities and organizations: Lists information on drama-theater groups, choral groups, marching bands, student-run campus newspapers, student-run radio stations, and social organizations (sororities, fraternities, eating clubs, etc.) and how many are represented on campus.

Campus security: Campus safety measures including 24-hour emergency response devices (telephones and alarms) and patrols by trained security personnel, student patrols, late-night transport-escort service, and controlled dormitory access (key, security card, etc.).

Student services: Information provided indicates services offered to students by the college, such as legal services, health clinics, personal-psychological counseling, and women's centers.

Athletics

Membership in one or more of the following athletic associations is indicated by initials.

NCAA: National Collegiate Athletic Association

NAIA: National Association of Intercollegiate Athletics

NCCAA: National Christian College Athletic Association

NSCAA: National Small College Athletic Association

NJCAA: National Junior College Athletic Association

CIS: Canadian Interuniversity Sports

The overall NCAA division in which all or most intercollegiate teams compete is designated by a roman numeral I, II, or III. All teams that do not compete in this division are listed as exceptions.

Sports offered by the college are divided into two groups: intercollegiate (**M** or **W** following the name of each sport indicates that it is offered for men or women) and intramural. An **s** in parentheses following an **M** or **W** for an intercollegiate sport indicates that athletic scholarships (or grants-in-aid) are offered for men or women in that sport, and a c indicates a club team as opposed to a varsity team.

Standardized Tests

The most commonly required standardized tests are the ACT Assessment, SAT, and SAT Subject Tests. These and other standardized tests may be used for selective

admission, as a basis for counseling or course placement, or for both purposes. This section notes if a test is used for admission or placement and whether it is required, required for some, or recommended.

In addition to the ACT Assessment and SAT, the following standardized entrance and placement examinations are referred to by their initials:

ABLE: Adult Basic Learning Examination

ACT ASSET: ACT Assessment of Skills for Successful Entry and Transfer

ACT PEP: ACT Proficiency Examination Program

CAT: California Achievement Tests

CELT: Comprehensive English Language Test

CPAt: Career Programs Assessment

CPT: Computerized Placement Test

DAT: Differential Aptitude Test

LSAT: Law School Admission Test

MAPS: Multiple Assessment Program Service

MCAT: Medical College Admission Test

MMPI: Minnesota Multiphasic Personality Inventory

OAT: Optometry Admission Test

PAA: Prueba de Aptitude Académica (Spanish-language version of the SAT)

PCAT: Pharmacy College Admission Test

PSAT: Preliminary SAT

SCAT: Scholastic College Aptitude Test

SRA: Scientific Research Association (administers verbal, arithmetical, and achievement tests)

TABE: Test of Adult Basic Education

TASP: Texas Academic Skills Program

TOEFL: Test of English as a Foreign Language (for international students whose native language is not English)

WPCT: Washington Pre-College Test

Costs

Costs are given for the 2006–07 academic year or for the 2005–06 academic year if 2006–07 figures were not yet available. Annual expenses may be expressed as a comprehensive fee (including full-time tuition, mandatory fees, and college room and board) or as separate figures for full-time tuition, fees, room and board, or room only. For public institutions where tuition differs according to residence, separate figures are given for area or state residents and for nonresidents. Part-time tuition is expressed in terms of a per-unit rate (per credit, per semester hour, etc.) as specified by the institution.

The tuition structure at some institutions is complex in that freshmen and sophomores may be charged a different rate from that for juniors and seniors, a professional or vocational division may have a different fee structure from the liberal arts division of the same institution, or part-time tuition may be prorated on a sliding scale according to the number of credit hours taken. Tuition and fees may vary according to academic program, campus/location, class time (day, evening, weekend), course/credit load, course level, degree level, reciprocity agreements, and student level. Room and board charges are reported as an average for one academic year and may vary according to the board plan selected, campus/location, type of housing facility, or student level. If no college-owned or -operated housing facilities are offered, the phrase college housing not available will appear in the Housing section of the Student Life paragraph.

Tuition payment plans that may be offered to undergraduates include tuition prepayment, installment payments, and deferred payment. A tuition prepayment plan gives a student the option of locking in the current tuition rate for the entire term of enrollment by paying the full amount in advance rather than year by year. Colleges that offer such a prepayment plan may also help the student to arrange financing.

The availability of full or partial undergraduate tuition waivers to minority students, children of alumni, employees or their children, adult students, and senior citizens may be listed.

Financial Aid

Financial aid information presented represents aid awarded to undergraduates for the 2005–06 academic year. Figures are given for the number of undergraduates who applied for aid, the number who were judged to have need, and the number who had their need met. The number of Federal Work-Study and/or part-time jobs and average earnings are listed, as well as the number of non-need-based awards that were made. Non-need-based awards are college-administered scholarships for which the college determines the recipient and amount of each award. These scholarships are awarded to full-time undergraduates on the basis of merit or personal attributes without regard to need, although they many certainly be given to students who also happen to need aid. The average percent of need met for those determined to have need, the average financial aid package awarded to undergraduates (the amount of scholarships, grants, work-study payments, or loans in the institutionally administered financial aid package divided by the number of students who received any financial aid-amounts used to pay the officially designated Expected Family Contribution (EFC), such as PLUS or other alternative loans, are excluded from the amounts reported), the average amount of need-based gift aid, and the average amount of non-need-based aid are given. Average indebtedness, which is the average per-borrower indebtedness of the last graduating undergraduate class

from amounts borrowed at this institution through any loan programs, excluding parent loans, is listed last.

Applying

Application and admission options include the following:

Early admission: Highly qualified students may matriculate before graduating from high school.

Early action plan: An admission plan that allows students to apply and be notified of an admission decision well in advance of the regular notification dates. If accepted, the candidate is not committed to enroll; students may reply to the offer under the college's regular reply policy.

Early decision plan: A plan that permits students to apply and be notified of an admission decision (and financial aid offer, if applicable) well in advance of the regular notification date. Applicants agree to accept an offer of admission and to withdraw their applications from other colleges. Candidates who are not accepted under early decision are automatically considered with the regular applicant pool, without prejudice.

Deferred entrance: The practice of permitting accepted students to postpone enrollment, usually for a period of one academic term or year.

Application fee: The fee required with an application is noted. This is typically nonrefundable, although under certain specified conditions it may be waived or returned.

Requirements: Other application requirements are grouped into three categories: required for all, required for some, and recommended. They may include an essay, standardized test scores, a high school transcript, a minimum high school grade point average (expressed as a number on a scale of 0 to 4.0, where 4.0 equals A, 3.0 equals B, etc.), letters of recommendation, an interview on campus or with local alumni, and, for certain types of schools or programs, special requirements such as a musical audition or an art portfolio.

Application deadlines and notification dates: Admission application deadlines and dates for notification of acceptance or rejection are given either as specific dates or as **rolling** and **continuous.** Rolling means that applications are processed as they are received, and qualified students are accepted as long as there are openings. Continuous means that applicants are notified of acceptance or rejection as applications are processed up until the date indicated or the actual beginning of classes. The application deadline and the notification date for transfers are given if they differ from the dates for freshmen. Early decision and early action application deadlines and notification dates are also indicated when relevant.

Admissions Contact

The name, title, and telephone number of the person to contact for application information are given at the end of the Profile. The admission office address is listed. Toll-free telephone numbers may also be included. The admission office fax number and e-mail address, if available, are listed, provided the school wanted them printed for use by prospective students.

Additional Information

Each college that has a **College Close-Up** in the guide will have a cross-reference appended to the Profile, referring you directly to that **College Close-Up.**

COLLEGE CLOSE-UPS

Nearly 100 two-page narrative descriptions provide an inside look at colleges and universities appearing in this section, shifting the focus to a variety of other factors, some of them intangible, that should also be considered. The descriptions presented in this section provide a wealth of statistics that are crucial components in the college decision-making equation—components such as tuition, financial aid, and major fields of study. Prepared exclusively by college officials, the descriptions are designed to help give students a better sense of the individuality of each institution, in terms that include campus environment, student activities, and lifestyle. Such quality-of-life intangibles can be the deciding factors in the college selection process. The absence from this section of any college or university does not constitute an editorial decision on the part of Thomson Peterson's. In essence, this section is an open forum for colleges and universities, on a voluntary basis, to communicate their particular message to prospective college students. The colleges included have paid a fee to Thomson Peterson's to provide this information. The **College Close-Ups** are edited to provide a consistent format across entries for your ease of comparison and are presented alphabetically by the official name of the institution.

INDEXES

Associate Degree Programs at Two- and Four-Year Colleges

These indexes present hundreds of undergraduate fields of study that are currently offered most widely according to the colleges' responses on *Thomson Peterson's Annual Survey of Undergraduate Institutions*. The majors appear in alphabetical order, each followed by an alphabetical list of the schools that offer an associate-level program in that field. Liberal Arts and Studies indicates a general program with no specified major. The terms used for the majors are those of the U.S. Department of Education Classification of Instructional Programs (CIPs). Many institutions, however, use different terms. Readers should visit www.petersons.com in order to contact a college and ask for its catalog or refer to the **College Close-Up** in this book for the school's exact terminology. In addition, although the term "major" is used in this guide, some colleges may use other terms, such as "concentration," "program of study," or "field."

DATA COLLECTION PROCEDURES

The data contained in the **Profiles of Two-Year Colleges** and **Indexes** were researched between fall 2005 and spring 2006 through *Thomson Peterson's Annual Survey of Undergraduate Institutions*. Questionnaires were sent to the more than 1,800 colleges that meet the outlined inclusion criteria. All data included in this edition have been submitted by officials (usually admission and financial aid officers, registrars, or institutional research personnel) at the colleges themselves. In addition, the great majority of institutions that submitted data were contacted directly by Thomson Peterson's research staff to verify unusual figures, resolve discrepancies, and obtain additional data. All usable information received in time for publication has been included. The omission of any particular item from the **Profiles of Two-Year Colleges** and **Indexes** listing signifies either that the item is not applicable to that institution or that data were not available. Because of the comprehensive editorial review that takes place in our offices and because all material comes directly from college officials, Thomson Peterson's has every reason to believe that the information presented in this guide is accurate at the time of printing. However, students should check with a specific college or university at the time of application to verify such figures as tuition and fees, which may have changed since the publication of this volume.

CRITERIA FOR INCLUSION IN THIS BOOK

Peterson's Two-Year Colleges 2007 covers accredited institutions in the United States, U.S. territories, and other countries that award the associate degree as their most popular undergraduate offering (a few also offer bachelor's, master's, or doctoral degrees). The term two-year college is the commonly used designation for institutions that grant the associate degree, since two years is the normal duration of the traditional associate degree program. However, some programs may be completed in one year, others require three years, and, of course, part-time programs may take a considerably longer period. Therefore, "two-year college" should be understood as a conventional term that accurately describes most of the institutions included in this guide but which should not be taken literally in all cases. Also included are some non-degree-granting institutions, usually branch campuses of a multicampus system, which offer the equivalent of the first two years of a bachelor's degree, transferable to a bachelor's degree–granting institution.

To be included in this guide, an institution must have full accreditation or be a candidate for accreditation (preaccreditation) status by an institutional or specialized accrediting body recognized by the U.S. Department of Education or the Council for Higher Education Accreditation (CHEA). Institutional accrediting bodies, which review each institution as a whole, include the six regional associations of schools and colleges (Middle States, New England, North Central, Northwest, Southern, and Western), each of which is responsible for a specified portion of the United States and its territories. Other institutional accrediting bodies are national in scope and accredit specific kinds of institutions (e.g., Bible colleges, independent colleges, and rabbinical and Talmudic schools). Program registration by the New York State Board of Regents is considered to be the equivalent of institutional accreditation, since the board requires that all programs offered by an institution meet its standards before recognition is granted. This guide also includes institutions outside the United States that are accredited by these U.S. accrediting bodies. There are recognized specialized or professional accrediting bodies in more than forty different fields, each of which is authorized to accredit institutions or specific programs in its particular field. For specialized institutions that offer programs in one field only, we designate this to be the equivalent of institutional accreditation. A full explanation of the accrediting process and complete information on recognized, institutional (regional and national) and specialized accrediting bodies can be found online at www.chea.org or at www.ed.gov//admins/finaid/accred/index.html.

Quick-Reference
Chart

Two-Year Colleges At-a-Glance

This chart includes the names and locations of accredited two-year colleges in the United States and U.S. territories and shows institutions' responses to the *Thomson Peterson's Annual Survey of Undergraduate Institutions*. If an institution submitted incomplete data, one or more columns opposite the institution's name is blank. An asterisk after the school name denotes a *Special Message* following the college's profile, and a dagger indicates that the institution has one or more entries in the *College Close-Ups* section. If a school does not appear, it did not report any of the information.

Y—Yes; N—No; R—Recommended; S—For Some

Institution	City	Degrees Awarded	Institutional Control	Student Body	Undergraduate Enrollment Fall 2005	Percent Attending Part-Time	Percent 25 Years of Age or Older	Percent of Grads Going on to Four-Year Colleges	High School Equivalency Certificate Accepted	Open Admissions	High School Transcript Required	Need-Based Aid Available	Part-Time Jobs Available	Career Counseling Available	Job Placement Services Available	College Housing Available	Number of Sports Offered	Number of Majors Offered
UNITED STATES																		
Alabama																		
Alabama Southern Community College	Monroeville	C,T	St	M/W	1,500													
Bessemer State Technical College	Bessemer	T	St	M/W	2,087													
Bevill State Community College	Sumiton	C,T	St	M/W	4,327	43												
Bishop State Community College	Mobile	C,T	St	M/W	4,883	51	51		Y	Y	Y	Y	Y			N	3	16
Calhoun Community College	Decatur	C,T	St	M/W	8,879													
Central Alabama Community College	Alexander City	C,T	St	M/W	1,790													
Chattahoochee Valley Community College	Phenix City	C,T	St	M/W	2,034		45	18	Y	Y	Y	Y	Y	Y	Y	N	2	24
Community College of the Air Force	Maxwell Air Force Base	T	Fed	PM	351,715		63		Y		Y				Y	Y	15	51
Enterprise-Ozark Community College	Enterprise	C,T	St	M/W	1,590	46												
Gadsden State Community College	Gadsden	C,T	St	M/W	5,426	45	34		Y	Y	Y	Y	Y	Y	Y	Y	7	21
Gadsden State Community College-Ayers Campus	Anniston	C,T	St	M/W	1,137	40												
George Corley Wallace State Community College	Selma	C,T	St	M/W	1,758													
George C. Wallace Community College	Dothan	C,T	St	M/W	3,500	45	43		Y	Y	Y	Y	Y	Y	Y	N	3	26
H. Councill Trenholm State Technical College	Montgomery	T	St	M/W	1,403	49	55		Y	Y	Y	Y	Y	Y	Y	N		31
ITT Technical Institute	Birmingham	T,B	Prop	M/W					N	Y	Y	Y	Y	Y	Y	N		
James H. Faulkner State Community College*	Bay Minette	C,T	St	M/W	3,067	37	39		Y	Y	Y	Y	Y	Y	Y	Y	6	18
Jefferson State Community College	Birmingham	C,T	St	M/W	7,173	56	36		Y	Y	S	Y	Y	Y	Y	N	8	23
J. F. Drake State Technical College	Huntsville	T	St	M/W	764	41	55		Y		Y		Y	Y	Y	N		7
Lawson State Community College	Birmingham	C,T	St	M/W	3,371	48	33	1	Y	Y	Y	Y	Y	Y	Y	N	11	44
Northeast Alabama Community College	Rainsville	C,T	St	M/W	2,015	51												
Northwest-Shoals Community College	Muscle Shoals	C	St	M/W	3,380	37	40		Y	Y	Y	Y	Y	Y	Y	Y	9	41
Prince Institute of Professional Studies	Montgomery	T	Ind	PW	94	40	50					Y	Y	Y			N		1
Reid State Technical College	Evergreen	T	St	M/W	620	37												
Remington College–Mobile Campus	Mobile	C,T,B	Prop	M/W	433		49			Y	Y	Y	Y	Y	Y	N		7
Shelton State Community College	Tuscaloosa	C,T	St	M/W	5,754	42	32		Y	Y	Y	Y	Y	Y	Y	N	6	14
Snead State Community College	Boaz	C,T	St	M/W		26	53		Y	Y	Y	Y	Y	Y	Y	Y	5	7
Southern Union State Community College	Wadley	C,T	St	M/W														
Alaska																		
Ilisagvik College	Barrow	C	St	M/W	263	81								Y				5
University of Alaska Anchorage, Matanuska-Susitna College	Palmer	C,T	St	M/W	1,326	71	82		Y	Y	Y	Y	Y	Y		N		8
American Samoa																		
American Samoa Community College	Pago Pago	C,T	Terr	M/W	1,537													
Arizona																		
Arizona Western College	Yuma	C,T	St-L	M/W	6,731	73			Y	Y		Y	Y	Y	Y	Y	9	43
Central Arizona College	Coolidge	C,T	Cou	M/W	6,388		71		Y			Y	Y	Y	Y	Y	7	26
Chandler-Gilbert Community College	Chandler	C,T	St-L	M/W	8,663													
Cochise College	Douglas	C,T	St-L	M/W	4,610	69	33		Y		R	Y	Y	Y	Y	Y	3	49
Coconino Community College	Flagstaff	C,T	St	M/W	3,689													
Diné College	Tsaile	C,T	Fed	M/W	1,825	54	63		Y	Y	Y	Y	Y	Y	Y	Y	2	14
Eastern Arizona College	Thatcher	C,T	St-L	M/W	5,239	73	19		Y		R	Y	Y	Y	Y	Y	10	50
Estrella Mountain Community College	Avondale	C,T	St-L	M/W	5,947	77												
Everest College	Phoenix	C,T,B	Prop	M/W	804	53	95	2	N	Y	Y	Y		Y	Y	N		5
GateWay Community College	Phoenix	C,T	St-L	M/W	9,377	90	31		Y		S	Y	Y	Y	Y	N	3	39
Glendale Community College	Glendale	C,T	St-L	M/W	20,070	70	44		Y		S	Y	Y	Y	Y	N	11	28
International Institute of the Americas	Mesa	T,B	Ind	M/W	174													5
International Institute of the Americas	Phoenix	T,B	Ind	M/W	205													5
International Institute of the Americas	Phoenix	T,B	Ind	M/W	240		76		Y	Y				Y	Y	N		5
International Institute of the Americas	Tucson	T,B	Ind	M/W	298													5
ITT Technical Institute	Tucson	T,B	Prop	M/W					N	Y	Y	Y	Y	Y	Y	N		12
Mohave Community College	Kingman	C,T	St	M/W	6,187	80												
Paradise Valley Community College	Phoenix	C,T	St-L	M/W	8,237													
The Paralegal Institute, Inc.	Phoenix	T	Prop		400													2
Phoenix College	Phoenix	C,T	St-L	M/W	12,549				Y			Y	Y	Y	Y	N	12	40
Pima Community College	Tucson	C,T	St-L	M/W	30,884	70	42	15	Y			Y	Y	Y	Y	N	16	48
Pima Medical Institute	Mesa	T	Prop	M/W	592													

This chart includes the names and locations of accredited two-year colleges in the United States and U.S. territories and shows institutions' responses to the *Thomson Peterson's Annual Survey of Undergraduate Institutions*. If an institution submitted incomplete data, one or more columns opposite the institution's name is blank.

An asterisk after the school name denotes a *Special Message* following the college's profile, and a dagger indicates that the institution has one or more entries in the *College Close-Ups* section. If a school does not appear, it did not report any of the information.

Y—Yes; N—No; R—Recommended; S—For Some

Column key: Deg = Degrees Awarded; Ctrl = Institutional Control; SB = Student Body; Enr = Undergraduate Enrollment Fall 2005; PT = Percent Attending Part-Time; 25+ = Percent 25 Years of Age or Older; 4Yr = Percent of Grads Going on to Four-Year Colleges; HSE = High School Equivalency Certificate Accepted; OA = Open Admissions; HST = High School Transcript Required; NBA = Need-Based Aid Available; PTJ = Part-Time Jobs Available; CC = Career Counseling Available; JP = Job Placement Services Available; CH = College Housing Available; Sp = Number of Sports Offered; Maj = Number of Majors Offered

Institution	Location	Deg	Ctrl	SB	Enr	PT	25+	4Yr	HSE	OA	HST	NBA	PTJ	CC	JP	CH	Sp	Maj
Pima Medical Institute	Tucson	T	Prop	M/W	711													
Scottsdale Community College	Scottsdale	C,T	St-L	M/W	11,261	70	43		Y				Y	Y	Y		N	14	25
South Mountain Community College	Phoenix	C,T	St-L	M/W	3,933													
Tohono O'odham Community College	Sells	C,T	Ind	M/W	171													
Universal Technical Institute	Avondale	T	Priv															
Yavapai College	Prescott	C,T	St-L	M/W	7,422	82	70	80	Y	Y	Y	Y	Y	Y	Y	Y		5	25
Arkansas																		
Arkansas Northeastern College	Blytheville	C,T	St	M/W	1,830	47	40	5	Y	Y	R	Y	Y	Y	Y	N		12
Arkansas State University–Beebe	Beebe	C,T	St	M/W	3,976	47	38		Y	Y	Y	Y	Y	Y	Y	Y	12	17
Arkansas State University–Mountain Home	Mountain Home	T	St	M/W	1,031	39	44		Y	Y	Y	Y	Y			N		11
Black River Technical College	Pocahontas	C,T	St	M/W	1,243	48												
Cossatot Community College of the University of Arkansas	De Queen	C,T	St	M/W	1,020				Y	Y	R	Y	Y	Y	Y	N		12
East Arkansas Community College	Forrest City	C,T	St	M/W	1,477	50	47		Y	Y	Y	Y	Y	Y	Y	Y		7
ITT Technical Institute	Little Rock	T,B	Prop	M/W					N	Y	Y	Y	Y	Y	Y	N		14
Mid-South Community College	West Memphis	C,T	St	M/W	1,467	69	48		Y	Y	Y	Y	Y	Y	Y	N		5
North Arkansas College	Harrison	C,T	St-L	M/W	2,187	48	40		Y	Y	S	Y	Y	Y	Y	N	11	24
Ouachita Technical College	Malvern	C,T	St	M/W	1,590	65	45		Y	Y	Y	Y	Y	Y	Y			16
Phillips Community College of the University of Arkansas	Helena	C,T	St-L	M/W	2,322													
Pulaski Technical College	North Little Rock	C,T	St	M/W	7,685	49	54			Y		Y	Y	Y	Y			8
Rich Mountain Community College	Mena	C,T	St-L	M/W	973													
South Arkansas Community College	El Dorado	C,T	St	M/W	1,368	55	43		Y			Y	Y	Y	Y	N	4	10
Southern Arkansas University Tech	Camden	C,T	St	M/W	1,767	69	54		Y	Y	S	Y		Y		Y	6	15
University of Arkansas Community College at Batesville	Batesville	C,T	St	M/W	1,317	40												
University of Arkansas Community College at Hope	Hope	C,T	St	M/W	1,213	44												
University of Arkansas Community College at Morrilton	Morrilton	C,T	St	M/W	1,514													
California																		
Allan Hancock College	Santa Maria	C,T	St-L	M/W	10,387	71			Y	Y	Y	Y	Y	Y	Y	N	10	50
Argosy University/Orange County†	Santa Ana	T,B,M,D	Prop	M/W	81	19			N	Y		Y	Y			N		4
Argosy University/San Diego†	San Diego	T	Prop	M/W														4
Argosy University/Santa Monica†	Santa Monica	T	Prop	M/W														4
Berkeley City College	Berkeley	C,T	St-L	M/W	4,500		65	90	Y		R	Y	Y					21
Brooks College	Long Beach	T	Prop	M/W	826	8	3		N	Y	Y		Y	Y	Y	Y		7
Cerro Coso Community College	Ridgecrest	C,T	St	M/W	5,020	76												
Citrus College	Glendora	C,T	St-L	M/W	12,393		25		Y	Y	Y	Y	Y	Y	Y	N	12	43
College of the Canyons	Santa Clarita	C,T	St-L	M/W	16,504	23	35		Y		R	Y	Y	Y	Y	N	11	46
College of the Siskiyous*	Weed	C,T	St-L	M/W	2,998		39	30	Y			Y	Y	Y	Y	Y	11	30
Columbia College	Sonora	C,T	St-L	M/W	2,691	65	68	91	Y	Y	S	Y	Y	Y	Y	Y	4	32
Compton Community College	Compton	C,T	St-L	M/W	7,900													
Contra Costa College	San Pablo	C,T	St-L	M/W	8,834	55												
De Anza College	Cupertino	C,T	St-L	M/W	23,344	62												
Deep Springs College	Deep Springs	C	Ind	M	27		0	46	N	N	Y					Y	10	1
Diablo Valley College	Pleasant Hill	C,T	St-L	M/W	20,688		38		Y		R	Y	Y	Y	Y	N	10	1
Evergreen Valley College	San Jose	C,T	St-L	M/W	11,751		52		Y			Y	Y	Y	Y	N	5	27
Fashion Careers College	San Diego	C,T	Prop	PW	101		9	0	N	Y	Y	Y	Y	Y	Y	N		2
Feather River College	Quincy	C,T	St-L	M/W	1,714	57	31		Y			Y	Y	Y	Y	Y	8	19
FIDM/The Fashion Institute of Design & Merchandising, Los Angeles Campus†	Los Angeles	C,T,B	Prop	M/W	3,522	21	18		N	Y	Y	Y	Y	Y	Y	N		9
FIDM/The Fashion Institute of Design & Merchandising, San Diego Campus	San Diego	C,T	Prop	M/W	272	14	10	18	N	Y			Y					7
FIDM/The Fashion Institute of Design & Merchandising, San Francisco Campus	San Francisco	C,T	Prop	PW	936	20	25		N	Y	Y		Y	Y	Y			8
Foothill College	Los Altos Hills	C,T	St-L	M/W	17,488		57	31	Y		R	Y	Y	Y	Y	N	9	52
Foundation College	San Diego	C,T	Ind	M/W	106													
Gavilan College	Gilroy	C,T	St-L	M/W	6,064		58		Y	Y		Y	Y	Y		N	8	38
Glendale Community College	Glendale	C,T	St-L	M/W	15,767	70												
Heald College-Concord	Concord	C,T	Ind	M/W	639	18			Y	Y	Y		Y	Y	Y	N		2
Heald College-Fresno	Fresno	C,T	Ind	M/W	729	25			Y	Y	Y	Y	Y	Y	Y	N		8
Heald College-Hayward	Hayward	C,T	Ind	M/W	864	26			Y	Y	Y	Y	Y	Y	Y	N		9
Heald College-Rancho Cordova	Rancho Cordova	C,T	Ind	M/W	471	26			Y	Y	Y	Y	Y	Y	Y	N		5
Heald College-Roseville	Roseville	C,T	Ind	M/W	528	29			Y	Y	Y	Y	Y	Y	Y	N		3
Heald College-Salinas	Salinas	C,T	Ind	M/W	414	21			Y	Y	Y		Y	Y	Y	N		5
Heald College-San Francisco	San Francisco	C,T	Ind	M/W	389	30			Y	Y	Y		Y	Y	Y	N		8
Heald College-San Jose	Milpitas	C,T	Ind	M/W	639	21			Y	Y	Y	Y	Y	Y	Y	N		6
Heald College-Stockton	Stockton	C,T	Ind	M/W	530	25			Y	Y	Y		Y	Y	Y	N		4
ITT Technical Institute	Anaheim	T,B	Prop	M/W					N	Y	Y	Y	Y	Y	Y	N		10
ITT Technical Institute	Lathrop	T,B	Prop	M/W					N	Y	Y	Y	Y	Y	Y	N		12
ITT Technical Institute	Oxnard	C,T,B	Prop	M/W					N	Y	Y	Y	Y	Y	Y	N		9
ITT Technical Institute	Rancho Cordova	T,B	Prop	M/W					N	Y	Y	Y	Y	Y	Y	N		12
ITT Technical Institute	San Bernardino	T,B	Prop	M/W					N	Y	Y	Y	Y	Y	Y	N		10

This chart includes the names and locations of accredited two-year colleges in the United States and U.S. territories and shows institutions' responses to the *Thomson Peterson's Annual Survey of Undergraduate Institutions.* If an institution submitted incomplete data, one or more columns opposite the institution's name is blank.

An asterisk after the school name denotes a *Special Message* following the college's profile, and a dagger indicates that the institution has one or more entries in the *College Close-Ups* section. If a school does not appear, it did not report any of the information.

Y—Yes; N—No; R—Recommended; S—For Some

Degrees Awarded: College Transfer Associate (C), County District City, State and Local; Terminal Associate (T), Bachelor's (B), Master's (M), Doctoral (D), First Professional (P)

Name	Location	Degrees Awarded	Institutional Control	Student Body	Undergraduate Enrollment Fall 2005	Percent Attending Part-Time	Percent 25 Years of Age or Older	Percent of Grade Going on to Four-Year Colleges	High School Equivalency Certificate Accepted	Open Admissions	High School Transcript Required	Need-Based Aid Available	Part-Time Jobs Available	Career Counseling Available	Job Placement Services Available	College Housing Available	Number of Sports Offered	Number of Majors Offered
ITT Technical Institute	San Diego	T,B	Prop	M/W					N	Y	Y		Y	Y	Y	N		10
ITT Technical Institute	Sylmar	T,B	Prop	M/W					N	Y	Y	Y	Y	Y	Y	N		11
ITT Technical Institute	Torrance	T,B	Prop	M/W					N	Y	Y	Y	Y	Y	Y	N		11
ITT Technical Institute	West Covina	T,B	Prop	M/W					N	Y	Y		Y	Y	Y	N		10
Long Beach City College	Long Beach	C,T	St	M/W	26,296	64	54	23	Y		R	Y	Y	Y	Y	N	18	69
MiraCosta College*	Oceanside	C,T	St	M/W	10,252		33	80	Y			Y	Y	Y	Y	N	4	54
Modesto Junior College	Modesto	C,T	St-L	M/W	18,240		53		Y		R	Y	Y	Y	Y		15	87
Mt. San Antonio College	Walnut	C,T	Dist	M/W	27,195	68			Y		S	Y	Y	Y	Y		14	72
MTI College of Business and Technology	Sacramento	C,T	Prop	M/W	600									Y	Y			5
Napa Valley College	Napa	C,T	St-L	M/W	6,908	72			Y			Y	Y	Y	Y			
Orange Coast College	Costa Mesa	C,T	St-L	M/W	24,350	56	34		Y			Y	Y	Y	Y	N	14	102
Palo Verde College	Blythe	C,T	St-L	M/W	3,648	88			Y		R	Y	Y	Y	Y	N		30
Pasadena City College	Pasadena	C,T	St-L	M/W	29,189	42			Y							N	11	105
Pima Medical Institute	Chula Vista	T	Prop	M/W	447													
Platt College San Diego*	San Diego	C,T,B	Prop	M/W	253		70	90	N	Y	Y					N		9
Professional Golfers Career College	Temecula	T	Ind	PM	318													
Riverside Community College District	Riverside	T	St-L	M/W	30,390	71	40		Y			Y	Y	Y	Y	N	16	22
Saddleback College	Mission Viejo	C	St-L	M/W	18,351	52	60		Y			Y	Y	Y	Y	N	12	84
The Salvation Army College for Officer Training at Crestmont	Rancho Palos Verdes	C,T	I-R	M/W	27	100			N	Y	Y					Y		1
San Diego City College	San Diego	C	St-L	M/W	14,591	63			Y			S	Y	Y	Y	N	16	68
San Diego Mesa College	San Diego	C	St-L	M/W	21,198	51			Y				Y	Y	Y	N	19	55
San Diego Miramar College	San Diego	C	St-L	M/W	8,080													
San Joaquin Delta College	Stockton	C,T	Dist	M/W	18,525	40			Y			Y	Y	Y	Y	N	18	82
San Joaquin Valley College	Visalia	C,T	Ind	M/W	3,352				Y	Y	Y	Y		Y	Y	N		22
Santa Barbara City College	Santa Barbara	T	St-L	M/W	15,740	59	25		Y	Y	R	Y	Y	Y	Y	N	10	79
Santa Rosa Junior College	Santa Rosa	C,T	St-L	M/W	23,682	56			Y			Y	Y	Y	Y	N	15	83
Skyline College	San Bruno	C,T	St-L	M/W	8,147	9			Y		S	Y	Y	Y	Y	N	8	47
Solano Community College	Suisun City	C,T	St-L	M/W	12,027													
Taft College	Taft	C	St-L	M/W	7,024	92												
Ventura College	Ventura	C,T	St-L	M/W	12,096	66	47		Y	Y	Y	Y	Y	Y	Y	N	12	29
Westwood College–Long Beach†	Long Beach	T,B	Prop	M/W	265													
WyoTech	Fremont	T	Prop	PM	1,364											N		3
Yuba College	Marysville	C	St-L	M/W	10,457	48			Y	Y	Y	Y	Y	Y	Y		9	58
Colorado																		
Arapahoe Community College	Littleton	C,T	St	M/W	7,560	69			Y			Y	Y	Y	Y	N	6	47
Argosy University/Denver†	Denver	T	Prop	M/W														4
Colorado Mountain College*†	Glenwood Springs	C,T	Dist	M/W	867		23		Y	Y	Y	Y	Y	Y	Y	Y	7	24
Colorado Mountain College, Alpine Campus	Steamboat Springs	C,T	Dist	M/W	1,104		21		Y	Y	Y	Y	Y	Y	Y	Y	6	21
Colorado Mountain College, Timberline Campus	Leadville	C,T	Dist	M/W	1,305		33		Y	Y	Y	Y	Y	Y	Y	Y	6	12
Colorado Northwestern Community College*	Rangely	C,T	St	M/W	2,242	78												1
Colorado School of Healing Arts	Lakewood	T	Prop	M/W	240	38							Y					1
Colorado School of Trades	Lakewood	T	Prop	M/W	125								Y	Y				1
Community College of Aurora	Aurora	C,T	St	M/W	5,525	73												
Community College of Denver	Denver	C,T	St	M/W	8,909	77	47		Y			Y	Y	Y	Y	N	23	19
Front Range Community College	Westminster	C,T	St	M/W	14,957	66	19		Y			Y	Y	Y	Y	N		25
IntelliTec College	Grand Junction	C	Prop	M/W	486								Y	Y	Y			11
ITT Technical Institute	Thornton	T,B	Prop	M/W					N	Y	Y	Y	Y	Y	Y	N		10
Otero Junior College	La Junta	C,T	St	M/W	1,636	53	49	36	Y	Y	R	Y	Y	Y	Y	Y	5	25
Pima Medical Institute	Denver	T	Prop	M/W	724													
Trinidad State Junior College	Trinidad	C,T	St	M/W	1,831	58	59		Y	Y	Y	Y	Y	Y	Y	Y	13	46
Westwood College–Denver North†	Denver	T,B	Prop	M/W	1,423	24												
Connecticut																		
Asnuntuck Community College	Enfield	C,T	St	M/W	1,483	65	50		Y	Y	Y	Y	Y	Y	Y	N		21
Briarwood College†	Southington	C,T,B	Prop	M/W	647	40	38	7	N	Y	Y	Y	Y	Y	Y	Y	3	22
Capital Community College	Hartford	C,T	St	M/W	3,573	74	56		Y	Y	R	Y	Y	Y	Y	N		20
Gateway Community College	New Haven	C,T	St	M/W	5,739	68	53	40	Y	Y	Y	Y	Y	Y	Y	N	4	33
Goodwin College	East Hartford	C,T	Prop	M/W	1,219	89	59		Y	Y	Y	Y	Y	Y	Y	N		17
International College of Hospitality Management*†	Suffield	C,T	Prop	M/W	116		14	35	N	Y	Y	Y	Y	Y	Y	Y	3	2
Manchester Community College	Manchester	C,T	St	M/W	6,135	56	35		Y	Y	Y	Y	Y	Y	Y	N	4	31
Middlesex Community College	Middletown	C,T	St	M/W	2,286	62	64		Y	Y	Y	Y	Y	Y	Y	N		25
Naugatuck Valley Community College	Waterbury	C,T	St	M/W	5,671	61	51		Y	Y	Y	Y				N		50
Northwestern Connecticut Community College	Winsted	C,T	St	M/W	1,569	66	36	30	Y	Y	Y					N		35
Norwalk Community College	Norwalk	C,T	St	M/W	6,036	51	41		Y	Y	Y	Y	Y	Y	Y	N		32
Quinebaug Valley Community College	Danielson	C,T	St	M/W	1,714	62	60		Y		Y	R,S	Y	Y	Y	Y		18
Three Rivers Community College	Norwich	C,T	St	M/W	3,624													
Tunxis Community College	Farmington	C,T	St	M/W	3,894	62	47		Y	Y	Y			Y	Y	N		23

This chart includes the names and locations of accredited two-year colleges in the United States and U.S. territories and shows institutions' responses to the *Thomson Peterson's Annual Survey of Undergraduate Institutions.* If an institution submitted incomplete data, one or more columns opposite the institution's name is blank. An asterisk after the school name denotes a *Special Message* following the college's profile, and a dagger indicates that the institution has one or more entries in the *College Close-Ups* section. If a school does not appear, it did not report any of the information.

Y—Yes; N—No; R—Recommended; S—For Some

Name	Location	Degrees Awarded	Institutional Control	Student Body	Undergraduate Enrollment Fall 2005	Percent Attending Part-Time	Percent 25 Years of Age or Older	Percent of Grads Going on to Four-Year Colleges	Open Admissions	High School Equivalency Certificate Accepted	High School Transcript Required	Need-Based Aid Available	Part-Time Jobs Available	Job Placement Services Available	Career Counseling Services Available	College Housing Available	Number of Sports Offered	Number of Majors Offered
Delaware																		
Delaware College of Art and Design	Wilmington	C,T	Ind	M/W	194	24	13		N	Y	Y			Y	Y	Y			6
Delaware Technical & Community College, Jack F. Owens Campus	Georgetown	T	St	M/W	3,936	59	48		Y		Y	Y	Y	Y	Y	N	2		36
Delaware Technical & Community College, Stanton/Wilmington Campus	Newark	T	St	M/W	7,473	63	49		Y		Y	Y	Y	Y	Y	N	5		43
Delaware Technical & Community College, Terry Campus	Dover	T	St	M/W	2,569	66	57		Y		Y	Y	Y	Y	Y	N			25
Florida																		
Brevard Community College	Cocoa	C,T	St	M/W	14,039	63	38	42	Y	Y	Y	Y	Y	Y	Y	N	5		37
Broward Community College	Fort Lauderdale	C,T	St	M/W	32,041	69	29	39	Y	Y	S	Y	Y	Y	Y	N	8		48
Brown Mackie College–Miami†	Miami	T	Prop	M/W	136						Y								6
Central Florida Community College	Ocala	C,T	St-L	M/W	5,978	59	41	33	Y	Y	Y	Y	Y	Y	Y	N	4		19
Chipola College	Marianna	C,T,B	St	M/W	2,249	54													
College of Business and Technology	Miami	C	Prop	M/W	250		70		Y		Y			Y	Y				7
Daytona Beach Community College	Daytona Beach	C,T	St	M/W	11,945	60													
Florida Community College at Jacksonville	Jacksonville	C,T	St	M/W	29,831	75	47	81	Y	Y	Y		Y	Y	Y	N	11		90
Florida Hospital College of Health Sciences	Orlando	T,B	Ind	M/W	1,403	57													
Florida Keys Community College	Key West	C,T	St	M/W	1,551														
Florida National College	Hialeah	C,T	Prop	M/W	1,871	8	60		Y	Y	Y	Y	Y	Y	Y	N			34
Florida Technical College	DeLand	C,T	Prop	M/W	260														7
Full Sail Real World Education†	Winter Park	T,B	Prop	PM	5,219		12		Y	Y	Y	Y	Y	Y	Y	N			7
Gulf Coast Community College	Panama City	C,T	St	M/W	6,058	63													
Hillsborough Community College	Tampa	C,T	St	M/W	22,149	68													
Indian River Community College	Fort Pierce	C,T	St	M/W	38,464														
ITT Technical Institute	Fort Lauderdale	T,B	Prop	M/W					N	Y	Y	Y	Y	Y	Y	N			10
ITT Technical Institute	Jacksonville	T,B	Prop	M/W					N	Y	Y	Y	Y	Y	Y	N			11
ITT Technical Institute	Lake Mary	T,B	Prop	M/W					N	Y	Y	Y	Y	Y	Y	N			11
ITT Technical Institute	Miami	T,B	Prop	M/W					N	Y	Y	Y	Y	Y	Y	N			11
ITT Technical Institute	Tampa	T,B	Prop	M/W					N	Y	Y	Y	Y	Y	Y	N			11
Keiser College	Fort Lauderdale	C,T,B	Prop	M/W	6,121	18													9
Keiser College	Miami	C,T,B	Prop	M/W	739		55	12						Y			N		9
Keiser College	Pembroke Pines	C,T,B	Prop	M/W															
Keiser College	Port St. Lucie	C,T	Prop	M/W															
Keiser College	West Palm Beach	C,T,B	Prop	M/W															
Lake City Community College	Lake City	C,T	St	M/W	2,736	60	52		Y	Y	S	Y	Y	Y	Y	Y	9		19
Lake-Sumter Community College	Leesburg	C,T	St-L	M/W	3,409	65	39		Y	Y	Y	Y	Y	Y	Y	N	4		14
Manatee Community College	Bradenton	C,T	St	M/W	9,767	61	41		Y	Y	Y	Y	Y	Y	Y	N	5		96
Miami Dade College*†	Miami	C,T,B	St-L	M/W	54,169	65	41	78	Y	Y	Y	Y	Y	Y	Y	N	10		136
Okaloosa-Walton College	Niceville	C,T,B	St-L	M/W	8,728		49		Y		Y	Y	Y	Y	Y	N	4		55
Palm Beach Community College	Lake Worth	C,T	St	M/W	22,666	69	37	90	Y		Y	Y	Y	Y	Y	N	9		67
Pasco-Hernando Community College	New Port Richey	C,T	St	M/W	7,346	64	42		Y	Y	Y	Y	Y	Y	Y	N	5		19
Polk Community College	Winter Haven	C,T	St	M/W	7,082	71	38		Y	Y	Y	Y	Y	Y	Y	N	5		21
Remington College–Tampa Campus	Tampa	C,B	Prop	M/W	685		32		Y	Y	Y	Y	Y	Y	Y				6
St. Petersburg College	St. Petersburg	C,T,B	St-L	M/W	24,102	67	46		Y	Y	Y	Y	Y	Y	Y	N	5		66
Santa Fe Community College	Gainesville	C,T	St-L	M/W	13,806	52													
Seminole Community College	Sanford	C,T	St-L	M/W	11,682	65	45		Y	Y	Y	Y	Y	Y	Y	N	6		50
South University	West Palm Beach	T,B,M	Prop	M/W	502	31	38	3	N	Y	Y	Y	Y	Y	Y	Y			15
Southwest Florida College	Fort Myers	T,B	Ind	M/W	1,263				Y	Y	R	Y	Y	Y	Y	N			7
Valencia Community College	Orlando	C,T	St	M/W	29,342		31	75	Y	Y	Y	Y	Y	Y	Y	Y			41
Georgia																		
Abraham Baldwin Agricultural College	Tifton	C,T	St	M/W	3,423	35	29		Y	Y	Y			Y	Y	Y	9		57
Albany Technical College	Albany	T	St	M/W	2,787	50			Y		Y			Y	Y	N			17
Altamaha Technical College	Jesup	T	St	M/W	859	60			Y		Y					N			9
Andrew College†	Cuthbert	C	I-R	M/W	331	1													
Appalachian Technical College	Jasper	T	St	M/W	1,047	60			Y		Y								9
Athens Technical College	Athens	T	St	M/W	3,805	62	40		Y		Y	Y	Y	Y	Y	N			28
Atlanta Metropolitan College	Atlanta	C,T	St	M/W	1,748	51	43		N	Y	Y			Y	Y	N	2		32
Atlanta Technical College	Atlanta	T	St	M/W	3,523	56			Y		Y					N			11
Augusta Technical College	Augusta	T	St	M/W	4,171	52	49		Y		Y	Y	Y	Y	Y	N			24
Bainbridge College	Bainbridge	C,T	St	M/W	2,475		47	30	Y	S	Y	Y	Y	Y	Y	N	2		34
Brown Mackie College–Atlanta†	Norcross	T	Prop	M/W	150					Y	Y								5
Central Georgia Technical College	Macon	T	St	M/W	6,047	49	59		Y		Y	Y	Y	Y	Y	N			28
Chattahoochee Technical College	Marietta	T	St	M/W	6,243	64	52		Y		Y	Y	Y	Y	Y	N			23
Coastal Georgia Community College	Brunswick	C,T	St	M/W	3,062	67	50			Y	Y	Y	Y	Y	Y	N	6		35
Columbus Technical College	Columbus	T	St	M/W	3,530	56			Y		Y	Y	Y	Y	Y	N			24
Coosa Valley Technical College	Rome	T	St	M/W	2,893	58			Y		Y					N			13
Darton College	Albany	C,T	St	M/W	4,126	54													
DeKalb Technical College	Clarkston	T	St	M/W	4,083	62	64		Y		Y	Y	Y	Y	Y	N			28

This chart includes the names and locations of accredited two-year colleges in the United States and U.S. territories and shows institutions' responses to the *Thomson Peterson's Annual Survey of Undergraduate Institutions.* If an institution submitted incomplete data, one or more columns opposite the institution's name is blank. An asterisk after the school name denotes a *Special Message* following the college's profile, and a dagger indicates that the institution has one or more entries in the *College Close-Ups* section. If a school does not appear, it did not report any of the information.

Y—Yes; N—No; R—Recommended; S—For Some

Name	Location	Degrees Awarded	Institutional Control	Student Body	Undergraduate Enrollment Fall 2005	Percent Attending Part-Time	Percent 25 Years of Age or Older	Percent of Grads Going on to Four-Year Colleges	Open Admissions	High School Equivalency Certificate Accepted	High School Transcript Required	Need-Based Aid Available	Part-Time Jobs Available	Job Placement Services Available	Career Counseling Services Available	College Housing Available	Number of Sports Offered	Number of Majors Offered
East Central Technical College	Fitzgerald	T	St	M/W	1,238	55				Y		Y					N		5
Flint River Technical College	Thomaston	T	St	M/W	805	47				Y		Y					N		11
Gainesville College	Oakwood	C,T,B	St	M/W	5,985	41	11	80	N	Y	Y	Y	Y	Y	Y	Y	N	10	35
Georgia Aviation & Technical College	Eastman	T	St	M/W	252	37				Y		Y					N		3
Georgia Highlands College	Rome	C,T	St	M/W	3,817	46	35		N	Y	Y	Y	Y	Y			N	12	40
Gordon College	Barnesville	C,T	St	M/W	3,449	33													
Griffin Technical College	Griffin	T	St	M/W	3,407	56	49			Y		Y	Y		Y	Y	N		23
Gwinnett Technical College	Lawrenceville	T	St	M/W	4,204	62	80			Y		Y	Y	Y			N		27
Heart of Georgia Technical College	Dublin	T	St	M/W	1,755	67				Y		Y					N		9
Herzing College	Atlanta	T,B	Prop	M/W	276		56		N	Y	Y	Y					N		6
Interactive College of Technology	Chamblee	T	Prop	M/W	1,069	1	56		Y	Y	Y				Y	Y			6
ITT Technical Institute	Duluth	T,B	Prop	M/W					N	Y	Y	Y		Y	Y	Y	N		9
ITT Technical Institute	Kennesaw	T,B		M/W							Y								6
Lanier Technical College	Oakwood	T	St	M/W	3,196	61				Y		Y					N		22
Middle Georgia College*	Cochran	C,T	St	M/W	2,677	32	26		N	Y	Y	Y	Y	Y	Y	Y	Y	9	15
Middle Georgia Technical College	Warner Robbins	T	St	M/W	2,351	54				Y		Y	Y	Y			N		11
Moultrie Technical College	Moultrie	T	St	M/W	1,951	57				Y		Y					N		10
North Georgia Technical College	Clarkesville	T	St	M/W	1,812	46				Y		Y					Y		11
North Metro Technical College	Acworth	T	St	M/W	1,903	58				Y		Y					N		10
Northwestern Technical College	Rock Springs	T	St	M/W	2,303	61	60			Y		Y	Y		Y	Y	N		17
Ogeechee Technical College	Statesboro	T	St	M/W	1,950	48	39			Y		Y					N		24
Okefenokee Technical College	Waycross	T	St	M/W	1,731	66				Y		Y					N		11
Sandersville Technical College	Sandersville	T	St	M/W	765	69				Y		Y					N		5
Savannah Technical College	Savannah	T	St	M/W	3,786	58	59			Y		Y	Y	Y		Y	N		16
Southeastern Technical College	Vidalia	T	St	M/W	982	54				Y		Y					N		14
South Georgia Technical College	Americus	T	St	M/W	1,669	47				Y		Y					Y	1	15
Southwest Georgia Technical College	Thomasville	T	St	M/W	1,491	61	74			Y		Y	Y	Y	Y	Y	N		12
Swainsboro Technical College	Swainsboro	T	St	M/W	684	58				Y		Y					N		10
Truett-McConnell College	Cleveland	C,T,B	I-R	M/W	375	9	4		N	Y	Y	Y	Y	Y			Y	9	7
Valdosta Technical College	Valdosta	T	St	M/W	2,444	59	29			Y		Y			Y	Y	N		16
West Central Technical College	Waco	T	St	M/W	2,888	70	13			Y		Y	Y	Y	Y	Y	N		21
West Georgia Technical College	LaGrange	T	St	M/W	1,858	55	60			Y		Y	Y	Y			N		17
Westwood College–Atlanta Northlake†	Atlanta	C,T,B	Prop	M/W	220							Y							7
Young Harris College	Young Harris	C	I-R	M/W	533	5	1	93	N	Y	Y	Y	Y	Y			Y	14	36
Guam																		
Guam Community College	Barrigada	T	Terr	M/W	2,841	82	47			Y	Y	Y	Y	Y	Y		N		29
Hawaii																		
Hawaii Business College	Honolulu	C,T	Ind	M/W	303														
Hawaii Tokai International College	Honolulu	C	Ind	M/W	54		17	88	N	Y	Y	Y					Y		2
Heald College-Honolulu	Honolulu	C,T	Ind	M/W	807	27				Y	Y	Y	Y	Y	Y	Y	N		8
Kapiolani Community College	Honolulu	C,T	St	M/W	7,174	61	40			Y		Y	Y	Y	Y	Y	N	2	17
Kauai Community College	Lihue	C	St	M/W	1,210					Y		R,S	Y	Y	Y	Y	N	3	11
TransPacific Hawaii College	Honolulu	C	Ind	PW	240		0	82	Y	Y	Y				Y		N	3	1
Windward Community College	Kaneohe	C,T	St	M/W	1,761														
Idaho																		
Apollo College	Boise	C,T	Prop	M/W	469	5													
College of Southern Idaho	Twin Falls	C,T	St-L	M/W	7,105	55													
Eastern Idaho Technical College	Idaho Falls	T	St	M/W	755	70	47			Y	Y	Y	Y	Y	Y	Y	N		12
ITT Technical Institute	Boise	T,B	Prop	M/W						N	Y	Y	Y	Y	Y	Y	N		13
North Idaho College	Coeur d'Alene	C,T	St-L	M/W	4,099	39	36		N	Y	S	Y	Y	Y	Y	Y	18	68
Illinois																		
Black Hawk College	Moline	C,T	St-L	M/W	6,600	52													
Brown Mackie College–Moline†	Moline		Prop	M/W	119									Y					
Career Colleges of Chicago	Chicago	T	Prop	PW	144	76													
City Colleges of Chicago, Wilbur Wright College	Chicago	C,T	St-L	M/W	7,365		43	33	Y	Y			Y	Y	Y	Y	N	6	30
College of DuPage	Glen Ellyn	C,T	St-L	M/W	27,117	68	34	76	Y				Y	Y	Y	Y	N	16	85
College of Lake County	Grayslake	C,T	Dist	M/W	15,745	71	41		Y		S	Y	Y	Y	Y	N	9	40
Danville Area Community College	Danville	C,T	St-L	M/W	3,000														
Elgin Community College	Elgin	C,T	St-L'	M/W	10,851	69													
Fox College	Oak Lawn		Prop	M/W	251														
Heartland Community College	Normal	C,T	St-L	M/W	4,667		38	94	Y	Y	R	Y	Y	Y	Y	N		37
Highland Community College	Freeport	C,T	St-L	M/W	2,406	53	58	80	Y	Y	S	Y	Y	Y	Y	N	6	43
Illinois Central College	East Peoria	C,T	St-L	M/W	12,343		55	89	Y	Y	Y	Y	Y	Y	Y	Y	8	37
Illinois Eastern Community Colleges, Frontier Community College	Fairfield	C,T	St-L	M/W	2,164	88	56			Y	Y	Y	Y	Y	Y	Y	N		8
Illinois Eastern Community Colleges, Lincoln Trail College	Robinson	C,T	St-L	M/W	1,532	67	54			Y	Y	Y	Y	Y	Y	Y	N	4	14

This chart includes the names and locations of accredited two-year colleges in the United States and U.S. territories and shows institutions' responses to the *Thomson Peterson's Annual Survey of Undergraduate Institutions*. If an institution submitted incomplete data, one or more columns opposite the institution's name is blank. An asterisk after the school name denotes a *Special Message* following the college's profile, and a dagger indicates that the institution has one or more entries in the *College Close-Ups* section. If a school does not appear, it did not report any of the information.

Y—Yes; N—No; R—Recommended; S—For Some

Institution	Location	Degrees Awarded	Institutional Control	Student Body	Undergraduate Enrollment Fall 2005	Percent Attending Part-Time	Percent 25 Years of Age or Older	Percent of Grads Going on to Four-Year Colleges	High School Equivalency Certificate Accepted	High School Transcript Required	Open Admissions	Need-Based Aid Available	Part-Time Jobs Available	Job Placement Services Available	Career Counseling Available	College Housing Available	Number of Sports Offered	Number of Majors Offered
Illinois Eastern Community Colleges, Olney Central College	Olney	C,T	St-L	M/W	1,701	55	64		Y	Y	Y	Y	Y	Y	Y	N	4	19
Illinois Eastern Community Colleges, Wabash Valley College	Mount Carmel	C,T	St-L	M/W	3,155	80	53		Y	Y	Y	Y	Y	Y	Y	N	6	20
Illinois Valley Community College	Oglesby	C,T	Dist	M/W	4,315		6		Y		Y	Y	Y	Y	Y	N	4	26
ITT Technical Institute	Burr Ridge	T,B	Prop	M/W					N	Y	Y	Y	Y	Y	Y	N		7
ITT Technical Institute	Matteson	T,B	Prop	M/W					N	Y	Y	Y	Y	Y	Y	N		7
ITT Technical Institute	Mount Prospect	T,B	Prop	M/W					N	Y	Y	Y	Y	Y	Y	N		7
John A. Logan College	Carterville	C	St-L	M/W	5,501													
John Wood Community College	Quincy	C,T	Dist	M/W	2,530	53	32		Y	Y	Y	Y	Y	Y	Y	N	5	35
Joliet Junior College	Joliet	C,T	St-L	M/W	13,022	62	44	77	Y		Y	Y	Y	Y	Y	Y	6	51
Kaskaskia College	Centralia	C,T	St-L	M/W	4,742	60	42		Y	Y	Y	Y	Y	Y		N	6	21
Lake Land College	Mattoon	C,T	St-L	M/W	7,038		36		Y		R	Y	Y	Y	Y	N	8	37
Lewis and Clark Community College	Godfrey	C,T	Dist	M/W	7,446													
Lincoln College†	Lincoln	C	Ind	M/W	758	8	3	89	N	Y	Y	Y	Y	Y	Y	Y	17	72
Lincoln College–Normal†	Normal	C,T,B	Ind	M/W	520	33	8	89	N	Y	Y	Y	Y	Y	Y	Y	13	31
Lincoln Land Community College	Springfield	C,T	Dist	M/W	6,847	61	39		Y		R	Y	Y	Y	Y	N	6	29
Moraine Valley Community College	Palos Hills	C,T	St-L	M/W	15,929	58	36	85	Y		Y	Y	Y	Y	Y	N	9	28
Morrison Institute of Technology†	Morrison	C,T	Ind	PM	126		8	20	Y	Y	Y	Y	Y	Y	Y	Y	5	6
Parkland College	Champaign	C,T	Dist	M/W	9,752	53	31		Y	Y	R	Y	Y	Y	Y	N	7	60
Prairie State College	Chicago Heights	C,T	St-L	M/W	5,083	66	50		Y		Y	Y	Y	Y	Y	N	9	24
Richland Community College	Decatur	C,T	Dist	M/W	3,034		40	37	Y	Y	Y	Y	Y	Y	Y	N		27
Rock Valley College	Rockford	C,T	Dist	M/W	8,145	57	43		Y		Y	Y	Y	Y	Y	N	8	22
Sauk Valley Community College	Dixon	C,T	Dist	M/W	2,745	58	50		Y		R	Y	Y	Y	Y	N	5	52
Shawnee Community College	Ullin	C,T	St-L	M/W	3,191	70												
Southwestern Illinois College	Belleville	C,T	Dist	M/W	14,479	63	45		Y	Y	Y	Y	Y	Y	Y	N	7	43
Spoon River College	Canton	C,T	St	M/W	2,333		36		Y	Y	Y	Y	Y	Y		N	5	41
Springfield College in Illinois	Springfield	C	I-R	M/W	552	51	6	86	N	Y	Y	Y				Y	7	16
Triton College	River Grove	C,T	St	M/W	11,021	65	45		Y	Y	Y	Y	Y	Y	Y	N	7	66
Waubonsee Community College	Sugar Grove	C,T	Dist	M/W	8,834	70	21	85	Y			Y	Y			N	11	46
William Rainey Harper College	Palatine	C,T	St-L	M/W	15,026	59	32	67	Y	Y	Y	Y	Y	Y	Y	N	15	70
Indiana																		
Ancilla College	Donaldson	C,T	I-R	M/W	624	36	40	59	Y	Y	Y	Y	Y	Y	Y	N	4	34
Aviation Institute of Maintenance–Indianapolis	Indianapolis		Prop															
Brown Mackie College–Fort Wayne†	Fort Wayne	T	Prop	M/W	706				Y	Y	Y	Y	Y					7
Brown Mackie College–Merrillville†	Merrillville	T	Prop	M/W	585		40		Y	Y	Y	Y	Y	Y	Y	N		9
Brown Mackie College–Michigan City†	Michigan City	C,T	Prop	M/W	461		44		N	Y	Y	Y	Y	Y	Y	N		7
Brown Mackie College–South Bend†	South Bend	C,T	Prop	PW	619		65		N	Y	Y	Y		Y	Y	N		5
Davenport University	Granger	C,T,B	Ind	M/W														
Davenport University	Hammond	C,T	Ind	M/W														
Davenport University	Merrillville	C,T,B	Ind	M/W														
Holy Cross College	Notre Dame	C,B	I-R	M/W	369	11	2	85	N	Y	Y	Y	Y	Y		Y	14	1
Indiana Business College	Anderson	T	Prop	M/W	235				N	Y	Y			Y	Y			9
Indiana Business College	Columbus	T	Prop	M/W	273				N		Y	Y	Y	Y	Y			8
Indiana Business College	Evansville	T	Prop	M/W	295				N		Y	Y	Y	Y	Y			7
Indiana Business College	Fort Wayne	T	Prop	M/W	384				N	Y	Y	Y	Y	Y	Y			6
Indiana Business College†	Indianapolis	T	Prop	M/W	782				N	Y	Y	Y	Y	Y	Y	N		14
Indiana Business College	Indianapolis	T	Prop	M/W	584					Y								6
Indiana Business College	Indianapolis	T	Prop	M/W	86					Y								7
Indiana Business College	Lafayette	T	Prop	M/W	215				N	Y		Y		Y	Y			9
Indiana Business College	Marion	T	Prop	M/W	120				N	Y	Y			Y	Y			5
Indiana Business College	Muncie	T	Prop	M/W	310			0	N	Y	Y		Y	Y	Y	N		11
Indiana Business College	Terre Haute	T	Prop	M/W	220				N	Y	Y			Y	Y			8
Indiana Business College-Medical	Indianapolis	T	Prop	M/W	584				N	Y				Y	Y			6
International Business College	Indianapolis	T	Prop	M/W	289		1		Y	Y	Y	Y		Y	Y	Y		10
ITT Technical Institute	Fort Wayne	T,B	Prop	M/W					N	Y	Y	Y	Y	Y	Y	N		13
ITT Technical Institute	Indianapolis	T,B	Prop	M/W					N	Y	Y	Y	Y	Y	Y	N		16
ITT Technical Institute	Newburgh	T,B	Prop	M/W					N	Y	Y	Y	Y	Y	Y	N		14
Ivy Tech Community College–Bloomington	Bloomington	C,T	St	M/W	3,565	54	47		Y		Y	Y	Y	Y	Y			23
Ivy Tech Community College–Central Indiana	Indianapolis	C,T	St	M/W	11,590	69	57		Y		Y	Y	Y	Y	Y	N	6	38
Ivy Tech Community College–Columbus	Columbus	C,T	St	M/W	2,216	65	58		Y		Y	Y	Y	Y	Y	N		28
Ivy Tech Community College–East Central	Muncie	C,T	St	M/W	5,943	57	57		Y		Y	Y	Y	Y	Y	N		38
Ivy Tech Community College–Kokomo	Kokomo	C,T	St	M/W	3,248	68	59		Y		Y	Y	Y	Y	Y	N		31
Ivy Tech Community College–Lafayette	Lafayette	C,T	St	M/W	5,970	60	50		Y		Y	Y	Y	Y	Y	N		37
Ivy Tech Community College–North Central	South Bend	C,T	St	M/W	5,228	77	61		Y		Y	Y	Y	Y	Y	N		42
Ivy Tech Community College–Northeast	Fort Wayne	C,T	St	M/W	6,082	65	60		Y		Y	Y	Y	Y	Y	N		39
Ivy Tech Community College–Northwest	Gary	C,T	St	M/W	4,815	71	64		Y		Y	Y	Y	Y	Y	N		40
Ivy Tech Community College–Southeast	Madison	C,T	St	M/W	1,766	64	56		Y		Y	Y	Y	Y	Y	N		14
Ivy Tech Community College–Southern Indiana	Sellersburg	C,T	St	M/W	3,112	71	61		Y		Y	Y	Y	Y	Y	N		28
Ivy Tech Community College–Southwest	Evansville	C,T	St	M/W	4,858	69	51		Y		Y	Y	Y	Y	Y	N		38
Ivy Tech Community College–Wabash Valley	Terre Haute	C,T	St	M/W	4,992	57	55		Y		Y	Y	Y	Y	Y	N	2	40

This chart includes the names and locations of accredited two-year colleges in the United States and U.S. territories and shows institutions' responses to the *Thomson Peterson's Annual Survey of Undergraduate Institutions*. If an institution submitted incomplete data, one or more columns opposite the institution's name is blank.
An asterisk after the school name denotes a *Special Message* following the college's profile, and a dagger indicates that the institution has one or more entries in the *College Close-Ups* section. If a school does not appear, it did not report any of the information.

Y—Yes; N—No; R—Recommended; S—For Some

Institution	Location	Degrees Awarded	Institutional Control	Student Body	Undergrad Enrollment Fall 2005	Percent Attending Part-Time	Percent 25 Years of Age or Older	Percent of Grads Going on to Four-Year Colleges	High School Equivalency Certificate Accepted	Open Admissions	High School Transcript Required	Need-Based Aid Required	Part-Time Jobs Available	Career Counseling Available	Job Placement Services Available	College Housing Available	Number of Sports Offered	Number of Majors Offered
Ivy Tech Community College–Whitewater	Richmond	C,T	St	M/W	1,832	69	62		Y		Y	Y	Y	Y	Y	N	1	26
Iowa																		
Clinton Community College	Clinton	C,T	St-L	M/W	1,298	55												
Des Moines Area Community College	Ankeny	C,T	St-L	M/W	13,719	56												
Ellsworth Community College	Iowa Falls	C,T	St-L	M/W	930													
Hamilton College	Cedar Falls	C,T,B			695	22								Y				12
Hamilton College	Cedar Rapids	C,T,B	Prop	M/W	511	14	47		N	Y	Y	Y	Y	Y	Y	N		8
Hawkeye Community College	Waterloo	C,T	St-L	M/W	5,272	48	27	62	Y	Y	Y	Y	Y	Y	Y	N	5	55
Indian Hills Community College	Ottumwa	C,T	St-L	M/W	2,867	29												
Iowa Central Community College	Fort Dodge	C,T	St-L	M/W	4,567													
Iowa Lakes Community College	Estherville	C,T	St-L	M/W	2,993	54												
Iowa Western Community College	Council Bluffs	C,T	Dist	M/W	4,299													
Muscatine Community College	Muscatine	C,T	St	M/W	1,280	57												
Northeast Iowa Community College	Calmar	C,T	St-L	M/W	4,833	56	36		Y	Y	R	Y	Y	Y	Y	N	9	13
North Iowa Area Community College	Mason City	C,T	St-L	M/W	3,133	46	22	70	Y	Y	Y	Y	Y	Y	Y	Y	15	29
St. Luke's College	Sioux City	T	Ind	M/W	155	17	45	61	N	Y	Y	Y	Y			Y		3
Scott Community College	Bettendorf	C,T	St-L	M/W	4,697	53												
Southwestern Community College	Creston	C,T	St	M/W	1,254	47												
Vatterott College	Des Moines	T,B	Prop	M/W										Y				5
Western Iowa Tech Community College	Sioux City	C,T	St	M/W	5,334	61	30		Y	Y	Y	Y	Y	Y	Y	Y	8	26
Kansas																		
Allen County Community College	Iola	C,T	St-L	M/W	2,256	63	35	60	Y	Y	Y	Y	Y	Y	Y		11	69
Barton County Community College	Great Bend	C,T	St-L	M/W	3,821	75	47		Y	Y	R	Y	Y	Y	Y	Y	14	84
Brown Mackie College–Kansas City†	Lenexa	T	Prop	M/W	370		60		Y	Y	Y	Y	Y	Y	Y	N		16
Brown Mackie College–Salina†	Salina	C,T	Prop	M/W	367		38	27	Y	Y	Y	Y	Y	Y	Y	N	3	7
Butler Community College	El Dorado	C,T	St-L	M/W	8,863	59	42	95	Y	Y	Y	Y	Y	Y	Y	Y	12	41
Cloud County Community College	Concordia	C,T	St-L	M/W	3,521													
Coffeyville Community College	Coffeyville	C,T	St-L	M/W	1,766	62												
Colby Community College*	Colby	C,T	St-L	M/W	1,784		22	60	Y	Y	Y	Y	Y	Y	Y	Y	10	58
Cowley County Community College and Area Vocational–Technical School	Arkansas City	C,T	St-L	M/W	4,679	49	19		Y	Y	Y	Y	Y	Y		Y	8	42
Dodge City Community College	Dodge City	C,T	St-L	M/W	1,956													
Fort Scott Community College	Fort Scott	C,T	St-L	M/W	1,923													
Garden City Community College	Garden City	C,T	Cou	M/W	2,174	57												
Hesston College	Hesston	C,T	I-R	M/W	477	13	50		Y	Y	Y	Y	Y	Y	Y	Y	7	8
Highland Community College	Highland	C,T	St-L	M/W	3,040													
Hutchinson Community College and Area Vocational School	Hutchinson	C,T	St-L	M/W	4,869	60	32	70	Y	Y	R	Y	Y	Y	Y	Y	14	40
Independence Community College	Independence	C,T	St	M/W	906	47	44		Y	Y	Y	Y	Y	Y	Y	Y	8	40
Johnson County Community College	Overland Park	C,T	St-L	M/W	18,612	66												
Kansas City Kansas Community College	Kansas City	C,T	St-L	M/W	5,419	64	49		Y	Y	Y	Y	Y	Y		N	8	22
Manhattan Area Technical College	Manhattan	T	St-L	M/W	401	19	32				Y	R,S			Y	N		12
Northeast Kansas Technical College	Atchison		St	M/W														
Pratt Community College	Pratt	C,T	St-L	M/W	1,546	60				Y	Y	Y	Y	Y		Y	10	63
Seward County Community College	Liberal	C,T	St-L	M/W	2,325													
Wichita Area Technical College	Wichita	C,T	Dist	M/W	1,044	70								S				4
Kentucky																		
Ashland Community and Technical College	Ashland	C,T	St	M/W	2,565													
Big Sandy Community and Technical College	Prestonsburg	C,T	St	M/W	4,406													
Bowling Green Technical College	Bowling Green		St	M/W														
Brown Mackie College–Hopkinsville†	Hopkinsville	C	Prop	PW	146									Y	Y	Y		8
Brown Mackie College–Louisville†	Louisville	T	Prop	M/W	315		63		N	Y	Y	Y	Y	Y	Y	N		11
Brown Mackie College–Northern Kentucky†	Fort Mitchell	C,T	Prop	M/W	465		59		Y	Y			Y	Y	Y	N		10
Elizabethtown Community and Technical College	Elizabethtown	C,T	St	M/W	3,615	54												
Gateway Community and Technical College	Covington	C	St	M/W	2,597													
Hazard Community and Technical College	Hazard	C,T	St	M/W	3,500													
Henderson Community College	Henderson	C,T	St	M/W	2,241													
Hopkinsville Community College	Hopkinsville	C,T	St	M/W	3,104	54												
ITT Technical Institute	Louisville	T,B	Prop	M/W					N	Y	Y	Y	Y	Y	Y	N		11
Jefferson Community and Technical College	Louisville	C,T	St	M/W	14,240	65	41		Y				Y	Y	Y	N		18
National College of Business & Technology	Danville	T	Prop	M/W	326													
National College of Business & Technology	Florence	T	Prop	M/W	189													
National College of Business & Technology	Lexington	T	Prop	M/W	378													
National College of Business & Technology	Louisville	T	Prop	M/W	678													
National College of Business & Technology	Pikeville	T	Prop	M/W	219													
National College of Business & Technology	Richmond	T	Prop	M/W	363													
Owensboro Community and Technical College	Owensboro	C,T	St	M/W	3,664	50												
Somerset Community College	Somerset	C,T	St	M/W	5,850													

This chart includes the names and locations of accredited two-year colleges in the United States and U.S. territories and shows institutions' responses to the *Thomson Peterson's Annual Survey of Undergraduate Institutions*. If an institution submitted incomplete data, one or more columns opposite the institution's name is blank.
An asterisk after the school name denotes a *Special Message* following the college's profile, and a dagger indicates that the institution has one or more entries in the *College Close-Ups* section. If a school does not appear, it did not report any of the information.

Y—Yes; N—No; R—Recommended; S—For Some

Name	Location	Degrees Awarded	Institutional Control	Student Body	Undergraduate Enrollment Fall 2005	Percent Attending Part-Time	Percent 25 Years of Age or Older	Percent of Grads Going on to Four-Year Colleges	High School Equivalency Certificate Accepted	High School Transcript Required	Open Admissions	Need-Based Aid Available	Part-Time Jobs Available	Career Counseling Available	Job Placement Services Available	College Housing Available	Number of Sports Available	Number of Majors Offered
Southeast Kentucky Community and Technical College	Cumberland	C,T	St	M/W	4,519													
Spencerian College	Louisville	C,T	Prop	M/W	1,326													
Spencerian College–Lexington	Lexington	T	Prop	M/W	376													
West Kentucky Community and Technical College	Paducah	C,T	St	M/W	3,545													
Louisiana																		
Baton Rouge Community College	Baton Rouge	C,T	St	M/W	5,761													
Bossier Parish Community College	Bossier City	C,T	St	M/W	4,121													
Delgado Community College	New Orleans	C,T	St	M/W	16,501	55	42		Y	Y	R,S	Y	Y	Y	Y	N	8	44
ITI Technical College	Baton Rouge	T	Prop	M/W	351	36					Y							6
ITT Technical Institute	St. Rose	T,B	Prop	M/W	541				N	Y	Y	Y	Y	Y	Y	N		11
Louisiana State University at Alexandria	Alexandria	C,T,B	St	M/W	2,988	47	41		Y	Y	Y	Y	Y	Y	Y	N	4	20
Louisiana Technical College	Baton Rouge	C	St	M/W	13,414	46								Y		N		28
Remington College–Lafayette Campus	Lafayette	T	Prop	M/W	367		40		N	Y	Y	Y	Y		Y	N		11
River Parishes Community College	Sorrento	C	St	M/W	724													
Maine																		
Andover College*	Portland	T	Prop	M/W	502													
Beal College	Bangor	T	Prop	M/W	373	36	54		Y	Y	Y	Y		Y	Y	N		10
Central Maine Medical Center School of Nursing	Lewiston	T	Ind	PW	114	81												
Eastern Maine Community College	Bangor	C,T	St	M/W	1,790	58												
Kennebec Valley Community College	Fairfield	C,T	St	M/W	1,782	71	66		Y	Y	Y	Y	Y	Y	Y	N	4	36
Northern Maine Community College	Presque Isle	C,T	St-R	M/W	921	34	45		Y	Y	Y	Y	Y	Y	Y	Y	13	20
Southern Maine Community College	South Portland	C,T	St	M/W	4,103	48												
Maryland																		
Allegany College of Maryland	Cumberland	C,T	St-L	M/W	3,666	43	35	80	Y	Y	Y	Y	Y	Y	Y	N	6	26
Anne Arundel Community College	Arnold	C,T	St-L	M/W	14,290	67												
Baltimore City Community College	Baltimore	C,T	St	M/W	7,095													
Baltimore International College†	Baltimore	C,T,B,M	Ind	M/W	516	6	24		N	Y	Y	Y	Y	Y	Y	Y		4
Carroll Community College	Westminster	C,T	St-L	M/W	3,115	57	31		Y			Y	Y	Y	Y	N		15
Cecil Community College	North East	C	Cou	M/W	1,916	64	31		Y	Y	Y	Y	Y	Y		N	6	34
College of Southern Maryland	La Plata	C,T	St-L	M/W	7,546	66	37		Y			R		Y	Y	N	7	28
The Community College of Baltimore County	Baltimore	C,T	Cou	M/W	19,622	64												
Frederick Community College	Frederick	C,T	St-L	M/W	4,822	62	60		Y			Y	Y	Y	Y	N	6	44
Garrett College	McHenry	C,T	St-L	M/W	613	41												
Hagerstown Business College	Hagerstown	T	Prop	M/W	932		55		Y	Y		Y		Y	Y	Y		13
Hagerstown Community College	Hagerstown	C,T	St-L	M/W	3,521	66	37		Y			S	Y	Y	Y	N	12	24
Harford Community College	Bel Air	C,T	St-L	M/W	5,492	61												
Howard Community College	Columbia	C,T	St-L	M/W	6,842	43		76	Y			S	Y	Y	Y	N	9	55
ITT Technical Institute	Owings Mills	T,B		M/W											Y			9
TESST College of Technology	Towson	T	Prop	M/W											Y			11
Wor-Wic Community College	Salisbury	C,T	St-L	M/W	3,043	68	47		Y			R		Y	Y	N		17
Massachusetts																		
Bay State College†	Boston	C,T,B	Ind	M/W	757		12		N	Y		Y	Y	Y	Y	Y		18
Benjamin Franklin Institute of Technology†	Boston	C,T,B	Ind	PM	386	10	38		Y	Y	Y		Y	Y	Y	N	2	11
Berkshire Community College	Pittsfield	C,T	St	M/W	2,328	60	40	47	Y	Y		Y	Y	Y		N		28
Bristol Community College	Fall River	C,T	St	M/W	6,873	55	35	43	Y	Y	Y	Y	Y	Y		N		49
Bunker Hill Community College†	Boston	C,T	St	M/W	7,837	70	52	35	Y	Y	Y	Y	Y	Y	Y	N	7	40
Cape Cod Community College	West Barnstable	C,T	St	M/W	4,243	65												
Dean College	Franklin	C,T,B	Ind	M/W	1,249	26	3	90	N	Y		Y	Y	Y	Y	Y	11	12
Fisher College	Boston	C,T,B	Ind	M/W	507	47	50		N	Y		Y	Y	Y	Y	Y	3	11
Greenfield Community College	Greenfield	C,T	St	M/W	2,217	55	46		Y	Y	S	Y	Y		Y	N		29
Holyoke Community College	Holyoke	C,T	St	M/W	6,258	51	31		Y	Y	Y	Y	Y	Y	Y	N	8	40
ITT Technical Institute	Norwood	T	Prop	M/W					N	Y		Y	Y	Y	Y	N		6
ITT Technical Institute	Woburn	T	Prop	M/W					Y	Y		Y	Y	Y		N		6
Massachusetts Bay Community College†	Wellesley Hills	C,T	St	M/W	5,015	57	42		Y	Y			Y	Y	Y	N	9	30
Mount Wachusett Community College*	Gardner	C,T	St	M/W	4,170	53	42	61	Y	Y	Y	Y	Y	Y		N		35
New England College of Finance	Boston	T	Ind	PW	412	22	50		Y	Y	Y					N		6
Northern Essex Community College*	Haverhill	C,T	St	M/W	6,362	51	40		Y	Y	Y	Y	Y	Y		N	10	59
North Shore Community College	Danvers	C,T	St	M/W	6,604	58	45	57	Y	Y	S	Y	Y	Y		N		42
Quinsigamond Community College	Worcester	C,T	St	M/W	5,970	54	45	40	Y	Y	Y	Y	Y	Y		N	11	27
Springfield Technical Community College	Springfield	C,T	St	M/W	5,823	54	42		Y	Y	Y	Y	Y	Y		N	9	57
Michigan																		
Alpena Community College	Alpena	C,T	St-L	M/W	1,937	49												
Bay de Noc Community College	Escanaba	C,T	Cou	M/W	2,549													
Bay Mills Community College	Brimley	C	Dist	M/W	489													
Davenport University	Alma	C,T,B	Ind	M/W														

This chart includes the names and locations of accredited two-year colleges in the United States and U.S. territories and shows institutions' responses to the *Thomson Peterson's Annual Survey of Undergraduate Institutions*. If an institution submitted incomplete data, one or more columns opposite the institution's name is blank.
An asterisk after the school name denotes a *Special Message* following the college's profile, and a dagger indicates that the institution has one or more entries in the *College Close-Ups* section. If a school does not appear, it did not report any of the information.

Y—Yes; N—No; R—Recommended; S—For Some

College	City	Degrees Awarded	Institutional Control	Student Body	Undergraduate Enrollment Fall 2005	Percent Attending Part-Time	Percent 25 Years of Age or Older	Percent of Grads Going on to Four-Year Colleges	High School Equivalency Certificate Accepted	Open Admissions	High School Transcript Required	Need-Based Aid Available	Part-Time Jobs Available	Career Counseling Available	Job Placement Services Available	College Housing Available	Number of Sports Offered	Number of Majors Offered
Davenport University	Bad Axe	C,T,B	Ind	M/W														
Davenport University	Bay City	C,T,B	Ind	M/W														
Davenport University	Caro	C,T,B	Ind	M/W														
Davenport University	Midland	C,T,B	Ind	M/W														
Davenport University	Romeo	C,T,B	Ind	M/W														
Davenport University	Saginaw	C,T,B	Ind	M/W														
Delta College	University Center	C,T	Dist	M/W	10,210	61	34		Y		R	Y	Y	Y	Y	N	8	71
Glen Oaks Community College	Centreville	C,T	St-L	M/W	1,710	61												
Gogebic Community College	Ironwood	C,T	St-L	M/W	981	47												
Grand Rapids Community College	Grand Rapids	C,T	Dist	M/W	14,798	56	28	78	Y	Y	Y	Y	Y	Y	Y	N	14	30
Henry Ford Community College	Dearborn	C,T	Dist	M/W	12,123													
ITT Technical Institute	Canton	T	Prop	M/W					N	Y	Y	Y	Y	Y	Y	N		8
ITT Technical Institute	Grand Rapids	T	Prop	M/W					N	Y	Y	Y	Y	Y	Y	N		8
ITT Technical Institute	Troy	T	Prop	M/W					N	Y	Y	Y	Y	Y	Y	N		8
Jackson Community College	Jackson	C,T	Cou	M/W	5,870	64	44		Y	Y		Y	Y			N		26
Kalamazoo Valley Community College	Kalamazoo	C,T	St-L	M/W	10,634	63												
Kellogg Community College	Battle Creek	C,T	St-L	M/W	6,200	68	47		Y		S	Y	Y	Y	Y	N	5	73
Lake Michigan College	Benton Harbor	C,T	Dist	M/W	4,043	69	56		Y	Y	Y	Y	Y	Y	Y	N	4	25
Lansing Community College	Lansing	C,T	St-L	M/W	20,057	69	18		Y		S	Y	Y	Y	Y	N	9	104
Macomb Community College	Warren	C,T	Dist	M/W	20,596	63	45		Y			Y	Y	Y	Y	N	11	73
Mid Michigan Community College	Harrison	C,T	St-L	M/W	3,232	55												
Montcalm Community College	Sidney	C,T	St-L	M/W	2,080	68												
Mott Community College	Flint	C,T	Dist	M/W	10,299	64	46		Y		Y	Y	Y	Y	Y	N	6	50
Muskegon Community College	Muskegon	C,T	St-L	M/W	5,000													
Northwestern Michigan College	Traverse City	C,T	St-L	M/W	4,609	56												
Oakland Community College	Bloomfield Hills	C,T	St-L	M/W	24,287	68	47		Y		R	Y	Y	Y	Y	N	8	90
Saginaw Chippewa Tribal College	Mount Pleasant	C,T	Ind	M/W	123	65								Y				3
Schoolcraft College	Livonia	C,T	Dist	M/W	10,213	67												
Southwestern Michigan College	Dowagiac	C,T	St-L	M/W	2,676	62	40		Y	Y	Y	Y	Y	Y	Y	N	14	27
Wayne County Community College District	Detroit	C,T	St-L	M/W	11,673													
Minnesota																		
Academy College	Minneapolis	C,T,B	Prop	M/W	320													
Alexandria Technical College	Alexandria	C,T	St	M/W	1,971		23		Y	Y	Y	Y	Y	Y	Y	N	5	50
Anoka-Ramsey Community College	Coon Rapids	C,T	St	M/W	5,606													
Anoka-Ramsey Community College, Cambridge Campus	Cambridge	C,T	St	M/W	1,777													
Argosy University/Twin Cities†	Eagan	T,B,M,D	Prop	M/W	1,100		69		N	Y	Y	Y	Y	Y	Y	N		7
Brown College	Mendota Heights	C,T,B	Prop	M/W	2,054	8			N	Y	Y	Y	Y	Y	Y	N		14
Central Lakes College	Brainerd	C,T	St	M/W	2,768		33		Y	Y	Y	Y	Y	Y			9	10
Century College	White Bear Lake	C,T	St	M/W	8,553	53	33		Y		Y	Y	Y	Y		N	5	36
Globe College	Oakdale	T,B	Priv	M/W	845		48		Y	Y	Y			Y	Y			19
Herzing College	Minneapolis	T,B	Prop	PW	346	41												19
Hibbing Community College	Hibbing	C,T	St	M/W	1,176		55		Y	Y	Y	Y	Y	Y		Y	11	19
Itasca Community College	Grand Rapids	C,T	St	M/W	1,137		20	75	Y	Y	Y	Y	Y	Y		Y	9	30
ITT Technical Institute	Eden Prairie	T,B	Prop	M/W										Y				8
Lake Superior College	Duluth	C,T	St	M/W	4,200		33		Y		S	Y	Y	Y	Y	N	3	32
McNally Smith College of Music	Saint Paul	C,T,B	Prop	M/W	471	20	10		Y	Y	Y			Y	Y	N		4
Mesabi Range Community and Technical College	Virginia	C,T	St	M/W	1,371		32	80	Y	Y		Y	Y	Y	Y	Y	13	16
Minneapolis Business College	Roseville	T	Prop	PW	350		1				Y				Y			7
Minneapolis Community and Technical College	Minneapolis	C,T	St	M/W	7,091													
Minnesota School of Business–Brooklyn Center	Brooklyn Center	T,B,M	Prop	M/W	809				Y	Y	Y					N		16
Minnesota School of Business–Plymouth	Minneapolis	T,B,M	Prop	M/W	500				Y	Y	Y			Y	Y	N		15
Minnesota School of Business–Richfield	Richfield	T,B,M	Prop	M/W	944		40		Y	Y	Y	Y		Y	Y	N		15
Minnesota School of Business–St. Cloud	Waite Park	T,B,M	Prop	M/W	609				Y	Y	Y			Y	Y	N		15
Minnesota School of Business–Shakopee	Shakopee	T,B,M	Prop	M/W	360				Y	Y	Y			Y	Y	N		12
Minnesota State College–Southeast Technical	Winona	C,T	St	M/W	1,817	42												
Minnesota State Community and Technical College–Fergus Falls	Fergus Falls	C,T	St	M/W	5,631	36	20	81	Y	Y	Y	Y	Y	Y	Y	Y	13	40
Minnesota West Community and Technical College	Pipestone	C,T	St	M/W	2,783	48	43		Y	Y	Y	Y	Y	Y	Y	N	7	8
Normandale Community College	Bloomington	C,T	St	M/W	8,261		34	70	Y	Y	S	Y	Y	Y	Y	N	13	28
North Hennepin Community College	Brooklyn Park	C,T	St	M/W	6,382		35		Y		R	Y	Y	Y	Y	N	7	16
Northland Community and Technical College–East Grand Forks	East Grand Forks	C,T	St	M/W	1,442													
Northland Community and Technical College–Thief River Falls	Thief River Falls	C,T	St	M/W	3,652		26	76	Y	Y	Y	Y	Y	Y	Y	N	8	46
Northwest Technical College	Bemidji	T	St	M/W	4,500													
Rainy River Community College	International Falls	C,T	St	M/W	384													
Rasmussen College Eden Prarie	Eden Prarie	T	Prop	M/W	363	42	80		N	Y	Y	Y	Y	Y	Y	N		8
Rasmussen College Mankato	Mankato	T	Prop	PW	463		40		N	Y	Y	Y	Y	Y	Y	N		32
Rasmussen College St. Cloud	St. Cloud	C,T	Prop	PW	533	53												
Riverland Community College	Austin	C,T	St	M/W	3,600		42	68	Y	Y	Y	Y	Y	Y	Y	Y	5	28
Rochester Community and Technical College	Rochester	C,T,B	St	M/W	5,862													

This chart includes the names and locations of accredited two-year colleges in the United States and U.S. territories and shows institutions' responses to the *Thomson Peterson's Annual Survey of Undergraduate Institutions*. If an institution submitted incomplete data, one or more columns opposite the institution's name is blank. An asterisk after the school name denotes a *Special Message* following the college's profile, and a dagger indicates that the institution has one or more entries in the *College Close-Ups* section. If a school does not appear, it did not report any of the information.

Degrees Awarded: College Transfer Associate (C), Terminal Associate (T), Bachelor's (B), Master's (M), Doctoral (D), First Professional (F)

Y—Yes; N—No; R—Recommended; S—For Some

Institution	Location	Degrees Awarded	Institutional Control	Student Body	Undergraduate Enrollment Fall 2005	Percent Attending Part-Time	Percent 25 Years or Older	Percent of Grads Going on to Four-Year Colleges	HS Equivalency Certificate Accepted	Open Admissions	HS Transcript Required	Need-Based Aid Available	Part-Time Jobs Available	Job Placement Services Available	Career Counseling Available	College Housing Available	Number of Sports Offered	Number of Majors Offered
St. Cloud Technical College	St. Cloud	T	St	M/W	3,348	35	25		Y	Y	Y	Y	Y	Y	Y	N	5	52
Saint Paul College–A Community & Technical College	St. Paul	C,T	St-R	M/W	5,169	70			Y	Y	S	Y	Y	Y	Y	N		13
South Central Technical College	North Mankato	C,T	St	M/W	2,350													
Vermilion Community College	Ely	C,T	St	M/W	745		10		Y	Y	Y	Y	Y	Y	Y	Y	14	77
Mississippi																		
Coahoma Community College	Clarksdale	C,T	St-L	M/W	1,946	7	10		Y	Y	Y	Y	Y	Y	Y	Y	3	28
Copiah-Lincoln Community College	Wesson	C,T	St-L	M/W	2,161		22		Y	Y	Y	Y	Y	Y	Y	Y	8	45
Copiah-Lincoln Community College–Natchez Campus	Natchez	C,T	St-L	M/W	900	38												
East Central Community College	Decatur	C,T	St-L	M/W	2,382													
East Mississippi Community College	Scooba	C,T	St-L	M/W	3,417													
Hinds Community College	Raymond	C,T	St-L	M/W	9,961	28												
Holmes Community College	Goodman	C,T	St-L	M/W	4,494	28												
Itawamba Community College	Fulton	C,T	St-L	M/W	4,000													
Meridian Community College	Meridian	C,T	St-L	M/W	3,572	30		75	Y	Y	Y	Y	Y	Y	Y	Y	11	21
Mississippi Gulf Coast Community College	Perkinston	C,T	Dist	M/W	7,806	33		0	Y	Y	Y	Y	Y	Y	Y	Y	9	46
Southwest Mississippi Community College	Summit	C,T	St-L	M/W	1,894		31		Y	Y	Y	Y	Y	Y	Y	Y	6	38
Missouri																		
Aviation Institute of Maintenance–Kansas City	Kansas City	T	Prop															1
Blue River Community College	Independence	C,T	St-L	M/W	2,662	60	32		Y	Y			Y	Y	Y	N		9
Cottey College†	Nevada	C	Ind	W	308		1	100	N	Y	Y	Y	Y			Y	12	2
Crowder College	Neosho	C,T	St-L	M/W	2,615	50	23		Y	Y	Y	Y	Y	Y	Y	Y	3	35
East Central College	Union	C,T	Dist	M/W	3,486	58	25	65	Y	Y	Y	Y	Y	Y		N	2	71
Hickey College*	St. Louis	T,B	Prop	M/W	610				Y	Y	Y				Y			9
ITT Technical Institute	Arnold	T,B	Prop	M/W					N	Y	Y	Y	Y	Y	Y	N		14
ITT Technical Institute	Earth City	T,B	Prop	M/W					N	Y	Y	Y	Y	Y	Y	N		12
ITT Technical Institute	Kansas City	T,B		M/W								Y						6
Linn State Technical College	Linn	T	St	PM	878	11	13		Y	Y	Y		Y	Y	Y	Y	8	16
Longview Community College	Lee's Summit	C,T	St-L	M/W	5,667	57	29		Y	Y			Y	Y	Y	N	5	25
Maple Woods Community College	Kansas City	C,T	St-L	M/W	4,442	59	26		Y	Y			Y	Y	Y	N	3	19
Metro Business College	Jefferson City	T	Prop	M/W	155	10									Y			2
Metropolitan Community College-Business & Technology College	Kansas City	C,T	St-L	PM	602	80	64									N		43
Mineral Area College	Park Hills	C,T	Dist	M/W	2,820	43												
Missouri State University–West Plains	West Plains	C,T	St	M/W	1,675	47	10		Y	Y	S	Y	Y	Y	Y	Y	2	18
Moberly Area Community College	Moberly	C,T	St-L	M/W	3,835	53	24		Y	Y	Y	Y	Y	Y	Y	Y	3	15
North Central Missouri College	Trenton	C,T	Dist	M/W	1,342	48	25		Y	Y	Y	Y	Y	Y	Y	Y	3	21
Penn Valley Community College	Kansas City	C,T	St-L	M/W	4,627	69	54		Y	Y	Y	Y	Y	Y	Y	N	1	31
Ranken Technical College	St. Louis	C,T,B	Ind	PM	1,423	48												
Saint Charles Community College	St. Peters	C,T	St	M/W	6,870	51	52		Y	Y	R,S	Y	Y	Y	Y	N	6	22
St. Louis Community College at Florissant Valley	St. Louis	C,T	Dist	M/W		53			Y	Y	Y	Y	Y	Y	Y	N	7	48
St. Louis Community College at Forest Park	St. Louis	C,T	Dist	M/W	7,610													
St. Louis Community College at Meramec	Kirkwood	C,T	Dist	M/W	12,607													
Three Rivers Community College	Poplar Bluff	C,T	St-L	M/W	2,935	45	38	40	Y	Y	Y	Y	Y	Y	Y	Y	5	24
Vatterott College	St. Joseph	T	Prop	M/W														
Vatterott College	Springfield	T	Prop	M/W														
Wentworth Military Academy and Junior College	Lexington	C	Ind	M/W	561	58	10	76	N	Y	Y	Y	Y	Y		Y	13	1
Montana																		
Blackfeet Community College	Browning	C,T	Ind	M/W	503	16												
Dawson Community College	Glendive	C,T	St-L	M/W	539	27												
Flathead Valley Community College	Kalispell	C,T	St-L	M/W	2,100	54												
Fort Peck Community College	Poplar	C,T	Dist	M/W	428													
Nebraska																		
Central Community College–Columbus Campus	Columbus	C,T	St-L	M/W	1,999	78	50		Y	Y	Y	Y	Y	Y	Y	Y	5	22
Central Community College–Grand Island Campus	Grand Island	C,T	St-L	M/W	2,916	86	57		Y	Y	Y	Y	Y	Y	Y	Y	3	22
Central Community College–Hastings Campus	Hastings	C,T	St-L	M/W	2,534	63	44		Y	Y	Y	Y	Y	Y	Y	Y	6	36
The Creative Center	Omaha	T	Prop	M/W														
ITT Technical Institute	Omaha	T,B	Prop	M/W					N	Y	Y			Y	Y	N		14
Metropolitan Community College*	Omaha	C,T	St-L	M/W	12,461	61	47		Y		R	Y	Y	Y	Y	N		33
Nebraska Indian Community College	Macy	C,T	Fed	M/W	190	49												
Northeast Community College	Norfolk	C,T	St-L	M/W	5,101	58	39	21	Y	Y	R		Y	Y	Y	Y	8	76
Southeast Community College, Lincoln Campus	Lincoln	C,T	Dist	M/W	7,917	48												
Southeast Community College, Milford Campus	Milford	T	Dist	PM	922	3												
Nevada																		
Career College of Northern Nevada	Reno	T	Prop	M/W	283				Y	Y	Y	Y	Y	Y	Y	N		6
Community College of Southern Nevada	North Las Vegas	C	St	M/W	34,204	77												

This chart includes the names and locations of accredited two-year colleges in the United States and U.S. territories and shows institutions' responses to the *Thomson Peterson's Annual Survey of Undergraduate Institutions.* If an institution submitted incomplete data, one or more columns opposite the institution's name is blank.
An asterisk after the school name denotes a *Special Message* following the college's profile, and a dagger indicates that the institution has one or more entries in the *College Close-Ups* section. If a school does not appear, it did not report any of the information.

Y—Yes; N—No; R—Recommended; S—For Some

Name	Location	Degrees Awarded	Institutional Control	Student Body	Undergrad Enrollment Fall 2005	% Attending Part-Time	% 25 or Older	% Grads to 4-Year	HS Equivalency Accepted	Open Admissions	HS Transcript Required	Need-Based Aid Available	Part-Time Jobs Available	Career Counseling Available	Job Placement Services Available	College Housing Available	Number of Sports Offered	Number of Majors Offered
Great Basin College	Elko	C,T,B	St	M/W	3,095	72	60		Y		Y	Y	Y	Y	Y	Y	4	27
ITT Technical Institute	Henderson	T,B	Prop	M/W					N	Y	Y	Y	Y	Y	Y	N		10
Pima Medical Institute	Las Vegas	T	Prop	M/W	329													10
Truckee Meadows Community College	Reno	C,T	St	M/W	9,697	80												
Western Nevada Community College	Carson City	C,T	St	M/W	4,897													
New Hampshire																		
Hesser College†	Manchester	C,T,B	Prop	M/W	3,398	38												
McIntosh College†	Dover	C,T	Prop	M/W	750													
New Hampshire Community Technical College, Manchester/Stratham	Manchester	C,T	St	M/W	2,944			9	N	Y	Y	Y	Y	Y	Y	N	8	23
New Hampshire Community Technical College, Nashua/Claremont	Nashua	C,T	St	M/W	1,639				N	Y	Y	Y	Y	Y	Y	N	4	31
New Hampshire Technical Institute	Concord	C	St	M/W	3,650		50	18		Y	Y	Y	Y	Y	Y	Y	5	32
New Jersey																		
Assumption College for Sisters	Mendham	C	I-R	W	37	19	86	100	N	Y	Y	Y					N	2
Atlantic Cape Community College†	Mays Landing	C,T	Cou	M/W	6,515	54												
Bergen Community College	Paramus	C,T	Cou	M/W	14,812	49	31	80	Y		Y	Y	Y	Y	Y	N	10	55
Berkeley College	West Paterson	C,T,B	Prop	M/W	2,422	16	26		N	Y	Y	Y	Y	Y	Y	Y	5	11
Brookdale Community College	Lincroft	C,T	Cou	M/W	12,724	48												
Cumberland County College	Vineland	C,T	St-L	M/W	3,176													
Essex County College	Newark	C,T	Cou	M/W	10,435	46	50	65	Y		Y	Y	Y	Y	Y	N	6	48
Hudson County Community College	Jersey City	C,T	St-L	M/W	6,489	34												
Mercer County Community College	Trenton	C,T	St-L	M/W	8,928	62	41	64	Y		Y	Y	Y	Y	Y	N	9	51
Middlesex County College†	Edison	C,T	Cou	M/W	11,276		44		Y	Y	Y	Y	Y	Y	Y	N	10	68
Ocean County College	Toms River	C,T	Cou	M/W	8,449	52			Y		S	Y	Y	Y	Y	N	9	27
Raritan Valley Community College	Somerville	C,T	Cou	M/W	6,251	59	40		Y	Y	Y	Y	Y	Y	Y	N	4	46
Salem Community College	Carneys Point	C,T	Cou	M/W	1,251	52	52		Y		Y	Y	Y	Y	Y	N	4	30
Sussex County Community College	Newton	C,T	St-L	M/W	3,461	51	41		Y		Y	Y	Y	Y	Y	N	6	20
Union County College	Cranford	C,T	St-L	M/W	10,976	51	50		Y	Y	Y	Y	Y	Y	Y	N	6	35
New Mexico																		
Central New Mexico Community College	Albuquerque	C,T	St	M/W	23,107	70	54		Y		R	Y	Y	Y	Y	N		35
Clovis Community College	Clovis	C,T	St	M/W	3,937	83	52		Y	Y	Y	Y	Y	Y	Y	N	5	36
Doña Ana Branch Community College	Las Cruces	C,T	St-L	M/W	6,347	43												
Institute of American Indian Arts	Santa Fe	C,B	Fed	M/W	183	15												
International Institute of the Americas	Albuquerque	T,B	Ind	M/W	232													4
ITT Technical Institute	Albuquerque	T,B	Prop	M/W					N	Y	Y	Y	Y	Y	Y	Y		10
Luna Community College	Las Vegas	C,T	St	M/W	2,041	75												
New Mexico Military Institute*†	Roswell	C	St	PM	455		0	89	Y		Y	Y	Y	Y		Y	17	28
New Mexico State University–Alamogordo	Alamogordo	C,T	St	M/W	1,915	63	70		Y	Y	Y	Y	Y	Y	Y	N	2	16
Pima Medical Institute	Albuquerque	T	Prop	M/W	576													
San Juan College	Farmington	C,T	St	M/W	5,064	49	37		Y		Y	Y	Y	Y	Y	N	16	52
New York																		
Adirondack Community College	Queensbury	C,T	St-L	M/W	3,200													
American Academy of Dramatic Arts†	New York	T	Ind	M/W	220		14		N	Y	YS	Y	Y	Y	Y	N		1
The Art Institute of New York City†	New York	C,T	Prop	M/W	1,477		40	1	Y	Y	Y	Y	Y	Y	Y	N		5
Berkeley College-New York City Campus	New York	C,T,B	Prop	M/W	2,321	8	31		N	Y	Y	Y	Y	Y	Y	Y		8
Berkeley College-Westchester Campus	White Plains	C,T,B	Prop	M/W	610	8	20		N	Y	Y	Y	Y	Y	Y	Y		8
Borough of Manhattan Community College of the City University of New York	New York	C,T	St-L	M/W	18,776	42	42	57	Y	Y	Y	Y	Y	Y	Y	N	4	17
Bronx Community College of the City University of New York	Bronx	C,T	St-L	M/W	8,470	40	48		Y	Y	Y		Y	Y	Y	N	6	27
Broome Community College	Binghamton	C,T	St-L	M/W	6,231	37	10	56	Y	Y	Y	Y	Y	Y	Y	N	10	35
Bryant and Stratton College	Albany	T	Prop	M/W	470	25	51		N		Y	Y	Y	Y	Y	N		9
Bryant and Stratton College	Rochester	T	Prop	M/W	297	20	60		N		Y	Y	Y	Y	Y	N		11
Bryant and Stratton College	Rochester	T	Prop	M/W	194	22	97		N		Y	Y	Y	Y	Y	N	3	7
Bryant and Stratton College	Syracuse	T	Prop	M/W	636	22	26		N		Y	Y	Y	Y	Y	Y	1	9
Bryant and Stratton College, Amherst Campus	Clarence	T,B	Prop	M/W	403	40	56		N		Y	Y	Y	Y	Y	N		8
Bryant and Stratton College, Buffalo Campus	Buffalo	T	Prop	M/W	603	18	46		N		Y	Y	Y	Y	Y	N		8
Bryant and Stratton College, Lackawanna Campus	Lackawanna	T	Prop	M/W	269	30	49	4	N		Y	Y	Y	Y	Y	N		8
Cayuga County Community College	Auburn	C,T	St-L	M/W	3,896	43												
Clinton Community College	Plattsburgh	C,T	St-L	M/W	2,192	43												
The College of Westchester†	White Plains	T	Prop	M/W	1,039	20	48		N	Y	Y	Y	Y	Y	Y	N		26
Columbia-Greene Community College	Hudson	C,T	St-L	M/W	1,715	45												
Corning Community College	Corning	C,T	St-L	M/W	5,310	50	41	74	Y	Y	Y	Y	Y	Y	Y	N	11	44
Crouse Hospital School of Nursing	Syracuse	C,T	Ind	M/W	252	44												
Dutchess Community College	Poughkeepsie	C,T	St-L	M/W	7,810													
Elmira Business Institute	Elmira	C,T	Priv	PW	361	22	70		Y		Y	Y		Y	Y	N		5
Erie Community College	Buffalo	C,T	St-L	M/W	2,949	26	44	29	Y	Y	Y	Y	Y	Y	Y	N	14	19

This chart includes the names and locations of accredited two-year colleges in the United States and U.S. territories and shows institutions' responses to the *Thomson Peterson's Annual Survey of Undergraduate Institutions.* If an institution submitted incomplete data, one or more columns opposite the institution's name is blank. An asterisk after the school name denotes a *Special Message* following the college's profile, and a dagger indicates that the institution has one or more entries in the *College Close-Ups* section. If a school does not appear, it did not report any of the information.

Legend: Degrees Awarded — Bachelor's (B), Master's (M), Doctoral (D), First Professional (F), College Transfer Associate (C), Terminal Associate (T). Institutional Control — County District City (C), State and Local (St-L), State-Related, Federal, State (St), Commonwealth, Independent (Ind), Independent-Religious (I-R), Proprietary (Prop), Territory. Student Body — Men, Primarily Men (PM), Women, Primarily Women (PW), Coed (M/W).

Y—Yes; N—No; R—Recommended; S—For Some

College	Location	Degrees Awarded	Inst. Control	Student Body	Undergrad Enrollment Fall 2005	% Attending Part-Time	% 25 Years of Age or Older	% of Grads Going on to Four-Year Colleges	Open Admissions	HS Equivalency Certificate Accepted	HS Transcript Required	Need-Based Aid Available	Part-Time Jobs Available	Career Counseling Available	Job Placement Services Available	College Housing Available	Number of Sports Offered	Number of Majors Offered
Erie Community College, North Campus	Williamsville	C,T	St-L	M/W	5,641	33	29	35	Y	Y	Y	Y		Y	Y	Y	N	14	26
Erie Community College, South Campus	Orchard Park	C,T	St-L	M/W	4,067	38	20	39	Y	Y	Y	Y		Y	Y	Y	N	14	20
Eugenio María de Hostos Community College of the City University of New York	Bronx	C,T	St-L	M/W	4,340	33													
Fashion Institute of Technology†	New York	C,T,B,M	St-L	PW	10,199	35	28	53	N	Y	Y	Y		Y	Y	Y	Y	5	21
Finger Lakes Community College	Canandaigua	C,T	St-L	M/W	4,910	47	32		Y	Y	Y	Y	Y	Y	Y	Y	N	8	49
Fiorello H. LaGuardia Community College of the City University of New York*	Long Island City	C,T	St-L	M/W	13,489	45	40	50	Y	Y	Y	Y	Y	Y	Y	Y	N	6	33
Fulton-Montgomery Community College	Johnstown	C,T	St-L	M/W	2,071	32													
Genesee Community College	Batavia	C,T	St-L	M/W	6,490	52	19	64	Y	Y	Y	Y		Y	Y	Y	Y	15	37
Herkimer County Community College	Herkimer	C,T	St-L	M/W	3,477														
Hudson Valley Community College	Troy	C,T	St-L	M/W	12,205		35	37	Y	Y	Y	Y		Y	Y	Y	N	16	41
Island Drafting and Technical Institute	Amityville	C,T	Prop	PM	185		56		Y	Y	R	Y		Y	Y	Y	N		8
ITT Technical Institute	Albany	T	Prop						N	Y	Y	Y	Y	Y	Y	Y	N		7
ITT Technical Institute	Getzville	T	Prop	M/W					N	Y	Y	Y	Y	Y	Y	Y	N		6
ITT Technical Institute	Liverpool	T	Prop	M/W					N	Y	Y	Y	Y	Y	Y	Y	N		4
Jamestown Community College	Jamestown	C,T	St-L	M/W	3,672	33	32		Y	Y	Y	Y		Y	Y	Y	N	10	22
Jefferson Community College	Watertown	C,T	St-L	M/W	3,545	49	37	61	N	Y	Y	Y		Y	Y	Y	N	9	29
Kingsborough Community College of the City University of New York	Brooklyn	C,T	St-L	M/W	15,265	48	31	75	Y	Y	Y	Y		Y	Y	Y	N	7	38
Long Island Business Institute	Commack	C	Prop	PW	890	24	95	0	Y	Y	Y			Y	Y	N			4
Long Island College Hospital School of Nursing	Brooklyn	C,T	Ind	PW	147	50	81		N	Y	Y	Y	Y				N		1
Maria College*†	Albany	C,T	Ind	M/W	788	65	75	18	N	Y	Y	Y	Y	Y	Y	Y	N		12
Mohawk Valley Community College†	Utica	C,T	St-L	M/W	5,984	37	26	71	Y	Y	Y	Y	Y	Y	Y	Y	Y	17	73
Monroe College*	Bronx	C,T,B,M	Prop	M/W	4,285	15	46	26	N		Y	Y	Y	Y	Y	Y	Y	7	8
Nassau Community College	Garden City	C,T	St-L	M/W	20,979	36	20	65		Y	Y	Y	Y	Y	Y	Y	N	19	55
Niagara County Community College	Sanborn	C,T	St-L	M/W	5,572	35	31	62	Y	Y	Y	Y	Y	Y	Y	Y	N	10	36
North Country Community College	Saranac Lake	C,T	St-L	M/W	1,605	38	33	34	Y	Y	Y	Y	Y	Y	Y	Y	Y	12	14
Orange County Community College	Middletown	C,T	St-L	M/W	6,441	48	29	62	Y	Y	Y	Y	Y	Y	Y	Y	N	10	40
Phillips Beth Israel School of Nursing	New York	C,T	Ind	PW	200		65	10	N	Y	Y	Y		Y			N		2
Queensborough Community College of the City University of New York	Bayside	C,T	St-L	M/W	12,798	52													
Rockland Community College	Suffern	C,T	St-L	M/W	6,549	44													
Saint Joseph's Hospital Health Center School of Nursing	Syracuse	T	Ind	PW	293		51		Y	Y	Y		Y	Y	Y	Y			1
State University of New York College of Environmental Science & Forestry, Ranger School†	Wanakena	C,T	St	PM	43		20	38	N	N	R	Y	Y	Y	Y	Y	Y	7	2
State University of New York College of Technology at Alfred	Alfred	C,T,B	St	M/W	3,377		23	83	N	Y	Y	Y	Y	Y	Y	Y	Y	22	57
State University of New York College of Technology at Canton	Canton	C,T,B	St	M/W	2,518	18													
State University of New York College of Technology at Delhi	Delhi	C,T,B	St	M/W	2,557		19	81	N	Y	Y	Y	Y	Y	Y	Y	Y	17	33
Sullivan County Community College	Loch Sheldrake	C,T	St-L	M/W	1,684	37	31		Y	Y	Y	Y	Y	Y	Y		14	31
Tompkins Cortland Community College	Dryden	C,T	St-L	M/W	3,174	32	37		Y		Y	Y	Y	Y	Y	Y	16	45
Villa Maria College of Buffalo	Buffalo	C,T,B	I-R	M/W	502	21	40	59		Y	Y	Y		Y	Y			12
Westchester Community College	Valhalla	C,T	St-L	M/W	11,564	40			Y	Y	Y	Y		Y	Y	N	11	52
Wood Tobe–Coburn School	New York	T	Prop	PW	269	1			N	Y	Y	Y		Y	Y			9
North Carolina																		
Alamance Community College	Graham	C,T	St	M/W	4,285	59	47	1	Y	Y	Y	Y		Y	Y	N	4	33
The Art Institute of Charlotte†	Charlotte	T,B	Prop	M/W	819	31			N	Y	Y		Y	Y	Y			
Asheville-Buncombe Technical Community College	Asheville	C,T	St	M/W	5,627	64													
Beaufort County Community College	Washington	C,T	St	M/W	1,424		58	75	Y										21
Bladen Community College	Dublin	C,T	St-L	M/W	1,407	40	62	81	Y	Y	Y	Y		Y	Y	N		15
Blue Ridge Community College	Flat Rock	C	St-L	M/W	1,959	60													
Brunswick Community College	Supply	C,T	St	M/W	1,003	51													
Caldwell Community College and Technical Institute	Hudson	C,T	St	M/W	3,744	66	44		Y	Y	Y	Y		Y	Y	N	4	25
Cape Fear Community College	Wilmington	C,T	St	M/W	7,501	58	11	85	Y	Y	Y	Y		Y	Y	N	7	31
Carolinas College of Health Sciences	Charlotte	T	Ind	PW	458	68													
Carteret Community College	Morehead City	C,T	St	M/W	1,659	61	53		Y	Y	Y		Y	Y	N	2	18
Catawba Valley Community College	Hickory	C,T	St-L	M/W	3,943	61													
Central Carolina Community College	Sanford	C,T	St-L	M/W	4,857	62													
Central Piedmont Community College	Charlotte	C,T	St-L	M/W	16,631	63	50	46	Y	Y	Y	Y		Y	Y	N	1	69
Cleveland Community College	Shelby	C,T	St	M/W	3,047	59	47	50	Y	Y	Y	Y		Y	Y	N		31
Coastal Carolina Community College	Jacksonville	C,T	St-L	M/W	4,111	50	45		Y	Y	Y		Y	Y	N		19
College of The Albemarle	Elizabeth City	C,T	St	M/W	2,071	59	56	84	Y	Y	Y	Y		Y	Y	N	14	26
Craven Community College	New Bern	C,T	St	M/W	2,555														
Davidson County Community College	Lexington	C,T	St-L	M/W	2,303	64													
Durham Technical Community College	Durham	C,T	St	M/W	5,642	74													
ECPI Technical College	Raleigh	T	Prop	M/W	550		51		Y	Y		Y	Y	N		8
Edgecombe Community College	Tarboro	C,T	St-L	M/W	2,553	63													
Fayetteville Technical Community College	Fayetteville	C,T	St	M/W	9,950	69	59		Y	Y	S	Y		Y	Y	N	3	53
Forsyth Technical Community College	Winston-Salem	C,T	St	M/W	6,978	64	51		Y	Y	Y	Y		Y	Y	N	4	38
Gaston College	Dallas	C,T	St-L	M/W	5,048	51	52	42	Y	Y	S	Y		Y	Y	N		22

This chart includes the names and locations of accredited two-year colleges in the United States and U.S. territories and shows institutions' responses to the *Thomson Peterson's Annual Survey of Undergraduate Institutions*. If an institution submitted incomplete data, one or more columns opposite the institution's name is blank.
An asterisk after the school name denotes a *Special Message* following the college's profile, and a dagger indicates that the institution has one or more entries in the *College Close-Ups* section. If a school does not appear, it did not report any of the information.

Y—Yes; N—No; R—Recommended; S—For Some

Name	City	Degrees Awarded	Institutional Control	Student Body	Undergraduate Enrollment Fall 2005	Percent Attending Part-Time	Percent 25 Years of Age or Older	Percent of Grads Going on to Four-Year Colleges	High School Equivalency Certificate Accepted	Open Admissions	High School Transcript Required	Need-Based Aid Available	Part-Time Jobs Available	Career Counseling Available	Job Placement Services Available	College Housing Available	Number of Sports Offered	Number of Majors Offered
Guilford Technical Community College	Jamestown	C,T	St-L	M/W	8,491	65												
Halifax Community College	Weldon	C,T	St-L	M/W	1,580													
Haywood Community College	Clyde	C,T	St-L	M/W	1,988	56												
Isothermal Community College	Spindale	C,T	St	M/W	2,005	51												
James Sprunt Community College	Kenansville	C,T	St	M/W	1,370	53	51	68	Y	Y	Y	Y	Y	Y	Y	N	2	13
Johnston Community College	Smithfield	C,T	St	M/W	4,095	60	43		Y	Y	Y	Y	Y	Y	Y	N	4	19
Mayland Community College	Spruce Pine	C,T	St-L	M/W	1,019	52												
McDowell Technical Community College	Marion	C,T	St	M/W	1,078													
Montgomery Community College	Troy	C,T	St	M/W	850	54	57		Y	Y	Y	Y	Y	Y	Y	N		11
Piedmont Community College	Roxboro	C,T	St	M/W	2,189	62												
Randolph Community College	Asheboro	C,T	St	M/W	2,291													
Richmond Community College	Hamlet	C,T	St	M/W	1,472	53	57		Y	Y	Y	Y	Y	Y	Y	N		16
Roanoke-Chowan Community College	Ahoskie	C,T	St	M/W	1,014	52												
Rockingham Community College	Wentworth	C,T	St	M/W	2,036	70			Y	Y		Y	Y	Y	Y	N	8	32
Rowan-Cabarrus Community College	Salisbury	C,T	St	M/W	5,200	57												
Sandhills Community College	Pinehurst	C,T	St-L	M/W	3,502													
Southeastern Community College	Whiteville	C,T	St	M/W	1,825		45		Y	Y	Y	Y	Y	Y	Y	N	4	21
Southwestern Community College	Sylva	C,T	St	M/W	2,014	55												
Stanly Community College	Albemarle	C,T	St	M/W	2,000													
Surry Community College	Dobson	C,T	St	M/W	3,600													
Tri-County Community College	Murphy	C,T	St	M/W	1,155		65	40	Y	Y	Y	Y	Y	Y	Y	N		11
Vance-Granville Community College	Henderson	C,T	St	M/W	4,057	58	53		Y	Y	Y	Y	Y	Y	Y	N	2	30
Wake Technical Community College	Raleigh	C,T	St-L	M/W	11,372	66												
Wilkes Community College	Wilkesboro	C,T	St	M/W	2,617	49	44	70	Y	Y	Y	Y	Y	Y	Y	N	4	23
Wilson Technical Community College	Wilson	C,T	St	M/W	1,925	54	61	80	Y	Y	Y	Y	Y	Y	Y	N		18
North Dakota																		
Aakers Business College	Fargo	C,T,B	Prop	M/W	577	45							Y					7
Bismarck State College	Bismarck	C,T	St	M/W	3,541	34												
Lake Region State College	Devils Lake	C,T	St	M/W	1,471	72	21		Y	Y	Y	Y	Y	Y	Y	Y	8	35
North Dakota State College of Science	Wahpeton	C,T	St	M/W	2,468	21	18	81	Y	Y	Y	Y	Y	Y	Y	Y	8	31
United Tribes Technical College	Bismarck	C,T	Fed	M/W	885	28			Y	Y	Y	Y	Y	Y	Y	Y	3	22
Williston State College	Williston	C,T	St	M/W	947	41	28	80	Y	Y	Y	Y	Y			Y	3	15
Ohio																		
The Art Institute of Cincinnati	Cincinnati	C	Prop	M/W	74													
The Art Institute of Ohio–Cincinnati†	Cincinnati	C,T	Prop	M/W	229		62		Y	Y	Y			Y	Y			2
Belmont Technical College	St. Clairsville	T	St	M/W	1,740	32												
Bowling Green State University–Firelands College	Huron	C,T	St	M/W	1,918	46												
Brown Mackie College–Akron†	Akron	T	Prop	M/W	521		70	9	N		Y		Y	Y	Y	N		9
Brown Mackie College–Cincinnati†	Cincinnati	T	Prop	M/W	971		55		Y		Y	Y	Y	Y	Y	N		10
Brown Mackie College–Findlay†	Findlay	T	Prop	M/W	632	27	80		Y		Y	Y	Y	Y	Y	N		9
Brown Mackie College–North Canton†	North Canton	T	Prop	M/W	1,131				N		Y	Y		Y	Y	N		10
Bryant and Stratton College	Parma	T,B	Prop	M/W	329	44	51	2	N		Y	Y		Y	Y	N		11
Chatfield College	St. Martin	C,T	I-R	PW	230		50	39	Y	Y	Y	Y	Y			N		4
Cincinnati College of Mortuary Science	Cincinnati	T,B	Ind	M/W	133		55		N		Y	Y		Y	Y	N	4	1
Cincinnati State Technical and Community College	Cincinnati	C,T	St	M/W	8,470	59	45	31	Y		Y	Y	Y	Y	Y	N	4	65
Clark State Community College	Springfield	C,T	St	M/W	3,504	55			Y		Y	Y	Y	Y	Y	N	4	37
Cleveland Institute of Electronics	Cleveland	T	Prop	PM	2,602		85		Y	Y	Y					N		
Columbus State Community College	Columbus	C,T	St	M/W	21,872	61												
Cuyahoga Community College	Cleveland	C,T	St-L	M/W	25,358	59	42		Y		S	Y	Y	Y	Y	N	8	32
Davis College	Toledo	T	Prop	M/W	451	50	70		N		Y	Y	Y	Y	Y	N		14
Edison State Community College	Piqua	C,T	St	M/W	3,000	66												
Gallipolis Career College	Gallipolis	T	Ind	PW	154	6			N		Y	Y		Y	Y	N		9
International College of Broadcasting	Dayton	C,T	Priv	M/W	87													
ITT Technical Institute	Dayton	T	Prop	M/W					N		Y	Y	Y	Y	Y	N		9
ITT Technical Institute	Hilliard	T	Prop	M/W							Y							7
ITT Technical Institute	Norwood	C	Prop	M/W					N		Y	Y	Y	Y	Y	N		9
ITT Technical Institute	Strongsville	T	Prop	M/W					N		Y	Y	Y	Y	Y	N		9
ITT Technical Institute	Warrensville Heights	T		M/W							Y							6
ITT Technical Institute	Youngstown	T	Prop	M/W					N		Y	Y	Y	Y	Y	N		6
Jefferson Community College	Steubenville	C,T	St-L	M/W	1,697	46	43		Y		S	Y	Y	Y	Y	N	6	25
Kent State University, Geauga Campus	Burton	C,B	St	M/W	918	66	39		Y		Y	Y	Y	Y		N	4	8
Kent State University, Trumbull Campus	Warren	C,T,B	St	M/W	2,036	56	54		Y		Y	Y	Y	Y		N	4	12
Kent State University, Tuscarawas Campus	New Philadelphia	C,T,B,M	St	M/W	1,905	51	29		Y		Y	Y	Y	Y	Y	N	2	16
Mercy College of Northwest Ohio	Toledo	C,B	I-R	PW	756	47	51		N		Y	Y	Y	Y	Y	Y		6
Miami University Hamilton	Hamilton	C,T,B,M	St	M/W	3,330	27												
North Central State College	Mansfield	T	St	M/W	3,333													
Northwest State Community College	Archbold	C,T	St	M/W	3,145	65												
Ohio Business College	Sandusky	C	Prop	M/W	192	18									Y			8

Two-Year Colleges At-a-Glance

This chart includes the names and locations of accredited two-year colleges in the United States and U.S. territories and shows institutions' responses to the *Thomson Peterson's Annual Survey of Undergraduate Institutions.* If an institution submitted incomplete data, one or more columns opposite the institution's name is blank.

An asterisk after the school name denotes a *Special Message* following the college's profile, and a dagger indicates that the institution has one or more entries in the *College Close-Ups* section. If a school does not appear, it did not report any of the information.

Degrees Awarded: College Transfer Associate (C), Terminal Associate (T), Bachelor's (B), Master's (M), Doctoral (D), First Professional (F)
Institutional Control: County, District, City; State and Local; State-Related; Independent; Independent-Religious; Federal; State; Commonwealth; Territory; Proprietary
Student Body: Men, Primarily Men; Women, Primarily Women; Coed

Legend: Y—Yes; N—No; R—Recommended; S—For Some

Institution	Location	Degrees Awarded	Inst. Control	Student Body	Undergrad Enrollment Fall 2005	% 25 Yrs or Older	% Attending Part-Time	% Grads to Four-Year	HS Equiv. Cert. Accepted	Open Admissions	HS Transcript Required	Need-Based Aid Avail.	Part-Time Jobs Avail.	Career Counseling Avail.	Job Placement Svcs Avail.	College Housing Avail.	No. of Sports Avail.	No. of Majors Offered
Ohio Institute of Photography and Technology	Dayton	T	Prop	M/W	740	33		5	N	Y	Y	Y	Y	Y	Y	N		4
The Ohio State University Agricultural Technical Institute	Wooster	C,T	St	M/W	821	12	10		Y	Y	Y		Y	Y	Y	Y	5	36
Owens Community College	Toledo	C,T	St	M/W	20,244	63	50		Y		Y	R	Y	Y	Y	N	11	25
Remington College–Cleveland Campus	Cleveland	C	Prop	M/W	676													
Remington College–Cleveland West Campus	North Olmstead	T	Prop	M/W	399													3
RETS Tech Center	Centerville	C,T	Prop	M/W	556													
School of Advertising Art	Kettering	C,T	Prop	M/W	146	3	1					Y		Y		N		1
Sinclair Community College	Dayton	C,T	St-L	M/W	19,563	61	47	53	Y		S	Y	Y	Y	Y	N	5	89
Southern State Community College	Hillsboro	C,T	St	M/W	2,307				Y	Y	R	Y	Y	Y	Y	N	5	15
Stark State College of Technology	North Canton	C,T	St-L	M/W	6,857	67	55		Y	Y	Y	Y	Y	Y	Y	Y		49
The University of Akron–Wayne College	Orrville	C,T	St	M/W	1,737	47	41	75	Y	Y	S	Y	Y	Y	Y	Y	4	20
University of Cincinnati Raymond Walters College	Cincinnati	C,T	St	M/W	4,421	51												
University of Northwestern Ohio*	Lima	C,B	Ind	M/W	2,915	10	18	40	Y	Y	Y	Y	Y	Y	Y	Y	3	16
Oklahoma																		
Carl Albert State College	Poteau	C,T	St	M/W	2,501	41			Y			Y	Y	Y	Y	Y	6	27
Community Care College	Tulsa	T	Prop	M/W	525	2								Y				8
ITT Technical Institute	Tulsa	T,B		M/W										Y				7
Seminole State College	Seminole	C,T	St	M/W	2,584	19	47		Y		Y	Y	Y		Y		5	18
Southwestern Oklahoma State University at Sayre	Sayre	C,T	St-L	M/W	549	40	50	75	Y	Y	Y	Y	Y	Y		N		10
Tulsa Community College	Tulsa	C,T	St	M/W	16,803	63	59	3	Y	Y	Y	Y	Y	Y	Y	N	10	158
Tulsa Welding School	Tulsa	C,T	Prop	PM	362	37								Y	Y	N		1
Vatterott College	Oklahoma City	T,F	Prop	PW	249													
Vatterott College	Tulsa	T	Prop	PW	226													4
Western Oklahoma State College	Altus	C,T	St	M/W	2,061	58	65	25	Y	Y	Y	Y	Y			Y	8	12
Oregon																		
Blue Mountain Community College	Pendleton	C,T	St-L	M/W	1,878	54												
Central Oregon Community College*	Bend	C,T	Dist	M/W	4,048	62	41	50	N			Y	Y	Y	Y	Y	13	38
Chemeketa Community College	Salem	C,T	St-L	M/W	15,000	45			Y		S	Y	Y	Y	Y	N	5	48
Clackamas Community College	Oregon City	C,T	Dist	M/W	7,329	69												
Clatsop Community College	Astoria	C,T	Cou	M/W	1,824	76	50	30	Y		R	Y	Y	Y		N		12
Columbia Gorge Community College	The Dalles	C,T	St	M/W														
Heald College-Portland	Portland	C,T	Ind	M/W	206	28			Y	Y	Y	Y	Y	Y				5
ITT Technical Institute	Portland	T,B	Prop	M/W					N	Y	Y	Y	Y	Y	Y	N		13
Lane Community College	Eugene	C,T	St-L	M/W	11,834													
Linn-Benton Community College	Albany	C,T	St-L	M/W	5,289	46	43		Y		S	Y	Y	Y		N	5	61
Oregon Coast Community College	Newport	C	Pub	M/W	599	88	58		Y					Y		N		4
Pioneer Pacific College	Wilsonville	C,B	Prop	M/W	1,132	1	64		Y	Y	Y	Y		Y	Y	N		10
Rogue Community College	Grants Pass	C,T	St-L	M/W	4,224	68	55		Y		Y	Y	Y			N	4	19
Southwestern Oregon Community College	Coos Bay	C,T	St-L	M/W	1,980	51	45		Y		S	Y				Y	10	30
Tillamook Bay Community College	Tillamook	C,T	Dist	M/W	299	76	46				R					N		14
Treasure Valley Community College	Ontario	C,T	St-L	M/W	1,946	46	45		Y			Y	Y	Y	Y	Y	6	40
Umpqua Community College	Roseburg	C,T	St-L	M/W	2,141													
Pennsylvania																		
Antonelli Institute	Erdenheim	T	Prop	M/W	189	3	8	0	Y	Y	Y	Y	Y	Y	Y	Y		2
The Art Institute of Philadelphia	Philadelphia	T,B	Prop	M/W	3,374	28	20		N	Y	Y	Y	Y	Y	Y	Y	2	13
Berks Technical Institute	Wyomissing	C,T	Prop	M/W	650	25			Y	Y	Y		Y	Y		N		8
Bradley Academy for the Visual Arts†	York	T	Prop	M/W	596	7	11		N	Y	Y	Y	Y	Y	Y	N		10
Bucks County Community College	Newtown	C,T	Cou	M/W	9,596	58	37		Y	Y	Y		Y	Y		N	8	55
Business Institute of Pennsylvania	Meadville	T	Prop	PW	68									Y		N		7
Business Institute of Pennsylvania	Sharon	T	Prop	PW	106	8												
Butler County Community College	Butler	C,T	Cou	M/W	3,809	48	40		Y	Y	Y		Y	Y	Y	N	11	49
Cambria-Rowe Business College	Johnstown	C,T	Prop	PW	230	51	3		N	Y	Y	Y		Y	Y	N		5
Career Training Academy	New Kensington	C,T	Prop		337									Y				2
Commonwealth Technical Institute	Johnstown	T	St	M/W	275				Y	Y	R,S			Y				7
Community College of Allegheny County†	Pittsburgh	C,T	Cou	M/W	18,404	59	48	39	Y		R	Y	Y	Y	Y	N	15	116
Community College of Beaver County	Monaca	C,T	St	M/W	2,500													
Community College of Philadelphia	Philadelphia	C,T	St-L	M/W	22,851													
Consolidated School of Business	Lancaster	T	Prop	PW	173	23			Y	Y	Y		Y	Y	N			7
Consolidated School of Business	York	T	Prop	PW	176	41			Y	Y	Y		Y	Y	N			7
Delaware County Community College	Media	C,T	St-L	M/W	10,608	60												
Erie Business Center, Main	Erie	T	Prop	M/W	393	29	38		N	Y	Y	Y			Y	N		15
Erie Business Center South	New Castle	C,T	Prop	PW	100													
Harcum College†	Bryn Mawr	C,T	Ind	PW	573	33												
Harrisburg Area Community College	Harrisburg	C,T	St-L	M/W	16,899	61	48	67	Y			Y	Y	Y	Y	N	11	86
ICM School of Business & Medical Careers	Pittsburgh	C,T	Prop	M/W	1,095	3												
Keystone College†	La Plume	C,T,B	Ind	M/W	1,638	25	28	71	N	Y	Y	Y	Y	Y	Y	Y	16	65
Lackawanna College	Scranton	C,T	Ind	M/W	1,197	37	33	57	Y	Y	Y	Y	Y	Y	Y	Y	7	23

This chart includes the names and locations of accredited two-year colleges in the United States and U.S. territories and shows institutions' responses to the *Thomson Peterson's Annual Survey of Undergraduate Institutions*. If an institution submitted incomplete data, one or more columns opposite the institution's name is blank.

An asterisk after the school name denotes a *Special Message* following the college's profile, and a dagger indicates that the institution has one or more entries in the *College Close-Ups* section. If a school does not appear, it did not report any of the information.

Y—Yes; N—No; R—Recommended; S—For Some

Institution	Location	Degrees Awarded	Institutional Control	Student Body	Undergraduate Enrollment Fall 2005	Percent Attending Part-Time	Percent 25 Years of Age or Older	Percent of Grads Going on to Four-Year Colleges	High School Equivalency Certificate Accepted	Open Admissions	High School Transcript Required	Need-Based Aid Available	Part-Time Jobs Available	Career Counseling Available	Job Placement Services Available	College Housing Available	Number of Sports Offered	Number of Majors Offered
Laurel Business Institute	Uniontown	C,T	Prop	M/W	297				Y	Y	Y	Y	Y	Y	Y	N		28
Lehigh Carbon Community College	Schnecksville	C,T	St-L	M/W	6,674	61												
Lehigh Valley College†	Center Valley	T	Prop	M/W	1,236	55		0	Y	Y	Y	Y	Y	Y	Y	N		14
Luzerne County Community College	Nanticoke	C,T	Cou	M/W	6,170	52	43		Y	Y	R	Y	Y	Y	Y	N	10	75
Manor College*†	Jenkintown	C,T	I-R	M/W	865	50	41		N	Y	Y	Y	Y	Y	Y	Y	3	27
Montgomery County Community College	Blue Bell	C,T	Cou	M/W	10,874	56	27	74	Y	Y	S	Y	Y	Y	Y	N	12	53
Newport Business Institute	Lower Burrell	T	Prop	M/W	79	40	4		Y	Y	Y	Y		Y	Y	N		13
Newport Business Institute	Williamsport	T	Prop	PW	104	1	48	0	N	Y	Y	Y		Y	Y	N		4
Northampton County Area Community College	Bethlehem	C,T	St-L	M/W	8,754	58	41	68	N	Y	Y	Y	Y	Y	Y	Y	12	57
Oakbridge Academy of Arts	Lower Burrell	C,T	Prop	M/W	66		28		N	Y	Y	Y		Y	Y	N		3
Orleans Technical Institute-Center City Campus	Philadelphia	C,T	Prop	PW	135	36												
Penn Foster Career School	Scranton	T	Prop	M/W	18,881		76		Y	Y	Y					N		13
Pennsylvania College of Technology†	Williamsport	C,T,B	St-R	M/W	6,537	16	19		Y	Y	Y	Y	Y	Y	Y	Y	18	108
Pennsylvania Culinary Institute	Pittsburgh	T	Prop	M/W	1,040													
Pennsylvania Highland Community College	Johnstown	C,T	St-L	M/W	1,327	55												
Pennsylvania Institute of Technology	Media	C,T	Ind	M/W	384	30	51			Y	Y	Y	Y	Y	Y	N	2	10
The Pennsylvania State University Beaver Campus of the Commonwealth College	Monaca	C,T,B	St-R	M/W	632	14	11		N	Y	Y	Y	Y	Y	Y	Y	10	118
The Pennsylvania State University Delaware County Campus of the Commonwealth College	Media	T,B	St-R	M/W	1,589	15	10		N	Y	Y	Y	Y	Y	Y	N	10	120
The Pennsylvania State University DuBois Campus of the Commonwealth College	DuBois	C,T,B	St-R	M/W	804	26	34		N	Y	Y	Y	Y	Y	Y	N	7	127
The Pennsylvania State University Fayette Campus of the Commonwealth College	Uniontown	C,T,B	St-R	M/W	995	27	39		N	Y	Y	Y	Y	Y	Y	N	11	124
The Pennsylvania State University Hazleton Campus of the Commonwealth College	Hazleton	C,T,B	St-R	M/W	1,065	5	6		N	Y	Y	Y	Y	Y	Y	Y	8	125
The Pennsylvania State University, Lehigh Valley Campus of the Berks-Lehigh Valley College	Fogelsville	T,B	St-R	M/W	644	24												
The Pennsylvania State University McKeesport Campus of the Commonwealth College	McKeesport	T,B	St-R	M/W	682	13	8		N	Y	Y	Y	Y	Y	Y	Y	12	119
The Pennsylvania State University Mont Alto Campus of the Commonwealth College	Mont Alto	T,B	St-R	M/W	932	28	26		N	Y	Y	Y	Y	Y	Y	Y	10	120
The Pennsylvania State University New Kensington Campus of the Commonwealth College	New Kensington	C,T,B	St-R	M/W	880	29	23		N	Y	Y	Y	Y	Y	Y	N	13	124
The Pennsylvania State University Schuylkill Campus of the Capital College	Schuylkill Haven	C,T,B	St-R	M/W	924	16												
The Pennsylvania State University Shenango Campus of the Commonwealth College	Sharon	C,T,B	St-R	M/W	855	41	50		N	Y	Y	Y	Y	Y	Y	N	7	124
The Pennsylvania State University Wilkes-Barre Campus of the Commonwealth College	Lehman	C,T,B	St-R	M/W	666	20	14		N	Y	Y	Y	Y	Y	Y	N	11	122
The Pennsylvania State University Worthington Scranton Campus of the Commonwealth College	Dunmore	T,B	St-R	M/W	1,241	23	26		N	Y	Y	Y	Y	Y	Y	N	10	119
The Pennsylvania State University York Campus of the Commonwealth College	York	C,T,B	St-R	M/W	1,415	42	31		N	Y	Y	Y	Y	Y	Y	N	10	126
Pittsburgh Institute of Mortuary Science, Incorporated	Pittsburgh	C,T	Ind	M/W	192	6	48	6	Y	Y	Y	Y		Y	Y	N		1
Rosedale Technical Institute	Pittsburgh	T	Ind	PM	200													3
Schuylkill Institute of Business and Technology	Pottsville	C,T	Prop	M/W	136		45		Y	Y	Y			Y	Y	N		8
South Hills School of Business & Technology	State College	C,T	Prop	M/W	663	8	39	2	N	Y	Y	Y		Y	Y	N		12
Thaddeus Stevens College of Technology	Lancaster	C,T	St	M/W	660													
Thompson Institute	Harrisburg	T,B	Prop	M/W	485													
Triangle Tech, Inc.–DuBois School	DuBois	T	Prop	PM	246		40		N	Y	Y		Y	Y	Y			4
Triangle Tech, Inc.–Greensburg School	Greensburg	T	Prop	PM	271		49		N	Y	Y	Y	Y	Y	Y	N		8
Triangle Tech, Inc.–Pittsburgh School	Pittsburgh	C,T	Prop	PM	377													
University of Pittsburgh at Titusville	Titusville	C,T	St-R	M/W	547	24		100	N	Y	Y	Y	Y	Y	Y	Y	11	8
Valley Forge Military College*†	Wayne	C	Ind	M/W	165			98	N	Y	Y	Y	Y		Y	Y	14	5
Westmoreland County Community College	Youngwood	C,T	Cou	M/W	6,133	56	45		Y	Y		Y	Y	Y	Y	N	12	53
The Williamson Free School of Mechanical Trades	Media	T	Ind	M	251		0	19	N	Y	Y	Y		Y	Y	Y	14	8
WyoTech	Blairsville	T	Prop	PM										Y				
Puerto Rico																		
Instituto Comercial de Puerto Rico Junior College	San Juan	T	Prop	M/W	1,270	14												
Rhode Island																		
Community College of Rhode Island	Warwick	C,T	St	M/W	16,293	65												
South Carolina																		
Aiken Technical College	Aiken	C,T	St-L	M/W	2,516	44	40	35	Y	Y	Y	Y	Y	Y	Y	N	2	16
Central Carolina Technical College	Sumter	C,T	St	M/W	3,244	71	46	11	Y	Y	Y	Y	Y	Y	Y	N		17
Denmark Technical College	Denmark	C,T	St	M/W	1,408	31	20		Y	Y	Y	Y	Y	Y	Y	Y	5	8
Forrest Junior College	Anderson	C,T	Prop	PW	165													
Horry-Georgetown Technical College	Conway	C,T	St-L	M/W	5,362	54			Y		S	Y	Y	Y	Y	N		25
ITT Technical Institute	Greenville	T,B	Prop	M/W					N	Y	Y	Y	Y	Y	Y	N		9

Two-Year Colleges At-a-Glance

This chart includes the names and locations of accredited two-year colleges in the United States and U.S. territories and shows institutions' responses to the *Thomson Peterson's Annual Survey of Undergraduate Institutions*. If an institution submitted incomplete data, one or more columns opposite the institution's name is blank. An asterisk after the school name denotes a *Special Message* following the college's profile, and a dagger indicates that the institution has one or more entries in the *College Close-Ups* section. If a school does not appear, it did not report any of the information.

Y—Yes; N—No; R—Recommended; S—For Some

Institution	Location	Degrees Awarded	Institutional Control	Student Body	Undergraduate Enrollment Fall 2005	Percent Attending Part-Time	Percent 25 Years of Age or Older	Percent of Grads Going on to Four-Year Colleges	High School Equivalency Certificate Accepted	High School Transcript Required	Open Admissions	Need-Based Aid Available	Part-Time Jobs Available	Career Counseling Available	Job Placement Services Available	College Housing Available	Number of Sports Offered	Number of Majors Offered
Midlands Technical College	Columbia	C,T	St-L	M/W	10,779	56	40		Y	Y	R	Y	Y	Y	Y	N	4	49
Northeastern Technical College	Cheraw	C,T	St-L	M/W	1,115													
Spartanburg Methodist College	Spartanburg	C,T	I-R	M/W	779	8	6	93	N	Y	Y	Y	Y	Y	Y	Y	13	4
Spartanburg Technical College	Spartanburg	C,T	St	M/W	4,409		43		Y	Y	Y	Y	Y	Y	Y	N		24
Technical College of the Lowcountry	Beaufort	C,T	St	M/W	1,765													
Tri-County Technical College	Pendleton	C,T	St	M/W	4,100													
Trident Technical College	Charleston	C,T	St-L	M/W	11,795	55	47		Y	Y	S	Y	Y	Y	Y	N		40
University of South Carolina Sumter	Sumter	C	St	M/W	1,020	43	30		N	Y	Y	Y	Y	Y		N	10	2
University of South Carolina Union	Union	C	St	M/W	321	50	35		N	Y	Y	Y	Y			N		2
York Technical College	Rock Hill	C,T	St	M/W	4,153	51	39		Y		S	Y	Y	Y	Y	N		35
South Dakota																		
Kilian Community College	Sioux Falls	C,T	Ind	M/W	538	80	52		Y	Y	Y	Y	Y	Y	Y	N		13
Sisseton-Wahpeton Community College	Sisseton	C,T	Fed	M/W	274	46												
Southeast Technical Institute	Sioux Falls	T	St	M/W	2,320		28		N	Y	Y	Y	Y	Y	Y	Y	2	50
Tennessee																		
Chattanooga State Technical Community College	Chattanooga	C,T	St	M/W	7,836	55	44		Y	Y	Y	Y	Y	Y	Y	N	3	63
Cleveland State Community College	Cleveland	C,T	St	M/W	3,027	48	43	40	Y	Y	Y	Y	Y	Y	Y	N	10	11
Columbia State Community College	Columbia	C,T	St	M/W	4,613	47												
Dyersburg State Community College	Dyersburg	C,T	St	M/W	2,457	42	42		Y	Y	Y	Y	Y	Y	Y	N	4	8
Fountainhead College of Technology	Knoxville	C,T,B	Prop	M/W	120		20		Y	Y	R	Y		Y	Y	N		6
ITT Technical Institute	Knoxville	T,B	Prop	M/W					N	Y	Y	Y		Y	Y	N		14
ITT Technical Institute	Memphis	T,B	Prop	M/W					N	Y	Y	Y		Y	Y	N		12
ITT Technical Institute	Nashville	T,B	Prop	M/W					N	Y	Y	Y		Y	Y	N		14
Jackson State Community College	Jackson	C,T	St	M/W	3,866	47	43	67	Y	Y	S	Y	Y	Y	Y	N	8	15
Mid-America Baptist Theological Seminary	Germantown	T,M,D,F	I-R	PM	62	40			Y	Y	S	Y		Y	Y	Y		1
Motlow State Community College	Tullahoma	C,T	St	M/W	3,407	41	31	69	Y	Y	Y	Y	Y	Y	Y	N	9	4
Nashville Auto Diesel College	Nashville	T	Prop	PM	1,306		5		N	Y	Y	Y		Y	Y	Y		3
Nashville State Technical Community College	Nashville	C,T	St	M/W	7,021	66												
National College of Business & Technology	Bristol	T	Prop	M/W	319													
National College of Business & Technology	Nashville	T	Prop	M/W	466													
North Central Institute	Clarksville	T	Prop	PM	130	60	50		Y	Y	R	Y		Y	Y	N		2
Northeast State Technical Community College	Blountville	C,T	St	M/W	4,860	46	47	90	Y	Y	Y	Y	Y	Y	Y	N	3	22
Pellissippi State Technical Community College	Knoxville	C,T	St	M/W	7,686	49	40		Y	Y	Y	Y	Y	Y	Y	N	6	39
Roane State Community College	Harriman	C,T	St	M/W	5,155	44	45		Y	Y	Y	Y	Y	Y	Y	N	9	39
Southwest Tennessee Community College	Memphis	C,T	St	M/W	11,556	51	50		Y	Y	Y	Y	Y	Y	Y	Y		31
Volunteer State Community College	Gallatin	C,T	St	M/W	7,150	51	39		Y	Y	Y	Y	Y	Y	Y	N	3	11
Walters State Community College	Morristown	C,T	St	M/W	5,964	48												
Texas																		
Alvin Community College	Alvin	C,T	St-L	M/W	3,932	59												
Amarillo College	Amarillo	C,T	St-L	M/W	10,196													
Austin Community College	Austin	C,T	Dist	M/W	31,908	72	39		Y	Y			Y	Y	Y	N	6	75
Brazosport College	Lake Jackson	C,T	St-L	M/W	3,503	52	42	35	Y	Y	S	Y		Y	Y	N	11	75
Cedar Valley College	Lancaster	C,T	St	M/W	4,290	66	42		Y	Y	R	Y	Y	Y	Y	N	5	16
Central Texas College	Killeen	C,T	St-L	M/W	18,351	84												
Clarendon College	Clarendon	C,T	St-L	M/W	1,123	50			Y	Y		Y	Y			Y	6	42
Coastal Bend College	Beeville	C,T	Cou	M/W	3,366	59	42		Y	Y	Y	Y	Y	Y	Y	Y	13	67
College of the Mainland	Texas City	C,T	St-L	M/W	3,999	65	41		Y	Y	S	Y	Y	Y	Y	N	11	25
Collin County Community College District	Plano	C,T	St-L	M/W	18,457	61	37		Y	Y		Y	Y	Y	Y	N	3	31
Commonwealth Institute of Funeral Service	Houston	T	Ind	M/W	164	4												
Cy-Fair College	Houston	C,T	St-L	M/W	8,540	78												
Dallas Institute of Funeral Service	Dallas	C,T	Ind	M/W	247		52		Y	Y	Y	Y				N		1
Eastfield College	Mesquite	C,T	St-L	M/W	12,111	81	35	60	Y	Y	R	Y	Y	Y	Y	N	8	29
El Centro College	Dallas	C,T	Cou	M/W	6,089	75	51	30	Y	Y	S	Y	Y	Y	Y	N	4	46
El Paso Community College	El Paso	C,T	Cou	M/W	19,953													
Frank Phillips College	Borger	C,T	St-L	M/W	1,100													
Galveston College	Galveston	C,T	St-L	M/W	2,230	62	45		Y	Y	S	Y	Y	Y	Y	N	5	32
Houston Community College System	Houston	C,T	St-L	M/W	39,516	69		25	Y		S	Y	Y	Y	Y	N		65
Howard College	Big Spring	C,T	St-L	M/W	2,725	57	58		Y	Y	Y	Y	Y	Y	Y	Y	8	31
ITT Technical Institute	Arlington	T	Prop	M/W					N	Y	Y	Y		Y	Y	N		6
ITT Technical Institute	Austin	T	Prop	M/W					N	Y	Y	Y		Y	Y	N		6
ITT Technical Institute	Houston	T	Prop	M/W					N	Y	Y	Y		Y	Y	N		6
ITT Technical Institute	Houston	T	Prop	M/W					N	Y	Y	Y		Y	Y	N		6
ITT Technical Institute	Houston	T	Prop	M/W	585				N	Y	Y	Y		Y	Y	N		6
ITT Technical Institute	Richardson	T	Prop	M/W					N	Y	Y	Y		Y	Y	N		6
ITT Technical Institute	San Antonio	T	Prop	M/W					N	Y	Y	Y		Y	Y	N		6
Jacksonville College	Jacksonville	C,T	I-R	M/W	300	27	12		Y	Y		Y	Y	Y		Y	4	2
KD Studio	Dallas	T	Prop	M/W	152		20	5	Y	Y	Y	Y		Y		N		2

This chart includes the names and locations of accredited two-year colleges in the United States and U.S. territories and shows institutions' responses to the *Thomson Peterson's Annual Survey of Undergraduate Institutions*. If an institution submitted incomplete data, one or more columns opposite the institution's name is blank. An asterisk after the school name denotes a *Special Message* following the college's profile, and a dagger indicates that the institution has one or more entries in the *College Close-Ups* section. If a school does not appear, it did not report any of the information.

Y—Yes; N—No; R—Recommended; S—For Some

College	City	Degrees Awarded	Institutional Control	Student Body	Undergraduate Enrollment Fall 2005	Percent Attending Part-Time	Percent 25 Years of Age or Older	Percent of Grads Going on to Four-Year Colleges	High School Equivalency Certificate Accepted	Open Admissions	High School Transcript Accepted	Need-Based Aid Available	Part-Time Jobs Available	Career Counseling Available	Job Placement Services Available	College Housing Available	Number of Sports Offered	Number of Majors Offered
Kilgore College	Kilgore	C,T	St-L	M/W	4,957	45												
Kingwood College	Kingwood	C,T	St-L	M/W	6,842	81	35		Y	Y	Y	Y	Y	Y		N	1	17
Lamar State College–Orange	Orange	C,T	St	M/W	2,143	57	38		Y	Y	Y	Y	Y	Y		N	4	16
Lamar State College–Port Arthur	Port Arthur	C,T	St	M/W	2,530	61	41		Y		Y	Y	Y	Y	Y	N		24
Laredo Community College	Laredo	C,T	St-L	M/W	8,298	61	35		Y		Y	Y	Y	Y	Y	Y	7	29
McLennan Community College	Waco	C,T	Cou	M/W	7,562	56												
Midland College	Midland	C,T,B	St-L	M/W	5,531	63	16		Y		Y	Y	Y	Y	Y	Y	11	59
Montgomery College	Conroe	C,T	St-L	M/W	8,306	64	30		Y	Y		Y	Y	Y	Y	N		18
Mountain View College	Dallas	C,T	St-L	M/W	6,496		41		Y	Y	Y	Y	Y	Y	Y	N	4	16
MTI College of Business and Technology	Houston	T	Prop	M/W	217													
MTI College of Business and Technology	Houston	T	Prop		718													
North Lake College	Irving	C,T	Cou	M/W	8,779	67												
Northwest Vista College	San Antonio	C,T	St-L	M/W	8,463													16
Odessa College	Odessa	C,T	St-L	M/W	4,569	61												
Palo Alto College	San Antonio	C,T	St-L	M/W	8,070		35		Y	Y	Y	Y	Y	Y	Y	N	4	38
Panola College	Carthage	C,T	St-L	M/W	1,927	51	30		Y	Y	R,S	Y	Y	Y		Y	7	5
St. Philip's College	San Antonio	C,T	Dist	M/W	9,792	57	48		Y	Y	Y	Y	Y	Y	Y	N	6	73
San Antonio College	San Antonio	C,T	St-L	M/W	22,226	61												
South Plains College	Levelland	C,T	St-L	M/W	9,273	49	39	90	Y		Y	Y	Y	Y	Y	Y	10	59
South Texas College	McAllen	C,T,B	Dist	M/W	16,225	62	35		Y	Y	Y	Y	Y	Y		N	10	26
Tarrant County College District	Fort Worth	C,T	Cou	M/W	34,892	65	38	65	Y			Y	Y	Y	Y	N	6	43
Temple College	Temple	C,T	Dist	M/W	4,068	62												
Texas State Technical College Waco	Waco	C,T	St	M/W	4,452	33	18		Y	Y	Y	Y	Y	Y	Y	Y	7	44
Tomball College	Tomball	C,T	St-L	M/W	7,647	81	32		Y	Y		Y	Y	Y		N		10
Trinity Valley Community College	Athens	C,T	St-L	M/W	5,821	58	48		Y	Y		Y	Y	Y	Y	Y	6	54
Weatherford College	Weatherford	C,T	St-L	M/W	4,552				Y	Y		Y	Y	Y	Y	Y	4	15
Western Technical College	El Paso	C,T	Priv	M/W	825				Y	Y				Y	Y	N		3
Wharton County Junior College	Wharton	C,T	St-L	M/W	6,029		30		Y	Y	Y	Y	Y	Y	Y	Y	2	29
Utah																		
College of Eastern Utah	Price	C,T	St	M/W	2,294	43	26	60	Y	Y	R	Y	Y	Y	Y	Y	7	15
Dixie State College of Utah	St. George	C,T,B	St	M/W	8,992	62	21		Y	Y	Y	Y	Y	Y	Y	Y	9	79
ITT Technical Institute	Murray	T,B	Prop	M/W					N	Y	Y	Y	Y	Y	Y	N		12
Salt Lake Community College	Salt Lake City	C,T	St	M/W	24,111	66	37		Y			Y	Y	Y	Y	N	6	63
Snow College	Ephraim	C,T	St	M/W	3,333	26	14		Y	Y	Y	Y	Y	Y		Y	12	66
Utah Career College	West Jordan	C	Prop	M/W	570	73	53						Y	Y		N		9
Vermont																		
Community College of Vermont	Waterbury	C,T	St	M/W	5,801													
Landmark College†	Putney	C,T	Ind	M/W	371	37	7	90	N	Y	Y	Y	Y			Y	13	1
New England Culinary Institute at Essex	Essex Junction	B	Prop	M/W	501							Y						3
Virginia																		
Aviation Institute of Maintenance–Manassas	Manassas	T	Prop															1
Aviation Institute of Maintenance–Virginia Beach	Virginia Beach	T	Prop															1
Blue Ridge Community College	Weyers Cave	C,T	St	M/W	3,804	60	36		Y	Y	S	Y	Y	Y	Y	N	1	10
Bryant and Stratton College, Richmond	Richmond	T,B	Prop	M/W	421	67	75		N	Y	Y		Y	Y	Y	N		11
Dabney S. Lancaster Community College	Clifton Forge	C,T	St	M/W	1,453		59	60	Y	Y		Y		Y	Y	N	9	17
Danville Community College	Danville	C,T	St	M/W	4,089	67												
Eastern Shore Community College	Melfa	C,T	St	M/W	807													
ECPI College of Technology	Newport News	T,B	Prop	M/W	556		64		N	Y	Y	Y	Y	Y	Y	N		17
ECPI College of Technology	Virginia Beach	T,B	Prop	M/W	4,391	2	50		Y	Y	Y	Y	Y	Y	Y	Y		20
ECPI Technical College	Roanoke	T,B	Prop	M/W	300		47		N	Y	Y	Y	Y	Y	Y	N		21
ECPI Technical College	Glen Allen	T,B	Prop	M/W	473		48			Y						N		6
ECPI Technical College	Richmond	T,B	Prop	M/W	400		46		N	Y	Y	Y	Y	Y	Y	N		25
Germanna Community College	Locust Grove	C,T	St	M/W	4,799	72	53		Y		S	Y	Y	Y	Y	N	7	9
ITT Technical Institute	Chantilly	T,B	Prop	M/W					N	Y	Y	Y	Y	Y	Y	N		11
ITT Technical Institute	Norfolk	T,B	Prop	M/W					N	Y	Y	Y	Y	Y	Y	N		13
ITT Technical Institute	Richmond	T,B	Prop	M/W					N	Y	Y	Y	Y	Y	Y	N		10
ITT Technical Institute	Springfield	T,B	Prop	M/W					N	Y	Y	Y	Y	Y	Y	N		9
John Tyler Community College	Chester	C,T	St	M/W	6,314	75	51		Y			R	Y	Y		N	4	14
J. Sargeant Reynolds Community College	Richmond	C,T	St	M/W	11,678	75												
Lord Fairfax Community College	Middletown	C,T	St	M/W	5,492	72	49		Y		R	Y	Y	Y		N		21
National College of Business & Technology	Bluefield	T	Prop	M/W	203													
National College of Business & Technology	Charlottesville	T	Prop	M/W	163													
National College of Business & Technology	Harrisonburg	T	Prop	M/W	233													
National College of Business & Technology	Lynchburg	T	Prop	M/W	383													
National College of Business & Technology	Martinsville	T	Prop	M/W	383													
National College of Business & Technology	Salem	C,T,B,M	Prop	M/W	756													
Northern Virginia Community College	Annandale	C,T	St	M/W	39,353													

Two-Year Colleges At-a-Glance

This chart includes the names and locations of accredited two-year colleges in the United States and U.S. territories and shows institutions' responses to the *Thomson Peterson's Annual Survey of Undergraduate Institutions*. If an institution submitted incomplete data, one or more columns opposite the institution's name is blank. An asterisk after the school name denotes a *Special Message* following the college's profile, and a dagger indicates that the institution has one or more entries in the *College Close-Ups* section. If a school does not appear, it did not report any of the information.

Y—Yes; N—No; R—Recommended; S—For Some

Column headers (left to right): Degrees Awarded [College Transfer Associate (C), Terminal Associate (T), Bachelor's (B), Master's (M), Doctoral (D), First Professional (P)]; Institutional Control [County District City, State and Local, State-Related, Federal, State, Commonwealth/Territory, Independent, Independent-Religious, Proprietary]; Student Body [Men, Primarily Men, Women, Primarily Women, Coed]; Undergraduate Enrollment Fall 2005; Percent Attending Part-Time; Percent 25 Years of Age or Older; Percent of Grads Going on to Four-Year Colleges; High School Equivalency Certificate Accepted; Open Admissions; High School Transcript Required; Need-Based Aid Available; Part-Time Jobs Available; Career Counseling Available; Job Placement Services Available; College Housing Available; Number of Sports Offered; Number of Majors Offered

Institution	Location	Degrees	Control	Body	Enroll	% PT	% 25+	% Grads→4yr	HS Equiv	Open Adm	HS Transcript	Need Aid	PT Jobs	Career Couns	Job Place	Housing	Sports	Majors
Patrick Henry Community College	Martinsville	C,T	St	M/W	3,456													
Piedmont Virginia Community College	Charlottesville	C,T	St	M/W	4,163	74	44	23	Y	Y	S	Y	Y	Y	Y	N	11	30
Richard Bland College of The College of William and Mary	Petersburg	C	St	M/W	1,437	43	18	68	N	Y	Y	Y	Y			N	5	1
Southside Virginia Community College	Alberta	C,T	St	M/W	4,686	71	46		Y	Y	Y	Y	Y	Y	Y	N	5	14
Southwest Virginia Community College	Richlands	C,T	St	M/W	3,666	59	57		Y	Y	Y	Y	Y	Y	Y	N	10	18
Thomas Nelson Community College	Hampton	C,T	St	M/W	8,595	69			Y		Y	Y	Y	Y	Y		5	22
Tidewater Community College	Norfolk	C,T	St	M/W	23,718			53	Y			Y	Y	Y	Y	N	5	26
Westwood College–Arlington Ballston Campus†	Arlington	T,B	Prop	M/W														
Washington																		
The Art Institute of Seattle†	Seattle	T,B	Prop	M/W	2,492	48	52			Y	Y	Y	Y	Y	Y	Y	1	11
Big Bend Community College	Moses Lake	C,T	St	M/W	1,800	34	30		Y		S	Y	Y	Y	Y	Y	4	14
Cascadia Community College	Bothell	C,T	St	M/W	1,889	50												
Centralia College	Centralia	C,T	St	M/W	3,827		55		Y	Y	Y		Y	Y	Y	N	5	66
Clark College	Vancouver	C,T	St	M/W	9,820	57	36	67	Y		S	Y	Y	Y	Y	N	9	35
Clover Park Technical College	Lakewood	T	St	M/W	8,488	78												
Crown College	Tacoma	C,T,B	Prop	M/W	218		59			Y	Y	Y	Y	Y	Y	N		4
DigiPen Institute of Technology	Redmond	T,B,M	Prop	M/W	657	6								Y				2
Edmonds Community College	Lynnwood	C,T	St-L	M/W	7,581	55	11	25	Y			Y	Y	Y	Y	N	10	51
Everett Community College	Everett	C,T	St	M/W	7,188	55												
Green River Community College	Auburn	C,T	St	M/W	6,621	41												
Highline Community College*	Des Moines	C,T	St	M/W	6,372	49	52		Y			Y	Y	Y	Y	N	7	48
ITT Technical Institute	Bothell	T,B	Prop	M/W					N	Y	Y	Y	Y	Y	Y	N		12
ITT Technical Institute	Seattle	T,B	Prop	M/W					N	Y	Y	Y	Y	Y	Y	N		10
ITT Technical Institute	Spokane	T,B	Prop	M/W					N	Y	Y	Y	Y	Y	Y	N		10
Lower Columbia College	Longview	C,T	St	M/W	3,073	43	36		Y		R	Y	Y	Y		N	5	79
North Seattle Community College	Seattle	C,T	St	M/W	5,959	52	55	40	Y		Y	Y	Y	Y	Y	N	1	27
Northwest Indian College	Bellingham	C,T	Fed	M/W	1,189		75	40			Y	Y	Y	Y	Y	N	3	9
Olympic College	Bremerton	C,T	St	M/W	6,390	49												
Peninsula College	Port Angeles	C,T	St	M/W	4,256	67	66		Y		S	Y	Y	Y	Y	Y	11	19
Pima Medical Institute	Seattle	T	Prop	M/W	289													
Seattle Central Community College	Seattle	C,T	St	M/W	9,418		63					Y	Y	Y		N	6	25
Shoreline Community College	Shoreline	C	St	M/W	8,591													
Spokane Community College	Spokane	C,T	St	M/W	6,152	15	40		Y	Y	R	Y	Y	Y	Y	N	12	53
Spokane Falls Community College	Spokane	C,T	St	M/W	5,649		28		Y	Y	R	Y	Y	Y	Y	N	11	31
Tacoma Community College	Tacoma	C,T	St	M/W	6,056													
Walla Walla Community College	Walla Walla	C,T	St	M/W	4,440	51												
Whatcom Community College	Bellingham	C,T	St	M/W	4,173													
Yakima Valley Community College	Yakima	C,T	St	M/W	6,225		46		Y	Y	R,S	Y	Y	Y		Y	6	38
West Virginia																		
Community & Technical College at West Virginia University Institute of Technology	Montgomery	T	Cou	M/W														
Community and Technical College of Shepherd	Martinsburg	C,T	Cou	M/W	1,711	75								Y				15
Eastern West Virginia Community and Technical College	Moorefield	C,T	St	M/W	882	92										N		8
Fairmont State Community & Technical College†	Fairmont	C,T	St	M/W	3,355	44												
Marshall Community and Technical College	Huntington	T	Cou	M/W	2,589	50	55		Y	Y	Y				Y	Y	Y		23
Mountain State College	Parkersburg	T	Prop	PW	166		55		N	Y		Y	Y	Y	Y	N		6
New River Community and Technical College	Beckley	C,T	Cou	M/W														
Southern West Virginia Community and Technical College	Mount Gay	C,T	St	M/W	1,982	37	38		Y	Y	Y	Y	Y	Y	Y	N		16
Valley College	Martinsburg	T	Prop	PW	47									Y				1
West Virginia Business College	Wheeling	T	Prop	PW	78		50							Y		Y		4
West Virginia Northern Community College	Wheeling	C,T	St	M/W	2,842	50	94	33	Y	Y	S	Y	Y	Y	Y	N	4	18
West Virginia State Community and Technical College	Institute	C,T	Cou	M/W														
West Virginia University at Parkersburg	Parkersburg	C,T,B	St	M/W	3,722	42												
Wisconsin																		
Bryant and Stratton College	Milwaukee	T,B	Prop	M/W	488			9	N	Y	Y	Y	Y	Y	Y	N		8
Fox Valley Technical College	Appleton	C,T	St-L	M/W	7,855	79	51	10	Y	Y	Y	Y	Y	Y	Y	N	7	35
Herzing College	Madison	C,T,B	Prop	PM	650													
ITT Technical Institute	Green Bay	T,B	Prop	M/W					N	Y	Y	Y	Y	Y	Y	N		13
ITT Technical Institute	Greenfield	T,B	Prop	M/W	548				N	Y	Y	Y	Y	Y	Y	N		11
Lac Courte Oreilles Ojibwa Community College	Hayward	C,T	Fed	M/W	505	42	75	15	Y	Y	Y	Y	Y	Y	Y	N	4	9
Lakeshore Technical College	Cleveland	C,T	St-L	M/W	2,939	74	55		Y	Y	S	Y	Y	Y	Y	N		21
Milwaukee Area Technical College	Milwaukee	C,T	Dist	M/W	55,992													
Moraine Park Technical College	Fond du Lac	C,T	St-L	M/W	7,509	84	51		Y			R	Y					40
Southwest Wisconsin Technical College	Fennimore	T	St-L	M/W	1,861	58												
University of Wisconsin–Baraboo/Sauk County	Baraboo	C,T	St	M/W	548		19	80	N	Y	Y	Y	Y			N	9	1
University of Wisconsin–Barron County	Rice Lake	C	St	M/W	616													
University of Wisconsin–Manitowoc	Manitowoc	C,T	St	M/W	643		23	90	N	Y	Y	Y	Y			N	5	1

This chart includes the names and locations of accredited two-year colleges in the United States and U.S. territories and shows institutions' responses to the *Thomson Peterson's Annual Survey of Undergraduate Institutions.* If an institution submitted incomplete data, one or more columns opposite the institution's name is blank.

An asterisk after the school name denotes a *Special Message* following the college's profile, and a dagger indicates that the institution has one or more entries in the *College Close-Ups* section. If a school does not appear, it did not report any of the information.

Y—Yes; N—No; R—Recommended; S—For Some

Name	City	Degrees Awarded	Institutional Control	Student Body	Undergraduate Enrollment Fall 2005	Percent Attending Part-Time	Percent 25 Years of Age or Older	Percent of Grads Going on to Four-Year Colleges	High School Equivalency Certificate Accepted	Open Admissions	High School Transcript Required	Need-Based Aid Available	Part-Time Jobs Available	Career Counseling Available	Job Placement Services Available	College Housing Available	Number of Sports Offered	Number of Majors Offered
University of Wisconsin–Marathon County	Wausau	C	St	M/W	1,303	32												
University of Wisconsin–Marinette	Marinette	C	St	M/W	486													
University of Wisconsin–Richland	Richland Center	C	St	M/W	464	33	16		N	Y	Y	Y	Y	Y		Y	9	2
University of Wisconsin–Rock County	Janesville	C	St	M/W	880	15												
University of Wisconsin–Sheboygan	Sheboygan	C	St	M/W	731													
University of Wisconsin–Washington County	West Bend	C	St	M/W	951	30	16		N	Y	Y	Y	Y	Y		N	7	1
University of Wisconsin–Waukesha	Waukesha	C	St	M/W	2,064		16	95	N	Y	Y	Y	Y	Y		N	9	1
Waukesha County Technical College	Pewaukee	T	St-L	M/W	6,386	75	90		Y		Y	Y	Y	Y	Y	N	7	34
Western Technical College	La Crosse	C,T	Dist	M/W	4,765		16		Y	Y	Y	Y	Y	Y	Y	Y	3	45
Wisconsin Indianhead Technical College	Shell Lake	T	Dist	M/W	3,533	56	45											25
Wyoming																		
Casper College	Casper	C,T	Dist	M/W	4,285	56	45		Y	Y	Y	Y	Y	Y	Y	Y	12	73
Central Wyoming College	Riverton	C,T	St-L	M/W	1,637	57	41		Y	Y	R	Y	Y	Y	Y	Y	12	41
Eastern Wyoming College	Torrington	C,T	St-L	M/W	1,346	61	32		Y	Y	R	Y	Y	Y	Y	Y	12	45
Laramie County Community College	Cheyenne	C,T	St	M/W	4,603	63	45	46	Y	Y	Y	Y	Y	Y	Y	Y	10	78
Sheridan College–Sheridan and Gillette	Sheridan	C,T	St-L	M/W	2,895	64	38		Y	Y	R,S	Y	Y	Y	Y	Y	8	42
Western Wyoming Community College	Rock Springs	C,T	St-L	M/W	2,654	59												
OTHER COUNTRIES																		
Palau																		
Palau Community College	Koror	C,T	Terr	M/W	651	34	33		Y	Y	Y	Y	Y	Y	Y	Y	7	14

Profiles of Two-Year
COLLEGES

U.S. AND U.S. TERRITORIES

ALABAMA

ALABAMA SOUTHERN COMMUNITY COLLEGE

Monroeville, Alabama   **www.ascc.edu/**

- **State-supported** 2-year, founded 1965, part of Alabama College System
- **Rural** 80-acre campus
- **Coed**

Undergraduates Students come from 5 states and territories.
Academics *Calendar:* semesters. *Degree:* certificates and associate. *Special study options:* academic remediation for entering students, adult/continuing education programs, advanced placement credit, honors programs, part-time degree program, summer session for credit.
Student Life *Campus security:* 24-hour patrols.
Athletics Member NJCAA.
Standardized Tests *Required:* ACT COMPASS (for placement). *Recommended:* ACT (for placement).
Applying *Options:* early admission. *Required:* high school transcript.
Director of Admissions Ms. Jana S. Horton, Registrar, Alabama Southern Community College, PO Box 2000, Monroeville, AL 36461. *Phone:* 251-575-3156 Ext. 252. *E-mail:* jhorton@ascc.edu.

BESSEMER STATE TECHNICAL COLLEGE

Bessemer, Alabama   **www.bessemertech.com/**

- **State-supported** 2-year, founded 1966, part of Alabama College System
- **Small-town** 60-acre campus with easy access to Birmingham
- **Endowment** $43,950
- **Coed**

Undergraduates 39% African American, 0.3% Asian American or Pacific Islander, 0.3% Hispanic American, 0.1% Native American.
Academics *Calendar:* semesters. *Degree:* certificates, diplomas, and associate. *Special study options:* academic remediation for entering students, advanced placement credit, internships, part-time degree program, services for LD students.
Student Life *Campus security:* 24-hour patrols, student patrols.
Standardized Tests *Required:* ACT ASSET (for admission).
Financial Aid Of all full-time matriculated undergraduates who enrolled in 2004, 65 Federal Work-Study jobs (averaging $3000). 5 state and other part-time jobs.
Applying *Required:* high school transcript.
Director of Admissions Director of Admissions, Bessemer State Technical College, PO Box 308, Bessemer, AL 35021-0308. *Phone:* 205-428-6391. *Toll-free phone:* 800-235-5368.

BEVILL STATE COMMUNITY COLLEGE

Sumiton, Alabama   **www.bscc.edu/**

- **State-supported** 2-year, founded 1969, part of Alabama College System
- **Rural** 23-acre campus with easy access to Birmingham
- **Coed**

Undergraduates 2,465 full-time, 1,862 part-time. Students come from 4 states and territories, 12% African American, 0.4% Asian American or Pacific Islander, 0.3% Hispanic American, 0.2% Native American. *Retention:* 64% of 2003 full-time freshmen returned.
Faculty *Student/faculty ratio:* 16:1.

Academics *Calendar:* semesters. *Degree:* certificates and associate. *Special study options:* academic remediation for entering students, adult/continuing education programs, advanced placement credit, cooperative education, honors programs, off-campus study, part-time degree program, services for LD students, summer session for credit.
Athletics Member NJCAA.
Standardized Tests *Required:* ACT ASSET (for placement). *Required for some:* ACT (for placement).
Financial Aid Of all full-time matriculated undergraduates who enrolled in 2004, 126 Federal Work-Study jobs (averaging $1283).
Applying *Options:* early admission, deferred entrance. *Required:* high school transcript.
Director of Admissions Ms. Melissa Stowe, Enrollment Supervisor, Bevill State Community College, PO Box 800, Sumiton, AL 35148. *Phone:* 205-932-3221 Ext. 5101.

BISHOP STATE COMMUNITY COLLEGE

Mobile, Alabama   **www.bscc.cc.al.us/**

- **State-supported** 2-year, founded 1965, part of Alabama College System
- **Urban** 9-acre campus
- **Coed**, 4,883 undergraduate students, 49% full-time, 66% women, 34% men

Undergraduates 2,381 full-time, 2,502 part-time. Students come from 9 states and territories, 4% are from out of state, 63% African American, 1% Asian American or Pacific Islander, 0.6% Hispanic American, 0.8% Native American, 12% transferred in.
Freshmen *Admission:* 689 applied, 689 admitted, 689 enrolled.
Faculty *Total:* 189, 60% full-time, 78% with terminal degrees. *Student/faculty ratio:* 14:1.
Majors Accounting technology and bookkeeping; administrative assistant and secretarial science; civil engineering technology; computer and information sciences; drafting and design technology; electrical, electronic and communications engineering technology; engineering technology; funeral service and mortuary science; general studies; graphic and printing equipment operation/production; health information/medical records technology; instrumentation technology; liberal arts and sciences/liberal studies; nursing (registered nurse training); physical therapist assistant; special education (hearing impaired).
Academics *Calendar:* semesters. *Degree:* certificates and associate. *Special study options:* academic remediation for entering students, adult/continuing education programs, cooperative education, internships, part-time degree program, services for LD students, summer session for credit.
Library Minnie Slade Bishop Library with 56,687 titles, 265 serial subscriptions, 8,607 audiovisual materials.
Computers on Campus 96 computers available on campus for general student use. Internet access, at least one staffed computer lab available.
Student Life *Housing:* college housing not available. *Activities and Organizations:* drama/theater group, student-run radio station, choral group, Student Government Association, Health Occupations Students of America, Phi Beta Lambda, Phi Theta Kappa, Vocational Industrial Clubs of America. *Campus security:* 24-hour emergency response devices and patrols. *Student services:* health clinic.
Athletics Member NJCAA. *Intercollegiate sports:* baseball M, basketball M(s)/W(s), softball W(s).
Costs (2005–06) *Tuition:* state resident $1728 full-time, $72 per credit hour part-time; nonresident $3456 full-time, $144 per credit hour part-time. *Required fees:* $432 full-time, $18 per credit hour part-time.
Financial Aid Of all full-time matriculated undergraduates who enrolled in 2004, 299 Federal Work-Study jobs (averaging $2400).
Applying *Options:* common application, early admission, deferred entrance. *Required:* high school transcript. *Application deadline:* rolling (freshmen), rolling (transfers). *Notification:* continuous until 9/17 (freshmen).
Freshmen Application Contact Dr. Terry Hazzard, Dean of Students, Bishop State Community College, 351 North Broad Street, Mobile, AL 36603-5898. *Phone:* 251-690-6419. *Fax:* 251-438-5403. *E-mail:* info@bishop.edu.

CALHOUN COMMUNITY COLLEGE
Decatur, Alabama   www.calhoun.edu/

- **State-supported** 2-year, founded 1965, part of Alabama College System
- **Suburban** campus
- **Coed**

Undergraduates Students come from 9 states and territories, 16 other countries, 1% are from out of state, 19% African American, 1% Asian American or Pacific Islander, 2% Hispanic American, 2% Native American, 0.2% international.

Faculty *Student/faculty ratio:* 21:1.

Academics *Calendar:* semesters. *Degree:* certificates and associate. *Special study options:* academic remediation for entering students, accelerated degree program, adult/continuing education programs, advanced placement credit, cooperative education, distance learning, English as a second language, independent study, part-time degree program, services for LD students, summer session for credit.

Student Life *Campus security:* 24-hour patrols.

Standardized Tests *Required for some:* SAT or ACT (for admission).

Costs (2005–06) *Tuition:* state resident $3040 full-time, $71 per semester hour part-time; nonresident $5312 full-time, $142 per semester hour part-time. *Required fees:* $768 full-time, $24 per semester hour part-time.

Financial Aid Of all full-time matriculated undergraduates who enrolled in 2004, 50 Federal Work-Study jobs (averaging $3000).

Applying *Required for some:* high school transcript.

Freshmen Application Contact Ms. Patricia Landers, Admissions Receptionist, Calhoun Community College, PO Box 2216, 6250 Highway 31 North, Decatur, AL 35609-2216. *Phone:* 256-306-2593. *Toll-free phone:* 800-626-3628 Ext. 2594.

CENTRAL ALABAMA COMMUNITY COLLEGE
Alexander City, Alabama   www.cacc.cc.al.us/

- **State-supported** 2-year, founded 1965, part of Alabama College System
- **Small-town** 100-acre campus
- **Coed**

Undergraduates Students come from 6 states and territories, 25% African American, 0.4% Asian American or Pacific Islander, 0.7% Hispanic American, 0.2% Native American.

Faculty *Student/faculty ratio:* 15:1.

Academics *Calendar:* semesters. *Degree:* certificates and associate. *Special study options:* academic remediation for entering students, adult/continuing education programs, advanced placement credit, cooperative education, distance learning, internships, part-time degree program, services for LD students, summer session for credit.

Student Life *Campus security:* evening security.

Athletics Member NJCAA.

Standardized Tests *Required for some:* SAT or ACT (for admission).

Applying *Options:* common application, early admission. *Required:* high school transcript. *Required for some:* 3 letters of recommendation, interview.

Freshmen Application Contact Ms. Bettie Macmillan, Admission, Central Alabama Community College, PO Box 699, Alexander City, AL 35011-0699. *Phone:* 256-234-6346 Ext. 6232. *Toll-free phone:* 800-643-2657 Ext. 6232.

CHATTAHOOCHEE VALLEY COMMUNITY COLLEGE
Phenix City, Alabama   www.cv.edu/

- **State-supported** 2-year, founded 1974
- **Small-town** 103-acre campus
- **Endowment** $42,791
- **Coed,** 2,034 undergraduate students, 48% full-time, 66% women, 34% men

Undergraduates 972 full-time, 1,062 part-time. Students come from 6 states and territories, 10 other countries, 43% African American, 0.6% Asian American or Pacific Islander, 2% Hispanic American, 0.0% Native American. *Retention:* 66% of 2003 full-time freshmen returned.

Faculty *Total:* 88, 32% full-time.

Majors Administrative assistant and secretarial science; agriculture; biology/biological sciences; business administration and management; chemistry; clinical laboratory science/medical technology; criminal justice/law enforcement administration; data processing and data processing technology; dramatic/theater arts; elementary education; fire science; forestry; industrial radiologic technology; information science/studies; legal administrative assistant/secretary; liberal arts and sciences/liberal studies; mathematics; music; music teacher education; nursing (licensed practical/vocational nurse training); nursing (registered nurse training); physical education teaching and coaching; physics; pre-engineering.

Academics *Calendar:* semesters. *Degree:* certificates and associate. *Special study options:* academic remediation for entering students, adult/continuing education programs, advanced placement credit, distance learning, honors programs, off-campus study, part-time degree program, services for LD students, student-designed majors, summer session for credit.

Library Estelle Bain Owens Learning Resource Center and Library with 54,129 titles, 90 serial subscriptions, 853 audiovisual materials, a Web page.

Computers on Campus 55 computers available on campus for general student use. A campuswide network can be accessed from off campus. Internet access, at least one staffed computer lab available.

Student Life *Housing:* college housing not available. *Activities and Organizations:* drama/theater group, choral group. *Campus security:* 24-hour emergency response devices and patrols. *Student services:* personal/psychological counseling.

Athletics Member NJCAA. *Intercollegiate sports:* baseball M(s), softball W(s).

Financial Aid Of all full-time matriculated undergraduates who enrolled in 2004, 40 Federal Work-Study jobs (averaging $2000). 10 state and other part-time jobs (averaging $2000).

Applying *Options:* common application, early admission. *Required:* high school transcript. *Application deadline:* rolling (freshmen), rolling (transfers). *Notification:* continuous (freshmen).

Freshmen Application Contact Ms. Rita Cherry, Admissions Clerk, Chattahoochee Valley Community College, PO Box 1000, Phenix City, AL 36869. *Phone:* 334-291-4995. *Toll-free phone:* 800-842-2822. *Fax:* 334-291-4994. *E-mail:* information@cv.edu.

COMMUNITY COLLEGE OF THE AIR FORCE
Maxwell Air Force Base, Alabama   www.au.af.mil/au/ccaf/

- **Federally supported** 2-year, founded 1972
- **Suburban** campus
- **Coed, primarily men,** 351,715 undergraduate students, 100% full-time, 19% women, 81% men

Undergraduates 351,715 full-time. 15% African American, 4% Asian American or Pacific Islander, 1% Native American.
Freshmen *Admission:* 24,377 applied, 24,377 admitted, 24,377 enrolled.

Faculty *Total:* 6,720, 100% full-time. *Student/faculty ratio:* 28:1.

Majors Aeronautics/aviation/aerospace science and technology; airframe mechanics and aircraft maintenance technology; air traffic control; apparel and textile marketing management; atmospheric sciences and meteorology; automobile/automotive mechanics technology; avionics maintenance technology; biomedical technology; cardiovascular technology; clinical/medical laboratory technology; commercial and advertising art; communications technology; construction engineering technology; criminal justice/law enforcement administration; dental assisting; dental laboratory technology; dietetics; educational/instructional media design; educational leadership and administration; electrical, electronic and communications engineering technology; environmental health; environmental studies; finance; fire science; health/health care administration; hematology technology; hotel/motel administration; human resources management; industrial technology; legal assistant/paralegal; logistics and materials management; management information systems; medical physiology; medical radiologic technology; mental health/rehabilitation; metallurgical technology; military technologies; music performance; nuclear medical technology; occupational safety and health technology; office management; ophthalmic laboratory technology; parks, recreation and leisure; pharmacy technician; physical therapist assistant; public relations/image management; purchasing, procurement/acquisitions and contracts management; security and loss prevention; social work; surgical technology; vehicle/equipment operation.

Academics *Calendar:* continuous. *Degrees:* certificates and associate (courses conducted at 125 branch locations worldwide for members of the U.S. Air Force). *Special study options:* academic remediation for entering students, adult/continuing education programs, advanced placement credit, distance learning, independent study, internships.

Community College of the Air Force (continued)

Library Air Force Library Service with 5.0 million titles, 56,654 serial subscriptions, an OPAC, a Web page.

Computers on Campus Internet access available.

Student Life *Housing:* on-campus residence required for freshman year. *Options:* coed. Campus housing is university owned, leased by the school and is provided by a third party. Freshman applicants given priority for college housing. *Campus security:* 24-hour emergency response devices and patrols. *Student services:* health clinic, personal/psychological counseling, legal services.

Athletics *Intramural sports:* badminton M/W, baseball M, basketball M/W, bowling M/W, cross-country running M/W, football M, golf M/W, racquetball M/W, softball M/W, squash M/W, table tennis M/W, tennis M/W, track and field M/W, volleyball M/W, weight lifting M/W.

Standardized Tests *Required:* Armed Services Vocational Aptitude Battery (for admission).

Costs (2006–07) *Tuition:* Tuition, room and board, and medical and dental care are provided by the U.S. government. Each student receives a salary from which to pay for uniforms, supplies, and personal expenses.

Applying *Options:* electronic application. *Required:* high school transcript, letters of recommendation, interview, pass military physical, be of good character, no criminal record. *Application deadline:* rolling (freshmen), rolling (transfers). *Notification:* continuous (freshmen).

Freshmen Application Contact C.M. Sgt. Robert McAlexander, Director of Admissions/Registrar, Community College of the Air Force, 130 West Maxwell Boulevard, Building 836, Maxwell Air Force Base, Maxwell AFB, AL 36112-6613. *Phone:* 334-953-6436. *Fax:* 334-953-8211. *E-mail:* ronald.hall@maxwell.af.mil.

ENTERPRISE-OZARK COMMUNITY COLLEGE

Enterprise, Alabama **www.eocc.edu/**

- **State-supported** 2-year, founded 1965, part of Alabama College System
- **Small-town** 100-acre campus
- **Coed**

Undergraduates 866 full-time, 724 part-time. 21% African American, 3% Asian American or Pacific Islander, 4% Hispanic American, 1% Native American.

Academics *Calendar:* semesters. *Degree:* certificates and associate. *Special study options:* academic remediation for entering students, adult/continuing education programs, advanced placement credit, English as a second language, honors programs, internships, part-time degree program, services for LD students, summer session for credit.

Student Life *Campus security:* security personnel.

Athletics Member NJCAA.

Standardized Tests *Recommended:* SAT or ACT (for placement).

Financial Aid Of all full-time matriculated undergraduates who enrolled in 2004, 99 Federal Work-Study jobs (averaging $2000).

Applying *Options:* early admission, deferred entrance. *Required:* high school transcript.

Director of Admissions Mr. Gary Deas, Associate Dean of Students/Registrar, Enterprise-Ozark Community College, PO Box 1300, Enterprise, AL 36331. *Phone:* 334-347-2623 Ext. 2233. *E-mail:* gdeas@eocc.edu.

GADSDEN STATE COMMUNITY COLLEGE

Gadsden, Alabama **www.gadsdenstate.edu/**

- **State-supported** 2-year, founded 1965, part of Alabama College System
- **Small-town** 275-acre campus with easy access to Birmingham
- **Endowment** $1.3 million
- **Coed,** 5,426 undergraduate students, 55% full-time, 62% women, 38% men

Undergraduates 2,964 full-time, 2,462 part-time. Students come from 4 states and territories, 32 other countries, 4% are from out of state, 19% African American, 2% Asian American or Pacific Islander, 2% Hispanic American, 0.4% Native American.

Freshmen *Admission:* 1,680 applied, 1,680 admitted, 1,658 enrolled.

Faculty *Total:* 295, 48% full-time, 3% with terminal degrees.

Majors Administrative assistant and secretarial science; child care and support services management; civil engineering technology; clinical/medical laboratory technology; computer and information sciences; court reporting; criminal justice/police science; emergency medical technology (EMT paramedic); general retailing/wholesaling; general studies; heating, air conditioning and refrigeration technology; legal assistant/paralegal; liberal arts and sciences/liberal studies; mechanical engineering/mechanical technology; medical radiologic technology; nursing (registered nurse training); physical education teaching and coaching; radio and television broadcasting technology; substance abuse/addiction counseling; telecommunications; tool and die technology.

Academics *Calendar:* semesters. *Degree:* certificates and associate. *Special study options:* academic remediation for entering students, adult/continuing education programs, advanced placement credit, cooperative education, English as a second language, external degree program, part-time degree program, services for LD students, summer session for credit.

Library Meadows Library with 72,915 titles, 303 serial subscriptions.

Computers on Campus 200 computers available on campus for general student use. A campuswide network can be accessed. Internet access, at least one staffed computer lab available.

Student Life *Housing Options:* coed. *Activities and Organizations:* drama/theater group, student-run newspaper, radio station, choral group, Science, Math, and Engineering Club, Student Government Association, Circle K, Phi Beta Lambda, VICA. *Campus security:* 24-hour patrols. *Student services:* women's center.

Athletics Member NJCAA. *Intercollegiate sports:* baseball M(s), basketball M(s)/W(s), cross-country running W(s), golf M(s), softball W(s), tennis M(s), volleyball W(s). *Intramural sports:* basketball M/W, volleyball M/W.

Costs (2006–07) *Tuition:* state resident $90 per credit hour part-time; nonresident $161 per credit hour part-time.

Financial Aid Of all full-time matriculated undergraduates who enrolled in 2004, 95 Federal Work-Study jobs (averaging $1364).

Applying *Options:* early admission, deferred entrance. *Required:* high school transcript. *Application deadline:* rolling (freshmen), rolling (transfers).

Freshmen Application Contact Dr. Teresa Rhea, Admissions and Records, Gadsden State Community College, Admissions, Allen Hall, PO Box 227, Gadsden, AL 35902-0227. *Phone:* 256-549-8210. *Toll-free phone:* 800-226-5563. *Fax:* 256-549-8205. *E-mail:* info@gadsdenstate.edu.

GADSDEN STATE COMMUNITY COLLEGE-AYERS CAMPUS

Anniston, Alabama **www.gadsdenstate.edu/**

- **State-supported** 2-year, founded 1966
- **Small-town** 25-acre campus with easy access to Birmingham
- **Coed**

Undergraduates 686 full-time, 451 part-time. Students come from 2 states and territories, 31% African American, 0.5% Hispanic American, 0.6% Native American.

Faculty *Student/faculty ratio:* 18:1.

Academics *Calendar:* semesters. *Degree:* certificates and associate. *Special study options:* advanced placement credit, part-time degree program, services for LD students.

Student Life *Campus security:* late-night transport/escort service.

Standardized Tests *Required:* ACT ASSET (for placement).

Financial Aid Of all full-time matriculated undergraduates who enrolled in 2004, 25 Federal Work-Study jobs (averaging $2500).

Applying *Options:* deferred entrance. *Required:* high school transcript.

Freshmen Application Contact Mrs. Michele Conger, Director of Admissions and Records, Gadsden State Community College-Ayers Campus, 1801 Coleman Road, Anniston, AL 36207. *Phone:* 256-835-5400.

GEORGE CORLEY WALLACE STATE COMMUNITY COLLEGE

Selma, Alabama **www.wccs.edu/**

- **State-supported** 2-year, founded 1966, part of Alabama College System
- **Small-town** campus
- **Coed**

Faculty *Student/faculty ratio:* 17:1.

Academics *Calendar:* semesters. *Degree:* certificates, diplomas, and associate. *Special study options:* academic remediation for entering students, adult/

Alabama

continuing education programs, advanced placement credit, independent study, part-time degree program, services for LD students, summer session for credit.
Student Life *Campus security:* 24-hour patrols.
Athletics Member NJCAA.
Standardized Tests *Required:* ACT ASSET (for placement).
Costs (2005–06) *Tuition:* state resident $2160 full-time, $90 per credit hour part-time; nonresident $4320 full-time, $180 per credit hour part-time.
Financial Aid Of all full-time matriculated undergraduates who enrolled in 2004, 50 Federal Work-Study jobs (averaging $3000).
Applying *Options:* common application, early admission, deferred entrance.
Director of Admissions Ms. Sunette Newman, Registrar, George Corley Wallace State Community College, 3000 Earl Goodwin Parkway, Selma, AL 36702-2530. *Phone:* 334-876-9305.

GEORGE C. WALLACE COMMUNITY COLLEGE
Dothan, Alabama   www.wallace.edu/

- **State-supported** 2-year, founded 1949
- **Rural** 200-acre campus
- **Endowment** $446,000
- **Coed,** 3,500 undergraduate students, 55% full-time, 64% women, 36% men

Undergraduates 1,919 full-time, 1,581 part-time. Students come from 31 states and territories, 4 other countries, 4% are from out of state, 27% African American, 2% Asian American or Pacific Islander, 1% Hispanic American, 0.4% Native American.
Freshmen *Admission:* 838 enrolled.
Faculty *Total:* 241, 52% full-time. *Student/faculty ratio:* 7:1.
Majors Accounting; administrative assistant and secretarial science; automobile/automotive mechanics technology; business administration and management; carpentry; clinical/medical laboratory technology; commercial and advertising art; computer science; criminal justice/police science; data processing and data processing technology; drafting and design technology; electrical, electronic and communications engineering technology; emergency medical technology (EMT paramedic); heating, air conditioning, ventilation and refrigeration maintenance technology; industrial mechanics and maintenance technology; laser and optical technology; liberal arts and sciences/liberal studies; machine tool technology; medical administrative assistant and medical secretary; medical/clinical assistant; nursing (licensed practical/vocational nurse training); nursing (registered nurse training); physical therapist assistant; radiologic technology/science; respiratory care therapy; welding technology.
Academics *Calendar:* semesters. *Degree:* certificates and associate. *Special study options:* academic remediation for entering students, adult/continuing education programs, advanced placement credit, cooperative education, internships, off-campus study, part-time degree program, summer session for credit.
Library 45,353 titles, 399 serial subscriptions.
Computers on Campus 75 computers available on campus for general student use. At least one staffed computer lab available.
Student Life *Housing:* college housing not available. *Activities and Organizations:* drama/theater group, student-run newspaper. *Student services:* personal/psychological counseling.
Athletics Member NJCAA. *Intercollegiate sports:* basketball M(s)/W(s), tennis M(s)/W(s). *Intramural sports:* basketball M/W, tennis M/W, volleyball M/W.
Costs (2006–07) *Tuition:* state resident $2160 full-time, $72 per credit hour part-time; nonresident $4320 full-time, $144 per credit hour part-time. *Required fees:* $540 full-time, $18 per credit hour part-time.
Financial Aid Of all full-time matriculated undergraduates who enrolled in 2004, 83 Federal Work-Study jobs (averaging $2217).
Applying *Options:* early admission. *Required:* high school transcript. *Application deadline:* rolling (freshmen), rolling (transfers).
Freshmen Application Contact Dr. Brenda Barnes, Assistant Dean of Student Affairs, George C. Wallace Community College, 1141 Wallace Drive, Dothan, AL 36303-9234. *Phone:* 334-983-3521 Ext. 283. *Toll-free phone:* 800-543-2426. *Fax:* 334-983-3600. *E-mail:* bbarnes@wallace.edu.

H. COUNCILL TRENHOLM STATE TECHNICAL COLLEGE
Montgomery, Alabama   www.trenholmtech.cc.al.us/

- **State-supported** 2-year, founded 1962, part of Alabama Department of Post Secondary Education
- **Urban** 78-acre campus
- **Coed,** 1,403 undergraduate students, 51% full-time, 51% women, 49% men

Undergraduates 711 full-time, 692 part-time. Students come from 1 other state, 60% African American, 0.6% Asian American or Pacific Islander, 0.4% Hispanic American, 0.1% Native American.
Freshmen *Admission:* 1,204 applied, 509 admitted, 385 enrolled.
Faculty *Total:* 111, 58% full-time. *Student/faculty ratio:* 10:1.
Majors Accounting technology and bookkeeping; administrative assistant and secretarial science; automobile/automotive mechanics technology; automotive engineering technology; carpentry; child care and support services management; clothing/textiles; computer and information sciences; construction engineering technology; cosmetology; culinary arts; dental assisting; dental laboratory technology; drafting and design technology; electrical, electronic and communications engineering technology; electrician; emergency medical technology (EMT paramedic); graphic and printing equipment operation/production; graphic communications related; heating, air conditioning, ventilation and refrigeration maintenance technology; heavy equipment maintenance technology; industrial electronics technology; industrial mechanics and maintenance technology; information science/studies; instrumentation technology; machine tool technology; massage therapy; medical/clinical assistant; pipefitting and sprinkler fitting; tool and die technology; welding technology.
Academics *Calendar:* semesters. *Degree:* certificates, diplomas, and associate. *Special study options:* academic remediation for entering students, adult/continuing education programs, advanced placement credit, cooperative education, internships, part-time degree program, services for LD students, summer session for credit.
Library Main Library plus 1 other with 2,945 titles, 80 serial subscriptions, 206 audiovisual materials, an OPAC, a Web page.
Computers on Campus 443 computers available on campus for general student use. A campuswide network can be accessed. Internet access, at least one staffed computer lab available.
Student Life *Housing:* college housing not available. *Campus security:* 24-hour emergency response devices and patrols.
Costs (2005–06) *One-time required fee:* $35. *Tuition:* state resident $2160 full-time, $71 per hour part-time; nonresident $4320 full-time, $142 per hour part-time. *Required fees:* $540 full-time, $19 per hour part-time.
Applying *Options:* early admission. *Required:* high school transcript. *Application deadline:* rolling (freshmen), rolling (transfers).
Freshmen Application Contact Ms. Tennie McBryde, Registrar, H. Councill Trenholm State Technical College, 1225 Air Base Boulevard, Montgomery, AL 36108. *Phone:* 334-420-4306. *Fax:* 334-420-4201. *E-mail:* tmcbryde@trenholmtech.cc.al.us.

HERZING COLLEGE
Birmingham, Alabama   www.herzing.edu/birmingham/
Director of Admissions Ms. Tess Anderson, Admissions Coordinator, Herzing College, 280 West Valley Avenue, Birmingham, AL 35209. *Phone:* 205-916-2800. *E-mail:* admiss@bhm.herzing.edu.

ITT TECHNICAL INSTITUTE
Birmingham, Alabama   www.itt-tech.edu/

- **Proprietary** primarily 2-year, founded 1994, part of ITT Educational Services, Inc
- **Suburban** campus
- **Coed**

Academics *Calendar:* quarters. *Degrees:* associate and bachelor's.
Library a Web page.
Computers on Campus Internet access, at least one staffed computer lab available.
Student Life *Housing:* college housing not available. *Activities and Organizations:* student-run newspaper. *Campus security:* 24-hour emergency response devices.

ITT Technical Institute (continued)

Standardized Tests *Required:* Wonderlic aptitude test (for admission).

Costs (2005–06) *Tuition:* Please see school catalog for specific information.

Applying *Options:* deferred entrance. *Application fee:* $100. *Required:* high school transcript, interview. *Recommended:* letters of recommendation. *Application deadline:* rolling (freshmen), rolling (transfers). *Notification:* continuous (freshmen).

Freshmen Application Contact Jesse L. Johnson, Director of Recruitment, ITT Technical Institute, 6270 Park South Drive, Bessemer, AL 35022. *Phone:* 205-497-5700. *Toll-free phone:* 800-488-7033. *Fax:* 205-497-5799.

JAMES H. FAULKNER STATE COMMUNITY COLLEGE

Bay Minette, Alabama   **www.faulknerstate.edu/**

- **State-supported** 2-year, founded 1965, part of Alabama College System
- **Small-town** 105-acre campus
- **Coed,** 3,067 undergraduate students, 63% full-time, 61% women, 39% men

Faulkner State Community College (FSCC), accredited by the Southern Association of Colleges and Schools, offers both transfer and certificate programs. The main campus is located in Bay Minette, Alabama, with branches in Fairhope and Gulf Shores, Alabama. FSCC serves the entire Gulf Coast area. For information, prospective students should call 800-231-3752 (toll-free).

Undergraduates 1,925 full-time, 1,142 part-time. 3% are from out of state, 13% African American, 0.5% Asian American or Pacific Islander, 0.6% Hispanic American, 1% Native American, 9% live on campus.

Freshmen *Admission:* 853 enrolled.

Faculty *Total:* 158, 39% full-time. *Student/faculty ratio:* 15:1.

Majors Administrative assistant and secretarial science; agricultural economics; business administration and management; commercial and advertising art; computer and information sciences; criminal justice/law enforcement administration; dental assisting; environmental engineering technology; general studies; hospitality administration; landscaping and groundskeeping; legal assistant/paralegal; liberal arts and sciences/liberal studies; mass communications; nursing (licensed practical/vocational nurse training); nursing (registered nurse training); parks, recreation and leisure facilities management; surgical technology.

Academics *Calendar:* semesters. *Degree:* certificates and associate. *Special study options:* academic remediation for entering students, adult/continuing education programs, advanced placement credit, cooperative education, honors programs, internships, part-time degree program, services for LD students.

Library Austin R. Meadows Library with 53,100 titles, 200 serial subscriptions, 2,513 audiovisual materials, an OPAC.

Computers on Campus 208 computers available on campus for general student use. A campuswide network can be accessed. Internet access, at least one staffed computer lab available.

Student Life *Housing Options:* men-only, women-only. *Activities and Organizations:* drama/theater group, student-run newspaper, choral group, Student Government Association, Pow-Wow Leadership Society, Phi Theta Kappa, Association of Computational Machinery, Phi Beta Lambda, national fraternities. *Campus security:* 24-hour patrols, controlled dormitory access. *Student services:* personal/psychological counseling.

Athletics Member NJCAA. *Intercollegiate sports:* baseball M(s), basketball M(s)/W(s), golf M(s), softball W(s), tennis M(s)/W(s), volleyball W(s). *Intramural sports:* basketball M, tennis M/W, volleyball M/W.

Costs (2006–07) *Tuition:* state resident $2790 full-time, $93 per credit hour part-time; nonresident $4920 full-time, $164 per credit hour part-time. *Room and board:* $2931.

Applying *Options:* early admission, deferred entrance. *Required:* high school transcript. *Application deadline:* rolling (freshmen), rolling (transfers). *Notification:* continuous until 8/18 (freshmen).

Freshmen Application Contact Ms. Peggy Duck, Director of High School Relations/Student Activities, James H. Faulkner State Community College, 1900 Highway 31 South, Bay Minette, AL 36507. *Phone:* 251-580-2152. *Toll-free phone:* 800-231-3752 Ext. 2111.

JEFFERSON DAVIS COMMUNITY COLLEGE

Brewton, Alabama   **www.jdcc.edu/**

Director of Admissions Ms. Robin Sessions, Coordinator of Admissions and Records, Jefferson Davis Community College, PO Box 958, Brewton, AL 36427. *Phone:* 251-867-4832.

JEFFERSON STATE COMMUNITY COLLEGE

Birmingham, Alabama   **www.jeffstateonline.com**

- **State-supported** 2-year, founded 1965, part of Alabama College System
- **Suburban** 234-acre campus
- **Coed,** 7,173 undergraduate students, 44% full-time, 62% women, 38% men

Undergraduates 3,129 full-time, 4,044 part-time. Students come from 28 states and territories, 61 other countries, 1% are from out of state, 21% African American, 2% Asian American or Pacific Islander, 1% Hispanic American, 0.3% Native American, 2% international, 8% transferred in.

Freshmen *Admission:* 1,260 enrolled. *Average high school GPA:* 2.76.

Faculty *Total:* 397, 31% full-time, 15% with terminal degrees. *Student/faculty ratio:* 21:1.

Majors Accounting technology and bookkeeping; administrative assistant and secretarial science; agricultural business and management; banking and financial support services; biomedical technology; business/commerce; child care and support services management; clinical/medical laboratory technology; computer and information sciences; construction engineering technology; criminal justice/police science; fire services administration; funeral service and mortuary science; general studies; home furnishings and equipment installation; hospitality administration; liberal arts and sciences/liberal studies; medical radiologic technology; nursing (registered nurse training); physical therapist assistant; radio and television broadcasting technology; robotics technology; veterinary technology.

Academics *Calendar:* semesters. *Degree:* certificates and associate. *Special study options:* academic remediation for entering students, adult/continuing education programs, advanced placement credit, distance learning, honors programs, independent study, internships, part-time degree program, services for LD students, summer session for credit. *ROTC:* Army (c), Air Force (c).

Library James B. Allen Library plus 1 other with 77,015 titles, 242 serial subscriptions, 3,349 audiovisual materials, an OPAC.

Computers on Campus A campuswide network can be accessed from off campus. Internet access, online (class) registration, at least one staffed computer lab available.

Student Life *Housing:* college housing not available. *Activities and Organizations:* drama/theater group, student-run newspaper, radio station, choral group, Student Government Association, Phi Theta Kappa, Baptist Campus Ministries, Jefferson State Ambassadors, Students in Free Enterprise (SIFE). *Campus security:* 24-hour patrols. *Student services:* women's center.

Athletics Member NJCAA. *Intercollegiate sports:* baseball M(s), softball W(s). *Intramural sports:* badminton M/W, basketball M/W, bowling M/W, soccer M/W, softball M/W, tennis M/W, volleyball M/W.

Costs (2005–06) *Tuition:* state resident $2130 full-time, $71 per semester hour part-time; nonresident $4260 full-time, $143 per semester hour part-time. *Required fees:* $930 full-time, $31 per semester hour part-time. *Waivers:* senior citizens and employees or children of employees.

Financial Aid Of all full-time matriculated undergraduates who enrolled in 2004, 189 Federal Work-Study jobs (averaging $1926).

Applying *Options:* electronic application, early admission, deferred entrance. *Required for some:* high school transcript. *Application deadline:* rolling (freshmen). *Notification:* continuous (freshmen).

Freshmen Application Contact Mr. Michael Hobbs, Director of Enrollment Services, Jefferson State Community College, 2601 Carson Road, Birmingham, AL 35215-3098. *Phone:* 205-853-1200 Ext. 7991. *Toll-free phone:* 800-239-5900. *Fax:* 205-856-6070.

J. F. DRAKE STATE TECHNICAL COLLEGE

Huntsville, Alabama   www.drakestate.edu/

- **State-supported** 2-year, founded 1961, part of State of Alabama Department of Postsecondary Education
- **Urban** 6-acre campus with easy access to Huntsville
- **Coed,** 764 undergraduate students, 59% full-time, 49% women, 51% men

Undergraduates 454 full-time, 310 part-time. Students come from 1 other state, 4% are from out of state, 57% African American, 0.9% Asian American or Pacific Islander, 2% Hispanic American, 0.3% Native American.
Freshmen *Admission:* 628 applied, 378 admitted, 212 enrolled.
Faculty *Total:* 67, 37% full-time, 6% with terminal degrees. *Student/faculty ratio:* 21:1.
Majors Accounting; administrative assistant and secretarial science; commercial and advertising art; drafting and design technology; electrical, electronic and communications engineering technology; information science/studies; machine tool technology.
Academics *Calendar:* semesters. *Degree:* certificates, diplomas, and associate. *Special study options:* academic remediation for entering students, cooperative education, internships, part-time degree program, services for LD students.
Computers on Campus 380 computers available on campus for general student use. At least one staffed computer lab available.
Student Life *Housing:* college housing not available. *Activities and Organizations:* student-run newspaper, Phi Beta Lambda, Vocational Industrial Clubs of America. *Campus security:* 24-hour patrols.
Costs (2005–06) *Tuition:* state resident $2700 full-time, $72 per semester hour part-time; nonresident $5400 full-time, $144 per semester hour part-time. *Required fees:* $540 full-time, $18 per semester hour part-time. *Waivers:* employees or children of employees.
Applying *Options:* deferred entrance. *Required:* high school transcript. *Application deadline:* rolling (freshmen).
Freshmen Application Contact Mrs. Shirley Clemons, Registrar, J. F. Drake State Technical College, 3421 Meridian Street, Huntsville, AL 35811. *Phone:* 256-539-8161. *Toll-free phone:* 888-413-7253. *Fax:* 256-551-3142. *E-mail:* clemons@drakestate.edu.

LAWSON STATE COMMUNITY COLLEGE

Birmingham, Alabama   www.lawsonstate.edu/

- **State-supported** 2-year, founded 1949, part of Alabama College System
- **Urban** 30-acre campus
- **Coed,** 3,371 undergraduate students, 52% full-time, 65% women, 35% men

Undergraduates 1,740 full-time, 1,631 part-time. Students come from 2 states and territories, 1% are from out of state, 83% African American, 0.4% Asian American or Pacific Islander, 0.4% Hispanic American, 0.1% Native American, 2% transferred in. *Retention:* 68% of 2003 full-time freshmen returned.
Freshmen *Admission:* 1,738 applied, 862 admitted, 862 enrolled.
Faculty *Total:* 219, 45% full-time. *Student/faculty ratio:* 16:1.
Majors Accounting; administrative assistant and secretarial science; art; biology/biological sciences; business administration and management; business teacher education; carpentry; chemistry; clinical laboratory science/medical technology; clothing/textiles; computer and information sciences related; cosmetology; crafts, folk art and artisanry; criminal justice/law enforcement administration; criminal justice/police science; dietetics; drafting and design technology; education; electrical, electronic and communications engineering technology; English; fire science; health and physical education; heavy equipment maintenance technology; history; hydrology and water resources science; information science/studies; legal administrative assistant/secretary; liberal arts and sciences/liberal studies; library science; mathematics; music; nursing (registered nurse training); parks, recreation and leisure; physical sciences; physical therapy; political science and government; pre-engineering; pre-law studies; psychology; radio and television; social sciences; social work; sociology; urban studies/affairs.
Academics *Calendar:* semesters. *Degree:* certificates and associate. *Special study options:* academic remediation for entering students, adult/continuing education programs, cooperative education, distance learning, freshman honors college, honors programs, internships, part-time degree program, summer session for credit.
Library Lawson State Library with 31,998 titles, 170 serial subscriptions, 506 audiovisual materials, an OPAC.

Computers on Campus 140 computers available on campus for general student use. A campuswide network can be accessed. Internet access, online (class) registration, at least one staffed computer lab available.
Student Life *Housing:* college housing not available. *Activities and Organizations:* choral group. *Campus security:* 24-hour emergency response devices and patrols, student patrols.
Athletics Member NJCAA. *Intercollegiate sports:* baseball W, basketball M/W, cross-country running M(s), equestrian sports M, volleyball W(s). *Intramural sports:* basketball M/W, softball M/W, swimming and diving M/W, table tennis M/W, tennis M/W, track and field M/W, volleyball W, weight lifting M.
Costs (2006–07) *Tuition:* state resident $2160 full-time, $72 per credit part-time; nonresident $4320 full-time, $144 per credit part-time. *Required fees:* $540 full-time.
Financial Aid Of all full-time matriculated undergraduates who enrolled in 2004, 91 Federal Work-Study jobs (averaging $3000).
Applying *Options:* common application, early admission, deferred entrance. *Required:* high school transcript. *Application deadline:* rolling (freshmen), rolling (transfers). *Notification:* continuous (freshmen).
Freshmen Application Contact Mr. Darren Allen, Director of Admissions and Records, Lawson State Community College, 3060 Wilson Road, SW, Birmingham, AL 35221-1798. *Phone:* 205-929-6361. *Fax:* 205-923-7106. *E-mail:* dallen@lawsonstate.edu.

LURLEEN B. WALLACE COMMUNITY COLLEGE

Andalusia, Alabama   www.lbwcc.edu/

Director of Admissions Mrs. Judy Hall, Director of Student Services, Lurleen B. Wallace Community College, PO Box 1418, Andalusia, AL 36420. *Phone:* 334-222-6591 Ext. 271.

MARION MILITARY INSTITUTE

Marion, Alabama   www.marionmilitary.org/

Director of Admissions Dan Sumlin, Director of Admissions, Marion Military Institute, 1101 Washington Street, Marion, AL 36756. *Phone:* 800-664-1842 Ext. 306. *Toll-free phone:* 800-664-1842 Ext. 307.

NORTHEAST ALABAMA COMMUNITY COLLEGE

Rainsville, Alabama   www.nacc.edu/

- **State-supported** 2-year, founded 1963, part of Alabama College System
- **Rural** 100-acre campus
- **Coed**

Undergraduates 978 full-time, 1,037 part-time. Students come from 3 states and territories, 2% are from out of state, 2% African American, 0.2% Asian American or Pacific Islander, 1% Hispanic American, 5% Native American. *Retention:* 62% of 2003 full-time freshmen returned.
Faculty *Student/faculty ratio:* 32:1.
Academics *Calendar:* quarters. *Degree:* certificates and associate. *Special study options:* academic remediation for entering students, accelerated degree program, adult/continuing education programs, advanced placement credit, honors programs, part-time degree program, services for LD students, summer session for credit.
Student Life *Campus security:* 24-hour emergency response devices and patrols, late-night transport/escort service.
Standardized Tests *Required:* ACT ASSET, ACT COMPASS (for placement).
Costs (2005–06) *Tuition:* state resident $2700 full-time, $90 per credit hour part-time; nonresident $4860 full-time, $161 per credit hour part-time. Part-time tuition and fees vary according to location.
Financial Aid Of all full-time matriculated undergraduates who enrolled in 2004, 40 Federal Work-Study jobs (averaging $2500).
Applying *Options:* early admission, deferred entrance.
Freshmen Application Contact Dr. Joe Burke, Director of Admissions, Northeast Alabama Community College, PO Box 159, Rainsville, AL 35986. *Phone:* 256-228-6001.

NORTHWEST-SHOALS COMMUNITY COLLEGE

Muscle Shoals, Alabama   www.nwscc.edu/

- **State-supported** 2-year, founded 1963, part of State of Alabama Department of Postsecondary Education
- **Small-town** 205-acre campus
- **Coed,** 3,380 undergraduate students, 63% full-time, 61% women, 39% men

Undergraduates 2,132 full-time, 1,248 part-time. Students come from 8 states and territories, 5 other countries, 1% are from out of state, 12% African American, 0.1% Asian American or Pacific Islander, 0.9% Hispanic American, 2% Native American, 2% live on campus.
Freshmen *Admission:* 1,576 applied, 1,082 admitted, 744 enrolled.
Faculty *Total:* 254, 30% full-time, 4% with terminal degrees. *Student/faculty ratio:* 19:1.
Majors Accounting; administrative assistant and secretarial science; agricultural teacher education; art; business administration and management; child development; clinical laboratory science/medical technology; computer and information sciences; computer engineering technology; computer programming; computer science; computer typography and composition equipment operation; criminal justice/law enforcement administration; criminal justice/police science; drafting and design technology; education; electrical, electronic and communications engineering technology; elementary education; environmental biology; environmental science; fire science; forestry; general studies; industrial electronics technology; industrial mechanics and maintenance technology; information science/studies; liberal arts and sciences/liberal studies; medical laboratory technology; multi-/interdisciplinary studies related; nursing (licensed practical/vocational nurse training); nursing (registered nurse training); pre-dentistry studies; pre-engineering; pre-law studies; pre-nursing studies; pre-pharmacy studies; pre-veterinary studies; secondary education; veterinary sciences; water quality and wastewater treatment management and recycling technology; welding technology.
Academics *Calendar:* semesters. *Degree:* certificates, diplomas, and associate. *Special study options:* academic remediation for entering students, accelerated degree program, adult/continuing education programs, advanced placement credit, cooperative education, honors programs, internships, part-time degree program, summer session for credit. *ROTC:* Army (b).
Library Larry W. McCoy Learning Resource Center and James Glasgow Library with 57,827 titles, 268 serial subscriptions, 1,428 audiovisual materials.
Computers on Campus 620 computers available on campus for general student use. A campuswide network can be accessed from off campus. Internet access, at least one staffed computer lab available.
Student Life *Housing Options:* coed. Campus housing is university owned. *Activities and Organizations:* choral group, Student Government Association, Science Club, Phi Theta Kappa, Baptist Campus Ministry, Northwest-Shoals Singers. *Campus security:* 24-hour emergency response devices and patrols. *Student services:* personal/psychological counseling.
Athletics Member NJCAA. *Intercollegiate sports:* baseball M(s), basketball M(s)/W(s), cheerleading M(s)/W(s), cross-country running M(s), golf M(s), softball W(s), tennis W(s), volleyball W(s). *Intramural sports:* basketball M/W, softball M/W, table tennis M/W, tennis M/W, volleyball M/W.
Costs (2006–07) *Tuition:* state resident $2130 full-time, $71 per credit hour part-time; nonresident $4260 full-time, $142 per credit hour part-time. *Required fees:* $750 full-time, $25 per credit hour part-time. *Room and board:* room only: $1675.
Financial Aid *Financial aid deadline:* 6/1.
Applying *Options:* common application. *Required:* high school transcript. *Application deadline:* rolling (freshmen), rolling (transfers).
Freshmen Application Contact Dr. Karen Berryhill, Vice President of Student Development Services, Northwest-Shoals Community College, PO Box 2545, Muscle Shoals, AL 35662. *Phone:* 256-331-5261. *Toll-free phone:* 800-645-8967. *Fax:* 256-331-5366.

PRINCE INSTITUTE OF PROFESSIONAL STUDIES

Montgomery, Alabama   www.princeinstitute.edu/

- **Independent** 2-year
- **Suburban** campus
- **Endowment** $6040
- **Coed, primarily women,** 94 undergraduate students, 60% full-time, 100% women

Undergraduates 56 full-time, 38 part-time. 1% are from out of state, 17% African American.
Freshmen *Admission:* 9 applied, 9 admitted, 4 enrolled.
Faculty *Total:* 7, 71% full-time, 43% with terminal degrees. *Student/faculty ratio:* 15:1.
Majors Court reporting.
Academics *Calendar:* quarters. *Degree:* certificates and associate.
Student Life *Housing:* college housing not available. *Student services:* personal/psychological counseling.
Costs (2006–07) *Tuition:* $8448 full-time. *Required fees:* $340 full-time.
Applying *Application fee:* $90. *Required:* high school transcript, interview. *Application deadline:* 10/1 (freshmen).
Freshmen Application Contact Ms. Sherry Hill, Director of Admissions, Prince Institute of Professional Studies, 7735 Atlanta Highway, Montgomery, AL 36117. *Phone:* 334-271-1670. *Toll-free phone:* 877-853-5569. *Fax:* 334-271-1671. *E-mail:* admissions@princeinstitute.edu.

REID STATE TECHNICAL COLLEGE

Evergreen, Alabama   www.rstc.cc.al.us/

- **State-supported** 2-year, founded 1966, part of Alabama College System
- **Rural** 26-acre campus
- **Coed**

Undergraduates 390 full-time, 230 part-time. Students come from 2 states and territories, 1% are from out of state, 54% African American, 0.6% Hispanic American, 1% Native American.
Faculty *Student/faculty ratio:* 16:1.
Academics *Calendar:* semesters. *Degree:* certificates, diplomas, and associate. *Special study options:* academic remediation for entering students, adult/continuing education programs, double majors, independent study, internships, part-time degree program, services for LD students, summer session for credit.
Student Life *Campus security:* 24-hour emergency response devices, day and evening security guard.
Standardized Tests *Required:* ACT ASSET, Ability-To-Benefit Admissions Test (for placement).
Financial Aid Of all full-time matriculated undergraduates who enrolled in 2004, 35 Federal Work-Study jobs (averaging $1500).
Applying *Options:* common application, early admission. *Required:* high school transcript.
Freshmen Application Contact Ms. Alesia Stuart, Public Relations/Marketing, Reid State Technical College, PO Box 588, Intersection of I-95 and Highway 83, Evergreen, AL 36401-0588. *Phone:* 251-578-1313 Ext. 108.

REMINGTON COLLEGE—MOBILE CAMPUS

Mobile, Alabama   www.remingtoncollege.edu/

- **Proprietary** primarily 2-year, part of Education America
- **Suburban** 5-acre campus
- **Coed,** 433 undergraduate students, 100% full-time, 39% women, 61% men

Undergraduates 433 full-time. Students come from 3 states and territories, 4% are from out of state, 47% African American, 0.9% Asian American or Pacific Islander, 1% Hispanic American, 1% Native American. *Retention:* 90% of 2003 full-time freshmen returned.
Freshmen *Admission:* 119 applied, 114 admitted.
Faculty *Total:* 41, 73% full-time, 10% with terminal degrees. *Student/faculty ratio:* 16:1.

Majors Computer and information sciences; computer engineering technology; computer systems networking and telecommunications; drafting and design technology; information science/studies; operations management; web/multimedia management and webmaster.

Academics *Calendar:* quarters. *Degrees:* diplomas, associate, and bachelor's. *Special study options:* adult/continuing education programs, cooperative education, services for LD students.

Library SCT plus 1 other.

Computers on Campus Internet access available.

Student Life *Housing:* college housing not available. *Activities and Organizations:* Association of Information Technology Professionals, Instrumentation Technology Association.

Standardized Tests *Required:* Wonderlic aptitude test (for admission).

Costs (2006–07) *Tuition:* $34,200 full-time. *Required fees:* $50 full-time.

Financial Aid Of all full-time matriculated undergraduates who enrolled in 2004, 500 applied for aid, 500 were judged to have need. *Average percent of need met:* 45%. *Average financial aid package:* $7043. *Average need-based loan:* $3000. *Average need-based gift aid:* $7043. *Average indebtedness upon graduation:* $14,000.

Applying *Application fee:* $50. *Required:* high school transcript, interview.

Freshmen Application Contact Mr. Chris Jones, Director of Recruitment, Remington College–Mobile Campus, 828 Downtowner Loop West, Mobile, AL 36609. *Phone:* 251-343-8200 Ext. 208. *Toll-free phone:* 800-866-0850. *Fax:* 251-343-0577.

SHELTON STATE COMMUNITY COLLEGE
Tuscaloosa, Alabama   www.sheltonstate.edu/

- **State-supported** 2-year, founded 1979, part of Alabama College System
- **Small-town** 30-acre campus with easy access to Birmingham
- **Coed,** 5,754 undergraduate students, 58% full-time, 53% women, 47% men

Undergraduates 3,363 full-time, 2,391 part-time. Students come from 11 states and territories, 2% are from out of state, 29% African American, 1% Asian American or Pacific Islander, 0.9% Hispanic American, 0.4% Native American, 35% transferred in.
Freshmen *Admission:* 2,201 applied, 2,201 admitted, 1,741 enrolled.

Faculty *Total:* 199, 41% full-time, 6% with terminal degrees. *Student/faculty ratio:* 30:1.

Majors Administrative assistant and secretarial science; culinary arts; diesel mechanics technology; drafting and design technology; electrical, electronic and communications engineering technology; emergency medical technology (EMT paramedic); heating, air conditioning, ventilation and refrigeration maintenance technology; industrial electronics technology; liberal arts and sciences/liberal studies; machine tool technology; medical administrative assistant and medical secretary; nursing (registered nurse training); respiratory care therapy; welding technology.

Academics *Calendar:* semesters. *Degree:* certificates, diplomas, and associate. *Special study options:* academic remediation for entering students, accelerated degree program, adult/continuing education programs, advanced placement credit, distance learning, honors programs, part-time degree program, services for LD students, summer session for credit. *ROTC:* Army (c), Air Force (c).

Library Brooks-Cork Library plus 1 other with 50,123 titles, 361 serial subscriptions, 3,247 audiovisual materials, an OPAC, a Web page.

Computers on Campus 150 computers available on campus for general student use. A campuswide network can be accessed from off campus. Internet access, online (class) registration, at least one staffed computer lab available.

Student Life *Housing:* college housing not available. *Activities and Organizations:* drama/theater group, student-run newspaper, choral group, PTK, Student Government Association, African American Cultural Association. *Campus security:* 24-hour emergency response devices and patrols.

Athletics Member NJCAA. *Intercollegiate sports:* baseball M(s), basketball M(s)/W(s), cheerleading M(s)/W(s), soccer W(s), softball W(s). *Intramural sports:* fencing M/W.

Costs (2005–06) *Tuition:* state resident $2130 full-time, $71 per credit hour part-time; nonresident $4290 full-time, $143 per credit hour part-time. *Required fees:* $570 full-time, $18 per credit hour part-time. *Payment plan:* deferred payment. *Waivers:* senior citizens and employees or children of employees.

Financial Aid Of all full-time matriculated undergraduates who enrolled in 2004, 95 Federal Work-Study jobs (averaging $3807). 35 state and other part-time jobs (averaging $3477).

Applying *Options:* electronic application. *Required:* high school transcript. *Application deadline:* rolling (freshmen), rolling (transfers).

Freshmen Application Contact Ms. Loretta Jones, Assistant to the Dean of Students, Shelton State Community College, Shelton State Community College, 9500 Old Greensboro Road, Tuscaloosa, AL 35405. *Phone:* 205-391-2236. *Fax:* 205-391-3910.

SNEAD STATE COMMUNITY COLLEGE
Boaz, Alabama   www.snead.edu/

- **State-supported** 2-year, founded 1898, part of Alabama College System
- **Small-town** 42-acre campus with easy access to Birmingham
- **Endowment** $1.6 million
- **Coed**

Undergraduates Students come from 6 states and territories, 1% are from out of state, 2% live on campus.

Majors Business administration and management; child care and support services management; computer and information sciences; data processing and data processing technology; engineering technology; general studies; liberal arts and sciences/liberal studies.

Academics *Calendar:* semesters. *Degree:* certificates and associate. *Special study options:* academic remediation for entering students, accelerated degree program, adult/continuing education programs, advanced placement credit, distance learning, independent study, internships, part-time degree program, services for LD students, student-designed majors, summer session for credit.

Library McCain Learning Resource Center with 40,690 titles, 223 serial subscriptions, 1,699 audiovisual materials, an OPAC, a Web page.

Computers on Campus 250 computers available on campus for general student use. A campuswide network can be accessed from off campus. Internet access, online (class) registration, at least one staffed computer lab available.

Student Life *Housing Options:* coed. Campus housing is university owned. *Activities and Organizations:* student-run newspaper, choral group, Phi Theta Kappa, Snead Agricultural Organization, North American Veterinary Technician Association, Ambassadors, Baptist Campus Ministry. *Campus security:* 24-hour patrols, student patrols. *Student services:* personal/psychological counseling.

Athletics Member NJCAA. *Intercollegiate sports:* baseball M(s), basketball M(s)/W(s), softball W(s), tennis W(s). *Intramural sports:* basketball M/W, softball M/W, volleyball M/W.

Costs (2005–06) *Tuition:* state resident $2304 full-time, $72 per semester hour part-time; nonresident $4608 full-time, $144 per semester hour part-time. *Required fees:* $704 full-time, $22 per semester hour part-time.

Financial Aid Of all full-time matriculated undergraduates who enrolled in 2004, 41 Federal Work-Study jobs.

Applying *Options:* early admission, deferred entrance. *Required:* high school transcript. *Required for some:* interview. *Application deadlines:* 8/24 (freshmen), 8/24 (transfers). *Notification:* 8/20 (freshmen).

Freshmen Application Contact Dr. Greg Chapman, Director of Instruction, Snead State Community College, PO Box 734, Boaz, AL 35957-0734. *Phone:* 256-840-4111. *Fax:* 256-593-7180. *E-mail:* gchapman@snead.edu.

SOUTHERN UNION STATE COMMUNITY COLLEGE
Wadley, Alabama   www.suscc.cc.al.us/

- **State-supported** 2-year, founded 1922, part of Alabama College System
- **Rural** campus
- **Coed**

Undergraduates 6% live on campus.

Faculty *Student/faculty ratio:* 19:1.

Academics *Calendar:* quarters. *Degree:* certificates, diplomas, and associate. *Special study options:* academic remediation for entering students, adult/continuing education programs, advanced placement credit, cooperative education, internships, part-time degree program, services for LD students, summer session for credit. *ROTC:* Air Force (c).

Student Life *Campus security:* 24-hour patrols, controlled dormitory access.

Athletics Member NSCAA, NJCAA.

Financial Aid Of all full-time matriculated undergraduates who enrolled in 2004, 150 Federal Work-Study jobs (averaging $1000). 35 state and other part-time jobs (averaging $1000).

Applying *Options:* common application, early admission, deferred entrance. *Required:* high school transcript.

Southern Union State Community College (continued)

Director of Admissions Mrs. Susan Salatto, Director of Student Development, Southern Union State Community College, PO Box 1000, Roberts Street, Wadley, AL 36276. *Phone:* 256-395-2211.

VC TECH
Pelham, Alabama

VIRGINIA COLLEGE AT HUNTSVILLE
Huntsville, Alabama   **www.vc.edu/**

Director of Admissions Ms. Pat Foster, Director of Admissions, Virginia College at Huntsville, 2800-A Bob Wallace Avenue, Huntsville, AL 35805. *Phone:* 205-533-7387.

WALLACE STATE COMMUNITY COLLEGE
Hanceville, Alabama   **www.wallacestate.edu/**

Director of Admissions Ms. Linda Sperling, Director of Admissions, Wallace State Community College, PO Box 2000, Hanceville, AL 35077-2000. *Phone:* 256-352-8278.

ALASKA

CHARTER COLLEGE
Anchorage, Alaska   **www.chartercollege.org/**

Director of Admissions Ms. Lily Sirianni, Vice President, Charter College, 2221 East Northern Lights Boulevard, Suite 120, Anchorage, AK 99508-4157. *Phone:* 907-277-1000. *Toll-free phone:* 800-279-1008.

ILISAGVIK COLLEGE
Barrow, Alaska   **www.ilisagvik.cc/**

- **State-supported** 2-year, founded 1995
- **Endowment** $155,880
- **Coed,** 263 undergraduate students, 19% full-time, 47% women, 53% men
- 100% of applicants were admitted

Undergraduates 49 full-time, 214 part-time. 0.4% African American, 3% Asian American or Pacific Islander, 0.8% Hispanic American, 90% Native American.
Freshmen *Admission:* 214 applied, 214 admitted, 61 enrolled.
Faculty *Total:* 12, 100% full-time, 25% with terminal degrees. *Student/faculty ratio:* 10:1.
Majors Accounting technology and bookkeeping; business/commerce; computer/technical support; construction trades; general studies.
Academics *Calendar:* semesters. *Degree:* certificates, diplomas, and associate.
Student Life *Student services:* women's center.
Standardized Tests *Required:* ACT ASSET (for admission).
Costs (2006–07) *Tuition:* area resident $1440 full-time, $60 per credit hour part-time; state resident $2880 full-time, $120 per credit hour part-time; nonresident $2880 full-time, $120 per credit hour part-time. *Required fees:* $100 full-time, $50 per term part-time. *Room and board:* room only: $4000.

Applying *Required:* essay or personal statement, high school transcript, minimum 2.0. GPA. *Application deadline:* 8/1 (freshmen).
Freshmen Application Contact Ms. Beverly Patkotak Grinage, President, Ilisagvik College, UIC/Narl, Barrow, AK 99723. *Phone:* 907-852-1820. *Toll-free phone:* 800-478-7337. *Fax:* 907-852-1821. *E-mail:* beverly.grinage@ilisagvik.cc.

UNIVERSITY OF ALASKA ANCHORAGE, KENAI PENINSULA COLLEGE
Soldotna, Alaska   **www.kpc.alaska.edu/**

Freshmen Application Contact Ms. Shelly Love, Admission and Registration Coordinator, University of Alaska Anchorage, Kenai Peninsula College, 34820 College Drive, Soldotna, AK 99669-9798. *Phone:* 907-262-0311.

UNIVERSITY OF ALASKA ANCHORAGE, KODIAK COLLEGE
Kodiak, Alaska   **www.koc.alaska.edu/**

Director of Admissions Ms. Karen Hamer, Registrar, University of Alaska Anchorage, Kodiak College, 117 Benny Benson Drive, Kodiak, AK 99615. *Phone:* 907-486-1235.

UNIVERSITY OF ALASKA ANCHORAGE, MATANUSKA-SUSITNA COLLEGE
Palmer, Alaska   **www.matsu.alaska.edu/**

- **State-supported** 2-year, founded 1958, part of University of Alaska System
- **Small-town** 950-acre campus with easy access to Anchorage
- **Coed,** 1,326 undergraduate students, 29% full-time, 68% women, 32% men

Undergraduates 384 full-time, 942 part-time. Students come from 51 states and territories, 18 other countries, 2% African American, 0.8% Asian American or Pacific Islander, 3% Hispanic American, 4% Native American, 0.2% international. *Retention:* 67% of 2003 full-time freshmen returned.
Freshmen *Admission:* 93 enrolled.
Faculty *Total:* 96, 22% full-time, 9% with terminal degrees. *Student/faculty ratio:* 14:1.
Majors Accounting; administrative assistant and secretarial science; business administration and management; electrical, electronic and communications engineering technology; fire science; heating, air conditioning, ventilation and refrigeration maintenance technology; human services; liberal arts and sciences/liberal studies.
Academics *Calendar:* semesters. *Degree:* certificates and associate. *Special study options:* academic remediation for entering students, adult/continuing education programs, advanced placement credit, cooperative education, distance learning, double majors, independent study, internships, off-campus study, part-time degree program, summer session for credit.
Library Al Okeson Library with 50,000 titles, 280 serial subscriptions, 1,840 audiovisual materials, an OPAC, a Web page.
Computers on Campus 207 computers available on campus for general student use. A campuswide network can be accessed from off campus. Internet access, online (class) registration, at least one staffed computer lab available. Computer purchase or lease plan available.
Student Life *Housing:* college housing not available. *Activities and Organizations:* student-run newspaper, choral group, student government, Math Club. *Campus security:* 24-hour patrols.
Costs (2006–07) *Tuition:* state resident $2880 full-time; nonresident $9576 full-time. *Required fees:* $250 full-time.
Financial Aid Of all full-time matriculated undergraduates who enrolled in 2004, 8 Federal Work-Study jobs (averaging $3000).
Applying *Application fee:* $40. *Required:* high school transcript. *Application deadline:* 11/1 (freshmen). *Notification:* 12/1 (freshmen).
Freshmen Application Contact Ms. Sandra Gravley, Student Services Manager, University of Alaska Anchorage, Matanuska-Susitna College, PO Box 2889, Palmer, AK 99645-2889. *Phone:* 907-745-9712. *Fax:* 907-745-9747. *E-mail:* info@matsu.alaska.edu.

UNIVERSITY OF ALASKA, PRINCE WILLIAM SOUND COMMUNITY COLLEGE

Valdez, Alaska www.pwscc.edu/

Freshmen Application Contact Mr. Nathan J. Platt, Director of Student Services, University of Alaska, Prince William Sound Community College, PO Box 97, Valdez, AK 99686-0097. *Phone:* 907-834-1631. *Toll-free phone:* 800-478-8800 Ext. 1600. *E-mail:* studentservices@pwscc.edu.

UNIVERSITY OF ALASKA SOUTHEAST, KETCHIKAN CAMPUS

Ketchikan, Alaska www.ketch.alaska.edu/

Director of Admissions Mrs. Gail Klein, Student Services Coordinator, University of Alaska Southeast, Ketchikan Campus, 2600 7th Avenue, Ketchikan, AK 99901-5798. *Phone:* 907-228-4508. *Fax:* 907-225-3624. *E-mail:* knblj@acad1.alaska.edu.

UNIVERSITY OF ALASKA SOUTHEAST, SITKA CAMPUS

Sitka, Alaska www.uas.alaska.edu/

Director of Admissions Mr. Tim Schroeder, Coordinator of Admissions, University of Alaska Southeast, Sitka Campus, 1332 Seward Avenue, Sitka, AK 99835-9418. *Phone:* 907-747-7703. *Toll-free phone:* 800-478-6653.

AMERICAN SAMOA

AMERICAN SAMOA COMMUNITY COLLEGE

Pago Pago, American Samoa www.ascc.as/

- **Territory-supported** 2-year, founded 1969
- **Rural** 20-acre campus
- **Coed**

Undergraduates Students come from 2 other countries.
Academics *Calendar:* semesters. *Degree:* certificates and associate. *Special study options:* academic remediation for entering students, adult/continuing education programs, off-campus study, part-time degree program, summer session for credit.
Standardized Tests *Required:* Michigan Test of English Language Proficiency (for placement). *Recommended:* SAT or ACT (for placement).
Applying *Options:* deferred entrance.
Director of Admissions Mrs. Sina P. Ward, Registrar, American Samoa Community College, PO Box 2609, Pago Pago, AS 96799. *Phone:* 684-699-1141.

ARIZONA

APOLLO COLLEGE—PHOENIX, INC.

Phoenix, Arizona www.apollocollege.com/

Director of Admissions Mr. Randy Utley, Campus Director, Apollo College–Phoenix, Inc., 2701 West Bethany Home Road, Phoenix, AZ 85051. *Phone:*

602-864-1571. *Toll-free phone:* 800-36-TRAIN. *Fax:* 602-864-8207. *E-mail:* rutley@apollocollege.com.

APOLLO COLLEGE—TRI-CITY, INC.

Mesa, Arizona www.apollocollege.com/

Director of Admissions Mr. James Norris Miller, Campus Director, Apollo College–Tri-City, Inc., 630 West Southern Avenue, Mesa, AZ 85210-5004. *Phone:* 480-831-6585. *Toll-free phone:* 800-36-TRAIN. *E-mail:* jmiller@apollocollege.com.

APOLLO COLLEGE—TUCSON, INC.

Tucson, Arizona www.apollocollege.com/

Director of Admissions Ms. Jenell McKinney, Campus Director, Apollo College–Tucson, Inc., 3870 North Oracle Road, Tucson, AZ 85705-3227. *Phone:* 520-888-5885. *Toll-free phone:* 800-36-TRAIN. *Fax:* 520-887-3005. *E-mail:* jmckinney@apollocollege.com.

▶ See page 464 for the College Close-Up.

APOLLO COLLEGE—WESTSIDE, INC.

Phoenix, Arizona www.apollocollege.com/

Director of Admissions Ms. Cindy Nestor, Vice President, Apollo College–Westside, Inc., 2701 West Bethany Home Road, Phoenix, AZ 85017. *Phone:* 602-433-1222 Ext. 251. *Toll-free phone:* 800-36-TRAIN. *Fax:* 602-433-1222. *E-mail:* cnestor@apollocollege.com.

ARIZONA AUTOMOTIVE INSTITUTE

Glendale, Arizona www.azautoinst.com/

Director of Admissions Mr. Mark LaCara, Director of Admissions, Arizona Automotive Institute, 6829 North 46th Avenue, Glendale, AZ 85301-3597. *Phone:* 623-934-7273 Ext. 211. *Fax:* 623-937-5000.

ARIZONA COLLEGE OF ALLIED HEALTH

Glendale, Arizona

ARIZONA WESTERN COLLEGE

Yuma, Arizona www.azwestern.edu/

- **State and locally supported** 2-year, founded 1962, part of Arizona State Community College System
- **Rural** 640-acre campus
- **Coed,** 6,731 undergraduate students, 27% full-time, 60% women, 40% men

Undergraduates 1,849 full-time, 4,882 part-time. Students come from 26 states and territories, 7% are from out of state, 3% African American, 2% Asian American or Pacific Islander, 53% Hispanic American, 2% Native American, 10% international, 6% live on campus. *Retention:* 50% of 2003 full-time freshmen returned.
Freshmen *Admission:* 1,456 enrolled.
Faculty *Total:* 344, 32% full-time, 8% with terminal degrees. *Student/faculty ratio:* 16:1.
Majors Administrative assistant and secretarial science; agricultural business and management; agriculture; art; automobile/automotive mechanics technology; biological and physical sciences; biology/biological sciences; broadcast journalism; business administration and management; chemistry; computer science; criminal justice/law enforcement administration; criminal justice/police science; developmental and child psychology; drafting and design technology;

Arizona Western College (continued)

dramatic/theater arts; education; electrical, electronic and communications engineering technology; engineering technology; English; environmental studies; family and consumer economics related; fire science; geology/earth science; health science; heating, air conditioning, ventilation and refrigeration maintenance technology; hospitality administration; hospitality administration related; human services; information science/studies; marketing/marketing management; massage therapy; mathematics; music; nursing (licensed practical/vocational nurse training); nursing (registered nurse training); physical education teaching and coaching; physics; radiologic technology/science; social sciences; Spanish; water quality and wastewater treatment management and recycling technology; welding technology.

Academics *Calendar:* semesters. *Degree:* certificates and associate. *Special study options:* academic remediation for entering students, adult/continuing education programs, advanced placement credit, cooperative education, distance learning, English as a second language, honors programs, independent study, part-time degree program, summer session for credit.

Library Arizona Western College Library with 698 serial subscriptions, 10,800 audiovisual materials, an OPAC, a Web page.

Computers on Campus 500 computers available on campus for general student use. A campuswide network can be accessed from off campus. Internet access, at least one staffed computer lab available.

Student Life *Housing Options:* coed. Campus housing is university owned. *Activities and Organizations:* drama/theater group, student-run newspaper, radio and television station, choral group, Associated Students Governing Board, MECHA, Umoja, Honors Club, UVU. *Campus security:* 24-hour emergency response devices and patrols, student patrols, late-night transport/escort service. *Student services:* health clinic, personal/psychological counseling.

Athletics Member NJCAA. *Intercollegiate sports:* baseball M(s), basketball M(s), football M(s), soccer M(s), softball W(s), volleyball W(s). *Intramural sports:* badminton M/W, basketball M/W, football M, soccer M, softball M/W, swimming and diving M/W, table tennis M/W, volleyball M/W.

Costs (2006–07) *Tuition:* state resident $1200 full-time, $40 per credit hour part-time; nonresident $5760 full-time, $46 per credit hour part-time. *Room and board:* $4468; room only: $1790.

Financial Aid Of all full-time matriculated undergraduates who enrolled in 2004, 350 Federal Work-Study jobs (averaging $1500). 100 state and other part-time jobs (averaging $1800).

Applying *Options:* common application, early admission, deferred entrance. *Application deadline:* rolling (freshmen), rolling (transfers).

Freshmen Application Contact Mr. Bryan Doak, Dean of Enrollment Services, Arizona Western College, PO Box 929, Yuma, AZ 85366. *Phone:* 928-317-7617. *Toll-free phone:* 888-293-0392. *Fax:* 928-344-7730. *E-mail:* bryan.doak@azwestern.edu.

THE BRYMAN SCHOOL

Phoenix, Arizona   www.brymanschool.edu/

Director of Admissions Ms. Vicki Maurer, Admission Manager, The Bryman School, 2250 W. Peoria Avenue, Phoenix, AZ 85029. *Phone:* 602-274-4300. *Toll-free phone:* 800-729-4819.

CENTRAL ARIZONA COLLEGE

Coolidge, Arizona   www.cac.cc.az.us/

- **County-supported** 2-year, founded 1961
- **Rural** 709-acre campus with easy access to Phoenix
- **Coed,** 6,388 undergraduate students, 30% full-time, 60% women, 40% men

Undergraduates 1,928 full-time, 4,460 part-time. Students come from 6 other countries, 5% African American, 1% Asian American or Pacific Islander, 32% Hispanic American, 6% Native American, 0.5% international, 17% live on campus.

Freshmen *Admission:* 2,469 applied, 1,801 admitted.

Faculty *Total:* 330, 28% full-time. *Student/faculty ratio:* 17:1.

Majors Accounting; administrative assistant and secretarial science; agriculture; automobile/automotive mechanics technology; business administration and management; child development; civil engineering technology; computer and information sciences; computer science; corrections; criminal justice/law enforcement administration; dietetics; emergency medical technology (EMT paramedic); engineering; health aide; hotel/motel administration; industrial technology; kindergarten/preschool education; legal administrative assistant/secretary; liberal arts and sciences/liberal studies; marketing/marketing management; materi-

als science; medical administrative assistant and medical secretary; medical transcription; nursing (licensed practical/vocational nurse training); nursing (registered nurse training).

Academics *Calendar:* semesters. *Degree:* certificates and associate. *Special study options:* academic remediation for entering students, adult/continuing education programs, distance learning, honors programs, independent study, part-time degree program, services for LD students, student-designed majors, summer session for credit.

Library Learning Resource Center with 99,480 titles, 494 serial subscriptions.

Computers on Campus Internet access, at least one staffed computer lab available.

Student Life *Housing Options:* Campus housing is university owned. *Activities and Organizations:* drama/theater group, student-run newspaper, choral group. *Campus security:* 24-hour emergency response devices and patrols. *Student services:* personal/psychological counseling.

Athletics Member NJCAA. *Intercollegiate sports:* baseball M(s), basketball M(s)/W(s), cross-country running M(s)/W(s), equestrian sports M(s)/W(s), golf M(s), softball W(s), track and field M(s)/W(s).

Costs (2005–06) *Tuition:* state resident $1316 full-time, $47 per credit part-time; nonresident $6356 full-time, $94 per credit part-time. Part-time tuition and fees vary according to course level. *Required fees:* $16 full-time, $8 per term part-time. *Room and board:* $4160. Room and board charges vary according to housing facility. *Payment plan:* installment. *Waivers:* employees or children of employees.

Financial Aid Of all full-time matriculated undergraduates who enrolled in 2004, 68 Federal Work-Study jobs (averaging $1310).

Applying *Options:* common application, early admission, deferred entrance. *Application deadline:* rolling (freshmen), rolling (transfers). *Notification:* continuous (freshmen).

Freshmen Application Contact Ms. Doris Helmich, Interim Dean of Enrollment and Student Services, Central Arizona College, 8470 North Overfield Road, Coolidge, AZ 85228. *Phone:* 520-426-4406. *Toll-free phone:* 800-237-9814. *Fax:* 520-426-4271. *E-mail:* leonor_verduzoo@centralaz.edu.

CHANDLER-GILBERT COMMUNITY COLLEGE

Chandler, Arizona   www.cgc.maricopa.edu/

- **State and locally supported** 2-year, founded 1985, part of Maricopa County Community College District System
- **Rural** 80-acre campus with easy access to Phoenix
- **Endowment** $315,961
- **Coed**

Undergraduates Students come from 38 states and territories, 5 other countries, 4% are from out of state, 4% African American, 3% Asian American or Pacific Islander, 16% Hispanic American, 4% Native American, 1% international.

Faculty *Student/faculty ratio:* 19:1.

Academics *Calendar:* semesters. *Degree:* certificates, diplomas, and associate. *Special study options:* academic remediation for entering students, advanced placement credit, English as a second language, freshman honors college, honors programs, part-time degree program, summer session for credit.

Student Life *Campus security:* 24-hour emergency response devices and patrols, late-night transport/escort service.

Standardized Tests *Required for some:* ACT ASSET.

Applying *Options:* common application, electronic application.

Director of Admissions Ms. Irene Pearl, Supervisor of Admissions and Records, Chandler-Gilbert Community College, 2626 East Pecos Road, Chandler, AZ 85225-2479. *Phone:* 480-732-7307.

CHAPARRAL COLLEGE

Tucson, Arizona   www.chap-col.edu/

Director of Admissions Ms. Becki Rossini, Director of Admissions, Chaparral College, 4585 East Speedway, # 204, Tucson, AZ 85712. *Phone:* 520-327-6866.

COCHISE COLLEGE
Douglas, Arizona www.cochise.edu/

- **State and locally supported** 2-year, founded 1962, part of Cochise College
- **Rural** 500-acre campus
- **Endowment** $1.3 million
- **Coed,** 4,610 undergraduate students, 31% full-time, 60% women, 40% men

Undergraduates 1,440 full-time, 3,170 part-time. Students come from 4 states and territories, 8 other countries, 5% are from out of state, 7% African American, 3% Asian American or Pacific Islander, 37% Hispanic American, 1% Native American, 0.2% international, 0.5% transferred in, 17% live on campus. Freshmen *Admission:* 759 applied, 759 admitted, 759 enrolled.
Faculty *Total:* 368, 25% full-time. *Student/faculty ratio:* 13:1.
Majors Administrative assistant and secretarial science; agricultural business and management; airframe mechanics and aircraft maintenance technology; airline pilot and flight crew; anthropology; art; avionics maintenance technology; biology/biological sciences; business administration and management; chemistry; communication/speech communication and rhetoric; computer and information systems security; computer programming; computer science; computer systems networking and telecommunications; criminal justice/police science; culinary arts; data processing and data processing technology; early childhood education; economics; education; electrical, electronic and communications engineering technology; emergency medical technology (EMT paramedic); English; family psychology; fire science; foreign languages and literatures; general studies; health and physical education; health services/allied health/health sciences; history; hospitality administration; humanities; human services; information science/studies; journalism; language interpretation and translation; liberal arts and sciences/liberal studies; manufacturing engineering; mathematics; military technologies; nursing (registered nurse training); physical education teaching and coaching; political science and government; pre-nursing studies; psychology; social work; sociology; welding technology.
Academics *Calendar:* semesters. *Degree:* certificates and associate. *Special study options:* academic remediation for entering students, accelerated degree program, cooperative education, distance learning, English as a second language, independent study, internships, part-time degree program, services for LD students, summer session for credit.
Library 42,876 titles, 182 serial subscriptions, a Web page.
Computers on Campus 84 computers available on campus for general student use. Internet access, at least one staffed computer lab available.
Student Life *Housing Options:* Campus housing is university owned. *Activities and Organizations:* choral group, student government, Phi Theta Kappa. *Campus security:* 24-hour emergency response devices and patrols, controlled dormitory access. *Student services:* health clinic, personal/psychological counseling.
Athletics Member NJCAA. *Intercollegiate sports:* baseball M(s), basketball M(s)/W(s), soccer W(s). *Intramural sports:* basketball M.
Costs (2006–07) *Tuition:* state resident $1350 full-time, $45 per credit hour part-time; nonresident $6300 full-time, $65 per credit hour part-time. *Required fees:* $60 full-time, $30 per term part-time. *Room and board:* $3562.
Financial Aid Of all full-time matriculated undergraduates who enrolled in 2004, 137 Federal Work-Study jobs (averaging $1070).
Applying *Options:* early admission, deferred entrance. *Recommended:* high school transcript. *Application deadline:* rolling (freshmen), rolling (transfers). *Notification:* continuous (freshmen).
Freshmen Application Contact Ms. Pati Mapp, Admissions Counselor, Cochise College, 4190 West Highway 80, Douglas, AZ 85607-9724. *Phone:* 520-364-0336. *Toll-free phone:* 800-966-7946. *Fax:* 520-364-0236. *E-mail:* info@tron.cochise.cc.az.us.

COCHISE COLLEGE
Sierra Vista, Arizona www.cochise.cc.az.us/

Freshmen Application Contact Ms. Debbie Quick, Admissions Officer, Cochise College, 901 North Colombo, Sierra Vista, AZ 85635-2317. *Phone:* 520-515-5412. *Toll-free phone:* 800-593-9567.

COCONINO COMMUNITY COLLEGE
Flagstaff, Arizona www.coconino.edu/

- **State-supported** 2-year, founded 1991
- **Small-town** 5-acre campus
- **Endowment** $11,275
- **Coed**

Academics *Calendar:* semesters. *Degree:* certificates and associate. *Special study options:* academic remediation for entering students, adult/continuing education programs, advanced placement credit, part-time degree program, services for LD students, summer session for credit.
Student Life *Campus security:* 24-hour patrols.
Costs (2005–06) *Tuition:* state resident $1344 full-time, $56 per credit hour part-time; nonresident $5376 full-time, $224 per credit hour part-time.
Financial Aid Of all full-time matriculated undergraduates who enrolled in 2004, 25 Federal Work-Study jobs (averaging $4000).
Applying *Application fee:* $10. *Required for some:* high school transcript.
Director of Admissions Mr. Steve Miller, Director of Admissions/Registrar, Coconino Community College, 3000 North Fourth Street, Flagstaff, AZ 86003. *Phone:* 928-527-1222. *Toll-free phone:* 800-350-7122. *E-mail:* smiller@coco.cc.az.us.

COLLEGEAMERICA—FLAGSTAFF
Flagstaff, Arizona www.collegeamerica.com/

Director of Admissions Mr. Pescal Berlioux, Executive Director, CollegeAmerica–Flagstaff, 5200 East Cortland Boulevard, Suite A-19, Flagstaff, AZ 86004. *Phone:* 800-977-5455. *Fax:* 928-526-5391. *E-mail:* pberlioux@collegeamerica.edu.

DINÉ COLLEGE
Tsaile, Arizona www.dinecollege.edu/

- **Federally supported** 2-year, founded 1968
- **Rural** 1200-acre campus
- **Endowment** $3.5 million
- **Coed,** 1,825 undergraduate students, 46% full-time, 76% women, 24% men

Undergraduates 843 full-time, 982 part-time. Students come from 1 other state, 3 other countries, 0.2% African American, 0.3% Asian American or Pacific Islander, 98% Native American, 12% transferred in, 8% live on campus. Freshmen *Admission:* 388 enrolled.
Faculty *Total:* 156, 42% full-time.
Majors Administrative assistant and secretarial science; American Indian/Native American studies; art; business administration and management; computer science; elementary education; geology/earth science; health science; information science/studies; kinesiology and exercise science; liberal arts and sciences/liberal studies; pre-engineering; social sciences; social work.
Academics *Calendar:* semesters. *Degree:* certificates and associate. *Special study options:* academic remediation for entering students, adult/continuing education programs, off-campus study, part-time degree program, services for LD students, summer session for credit.
Library Tsaile-Navajo Community College Library plus 1 other with 50,000 titles, 329 serial subscriptions, a Web page.
Computers on Campus 262 computers available on campus for general student use. A campuswide network can be accessed from off campus. Internet access, at least one staffed computer lab available.
Student Life *Housing Options:* coed. Campus housing is university owned. *Activities and Organizations:* Associate Students of Navajo Community College, Bar-N-Rodeo Club, Red Dawn Indian Club, Native American Church. *Campus security:* 24-hour emergency response devices and patrols, student patrols, late-night transport/escort service. *Student services:* health clinic, personal/psychological counseling.
Athletics Member NSCAA, NJCAA. *Intercollegiate sports:* archery M/W, cross-country running M(s)/W(s).
Costs (2006–07) *Tuition:* state resident $720 full-time, $30 per hour part-time; nonresident $720 full-time, $30 per hour part-time. *Room and board:* $3764; room only: $1180.
Financial Aid Of all full-time matriculated undergraduates who enrolled in 2004, 100 Federal Work-Study jobs (averaging $650).

Diné College (continued)

Applying *Options:* common application, early admission. *Required:* high school transcript, certificate of Indian Blood form for Native American Students. *Application deadline:* rolling (freshmen), rolling (transfers). *Notification:* continuous (freshmen).

Freshmen Application Contact Mrs. Louise Litzin, Registrar, Diné College, PO Box 67, Tsaile, AZ 86556. *Phone:* 928-724-6633. *Fax:* 928-724-3349. *E-mail:* louise@dinecollege.edu.

EASTERN ARIZONA COLLEGE

Thatcher, Arizona   **www.eac.edu/**

- **State and locally supported** 2-year, founded 1888, part of Arizona State Community College System
- **Small-town** campus
- **Endowment** $1.6 million
- **Coed,** 5,239 undergraduate students, 27% full-time, 59% women, 41% men

Undergraduates 1,413 full-time, 3,826 part-time. Students come from 29 states and territories, 6% are from out of state, 4% African American, 2% Asian American or Pacific Islander, 28% Hispanic American, 14% Native American, 1% international, 5% live on campus. *Retention:* 43% of 2003 full-time freshmen returned.

Freshmen *Admission:* 2,287 applied, 2,287 admitted, 1,197 enrolled.

Faculty *Total:* 298, 30% full-time, 4% with terminal degrees. *Student/faculty ratio:* 17:1.

Majors Agribusiness; agriculture; anthropology; art; art teacher education; automobile/automotive mechanics technology; biology/biological sciences; business administration and management; business, management, and marketing related; business operations support and secretarial services related; business teacher education; chemistry; child care provision; civil engineering technology; commercial and advertising art; corrections; criminal justice/law enforcement administration; criminal justice/police science; data entry/microcomputer applications; drafting and design technology; dramatic/theater arts; elementary education; emergency medical technology (EMT paramedic); English; entrepreneurship; foreign languages and literatures; forestry; geology/earth science; health and physical education; health/medical preparatory programs related; history; information science/studies; liberal arts and sciences/liberal studies; machine shop technology; management information systems and services related; mathematics; mining technology; music; nursing (registered nurse training); physics; political science and government; pre-law studies; pre-medical studies; pre-pharmacy studies; psychology; secondary education; sociology; technology/industrial arts teacher education; welding technology; wildlife biology.

Academics *Calendar:* semesters. *Degree:* certificates and associate. *Special study options:* academic remediation for entering students, adult/continuing education programs, advanced placement credit, cooperative education, double majors, independent study, part-time degree program, services for LD students, study abroad, summer session for credit.

Library Alumni Library plus 1 other with an OPAC, a Web page.

Computers on Campus 458 computers available on campus for general student use. A campuswide network can be accessed from student residence rooms and from off campus. Internet access, online (class) registration, at least one staffed computer lab available.

Student Life *Housing Options:* men-only, women-only. Campus housing is university owned. *Activities and Organizations:* drama/theater group, choral group, marching band, Latter-Day Saints Student Association, Criminal Justice Student Association, Multicultural Council, Phi Theta Kappa, Mark Allen Dorm Club. *Campus security:* late-night transport/escort service, controlled dormitory access, 20-hour patrols by trained security personnel. *Student services:* personal/psychological counseling.

Athletics Member NJCAA. *Intercollegiate sports:* baseball M(s), basketball M(s)/W(s), football M(s), golf M/W, softball W(s), volleyball W(s). *Intramural sports:* basketball M/W, racquetball M/W, swimming and diving M/W, table tennis M/W, tennis M/W, volleyball M/W.

Costs (2006–07) *Tuition:* state resident $1220 full-time, $50 per credit part-time; nonresident $6460 full-time, $100 per credit part-time. *Room and board:* $4320.

Financial Aid Of all full-time matriculated undergraduates who enrolled in 2004, 314 Federal Work-Study jobs (averaging $1800). 145 state and other part-time jobs (averaging $1800).

Applying *Options:* electronic application, early admission, deferred entrance. *Recommended:* high school transcript. *Application deadline:* rolling (freshmen), rolling (transfers). *Notification:* continuous (freshmen).

Freshmen Application Contact Mr. Jeff Savage, Coordinator of Recruitment, Eastern Arizona College, 615 North Stadium Avenue, Thatcher, AZ 85552-0769. *Phone:* 928-426-8247. *Toll-free phone:* 800-678-3808. *Fax:* 928-428-8462. *E-mail:* admissions@eac.edu.

ESTRELLA MOUNTAIN COMMUNITY COLLEGE

Avondale, Arizona   **www.emc.maricopa.edu/**

- **State and locally supported** 2-year, part of Maricopa County Community College District System
- **Urban** campus with easy access to Phoenix
- **Coed**

Undergraduates 1,372 full-time, 4,575 part-time. 7% African American, 3% Asian American or Pacific Islander, 31% Hispanic American, 2% Native American, 0.8% international.

Faculty *Student/faculty ratio:* 20:1.

Academics *Calendar:* semesters. *Degree:* certificates and associate.

Financial Aid Of all full-time matriculated undergraduates who enrolled in 2004, 50 Federal Work-Study jobs (averaging $3000).

Director of Admissions Dr. Ernesto Laura, Dean of Student Services, Estrella Mountain Community College, 3000 North Dysart Road, Avondale, AZ 85323-1000. *Phone:* 623-935-8808.

EVEREST COLLEGE

Phoenix, Arizona   **www.everest-college.com/**

- **Proprietary** primarily 2-year, founded 1982
- **Urban** campus
- **Coed,** 804 undergraduate students, 47% full-time, 80% women, 20% men

Undergraduates 378 full-time, 426 part-time. Students come from 2 states and territories, 25% are from out of state, 11% African American, 2% Asian American or Pacific Islander, 28% Hispanic American, 4% Native American. *Retention:* 65% of 2003 full-time freshmen returned.

Freshmen *Admission:* 526 applied, 382 admitted, 376 enrolled.

Faculty *Total:* 34, 21% full-time, 26% with terminal degrees. *Student/faculty ratio:* 24:1.

Majors Accounting; business/commerce; criminal justice/police science; legal assistant/paralegal; medical/clinical assistant.

Academics *Calendar:* 6 or 12 week terms. *Degrees:* diplomas, associate, and bachelor's. *Special study options:* adult/continuing education programs, distance learning, double majors, internships, summer session for credit.

Library Academy of Business College Library with 57 serial subscriptions, a Web page.

Computers on Campus 50 computers available on campus for general student use. Internet access, at least one staffed computer lab available.

Student Life *Housing:* college housing not available. *Activities and Organizations:* Collegiate Secretaries International, Toastmasters. *Campus security:* 24-hour emergency response devices and patrols. *Student services:* personal/psychological counseling.

Costs (2006–07) *Tuition:* $13,111 full-time, $259 per quarter hour part-time. *Required fees:* $100 full-time, $25 per term part-time.

Applying *Options:* deferred entrance. *Required:* high school transcript, minimum 2.0 GPA, interview. *Required for some:* essay or personal statement. *Application deadline:* rolling (freshmen). *Notification:* continuous (freshmen).

Freshmen Application Contact Ms. Melissa Agee, Director of Admissions, Everest College, 10400 North 25th Avenue, Suite 190, Phoenix, AZ 85021. *Phone:* 602-942-4141. *Fax:* 602-943-0960. *E-mail:* magee@cci.edu.

GATEWAY COMMUNITY COLLEGE

Phoenix, Arizona   **www.gwc.maricopa.edu/**

- **State and locally supported** 2-year, founded 1968, part of Maricopa County Community College District System
- **Urban** 20-acre campus
- **Coed,** 9,377 undergraduate students, 10% full-time, 47% women, 53% men

Undergraduates 976 full-time, 8,401 part-time. Students come from 50 states and territories, 26 other countries, 3% are from out of state, 8% African American, 2% Asian American or Pacific Islander, 21% Hispanic American, 4% Native American.

Freshmen *Admission:* 1,482 enrolled.

Faculty *Total:* 259, 27% full-time. *Student/faculty ratio:* 25:1.

Majors Accounting; aeronautical/aerospace engineering technology; automobile/automotive mechanics technology; business/commerce; carpentry; computer and information sciences; computer and information sciences related; computer programming (specific applications); computer programming (vendor/product certification); construction engineering technology; court reporting; diagnostic medical sonography and ultrasound technology; economics; education; electromechanical technology; finance; general studies; health/health care administration; heating, air conditioning and refrigeration technology; heating, air conditioning, ventilation and refrigeration maintenance technology; industrial technology; information technology; international business/trade/commerce; liberal arts and sciences/liberal studies; management science; materials science; medical radiologic technology; nuclear medical technology; nursing (registered nurse training); occupational safety and health technology; office occupations and clerical services; physical therapist assistant; pipefitting and sprinkler fitting; psychology; real estate; respiratory care therapy; social work; surgical technology; system administration.

Academics *Calendar:* semesters. *Degree:* certificates and associate. *Special study options:* academic remediation for entering students, accelerated degree program, adult/continuing education programs, advanced placement credit, cooperative education, distance learning, English as a second language, honors programs, independent study, internships, part-time degree program, services for LD students, summer session for credit. *ROTC:* Army (c), Air Force (c).

Library Gateway Library with 50,000 titles, 300 serial subscriptions, an OPAC.

Computers on Campus 300 computers available on campus for general student use. Internet access, online (class) registration, at least one staffed computer lab available.

Student Life *Housing:* college housing not available. *Activities and Organizations:* Associated Students, African-American Students Association, MECHA SAMO THRACE, Volunteer Committee, VA Club. *Campus security:* 24-hour emergency response devices and patrols, student patrols, late-night transport/escort service. *Student services:* personal/psychological counseling, women's center.

Athletics Member NJCAA. *Intercollegiate sports:* cross-country running M/W, golf M/W, tennis M/W.

Costs (2006–07) *Tuition:* area resident $1560 full-time, $65 per credit part-time; state resident $6720 full-time, $85 per credit part-time; nonresident $6720 full-time, $85 per credit part-time. *Required fees:* $30 full-time.

Applying *Options:* common application, electronic application, early admission, deferred entrance. *Required for some:* high school transcript. *Application deadline:* rolling (freshmen), rolling (transfers). *Notification:* continuous (freshmen).

Freshmen Application Contact Ms. Cathy Gibson, Director of Admissions and Records, GateWay Community College, 108 North 40th Street, Phoenix, AZ 85034. *Phone:* 602-286-8052. *Fax:* 602-286-8200. *E-mail:* cathy.gibson@gwmail.maricopa.edu.

GLENDALE COMMUNITY COLLEGE
Glendale, Arizona **www.gc.maricopa.edu/**

- **State and locally supported** 2-year, founded 1965, part of Maricopa County Community College District System
- **Suburban** 160-acre campus with easy access to Phoenix
- **Endowment** $353,507
- **Coed,** 20,070 undergraduate students, 30% full-time, 56% women, 44% men

Undergraduates 6,108 full-time, 13,962 part-time. Students come from 50 states and territories, 3% are from out of state, 7% African American, 4% Asian American or Pacific Islander, 22% Hispanic American, 2% Native American, 1% international, 28% transferred in. *Retention:* 60% of 2003 full-time freshmen returned.

Freshmen *Admission:* 856 enrolled.

Faculty *Total:* 912, 30% full-time. *Student/faculty ratio:* 22:1.

Majors Accounting technology and bookkeeping; administrative assistant and secretarial science; agribusiness; applied horticulture; architectural drafting and CAD/CADD; automobile/automotive mechanics technology; business administration and management; business/commerce; cinematography and film/video production; commercial and advertising art; computer systems networking and telecommunications; consumer merchandising/retailing management; criminal justice/law enforcement administration; criminal justice/police science; electrical, electronic and communications engineering technology; emergency medical technology (EMT paramedic); engineering technology; fire science; human services; industrial technology; kindergarten/preschool education; landscaping and groundskeeping; liberal arts and sciences/liberal studies; management information systems; nursing assistant/aide and patient care assistant; nursing (registered nurse training); public relations/image management; real estate.

Academics *Calendar:* semesters. *Degree:* certificates and associate. *Special study options:* academic remediation for entering students, adult/continuing

---

education programs, advanced placement credit, cooperative education, distance learning, double majors, English as a second language, freshman honors college, honors programs, internships, off-campus study, part-time degree program, services for LD students, summer session for credit. *ROTC:* Army (c), Air Force (c).

Library Library/Media Center plus 1 other with 79,006 titles, 406 serial subscriptions, 3,807 audiovisual materials, an OPAC, a Web page.

Computers on Campus 1500 computers available on campus for general student use. A campuswide network can be accessed from off campus. Internet access, online (class) registration, at least one staffed computer lab available.

Student Life *Housing:* college housing not available. *Activities and Organizations:* drama/theater group, student-run newspaper, choral group, marching band, LDS Student Association, Phi Theta Kappa International Honor Society, band, Glendale Association of Student Nurses, Inter-Varsity Christian Fellowship. *Campus security:* 24-hour patrols, student patrols, late-night transport/escort service. *Student services:* personal/psychological counseling, legal services.

Athletics Member NJCAA. *Intercollegiate sports:* baseball M(s), basketball M(s)/W(s), cross-country running M(s)/W(s), football M(s), golf M(s), soccer M(s)/W(s), softball W(s), tennis M(s)/W(s), track and field M(s)/W(s), volleyball W(s). *Intramural sports:* golf M, racquetball M/W, softball W, tennis M/W, volleyball W.

Costs (2006–07) *Tuition:* area resident $1560 full-time, $65 per credit hour part-time; state resident $6720 full-time, $280 per credit hour part-time; nonresident $6720 full-time, $280 per credit hour part-time. *Required fees:* $30 full-time, $15 per term part-time.

Financial Aid Of all full-time matriculated undergraduates who enrolled in 2004, 350 Federal Work-Study jobs (averaging $1700).

Applying *Options:* common application, electronic application. *Required for some:* high school transcript. *Application deadlines:* 8/23 (freshmen), 8/23 (transfers). *Notification:* continuous until 8/23 (freshmen).

Freshmen Application Contact Ms. Mary Lou Massal, Dean of Enrollment Services, Glendale Community College, 6000 West Olive Avenue, Glendale, AZ 85302. *Phone:* 623-435-3305. *Toll-free phone:* 623-845-3000. *Fax:* 623-845-3303. *E-mail:* info@gc.maricopa.edu.

HIGH-TECH INSTITUTE
Phoenix, Arizona **www.high-techinstitute.com/**

Freshmen Application Contact Mr. Glen Husband, Vice President of Admissions, High-Tech Institute, 1515 East Indian School Road, Phoenix, AZ 85014-4901. *Phone:* 602-279-9700.

INTERNATIONAL INSTITUTE OF THE AMERICAS
Mesa, Arizona **www.aibtonline.com/**

- **Independent** primarily 2-year, founded 1982
- **Coed,** 174 undergraduate students, 100% full-time, 84% women, 16% men

Undergraduates 174 full-time. 7% African American, 29% Hispanic American, 17% Native American.

Faculty *Total:* 25, 28% full-time, 16% with terminal degrees. *Student/faculty ratio:* 13:1.

Majors Accounting; business administration and management; criminal justice/law enforcement administration; health/health care administration; legal assistant/paralegal.

Academics *Calendar:* semesters. *Degrees:* diplomas, associate, and bachelor's.

Costs (2005–06) *One-time required fee:* $200. *Tuition:* $9850 full-time. *Required fees:* $350 full-time.

Applying *Required:* interview. *Application deadline:* rolling (freshmen), rolling (out-of-state freshmen), rolling (transfers). *Notification:* continuous (freshmen), continuous (out-of-state freshmen).

Freshmen Application Contact Ms. Meredith Kiljan, Campus Director, International Institute of the Americas, 925 South Gilbert Road, Suite 201, Mesa, AZ 85204-4448. *Phone:* 480-545-8755. *Toll-free phone:* 888-886-2428. *Fax:* 480-926-1371. *E-mail:* mkiljan@iia.edu.

INTERNATIONAL INSTITUTE OF THE AMERICAS
Phoenix, Arizona www.aibtonline.com/

- **Independent** primarily 2-year, founded 1979
- **Coed,** 205 undergraduate students, 100% full-time, 85% women, 15% men

Undergraduates 205 full-time. 15% African American, 0.5% Asian American or Pacific Islander, 37% Hispanic American, 5% Native American.
Faculty *Total:* 20, 50% full-time, 20% with terminal degrees. *Student/faculty ratio:* 15:1.
Majors Accounting; business administration and management; criminal justice/law enforcement administration; health/health care administration; legal assistant/paralegal.
Academics *Calendar:* semesters. *Degrees:* diplomas, associate, and bachelor's.
Costs (2005–06) *One-time required fee:* $200. *Tuition:* $9850 full-time. *Required fees:* $350 full-time.
Applying *Required:* interview. *Application deadline:* rolling (freshmen), rolling (out-of-state freshmen), rolling (transfers). *Notification:* continuous (freshmen), continuous (out-of-state freshmen).
Freshmen Application Contact Dr. Lori Ebert, Campus Director, International Institute of the Americas, 4136 North 75th Avenue, Suite 211, Phoenix, AZ 85033-3196. *Phone:* 623-849-8208. *Toll-free phone:* 888-884-2428. *Fax:* 623-849-0110. *E-mail:* lebert@iia.edu.

INTERNATIONAL INSTITUTE OF THE AMERICAS
Phoenix, Arizona www.aibtonline.com/

- **Independent** primarily 2-year, founded 1979
- **Urban** campus
- **Coed,** 240 undergraduate students, 100% full-time, 92% women, 8% men

Undergraduates 240 full-time. Students come from 7 states and territories, 15% African American, 0.4% Asian American or Pacific Islander, 30% Hispanic American, 4% Native American.
Faculty *Total:* 26, 54% full-time, 19% with terminal degrees. *Student/faculty ratio:* 13:1.
Majors Accounting; business administration and management; health/health care administration; legal assistant/paralegal; nursing (registered nurse training).
Academics *Calendar:* semesters. *Degrees:* diplomas, associate, and bachelor's. *Special study options:* accelerated degree program, adult/continuing education programs, cooperative education, distance learning, internships, summer session for credit.
Library Learning Resource Center with 1,974 titles, 1,750 serial subscriptions, 120 audiovisual materials, an OPAC, a Web page.
Computers on Campus 421 computers available on campus for general student use. A campuswide network can be accessed. Internet access, online (class) registration, at least one staffed computer lab available.
Student Life *Housing:* college housing not available. *Campus security:* 24-hour emergency response devices.
Costs (2005–06) *One-time required fee:* $200. *Tuition:* $9850 full-time. *Required fees:* $350 full-time.
Applying *Options:* electronic application, early admission, deferred entrance. *Required:* interview. *Application deadline:* rolling (freshmen), rolling (out-of-state freshmen), rolling (transfers). *Notification:* continuous (freshmen), continuous (out-of-state freshmen).
Freshmen Application Contact Mr. Lynn McConnell, Campus Director, International Institute of the Americas, 6049 North 43 Avenue, Phoenix, AZ 85019. *Phone:* 602-242-6265. *Toll-free phone:* 800-793-2428. *Fax:* 602-973-2572. *E-mail:* lmcconnell@iia.edu.

INTERNATIONAL INSTITUTE OF THE AMERICAS
Tucson, Arizona www.aibtonline.com/

- **Independent** primarily 2-year, founded 1979
- **Coed,** 298 undergraduate students, 100% full-time, 84% women, 16% men

Undergraduates 298 full-time. 12% African American, 1% Asian American or Pacific Islander, 46% Hispanic American, 6% Native American.
Faculty *Total:* 23, 87% full-time, 13% with terminal degrees. *Student/faculty ratio:* 14:1.
Majors Accounting; business administration and management; criminal justice/law enforcement administration; health/health care administration; legal assistant/paralegal.
Academics *Calendar:* semesters. *Degrees:* diplomas, associate, and bachelor's.
Applying *Required:* interview. *Application deadline:* rolling (freshmen), rolling (out-of-state freshmen), rolling (transfers). *Notification:* continuous (freshmen), continuous (out-of-state freshmen).
Freshmen Application Contact Ms. Leigh Anne Pechota, Campus Director, International Institute of the Americas, 5441 East 22nd Street, Suite 125, Tucson, AZ 85711-5444. *Phone:* 520-748-9799. *Toll-free phone:* 888-292-2428. *Fax:* 520-748-9355. *E-mail:* lpechota@iia.edu.

ITT TECHNICAL INSTITUTE
Phoenix, Arizona www.itt-tech.edu/

Freshmen Application Contact Mr. Gene McWhorter, Director of Recruitment, ITT Technical Institute, 4837 East McDowell Road, Phoenix, AZ 85008. *Phone:* 602-252-2331. *Toll-free phone:* 800-879-4881.

ITT TECHNICAL INSTITUTE
Tucson, Arizona www.itt-tech.edu/

- **Proprietary** primarily 2-year, founded 1984, part of ITT Educational Services, Inc
- **Urban** 3-acre campus
- **Coed**

Majors Animation, interactive technology, video graphics and special effects; business administration and management; CAD/CADD drafting/design technology; computer programming; computer software technology; computer systems networking and telecommunications; criminal justice/law enforcement administration; e-commerce; electrical, electronic and communications engineering technology; system, networking, and LAN/WAN management; web/multimedia management and webmaster; web page, digital/multimedia and information resources design.
Academics *Calendar:* quarters. *Degrees:* associate and bachelor's.
Library a Web page.
Computers on Campus Internet access, at least one staffed computer lab available.
Student Life *Housing:* college housing not available.
Standardized Tests *Required:* Wonderlic aptitude test (for admission).
Costs (2005–06) *Tuition:* Please see school catalog for specific information.
Applying *Options:* deferred entrance. *Application fee:* $100. *Required:* high school transcript, interview. *Recommended:* letters of recommendation. *Application deadline:* rolling (freshmen), rolling (transfers). *Notification:* continuous (freshmen).
Freshmen Application Contact Ms. Linda Lemken, Director of Recruitment, ITT Technical Institute, 1455 West River Road, Tucson, AZ 85704. *Phone:* 520-408-7488. *Toll-free phone:* 800-870-9730.

LAMSON COLLEGE
Tempe, Arizona www.lamsoncollege.com/

Director of Admissions Mr. Chico Chavez, Director of Admissions, Lamson College, 1126 North Scottsdale Road, Suite 17, Tempe, AZ 85281. *Phone:* 480-898-7000. *Toll-free phone:* 800-898-7017.

LONG TECHNICAL COLLEGE

Phoenix, Arizona   www.longtechnicalcollege.com/

Director of Admissions Mr. Michael S. Savely, Executive Director, Long Technical College, 13450 North Black Canyon Highway, Suite 104, Phoenix, AZ 85029. *Phone:* 602-548-1955. *Toll-free phone:* 877-548-1955. *Fax:* 602-548-1956. *E-mail:* msavely@longtechnicalcollege.com.

MESA COMMUNITY COLLEGE

Mesa, Arizona   www.mc.maricopa.edu/

Director of Admissions Ms. Carol Petersen, Director, Admissions and Records, Mesa Community College, 1833 West Southern Avenue, Mesa, AZ 85202-4866. *Phone:* 480-461-7478. *E-mail:* admissions@mc.maricopa.edu.

MOHAVE COMMUNITY COLLEGE

Kingman, Arizona   www.mohave.edu/

- **State-supported** 2-year, founded 1971
- **Small-town** 160-acre campus
- **Coed**

Undergraduates 1,208 full-time, 4,979 part-time. Students come from 8 states and territories, 8% are from out of state, 0.7% African American, 2% Asian American or Pacific Islander, 13% Hispanic American, 2% Native American.
Faculty *Student/faculty ratio:* 13:1.
Academics *Calendar:* semesters. *Degree:* certificates and associate. *Special study options:* academic remediation for entering students, adult/continuing education programs, distance learning, English as a second language, independent study, part-time degree program, summer session for credit.
Student Life *Campus security:* 24-hour emergency response devices, late-night transport/escort service.
Costs (2005–06) *Tuition:* state resident $1104 full-time, $46 per credit hour part-time; nonresident $3312 full-time, $138 per credit hour part-time. Part-time tuition and fees vary according to course load.
Applying *Options:* early admission, deferred entrance. *Required for some:* high school transcript, interview. *Recommended:* minimum 2.0 GPA.
Director of Admissions Mr. John Wilson, Registrar/Director of Enrollment Services, Mohave Community College, 1971 Jagerson Avenue, Kingman, AZ 86401. *Phone:* 928-757-0847. *Toll-free phone:* 888-664-2832.

NORTHLAND PIONEER COLLEGE

Holbrook, Arizona   www.npc.edu/

Director of Admissions Ms. Dawn Edgmon, Coordinator of Admissions, Northland Pioneer College, PO Box 610, Holbrook, AZ 86025-0610. *Phone:* 928-536-6257. *Toll-free phone:* 800-266-7845.

PARADISE VALLEY COMMUNITY COLLEGE

Phoenix, Arizona   www.pvc.maricopa.edu/

- **State and locally supported** 2-year, founded 1985, part of Maricopa County Community College District System
- **Urban** campus
- **Coed**

Undergraduates 2,118 full-time, 6,119 part-time. 3% African American, 3% Asian American or Pacific Islander, 10% Hispanic American, 1% Native American.
Academics *Calendar:* semesters. *Degree:* certificates and associate. *Special study options:* academic remediation for entering students, adult/continuing education programs, advanced placement credit, cooperative education, distance learning, honors programs, services for LD students, summer session for credit.
Student Life *Campus security:* 24-hour emergency response devices, late-night transport/escort service.
Athletics Member NJCAA.

Financial Aid Of all full-time matriculated undergraduates who enrolled in 2004, 50 Federal Work-Study jobs (averaging $2500).
Applying *Options:* early admission.
Director of Admissions Dr. Shirley Green, Associate Dean of Student Services, Paradise Valley Community College, 18401 North 32nd Street, Phoenix, AZ 85032. *Phone:* 602-787-7020.

THE PARALEGAL INSTITUTE, INC.

Phoenix, Arizona   www.theparalegalinstitute.com/

- **Proprietary** 2-year, founded 1974
- **400 undergraduate students**
- **25% of applicants were admitted**

Freshmen *Admission:* 500 applied, 125 admitted.
Faculty *Total:* 4, 25% full-time.
Majors Criminal justice/law enforcement administration; legal assistant/paralegal.
Academics *Degree:* diplomas and associate.
Costs (2005–06) *Tuition:* Contact school as tuition and fees vary according to program.
Freshmen Application Contact Patricia Yancy, Director of Admissions, The Paralegal Institute, Inc., 2933 West Indian School Road, Drawer 11408, Phoenix, AZ 85061-1408. *Phone:* 602-212-0501. *Toll-free phone:* 800-354-1254. *Fax:* 602-212-0502. *E-mail:* paralegalinst@mindspring.com.

PHOENIX COLLEGE

Phoenix, Arizona   www.pc.maricopa.edu/

- **State and locally supported** 2-year, founded 1920, part of Maricopa County Community College District System
- **Urban** 52-acre campus
- **Coed,** 12,549 undergraduate students

Undergraduates Students come from 42 states and territories, 2% are from out of state, 8% African American, 2% Asian American or Pacific Islander, 32% Hispanic American, 4% Native American.
Faculty *Total:* 104, 100% full-time.
Majors Accounting; administrative assistant and secretarial science; architectural engineering technology; art; behavioral sciences; business administration and management; civil engineering technology; clinical laboratory science/medical technology; clinical/medical laboratory technology; computer and information sciences; computer graphics; construction engineering technology; corrections; criminal justice/police science; criminal justice/safety; data processing and data processing technology; dental hygiene; drafting and design technology; emergency medical technology (EMT paramedic); family and consumer sciences/human sciences; fashion/apparel design; finance; fire science; health information/medical records administration; information science/studies; interior design; legal administrative assistant/secretary; legal assistant/paralegal; liberal arts and sciences/liberal studies; management science; marketing/marketing management; mass communication/media; mechanical design technology; medical administrative assistant and medical secretary; medical/clinical assistant; medical laboratory technology; nursing (registered nurse training); real estate; special products marketing; tourism and travel services management.
Academics *Calendar:* semesters. *Degree:* certificates, diplomas, and associate. *Special study options:* academic remediation for entering students, adult/continuing education programs, advanced placement credit, cooperative education, English as a second language, freshman honors college, honors programs, internships, part-time degree program, services for LD students, study abroad, summer session for credit. *ROTC:* Army (c), Air Force (c).
Library Fannin Library with 83,000 titles, 394 serial subscriptions.
Computers on Campus 250 computers available on campus for general student use. A campuswide network can be accessed from off campus. Internet access, at least one staffed computer lab available.
Student Life *Housing:* college housing not available. *Activities and Organizations:* drama/theater group, student-run newspaper, choral group, Black Student Union, NASA (Native American Club), Asian American Club, MECHA (Mexican Club). *Campus security:* 24-hour emergency response devices, student patrols, late-night transport/escort service. *Student services:* personal/psychological counseling, women's center, legal services.
Athletics Member NJCAA. *Intercollegiate sports:* baseball M(s), basketball M(s)/W(s), cross-country running M(s)/W(s), football M(s), golf M(s)/W(s), soccer M/W, softball W(s), tennis M(s)/W(s), track and field M(s)/W(s), volleyball W(s). *Intramural sports:* skiing (cross-country) M(c)/W(c), skiing (downhill) M(c)/W(c).

Phoenix College (continued)

Costs (2006–07) *Tuition:* state resident $1560 full-time, $65 per credit hour part-time; nonresident $6720 full-time, $280 per credit hour part-time. *Required fees:* $30 full-time, $15 per term part-time.

Financial Aid Of all full-time matriculated undergraduates who enrolled in 2004, 350 Federal Work-Study jobs (averaging $2800).

Applying *Options:* common application, electronic application, early admission, deferred entrance. *Application deadline:* rolling (freshmen), rolling (transfers). *Notification:* continuous (freshmen).

Freshmen Application Contact Ms. Mary Blackwell, Director of Admissions, Registration and Records, Phoenix College, Phoenix, AZ 85013. *Phone:* 602-285-7500. *Fax:* 602-285-7813. *E-mail:* mblackwell@pcmail.maricopa.edu.

PIMA COMMUNITY COLLEGE

Tucson, Arizona — **www.pima.edu/**

- **State and locally supported** 2-year, founded 1966
- **Urban** 483-acre campus
- **Endowment** $2.7 million
- **Coed,** 30,884 undergraduate students, 30% full-time, 57% women, 43% men

Undergraduates 9,187 full-time, 21,697 part-time. Students come from 40 states and territories, 64 other countries, 5% are from out of state, 4% African American, 3% Asian American or Pacific Islander, 31% Hispanic American, 3% Native American, 1% international, 9% transferred in. Freshmen *Admission:* 5,456 applied, 5,456 admitted, 5,456 enrolled. *Test scores:* ACT scores over 18: 52%; ACT scores over 24: 14%; ACT scores over 30: 2%.

Faculty *Total:* 1,375, 23% full-time. *Student/faculty ratio:* 21:1.

Majors Accounting; administrative assistant and secretarial science; aircraft powerplant technology; American Indian/Native American studies; anthropology; architectural drafting and CAD/CADD; automobile/automotive mechanics technology; building/construction finishing, management, and inspection related; building/property maintenance and management; business administration and management; child care and support services management; child care provision; computer and information sciences; computer engineering technology; computer systems analysis; computer systems networking and telecommunications; computer technology/computer systems technology; construction engineering technology; criminal justice/police science; criminal justice/safety; dental hygiene; dental laboratory technology; design and visual communications; dramatic/theater arts; electrical, electronic and communications engineering technology; elementary education; emergency medical technology (EMT paramedic); environmental engineering technology; fire science; general studies; hospitality administration; industrial technology; international business/trade/commerce; legal assistant/paralegal; liberal arts and sciences/liberal studies; machine shop technology; medical radiologic technology; music; nursing (registered nurse training); pharmacy technician; political science and government; real estate; respiratory care therapy; restaurant, culinary, and catering management; security and protective services related; sign language interpretation and translation; sociology; veterinary/animal health technology; welding technology.

Academics *Calendar:* semesters. *Degrees:* certificates, associate, and post-bachelor's certificates. *Special study options:* academic remediation for entering students, accelerated degree program, adult/continuing education programs, advanced placement credit, cooperative education, distance learning, double majors, English as a second language, freshman honors college, honors programs, independent study, internships, part-time degree program, services for LD students, student-designed majors, summer session for credit. *ROTC:* Army (c), Navy (c), Air Force (c).

Library Pima College Library with 217,049 titles, 984 serial subscriptions, 24,005 audiovisual materials, an OPAC, a Web page.

Computers on Campus 2500 computers available on campus for general student use. A campuswide network can be accessed from off campus. Internet access, online (class) registration, at least one staffed computer lab available.

Student Life *Housing:* college housing not available. *Activities and Organizations:* drama/theater group, student-run newspaper, choral group. *Campus security:* 24-hour emergency response devices and patrols, late-night transport/escort service. *Student services:* personal/psychological counseling, women's center.

Athletics Member NJCAA. *Intercollegiate sports:* baseball M(s), basketball M(s)/W(s), cheerleading W, cross-country running M(s)/W(s), football M(s), golf M(s)/W(s), soccer M(s)/W(s), softball W(s), tennis M(s)/W(s), track and field M(s)/W(s), volleyball W(s). *Intramural sports:* badminton M/W, basketball M/W, cross-country running M/W, equestrian sports M(c)/W(c), football M, golf M/W, ice hockey M(c), racquetball M/W, tennis M/W, track and field M/W, volleyball M/W, wrestling M(c).

Costs (2006–07) *Tuition:* state resident $1104 full-time, $46 per credit part-time; nonresident $5544 full-time, $78 per credit part-time. *Required fees:* $80 full-time, $3 per credit part-time, $10 per term part-time.

Applying *Options:* common application, early admission. *Application fee:* $5. *Application deadline:* rolling (freshmen), rolling (transfers).

Freshmen Application Contact Dr. Wendy Kilgore, Director of Enrollment Services and Registration, Pima Community College, 4905B East Broadway Boulevard, Tucson, AZ 85709-1120. *Phone:* 520-206-4640. *Fax:* 520-206-4790. *E-mail:* wendy.kilgore@pima.edu.

PIMA MEDICAL INSTITUTE

Mesa, Arizona — **www.pimamedical.com/**

- **Proprietary** 2-year, founded 1985, part of Vocational Training Institutes, Inc
- **Urban** campus
- **Coed**

Faculty *Student/faculty ratio:* 15:1.

Academics *Calendar:* modular. *Degree:* certificates and associate.

Standardized Tests *Required:* Wonderlic aptitude test (for admission).

Costs (2005–06) *Tuition:* Tuition varies depending on course.

Applying *Required:* interview. *Required for some:* high school transcript.

Freshmen Application Contact Admissions Office, Pima Medical Institute, Pima Medical Institute, 957 South Dobson Road, Mesa, AZ 85202. *Phone:* 480-644-0267 Ext. 225. *Toll-free phone:* 888-898-9048.

PIMA MEDICAL INSTITUTE

Tucson, Arizona — **www.pmi.edu**

- **Proprietary** 2-year, founded 1972, part of Vocational Training Institutes, Inc
- **Urban** campus
- **Coed**

Undergraduates 711 full-time.

Faculty *Student/faculty ratio:* 13:1.

Academics *Calendar:* modular. *Degree:* certificates and associate. *Special study options:* academic remediation for entering students, accelerated degree program, adult/continuing education programs, cooperative education, internships.

Standardized Tests *Required:* Wonderlic Scholastic Level Exam (for admission).

Costs (2005–06) *Tuition:* Tuition varies depending on course.

Applying *Options:* common application, early admission. *Application fee:* $150. *Required:* interview. *Required for some:* high school transcript.

Freshmen Application Contact Admissions Office, Pima Medical Institute, Pima Medical Institute, 3350 East Grant Road, Tucson, AZ 85716-2800. *Phone:* 520-326-1600 Ext. 5112. *Toll-free phone:* 888-898-9048.

THE REFRIGERATION SCHOOL

Phoenix, Arizona — **www.refrigerationschool.com/**

Director of Admissions Ms. Mary Simmons, Admissions Director, The Refrigeration School, 4210 East Washington Street, Phoenix, AZ 85034-1816. *Phone:* 602-275-7133.

RIO SALADO COLLEGE

Tempe, Arizona — **www.rio.maricopa.edu/**

Freshmen Application Contact Ms. Ruby Miller, Supervisor of Admissions and Records, Rio Salado College, 2323 West 14th Street, Tempe, AZ 85281-6950. *Phone:* 480-517-8152. *Toll-free phone:* 800-729-1197.

SCOTTSDALE COMMUNITY COLLEGE

Scottsdale, Arizona www.sc.maricopa.edu/

- **State and locally supported** 2-year, founded 1969, part of Maricopa County Community College District System
- **Urban** 160-acre campus with easy access to Phoenix
- **Coed,** 11,261 undergraduate students, 30% full-time, 55% women, 45% men

Undergraduates 3,342 full-time, 7,919 part-time. Students come from 49 other countries, 3% are from out of state, 4% African American, 2% Asian American or Pacific Islander, 11% Hispanic American, 5% Native American, 1% international.
Freshmen *Admission:* 517 applied, 517 admitted, 517 enrolled.
Faculty *Total:* 644, 26% full-time, 10% with terminal degrees. *Student/faculty ratio:* 18:1.
Majors Accounting; administrative assistant and secretarial science; business administration and management; criminal justice/law enforcement administration; culinary arts; dramatic/theater arts; electrical, electronic and communications engineering technology; emergency medical technology (EMT paramedic); environmental design/architecture; equestrian studies; fashion merchandising; finance; fire science; hospitality administration; hotel/motel administration; information science/studies; interior design; kindergarten/preschool education; mathematics; medical administrative assistant and medical secretary; nursing (registered nurse training); photography; public administration; real estate; special products marketing.
Academics *Calendar:* semesters. *Degree:* certificates, diplomas, and associate. *Special study options:* academic remediation for entering students, adult/continuing education programs, advanced placement credit, cooperative education, English as a second language, honors programs, off-campus study, part-time degree program, services for LD students, student-designed majors, summer session for credit.
Library an OPAC, a Web page.
Computers on Campus 75 computers available on campus for general student use. A campuswide network can be accessed. Internet access, online (class) registration, at least one staffed computer lab available.
Student Life *Housing:* college housing not available. *Activities and Organizations:* drama/theater group, student-run newspaper, radio station, choral group. *Campus security:* 24-hour emergency response devices and patrols, student patrols, late-night transport/escort service, 24-hour automatic surveillance cameras. *Student services:* personal/psychological counseling.
Athletics Member NJCAA. *Intercollegiate sports:* baseball M, basketball M/W, cross-country running M/W, football M, golf M/W, soccer M/W, softball W, tennis M/W, track and field M/W, volleyball W. *Intramural sports:* archery M/W, badminton M/W, basketball M/W, bowling M/W, racquetball M/W, track and field M/W, volleyball M/W.
Costs (2006–07) *Tuition:* area resident $1980 full-time, $65 per credit hour part-time; state resident $8430 full-time, $90 per credit hour part-time; nonresident $8430 full-time, $90 per credit hour part-time. *Required fees:* $15 full-time.
Financial Aid Of all full-time matriculated undergraduates who enrolled in 2004, 75 Federal Work-Study jobs (averaging $2000). *Financial aid deadline:* 7/15.
Applying *Options:* early admission. *Application deadline:* rolling (freshmen). *Notification:* continuous (freshmen).
Freshmen Application Contact Ms. Fran Watkins, Director of Admissions and Records, Scottsdale Community College, 9000 East Chaparral Road, Scottsdale, AZ 85256. *Phone:* 602-423-6133. *Fax:* 480-423-6200. *E-mail:* fran.watkins@sccmail.maricopa.edu.

SCOTTSDALE CULINARY INSTITUTE

Scottsdale, Arizona www.scichefs.com/

Director of Admissions Mr. Jon Alberts, President, Scottsdale Culinary Institute, 8100 East Camelback Road, Suite 1001, Scottsdale, AZ 85251-3940. *Toll-free phone:* 800-848-2433.

SOUTH MOUNTAIN COMMUNITY COLLEGE

Phoenix, Arizona www.smc.maricopa.edu/

- **State and locally supported** 2-year, founded 1979, part of Maricopa County Community College District System
- **Suburban** 108-acre campus
- **Coed**

Undergraduates 2% are from out of state, 14% African American, 2% Asian American or Pacific Islander, 43% Hispanic American, 4% Native American.
Academics *Calendar:* semesters. *Degree:* certificates and associate. *Special study options:* academic remediation for entering students, adult/continuing education programs, advanced placement credit, cooperative education, English as a second language, honors programs, part-time degree program, services for LD students, summer session for credit. *ROTC:* Air Force (c).
Student Life *Campus security:* late-night transport/escort service, 18-hour patrols, campus lockdown.
Athletics Member NJCAA.
Costs (2005–06) *Tuition:* area resident $1440 full-time; state resident $6192 full-time; nonresident $6192 full-time. *Required fees:* $10 full-time.
Financial Aid Of all full-time matriculated undergraduates who enrolled in 2004, 36 Federal Work-Study jobs (averaging $2000).
Director of Admissions Mr. Tony Bracamonte, Senior Associate Dean of Enrollment Services, South Mountain Community College, 7050 South 24th Street, Phoenix, AZ 85042. *Phone:* 602-243-8120.

SOUTHWEST INSTITUTE OF HEALING ARTS

Tempe, Arizona www.swiha.org/

Director of Admissions Katie Yearous, Student Advisor, Southwest Institute of Healing Arts, 1100 East Apache Boulevard, Tempe, AZ 85281. *Phone:* 480-994-9244. *Toll-free phone:* 888-504-9106. *E-mail:* joannl@swiha.net.

TOHONO O'ODHAM COMMUNITY COLLEGE

Sells, Arizona www.tocc.cc.az.us/

- **Independent** 2-year, founded 1998
- **Coed**

Undergraduates Students come from 1 other state, 97% Native American.
Academics *Calendar:* semesters. *Degree:* certificates, diplomas, and associate.
Applying *Application fee:* $25 (non-residents).
Director of Admissions Tohono O'odham Community College, PO Box 3129, Sells, AZ 85634. *Phone:* 520-383-8401. *Fax:* 520-383-8403. *E-mail:* tocc@tocc.cc.az.us.

UNIVERSAL TECHNICAL INSTITUTE

Avondale, Arizona

- **Private** 2-year

Faculty *Student/faculty ratio:* 30:1.
Academics *Degree:* associate.
Applying *Required:* interview.

YAVAPAI COLLEGE

Prescott, Arizona www2.yc.edu/

- **State and locally supported** 2-year, founded 1966, part of Arizona State Community College System
- **Small-town** 100-acre campus
- **Coed,** 7,422 undergraduate students, 18% full-time, 62% women, 38% men

Undergraduates 1,322 full-time, 6,100 part-time. Students come from 30 states and territories, 18% are from out of state, 1% African American, 1% Asian American or Pacific Islander, 7% Hispanic American, 4% Native American, 5% live on campus.
Freshmen *Admission:* 672 enrolled.
Faculty *Total:* 372, 29% full-time. *Student/faculty ratio:* 15:1.
Majors Accounting; administrative assistant and secretarial science; agribusiness; agricultural business and management; agriculture; aquaculture; architectural drafting and CAD/CADD; automobile/automotive mechanics technology; business administration and management; commercial and advertising art; construction engineering technology; criminal justice/police science; education related; equestrian studies; film/cinema studies; fine arts related; fire science; graphic design; gunsmithing; horse husbandry/equine science and management; information science/studies; legal administrative assistant/secretary; legal assistant/paralegal; liberal arts and sciences/liberal studies; nursing (registered nurse training).
Academics *Calendar:* semesters. *Degree:* certificates and associate. *Special study options:* academic remediation for entering students, adult/continuing education programs, advanced placement credit, cooperative education, distance learning, English as a second language, honors programs, independent study, internships, off-campus study, part-time degree program, services for LD students, summer session for credit. *ROTC:* Army (c), Air Force (c).
Library Yavapai College Library with 81,144 titles, 1,091 serial subscriptions, an OPAC, a Web page.
Computers on Campus 677 computers available on campus for general student use. A campuswide network can be accessed from student residence rooms and from off campus. Internet access, at least one staffed computer lab available.
Student Life *Housing Options:* coed. Campus housing is university owned. *Activities and Organizations:* drama/theater group, student-run newspaper, choral group, Re-Entry Club, Student Nurses Association, Native American Club, International Club, VICA. *Campus security:* 24-hour emergency response devices and patrols, student patrols, late-night transport/escort service, controlled dormitory access. *Student services:* health clinic, personal/psychological counseling, women's center.
Athletics Member NJCAA. *Intercollegiate sports:* baseball M(s), basketball M(s)/W(s), cross-country running W(s), soccer M(s), volleyball W(s).
Costs (2006–07) *Tuition:* state resident $1080 full-time, $45 per credit part-time; nonresident $6880 full-time, $56 per credit part-time.
Applying *Options:* early admission, deferred entrance. *Required:* high school transcript. *Required for some:* essay or personal statement, letters of recommendation. *Application deadline:* rolling (freshmen), rolling (transfers).
Freshmen Application Contact Mr. David Vanness, Admissions, Registration, and Records Manager, Yavapai College, 1100 East Sheldon Street, Prescott, AZ 86301-3297. *Phone:* 928-776-2188. *Toll-free phone:* 800-922-6787. *Fax:* 520-776-2151. *E-mail:* registration@yc.edu.

ARKANSAS

ARKANSAS NORTHEASTERN COLLEGE

Blytheville, Arkansas www.anc.edu/

- **State-supported** 2-year, founded 1975
- **Rural** 80-acre campus with easy access to Memphis
- **Endowment** $187,500
- **Coed,** 1,830 undergraduate students, 53% full-time, 66% women, 34% men

Undergraduates 962 full-time, 868 part-time. Students come from 3 states and territories, 17% are from out of state, 29% African American, 1% Asian American

or Pacific Islander, 0.9% Hispanic American, 0.2% Native American, 5% transferred in. *Retention:* 50% of 2003 full-time freshmen returned.
Freshmen *Admission:* 513 applied, 513 admitted, 370 enrolled. *Average high school GPA:* 2.85.
Faculty *Total:* 173, 42% full-time, 4% with terminal degrees. *Student/faculty ratio:* 18:1.
Majors Agriculture; applied horticulture; business/commerce; criminal justice/police science; general studies; industrial mechanics and maintenance technology; industrial production technologies related; industrial technology; marketing/marketing management; metallurgical technology; middle school education; nursing (registered nurse training).
Academics *Calendar:* semesters. *Degree:* certificates and associate. *Special study options:* academic remediation for entering students, adult/continuing education programs, advanced placement credit, distance learning, double majors, part-time degree program, summer session for credit.
Library Adams/Vines Library with 15,493 titles, 165 serial subscriptions, 682 audiovisual materials, an OPAC.
Computers on Campus 280 computers available on campus for general student use. A campuswide network can be accessed. Internet access, at least one staffed computer lab available.
Student Life *Housing:* college housing not available. *Activities and Organizations:* choral group, Gamma Beta Phi, Association of Childhood Education International, Nursing Club, Cultural Diversity, Adult Student Association. *Campus security:* 24-hour patrols.
Costs (2005–06) *Tuition:* area resident $1410 full-time, $47 per semester hour part-time; state resident $1710 full-time, $57 per semester hour part-time; nonresident $3210 full-time, $107 per semester hour part-time. *Required fees:* $220 full-time, $6 per semester hour part-time, $20 per term part-time. *Payment plans:* installment, deferred payment. *Waivers:* senior citizens and employees or children of employees.
Financial Aid Of all full-time matriculated undergraduates who enrolled in 2004, 42 Federal Work-Study jobs (averaging $2500).
Applying *Options:* deferred entrance. *Recommended:* high school transcript. *Application deadline:* rolling (freshmen), rolling (transfers). *Notification:* continuous (freshmen).
Freshmen Application Contact Mrs. Leslie Wells, Admissions Counselor, Arkansas Northeastern College, PO Box 1109, Blytheville, AR 72316. *Phone:* 870-762-1020 Ext. 1118. *Fax:* 870-763-1654. *E-mail:* lwells@anc.edu.

ARKANSAS STATE UNIVERSITY—BEEBE

Beebe, Arkansas www.asub.edu/

- **State-supported** 2-year, founded 1927, part of Arkansas State University System
- **Small-town** 320-acre campus with easy access to Memphis
- **Coed,** 3,976 undergraduate students, 53% full-time, 57% women, 43% men

Undergraduates 2,124 full-time, 1,852 part-time. Students come from 25 states and territories, 5% African American, 1% Asian American or Pacific Islander, 2% Hispanic American, 1% Native American, 0.1% international, 2% transferred in, 12% live on campus.
Freshmen *Admission:* 904 enrolled. *Average high school GPA:* 2.75.
Faculty *Total:* 97, 65% full-time, 22% with terminal degrees. *Student/faculty ratio:* 30:1.
Majors Agriculture; animal sciences; business administration and management; clinical/medical laboratory technology; computer programming (vendor/product certification); computer systems networking and telecommunications; computer technology/computer systems technology; drafting and design technology; electrical, electronic and communications engineering technology; general studies; health/medical preparatory programs related; industrial mechanics and maintenance technology; information technology; liberal arts and sciences/liberal studies; nursing (registered nurse training); quality control technology; vehicle maintenance and repair technologies related.
Academics *Calendar:* semesters. *Degree:* certificates and associate. *Special study options:* academic remediation for entering students, adult/continuing education programs, advanced placement credit, distance learning, honors programs, part-time degree program, summer session for credit.
Library Abington Library with 90,000 titles, 500 serial subscriptions, 10 audiovisual materials.
Computers on Campus 375 computers available on campus for general student use. A campuswide network can be accessed from off campus. Internet access, at least one staffed computer lab available.
Student Life *Housing Options:* men-only, women-only. Campus housing is university owned. *Activities and Organizations:* drama/theater group, choral group, Student Arkansas Education Association, Art Club, Agri Club, Social Science Club, Leadership Council. *Campus security:* 24-hour emergency response devices and patrols. *Student services:* personal/psychological counseling.

Athletics *Intramural sports:* archery M/W, badminton M/W, basketball M/W, football M/W, golf M/W, racquetball M/W, softball M/W, squash M/W, table tennis M/W, tennis M/W, track and field M/W, volleyball M/W.

Standardized Tests *Recommended:* ACT (for placement).

Costs (2005–06) *Tuition:* state resident $1824 full-time; nonresident $3000 full-time. *Room and board:* $2480.

Financial Aid Of all full-time matriculated undergraduates who enrolled in 2004, 36 Federal Work-Study jobs (averaging $1800). 112 state and other part-time jobs (averaging $750).

Applying *Options:* common application, deferred entrance. *Required:* high school transcript. *Application deadline:* rolling (freshmen). *Notification:* continuous (freshmen).

Director of Admissions Mr. James Washburn, Director of Admissions, Arkansas State University–Beebe, PO Box 1000, Beebe, AR 72012-1000. *Phone:* 501-882-8280. *Toll-free phone:* 800-632-9985.

ARKANSAS STATE UNIVERSITY– MOUNTAIN HOME

Mountain Home, Arkansas www.asumh.edu/

- **State-supported** 2-year, part of Arkansas State University
- **Small-town** 136-acre campus
- **Coed,** 1,031 undergraduate students, 61% full-time, 67% women, 33% men

Undergraduates 625 full-time, 406 part-time. Students come from 11 states and territories, 3 other countries, 0.1% are from out of state, 15% transferred in. *Retention:* 46% of 2003 full-time freshmen returned.

Freshmen *Admission:* 735 applied, 383 admitted, 305 enrolled. *Average high school GPA:* 2.30. *Test scores:* ACT scores over 18: 84%; ACT scores over 24: 24%.

Faculty *Total:* 62, 61% full-time, 24% with terminal degrees. *Student/faculty ratio:* 20:1.

Majors Audiology and hearing sciences; business automation/technology/data entry; criminal justice/law enforcement administration; criminal justice/safety; emergency medical technology (EMT paramedic); forensic science and technology; funeral service and mortuary science; information science/studies; liberal arts and sciences/liberal studies; middle school education; opticianry.

Academics *Calendar:* semesters. *Degree:* certificates and associate. *Special study options:* academic remediation for entering students, advanced placement credit, cooperative education, distance learning, independent study, part-time degree program, services for LD students, summer session for credit.

Library Norma Wood Library with 30,682 titles, 6,634 serial subscriptions, 2,150 audiovisual materials, an OPAC, a Web page.

Computers on Campus 60 computers available on campus for general student use. A campuswide network can be accessed from off campus. Internet access, online (class) registration, at least one staffed computer lab available.

Student Life *Housing:* college housing not available. *Activities and Organizations:* choral group, Phi Theta Kappa, Circle K, Criminal Justice Club, Mortuary Science Club, Student Ambassadors.

Standardized Tests *Recommended:* ACT (for admission), SAT Subject Tests (for admission), COMPASS, ASSET.

Costs (2006–07) *Tuition:* state resident $2130 full-time, $71 per credit part-time; nonresident $3660 full-time, $122 per credit part-time. *Required fees:* $240 full-time, $8 per credit part-time.

Financial Aid Of all full-time matriculated undergraduates who enrolled in 2004, 14 Federal Work-Study jobs (averaging $3200).

Applying *Required:* high school transcript. *Recommended:* placement scores. *Notification:* continuous (freshmen).

Freshmen Application Contact Mr. Jeff Obert, Recruiter, Arkansas State University–Mountain Home, 1600 South College Street, Mountain Home, AR 72653. *Phone:* 870-508-6262. *Fax:* 870-508-6287. *E-mail:* jobert@asumh.edu.

ARKANSAS STATE UNIVERSITY– NEWPORT

Newport, Arkansas www.asun.edu/

Director of Admissions Ms. Tara Byrd, Registrar, Director of Admissions, Arkansas State University–Newport, 7648 Victory Boulevard, Newport, AR 72112. *Phone:* 870-512-7800. *Toll-free phone:* 800-976-1676.

BLACK RIVER TECHNICAL COLLEGE

Pocahontas, Arkansas www.blackrivertech.edu/

- **State-supported** 2-year, founded 1972
- **Small-town** 55-acre campus
- **Coed**

Undergraduates 652 full-time, 591 part-time. Students come from 2 states and territories.

Faculty *Student/faculty ratio:* 16:1.

Academics *Calendar:* semesters. *Degree:* associate. *Special study options:* academic remediation for entering students, cooperative education, honors programs, internships, part-time degree program, services for LD students, student-designed majors, summer session for credit.

Student Life *Campus security:* night patrol.

Standardized Tests *Required for some:* ACT, ACT ASSET, or SAT.

Applying *Options:* common application. *Required for some:* high school transcript, interview.

Director of Admissions Mr. Jim Ulmer, Director of Admissions, Black River Technical College, 1410 Highway 304 East, Pocahontas, AR 72455. *Phone:* 870-892-4565. *Toll-free phone:* 800-919-3086.

COSSATOT COMMUNITY COLLEGE OF THE UNIVERSITY OF ARKANSAS

De Queen, Arkansas www.cccua.edu/

- **State-supported** 2-year, founded 1991, part of University of Arkansas System
- **Rural** campus
- **Endowment** $110,096
- **Coed,** 1,020 undergraduate students

Undergraduates Students come from 6 states and territories, 2% are from out of state, 10% African American, 1% Asian American or Pacific Islander, 10% Hispanic American, 2% Native American.

Freshmen *Admission:* 361 applied, 301 admitted.

Faculty *Total:* 74, 46% full-time, 3% with terminal degrees. *Student/faculty ratio:* 12:1.

Majors Automobile/automotive mechanics technology; business administration and management; carpentry; computer management; emergency medical technology (EMT paramedic); environmental studies; industrial technology; liberal arts and sciences/liberal studies; medical/clinical assistant; occupational safety and health technology; welding technology; wood science and wood products/pulp and paper technology.

Academics *Calendar:* semesters. *Degree:* certificates and associate. *Special study options:* academic remediation for entering students, adult/continuing education programs, advanced placement credit, cooperative education, distance learning, double majors, English as a second language, external degree program, independent study, internships, off-campus study, part-time degree program, services for LD students, summer session for credit.

Library Kimbell Library.

Computers on Campus Internet access, online (class) registration available.

Student Life *Housing:* college housing not available.

Costs (2005–06) *Tuition:* area resident $1350 full-time, $45 per credit hour part-time; state resident $1650 full-time, $55 per credit hour part-time; nonresident $4950 full-time, $165 per credit hour part-time. Full-time tuition and fees vary according to course load and program. Part-time tuition and fees vary according to course load and program. *Required fees:* $250 full-time, $15 per course part-time, $53 per term part-time. *Payment plan:* installment. *Waivers:* senior citizens and employees or children of employees.

Financial Aid Of all full-time matriculated undergraduates who enrolled in 2004, 14 Federal Work-Study jobs (averaging $2700).

Applying *Options:* common application, electronic application. *Recommended:* high school transcript.

Freshmen Application Contact Ms. Nancy Cowling, Admissions Advisor, Cossatot Community College of the University of Arkansas, PO Box 960, DeQueen, AR 71832. *Phone:* 870-584-4471. *Toll-free phone:* 800-844-4471. *Fax:* 870-642-8766. *E-mail:* ncowling@cccua.edu.

CROWLEY'S RIDGE COLLEGE

Paragould, Arkansas www.crowleysridgecollege.edu/

Director of Admissions Mrs. Nancy Joneshill, Director of Admissions, Crowley's Ridge College, 100 College Drive, Paragould, AR 72450. *Phone:*

Crowley's Ridge College (continued)
870-236-6901 Ext. 14. *Toll-free phone:* 800-264-1096. *Fax:* 870-236-7748. *E-mail:* njoneshi@crowleysridgecollege.edu.

EAST ARKANSAS COMMUNITY COLLEGE

Forrest City, Arkansas   www.eacc.edu/

- **State-supported** 2-year, founded 1974
- **Small-town** 40-acre campus with easy access to Memphis
- **Endowment** $217,500
- **Coed,** 1,477 undergraduate students, 50% full-time, 67% women, 33% men

Undergraduates 745 full-time, 732 part-time. Students come from 4 states and territories, 1% are from out of state, 41% African American, 0.7% Asian American or Pacific Islander, 1% Hispanic American, 0.2% Native American, 0.1% international.
Freshmen *Admission:* 276 admitted, 276 enrolled. *Test scores:* ACT scores over 18: 52%; ACT scores over 24: 4%.
Faculty *Total:* 91, 42% full-time. *Student/faculty ratio:* 17:1.
Majors Business administration and management; computer engineering technology; criminal justice/law enforcement administration; criminal justice/police science; drafting and design technology; liberal arts and sciences/liberal studies; nursing (licensed practical/vocational nurse training).
Academics *Calendar:* semesters. *Degree:* certificates and associate. *Special study options:* academic remediation for entering students, adult/continuing education programs, advanced placement credit, honors programs, part-time degree program, services for LD students, summer session for credit.
Library Learning Resource Center plus 1 other with 21,908 titles, 109 serial subscriptions.
Computers on Campus 26 computers available on campus for general student use. At least one staffed computer lab available.
Student Life *Housing:* college housing not available. *Activities and Organizations:* drama/theater group, choral group, Gamma Beta Phi, Baptist Student Union, Student Activities Committee, Lambda Alpha Epsilon. *Campus security:* 24-hour emergency response devices, 16-hour patrols by trained security personnel. *Student services:* personal/psychological counseling.
Costs (2006–07) *Tuition:* area resident $1470 full-time, $49 per credit hour part-time; state resident $1710 full-time, $57 per credit hour part-time; nonresident $2070 full-time, $69 per credit hour part-time. *Required fees:* $150 full-time, $5 per credit hour part-time.
Financial Aid Of all full-time matriculated undergraduates who enrolled in 2004, 74 Federal Work-Study jobs (averaging $1104).
Applying *Options:* early admission, deferred entrance. *Required:* high school transcript. *Application deadline:* rolling (freshmen), rolling (transfers). *Notification:* continuous (freshmen).
Freshmen Application Contact Ms. DeAnna Adams, Director of Enrollment Management/Institutional Research, East Arkansas Community College, 1700 Newcastle Road, Forrest City, AR 72335-2204. *Phone:* 870-633-4480 Ext. 219. *Toll-free phone:* 877-797-3222. *Fax:* 870-633-3840. *E-mail:* dadams@eacc.edu.

ITT TECHNICAL INSTITUTE

Little Rock, Arkansas   www.itt-tech.edu/

- **Proprietary** primarily 2-year, founded 1993, part of ITT Educational Services, Inc
- **Urban** campus
- **Coed**

Majors Accounting and business/management; animation, interactive technology, video graphics and special effects; business administration and management; CAD/CADD drafting/design technology; computer and information systems security; computer programming; computer software technology; computer systems networking and telecommunications; criminal justice/law enforcement administration; e-commerce; electrical, electronic and communications engineering technology; system, networking, and LAN/WAN management; web/multimedia management and webmaster; web page, digital/multimedia and information resources design.
Academics *Calendar:* quarters. *Degrees:* associate and bachelor's.
Library a Web page.
Computers on Campus Internet access, at least one staffed computer lab available.
Student Life *Housing:* college housing not available.
Standardized Tests *Required:* Wonderlic aptitude test (for admission).

Costs (2005–06) *Tuition:* Please see school catalog for specific information.
Applying *Options:* deferred entrance. *Application fee:* $100. *Required:* high school transcript, interview. *Recommended:* letters of recommendation. *Application deadline:* rolling (freshmen), rolling (transfers). *Notification:* continuous (freshmen).
Freshmen Application Contact Mr. Reed W. Thompson, Director of Recruitment, ITT Technical Institute, 4520 South University Avenue, Little Rock, AR 72204. *Phone:* 501-565-5550. *Toll-free phone:* 800-359-4429.

MID-SOUTH COMMUNITY COLLEGE

West Memphis, Arkansas   www.midsouthcc.edu/

- **State-supported** 2-year, founded 1993
- **Suburban** 80-acre campus with easy access to Memphis
- **Endowment** $894,155
- **Coed,** 1,467 undergraduate students, 31% full-time, 65% women, 35% men

Undergraduates 457 full-time, 1,010 part-time. Students come from 2 other countries, 5% are from out of state, 49% African American, 0.7% Asian American or Pacific Islander, 1% Hispanic American, 0.2% Native American, 0.4% international, 5% transferred in. *Retention:* 41% of 2003 full-time freshmen returned.
Freshmen *Admission:* 214 applied, 214 admitted, 210 enrolled. *Test scores:* ACT scores over 18: 60%; ACT scores over 24: 9%.
Faculty *Total:* 99, 34% full-time, 5% with terminal degrees. *Student/faculty ratio:* 15:1.
Majors Computer and information sciences; liberal arts and sciences/liberal studies; management information systems and services related; multi-/interdisciplinary studies related; web/multimedia management and webmaster.
Academics *Calendar:* semesters. *Degree:* certificates and associate. *Special study options:* academic remediation for entering students, adult/continuing education programs, distance learning, independent study, internships, part-time degree program, summer session for credit.
Library Mid-South Community College Library/Media Center with 14,672 titles, 88 serial subscriptions, 2,151 audiovisual materials, an OPAC, a Web page.
Computers on Campus 280 computers available on campus for general student use. A campuswide network can be accessed from off campus. Internet access, at least one staffed computer lab available.
Student Life *Housing:* college housing not available. *Activities and Organizations:* choral group, Phi Theta Kappa, Baptist Collegiate Ministry, Campus Ministry International, Student Ambassador, Skills-USA-Vica. *Campus security:* 24-hour emergency response devices, security during class hours.
Standardized Tests *Required for some:* ACT (for admission), ASSET, COMPASS.
Costs (2005–06) *Tuition:* area resident $1410 full-time, $47 per credit part-time; state resident $1740 full-time, $58 per credit part-time; nonresident $3150 full-time, $105 per credit part-time. Full-time tuition and fees vary according to course load and reciprocity agreements. Part-time tuition and fees vary according to course load and reciprocity agreements. *Required fees:* $210 full-time, $7 per credit part-time. *Payment plan:* installment. *Waivers:* senior citizens and employees or children of employees.
Financial Aid Of all full-time matriculated undergraduates who enrolled in 2004, 29 Federal Work-Study jobs (averaging $1914).
Applying *Options:* common application, electronic application, early admission. *Required:* high school transcript. *Application deadline:* rolling (freshmen), rolling (transfers). *Notification:* continuous (freshmen).
Freshmen Application Contact Ms. Leslie Anderson, Registrar, Mid-South Community College, 2000 West Broadway, West Memphis, AR 72301. *Phone:* 870-733-6732. *Fax:* 870-733-6719. *E-mail:* landerson@midsouthcc.edu.

NATIONAL PARK COMMUNITY COLLEGE

Hot Springs, Arkansas   www.npcc.edu/

Director of Admissions Dr. Allen B. Moody, Director of Institutional Services/Registrar, National Park Community College, 101 College Drive, Hot Springs, AR 71913. *Phone:* 501-760-4222. *E-mail:* bmoody@npcc.edu.

NORTH ARKANSAS COLLEGE
Harrison, Arkansas   **www.northark.edu/**

- **State and locally supported** 2-year, founded 1974
- **Small-town** 40-acre campus
- **Endowment** $333,030
- **Coed,** 2,187 undergraduate students, 52% full-time, 62% women, 38% men

Undergraduates 1,138 full-time, 1,049 part-time. Students come from 14 states and territories, 2% are from out of state, 0.6% African American, 0.8% Asian American or Pacific Islander, 2% Hispanic American, 0.8% Native American, 5% transferred in. *Retention:* 48% of 2003 full-time freshmen returned. Freshmen *Admission:* 737 applied, 737 admitted, 474 enrolled. *Test scores:* ACT scores over 18: 74%; ACT scores over 24: 12%; ACT scores over 30: 1%.

Faculty *Total:* 156, 42% full-time, 9% with terminal degrees. *Student/faculty ratio:* 16:1.

Majors Administrative assistant and secretarial science; agricultural business and management; agriculture; automobile/automotive mechanics technology; biomedical technology; business/commerce; clinical/medical laboratory assistant; clinical/medical laboratory technology; computer and information sciences; criminal justice/law enforcement administration; criminal justice/police science; drafting/design technology; electrical, electronic and communications engineering technology; electromechanical and instrumentation and maintenance technologies related; electromechanical technology; emergency medical technology (EMT paramedic); forensic science and technology; industrial technology; institutional food workers; liberal arts and sciences/liberal studies; medical radiologic technology; middle school education; nursing (registered nurse training); surgical technology.

Academics *Calendar:* semesters. *Degree:* certificates and associate. *Special study options:* academic remediation for entering students, adult/continuing education programs, advanced placement credit, distance learning, freshman honors college, honors programs, independent study, part-time degree program, services for LD students, summer session for credit.

Library North Arkansas College Library plus 1 other with 29,969 titles, 340 serial subscriptions, 2,879 audiovisual materials, an OPAC, a Web page.

Computers on Campus 200 computers available on campus for general student use. A campuswide network can be accessed from off campus. Internet access, at least one staffed computer lab available.

Student Life *Housing:* college housing not available. *Activities and Organizations:* drama/theater group, choral group, Phi Beta Lambda, Phi Theta Kappa, Student Nurses Association, Vocational Industrial Clubs, Baptist Student Union. *Campus security:* 24-hour patrols. *Student services:* personal/psychological counseling.

Athletics Member NJCAA. *Intercollegiate sports:* baseball M, basketball M(s)/W(s), softball W. *Intramural sports:* archery M/W, badminton M/W, baseball M/W, football M/W, golf M/W, racquetball M/W, softball W, table tennis M/W, tennis M/W, volleyball M/W.

Costs (2005–06) *Tuition:* area resident $1590 full-time, $53 per credit hour part-time; state resident $2130 full-time, $71 per credit hour part-time; nonresident $4110 full-time, $137 per credit hour part-time. *Required fees:* $150 full-time.

Financial Aid Of all full-time matriculated undergraduates who enrolled in 2004, 107 Federal Work-Study jobs (averaging $1103).

Applying *Options:* deferred entrance. *Required for some:* high school transcript. *Application deadline:* rolling (freshmen), rolling (transfers). *Notification:* continuous (freshmen).

Freshmen Application Contact Ms. Charla McDonald, Director of Admissions, North Arkansas College, 1515 Pioneer Drive, Harrison, AR 72601. *Phone:* 870-391-3221. *Toll-free phone:* 800-679-6622. *Fax:* 870-391-3339. *E-mail:* charlam@northard.edu.

NORTHWEST ARKANSAS COMMUNITY COLLEGE
Bentonville, Arkansas   **www.nwacc.edu/**

Director of Admissions Dr. Charles Mullins, Director of Admissions, NorthWest Arkansas Community College, One College Drive, Bentonville, AR 72712. *Phone:* 479-636-9222 Ext. 4231. *Toll-free phone:* 800-995-6922.

OUACHITA TECHNICAL COLLEGE
Malvern, Arkansas   **www.otcweb.edu/**

- **State-supported** 2-year, founded 1972
- **Small-town** 11-acre campus
- **Coed,** 1,590 undergraduate students, 35% full-time, 51% women, 49% men

Undergraduates 556 full-time, 1,034 part-time. Students come from 2 states and territories, 2 other countries, 0.1% are from out of state, 12% African American, 0.9% Asian American or Pacific Islander, 1% Hispanic American, 0.6% Native American, 0.3% international, 6% transferred in. *Retention:* 50% of 2003 full-time freshmen returned.

Freshmen *Admission:* 325 applied, 325 admitted, 210 enrolled. *Average high school GPA:* 2.67. *Test scores:* ACT scores over 18: 62%; ACT scores over 24: 9%.

Faculty *Total:* 99, 33% full-time, 12% with terminal degrees. *Student/faculty ratio:* 16:1.

Majors Accounting; administrative assistant and secretarial science; automobile/automotive mechanics technology; business administration and management; child care and support services management; computer and information sciences; criminal justice/law enforcement administration; general studies; industrial arts; industrial technology; legal administrative assistant/secretary; legal assistant/paralegal; liberal arts and sciences/liberal studies; machine tool technology; management information systems; marketing/marketing management; medical administrative assistant and medical secretary; nursing (licensed practical/vocational nurse training).

Academics *Calendar:* semesters. *Degree:* certificates and associate. *Special study options:* academic remediation for entering students, accelerated degree program, advanced placement credit, cooperative education, distance learning, double majors, independent study, internships, part-time degree program, services for LD students, summer session for credit.

Library Ouachita Technical College Library/Learning Resource Center with 8,000 titles, 100 serial subscriptions, 1,200 audiovisual materials, an OPAC, a Web page.

Computers on Campus 125 computers available on campus for general student use. A campuswide network can be accessed from off campus. Internet access, at least one staffed computer lab available.

Student Life *Housing:* college housing not available. *Campus security:* 24-hour patrols. *Student services:* personal/psychological counseling.

Standardized Tests *Recommended:* SAT or ACT (for admission), ACT COMPASS or ACT ASSET.

Costs (2006–07) *One-time required fee:* $35. *Tuition:* state resident $1560 full-time, $52 per credit hour part-time; nonresident $3120 full-time, $104 per credit hour part-time. *Required fees:* $420 full-time, $14 per credit hour part-time.

Financial Aid Of all full-time matriculated undergraduates who enrolled in 2004, 18 Federal Work-Study jobs (averaging $2400).

Applying *Options:* electronic application, early admission, deferred entrance. *Required:* high school transcript. *Application deadline:* rolling (freshmen), rolling (transfers).

Freshmen Application Contact Mr. Vaughn Kesterson, Counselor, Ouachita Technical College, One College Circle, Malvern, AR 72104. *Phone:* 501-337-5000 Ext. 1117. *Toll-free phone:* 800-337-0266. *Fax:* 501-337-9382. *E-mail:* vkesterson@otcweb.edu.

OZARKA COLLEGE
Melbourne, Arkansas   **www.ozarka.edu/**

Freshmen Application Contact Mr. Randy Scaggs, Counselor and Recruiter, Ozarka College, PO Box 12, 218 College Drive, Melbourne, AR 72556. *Phone:* 870-368-7371 Ext. 2028. *Toll-free phone:* 800-821-4335.

PHILLIPS COMMUNITY COLLEGE OF THE UNIVERSITY OF ARKANSAS
Helena, Arkansas   **www.pccua.edu/**

- **State and locally supported** 2-year, founded 1965, part of University of Arkansas System
- **Small-town** 80-acre campus with easy access to Memphis
- **Coed**

Academics *Calendar:* semesters. *Degree:* certificates and associate. *Special study options:* academic remediation for entering students, adult/continuing

Phillips Community College of the University of Arkansas (continued)
education programs, advanced placement credit, part-time degree program, services for LD students, summer session for credit.

Student Life *Campus security:* 24-hour patrols.

Standardized Tests *Required:* ACT (for placement), ACT ASSET (for placement).

Costs (2005–06) *Tuition:* area resident $750 full-time, $50 per semester hour part-time; state resident $885 full-time, $59 per semester hour part-time; nonresident $1455 full-time, $97 per semester hour part-time.

Applying *Options:* early admission.

Director of Admissions Mr. Lynn Boone, Registrar, Phillips Community College of the University of Arkansas, PO Box 785, Helena, AR 72342-0785. *Phone:* 870-338-6474.

PULASKI TECHNICAL COLLEGE

North Little Rock, Arkansas   **www.pulaskitech.edu/**

- **State-supported** 2-year, founded 1945
- **Urban** 40-acre campus with easy access to Little Rock
- **Coed,** 7,685 undergraduate students, 51% full-time, 67% women, 33% men

Undergraduates 3,953 full-time, 3,732 part-time. Students come from 3 states and territories, 1% are from out of state, 46% African American, 1% Asian American or Pacific Islander, 1% Hispanic American, 0.5% Native American, 0.3% international. *Retention:* 46% of 2003 full-time freshmen returned. Freshmen *Admission:* 2,268 applied, 2,268 admitted, 1,302 enrolled. *Average high school GPA:* 2.55.

Faculty *Total:* 455, 24% full-time, 18% with terminal degrees. *Student/faculty ratio:* 25:1.

Majors Administrative assistant and secretarial science; computer engineering technology; drafting and design technology; electromechanical technology; industrial technology; information science/studies; occupational therapist assistant; respiratory care therapy.

Academics *Calendar:* semesters. *Degree:* certificates and associate. *Special study options:* academic remediation for entering students, advanced placement credit, distance learning, part-time degree program, services for LD students, summer session for credit.

Library Ottenheimer Library with 16,378 titles, 234 serial subscriptions, 1,520 audiovisual materials, an OPAC, a Web page.

Computers on Campus 75 computers available on campus for general student use. A campuswide network can be accessed. Internet access, online (class) registration, at least one staffed computer lab available.

Student Life *Housing:* college housing not available. *Activities and Organizations:* drama/theater group. *Campus security:* security personnel 7 a.m. to 11 p.m.

Costs (2006–07) *Tuition:* state resident $2161 full-time, $72 per credit hour part-time; nonresident $3570 full-time, $119 per credit hour part-time. *Required fees:* $255 full-time, $8 per credit hour part-time, $15 per credit hour part-time.

Applying *Options:* common application, electronic application. *Required:* high school transcript. *Application deadline:* rolling (freshmen).

Freshmen Application Contact Ms. Janice Hurd, Admissions Department, Pulaski Technical College, 3000 West Scenic Drive, North Little Rock, AR 72118. *Phone:* 501-812-2231. *Fax:* 501-812-2316. *E-mail:* jhurd@pulaskitech.edu.

REMINGTON COLLEGE—LITTLE ROCK CAMPUS

Little Rock, Arkansas   **www.remingtoncollege.edu/**

Director of Admissions Mr. David Caldwell, Campus President, Remington College–Little Rock Campus, 8901 Kanis Road, Little Rock, AR 72205. *Phone:* 501-312-0007. *Fax:* 501-225-3819. *E-mail:* david.caldwell@remingtoncollege.edu.

RICH MOUNTAIN COMMUNITY COLLEGE

Mena, Arkansas   **www.rmcc.edu/**

- **State and locally supported** 2-year, founded 1983
- **Small-town** 40-acre campus
- **Endowment** $301,360
- **Coed**

Undergraduates 348 full-time, 625 part-time. Students come from 2 states and territories, 2 other countries, 2% are from out of state, 1% Asian American or Pacific Islander, 0.8% Hispanic American, 2% Native American.

Faculty *Student/faculty ratio:* 18:1.

Academics *Calendar:* semesters. *Degree:* certificates and associate. *Special study options:* academic remediation for entering students, adult/continuing education programs, advanced placement credit, distance learning, double majors, English as a second language, part-time degree program, services for LD students, summer session for credit.

Student Life *Campus security:* administrator on night duty.

Costs (2005–06) *Tuition:* area resident $960 full-time, $40 per semester hour part-time; state resident $1200 full-time, $50 per semester hour part-time; nonresident $3600 full-time, $150 per semester hour part-time. *Required fees:* $72 full-time, $3 per semester hour part-time.

Financial Aid Of all full-time matriculated undergraduates who enrolled in 2004, 12 Federal Work-Study jobs (averaging $1500).

Applying *Options:* common application, early admission. *Required:* high school transcript.

Director of Admissions Dr. Steve Rook, Dean of Students, Rich Mountain Community College, 1100 College Drive, Mena, AR 71953. *Phone:* 479-394-7622 Ext. 1400.

SOUTH ARKANSAS COMMUNITY COLLEGE

El Dorado, Arkansas   **www.southark.edu/**

- **State-supported** 2-year, founded 1975, part of Arkansas Department of Higher Education
- **Small-town** 4-acre campus
- **Coed,** 1,368 undergraduate students, 45% full-time, 71% women, 29% men

Undergraduates 612 full-time, 756 part-time. Students come from 2 states and territories, 6% are from out of state, 32% African American, 0.3% Asian American or Pacific Islander, 1% Hispanic American, 0.5% Native American. *Retention:* 46% of 2003 full-time freshmen returned. Freshmen *Admission:* 183 enrolled.

Faculty *Student/faculty ratio:* 13:1.

Majors Administrative assistant and secretarial science; business/commerce; clinical/medical laboratory technology; criminal justice/police science; emergency medical technology (EMT paramedic); general studies; industrial technology; management information systems; medical radiologic technology; physical therapist assistant.

Academics *Calendar:* semesters. *Degree:* certificates and associate. *Special study options:* academic remediation for entering students, adult/continuing education programs, advanced placement credit, internships, part-time degree program, services for LD students, summer session for credit.

Library South Arkansas Community College Library with 22,652 titles, 223 serial subscriptions.

Computers on Campus 75 computers available on campus for general student use. A campuswide network can be accessed. Internet access, at least one staffed computer lab available.

Student Life *Housing:* college housing not available. *Activities and Organizations:* choral group. *Campus security:* security guard. *Student services:* personal/psychological counseling.

Athletics *Intramural sports:* badminton M/W, basketball M/W, tennis M/W, volleyball M/W.

Standardized Tests *Required for some:* ACT COMPASS. *Recommended:* SAT or ACT (for admission).

Costs (2006–07) *Tuition:* area resident $1710 full-time; state resident $1950 full-time; nonresident $3600 full-time.

Financial Aid Of all full-time matriculated undergraduates who enrolled in 2004, 45 Federal Work-Study jobs (averaging $1300).

Applying *Options:* early admission, deferred entrance. *Required:* high school transcript. *Application deadline:* 8/25 (freshmen), rolling (transfers).

Freshmen Application Contact Dean Inman, Director of Enrollment Services, South Arkansas Community College, PO Box 7010, El Dorado, AR

71731-7010. *Phone:* 870-864-7142. *Toll-free phone:* 800-955-2289 Ext. 142. *Fax:* 870-864-7109. *E-mail:* dinman@southark.edu.

SOUTHEAST ARKANSAS COLLEGE
Pine Bluff, Arkansas   www.seark.edu/

Director of Admissions Ms. Barbara Dunn, Coordinator of Admissions and Enrollment Management, Southeast Arkansas College, 1900 Hazel Street, Pine Bluff, AR 71603. *Phone:* 870-543-5957. *Toll-free phone:* 888-SEARK TC. *E-mail:* main@seark.edu.

SOUTHERN ARKANSAS UNIVERSITY TECH
Camden, Arkansas   www.sautech.edu/

- **State-supported** 2-year, founded 1967, part of Arkansas Department of Higher Education
- **Rural** 96-acre campus
- **Coed,** 1,767 undergraduate students, 31% full-time, 43% women, 57% men

Undergraduates 554 full-time, 1,213 part-time. Students come from 6 states and territories, 1% are from out of state, 25% African American, 0.3% Asian American or Pacific Islander, 0.7% Hispanic American, 0.5% Native American, 2% transferred in.
Freshmen *Admission:* 555 applied, 555 admitted, 165 enrolled. *Average high school GPA:* 2.70. *Test scores:* ACT scores over 18: 72%; ACT scores over 24: 8%.
Faculty *Total:* 81, 47% full-time, 7% with terminal degrees. *Student/faculty ratio:* 21:1.
Majors Airframe mechanics and aircraft maintenance technology; business administration and management; computer and information sciences; computer and information sciences and support services related; emergency medical technology (EMT paramedic); engineering technologies related; environmental engineering technology; fire science; general studies; industrial mechanics and maintenance technology; industrial technology; office management; teaching assistants/aides related; web/multimedia management and webmaster; Web page, digital/multimedia and information resources design.
Academics *Calendar:* semesters. *Degree:* certificates and associate. *Special study options:* academic remediation for entering students, adult/continuing education programs, advanced placement credit, distance learning, double majors, honors programs, independent study, internships, off-campus study, part-time degree program, summer session for credit.
Library Southern Arkansas University Tech Learning Resource Center with 17,389 titles, 115 serial subscriptions, 960 audiovisual materials, an OPAC.
Computers on Campus 200 computers available on campus for general student use. A campuswide network can be accessed. Internet access, at least one staffed computer lab available.
Student Life *Housing Options:* Campus housing is university owned. *Activities and Organizations:* student-run radio station, Phi Beta Lambda, SAU Tech Ambassadors, Allied Health Student Club, Computer Club, Phi Theta Kappa. *Campus security:* 24-hour emergency response devices, patrols by trained security personnel. *Student services:* personal/psychological counseling.
Athletics *Intramural sports:* basketball M/W, football M/W, soccer M/W, softball M/W, table tennis M/W, volleyball M/W.
Costs (2006–07) *Tuition:* state resident $1638 full-time, $63 per hour part-time; nonresident $2184 full-time, $84 per hour part-time. *Required fees:* $574 full-time, $21 per credit hour part-time. *Room and board:* $3413; room only: $2100.
Financial Aid Of all full-time matriculated undergraduates who enrolled in 2004, 21 Federal Work-Study jobs (averaging $1274).
Applying *Options:* deferred entrance. *Required for some:* high school transcript. *Application deadline:* 8/15 (freshmen), rolling (transfers). *Notification:* continuous (freshmen).
Freshmen Application Contact Mrs. Beverly Clark, Admissions Secretary, Southern Arkansas University Tech, PO Box 3499, East Camden, AR 71711. *Phone:* 870-574-4558. *Fax:* 870-574-4478. *E-mail:* bclark@sautech.edu.

UNIVERSITY OF ARKANSAS COMMUNITY COLLEGE AT BATESVILLE
Batesville, Arkansas   www.uaccb.edu/

- **State-supported** 2-year, part of University of Arkansas System
- **Small-town** campus
- **Coed**

Undergraduates 784 full-time, 533 part-time. 3% African American, 0.5% Asian American or Pacific Islander, 1% Hispanic American, 0.5% Native American, 0.1% international, 9% transferred in. *Retention:* 57% of 2003 full-time freshmen returned.
Faculty *Student/faculty ratio:* 13:1.
Academics *Calendar:* semesters. *Degree:* certificates and associate. *Special study options:* academic remediation for entering students, adult/continuing education programs, advanced placement credit, cooperative education, distance learning, double majors, English as a second language, external degree program, independent study, internships, off-campus study, part-time degree program, services for LD students, student-designed majors, summer session for credit.
Student Life *Campus security:* security cameras.
Financial Aid Of all full-time matriculated undergraduates who enrolled in 2004, 49 Federal Work-Study jobs (averaging $1311).
Applying *Options:* common application.
Director of Admissions Mr. Andy Thomas, Director of Admissions, University of Arkansas Community College at Batesville, PO Box 3350, Batesville, AR 72503. *Phone:* 870-612-2010. *Toll-free phone:* 800-508-7878.

UNIVERSITY OF ARKANSAS COMMUNITY COLLEGE AT HOPE
Hope, Arkansas   www.uacch.edu/

- **State-supported** 2-year, founded 1966, part of University of Arkansas System
- **Rural** 60-acre campus
- **Coed**

Undergraduates 676 full-time, 537 part-time. Students come from 4 states and territories, 30% African American, 0.7% Asian American or Pacific Islander, 1% Hispanic American, 0.7% Native American, 0.2% international.
Faculty *Student/faculty ratio:* 19:1.
Academics *Calendar:* semesters. *Degree:* certificates, diplomas, and associate. *Special study options:* academic remediation for entering students, accelerated degree program, distance learning, English as a second language, independent study, internships, part-time degree program, summer session for credit.
Student Life *Campus security:* on-campus security during class hours.
Standardized Tests *Required for some:* ACT ASSET. *Recommended:* ACT (for placement), ACT ASSET.
Financial Aid Of all full-time matriculated undergraduates who enrolled in 2004, 26 Federal Work-Study jobs (averaging $2472).
Applying *Options:* early admission. *Required:* high school transcript.
Director of Admissions Ms. Danita Ormand, Director of Enrollment Services, University of Arkansas Community College at Hope, AR 71802-0140. *Phone:* 870-777-5722 Ext. 1267.

UNIVERSITY OF ARKANSAS COMMUNITY COLLEGE AT MORRILTON
Morrilton, Arkansas   www.uaccm.edu/

- **State-supported** 2-year, founded 1961, part of University of Arkansas System
- **Rural** 63-acre campus
- **Coed**

Undergraduates Students come from 1 other state, 8% African American, 0.5% Asian American or Pacific Islander, 2% Hispanic American, 0.4% Native American.
Faculty *Student/faculty ratio:* 19:1.
Academics *Calendar:* semesters. *Degree:* certificates and associate. *Special study options:* academic remediation for entering students, advanced placement credit, distance learning, double majors, internships, off-campus study, part-time degree program, services for LD students, student-designed majors, summer session for credit.

University of Arkansas Community College at Morrilton (continued)

Student Life *Campus security:* 24-hour emergency response devices.

Standardized Tests *Required:* ACT (for placement), ACT ASSET or ACT COMPASS (for placement).

Costs (2005–06) *Tuition:* area resident $1920 full-time, $64 per credit hour part-time; state resident $2100 full-time, $70 per credit hour part-time; nonresident $3060 full-time, $102 per credit hour part-time. Full-time tuition and fees vary according to course load. Part-time tuition and fees vary according to course load. *Required fees:* $210 full-time, $7 per hour part-time.

Financial Aid Of all full-time matriculated undergraduates who enrolled in 2004, 20 Federal Work-Study jobs (averaging $1000). *Financial aid deadline:* 7/23.

Applying *Options:* early admission, deferred entrance. *Required:* high school transcript. *Required for some:* immunization records.

Director of Admissions Dr. Gary Gaston, Vice Chancellor for Student Services, University of Arkansas Community College at Morrilton, One Bruce Street, Morrilton, AR 72110. *Phone:* 501-977-2014. *Toll-free phone:* 800-264-1094.

CALIFORNIA

ALLAN HANCOCK COLLEGE

Santa Maria, California   www.hancockcollege.edu/

- **State and locally supported** 2-year, founded 1920
- **Small-town** 120-acre campus
- **Endowment** $1.1 million
- **Coed,** 10,387 undergraduate students, 29% full-time, 55% women, 45% men

Undergraduates 2,996 full-time, 7,391 part-time. Students come from 27 states and territories, 12 other countries, 4% African American, 3% Asian American or Pacific Islander, 33% Hispanic American, 1% Native American, 0.1% international.

Freshmen *Admission:* 715 enrolled.

Faculty *Total:* 594, 26% full-time. *Student/faculty ratio:* 17:1.

Majors Accounting; administrative assistant and secretarial science; aerospace, aeronautical and astronautical engineering; agribusiness; applied art; architectural engineering technology; art; automobile/automotive mechanics technology; biology/biological sciences; business administration and management; chemistry; civil engineering technology; commercial and advertising art; computer engineering technology; computer science; cosmetology; criminal justice/police science; dance; dental assisting; dietetics; electrical, electronic and communications engineering technology; engineering; engineering technology; English; environmental engineering technology; family and consumer economics related; fashion/apparel design; film/cinema studies; fire science; heavy equipment maintenance technology; human services; information science/studies; interior design; international relations and affairs; kindergarten/preschool education; legal administrative assistant/secretary; liberal arts and sciences/liberal studies; machine tool technology; medical/clinical assistant; music; nursing (licensed practical/vocational nurse training); nursing (registered nurse training); parks, recreation and leisure; photography; physical education teaching and coaching; physical therapy; physics; social sciences; Spanish; welding technology.

Academics *Calendar:* semesters. *Degree:* certificates and associate. *Special study options:* adult/continuing education programs, advanced placement credit, cooperative education, distance learning, English as a second language, part-time degree program, services for LD students, study abroad, summer session for credit.

Library Learning Resources Center with 47,370 titles, 397 serial subscriptions, 2,463 audiovisual materials, an OPAC, a Web page.

Computers on Campus 200 computers available on campus for general student use. Internet access, at least one staffed computer lab available.

Student Life *Housing:* college housing not available. *Activities and Organizations:* drama/theater group, student-run newspaper, choral group, MECHA, AHC Student Club, Club Med (medical), Hancock Christian Fellowship, Vocational Industrial Clubs of America. *Campus security:* 24-hour emergency response devices and patrols, student patrols, late-night transport/escort service. *Student services:* health clinic, personal/psychological counseling, legal services.

Athletics *Intercollegiate sports:* baseball M, basketball M/W, cross-country running M/W, football M, golf M, soccer M/W, softball W, tennis M/W, track and field M/W, volleyball W.

Costs (2006–07) *Tuition:* state resident $0 full-time; nonresident $4956 full-time, $177 per unit part-time. *Required fees:* $792 full-time, $27 per unit part-time.

Financial Aid Of all full-time matriculated undergraduates who enrolled in 2004, 250 Federal Work-Study jobs (averaging $3000).

Applying *Options:* early admission. *Required:* high school transcript. *Application deadline:* rolling (freshmen), rolling (transfers). *Notification:* continuous (freshmen).

Freshmen Application Contact Ms. Marian Quaid Maltagliati, Interim Director of Admissions and Records, Allan Hancock College, 800 South College Drive, Santa Maria, CA 93454-6399. *Phone:* 805-922-6966 Ext. 3272. *Toll-free phone:* 866-342-5242. *Fax:* 805-922-3477.

AMERICAN ACADEMY OF DRAMATIC ARTS/HOLLYWOOD

Hollywood, California   www.aada.org/

Director of Admissions Mr. Dan Justin, Director of Admissions, American Academy of Dramatic Arts/Hollywood, 1336 North LaBrea Avenue, Hollywood, CA 90028. *Toll-free phone:* 800-222-2867.

AMERICAN RIVER COLLEGE

Sacramento, California   www.arc.losrios.edu/

Director of Admissions Ms. Robin Neal, Dean of Enrollment Services, American River College, 4700 College Oak Drive, Sacramento, CA 95841-4286. *Phone:* 916-484-8171. *E-mail:* esposic@arc.losrios.cc.ca.us.

ANTELOPE VALLEY COLLEGE

Lancaster, California   www.avc.edu/

Director of Admissions Office of Admissions, Antelope Valley College, 3041 West Avenue K, Lancaster, CA 93536-5426. *Phone:* 661-722-6300.

ARGOSY UNIVERSITY/ORANGE COUNTY

Santa Ana, California   www.argosyu.edu/

- **Urban** campus with easy access to Los Angeles and San Diego
- **Coed,** 81 undergraduate students, 81% full-time, 59% women, 41% men

Undergraduates 66 full-time, 15 part-time. 62% transferred in.

Faculty *Total:* 81, 14% full-time, 90% with terminal degrees. *Student/faculty ratio:* 22:1.

Majors Business administration, management and operations related; criminal justice/law enforcement administration; medical/clinical assistant; paralegal/legal assistant.

Academics *Calendar:* semesters. *Degrees:* associate, bachelor's, master's, and doctoral. *Special study options:* academic remediation for entering students, distance learning, part-time degree program, services for LD students.

Library Carrie Lixey with 1,200 titles, 50 serial subscriptions, an OPAC.

Computers on Campus 12 computers available on campus for general student use. Internet access, online (class) registration, at least one staffed computer lab available.

Student Life *Housing:* college housing not available.

Financial Aid Of all full-time matriculated undergraduates who enrolled in 2003, 28 applied for aid, 23 were judged to have need. 3 Federal Work-Study jobs (averaging $4660). *Average financial aid package:* $3586. *Average need-based loan:* $2185. *Average need-based gift aid:* $2349.

Applying *Options:* common application, electronic application, early admission, deferred entrance. *Application fee:* $50.

Director of Admissions Admissions Director, Argosy University/Orange County, 3501 West Sunflower Avenue, Suite 110, Santa Ana, CA 92704. *Toll-free phone:* 800-716-9598. *Fax:* 714-437-1697. *E-mail:* auadmissions@argosyu.edu.

▶ **See page 468 for the College Close-Up.**

ARGOSY UNIVERSITY/SAN DIEGO

San Diego, California   www.argosyu.edu/sandiego/

- **Proprietary** 2-year
- **Coed**

Majors Business administration, management and operations related; criminal justice/law enforcement administration; medical/clinical assistant; paralegal/legal assistant.

Academics *Degree:* associate.

Director of Admissions Admissions Director, Argosy University/San Diego, 7650 Mission Valley Road, San Diego, CA 92108. *Toll-free phone:* 866-505-0333. *E-mail:* auadmissions@argosyu.edu.

▶ **See page 470 for the College Close-Up.**

ARGOSY UNIVERSITY/SANTA MONICA

Santa Monica, California   www.argosyu.edu/santamonica/

- **Proprietary** comprehensive
- **Coed**

Majors Business administration, management and operations related; criminal justice/law enforcement administration; medical/clinical assistant; paralegal/legal assistant.

Academics *Degree:* associate.

Freshmen Application Contact Argosy University/Santa Monica, 2900 31st Street, Santa Monica, CA 90405. *Phone:* 310-866-4000. *Toll-free phone:* 866-505-0332.

▶ **See page 472 for the College Close-Up.**

AVIATION & ELECTRONIC SCHOOLS OF AMERICA

Colfax, California

BAKERSFIELD COLLEGE

Bakersfield, California   www.bakersfieldcollege.edu/

Director of Admissions Ms. Sue Vaughn, Director of Enrollment Services, Bakersfield College, 1801 Panorama Drive, Bakersfield, CA 93305-1299. *Phone:* 661-395-4301. *E-mail:* svaughn@bc.cc.ca.us.

BARSTOW COLLEGE

Barstow, California   www.barstow.edu/

Director of Admissions Mr. Don Low, Interim Vice President, Barstow College, 2700 Barstow Road, Barstow, CA 92311-6699.

BERKELEY CITY COLLEGE

Berkeley, California   www.peralta.cc.ca.us/

- **State and locally supported** 2-year, founded 1974
- **Urban** campus with easy access to San Francisco
- **Coed,** 4,500 undergraduate students

Undergraduates 1% are from out of state, 23% African American, 12% Asian American or Pacific Islander, 11% Hispanic American, 0.7% Native American, 5% international.

Faculty *Total:* 164, 21% full-time. *Student/faculty ratio:* 25:1.

Majors Accounting; art; biology/biotechnology laboratory technician; business administration and management; business/commerce; computer and information sciences; computer and information sciences related; computer and information systems security; computer graphics; computer software and media applications related; creative writing; data entry/microcomputer applications related; English; English composition; fine/studio arts; general studies; liberal arts and sciences/liberal studies; medical administrative assistant and medical secretary; office management; Spanish; web page, digital/multimedia and information resources design.

Academics *Calendar:* semesters. *Degree:* certificates and associate. *Special study options:* academic remediation for entering students, adult/continuing education programs, English as a second language, independent study, internships, off-campus study, part-time degree program, services for LD students, student-designed majors, study abroad, summer session for credit.

Library Vista Community College Library with a Web page.

Computers on Campus 50 computers available on campus for general student use. A campuswide network can be accessed. Internet access, online (class) registration, at least one staffed computer lab available.

Student Life *Housing:* college housing not available. *Activities and Organizations:* drama/theater group, student-run newspaper. *Student services:* personal/psychological counseling.

Costs (2006–07) *Tuition:* nonresident $172 per unit part-time. *Required fees:* $26 per unit part-time.

Financial Aid Of all full-time matriculated undergraduates who enrolled in 2004, 50 Federal Work-Study jobs (averaging $3000). 20 state and other part-time jobs (averaging $2000).

Applying *Options:* common application, electronic application, early admission, deferred entrance. *Recommended:* high school transcript. *Application deadline:* rolling (freshmen). *Notification:* continuous (freshmen).

Freshmen Application Contact Dr. Mario Rivas, Vice President of Student Services, Berkeley City College, 2020 Milvia Street, Berkeley, CA 94704. *Phone:* 510-981-2820. *Fax:* 510-841-7333. *E-mail:* sfogarino@peralta.edu.

BROOKS COLLEGE

Long Beach, California   www.brookscollege.edu/

- **Proprietary** 2-year, founded 1971
- **Suburban** 7-acre campus with easy access to Los Angeles
- **Coed,** 826 undergraduate students, 92% full-time, 65% women, 35% men

Undergraduates 757 full-time, 69 part-time. Students come from 17 other countries, 39% are from out of state, 6% African American, 5% Asian American or Pacific Islander, 18% Hispanic American, 0.5% Native American, 60% live on campus.

Freshmen *Admission:* 312 enrolled.

Faculty *Total:* 75.

Majors Animation, interactive technology, video graphics and special effects; clothing/textiles; commercial and advertising art; fashion/apparel design; fashion merchandising; interior design; telecommunications technology.

Academics *Calendar:* quarters. *Degree:* diplomas and associate. *Special study options:* academic remediation for entering students, cooperative education, internships, services for LD students, summer session for credit.

Library 15,000 titles, 80 serial subscriptions.

Computers on Campus 50 computers available on campus for general student use. At least one staffed computer lab available.

Student Life *Campus security:* 24-hour emergency response devices and patrols, controlled dormitory access. *Student services:* personal/psychological counseling.

Applying *Options:* deferred entrance. *Application fee:* $50. *Required:* essay or personal statement, high school transcript, minimum 2.0 GPA, letters of recommendation, interview. *Recommended:* portfolio. *Application deadline:* rolling (freshmen), rolling (transfers). *Notification:* continuous (freshmen).

Freshmen Application Contact Ms. Christina Varon, Director of Admissions, Brooks College, 4825 East Pacific Coast Highway, Long Beach, CA 90804-3291. *Phone:* 562-498-2441 Ext. 265. *Toll-free phone:* 800-421-3775. *Fax:* 562-597-7412. *E-mail:* info@brookscollege.edu.

BROOKS COLLEGE
Sunnyvale, California

BROWN MACKIE COLLEGE—ORANGE COUNTY
Santa Anna, California

BRYMAN COLLEGE
City of Industry, California

BRYMAN COLLEGE
Ontario, California

BUTTE COLLEGE
Oroville, California　　　　www.butte.edu/

Freshmen Application Contact Ms. Nancy Jenson, Registrar, Butte College, 3536 Butte Campus Drive, Oroville, CA 95965. *Phone:* 530-895-2361.

CABRILLO COLLEGE
Aptos, California　　　　www.cabrillo.edu/

Director of Admissions Ms. Gloria Garing, Director of Admissions and Records, Cabrillo College, 6500 Soquel Drive, Aptos, CA 95003. *Phone:* 831-479-6201.

CALIFORNIA CULINARY ACADEMY
San Francisco, California　　　www.baychef.com/

Director of Admissions Ms. Nancy Seyfert, Vice President of Admissions, California Culinary Academy, 625 Polk Street, San Francisco, CA 94102-3368. *Phone:* 800-229-2433 Ext. 275. *Toll-free phone:* 800-229-2433 (in-state); 800-BAYCHEF (out-of-state).

CALIFORNIA SCHOOL OF CULINARY ARTS
Pasadena, California

CAÑADA COLLEGE
Redwood City, California　　　www.canadacollege.net/

Freshmen Application Contact Mr. Jose Romero, Lead Records Clerk, Cañada College, 4200 Farm Hill Boulevard, Redwood City, CA 94061. *Phone:* 650-306-3395.

CERRITOS COLLEGE
Norwalk, California　　　　www.cerritos.edu/

Director of Admissions Ms. Stephanie Murguia, Director of Admissions and Records, Cerritos College, 11110 Alondra Boulevard, Norwalk, CA 90650-6298. *Phone:* 562-860-2451. *E-mail:* smurguia@cerritos.edu.

CERRO COSO COMMUNITY COLLEGE
Ridgecrest, California　　　　www.cerrocoso.edu/

- **State-supported** 2-year, founded 1973, part of Kern Community College District System
- **Small-town** 320-acre campus
- **Coed**

Undergraduates 1,218 full-time, 3,802 part-time. Students come from 30 states and territories, 2% are from out of state, 6% African American, 6% Asian American or Pacific Islander, 12% Hispanic American, 3% Native American, 0.4% international, 4% transferred in. *Retention:* 51% of 2003 full-time freshmen returned.
Faculty *Student/faculty ratio:* 14:1.
Academics *Calendar:* semesters. *Degree:* certificates and associate. *Special study options:* academic remediation for entering students, adult/continuing education programs, cooperative education, distance learning, English as a second language, honors programs, part-time degree program, services for LD students, summer session for credit.
Student Life *Campus security:* patrols by trained security personnel.
Standardized Tests *Required for some:* ACT ASSET.
Costs (2005–06) *Tuition:* state resident $0 full-time; nonresident $5010 full-time, $162 per unit part-time. *Required fees:* $780 full-time, $26 per unit part-time.
Financial Aid Of all full-time matriculated undergraduates who enrolled in 2004, 150 Federal Work-Study jobs (averaging $2000).
Applying *Options:* early admission. *Recommended:* high school transcript.
Director of Admissions Mr. Robert Weisenthal, Associate Dean for Student Life, Cerro Coso Community College, 3000 College Heights Boulevard, Ridgecrest, CA 93555. *Phone:* 760-384-6291.

CHABOT COLLEGE
Hayward, California　　　www.chabotcollege.edu/

Director of Admissions Ms. Judy Young, Director of Admissions and Records, Chabot College, 25555 Hesperian Boulevard, Hayward, CA 94545. *Phone:* 510-723-6700.

CHAFFEY COLLEGE
Rancho Cucamonga, California　　　www.chaffey.edu/

Director of Admissions Ms. Cecilia Carerra, Director of Admissions, Registration, and Records, Chaffey College, 5885 Haven Avenue, Rancho Cucamonga, CA 91737-3002. *Phone:* 909-941-2631. *Fax:* 909-466-2820.

CITRUS COLLEGE
Glendora, California　　　www.citruscollege.edu/

- **State and locally supported** 2-year, founded 1915, part of California Community College System
- **Small-town** 104-acre campus with easy access to Los Angeles
- **Coed,** 12,393 undergraduate students

Faculty *Total:* 393, 35% full-time. *Student/faculty ratio:* 29:1.
Majors Administrative assistant and secretarial science; art; automobile/automotive mechanics technology; behavioral sciences; biology/biological sciences; business administration and management; computer and information sciences related; computer science; cosmetology; criminal justice/law enforcement administration; criminal justice/police science; dance; data processing and data processing technology; dental assisting; drafting and design technology;

dramatic/theater arts; electrical, electronic and communications engineering technology; engineering; engineering technology; English; French; German; health and physical education; hydrology and water resources science; Japanese; journalism; liberal arts and sciences/liberal studies; library assistant; library science; mathematics; mechanical engineering/mechanical technology; modern languages; music; natural sciences; nursing (licensed practical/vocational nurse training); photography; physical education teaching and coaching; physical sciences; public administration; real estate; social sciences; Spanish; visual and performing arts.

Academics *Calendar:* semesters. *Degree:* certificates, diplomas, and associate. *Special study options:* academic remediation for entering students, advanced placement credit, cooperative education, distance learning, English as a second language, honors programs, part-time degree program, services for LD students, study abroad, summer session for credit.

Library Hayden Library with 45,091 titles, 133 serial subscriptions, 4,752 audiovisual materials, an OPAC, a Web page.

Computers on Campus 1100 computers available on campus for general student use. A campuswide network can be accessed. Internet access, online (class) registration, at least one staffed computer lab available.

Student Life *Housing:* college housing not available. *Activities and Organizations:* drama/theater group, student-run newspaper, choral group, Student Government, AGS Honor Society, International Student Association, Cosmetology Club. *Campus security:* 24-hour patrols, student patrols, late-night transport/escort service. *Student services:* health clinic, personal/psychological counseling, legal services.

Athletics *Intercollegiate sports:* baseball M, basketball M/W, cross-country running M/W, football M, golf M/W, soccer M/W, softball W, swimming and diving M/W, tennis M/W, track and field M/W, volleyball W, water polo M/W.

Costs (2005–06) *Tuition:* state resident $0 full-time; nonresident $4954 full-time, $150 per unit part-time. Full-time tuition and fees vary according to course load. Part-time tuition and fees vary according to course load. *Required fees:* $754 full-time, $26 per unit part-time.

Financial Aid Of all full-time matriculated undergraduates who enrolled in 2004, 141 Federal Work-Study jobs (averaging $5500).

Applying *Required:* high school transcript.

Freshmen Application Contact Admissions and Records, Citrus College, 1000 West Foothill Boulevard, Glendora, CA 91741-1899. *Phone:* 626-914-8511. *Fax:* 626-914-8613. *E-mail:* admissions@citruscollege.edu.

CITY COLLEGE OF SAN FRANCISCO
San Francisco, California　　　　　**www.ccsf.edu/**

Director of Admissions Mr. Robert Balesteri, Dean of Admissions and Records, City College of San Francisco, 50 Phelan Avenue, San Francisco, CA 94112-1821. *Phone:* 415-239-3291.

COASTLINE COMMUNITY COLLEGE
Fountain Valley, California　　　　　**coastline.cccd.edu/**

Freshmen Application Contact Jennifer McDonald, Director of Admissions and Records, Coastline Community College, 11460 Warner Avenue, Fountain Valley, CA 92708. *Phone:* 714-241-6163.

COLEMAN COLLEGE
San Marcos, California　　　　　**www.coleman.edu/**

Director of Admissions Mr. James Warner, Senior Admissions Officer, Coleman College, 1284 West San Marcos Boulevard, San Marcos, CA 92069. *Phone:* 760-747-3990. *Fax:* 760-752-9808.

COLLEGE OF ALAMEDA
Alameda, California　　　　　**www.peralta.cc.ca.us/**

Freshmen Application Contact Ms. Barbara Simmons, District Admissions Officer, College of Alameda, 555 Atlantic Avenue, Alameda, CA 94501-2109. *Phone:* 510-466-7370. *E-mail:* hperdue@peralta.cc.ca.us.

COLLEGE OF MARIN
Kentfield, California　　　　　**www.marin.cc.ca.us/**

Director of Admissions Ms. Gina Longo, Secretary to the Dean of Enrollment Services, College of Marin, 835 College Avenue, Kentfield, CA 94904. *Phone:* 415-485-9417.

COLLEGE OF SAN MATEO
San Mateo, California　　　　　**www.collegeofsanmateo.edu/**

Director of Admissions Mr. Henry Villareal, Dean of Admissions and Records, College of San Mateo, 1700 West Hillsdale Boulevard, San Mateo, CA 94402-3784. *Phone:* 650-574-6594. *E-mail:* csmadmission@smcccd.cc.ca.us.

COLLEGE OF THE CANYONS
Santa Clarita, California　　　　　**www.canyons.edu/**

- **State and locally supported** 2-year, founded 1969, part of California Community College System
- **Suburban** 158-acre campus with easy access to Los Angeles
- **Coed,** 16,504 undergraduate students, 77% full-time, 42% women, 58% men

Undergraduates 12,679 full-time, 3,825 part-time. Students come from 15 states and territories, 3% are from out of state, 4% African American, 9% Asian American or Pacific Islander, 23% Hispanic American, 0.7% Native American, 1% international, 3% transferred in. *Retention:* 51% of 2003 full-time freshmen returned.

Freshmen *Admission:* 1,596 enrolled.

Faculty *Total:* 591, 29% full-time. *Student/faculty ratio:* 27:1.

Majors Accounting; administrative assistant and secretarial science; art; biological and physical sciences; biology/biological sciences; business administration and management; chemistry; child development; cinematography and film/video production; computer and information sciences related; computer engineering related; computer science; criminal justice/law enforcement administration; criminal justice/police science; developmental and child psychology; drafting and design technology; electrical, electronic and communications engineering technology; English; French; geography; geology/earth science; German; health science; history; hotel/motel administration; humanities; hydrology and water resources science; information science/studies; interior design; journalism; kindergarten/preschool education; liberal arts and sciences/liberal studies; mathematics; natural sciences; nursing (licensed practical/vocational nurse training); nursing (registered nurse training); physical education teaching and coaching; physical sciences; political science and government; pre-engineering; psychology; quality control technology; real estate; social sciences; Spanish; welding technology.

Academics *Calendar:* semesters. *Degree:* certificates and associate. *Special study options:* academic remediation for entering students, adult/continuing education programs, advanced placement credit, cooperative education, distance learning, double majors, English as a second language, honors programs, independent study, internships, off-campus study, part-time degree program, services for LD students, study abroad, summer session for credit.

Library College of the Canyons Library with 40,646 titles, 233 serial subscriptions, 29,955 audiovisual materials, an OPAC, a Web page.

Computers on Campus 650 computers available on campus for general student use. A campuswide network can be accessed. Internet access, at least one staffed computer lab available.

Student Life *Housing:* college housing not available. *Activities and Organizations:* drama/theater group, student-run newspaper, choral group, HITE, Phi Theta Kappa, Alpha Gamma Sigma, MECHA, Biology Club. *Campus security:* student patrols, late-night transport/escort service. *Student services:* health clinic, personal/psychological counseling.

Athletics *Intercollegiate sports:* baseball M, basketball M/W, cross-country running M/W, football M, golf M, soccer W, softball W, swimming and diving M/W, track and field M/W, volleyball W, water polo M.

Costs (2005–06) *Tuition:* state resident $0 full-time; nonresident $5168 full-time, $171 per unit part-time. *Required fees:* $818 full-time, $26 per unit part-time.

Applying *Options:* electronic application, early admission. *Recommended:* high school transcript. *Application deadlines:* 8/22 (freshmen), 8/22 (transfers). *Notification:* continuous until 8/22 (freshmen).

Freshmen Application Contact Ms. Deborah Rio, Director, Admissions and Records and Online Services, College of the Canyons, 26455 Rockwell Canyon

College of the Canyons (continued)
Road, Santa Clara, CA 91355. *Phone:* 661-362-3280. *Toll-free phone:* 888-206-7827. *Fax:* 661-254-7996. *E-mail:* debbie.rio@canyons.edu.

COLLEGE OF THE DESERT

Palm Desert, California   desert.cc.ca.us/

Freshmen Application Contact Ms. Kathi Westerfield, Registrar, College of the Desert, 43-500 Monterey Avenue, Palm Desert, CA 92260-9305. *Phone:* 760-773-2519. *Toll-free phone:* 760-773-2516.

COLLEGE OF THE REDWOODS

Eureka, California   www.redwoods.edu/

Freshmen Application Contact Ms. Sue Bailey, Director of Enrollment Management, College of the Redwoods, 7351 Tompkins Hill Road, Eureka, CA 95501-9300. *Phone:* 707-476-4168. *Toll-free phone:* 800-641-0400.

COLLEGE OF THE SEQUOIAS

Visalia, California   www.cos.edu/

Director of Admissions Mr. Don Mast, Associate Dean of Admissions/Registrar, College of the Sequoias, 915 South Mooney Boulevard, Visalia, CA 93277-2234. *Phone:* 559-737-4844.

COLLEGE OF THE SISKIYOUS

Weed, California   www.siskiyous.edu/

- **State and locally supported** 2-year, founded 1957, part of California Community College System
- **Rural** 260-acre campus
- **Coed,** 2,998 undergraduate students

The College of the Siskiyous (COS) is located at the base of Mt. Shasta in northern California, 60 miles south of the Oregon border, and provides many recreational opportunities. COS offers excellent transfer and vocational programs, support services, on-campus residence halls, and athletic programs. Small class sizes and individualized instruction provide a supportive environment that encourages learning. For more information, prospective students may visit COS online at http://www.siskiyous.edu.

Undergraduates Students come from 18 states and territories, 6 other countries, 27% are from out of state, 3% African American, 3% Asian American or Pacific Islander, 7% Hispanic American, 4% Native American, 0.5% international, 10% live on campus.
Freshmen *Admission:* 389 applied, 389 admitted.
Faculty *Total:* 151, 32% full-time. *Student/faculty ratio:* 21:1.
Majors Accounting; biology/biological sciences; biology teacher education; business administration and management; chemistry; chemistry teacher education; computer graphics; computer programming; computer science; computer/technical support; criminal justice/law enforcement administration; English; English language and literature related; English/language arts teacher education; fire science; geology/earth science; history; history related; information technology; intermedia/multimedia; kindergarten/preschool education; legal assistant/paralegal; legal studies; mathematics; philosophy; physical sciences; physics; physics teacher education; web/multimedia management and webmaster; web page, digital/multimedia and information resources design.
Academics *Calendar:* semesters. *Degree:* certificates and associate. *Special study options:* academic remediation for entering students, adult/continuing education programs, advanced placement credit, cooperative education, distance learning, double majors, English as a second language, honors programs, independent study, internships, part-time degree program, services for LD students, student-designed majors, summer session for credit.
Library College of the Siskiyous Library with 34,708 titles, 148 serial subscriptions, 9,433 audiovisual materials, an OPAC, a Web page.
Computers on Campus 260 computers available on campus for general student use. A campuswide network can be accessed from off campus. Internet access, at least one staffed computer lab available.
Student Life *Housing Options:* coed, men-only. Campus housing is university owned. *Activities and Organizations:* drama/theater group, student-run newspa-

per, television station, choral group, Associated Student Body, Latino Student Union, Phi Theta Kappa, Black Student Union, American Indian Alliance. *Campus security:* 24-hour emergency response devices, controlled dormitory access. *Student services:* health clinic, personal/psychological counseling, women's center, legal services.
Athletics Member NJCAA. *Intercollegiate sports:* baseball M, basketball M/W, cross-country running M/W, football M, softball W, track and field M/W, volleyball W. *Intramural sports:* basketball M/W, cheerleading M/W, skiing (cross-country) M/W, skiing (downhill) M/W, tennis M/W, volleyball W.
Costs (2005–06) *Tuition:* nonresident $174 per unit part-time. *Required fees:* $26 per unit part-time, $12 per term part-time.
Financial Aid Of all full-time matriculated undergraduates who enrolled in 2004, 51 Federal Work-Study jobs (averaging $1897). 30 state and other part-time jobs (averaging $2000).
Applying *Options:* early admission, deferred entrance. *Application deadline:* rolling (freshmen), rolling (transfers). *Notification:* continuous (freshmen).
Freshmen Application Contact Ms. Christina Bruck, Recruitment and Outreach Coordinator, College of the Siskiyous, 800 College Avenue, Weed, CA 96094. *Phone:* 530-938-5847. *Toll-free phone:* 888-397-4339 Ext. 5847.

COLUMBIA COLLEGE

Sonora, California   www.gocolumbia.org/

- **State and locally supported** 2-year, founded 1968, part of Yosemite Community College District System
- **Rural** 200-acre campus
- **Coed,** 2,691 undergraduate students, 35% full-time, 55% women, 45% men

Undergraduates 940 full-time, 1,751 part-time. Students come from 7 states and territories, 5% are from out of state, 1% African American, 2% Asian American or Pacific Islander, 7% Hispanic American, 3% Native American, 0.1% international.
Freshmen *Admission:* 242 applied, 242 admitted, 242 enrolled.
Faculty *Total:* 167, 34% full-time. *Student/faculty ratio:* 16:1.
Majors Administrative assistant and secretarial science; anthropology; art; automobile/automotive mechanics technology; biology/biological sciences; business administration and management; chemistry; computer science; culinary arts; developmental and child psychology; dramatic/theater arts; English; environmental studies; fire science; food services technology; forestry technology; geology/earth science; health teacher education; history; hotel/motel administration; humanities; liberal arts and sciences/liberal studies; mathematics; music; natural resources management and policy; photography; physical education teaching and coaching; physical sciences; physics; psychology; sociology; special products marketing.
Academics *Calendar:* semesters. *Degree:* certificates and associate. *Special study options:* academic remediation for entering students, adult/continuing education programs, advanced placement credit, cooperative education, distance learning, double majors, English as a second language, independent study, internships, part-time degree program, services for LD students, summer session for credit.
Library Columbia College Library with 34,892 titles, 320 serial subscriptions, 4,852 audiovisual materials, an OPAC, a Web page.
Computers on Campus 85 computers available on campus for general student use. Internet access, at least one staffed computer lab available.
Student Life *Housing Options:* Campus housing is provided by a third party. *Activities and Organizations:* drama/theater group, student-run newspaper, choral group, International Club, Jazz Club, Ecology Action Club, Christian Club. *Campus security:* 24-hour emergency response devices and patrols, late-night transport/escort service. *Student services:* health clinic, personal/psychological counseling.
Athletics Member NJCAA. *Intercollegiate sports:* basketball M, cross-country running M/W, tennis M/W, volleyball W.
Costs (2006–07) *Tuition:* state resident $0 full-time; nonresident $4286 full-time, $177 per unit part-time. *Required fees:* $662 full-time, $26 per unit part-time, $24 per term part-time. *Room and board:* $6115.
Financial Aid Of all full-time matriculated undergraduates who enrolled in 2004, 42 Federal Work-Study jobs (averaging $2350).
Applying *Options:* common application, electronic application, early admission. *Required for some:* high school transcript. *Application deadline:* rolling (freshmen), rolling (transfers). *Notification:* continuous (freshmen).
Freshmen Application Contact Dr. Kathleen Smith, Director Student Success/Matriculation, Columbia College, Columbia College, 11600 Columbia College Drive, Sonora, CA 95370. *Phone:* 209-588-5234. *Fax:* 209-588-5337. *E-mail:* smithk@yosemite.cc.ca.us.

COMPTON COMMUNITY COLLEGE
Compton, California www.compton.edu/

- **State and locally supported** 2-year, founded 1927, part of California Community College System
- **Urban** 83-acre campus with easy access to Los Angeles
- **Coed**

Undergraduates Students come from 4 states and territories, 25 other countries.

Academics *Calendar:* semesters. *Degree:* associate. *Special study options:* academic remediation for entering students, adult/continuing education programs, advanced placement credit, English as a second language, honors programs, part-time degree program, services for LD students, summer session for credit.

Student Life *Campus security:* 24-hour patrols.

Financial Aid Of all full-time matriculated undergraduates who enrolled in 2004, 300 Federal Work-Study jobs (averaging $3000).

Applying *Options:* early admission.

Director of Admissions Mr. Phillip Glezer, Interim Associate Dean, Admissions and Records, Compton Community College, 1111 East Artesia Boulevard, Compton, CA 91221. *Phone:* 310-900-1600 Ext. 2047.

CONCORDE CAREER INSTITUTE
North Hollywood, California

CONTRA COSTA COLLEGE
San Pablo, California www.contracosta.edu/

- **State and locally supported** 2-year, founded 1948, part of Contra Costa Community College District and California Community College System
- **Small-town** 83-acre campus with easy access to San Francisco
- **Coed**

Undergraduates 3,973 full-time, 4,861 part-time. Students come from 5 states and territories, 16 other countries, 28% African American, 15% Asian American or Pacific Islander, 28% Hispanic American, 0.6% Native American, 2% international.

Academics *Calendar:* semesters. *Degree:* certificates and associate. *Special study options:* academic remediation for entering students, adult/continuing education programs, cooperative education, English as a second language, honors programs, off-campus study, part-time degree program, services for LD students, study abroad, summer session for credit. *ROTC:* Army (c), Air Force (c).

Student Life *Campus security:* 24-hour patrols.

Standardized Tests *Recommended:* SAT or ACT (for placement).

Financial Aid Of all full-time matriculated undergraduates who enrolled in 2004, 100 Federal Work-Study jobs (averaging $3000).

Applying *Options:* common application, early admission.

Freshmen Application Contact Mrs. Linda Ames, Admissions and Records Supervisor, Contra Costa College, 2600 Mission Bell Drive, San Pablo, CA 94806-3195. *Phone:* 510-235-7800 Ext. 4211.

COPPER MOUNTAIN COLLEGE
Joshua Tree, California www.cmccd.cc.ca.us/

Director of Admissions Dr. Laraine Turk, Associate Dean of Student Services, Copper Mountain College, 6162 Rotary Way, Joshua Tree, CA 92252. *Phone:* 760-366-5290.

COSUMNES RIVER COLLEGE
Sacramento, California

COSUMNES RIVER COLLEGE
Sacramento, California www.crc.losrios.edu/

Freshmen Application Contact Ms. Dianna L. Moore, Supervisor of Admissions Records, Cosumnes River College, 8401 Center Parkway, Sacramento, CA 95823-5799. *Phone:* 916-688-7423.

CRAFTON HILLS COLLEGE
Yucaipa, California www.craftonhills.edu/

Director of Admissions Mr. Marco Cota, Interim Director of Admissions, Crafton Hills College, 11711 Sand Canyon Road, Yucaipa, CA 92399. *Phone:* 909-389-3355.

CUESTA COLLEGE
San Luis Obispo, California www.cuesta.edu/

Freshmen Application Contact Ms. Juileta Siu, Admissions Clerk, Cuesta College, PO Box 8106, Highway 1, San Luis Obispo, CA 93403-8106. *Phone:* 805-546-3140.

CUYAMACA COLLEGE
El Cajon, California www.cuyamaca.net/

Director of Admissions Dr. Beth Appenzeller, Dean of Admissions and Records, Cuyamaca College, 900 Rancho San Diego Parkway, El Cajon, CA 92019-4304. *Phone:* 619-660-4302.

CYPRESS COLLEGE
Cypress, California www.cypress.cc.ca.us/

Director of Admissions Mr. David Wassenaar, Dean of Admissions and Records, Cypress College, 9200 Valley View, Cypress, CA 90630. *Phone:* 714-484-7435. *E-mail:* dwassenaar@cypresscollege.edu.

DE ANZA COLLEGE
Cupertino, California www.deanza.fhda.edu/

- **State and locally supported** 2-year, founded 1967, part of California Community College System
- **Small-town** 112-acre campus with easy access to San Francisco and San Jose
- **Coed**

Undergraduates 8,860 full-time, 14,484 part-time. Students come from 48 states and territories, 79 other countries, 6% African American, 33% Asian American or Pacific Islander, 15% Hispanic American, 0.5% Native American, 6% international.

Academics *Calendar:* quarters. *Degree:* certificates, diplomas, and associate. *Special study options:* academic remediation for entering students, adult/continuing education programs, advanced placement credit, cooperative education, English as a second language, external degree program, honors programs, internships, part-time degree program, services for LD students, study abroad, summer session for credit. *ROTC:* Army (c), Air Force (c).

Student Life *Campus security:* 24-hour emergency response devices, student patrols, late-night transport/escort service.

De Anza College (continued)

Standardized Tests *Required for some:* SAT (for placement), CPT, DTLS, DTMS.

Costs (2005–06) *Tuition:* state resident $0 full-time; nonresident $3636 full-time, $101 per unit part-time. *Required fees:* $818 full-time, $17 per unit part-time.

Applying *Options:* common application, early admission. *Application fee:* $22.

Director of Admissions Ms. Kathleen Kayne, Director of Records and Admissions, De Anza College, 21250 Stevens Creek Boulevard, Cupertino, CA 95014. *Phone:* 408-864-8292. *E-mail:* webregda@mercury.fhda.edu.

DEEP SPRINGS COLLEGE

Deep Springs, California　　　　**www.deepsprings.edu/**

- **Independent** 2-year, founded 1917
- **Rural** 3000-acre campus
- **Endowment** $9.0 million
- **Men only,** 27 undergraduate students, 100% full-time

Undergraduates 27 full-time. Students come from 14 states and territories, 3 other countries, 85% are from out of state, 4% international, 100% live on campus. *Retention:* 87% of 2003 full-time freshmen returned.
Freshmen Admission: 160 applied, 12 admitted. *Average high school GPA:* 3.87. *Test scores:* SAT verbal scores over 500: 100%; SAT math scores over 500: 100%; SAT verbal scores over 600: 100%; SAT math scores over 600: 90%; SAT verbal scores over 700: 90%; SAT math scores over 700: 70%.

Faculty *Total:* 9, 56% full-time, 78% with terminal degrees. *Student/faculty ratio:* 3:1.

Majors Liberal arts and sciences/liberal studies.

Academics *Calendar:* 6 seven-week terms. *Degree:* associate. *Special study options:* accelerated degree program, cooperative education, freshman honors college, honors programs, independent study, internships, student-designed majors, summer session for credit.

Library Mossner Library of Deep Springs with 20,000 titles, 60 serial subscriptions, an OPAC, a Web page.

Computers on Campus 6 computers available on campus for general student use.

Student Life *Housing:* on-campus residence required through sophomore year. *Options:* men-only. Campus housing is university owned. *Activities and Organizations:* drama/theater group, choral group, Student Self-Government, Labor Program, Applications Committee, Review Committee, Curriculum Committee. *Student services:* personal/psychological counseling, legal services.

Athletics *Intramural sports:* archery M, basketball M, cross-country running M, equestrian sports M, football M, riflery M, soccer M, swimming and diving M, water polo M, weight lifting M.

Standardized Tests *Required:* SAT and SAT Subject Tests or ACT (for admission).

Applying *Options:* common application. *Required:* essay or personal statement, high school transcript, letters of recommendation, interview. *Application deadlines:* 11/15 (freshmen), 11/15 (transfers). *Notification:* 4/15 (freshmen).

Freshmen Application Contact Dr. F. Ross Peterson, President, Deep Springs College, HC 72, Box 45001, Dyer, NV 89010-9803. *Phone:* 760-872-2000. *E-mail:* apcom@deepsprings.edu.

DIABLO VALLEY COLLEGE

Pleasant Hill, California　　　　**www.dvc.edu/**

- **State and locally supported** 2-year, founded 1949, part of Contra Costa Community College District, part of California Community Colleges
- **Suburban** 100-acre campus with easy access to San Francisco
- **Coed,** 20,688 undergraduate students, 33% full-time, 53% women, 47% men

Undergraduates 6,848 full-time, 13,840 part-time. Students come from 16 states and territories, 0.2% are from out of state, 6% African American, 18% Asian American or Pacific Islander, 13% Hispanic American, 0.7% Native American.

Faculty *Total:* 831, 31% full-time. *Student/faculty ratio:* 15:1.

Majors Liberal arts and sciences/liberal studies.

Academics *Calendar:* semesters. *Degree:* certificates and associate. *Special study options:* academic remediation for entering students, adult/continuing education programs, advanced placement credit, cooperative education, part-

time degree program, services for LD students, student-designed majors, study abroad, summer session for credit. *ROTC:* Air Force (c).

Library 88,286 titles, 298 serial subscriptions.

Computers on Campus 450 computers available on campus for general student use. A campuswide network can be accessed from off campus. Internet access, online (class) registration, at least one staffed computer lab available.

Student Life *Housing:* college housing not available. *Activities and Organizations:* drama/theater group, student-run newspaper, choral group. *Campus security:* 24-hour emergency response devices and patrols, student patrols. *Student services:* women's center.

Athletics *Intercollegiate sports:* basketball M/W, cross-country running M/W, football M, soccer W, softball W, swimming and diving M/W, tennis M/W, track and field M/W, volleyball W, water polo M/W.

Costs (2005–06) *Tuition:* state resident $0 full-time; nonresident $5190 full-time, $173 per unit part-time. *Required fees:* $799 full-time, $26 per unit part-time, $19 per term part-time.

Financial Aid Of all full-time matriculated undergraduates who enrolled in 2004, 67 Federal Work-Study jobs (averaging $3000). *Financial aid deadline:* 5/23.

Applying *Options:* early admission. *Recommended:* high school transcript. *Application deadline:* 8/15 (freshmen), rolling (transfers).

Freshmen Application Contact Judith Watkins, Supervisor of Admissions and Records, Diablo Valley College, 321 Golf Club Road, Pleasant Hill, CA 94523-1529. *Phone:* 925-685-1230 Ext. 2561. *Fax:* 925-609-8085.

DON BOSCO TECHNICAL INSTITUTE

Rosemead, California　　　　**www.boscotech.edu/**

Director of Admissions Director of College Admissions, Don Bosco Technical Institute, 1151 San Gabriel Boulevard, Rosemead, CA 91770-4299. *Phone:* 626-940-2036. *E-mail:* gr8piper@aol.com.

EAST LOS ANGELES COLLEGE

Monterey Park, California　　　　**www.elac.edu/**

Director of Admissions Mr. Jeremy Allred, Associate Dean of Admissions, East Los Angeles College, 1301 Avenida Cesar Chavez, Monterey Park, CA 91754-6001. *Phone:* 323-265-8801.

EL CAMINO COLLEGE

Torrance, California　　　　**www.elcamino.edu/**

Director of Admissions Mr. William Robinson, Director of Admissions, El Camino College, 16007 Crenshaw Boulevard, Torrance, CA 90506. *Phone:* 310-660-3418. *Toll-free phone:* 866-ELCAMINO.

EMPIRE COLLEGE

Santa Rosa, California　　　　**www.empcol.com/**

Freshmen Application Contact Ms. Dahnja Barker, Admissions Officer, Empire College, 3035 Cleveland Avenue, Santa Rosa, CA 95403. *Phone:* 707-546-4000.

EVEREST COLLEGE
Rancho Cucamonga, California

EVERGREEN VALLEY COLLEGE
San Jose, California　　　　　www.evc.edu/

- **State and locally supported** 2-year, founded 1975, part of California Community College System
- **Urban** 175-acre campus
- **Coed,** 11,751 undergraduate students, 100% full-time, 52% women, 48% men

Undergraduates 11,751 full-time. Students come from 23 states and territories, 11 other countries, 1% are from out of state, 5% African American, 40% Asian American or Pacific Islander, 29% Hispanic American, 0.8% Native American, 1% international.
Freshmen *Admission:* 2,186 applied, 2,186 admitted.
Faculty *Total:* 301, 42% full-time.
Majors Accounting; applied art; automobile/automotive mechanics technology; biology/biological sciences; business administration and management; business/commerce; computer and information sciences; computer graphics; criminal justice/law enforcement administration; data processing and data processing technology; desktop publishing and digital imaging design; drafting and design technology; electrical, electronic and communications engineering technology; engineering; English; family and consumer economics related; fashion merchandising; general studies; industrial technology; information science/studies; interdisciplinary studies; legal assistant/paralegal; liberal arts and sciences/liberal studies; management information systems; mental health/rehabilitation; nursing (registered nurse training); pre-engineering.
Academics *Calendar:* semesters. *Degree:* certificates and associate. *Special study options:* academic remediation for entering students, accelerated degree program, adult/continuing education programs, advanced placement credit, cooperative education, distance learning, English as a second language, freshman honors college, honors programs, independent study, off-campus study, part-time degree program, services for LD students, summer session for credit. *ROTC:* Army (c).
Library Evergreen Valley College Library with 42,782 titles, 368 serial subscriptions.
Computers on Campus 415 computers available on campus for general student use. At least one staffed computer lab available.
Student Life *Housing:* college housing not available. *Activities and Organizations:* drama/theater group, choral group, Affirm, Edlace, Phi Theta Kappa, Vietnamese Student Association. *Campus security:* 24-hour emergency response devices, late-night transport/escort service, patrols by trained security personnel. *Student services:* health clinic, personal/psychological counseling.
Athletics *Intercollegiate sports:* soccer M. *Intramural sports:* basketball M/W, racquetball M/W, soccer M, tennis M/W, volleyball M/W.
Costs (2006–07) *Tuition:* state resident $0 full-time; nonresident $4872 full-time, $177 per unit part-time. *Required fees:* $664 full-time, $26 per unit part-time.
Financial Aid Of all full-time matriculated undergraduates who enrolled in 2004, 107 Federal Work-Study jobs (averaging $3000). 6 state and other part-time jobs (averaging $1500).
Applying *Options:* early admission. *Application deadline:* rolling (freshmen), rolling (transfers). *Notification:* continuous (freshmen).
Freshmen Application Contact Ms. Kathleen Moberg, Director of Admissions and Records, Evergreen Valley College, 3095 Yerba Buena Road, San Jose, CA 95135-1598. *Phone:* 408-270-6423. *Fax:* 408-223-9351.

FASHION CAREERS COLLEGE
San Diego, California　　　www.fashioncollege.com/

- **Proprietary** 2-year, founded 1979
- **Urban** campus
- **Coed, primarily women,** 101 undergraduate students, 100% full-time, 88% women, 12% men

Undergraduates 101 full-time. Students come from 18 states and territories, 3 other countries, 27% are from out of state, 7% African American, 4% Asian American or Pacific Islander, 31% Hispanic American, 2% international. *Reten-*

tion: 75% of 2003 full-time freshmen returned.
Freshmen *Admission:* 27 applied, 27 admitted, 27 enrolled.
Faculty *Total:* 9. *Student/faculty ratio:* 32:1.
Majors Fashion/apparel design; fashion merchandising.
Academics *Calendar:* quarters. *Degree:* certificates and associate. *Special study options:* adult/continuing education programs, cooperative education, double majors, internships.
Library Fashion Careers of California Library with 800 titles, 14 serial subscriptions, 175 audiovisual materials.
Computers on Campus 36 computers available on campus for general student use. Internet access, at least one staffed computer lab available.
Student Life *Housing:* college housing not available. *Campus security:* 24-hour emergency response devices.
Standardized Tests *Required:* Wonderlic aptitude test (for admission).
Costs (2005–06) *Tuition:* $15,900 full-time, $400 per credit part-time. *Required fees:* $325 full-time.
Financial Aid Of all full-time matriculated undergraduates who enrolled in 2004, 10 Federal Work-Study jobs (averaging $1200).
Applying *Options:* common application, electronic application. *Application fee:* $25. *Required:* essay or personal statement, high school transcript, interview. *Application deadline:* rolling (freshmen), rolling (transfers). *Notification:* continuous (freshmen).
Freshmen Application Contact Ms. Karen Rogue, Admissions Representative, Fashion Careers College, 1923 Morena Boulevard, San Diego, CA 92110. *Phone:* 619-275-4700 Ext. 314. *Toll-free phone:* 888-FCCC999. *Fax:* 619-275-0635. *E-mail:* karen@fashioncareerscollege.com.

FEATHER RIVER COLLEGE
Quincy, California　　　　　www.frc.edu/

- **State and locally supported** 2-year, founded 1968, part of California Community College System
- **Rural** 150-acre campus
- **Coed,** 2,173 undergraduate students, 55% full-time, 51% women, 49% men

Undergraduates 1,191 full-time, 982 part-time. Students come from 24 states and territories, 6 other countries, 23% are from out of state, 3% transferred in, 24% live on campus. *Retention:* 62% of 2003 full-time freshmen returned.
Freshmen *Admission:* 189 applied, 189 admitted, 225 enrolled.
Faculty *Total:* 93, 29% full-time. *Student/faculty ratio:* 18:1.
Majors Administrative assistant and secretarial science; animal/livestock husbandry and production; biology/biological sciences; business/commerce; child care and support services management; child care/guidance; construction engineering technology; criminal justice/law enforcement administration; English; forestry; history; liberal arts and sciences/liberal studies; mathematics; natural resources management; nursing (licensed practical/vocational nurse training); parks, recreation and leisure facilities management; parks, recreation, and leisure related; physical sciences; social sciences.
Academics *Calendar:* semesters. *Degree:* certificates, diplomas, and associate. *Special study options:* academic remediation for entering students, adult/continuing education programs, advanced placement credit, cooperative education, distance learning, double majors, honors programs, independent study, part-time degree program, services for LD students, summer session for credit.
Library Feather River Library with 20,782 titles, 4,122 serial subscriptions, 1,762 audiovisual materials, an OPAC.
Computers on Campus 146 computers available on campus for general student use. A campuswide network can be accessed. Internet access, at least one staffed computer lab available.
Student Life *Housing Options:* coed. Campus housing is university owned. *Activities and Organizations:* drama/theater group, choral group, Mountain Ultimate Disc (MUD), Varsity Club, Feather River Outings Group, SIFE, Chess Club. *Campus security:* student patrols.
Athletics *Intercollegiate sports:* baseball M, basketball M/W, equestrian sports M/W, football M, soccer M/W, softball W. *Intramural sports:* cheerleading W(c), ultimate Frisbee M(c)/W(c).
Costs (2005–06) *Tuition:* state resident $0 full-time; nonresident $5250 full-time, $175 per unit part-time. *Required fees:* $806 full-time, $27 per unit part-time, $13 per term part-time. *Room and board:* room only: $3865. Room and board charges vary according to housing facility. *Payment plan:* deferred payment.
Financial Aid Of all full-time matriculated undergraduates who enrolled in 2004, 22 Federal Work-Study jobs (averaging $750). 103 state and other part-time jobs (averaging $1504).
Applying *Options:* electronic application.

Feather River College (continued)
Freshmen Application Contact Ms. Karen Hayden, Registrar, Feather River College, 570 Golden Eagle Avenue, Quincy, CA 95971. *Phone:* 530-283-0202 Ext. 285. *Toll-free phone:* 800-442-9799 Ext. 286. *Fax:* 530-283-9961. *E-mail:* info@frc.edu.

FIDM/THE FASHION INSTITUTE OF DESIGN & MERCHANDISING, LOS ANGELES CAMPUS

Los Angeles, California   www.fidm.edu/

- **Proprietary** primarily 2-year, founded 1969, part of Fashion Institute of Design and Merchandising
- **Urban** campus
- **Coed,** 3,522 undergraduate students, 79% full-time, 90% women, 10% men

Undergraduates 2,778 full-time, 744 part-time. Students come from 40 states and territories, 30 other countries, 29% are from out of state, 5% African American, 16% Asian American or Pacific Islander, 20% Hispanic American, 0.3% Native American, 7% international.
Freshmen *Admission:* 1,052 admitted, 895 enrolled.
Faculty *Total:* 213, 26% full-time. *Student/faculty ratio:* 26:1.
Majors Apparel and accessories marketing; apparel and textiles; business administration and management; commercial and advertising art; consumer merchandising/retailing management; design and visual communications; fashion/apparel design; fashion merchandising; interior design.
Academics *Calendar:* quarters. *Degrees:* associate and bachelor's (also includes Orange County Campus). *Special study options:* academic remediation for entering students, adult/continuing education programs, advanced placement credit, cooperative education, distance learning, English as a second language, independent study, internships, part-time degree program, services for LD students, study abroad, summer session for credit.
Library Resource and Research Center with 19,099 titles, 369 serial subscriptions, 3,607 audiovisual materials, an OPAC.
Computers on Campus 322 computers available on campus for general student use. A campuswide network can be accessed from student residence rooms and from off campus. Internet access, online (class) registration, at least one staffed computer lab available.
Student Life *Housing:* college housing not available. *Options:* Campus housing is provided by a third party. *Activities and Organizations:* student-run newspaper, ASID (student chapter), International Club, DECA, Association of Manufacturing Students, Honor Society. *Campus security:* 24-hour emergency response devices and patrols, late-night transport/escort service. *Student services:* personal/psychological counseling.
Standardized Tests *Required:* Wonderlic Aptitude Test (for admission).
Costs (2006–07) *Tuition:* $17,415 full-time, $387 per unit part-time. *Required fees:* $500 full-time.
Financial Aid Of all full-time matriculated undergraduates who enrolled in 2004, 88 Federal Work-Study jobs (averaging $2935).
Applying *Options:* common application, electronic application, deferred entrance. *Application fee:* $225. *Required:* essay or personal statement, high school transcript, 3 letters of recommendation, interview, major-determined project. *Required for some:* 3 letters of recommendation, interview, major-determined project. *Application deadline:* rolling (freshmen), rolling (transfers).
Freshmen Application Contact Ms. Susan Aronson, Director of Admissions, FIDM/The Fashion Institute of Design & Merchandising, Los Angeles Campus, FIDM LA, 919 South Grand Avenue, Los Angeles, CA 90015. *Phone:* 213-624-1200 Ext. 5400. *Toll-free phone:* 800-624-1200. *Fax:* 213-624-4799. *E-mail:* info@fidm.com.

▶ See page 544 for the College Close-Up.

FIDM/THE FASHION INSTITUTE OF DESIGN & MERCHANDISING, ORANGE COUNTY CAMPUS

Irvine, California   www.fidm.com/

Freshmen Application Contact Admissions, FIDM/The Fashion Institute of Design & Merchandising, Orange County Campus, 17590 Gillette Avenue, Irvine, CA 92614-5610. *Phone:* 949-851-6200. *Toll-free phone:* 888-974-3436. *Fax:* 949-851-6808.

FIDM/THE FASHION INSTITUTE OF DESIGN & MERCHANDISING, SAN DIEGO CAMPUS

San Diego, California   www.fidm.com/

- **Proprietary** 2-year, founded 1985, part of Fashion Institute of Design and Merchandising
- **Urban** campus
- **Coed,** 272 undergraduate students, 86% full-time, 95% women, 5% men

Undergraduates 235 full-time, 37 part-time. Students come from 15 states and territories, 1 other country, 19% are from out of state, 4% African American, 11% Asian American or Pacific Islander, 23% Hispanic American, 0.4% Native American, 1% international.
Freshmen *Admission:* 150 admitted, 150 enrolled.
Faculty *Total:* 29, 10% full-time. *Student/faculty ratio:* 20:1.
Majors Apparel and accessories marketing; commercial and advertising art; consumer merchandising/retailing management; design and visual communications; fashion/apparel design; fashion merchandising; interior design.
Academics *Calendar:* quarters. *Degree:* associate. *Special study options:* academic remediation for entering students, adult/continuing education programs, advanced placement credit, cooperative education, distance learning, English as a second language, independent study, internships, part-time degree program, services for LD students, study abroad, summer session for credit.
Library Resource and Research Center with 2,642 titles, 100 serial subscriptions, 915 audiovisual materials, an OPAC.
Computers on Campus 32 computers available on campus for general student use. A campuswide network can be accessed from student residence rooms and from off campus. Internet access, online (class) registration, at least one staffed computer lab available.
Student Life *Housing:* college housing not available. *Options:* Campus housing is provided by a third party. *Activities and Organizations:* ASID (student chapter), DECA, Honor Society, Phi Theta Kappa. *Campus security:* 24-hour emergency response devices and patrols. *Student services:* personal/psychological counseling.
Costs (2006–07) *Tuition:* $17,415 full-time, $387 per unit part-time. *Required fees:* $500 full-time.
Applying *Options:* common application, electronic application, deferred entrance. *Application fee:* $225. *Required:* essay or personal statement, 3 letters of recommendation, interview, major-determined project. *Required for some:* 3 letters of recommendation, interview, major-determined project. *Recommended:* minimum 2.5 GPA. *Application deadline:* rolling (freshmen), rolling (transfers).
Freshmen Application Contact Ms. Susan Aronson, Director of Admissions, FIDM/The Fashion Institute of Design & Merchandising, San Diego Campus, FIDM San Diego, 1010 2nd Avenue, San Diego, CA 92101. *Phone:* 213-624-1200 Ext. 5400. *Toll-free phone:* 800-243-3436. *Fax:* 619-232-4322. *E-mail:* info@fidm.com.

FIDM/THE FASHION INSTITUTE OF DESIGN & MERCHANDISING, SAN FRANCISCO CAMPUS

San Francisco, California   www.fidm.edu/

- **Proprietary** 2-year, founded 1973, part of Fashion Institute of Design and Merchandising
- **Urban** campus
- **Coed, primarily women,** 936 undergraduate students, 80% full-time, 93% women, 7% men

Undergraduates 747 full-time, 189 part-time. Students come from 15 states and territories, 20 other countries, 6% are from out of state, 5% African American, 18% Asian American or Pacific Islander, 17% Hispanic American, 0.7% Native American, 2% international.
Freshmen *Admission:* 289 admitted, 289 enrolled.
Faculty *Total:* 71, 20% full-time.
Majors Apparel and accessories marketing; apparel and textiles; commercial and advertising art; consumer merchandising/retailing management; design and visual communications; fashion/apparel design; fashion merchandising; interior design.
Academics *Calendar:* quarters. *Degree:* associate. *Special study options:* academic remediation for entering students, adult/continuing education programs, advanced placement credit, cooperative education, distance learning,

English as a second language, honors programs, independent study, internships, off-campus study, part-time degree program, services for LD students, study abroad, summer session for credit.

Library Resource and Research Center with 5,073 titles, 173 serial subscriptions, 616 audiovisual materials, an OPAC.

Computers on Campus 81 computers available on campus for general student use. A campuswide network can be accessed from student residence rooms and from off campus. Internet access, online (class) registration, at least one staffed computer lab available.

Student Life *Housing:* college housing not available. *Options:* Campus housing is provided by a third party. *Activities and Organizations:* ASID (student chapter), DECA, Visual Design Form, Honor Society. *Campus security:* 24-hour emergency response devices and patrols. *Student services:* personal/psychological counseling.

Standardized Tests *Required:* Wonderlic aptitude test (for admission).

Costs (2006–07) *Tuition:* $17,415 full-time, $387 per unit part-time.

Applying *Options:* common application, electronic application, deferred entrance. *Application fee:* $225. *Required:* essay or personal statement, high school transcript, 3 letters of recommendation, interview, major-determined project. *Required for some:* 3 letters of recommendation, interview, major-determined project. *Recommended:* minimum 2.0 GPA. *Application deadline:* rolling (freshmen), rolling (transfers).

Freshmen Application Contact Ms. Susan Aronson, Director of Admissions, FIDM/The Fashion Institute of Design & Merchandising, San Francisco Campus, 55 Stockton Street, San Francisco, CA 94108. *Phone:* 213-624-1200 Ext. 5400. *Toll-free phone:* 800-711-7175. *Fax:* 415-296-7299. *E-mail:* info@fidm.com.

FOLSOM LAKE COLLEGE

Folsom, California   **www.flc.losrios.edu/**

Freshmen Application Contact Folsom Lake College, 100 Scholar Way, Folsom, CA 95630. *Phone:* 916-608-6500.

FOOTHILL COLLEGE

Los Altos Hills, California   **www.foothill.edu/**

- **State and locally supported** 2-year, founded 1958, part of Foothill-DeAnza Community College District
- **Suburban** 122-acre campus with easy access to San Jose
- **Coed,** 17,488 undergraduate students

Undergraduates Students come from 51 states and territories, 101 other countries, 2% are from out of state, 3% African American, 24% Asian American or Pacific Islander, 12% Hispanic American, 0.4% Native American, 5% international.

Freshmen *Admission:* 5,284 applied, 5,284 admitted.

Faculty *Total:* 616, 32% full-time. *Student/faculty ratio:* 28:1.

Majors Accounting; American studies; anthropology; art; art history, criticism and conservation; athletic training; avionics maintenance technology; biology/biological sciences; biology/biotechnology laboratory technician; business administration and management; chemistry; child development; classics and languages, literatures and linguistics; creative writing; cultural studies; dental assisting; dental hygiene; diagnostic medical sonography and ultrasound technology; economics; electrical, electronic and communications engineering technology; emergency medical technology (EMT paramedic); English; fine/studio arts; history; international business/trade/commerce; landscape architecture; legal studies; linguistics; literature; mathematics; medical radiologic technology; music; ornamental horticulture; philosophy; photography; physical education teaching and coaching; physician assistant; physics; plant nursery management; political science and government; psychology; radio and television; radiologic technology/science; real estate; respiratory care therapy; social sciences; sociology; Spanish; speech and rhetoric; tourism and travel services management; veterinary technology; women's studies.

Academics *Calendar:* quarters. *Degree:* certificates and associate. *Special study options:* academic remediation for entering students, accelerated degree program, adult/continuing education programs, advanced placement credit, cooperative education, distance learning, English as a second language, honors programs, independent study, internships, off-campus study, part-time degree program, services for LD students, student-designed majors, study abroad, summer session for credit. *ROTC:* Army (c), Air Force (c).

Library Hubert H. Semans Library with 70,000 titles, 450 serial subscriptions, an OPAC, a Web page.

Computers on Campus 400 computers available on campus for general student use. A campuswide network can be accessed from off campus. Internet access, online (class) registration, at least one staffed computer lab available.

Student Life *Housing:* college housing not available. *Activities and Organizations:* drama/theater group, student-run newspaper, radio station, choral group, Alpha Gamma Sigma, student government. *Campus security:* 24-hour emergency response devices and patrols, late-night transport/escort service. *Student services:* health clinic, personal/psychological counseling, legal services.

Athletics Member NJCAA. *Intercollegiate sports:* basketball M/W, football M, golf M/W, soccer M/W, softball W, swimming and diving M/W, tennis M, volleyball W, water polo M/W.

Costs (2006–07) *Tuition:* nonresident $4500 full-time, $100 per unit part-time. *Required fees:* $780 full-time, $17 per unit part-time, $29 per term part-time.

Financial Aid Of all full-time matriculated undergraduates who enrolled in 2004, 80 Federal Work-Study jobs (averaging $1300). 210 state and other part-time jobs.

Applying *Options:* electronic application. *Recommended:* high school transcript. *Application deadline:* 9/15 (freshmen), rolling (transfers). *Notification:* continuous (freshmen).

Freshmen Application Contact Ms. Penny Johnson, Dean, Counseling and Student Services, Foothill College, Admissions and Records, 12345 El Monte Road, Los Altos Hills, CA 94022. *Phone:* 650-949-7326. *Fax:* 650-949-7375.

FOUNDATION COLLEGE

San Diego, California   **www.foundationcollege.org/**

- **Independent** 2-year
- **Urban** campus
- **Coed**

Undergraduates 106 full-time. 18% African American, 18% Asian American or Pacific Islander, 20% Hispanic American, 3% Native American.

Faculty *Student/faculty ratio:* 8:1.

Academics *Calendar:* continuous. *Degree:* certificates and associate.

Costs (2005–06) *Tuition:* $17,940 full-time, $260 per credit part-time. *Required fees:* $1200 full-time, $120 per course part-time.

Director of Admissions Peggy Aplin, Admissions Manager, Foundation College, 5353 Mission Center Road, Suite 100, San Diego, CA 92108-1306. *Phone:* 619-683-3273 Ext. 105. *Toll-free phone:* 888-707-3273.

FRESNO CITY COLLEGE

Fresno, California   **www.fresnocitycollege.com/**

Freshmen Application Contact Ms. Stephanie Pauhi, Office Assistant, Fresno City College, 1101 East University Avenue, Fresno, CA 93741. *Phone:* 559-442-8225.

FULLERTON COLLEGE

Fullerton, California   **www.fullcoll.edu/**

Director of Admissions Mr. Peter Fong, Dean of Admissions and Records, Fullerton College, 321 East Chapman Avenue, Fullerton, CA 92832-2095. *Phone:* 714-992-7582.

GAVILAN COLLEGE

Gilroy, California   **www.gavilan.edu/**

- **State and locally supported** 2-year, founded 1919, part of California Community College System
- **Rural** 150-acre campus with easy access to San Jose
- **Coed,** 6,064 undergraduate students, 20% full-time, 57% women, 43% men

Undergraduates 1,212 full-time, 4,852 part-time. Students come from 6 states and territories, 11 other countries, 4% are from out of state, 2% African American, 6% Asian American or Pacific Islander, 41% Hispanic American, 0.7% Native American, 0.1% international.

Freshmen *Admission:* 1,926 admitted.

Faculty *Total:* 164, 45% full-time.

Majors Accounting; administrative assistant and secretarial science; art; avionics maintenance technology; biological and physical sciences; biology/biological

Gavilan College (continued)

sciences; business administration and management; chemistry; child development; computer and information sciences related; computer graphics; computer programming; computer science; corrections; cosmetology; criminal justice/law enforcement administration; criminal justice/police science; developmental and child psychology; digital communication and media/multimedia; drafting and design technology; English; history; information science/studies; journalism; kindergarten/preschool education; liberal arts and sciences/liberal studies; mathematics; music; natural sciences; nursing (licensed practical/vocational nurse training); nursing (registered nurse training); physical education teaching and coaching; political science and government; pre-engineering; psychology; social sciences; sociology; Spanish.

Academics *Calendar:* semesters. *Degree:* certificates, diplomas, and associate. *Special study options:* academic remediation for entering students, adult/continuing education programs, advanced placement credit, cooperative education, distance learning, English as a second language, honors programs, independent study, internships, part-time degree program, services for LD students, study abroad, summer session for credit.

Library 55,440 titles, 205 serial subscriptions.

Computers on Campus 31 computers available on campus for general student use. A campuswide network can be accessed. Internet access, at least one staffed computer lab available.

Student Life *Housing:* college housing not available. *Activities and Organizations:* drama/theater group, student-run newspaper, marching band, Student Government. *Campus security:* 24-hour emergency response devices and patrols, late-night transport/escort service. *Student services:* health clinic, personal/psychological counseling.

Athletics *Intercollegiate sports:* baseball W, basketball M/W, football M, golf M, soccer M/W, softball W, tennis M, volleyball W.

Costs (2006–07) *Tuition:* state resident $0 full-time; nonresident $4800 full-time. *Required fees:* $676 full-time, $26 per semester part-time.

Financial Aid Of all full-time matriculated undergraduates who enrolled in 2004, 50 Federal Work-Study jobs (averaging $2000). *Financial aid deadline:* 6/30.

Applying *Application deadline:* rolling (freshmen), rolling (transfers). *Notification:* continuous (freshmen).

Freshmen Application Contact Ms. Joy Parker, Director of Admissions, Gavilan College, 5055 Santa Teresa Boulevard, Gilroy, CA 95020. *Phone:* 408-848-4735. *Fax:* 408-846-4940.

GLENDALE COMMUNITY COLLEGE

Glendale, California   www.glendale.edu/

- **State and locally supported** 2-year, founded 1927, part of California Community College System
- **Urban** 119-acre campus with easy access to Los Angeles
- **Endowment** $5.3 million
- **Coed**

Undergraduates 4,712 full-time, 11,055 part-time. Students come from 56 states and territories, 121 other countries, 1% are from out of state, 3% African American, 9% Asian American or Pacific Islander, 22% Hispanic American, 0.5% Native American, 27% international, 5% transferred in.

Academics *Calendar:* semesters. *Degree:* certificates and associate. *Special study options:* academic remediation for entering students, adult/continuing education programs, advanced placement credit, cooperative education, distance learning, English as a second language, honors programs, independent study, internships, part-time degree program, services for LD students, study abroad, summer session for credit.

Student Life *Campus security:* student patrols, late-night transport/escort service.

Standardized Tests *Recommended:* CPT.

Costs (2005–06) *Tuition:* state resident $0 full-time; nonresident $3600 full-time, $150 per unit part-time. Full-time tuition and fees vary according to course load. Part-time tuition and fees vary according to course load. *Required fees:* $740 full-time, $26 per unit part-time.

Financial Aid Of all full-time matriculated undergraduates who enrolled in 2004, 300 Federal Work-Study jobs (averaging $2500).

Applying *Options:* common application, electronic application, early admission, deferred entrance. *Recommended:* high school transcript.

Director of Admissions Ms. Sharon Combs, Dean, Admissions and Records, Glendale Community College, 1500 North Verdugo Road, Glendale, CA 91208. *Phone:* 818-551-5115.

GOLDEN WEST COLLEGE

Huntington Beach, California   www.gwc.cccd.edu/

Director of Admissions Ms. Shirley Donnelly, Director of Enrollment Services, Golden West College, 15744 Golden West Street, Huntington Beach, CA 92647. *Phone:* 714-892-7711 Ext. 58196.

GROSSMONT COLLEGE

El Cajon, California   www.grossmont.edu/

Freshmen Application Contact Ms. Sharon Clark, Registrar, Grossmont College, El Cajon, CA 92020-1799. *Phone:* 619-644-7170.

HARTNELL COLLEGE

Salinas, California   www.hartnell.edu/

Director of Admissions Ms. Mary Dominguez, Director of Admissions, Hartnell College, 156 Homestead Avenue, Salinas, CA 93901-1697. *Phone:* 831-755-6711.

HEALD COLLEGE-CONCORD

Concord, California   www.heald.edu/

- **Independent** 2-year, founded 1863
- **Small-town** 5-acre campus with easy access to San Francisco
- **Coed,** 639 undergraduate students, 82% full-time, 67% women, 33% men

Undergraduates 524 full-time, 115 part-time. 5% African American, 3% Asian American or Pacific Islander, 5% Hispanic American.
Freshmen *Admission:* 172 enrolled.

Faculty *Total:* 44, 57% full-time, 100% with terminal degrees. *Student/faculty ratio:* 18:1.

Majors Computer engineering technology; electrical, electronic and communications engineering technology.

Academics *Calendar:* quarters. *Degree:* certificates, diplomas, and associate. *Special study options:* academic remediation for entering students, advanced placement credit, internships, part-time degree program, summer session for credit.

Library Learning Resource Center with an OPAC.

Computers on Campus Internet access, at least one staffed computer lab available.

Student Life *Housing:* college housing not available. *Campus security:* 24-hour emergency response devices.

Standardized Tests *Required:* COMPASS (for admission).

Applying *Options:* electronic application, early admission, deferred entrance. *Application fee:* $40. *Required:* high school transcript, interview. *Application deadline:* rolling (freshmen), rolling (transfers). *Notification:* continuous (freshmen).

Freshmen Application Contact Director of Admissions, Heald College-Concord, 5130 Commercial Circle, Concord, CA 94520. *Phone:* 925-288-5800. *Toll-free phone:* 800-755-3550. *Fax:* 925-288-5896. *E-mail:* info@heald.edu.

HEALD COLLEGE-FRESNO

Fresno, California   www.heald.edu/

- **Independent** 2-year, founded 1863
- **Suburban** 3-acre campus
- **Coed,** 729 undergraduate students, 75% full-time, 62% women, 38% men

Undergraduates 547 full-time, 182 part-time. 2% African American, 3% Asian American or Pacific Islander, 11% Hispanic American, 0.1% Native American.
Freshmen *Admission:* 227 enrolled.

Faculty *Total:* 38, 68% full-time, 100% with terminal degrees. *Student/faculty ratio:* 20:1.

Majors Accounting; administrative assistant and secretarial science; business administration and management; computer engineering technology; electrical, electronic and communications engineering technology; information science/studies; legal administrative assistant/secretary; medical administrative assistant and medical secretary.

Academics *Calendar:* quarters. *Degree:* certificates, diplomas, and associate. *Special study options:* academic remediation for entering students, advanced placement credit, internships, part-time degree program, summer session for credit.

Library Learning Resource Center with an OPAC.

Computers on Campus Internet access, at least one staffed computer lab available.

Student Life *Housing:* college housing not available.

Standardized Tests *Required:* COMPASS (for admission).

Applying *Options:* electronic application, early admission, deferred entrance. *Application fee:* $40. *Required:* high school transcript, interview. *Application deadline:* rolling (freshmen), rolling (transfers). *Notification:* continuous (freshmen).

Freshmen Application Contact Director of Admissions, Heald College-Fresno, 255 West Bullard Avenue, Fresno, CA 93704-1706. *Phone:* 559-438-4222. *Toll-free phone:* 800-755-3550. *E-mail:* info@heald.edu.

HEALD COLLEGE-HAYWARD
Hayward, California   **www.heald.edu/**

- **Independent** 2-year, founded 1863
- **Urban** campus with easy access to San Francisco
- **Coed,** 864 undergraduate students, 74% full-time, 65% women, 35% men

Undergraduates 637 full-time, 227 part-time. 6% African American, 6% Asian American or Pacific Islander, 9% Hispanic American, 0.3% Native American. Freshmen *Admission:* 215 enrolled.

Faculty *Total:* 36, 64% full-time, 100% with terminal degrees. *Student/faculty ratio:* 26:1.

Majors Accounting; administrative assistant and secretarial science; computer and information sciences related; computer/information technology services administration related; computer management; computer programming (vendor/product certification); computer science; legal administrative assistant/secretary; medical administrative assistant and medical secretary.

Academics *Calendar:* quarters. *Degree:* certificates, diplomas, and associate. *Special study options:* academic remediation for entering students, advanced placement credit, internships, part-time degree program, summer session for credit.

Library Learning Resource Center (LRC) with an OPAC.

Computers on Campus Internet access, at least one staffed computer lab available.

Student Life *Housing:* college housing not available. *Campus security:* 24-hour emergency response devices and patrols.

Standardized Tests *Required:* COMPASS (for admission).

Applying *Options:* electronic application, early admission, deferred entrance. *Application fee:* $40. *Required:* high school transcript, interview. *Application deadline:* rolling (freshmen), rolling (transfers). *Notification:* continuous (freshmen).

Freshmen Application Contact Director of Admissions, Heald College-Hayward, 25500 Industrial Boulevard, Hayward, CA 94545. *Phone:* 510-783-2100. *Toll-free phone:* 800-755-3550. *Fax:* 510-783-3287. *E-mail:* info@heald.edu.

HEALD COLLEGE-RANCHO CORDOVA
Rancho Cordova, California   **www.heald.edu/**

- **Independent** 2-year, founded 1863
- **Suburban** 1-acre campus with easy access to Sacramento
- **Coed,** 471 undergraduate students, 74% full-time, 66% women, 34% men

Undergraduates 349 full-time, 122 part-time. 12% African American, 9% Asian American or Pacific Islander, 13% Hispanic American, 0.2% Native American. Freshmen *Admission:* 120 enrolled.

Faculty *Total:* 22, 86% full-time, 100% with terminal degrees. *Student/faculty ratio:* 20:1.

Majors Accounting; administrative assistant and secretarial science; business administration and management; legal administrative assistant/secretary; medical administrative assistant and medical secretary.

Academics *Calendar:* quarters. *Degree:* certificates, diplomas, and associate. *Special study options:* academic remediation for entering students, advanced placement credit, internships, part-time degree program, summer session for credit.

Library Learning Resource Center with an OPAC.

Computers on Campus Internet access, at least one staffed computer lab available.

Student Life *Housing:* college housing not available. *Campus security:* late-night transport/escort service.

Standardized Tests *Required:* COMPASS (for admission).

Applying *Options:* electronic application, early admission, deferred entrance. *Application fee:* $40. *Required:* high school transcript, interview. *Application deadline:* rolling (freshmen), rolling (transfers). *Notification:* continuous (freshmen).

Freshmen Application Contact Director of Admissions, Heald College-Rancho Cordova, 2910 Prospect Park Drive, Rancho Cordova, CA 95670-6005. *Phone:* 916-638-1616. *Toll-free phone:* 800-755-3550. *Fax:* 916-853-8282. *E-mail:* info@heald.edu.

HEALD COLLEGE-ROSEVILLE
Roseville, California   **www.heald.edu/**

- **Independent** 2-year, founded 1863
- **Urban** 5-acre campus
- **Coed,** 528 undergraduate students, 71% full-time, 61% women, 39% men

Undergraduates 376 full-time, 152 part-time. 1% African American, 2% Asian American or Pacific Islander, 7% Hispanic American, 0.8% Native American. Freshmen *Admission:* 119 enrolled.

Faculty *Total:* 23, 91% full-time, 100% with terminal degrees. *Student/faculty ratio:* 19:1.

Majors Business administration and management; computer engineering technology; electrical, electronic and communications engineering technology.

Academics *Calendar:* quarters. *Degree:* certificates, diplomas, and associate. *Special study options:* academic remediation for entering students, advanced placement credit, internships, part-time degree program, summer session for credit.

Library Learning Resource Center with an OPAC.

Computers on Campus Internet access, at least one staffed computer lab available.

Student Life *Housing:* college housing not available. *Campus security:* 24-hour emergency response devices, evening security guard.

Standardized Tests *Required:* COMPASS (for admission).

Financial Aid Of all full-time matriculated undergraduates who enrolled in 2004, 35 Federal Work-Study jobs.

Applying *Options:* electronic application, early admission, deferred entrance. *Application fee:* $40. *Required:* high school transcript, interview.

Freshmen Application Contact Director of Admissions, Heald College-Roseville, 7 Sierra Gate Plaza, Roseville, CA 95678. *Phone:* 916-789-8600. *Toll-free phone:* 800-755-3550. *E-mail:* info@heald.edu.

HEALD COLLEGE-SALINAS
Salinas, California   **www.heald.edu/**

- **Independent** 2-year, founded 1863
- **Small-town** campus with easy access to San Jose
- **Coed,** 414 undergraduate students, 79% full-time, 67% women, 33% men

Undergraduates 329 full-time, 85 part-time. 3% African American, 0.5% Asian American or Pacific Islander, 18% Hispanic American. Freshmen *Admission:* 120 enrolled.

Faculty *Total:* 18, 78% full-time, 100% with terminal degrees. *Student/faculty ratio:* 24:1.

Majors Accounting; business administration and management; hospitality administration; legal administrative assistant/secretary; medical administrative assistant and medical secretary.

Heald College-Salinas (continued)

Academics *Calendar:* quarters. *Degree:* certificates, diplomas, and associate. *Special study options:* academic remediation for entering students, advanced placement credit, internships, part-time degree program, summer session for credit.

Library Learning Resource Center with an OPAC.

Computers on Campus Internet access, at least one staffed computer lab available.

Student Life *Housing:* college housing not available. *Campus security:* 24-hour emergency response devices, evening security personnel.

Standardized Tests *Required:* COMPASS (for admission).

Applying *Options:* electronic application, early admission, deferred entrance. *Application fee:* $40. *Required:* high school transcript, interview. *Application deadline:* rolling (freshmen), rolling (transfers). *Notification:* continuous (freshmen).

Freshmen Application Contact Director of Admissions, Heald College-Salinas, 1450 North Main Street, Salinas, CA 93906. *Phone:* 831-443-1700. *Toll-free phone:* 800-755-3550. *Fax:* 831-443-1050. *E-mail:* info@heald.edu.

HEALD COLLEGE-SAN FRANCISCO

San Francisco, California   **www.heald.edu/**

- **Independent** 2-year, founded 1863
- **Urban** campus
- **Coed,** 389 undergraduate students, 70% full-time, 55% women, 45% men

Undergraduates 273 full-time, 116 part-time. 5% African American, 5% Asian American or Pacific Islander, 5% Hispanic American, 0.3% Native American.

Freshmen *Admission:* 63 enrolled.

Faculty *Total:* 24, 75% full-time, 100% with terminal degrees. *Student/faculty ratio:* 16:1.

Majors Accounting; administrative assistant and secretarial science; computer engineering technology; computer systems networking and telecommunications; electrical, electronic and communications engineering technology; hospitality administration; legal administrative assistant/secretary; medical administrative assistant and medical secretary.

Academics *Calendar:* quarters. *Degree:* certificates, diplomas, and associate. *Special study options:* academic remediation for entering students, advanced placement credit, internships, part-time degree program, summer session for credit.

Library Learning Resource Center with an OPAC.

Computers on Campus Internet access, at least one staffed computer lab available.

Student Life *Housing:* college housing not available.

Standardized Tests *Required:* COMPASS (for admission).

Applying *Options:* electronic application, early admission, deferred entrance. *Application fee:* $40. *Required:* high school transcript, interview. *Application deadline:* rolling (freshmen), rolling (transfers). *Notification:* continuous (freshmen).

Freshmen Application Contact Director of Admissions, Heald College-San Francisco, 350 Mission Street, San Francisco, CA 94105. *Phone:* 415-808-3000. *Toll-free phone:* 800-755-3550. *Fax:* 415-808-3003. *E-mail:* info@heald.edu.

HEALD COLLEGE-SAN JOSE

Milpitas, California   **www.heald.edu/**

- **Independent** 2-year, founded 1863
- **Small-town** 5-acre campus with easy access to San Jose
- **Coed,** 639 undergraduate students, 79% full-time, 63% women, 37% men

Undergraduates 502 full-time, 137 part-time. 11% African American, 19% Asian American or Pacific Islander, 39% Hispanic American, 0.3% Native American.

Freshmen *Admission:* 140 enrolled.

Faculty *Total:* 32, 78% full-time, 100% with terminal degrees. *Student/faculty ratio:* 20:1.

Majors Accounting; computer engineering technology; computer science; electrical, electronic and communications engineering technology; legal administrative assistant/secretary; telecommunications.

Academics *Calendar:* quarters. *Degree:* certificates, diplomas, and associate. *Special study options:* academic remediation for entering students, advanced placement credit, internships, part-time degree program, summer session for credit.

Library Learning Resource Center with an OPAC.

Computers on Campus Internet access, at least one staffed computer lab available.

Student Life *Housing:* college housing not available.

Standardized Tests *Required:* COMPASS (for admission).

Financial Aid Of all full-time matriculated undergraduates who enrolled in 2004, 20 Federal Work-Study jobs.

Applying *Options:* electronic application, early admission, deferred entrance. *Application fee:* $40. *Required:* high school transcript, interview. *Application deadline:* rolling (freshmen), rolling (transfers). *Notification:* continuous (freshmen).

Freshmen Application Contact Director of Admissions, Heald College-San Jose, 341 Great Mall Parkway, Milpitas, CA 95035. *Phone:* 408-934-4900. *Toll-free phone:* 800-755-3550. *Fax:* 408-934-7777. *E-mail:* info@heald.edu.

HEALD COLLEGE-STOCKTON

Stockton, California   **www.heald.edu/**

- **Independent** 2-year, founded 1863
- **Coed,** 530 undergraduate students, 75% full-time, 74% women, 26% men

Undergraduates 398 full-time, 132 part-time. 4% African American, 8% Asian American or Pacific Islander, 17% Hispanic American, 0.2% Native American.

Freshmen *Admission:* 149 enrolled.

Faculty *Total:* 37, 54% full-time, 100% with terminal degrees. *Student/faculty ratio:* 17:1.

Majors Accounting; computer management; computer systems analysis; data processing and data processing technology.

Academics *Calendar:* quarters. *Degree:* certificates, diplomas, and associate. *Special study options:* academic remediation for entering students, advanced placement credit, internships, part-time degree program, summer session for credit.

Library Learning Resource Center with an OPAC.

Computers on Campus Internet access, at least one staffed computer lab available.

Student Life *Housing:* college housing not available.

Standardized Tests *Required:* COMPASS (for admission).

Applying *Options:* electronic application, early admission, deferred entrance. *Application fee:* $40. *Required:* high school transcript, interview. *Application deadline:* rolling (freshmen), rolling (transfers). *Notification:* continuous (freshmen).

Freshmen Application Contact Director of Admissions, Heald College-Stockton, 1605 East March Lane, Stockton, CA 95210. *Phone:* 209-473-5200. *Toll-free phone:* 800-755-3550. *Fax:* 209-477-2739. *E-mail:* info@heald.edu.

HIGH-TECH INSTITUTE

Sacramento, California   **www.high-techinstitute.com/**

Director of Admissions Mr. Richard Dyer, School Director, High-Tech Institute, 1111 Howe Avenue, #250, Sacramento, CA 95825. *Phone:* 916-929-9700. *Toll-free phone:* 800-987-0110. *Fax:* 916-929-9703. *E-mail:* rdyer@hightechschools.com.

IMPERIAL VALLEY COLLEGE

Imperial, California   **www.imperial.cc.ca.us/**

Director of Admissions Mrs. Sandra Standiford, Dean of Admissions, Imperial Valley College, PO Box 158, Imperial, CA 92251. *Phone:* 760-352-8320 Ext. 200.

IRVINE VALLEY COLLEGE

Irvine, California   **www.ivc.edu/**

Director of Admissions Mr. John Edwards, Director of Admissions, Records and Enrollment Services, Irvine Valley College, 5500 Irvine Center Drive, Irvine, CA 92618. *Phone:* 949-451-5416.

ITT TECHNICAL INSTITUTE
Anaheim, California   www.itt-tech.edu/

- **Proprietary** primarily 2-year, founded 1982, part of ITT Educational Services, Inc
- **Suburban** 5-acre campus with easy access to Los Angeles
- **Coed**

Majors Animation, interactive technology, video graphics and special effects; business administration and management; CAD/CADD drafting/design technology; computer and information systems security; computer systems networking and telecommunications; criminal justice/law enforcement administration; e-commerce; electrical, electronic and communications engineering technology; system, networking, and LAN/WAN management; web page, digital/multimedia and information resources design.
Academics *Calendar:* quarters. *Degrees:* associate and bachelor's.
Library a Web page.
Computers on Campus Internet access, at least one staffed computer lab available.
Student Life *Housing:* college housing not available. *Activities and Organizations:* student-run newspaper.
Standardized Tests *Required:* Wonderlic aptitude test (for admission).
Costs (2005–06) *Tuition:* Please see school catalog for specific information.
Financial Aid Of all full-time matriculated undergraduates who enrolled in 2004, 20 Federal Work-Study jobs (averaging $5000).
Applying *Options:* deferred entrance. *Application fee:* $100. *Required:* high school transcript, interview. *Recommended:* letters of recommendation. *Application deadline:* rolling (freshmen), rolling (transfers). *Notification:* continuous (freshmen).
Freshmen Application Contact Sheryl Schulgen, Director of Recruitment, ITT Technical Institute, 525 North Muller Avenue, Anaheim, CA 92801. *Phone:* 714-535-3700. *Fax:* 714-535-1802.

ITT TECHNICAL INSTITUTE
Lathrop, California   www.itt-tech.edu/

- **Proprietary** primarily 2-year, part of ITT Educational Services
- **Coed**

Majors Animation, interactive technology, video graphics and special effects; business administration and management; CAD/CADD drafting/design technology; computer and information systems security; computer programming; computer software technology; computer systems networking and telecommunications; criminal justice/law enforcement administration; e-commerce; electrical, electronic and communications engineering technology; system, networking, and LAN/WAN management; web page, digital/multimedia and information resources design.
Academics *Calendar:* quarters. *Degrees:* associate and bachelor's.
Library a Web page.
Computers on Campus Internet access, at least one staffed computer lab available.
Student Life *Housing:* college housing not available.
Standardized Tests *Required:* Wonderlic aptitude test (for admission).
Costs (2005–06) *Tuition:* Please see school catalog for specific information.
Applying *Options:* deferred entrance. *Application fee:* $100. *Required:* high school transcript, interview. *Recommended:* letters of recommendation. *Application deadline:* rolling (freshmen), rolling (transfers). *Notification:* continuous (freshmen).
Freshmen Application Contact Ms. Kathy Paradis, Director of Recruitment, ITT Technical Institute, 16916 South Harlan Road, Lathrop, CA 95330. *Phone:* 209-858-0077. *Toll-free phone:* 800-346-1786.

ITT TECHNICAL INSTITUTE
Oxnard, California   www.itt-tech.edu/

- **Proprietary** primarily 2-year, founded 1993, part of ITT Educational Services, Inc
- **Urban** campus with easy access to Los Angeles
- **Coed**

Majors Animation, interactive technology, video graphics and special effects; business administration and management; CAD/CADD drafting/design technology; computer and information systems security; criminal justice/law enforce-ment administration; e-commerce; electrical, electronic and communications engineering technology; system, networking, and LAN/WAN management; web page, digital/multimedia and information resources design.
Academics *Calendar:* quarters. *Degrees:* associate and bachelor's.
Library a Web page.
Computers on Campus Internet access, at least one staffed computer lab available.
Student Life *Housing:* college housing not available. *Campus security:* 24-hour emergency response devices and patrols.
Standardized Tests *Required:* Wonderlic aptitude test (for admission).
Costs (2005–06) *Tuition:* Please see school catalog for specific information.
Applying *Options:* deferred entrance. *Application fee:* $100. *Required:* high school transcript, interview. *Recommended:* letters of recommendation. *Application deadline:* rolling (freshmen), rolling (transfers). *Notification:* continuous (freshmen).
Freshmen Application Contact Mrs. Claudia Wilroy, Director of Recruitment, ITT Technical Institute, 2051 Solar Drive, Building B, Oxnard, CA 93036. *Phone:* 805-988-0143. *Toll-free phone:* 800-530-1582.

ITT TECHNICAL INSTITUTE
Rancho Cordova, California   www.itt-tech.edu/

- **Proprietary** primarily 2-year, founded 1954, part of ITT Educational Services, Inc
- **Urban** 5-acre campus
- **Coed**

Majors Animation, interactive technology, video graphics and special effects; business administration and management; CAD/CADD drafting/design technology; computer and information systems security; computer programming; computer systems networking and telecommunications; criminal justice/law enforcement administration; e-commerce; electrical, electronic and communications engineering technology; system, networking, and LAN/WAN management; web/multimedia management and webmaster; web page, digital/multimedia and information resources design.
Academics *Calendar:* quarters. *Degrees:* associate and bachelor's.
Library a Web page.
Computers on Campus Internet access, at least one staffed computer lab available.
Student Life *Housing:* college housing not available.
Standardized Tests *Required:* Wonderlic aptitude test (for admission).
Costs (2005–06) *Tuition:* Please see school catalog for specific information.
Applying *Options:* deferred entrance. *Application fee:* $100. *Required:* high school transcript, interview. *Recommended:* letters of recommendation. *Application deadline:* rolling (freshmen), rolling (transfers). *Notification:* continuous (freshmen).
Freshmen Application Contact Mr. Vance Klinke, Director of Recruitment, ITT Technical Institute, 10863 Gold Center Drive, Rancho Cordova, CA 95670. *Phone:* 916-851-3900. *Toll-free phone:* 800-488-8466.

ITT TECHNICAL INSTITUTE
San Bernardino, California   www.itt-tech.edu/

- **Proprietary** primarily 2-year, founded 1987, part of ITT Educational Services, Inc
- **Urban** campus with easy access to Los Angeles
- **Coed**

Majors Animation, interactive technology, video graphics and special effects; business administration and management; CAD/CADD drafting/design technology; computer and information systems security; computer programming; criminal justice/law enforcement administration; e-commerce; electrical, electronic and communications engineering technology; system, networking, and LAN/WAN management; web page, digital/multimedia and information resources design.
Academics *Calendar:* quarters. *Degrees:* associate and bachelor's.
Library a Web page.
Computers on Campus Internet access, at least one staffed computer lab available.
Student Life *Housing:* college housing not available.
Standardized Tests *Required:* Wonderlic aptitude test (for admission).
Costs (2005–06) *Tuition:* Please see school catalog for specific information.

ITT Technical Institute (continued)

Applying *Options:* deferred entrance. *Application fee:* $100. *Required:* high school transcript, interview. *Recommended:* letters of recommendation. *Application deadline:* rolling (freshmen), rolling (transfers). *Notification:* continuous (freshmen).

Freshmen Application Contact Ms. Laura Brozeck, Director of Recruitment, ITT Technical Institute, 670 East Carnegie Drive, San Bernardino, CA 92408. *Phone:* 909-806-4600. *Toll-free phone:* 800-888-3801.

ITT TECHNICAL INSTITUTE
San Diego, California
www.itt-tech.edu/

- **Proprietary** primarily 2-year, founded 1981, part of ITT Educational Services, Inc
- **Suburban** campus
- **Coed**

Majors Animation, interactive technology, video graphics and special effects; business administration and management; CAD/CADD drafting/design technology; computer and information systems security; computer programming; criminal justice/law enforcement administration; e-commerce; electrical, electronic and communications engineering technology; system, networking, and LAN/WAN management; web page, digital/multimedia and information resources design.

Academics *Calendar:* quarters. *Degrees:* associate and bachelor's.

Library a Web page.

Computers on Campus Internet access, at least one staffed computer lab available.

Student Life *Housing:* college housing not available.

Standardized Tests *Required:* Wonderlic aptitude test (for admission).

Costs (2005–06) *Tuition:* Please see school catalog for specific information.

Applying *Options:* deferred entrance. *Application fee:* $100. *Required:* high school transcript, interview. *Recommended:* letters of recommendation. *Application deadline:* rolling (freshmen), rolling (transfers). *Notification:* continuous (freshmen).

Freshmen Application Contact Ron Begora, Director of Recruitment, ITT Technical Institute, 9680 Granite Ridge Drive, San Diego, CA 92123. *Phone:* 858-571-8500. *Toll-free phone:* 800-883-0380.

ITT TECHNICAL INSTITUTE
Sylmar, California
www.itt-tech.edu/

- **Proprietary** primarily 2-year, founded 1982, part of ITT Educational Services, Inc
- **Urban** campus with easy access to Los Angeles
- **Coed**

Majors Animation, interactive technology, video graphics and special effects; business administration and management; CAD/CADD drafting/design technology; computer and information systems security; computer programming; computer systems networking and telecommunications; criminal justice/law enforcement administration; e-commerce; electrical, electronic and communications engineering technology; system, networking, and LAN/WAN management; web page, digital/multimedia and information resources design.

Academics *Calendar:* quarters. *Degrees:* associate and bachelor's.

Library a Web page.

Computers on Campus Internet access, at least one staffed computer lab available.

Student Life *Housing:* college housing not available.

Standardized Tests *Required:* Wonderlic aptitude test (for admission).

Costs (2005–06) *Tuition:* Please see school catalog for specific information.

Applying *Options:* deferred entrance. *Application fee:* $100. *Required:* high school transcript, interview. *Recommended:* letters of recommendation. *Application deadline:* rolling (freshmen), rolling (transfers). *Notification:* continuous (freshmen).

Freshmen Application Contact Ms. Kelly Christensen, Director of Recruitment, ITT Technical Institute, 12669 Encinitas Avenue, Sylmar, CA 91342. *Phone:* 818-364-5151. *Toll-free phone:* 800-363-2086.

ITT TECHNICAL INSTITUTE
Torrance, California
www.itt-tech.edu/

- **Proprietary** primarily 2-year, founded 1987, part of ITT Educational Services, Inc
- **Urban** campus with easy access to Los Angeles
- **Coed**

Majors Animation, interactive technology, video graphics and special effects; business administration and management; CAD/CADD drafting/design technology; computer and information systems security; computer software technology; computer systems networking and telecommunications; criminal justice/law enforcement administration; e-commerce; electrical, electronic and communications engineering technology; system, networking, and LAN/WAN management; web page, digital/multimedia and information resources design.

Academics *Calendar:* quarters. *Degrees:* associate and bachelor's.

Library a Web page.

Computers on Campus Internet access, at least one staffed computer lab available.

Student Life *Housing:* college housing not available.

Standardized Tests *Required:* Wonderlic aptitude test (for admission).

Costs (2005–06) *Tuition:* Please see school catalog for specific information.

Financial Aid Of all full-time matriculated undergraduates who enrolled in 2004, 6 Federal Work-Study jobs (averaging $4000).

Applying *Options:* deferred entrance. *Application fee:* $100. *Required:* high school transcript, interview. *Recommended:* letters of recommendation. *Application deadline:* rolling (freshmen), rolling (transfers). *Notification:* continuous (freshmen).

Freshmen Application Contact Mr. Freddie Polk, Director of Recruitment, ITT Technical Institute, 20050 South Vermont Avenue, Torrance, CA 90502. *Phone:* 310-380-1555.

ITT TECHNICAL INSTITUTE
West Covina, California
www.itt-tech.edu/

- **Proprietary** primarily 2-year, founded 1982, part of ITT Educational Services, Inc
- **Suburban** 4-acre campus with easy access to Los Angeles
- **Coed**

Majors Animation, interactive technology, video graphics and special effects; business administration and management; CAD/CADD drafting/design technology; computer and information systems security; criminal justice/law enforcement administration; e-commerce; electrical, electronic and communications engineering technology; robotics technology; system, networking, and LAN/WAN management; web page, digital/multimedia and information resources design.

Academics *Calendar:* quarters. *Degrees:* associate and bachelor's.

Library a Web page.

Computers on Campus Internet access, at least one staffed computer lab available.

Student Life *Housing:* college housing not available.

Standardized Tests *Required:* Wonderlic aptitude test (for admission).

Costs (2005–06) *Tuition:* Please see school catalog for specific information.

Financial Aid Of all full-time matriculated undergraduates who enrolled in 2004, 20 Federal Work-Study jobs (averaging $4500).

Applying *Options:* deferred entrance. *Application fee:* $100. *Required:* high school transcript, interview. *Recommended:* letters of recommendation. *Application deadline:* rolling (freshmen), rolling (transfers). *Notification:* continuous (freshmen).

Freshmen Application Contact Mr. George Gaines, Director of Recruitment, ITT Technical Institute, 1530 West Cameron Avenue, West Covina, CA 91790. *Phone:* 626-960-8681. *Toll-free phone:* 800-414-6522.

LAKE TAHOE COMMUNITY COLLEGE
South Lake Tahoe, California
www.ltcc.edu/

Director of Admissions Ms. Linda M. Stevenson, Director of Admissions and Records, Lake Tahoe Community College, One College Drive, South Lake Tahoe, CA 96150-4524. *Phone:* 530-541-4660 Ext. 282.

LANEY COLLEGE

Oakland, California   www.peralta.cc.ca.us/

Freshmen Application Contact Mrs. Barbara Simmons, District Admissions Officer, Laney College, 900 Fallon Street, Oakland, CA 94607-4893. *Phone:* 510-466-7369.

LAS POSITAS COLLEGE

Livermore, California   www.clpccd.cc.ca.us/lpc/

Director of Admissions Mrs. Sylvia R. Rodriguez, Director of Admissions and Records, Las Positas College, 3033 Collier Canyon Road, Livermore, CA 94551-7650. *Phone:* 925-373-4942.

LASSEN COMMUNITY COLLEGE DISTRICT

Susanville, California   www.lassencollege.edu/

Director of Admissions Mr. Chris J. Alberico, Registrar, Lassen Community College District, Highway 139, PO Box 3000, Susanville, CA 96130. *Phone:* 530-257-6181 Ext. 132.

LONG BEACH CITY COLLEGE

Long Beach, California   www.lbcc.edu/

- **State-supported** 2-year, founded 1927, part of California Community College System
- **Urban** 40-acre campus with easy access to Los Angeles
- **Coed,** 26,296 undergraduate students, 36% full-time, 56% women, 44% men

Undergraduates 9,580 full-time, 16,716 part-time. 1% are from out of state, 14% African American, 15% Asian American or Pacific Islander, 37% Hispanic American, 0.8% Native American, 3% transferred in. Freshmen *Admission:* 2,001 enrolled.

Faculty *Total:* 1,133, 31% full-time. *Student/faculty ratio:* 24:1.

Majors Accounting; administrative assistant and secretarial science; advertising; airline pilot and flight crew; architectural engineering technology; art; automobile/automotive mechanics technology; aviation/airway management; avionics maintenance technology; biology/biological sciences; business administration and management; carpentry; computer programming; computer typography and composition equipment operation; consumer merchandising/retailing management; criminal justice/law enforcement administration; culinary arts; dance; data processing and data processing technology; developmental and child psychology; dietetics; drafting and design technology; dramatic/theater arts; electrical, electronic and communications engineering technology; engineering; English; family and consumer economics related; family and consumer sciences/human sciences; fashion/apparel design; fashion merchandising; film/cinema studies; fire science; food services technology; French; German; heating, air conditioning, ventilation and refrigeration maintenance technology; heavy equipment maintenance technology; horticultural science; hotel/motel administration; human services; industrial arts; industrial radiologic technology; industrial technology; interior design; international business/trade/commerce; journalism; kindergarten/preschool education; legal administrative assistant/secretary; liberal arts and sciences/liberal studies; machine tool technology; marketing/marketing management; mathematics; medical administrative assistant and medical secretary; medical/clinical assistant; music; nursing (registered nurse training); ornamental horticulture; photography; physical education teaching and coaching; physical sciences; pre-engineering; radio and television; real estate; social sciences; Spanish; special products marketing; speech and rhetoric; tourism and travel services management; welding technology.

Academics *Calendar:* semesters. *Degree:* certificates and associate. *Special study options:* academic remediation for entering students, adult/continuing education programs, advanced placement credit, distance learning, English as a second language, honors programs, internships, part-time degree program, services for LD students, summer session for credit.

Library Long Beach City College Library plus 1 other with 151,367 titles, 471 serial subscriptions, 3,150 audiovisual materials, an OPAC, a Web page.

Computers on Campus 200 computers available on campus for general student use. Internet access, online (class) registration, at least one staffed computer lab available.

Student Life *Housing:* college housing not available. *Activities and Organizations:* drama/theater group, student-run newspaper, radio and television station, choral group, American Criminal Justice Association, AGS Scholarship Organization, American Association of Future Firefighters, Vietnamese Club, Network Christian Fellowship. *Campus security:* 24-hour emergency response devices and patrols, student patrols, late-night transport/escort service. *Student services:* health clinic, personal/psychological counseling, women's center, legal services.

Athletics Member NJCAA. *Intercollegiate sports:* badminton M/W, baseball M, basketball M/W, cross-country running M/W, football M, golf M/W, soccer M/W, softball W, swimming and diving M/W, tennis M/W, track and field M/W, volleyball M/W, water polo M/W. *Intramural sports:* archery M/W, basketball M/W, bowling M/W, football M/W, golf M/W, racquetball M/W, soccer M/W, softball M/W, swimming and diving M/W, tennis M/W, track and field M/W, volleyball M/W, weight lifting M, wrestling M.

Costs (2006–07) *Tuition:* state resident $0 full-time; nonresident $3840 full-time, $160 per unit part-time. *Required fees:* $692 full-time, $26 per unit part-time, $34 per term part-time.

Financial Aid Of all full-time matriculated undergraduates who enrolled in 2004, 275 Federal Work-Study jobs (averaging $4400). 225 state and other part-time jobs (averaging $4400).

Applying *Options:* early admission. *Recommended:* high school transcript. *Application deadline:* rolling (freshmen).

Director of Admissions Mr. Ross Miyashiro, Dean of Admissions and Records, Long Beach City College, 4901 East Carson Boulevard, Long Beach, CA 90808. *Phone:* 562-938-4130.

LOS ANGELES CITY COLLEGE

Los Angeles, California   www.lacc.cc.ca.us/

Freshmen Application Contact Elaine Geismar, Director of Student Assistance Center, Los Angeles City College, 855 North Vermont Avenue, Los Angeles, CA 90029. *Phone:* 323-953-4340.

LOS ANGELES COUNTY COLLEGE OF NURSING AND ALLIED HEALTH

Los Angeles, California   www.ladhs.org/lacusc/lacnah/

Director of Admissions Ms. Maria Caballero, Manager, Admissions, Los Angeles County College of Nursing and Allied Health, 1237 North Mission Road, Los Angeles, CA 90033. *Phone:* 323-226-4911.

LOS ANGELES HARBOR COLLEGE

Wilmington, California   www.lahc.edu/

Director of Admissions Mr. David Ching, Dean of Admissions and Records, Los Angeles Harbor College, 1111 Figueroa Place, Wilmington, CA 90744-2397. *Phone:* 310-233-4091.

LOS ANGELES MISSION COLLEGE

Sylmar, California   www.lamission.cc.ca.us/

Freshmen Application Contact Ms. Angela Merrill, Admissions Supervisor, Los Angeles Mission College, 13356 Eldridge Avenue, Sylmar, CA 91342-3245. *Phone:* 818-364-7658.

LOS ANGELES PIERCE COLLEGE

Woodland Hills, California   www.lapc.cc.ca.us/

Director of Admissions Ms. Shelley L. Gerstl, Dean of Admissions and Records, Los Angeles Pierce College, 6201 Winnetka Avenue, Woodland Hills, CA 91371-0001. *Phone:* 818-719-6448.

LOS ANGELES SOUTHWEST COLLEGE
Los Angeles, California   www.lasc.cc.ca.us/

Director of Admissions Dr. Lawrence Jarmon, Vice President of Student Services, Los Angeles Southwest College, 1600 West Imperial Highway, Los Angeles, CA 90047-4810. *Phone:* 323-241-5279.

LOS ANGELES TRADE-TECHNICAL COLLEGE
Los Angeles, California   www.lattc.edu/

Director of Admissions Mrs. Rosemary Royal, Dean of Enrollment Management, Los Angeles Trade-Technical College, 400 West Washington Boulevard, Los Angeles, CA 90015. *Phone:* 213-763-5301.

LOS ANGELES VALLEY COLLEGE
Van Nuys, California   www.lavc.cc.ca.us/

Director of Admissions Mr. Florentino Manzano, Associate Dean, Los Angeles Valley College, 5800 Fulton Avenue, Valley Glen, CA 91401. *Phone:* 818-947-2353. *E-mail:* manzanf@lavc.edu.

LOS MEDANOS COLLEGE
Pittsburg, California   www.losmedanos.net/

Freshmen Application Contact Ms. Gail Newman, Director of Admissions and Records, Los Medanos College, 2700 East Leland Road, Pittsburg, CA 94565-5197. *Phone:* 925-439-2181 Ext. 7500.

MARIC COLLEGE
Anaheim, California

MARIC COLLEGE
North Hollywood, California   www.mariccollege.edu/

Director of Admissions Mr. Mark Newman, Executive Director, Maric College, 6180 Laurel Canyon Boulevard, Suite 101, North Hollywood, CA 91606. *Phone:* 818-763-2563 Ext. 240. *Toll-free phone:* 800-404-9729. *Fax:* 818-763-1623. *E-mail:* mark@moderntec.com.

MARIC COLLEGE
Panorama City, California

MARIC COLLEGE
Sacramento, California   www.californiacollege.com/

Director of Admissions Mr. Charles Reese, Director of Admissions, Maric College, 4330 Watt Avenue,Suite 400, Sacramento, CA 95821. *Phone:* 916-649-8168. *Toll-free phone:* 800-955-8168.

MARIC COLLEGE
Salida, California   www.mariccollege.edu/

Director of Admissions Mrs. Linda Stovall, Chief Admission Officer, Maric College, 5172 Kiernan Court, Salida, CA 95368. *Phone:* 209-543-7000.

MARIC COLLEGE
San Diego, California   www.mariccollege.edu/

Freshmen Application Contact Admissions, Maric College, 3666 Kearny Villa Road, Suite 100, San Diego, CA 92123-1995. *Phone:* 858-654-3601. *Toll-free phone:* 800-400-8232.

MARYMOUNT COLLEGE, PALOS VERDES, CALIFORNIA
Rancho Palos Verdes, California   www.marymountpv.edu/

Director of Admissions Ms. Nina Lococo, Dean of Admission and School Relations, Marymount College, Palos Verdes, California, 30800 Palos Verdes Drive East, Rancho Palos Verdes, CA 90815. *Phone:* 310-377-5501 Ext. 182. *E-mail:* admission@marymountpv.edu.

MENDOCINO COLLEGE
Ukiah, California   www.mendocino.cc.ca.us/

Director of Admissions Ms. Kristie A. Taylor, Director of Admissions and Records, Mendocino College, 1000 Hensley Creek Road, Ukiah, CA 95482-0300. *Phone:* 707-468-3103. *Fax:* 707-468-3430. *E-mail:* ktaylor@mendocino.cc.ca.us.

MERCED COLLEGE
Merced, California   www.mccd.edu/

Freshmen Application Contact Ms. Helen Torres, Admissions Clerk, Merced College, 3600 M Street, Merced, CA 95348-2898. *Phone:* 209-384-6187.

MERRITT COLLEGE
Oakland, California   www.merritt.edu/

Freshmen Application Contact Ms. Barbara Simmons, District Admissions Officer, Merritt College, 12500 Campus Drive, Oakland, CA 94619-3196. *Phone:* 510-466-7369. *E-mail:* hperdue@peralta.cc.ca.us.

MIRACOSTA COLLEGE
Oceanside, California   www.miracosta.edu/

- **State-supported** 2-year, founded 1934, part of California Community College System
- **Suburban** 131-acre campus with easy access to San Diego
- **Endowment** $894,495
- **Coed,** 10,252 undergraduate students

MiraCosta College's campuses in Oceanside and Cardiff are minutes from the beach. MiraCosta offers a strong university transfer program, including transfer admission guarantees. Courses of special interest include computer science, horticulture, multimedia, and music technology. Facilities include technology hubs at both campuses and a wellness center at the Oceanside campus.

Undergraduates Students come from 37 states and territories, 44 other countries, 2% are from out of state.
Faculty *Total:* 529, 26% full-time. *Student/faculty ratio:* 23:1.

Majors Accounting; administrative assistant and secretarial science; African studies; architectural engineering technology; art; automobile/automotive mechanics technology; behavioral sciences; biology/biological sciences; business administration and management; chemistry; child care and support services management; computer engineering technology; consumer/homemaking education; cosmetology; criminal justice/law enforcement administration; criminal justice/police science; dance; developmental and child psychology; drafting and design technology; dramatic/theater arts; economics; English; French; general studies; history; horticultural science; hotel/motel administration; humanities; industrial technology; information science/studies; institutional food workers; Japanese; journalism; kindergarten/preschool education; landscaping and groundskeeping; liberal arts and sciences/liberal studies; machine tool technology; marketing; marketing management; mathematics; music; nursing (licensed practical/vocational nurse training); ornamental horticulture; philosophy; physical sciences; physics; political science and government; psychology; real estate; social sciences; sociology; Spanish; speech and rhetoric; teacher assistant/aide; tourism and travel services management.

Academics *Calendar:* semesters. *Degree:* certificates, diplomas, and associate. *Special study options:* academic remediation for entering students, accelerated degree program, adult/continuing education programs, advanced placement credit, cooperative education, distance learning, double majors, English as a second language, freshman honors college, honors programs, independent study, internships, part-time degree program, services for LD students, student-designed majors, study abroad, summer session for credit.

Library MiraCosta College Library with 113,810 titles, 272 serial subscriptions, 5,340 audiovisual materials, an OPAC, a Web page.

Computers on Campus 753 computers available on campus for general student use. A campuswide network can be accessed from off campus that provide access to course listing. Internet access, at least one staffed computer lab available.

Student Life *Housing:* college housing not available. *Activities and Organizations:* drama/theater group, student-run newspaper, choral group, African-American Student Alliance, Spanish Club, Cultural Exchange Program, Phi Theta Kappa, Friends of EOPS. *Campus security:* 24-hour emergency response devices, student patrols, late-night transport/escort service, trained security personnel during class hours. *Student services:* health clinic, personal/psychological counseling, women's center.

Athletics Member NJCAA. *Intercollegiate sports:* basketball M, cross-country running M/W, soccer W, track and field W. *Intramural sports:* soccer M/W.

Costs (2006–07) *Tuition:* state resident $0 full-time; nonresident $4800 full-time, $160 per unit part-time. *Required fees:* $804 full-time, $26 per unit part-time.

Financial Aid Of all full-time matriculated undergraduates who enrolled in 2004, 83 Federal Work-Study jobs (averaging $1315).

Applying *Options:* early admission, deferred entrance. *Application deadline:* rolling (freshmen), rolling (transfers).

Freshmen Application Contact Admissions and Records Assistant, MiraCosta College, One Barnard Drive, Oceanside, CA 92056. *Phone:* 760-795-6620. *Toll-free phone:* 888-201-8480.

MISSION COLLEGE
Santa Clara, California   www.missioncollege.org/

Director of Admissions Dr. Sam Bersolo, Interim Vice President of Student Services, Mission College, 3000 Mission College Boulevard, Santa Clara, CA 95054-1897. *Phone:* 408-855-5195.

MODESTO JUNIOR COLLEGE
Modesto, California   www.mjc.edu/

- **State and locally supported** 2-year, founded 1921, part of Yosemite Community College District System
- **Urban** 229-acre campus
- **Endowment** $817,811
- **Coed,** 18,240 undergraduate students

Freshmen *Admission:* 11,385 applied, 11,385 admitted.
Faculty *Total:* 534, 53% full-time. *Student/faculty ratio:* 40:1.
Majors Accounting; administrative assistant and secretarial science; agricultural business and management; agricultural mechanization; agricultural production; agriculture; agronomy and crop science; animal sciences; apparel and textiles; architectural engineering technology; art; autobody/collision and repair technology; automobile/automotive mechanics technology; banking and financial support services; behavioral sciences; biology/biological sciences; building/home/construction inspection; business administration and management; child

care and support services management; child care provision; child development; commercial and advertising art; communications systems installation and repair technology; computer graphics; computer/information technology services administration related; computer installation and repair technology; computer science; construction management; corrections; criminal justice/law enforcement administration; criminal justice/police science; dairy science; data entry/microcomputer applications; dental assisting; drafting and design technology; dramatic/theater arts; electrical, electronic and communications engineering technology; electrical/electronics equipment installation and repair; emergency medical technology (EMT paramedic); engineering; English; family and consumer economics related; fashion merchandising; finance; fire science; food science; food services technology; foreign languages and literatures; forestry; forestry technology; general studies; graphic and printing equipment operation/production; heating, air conditioning, ventilation and refrigeration maintenance technology; housing and human environments; humanities; human services; industrial arts; industrial electronics technology; interior design; kindergarten/preschool education; landscape architecture; machine shop technology; machine tool technology; management information systems; marketing/marketing management; mass communication/media; mathematics; medical/clinical assistant; music; nursing assistant/aide and patient care assistant; nursing (registered nurse training); office management; office occupations and clerical services; ornamental horticulture; parks, recreation and leisure facilities management; photography; physical education teaching and coaching; plant nursery management; poultry science; radio and television; real estate; respiratory care therapy; social sciences; special products marketing; speech and rhetoric; welding technology; word processing.

Academics *Calendar:* semesters. *Degree:* certificates and associate. *Special study options:* academic remediation for entering students, adult/continuing education programs, advanced placement credit, cooperative education, distance learning, English as a second language, honors programs, independent study, part-time degree program, services for LD students, study abroad, summer session for credit.

Library Modesto Junior College Library with 69,865 titles, 4,161 audiovisual materials, an OPAC, a Web page.

Computers on Campus 95 computers available on campus for general student use. A campuswide network can be accessed from off campus. Internet access, at least one staffed computer lab available.

Student Life *Housing:* college housing not available. *Activities and Organizations:* drama/theater group, student-run newspaper, radio and television station, choral group, Young Farmers, Red Nations, Psychology Club, Alpha Gamma Sigma, MECHA. *Campus security:* 24-hour emergency response devices and patrols, late-night transport/escort service. *Student services:* health clinic, personal/psychological counseling.

Athletics *Intercollegiate sports:* baseball M, basketball M/W, cross-country running M/W, football M, golf M, gymnastics W, soccer M/W, softball W, swimming and diving M/W, tennis M/W, track and field M/W, volleyball W, water polo M/W, wrestling M. *Intramural sports:* basketball M/W, football M, softball W, table tennis M/W, tennis M/W, volleyball M/W.

Costs (2006–07) *Tuition:* state resident $0 full-time; nonresident $3840 full-time, $160 per unit part-time. *Required fees:* $664 full-time, $26 per unit part-time, $40 per year part-time.

Financial Aid Of all full-time matriculated undergraduates who enrolled in 2004, 152 Federal Work-Study jobs (averaging $2732). 62 state and other part-time jobs (averaging $1655).

Applying *Options:* electronic application. *Recommended:* high school transcript. *Application deadline:* rolling (freshmen), rolling (transfers). *Notification:* continuous (freshmen).

Freshmen Application Contact Ms. Susie Agostini, Dean of Matriculation, Admissions, and Records, Modesto Junior College, 435 College Avenue, Modesto, CA 95350. *Phone:* 209-575-6470. *Fax:* 209-575-6859. *E-mail:* mjcadmissions@mail.yosemite.cc.ca.us.

MONTEREY PENINSULA COLLEGE
Monterey, California   www.mpc.edu/

Director of Admissions Ms. Vera Coleman, Registrar, Monterey Peninsula College, 980 Fremont Street, Monterey, CA 93940. *Phone:* 831-646-4007. *E-mail:* vcoleman@mpc.edu.

MOORPARK COLLEGE
Moorpark, California   www.moorpark.cc.ca.us/

Freshmen Application Contact Ms. Kathy Colborn, Registrar, Moorpark College, 7075 Campus Road, Moorpark, CA 93021-2899. *Phone:* 805-378-1415.

MT. SAN ANTONIO COLLEGE

Walnut, California www.mtsac.edu/

- **District-supported** 2-year, founded 1946, part of California Community College System
- **Suburban** 421-acre campus with easy access to Los Angeles
- **Coed,** 27,195 undergraduate students, 32% full-time, 55% women, 45% men

Undergraduates 8,567 full-time, 18,628 part-time. Students come from 51 states and territories, 6% African American, 24% Asian American or Pacific Islander, 44% Hispanic American, 0.5% Native American, 1% international. Freshmen *Admission:* 3,089 enrolled.

Faculty *Total:* 1,222, 30% full-time.

Majors Accounting; administrative assistant and secretarial science; advertising; agricultural business and management; agricultural mechanization; agriculture; agronomy and crop science; airframe mechanics and aircraft maintenance technology; airline pilot and flight crew; air traffic control; animal sciences; apparel and textiles; architectural engineering technology; avionics maintenance technology; business administration and management; business teacher education; child development; civil engineering technology; commercial and advertising art; computer engineering technology; computer graphics; computer science; construction management; corrections; criminal justice/police science; dairy science; data processing and data processing technology; drafting and design technology; electrical, electronic and communications engineering technology; emergency medical technology (EMT paramedic); engineering technology; family and consumer sciences/human sciences; fashion merchandising; finance; fire science; forestry technology; heating, air conditioning, ventilation and refrigeration maintenance technology; horticultural science; hotel/motel administration; industrial arts; industrial design; industrial radiologic technology; interior design; journalism; kindergarten/preschool education; landscape architecture; legal administrative assistant/secretary; legal assistant/paralegal; liberal arts and sciences/liberal studies; machine tool technology; marketing/marketing management; materials science; mechanical design technology; medical administrative assistant and medical secretary; mental health/rehabilitation; nursing (registered nurse training); occupational safety and health technology; ornamental horticulture; parks, recreation and leisure; parks, recreation and leisure facilities management; photography; physical sciences related; pre-engineering; quality control technology; radio and television; real estate; respiratory care therapy; sign language interpretation and translation; survey technology; transportation technology; welding technology; wildlife and wildlands science and management.

Academics *Calendar:* semesters. *Degree:* certificates, diplomas, and associate. *Special study options:* academic remediation for entering students, adult/continuing education programs, cooperative education, distance learning, English as a second language, honors programs, part-time degree program, services for LD students, study abroad, summer session for credit.

Library Learning Resources Center with 64,291 titles, 753 serial subscriptions, 6,494 audiovisual materials, an OPAC, a Web page.

Computers on Campus 1200 computers available on campus for general student use. A campuswide network can be accessed from off campus. Internet access, at least one staffed computer lab available.

Student Life *Activities and Organizations:* drama/theater group, student-run radio station, choral group, Alpha Gamma Sigma, Muslim Student Association, student government, Asian Student Association, Kasama-Filipino Student Organization. *Campus security:* 24-hour emergency response devices and patrols, late-night transport/escort service. *Student services:* health clinic, personal/psychological counseling, women's center, legal services.

Athletics *Intercollegiate sports:* badminton W, baseball M, basketball M/W, cross-country running M/W, football M, golf M/W, soccer M/W, softball W, swimming and diving M/W, tennis M/W, track and field M/W, volleyball M/W, water polo M/W, wrestling M.

Costs (2005–06) *Tuition:* state resident $0 full-time; nonresident $4248 full-time, $177 per term part-time. *Required fees:* $672 full-time, $26 per unit part-time, $24 per term part-time.

Financial Aid Of all full-time matriculated undergraduates who enrolled in 2004, 250 Federal Work-Study jobs (averaging $2898).

Applying *Options:* early admission, deferred entrance. *Required for some:* high school transcript. *Notification:* continuous (freshmen).

Freshmen Application Contact Mr. James Ocampo, Interim Director of Admissions and Records, Mt. San Antonio College, 1100 North Grand Avenue, Walnut, CA 91789. *Phone:* 909-594-5611 Ext. 4415. *Toll-free phone:* 800-672-2463 Ext. 4415. *E-mail:* admissions@mtsac.edu.

MT. SAN JACINTO COLLEGE

San Jacinto, California www.msjc.edu/

Freshmen Application Contact Ms. Susan Loomis, Supervisor, Enrollment Services, Mt. San Jacinto College, 1499 North State Street, San Jacinto, CA 92583-2399. *Phone:* 909-672-6752 Ext. 2401. *Toll-free phone:* 800-624-5561 Ext. 1410.

MTI COLLEGE OF BUSINESS AND TECHNOLOGY

Sacramento, California www.mticollege.com/

- **Proprietary** 2-year, founded 1965
- **Coed,** 600 undergraduate students

Majors Accounting; business administration and management; computer technology/computer systems technology; legal administrative assistant/secretary; medical office management.

Academics *Calendar:* continuous. *Degree:* diplomas and associate.

Standardized Tests *Required:* MTI Assessment (for admission).

Financial Aid Of all full-time matriculated undergraduates who enrolled in 2004, 35 Federal Work-Study jobs (averaging $1722).

Applying *Application fee:* $75.

Freshmen Application Contact Ms. Marije Miller, Director of Admissions, MTI College of Business and Technology, 5221 Madison Avenue, Sacramento, CA 95841. *Phone:* 916-339-1500. *Fax:* 916-339-0305. *E-mail:* mmiller@mticollege.edu.

NAPA VALLEY COLLEGE

Napa, California www.napavalley.edu/

- **State and locally supported** 2-year, founded 1942, part of California Community College System
- **Suburban** 188-acre campus with easy access to San Francisco
- **Coed**

Undergraduates 1,909 full-time, 4,999 part-time. 8% African American, 18% Asian American or Pacific Islander, 20% Hispanic American, 1% Native American. *Retention:* 66% of 2003 full-time freshmen returned.

Faculty *Student/faculty ratio:* 22:1.

Academics *Calendar:* semesters. *Degree:* certificates and associate. *Special study options:* academic remediation for entering students, advanced placement credit, cooperative education, distance learning, English as a second language, part-time degree program, services for LD students, study abroad, summer session for credit.

Student Life *Campus security:* late-night transport/escort service.

Athletics Member NJCAA.

Standardized Tests *Required for some:* SAT or ACT (for placement).

Costs (2005–06) *Tuition:* state resident $0 full-time; nonresident $3624 full-time, $151 per unit part-time. Full-time tuition and fees vary according to course load. Part-time tuition and fees vary according to course load. *Required fees:* $648 full-time, $26 per unit part-time, $12 per term part-time.

Financial Aid *Financial aid deadline:* 3/2.

Applying *Required for some:* high school transcript.

Director of Admissions Dr. Edward Shenk, Vice President of Student Services, Napa Valley College, 2277 Napa-Vallejo Highway, Napa, CA 94558-6236. *Phone:* 707-253-3000. *E-mail:* eshenk@napavalley.edu.

NATIONAL POLYTECHNIC COLLEGE OF ENGINEERING AND OCEANEERING

Wilmington, California www.coo.edu/

Director of Admissions Ms. Deborah Montgomery, Director of Admissions, National Polytechnic College of Engineering and Oceaneering, 272 South Fries Avenue, Wilmington, CA 90744-6399. *Phone:* 310-834-2501 Ext. 237. *Toll-free phone:* 800-432-DIVE Ext. 237.

NORTHROP RICE AVIATION INSTITUTE OF TECHNOLOGY

Inglewood, California   www.nrait.edu/

Director of Admissions Mr. James Michael Rice, Chief Administrative Officer, Northrop Rice Aviation Institute of Technology, 1155 West Arbor Vitae Street, Suite 115, Inglewood, CA 90301-2904. *Phone:* 310-568-8541. *Fax:* 310-568-8542. *E-mail:* info@nrait.edu.

NORTHWESTERN TECHNICAL COLLEGE

Sacramento, California   www.ntcollege.com/

Director of Admissions Mr. Robert Naylor, Director of Admissions, Northwestern Technical College, 1825 Bell Street, #100, Sacramento, CA 95825. *Phone:* 916-649-2400. *Toll-free phone:* 866-649-2400. *E-mail:* rnaylor@ntcollege.com.

OHLONE COLLEGE

Fremont, California   www.ohlone.edu/

Director of Admissions Ms. Allison Hill, Director, Admissions and Records, Ohlone College, 43600 Mission Boulevard, Fremont, CA 94539-5884. *Phone:* 510-659-6108. *Fax:* 510-659-7321.

ORANGE COAST COLLEGE

Costa Mesa, California   www.orangecoastcollege.com/

- **State and locally supported** 2-year, founded 1947, part of Coast Community College District System
- **Suburban** 200-acre campus with easy access to Los Angeles
- **Endowment** $5.1 million
- **Coed,** 24,350 undergraduate students, 44% full-time, 50% women, 50% men

Undergraduates 10,671 full-time, 13,679 part-time. Students come from 52 states and territories, 76 other countries, 2% are from out of state, 2% African American, 24% Asian American or Pacific Islander, 18% Hispanic American, 0.6% Native American, 2% international, 8% transferred in. *Retention:* 79% of 2003 full-time freshmen returned.
Freshmen *Admission:* 4,193 enrolled.
Faculty *Total:* 940, 32% full-time. *Student/faculty ratio:* 20:1.
Majors Accounting; administrative assistant and secretarial science; aeronautics/aviation/aerospace science and technology; airline pilot and flight crew; anthropology; architectural engineering technology; art; athletic training; avionics maintenance technology; behavioral sciences; biology/biological sciences; building/home/construction inspection; business administration and management; cardiovascular technology; chemistry; child care and support services management; child care provision; cinematography and film/video production; clinical laboratory science/medical technology; commercial and advertising art; communications technology; computer engineering technology; computer graphics; computer programming; computer programming (specific applications); computer typography and composition equipment operation; construction engineering technology; culinary arts; cultural studies; dance; data entry/microcomputer applications related; data processing and data processing technology; dental hygiene; dietetics; drafting and design technology; dramatic/theater arts; economics; electrical and power transmission installation; electrical, electronic and communications engineering technology; electrical/electronics equipment installation and repair; emergency medical technology (EMT paramedic); engineering; English; family and consumer economics related; family and consumer sciences/human sciences; fashion merchandising; film/cinema studies; food science; food services technology; foods, nutrition, and wellness; French; general retailing/wholesaling; geography; geology/earth science; German; health science; heating, air conditioning, ventilation and refrigeration maintenance technology; history; horticultural science; hotel/motel administration; housing and human environments; human development and family studies; humanities; industrial design; industrial radiologic technology; information science/studies; interior design; journalism; kindergarten/preschool education; kinesiology and exercise science; legal administrative assistant/secretary; liberal arts and sciences/liberal studies; machine shop technology; machine tool technology; marine technology; marketing/marketing management; mass communication/media; mathematics; medical

administrative assistant and medical secretary; medical/clinical assistant; music; musical instrument fabrication and repair; music management and merchandising; natural sciences; nuclear medical technology; ornamental horticulture; philosophy; photography; physical education teaching and coaching; physics; political science and government; religious studies; respiratory care therapy; restaurant, culinary, and catering management; retailing; selling skills and sales; social sciences; sociology; Spanish; special products marketing; welding technology; word processing.
Academics *Calendar:* semesters plus summer session. *Degree:* certificates and associate. *Special study options:* academic remediation for entering students, adult/continuing education programs, advanced placement credit, cooperative education, distance learning, double majors, English as a second language, external degree program, freshman honors college, honors programs, internships, off-campus study, part-time degree program, services for LD students, student-designed majors, study abroad, summer session for credit. *ROTC:* Army (c), Air Force (c).
Library Norman E. Watson Library with 84,447 titles, 420 serial subscriptions, 2,510 audiovisual materials, an OPAC, a Web page.
Computers on Campus 1515 computers available on campus for general student use. A campuswide network can be accessed from off campus. Internet access, at least one staffed computer lab available.
Student Life *Housing:* college housing not available. *Activities and Organizations:* drama/theater group, student-run newspaper, choral group, Vietnamese Student Association, International Club, Adventurist Souls, Muslim Student Association. *Campus security:* 24-hour emergency response devices and patrols, student patrols, late-night transport/escort service. *Student services:* health clinic, personal/psychological counseling, legal services.
Athletics *Intercollegiate sports:* baseball M, basketball M/W, bowling M(c)/W(c), crew M/W, cross-country running M/W, football M, golf M/W, soccer M/W, softball W, swimming and diving M/W, tennis M/W, track and field M/W, volleyball M/W, water polo M/W.
Costs (2006–07) *Tuition:* nonresident $152 per unit part-time. *Required fees:* $26 per unit part-time, $28 per term part-time.
Financial Aid Of all full-time matriculated undergraduates who enrolled in 2004, 108 Federal Work-Study jobs (averaging $3000). *Financial aid deadline:* 5/28.
Applying *Options:* common application. *Application deadline:* rolling (freshmen), rolling (transfers). *Notification:* continuous (freshmen).
Freshmen Application Contact Ms. Nancy Kidder, Administrative Dean of Admissions and Records, Orange Coast College, 2701 Fairview Road, Costa Mesa, CA 92626. *Phone:* 714-432-5788. *Fax:* 714-432-5072. *E-mail:* nkidder@cccd.edu.

OXNARD COLLEGE

Oxnard, California   www.oxnard.cc.ca.us/

Director of Admissions Ms. Susan O. Brent, Registrar, Oxnard College, 4000 South Rose Avenue, Oxnard, CA 93033-6699. *Phone:* 805-986-5843.

PALOMAR COLLEGE

San Marcos, California   www.palomar.edu/

Director of Admissions Mr. Herman Lee, Director of Enrollment Services, Palomar College, 1140 West Mission Road, San Marcos, CA 92069-1487. *Phone:* 760-744-1150 Ext. 2171. *E-mail:* hlee@palomar.edu.

PALO VERDE COLLEGE

Blythe, California   www.paloverde.edu/

- **State and locally supported** 2-year, founded 1947, part of California Community College System
- **Small-town** 10-acre campus
- **Coed,** 3,648 undergraduate students, 100% full-time, 36% women, 64% men

Undergraduates 3,648 full-time. Students come from 4 states and territories, 3 other countries, 9% African American, 4% Asian American or Pacific Islander, 30% Hispanic American, 2% Native American.
Freshmen *Admission:* 300 applied, 300 admitted.
Faculty *Total:* 161, 20% full-time.
Majors Accounting; administrative assistant and secretarial science; agriculture; automobile/automotive mechanics technology; behavioral sciences; biology/

Palo Verde College (continued)

biological sciences; business administration and management; child guidance; computer and information sciences; construction trades related; criminal justice/law enforcement administration; criminal justice/police science; developmental and child psychology; economics; education; English; entrepreneurship; forestry; general studies; health science; history; interior design; kindergarten/preschool education; liberal arts and sciences/liberal studies; marketing/marketing management; political science and government; pre-engineering; psychology; sociology; transportation and materials moving related.

Academics *Calendar:* semesters. *Degree:* associate. *Special study options:* academic remediation for entering students, adult/continuing education programs, advanced placement credit, English as a second language, internships, part-time degree program, services for LD students, summer session for credit.

Library Palo Verde College Library with 21,457 titles, 165 serial subscriptions.

Computers on Campus 25 computers available on campus for general student use. At least one staffed computer lab available.

Student Life *Housing:* college housing not available. *Activities and Organizations:* drama/theater group, student-run newspaper, Extended Opportunity Program and Services Club, Associated Student Body. *Campus security:* student patrols, security personnel during open hours. *Student services:* personal/psychological counseling.

Costs (2005–06) *Tuition:* nonresident $4248 full-time, $177 per unit part-time. *Required fees:* $624 full-time, $26 per unit part-time.

Financial Aid Of all full-time matriculated undergraduates who enrolled in 2004, 30 Federal Work-Study jobs (averaging $1000).

Applying *Options:* early admission. *Recommended:* high school transcript. *Application deadline:* rolling (freshmen), rolling (transfers). *Notification:* continuous (freshmen).

Freshmen Application Contact Ms. Pat Koester, Vice President of Student Services, Palo Verde College, 1 College Drive, Blythe, CA 92225. *Phone:* 760-921-5409. *Fax:* 760-921-3608.

PASADENA CITY COLLEGE

Pasadena, California   www.pasadena.edu/

- **State and locally supported** 2-year, founded 1924, part of California Community College System
- **Urban** 55-acre campus with easy access to Los Angeles
- **Coed,** 29,189 undergraduate students, 100% full-time, 56% women, 44% men

Undergraduates 29,189 full-time. Students come from 15 states and territories, 6% African American, 30% Asian American or Pacific Islander, 34% Hispanic American, 0.6% Native American.

Faculty *Total:* 1,325, 30% full-time. *Student/faculty ratio:* 20:1.

Majors Accounting; administrative assistant and secretarial science; advertising; African-American/Black studies; African studies; airline pilot and flight crew; anthropology; architectural engineering technology; art; art history, criticism and conservation; astronomy; automobile/automotive mechanics technology; aviation/airway management; avionics maintenance technology; biological and physical sciences; biology/biological sciences; broadcast journalism; business administration and management; business teacher education; carpentry; ceramic arts and ceramics; ceramic sciences and engineering; chemistry; civil engineering technology; communications technology; computer engineering technology; computer programming; computer science; computer typography and composition equipment operation; construction engineering technology; cosmetology; criminal justice/law enforcement administration; cultural studies; data processing and data processing technology; dental hygiene; developmental and child psychology; drafting and design technology; dramatic/theater arts; drawing; economics; electrical, electronic and communications engineering technology; engineering; engineering technology; English; fashion merchandising; fiber, textile and weaving arts; finance; fire science; forestry technology; French; geography; geology/earth science; German; Hispanic-American, Puerto Rican, and Mexican-American/Chicano studies; history; human services; industrial radiologic technology; information science/studies; interdisciplinary studies; interior design; journalism; kindergarten/preschool education; landscape architecture; Latin American studies; legal administrative assistant/secretary; legal studies; liberal arts and sciences/liberal studies; library science; machine tool technology; marketing/marketing management; mass communication/media; mathematics; mechanical engineering/mechanical technology; medical/clinical assistant; metal and jewelry arts; Mexican-American studies; modern languages; music; music therapy; nursing (licensed practical/vocational nurse training); nursing (registered nurse training); occupational therapy; parks, recreation and leisure; pharmacy; philosophy; photography; physical education teaching and coaching; physical sciences; physics; political science and government; psychology; radio and television; real estate; religious studies; sign language interpretation and translation; social sciences; sociology; Spanish; speech and rhetoric; statistics; teacher assistant/aide; telecommunications; tourism and travel services management; veterinary sciences; welding technology.

Academics *Calendar:* semesters. *Degree:* certificates and associate. *Special study options:* academic remediation for entering students, adult/continuing education programs, advanced placement credit, English as a second language, honors programs, part-time degree program, services for LD students, student-designed majors, study abroad, summer session for credit.

Library Pasadena City College Library plus 1 other with 120,000 titles, 350 serial subscriptions, an OPAC.

Computers on Campus 300 computers available on campus for general student use. At least one staffed computer lab available.

Student Life *Housing:* college housing not available. *Activities and Organizations:* drama/theater group, student-run newspaper, radio station, choral group, marching band. *Campus security:* 24-hour emergency response devices and patrols, late-night transport/escort service, cadet patrols. *Student services:* health clinic, personal/psychological counseling, women's center.

Athletics *Intercollegiate sports:* baseball M, basketball M/W, cross-country running M/W, football M, soccer M/W, softball W, swimming and diving M/W, tennis M/W, track and field M/W, volleyball W, water polo M.

Costs (2006–07) *Tuition:* state resident $0 full-time; nonresident $5000 full-time, $160 per unit part-time. *Required fees:* $780 full-time, $26 per unit part-time.

Applying *Options:* early admission, deferred entrance. *Application deadline:* rolling (freshmen), rolling (transfers). *Notification:* continuous (freshmen).

Freshmen Application Contact Ms. Carol Kaser, Supervisor of Admissions and Records, Pasadena City College, 1570 East Colorado Boulevard, Pasadena, CA 91106. *Phone:* 626-585-7397. *Fax:* 626-585-7915.

PIMA MEDICAL INSTITUTE

Chula Vista, California   www.pmi.edu

- **Proprietary** 2-year, administratively affiliated with Vocational Training Institutes, Inc
- **Urban** campus
- **Coed**

Undergraduates 447 full-time. Students come from 1 other state.

Faculty *Student/faculty ratio:* 14:1.

Academics *Calendar:* modular. *Degree:* certificates and associate. *Special study options:* cooperative education, internships.

Standardized Tests *Required:* Wonderlic Scholastic Level Exam (for admission).

Costs (2005–06) *Tuition:* No tuition increase for student's term of enrollment. Tuition varies depending on course. *Payment plans:* tuition prepayment, installment.

Applying *Options:* common application. *Application fee:* $100. *Required:* high school transcript, interview.

Freshmen Application Contact Admissions Office, Pima Medical Institute, Pima Medical Institute, 780 Bay Boulevard, Suite 101, Chula Vista, CA 91910. *Phone:* 619-425-3200. *Toll-free phone:* 888-898-9048.

PLATT COLLEGE

Cerritos, California   www.platt.edu/

Freshmen Application Contact Ms. Ilene Holt, Dean of Student Services, Platt College, 10900 East 183rd Street, Suite 290, Cerritos, CA 90703-5342. *Phone:* 562-809-5100. *Toll-free phone:* 800-807-5288.

PLATT COLLEGE

Newport Beach, California   www.plattcollege.edu/

Director of Admissions Ms. Lisa Rhodes, President, Platt College, 3901 MacArthur Boulevard, Suite 101, Newport Beach, CA 92660. *Phone:* 949-833-2300 Ext. 222. *Toll-free phone:* 888-866-6697 Ext. 230.

PLATT COLLEGE

Ontario, California   www.plattcollege.edu/

Director of Admissions Ms. Jennifer Abandonato, Director of Admissions, Platt College, 3700 Inland Empire Boulevard, Ontario, CA 91764. *Phone:* 909-941-9410. *Toll-free phone:* 888-866-6697.

PLATT COLLEGE–LOS ANGELES, INC

Alhambra, California　　　　www.plattcollege.edu/

Director of Admissions Mr. Detroit Whiteside, Director of Admissions, Platt College–Los Angeles, Inc, 7470 North Figueroa Street, Los Angeles, CA 90041-1717. *Phone:* 323-258-8050. *Toll-free phone:* 888-866-6697.

PLATT COLLEGE SAN DIEGO

San Diego, California　　　　www.platt.edu/

- **Proprietary** primarily 2-year, founded 1879
- **Suburban** campus with easy access to San Diego
- **Coed,** 253 undergraduate students, 100% full-time, 24% women, 76% men

Platt College offers a B.S. degree in media arts; A.A.S. degrees in multimedia design and graphic design; specialized diplomas in DV production, 3-D animation, and Web design; and diplomas in multimedia and graphic design. Career services assistance and financial aid (for those who qualify) are available. For further information, students should call 866-PLATTCOLLEGE (toll-free) or visit http://www.platt.edu.

Undergraduates 253 full-time. Students come from 4 states and territories, 2 other countries, 5% are from out of state, 6% African American, 8% Asian American or Pacific Islander, 20% Hispanic American. *Retention:* 72% of 2003 full-time freshmen returned.
Freshmen *Admission:* 106 admitted, 106 enrolled.
Faculty *Total:* 30, 17% full-time, 3% with terminal degrees. *Student/faculty ratio:* 20:1.
Majors Animation, interactive technology, video graphics and special effects; commercial and advertising art; computer graphics; computer software and media applications related; digital communication and media/multimedia; graphic design; intermedia/multimedia; web/multimedia management and webmaster; Web page, digital/multimedia and information resources design.
Academics *Calendar:* continuous. *Degrees:* certificates, diplomas, associate, and bachelor's.
Student Life *Housing:* college housing not available. *Campus security:* 24-hour emergency response devices, video camera. *Student services:* personal/psychological counseling.
Costs (2006–07) *Tuition:* $17,226 full-time. *Required fees:* $110 full-time.
Applying *Application fee:* $110. *Required:* high school transcript, interview, Wonderlic aptitude test.
Freshmen Application Contact Mr. Craig Hinson, Admissions Representative, Platt College San Diego, 6250 El Cajon Boulevard, San Diego, CA 92115-3919. *Phone:* 619-265-0107. *Toll-free phone:* 866-752-8826. *Fax:* 619-265-8655. *E-mail:* chinson@platt.edu.

PORTERVILLE COLLEGE

Porterville, California　　　　www.pc.cc.ca.us/

Director of Admissions Ms. Judy Pope, Director of Admissions and Records/Registrar, Porterville College, 100 East College Avenue, Porterville, CA 93257-6058. *Phone:* 559-791-2222.

PROFESSIONAL GOLFERS CAREER COLLEGE

Temecula, California　　　　www.golfcollege.edu/

- **Independent** 2-year
- **Coed, primarily men**
- 100% of applicants were admitted

Undergraduates 318 full-time. Students come from 50 states and territories, 13 other countries, 75% are from out of state, 1% African American, 26% Asian American or Pacific Islander, 4% Hispanic American, 2% Native American.
Faculty *Student/faculty ratio:* 15:1.
Academics *Calendar:* semesters. *Degree:* associate. *Special study options:* English as a second language.

Costs (2005–06) *Tuition:* $14,370 full-time. Full-time tuition and fees vary according to student level. *Required fees:* $475 full-time. *Room only:* $2525. Room and board charges vary according to location.
Applying *Options:* early admission, deferred entrance. *Application fee:* $75. *Required:* high school transcript, 4 letters of recommendation.
Director of Admissions Mr. David Ober, Director of Admissions, Professional Golfers Career College, PO Box 892319, 261 Ynez Road, Temecula, CA 92589-2319. *Phone:* 951-693-2963 Ext. 19. *Toll-free phone:* 800-877-4380.

QUEEN OF THE HOLY ROSARY COLLEGE

Mission San Jose, California　　　　www.msjdominicans.org/college.html

Director of Admissions Sr. Mary Paul Mehegan, Dean of the College, Queen of the Holy Rosary College, 43326 Mission Boulevard, PO Box 3908, Mission San Jose, CA 94539. *Phone:* 510-657-2468 Ext. 322.

REEDLEY COLLEGE

Reedley, California　　　　www.reedleycollege.com/

Director of Admissions Ms. Leticia Alvarez, Admissions and Records Manager, Reedley College, 995 North Reed Avenue, Reedley, CA 93654. *Phone:* 559-638-0323 Ext. 3624.

RIO HONDO COLLEGE

Whittier, California　　　　www.rh.cc.ca.us/

Director of Admissions Ms. Judy G. Pearson, Director of Admissions and Records, Rio Hondo College, 3600 Workman Mill Road, Whittier, CA 90601-1699. *Phone:* 562-692-0921 Ext. 3153.

RIVERSIDE COMMUNITY COLLEGE DISTRICT

Riverside, California　　　　www.rcc.edu/

- **State and locally supported** 2-year, founded 1916, part of California Community College System
- **Suburban** 108-acre campus with easy access to Los Angeles
- **Coed,** 30,390 undergraduate students, 29% full-time, 57% women, 43% men

Undergraduates 8,701 full-time, 21,689 part-time. Students come from 23 states and territories, 60 other countries, 14% African American, 11% Asian American or Pacific Islander, 35% Hispanic American, 0.6% Native American, 2% transferred in.
Freshmen *Admission:* 1,081 applied, 1,081 admitted, 1,081 enrolled.
Faculty *Total:* 1,376, 23% full-time. *Student/faculty ratio:* 22:1.
Majors Autobody/collision and repair technology; automobile/automotive mechanics technology; business administration and management; cinematography and film/video production; computer programming; computer programming related; construction engineering technology; cosmetology; criminal justice/law enforcement administration; culinary arts; fire science; graphic and printing equipment operation/production; heating, air conditioning and refrigeration technology; liberal arts and sciences/liberal studies; nursing (licensed practical/vocational nurse training); nursing (registered nurse training); office management; paralegal/legal assistant; photography; retail management; sign language interpretation and translation; welding technology.
Academics *Calendar:* semesters. *Degree:* certificates and associate. *Special study options:* academic remediation for entering students, adult/continuing education programs, advanced placement credit, distance learning, double majors, English as a second language, internships, part-time degree program, services for LD students, study abroad, summer session for credit. *ROTC:* Army (c), Air Force (c).
Library Digital Library Learning Resource Center with 101,243 titles, 911 serial subscriptions, 5,417 audiovisual materials, an OPAC, a Web page.

Riverside Community College District (continued)

Computers on Campus 200 computers available on campus for general student use. A campuswide network can be accessed from off campus. Internet access, at least one staffed computer lab available.

Student Life *Housing:* college housing not available. *Activities and Organizations:* drama/theater group, student-run newspaper, radio station, choral group, marching band, Marching Tigers Band, Wind Ensemble, Student Nurses Organization, Gospel Singers, Alpha Gamma Sigma. *Campus security:* 24-hour patrols, late-night transport/escort service. *Student services:* health clinic, personal/psychological counseling.

Athletics *Intercollegiate sports:* baseball M, basketball M/W, cross-country running M/W, football M, golf M, soccer M/W, softball W, swimming and diving M/W, tennis M/W, track and field M/W, volleyball W, water polo M/W. *Intramural sports:* badminton M/W, basketball M/W, bowling M/W, football M, golf M/W, racquetball M/W, soccer M/W, tennis M/W, volleyball M/W, weight lifting M/W.

Costs (2005–06) *Tuition:* state resident $0 full-time; nonresident $6090 full-time, $203 per unit part-time. *Required fees:* $820 full-time, $26 per unit part-time, $20 per term part-time.

Applying *Required:* high school transcript. *Application deadline:* rolling (freshmen), rolling (transfers). *Notification:* continuous (freshmen).

Freshmen Application Contact Ms. Lorraine Anderson, District Dean of Admissions and Records, Riverside Community College District, 4800 Magnolia Avenue, Riverside, CA 92506. *Phone:* 951-222-8600. *Fax:* 951-222-8037. *E-mail:* admissions@rcc.edu.

SACRAMENTO CITY COLLEGE

Sacramento, California　　　　**www.scc.losrios.edu/**

Director of Admissions Mr. Sam T. Sandusky, Dean, Student Services, Sacramento City College, 3835 Freeport Boulevard, Sacramento, CA 95822-1386. *Phone:* 916-558-2438.

SADDLEBACK COLLEGE

Mission Viejo, California　　　　**www.saddleback.cc.ca.us/**

- **State and locally supported** 2-year, founded 1967
- **Suburban** 200-acre campus with easy access to Los Angeles and San Diego
- **Coed,** 18,351 undergraduate students, 35% full-time, 56% women, 44% men

Undergraduates 6,337 full-time, 12,014 part-time. Students come from 37 states and territories, 23 other countries, 2% African American, 11% Asian American or Pacific Islander, 14% Hispanic American, 0.6% Native American, 1% international.

Faculty *Total:* 754, 29% full-time.

Majors Accounting; administrative assistant and secretarial science; American studies; anthropology; architectural engineering technology; art; astronomy; automobile/automotive mechanics technology; biology/biological sciences; business administration and management; carpentry; chemical engineering; chemistry; child development; cinematography and film/video production; commercial and advertising art; computer and information sciences; computer programming; computer science; computer typography and composition equipment operation; construction engineering technology; consumer merchandising/retailing management; consumer services and advocacy; cosmetology; developmental and child psychology; drafting and design technology; dramatic/theater arts; economics; electrical, electronic and communications engineering technology; emergency medical technology (EMT paramedic); engineering; environmental studies; family and community services; family and consumer sciences/human sciences; fashion/apparel design; fashion merchandising; food science; food services technology; foods, nutrition, and wellness; geography; geology/earth science; gerontology; history; horticultural science; human development and family studies; humanities; human services; industrial arts; information science/studies; interior design; journalism; kindergarten/preschool education; landscape architecture; legal administrative assistant/secretary; legal assistant/paralegal; legal studies; liberal arts and sciences/liberal studies; literature; marine science/merchant marine officer; marine technology; mathematics; medical/clinical assistant; music; natural sciences; nursing (registered nurse training); ornamental horticulture; philosophy; photography; physical education teaching and coaching; physical sciences; physics; political science and government; pre-engineering; psychology; radio and television; real estate; social sciences; sociology; special products marketing; speech and rhetoric; substance abuse/addiction counseling; teacher assistant/aide; tourism and travel services management; women's studies.

Academics *Calendar:* semesters. *Degree:* certificates and associate. *Special study options:* academic remediation for entering students, adult/continuing education programs, advanced placement credit, cooperative education, distance learning, English as a second language, honors programs, off-campus study, part-time degree program, services for LD students, study abroad, summer session for credit.

Library James B. Utt Memorial Library with 109,000 titles, 132 serial subscriptions.

Computers on Campus 200 computers available on campus for general student use. A campuswide network can be accessed. Internet access, at least one staffed computer lab available.

Student Life *Housing:* college housing not available. *Activities and Organizations:* drama/theater group, student-run newspaper, radio station, choral group. *Campus security:* 24-hour emergency response devices and patrols, late-night transport/escort service. *Student services:* health clinic, personal/psychological counseling, women's center, legal services.

Athletics *Intercollegiate sports:* baseball M, basketball M/W, cross-country running M/W, football M, golf M/W, softball W, swimming and diving M/W, tennis M/W, track and field M/W, volleyball W, water polo M/W. *Intramural sports:* soccer M/W.

Costs (2006–07) *Tuition:* nonresident $178 per unit part-time. *Required fees:* $26 per unit part-time, $14 per term part-time.

Financial Aid Of all full-time matriculated undergraduates who enrolled in 2004, 125 Federal Work-Study jobs (averaging $4000). 125 state and other part-time jobs.

Applying *Options:* early admission. *Application deadline:* rolling (freshmen), rolling (transfers).

Freshmen Application Contact Admissions Office, Saddleback College, 28000 Marguerite Parkway, Mission Viejo, CA 92692-3635. *Phone:* 949-582-4555. *Fax:* 949-347-8315. *E-mail:* earaiza@saddleback.edu.

SAGE COLLEGE

Moreno Valley, California

THE SALVATION ARMY COLLEGE FOR OFFICER TRAINING AT CRESTMONT

Rancho Palos Verdes, California　　　　**www.crestmont.edu/**

- **Independent religious** 2-year, founded 1878, administratively affiliated with The Salvation Army
- **Suburban** 44-acre campus with easy access to Los Angeles
- **Endowment** $85.5 million
- **Coed,** 27 undergraduate students, 100% full-time, 52% women, 48% men

Undergraduates 27 full-time. Students come from 14 states and territories, 1 other country, 67% are from out of state, 7% African American, 15% Asian American or Pacific Islander, 30% Hispanic American, 7% international, 100% live on campus. *Retention:* 98% of 2003 full-time freshmen returned. Freshmen *Admission:* 21 applied, 14 admitted, 5 enrolled.

Faculty *Total:* 35, 37% full-time, 23% with terminal degrees. *Student/faculty ratio:* 1:1.

Majors Divinity/ministry.

Academics *Calendar:* quarters. *Degree:* associate. *Special study options:* academic remediation for entering students, accelerated degree program, cooperative education, distance learning, English as a second language, external degree program, independent study, internships, off-campus study, student-designed majors.

Library The Salvation Army Elfman Memorial Library with 35,700 titles, 125 serial subscriptions, an OPAC.

Computers on Campus 65 computers available on campus for general student use. A campuswide network can be accessed from student residence rooms and from off campus. Internet access, at least one staffed computer lab available. Computer purchase or lease plan available.

Student Life *Housing:* on-campus residence required through sophomore year. *Options:* Campus housing is university owned. *Activities and Organizations:* drama/theater group, choral group. *Campus security:* 24-hour emergency response devices and patrols. *Student services:* health clinic, personal/psychological counseling.

Costs (2006–07) *Comprehensive fee:* $10,600 includes full-time tuition ($1500), mandatory fees ($850), and room and board ($8250).

Applying *Application fee:* $15. *Required:* essay or personal statement, high school transcript, 2 letters of recommendation, interview. *Application deadline:* 6/1 (freshmen). *Notification:* 8/20 (freshmen).

Freshmen Application Contact Capt. Kevin Jackson, Director of Curriculum, The Salvation Army College for Officer Training at Crestmont, 30840 Hawthorne Boulevard, Rancho Palos Verdes, CA 90275. *Phone:* 310-544-6442. *Toll-free phone:* 310-544-6440. *Fax:* 310-265-6520.

SAN BERNARDINO VALLEY COLLEGE

San Bernardino, California　　**www.valleycollege.edu/**

Director of Admissions Ms. Helena Johnson, Director of Admissions and Records, San Bernardino Valley College, 701 South Mt Vernon Avenue, San Bernardino, CA 92410-2748. *Phone:* 909-384-4401.

SAN DIEGO CITY COLLEGE

San Diego, California　　**www.sdcity.edu/**

- **State and locally supported** 2-year, founded 1914, part of San Diego Community College District System
- **Urban** 56-acre campus
- **Coed,** 14,591 undergraduate students

Undergraduates 14% African American, 12% Asian American or Pacific Islander, 30% Hispanic American, 1% Native American.
Freshmen *Admission:* 3,646 admitted.
Faculty *Total:* 485, 33% full-time, 26% with terminal degrees. *Student/faculty ratio:* 35:1.
Majors Accounting; administrative assistant and secretarial science; African-American/Black studies; anthropology; art; artificial intelligence and robotics; automobile/automotive mechanics technology; behavioral sciences; biology/biological sciences; business administration and management; carpentry; commercial and advertising art; computer engineering technology; consumer services and advocacy; cosmetology; court reporting; data processing and data processing technology; developmental and child psychology; drafting and design technology; dramatic/theater arts; electrical, electronic and communications engineering technology; emergency medical technology (EMT paramedic); engineering technology; English; environmental engineering technology; fashion merchandising; finance; graphic and printing equipment operation/production; Hispanic-American, Puerto Rican, and Mexican-American/Chicano studies; hospitality administration; industrial arts; industrial technology; insurance; interior design; journalism; labor and industrial relations; Latin American studies; legal administrative assistant/secretary; legal assistant/paralegal; liberal arts and sciences/liberal studies; machine tool technology; marketing/marketing management; mathematics; modern languages; music; nursing (licensed practical/vocational nurse training); nursing (registered nurse training); occupational safety and health technology; parks, recreation and leisure; photography; physical education teaching and coaching; physical sciences; political science and government; postal management; pre-engineering; psychology; radio and television; real estate; social sciences; social work; sociology; special products marketing; speech and rhetoric; teacher assistant/aide; telecommunications; tourism and travel services management; transportation technology; welding technology.
Academics *Calendar:* semesters. *Degree:* certificates and associate. *Special study options:* academic remediation for entering students, adult/continuing education programs, cooperative education, distance learning, English as a second language, external degree program, honors programs, independent study, off-campus study, part-time degree program, services for LD students, student-designed majors, summer session for credit. *ROTC:* Air Force (c).
Library San Diego City College Library with 73,000 titles, 337 serial subscriptions, an OPAC.
Computers on Campus 121 computers available on campus for general student use. A campuswide network can be accessed from student residence rooms and from off campus. Internet access, online (class) registration, at least one staffed computer lab available.
Student Life *Housing:* college housing not available. *Activities and Organizations:* drama/theater group, student-run newspaper, radio station, choral group, Alpha Gamma Sigma, Association of United Latin American Students, MECHA, Afrikan Student Union, Student Nurses Association. *Campus security:* 24-hour emergency response devices and patrols, late-night transport/escort service. *Student services:* health clinic, personal/psychological counseling.
Athletics Member NJCAA. *Intercollegiate sports:* baseball M, basketball M/W, cross-country running M/W, football M, golf M/W, soccer M/W, softball W, tennis M/W, track and field M/W, volleyball M/W. *Intramural sports:* archery M/W, badminton M/W, baseball M, basketball M/W, bowling M/W, racquetball

M/W, soccer M/W, softball W, swimming and diving M/W, tennis M/W, track and field M/W, volleyball M/W, weight lifting M/W.
Costs (2006–07) *Tuition:* state resident $0 full-time; nonresident $4800 full-time, $186 per unit part-time. *Required fees:* $806 full-time, $26 per unit part-time, $13 per term part-time.
Financial Aid Of all full-time matriculated undergraduates who enrolled in 2004, 100 Federal Work-Study jobs (averaging $4000).
Applying *Options:* electronic application. *Required for some:* high school transcript. *Application deadline:* rolling (freshmen), rolling (transfers).
Freshmen Application Contact Ms. Lou Humphries, Supervisor of Admissions and Records, San Diego City College, 1313 Twelfth Avenue, San Diego, CA 92101-4787. *Phone:* 619-388-3474. *Fax:* 619-388-3505. *E-mail:* lhumphri@sdccd.edu.

SAN DIEGO GOLF ACADEMY

Vista, California　　**www.sdgagolf.com/**

Director of Admissions Ms. Deborah Wells, Admissions Coordinator, San Diego Golf Academy, 1910 Shadowridge Drive, Suite 111, Vista, CA 92083. *Phone:* 760-414-1501. *Toll-free phone:* 800-342-7342. *E-mail:* sdga@sdgagolf.com.

SAN DIEGO MESA COLLEGE

San Diego, California　　**www.sandiegomesacollege.net/**

- **State and locally supported** 2-year, founded 1964, part of San Diego Community College District System
- **Suburban** 104-acre campus
- **Coed,** 21,198 undergraduate students, 100% full-time, 54% women, 46% men

Undergraduates 21,198 full-time. 6% African American, 16% Asian American or Pacific Islander, 17% Hispanic American, 0.9% Native American.
Freshmen *Admission:* 1,678 applied, 1,678 admitted.
Faculty *Total:* 840, 34% full-time.
Majors Accounting; administrative assistant and secretarial science; African-American/Black studies; architectural engineering technology; architecture; art; biology/biological sciences; business administration and management; chemistry; child care provision; clinical/medical laboratory technology; computer and information sciences; computer programming related; computer programming (specific applications); computer science; computer software and media applications related; construction engineering technology; data entry/microcomputer applications related; dental assisting; engineering; English; fashion/apparel design; fashion merchandising; foods and nutrition related; foods, nutrition, and wellness; French; geography; health information/medical records administration; Hispanic-American, Puerto Rican, and Mexican-American/Chicano studies; hospitality and recreation marketing; hotel/motel administration; industrial radiologic technology; interior design; intermedia/multimedia; landscape architecture; legal administrative assistant/secretary; liberal arts and sciences/liberal studies; marketing/marketing management; marketing research; mathematics; medical/clinical assistant; music; physical education teaching and coaching; physical sciences; physical therapist assistant; physics; psychology; real estate; social sciences; sociology; Spanish; speech and rhetoric; tourism and travel services management; tourism and travel services marketing; veterinary technology.
Academics *Calendar:* semesters. *Degree:* certificates, diplomas, and associate. *Special study options:* academic remediation for entering students, adult/continuing education programs, English as a second language, external degree program, honors programs, independent study, part-time degree program, services for LD students, summer session for credit.
Library 84,353 titles, 657 serial subscriptions.
Computers on Campus 350 computers available on campus for general student use. Internet access, at least one staffed computer lab available.
Student Life *Housing:* college housing not available. *Activities and Organizations:* drama/theater group, student-run newspaper, choral group, Alpha Gamma Sigma, Black Students Association, MECHA, Gay and Lesbian Student Group, Vietnamese Student Association. *Campus security:* 24-hour emergency response devices and patrols, late-night transport/escort service. *Student services:* health clinic, personal/psychological counseling.
Athletics *Intercollegiate sports:* baseball M, basketball M/W, cross-country running M/W, football M, soccer M/W, softball W, swimming and diving M/W, tennis M/W, track and field M/W, volleyball M/W, water polo M/W. *Intramural sports:* badminton M/W, basketball M/W, bowling M/W, fencing M/W, football M, golf M/W, gymnastics M/W, racquetball M/W, skiing (downhill) M, soccer M/W, softball M/W, swimming and diving M/W, tennis M/W, volleyball M/W, weight lifting M/W.

San Diego Mesa College (continued)

Financial Aid Of all full-time matriculated undergraduates who enrolled in 2004, 237 Federal Work-Study jobs (averaging $5000). *Financial aid deadline:* 6/30.

Applying *Options:* early admission. *Application deadline:* rolling (freshmen). *Notification:* continuous (freshmen).

Freshmen Application Contact Ms. Dominga Arellano, Senior Student Services Assistant, San Diego Mesa College, 7250 Mesa College Drive, San Diego, CA 92111. *Phone:* 619-388-2686. *Fax:* 619-388-3960. *E-mail:* darellano@sdccd.edu.

SAN DIEGO MIRAMAR COLLEGE

San Diego, California   **www.miramar.sdccd.cc.ca.us/**

- **State and locally supported** 2-year, founded 1969, part of San Diego Community College District System
- **Suburban** 120-acre campus
- **Coed**

Undergraduates 6% African American, 20% Asian American or Pacific Islander, 16% Hispanic American, 1% Native American.

Academics *Calendar:* semesters. *Degree:* associate. *Special study options:* academic remediation for entering students, accelerated degree program, adult/continuing education programs, advanced placement credit, cooperative education, distance learning, double majors, English as a second language, honors programs, independent study, part-time degree program, services for LD students, student-designed majors, study abroad, summer session for credit.

Student Life *Campus security:* 24-hour emergency response devices and patrols.

Costs (2005–06) *Tuition:* state resident $0 full-time; nonresident $4492 full-time, $186 per unit part-time. *Required fees:* $652 full-time, $26 per unit part-time.

Financial Aid Of all full-time matriculated undergraduates who enrolled in 2004, 39 Federal Work-Study jobs (averaging $1500).

Applying *Options:* electronic application.

Freshmen Application Contact Ms. Dana Andras, Admissions Supervisor, San Diego Miramar College, 10440 Black Mountain Road, San Diego, CA 92126-2999. *Phone:* 619-536-7854. *E-mail:* dmaxwell@sdccd.cc.ca.us.

SAN JOAQUIN DELTA COLLEGE

Stockton, California   **www.deltacollege.edu/**

- **District-supported** 2-year, founded 1935, part of California Community College System
- **Urban** 165-acre campus with easy access to Sacramento
- **Coed,** 18,525 undergraduate students

Undergraduates Students come from 15 states and territories, 9% African American, 20% Asian American or Pacific Islander, 27% Hispanic American, 1% Native American. *Retention:* 25% of 2003 full-time freshmen returned. Freshmen *Admission:* 20,530 applied, 20,530 admitted.

Faculty *Total:* 615, 34% full-time. *Student/faculty ratio:* 33:1.

Majors Accounting; agricultural business and management; agricultural mechanization; agriculture; animal sciences; anthropology; art; automobile/automotive mechanics technology; behavioral sciences; biology/biological sciences; botany/plant biology; broadcast journalism; business administration and management; business/managerial economics; carpentry; chemistry; child development; civil engineering technology; commercial and advertising art; computer engineering technology; computer programming; computer science; construction engineering technology; corrections; criminal justice/police science; culinary arts; dance; developmental and child psychology; drafting and design technology; dramatic/theater arts; drawing; economics; electrical, electronic and communications engineering technology; emergency medical technology (EMT paramedic); engineering; engineering related; engineering technology; English; family and consumer sciences/human sciences; fashion merchandising; fire science; food services technology; French; geology/earth science; German; graphic and printing equipment operation/production; health science; heating, air conditioning, ventilation and refrigeration maintenance technology; history; humanities; industrial radiologic technology; interior design; Italian; Japanese; journalism; kindergarten/preschool education; liberal arts and sciences/liberal studies; literature; machine tool technology; marketing/marketing management; mathematics; mechanical engineering/mechanical technology; music; natural resources management and policy; natural sciences; nursing (licensed practical/vocational nurse training); nursing (registered nurse training); ornamental horticulture; philosophy; photography; physical education teaching and coaching; physical

sciences; political science and government; psychiatric/mental health services technology; psychology; public administration; religious studies; social sciences; sociology; Spanish; special products marketing; speech and rhetoric.

Academics *Calendar:* semesters. *Degree:* certificates and associate. *Special study options:* academic remediation for entering students, adult/continuing education programs, advanced placement credit, cooperative education, distance learning, English as a second language, honors programs, independent study, part-time degree program, services for LD students, summer session for credit.

Library Goleman Library plus 1 other with 92,398 titles, 605 serial subscriptions, an OPAC, a Web page.

Computers on Campus 400 computers available on campus for general student use. A campuswide network can be accessed from off campus. Internet access, online (class) registration, at least one staffed computer lab available.

Student Life *Housing:* college housing not available. *Activities and Organizations:* drama/theater group, student-run newspaper, radio station, choral group, Alpha Gamma Sigma, Fashion Club, International Club, Badminton Club. *Campus security:* 24-hour emergency response devices and patrols, late-night transport/escort service. *Student services:* personal/psychological counseling, legal services.

Athletics Member NJCAA. *Intercollegiate sports:* baseball M, basketball M/W, cross-country running M/W, fencing M/W, football M, golf M/W, soccer M/W, softball W, swimming and diving M/W, tennis M/W, track and field M/W, volleyball W, water polo M/W, wrestling M. *Intramural sports:* badminton M/W, basketball M/W, bowling M/W, soccer M/W, swimming and diving M/W, tennis M/W, ultimate Frisbee M/W, volleyball M/W, weight lifting M/W.

Costs (2005–06) *Tuition:* state resident $0 full-time; nonresident $5250 full-time, $175 per unit part-time. *Required fees:* $780 full-time, $26 per unit part-time. *Payment plan:* installment. *Waivers:* employees or children of employees.

Financial Aid Of all full-time matriculated undergraduates who enrolled in 2004, 315 Federal Work-Study jobs (averaging $3100). 210 state and other part-time jobs (averaging $1172).

Applying *Options:* common application, electronic application, early admission. *Application deadline:* rolling (freshmen), rolling (transfers). *Notification:* continuous (freshmen).

Freshmen Application Contact Ms. Catherine Mooney, Registrar, San Joaquin Delta College, 5151 Pacific Avenue, Stockton, CA 95207. *Phone:* 209-954-5635. *Fax:* 209-954-5769. *E-mail:* admissions@deltacollege.edu.

SAN JOAQUIN VALLEY COLLEGE

Visalia, California   **www.sjvc.edu**

- **Independent** 2-year, founded 1977
- **Small-town** campus
- **Coed,** 3,352 undergraduate students, 100% full-time, 75% women, 25% men

Undergraduates 3,351 full-time, 1 part-time. 6% are from out of state, 8% African American, 6% Asian American or Pacific Islander, 42% Hispanic American, 0.9% Native American.

Freshmen *Admission:* 3,471 applied, 3,351 admitted, 1,088 enrolled.

Faculty *Total:* 512, 54% full-time. *Student/faculty ratio:* 10:1.

Majors Aircraft powerplant technology; airframe mechanics and aircraft maintenance technology; business/commerce; computer systems networking and telecommunications; computer/technical support; construction management; corrections; criminal justice/law enforcement administration; dental assisting; dental hygiene; heating, air conditioning, ventilation and refrigeration maintenance technology; industrial mechanics and maintenance technology; medical administrative assistant and medical secretary; medical/clinical assistant; medical insurance/medical billing; medical office management; nursing (licensed practical/vocational nurse training); nursing (registered nurse training); operations management; pharmacy technician; respiratory care therapy; security and loss prevention; surgical technology; veterinary technology.

Academics *Calendar:* semesters. *Degree:* certificates and associate. *Special study options:* academic remediation for entering students.

Library SJVC Visalia Campus Library with 4,720 titles, 53 serial subscriptions, 125 audiovisual materials.

Computers on Campus 740 computers available on campus for general student use. A campuswide network can be accessed. At least one staffed computer lab available.

Student Life *Housing:* college housing not available. *Activities and Organizations:* Associated Student Body, Students in Free Enterprise, American Medical Technologists. *Campus security:* late-night transport/escort service, full-time security personnel. *Student services:* health clinic, personal/psychological counseling, women's center.

Costs (2006–07) *Tuition:* $11,475 full-time, $348 per unit part-time.

Applying *Required:* high school transcript. *Required for some:* essay or personal statement, minimum X GPA, letters of recommendation, interview. *Application deadline:* rolling (freshmen), rolling (transfers). *Notification:* continuous (freshmen).

Freshmen Application Contact Mr. Joseph Holt, Director of Marketing and Admissions, San Joaquin Valley College, 8400 West Mineral King Avenue, Visalia, CA 93291. *Fax:* 559-734-9048. *E-mail:* josephh@sjvc.edu.

SAN JOSE CITY COLLEGE
San Jose, California   www.sjcc.edu/

Director of Admissions Mr. Carlo Santos, Director of Admissions/Registrar, San Jose City College, 2100 Moorpark Avenue, San Jose, CA 95128-2799. *Phone:* 408-288-3707.

SANTA ANA COLLEGE
Santa Ana, California   www.sac.edu/

Freshmen Application Contact Mrs. Christie Steward, Admissions Clerk, Santa Ana College, 1530 West 17th Street, Santa Ana, CA 92704. *Phone:* 714-564-6053.

SANTA BARBARA CITY COLLEGE
Santa Barbara, California   www.sbcc.edu/

- **State and locally supported** 2-year, founded 1908, part of California Community College System
- **Small-town** 65-acre campus
- **Coed,** 15,740 undergraduate students, 41% full-time, 53% women, 47% men

Undergraduates 6,488 full-time, 9,252 part-time. Students come from 49 states and territories, 59 other countries, 6% are from out of state, 3% African American, 5% Asian American or Pacific Islander, 23% Hispanic American, 0.9% Native American, 6% international, 5% transferred in.

Freshmen *Admission:* 2,768 applied, 2,768 admitted, 1,731 enrolled.

Faculty *Total:* 738, 35% full-time. *Student/faculty ratio:* 29:1.

Majors Accounting; acting; administrative assistant and secretarial science; African-American/Black studies; American Indian/Native American studies; anthropology; applied horticulture; art history, criticism and conservation; athletic training; automobile/automotive mechanics technology; biology/biological sciences; biomedical technology; biotechnology; business administration and management; chemistry; child care and support services management; commercial and advertising art; communication/speech communication and rhetoric; computer engineering; computer science; cosmetology; criminal justice/law enforcement administration; culinary arts related; cultural studies; drafting and design technology; dramatic/theater arts; economics; electrical, electronic and communications engineering technology; electrical/electronics equipment installation and repair; engineering; engineering technology; English; environmental/environmental health engineering; environmental studies; film/cinema studies; finance; fine/studio arts; foodservice systems administration; French; geography; geology/earth science; health information/medical records technology; Hispanic-American, Puerto Rican, and Mexican-American/Chicano studies; history; hotel/motel administration; industrial engineering; industrial technology; information science/studies; information technology; institutional food workers; interior design; international relations and affairs; kindergarten/preschool education; kinesiology and exercise science; landscaping and groundskeeping; legal studies; liberal arts and sciences/liberal studies; marine technology; marketing/marketing management; mathematics; medical radiologic technology; music; nursing (licensed practical/vocational nurse training); nursing (registered nurse training); ornamental horticulture; parks, recreation and leisure; philosophy; physical education teaching and coaching; physics; political science and government; psychology; real estate; sales, distribution and marketing; selling skills and sales; sociology; Spanish; system administration; theater design and technology; therapeutic recreation.

Academics *Calendar:* semesters. *Degree:* certificates and associate. *Special study options:* academic remediation for entering students, adult/continuing education programs, advanced placement credit, cooperative education, distance learning, double majors, English as a second language, honors programs, independent study, internships, part-time degree program, services for LD students, study abroad, summer session for credit. *ROTC:* Army (c).

Library Eli Luria Library with 121,622 titles, 3,325 serial subscriptions, 9,230 audiovisual materials, an OPAC, a Web page.

Computers on Campus 1465 computers available on campus for general student use. A campuswide network can be accessed from off campus. Internet access, at least one staffed computer lab available.

Student Life *Housing:* college housing not available. *Activities and Organizations:* drama/theater group, student-run newspaper, choral group, MECHA, International-Cultural Exchange Club, Geology Club, Computer Club, Future Teachers Club. *Campus security:* 24-hour emergency response devices and patrols, late-night transport/escort service. *Student services:* health clinic, personal/psychological counseling.

Athletics *Intercollegiate sports:* baseball M, basketball M/W, cross-country running M/W, football M, golf M/W, soccer M/W, softball W, tennis M/W, track and field M/W, volleyball M/W.

Costs (2005–06) *Tuition:* state resident $0 full-time; nonresident $5310 full-time, $151 per unit part-time. Full-time tuition and fees vary according to course load. Part-time tuition and fees vary according to course load. *Required fees:* $831 full-time, $26 per unit part-time, $51 per year part-time. *Waivers:* employees or children of employees.

Applying *Options:* early admission. *Recommended:* high school transcript. *Application deadlines:* 8/26 (freshmen), 8/26 (transfers). *Notification:* continuous (freshmen).

Freshmen Application Contact Ms. Allison Curtis, Director of Admissions and Records, Santa Barbara City College, 721 Cliff Drive, Santa Barbara, CA 93109. *Phone:* 805-965-0581 Ext. 2352. *Fax:* 805-962-0497. *E-mail:* admissions@sbcc.edu.

SANTA MONICA COLLEGE
Santa Monica, California   www.smc.edu/

Director of Admissions Ms. Teresita Rodriguez, Dean of Enrollment Services, Santa Monica College, 1900 Pico Boulevard, Santa Monica, CA 90405-1628. *Phone:* 310-434-4880 Ext. 4774.

▶ **See page 594 for the College Close-Up.**

SANTA ROSA JUNIOR COLLEGE
Santa Rosa, California   www.santarosa.edu/

- **State and locally supported** 2-year, founded 1918, part of California Community College System
- **Urban** 93-acre campus with easy access to San Francisco
- **Endowment** $15.7 million
- **Coed,** 23,682 undergraduate students

Undergraduates Students come from 29 states and territories, 39 other countries, 2% are from out of state.

Freshmen *Admission:* 4,434 applied, 4,434 admitted.

Faculty *Total:* 1,566, 19% full-time, 11% with terminal degrees. *Student/faculty ratio:* 19:1.

Majors Advertising; aeronautical/aerospace engineering technology; agricultural business and management; agricultural mechanization; agriculture; animal health; animal physiology; animal sciences; anthropology; art; astronomy; athletic training; atmospheric sciences and meteorology; behavioral sciences; biology/biological sciences; botany/plant biology; business administration and management; chemistry; child guidance; civil engineering; communication/speech communication and rhetoric; computer science; construction management; criminal justice/law enforcement administration; culinary arts; cultural studies; dance; dental hygiene; dietetics; dramatic/theater arts; economics; education; electrical, electronic and communications engineering technology; emergency medical technology (EMT paramedic); engineering; engineering technology; English; environmental science; environmental studies; ethnic, cultural minority, and gender studies related; family and consumer sciences/human sciences; film/cinema studies; fire science; fishing and fisheries sciences and management; floriculture/floristry management; geography; geology/earth science; gerontological services; graphic design; health and physical education related; history; horse husbandry/equine science and management; hotel/motel administration; human services; industrial design; interior design; journalism; landscape architecture; Latin American studies; liberal arts and sciences/liberal studies; mathematics; mechanics and repair; music; natural resources/conservation; natural resources management and policy; nursing (registered nurse training); oceanography (chemical and physical); ophthalmic laboratory technology; philosophy; physical education teaching and coaching; physical sciences; physician assistant; physics; political science and government; precision production trades; pre-pharmacy studies; psychology; social sciences; sociology; speech-language pathology; surveying engineering; wildlife and wildlands science and management; women's studies.

Santa Rosa Junior College (continued)

Academics *Calendar:* semesters. *Degree:* certificates and associate. *Special study options:* academic remediation for entering students, adult/continuing education programs, advanced placement credit, cooperative education, distance learning, English as a second language, independent study, internships, off-campus study, part-time degree program, services for LD students, study abroad, summer session for credit. *ROTC:* Army (c).

Library Plover Library plus 1 other with 119,803 titles, 393 serial subscriptions, 9,430 audiovisual materials, an OPAC, a Web page.

Computers on Campus 1325 computers available on campus for general student use. A campuswide network can be accessed from off campus that provide access to library databases. Internet access, online (class) registration, at least one staffed computer lab available.

Student Life *Housing:* college housing not available. *Activities and Organizations:* drama/theater group, student-run newspaper, choral group, International Club, MECHA, Alpha Gamma Sigma, Asian/Pacific Island Association, Phi Theta Kappa. *Campus security:* 24-hour emergency response devices and patrols. *Student services:* health clinic, personal/psychological counseling.

Athletics Member NJCAA. *Intercollegiate sports:* baseball M, basketball M/W, cross-country running M/W, football M, golf M, ice hockey M(c), rugby M(c), soccer M/W, softball W, swimming and diving M/W, tennis M/W, track and field M/W, volleyball W, water polo M/W, wrestling M.

Costs (2006–07) *Tuition:* state resident $0 full-time; nonresident $5630 full-time. *Required fees:* $746 full-time, $26 per unit part-time.

Financial Aid Of all full-time matriculated undergraduates who enrolled in 2004, 228 Federal Work-Study jobs (averaging $3500).

Applying *Options:* electronic application, early admission. *Application deadline:* rolling (freshmen), rolling (transfers). *Notification:* continuous (freshmen).

Freshmen Application Contact Diane Traversi, Director of Enrollment Services, Santa Rosa Junior College, 1501 Mendocino Avenue, Santa Rosa, CA 95401. *Phone:* 707-527-4685. *Fax:* 707-527-4798. *E-mail:* admininfo@santarosa.edu.

SANTIAGO CANYON COLLEGE

Orange, California　　　　　**www.sccollege.edu/**

Freshmen Application Contact Denise Pennock, Admissions and Records, Santiago Canyon College, 8045 East Chapman, Orange, CA 92669. *Phone:* 714-564-4000.

SHASTA COLLEGE

Redding, California　　　　　**www.shastacollege.edu/**

Director of Admissions Ms. Cassandra Ryan, Admissions and Records Office Director, Shasta College, PO Box 496006, Redding, CA 96049-6006. *Phone:* 530-225-4841.

SIERRA COLLEGE

Rocklin, California　　　　　**www.sierracollege.edu/**

Director of Admissions Ms. Carla Epting-Davis, Associate Dean of Student Services, Sierra College, 5000 Rocklin Road, Rocklin, CA 93677-3397. *Phone:* 916-789-2939.

SKYLINE COLLEGE

San Bruno, California　　　　　**skylinecollege.net/**

- **State and locally supported** 2-year, founded 1969, part of San Mateo County Community College District System
- **Suburban** 125-acre campus with easy access to San Francisco
- **Coed,** 8,147 undergraduate students

Undergraduates Students come from 9 other countries, 2% are from out of state.

Freshmen *Admission:* 736 admitted.

Faculty *Total:* 300, 29% full-time. *Student/faculty ratio:* 27:1.

Majors Accounting; administrative assistant and secretarial science; anthropology; applied art; art; art history, criticism and conservation; automobile/automotive mechanics technology; biological and physical sciences; biology/

biological sciences; business administration and management; chemistry; computer programming; computer science; cosmetology; criminal justice/law enforcement administration; criminal justice/police science; data processing and data processing technology; economics; emergency medical technology (EMT paramedic); English; family and consumer sciences/human sciences; fashion merchandising; finance; fine/studio arts; French; history; hotel/motel administration; journalism; legal administrative assistant/secretary; legal assistant/paralegal; liberal arts and sciences/liberal studies; literature; mathematics; music; parks, recreation and leisure; philosophy; physical education teaching and coaching; physics; political science and government; psychology; respiratory care therapy; social sciences; sociology; Spanish; speech and rhetoric; surgical technology; telecommunications.

Academics *Calendar:* semesters. *Degree:* certificates and associate. *Special study options:* academic remediation for entering students, adult/continuing education programs, advanced placement credit, cooperative education, distance learning, English as a second language, honors programs, part-time degree program, services for LD students, study abroad, summer session for credit.

Library Skyline College Library with 50,000 titles, 230 serial subscriptions, an OPAC.

Computers on Campus 220 computers available on campus for general student use. A campuswide network can be accessed from off campus that provide access to course registration, student account and grade information. Internet access, online (class) registration, at least one staffed computer lab available.

Student Life *Housing:* college housing not available. *Activities and Organizations:* student-run newspaper, choral group. *Campus security:* security guards during open hours. *Student services:* health clinic, personal/psychological counseling.

Athletics Member NJCAA. *Intercollegiate sports:* baseball M, basketball M, cross-country running M/W, soccer M, softball W, track and field M/W, volleyball W, wrestling M.

Costs (2006–07) *Required fees:* $1536 full-time, $26 per unit part-time.

Financial Aid Of all full-time matriculated undergraduates who enrolled in 2004, 125 Federal Work-Study jobs (averaging $4000).

Applying *Required for some:* high school transcript. *Application deadlines:* rolling (freshmen), 8/19 (transfers).

Freshmen Application Contact Terry Stats, Admissions Office, Skyline College, 3300 College Drive, San Bruno, CA 94066-1698. *Phone:* 650-738-4251. *E-mail:* stats@smccd.net.

SOLANO COMMUNITY COLLEGE

Suisun City, California　　　　　**www.solano.edu/**

- **State and locally supported** 2-year, founded 1945, part of California Community College System
- **Rural** 192-acre campus with easy access to Sacramento and San Francisco
- **Coed**

Undergraduates Students come from 43 states and territories, 6 other countries, 1% are from out of state, 15% African American, 18% Asian American or Pacific Islander, 14% Hispanic American, 1% Native American, 0.2% international.

Faculty *Student/faculty ratio:* 27:1.

Academics *Calendar:* semesters. *Degree:* certificates, diplomas, and associate. *Special study options:* academic remediation for entering students, adult/continuing education programs, advanced placement credit, cooperative education, distance learning, double majors, English as a second language, honors programs, independent study, off-campus study, part-time degree program, services for LD students, study abroad, summer session for credit.

Student Life *Campus security:* 24-hour patrols, student patrols, late-night transport/escort service.

Financial Aid Of all full-time matriculated undergraduates who enrolled in 2004, 125 Federal Work-Study jobs (averaging $2000). 30 state and other part-time jobs (averaging $2000).

Applying *Options:* electronic application, early admission, deferred entrance.

Director of Admissions Mr. Gerald Fisher, Dean of Admissions and Records, Solano Community College, 4000 Suisun Valley Road, Fairfield, CA 94534. *Phone:* 707-864-7113. *E-mail:* admissions@solano.cc.ca.us.

SONOMA COLLEGE

Petaluma, California　　　　　**www.sonomacollege.com/**

Director of Admissions Ms. Delores Ford, Chief Operating Officer/Campus Director, Sonoma College, 130 Avram Avenue, Rhonert Park, CA 94928. *Phone:* 707-664-9267 Ext. 12. *Toll-free phone:* 800-437-9474. *Fax:* 707-664-9237.

SONOMA COLLEGE

San Francisco, California   www.sonomacollege.com/

Director of Admissions Sonoma College, 78 First Street, San Francisco, CA 94105. *Toll-free phone:* 888-649-7801.

SOUTH COAST COLLEGE

Orange, California   www.southcoastcollege.com/

Director of Admissions South Coast College, 2011 West Chapman Avenue, Orange, CA 92868. *Toll-free phone:* 800-337-8366.

SOUTHERN CALIFORNIA INSTITUTE OF TECHNOLOGY

Anaheim, California   www.scitcollege.com/

Director of Admissions Director of Admissions, Southern California Institute of Technology, 1900 West Crescent Avenue, Building B, Anaheim, CA 92801. *Phone:* 714-520-5552.

SOUTHWESTERN COLLEGE

Chula Vista, California   www.swc.cc.ca.us/

Director of Admissions Ms. Georgia A. Copeland, Director of Admissions and Records, Southwestern College, 900 Otay Lakes Road, Chula Vista, CA 91910. *Phone:* 619-482-6550.

TAFT COLLEGE

Taft, California   www.taftcollege.edu/

- **State and locally supported** 2-year, founded 1922, part of California Community College System
- **Small-town** 15-acre campus
- **Endowment** $14,405
- **Coed**

Undergraduates 561 full-time, 6,463 part-time. Students come from 16 states and territories, 5% are from out of state, 14% African American, 4% Asian American or Pacific Islander, 24% Hispanic American, 2% Native American, 11% transferred in, 6% live on campus.

Faculty *Student/faculty ratio:* 18:1.

Academics *Calendar:* semesters. *Degree:* certificates and associate. *Special study options:* academic remediation for entering students, adult/continuing education programs, advanced placement credit, distance learning, English as a second language, honors programs, independent study, part-time degree program, services for LD students, summer session for credit.

Student Life *Campus security:* controlled dormitory access, parking lot security.

Costs (2005–06) *Tuition:* state resident $0 full-time; nonresident $4530 full-time, $151 per unit part-time. Full-time tuition and fees vary according to course load. Part-time tuition and fees vary according to course load. *Required fees:* $780 full-time, $26 per unit part-time. *Room and board:* $3146; room only: $1294.

Financial Aid Of all full-time matriculated undergraduates who enrolled in 2004, 63 Federal Work-Study jobs (averaging $1500).

Applying *Options:* electronic application. *Required for some:* high school transcript.

Director of Admissions Ms. Gayle Roberts, Director of Financial Aid and Admissions, Taft College, 29 Emmons Park Drive, Taft, CA 93268. *Phone:* 661-763-7763.

VENTURA COLLEGE

Ventura, California   www.venturacollege.edu/

- **State and locally supported** 2-year, founded 1925, part of California Community College System
- **Suburban** 103-acre campus with easy access to Los Angeles
- **Coed,** 12,096 undergraduate students, 34% full-time, 57% women, 43% men

Undergraduates 4,112 full-time, 7,984 part-time. Students come from 25 states and territories, 11% are from out of state, 2% African American, 7% Asian American or Pacific Islander, 38% Hispanic American, 1% Native American, 20% transferred in.

Freshmen *Admission:* 2,652 applied, 738 enrolled.

Faculty *Total:* 519, 26% full-time. *Student/faculty ratio:* 22:1.

Majors Accounting; agriculture; automobile/automotive mechanics technology; biology/biological sciences; business administration and management; ceramic arts and ceramics; commercial and advertising art; computer and information sciences; construction engineering technology; criminal justice/law enforcement administration; dramatic/theater arts; engineering; fashion/apparel design; fine/studio arts; hydrology and water resources science; journalism; liberal arts and sciences/liberal studies; machine tool technology; medical/clinical assistant; medical transcription; music; natural resources management and policy; nursing (registered nurse training); parks, recreation and leisure; physical sciences; plant sciences; real estate; tool and die technology; welding technology.

Academics *Calendar:* semesters. *Degree:* certificates, diplomas, and associate. *Special study options:* academic remediation for entering students, adult/continuing education programs, advanced placement credit, English as a second language, independent study, internships, part-time degree program, services for LD students, summer session for credit.

Library Ventura College Library with 63,529 titles, 341 serial subscriptions, an OPAC, a Web page.

Computers on Campus 40 computers available on campus for general student use. Internet access, online (class) registration, at least one staffed computer lab available.

Student Life *Housing:* college housing not available. *Activities and Organizations:* drama/theater group, student-run newspaper, choral group, Pan American Student Union, MECHA, Automotive Technology Club, Campus Christian Fellowship, Asian-American Club. *Campus security:* 24-hour emergency response devices and patrols, student patrols. *Student services:* health clinic, personal/psychological counseling, women's center.

Athletics *Intercollegiate sports:* baseball M, basketball M/W, cross-country running M/W, football M, golf M, soccer M/W, softball W, swimming and diving M/W, tennis M/W, track and field M/W, volleyball W, water polo M/W.

Costs (2006–07) *Tuition:* state resident $0 full-time; nonresident $4650 full-time. *Required fees:* $850 full-time.

Financial Aid Of all full-time matriculated undergraduates who enrolled in 2004, 70 Federal Work-Study jobs.

Applying *Required:* high school transcript.

Freshmen Application Contact Ms. Susan Bricker, Registrar, Ventura College, 4667 Telegraph Road, Ventura, CA 93003-3899. *Phone:* 805-654-6456. *Fax:* 805-654-6466. *E-mail:* sbricker@vcccd.net.

VICTOR VALLEY COLLEGE

Victorville, California   www.vvc.edu/

Director of Admissions Ms. Becky Millen, Director of Admissions and Records, Victor Valley College, 18422 Bear Valley Road, Victorville, CA 92392. *Phone:* 760-245-4271 Ext. 2668.

WESTERN CAREER COLLEGE

Emeryville, California   www.westerncollege.edu/

Director of Admissions Ms. Marianne Dulay, Admissions Representative, Western Career College, 1400 65th Street, Suite 200, Emeryville, CA 94608. *Phone:* 510-601-0133 Ext. 14. *Toll-free phone:* 800-750-5627.

WESTERN CAREER COLLEGE
Fremont, California www.westerncollege.edu/

Director of Admissions Mr. Anton Croos, Admissions Director, Western Career College, 41350 Christy Street, Fremont, CA 94538. *Phone:* 510-623-9966 Ext. 212. *Toll-free phone:* 800-750-5627.

WESTERN CAREER COLLEGE
Pleasant Hill, California

▶ **See page 602 for the College Close-Up.**

WESTERN CAREER COLLEGE
Sacramento, California

WESTERN CAREER COLLEGE
San Jose, California www.westerncollege.edu/

Director of Admissions Ms. Patricia Fraser, Admissions Director, Western Career College, 6201 San Ignacio Avenue, San Jose, CA 95119. *Phone:* 408-360-0840 Ext. 247. *Toll-free phone:* 800-750-5627.

WESTERN CAREER COLLEGE
San Leandro, California

WESTERN CAREER COLLEGE
Walnut Creek,
California www.westerncollege.edu/campus_locations/antioch_campus.html

Director of Admissions Mr. Mark Millen, Admissions Director, Western Career College, 2800 Mitchell Drive, Walnut Creek, CA 94598. *Phone:* 925-280-0235 Ext. 37. *Toll-free phone:* 888-203-9947.

WEST HILLS COMMUNITY COLLEGE
Coalinga, California www.westhillscollege.com/

Director of Admissions Mrs. Darlene Georgatos, Director of Admissions and Records, West Hills Community College, 300 Cherry Lane, Coalinga, CA 93210-1399. *Phone:* 559-934-3204. *Toll-free phone:* 800-266-1114. *E-mail:* darlenegeorgatos@westhillcollege.com.

WEST LOS ANGELES COLLEGE
Culver City, California www.wlac.cc.ca.us/

Director of Admissions Mr. Len Isaksen, Director of Admissions, West Los Angeles College, 4800 Freshman Drive, Culver City, CA 90230-3519. *Phone:* 310-287-4255.

WEST VALLEY COLLEGE
Saratoga, California www.westvalley.edu/

Freshmen Application Contact Mr. Albert Moore, Admissions and Records Supervisor, West Valley College, 14000 Fruitvale Avenue, Saratoga, CA 95070-5698. *Phone:* 408-741-2533.

WESTWOOD COLLEGE–ANAHEIM
Anaheim, California www.westwood.edu/

Director of Admissions Mr. Paul Sallenbach, Director of Admissions, Westwood College–Anaheim, 2461 West La Palma Avenue, Anaheim, CA 92801-2610. *Phone:* 714-226-9990. *Toll-free phone:* 877-650-6050.

▶ **See page 604 for the College Close-Up.**

WESTWOOD COLLEGE–INLAND EMPIRE
Upland, California www.westwood.edu/

Director of Admissions Mr. Lyle Seavers, Director of Admissions, Westwood College–Inland Empire, 20 West 7th Street, Upland, CA 91786-7148. *Phone:* 909-931-7550. *Toll-free phone:* 866-288-9488.

▶ **See page 632 for the College Close-Up.**

WESTWOOD COLLEGE–LONG BEACH
Long Beach, California www.westwood.edu

- **Proprietary** primarily 2-year, founded 2002, part of AITU Colleges
- **Urban** 1-acre campus with easy access to Los Angeles
- **Coed**

Undergraduates 265 full-time. Students come from 4 states and territories, 2% are from out of state, 14% African American, 8% Asian American or Pacific Islander, 48% Hispanic American, 0.4% Native American, 0.4% international.
Faculty *Student/faculty ratio:* 15:1.
Academics *Calendar:* continuous. *Degrees:* associate and bachelor's. *Special study options:* accelerated degree program, adult/continuing education programs, advanced placement credit, cooperative education, external degree program, freshman honors college, honors programs, independent study, internships, off-campus study, part-time degree program, services for LD students, student-designed majors.
Student Life *Campus security:* 24-hour emergency response devices and patrols, late-night transport/escort service.
Standardized Tests *Required:* ACCUPLACER (for admission). *Recommended:* SAT or ACT (for admission).
Applying *Options:* common application, electronic application. *Application fee:* $100. *Required:* high school transcript, interview.
Director of Admissions Jesse Kamekona, Director of Admissions, Westwood College–Long Beach, 3901 Via Oro Avenue, Suite 103, Long Beach, CA 90810. *Phone:* 310-522-2088 Ext. 100. *Toll-free phone:* 888-403-3308.

▶ **See page 634 for the College Close-Up.**

WESTWOOD COLLEGE–LOS ANGELES
Los Angeles, California www.westwood.edu/

Director of Admissions Mr. Ron Milman, Director of Admissions, Westwood College–Los Angeles, 3460 Wilshire Boulevard, Suite 700, Los Angeles, CA 90010-2210. *Phone:* 213-739-9999. *Toll-free phone:* 877-377-4600.

▶ **See page 636 for the College Close-Up.**

WYOTECH
Fremont, California
www.wyotech.com/

- **Proprietary** 2-year, founded 1966
- **Coed, primarily men,** 1,364 undergraduate students, 100% full-time, 2% women, 98% men
- 81% of applicants were admitted

Undergraduates 1,364 full-time. 8% African American, 27% Asian American or Pacific Islander, 34% Hispanic American, 0.7% Native American. Freshmen *Admission:* 307 applied, 250 admitted.

Faculty *Total:* 59, 100% full-time. *Student/faculty ratio:* 23:1.

Majors Automobile/automotive mechanics technology; automotive engineering technology; heating, air conditioning, ventilation and refrigeration maintenance technology.

Academics *Calendar:* continuous. *Degree:* certificates, diplomas, and associate.

Student Life *Housing:* college housing not available.

Standardized Tests *Required:* CPAt or ATB Entrance Exam (for admission).

Costs (2006–07) *Tuition:* $24,525 full-time. *Required fees:* $50 full-time.

Freshmen Application Contact Admissions Department, WyoTech, 200 Whitney Place, Fremont, CA 94539-7663. *Phone:* 510-580-3507. *Toll-free phone:* 800-248-8585. *Fax:* 510-490-8599.

WYOTECH
West Sacramento, California

YUBA COLLEGE
Marysville, California
www.yccd.edu/

- **State and locally supported** 2-year, founded 1927, part of California Community College System
- **Rural** 160-acre campus with easy access to Sacramento
- **Endowment** $3.7 million
- **Coed,** 10,457 undergraduate students, 60% full-time, 65% women, 35% men

Undergraduates 6,294 full-time, 4,163 part-time. 3% African American, 11% Asian American or Pacific Islander, 28% Hispanic American, 2% Native American.

Freshmen *Admission:* 2,021 applied, 2,021 admitted.

Faculty *Total:* 510, 26% full-time.

Majors Accounting; administrative assistant and secretarial science; advertising; African-American/Black studies; agricultural business and management; agricultural mechanization; agriculture; agronomy and crop science; animal sciences; art; automobile/automotive mechanics technology; biological and physical sciences; biology/biological sciences; business administration and management; chemistry; child development; communication/speech communication and rhetoric; computer and information sciences related; computer science; corrections; cosmetology; criminal justice/law enforcement administration; criminal justice/police science; cultural studies; dramatic/theater arts; education; electrical, electronic and communications engineering technology; elementary education; English; family and consumer economics related; family and consumer sciences/human sciences; fire science; health teacher education; Hispanic-American, Puerto Rican, and Mexican-American/Chicano studies; history; human services; industrial radiologic technology; industrial technology; kindergarten/preschool education; machine tool technology; mass communication/media; mathematics; music; nursing (licensed practical/vocational nurse training); nursing (registered nurse training); philosophy; photography; physical education teaching and coaching; pre-engineering; psychiatric/mental health services technology; psychology; robotics technology; social sciences; substance abuse/addiction counseling; veterinary technology; welding technology; women's studies; word processing.

Academics *Calendar:* semesters. *Degree:* certificates and associate. *Special study options:* academic remediation for entering students, advanced placement credit, distance learning, double majors, English as a second language, part-time degree program, services for LD students, summer session for credit.

Library Learning Resource Center and Library plus 1 other with 65,000 titles, 1,300 serial subscriptions, 9,419 audiovisual materials, an OPAC.

Computers on Campus 200 computers available on campus for general student use. A campuswide network can be accessed from student residence rooms and from off campus. Internet access, online (class) registration, at least one staffed computer lab available.

Student Life *Activities and Organizations:* drama/theater group, choral group. *Campus security:* 24-hour patrols, student patrols. *Student services:* health clinic, personal/psychological counseling, women's center.

Athletics Member NCAA. *Intercollegiate sports:* baseball M(s), basketball M/W, cross-country running M/W, football M, soccer M/W, softball W, tennis M/W, track and field M/W, volleyball W.

Costs (2005–06) *Tuition:* state resident $0 full-time. *Required fees:* $780 full-time, $26 per unit part-time.

Financial Aid Of all full-time matriculated undergraduates who enrolled in 2004, 290 Federal Work-Study jobs (averaging $2400). 50 state and other part-time jobs (averaging $1000).

Applying *Options:* common application, electronic application. *Required:* high school transcript. *Application deadline:* rolling (freshmen), rolling (transfers).

Director of Admissions Dr. David Farrell, Dean of Student Development, Yuba College, 2088 North Beale Road, Marysville, CA 95901. *Phone:* 530-741-6705.

COLORADO

AIMS COMMUNITY COLLEGE
Greeley, Colorado
www.aims.edu/

Freshmen Application Contact Ms. Susie Gallardo, Admissions Technician, Aims Community College, Box 69, Greeley, CO 80632-0069. *Phone:* 970-330-8008 Ext. 6624. *E-mail:* wgreen@chiron.aims.edu.

ARAPAHOE COMMUNITY COLLEGE
Littleton, Colorado
www.arapahoe.edu/

- **State-supported** 2-year, founded 1965, part of Community Colleges of Colorado
- **Suburban** 52-acre campus with easy access to Denver
- **Coed,** 7,560 undergraduate students, 31% full-time, 63% women, 37% men

Undergraduates 2,312 full-time, 5,248 part-time. Students come from 35 other countries, 3% African American, 3% Asian American or Pacific Islander, 9% Hispanic American, 1% Native American, 1% international.

Freshmen *Admission:* 2,017 applied, 2,017 admitted, 1,274 enrolled. *Average high school GPA:* 2.0.

Faculty *Total:* 414, 28% full-time. *Student/faculty ratio:* 19:1.

Majors Accounting technology and bookkeeping; administrative assistant and secretarial science; architectural engineering technology; automobile/automotive mechanics technology; biological and physical sciences; building/home/construction inspection; business administration and management; child care and support services management; child care provision; clinical laboratory science/medical technology; clinical/medical laboratory technology; commercial and advertising art; communications systems installation and repair technology; communications technology; computer graphics; computer/information technology services administration related; computer programming; computer programming related; computer programming (specific applications); computer science; computer software and media applications related; computer systems networking and telecommunications; computer/technical support; construction management; consumer merchandising/retailing management; criminal justice/law enforcement administration; criminal justice/police science; data modeling/warehousing and database administration; drafting and design technology; electrical, electronic and communications engineering technology; emergency medical technology (EMT paramedic); environmental engineering technology; finance; food services technology; funeral service and mortuary science; health information/medical records administration; information science/studies; legal administrative assistant/secretary; legal assistant/paralegal; liberal arts and sciences/liberal studies; management information systems; marketing/marketing management; mechanical design technology; medical/clinical assistant; nursing (registered

Arapahoe Community College (continued)

nurse training); physical therapy; tourism and travel services management; web page, digital/multimedia and information resources design.

Academics *Calendar:* semesters. *Degree:* certificates, diplomas, and associate. *Special study options:* academic remediation for entering students, accelerated degree program, adult/continuing education programs, advanced placement credit, cooperative education, distance learning, double majors, English as a second language, honors programs, independent study, internships, off-campus study, part-time degree program, services for LD students, student-designed majors, study abroad, summer session for credit. *ROTC:* Army (c), Air Force (c).

Library Weber Center for Learning Resources plus 1 other with 45,000 titles, 441 serial subscriptions, an OPAC, a Web page.

Computers on Campus 200 computers available on campus for general student use. A campuswide network can be accessed from off campus. Internet access, at least one staffed computer lab available.

Student Life *Housing:* college housing not available. *Activities and Organizations:* drama/theater group, student-run newspaper, choral group. *Campus security:* 24-hour emergency response devices and patrols, late-night transport/escort service. *Student services:* personal/psychological counseling.

Athletics Member NJCAA. *Intramural sports:* skiing (cross-country) M/W, skiing (downhill) M/W, soccer M/W, swimming and diving M/W, tennis M/W, volleyball M/W.

Costs (2006–07) *Tuition:* state resident $1619 full-time, $90 per credit hour part-time; nonresident $8000 full-time, $369 per credit hour part-time. *Required fees:* $81 full-time.

Financial Aid Of all full-time matriculated undergraduates who enrolled in 2004, 100 Federal Work-Study jobs (averaging $4200). 200 state and other part-time jobs (averaging $4200).

Applying *Options:* common application, electronic application, early admission, deferred entrance. *Application deadline:* rolling (freshmen), rolling (transfers).

Freshmen Application Contact Mr. Howard Fukaye, Admissions Specialist, Arapahoe Community College, 5900 South Santa Fe Drive, PO Box 9002, Littleton, CO 80160-9002. *Phone:* 303-797-5622. *Fax:* 303-797-5970. *E-mail:* hfukaye@arapahoe.edu.

ARGOSY UNIVERSITY/DENVER

Denver, Colorado   www.argosyu.edu/

- **Proprietary** 2-year
- **Coed**

Majors Business administration, management and operations related; criminal justice/law enforcement administration; medical/clinical assistant; paralegal/legal assistant.

Academics *Degree:* associate.

Director of Admissions Admissions Director, Argosy University/Denver, 1200 Lincoln Street, Denver, CO 80203. *Toll-free phone:* 866-431-5981. *E-mail:* auadmissions@argosyu.edu.

▶ **See page 466 for the College Close-Up.**

BEL–REA INSTITUTE OF ANIMAL TECHNOLOGY

Denver, Colorado   www.bel-rea.com/

Director of Admissions Ms. Paulette Kaufman, Director, Bel–Rea Institute of Animal Technology, 1681 South Dayton Street, Denver, CO 80247. *Phone:* 303-751-8700. *Toll-free phone:* 800-950-8001.

BLAIR COLLEGE

Colorado Springs, Colorado   blair-college.com/

Director of Admissions Ms. Dawn Collins, Director of Admissions, Blair College, 1815 Jet Wing Drive, Colorado Springs, CO 80916. *Phone:* 719-630-6580. *Toll-free phone:* 888-741-4271. *Fax:* 719-574-4493. *E-mail:* dcollins@cci.edu.

BOULDER COLLEGE OF MASSAGE THERAPY

Boulder, Colorado

CAMBRIDGE COLLEGE

Aurora, Colorado

COLLEGEAMERICA–COLORADO SPRINGS

Colorado Spring, Colorado

COLLEGEAMERICA–DENVER

Denver, Colorado   www.collegeamerica.com/

Director of Admissions Barbara W. Thomas, President, CollegeAmerica–Denver, 1385 South Colorado Boulevard, Denver, CO 80222-1912. *Phone:* 303-691-9756. *Toll-free phone:* 800-97-SKILLS. *Fax:* 303-695-6059. *E-mail:* collegeamerica@aol.com.

COLLEGEAMERICA–FORT COLLINS

Fort Collins, Colorado   www.collegeamerica.edu/

Director of Admissions Ms. Anna DiTorrice-Mull, Director of Admissions, CollegeAmerica–Fort Collins, 4601 South Mason Street, Fort Collins, CO 80525. *Phone:* 970-223-6060 Ext. 8002. *Toll-free phone:* 800-97-SKILLS.

COLORADO MOUNTAIN COLLEGE

Glenwood Springs, Colorado   www.coloradomtn.edu/

- **District-supported** 2-year, founded 1965, part of Colorado Mountain College District System
- **Rural** 680-acre campus
- **Coed,** 867 undergraduate students

Colorado Mountain College (CMC) offers high-quality instruction in a centered environment. Degree choices range from occupational to transfer options. CMC's Associate of Arts and Associate of Science degrees are part of the State Transfer Guarantee to any 4-year public college/university in Colorado. CMC also offers specialized occupational programs in culinary areas, graphic design, natural resources, outdoor leadership, photography, the ski industry, and veterinary technology.

Undergraduates Students come from 38 states and territories, 20% are from out of state, 0.3% African American, 1% Asian American or Pacific Islander, 11% Hispanic American, 0.8% Native American, 0.1% international, 44% live on campus.

Freshmen *Admission:* 579 applied, 579 admitted. *Average high school GPA:* 2.40.

Faculty *Total:* 22. *Student/faculty ratio:* 17:1.

Majors Accounting; behavioral sciences; biological and physical sciences; biology/biological sciences; business administration and management; commercial and advertising art; computer engineering technology; computer systems networking and telecommunications; computer/technical support; criminal justice/law enforcement administration; data entry/microcomputer applications related; dramatic/theater arts; English; humanities; liberal arts and sciences/liberal studies; mathematics; natural sciences; nursing (licensed practical/vocational nurse training); nursing (registered nurse training); photography; psychology; social sciences; therapeutic recreation; veterinary technology.

Academics *Calendar:* semesters. *Degree:* certificates and associate. *Special study options:* academic remediation for entering students, adult/continuing education programs, advanced placement credit, cooperative education, distance learning, honors programs, independent study, internships, part-time degree program, services for LD students, study abroad, summer session for credit.

Library Quigley Library with 36,000 titles, 186 serial subscriptions, an OPAC, a Web page.

Computers on Campus 65 computers available on campus for general student use. A campuswide network can be accessed from student residence rooms. Internet access, at least one staffed computer lab available.

Student Life *Housing:* on-campus residence required for freshman year. *Options:* coed. Campus housing is university owned. Freshman applicants given priority for college housing. *Activities and Organizations:* drama/theater group, student-run newspaper, student government, outdoor activities, World Awareness Society, Peer Mentors, Student Activities Board. *Campus security:* 24-hour emergency response devices, controlled dormitory access. *Student services:* health clinic, personal/psychological counseling.

Athletics Member NJCAA. *Intercollegiate sports:* soccer M/W. *Intramural sports:* basketball M/W, rock climbing M/W, skiing (cross-country) M/W, skiing (downhill) M/W, ultimate Frisbee M/W, volleyball M/W.

Standardized Tests *Recommended:* SAT or ACT (for admission).

Costs (2006–07) *Tuition:* area resident $1290 full-time, $43 per credit part-time; state resident $2160 full-time, $72 per credit part-time; nonresident $6930 full-time, $231 per credit part-time. *Required fees:* $180 full-time. *Room and board:* $6600; room only: $3400.

Applying *Options:* early admission, deferred entrance. *Required:* high school transcript. *Application deadline:* rolling (freshmen), rolling (transfers).

Freshmen Application Contact Ms. Cris Hauskins, Admissions Assistant, Colorado Mountain College, PO Box 10001, Department PG, Glenwood Springs, CO 81601. *Phone:* 970-947-8276. *Toll-free phone:* 800-621-8559. *E-mail:* joinus@coloradomtn.edu.

▶ **See page 532 for the College Close-Up.**

COLORADO MOUNTAIN COLLEGE, ALPINE CAMPUS

Steamboat Springs, Colorado　　　**www.coloradomtn.edu/**

- **District-supported** 2-year, founded 1965, part of Colorado Mountain College District System
- **Rural** 10-acre campus
- **Coed,** 1,104 undergraduate students, 41% full-time, 47% women, 53% men

Undergraduates 454 full-time, 650 part-time. Students come from 49 states and territories, 15% are from out of state, 0.7% African American, 2% Asian American or Pacific Islander, 11% Hispanic American, 1% Native American, 1% international, 44% live on campus.

Freshmen *Admission:* 579 applied, 579 admitted. *Average high school GPA:* 2.40.

Faculty *Total:* 19.

Majors Accounting; behavioral sciences; biological and physical sciences; biology/biological sciences; business administration and management; computer engineering technology; consumer merchandising/retailing management; data entry/microcomputer applications related; English; fine/studio arts; geology/earth science; hospitality administration; hotel/motel administration; humanities; liberal arts and sciences/liberal studies; marketing/marketing management; mathematics; parks, recreation and leisure facilities management; physical sciences; pre-engineering; social sciences.

Academics *Calendar:* semesters. *Degree:* certificates and associate. *Special study options:* academic remediation for entering students, adult/continuing education programs, advanced placement credit, cooperative education, distance learning, honors programs, independent study, internships, part-time degree program, services for LD students, study abroad, summer session for credit.

Library 17,000 titles, 192 serial subscriptions, an OPAC, a Web page.

Computers on Campus 60 computers available on campus for general student use. A campuswide network can be accessed from student residence rooms. Internet access, at least one staffed computer lab available.

Student Life *Housing:* on-campus residence required for freshman year. *Options:* coed. Campus housing is university owned. *Activities and Organizations:* student-run newspaper, student government, Forensics Team, Ski Club, International Club, Phi Theta Kappa. *Campus security:* 24-hour emergency response devices, controlled dormitory access. *Student services:* health clinic, personal/psychological counseling.

Athletics *Intercollegiate sports:* skiing (downhill) M/W. *Intramural sports:* basketball M/W, skiing (cross-country) M/W, skiing (downhill) M/W, soccer M/W, ultimate Frisbee M/W, volleyball M/W.

Standardized Tests *Recommended:* SAT or ACT (for admission).

Costs (2006–07) *Tuition:* area resident $1290 full-time, $43 per credit part-time; state resident $2160 full-time, $72 per credit part-time; nonresident $6930 full-time, $231 per credit part-time. *Required fees:* $180 full-time. *Room and board:* $6600; room only: $3400.

Applying *Options:* early admission, deferred entrance. *Required:* high school transcript. *Application deadline:* rolling (freshmen), rolling (transfers).

Freshmen Application Contact Ms. Janice Bell, Admissions Assistant, Colorado Mountain College, Alpine Campus, PO Box 10001, Department PG, Glenwood Springs, CO 81602. *Phone:* 970-870-4417 Ext. 4417. *Toll-free phone:* 800-621-8559. *E-mail:* joinus@coloradomtn.edu.

COLORADO MOUNTAIN COLLEGE, TIMBERLINE CAMPUS

Leadville, Colorado　　　**www.coloradomtn.edu/**

- **District-supported** 2-year, founded 1965, part of Colorado Mountain College District System
- **Rural** 200-acre campus
- **Coed,** 1,305 undergraduate students

Undergraduates Students come from 48 states and territories, 20% are from out of state, 0.1% African American, 0.4% Asian American or Pacific Islander, 17% Hispanic American, 0.2% Native American, 30% live on campus.

Freshmen *Admission:* 242 applied, 242 admitted. *Average high school GPA:* 2.40.

Faculty *Total:* 14.

Majors Accounting; business/commerce; corrections; criminal justice/law enforcement administration; early childhood education; environmental studies; general studies; historic preservation and conservation; land use planning and management; liberal arts and sciences/liberal studies; parks, recreation and leisure; parks, recreation and leisure facilities management.

Academics *Calendar:* semesters. *Degree:* certificates and associate. *Special study options:* academic remediation for entering students, adult/continuing education programs, advanced placement credit, cooperative education, distance learning, English as a second language, honors programs, independent study, internships, part-time degree program, services for LD students, study abroad, summer session for credit.

Library 25,000 titles, 185 serial subscriptions.

Computers on Campus 30 computers available on campus for general student use. A campuswide network can be accessed from student residence rooms. Internet access, at least one staffed computer lab available.

Student Life *Housing:* on-campus residence required for freshman year. *Options:* coed. Freshman applicants given priority for college housing. *Activities and Organizations:* Environmental Club, Outdoor Club, Student Activities Board. *Campus security:* 24-hour emergency response devices, controlled dormitory access. *Student services:* health clinic, personal/psychological counseling.

Athletics *Intramural sports:* basketball M, rock climbing M/W, skiing (cross-country) M/W, skiing (downhill) M/W, soccer M/W, volleyball M/W.

Costs (2006–07) *Tuition:* area resident $1290 full-time, $43 per credit part-time; state resident $2160 full-time, $72 per credit part-time; nonresident $6930 full-time, $231 per credit part-time. *Required fees:* $180 full-time. *Room and board:* $6600; room only: $3400.

Applying *Options:* early admission, deferred entrance. *Required:* high school transcript. *Application deadline:* rolling (freshmen), rolling (transfers).

Freshmen Application Contact Ms. Virginia Espinoza, Admissions Assistant, Colorado Mountain College, Timberline Campus, PO Box 10001, Department PG, Glenwood Springs, CO 81602. *Phone:* 719-486-4291. *Toll-free phone:* 800-621-8559. *E-mail:* joinus@coloradomtn.edu.

COLORADO NORTHWESTERN COMMUNITY COLLEGE

Rangely, Colorado　　　**www.cncc.edu/**

- **State-supported** 2-year, founded 1962, part of Colorado Community College and Occupational Education System
- **Rural** 150-acre campus
- **Endowment** $27,000
- **Coed**

Colorado Northwestern Community College's residential campus in Rangely, provides athletics and outdoor recreation opportunities. The Rangely and

Colorado Northwestern Community College (continued)

Craig campuses offer A.A. and A.S. degrees and vocational programs, such as aviation, construction technology, criminal justice, dental hygiene, nursing, and power plant and petroleum technology. Prospective students should visit http://www.cncc.edu or call 800-562-1105 (toll-free) for more information.

Undergraduates 499 full-time, 1,743 part-time. Students come from 28 states and territories, 3 other countries, 5% are from out of state, 0.8% African American, 0.6% Asian American or Pacific Islander, 5% Hispanic American, 1% Native American, 0.3% international, 7% transferred in, 62% live on campus. *Retention:* 55% of 2003 full-time freshmen returned.

Faculty *Student/faculty ratio:* 9:1.

Academics *Calendar:* semesters. *Degree:* certificates and associate. *Special study options:* academic remediation for entering students, adult/continuing education programs, advanced placement credit, distance learning, double majors, independent study, internships, part-time degree program, services for LD students, student-designed majors, summer session for credit.

Student Life *Campus security:* student patrols, late-night transport/escort service.

Athletics Member NJCAA.

Financial Aid Of all full-time matriculated undergraduates who enrolled in 2004, 35 Federal Work-Study jobs (averaging $1000). 80 state and other part-time jobs (averaging $1600).

Applying *Options:* early admission, deferred entrance. *Required:* high school transcript. *Required for some:* essay or personal statement, 3 letters of recommendation, interview.

Director of Admissions Mr. Gene Bilodeau, Registrar, Colorado Northwestern Community College, 500 Kennedy Drive, Rangely, CO 81648. *Phone:* 970-824-1103. *Toll-free phone:* 970-675-3221 Ext. 218 (in-state); 800-562-1105 Ext. 218 (out-of-state). *E-mail:* gene.bilodeau@cncc.edu.

COLORADO SCHOOL OF HEALING ARTS
Lakewood, Colorado www.csha.net/

- **Proprietary** 2-year, founded 1986
- **Coed,** 240 undergraduate students, 62% full-time, 86% women, 14% men

Undergraduates 149 full-time, 91 part-time. 3% African American, 0.8% Asian American or Pacific Islander, 9% Hispanic American, 2% Native American, 1% international.
Freshmen *Admission:* 26 applied, 26 admitted, 26 enrolled.

Faculty *Total:* 35, 11% full-time, 9% with terminal degrees. *Student/faculty ratio:* 13:1.

Majors Massage therapy.

Academics *Calendar:* quarters. *Degree:* certificates and associate.

Student Life *Student services:* personal/psychological counseling.

Costs (2006–07) *Tuition:* $8925 full-time, $13 per quarter hour part-time. *Required fees:* $1236 full-time.

Applying *Application fee:* $50. *Required:* high school transcript, interview. *Application deadline:* 10/1 (freshmen).

Freshmen Application Contact Ms. Chris Smith, Colorado School of Healing Arts, 7655 West Mississippi Avenue, Suite 100, Lakewood, CO 80226. *Phone:* 303-986-2320. *Toll-free phone:* 800-233-7114. *Fax:* 303-980-6594.

COLORADO SCHOOL OF TRADES
Lakewood, Colorado www.schooloftrades.com/

- **Proprietary** 2-year
- **Coed,** 125 undergraduate students, 100% full-time, 2% women, 98% men
- **87%** of applicants were admitted

Undergraduates 125 full-time. 88% are from out of state.
Freshmen *Admission:* 174 applied, 152 admitted, 20 enrolled.

Faculty *Total:* 10. *Student/faculty ratio:* 12:1.

Majors Gunsmithing.

Academics *Degree:* associate.

Costs (2006–07) *Tuition:* $16,200 full-time. *Required fees:* $154 full-time.

Applying *Application fee:* $25. *Required:* essay or personal statement, high school transcript, interview.

Director of Admissions Mr. Robert Martin, Director, Colorado School of Trades, 1575 Hoyt Street, Lakewood, CO 80215-2996. *Toll-free phone:* 800-234-4594.

COMMUNITY COLLEGE OF AURORA
Aurora, Colorado www.ccaurora.edu/

- **State-supported** 2-year, founded 1983
- **Suburban** campus with easy access to Denver
- **Coed**

Undergraduates 1,502 full-time, 4,023 part-time. 20% African American, 7% Asian American or Pacific Islander, 11% Hispanic American, 1% Native American, 1% transferred in.

Faculty *Student/faculty ratio:* 16:1.

Academics *Calendar:* semesters. *Degree:* certificates and associate. *Special study options:* academic remediation for entering students, adult/continuing education programs, distance learning, English as a second language, external degree program, independent study, internships, off-campus study, part-time degree program, services for LD students, summer session for credit.

Student Life *Campus security:* late-night transport/escort service.

Standardized Tests *Recommended:* SAT or ACT (for placement).

Costs (2005–06) *Tuition:* state resident $2184 full-time, $73 per credit hour part-time; nonresident $11,286 full-time, $376 per credit hour part-time. *Required fees:* $128 full-time, $3 per credit hour part-time, $22 per term part-time.

Financial Aid Of all full-time matriculated undergraduates who enrolled in 2004, 61 Federal Work-Study jobs (averaging $2357). 91 state and other part-time jobs (averaging $2431).

Applying *Options:* early admission.

Freshmen Application Contact Ms. Connie Simpson, Director of Registrations, Records, and Admission, Community College of Aurora, 16000 East CentreTech Parkway, Aurora, CO 80011-9036. *Phone:* 303-360-4700.

COMMUNITY COLLEGE OF DENVER
Denver, Colorado www.ccd.edu/

- **State-supported** 2-year, founded 1970, part of Community Colleges of Colorado
- **Urban** 171-acre campus
- **Coed,** 8,909 undergraduate students, 23% full-time, 63% women, 37% men

Undergraduates 2,041 full-time, 6,868 part-time. Students come from 35 states and territories, 0.4% are from out of state, 17% African American, 6% Asian American or Pacific Islander, 26% Hispanic American, 2% Native American, 6% international, 2% transferred in.
Freshmen *Admission:* 1,127 enrolled.

Faculty *Total:* 441, 15% full-time. *Student/faculty ratio:* 23:1.

Majors Accounting; administrative assistant and secretarial science; business administration and management; computer and information sciences; dental hygiene; drafting; electroneurodiagnostic/electroencephalographic technology; general studies; graphic design; human services; nursing (licensed practical/vocational nurse training); nursing (registered nurse training); office management; paralegal/legal assistant; radiologic technology/science; safety/security technology; teacher assistant/aide; veterinary technology; welding technology.

Academics *Calendar:* semesters. *Degree:* certificates and associate. *Special study options:* academic remediation for entering students, accelerated degree program, adult/continuing education programs, advanced placement credit, cooperative education, distance learning, double majors, English as a second language, freshman honors college, honors programs, independent study, internships, off-campus study, part-time degree program, services for LD students, study abroad, summer session for credit. *ROTC:* Army (c).

Library Auraria Library plus 1 other with 683,045 titles, 3,233 serial subscriptions, 16,821 audiovisual materials, an OPAC, a Web page.

Computers on Campus 1142 computers available on campus for general student use. A campuswide network can be accessed from off campus. Internet access, at least one staffed computer lab available.

Student Life *Housing:* college housing not available. *Activities and Organizations:* student-run newspaper, Trio Advocates for Multicultural Students, Student Alliance for Human Services, Ad Hoc Nursing, Black Men on Campus, Auraria Fine Arts. *Campus security:* 24-hour emergency response devices and patrols, late-night transport/escort service. *Student services:* health clinic, personal/psychological counseling.

Athletics *Intramural sports:* archery M/W, badminton M/W, basketball M/W, bowling M/W, cross-country running M/W, equestrian sports M/W, fencing M/W, field hockey M/W, football M/W, golf M/W, gymnastics M/W, racquetball M/W, riflery M/W, rugby M/W, skiing (cross-country) M/W, skiing (downhill) M/W, soccer M/W, swimming and diving M/W, table tennis M/W, tennis M/W, track and field M/W, volleyball M/W, weight lifting M/W.

Costs (2006–07) *Tuition:* state resident $2237 full-time, $75 per credit part-time; nonresident $10,355 full-time, $345 per credit part-time. *Required fees:* $612 full-time.

Financial Aid Of all full-time matriculated undergraduates who enrolled in 2004, 95 Federal Work-Study jobs (averaging $2442). 305 state and other part-time jobs (averaging $2156).

Applying *Options:* common application, electronic application, early admission, deferred entrance. *Application deadline:* rolling (freshmen), rolling (transfers).

Freshmen Application Contact Ms. Emita Samuels, Dean of Enrollment Services, Community College of Denver, PO Box 173363, 1111 West Colfax Avenue, Denver, CO 80217-3363. *Phone:* 303-556-6325. *E-mail:* enrollment_services@ccd.edu.

DENVER ACADEMY OF COURT REPORTING
Westminster, Colorado   **www.dacr.org/**

Director of Admissions Mr. Howard Brookner, Director of Admissions, Denver Academy of Court Reporting, 7290 Samuel Drive, Suite 200, Denver, CO 80221-2792. *Phone:* 303-427-5292 Ext. 14. *Toll-free phone:* 800-574-2087.

DENVER AUTOMOTIVE AND DIESEL COLLEGE
Denver, Colorado   **www.dadc.com/**

Director of Admissions Mr. John Chalupa, Director of Admissions, Denver Automotive and Diesel College, 460 South Lipan Street, Denver, CO 80223-2025. *Phone:* 303-722-5724. *Toll-free phone:* 800-347-3232.

DENVER CAREER COLLEGE
Thornton, Colorado

FRONT RANGE COMMUNITY COLLEGE
Westminster, Colorado   **frcc.cc.co.us/**

- **State-supported** 2-year, founded 1968, part of Community Colleges of Colorado System
- **Suburban** 90-acre campus with easy access to Denver
- **Coed,** 14,957 undergraduate students, 34% full-time, 59% women, 41% men

Undergraduates 5,149 full-time, 9,808 part-time. Students come from 40 states and territories, 104 other countries, 2% are from out of state, 1% African American, 3% Asian American or Pacific Islander, 11% Hispanic American, 1% Native American, 0.9% international.

Freshmen *Admission:* 6,269 applied, 6,269 admitted, 3,160 enrolled.

Faculty *Total:* 1,001, 17% full-time, 2% with terminal degrees. *Student/faculty ratio:* 16:1.

Majors Accounting; architectural engineering technology; automotive engineering technology; business administration and management; business automation/technology/data entry; computer and information sciences; construction trades; dietetic technician; drafting/design engineering technologies related; early childhood education; electrical/electronics maintenance and repair technology related; general studies; heating, air conditioning and refrigeration technology; intermedia/multimedia; landscaping and groundskeeping; language interpretation and translation; liberal arts and sciences/liberal studies; machine tool technology; medical staff services technology; nursing assistant/aide and patient care assistant; nursing (registered nurse training); paralegal/legal assistant; restaurant/food services management; veterinary technology; welding technology.

Academics *Calendar:* semesters. *Degree:* certificates and associate. *Special study options:* academic remediation for entering students, adult/continuing education programs, advanced placement credit, cooperative education, distance learning, double majors, English as a second language, external degree program, freshman honors college, honors programs, internships, off-campus study, part-time degree program, services for LD students, student-designed majors, study abroad, summer session for credit. *ROTC:* Army (c), Air Force (c).

Library College Hill Library with an OPAC, a Web page.

Computers on Campus 62 computers available on campus for general student use. A campuswide network can be accessed from off campus that provide access to online courses. Internet access, online (class) registration, at least one staffed computer lab available.

Student Life *Housing:* college housing not available. *Activities and Organizations:* drama/theater group, student-run newspaper, Student Government Association, Student Colorado Registry of Interpreters for the Deaf, Alpha Mu Psi, Alpha Tau Kappa, Hispanic Club. *Campus security:* 24-hour patrols, late-night transport/escort service. *Student services:* personal/psychological counseling.

Costs (2005–06) *Tuition:* state resident $1746 full-time, $72 per credit part-time; nonresident $8284 full-time, $345 per credit part-time. *Required fees:* $223 full-time, $4 per credit part-time, $40 per term part-time.

Financial Aid Of all full-time matriculated undergraduates who enrolled in 2004, 165 Federal Work-Study jobs (averaging $1316). 277 state and other part-time jobs (averaging $1635).

Applying *Options:* common application, electronic application, early admission, deferred entrance. *Application deadline:* rolling (freshmen), rolling (transfers).

Freshmen Application Contact Ms. Yolanda Espinoza, Registrar, Front Range Community College, 3645 West 112th Avenue, Westminster, CO 80031. *Phone:* 303-404-5000.

HERITAGE COLLEGE
Denver, Colorado

INSTITUTE OF BUSINESS & MEDICAL CAREERS
Fort Collins, Colorado   **www.ibmcedu.com/**

Director of Admissions Mr. Steve Steele, Vice President of Operations, Institute of Business & Medical Careers, 1609 Oakridge Drive, Fort Collins, CO 80525. *Phone:* 970-223-2669 Ext. 102. *Toll-free phone:* 800-495-2669.

INTELLITEC COLLEGE
Colorado Springs, Colorado   **www.intelliteccollege.edu/**

Director of Admissions Ms. Ellen Pitrone, Director of Admissions, IntelliTec College, 2315 East Pikes Peak Avenue, Colorado Springs, CO 80909-6030. *Phone:* 719-632-7626. *Toll-free phone:* 800-748-2282.

INTELLITEC COLLEGE
Grand Junction, Colorado   **www.intelliteccollege.edu/**

- **Proprietary** 2-year
- **Small-town** campus
- **Coed,** 486 undergraduate students, 100% full-time, 83% women, 17% men

Undergraduates 486 full-time. 2% African American, 28% Hispanic American, 0.6% Native American.

Freshmen *Admission:* 256 applied, 256 admitted, 256 enrolled.

Faculty *Total:* 46, 57% full-time.

Majors Architectural drafting; clinical/medical laboratory assistant; computer and information sciences; computer systems networking and telecommunications; data entry/microcomputer applications; electrical, electronic and communications engineering technology; heating, air conditioning, ventilation and refrigeration maintenance technology; massage therapy; mechanical drafting; medical administrative assistant and medical secretary; system administration.

Academics *Calendar:* continuous. *Degree:* certificates, diplomas, and associate.

Costs (2006–07) *Tuition:* $5940 full-time.

Applying *Required:* high school transcript, interview.

IntelliTec College (continued)
Freshmen Application Contact Admissions, IntelliTec College, 772 Horizon Drive, Grand Junction, CO 81506. *Phone:* 970-245-8101. *Fax:* 970-243-8074.

INTELLITEC MEDICAL INSTITUTE
Colorado Springs, Colorado
www.intelliteccollege.edu/

Director of Admissions Michelle Squibb, Admissions Representative, IntelliTec Medical Institute, 2345 North Academy Boulevard, Colorado Springs, CO 80909. *Phone:* 719-596-7400.

ITT TECHNICAL INSTITUTE
Thornton, Colorado
www.itt-tech.edu/

- **Proprietary** primarily 2-year, founded 1984, part of ITT Educational Services, Inc
- **Suburban** 2-acre campus with easy access to Denver
- **Coed**

Majors Animation, interactive technology, video graphics and special effects; business administration and management; CAD/CADD drafting/design technology; computer and information systems security; computer programming; criminal justice/law enforcement administration; electrical, electronic and communications engineering technology; system, networking, and LAN/WAN management; web/multimedia management and webmaster; web page, digital/multimedia and information resources design.
Academics *Calendar:* quarters. *Degrees:* associate and bachelor's.
Library a Web page.
Computers on Campus Internet access, at least one staffed computer lab available.
Student Life *Housing:* college housing not available. *Activities and Organizations:* student-run newspaper.
Standardized Tests *Required:* Wonderlic aptitude test (for admission).
Costs (2005–06) *Tuition:* Please see school catalog for specific information.
Applying *Options:* deferred entrance. *Application fee:* $100. *Required:* high school transcript, interview. *Recommended:* letters of recommendation. *Application deadline:* rolling (freshmen), rolling (transfers). *Notification:* continuous (freshmen).
Freshmen Application Contact Ms. Tracy Arnett, Director of Recruitment, ITT Technical Institute, 500 East 84th Avenue, Thornton, CO 80229. *Phone:* 303-288-4488. *Toll-free phone:* 800-395-4488.

LAMAR COMMUNITY COLLEGE
Lamar, Colorado
www.lamarcc.edu/

Freshmen Application Contact Director of Admissions, Lamar Community College, 2401 South Main Street, Lamar, CO 81052-3999. *Phone:* 719-336-1590. *Toll-free phone:* 800-968-6920.

MORGAN COMMUNITY COLLEGE
Fort Morgan, Colorado
www.morgancc.edu/

Freshmen Application Contact Ms. Jody Brown, Student Services, Morgan Community College, Student Services, 17800 Road 20, Fort Morgan, CO 80701. *Phone:* 970-542-3156. *Toll-free phone:* 800-622-0216.

NORTHEASTERN JUNIOR COLLEGE
Sterling, Colorado
www.njc.edu/

Freshmen Application Contact Ms. Tina Joyce, Director of Admissions, Northeastern Junior College, 100 College Avenue, Sterling, CO 80751. *Phone:* 970-521-7000. *Toll-free phone:* 800-626-4637.

OTERO JUNIOR COLLEGE
La Junta, Colorado
www.ojc.edu/

- **State-supported** 2-year, founded 1941, part of Colorado Community College and Occupational Education System
- **Rural** 50-acre campus
- **Coed,** 1,636 undergraduate students, 47% full-time, 61% women, 39% men

Undergraduates 771 full-time, 865 part-time. Students come from 12 states and territories, 2% are from out of state, 2% African American, 0.7% Asian American or Pacific Islander, 30% Hispanic American, 2% Native American, 0.4% international, 15% transferred in, 14% live on campus.
Freshmen *Admission:* 347 enrolled.
Faculty *Total:* 78, 46% full-time.
Majors Administrative assistant and secretarial science; agricultural business and management; automobile/automotive mechanics technology; biological and physical sciences; biology/biological sciences; business administration and management; child development; computer management; data processing and data processing technology; dramatic/theater arts; elementary education; history; humanities; kindergarten/preschool education; legal administrative assistant/secretary; liberal arts and sciences/liberal studies; literature; mathematics; medical administrative assistant and medical secretary; modern languages; nursing (registered nurse training); political science and government; pre-engineering; psychology; social sciences.
Academics *Calendar:* semesters. *Degree:* certificates and associate. *Special study options:* academic remediation for entering students, adult/continuing education programs, advanced placement credit, distance learning, external degree program, internships, part-time degree program, summer session for credit.
Library Wheeler Library with 36,701 titles, 183 serial subscriptions, an OPAC.
Computers on Campus 100 computers available on campus for general student use. A campuswide network can be accessed from student residence rooms. Internet access, at least one staffed computer lab available.
Student Life *Housing:* on-campus residence required for freshman year. *Options:* coed. Campus housing is university owned. *Activities and Organizations:* drama/theater group, student-run newspaper, choral group. *Campus security:* 24-hour patrols, late-night transport/escort service. *Student services:* personal/psychological counseling.
Athletics Member NJCAA. *Intercollegiate sports:* baseball M(s), basketball M(s)/W(s), golf M(s)/W(s), softball W(s), volleyball W(s). *Intramural sports:* basketball M, volleyball M/W.
Costs (2006–07) *Tuition:* state resident $1788 full-time, $75 per credit part-time; nonresident $6626 full-time, $276 per credit part-time. *Required fees:* $184 full-time. *Room and board:* $4512.
Financial Aid Of all full-time matriculated undergraduates who enrolled in 2004, 30 Federal Work-Study jobs (averaging $2000). 100 state and other part-time jobs (averaging $2000).
Applying *Options:* electronic application, early admission. *Recommended:* high school transcript. *Application deadlines:* 8/30 (freshmen), 8/30 (transfers). *Notification:* continuous (freshmen).
Freshmen Application Contact Mr. Brad Franz, Vice President for Student Services, Otero Junior College, 1802 Colorado Avenue, La Junta, CO 81050-3415. *Phone:* 719-384-6833. *Fax:* 719-384-6933. *E-mail:* j_schiro@ojc.cccoes.edu.

PARKS COLLEGE
Aurora, Colorado
www.parks-college.com/

Director of Admissions Mr. Rick Harding, Director of Admissions, Parks College, 14280 East Jewell Avenue, Suite 100, Aurora, CO 80014. *Phone:* 303-745-6244. *Fax:* 303-745-6245. *E-mail:* rharding@cci.edu.

PARKS COLLEGE
Denver, Colorado
www.parks-college.com/

Director of Admissions Ms. JoAnn Q. Navarro, Director of Admissions, Parks College, 9065 Grant Street, Denver, CO 80229-4339. *Phone:* 303-457-2757. *Fax:* 303-457-4030. *E-mail:* jqnira@cci.edu.

PIKES PEAK COMMUNITY COLLEGE

Colorado Springs, Colorado   **www.ppcc.edu/**

Director of Admissions Mr. Troy Nelson, Associate Director, Enrollment Services, Admissions, Pikes Peak Community College, 5675 South Academy Boulevard, Colorado Springs, CO 80906-5498. *Phone:* 719-540-7041. *Toll-free phone:* 866-411-7722.

PIMA MEDICAL INSTITUTE

Denver, Colorado   **www.pmi.edu**

- **Proprietary** 2-year, founded 1988, part of Vocational Training Institutes, Inc
- **Urban** campus
- **Coed**

Faculty *Student/faculty ratio:* 15:1.
Academics *Calendar:* modular. *Degree:* certificates and associate. *Special study options:* academic remediation for entering students, cooperative education, internships.
Standardized Tests *Required:* Wonderlic Scholastic Level Exam (for admission).
Costs (2005–06) *Tuition:* Tuition varies depending on course.
Applying *Required:* interview. *Required for some:* high school transcript.
Freshmen Application Contact Admissions Office, Pima Medical Institute, Pima Medical Institute, 1701 West 72nd Avenue, Suite 130, Denver, CO 80221. *Phone:* 303-426-1800. *Toll-free phone:* 888-898-9048.

PLATT COLLEGE

Aurora, Colorado   **www.plattcolorado.edu/**

Freshmen Application Contact Admissions Office, Platt College, 3100 South Parker Road, Suite 200, Aurora, CO 80014-3141. *Phone:* 303-369-5151.

PUEBLO COMMUNITY COLLEGE

Pueblo, Colorado   **www.pueblocc.edu/**

Director of Admissions Ms. Mary Santoro, Director of Admissions and Records, Pueblo Community College, 900 West Orman Avenue, Pueblo, CO 81004. *Phone:* 719-549-3010.

RED ROCKS COMMUNITY COLLEGE

Lakewood, Colorado   **www.rrcc.edu/**

Freshmen Application Contact Ms. Judy Beckmann, Director of Student Recruitment, Red Rocks Community College, 13300 West 6th Avenue Box 5, Lakewood, CO 80228-1255. *Phone:* 303-914-6234.

TRINIDAD STATE JUNIOR COLLEGE

Trinidad, Colorado   **www.trinidadstate.edu/**

- **State-supported** 2-year, founded 1925, part of Colorado Community College and Occupational Education System
- **Small-town** 17-acre campus
- **Endowment** $4.7 million
- **Coed**, 1,831 undergraduate students, 42% full-time, 60% women, 40% men

Undergraduates 775 full-time, 1,056 part-time. Students come from 33 states and territories, 5 other countries, 8% are from out of state, 2% transferred in, 30% live on campus. *Retention:* 50% of 2003 full-time freshmen returned. Freshmen *Admission:* 841 applied, 841 admitted, 431 enrolled.
Faculty *Total:* 140, 29% full-time, 100% with terminal degrees. *Student/faculty ratio:* 16:1.

Majors Accounting; administrative assistant and secretarial science; aquaculture; art teacher education; automobile/automotive mechanics technology; biological and physical sciences; biology/biological sciences; business administration and management; carpentry; chemistry; civil engineering technology; commercial and advertising art; computer and information sciences related; computer science; computer systems networking and telecommunications; construction engineering technology; corrections; cosmetology; criminal justice/police science; data processing and data processing technology; design and visual communications; digital communication and media/multimedia; drafting and design technology; dramatic/theater arts; education; engineering; English; farm and ranch management; forestry; gunsmithing; heavy equipment maintenance technology; industrial technology; information science/studies; information technology; kindergarten/preschool education; liberal arts and sciences/liberal studies; management information systems; music; natural resources management and policy; nursing assistant/aide and patient care assistant; nursing (licensed practical/vocational nurse training); nursing (registered nurse training); occupational safety and health technology; physical education teaching and coaching; pre-engineering; psychology.
Academics *Calendar:* semesters. *Degree:* certificates, diplomas, and associate. *Special study options:* academic remediation for entering students, accelerated degree program, adult/continuing education programs, advanced placement credit, cooperative education, distance learning, double majors, English as a second language, honors programs, independent study, internships, part-time degree program, services for LD students, student-designed majors, summer session for credit.
Library Frendenthal Library plus 1 other with 54,255 titles, 105 serial subscriptions, 1,574 audiovisual materials, an OPAC.
Computers on Campus 125 computers available on campus for general student use. A campuswide network can be accessed from student residence rooms and from off campus. Internet access, online (class) registration, at least one staffed computer lab available.
Student Life *Housing Options:* coed, men-only, women-only. Campus housing is university owned. *Activities and Organizations:* drama/theater group, student-run newspaper, choral group, student association, International Club, Gunsmithing Club, Nursing Club, Cosmetology Club. *Campus security:* 24-hour emergency response devices and patrols, late-night transport/escort service.
Athletics Member NJCAA. *Intercollegiate sports:* baseball M(s), basketball M(s), softball W, volleyball W(s). *Intramural sports:* badminton M/W, basketball M, bowling M/W, football M/W, riflery M/W, skiing (cross-country) M/W, skiing (downhill) M/W, softball M/W, table tennis M/W, tennis M/W, volleyball M/W, weight lifting M/W.
Costs (2005–06) *Tuition:* state resident $2183 full-time, $73 per credit part-time; nonresident $8280 full-time, $276 per credit part-time. *Required fees:* $528 full-time, $14 per credit part-time. *Room and board:* $4298; room only: $1048. Room and board charges vary according to board plan. *Payment plan:* installment. *Waivers:* senior citizens and employees or children of employees.
Financial Aid Of all full-time matriculated undergraduates who enrolled in 2004, 30 Federal Work-Study jobs (averaging $2040). 40 state and other part-time jobs (averaging $2040).
Applying *Options:* common application, electronic application, deferred entrance. *Required:* high school transcript. *Application deadline:* rolling (freshmen), rolling (transfers). *Notification:* continuous (freshmen).
Freshmen Application Contact Mr. Alex Borja, Admissions Counselor, Trinidad State Junior College, 600 Prospect, Trinidad, CO 81082-2396. *Phone:* 719-846-5545. *Toll-free phone:* 800-621-8752. *Fax:* 719-846-5620. *E-mail:* alex.borja@trinidadstate.edu.

WESTWOOD COLLEGE—DENVER NORTH

Denver, Colorado   **www.westwood.edu/**

- **Proprietary** primarily 2-year, founded 1953
- **Suburban** 11-acre campus
- **Coed**

Undergraduates 1,086 full-time, 337 part-time. Students come from 38 states and territories, 2 other countries, 16% are from out of state, 3% African American, 3% Asian American or Pacific Islander, 16% Hispanic American, 2% Native American, 0.1% international, 0.2% transferred in. *Retention:* 28% of 2003 full-time freshmen returned.
Faculty *Student/faculty ratio:* 13:1.
Academics *Calendar:* 5 terms. *Degrees:* diplomas, associate, and bachelor's. *Special study options:* academic remediation for entering students, accelerated degree program, advanced placement credit, distance learning, independent study, internships, part-time degree program, services for LD students, summer session for credit.
Student Life *Campus security:* 24-hour emergency response devices.
Standardized Tests *Required for some:* ACCUPLACER. *Recommended:* SAT or ACT (for admission), SAT and SAT Subject Tests or ACT (for admission).

Westwood College–Denver North (continued)

Costs (2005–06) *Tuition:* $2796 per term part-time. Full-time tuition and fees vary according to course load and program. Part-time tuition and fees vary according to course load and program. *Required fees:* $425 per credit part-time, $120 per term part-time.

Applying *Options:* common application, deferred entrance. *Application fee:* $100. *Required:* high school transcript, interview. *Required for some:* ACCUPLACER.

Freshmen Application Contact Ms. Dianne Hopkins, New Student Coordinator, Westwood College–Denver North, 7350 North Broadway, Denver, CO 80221-3653. *Phone:* 303-650-5050 Ext. 325. *Toll-free phone:* 800-992-5050.

▶ See page 624 for the College Close-Up.

WESTWOOD COLLEGE–DENVER SOUTH
Denver, Colorado   www.westwood.edu/

Director of Admissions Mr. Ron DeJong, Director of Admissions, Westwood College–Denver South, 3150 South Sheridan Boulevard, Denver, CO 80227-5548. *Phone:* 303-934-2790.

▶ See page 626 for the College Close-Up.

CONNECTICUT

ASNUNTUCK COMMUNITY COLLEGE
Enfield, Connecticut   www.acc.commnet.edu/

- **State-supported** 2-year, founded 1972, part of Connecticut Community College System
- **Suburban** 4-acre campus
- **Coed,** 1,483 undergraduate students, 35% full-time, 59% women, 41% men

Undergraduates 526 full-time, 957 part-time. Students come from 3 states and territories, 4% are from out of state, 5% African American, 2% Asian American or Pacific Islander, 3% Hispanic American, 0.3% Native American, 0.1% international, 3% transferred in.
Freshmen *Admission:* 303 applied, 303 admitted, 199 enrolled.

Faculty *Total:* 115, 22% full-time. *Student/faculty ratio:* 16:1.

Majors Accounting; administrative assistant and secretarial science; banking and financial support services; business administration and management; business automation/technology/data entry; communication and media related; computer and information sciences; criminal justice/safety; early childhood education; engineering science; fine/studio arts; general studies; human services; industrial technology; legal administrative assistant; liberal arts and sciences/liberal studies; machine tool technology; mass communication/media; medical office assistant; radio and television; special products marketing.

Academics *Calendar:* semesters. *Degree:* certificates and associate. *Special study options:* academic remediation for entering students, adult/continuing education programs, advanced placement credit, distance learning, double majors, English as a second language, independent study, internships, part-time degree program, services for LD students, student-designed majors, study abroad, summer session for credit.

Library ACTC Learning Resource Center with 31,700 titles, 257 serial subscriptions, 2,570 audiovisual materials, an OPAC.

Computers on Campus 90 computers available on campus for general student use. A campuswide network can be accessed from off campus. Internet access, at least one staffed computer lab available.

Student Life *Housing:* college housing not available. *Activities and Organizations:* drama/theater group, student-run newspaper, radio station, Phi Theta Kappa, Drama Club, Outdoor Club, Poetry Club, Ski Club. *Campus security:* 24-hour patrols, late-night transport/escort service. *Student services:* women's center.

Costs (2006–07) *Tuition:* state resident $2352 full-time, $98 per credit part-time; nonresident $7976 full-time, $294 per credit part-time. *Required fees:* $320 full-time, $58 per credit part-time.

Financial Aid Of all full-time matriculated undergraduates who enrolled in 2004, 23 Federal Work-Study jobs (averaging $3000). 5 state and other part-time jobs (averaging $3000).

Applying *Options:* deferred entrance. *Application fee:* $20. *Required:* high school transcript. *Application deadline:* rolling (freshmen), rolling (transfers). *Notification:* continuous (freshmen).

Freshmen Application Contact Ms. Donna Shaw, Director of Admissions, Asnuntuck Community College, 170 Elm Street, Enfield, CT 06082-3800. *Phone:* 860-253-3018. *Toll-free phone:* 800-501-3967. *Fax:* 860-253-3014. *E-mail:* dshaw@acc.commnet.edu.

BRIARWOOD COLLEGE
Southington, Connecticut   www.briarwood.edu

- **Proprietary** primarily 2-year, founded 1966
- **Small-town** 32-acre campus with easy access to Boston and Hartford
- **Endowment** $27,595
- **Coed,** 647 undergraduate students, 60% full-time, 74% women, 26% men

Undergraduates 389 full-time, 258 part-time. Students come from 11 states and territories, 2 other countries, 7% are from out of state, 22% African American, 0.8% Asian American or Pacific Islander, 11% Hispanic American, 0.2% Native American, 1% international, 13% transferred in, 21% live on campus.
Freshmen *Admission:* 607 applied, 442 admitted, 165 enrolled. *Test scores:* SAT verbal scores over 500: 16%; SAT math scores over 500: 19%; SAT verbal scores over 600: 3%; SAT math scores over 600: 16%; SAT verbal scores over 700: 3%; SAT math scores over 700: 16%.

Faculty *Total:* 95, 31% full-time. *Student/faculty ratio:* 10:1.

Majors Accounting; administrative assistant and secretarial science; biotechnology; business administration and management; child development; communication/speech communication and rhetoric; criminal justice/law enforcement administration; dental assisting; dietetics; fashion merchandising; funeral service and mortuary science; general studies; health information/medical records administration; hotel/motel administration; legal administrative assistant/secretary; legal assistant/paralegal; medical administrative assistant and medical secretary; medical/clinical assistant; medical office management; occupational therapist assistant; radio and television broadcasting technology; tourism and travel services management.

Academics *Calendar:* semesters. *Degrees:* certificates, diplomas, associate, and bachelor's. *Special study options:* academic remediation for entering students, accelerated degree program, adult/continuing education programs, advanced placement credit, double majors, English as a second language, independent study, internships, part-time degree program, services for LD students, summer session for credit.

Library Pupillo Library with 11,500 titles, 154 serial subscriptions, 130 audiovisual materials, a Web page.

Computers on Campus 54 computers available on campus for general student use. Internet access, online (class) registration, at least one staffed computer lab available.

Student Life *Housing Options:* coed. Freshman applicants given priority for college housing. *Activities and Organizations:* student-run radio station, student government, Yearbook Committee, Student Ambassador Club, F.A.M.E. (Fashion Merchandising Club). *Campus security:* 24-hour patrols, late-night transport/escort service. *Student services:* personal/psychological counseling.

Athletics *Intramural sports:* basketball M, soccer W, softball M/W.

Costs (2005–06) *Tuition:* $15,200 full-time, $500 per credit part-time. Full-time tuition and fees vary according to program. Part-time tuition and fees vary according to course load and program. No tuition increase for student's term of enrollment. *Required fees:* $220 full-time, $125 per term part-time. *Room only:* $3320. *Payment plan:* installment. *Waivers:* employees or children of employees.

Financial Aid Of all full-time matriculated undergraduates who enrolled in 2004, 33 Federal Work-Study jobs (averaging $600). 30 state and other part-time jobs.

Applying *Options:* common application, electronic application. *Application fee:* $25. *Required:* high school transcript. *Required for some:* essay or personal statement, letters of recommendation, interview. *Application deadline:* rolling (freshmen), rolling (transfers).

Freshmen Application Contact Ms. Donna Yamanis, Director of Enrollment Management, Briarwood College, 2279 Mount Vernon Road, Southington, CT 06489. *Phone:* 860-628-4751 Ext. 133. *Toll-free phone:* 800-952-2444. *Fax:* 860-628-6444.

▶ See page 494 for the College Close-Up.

CAPITAL COMMUNITY COLLEGE

Hartford, Connecticut   **www.ccc.commnet.edu/**

- **State-supported** 2-year, founded 1946, part of Connecticut Community College System
- **Urban** 10-acre campus
- **Coed,** 3,573 undergraduate students, 26% full-time, 72% women, 28% men

Undergraduates 927 full-time, 2,646 part-time. Students come from 3 states and territories, 39% African American, 4% Asian American or Pacific Islander, 27% Hispanic American, 0.3% Native American, 0.8% international. Freshmen *Admission:* 693 enrolled.

Faculty *Total:* 63.

Majors Accounting; administrative assistant and secretarial science; business administration and management; computer and information sciences; computer and information sciences related; computer engineering technology; data entry/microcomputer applications related; electrical, electronic and communications engineering technology; emergency medical technology (EMT paramedic); fire protection and safety technology; fire services administration; information technology; kindergarten/preschool education; liberal arts and sciences/liberal studies; medical/clinical assistant; medical radiologic technology; nursing (registered nurse training); physical therapist assistant; social work; web page, digital/multimedia and information resources design.

Academics *Calendar:* semesters. *Degree:* certificates and associate. *Special study options:* academic remediation for entering students, accelerated degree program, adult/continuing education programs, advanced placement credit, distance learning, double majors, English as a second language, independent study, internships, part-time degree program, services for LD students, summer session for credit.

Library Arthur C. Banks, Jr. Library plus 1 other with 46,760 titles, 359 serial subscriptions, 2,409 audiovisual materials, an OPAC, a Web page.

Computers on Campus 180 computers available on campus for general student use. A campuswide network can be accessed from off campus. Internet access, at least one staffed computer lab available.

Student Life *Housing:* college housing not available. *Activities and Organizations:* drama/theater group, student-run television station, choral group, Latin American Student Association, Student Senate, Senior Renewal Club, Early Childhood Club, Pre-Professional Club. *Campus security:* late-night transport/escort service, security staff during hours of operation, emergency telephones 7 a.m.—11 p.m. *Student services:* personal/psychological counseling.

Costs (2005–06) *Tuition:* state resident $2352 full-time, $98 per credit hour part-time; nonresident $7056 full-time, $294 per credit hour part-time. *Required fees:* $320 full-time.

Financial Aid Of all full-time matriculated undergraduates who enrolled in 2004, 87 Federal Work-Study jobs (averaging $3000). 160 state and other part-time jobs (averaging $3000).

Applying *Application fee:* $20. *Recommended:* high school transcript. *Application deadline:* rolling (freshmen), rolling (transfers). *Notification:* continuous until 9/1 (freshmen).

Freshmen Application Contact Ms. Jackie Phillips, Director of the Welcome and Advising Center, Capital Community College, 950 Main Street, Hartford, CT 06103. *Phone:* 860-906-5078. *Toll-free phone:* 800-894-6126. *E-mail:* mballjdavis@ccc.commnet.edu.

GATEWAY COMMUNITY COLLEGE

New Haven, Connecticut   **www.gwcc.commnet.edu/**

- **State-supported** 2-year, founded 1992, part of Connecticut Community College System
- **Urban** 5-acre campus with easy access to New York City
- **Coed,** 5,739 undergraduate students, 32% full-time, 63% women, 37% men

Undergraduates 1,809 full-time, 3,930 part-time. Students come from 8 states and territories, 60 other countries, 0.1% are from out of state, 26% African American, 3% Asian American or Pacific Islander, 13% Hispanic American, 0.2% Native American, 0.9% international, 7% transferred in. Freshmen *Admission:* 3,381 applied, 3,172 admitted, 1,487 enrolled.

Faculty *Total:* 303, 24% full-time, 5% with terminal degrees. *Student/faculty ratio:* 21:1.

Majors Accounting; automobile/automotive mechanics technology; avionics maintenance technology; biomedical technology; business administration and management; computer and information sciences related; computer engineering related; computer engineering technology; computer graphics; computer typography and composition equipment operation; consumer merchandising/retailing

management; data entry/microcomputer applications; data processing and data processing technology; dietetics; electrical, electronic and communications engineering technology; engineering technology; fashion merchandising; fire science; gerontology; hotel/motel administration; human services; industrial radiologic technology; industrial technology; kindergarten/preschool education; legal administrative assistant/secretary; liberal arts and sciences/liberal studies; mechanical engineering/mechanical technology; medical administrative assistant and medical secretary; mental health/rehabilitation; nuclear medical technology; special products marketing; substance abuse/addiction counseling; word processing.

Academics *Calendar:* semesters. *Degree:* certificates and associate. *Special study options:* academic remediation for entering students, adult/continuing education programs, advanced placement credit, distance learning, English as a second language, external degree program, independent study, internships, off-campus study, part-time degree program, services for LD students, summer session for credit.

Library 54,802 titles, 532 serial subscriptions, 9,902 audiovisual materials, an OPAC.

Computers on Campus 385 computers available on campus for general student use. A campuswide network can be accessed from off campus. Internet access, online (class) registration, at least one staffed computer lab available.

Student Life *Housing:* college housing not available. *Campus security:* late-night transport/escort service.

Athletics Member NJCAA. *Intercollegiate sports:* baseball M, basketball M/W, soccer M, softball W.

Costs (2006–07) *Tuition:* state resident $2352 full-time, $98 per credit part-time; nonresident $7056 full-time, $294 per credit part-time. *Required fees:* $320 full-time.

Financial Aid Of all full-time matriculated undergraduates who enrolled in 2004, 60 Federal Work-Study jobs (averaging $6000).

Applying *Options:* early admission, deferred entrance. *Application fee:* $20. *Required:* high school transcript. *Required for some:* essay or personal statement, interview. *Application deadlines:* 9/1 (freshmen), 9/1 (transfers). *Notification:* continuous until 9/1 (freshmen).

Freshmen Application Contact Ms. Catherine Surface, Director of Admissions, Gateway Community College, 60 Sargent Drive, New Haven, CT 06511. *Phone:* 203-789-7043. *Toll-free phone:* 800-390-7723. *Fax:* 203-285-2018. *E-mail:* gateway_ctc@commnet.edu.

GIBBS COLLEGE

Norwalk, Connecticut   **www.gibbscollege.com/**

Director of Admissions Mr. Ted Havelka, Vice President of Admissions/Marketing, Gibbs College, 148 East Avenue, Norwalk, CT 06851. *Phone:* 203-633-2311. *Toll-free phone:* 800-845-5333.

GOODWIN COLLEGE

East Hartford, Connecticut   **www.goodwin.edu/**

- **Proprietary** 2-year
- **Urban** campus with easy access to Hartford
- **Endowment** $1.0 million
- **Coed,** 1,219 undergraduate students, 11% full-time, 89% women, 11% men

Undergraduates 132 full-time, 1,087 part-time. Students come from 1 other state, 1% are from out of state, 30% African American, 1% Asian American or Pacific Islander, 14% Hispanic American, 0.4% Native American, 10% transferred in. Freshmen *Admission:* 360 applied, 325 admitted, 196 enrolled. *Average high school GPA:* 2.8.

Faculty *Total:* 98, 22% full-time, 5% with terminal degrees. *Student/faculty ratio:* 10:1.

Majors Accounting technology and bookkeeping; business administration and management; business/commerce; computer and information sciences; early childhood education; emergency medical technology (EMT paramedic); entrepreneurship; histologic technician; human services; medical administrative assistant and medical secretary; medical/clinical assistant; medical insurance coding; medical insurance/medical billing; nursing (registered nurse training); respiratory care therapy; security and protective services related; teacher assistant/aide.

Academics *Calendar:* semesters. *Degree:* certificates, diplomas, and associate. *Special study options:* academic remediation for entering students, accelerated degree program, adult/continuing education programs, advanced placement credit, cooperative education, distance learning, double majors, English as a second language, external degree program, honors programs, independent study,

Goodwin College (continued)

internships, off-campus study, part-time degree program, services for LD students, summer session for credit.

Library Goodwin College Library with 6,000 titles, 1,300 serial subscriptions, 506 audiovisual materials, an OPAC.

Computers on Campus 220 computers available on campus for general student use. A campuswide network can be accessed from off campus. Internet access, at least one staffed computer lab available.

Student Life *Housing:* college housing not available. *Campus security:* evening security patrolman.

Costs (2006–07) *Tuition:* $13,570 full-time, $425 per credit part-time. *Required fees:* $300 full-time.

Applying *Options:* common application, electronic application, deferred entrance. *Application fee:* $50. *Required:* essay or personal statement, high school transcript, minimum 2.0 GPA, medical exam. *Recommended:* 2 letters of recommendation, interview. *Notification:* continuous until 8/1 (freshmen).

Freshmen Application Contact Mr. Daniel P. Noonan, Director of Enrollment, Goodwin College, 745 Burnside Avenue, East Hartford, CT 06108. *Phone:* 860-528-4111 Ext. 6902. *Toll-free phone:* 800-889-3282. *Fax:* 860-291-8285. *E-mail:* dnoonan@goodwin.edu.

HOUSATONIC COMMUNITY COLLEGE

Bridgeport, Connecticut   www.hctc.commnet.edu/

Director of Admissions Ms. Delores Y. Curtis, Director of Admissions, Housatonic Community College, 900 Lafayette Boulevard, Bridgeport, CT 06604-4704. *Phone:* 203-332-5102.

INTERNATIONAL COLLEGE OF HOSPITALITY MANAGEMENT

Suffield, Connecticut   www.ichm.edu/

- **Proprietary** 2-year, founded 1992
- **Small-town** 56-acre campus with easy access to New York City or Boston, MA
- **Coed,** 116 undergraduate students, 100% full-time, 59% women, 41% men

The International College of Hospitality Management is the only Swiss college of hospitality management in the United States. The Swiss tradition of *hôtellerie*, combined with practical experience obtained on paid internships in the best American hospitality properties, prepares students for managerial positions in the fastest-growing industry in the world.

Undergraduates 116 full-time. Students come from 6 states and territories, 34 other countries, 50% are from out of state, 6% African American, 16% Asian American or Pacific Islander, 7% Hispanic American, 51% international, 16% transferred in, 90% live on campus.

Freshmen *Admission:* 35 applied, 27 admitted, 27 enrolled.

Faculty *Total:* 13, 54% full-time, 8% with terminal degrees.

Majors Culinary arts; hospitality administration.

Academics *Calendar:* continuous. *Degree:* certificates and associate. *Special study options:* academic remediation for entering students, accelerated degree program, adult/continuing education programs, advanced placement credit, cooperative education, distance learning, English as a second language, independent study, internships, part-time degree program, services for LD students, study abroad.

Library International College of Hospitality Management Library with 10,000 titles, 50 serial subscriptions, an OPAC.

Computers on Campus 23 computers available on campus for general student use. A campuswide network can be accessed from off campus. Internet access, at least one staffed computer lab available.

Student Life *Housing Options:* coed. *Activities and Organizations:* student-run newspaper, student committee, student newsletter, yearbook committee, Ritz Guild, Student Ambassadors. *Campus security:* 24-hour emergency response devices, student patrols, late-night transport/escort service, controlled dormitory access, weekend patrols by trained security personnel. *Student services:* health clinic, personal/psychological counseling.

Athletics *Intramural sports:* basketball M/W, soccer M/W, volleyball M/W.

Standardized Tests *Recommended:* SAT (for admission).

Costs (2005–06) *Comprehensive fee:* $20,878 includes full-time tuition ($15,900) and room and board ($4978). *Room and board:* Room and board charges vary according to board plan. *Payment plans:* installment, deferred payment.

Applying *Options:* common application, electronic application, deferred entrance. *Application fee:* $100. *Required:* high school transcript, 2 letters of recommendation. *Required for some:* essay or personal statement, interview. *Recommended:* interview. *Application deadline:* rolling (freshmen), rolling (transfers). *Notification:* continuous (freshmen).

Freshmen Application Contact Mrs. Tina Merullo, Admissions, International College of Hospitality Management, 1760 Mapleton Avenue, Suffield, CT 06078. *Phone:* 860-668-3515 Ext. 126. *Toll-free phone:* 800-955-0809. *Fax:* 860-668-7369. *E-mail:* admissions@ichm.edu.

▶ **See page 554 for the College Close-Up.**

MANCHESTER COMMUNITY COLLEGE

Manchester, Connecticut   www.mcc.commnet.edu/

- **State-supported** 2-year, founded 1963, part of Connecticut Community College System
- **Small-town** 160-acre campus with easy access to Hartford
- **Coed,** 6,135 undergraduate students, 44% full-time, 56% women, 44% men

Undergraduates 2,713 full-time, 3,422 part-time. Students come from 5 states and territories, 12% African American, 4% Asian American or Pacific Islander, 10% Hispanic American, 0.2% Native American, 0.7% international, 11% transferred in. *Retention:* 60% of 2003 full-time freshmen returned.

Freshmen *Admission:* 2,016 applied, 2,016 admitted, 1,255 enrolled.

Faculty *Total:* 353, 27% full-time. *Student/faculty ratio:* 21:1.

Majors Accounting; administrative assistant and secretarial science; business administration and management; clinical/medical laboratory technology; commercial and advertising art; communication/speech communication and rhetoric; criminal justice/law enforcement administration; dramatic/theater arts; engineering science; fine/studio arts; general studies; hotel/motel administration; human services; industrial engineering; industrial technology; information science/studies; journalism; kindergarten/preschool education; legal administrative assistant/secretary; legal assistant/paralegal; liberal arts and sciences/liberal studies; management information systems; marketing/marketing management; medical administrative assistant and medical secretary; music; occupational therapist assistant; physical therapist assistant; respiratory care therapy; social work; surgical technology; teacher assistant/aide.

Academics *Calendar:* semesters. *Degree:* certificates and associate. *Special study options:* academic remediation for entering students, adult/continuing education programs, cooperative education, distance learning, double majors, English as a second language, independent study, internships, off-campus study, part-time degree program, services for LD students, student-designed majors, summer session for credit.

Library 45,265 titles, 493 serial subscriptions, 2,481 audiovisual materials.

Student Life *Housing:* college housing not available. *Activities and Organizations:* drama/theater group, student-run newspaper, choral group. *Student services:* women's center.

Athletics Member NJCAA. *Intercollegiate sports:* baseball M, basketball M/W, soccer M/W, softball W.

Costs (2005–06) *Tuition:* state resident $2232 full-time, $93 per credit hour part-time; nonresident $6696 full-time, $279 per credit hour part-time.

Financial Aid Of all full-time matriculated undergraduates who enrolled in 2004, 100 Federal Work-Study jobs (averaging $2000). 25 state and other part-time jobs (averaging $2000).

Applying *Options:* electronic application, deferred entrance. *Application fee:* $20. *Required:* high school transcript. *Application deadline:* rolling (freshmen), rolling (transfers). *Notification:* continuous (freshmen).

Director of Admissions Mr. Peter Harris, Director of Admissions, Manchester Community College, PO Box 1046, MS #12, Manchester, CT 06045-1046. *Phone:* 860-512-3210.

MIDDLESEX COMMUNITY COLLEGE

Middletown, Connecticut   www.mxcc.commnet.edu/

- **State-supported** 2-year, founded 1966, part of Connecticut Community College System
- **Suburban** 38-acre campus with easy access to Hartford
- **Coed,** 2,286 undergraduate students, 38% full-time, 65% women, 35% men

Undergraduates 876 full-time, 1,410 part-time. Students come from 4 states and territories, 1% are from out of state, 7% African American, 3% Asian American or Pacific Islander, 8% Hispanic American, 0.1% Native American, 0.3% international. *Retention:* 44% of 2003 full-time freshmen returned.

Freshmen *Admission:* 671 applied, 671 admitted, 432 enrolled.

Faculty *Total:* 125, 31% full-time. *Student/faculty ratio:* 18:1.

Majors Accounting; administrative assistant and secretarial science; biological and physical sciences; biology/biotechnology laboratory technician; broadcast journalism; business administration and management; commercial and advertising art; computer programming; engineering science; engineering technology; environmental studies; fine/studio arts; human services; industrial radiologic technology; intermedia/multimedia; legal administrative assistant/secretary; liberal arts and sciences/liberal studies; marketing/marketing management; mass communication/media; medical administrative assistant and medical secretary; mental health/rehabilitation; ophthalmic laboratory technology; pre-engineering; radio and television; substance abuse/addiction counseling.

Academics *Calendar:* semesters. *Degree:* certificates and associate. *Special study options:* academic remediation for entering students, advanced placement credit, cooperative education, distance learning, double majors, English as a second language, honors programs, independent study, internships, off-campus study, part-time degree program, services for LD students, summer session for credit. *ROTC:* Army (b).

Library Jean Burr Smith Library with 45,000 titles, 180 serial subscriptions, an OPAC, a Web page.

Computers on Campus 50 computers available on campus for general student use. A campuswide network can be accessed from off campus. Internet access, at least one staffed computer lab available.

Student Life *Housing:* college housing not available. *Activities and Organizations:* Collegiate Secretaries International, Minority Opportunities in Education, Radio Club. *Campus security:* 24-hour patrols. *Student services:* personal/psychological counseling.

Costs (2006–07) *Tuition:* state resident $2232 full-time, $93 per credit part-time; nonresident $6696 full-time, $279 per credit part-time. *Required fees:* $304 full-time, $3 per credit part-time, $53 per term part-time.

Financial Aid Of all full-time matriculated undergraduates who enrolled in 2004, 50 Federal Work-Study jobs (averaging $5000). 2 state and other part-time jobs (averaging $5000).

Applying *Options:* early admission, deferred entrance. *Application fee:* $20. *Required:* high school transcript, CPT. *Application deadline:* rolling (freshmen), rolling (transfers).

Freshmen Application Contact Mensimah Shabazz, Director of Admissions, Middlesex Community College, 100 Training Hill Road, Middletown, CT 06457-4889. *Phone:* 860-343-5742. *Fax:* 860-344-7488. *E-mail:* mshabazz@mxcc.commnet.edu.

NAUGATUCK VALLEY COMMUNITY COLLEGE

Waterbury, Connecticut   **www.nvcc.commnet.edu/**

- **State-supported** 2-year, founded 1992, part of Connecticut Community–Technical College System
- **Urban** 110-acre campus
- **Coed,** 5,671 undergraduate students, 39% full-time, 60% women, 40% men

Undergraduates 2,215 full-time, 3,456 part-time. 7% are from out of state, 8% African American, 3% Asian American or Pacific Islander, 11% Hispanic American, 0.4% Native American, 0.4% international, 0.1% transferred in.
Freshmen *Admission:* 3,358 applied, 1,406 admitted, 1,173 enrolled.

Faculty *Total:* 210. *Student/faculty ratio:* 5:1.

Majors Accounting; administrative assistant and secretarial science; American studies; automobile/automotive mechanics technology; biological and physical sciences; business administration and management; chemical engineering; computer/information technology services administration related; computer programming; computer programming (specific applications); criminal justice/law enforcement administration; drafting and design technology; electrical, electronic and communications engineering technology; engineering technology; environmental studies; finance; fire science; gerontology; history; horticultural science; hospitality administration; hotel/motel administration; human services; industrial radiologic technology; industrial technology; information science/studies; information technology; international relations and affairs; kindergarten/preschool education; kinesiology and exercise science; legal administrative assistant/secretary; legal assistant/paralegal; liberal arts and sciences/liberal studies; marketing/marketing management; mathematics; mechanical engineering; mechanical technology; medical administrative assistant and medical secretary; mental health/rehabilitation; music; natural sciences; nursing (registered nurse training); physical sciences; physical therapist assistant; pre-engineering; quality control technology; social work; special products marketing; substance abuse/addiction counseling; system administration; word processing.

Academics *Calendar:* semesters. *Degree:* certificates and associate. *Special study options:* academic remediation for entering students, accelerated degree

program, adult/continuing education programs, advanced placement credit, cooperative education, English as a second language, external degree program, independent study, internships, off-campus study, part-time degree program, services for LD students, student-designed majors, study abroad, summer session for credit.

Library Max R. Traurig Learning Resource Center with 35,000 titles, 520 serial subscriptions, an OPAC, a Web page.

Computers on Campus 450 computers available on campus for general student use. A campuswide network can be accessed. Internet access, at least one staffed computer lab available.

Student Life *Housing:* college housing not available. *Activities and Organizations:* drama/theater group, student-run newspaper, choral group, Student Senate, Choral Society, Automotive Technician Club, Human Service Club, Legal Assistant Club. *Campus security:* 24-hour emergency response devices and patrols, late-night transport/escort service, security escort service. *Student services:* health clinic, personal/psychological counseling.

Athletics Member NJCAA.

Standardized Tests *Required:* ACCUPLACER (for admission).

Costs (2006–07) *Tuition:* state resident $2672 full-time; nonresident $7976 full-time.

Financial Aid Of all full-time matriculated undergraduates who enrolled in 2004, 70 Federal Work-Study jobs (averaging $1942). 16 state and other part-time jobs (averaging $1660).

Applying *Options:* deferred entrance. *Application fee:* $20. *Required:* high school transcript. *Required for some:* interview. *Application deadline:* rolling (freshmen), rolling (transfers). *Notification:* continuous (freshmen).

Freshmen Application Contact Ms. Lucretia Sveda, Director of Enrollment Services, Naugatuck Valley Community College, Waterbury, CT 06708. *Phone:* 203-575-8016. *Fax:* 203-596-8766. *E-mail:* lsveda@nvcc.commnet.edu.

NORTHWESTERN CONNECTICUT COMMUNITY COLLEGE

Winsted, Connecticut   **www.nwctc.commnet.edu/**

- **State-supported** 2-year, founded 1965, part of Connecticut Community–Technical College System
- **Small-town** 5-acre campus with easy access to Hartford
- **Coed,** 1,569 undergraduate students, 34% full-time, 68% women, 32% men

Undergraduates 527 full-time, 1,042 part-time. Students come from 6 states and territories, 1% are from out of state, 2% African American, 2% Asian American or Pacific Islander, 3% Hispanic American, 0.3% Native American, 0.1% international, 6% transferred in. *Retention:* 56% of 2003 full-time freshmen returned.
Freshmen *Admission:* 390 applied, 390 admitted, 296 enrolled.

Faculty *Total:* 113, 24% full-time. *Student/faculty ratio:* 16:1.

Majors Accounting; administrative assistant and secretarial science; art; behavioral sciences; biology/biological sciences; business administration and management; child development; commercial and advertising art; communications technology; computer engineering technology; computer graphics; computer programming; computer science; criminal justice/law enforcement administration; criminal justice/police science; electrical, electronic and communications engineering technology; engineering; English; health science; human services; information science/studies; kindergarten/preschool education; legal assistant/paralegal; liberal arts and sciences/liberal studies; mathematics; medical/clinical assistant; parks, recreation and leisure; parks, recreation and leisure facilities management; physical sciences; pre-engineering; sign language interpretation and translation; social sciences; substance abuse/addiction counseling; therapeutic recreation; veterinary technology.

Academics *Calendar:* semesters. *Degree:* certificates and associate. *Special study options:* academic remediation for entering students, adult/continuing education programs, advanced placement credit, cooperative education, distance learning, double majors, English as a second language, independent study, internships, part-time degree program, services for LD students, summer session for credit.

Library Northwestern Connecticut Community–Technical College Learning Center with 37,666 titles, 267 serial subscriptions, 1,599 audiovisual materials, an OPAC.

Computers on Campus 90 computers available on campus for general student use. A campuswide network can be accessed from off campus. Internet access, at least one staffed computer lab available.

Student Life *Housing:* college housing not available. *Activities and Organizations:* student-run newspaper, Ski Club, Student Senate, Deaf Club, Recreation Club, Early Childhood Educational Club. *Campus security:* evening security patrols.

Connecticut

Northwestern Connecticut Community College (continued)

Costs (2006–07) *Tuition:* state resident $2672 full-time, $156 per semester hour part-time; nonresident $7976 full-time, $458 per semester hour part-time.
Applying *Options:* deferred entrance. *Application fee:* $20. *Application deadline:* rolling (freshmen), rolling (transfers). *Notification:* continuous (freshmen).
Director of Admissions Ms. Beverly Chrzan, Director of Admissions, Northwestern Connecticut Community College, Park Place East, Winsted, CT 06098. *Phone:* 860-738-6329.

NORWALK COMMUNITY COLLEGE
Norwalk, Connecticut　　　**www.ncc.commnet.edu/**

- **State-supported** 2-year, founded 1961, part of Connecticut Community College System
- **Suburban** 30-acre campus with easy access to New York City
- **Endowment** $11.0 million
- **Coed,** 6,036 undergraduate students, 33% full-time, 63% women, 37% men

Undergraduates 2,016 full-time, 4,020 part-time. Students come from 4 states and territories, 30 other countries, 1% are from out of state, 19% African American, 5% Asian American or Pacific Islander, 19% Hispanic American, 0.2% Native American.
Freshmen *Admission:* 3,391 applied.
Faculty *Total:* 349, 26% full-time. *Student/faculty ratio:* 20:1.
Majors Accounting; administrative assistant and secretarial science; architectural engineering technology; art; business administration and management; commercial and advertising art; computer and information sciences related; computer programming related; construction engineering technology; criminal justice/law enforcement administration; data processing and data processing technology; electrical, electronic and communications engineering technology; engineering science; engineering technology; finance; fine/studio arts; fire science; general studies; hotel/motel administration; human services; information science/studies; kindergarten/preschool education; legal assistant/paralegal; liberal arts and sciences/liberal studies; marketing/marketing management; mass communication/media; nursing (registered nurse training); parks, recreation and leisure; respiratory care therapy; sales, distribution and marketing; substance abuse/addiction counseling; therapeutic recreation.
Academics *Calendar:* semesters. *Degree:* certificates and associate. *Special study options:* academic remediation for entering students, adult/continuing education programs, advanced placement credit, cooperative education, distance learning, English as a second language, freshman honors college, honors programs, independent study, internships, part-time degree program, services for LD students, summer session for credit.
Library Everett I. L. Baker Library with 66,080 titles, 221 serial subscriptions, 2,988 audiovisual materials, an OPAC, a Web page.
Computers on Campus 500 computers available on campus for general student use. A campuswide network can be accessed from off campus. Internet access, online (class) registration, at least one staffed computer lab available.
Student Life *Housing:* college housing not available. *Activities and Organizations:* drama/theater group, student-run newspaper, choral group, African Culture Club, Archaeology Club, Hay Motivo Club, Art Club, Phi Theta Kappa. *Campus security:* 24-hour emergency response devices and patrols, student patrols, late-night transport/escort service, patrols by security. *Student services:* women's center.
Costs (2006–07) *Tuition:* state resident $2352 full-time, $98 per credit part-time; nonresident $7056 full-time, $294 per credit part-time. *Required fees:* $320 full-time, $20 per credit part-time, $160 per term part-time.
Financial Aid Of all full-time matriculated undergraduates who enrolled in 2004, 42 Federal Work-Study jobs (averaging $2581). 60 state and other part-time jobs (averaging $2046).
Applying *Options:* deferred entrance. *Application fee:* $20. *Required:* high school transcript. *Application deadline:* rolling (freshmen), rolling (transfers). *Notification:* continuous (freshmen).
Freshmen Application Contact Mr. Curtis Antrum, Admissions Counselor, Norwalk Community College, 188 Richards Avenue, Norwalk, CT 06854-1655. *Phone:* 203-857-7060. *Toll-free phone:* 888-462-6282. *Fax:* 203-857-3335. *E-mail:* admissions@commnet.edu.

QUINEBAUG VALLEY COMMUNITY COLLEGE
Danielson, Connecticut　　　**www.qvcc.commnet.edu/**

- **State-supported** 2-year, founded 1971, part of Connecticut Community College System
- **Rural** 60-acre campus
- **Coed,** 1,714 undergraduate students, 38% full-time, 68% women, 32% men

Undergraduates 643 full-time, 1,071 part-time. Students come from 3 states and territories, 1% are from out of state, 2% African American, 1% Asian American or Pacific Islander, 10% Hispanic American, 0.8% Native American, 9% transferred in.
Freshmen *Admission:* 586 applied, 576 admitted, 338 enrolled.
Faculty *Total:* 122, 17% full-time. *Student/faculty ratio:* 18:1.
Majors Accounting; administrative assistant and secretarial science; art; avionics maintenance technology; business administration and management; computer and information sciences related; computer graphics; computer systems networking and telecommunications; data entry/microcomputer applications; engineering technology; human services; liberal arts and sciences/liberal studies; medical/clinical assistant; plastics engineering technology; pre-engineering; substance abuse/addiction counseling; system administration; word processing.
Academics *Calendar:* semesters. *Degree:* certificates and associate. *Special study options:* academic remediation for entering students, adult/continuing education programs, advanced placement credit, distance learning, English as a second language, external degree program, internships, part-time degree program, services for LD students, summer session for credit.
Library Audrey Beck Library with 31,000 titles, 130 serial subscriptions, an OPAC.
Computers on Campus 80 computers available on campus for general student use. A campuswide network can be accessed. Internet access, at least one staffed computer lab available.
Student Life *Housing:* college housing not available. *Campus security:* evening security guard.
Costs (2005–06) *Tuition:* state resident $2112 full-time; nonresident $6336 full-time. Full-time tuition and fees vary according to reciprocity agreements. Part-time tuition and fees vary according to reciprocity agreements. *Required fees:* $294 full-time. *Payment plans:* installment, deferred payment. *Waivers:* employees or children of employees.
Financial Aid Of all full-time matriculated undergraduates who enrolled in 2004, 38 Federal Work-Study jobs (averaging $1400). 24 state and other part-time jobs (averaging $1350).
Applying *Options:* common application, electronic application, early admission, deferred entrance. *Application fee:* $20. *Required for some:* high school transcript. *Recommended:* high school transcript. *Application deadlines:* 9/1 (freshmen), 9/1 (transfers). *Notification:* continuous until 9/1 (freshmen).
Freshmen Application Contact Dr. Toni Moumouris, Director of Admissions, Quinebaug Valley Community College, 742 Upper Maple Street, Danielson, CT 06239. *Phone:* 860-774-1130 Ext. 318. *Fax:* 860-774-7768. *E-mail:* qu_isd@commnet.edu.

ST. VINCENT'S COLLEGE
Bridgeport, Connecticut　　　**www.stvincentscollege.edu/**
Director of Admissions Mr. Joseph Marrone, Director of Admissions and Recruitment Marketing, St. Vincent's College, 2800 Main Street, Bridgeport, CT 06606-4292. *Phone:* 203-576-5515. *Fax:* 203-576-5893. *E-mail:* jmarrone@stvincentscollege.edu.

THREE RIVERS COMMUNITY COLLEGE
Norwich, Connecticut　　　**www.trcc.commnet.edu/**

- **State-supported** 2-year, founded 1963, part of Connecticut Community–Technical College System
- **Small-town** 40-acre campus with easy access to Hartford
- **Coed**

Undergraduates Students come from 6 states and territories, 1% are from out of state, 7% African American, 2% Asian American or Pacific Islander, 5% Hispanic American, 2% Native American, 0.4% international.
Academics *Calendar:* semesters. *Degrees:* certificates and associate (engineering technology programs are offered on the Thames Valley Campus; liberal arts,

transfer and career programs are offered on the Mohegan Campus). *Special study options:* academic remediation for entering students, adult/continuing education programs, advanced placement credit, cooperative education, double majors, English as a second language, external degree program, independent study, internships, part-time degree program, services for LD students, student-designed majors, study abroad, summer session for credit.

Student Life *Campus security:* late-night transport/escort service, 14 hour patrols by trained security personnel.

Standardized Tests *Required:* ACCUPLACER (for placement).

Costs (2005–06) *Tuition:* state resident $2232 full-time, $93 per semester hour part-time; nonresident $7264 full-time, $279 per semester hour part-time. *Required fees:* $304 full-time.

Financial Aid Of all full-time matriculated undergraduates who enrolled in 2004, 40 Federal Work-Study jobs (averaging $3000). 80 state and other part-time jobs (averaging $3000).

Applying *Options:* early admission, deferred entrance. *Application fee:* $20. *Required for some:* minimum 3.0 GPA. *Recommended:* high school transcript.

Freshmen Application Contact Ms. Aida Garcia, Admissions and Recruitment Counselor, Mohegan Campus, Three Rivers Community College, Mahan Drive, Norwich, CT 06360. *Phone:* 860-892-5762. *E-mail:* info3rivers@trcc.commnet.edu.

TUNXIS COMMUNITY COLLEGE

Farmington, Connecticut www.tunxis.commnet.edu/

- **State-supported** 2-year, founded 1969, part of Connecticut Community College System
- **Suburban** 12-acre campus with easy access to Hartford
- **Coed,** 3,894 undergraduate students, 38% full-time, 61% women, 39% men

Undergraduates 1,488 full-time, 2,406 part-time. Students come from 6 states and territories, 2% are from out of state, 6% African American, 3% Asian American or Pacific Islander, 10% Hispanic American, 0.4% Native American, 0.8% international. *Retention:* 56% of 2003 full-time freshmen returned.

Freshmen *Admission:* 604 enrolled.

Faculty *Total:* 234, 26% full-time, 12% with terminal degrees. *Student/faculty ratio:* 19:1.

Majors Accounting; administrative assistant and secretarial science; applied art; art; business administration and management; commercial and advertising art; corrections; criminal justice/law enforcement administration; data processing and data processing technology; dental hygiene; engineering; engineering technology; fashion merchandising; forensic science and technology; human services; information science/studies; kindergarten/preschool education; legal administrative assistant/secretary; liberal arts and sciences/liberal studies; marketing/marketing management; medical administrative assistant and medical secretary; physical therapy; substance abuse/addiction counseling.

Academics *Calendar:* semesters. *Degree:* certificates and associate. *Special study options:* academic remediation for entering students, adult/continuing education programs, English as a second language, part-time degree program, summer session for credit.

Library Tunxis Community College Library with 33,866 titles, 285 serial subscriptions, 3,571 audiovisual materials, an OPAC.

Computers on Campus 274 computers available on campus for general student use. A campuswide network can be accessed from off campus. Internet access, at least one staffed computer lab available.

Student Life *Housing:* college housing not available. *Activities and Organizations:* student-run newspaper, Phi Theta Kappa, Student American Dental Hygiene Association (SADHA), Human Services Club, student newspaper, Bible Club. *Campus security:* 24-hour patrols. *Student services:* health clinic.

Costs (2006–07) *Tuition:* $98 per credit hour part-time; state resident $2352 full-time; nonresident $7056 full-time, $294 per credit hour part-time. *Required fees:* $320 full-time, $178 per term part-time.

Applying *Options:* common application, deferred entrance. *Application fee:* $20. *Required:* high school transcript. *Application deadline:* rolling (freshmen), rolling (transfers).

Freshmen Application Contact Kelly Pittman, Academic Advisor, Tunxis Community College, 271 Scott Swamp Road, Farmington, CT 06032. *Phone:* 860-255-3544. *Fax:* 860-255-3559. *E-mail:* kpittman@txcc.commnet.edu.

DELAWARE COLLEGE OF ART AND DESIGN

Wilmington, Delaware www.dcad.edu/

- **Independent** 2-year, founded 1997, administratively affiliated with Corcoran College of Art and Design
- **Urban** 1-acre campus
- **Endowment** $65,295
- **Coed,** 194 undergraduate students, 76% full-time, 51% women, 49% men

Undergraduates 148 full-time, 46 part-time. Students come from 9 states and territories, 45% are from out of state, 9% African American, 1% Asian American or Pacific Islander, 4% Hispanic American, 0.5% Native American, 1% international, 11% transferred in, 50% live on campus.

Freshmen *Admission:* 322 applied, 186 admitted, 108 enrolled. *Average high school GPA:* 2.5.

Faculty *Total:* 20, 25% full-time, 80% with terminal degrees. *Student/faculty ratio:* 5:1.

Majors Animation, interactive technology, video graphics and special effects; fine/studio arts; graphic design; illustration; interior design; photography.

Academics *Calendar:* semesters. *Degree:* associate. *Special study options:* academic remediation for entering students, adult/continuing education programs, advanced placement credit, double majors, off-campus study, part-time degree program, services for LD students, study abroad, summer session for credit.

Library Information Resource Center plus 1 other with 8,000 titles, 76 serial subscriptions, 500 audiovisual materials, an OPAC.

Computers on Campus 68 computers available on campus for general student use. A campuswide network can be accessed from student residence rooms and from off campus that provide access to access to e-mail, student Web space. Internet access, at least one staffed computer lab available. Computer purchase or lease plan available.

Student Life *Housing Options:* coed. Campus housing is leased by the school. Freshman applicants given priority for college housing.

Costs (2006–07) *Tuition:* $14,070 full-time, $595 per credit part-time. *Required fees:* $200 per term part-time. *Room only:* $5490.

Applying *Options:* common application, electronic application, deferred entrance. *Application fee:* $25. *Required:* essay or personal statement, high school transcript, minimum 2 GPA, interview, portfolio. *Required for some:* letters of recommendation. *Application deadline:* rolling (freshmen), rolling (transfers). *Notification:* continuous until 8/15 (freshmen).

Freshmen Application Contact Krista Rothwell, Admissions Recruiter, Delaware College of Art and Design, 600 North Market Street, Wilmington, DE 19801. *Phone:* 302-622-8000 Ext. 111. *Fax:* 302-622-8870. *E-mail:* admissions@dcad.edu.

DELAWARE TECHNICAL & COMMUNITY COLLEGE, JACK F. OWENS CAMPUS

Georgetown, Delaware www.dtcc.edu/

- **State-supported** 2-year, founded 1967, part of Delaware Technical and Community College System
- **Small-town** 120-acre campus
- **Coed,** 3,936 undergraduate students, 41% full-time, 67% women, 33% men

Undergraduates 1,600 full-time, 2,336 part-time. Students come from 3 states and territories, 9 other countries, 6% are from out of state, 15% African American, 0.9% Asian American or Pacific Islander, 3% Hispanic American, 0.3% Native American, 6% international.

Freshmen *Admission:* 1,122 applied, 816 admitted, 750 enrolled.

Faculty *Total:* 280, 37% full-time. *Student/faculty ratio:* 15:1.

Majors Accounting; administrative assistant and secretarial science; agricultural business and management; architectural engineering technology; automobile/automotive mechanics technology; business administration and management; carpentry; chemical engineering; child development; civil engineering technology; clinical/medical laboratory technology; computer programming; construc-

Delaware Technical & Community College, Jack F.
Owens Campus (continued)

tion management; consumer merchandising/retailing management; criminal justice/law enforcement administration; data processing and data processing technology; drafting and design technology; electrical, electronic and communications engineering technology; emergency medical technology (EMT paramedic); engineering; engineering technology; environmental engineering technology; heavy equipment maintenance technology; hospitality administration; hotel/motel administration; human services; journalism; legal administrative assistant/secretary; marketing/marketing management; medical administrative assistant and medical secretary; medical/clinical assistant; medical laboratory technology; nursing (licensed practical/vocational nurse training); nursing (registered nurse training); veterinary technology; welding technology.

Academics *Calendar:* semesters. *Degree:* certificates, diplomas, and associate. *Special study options:* academic remediation for entering students, adult/continuing education programs, cooperative education, distance learning, English as a second language, external degree program, internships, part-time degree program, services for LD students, student-designed majors, summer session for credit.

Library Stephen J. Betze Library plus 1 other with 72,657 titles, 514 serial subscriptions, an OPAC.

Computers on Campus 400 computers available on campus for general student use. A campuswide network can be accessed. Online (class) registration, at least one staffed computer lab available.

Student Life *Housing:* college housing not available. *Activities and Organizations:* student-run radio station, Student Government Association, Student Nursing Association, Phi Beta Kappa, Occupational Therapy Assistant Club, Physical Therapy Assistant Club. *Campus security:* 24-hour patrols, late-night transport/escort service.

Athletics Member NJCAA. *Intercollegiate sports:* baseball M(s), softball W.

Costs (2005–06) *Tuition:* state resident $1956 full-time, $82 per credit hour part-time; nonresident $4890 full-time, $204 per credit hour part-time. *Required fees:* $204 full-time, $6 per credit hour part-time, $21 per term part-time. *Payment plan:* deferred payment. *Waivers:* senior citizens and employees or children of employees.

Financial Aid Of all full-time matriculated undergraduates who enrolled in 2004, 250 Federal Work-Study jobs (averaging $2000).

Applying *Options:* early admission. *Application fee:* $10. *Required:* high school transcript. *Application deadline:* rolling (freshmen), rolling (transfers). *Notification:* continuous (freshmen).

Freshmen Application Contact Ms. Claire McDonald, Admissions Counselor, Delaware Technical & Community College, Jack F. Owens Campus, PO Box 610, Georgetown, DE 19947. *Phone:* 302-856-5400. *Fax:* 302-856-9461.

DELAWARE TECHNICAL & COMMUNITY COLLEGE, STANTON/WILMINGTON CAMPUS

Newark, Delaware www.dtcc.edu/

- **State-supported** 2-year, founded 1968, part of Delaware Technical and Community College System
- **Coed,** 7,473 undergraduate students, 37% full-time, 63% women, 37% men

Undergraduates 2,767 full-time, 4,706 part-time. Students come from 13 states and territories, 45 other countries, 8% are from out of state, 23% African American, 3% Asian American or Pacific Islander, 5% Hispanic American, 0.4% Native American, 2% international.
Freshmen *Admission:* 1,965 applied, 1,445 admitted, 1,410 enrolled.
Faculty *Total:* 525, 31% full-time. *Student/faculty ratio:* 15:1.
Majors Accounting; administrative assistant and secretarial science; architectural engineering technology; banking and financial support services; biomedical technology; business administration and management; chemical engineering; civil engineering technology; corrections; criminal justice/law enforcement administration; criminal justice/police science; culinary arts; data processing and data processing technology; dental hygiene; diagnostic medical sonography and ultrasound technology; drafting and design technology; electrical, electronic and communications engineering technology; emergency medical technology (EMT paramedic); engineering; fire science; food services technology; gerontology; hotel/motel administration; human services; industrial radiologic technology; industrial technology; information science/studies; instrumentation technology; kindergarten/preschool education; kinesiology and exercise science; management information systems; marketing/marketing management; mechanical engineering/mechanical technology; medical administrative assistant and medical secretary; nuclear medical technology; nursing (registered nurse training); occupational safety and health technology; occupational therapist assistant;

physical therapist assistant; respiratory care therapy; sign language interpretation and translation; substance abuse/addiction counseling; transportation technology.
Academics *Calendar:* semesters. *Degree:* certificates, diplomas, and associate. *Special study options:* academic remediation for entering students, adult/continuing education programs, cooperative education, English as a second language, external degree program, part-time degree program, services for LD students, summer session for credit.
Library 60,066 titles, 793 serial subscriptions, an OPAC.
Computers on Campus 200 computers available on campus for general student use. A campuswide network can be accessed. At least one staffed computer lab available.
Student Life *Housing:* college housing not available. *Campus security:* 24-hour patrols, late-night transport/escort service.
Athletics Member NJCAA. *Intercollegiate sports:* basketball M, soccer M, softball W, tennis M/W, volleyball M/W. *Intramural sports:* basketball M, tennis M/W.
Costs (2005–06) *Tuition:* state resident $1956 full-time, $82 per credit hour part-time; nonresident $4890 full-time, $204 per credit hour part-time. *Required fees:* $204 full-time, $6 per credit hour part-time, $21 per term part-time. *Payment plan:* deferred payment. *Waivers:* senior citizens and employees or children of employees.
Applying *Options:* early admission. *Application fee:* $10. *Required:* high school transcript. *Application deadline:* rolling (freshmen), rolling (transfers). *Notification:* continuous (freshmen).
Freshmen Application Contact Ms. Rebecca Bailey, Admissions Coordinator, Wilmington, Delaware Technical & Community College, Stanton/Wilmington Campus, 333 Shipley Street, Wilmington, DE 19713. *Phone:* 302-571-5366. *Fax:* 302-577-2548.

DELAWARE TECHNICAL & COMMUNITY COLLEGE, TERRY CAMPUS

Dover, Delaware www.dtcc.edu/terry/

- **State-supported** 2-year, founded 1972, part of Delaware Technical and Community College System
- **Small-town** 70-acre campus with easy access to Philadelphia
- **Coed,** 2,569 undergraduate students, 34% full-time, 71% women, 29% men

Undergraduates 875 full-time, 1,694 part-time. Students come from 10 states and territories, 10 other countries, 3% are from out of state, 24% African American, 2% Asian American or Pacific Islander, 3% Hispanic American, 0.4% Native American, 1% international, 10% transferred in.
Freshmen *Admission:* 691 applied, 555 admitted, 535 enrolled.
Faculty *Total:* 184, 35% full-time. *Student/faculty ratio:* 14:1.
Majors Accounting; administrative assistant and secretarial science; aeronautics/aviation/aerospace science and technology; architectural engineering technology; aviation/airway management; avionics maintenance technology; business administration and management; civil engineering technology; computer engineering technology; computer programming; construction engineering technology; construction management; corrections; criminal justice/law enforcement administration; data processing and data processing technology; drafting and design technology; electrical, electronic and communications engineering technology; electromechanical technology; engineering technology; human services; industrial technology; kindergarten/preschool education; nursing (licensed practical/vocational nurse training); nursing (registered nurse training); survey technology.
Academics *Calendar:* semesters. *Degree:* certificates, diplomas, and associate. *Special study options:* academic remediation for entering students, adult/continuing education programs, cooperative education, English as a second language, internships, part-time degree program, services for LD students, summer session for credit.
Library 9,663 titles, 245 serial subscriptions, an OPAC.
Computers on Campus 125 computers available on campus for general student use. A campuswide network can be accessed. At least one staffed computer lab available.
Student Life *Housing:* college housing not available. *Activities and Organizations:* Students of Kolor, Human Services Organization, Phi Theta Kappa, Alpha Beta Gamma. *Campus security:* late-night transport/escort service.
Costs (2005–06) *Tuition:* state resident $1956 full-time, $82 per credit hour part-time; nonresident $4890 full-time, $204 per credit hour part-time. *Required fees:* $204 full-time, $6 per credit hour part-time, $21 per term part-time. *Payment plan:* deferred payment. *Waivers:* senior citizens and employees or children of employees.
Financial Aid Of all full-time matriculated undergraduates who enrolled in 2004, 50 Federal Work-Study jobs (averaging $1500).

Applying *Options:* early admission. *Application fee:* $10. *Required:* high school transcript. *Application deadline:* rolling (freshmen), rolling (transfers). *Notification:* continuous (freshmen).

Freshmen Application Contact Mrs. Maria Harris, Admissions Officer, Delaware Technical & Community College, Terry Campus, 100 Campus Drive, Dover, DE 19904. *Phone:* 302-857-1020. *Fax:* 302-857-1296. *E-mail:* mharris@outland.dtcc.edu.

FLORIDA

ANGLEY COLLEGE
Deland, Florida
www.angley.edu

ATI CAREER TRAINING CENTER
Fort Lauderdale, Florida
www.aticareertraining.com/

Director of Admissions Ms. Wendy Hopkins Goffinet, Director of Admissions, ATI Career Training Center, 2880 NW 62nd Street, Fort Lauderdale, FL 33309-9731. *Phone:* 954-973-4760.

ATI CAREER TRAINING CENTER
Miami, Florida
www.aticareertraining.com/

Director of Admissions Ms. Mary Fernandez, Director of Admissions, ATI Career Training Center, 1 NE 19th Street, Miami, FL 33132. *Phone:* 305-573-1600.

ATI CAREER TRAINING CENTER
Oakland Park, Florida

ATI HEALTH EDUCATION CENTER
Miami, Florida
www.aticareertraining.com/

Director of Admissions Mrs. Barbara Woosley, Director, ATI Health Education Center, 1395 NW 167th Street, Suite 200, Miami, FL 33169-5742. *Phone:* 305-628-1000. *Fax:* 305-628-1461. *E-mail:* bwoolsey@atienterprises.edu.

BREVARD COMMUNITY COLLEGE
Cocoa, Florida
www.brevardcc.edu/

- **State-supported** 2-year, founded 1960, part of Florida Community College System
- **Suburban** 100-acre campus with easy access to Orlando
- **Coed,** 14,039 undergraduate students, 37% full-time, 61% women, 39% men

Undergraduates 5,129 full-time, 8,910 part-time. Students come from 34 states and territories, 72 other countries, 9% African American, 3% Asian American or Pacific Islander, 7% Hispanic American, 0.6% Native American, 0.8% international.

Freshmen *Admission:* 5,350 applied, 5,350 admitted, 2,691 enrolled.

Faculty *Total:* 1,042, 19% full-time. *Student/faculty ratio:* 18:1.

Majors Accounting; business administration and management; chemical engineering; clinical/medical laboratory technology; computer engineering technology; computer/information technology services administration related; computer programming; computer programming (specific applications); computer software and media applications related; computer systems analysis; computer systems networking and telecommunications; corrections; criminal justice/law enforcement administration; criminal justice/police science; culinary arts; dental hygiene; digital communication and media/multimedia; drafting and design technology; early childhood education; electrical, electronic and communications engineering technology; electrical/electronics drafting and CAD/CADD; emergency medical technology (EMT paramedic); fire science; international business/trade/commerce; legal assistant/paralegal; liberal arts and sciences/liberal studies; manufacturing technology; medical administrative assistant and medical secretary; medical/clinical assistant; nursing (registered nurse training); radio and television; radiologic technology/science; surgical technology; system administration; system, networking, and LAN/WAN management; veterinary technology; web page, digital/multimedia and information resources design.

Academics *Calendar:* semesters. *Degree:* certificates and associate. *Special study options:* academic remediation for entering students, accelerated degree program, adult/continuing education programs, advanced placement credit, cooperative education, distance learning, double majors, English as a second language, external degree program, honors programs, independent study, internships, part-time degree program, services for LD students, study abroad, summer session for credit. *ROTC:* Army (b), Air Force (b).

Library UCF Library with 213,873 titles, 904 serial subscriptions, 17,904 audiovisual materials, an OPAC, a Web page.

Computers on Campus 125 computers available on campus for general student use. A campuswide network can be accessed from off campus. Online (class) registration, at least one staffed computer lab available.

Student Life *Housing:* college housing not available. *Activities and Organizations:* drama/theater group, student-run newspaper, television station, choral group, Phi Theta Kappa, ROTORACT, African-American Student Union, Student Government Association, Psi Beta. *Campus security:* 24-hour emergency response devices and patrols, late-night transport/escort service. *Student services:* women's center.

Athletics Member NJCAA. *Intercollegiate sports:* baseball M(s), basketball M(s)/W(s), golf M(s), softball W(s), volleyball W(s).

Costs (2005–06) *Tuition:* state resident $1542 full-time, $64 per credit hour part-time; nonresident $5664 full-time, $236 per credit hour part-time. *Waivers:* senior citizens and employees or children of employees.

Financial Aid Of all full-time matriculated undergraduates who enrolled in 2004, 200 Federal Work-Study jobs (averaging $2244). 200 state and other part-time jobs (averaging $2000).

Applying *Options:* common application, electronic application. *Application fee:* $30. *Required:* high school transcript. *Application deadline:* rolling (freshmen), rolling (transfers). *Notification:* continuous (freshmen).

Freshmen Application Contact Ms. Stephanie Burnette, Registrar, Brevard Community College, 1519 Clearlake Road, Cocoa, FL 32922-6597. *Phone:* 321-433-7271. *Fax:* 321-433-7172. *E-mail:* cocoaadmissions@brevardcc.edu.

BROWARD COMMUNITY COLLEGE
Fort Lauderdale, Florida
www.broward.edu/

- **State-supported** 2-year, founded 1960, part of Florida Community College System
- **Urban** campus with easy access to Miami
- **Coed,** 32,041 undergraduate students, 31% full-time, 62% women, 38% men

Undergraduates 10,044 full-time, 21,997 part-time. Students come from 100 other countries, 5% are from out of state, 27% African American, 3% Asian American or Pacific Islander, 24% Hispanic American, 0.3% Native American, 9% international.

Freshmen *Admission:* 4,630 applied, 4,630 admitted, 4,630 enrolled. *Test scores:* SAT verbal scores over 500: 22%; SAT math scores over 500: 28%; SAT verbal scores over 600: 3%; SAT math scores over 600: 4%.

Faculty *Total:* 1,561, 28% full-time, 24% with terminal degrees.

Majors Accounting; administrative assistant and secretarial science; airline pilot and flight crew; architectural engineering technology; automobile/automotive mechanics technology; aviation/airway management; avionics maintenance technology; business administration and management; child development; civil engineering technology; clinical laboratory science/medical technology; clinical/medical laboratory technology; computer engineering technology; computer programming; computer science; construction management; corrections; criminal justice/law enforcement administration; criminal justice/police science; data processing and data processing technology; dental hygiene; electrical, electronic

Broward Community College (continued)

and communications engineering technology; elementary education; emergency medical technology (EMT paramedic); engineering science; environmental engineering technology; finance; fire science; hotel/motel administration; industrial radiologic technology; information science/studies; insurance; interior design; kindergarten/preschool education; legal administrative assistant/secretary; legal assistant/paralegal; liberal arts and sciences/liberal studies; marketing/marketing management; mechanical engineering/mechanical technology; medical administrative assistant and medical secretary; medical/clinical assistant; nuclear medical technology; nursing (registered nurse training); physical therapy; pre-engineering; respiratory care therapy; special products marketing; tourism and travel services management.

Academics *Calendar:* trimesters. *Degree:* certificates, diplomas, and associate. *Special study options:* academic remediation for entering students, adult/continuing education programs, advanced placement credit, cooperative education, English as a second language, honors programs, part-time degree program, services for LD students, student-designed majors, study abroad, summer session for credit. *ROTC:* Army (b).

Library South Regional/Broward Community College Library with 200,000 titles, 600 serial subscriptions, an OPAC.

Computers on Campus Online (class) registration available.

Student Life *Housing:* college housing not available. *Activities and Organizations:* drama/theater group, student-run newspaper, choral group. *Campus security:* 24-hour emergency response devices and patrols, late-night transport/escort service. *Student services:* personal/psychological counseling, women's center.

Athletics Member NJCAA. *Intercollegiate sports:* baseball M(s), basketball M(s)/W(s), soccer W, softball W(s), swimming and diving M(s)/W(s), tennis W(s), volleyball W(s), wrestling M(s). *Intramural sports:* baseball M, basketball M/W, tennis W.

Standardized Tests *Required for some:* SAT and SAT Subject Tests or ACT (for admission).

Costs (2006–07) *Tuition:* state resident $1574 full-time, $63 per credit hour part-time; nonresident $6294 full-time, $229 per credit hour part-time. *Required fees:* $318 full-time.

Financial Aid *Financial aid deadline:* 7/1.

Applying *Options:* common application, early admission, deferred entrance. *Application fee:* $35. *Required for some:* high school transcript, minimum 2.75 GPA.

Freshmen Application Contact Barbara Bryan PhD, Associate Vice President for Student Affairs/College Registrar, Broward Community College, 225 East Las Olas Boulevard, Fort Lauderdale, FL 33301-2298. *Phone:* 954-761-7465. *Fax:* 954-201-7466.

BROWN MACKIE COLLEGE–MIAMI
Miami, Florida

www.brownmackie.edu/locations.asp?locid=25

- **Proprietary** 2-year
- **Coed,** 136 undergraduate students, 100% full-time, 71% women, 29% men
- 53% of applicants were admitted

Undergraduates 136 full-time. 65% African American, 3% Asian American or Pacific Islander, 27% Hispanic American.
Freshmen *Admission:* 325 applied, 172 admitted, 75 enrolled.

Faculty *Total:* 9, 100% with terminal degrees.

Majors Accounting technology and bookkeeping; business administration and management; computer software technology; criminal justice/safety; medical/clinical assistant; paralegal/legal assistant.

Academics *Degree:* diplomas and associate.

Student Life *Activities and Organizations:* national sororities. *Student services:* personal/psychological counseling.

Costs (2005–06) *Comprehensive fee:* $19,272 includes full-time tuition ($10,992), mandatory fees ($480), and room and board ($7800).

Applying *Required:* high school transcript, interview. *Application deadline:* rolling (freshmen), rolling (transfers). *Notification:* continuous (freshmen).

Freshmen Application Contact Ms. Jessica Rivera, Student Records Officer, Brown Mackie College–Miami, 1501 Biscayne Boulevard, Miami, FL 33132. *Phone:* 305-341-6612. *Toll-free phone:* 866-505-0335. *Fax:* 305-373-8814. *E-mail:* jrivera@brownmackie.edu.

▶ **See page 514 for the College Close-Up.**

CENTRAL FLORIDA COLLEGE
Winter Park, Florida

CENTRAL FLORIDA COMMUNITY COLLEGE
Ocala, Florida   www.cf.edu/

- **State and locally supported** 2-year, founded 1957, part of Florida Community College System
- **Small-town** 139-acre campus
- **Endowment** $14.8 million
- **Coed,** 5,978 undergraduate students, 41% full-time, 66% women, 34% men

Undergraduates 2,476 full-time, 3,502 part-time. Students come from 20 states and territories, 11% African American, 2% Asian American or Pacific Islander, 7% Hispanic American, 0.7% Native American, 0.6% international. Freshmen *Admission:* 1,188 admitted, 1,188 enrolled.

Faculty *Total:* 605, 20% full-time. *Student/faculty ratio:* 13:1.

Majors Accounting technology and bookkeeping; automobile/automotive mechanics technology; business/commerce; drafting and design technology; early childhood education; emergency medical technology (EMT paramedic); fire science; health information/medical records technology; human services; information technology; landscaping and groundskeeping; liberal arts and sciences/liberal studies; marketing/marketing management; nursing (registered nurse training); office management; parks, recreation and leisure; physical therapist assistant; restaurant, culinary, and catering management; veterinary/animal health technology.

Academics *Calendar:* semesters. *Degree:* certificates and associate. *Special study options:* academic remediation for entering students, adult/continuing education programs, advanced placement credit, cooperative education, distance learning, English as a second language, freshman honors college, honors programs, independent study, internships, part-time degree program, services for LD students, summer session for credit.

Library Learning Resources Center plus 1 other with 54,491 titles, 367 serial subscriptions, an OPAC.

Computers on Campus 737 computers available on campus for general student use. A campuswide network can be accessed from off campus. Internet access, online (class) registration, at least one staffed computer lab available.

Student Life *Housing:* college housing not available. *Options:* Campus housing is provided by a third party. *Activities and Organizations:* drama/theater group, student-run newspaper, choral group, Student Activities Board, African-American Student Union, ROC (Realizing Our Cause), Gay Straight Alliance, Musagettas. *Campus security:* 24-hour emergency response devices and patrols, student patrols, late-night transport/escort service. *Student services:* personal/psychological counseling.

Athletics Member NJCAA. *Intercollegiate sports:* baseball M(s), basketball M(s)/W(s), softball W(s), tennis W(s).

Costs (2005–06) *Tuition:* state resident $1961 full-time, $65 per credit hour part-time; nonresident $7177 full-time, $239 per credit hour part-time. *Room and board:* $5562.

Financial Aid Of all full-time matriculated undergraduates who enrolled in 2004, 103 Federal Work-Study jobs (averaging $1500).

Applying *Options:* common application, early admission. *Application fee:* $20. *Required:* high school transcript. *Application deadline:* rolling (freshmen), rolling (transfers). *Notification:* continuous (freshmen).

Freshmen Application Contact Ms. Christy Jones, Registrar, Central Florida Community College, PO Box 1388, 3001 SW College Road, Ocala, FL 34474-1388. *Phone:* 352-237-2111 Ext. 1398. *Fax:* 352-873-5882. *E-mail:* jonesch@cf.edu.

CENTRAL FLORIDA INSTITUTE
Palm Harbor, Florida   www.cfinstitute.com/

Director of Admissions Carol Bruno, Director of Admissions, Central Florida Institute, 60522 US Highway 19 North, Suite 200, Palm Harbor, FL 34684. *Phone:* 727-786-4707.

CHIPOLA COLLEGE

Marianna, Florida   www.chipola.edu/

- **State-supported** primarily 2-year, founded 1947
- **Rural** 105-acre campus
- **Coed**

Undergraduates 1,030 full-time, 1,219 part-time. Students come from 13 states and territories, 7 other countries, 3% are from out of state, 19% African American, 0.9% Asian American or Pacific Islander, 2% Hispanic American, 0.7% Native American, 4% transferred in.

Faculty *Student/faculty ratio:* 24:1.

Academics *Calendar:* semesters. *Degrees:* certificates, associate, and bachelor's. *Special study options:* academic remediation for entering students, adult/continuing education programs, advanced placement credit, distance learning, honors programs, independent study, part-time degree program, services for LD students, summer session for credit.

Student Life *Campus security:* night security personnel.

Athletics Member NJCAA.

Standardized Tests *Required:* SAT or ACT (for placement).

Applying *Options:* early admission. *Required:* high school transcript.

Director of Admissions Dr. Jayne Roberts, Dean of Enrollment Services and Register, Chipola College, Marianna, FL 32446. *Phone:* 850-718-2209 Ext. 2209. *E-mail:* robertsj@chipola.edu.

CITY COLLEGE

Casselberry, Florida   www.citycollege.edu/

Director of Admissions Ms. Yvonne C. Hunter, Director of Admissions, City College, 853 Semoran Boulevard, Suite 200, Casselberry, FL 32707-5342. *Phone:* 407-831-9816. *Fax:* 407-831-1147. *E-mail:* yhunter@citycollege.edu.

CITY COLLEGE

Fort Lauderdale, Florida   www.citycollege.edu/

Director of Admissions Mr. Michael Beauregard, Vice President, City College, 1401 West Cypress Creek Road, Fort Lauderdale, FL 33309. *Phone:* 954-492-5353.

CITY COLLEGE

Gainesville, Florida

CITY COLLEGE

Miami, Florida   www.citycollege.edu/

Director of Admissions Admissions, City College, 9300 South Dadeland Boulevard, Miami, FL 33156.

COLLEGE OF BUSINESS AND TECHNOLOGY

Miami, Florida   www.cbt.edu/

- **Proprietary** 2-year, founded 1988
- **Endowment** $3.5 million
- **Coed**, 250 undergraduate students

Undergraduates Students come from 7 states and territories, 90% Hispanic American.

Freshmen *Admission:* 350 applied, 250 admitted. *Average high school GPA:* 2.80.

Faculty *Total:* 15, 67% full-time, 20% with terminal degrees. *Student/faculty ratio:* 10:1.

Majors Accounting; business administration and management; business systems networking/ telecommunications; computer graphics; heating, air conditioning, ventilation and refrigeration maintenance technology; medical/clinical assistant; system, networking, and LAN/WAN management.

Academics *Calendar:* semesters. *Degree:* certificates, diplomas, and associate. *Special study options:* academic remediation for entering students, accelerated degree program, adult/continuing education programs, advanced placement credit, cooperative education, distance learning, double majors, English as a second language, honors programs, independent study, internships, off-campus study, part-time degree program, services for LD students, summer session for credit.

Library The Bill Clinton Library plus 1 other with 700,000 titles, 200,000 serial subscriptions, 1,200 audiovisual materials, an OPAC, a Web page.

Computers on Campus 560 computers available on campus for general student use. A campuswide network can be accessed from student residence rooms and from off campus. Internet access, online (class) registration, at least one staffed computer lab available. Computer purchase or lease plan available.

Student Life *Housing Options:* Campus housing is provided by a third party. *Activities and Organizations:* student-run newspaper.

Costs (2006–07) *Tuition:* $10,500 full-time, $278 per semester hour part-time. *Required fees:* $200 full-time. *Room only:* $6000.

Applying *Options:* common application, electronic application. *Application fee:* $100. *Required:* essay or personal statement, high school transcript, minimum 2.6 GPA, 2 letters of recommendation, interview. *Application deadline:* 6/15 (freshmen).

Freshmen Application Contact Ms. Ivis Delgado, Admissions Representative, College of Business and Technology, 8991 Southwest 107 Avenue, Suite 200, Miami, FL 33176. *Phone:* 305-273-4499 Ext. 2204. *Fax:* 305-485-4411. *E-mail:* admissions@cbt.edu.

DAYTONA BEACH COMMUNITY COLLEGE

Daytona Beach, Florida   www.dbcc.edu/

- **State-supported** 2-year, founded 1958, part of Florida Community College System
- **Suburban** 100-acre campus with easy access to Orlando
- **Endowment** $3.1 million
- **Coed**

Undergraduates 4,776 full-time, 7,169 part-time. Students come from 51 states and territories, 52 other countries, 5% are from out of state, 12% African American, 2% Asian American or Pacific Islander, 7% Hispanic American, 0.5% Native American, 1% international, 6% transferred in.

Faculty *Student/faculty ratio:* 17:1.

Academics *Calendar:* semesters. *Degree:* certificates and associate. *Special study options:* academic remediation for entering students, adult/continuing education programs, advanced placement credit, cooperative education, English as a second language, honors programs, internships, part-time degree program, services for LD students, study abroad, summer session for credit. *ROTC:* Army (c), Air Force (c).

Student Life *Campus security:* 24-hour patrols, late-night transport/escort service.

Athletics Member NJCAA.

Standardized Tests *Required:* ACT ASSET, CPT (for placement).

Financial Aid Of all full-time matriculated undergraduates who enrolled in 2004, 193 Federal Work-Study jobs (averaging $1542).

Applying *Options:* common application, early admission, deferred entrance. *Required:* high school transcript.

Director of Admissions Mr. Thomas LoBasso, Dean of Enrollment Development, Daytona Beach Community College, PO Box 2811, Daytona Beach, FL 32120-2811. *Phone:* 386-506-3732.

EDISON COLLEGE

Fort Myers, Florida   www.edison.edu/

Freshmen Application Contact Ms. Pat Armstrong, Admissions Specialist, Edison College, PO Box 60210, Fort Myers, FL 33906-6210. *Phone:* 941-489-9121. *Toll-free phone:* 800-749-2ECC. *E-mail:* inquiry@eccrs.edison.cc.fl.us.

FLORIDA CAREER COLLEGE

Miami, Florida   **www.careercollege.edu/**

Director of Admissions Mr. David Knobel, President, Florida Career College, 1321 Southwest 107 Avenue, Miami, FL 33174. *Phone:* 305-553-6065.

FLORIDA COLLEGE OF NATURAL HEALTH

Bradenton, Florida   **www.fcnh.com/**

Director of Admissions Ms. Karen Curry, Director, Florida College of Natural Health, 616 67th Street Circle East, Bradenton, FL 34208. *Phone:* 941-954-8999. *Toll-free phone:* 800-966-7117. *Fax:* 941-954-8991. *E-mail:* sarasota@fcnh.com.

FLORIDA COLLEGE OF NATURAL HEALTH

Maitland, Florida   **www.fcnh.com/**

Director of Admissions Mr. Steve Richards, Campus Director, Florida College of Natural Health, 2600 Lake Lucien Drive, Suite 140, Maitland, FL 32751. *Phone:* 407-261-0319. *Toll-free phone:* 800-393-7337. *Fax:* 407-261-0342. *E-mail:* orlando@fcnh.com.

FLORIDA COLLEGE OF NATURAL HEALTH

Miami, Florida   **www.fcnh.com/**

Director of Admissions Ms. Lissette Vidal, Admissions Coordinator, Florida College of Natural Health, 7925 Northwest 12th Street, Suite 201, Miami, FL 33126. *Phone:* 305-597-9599. *Toll-free phone:* 800-599-9599. *Fax:* 305-597-9110. *E-mail:* miami@fcnh.com.

FLORIDA COLLEGE OF NATURAL HEALTH

Pompano Beach, Florida   **www.fcnh.com/**

Director of Admissions Mr. Peter Hogaboom, Campus Director, Florida College of Natural Health, 2001 West Sample Road, Suite 100, Pompano Beach, FL 33064. *Phone:* 954-975-6400. *Toll-free phone:* 800-541-9299. *Fax:* 954-975-9633. *E-mail:* adrener@fcnh.com.

FLORIDA COMMUNITY COLLEGE AT JACKSONVILLE

Jacksonville, Florida   **www.fccj.edu/**

- **State-supported** 2-year, founded 1963, part of Florida Community College System
- **Urban** 656-acre campus
- **Endowment** $3.9 million
- **Coed,** 29,831 undergraduate students, 25% full-time, 42% women, 58% men

Undergraduates 7,462 full-time, 22,369 part-time. Students come from 19 states and territories, 108 other countries, 23% are from out of state, 28% African American, 4% Asian American or Pacific Islander, 6% Hispanic American, 0.3% Native American, 20% transferred in.
Freshmen *Admission:* 700 applied, 700 admitted, 700 enrolled. *Test scores:* SAT verbal scores over 500: 37%; SAT math scores over 500: 29%; ACT scores over 18: 40%; SAT verbal scores over 600: 4%; SAT math scores over 600: 4%; ACT scores over 24: 6%; SAT verbal scores over 700: 1%.

Faculty *Total:* 1,134, 32% full-time, 10% with terminal degrees. *Student/faculty ratio:* 21:1.

Majors Accounting; administrative assistant and secretarial science; aircraft powerplant technology; airframe mechanics and aircraft maintenance technology; airline pilot and flight crew; architectural drafting and CAD/CADD; architectural engineering technology; autobody/collision and repair technology; automobile/automotive mechanics technology; aviation/airway management; banking and financial support services; biomedical technology; business administration and management; child care and support services management; child care provision; civil engineering technology; commercial and advertising art; computer and information sciences; computer and information sciences related; computer and information systems security; computer engineering technology; computer graphics; computer hardware engineering; computer/information technology services administration related; computer programming; computer programming related; computer programming (specific applications); computer programming (vendor/product certification); computer software and media applications related; computer software engineering; computer systems analysis; computer systems networking and telecommunications; computer/technical support; construction engineering technology; criminal justice/law enforcement administration; criminal justice/police science; culinary arts; data entry/microcomputer applications; data entry/microcomputer applications related; data modeling/warehousing and database administration; dental hygiene; design and visual communications; diagnostic medical sonography and ultrasound technology; dietetics; dietitian assistant; drafting and design technology; electrical, electronic and communications engineering technology; emergency medical technology (EMT paramedic); engineering technology; fashion merchandising; fire protection and safety technology; fire science; foodservice systems administration; health information/medical records administration; hospitality administration; hospitality and recreation marketing; hotel/motel administration; human services; information science/studies; information technology; instrumentation technology; insurance; interior design; legal assistant/paralegal; liberal arts and sciences/liberal studies; machine shop technology; marketing/marketing management; masonry; medical laboratory technology; medical office management; medical radiologic technology; nuclear/nuclear power technology; nursing (registered nurse training); office management; office occupations and clerical services; physical therapist assistant; printmaking; real estate; respiratory care therapy; retailing; sign language interpretation and translation; substance abuse/addiction counseling; system administration; theater design and technology; tourism and travel services marketing; visual and performing arts related; water quality and wastewater treatment management and recycling technology; web/multimedia management and webmaster; web page, digital/multimedia and information resources design; word processing.

Academics *Calendar:* semesters. *Degree:* certificates, diplomas, and associate. *Special study options:* academic remediation for entering students, accelerated degree program, adult/continuing education programs, advanced placement credit, cooperative education, distance learning, double majors, English as a second language, honors programs, independent study, internships, off-campus study, part-time degree program, services for LD students, study abroad, summer session for credit. *ROTC:* Navy (c).

Library Main Library plus 6 others with 412,856 titles, 4,137 serial subscriptions, 15,286 audiovisual materials, an OPAC, a Web page.

Computers on Campus 2500 computers available on campus for general student use. A campuswide network can be accessed from off campus. Internet access, online (class) registration, at least one staffed computer lab available.

Student Life *Housing:* college housing not available. *Activities and Organizations:* drama/theater group, student-run newspaper, radio and television station, choral group, Phi Theta Kappa, Troupe de Kent, Forensic Team, Brain Bowl Team, International Student Association. *Campus security:* 24-hour emergency response devices and patrols, student patrols, late-night transport/escort service. *Student services:* personal/psychological counseling, women's center.

Athletics Member NJCAA. *Intercollegiate sports:* baseball M(s), basketball M(s)/W(s), softball W(s), tennis W(s), volleyball W(s). *Intramural sports:* badminton M/W, basketball M/W, bowling M/W, football M/W, golf M/W, soccer M/W, softball M/W, table tennis M/W, tennis M/W, volleyball M/W.

Costs (2005–06) *Tuition:* state resident $1518 full-time, $63 per credit part-time; nonresident $5742 full-time, $239 per credit part-time.

Applying *Options:* common application, early admission, deferred entrance. *Application fee:* $15. *Required:* high school transcript. *Application deadline:* rolling (freshmen), rolling (transfers).

Freshmen Application Contact Mr. Peter Biegel, District Director of Enrollment Services and Registrar, Florida Community College at Jacksonville, 501 West State Street, Jacksonville, FL 32202. *Phone:* 904-632-3131. *Fax:* 904-632-5105. *E-mail:* admissions@fccj.edu.

FLORIDA CULINARY INSTITUTE

West Palm Beach, Florida   www.floridaculinary.com/

Director of Admissions Mr. David Conway, Associate Director of Admissions, Florida Culinary Institute, 2400 Metrocentre Boulevard, West Palm Beach, FL 33407. *Phone:* 561-842-8324 Ext. 202. *Toll-free phone:* 800-826-9986. *E-mail:* info@floridaculinary.com.

FLORIDA HOSPITAL COLLEGE OF HEALTH SCIENCES

Orlando, Florida   www.fhchs.edu/

- **Independent** primarily 2-year
- **Urban** 9-acre campus
- **Endowment** $1.0 million
- **Coed**

Undergraduates 609 full-time, 794 part-time. Students come from 8 states and territories, 23 other countries, 14% African American, 9% Asian American or Pacific Islander, 15% Hispanic American, 0.7% Native American, 8% live on campus.
Academics *Calendar:* semesters. *Degrees:* certificates, associate, and bachelor's. *Special study options:* academic remediation for entering students, advanced placement credit, distance learning, independent study, services for LD students. *ROTC:* Air Force (c).
Student Life *Campus security:* 24-hour emergency response devices and patrols, late-night transport/escort service, controlled dormitory access.
Standardized Tests *Required for some:* SAT or ACT (for admission).
Costs (2005–06) *Tuition:* $8060 full-time, $230 per credit part-time. *Required fees:* $570 full-time. *Room only:* $1760.
Financial Aid *Financial aid deadline:* 7/18.
Applying *Options:* common application, electronic application. *Application fee:* $20. *Required:* minimum 2.7 GPA. *Required for some:* essay or personal statement, high school transcript, 3 letters of recommendation.
Director of Admissions Ms. Fiona Ghosn, Director of Admissions, Florida Hospital College of Health Sciences, 800 Lake Estelle Drive, Orlando, FL 32803. *Phone:* 407-303-9798 Ext. 9624. *Toll-free phone:* 800-500-7747.

FLORIDA KEYS COMMUNITY COLLEGE

Key West, Florida   www.fkcc.edu/

- **State-supported** 2-year, founded 1965, part of Florida Community College System
- **Small-town** 20-acre campus
- **Endowment** $658,235
- **Coed**

Undergraduates 1% are from out of state.
Faculty *Student/faculty ratio:* 11:1.
Academics *Calendar:* trimesters. *Degree:* certificates and associate. *Special study options:* academic remediation for entering students, adult/continuing education programs, advanced placement credit, cooperative education, distance learning, double majors, English as a second language, independent study, internships, part-time degree program, services for LD students, student-designed majors, summer session for credit.
Student Life *Campus security:* 24-hour patrols.
Standardized Tests *Required for some:* SAT or ACT (for placement).
Financial Aid Of all full-time matriculated undergraduates who enrolled in 2004, 30 Federal Work-Study jobs (averaging $2000).
Applying *Options:* early admission, deferred entrance. *Application fee:* $20. *Required for some:* high school transcript.
Director of Admissions Ms. Cheryl A. Malsheimer, Director of Admissions and Records, Florida Keys Community College, 5901 College Road, Key West, FL 33040. *Phone:* 305-296-9081 Ext. 201.

FLORIDA METROPOLITAN UNIVERSITY— ORANGE PARK CAMPUS

Orange Park, Florida   www.fmu.edu

FLORIDA NATIONAL COLLEGE

Hialeah, Florida   www.fnc.edu/

- **Proprietary** 2-year, founded 1982
- **Urban** campus with easy access to Miami
- **Coed,** 1,871 undergraduate students, 92% full-time, 67% women, 33% men

Undergraduates 1,723 full-time, 148 part-time. Students come from 1 other state, 4% African American, 1% Asian American or Pacific Islander, 91% Hispanic American, 0.3% Native American, 2% international.
Freshmen *Admission:* 591 applied, 423 admitted, 423 enrolled.
Faculty *Total:* 76, 57% full-time, 22% with terminal degrees. *Student/faculty ratio:* 24:1.
Majors Accounting; administrative assistant and secretarial science; allied health and medical assisting services related; business administration and management; computer and information systems security; computer graphics; computer programming; computer programming related; computer programming (specific applications); computer science; computer systems networking and telecommunications; computer/technical support; data entry/microcomputer applications; data entry/microcomputer applications related; data processing and data processing technology; dental hygiene; diagnostic medical sonography and ultrasound technology; education; health services/allied health/health sciences; hospitality administration; legal administrative assistant/secretary; legal assistant/paralegal; legal professions and studies related; legal studies; liberal arts and sciences/liberal studies; medical administrative assistant and medical secretary; medical/clinical assistant; radiologic technology/science; system administration; technical and business writing; tourism and travel services management; tourism promotion; web page, digital/multimedia and information resources design; word processing.
Academics *Calendar:* semesters. *Degree:* certificates, diplomas, and associate. *Special study options:* academic remediation for entering students, adult/continuing education programs, cooperative education, English as a second language, services for LD students, student-designed majors, summer session for credit.
Library Hialeah Campus Library with 23,507 titles, 87 serial subscriptions, 3,337 audiovisual materials, an OPAC, a Web page.
Computers on Campus 152 computers available on campus for general student use. A campuswide network can be accessed from off campus. Internet access available.
Student Life *Housing:* college housing not available. *Activities and Organizations:* student-run newspaper, Student Government Association. *Campus security:* 24-hour emergency response devices.
Costs (2006–07) *Tuition:* $10,200 full-time, $340 per credit part-time. *Required fees:* $760 full-time.
Financial Aid Of all full-time matriculated undergraduates who enrolled in 2004, 20 Federal Work-Study jobs (averaging $8050).
Applying *Options:* common application, deferred entrance. *Required:* high school transcript. *Application deadline:* rolling (freshmen), rolling (transfers). *Notification:* continuous (freshmen).
Freshmen Application Contact Ms. Maria C. Reguerio, Vice President, Florida National College, 4425 West 20 Avenue, Hialeah, FL 33012. *Phone:* 305-821-3333 Ext. 3. *Fax:* 305-362-0595. *E-mail:* admissions@fnc.edu.

THE FLORIDA SCHOOL OF MIDWIFERY

Gainseville, Florida   www.midwiferyschool.org/

Director of Admissions Ms. Gloria Huffman, Director of Finance, The Florida School of Midwifery, PO Box 5505, Gainesville, FL 32627-5505. *Phone:* 352-338-0766.

FLORIDA TECHNICAL COLLEGE
Auburndale, Florida
www.flatech.edu/

Director of Admissions Mr. Charles Owens, Admissions Office, Florida Technical College, 298 Havendale Boulevard, Auburndale, FL 33823. *Phone:* 863-967-8822.

FLORIDA TECHNICAL COLLEGE
DeLand, Florida
www.flatech.edu/

- **Proprietary** 2-year
- **Coed,** 260 undergraduate students, 100% full-time, 58% women, 42% men

Undergraduates 260 full-time.
Freshmen *Admission:* 260 enrolled.
Faculty *Total:* 13, 85% full-time. *Student/faculty ratio:* 22:1.
Majors CAD/CADD drafting/design technology; computer science; criminal justice/safety; medical administrative assistant and medical secretary; medical/clinical assistant; paralegal/legal assistant; web page, digital/multimedia and information resources design.
Academics *Calendar:* quarters. *Degree:* associate.
Applying *Application fee:* $25.
Freshmen Application Contact Mr. Bill Atkinson, Director, Florida Technical College, 1450 South Woodland Boulevard, 3rd Floor, DeLand, FL 32720. *Phone:* 386-734-3303. *Fax:* 386-734-5150.

FLORIDA TECHNICAL COLLEGE
Jacksonville, Florida
www.flatech.edu/

Director of Admissions Mr. Bryan Gulebiam, Director of Admissions, Florida Technical College, 8711 Lone Star Road, Jacksonville, FL 32211. *Phone:* 407-678-5600.

FLORIDA TECHNICAL COLLEGE
Orlando, Florida
www.flatech.edu/

Director of Admissions Ms. Jeanette E. Muschlitz, Director of Admissions, Florida Technical College, 1819 North Semoran Boulevard, Orlando, FL 32807-3546. *Phone:* 407-678-5600.

FULL SAIL REAL WORLD EDUCATION
Winter Park, Florida
www.fullsail.com

- **Proprietary** primarily 2-year, founded 1979
- **Suburban** campus with easy access to Orlando
- **Coed, primarily men,** 5,219 undergraduate students, 100% full-time, 11% women, 89% men

Undergraduates 5,219 full-time. Students come from 47 states and territories, 6 other countries, 70% are from out of state, 11% African American, 3% Asian American or Pacific Islander, 10% Hispanic American, 0.7% Native American, 1% international.
Freshmen *Admission:* 2,954 applied, 2,025 admitted, 1,596 enrolled.
Faculty *Total:* 482. *Student/faculty ratio:* 10:1.
Majors Animation, interactive technology, video graphics and special effects; business, management, and marketing related; computer graphics; design and applied arts related; dramatic/theater arts and stagecraft related; film/video and photographic arts related; recording arts technology.
Academics *Calendar:* modular. *Degrees:* associate and bachelor's. *Special study options:* academic remediation for entering students, cooperative education, internships, services for LD students, summer session for credit.
Library Full Sail Library plus 1 other with 2,531 titles, 84 serial subscriptions, 784 audiovisual materials, an OPAC.
Computers on Campus A campuswide network can be accessed from off campus. Internet access, at least one staffed computer lab available.

Student Life *Housing:* college housing not available. *Options:* Campus housing is provided by a third party. *Activities and Organizations:* Student Chapter of Audio Engineering Society. *Campus security:* 24-hour patrols. *Student services:* personal/psychological counseling.
Financial Aid Of all full-time matriculated undergraduates who enrolled in 2004, 212 Federal Work-Study jobs (averaging $561).
Applying *Options:* common application, electronic application. *Application fee:* $150. *Required:* high school transcript. *Required for some:* minimum "A" average in Algebra II. *Application deadline:* rolling (freshmen).
Freshmen Application Contact Ms. Mary Beth Plank, Director of Admissions, Full Sail Real World Education, 3300 University Boulevard, Winter Park, FL 32792. *Phone:* 407-679-6333 Ext. 2122. *Toll-free phone:* 800-226-7625. *E-mail:* admissions@fullsail.com.

▶ See page 546 for the College Close-Up.

GULF COAST COLLEGE
Tampa, Florida
gulfcoastcollege.com/

Director of Admissions Mr. Todd A. Matthews Sr., Regional Vice President, Gulf Coast College, 3910 US Hwy 301 North, Suite 200, Tampa, FL 33619. *Phone:* 813-620-1446. *Toll-free phone:* 888-729-7247.

GULF COAST COMMUNITY COLLEGE
Panama City, Florida
www.gulfcoast.edu/

- **State-supported** 2-year, founded 1957
- **Suburban** 80-acre campus
- **Endowment** $13.9 million
- **Coed**

Undergraduates 2,248 full-time, 3,810 part-time. Students come from 28 states and territories, 8 other countries, 12% African American, 2% Asian American or Pacific Islander, 3% Hispanic American, 0.7% Native American, 0.7% international.
Faculty *Student/faculty ratio:* 14:1.
Academics *Calendar:* semesters. *Degree:* certificates and associate. *Special study options:* academic remediation for entering students, accelerated degree program, adult/continuing education programs, advanced placement credit, cooperative education, distance learning, double majors, English as a second language, external degree program, honors programs, independent study, off-campus study, part-time degree program, services for LD students, summer session for credit.
Student Life *Campus security:* patrols by trained security personnel during campus hours.
Athletics Member NJCAA.
Standardized Tests *Required:* CPT (for placement).
Costs (2005–06) *Tuition:* state resident $1446 full-time, $48 per credit part-time; nonresident $6232 full-time, $208 per credit part-time. Full-time tuition and fees vary according to course load. Part-time tuition and fees vary according to course load. *Required fees:* $309 full-time, $10 per credit part-time.
Financial Aid Of all full-time matriculated undergraduates who enrolled in 2004, 145 Federal Work-Study jobs (averaging $3200). 60 state and other part-time jobs (averaging $2600).
Applying *Options:* electronic application, early admission, deferred entrance. *Required:* high school transcript.
Freshmen Application Contact Mrs. Jackie Kuczenski, Administrative Secretary of Admissions, Gulf Coast Community College, 5230 West Highway 98, Panama City, FL 32401. *Phone:* 850-769-1551 Ext. 4892. *Toll-free phone:* 800-311-3628.

HERZING COLLEGE
Winter Park, Florida
www.herzing.edu/

Director of Admissions Ms. Karen Mohamad, Director of Admissions, Herzing College, 1595 South Semoran Boulevard, Suite 1501, Winter Park, FL 32792-5509. *Phone:* 407-478-0500. *Fax:* 407-380-0269.

HIGH-TECH INSTITUTE
Orlando, Florida   www.high-techinstitute.com

HILLSBOROUGH COMMUNITY COLLEGE
Tampa, Florida   www.hccfl.edu/

- **State-supported** 2-year, founded 1968, part of Florida Community College System
- **Urban** campus
- **Endowment** $1.6 million
- **Coed**

Undergraduates 7,009 full-time, 15,140 part-time. Students come from 40 states and territories, 100 other countries, 4% are from out of state, 19% African American, 4% Asian American or Pacific Islander, 19% Hispanic American, 0.4% Native American, 0.8% international, 19% transferred in. *Retention:* 57% of 2003 full-time freshmen returned.

Faculty *Student/faculty ratio:* 28:1.

Academics *Calendar:* semesters. *Degree:* certificates and associate. *Special study options:* academic remediation for entering students, adult/continuing education programs, advanced placement credit, cooperative education, distance learning, English as a second language, honors programs, off-campus study, part-time degree program, services for LD students, summer session for credit. *ROTC:* Army (c), Air Force (c).

Student Life *Campus security:* 24-hour emergency response devices and patrols.

Athletics Member NJCAA.

Standardized Tests *Required for some:* CPT.

Applying *Options:* common application, early admission. *Application fee:* $20. *Required:* high school transcript.

Director of Admissions Ms. Kathy G. Cecil, Admissions, Registration, and Records Officer, Hillsborough Community College, PO Box 31127, Tampa, FL 33631-3127. *Phone:* 813-253-7027.

INDIAN RIVER COMMUNITY COLLEGE
Fort Pierce, Florida   www.ircc.edu/

- **State-supported** 2-year, founded 1960, part of Florida Community College System
- **Small-town** 133-acre campus
- **Coed**

Undergraduates Students come from 33 states and territories, 2% are from out of state, 17% African American, 1% Asian American or Pacific Islander, 12% Hispanic American, 0.4% Native American.

Academics *Calendar:* semesters. *Degree:* certificates, diplomas, and associate. *Special study options:* academic remediation for entering students, adult/continuing education programs, advanced placement credit, distance learning, English as a second language, independent study, part-time degree program, services for LD students, summer session for credit.

Student Life *Campus security:* 24-hour patrols.

Athletics Member NJCAA.

Standardized Tests *Required:* SAT, ACT, or CPT (for placement).

Financial Aid Of all full-time matriculated undergraduates who enrolled in 2004, 130 Federal Work-Study jobs (averaging $1500).

Applying *Options:* early admission, deferred entrance. *Required:* high school transcript.

Director of Admissions Mrs. Linda Hays, Dean of Educational Services, Indian River Community College, 3209 Virginia Avenue, Fort Pierce, FL 34981-5596. *Phone:* 772-462-4740.

ITT TECHNICAL INSTITUTE
Fort Lauderdale, Florida   www.itt-tech.edu/

- **Proprietary** primarily 2-year, founded 1991, part of ITT Educational Services, Inc
- **Suburban** campus with easy access to Miami
- **Coed**

Majors Animation, interactive technology, video graphics and special effects; business administration and management; CAD/CADD drafting/design technology; computer and information systems security; computer programming; criminal justice/law enforcement administration; electrical, electronic and communications engineering technology; system, networking, and LAN/WAN management; web/multimedia management and webmaster; web page, digital/multimedia and information resources design.

Academics *Calendar:* quarters. *Degrees:* associate and bachelor's.

Library a Web page.

Computers on Campus Internet access, at least one staffed computer lab available.

Student Life *Housing:* college housing not available.

Standardized Tests *Required:* Wonderlic aptitude test (for admission).

Costs (2005–06) *Tuition:* Please see school catalog for specific information.

Applying *Options:* deferred entrance. *Application fee:* $100. *Required:* high school transcript, interview. *Recommended:* letters of recommendation. *Application deadline:* rolling (freshmen), rolling (transfers). *Notification:* continuous (freshmen).

Freshmen Application Contact Ms. Lori Glaser, Director of Recruitment, ITT Technical Institute, 3401 South University Drive, Fort Lauderdale, FL 33328. *Phone:* 954-476-9300. *Toll-free phone:* 800-488-7797.

ITT TECHNICAL INSTITUTE
Jacksonville, Florida   www.itt-tech.edu/

- **Proprietary** primarily 2-year, founded 1991, part of ITT Educational Services, Inc
- **Urban** 1-acre campus
- **Coed**

Majors Animation, interactive technology, video graphics and special effects; business administration and management; CAD/CADD drafting/design technology; computer and information systems security; computer programming; criminal justice/law enforcement administration; e-commerce; electrical, electronic and communications engineering technology; system, networking, and LAN/WAN management; web/multimedia management and webmaster; web page, digital/multimedia and information resources design.

Academics *Calendar:* quarters. *Degrees:* associate and bachelor's.

Library a Web page.

Computers on Campus Internet access, at least one staffed computer lab available.

Student Life *Housing:* college housing not available.

Standardized Tests *Required:* Wonderlic aptitude test (for admission).

Costs (2005–06) *Tuition:* Please see school catalog for specific information.

Financial Aid Of all full-time matriculated undergraduates who enrolled in 2004, 5 Federal Work-Study jobs.

Applying *Options:* deferred entrance. *Application fee:* $100. *Required:* high school transcript, interview. *Recommended:* letters of recommendation. *Application deadline:* rolling (freshmen), rolling (transfers). *Notification:* continuous (freshmen).

Freshmen Application Contact Mr. Jorge Torres, Director of Recruitment, ITT Technical Institute, 6600-10 Youngerman Circle, Jacksonville, FL 32244. *Phone:* 904-573-9100. *Toll-free phone:* 800-318-1264.

ITT TECHNICAL INSTITUTE
Lake Mary, Florida   www.itt-tech.edu/

- **Proprietary** primarily 2-year, founded 1989, part of ITT Educational Services, Inc
- **Suburban** 1-acre campus with easy access to Orlando
- **Coed**

Majors Animation, interactive technology, video graphics and special effects; business administration and management; CAD/CADD drafting/design technol-

Florida

ITT Technical Institute (continued)

ogy; computer and information systems security; computer programming; computer systems networking and telecommunications; criminal justice/law enforcement administration; electrical, electronic and communications engineering technology; system, networking, and LAN/WAN management; web/multimedia management and webmaster; web page, digital/multimedia and information resources design.

Academics *Calendar:* quarters. *Degrees:* associate and bachelor's.

Library a Web page.

Computers on Campus Internet access, at least one staffed computer lab available.

Student Life *Housing:* college housing not available. *Activities and Organizations:* student-run newspaper.

Standardized Tests *Required:* Wonderlic aptitude test (for admission).

Costs (2005–06) *Tuition:* Please see school catalog for specific information.

Applying *Options:* deferred entrance. *Application fee:* $100. *Required:* high school transcript, interview. *Recommended:* letters of recommendation. *Application deadline:* rolling (freshmen), rolling (transfers). *Notification:* continuous (freshmen).

Freshmen Application Contact Mr. Larry Johnson, Director of Recruitment, ITT Technical Institute, 1400 International Pkwy South, Lake Mary, FL 32746. *Phone:* 407-660-2900. *Toll-free phone:* 866-489-8441. *Fax:* 407-660-2566.

ITT TECHNICAL INSTITUTE
Miami, Florida   www.itt-tech.edu/

- **Proprietary** primarily 2-year, founded 1996, part of ITT Educational Services, Inc
- **Coed**

Majors Accounting and business/management; animation, interactive technology, video graphics and special effects; business administration and management; computer and information systems security; computer programming; computer systems networking and telecommunications; criminal justice/law enforcement administration; electrical, electronic and communications engineering technology; system, networking, and LAN/WAN management; web/multimedia management and webmaster; web page, digital/multimedia and information resources design.

Academics *Calendar:* quarters. *Degrees:* associate and bachelor's.

Library a Web page.

Computers on Campus Internet access, at least one staffed computer lab available.

Student Life *Housing:* college housing not available.

Standardized Tests *Required:* Wonderlic aptitude test (for admission).

Costs (2005–06) *Tuition:* Please see school catalog for specific information.

Applying *Options:* deferred entrance. *Application fee:* $100. *Required:* high school transcript, interview. *Recommended:* letters of recommendation. *Application deadline:* rolling (freshmen), rolling (transfers). *Notification:* continuous (freshmen).

Freshmen Application Contact Mr. Alan Arellano, Director of Recruitment, ITT Technical Institute, 7955 NW 12th Street, Suite 119, Miami, FL 33126. *Phone:* 305-477-3080.

ITT TECHNICAL INSTITUTE
Tampa, Florida   www.itt-tech.edu/

- **Proprietary** primarily 2-year, founded 1981, part of ITT Educational Services, Inc
- **Suburban** campus with easy access to St. Petersburg
- **Coed**

Majors Animation, interactive technology, video graphics and special effects; business administration and management; CAD/CADD drafting/design technology; computer and information systems security; computer programming; criminal justice/law enforcement administration; e-commerce; electrical, electronic and communications engineering technology; system, networking, and LAN/WAN management; web/multimedia management and webmaster; web page, digital/multimedia and information resources design.

Academics *Calendar:* quarters. *Degrees:* associate and bachelor's.

Library a Web page.

Computers on Campus Internet access, at least one staffed computer lab available.

Student Life *Housing:* college housing not available.

Standardized Tests *Required:* Wonderlic aptitude test (for admission).

Costs (2005–06) *Tuition:* Please see school catalog for specific information.

Applying *Options:* deferred entrance. *Application fee:* $100. *Required:* high school transcript, interview. *Recommended:* letters of recommendation. *Application deadline:* rolling (freshmen), rolling (transfers). *Notification:* continuous (freshmen).

Freshmen Application Contact Mr. Joseph E. Rostkowski, Director of Recruitment, ITT Technical Institute, 4809 Memorial Highway, Tampa, FL 33634. *Phone:* 813-885-2244. *Toll-free phone:* 800-825-2831.

KEISER COLLEGE
Daytona Beach, Florida   www.keisercollege.edu/

Director of Admissions Ms. Heather Armstrong, Director of Admissions, Keiser College, 1800 West International Speedway, Building 3, Daytona Beach, FL 32114. *Phone:* 386-274-5060. *Toll-free phone:* 800-749-4456. *Fax:* 386-274-2725.

KEISER COLLEGE
Fort Lauderdale, Florida   www.keisercollege.edu

- **Proprietary** primarily 2-year, founded 1977
- **Suburban** 4-acre campus with easy access to Miami
- **Coed**

Undergraduates 5,043 full-time, 1,078 part-time. Students come from 25 other countries, 26% African American, 1% Asian American or Pacific Islander, 17% Hispanic American, 0.5% Native American, 1% international.

Academics *Calendar:* 3 semesters per year. *Degrees:* diplomas, associate, and bachelor's (profile includes data from Daytona Beach, Melbourne, Sarasota, Tallahassee, and Lakeland campuses). *Special study options:* adult/continuing education programs, distance learning, independent study, internships.

Student Life *Campus security:* security guard after 8 p.m.

Standardized Tests *Required:* SAT, ACT, or Otis-Lennon School Ability Test (for admission).

Costs (2005–06) *Tuition:* Tuition varies by program. Contact institution.

Applying *Options:* deferred entrance. *Application fee:* $55. *Required:* high school transcript, minimum 2.0 GPA, interview.

Director of Admissions Mr. Brian Woods, Vice President of Enrollment Management, Keiser College, 1500 Northwest 49th Street, Fort Lauderdale, FL 33309. *Phone:* 954-776-4476. *Toll-free phone:* 800-749-4456. *Fax:* 954-351-4030. *E-mail:* admissions@keisercollege.edu.

KEISER COLLEGE
Lakeland, Florida   www.keisercollege.edu/

Director of Admissions Mr. Walter Bequette, Director of Admissions, Keiser College, 3515 Aviation Drive, Lakeland, FL 33811. *Phone:* 863-701-7789.

KEISER COLLEGE
Melbourne, Florida   www.keisercollege.edu/

Director of Admissions Ms. Susan Zeigelhofer, Director of Admissions, Keiser College, 900 South Babcock Street, Melbourne, FL 32901-1461. *Phone:* 954-776-4456. *Toll-free phone:* 800-749-4456. *Fax:* 954-771-4894.

KEISER COLLEGE
Miami, Florida   www.keisercollege.edu/

- **Proprietary** primarily 2-year
- **Coed,** 739 undergraduate students, 100% full-time, 58% women, 42% men

Undergraduates 739 full-time. Students come from 3 states and territories, 10% African American, 78% Hispanic American, 0.7% international.

Freshmen *Admission:* 739 enrolled.

Faculty *Total:* 47, 85% full-time, 9% with terminal degrees. *Student/faculty ratio:* 18:1.

Majors Business administration and management; computer systems networking and telecommunications; criminal justice/law enforcement administration; health and medical administrative services related; health services/allied health/health sciences; legal assistant/paralegal; medical office assistant; nursing (registered nurse training); radiologic technology/science.

Academics *Calendar:* 3 semesters per year. *Degrees:* associate and bachelor's.

Student Life *Housing:* college housing not available. *Activities and Organizations:* Student Ambassador Program. *Campus security:* 24-hour patrols.

Standardized Tests *Recommended:* SAT or ACT (for admission).

Costs (2005–06) *Tuition:* $11,032 full-time. *Required fees:* $400 full-time. *Payment plan:* installment.

Applying *Application fee:* $55. *Required:* high school transcript, interview.

Freshmen Application Contact Mr. Ted Weiner, Director of Admissions, Keiser College, 8505 Mills Drive, Miami, FL 33183. *Phone:* 305-596-2226. *Fax:* 305-596-7077. *E-mail:* tedw@keisercollege.edu.

KEISER COLLEGE
Orlando, Florida   www.keisercollege.edu

KEISER COLLEGE
Pembroke Pines, Florida   www.keisercollege.edu

KEISER COLLEGE
Port St. Lucie, Florida   www.keisercollege.edu

KEISER COLLEGE
Sarasota, Florida   www.keisercollege.edu/

Director of Admissions Brandon Barnhill, Director of Admissions, Keiser College, 6151 Lake Osprey Drive, Sarasota, FL 34240. *Phone:* 941-907-3900. *Toll-free phone:* 866-KEISER2. *Fax:* 941-907-2016.

KEISER COLLEGE
Tallahassee, Florida   www.keisercollege.edu/

Director of Admissions Phil Hooks, Director of Admissions, Keiser College, 1700 Halstead Boulevard, Tallahassee, FL 32308. *Phone:* 850-906-9494. *Toll-free phone:* 800-749-4456. *Fax:* 850-906-9497.

KEISER COLLEGE
West Palm Beach, Florida   www.keisercollege.edu

KEY COLLEGE
Fort Lauderdale, Florida   www.keycollege.edu/

Director of Admissions Mr. Ronald H. Dooley, President and Director of Admissions, Key College, 5225 West Broward Boulevard, Ft. Lauderdale, FL 33317. *Phone:* 954-581-2223 Ext. 23. *Toll-free phone:* 800-581-8292.

LAKE CITY COMMUNITY COLLEGE
Lake City, Florida   www.lakecity.cc.fl.us/

- **State-supported** 2-year, founded 1962, part of Florida Community College System
- **Small-town** 132-acre campus with easy access to Jacksonville
- **Endowment** $3.3 million
- **Coed,** 2,736 undergraduate students, 40% full-time, 64% women, 36% men

Undergraduates 1,084 full-time, 1,652 part-time. Students come from 18 states and territories, 7 other countries, 11% African American, 2% Asian American or Pacific Islander, 2% Hispanic American, 0.2% Native American, 0.5% international, 2% live on campus. Freshmen *Admission:* 1,162 applied, 657 admitted, 657 enrolled.

Faculty *Total:* 165, 33% full-time, 24% with terminal degrees. *Student/faculty ratio:* 18:1.

Majors Administrative assistant and secretarial science; business administration and management; clinical/medical laboratory technology; computer hardware engineering; computer programming; computer programming (specific applications); computer programming (vendor/product certification); computer software engineering; criminal justice/law enforcement administration; electrical, electronic and communications engineering technology; emergency medical technology (EMT paramedic); forest/forest resources management; forestry technology; landscaping and groundskeeping; liberal arts and sciences/liberal studies; nursing (registered nurse training); physical therapist assistant; turf and turfgrass management; web page, digital/multimedia and information resources design.

Academics *Calendar:* semesters. *Degree:* certificates, diplomas, and associate. *Special study options:* academic remediation for entering students, adult/continuing education programs, advanced placement credit, cooperative education, distance learning, English as a second language, independent study, internships, part-time degree program, services for LD students, study abroad, summer session for credit.

Library Learning Resources Center with 42,000 titles, 180 serial subscriptions, an OPAC.

Computers on Campus 150 computers available on campus for general student use. A campuswide network can be accessed. Internet access, at least one staffed computer lab available.

Student Life *Housing Options:* coed. *Activities and Organizations:* drama/theater group, choral group, student government, Florida Turf Grass Association, Florida Student Nurses Association, Phi Theta Kappa, Multicultural Student Union. *Campus security:* 24-hour patrols.

Athletics Member NJCAA. *Intercollegiate sports:* baseball M(s), golf W(s), softball W(s). *Intramural sports:* basketball M, racquetball M/W, softball M/W, table tennis M/W, tennis M/W, volleyball M/W, weight lifting M/W.

Costs (2006–07) *Tuition:* state resident $2037 full-time; nonresident $7290 full-time. *Room and board:* $4535.

Financial Aid Of all full-time matriculated undergraduates who enrolled in 2004, 58 Federal Work-Study jobs (averaging $975).

Applying *Options:* early admission, deferred entrance. *Application fee:* $15. *Required for some:* high school transcript. *Application deadline:* rolling (freshmen), rolling (transfers). *Notification:* continuous (freshmen).

Freshmen Application Contact Vince Rice, Director of Postsecondary Transition, Lake City Community College, Route 19, Box 1030, Lake City, FL 32025-8703. *Phone:* 386-754-4288. *Fax:* 386-755-1521. *E-mail:* admissions@mail.lakecity.cc.fl.us.

LAKE-SUMTER COMMUNITY COLLEGE
Leesburg, Florida
www.lscc.edu/

- **State and locally supported** 2-year, founded 1962, part of Florida Department of Education
- **Suburban** 110-acre campus with easy access to Orlando
- **Endowment** $3.3 million
- **Coed,** 3,409 undergraduate students, 35% full-time, 66% women, 34% men

Undergraduates 1,208 full-time, 2,201 part-time. Students come from 8 states and territories, 6 other countries, 1% are from out of state, 10% African American, 2% Asian American or Pacific Islander, 9% Hispanic American, 0.4% Native American, 0.7% international, 28% transferred in.

Freshmen *Admission:* 1,088 applied, 1,088 admitted, 607 enrolled.

Faculty *Total:* 168, 29% full-time, 12% with terminal degrees. *Student/faculty ratio:* 20:1.

Majors Business administration and management; commercial and advertising art; computer and information sciences related; computer science; criminal justice/law enforcement administration; emergency medical technology (EMT paramedic); fire science; health information/medical records administration; legal assistant/paralegal; liberal arts and sciences/liberal studies; nursing (registered nurse training); office management; sport and fitness administration/management; theater design and technology.

Academics *Calendar:* semesters. *Degree:* certificates, diplomas, and associate. *Special study options:* academic remediation for entering students, adult/continuing education programs, advanced placement credit, cooperative education, distance learning, double majors, independent study, off-campus study, part-time degree program, services for LD students, summer session for credit.

Library Lake-Sumter Community College Library with 69,465 titles, 528 serial subscriptions, 1,262 audiovisual materials, an OPAC, a Web page.

Computers on Campus 537 computers available on campus for general student use. A campuswide network can be accessed from off campus. Internet access, online (class) registration, at least one staffed computer lab available.

Student Life *Housing:* college housing not available. *Activities and Organizations:* drama/theater group, student-run newspaper, television station, choral group, Phi Theta Kappa, Baptist Collegiate Ministry, Environmental Society, Nursing Students' Association. *Campus security:* 24-hour emergency response devices. *Student services:* women's center.

Athletics Member NJCAA. *Intercollegiate sports:* baseball M(s), softball W(s), volleyball W(s). *Intramural sports:* basketball M/W, softball W, volleyball W.

Costs (2005–06) *Tuition:* state resident $1932 full-time, $64 per credit hour part-time; nonresident $7108 full-time, $237 per credit hour part-time. Full-time tuition and fees vary according to course load. Part-time tuition and fees vary according to course load. *Required fees:* $30 full-time, $1 per credit hour part-time. *Waivers:* employees or children of employees.

Applying *Application fee:* $25. *Required:* high school transcript. *Application deadline:* rolling (freshmen), rolling (transfers). *Notification:* continuous (freshmen).

Freshmen Application Contact Ms. Amy Whitely, Enrollment Specialist, Lake-Sumter Community College, 9501 US Highway 441, Leesburg, FL 34788-8751. *Phone:* 352-365-3561. *Fax:* 352-365-3553. *E-mail:* admissinquiry@lscc.edu.

MANATEE COMMUNITY COLLEGE
Bradenton, Florida
www.mccfl.edu/

- **State-supported** 2-year, founded 1957, part of Florida Community College System
- **Suburban** 100-acre campus with easy access to Tampa–St. Petersburg
- **Coed,** 9,767 undergraduate students, 39% full-time, 62% women, 38% men

Undergraduates 3,855 full-time, 5,912 part-time. Students come from 47 states and territories, 86 other countries, 4% are from out of state, 10% African American, 2% Asian American or Pacific Islander, 7% Hispanic American, 0.3% Native American, 2% international, 6% transferred in. *Retention:* 64% of 2003 full-time freshmen returned.

Freshmen *Admission:* 2,281 enrolled. *Test scores:* SAT verbal scores over 500: 37%; SAT math scores over 500: 37%; ACT scores over 18: 64%; SAT verbal scores over 600: 8%; SAT math scores over 600: 7%; ACT scores over 24: 11%; ACT scores over 30: 1%.

Faculty *Total:* 463, 27% full-time, 11% with terminal degrees. *Student/faculty ratio:* 23:1.

Majors Accounting; administrative assistant and secretarial science; advertising; African-American/Black studies; American government and politics; Ameri-

can studies; art; art history, criticism and conservation; Asian studies; astronomy; biology/biological sciences; biology teacher education; business administration and management; business/commerce; business/managerial economics; chemistry; chemistry teacher education; child guidance; civil engineering technology; commercial and advertising art; community health services counseling; computer and information sciences; computer and information sciences related; computer engineering technology; computer graphics; computer programming; computer programming related; construction engineering technology; criminal justice/safety; dietetics; drafting and design technology; dramatic/theater arts; economics; electrical, electronic and communications engineering technology; engineering; English; English/language arts teacher education; European studies (Central and Eastern); family and consumer sciences/home economics teacher education; finance; fine/studio arts; fire science; foreign language teacher education; French; German; health/health care administration; health teacher education; history; hospital and health care facilities administration; humanities; information science/studies; jazz/jazz studies; Jewish/Judaic studies; journalism; kindergarten/preschool education; Latin American studies; legal assistant/paralegal; liberal arts and sciences/liberal studies; mass communication/media; mathematics teacher education; medical radiologic technology; music; music performance; music teacher education; music theory and composition; nursing (registered nurse training); occupational therapist assistant; occupational therapy; philosophy; physical education teaching and coaching; physical therapist assistant; physical therapy; physician assistant; physics; physics teacher education; pre-pharmacy studies; psychology; public administration; radio and television; radio and television broadcasting technology; radiologic technology/science; religious studies; respiratory care therapy; Russian studies; science teacher education; social psychology; social sciences; social studies teacher education; social work; Spanish; speech and rhetoric; statistics; technology/industrial arts teacher education; trade and industrial teacher education; vocational rehabilitation counseling; women's studies.

Academics *Calendar:* semesters. *Degree:* certificates and associate. *Special study options:* academic remediation for entering students, advanced placement credit, cooperative education, distance learning, English as a second language, honors programs, independent study, part-time degree program, services for LD students, summer session for credit.

Library Sara Harlee Library plus 1 other with 65,386 titles, 378 serial subscriptions, 14,617 audiovisual materials, an OPAC, a Web page.

Computers on Campus 1000 computers available on campus for general student use. A campuswide network can be accessed from off campus. Internet access, online (class) registration, at least one staffed computer lab available.

Student Life *Housing:* college housing not available. *Activities and Organizations:* drama/theater group, student-run newspaper, choral group, Student Government Association, Phi Theta Kappa, American Chemical Society Student Affiliate, Campus Ministry, Medical Community Club. *Campus security:* 24-hour emergency response devices and patrols, late-night transport/escort service.

Athletics Member NJCAA. *Intercollegiate sports:* baseball M(s), basketball M(s), softball W(s), volleyball W(s). *Intramural sports:* basketball M/W, softball M/W, volleyball M/W, weight lifting M/W.

Costs (2005–06) *Tuition:* state resident $1983 full-time, $66 per credit part-time; nonresident $7352 full-time, $245 per credit part-time.

Financial Aid Of all full-time matriculated undergraduates who enrolled in 2004, 82 Federal Work-Study jobs (averaging $2800). *Financial aid deadline:* 8/15.

Applying *Options:* early admission. *Application fee:* $40. *Required:* high school transcript. *Application deadlines:* 8/20 (freshmen), 8/20 (transfers). *Notification:* continuous (freshmen).

Freshmen Application Contact Ms. MariLynn Paro, Registrar, Manatee Community College, PO Box 1849, Bradenton, FL 34206. *Phone:* 941-752-5031. *Fax:* 941-727-6380.

MEDVANCE INSTITUTE
Atlantis, Florida
www.medvance.org/

Director of Admissions Ms. Brenda Cortez, Campus Director, MedVance Institute, 170 JFK Drive, Atlantis, FL 33462. *Phone:* 561-304-3466. *Toll-free phone:* 888-86-GO-MED. *Fax:* 561-304-3471. *E-mail:* bcortez@medvance.org.

MIAMI DADE COLLEGE
Miami, Florida   www.mdc.edu/

- **State and locally supported** primarily 2-year, founded 1960, part of Florida Community College System
- **Urban** campus
- **Endowment** $109.2 million
- **Coed,** 54,169 undergraduate students, 35% full-time, 62% women, 38% men

Miami Dade College offers undergraduate study in more than 200 academic areas and professions. The College is internationally recognized as an educational leader in undergraduate programs that are innovative and diverse within a multicultural, multiethnic environment. Annually, more than 163,000 credit- and noncredit-seeking students are enrolled at eight major campuses and numerous outreach centers.

Undergraduates 18,836 full-time, 35,333 part-time. Students come from 43 states and territories, 160 other countries, 1% are from out of state, 21% African American, 1% Asian American or Pacific Islander, 64% Hispanic American, 0.1% Native American, 3% international, 2% transferred in. Freshmen *Admission:* 20,445 applied, 20,445 admitted, 10,409 enrolled. *Test scores:* SAT verbal scores over 500: 18%; SAT math scores over 500: 18%; ACT scores over 18: 32%; SAT verbal scores over 600: 2%; SAT math scores over 600: 2%; ACT scores over 24: 2%.

Faculty *Total:* 2,103, 34% full-time, 16% with terminal degrees. *Student/faculty ratio:* 26:1.

Majors Accounting technology and bookkeeping; administrative assistant and secretarial science; aeronautics/aviation/aerospace science and technology; agriculture; airline pilot and flight crew; air traffic control; American studies; anthropology; architectural drafting and CAD/CADD; architectural engineering technology; art; Asian studies; audiology and speech-language pathology; aviation/airway management; behavioral sciences; biology/biological sciences; biology teacher education; biomedical technology; business administration and management; chemistry; chemistry teacher education; child development; cinematography and film/video production; civil engineering technology; clinical/medical laboratory technology; commercial and advertising art; computer engineering technology; computer graphics; computer programming; computer science; computer software technology; computer technology/computer systems technology; construction engineering technology; court reporting; criminal justice/law enforcement administration; criminal justice/police science; dance; data processing and data processing technology; dental hygiene; diagnostic medical sonography and ultrasound technology; dietetics; dietetic technician; drafting and design technology; dramatic/theater arts; economics; education; education (specific subject areas) related; electrical and electronic engineering technologies related; electrical, electronic and communications engineering technology; elementary education; emergency medical technology (EMT paramedic); engineering; engineering related; engineering technology; English; environmental engineering technology; finance; fire science; food science; forestry; French; funeral service and mortuary science; general studies; geology/earth science; German; health information/medical records administration; health/medical preparatory programs related; health professions related; heating, air conditioning and refrigeration technology; heating, air conditioning, ventilation and refrigeration maintenance technology; histologic technician; history; horticultural science; hospitality administration; humanities; human services; industrial technology; information science/studies; interior design; international relations and affairs; Italian; journalism; kindergarten/preschool education; landscaping and groundskeeping; Latin American studies; legal administrative assistant/secretary; legal assistant/paralegal; literature; management information systems; marketing/marketing management; mass communication/media; mathematics; mathematics teacher education; medical/clinical assistant; middle school education; music; music performance; music teacher education; natural sciences; non-profit management; nuclear medical technology; nursing (registered nurse training); ophthalmic technology; ornamental horticulture; parks, recreation and leisure; philosophy; photographic and film/video technology; photography; physical education teaching and coaching; physical sciences; physical therapist assistant; physics; physics teacher education; plant nursery management; political science and government; Portuguese; pre-engineering; psychology; public administration; radio and television; radio and television broadcasting technology; radiologic technology/science; recording arts technology; respiratory care therapy; respiratory therapy technician; science teacher education; sign language interpretation and translation; social sciences; social work; sociology; Spanish; special education; substance abuse/addiction counseling; teacher assistant/aide; telecommunications technology; tourism and travel services management.

Academics *Calendar:* 16-16-6-6. *Degrees:* certificates, associate, and bachelor's. *Special study options:* academic remediation for entering students, adult/continuing education programs, advanced placement credit, cooperative education, distance learning, English as a second language, freshman honors college, honors programs, independent study, internships, part-time degree program, services for LD students, study abroad, summer session for credit. *ROTC:* Army (c), Air Force (c).

Library Main Library plus 8 others with 327,417 titles, 4,916 serial subscriptions, 17,186 audiovisual materials, an OPAC, a Web page.

Computers on Campus 6750 computers available on campus for general student use. A campuswide network can be accessed from off campus that provide access to admissions; grades; student feedback of faculty; financial aid. Internet access, online (class) registration, at least one staffed computer lab available. Computer purchase or lease plan available.

Student Life *Housing:* college housing not available. *Activities and Organizations:* drama/theater group, student-run newspaper, radio station, choral group, Welcome Back, Hispanic Heritage Month, Black History Month, Paella Festival. *Campus security:* 24-hour patrols. *Student services:* personal/psychological counseling.

Athletics Member NJCAA. *Intercollegiate sports:* baseball M(s), basketball M(s)/W(s), softball W(s), volleyball W(s). *Intramural sports:* basketball M/W, racquetball M/W, soccer M/W, softball M/W, swimming and diving M/W, tennis M/W, track and field M/W, volleyball M/W, weight lifting M/W.

Costs (2005–06) *Tuition:* state resident $1620 full-time, $54 per credit part-time; nonresident $5997 full-time, $200 per credit part-time. *Required fees:* $302 full-time.

Financial Aid Of all full-time matriculated undergraduates who enrolled in 2004, 800 Federal Work-Study jobs (averaging $5000). 125 state and other part-time jobs (averaging $5000).

Applying *Options:* electronic application, early admission. *Application fee:* $20. *Required:* high school transcript. *Application deadline:* rolling (freshmen). *Notification:* continuous (freshmen).

Freshmen Application Contact Mr. Steven Kelly, College Registrar, Miami Dade College, 11011 SW 104th Street, Miami, FL 33176. *Phone:* 305-237-0633. *Fax:* 305-237-2964. *E-mail:* skelly@mdc.edu.

▶ **See page 576 for the College Close-Up.**

NATIONAL SCHOOL OF TECHNOLOGY, INC.
Fort Lauderdale, Florida   www.nst.cc/

Director of Admissions Ashly Miller, Director of Admissions, National School of Technology, Inc., 1040 Bayview Drive, Fort Lauderdale, FL 33304. *Phone:* 954-630-0066. *Fax:* 954-630-0076. *E-mail:* amiller@cci.edu.

NATIONAL SCHOOL OF TECHNOLOGY, INC.
Hialeah, Florida   www.nst.cc/

Director of Admissions Mr. Daniel Alonso, Director of Admissions, National School of Technology, Inc., 4410 West 16th Avenue, Suite 52, Hialeah, FL 33012. *Phone:* 305-558-9500. *Fax:* 305-558-4419. *E-mail:* dalonso@cci.edu.

NATIONAL SCHOOL OF TECHNOLOGY, INC.
Miami, Florida   www.nst.cc/

Director of Admissions Ms. Amber Stenbeck, Director of Admissions, National School of Technology, Inc., 111 Northwest 183rd Street, 2nd Floor, Miami, FL 33169. *Phone:* 305-386-9900.

NATIONAL SCHOOL OF TECHNOLOGY, INC.
North Miami Beach, Florida   www.nst.cc/

Director of Admissions Mr. Walter McQuade, Director of Admissions, National School of Technology, Inc., 16150 Northeast 17th Avenue, North Miami Beach, FL 33162-4744. *Phone:* 305-949-9500.

NEW ENGLAND INSTITUTE OF TECHNOLOGY AT PALM BEACH

West Palm Beach, Florida   **newenglandtech.com/**

Director of Admissions Mr. Kevin Cassidy, Director of Admissions, New England Institute of Technology at Palm Beach, 1126 53rd Court, West Palm Beach, FL 33407-2384. *Phone:* 561-842-8324 Ext. 117. *Toll-free phone:* 800-826-9986. *Fax:* 561-842-9503.

NORTH FLORIDA COMMUNITY COLLEGE

Madison, Florida   **www.nfcc.edu/**

Freshmen Application Contact Mrs. Betty Starling, Admissions Assistant, North Florida Community College, 1000 Turner Davis Drive, Madison, FL 32340-1602. *Phone:* 850-973-1622.

OKALOOSA-WALTON COLLEGE

Niceville, Florida   **www.owc.edu/**

- **State and locally supported** primarily 2-year, founded 1963, part of Florida Community College System
- **Small-town** 264-acre campus
- **Endowment** $21.0 million
- **Coed,** 8,728 undergraduate students

Undergraduates Students come from 18 states and territories, 10% African American.

Faculty *Total:* 243, 34% full-time. *Student/faculty ratio:* 20:1.

Majors Accounting; administrative assistant and secretarial science; art; atmospheric sciences and meteorology; automobile/automotive mechanics technology; avionics maintenance technology; biological and physical sciences; biology/biological sciences; business administration and management; chemistry; child development; clinical laboratory science/medical technology; commercial and advertising art; computer engineering related; computer programming; computer programming (specific applications); computer science; computer systems networking and telecommunications; construction engineering technology; criminal justice/law enforcement administration; criminal justice/police science; data entry/microcomputer applications; dietetics; divinity/ministry; drafting and design technology; education; electrical, electronic and communications engineering technology; elementary education; engineering; family and consumer sciences/home economics teacher education; fashion merchandising; finance; foods, nutrition, and wellness; heating, air conditioning, ventilation and refrigeration maintenance technology; hotel/motel administration; humanities; human resources management; information technology; interior design; kindergarten/preschool education; legal assistant/paralegal; legal studies; liberal arts and sciences/liberal studies; mathematics; modern languages; music; nursing (registered nurse training); physical education teaching and coaching; physics; purchasing, procurement/acquisitions and contracts management; real estate; social sciences; social work; welding technology; word processing.

Academics *Calendar:* semesters plus summer sessions. *Degrees:* certificates, associate, and bachelor's. *Special study options:* academic remediation for entering students, adult/continuing education programs, advanced placement credit, distance learning, English as a second language, independent study, part-time degree program, services for LD students, summer session for credit. *ROTC:* Army (c).

Library Okaloosa-Walton Community College Learning Resource Center with 84,991 titles, 365 serial subscriptions, 10,800 audiovisual materials, an OPAC, a Web page.

Computers on Campus 643 computers available on campus for general student use. A campuswide network can be accessed. Internet access, online (class) registration, at least one staffed computer lab available.

Student Life *Housing:* college housing not available. *Activities and Organizations:* drama/theater group, choral group. *Campus security:* 24-hour patrols. *Student services:* health clinic.

Athletics Member NJCAA. *Intercollegiate sports:* baseball M(s), basketball M(s)/W(s), softball W(s). *Intramural sports:* baseball M, basketball M/W, soccer M(c)/W(c), softball W.

Standardized Tests *Required:* ACT, SAT I, ACT ASSET, MAPS, or Florida College Entry Placement Test (for admission).

Costs (2005–06) *Tuition:* state resident $1774 full-time, $55 per credit part-time; nonresident $6661 full-time, $208 per credit part-time.

Financial Aid Of all full-time matriculated undergraduates who enrolled in 2004, 81 Federal Work-Study jobs (averaging $1500). 11 state and other part-time jobs (averaging $1460).

Applying *Options:* early admission, deferred entrance. *Required:* high school transcript. *Application deadline:* rolling (freshmen), rolling (transfers). *Notification:* continuous (freshmen).

Freshmen Application Contact Ms. Christine Bishop, Registrar/Division Director Enrollment Services, Okaloosa-Walton College, 100 College Boulevard, Niceville, FL 32578. *Phone:* 850-729-5373. *Fax:* 850-729-5323. *E-mail:* registrar@owc.edu.

ORLANDO CULINARY ACADEMY

Orlando, Florida

PALM BEACH COMMUNITY COLLEGE

Lake Worth, Florida   **www.pbcc.edu/**

- **State-supported** 2-year, founded 1933, part of Florida Community College System
- **Urban** 150-acre campus with easy access to West Palm Beach
- **Endowment** $14.4 million
- **Coed,** 22,666 undergraduate students, 31% full-time, 62% women, 38% men

Undergraduates 6,917 full-time, 15,749 part-time. Students come from 49 states and territories, 138 other countries, 5% are from out of state, 22% African American, 3% Asian American or Pacific Islander, 15% Hispanic American, 0.3% Native American, 3% international, 10% transferred in.
Freshmen *Admission:* 27,824 applied, 27,824 admitted, 2,485 enrolled.

Faculty *Total:* 1,024, 23% full-time, 15% with terminal degrees. *Student/faculty ratio:* 22:1.

Majors Accounting; administrative assistant and secretarial science; airline pilot and flight crew; art; art history, criticism and conservation; biology/biological sciences; botany/plant biology; business administration and management; ceramic arts and ceramics; chemistry; clothing/textiles; commercial and advertising art; computer programming; computer programming (specific applications); computer science; computer/technical support; construction management; criminal justice/law enforcement administration; criminal justice/police science; data processing and data processing technology; dental hygiene; drafting and design technology; dramatic/theater arts; economics; education; electrical, electronic and communications engineering technology; elementary education; English; family and consumer sciences/human sciences; fashion/apparel design; fashion merchandising; finance; fire science; foods, nutrition, and wellness; health teacher education; history; hotel/motel administration; industrial radiologic technology; interior design; journalism; kindergarten/preschool education; legal administrative assistant/secretary; liberal arts and sciences/liberal studies; literature; marketing/marketing management; mass communication/media; mathematics; music; nursing (registered nurse training); occupational therapy; philosophy; photography; physical education teaching and coaching; physical sciences; physical therapy; political science and government; pre-engineering; psychology; religious studies; social sciences; social work; special products marketing; survey technology; system administration; web page, digital/multimedia and information resources design; word processing; zoology/animal biology.

Academics *Calendar:* semesters. *Degree:* certificates and associate. *Special study options:* academic remediation for entering students, adult/continuing education programs, advanced placement credit, cooperative education, distance learning, double majors, English as a second language, freshman honors college, honors programs, independent study, internships, off-campus study, part-time degree program, services for LD students, student-designed majors, study abroad, summer session for credit.

Library Harold C. Manor Library plus 3 others with 151,000 titles, 1,474 serial subscriptions, 9,700 audiovisual materials, an OPAC, a Web page.

Computers on Campus 2300 computers available on campus for general student use. A campuswide network can be accessed from off campus. Internet access, online (class) registration, at least one staffed computer lab available.

Student Life *Activities and Organizations:* drama/theater group, student-run newspaper, choral group, student government, Phi Theta Kappa, Students for International Understanding, Black Student Union, Drama Club, national fraternities. *Campus security:* 24-hour emergency response devices and patrols. *Student services:* health clinic, women's center.

Athletics Member NJCAA. *Intercollegiate sports:* baseball M(s), basketball M(s)/W(s), softball W(s), volleyball M(s)/W(s). *Intramural sports:* basketball M/W, bowling M/W, football M/W, racquetball M/W, soccer M, tennis M/W, volleyball M/W.
Costs (2005–06) *Tuition:* $63 per hour part-time; state resident $1890 full-time, $63 per hour part-time; nonresident $6892 full-time, $230 per hour part-time. *Required fees:* $10 full-time.
Applying *Options:* electronic application, early admission, deferred entrance. *Application fee:* $20. *Application deadlines:* 8/20 (freshmen), 8/20 (transfers). *Notification:* continuous until 8/20 (freshmen).
Freshmen Application Contact Ms. Anne Guiler, Coordinator of Distance Learning, Palm Beach Community College, 4200 Congress Avenue, Lake Worth, FL 33461. *Phone:* 561-868-3032. *Fax:* 561-868-3584. *E-mail:* enrollmt@pbcc.edu.

PASCO-HERNANDO COMMUNITY COLLEGE
New Port Richey, Florida   www.phcc.edu/

- **State-supported** 2-year, founded 1972, part of Florida Community College System
- **Small-town** 142-acre campus with easy access to Tampa
- **Endowment** $20.3 million
- **Coed,** 7,346 undergraduate students, 36% full-time, 66% women, 34% men

Undergraduates 2,670 full-time, 4,676 part-time. Students come from 11 states and territories, 10 other countries, 1% are from out of state, 4% African American, 2% Asian American or Pacific Islander, 8% Hispanic American, 0.7% Native American, 0.5% international, 5% transferred in.
Freshmen *Admission:* 2,670 admitted, 1,766 enrolled.
Faculty *Total:* 315, 31% full-time, 15% with terminal degrees. *Student/faculty ratio:* 25:1.
Majors Business administration and management; computer programming related; computer programming (specific applications); computer systems networking and telecommunications; computer technology/computer systems technology; criminal justice/law enforcement administration; dental hygiene; drafting and design technology; e-commerce; emergency medical technology (EMT paramedic); human services; information technology; legal assistant/paralegal; liberal arts and sciences/liberal studies; marketing/marketing management; nursing (registered nurse training); physical therapist assistant; radiologic technology/science; web page, digital/multimedia and information resources design.
Academics *Calendar:* semesters. *Degree:* certificates, diplomas, and associate. *Special study options:* academic remediation for entering students, accelerated degree program, adult/continuing education programs, advanced placement credit, cooperative education, distance learning, double majors, honors programs, independent study, internships, off-campus study, part-time degree program, services for LD students, summer session for credit. *ROTC:* Army (c).
Library Pottberg Library plus 2 others with 67,852 titles, 351 serial subscriptions, 4,357 audiovisual materials, an OPAC, a Web page.
Computers on Campus 974 computers available on campus for general student use. A campuswide network can be accessed. Online (class) registration, at least one staffed computer lab available. Computer purchase or lease plan available.
Student Life *Housing:* college housing not available. *Activities and Organizations:* drama/theater group, choral group, Student Government Association, Phi Theta Kappa, Phi Beta Lambda, Human Services, PHCC Cares. *Campus security:* 24-hour patrols.
Athletics Member NJCAA. *Intercollegiate sports:* baseball M(s), basketball M(s), softball W(s), tennis W(s), volleyball W(s).
Costs (2005–06) *Tuition:* state resident $1872 full-time, $62 per credit part-time; nonresident $7222 full-time, $241 per credit part-time.
Financial Aid Of all full-time matriculated undergraduates who enrolled in 2004, 45 Federal Work-Study jobs (averaging $2133).
Applying *Options:* electronic application. *Application fee:* $20. *Required:* high school transcript. *Application deadline:* rolling (freshmen), rolling (transfers). *Notification:* continuous (freshmen).
Freshmen Application Contact Ms. Debra Bullard, Director of Admissions and Student Records, Pasco-Hernando Community College, 10230 Ridge Road, New Port Richey, FL 34654-5199. *Phone:* 727-816-3261. *Fax:* 727-816-3389. *E-mail:* bullard@phcc.edu.

PENSACOLA JUNIOR COLLEGE
Pensacola, Florida   www.pjc.edu/

Freshmen Application Contact Ms. Martha Caughey, Registrar, Pensacola Junior College, 1000 College Boulevard, Pensacola, FL 32504-8998. *Phone:* 850-484-1600. *Fax:* 850-484-1829.

POLK COMMUNITY COLLEGE
Winter Haven, Florida   www.polk.edu/

- **State-supported** 2-year, founded 1964, part of Florida Community College System
- **Suburban** 98-acre campus with easy access to Orlando and Tampa
- **Endowment** $11.1 million
- **Coed,** 7,082 undergraduate students, 29% full-time, 66% women, 34% men

Undergraduates 2,037 full-time, 5,045 part-time. Students come from 25 states and territories, 73 other countries, 10% are from out of state, 13% African American, 2% Asian American or Pacific Islander, 8% Hispanic American, 0.3% Native American, 4% international.
Freshmen *Admission:* 1,125 applied, 1,125 admitted, 1,125 enrolled.
Faculty *Total:* 446, 27% full-time, 8% with terminal degrees. *Student/faculty ratio:* 16:1.
Majors Accounting technology and bookkeeping; business administration and management; child development; corrections; criminal justice/law enforcement administration; data processing and data processing technology; emergency medical technology (EMT paramedic); finance; fire science; health information/medical records administration; information science/studies; legal administrative assistant/secretary; liberal arts and sciences/liberal studies; marketing/marketing management; medical administrative assistant and medical secretary; nursing (registered nurse training); occupational therapist assistant; physical therapist assistant; pre-engineering; radiologic technology/science; respiratory care therapy.
Academics *Calendar:* semesters 16-16-6-6. *Degree:* certificates and associate. *Special study options:* academic remediation for entering students, accelerated degree program, adult/continuing education programs, advanced placement credit, cooperative education, distance learning, double majors, English as a second language, independent study, part-time degree program, services for LD students, student-designed majors, summer session for credit. *ROTC:* Army (c).
Library Polk Community College Library with 181,000 titles, 325 serial subscriptions, 4,527 audiovisual materials, an OPAC, a Web page.
Computers on Campus 171 computers available on campus for general student use. A campuswide network can be accessed. Internet access, online (class) registration, at least one staffed computer lab available.
Student Life *Housing:* college housing not available. *Activities and Organizations:* drama/theater group, student-run newspaper, choral group. *Campus security:* 24-hour emergency response devices and patrols.
Athletics Member NJCAA. *Intercollegiate sports:* baseball M(s), basketball M(s), soccer W(s), softball W(s), volleyball W(s).
Costs (2005–06) *Tuition:* state resident $1901 full-time, $63 per credit hour part-time; nonresident $7044 full-time, $235 per credit hour part-time. *Waivers:* employees or children of employees.
Financial Aid Of all full-time matriculated undergraduates who enrolled in 2004, 16 Federal Work-Study jobs (averaging $400).
Applying *Options:* early admission, deferred entrance. *Application fee:* $20. *Required:* high school transcript. *Application deadline:* rolling (freshmen), rolling (transfers). *Notification:* continuous (freshmen).
Freshmen Application Contact Ms. Barbara Guthrie, Registrar, Polk Community College, 999 Avenue H North East, Winter Haven, FL 33881. *Phone:* 863-297-1016. *Fax:* 863-297-1060. *E-mail:* bguthrie@polk.edu.

REMINGTON COLLEGE—JACKSONVILLE CAMPUS
Jacksonville, Florida   www.remingtoncollege.edu/

Director of Admissions Mr. Tony Galang, Campus President, Remington College–Jacksonville Campus, 7011 A.C. Skinner Parkway, Jacksonville, FL 32256. *Phone:* 904-296-3435 Ext. 218. *Fax:* 904-296-9097. *E-mail:* tony.galang@remingtoncollege.edu.

REMINGTON COLLEGE–PINELLAS CAMPUS

Largo, Florida www.remingtoncollege.edu/

Director of Admissions Ms. Edna Higgins, Campus President, Remington College–Pinellas Campus, 8550 Ulmerton Road, Largo, FL 33771. *Phone:* 727-532-1999. *Toll-free phone:* 888-900-2343. *Fax:* 727-530-7710.

REMINGTON COLLEGE–TAMPA CAMPUS

Tampa, Florida www.remingtoncollege.edu/

- **Proprietary** primarily 2-year, founded 1948
- **Urban** 10-acre campus
- **Coed,** 685 undergraduate students, 100% full-time, 52% women, 48% men

Undergraduates 685 full-time. 36% African American, 1% Asian American or Pacific Islander, 18% Hispanic American, 0.9% Native American, 3% international.

Faculty *Total:* 26, 69% full-time. *Student/faculty ratio:* 15:1.

Majors Business administration and management; computer technology/ computer systems technology; criminal justice/safety; electrical, electronic and communications engineering technology; information science/studies; operations management.

Academics *Calendar:* quarters. *Degrees:* diplomas, associate, and bachelor's. *Special study options:* academic remediation for entering students, accelerated degree program, internships.

Library Tampa Technical Institute Library with 4,100 titles, 124 serial subscriptions, 340 audiovisual materials, an OPAC.

Computers on Campus 200 computers available on campus for general student use. A campuswide network can be accessed. Internet access, at least one staffed computer lab available.

Student Life *Housing:* college housing not available. *Activities and Organizations:* national fraternities. *Campus security:* late-night transport/escort service.

Standardized Tests *Required:* Wonderlic aptitude test (for admission).

Financial Aid Of all full-time matriculated undergraduates who enrolled in 2004, 12 Federal Work-Study jobs (averaging $8000).

Applying *Options:* common application, deferred entrance. *Application fee:* $50. *Required:* high school transcript, interview. *Application deadline:* rolling (freshmen), rolling (transfers).

Freshmen Application Contact Mr. James Royster, Director of Admissions, Remington College–Tampa Campus, 2410 East Busch Boulevard, Tampa, FL 33612. *Phone:* 813-935-5700. *Toll-free phone:* 800-992-4850. *Fax:* 813-935-7415.

ST. JOHNS RIVER COMMUNITY COLLEGE

Palatka, Florida www.sjrcc.cc.fl.us/

Director of Admissions Mr. O'Neal Williams, Dean of Admissions and Records, St. Johns River Community College, 5001 Saint Johns Avenue, Palatka, FL 32177-3897. *Phone:* 386-312-4032. *Fax:* 386-312-4289.

ST. PETERSBURG COLLEGE

St. Petersburg, Florida www.spjc.edu/

- **State and locally supported** primarily 2-year, founded 1927
- **Suburban** campus
- **Endowment** $13.4 million
- **Coed,** 24,102 undergraduate students, 33% full-time, 63% women, 37% men

Undergraduates 8,012 full-time, 16,090 part-time. Students come from 45 states and territories, 30 other countries, 4% are from out of state, 11% African American, 3% Asian American or Pacific Islander, 6% Hispanic American, 0.7% Native American, 1% international.

Freshmen *Admission:* 3,919 applied, 3,919 admitted, 3,485 enrolled.

Faculty *Total:* 1,912, 16% full-time, 12% with terminal degrees.

Majors Accounting technology and bookkeeping; architectural engineering technology; aviation/airway management; biology teacher education; business administration and management; business teacher education; clinical/medical laboratory technology; commercial and advertising art; computer engineering technology; computer/information technology services administration related; computer systems networking and telecommunications; construction engineering technology; corrections; corrections administration; criminalistics and criminal science; criminal justice/law enforcement administration; criminal justice/police science; data modeling/warehousing and database administration; dental hygiene; drafting and design technology; early childhood education; education; electrical, electronic and communications engineering technology; electromechanical and instrumentation and maintenance technologies related; elementary education; emergency medical technology (EMT paramedic); engineering/industrial management; fire protection and safety technology; fire science; funeral service and mortuary science; graphic design; health/health care administration; health information/medical records administration; hospitality administration; human services; hydrology and water resources science; industrial radiologic technology; industrial technology; information technology; international business/trade/ commerce; kindergarten/preschool education; legal administrative assistant/ secretary; legal assistant/paralegal; liberal arts and sciences/liberal studies; manufacturing technology; marketing/marketing management; mathematics teacher education; nursing (registered nurse training); orthotics/prosthetics; physical therapist assistant; plastics engineering technology; quality control technology; radiologic technology/science; respiratory care therapy; security and loss prevention; security and protective services related; sign language interpretation and translation; special education; substance abuse/addiction counseling; technology/industrial arts teacher education; telecommunications technology; tourism and travel services management; veterinary/animal health technology; veterinary technology; web/multimedia management and webmaster; web page, digital/multimedia and information resources design.

Academics *Calendar:* semesters. *Degrees:* certificates, diplomas, associate, and bachelor's. *Special study options:* academic remediation for entering students, adult/continuing education programs, advanced placement credit, cooperative education, distance learning, English as a second language, freshman honors college, honors programs, internships, part-time degree program, services for LD students, summer session for credit.

Library M. M. Bennett Library plus 5 others with 222,990 titles, 1,393 serial subscriptions, 16,543 audiovisual materials, an OPAC, a Web page.

Computers on Campus 2951 computers available on campus for general student use. A campuswide network can be accessed from off campus. Internet access, online (class) registration, at least one staffed computer lab available. Computer purchase or lease plan available.

Student Life *Housing:* college housing not available. *Activities and Organizations:* drama/theater group, student-run newspaper. *Campus security:* late-night transport/escort service. *Student services:* women's center.

Athletics Member NJCAA. *Intercollegiate sports:* baseball M(s), basketball M(s)/W(s), softball W(s), volleyball W(s). *Intramural sports:* basketball M, bowling M/W, volleyball M/W.

Costs (2005–06) *Tuition:* state resident $1646 full-time, $55 per credit part-time; nonresident $6587 full-time, $219 per credit part-time. Full-time tuition and fees vary according to degree level and program. Part-time tuition and fees vary according to degree level and program. *Required fees:* $337 full-time, $25 per credit part-time. *Payment plan:* deferred payment. *Waivers:* senior citizens and employees or children of employees.

Financial Aid Of all full-time matriculated undergraduates who enrolled in 2004, 350 Federal Work-Study jobs (averaging $2500).

Applying *Options:* common application, electronic application, early admission, deferred entrance. *Application fee:* $35. *Required:* high school transcript. *Application deadline:* rolling (freshmen). *Notification:* continuous (freshmen).

Freshmen Application Contact Mr. Martyn Clay, Admissions Director/ Registrar, St. Petersburg College, PO Box 13489, St. Petersburg, FL 33733-3489. *Phone:* 727-712-5892. *Fax:* 727-712-5872. *E-mail:* information@spcollege.edu.

SANFORD-BROWN INSTITUTE
Jacksonville, Florida   www.sbjacksonville.com

SANFORD-BROWN INSTITUTE
Lauderdale Lakes, Florida   www.sbftlauderdale.com

SANFORD-BROWN INSTITUTE
Tampa, Florida   www.sbtampa.com

SANTA FE COMMUNITY COLLEGE
Gainesville, Florida   www.sfcc.edu/

- **State and locally supported** 2-year, founded 1966, part of Florida Community College System
- **Suburban** 175-acre campus with easy access to Jacksonville
- **Coed**

Undergraduates 6,560 full-time, 7,246 part-time. Students come from 46 states and territories, 80 other countries, 3% are from out of state, 12% African American, 3% Asian American or Pacific Islander, 8% Hispanic American, 0.7% Native American, 3% international, 11% transferred in. *Retention:* 61% of 2003 full-time freshmen returned.
Academics *Calendar:* semesters. *Degrees:* certificates and associate (offers bachelor's degrees in conjunction with Saint Leo College). *Special study options:* academic remediation for entering students, adult/continuing education programs, advanced placement credit, cooperative education, distance learning, English as a second language, honors programs, independent study, part-time degree program, services for LD students, student-designed majors, summer session for credit. *ROTC:* Army (c), Air Force (c).
Student Life *Campus security:* 24-hour emergency response devices and patrols.
Athletics Member NJCAA.
Standardized Tests *Required:* SAT, ACT, or CPT (for placement).
Costs (2005–06) *Tuition:* state resident $1755 full-time, $59 per credit hour part-time; nonresident $6540 full-time, $218 per credit hour part-time.
Financial Aid Of all full-time matriculated undergraduates who enrolled in 2004, 190 Federal Work-Study jobs.
Applying *Options:* early admission. *Application fee:* $30. *Required:* high school transcript.
Director of Admissions Ms. Margaret Karrh, Registrar, Santa Fe Community College, 3000 Northwest 83rd Street, Gainesville, FL 32606-6200. *Phone:* 352-395-5857. *E-mail:* information@santafe.cc.fl.us.

SEMINOLE COMMUNITY COLLEGE
Sanford, Florida   www.scc-fl.edu/

- **State and locally supported** 2-year, founded 1966
- **Small-town** 200-acre campus with easy access to Orlando
- **Endowment** $5.3 million
- **Coed,** 11,582 undergraduate students, 35% full-time, 60% women, 40% men

Undergraduates 4,079 full-time, 7,603 part-time. Students come from 18 states and territories, 123 other countries, 13% African American, 3% Asian American or Pacific Islander, 13% Hispanic American, 0.4% Native American, 5% international, 20% transferred in.
Freshmen *Admission:* 1,726 enrolled.

Faculty *Total:* 809, 25% full-time, 11% with terminal degrees. *Student/faculty ratio:* 11:1.
Majors Accounting; administrative assistant and secretarial science; architectural engineering technology; automobile/automotive mechanics technology; banking and financial support services; business administration and management; child development; civil engineering technology; computer and information sciences related; computer and information systems security; computer engineering related; computer engineering technology; computer graphics; computer hardware engineering; computer/information technology services administration related; computer programming; computer programming related; computer programming (specific applications); computer programming (vendor/product certification); computer software and media applications related; computer software engineering; computer systems networking and telecommunications; computer/technical support; construction engineering technology; construction management; criminal justice/law enforcement administration; data entry/microcomputer applications; data entry/microcomputer applications related; data modeling/warehousing and database administration; data processing and data processing technology; drafting and design technology; electrical, electronic and communications engineering technology; emergency medical technology (EMT paramedic); finance; fire science; industrial technology; information science/studies; information technology; interior design; legal assistant/paralegal; liberal arts and sciences/liberal studies; marketing/marketing management; nursing (registered nurse training); physical therapy; respiratory care therapy; system administration; telecommunications; web/multimedia management and webmaster; web page, digital/multimedia and information resources design; word processing.
Academics *Calendar:* semesters. *Degree:* certificates, diplomas, and associate. *Special study options:* academic remediation for entering students, accelerated degree program, adult/continuing education programs, advanced placement credit, cooperative education, distance learning, double majors, English as a second language, external degree program, honors programs, independent study, internships, part-time degree program, services for LD students, study abroad, summer session for credit. *ROTC:* Army (b).
Library Seminole Community College Library plus 2 others with 102,744 titles, 353 serial subscriptions, 8,913 audiovisual materials, an OPAC, a Web page.
Computers on Campus 56 computers available on campus for general student use. A campuswide network can be accessed from off campus. Internet access, online (class) registration, at least one staffed computer lab available.
Student Life *Housing:* college housing not available. *Activities and Organizations:* drama/theater group, student-run newspaper, choral group, Phi Beta Lambda, Phi Theta Kappa, Student Government Association, International Student Organization. *Campus security:* 24-hour emergency response devices and patrols. *Student services:* personal/psychological counseling.
Athletics Member NJCAA. *Intercollegiate sports:* baseball M(s), basketball M(s)/W(s), softball W(s). *Intramural sports:* basketball M/W, golf M, tennis M/W, volleyball M/W.
Costs (2005–06) *Tuition:* state resident $1592 full-time, $53 per credit hour part-time; nonresident $6125 full-time, $214 per credit hour part-time. *Required fees:* $488 full-time, $16 per credit hour part-time.
Applying *Options:* early admission, deferred entrance. *Required:* high school transcript, minimum 2.0 GPA. *Application deadline:* rolling (freshmen), rolling (transfers). *Notification:* continuous (freshmen).
Freshmen Application Contact Ms. Pamela Mennechey, Director of Admissions, Seminole Community College, 100 Weldon Boulevard, Sanford, FL 32773-6199. *Phone:* 407-708-2050. *Fax:* 407-708-2395. *E-mail:* admissions@scc-fl.edu.

SOUTH FLORIDA COMMUNITY COLLEGE
Avon Park, Florida   www.sfcc.cc.fl.us/

Director of Admissions Ms. Annie Alexander-Harvey, Dean of Student Services, South Florida Community College, 600 West College Drive, Avon Park, FL 33825-9356. *Phone:* 863-453-6661 Ext. 7107.

SOUTH UNIVERSITY
West Palm Beach, Florida   www.southuniversity.edu

- **Proprietary** primarily 2-year, founded 1899, part of Education Management Corporation
- **Suburban** 1-acre campus with easy access to Miami
- **Coed,** 502 undergraduate students, 69% full-time, 86% women, 14% men

Undergraduates 347 full-time, 155 part-time. Students come from 1 other state, 4 other countries, 51% African American, 0.8% Asian American or Pacific

South University (continued)

Islander, 9% Hispanic American, 0.2% Native American, 1% international. *Retention:* 60% of 2003 full-time freshmen returned.

Freshmen *Admission:* 53 admitted, 53 enrolled.

Faculty *Total:* 58, 31% full-time, 5% with terminal degrees. *Student/faculty ratio:* 13:1.

Majors Accounting; administrative assistant and secretarial science; business administration and management; health/health care administration; health services/allied health/health sciences; information science/studies; information technology; legal administrative assistant/secretary; legal assistant/paralegal; legal studies; medical/clinical assistant; nursing (registered nurse training); nursing science; physical therapist assistant; pre-nursing studies.

Academics *Calendar:* quarters. *Degrees:* associate, bachelor's, and master's. *Special study options:* academic remediation for entering students, adult/continuing education programs, advanced placement credit, double majors, internships, part-time degree program.

Library South University Library plus 3 others with 8,400 titles, 67 serial subscriptions.

Computers on Campus 53 computers available on campus for general student use. A campuswide network can be accessed. Internet access, at least one staffed computer lab available.

Student Life *Housing:* college housing not available. *Activities and Organizations:* Pro Bono Club. *Campus security:* evening security personnel. *Student services:* personal/psychological counseling.

Standardized Tests *Recommended:* SAT or ACT (for admission).

Costs (2006–07) *Tuition:* $11,475 full-time, $2995 per term part-time.

Financial Aid Of all full-time matriculated undergraduates who enrolled in 2004, 14 Federal Work-Study jobs (averaging $1530).

Applying *Options:* common application, electronic application, early admission, deferred entrance. *Application fee:* $25. *Required:* high school transcript. *Required for some:* letters of recommendation, interview. *Application deadline:* rolling (freshmen), rolling (transfers). *Notification:* continuous (freshmen).

Freshmen Application Contact South University, 1760 North Congress Avenue, West Palm Beach, FL 33409-5178. *Phone:* 561-697-9200. *Toll-free phone:* 866-629-2902 (in-state); 866-629-9200 (out-of-state). *Fax:* 561-697-9944. *E-mail:* wpbfdesk@southuniversity.edu.

SOUTHWEST FLORIDA COLLEGE

Fort Myers, Florida   **www.swfc.edu/**

- **Independent** primarily 2-year, founded 1940
- **Urban** campus
- **Coed,** 1,263 undergraduate students

Freshmen *Admission:* 954 admitted.

Majors Accounting; administrative assistant and secretarial science; business administration and management; court reporting; information science/studies; legal assistant/paralegal; medical/clinical assistant.

Academics *Calendar:* quarters. *Degrees:* diplomas, associate, and bachelor's. *Special study options:* academic remediation for entering students, cooperative education, internships.

Library Learning Resource Center with 1,000 titles, 20 serial subscriptions, a Web page.

Computers on Campus 80 computers available on campus for general student use. A campuswide network can be accessed from off campus. Internet access, at least one staffed computer lab available.

Student Life *Housing:* college housing not available. *Campus security:* day and evening security guards.

Financial Aid Of all full-time matriculated undergraduates who enrolled in 2004, 10 Federal Work-Study jobs (averaging $5000).

Applying *Options:* common application. *Recommended:* high school transcript. *Application deadline:* rolling (freshmen), rolling (transfers). *Notification:* continuous (freshmen).

Freshmen Application Contact Ms. Carmen King, Director of Admissions, Southwest Florida College, 1685 Medical Lane, Fort Myers, FL 33907. *Phone:* 239-939-4766. *Toll-free phone:* 866-SWFC-NOW. *Fax:* 239-936-4040.

SOUTHWEST FLORIDA COLLEGE

Tampa, Florida   **www.swfc.edu/**

Director of Admissions Admissions, Southwest Florida College, 3910 Riga Boulevard, Tampa, FL 33619. *Phone:* 813-630-4401. *Toll-free phone:* 877-907-2456.

TALLAHASSEE COMMUNITY COLLEGE

Tallahassee, Florida   **www.tcc.fl.edu/**

Freshmen Application Contact Ms. Sharon Jefferson, Director of Enrollment Services, Tallahassee Community College, 444 Appleyard Drive, Tallahassee, FL 32304-2895. *Phone:* 850-201-8555. *E-mail:* enroll@mail.tallahassee.cc.fl.us.

VALENCIA COMMUNITY COLLEGE

Orlando, Florida   **www.valencia.cc.fl.us/**

- **State-supported** 2-year, founded 1967, part of Florida Community College System
- **Urban** campus
- **Endowment** $14.4 million
- **Coed,** 29,342 undergraduate students

Undergraduates Students come from 40 states and territories, 92 other countries, 4% are from out of state, 15% African American, 6% Asian American or Pacific Islander, 23% Hispanic American, 0.5% Native American.

Freshmen *Admission:* 11,409 applied. *Test scores:* SAT verbal scores over 500: 70%; SAT math scores over 500: 58%; SAT verbal scores over 600: 13%; SAT math scores over 600: 5%; SAT verbal scores over 700: 1%; SAT math scores over 700: 1%.

Faculty *Total:* 1,190, 33% full-time. *Student/faculty ratio:* 21:1.

Majors Accounting; administrative assistant and secretarial science; business administration and management; cardiovascular technology; cinematography and film/video production; civil engineering technology; commercial and advertising art; computer programming; computer programming related; computer programming (specific applications); construction engineering technology; criminal justice/law enforcement administration; culinary arts; data entry/microcomputer applications; dental hygiene; diagnostic medical sonography and ultrasound technology; drafting and design technology; dramatic/theater arts; electrical, electronic and communications engineering technology; emergency medical technology (EMT paramedic); environmental engineering technology; fire science; hospitality administration; human resources management; industrial technology; information technology; legal administrative assistant/secretary; legal assistant/paralegal; liberal arts and sciences/liberal studies; marketing/marketing management; medical administrative assistant and medical secretary; medical radiologic technology; nursing (registered nurse training); office management; ornamental horticulture; physical education teaching and coaching; pre-engineering; respiratory care therapy; survey technology; tourism and travel services management; word processing.

Academics *Calendar:* semesters. *Degree:* certificates, diplomas, and associate. *Special study options:* academic remediation for entering students, accelerated degree program, adult/continuing education programs, advanced placement credit, cooperative education, distance learning, double majors, English as a second language, honors programs, independent study, internships, part-time degree program, services for LD students, student-designed majors, summer session for credit. *ROTC:* Army (c).

Library Learning Resources Center plus 3 others with 101,000 titles, 650 serial subscriptions, 15,500 audiovisual materials, an OPAC, a Web page.

Computers on Campus 1927 computers available on campus for general student use. A campuswide network can be accessed. At least one staffed computer lab available.

Student Life *Housing:* college housing not available. *Activities and Organizations:* drama/theater group, student-run newspaper, choral group, Phi Theta Kappa, Valencia Intercultural Student Association, Student Government Association, Latin American Student Association, Valencia Student Nurses Association. *Campus security:* 24-hour emergency response devices and patrols, student patrols, late-night transport/escort service. *Student services:* personal/psychological counseling.

Costs (2005–06) *Tuition:* state resident $1673 full-time, $66 per credit hour part-time; nonresident $6287 full-time, $248 per credit hour part-time.

Financial Aid Of all full-time matriculated undergraduates who enrolled in 2004, 238 Federal Work-Study jobs (averaging $2400).

Applying *Options:* early admission. *Application fee:* $25. *Required:* high school transcript. *Application deadlines:* 8/12 (freshmen), 8/12 (out-of-state freshmen), 8/12 (transfers).

Freshmen Application Contact Dr. Renee Simpson, Director of Admissions and Records, Valencia Community College, PO Box 3028, Orlando, FL 32802-3028. *Phone:* 407-582-1511. *Fax:* 407-582-1866. *E-mail:* rsimpson@valenciacc.edu.

WEBSTER COLLEGE

Holiday, Florida   www.webstercollege.com/

Director of Admissions Ms. Claire L. Walker, Senior Admissions Representative, Webster College, 2127 Grand Boulevard, Holiday, FL 34690. *Phone:* 727-942-0069. *Toll-free phone:* 888-729-7247.

WEBSTER COLLEGE

Ocala, Florida   www.webstercollege.com/

Freshmen Application Contact Admissions Office, Webster College, 1530 SW Third Avenue, Ocala, FL 34474. *Phone:* 352-629-1941.

GEORGIA

ABRAHAM BALDWIN AGRICULTURAL COLLEGE

Tifton, Georgia   www.abac.edu/

- **State-supported** 2-year, founded 1933, part of University System of Georgia
- **Small-town** 390-acre campus
- **Endowment** $4.3 million
- **Coed,** 3,423 undergraduate students, 65% full-time, 58% women, 42% men

Undergraduates 2,237 full-time, 1,186 part-time. Students come from 10 states and territories, 17% African American, 0.6% Asian American or Pacific Islander, 3% Hispanic American, 0.1% Native American, 1% international, 28% live on campus.
Freshmen *Admission:* 2,114 applied, 1,263 admitted, 1,116 enrolled. *Average high school GPA:* 2.8.
Faculty *Total:* 154, 65% full-time, 24% with terminal degrees. *Student/faculty ratio:* 22:1.
Majors Accounting; administrative assistant and secretarial science; agricultural business and management; agricultural economics; agricultural mechanization; agriculture; animal sciences; art; biological and physical sciences; biology/biological sciences; business administration and management; chemistry; child development; computer engineering technology; computer programming; computer science; computer typography and composition equipment operation; criminal justice/law enforcement administration; criminal justice/police science; data processing and data processing technology; ecology; education; elementary education; English; environmental design/architecture; family and consumer sciences/human sciences; farm and ranch management; fashion merchandising; fish/game management; forestry; forestry technology; history; horticultural science; hospitality administration; humanities; journalism; kindergarten/preschool education; landscaping and groundskeeping; liberal arts and sciences/liberal studies; marketing/marketing management; mathematics; music; nursing (registered nurse training); ornamental horticulture; parks, recreation and leisure facilities management; pharmacy technician; physical education teaching and coaching; physical sciences; political science and government; poultry science; pre-engineering; psychology; social sciences; social work; sociology; speech and rhetoric; wildlife and wildlands science and management.
Academics *Calendar:* semesters. *Degree:* certificates and associate. *Special study options:* academic remediation for entering students, adult/continuing education programs, advanced placement credit, English as a second language, honors programs, internships, off-campus study, part-time degree program, services for LD students, summer session for credit.
Library Baldwin Library with 69,986 titles, 431 serial subscriptions.
Computers on Campus 158 computers available on campus for general student use. Internet access, at least one staffed computer lab available.
Student Life *Housing:* on-campus residence required for freshman year. *Options:* coed. *Activities and Organizations:* drama/theater group, student-run newspaper, radio station, choral group, Rodeo Club, Baptist Student Union, Forestry/Wildlife Club. *Campus security:* 24-hour emergency response devices

and patrols, late-night transport/escort service. *Student services:* health clinic, personal/psychological counseling.
Athletics Member NJCAA. *Intercollegiate sports:* baseball M(s), basketball M(s), golf M, soccer W, softball W(s), tennis M(s)/W(s). *Intramural sports:* basketball M/W, bowling M/W, football M/W, golf M/W, soccer M/W, softball M/W, tennis M/W, volleyball M/W.
Costs (2005–06) *Tuition:* state resident $1542 full-time, $65 per credit hour part-time; nonresident $6166 full-time, $257 per credit hour part-time. *Required fees:* $232 full-time, $52 per term part-time. *Room and board:* $5040.
Financial Aid Of all full-time matriculated undergraduates who enrolled in 2004, 158 Federal Work-Study jobs (averaging $1675).
Applying *Options:* common application, early admission, deferred entrance. *Application fee:* $20. *Required:* high school transcript, minimum 2.0 GPA, college prep curriculum. *Required for some:* minimum 2.2 GPA. *Application deadline:* 9/24 (freshmen).
Freshmen Application Contact Ms. Beth Saxon, Director of Enrollment Services, Abraham Baldwin Agricultural College, 2802 Moore Highway, Tifton, GA 31793. *Phone:* 229-391-5001. *Toll-free phone:* 800-733-3653. *Fax:* 229-386-7181. *E-mail:* esaxon@abac.edu.

ALBANY TECHNICAL COLLEGE

Albany, Georgia   www.albanytech.edu/

- **State-supported** 2-year, founded 1961
- **Coed,** 2,787 undergraduate students, 50% full-time, 64% women, 36% men

Undergraduates 1,390 full-time, 1,397 part-time. 66% African American, 0.3% Asian American or Pacific Islander, 0.8% Hispanic American, 0.2% Native American.
Freshmen *Admission:* 480 enrolled.
Faculty *Total:* 91, 100% full-time.
Majors Accounting; child care and guidance related; child development; computer and information sciences; corrections and criminal justice related; culinary arts; drafting and design technology; electrical and electronic engineering technologies related; forestry technology; gerontological services; hotel and restaurant management; industrial technology; manufacturing technology; marketing/marketing management; medical radiologic technology; pharmacy technician; tourism and travel services management.
Academics *Calendar:* quarters. *Degree:* certificates, diplomas, and associate. *Special study options:* academic remediation for entering students, adult/continuing education programs, advanced placement credit, distance learning, internships, part-time degree program, services for LD students.
Library Albany Technical College Library and Media Center plus 1 other with 42,000 titles, 40 serial subscriptions, 520 audiovisual materials, an OPAC, a Web page.
Computers on Campus 500 computers available on campus for general student use. A campuswide network can be accessed from off campus. Online (class) registration, at least one staffed computer lab available. Computer purchase or lease plan available.
Student Life *Housing:* college housing not available.
Standardized Tests *Required:* ACT COMPASS or ASSET (for admission).
Costs (2006–07) *Tuition:* state resident $1116 full-time, $31 per credit hour part-time; nonresident $2232 full-time, $62 per credit hour part-time.
Applying *Options:* common application, electronic application, deferred entrance. *Application fee:* $15. *Required:* high school transcript.
Director of Admissions Lynderia S. Cheevers, Director of Admissions, Albany Technical College, 1704 South Slappey Boulevard, Albany, GA 31701. *Phone:* 229-430-3520. *Fax:* 229-430-6180. *E-mail:* lcheevers@albanytech.edu.

ALTAMAHA TECHNICAL COLLEGE

Jesup, Georgia   www.altamahatech.edu/

- **State-supported** 2-year
- **Coed,** 859 undergraduate students, 40% full-time, 58% women, 42% men

Undergraduates 342 full-time, 517 part-time. 27% African American, 0.2% Asian American or Pacific Islander, 2% Hispanic American, 0.1% Native American.
Freshmen *Admission:* 224 enrolled.
Faculty *Total:* 106, 39% full-time.
Majors Administrative assistant and secretarial science; child development; computer programming; computer systems networking and telecommunications;

Altamaha Technical College (continued)

criminal justice/safety; information science/studies; machine tool technology; manufacturing technology; marketing/marketing management.

Academics *Calendar:* quarters. *Degree:* certificates, diplomas, and associate. *Special study options:* academic remediation for entering students, advanced placement credit, distance learning, internships, services for LD students.

Library 4,435 titles, 90 serial subscriptions, 292 audiovisual materials.

Student Life *Housing:* college housing not available.

Standardized Tests *Required:* ACT COMPASS or ASSET (for placement).

Costs (2006–07) *Tuition:* state resident $1116 full-time, $31 per credit hour part-time; nonresident $2232 full-time, $62 per credit hour part-time.

Applying *Options:* deferred entrance. *Application fee:* $15. *Required:* high school transcript.

Director of Admissions Lillian Burns, Admissions Director, Altamaha Technical College, 1777 West Cherry Street, Jesup, GA 31545. *Phone:* 912-427-5817. *Fax:* 912-427-5823. *E-mail:* lburns@altamahatech.edu.

ANDREW COLLEGE

Cuthbert, Georgia   www.andrewcollege.edu/

- **Independent United Methodist** 2-year, founded 1854
- **Small-town** 40-acre campus
- **Endowment** $7.0 million
- **Coed**

Undergraduates 328 full-time, 3 part-time. Students come from 11 states and territories, 10 other countries, 16% are from out of state, 45% African American, 0.9% Asian American or Pacific Islander, 4% Hispanic American, 6% international, 6% transferred in, 90% live on campus.

Faculty *Student/faculty ratio:* 12:1.

Academics *Calendar:* semesters. *Degree:* certificates and associate. *Special study options:* academic remediation for entering students, advanced placement credit, English as a second language, honors programs, part-time degree program, services for LD students, summer session for credit.

Student Life *Campus security:* 24-hour patrols, controlled dormitory access, night patrols by trained security personnel.

Athletics Member NJCAA.

Standardized Tests *Required:* SAT or ACT (for admission).

Costs (2006–07) *Comprehensive fee:* $15,980 includes full-time tuition ($9814) and room and board ($6166).

Financial Aid Of all full-time matriculated undergraduates who enrolled in 2004, 72 Federal Work-Study jobs (averaging $772).

Applying *Options:* electronic application, early admission, deferred entrance. *Application fee:* $20. *Required:* high school transcript. *Required for some:* essay or personal statement, 1 letter of recommendation, interview. *Recommended:* minimum 2.0 GPA.

Freshmen Application Contact Ms. Janna Powell, Director of Admission, Andrew College, 413 College Street, Cuthbert, GA 39840. *Phone:* 229-732-5986. *Toll-free phone:* 800-664-9250. *Fax:* 229-732-2176. *E-mail:* admissions@andrewcollege.edu.

▶ **See page 462 for the College Close-Up.**

APPALACHIAN TECHNICAL COLLEGE

Jasper, Georgia   www.appalachiantech.edu/

- **State-supported** 2-year, founded 1965
- **Coed,** 1,047 undergraduate students, 40% full-time, 68% women, 32% men

Undergraduates 414 full-time, 633 part-time. 2% African American, 0.5% Asian American or Pacific Islander, 0.8% Hispanic American, 0.3% Native American.

Freshmen *Admission:* 276 enrolled.

Faculty *Total:* 77, 40% full-time.

Majors Accounting; administrative assistant and secretarial science; business administration and management; child development; computer systems networking and telecommunications; criminal justice/safety; forensic science and technology; information science/studies; paralegal/legal assistant.

Academics *Calendar:* quarters. *Degree:* certificates, diplomas, and associate. *Special study options:* academic remediation for entering students, advanced placement credit, distance learning, internships, services for LD students.

Student Life *Housing:* college housing not available.

Standardized Tests *Required:* ACT COMPASS or ASSET (for admission).

Costs (2006–07) *Tuition:* state resident $1116 full-time, $31 per credit hour part-time; nonresident $2232 full-time, $62 per credit hour part-time.

Applying *Options:* deferred entrance. *Application fee:* $15. *Required:* high school transcript.

Director of Admissions Nina Faix, Admissions Officer, Appalachian Technical College, 100 Campus Drive, Jasper, GA 30143-1253. *Phone:* 706-253-4537. *Fax:* 706-253-4433. *E-mail:* nfaix@appalachiantech.edu.

ASHWORTH COLLEGE

Norcross, Georgia   www.ashworthcollege.com/

Director of Admissions Mr. John Graves, Dean of Undergraduate Studies, Ashworth College, 430 Technology Parkway, Norcross, GA 30092. *Toll-free phone:* 800-223-4542.

ATHENS TECHNICAL COLLEGE

Athens, Georgia   www.athenstech.edu/

- **State-supported** 2-year, founded 1958, part of Georgia Department of Technical and Adult Education
- **Suburban** 41-acre campus with easy access to Atlanta
- **Coed,** 3,805 undergraduate students, 38% full-time, 68% women, 32% men

Undergraduates 1,436 full-time, 2,369 part-time. Students come from 2 states and territories, 23% African American, 4% Asian American or Pacific Islander, 2% Hispanic American, 0.1% Native American.

Freshmen *Admission:* 443 enrolled.

Faculty *Total:* 289, 28% full-time.

Majors Accounting; administrative assistant and secretarial science; biology/biotechnology laboratory technician; child development; clinical laboratory science/medical technology; communications technology; computer programming; computer systems networking and telecommunications; criminal justice/law enforcement administration; dental assisting; dental hygiene; diagnostic medical sonography and ultrasound technology; electrical, electronic and communications engineering technology; emergency medical technology (EMT paramedic); hotel and restaurant management; information science/studies; legal assistant/paralegal; logistics and materials management; marketing/marketing management; medical laboratory technology; medical radiologic technology; nursing (licensed practical/vocational nurse training); nursing (registered nurse training); physical therapy; respiratory care therapy; surgical technology; tourism and travel services management; veterinary technology.

Academics *Calendar:* quarters. *Degree:* certificates, diplomas, and associate. *Special study options:* academic remediation for entering students, adult/continuing education programs, advanced placement credit, distance learning, internships, part-time degree program, services for LD students, summer session for credit.

Library 33,891 titles, 538 serial subscriptions, 3,279 audiovisual materials.

Computers on Campus 277 computers available on campus for general student use. A campuswide network can be accessed. Internet access, online (class) registration, at least one staffed computer lab available.

Student Life *Housing:* college housing not available. *Activities and Organizations:* Athens Technical Student Advisory Council, Phi Theta Kappa, Delta Epsilon Chi, Radiological Technology Society, Organized Black Students Encouraging Unity and Excellence. *Campus security:* 24-hour patrols.

Standardized Tests *Required:* ACT COMPASS or ASSET (for admission).

Costs (2006–07) *Tuition:* state resident $1116 full-time, $31 per credit hour part-time; nonresident $2232 full-time, $62 per credit hour part-time.

Financial Aid Of all full-time matriculated undergraduates who enrolled in 2004, 34 Federal Work-Study jobs (averaging $3090).

Applying *Options:* deferred entrance. *Application fee:* $15. *Required:* high school transcript.

Director of Admissions Mr. Lenzy Reid, Director of Admissions, Athens Technical College, 800 US Highway 29 North, Athens, GA 30601-1500. *Phone:* 706-355-5124. *Fax:* 706-369-5756. *E-mail:* lreid@athenstech.org.

ATLANTA METROPOLITAN COLLEGE
Atlanta, Georgia   **www.atlm.edu/**

- **State-supported** 2-year, founded 1974, part of University System of Georgia
- **Urban** 68-acre campus
- **Coed,** 1,748 undergraduate students, 49% full-time, 64% women, 36% men

Undergraduates 860 full-time, 888 part-time. Students come from 33 states and territories, 39 other countries, 8% are from out of state, 94% African American, 0.7% Asian American or Pacific Islander, 0.6% Hispanic American, 0.1% Native American, 3% international, 8% transferred in. Freshmen *Admission:* 1,422 applied, 813 admitted, 276 enrolled.

Faculty *Total:* 72, 61% full-time, 35% with terminal degrees. *Student/faculty ratio:* 23:1.

Majors African-American/Black studies; art; biology/biological sciences; business administration and management; chemistry; child development; communication/speech communication and rhetoric; computer and information sciences; computer/information technology services administration related; computer science; criminal justice/law enforcement administration; education (multiple levels); engineering technology; English; foreign languages and literatures; general studies; health and physical education; health services/allied health/health sciences; history; human services; information science/studies; information technology; mathematics; music; nursing (licensed practical/vocational nurse training); operations management; physics; political science and government; psychology; social work; speech and rhetoric.

Academics *Calendar:* semesters. *Degree:* certificates and associate. *Special study options:* academic remediation for entering students, adult/continuing education programs, cooperative education, part-time degree program, services for LD students, study abroad, summer session for credit.

Library Atlanta Metropolitan College Library plus 1 other with 48,719 titles, 113 serial subscriptions, 3,874 audiovisual materials, an OPAC, a Web page.

Computers on Campus 585 computers available on campus for general student use. A campuswide network can be accessed from off campus. Internet access, at least one staffed computer lab available.

Student Life *Housing:* college housing not available. *Activities and Organizations:* drama/theater group, student-run newspaper, choral group, International Students Organization, Drama Club, choir, Criminal Justice Club, Study Abroad Club. *Campus security:* 24-hour emergency response devices and patrols. *Student services:* personal/psychological counseling.

Athletics Member NJCAA. *Intercollegiate sports:* basketball M(s)/W(s), cheerleading M/W.

Costs (2005–06) *Tuition:* state resident $1560 full-time, $65 per credit hour part-time; nonresident $6168 full-time, $257 per credit hour part-time. *Required fees:* $230 full-time, $115 per term part-time.

Applying *Options:* common application, electronic application. *Application fee:* $20. *Required:* high school transcript. *Application deadlines:* 7/15 (freshmen), 7/15 (transfers). *Notification:* continuous until 8/12 (freshmen).

Freshmen Application Contact Ms. Audrey Reid, Director, Office of Admissions, Atlanta Metropolitan College, 1630 Metropolitan Parkway, SW, Atlanta, GA 30310-4498. *Phone:* 404-756-4004. *Fax:* 404-756-4407. *E-mail:* admissions@atlm.edu.

ATLANTA TECHNICAL COLLEGE
Atlanta, Georgia   **www.atlantatech.org/**

- **State-supported** 2-year, founded 1945
- **Coed,** 3,523 undergraduate students, 44% full-time, 60% women, 40% men

Undergraduates 1,535 full-time, 1,988 part-time. 88% African American, 2% Asian American or Pacific Islander, 0.9% Hispanic American, 0.1% Native American. Freshmen *Admission:* 667 enrolled.

Faculty *Total:* 188, 46% full-time.

Majors Accounting; child development; computer programming; culinary arts; dental hygiene; health information/medical records technology; hotel and restaurant management; information technology; marketing/marketing management; paralegal/legal assistant; tourism and travel services management.

Academics *Calendar:* quarters. *Degree:* certificates, diplomas, and associate. *Special study options:* academic remediation for entering students, advanced placement credit, distance learning, internships, services for LD students.

Student Life *Housing:* college housing not available.

Standardized Tests *Required:* ACT COMPASS or ASSET (for admission).

Costs (2006–07) *Tuition:* state resident $1116 full-time, $31 per credit hour part-time; nonresident $2232 full-time, $62 per credit hour part-time.

Applying *Options:* deferred entrance. *Application fee:* $15. *Required:* high school transcript.

Director of Admissions Jill Triplett, Admissions Officer, Atlanta Technical College, 1560 Metropolitan Parkway SW, Atlanta, GA 30310. *Phone:* 404-225-4446. *Fax:* 404-225-4721. *E-mail:* jtriplet@atlantatech.edu.

AUGUSTA TECHNICAL COLLEGE
Augusta, Georgia   **www.augustatech.edu/**

- **State-supported** 2-year, founded 1961, part of Georgia Department of Technical and Adult Education
- **Urban** 70-acre campus
- **Coed,** 4,171 undergraduate students, 48% full-time, 62% women, 38% men

Undergraduates 1,986 full-time, 2,185 part-time. Students come from 2 states and territories, 50% African American, 2% Asian American or Pacific Islander, 3% Hispanic American, 0.5% Native American, 0.1% international. Freshmen *Admission:* 704 enrolled.

Faculty *Total:* 376, 36% full-time.

Majors Accounting; administrative assistant and secretarial science; biotechnology; business administration and management; cardiovascular technology; child development; computer programming; computer systems networking and telecommunications; criminal justice/safety; culinary arts; e-commerce; electrical, electronic and communications engineering technology; emergency medical technology (EMT paramedic); fire science; information science/studies; marketing/marketing management; mechanical engineering/mechanical technology; medical radiologic technology; occupational therapist assistant; parks, recreation and leisure facilities management; pharmacy technician; respiratory care therapy; respiratory therapy technician; surgical technology.

Academics *Calendar:* quarters. *Degree:* certificates, diplomas, and associate. *Special study options:* academic remediation for entering students, advanced placement credit, cooperative education, distance learning, internships, part-time degree program, services for LD students, summer session for credit.

Library Information Technology Center with 70,816 titles, 445 serial subscriptions, 7,733 audiovisual materials, an OPAC, a Web page.

Computers on Campus 339 computers available on campus for general student use. A campuswide network can be accessed from off campus. Internet access, at least one staffed computer lab available.

Student Life *Housing:* college housing not available. *Activities and Organizations:* VICA, professional organizations. *Campus security:* 24-hour emergency response devices, 12-hour patrols by trained security personnel.

Standardized Tests *Required:* ACT COMPASS or ASSET (for admission).

Costs (2006–07) *Tuition:* state resident $1116 full-time, $31 per credit hour part-time; nonresident $2232 full-time, $62 per credit hour part-time.

Applying *Options:* deferred entrance. *Application fee:* $15. *Required:* high school transcript.

Director of Admissions Mr. Brian Roberts, Director of Admissions and Counseling, Augusta Technical College, 3200 Augusta Tech Drive, Augusta, GA 30906. *Phone:* 706-771-4027. *Fax:* 706-771-4034. *E-mail:* bcrobert@augustatech.edu.

BAINBRIDGE COLLEGE
Bainbridge, Georgia   **www.bainbridge.edu/**

- **State-supported** 2-year, founded 1972, part of University System of Georgia
- **Small-town** 160-acre campus
- **Coed,** 2,475 undergraduate students, 39% full-time, 70% women, 30% men

Undergraduates 954 full-time, 1,521 part-time. Students come from 5 states and territories, 1% are from out of state, 51% African American, 3% Asian American or Pacific Islander, 0.6% Hispanic American, 0.2% Native American. Freshmen *Admission:* 1,330 applied, 1,033 admitted.

Faculty *Total:* 130, 48% full-time, 17% with terminal degrees.

Majors Accounting; administrative assistant and secretarial science; agriculture; art; automobile/automotive mechanics technology; biology/biological sciences; business administration and management; business teacher education; chemistry; criminal justice/law enforcement administration; data processing and data processing technology; drafting and design technology; dramatic/theater arts; education; electrical, electronic and communications engineering technology; elementary education; English; family and consumer sciences/human sci-

Bainbridge College (continued)

ences; forestry; health teacher education; history; information science/studies; journalism; kindergarten/preschool education; liberal arts and sciences/liberal studies; marketing/marketing management; mathematics; nursing (licensed practical/vocational nurse training); nursing (registered nurse training); political science and government; psychology; sociology; speech and rhetoric; welding technology.

Academics *Calendar:* semesters. *Degree:* certificates and associate. *Special study options:* academic remediation for entering students, adult/continuing education programs, advanced placement credit, distance learning, double majors, independent study, part-time degree program, services for LD students, study abroad, summer session for credit.

Library Bainbridge College Library with 37,387 titles, 180 serial subscriptions, 1,795 audiovisual materials, an OPAC.

Computers on Campus 250 computers available on campus for general student use. A campuswide network can be accessed. Internet access, online (class) registration, at least one staffed computer lab available.

Student Life *Housing:* college housing not available. *Activities and Organizations:* drama/theater group, Phi Theta Kappa, Alpha Beta Gamma, Drama Club, Delta Club, Sigma Kappa Delta. *Campus security:* 24-hour patrols.

Athletics *Intramural sports:* table tennis M/W, volleyball M/W.

Standardized Tests *Required for some:* SAT or ACT (for admission), ACT COMPASS.

Costs (2005–06) *Tuition:* state resident $1542 full-time, $65 per credit hour part-time; nonresident $6166 full-time, $257 per credit hour part-time. *Required fees:* $124 full-time. *Waivers:* senior citizens.

Applying *Options:* electronic application, early admission. *Required for some:* high school transcript, minimum 1.8 GPA, 3 letters of recommendation, interview, immunizations, or waivers; medical records and criminal background checks. *Application deadlines:* 8/1 (freshmen), 8/1 (transfers). *Notification:* continuous (freshmen).

Freshmen Application Contact Mrs. Connie Snyder, Director of Admissions and Records, Bainbridge College, 2500 East Shotwell Street, Bainbridge, GA 39819. *Phone:* 229-248-2504. *Fax:* 229-248-2525. *E-mail:* csnyder@bainbridge.edu.

BAUDER COLLEGE

Atlanta, Georgia   **www.bauder.edu/**

Freshmen Application Contact Ms. Lillie Lanier, Admissions Representative, Bauder College, Phipps Plaza, 3500 Peachtree Road NE, Atlanta, GA 30326. *Phone:* 404-237-7573. *Toll-free phone:* 404-237-7573 (in-state); 800-241-3797 (out-of-state).

BROWN MACKIE COLLEGE—ATLANTA

**Norcross,
Georgia**   **www.brownmackie.edu/locations.asp?locid=3**

- **Proprietary** 2-year
- **Coed,** 150 undergraduate students, 100% full-time, 73% women, 27% men

Undergraduates 150 full-time. 35% are from out of state, 76% African American, 2% Hispanic American.
Freshmen *Admission:* 105 enrolled.

Faculty *Total:* 8, 50% full-time, 75% with terminal degrees. *Student/faculty ratio:* 19:1.

Majors Accounting technology and bookkeeping; business administration and management; computer software technology; criminal justice/safety; paralegal/legal assistant.

Academics *Degree:* diplomas and associate.

Student Life *Activities and Organizations:* student-run newspaper. *Student services:* health clinic, personal/psychological counseling.

Costs (2006–07) *Tuition:* $6084 full-time, $169 per credit hour part-time. *Required fees:* $360 full-time, $10 per credit hour part-time.

Applying *Required:* high school transcript, interview. *Application deadline:* rolling (freshmen), rolling (transfers). *Notification:* continuous (freshmen).

Freshmen Application Contact Mr. Abul Hussain, Brown Mackie College–Atlanta, 4975 Jimmy Carter Boulevard, Suite 600, Norcross, GA 30093. *Phone:* 770-510-2318. *Fax:* 770-638-0479. *E-mail:* bmcatadm@brownmackie.edu.

▶ **See page 498 for the College Close-Up.**

CENTRAL GEORGIA TECHNICAL COLLEGE

Macon, Georgia   **www.cgtcollege.org/**

- **State-supported** 2-year, founded 1966, part of Georgia Department of Technical and Adult Education
- **Suburban** 152-acre campus
- **Coed,** 6,047 undergraduate students, 51% full-time, 68% women, 32% men

Undergraduates 3,057 full-time, 2,990 part-time. Students come from 5 states and territories, 1 other country, 59% African American, 0.5% Asian American or Pacific Islander, 0.7% Hispanic American, 0.4% Native American, 21% transferred in.
Freshmen *Admission:* 899 enrolled.

Faculty *Total:* 484, 23% full-time.

Majors Accounting; administrative assistant and secretarial science; banking and financial support services; business administration and management; cabinetmaking and millwork; cardiovascular technology; carpentry; child care and support services management; child development; clinical/medical laboratory technology; computer programming; computer systems networking and telecommunications; criminal justice/safety; dental hygiene; drafting and design technology; e-commerce; electrical, electronic and communications engineering technology; gerontological services; hotel and restaurant management; industrial technology; information science/studies; marketing/marketing management; medical laboratory technology; medical radiologic technology; paralegal/legal assistant; tourism and travel services management; veterinary technology; web page, digital/multimedia and information resources design.

Academics *Calendar:* quarters. *Degree:* certificates, diplomas, and associate. *Special study options:* academic remediation for entering students, advanced placement credit, distance learning, external degree program, internships, off-campus study, part-time degree program, services for LD students.

Library 16,500 titles, 300 serial subscriptions, 1,800 audiovisual materials, an OPAC, a Web page.

Computers on Campus Internet access, at least one staffed computer lab available.

Student Life *Housing:* college housing not available. *Activities and Organizations:* Skills USA-VICA, student government. *Campus security:* 24-hour patrols.

Standardized Tests *Required:* ACT COMPASS or ASSET (for admission).

Costs (2006–07) *Tuition:* state resident $1116 full-time, $61 per credit hour part-time; nonresident $2232 full-time, $62 per credit hour part-time.

Financial Aid Of all full-time matriculated undergraduates who enrolled in 2004, 175 Federal Work-Study jobs (averaging $2000). *Financial aid deadline:* 9/1.

Applying *Options:* deferred entrance. *Application fee:* $15. *Required:* high school transcript.

Director of Admissions Amy McDonald, Admissions Director, Central Georgia Technical College, 3300 Macon Tech Drive, Macon, GA 31206. *Phone:* 478-757-3408. *Fax:* 478-757-3454. *E-mail:* amymc@cgtcollege.edu.

CHATTAHOOCHEE TECHNICAL COLLEGE

Marietta, Georgia   **www.chattcollege.com**

- **State-supported** 2-year, founded 1961, part of Georgia Department of Technical and Adult Education
- **Suburban** campus with easy access to Atlanta
- **Coed,** 6,243 undergraduate students, 36% full-time, 54% women, 46% men

Undergraduates 2,260 full-time, 3,983 part-time. 33% African American, 2% Asian American or Pacific Islander, 4% Hispanic American, 0.3% Native American, 2% international.
Freshmen *Admission:* 964 enrolled.

Faculty *Total:* 300, 22% full-time.

Majors Accounting; administrative assistant and secretarial science; automobile/automotive mechanics technology; biomedical technology; business administration and management; child development; civil engineering technology; computer and information systems security; computer programming; computer systems networking and telecommunications; criminal justice/safety; culinary arts; drafting and design technology; electrical, electronic and communications engineering technology; fire science; horticultural science; information science/studies; logistics and materials management; marketing/marketing management; medical laboratory technology; medical radiologic technology; parks, recreation and leisure facilities management; web page, digital/multimedia and information resources design.

Academics *Calendar:* quarters. *Degree:* certificates, diplomas, and associate. *Special study options:* academic remediation for entering students, advanced placement credit, distance learning, internships, part-time degree program, services for LD students, study abroad.

Library 22,127 titles, 292 serial subscriptions, 1,826 audiovisual materials, a Web page.

Computers on Campus 200 computers available on campus for general student use. At least one staffed computer lab available.

Student Life *Housing:* college housing not available. *Activities and Organizations:* student government, Vocational Industrial Clubs of America, Institute for Electrical and Electronic Engineers, National Technical-Vocational Honor Society, Phi Beta Lambda. *Campus security:* full-time day and evening security.

Standardized Tests *Required:* ACT COMPASS or ASSET (for admission).

Costs (2006–07) *Tuition:* state resident $1116 full-time, $31 per credit hour part-time; nonresident $2232 full-time, $62 per credit hour part-time.

Financial Aid Of all full-time matriculated undergraduates who enrolled in 2004, 40 Federal Work-Study jobs (averaging $2500).

Applying *Options:* deferred entrance. *Application fee:* $15. *Required:* high school transcript.

Director of Admissions Admissions Director, Chattahoochee Technical College, 980 South Cobb Drive, Marietta, GA 30060-3398. *Phone:* 770-528-4465. *Fax:* 770-528-4580.

COASTAL GEORGIA COMMUNITY COLLEGE

Brunswick, Georgia   **www.cgcc.edu/**

- **State-supported** 2-year, founded 1961, part of University System of Georgia
- **Small-town** 193-acre campus with easy access to Jacksonville
- **Endowment** $88,674
- **Coed,** 3,062 undergraduate students, 33% full-time, 69% women, 31% men

Undergraduates 1,002 full-time, 2,060 part-time. Students come from 8 states and territories, 4% are from out of state, 30% African American, 1% Asian American or Pacific Islander, 2% Hispanic American, 0.4% Native American, 0.4% international, 5% transferred in.

Freshmen *Admission:* 1,866 applied, 1,006 admitted, 808 enrolled. *Average high school GPA:* 2.30.

Faculty *Total:* 140, 52% full-time, 8% with terminal degrees. *Student/faculty ratio:* 18:1.

Majors Agricultural business and management; art; biology/biological sciences; business administration and management; chemistry; clinical/medical laboratory technology; computer science; criminal justice/law enforcement administration; dental hygiene; education (multiple levels); English; foreign languages and literatures; forestry; geology/earth science; health and physical education; history; liberal arts and sciences/liberal studies; mathematics; medical radiologic technology; nursing (registered nurse training); occupational therapy; parks, recreation and leisure facilities management; philosophy; physical therapy; physician assistant; physics; political science and government; pre-dentistry studies; pre-engineering; pre-medical studies; pre-pharmacy studies; pre-veterinary studies; psychology; respiratory care therapy; sociology.

Academics *Calendar:* semesters. *Degree:* certificates and associate. *Special study options:* academic remediation for entering students, adult/continuing education programs, advanced placement credit, distance learning, double majors, part-time degree program, services for LD students, study abroad, summer session for credit.

Library Clara Wood Gould Memorial Library with 535 serial subscriptions, 1,151 audiovisual materials, an OPAC.

Computers on Campus 250 computers available on campus for general student use. A campuswide network can be accessed from off campus. Internet access, at least one staffed computer lab available.

Student Life *Housing:* college housing not available. *Activities and Organizations:* student-run newspaper, Association of Nursing Students, Minority Advisement and Social Development Association, Student Government Association, Baptist Student Union, Phi Theta Kappa. *Campus security:* 24-hour patrols, late-night transport/escort service. *Student services:* personal/psychological counseling.

Athletics Member NJCAA. *Intercollegiate sports:* basketball M(s), softball W(s). *Intramural sports:* basketball M/W, soccer M/W, swimming and diving M/W, tennis M/W, volleyball M/W.

Costs (2005–06) *Tuition:* state resident $1468 full-time, $62 per credit hour part-time; nonresident $245 per credit hour part-time. *Required fees:* $212 full-time, $52 per term part-time.

Financial Aid Of all full-time matriculated undergraduates who enrolled in 2004, 80 Federal Work-Study jobs (averaging $1500).

Applying *Options:* common application, electronic application, deferred entrance. *Application fee:* $20. *Required:* high school transcript, minimum 2.0 GPA, immunization records. *Application deadlines:* 8/15 (freshmen), 8/15 (transfers). *Notification:* continuous (freshmen).

Freshmen Application Contact Lisa Lessig, Director of Admissions/Registrar, Coastal Georgia Community College, 3700 Altama Avenue, Brunswick, GA 31525. *Phone:* 912-264-7253. *Toll-free phone:* 800-675-7235. *Fax:* 912-262-3072. *E-mail:* admiss@cgcc.edu.

COLUMBUS TECHNICAL COLLEGE

Columbus, Georgia   **www.columbustech.edu**

- **State-supported** 2-year, founded 1961, part of Georgia Department of Technical and Adult Education
- **Urban** campus with easy access to Atlanta
- **Coed,** 3,530 undergraduate students, 44% full-time, 64% women, 36% men

Undergraduates 1,536 full-time, 1,994 part-time. Students come from 9 states and territories, 48% African American, 2% Asian American or Pacific Islander, 3% Hispanic American, 0.7% Native American.

Freshmen *Admission:* 852 enrolled.

Faculty *Total:* 230, 33% full-time.

Majors Accounting; administrative assistant and secretarial science; automobile/automotive mechanics technology; child development; computer engineering related; computer systems networking and telecommunications; dental hygiene; diagnostic medical sonography and ultrasound technology; drafting and design technology; electrical, electronic and communications engineering technology; emergency medical technology (EMT paramedic); health information/medical records technology; horticultural science; industrial technology; information science/studies; machine tool technology; mechanical engineering/mechanical technology; medical office management; medical radiologic technology; nursing (registered nurse training); pharmacy technician; respiratory therapy technician; surgical technology; web page, digital/multimedia and information resources design.

Academics *Calendar:* quarters. *Degree:* certificates, diplomas, and associate. *Special study options:* academic remediation for entering students, adult/continuing education programs, advanced placement credit, distance learning, internships, part-time degree program, services for LD students.

Library Columbus Technical College Library with 26,072 titles, 49 serial subscriptions, 533 audiovisual materials.

Computers on Campus 50 computers available on campus for general student use. A campuswide network can be accessed from off campus. Internet access, at least one staffed computer lab available.

Student Life *Housing:* college housing not available. *Campus security:* security patrols during class hours.

Standardized Tests *Required:* ACT COMPASS or ASSET (for admission).

Costs (2006–07) *Tuition:* state resident $1116 full-time, $31 per credit hour part-time; nonresident $2232 full-time, $62 per credit hour part-time.

Financial Aid Of all full-time matriculated undergraduates who enrolled in 2004, 6 Federal Work-Study jobs (averaging $2000).

Applying *Options:* common application, deferred entrance. *Application fee:* $15. *Required:* high school transcript.

Director of Admissions Nichole Kennedy, Admissions Director, Columbus Technical College, 928 Manchester Expressway, Columbus, GA 31904-6572. *Phone:* 706-649-1174. *Fax:* 706-649-1804. *E-mail:* nkennedy@columbustech.edu.

COOSA VALLEY TECHNICAL COLLEGE

Rome, Georgia   **www.coosavalleytech.edu/**

- **State-supported** 2-year, founded 1962
- **Coed,** 2,893 undergraduate students, 42% full-time, 64% women, 36% men

Undergraduates 1,219 full-time, 1,674 part-time. 11% African American, 0.8% Asian American or Pacific Islander, 1% Hispanic American, 0.5% Native American.

Freshmen *Admission:* 701 enrolled.

Faculty *Total:* 191, 38% full-time.

Majors Accounting; child development; computer programming; criminal justice/safety; environmental engineering technology; fire science; information science/studies; marketing/marketing management; medical office management; paralegal/legal assistant; respiratory therapy technician; surgical technology; web page, digital/multimedia and information resources design.

Coosa Valley Technical College (continued)

Academics *Calendar:* quarters. *Degree:* certificates, diplomas, and associate. *Special study options:* academic remediation for entering students, advanced placement credit, distance learning, internships, services for LD students.

Student Life *Housing:* college housing not available.

Standardized Tests *Required:* ACT COMPASS or ASSET (for admission).

Costs (2006–07) *Tuition:* state resident $1116 full-time, $31 per credit hour part-time; nonresident $2232 full-time, $62 per credit hour part-time.

Applying *Options:* deferred entrance. *Application fee:* $15. *Required:* high school transcript.

Director of Admissions Stuart Phillips, Admissions Director, Coosa Valley Technical College, One Maurice Culberson Drive, Rome, GA 30161. *Phone:* 706-624-1117. *Fax:* 706-624-1120. *E-mail:* sphillip@coosavalleytech.edu.

DARTON COLLEGE

Albany, Georgia   **www.darton.edu/**

- **State-supported** 2-year, founded 1965, part of University System of Georgia
- **Suburban** 185-acre campus
- **Coed**

Undergraduates 1,904 full-time, 2,222 part-time. Students come from 6 other countries, 4% are from out of state, 43% African American, 1% Asian American or Pacific Islander, 0.9% Hispanic American, 0.1% Native American, 0.8% international, 5% transferred in. *Retention:* 63% of 2003 full-time freshmen returned.

Faculty *Student/faculty ratio:* 20:1.

Academics *Calendar:* semesters. *Degree:* certificates and associate. *Special study options:* academic remediation for entering students, accelerated degree program, adult/continuing education programs, advanced placement credit, cooperative education, distance learning, double majors, English as a second language, honors programs, independent study, part-time degree program, services for LD students, student-designed majors, study abroad, summer session for credit. *ROTC:* Army (c).

Student Life *Campus security:* 24-hour patrols, student patrols, late-night transport/escort service.

Athletics Member NJCAA.

Standardized Tests *Required for some:* SAT or ACT (for admission), SAT Subject Tests (for admission).

Costs (2005–06) *Tuition:* state resident $1542 full-time, $65 per credit hour part-time; nonresident $6166 full-time, $257 per credit hour part-time. Full-time tuition and fees vary according to course load. Part-time tuition and fees vary according to course load. *Required fees:* $300 full-time, $150 per term part-time.

Financial Aid Of all full-time matriculated undergraduates who enrolled in 2004, 60 Federal Work-Study jobs.

Applying *Options:* common application, electronic application, early admission. *Application fee:* $20. *Required:* high school transcript, minimum 1.8 GPA, proof of immunization.

Freshmen Application Contact Assistant Director, Admissions, Darton College, 2400 Gillionville Road, Albany, GA 31707. *Phone:* 229-430-6740. *E-mail:* darton@cavalier.dartnet.peachnet.edu.

DEKALB TECHNICAL COLLEGE

Clarkston, Georgia   **www.dekalbtech.edu/**

- **State-supported** 2-year, founded 1961, part of Georgia Department of Technical and Adult Education
- **Suburban** 17-acre campus with easy access to Atlanta
- **Coed,** 4,083 undergraduate students, 38% full-time, 63% women, 37% men

Undergraduates 1,535 full-time, 2,548 part-time. Students come from 2 states and territories, 72% African American, 4% Asian American or Pacific Islander, 2% Hispanic American, 0.1% Native American.

Freshmen *Admission:* 647 enrolled.

Faculty *Total:* 459, 21% full-time, 0.2% with terminal degrees. *Student/faculty ratio:* 15:1.

Majors Accounting; administrative assistant and secretarial science; automobile/automotive mechanics technology; business/commerce; clinical/medical laboratory technology; computer engineering technology; computer programming; computer systems networking and telecommunications; criminal justice/safety; drafting and design technology; electrical, electronic and communications engineering technology; electromechanical technology; engineering technology; heat-

ing, air conditioning and refrigeration technology; industrial technology; information science/studies; instrumentation technology; legal administrative assistant/secretary; machine tool technology; marketing/marketing management; medical/clinical assistant; medical laboratory technology; operations management; ophthalmic laboratory technology; optician/vision care technology; opticianry; paralegal/legal assistant; surgical technology; telecommunications.

Academics *Calendar:* quarters. *Degree:* certificates, diplomas, and associate. *Special study options:* academic remediation for entering students, adult/continuing education programs, advanced placement credit, distance learning, internships, part-time degree program, services for LD students, summer session for credit.

Library an OPAC, a Web page.

Computers on Campus 500 computers available on campus for general student use. A campuswide network can be accessed. Internet access, online (class) registration, at least one staffed computer lab available.

Student Life *Housing:* college housing not available. *Activities and Organizations:* Student Government Association, Phi Beta Lambda, National Vocational-Technical Honor Society, Collegiate Secretaries International, Epsilon Delta Phi. *Campus security:* security during class hours.

Standardized Tests *Required:* ACT COMPASS or ASSET (for admission).

Costs (2006–07) *Tuition:* state resident $1116 full-time, $31 per credit hour part-time; nonresident $2232 full-time, $62 per credit hour part-time.

Financial Aid Of all full-time matriculated undergraduates who enrolled in 2004, 50 Federal Work-Study jobs (averaging $4000).

Applying *Options:* common application, deferred entrance. *Application fee:* $15. *Required:* high school transcript.

Freshmen Application Contact Mr. Terry Richardson, Coordinator of Admissions, DeKalb Technical College, 495 North Indian Creek Drive, Clarkston, GA 30021-2397. *Phone:* 404-297-9522 Ext. 1229. *Fax:* 404-294-4234. *E-mail:* admissonsclark@dekalbtech.org.

EAST CENTRAL TECHNICAL COLLEGE

Fitzgerald, Georgia   **www.eastcentraltech.edu/**

- **State-supported** 2-year, founded 1968
- **Rural** 30-acre campus
- **Coed,** 1,238 undergraduate students, 45% full-time, 70% women, 30% men

Undergraduates 561 full-time, 677 part-time. 37% African American, 0.1% Asian American or Pacific Islander, 1% Hispanic American.

Freshmen *Admission:* 265 enrolled.

Faculty *Total:* 90, 52% full-time.

Majors Administrative assistant and secretarial science; child development; computer systems networking and telecommunications; criminal justice/safety; information science/studies.

Academics *Calendar:* quarters. *Degree:* certificates, diplomas, and associate. *Special study options:* academic remediation for entering students, cooperative education, distance learning, internships, services for LD students.

Student Life *Housing:* college housing not available.

Standardized Tests *Required:* ACT COMPASS or ASSET (for admission).

Costs (2006–07) *Tuition:* state resident $1116 full-time, $31 per credit hour part-time; nonresident $2232 full-time, $62 per credit hour part-time.

Applying *Options:* deferred entrance. *Application fee:* $15. *Required:* high school transcript.

Director of Admissions Ms. Connie Coffey, Admissions Director, East Central Technical College, 667 Perry House Road, Fitzgerald, GA 31750. *Phone:* 229-468-2033. *Fax:* 229-468-2110. *E-mail:* ccoffey@ectcollege.org.

EAST GEORGIA COLLEGE

Swainsboro, Georgia   **www.ega.edu/**

Freshmen Application Contact Ms. Linda Connelly, Office Coordinator, East Georgia College, 131 College Circle, Swainsboro, GA 30401. *Phone:* 478-289-2019.

EMORY UNIVERSITY, OXFORD COLLEGE

Oxford, Georgia   **www.emory.edu/OXFORD/**

Director of Admissions Ms. Jennifer B. Taylor, Associate Dean of Admission and Financial Aid, Emory University, Oxford College, 100 Hamill Street, PO Box 1418, Oxford, GA 30054. *Phone:* 770-784-8328. *Toll-free phone:* 800-723-8328.

FLINT RIVER TECHNICAL COLLEGE

Thomaston, Georgia   **www.flintrivertech.edu/**

- **State-supported** 2-year, founded 1961
- **Coed,** 805 undergraduate students, 53% full-time, 75% women, 25% men

Undergraduates 425 full-time, 380 part-time. 48% African American, 0.1% Asian American or Pacific Islander, 0.5% Hispanic American, 0.1% Native American.
Freshmen *Admission:* 207 enrolled.
Faculty *Total:* 88, 33% full-time.
Majors Accounting; administrative assistant and secretarial science; child development; computer and information systems security; computer systems networking and telecommunications; criminal justice/safety; electrical, electronic and communications engineering technology; information science/studies; manufacturing technology; medical laboratory technology; web page, digital/multimedia and information resources design.
Academics *Calendar:* quarters. *Degree:* certificates, diplomas, and associate. *Special study options:* academic remediation for entering students, advanced placement credit, cooperative education, distance learning, internships, services for LD students.
Library 2,653 titles, 82 serial subscriptions, 202 audiovisual materials.
Student Life *Housing:* college housing not available.
Standardized Tests *Required:* ACT COMPASS or ASSET (for admission).
Costs (2006–07) *Tuition:* state resident $1116 full-time, $31 per credit hour part-time; nonresident $2232 full-time, $62 per credit hour part-time.
Applying *Options:* deferred entrance. *Application fee:* $15. *Required:* high school transcript.
Director of Admissions Mr. Gary Williams, Admissions Director, Flint River Technical College, 1533 US Highway 19 South, Thomaston, GA 30286-4752. *Phone:* 706-646-6148. *Toll-free phone:* 800-752-9681. *Fax:* 706-646-6152. *E-mail:* gwilliams@flintrivertech.edu.

GAINESVILLE COLLEGE

Oakwood, Georgia   **www.gc.peachnet.edu/**

- **State-supported** primarily 2-year, founded 1964, part of University System of Georgia
- **Small-town** 220-acre campus with easy access to Atlanta
- **Endowment** $9.2 million
- **Coed,** 5,985 undergraduate students, 59% full-time, 54% women, 46% men

Undergraduates 3,550 full-time, 2,435 part-time. Students come from 22 states and territories, 12 other countries, 4% are from out of state, 4% African American, 2% Asian American or Pacific Islander, 4% Hispanic American, 0.4% Native American, 2% international.
Freshmen *Admission:* 3,171 applied, 2,670 admitted, 1,780 enrolled. *Average high school GPA:* 2.9. *Test scores:* SAT verbal scores over 500: 42%; SAT math scores over 500: 42%; SAT verbal scores over 600: 9%; SAT math scores over 600: 10%; SAT verbal scores over 700: 1%; SAT math scores over 700: 1%.
Faculty *Total:* 131, 63% with terminal degrees. *Student/faculty ratio:* 24:1.
Majors Anthropology; biology/biological sciences; business administration and management; chemistry; computer science; criminal justice/law enforcement administration; dramatic/theater arts; early childhood education; elementary education; engineering technology; English; environmental design/architecture; foreign languages and literatures; forestry; general studies; geography; geology/earth science; history; information technology; journalism; kinesiology and exercise science; mass communication/media; mathematics; middle school education; music; physics; political science and government; pre-medical studies; pre-nursing studies; pre-pharmacy studies; psychology; secondary education; social work; sociology; sport and fitness administration/management.
Academics *Calendar:* semesters. *Degrees:* associate and bachelor's. *Special study options:* academic remediation for entering students, adult/continuing education programs, advanced placement credit, distance learning, double majors, English as a second language, honors programs, internships, off-campus study, part-time degree program, services for LD students, summer session for credit.
Library John Harrison Hosch Library with 70,000 titles, 398 serial subscriptions, an OPAC, a Web page.
Computers on Campus 500 computers available on campus for general student use. A campuswide network can be accessed from off campus. Internet access, online (class) registration, at least one staffed computer lab available.
Student Life *Housing:* college housing not available. *Activities and Organizations:* drama/theater group, student-run newspaper, choral group, student newspaper, Baptist Student Union, Student Government Association, Pre-Law/

Political Science Club. *Campus security:* 24-hour patrols. *Student services:* personal/psychological counseling.
Athletics *Intramural sports:* badminton M/W, basketball M/W, bowling M/W, football M/W, golf M/W, soccer M, softball M/W, tennis M/W, volleyball M/W, water polo M/W.
Standardized Tests *Recommended:* SAT or ACT (for admission).
Costs (2005–06) *Tuition:* state resident $1542 full-time, $65 per credit hour part-time; nonresident $6166 full-time, $257 per credit hour part-time. *Required fees:* $164 full-time.
Financial Aid Of all full-time matriculated undergraduates who enrolled in 2004, 40 Federal Work-Study jobs (averaging $2000). *Financial aid deadline:* 6/1.
Applying *Options:* early admission. *Application fee:* $35. *Required:* high school transcript. *Application deadlines:* 7/1 (freshmen), 7/1 (transfers).
Freshmen Application Contact W. Palmour, Director of Admissions, Gainesville College, PO Box 1358, Gainesville, GA 30503. *Phone:* 770-718-3641. *Fax:* 770-718-3751. *E-mail:* mpalmour@gsc.edu.

GEORGIA AVIATION & TECHNICAL COLLEGE

Eastman, Georgia   **www.gavtc.org/**

- **State-supported** 2-year, founded 1995
- **Coed,** 252 undergraduate students, 63% full-time, 14% women, 86% men

Undergraduates 158 full-time, 94 part-time. 6% African American, 0.4% Asian American or Pacific Islander, 0.8% Hispanic American, 0.8% Native American.
Freshmen *Admission:* 63 enrolled.
Faculty *Total:* 23, 100% full-time.
Majors Airline pilot and flight crew; air traffic control; aviation/airway management.
Academics *Calendar:* quarters. *Degree:* certificates, diplomas, and associate. *Special study options:* academic remediation for entering students, advanced placement credit, cooperative education, internships, services for LD students.
Student Life *Housing:* college housing not available.
Standardized Tests *Required:* ACT COMPASS or ASSET (for admission).
Costs (2006–07) *Tuition:* state resident $1116 full-time, $31 per credit hour part-time; nonresident $2232 full-time, $62 per credit hour part-time.
Applying *Options:* deferred entrance. *Application fee:* $15. *Required:* high school transcript.
Director of Admissions Teresa Spires, Georgia Aviation & Technical College, 71 Airport Road—Heart of Georgia Regional Airport, Eastman, GA 31023. *Phone:* 478-374-6980. *Fax:* 478-374-6641. *E-mail:* tspires@gaaviationtech.edu.

GEORGIA HIGHLANDS COLLEGE

Rome, Georgia   **www.highlands.edu/**

- **State-supported** 2-year, founded 1970, part of University System of Georgia
- **Small-town** 226-acre campus with easy access to Atlanta
- **Endowment** $443,000
- **Coed,** 3,817 undergraduate students, 54% full-time, 65% women, 35% men

Undergraduates 2,059 full-time, 1,758 part-time. 14% are from out of state, 11% African American, 2% Asian American or Pacific Islander, 3% Hispanic American, 0.2% Native American.
Freshmen *Admission:* 2,079 applied, 1,739 admitted, 1,021 enrolled. *Average high school GPA:* 2.7.
Faculty *Total:* 254, 35% full-time, 17% with terminal degrees. *Student/faculty ratio:* 40:1.
Majors Accounting; agriculture; art; automobile/automotive mechanics technology; biological and physical sciences; business administration and management; clinical laboratory science/medical technology; computer programming; criminal justice/police science; criminal justice/safety; dental hygiene; economics; electrical, electronic and communications engineering technology; emergency medical technology (EMT paramedic); English; foreign languages and literatures; forestry; geology/earth science; history; horticultural science; hotel/motel administration; human services; information science/studies; journalism; kindergarten/preschool education; legal assistant/paralegal; liberal arts and sciences/liberal studies; marketing/marketing management; nursing (registered

Georgia Highlands College (continued)

nurse training); occupational therapy; philosophy; physical therapist assistant; physical therapy; physician assistant; political science and government; psychology; radiologic technology/science; respiratory care therapy; secondary education; sociology.

Academics *Calendar:* semesters. *Degree:* certificates, diplomas, and associate. *Special study options:* academic remediation for entering students, advanced placement credit, cooperative education, distance learning, double majors, honors programs, independent study, part-time degree program, services for LD students, study abroad, summer session for credit.

Library Georgia Highlands Library plus 1 other with 65,090 titles, 267 serial subscriptions, 9,207 audiovisual materials, an OPAC, a Web page.

Computers on Campus A campuswide network can be accessed from off campus. Internet access, online (class) registration, at least one staffed computer lab available.

Student Life *Housing:* college housing not available. *Activities and Organizations:* student-run newspaper, Floyd Association of Nursing Students, Health, Physical Education, and Recreation Club, Black Awareness Society, Political Science Association. *Campus security:* 24-hour patrols. *Student services:* personal/psychological counseling.

Athletics *Intramural sports:* basketball M/W, bowling M/W, football M/W, golf M/W, sailing M/W, soccer M/W, softball M/W, table tennis M/W, tennis M/W, ultimate Frisbee M/W, volleyball M/W, weight lifting M/W.

Standardized Tests *Recommended:* SAT or ACT (for admission).

Costs (2005–06) *Tuition:* state resident $1542 full-time, $65 per hour part-time; nonresident $6168 full-time, $257 per hour part-time. Part-time tuition and fees vary according to course load. *Required fees:* $198 full-time, $99 per term part-time. *Waivers:* senior citizens.

Financial Aid Of all full-time matriculated undergraduates who enrolled in 2004, 50 Federal Work-Study jobs (averaging $3500).

Applying *Options:* common application, electronic application, early admission, deferred entrance. *Application fee:* $20. *Required:* high school transcript, minimum 2.0 GPA. *Required for some:* minimum 2.2 GPA. *Application deadline:* rolling (freshmen), rolling (transfers). *Notification:* continuous (freshmen), continuous (out-of-state freshmen).

Freshmen Application Contact Todd Jones, Director of Admissions, Georgia Highlands College, 3175 Cedartown Highway, Rome, GA 30162. *Phone:* 706-295-6339. *Toll-free phone:* 800-332-2406. *Fax:* 706-295-6610. *E-mail:* tjones@highlands.edu.

GEORGIA MEDICAL INSTITUTE—DEKALB
Atlanta, Georgia   www.georgia-med.com/

Director of Admissions Ms. Trish Sherwood, Director of Admissions, Georgia Medical Institute–DeKalb, 1706 Northeast Expressway, Atlanta, GA 30329. *Phone:* 404-327-8787.

GEORGIA MILITARY COLLEGE
Milledgeville, Georgia   www.gmc.cc.ga.us/

Director of Admissions Mrs. Donna W. Findley, Director of Admissions, Georgia Military College, 201 East Greene Street, Milledgeville, GA 31061-3398. *Phone:* 478-445-2751. *Toll-free phone:* 800-342-0413.

GEORGIA PERIMETER COLLEGE
Decatur, Georgia   www.gpc.edu/

Director of Admissions Ms. Erin Hart, Director of Enrollment Management, Georgia Perimeter College, 555 North Indian Creek Drive, Clarkston, GA 30021-2396. *Phone:* 404-299-4551. *Toll-free phone:* 888-696-2780. *Fax:* 404-299-4574.

GORDON COLLEGE
Barnesville, Georgia   www.gdn.edu/

- **State-supported** 2-year, founded 1852, part of University System of Georgia
- **Small-town** 125-acre campus with easy access to Atlanta
- **Endowment** $4.5 million
- **Coed**

Undergraduates 2,297 full-time, 1,152 part-time. Students come from 12 other countries, 1% are from out of state, 27% African American, 2% Asian American or Pacific Islander, 1% Hispanic American, 0.1% Native American, 0.6% international, 20% live on campus.

Faculty *Student/faculty ratio:* 25:1.

Academics *Calendar:* semesters. *Degree:* certificates and associate. *Special study options:* academic remediation for entering students, accelerated degree program, adult/continuing education programs, advanced placement credit, cooperative education, honors programs, off-campus study, part-time degree program, services for LD students, summer session for credit.

Student Life *Campus security:* 24-hour patrols, late-night transport/escort service.

Athletics Member NJCAA.

Standardized Tests *Required:* SAT or ACT (for admission).

Financial Aid Of all full-time matriculated undergraduates who enrolled in 2004, 75 Federal Work-Study jobs (averaging $1850).

Applying *Options:* electronic application, early admission, deferred entrance. *Application fee:* $20. *Required:* high school transcript, minimum 1.8 GPA, minimum SAT score of 830 and 15 CPC credits.

Freshmen Application Contact Mr. Brian Gipson, Director of Admissions, Gordon College, 419 College Drive, Barnesville, GA 30204. *Phone:* 770-358-5023. *Toll-free phone:* 800-282-6504.

GRIFFIN TECHNICAL COLLEGE
Griffin, Georgia   www.griffintech.edu

- **State-supported** 2-year, founded 1965, part of Georgia Department of Technical and Adult Education
- **Small-town** 10-acre campus with easy access to Atlanta
- **Coed,** 3,407 undergraduate students, 44% full-time, 63% women, 37% men

Undergraduates 1,494 full-time, 1,913 part-time. 37% African American, 1% Asian American or Pacific Islander, 1% Hispanic American, 0.3% Native American.

Freshmen *Admission:* 665 enrolled.

Faculty *Total:* 240, 28% full-time.

Majors Accounting; administrative assistant and secretarial science; automobile/automotive mechanics technology; business administration and management; child development; computer and information systems security; computer programming; computer systems networking and telecommunications; criminal justice/safety; drafting and design technology; electrical, electronic and communications engineering technology; emergency medical technology (EMT paramedic); heating, air conditioning and refrigeration technology; horticultural science; industrial technology; manufacturing technology; marketing/marketing management; medical radiologic technology; paralegal/legal assistant; pharmacy technician; respiratory therapy technician; surgical technology; web page, digital/multimedia and information resources design.

Academics *Calendar:* quarters. *Degree:* certificates, diplomas, and associate. *Special study options:* academic remediation for entering students, adult/continuing education programs, advanced placement credit, distance learning, honors programs, internships, part-time degree program, services for LD students.

Library Griffin Technical College Library with 12,493 titles, 188 serial subscriptions, 1,326 audiovisual materials, an OPAC, a Web page.

Computers on Campus 500 computers available on campus for general student use. A campuswide network can be accessed. Internet access, online (class) registration, at least one staffed computer lab available.

Student Life *Housing:* college housing not available. *Activities and Organizations:* Phi Beta Lambda, Vocational Industrial Clubs of America, student government.

Standardized Tests *Required:* ACT COMPASS or ASSET (for admission).

Costs (2006–07) *Tuition:* state resident $1116 full-time, $31 per credit hour part-time; nonresident $2232 full-time, $62 per credit hour part-time.

Applying *Options:* deferred entrance. *Application fee:* $15. *Required:* high school transcript.

Director of Admissions Christine James-Brown, Admissions Officer, Griffin Technical College, 501 Varsity Road, Griffin, GA 30223-2042. *Phone:* 770-228-7371. *Fax:* 770-229-3227. *E-mail:* cbrown@griftec.org.

GUPTON-JONES COLLEGE OF FUNERAL SERVICE
Decatur, Georgia   www.gupton-jones.edu/

Freshmen Application Contact Ms. Beverly Wheaton, Registrar, Gupton-Jones College of Funeral Service, 5141 Snapfinger Woods Drive, Decatur, GA 30035. *Phone:* 770-593-2257. *Toll-free phone:* 800-848-5352.

GWINNETT TECHNICAL COLLEGE
Lawrenceville, Georgia   www.gwinnetttech.edu/

- **State-supported** 2-year, founded 1984
- **Suburban** 93-acre campus with easy access to Atlanta
- **Coed,** 4,204 undergraduate students, 38% full-time, 55% women, 45% men

Undergraduates 1,617 full-time, 2,587 part-time. 26% African American, 6% Asian American or Pacific Islander, 6% Hispanic American, 0.1% Native American.

Freshmen *Admission:* 469 enrolled.

Faculty *Total:* 206, 34% full-time.

Majors Accounting; administrative assistant and secretarial science; automobile/automotive mechanics technology; business administration and management; computer programming; computer science; computer systems networking and telecommunications; construction management; drafting and design technology; electrical, electronic and communications engineering technology; emergency medical technology (EMT paramedic); horticultural science; hotel/motel administration; information science/studies; interior design; machine tool technology; management information systems; marketing/marketing management; medical/clinical assistant; medical radiologic technology; ornamental horticulture; photography; physical therapist assistant; physical therapy; respiratory care therapy; tourism and travel services management; veterinary/animal health technology.

Academics *Calendar:* quarters. *Degree:* certificates, diplomas, and associate. *Special study options:* academic remediation for entering students, adult/continuing education programs, advanced placement credit, internships, part-time degree program, services for LD students, summer session for credit.

Library Gwinnett Technical Institute Media Center with 19,547 titles, 246 serial subscriptions, 2,289 audiovisual materials.

Computers on Campus 264 computers available on campus for general student use. Internet access, at least one staffed computer lab available.

Student Life *Housing:* college housing not available. *Campus security:* patrols by campus police.

Standardized Tests *Required:* ACT COMPASS or ASSET (for admission), ACT COMPASS or ASSET (for placement).

Costs (2006–07) *Tuition:* state resident $1116 full-time, $31 per credit hour part-time; nonresident $2232 full-time, $62 per credit hour part-time.

Financial Aid Of all full-time matriculated undergraduates who enrolled in 2004, 20 Federal Work-Study jobs (averaging $2100).

Applying *Options:* deferred entrance. *Application fee:* $20. *Required:* high school transcript.

Director of Admissions Michelle McIntire, Admissions Director, Gwinnett Technical College, PO Box 1505, 5150 Sugarloaf Parkway, Lawrenceville, GA 30043-5702. *Phone:* 770-962-7580 Ext. 434. *Fax:* 770-685-1267. *E-mail:* mmcintire@gwinnett.tec.ga.us.

HEART OF GEORGIA TECHNICAL COLLEGE
Dublin, Georgia   www.hgtc.org/

- **State-supported** 2-year, founded 1984
- **Small-town** campus with easy access to Atlanta
- **Coed,** 1,755 undergraduate students, 33% full-time, 56% women, 44% men

Undergraduates 576 full-time, 1,179 part-time. 44% African American, 0.6% Asian American or Pacific Islander, 2% Hispanic American, 0.2% Native American, 0.1% international.

Freshmen *Admission:* 369 enrolled.

Faculty *Total:* 186, 34% full-time.

Majors Business, management, and marketing related; child development; criminal justice/safety; electrical, electronic and communications engineering technology; health information/medical records technology; machine tool technology; marketing/marketing management; medical radiologic technology; respiratory therapy technician.

Academics *Calendar:* quarters. *Degree:* certificates, diplomas, and associate. *Special study options:* academic remediation for entering students, advanced placement credit, cooperative education, distance learning, internships, services for LD students.

Student Life *Housing:* college housing not available.

Standardized Tests *Required:* ACT COMPASS or ASSET (for admission).

Costs (2006–07) *Tuition:* state resident $1116 full-time, $31 per credit hour part-time; nonresident $2232 full-time, $62 per credit hour part-time.

Applying *Options:* deferred entrance. *Application fee:* $15. *Required:* high school transcript.

Director of Admissions Ms. Lisa Kelly, Director of Admissions, Heart of Georgia Technical College, 560 Pinehill Road, Dublin, GA 31021. *Phone:* 478-274-7837. *Fax:* 478-296-6113. *E-mail:* lisak@hgtc.org.

HERZING COLLEGE
Atlanta, Georgia   www.herzing.edu/atlanta/

- **Proprietary** primarily 2-year, founded 1949, part of Herzing Institutes, Inc
- **Urban** campus
- **Coed,** 276 undergraduate students, 58% full-time, 54% women, 46% men

Undergraduates 161 full-time, 115 part-time. Students come from 5 states and territories, 73% African American, 4% Asian American or Pacific Islander, 3% Hispanic American, 0.7% Native American.

Freshmen *Admission:* 279 applied, 209 admitted.

Faculty *Total:* 25, 40% full-time, 28% with terminal degrees. *Student/faculty ratio:* 8:1.

Majors Business administration and management; computer and information sciences; electrical, electronic and communications engineering technology; information science/studies; securities services administration; system, networking, and LAN/WAN management.

Academics *Calendar:* semesters. *Degrees:* certificates, diplomas, associate, and bachelor's. *Special study options:* academic remediation for entering students, English as a second language, honors programs, internships.

Library Loretta Herzing Library with 6,000 titles, 25 serial subscriptions, a Web page.

Computers on Campus 125 computers available on campus for general student use. A campuswide network can be accessed.

Student Life *Housing:* college housing not available. *Campus security:* 24-hour patrols. *Student services:* personal/psychological counseling, women's center.

Standardized Tests *Required:* Wonderlic aptitude test (for admission).

Costs (2006–07) *Tuition:* $11,200 full-time, $350 per credit hour part-time. *Required fees:* $125 full-time, $30 per credit hour part-time, $25 per term part-time.

Applying *Application fee:* $25. *Required:* high school transcript, interview. *Application deadline:* rolling (freshmen), rolling (transfers). *Notification:* continuous (freshmen).

Freshmen Application Contact Mrs. Rose White, Director of Admissions, Herzing College, 3355 Lenox Road, Suite 100, Atlanta, GA 30326. *Phone:* 404-816-4533. *Toll-free phone:* 800-573-4533. *Fax:* 404-816-5576. *E-mail:* info@ath.herzing.edu.

HIGH-TECH INSTITUTE
Marietta, Georgia   www.high-techinstitute.com/

Director of Admissions Frank Webster, Office Manager, High-Tech Institute, 1090 Northchase Parkway, Suite 150, Marietta, GA 30067. *Phone:* 770-988-9877. *Toll-free phone:* 800-987-0110. *Fax:* 770-988-8824. *E-mail:* ckusema@hightechschools.com.

INTERACTIVE COLLEGE OF TECHNOLOGY
Chamblee, Georgia   www.ict-ils.edu/

- **Proprietary** 2-year, part of Interactive Learning Systems
- **Coed,** 1,069 undergraduate students, 99% full-time, 49% women, 51% men

Undergraduates 1,063 full-time, 6 part-time. Students come from 3 states and territories, 80 other countries.

Freshmen *Admission:* 104 enrolled.

Faculty *Total:* 62, 29% full-time, 8% with terminal degrees. *Student/faculty ratio:* 18:1.

Academics *Degree:* certificates, diplomas, and associate. *Special study options:* academic remediation for entering students, accelerated degree program, adult/

Interactive College of Technology (continued)

continuing education programs, advanced placement credit, double majors, English as a second language, independent study, internships, part-time degree program.

Library 1,600 titles, 43 serial subscriptions, an OPAC.

Computers on Campus 164 computers available on campus for general student use. A campuswide network can be accessed from student residence rooms. Internet access, at least one staffed computer lab available.

Costs (2006–07) *Tuition:* $6480 full-time.

Applying *Application fee:* $50. *Required:* high school transcript. *Recommended:* high school transcript, interview. *Application deadline:* rolling (freshmen).

Freshmen Application Contact Ms. Nicole Caruso, Associate Dean of Admissions, Interactive College of Technology, 5303 New Peachtree Road, Chamblee, GA 30341. *Phone:* 770-216-2960. *Toll-free phone:* 800-550-3475. *Fax:* 770-216-2989.

ITT TECHNICAL INSTITUTE

Duluth, Georgia   www.itt-tech.edu/

- **Proprietary** primarily 2-year, founded 2003, part of ITT Educational Services, Inc
- **Coed**

Majors Animation, interactive technology, video graphics and special effects; business administration and management; CAD/CADD drafting/design technology; computer and information systems security; criminal justice/law enforcement administration; e-commerce; electrical, electronic and communications engineering technology; system, networking, and LAN/WAN management; web page, digital/multimedia and information resources design.

Academics *Calendar:* quarters. *Degrees:* associate and bachelor's.

Library a Web page.

Computers on Campus Internet access, at least one staffed computer lab available.

Student Life *Housing:* college housing not available.

Standardized Tests *Required:* Wonderlic aptitude test (for admission).

Costs (2005–06) *Tuition:* Please see school catalog for specific information.

Applying *Options:* deferred entrance. *Application fee:* $100. *Required:* high school transcript, interview. *Recommended:* letters of recommendation. *Application deadline:* rolling (freshmen), rolling (transfers). *Notification:* continuous (freshmen).

Freshmen Application Contact Finny Knight, Director of Recruitment, ITT Technical Institute, 10700 Abbotts Bridge Road, Suite 190, Duluth, GA 30097. *Phone:* 678-957-8510. *Toll-free phone:* 866-489-8818.

ITT TECHNICAL INSTITUTE

Kennesaw, Georgia   www.itt-tech.edu/

- primarily 2-year
- **Coed**

Majors Business administration and management; CAD/CADD drafting/design technology; criminal justice/law enforcement administration; electrical, electronic and communications engineering technology; system, networking, and LAN/WAN management; web page, digital/multimedia and information resources design.

Academics *Calendar:* quarters. *Degrees:* associate and bachelor's.

Standardized Tests *Required:* Wonderlic aptitude test (for admission).

Costs (2005–06) *Tuition:* Please see school catalog for specific information.

Applying *Application fee:* $100. *Required:* high school transcript, interview. *Recommended:* letters of recommendation. *Application deadline:* rolling (freshmen), rolling (transfers). *Notification:* continuous (freshmen).

Freshmen Application Contact Mr. John E. Bagley, ITT Technical Institute, 1000 Cobb Place Boulevard NW, Kennesaw, GA 30144. *Phone:* 770-426-2300.

LANIER TECHNICAL COLLEGE

Oakwood, Georgia   www.laniertech.edu/

- **State-supported** 2-year, founded 1964
- **Coed**, 3,196 undergraduate students, 39% full-time, 64% women, 36% men

Undergraduates 1,248 full-time, 1,948 part-time. 11% African American, 2% Asian American or Pacific Islander, 4% Hispanic American, 0.2% Native American.

Freshmen *Admission:* 844 enrolled.

Faculty *Total:* 262, 27% full-time.

Majors Accounting; administrative assistant and secretarial science; banking and financial support services; child development; computer and information systems security; computer programming; computer science; computer systems networking and telecommunications; criminal justice/safety; drafting and design technology; electrical, electronic and communications engineering technology; fire science; health professions related; industrial technology; information science/studies; interior design; marketing/marketing management; medical laboratory technology; medical radiologic technology; occupational safety and health technology; surgical technology; web page, digital/multimedia and information resources design.

Academics *Calendar:* quarters. *Degree:* certificates, diplomas, and associate. *Special study options:* academic remediation for entering students, advanced placement credit, distance learning, services for LD students.

Library 7,096 titles, 154 serial subscriptions, 570 audiovisual materials.

Student Life *Housing:* college housing not available.

Standardized Tests *Required:* ACT COMPASS or ASSET (for admission).

Costs (2006–07) *Tuition:* state resident $1116 full-time, $31 per credit hour part-time; nonresident $2232 full-time, $62 per credit hour part-time.

Applying *Options:* deferred entrance. *Application fee:* $15. *Required:* high school transcript.

Director of Admissions Mike Marlowe, Admissions Director, Lanier Technical College, 2990 Landrum Education Drive, Oakwood, GA 30566. *Phone:* 770-531-6332. *Fax:* 770-531-6328. *E-mail:* mike@laniertech.edu.

LE CORDON BLEU COLLEGE OF CULINARY ARTS, ATLANTA

Tucker, Georgia

MIDDLE GEORGIA COLLEGE

Cochran, Georgia   www.mgc.edu/

- **State-supported** 2-year, founded 1884, part of University System of Georgia
- **Small-town** 165-acre campus
- **Endowment** $1.0 million
- **Coed**, 2,677 undergraduate students, 68% full-time, 59% women, 41% men

Middle Georgia College is a 2-year, residential public college with a student population of approximately 2,600. Transfer programs are offered in more than 100 academic disciplines, including engineering, nursing, business, and education. Numerous clubs and organizations, as well as intercollegiate athletics for men and women, enrich student life.

Undergraduates 1,808 full-time, 869 part-time. Students come from 37 states and territories, 5% are from out of state, 34% African American, 0.7% Asian American or Pacific Islander, 1% Hispanic American, 0.3% Native American, 0.4% international, 15% transferred in, 32% live on campus.

Freshmen *Admission:* 1,771 applied, 1,613 admitted, 890 enrolled. *Average high school GPA:* 2.82. *Test scores:* SAT verbal scores over 500: 33%; SAT math scores over 500: 38%; ACT scores over 18: 31%; SAT verbal scores over 600: 6%; SAT math scores over 600: 10%; ACT scores over 24: 5%; SAT verbal scores over 700: 1%; SAT math scores over 700: 1%.

Faculty *Total:* 129, 60% full-time, 24% with terminal degrees. *Student/faculty ratio:* 22:1.

Majors Business administration and management; computer and information sciences related; computer engineering related; computer/information technology services administration related; computer science; criminal justice/police science; data processing and data processing technology; fashion merchandising; information science/studies; liberal arts and sciences/liberal studies; nursing (registered nurse training); occupational therapist assistant; physical therapist assistant; public administration; survey technology.

Academics *Calendar:* semesters. *Degree:* certificates and associate. *Special study options:* academic remediation for entering students, accelerated degree program, adult/continuing education programs, advanced placement credit, cooperative education, distance learning, honors programs, part-time degree program, services for LD students, study abroad, summer session for credit.

Library Roberts Memorial Library with 110,000 titles, 147 serial subscriptions, 5,119 audiovisual materials, an OPAC, a Web page.

Computers on Campus 439 computers available on campus for general student use. A campuswide network can be accessed from student residence rooms and from off campus. Internet access, online (class) registration, at least one staffed computer lab available.

Student Life *Housing:* on-campus residence required through sophomore year. *Options:* men-only, women-only. Campus housing is university owned. Freshman campus housing is guaranteed. *Activities and Organizations:* drama/theater group, student-run newspaper, choral group, marching band, Baptist Student Union, Student Government Association, MGC Ambassadors, Encore Productions, United Voices of Praise. *Campus security:* 24-hour emergency response devices and patrols, student patrols, late-night transport/escort service, controlled dormitory access, patrols by police officers. *Student services:* health clinic, personal/psychological counseling.

Athletics Member NJCAA. *Intercollegiate sports:* baseball M(s), basketball M(s)/W(s), soccer M(s)/W(s), softball W(s). *Intramural sports:* badminton M/W, basketball M/W, football M/W, golf M/W, softball M/W, swimming and diving M/W, tennis M/W.

Costs (2005–06) *Tuition:* state resident $1542 full-time, $65 per credit hour part-time; nonresident $6166 full-time, $257 per credit hour part-time. Full-time tuition and fees vary according to location. Part-time tuition and fees vary according to location. *Required fees:* $424 full-time. *Room and board:* $4200; room only: $1950. Room and board charges vary according to board plan and housing facility.

Financial Aid Of all full-time matriculated undergraduates who enrolled in 2004, 91 Federal Work-Study jobs (averaging $692).

Applying *Options:* common application, electronic application, early admission, deferred entrance. *Application fee:* $20. *Required:* high school transcript, minimum 2.0 GPA. *Required for some:* essay or personal statement, minimum 3.5 GPA, letters of recommendation, interview. *Application deadline:* rolling (freshmen), rolling (transfers). *Notification:* continuous (freshmen).

Freshmen Application Contact Ms. Jennifer Brannon, Director of Admissions, Middle Georgia College, 1100 2nd Street, SE, Cochran, GA 31014. *Phone:* 478-934-3138. *Fax:* 478-934-3403. *E-mail:* admissions@mgc.edu.

MIDDLE GEORGIA TECHNICAL COLLEGE

Warner Robbins, Georgia www.middlegatech.edu/

- **State-supported** 2-year, founded 1973
- **Coed,** 2,351 undergraduate students, 46% full-time, 52% women, 48% men

Undergraduates 1,078 full-time, 1,273 part-time. 39% African American, 1% Asian American or Pacific Islander, 2% Hispanic American, 0.4% Native American.
Freshmen *Admission:* 737 enrolled.
Faculty *Total:* 235, 47% full-time.
Majors Accounting; administrative assistant and secretarial science; airframe mechanics and aircraft maintenance technology; child development; computer systems networking and telecommunications; dental hygiene; drafting and design technology; information science/studies; marketing/marketing management; medical radiologic technology; web page, digital/multimedia and information resources design.
Academics *Calendar:* quarters. *Degree:* certificates, diplomas, and associate. *Special study options:* academic remediation for entering students, advanced placement credit, cooperative education, distance learning, internships, services for LD students.
Library 2,124 titles, 69 serial subscriptions, 211 audiovisual materials.
Student Life *Housing:* college housing not available.
Standardized Tests *Required:* ACT COMPASS or ASSET (for admission).
Costs (2006–07) *Tuition:* state resident $1116 full-time, $31 per credit hour part-time; nonresident $2232 full-time, $62 per credit hour part-time.
Applying *Options:* deferred entrance. *Application fee:* $15. *Required:* high school transcript.
Director of Admissions Craig B. Jackson, Director of Admissions, Middle Georgia Technical College, 80 Cohen Walker Drive, Warner Robins, GA 31088. *Phone:* 478-988-6843. *Toll-free phone:* 800-474-1031. *Fax:* 478-988-6813. *E-mail:* cjackson@middlegatech.edu.

MOULTRIE TECHNICAL COLLEGE

Moultrie, Georgia www.moultrietech.edu/

- **State-supported** 2-year, founded 1964
- **Coed,** 1,951 undergraduate students, 43% full-time, 64% women, 36% men

Undergraduates 831 full-time, 1,120 part-time. 35% African American, 0.2% Asian American or Pacific Islander, 2% Hispanic American, 0.2% Native American.
Freshmen *Admission:* 398 enrolled.
Faculty *Total:* 96, 49% full-time.
Majors Accounting; administrative assistant and secretarial science; child development; civil engineering technology; computer systems networking and telecommunications; criminal justice/safety; electrical, electronic and communications engineering technology; information science/studies; marketing/marketing management; web page, digital/multimedia and information resources design.
Academics *Calendar:* quarters. *Degree:* certificates, diplomas, and associate. *Special study options:* academic remediation for entering students, advanced placement credit, distance learning, internships, services for LD students.
Student Life *Housing:* college housing not available.
Standardized Tests *Required:* ACT COMPASS or ASSET (for admission).
Costs (2006–07) *Tuition:* state resident $1116 full-time, $31 per credit hour part-time; nonresident $2232 full-time, $62 per credit hour part-time.
Applying *Options:* deferred entrance. *Application fee:* $15. *Required:* high school transcript.
Director of Admissions Leigh Wallace, Admissions Director, Moultrie Technical College, 800 Veterans Parkway North, Moultrie, GA 31788. *Phone:* 229-891-4144. *Fax:* 229-891-7010. *E-mail:* lwallace@moultrietech.edu.

NORTH GEORGIA TECHNICAL COLLEGE

Clarkesville, Georgia www.northgatech.edu/

- **State-supported** 2-year, founded 1943
- **Coed,** 1,812 undergraduate students, 54% full-time, 62% women, 38% men

Undergraduates 974 full-time, 838 part-time. 6% African American, 1% Asian American or Pacific Islander, 1% Hispanic American, 0.2% Native American.
Freshmen *Admission:* 482 enrolled.
Faculty *Total:* 189, 36% full-time.
Majors Administrative assistant and secretarial science; computer systems networking and telecommunications; criminal justice/safety; culinary arts; heating, air conditioning and refrigeration technology; horticultural science; industrial technology; medical laboratory technology; parks, recreation and leisure facilities management; turf and turfgrass management; web page, digital/multimedia and information resources design.
Academics *Calendar:* quarters. *Degree:* certificates, diplomas, and associate. *Special study options:* academic remediation for entering students, advanced placement credit, distance learning, internships, services for LD students.
Library 15,684 titles, 162 serial subscriptions, 990 audiovisual materials.
Standardized Tests *Required:* ACT COMPASS or ASSET (for admission).
Costs (2006–07) *Tuition:* state resident $1116 full-time, $31 per credit hour part-time; nonresident $2232 full-time, $62 per credit hour part-time.
Applying *Options:* deferred entrance. *Application fee:* $15. *Required:* high school transcript.
Director of Admissions Gail Taylor, Admissions Director, North Georgia Technical College, PO Box 65, 1500 Georgia Highway 197, Clarkesville, GA 30523. *Phone:* 706-754-7724. *Fax:* 706-754-7777. *E-mail:* gtaylor@northgatech.edu.

NORTH METRO TECHNICAL COLLEGE

Acworth, Georgia www.northmetrotech.edu/

- **State-supported** 2-year, founded 1989
- **Coed,** 1,903 undergraduate students, 42% full-time, 60% women, 40% men

Undergraduates 790 full-time, 1,113 part-time. 15% African American, 1% Asian American or Pacific Islander, 2% Hispanic American, 0.5% Native American.
Freshmen *Admission:* 414 enrolled.

North Metro Technical College (continued)

Faculty *Total:* 110, 31% full-time.

Majors Accounting; administrative assistant and secretarial science; child development; computer systems networking and telecommunications; design and visual communications; electrical, electronic and communications engineering technology; horticultural science; marketing/marketing management; medical radiologic technology; web page, digital/multimedia and information resources design.

Academics *Calendar:* quarters. *Degree:* certificates, diplomas, and associate. *Special study options:* academic remediation for entering students, advanced placement credit, distance learning, internships, services for LD students.

Student Life *Housing:* college housing not available.

Standardized Tests *Required:* ACT COMPASS or ASSET (for admission).

Costs (2006–07) *Tuition:* state resident $1116 full-time, $31 per credit hour part-time; nonresident $2232 full-time, $62 per credit hour part-time.

Applying *Options:* deferred entrance. *Application fee:* $15. *Required:* high school transcript.

Director of Admissions Missy Cusack, Admissions Director, North Metro Technical College, 5198 Ross Road, Acworth, GA 30102-3012. *Phone:* 770-975-4079. *Fax:* 770-975-4142. *E-mail:* mcusack@northmetrotech.edu.

NORTHWESTERN TECHNICAL COLLEGE

Rock Springs, Georgia   **www.northwesterntech.edu/**

- **State-supported** 2-year, founded 1966, part of Georgia Department of Technical and Adult Education
- **Rural** campus
- **Coed,** 2,303 undergraduate students, 39% full-time, 70% women, 30% men

Undergraduates 891 full-time, 1,412 part-time. Students come from 3 states and territories, 4% African American, 0.4% Asian American or Pacific Islander, 1% Hispanic American, 0.5% Native American.

Freshmen *Admission:* 285 enrolled.

Faculty *Total:* 110, 45% full-time.

Majors Accounting; administrative assistant and secretarial science; automobile/automotive mechanics technology; cardiovascular technology; child development; computer systems networking and telecommunications; criminal justice/safety; drafting and design technology; electrical, electronic and communications engineering technology; health information/medical records technology; information science/studies; nursing (registered nurse training); occupational therapist assistant; pharmacy technician; social work; surgical technology; web page, digital/multimedia and information resources design.

Academics *Calendar:* quarters. *Degree:* certificates, diplomas, and associate. *Special study options:* academic remediation for entering students, adult/continuing education programs, advanced placement credit, distance learning, internships, part-time degree program, services for LD students, summer session for credit.

Library Northwestern Technical Institute Library with 350,000 titles, 180 serial subscriptions, 20,000 audiovisual materials, an OPAC, a Web page.

Computers on Campus 270 computers available on campus for general student use. A campuswide network can be accessed from off campus. Internet access, online (class) registration, at least one staffed computer lab available.

Student Life *Housing:* college housing not available.

Standardized Tests *Required:* ACT COMPASS or ASSET (for admission).

Costs (2006–07) *Tuition:* state resident $1116 full-time, $31 per credit hour part-time; nonresident $2232 full-time, $62 per credit hour part-time.

Financial Aid Of all full-time matriculated undergraduates who enrolled in 2004, 30 Federal Work-Study jobs (averaging $4800).

Applying *Options:* deferred entrance. *Application fee:* $15. *Required:* high school transcript.

Director of Admissions Mrs. Carolyn Solmon, Director of Admissions and Career Planning, Northwestern Technical College, 265 Bicentennial Trail, PO Box 569, Rock Springs, GA 30739. *Phone:* 706-764-3511. *Toll-free phone:* 800-735-5726. *Fax:* 706-764-3707. *E-mail:* csolmon@northwesterntech.edu.

OGEECHEE TECHNICAL COLLEGE

Statesboro, Georgia   **www.ogeecheetech.edu**

- **State-supported** 2-year, founded 1989, part of Georgia Department of Technical and Adult Education
- **Small-town** campus
- **Coed,** 1,950 undergraduate students, 52% full-time, 69% women, 31% men

Undergraduates 1,008 full-time, 942 part-time. 33% African American, 0.5% Asian American or Pacific Islander, 1% Hispanic American, 0.5% Native American.

Freshmen *Admission:* 360 enrolled.

Faculty *Total:* 142, 51% full-time.

Majors Accounting; administrative assistant and secretarial science; agribusiness; automobile/automotive mechanics technology; banking and financial support services; child development; computer systems networking and telecommunications; construction trades; culinary arts; dental hygiene; forestry technology; funeral service and mortuary science; health information/medical records technology; hotel and restaurant management; information science/studies; interior design; marketing/marketing management; opticianry; paralegal/legal assistant; tourism and travel services management; veterinary technology; water quality and wastewater treatment management and recycling technology; wildlife and wildlands science and management; wood science and wood products/pulp and paper technology.

Academics *Calendar:* quarters. *Degree:* certificates, diplomas, and associate. *Special study options:* academic remediation for entering students, advanced placement credit, distance learning, internships, services for LD students.

Library 2,477 titles, 109 serial subscriptions, 276 audiovisual materials.

Student Life *Housing:* college housing not available.

Standardized Tests *Required:* ACT COMPASS or ASSET (for admission).

Costs (2006–07) *Tuition:* state resident $31 per credit hour part-time; nonresident $62 per credit hour part-time.

Applying *Options:* deferred entrance. *Application fee:* $15. *Required:* high school transcript.

Director of Admissions Mr. Ryan Foley, Admissions Director, Ogeechee Technical College, 1 Joe Kennedy Boulevard, Statesboro, GA 30458. *Phone:* 912-871-1600. *Toll-free phone:* 800-646-1316. *Fax:* 912-486-7413. *E-mail:* rfoley@ogeecheetech.edu.

OKEFENOKEE TECHNICAL COLLEGE

Waycross, Georgia   **www.okefenokeetech.org/**

- **State-supported** 2-year
- **Small-town** campus
- **Coed,** 1,731 undergraduate students, 34% full-time, 68% women, 32% men

Undergraduates 595 full-time, 1,136 part-time. 25% African American, 0.6% Asian American or Pacific Islander, 0.7% Hispanic American, 0.7% Native American.

Freshmen *Admission:* 306 enrolled.

Faculty *Total:* 113, 42% full-time.

Majors Administrative assistant and secretarial science; child development; clinical/medical laboratory technology; computer systems networking and telecommunications; computer technology/computer systems technology; criminal justice/police science; forestry technology; information science/studies; occupational safety and health technology; respiratory therapy technician; surgical technology.

Academics *Calendar:* quarters. *Degree:* certificates, diplomas, and associate. *Special study options:* academic remediation for entering students, advanced placement credit, distance learning, internships, services for LD students.

Library 1,714 titles.

Student Life *Housing:* college housing not available.

Standardized Tests *Required:* ACT COMPASS or ASSET (for admission).

Costs (2006–07) *Tuition:* state resident $1116 full-time, $31 per credit hour part-time; nonresident $2232 full-time, $62 per credit hour part-time.

Applying *Options:* deferred entrance. *Application fee:* $15. *Required:* high school transcript.

Director of Admissions Reba Smith, Director of Admissions, Okefenokee Technical College, 1701 Carswell Avenue, Waycross, GA 31503. *Phone:* 912-287-5806. *Fax:* 912-284-2508. *E-mail:* reba@okefenokeetech.org.

SANDERSVILLE TECHNICAL COLLEGE
Sandersville, Georgia   **www.sandersvilletech.org/**

- **State-supported** 2-year
- **Coed,** 765 undergraduate students, 31% full-time, 65% women, 35% men

Undergraduates 237 full-time, 528 part-time. 65% African American, 0.3% Asian American or Pacific Islander, 0.1% Hispanic American, 0.4% Native American.
Freshmen *Admission:* 176 enrolled.
Faculty *Total:* 100, 30% full-time.
Majors Accounting; administrative assistant and secretarial science; child development; computer systems networking and telecommunications; information science/studies.
Academics *Calendar:* quarters. *Degree:* certificates, diplomas, and associate. *Special study options:* academic remediation for entering students, advanced placement credit, distance learning, internships, services for LD students.
Student Life *Housing:* college housing not available.
Standardized Tests *Required:* ACT COMPASS or ASSET (for admission).
Costs (2006–07) *Tuition:* state resident $1116 full-time, $31 per credit hour part-time; nonresident $2232 full-time, $62 per credit hour part-time.
Applying *Options:* deferred entrance. *Application fee:* $15. *Required:* high school transcript.
Director of Admissions Patrick Wilson, Admissions Director, Sandersville Technical College, 1189 Deepstep Road, Sandersville, GA 31082. *Phone:* 478-553-2065. *Fax:* 478-553-2118. *E-mail:* pwilson@sandervilletech.edu.

SAVANNAH RIVER COLLEGE
Augusta, Georgia

SAVANNAH TECHNICAL COLLEGE
Savannah, Georgia   **www.savannahtech.edu/**

- **State-supported** 2-year, founded 1929, part of Georgia Department of Technical and Adult Education
- **Urban** 15-acre campus
- **Coed,** 3,786 undergraduate students, 42% full-time, 69% women, 31% men

Undergraduates 1,577 full-time, 2,209 part-time. Students come from 4 states and territories, 57% African American, 2% Asian American or Pacific Islander, 3% Hispanic American, 0.4% Native American, 2% international, 3% transferred in.
Freshmen *Admission:* 783 enrolled.
Faculty *Total:* 290, 21% full-time.
Majors Accounting; administrative assistant and secretarial science; automobile/automotive mechanics technology; child development; computer systems networking and telecommunications; criminal justice/safety; culinary arts; electrical, electronic and communications engineering technology; fire science; heating, air conditioning and refrigeration technology; hotel and restaurant management; industrial technology; information technology; marketing/marketing management; surgical technology; tourism and travel services management.
Academics *Calendar:* quarters. *Degree:* certificates, diplomas, and associate. *Special study options:* academic remediation for entering students, advanced placement credit, distance learning, internships, part-time degree program, services for LD students, summer session for credit.
Library 20,804 titles, 160 serial subscriptions, 3,150 audiovisual materials, an OPAC, a Web page.
Computers on Campus Internet access, at least one staffed computer lab available.
Student Life *Housing:* college housing not available. *Activities and Organizations:* Phi Beta Lambda, Vocational Industrial Clubs of America (VICA).
Standardized Tests *Required:* ACT COMPASS or ASSET (for admission).
Costs (2006–07) *Tuition:* state resident $1116 full-time, $31 per credit hour part-time; nonresident $2232 full-time, $62 per credit hour part-time.
Applying *Options:* deferred entrance. *Application fee:* $15. *Required:* high school transcript.

Director of Admissions Angela Southerland, Admissions Director, Savannah Technical College, 5717 White Bluff Road, Savannah, GA 31405. *Phone:* 912-303-1772. *Toll-free phone:* 800-769-6362. *Fax:* 912-303-1781. *E-mail:* asoutherland@savannahtech.edu.

SOUTHEASTERN TECHNICAL COLLEGE
Vidalia, Georgia   **www.southeasterntech.edu/**

- **State-supported** 2-year, founded 1989
- **Coed,** 982 undergraduate students, 46% full-time, 73% women, 27% men

Undergraduates 447 full-time, 535 part-time. 29% African American, 0.2% Asian American or Pacific Islander, 2% Hispanic American, 0.3% Native American.
Freshmen *Admission:* 202 enrolled.
Faculty *Total:* 102, 39% full-time.
Majors Accounting; administrative assistant and secretarial science; child development; computer systems networking and telecommunications; criminal justice/safety; dental hygiene; design and visual communications; electrical, electronic and communications engineering technology; information science/studies; marketing/marketing management; medical laboratory technology; medical radiologic technology; respiratory therapy technician; web page, digital/multimedia and information resources design.
Academics *Calendar:* quarters. *Degree:* certificates, diplomas, and associate. *Special study options:* academic remediation for entering students, advanced placement credit, distance learning, internships, services for LD students.
Student Life *Housing:* college housing not available.
Standardized Tests *Required:* ACT COMPASS or ASSET (for admission).
Costs (2006–07) *Tuition:* state resident $1116 full-time, $31 per credit hour part-time; nonresident $2232 full-time, $62 per credit hour part-time.
Applying *Options:* deferred entrance. *Application fee:* $15. *Required:* high school transcript.
Director of Admissions Christopher P. Carroll, Admissions Director, Southeastern Technical College, 3001 East First Street, Vidalia, GA 30474. *Phone:* 912-538-3121. *Fax:* 912-538-3156. *E-mail:* ccarroll@southeasterntech.edu.

SOUTH GEORGIA COLLEGE
Douglas, Georgia   **www.sga.edu/**
Director of Admissions Dr. Randy L. Braswell, Director of Admissions, Records, and Research, South Georgia College, 100 West College Park Drive, Douglas, GA 31533-5098. *Phone:* 912-389-4200. *Toll-free phone:* 800-342-6364. *E-mail:* rbraswell@sga.edu.

SOUTH GEORGIA TECHNICAL COLLEGE
Americus, Georgia   **www.southgatech.edu/**

- **State-supported** 2-year, founded 1948
- **Coed,** 1,669 undergraduate students, 53% full-time, 52% women, 48% men

Undergraduates 886 full-time, 783 part-time. 59% African American, 0.4% Asian American or Pacific Islander, 0.7% Hispanic American, 0.1% Native American.
Freshmen *Admission:* 479 enrolled.
Faculty *Total:* 143, 48% full-time.
Majors Accounting; administrative assistant and secretarial science; child development; computer systems networking and telecommunications; criminal justice/safety; culinary arts; drafting and design technology; electrical, electronic and communications engineering technology; heating, air conditioning and refrigeration technology; horticultural science; industrial technology; information science/studies; manufacturing technology; marketing/marketing management; paralegal/legal assistant.
Academics *Calendar:* quarters. *Degree:* certificates, diplomas, and associate. *Special study options:* academic remediation for entering students, advanced placement credit, cooperative education, distance learning, internships, services for LD students.
Athletics Member NJCAA. *Intercollegiate sports:* basketball M/W.
Standardized Tests *Required:* ACT COMPASS or ASSET (for admission).
Costs (2006–07) *Tuition:* state resident $1116 full-time, $31 per credit hour part-time; nonresident $2232 full-time, $62 per credit hour part-time.

South Georgia Technical College (continued)

Applying *Options:* deferred entrance. *Application fee:* $15. *Required:* high school transcript.

Director of Admissions Karen Werling, Admissions Director, South Georgia Technical College, 900 South Georgia Tech Parkway, Americus, GA 31709-8104. *Phone:* 229-931-2299. *Fax:* 229-931-5001. *E-mail:* kwerling@southgatech.edu.

SOUTHWEST GEORGIA TECHNICAL COLLEGE

Thomasville, Georgia   **www.southwestgatech.edu/**

- **State-supported** 2-year, founded 1963, part of Georgia Department of Technical and Adult Education
- **Coed,** 1,491 undergraduate students, 39% full-time, 73% women, 27% men

Undergraduates 588 full-time, 903 part-time. 41% African American, 0.3% Asian American or Pacific Islander, 0.9% Hispanic American, 0.7% Native American, 0.1% international.
Freshmen *Admission:* 242 enrolled.

Faculty *Total:* 62, 100% full-time.

Majors Accounting; administrative assistant and secretarial science; agricultural mechanization; child development; computer systems networking and telecommunications; criminal justice/safety; information science/studies; medical laboratory technology; medical radiologic technology; nursing (registered nurse training); respiratory care therapy; surgical technology.

Academics *Calendar:* quarters. *Degree:* certificates, diplomas, and associate. *Special study options:* academic remediation for entering students, advanced placement credit, cooperative education, distance learning, internships, part-time degree program, services for LD students, summer session for credit.

Library 19,767 titles, 113 serial subscriptions, 920 audiovisual materials, an OPAC, a Web page.

Computers on Campus 430 computers available on campus for general student use. A campuswide network can be accessed. Internet access, online (class) registration available.

Student Life *Housing:* college housing not available.

Standardized Tests *Required:* ACT COMPASS or ASSET (for admission).

Costs (2006–07) *Tuition:* state resident $1116 full-time, $31 per credit hour part-time; nonresident $2232 full-time, $62 per credit hour part-time.

Applying *Options:* electronic application, deferred entrance. *Application fee:* $20. *Required:* high school transcript.

Freshmen Application Contact Admissions Office, Southwest Georgia Technical College, 15689 US Highway 19 N, Thomasville, GA 31792. *Phone:* 229-225-5060. *E-mail:* info@southwestgatech.edu.

SWAINSBORO TECHNICAL COLLEGE

Swainsboro, Georgia   **www.swainsborotech.edu/**

- **State-supported** 2-year, founded 1963
- **Coed,** 684 undergraduate students, 42% full-time, 75% women, 25% men

Undergraduates 286 full-time, 398 part-time. 43% African American, 0.4% Asian American or Pacific Islander, 0.3% Hispanic American, 0.3% Native American.
Freshmen *Admission:* 117 enrolled.

Faculty *Total:* 79, 52% full-time.

Majors Accounting; administrative assistant and secretarial science; child development; computer systems networking and telecommunications; criminal justice/safety; drafting and design technology; electrical, electronic and communications engineering technology; fish/game management; forestry technology; information science/studies.

Academics *Calendar:* quarters. *Degree:* certificates, diplomas, and associate. *Special study options:* advanced placement credit, cooperative education, distance learning, internships, services for LD students.

Student Life *Housing:* college housing not available.

Standardized Tests *Required:* ACT COMPASS or ASSET (for admission).

Costs (2006–07) *Tuition:* state resident $1116 full-time, $31 per credit hour part-time; nonresident $2232 full-time, $62 per credit hour part-time.

Applying *Options:* deferred entrance. *Application fee:* $15. *Required:* high school transcript.

Director of Admissions Mitchell Fagler, Admissions Director, Swainsboro Technical College, 346 Kite Road, Swainsboro, GA 30401. *Phone:* 478-289-2259. *Fax:* 478-289-2263. *E-mail:* mfagler@swainsborotech.edu.

TRUETT-McCONNELL COLLEGE

Cleveland, Georgia   **www.truett.edu/**

- **Independent Baptist** primarily 2-year, founded 1946
- **Rural** 310-acre campus with easy access to Atlanta
- **Coed,** 375 undergraduate students, 91% full-time, 46% women, 54% men

Undergraduates 340 full-time, 35 part-time. Students come from 4 states and territories, 4 other countries, 3% are from out of state, 11% African American, 2% Asian American or Pacific Islander, 3% Hispanic American, 0.3% Native American, 5% transferred in, 73% live on campus. *Retention:* 55% of 2003 full-time freshmen returned.
Freshmen *Admission:* 604 applied, 254 admitted, 171 enrolled. *Average high school GPA:* 2.93. *Test scores:* SAT verbal scores over 500: 30%; SAT math scores over 500: 32%; ACT scores over 18: 47%; SAT verbal scores over 600: 8%; SAT math scores over 600: 3%; ACT scores over 24: 1%; SAT verbal scores over 700: 1%.

Faculty *Total:* 44, 57% full-time. *Student/faculty ratio:* 11:1.

Majors Business/commerce; Christian studies; education; general studies; humanities; liberal arts and sciences/liberal studies; music.

Academics *Calendar:* semesters. *Degrees:* associate and bachelor's. *Special study options:* academic remediation for entering students, accelerated degree program, advanced placement credit, double majors, honors programs, part-time degree program, services for LD students, study abroad, summer session for credit.

Library Cofer Library with 30,779 titles, 155 serial subscriptions, 2,522 audiovisual materials, an OPAC.

Computers on Campus 38 computers available on campus for general student use. A campuswide network can be accessed from student residence rooms and from off campus. Internet access, at least one staffed computer lab available.

Student Life *Housing Options:* men-only, women-only. Campus housing is university owned. *Activities and Organizations:* choral group, intramurals, Baptist Student Union, College Choir, Student Government Association, Fellowship of Christian Athletes (FCA). *Campus security:* 24-hour weekday patrols, 10-hour weekend patrols by trained security personnel.

Athletics Member NJCAA. *Intercollegiate sports:* baseball M(s), basketball M(s)/W(s), cross-country running M(s)/W(s), golf M, soccer M(s)/W(s), softball W(s). *Intramural sports:* basketball M/W, football M/W, ultimate Frisbee M/W, volleyball M/W.

Standardized Tests *Required:* SAT or ACT (for admission).

Costs (2006–07) *Comprehensive fee:* $17,450 includes full-time tuition ($11,950), mandatory fees ($500), and room and board ($5000). Part-time tuition: $398 per credit hour. *Required fees:* $250 per term part-time. *Room and board:* college room only: $2300.

Applying *Options:* early admission, deferred entrance. *Application fee:* $25. *Required:* high school transcript, minimum 2.0 GPA, minimum SAT score of 720 or ACT score of 15. *Required for some:* letters of recommendation, interview. *Application deadlines:* 8/1 (freshmen), 8/1 (transfers). *Notification:* continuous (freshmen).

Freshmen Application Contact Ms. Penny Loggins, Dean for Admissions, Truett-McConnell College, 100 Alumni Drive, Cleveland, GA 30528-9799. *Phone:* 706-865-2134 Ext. 210. *Toll-free phone:* 800-226-8621. *Fax:* 706-865-7615. *E-mail:* admissions@truett.edu.

VALDOSTA TECHNICAL COLLEGE

Valdosta, Georgia   **www.valdostatech.edu/**

- **State-supported** 2-year, founded 1963, part of Georgia Department of Technical and Adult Education
- **Suburban** 18-acre campus
- **Coed,** 2,444 undergraduate students, 41% full-time, 64% women, 36% men

Undergraduates 992 full-time, 1,452 part-time. Students come from 2 states and territories, 39% African American, 1% Asian American or Pacific Islander, 1% Hispanic American, 0.5% Native American, 4% transferred in.
Freshmen *Admission:* 451 enrolled.

Faculty *Total:* 186, 36% full-time.

Majors Accounting; administrative assistant and secretarial science; banking and financial support services; child development; computer and information systems security; computer programming; computer systems networking and telecommunications; criminal justice/safety; drafting and design technology; e-commerce; fire science; machine tool technology; marketing/marketing management; medical laboratory technology; medical radiologic technology; web page, digital/multimedia and information resources design.

Academics *Calendar:* quarters. *Degree:* certificates, diplomas, and associate. *Special study options:* academic remediation for entering students, advanced placement credit, distance learning, external degree program, internships, services for LD students.

Library Valdosta Technical College Library plus 1 other with 3,373 titles, 109 serial subscriptions, 225 audiovisual materials, an OPAC.

Computers on Campus 564 computers available on campus for general student use. A campuswide network can be accessed from off campus. Internet access, online (class) registration, at least one staffed computer lab available.

Student Life *Housing:* college housing not available.

Standardized Tests *Required:* ACT COMPASS or ASSET (for admission).

Costs (2006–07) *Tuition:* state resident $1116 full-time, $31 per credit hour part-time; nonresident $2232 full-time, $62 per credit hour part-time.

Applying *Options:* common application, deferred entrance. *Application fee:* $15. *Required:* high school transcript.

Freshmen Application Contact Valdosta Technical College, Student Customer Services, PO Box 928, 4089 Val Tech Road, Valdosta, GA 31603-0928. *Phone:* 229-333-1394.

WAYCROSS COLLEGE

Waycross, Georgia   **www.waycross.edu/**

Freshmen Application Contact Mrs. Susan Dukes, Assistant Director for Admissions, Waycross College, 2001 South Georgia Parkway, Waycross, GA 31503. *Phone:* 912-285-6133.

WEST CENTRAL TECHNICAL COLLEGE

Waco, Georgia   **www.westcentraltech.edu/**

- **State-supported** 2-year, founded 1968, part of Georgia Department of Technical and Adult Education
- **Coed,** 2,888 undergraduate students, 30% full-time, 71% women, 29% men

Undergraduates 877 full-time, 2,011 part-time. 47% are from out of state, 22% African American, 0.8% Asian American or Pacific Islander, 1% Hispanic American, 0.5% Native American. Freshmen *Admission:* 455 enrolled.

Faculty *Total:* 310, 27% full-time.

Majors Accounting; administrative assistant and secretarial science; business administration and management; child development; computer and information sciences related; computer programming (specific applications); computer systems networking and telecommunications; criminal justice/safety; data entry/microcomputer applications; dental hygiene; electrical, electronic and communications engineering technology; heavy equipment maintenance technology; industrial radiologic technology; information science/studies; manufacturing technology; marketing/marketing management; medical laboratory technology; medical radiologic technology; nursing (registered nurse training); web page, digital/multimedia and information resources design; word processing.

Academics *Calendar:* quarters. *Degree:* certificates, diplomas, and associate. *Special study options:* academic remediation for entering students, adult/continuing education programs, advanced placement credit, distance learning, external degree program, internships, part-time degree program, services for LD students.

Library 18,462 titles, 1,635 audiovisual materials.

Computers on Campus 109 computers available on campus for general student use. At least one staffed computer lab available.

Student Life *Housing:* college housing not available.

Standardized Tests *Required:* ACT COMPASS or ASSET (for admission).

Costs (2006–07) *Tuition:* state resident $1116 full-time, $31 per credit hour part-time; nonresident $2232 full-time, $62 per credit hour part-time.

Financial Aid Of all full-time matriculated undergraduates who enrolled in 2004, 45 Federal Work-Study jobs (averaging $1000).

Applying *Options:* electronic application, deferred entrance. *Application fee:* $25. *Required:* high school transcript.

Director of Admissions Mrs. Mary Alderhold, Director of Student Services, West Central Technical College, 176 Murphy Campus Boulevard, Waco, GA 30182. *Phone:* 770-537-5712. *Fax:* 770-537-7995. *E-mail:* malderhold@westcentral.edu.

WEST GEORGIA TECHNICAL COLLEGE

LaGrange, Georgia   **www.westgatech.edu/**

- **State-supported** 2-year, founded 1966, part of Georgia Department of Technical and Adult Education
- **Coed,** 1,858 undergraduate students, 45% full-time, 62% women, 38% men

Undergraduates 843 full-time, 1,015 part-time. Students come from 2 states and territories, 41% African American, 0.5% Asian American or Pacific Islander, 1% Hispanic American, 0.4% Native American, 7% transferred in. Freshmen *Admission:* 427 enrolled.

Faculty *Total:* 142, 32% full-time.

Majors Accounting; administrative assistant and secretarial science; automobile/automotive mechanics technology; child development; computer systems networking and telecommunications; criminal justice/safety; electrical, electronic and communications engineering technology; fire science; health information/medical records technology; industrial technology; information science/studies; marketing/marketing management; medical radiologic technology; pharmacy technician; plastics engineering technology; social work; web page, digital/multimedia and information resources design.

Academics *Calendar:* quarters. *Degree:* certificates, diplomas, and associate. *Special study options:* academic remediation for entering students, advanced placement credit, distance learning, internships, services for LD students.

Library 19,683 titles, 218 serial subscriptions, 525 audiovisual materials.

Student Life *Housing:* college housing not available. *Activities and Organizations:* Student Government Association, Vocational Industrial Clubs of America, Phi Beta Lambda. *Campus security:* 24-hour emergency response devices.

Standardized Tests *Required:* ACT COMPASS or ASSET (for admission).

Costs (2006–07) *Tuition:* state resident $1116 full-time, $31 per credit hour part-time; nonresident $2232 full-time, $62 per credit hour part-time.

Financial Aid Of all full-time matriculated undergraduates who enrolled in 2004, 68 Federal Work-Study jobs (averaging $800).

Applying *Options:* deferred entrance. *Application fee:* $15. *Required:* high school transcript.

Director of Admissions Lori Basham, Admissions Director, West Georgia Technical College, 303 Fort Drive, LaGrange, GA 30240. *Phone:* 706-837-4244. *Fax:* 706-845-4340. *E-mail:* lbasham@westgatech.edu.

WESTWOOD COLLEGE—ATLANTA MIDTOWN

Atlanta, Georgia   **www.westwood.edu/**

Director of Admissions Rory Laney, Director of Admissions, Westwood College–Atlanta Midtown, 1100 Spring Street, Ste. 101A, Atlanta, GA 30309. *Phone:* 404-870-8982.

▶ **See page 610 for the College Close-Up.**

WESTWOOD COLLEGE—ATLANTA NORTHLAKE

Atlanta, Georgia   **www.westwood.edu/**

- **Proprietary** 4-year
- **Coed,** 220 undergraduate students

Undergraduates 1% are from out of state, 60% African American, 3% Asian American or Pacific Islander, 3% Hispanic American.

Faculty *Student/faculty ratio:* 12:1.

Majors Animation, interactive technology, video graphics and special effects; architectural drafting and CAD/CADD; computer systems networking and telecommunications; design and visual communications; e-commerce; graphic design; interior design.

Academics *Degrees:* diplomas, associate, and bachelor's.

Applying *Required:* high school transcript, entrance assessment.

Director of Admissions Westwood College–Atlanta Northlake, 2220 Parklake Drive, Suite 175, Atlanta, GA 30345.

▶ **See page 612 for the College Close-Up.**

YOUNG HARRIS COLLEGE
Young Harris, Georgia   **www.yhc.edu/**

- **Independent United Methodist** 2-year, founded 1886
- **Rural** campus
- **Endowment** $110.4 million
- **Coed,** 533 undergraduate students, 95% full-time, 54% women, 46% men

Undergraduates 508 full-time, 25 part-time. Students come from 12 states and territories, 5 other countries, 6% are from out of state, 2% African American, 0.9% Asian American or Pacific Islander, 2% Hispanic American, 0.4% international, 4% transferred in, 90% live on campus. *Retention:* 63% of 2003 full-time freshmen returned.

Freshmen *Admission:* 1,421 applied, 821 admitted, 281 enrolled. *Average high school GPA:* 3.27. *Test scores:* SAT verbal scores over 500: 65%; SAT math scores over 500: 62%; ACT scores over 18: 81%; SAT verbal scores over 600: 17%; SAT math scores over 600: 16%; ACT scores over 24: 30%; SAT verbal scores over 700: 1%; SAT math scores over 700: 2%; ACT scores over 30: 2%.

Faculty *Total:* 54, 93% full-time, 76% with terminal degrees. *Student/faculty ratio:* 14:1.

Majors Agriculture; art; art teacher education; biological and physical sciences; biology/biological sciences; business administration and management; chemistry; clinical laboratory science/medical technology; computer science; criminal justice/law enforcement administration; dramatic/theater arts; education; English; French; geology/earth science; health teacher education; history; hospitality administration; international business/trade/commerce; journalism; liberal arts and sciences/liberal studies; mathematics; music; music related; music teacher education; natural sciences; nursing (registered nurse training); parks, recreation and leisure; physical therapy; physics; political science and government; pre-engineering; psychology; religious studies; sociology; Spanish.

Academics *Calendar:* semesters. *Degree:* associate. *Special study options:* academic remediation for entering students, accelerated degree program, advanced placement credit, double majors, internships, part-time degree program, summer session for credit.

Library J. Lon Duckworth Library with 55,201 titles, 260 serial subscriptions, 1,850 audiovisual materials, an OPAC, a Web page.

Computers on Campus 85 computers available on campus for general student use. A campuswide network can be accessed from student residence rooms and from off campus. Internet access, at least one staffed computer lab available.

Student Life *Housing:* on-campus residence required through sophomore year. *Options:* coed, men-only, women-only. *Activities and Organizations:* drama/theater group, student-run newspaper, choral group, Wesley Fellowship, BSU, Quantrek (outdoor club), intramurals. *Campus security:* 24-hour emergency response devices and patrols. *Student services:* health clinic, personal/psychological counseling.

Athletics Member NJCAA. *Intercollegiate sports:* baseball M(s), soccer M(s)/W(s), softball W(s), tennis W(s). *Intramural sports:* badminton M/W, basketball M/W, bowling M/W, football M/W, golf M/W, skiing (downhill) M/W, softball M/W, swimming and diving M/W, tennis M/W, ultimate Frisbee M/W, volleyball M/W, weight lifting M/W.

Standardized Tests *Required:* SAT or ACT (for admission).

Costs (2006–07) *Comprehensive fee:* $19,510 includes full-time tuition ($14,730) and room and board ($4780). Part-time tuition: $500 per hour. *Room and board:* college room only: $1970.

Financial Aid Of all full-time matriculated undergraduates who enrolled in 2004, 89 Federal Work-Study jobs (averaging $1000). 242 state and other part-time jobs (averaging $1000).

Applying *Options:* electronic application, early admission, deferred entrance. *Application fee:* $30. *Required:* high school transcript, minimum 2.5 GPA. *Required for some:* letters of recommendation. *Recommended:* interview. *Application deadline:* rolling (freshmen), rolling (transfers). *Notification:* continuous (freshmen).

Freshmen Application Contact Mr. Clinton G. Hobbs, Vice President for Enrollment Management, Young Harris College, PO Box 116, Young Harris, GA 30582-0098. *Phone:* 706-379-3111 Ext. 5147. *Toll-free phone:* 800-241-3754. *Fax:* 706-379-3108. *E-mail:* admissions@yhc.edu.

GUAM

GUAM COMMUNITY COLLEGE
Barrigada, Guam   **www.guamcc.net/**

- **Territory-supported** 2-year, founded 1977
- **Suburban** 22-acre campus
- **Endowment** $6.4 million
- **Coed,** 2,841 undergraduate students, 18% full-time, 64% women, 36% men

Undergraduates 504 full-time, 2,337 part-time. Students come from 10 other countries, 0.7% African American, 90% Asian American or Pacific Islander, 0.6% Hispanic American, 0.1% Native American, 2% international.

Freshmen *Admission:* 410 enrolled.

Faculty *Total:* 120, 62% full-time.

Majors Accounting; administrative assistant and secretarial science; architectural engineering technology; automobile/automotive mechanics technology; business administration and management; child development; civil engineering technology; computer programming (vendor/product certification); computer science; corrections; criminal justice/law enforcement administration; criminal justice/police science; education; electrical, electronic and communications engineering technology; fire science; hospitality administration; hospitality and recreation marketing; hotel/motel administration; kindergarten/preschool education; marketing/marketing management; marketing research; medical/clinical assistant; operations management; safety/security technology; sign language interpretation and translation; tourism and travel services management; tourism and travel services marketing; tourism promotion; vehicle and vehicle parts and accessories marketing.

Academics *Calendar:* semesters. *Degree:* certificates, diplomas, and associate. *Special study options:* academic remediation for entering students, adult/continuing education programs, cooperative education, double majors, English as a second language, honors programs, independent study, internships, off-campus study, part-time degree program, services for LD students, summer session for credit. *ROTC:* Army (c).

Library 15,806 titles, 375 serial subscriptions, 1,567 audiovisual materials, an OPAC.

Computers on Campus 220 computers available on campus for general student use. A campuswide network can be accessed. Internet access, at least one staffed computer lab available.

Student Life *Housing:* college housing not available. *Activities and Organizations:* Council of Post Secondary Student Association (COPSA), Phi Theta Kappa. *Campus security:* 12-hour patrols by trained security personnel. *Student services:* health clinic, personal/psychological counseling.

Costs (2006–07) *Tuition:* area resident $2100 full-time; nonresident $2850 full-time. *Required fees:* $244 full-time.

Financial Aid Of all full-time matriculated undergraduates who enrolled in 2004, 83 Federal Work-Study jobs (averaging $940).

Applying *Options:* common application, early admission. *Required:* high school transcript. *Application deadline:* rolling (freshmen). *Notification:* continuous (freshmen).

Freshmen Application Contact Mr. Patrick L. Clymer, Registrar, Guam Community College, PO Box 23069, Sesame Street, Barrigada, GU 96921, Guam. *Phone:* 671-735-5531. *Fax:* 671-735-5531. *E-mail:* pclymer@guamcc.edu.

HAWAII

HAWAII BUSINESS COLLEGE
Honolulu, Hawaii   **www.hbc.edu/**

- **Independent** 2-year, founded 1973
- **Urban** campus
- **Coed**

Undergraduates 279 full-time, 24 part-time. 7% African American, 78% Asian American or Pacific Islander, 2% Hispanic American, 1% Native American, 1% international.

Faculty *Student/faculty ratio:* 15:1.
Academics *Calendar:* quarters. *Degree:* certificates, diplomas, and associate. *Special study options:* academic remediation for entering students, adult/continuing education programs, advanced placement credit, cooperative education, double majors, English as a second language, external degree program, independent study, internships, part-time degree program, summer session for credit.
Standardized Tests *Required:* Wonderlic Basic Skills Test (for placement).
Applying *Options:* deferred entrance. *Application fee:* $30. *Required:* high school transcript. *Required for some:* essay or personal statement, interview.
Director of Admissions Seira Puletasi, Registrar, Hawaii Business College, 33 South King Street, Fourth Floor, Honolulu, HI 96813. *Phone:* 808-524-4014 Ext. 136.

HAWAII COMMUNITY COLLEGE

Hilo, Hawaii   www.hawcc.hawaii.edu/

Director of Admissions Mrs. Tammy M. Tanaka, Admissions Specialist, Hawaii Community College, 200 West Kawili Street, Hilo, HI 96720-4091. *Phone:* 808-974-7661.

HAWAII TOKAI INTERNATIONAL COLLEGE

Honolulu, Hawaii   www.tokai.edu/

- **Independent** 2-year, founded 1992, part of Tokai University Educational System (Japan)
- **Urban** campus
- **Coed,** 54 undergraduate students, 100% full-time, 46% women, 54% men

Undergraduates 54 full-time. Students come from 1 other state, 3 other countries, 100% Asian American or Pacific Islander, 60% live on campus. *Retention:* 83% of 2003 full-time freshmen returned.
Freshmen *Admission:* 2 applied, 2 admitted, 2 enrolled.
Faculty *Total:* 24, 42% full-time, 29% with terminal degrees. *Student/faculty ratio:* 4:1.
Majors Japanese; Japanese studies.
Academics *Calendar:* quarters. *Degree:* certificates, diplomas, and associate. *Special study options:* English as a second language, summer session for credit.
Library The Learning Center with 7,000 titles, 100 serial subscriptions, 500 audiovisual materials, an OPAC, a Web page.
Computers on Campus 45 computers available on campus for general student use. A campuswide network can be accessed from student residence rooms and from off campus. Internet access, at least one staffed computer lab available.
Student Life *Housing:* on-campus residence required for freshman year. *Options:* coed. *Activities and Organizations:* student-run newspaper, Basketball Club, Hula Club, Martial Arts Club, Chinese and Japanese Culture Club, fishing. *Campus security:* 24-hour patrols.
Costs (2006–07) *Tuition:* $375 per credit part-time.
Applying *Options:* deferred entrance. *Application fee:* $50. *Required:* essay or personal statement, high school transcript, interview. *Application deadline:* 9/1 (freshmen). *Notification:* continuous (freshmen).
Freshmen Application Contact Mr. Derrick Kerr, Director, Student Services, Hawaii Tokai International College, 2241 Kapiolani Boulevard, Honolulu, HI 96826. *Phone:* 808-983-4154. *Fax:* 808-983-4107. *E-mail:* htc!@tokai.edu.

HEALD COLLEGE-HONOLULU

Honolulu, Hawaii   www.heald.edu/

- **Independent** 2-year, founded 1863
- **Urban** campus
- **Coed,** 807 undergraduate students, 73% full-time, 62% women, 38% men

Undergraduates 591 full-time, 216 part-time. 3% African American, 80% Asian American or Pacific Islander, 2% Hispanic American, 0.2% Native American.
Freshmen *Admission:* 237 enrolled.
Faculty *Total:* 61, 49% full-time, 100% with terminal degrees. *Student/faculty ratio:* 17:1.

Majors Accounting; administrative assistant and secretarial science; business administration and management; electrical, electronic and communications engineering technology; information science/studies; legal administrative assistant/secretary; medical administrative assistant and medical secretary; tourism and travel services management.
Academics *Calendar:* quarters. *Degree:* certificates, diplomas, and associate. *Special study options:* academic remediation for entering students, advanced placement credit, internships, part-time degree program, summer session for credit.
Library Learning Resource Center with an OPAC.
Computers on Campus Internet access, at least one staffed computer lab available.
Student Life *Housing:* college housing not available.
Standardized Tests *Required:* COMPASS (for admission).
Applying *Options:* electronic application, early admission, deferred entrance. *Application fee:* $40. *Required:* high school transcript, interview. *Application deadline:* rolling (freshmen), rolling (transfers). *Notification:* continuous (freshmen).
Freshmen Application Contact Director of Admissions, Heald College-Honolulu, 1500 Kapiolani Boulevard, Suite 201, Honolulu, HI 96814. *Phone:* 808-955-1500. *Toll-free phone:* 800-755-3550. *Fax:* 808-955-6964. *E-mail:* info@heald.edu.

HONOLULU COMMUNITY COLLEGE

Honolulu, Hawaii   www.honolulu.hawaii.edu/

Freshmen Application Contact Admissions Office, Honolulu Community College, 874 Dillingham Boulevard, Honolulu, HI 96817. *Phone:* 808-845-9129. *E-mail:* admission@hccadb.hcc.hawaii.edu.

KAPIOLANI COMMUNITY COLLEGE

Honolulu, Hawaii   www.kcc.hawaii.edu/

- **State-supported** 2-year, founded 1957, part of University of Hawaii System
- **Urban** 52-acre campus
- **Coed,** 7,174 undergraduate students, 39% full-time, 58% women, 42% men

Undergraduates 2,833 full-time, 4,341 part-time. Students come from 27 states and territories, 59 other countries, 0.9% African American, 75% Asian American or Pacific Islander, 2% Hispanic American, 0.2% Native American, 7% international, 18% transferred in.
Freshmen *Admission:* 1,455 applied, 1,334 admitted, 787 enrolled.
Faculty *Total:* 344, 58% full-time.
Majors Accounting; clinical/medical laboratory technology; culinary arts; data processing and data processing technology; hotel/motel administration; industrial radiologic technology; legal administrative assistant/secretary; legal assistant/paralegal; liberal arts and sciences/liberal studies; marketing/marketing management; medical/clinical assistant; nursing (registered nurse training); occupational therapy; physical therapy; respiratory care therapy; special products marketing; tourism and travel services management.
Academics *Calendar:* semesters. *Degree:* certificates and associate. *Special study options:* academic remediation for entering students, adult/continuing education programs, advanced placement credit, cooperative education, distance learning, English as a second language, honors programs, internships, off-campus study, part-time degree program, services for LD students, student-designed majors, summer session for credit. *ROTC:* Army (c), Air Force (c).
Library Lama Library with 50,000 titles, 600 serial subscriptions.
Computers on Campus 175 computers available on campus for general student use. A campuswide network can be accessed from off campus. Internet access, at least one staffed computer lab available.
Student Life *Housing:* college housing not available. *Activities and Organizations:* student-run newspaper, choral group, Hawaiian Club, Phi Theta Kappa, Chinese Club, Hospitality Industry, Bayanihan. *Campus security:* 24-hour patrols.
Athletics *Intramural sports:* bowling M/W, volleyball M/W.
Costs (2006–07) *Tuition:* state resident $1344 full-time, $56 per credit hour part-time; nonresident $5976 full-time, $249 per credit hour part-time. *Required fees:* $60 full-time, $2 per credit hour part-time, $10 per term part-time.
Financial Aid Of all full-time matriculated undergraduates who enrolled in 2004, 30 Federal Work-Study jobs (averaging $2275). 440 state and other part-time jobs (averaging $1762).
Applying *Options:* early admission. *Application deadlines:* 7/1 (freshmen), 7/1 (transfers). *Notification:* continuous until 8/15 (freshmen).

Kapiolani Community College (continued)

Freshmen Application Contact Ms. Cynthia Suzuki, Chief Admissions Officer, Kapiolani Community College, 4303 Diamond Head Road, Honolulu, HI 96816-4421. *Phone:* 808-734-9897. *E-mail:* cio@leahi.kcc.hawaii.edu.

KAUAI COMMUNITY COLLEGE

Lihue, Hawaii   kauai.hawaii.edu/

- **State-supported** 2-year, founded 1965, part of University of Hawaii System
- **Small-town** 100-acre campus
- **Coed,** 1,210 undergraduate students

Majors Accounting; administrative assistant and secretarial science; autobody/collision and repair technology; automobile/automotive mechanics technology; carpentry; culinary arts; electrical, electronic and communications engineering technology; hospitality administration; kindergarten/preschool education; liberal arts and sciences/liberal studies; nursing (registered nurse training).
Academics *Calendar:* semesters. *Degree:* certificates and associate. *Special study options:* accelerated degree program, advanced placement credit, cooperative education, distance learning, English as a second language, internships, part-time degree program, services for LD students, summer session for credit.
Library S. W. Wilcox II Learning Resource Center plus 1 other with 51,875 titles, 165 serial subscriptions, 1,248 audiovisual materials, an OPAC, a Web page.
Computers on Campus 173 computers available on campus for general student use. A campuswide network can be accessed. Internet access, at least one staffed computer lab available.
Student Life *Housing:* college housing not available. *Activities and Organizations:* student-run newspaper, choral group, Food Service Club, Hui O Hana Po'okela (Hoper Club), Nursing Club, Phi Theta Kappa, Pamantasan Club. *Campus security:* student patrols, 6-hour evening patrols by trained security personnel. *Student services:* health clinic, personal/psychological counseling.
Athletics *Intramural sports:* basketball M/W, golf M/W, tennis M/W.
Costs (2005–06) *Tuition:* state resident $1176 full-time, $49 per credit part-time; nonresident $5808 full-time, $242 per credit part-time. Full-time tuition and fees vary according to course load. Part-time tuition and fees vary according to course load. *Required fees:* $15 full-time, $1 per credit part-time. *Waivers:* minority students, senior citizens, and employees or children of employees.
Financial Aid Of all full-time matriculated undergraduates who enrolled in 2004, 10 Federal Work-Study jobs (averaging $3000). 30 state and other part-time jobs (averaging $3000).
Applying *Options:* common application, early admission. *Required for some:* high school transcript. *Recommended:* high school transcript. *Application deadlines:* 8/1 (freshmen), 8/1 (transfers). *Notification:* continuous until 8/1 (freshmen).
Freshmen Application Contact Mr. Leighton Oride, Admissions Officer and Registrar, Kauai Community College, 3-1901 Kaumualii Highway, Lihue, HI 96766. *Phone:* 808-245-8225. *Fax:* 808-245-8297. *E-mail:* arkauai@hawaii.edu.

LEEWARD COMMUNITY COLLEGE

Pearl City, Hawaii   www.lcc.hawaii.edu/

Freshmen Application Contact Ms. Veda Tokashiki, Clerk, Leeward Community College, 96-045 Ala Ike, Pearl City, HI 96782-3393. *Phone:* 808-455-0217.

MAUI COMMUNITY COLLEGE

Kahului, Hawaii   mauicc.hawaii.edu/

Director of Admissions Mr. Stephen Kameda, Director of Admissions and Records, Maui Community College, 310 Kaahumanu Avenue, Kahului, HI 96732. *Phone:* 808-984-3267. *Toll-free phone:* 800-479-6692. *Fax:* 808-242-9618. *E-mail:* kameda@hawaii.edu.

TRANSPACIFIC HAWAII COLLEGE

Honolulu, Hawaii   www.transpacific.org/

- **Independent** 2-year, founded 1977
- **Suburban** campus
- **Endowment** $1.0 million
- **Coed, primarily women,** 240 undergraduate students, 100% full-time, 60% women, 40% men

Undergraduates 240 full-time. Students come from 3 other countries, 100% international, 2% transferred in.
Freshmen *Admission:* 110 applied, 98 admitted, 98 enrolled.
Faculty *Total:* 45, 36% full-time, 36% with terminal degrees. *Student/faculty ratio:* 5:1.
Majors Liberal arts and sciences/liberal studies.
Academics *Calendar:* quarters. *Degrees:* associate (majority of students are from outside of U.S. and participate in intensive ESL program in preparation for transfer to a 4-year institution). *Special study options:* academic remediation for entering students, accelerated degree program, English as a second language, independent study.
Library TransPacific Hawaii College Library with 606 titles, 6 serial subscriptions, 50 audiovisual materials, an OPAC, a Web page.
Computers on Campus 41 computers available on campus for general student use. A campuswide network can be accessed. Internet access, at least one staffed computer lab available.
Student Life *Housing:* college housing not available. *Activities and Organizations:* student-run newspaper, Basketball Club, Volleyball Club, Hula Club, Swim Club, Surfing Club. *Campus security:* 24-hour emergency response devices. *Student services:* personal/psychological counseling.
Athletics *Intramural sports:* basketball M/W, swimming and diving M/W, tennis M/W.
Costs (2006–07) *Tuition:* $16,250 full-time.
Applying *Options:* common application, electronic application, early admission, deferred entrance. *Application fee:* $50. *Required:* essay or personal statement, high school transcript. *Required for some:* interview. *Application deadline:* 8/5 (freshmen).
Freshmen Application Contact Dr. John Norris, President, TransPacific Hawaii College, 5257 Kalanianaole Highway, Honolulu, HI 96821. *Phone:* 808-377-5402 Ext. 313. *Fax:* 808-373-4754. *E-mail:* jnorris@transpacific.org.

WINDWARD COMMUNITY COLLEGE

Kaneohe, Hawaii   www.wcc.hawaii.edu/

- **State-supported** 2-year, founded 1972, part of University of Hawaii System
- **Small-town** 78-acre campus with easy access to Honolulu
- **Coed**

Undergraduates 6% are from out of state.
Academics *Calendar:* semesters. *Degree:* certificates and associate. *Special study options:* academic remediation for entering students, adult/continuing education programs, advanced placement credit, cooperative education, distance learning, independent study, part-time degree program, services for LD students, summer session for credit. *ROTC:* Army (c), Air Force (c).
Costs (2005–06) *Tuition:* state resident $1176 full-time, $49 per credit part-time; nonresident $5808 full-time, $242 per credit part-time. *Required fees:* $40 full-time.
Applying *Options:* early admission. *Application fee:* $25.
Director of Admissions Mr. Russell Chan, Registrar, Windward Community College, 45-720 Keaahala Road, Kaneohe, HI 96744. *Phone:* 808-235-7400.

IDAHO

APOLLO COLLEGE
Boise, Idaho **www.apolloboise.com/**

- **Proprietary** 2-year, founded 1980, administratively affiliated with U.S. Education Corporation
- **Coed**

Undergraduates 444 full-time, 25 part-time. Students come from 5 states and territories, 21% are from out of state, 0.9% African American, 2% Asian American or Pacific Islander, 9% Hispanic American, 0.9% Native American, 1% transferred in.

Faculty *Student/faculty ratio:* 10:1.

Academics *Calendar:* semesters. *Degree:* certificates, diplomas, and associate.

Student Life *Campus security:* 24-hour patrols.

Standardized Tests *Required:* Wonderlic aptitude test (for admission).

Applying *Required:* high school transcript, 3 letters of recommendation, interview. *Required for some:* essay or personal statement.

Director of Admissions Kevin Price, Director of Admissions, Apollo College, 1200 North Liberty, Boise, ID 83704. *Phone:* 208-377-8080 Ext. 35. *Toll-free phone:* 800-473-4365.

BRIGHAM YOUNG UNIVERSITY —IDAHO
Rexburg, Idaho **www.byui.edu/**

Freshmen Application Contact Mr. Steven Davis, Assistant Director of Admissions, Brigham Young University —Idaho, 120 Kimball, Rexburg, ID 83460-1615. *Phone:* 208-356-1026. *E-mail:* daviss@byui.edu.

COLLEGE OF SOUTHERN IDAHO
Twin Falls, Idaho **www.csi.edu/**

- **State and locally supported** 2-year, founded 1964
- **Small-town** 287-acre campus
- **Endowment** $15.0 million
- **Coed**

Undergraduates 3,175 full-time, 3,930 part-time. Students come from 29 states and territories, 27 other countries, 3% are from out of state, 0.5% African American, 0.9% Asian American or Pacific Islander, 9% Hispanic American, 0.8% Native American, 4% international, 10% live on campus.

Faculty *Student/faculty ratio:* 26:1.

Academics *Calendar:* semesters. *Degree:* certificates, diplomas, and associate. *Special study options:* academic remediation for entering students, adult/continuing education programs, advanced placement credit, cooperative education, distance learning, English as a second language, honors programs, independent study, internships, part-time degree program, services for LD students, summer session for credit.

Student Life *Campus security:* 24-hour emergency response devices and patrols, controlled dormitory access.

Athletics Member NJCAA.

Standardized Tests *Required:* ACT COMPASS (for admission). *Required for some:* ACT (for admission).

Costs (2005–06) *Tuition:* state resident $1900 full-time, $95 per credit part-time; nonresident $5300 full-time, $265 per credit part-time. *Room and board:* $3870. Room and board charges vary according to board plan.

Financial Aid Of all full-time matriculated undergraduates who enrolled in 2004, 250 Federal Work-Study jobs (averaging $2000). 100 state and other part-time jobs (averaging $2000).

Applying *Options:* common application. *Required:* high school transcript. *Required for some:* letters of recommendation, interview.

Director of Admissions Dr. John S. Martin, Director of Admissions, Registration, and Records, College of Southern Idaho, PO Box 1238, 315 Falls Avenue, Twin Falls, ID 83303. *Phone:* 208-732-6232. *Toll-free phone:* 800-680-0274. *Fax:* 208-736-3014.

EASTERN IDAHO TECHNICAL COLLEGE
Idaho Falls, Idaho **www.eitc.edu/**

- **State-supported** 2-year, founded 1970
- **Small-town** 40-acre campus
- **Endowment** $1.4 million
- **Coed**, 755 undergraduate students, 30% full-time, 71% women, 29% men

Undergraduates 229 full-time, 526 part-time. Students come from 5 states and territories, 0.9% African American, 0.6% Asian American or Pacific Islander, 6% Hispanic American, 0.5% Native American, 11% transferred in. *Retention:* 50% of 2003 full-time freshmen returned.

Freshmen *Admission:* 631 applied, 262 admitted, 141 enrolled.

Faculty *Total:* 111, 37% full-time, 0.9% with terminal degrees. *Student/faculty ratio:* 12:1.

Majors Accounting; administrative assistant and secretarial science; automobile/automotive mechanics technology; computer systems networking and telecommunications; desktop publishing and digital imaging design; diesel mechanics technology; electrical, electronic and communications engineering technology; legal assistant/paralegal; marketing/marketing management; medical/clinical assistant; surgical technology; welding technology.

Academics *Calendar:* semesters. *Degree:* certificates and associate. *Special study options:* academic remediation for entering students, adult/continuing education programs, cooperative education, distance learning, internships, part-time degree program, services for LD students, summer session for credit.

Library Richard and Lila Jordan Library plus 1 other with 18,000 titles, 125 serial subscriptions, 150 audiovisual materials, an OPAC, a Web page.

Computers on Campus 105 computers available on campus for general student use. A campuswide network can be accessed. Internet access, at least one staffed computer lab available.

Student Life *Housing:* college housing not available. *Campus security:* 24-hour patrols. *Student services:* personal/psychological counseling.

Costs (2006–07) *Tuition:* state resident $1578 full-time, $79 per credit part-time; nonresident $5784 full-time, $158 per credit part-time. *Required fees:* $124 full-time, $15 per term part-time.

Financial Aid Of all full-time matriculated undergraduates who enrolled in 2004, 37 Federal Work-Study jobs (averaging $1176). 11 state and other part-time jobs (averaging $1619).

Applying *Options:* deferred entrance. *Application fee:* $10. *Required:* high school transcript, interview, COMPASS. *Required for some:* essay or personal statement. *Application deadline:* 8/21 (freshmen).

Freshmen Application Contact Dr. Steve Albiston, Dean of Students, Eastern Idaho Technical College, 1600 South 25th East, Idaho Falls, ID 83404. *Phone:* 208-524-3000 Ext. 3366. *Toll-free phone:* 800-662-0261 Ext. 3371. *Fax:* 208-525-7026. *E-mail:* salbisto@eitc.edu.

ITT TECHNICAL INSTITUTE
Boise, Idaho **www.itt-tech.edu/**

- **Proprietary** primarily 2-year, founded 1906, part of ITT Educational Services, Inc
- **Urban** 1-acre campus
- **Coed**

Majors Animation, interactive technology, video graphics and special effects; business administration and management; CAD/CADD drafting/design technology; computer and information systems security; computer programming; computer software technology; computer systems networking and telecommunications; criminal justice/law enforcement administration; e-commerce; electrical, electronic and communications engineering technology; system, networking, and LAN/WAN management; web/multimedia management and webmaster; web page, digital/multimedia and information resources design.

Academics *Calendar:* quarters. *Degrees:* associate and bachelor's.

Library a Web page.

Computers on Campus Internet access, at least one staffed computer lab available.

Student Life *Housing:* college housing not available.

Standardized Tests *Required:* Wonderlic aptitude test (for admission).

Costs (2005–06) *Tuition:* Please see school catalog for specific information.

Financial Aid Of all full-time matriculated undergraduates who enrolled in 2004, 9 Federal Work-Study jobs (averaging $5500).

Applying *Options:* deferred entrance. *Application fee:* $100. *Required:* high school transcript, interview. *Recommended:* letters of recommendation. *Application deadline:* rolling (freshmen), rolling (transfers). *Notification:* continuous (freshmen).

ITT Technical Institute (continued)
Freshmen Application Contact Terry G. Lowder, Director of Recruitment, ITT Technical Institute, 12302 West Explorer Drive, Boise, ID 83713. *Phone:* 208-322-8844. *Toll-free phone:* 800-666-4888. *Fax:* 208-322-0173.

NORTH IDAHO COLLEGE
Coeur d'Alene, Idaho
www.nic.edu/

- **State and locally supported** 2-year, founded 1933
- **Small-town** 42-acre campus
- **Endowment** $5.4 million
- **Coed,** 4,099 undergraduate students, 61% full-time, 62% women, 38% men

Undergraduates 2,492 full-time, 1,607 part-time. Students come from 27 states and territories, 16 other countries, 0.4% African American, 0.9% Asian American or Pacific Islander, 2% Hispanic American, 2% Native American, 14% transferred in.
Freshmen *Admission:* 3,148 applied, 1,855 admitted, 1,015 enrolled. *Average high school GPA:* 2.84.
Faculty *Total:* 297, 52% full-time, 6% with terminal degrees. *Student/faculty ratio:* 14:1.
Majors Administrative assistant and secretarial science; agriculture; American Indian/Native American studies; anthropology; art; astronomy; athletic training; automobile/automotive mechanics technology; biological and physical sciences; biology/biological sciences; botany/plant biology; business administration and management; business teacher education; carpentry; chemistry; clinical laboratory science/medical technology; commercial and advertising art; computer and information sciences related; computer programming; computer science; computer/technical support; criminal justice/law enforcement administration; criminal justice/police science; culinary arts; developmental and child psychology; drafting and design technology; dramatic/theater arts; education; electrical, electronic and communications engineering technology; elementary education; engineering; English; environmental health; fish/game management; forestry; French; geology/earth science; German; health/health care administration; heating, air conditioning, ventilation and refrigeration maintenance technology; heavy equipment maintenance technology; history; hospitality administration; human services; journalism; legal administrative assistant/secretary; legal assistant/paralegal; liberal arts and sciences/liberal studies; machine tool technology; marine technology; mass communication/media; mathematics; medical administrative assistant and medical secretary; music; music teacher education; nursing (licensed practical/vocational nurse training); nursing (registered nurse training); physical sciences; physics; political science and government; psychology; social sciences; sociology; Spanish; welding technology; wildlife and wildlands science and management; wildlife biology; zoology/animal biology.
Academics *Calendar:* semesters. *Degree:* certificates and associate. *Special study options:* academic remediation for entering students, adult/continuing education programs, advanced placement credit, cooperative education, distance learning, English as a second language, independent study, internships, off-campus study, part-time degree program, services for LD students, summer session for credit.
Library Molstead Library Computer Center with 60,893 titles, 751 serial subscriptions, an OPAC, a Web page.
Computers on Campus 145 computers available on campus for general student use. A campuswide network can be accessed. Internet access, at least one staffed computer lab available.
Student Life *Housing Options:* Campus housing is university owned. *Activities and Organizations:* drama/theater group, student-run newspaper, choral group, Ski Club, Fusion, Baptist student ministries, Journalism Club, Phi Theta Kappa. *Campus security:* 24-hour emergency response devices and patrols, late-night transport/escort service. *Student services:* health clinic, personal/psychological counseling, women's center, legal services.
Athletics Member NJCAA. *Intercollegiate sports:* basketball M(s)/W(s), cheerleading M(s)/W(s), soccer M(s)/W(s), softball W(s), volleyball W(s), wrestling M(s). *Intramural sports:* basketball M/W, bowling M/W, cheerleading M/W, crew M(c)/W(c), cross-country running M(c)/W(c), football M/W, golf M/W, racquetball M/W, sailing M(c)/W(c), skiing (cross-country) M(c)/W(c), skiing (downhill) M(c)/W(c), soccer M(c)/W(c), softball M/W, table tennis M/W, tennis M/W, track and field M(c)/W(c), volleyball M/W.
Costs (2005–06) *Tuition:* area resident $1068 full-time, $67 per credit part-time; state resident $2068 full-time, $129 per credit part-time; nonresident $5620 full-time, $351 per credit part-time. Full-time tuition and fees vary according to course load, program, and reciprocity agreements. *Required fees:* $820 full-time, $60 per credit part-time. *Room and board:* $5010; room only: $3210. Room and board charges vary according to board plan and housing facility. *Waivers:* senior citizens and employees or children of employees.
Financial Aid Of all full-time matriculated undergraduates who enrolled in 2004, 142 Federal Work-Study jobs (averaging $1425). 106 state and other part-time jobs (averaging $1327).

Applying *Options:* electronic application, early admission, deferred entrance. *Application fee:* $25. *Required for some:* essay or personal statement, high school transcript, county residency certificate. *Application deadlines:* 8/20 (freshmen), 8/20 (transfers).
Freshmen Application Contact Dr. Candace Wheeler, Director of Distance Education, North Idaho College, 1000 West Garden Avenue, Coeur d'Alene, ID 83814-2199. *Phone:* 208-769-3436. *Toll-free phone:* 877-404-4536 Ext. 3311. *Fax:* 208-769-3399. *E-mail:* admit@nic.edu.

ILLINOIS

BLACK HAWK COLLEGE
Moline, Illinois
www.bhc.edu/

- **State and locally supported** 2-year, founded 1946, part of Black Hawk College District System
- **Urban** 161-acre campus
- **Coed**

Undergraduates 3,138 full-time, 3,462 part-time. Students come from 5 states and territories, 3% are from out of state, 7% African American, 0.8% Asian American or Pacific Islander, 7% Hispanic American, 0.5% Native American, 0.1% transferred in. *Retention:* 62% of 2003 full-time freshmen returned.
Faculty *Student/faculty ratio:* 18:1.
Academics *Calendar:* semesters. *Degree:* certificates and associate. *Special study options:* academic remediation for entering students, accelerated degree program, adult/continuing education programs, advanced placement credit, cooperative education, distance learning, English as a second language, independent study, internships, off-campus study, part-time degree program, services for LD students, study abroad, summer session for credit.
Student Life *Campus security:* 24-hour patrols.
Athletics Member NJCAA.
Standardized Tests *Required for some:* ACT (for placement), COMPASS.
Costs (2005–06) *Tuition:* area resident $1860 full-time, $62 per credit hour part-time; state resident $4200 full-time, $140 per credit hour part-time; nonresident $7770 full-time, $259 per credit hour part-time. Full-time tuition and fees vary according to program and reciprocity agreements. Part-time tuition and fees vary according to program and reciprocity agreements. *Required fees:* $210 full-time, $7 per credit hour part-time. *Payment plans:* installment, deferred payment.
Financial Aid Of all full-time matriculated undergraduates who enrolled in 2004, 173 Federal Work-Study jobs (averaging $1531). 196 state and other part-time jobs (averaging $1228).
Applying *Options:* early admission, deferred entrance. *Required:* high school transcript.
Freshmen Application Contact Ms. Rose Hernandez, Coordinator of Recruitment, Black Hawk College, 6600 34th Avenue, Moline, IL 61265. *Phone:* 309-796-5342.

BROWN MACKIE COLLEGE—MOLINE
Moline, Illinois
www.brownmackie.edu/locations.asp?locid=21

- **Coed,** 119 undergraduate students

Faculty *Student/faculty ratio:* 10:1.
Academics *Degree:* diplomas.
Costs (2005–06) *Tuition:* Contact institution directly for tuition and fees.
Applying *Required:* high school transcript, interview.
Director of Admissions Ms. Ann M. Sandoval, Brown Mackie College–Moline, 1527 47th Avenue, Moline, IL 61265-7062. *Phone:* 309-762-2100. *Fax:* 309-762-2374. *E-mail:* asandoral@brownmackie.edu.

▶ **See page 518 for the College Close-Up.**

CAREER COLLEGES OF CHICAGO

Chicago, Illinois   www.careerchi.com/

- **Proprietary** 2-year, founded 1950
- **Urban** campus
- **Coed, primarily women**

Undergraduates 35 full-time, 109 part-time. Students come from 1 other state.
Faculty *Student/faculty ratio:* 11:1.
Academics *Calendar:* quarters. *Degree:* certificates and associate. *Special study options:* advanced placement credit, internships, part-time degree program, summer session for credit.
Student Life *Campus security:* 24-hour emergency response devices, guard on duty during building hours.
Standardized Tests *Recommended:* ACT (for admission).
Financial Aid *Financial aid deadline:* 6/1.
Applying *Options:* deferred entrance. *Application fee:* $40. *Required:* high school transcript, interview.
Freshmen Application Contact Ms. Rosa Alvarado, Admissions Assistant, Career Colleges of Chicago, 11 East Adams Street, Chicago, IL 60603. *Phone:* 312-895-6306.

CARL SANDBURG COLLEGE

Galesburg, Illinois   www.sandburg.edu/

Director of Admissions Ms. Carol Kreider, Director of Admissions and Records, Carl Sandburg College, 2400 Tom L. Wilson Boulevard, Galesburg, IL 61401-9576. *Phone:* 309-341-5234.

CITY COLLEGES OF CHICAGO, HAROLD WASHINGTON COLLEGE

Chicago, Illinois   hwashington.ccc.edu/

Director of Admissions Mr. Terry Pendleton, Admissions Coordinator, City Colleges of Chicago, Harold Washington College, 30 East Lake Street, Chicago, IL 60601-2449. *Phone:* 312-553-6006.

CITY COLLEGES OF CHICAGO, HARRY S. TRUMAN COLLEGE

Chicago, Illinois   www.trumancollege.cc/

Director of Admissions Mrs. Kelly O'Malley, Assistant Dean, Student Services, City Colleges of Chicago, Harry S. Truman College, 1145 West Wilson Avenue, Chicago, IL 60640-5616. *Phone:* 773-907-4720.

CITY COLLEGES OF CHICAGO, KENNEDY-KING COLLEGE

Chicago, Illinois   kennedyking.ccc.edu/

Freshmen Application Contact Ms. Joyce Collins, Clerical Supervisor for Admissions and Records, City Colleges of Chicago, Kennedy-King College, 6800 South Wentworth Avenue, Chicago, IL 60621. *Phone:* 773-602-5000 Ext. 5055.

CITY COLLEGES OF CHICAGO, MALCOLM X COLLEGE

Chicago, Illinois   malcolmx.ccc.edu/

Director of Admissions Mr. Ghingo Brooks, Vice President of Enrollment Management and Student Services, City Colleges of Chicago, Malcolm X College, 1900 West Van Buren Street, Chicago, IL 60612. *Phone:* 312-850-7120.

CITY COLLEGES OF CHICAGO, OLIVE-HARVEY COLLEGE

Chicago, Illinois   oliveharvey.ccc.edu/

Director of Admissions Ms. Ernestine Taylor, Director of Admissions, City Colleges of Chicago, Olive-Harvey College, 10001 South Woodlawn, Chicago, IL 60628-1696. *Phone:* 773-291-6359.

CITY COLLEGES OF CHICAGO, RICHARD J. DALEY COLLEGE

Chicago, Illinois   daley.ccc.edu/

Freshmen Application Contact Ms. Karla Reynolds, Registrar, City Colleges of Chicago, Richard J. Daley College, 7500 South Pulaski Road, Chicago, IL 60652-1242. *Phone:* 773-838-7599. *E-mail:* kreynolds@ccc.edu.

CITY COLLEGES OF CHICAGO, WILBUR WRIGHT COLLEGE

Chicago, Illinois   wright.ccc.edu/

- **State and locally supported** 2-year, founded 1934, part of City Colleges of Chicago
- **Urban** 20-acre campus with easy access to Chicago, Illinois
- **Coed,** 7,365 undergraduate students, 30% full-time, 58% women, 42% men

Undergraduates 2,211 full-time, 5,154 part-time. 10% African American, 10% Asian American or Pacific Islander, 40% Hispanic American, 1% Native American.
Freshmen *Admission:* 2,825 applied, 2,825 admitted. *Average high school GPA:* 2.5.
Faculty *Total:* 257, 42% full-time, 28% with terminal degrees. *Student/faculty ratio:* 22:1.
Majors Accounting; architectural engineering technology; architectural technology; art; biological and physical sciences; business administration and management; computer and information sciences; computer and information systems security; criminal justice/police science; data processing and data processing technology; elementary education; engineering; English; environmental engineering technology; environmental science; general studies; gerontology; Hispanic-American, Puerto Rican, and Mexican-American/Chicano studies; journalism; liberal arts and sciences/liberal studies; library science; machine tool technology; marketing/marketing management; medical radiologic technology; modern languages; music; occupational therapy; physical sciences; pre-engineering; speech and rhetoric.
Academics *Calendar:* semesters. *Degree:* certificates and associate. *Special study options:* academic remediation for entering students, accelerated degree program, adult/continuing education programs, distance learning, English as a second language, part-time degree program, summer session for credit.
Library Learning Resource Center plus 1 other with 60,000 titles, 350 serial subscriptions.
Computers on Campus 700 computers available on campus for general student use. A campuswide network can be accessed. Internet access, at least one staffed computer lab available.
Student Life *Housing:* college housing not available. *Activities and Organizations:* drama/theater group, student-run newspaper, choral group, student government, Circle K, Phi Theta Kappa, Black Student Union. *Campus security:* 24-hour emergency response devices and patrols, student patrols, late-night transport/escort service. *Student services:* legal services.
Athletics Member NJCAA. *Intercollegiate sports:* basketball M(s)/W(s), wrestling M(s). *Intramural sports:* basketball M, cross-country running M/W, golf M/W, volleyball M/W, weight lifting M/W, wrestling M/W.
Costs (2006–07) *Tuition:* area resident $2304 full-time, $72 per credit hour part-time; state resident $5787 full-time, $181 per credit hour part-time; nonresident $9332 full-time, $292 per credit hour part-time. *Required fees:* $250 full-time, $75 per term part-time.
Financial Aid Of all full-time matriculated undergraduates who enrolled in 2004, 67 Federal Work-Study jobs (averaging $1000).
Applying *Options:* common application, early admission, deferred entrance. *Application deadline:* rolling (freshmen), rolling (transfers). *Notification:* continuous (freshmen).

City Colleges of Chicago, Wilbur Wright College (continued)

Freshmen Application Contact Ms. Amy Aiello, Assistant Dean of Student Services, City Colleges of Chicago, Wilbur Wright College, 4300 North Narragansett, Chicago, IL 60634. *Phone:* 773-481-8207.

COLLEGE OF DuPAGE

Glen Ellyn, Illinois   **www.cod.edu/**

- **State and locally supported** 2-year, founded 1967, part of Illinois Community College Board
- **Suburban** 297-acre campus with easy access to Chicago
- **Endowment** $10.5 million
- **Coed,** 27,117 undergraduate students, 32% full-time, 55% women, 45% men

Undergraduates 8,784 full-time, 18,333 part-time. Students come from 19 states and territories, 6% African American, 12% Asian American or Pacific Islander, 14% Hispanic American, 0.3% Native American, 7% transferred in. *Retention:* 65% of 2003 full-time freshmen returned.
Freshmen *Admission:* 3,158 admitted, 3,158 enrolled.
Faculty *Total:* 1,297, 23% full-time, 17% with terminal degrees. *Student/faculty ratio:* 21:1.
Majors Accounting; administrative assistant and secretarial science; automobile/automotive mechanics technology; baking and pastry arts; biological and physical sciences; building/property maintenance and management; business administration and management; child care and support services management; child care provision; child development; cinematography and film/video production; commercial and advertising art; communications systems installation and repair technology; communications technology; computer installation and repair technology; computer programming (specific applications); computer typography and composition equipment operation; corrections; criminal justice/law enforcement administration; criminal justice/police science; culinary arts; data entry/microcomputer applications related; dental hygiene; design and visual communications; desktop publishing and digital imaging design; drafting and design technology; electrical, electronic and communications engineering technology; electrical/electronics equipment installation and repair; electromechanical technology; emergency medical technology (EMT paramedic); engineering; fashion and fabric consulting; fashion/apparel design; fashion merchandising; fire science; graphic and printing equipment operation/production; health/health care administration; health information/medical records administration; health information/medical records technology; heating, air conditioning, ventilation and refrigeration maintenance technology; hospital and health care facilities administration; hospitality administration; hotel/motel administration; human services; industrial electronics technology; industrial technology; interior design; landscaping and groundskeeping; legal administrative assistant/secretary; liberal arts and sciences/liberal studies; library assistant; library science; machine tool technology; manufacturing technology; marketing/marketing management; massage therapy; mechanical design technology; medical radiologic technology; merchandising; nuclear medical technology; nursing (registered nurse training); occupational therapist assistant; occupational therapy; office management; ornamental horticulture; photography; physical therapist assistant; plastics engineering technology; precision production trades; real estate; respiratory care therapy; restaurant, culinary, and catering management; retailing; robotics technology; sales, distribution and marketing; selling skills and sales; speech-language pathology; substance abuse/addiction counseling; surgical technology; tourism and travel services management; tourism and travel services marketing; tourism promotion; transportation technology; welding technology.
Academics *Calendar:* quarters. *Degree:* certificates and associate. *Special study options:* academic remediation for entering students, accelerated degree program, adult/continuing education programs, advanced placement credit, cooperative education, distance learning, double majors, English as a second language, external degree program, honors programs, independent study, internships, off-campus study, part-time degree program, services for LD students, student-designed majors, study abroad, summer session for credit.
Library College of DuPage Library with 203,300 titles, 6,005 serial subscriptions, 33,600 audiovisual materials, an OPAC, a Web page.
Computers on Campus 2403 computers available on campus for general student use. A campuswide network can be accessed from off campus. Internet access, online (class) registration, at least one staffed computer lab available. Computer purchase or lease plan available.
Student Life *Housing:* college housing not available. *Activities and Organizations:* drama/theater group, student-run newspaper, choral group, Latino Ethnic Awareness Association, The Christian Group, Phi Theta Kappa, International Students Organization, Muslim Student Association. *Campus security:* 24-hour emergency response devices and patrols, student patrols, late-night transport/escort service. *Student services:* health clinic, personal/psychological counseling.
Athletics Member NJCAA. *Intercollegiate sports:* baseball M, basketball M/W, cheerleading M/W, cross-country running M/W, football M, golf M, soccer M/W, softball W, swimming and diving M/W, tennis M/W, track and field M/W,

volleyball W. *Intramural sports:* basketball M/W, bowling M/W, golf M/W, ice hockey M(c), racquetball M/W, soccer M/W, softball M/W, swimming and diving M/W, tennis M/W, volleyball M/W, weight lifting M/W.
Costs (2006–07) *Tuition:* area resident $2850 full-time, $96 per semester hour part-time; state resident $6690 full-time, $223 per semester hour part-time; nonresident $8400 full-time, $280 per semester hour part-time. *Required fees:* $634 full-time.
Applying *Options:* early admission, deferred entrance. *Application fee:* $10. *Application deadline:* rolling (freshmen), rolling (transfers). *Notification:* continuous (freshmen).
Freshmen Application Contact Mrs. Christine A. Legner, Coordinator of Admission Services, College of DuPage, SRC 2046, 425 Fawell Boulevard, Glen Ellyn, IL 60137-6599. *Phone:* 630-942-2442. *Fax:* 630-790-2686. *E-mail:* protis@cdnet.cod.edu.

COLLEGE OF LAKE COUNTY

Grayslake, Illinois   **www.clcillinois.edu/**

- **District-supported** 2-year, founded 1967, part of Illinois Community College Board
- **Suburban** 226-acre campus with easy access to Chicago and Milwaukee
- **Endowment** $2.6 million
- **Coed,** 15,745 undergraduate students, 29% full-time, 57% women, 43% men

Undergraduates 4,514 full-time, 11,231 part-time. Students come from 22 states and territories, 42 other countries, 1% are from out of state, 9% African American, 6% Asian American or Pacific Islander, 16% Hispanic American, 0.3% Native American, 2% international, 8% transferred in. *Retention:* 60% of 2003 full-time freshmen returned.
Freshmen *Admission:* 1,959 applied, 1,959 admitted, 1,959 enrolled.
Faculty *Total:* 794, 22% full-time, 10% with terminal degrees. *Student/faculty ratio:* 20:1.
Majors Accounting technology and bookkeeping; administrative assistant and secretarial science; architectural drafting; art; automobile/automotive mechanics technology; biological and physical sciences; business administration and management; business automation/technology/data entry; business computer programming; business systems networking/ telecommunications; chemical technology; child care provision; civil engineering technology; computer installation and repair technology; construction engineering technology; criminal justice/police science; dental hygiene; electrical, electronic and communications engineering technology; electrician; engineering; fire protection and safety technology; heating, air conditioning, ventilation and refrigeration maintenance technology; industrial mechanics and maintenance technology; landscaping and groundskeeping; liberal arts and sciences/liberal studies; machine shop technology; mechanical engineering/mechanical technology; medical office management; medical radiologic technology; music; music teacher education; natural resources management and policy; nursing (registered nurse training); ornamental horticulture; restaurant, culinary, and catering management; sales operations; social work; substance abuse/addiction counseling; technical and business writing; turf and turfgrass management.
Academics *Calendar:* semesters. *Degree:* certificates and associate. *Special study options:* academic remediation for entering students, adult/continuing education programs, advanced placement credit, cooperative education, distance learning, double majors, English as a second language, honors programs, independent study, internships, off-campus study, part-time degree program, services for LD students, student-designed majors, study abroad, summer session for credit.
Library College of Lake County Library plus 1 other with 106,842 titles, 766 serial subscriptions, 7,433 audiovisual materials, an OPAC, a Web page.
Computers on Campus 1500 computers available on campus for general student use. A campuswide network can be accessed from off campus. Internet access, online (class) registration, at least one staffed computer lab available.
Student Life *Housing:* college housing not available. *Activities and Organizations:* drama/theater group, student-run newspaper, radio station, choral group, Latino Alliance, Asian Student Alliance, Black Student Union, International Student Council, Phi Theta Kappa. *Campus security:* 24-hour emergency response devices and patrols, late-night transport/escort service. *Student services:* health clinic, personal/psychological counseling, women's center.
Athletics Member NJCAA. *Intercollegiate sports:* baseball M(s), basketball M(s)/W(s), cross-country running M(s)/W(s), golf M(s), soccer M(s)/W(s), softball W(s), tennis M(s)/W(s), volleyball W(s). *Intramural sports:* cheerleading W, golf M/W.
Costs (2006–07) *Tuition:* area resident $2130 full-time, $71 per credit hour part-time; state resident $5880 full-time, $196 per credit hour part-time; nonresident $8010 full-time, $267 per credit hour part-time. *Required fees:* $270 full-time, $9 per credit hour part-time.

Financial Aid Of all full-time matriculated undergraduates who enrolled in 2004, 68 Federal Work-Study jobs (averaging $1856). 178 state and other part-time jobs (averaging $1937).
Applying *Options:* common application, electronic application, early admission, deferred entrance. *Required for some:* high school transcript, interview. *Application deadline:* rolling (freshmen), rolling (transfers). *Notification:* continuous (freshmen).
Freshmen Application Contact Mr. Melvin Allen, Director, Student Recruitment, College of Lake County, 19351 West Washington Street, Grayslake, IL 60030-1198. *Phone:* 847-543-2383. *Fax:* 847-543-3061. *E-mail:* mallen@ clcillinois.edu.

THE COLLEGE OF OFFICE TECHNOLOGY
Chicago, Illinois   **www.cotedu.com/**

Director of Admissions Mr. William Bolton, Director of Admissions, The College of Office Technology, 1514-20 West Division Street, Second Floor, Chicago, IL 60622. *Phone:* 773-278-0042. *E-mail:* bbolton@cotedu.com.

THE COOKING AND HOSPITALITY INSTITUTE OF CHICAGO
Chicago, Illinois   **www.chicnet.org/**

Director of Admissions Mr. Alan Schultz, Director of Admissions, The Cooking and Hospitality Institute of Chicago, 361 West Chestnut, Chicago, IL 60610. *Phone:* 312-873-2064. *Toll-free phone:* 877-828-7772.

▶ **See page 536 for the College Close-Up.**

DANVILLE AREA COMMUNITY COLLEGE
Danville, Illinois   **www.dacc.cc.il.us/**

- **State and locally supported** 2-year, founded 1946, part of Illinois Community College Board
- **Small-town** 50-acre campus
- **Endowment** $978,329
- **Coed**

Undergraduates Students come from 4 states and territories, 1% are from out of state, 10% African American, 0.7% Asian American or Pacific Islander, 3% Hispanic American, 0.1% Native American.
Faculty *Student/faculty ratio:* 20:1.
Academics *Calendar:* semesters. *Degree:* certificates and associate. *Special study options:* academic remediation for entering students, adult/continuing education programs, advanced placement credit, cooperative education, distance learning, double majors, English as a second language, independent study, internships, part-time degree program, services for LD students, summer session for credit.
Student Life *Campus security:* 24-hour patrols.
Athletics Member NJCAA.
Standardized Tests *Required for some:* ACT ASSET.
Costs (2005–06) *Tuition:* state resident $1392 full-time, $58 per credit hour part-time; nonresident $3600 full-time, $150 per credit hour part-time. *Required fees:* $144 full-time, $6 per credit hour part-time.
Financial Aid Of all full-time matriculated undergraduates who enrolled in 2004, 119 Federal Work-Study jobs (averaging $4300). 100 state and other part-time jobs (averaging $4000).
Applying *Options:* early admission, deferred entrance. *Required:* high school transcript.
Director of Admissions Ms. Stacy L. Ehmen, Director of Admissions of Records/Registrar, Danville Area Community College, 2000 East Main Street, Danville, IL 61832-5199. *Phone:* 217-443-8800.

ELGIN COMMUNITY COLLEGE
Elgin, Illinois   **www.elgin.edu/**

- **State and locally supported** 2-year, founded 1949, part of Illinois Community College Board
- **Suburban** 145-acre campus with easy access to Chicago
- **Coed**

Undergraduates 3,348 full-time, 7,503 part-time. Students come from 4 states and territories, 22 other countries, 1% are from out of state, 5% African American,

6% Asian American or Pacific Islander, 16% Hispanic American, 0.2% Native American, 0.3% international, 29% transferred in.
Faculty *Student/faculty ratio:* 23:1.
Academics *Calendar:* semesters. *Degree:* certificates, diplomas, and associate. *Special study options:* academic remediation for entering students, accelerated degree program, adult/continuing education programs, advanced placement credit, cooperative education, distance learning, double majors, English as a second language, honors programs, independent study, internships, off-campus study, part-time degree program, services for LD students, student-designed majors, summer session for credit.
Student Life *Campus security:* 24-hour patrols.
Athletics Member NJCAA.
Standardized Tests *Recommended:* ACT (for placement).
Costs (2005–06) *Tuition:* area resident $2250 full-time, $75 per credit hour part-time; state resident $7666 full-time, $256 per credit hour part-time; nonresident $9947 full-time, $332 per credit hour part-time. *Required fees:* $10 full-time, $5 per term part-time.
Applying *Options:* early admission. *Application fee:* $15. *Required for some:* high school transcript.
Director of Admissions Ms. Kelly Sinclair, Admissions, Recruitment, and Student Life, Elgin Community College, 1700 Spartan Drive, Elgin, IL 60123. *Phone:* 847-214-7414.

FOX COLLEGE
Oak Lawn, Illinois   **www.foxcollege.com/**

- **Proprietary** 2-year, founded 1932
- **Coed**

Undergraduates 251 full-time. 8% African American, 0.5% Asian American or Pacific Islander, 54% Hispanic American.
Costs (2005–06) *Tuition:* $12,720 full-time.
Director of Admissions Ms. Susan Szala, Director of Admissions, Fox College, 4201 West 93rd Street, Oak Lawn, IL 60453. *Phone:* 708-636-7700. *Toll-free phone:* 866-636-7711. *Fax:* 708-636-8078. *E-mail:* sszala@ foxcollege.edu.

GEM CITY COLLEGE
Quincy, Illinois   **www.gemcitycollege.com/**

Director of Admissions Admissions Director, Gem City College, PO Box 179, Quincy, IL 62306-0179. *Phone:* 217-222-0391.

HEARTLAND COMMUNITY COLLEGE
Normal, Illinois   **www.heartland.edu/**

- **State and locally supported** 2-year, founded 1990, part of Illinois Community College Board
- **Urban** campus
- **Coed,** 4,667 undergraduate students

Undergraduates Students come from 5 states and territories, 2 other countries, 1% are from out of state. *Retention:* 55% of 2003 full-time freshmen returned.
Freshmen *Admission:* 1,051 admitted.
Faculty *Total:* 253, 28% full-time. *Student/faculty ratio:* 19:1.
Majors Administrative assistant and secretarial science; biological and physical sciences; business administration and management; business and personal/financial services marketing; child care provision; child development; computer and information sciences; computer and information sciences related; computer engineering technology; computer programming; computer programming (specific applications); computer programming (vendor/product certification); computer science; computer systems networking and telecommunications; computer/technical support; corrections; data entry/microcomputer applications; data entry/microcomputer applications related; drafting and design technology; electrical, electronic and communications engineering technology; engineering; heating, air conditioning, ventilation and refrigeration maintenance technology; industrial mechanics and maintenance technology; industrial technology; information science/studies; information technology; kindergarten/preschool education; liberal arts and sciences/liberal studies; machine tool technology; management information systems; mechanical design technology; nursing (licensed practical/vocational nurse training); nursing (registered nurse training); quality control

Heartland Community College (continued)

technology; system administration; web page, digital/multimedia and information resources design; welding technology.

Academics *Calendar:* semesters. *Degree:* certificates and associate. *Special study options:* academic remediation for entering students, adult/continuing education programs, advanced placement credit, cooperative education, distance learning, double majors, English as a second language, independent study, internships, part-time degree program, services for LD students, study abroad, summer session for credit. *ROTC:* Army (c).

Library Heartland Community College Library with 5,000 titles, 188 serial subscriptions, 4,000 audiovisual materials, an OPAC, a Web page.

Computers on Campus 400 computers available on campus for general student use. A campuswide network can be accessed. Internet access, at least one staffed computer lab available.

Student Life *Housing:* college housing not available. *Activities and Organizations:* drama/theater group, student-run newspaper, choral group, Environmental Club, Early Childhood Club, student government, Nursing Club, Phi Theta Kappa. *Campus security:* 24-hour emergency response devices and patrols. *Student services:* personal/psychological counseling.

Standardized Tests *Required for some:* ACT COMPASS. *Recommended:* SAT (for placement), ACT (for placement).

Costs (2006–07) *Tuition:* area resident $2010 full-time, $67 per semester hour part-time; state resident $4020 full-time, $134 per semester hour part-time; nonresident $6030 full-time, $201 per semester hour part-time. *Required fees:* $90 full-time, $3 per semester hour part-time.

Financial Aid Of all full-time matriculated undergraduates who enrolled in 2004, 65 Federal Work-Study jobs (averaging $1500).

Applying *Recommended:* high school transcript. *Application deadline:* rolling (freshmen), rolling (transfers). *Notification:* continuous (freshmen).

Freshmen Application Contact Ms. Christine M. Riley, Director of Advisement and Enrollment Services, Heartland Community College, 1500 West Raab Road, Normal, IL 61761. *Phone:* 309-268-8000.

HIGHLAND COMMUNITY COLLEGE

Freeport, Illinois   **www.highland.edu/**

- **State and locally supported** 2-year, founded 1962, part of Illinois Community College Board
- **Rural** 240-acre campus
- **Endowment** $5.6 million
- **Coed,** 2,406 undergraduate students, 47% full-time, 63% women, 37% men

Undergraduates 1,134 full-time, 1,272 part-time. Students come from 8 states and territories, 2% are from out of state, 9% African American, 1% Asian American or Pacific Islander, 2% Hispanic American, 0.1% Native American, 0.2% international. *Retention:* 65% of 2003 full-time freshmen returned.

Freshmen *Admission:* 665 applied, 665 admitted, 508 enrolled. *Test scores:* ACT scores over 18: 69%; ACT scores over 24: 22%.

Faculty *Total:* 190, 25% full-time, 3% with terminal degrees. *Student/faculty ratio:* 16:1.

Majors Accounting; administrative assistant and secretarial science; agricultural business and management; agricultural mechanization; art; automobile/automotive mechanics technology; biological and physical sciences; business administration and management; chemistry; child care and support services management; child care provision; child development; commercial and advertising art; computer and information sciences related; computer programming (specific applications); computer science; computer/technical support; data processing and data processing technology; drafting and design technology; dramatic/theater arts; education; electrical, electronic and communications engineering technology; engineering; engineering science; engineering technology; geology/earth science; history; human services; kindergarten/preschool education; liberal arts and sciences/liberal studies; marketing/marketing management; mathematics; mechanical engineering/mechanical technology; music teacher education; nursing (registered nurse training); physical sciences; physics; political science and government; pre-engineering; psychology; sociology; speech/theater education; web page, digital/multimedia and information resources design.

Academics *Calendar:* semesters. *Degree:* certificates and associate. *Special study options:* academic remediation for entering students, adult/continuing education programs, advanced placement credit, distance learning, English as a second language, external degree program, independent study, internships, part-time degree program, services for LD students, student-designed majors, summer session for credit.

Library Highland Library plus 1 other with 47,000 titles, 3,980 serial subscriptions, 2,776 audiovisual materials, an OPAC, a Web page.

Computers on Campus 200 computers available on campus for general student use. A campuswide network can be accessed. Internet access, at least one staffed computer lab available.

Student Life *Housing:* college housing not available. *Activities and Organizations:* drama/theater group, student-run newspaper, choral group, Phi Theta Kappa, Royal Scots, Prairie Wind, intramurals, Collegiate Choir. *Campus security:* 24-hour patrols. *Student services:* personal/psychological counseling.

Athletics Member NJCAA. *Intercollegiate sports:* baseball M(s)/W(s), basketball M(s)/W(s), golf M(s)/W(s), softball W(s), volleyball W(s). *Intramural sports:* basketball M/W, racquetball M/W, volleyball M/W.

Costs (2006–07) *Tuition:* area resident $1608 full-time, $67 per credit part-time; state resident $2880 full-time, $120 per credit part-time; nonresident $2880 full-time, $120 per credit part-time. *Required fees:* $120 full-time, $5 per credit part-time.

Financial Aid Of all full-time matriculated undergraduates who enrolled in 2004, 50 Federal Work-Study jobs (averaging $2000). 50 state and other part-time jobs (averaging $2000).

Applying *Options:* early admission, deferred entrance. *Required for some:* high school transcript. *Application deadline:* rolling (freshmen), rolling (transfers).

Freshmen Application Contact Mr. Karl Richards, Dean of Enrollment Services, Highland Community College, 2998 West Pearl City Road, Freeport, IL 61032. *Phone:* 815-235-6121 Ext. 3486. *Fax:* 815-235-6130.

ILLINOIS CENTRAL COLLEGE

East Peoria, Illinois   **www.icc.edu/**

- **State and locally supported** 2-year, founded 1967, part of Illinois Community College Board
- **Suburban** 430-acre campus
- **Coed,** 12,343 undergraduate students, 40% full-time, 56% women, 44% men

Undergraduates 4,907 full-time, 7,436 part-time. Students come from 20 other countries, 10% African American, 2% Asian American or Pacific Islander, 2% Hispanic American, 0.4% Native American, 0.6% international.

Faculty *Total:* 658, 26% full-time.

Majors Accounting; administrative assistant and secretarial science; agricultural business and management; agricultural mechanization; architectural engineering technology; artificial intelligence and robotics; automobile/automotive mechanics technology; biological and physical sciences; business administration and management; clinical/medical laboratory technology; commercial and advertising art; court reporting; criminal justice/police science; data processing and data processing technology; dental hygiene; developmental and child psychology; electrical, electronic and communications engineering technology; engineering technology; finance; fire science; health/health care administration; health information/medical records administration; horticultural science; industrial radiologic technology; industrial technology; interior design; legal assistant/paralegal; liberal arts and sciences/liberal studies; library science; marketing/marketing management; mechanical design technology; nursing (registered nurse training); occupational therapy; physical therapy; real estate; respiratory care therapy; welding technology.

Academics *Calendar:* semesters. *Degree:* certificates and associate. *Special study options:* academic remediation for entering students, adult/continuing education programs, advanced placement credit, English as a second language, honors programs, internships, part-time degree program, services for LD students, summer session for credit.

Library 82,492 titles, 563 serial subscriptions.

Computers on Campus 250 computers available on campus for general student use. A campuswide network can be accessed from off campus. Internet access, at least one staffed computer lab available.

Student Life *Activities and Organizations:* drama/theater group, student-run newspaper, choral group, Student Association for the Environment, Horticulture Club. *Student services:* health clinic, personal/psychological counseling.

Athletics Member NJCAA. *Intercollegiate sports:* baseball M(s), basketball M(s)/W(s), golf M/W, soccer M/W, softball W(s), volleyball W(s). *Intramural sports:* basketball M/W, soccer M/W, table tennis M/W, tennis M/W, volleyball M/W.

Costs (2006–07) *Tuition:* area resident $2240 full-time, $70 per semester hour part-time; state resident $4960 full-time, $155 per semester hour part-time; nonresident $4960 full-time, $155 per semester hour part-time. *Room and board:* room only: $3978.

Applying *Options:* early admission. *Required:* high school transcript. *Application deadline:* rolling (freshmen), rolling (transfers). *Notification:* continuous (freshmen).

Freshmen Application Contact Mr. John Avendano, Vice President of Academic Affairs and Student Development, Illinois Central College, One College Drive, East Peoria, IL 61635-0001. *Phone:* 309-694-5784. *Toll-free phone:* 800-422-2293. *Fax:* 309-694-5450. *E-mail:* info@icc.edu.

ILLINOIS EASTERN COMMUNITY COLLEGES, FRONTIER COMMUNITY COLLEGE

Fairfield, Illinois www.iecc.edu/fcc/

- **State and locally supported** 2-year, founded 1976, part of Illinois Eastern Community College System
- **Rural** 8-acre campus
- **Coed,** 2,164 undergraduate students, 12% full-time, 66% women, 34% men

Undergraduates 249 full-time, 1,915 part-time. 0.2% African American, 1% Asian American or Pacific Islander, 0.3% Hispanic American, 0.1% Native American.
Freshmen *Admission:* 27 enrolled.
Faculty *Total:* 235, 2% full-time.
Majors Administrative assistant and secretarial science; biological and physical sciences; business automation/technology/data entry; corrections; general studies; liberal arts and sciences/liberal studies; nursing (registered nurse training); quality control technology.
Academics *Calendar:* semesters. *Degree:* certificates and associate. *Special study options:* academic remediation for entering students, adult/continuing education programs, advanced placement credit, cooperative education, distance learning, double majors, English as a second language, external degree program, independent study, part-time degree program, services for LD students, student-designed majors, summer session for credit.
Library 19,088 titles, 7,664 serial subscriptions, 2,679 audiovisual materials.
Computers on Campus 42 computers available on campus for general student use. At least one staffed computer lab available.
Student Life *Housing:* college housing not available.
Costs (2006–07) *Tuition:* area resident $1696 full-time, $53 per credit hour part-time; state resident $5908 full-time, $185 per credit hour part-time; nonresident $7314 full-time, $229 per credit hour part-time. *Required fees:* $106 full-time, $3 per credit hour part-time.
Applying *Options:* early admission, deferred entrance. *Application fee:* $10. *Required:* high school transcript. *Application deadline:* rolling (freshmen), rolling (transfers). *Notification:* continuous (freshmen).
Freshmen Application Contact Mrs. Suzanne Brooks, Coordinator of Registration and Records, Illinois Eastern Community Colleges, Frontier Community College, 2 Frontier Drive, Fairfield, IL 62837. *Phone:* 618-842-3711 Ext. 4111. *Fax:* 618-842-6340.

ILLINOIS EASTERN COMMUNITY COLLEGES, LINCOLN TRAIL COLLEGE

Robinson, Illinois www.iecc.edu/ltc/

- **State and locally supported** 2-year, founded 1969, part of Illinois Eastern Community College System
- **Rural** 120-acre campus
- **Coed,** 1,532 undergraduate students, 33% full-time, 48% women, 52% men

Undergraduates 505 full-time, 1,027 part-time. 15% African American, 2% Asian American or Pacific Islander, 4% Hispanic American, 0.2% Native American, 0.3% international.
Freshmen *Admission:* 257 enrolled.
Faculty *Total:* 86, 30% full-time.
Majors Biological and physical sciences; building/property maintenance and management; business automation/technology/data entry; corrections; culinary arts; general studies; heating, air conditioning, ventilation and refrigeration maintenance technology; liberal arts and sciences/liberal studies; mechanical engineering/mechanical technology; music; music teacher education; quality control technology; teacher assistant/aide; telecommunications.
Academics *Calendar:* semesters. *Degree:* certificates and associate. *Special study options:* academic remediation for entering students, adult/continuing education programs, advanced placement credit, cooperative education, distance learning, double majors, English as a second language, external degree program, independent study, internships, part-time degree program, services for LD students, student-designed majors, summer session for credit.
Library Eagleton Learning Resource Center with 16,654 titles, 7,391 serial subscriptions, 2,029 audiovisual materials.
Computers on Campus 96 computers available on campus for general student use. At least one staffed computer lab available.

Student Life *Housing:* college housing not available. *Activities and Organizations:* drama/theater group, choral group, national fraternities. *Student services:* personal/psychological counseling.
Athletics Member NJCAA. *Intercollegiate sports:* baseball M(s), basketball M(s)/W(s), softball W(s), volleyball W(s). *Intramural sports:* baseball M, basketball M, softball W, volleyball M/W.
Costs (2006–07) *Tuition:* area resident $1696 full-time, $53 per credit hour part-time; state resident $5908 full-time, $185 per credit hour part-time; nonresident $7314 full-time, $229 per credit hour part-time. *Required fees:* $106 full-time, $3 per credit hour part-time.
Applying *Options:* early admission, deferred entrance. *Application fee:* $10. *Required:* high school transcript. *Application deadline:* rolling (freshmen), rolling (transfers). *Notification:* continuous (freshmen).
Freshmen Application Contact Ms. Becky Mikeworth, Illinois Eastern Community Colleges, Lincoln Trail College, 11220 State Highway 1, Robinson, IL 62454. *Phone:* 618-544-8657 Ext. 1137. *Fax:* 618-544-7423.

ILLINOIS EASTERN COMMUNITY COLLEGES, OLNEY CENTRAL COLLEGE

Olney, Illinois www.iecc.edu/occ/

- **State and locally supported** 2-year, founded 1962, part of Illinois Eastern Community College System
- **Rural** 128-acre campus
- **Coed,** 1,701 undergraduate students, 45% full-time, 57% women, 43% men

Undergraduates 758 full-time, 943 part-time. 0.8% African American, 1% Asian American or Pacific Islander, 0.6% Hispanic American, 0.1% Native American, 0.1% international.
Freshmen *Admission:* 159 enrolled.
Faculty *Total:* 118, 41% full-time.
Majors Accounting; administrative assistant and secretarial science; autobody/collision and repair technology; automobile/automotive mechanics technology; biological and physical sciences; business automation/technology/data entry; cabinetmaking and millwork; corrections; criminal justice/police science; general studies; heavy equipment maintenance technology; industrial mechanics and maintenance technology; liberal arts and sciences/liberal studies; medical administrative assistant and medical secretary; medical radiologic technology; music; music teacher education; nursing (licensed practical/vocational nurse training); nursing (registered nurse training).
Academics *Calendar:* semesters. *Degree:* certificates and associate. *Special study options:* academic remediation for entering students, adult/continuing education programs, advanced placement credit, cooperative education, distance learning, double majors, English as a second language, external degree program, independent study, internships, part-time degree program, services for LD students, student-designed majors, summer session for credit.
Library Anderson Learning Resources Center with 22,976 titles, 81 serial subscriptions, 693 audiovisual materials.
Computers on Campus 125 computers available on campus for general student use. At least one staffed computer lab available.
Student Life *Housing:* college housing not available. *Activities and Organizations:* drama/theater group, student-run newspaper, choral group. *Student services:* personal/psychological counseling, women's center.
Athletics Member NJCAA. *Intercollegiate sports:* baseball M(s), basketball M(s)/W(s), softball W(s), volleyball W(s). *Intramural sports:* baseball M, basketball M/W, softball W.
Costs (2006–07) *Tuition:* area resident $1696 full-time, $53 per credit hour part-time; state resident $5908 full-time, $185 per credit hour part-time; nonresident $7314 full-time, $229 per credit hour part-time. *Required fees:* $106 full-time, $3 per credit hour part-time.
Applying *Options:* early admission, deferred entrance. *Application fee:* $10. *Required:* high school transcript. *Application deadline:* rolling (freshmen), rolling (transfers). *Notification:* continuous (freshmen).
Freshmen Application Contact Ms. Chris Webber, Assistant Dean for Student Services, Illinois Eastern Community Colleges, Olney Central College, 305 North West Street, Olney, IL 62450. *Phone:* 618-395-7777 Ext. 2005. *Fax:* 618-392-5212.

ILLINOIS EASTERN COMMUNITY COLLEGES, WABASH VALLEY COLLEGE

Mount Carmel, Illinois www.iecc.edu/wvc/

- **State and locally supported** 2-year, founded 1960, part of Illinois Eastern Community College System
- **Rural** 40-acre campus
- **Coed,** 3,155 undergraduate students, 20% full-time, 39% women, 61% men

Undergraduates 631 full-time, 2,524 part-time. 3% African American, 1% Asian American or Pacific Islander, 0.9% Hispanic American, 0.2% Native American, 0.1% international. **Freshmen** *Admission:* 163 enrolled.

Faculty *Total:* 186, 20% full-time.

Majors Administrative assistant and secretarial science; agricultural business and management; agricultural production; biological and physical sciences; business administration and management; business automation/technology/data entry; child development; corrections; court reporting; diesel mechanics technology; electrical, electronic and communications engineering technology; general studies; industrial technology; liberal arts and sciences/liberal studies; machine shop technology; manufacturing technology; mining technology; radio and television; social work.

Academics *Calendar:* semesters. *Degree:* certificates and associate. *Special study options:* academic remediation for entering students, adult/continuing education programs, advanced placement credit, cooperative education, distance learning, double majors, English as a second language, external degree program, independent study, internships, part-time degree program, services for LD students, student-designed majors, summer session for credit.

Library Bauer Media Center with 34,589 titles, 7,665 serial subscriptions, 1,629 audiovisual materials.

Computers on Campus 100 computers available on campus for general student use. At least one staffed computer lab available.

Student Life *Housing:* college housing not available. *Activities and Organizations:* drama/theater group, student-run newspaper, radio and television station, choral group.

Athletics Member NJCAA. *Intercollegiate sports:* baseball M(s), basketball M(s)/W(s), softball W(s), tennis M, volleyball W(s). *Intramural sports:* baseball M, basketball M/W, cross-country running M/W, softball W, volleyball M/W.

Costs (2006–07) *Tuition:* area resident $1696 full-time, $53 per credit hour part-time; state resident $5908 full-time, $185 per credit hour part-time; nonresident $7314 full-time, $229 per credit hour part-time. *Required fees:* $106 full-time, $3 per credit hour part-time.

Applying *Options:* early admission, deferred entrance. *Application fee:* $10. *Required:* high school transcript. *Application deadline:* rolling (freshmen), rolling (transfers). *Notification:* continuous (freshmen).

Freshmen Application Contact Mrs. Diana Spear, Assistant Dean for Student Services, Illinois Eastern Community Colleges, Wabash Valley College, 2200 College Drive, Mt. Carmel, IL 62863. *Phone:* 618-262-8641 Ext. 3101. *Fax:* 618-262-8641.

ILLINOIS VALLEY COMMUNITY COLLEGE

Oglesby, Illinois www.ivcc.edu/

- **District-supported** 2-year, founded 1924, part of Illinois Community College Board
- **Rural** 410-acre campus with easy access to Chicago
- **Coed,** 4,315 undergraduate students

Faculty *Total:* 189, 36% full-time.

Majors Accounting; administrative assistant and secretarial science; agricultural business and management; agriculture; automobile/automotive mechanics technology; business administration and management; carpentry; child development; computer programming; computer systems networking and telecommunications; criminal justice/law enforcement administration; criminal justice/police science; data processing and data processing technology; drafting and design technology; education; electrical, electronic and communications engineering technology; elementary education; English; industrial technology; journalism; liberal arts and sciences/liberal studies; marketing/marketing management; mechanical design technology; mechanical engineering/mechanical technology; nursing (registered nurse training); pre-engineering.

Academics *Calendar:* semesters. *Degree:* associate. *Special study options:* academic remediation for entering students, adult/continuing education programs, advanced placement credit, distance learning, English as a second language, honors programs, independent study, internships, off-campus study,

part-time degree program, services for LD students, student-designed majors, study abroad, summer session for credit.

Library Jacobs Library with 58,250 titles, 504 serial subscriptions.

Computers on Campus 420 computers available on campus for general student use.

Student Life *Housing:* college housing not available. *Activities and Organizations:* drama/theater group, student-run newspaper, choral group. *Campus security:* 24-hour patrols. *Student services:* personal/psychological counseling.

Athletics *Intercollegiate sports:* basketball M/W, golf M, tennis M/W. *Intramural sports:* basketball M, volleyball W.

Standardized Tests *Recommended:* ACT (for placement).

Costs (2006–07) *Tuition:* $63 per credit hour part-time; state resident $214 per credit hour part-time; nonresident $247 per credit hour part-time.

Financial Aid Of all full-time matriculated undergraduates who enrolled in 2004, 81 Federal Work-Study jobs (averaging $955).

Applying *Options:* early admission, deferred entrance. *Required:* high school transcript. *Application deadline:* rolling (freshmen), rolling (transfers). *Notification:* continuous (freshmen).

Freshmen Application Contact Ms. Tracy Morris, Director of Admissions and Records, Illinois Valley Community College, 815 North Orlando Smith Avenue Oglesby, Oglesby, IL 61348. *Phone:* 815-224-0437. *Fax:* 815-224-3033. *E-mail:* tracy_morris@ivcc.edu.

ITT TECHNICAL INSTITUTE

Burr Ridge, Illinois www.itt-tech.edu/

- **Proprietary** primarily 2-year, part of ITT Educational Services, Inc
- **Coed**

Majors Computer and information systems security; computer programming; e-commerce; electrical, electronic and communications engineering technology; system, networking, and LAN/WAN management; web/multimedia management and webmaster; web page, digital/multimedia and information resources design.

Academics *Calendar:* quarters. *Degrees:* associate and bachelor's.

Library a Web page.

Computers on Campus Internet access, at least one staffed computer lab available.

Student Life *Housing:* college housing not available.

Standardized Tests *Required:* Wonderlic aptitude test (for admission).

Costs (2005–06) *Tuition:* Please see school catalog for specific information.

Applying *Options:* deferred entrance. *Application fee:* $100. *Required:* high school transcript, interview. *Recommended:* letters of recommendation. *Application deadline:* rolling (freshmen), rolling (transfers). *Notification:* continuous (freshmen).

Freshmen Application Contact Mr. Andrew Mical, Director of Recruitment, ITT Technical Institute, 7040 High Grove Boulevard, Burr Ridge, IL 60527. *Phone:* 630-455-6470. *Toll-free phone:* 877-488-0001. *Fax:* 630-455-6476.

ITT TECHNICAL INSTITUTE

Matteson, Illinois www.itt-tech.edu/

- **Proprietary** primarily 2-year, founded 1993, part of ITT Educational Services, Inc
- **Suburban** campus with easy access to Chicago
- **Coed**

Majors CAD/CADD drafting/design technology; computer programming; e-commerce; electrical, electronic and communications engineering technology; system, networking, and LAN/WAN management; web/multimedia management and webmaster; web page, digital/multimedia and information resources design.

Academics *Calendar:* quarters. *Degrees:* associate and bachelor's.

Library a Web page.

Computers on Campus Internet access, at least one staffed computer lab available.

Student Life *Housing:* college housing not available.

Standardized Tests *Required:* Wonderlic aptitude test (for admission).

Costs (2005–06) *Tuition:* Please see school catalog for specific information.

Financial Aid Of all full-time matriculated undergraduates who enrolled in 2004, 6 Federal Work-Study jobs (averaging $4000).

Applying *Options:* deferred entrance. *Application fee:* $100. *Required:* high school transcript, interview. *Recommended:* letters of recommendation. *Application deadline:* rolling (freshmen), rolling (transfers). *Notification:* continuous (freshmen).

Freshmen Application Contact Mr. James Tannheimer, ITT Technical Institute, 600 Holiday Plaza Drive, Matteson, IL 60443. *Phone:* 708-747-2571.

ITT TECHNICAL INSTITUTE
Mount Prospect, Illinois   www.itt-tech.edu/

- **Proprietary** primarily 2-year, founded 1986, part of ITT Educational Services, Inc
- **Suburban** 1-acre campus with easy access to Chicago
- **Coed**

Majors CAD/CADD drafting/design technology; computer and information systems security; computer programming; e-commerce; electrical, electronic and communications engineering technology; system, networking, and LAN/WAN management; web page, digital/multimedia and information resources design.
Academics *Calendar:* quarters. *Degrees:* associate and bachelor's.
Library a Web page.
Computers on Campus Internet access, at least one staffed computer lab available.
Student Life *Housing:* college housing not available.
Standardized Tests *Required:* Wonderlic aptitude test (for admission).
Costs (2005–06) *Tuition:* Please see school catalog for specific information.
Applying *Options:* deferred entrance. *Application fee:* $100. *Required:* high school transcript, interview. *Recommended:* letters of recommendation. *Application deadline:* rolling (freshmen), rolling (transfers). *Notification:* continuous (freshmen).
Freshmen Application Contact Mr. Cesar Rodriguez Jr., Director of Recruitment, ITT Technical Institute, 1401 Feehanville Drive, Mount Prospect, IL 60056. *Phone:* 847-375-8800.

JOHN A. LOGAN COLLEGE
Carterville, Illinois   www.jalc.edu/

- **State and locally supported** 2-year, founded 1967, part of Illinois Community College Board
- **Rural** 160-acre campus
- **Endowment** $19,000
- **Coed**

Undergraduates Students come from 41 states and territories, 20 other countries.
Academics *Calendar:* semesters. *Degree:* certificates and associate. *Special study options:* academic remediation for entering students, adult/continuing education programs, advanced placement credit, cooperative education, distance learning, internships, off-campus study, part-time degree program, services for LD students, study abroad, summer session for credit. *ROTC:* Army (c), Air Force (c).
Student Life *Campus security:* 24-hour emergency response devices and patrols.
Athletics Member NJCAA.
Standardized Tests *Required:* ACT ASSET (for placement). *Recommended:* SAT or ACT (for placement).
Costs (2005–06) *Tuition:* area resident $1900 full-time, $61 per credit hour part-time; state resident $6000 full-time, $169 per credit hour part-time; nonresident $9000 full-time, $255 per credit hour part-time.
Applying *Options:* electronic application, early admission. *Required:* high school transcript.
Director of Admissions Mr. Terry Crain, Dean of Student Services, John A. Logan College, 700 Logan College Road, Carterville, IL 62918-9900. *Phone:* 618-985-3741 Ext. 8382. *E-mail:* terry.crain@jalc.edu.

JOHN WOOD COMMUNITY COLLEGE
Quincy, Illinois   www.jwcc.edu/

- **District-supported** 2-year, founded 1974, part of Illinois Community College Board
- **Small-town** campus
- **Coed,** 2,530 undergraduate students, 47% full-time, 63% women, 37% men

Undergraduates 1,197 full-time, 1,333 part-time. Students come from 4 states and territories, 3 other countries, 9% are from out of state, 4% African American,

0.8% Asian American or Pacific Islander, 0.8% Hispanic American, 0.3% Native American, 0.2% international, 6% transferred in.
Freshmen *Admission:* 711 applied, 711 admitted, 545 enrolled. *Test scores:* ACT scores over 18: 66%; ACT scores over 24: 14%; ACT scores over 30: 1%.
Faculty *Total:* 190, 27% full-time, 6% with terminal degrees. *Student/faculty ratio:* 15:1.
Majors Accounting; accounting technology and bookkeeping; administrative assistant and secretarial science; agricultural business and management; agricultural production; animal/livestock husbandry and production; applied horticulture; biological and physical sciences; business administration and management; business/commerce; child guidance; clinical/medical laboratory technology; computer programming (specific applications); criminal justice/police science; early childhood education; electrical, electronic and communications engineering technology; electrician; emergency medical technology (EMT paramedic); executive assistant/executive secretary; fire protection and safety technology; general studies; health and physical education; hotel/motel administration; industrial electronics technology; industrial mechanics and maintenance technology; legal administrative assistant/secretary; liberal arts and sciences/liberal studies; mechanical drafting and CAD/CADD; medical administrative assistant and medical secretary; medical radiologic technology; nursing (registered nurse training); psychology; restaurant, culinary, and catering management; sales, distribution and marketing; sociology.
Academics *Calendar:* semesters. *Degree:* certificates and associate. *Special study options:* academic remediation for entering students, adult/continuing education programs, advanced placement credit, cooperative education, distance learning, English as a second language, external degree program, independent study, internships, off-campus study, part-time degree program, services for LD students, student-designed majors, study abroad, summer session for credit.
Library 18,000 titles, 160 serial subscriptions, 2,200 audiovisual materials, an OPAC, a Web page.
Computers on Campus 250 computers available on campus for general student use. A campuswide network can be accessed. Internet access, at least one staffed computer lab available.
Student Life *Housing:* college housing not available. *Activities and Organizations:* choral group. *Campus security:* 24-hour emergency response devices, late-night transport/escort service.
Athletics Member NJCAA. *Intercollegiate sports:* baseball M(s), basketball M(s)/W(s), golf M(s), softball W(s), volleyball W(s). *Intramural sports:* basketball M/W, volleyball M/W.
Standardized Tests *Recommended:* ACT (for admission).
Costs (2005–06) *Tuition:* area resident $2280 full-time, $76 per credit hour part-time; state resident $5280 full-time, $176 per credit hour part-time. *Required fees:* $150 full-time, $5 per credit hour part-time.
Financial Aid Of all full-time matriculated undergraduates who enrolled in 2004, 360 Federal Work-Study jobs (averaging $364).
Applying *Options:* common application, early admission. *Required:* high school transcript. *Application deadline:* rolling (freshmen), rolling (transfers). *Notification:* continuous (freshmen).
Freshmen Application Contact Mr. Mark McNett, Director of Admissions, John Wood Community College, 1301 South 48th Street, Quincy, IL 62305-8736. *Phone:* 217-641-4339. *Fax:* 217-224-4208. *E-mail:* admissions@jwcc.edu.

JOLIET JUNIOR COLLEGE
Joliet, Illinois   www.jjc.edu/

- **State and locally supported** 2-year, founded 1901, part of Illinois Community College Board
- **Suburban** campus with easy access to Chicago
- **Endowment** $9.6 million
- **Coed,** 13,022 undergraduate students, 38% full-time, 59% women, 41% men

Undergraduates 4,895 full-time, 8,127 part-time. Students come from 12 states and territories, 0.3% are from out of state, 10% African American, 2% Asian American or Pacific Islander, 9% Hispanic American, 0.3% Native American, 0.1% international, 2% transferred in.
Freshmen *Admission:* 4,484 applied, 4,484 admitted, 2,334 enrolled.
Faculty *Total:* 562, 33% full-time. *Student/faculty ratio:* 24:1.
Majors Accounting; administrative assistant and secretarial science; agricultural business and management; animal physiology; art; automobile/automotive mechanics technology; biology/biological sciences; business administration and management; business automation/technology/data entry; business/managerial economics; chemistry; clinical laboratory science/medical technology; computer and information sciences; computer programming; computer programming (specific applications); computer systems networking and telecommunications; computer/technical support; construction engineering technology; corrections; criminal justice/law enforcement administration; criminal justice/police science; culinary arts; ecology; education; electrical, electronic and communications

Joliet Junior College (continued)

engineering technology; electrical/electronics drafting and CAD/CADD; emergency medical technology (EMT paramedic); fashion merchandising; fire science; geography; greenhouse management; horticultural science; hospitality administration; industrial technology; interior design; landscaping and groundskeeping; marketing/marketing management; massage therapy; mathematics; mechanical design technology; medical administrative assistant and medical secretary; nuclear/nuclear power technology; nursing (registered nurse training); plant nursery management; real estate; special products marketing; teacher assistant/aide; turf and turfgrass management; veterinary/animal health technology; web page, digital/multimedia and information resources design; welding technology.

Academics *Calendar:* semesters. *Degree:* certificates, diplomas, and associate. *Special study options:* academic remediation for entering students, adult/continuing education programs, advanced placement credit, distance learning, English as a second language, honors programs, independent study, internships, part-time degree program, services for LD students, summer session for credit.

Library Learning Resource Center with 60,364 titles, 360 serial subscriptions, an OPAC.

Computers on Campus A campuswide network can be accessed from off campus. Internet access, at least one staffed computer lab available.

Student Life *Housing Options:* Campus housing is provided by a third party. *Activities and Organizations:* drama/theater group, student-run newspaper, choral group, Phi Theta Kappa, JC Players, Nursing Student Association, Student Agricultural Association, Inter-Varsity Christian Fellowship, national fraternities. *Campus security:* 24-hour emergency response devices and patrols, student patrols, late-night transport/escort service. *Student services:* personal/psychological counseling, women's center.

Athletics Member NJCAA. *Intercollegiate sports:* basketball M/W, football M, golf M, softball W, tennis M/W, volleyball W.

Costs (2006–07) *Tuition:* area resident $1800 full-time, $60 per hour part-time; state resident $6248 full-time, $208 per hour part-time; nonresident $7149 full-time, $238 per hour part-time. *Required fees:* $390 full-time, $13 per hour part-time.

Financial Aid Of all full-time matriculated undergraduates who enrolled in 2004, 96 Federal Work-Study jobs (averaging $1168). 254 state and other part-time jobs (averaging $1778).

Applying *Options:* early admission, deferred entrance. *Required:* high school transcript. *Application deadline:* rolling (freshmen), rolling (transfers).

Freshmen Application Contact Ms. Jennifer Kloberdanz, Dean of Admissions and Financial Aid, Joliet Junior College, 1215 Houbolt Road, Joliet, IL 60431. *Phone:* 815-280-2493. *Fax:* 815-280-6740. *E-mail:* admission@jjc.edu.

KANKAKEE COMMUNITY COLLEGE

Kankakee, Illinois   **www.kcc.cc.il.us/**

Director of Admissions Ms. Michelle Driscoll, Kankakee Community College, Box 888, Kankakee, IL 60901. *Phone:* 815-802-8520.

KASKASKIA COLLEGE

Centralia, Illinois   **www.kaskaskia.edu/**

- **State and locally supported** 2-year, founded 1966, part of Illinois Community College Board
- **Rural** 195-acre campus with easy access to St. Louis
- **Endowment** $606,505
- **Coed,** 4,742 undergraduate students, 40% full-time, 58% women, 42% men

Undergraduates 1,908 full-time, 2,834 part-time. Students come from 23 states and territories, 2 other countries, 1% are from out of state, 7% African American, 0.4% Asian American or Pacific Islander, 2% Hispanic American, 0.3% Native American, 0.2% international, 21% transferred in. Freshmen *Admission:* 514 applied, 514 admitted, 484 enrolled.

Faculty *Total:* 246, 29% full-time, 3% with terminal degrees. *Student/faculty ratio:* 22:1.

Majors Agricultural business and management; applied horticulture; architectural drafting and CAD/CADD; autobody/collision and repair technology; automobile/automotive mechanics technology; biological and physical sciences; business administration and management; business automation/technology/data entry; carpentry; computer programming (specific applications); criminal justice/police science; culinary arts; electrical, electronic and communications engineering technology; executive assistant/executive secretary; general studies; industrial mechanics and maintenance technology; liberal arts and sciences/liberal studies;

medical radiologic technology; nursing (registered nurse training); physical therapist assistant; respiratory care therapy.

Academics *Calendar:* semesters. *Degree:* certificates and associate. *Special study options:* academic remediation for entering students, accelerated degree program, adult/continuing education programs, cooperative education, distance learning, double majors, English as a second language, honors programs, independent study, internships, off-campus study, part-time degree program, services for LD students, study abroad, summer session for credit.

Library Kaskaskia College Library with 23,685 titles, 165 serial subscriptions, 480 audiovisual materials, an OPAC, a Web page.

Computers on Campus 129 computers available on campus for general student use. A campuswide network can be accessed from off campus. Internet access, at least one staffed computer lab available.

Student Life *Housing:* college housing not available. *Activities and Organizations:* drama/theater group, student-run newspaper, choral group, Phi Theta Kappa, Administration of Justice, Student Radiology Club, Cosmetology Club, Vocal Music Club. *Campus security:* 24-hour patrols, late-night transport/escort service. *Student services:* personal/psychological counseling.

Athletics Member NJCAA. *Intercollegiate sports:* baseball M(s), basketball M(s)/W(s), cheerleading M(s)/W(s), golf M(s), softball W(s), volleyball W(s).

Standardized Tests *Recommended:* ACT (for admission), ASSET.

Costs (2005–06) *Tuition:* area resident $1590 full-time, $53 per credit hour part-time; state resident $3030 full-time, $101 per credit hour part-time; nonresident $7038 full-time, $235 per credit hour part-time. Full-time tuition and fees vary according to location. Part-time tuition and fees vary according to location. *Required fees:* $210 full-time, $7 per credit hour part-time. *Payment plan:* installment. *Waivers:* senior citizens and employees or children of employees.

Applying *Options:* common application, early admission, deferred entrance. *Required:* high school transcript. *Required for some:* interview. *Application deadline:* rolling (freshmen), rolling (transfers). *Notification:* continuous (freshmen).

Freshmen Application Contact Ms. Sharon Conners, Director of Admissions, Kaskaskia College, 27210 College Road, Centralia, IL 62801. *Phone:* 618-545-3000. *Toll-free phone:* 800-642-0859. *Fax:* 618-532-1990. *E-mail:* sconners@kaskaskia.edu.

KISHWAUKEE COLLEGE

Malta, Illinois   **www.kishwaukeecollege.edu/**

Freshmen Application Contact Ms. Sally Misciasci, Admission Analyst, Kishwaukee College, 21193 Malta Road, Malta, IL 60150-9699. *Phone:* 815-825-2086 Ext. 400.

LAKE LAND COLLEGE

Mattoon, Illinois   **www.lakelandcollege.edu/**

- **State and locally supported** 2-year, founded 1966, part of Illinois Community College Board
- **Rural** 304-acre campus
- **Endowment** $2.7 million
- **Coed,** 7,038 undergraduate students, 44% full-time, 48% women, 52% men

Undergraduates 3,108 full-time, 3,930 part-time. Students come from 23 other countries, 5% are from out of state, 9% African American, 0.7% Asian American or Pacific Islander, 2% Hispanic American, 0.2% Native American, 0.6% international.
Freshmen *Admission:* 2,159 applied, 2,159 admitted.

Faculty *Total:* 191, 61% full-time, 5% with terminal degrees. *Student/faculty ratio:* 21:1.

Majors Accounting technology and bookkeeping; administrative assistant and secretarial science; agricultural business and management; agricultural mechanization; agricultural production; architectural engineering technology; automobile/automotive mechanics technology; biological and physical sciences; business administration and management; child care and support services management; civil engineering technology; computer programming (specific applications); computer systems networking and telecommunications; corrections; criminal justice/police science; dental hygiene; desktop publishing and digital imaging design; drafting and design technology; electrical, electronic and communications engineering technology; electromechanical technology; executive assistant/executive secretary; general studies; graphic and printing equipment operation/production; human services; industrial technology; information technology; legal administrative assistant/secretary; liberal arts and sciences/liberal studies; marketing/marketing management; medical administrative assistant and medical secretary; nursing (registered nurse training); office management; physical therapist assistant; printing press operation; radio and television; social work; telecommunications.

Academics *Calendar:* semesters. *Degree:* certificates and associate. *Special study options:* academic remediation for entering students, accelerated degree program, adult/continuing education programs, cooperative education, distance learning, English as a second language, external degree program, honors programs, internships, part-time degree program, services for LD students, summer session for credit.

Library Virgil H. Judge Learning Resource Center with 36,912 titles, 193 serial subscriptions, 1,446 audiovisual materials, an OPAC.

Computers on Campus 100 computers available on campus for general student use. A campuswide network can be accessed. Internet access, online (class) registration, at least one staffed computer lab available.

Student Life *Housing:* college housing not available. *Activities and Organizations:* student-run newspaper, radio station, choral group, Agriculture Production and Management Club, Cosmetology Club, Agriculture Transfer Club, Phi Theta Kappa, Civil Engineering Technology Club. *Campus security:* 24-hour patrols. *Student services:* personal/psychological counseling.

Athletics Member NJCAA. *Intercollegiate sports:* baseball M(s), basketball M(s)/W(s), cheerleading W, softball W(s), tennis M(s)/W, volleyball W(s). *Intramural sports:* basketball M/W, bowling M/W, golf M/W, softball M/W, volleyball M/W.

Costs (2005–06) *Tuition:* area resident $1545 full-time, $52 per credit hour part-time; state resident $3595 full-time, $120 per credit hour part-time; nonresident $7568 full-time, $252 per credit hour part-time. *Required fees:* $358 full-time, $12 per credit hour part-time. *Payment plan:* deferred payment. *Waivers:* senior citizens.

Financial Aid Of all full-time matriculated undergraduates who enrolled in 2004, 120 Federal Work-Study jobs (averaging $1400).

Applying *Options:* common application, electronic application, early admission. *Required for some:* letters of recommendation. *Recommended:* high school transcript. *Application deadline:* rolling (freshmen), rolling (transfers). *Notification:* continuous (freshmen).

Freshmen Application Contact Mr. Jon VanDyke, Dean of Admission Services, Lake Land College, Mattoon, IL 61938-9366. *Phone:* 217-234-5378. *Toll-free phone:* 800-252-4121.

LEWIS AND CLARK COMMUNITY COLLEGE

Godfrey, Illinois **www.lc.edu/**

- **District-supported** 2-year, founded 1970, part of Illinois Community College Board
- **Small-town** 275-acre campus with easy access to St. Louis
- **Coed**

Undergraduates 2,377 full-time, 5,069 part-time. Students come from 3 states and territories, 4 other countries, 1% are from out of state, 6% African American, 0.3% Asian American or Pacific Islander, 0.6% Hispanic American, 0.2% Native American, 0.4% international.

Academics *Calendar:* semesters. *Degree:* certificates and associate. *Special study options:* academic remediation for entering students, adult/continuing education programs, advanced placement credit, cooperative education, distance learning, double majors, English as a second language, independent study, internships, off-campus study, part-time degree program, services for LD students, summer session for credit. *ROTC:* Army (b).

Student Life *Campus security:* 24-hour emergency response devices and patrols.

Athletics Member NJCAA.

Applying *Options:* early admission, deferred entrance. *Required for some:* interview. *Recommended:* high school transcript.

Director of Admissions Ms. Peggy Hudson, Director of Enrollment Center for Admissions Services, Lewis and Clark Community College, Enrollment Center, 5800 Godfrey Road, Godfrey, IL 62035. *Phone:* 618-468-5100. *Toll-free phone:* 800-500-LCCC.

LINCOLN COLLEGE

Lincoln, Illinois **www.lincolncollege.edu/**

- **Independent** 2-year, founded 1865
- **Small-town** 42-acre campus
- **Endowment** $14.0 million
- **Coed,** 758 undergraduate students, 92% full-time, 46% women, 54% men

Undergraduates 700 full-time, 58 part-time. Students come from 15 states and territories, 9% are from out of state, 2% transferred in, 90% live on campus. Freshmen *Admission:* 835 applied, 544 admitted, 380 enrolled. *Average high school GPA:* 2.59. *Test scores:* ACT scores over 18: 48%; ACT scores over 24: 8%.

Faculty *Total:* 53, 64% full-time. *Student/faculty ratio:* 16:1.

Majors Accounting; applied art; applied mathematics; art history, criticism and conservation; art teacher education; behavioral sciences; biological and physical sciences; biology/biological sciences; botany/plant biology; broadcast journalism; business administration and management; business/managerial economics; business teacher education; ceramic arts and ceramics; chemistry; commercial and advertising art; computer programming; computer science; computer typography and composition equipment operation; corrections; cosmetology; creative writing; criminal justice/law enforcement administration; criminal justice/police science; criminology; dance; data processing and data processing technology; developmental and child psychology; dramatic/theater arts; drawing; economics; education; elementary education; English; fine/studio arts; foods, nutrition, and wellness; geography; geology/earth science; history; human development and family studies; humanities; jazz/jazz studies; journalism; kindergarten/preschool education; liberal arts and sciences/liberal studies; marine biology and biological oceanography; marketing/marketing management; mass communication/media; mathematics; middle school education; music; music history, literature, and theory; music management and merchandising; nursing (licensed practical/vocational nurse training); nursing (registered nurse training); painting; philosophy; photography; physical education teaching and coaching; physical sciences; piano and organ; political science and government; psychology; radio and television; religious education; sociology; Spanish; statistics; tourism and travel services management; voice and opera; western civilization; zoology/animal biology.

Academics *Calendar:* semesters. *Degree:* associate. *Special study options:* academic remediation for entering students, accelerated degree program, freshman honors college, honors programs, independent study, part-time degree program, summer session for credit.

Library McKinstry Library with 42,500 titles, 380 serial subscriptions, an OPAC, a Web page.

Computers on Campus 72 computers available on campus for general student use. Internet access, at least one staffed computer lab available.

Student Life *Housing:* on-campus residence required through sophomore year. *Options:* men-only, women-only. Campus housing is university owned. *Activities and Organizations:* drama/theater group, student-run newspaper, radio station, choral group, Admissions Ambassadors, Phi Beta Kappa, Connections, SHOS, Spanish Club. *Campus security:* 24-hour emergency response devices and patrols, controlled dormitory access. *Student services:* health clinic.

Athletics Member NJCAA. *Intercollegiate sports:* baseball M(s), basketball M(s)/W(s), golf M(s)/W(s), soccer M(s)/W(s), softball W(s), swimming and diving M(s)/W(s), tennis M/W, volleyball W(s), wrestling M(s). *Intramural sports:* basketball M/W, bowling M/W, equestrian sports M/W, football M, golf M/W, racquetball M/W, soccer M, softball M/W, swimming and diving M/W, table tennis M/W, track and field M/W, volleyball M/W, water polo M/W, weight lifting M/W, wrestling M.

Standardized Tests *Required:* SAT or ACT (for admission).

Costs (2006–07) *Comprehensive fee:* $21,370 includes full-time tuition ($15,000), mandatory fees ($570), and room and board ($5800). Part-time tuition: $500 per credit. *Required fees:* $19 per credit part-time. *Room and board:* college room only: $2200.

Financial Aid Of all full-time matriculated undergraduates who enrolled in 2004, 200 Federal Work-Study jobs (averaging $900).

Applying *Options:* early admission, deferred entrance. *Application fee:* $25. *Required:* high school transcript. *Required for some:* 1 letter of recommendation. *Recommended:* interview. *Application deadline:* rolling (freshmen), rolling (transfers).

Director of Admissions Mr. Tony Schilling, Director of Admissions, Lincoln College, 300 Keokuk Street, Lincoln, IL 62656-1699. *Toll-free phone:* 800-569-0556.

► **See page 564 for the College Close-Up.**

LINCOLN COLLEGE—NORMAL
Normal, Illinois   www.lincolncollege.edu/normal/

- **Independent** primarily 2-year, founded 1865
- **Suburban** 10-acre campus
- **Endowment** $14.0 million
- **Coed,** 520 undergraduate students, 67% full-time, 62% women, 38% men

Undergraduates 350 full-time, 170 part-time. Students come from 6 states and territories, 3 other countries, 6% are from out of state, 17% African American, 2% Hispanic American, 1% international, 10% transferred in, 40% live on campus. Freshmen *Admission:* 225 enrolled. *Average high school GPA:* 2.40. *Test scores:* ACT scores over 18: 80%; ACT scores over 24: 15%.

Faculty *Total:* 50, 18% full-time, 16% with terminal degrees. *Student/faculty ratio:* 14:1.

Majors Accounting; applied art; art teacher education; behavioral sciences; business administration and management; business teacher education; commercial and advertising art; computer graphics; computer management; computer programming; computer science; computer typography and composition equipment operation; corrections; data processing and data processing technology; drawing; economics; education; humanities; information science/studies; legal administrative assistant/secretary; legal assistant/paralegal; liberal arts and sciences/liberal studies; marketing/marketing management; medical administrative assistant and medical secretary; nursing (licensed practical/vocational nurse training); nursing (registered nurse training); philosophy; physical education teaching and coaching; psychology; social sciences; tourism and travel services management.

Academics *Calendar:* semesters. *Degrees:* certificates, associate, and bachelor's. *Special study options:* academic remediation for entering students, adult/continuing education programs, cooperative education, honors programs, internships, part-time degree program, summer session for credit.

Library Milner Library at Illinois State University plus 1 other with 1.8 million titles, 25,000 audiovisual materials, an OPAC, a Web page.

Computers on Campus 50 computers available on campus for general student use. A campuswide network can be accessed from student residence rooms and from off campus. Internet access, at least one staffed computer lab available.

Student Life *Housing:* on-campus residence required for freshman year. *Options:* coed. Campus housing is university owned. *Activities and Organizations:* Phi Theta Kappa, Student Ambassadors. *Campus security:* 24-hour emergency response devices and patrols, student patrols, late-night transport/escort service, controlled dormitory access. *Student services:* health clinic.

Athletics Member NJCAA. *Intercollegiate sports:* baseball M, basketball M/W, golf M/W, soccer M/W, softball W, swimming and diving M/W, volleyball W, wrestling M. *Intramural sports:* bowling M/W, football M, ice hockey M, lacrosse M, tennis M/W.

Standardized Tests *Required for some:* SAT or ACT (for admission).

Costs (2006–07) *Tuition:* $1500 full-time, $413 per credit hour part-time. *Required fees:* $810 full-time, $8 per credit hour part-time, $35 per term part-time. *Room only:* $3200.

Applying *Options:* common application, electronic application, deferred entrance. *Application fee:* $25. *Required:* high school transcript, interview. *Required for some:* 2 letters of recommendation. *Application deadline:* rolling (freshmen), rolling (transfers).

Freshmen Application Contact Mr. Joe Hendrix, Dean of Student Affairs, Lincoln College–Normal, 715 West Raab Road, Normal, IL 61761. *Phone:* 309-454-0500 Ext. 4315. *Toll-free phone:* 800-569-0558. *E-mail:* ncadmissionsinfo@lincolncollege.edu.

▶ **See page 566 for the College Close-Up.**

LINCOLN LAND COMMUNITY COLLEGE
Springfield, Illinois   www.llcc.edu/

- **District-supported** 2-year, founded 1967, part of Illinois Community College Board
- **Suburban** 441-acre campus with easy access to St. Louis
- **Endowment** $1.7 million
- **Coed,** 6,847 undergraduate students, 39% full-time, 59% women, 41% men

Undergraduates 2,700 full-time, 4,147 part-time. Students come from 4 states and territories, 3 other countries, 7% African American, 1% Asian American or Pacific Islander, 2% Hispanic American, 0.4% Native American, 0.2% international, 3% transferred in. *Retention:* 46% of 2003 full-time freshmen returned. Freshmen *Admission:* 765 applied, 765 admitted, 765 enrolled. *Average high school GPA:* 2.94. *Test scores:* ACT scores over 18: 63%; ACT scores over 24: 17%; ACT scores over 30: 1%.

Faculty *Total:* 388, 32% full-time, 30% with terminal degrees. *Student/faculty ratio:* 19:1.

Majors Administrative assistant and secretarial science; agricultural production; architectural drafting and CAD/CADD; art; automobile/automotive mechanics technology; biological and physical sciences; business administration and management; business automation/technology/data entry; child care provision; child guidance; computer programming (specific applications); computer systems networking and telecommunications; criminal justice/police science; electrical, electronic and communications engineering technology; fire protection and safety technology; general studies; hotel/motel administration; landscaping and groundskeeping; legal administrative assistant/secretary; liberal arts and sciences/liberal studies; literature; medical radiologic technology; music; nursing (registered nurse training); occupational therapist assistant; physical therapist assistant; pre-engineering; respiratory care therapy; selling skills and sales.

Academics *Calendar:* semesters. *Degree:* certificates and associate. *Special study options:* academic remediation for entering students, accelerated degree program, adult/continuing education programs, advanced placement credit, distance learning, English as a second language, external degree program, honors programs, independent study, internships, off-campus study, part-time degree program, services for LD students, study abroad, summer session for credit.

Library Learning Resource Center with 65,000 titles, 10,000 serial subscriptions, 3,300 audiovisual materials, an OPAC, a Web page.

Computers on Campus 130 computers available on campus for general student use. A campuswide network can be accessed from off campus. Internet access, online (class) registration, at least one staffed computer lab available.

Student Life *Housing:* college housing not available. *Activities and Organizations:* drama/theater group, student-run newspaper, choral group, Student Senate, Phi Theta Kappa, Model Illinois Government, student newspaper, Madrigals. *Campus security:* 24-hour emergency response devices and patrols, late-night transport/escort service. *Student services:* health clinic, personal/psychological counseling, women's center.

Athletics Member NJCAA. *Intercollegiate sports:* baseball M(s), basketball M(s)/W(s), soccer M(s), softball W(s), volleyball W(s). *Intramural sports:* basketball M/W, tennis M/W.

Costs (2005–06) *Tuition:* area resident $1890 full-time, $63 per credit hour part-time; state resident $7980 full-time, $266 per credit hour part-time; nonresident $9510 full-time, $317 per credit hour part-time. Full-time tuition and fees vary according to course load. Part-time tuition and fees vary according to course load. *Required fees:* $165 full-time, $6 per credit hour part-time. *Payment plan:* installment. *Waivers:* senior citizens and employees or children of employees.

Applying *Options:* common application, early admission, deferred entrance. *Recommended:* high school transcript. *Application deadline:* rolling (freshmen), rolling (transfers). *Notification:* continuous (freshmen).

Freshmen Application Contact Mr. Ron Gregoire, Executive Director of Admissions and Records, Lincoln Land Community College, 5250 Shepherd Road, PO Box 19256, Springfield, IL 62794-9256. *Phone:* 217-786-2243. *Toll-free phone:* 800-727-4161 Ext. 298. *Fax:* 217-786-2492. *E-mail:* ron.gregoire@llcc.edu.

MACCORMAC COLLEGE
Chicago, Illinois   www.maccormac.edu/

Director of Admissions Ms. Rosa Medina, Coordinator of Admissions, MacCormac College, 506 South Wabash Avenue, Chicago, IL 60605-1667. *Phone:* 312-922-1884 Ext. 106.

MCHENRY COUNTY COLLEGE
Crystal Lake, Illinois   www.mchenry.edu/

Freshmen Application Contact Fran Duwaldt, Coordinator of Admissions, McHenry County College, 8900 US Highway 14, Crystal Lake, IL 60012. *Phone:* 815-479-7620. *Toll-free phone:* 815-455-8530.

MORAINE VALLEY COMMUNITY COLLEGE
Palos Hills, Illinois   www.morainevalley.edu/

- **State and locally supported** 2-year, founded 1967, part of Illinois Community College Board
- **Suburban** 294-acre campus with easy access to Chicago
- **Endowment** $12.3 million
- **Coed,** 15,929 undergraduate students, 42% full-time, 58% women, 42% men

Undergraduates 6,654 full-time, 9,275 part-time. Students come from 10 states and territories, 34 other countries, 9% African American, 2% Asian American or Pacific Islander, 10% Hispanic American, 0.3% Native American, 2% international, 1% transferred in. *Retention:* 65% of 2003 full-time freshmen returned.
Freshmen *Admission:* 3,961 applied, 3,961 admitted, 2,009 enrolled. *Test scores:* ACT scores over 18: 66%; ACT scores over 24: 15%; ACT scores over 30: 3%.
Faculty *Total:* 761, 22% full-time. *Student/faculty ratio:* 36:1.
Majors Administrative assistant and secretarial science; automobile/automotive mechanics technology; biological and physical sciences; business administration and management; business/commerce; child care provision; computer programming (specific applications); computer systems networking and telecommunications; corrections; criminal justice/police science; design and visual communications; entrepreneurship; fire protection and safety technology; health information/medical records technology; human resources management; instrumentation technology; liberal arts and sciences/liberal studies; mechanical engineering/mechanical technology; medical radiologic technology; nursing (registered nurse training); parks, recreation and leisure facilities management; respiratory care therapy; restaurant, culinary, and catering management; retailing; selling skills and sales; therapeutic recreation; tourism and travel services marketing; visual and performing arts.
Academics *Calendar:* semesters. *Degree:* certificates and associate. *Special study options:* academic remediation for entering students, accelerated degree program, adult/continuing education programs, advanced placement credit, cooperative education, distance learning, double majors, English as a second language, external degree program, honors programs, independent study, internships, off-campus study, part-time degree program, services for LD students, study abroad, summer session for credit.
Library Robert E. Turner Learning Resources Center/Library plus 1 other with 77,164 titles, 399 serial subscriptions, 22,092 audiovisual materials, an OPAC, a Web page.
Computers on Campus 1200 computers available on campus for general student use. A campuswide network can be accessed from off campus. Internet access, online (class) registration, at least one staffed computer lab available.
Student Life *Housing:* college housing not available. *Activities and Organizations:* drama/theater group, student-run newspaper, choral group, student newspaper, Speech Team, Alliance of Latin American Students, Phi Theta Kappa, Arab Student Union. *Campus security:* 24-hour emergency response devices and patrols, late-night transport/escort service, safety and security programs. *Student services:* personal/psychological counseling, women's center.
Athletics Member NJCAA. *Intercollegiate sports:* baseball M(s), basketball M(s)/W(s), cross-country running M(s)/W(s), golf M(s), soccer M(s)/W(s), softball W, tennis M/W(s), volleyball W(s). *Intramural sports:* badminton M/W, basketball M/W, softball W, volleyball W.
Costs (2005–06) *Tuition:* area resident $1920 full-time, $64 per credit hour part-time; state resident $5970 full-time, $199 per credit hour part-time; nonresident $7260 full-time, $242 per credit hour part-time. *Required fees:* $152 full-time, $5 per credit hour part-time, $1 per term part-time. *Payment plan:* installment. *Waivers:* senior citizens and employees or children of employees.
Financial Aid Of all full-time matriculated undergraduates who enrolled in 2004, 84 Federal Work-Study jobs (averaging $1900). 150 state and other part-time jobs (averaging $800).
Applying *Options:* electronic application, early admission, deferred entrance. *Required:* high school transcript. *Application deadline:* rolling (freshmen), rolling (transfers). *Notification:* continuous (freshmen).
Freshmen Application Contact Ms. Claudia Roselli, Director, Admissions and Recruitment, Moraine Valley Community College, 9000 West College Parkway, Palos Hills, IL 60465-0937. *Phone:* 708-974-5357. *Fax:* 708-974-0681. *E-mail:* roselli@morainevalley.edu.

MORRISON INSTITUTE OF TECHNOLOGY
Morrison, Illinois   www.morrison.tec.il.us/

- **Independent** 2-year, founded 1973
- **Small-town** 17-acre campus
- **Endowment** $76,000
- **Coed, primarily men,** 126 undergraduate students

Undergraduates Students come from 4 states and territories, 6% are from out of state, 4% African American, 3% Hispanic American, 55% live on campus.
Freshmen *Average high school GPA:* 2.3. *Test scores:* ACT scores over 18: 72%; ACT scores over 24: 10%; ACT scores over 30: 2%.
Faculty *Total:* 11, 91% full-time. *Student/faculty ratio:* 12:1.
Majors CAD/CADD drafting/design technology; construction engineering technology; drafting and design technology; engineering technology; mechanical drafting and CAD/CADD; survey technology.
Academics *Calendar:* semesters. *Degree:* associate. *Special study options:* academic remediation for entering students, double majors, internships, part-time degree program.
Library Milikan Library with 7,946 titles, 39 serial subscriptions.
Computers on Campus 60 computers available on campus for general student use. A campuswide network can be accessed from student residence rooms. Internet access, at least one staffed computer lab available. Computer purchase or lease plan available.
Student Life *Housing:* on-campus residence required for freshman year. *Options:* coed. Freshman applicants given priority for college housing. *Campus security:* late-night transport/escort service, controlled dormitory access.
Athletics *Intramural sports:* basketball M, bowling M/W, softball M/W, table tennis M/W, volleyball M/W.
Standardized Tests *Recommended:* SAT or ACT (for admission).
Costs (2006–07) *Tuition:* $12,100 full-time, $505 per credit part-time. *Required fees:* $560 full-time, $125 per term part-time. *Room only:* $2600.
Financial Aid Of all full-time matriculated undergraduates who enrolled in 2004, 25 Federal Work-Study jobs (averaging $2000).
Applying *Options:* common application, deferred entrance. *Application fee:* $100. *Required:* high school transcript, proof of immunization. *Application deadline:* rolling (freshmen). *Notification:* continuous until 9/1 (freshmen).
Freshmen Application Contact Mrs. Tammy Pruis, Admission Secretary, Morrison Institute of Technology, 701 Portland Avenue, Morrison, IL 61270. *Phone:* 815-772-7218. *E-mail:* admissions@morrison.tec.il.us.

▶ **See page 582 for the College Close-Up.**

MORTON COLLEGE
Cicero, Illinois   www.morton.edu/

Director of Admissions Ms. Jill Caccamo-Beer, Director of Enrollment Management, Morton College, 3801 South Central Avenue, Cicero, IL 60804. *Phone:* 708-656-8000 Ext. 400.

NORTHWESTERN BUSINESS COLLEGE
Chicago, Illinois   www.northwesternbc.edu/

Director of Admissions Mr. Mark Sliz, Director of Admissions, Northwestern Business College, 4839 North Milwaukee Avenue, Chicago, IL 60630. *Phone:* 773-481-3730. *Toll-free phone:* 800-396-5613.

▶ **See page 588 for the College Close-Up.**

OAKTON COMMUNITY COLLEGE
Des Plaines, Illinois   www.oakton.edu/

Freshmen Application Contact Mr. Dale Cohen, Admissions Specialist, Oakton Community College, 1600 East Golf Road, Des Plaines, IL 60016. *Phone:* 847-635-1703. *E-mail:* dcohen@oakton.edu.

PARKLAND COLLEGE
Champaign, Illinois   www.parkland.edu/

- **District-supported** 2-year, founded 1967, part of Illinois Community College Board
- **Suburban** 233-acre campus
- **Coed,** 9,752 undergraduate students, 47% full-time, 54% women, 46% men

Undergraduates 4,536 full-time, 5,216 part-time. Students come from 30 states and territories, 14 other countries, 1% are from out of state, 13% African American, 4% Asian American or Pacific Islander, 3% Hispanic American, 0.5% Native American, 4% international, 6% transferred in.
Freshmen *Admission:* 4,097 applied, 2,122 admitted, 1,519 enrolled. *Test scores:* ACT scores over 18: 62%; ACT scores over 24: 17%; ACT scores over 30: 1%.
Faculty *Total:* 535, 31% full-time, 12% with terminal degrees. *Student/faculty ratio:* 17:1.
Majors Accounting technology and bookkeeping; administrative assistant and secretarial science; advertising; agricultural business and management; agricultural mechanization; art; art teacher education; autobody/collision and repair technology; automobile/automotive mechanics technology; biological and physical sciences; biomedical technology; business administration and management; business automation/technology/data entry; child care provision; computer and information sciences; computer graphics; computer/information technology services administration related; computer programming; computer programming (specific applications); computer programming (vendor/product certification); computer science; computer software and media applications related; computer systems networking and telecommunications; computer/technical support; construction management; consumer merchandising/retailing management; criminal justice/safety; data entry/microcomputer applications; dental hygiene; design and visual communications; early childhood education; electroneurodiagnostic/electroencephalographic technology; elementary education; engineering science; English; general studies; graphic design; history; human services; industrial technology; information science/studies; landscaping and groundskeeping; liberal arts and sciences/liberal studies; mass communication/media; medical radiologic technology; music performance; music teacher education; nursing (registered nurse training); occupational therapist assistant; radio and television; radio and television broadcasting technology; respiratory care therapy; sales and marketing/marketing and distribution teacher education; secondary education; speech-language pathology; surgical technology; system administration; theater/theater arts management; veterinary/animal health technology; web page, digital/multimedia and information resources design.
Academics *Calendar:* semesters. *Degree:* certificates and associate. *Special study options:* academic remediation for entering students, accelerated degree program, adult/continuing education programs, advanced placement credit, cooperative education, distance learning, double majors, English as a second language, honors programs, independent study, internships, off-campus study, part-time degree program, services for LD students, student-designed majors, study abroad, summer session for credit. *ROTC:* Army (c), Navy (c), Air Force (c).
Library Parkland College Library with 122,676 titles, 300 serial subscriptions, 8,115 audiovisual materials, an OPAC, a Web page.
Computers on Campus 800 computers available on campus for general student use. A campuswide network can be accessed. Internet access, online (class) registration, at least one staffed computer lab available.
Student Life *Housing:* college housing not available. *Activities and Organizations:* drama/theater group, student-run newspaper, radio and television station, choral group. *Campus security:* 24-hour emergency response devices and patrols, late-night transport/escort service. *Student services:* personal/psychological counseling.
Athletics Member NJCAA. *Intercollegiate sports:* baseball M(s), basketball M(s)/W(s), golf M(s), soccer M(s)/W(s), softball W(s), volleyball W(s). *Intramural sports:* basketball M/W, bowling M/W, softball M/W, volleyball M/W.
Standardized Tests *Required for some:* ACT (for admission).
Costs (2006–07) *Tuition:* area resident $2220 full-time, $72 per credit hour part-time; state resident $6360 full-time, $212 per credit hour part-time; nonresident $9450 full-time, $315 per credit hour part-time.
Financial Aid Of all full-time matriculated undergraduates who enrolled in 2004, 100 Federal Work-Study jobs (averaging $2000).
Applying *Options:* deferred entrance. *Recommended:* high school transcript. *Application deadline:* rolling (freshmen), rolling (transfers). *Notification:* continuous (freshmen).
Freshmen Application Contact Admissions Representative, Parkland College, 2400 West Bradley Avenue, Champaign, IL 61821-1899. *Phone:* 217-351-2482. *Toll-free phone:* 800-346-8089. *Fax:* 217-351-2640. *E-mail:* mhenry@parkland.edu.

PRAIRIE STATE COLLEGE
Chicago Heights, Illinois   www.prairiestate.edu/

- **State and locally supported** 2-year, founded 1958, part of Illinois Community College Board
- **Suburban** 68-acre campus with easy access to Chicago
- **Endowment** $573,000
- **Coed,** 5,083 undergraduate students, 34% full-time, 62% women, 38% men

Undergraduates 1,714 full-time, 3,369 part-time. Students come from 4 states and territories, 4% are from out of state, 47% African American, 1% Asian American or Pacific Islander, 10% Hispanic American, 0.6% Native American, 0.2% international, 0.4% transferred in. *Retention:* 48% of 2003 full-time freshmen returned.
Freshmen *Admission:* 836 applied, 836 admitted, 836 enrolled.
Faculty *Total:* 363, 22% full-time. *Student/faculty ratio:* 16:1.
Majors Autobody/collision and repair technology; automobile/automotive mechanics technology; child guidance; computer and information sciences; computer graphics; criminal justice/law enforcement administration; dental hygiene; electrical, electronic and communications engineering technology; executive assistant/executive secretary; finance; fire science; human resources management; industrial technology; interior design; liberal arts and sciences/liberal studies; logistics and materials management; management science; mechanical design technology; mental health/rehabilitation; nursing (registered nurse training); photography; substance abuse/addiction counseling; teacher assistant/aide; tool and die technology.
Academics *Calendar:* semesters. *Degree:* certificates and associate. *Special study options:* academic remediation for entering students, adult/continuing education programs, advanced placement credit, distance learning, English as a second language, honors programs, internships, part-time degree program, services for LD students, student-designed majors, summer session for credit.
Library Learning Resource Center with 45,000 titles, 515 serial subscriptions, 4,000 audiovisual materials, an OPAC.
Computers on Campus 300 computers available on campus for general student use. A campuswide network can be accessed. Internet access, at least one staffed computer lab available.
Student Life *Activities and Organizations:* drama/theater group, student-run newspaper, choral group, Phi Theta Kappa, Black Student Union, Student Government Association, student newspaper, Mental Health Club. *Campus security:* 24-hour emergency response devices and patrols, student patrols, late-night transport/escort service. *Student services:* personal/psychological counseling.
Athletics Member NJCAA. *Intercollegiate sports:* baseball M(s), basketball M(s)/W(s), football M(s), golf M(s)/W(s), soccer M/W, softball M/W(s), tennis W(s). *Intramural sports:* basketball M/W, soccer M/W, softball W, table tennis M/W, volleyball W.
Costs (2005–06) *Tuition:* area resident $1824 full-time, $67 per credit hour part-time; state resident $5280 full-time, $211 per credit hour part-time; nonresident $7200 full-time, $291 per credit hour part-time. Full-time tuition and fees vary according to course load. Part-time tuition and fees vary according to course load. *Required fees:* $236 full-time, $9 per credit hour part-time, $10 per term part-time. *Room and board:* $4500. Room and board charges vary according to location. *Payment plans:* installment, deferred payment. *Waivers:* senior citizens and employees or children of employees.
Financial Aid Of all full-time matriculated undergraduates who enrolled in 2004, 60 Federal Work-Study jobs (averaging $2500).
Applying *Options:* common application, deferred entrance. *Application fee:* $10. *Required:* high school transcript. *Application deadline:* rolling (freshmen), rolling (transfers).
Freshmen Application Contact Ms. Marietta Turner, Director, Admissions, Enrollment and Career Development Services, Prairie State College, 202 South Halsted Street, Chicago Heights, IL 60411. *Phone:* 708-709-3513. *Toll-free phone:* 708-709-3516. *E-mail:* webmaster@prairiestate.edu.

REND LAKE COLLEGE
Ina, Illinois   www.rlc.edu/

Freshmen Application Contact Ms. Lisa Price, Director, Counseling, Rend Lake College, 468 North Ken Gray Parkway, Ina, IL 62846-9801. *Phone:* 618-437-5321 Ext. 205. *Toll-free phone:* 800-369-5321.

RICHLAND COMMUNITY COLLEGE

Decatur, Illinois www.richland.edu/

- **District-supported** 2-year, founded 1971, part of Illinois Community College Board
- **Small-town** 117-acre campus
- **Endowment** $4.8 million
- **Coed,** 3,034 undergraduate students, 35% full-time, 66% women, 34% men

Undergraduates 1,048 full-time, 1,986 part-time. Students come from 1 other state, 12% African American, 0.9% Asian American or Pacific Islander, 0.9% Hispanic American, 0.5% Native American, 0.1% international. *Retention:* 53% of 2003 full-time freshmen returned.

Freshmen *Admission:* 769 applied, 769 admitted. *Test scores:* ACT scores over 18: 74%; ACT scores over 24: 22%; ACT scores over 30: 2%.

Faculty *Total:* 217, 31% full-time, 5% with terminal degrees. *Student/faculty ratio:* 14:1.

Majors Accounting; administrative assistant and secretarial science; agricultural business and management; automobile/automotive mechanics technology; biological and physical sciences; business administration and management; child development; computer and information sciences related; computer graphics; computer programming (specific applications); construction engineering technology; criminal justice/police science; data entry/microcomputer applications; data entry/microcomputer applications related; drafting and design technology; electrical, electronic and communications engineering technology; fire science; food services technology; industrial technology; information science/studies; insurance; legal administrative assistant/secretary; liberal arts and sciences/ liberal studies; medical administrative assistant and medical secretary; nursing (registered nurse training); pre-engineering; word processing.

Academics *Calendar:* semesters. *Degree:* certificates and associate. *Special study options:* academic remediation for entering students, adult/continuing education programs, advanced placement credit, distance learning, English as a second language, freshman honors college, honors programs, part-time degree program, services for LD students, student-designed majors, summer session for credit.

Library Kitty Lindsay Library with 39,452 titles, 275 serial subscriptions, 2,910 audiovisual materials, an OPAC, a Web page.

Computers on Campus 150 computers available on campus for general student use. Internet access, online (class) registration, at least one staffed computer lab available.

Student Life *Housing:* college housing not available. *Activities and Organizations:* student-run newspaper, Student Senate, Forensics Club, Drama Club, Black Student Association, Student Activities Board. *Campus security:* 24-hour emergency response devices and patrols. *Student services:* personal/psychological counseling.

Standardized Tests *Recommended:* ACT (for admission).

Costs (2006–07) *Tuition:* area resident $1785 full-time, $60 per credit hour part-time; state resident $7566 full-time, $258 per credit hour part-time; nonresident $11,490 full-time, $383 per credit hour part-time. *Required fees:* $155 full-time, $5 per credit hour part-time, $10 per term part-time.

Financial Aid Of all full-time matriculated undergraduates who enrolled in 2004, 43 Federal Work-Study jobs (averaging $1339). 129 state and other part-time jobs (averaging $578).

Applying *Options:* early admission. *Required:* high school transcript. *Application deadline:* rolling (freshmen), rolling (transfers).

Freshmen Application Contact Ms. JoAnn Wireg, Director of Admissions and Records, Richland Community College, One College Park, Decatur, IL 62521. *Phone:* 217-875-7200 Ext. 284. *Fax:* 217-875-7783. *E-mail:* jwireg@ richland.edu.

ROCKFORD BUSINESS COLLEGE

Rockford, Illinois www.rbcsuccess.com/

Director of Admissions Ms. Barbara Holliman, Director of Admissions, Rockford Business College, 730 North Church Street, Rockford, IL 61103. *Phone:* 815-965-8616 Ext. 16.

ROCK VALLEY COLLEGE

Rockford, Illinois www.rockvalleycollege.edu/

- **District-supported** 2-year, founded 1964, part of Illinois Community College Board
- **Suburban** 217-acre campus with easy access to Chicago
- **Coed,** 8,145 undergraduate students, 43% full-time, 59% women, 41% men

Undergraduates 3,508 full-time, 4,637 part-time. Students come from 2 states and territories, 3 other countries, 1% are from out of state, 9% African American, 3% Asian American or Pacific Islander, 6% Hispanic American, 0.4% Native American, 0.3% international.

Freshmen *Admission:* 1,118 enrolled.

Faculty *Total:* 291, 48% full-time, 13% with terminal degrees. *Student/faculty ratio:* 21:1.

Majors Accounting; automobile/automotive mechanics technology; avionics maintenance technology; business administration and management; child development; computer engineering technology; computer science; construction engineering technology; criminal justice/law enforcement administration; dental hygiene; electrical, electronic and communications engineering technology; fire science; human services; industrial design; industrial technology; liberal arts and sciences/liberal studies; marketing/marketing management; mechanical design technology; nursing (registered nurse training); pre-engineering; quality control technology; respiratory care therapy; welding technology.

Academics *Calendar:* semesters. *Degree:* certificates and associate. *Special study options:* academic remediation for entering students, adult/continuing education programs, advanced placement credit, cooperative education, distance learning, English as a second language, honors programs, independent study, internships, part-time degree program, services for LD students, student-designed majors, study abroad, summer session for credit.

Library Educational Resource Center with 67,168 titles, an OPAC, a Web page.

Computers on Campus 130 computers available on campus for general student use. A campuswide network can be accessed from off campus. Internet access, online (class) registration, at least one staffed computer lab available.

Student Life *Housing:* college housing not available. *Activities and Organizations:* drama/theater group, student-run newspaper, choral group, Black Student Alliance, Phi Theta Kappa, Adults on Campus, Inter-Varsity Club, Christian Fellowship. *Campus security:* 24-hour emergency response devices and patrols, late-night transport/escort service. *Student services:* personal/psychological counseling.

Athletics Member NJCAA. *Intercollegiate sports:* baseball M, basketball M/W, football M, golf M, softball W, tennis M/W, volleyball W. *Intramural sports:* basketball M/W, skiing (downhill) M/W.

Costs (2006–07) *Tuition:* area resident $1830 full-time, $61 per credit part-time; state resident $7350 full-time, $245 per credit part-time; nonresident $12,030 full-time, $401 per credit part-time.

Financial Aid Of all full-time matriculated undergraduates who enrolled in 2004, 120 Federal Work-Study jobs (averaging $1800).

Applying *Required:* high school transcript. *Application deadlines:* 8/29 (freshmen), 8/29 (transfers). *Notification:* continuous (freshmen).

Freshmen Application Contact Ms. Lisa Allman, Coordinator of Admissions and Records, Rock Valley College, 3301 North Mulford Road, Rockford, IL 61114-5699. *Phone:* 815-921-4262. *Toll-free phone:* 800-973-7821. *Fax:* 815-921-4267. *E-mail:* s.ullrick@rvc.cc.il.us.

SAUK VALLEY COMMUNITY COLLEGE

Dixon, Illinois www.svcc.edu/

- **District-supported** 2-year, founded 1965, part of Illinois Community College Board
- **Rural** 165-acre campus
- **Coed,** 2,745 undergraduate students, 42% full-time, 62% women, 38% men

Undergraduates 1,154 full-time, 1,591 part-time. 2% African American, 0.9% Asian American or Pacific Islander, 7% Hispanic American, 0.2% Native American.

Freshmen *Admission:* 1,327 applied, 1,327 admitted, 354 enrolled. *Test scores:* ACT scores over 18: 75%; ACT scores over 24: 18%.

Faculty *Total:* 157, 33% full-time, 10% with terminal degrees. *Student/faculty ratio:* 19:1.

Majors Accounting; administrative assistant and secretarial science; architecture; art; athletic training; biology/biological sciences; business administration and management; chemistry; chiropractic assistant; communication/speech communication and rhetoric; computer and information sciences related; corrections;

Sauk Valley Community College (continued)

criminal justice/law enforcement administration; criminal justice/police science; dramatic/theater arts; early childhood education; economics; education; electrical, electronic and communications engineering technology; elementary education; English; French; heating, air conditioning, ventilation and refrigeration maintenance technology; history; human services; industrial radiologic technology; legal administrative assistant/secretary; liberal arts and sciences/liberal studies; marketing/marketing management; mathematics; mechanical engineering/ mechanical technology; medical office assistant; music; nursing (registered nurse training); occupational therapy; optometric technician; physical education teaching and coaching; physical therapy; physics; political science and government; pre-dentistry studies; pre-medical studies; pre-pharmacy studies; pre-veterinary studies; psychology; public administration and social service professions related; secondary education; social work; sociology; Spanish; special education; speech and rhetoric.

Academics *Calendar:* semesters. *Degree:* certificates and associate. *Special study options:* academic remediation for entering students, accelerated degree program, adult/continuing education programs, cooperative education, distance learning, English as a second language, honors programs, independent study, internships, off-campus study, part-time degree program, services for LD students, student-designed majors.

Library Learning Resource Center plus 1 other with 55,000 titles, 268 serial subscriptions.

Computers on Campus 100 computers available on campus for general student use. A campuswide network can be accessed. Internet access, at least one staffed computer lab available.

Student Life *Housing:* college housing not available. *Activities and Organizations:* drama/theater group, choral group. *Campus security:* 24-hour emergency response devices and patrols, late-night transport/escort service. *Student services:* personal/psychological counseling.

Athletics Member NJCAA. *Intercollegiate sports:* baseball M(s), basketball M(s)/W(s), cross-country running M(s)/W(s), softball W(s), tennis M(s)/W(s). *Intramural sports:* basketball M/W.

Standardized Tests *Recommended:* ACT (for admission).

Costs (2006–07) *Tuition:* area resident $2418 full-time, $74 per credit hour part-time; state resident $9065 full-time, $259 per credit hour part-time; nonresident $9375 full-time, $293 per credit hour part-time.

Financial Aid Of all full-time matriculated undergraduates who enrolled in 2004, 150 Federal Work-Study jobs (averaging $3000).

Applying *Options:* early admission, deferred entrance. *Recommended:* high school transcript. *Application deadline:* rolling (freshmen), rolling (transfers). *Notification:* continuous (freshmen).

Freshmen Application Contact Ms. Pamela Clodfelter, Director of Admissions, Records, and Placement, Sauk Valley Community College, 173 Illinois Route 2, Dixon, IL 61021. *Phone:* 815-288-5511 Ext. 310. *Fax:* 815-288-3190. *E-mail:* skyhawk@svcc.edu.

SHAWNEE COMMUNITY COLLEGE
Ullin, Illinois   **www.shawneecc.edu/**

- **State and locally supported** 2-year, founded 1967, part of Illinois Community College Board
- **Rural** 163-acre campus
- **Coed**

Undergraduates 943 full-time, 2,248 part-time. Students come from 3 states and territories, 22% African American, 0.7% Asian American or Pacific Islander, 1% Hispanic American, 0.6% Native American.

Academics *Calendar:* semesters. *Degree:* certificates and associate. *Special study options:* academic remediation for entering students, accelerated degree program, adult/continuing education programs, English as a second language, internships, part-time degree program, services for LD students, summer session for credit.

Student Life *Campus security:* student patrols.

Athletics Member NJCAA.

Standardized Tests *Required:* ACT ASSET (for placement). *Required for some:* ACT (for placement). *Recommended:* ACT (for placement).

Financial Aid Of all full-time matriculated undergraduates who enrolled in 2004, 60 Federal Work-Study jobs (averaging $2000). 50 state and other part-time jobs (averaging $2000).

Applying *Options:* common application, early admission, deferred entrance. *Required:* high school transcript.

Director of Admissions Ms. Dee Blakely, Director of Admissions, Shawnee Community College, 8364 Shawnee College Road, Ullin, IL 62992-2206. *Phone:* 618-634-3200 Ext. 3247. *Toll-free phone:* 800-481-2242.

SOUTHEASTERN ILLINOIS COLLEGE
Harrisburg, Illinois   **www.sic.edu/**

Freshmen Application Contact Dr. David Nudo, Director of Counseling, Southeastern Illinois College, 3575 College Road, Harrisburg, IL 62946-4925. *Phone:* 618-252-5400 Ext. 2430. *Toll-free phone:* 866-338-2742.

SOUTH SUBURBAN COLLEGE
South Holland, Illinois   **www.southsuburbancollege.edu/**

Director of Admissions Ms. Jazaer Farrar, Director of New Student Services, South Suburban College, 15800 South State Street, South Holland, IL 60473-1270. *Phone:* 708-596-2000 Ext. 2291.

SOUTHWESTERN ILLINOIS COLLEGE
Belleville, Illinois   **www.southwestern.cc.il.us/**

- **District-supported** 2-year, founded 1946, part of Illinois Community College Board
- **Suburban** 150-acre campus with easy access to St. Louis
- **Endowment** $3.1 million
- **Coed,** 14,479 undergraduate students, 37% full-time, 57% women, 43% men

Undergraduates 5,296 full-time, 9,183 part-time. Students come from 6 states and territories, 19 other countries, 18% African American, 2% Asian American or Pacific Islander, 3% Hispanic American, 0.6% Native American, 0.1% international, 43% transferred in.

Freshmen *Admission:* 1,006 admitted, 1,006 enrolled.

Faculty *Total:* 829, 15% full-time. *Student/faculty ratio:* 17:1.

Majors Accounting; administrative assistant and secretarial science; airframe mechanics and aircraft maintenance technology; autobody/collision and repair technology; avionics maintenance technology; banking and financial support services; business administration and management; carpentry; child development; clinical/medical laboratory technology; construction engineering technology; construction management; criminal justice/law enforcement administration; data processing and data processing technology; desktop publishing and digital imaging design; drafting and design technology; electrical, electronic and communications engineering technology; elementary education; engineering technology; fine/studio arts; fire science; health information/medical records administration; heating, air conditioning, ventilation and refrigeration maintenance technology; horticultural science; hospitality administration; industrial radiologic technology; information science/studies; instrumentation technology; legal administrative assistant/secretary; legal assistant/paralegal; liberal arts and sciences/liberal studies; machine tool technology; marketing/marketing management; medical administrative assistant and medical secretary; medical/clinical assistant; metallurgical technology; nursing (registered nurse training); physical education teaching and coaching; physical therapist assistant; pre-pharmacy studies; real estate; sign language interpretation and translation; welding technology.

Academics *Calendar:* semesters. *Degree:* certificates, diplomas, and associate. *Special study options:* academic remediation for entering students, accelerated degree program, adult/continuing education programs, advanced placement credit, cooperative education, distance learning, double majors, English as a second language, internships, off-campus study, part-time degree program, services for LD students, study abroad, summer session for credit. *ROTC:* Army (c), Air Force (c).

Library Belleville Area College Library with 82,537 titles, 638 serial subscriptions, 2,688 audiovisual materials, an OPAC, a Web page.

Computers on Campus 348 computers available on campus for general student use. A campuswide network can be accessed. Internet access, at least one staffed computer lab available.

Student Life *Housing:* college housing not available. *Activities and Organizations:* drama/theater group, student-run newspaper, choral group, College Activities Board, Phi Theta Kappa, Student Nurses Association, Horticulture Club, Data Processing Management Association. *Campus security:* 24-hour emergency response devices and patrols, student patrols, late-night transport/escort service. *Student services:* personal/psychological counseling, women's center.

Athletics Member NJCAA. *Intercollegiate sports:* baseball M(s), basketball M(s)/W(s), soccer M(s), softball W(s), tennis M(s)/W(s), volleyball W(s). *Intramural sports:* basketball M/W, bowling M/W, softball M/W, tennis M/W, volleyball M/W.

Standardized Tests *Required for some:* ACT ASSET or ACT COMPASS, ACT ASSET or ACT COMPASS.

Costs (2006–07) *Tuition:* area resident $1890 full-time, $63 per credit hour part-time; state resident $5220 full-time, $174 per credit hour part-time; nonresident $8070 full-time, $269 per credit hour part-time.

Financial Aid Of all full-time matriculated undergraduates who enrolled in 2004, 170 Federal Work-Study jobs (averaging $1537). 179 state and other part-time jobs (averaging $1004).

Applying *Options:* early admission, deferred entrance. *Application fee:* $10. *Required:* high school transcript. *Application deadline:* rolling (freshmen), rolling (transfers).

Freshmen Application Contact Mike Leiker, Director of Admissions, Southwestern Illinois College, 2500 Carlyle Road, Belleville, IL 62221-5899. *Phone:* 618-235-2700 Ext. 5400. *Toll-free phone:* 800-222-5131. *Fax:* 618-277-0631.

SPOON RIVER COLLEGE

Canton, Illinois   **www.spoonrivercollege.net/**

- **State-supported** 2-year, founded 1959, part of Illinois Community College Board
- **Rural** 160-acre campus
- **Endowment** $98,726
- **Coed,** 2,333 undergraduate students, 45% full-time, 55% women, 45% men

Undergraduates 1,053 full-time, 1,280 part-time. Students come from 6 states and territories, 0.5% are from out of state, 5% African American, 1% Asian American or Pacific Islander, 0.9% Hispanic American, 0.5% Native American, 0.1% international.

Freshmen *Test scores:* ACT scores over 18: 64%; ACT scores over 24: 12%.

Faculty *Total:* 142, 29% full-time, 7% with terminal degrees. *Student/faculty ratio:* 20:1.

Majors Accounting; administrative assistant and secretarial science; agricultural mechanization; agricultural teacher education; art; automobile/automotive mechanics technology; biological and physical sciences; biology/biological sciences; botany/plant biology; business administration and management; business teacher education; chemistry; child development; criminal justice/law enforcement administration; criminal justice/police science; dramatic/theater arts; education; electrical, electronic and communications engineering technology; English; finance; health science; history; industrial technology; information science/studies; kindergarten/preschool education; legal administrative assistant/secretary; liberal arts and sciences/liberal studies; mass communication/media; mathematics; medical administrative assistant and medical secretary; nursing (registered nurse training); physical education teaching and coaching; physical sciences; physics; political science and government; pre-engineering; psychology; social sciences; sociology; speech and rhetoric; zoology/animal biology.

Academics *Calendar:* semesters. *Degree:* certificates and associate. *Special study options:* accelerated degree program, adult/continuing education programs, advanced placement credit, distance learning, English as a second language, freshman honors college, honors programs, internships, part-time degree program, services for LD students, summer session for credit. *ROTC:* Army (b).

Library Learning Resource Center with 34,799 titles, 121 serial subscriptions, 3,213 audiovisual materials, an OPAC.

Computers on Campus 34 computers available on campus for general student use. A campuswide network can be accessed. At least one staffed computer lab available.

Student Life *Housing:* college housing not available. *Activities and Organizations:* drama/theater group, Student Senate, PEACE, Peer Ambassadors. *Campus security:* 24-hour emergency response devices. *Student services:* personal/psychological counseling.

Athletics Member NJCAA. *Intercollegiate sports:* baseball M(s), basketball M(s)/W(s), softball W(s), track and field M(s)/W(s), volleyball W(s).

Costs (2005–06) *Tuition:* area resident $1845 full-time, $62 per credit hour part-time; state resident $3465 full-time, $116 per credit hour part-time; nonresident $4545 full-time, $152 per credit hour part-time. Full-time tuition and fees vary according to course load. Part-time tuition and fees vary according to course load. *Required fees:* $255 full-time, $9 per credit hour part-time. *Payment plan:* installment. *Waivers:* senior citizens and employees or children of employees.

Applying *Options:* early admission. *Required:* high school transcript. *Application deadline:* rolling (freshmen), rolling (transfers).

Freshmen Application Contact Dr. Sharon Wrenn, Dean of Student Services, Spoon River College, 23235 North County 22, Canton, IL 61520-9801. *Phone:* 309-649-6305. *Toll-free phone:* 800-334-7337. *Fax:* 309-649-6235. *E-mail:* info@spoonrivercollege.edu.

SPRINGFIELD COLLEGE IN ILLINOIS

Springfield, Illinois   **www.sci.edu/**

- **Independent** 2-year, founded 1929, affiliated with Roman Catholic Church
- **Urban** 8-acre campus
- **Endowment** $694,388
- **Coed,** 552 undergraduate students, 49% full-time, 68% women, 32% men

Undergraduates 271 full-time, 281 part-time. Students come from 13 states and territories, 8 other countries, 3% are from out of state, 15% African American, 0.2% Asian American or Pacific Islander, 0.7% Hispanic American, 0.2% Native American, 0.9% international, 6% transferred in.

Freshmen *Admission:* 243 applied, 209 admitted, 130 enrolled. *Average high school GPA:* 3.00. *Test scores:* ACT scores over 18: 67%; ACT scores over 24: 19%; ACT scores over 30: 1%.

Faculty *Total:* 71, 30% full-time, 11% with terminal degrees. *Student/faculty ratio:* 12:1.

Majors Art; business administration and management; computer science; education; forensic science and technology; general studies; liberal arts and sciences/liberal studies; mass communication/media; mathematics; pre-dentistry studies; pre-law studies; pre-medical studies; pre-nursing studies; pre-pharmacy studies; pre-veterinary studies; social work.

Academics *Calendar:* semesters. *Degrees:* associate (the college partners with Benedictine University, which offers baccalaureate and master degree programs at Springfield College's campus). *Special study options:* academic remediation for entering students, adult/continuing education programs, advanced placement credit, off-campus study, part-time degree program, student-designed majors, summer session for credit.

Library Charles E. Becker Library plus 1 other with 19,951 titles, 146 serial subscriptions, 2,490 audiovisual materials, an OPAC, a Web page.

Computers on Campus 25 computers available on campus for general student use. A campuswide network can be accessed. Internet access, at least one staffed computer lab available.

Student Life *Housing Options:* coed. *Activities and Organizations:* student-run newspaper, Phi Theta Kappa, Student Ambassadors, Student Activity Council, Sculpture Club, Pep/Poms, national fraternities. *Campus security:* 24-hour emergency response devices. *Student services:* personal/psychological counseling.

Athletics Member NJCAA. *Intercollegiate sports:* baseball M(s), golf M, soccer M(s)/W(s), softball W(s), volleyball W(s). *Intramural sports:* basketball M, tennis W, volleyball W.

Standardized Tests *Required:* SAT and SAT Subject Tests or ACT (for admission).

Costs (2006–07) *Comprehensive fee:* $15,400 includes full-time tuition ($7490), mandatory fees ($1990), and room and board ($5920). Part-time tuition: $312 per hour.

Financial Aid Of all full-time matriculated undergraduates who enrolled in 2004, 30 Federal Work-Study jobs (averaging $1700).

Applying *Options:* common application. *Application fee:* $20. *Required:* high school transcript. *Required for some:* interview. *Recommended:* minimum 2.0 GPA. *Application deadline:* rolling (freshmen), rolling (transfers). *Notification:* continuous (freshmen).

Director of Admissions Ms. Kim Fontana, Director of Admissions, Springfield College in Illinois, 1500 North Fifth Street, Springfield, IL 62702-2694. *Phone:* 217-525-1420 Ext. 241. *Toll-free phone:* 800-635-7289.

TAYLOR BUSINESS INSTITUTE

Chicago, Illinois

Director of Admissions Mr. Rashed Jahangir, Taylor Business Institute, 200 North Michigan Avenue, Suite 301, Chicago, IL 60601.

TRITON COLLEGE

River Grove, Illinois   **www.triton.cc.il.us/**

- **State-supported** 2-year, founded 1964, part of Illinois Community College Board
- **Suburban** 100-acre campus with easy access to Chicago
- **Coed,** 11,021 undergraduate students, 35% full-time, 55% women, 45% men

Undergraduates 3,831 full-time, 7,190 part-time. Students come from 26 other countries, 2% are from out of state, 21% African American, 5% Asian

Triton College (continued)

American or Pacific Islander, 17% Hispanic American, 0.3% Native American, 0.2% international.

Freshmen *Admission:* 5,492 applied, 5,492 admitted, 2,089 enrolled.

Faculty *Total:* 597, 21% full-time, 18% with terminal degrees. *Student/faculty ratio:* 22:1.

Majors Accounting; administrative assistant and secretarial science; architectural engineering technology; art; automobile/automotive mechanics technology; baking and pastry arts; business administration and management; child care provision; commercial and advertising art; computer and information systems security; computer engineering technology; computer graphics; computer programming related; computer science; computer software and media applications related; computer systems networking and telecommunications; computer/technical support; computer typography and composition equipment operation; construction engineering technology; construction management; consumer merchandising/retailing management; court reporting; criminal justice/law enforcement administration; criminal justice/police science; culinary arts; data processing and data processing technology; drafting and design technology; dramatic/theater arts; electrical, electronic and communications engineering technology; engineering technology; fashion merchandising; fire science; graphic and printing equipment operation/production; heating, air conditioning, ventilation and refrigeration maintenance technology; hospitality administration; hotel/motel administration; industrial technology; information science/studies; interdisciplinary studies; interior design; international business/trade/commerce; kindergarten/preschool education; landscape architecture; landscaping and groundskeeping; legal administrative assistant/secretary; liberal arts and sciences/liberal studies; machine tool technology; management information systems; marketing/marketing management; music; nuclear medical technology; nursing (licensed practical/vocational nurse training); nursing (registered nurse training); ophthalmic laboratory technology; ophthalmic technology; opticianry; ornamental horticulture; radiologic technology/science; real estate; respiratory care therapy; substance abuse/addiction counseling; system administration; transportation technology; web/multimedia management and webmaster; web page, digital/multimedia and information resources design; welding technology.

Academics *Calendar:* semesters. *Degree:* certificates and associate. *Special study options:* academic remediation for entering students, adult/continuing education programs, advanced placement credit, cooperative education, distance learning, English as a second language, freshman honors college, honors programs, internships, part-time degree program, student-designed majors, summer session for credit.

Library Learning Resource Center with 70,859 titles, 1,247 serial subscriptions.

Computers on Campus 350 computers available on campus for general student use. At least one staffed computer lab available.

Student Life *Housing:* college housing not available. *Activities and Organizations:* drama/theater group, student-run newspaper, radio station, choral group, student government, Program Board. *Campus security:* 24-hour emergency response devices and patrols. *Student services:* health clinic, personal/psychological counseling.

Athletics Member NJCAA. *Intercollegiate sports:* baseball M, basketball M/W, soccer M, softball W, swimming and diving W, volleyball W, wrestling M.

Costs (2006–07) *Tuition:* area resident $1680 full-time, $56 per semester hour part-time; state resident $5244 full-time, $175 per semester hour part-time; nonresident $6670 full-time, $222 per semester hour part-time. *Required fees:* $250 full-time, $5 per credit hour part-time, $30 per term part-time.

Financial Aid Of all full-time matriculated undergraduates who enrolled in 2004, 250 Federal Work-Study jobs (averaging $2000).

Applying *Options:* deferred entrance. *Required:* high school transcript. *Application deadline:* rolling (freshmen), rolling (transfers).

Freshmen Application Contact Mr. Doug Olson, Dean of Student Services, Triton College, 2000 Fifth Avenue, River Grove, IL 60171. *Phone:* 708-456-0300 Ext. 3230. *Toll-free phone:* 800-942-7404. *Fax:* 708-583-3121. *E-mail:* dolson@triton.edu.

WAUBONSEE COMMUNITY COLLEGE
Sugar Grove, Illinois   www.waubonsee.edu/

- **District-supported** 2-year, founded 1966, part of Illinois Community College Board
- **Rural** 243-acre campus with easy access to Chicago
- **Endowment** $1.6 million
- **Coed,** 8,834 undergraduate students, 30% full-time, 57% women, 43% men

Undergraduates 2,624 full-time, 6,210 part-time. Students come from 1 other state, 2 other countries, 7% African American, 2% Asian American or Pacific Islander, 17% Hispanic American, 0.3% Native American, 0.0% international, 2% transferred in. *Retention:* 63% of 2003 full-time freshmen returned.

Freshmen *Admission:* 916 applied, 916 admitted, 916 enrolled.

Faculty *Total:* 877, 10% full-time. *Student/faculty ratio:* 17:1.

Majors Accounting technology and bookkeeping; administrative assistant and secretarial science; art; art teacher education; autobody/collision and repair technology; automobile/automotive mechanics technology; banking and financial support services; biological and physical sciences; business administration and management; business automation/technology/data entry; CAD/CADD drafting/design technology; child care provision; communication/speech communication and rhetoric; computer and information sciences; computer and information sciences related; computer programming (specific applications); criminal justice/police science; design and visual communications; electrical, electronic and communications engineering technology; engineering; entrepreneurship; executive assistant/executive secretary; fire protection and safety technology; general studies; graphic design; heating, air conditioning, ventilation and refrigeration maintenance technology; industrial mechanics and maintenance technology; industrial technology; kindergarten/preschool education; liberal arts and sciences/liberal studies; logistics and materials management; machine tool technology; massage therapy; mass communication/media; medical/clinical assistant; music; music teacher education; nursing assistant/aide and patient care assistant; nursing (registered nurse training); operations management; quality control technology; retailing; robotics technology; sign language interpretation and translation; social work; tourism and travel services marketing.

Academics *Calendar:* semesters. *Degree:* certificates and associate. *Special study options:* academic remediation for entering students, accelerated degree program, advanced placement credit, distance learning, honors programs, independent study, internships, part-time degree program, services for LD students, study abroad, summer session for credit. *ROTC:* Army (c).

Library Todd Library with 53,679 titles, 562 serial subscriptions, 6,388 audiovisual materials, an OPAC, a Web page.

Computers on Campus 160 computers available on campus for general student use. A campuswide network can be accessed from off campus. Internet access, online (class) registration, at least one staffed computer lab available.

Student Life *Housing:* college housing not available. *Activities and Organizations:* drama/theater group, student-run newspaper, choral group, Phi Theta Kappa, VICA, Alpha Sigma Lamda, Latinos Unidos, Christian Fellowship. *Campus security:* 24-hour emergency response devices and patrols, late-night transport/escort service.

Athletics Member NJCAA. *Intercollegiate sports:* baseball M, basketball M(s)/W(s), cross-country running M(s)/W(s), golf M(s), soccer M(s), softball W(s), tennis M(s)/W(s), volleyball W(s), wrestling M(s). *Intramural sports:* basketball M/W, bowling M/W, golf M/W, table tennis M/W.

Costs (2006–07) *Tuition:* area resident $2010 full-time, $67 per semester hour part-time; state resident $6300 full-time, $210 per semester hour part-time; nonresident $7110 full-time, $237 per semester hour part-time. *Required fees:* $90 full-time, $3 per semester hour part-time.

Financial Aid Of all full-time matriculated undergraduates who enrolled in 2004, 23 Federal Work-Study jobs (averaging $2000).

Applying *Application deadline:* rolling (freshmen), rolling (transfers).

Freshmen Application Contact Ms. Faith Marston, Recruitment and Retention Manager, Waubonsee Community College, Route 47 at Waubonsee Drive, Sugar Grove, IL 60554. *Phone:* 630-466-7900 Ext. 2938. *Fax:* 630-466-4964. *E-mail:* recruitment@waubonsee.edu.

WESTWOOD COLLEGE–CHICAGO DUPAGE
Woodridge, Illinois   www.westwood.edu/

Director of Admissions Mr. Scott Kawall, Director of Admissions, Westwood College–Chicago Du Page, 7155 James Avenue, Woodridge, IL 60517-2321. *Phone:* 630-434-8244. *Toll-free phone:* 888-721-7646.

► **See page 614 for the College Close-Up.**

WESTWOOD COLLEGE–CHICAGO LOOP CAMPUS
Chicago, Illinois   www.westwood.edu/

Director of Admissions Gus Pyrolis, Acting Director of Admissions, Westwood College–Chicago Loop Campus, 17 North State Street, Suite 1500, Chicago, IL 60602. *Phone:* 312-739-0850.

► **See page 616 for the College Close-Up.**

WESTWOOD COLLEGE—CHICAGO O'HARE AIRPORT

Schiller Park, Illinois   **www.westwood.edu/**

Director of Admissions Mr. David Traub, Director of Admissions, Westwood College–Chicago O'Hare Airport, 4825 North Scott Street, Suite 100, Schiller Park, IL 60176-1209. *Phone:* 847-928-0200 Ext. 100. *Toll-free phone:* 877-877-8857.

▶ **See page 618 for the College Close-Up.**

WESTWOOD COLLEGE—CHICAGO RIVER OAKS

Calumet City, Illinois   **www.westwood.edu/**

Director of Admissions Tash Uray, Director of Admissions, Westwood College–Chicago River Oaks, 80 River Oaks Drive, Suite D-49, Calumet City, IL 60409-5820. *Phone:* 708-832-1988. *Toll-free phone:* 888-549-6873.

▶ **See page 620 for the College Close-Up.**

WILLIAM RAINEY HARPER COLLEGE

Palatine, Illinois   **www.harpercollege.edu/**

- **State and locally supported** 2-year, founded 1965, part of Illinois Community College Board
- **Suburban** 200-acre campus with easy access to Chicago
- **Coed,** 15,026 undergraduate students, 41% full-time, 57% women, 43% men

Undergraduates 6,174 full-time, 8,852 part-time. Students come from 13 states and territories, 31 other countries, 1% are from out of state, 4% African American, 12% Asian American or Pacific Islander, 14% Hispanic American, 0.3% Native American, 0.6% international, 3% transferred in. *Retention:* 70% of 2003 full-time freshmen returned.

Freshmen *Admission:* 4,887 applied, 4,887 admitted, 2,494 enrolled.

Faculty *Total:* 830, 23% full-time. *Student/faculty ratio:* 22:1.

Majors Accounting; administrative assistant and secretarial science; architectural engineering technology; art; biological and physical sciences; biology/biological sciences; botany/plant biology; business administration and management; child development; computer and information sciences; computer engineering technology; computer management; computer programming; computer science; computer typography and composition equipment operation; criminal justice/law enforcement administration; criminal justice/police science; culinary arts; data processing and data processing technology; dental hygiene; dietetics; drafting and design technology; electrical, electronic and communications engineering technology; engineering; fashion/apparel design; fashion merchandising; finance; fire science; health teacher education; heating, air conditioning, ventilation and refrigeration maintenance technology; horticultural science; hospitality administration; hotel/motel administration; humanities; human resources management; industrial technology; information science/studies; insurance; interior design; international business/trade/commerce; journalism; kindergarten/preschool education; kinesiology and exercise science; landscape architecture; landscaping and groundskeeping; legal administrative assistant/secretary; legal assistant/paralegal; liberal arts and sciences/liberal studies; machine tool technology; management information systems; marketing/marketing management; materials science; mathematics; mechanical design technology; mechanical engineering/mechanical technology; medical administrative assistant and medical secretary; medical/clinical assistant; music; nursing (licensed practical/vocational nurse training); nursing (registered nurse training); parks, recreation and leisure facilities management; physical education teaching and coaching; physical sciences; pre-engineering; purchasing, procurement/acquisitions and contracts management; quality control technology; real estate; rehabilitation therapy; sign language interpretation and translation; social sciences.

Academics *Calendar:* semesters. *Degree:* certificates and associate. *Special study options:* academic remediation for entering students, adult/continuing education programs, advanced placement credit, cooperative education, distance learning, English as a second language, honors programs, independent study, internships, part-time degree program, services for LD students, study abroad, summer session for credit.

Library Harper College Library with 143,817 titles, 6,606 serial subscriptions, 33,049 audiovisual materials, an OPAC, a Web page.

Computers on Campus 206 computers available on campus for general student use. A campuswide network can be accessed from off campus. Internet access, online (class) registration, at least one staffed computer lab available.

Student Life *Housing:* college housing not available. *Activities and Organizations:* drama/theater group, student-run newspaper, radio station, choral group, student radio station, Program Board, Student Senate, Nursing Club, Phi Theta Kappa. *Campus security:* 24-hour emergency response devices and patrols, late-night transport/escort service. *Student services:* health clinic, personal/psychological counseling, women's center, legal services.

Athletics Member NJCAA. *Intercollegiate sports:* baseball M, basketball M/W, cross-country running M/W, football M, soccer M/W, softball W, track and field M/W, volleyball W, wrestling M. *Intramural sports:* baseball M, basketball M/W, bowling M, racquetball M/W, skiing (cross-country) M/W, skiing (downhill) M/W, softball M/W, table tennis M/W, tennis M/W, volleyball M/W.

Costs (2005–06) *Tuition:* area resident $1800 full-time, $75 per credit hour part-time; state resident $6600 full-time, $275 per credit hour part-time; nonresident $8256 full-time, $344 per credit hour part-time. *Required fees:* $450 full-time.

Financial Aid Of all full-time matriculated undergraduates who enrolled in 2004, 85 Federal Work-Study jobs (averaging $1210).

Applying *Options:* electronic application, early admission, deferred entrance. *Application fee:* $25. *Required:* high school transcript. *Application deadline:* rolling (freshmen), rolling (transfers). *Notification:* continuous (freshmen).

Freshmen Application Contact Director of Outreach, William Rainey Harper College, 1200 West Algonquin Road, Palatine, IL 60067. *Phone:* 847-925-6206. *Fax:* 847-925-6044.

WORSHAM COLLEGE OF MORTUARY SCIENCE

Wheeling, Illinois   **www.worshamcollege.com/**

Director of Admissions Ms. Stephanie Kann, President, Worsham College of Mortuary Science, 495 Northgate Parkway, Wheeling, IL 60090-2646. *Phone:* 847-808-8444.

INDIANA

AMERICAN TRANS AIR AVIATION TRAINING ACADEMY

Indianapolis, Indiana

ANCILLA COLLEGE

Donaldson, Indiana   **www.ancilla.edu/**

- **Independent Roman Catholic** 2-year, founded 1937
- **Rural** 63-acre campus with easy access to Chicago
- **Endowment** $1.9 million
- **Coed,** 624 undergraduate students, 64% full-time, 73% women, 27% men

Undergraduates 397 full-time, 227 part-time. Students come from 10 states and territories, 1% are from out of state, 6% African American, 0.2% Asian American or Pacific Islander, 3% Hispanic American, 1% Native American, 0.2% international, 9% transferred in. *Retention:* 55% of 2003 full-time freshmen returned.

Freshmen *Admission:* 574 applied, 547 admitted, 151 enrolled. *Average high school GPA:* 2.50. *Test scores:* SAT verbal scores over 500: 13%; SAT math scores over 500: 23%; ACT scores over 18: 41%; SAT verbal scores over 600: 2%; ACT scores over 24: 1%.

Faculty *Total:* 50, 44% full-time, 22% with terminal degrees. *Student/faculty ratio:* 15:1.

Majors Art; art teacher education; behavioral sciences; biological and physical sciences; biology/biological sciences; biology teacher education; business administration and management; business/commerce; business operations support and

Ancilla College (continued)

secretarial services related; chemistry; chemistry teacher education; computer programming; computer software and media applications related; computer systems networking and telecommunications; criminal justice/law enforcement administration; criminal justice/safety; early childhood education; elementary education; English; English/language arts teacher education; fine arts related; fine/studio arts; graphic design; health/medical preparatory programs related; health services/allied health/health sciences; history; history teacher education; humanities; liberal arts and sciences/liberal studies; mathematics; mathematics teacher education; nursing (registered nurse training); piano and organ; social sciences.

Academics *Calendar:* semesters. *Degree:* certificates and associate. *Special study options:* academic remediation for entering students, accelerated degree program, adult/continuing education programs, advanced placement credit, cooperative education, double majors, independent study, internships, part-time degree program, services for LD students, student-designed majors, summer session for credit.

Library Ball Library with 27,859 titles, 152 serial subscriptions, 1,499 audiovisual materials, an OPAC, a Web page.

Computers on Campus 82 computers available on campus for general student use. A campuswide network can be accessed. Internet access, at least one staffed computer lab available. Computer purchase or lease plan available.

Student Life *Housing:* college housing not available. *Activities and Organizations:* student-run newspaper, Student Senate, Scripta Literary Magazine, Ancilla student ambassadors. *Campus security:* 24-hour patrols, late-night transport/escort service. *Student services:* personal/psychological counseling.

Athletics Member NJCAA. *Intercollegiate sports:* baseball M(s), basketball M(s)/W(s), softball W(s), volleyball W(s).

Standardized Tests *Required:* SAT and SAT Subject Tests or ACT (for admission). *Recommended:* SAT (for admission), SAT or ACT (for admission).

Costs (2006–07) *Tuition:* $10,800 full-time, $360 per credit hour part-time. *Required fees:* $230 full-time, $55 per term part-time.

Financial Aid Of all full-time matriculated undergraduates who enrolled in 2004, 28 Federal Work-Study jobs (averaging $1820). 16 state and other part-time jobs (averaging $1000). *Financial aid deadline:* 3/1.

Applying *Options:* common application, electronic application. *Application fee:* $25. *Required:* high school transcript. *Recommended:* interview. *Application deadline:* rolling (freshmen), rolling (transfers).

Freshmen Application Contact Erin Wittmeyer, Director of Admissions, Ancilla College, 9601 Union Road, Donaldson, IN 46513. *Phone:* 574-936-8898 Ext. 350. *Toll-free phone:* 866-262-4552 Ext. 350. *Fax:* 574-935-1773. *E-mail:* admissions@ancilla.edu.

AVIATION INSTITUTE OF MAINTENANCE—INDIANAPOLIS

Indianapolis, Indiana
www.aviationmaintenance.edu/aviation-indianapolis.asp

- **Proprietary** 2-year

Faculty *Total:* 25.

Academics *Calendar:* quarters.

Costs (2005–06) *Tuition:* Tuition and fees for Associates degree, $34,560.

Applying *Application fee:* $25. *Required:* High school diploma or GED.

Director of Admissions Mr. Andrew Duncan, School Director, Aviation Institute of Maintenance—Indianapolis, 7251 W. McCarty Street, Indianapolis, IN 46241. *Phone:* 317-243-4519. *Toll-free phone:* 888-349-5387. *E-mail:* directorami@aviationmaintenance.edu.

BROWN MACKIE COLLEGE—FORT WAYNE

Fort Wayne, Indiana
www.brownmackie.edu/locations.asp?locid=1

- **Proprietary** 2-year
- **Coed,** 706 undergraduate students, 100% full-time, 86% women, 14% men

Undergraduates 706 full-time. 3% are from out of state, 30% African American, 0.3% Asian American or Pacific Islander, 4% Hispanic American. Freshmen *Admission:* 933 applied, 605 admitted, 209 enrolled.

Faculty *Total:* 47, 40% full-time, 6% with terminal degrees. *Student/faculty ratio:* 13:1.

Majors Accounting technology and bookkeeping; business administration and management; computer software technology; criminal justice/police science; legal assistant/paralegal; medical/clinical assistant; occupational therapist assistant.

Academics *Calendar:* quarters. *Degree:* certificates, diplomas, and associate.

Student Life *Student services:* personal/psychological counseling.

Costs (2005–06) *Tuition:* $8592 full-time, $179 per credit hour part-time. *Required fees:* $480 full-time, $10 per credit hour part-time.

Applying *Required:* high school transcript, interview, Verify High School Grad or Equivalent. *Application deadline:* rolling (freshmen), rolling (transfers). *Notification:* continuous (freshmen).

Freshmen Application Contact Mr. Ken Taboh, Brown Mackie College–Fort Wayne, 4422 East State Boulevard, Fort Wayne, IN 46815. *Phone:* 260-481-5038. *Fax:* 260-484-2678. *E-mail:* ktaboh@brownmackie.edu.

▶ **See page 504 for the College Close-Up.**

BROWN MACKIE COLLEGE—MERRILLVILLE

Merrillville, Indiana
www.brownmackie.edu/locations.asp?locid=19

- **Proprietary** 2-year, founded 1890, part of American Education Centers
- **Small-town** 2-acre campus with easy access to Chicago
- **Coed,** 585 undergraduate students, 100% full-time, 80% women, 20% men

Undergraduates 585 full-time. 4% are from out of state, 42% African American, 0.2% Asian American or Pacific Islander, 8% Hispanic American, 0.2% Native American.

Freshmen *Admission:* 425 enrolled.

Faculty *Total:* 63, 41% full-time. *Student/faculty ratio:* 15:1.

Majors Accounting technology and bookkeeping; business administration and management; computer software technology; criminal justice/safety; gerontology; legal assistant/paralegal; medical/clinical assistant; medical office management; surgical technology.

Academics *Calendar:* quarters. *Degree:* certificates and associate. *Special study options:* internships, student-designed majors, summer session for credit.

Computers on Campus 150 computers available on campus for general student use. At least one staffed computer lab available.

Student Life *Housing:* college housing not available. *Campus security:* 24-hour emergency response devices.

Costs (2005–06) *Tuition:* $8592 full-time, $179 per credit hour part-time.

Financial Aid Of all full-time matriculated undergraduates who enrolled in 2004, 2 Federal Work-Study jobs.

Applying *Options:* common application, early admission, deferred entrance. *Required:* high school transcript, interview. *Application deadline:* rolling (freshmen), rolling (transfers). *Notification:* continuous (freshmen).

Freshmen Application Contact Mr. Don Richardson, Director of Admissions, Brown Mackie College–Merrillville, 1000 East 80th Place, Suite 101, N, Merrillville, IN 46410. *Phone:* 800-258-3321. *Fax:* 219-738-1076. *E-mail:* admissions@brownmackie.edu.

▶ **See page 512 for the College Close-Up.**

BROWN MACKIE COLLEGE—MICHIGAN CITY

Michigan City, Indiana
www.brownmackie.edu/locations.asp?locid=20

- **Proprietary** 2-year, founded 1890, part of Commonwealth Business College, Inc
- **Rural** 2-acre campus with easy access to Chicago
- **Coed,** 461 undergraduate students, 100% full-time, 79% women, 21% men

Undergraduates 461 full-time. Students come from 2 states and territories, 2% are from out of state, 18% African American, 0.4% Asian American or Pacific Islander, 3% Hispanic American.

Freshmen *Admission:* 461 applied, 461 admitted, 243 enrolled. *Average high school GPA:* 2.0.

Faculty *Total:* 15, 20% full-time. *Student/faculty ratio:* 13:1.

Majors Accounting technology and bookkeeping; business administration and management; computer software technology; criminal justice/safety; legal administrative assistant/secretary; medical administrative assistant and medical secretary; medical/clinical assistant.

Academics *Calendar:* quarters. *Degree:* diplomas and associate. *Special study options:* adult/continuing education programs, advanced placement credit, internships, part-time degree program, student-designed majors, summer session for credit.

Computers on Campus 24 computers available on campus for general student use. At least one staffed computer lab available.

Student Life *Housing:* college housing not available. *Activities and Organizations:* student-run newspaper. *Campus security:* 24-hour emergency response devices.

Costs (2005–06) *Tuition:* $6444 full-time, $179 per credit hour part-time. *Required fees:* $960 full-time.

Applying *Options:* early admission, deferred entrance. *Required:* high school transcript. *Application deadline:* rolling (freshmen), rolling (transfers). *Notification:* continuous (freshmen).

Director of Admissions Ms. Sheryl Elston, Director of Admissions, Brown Mackie College–Michigan City, 325 East US Highway 20, Michigan City, IN 46360. *Phone:* 219-877-3100. *Toll-free phone:* 800-519-2416. *Fax:* 219-877-3110. *E-mail:* selston@brownmackie.edu.

▶ See page 516 for the College Close-Up.

BROWN MACKIE COLLEGE–SOUTH BEND

South Bend, Indiana   www.brownmackie.edu/locations.asp?locid=2

- **Proprietary** 2-year, founded 1882, part of American Education Centers
- **Urban** 5-acre campus with easy access to Chicago
- **Coed, primarily women,** 619 undergraduate students, 100% full-time, 87% women, 13% men

Undergraduates 619 full-time. Students come from 2 states and territories, 10% are from out of state, 29% African American, 0.8% Asian American or Pacific Islander, 4% Hispanic American, 5% transferred in.
Freshmen *Admission:* 29 applied, 29 admitted, 29 enrolled. *Average high school GPA:* 2.0.

Faculty *Total:* 52, 35% full-time, 2% with terminal degrees. *Student/faculty ratio:* 12:1.

Majors Accounting technology and bookkeeping; business administration and management; computer software technology; criminal justice/safety; legal assistant/paralegal; medical/clinical assistant; occupational therapist assistant; physical therapist assistant.

Academics *Calendar:* quarters. *Degree:* certificates and associate. *Special study options:* academic remediation for entering students, accelerated degree program, adult/continuing education programs, double majors, summer session for credit.

Library Michiana College Library with 1,409 titles, 65 serial subscriptions, 65 audiovisual materials.

Computers on Campus 8 computers available on campus for general student use. Internet access available.

Student Life *Housing:* college housing not available. *Activities and Organizations:* Business Club, Medical Assisting Club, Legal Club, Physical Therapy Assistant Club, Occupational Therapy Assistant Club. *Campus security:* 24-hour emergency response devices. *Student services:* personal/psychological counseling.

Costs (2005–06) *Comprehensive fee:* $12,402 includes full-time tuition ($6444), mandatory fees ($360), and room and board ($5598). Part-time tuition: $179 per credit hour. *Required fees:* $10 per credit hour part-time.

Applying *Options:* common application, deferred entrance. *Required:* essay or personal statement, high school transcript, interview. *Required for some:* minimum 2.0 GPA, 2 letters of recommendation. *Application deadline:* rolling (freshmen), rolling (transfers). *Notification:* continuous (freshmen).

Freshmen Application Contact Ms. Katie Marsico, Admissions Representative; High School, Brown Mackie College–South Bend, 1030 East Jefferson Boulevard, South Bend, IN 46617-3123. *Phone:* 574-237-0774. *Toll-free phone:* 800-743-2447. *Fax:* 574-237-3585. *E-mail:* kmarsico@brownmackie.edu.

▶ See page 526 for the College Close-Up.

COLLEGE OF COURT REPORTING

Hobart, Indiana   www.ccredu.com/

Director of Admissions Ms. Stacy Drohosky, Director of Admissions, College of Court Reporting, 111 West Tenth Street, Suite 111, Hobart, IN 46342. *Phone:* 219-942-1459 Ext. 226. *Fax:* 219-942-1631. *E-mail:* sdrohoskie@ccvedu.com.

DAVENPORT UNIVERSITY

Granger, Indiana   www.davenport.edu/

- **Independent** primarily 2-year, founded 1977, part of Davenport Educational System
- **Coed**

Faculty *Student/faculty ratio:* 16:1.

Academics *Calendar:* semesters. *Degrees:* diplomas, associate, and bachelor's. *Special study options:* accelerated degree program, distance learning, English as a second language, independent study, internships, student-designed majors.

Applying *Options:* deferred entrance. *Application fee:* $25.

Director of Admissions Admissions, Davenport University, 415 East Fulton Street, Grand Rapids, MI 49503. *Toll-free phone:* 800-632-9569.

DAVENPORT UNIVERSITY

Hammond, Indiana   www.davenport.edu/

- **Independent** 2-year, founded 1977, part of Davenport Educational System
- **Coed**

Faculty *Student/faculty ratio:* 16:1.

Academics *Calendar:* semesters. *Degree:* diplomas and associate. *Special study options:* accelerated degree program, distance learning, English as a second language, independent study, internships, student-designed majors.

Costs (2005–06) *Tuition:* $7080 full-time, $295 per credit hour part-time. *Required fees:* $120 full-time.

Applying *Options:* deferred entrance. *Application fee:* $25.

Director of Admissions Admissions, Davenport University, 415 East Fulton Street, Grand Rapids, MI 49503. *Toll-free phone:* 800-632-9569.

DAVENPORT UNIVERSITY

Merrillville, Indiana   www.davenport.edu/

- **Independent** primarily 2-year, founded 1977, part of Davenport Educational System
- **Coed**

Faculty *Student/faculty ratio:* 16:1.

Academics *Calendar:* semesters. *Degrees:* diplomas, associate, and bachelor's. *Special study options:* accelerated degree program, distance learning, English as a second language, independent study, internships, student-designed majors.

Costs (2005–06) *Tuition:* $7080 full-time, $295 per credit hour part-time. *Required fees:* $120 full-time.

Applying *Options:* deferred entrance. *Application fee:* $25.

Director of Admissions Admissions, Davenport University, 415 East Fulton Street, Grand Rapids, MI 49503. *Toll-free phone:* 800-632-9569.

HOLY CROSS COLLEGE

Notre Dame, Indiana

- **Independent Roman Catholic** primarily 2-year, founded 1966
- **Urban** 150-acre campus
- **Coed,** 369 undergraduate students, 89% full-time, 39% women, 61% men

Undergraduates 328 full-time, 41 part-time. Students come from 37 states and territories, 12 other countries, 42% are from out of state, 3% African American,

Holy Cross College (continued)

2% Asian American or Pacific Islander, 7% Hispanic American, 1% international, 10% transferred in, 54% live on campus. *Retention:* 53% of 2003 full-time freshmen returned.

Freshmen *Admission:* 459 applied, 159 enrolled. *Average high school GPA:* 3.10.

Faculty *Total:* 38, 68% full-time, 32% with terminal degrees. *Student/faculty ratio:* 12:1.

Majors Liberal arts and sciences/liberal studies.

Academics *Calendar:* semesters. *Degrees:* associate and bachelor's. *Special study options:* academic remediation for entering students, advanced placement credit, English as a second language, freshman honors college, internships, off-campus study, part-time degree program, summer session for credit. *ROTC:* Army (c), Air Force (c).

Library Holy Cross Library with 15,000 titles, 160 serial subscriptions, an OPAC.

Computers on Campus 60 computers available on campus for general student use. A campuswide network can be accessed from student residence rooms and from off campus. Internet access, at least one staffed computer lab available.

Student Life *Housing Options:* coed, men-only, women-only. *Activities and Organizations:* drama/theater group, student-run newspaper, choral group, marching band, Student Advisory Committee, Campus Ministry, Volunteers in Support of Admissions, intramural athletics. *Campus security:* 24-hour emergency response devices, 24-hour patrols by trained personnel on certain days. *Student services:* personal/psychological counseling.

Athletics *Intercollegiate sports:* basketball M, crew M/W, cross-country running M/W, lacrosse M, soccer M/W. *Intramural sports:* basketball M/W, football M/W, golf M/W, lacrosse M, rugby M, skiing (downhill) M, soccer M, softball M/W, table tennis M/W, tennis M/W, ultimate Frisbee M/W, volleyball M/W.

Standardized Tests *Required:* SAT or ACT (for admission).

Costs (2006–07) *Comprehensive fee:* $23,500 includes full-time tuition ($14,500), mandatory fees ($1000), and room and board ($8000). Part-time tuition: $365 per hour.

Financial Aid Of all full-time matriculated undergraduates who enrolled in 2004, 54 Federal Work-Study jobs (averaging $857).

Applying *Options:* common application, electronic application, deferred entrance. *Application fee:* $50. *Required:* essay or personal statement, high school transcript, minimum 2.5 GPA. *Required for some:* letters of recommendation. *Recommended:* interview. *Application deadline:* rolling (freshmen), rolling (transfers).

Freshmen Application Contact Office of Admissions, Holy Cross College, PO Box 308, Notre Dame, IN 46556. *Phone:* 574-239-8400. *Fax:* 574-239-8323. *E-mail:* vduke@hcc-nd.edu.

INDIANA BUSINESS COLLEGE
Anderson, Indiana   www.ibcschools.edu/

- **Proprietary** 2-year, founded 1902
- **Coed,** 235 undergraduate students

Faculty *Student/faculty ratio:* 20:1.

Majors Accounting; administrative assistant and secretarial science; business administration and management; business administration, management and operations related; criminal justice/safety; health information/medical records technology; human resources management; medical/clinical assistant; medical insurance/medical billing.

Academics *Calendar:* quarters. *Degree:* certificates, diplomas, and associate. *Special study options:* adult/continuing education programs, cooperative education, distance learning, double majors, internships, part-time degree program.

Computers on Campus Internet access available.

Standardized Tests *Required:* Wonderlic Scholastic Level Exam (SLE) (for admission).

Costs (2005–06) *Tuition:* Contact campus as full and part-time tuition depends on program.

Applying *Options:* electronic application, early admission. *Application fee:* $50. *Required:* high school transcript, interview. *Application deadline:* rolling (freshmen), rolling (transfers). *Notification:* continuous (freshmen).

Freshmen Application Contact Mr. Troy Robertson, Indiana Business College, 140 East 53rd Street, Anderson, IN 46013. *Phone:* 765-644-7514. *Toll-free phone:* 800-IBC-GRAD. *Fax:* 765-664-5724.

INDIANA BUSINESS COLLEGE
Columbus, Indiana   www.ibcschools.edu/

- **Proprietary** 2-year
- **Coed,** 273 undergraduate students

Faculty *Student/faculty ratio:* 20:1.

Majors Accounting; administrative assistant and secretarial science; business administration and management; business administration, management and operations related; criminal justice/safety; human resources management; medical/clinical assistant; medical insurance/medical billing.

Academics *Calendar:* quarters. *Degree:* certificates, diplomas, and associate. *Special study options:* adult/continuing education programs, cooperative education, distance learning, double majors, internships, part-time degree program.

Computers on Campus Internet access available.

Standardized Tests *Required:* Wonderlic Scholastic Level Exam (SLE) (for admission).

Costs (2005–06) *Tuition:* Contact campus as full and part-time tuition depends on program.

Applying *Options:* electronic application. *Application fee:* $50. *Required:* high school transcript, interview. *Application deadline:* rolling (freshmen), rolling (transfers). *Notification:* continuous (freshmen).

Freshmen Application Contact Ms. Angela Rentmeesters, Executive Director, Indiana Business College, 2222 Poshard Drive, Columbus, IN 47203. *Phone:* 812-379-9000. *Toll-free phone:* 800-IBC-GRAD. *Fax:* 812-375-0414.

INDIANA BUSINESS COLLEGE
Evansville, Indiana   www.ibcschools.edu/

- **Proprietary** 2-year
- **Coed,** 295 undergraduate students

Faculty *Student/faculty ratio:* 20:1.

Majors Accounting; administrative assistant and secretarial science; business administration and management; criminal justice/safety; human resources management; information technology; medical/clinical assistant; medical insurance coding; medical insurance/medical billing.

Academics *Calendar:* quarters. *Degree:* certificates, diplomas, and associate. *Special study options:* adult/continuing education programs, cooperative education, distance learning, double majors, internships, part-time degree program.

Computers on Campus Internet access available.

Standardized Tests *Required:* Wonderlic Scholastic Level Exam (SLE) (for admission).

Costs (2005–06) *Tuition:* Contact campus as full and part-time tuition depends on program.

Applying *Options:* electronic application. *Application fee:* $50. *Required:* high school transcript, interview. *Application deadline:* rolling (freshmen), rolling (transfers). *Notification:* continuous (freshmen).

Freshmen Application Contact Mr. Steve Hardin, Regional Director, Indiana Business College, 4601 Theater Drive, Evansville, IN 47715. *Phone:* 812-476-6000. *Toll-free phone:* 800-IBC-GRAD. *Fax:* 812-471-8576.

INDIANA BUSINESS COLLEGE
Fort Wayne, Indiana   www.ibcschools.edu/

- **Proprietary** 2-year
- **Coed,** 384 undergraduate students

Faculty *Student/faculty ratio:* 20:1.

Majors Accounting; administrative assistant and secretarial science; business administration and management; criminal justice/safety; human resources management; medical/clinical assistant; medical insurance/medical billing; surgical technology.

Academics *Calendar:* quarters. *Degree:* certificates, diplomas, and associate. *Special study options:* adult/continuing education programs, cooperative education, distance learning, double majors, internships, part-time degree program.

Computers on Campus Internet access available.

Standardized Tests *Required:* Wonderlic Scholastic Level Exam (SLE) (for admission).

Costs (2005–06) *Tuition:* Contact campus as full and part-time tuition depends on program.

Applying *Options:* electronic application. *Application fee:* $50. *Required:* high school transcript, interview. *Application deadline:* rolling (freshmen), rolling (transfers). *Notification:* continuous (freshmen).
Freshmen Application Contact Ms. Janet Herman, Executive Director, Indiana Business College, 6413 North Clinton Street, Fort Wayne, IN 46825. *Phone:* 260-471-7667. *Toll-free phone:* 260-471-6918. *Fax:* 260-471-6918.

INDIANA BUSINESS COLLEGE
Indianapolis, Indiana　　　　**www.ibcschools.edu/**

- **Proprietary** 2-year, founded 1902
- **Urban** 1-acre campus
- **Coed,** 782 undergraduate students

Faculty *Student/faculty ratio:* 20:1.
Majors Accounting; administrative assistant and secretarial science; business administration and management; business administration, management and operations related; computer and information sciences; computer and information sciences and support services related; computer programming; computer programming (specific applications); criminal justice/safety; fashion merchandising; human resources management; information technology; legal administrative assistant/secretary; management information systems and services related; medical/clinical assistant.
Academics *Calendar:* quarters. *Degree:* certificates, diplomas, and associate. *Special study options:* adult/continuing education programs, cooperative education, distance learning, double majors, internships, part-time degree program, summer session for credit.
Computers on Campus Internet access, online (class) registration available.
Student Life *Housing:* college housing not available. *Activities and Organizations:* Student Advisory Board, Student Ambassadors, Phi Beta Lambda. *Campus security:* 24-hour patrols.
Standardized Tests *Required:* Wonderlic Scholastic Level Exam (SLE) (for admission).
Costs (2005–06) *Tuition:* Contact campus as full and part-time tuition depends on program.
Applying *Options:* electronic application. *Application fee:* $50. *Required:* high school transcript, interview. *Application deadline:* rolling (freshmen), rolling (transfers). *Notification:* continuous (freshmen).
Freshmen Application Contact Ms. Pat Mozley, Regional Director, Indiana Business College, 550 East Washington Street, Indianapolis, IN 46204. *Phone:* 317-264-5656. *Toll-free phone:* 800-IBC-GRAD. *Fax:* 317-264-5650.
▶ **See page 552 for the College Close-Up.**

INDIANA BUSINESS COLLEGE
Indianapolis, Indiana
　　　　www.ibcschools.edu/campuses/northwest.asp

- **Proprietary** 2-year
- **Coed,** 584 undergraduate students

Faculty *Student/faculty ratio:* 20:1.
Majors Accounting; administrative assistant and secretarial science; business administration and management; criminal justice/safety; human resources management; massage therapy; medical/clinical assistant; medical insurance coding; medical insurance/medical billing; medical laboratory technology; surgical technology.
Academics *Calendar:* quarters. *Degree:* certificates, diplomas, and associate.
Standardized Tests *Required:* Wonderlic Scholastic Level Exam (for admission).
Costs (2005–06) *Tuition:* Contact campus as full and part-time tuition depends on program.
Applying *Application fee:* $50. *Required:* high school transcript, interview. *Application deadline:* rolling (freshmen), rolling (transfers). *Notification:* continuous (freshmen).
Freshmen Application Contact Mr. Gary McGee, Senior Regional Director, Indiana Business College, 6300 Technology Center Drive, Indianapolis, IN 46278. *Phone:* 317-375-8000. *Fax:* 317-351-1871.

INDIANA BUSINESS COLLEGE
Indianapolis, Indiana
　　　　www.ibcschools.edu/Campuses/northwest.asp

- **Proprietary** 2-year
- **Coed,** 86 undergraduate students

Majors Accounting; administrative assistant and secretarial science; business administration and management; medical/clinical assistant; medical insurance coding; medical insurance/medical billing; surgical technology.
Academics *Calendar:* quarters. *Degree:* certificates, diplomas, and associate.
Standardized Tests *Required:* Wonderlic Scholastic Level Exam (for admission).
Costs (2005–06) *Tuition:* Contact campus as full and part-time tuition depends on program.
Applying *Application fee:* $50. *Required:* high school transcript, interview. *Application deadline:* rolling (freshmen), rolling (transfers). *Notification:* continuous (freshmen).
Freshmen Application Contact Mr. Marc Konesco, Executive Director, Indiana Business College, 6300 Technology Center Drive, Indianapolis, IN 46278. *Phone:* 317-873-6500. *Fax:* 317-733-6266.

INDIANA BUSINESS COLLEGE
Lafayette, Indiana　　　　**www.ibcschools.edu/**

- **Proprietary** 2-year
- **Coed,** 215 undergraduate students

Faculty *Student/faculty ratio:* 20:1.
Majors Accounting; administrative assistant and secretarial science; business administration and management; business administration, management and operations related; computer and information sciences and support services related; criminal justice/safety; human resources management; information technology; medical/clinical assistant; medical insurance coding; medical insurance/medical billing.
Academics *Calendar:* quarters. *Degree:* certificates, diplomas, and associate. *Special study options:* adult/continuing education programs, cooperative education, distance learning, double majors, internships, part-time degree program.
Computers on Campus Internet access available.
Standardized Tests *Required:* Wonderlic Scholastic Level Exam (SLE) (for admission).
Costs (2005–06) *Tuition:* Contact campus as full and part-time tuition depends on program.
Applying *Options:* electronic application. *Application fee:* $50. *Required:* high school transcript, interview. *Application deadline:* rolling (freshmen), rolling (transfers). *Notification:* continuous (freshmen).
Freshmen Application Contact Mr. Greg Reger, Executive Director, Indiana Business College, 2 Executive Drive, Lafayette, IN 47905. *Phone:* 765-447-9550. *Toll-free phone:* 800-IBC-GRAD. *Fax:* 765-447-0868.

INDIANA BUSINESS COLLEGE
Marion, Indiana　　　　**www.ibcschools.edu/**

- **Proprietary** 2-year
- **Coed,** 120 undergraduate students

Faculty *Student/faculty ratio:* 20:1.
Majors Accounting; administrative assistant and secretarial science; business administration and management; criminal justice/safety; human resources management; medical/clinical assistant; medical insurance coding.
Academics *Calendar:* quarters. *Degree:* certificates, diplomas, and associate. *Special study options:* adult/continuing education programs, cooperative education, distance learning, double majors, internships, part-time degree program.
Computers on Campus Internet access available.
Standardized Tests *Required:* Wonderlic Scholastic Level Exam (SLE) (for admission).
Costs (2005–06) *Tuition:* Contact campus as full and part-time tuition depends on program.
Applying *Options:* electronic application. *Application fee:* $50. *Required:* high school transcript, interview. *Application deadline:* rolling (freshmen), rolling (transfers). *Notification:* continuous (freshmen).

Indiana Business College (continued)

Freshmen Application Contact Mr. Richard Herman, Executive Director, Indiana Business College, 830 North Miller Avenue, Marion, IN 46952. *Phone:* 765-662-7497. *Toll-free phone:* 800-IBC-GRAD. *Fax:* 765-651-9421.

INDIANA BUSINESS COLLEGE
Muncie, Indiana   www.ibcschools.edu/

- **Proprietary** 2-year
- **Coed,** 310 undergraduate students

Faculty *Student/faculty ratio:* 20:1.

Majors Accounting; administrative assistant and secretarial science; business administration and management; business administration, management and operations related; computer and information sciences and support services related; computer programming (specific applications); criminal justice/safety; health information/medical records technology; human resources management; information technology; management information systems and services related; medical office assistant.

Academics *Calendar:* quarters. *Degree:* certificates, diplomas, and associate. *Special study options:* cooperative education, distance learning, double majors, internships, part-time degree program.

Computers on Campus Internet access available.

Student Life *Housing:* college housing not available. *Activities and Organizations:* Phi Beta Lambda.

Standardized Tests *Required:* Wonderlic Scholastic Level Exam (SLE) (for admission).

Costs (2005–06) *Tuition:* Contact campus as full and part-time tuition depends on program.

Applying *Options:* electronic application. *Application fee:* $50. *Required:* high school transcript, interview. *Application deadline:* rolling (freshmen), rolling (transfers). *Notification:* continuous (freshmen).

Freshmen Application Contact Nikki Adams, Indiana Business College, 411 West Riggin Road, Muncie, IN 47303. *Phone:* 765-288-8681. *Toll-free phone:* 800-IBC-GRAD. *Fax:* 765-288-8797.

INDIANA BUSINESS COLLEGE
Terre Haute, Indiana   www.ibcschools.edu/

- **Proprietary** 2-year, founded 1902
- **Coed,** 220 undergraduate students

Faculty *Student/faculty ratio:* 20:1.

Majors Accounting; administrative assistant and secretarial science; business administration and management; business administration, management and operations related; criminal justice/safety; human resources management; medical/clinical assistant; medical insurance/medical billing.

Academics *Calendar:* quarters. *Degree:* certificates, diplomas, and associate. *Special study options:* adult/continuing education programs, cooperative education, distance learning, double majors, internships, part-time degree program.

Computers on Campus Internet access available.

Standardized Tests *Required:* Wonderlic Scholastic Level Exam (SLE) (for admission).

Costs (2005–06) *Tuition:* Contact campus as full and part-time tuition depends on program.

Applying *Options:* electronic application. *Application fee:* $50. *Required:* high school transcript, interview, Wonderlic Scholastic Level Exam. *Application deadline:* rolling (freshmen), rolling (transfers). *Notification:* continuous (freshmen).

Freshmen Application Contact Ms. Laura Hale, Executive Director, Indiana Business College, 3175 South Third Place, Terre Haute, IN 47802. *Phone:* 812-232-4458. *Toll-free phone:* 800-IBC-GRAD. *Fax:* 812-234-2361.

INDIANA BUSINESS COLLEGE-MEDICAL
Indianapolis, Indiana   www.ibcschools.edu/

- **Proprietary** 2-year
- **Coed,** 584 undergraduate students

Faculty *Student/faculty ratio:* 20:1.

Majors Clinical/medical laboratory technology; massage therapy; medical/clinical assistant; medical insurance coding; medical insurance/medical billing; surgical technology.

Academics *Calendar:* quarters. *Degree:* certificates, diplomas, and associate. *Special study options:* adult/continuing education programs, cooperative education, distance learning, double majors, internships, part-time degree program.

Computers on Campus Internet access available.

Standardized Tests *Required:* Wonderlic Scholastic Level Exam (SLE) (for admission).

Costs (2006–07) *Tuition:* Contact campus as full and part-time tuition depends on program.

Applying *Options:* electronic application. *Application fee:* $50. *Required:* high school transcript, interview. *Application deadline:* rolling (freshmen), rolling (transfers). *Notification:* continuous (freshmen).

Freshmen Application Contact Mr. Gary McGee, Senior Regional Director, Indiana Business College-Medical, 8150 Brookville Road, Indianapolis, IN 46239. *Phone:* 317-375-8000. *Toll-free phone:* 800-IBC-6611. *Fax:* 317-351-1871.

INTERNATIONAL BUSINESS COLLEGE
Fort Wayne, Indiana   www.ibcfortwayne.edu/

Director of Admissions Mr. Steve Kinzer, School Director, International Business College, 5699 Coventry Lane, Fort Wayne, IN 46804. *Phone:* 219-459-4513. *Toll-free phone:* 800-589-6363.

INTERNATIONAL BUSINESS COLLEGE
Indianapolis, Indiana   www.intlbusinesscollege.com/

- **Proprietary** 2-year, administratively affiliated with Bradford Schools, Charlotte, NC
- **Coed,** 289 undergraduate students, 100% full-time, 71% women, 29% men

Undergraduates 289 full-time. 14% African American, 0.7% Asian American or Pacific Islander, 3% Hispanic American.

Freshmen *Admission:* 597 applied, 559 admitted, 167 enrolled.

Faculty *Total:* 15, 40% full-time, 40% with terminal degrees. *Student/faculty ratio:* 20:1.

Majors Accounting technology and bookkeeping; administrative assistant and secretarial science; computer programming; computer/technical support; graphic design; legal administrative assistant; medical/clinical assistant; paralegal/legal assistant; system, networking, and LAN/WAN management; tourism/travel marketing.

Academics *Calendar:* semesters. *Degree:* diplomas and associate. *Special study options:* academic remediation for entering students, internships.

Computers on Campus 125 computers available on campus for general student use. Internet access, at least one staffed computer lab available.

Student Life *Housing Options:* Campus housing is leased by the school. Freshman applicants given priority for college housing.

Costs (2006–07) *Tuition:* $11,960 full-time. *Room only:* $6100.

Applying *Options:* common application, electronic application. *Application fee:* $50. *Required:* high school transcript. *Required for some:* paralegal test. *Application deadline:* rolling (freshmen). *Notification:* continuous (freshmen).

Freshmen Application Contact Ms. Kathy Chiudioni, Director of Admissions, International Business College, 7205 Shadeland Station, Indianapolis, IN 46256. *Phone:* 317-213-2320. *Fax:* 317-841-6419. *E-mail:* info@intlbusinesscollege.com.

ITT TECHNICAL INSTITUTE
Fort Wayne, Indiana   www.itt-tech.edu/

- **Proprietary** primarily 2-year, founded 1967, part of ITT Educational Services, Inc
- **Coed**

Majors Accounting and business/management; animation, interactive technology, video graphics and special effects; business administration and management; CAD/CADD drafting/design technology; computer and information systems security; computer programming; computer systems networking and telecommunications; criminal justice/law enforcement administration; e-commerce; electrical, electronic and communications engineering technology; robotics technology; system, networking, and LAN/WAN management; web page, digital/multimedia and information resources design.

Academics *Calendar:* quarters. *Degrees:* associate and bachelor's.

Library a Web page.

Computers on Campus Internet access, at least one staffed computer lab available.

Student Life *Housing:* college housing not available.

Standardized Tests *Required:* Wonderlic aptitude test (for admission).

Costs (2005–06) *Tuition:* Please see school catalog for specific information.

Applying *Options:* deferred entrance. *Application fee:* $100. *Required:* high school transcript, interview. *Recommended:* letters of recommendation. *Application deadline:* rolling (freshmen), rolling (transfers). *Notification:* continuous (freshmen).

Freshmen Application Contact Ms. Bethanne Taylor, ITT Technical Institute, 2810 Dupont Commerce Court, Fort Wayne, IN 46825. *Phone:* 260-497-6200. *Toll-free phone:* 800-866-4488. *Fax:* 260-497-6299.

ITT TECHNICAL INSTITUTE
Indianapolis, Indiana www.itt-tech.edu/

- **Proprietary** founded 1966, part of ITT Educational Services, Inc
- **Suburban** 10-acre campus
- **Coed**

Majors Accounting and business/management; animation, interactive technology, video graphics and special effects; business administration and management; CAD/CADD drafting/design technology; computer and information systems security; computer programming; computer software technology; computer systems networking and telecommunications; criminal justice/law enforcement administration; e-commerce; electrical, electronic and communications engineering technology; information technology; robotics technology; system, networking, and LAN/WAN management; web/multimedia management and webmaster; web page, digital/multimedia and information resources design.

Academics *Calendar:* quarters. *Degrees:* diplomas, associate, and bachelor's. *Special study options:* distance learning.

Library a Web page.

Computers on Campus Internet access, at least one staffed computer lab available.

Student Life *Housing:* college housing not available. *Activities and Organizations:* student-run newspaper.

Standardized Tests *Required:* Wonderlic aptitude test (for admission).

Costs (2005–06) *Tuition:* Please see school catalog for specific information.

Applying *Options:* deferred entrance. *Application fee:* $100. *Required:* high school transcript, interview. *Recommended:* letters of recommendation. *Application deadline:* rolling (freshmen), rolling (transfers). *Notification:* continuous (freshmen).

Freshmen Application Contact Mr. James Mills, ITT Technical Institute, 9511 Angola Court, Indianapolis, IN 46268. *Phone:* 317-875-8640. *Toll-free phone:* 800-937-4488.

ITT TECHNICAL INSTITUTE
Newburgh, Indiana www.itt-tech.edu/

- **Proprietary** primarily 2-year, founded 1966, part of ITT Educational Services, Inc
- **Coed**

Majors Animation, interactive technology, video graphics and special effects; business administration and management; CAD/CADD drafting/design technology; computer and information systems security; computer programming; computer software technology; computer systems networking and telecommunications; criminal justice/law enforcement administration; e-commerce; electrical, electronic and communications engineering technology; robotics technology; system, networking, and LAN/WAN management; web/multimedia management and webmaster; web page, digital/multimedia and information resources design.

Academics *Calendar:* quarters. *Degrees:* associate and bachelor's.

Library a Web page.

Computers on Campus Internet access, at least one staffed computer lab available.

Student Life *Housing:* college housing not available.

Standardized Tests *Required:* Wonderlic aptitude test (for admission).

Costs (2005–06) *Tuition:* Please see school catalog for specific information.

Applying *Options:* deferred entrance. *Application fee:* $100. *Required:* high school transcript, interview. *Recommended:* letters of recommendation. *Application deadline:* rolling (freshmen), rolling (transfers). *Notification:* continuous (freshmen).

Freshmen Application Contact Mr. Thomas Montgomery, Director of Recruitment, ITT Technical Institute, 10999 Stahl Road, Newburgh, IN 47630. *Phone:* 812-858-1600. *Toll-free phone:* 800-832-4488.

IVY TECH COMMUNITY COLLEGE–BLOOMINGTON
Bloomington, Indiana www.ivytech.edu/

- **State-supported** 2-year, founded 2001, part of Ivy Tech State College System
- **Endowment** $15.9 million
- **Coed,** 3,565 undergraduate students, 46% full-time, 61% women, 39% men

Undergraduates 1,639 full-time, 1,926 part-time. 3% African American, 0.7% Asian American or Pacific Islander, 1% Hispanic American, 0.3% Native American, 0.1% international, 4% transferred in.

Freshmen *Admission:* 899 applied, 899 admitted, 618 enrolled.

Faculty *Total:* 275, 17% full-time.

Majors Accounting technology and bookkeeping; building/property maintenance and management; business administration and management; business automation/technology/data entry; cabinetmaking and millwork; child care and support services management; computer and information sciences; criminal justice/safety; early childhood education; electrical, electronic and communications engineering technology; electrician; emergency medical technology (EMT paramedic); executive assistant/executive secretary; general studies; heating, air conditioning, ventilation and refrigeration maintenance technology; human services; industrial technology; legal assistant/paralegal; liberal arts and sciences/liberal studies; library assistant; machine tool technology; mechanic and repair technologies related; mechanics and repair; nursing (registered nurse training); pipefitting and sprinkler fitting; psychiatric/mental health services technology; tool and die technology.

Academics *Calendar:* semesters. *Degree:* certificates and associate. *Special study options:* academic remediation for entering students, adult/continuing education programs, advanced placement credit, distance learning, external degree program, internships, part-time degree program, services for LD students, summer session for credit.

Library 5,516 titles, 97 serial subscriptions, 1,281 audiovisual materials, an OPAC, a Web page.

Computers on Campus 221 computers available on campus for general student use. Internet access, online (class) registration available.

Student Life *Activities and Organizations:* Student Government, Phi Theta Kappa. *Campus security:* late-night transport/escort service.

Costs (2005–06) *Tuition:* state resident $2520 full-time, $84 per credit part-time; nonresident $5108 full-time, $170 per credit part-time. *Required fees:* $70 full-time, $35 per term part-time.

Financial Aid Of all full-time matriculated undergraduates who enrolled in 2004, 51 Federal Work-Study jobs (averaging $3259).

Applying *Options:* deferred entrance. *Required:* high school transcript. *Required for some:* interview. *Application deadline:* rolling (freshmen), rolling (transfers). *Notification:* continuous (freshmen).

Freshmen Application Contact Dr. Rebecca Nickoli, Executive Director of Educational Systems, Ivy Tech Community College–Bloomington, 200 Daniels Way, Bloomington, IN 47404-1511. *Phone:* 317-921-4515. *Fax:* 812-330-6200. *E-mail:* nfrederi@ivytech.edu.

IVY TECH COMMUNITY COLLEGE–CENTRAL INDIANA
Indianapolis, Indiana www.ivytech.edu/

- **State-supported** 2-year, founded 1963
- **Urban** 10-acre campus
- **Endowment** $15,900
- **Coed,** 11,590 undergraduate students, 31% full-time, 59% women, 41% men

Undergraduates 3,581 full-time, 8,009 part-time. 25% African American, 1% Asian American or Pacific Islander, 2% Hispanic American, 0.5% Native American, 0.2% international, 6% transferred in.

Freshmen *Admission:* 2,926 applied, 2,926 admitted, 1,846 enrolled.

Ivy Tech Community College–Central Indiana (continued)

Faculty *Total:* 662, 21% full-time.

Majors Accounting technology and bookkeeping; automobile/automotive mechanics technology; biotechnology; building/property maintenance and management; business administration and management; business automation/technology/data entry; cabinetmaking and millwork; carpentry; child care and support services management; child guidance; computer and information sciences; criminal justice/safety; design and visual communications; drafting and design technology; early childhood education; electrical, electronic and communications engineering technology; electrician; executive assistant/executive secretary; general studies; heating, air conditioning, ventilation and refrigeration maintenance technology; hospitality administration related; human services; industrial production technologies related; industrial technology; legal assistant/paralegal; liberal arts and sciences/liberal studies; machine shop technology; machine tool technology; masonry; mechanics and repair; medical/clinical assistant; medical radiologic technology; nursing (registered nurse training); occupational safety and health technology; occupational therapist assistant; painting and wall covering; pipefitting and sprinkler fitting; psychiatric/mental health services technology; respiratory care therapy; sheet metal technology; surgical technology; tool and die technology.

Academics *Calendar:* semesters. *Degree:* certificates and associate. *Special study options:* academic remediation for entering students, adult/continuing education programs, advanced placement credit, cooperative education, distance learning, English as a second language, internships, off-campus study, part-time degree program, services for LD students, summer session for credit.

Library 20,247 titles, 138 serial subscriptions, 2,135 audiovisual materials, an OPAC, a Web page.

Computers on Campus 407 computers available on campus for general student use. Internet access, online (class) registration, at least one staffed computer lab available.

Student Life *Housing:* college housing not available. *Activities and Organizations:* student-run newspaper, Student Government, Phi Theta Kappa, Human Services Club, Administrative Office Assistants Club, Radiology Club. *Campus security:* 24-hour emergency response devices and patrols, late-night transport/escort service. *Student services:* personal/psychological counseling.

Athletics *Intramural sports:* baseball M, basketball M/W, cheerleading W, golf M/W, softball W, volleyball M/W.

Costs (2005–06) *Tuition:* state resident $2520 full-time, $84 per credit part-time; nonresident $5108 full-time, $170 per credit part-time. *Required fees:* $70 full-time, $35 per term part-time.

Financial Aid Of all full-time matriculated undergraduates who enrolled in 2004, 92 Federal Work-Study jobs (averaging $3766).

Applying *Options:* early admission, deferred entrance. *Required:* high school transcript. *Required for some:* interview. *Application deadline:* rolling (freshmen), rolling (transfers). *Notification:* continuous (freshmen).

Freshmen Application Contact Ms. Tracy Funk, Counselor, Ivy Tech Community College–Central Indiana, One West 26th Street, Indianapolis, IN 46208-4777. *Phone:* 317-921-4371. *Toll-free phone:* 888-IVYLINE. *Fax:* 317-921-4753. *E-mail:* tfunk@ivytech.edu.

IVY TECH COMMUNITY COLLEGE– COLUMBUS

Columbus, Indiana **www.ivytech.edu/**

- **State-supported** 2-year, founded 1963, part of Ivy Tech State College System
- **Small-town** campus with easy access to Indianapolis
- **Endowment** $15.9 million
- **Coed,** 2,216 undergraduate students, 35% full-time, 71% women, 29% men

Undergraduates 777 full-time, 1,439 part-time. 2% African American, 0.7% Asian American or Pacific Islander, 0.8% Hispanic American, 0.2% Native American, 0.1% international, 8% transferred in.

Freshmen *Admission:* 506 applied, 506 admitted, 283 enrolled.

Faculty *Total:* 193, 20% full-time.

Majors Accounting technology and bookkeeping; automobile/automotive mechanics technology; building/property maintenance and management; business administration and management; business automation/technology/data entry; cabinetmaking and millwork; child care and support services management; computer and information sciences; design and visual communications; drafting and design technology; early childhood education; electrical and power transmission installation; electrical, electronic and communications engineering technology; executive assistant/executive secretary; general studies; heating, air conditioning, ventilation and refrigeration maintenance technology; human services; industrial technology; legal assistant/paralegal; liberal arts and sciences/liberal studies; library assistant; machine tool technology; masonry; mechanic

and repair technologies related; mechanics and repair; medical/clinical assistant; medical radiologic technology; pipefitting and sprinkler fitting; psychiatric/mental health services technology; robotics technology; surgical technology; tool and die technology.

Academics *Calendar:* semesters. *Degree:* certificates and associate. *Special study options:* academic remediation for entering students, adult/continuing education programs, advanced placement credit, distance learning, internships, part-time degree program, services for LD students, summer session for credit.

Library 7,855 titles, 13,382 serial subscriptions, 989 audiovisual materials, an OPAC, a Web page.

Computers on Campus 185 computers available on campus for general student use. Internet access, online (class) registration, at least one staffed computer lab available.

Student Life *Housing:* college housing not available. *Activities and Organizations:* Student Government, Phi Theta Kappa, LPN Club. *Campus security:* late-night transport/escort service, trained evening security personnel, escort service.

Costs (2005–06) *Tuition:* state resident $2520 full-time, $84 per credit part-time; nonresident $5108 full-time, $170 per credit part-time. *Required fees:* $70 full-time, $35 per term part-time.

Financial Aid Of all full-time matriculated undergraduates who enrolled in 2004, 26 Federal Work-Study jobs (averaging $1694).

Applying *Options:* early admission, deferred entrance. *Required:* high school transcript. *Required for some:* interview. *Application deadline:* rolling (freshmen), rolling (transfers). *Notification:* continuous (freshmen).

Freshmen Application Contact Mr. Neil Bagadiong, Assistant Director of Student Affairs, Ivy Tech Community College–Columbus, 4475 Central Avenue, Columbus, IN 47203-1868. *Phone:* 317-921-4515. *Toll-free phone:* 800-922-4838. *Fax:* 812-372-0331. *E-mail:* nbagadio@ivytech.edu.

IVY TECH COMMUNITY COLLEGE–EAST CENTRAL

Muncie, Indiana **www.ivytech.edu/**

- **State-supported** 2-year, founded 1968, part of Ivy Tech State College System
- **Suburban** 15-acre campus with easy access to Indianapolis
- **Endowment** $15.9 million
- **Coed,** 5,943 undergraduate students, 43% full-time, 65% women, 35% men

Undergraduates 2,551 full-time, 3,392 part-time. 8% African American, 0.3% Asian American or Pacific Islander, 1% Hispanic American, 0.3% Native American, 4% transferred in.

Freshmen *Admission:* 1,146 applied, 1,146 admitted, 899 enrolled.

Faculty *Total:* 445, 20% full-time.

Majors Accounting technology and bookkeeping; automobile/automotive mechanics technology; building/property maintenance and management; business administration and management; business automation/technology/data entry; cabinetmaking and millwork; carpentry; child care and support services management; computer and information sciences; construction trades; construction trades related; criminal justice/safety; early childhood education; electrical, electronic and communications engineering technology; electrician; executive assistant/executive secretary; general studies; heating, air conditioning, ventilation and refrigeration maintenance technology; hospitality administration; hospitality administration related; human services; industrial mechanics and maintenance technology; industrial production technologies related; industrial technology; legal assistant/paralegal; liberal arts and sciences/liberal studies; library assistant; machine tool technology; masonry; medical/clinical assistant; medical radiologic technology; nursing (registered nurse training); painting and wall covering; physical therapist assistant; pipefitting and sprinkler fitting; psychiatric/mental health services technology; surgical technology; tool and die technology.

Academics *Calendar:* semesters. *Degree:* certificates and associate. *Special study options:* academic remediation for entering students, adult/continuing education programs, advanced placement credit, distance learning, internships, part-time degree program, services for LD students.

Library 5,779 titles, 145 serial subscriptions, 6,266 audiovisual materials, an OPAC, a Web page.

Computers on Campus 270 computers available on campus for general student use. A campuswide network can be accessed from off campus. Internet access, online (class) registration, at least one staffed computer lab available.

Student Life *Housing:* college housing not available. *Activities and Organizations:* Business Professionals of America, Skills USA-VICA, Student Government, Phi Theta Kappa, Human Services Club.

Costs (2005–06) *Tuition:* state resident $2520 full-time, $84 per credit part-time; nonresident $5108 full-time, $170 per credit part-time. *Required fees:* $70 full-time, $35 per term part-time.

Financial Aid Of all full-time matriculated undergraduates who enrolled in 2004, 65 Federal Work-Study jobs (averaging $2666).

Applying *Options:* early admission, deferred entrance. *Required:* high school transcript. *Required for some:* interview. *Application deadline:* rolling (freshmen), rolling (transfers). *Notification:* continuous (freshmen).

Freshmen Application Contact Ms. Mary Lewellen, Ivy Tech Community College–East Central, 4301 South Cowan Road, Muncie, IN 47302-9448. *Phone:* 317-921-4515. *Toll-free phone:* 800-589-8324. *Fax:* 765-289-2292. *E-mail:* mlewelle@ivytech.edu.

IVY TECH COMMUNITY COLLEGE– KOKOMO

Kokomo, Indiana   **www.ivytech.edu/**

- **State-supported** 2-year, founded 1968, part of Ivy Tech State College System
- **Small-town** 20-acre campus with easy access to Indianapolis
- **Endowment** $15.9 million
- **Coed,** 3,248 undergraduate students, 32% full-time, 64% women, 36% men

Undergraduates 1,031 full-time, 2,217 part-time. 4% African American, 0.4% Asian American or Pacific Islander, 2% Hispanic American, 0.9% Native American, 0.2% transferred in.

Freshmen *Admission:* 1,083 applied, 1,083 admitted, 588 enrolled.

Faculty *Total:* 255, 23% full-time.

Majors Accounting technology and bookkeeping; automobile/automotive mechanics technology; building/property maintenance and management; business administration and management; business automation/technology/data entry; cabinetmaking and millwork; child care and support services management; computer and information sciences; construction trades related; criminal justice/safety; drafting and design technology; early childhood education; electrical, electronic and communications engineering technology; electrician; emergency medical technology (EMT paramedic); executive assistant/executive secretary; general studies; heating, air conditioning, ventilation and refrigeration maintenance technology; human services; industrial technology; legal assistant/paralegal; liberal arts and sciences/liberal studies; library assistant; machine tool technology; mechanic and repair technologies related; mechanics and repair; medical/clinical assistant; pipefitting and sprinkler fitting; psychiatric/mental health services technology; surgical technology; tool and die technology.

Academics *Calendar:* semesters. *Degree:* certificates and associate. *Special study options:* academic remediation for entering students, adult/continuing education programs, advanced placement credit, distance learning, internships, part-time degree program, services for LD students, summer session for credit.

Library 5,177 titles, 99 serial subscriptions, 772 audiovisual materials, an OPAC, a Web page.

Computers on Campus 320 computers available on campus for general student use. A campuswide network can be accessed from off campus. Internet access, online (class) registration, at least one staffed computer lab available.

Student Life *Housing:* college housing not available. *Activities and Organizations:* student-run newspaper, Student Government, Collegiate Secretaries International, Licensed Practical Nursing Club, Phi Theta Kappa. *Campus security:* 24-hour emergency response devices, late-night transport/escort service. *Student services:* personal/psychological counseling.

Costs (2005–06) *Tuition:* state resident $2520 full-time, $84 per credit part-time; nonresident $5108 full-time, $170 per credit part-time. *Required fees:* $70 full-time, $35 per term part-time.

Financial Aid Of all full-time matriculated undergraduates who enrolled in 2004, 45 Federal Work-Study jobs (averaging $1829).

Applying *Options:* early admission. *Required:* high school transcript. *Required for some:* interview. *Application deadline:* rolling (freshmen), rolling (transfers). *Notification:* continuous (freshmen).

Freshmen Application Contact Ms. Alayne Cook, Assistant Director of Admissions, Ivy Tech Community College–Kokomo, 1815 East Morgan Street, Kokomo, IN 46903-1373. *Phone:* 317-921-4515. *Toll-free phone:* 800-459-0561. *Fax:* 765-454-5111. *E-mail:* acook@ivytech.edu.

IVY TECH COMMUNITY COLLEGE– LAFAYETTE

Lafayette, Indiana   **www.ivytech.edu/**

- **State-supported** 2-year, founded 1968, part of Ivy Tech State College System
- **Suburban** campus with easy access to Indianapolis
- **Endowment** $15.9 million
- **Coed,** 5,970 undergraduate students, 40% full-time, 51% women, 49% men

Undergraduates 2,374 full-time, 3,596 part-time. 3% African American, 1% Asian American or Pacific Islander, 4% Hispanic American, 0.3% Native American, 0.1% international, 4% transferred in.

Freshmen *Admission:* 1,326 applied, 1,326 admitted, 685 enrolled.

Faculty *Total:* 325, 20% full-time.

Majors Accounting; accounting technology and bookkeeping; automobile/automotive mechanics technology; biotechnology; building/property maintenance and management; business administration and management; business automation/technology/data entry; cabinetmaking and millwork; carpentry; child care and support services management; computer and information sciences; drafting and design technology; early childhood education; electrical, electronic and communications engineering technology; electrician; executive assistant/executive secretary; general studies; heating, air conditioning, ventilation and refrigeration maintenance technology; human services; industrial production technologies related; industrial technology; ironworking; legal assistant/paralegal; liberal arts and sciences/liberal studies; library assistant; lineworker; machine tool technology; masonry; mechanic and repair technologies related; mechanics and repair; medical/clinical assistant; nursing (registered nurse training); painting and wall covering; pipefitting and sprinkler fitting; psychiatric/mental health services technology; quality control and safety technologies related; quality control technology; respiratory care therapy; robotics technology; sheet metal technology; surgical technology; tool and die technology.

Academics *Calendar:* semesters. *Degree:* certificates and associate. *Special study options:* academic remediation for entering students, advanced placement credit, distance learning, internships, part-time degree program, services for LD students, summer session for credit.

Library 8,043 titles, 200 serial subscriptions, 2,234 audiovisual materials, an OPAC, a Web page.

Computers on Campus 267 computers available on campus for general student use. A campuswide network can be accessed. Internet access, online (class) registration, at least one staffed computer lab available.

Student Life *Housing:* college housing not available. *Activities and Organizations:* student-run newspaper, Student Government, Phi Theta Kappa, LPN Club, Accounting Club, Student Computer Technology Association. *Student services:* personal/psychological counseling.

Costs (2005–06) *Tuition:* state resident $2520 full-time, $84 per credit part-time; nonresident $5108 full-time, $170 per credit part-time. *Required fees:* $70 full-time, $35 per term part-time.

Financial Aid Of all full-time matriculated undergraduates who enrolled in 2004, 65 Federal Work-Study jobs (averaging $2222). 1 state and other part-time job (averaging $2436).

Applying *Required:* high school transcript. *Required for some:* interview. *Application deadline:* rolling (freshmen), rolling (transfers). *Notification:* continuous (freshmen).

Freshmen Application Contact Ms. Judy Doppelfeld, Director of Admissions, Ivy Tech Community College–Lafayette, 3101 South Creagy Lane, PO Box 6299, Lafayette, IN 47903. *Phone:* 317-921-4515. *Toll-free phone:* 800-669-4882. *Fax:* 765-772-9107. *E-mail:* jdopplef@ivytech.edu.

IVY TECH COMMUNITY COLLEGE– NORTH CENTRAL

South Bend, Indiana   **www.ivytech.edu/**

- **State-supported** 2-year, founded 1968, part of Ivy Tech State College System
- **Suburban** 4-acre campus
- **Endowment** $15.9 million
- **Coed,** 5,228 undergraduate students, 23% full-time, 58% women, 42% men

Undergraduates 1,225 full-time, 4,003 part-time. 2% are from out of state, 14% African American, 0.9% Asian American or Pacific Islander, 5% Hispanic American, 0.5% Native American, 0.3% international, 2% transferred in.

Freshmen *Admission:* 1,113 applied, 1,113 admitted, 821 enrolled.

Ivy Tech Community College–North Central (continued)

Faculty *Total:* 311, 23% full-time.

Majors Accounting technology and bookkeeping; automobile/automotive mechanics technology; biotechnology; building/property maintenance and management; business administration and management; business automation/technology/data entry; cabinetmaking and millwork; carpentry; child care and support services management; clinical/medical laboratory technology; computer and information sciences; criminal justice/safety; design and visual communications; early childhood education; educational/instructional media design; electrical, electronic and communications engineering technology; electrician; emergency medical technology (EMT paramedic); executive assistant/executive secretary; general studies; heating, air conditioning, ventilation and refrigeration maintenance technology; hospitality administration; human services; industrial production technologies related; industrial technology; interior design; ironworking; legal assistant/paralegal; liberal arts and sciences/liberal studies; library assistant; machine tool technology; masonry; mechanic and repair technologies related; mechanics and repair; medical/clinical assistant; nursing (registered nurse training); painting and wall covering; pipefitting and sprinkler fitting; robotics technology; sheet metal technology; telecommunications technology; tool and die technology.

Academics *Calendar:* semesters. *Degree:* certificates and associate. *Special study options:* academic remediation for entering students, adult/continuing education programs, advanced placement credit, distance learning, English as a second language, internships, off-campus study, part-time degree program, services for LD students, summer session for credit.

Library 6,246 titles, 90 serial subscriptions, 689 audiovisual materials, an OPAC, a Web page.

Computers on Campus 426 computers available on campus for general student use. Internet access, online (class) registration, at least one staffed computer lab available.

Student Life *Housing:* college housing not available. *Activities and Organizations:* Phi Theta Kappa, Student Government, LPN Club. *Campus security:* 24-hour emergency response devices and patrols, late-night transport/escort service, security during open hours. *Student services:* personal/psychological counseling, women's center.

Costs (2005–06) *Tuition:* state resident $2520 full-time, $84 per credit part-time; nonresident $5108 full-time, $170 per credit part-time. *Required fees:* $70 full-time, $35 per term part-time.

Financial Aid Of all full-time matriculated undergraduates who enrolled in 2004, 100 Federal Work-Study jobs (averaging $1538).

Applying *Options:* early admission, deferred entrance. *Required:* high school transcript. *Required for some:* interview. *Application deadline:* rolling (freshmen), rolling (transfers). *Notification:* continuous (freshmen).

Freshmen Application Contact Ms. Pam Decker, Director of Admissions, Ivy Tech Community College–North Central, 220 Dean Johnson Boulevard, South Bend, IN 46601-3415. *Phone:* 574-289-7001. *Fax:* 219-236-7177. *E-mail:* pdecker@ivytech.edu.

IVY TECH COMMUNITY COLLEGE–NORTHEAST

Fort Wayne, Indiana   www.ivytech.edu/

- **State-supported** 2-year, founded 1969, part of Ivy Tech State College System
- **Urban** 22-acre campus
- **Endowment** $15.9 million
- **Coed,** 6,082 undergraduate students, 35% full-time, 61% women, 39% men

Undergraduates 2,120 full-time, 3,962 part-time. 1% are from out of state, 15% African American, 1% Asian American or Pacific Islander, 2% Hispanic American, 0.5% Native American, 0.1% international, 3% transferred in.
Freshmen *Admission:* 841 applied, 841 admitted, 608 enrolled.

Faculty *Total:* 435, 20% full-time.

Majors Accounting technology and bookkeeping; automobile/automotive mechanics technology; building/property maintenance and management; business administration and management; business automation/technology/data entry; cabinetmaking and millwork; child care and support services management; computer and information sciences; construction trades; construction trades related; drafting and design technology; early childhood education; electrical, electronic and communications engineering technology; electrician; executive assistant/executive secretary; general studies; heating, air conditioning, ventilation and refrigeration maintenance technology; hospitality administration; hospitality administration related; human services; industrial production technologies related; industrial technology; ironworking; legal assistant/paralegal; liberal arts and sciences/liberal studies; library assistant; machine tool technology; masonry; massage therapy; mechanics and repair; medical/clinical assistant; occupational

safety and health technology; painting and wall covering; pipefitting and sprinkler fitting; psychiatric/mental health services technology; respiratory care therapy; robotics technology; sheet metal technology; tool and die technology.

Academics *Calendar:* semesters. *Degree:* certificates and associate. *Special study options:* adult/continuing education programs, advanced placement credit, distance learning, English as a second language, internships, part-time degree program, services for LD students, summer session for credit.

Library 18,389 titles, 110 serial subscriptions, 3,397 audiovisual materials, an OPAC, a Web page.

Computers on Campus 382 computers available on campus for general student use. Internet access, online (class) registration, at least one staffed computer lab available.

Student Life *Housing:* college housing not available. *Activities and Organizations:* student-run newspaper, Student Government, LPN Club, Phi Theta Kappa. *Campus security:* 24-hour emergency response devices and patrols, late-night transport/escort service.

Costs (2005–06) *Tuition:* state resident $2520 full-time, $84 per credit part-time; nonresident $5108 full-time, $170 per credit part-time. *Required fees:* $70 full-time, $35 per term part-time.

Financial Aid Of all full-time matriculated undergraduates who enrolled in 2004, 40 Federal Work-Study jobs (averaging $4041).

Applying *Options:* early admission. *Required:* high school transcript. *Required for some:* interview. *Application deadline:* rolling (freshmen), rolling (transfers). *Notification:* continuous (freshmen).

Freshmen Application Contact Dr. Rebecca Nickoli, Executive Director of Educational Systems, Ivy Tech Community College–Northeast, 3800 N. Anthony Boulevard, Ft. Wayne, IN 46805-1489. *Phone:* 317-921-4515. *Toll-free phone:* 800-859-4882. *Fax:* 260-480-4177. *E-mail:* sscheer@ivytech.edu.

IVY TECH COMMUNITY COLLEGE–NORTHWEST

Gary, Indiana   www.ivytech.edu/

- **State-supported** 2-year, founded 1963, part of Ivy Tech State College System
- **Urban** 13-acre campus with easy access to Chicago
- **Endowment** $15.9 million
- **Coed,** 4,815 undergraduate students, 29% full-time, 66% women, 34% men

Undergraduates 1,395 full-time, 3,420 part-time. 30% African American, 0.7% Asian American or Pacific Islander, 9% Hispanic American, 0.2% Native American, 0.1% international, 5% transferred in.
Freshmen *Admission:* 738 applied, 738 admitted, 585 enrolled.

Faculty *Total:* 419, 22% full-time.

Majors Accounting technology and bookkeeping; automobile/automotive mechanics technology; building/construction finishing, management, and inspection related; building/property maintenance and management; business administration and management; business automation/technology/data entry; cabinetmaking and millwork; carpentry; child care and support services management; computer and information sciences; construction trades; criminal justice/safety; drafting and design technology; early childhood education; electrical, electronic and communications engineering technology; electrician; executive assistant/executive secretary; funeral service and mortuary science; general studies; heating, air conditioning, ventilation and refrigeration maintenance technology; hospitality administration; human services; industrial technology; ironworking; legal assistant/paralegal; liberal arts and sciences/liberal studies; library assistant; machine tool technology; masonry; mechanics and repair; medical/clinical assistant; nursing (registered nurse training); occupational safety and health technology; painting and wall covering; pipefitting and sprinkler fitting; psychiatric/mental health services technology; respiratory care therapy; sheet metal technology; stationary energy sources installation; surgical technology; telecommunications technology; tool and die technology.

Academics *Calendar:* semesters. *Degree:* certificates and associate. *Special study options:* academic remediation for entering students, adult/continuing education programs, advanced placement credit, distance learning, internships, part-time degree program, services for LD students, summer session for credit.

Library 13,805 titles, 160 serial subscriptions, 4,295 audiovisual materials, an OPAC, a Web page.

Computers on Campus 267 computers available on campus for general student use. Internet access, online (class) registration, at least one staffed computer lab available.

Student Life *Housing:* college housing not available. *Activities and Organizations:* Phi Theta Kappa, LPN Club, Computer Club, Student Government, Business Club. *Campus security:* 24-hour emergency response devices, late-night transport/escort service.

Costs (2005–06) *Tuition:* state resident $2520 full-time, $84 per credit part-time; nonresident $5108 full-time, $170 per credit part-time. *Required fees:* $70 full-time, $35 per term part-time.

Financial Aid Of all full-time matriculated undergraduates who enrolled in 2004, 74 Federal Work-Study jobs (averaging $2131).

Applying *Options:* deferred entrance. *Required:* high school transcript. *Required for some:* interview. *Application deadline:* rolling (freshmen), rolling (transfers). *Notification:* continuous (freshmen).

Freshmen Application Contact Dr. Rebecca Nickoli, Executive Director of Educational Systems, Ivy Tech Community College–Northwest, 1440 East 35th Avenue, Gary, IN 46409-1499. *Phone:* 317-921-4515. *Toll-free phone:* 800-843-4882. *Fax:* 219-981-4415. *E-mail:* tlewis@ivytech.edu.

IVY TECH COMMUNITY COLLEGE— SOUTHEAST

Madison, Indiana　　　　　　**www.ivytech.edu/**

- **State-supported** 2-year, founded 1963, part of Ivy Tech State College System
- **Small-town** 5-acre campus with easy access to Louisville
- **Endowment** $15.9 million
- **Coed,** 1,766 undergraduate students, 36% full-time, 72% women, 28% men

Undergraduates 630 full-time, 1,136 part-time. 2% are from out of state, 0.9% African American, 0.3% Asian American or Pacific Islander, 0.6% Hispanic American, 0.1% Native American, 0.1% international, 2% transferred in. Freshmen *Admission:* 280 applied, 280 admitted, 266 enrolled.

Faculty *Total:* 148, 24% full-time.

Majors Accounting technology and bookkeeping; business administration and management; business automation/technology/data entry; child care and support services management; computer and information sciences; early childhood education; electrical, electronic and communications engineering technology; executive assistant/executive secretary; general studies; human services; industrial technology; legal assistant/paralegal; liberal arts and sciences/liberal studies; library assistant; medical/clinical assistant; nursing (licensed practical/vocational nurse training); nursing (registered nurse training); psychiatric/mental health services technology.

Academics *Calendar:* semesters. *Degree:* certificates and associate. *Special study options:* academic remediation for entering students, advanced placement credit, distance learning, internships, part-time degree program, services for LD students, summer session for credit.

Library 9,027 titles, 14,299 serial subscriptions, 1,341 audiovisual materials, an OPAC, a Web page.

Computers on Campus 123 computers available on campus for general student use. A campuswide network can be accessed. Internet access, online (class) registration, at least one staffed computer lab available.

Student Life *Housing:* college housing not available. *Activities and Organizations:* Student Government, Phi Theta Kappa, LPN Club. *Campus security:* 24-hour emergency response devices.

Costs (2005–06) *Tuition:* state resident $2520 full-time, $84 per credit part-time; nonresident $5108 full-time, $170 per credit part-time. *Required fees:* $70 full-time, $35 per term part-time.

Financial Aid Of all full-time matriculated undergraduates who enrolled in 2004, 26 Federal Work-Study jobs (averaging $1696).

Applying *Required:* high school transcript. *Required for some:* interview. *Application deadline:* rolling (freshmen), rolling (transfers). *Notification:* continuous (freshmen).

Freshmen Application Contact Ms. Cindy Hutcherson, Assistant Director of Admission/Career Counselor, Ivy Tech Community College–Southeast, 590 Ivy Tech Drive, Madison, IN 47250-1881. *Phone:* 812-265-2580. *Toll-free phone:* 800-403-2190. *Fax:* 812-265-4028. *E-mail:* chutcher@ivytech.edu.

IVY TECH COMMUNITY COLLEGE— SOUTHERN INDIANA

Sellersburg, Indiana　　　　　　**www.ivytech.edu/**

- **State-supported** 2-year, founded 1968, part of Ivy Tech State College System
- **Small-town** 63-acre campus with easy access to Louisville
- **Endowment** $15.9 million
- **Coed,** 3,112 undergraduate students, 29% full-time, 52% women, 48% men

Undergraduates 904 full-time, 2,208 part-time. 25% are from out of state, 5% African American, 0.5% Asian American or Pacific Islander, 0.5% Hispanic American, 0.6% Native American, 5% transferred in. Freshmen *Admission:* 742 applied, 742 admitted, 493 enrolled.

Faculty *Total:* 173, 27% full-time.

Majors Accounting technology and bookkeeping; automobile/automotive mechanics technology; building/property maintenance and management; business administration and management; business automation/technology/data entry; cabinetmaking and millwork; carpentry; child care and support services management; computer and information sciences; design and visual communications; early childhood education; electrical, electronic and communications engineering technology; electrician; executive assistant/executive secretary; general studies; heating, air conditioning, ventilation and refrigeration maintenance technology; human services; industrial technology; legal assistant/paralegal; liberal arts and sciences/liberal studies; library assistant; machine tool technology; masonry; mechanics and repair; medical/clinical assistant; nursing (registered nurse training); pipefitting and sprinkler fitting; psychiatric/mental health services technology; respiratory care therapy; sheet metal technology; tool and die technology.

Academics *Calendar:* semesters. *Degree:* certificates and associate. *Special study options:* academic remediation for entering students, adult/continuing education programs, advanced placement credit, cooperative education, distance learning, internships, part-time degree program, services for LD students, summer session for credit.

Library 7,634 titles, 66 serial subscriptions, 648 audiovisual materials, an OPAC, a Web page.

Computers on Campus 187 computers available on campus for general student use. A campuswide network can be accessed. Internet access, online (class) registration, at least one staffed computer lab available.

Student Life *Housing:* college housing not available. *Activities and Organizations:* Phi Theta Kappa, Practical Nursing Club, Medical Assistant Club, Accounting Club, Student Government. *Campus security:* late-night transport/escort service.

Costs (2005–06) *Tuition:* state resident $2520 full-time, $84 per credit part-time; nonresident $5108 full-time, $170 per credit part-time. *Required fees:* $70 full-time, $35 per term part-time.

Financial Aid Of all full-time matriculated undergraduates who enrolled in 2004, 20 Federal Work-Study jobs (averaging $5007). 1 state and other part-time job (averaging $6080).

Applying *Options:* early admission, deferred entrance. *Required:* high school transcript. *Required for some:* interview. *Application deadline:* rolling (freshmen), rolling (transfers). *Notification:* continuous (freshmen).

Freshmen Application Contact Ms. Mindy Steinberg, Director of Admissions, Ivy Tech Community College–Southern Indiana, 8204 Highway 311, Sellersburg, IN 47172-1897. *Phone:* 812-246-3301. *Toll-free phone:* 800-321-9021. *Fax:* 812-246-9905. *E-mail:* msteinbe@ivytech.edu.

IVY TECH COMMUNITY COLLEGE— SOUTHWEST

Evansville, Indiana　　　　　　**www.ivytech.edu/**

- **State-supported** 2-year, founded 1963, part of Ivy Tech State College System
- **Suburban** 15-acre campus
- **Endowment** $15.9 million
- **Coed,** 4,858 undergraduate students, 31% full-time, 54% women, 46% men

Undergraduates 1,526 full-time, 3,332 part-time. 2% are from out of state, 8% African American, 0.5% Asian American or Pacific Islander, 1% Hispanic American, 0.3% Native American, 4% transferred in. Freshmen *Admission:* 1,038 applied, 1,038 admitted, 606 enrolled.

Faculty *Total:* 308, 23% full-time.

Majors Accounting technology and bookkeeping; automobile/automotive mechanics technology; boilermaking; building/property maintenance and man-

Ivy Tech Community College–Southwest (continued)

agement; business administration and management; business automation/technology/data entry; cabinetmaking and millwork; carpentry; child care and support services management; computer and information sciences; construction/heavy equipment/earthmoving equipment operation; criminal justice/safety; design and visual communications; early childhood education; electrical, electronic and communications engineering technology; electrician; emergency medical technology (EMT paramedic); executive assistant/executive secretary; general studies; graphic design; heating, air conditioning, ventilation and refrigeration maintenance technology; human services; industrial production technologies related; industrial technology; interior design; ironworking; legal assistant/paralegal; liberal arts and sciences/liberal studies; library assistant; machine tool technology; masonry; mechanic and repair technologies related; mechanics and repair; medical/clinical assistant; nursing (registered nurse training); painting and wall covering; pipefitting and sprinkler fitting; psychiatric/mental health services technology; robotics technology; sheet metal technology; surgical technology; tool and die technology.

Academics *Calendar:* semesters. *Degree:* certificates and associate. *Special study options:* academic remediation for entering students, advanced placement credit, cooperative education, distance learning, independent study, internships, part-time degree program, services for LD students, summer session for credit.

Library 7,082 titles, 107 serial subscriptions, 1,755 audiovisual materials, an OPAC, a Web page.

Computers on Campus 362 computers available on campus for general student use. Internet access, online (class) registration, at least one staffed computer lab available.

Student Life *Housing:* college housing not available. *Activities and Organizations:* Student Government, Phi Theta Kappa, LPN Club, National Association of Industrial Technology, Design Club. *Campus security:* late-night transport/escort service.

Costs (2005–06) *Tuition:* state resident $2520 full-time, $84 per credit part-time; nonresident $5108 full-time, $170 per credit part-time. *Required fees:* $70 full-time, $35 per term part-time.

Financial Aid Of all full-time matriculated undergraduates who enrolled in 2004, 65 Federal Work-Study jobs (averaging $2264).

Applying *Options:* early admission, deferred entrance. *Required:* high school transcript. *Required for some:* interview. *Application deadline:* rolling (freshmen), rolling (transfers). *Notification:* continuous (freshmen).

Freshmen Application Contact Ms. Denise Johnson-Kincade, Director of Admissions, Ivy Tech Community College–Southwest, 3501 First Avenue, Evansville, IN 47710-3398. *Phone:* 317-921-4515. *Fax:* 812-429-1483. *E-mail:* ajohnson@ivytech.edu.

IVY TECH COMMUNITY COLLEGE–WABASH VALLEY

Terre Haute, Indiana   www.ivytech.edu/

- **State-supported** 2-year, founded 1966, part of Ivy Tech State College System
- **Suburban** 55-acre campus with easy access to Indianapolis
- **Endowment** $15.9 million
- **Coed,** 4,992 undergraduate students, 43% full-time, 57% women, 43% men

Undergraduates 2,169 full-time, 2,823 part-time. 2% are from out of state, 3% African American, 0.4% Asian American or Pacific Islander, 0.3% Hispanic American, 0.6% Native American, 3% transferred in.
Freshmen *Admission:* 1,300 applied, 1,300 admitted, 710 enrolled.
Faculty *Total:* 313, 25% full-time.

Majors Accounting technology and bookkeeping; airframe mechanics and aircraft maintenance technology; allied health diagnostic, intervention, and treatment professions related; automobile/automotive mechanics technology; building/property maintenance and management; business administration and management; cabinetmaking and millwork; carpentry; child care and support services management; clinical/medical laboratory technology; computer and information sciences; construction/heavy equipment/earthmoving equipment operation; criminal justice/safety; design and visual communications; early childhood education; electrical, electronic and communications engineering technology; electrician; emergency medical technology (EMT paramedic); executive assistant/executive secretary; general studies; heating, air conditioning, ventilation and refrigeration maintenance technology; human services; industrial production technologies related; industrial technology; ironworking; legal assistant/paralegal; liberal arts and sciences/liberal studies; library assistant; machine tool technology; masonry; mechanics and repair; medical/clinical assistant; medical radiologic technology; nursing (registered nurse training); occupational safety and health technology; office management; painting and wall covering; pipefitting and sprinkler fitting; psychiatric/mental health services technology; quality

control and safety technologies related; robotics technology; sheet metal technology; surgical technology; tool and die technology.

Academics *Calendar:* semesters. *Degree:* certificates and associate. *Special study options:* academic remediation for entering students, adult/continuing education programs, advanced placement credit, distance learning, internships, part-time degree program, services for LD students, summer session for credit.

Library 4,403 titles, 77 serial subscriptions, 406 audiovisual materials, an OPAC, a Web page.

Computers on Campus 305 computers available on campus for general student use. A campuswide network can be accessed. Internet access, online (class) registration, at least one staffed computer lab available.

Student Life *Housing:* college housing not available. *Activities and Organizations:* Student Government, Phi Theta Kappa, LPN Club, National Association of Industrial Technology. *Campus security:* 24-hour emergency response devices. *Student services:* personal/psychological counseling, women's center.

Athletics *Intramural sports:* basketball M/W, volleyball M/W.

Costs (2005–06) *Tuition:* state resident $2520 full-time, $84 per credit part-time; nonresident $5180 full-time, $170 per credit part-time. *Required fees:* $70 full-time, $35 per term part-time.

Financial Aid Of all full-time matriculated undergraduates who enrolled in 2004, 51 Federal Work-Study jobs (averaging $2110). 1 state and other part-time job (averaging $2963).

Applying *Options:* early admission, deferred entrance. *Required:* high school transcript. *Required for some:* interview. *Application deadline:* rolling (freshmen), rolling (transfers). *Notification:* continuous (freshmen).

Freshmen Application Contact Mr. Michael Fisher, Ivy Tech Community College–Wabash Valley, 7999 U.S. Highway 41 South, Terre Haute, IN 47802-4898. *Phone:* 317-921-4515. *Toll-free phone:* 800-377-4882. *Fax:* 812-299-5723. *E-mail:* mfisher@ivytech.edu.

IVY TECH COMMUNITY COLLEGE–WHITEWATER

Richmond, Indiana   www.ivytech.edu/

- **State-supported** 2-year, founded 1963, part of Ivy Tech State College System
- **Small-town** 23-acre campus with easy access to Indianapolis
- **Endowment** $15.9 million
- **Coed,** 1,832 undergraduate students, 31% full-time, 74% women, 26% men

Undergraduates 570 full-time, 1,262 part-time. 4% are from out of state, 5% African American, 0.2% Asian American or Pacific Islander, 0.8% Hispanic American, 0.3% Native American, 2% transferred in.
Freshmen *Admission:* 347 applied, 347 admitted, 221 enrolled.
Faculty *Total:* 175, 17% full-time.

Majors Accounting technology and bookkeeping; automobile/automotive mechanics technology; building/property maintenance and management; business administration and management; business automation/technology/data entry; cabinetmaking and millwork; child care and support services management; computer and information sciences; construction trades; construction trades related; early childhood education; electrical, electronic and communications engineering technology; electrician; executive assistant/executive secretary; general studies; heating, air conditioning, ventilation and refrigeration maintenance technology; human services; industrial production technologies related; industrial technology; legal assistant/paralegal; liberal arts and sciences/liberal studies; library assistant; machine tool technology; mechanics and repair; medical/clinical assistant; nursing (registered nurse training); pipefitting and sprinkler fitting; psychiatric/mental health services technology; robotics technology; tool and die technology.

Academics *Calendar:* semesters. *Degree:* certificates and associate. *Special study options:* academic remediation for entering students, adult/continuing education programs, advanced placement credit, distance learning, independent study, internships, off-campus study, part-time degree program, services for LD students, summer session for credit.

Computers on Campus 169 computers available on campus for general student use. A campuswide network can be accessed. Internet access, online (class) registration, at least one staffed computer lab available.

Student Life *Housing:* college housing not available. *Activities and Organizations:* student-run newspaper, Student Government, Phi Theta Kappa, LPN Club, CATS 2000, Business Professionals of America. *Campus security:* 24-hour emergency response devices, late-night transport/escort service. *Student services:* personal/psychological counseling.

Athletics *Intramural sports:* softball M/W.

Costs (2005–06) *Tuition:* state resident $2520 full-time, $84 per credit part-time; nonresident $15,108 full-time, $170 per credit part-time. *Required fees:* $70 full-time, $35 per term part-time.

Financial Aid Of all full-time matriculated undergraduates who enrolled in 2004, 14 Federal Work-Study jobs (averaging $3106). 1 state and other part-time job (averaging $3380).

Applying *Options:* early admission. *Required:* high school transcript. *Required for some:* interview. *Application deadline:* rolling (freshmen), rolling (transfers). *Notification:* continuous (freshmen).

Freshmen Application Contact Mr. Jeff Plasterer, Director of Admissions, Ivy Tech Community College–Whitewater, 2325 Chester Boulevard, Richmond, IN 47374-1298. *Phone:* 317-921-4515. *Toll-free phone:* 800-659-4562. *Fax:* 765-962-8741. *E-mail:* jplaster@ivytech.edu.

LINCOLN TECHNICAL INSTITUTE
Indianapolis, Indiana   www.lincolntech.com/

Director of Admissions Ms. Cindy Ryan, Director of Admissions, Lincoln Technical Institute, 1201 Stadium Drive, Indianapolis, IN 46202-2194. *Phone:* 317-632-5553. *Toll-free phone:* 800-554-4465.

MID-AMERICA COLLEGE OF FUNERAL SERVICE
Jeffersonville, Indiana   www.mid-america.edu/

Freshmen Application Contact Mr. Richard Nelson, Dean of Students, Mid-America College of Funeral Service, 3111 Hamburg Pike, Jeffersonville, IN 47130-9630. *Phone:* 812-288-8878. *Toll-free phone:* 800-221-6158.

PROFESSIONAL CAREERS INSTITUTE
Indianapolis, Indiana   www.pcicareers.com/

Director of Admissions Ms. Paulette M. Clay, Director of Admissions, Professional Careers Institute, 7302 Woodland Drive, Indianapolis, IN 46217. *Phone:* 317-299-6001 Ext. 320.

SAWYER COLLEGE
Hammond, Indiana   www.sawyercollege.edu/

Director of Admissions Director, Sawyer College, 6040 Hohman Avenue, Hammond, IN 46320. *Phone:* 219-844-0100.

SAWYER COLLEGE
Merrillville, Indiana

VINCENNES UNIVERSITY
Vincennes, Indiana   www.vinu.edu/

Director of Admissions Mr. Chris M. Crews, Director of Admissions, Vincennes University, 1002 North First Street, Vincennes, IN 47591. *Phone:* 812-888-4313. *Toll-free phone:* 800-742-9198.

VINCENNES UNIVERSITY JASPER CAMPUS
Jasper, Indiana   vujc.vinu.edu/

Director of Admissions Ms. LouAnn Gilbert, Director, Vincennes University Jasper Campus, Jasper, IN 47546. *Phone:* 812-482-3030. *Toll-free phone:* 800-809-VUJC. *E-mail:* lgilbert@indian.vinu.edu.

AIB COLLEGE OF BUSINESS
Des Moines, Iowa   www.aib.edu/

Director of Admissions Ms. Gail Cline, Director of Admissions, AIB College of Business, Keith Fenton Administration Building, 2500 Fleur Drive, Des Moines, IA 50321-1799. *Phone:* 515-244-4221 Ext. 5634. *Toll-free phone:* 800-444-1921. *Fax:* 515-244-6773. *E-mail:* clineg@aib.edu.

CLINTON COMMUNITY COLLEGE
Clinton, Iowa   www.eicc.edu/ccc/

- **State and locally supported** 2-year, founded 1946, part of Eastern Iowa Community College District
- **Small-town** 20-acre campus
- **Coed**

Undergraduates 590 full-time, 708 part-time. Students come from 9 states and territories, 8% are from out of state, 3% African American, 0.5% Asian American or Pacific Islander, 2% Hispanic American, 0.8% Native American, 0.4% international.

Academics *Calendar:* semesters. *Degree:* certificates, diplomas, and associate. *Special study options:* academic remediation for entering students, adult/continuing education programs, advanced placement credit, cooperative education, distance learning, double majors, English as a second language, independent study, internships, part-time degree program, services for LD students, study abroad, summer session for credit.

Athletics Member NJCAA.

Financial Aid Of all full-time matriculated undergraduates who enrolled in 2004, 54 Federal Work-Study jobs (averaging $3000).

Applying *Options:* early admission, deferred entrance. *Required:* high school transcript.

Director of Admissions Mr. Neil Mandsager, Executive Director of Enrollment Management and Marketing, Clinton Community College, 1000 Lincoln Boulevard, Clinton, IA 52732-6299. *Phone:* 563-244-7007.

DES MOINES AREA COMMUNITY COLLEGE
Ankeny, Iowa   www.dmacc.edu/

- **State and locally supported** 2-year, founded 1966, part of Iowa Area Community Colleges System
- **Small-town** 362-acre campus
- **Endowment** $1.8 million
- **Coed**

Undergraduates 6,002 full-time, 7,717 part-time. Students come from 31 states and territories, 53 other countries, 1% are from out of state, 4% African American, 3% Asian American or Pacific Islander, 2% Hispanic American, 0.3% Native American, 2% international, 3% transferred in.

Faculty *Student/faculty ratio:* 50:1.

Academics *Calendar:* semesters. *Degrees:* certificates, diplomas, and associate (profile also includes information from the Boone, Carroll, Des Moines, and Newton campuses). *Special study options:* academic remediation for entering students, adult/continuing education programs, advanced placement credit, cooperative education, distance learning, English as a second language, honors programs, off-campus study, part-time degree program, services for LD students, student-designed majors, summer session for credit.

Student Life *Campus security:* 24-hour emergency response devices and patrols, late-night transport/escort service.

Athletics Member NJCAA.

Standardized Tests *Required:* ACT COMPASS (for placement). *Recommended:* ACT (for placement).

Costs (2005–06) *Tuition:* state resident $2850 full-time, $95 per credit hour part-time; nonresident $5700 full-time, $190 per credit hour part-time. Full-time tuition and fees vary according to course load. Part-time tuition and fees vary according to course load.

Financial Aid Of all full-time matriculated undergraduates who enrolled in 2004, 377 Federal Work-Study jobs (averaging $1055).

Applying *Options:* electronic application, early admission, deferred entrance. *Required for some:* high school transcript, interview.

Director of Admissions Mr. Keith Knowles, Director of Admissions and Assessment, Des Moines Area Community College, Building 1, 2006 South Ankeny Boulevard, Ankeny, IA 50021. *Phone:* 515-964-6216. *Toll-free phone:* 800-362-2127.

ELLSWORTH COMMUNITY COLLEGE

Iowa Falls, Iowa   **www.iavalley.cc.ia.us/ecc/**

- **State and locally supported** 2-year, founded 1890, part of Iowa Valley Community College District System
- **Small-town** 10-acre campus
- **Endowment** $2.3 million
- **Coed**

Undergraduates 627 full-time, 303 part-time. Students come from 18 states and territories, 4 other countries, 9% are from out of state, 8% African American, 0.3% Asian American or Pacific Islander, 4% Hispanic American, 2% international, 38% live on campus.

Faculty *Student/faculty ratio:* 17:1.

Academics *Calendar:* semesters. *Degree:* diplomas and associate. *Special study options:* academic remediation for entering students, adult/continuing education programs, advanced placement credit, cooperative education, distance learning, honors programs, internships, part-time degree program, services for LD students, student-designed majors, summer session for credit.

Student Life *Campus security:* 24-hour emergency response devices and patrols.

Athletics Member NJCAA.

Standardized Tests *Required for some:* ACT (for placement), COMPASS. *Recommended:* ACT (for placement).

Financial Aid Of all full-time matriculated undergraduates who enrolled in 2004, 95 Federal Work-Study jobs (averaging $1200). 40 state and other part-time jobs (averaging $1200).

Applying *Options:* electronic application, early admission, deferred entrance. *Required:* high school transcript.

Director of Admissions Mrs. Nancy Walters, Registrar, Ellsworth Community College, 1100 College Avenue, Iowa Falls, IA 50126-1199. *Phone:* 641-648-4611. *Toll-free phone:* 800-ECC-9235.

HAMILTON COLLEGE

Cedar Falls, Iowa   **www.hamiltoncf.com/**

- primarily 2-year
- 695 undergraduate students, 78% full-time

Undergraduates 541 full-time, 154 part-time. 10% African American, 1% Hispanic American, 0.3% Native American.

Freshmen *Admission:* 94 enrolled.

Faculty *Total:* 37, 46% full-time, 8% with terminal degrees. *Student/faculty ratio:* 25:1.

Majors Accounting; business, management, and marketing related; business systems networking/ telecommunications; computer programming; computer systems networking and telecommunications; criminal justice/safety; executive assistant/executive secretary; legal assistant/paralegal; management information systems; medical/clinical assistant; multi-/interdisciplinary studies related; tourism and travel services marketing.

Academics *Calendar:* quarters. *Degrees:* associate and bachelor's.

Student Life *Activities and Organizations:* student-run newspaper.

Standardized Tests *Required:* Wonderlic (for admission).

Costs (2006–07) *One-time required fee:* $25. *Tuition:* contact school as costs vary with program selected. Tuition includes books.

Applying *Application fee:* $20. *Required:* essay or personal statement, high school transcript, letters of recommendation, interview. *Application deadline:* rolling (freshmen).

Freshmen Application Contact Ms. Jill Lines, Director of Admissions, Hamilton College, 7009 Nordic Drive, Cedar Falls, IA 50613. *Phone:* 319-277-0220. *Toll-free phone:* 800-728-1220. *Fax:* 319-268-0978. *E-mail:* jilines@hamiltoncf.com.

HAMILTON COLLEGE

Cedar Rapids, Iowa   **www.hamiltonia.edu/**

- **Proprietary** primarily 2-year, founded 1900
- **Suburban** 4-acre campus
- **Coed,** 511 undergraduate students, 86% full-time, 60% women, 40% men

Undergraduates 440 full-time, 71 part-time. Students come from 1 other state, 3% African American, 2% Asian American or Pacific Islander, 1% Hispanic American, 0.6% Native American. *Retention:* 52% of 2003 full-time freshmen returned.

Freshmen *Admission:* 278 enrolled.

Faculty *Total:* 40, 18% full-time, 3% with terminal degrees. *Student/faculty ratio:* 25:1.

Majors Accounting; administrative assistant and secretarial science; business administration and management; criminal justice/law enforcement administration; general studies; management information systems; medical/clinical assistant; tourism and travel services management.

Academics *Calendar:* quarters. *Degrees:* certificates, diplomas, associate, and bachelor's (branch locations in Des Moines, Mason City, and Cedar Falls with significant enrollment not reflected in profile). *Special study options:* academic remediation for entering students, adult/continuing education programs, cooperative education, distance learning, internships, part-time degree program.

Library Hamilton College Library with 5,500 titles, 40 serial subscriptions, an OPAC, a Web page.

Computers on Campus 50 computers available on campus for general student use. A campuswide network can be accessed from off campus. Internet access, at least one staffed computer lab available.

Student Life *Housing:* college housing not available. *Activities and Organizations:* Phi Beta Lambda, Travel Club, Student Senate. *Campus security:* 24-hour emergency response devices.

Standardized Tests *Required:* Wonderlic (for admission).

Costs (2006–07) *Tuition:* $17,040 full-time, $355 per credit hour part-time.

Financial Aid Of all full-time matriculated undergraduates who enrolled in 2004, 10 Federal Work-Study jobs (averaging $889). 3 state and other part-time jobs (averaging $1885).

Applying *Options:* common application, early admission, deferred entrance. *Application fee:* $50. *Required:* high school transcript, interview. *Application deadline:* rolling (freshmen).

Freshmen Application Contact Ms. Niki Donahue, Director of Admissions, Hamilton College, 1924 D Street SW, Cedar Rapids, IA 52404. *Phone:* 319-363-0481. *Toll-free phone:* 800-728-0481. *Fax:* 319-363-3812.

HAMILTON COLLEGE

Council Bluffs, Iowa

HAWKEYE COMMUNITY COLLEGE

Waterloo, Iowa   **www.hawkeyecollege.edu/**

- **State and locally supported** 2-year, founded 1966
- **Rural** 320-acre campus
- **Coed,** 5,272 undergraduate students, 52% full-time, 56% women, 44% men

Undergraduates 2,751 full-time, 2,521 part-time. Students come from 18 states and territories, 10 other countries, 1% are from out of state, 7% African American, 1% Asian American or Pacific Islander, 2% Hispanic American, 0.3% Native American, 11% transferred in.

Freshmen *Admission:* 2,311 enrolled. *Average high school GPA:* 2.5.

Faculty *Total:* 357, 32% full-time. *Student/faculty ratio:* 16:1.

Majors Accounting; administrative assistant and secretarial science; agricultural business and management; agricultural mechanization; agronomy and crop science; animal sciences; architectural engineering technology; autobody/collision and repair technology; automobile/automotive mechanics technology; avionics maintenance technology; biology/biological sciences; business administration and management; business/commerce; child development; civil engineering technology; clinical/medical laboratory technology; commercial and advertising art; computer engineering technology; computer/information technology services administration related; computer systems networking and telecommunications; computer/technical support; corrections; criminal justice/law enforcement administration; criminal justice/police science; data entry/ microcomputer applications related; dental hygiene; drafting and design technology; education; engineering technology; farm and ranch management; fire science; food science; heavy equipment maintenance technology; horticultural science; information technology; interdisciplinary studies; interior design; liberal arts and sciences/liberal studies; machine tool technology; marketing/marketing management; mechanical design technology; mechanical engineering/mechanical technology; medical administrative assistant and medical secretary; natural resources management and policy; nursing (registered nurse training); ornamental horticulture; parks, recreation and leisure facilities management; photography; respiratory care therapy; survey technology; system administration; tool and die technology; web/multimedia management and webmaster; web page, digital/ multimedia and information resources design; word processing.

Academics *Calendar:* semesters. *Degree:* certificates, diplomas, and associate. *Special study options:* academic remediation for entering students, adult/ continuing education programs, advanced placement credit, cooperative education, distance learning, English as a second language, external degree program, part-time degree program, services for LD students, summer session for credit. *ROTC:* Army (c).

Library Hawkeye Community College Library with 37,155 titles, 482 serial subscriptions, 2,078 audiovisual materials, an OPAC, a Web page.

Computers on Campus 300 computers available on campus for general student use. A campuswide network can be accessed. Internet access, online (class) registration, at least one staffed computer lab available.

Student Life *Housing:* college housing not available. *Options:* Campus housing is provided by a third party. *Activities and Organizations:* Student Senate, Phi Theta Kappa, Environmental Conservation Club/Ag Club, Law Enforcement/Criminal Justice, Fashion Merchandising. *Campus security:* 24-hour patrols. *Student services:* personal/psychological counseling, women's center.

Athletics *Intramural sports:* basketball M/W, bowling M/W, golf M/W, softball M/W, volleyball M/W.

Standardized Tests *Required for some:* ACT (for admission).

Costs (2005–06) *Tuition:* state resident $2940 full-time, $98 per credit part-time; nonresident $5880 full-time, $196 per credit part-time. *Required fees:* $300 full-time, $10 per credit part-time.

Applying *Options:* electronic application, deferred entrance. *Required:* high school transcript. *Application deadline:* rolling (freshmen), rolling (transfers). *Notification:* continuous (freshmen).

Freshmen Application Contact Ms. Holly Grimm, Admissions Coordinator, Hawkeye Community College, PO Box 8015, Waterloo, IA 50704-8015. *Phone:* 319-296-4277. *Toll-free phone:* 800-670-4769. *Fax:* 319-296-2505. *E-mail:* admission@hawkeyecollege.edu.

INDIAN HILLS COMMUNITY COLLEGE
Ottumwa, Iowa   www.ihcc.cc.ia.us/

- **State and locally supported** 2-year, founded 1966, part of Iowa Area Community Colleges System
- **Small-town** 400-acre campus
- **Coed**

Undergraduates 2,046 full-time, 821 part-time. Students come from 16 states and territories, 7% are from out of state, 0.4% transferred in, 15% live on campus.

Academics *Calendar:* quarters. *Degree:* certificates, diplomas, and associate. *Special study options:* academic remediation for entering students, adult/ continuing education programs, cooperative education, English as a second language, honors programs, internships, part-time degree program, services for LD students, student-designed majors, summer session for credit.

Student Life *Campus security:* 24-hour emergency response devices and patrols.

Athletics Member NJCAA.

Standardized Tests *Required:* ACT ASSET (for placement). *Required for some:* ACT (for placement).

Financial Aid Of all full-time matriculated undergraduates who enrolled in 2004, 123 Federal Work-Study jobs (averaging $742). 62 state and other part-time jobs (averaging $823).

Applying *Options:* common application, early admission. *Required for some:* high school transcript.

Freshmen Application Contact Mrs. Jane Sapp, Admissions Officer, Indian Hills Community College, 525 Grandview Avenue, Building #1, Ottumwa, IA 52501-1398. *Phone:* 641-683-5155. *Toll-free phone:* 800-726-2585.

IOWA CENTRAL COMMUNITY COLLEGE
Fort Dodge, Iowa   www.iccc.cc.ia.us/

- **State and locally supported** 2-year, founded 1966, part of Iowa Department of Education Division of Community Colleges
- **Small-town** 110-acre campus
- **Coed**

Undergraduates Students come from 25 states and territories, 18 other countries, 5% are from out of state, 22% live on campus.

Faculty *Student/faculty ratio:* 18:1.

Academics *Calendar:* semesters. *Degree:* certificates, diplomas, and associate. *Special study options:* academic remediation for entering students, adult/ continuing education programs, advanced placement credit, cooperative education, distance learning, independent study, internships, part-time degree program, services for LD students, study abroad, summer session for credit.

Student Life *Campus security:* 24-hour emergency response devices and patrols, student patrols, late-night transport/escort service, controlled dormitory access.

Athletics Member NJCAA.

Standardized Tests *Required:* SAT or ACT (for placement), ACT ASSET or ACT COMPASS (for placement).

Costs (2005–06) *Tuition:* state resident $2790 full-time, $93 per credit part-time; nonresident $4135 full-time, $140 per credit part-time. *Required fees:* $300 full-time, $10 per credit part-time.

Applying *Options:* early admission, deferred entrance. *Required:* high school transcript.

Director of Admissions Mr. Brian K. Dioguardi, Director of Admissions, Iowa Central Community College, 330 Avenue M, Ft. Dodge, IA 50501. *Phone:* 515-576-0099 Ext. 2471. *Toll-free phone:* 800-362-2793.

IOWA LAKES COMMUNITY COLLEGE
Estherville, Iowa   www.iowalakes.edu/

- **State and locally supported** 2-year, founded 1967, part of Iowa Area Community Colleges System
- **Small-town** 20-acre campus
- **Endowment** $63,000
- **Coed**

Undergraduates 1,371 full-time, 1,622 part-time. Students come from 12 states and territories, 2 other countries, 13% are from out of state, 0.5% African American, 0.3% Asian American or Pacific Islander, 0.7% Hispanic American, 0.3% Native American, 0.4% international, 4% transferred in, 24% live on campus.

Faculty *Student/faculty ratio:* 19:1.

Academics *Calendar:* semesters. *Degree:* certificates, diplomas, and associate. *Special study options:* academic remediation for entering students, accelerated degree program, adult/continuing education programs, advanced placement credit, cooperative education, distance learning, honors programs, independent study, internships, part-time degree program, services for LD students, study abroad, summer session for credit.

Student Life *Campus security:* 24-hour emergency response devices, student patrols.

Athletics Member NJCAA.

Standardized Tests *Required for some:* ACT (for placement), ACT ASSET, ACT COMPASS.

Costs (2005–06) *Tuition:* state resident $3296 full-time; nonresident $3360 full-time. Full-time tuition and fees vary according to course load and program. Part-time tuition and fees vary according to course load and program. *Required fees:* $452 full-time. *Room and board:* $4120. Room and board charges vary according to board plan.

Financial Aid Of all full-time matriculated undergraduates who enrolled in 2004, 210 Federal Work-Study jobs (averaging $800).

Applying *Options:* deferred entrance. *Required:* high school transcript. *Required for some:* letters of recommendation, interview.

Freshmen Application Contact Ms. Anne Stansbury, Assistant Director Admissions, Iowa Lakes Community College, 3200 College Drive, Emmetsburg, IA 50536. *Phone:* 712-852-5254. *Toll-free phone:* 800-521-5054.

IOWA WESTERN COMMUNITY COLLEGE

Council Bluffs, Iowa   **www.iwcc.edu/**

- **District-supported** 2-year, founded 1966, part of Iowa Department of Education Division of Community Colleges
- **Suburban** 282-acre campus with easy access to Omaha
- **Coed**

Undergraduates 2,152 full-time, 2,147 part-time. Students come from 27 states and territories, 10 other countries, 2% African American, 1% Asian American or Pacific Islander, 1% Hispanic American, 0.6% Native American, 2% international, 19% live on campus.
Academics *Calendar:* semesters. *Degree:* certificates, diplomas, and associate. *Special study options:* academic remediation for entering students, adult/continuing education programs, cooperative education, distance learning, English as a second language, independent study, internships, part-time degree program, services for LD students, summer session for credit. *ROTC:* Army (c), Air Force (c).
Student Life *Campus security:* 24-hour patrols, late-night transport/escort service.
Athletics Member NJCAA.
Standardized Tests *Required:* SAT Reasoning Test or ACT or ACT ASSET or ACT COMPASS (for placement).
Costs (2005–06) *Tuition:* state resident $3200 full-time, $100 per credit part-time; nonresident $4800 full-time, $150 per credit part-time. *Required fees:* $320 full-time, $10 per credit part-time. *Room and board:* $4350. Room and board charges vary according to board plan and housing facility. *Payment plans:* installment, deferred payment.
Applying *Options:* early admission, deferred entrance. *Required:* high school transcript.
Freshmen Application Contact Mrs. Tammy Young, Director of Admissions, Iowa Western Community College, 2700 College Road, Box 4-C, Council Bluffs, IA 51502. *Phone:* 712-325-3288. *Toll-free phone:* 800-432-5852.

KAPLAN UNIVERSITY

Davenport, Iowa   **www.kaplancollegeia.com/**

Director of Admissions Mr. Robert Hoffmann, Director of Admissions, Kaplan University, 1801 East Kimberly Road, Suite 1, Davenport, IA 52807. *Phone:* 563-441-2496. *Toll-free phone:* 800-747-1035. *Fax:* 563-355-1320.

KIRKWOOD COMMUNITY COLLEGE

Cedar Rapids, Iowa   **www.kirkwood.cc.ia.us/**

Director of Admissions Mr. Doug Bannon, Director of Admissions, Kirkwood Community College, PO Box 2068, Cedar Rapids, IA 52406-2068. *Phone:* 319-398-5517. *Toll-free phone:* 800-332-2055. *E-mail:* dbannon@kirkwood.cc.ia.us.

MARSHALLTOWN COMMUNITY COLLEGE

Marshalltown,
Iowa   **www.marshalltowncommunitycollege.com/**

Director of Admissions Ms. Deana Trawny, Director of Admissions, Marshalltown Community College, 3700 South Center Street, Marshalltown, IA 50158. *Phone:* 641-752-7106 Ext. 391. *Toll-free phone:* 866-622-4748. *Fax:* 641-752-8149. *E-mail:* dtrawny@iavalley.cc.ia.us.

MUSCATINE COMMUNITY COLLEGE

Muscatine, Iowa   **www.eicc.edu/**

- **State-supported** 2-year, founded 1929, part of Eastern Iowa Community College District
- **Small-town** 25-acre campus
- **Coed**

Undergraduates 552 full-time, 728 part-time. Students come from 6 states and territories, 4% are from out of state, 1% African American, 0.5% Asian American or Pacific Islander, 10% Hispanic American, 0.5% Native American, 0.6% international.

Academics *Calendar:* semesters. *Degree:* certificates, diplomas, and associate. *Special study options:* academic remediation for entering students, adult/continuing education programs, advanced placement credit, cooperative education, distance learning, double majors, English as a second language, honors programs, independent study, internships, part-time degree program, services for LD students, study abroad, summer session for credit.
Athletics Member NJCAA.
Standardized Tests *Required:* ACT or DTLS, DTMS (for placement).
Financial Aid Of all full-time matriculated undergraduates who enrolled in 2004, 52 Federal Work-Study jobs (averaging $3000).
Applying *Options:* early admission, deferred entrance. *Required:* high school transcript.
Director of Admissions Neil Mandsager, Executive Director of Enrollment Management and Marketing, Muscatine Community College, 152 Colorado Street, Muscatine, IA 52761-5396. *Phone:* 563-288-6012. *Toll-free phone:* 800-351-4669.

NORTHEAST IOWA COMMUNITY COLLEGE

Calmar, Iowa   **www.nicc.edu/**

- **State and locally supported** 2-year, founded 1966, part of Iowa Area Community Colleges System
- **Small-town** 210-acre campus
- **Coed,** 4,833 undergraduate students, 44% full-time, 62% women, 38% men

Undergraduates 2,140 full-time, 2,693 part-time. Students come from 5 states and territories, 13% are from out of state, 1% African American, 0.5% Asian American or Pacific Islander, 0.7% Hispanic American, 0.2% Native American, 0.3% international.
Freshmen *Admission:* 1,161 applied, 771 admitted, 284 enrolled.
Faculty *Total:* 180, 63% full-time, 11% with terminal degrees. *Student/faculty ratio:* 15:1.
Majors Accounting; agricultural business and management; clinical/medical laboratory technology; computer engineering technology; construction engineering technology; dairy science; electrical, electronic and communications engineering technology; health information/medical records administration; liberal arts and sciences/liberal studies; marketing/marketing management; mechanical design technology; nursing (registered nurse training); trade and industrial teacher education.
Academics *Calendar:* semesters. *Degree:* certificates, diplomas, and associate. *Special study options:* academic remediation for entering students, adult/continuing education programs, cooperative education, distance learning, double majors, English as a second language, independent study, internships, off-campus study, services for LD students, student-designed majors, study abroad, summer session for credit.
Library Wilder Resource Center plus 1 other with 18,634 titles, 302 serial subscriptions, an OPAC.
Computers on Campus 4000 computers available on campus for general student use. A campuswide network can be accessed from off campus. Internet access, at least one staffed computer lab available.
Student Life *Housing:* college housing not available. *Activities and Organizations:* student-run newspaper. *Campus security:* security personnel on week nights. *Student services:* personal/psychological counseling.
Athletics *Intramural sports:* basketball M/W, bowling M/W, football M/W, golf M/W, skiing (cross-country) M/W, skiing (downhill) M/W, swimming and diving M/W, tennis M/W, volleyball M/W.
Costs (2005–06) *Tuition:* state resident $3590 full-time, $105 per credit part-time; nonresident $3590 full-time, $105 per credit part-time. *Required fees:* $442 full-time, $13 per credit part-time.
Financial Aid Of all full-time matriculated undergraduates who enrolled in 2004, 154 Federal Work-Study jobs (averaging $1248). 45 state and other part-time jobs (averaging $980).
Applying *Recommended:* high school transcript. *Application deadline:* rolling (freshmen), rolling (transfers). *Notification:* continuous (freshmen).
Freshmen Application Contact Ms. Martha Keune, Admissions Representative, Northeast Iowa Community College, PO Box 400, Calmar, IA 52132. *Phone:* 563-562-3263 Ext. 307. *Toll-free phone:* 800-728-CALMAR. *Fax:* 563-562-4369. *E-mail:* keunem@nicc.edu.

NORTH IOWA AREA COMMUNITY COLLEGE

Mason City, Iowa   **www.niacc.edu/**

- **State and locally supported** 2-year, founded 1918, part of Iowa Community Colleges System
- **Rural** 320-acre campus
- **Coed,** 3,133 undergraduate students, 54% full-time, 56% women, 44% men

Undergraduates 1,698 full-time, 1,435 part-time. Students come from 25 states and territories, 7 other countries, 4% are from out of state, 3% African American, 1% Asian American or Pacific Islander, 2% Hispanic American, 0.3% Native American, 0.5% international, 57% transferred in, 15% live on campus. *Retention:* 68% of 2003 full-time freshmen returned.
Freshmen *Admission:* 835 enrolled. *Average high school GPA:* 2.68. *Test scores:* ACT scores over 18: 74%; ACT scores over 24: 22%; ACT scores over 30: 6%.
Faculty *Total:* 195, 43% full-time, 5% with terminal degrees. *Student/faculty ratio:* 13:1.
Majors Accounting; accounting technology and bookkeeping; administrative assistant and secretarial science; agricultural business technology; agricultural economics; agricultural production; automobile/automotive mechanics technology; business administration and management; carpentry; clinical/medical laboratory technology; computer and information sciences; criminal justice/police science; electrical, electronic and communications engineering technology; emergency medical technology (EMT paramedic); entrepreneurship; fire services administration; heating, air conditioning, ventilation and refrigeration maintenance technology; industrial electronics technology; liberal arts and sciences/liberal studies; machine shop technology; machine tool technology; medical/clinical assistant; nursing assistant/aide and patient care assistant; nursing (licensed practical/vocational nurse training); nursing (registered nurse training); physical therapist assistant; sport and fitness administration/management; tool and die technology; welding technology.
Academics *Calendar:* semesters. *Degree:* certificates, diplomas, and associate. *Special study options:* academic remediation for entering students, advanced placement credit, cooperative education, distance learning, double majors, English as a second language, external degree program, honors programs, independent study, internships, off-campus study, part-time degree program, services for LD students, student-designed majors, summer session for credit.
Library North Iowa Area Community College Library with 29,540 titles, 413 serial subscriptions, 7,773 audiovisual materials, an OPAC, a Web page.
Computers on Campus 365 computers available on campus for general student use. A campuswide network can be accessed from off campus. Internet access, at least one staffed computer lab available.
Student Life *Housing:* on-campus residence required for freshman year. *Options:* coed. Campus housing is provided by a third party. Freshman applicants given priority for college housing. *Activities and Organizations:* student-run newspaper, choral group, Student Senate, school newspaper, intramurals, choral groups, band/orchestra. *Campus security:* 24-hour emergency response devices, controlled dormitory access. *Student services:* personal/psychological counseling.
Athletics Member NJCAA. *Intercollegiate sports:* baseball M(s), basketball M(s)/W(s), cross-country running W(s), football M(s), golf M(s)/W(s), soccer M(s)/W(s), softball W(s), track and field M(s)/W(s), volleyball W(s). *Intramural sports:* basketball M/W, bowling M/W, cheerleading W, football M, skiing (downhill) M/W, soccer M/W, softball W, table tennis M/W, tennis M/W, volleyball M/W, weight lifting M/W.
Costs (2005–06) *Tuition:* state resident $2790 full-time, $93 per credit part-time; nonresident $4184 full-time, $140 per credit part-time. *Required fees:* $174 full-time, $11 per credit part-time. *Room and board:* $3920.
Financial Aid Of all full-time matriculated undergraduates who enrolled in 2004, 125 Federal Work-Study jobs (averaging $2000).
Applying *Options:* common application, electronic application. *Required:* high school transcript. *Application deadline:* rolling (freshmen), rolling (transfers). *Notification:* continuous (freshmen).
Freshmen Application Contact Ms. Rachel McGuire, Director of Admissions, North Iowa Area Community College, 500 College Drive, Mason City, IA 50401. *Phone:* 641-422-4104. *Toll-free phone:* 888-GO NIACC Ext. 4245. *Fax:* 641-422-4385. *E-mail:* request@niacc.edu.

NORTHWEST IOWA COMMUNITY COLLEGE

Sheldon, Iowa   **www.nwicc.edu/**

Director of Admissions Ms. Lisa Story, Director of Enrollment Management, Northwest Iowa Community College, 603 West Park Street, Sheldon, IA 51201-1046. *Phone:* 712-324-5061 Ext. 115. *Toll-free phone:* 800-352-4907.

ST. LUKE'S COLLEGE

Sioux City, Iowa   **stlukescollege.edu/**

- **Independent** 2-year, part of St. Luke's Regional Medical Center
- **Rural** campus
- **Endowment** $883,130
- **Coed,** 155 undergraduate students, 83% full-time, 90% women, 10% men

Undergraduates 128 full-time, 27 part-time. Students come from 8 states and territories, 28% are from out of state, 0.6% African American, 1% Hispanic American, 2% Native American, 7% transferred in, 15% live on campus. *Retention:* 83% of 2003 full-time freshmen returned.
Freshmen *Admission:* 21 enrolled. *Average high school GPA:* 3.02. *Test scores:* ACT scores over 18: 100%; ACT scores over 24: 50%.
Faculty *Total:* 16, 63% full-time, 31% with terminal degrees. *Student/faculty ratio:* 11:1.
Majors Nursing (registered nurse training); radiologic technology/science; respiratory care therapy.
Academics *Calendar:* semesters. *Degree:* certificates and associate. *Special study options:* advanced placement credit, cooperative education, part-time degree program, summer session for credit.
Library St. Luke's Library plus 1 other with 2,038 titles, 119 serial subscriptions, 324 audiovisual materials, an OPAC, a Web page.
Computers on Campus 10 computers available on campus for general student use. A campuswide network can be accessed. Internet access, at least one staffed computer lab available.
Student Life *Housing Options:* coed. Campus housing is university owned. *Campus security:* 24-hour emergency response devices and patrols, late-night transport/escort service. *Student services:* health clinic, personal/psychological counseling.
Standardized Tests *Required:* ACT (for admission).
Costs (2006–07) *Tuition:* $11,900 full-time, $340 per credit part-time. *Required fees:* $600 full-time.
Financial Aid Of all full-time matriculated undergraduates who enrolled in 2004, 16 Federal Work-Study jobs (averaging $1453).
Applying *Options:* electronic application, early admission, early action. *Application fee:* $25. *Required:* essay or personal statement, high school transcript, minimum 2.50 GPA, interview, minimum ACT score of 19. *Application deadline:* 8/1 (freshmen).
Freshmen Application Contact Ms. Sherry McCarthy, Admissions Coordinator, St. Luke's College, 2720 Stone Park Boulevard, Sioux City, IA 51104. *Phone:* 712-279-3149. *Toll-free phone:* 800-352-4660 Ext. 3149. *Fax:* 712-233-8017. *E-mail:* mccartsj@stlukes.org.

SCOTT COMMUNITY COLLEGE

Bettendorf, Iowa   **www.eicc.edu/scc/**

- **State and locally supported** 2-year, founded 1966, part of Eastern Iowa Community College District
- **Urban** campus
- **Coed**

Undergraduates 2,212 full-time, 2,485 part-time. Students come from 36 states and territories, 8% are from out of state, 8% African American, 2% Asian American or Pacific Islander, 4% Hispanic American, 0.6% Native American, 1% international.
Faculty *Student/faculty ratio:* 20:1.
Academics *Calendar:* semesters. *Degree:* certificates, diplomas, and associate. *Special study options:* academic remediation for entering students, adult/continuing education programs, advanced placement credit, cooperative education, distance learning, double majors, English as a second language, honors programs, independent study, internships, off-campus study, part-time degree program, services for LD students, study abroad, summer session for credit.

Scott Community College (continued)

Student Life *Campus security:* 24-hour emergency response devices.

Athletics Member NJCAA.

Standardized Tests *Required:* ACT (for placement), College Board Diagnostic Tests (for placement).

Financial Aid Of all full-time matriculated undergraduates who enrolled in 2004, 72 Federal Work-Study jobs (averaging $3000).

Applying *Options:* early admission, deferred entrance. *Required:* high school transcript.

Director of Admissions Mr. Neil Mandsager, Executive Director of Enrollment Management and Marketing, Scott Community College, 500 Belmont Road, Bettendorf, IA 52722-6804. *Phone:* 563-441-4007. *Toll-free phone:* 800-895-0811.

SOUTHEASTERN COMMUNITY COLLEGE, NORTH CAMPUS

West Burlington, Iowa **www.secc.cc.ia.us/**

Freshmen Application Contact Ms. Stacy White, Admissions, Southeastern Community College, North Campus, 1015 South Gear Avenue, PO Box 180, West Burlington, IA 52655-0180. *Phone:* 319-752-2731 Ext. 8137. *Toll-free phone:* 866-722-4692.

SOUTHEASTERN COMMUNITY COLLEGE, SOUTH CAMPUS

Keokuk, Iowa **www.secc.cc.ia.us/**

Director of Admissions Ms. Kari Bevans, Admissions Coordinator, Southeastern Community College, South Campus, PO Box 6007, 335 Messenger Road, Keokuk, IA 52632. *Phone:* 319-752-2731. *Toll-free phone:* 866-722-4692 Ext. 8416.

SOUTHWESTERN COMMUNITY COLLEGE

Creston, Iowa **www.swcc.cc.ia.us/**

- **State-supported** 2-year, founded 1966, part of Iowa Department of Education Division of Community Colleges
- **Rural** 420-acre campus
- **Endowment** $691,031
- **Coed**

Undergraduates 666 full-time, 588 part-time. Students come from 11 states and territories, 4 other countries, 4% are from out of state, 2% African American, 0.2% Asian American or Pacific Islander, 1% Hispanic American, 0.5% international, 5% transferred in, 5% live on campus.

Faculty *Student/faculty ratio:* 14:1.

Academics *Calendar:* semesters. *Degree:* diplomas and associate. *Special study options:* academic remediation for entering students, adult/continuing education programs, advanced placement credit, cooperative education, independent study, internships, part-time degree program, services for LD students, student-designed majors, summer session for credit.

Student Life *Campus security:* 24-hour emergency response devices and patrols, controlled dormitory access.

Athletics Member NJCAA.

Standardized Tests *Required for some:* SAT or ACT (for admission), ACT COMPASS.

Costs (2005–06) *Tuition:* state resident $3104 full-time, $97 per credit hour part-time; nonresident $4560 full-time, $143 per credit hour part-time. *Required fees:* $384 full-time, $13 per credit hour part-time. *Room and board:* $3700.

Financial Aid Of all full-time matriculated undergraduates who enrolled in 2004, 84 Federal Work-Study jobs (averaging $1075). 42 state and other part-time jobs (averaging $1080).

Applying *Options:* common application, electronic application, early admission. *Required:* high school transcript.

Director of Admissions Ms. Lisa Carstens, Admissions Coordinator, Southwestern Community College, 1501 West Townline Street, Creston, IA 50801. *Phone:* 641-782-7081. *Toll-free phone:* 800-247-4023. *E-mail:* carstens@swcc.cc.ia.us.

VATTEROTT COLLEGE

Des Moines, Iowa **www.vatterott-college.edu/**

- **Proprietary** primarily 2-year
- **Urban** 25-acre campus
- **Coed**

Undergraduates 6% African American, 3% Asian American or Pacific Islander, 3% Hispanic American.

Faculty *Total:* 14, 57% full-time. *Student/faculty ratio:* 15:1.

Majors CAD/CADD drafting/design technology; computer technology/computer systems technology; dental assisting; medical/clinical assistant; medical office management.

Academics *Calendar:* ten week periods. *Degrees:* certificates, diplomas, associate, and bachelor's.

Applying *Required:* high school transcript, interview.

Freshmen Application Contact Mr. Henry Franken, Co-Director, Vatterott College, 6100 Thornton Avenue, Suite 290, Des Moines, IA 50321. *Phone:* 515-309-9000. *Toll-free phone:* 800-353-7264. *Fax:* 515-309-0366.

WESTERN IOWA TECH COMMUNITY COLLEGE

Sioux City, Iowa **www.witcc.edu/**

- **State-supported** 2-year, founded 1966, part of Iowa Department of Education Division of Community Colleges
- **Urban** 143-acre campus
- **Endowment** $337,763
- **Coed,** 5,334 undergraduate students, 39% full-time, 56% women, 44% men

Undergraduates 2,086 full-time, 3,248 part-time. 10% are from out of state, 2% African American, 2% Asian American or Pacific Islander, 6% Hispanic American, 2% Native American, 0.1% international, 7% transferred in, 2% live on campus.

Freshmen *Admission:* 581 applied, 581 admitted, 431 enrolled. *Average high school GPA:* 2.63. *Test scores:* ACT scores over 18: 55%; ACT scores over 24: 8%.

Faculty *Total:* 306, 29% full-time, 4% with terminal degrees. *Student/faculty ratio:* 20:1.

Majors Agricultural/farm supplies retailing and wholesaling; architectural engineering technology; autobody/collision and repair technology; automobile/automotive mechanics technology; biomedical technology; business administration and management; child care and support services management; clinical/medical laboratory technology; computer programming (specific applications); computer typography and composition equipment operation; criminal justice/law enforcement administration; diesel mechanics technology; electrical, electronic and communications engineering technology; emergency medical technology (EMT paramedic); executive assistant/executive secretary; heating, air conditioning, ventilation and refrigeration maintenance technology; legal administrative assistant/secretary; liberal arts and sciences/liberal studies; machine tool technology; medical administrative assistant and medical secretary; nursing assistant/aide and patient care assistant; nursing (registered nurse training); occupational therapist assistant; physical therapist assistant; tool and die technology; turf and turfgrass management.

Academics *Calendar:* semesters. *Degree:* certificates, diplomas, and associate. *Special study options:* academic remediation for entering students, accelerated degree program, adult/continuing education programs, distance learning, double majors, English as a second language, honors programs, independent study, internships, part-time degree program, services for LD students, summer session for credit.

Library Western Iowa Tech Community College Library Services with 25,696 titles, 1,886 serial subscriptions, 3,456 audiovisual materials, an OPAC.

Computers on Campus 640 computers available on campus for general student use. A campuswide network can be accessed from student residence rooms and from off campus. Internet access, at least one staffed computer lab available.

Student Life *Activities and Organizations:* Student Senate. *Campus security:* 24-hour emergency response devices and patrols. *Student services:* health clinic, personal/psychological counseling.

Athletics *Intramural sports:* basketball M/W, bowling M/W, football M/W, golf M/W, skiing (downhill) M/W, softball W, volleyball M/W, weight lifting M/W.

Costs (2005–06) *Tuition:* state resident $93 per credit hour part-time; nonresident $133 per credit hour part-time. *Required fees:* $15 per credit hour part-time. *Payment plan:* installment.

Applying *Options:* early admission, deferred entrance. *Application fee:* $20. *Required:* high school transcript. *Application deadline:* rolling (freshmen), rolling (transfers). *Notification:* continuous (freshmen).
Freshmen Application Contact Western Iowa Tech Community College, 4647 Stone Avenue, Sioux City, IA 51102-5199. *Phone:* 712-274-6403. *Toll-free phone:* 800-352-4649 Ext. 6403. *Fax:* 712-274-6441.

KANSAS

ALLEN COUNTY COMMUNITY COLLEGE
Iola, Kansas   **www.allencc.net/**

- **State and locally supported** 2-year, founded 1923, part of Kansas State Board of Regents
- **Small-town** 88-acre campus
- **Endowment** $2.7 million
- **Coed,** 2,256 undergraduate students, 37% full-time, 63% women, 37% men

Undergraduates 824 full-time, 1,432 part-time. Students come from 17 states and territories, 16 other countries, 4% are from out of state, 4% African American, 0.6% Asian American or Pacific Islander, 3% Hispanic American, 1% Native American, 1% international, 76% transferred in, 10% live on campus. *Retention:* 56% of 2003 full-time freshmen returned.
Freshmen *Admission:* 893 applied, 893 admitted, 628 enrolled. *Average high school GPA:* 2.97. *Test scores:* ACT scores over 18: 64%; ACT scores over 24: 14%; ACT scores over 30: 2%.
Faculty *Total:* 32, 91% with terminal degrees. *Student/faculty ratio:* 17:1.
Majors Accounting; administrative assistant and secretarial science; agricultural production; architecture; art; athletic training; banking and financial support services; biology/biological sciences; business administration and management; business/commerce; business teacher education; chemistry; child development; computer science; computer systems networking and telecommunications; criminal justice/law enforcement administration; data processing and data processing technology; drafting and design technology; dramatic/theater arts; economics; electrical, electronic and communications engineering technology; electrical, electronics and communications engineering; elementary education; emergency medical technology (EMT paramedic); engineering; engineering technology; English composition; equestrian studies; family and consumer sciences/human sciences; farm and ranch management; forestry; funeral service and mortuary science; general studies; geography; health aide; health and physical education; history; home health aide/home attendant; hospital and health care facilities administration; humanities; industrial arts; industrial technology; information science/studies; journalism; language interpretation and translation; library science; mathematics; music; nuclear/nuclear power technology; nursing assistant/aide and patient care assistant; parks, recreation and leisure facilities management; philosophy; physical therapy; physics; political science and government; postal management; pre-dentistry studies; pre-law studies; pre-medical studies; pre-pharmacy studies; pre-veterinary studies; psychology; religious studies; secondary education; social work; sociology; speech and rhetoric; technology/industrial arts teacher education; wood science and wood products/pulp and paper technology.
Academics *Calendar:* semesters. *Degree:* certificates and associate. *Special study options:* academic remediation for entering students, adult/continuing education programs, cooperative education, part-time degree program, services for LD students, student-designed majors, summer session for credit.
Library Learning Resource Center with 49,416 titles, 159 serial subscriptions, an OPAC.
Computers on Campus 65 computers available on campus for general student use. A campuswide network can be accessed. Internet access, at least one staffed computer lab available.
Student Life *Housing:* on-campus residence required through sophomore year. *Options:* coed. Campus housing is university owned. *Activities and Organizations:* drama/theater group, student-run newspaper, choral group, intramurals, Student Senate, Biology Club, student newspaper, Phi Theta Kappa. *Campus security:* controlled dormitory access. *Student services:* personal/psychological counseling.
Athletics Member NJCAA. *Intercollegiate sports:* baseball M(s), basketball M(s)/W(s), cross-country running M(s)/W(s), golf M(s), soccer M(s)/W(s), softball W(s), track and field M(s)/W(s), volleyball W(s). *Intramural sports:*

basketball M/W, football M/W, soccer M/W, softball M/W, table tennis M/W, tennis M/W, volleyball M/W.
Costs (2006–07) *Tuition:* area resident $1184 full-time, $37 per hour part-time; state resident $1280 full-time, $40 per hour part-time; nonresident $1280 full-time, $40 per hour part-time. *Required fees:* $512 full-time, $16 per hour part-time. *Room and board:* $3600; room only: $2600.
Financial Aid Of all full-time matriculated undergraduates who enrolled in 2004, 25 Federal Work-Study jobs (averaging $1650). 80 state and other part-time jobs (averaging $1650).
Applying *Options:* common application, early admission, deferred entrance. *Required:* high school transcript. *Application deadlines:* 8/24 (freshmen), 8/24 (transfers). *Notification:* continuous (freshmen).
Freshmen Application Contact Mr. Randall Weber, Director of Admissions, Allen County Community College, 1801 North Cottonwood, Iola, KS 66749. *Phone:* 620-365-5116 Ext. 267. *Fax:* 620-365-7406.

BARTON COUNTY COMMUNITY COLLEGE
Great Bend, Kansas   **www.bartonccc.edu/**

- **State and locally supported** 2-year, founded 1969, part of Kansas Board of Regents
- **Rural** 140-acre campus
- **Endowment** $4.3 million
- **Coed,** 3,821 undergraduate students, 25% full-time, 52% women, 48% men

Undergraduates 943 full-time, 2,878 part-time. Students come from 40 states and territories, 15 other countries, 17% are from out of state, 13% African American, 2% Asian American or Pacific Islander, 6% Hispanic American, 1% Native American, 2% international, 3% transferred in, 4% live on campus. *Retention:* 65% of 2003 full-time freshmen returned.
Freshmen *Admission:* 1,487 enrolled. *Test scores:* SAT verbal scores over 500: 25%; SAT math scores over 500: 25%; ACT scores over 18: 67%; ACT scores over 24: 16%; ACT scores over 30: 1%.
Faculty *Total:* 180, 40% full-time, 4% with terminal degrees. *Student/faculty ratio:* 18:1.
Majors Accounting; administrative assistant and secretarial science; agricultural business and management; agriculture; anthropology; architecture; art; athletic training; automobile/automotive mechanics technology; banking and financial support services; biology/biological sciences; business administration and management; business computer programming; chemistry; child care and support services management; chiropractic assistant; clinical/medical laboratory technology; communication/speech communication and rhetoric; computer/information technology services administration related; computer science; computer systems networking and telecommunications; criminal justice/police science; crop production; cytotechnology; dance; dental hygiene; dietitian assistant; dramatic/theater arts; early childhood education; economics; elementary education; emergency medical technology (EMT paramedic); engineering technology; English; fire science; forestry; funeral service and mortuary science; general studies; geology/earth science; graphic design; hazardous materials management and waste technology; health information/medical records administration; history; home health aide; human resources management and services related; information science/studies; journalism; kinesiology and exercise science; liberal arts and sciences/liberal studies; livestock management; marketing/marketing management; mathematics; medical administrative assistant and medical secretary; medical/clinical assistant; military studies; modern languages; music; nursing (registered nurse training); occupational therapy; optometric technician; pharmacy; philosophy; physical education teaching and coaching; physical sciences; physical therapist assistant; physical therapy; physician assistant; physics; political science and government; pre-dentistry studies; pre-engineering; pre-law studies; pre-medical studies; pre-veterinary studies; psychology; public administration; radiologic technology/science; religious studies; respiratory care therapy; secondary education; social work; sociology; sport and fitness administration/management; wildlife and wildlands science and management.
Academics *Calendar:* semesters. *Degree:* certificates and associate. *Special study options:* academic remediation for entering students, accelerated degree program, adult/continuing education programs, advanced placement credit, cooperative education, distance learning, English as a second language, external degree program, honors programs, independent study, internships, part-time degree program, services for LD students, student-designed majors, summer session for credit.
Library Barton County Community College Library with 26,322 titles, 179 serial subscriptions, 1,529 audiovisual materials, an OPAC, a Web page.
Computers on Campus 350 computers available on campus for general student use. A campuswide network can be accessed from student residence rooms and from off campus. Internet access, online (class) registration, at least one staffed computer lab available.
Student Life *Housing:* on-campus residence required for freshman year. *Options:* coed, disabled students. Campus housing is university owned. Fresh-

Barton County Community College (continued)

man campus housing is guaranteed. *Activities and Organizations:* drama/theater group, student-run newspaper, choral group, Danceline, Business Professionals, Psychology Club, Agriculture Club, Cougarettes. *Campus security:* 24-hour emergency response devices and patrols. *Student services:* health clinic, personal/ psychological counseling.

Athletics Member NJCAA. *Intercollegiate sports:* baseball M(s), basketball M(s)/W(s), cheerleading M(s)/W, cross-country running M(s)/W(s), golf M(s), soccer M(s)/W(s), softball W(s), tennis M(s)/W(s), track and field M(s)/W(s), volleyball W(s). *Intramural sports:* basketball M/W, bowling M/W, football M/W, golf M/W, swimming and diving M/W, table tennis M/W, tennis M/W, track and field M/W, volleyball M/W.

Costs (2006–07) *Tuition:* state resident $1568 full-time, $49 per credit hour part-time; nonresident $2176 full-time, $68 per credit hour part-time. *Required fees:* $576 full-time, $18 per credit hour part-time. *Room and board:* $3854.

Financial Aid Of all full-time matriculated undergraduates who enrolled in 2004, 102 Federal Work-Study jobs (averaging $2400).

Applying *Options:* common application, electronic application, early admission. *Recommended:* high school transcript. *Application deadline:* rolling (freshmen), rolling (transfers).

Freshmen Application Contact Mr. Todd Moore, Director of Admissions and Marketing, Barton County Community College, 245 Northeast 30th Road, Great Bend, KS 67530. *Phone:* 620-792-9241. *Toll-free phone:* 800-722-6842. *Fax:* 620-786-1160. *E-mail:* admissions@bartonccc.edu.

BROWN MACKIE COLLEGE–KANSAS CITY

Lenexa, Kansas   www.bmcaec.com/

- **Proprietary** 2-year, founded 1892, part of The Brown Mackie College
- **Suburban** 3-acre campus with easy access to Kansas City
- **Coed,** 370 undergraduate students, 100% full-time, 77% women, 23% men

Undergraduates 370 full-time. Students come from 2 states and territories, 35% are from out of state, 26% African American, 1% Asian American or Pacific Islander, 8% Hispanic American, 2% Native American.
Freshmen *Admission:* 111 enrolled.

Faculty *Total:* 21, 38% full-time, 33% with terminal degrees.

Majors Accounting; business administration and management; computer programming related; computer/technical support; computer typography and composition equipment operation; data entry/microcomputer applications; data entry/ microcomputer applications related; dental hygiene; health information/medical records administration; health unit coordinator/ward clerk; health unit management/ ward supervision; information technology; legal assistant/paralegal; medical administrative assistant and medical secretary; medical/clinical assistant; system administration.

Academics *Calendar:* quarters. *Degree:* certificates, diplomas, and associate. *Special study options:* academic remediation for entering students, adult/ continuing education programs, summer session for credit.

Library The Brown Mackie College Library plus 1 other with 48 serial subscriptions, an OPAC, a Web page.

Computers on Campus 185 computers available on campus for general student use. A campuswide network can be accessed from off campus. Internet access, at least one staffed computer lab available.

Student Life *Housing:* college housing not available. *Activities and Organizations:* Coffee Club (service and social organization). *Campus security:* 24-hour emergency response devices. *Student services:* personal/psychological counseling.

Costs (2006–07) *Tuition:* $7164 full-time. *Required fees:* $432 full-time.

Applying *Options:* deferred entrance. *Required:* high school transcript, interview. *Required for some:* essay or personal statement. *Recommended:* essay or personal statement, minimum 2.0 GPA. *Application deadline:* rolling (freshmen), rolling (transfers). *Notification:* continuous (freshmen).

Freshmen Application Contact Ms. Dorie E. White, Brown Mackie College–Kansas City, 9705 Lenexa Drive, Lenexa, KS 66215. *Phone:* 913-768-1900. *Toll-free phone:* 800-635-9101. *Fax:* 913-495-9555.

▶ See page 508 for the College Close-Up.

BROWN MACKIE COLLEGE–SALINA

Salina, Kansas www.brownmackie.edu/locations.asp?locid=13

- **Proprietary** 2-year, founded 1892
- **Small-town** 10-acre campus with easy access to Wichita
- **Coed,** 367 undergraduate students, 100% full-time, 68% women, 32% men

Undergraduates 367 full-time. Students come from 10 states and territories, 2 other countries, 26% are from out of state, 12% African American, 1% Asian American or Pacific Islander, 8% Hispanic American, 3% transferred in. Freshmen *Admission:* 136 applied, 130 admitted, 113 enrolled.

Faculty *Total:* 16, 38% full-time, 13% with terminal degrees. *Student/faculty ratio:* 15:1.

Majors Accounting; business administration and management; computer and information sciences; criminal justice/law enforcement administration; legal assistant/paralegal; medical office management; medical transcription.

Academics *Calendar:* modular. *Degree:* certificates, diplomas, and associate. *Special study options:* academic remediation for entering students, adult/ continuing education programs, advanced placement credit, cooperative education, independent study, services for LD students, summer session for credit.

Library Brown Mackie College Library plus 1 other with 14,788 titles, 45 serial subscriptions, 195 audiovisual materials, an OPAC, a Web page.

Computers on Campus 162 computers available on campus for general student use. Internet access, at least one staffed computer lab available.

Student Life *Housing:* college housing not available. *Activities and Organizations:* student-run newspaper, Student Senate, Athletic Booster Club.

Athletics Member NJCAA. *Intercollegiate sports:* baseball M(s), basketball M(s)/W(s), softball W(s).

Costs (2006–07) *Tuition:* $9072 full-time. *Required fees:* $576 full-time.

Financial Aid Of all full-time matriculated undergraduates who enrolled in 2004, 10 Federal Work-Study jobs (averaging $1500).

Applying *Options:* common application, deferred entrance. *Required:* high school transcript, interview. *Application deadline:* rolling (freshmen), rolling (transfers). *Notification:* continuous (freshmen).

Freshmen Application Contact Brown Mackie College–Salina, 2106 South 9th Street, Salina, KS 67401. *Phone:* 785-825-5422. *Toll-free phone:* 800-365-0433. *Fax:* 785-827-7623.

▶ See page 524 for the College Close-Up.

BUTLER COMMUNITY COLLEGE

El Dorado, Kansas   www.butlercc.edu/

- **State and locally supported** 2-year, founded 1927, part of Kansas Board of Regents
- **Small-town** 80-acre campus
- **Coed,** 8,863 undergraduate students, 41% full-time, 60% women, 40% men

Undergraduates 3,658 full-time, 5,205 part-time. Students come from 28 states and territories, 21 other countries, 5% are from out of state, 12% African American, 2% Asian American or Pacific Islander, 6% Hispanic American, 2% Native American, 3% international, 5% transferred in, 4% live on campus. *Retention:* 57% of 2003 full-time freshmen returned.
Freshmen *Admission:* 1,445 enrolled. *Test scores:* ACT scores over 18: 75%; ACT scores over 24: 23%; ACT scores over 30: 1%.

Faculty *Total:* 613, 23% full-time, 2% with terminal degrees. *Student/faculty ratio:* 18:1.

Majors Accounting; administrative assistant and secretarial science; agricultural business and management; art; automobile/automotive mechanics technology; biology/biological sciences; business administration and management; chemistry; child development; computer and information sciences; computer science; criminal justice/police science; data processing and data processing technology; drafting and design technology; dramatic/theater arts; electrical, electronic and communications engineering technology; English; farm and ranch management; fire science; health information/medical records administration; history; hotel/motel administration; journalism; kindergarten/preschool education; liberal arts and sciences/liberal studies; marketing/marketing management; mass communication/media; mathematics; medical administrative assistant and medical secretary; music; music performance; nursing (registered nurse training); physical education teaching and coaching; physical therapy; physics; political science and government; pre-engineering; psychology; sociology; substance abuse/addiction counseling; welding technology.

Academics *Calendar:* semesters. *Degree:* certificates and associate. *Special study options:* academic remediation for entering students, accelerated degree program, adult/continuing education programs, advanced placement credit, cooperative education, distance learning, double majors, English as a second language, honors programs, independent study, part-time degree program, services for LD students, student-designed majors, summer session for credit.

Library L.W. Nixon Library with 38,000 titles, 220 serial subscriptions, 914 audiovisual materials, an OPAC, a Web page.

Computers on Campus 90 computers available on campus for general student use. Internet access, at least one staffed computer lab available.

Student Life *Housing Options:* coed, men-only, women-only. Campus housing is university owned. *Activities and Organizations:* drama/theater group, student-run newspaper, radio and television station, choral group, Agriculture Club, Art Club, Campus Crusade for Christ, Grizzly Ambassadors, intramurals. *Campus security:* 24-hour emergency response devices and patrols, controlled dormitory access, video cameras at dormitory entrances and parking lot. *Student services:* personal/psychological counseling.

Athletics Member NJCAA. *Intercollegiate sports:* baseball M(s), basketball M(s)/W(s), cross-country running M(s)/W(s), football M(s), soccer W(s), softball W(s), tennis M(s)/W(s), track and field M(s)/W(s), volleyball W(s). *Intramural sports:* basketball M/W, bowling M/W, cheerleading M/W, football M, soccer W, softball W, table tennis M/W, tennis M/W, track and field M/W, volleyball W.

Costs (2005–06) *Tuition:* state resident $1756 full-time, $55 per credit hour part-time; nonresident $3164 full-time, $99 per credit hour part-time. *Required fees:* $448 full-time, $14 per credit hour part-time. *Room and board:* $4335. Room and board charges vary according to housing facility. *Payment plan:* installment. *Waivers:* employees or children of employees.

Financial Aid Of all full-time matriculated undergraduates who enrolled in 2004, 210 Federal Work-Study jobs (averaging $1800).

Applying *Options:* early admission, deferred entrance. *Required:* high school transcript. *Application deadlines:* 8/19 (freshmen), 8/20 (transfers). *Notification:* continuous (freshmen).

Freshmen Application Contact Mr. Paul Kyle, Director of Enrollment Management, Butler Community College, 901 South Haverhill Road, El Dorado, KS 67042. *Phone:* 316-321-2222 Ext. 3255. *Fax:* 316-322-3109. *E-mail:* admissions@butlercc.edu.

CLOUD COUNTY COMMUNITY COLLEGE
Concordia, Kansas www.cloud.edu/

- **State and locally supported** 2-year, founded 1965, part of Kansas Community College System
- **Rural** 35-acre campus
- **Coed**

Undergraduates Students come from 12 states and territories, 5 other countries, 6% African American, 0.9% Asian American or Pacific Islander, 2% Hispanic American, 0.9% Native American, 0.4% international.

Academics *Calendar:* semesters. *Degree:* certificates, diplomas, and associate. *Special study options:* academic remediation for entering students, adult/continuing education programs, advanced placement credit, cooperative education, internships, part-time degree program, services for LD students, summer session for credit.

Student Life *Campus security:* 24-hour emergency response devices.

Athletics Member NJCAA.

Standardized Tests *Required:* ACT ASSET (for placement). *Recommended:* ACT (for placement).

Costs (2005–06) *Tuition:* state resident $1560 full-time, $52 per credit hour part-time; nonresident $2220 full-time, $74 per credit hour part-time. *Required fees:* $540 full-time, $18 per credit hour part-time. *Room and board:* $3780.

Financial Aid Of all full-time matriculated undergraduates who enrolled in 2004, 122 Federal Work-Study jobs (averaging $800).

Applying *Options:* common application, early admission, deferred entrance. *Required:* high school transcript.

Director of Admissions Chris Burlew, Director of Admissions, Cloud County Community College, 2221 Campus Drive, PO Box 1002, Concordia, KS 66901-1002. *Phone:* 785-243-1435 Ext. 214. *Toll-free phone:* 800-729-5101.

COFFEYVILLE COMMUNITY COLLEGE
Coffeyville, Kansas www.coffeyville.edu/

- **State and locally supported** 2-year, founded 1923, part of Kansas Board of Regents
- **Small-town** 39-acre campus with easy access to Tulsa
- **Endowment** $2.8 million
- **Coed**

Undergraduates 665 full-time, 1,101 part-time. Students come from 19 states and territories, 4 other countries, 8% are from out of state, 12% African American, 0.3% Asian American or Pacific Islander, 2% Hispanic American, 2% Native American, 1% international, 38% transferred in, 27% live on campus.

Faculty *Student/faculty ratio:* 20:1.

Academics *Calendar:* semesters. *Degree:* certificates and associate. *Special study options:* academic remediation for entering students, adult/continuing education programs, advanced placement credit, cooperative education, distance learning, double majors, English as a second language, honors programs, internships, part-time degree program, services for LD students, student-designed majors, summer session for credit.

Student Life *Campus security:* 24-hour patrols, late-night transport/escort service.

Athletics Member NJCAA.

Standardized Tests *Required:* ACT (for placement), ACT COMPASS (for placement).

Costs (2005–06) *Tuition:* state resident $896 full-time, $28 per credit hour part-time; nonresident $2176 full-time, $68 per credit hour part-time. *Required fees:* $704 full-time, $22 per credit hour part-time. *Room and board:* $3380.

Financial Aid Of all full-time matriculated undergraduates who enrolled in 2004, 120 Federal Work-Study jobs (averaging $1000).

Applying *Options:* common application, early admission, deferred entrance. *Required:* high school transcript.

Freshmen Application Contact Ms. Kim Lay, Coordinator/Advisor of Enrollment Services, Coffeyville Community College, 400 West 11th, Coffeyville, KS 67337. *Phone:* 620-252-7155.

COLBY COMMUNITY COLLEGE
Colby, Kansas www.colbycc.edu/

- **State and locally supported** 2-year, founded 1964, part of Kansas Board of Regents
- **Small-town** 80-acre campus
- **Endowment** $3.2 million
- **Coed**, 1,784 undergraduate students

Colby Community College offers 2-year career programs in veterinary technology, beef and equine production, criminal justice, physical therapist assistant studies, nursing, office technology, mid-management, dental hygiene, computer science, information systems, radio broadcasting, and television production; transfer curricula in health, education, arts and letters, behavioral science, business, graphic arts, and math/science; and preprofessional options in law, engineering, and medicine. A College-owned farm is operated by agriculture students.

Undergraduates Students come from 14 states and territories, 5 other countries, 13% are from out of state, 1% African American, 0.6% Asian American or Pacific Islander, 2% Hispanic American, 0.2% Native American, 2% international, 30% live on campus.

Freshmen *Admission:* 647 applied, 647 admitted. *Average high school GPA:* 3.28.

Faculty *Total:* 60, 100% full-time. *Student/faculty ratio:* 19:1.

Majors Accounting; agricultural business and management; agricultural economics; agricultural teacher education; agriculture; agronomy and crop science; animal sciences; behavioral sciences; biological and physical sciences; biology/biological sciences; broadcast journalism; business administration and management; business/managerial economics; business teacher education; chemistry; child development; commercial and advertising art; computer and information sciences related; computer science; criminal justice/law enforcement administration; dental hygiene; dramatic/theater arts; education; English; family and consumer sciences/human sciences; farm and ranch management; foods, nutrition, and wellness; forestry; geology/earth science; history; humanities; journalism; kindergarten/preschool education; liberal arts and sciences/liberal studies; library science; marketing/marketing management; mass communication/media; mathematics; music; music teacher education; nursing (licensed practical/vocational nurse training); nursing (registered nurse training); pharmacy; physical education teaching and coaching; physical therapist assistant; physical

Colby Community College (continued)

therapy; political science and government; pre-engineering; psychology; radio and television; range science and management; science teacher education; social work; sociology; veterinary sciences; veterinary technology; wildlife biology; zoology/animal biology.

Academics *Calendar:* semesters. *Degree:* certificates, diplomas, and associate. *Special study options:* academic remediation for entering students, adult/continuing education programs, advanced placement credit, cooperative education, distance learning, double majors, honors programs, internships, part-time degree program, services for LD students, student-designed majors, summer session for credit.

Library Davis Library with 32,000 titles, 350 serial subscriptions, an OPAC.

Computers on Campus 178 computers available on campus for general student use. A campuswide network can be accessed from student residence rooms and from off campus. Internet access, at least one staffed computer lab available.

Student Life *Housing:* on-campus residence required for freshman year. *Options:* men-only, women-only. Campus housing is university owned. *Activities and Organizations:* drama/theater group, student-run newspaper, radio and television station, choral group, marching band, KSNEA, Physical Therapist Assistants Club, Block and Bridle, SVTA, COPNS. *Campus security:* 24-hour emergency response devices and patrols. *Student services:* health clinic, personal/psychological counseling.

Athletics Member NJCAA. *Intercollegiate sports:* baseball M(s), basketball M(s)/W(s), cheerleading W, cross-country running M(s)/W(s), equestrian sports M/W, golf M(s)/W(s), softball W(s), track and field M(s)/W(s), volleyball W(s), wrestling M(s). *Intramural sports:* basketball M/W, softball M/W, volleyball M/W.

Costs (2006–07) *Tuition:* state resident $1536 full-time, $48 per credit hour part-time; nonresident $2784 full-time, $87 per credit hour part-time. *Required fees:* $768 full-time, $24 per credit hour part-time. *Room and board:* $3632.

Financial Aid Of all full-time matriculated undergraduates who enrolled in 2004, 95 Federal Work-Study jobs (averaging $1500). 30 state and other part-time jobs (averaging $2000).

Applying *Options:* early admission, deferred entrance. *Required:* high school transcript. *Application deadline:* rolling (freshmen), rolling (transfers). *Notification:* continuous (freshmen).

Freshmen Application Contact Ms. Nikol Nolan, Admissions Director, Colby Community College, 1255 South Range, Colby, KS 67701-4099. *Phone:* 785-462-3984 Ext. 246. *Toll-free phone:* 888-634-9350 Ext. 690. *Fax:* 785-460-4691. *E-mail:* leasa@colbycc.edu.

COWLEY COUNTY COMMUNITY COLLEGE AND AREA VOCATIONAL–TECHNICAL SCHOOL

Arkansas City, Kansas　　　　　**www.cowley.cc.ks.us/**

- **State and locally supported** 2-year, founded 1922, part of Kansas State Board of Education
- **Small-town** 19-acre campus
- **Endowment** $3.0 million
- **Coed,** 4,679 undergraduate students, 51% full-time, 59% women, 41% men

Undergraduates 2,386 full-time, 2,293 part-time. Students come from 16 states and territories, 12 other countries, 6% are from out of state, 8% African American, 5% Asian American or Pacific Islander, 4% Hispanic American, 0.9% Native American, 0.9% international, 7% live on campus.

Freshmen *Admission:* 1,185 applied, 1,185 admitted, 1,185 enrolled. *Average high school GPA:* 2.89. *Test scores:* ACT scores over 18: 71%; ACT scores over 24: 12%; ACT scores over 30: 1%.

Faculty *Total:* 216, 21% full-time. *Student/faculty ratio:* 31:1.

Majors Accounting; administrative assistant and secretarial science; agricultural mechanization; agriculture; agronomy and crop science; airframe mechanics and aircraft maintenance technology; art; automobile/automotive mechanics technology; business administration and management; chemistry; child development; computer graphics; consumer merchandising/retailing management; corrections; cosmetology; criminal justice/law enforcement administration; criminal justice/police science; drafting and design technology; dramatic/theater arts; education; elementary education; emergency medical technology (EMT paramedic); engineering technology; family and consumer economics related; farm and ranch management; hotel/motel administration; industrial arts; industrial radiologic technology; journalism; liberal arts and sciences/liberal studies; machine tool technology; marketing/marketing management; music; parks, recreation and leisure; physical education teaching and coaching; physical therapy; pre-engineering; religious studies; sign language interpretation and translation; social work; technology/industrial arts teacher education; welding technology.

Academics *Calendar:* semesters. *Degree:* certificates, diplomas, and associate. *Special study options:* academic remediation for entering students, accelerated degree program, adult/continuing education programs, advanced placement credit, cooperative education, distance learning, external degree program, independent study, part-time degree program, student-designed majors, summer session for credit.

Library Renn Memorial Library with 26,000 titles, 100 serial subscriptions.

Computers on Campus 53 computers available on campus for general student use. A campuswide network can be accessed. Internet access, at least one staffed computer lab available.

Student Life *Housing Options:* coed, men-only, women-only. *Activities and Organizations:* drama/theater group, student-run newspaper, choral group, Volunteer Club, Peers Advocating for Wellness, Phi Theta Kappa, Student Government Association, Phi Beta Lambda. *Campus security:* student patrols, late-night transport/escort service, residence hall entrances are locked at night. *Student services:* health clinic, personal/psychological counseling.

Athletics Member NJCAA. *Intercollegiate sports:* baseball M(s), basketball M(s)/W(s), golf M(s), softball W(s), tennis M(s)/W(s), volleyball W(s). *Intramural sports:* basketball M/W, bowling M/W, softball M/W, table tennis M/W, tennis M/W, volleyball M/W.

Standardized Tests *Recommended:* ACT (for admission).

Costs (2006–07) *Tuition:* area resident $1290 full-time, $43 per credit hour part-time; state resident $1440 full-time, $48 per credit hour part-time; nonresident $3000 full-time, $100 per credit hour part-time. *Required fees:* $570 full-time, $19 per credit hour part-time. *Room and board:* $3530.

Financial Aid Of all full-time matriculated undergraduates who enrolled in 2004, 50 Federal Work-Study jobs (averaging $1500). 75 state and other part-time jobs (averaging $2000).

Applying *Options:* early admission, deferred entrance. *Required:* high school transcript. *Application deadline:* rolling (freshmen), rolling (transfers).

Freshmen Application Contact Ms. Sue Saia, Associate Dean of Admissions, Cowley County Community College and Area Vocational–Technical School, 125 South Second, PO Box 1147, Arkansas City, KS 67005-1147. *Phone:* 620-441-5245. *Toll-free phone:* 800-593-CCCC. *Fax:* 620-441-5264. *E-mail:* admissions@cowley.cc.ks.us.

DODGE CITY COMMUNITY COLLEGE

Dodge City, Kansas　　　　　**www.dccc.cc.ks.us/**

- **State and locally supported** 2-year, founded 1935, part of Kansas State Board of Education
- **Small-town** 143-acre campus
- **Coed**

Undergraduates Students come from 20 states and territories, 5 other countries, 20% live on campus.

Academics *Calendar:* semesters. *Degree:* certificates and associate. *Special study options:* academic remediation for entering students, adult/continuing education programs, advanced placement credit, cooperative education, English as a second language, external degree program, internships, part-time degree program, student-designed majors, summer session for credit.

Athletics Member NJCAA.

Standardized Tests *Required:* ACT ASSET (for placement).

Costs (2005–06) *Tuition:* state resident $1120 full-time, $35 per credit hour part-time; nonresident $1344 full-time, $42 per credit hour part-time. Full-time tuition and fees vary according to course load. Part-time tuition and fees vary according to course load. *Required fees:* $806 full-time, $23 per credit hour part-time, $35 per term part-time. *Room and board:* $4060.

Applying *Options:* common application, early admission, deferred entrance. *Required:* high school transcript.

Director of Admissions Mr. Corbin Strobel, Director of Admissions, Placement, Testing and Student Services Marketing, Dodge City Community College, 2501 North 14th Avenue, Dodge City, KS 67801-2399. *Phone:* 316-225-1321. *Toll-free phone:* 800-742-9519. *E-mail:* admin@dccc.dodge-city.cc.ks.us.

DONNELLY COLLEGE

Kansas City, Kansas　　　　　**www.donnelly.edu/**

Director of Admissions Mr. Kevin Kelley, Vice President of Enrollment Management, Donnelly College, 608 North 18th Street, Kansas City, KS 66102. *Phone:* 913-621-8769.

FLINT HILLS TECHNICAL COLLEGE
Emporia, Kansas

FORT SCOTT COMMUNITY COLLEGE
Fort Scott, Kansas · www.fortscott.edu/

- **State and locally supported** 2-year, founded 1919
- **Small-town** 147-acre campus
- **Coed**

Undergraduates Students come from 24 states and territories, 6% African American, 0.5% Asian American or Pacific Islander, 1% Hispanic American, 1% Native American, 0.3% international, 9% live on campus.
Faculty *Student/faculty ratio:* 26:1.
Academics *Calendar:* semesters. *Degree:* certificates and associate. *Special study options:* academic remediation for entering students, adult/continuing education programs, advanced placement credit, cooperative education, distance learning, English as a second language, external degree program, independent study, internships, part-time degree program, services for LD students, student-designed majors, study abroad, summer session for credit. *ROTC:* Army (c).
Student Life *Campus security:* controlled dormitory access, evening security from 9 pm to 6am.
Athletics Member NJCAA.
Standardized Tests *Required:* ACT ASSET (for placement). *Required for some:* ACT (for placement).
Applying *Options:* early admission, deferred entrance.
Director of Admissions Mrs. Mert Barrows, Director of Admissions, Fort Scott Community College, 2108 South Horton, Fort Scott, KS 66701. *Phone:* 316-223-2700 Ext. 353. *Toll-free phone:* 800-874-3722.

GARDEN CITY COMMUNITY COLLEGE
Garden City, Kansas · www.gcccks.edu/

- **County-supported** 2-year, founded 1919, part of Kansas Board of Regents
- **Rural** 63-acre campus
- **Endowment** $4.9 million
- **Coed**

Undergraduates 925 full-time, 1,249 part-time. Students come from 31 states and territories, 7% are from out of state, 9% African American, 2% Asian American or Pacific Islander, 20% Hispanic American, 0.6% Native American, 0.6% international, 12% live on campus. *Retention:* 78% of 2003 full-time freshmen returned.
Faculty *Student/faculty ratio:* 17:1.
Academics *Calendar:* semesters. *Degree:* certificates and associate. *Special study options:* academic remediation for entering students, adult/continuing education programs, advanced placement credit, distance learning, English as a second language, external degree program, part-time degree program, services for LD students, student-designed majors, summer session for credit.
Student Life *Campus security:* 24-hour emergency response devices and patrols, student patrols, late-night transport/escort service, controlled dormitory access.
Athletics Member NJCAA.
Standardized Tests *Required:* ACT COMPASS (for placement).
Costs (2005–06) *Tuition:* state resident $1248 full-time, $39 per credit hour part-time; nonresident $2080 full-time, $65 per credit hour part-time. Full-time tuition and fees vary according to course load and location. Part-time tuition and fees vary according to course load and location. *Required fees:* $672 full-time, $21 per credit hour part-time. *Room and board:* $4500. Room and board charges vary according to housing facility.
Financial Aid Of all full-time matriculated undergraduates who enrolled in 2004, 90 Federal Work-Study jobs (averaging $1000). 100 state and other part-time jobs (averaging $900).
Applying *Required:* high school transcript.
Director of Admissions Ms. Nikki Geier, Director of Admissions, Garden City Community College, 801 Campus Drive, Garden City, KS 67846. *Phone:* 620-276-7611 Ext. 531.

HESSTON COLLEGE
Hesston, Kansas · www.hesston.edu/

- **Independent Mennonite** 2-year, founded 1909
- **Small-town** 50-acre campus with easy access to Wichita
- **Coed,** 477 undergraduate students, 87% full-time, 50% women, 50% men

Undergraduates 414 full-time, 63 part-time. Students come from 30 states and territories, 13 other countries, 50% are from out of state, 4% African American, 1% Asian American or Pacific Islander, 3% Hispanic American, 0.6% Native American, 9% international, 9% transferred in, 74% live on campus. *Retention:* 76% of 2003 full-time freshmen returned.
Freshmen *Admission:* 710 applied, 592 admitted, 195 enrolled. *Average high school GPA:* 3.35. *Test scores:* SAT verbal scores over 500: 58%; SAT math scores over 500: 52%; ACT scores over 18: 80%; SAT verbal scores over 600: 20%; SAT math scores over 600: 19%; ACT scores over 24: 34%; SAT verbal scores over 700: 1%; SAT math scores over 700: 1%; ACT scores over 30: 4%.
Faculty *Total:* 44, 43% full-time, 18% with terminal degrees.
Majors Aeronautics/aviation/aerospace science and technology; biblical studies; business administration and management; computer/information technology services administration related; kindergarten/preschool education; liberal arts and sciences/liberal studies; nursing (registered nurse training); pastoral studies/counseling.
Academics *Calendar:* semesters. *Degree:* associate. *Special study options:* academic remediation for entering students, advanced placement credit, cooperative education, double majors, English as a second language, independent study, internships, part-time degree program, services for LD students, summer session for credit.
Library Mary Miller Library with 35,000 titles, 234 serial subscriptions, 2,409 audiovisual materials, an OPAC, a Web page.
Computers on Campus 67 computers available on campus for general student use. A campuswide network can be accessed from student residence rooms and from off campus. Internet access, at least one staffed computer lab available.
Student Life *Housing:* on-campus residence required through sophomore year. *Options:* men-only, women-only. Campus housing is university owned. Freshman campus housing is guaranteed. *Activities and Organizations:* drama/theater group, student-run newspaper, choral group. *Campus security:* 24-hour emergency response devices. *Student services:* personal/psychological counseling.
Athletics Member NJCAA. *Intercollegiate sports:* baseball M(s), basketball M(s)/W(s), soccer M(s), softball W(s), tennis M(s)/W(s), volleyball W(s). *Intramural sports:* basketball M/W, golf M(c)/W(c), soccer M/W, softball W, tennis M/W, volleyball M/W.
Standardized Tests *Required:* SAT or ACT (for admission).
Costs (2006–07) *Comprehensive fee:* $22,354 includes full-time tuition ($16,246), mandatory fees ($250), and room and board ($5858). Part-time tuition: $676 per hour. *Required fees:* $60 per term part-time.
Financial Aid Of all full-time matriculated undergraduates who enrolled in 2004, 120 Federal Work-Study jobs (averaging $800).
Applying *Options:* electronic application, early admission, deferred entrance. *Application fee:* $15. *Required:* high school transcript, 2 letters of recommendation. *Required for some:* interview. *Application deadline:* rolling (freshmen), rolling (transfers).
Freshmen Application Contact Mr. Clark Roth, Vice President for Admissions, Hesston College, Box 3000, Hesston, KS 67062. *Phone:* 620-327-8222. *Toll-free phone:* 800-995-2757. *Fax:* 620-327-8300. *E-mail:* admissions@hesston.edu.

HIGHLAND COMMUNITY COLLEGE
Highland, Kansas · www.highlandcc.edu/

- **State and locally supported** 2-year, founded 1858, part of Kansas Community College System
- **Rural** 20-acre campus
- **Coed**

Undergraduates Students come from 9 states and territories.
Academics *Calendar:* semesters. *Degree:* certificates and associate. *Special study options:* academic remediation for entering students, adult/continuing education programs, advanced placement credit, cooperative education, internships, off-campus study, part-time degree program, services for LD students, student-designed majors, summer session for credit. *ROTC:* Army (c).
Athletics Member NJCAA.
Standardized Tests *Required:* ACT ASSET (for placement). *Recommended:* ACT (for placement).

Highland Community College (continued)

Costs (2005–06) *Tuition:* area resident $888 full-time, $37 per credit hour part-time; state resident $1080 full-time, $45 per credit hour part-time; nonresident $2280 full-time, $95 per credit hour part-time. *Required fees:* $1056 full-time, $44 per credit hour part-time. *Room and board:* $3872; room only: $2242.

Financial Aid Of all full-time matriculated undergraduates who enrolled in 2004, 75 Federal Work-Study jobs (averaging $1200). 25 state and other part-time jobs (averaging $1000).

Applying *Options:* early admission. *Required:* high school transcript.

Director of Admissions Ms. Cheryl Rasmussen, Vice President of Student Services, Highland Community College, 606 West Main Street, Highland, KS 66035-4165. *Phone:* 785-442-6020. *Fax:* 785-442-6106.

HUTCHINSON COMMUNITY COLLEGE AND AREA VOCATIONAL SCHOOL
Hutchinson, Kansas   www.hutchcc.edu/

- **State and locally supported** 2-year, founded 1928, part of Kansas Board of Regents
- **Small-town** 47-acre campus
- **Endowment** $3.6 million
- **Coed,** 4,869 undergraduate students, 40% full-time, 57% women, 43% men

Undergraduates 1,956 full-time, 2,913 part-time. Students come from 34 states and territories, 18 other countries, 7% are from out of state, 4% African American, 0.8% Asian American or Pacific Islander, 4% Hispanic American, 0.7% Native American, 0.4% international, 10% transferred in, 11% live on campus. *Retention:* 56% of 2003 full-time freshmen returned.
Freshmen *Admission:* 2,940 applied, 2,940 admitted, 1,059 enrolled. *Average high school GPA:* 2.84. *Test scores:* ACT scores over 18: 74%; ACT scores over 24: 18%.
Faculty *Total:* 333, 34% full-time, 5% with terminal degrees. *Student/faculty ratio:* 16:1.
Majors Administrative assistant and secretarial science; agricultural mechanization; agriculture; autobody/collision and repair technology; automobile/automotive mechanics technology; biology/biological sciences; business and personal/financial services marketing; business/commerce; carpentry; child care and support services management; communication/speech communication and rhetoric; communications technology; computer and information sciences; criminal justice/police science; drafting and design technology; education; educational/instructional media design; electrical/electronics equipment installation and repair; emergency medical technology (EMT paramedic); engineering; English; family and consumer sciences/human sciences; farm and ranch management; fire science; foreign languages and literatures; health information/medical records technology; legal assistant/paralegal; liberal arts and sciences/liberal studies; machine tool technology; management information systems; manufacturing technology; mathematics; medical radiologic technology; nursing (registered nurse training); physical sciences; psychology; retailing; social sciences; visual and performing arts; welding technology.
Academics *Calendar:* semesters. *Degree:* certificates and associate. *Special study options:* academic remediation for entering students, adult/continuing education programs, advanced placement credit, cooperative education, distance learning, double majors, English as a second language, honors programs, independent study, internships, part-time degree program, services for LD students, student-designed majors, summer session for credit. *ROTC:* Army (c).
Library John F. Kennedy Library plus 1 other with 41,812 titles, 245 serial subscriptions, 3,039 audiovisual materials, an OPAC, a Web page.
Computers on Campus 475 computers available on campus for general student use. A campuswide network can be accessed from off campus. Internet access, at least one staffed computer lab available.
Student Life *Housing Options:* men-only, women-only. Campus housing is university owned. *Activities and Organizations:* drama/theater group, student-run newspaper, choral group, Student Government Association, Black Cultural Society, Hispanic-American Leadership Organization, Hutchinson Christian Fellowship, Campus Crusade for Christ. *Campus security:* 24-hour emergency response devices and patrols, student patrols, late-night transport/escort service, controlled dormitory access. *Student services:* health clinic, personal/psychological counseling.
Athletics Member NJCAA. *Intercollegiate sports:* baseball M(s), basketball M(s)/W(s), cheerleading M(s)/W(s), cross-country running M(s)/W(s), football M(s), golf M(s), soccer W(s), softball W(s), tennis M(s)/W(s), track and field M(s)/W(s), volleyball W(s). *Intramural sports:* badminton M/W, basketball M/W, bowling M/W, football M/W, racquetball M/W, soccer M/W, tennis M/W, track and field M/W, volleyball M/W.
Costs (2005–06) *Tuition:* $50 per hour part-time; state resident $1600 full-time, $50 per hour part-time; nonresident $2816 full-time, $88 per hour

part-time. *Required fees:* $480 full-time, $15 per hour part-time. *Room and board:* $4060. Room and board charges vary according to board plan. *Payment plan:* installment.
Applying *Options:* electronic application, early admission, deferred entrance. *Required for some:* interview. *Recommended:* high school transcript. *Application deadline:* rolling (freshmen), rolling (transfers).
Freshmen Application Contact Mr. Corbin Strobel, Director of Admissions, Hutchinson Community College and Area Vocational School, 1300 North Plum, Hutchinson, KS 67501. *Phone:* 620-665-3536. *Toll-free phone:* 800-289-3501 Ext. 3536. *Fax:* 620-665-3301. *E-mail:* strobelc@hutchcc.edu.

INDEPENDENCE COMMUNITY COLLEGE
Independence, Kansas   www.indycc.edu/

- **State-supported** 2-year, founded 1925, part of Kansas State Board of Education
- **Small-town** 68-acre campus
- **Coed,** 906 undergraduate students, 53% full-time, 54% women, 46% men

Undergraduates 478 full-time, 428 part-time. Students come from 18 states and territories, 17 other countries, 9% are from out of state, 2% African American, 4% Asian American or Pacific Islander, 2% Hispanic American, 2% Native American, 0.9% international, 10% live on campus.
Freshmen *Admission:* 177 enrolled.
Faculty *Total:* 94, 31% full-time, 5% with terminal degrees. *Student/faculty ratio:* 17:1.
Majors Accounting; administrative assistant and secretarial science; art teacher education; athletic training; biological and physical sciences; biology/biological sciences; business administration and management; business teacher education; chemistry; child development; civil engineering technology; cosmetology; data processing and data processing technology; drafting and design technology; electrical, electronic and communications engineering technology; elementary education; emergency medical technology (EMT paramedic); engineering; engineering technology; English; finance; French; history; humanities; kindergarten/preschool education; liberal arts and sciences/liberal studies; mathematics; modern languages; music; music management and merchandising; music teacher education; natural sciences; physical education teaching and coaching; physical sciences; political science and government; pre-engineering; psychology; science teacher education; sociology; Spanish.
Academics *Calendar:* semesters. *Degree:* certificates and associate. *Special study options:* academic remediation for entering students, adult/continuing education programs, advanced placement credit, cooperative education, English as a second language, honors programs, internships, part-time degree program, summer session for credit.
Library Independence Community College Library plus 1 other with 32,408 titles, 166 serial subscriptions.
Computers on Campus 75 computers available on campus for general student use. A campuswide network can be accessed from student residence rooms and from off campus. Internet access, online (class) registration, at least one staffed computer lab available.
Student Life *Housing:* on-campus residence required through sophomore year. *Options:* Campus housing is university owned. Freshman campus housing is guaranteed. *Activities and Organizations:* drama/theater group, student-run newspaper, choral group, Student Senate, Phi Theta Kappa, Student Ambassadors, Campus Christians, multicultural student organization. *Campus security:* night patrol. *Student services:* personal/psychological counseling.
Athletics Member NJCAA. *Intercollegiate sports:* baseball M(s), basketball M(s)/W(s), cheerleading M(s)/W(s), football M(s), softball W(s), tennis M(s)/W(s), track and field M(s)/W(s), volleyball W(s). *Intramural sports:* basketball M/W.
Standardized Tests *Recommended:* SAT or ACT (for placement).
Costs (2006–07) *Tuition:* area resident $800 full-time, $25 per credit hour part-time; state resident $800 full-time, $25 per credit hour part-time; nonresident $2080 full-time, $65 per credit hour part-time. *Required fees:* $800 full-time, $25 per credit hour part-time. *Room and board:* $4100.
Financial Aid Of all full-time matriculated undergraduates who enrolled in 2004, 85 Federal Work-Study jobs (averaging $900).
Applying *Options:* common application, electronic application, early admission. *Required:* high school transcript. *Application deadline:* rolling (freshmen), rolling (transfers).
Director of Admissions Ms. Sally A. Ciufulescu, Director of Admissions, Independence Community College, PO Box 708, Independence, KS 67301. *Phone:* 620-332-5400. *Toll-free phone:* 800-842-6063. *Fax:* 620-331-0946. *E-mail:* sciufulescu@indycc.edu.

JOHNSON COUNTY COMMUNITY COLLEGE

Overland Park, Kansas www.johnco.cc.ks.us/

- **State and locally supported** 2-year, founded 1967, part of Kansas State Board of Education
- **Suburban** 220-acre campus with easy access to Kansas City
- **Endowment** $4.4 million
- **Coed**

Undergraduates 6,378 full-time, 12,234 part-time. Students come from 26 states and territories, 36 other countries, 5% are from out of state, 4% African American, 4% Asian American or Pacific Islander, 3% Hispanic American, 0.7% Native American, 1% international, 1% transferred in.

Faculty *Student/faculty ratio:* 21:1.

Academics *Calendar:* semesters. *Degree:* certificates and associate. *Special study options:* academic remediation for entering students, adult/continuing education programs, advanced placement credit, cooperative education, distance learning, double majors, English as a second language, honors programs, independent study, internships, off-campus study, part-time degree program, services for LD students, student-designed majors, summer session for credit.

Student Life *Campus security:* 24-hour emergency response devices and patrols, late-night transport/escort service.

Athletics Member NJCAA.

Standardized Tests *Required for some:* ACT (for placement), ACT ASSET.

Costs (2005–06) *Tuition:* area resident $1920 full-time, $64 per credit hour part-time; state resident $2370 full-time, $79 per credit hour part-time; nonresident $4350 full-time, $145 per credit hour part-time. Full-time tuition and fees vary according to course load. Part-time tuition and fees vary according to course load.

Financial Aid Of all full-time matriculated undergraduates who enrolled in 2004, 85 Federal Work-Study jobs (averaging $4000).

Applying *Options:* early admission. *Application fee:* $10. *Required for some:* high school transcript.

Director of Admissions Dr. Charles J. Carlsen, President, Johnson County Community College, 12345 College Park Boulevard, Overland Park, KS 66210. *Phone:* 913-469-8500 Ext. 3806.

KANSAS CITY KANSAS COMMUNITY COLLEGE

Kansas City, Kansas www.kckcc.edu/

- **State and locally supported** 2-year, founded 1923
- **Urban** 148-acre campus
- **Coed,** 5,419 undergraduate students, 36% full-time, 65% women, 35% men

Undergraduates 1,925 full-time, 3,494 part-time. Students come from 29 states and territories, 23 other countries, 5% are from out of state, 25% African American, 2% Asian American or Pacific Islander, 7% Hispanic American, 1% Native American, 2% international, 7% transferred in.

Freshmen *Admission:* 690 admitted, 690 enrolled.

Faculty *Total:* 352, 31% full-time. *Student/faculty ratio:* 14:1.

Majors Administrative assistant and secretarial science; business administration and management; child care and support services management; computer engineering technology; criminal justice/police science; data processing and data processing technology; drafting and design technology; emergency medical technology (EMT paramedic); fire science; funeral service and mortuary science; hazardous materials management and waste technology; international business/trade/commerce; legal assistant/paralegal; liberal arts and sciences and humanities related; liberal arts and sciences/liberal studies; nursing (registered nurse training); physical therapist assistant; recording arts technology; respiratory care therapy; respiratory therapy technician; substance abuse/addiction counseling; web page, digital/multimedia and information resources design.

Academics *Calendar:* semesters. *Degree:* certificates, diplomas, and associate. *Special study options:* academic remediation for entering students, adult/continuing education programs, advanced placement credit, cooperative education, distance learning, English as a second language, external degree program, freshman honors college, honors programs, independent study, internships, part-time degree program, services for LD students, summer session for credit.

Library Kansas City Kansas Community College Library with 65,000 titles, 200 serial subscriptions, 12,000 audiovisual materials, an OPAC, a Web page.

Computers on Campus 775 computers available on campus for general student use. A campuswide network can be accessed from off campus. Internet access, online (class) registration, at least one staffed computer lab available.

Student Life *Housing:* college housing not available. *Activities and Organizations:* drama/theater group, student-run newspaper, choral group, Student Senate, Phi Theta Kappa, Drama Club, The African American Student Union, Christian Student Union. *Campus security:* 24-hour emergency response devices and patrols, student patrols, late-night transport/escort service. *Student services:* health clinic, personal/psychological counseling, women's center.

Athletics Member NJCAA. *Intercollegiate sports:* baseball M(s), basketball M(s)/W(s), cross-country running M(s)/W(s), golf M(s), soccer M(s), softball W(s), track and field M(s)/W(s), volleyball W(s).

Costs (2005–06) *Tuition:* state resident $1470 full-time, $49 per credit hour part-time; nonresident $4410 full-time, $147 per credit hour part-time. Full-time tuition and fees vary according to course load. Part-time tuition and fees vary according to course load. *Required fees:* $300 full-time, $10 per credit hour part-time. *Payment plan:* installment. *Waivers:* employees or children of employees.

Financial Aid Of all full-time matriculated undergraduates who enrolled in 2004, 125 Federal Work-Study jobs (averaging $3000).

Applying *Options:* common application, electronic application. *Required:* high school transcript. *Application deadline:* rolling (freshmen), rolling (transfers). *Notification:* continuous (freshmen).

Freshmen Application Contact Ms. Sherri Neff, Assistant Director of Admissions, Kansas City Kansas Community College, 7250 State Avenue, Kansas City, KS 66112. *Phone:* 913-288-7201. *Fax:* 913-288-7648. *E-mail:* admiss@toto.net.

LABETTE COMMUNITY COLLEGE

Parsons, Kansas www.labette.edu/

Freshmen Application Contact Mr. Jeff Almond, Director of Admission, Labette Community College, 200 South 14th Street, Parsons, KS 67357. *Phone:* 620-421-6700 Ext. 1228. *Toll-free phone:* 888-LABETTE.

MANHATTAN AREA TECHNICAL COLLEGE

Manhattan, Kansas www.matc.net/

- **State and locally supported** 2-year, founded 1965
- **Suburban** 19-acre campus
- **Coed,** 401 undergraduate students, 81% full-time, 35% women, 65% men

Undergraduates 324 full-time, 77 part-time. 4% African American, 1% Asian American or Pacific Islander, 4% Hispanic American, 2% Native American, 37% transferred in.

Freshmen *Admission:* 126 admitted, 125 enrolled.

Faculty *Total:* 35, 77% full-time. *Student/faculty ratio:* 11:1.

Majors Autobody/collision and repair technology; automobile/automotive mechanics technology; building/construction finishing, management, and inspection related; computer systems networking and telecommunications; computer technology/computer systems technology; drafting and design technology; electrical and power transmission installation related; heating, air conditioning and refrigeration technology; management information systems; nursing (licensed practical/vocational nurse training); nursing (registered nurse training); welding technology.

Academics *Calendar:* semesters. *Degree:* certificates, diplomas, and associate.

Library Matc Library with an OPAC.

Computers on Campus A campuswide network can be accessed. Internet access, at least one staffed computer lab available.

Student Life *Housing:* college housing not available.

Costs (2006–07) *Tuition:* state resident $2035 full-time, $55 per credit hour part-time. *Required fees:* $400 full-time, $10 per credit hour part-time.

Applying *Application fee:* $40. *Required for some:* high school transcript. *Recommended:* high school transcript.

Freshmen Application Contact Mr. Rick Smith, Coordinator of Admissions and Recruitment, Manhattan Area Technical College, 3136 Dickens Avenue, Manhattan, KS 66503-2499. *Phone:* 785-587-2800 Ext. 104. *Toll-free phone:* 800-352-7575. *Fax:* 913-587-2804.

NATIONAL AMERICAN UNIVERSITY
Overland Park, Kansas

NEOSHO COUNTY COMMUNITY COLLEGE
Chanute, Kansas   www.neosho.edu/

Director of Admissions Ms. Lisa Last, Director of Admission/Registrar, Neosho County Community College, 800 West 14th Street, Chanute, KS 66720-2699. *Phone:* 620-431-2820 Ext. 213. *Toll-free phone:* 800-729-6222. *Fax:* 620-431-0082. *E-mail:* llast@neosho.edu.

NORTH CENTRAL KANSAS TECHNICAL COLLEGE
Beloit, Kansas   www.ncktc.tec.ks.us/

Director of Admissions Ms. Judy Heidrick, Director of Admissions, North Central Kansas Technical College, PO Box 507, Beloit, KS 67420. *Toll-free phone:* 800-658-4655. *E-mail:* jheidrick@ncktc.tec.ks.us.

NORTHEAST KANSAS TECHNICAL COLLEGE
Atchison, Kansas

- **State-supported** 2-year, founded 1965
- **Coed**

Academics *Calendar:* semesters.

NORTHWEST KANSAS TECHNICAL COLLEGE
Goodland, Kansas

PRATT COMMUNITY COLLEGE
Pratt, Kansas   www.prattcc.edu/

- **State and locally supported** 2-year, founded 1938, part of Kansas Board of Regents
- **Rural** 80-acre campus with easy access to Wichita
- **Coed,** 1,546 undergraduate students, 40% full-time, 52% women, 48% men

Undergraduates 625 full-time, 921 part-time. Students come from 21 states and territories, 16% are from out of state, 5% African American, 0.8% Asian American or Pacific Islander, 5% Hispanic American, 0.8% Native American, 2% international, 22% live on campus. *Retention:* 51% of 2003 full-time freshmen returned.
Freshmen *Admission:* 904 applied, 904 admitted, 258 enrolled.
Faculty *Total:* 120, 34% full-time, 7% with terminal degrees. *Student/faculty ratio:* 14:1.
Majors Accounting; administrative assistant and secretarial science; agricultural business and management; agricultural economics; agricultural mechanization; agricultural teacher education; agriculture; animal/livestock husbandry and production; animal sciences; applied art; art; art teacher education; athletic training; automobile/automotive mechanics technology; biological and physical sciences; biology/biological sciences; broadcast journalism; business administration and management; business teacher education; chemistry; child development;

commercial and advertising art; computer systems networking and telecommunications; computer/technical support; computer typography and composition equipment operation; counselor education/school counseling and guidance; data entry/microcomputer applications; data entry/microcomputer applications related; education (K-12); elementary education; energy management and systems technology; English; family and consumer sciences/human sciences; farm and ranch management; fine/studio arts; fish/game management; health teacher education; history; humanities; human services; industrial arts; kindergarten/preschool education; liberal arts and sciences/liberal studies; literature; marketing/marketing management; mass communication/media; mathematics; music; nursing (registered nurse training); physical education teaching and coaching; pre-engineering; professional studies; psychology; social sciences; social work; sociology; speech and rhetoric; speech/theater education; trade and industrial teacher education; welding technology; wildlife and wildlands science and management; wildlife biology; word processing.
Academics *Calendar:* semesters. *Degree:* certificates and associate. *Special study options:* academic remediation for entering students, adult/continuing education programs, advanced placement credit, cooperative education, distance learning, internships, part-time degree program, summer session for credit.
Library 33,000 titles, 250 serial subscriptions, 1,200 audiovisual materials, an OPAC, a Web page.
Computers on Campus 100 computers available on campus for general student use. A campuswide network can be accessed from off campus. Internet access, at least one staffed computer lab available.
Student Life *Housing:* on-campus residence required through sophomore year. *Options:* coed, men-only, women-only. Campus housing is university owned. *Activities and Organizations:* drama/theater group, student-run newspaper, choral group, Phi Theta Kappa, Student Senate, Baptist Student Union, Block and Bridle, Business Professionals Club. *Campus security:* 24-hour patrols, late-night transport/escort service, controlled dormitory access. *Student services:* health clinic, personal/psychological counseling.
Athletics Member NJCAA. *Intercollegiate sports:* baseball M(s), basketball M(s)/W(s), cheerleading W(s), cross-country running M(s)/W(s), golf M(s)/W(s), softball W(s), track and field M(s)/W(s), volleyball W(s). *Intramural sports:* basketball M/W, softball M/W, table tennis M/W, volleyball M/W, weight lifting M/W.
Standardized Tests *Required for some:* ASSET.
Costs (2006–07) *Tuition:* state resident $1344 full-time, $42 per credit hour part-time; nonresident $1344 full-time, $42 per credit hour part-time. *Required fees:* $928 full-time, $29 per credit hour part-time. *Room and board:* $3768.
Financial Aid Of all full-time matriculated undergraduates who enrolled in 2004, 77 Federal Work-Study jobs (averaging $800). 13 state and other part-time jobs (averaging $800). *Financial aid deadline:* 8/1.
Applying *Options:* common application, early admission. *Required:* high school transcript. *Application deadline:* rolling (freshmen), rolling (transfers).
Freshmen Application Contact Ms. Yolanda Mendoza, Student Services, Pratt Community College, 348 Northeast State Road 61, Pratt, KS 67124. *Phone:* 620-450-2217. *Toll-free phone:* 800-794-3091. *Fax:* 620-672-5288. *E-mail:* yolandam@prattcc.edu.

SEWARD COUNTY COMMUNITY COLLEGE
Liberal, Kansas   www.sccc.edu/

- **State and locally supported** 2-year, founded 1969, part of Kansas State Board of Regents
- **Rural** 120-acre campus
- **Endowment** $8.5 million
- **Coed**

Undergraduates 538 full-time, 1,787 part-time. Students come from 8 states and territories, 7 other countries, 11% are from out of state, 21% live on campus.
Faculty *Student/faculty ratio:* 18:1.
Academics *Calendar:* semesters. *Degree:* certificates, diplomas, and associate. *Special study options:* academic remediation for entering students, adult/continuing education programs, cooperative education, distance learning, English as a second language, external degree program, internships, part-time degree program, student-designed majors, summer session for credit.
Student Life *Campus security:* 24-hour patrols, late-night transport/escort service.
Athletics Member NJCAA.
Standardized Tests *Recommended:* SAT or ACT (for placement).
Financial Aid Of all full-time matriculated undergraduates who enrolled in 2004, 60 Federal Work-Study jobs (averaging $1854). 168 state and other part-time jobs (averaging $1854).

Applying *Options:* early admission, deferred entrance. *Required:* high school transcript. *Required for some:* minimum 2.0 GPA, 1 letter of recommendation, interview.
Director of Admissions Dr. Gerald Harris, Dean of Student Services, Seward County Community College, PO Box 1137, Liberal, KS 67905-1137. *Phone:* 620-624-1951 Ext. 617. *Toll-free phone:* 800-373-9951 Ext. 710.

WICHITA AREA TECHNICAL COLLEGE
Wichita, Kansas www.wichitatech.com/

- **District-supported** 2-year, founded 1963
- **Urban** campus
- **Coed,** 1,044 undergraduate students, 30% full-time, 46% women, 54% men

Undergraduates 313 full-time, 731 part-time. 16% African American, 5% Asian American or Pacific Islander, 7% Hispanic American, 2% Native American, 0.1% international.
Freshmen *Admission:* 719 applied, 350 admitted, 337 enrolled.
Faculty *Total:* 51, 71% full-time. *Student/faculty ratio:* 14:1.
Majors Automobile/automotive mechanics technology; clinical/medical laboratory technology; interior design; mechanical engineering/mechanical technology.
Academics *Calendar:* semesters. *Degree:* certificates, diplomas, and associate.
Standardized Tests *Required for some:* WorkKeys & COMPASS.
Costs (2006–07) *Tuition:* state resident $2970 full-time, $99 per credit part-time; nonresident $11,730 full-time, $345 per credit part-time. *Required fees:* $236 full-time, $118 per term part-time.
Applying *Application fee:* $16. *Required for some:* high school transcript. *Application deadline:* rolling (freshmen), rolling (transfers).
Freshmen Application Contact Ms. Jessica Ross, Director, Admissions, Wichita Area Technical College, 301 South Grove Street, Wichita, KS 67211. *Phone:* 316-677-9400. *Fax:* 316-677-9555. *E-mail:* info@watc.edu.

KENTUCKY

ASHLAND COMMUNITY AND TECHNICAL COLLEGE
Ashland, Kentucky www.ashland.kctcs.edu/

- **State-supported** 2-year, founded 1937, part of Kentucky Community and Technical College System
- **Small-town** 47-acre campus
- **Endowment** $870,926
- **Coed**

Undergraduates Students come from 6 states and territories, 10% are from out of state. *Retention:* 44% of 2003 full-time freshmen returned.
Faculty *Student/faculty ratio:* 19:1.
Academics *Calendar:* semesters. *Degree:* certificates, diplomas, and associate. *Special study options:* academic remediation for entering students, adult/continuing education programs, advanced placement credit, cooperative education, distance learning, honors programs, internships, off-campus study, part-time degree program, services for LD students, summer session for credit.
Student Life *Campus security:* 24-hour emergency response devices and patrols, late-night transport/escort service, electronic surveillance of bookstore and business office.
Standardized Tests *Required:* ACT COMPASS (for placement). *Recommended:* ACT (for placement).
Costs (2005–06) *Tuition:* state resident $2940 full-time, $98 per credit hour part-time; nonresident $8820 full-time, $294 per credit hour part-time. Full-time tuition and fees vary according to reciprocity agreements. Part-time tuition and fees vary according to reciprocity agreements.
Financial Aid Of all full-time matriculated undergraduates who enrolled in 2004, 12 Federal Work-Study jobs (averaging $2500). 1 state and other part-time job (averaging $1000).

Applying *Options:* common application, early admission, deferred entrance. *Required:* high school transcript.
Director of Admissions Mr. Steven D. Flouhouse, Dean of Students, Ashland Community and Technical College, 1400 College Drive, Ashland, KY 41101. *Phone:* 606-326-2114. *Toll-free phone:* 800-370-7191. *E-mail:* steve.flouhouse@kctcs.edu.

BECKFIELD COLLEGE
Florence, Kentucky www.beckfield.edu/

Director of Admissions Mr. Ken Leeds, Director of Admissions, Beckfield College, 16 Spiral Drive, Florence, KY 41042. *Phone:* 859-371-9393. *E-mail:* kleeds@beckfield.org.

BIG SANDY COMMUNITY AND TECHNICAL COLLEGE
Prestonsburg, Kentucky www.bigsandy.kctcs.edu/

- **State-supported** 2-year, founded 1964, part of Kentucky Community and Technical College System
- **Rural** 50-acre campus
- **Endowment** $700,000
- **Coed**

Undergraduates Students come from 1 other state, 0.8% African American, 0.2% Asian American or Pacific Islander, 0.2% Hispanic American, 0.1% Native American.
Academics *Calendar:* semesters. *Degree:* associate. *Special study options:* academic remediation for entering students, adult/continuing education programs, advanced placement credit, cooperative education, distance learning, independent study, off-campus study, part-time degree program, services for LD students, summer session for credit.
Student Life *Campus security:* 24-hour emergency response devices.
Standardized Tests *Required:* ACT (for placement). *Recommended:* ACT ASSET.
Costs (2005–06) *Tuition:* area resident $2940 full-time, $98 per credit hour part-time; state resident $3540 full-time, $118 per credit hour part-time; nonresident $8820 full-time, $294 per credit hour part-time.
Financial Aid Of all full-time matriculated undergraduates who enrolled in 2004, 112 Federal Work-Study jobs (averaging $1749).
Applying *Options:* common application, early admission, deferred entrance. *Required:* high school transcript.
Director of Admissions Mr. Jim Glover, Director of Admissions, Big Sandy Community and Technical College, One Bert T. Combs Drive, Prestonsburg, KY 41653-1815. *Phone:* 606-886-3863 Ext. 220. *Toll-free phone:* 888-641-4132. *E-mail:* ccsprerg@kctcs.edu.

BOWLING GREEN TECHNICAL COLLEGE
Bowling Green, Kentucky

- **State-supported** 2-year, founded 1938
- **Coed**

Academics *Calendar:* semesters.

BROWN MACKIE COLLEGE—HOPKINSVILLE
Hopkinsville, Kentucky www.brownmackie.edu/locations.asp?locid=17

- **Proprietary** 2-year
- **Small-town** campus
- **Coed, primarily women,** 146 undergraduate students, 100% full-time, 88% women, 12% men

Undergraduates 146 full-time. 25% African American, 0.7% Asian American or Pacific Islander, 3% Hispanic American, 0.7% Native American.
Freshmen *Admission:* 89 applied, 89 admitted, 75 enrolled.

Brown Mackie College–Hopkinsville (continued)

Faculty *Total:* 10, 30% full-time, 20% with terminal degrees. *Student/faculty ratio:* 15:1.

Majors Accounting technology and bookkeeping; business administration and management; computer programming; computer programming (specific applications); computer software technology; criminal justice/safety; medical/clinical assistant; paralegal/legal assistant.

Academics *Calendar:* quarters. *Degree:* diplomas and associate.

Costs (2005–06) *Tuition:* $8592 full-time, $179 per credit hour part-time. *Required fees:* $480 full-time, $10 per credit hour part-time.

Financial Aid Of all full-time matriculated undergraduates who enrolled in 2004, 12 Federal Work-Study jobs.

Applying *Required:* high school transcript. *Recommended:* interview. *Application deadline:* rolling (freshmen), rolling (transfers). *Notification:* continuous (freshmen).

Freshmen Application Contact Ms. Elizabeth Ashy, Dean of Academic Affairs, Brown Mackie College–Hopkinsville, 4001 Fort Campbell Boulevard, Hopkinsville, KY 42240-4962. *Phone:* 270-886-1302. *Toll-free phone:* 800-359-4753. *Fax:* 270-886-3544. *E-mail:* eashy@brownmackie.edu.

▶ See page 506 for the College Close-Up.

BROWN MACKIE COLLEGE–LOUISVILLE

**Louisville,
Kentucky** www.brownmackie.edu/locations.asp?locid=18

- **Proprietary** 2-year, founded 1972
- **Suburban** campus
- **Coed,** 315 undergraduate students, 100% full-time, 54% women, 46% men

Undergraduates 315 full-time. Students come from 3 states and territories, 1 other country, 7% are from out of state, 34% African American, 0.6% Asian American or Pacific Islander, 2% Hispanic American, 0.6% Native American. Freshmen *Admission:* 128 applied, 92 admitted.

Faculty *Total:* 17, 41% full-time, 47% with terminal degrees. *Student/faculty ratio:* 18:1.

Majors Accounting technology and bookkeeping; business administration and management; computer systems networking and telecommunications; criminal justice/safety; gerontology; graphic design; health/health care administration; industrial electronics technology; medical/clinical assistant; paralegal/legal assistant; pharmacy technician.

Academics *Calendar:* quarters. *Degree:* associate. *Special study options:* academic remediation for entering students.

Library Main Library plus 1 other with 1,210 titles, 23 serial subscriptions.

Computers on Campus 3 computers available on campus for general student use. A campuswide network can be accessed. At least one staffed computer lab available.

Student Life *Housing:* college housing not available. *Campus security:* 24-hour emergency response devices, evening security guards, electronically operated building access. *Student services:* personal/psychological counseling.

Costs (2006–07) *Tuition:* $8592 full-time. *Required fees:* $480 full-time.

Applying *Options:* early admission, deferred entrance. *Required:* high school transcript, interview. *Application deadline:* rolling (freshmen), rolling (transfers). *Notification:* continuous (freshmen).

Freshmen Application Contact Ms. Kathleen Belanger, Director of Admissions, Brown Mackie College–Louisville, 300 Highrise Drive, Louisville, KY 40213. *Phone:* 502-968-7191. *Toll-free phone:* 800-999-7387. *Fax:* 502-968-9956. *E-mail:* bmcloadm@brownmackie.edu.

▶ See page 510 for the College Close-Up.

BROWN MACKIE COLLEGE–NORTHERN KENTUCKY

Fort Mitchell, Kentucky www.brownmackie.edu

- **Proprietary** 2-year, founded 1927, part of American Education Centers, Inc
- **Suburban** 5-acre campus with easy access to Cincinnati
- **Coed,** 465 undergraduate students, 100% full-time, 70% women, 30% men

Undergraduates 465 full-time. Students come from 3 states and territories, 12% are from out of state, 8% African American, 0.9% Asian American or Pacific Islander, 1% Hispanic American. *Retention:* 81% of 2003 full-time freshmen returned.

Freshmen *Admission:* 500 applied, 465 enrolled.

Faculty *Student/faculty ratio:* 14:1.

Majors Accounting technology and bookkeeping; business administration and management; CAD/CADD drafting/design technology; computer programming (specific applications); computer software technology; criminal justice/law enforcement administration; medical/clinical assistant; paralegal/legal assistant; pharmacy technician; system, networking, and LAN/WAN management.

Academics *Calendar:* quarters. *Degree:* certificates, diplomas, and associate. *Special study options:* academic remediation for entering students, adult/continuing education programs, internships, part-time degree program, summer session for credit.

Library 1,500 titles, 50 serial subscriptions.

Computers on Campus 50 computers available on campus for general student use. Internet access, at least one staffed computer lab available.

Student Life *Housing:* college housing not available. *Campus security:* 24-hour emergency response devices, late-night transport/escort service. *Student services:* personal/psychological counseling.

Applying *Options:* common application. *Required:* interview. *Application deadline:* rolling (freshmen), rolling (transfers). *Notification:* continuous (freshmen).

Freshmen Application Contact Admissions, Brown Mackie College–Northern Kentucky, 309 Buttermilk Pike, Fort Mitchell, KY 41017. *Phone:* 859-341-5627. *Toll-free phone:* 800-888-1445. *Fax:* 859-341-6483.

▶ See page 522 for the College Close-Up.

DAYMAR COLLEGE

Louisville, Kentucky www.daymarcollege.edu/

Director of Admissions Mr. Patrick Carney, Director of Admissions, Daymar College, 4400 Breckenridge Lane, Suite 415, Louisville, KY 40218.

DAYMAR COLLEGE

Owensboro, Kentucky www.daymarcollege.edu/

Director of Admissions Ms. Vickie McDougal, Director of Admissions, Daymar College, 3361 Buckland Square, PO Box 22150, Owensboro, KY 42303. *Phone:* 270-926-4040. *Toll-free phone:* 800-960-4090. *E-mail:* mdowney@ojcb.com.

DRAUGHONS JUNIOR COLLEGE

Bowling Green, Kentucky www.draughons.edu/

Freshmen Application Contact Amye Melton, Admissions Director, Draughons Junior College, 2421 Fitzgerald Industrial Drive, Bowling Green, KY 42101. *Phone:* 270-843-6750.

ELIZABETHTOWN COMMUNITY AND TECHNICAL COLLEGE

Elizabethtown, Kentucky www.elizabethtown.kctcs.edu/

- **State-supported** 2-year, founded 1964, part of Kentucky Community and Technical College System
- **Small-town** 40-acre campus with easy access to Louisville
- **Coed**

Undergraduates 1,645 full-time, 1,970 part-time. Students come from 10 states and territories, 11% African American, 2% Asian American or Pacific Islander, 3% Hispanic American, 0.6% Native American.

Academics *Calendar:* semesters. *Degree:* certificates, diplomas, and associate. *Special study options:* academic remediation for entering students, adult/continuing education programs, advanced placement credit, cooperative education, external degree program, internships, off-campus study, part-time degree program, services for LD students, summer session for credit.

Student Life *Campus security:* late night security.

Standardized Tests *Required for some:* ACT (for admission).

Costs (2005–06) *Tuition:* state resident $2352 full-time, $98 per credit hour part-time; nonresident $7056 full-time, $294 per credit hour part-time. Full-time tuition and fees vary according to course load. Part-time tuition and fees vary according to course load.

Financial Aid Of all full-time matriculated undergraduates who enrolled in 2004, 20 Federal Work-Study jobs (averaging $2000).

Applying *Options:* common application, early admission. *Required:* essay or personal statement, high school transcript.

Director of Admissions Dr. Dale Buckles, Dean of Student Affairs, Elizabethtown Community and Technical College, 600 College Street Road, Elizabethtown, KY 42701. *Phone:* 270-769-2371 Ext. 68431. *Toll-free phone:* 877-246-2322.

ELIZABETHTOWN TECHNICAL COLLEGE
Elizabethtown, Kentucky

GATEWAY COMMUNITY AND TECHNICAL COLLEGE
Covington, Kentucky   www.gateway.kctcs.edu/

- **State-supported** 2-year, founded 1961
- **Coed**

Academics *Calendar:* semesters. *Degree:* certificates, diplomas, and associate.

Standardized Tests *Required:* ACT or ACT COMPASS (for placement).

Costs (2005–06) *Tuition:* state resident $2940 full-time, $98 per credit hour part-time; nonresident $8820 full-time, $294 per credit hour part-time.

Director of Admissions Mr. Paul Brinkman, Dean of Student Affairs, Gateway Community and Technical College, 1025 Amsterdam Road, Covington, KY 41011.

HAZARD COMMUNITY AND TECHNICAL COLLEGE
Hazard, Kentucky   www.hazard.kctcs.edu/

- **State-supported** 2-year, founded 1968, part of Kentucky Community and Technical College System
- **Rural** 34-acre campus
- **Coed**

Undergraduates Students come from 3 states and territories, 5% are from out of state.

Academics *Calendar:* semesters. *Degree:* certificates, diplomas, and associate. *Special study options:* academic remediation for entering students, adult/continuing education programs, honors programs, part-time degree program, summer session for credit.

Student Life *Campus security:* late-night transport/escort service.

Standardized Tests *Required:* ACT (for placement).

Applying *Options:* common application, early admission. *Required:* high school transcript.

Freshmen Application Contact Mr. Steve Jones, Director of Admissions, Hazard Community and Technical College, 1 Community College Drive, Hazard, KY 41701-2403. *Phone:* 606-436-5721 Ext. 8076. *Toll-free phone:* 800-246-7521.

HENDERSON COMMUNITY COLLEGE
Henderson, Kentucky   www.henderson.kctcs.edu/

- **State-supported** 2-year, founded 1963, part of Kentucky Community and Technical College System
- **Small-town** 120-acre campus
- **Coed**

Undergraduates 690 full-time, 1,551 part-time. Students come from 12 states and territories, 1% are from out of state, 5% African American, 0.3% Asian American or Pacific Islander, 0.6% Hispanic American, 0.8% Native American.

Faculty *Student/faculty ratio:* 13:1.

Academics *Calendar:* semesters. *Degree:* associate. *Special study options:* academic remediation for entering students, accelerated degree program, adult/continuing education programs, advanced placement credit, cooperative education, distance learning, double majors, English as a second language, external degree program, independent study, internships, off-campus study, part-time degree program, summer session for credit.

Student Life *Campus security:* 24-hour emergency response devices.

Standardized Tests *Required:* ACT (for admission), ACT COMPASS (for admission).

Costs (2005–06) *Tuition:* state resident $2490 full-time, $98 per credit hour part-time; nonresident $8820 full-time, $294 per credit hour part-time. Full-time tuition and fees vary according to course load. Part-time tuition and fees vary according to course load.

Financial Aid Of all full-time matriculated undergraduates who enrolled in 2004, 31 Federal Work-Study jobs.

Applying *Options:* common application. *Required:* high school transcript. *Required for some:* essay or personal statement, letters of recommendation, interview.

Freshmen Application Contact Ms. Teresa Hamiton, Admissions Counselor, Henderson Community College, 2660 South Green Street, Henderson, KY 42420-4623. *Phone:* 270-827-1867 Ext. 354.

HOPKINSVILLE COMMUNITY COLLEGE
Hopkinsville, Kentucky   www.hopcc.kctcs.edu/

- **State-supported** 2-year, founded 1965, part of Kentucky Community and Technical College System
- **Small-town** 70-acre campus with easy access to Nashville
- **Endowment** $2.4 million
- **Coed**

Undergraduates 1,413 full-time, 1,691 part-time. Students come from 3 states and territories, 1 other country, 25% are from out of state, 22% African American, 1% Asian American or Pacific Islander, 4% Hispanic American, 0.4% Native American, 61% transferred in. *Retention:* 55% of 2003 full-time freshmen returned.

Faculty *Student/faculty ratio:* 23:1.

Academics *Calendar:* semesters. *Degree:* certificates, diplomas, and associate. *Special study options:* academic remediation for entering students, adult/continuing education programs, advanced placement credit, distance learning, honors programs, independent study, part-time degree program, services for LD students, summer session for credit.

Student Life *Campus security:* 24-hour emergency response devices, late-night transport/escort service.

Standardized Tests *Required:* ACT (for placement), ACT COMPASS (for placement).

Costs (2005–06) *Tuition:* state resident $2940 full-time, $98 per credit hour part-time; nonresident $8820 full-time, $294 per credit hour part-time. Full-time tuition and fees vary according to location and reciprocity agreements. Part-time tuition and fees vary according to location and reciprocity agreements.

Financial Aid Of all full-time matriculated undergraduates who enrolled in 2004, 30 Federal Work-Study jobs (averaging $1500). *Financial aid deadline:* 6/30.

Applying *Options:* common application, early admission, deferred entrance. *Required for some:* high school transcript, interview.

Director of Admissions Ms. Ruth Ann Rettie, Registrar, Hopkinsville Community College, North Drive, PO Box 2100, Hopkinsville, KY 42241-2100. *Phone:* 270-886-3921 Ext. 6197.

ITT TECHNICAL INSTITUTE
Louisville, Kentucky   www.itt-tech.edu/

- **Proprietary** primarily 2-year, founded 1993, part of ITT Educational Services, Inc
- **Suburban** campus
- **Coed**

Majors Animation, interactive technology, video graphics and special effects; business administration and management; CAD/CADD drafting/design technology; computer and information systems security; computer programming; criminal justice/law enforcement administration; e-commerce; electrical, electronic and communications engineering technology; system, networking, and LAN/WAN management; web/multimedia management and webmaster; web page, digital/multimedia and information resources design.

ITT Technical Institute (continued)

Academics *Calendar:* quarters. *Degrees:* associate and bachelor's.

Library a Web page.

Computers on Campus Internet access, at least one staffed computer lab available.

Student Life *Housing:* college housing not available.

Standardized Tests *Required:* Wonderlic aptitude test (for admission).

Costs (2005–06) *Tuition:* Please see school catalog for specific information.

Applying *Options:* deferred entrance. *Application fee:* $100. *Required:* high school transcript, interview. *Recommended:* letters of recommendation. *Application deadline:* rolling (freshmen), rolling (transfers). *Notification:* continuous (freshmen).

Freshmen Application Contact Mr. Michael Alcorn, Director of Recruitment, ITT Technical Institute, 10509 Timberwood Circle, Louisville, KY 40223. *Phone:* 502-327-7424. *Toll-free phone:* 888-790-7427.

JEFFERSON COMMUNITY AND TECHNICAL COLLEGE

Louisville, Kentucky   www.jctc.kctcs.edu/

- **State-supported** 2-year, founded 1968, part of Kentucky Community and Technical College System
- **Urban** 10-acre campus
- **Endowment** $1.1 million
- **Coed,** 14,240 undergraduate students, 35% full-time, 51% women, 49% men

Undergraduates 4,941 full-time, 9,299 part-time. Students come from 11 states and territories, 3% are from out of state, 16% African American, 1% Asian American or Pacific Islander, 2% Hispanic American, 0.3% Native American, 0.3% international, 11% transferred in.

Freshmen *Admission:* 2,292 enrolled.

Faculty *Total:* 661, 46% full-time. *Student/faculty ratio:* 19:1.

Majors Accounting; business administration and management; child development; commercial and advertising art; culinary arts; data processing and data processing technology; electrical, electronic and communications engineering technology; health information/medical records technology; liberal arts and sciences/liberal studies; mechanical engineering/mechanical technology; medical radiologic technology; nuclear medical technology; nursing (registered nurse training); physical therapy; real estate; respiratory care therapy; social work; welding technology.

Academics *Calendar:* semesters. *Degree:* certificates, diplomas, and associate. *Special study options:* academic remediation for entering students, adult/continuing education programs, advanced placement credit, cooperative education, distance learning, English as a second language, external degree program, honors programs, independent study, internships, off-campus study, part-time degree program, services for LD students, summer session for credit. *ROTC:* Army (c).

Library John T. Smith Learning Resource Center plus 2 others with 76,578 titles, 391 serial subscriptions, 15,103 audiovisual materials, an OPAC, a Web page.

Computers on Campus 895 computers available on campus for general student use. A campuswide network can be accessed from off campus. Internet access, at least one staffed computer lab available.

Student Life *Housing:* college housing not available. *Activities and Organizations:* drama/theater group, student-run newspaper. *Campus security:* 24-hour emergency response devices and patrols, late-night transport/escort service. *Student services:* personal/psychological counseling.

Costs (2006–07) *Tuition:* state resident $3270 full-time, $109 per credit hour part-time; nonresident $9810 full-time, $327 per credit hour part-time. *Required fees:* $50 full-time, $25 per term part-time.

Financial Aid Of all full-time matriculated undergraduates who enrolled in 2004, 50 Federal Work-Study jobs (averaging $4000).

Applying *Options:* early admission. *Application deadline:* rolling (freshmen), rolling (transfers). *Notification:* continuous (freshmen).

Freshmen Application Contact Ms. Melanie Vaughan-Cooke, Jefferson Community and Technical College, 109 East Broadway, Louisville, KY 40202. *Phone:* 502-213-4000. *Fax:* 502-213-2540.

LEXINGTON COMMUNITY COLLEGE

Lexington, Kentucky   www.uky.edu/lcc/

Director of Admissions Mrs. Shelbie Hugle, Director of Admission Services, Lexington Community College, 200 Oswald Building, Cooper Drive, Lexington,

KY 40506-0235. *Phone:* 859-257-4872 Ext. 4197. *Toll-free phone:* 866-744-4872 Ext. 5111. *E-mail:* shugl00@uky.edu.

LOUISVILLE TECHNICAL INSTITUTE

Louisville, Kentucky   www.louisvilletech.com/

Director of Admissions Mr. David Ritz, Director of Admissions, Louisville Technical Institute, 3901 Atkinson Square Drive, Louisville, KY 40218. *Phone:* 502-456-6509. *Toll-free phone:* 800-884-6528. *Fax:* 502-456-2351.

MADISONVILLE COMMUNITY COLLEGE

Madisonville, Kentucky   www.madcc.kctcs.edu/

Director of Admissions Mr. Jay Parent, Registrar, Madisonville Community College, 2000 College Drive, Madisonville, KY 42431. *Phone:* 270-821-2250.

MAYSVILLE COMMUNITY AND TECHNICAL COLLEGE

Maysville, Kentucky   www.maycc.kctcs.net/

Director of Admissions Ms. Patee Massie, Registrar, Maysville Community and Technical College, 1755 US 68, Maysville, KY 41056. *Phone:* 606-759-7141 Ext. 6184. *Fax:* 606-759-5818. *E-mail:* ccsmayrg@ukcc.uky.edu.

NATIONAL COLLEGE OF BUSINESS & TECHNOLOGY

Danville, Kentucky   www.ncbt.edu/

- **Proprietary** 2-year, founded 1962, part of National College of Business and Technology
- **Coed**

Faculty *Student/faculty ratio:* 10:1.

Academics *Calendar:* quarters. *Degree:* diplomas and associate. *Special study options:* advanced placement credit, double majors, honors programs, internships, part-time degree program, services for LD students, summer session for credit.

Costs (2005–06) *Tuition:* $6408 full-time, $178 per credit hour part-time. *Required fees:* $75 full-time, $15 per term part-time. *Payment plans:* installment, deferred payment.

Financial Aid Of all full-time matriculated undergraduates who enrolled in 2004, 1 Federal Work-Study job.

Applying *Options:* common application, electronic application. *Application fee:* $30. *Required:* high school transcript.

Director of Admissions Ms. Stacie Catlett, Campus Director, National College of Business & Technology, 115 East Lexington Avenue, Danville, KY 40422. *Phone:* 859-236-6991. *Toll-free phone:* 800-664-1886.

NATIONAL COLLEGE OF BUSINESS & TECHNOLOGY

Florence, Kentucky   www.ncbt.edu/

- **Proprietary** 2-year, founded 1941, part of National College of Business and Technology
- **Suburban** campus
- **Coed**

Faculty *Student/faculty ratio:* 12:1.

Academics *Calendar:* quarters. *Degree:* diplomas and associate. *Special study options:* advanced placement credit, double majors, honors programs, internships, part-time degree program, services for LD students, summer session for credit.

Student Life *Campus security:* 24-hour emergency response devices.

Costs (2005–06) *Tuition:* $6408 full-time, $178 per credit hour part-time. *Required fees:* $75 full-time, $15 per term part-time.
Financial Aid Of all full-time matriculated undergraduates who enrolled in 2004, 3 Federal Work-Study jobs.
Applying *Options:* electronic application. *Application fee:* $30. *Required for some:* high school transcript. *Recommended:* interview.
Director of Admissions Ron Thomas, Campus Director, National College of Business & Technology, 7627 Ewing Boulevard, Florence, KY 41042. *Phone:* 859-525-6510. *Toll-free phone:* 800-664-1886.

NATIONAL COLLEGE OF BUSINESS & TECHNOLOGY
Lexington, Kentucky   www.ncbt.edu/

- **Proprietary** 2-year, founded 1947, part of National College of Business and Technology
- **Urban** campus
- **Coed**

Faculty *Student/faculty ratio:* 12:1.
Academics *Calendar:* quarters. *Degree:* diplomas and associate. *Special study options:* advanced placement credit, double majors, honors programs, internships, part-time degree program, summer session for credit.
Costs (2005–06) *Tuition:* $6408 full-time, $178 per credit hour part-time. *Required fees:* $75 full-time, $15 per term part-time.
Financial Aid Of all full-time matriculated undergraduates who enrolled in 2004, 6 Federal Work-Study jobs.
Applying *Options:* electronic application. *Application fee:* $30. *Required:* high school transcript.
Director of Admissions Kim Thomasson, Campus Director, National College of Business & Technology, 628 East Main Street, Lexington, KY 40508-2312. *Phone:* 859-266-0401. *Toll-free phone:* 800-664-1886.

NATIONAL COLLEGE OF BUSINESS & TECHNOLOGY
Louisville, Kentucky   www.ncbt.edu/

- **Proprietary** 2-year, founded 1990, part of National College of Business and Technology
- **Coed**

Faculty *Student/faculty ratio:* 10:1.
Academics *Calendar:* quarters. *Degree:* diplomas and associate. *Special study options:* advanced placement credit, double majors, honors programs, internships, part-time degree program, services for LD students, summer session for credit.
Costs (2005–06) *Tuition:* $6408 full-time, $178 per credit hour part-time. Full-time tuition and fees vary according to course load. Part-time tuition and fees vary according to course load. *Required fees:* $75 full-time, $15 per term part-time. *Payment plans:* installment, deferred payment.
Financial Aid Of all full-time matriculated undergraduates who enrolled in 2004, 2 Federal Work-Study jobs.
Applying *Options:* electronic application. *Application fee:* $30. *Required for some:* high school transcript. *Recommended:* interview.
Director of Admissions Mike Fiore, Campus Director, National College of Business & Technology, 3950 Dixie Highway, Louisville, KY 40216. *Phone:* 502-447-7634. *Toll-free phone:* 800-664-1886.

NATIONAL COLLEGE OF BUSINESS & TECHNOLOGY
Pikeville, Kentucky   www.ncbt.edu/

- **Proprietary** 2-year, founded 1976, part of National College of Business and Technology
- **Rural** campus
- **Coed**

Faculty *Student/faculty ratio:* 10:1.

Academics *Calendar:* quarters. *Degree:* diplomas and associate. *Special study options:* advanced placement credit, double majors, honors programs, internships, part-time degree program, services for LD students, summer session for credit.
Costs (2005–06) *Tuition:* $6408 full-time, $178 per credit hour part-time. *Required fees:* $75 full-time, $15 per term part-time.
Financial Aid Of all full-time matriculated undergraduates who enrolled in 2004, 4 Federal Work-Study jobs.
Applying *Application fee:* $30. *Required for some:* high school transcript. *Recommended:* interview.
Director of Admissions Mr. Jerry Lafferty, Campus Director, National College of Business & Technology, 288 South Mayo Trail, Suite 2, Pikeville, KY 41501. *Phone:* 606-432-5477. *Toll-free phone:* 800-664-1886.

NATIONAL COLLEGE OF BUSINESS & TECHNOLOGY
Richmond, Kentucky   www.ncbt.edu/

- **Proprietary** 2-year, founded 1951, part of National College of Business and Technology
- **Suburban** campus
- **Coed**

Faculty *Student/faculty ratio:* 12:1.
Academics *Calendar:* quarters. *Degree:* diplomas and associate. *Special study options:* advanced placement credit, double majors, honors programs, internships, part-time degree program, summer session for credit.
Costs (2005–06) *Tuition:* $6408 full-time, $178 per credit hour part-time. *Required fees:* $75 full-time, $15 per term part-time.
Financial Aid Of all full-time matriculated undergraduates who enrolled in 2004, 1 Federal Work-Study job.
Applying *Options:* electronic application. *Application fee:* $30. *Required for some:* high school transcript. *Recommended:* interview.
Director of Admissions Ms. Keeley Gadd, Campus Director, National College of Business & Technology, 139 Killarney Lane, Richmond, KY 40475. *Phone:* 859-623-8956. *Toll-free phone:* 800-664-1886.

OWENSBORO COMMUNITY AND TECHNICAL COLLEGE
Owensboro, Kentucky   www.octc.kctcs.edu/

- **State-supported** 2-year, founded 1986, part of Kentucky Community and Technical College System
- **Suburban** 102-acre campus
- **Endowment** $109,305
- **Coed**

Undergraduates 1,848 full-time, 1,816 part-time. Students come from 6 states and territories, 2 other countries, 5% are from out of state, 3% African American, 0.5% Asian American or Pacific Islander, 0.3% Hispanic American, 0.2% Native American, 2% transferred in.
Faculty *Student/faculty ratio:* 21:1.
Academics *Calendar:* semesters. *Degree:* certificates and associate. *Special study options:* academic remediation for entering students, adult/continuing education programs, advanced placement credit, cooperative education, distance learning, double majors, external degree program, honors programs, internships, off-campus study, part-time degree program, study abroad, summer session for credit.
Student Life *Campus security:* 24-hour emergency response devices, late-night transport/escort service.
Standardized Tests *Required:* ACT (for placement). *Required for some:* ACT COMPASS.
Financial Aid Of all full-time matriculated undergraduates who enrolled in 2004, 60 Federal Work-Study jobs (averaging $2500). *Financial aid deadline:* 4/1.
Applying *Required:* high school transcript.
Director of Admissions Ms. Barbara Tipmore, Admissions Counselor, Owensboro Community and Technical College, 4800 New Hartford Road, Owensboro, KY 42303. *Phone:* 270-686-4527. *Toll-free phone:* 866-755-6282.

PADUCAH TECHNICAL COLLEGE

Paducah, Kentucky   **www.ptc-ky.com/**

Director of Admissions Mr. Arnold Harris, Director of Admissions, Paducah Technical College, 509 South 30th Street, PO Box 8252, Paducah, KY 42001. *Phone:* 502-444-9676. *Toll-free phone:* 800-995-4438.

ROWAN TECHNICAL COLLEGE

Morehead, Kentucky   **www.rowtc.kctcs.edu/**

Director of Admissions Patee Massie, Registrar, Rowan Technical College, 609 Viking Drive, Morehead, KY 40351. *Phone:* 606-759-7141 Ext. 66184.

ST. CATHARINE COLLEGE

St. Catharine, Kentucky   **www.sccky.edu/**

Director of Admissions Ms. Amy C. Carrico, Director of Admissions, St. Catharine College, 2735 Bardstown Road, St. Catharine, KY 40061. *Phone:* 859-336-5082. *Toll-free phone:* 800-599-2000 Ext. 1227.

SOMERSET COMMUNITY COLLEGE

Somerset, Kentucky   **www.somerset.kctcs.edu/**

- **State-supported** 2-year, founded 1965, part of Kentucky Community and Technical College System
- **Small-town** 70-acre campus
- **Endowment** $419,000
- **Coed**

Undergraduates Students come from 3 states and territories, 0.7% African American, 0.2% Asian American or Pacific Islander, 0.3% Hispanic American, 0.2% Native American. *Retention:* 60% of 2003 full-time freshmen returned.
Faculty *Student/faculty ratio:* 19:1.
Academics *Calendar:* semesters. *Degree:* certificates, diplomas, and associate. *Special study options:* academic remediation for entering students, adult/continuing education programs, advanced placement credit, cooperative education, distance learning, double majors, English as a second language, independent study, internships, part-time degree program, services for LD students, summer session for credit.
Standardized Tests *Required:* ACT (for placement).
Financial Aid Of all full-time matriculated undergraduates who enrolled in 2004, 40 Federal Work-Study jobs (averaging $2500). 25 state and other part-time jobs (averaging $2500).
Applying *Options:* common application, early admission. *Required:* high school transcript.
Freshmen Application Contact Mr. Sean Ayers, Recruiter, Somerset Community College, 808 Monticello Street, Somerset, KY 42501. *Phone:* 606-679-8501 Ext. 3778. *Toll-free phone:* 877-629-9722.

SOUTHEAST KENTUCKY COMMUNITY AND TECHNICAL COLLEGE

Cumberland, Kentucky   **www.soucc.kctcs.net/**

- **State-supported** 2-year, founded 1960, part of Kentucky Community and Technical College System
- **Small-town** 150-acre campus
- **Endowment** $1.8 million
- **Coed**

Undergraduates 1,939 full-time, 2,580 part-time. 1% African American, 0.2% Asian American or Pacific Islander, 0.3% Hispanic American, 0.2% Native American.
Faculty *Student/faculty ratio:* 20:1.
Academics *Calendar:* semesters. *Degree:* certificates, diplomas, and associate. *Special study options:* academic remediation for entering students, acceler-ated degree program, adult/continuing education programs, advanced placement credit, distance learning, internships, part-time degree program, summer session for credit.
Costs (2005–06) *Tuition:* state resident $2352 full-time, $98 per credit hour part-time; nonresident $7056 full-time, $294 per credit hour part-time. *Required fees:* $164 full-time.
Financial Aid Of all full-time matriculated undergraduates who enrolled in 2004, 90 Federal Work-Study jobs (averaging $635).
Applying *Required:* high school transcript.
Director of Admissions Ms. Cookie Baker, Director of Admissions, Southeast Kentucky Community and Technical College, 700 College Road, Cumberland, KY 40823. *Phone:* 606-589-2145 Ext. 13018. *Toll-free phone:* 888-274-SECC Ext. 2108.

SOUTHWESTERN COLLEGE OF BUSINESS

Florence, Kentucky   **www.swcollege.net/**

Director of Admissions Mr. Bruce Budesheim, Director, Southwestern College of Business, 8095 Connector Drive, Florence, KY 41042. *Phone:* 859-341-6633. *Fax:* 859-341-6749. *E-mail:* bbudesheim@swcollege.net.

SPENCERIAN COLLEGE

Louisville, Kentucky   **www.spencerian.edu/**

- **Proprietary** 2-year, founded 1892, part of The Sullivan University System
- **Urban** 10-acre campus
- **Coed**

Undergraduates 1,326 full-time. Students come from 11 states and territories, 16% are from out of state, 25% African American, 0.7% Asian American or Pacific Islander, 0.3% Hispanic American, 0.6% Native American.
Faculty *Student/faculty ratio:* 14:1.
Academics *Calendar:* quarters. *Degree:* certificates, diplomas, and associate. *Special study options:* academic remediation for entering students, accelerated degree program, advanced placement credit, cooperative education, distance learning, double majors, external degree program, honors programs, independent study, internships, part-time degree program, services for LD students.
Student Life *Campus security:* 24-hour emergency response devices.
Standardized Tests *Recommended:* SAT or ACT (for admission).
Costs (2005–06) *Tuition:* $12,120 full-time, $202 per credit hour part-time. *Required fees:* $575 full-time, $30 per course part-time. *Room only:* $3960.
Applying *Options:* common application, electronic application. *Application fee:* $90. *Required:* high school transcript, interview. *Required for some:* essay or personal statement, letters of recommendation.
Director of Admissions Terri D. Thomas, Director of Admissions, Spencerian College, 4627 Dixie Highway, Louisville, KY 40299. *Phone:* 502-447-1000 Ext. 7808. *Toll-free phone:* 800-264-1799.

SPENCERIAN COLLEGE—LEXINGTON

Lexington, Kentucky   **www.spencerian.edu/**

- **Proprietary** 2-year, part of Sullivan Colleges System
- **Urban** campus with easy access to Louisville
- **Coed**

Undergraduates 306 full-time, 70 part-time. Students come from 1 other state, 1 other country, 6% African American, 2% Hispanic American, 0.3% Native American, 0.3% international, 13% live on campus.
Faculty *Student/faculty ratio:* 9:1.
Academics *Calendar:* quarters. *Degree:* certificates, diplomas, and associate. *Special study options:* academic remediation for entering students, cooperative education, independent study, part-time degree program, services for LD students, summer session for credit.
Student Life *Campus security:* 24-hour emergency response devices.
Standardized Tests *Required for some:* CPAt.
Applying *Options:* common application. *Application fee:* $90. *Required:* high school transcript, interview.

Freshmen Application Contact Ms. Georgia Mullins, Admissions Representative, Spencerian College–Lexington, 2355 Harrodsburg Road, Lexington, KY 40504. *Phone:* 800-456-3253 Ext. 8010. *Toll-free phone:* 800-456-3253.

WEST KENTUCKY COMMUNITY AND TECHNICAL COLLEGE
Paducah, Kentucky   **www.westkentucky.kctcs.edu/**

- **State-supported** 2-year, founded 1932, part of University of Kentucky Community College System
- **Small-town** 117-acre campus
- **Coed**

Undergraduates 1,455 full-time, 2,090 part-time. Students come from 12 states and territories, 6% African American, 0.4% Asian American or Pacific Islander, 0.6% Hispanic American, 0.4% Native American.
Faculty *Student/faculty ratio:* 15:1.
Academics *Calendar:* semesters. *Degree:* certificates, diplomas, and associate. *Special study options:* academic remediation for entering students, adult/continuing education programs, cooperative education, honors programs, internships, part-time degree program, services for LD students, summer session for credit.
Student Life *Campus security:* 14-hour patrols by trained security personnel.
Standardized Tests *Required for some:* ACT (for placement).
Costs (2005–06) *Tuition:* $98 per credit hour part-time; state resident $118 per credit hour part-time; nonresident $294 per credit hour part-time.
Financial Aid Of all full-time matriculated undergraduates who enrolled in 2004, 50 Federal Work-Study jobs (averaging $1650).
Applying *Options:* early admission. *Required for some:* high school transcript.
Freshmen Application Contact Mr. Jerry Anderson, Admissions Counselor, West Kentucky Community and Technical College, 4810 Alben Barkley Drive, PO Box 7380, Paducah, KY 42002-7380. *Phone:* 270-554-9200.

LOUISIANA

BATON ROUGE COMMUNITY COLLEGE
Baton Rouge, Louisiana   **www.brcc.cc.la.us/**

- **State-supported** 2-year, founded 1995
- **Coed**

Academics *Calendar:* semesters. *Degree:* associate.
Costs (2005–06) *Tuition:* state resident $1656 full-time; nonresident $4464 full-time. Full-time tuition and fees vary according to course load. Part-time tuition and fees vary according to course load. *Required fees:* $432 full-time. *Payment plans:* installment, deferred payment.
Director of Admissions Ms. Michelle L. Hill, Associate Dean, Enrollment Services, Baton Rouge Community College, 5310 Florida Boulevard, Baton Rouge, LA 70806. *Phone:* 225-216-8700. *Toll-free phone:* 800-601-4558.

BATON ROUGE SCHOOL OF COMPUTERS
Baton Rouge, Louisiana

BLUE CLIFF COLLEGE—LAFAYETTE
Lafayette, Louisiana

BLUE CLIFF COLLEGE—SHREVEPORT
Shreveport, Louisiana

BOSSIER PARISH COMMUNITY COLLEGE
Bossier City, Louisiana   **www.bpcc.edu/**

- **State-supported** 2-year, founded 1967, part of University of Louisiana System
- **Urban** 64-acre campus
- **Coed**

Undergraduates 24% African American, 0.9% Asian American or Pacific Islander, 2% Hispanic American, 0.1% Native American.
Academics *Calendar:* semesters. *Degree:* certificates, diplomas, and associate. *Special study options:* academic remediation for entering students, adult/continuing education programs, advanced placement credit, distance learning, double majors, part-time degree program, services for LD students, summer session for credit.
Student Life *Campus security:* student patrols.
Athletics Member NJCAA.
Standardized Tests *Required:* ACT (for placement).
Costs (2005–06) *Tuition:* state resident $1720 full-time, $254 per credit part-time; nonresident $3860 full-time, $414 per credit part-time. *Required fees:* $448 full-time, $19 per credit part-time, $55 per term part-time.
Financial Aid Of all full-time matriculated undergraduates who enrolled in 2004, 53 Federal Work-Study jobs.
Applying *Options:* early admission. *Application fee:* $15. *Required:* high school transcript.
Director of Admissions Ms. Ann Jempole, Director of Admissions, Bossier Parish Community College, 2719 Airline Drive North, Bossier City, LA 71111-5801. *Phone:* 318-678-6166.

BRYMAN COLLEGE
New Orleans, Louisiana

CAMELOT COLLEGE
Baton Rouge, Louisiana   **www.camelotcollege.com/**

Director of Admissions Rev. Ronny L. Williams, President, Camelot College, 2618 Wooddale Boulevard, Suite A, Baton Rouge, LA 70805. *Phone:* 225-928-3005. *Toll-free phone:* 800-470-3320. *Fax:* 225-927-3794. *E-mail:* home@camelotcollege.com.

CAMERON COLLEGE
New Orleans, Louisiana

CAREER TECHNICAL COLLEGE
Monroe, Louisiana

DELGADO COMMUNITY COLLEGE
New Orleans, Louisiana   www.dcc.edu/

- **State-supported** 2-year, founded 1921, part of Louisiana Community and Technical College System
- **Urban** 57-acre campus
- **Endowment** $1.0 million
- **Coed,** 16,501 undergraduate students, 45% full-time, 70% women, 30% men

Undergraduates 7,376 full-time, 9,125 part-time. Students come from 33 states and territories, 3 other countries, 0.3% are from out of state, 43% African American, 2% Asian American or Pacific Islander, 4% Hispanic American, 0.7% Native American. *Retention:* 53% of 2003 full-time freshmen returned. Freshmen *Admission:* 2,657 applied, 2,657 enrolled.
Faculty *Total:* 833, 43% full-time. *Student/faculty ratio:* 20:1.
Majors Accounting; administrative assistant and secretarial science; applied horticulture; architectural engineering technology; automobile/automotive mechanics technology; biological and physical sciences; biomedical technology; building/property maintenance and management; business administration and management; civil engineering technology; clinical/medical laboratory technology; commercial and advertising art; communication and journalism related; computer engineering technology; computer installation and repair technology; construction management; criminal justice/police science; data processing and data processing technology; dental hygiene; dental laboratory technology; dietetics; drafting and design technology; electrical, electronic and communications engineering technology; electrical/electronics equipment installation and repair; emergency medical technology (EMT paramedic); fine/studio arts; fire protection and safety technology; funeral service and mortuary science; general studies; health information/medical records technology; hospitality administration; institutional food workers; interior architecture; kindergarten/preschool education; machine shop technology; machine tool technology; medical radiologic technology; music; nursing (registered nurse training); occupational safety and health technology; occupational therapist assistant; physical therapist assistant; respiratory care therapy; sign language interpretation and translation.
Academics *Calendar:* semesters. *Degree:* certificates and associate. *Special study options:* academic remediation for entering students, advanced placement credit, cooperative education, distance learning, English as a second language, honors programs, off-campus study, part-time degree program, services for LD students, student-designed majors, summer session for credit. *ROTC:* Army (c), Air Force (c).
Library Moss Memorial Library with 110,000 titles, 1,299 serial subscriptions, an OPAC, a Web page.
Computers on Campus 950 computers available on campus for general student use. A campuswide network can be accessed from off campus. Internet access, at least one staffed computer lab available.
Student Life *Housing:* college housing not available. *Activities and Organizations:* drama/theater group, student-run newspaper, choral group, student government, Circle K, International Club, Phi Theta Kappa, Lambda Phi Nu. *Campus security:* 24-hour patrols, student patrols. *Student services:* health clinic, personal/psychological counseling.
Athletics Member NJCAA. *Intercollegiate sports:* baseball M(s), basketball M(s)/W(s), track and field W. *Intramural sports:* football M, golf M, soccer M, tennis M/W, volleyball M/W.
Standardized Tests *Required for some:* ACT (for placement). *Recommended:* ACT (for placement).
Costs (2005–06) *Tuition:* state resident $1482 full-time, $420 per term part-time; nonresident $4462 full-time, $1275 per term part-time. Part-time tuition and fees vary according to course load. *Required fees:* $362 full-time, $5 per credit part-time, $10 per term part-time. *Payment plan:* deferred payment. *Waivers:* senior citizens and employees or children of employees.

Financial Aid Of all full-time matriculated undergraduates who enrolled in 2004, 308 Federal Work-Study jobs (averaging $1375).
Applying *Application fee:* $15. *Required for some:* high school transcript. *Recommended:* high school transcript, proof of immunization. *Application deadline:* rolling (freshmen), rolling (transfers).
Director of Admissions Ms. Gwen Boute, Director of Admissions, Delgado Community College, 615 City Park Avenue, New Orleans, LA 70119. *Phone:* 504-483-4004. *E-mail:* jbolde@dcc.edu.

DELTA COLLEGE OF ARTS AND TECHNOLOGY
Baton Rouge, Louisiana   www.deltacollege.com/
Director of Admissions Ms. Beulah Laverghe-Brown, Admissions Director, Delta College of Arts and Technology, 7380 Exchange Place, Baton Rouge, LA 70806. *Phone:* 225-928-7770. *Fax:* 225-927-9096.

DELTA SCHOOL OF BUSINESS & TECHNOLOGY
Lake Charles, Louisiana   www.deltatech.edu/
Director of Admissions Mr. Gary J. Holt, President, Delta School of Business & Technology, 517 Broad Street, Lake Charles, LA 70601. *Phone:* 337-439-5765. *Fax:* 337-436-5151. *E-mail:* gholt@deltatech.edu.

ELAINE P. NUNEZ COMMUNITY COLLEGE
Chalmette, Louisiana   www.nunez.edu/
Director of Admissions Ms. Donna Clark, Dean of Student Affairs, Elaine P. Nunez Community College, 3710 Paris Road, Chalmette, LA 70043. *Phone:* 504-680-2457.

GRETNA CAREER COLLEGE
Gretna, Louisiana

HERZING COLLEGE
Kenner, Louisiana   www.herzing.edu/
Director of Admissions Genny Bordelon, Director of Admissions, Herzing College, 2400 Veterans Boulevard, Kenner, LA 70062. *Phone:* 504-733-0074. *Fax:* 504-733-0020.

ITI TECHNICAL COLLEGE
Baton Rouge, Louisiana   www.iticollege.edu/

- **Proprietary** 2-year, founded 1973
- **Suburban** 10-acre campus
- **Coed,** 351 undergraduate students, 64% full-time, 14% women, 86% men
- 85% of applicants were admitted

Undergraduates 226 full-time, 125 part-time. 1% are from out of state, 32% African American, 0.4% Asian American or Pacific Islander, 2% Hispanic American, 0.4% Native American.
Freshmen *Admission:* 435 applied, 371 admitted, 168 enrolled.
Faculty *Total:* 44, 50% full-time, 39% with terminal degrees. *Student/faculty ratio:* 10:1.

Majors Computer technology/computer systems technology; drafting and design technology; electrical, electronic and communications engineering technology; information technology; instrumentation technology; office occupations and clerical services.

Academics *Calendar:* continuous. *Degree:* certificates and associate.

Costs (2005–06) *Tuition:* Cost varies by program; contact school.

Applying *Required:* high school transcript, interview.

Freshmen Application Contact Mr. Joe Martin, President, ITI Technical College, 13944 Airline Highway, Baton Rouge, LA 70817. *Phone:* 225-752-4230 Ext. 213. *Toll-free phone:* 800-467-4484. *Fax:* 225-756-0903. *E-mail:* jmartin@iticollege.edu.

ITT TECHNICAL INSTITUTE

St. Rose, Louisiana
www.itt-tech.edu/

- **Proprietary** primarily 2-year, part of ITT Educational Services, Inc
- **Coed**, 541 undergraduate students

Majors Accounting and business/management; animation, interactive technology, video graphics and special effects; business administration and management; CAD/CADD drafting/design technology; computer and information systems security; computer programming; criminal justice/law enforcement administration; electrical, electronic and communications engineering technology; system, networking, and LAN/WAN management; web/multimedia management and webmaster; web page, digital/multimedia and information resources design.

Academics *Calendar:* quarters. *Degrees:* associate and bachelor's.

Library a Web page.

Computers on Campus Internet access, at least one staffed computer lab available.

Student Life *Housing:* college housing not available.

Standardized Tests *Required:* Wonderlic aptitude test (for admission).

Costs (2005–06) *Tuition:* Please see school catalog for specific information.

Applying *Options:* deferred entrance. *Application fee:* $100. *Required:* high school transcript, interview. *Recommended:* letters of recommendation. *Application deadline:* rolling (freshmen), rolling (transfers). *Notification:* continuous (freshmen).

Freshmen Application Contact Chaleta Cooper, Director of Recruitment, ITT Technical Institute, 140 James Drive East, Saint Rose, LA 70087. *Phone:* 504-463-0338. *Toll-free phone:* 866-463-0338.

LOUISIANA STATE UNIVERSITY AT ALEXANDRIA

Alexandria, Louisiana
www.lsua.edu/

- **State-supported** primarily 2-year, founded 1960, part of Louisiana State University System
- **Rural** 3114-acre campus
- **Endowment** $588,481
- **Coed**, 2,988 undergraduate students, 53% full-time, 74% women, 26% men

Undergraduates 1,572 full-time, 1,416 part-time. Students come from 14 states and territories, 6 other countries, 0.7% are from out of state, 19% African American, 0.8% Asian American or Pacific Islander, 0.8% Hispanic American, 2% Native American, 0.5% international, 9% transferred in.

Freshmen *Admission:* 668 applied, 516 admitted, 516 enrolled. *Test scores:* ACT scores over 18: 61%; ACT scores over 24: 11%.

Faculty *Total:* 180, 58% full-time, 34% with terminal degrees. *Student/faculty ratio:* 16:1.

Majors Behavioral sciences; biology/biological sciences; business administration and management; clinical laboratory science/medical technology; communication/speech communication and rhetoric; criminal justice/police science; early childhood education; elementary education; English; general studies; health services/allied health/health sciences; history; information technology; liberal arts and sciences/liberal studies; mathematics; medical radiologic technology; nursing (registered nurse training); psychology; radiologic technology/science; theater/theater arts management.

Academics *Calendar:* semesters. *Degrees:* certificates, associate, and bachelor's. *Special study options:* academic remediation for entering students, adult/continuing education programs, advanced placement credit, distance learning, part-time degree program, services for LD students, summer session for credit. *ROTC:* Army (c).

Library James C. Bolton Library with 154,935 titles, 354 serial subscriptions, 5,949 audiovisual materials, an OPAC, a Web page.

Computers on Campus 180 computers available on campus for general student use. A campuswide network can be accessed. Internet access, at least one staffed computer lab available.

Student Life *Housing:* college housing not available. *Activities and Organizations:* drama/theater group, student-run newspaper, choral group, Pentecostal Student Fellowship, Baptist Collegiate Ministries, Catholic Student Center, Student Government Association, Gamma Beta Phi, national fraternities. *Campus security:* 24-hour patrols. *Student services:* personal/psychological counseling.

Athletics *Intramural sports:* basketball M/W, football M/W, softball M/W, volleyball M/W.

Standardized Tests *Required:* ACT (for admission).

Costs (2006–07) *Tuition:* area resident $3092 full-time; state resident $128 per credit hour part-time; nonresident $5552 full-time, $231 per credit hour part-time.

Financial Aid Of all full-time matriculated undergraduates who enrolled in 2004, 53 Federal Work-Study jobs (averaging $1226). 76 state and other part-time jobs (averaging $1261).

Applying *Options:* early admission. *Application fee:* $20. *Required:* high school transcript. *Application deadline:* rolling (freshmen), rolling (transfers). *Notification:* continuous (freshmen).

Freshmen Application Contact Ms. Shelly Kieffer, Recruiter/Admissions Counselor, Louisiana State University at Alexandria, 8100 Highway 71 South, Alexandria, LA 71302-9121. *Phone:* 318-473-6508. *Toll-free phone:* 888-473-6417. *Fax:* 318-473-6418. *E-mail:* skieffer@isua.edu.

LOUISIANA STATE UNIVERSITY AT EUNICE

Eunice, Louisiana
www.lsue.edu/

Freshmen Application Contact Ms. Gracie Guillory, Director of Financial Aid, Louisiana State University at Eunice, PO Box 1129, Eunice, LA 70535-1129. *Phone:* 337-550-1282. *Toll-free phone:* 888-367-5783.

LOUISIANA TECHNICAL COLLEGE

Baton Rouge, Louisiana
www.ltc.edu/

- **State-supported** 2-year, founded 1930
- **Endowment** $286,936
- **Coed**, 13,414 undergraduate students, 54% full-time, 48% women, 52% men

Undergraduates 7,264 full-time, 6,150 part-time. 1% are from out of state, 37% African American, 0.9% Asian American or Pacific Islander, 1% Hispanic American, 0.7% Native American.

Freshmen *Admission:* 2,094 applied, 2,094 admitted, 2,094 enrolled.

Faculty *Total:* 1,353, 58% full-time. *Student/faculty ratio:* 10:1.

Majors Accounting technology and bookkeeping; administrative assistant and secretarial science; aircraft powerplant technology; automobile/automotive mechanics technology; child care provision; clinical/medical laboratory assistant; communications systems installation and repair technology; computer installation and repair technology; computer programming (specific applications); computer systems analysis; computer systems networking and telecommunications; criminal justice/safety; culinary arts; data processing and data processing technology; desktop publishing and digital imaging design; drafting and design technology; forestry technology; hotel/motel administration; industrial electronics technology; industrial production technologies related; instrumentation technology; precision systems maintenance and repair technologies related; printing press operation; respiratory therapy technician; surgical technology; survey technology; system administration; technical teacher education.

Academics *Degree:* certificates, diplomas, and associate.

Student Life *Housing:* college housing not available.

Costs (2006–07) *Tuition:* state resident $552 full-time, $23 per credit hour part-time; nonresident $1104 full-time, $46 per credit hour part-time. *Required fees:* $214 full-time, $9 per credit hour part-time, $5 per term part-time.

Applying *Application fee:* $5. *Required:* high school transcript.

Freshmen Application Contact Ms. Janice M. Bolden, Vice Chancellor of Student Affairs, Enrollment Management, and College Registrar, Louisiana Technical College, 150 3rd Street, Baton Rouge, LA 70801. *Toll-free phone:* 800-351-7611.

MEDVANCE INSTITUTE

Baton Rouge, Louisiana   www.medvance.org/

Director of Admissions Ms. Sheri Kirley, Associate Director of Admissions, MedVance Institute, 4173 Government Street, Baton Rouge, LA 70806. *Phone:* 225-248-1015.

METROPOLITAN COMMUNITY COLLEGE

Gretna, Louisiana

REMINGTON COLLEGE–BATON ROUGE CAMPUS

Baton Rouge, Louisiana   www.remingtoncollege.edu/

Director of Admissions Mr. Gregg Falcon, Campus President, Remington College–Baton Rouge Campus, 1900 North Lobdell, Baton Rouge, LA 70806. *Phone:* 225-922-3990. *Fax:* 225-922-9569. *E-mail:* gregg.falcon@remingtoncollege.edu.

REMINGTON COLLEGE–LAFAYETTE CAMPUS

Lafayette, Louisiana   www.remingtoncollege.edu/

- **Proprietary** 2-year, founded 1940, part of Education America Inc
- **Urban** 4-acre campus
- **Coed,** 367 undergraduate students, 100% full-time, 68% women, 32% men

Undergraduates 367 full-time. 50% African American, 2% Asian American or Pacific Islander, 2% Hispanic American, 0.5% Native American. Freshmen *Admission:* 114 applied, 114 admitted.

Faculty *Total:* 28, 57% full-time. *Student/faculty ratio:* 18:1.

Majors Business administration and management; computer programming; computer programming related; computer systems analysis; computer systems networking and telecommunications; computer/technical support; data entry/microcomputer applications related; electrical, electronic and communications engineering technology; legal assistant/paralegal; medical/clinical assistant; web page, digital/multimedia and information resources design.

Academics *Calendar:* continuous. *Degree:* diplomas and associate. *Special study options:* honors programs, independent study.

Library Remington College Library with 15,435 titles, 85 serial subscriptions, 182 audiovisual materials, an OPAC.

Computers on Campus 120 computers available on campus for general student use. A campuswide network can be accessed from off campus. Internet access, at least one staffed computer lab available.

Student Life *Housing:* college housing not available. *Campus security:* 24-hour emergency response devices.

Costs (2006–07) *Tuition:* $12,825 full-time.

Applying *Options:* early admission, deferred entrance. *Application fee:* $50. *Required:* high school transcript, interview.

Freshmen Application Contact Mr. Gary Schwartz, Director of Recruiting, Remington College–Lafayette Campus, 303 Rue Louis XIV, Lafayette, LA 70508. *Phone:* 337-981-9010. *Toll-free phone:* 800-736-2687. *Fax:* 337-983-7130.

REMINGTON COLLEGE–NEW ORLEANS CAMPUS

Metairie, Louisiana   www.remingtoncollege.edu/

Director of Admissions Mr. Roy Kimble, Director of Recruitment, Remington College–New Orleans Campus, 321 Veterans Memorial Boulevard, Metairie, LA 70005. *Phone:* 504-831-8889.

RIVER PARISHES COMMUNITY COLLEGE

Sorrento, Louisiana   rpcc.cc.la.us/

- **State-supported** 2-year, founded 1997
- **Coed**

Academics *Calendar:* semesters. *Degree:* certificates, diplomas, and associate.

Costs (2005–06) *Tuition:* state resident $1458 full-time, $66 per credit hour part-time; nonresident $4174 full-time, $66 per credit hour part-time. *Required fees:* $310 full-time, $40 per term part-time.

Applying *Application fee:* $10.

Director of Admissions Ms. Allison Dauzat, Dean of Students and Enrollment Management, River Parishes Community College, PO Box 310, 7384 John LeBlanc Boulevard, Sorrento, LA 70778. *Phone:* 225-675-8270. *Fax:* 225-675-5478. *E-mail:* adauzat@rpcc.cc.la.us.

SCHOOL OF URBAN MISSIONS–NEW ORLEANS

New Orleans, Louisiana

SOUTHERN UNIVERSITY AT SHREVEPORT

Shreveport, Louisiana   www.susla.edu/

Freshmen Application Contact Ms. Juanita Johnson, Acting Admissions Records Technician, Southern University at Shreveport, 3050 Martin Luther King, Jr. Drive, Shreveport, LA 71107. *Phone:* 318-674-3342. *Toll-free phone:* 800-458-1472 Ext. 342.

MAINE

ANDOVER COLLEGE

Portland, Maine   www.andovercollege.com/

- **Proprietary** 2-year, founded 1966
- **Urban** 2-acre campus
- **Coed**

Associate degrees offered at Portland and Lewiston campuses in twenty-four months or less include accounting, business administration, computer technology, criminal justice, early childhood education, medical assisting, office administration, paralegal studies, and travel and hospitality management. Certificates include early childhood education, medical transcription, office administration, paralegal studies, and travel and hospitality management. Facilities and services include five computer labs, all-digital high-speed Internet access, the Academic Assistance Center, internships, and lifetime placement services.

Undergraduates 490 full-time, 12 part-time. Students come from 4 states and territories, 3 other countries.

Faculty *Student/faculty ratio:* 19:1.

Academics *Calendar:* modular. *Degree:* certificates and associate. *Special study options:* academic remediation for entering students, adult/continuing education programs, cooperative education, independent study, internships, part-time degree program, summer session for credit.

Student Life *Campus security:* 24-hour emergency response devices.

Financial Aid Of all full-time matriculated undergraduates who enrolled in 2004, 25 Federal Work-Study jobs (averaging $3000).

Applying *Options:* common application, early admission, deferred entrance. *Application fee:* $25. *Required:* high school transcript. *Recommended:* interview.
Director of Admissions Mr. David Blessing, Director of Enrollment Management, Andover College, 901 Washington Avenue, Portland, ME 04103-2791. *Phone:* 207-774-6126 Ext. 261. *Toll-free phone:* 800-639-3110 Ext. 240 (in-state); 800-639-3110 Ext. 242 (out-of-state).

BEAL COLLEGE
Bangor, Maine   www.bealcollege.edu/

- **Proprietary** 2-year, founded 1891
- **Small-town** 4-acre campus
- **Coed,** 373 undergraduate students, 64% full-time, 85% women, 15% men

Undergraduates 239 full-time, 134 part-time. Students come from 2 states and territories, 1% African American, 0.8% Hispanic American, 0.8% Native American.
Freshmen *Admission:* 96 enrolled.
Faculty *Total:* 16, 38% full-time. *Student/faculty ratio:* 16:1.
Majors Accounting; administrative assistant and secretarial science; business administration and management; computer and information sciences; criminal justice/law enforcement administration; early childhood education; legal administrative assistant/secretary; medical administrative assistant and medical secretary; medical/clinical assistant; tourism and travel services management.
Academics *Calendar:* modular. *Degree:* certificates, diplomas, and associate. *Special study options:* academic remediation for entering students, accelerated degree program, adult/continuing education programs, advanced placement credit, double majors, internships, part-time degree program, summer session for credit.
Library Beal College Library with 7,275 titles, 100 serial subscriptions, a Web page.
Computers on Campus 85 computers available on campus for general student use. Internet access available.
Student Life *Housing:* college housing not available. *Activities and Organizations:* student-run newspaper, Sophomore Travel Club, Freshman Travel Club, yearbook staff.
Applying *Options:* deferred entrance. *Application fee:* $25. *Required:* high school transcript. *Recommended:* interview. *Application deadline:* rolling (freshmen), rolling (transfers).
Freshmen Application Contact Ms. Susan Palmer, Admissions Assistant, Beal College, 629 Main Street, Bangor, ME 04401. *Phone:* 207-947-4591. *Toll-free phone:* 800-660-7351. *Fax:* 207-947-0208.

CENTRAL MAINE COMMUNITY COLLEGE
Auburn, Maine   www.cmcc.edu/

Freshmen Application Contact Ms. Elizabeth Oken, Director of Admissions, Central Maine Community College, 1250 Turner Street, Auburn, ME 04210-6498. *Phone:* 207-755-5334 Ext. 334. *Toll-free phone:* 800-891-2002. *E-mail:* admissions@cmtc.mtcs.tec.me.us.

CENTRAL MAINE MEDICAL CENTER SCHOOL OF NURSING
Lewiston, Maine   www.cmmcson.edu/

- **Independent** 2-year, founded 1891
- **Urban** campus
- **Coed, primarily women**

Undergraduates 22 full-time, 92 part-time. Students come from 2 states and territories, 1% are from out of state, 0.9% Native American, 2% live on campus.
Faculty *Student/faculty ratio:* 5:1.
Academics *Calendar:* semesters. *Degree:* certificates and associate. *Special study options:* advanced placement credit, off-campus study.
Student Life *Campus security:* 24-hour emergency response devices and patrols, late-night transport/escort service, controlled dormitory access.
Standardized Tests *Required:* SAT (for admission).
Costs (2005–06) *Tuition:* $2898 full-time, $138 per credit part-time. *Required fees:* $1205 full-time, $20 per term part-time. *Room only:* $1500.

Applying *Application fee:* $40. *Required:* essay or personal statement, high school transcript, 2 letters of recommendation.
Freshmen Application Contact Mrs. Kathleen C. Jacques, Registrar, Central Maine Medical Center School of Nursing, 70 Middle Street, Lewiston, ME 04240-0305. *Phone:* 207-795-2858.

EASTERN MAINE COMMUNITY COLLEGE
Bangor, Maine   www.emcc.edu/

- **State-supported** 2-year, founded 1966, part of Maine Community College System
- **Small-town** 72-acre campus
- **Endowment** $1.5 million
- **Coed**

Undergraduates 744 full-time, 1,046 part-time. Students come from 2 states and territories, 1% are from out of state, 0.1% African American, 0.3% Asian American or Pacific Islander, 0.1% Hispanic American, 1% Native American, 20% live on campus.
Faculty *Student/faculty ratio:* 11:1.
Academics *Calendar:* semesters. *Degree:* certificates, diplomas, and associate. *Special study options:* academic remediation for entering students, adult/continuing education programs, advanced placement credit, part-time degree program, summer session for credit.
Student Life *Campus security:* late-night transport/escort service, controlled dormitory access.
Athletics Member NSCAA.
Standardized Tests *Required:* ACCUPLACER (for admission). *Required for some:* SAT (for admission).
Financial Aid Of all full-time matriculated undergraduates who enrolled in 2004, 100 Federal Work-Study jobs (averaging $1000).
Applying *Options:* deferred entrance. *Application fee:* $20. *Required:* essay or personal statement, high school transcript, letters of recommendation. *Required for some:* interview. *Recommended:* minimum 2.0 GPA.
Director of Admissions Ms. Veronica Delcort, Director of Admissions, Eastern Maine Community College, 354 Hogan Road, Bangor, ME 04401. *Phone:* 207-974-4680. *Toll-free phone:* 800-286-9357.

KENNEBEC VALLEY COMMUNITY COLLEGE
Fairfield, Maine   www.kvcc.me.edu/

- **State-supported** 2-year, founded 1970, part of Maine Community College System
- **Small-town** 58-acre campus
- **Endowment** $229,488
- **Coed,** 1,782 undergraduate students, 29% full-time, 69% women, 31% men

Undergraduates 523 full-time, 1,259 part-time. Students come from 4 states and territories, 0.2% African American, 0.5% Asian American or Pacific Islander, 2% Hispanic American, 0.7% Native American.
Freshmen *Admission:* 476 applied, 340 admitted, 303 enrolled.
Faculty *Total:* 216, 19% full-time. *Student/faculty ratio:* 22:1.
Majors Accounting; administrative assistant and secretarial science; biology/biological sciences; business administration and management; child care and support services management; child care provision; communications systems installation and repair technology; computer/information technology services administration related; computer installation and repair technology; computer management; computer programming related; computer science; computer software and media applications related; computer systems networking and telecommunications; data modeling/warehousing and database administration; drafting and design technology; education; electrical/electronics equipment installation and repair; emergency medical technology (EMT paramedic); executive assistant/executive secretary; general studies; health information/medical records administration; industrial electronics technology; industrial mechanics and maintenance technology; legal administrative assistant/secretary; liberal arts and sciences/liberal studies; machine tool technology; marketing/marketing management; medical/clinical assistant; nursing (registered nurse training); occupational therapist assistant; physical therapist assistant; respiratory care therapy; sales, distribution and marketing; web/multimedia management and webmaster; web page, digital/multimedia and information resources design; wood science and wood products/pulp and paper technology.

Kennebec Valley Community College (continued)

Academics *Calendar:* semesters. *Degree:* certificates, diplomas, and associate. *Special study options:* academic remediation for entering students, accelerated degree program, adult/continuing education programs, advanced placement credit, distance learning, external degree program, independent study, internships, part-time degree program, services for LD students, summer session for credit.

Library Lunder Library with 19,629 titles, 25,734 serial subscriptions, 1,373 audiovisual materials, an OPAC, a Web page.

Computers on Campus 250 computers available on campus for general student use. A campuswide network can be accessed from off campus. Internet access, at least one staffed computer lab available.

Student Life *Housing:* college housing not available. *Activities and Organizations:* Vocational Industrial Clubs of America (VICA) Skills USA, Student Senate, Phi Theta Kappa, Glee Club. *Campus security:* Evening security patrol. *Student services:* personal/psychological counseling.

Athletics *Intramural sports:* basketball M/W, bowling M/W, ultimate Frisbee M/W, volleyball M/W.

Standardized Tests *Required for some:* nursing exam, HOBET, ACCUPLACER. *Recommended:* SAT or ACT (for admission).

Costs (2006–07) *Tuition:* state resident $2220 full-time, $74 per credit part-time; nonresident $4650 full-time, $155 per credit part-time. *Required fees:* $600 full-time.

Financial Aid Of all full-time matriculated undergraduates who enrolled in 2004, 34 Federal Work-Study jobs (averaging $1207).

Applying *Options:* electronic application, deferred entrance. *Application fee:* $20. *Required:* essay or personal statement, high school transcript. *Required for some:* letters of recommendation, interview. *Application deadline:* rolling (freshmen), rolling (transfers). *Notification:* continuous (freshmen).

Freshmen Application Contact Mr. Jim Bourgoin, Director of Recruitment, Kennebec Valley Community College, 92 Western Avenue, Fairfield, ME 04937-1367. *Phone:* 207-453-5035. *Toll-free phone:* 800-528-5882 Ext. 5035. *Fax:* 207-453-5011. *E-mail:* admissions@kvcc.me.edu.

NORTHERN MAINE COMMUNITY COLLEGE

Presque Isle, Maine　　　　　www.nmtc.net/

- **State-related** 2-year, founded 1963, part of Maine Technical College System
- **Small-town** 86-acre campus
- **Coed,** 921 undergraduate students, 66% full-time, 53% women, 47% men

Undergraduates 605 full-time, 316 part-time. Students come from 5 states and territories, 1 other country, 4% are from out of state, 0.5% African American, 0.4% Asian American or Pacific Islander, 0.8% Hispanic American, 4% Native American, 4% international, 28% live on campus.
Freshmen *Admission:* 759 applied, 397 admitted, 222 enrolled.

Faculty *Total:* 87, 51% full-time.

Majors Accounting; administrative assistant and secretarial science; automobile/automotive mechanics technology; business administration and management; carpentry; computer engineering technology; computer programming; data processing and data processing technology; drafting and design technology; electrical, electronic and communications engineering technology; emergency medical technology (EMT paramedic); heating, air conditioning, ventilation and refrigeration maintenance technology; heavy equipment maintenance technology; industrial arts; instrumentation technology; kindergarten/preschool education; legal administrative assistant/secretary; medical administrative assistant and medical secretary; nursing (registered nurse training); pipefitting and sprinkler fitting.

Academics *Calendar:* semesters. *Degree:* certificates, diplomas, and associate. *Special study options:* academic remediation for entering students, adult/continuing education programs, advanced placement credit, cooperative education, double majors, independent study, internships, off-campus study, part-time degree program, services for LD students, summer session for credit.

Library Northern Maine Technical College Library with 11,200 titles, 233 serial subscriptions, 250 audiovisual materials, an OPAC, a Web page.

Computers on Campus A campuswide network can be accessed from student residence rooms and from off campus. Internet access, at least one staffed computer lab available.

Student Life *Housing Options:* coed. *Campus security:* 24-hour patrols. *Student services:* health clinic.

Athletics Member NSCAA. *Intercollegiate sports:* basketball M/W, cross-country running M/W, golf M/W, ice hockey M/W, soccer M/W. *Intramural*

sports: archery M/W, basketball M/W, football M/W, golf M, racquetball M/W, soccer M, softball M/W, table tennis M/W, tennis M/W, volleyball M/W, weight lifting M/W.

Standardized Tests *Required:* ACCUPLACER (for admission).

Costs (2006–07) *Tuition:* area resident $2390 full-time, $78 per credit hour part-time; state resident $115 per credit hour part-time; nonresident $4770 full-time, $159 per credit hour part-time. *Room and board:* $4040.

Financial Aid Of all full-time matriculated undergraduates who enrolled in 2004, 74 Federal Work-Study jobs (averaging $1950).

Applying *Options:* common application, electronic application, early admission. *Application fee:* $20. *Required:* high school transcript, interview. *Required for some:* letters of recommendation, Net Test/RN. *Recommended:* essay or personal statement, minimum 2.0 GPA. *Application deadline:* rolling (freshmen). *Notification:* continuous (freshmen).

Freshmen Application Contact Ms. Nancy Gagnon, Admissions Secretary, Northern Maine Community College, 33 Edgemont Drive, Presque Isle, ME 04769-2016. *Phone:* 207-768-2785. *Toll-free phone:* 800-535-6682. *Fax:* 207-768-2848. *E-mail:* ngagnon@nmcc.edu.

SOUTHERN MAINE COMMUNITY COLLEGE

South Portland, Maine　　　　　www.smccme.edu/

- **State-supported** 2-year, founded 1946, part of Maine Community College System
- **Small-town** 65-acre campus
- **Endowment** $513,726
- **Coed**

Undergraduates 2,135 full-time, 1,968 part-time. Students come from 9 states and territories, 6% are from out of state, 3% African American, 1% Asian American or Pacific Islander, 1% Hispanic American, 1% Native American, 0.5% international, 10% live on campus.

Faculty *Student/faculty ratio:* 18:1.

Academics *Calendar:* semesters. *Degree:* certificates, diplomas, and associate. *Special study options:* academic remediation for entering students, advanced placement credit, cooperative education, distance learning, double majors, English as a second language, internships, off-campus study, part-time degree program, services for LD students, study abroad, summer session for credit.

Student Life *Campus security:* 24-hour emergency response devices, student patrols, late-night transport/escort service.

Athletics Member NSCAA.

Standardized Tests *Required for some:* ACCUPLACER. *Recommended:* SAT (for placement).

Costs (2005–06) *Tuition:* state resident $2220 full-time; nonresident $4650 full-time. *Room and board:* $5824; room only: $2678.

Financial Aid Of all full-time matriculated undergraduates who enrolled in 2004, 130 Federal Work-Study jobs (averaging $1500).

Applying *Options:* electronic application. *Application fee:* $20. *Required:* high school transcript.

Director of Admissions David Tracy, Assistant Dean for Enrollment Services, Southern Maine Community College, Admissions, 2 Fort Road, South Portland, ME 04106. *Phone:* 207-741-5664. *Toll-free phone:* 877-282-2182.

WASHINGTON COUNTY COMMUNITY COLLEGE

Calais, Maine　　　　　www.wccc.me.edu/

Director of Admissions Mr. Kent Lyons, Admissions Counselor, Washington County Community College, RR#1, Box 22C River Road, Calais, ME 04619. *Phone:* 207-454-1000. *Toll-free phone:* 800-210-6932 Ext. 41049.

YORK COUNTY COMMUNITY COLLEGE

Wells, Maine　　　　　www.yccc.edu/

Director of Admissions Ms. Leisa Collins, Director of Admissions, York County Community College, 112 College Drive, Wells, ME 04090. *Phone:* 207-646-9282 Ext. 305. *Toll-free phone:* 800-580-3820. *E-mail:* admissions@yctc.net.

MARYLAND

ALLEGANY COLLEGE OF MARYLAND
Cumberland, Maryland   www.allegany.edu/

- **State and locally supported** 2-year, founded 1961, part of Maryland State Community Colleges System
- **Small-town** 311-acre campus
- **Endowment** $5.2 million
- **Coed**, 3,666 undergraduate students, 57% full-time, 69% women, 31% men

Undergraduates 2,073 full-time, 1,593 part-time. Students come from 21 states and territories, 42% are from out of state, 8% African American, 0.5% Asian American or Pacific Islander, 0.8% Hispanic American, 0.2% Native American.

Freshmen *Admission:* 2,098 applied, 2,089 admitted, 865 enrolled. *Test scores:* SAT verbal scores over 500: 23%; SAT math scores over 500: 26%; ACT scores over 18: 68%; SAT verbal scores over 600: 3%; SAT math scores over 600: 6%; ACT scores over 24: 6%.

Faculty *Total:* 230, 48% full-time, 11% with terminal degrees. *Student/faculty ratio:* 17:1.

Majors Accounting technology and bookkeeping; administrative assistant and secretarial science; automobile/automotive mechanics technology; business administration and management; clinical/medical laboratory assistant; clinical/medical laboratory technology; communications technology; computer engineering technology; cosmetology and personal grooming arts related; criminal justice/police science; culinary arts; dental hygiene; forest/forest resources management; health professions related; hospitality administration; legal assistant/paralegal; liberal arts and sciences/liberal studies; management information systems; marketing/marketing management; medical radiologic technology; nursing (registered nurse training); occupational therapist assistant; occupational therapy; physical therapist assistant; psychiatric/mental health services technology; respiratory care therapy.

Academics *Calendar:* semesters. *Degree:* certificates and associate. *Special study options:* academic remediation for entering students, adult/continuing education programs, advanced placement credit, distance learning, double majors, honors programs, independent study, internships, part-time degree program, summer session for credit. *ROTC:* Army (c).

Library Allegany College of Maryland Library with 86,636 titles, 313 serial subscriptions, 3,395 audiovisual materials, an OPAC, a Web page.

Computers on Campus 700 computers available on campus for general student use. A campuswide network can be accessed from off campus. Internet access, online (class) registration, at least one staffed computer lab available.

Student Life *Housing:* college housing not available. *Activities and Organizations:* choral group, SAHDA, Honors Club, EMT Club, Forestry Club. *Campus security:* 24-hour emergency response devices and patrols, late-night transport/escort service. *Student services:* personal/psychological counseling, women's center.

Athletics Member NJCAA. *Intercollegiate sports:* baseball M, basketball M/W, soccer M/W, softball W, tennis M/W, volleyball W.

Standardized Tests *Required for some:* ACT (for admission).

Costs (2005–06) *Tuition:* area resident $2700 full-time, $90 per credit part-time; state resident $5160 full-time, $172 per credit part-time; nonresident $6060 full-time, $202 per credit part-time. Full-time tuition and fees vary according to course load and location. Part-time tuition and fees vary according to course load and location. *Required fees:* $194 full-time, $8 per credit part-time, $41 per term part-time. *Waivers:* employees or children of employees.

Applying *Options:* electronic application, early admission. *Required:* high school transcript. *Application deadline:* rolling (freshmen), rolling (transfers).

Freshmen Application Contact Ms. Cathy Nolan, Director of Admissions and Registration, Allegany College of Maryland, 12401 Willowbrook Road, SE, Cumberland, MD 21502. *Phone:* 301-784-5000 Ext. 5202. *Fax:* 301-784-5220. *E-mail:* cnolan@allegany.edu.

ANNE ARUNDEL COMMUNITY COLLEGE
Arnold, Maryland   www.aacc.edu/

- **State and locally supported** 2-year, founded 1961
- **Suburban** 230-acre campus with easy access to Baltimore and Washington, DC
- **Endowment** $2.4 million
- **Coed**

Undergraduates 4,780 full-time, 9,510 part-time. Students come from 12 states and territories, 19 other countries, 0.8% are from out of state, 12% African American, 3% Asian American or Pacific Islander, 2% Hispanic American, 0.6% Native American, 0.7% international, 19% transferred in. *Retention:* 58% of 2003 full-time freshmen returned.

Faculty *Student/faculty ratio:* 18:1.

Academics *Calendar:* semesters. *Degree:* certificates and associate. *Special study options:* academic remediation for entering students, accelerated degree program, adult/continuing education programs, advanced placement credit, cooperative education, distance learning, English as a second language, freshman honors college, honors programs, independent study, internships, part-time degree program, services for LD students, summer session for credit. *ROTC:* Army (c), Air Force (c).

Student Life *Campus security:* 24-hour emergency response devices and patrols, student patrols, late-night transport/escort service.

Athletics Member NJCAA.

Standardized Tests *Recommended:* SAT or ACT (for placement).

Costs (2005–06) *Tuition:* area resident $1992 full-time, $83 per credit hour part-time; state resident $3816 full-time, $159 per credit hour part-time; nonresident $6768 full-time, $282 per credit hour part-time. Full-time tuition and fees vary according to course load. Part-time tuition and fees vary according to course load. *Required fees:* $232 full-time, $8 per credit hour part-time, $20 per term part-time.

Financial Aid Of all full-time matriculated undergraduates who enrolled in 2004, 104 Federal Work-Study jobs (averaging $1900). 55 state and other part-time jobs (averaging $1740).

Applying *Options:* early admission, deferred entrance.

Director of Admissions Mr. Thomas McGinn, Director of Enrollment Development and Admissions, Anne Arundel Community College, 101 College Parkway, Arnold, MD 21012-1895. *Phone:* 410-777-2240.

BALTIMORE CITY COMMUNITY COLLEGE
Baltimore, Maryland   www.bccc.state.md.us/

- **State-supported** 2-year, founded 1947
- **Urban** 19-acre campus
- **Endowment** $139,215
- **Coed**

Undergraduates Students come from 4 states and territories, 1% are from out of state.

Faculty *Student/faculty ratio:* 17:1.

Academics *Calendar:* semesters. *Degree:* certificates and associate. *Special study options:* academic remediation for entering students, adult/continuing education programs, advanced placement credit, cooperative education, distance learning, double majors, English as a second language, honors programs, internships, part-time degree program, services for LD students, study abroad, summer session for credit.

Standardized Tests *Recommended:* SAT Subject Tests (for placement).

Financial Aid Of all full-time matriculated undergraduates who enrolled in 2004, 331 Federal Work-Study jobs (averaging $1879).

Applying *Options:* common application, early admission, deferred entrance. *Application fee:* $10. *Required:* high school transcript. *Recommended:* interview.

Director of Admissions Mrs. Scheherazade Forman, Admissions Coordinator, Baltimore City Community College, 2901 Liberty Heights Avenue, Baltimore, MD 21215. *Phone:* 410-462-8300. *Toll-free phone:* 888-203-1261 Ext. 8300.

BALTIMORE INTERNATIONAL COLLEGE
Baltimore, Maryland   **www.bic.edu**

- **Independent** primarily 2-year, founded 1972
- **Urban** 6-acre campus with easy access to Washington, DC
- **Endowment** $83,144
- **Coed,** 516 undergraduate students, 94% full-time, 53% women, 47% men

Undergraduates 486 full-time, 30 part-time. Students come from 19 states and territories, 5 other countries, 12% are from out of state, 52% African American, 3% Asian American or Pacific Islander, 2% Hispanic American, 0.4% Native American, 1% international, 21% transferred in, 24% live on campus. *Retention:* 39% of 2003 full-time freshmen returned.
Freshmen *Admission:* 135 enrolled. *Average high school GPA:* 2.50. *Test scores:* SAT verbal scores over 700: 1%; SAT math scores over 700: 1%.
Faculty *Total:* 32, 44% full-time, 72% with terminal degrees.
Majors Baking and pastry arts; culinary arts; hospitality administration; restaurant, culinary, and catering management.
Academics *Calendar:* semesters. *Degrees:* certificates, associate, bachelor's, and master's. *Special study options:* academic remediation for entering students, accelerated degree program, adult/continuing education programs, advanced placement credit, cooperative education, double majors, honors programs, internships, off-campus study, study abroad.
Library George A. Piendak Library plus 1 other with 13,000 titles, 200 serial subscriptions, 1,000 audiovisual materials.
Computers on Campus 35 computers available on campus for general student use. A campuswide network can be accessed from off campus. Internet access, at least one staffed computer lab available.
Student Life *Housing:* on-campus residence required for freshman year. *Options:* coed. Campus housing is university owned. Freshman campus housing is guaranteed. *Activities and Organizations:* student-run newspaper, American Culinary Federation, Beta Iota Kappa. *Campus security:* late-night transport/escort service, controlled dormitory access. *Student services:* health clinic, personal/psychological counseling.
Standardized Tests *Required for some:* SAT or ACT (for admission), CPat or TOEFL.
Costs (2005–06) *Comprehensive fee:* $20,313 includes full-time tuition ($14,751), mandatory fees ($107), and room and board ($5455). *Room and board:* college room only: $3255. Room and board charges vary according to housing facility. *Payment plans:* tuition prepayment, installment. *Waivers:* employees or children of employees.
Applying *Options:* common application, electronic application, early action, deferred entrance. *Application fee:* $35. *Required:* high school transcript. *Required for some:* essay or personal statement. *Recommended:* letters of recommendation, interview. *Application deadline:* rolling (freshmen), rolling (transfers). *Notification:* continuous until 8/15 (freshmen).
Freshmen Application Contact Marti Hackett, Director of Admissions, Baltimore International College, Commerce Exchange, 17 Commerce Street, Baltimore, MD 21202-3230. *Phone:* 410-752-4710 Ext. 239. *Toll-free phone:* 800-624-9926 Ext. 120. *Fax:* 410-752-3730. *E-mail:* admissions@bic.edu.

► **See page 486 for the College Close-Up.**

CARROLL COMMUNITY COLLEGE
Westminster, Maryland   **www.carrollcc.edu/**

- **State and locally supported** 2-year, founded 1993, part of Maryland Higher Education Commission
- **Small-town** 80-acre campus with easy access to Baltimore
- **Endowment** $1.2 million
- **Coed,** 3,115 undergraduate students, 43% full-time, 64% women, 36% men

Undergraduates 1,327 full-time, 1,788 part-time. Students come from 3 states and territories, 4 other countries, 1% are from out of state, 3% African American, 2% Asian American or Pacific Islander, 2% Hispanic American, 0.4% Native American, 0.2% international.
Freshmen *Admission:* 711 applied, 711 admitted, 711 enrolled.
Faculty *Total:* 210, 29% full-time, 4% with terminal degrees. *Student/faculty ratio:* 17:1.
Majors Accounting; business administration and management; computer and information sciences; computer graphics; data processing and data processing technology; education (multiple levels); general studies; health science; human services; kindergarten/preschool education; liberal arts and sciences/liberal studies; mechanical design technology; music; nursing (registered nurse training); physical therapist assistant.

Academics *Calendar:* semesters plus winter session. *Degree:* certificates and associate. *Special study options:* academic remediation for entering students, advanced placement credit, distance learning, English as a second language, honors programs, independent study, internships, part-time degree program, services for LD students, summer session for credit.
Library Random House Learning Resources Center with 39,187 titles, 318 serial subscriptions, 3,151 audiovisual materials, an OPAC, a Web page.
Computers on Campus 674 computers available on campus for general student use. A campuswide network can be accessed. Internet access, at least one staffed computer lab available.
Student Life *Housing:* college housing not available. *Activities and Organizations:* drama/theater group, student-run newspaper, choral group, Student Government Organization, Carroll Community Chorus, Programming Board. *Campus security:* late-night transport/escort service. *Student services:* personal/psychological counseling.
Costs (2005–06) *Tuition:* area resident $3234 full-time, $92 per credit part-time; state resident $4476 full-time, $128 per credit part-time; nonresident $6788 full-time, $195 per credit part-time. *Payment plan:* installment. *Waivers:* senior citizens and employees or children of employees.
Financial Aid Of all full-time matriculated undergraduates who enrolled in 2004, 22 Federal Work-Study jobs (averaging $1772).
Applying *Options:* early admission. *Required:* high school transcript. *Application deadline:* rolling (freshmen), rolling (transfers). *Notification:* continuous (freshmen).
Freshmen Application Contact Ms. Candace Edwards, Coordinator of Admissions, Carroll Community College, 1601 Washington Road, Westminster, MD 21157. *Phone:* 410-386-8430. *Toll-free phone:* 888-221-9748. *Fax:* 410-386-8446. *E-mail:* cedwards@carrollcc.edu.

CECIL COMMUNITY COLLEGE
North East, Maryland   **www.cecilcc.edu/**

- **County-supported** 2-year, founded 1968
- **Small-town** 100-acre campus with easy access to Baltimore
- **Coed,** 1,916 undergraduate students, 36% full-time, 65% women, 35% men

Undergraduates 687 full-time, 1,229 part-time. Students come from 5 states and territories, 4 other countries, 9% are from out of state, 7% African American, 1% Asian American or Pacific Islander, 2% Hispanic American, 0.5% Native American, 0.3% international, 0.6% transferred in.
Freshmen *Admission:* 481 applied, 481 admitted, 475 enrolled.
Faculty *Total:* 192, 21% full-time, 7% with terminal degrees.
Majors Accounting; administrative assistant and secretarial science; air traffic control; art; artificial intelligence and robotics; biology/biological sciences; business administration and management; carpentry; computer engineering technology; computer graphics; computer programming; construction engineering technology; criminal justice/law enforcement administration; data processing and data processing technology; education; education (K-12); electrical, electronic and communications engineering technology; elementary education; general studies; hydrology and water resources science; information science/studies; information technology; kindergarten/preschool education; liberal arts and sciences/liberal studies; marketing/marketing management; mathematics; medical laboratory technology; nursing (registered nurse training); photography; physical sciences; physics; pipefitting and sprinkler fitting; transportation and materials moving related; welding technology.
Academics *Calendar:* semesters. *Degree:* certificates and associate. *Special study options:* academic remediation for entering students, adult/continuing education programs, advanced placement credit, cooperative education, distance learning, double majors, English as a second language, independent study, internships, part-time degree program, services for LD students, summer session for credit.
Library Cecil County Veteran's Memorial Library with 35,575 titles, 192 serial subscriptions, 1,148 audiovisual materials, an OPAC, a Web page.
Computers on Campus 69 computers available on campus for general student use. A campuswide network can be accessed from off campus. Internet access, online (class) registration, at least one staffed computer lab available.
Student Life *Housing:* college housing not available. *Activities and Organizations:* drama/theater group, student-run newspaper, student government, Nontraditional Student Organization, Student Nurses Association, student newspaper, national fraternities. *Campus security:* 24-hour emergency response devices, late-night transport/escort service. *Student services:* personal/psychological counseling, women's center.
Athletics Member NJCAA. *Intercollegiate sports:* baseball M(s), basketball M(s)/W(s), cheerleading W, softball W, volleyball W(s). *Intramural sports:* basketball M/W, tennis M/W.

Costs (2006–07) *Tuition:* area resident $2550 full-time, $85 per credit hour part-time; state resident $5250 full-time, $175 per credit hour part-time; nonresident $6600 full-time, $220 per credit hour part-time.

Financial Aid Of all full-time matriculated undergraduates who enrolled in 2004, 59 Federal Work-Study jobs (averaging $1421).

Applying *Options:* common application, electronic application, early admission, deferred entrance. *Required:* high school transcript. *Application deadline:* rolling (freshmen), rolling (transfers). *Notification:* continuous (freshmen).

Director of Admissions Dr. Diane Lane, Cecil Community College, One Seahawk Drive, North East, MD 21901. *Phone:* 410-287-1002. *Fax:* 410-287-1001. *E-mail:* dlane@cecilcc.edu.

CHESAPEAKE COLLEGE
Wye Mills, Maryland   www.chesapeake.edu/

Director of Admissions Ms. Kathy Petrichenko, Director of Admissions, Chesapeake College, PO Box 8, Wye Mills, MD 21679. *Phone:* 410-822-5400 Ext. 257.

COLLEGE OF SOUTHERN MARYLAND
La Plata, Maryland   www.csmd.edu/

- **State and locally supported** 2-year, founded 1958
- **Rural** 175-acre campus with easy access to Washington, DC
- **Coed,** 7,546 undergraduate students, 34% full-time, 66% women, 34% men

Undergraduates 2,599 full-time, 4,947 part-time. Students come from 10 states and territories, 1% are from out of state, 19% African American, 3% Asian American or Pacific Islander, 3% Hispanic American, 0.8% Native American, 45% transferred in.
Freshmen *Admission:* 2,731 applied, 1,491 admitted, 1,077 enrolled. *Average high school GPA:* 2.86.

Faculty *Total:* 433, 28% full-time. *Student/faculty ratio:* 9:1.

Majors Accounting; agribusiness; art; biology/biological sciences; biotechnology; business administration and management; communication/speech communication and rhetoric; computer programming; dramatic/theater arts; early childhood education; education; electrical, electronic and communications engineering technology; elementary education; emergency medical technology (EMT paramedic); English; fire protection and safety technology; history; human services; information science/studies; journalism; legal assistant/paralegal; liberal arts and sciences/liberal studies; massage therapy; music; nursing (licensed practical/vocational nurse training); nursing (registered nurse training); physical therapist assistant; social sciences.

Academics *Calendar:* semesters. *Degree:* certificates and associate. *Special study options:* academic remediation for entering students, accelerated degree program, adult/continuing education programs, advanced placement credit, cooperative education, distance learning, honors programs, internships, part-time degree program, services for LD students, study abroad, summer session for credit.

Library College of Southern Maryland Library with 44,896 titles, 166 serial subscriptions, 14,013 audiovisual materials, an OPAC, a Web page.

Computers on Campus 130 computers available on campus for general student use. A campuswide network can be accessed from off campus. Internet access, online (class) registration, at least one staffed computer lab available.

Student Life *Housing:* college housing not available. *Activities and Organizations:* drama/theater group, student-run newspaper, choral group, Spanish Club, Nursing Student Association, Science Club, Black Student Union, BACCHUS. *Campus security:* 24-hour emergency response devices and patrols. *Student services:* personal/psychological counseling, women's center.

Athletics Member NJCAA. *Intercollegiate sports:* baseball M, basketball M/W, golf M/W, soccer M/W, softball W, tennis M/W, volleyball W.

Costs (2005–06) *Tuition:* area resident $2650 full-time, $110 per credit part-time; state resident $4608 full-time, $192 per credit part-time; nonresident $5789 full-time, $241 per credit part-time. Full-time tuition and fees vary according to course load. Part-time tuition and fees vary according to course load. *Required fees:* $552 full-time. *Payment plan:* deferred payment. *Waivers:* senior citizens and employees or children of employees.

Financial Aid Of all full-time matriculated undergraduates who enrolled in 2004, 25 Federal Work-Study jobs (averaging $1200).

Applying *Options:* electronic application, early admission, deferred entrance. *Recommended:* high school transcript. *Application deadline:* rolling (freshmen), rolling (transfers). *Notification:* continuous (freshmen).

Freshmen Application Contact Ed Gunther, Information Center Coordinator, College of Southern Maryland, PO Box 910, La Plata, MD 20646-0910. *Phone:* 301-934-7520 Ext. 7764. *Toll-free phone:* 800-933-9177. *Fax:* 301-934-7698. *E-mail:* info@csmd.edu.

THE COMMUNITY COLLEGE OF BALTIMORE COUNTY
Baltimore, Maryland   www.ccbcmd.edu/

- **County-supported** 2-year, founded 1957
- **Suburban** 350-acre campus
- **Coed,** 19,622 undergraduate students, 36% full-time, 63% women, 37% men

Undergraduates 7,049 full-time, 12,573 part-time. 30% African American, 5% Asian American or Pacific Islander, 2% Hispanic American, 0.4% Native American, 3% international.
Freshmen *Admission:* 12,614 enrolled.

Faculty *Total:* 1,086, 33% full-time, 8% with terminal degrees. *Student/faculty ratio:* 20:1.

Academics *Calendar:* semesters. *Degree:* certificates and associate.

Student Life *Activities and Organizations:* student-run newspaper.

Costs (2005–06) *Tuition:* area resident $2610 full-time, $87 per hour part-time; state resident $4500 full-time, $150 per hour part-time; nonresident $6150 full-time, $205 per hour part-time. *Required fees:* $316 full-time, $316 per term part-time.

Freshmen Application Contact Diane Drake, Director of Admissions, The Community College of Baltimore County, 800 South Rolling Road, Baltimore, MD 21228-5381. *Phone:* 410-455-4392. *Fax:* 410-719-6546.

FREDERICK COMMUNITY COLLEGE
Frederick, Maryland   www.frederick.edu/

- **State and locally supported** 2-year, founded 1957
- **Small-town** 125-acre campus with easy access to Baltimore and Washington, DC
- **Endowment** $4.0 million
- **Coed,** 4,822 undergraduate students, 38% full-time, 62% women, 38% men

Undergraduates 1,855 full-time, 2,967 part-time. Students come from 9 states and territories, 1% are from out of state, 9% African American, 3% Asian American or Pacific Islander, 4% Hispanic American, 0.6% Native American, 56% transferred in.
Freshmen *Admission:* 1,547 enrolled.

Faculty *Total:* 378, 21% full-time.

Majors Accounting; art; biology/biological sciences; business administration and management; chemistry; child development; computer engineering technology; computer science; construction management; criminal justice/law enforcement administration; data processing and data processing technology; drafting and design technology; education; electrical, electronic and communications engineering technology; elementary education; emergency medical technology (EMT paramedic); engineering; English; finance; fire science; general studies; human services; information technology; international business/trade/commerce; kindergarten/preschool education; legal administrative assistant/secretary; legal assistant/paralegal; liberal arts and sciences/liberal studies; marketing/marketing management; mass communication/media; mathematics; mathematics teacher education; medical administrative assistant and medical secretary; medical laboratory technology; music teacher education; nuclear medical technology; nursing (registered nurse training); physical education teaching and coaching; physical sciences; political science and government; psychology; respiratory care therapy; Spanish language teacher education; surgical technology.

Academics *Calendar:* semesters. *Degree:* certificates and associate. *Special study options:* academic remediation for entering students, adult/continuing education programs, advanced placement credit, cooperative education, distance learning, external degree program, honors programs, independent study, off-campus study, part-time degree program, services for LD students, study abroad, summer session for credit. *ROTC:* Army (c).

Library FCC Library with 40,000 titles, 5,150 serial subscriptions, 1,400 audiovisual materials, an OPAC, a Web page.

Computers on Campus A campuswide network can be accessed from off campus. Internet access, online (class) registration, at least one staffed computer lab available.

Student Life *Housing:* college housing not available. *Activities and Organizations:* drama/theater group, student-run newspaper. *Campus security:* 24-hour

Frederick Community College (continued)

emergency response devices and patrols. *Student services:* personal/psychological counseling, women's center.

Athletics Member NJCAA. *Intercollegiate sports:* baseball M, basketball M/W, golf M/W, soccer M/W, softball W, volleyball W.

Costs (2006–07) *Tuition:* area resident $2088 full-time, $87 per credit hour part-time; state resident $4560 full-time, $190 per credit hour part-time; nonresident $6216 full-time, $259 per credit hour part-time. *Required fees:* $300 full-time, $11 per credit hour part-time, $37 per year part-time.

Financial Aid Of all full-time matriculated undergraduates who enrolled in 2004, 25 Federal Work-Study jobs (averaging $1368). 14 state and other part-time jobs (averaging $2715).

Applying *Options:* early admission, deferred entrance. *Application deadlines:* 9/1 (freshmen), 9/1 (transfers). *Notification:* continuous (freshmen).

Freshmen Application Contact Ms. Kathy Frawley, Associate Vice President, Registrar, Frederick Community College, Welcome and Registration Center, 7932 Opossumtown Pike, Frederick, MD 21702. *Phone:* 301-846-2401. *Fax:* 301-624-2799.

GARRETT COLLEGE
McHenry, Maryland   www.garrettcollege.edu/

- **State and locally supported** 2-year, founded 1966
- **Rural** 62-acre campus
- **Coed**

Undergraduates 360 full-time, 253 part-time. Students come from 12 states and territories, 1 other country, 20% are from out of state, 9% African American, 2% Hispanic American, 0.8% Native American, 2% international, 48% transferred in, 8% live on campus.

Faculty *Student/faculty ratio:* 13:1.

Academics *Calendar:* semesters. *Degree:* certificates and associate. *Special study options:* academic remediation for entering students, adult/continuing education programs, advanced placement credit, distance learning, double majors, external degree program, honors programs, independent study, internships, part-time degree program, services for LD students, summer session for credit.

Athletics Member NJCAA.

Standardized Tests *Recommended:* SAT or ACT (for placement).

Costs (2005–06) *Tuition:* area resident $2340 full-time, $78 per credit hour part-time; state resident $5460 full-time, $182 per credit hour part-time; nonresident $6540 full-time, $218 per credit hour part-time. *Required fees:* $570 full-time, $18 per credit hour part-time, $15 per semester part-time. *Room and board:* $4970; room only: $2550.

Financial Aid Of all full-time matriculated undergraduates who enrolled in 2004, 55 Federal Work-Study jobs (averaging $1018). 75 state and other part-time jobs (averaging $954).

Applying *Options:* common application, early admission, deferred entrance. *Required:* high school transcript, interview.

Freshmen Application Contact Robin Swearengen, Coordinator of Student Assistance Center, Garrett College, 687 Mosser Road, McHenry, MD 21541. *Phone:* 301-387-3044.

HAGERSTOWN BUSINESS COLLEGE
Hagerstown, Maryland   www.hagerstownbusinesscol.org/

- **Proprietary** 2-year, founded 1938, part of Kaplan Higher Education Corporation
- **Small-town** 8-acre campus with easy access to Baltimore and Washington, DC
- **Coed,** 932 undergraduate students, 83% full-time, 74% women, 26% men

Undergraduates 770 full-time, 162 part-time. 64% are from out of state, 10% African American, 1% Asian American or Pacific Islander, 2% Hispanic American, 0.1% Native American, 3% live on campus.

Faculty *Total:* 65, 31% full-time, 5% with terminal degrees. *Student/faculty ratio:* 18:1.

Majors Accounting; administrative assistant and secretarial science; business administration and management; computer and information systems security; criminal justice/law enforcement administration; data processing and data processing technology; health information/medical records administration; information science/studies; legal administrative assistant/secretary; legal assistant/paralegal; marketing/marketing management; medical administrative assistant and medical secretary; medical/clinical assistant.

Academics *Calendar:* quarters. *Degree:* certificates and associate. *Special study options:* academic remediation for entering students, accelerated degree program, adult/continuing education programs, advanced placement credit, internships, summer session for credit.

Library HBC library plus 1 other with 8,000 titles, 70 serial subscriptions, 400 audiovisual materials.

Computers on Campus 207 computers available on campus for general student use. A campuswide network can be accessed. Internet access, at least one staffed computer lab available.

Student Life *Housing Options:* coed. Campus housing is university owned. *Activities and Organizations:* Phi Beta Lambda, Association of Legal Students, Health Information Technology Students Organization, Student Government Association, Caduceus Club. *Campus security:* 24-hour emergency response devices. *Student services:* personal/psychological counseling.

Costs (2005–06) *Tuition:* Contact college for current tuition, fees, and room and board expenses.

Financial Aid Of all full-time matriculated undergraduates who enrolled in 2004, 21 Federal Work-Study jobs (averaging $1343).

Applying *Options:* early admission, deferred entrance. *Required:* high school transcript, interview. *Application deadline:* rolling (freshmen), rolling (transfers).

Freshmen Application Contact Mr. Jim Klein, Director of Admissions, Hagerstown Business College, 18618 Crestwood Drive, Hagerstown, MD 21742-2797. *Phone:* 301-739-2670. *Toll-free phone:* 800-422-2670. *Fax:* 301-791-7661. *E-mail:* info@hagerstownbusinesscol.org.

HAGERSTOWN COMMUNITY COLLEGE
Hagerstown, Maryland   www.hagerstowncc.edu/

- **State and locally supported** 2-year, founded 1946
- **Suburban** 187-acre campus with easy access to Baltimore and Washington, DC
- **Endowment** $5.7 million
- **Coed,** 3,521 undergraduate students, 34% full-time, 63% women, 37% men

Undergraduates 1,204 full-time, 2,317 part-time. Students come from 6 states and territories, 1 other country, 23% are from out of state, 7% African American, 1% Asian American or Pacific Islander, 2% Hispanic American, 0.5% Native American, 5% transferred in. *Retention:* 62% of 2003 full-time freshmen returned. Freshmen *Admission:* 1,373 applied, 1,373 admitted, 874 enrolled.

Faculty *Total:* 227, 30% full-time, 6% with terminal degrees. *Student/faculty ratio:* 14:1.

Majors Accounting technology and bookkeeping; animation, interactive technology, video graphics and special effects; business administration and management; business/commerce; child care and support services management; commercial and advertising art; computer and information sciences; criminal justice/police science; early childhood education; education; electromechanical technology; elementary education; emergency medical technology (EMT paramedic); engineering; health information/medical records administration; industrial technology; liberal arts and sciences and humanities related; liberal arts and sciences/liberal studies; management information systems; mechanical engineering/mechanical technology; medical radiologic technology; nursing (registered nurse training); psychiatric/mental health services technology; web page, digital/multimedia and information resources design.

Academics *Calendar:* semesters. *Degree:* certificates and associate. *Special study options:* academic remediation for entering students, accelerated degree program, adult/continuing education programs, advanced placement credit, cooperative education, distance learning, English as a second language, honors programs, independent study, internships, off-campus study, part-time degree program, services for LD students, student-designed majors, summer session for credit.

Library William Brish Library with 45,705 titles, 228 serial subscriptions, 1,585 audiovisual materials, an OPAC, a Web page.

Computers on Campus 500 computers available on campus for general student use. A campuswide network can be accessed from off campus. Internet access, online (class) registration, at least one staffed computer lab available. Computer purchase or lease plan available.

Student Life *Housing:* college housing not available. *Activities and Organizations:* drama/theater group, student-run newspaper, choral group, Phi Theta Kappa, Robinwood Players, Association of Nursing Students, Theta Lambda Upsilon, Art Club. *Campus security:* 24-hour patrols. *Student services:* health clinic, personal/psychological counseling.

Athletics Member NJCAA. *Intercollegiate sports:* baseball M(s), basketball M(s)/W(s), cross-country running M(s)/W(s), golf M/W, soccer M(s)/W, softball W(s), track and field M(s)/W(s), volleyball W(s). *Intramural sports:* cheerleading M/W, golf M/W, lacrosse M/W, table tennis M/W, tennis M/W.

Costs (2005–06) *Tuition:* area resident $2670 full-time, $89 per credit hour part-time; state resident $4260 full-time, $142 per credit hour part-time; nonresident $5580 full-time, $186 per credit hour part-time. Full-time tuition and fees vary according to course load. Part-time tuition and fees vary according to course load. *Required fees:* $280 full-time, $8 per credit hour part-time, $20 per semester part-time. *Payment plan:* installment. *Waivers:* senior citizens and employees or children of employees.

Financial Aid Of all full-time matriculated undergraduates who enrolled in 2004, 27 Federal Work-Study jobs (averaging $2955).

Applying *Options:* common application, electronic application, early admission, deferred entrance. *Required for some:* high school transcript, ACT composite score of 21, 1 lab chemistry and algebra for admission into nursing and radiography programs. *Application deadline:* rolling (freshmen), rolling (transfers). *Notification:* continuous (freshmen).

Freshmen Application Contact Dr. Daniel Bock, Assistant Director, Admissions, Records and Registration, Hagerstown Community College, 11400 Robinwood Drive, Hagerstown, MD 21742-6590. *Phone:* 301-790-2800 Ext. 335. *Fax:* 301-791-4165. *E-mail:* bockd@hagerstowncc.edu.

HARFORD COMMUNITY COLLEGE
Bel Air, Maryland
www.harford.edu/

- **State and locally supported** 2-year, founded 1957
- **Small-town** 331-acre campus with easy access to Baltimore
- **Endowment** $4.1 million
- **Coed**

Undergraduates 2,157 full-time, 3,335 part-time. Students come from 10 states and territories, 17 other countries, 1% are from out of state, 11% African American, 2% Asian American or Pacific Islander, 3% Hispanic American, 0.4% Native American, 0.4% international, 60% transferred in. *Retention:* 66% of 2003 full-time freshmen returned.

Faculty *Student/faculty ratio:* 20:1.

Academics *Calendar:* semesters. *Degree:* certificates, diplomas, and associate. *Special study options:* academic remediation for entering students, adult/continuing education programs, advanced placement credit, cooperative education, distance learning, double majors, English as a second language, independent study, internships, part-time degree program, services for LD students, student-designed majors, summer session for credit.

Student Life *Campus security:* 24-hour patrols, late-night transport/escort service.

Athletics Member NJCAA.

Standardized Tests *Required for some:* ACCUPLACER.

Costs (2005–06) *Tuition:* area resident $2250 full-time, $75 per credit part-time; state resident $4500 full-time, $150 per credit part-time; nonresident $6750 full-time, $225 per credit part-time. Full-time tuition and fees vary according to course load. Part-time tuition and fees vary according to course load. *Required fees:* $225 full-time, $8 per credit part-time. *Payment plans:* installment, deferred payment.

Financial Aid Of all full-time matriculated undergraduates who enrolled in 2004, 55 Federal Work-Study jobs (averaging $1800).

Applying *Options:* electronic application.

Freshmen Application Contact Ms. Donna Strasavich, Enrollment Specialist, Harford Community College, 401 Thomas Run Road, Bel Air, MD 21015-1698. *Phone:* 410-836-4311.

HOWARD COMMUNITY COLLEGE
Columbia, Maryland
www.howardcc.edu/

- **State and locally supported** 2-year, founded 1966
- **Suburban** 122-acre campus with easy access to Baltimore and Washington, DC
- **Endowment** $2.0 million
- **Coed,** 6,842 undergraduate students, 39% full-time, 59% women, 41% men

Undergraduates 2,636 full-time, 4,206 part-time. Students come from 4 states and territories, 1% are from out of state, 21% African American, 11% Asian American or Pacific Islander, 4% Hispanic American, 0.5% Native American.

Faculty *Total:* 487, 24% full-time. *Student/faculty ratio:* 18:1.

Majors Accounting; administrative assistant and secretarial science; applied art; architecture; art; biological and physical sciences; biomedical technology; biotechnology; business administration and management; cardiovascular technology; child development; clinical laboratory science/medical technology; computer and information sciences related; computer graphics; computer/information technology services administration related; computer science; computer systems networking and telecommunications; consumer merchandising/retailing management; criminal justice/law enforcement administration; data entry/microcomputer applications; dramatic/theater arts; electrical, electronic and communications engineering technology; elementary education; emergency medical technology (EMT paramedic); engineering; environmental studies; fashion merchandising; financial planning and services; general studies; health teacher education; information science/studies; information technology; kindergarten/preschool education; legal administrative assistant/secretary; liberal arts and sciences/liberal studies; medical administrative assistant and medical secretary; music; nuclear medical technology; nursing (licensed practical/vocational nurse training); nursing (registered nurse training); office management; ophthalmic/optometric services; photography; physical sciences; pre-dentistry studies; pre-medical studies; pre-pharmacy studies; pre-veterinary studies; psychology; secondary education; social sciences; sport and fitness administration/management; substance abuse/addiction counseling; telecommunications; theater design and technology.

Academics *Calendar:* semesters. *Degree:* certificates and associate. *Special study options:* academic remediation for entering students, adult/continuing education programs, advanced placement credit, cooperative education, distance learning, double majors, English as a second language, honors programs, off-campus study, part-time degree program, services for LD students, study abroad, summer session for credit.

Library Howard Community College Library with 40,380 titles, 1,201 serial subscriptions, 6,253 audiovisual materials, an OPAC, a Web page.

Computers on Campus 750 computers available on campus for general student use. Internet access, online (class) registration, at least one staffed computer lab available.

Student Life *Housing:* college housing not available. *Activities and Organizations:* drama/theater group, student-run newspaper, choral group, Secretarial Club, Nursing Club, Black Leadership Organization, student newspaper, Student Government Association. *Campus security:* 24-hour emergency response devices and patrols, late-night transport/escort service. *Student services:* personal/psychological counseling.

Athletics Member NJCAA. *Intercollegiate sports:* basketball M/W, cross-country running M/W, lacrosse M, soccer M/W, tennis M/W, track and field M/W, volleyball W. *Intramural sports:* baseball M, basketball M/W, lacrosse M, softball W.

Standardized Tests *Required for some:* SAT or ACT (for admission).

Costs (2006–07) *Tuition:* area resident $3300 full-time, $110 per credit part-time; state resident $5790 full-time, $193 per credit part-time; nonresident $7140 full-time, $238 per credit part-time. *Required fees:* $553 full-time, $18 per credit part-time.

Applying *Options:* electronic application, early admission, deferred entrance. *Application fee:* $25. *Required for some:* essay or personal statement, high school transcript, 2 letters of recommendation. *Application deadline:* rolling (freshmen), rolling (transfers). *Notification:* continuous (freshmen).

Freshmen Application Contact Ms. Christy Thomson, Assistant Director of Admissions, Howard Community College, 10901 Little Patuxent Parkway, Columbia, MD 21044-3197. *Phone:* 410-772-4856. *Fax:* 410-772-4589. *E-mail:* hsinfo@howardcc.edu.

ITT TECHNICAL INSTITUTE
Owings Mills, Maryland
www.itt-tech.edu/

- **primarily 2-year**
- **Coed**

Majors CAD/CADD drafting/design technology; computer and information systems security; computer programming; computer systems networking and telecommunications; e-commerce; electrical, electronic and communications engineering technology; system, networking, and LAN/WAN management; web/multimedia management and webmaster; web page, digital/multimedia and information resources design.

Academics *Calendar:* quarters. *Degrees:* associate and bachelor's.

Standardized Tests *Required:* Wonderlic aptitude test (for admission).

Costs (2005–06) *Tuition:* Please see school catalog for specific information.

Applying *Application fee:* $100. *Required:* high school transcript, interview. *Recommended:* letters of recommendation. *Application deadline:* rolling (freshmen), rolling (transfers). *Notification:* continuous (freshmen).

Freshmen Application Contact Mr. Tony Owens, Director of Recruitment, ITT Technical Institute, 11301 Red Run Boulevard, Owings Mills, MD 21117. *Phone:* 443-394-7115.

MONTGOMERY COLLEGE

Rockville, Maryland   www.montgomerycollege.org/

Director of Admissions Mr. Sherman Helberg, Acting Director of Admissions and Enrollment, Montgomery College, 51 Mannakee Street, Rockville, MD 20850. *Phone:* 301-279-5034.

PRINCE GEORGE'S COMMUNITY COLLEGE

Largo, Maryland   www.pgcc.edu/

Director of Admissions Ms. Vera Bagley, Director of Admissions and Records, Prince George's Community College, 301 Largo Road, Largo, MD 20774-2199. *Phone:* 301-322-0801.

TESST COLLEGE OF TECHNOLOGY

Baltimore, Maryland   www.tesst.com/

Director of Admissions Ms. Susan Sherwood, Director, TESST College of Technology, 1520 South Caton Avenue, Baltimore, MD 21227-1063. *Phone:* 410-644-6400. *Fax:* 410-644-6481. *E-mail:* ssherwood@tesst.com.

TESST COLLEGE OF TECHNOLOGY

Beltsville, Maryland   www.tesst.com/

Director of Admissions Ms. Mary Colling, Director of Admissions, TESST College of Technology, 4600 Powder Mill Road, Beltsville, MD 20705. *Phone:* 301-937-8448. *Fax:* 301-937-5327. *E-mail:* mcolling@tesst.com.

TESST COLLEGE OF TECHNOLOGY

Towson, Maryland   www.tesst.com/

- **Proprietary** 2-year, founded 1992
- **Coed**

Majors CAD/CADD drafting/design technology; computer maintenance technology; computer systems networking and telecommunications; criminal justice/safety; data entry/microcomputer applications; electrician; graphic design; heating, air conditioning and refrigeration technology; medical/clinical assistant; pharmacy technician; telecommunications technology.

Academics *Calendar:* quarters. *Degree:* associate.

Student Life *Activities and Organizations:* student-run newspaper.

Applying *Required:* high school transcript, interview.

Freshmen Application Contact Ms. Diane McRae, President, TESST College of Technology, 803 Glen Eagles Court, Towson, MD 21286. *Phone:* 410-296-5350. *Toll-free phone:* 800-48-TESST. *Fax:* 410-296-5356. *E-mail:* dmcrae@tesst.com.

WOR-WIC COMMUNITY COLLEGE

Salisbury, Maryland   www.worwic.edu/

- **State and locally supported** 2-year, founded 1976, part of Maryland State Community Colleges System
- **Small-town** 202-acre campus
- **Endowment** $4.0 million
- **Coed,** 3,043 undergraduate students, 32% full-time, 67% women, 33% men

Undergraduates 970 full-time, 2,073 part-time. Students come from 15 states and territories, 2% are from out of state, 25% African American, 2% Asian American or Pacific Islander, 2% Hispanic American, 0.3% Native American, 8% transferred in.

Freshmen *Admission:* 1,075 applied, 1,075 admitted, 678 enrolled.

Faculty *Total:* 168, 33% full-time, 11% with terminal degrees. *Student/faculty ratio:* 20:1.

Majors Accounting technology and bookkeeping; administrative assistant and secretarial science; business administration and management; business/commerce; child care and support services management; computer and information sciences; computer systems analysis; criminal justice/police science; electrical, electronic and communications engineering technology; elementary education; emergency medical technology (EMT paramedic); engineering technologies related; hospitality administration; liberal arts and sciences and humanities related; medical radiologic technology; nursing (registered nurse training); substance abuse/addiction counseling.

Academics *Calendar:* semesters. *Degree:* certificates and associate. *Special study options:* academic remediation for entering students, accelerated degree program, adult/continuing education programs, advanced placement credit, distance learning, double majors, English as a second language, honors programs, independent study, internships, part-time degree program, services for LD students, summer session for credit.

Library Patricia M. Hazel Media Center plus 2 others with 25 titles, 37 serial subscriptions, 272 audiovisual materials, a Web page.

Computers on Campus 478 computers available on campus for general student use. A campuswide network can be accessed from off campus. Internet access, at least one staffed computer lab available.

Student Life *Housing:* college housing not available. *Activities and Organizations:* drama/theater group, student-run newspaper, choral group, Student Government Association, Arts Club, Bioneer Club, Future Educators of America Club, student newspaper. *Campus security:* 24-hour emergency response devices, late-night transport/escort service, patrols by trained security personnel 9 a.m. to midnight. *Student services:* personal/psychological counseling.

Standardized Tests *Required for some:* ACT (for admission).

Costs (2006–07) *Tuition:* area resident $2250 full-time, $75 per credit hour part-time; state resident $5700 full-time, $190 per credit hour part-time; nonresident $6630 full-time, $221 per credit hour part-time. *Required fees:* $86 full-time, $2 per credit hour part-time, $13 per term part-time.

Applying *Options:* early admission. *Recommended:* high school transcript. *Application deadline:* rolling (freshmen), rolling (transfers).

Freshmen Application Contact Mr. Richard Webster, Director of Admissions, Wor-Wic Community College, 32000 Campus Drive, Salisbury, MD 21804. *Phone:* 410-334-2895. *Fax:* 410-334-2954. *E-mail:* admissions@worwic.edu.

MASSACHUSETTS

BAY STATE COLLEGE

Boston, Massachusetts   www.baystate.edu

- **Independent** primarily 2-year, founded 1946
- **Urban** campus
- **Coed,** 757 undergraduate students, 69% full-time, 78% women, 22% men

Undergraduates 522 full-time, 235 part-time. Students come from 11 states and territories, 11 other countries, 11% are from out of state, 18% African American, 8% Asian American or Pacific Islander, 10% Hispanic American, 0.9% international, 21% live on campus. *Retention:* 50% of 2003 full-time freshmen returned.

Freshmen *Admission:* 1,405 applied, 1,119 admitted. *Average high school GPA:* 2.00.

Faculty *Total:* 66, 29% full-time. *Student/faculty ratio:* 13:1.

Majors Accounting; administrative assistant and secretarial science; business administration and management; consumer merchandising/retailing management; criminal justice/law enforcement administration; early childhood education; fashion/apparel design; fashion merchandising; general studies; hospitality administration; legal administrative assistant/secretary; liberal arts and sciences/liberal studies; marketing/marketing management; medical administrative assistant and medical secretary; medical/clinical assistant; physical therapy; recording arts technology; tourism and travel services management.

Academics *Calendar:* semesters. *Degrees:* associate and bachelor's. *Special study options:* academic remediation for entering students, adult/continuing education programs, advanced placement credit, cooperative education, English as a second language, independent study, internships, part-time degree program.

Library Bay State College Library with 4,490 titles, 262 serial subscriptions, 471 audiovisual materials, an OPAC.

Computers on Campus 55 computers available on campus for general student use. A campuswide network can be accessed. At least one staffed computer lab available.

Student Life *Housing Options:* coed, women-only. Campus housing is provided by a third party. *Activities and Organizations:* Activities Club, Hospitality Travel Association, Fashion Club, Early Childhood Education Club, Student Medical Assisting Society. *Campus security:* late-night transport/escort service, controlled dormitory access, 14-hour patrols by trained security personnel. *Student services:* personal/psychological counseling.

Costs (2006–07) *Comprehensive fee:* $26,325 includes full-time tuition ($15,900), mandatory fees ($350), and room and board ($10,075). Part-time tuition: $1530 per course.

Financial Aid Of all full-time matriculated undergraduates who enrolled in 2004, 20 Federal Work-Study jobs (averaging $2600).

Applying *Options:* common application, early admission. *Application fee:* $40. *Required:* essay or personal statement, high school transcript. *Recommended:* minimum 2.0 GPA, interview. *Application deadline:* rolling (freshmen), rolling (transfers).

Freshmen Application Contact Ms. Pamela DellaPorta, Director of Admissions, Bay State College, 122 Commonwealth Avenue, Boston, MA 02116. *Phone:* 617-236-8006. *Toll-free phone:* 800-81-LEARN. *Fax:* 617-536-1735. *E-mail:* admissions@baystate.edu.

► **See page 488 for the College Close-Up.**

BENJAMIN FRANKLIN INSTITUTE OF TECHNOLOGY
Boston, Massachusetts   www.bfit.edu/

- **Independent** primarily 2-year, founded 1908
- **Urban** 3-acre campus
- **Endowment** $8.0 million
- **Coed, primarily men,** 386 undergraduate students

Undergraduates Students come from 12 states and territories, 38% African American, 12% Asian American or Pacific Islander, 13% Hispanic American, 0.3% Native American, 0.3% international.
Freshmen *Admission:* 668 applied, 608 admitted. *Average high school GPA:* 2.70.

Faculty *Total:* 42, 52% full-time. *Student/faculty ratio:* 11:1.

Majors Architectural engineering technology; automobile/automotive mechanics technology; automotive engineering technology; computer engineering technology; computer science; drafting and design technology; electrical and power transmission installation; electrical, electronic and communications engineering technology; engineering technology; heating, air conditioning and refrigeration technology; mechanical engineering/mechanical technology.

Academics *Calendar:* semesters. *Degrees:* certificates, associate, and bachelor's. *Special study options:* academic remediation for entering students, adult/continuing education programs, advanced placement credit, English as a second language, internships, off-campus study, part-time degree program, summer session for credit.

Library Lufkin Memorial Library with 10,000 titles, 90 serial subscriptions, an OPAC.

Computers on Campus 100 computers available on campus for general student use. A campuswide network can be accessed. Internet access, at least one staffed computer lab available.

Student Life *Housing:* college housing not available. *Activities and Organizations:* Society of Manufacturing Engineers, student government, Yearbook Committee, athletics, Institute of Electrical and electronic Engineers (IEEE). *Campus security:* 24-hour emergency response devices, student patrols. *Student services:* personal/psychological counseling.

Athletics Member NJCAA. *Intramural sports:* basketball M, soccer M.

Standardized Tests *Recommended:* SAT or ACT (for admission).

Costs (2006–07) *Tuition:* $12,750 full-time, $531 per credit part-time.

Applying *Options:* common application, electronic application, deferred entrance. *Application fee:* $20. *Required:* high school transcript. *Recommended:* essay or personal statement, minimum 2.0 GPA, letters of recommendation, interview. *Application deadline:* 8/15 (freshmen), rolling (transfers).

Freshmen Application Contact Ms. Andrea Dawes, Associate Director of Admissions, Benjamin Franklin Institute of Technology, 41 Berkeley Street, Boston, MA 02116-6296. *Phone:* 617-423-4630 Ext. 190. *Fax:* 617-482-3706. *E-mail:* adawes@bfit.edu.

► **See page 490 for the College Close-Up.**

BERKSHIRE COMMUNITY COLLEGE
Pittsfield, Massachusetts   www.berkshirecc.edu/

- **State-supported** 2-year, founded 1960, part of Massachusetts Public Higher Education System
- **Suburban** 100-acre campus
- **Endowment** $3.0 million
- **Coed,** 2,328 undergraduate students, 40% full-time, 63% women, 37% men

Undergraduates 923 full-time, 1,405 part-time. Students come from 4 states and territories, 14 other countries, 4% are from out of state, 4% African American, 2% Asian American or Pacific Islander, 3% Hispanic American, 0.7% Native American, 2% international, 13% transferred in.
Freshmen *Admission:* 399 applied, 399 admitted, 399 enrolled.

Faculty *Total:* 170, 32% full-time, 50% with terminal degrees. *Student/faculty ratio:* 14:1.

Majors Banking and financial support services; biology/biological sciences; business administration and management; business automation/technology/data entry; business/commerce; computer and information sciences; criminal justice/safety; dramatic/theater arts; early childhood education; electrical, electronic and communications engineering technology; engineering; engineering technology; environmental science; fire science; health professions related; hospitality administration; human services; international/global studies; liberal arts and sciences/liberal studies; music; nursing (registered nurse training); peace studies and conflict resolution; physical therapist assistant; respiratory care therapy; social work; surgical technology; system, networking, and LAN/WAN management; visual and performing arts.

Academics *Calendar:* semesters. *Degree:* certificates and associate. *Special study options:* academic remediation for entering students, adult/continuing education programs, advanced placement credit, distance learning, double majors, English as a second language, honors programs, independent study, internships, off-campus study, part-time degree program, services for LD students, student-designed majors, summer session for credit.

Library Jonathan Edwards Library plus 1 other with 74,271 titles, 319 serial subscriptions, 3,247 audiovisual materials, an OPAC, a Web page.

Computers on Campus 354 computers available on campus for general student use. A campuswide network can be accessed from off campus. Internet access, at least one staffed computer lab available. Computer purchase or lease plan available.

Student Life *Housing:* college housing not available. *Activities and Organizations:* drama/theater group, choral group, Mass PIRG, Student Nurse Organization, Student Senate, Diversity Club, LPN Organization. *Campus security:* 24-hour emergency response devices and patrols. *Student services:* personal/psychological counseling.

Athletics Member NJCAA.

Costs (2006–07) *Tuition:* state resident $780 full-time, $26 per credit part-time; nonresident $7800 full-time, $260 per credit part-time. *Required fees:* $2820 full-time, $94 per credit part-time.

Financial Aid Of all full-time matriculated undergraduates who enrolled in 2004, 72 Federal Work-Study jobs (averaging $1600).

Applying *Options:* common application, deferred entrance. *Application fee:* $10. *Required:* high school transcript. *Recommended:* interview. *Application deadline:* rolling (freshmen), rolling (transfers). *Notification:* continuous (freshmen).

Freshmen Application Contact Ms. Margo J. Handschu, Coordinator of Admissions, Berkshire Community College, 1350 West Street, Pittsfield, MA 01201-5786. *Phone:* 413-499-4660 Ext. 425. *Toll-free phone:* 800-816-1233 Ext. 242. *Fax:* 413-496-9511. *E-mail:* mhandsch@berkshirecc.edu.

BRISTOL COMMUNITY COLLEGE
Fall River, Massachusetts   www.bristol.mass.edu/

- **State-supported** 2-year, founded 1965
- **Urban** 105-acre campus with easy access to Boston
- **Endowment** $2.9 million
- **Coed,** 6,873 undergraduate students, 45% full-time, 63% women, 37% men

Undergraduates 3,097 full-time, 3,776 part-time. Students come from 7 states and territories, 25 other countries, 7% are from out of state, 5% African American, 2% Asian American or Pacific Islander, 3% Hispanic American, 0.6% Native American, 0.2% international, 5% transferred in.
Freshmen *Admission:* 3,684 applied, 2,961 admitted, 1,491 enrolled.

Faculty *Total:* 792, 40% full-time. *Student/faculty ratio:* 19:1.

Bristol Community College (continued)

Majors Accounting; administrative assistant and secretarial science; audiology and hearing sciences; business administration and management; business automation/technology/data entry; child care/guidance; civil engineering related; civil engineering technology; clinical/medical laboratory technology; communication/ speech communication and rhetoric; computer and information sciences; computer and information sciences related; computer programming; computer science; criminal justice/safety; culinary arts; data processing and data processing technology; dental hygiene; dramatic/theater arts and stagecraft related; early childhood education; electrical, electronic and communications engineering technology; elementary education; engineering related; engineering science; engineering technologies related; environmental engineering technology; environmental/ environmental health engineering; environmental science; finance and financial management services related; fine/studio arts; fire science; general studies; graphic design; health information/medical records technology; humanities; human services; information science/studies; information technology; legal administrative assistant/secretary; liberal arts and sciences/liberal studies; management information systems; marketing/marketing management; medical administrative assistant and medical secretary; nursing (registered nurse training); occupational therapist assistant; pre-engineering; retail management; web/multimedia management and webmaster.

Academics *Calendar:* semesters. *Degree:* certificates and associate. *Special study options:* academic remediation for entering students, adult/continuing education programs, cooperative education, distance learning, English as a second language, honors programs, independent study, internships, off-campus study, part-time degree program, services for LD students, student-designed majors, summer session for credit.

Library Learning Resources Center with 65,000 titles, 380 serial subscriptions, an OPAC, a Web page.

Computers on Campus 150 computers available on campus for general student use. A campuswide network can be accessed from off campus. Internet access, at least one staffed computer lab available.

Student Life *Housing:* college housing not available. *Activities and Organizations:* drama/theater group, student-run newspaper, International Club, MASS/ PIRG WaterWatch, Criminal Justice Society, Society for Students in Free Enterprise, Portuguese Club. *Campus security:* 24-hour emergency response devices and patrols, student patrols, late-night transport/escort service. *Student services:* health clinic, personal/psychological counseling, women's center.

Costs (2006–07) *Tuition:* state resident $576 full-time, $24 per credit part-time; nonresident $5520 full-time, $230 per credit part-time. *Required fees:* $2544 full-time, $99 per credit part-time, $30 per term part-time.

Financial Aid Of all full-time matriculated undergraduates who enrolled in 2004, 205 Federal Work-Study jobs (averaging $1627). 65 state and other part-time jobs (averaging $1478).

Applying *Options:* common application. *Application fee:* $10. *Required:* high school transcript. *Notification:* continuous (freshmen).

Freshmen Application Contact Mr. Rodney Clark, Director of Admissions, Bristol Community College, 777 Elsbree Street, Hudnall Administration Building, Fall River, MA 02720. *Phone:* 508-678-2811 Ext. 2177. *Fax:* 508-730-3265. *E-mail:* rclark@bristol.mass.edu.

BUNKER HILL COMMUNITY COLLEGE
Boston, Massachusetts   www.bhcc.mass.edu/

- **State-supported** 2-year, founded 1973
- **Urban** 21-acre campus
- **Endowment** $2.1 million
- **Coed,** 7,837 undergraduate students, 30% full-time, 60% women, 40% men

Undergraduates 2,388 full-time, 5,449 part-time. Students come from 18 states and territories, 93 other countries, 1% are from out of state, 29% African American, 14% Asian American or Pacific Islander, 14% Hispanic American, 0.8% Native American, 6% international, 3% transferred in.
Freshmen *Admission:* 3,697 applied, 2,559 admitted, 1,356 enrolled.

Faculty *Total:* 448, 27% full-time. *Student/faculty ratio:* 19:1.

Majors Accounting; art; business administration and management; cardiovascular technology; chemistry; communication/speech communication and rhetoric; computer and information sciences and support services related; computer programming; computer programming (specific applications); computer science; computer systems networking and telecommunications; criminal justice/law enforcement administration; culinary arts; data entry/microcomputer applications; design and visual communications; dramatic/theater arts; early childhood education; education; electrical/electronics maintenance and repair technology related; English; finance; fire protection and safety technology; general studies; health information/medical records administration; history; hospitality administration; hotel/motel administration; human services; international business/trade/ commerce; mass communication/media; mathematics; medical radiologic tech-

nology; nursing (registered nurse training); operations management; physics; psychology; sociology; tourism and travel services management; web page, digital/multimedia and information resources design.

Academics *Calendar:* semesters. *Degree:* certificates and associate. *Special study options:* academic remediation for entering students, advanced placement credit, cooperative education, distance learning, English as a second language, external degree program, honors programs, independent study, internships, part-time degree program, services for LD students, study abroad, summer session for credit.

Library Bunker Hill Community College Library with 65,953 titles, 330 serial subscriptions, 934 audiovisual materials, an OPAC, a Web page.

Computers on Campus 585 computers available on campus for general student use. A campuswide network can be accessed from off campus that provide access to online advising; academic support services. Internet access, online (class) registration, at least one staffed computer lab available.

Student Life *Housing:* college housing not available. *Activities and Organizations:* drama/theater group, student-run radio station, choral group, African-American Cultural Society, Asian-Pacific Students Association, Arab Students Association, Hospitality Club, Radio station. *Campus security:* 24-hour emergency response devices and patrols, late-night transport/escort service. *Student services:* health clinic, personal/psychological counseling.

Athletics Member NSCAA, NJCAA. *Intercollegiate sports:* baseball M, basketball M/W, golf M/W, soccer M/W, softball W. *Intramural sports:* basketball M/W, table tennis M/W, tennis M/W.

Costs (2006–07) *Tuition:* state resident $576 full-time, $24 per credit part-time; nonresident $5520 full-time, $230 per credit part-time. *Required fees:* $1824 full-time, $76 per credit part-time.

Financial Aid Of all full-time matriculated undergraduates who enrolled in 2004, 116 Federal Work-Study jobs (averaging $1500).

Applying *Options:* deferred entrance. *Application fee:* $10. *Required:* high school transcript. *Application deadline:* rolling (freshmen), rolling (transfers). *Notification:* continuous (freshmen).

Freshmen Application Contact Ms. Debra Boyer, Registrar/Director of Enrollment Services, Bunker Hill Community College, BHCC Enrollment Services Center, 250 New Rutherford Avenue, Boston, MA 02129. *Phone:* 617-228-2420. *Fax:* 617-228-2082.

▶ **See page 528 for the College Close-Up.**

CAPE COD COMMUNITY COLLEGE
West Barnstable, Massachusetts   www.capecod.mass.edu/

- **State-supported** 2-year, founded 1961, part of Massachusetts Public Higher Education System
- **Rural** 120-acre campus with easy access to Boston
- **Endowment** $3.8 million
- **Coed**

Undergraduates 1,470 full-time, 2,773 part-time. Students come from 24 states and territories, 5 other countries, 1% are from out of state, 4% African American, 0.9% Asian American or Pacific Islander, 2% Hispanic American, 1% Native American, 0.9% international, 10% transferred in.

Faculty *Student/faculty ratio:* 18:1.

Academics *Calendar:* semesters. *Degree:* certificates and associate. *Special study options:* academic remediation for entering students, adult/continuing education programs, advanced placement credit, cooperative education, distance learning, English as a second language, freshman honors college, honors programs, independent study, internships, off-campus study, part-time degree program, services for LD students, study abroad, summer session for credit.

Student Life *Campus security:* 24-hour patrols.

Costs (2005–06) *Tuition:* state resident $720 full-time, $24 per credit hour part-time; nonresident $6900 full-time, $230 per credit hour part-time. *Required fees:* $2940 full-time, $98 per credit hour part-time.

Financial Aid Of all full-time matriculated undergraduates who enrolled in 2004, 50 Federal Work-Study jobs (averaging $1650).

Applying *Options:* deferred entrance. *Application fee:* $10. *Required:* high school transcript. *Required for some:* essay or personal statement, letters of recommendation.

Director of Admissions Ms. Susan Kline-Symington, Director of Admissions, Cape Cod Community College, 2240 Lyanough Road, West Barnstable, MA 02668-1599. *Phone:* 508-362-2131 Ext. 4311. *Toll-free phone:* 877-846-3672.

DEAN COLLEGE
Franklin, Massachusetts

- **Independent** primarily 2-year, founded 1865
- **Small-town** 100-acre campus with easy access to Boston and Providence
- **Endowment** $20.7 million
- **Coed,** 1,249 undergraduate students, 74% full-time, 51% women, 49% men

Undergraduates 925 full-time, 324 part-time. Students come from 25 states and territories, 14 other countries, 48% are from out of state, 5% African American, 2% Asian American or Pacific Islander, 3% Hispanic American, 0.4% Native American, 7% international, 3% transferred in, 90% live on campus. *Retention:* 69% of 2003 full-time freshmen returned.
Freshmen *Admission:* 1,816 applied, 1,341 admitted, 545 enrolled. *Average high school GPA:* 2.0. *Test scores:* SAT verbal scores over 500: 26%; SAT math scores over 500: 23%; ACT scores over 18: 42%; SAT verbal scores over 600: 4%; SAT math scores over 600: 4%; ACT scores over 24: 10%.
Faculty *Total:* 97, 31% full-time, 14% with terminal degrees. *Student/faculty ratio:* 19:1.
Majors Athletic training; business administration and management; communication/speech communication and rhetoric; criminal justice/law enforcement administration; criminal justice/police science; dance; dramatic/theater arts; early childhood education; liberal arts and sciences/liberal studies; mathematics and computer science; physical education teaching and coaching; sport and fitness administration/management.
Academics *Calendar:* semesters. *Degrees:* certificates, associate, and bachelor's. *Special study options:* academic remediation for entering students, accelerated degree program, adult/continuing education programs, advanced placement credit, English as a second language, freshman honors college, honors programs, independent study, internships, off-campus study, part-time degree program, services for LD students, student-designed majors, summer session for credit.
Library E. Ross Anderson Library with 46,226 titles, 185 serial subscriptions.
Computers on Campus 150 computers available on campus for general student use. A campuswide network can be accessed from student residence rooms. At least one staffed computer lab available.
Student Life *Housing:* on-campus residence required through sophomore year. *Options:* coed. Campus housing is university owned. Freshman campus housing is guaranteed. *Activities and Organizations:* drama/theater group, student-run radio station, choral group, Emerging Leaders, College Success Staff, Student Ambassadors, student government, Phi Theta Kappa. *Campus security:* 24-hour emergency response devices and patrols, late-night transport/escort service, controlled dormitory access. *Student services:* health clinic, personal/psychological counseling.
Athletics Member NJCAA. *Intercollegiate sports:* baseball M(s), basketball M(s)/W(s), football M(s), golf M, lacrosse M(s)/W(s), soccer M(s)/W(s), softball W(s), volleyball W(s). *Intramural sports:* basketball M, football M, golf M, lacrosse M, skiing (cross-country) M/W, skiing (downhill) M/W, tennis M/W, volleyball M/W.
Standardized Tests *Required:* SAT or ACT (for admission).
Costs (2006–07) *One-time required fee:* $200. *Comprehensive fee:* $34,350 includes full-time tuition ($24,000) and room and board ($10,350). Part-time tuition: $690 per course. *Room and board:* college room only: $6550.
Applying *Options:* common application, electronic application, deferred entrance. *Application fee:* $35. *Required:* essay or personal statement, high school transcript, letters of recommendation. *Recommended:* minimum 2.0 GPA, interview. *Application deadline:* rolling (freshmen), rolling (transfers). *Notification:* continuous (freshmen).
Freshmen Application Contact Mr. Paul Vaccaro, Assistant Vice President for Enrollment Services and Dean of Admission, Dean College, 99 Main Street, Franklin, MA 02038. *Phone:* 508-541-1508. *Toll-free phone:* 877-TRY-DEAN. *Fax:* 508-541-8726. *E-mail:* admission@dean.edu.

FINE MORTUARY COLLEGE, LLC
Norwood, Massachusetts

FISHER COLLEGE
Boston, Massachusetts

- **Independent** primarily 2-year, founded 1903
- **Urban** campus
- **Endowment** $12.9 million
- **Coed,** 507 undergraduate students, 100% full-time, 66% women, 34% men

Undergraduates 507 full-time. Students come from 14 states and territories, 21 other countries, 21% are from out of state, 19% African American, 4% Asian American or Pacific Islander, 16% Hispanic American, 0.2% Native American, 11% international, 18% transferred in, 50% live on campus.
Freshmen *Admission:* 1,700 applied, 1,060 admitted, 254 enrolled. *Average high school GPA:* 2.52.
Faculty *Total:* 48, 50% full-time, 21% with terminal degrees. *Student/faculty ratio:* 18:1.
Majors Accounting; business administration and management; fashion/apparel design; fashion merchandising; health science; hospitality administration; humanities; kindergarten/preschool education; liberal arts and sciences/liberal studies; psychology; tourism and travel services management.
Academics *Calendar:* semesters. *Degrees:* associate and bachelor's. *Special study options:* academic remediation for entering students, adult/continuing education programs, advanced placement credit, English as a second language, internships, off-campus study, part-time degree program, summer session for credit.
Library Fisher College Library plus 1 other with 30,000 titles, 160 serial subscriptions, an OPAC.
Computers on Campus 112 computers available on campus for general student use. A campuswide network can be accessed from off campus. Internet access, at least one staffed computer lab available.
Student Life *Housing Options:* coed, women-only. *Activities and Organizations:* drama/theater group, choral group, Drama Club, student government, Student Activity Club, Inter-Cultural Club. *Campus security:* 24-hour emergency response devices and patrols, controlled dormitory access. *Student services:* health clinic, personal/psychological counseling, women's center.
Athletics Member NAIA. *Intercollegiate sports:* baseball M, basketball M/W, softball W.
Costs (2006–07) *Comprehensive fee:* $30,280 includes full-time tuition ($18,330), mandatory fees ($950), and room and board ($11,000).
Applying *Options:* deferred entrance. *Application fee:* $25. *Required:* high school transcript. *Required for some:* essay or personal statement, letters of recommendation, interview. *Recommended:* minimum 2.0 GPA. *Application deadline:* rolling (freshmen), rolling (transfers). *Notification:* continuous (freshmen).
Freshmen Application Contact Mr. Robert Melaragni, Director Admissions, Fisher College, 118 Beacon Street, Boston, MA 02116. *Phone:* 617-236-8800 Ext. 4401. *Toll-free phone:* 800-821-3050 (in-state); 800-446-1226 (out-of-state). *Fax:* 617-236-5473. *E-mail:* admissions@fisher.edu.

GIBBS COLLEGE
Boston, Massachusetts   www.katharinegibbs.com/

Director of Admissions Mr. Robert A. Andriola, Director of Admissions, Gibbs College, 126 Newbury Street, Boston, MA 02116-2904. *Phone:* 617-578-7150. *Toll-free phone:* 800-6SKILLS.

GREENFIELD COMMUNITY COLLEGE
Greenfield, Massachusetts   www.gcc.mass.edu/

- **State-supported** 2-year, founded 1962
- **Small-town** 120-acre campus
- **Coed,** 2,217 undergraduate students, 45% full-time, 63% women, 37% men

Undergraduates 994 full-time, 1,223 part-time. Students come from 5 states and territories, 7 other countries, 5% are from out of state, 3% African American,

Greenfield Community College (continued)

3% Asian American or Pacific Islander, 3% Hispanic American, 0.4% Native American, 12% transferred in.

Freshmen *Admission:* 727 applied, 727 admitted, 325 enrolled.

Faculty *Total:* 199, 28% full-time. *Student/faculty ratio:* 23:1.

Majors Accounting; administrative assistant and secretarial science; American studies; art; behavioral sciences; biological and physical sciences; business administration and management; commercial and advertising art; computer programming; criminal justice/law enforcement administration; education; engineering science; fire science; food science; human ecology; humanities; human services; industrial technology; information science/studies; kindergarten/preschool education; liberal arts and sciences/liberal studies; marketing/marketing management; mass communication/media; mathematics; natural resources management and policy; nursing (registered nurse training); parks, recreation and leisure; photography; pre-engineering.

Academics *Calendar:* semesters. *Degree:* certificates and associate. *Special study options:* academic remediation for entering students, adult/continuing education programs, advanced placement credit, cooperative education, distance learning, double majors, English as a second language, honors programs, independent study, internships, part-time degree program, services for LD students, summer session for credit.

Library Greenfield Community College Library with 52,690 titles, 356 serial subscriptions.

Computers on Campus 115 computers available on campus for general student use. A campuswide network can be accessed from off campus. Internet access, at least one staffed computer lab available.

Student Life *Housing:* college housing not available. *Activities and Organizations:* drama/theater group, choral group. *Campus security:* 24-hour emergency response devices and patrols, late-night transport/escort service. *Student services:* health clinic, personal/psychological counseling, women's center.

Standardized Tests *Required for some:* Psychological Corporation Practical Nursing Entrance Examination.

Costs (2005–06) *Tuition:* state resident $780 full-time, $26 per credit part-time; nonresident $8430 full-time, $281 per credit part-time. Full-time tuition and fees vary according to class time. Part-time tuition and fees vary according to class time. *Required fees:* $3227 full-time, $104 per credit part-time, $61 per semester part-time. *Payment plan:* installment. *Waivers:* senior citizens and employees or children of employees.

Applying *Application fee:* $10. *Required for some:* high school transcript, interview. *Application deadline:* rolling (freshmen), rolling (transfers).

Freshmen Application Contact Mr. Herbert Hentz, Assistant Director of Admission, Greenfield Community College, 1 College Drive, Greenfield, MA 01301-9739. *Phone:* 413-775-1000. *Fax:* 413-773-5129. *E-mail:* admission@gcc.mass.edu.

HOLYOKE COMMUNITY COLLEGE
Holyoke, Massachusetts   www.hcc.mass.edu/

- **State-supported** 2-year, founded 1946, part of Massachusetts Public Higher Education System
- **Suburban** 135-acre campus
- **Endowment** $5.8 million
- **Coed,** 6,258 undergraduate students, 49% full-time, 65% women, 35% men

Undergraduates 3,075 full-time, 3,183 part-time. Students come from 18 states and territories, 11 other countries, 1% are from out of state, 6% African American, 2% Asian American or Pacific Islander, 13% Hispanic American, 0.6% Native American, 0.4% international, 5% transferred in.

Freshmen *Admission:* 1,524 enrolled.

Faculty *Total:* 427, 26% full-time. *Student/faculty ratio:* 15:1.

Majors Accounting; administrative assistant and secretarial science; American studies; biology/biological sciences; business administration and management; business teacher education; chemistry; cinematography and film/video production; clinical laboratory science/medical technology; commercial and advertising art; computer typography and composition equipment operation; consumer merchandising/retailing management; criminal justice/police science; dramatic/theater arts; elementary education; engineering science; environmental studies; family and consumer sciences/human sciences; fine/studio arts; foods, nutrition, and wellness; general studies; health information/medical records administration; hospitality administration; hotel/motel administration; human services; information science/studies; international business/trade/commerce; kindergarten/preschool education; legal administrative assistant/secretary; liberal arts and sciences/liberal studies; mass communication/media; music; nursing (registered nurse training); photography; physics; pre-engineering; radiologic technology/science; sport and fitness administration/management; tourism and travel services management; veterinary sciences; veterinary technology; visual and performing arts.

Academics *Calendar:* semesters. *Degree:* certificates and associate. *Special study options:* academic remediation for entering students, adult/continuing education programs, advanced placement credit, cooperative education, English as a second language, honors programs, independent study, internships, off-campus study, part-time degree program, services for LD students, student-designed majors, study abroad, summer session for credit. *ROTC:* Army (c), Air Force (c).

Library Elaine Marieb Library with 75,222 titles, 365 serial subscriptions, 7,489 audiovisual materials, an OPAC, a Web page.

Computers on Campus 450 computers available on campus for general student use. A campuswide network can be accessed from off campus. Internet access, online (class) registration, at least one staffed computer lab available.

Student Life *Housing:* college housing not available. *Activities and Organizations:* drama/theater group, student-run newspaper, radio station, choral group, Drama Club, Music Club, Student Advisory Board. *Campus security:* 24-hour emergency response devices and patrols, student patrols, late-night transport/escort service. *Student services:* health clinic, personal/psychological counseling, women's center.

Athletics Member NJCAA. *Intercollegiate sports:* baseball M, basketball M/W, golf M/W, skiing (downhill) M(c)/W(c), soccer M/W, softball W, tennis M/W, volleyball W.

Costs (2006–07) *Tuition:* state resident $2570 full-time, $103 per credit part-time; nonresident $7514 full-time, $309 per credit part-time.

Applying *Options:* common application, electronic application, early admission, deferred entrance. *Application fee:* $10. *Required:* high school transcript. *Recommended:* interview. *Application deadline:* rolling (freshmen), rolling (transfers). *Notification:* continuous (freshmen).

Freshmen Application Contact Ms. Marcia Rosbury-Henne, Director of Admissions and Transfer Affairs, Holyoke Community College, Holyoke Community College, Attn: Admission Office, Holyoke, MA 01040. *Phone:* 413-552-2321. *Toll-free phone:* 888-530-8855 (in-state); 413-552-2850 (out-of-state). *Fax:* 413-552-2045. *E-mail:* admissions@hcc.mass.edu.

ITT TECHNICAL INSTITUTE
Norwood, Massachusetts   www.itt-tech.edu/

- **Proprietary** 2-year, founded 1990, part of ITT Educational Services, Inc
- **Suburban** campus with easy access to Boston
- **Coed**

Majors CAD/CADD drafting/design technology; computer programming; electrical, electronic and communications engineering technology; system, networking, and LAN/WAN management; web/multimedia management and webmaster; web page, digital/multimedia and information resources design.

Academics *Calendar:* quarters. *Degree:* associate.

Library a Web page.

Computers on Campus Internet access, at least one staffed computer lab available.

Student Life *Housing:* college housing not available.

Standardized Tests *Required:* Wonderlic aptitude test (for admission).

Costs (2005–06) *Tuition:* Please see school catalog for specific information.

Applying *Options:* deferred entrance. *Application fee:* $100. *Required:* high school transcript, interview. *Recommended:* letters of recommendation. *Application deadline:* rolling (freshmen), rolling (transfers). *Notification:* continuous (freshmen).

Freshmen Application Contact Mr. Thomas F. Ryan III, Director of Recruitment, ITT Technical Institute, 333 Providence Highway, Norwood, MA 02062. *Phone:* 781-278-7200. *Toll-free phone:* 800-879-8324.

ITT TECHNICAL INSTITUTE
Woburn, Massachusetts   www.itt-tech.edu/

- **Proprietary** 2-year, part of ITT Educational Services, Inc
- **Coed**

Majors CAD/CADD drafting/design technology; computer programming; electrical, electronic and communications engineering technology; system, networking, and LAN/WAN management; web/multimedia management and webmaster; web page, digital/multimedia and information resources design.

Academics *Calendar:* quarters. *Degree:* associate.

Library a Web page.

Computers on Campus Internet access, at least one staffed computer lab available.

Student Life *Housing:* college housing not available.
Standardized Tests *Required:* Wonderlic aptitude test (for admission).
Costs (2005–06) *Tuition:* Please see school catalog for specific information.
Applying *Options:* deferred entrance. *Application fee:* $100. *Required:* high school transcript, interview. *Recommended:* letters of recommendation. *Application deadline:* rolling (freshmen), rolling (transfers). *Notification:* continuous (freshmen).
Freshmen Application Contact Mr. Craig Morton, ITT Technical Institute, 10 Forbes Road, Woburn, MA 01801. *Phone:* 781-937-8324. *Toll-free phone:* 800-430-5097.

LABOURÉ COLLEGE

Boston, Massachusetts   www.laboure.edu/

Director of Admissions Ms. Gina M. Morrissette, Director of Admissions, Labouré College, 2120 Dorchester Avenue, Boston, MA 02124. *Phone:* 617-296-8300.

MARIAN COURT COLLEGE

Swampscott, Massachusetts   www.mariancourt.edu/

Director of Admissions Mrs. Lisa Emerson Parker, Director of Admissions, Marian Court College, 35 Little's Point Road, Swampscott, MA 01907-2840. *Phone:* 781-595-6768 Ext. 139. *Fax:* 781-595-3536. *E-mail:* lparker@mariancourt.edu.

MASSACHUSETTS BAY COMMUNITY COLLEGE

Wellesley Hills, Massachusetts   www.massbay.edu/

- **State-supported** 2-year, founded 1961
- **Suburban** 84-acre campus with easy access to Boston
- **Coed,** 5,015 undergraduate students, 43% full-time, 58% women, 42% men

Undergraduates 2,145 full-time, 2,870 part-time. Students come from 7 states and territories, 50 other countries, 2% are from out of state, 12% African American, 4% Asian American or Pacific Islander, 7% Hispanic American, 0.3% Native American, 2% international, 38% transferred in.
Freshmen *Admission:* 2,557 applied, 2,532 admitted, 1,353 enrolled.
Faculty *Total:* 336, 22% full-time. *Student/faculty ratio:* 19:1.
Majors Accounting; automotive engineering technology; biological and physical sciences; biology/biotechnology laboratory technician; business administration and management; business/commerce; chemical technology; child care and support services management; communication/speech communication and rhetoric; computer and information sciences; computer engineering technology; computer science; criminal justice/law enforcement administration; drafting and design technology; engineering technology; environmental engineering technology; forensic science and technology; general studies; hospitality administration; human services; information science/studies; international relations and affairs; legal assistant/paralegal; liberal arts and sciences/liberal studies; mechanical engineering/mechanical technology; medical radiologic technology; nursing (registered nurse training); physical therapist assistant; respiratory care therapy; social sciences.
Academics *Calendar:* semesters. *Degree:* certificates and associate. *Special study options:* academic remediation for entering students, adult/continuing education programs, advanced placement credit, cooperative education, distance learning, honors programs, internships, part-time degree program, services for LD students, summer session for credit.
Library Perkins Library with 50,333 titles, 291 serial subscriptions, 4,650 audiovisual materials, an OPAC, a Web page.
Computers on Campus 400 computers available on campus for general student use. A campuswide network can be accessed from off campus. Internet access, at least one staffed computer lab available.
Student Life *Housing:* college housing not available. *Activities and Organizations:* drama/theater group, student-run newspaper, Student Government Association, Latino Student Organization, New World Society Club, Mass Bay Players, Student Occupational Therapy Association. *Campus security:* 24-hour emergency response devices and patrols. *Student services:* health clinic, personal/psychological counseling.

Athletics Member NJCAA. *Intercollegiate sports:* baseball M, basketball M/W, cross-country running M/W, golf M/W, soccer M/W, softball W, tennis M/W, volleyball W. *Intramural sports:* ice hockey M, soccer M/W.
Costs (2006–07) *Tuition:* state resident $720 full-time; nonresident $6900 full-time.
Financial Aid Of all full-time matriculated undergraduates who enrolled in 2004, 30 Federal Work-Study jobs (averaging $3000).
Applying *Options:* electronic application, deferred entrance. *Application fee:* $20. *Application deadline:* rolling (freshmen), rolling (transfers). *Notification:* continuous (freshmen).
Freshmen Application Contact Ms. Donna Raposa, Director of Admissions, Massachusetts Bay Community College, 50 Oakland Street, Wellesley Hills, MA 02481. *Phone:* 781-239-2500. *Fax:* 781-239-1047. *E-mail:* info@massbay.edu.

▶ **See page 572 for the College Close-Up.**

MASSASOIT COMMUNITY COLLEGE

Brockton, Massachusetts   www.massasoit.mass.edu/

Director of Admissions Ms. Michelle Hughes, Director of Admissions, Massasoit Community College, 1 Massasoit Boulevard, Brockton, MA 02302-3996. *Phone:* 508-588-9100 Ext. 1412. *Toll-free phone:* 800-CAREERS.

MIDDLESEX COMMUNITY COLLEGE

Bedford, Massachusetts   www.middlesex.mass.edu/

Director of Admissions Ms. Laurie Dimitrov, Director, Admissions and Recruitment, Middlesex Community College, 33 Kearney Square, Lowell, MA 01852. *Phone:* 978-656-3207. *Toll-free phone:* 800-818-3434. *E-mail:* orellanad@middlesex.cc.ma.us.

MOUNT WACHUSETT COMMUNITY COLLEGE

Gardner, Massachusetts   www.mwcc.mass.edu/

- **State-supported** 2-year, founded 1963, part of Massachusetts Public Higher Education System
- **Small-town** 270-acre campus with easy access to Boston
- **Endowment** $1.7 million
- **Coed,** 4,170 undergraduate students, 47% full-time, 67% women, 33% men

Mount Wachusett Community College (MWCC) is a two-year public community college that offers more than forty associate degree and certificate programs and noncredit and professional development courses. At MWCC, students gain education and training to build new skills, start a career, or transfer to a four-year public or private college or university. Prospective students may visit the College's Web site at http://www.mwcc.edu.

Undergraduates 1,958 full-time, 2,212 part-time. Students come from 6 states and territories, 8 other countries, 5% are from out of state, 4% African American, 3% Asian American or Pacific Islander, 9% Hispanic American, 0.5% Native American, 2% international, 8% transferred in. *Retention:* 49% of 2003 full-time freshmen returned.
Freshmen *Admission:* 1,542 applied, 1,514 admitted, 1,028 enrolled.
Faculty *Total:* 221, 32% full-time. *Student/faculty ratio:* 22:1.
Majors Accounting; art; automobile/automotive mechanics technology; business administration and management; child development; computer graphics; computer technology/computer systems technology; criminal justice/law enforcement administration; dental hygiene; electrical, electronic and communications engineering technology; entrepreneurship; environmental studies; fine/studio arts; fire science; general studies; human services; industrial engineering; industrial technology; information science/studies; kinesiology and exercise science; legal assistant/paralegal; liberal arts and sciences/liberal studies; management information systems; manufacturing technology; massage therapy; medical/clinical assistant; nursing (licensed practical/vocational nurse training); nursing (registered nurse training); physical therapy; plastics engineering technology; radio/television broadcasting technology; sign language interpretation and translation; speech therapy; telecommunications; web page, digital/multimedia and information resources design.
Academics *Calendar:* semesters. *Degree:* certificates and associate. *Special study options:* academic remediation for entering students, adult/continuing

Mount Wachusett Community College (continued)

education programs, advanced placement credit, cooperative education, distance learning, double majors, English as a second language, honors programs, independent study, internships, part-time degree program, services for LD students, study abroad, summer session for credit.

Library Mount Wachusett Community College Library with 56,344 titles, 532 serial subscriptions, 2,185 audiovisual materials, an OPAC, a Web page.

Computers on Campus 415 computers available on campus for general student use. A campuswide network can be accessed. Internet access, online (class) registration, at least one staffed computer lab available.

Student Life *Housing:* college housing not available. *Activities and Organizations:* drama/theater group, student-run newspaper, choral group, Sophomore Nursing Club, Freshman Nursing Club, Alpha Beta Gamma, Physical Therapist Assistant Club, Multicultural Club. *Campus security:* 24-hour emergency response devices and patrols. *Student services:* health clinic, personal/psychological counseling, women's center.

Costs (2006–07) *Tuition:* state resident $750 full-time, $25 per credit part-time; nonresident $6900 full-time, $230 per credit part-time. *Required fees:* $3480 full-time, $111 per credit part-time, $55 per term part-time.

Financial Aid Of all full-time matriculated undergraduates who enrolled in 2004, 47 Federal Work-Study jobs (averaging $2228).

Applying *Options:* common application, early admission. *Application fee:* $10. *Required:* high school transcript. *Required for some:* essay or personal statement, 2 letters of recommendation. *Application deadline:* rolling (freshmen), rolling (transfers). *Notification:* continuous (freshmen).

Freshmen Application Contact John D. Walsh, Director of Admissions, Mount Wachusett Community College, 444 Green Street, Gardner, MA 01440-1000. *Phone:* 978-632-6600 Ext. 110. *Fax:* 978-630-9554. *E-mail:* admissions@mwcc.mass.edu.

NEW ENGLAND COLLEGE OF FINANCE
Boston, Massachusetts   www.finance.edu/

- **Independent** 2-year, founded 1909
- **Urban** campus
- **Coed, primarily women,** 412 undergraduate students, 76% women, 24% men

Undergraduates 412 part-time. Students come from 4 states and territories, 5% are from out of state, 9% African American, 8% Asian American or Pacific Islander, 9% Hispanic American, 0.5% Native American.

Faculty *Total:* 216. *Student/faculty ratio:* 11:1.

Majors Accounting; business administration and management; computer science; finance; management information systems; marketing/marketing management.

Academics *Calendar:* 8 week terms (6 per academic year). *Degrees:* certificates and associate (offers primarily part-time evening degree programs; bachelor's degree offered jointly with Bentley College, Assumption College, Providence College, University of Hartford, and University System College for Lifelong Learning). *Special study options:* academic remediation for entering students, adult/continuing education programs, distance learning, independent study, internships, part-time degree program, summer session for credit.

Computers on Campus 10 computers available on campus for general student use.

Student Life *Housing:* college housing not available. *Campus security:* reception desk in lobby of building.

Costs (2005–06) *Tuition:* $242 per semester hour part-time. *Payment plan:* installment.

Applying *Options:* common application. *Required:* essay or personal statement, high school transcript, 1 letter of recommendation, interview. *Application deadline:* rolling (freshmen), rolling (transfers). *Notification:* continuous (freshmen).

Freshmen Application Contact Mr. Robert Wagstaff, Registrar, New England College of Finance, 10 High Street, Suite 204, Boston, MA 02111-2645. *Phone:* 617-951-2350 Ext. 230. *Toll-free phone:* 888-696-NECF. *Fax:* 617-951-2533.

NORTHERN ESSEX COMMUNITY COLLEGE
Haverhill, Massachusetts   www.necc.mass.edu/

- **State-supported** 2-year, founded 1960
- **Suburban** 106-acre campus with easy access to Boston
- **Endowment** $2.1 million
- **Coed,** 6,362 undergraduate students, 36% full-time, 65% women, 35% men

Northern Essex Community College is a two-year public community college with an open and rolling admission process, offering more than seventy degree and certificate programs in arts and sciences, business, computer information sciences, electronic technology and engineering science, health, human services, and paralegal studies. Students can prepare for a career or begin a bachelor's degree through the Joint Admissions Program or transfer agreements with four-year colleges and universities.

Undergraduates 2,300 full-time, 4,062 part-time. Students come from 4 states and territories, 16% are from out of state, 2% African American, 2% Asian American or Pacific Islander, 20% Hispanic American, 0.3% Native American, 0.9% international. *Retention:* 54% of 2003 full-time freshmen returned. Freshmen *Admission:* 3,347 applied, 3,164 admitted.

Faculty *Total:* 497, 20% full-time. *Student/faculty ratio:* 20:1.

Majors Accounting; administrative assistant and secretarial science; biological and physical sciences; business administration and management; business teacher education; civil engineering technology; commercial and advertising art; computer and information sciences; computer engineering technology; computer graphics; computer programming; computer programming related; computer programming (specific applications); computer science; computer systems networking and telecommunications; computer typography and composition equipment operation; criminal justice/law enforcement administration; dance; data processing and data processing technology; dental assisting; dramatic/theater arts; education; electrical, electronic and communications engineering technology; elementary education; engineering science; finance; general studies; health information/medical records administration; history; hotel/motel administration; human services; industrial radiologic technology; international relations and affairs; journalism; kindergarten/preschool education; legal assistant/paralegal; liberal arts and sciences/liberal studies; machine tool technology; marketing/marketing management; materials science; medical administrative assistant and medical secretary; medical transcription; mental health/rehabilitation; music; nursing (registered nurse training); parks, recreation and leisure; physical education teaching and coaching; political science and government; radiologic technology/science; real estate; respiratory care therapy; respiratory therapy technician; sign language interpretation and translation; telecommunications technology; tourism and travel services management; web/multimedia management and webmaster; web page, digital/multimedia and information resources design; women's studies; word processing.

Academics *Calendar:* semesters. *Degree:* certificates and associate. *Special study options:* academic remediation for entering students, adult/continuing education programs, advanced placement credit, cooperative education, distance learning, double majors, English as a second language, freshman honors college, honors programs, independent study, internships, off-campus study, part-time degree program, services for LD students, study abroad, summer session for credit. *ROTC:* Air Force (c).

Library Bentley Library with 61,120 titles, 598 serial subscriptions, an OPAC.

Computers on Campus 250 computers available on campus for general student use. A campuswide network can be accessed from off campus. At least one staffed computer lab available.

Student Life *Housing:* college housing not available. *Activities and Organizations:* drama/theater group, student-run newspaper. *Campus security:* 24-hour emergency response devices and patrols. *Student services:* health clinic, personal/psychological counseling, women's center.

Athletics Member NJCAA. *Intercollegiate sports:* baseball M, basketball M/W, cross-country running M/W, volleyball M/W. *Intramural sports:* basketball M/W, cross-country running M/W, football M/W, golf M/W, racquetball M/W, skiing (cross-country) M/W, skiing (downhill) M/W, weight lifting M/W.

Standardized Tests *Required:* Psychological Corporation Aptitude Test for Practical Nursing (for admission).

Costs (2005–06) *Tuition:* state resident $3150 full-time, $105 per credit part-time; nonresident $3660 full-time, $346 per credit part-time. Full-time tuition and fees vary according to course load, degree level, program, and reciprocity agreements. Part-time tuition and fees vary according to course load, degree level, program, and reciprocity agreements. *Payment plan:* installment. *Waivers:* employees or children of employees.

Financial Aid Of all full-time matriculated undergraduates who enrolled in 2004, 113 Federal Work-Study jobs (averaging $1668).

Applying *Options:* early admission. *Required:* high school transcript. *Application deadline:* rolling (freshmen), rolling (transfers). *Notification:* continuous (freshmen).
Freshmen Application Contact Nora Sheridan, Director of Admissions, Northern Essex Community College, 100 Elliott Street, Haverhill,, MA 01830. *Phone:* 978-556-3616. *Toll-free phone:* 800-NECC-123. *Fax:* 978-556-3155.

NORTH SHORE COMMUNITY COLLEGE
Danvers, Massachusetts www.northshore.edu/

- **State-supported** 2-year, founded 1965
- **Suburban** campus with easy access to Boston
- **Endowment** $4.1 million
- **Coed,** 6,604 undergraduate students, 42% full-time, 63% women, 37% men

Undergraduates 2,764 full-time, 3,840 part-time. Students come from 5 states and territories, 8 other countries, 1% are from out of state, 8% African American, 3% Asian American or Pacific Islander, 12% Hispanic American, 0.3% Native American, 0.1% international, 9% transferred in.
Freshmen *Admission:* 3,061 applied, 2,765 admitted, 1,471 enrolled.
Faculty *Total:* 404, 33% full-time, 32% with terminal degrees. *Student/faculty ratio:* 18:1.
Majors Accounting; administrative assistant and secretarial science; airline pilot and flight crew; applied horticulture; biology/biotechnology laboratory technician; business administration and management; child development; computer and information sciences related; computer engineering technology; computer graphics; computer programming; computer programming (specific applications); computer science; criminal justice/law enforcement administration; culinary arts; data entry/microcomputer applications; engineering science; fire science; foods, nutrition, and wellness; forestry; gerontology; health science; hospitality administration; information science/studies; interdisciplinary studies; kindergarten/preschool education; landscaping and groundskeeping; legal administrative assistant/secretary; legal assistant/paralegal; liberal arts and sciences/liberal studies; marketing/marketing management; medical administrative assistant and medical secretary; medical radiologic technology; mental health/rehabilitation; nursing (registered nurse training); occupational therapy; physical therapist assistant; pre-engineering; respiratory care therapy; substance abuse/addiction counseling; tourism and travel services management; veterinary technology; Web page, digital/multimedia and information resources design.
Academics *Calendar:* semesters. *Degree:* certificates and associate. *Special study options:* academic remediation for entering students, adult/continuing education programs, advanced placement credit, cooperative education, distance learning, English as a second language, honors programs, independent study, internships, part-time degree program, services for LD students, summer session for credit.
Library Learning Resource Center plus 2 others with 97,818 titles, 408 serial subscriptions, 7,795 audiovisual materials, an OPAC.
Computers on Campus 380 computers available on campus for general student use. A campuswide network can be accessed. Internet access, online (class) registration, at least one staffed computer lab available.
Student Life *Housing:* college housing not available. *Activities and Organizations:* drama/theater group, student-run newspaper, Program Council, student government, performing arts, student newspaper, Phi Theta Kappa. *Campus security:* 24-hour emergency response devices and patrols, late-night transport/escort service. *Student services:* health clinic, personal/psychological counseling, women's center.
Costs (2005–06) *Tuition:* state resident $600 full-time, $25 per credit part-time; nonresident $6168 full-time, $257 per credit part-time. *Required fees:* $2184 full-time, $91 per credit part-time. *Payment plans:* installment, deferred payment. *Waivers:* senior citizens and employees or children of employees.
Applying *Options:* electronic application, early admission. *Required for some:* high school transcript, interview. *Application deadline:* rolling (freshmen), rolling (transfers). *Notification:* continuous (freshmen).
Freshmen Application Contact Dr. Joanne Light, Dean of Enrollment Services, North Shore Community College, PO Box 3340, Danvers, MA 01923. *Phone:* 978-762-4000 Ext. 4337. *Fax:* 978-762-4015. *E-mail:* info@northshore.edu.

QUINCY COLLEGE
Quincy, Massachusetts www.quincycollege.edu/

Freshmen Application Contact Michelle DeRosa, Admissions Officer, Quincy College, 34 Coddington Street, Quincy, MA 02169. *Phone:* 617-984-1700. *Toll-free phone:* 800-698-1700. *Fax:* 617-984-1779. *E-mail:* mderosa@quicycollege.edu.

QUINSIGAMOND COMMUNITY COLLEGE
Worcester, Massachusetts www.qcc.mass.edu/

- **State-supported** 2-year, founded 1963
- **Urban** 57-acre campus with easy access to Boston
- **Coed,** 5,970 undergraduate students, 46% full-time, 60% women, 40% men

Undergraduates 2,761 full-time, 3,209 part-time. Students come from 3 states and territories, 13 other countries, 8% African American, 3% Asian American or Pacific Islander, 9% Hispanic American, 0.5% Native American, 0.5% international, 4% transferred in.
Freshmen *Admission:* 1,433 applied, 1,433 admitted, 1,227 enrolled.
Faculty *Total:* 398, 27% full-time.
Majors Accounting; administrative assistant and secretarial science; art; automobile/automotive mechanics technology; business administration and management; commercial and advertising art; computer programming; computer technology/computer systems technology; consumer merchandising/retailing management; criminal justice/law enforcement administration; data processing and data processing technology; dental hygiene; electrical, electronic and communications engineering technology; emergency medical technology (EMT paramedic); fire science; general studies; hotel/motel administration; human services; information science/studies; kindergarten/preschool education; liberal arts and sciences/liberal studies; medical radiologic technology; nursing (registered nurse training); occupational therapist assistant; occupational therapy; respiratory care therapy; tourism and travel services management.
Academics *Calendar:* semesters. *Degree:* certificates and associate. *Special study options:* academic remediation for entering students, accelerated degree program, adult/continuing education programs, advanced placement credit, cooperative education, double majors, English as a second language, internships, off-campus study, part-time degree program, services for LD students, summer session for credit. *ROTC:* Army (c).
Library Quinsigamond Library plus 1 other with 54,000 titles, 310 serial subscriptions, 230 audiovisual materials, an OPAC.
Computers on Campus 200 computers available on campus for general student use. A campuswide network can be accessed from off campus. At least one staffed computer lab available.
Student Life *Housing:* college housing not available. *Activities and Organizations:* drama/theater group, student-run newspaper, Phi Theta Kappa, Nursing Club, Rad Tech Club, Gay Straight Alliance, Criminal Justice Club. *Campus security:* 24-hour emergency response devices and patrols, late-night transport/escort service. *Student services:* health clinic, personal/psychological counseling, women's center.
Athletics Member NJCAA. *Intercollegiate sports:* baseball M, basketball M/W, softball W. *Intramural sports:* archery M/W, badminton M/W, basketball M/W, cross-country running M/W, skiing (cross-country) M/W, skiing (downhill) M/W, swimming and diving M/W, tennis M/W, volleyball M/W.
Costs (2005–06) *Tuition:* state resident $576 full-time, $24 per credit part-time; nonresident $5520 full-time, $230 per credit part-time. *Required fees:* $2479 full-time, $96 per credit part-time, $85 per term part-time.
Financial Aid Of all full-time matriculated undergraduates who enrolled in 2004, 70 Federal Work-Study jobs (averaging $2200).
Applying *Options:* common application. *Application fee:* $20. *Required:* high school transcript. *Required for some:* interview. *Application deadline:* rolling (freshmen), rolling (transfers). *Notification:* continuous (freshmen).
Freshmen Application Contact Mr. Ronald C. Smith, Director of Admissions, Quinsigamond Community College, 670 West Boylston Street, Worcester, MA 01606-2092. *Phone:* 508-854-4262. *Fax:* 508-854-4357. *E-mail:* qccadm@qcc.mass.edu.

ROXBURY COMMUNITY COLLEGE
Roxbury Crossing, Massachusetts www.rcc.mass.edu/

Director of Admissions Milton Samuels, Director/Admissions, Roxbury Community College, 1234 Columbus Avenue, Roxbury Crossing, MA 02120-3400. *Phone:* 617-541-5310.

SPRINGFIELD TECHNICAL COMMUNITY COLLEGE
Springfield, Massachusetts   www.stcc.edu/

- **State-supported** 2-year, founded 1967
- **Urban** 34-acre campus
- **Coed,** 5,823 undergraduate students, 46% full-time, 58% women, 42% men

Undergraduates 2,658 full-time, 3,165 part-time. Students come from 10 states and territories, 4% are from out of state, 15% African American, 2% Asian American or Pacific Islander, 16% Hispanic American, 0.4% Native American, 0.9% international.
Freshmen *Admission:* 2,211 applied, 2,048 admitted, 1,093 enrolled.
Faculty *Total:* 435, 35% full-time. *Student/faculty ratio:* 15:1.
Majors Accounting; administrative assistant and secretarial science; architectural engineering technology; automotive engineering technology; biology/biological sciences; biotechnology; business administration and management; business/commerce; CAD/CADD drafting/design technology; chemistry; civil engineering technology; clinical/medical laboratory technology; commercial and advertising art; communications technologies and support services related; computer and information sciences and support services related; computer engineering technology; computer science; cosmetology; criminal justice/police science; dental hygiene; desktop publishing and digital imaging design; diagnostic medical sonography and ultrasound technology; electrical and electronic engineering technologies related; electrical, electronic and communications engineering technology; electromechanical technology; elementary education; engineering; entrepreneurship; finance; fine/studio arts; fire science; general studies; graphic design; health aide; heating, air conditioning and refrigeration technology; kindergarten/preschool education; landscaping and groundskeeping; laser and optical technology; liberal arts and sciences/liberal studies; logistics and materials management; marketing/marketing management; massage therapy; mathematics; mechanical engineering/mechanical technology; medical administrative assistant and medical secretary; medical/clinical assistant; medical insurance coding; medical radiologic technology; nuclear medical technology; nursing (registered nurse training); occupational therapist assistant; physical therapist assistant; quality control technology; rehabilitation and therapeutic professions related; respiratory care therapy; surgical technology; web/multimedia management and webmaster.
Academics *Calendar:* semesters. *Degree:* certificates and associate. *Special study options:* academic remediation for entering students, adult/continuing education programs, advanced placement credit, cooperative education, distance learning, English as a second language, honors programs, independent study, internships, off-campus study, part-time degree program, services for LD students, summer session for credit.
Library Springfield Technical Community College Library with 63,945 titles, 259 serial subscriptions, 17,586 audiovisual materials, an OPAC, a Web page.
Computers on Campus 1175 computers available on campus for general student use. A campuswide network can be accessed from off campus. Internet access, at least one staffed computer lab available.
Student Life *Housing:* college housing not available. *Activities and Organizations:* drama/theater group, student-run television station, Phi Theta Kappa Honor Society, Landscape Club, Dental Hygiene Club, Clinical Lab Club, Physical Therapist Assistant Club. *Campus security:* 24-hour emergency response devices and patrols, late-night transport/escort service. *Student services:* health clinic, personal/psychological counseling.
Athletics Member NJCAA. *Intercollegiate sports:* basketball M/W, golf M/W, soccer M/W, tennis M/W, wrestling M. *Intramural sports:* basketball M/W, cross-country running M/W, golf M/W, skiing (cross-country) M/W, volleyball M/W, weight lifting M/W.
Standardized Tests *Required for some:* SAT (for admission).
Costs (2005–06) *Tuition:* state resident $750 full-time, $25 per credit hour part-time; nonresident $7260 full-time, $242 per credit hour part-time. Full-time tuition and fees vary according to course load. Part-time tuition and fees vary according to course load. No tuition increase for student's term of enrollment. *Required fees:* $2604 full-time, $80 per credit hour part-time, $109 per term part-time. *Payment plan:* deferred payment. *Waivers:* senior citizens and employees or children of employees.
Financial Aid Of all full-time matriculated undergraduates who enrolled in 2004, 124 Federal Work-Study jobs (averaging $2400).
Applying *Application fee:* $10. *Required:* high school transcript. *Required for some:* interview. *Application deadline:* rolling (freshmen), rolling (transfers).
Freshmen Application Contact Mr. Ray Blair, Springfield Technical Community College, One Armory Square, Springfield, MA 01105. *Phone:* 413-781-7822 Ext. 4868. *E-mail:* rblair@stcc.edu.

URBAN COLLEGE OF BOSTON
Boston, Massachusetts   www.urbancollegeofboston.org/
Director of Admissions Dr. Henry J. Johnson, Director of Enrollment Services/Registrar, Urban College of Boston, 178 Tremont Street, Boston, MA 02111-1093. *Phone:* 617-292-4723 Ext. 6357.

MICHIGAN

ALPENA COMMUNITY COLLEGE
Alpena, Michigan   www.alpenacc.edu/

- **State and locally supported** 2-year, founded 1952
- **Small-town** 700-acre campus
- **Endowment** $3.3 million
- **Coed**

Undergraduates 984 full-time, 953 part-time. Students come from 4 states and territories, 0.8% African American, 0.5% Asian American or Pacific Islander, 0.2% Hispanic American, 0.4% Native American, 2% transferred in, 2% live on campus. *Retention:* 55% of 2003 full-time freshmen returned.
Faculty *Student/faculty ratio:* 17:1.
Academics *Calendar:* semesters. *Degree:* certificates and associate. *Special study options:* academic remediation for entering students, advanced placement credit, distance learning, double majors, internships, part-time degree program, services for LD students, summer session for credit.
Student Life *Campus security:* 24-hour emergency response devices.
Athletics Member NJCAA.
Standardized Tests *Required:* ACT COMPASS (for placement). *Recommended:* ACT (for placement).
Costs (2005–06) *Tuition:* area resident $2532 full-time, $68 per contact hour part-time; state resident $3545 full-time, $102 per contact hour part-time; nonresident $4550 full-time, $135 per contact hour part-time. *Required fees:* $500 full-time, $16 per contact hour part-time, $10 per term part-time. *Room and board:* room only: $3000.
Financial Aid Of all full-time matriculated undergraduates who enrolled in 2004, 80 Federal Work-Study jobs (averaging $1200). 20 state and other part-time jobs (averaging $800).
Applying *Options:* electronic application, early admission, deferred entrance. *Required:* high school transcript.
Director of Admissions Mr. Mike Kollien, Admissions Technician, Alpena Community College, 666 Johnson Street, Alpena, MI 49707-1495. *Phone:* 989-358-7339. *Toll-free phone:* 888-468-6222.

BAY DE NOC COMMUNITY COLLEGE
Escanaba, Michigan   www.baydenoc.cc.mi.us/

- **County-supported** 2-year, founded 1963, part of Michigan Department of Education
- **Rural** 150-acre campus
- **Endowment** $2.1 million
- **Coed**

Undergraduates Students come from 2 states and territories, 2 other countries, 1% are from out of state, 0.4% African American, 0.1% Asian American or Pacific Islander, 0.2% Hispanic American, 4% Native American, 0.1% international.
Academics *Calendar:* semesters. *Degree:* certificates and associate. *Special study options:* academic remediation for entering students, adult/continuing education programs, advanced placement credit, cooperative education, distance learning, internships, part-time degree program, summer session for credit.
Student Life *Campus security:* evening housing security personnel.
Standardized Tests *Required:* ACT COMPASS (for placement).
Financial Aid Of all full-time matriculated undergraduates who enrolled in 2004, 80 Federal Work-Study jobs (averaging $2500). 40 state and other part-time jobs (averaging $2500).

Applying *Options:* early admission. *Required:* high school transcript.
Freshmen Application Contact Ms. Cynthia Aird, Director of Admissions, Bay de Noc Community College, Student Center, 2001 North Lincoln Road, Escanaba, MI 49829-2511. *Phone:* 906-786-5802 Ext. 1276. *Toll-free phone:* 800-221-20C1 Ext. 1276.

BAY MILLS COMMUNITY COLLEGE
Brimley, Michigan   www.bmcc.edu/

- **District-supported** 2-year, founded 1984
- **Rural** campus
- **Coed**

Faculty *Student/faculty ratio:* 10:1.
Academics *Calendar:* semesters. *Degree:* certificates, diplomas, and associate. *Special study options:* academic remediation for entering students, internships, part-time degree program.
Student Life *Campus security:* 24-hour emergency response devices.
Standardized Tests *Required:* ACT ASSET (for placement).
Costs (2005–06) *Tuition:* state resident $2040 full-time, $85 per credit hour part-time. *Required fees:* $300 full-time, $10 per credit hour part-time, $30 per term part-time.
Financial Aid Of all full-time matriculated undergraduates who enrolled in 2004, 7 Federal Work-Study jobs (averaging $2466). 6 state and other part-time jobs (averagir.g $2634).
Applying *Options:* common application, early admission. *Required:* high school transcript.
Director of Admissions Ms. Elaine Lehre, Admissions Officer, Bay Mills Community College, 12214 West Lakeshore Drive, Brimley, MI 49715. *Phone:* 906-248-3354. *Toll-free phone:* 800-844-BMCC.

DAVENPORT UNIVERSITY
Alma, Michigan   www.davenport.edu/

- **Independent** primarily 2-year, founded 1977, part of Davenport Educational System
- **Coed**

Faculty *Student/faculty ratio:* 16:1.
Academics *Calendar:* semesters. *Degrees:* diplomas, associate, and bachelor's. *Special study options:* accelerated degree program, distance learning, English as a second language, independent study, internships, student-designed majors.
Costs (2005–06) *Tuition:* $6216 full-time, $259 per credit hour part-time. *Required fees:* $120 full-time.
Applying *Options:* deferred entrance. *Application fee:* $25.
Director of Admissions Admissions, Davenport University, 415 East Fulton Street, Grand Rapids, MI 49503. *Toll-free phone:* 800-632-9569.

DAVENPORT UNIVERSITY
Bad Axe, Michigan   www.davenport.edu/

- **Independent** primarily 2-year, founded 1996, part of Davenport Educational System
- **Coed**

Faculty *Student/faculty ratio:* 16:1.
Academics *Calendar:* semesters. *Degrees:* diplomas, associate, and bachelor's. *Special study options:* accelerated degree program, distance learning, English as a second language, independent study, internships, student-designed majors.
Costs (2005–06) *Tuition:* $6600 full-time, $275 per credit hour part-time. *Required fees:* $120 full-time.
Applying *Options:* deferred entrance. *Application fee:* $25.
Director of Admissions Admissions, Davenport University, 415 East Fulton Street, Grand Rapids, MI 49503. *Toll-free phone:* 800-632-9569.

DAVENPORT UNIVERSITY
Bay City, Michigan   www.davenport.edu/

- **Independent** primarily 2-year, founded 1996, part of Davenport Educational System
- **Coed**

Faculty *Student/faculty ratio:* 16:1.
Academics *Calendar:* semesters. *Degrees:* diplomas, associate, and bachelor's. *Special study options:* accelerated degree program, distance learning, English as a second language, independent study, internships, student-designed majors.
Costs (2005–06) *Tuition:* $6600 full-time, $275 per credit hour part-time. *Required fees:* $120 full-time.
Applying *Options:* deferred entrance. *Application fee:* $25.
Director of Admissions Admissions, Davenport University, 415 East Fulton Street, Grand Rapids, MI 49503. *Toll-free phone:* 800-632-9569.

DAVENPORT UNIVERSITY
Caro, Michigan   www.davenport.edu/

- **Independent** primarily 2-year, founded 1996, part of Davenport Educational System
- **Coed**

Faculty *Student/faculty ratio:* 16:1.
Academics *Calendar:* semesters. *Degrees:* diplomas, associate, and bachelor's. *Special study options:* accelerated degree program, distance learning, English as a second language, independent study, internships, student-designed majors.
Costs (2005–06) *Tuition:* $6600 full-time, $275 per credit hour part-time. *Required fees:* $120 full-time.
Applying *Options:* deferred entrance. *Application fee:* $25.
Director of Admissions Admissions, Davenport University, 415 East Fulton Street, Grand Rapids, MI 49503. *Toll-free phone:* 800-632-9569.

DAVENPORT UNIVERSITY
Midland, Michigan   www.davenport.edu/

- **Independent** primarily 2-year, founded 1996, part of Davenport Educational System
- **Urban** campus
- **Coed**

Faculty *Student/faculty ratio:* 16:1.
Academics *Calendar:* semesters. *Degrees:* certificates, associate, and bachelor's. *Special study options:* academic remediation for entering students, accelerated degree program, cooperative education, distance learning, double majors, English as a second language, independent study, internships, part-time degree program, student-designed majors, summer session for credit.
Student Life *Campus security:* 24-hour emergency response devices.
Costs (2005–06) *Tuition:* $6600 full-time, $275 per credit hour part-time. *Required fees:* $120 full-time.
Applying *Options:* deferred entrance. *Application fee:* $25. *Required:* high school transcript.
Director of Admissions Admissions, Davenport University, 415 East Fulton Street, Grand Rapids, MI 49503. *Toll-free phone:* 800-632-9569.

DAVENPORT UNIVERSITY
Romeo, Michigan   www.davenport.edu/

- **Independent** primarily 2-year, founded 1985, part of Davenport Educational System
- **Coed**

Faculty *Student/faculty ratio:* 16:1.
Academics *Calendar:* semesters. *Degrees:* diplomas, associate, and bachelor's. *Special study options:* accelerated degree program, distance learning, English as a second language, independent study, internships, student-designed majors.

Davenport University (continued)

Costs (2005–06) *Tuition:* $6216 full-time, $259 per credit hour part-time. *Required fees:* $120 full-time.

Applying *Options:* deferred entrance. *Application fee:* $25.

Director of Admissions Admissions, Davenport University, 415 East Fulton Street, Grand Rapids, MI 49503. *Toll-free phone:* 800-632-9569.

DAVENPORT UNIVERSITY

Saginaw, Michigan **www.davenport.edu/**

- **Independent** primarily 2-year, founded 1996, part of Davenport Educational System
- **Coed**

Faculty *Student/faculty ratio:* 16:1.

Academics *Calendar:* semesters. *Degrees:* diplomas, associate, and bachelor's. *Special study options:* accelerated degree program, distance learning, English as a second language, independent study, internships, student-designed majors.

Costs (2005–06) *Tuition:* $6600 full-time, $275 per credit hour part-time. *Required fees:* $120 full-time.

Applying *Options:* deferred entrance. *Application fee:* $25.

Director of Admissions Admissions, Davenport University, 415 East Fulton Street, Grand Rapids, MI 49503. *Toll-free phone:* 800-632-9569.

DELTA COLLEGE

University Center, Michigan **www.delta.edu/**

- **District-supported** 2-year, founded 1961
- **Rural** 640-acre campus
- **Endowment** $8.6 million
- **Coed,** 10,210 undergraduate students, 39% full-time, 56% women, 44% men

Undergraduates 3,938 full-time, 6,272 part-time. Students come from 22 other countries, 7% African American, 0.8% Asian American or Pacific Islander, 4% Hispanic American, 0.8% Native American, 0.9% international, 4% transferred in.

Freshmen *Admission:* 4,054 applied, 4,054 admitted, 1,428 enrolled.

Faculty *Total:* 511, 41% full-time. *Student/faculty ratio:* 20:1.

Majors Accounting; administrative assistant and secretarial science; apparel and textile marketing management; architectural engineering technology; art; automobile/automotive mechanics technology; avionics maintenance technology; business administration and management; carpentry; chemical engineering technology; child development; child guidance; computer and information systems security; computer science; construction engineering technology; construction management; construction trades; consumer merchandising/retailing management; corrections; cosmetology; criminal justice/law enforcement administration; criminal justice/police science; dental assisting; dental hygiene; diagnostic medical sonography and ultrasound technology; drafting and design technology; electrician; emergency medical technology (EMT paramedic); engineering technology; entrepreneurship; environmental engineering technology; executive assistant/executive secretary; family and consumer sciences/human sciences; fire science; heating, air conditioning and refrigeration technology; heating, air conditioning, ventilation and refrigeration maintenance technology; industrial arts; industrial radiologic technology; information technology; interior design; legal administrative assistant/secretary; legal assistant/paralegal; liberal arts and sciences/liberal studies; machine tool technology; marketing/marketing management; mechanical design technology; mechanical engineering/mechanical technology; mechanic and repair technologies related; medical administrative assistant and medical secretary; medical/clinical assistant; merchandising; nursing (licensed practical/vocational nurse training); nursing (registered nurse training); office management; office occupations and clerical services; physical therapist assistant; physician assistant; pipefitting and sprinkler fitting; psychology; public health education and promotion; radiologic technology/science; radio/television broadcasting technology; respiratory care therapy; retail management; security and loss prevention; surgical technology; tool and die technology; water quality and wastewater treatment management and recycling technology; web/multimedia management and webmaster; web page, digital/multimedia and information resources design; welding technology.

Academics *Calendar:* semesters. *Degree:* certificates and associate. *Special study options:* academic remediation for entering students, adult/continuing education programs, advanced placement credit, cooperative education, distance learning, double majors, external degree program, freshman honors college,

honors programs, independent study, internships, off-campus study, part-time degree program, services for LD students, student-designed majors, summer session for credit.

Library Library Learning Information Center with 93,167 titles, 400 serial subscriptions, 4,200 audiovisual materials, an OPAC, a Web page.

Computers on Campus 550 computers available on campus for general student use. A campuswide network can be accessed from off campus. Internet access, online (class) registration, at least one staffed computer lab available.

Student Life *Housing:* college housing not available. *Activities and Organizations:* student-run newspaper, radio and television station, intramural activities, Student Senate, Phi Theta Kappa, Inter-Varsity Christian Fellowship, DECA. *Campus security:* 24-hour emergency response devices and patrols, student patrols, late-night transport/escort service. *Student services:* personal/psychological counseling.

Athletics Member NJCAA. *Intercollegiate sports:* basketball M(s)/W(s), golf M(s), soccer M(s), softball W(s), volleyball W(s). *Intramural sports:* baseball M, basketball M/W, football M, golf M/W, racquetball M/W, soccer M/W, softball M/W, volleyball M/W.

Costs (2005–06) *Tuition:* area resident $1740 full-time, $73 per credit hour part-time; state resident $2496 full-time, $104 per credit hour part-time; nonresident $3564 full-time, $149 per credit hour part-time. *Required fees:* $192 full-time, $6 per credit part-time, $30 per term part-time. *Waivers:* senior citizens and employees or children of employees.

Financial Aid Of all full-time matriculated undergraduates who enrolled in 2004, 154 Federal Work-Study jobs (averaging $1575). 382 state and other part-time jobs (averaging $1865).

Applying *Options:* common application, electronic application, early admission, deferred entrance. *Application fee:* $20. *Required for some:* essay or personal statement. *Recommended:* high school transcript. *Application deadline:* rolling (freshmen), rolling (transfers).

Freshmen Application Contact Mr. Duff Zube, Director of Admissions, Delta College, 1961 Delta Road, University Center, MI 48710. *Phone:* 989-686-9449. *Toll-free phone:* 800-285-1705. *Fax:* 989-667-2202. *E-mail:* admit@delta.edu.

GLEN OAKS COMMUNITY COLLEGE

Centreville, Michigan **www.glenoaks.edu/**

- **State and locally supported** 2-year, founded 1965, part of Michigan Department of Career Development
- **Rural** 300-acre campus
- **Endowment** $1.4 million
- **Coed**

Undergraduates 659 full-time, 1,051 part-time. Students come from 3 states and territories, 6% are from out of state, 2% African American, 0.8% Asian American or Pacific Islander, 2% Hispanic American, 0.9% Native American, 0.1% international.

Faculty *Student/faculty ratio:* 16:1.

Academics *Calendar:* semesters. *Degree:* certificates and associate. *Special study options:* academic remediation for entering students, adult/continuing education programs, advanced placement credit, distance learning, internships, part-time degree program, services for LD students, summer session for credit.

Student Life *Campus security:* 24-hour emergency response devices.

Athletics Member NJCAA.

Standardized Tests *Required:* ACT ASSET (for placement).

Costs (2005–06) *Tuition:* area resident $1800 full-time, $60 per credit hour part-time; state resident $2670 full-time, $89 per credit hour part-time; nonresident $3450 full-time, $114 per credit hour part-time. *Required fees:* $255 full-time, $8 per credit hour part-time, $31 per term part-time.

Financial Aid Of all full-time matriculated undergraduates who enrolled in 2004, 70 Federal Work-Study jobs (averaging $1100). 38 state and other part-time jobs (averaging $1200).

Applying *Required:* high school transcript.

Freshmen Application Contact Ms. Beverly M. Andrews, Director of Admissions/Registrar, Glen Oaks Community College, 62249 Shimmel Road, Centreville, MI 49032-9719. *Phone:* 269-467-9945 Ext. 248. *Toll-free phone:* 888-994-7818.

GOGEBIC COMMUNITY COLLEGE

Ironwood, Michigan
www.gogebic.edu/

- **State and locally supported** 2-year, founded 1932, part of Michigan Department of Education
- **Small-town** 195-acre campus
- **Endowment** $675,000
- **Coed**

Undergraduates 517 full-time, 464 part-time. Students come from 7 states and territories, 4 other countries, 22% are from out of state, 0.6% African American, 0.4% Asian American or Pacific Islander, 0.8% Hispanic American, 3% Native American, 1% international, 3% transferred in.

Faculty *Student/faculty ratio:* 13:1.

Academics *Calendar:* semesters. *Degree:* certificates and associate. *Special study options:* academic remediation for entering students, adult/continuing education programs, advanced placement credit, cooperative education, distance learning, honors programs, internships, part-time degree program, services for LD students, summer session for credit.

Athletics Member NJCAA.

Costs (2005–06) *Tuition:* area resident $2294 full-time, $74 per credit part-time; state resident $2914 full-time, $94 per credit part-time; nonresident $3720 full-time, $120 per credit part-time. Full-time tuition and fees vary according to course load and reciprocity agreements. Part-time tuition and fees vary according to course load and reciprocity agreements. *Required fees:* $442 full-time, $5 per credit part-time.

Financial Aid Of all full-time matriculated undergraduates who enrolled in 2004, 75 Federal Work-Study jobs (averaging $1800). 50 state and other part-time jobs (averaging $1800).

Applying *Options:* electronic application, early admission, deferred entrance. *Application fee:* $10. *Required:* high school transcript.

Freshmen Application Contact Ms. Jeanne Graham, Director of Admissions, Gogebic Community College, E-4946 Jackson Road, Ironwood, MI 49938. *Phone:* 906-932-4231 Ext. 306. *Toll-free phone:* 800-682-5910 Ext. 207.

GRAND RAPIDS COMMUNITY COLLEGE

Grand Rapids, Michigan
www.grcc.edu/

- **District-supported** 2-year, founded 1914, part of Michigan Department of Education
- **Urban** 35-acre campus
- **Endowment** $10.3 million
- **Coed,** 14,798 undergraduate students, 44% full-time, 51% women, 49% men

Undergraduates 6,483 full-time, 8,315 part-time. Students come from 13 states and territories, 35 other countries, 0.9% are from out of state, 10% African American, 2% Asian American or Pacific Islander, 6% Hispanic American, 1% Native American, 0.7% international, 41% transferred in. *Retention:* 65% of 2003 full-time freshmen returned. Freshmen *Admission:* 6,454 applied, 5,971 admitted, 3,334 enrolled. *Average high school GPA:* 2.79.

Faculty *Total:* 648, 35% full-time, 8% with terminal degrees. *Student/faculty ratio:* 25:1.

Majors Administrative assistant and secretarial science; architectural engineering technology; art; automobile/automotive mechanics technology; business administration and management; computer engineering technology; computer programming; computer science; corrections; criminal justice/law enforcement administration; criminal justice/police science; culinary arts; dental hygiene; drafting and design technology; electrical, electronic and communications engineering technology; fashion merchandising; forestry; geology/earth science; heating, air conditioning, ventilation and refrigeration maintenance technology; industrial technology; legal administrative assistant/secretary; liberal arts and sciences/liberal studies; mass communication/media; medical administrative assistant and medical secretary; music; nursing (licensed practical/vocational nurse training); nursing (registered nurse training); plastics engineering technology; quality control technology; welding technology.

Academics *Calendar:* semesters. *Degree:* certificates and associate. *Special study options:* academic remediation for entering students, adult/continuing education programs, advanced placement credit, cooperative education, distance learning, English as a second language, off-campus study, part-time degree program, services for LD students, study abroad, summer session for credit.

Library Arthur Andrews Memorial Library plus 1 other with 101,077 titles, 10,552 serial subscriptions, an OPAC, a Web page.

Computers on Campus 1048 computers available on campus for general student use. A campuswide network can be accessed from off campus. Internet access, at least one staffed computer lab available.

Student Life *Housing:* college housing not available. *Activities and Organizations:* drama/theater group, student-run newspaper, choral group, Student Congress, Phi Theta Kappa, Hispanic Student Organization, Asian Student Organization, Service Learning Advisory Board, national fraternities, national sororities. *Campus security:* 24-hour emergency response devices, late-night transport/escort service. *Student services:* personal/psychological counseling.

Athletics Member NJCAA. *Intercollegiate sports:* baseball M/W(s), basketball M(s)/W(s), football M(s), golf M(s), softball W(s), swimming and diving M(s)/W(s), tennis M(s)/W(s), track and field M(s), volleyball W(s), wrestling M(s). *Intramural sports:* badminton M/W, basketball M/W, skiing (cross-country) M/W, skiing (downhill) M/W, soccer M/W, swimming and diving M/W, tennis M/W, volleyball M/W.

Standardized Tests *Required for some:* ACT ASSET. *Recommended:* SAT or ACT (for admission).

Costs (2006–07) *Tuition:* area resident $2205 full-time, $74 per contact hour part-time; state resident $4260 full-time, $142 per contact hour part-time; nonresident $6060 full-time, $202 per contact hour part-time. *Required fees:* $100 full-time, $70 per term part-time.

Financial Aid Of all full-time matriculated undergraduates who enrolled in 2004, 196 Federal Work-Study jobs (averaging $1799). 66 state and other part-time jobs (averaging $1348).

Applying *Options:* early admission, deferred entrance. *Application fee:* $20. *Required:* high school transcript. *Application deadline:* 8/30 (freshmen). *Notification:* continuous (freshmen).

Freshmen Application Contact Ms. Diane Patrick, Director of Admissions, Grand Rapids Community College, 143 Bostwick Avenue, NE, Grand Rapids, MI 49503-3201. *Phone:* 616-234-4100. *Fax:* 616-234-4005. *E-mail:* dpatrick@grcc.edu.

HENRY FORD COMMUNITY COLLEGE

Dearborn, Michigan
www.hfcc.edu/

- **District-supported** 2-year, founded 1938
- **Suburban** 75-acre campus with easy access to Detroit
- **Coed**

Undergraduates Students come from 3 states and territories, 17% African American, 2% Asian American or Pacific Islander, 3% Hispanic American, 0.8% Native American, 0.2% international.

Academics *Calendar:* semesters. *Degree:* certificates and associate. *Special study options:* academic remediation for entering students, adult/continuing education programs, advanced placement credit, cooperative education, freshman honors college, honors programs, internships, part-time degree program, services for LD students, summer session for credit.

Student Life *Campus security:* 24-hour emergency response devices and patrols, late-night transport/escort service.

Athletics Member NJCAA.

Standardized Tests *Recommended:* ACT (for placement).

Applying *Options:* early admission, deferred entrance. *Application fee:* $30. *Recommended:* high school transcript.

Freshmen Application Contact Ms. Dorothy A. Murphy, Coordinator of Recruitment, Henry Ford Community College, 5101 Evergreen Road, Dearborn, MI 48128-1495. *Phone:* 313-845-9766. *E-mail:* dorothy@mail.henryford.cc.mi.us.

ITT TECHNICAL INSTITUTE

Canton, Michigan
www.itt-tech.edu/

- **Proprietary** 2-year, founded 2002, part of ITT Educational Services, Inc
- **Coed**

Majors Business administration and management; CAD/CADD drafting/design technology; computer programming; criminal justice/law enforcement administration; electrical, electronic and communications engineering technology; system, networking, and LAN/WAN management; web/multimedia management and webmaster; web page, digital/multimedia and information resources design.

Academics *Calendar:* quarters. *Degree:* associate.

Library a Web page.

Computers on Campus Internet access, at least one staffed computer lab available.

Student Life *Housing:* college housing not available.

Standardized Tests *Required:* (for admission).

Costs (2005–06) *Tuition:* Please see school catalog for specific information.

ITT Technical Institute (continued)

Applying *Options:* deferred entrance. *Application fee:* $100. *Required:* high school transcript, interview. *Recommended:* letters of recommendation. *Application deadline:* rolling (freshmen), rolling (transfers). *Notification:* continuous (freshmen).

Freshmen Application Contact Mr. Rodney L. Cline, Director of Recruitment, ITT Technical Institute, 1905 South Haggerty Road, Canton, MI 48188. *Phone:* 784-397-7800. *Toll-free phone:* 800-247-4477.

ITT TECHNICAL INSTITUTE
Grand Rapids, Michigan   www.itt-tech.edu/

- **Proprietary** 2-year, part of ITT Educational Services, Inc
- **Coed**

Majors Business administration and management; CAD/CADD drafting/design technology; computer programming; criminal justice/law enforcement administration; electrical, electronic and communications engineering technology; system, networking, and LAN/WAN management; web/multimedia management and webmaster; web page, digital/multimedia and information resources design.

Academics *Calendar:* quarters. *Degree:* associate.

Library a Web page.

Computers on Campus Internet access, at least one staffed computer lab available.

Student Life *Housing:* college housing not available.

Standardized Tests *Required:* Wonderlic aptitude test (for admission).

Costs (2005–06) *Tuition:* Please see school catalog for specific information.

Applying *Options:* deferred entrance. *Application fee:* $100. *Required:* high school transcript, interview. *Recommended:* letters of recommendation. *Application deadline:* rolling (freshmen), rolling (transfers). *Notification:* continuous (freshmen).

Freshmen Application Contact Mr. Todd Peuler, Director of Recruitment, ITT Technical Institute, 4020 Sparks Drive SE, Grand Rapids, MI 49546. *Phone:* 616-956-1060. *Toll-free phone:* 800-632-4676.

ITT TECHNICAL INSTITUTE
Troy, Michigan   www.itt-tech.edu/

- **Proprietary** 2-year, founded 1987, part of ITT Educational Services, Inc
- **Coed**

Majors Business administration and management; CAD/CADD drafting/design technology; computer programming; criminal justice/law enforcement administration; electrical, electronic and communications engineering technology; system, networking, and LAN/WAN management; web/multimedia management and webmaster; web page, digital/multimedia and information resources design.

Academics *Calendar:* quarters. *Degree:* associate.

Library a Web page.

Computers on Campus Internet access, at least one staffed computer lab available.

Student Life *Housing:* college housing not available.

Standardized Tests *Required:* Wonderlic aptitude test (for admission).

Costs (2005–06) *Tuition:* Please see school catalog for specific information.

Applying *Options:* deferred entrance. *Application fee:* $100. *Required:* high school transcript, interview. *Recommended:* letters of recommendation. *Application deadline:* rolling (freshmen), rolling (transfers). *Notification:* continuous (freshmen).

Freshmen Application Contact Ms. Jennifer Hickey, ITT Technical Institute, 1522 East Big Beaver Road, Troy, MI 48083. *Phone:* 248-524-1800. *Toll-free phone:* 800-832-6817. *Fax:* 248-524-1965.

JACKSON COMMUNITY COLLEGE
Jackson, Michigan   www.jccmi.edu

- **County-supported** 2-year, founded 1928
- **Suburban** 580-acre campus with easy access to Detroit
- **Endowment** $10.7 million
- **Coed,** 5,870 undergraduate students, 36% full-time, 64% women, 36% men

Undergraduates 2,108 full-time, 3,762 part-time. 1% are from out of state, 5% African American, 0.8% Asian American or Pacific Islander, 4% Hispanic American, 0.7% Native American, 0.1% international. *Retention:* 65% of 2003 full-time freshmen returned.
Freshmen *Admission:* 267 enrolled. *Average high school GPA:* 2.26.

Faculty *Total:* 332, 28% full-time, 4% with terminal degrees. *Student/faculty ratio:* 19:1.

Majors Accounting and finance; administrative assistant and secretarial science; airline pilot and flight crew; automobile/automotive mechanics technology; business administration and management; computer and information sciences and support services related; construction trades related; corrections; criminal justice/law enforcement administration; data processing and data processing technology; diagnostic medical sonography and ultrasound technology; early childhood education; electrical, electronic and communications engineering technology; emergency medical technology (EMT paramedic); executive assistant/executive secretary; general studies; graphic design; heating, air conditioning and refrigeration technology; liberal arts and sciences/liberal studies; marketing/marketing management; medical/clinical assistant; medical insurance/medical billing; medical radiologic technology; medical transcription; nursing (licensed practical/vocational nurse training); nursing (registered nurse training).

Academics *Calendar:* semesters. *Degree:* certificates and associate. *Special study options:* academic remediation for entering students, adult/continuing education programs, advanced placement credit, cooperative education, distance learning, English as a second language, independent study, internships, part-time degree program, services for LD students, summer session for credit.

Library Atkinson Learning Resources Center plus 1 other with 67,000 titles, 300 serial subscriptions, 2,000 audiovisual materials, an OPAC, a Web page.

Computers on Campus 356 computers available on campus for general student use. A campuswide network can be accessed from off campus. Internet access, online (class) registration, at least one staffed computer lab available.

Student Life *Housing:* college housing not available. *Activities and Organizations:* drama/theater group, student-run newspaper, choral group. *Campus security:* 24-hour patrols.

Costs (2005–06) *Tuition:* area resident $1776 full-time, $74 per credit hour part-time; state resident $2496 full-time, $104 per credit hour part-time; nonresident $3192 full-time, $133 per credit hour part-time. Full-time tuition and fees vary according to location. Part-time tuition and fees vary according to location. *Required fees:* $384 full-time, $5 per credit hour part-time, $18 per term part-time. *Payment plan:* deferred payment. *Waivers:* senior citizens and employees or children of employees.

Financial Aid Of all full-time matriculated undergraduates who enrolled in 2004, 60 Federal Work-Study jobs (averaging $1304). 19 state and other part-time jobs (averaging $1192).

Applying *Options:* electronic application, early admission. *Application deadline:* rolling (freshmen), rolling (transfers). *Notification:* continuous (freshmen).

Freshmen Application Contact Ms. Julie Hand, Director of Enrollment Services Team Leader, Jackson Community College, 2111 Emmons Road, Jackson, MI 49201. *Phone:* 517-796-8425. *Toll-free phone:* 888-522-7344. *Fax:* 517-796-8631. *E-mail:* admissions@jccmi.edu.

KALAMAZOO VALLEY COMMUNITY COLLEGE
Kalamazoo, Michigan   www.kvcc.edu/

- **State and locally supported** 2-year, founded 1966
- **Suburban** 187-acre campus
- **Coed**

Undergraduates 3,959 full-time, 6,675 part-time. Students come from 3 states and territories, 46 other countries, 1% are from out of state, 9% African American, 1% Asian American or Pacific Islander, 3% Hispanic American, 0.9% Native American, 1% international.

Faculty *Student/faculty ratio:* 26:1.

Academics *Calendar:* semesters. *Degree:* certificates and associate. *Special study options:* academic remediation for entering students, advanced placement credit, cooperative education, distance learning, English as a second language, honors programs, independent study, internships, off-campus study, part-time degree program, services for LD students, student-designed majors, summer session for credit. *ROTC:* Army (c).

Student Life *Campus security:* 24-hour emergency response devices and patrols, late-night transport/escort service.

Athletics Member NJCAA.

Standardized Tests *Recommended:* ACT (for placement).

Costs (2005–06) *Tuition:* area resident $1320 full-time, $55 per credit part-time; state resident $2256 full-time, $94 per credit part-time; nonresident $3072 full-time, $128 per credit part-time.

Financial Aid Of all full-time matriculated undergraduates who enrolled in 2004, 65 Federal Work-Study jobs (averaging $1859). 10 state and other part-time jobs (averaging $1340).

Applying *Options:* early admission, deferred entrance.
Director of Admissions Mr. Michael McCall, Director of Admissions, Registration and Records, Kalamazoo Valley Community College, PO Box 4070, Kalamazoo, MI 49003-4070. *Phone:* 269-488-4207.

KELLOGG COMMUNITY COLLEGE

Battle Creek, Michigan www.kellogg.edu/

- **State and locally supported** 2-year, founded 1956, part of Michigan Department of Education
- **Urban** 120-acre campus
- **Endowment** $91,005
- **Coed,** 6,200 undergraduate students, 32% full-time, 63% women, 37% men

Undergraduates 1,954 full-time, 4,246 part-time. Students come from 3 states and territories, 11 other countries, 1% are from out of state, 7% African American, 1% Asian American or Pacific Islander, 2% Hispanic American, 0.7% Native American, 0.7% international, 3% transferred in.
Freshmen *Admission:* 2,085 applied, 1,817 admitted, 910 enrolled.
Faculty *Total:* 382, 24% full-time, 7% with terminal degrees. *Student/faculty ratio:* 22:1.
Majors Accounting; accounting technology and bookkeeping; administrative assistant and secretarial science; anthropology; art; art teacher education; biology/biological sciences; business administration and management; chemical technology; chemistry; clinical/medical laboratory technology; commercial and advertising art; communication/speech communication and rhetoric; computer engineering technology; computer graphics; computer programming; computer programming (specific applications); computer software and media applications related; corrections; criminal justice/police science; criminal justice/safety; data entry/microcomputer applications related; dental hygiene; drafting and design technology; dramatic/theater arts; elementary education; emergency medical technology (EMT paramedic); engineering; English; executive assistant/executive secretary; fire protection and safety technology; general studies; heating, air conditioning, ventilation and refrigeration maintenance technology; history; human services; industrial technology; international relations and affairs; journalism; kindergarten/preschool education; legal administrative assistant/secretary; legal assistant/paralegal; liberal arts and sciences/liberal studies; machine tool technology; mathematics; medical administrative assistant and medical secretary; medical radiologic technology; music; nursing (licensed practical/vocational nurse training); nursing (registered nurse training); philosophy; physical education teaching and coaching; physical therapist assistant; physics; pipefitting and sprinkler fitting; plastics engineering technology; political science and government; pre-law studies; pre-medical studies; pre-pharmacy studies; pre-theology/pre-ministerial studies; pre-veterinary studies; psychology; public relations/image management; radio and television broadcasting technology; robotics technology; secondary education; sheet metal technology; social work; sociology; special education; technology/industrial arts teacher education; welding technology; word processing.
Academics *Calendar:* semesters. *Degree:* certificates and associate. *Special study options:* academic remediation for entering students, accelerated degree program, adult/continuing education programs, advanced placement credit, distance learning, double majors, freshman honors college, honors programs, independent study, internships, off-campus study, part-time degree program, services for LD students, summer session for credit.
Library Emory W. Morris Learning Resource Center with 42,131 titles, 172 serial subscriptions, 4,145 audiovisual materials, an OPAC, a Web page.
Computers on Campus 550 computers available on campus for general student use. A campuswide network can be accessed from off campus. At least one staffed computer lab available.
Student Life *Housing:* college housing not available. *Activities and Organizations:* drama/theater group, student-run newspaper, choral group, Tech Club, Phi Theta Kappa, Student Nurses Association, Crude Arts Club, Art League. *Campus security:* 24-hour emergency response devices and patrols, late-night transport/escort service.
Athletics Member NJCAA. *Intercollegiate sports:* baseball M(s), basketball M(s)/W(s), soccer M, softball W(s), volleyball W(s).
Standardized Tests *Required for some:* ACT (for admission), SAT or ACT (for admission).
Costs (2006–07) *Tuition:* area resident $1950 full-time, $65 per credit hour part-time; state resident $3165 full-time, $106 per credit hour part-time; nonresident $4770 full-time, $159 per credit hour part-time. *Required fees:* $210 full-time, $7 per credit hour part-time.
Financial Aid Of all full-time matriculated undergraduates who enrolled in 2004, 41 Federal Work-Study jobs (averaging $2251). 43 state and other part-time jobs (averaging $2058).

Applying *Options:* common application, early admission, deferred entrance. *Required for some:* high school transcript, minimum 2.0 GPA. *Application deadline:* 8/30 (freshmen), rolling (transfers). *Notification:* continuous (freshmen).
Freshmen Application Contact Mr. Sedgwick Harris, Director of Admissions, Kellogg Community College, 450 North Avenue, Battle Creek, MI 49017. *Phone:* 269-965-3931 Ext. 2641. *Fax:* 269-965-4133.

KIRTLAND COMMUNITY COLLEGE

Roscommon, Michigan www.kirtland.edu/

Freshmen Application Contact Ms. Stacey Thompson, Registrar, Kirtland Community College, 10775 North St Helen Road, Roscommon, MI 48653-9699. *Phone:* 517-275-5121 Ext. 248.

LAKE MICHIGAN COLLEGE

Benton Harbor, Michigan www.lmc.cc.mi.us/

- **District-supported** 2-year, founded 1946, part of Michigan Department of Education
- **Small-town** 260-acre campus
- **Endowment** $5.0 million
- **Coed,** 4,043 undergraduate students, 31% full-time, 60% women, 40% men

Undergraduates 1,235 full-time, 2,808 part-time. Students come from 5 states and territories, 2% are from out of state, 15% African American, 2% Asian American or Pacific Islander, 4% Hispanic American, 1% Native American, 0.9% international.
Freshmen *Admission:* 826 applied, 629 admitted, 629 enrolled. *Average high school GPA:* 2.62. *Test scores:* SAT verbal scores over 500: 75%; SAT math scores over 500: 75%; ACT scores over 18: 66%; SAT math scores over 600: 25%; ACT scores over 24: 8%; ACT scores over 30: 2%.
Faculty *Total:* 227, 26% full-time. *Student/faculty ratio:* 18:1.
Majors Accounting technology and bookkeeping; administrative assistant and secretarial science; business administration and management; computer and information sciences; criminal justice/police science; data processing and data processing technology; dental assisting; drafting and design technology; early childhood education; electrical, electronic and communications engineering technology; electromechanical technology; graphic design; hospitality administration; industrial technology; legal administrative assistant/secretary; liberal arts and sciences/liberal studies; machine tool technology; marketing/marketing management; medical administrative assistant and medical secretary; medical office assistant; medical radiologic technology; nuclear/nuclear power technology; nursing (registered nurse training); plastics engineering technology; precision production trades.
Academics *Calendar:* semesters. *Degree:* certificates and associate. *Special study options:* academic remediation for entering students, adult/continuing education programs, honors programs, part-time degree program, student-designed majors, summer session for credit.
Library Lake Michigan College Library with 79,000 titles, 280 serial subscriptions.
Computers on Campus 124 computers available on campus for general student use.
Student Life *Housing:* college housing not available. *Activities and Organizations:* drama/theater group, choral group, Hospitality Club, International Club, Pride Club II, DECA. *Student services:* personal/psychological counseling, women's center.
Athletics Member NJCAA. *Intercollegiate sports:* baseball M(s), basketball M(s)/W(s), softball W(s), volleyball W(s).
Costs (2006–07) *Tuition:* area resident $2175 full-time, $73 per credit hour part-time; state resident $3060 full-time, $102 per credit hour part-time; nonresident $4080 full-time, $136 per credit hour part-time. *Required fees:* $930 full-time, $31 per credit hour part-time.
Financial Aid Of all full-time matriculated undergraduates who enrolled in 2004, 105 Federal Work-Study jobs (averaging $1200). 176 state and other part-time jobs (averaging $1200).
Applying *Options:* common application, early admission, deferred entrance. *Required:* high school transcript. *Required for some:* interview. *Application deadline:* rolling (freshmen), rolling (transfers). *Notification:* continuous (freshmen).
Freshmen Application Contact Ms. Julie Bruns, Assistant Registrar, Lake Michigan College, 2755 East Napier, Benton Harbor, MI 49022-1899. *Phone:* 616-927-8100 Ext. 5083. *Toll-free phone:* 800-252-1LMC. *E-mail:* bruns@lakemichigancollege.edu.

LANSING COMMUNITY COLLEGE

Lansing, Michigan   **www.lcc.edu/**

- **State and locally supported** 2-year, founded 1957, part of Michigan Department of Education
- **Urban** 28-acre campus
- **Endowment** $3.5 million
- **Coed,** 20,057 undergraduate students, 31% full-time, 55% women, 45% men

Undergraduates 6,154 full-time, 13,903 part-time. Students come from 29 states and territories, 69 other countries, 1% are from out of state, 9% African American, 2% Asian American or Pacific Islander, 4% Hispanic American, 0.9% Native American, 2% international.

Freshmen *Admission:* 3,322 applied, 3,322 admitted, 3,321 enrolled.

Faculty *Total:* 1,383, 16% full-time. *Student/faculty ratio:* 14:1.

Majors Accounting; administrative assistant and secretarial science; airline pilot and flight crew; architectural engineering technology; art; automobile/automotive mechanics technology; avionics maintenance technology; biological and physical sciences; biology/biological sciences; biology/biotechnology laboratory technician; broadcast journalism; business administration and management; carpentry; chemical engineering; chemistry; child development; cinematography and film/video production; civil engineering technology; clinical laboratory science/medical technology; commercial and advertising art; computer engineering technology; computer graphics; computer management; computer programming; computer typography and composition equipment operation; construction engineering technology; consumer merchandising/retailing management; corrections; court reporting; criminal justice/law enforcement administration; criminal justice/police science; dance; dental hygiene; developmental and child psychology; diagnostic medical sonography and ultrasound technology; drafting and design technology; dramatic/theater arts; education; electrical, electronic and communications engineering technology; electromechanical technology; elementary education; emergency medical technology (EMT paramedic); engineering; engineering technology; English; film/cinema studies; finance; fine/studio arts; fire science; geography; geology/earth science; gerontology; heating, air conditioning, ventilation and refrigeration maintenance technology; heavy equipment maintenance technology; horticultural science; hospitality administration; hotel/motel administration; human resources management; human services; industrial technology; information science/studies; international business/trade/commerce; journalism; kindergarten/preschool education; labor and industrial relations; landscape architecture; legal administrative assistant/secretary; legal assistant/paralegal; liberal arts and sciences/liberal studies; machine tool technology; management information systems; marketing/marketing management; mass communication/media; mathematics; mechanical design technology; mechanical engineering/mechanical technology; medical/clinical assistant; medical radiologic technology; music; nursing (licensed practical/vocational nurse training); nursing (registered nurse training); philosophy; photography; physical education teaching and coaching; pre-engineering; public administration; public relations/image management; quality control technology; radio and television; real estate; religious studies; respiratory care therapy; sign language interpretation and translation; social work; special products marketing; speech and rhetoric; surgical technology; survey technology; teacher assistant/aide; telecommunications; tourism and travel services management; veterinary technology; voice and opera; welding technology.

Academics *Calendar:* semesters. *Degree:* certificates and associate. *Special study options:* academic remediation for entering students, adult/continuing education programs, advanced placement credit, cooperative education, distance learning, double majors, English as a second language, external degree program, honors programs, independent study, internships, part-time degree program, services for LD students, study abroad, summer session for credit. *ROTC:* Army (c), Air Force (c).

Library Abel Sykes Technology and Learning Center plus 1 other with 98,125 titles, 600 serial subscriptions, 11,653 audiovisual materials, an OPAC, a Web page.

Computers on Campus 1146 computers available on campus for general student use. A campuswide network can be accessed from off campus. At least one staffed computer lab available.

Student Life *Housing:* college housing not available. *Activities and Organizations:* drama/theater group, student-run newspaper, radio station, choral group, Student Marketing, Legal Assistants Club, Student Nursing Club, Phi Theta Kappa, Student Advising Club, national fraternities, national sororities. *Campus security:* 24-hour emergency response devices and patrols, student patrols, late-night transport/escort service. *Student services:* personal/psychological counseling, women's center.

Athletics Member NJCAA. *Intercollegiate sports:* basketball M(s)/W(s), cross-country running M(s)/W(s), golf M(s), track and field M(s)/W(s), volleyball W(s). *Intramural sports:* baseball M, basketball M/W, cross-country running M/W, ice hockey M, soccer M/W, softball W, track and field M/W, volleyball W.

Costs (2006–07) *Tuition:* area resident $1975 full-time, $65 per contact hour part-time; state resident $3175 full-time, $105 per contact hour part-time;

nonresident $4375 full-time, $145 per contact hour part-time. *Required fees:* $50 full-time, $25 per term part-time.

Financial Aid Of all full-time matriculated undergraduates who enrolled in 2004, 125 Federal Work-Study jobs (averaging $2636). 122 state and other part-time jobs (averaging $2563).

Applying *Options:* common application, electronic application, early admission, deferred entrance. *Required for some:* essay or personal statement, high school transcript, 2 letters of recommendation, interview. *Application deadline:* rolling (freshmen), rolling (transfers).

Freshmen Application Contact Ms. Tammy Grossbauer, Director of Admissions/Registrar, Lansing Community College, PO Box 40010, Lansing, MI 48901-7210. *Phone:* 517-483-9886. *Toll-free phone:* 800-644-4LCC. *Fax:* 517-483-1170. *E-mail:* grossbt@lcc.edu.

LEWIS COLLEGE OF BUSINESS

Detroit, Michigan   **www.lewiscollege.edu/**

Freshmen Application Contact Ms. Frances Ambrose, Admissions Secretary, Lewis College of Business, 17370 Meyers Road, Detroit, MI 48235-1423. *Phone:* 313-862-6300.

MACOMB COMMUNITY COLLEGE

Warren, Michigan   **www.macomb.edu/**

- **District-supported** 2-year, founded 1954
- **Suburban** 384-acre campus with easy access to Detroit
- **Endowment** $8.0 million
- **Coed,** 20,596 undergraduate students, 37% full-time, 52% women, 48% men

Undergraduates 7,520 full-time, 13,076 part-time. Students come from 5 states and territories, 6% African American, 4% Asian American or Pacific Islander, 1% Hispanic American, 0.5% Native American, 1% international.

Freshmen *Admission:* 2,031 enrolled.

Faculty *Total:* 1,032, 22% full-time, 10% with terminal degrees. *Student/faculty ratio:* 28:1.

Majors Accounting; administrative assistant and secretarial science; agriculture; architectural drafting and CAD/CADD; automobile/automotive mechanics technology; automotive engineering technology; biology/biological sciences; business administration and management; business automation/technology/data entry; business/commerce; cabinetmaking and millwork; chemistry; child care and support services management; civil engineering technology; commercial and advertising art; communication/speech communication and rhetoric; computer programming; computer programming (specific applications); construction engineering technology; criminal justice/law enforcement administration; criminal justice/police science; culinary arts; drafting and design technology; electrical, electronic and communications engineering technology; electrical/electronics equipment installation and repair; electromechanical technology; emergency medical technology (EMT paramedic); energy management and systems technology; engineering related; finance; fire protection and safety technology; forensic science and technology; general studies; graphic and printing equipment operation/production; heating, air conditioning and refrigeration technology; heating, air conditioning, ventilation and refrigeration maintenance technology; industrial mechanics and maintenance technology; industrial technology; international/global studies; legal assistant/paralegal; legal studies; liberal arts and sciences/liberal studies; machine tool technology; manufacturing technology; marketing/marketing management; mathematics; mechanical design technology; mechanical drafting and CAD/CADD; mechanical engineering/mechanical technology; mechanic and repair technologies related; medical/clinical assistant; mental health/rehabilitation; metallurgical technology; music performance; nursing (registered nurse training); occupational therapist assistant; operations management; physical therapist assistant; plastics engineering technology; plumbing technology; pre-engineering; quality control technology; respiratory care therapy; robotics technology; safety/security technology; sheet metal technology; social psychology; surgical technology; survey technology; tool and die technology; veterinary/animal health technology; veterinary sciences; welding technology.

Academics *Calendar:* semesters. *Degree:* certificates and associate. *Special study options:* academic remediation for entering students, adult/continuing education programs, advanced placement credit, cooperative education, English as a second language, honors programs, internships, off-campus study, part-time degree program, services for LD students, student-designed majors, summer session for credit.

Library 159,226 titles, 4,240 serial subscriptions, an OPAC.

Computers on Campus 2000 computers available on campus for general student use. A campuswide network can be accessed from off campus. At least one staffed computer lab available.

Student Life *Housing:* college housing not available. *Activities and Organizations:* drama/theater group, Phi Beta Kappa, Adventure Unlimited, Alpha Rho Rho, SADD. *Campus security:* 24-hour emergency response devices and patrols, late-night transport/escort service, security phones in parking lots, surveillance cameras. *Student services:* health clinic, personal/psychological counseling.

Athletics Member NJCAA. *Intercollegiate sports:* baseball M(s), basketball M(s), cross-country running M(s)/W(s), soccer M(s), softball W(s), track and field M(s)/W(s), volleyball W(s). *Intramural sports:* baseball M, basketball M, bowling M/W, cross-country running M/W, football M/W, skiing (cross-country) M/W, skiing (downhill) M/W, volleyball M/W.

Costs (2006–07) *Tuition:* area resident $2108 full-time, $68 per credit hour part-time; state resident $3224 full-time, $104 per credit hour part-time; nonresident $4185 full-time, $135 per credit hour part-time. *Required fees:* $40 full-time, $20 per term part-time.

Financial Aid Of all full-time matriculated undergraduates who enrolled in 2004, 800 Federal Work-Study jobs (averaging $2800).

Applying *Options:* common application, early admission, deferred entrance. *Application deadline:* rolling (freshmen), rolling (transfers).

Freshmen Application Contact Mr. Richard P. Stevens, Coordinator of Admissions and Assessment, Macomb Community College, G312, 14500 East 12 Mile Road, Warren, MI 48088-3896. *Phone:* 586-445-7246. *Toll-free phone:* 866-622-6624. *Fax:* 586-445-7140. *E-mail:* stevensr@macomb.edu.

MID MICHIGAN COMMUNITY COLLEGE
Harrison, Michigan   **www.midmich.cc.mi.us/**

- **State and locally supported** 2-year, founded 1965, part of Michigan Department of Education
- **Rural** 560-acre campus
- **Coed**

Undergraduates 1,465 full-time, 1,767 part-time. Students come from 6 states and territories, 0.5% are from out of state, 2% African American, 0.7% Asian American or Pacific Islander, 2% Hispanic American, 2% Native American, 0.3% international, 6% transferred in. *Retention:* 8% of 2003 full-time freshmen returned.

Faculty *Student/faculty ratio:* 15:1.

Academics *Calendar:* semesters. *Degree:* certificates and associate. *Special study options:* academic remediation for entering students, adult/continuing education programs, advanced placement credit, cooperative education, distance learning, honors programs, independent study, internships, part-time degree program, services for LD students, summer session for credit.

Student Life *Campus security:* 24-hour emergency response devices.

Standardized Tests *Recommended:* ACT (for placement).

Costs (2005–06) *Tuition:* area resident $2000 full-time; state resident $3500 full-time; nonresident $6400 full-time. *Required fees:* $150 full-time.

Financial Aid Of all full-time matriculated undergraduates who enrolled in 2004, 50 Federal Work-Study jobs (averaging $3600). 50 state and other part-time jobs (averaging $3600).

Applying *Options:* early admission. *Required for some:* interview. *Recommended:* high school transcript.

Freshmen Application Contact Ms. Brenda Mather, Admissions Specialist, Mid Michigan Community College, 1375 South Clare Avenue, Harrison, MI 48625. *Phone:* 989-386-6661.

MONROE COUNTY COMMUNITY COLLEGE
Monroe, Michigan   **www.monroeccc.edu/**

Director of Admissions Mr. Randell W. Daniels, Director of Admissions and Guidance Services, Monroe County Community College, 155 South Raisinville Road, Monroe, MI 48161-9047. *Phone:* 734-384-4261. *Toll-free phone:* 877-YES MCCC.

MONTCALM COMMUNITY COLLEGE
Sidney, Michigan   **www.montcalm.edu/**

- **State and locally supported** 2-year, founded 1965, part of Michigan Department of Education
- **Rural** 240-acre campus with easy access to Grand Rapids
- **Endowment** $3.4 million
- **Coed**

Undergraduates 674 full-time, 1,406 part-time. Students come from 1 other state, 0.2% African American, 0.3% Asian American or Pacific Islander, 2% Hispanic American, 1% Native American, 6% transferred in.

Faculty *Student/faculty ratio:* 13:1.

Academics *Calendar:* semesters. *Degree:* certificates and associate. *Special study options:* academic remediation for entering students, adult/continuing education programs, advanced placement credit, cooperative education, distance learning, double majors, independent study, internships, off-campus study, part-time degree program, services for LD students, summer session for credit.

Standardized Tests *Required:* ACT ASSET, ACT COMPASS (for placement). *Recommended:* ACT (for placement).

Costs (2005–06) *Tuition:* area resident $1920 full-time, $64 per credit hour part-time; state resident $2940 full-time, $98 per credit hour part-time; nonresident $3810 full-time, $127 per credit hour part-time. Full-time tuition and fees vary according to course load. Part-time tuition and fees vary according to course load. *Required fees:* $165 full-time, $6 per credit hour part-time.

Financial Aid Of all full-time matriculated undergraduates who enrolled in 2004, 57 Federal Work-Study jobs (averaging $2000).

Applying *Options:* early admission, deferred entrance. *Recommended:* high school transcript.

Freshmen Application Contact Ms. Debra Alexander, Director of Admissions, Montcalm Community College, 2800 College Drive, Sidney, MI 48885. *Phone:* 989-328-1276. *Toll-free phone:* 877-328-2111. *E-mail:* admissions@montcalm.edu.

MOTT COMMUNITY COLLEGE
Flint, Michigan   **www.mcc.edu/**

- **District-supported** 2-year, founded 1923, part of Michigan Labor and Economic Growth Department
- **Urban** 20-acre campus with easy access to Detroit
- **Endowment** $35.1 million
- **Coed,** 10,299 undergraduate students, 36% full-time, 61% women, 39% men

Undergraduates 3,663 full-time, 6,636 part-time. Students come from 10 states and territories, 33 other countries, 18% African American, 0.8% Asian American or Pacific Islander, 2% Hispanic American, 1% Native American, 0.3% international, 3% transferred in.

Freshmen *Admission:* 2,838 applied, 1,101 admitted, 1,101 enrolled.

Faculty *Total:* 509, 29% full-time, 9% with terminal degrees. *Student/faculty ratio:* 22:1.

Majors Accounting technology and bookkeeping; administrative assistant and secretarial science; architectural engineering technology; autobody/collision and repair technology; automobile/automotive mechanics technology; business administration and management; business/commerce; communications technology; community health services counseling; computer and information sciences and support services related; computer systems networking and telecommunications; criminal justice/police science; culinary arts; dental assisting; dental hygiene; drafting and design technology; early childhood education; electrical, electronic and communications engineering technology; emergency medical technology (EMT paramedic); engineering technologies related; entrepreneurship; fire protection and safety technology; foodservice systems administration; general studies; graphic design; heating, air conditioning and refrigeration technology; histologic technician; information resources management; international business/trade/commerce; legal administrative assistant/secretary; liberal arts and sciences/liberal studies; management information systems; manufacturing technology; marketing/marketing management; mechanical drafting and CAD/CADD; mechanical engineering/mechanical technology; medical administrative assistant and medical secretary; medical radiologic technology; nursing (registered nurse training); occupational therapist assistant; office management; photography; physical therapist assistant; precision production related; quality control technology; respiratory care therapy; salon/beauty salon management; sign language interpretation and translation; survey technology; teacher assistant/aide.

Academics *Calendar:* semesters. *Degree:* certificates and associate. *Special study options:* academic remediation for entering students, accelerated degree program, adult/continuing education programs, advanced placement credit, coop-

Mott Community College (continued)

erative education, distance learning, double majors, English as a second language, honors programs, independent study, internships, part-time degree program, services for LD students, summer session for credit.

Library Charles Stewart Mott Library with 112,251 titles, 325 serial subscriptions, an OPAC, a Web page.

Computers on Campus 1290 computers available on campus for general student use. A campuswide network can be accessed from off campus. Internet access, online (class) registration, at least one staffed computer lab available.

Student Life *Housing:* college housing not available. *Activities and Organizations:* choral group, Criminal Justice Association, Phi Theta Kappa, Dental Assisting Club, Connoisseur's Club, Social Work Club. *Campus security:* 24-hour emergency response devices and patrols, student patrols, late-night transport/escort service. *Student services:* health clinic, personal/psychological counseling.

Athletics Member NJCAA. *Intercollegiate sports:* baseball M(s), basketball M(s)/W(s), cross-country running M(s)/W(s), golf M(s), softball W(s), volleyball W(s).

Costs (2006–07) *Tuition:* area resident $2385 full-time, $80 per contact hour part-time; state resident $3572 full-time, $119 per contact hour part-time; nonresident $4766 full-time, $159 per contact hour part-time. *Required fees:* $107 full-time, $54 per term part-time.

Financial Aid Of all full-time matriculated undergraduates who enrolled in 2004, 258 Federal Work-Study jobs (averaging $1000). 300 state and other part-time jobs (averaging $1000).

Applying *Options:* electronic application, early admission, deferred entrance. *Required:* high school transcript. *Application deadline:* 8/31 (freshmen).

Freshmen Application Contact Mr. Marc Payne, Executive Director of Admissions and Recruitment, Mott Community College, 1401 East Court Street, Flint, MI 48503. *Phone:* 810-762-0315. *Toll-free phone:* 800-852-8614. *Fax:* 810-232-9442. *E-mail:* inquiry@mcc.edu.

MUSKEGON COMMUNITY COLLEGE

Muskegon, Michigan   www.muskegon.cc.mi.us/

- **State and locally supported** 2-year, founded 1926, part of Michigan Department of Education
- **Urban** 112-acre campus with easy access to Grand Rapids
- **Coed**

Undergraduates Students come from 3 states and territories, 5 other countries.

Academics *Calendar:* semesters. *Degree:* associate. *Special study options:* academic remediation for entering students, adult/continuing education programs, cooperative education, honors programs, part-time degree program, student-designed majors, summer session for credit.

Athletics Member NJCAA.

Standardized Tests *Recommended:* SAT or ACT (for placement).

Financial Aid Of all full-time matriculated undergraduates who enrolled in 2004, 250 Federal Work-Study jobs (averaging $2500). 50 state and other part-time jobs (averaging $2500).

Applying *Options:* early admission, deferred entrance.

Freshmen Application Contact Ms. Lynda Schwartz, Admissions Coordinator, Muskegon Community College, 221 South Quarterline Road, Muskegon, MI 49442-1493. *Phone:* 231-773-9131 Ext. 366.

NORTH CENTRAL MICHIGAN COLLEGE

Petoskey, Michigan   www.ncmc.cc.mi.us/

Director of Admissions Ms. Julieanne Tobin, Director of Enrollment Management, North Central Michigan College, 1515 Howard Street, Petoskey, MI 49770-8717. *Phone:* 231-439-6511. *Toll-free phone:* 888-298-6605.

NORTHWESTERN MICHIGAN COLLEGE

Traverse City, Michigan   www.nmc.edu/

- **State and locally supported** 2-year, founded 1951
- **Small-town** 180-acre campus
- **Coed**

Undergraduates 2,011 full-time, 2,598 part-time. Students come from 19 states and territories, 2% are from out of state, 0.5% African American, 0.8%

Asian American or Pacific Islander, 1% Hispanic American, 2% Native American, 11% transferred in, 5% live on campus. *Retention:* 49% of 2003 full-time freshmen returned.

Faculty *Student/faculty ratio:* 23:1.

Academics *Calendar:* semesters. *Degree:* certificates and associate. *Special study options:* academic remediation for entering students, adult/continuing education programs, advanced placement credit, cooperative education, distance learning, honors programs, independent study, internships, part-time degree program, services for LD students, summer session for credit.

Student Life *Campus security:* 24-hour emergency response devices and patrols, student patrols, late-night transport/escort service, controlled dormitory access, well-lit campus.

Standardized Tests *Required:* ACT COMPASS (for placement).

Costs (2005–06) *Tuition:* area resident $2339 full-time, $69 per contact hour part-time; state resident $4077 full-time, $120 per contact hour part-time; nonresident $5087 full-time, $149 per contact hour part-time. Part-time tuition and fees vary according to course load. *Required fees:* $383 full-time, $10 per contact hour part-time, $16 per term part-time. *Room and board:* $6285. Room and board charges vary according to board plan and housing facility. *Payment plans:* installment, deferred payment.

Financial Aid Of all full-time matriculated undergraduates who enrolled in 2004, 66 Federal Work-Study jobs (averaging $1742). 5 state and other part-time jobs (averaging $1603).

Applying *Options:* common application, early admission, deferred entrance. *Application fee:* $15. *Required for some:* high school transcript. *Recommended:* minimum 2.0 GPA.

Director of Admissions Mr. James Bensley, Coordinator of Admissions, Northwestern Michigan College, 1701 East Front Street, Traverse City, MI 49686. *Phone:* 231-995-1034. *Toll-free phone:* 800-748-0566.

OAKLAND COMMUNITY COLLEGE

Bloomfield Hills, Michigan   www.oaklandcc.edu/

- **State and locally supported** 2-year, founded 1964, part of Michigan Department of Career Development
- **Suburban** 540-acre campus with easy access to Detroit
- **Endowment** $1.4 million
- **Coed,** 24,287 undergraduate students, 32% full-time, 58% women, 42% men

Undergraduates 7,705 full-time, 16,582 part-time. Students come from 12 states and territories, 73 other countries, 16% African American, 2% Asian American or Pacific Islander, 2% Hispanic American, 0.7% Native American, 8% international, 2% transferred in. *Retention:* 66% of 2003 full-time freshmen returned.

Freshmen *Admission:* 2,615 applied, 2,615 admitted, 1,704 enrolled.

Faculty *Total:* 945, 29% full-time. *Student/faculty ratio:* 27:1.

Majors Accounting; allied health diagnostic, intervention, and treatment professions related; applied horticulture; architectural engineering technology; architecture; automobile/automotive mechanics technology; aviation/airway management; business administration and management; business automation/technology/data entry; cabinetmaking and millwork; carpentry; ceramic arts and ceramics; child care and support services management; clinical/medical laboratory science and allied professions related; computer and information sciences; computer programming; computer technology/computer systems technology; construction management; consumer merchandising/retailing management; corrections and criminal justice related; cosmetology; court reporting; criminal justice/law enforcement administration; criminal justice/police science; culinary arts; dental hygiene; diagnostic medical sonography and ultrasound technology; electrical, electronic and communications engineering technology; electromechanical technology; electroneurodiagnostic/electroencephalographic technology; emergency medical technology (EMT paramedic); engineering; entrepreneurship; environmental control technologies related; fashion merchandising; fine arts related; fire science; foodservice systems administration; forensic science and technology; general studies; gerontology; graphic design; health and physical education related; health/health care administration; health professions related; heating, air conditioning and refrigeration technology; histologic technician; hotel/motel administration; industrial electronics technology; industrial technology; interior design; international business/trade/commerce; kinesiology and exercise science; landscape architecture; landscaping and groundskeeping; legal assistant/paralegal; liberal arts and sciences and humanities related; liberal arts and sciences/liberal studies; library assistant; machine tool technology; management information systems and services related; management science; manufacturing technology; marketing related; massage therapy; mechanical drafting and CAD/CADD; medical/clinical assistant; medical radiologic technology; medical transcription; mental and social health services and allied professions related; nuclear medical technology; nursing (licensed practical/vocational nurse training); nursing (registered nurse training); office management; operations management; ornamental horticulture; pharmacy technician; photography; precision metal working related; pre-engineering; radio and television broadcasting technology; respiratory care therapy; restaurant/food services management; robotics technology; salon/beauty salon management; sport and fitness administration/ management; surgical technology; tool and die technology; welding technology; woodworking related.

Academics *Calendar:* semesters. *Degrees:* certificates, associate, and post-bachelor's certificates. *Special study options:* academic remediation for entering students, adult/continuing education programs, advanced placement credit, cooperative education, distance learning, English as a second language, internships, off-campus study, part-time degree program, services for LD students, study abroad, summer session for credit.

Library Main Library plus 5 others with 243,137 titles, 2,139 serial subscriptions, 8,315 audiovisual materials, an OPAC, a Web page.

Computers on Campus 2065 computers available on campus for general student use. A campuswide network can be accessed from off campus. Internet access, online (class) registration, at least one staffed computer lab available.

Student Life *Housing:* college housing not available. *Activities and Organizations:* drama/theater group, choral group, Phi Theta Kappa, International Student Organization, organizations related to student majors. *Campus security:* 24-hour emergency response devices, late-night transport/escort service. *Student services:* personal/psychological counseling, women's center.

Athletics Member NJCAA. *Intercollegiate sports:* basketball M(s)/W(s), cross-country running M(s)/W(s), golf M(s), soccer M, softball W(s), tennis W(s), volleyball W(s). *Intramural sports:* basketball M/W, racquetball M/W, tennis W, volleyball M/W.

Costs (2006–07) *Tuition:* area resident $1704 full-time, $57 per credit hour part-time; state resident $2885 full-time, $96 per credit hour part-time; nonresident $4045 full-time, $135 per credit hour part-time. *Required fees:* $70 full-time, $35 per term part-time.

Financial Aid Of all full-time matriculated undergraduates who enrolled in 2004, 135 Federal Work-Study jobs (averaging $2800). 70 state and other part-time jobs (averaging $2800).

Applying *Options:* deferred entrance. *Recommended:* high school transcript, interview. *Application deadline:* rolling (freshmen), rolling (transfers). *Notification:* continuous (freshmen).

Freshmen Application Contact Dr. Maurice McCall, Registrar and Director of Enrollment Services, Oakland Community College, 2480 Opdyke Road, Bloomfield Hills, MI 48304-2266. *Phone:* 248-341-2186. *Fax:* 248-341-2099.

SAGINAW CHIPPEWA TRIBAL COLLEGE
Mount Pleasant, Michigan   www.sagchip.org/tribalcollege/

- **Independent** 2-year, founded 1998
- **Coed,** 123 undergraduate students, 35% full-time, 75% women, 25% men

Undergraduates 43 full-time, 80 part-time. 2% African American, 3% Hispanic American, 85% Native American.
Freshmen *Admission:* 36 applied, 36 admitted, 36 enrolled.
Faculty *Total:* 17, 24% full-time. *Student/faculty ratio:* 9:1.
Majors American Indian/Native American studies; business/commerce; liberal arts and sciences/liberal studies.
Academics *Calendar:* semesters. *Degree:* associate.
Student Life *Activities and Organizations:* student-run newspaper.
Costs (2006–07) *Tuition:* $1320 full-time, $55 per credit hour part-time. *Required fees:* $136 full-time, $68 per term part-time.
Applying *Required:* high school transcript.
Freshmen Application Contact Ms. Tracy Reed, Admissions Officer/Registrar/ Financial Aid, Saginaw Chippewa Tribal College, 2274 Enterprise Drive, Mount Pleasant, MI 48858. *Phone:* 989-775-4123. *Fax:* 989-775-4528. *E-mail:* treed@ sagchip.org.

ST. CLAIR COUNTY COMMUNITY COLLEGE
Port Huron, Michigan   www.sc4.edu/

Director of Admissions Mr. Pete Lacey, Registrar, St. Clair County Community College, 323 Erie Street, PO Box 5015, PO Box 5015, Port Huron, MI 48061-5015. *Phone:* 810-989-5500. *Toll-free phone:* 800-553-2427.

SCHOOLCRAFT COLLEGE
Livonia, Michigan   www.schoolcraft.edu/

- **District-supported** 2-year, founded 1961, part of Michigan Department of Education
- **Suburban** 183-acre campus with easy access to Detroit
- **Endowment** $8.9 million
- **Coed**

Undergraduates 3,377 full-time, 6,836 part-time. Students come from 4 states and territories, 1% are from out of state, 8% African American, 2% Asian American or Pacific Islander, 2% Hispanic American, 0.7% Native American, 0.2% international, 13% transferred in.
Faculty *Student/faculty ratio:* 27:1.
Academics *Calendar:* semesters. *Degree:* certificates and associate. *Special study options:* academic remediation for entering students, accelerated degree program, adult/continuing education programs, advanced placement credit, cooperative education, distance learning, part-time degree program, services for LD students, summer session for credit.
Student Life *Campus security:* 24-hour emergency response devices and patrols, late-night transport/escort service.
Athletics Member NJCAA.
Standardized Tests *Required:* ACT or CPT (for placement). *Recommended:* ACT (for placement).
Costs (2005–06) *Tuition:* area resident $1950 full-time, $65 per credit hour part-time; state resident $2910 full-time, $97 per credit hour part-time; nonresident $4290 full-time, $143 per credit hour part-time. *Required fees:* $130 full-time. *Payment plans:* installment, deferred payment.
Financial Aid Of all full-time matriculated undergraduates who enrolled in 2004, 42 Federal Work-Study jobs (averaging $1722).
Applying *Options:* early admission, deferred entrance. *Required for some:* high school transcript. *Recommended:* high school transcript.
Director of Admissions Ms. Cheryl Wright, Dean of Student Services, Schoolcraft College, 18600 Hagerty Road, Livonia, MI 48152-2696. *Phone:* 734-462-4426.

SOUTHWESTERN MICHIGAN COLLEGE
Dowagiac, Michigan   www.swmich.edu/

- **State and locally supported** 2-year, founded 1964, part of Michigan Department of Education
- **Rural** 240-acre campus
- **Coed,** 2,676 undergraduate students, 38% full-time, 65% women, 35% men

Undergraduates 1,015 full-time, 1,661 part-time. Students come from 4 states and territories, 29 other countries, 9% are from out of state, 9% African American, 1% Asian American or Pacific Islander, 4% Hispanic American, 0.7% Native American, 4% international.
Freshmen *Admission:* 459 applied, 459 admitted, 449 enrolled.
Faculty *Total:* 164, 27% full-time, 11% with terminal degrees. *Student/faculty ratio:* 19:1.
Majors Accounting technology and bookkeeping; administrative assistant and secretarial science; airframe mechanics and aircraft maintenance technology; automobile/automotive mechanics technology; business administration and management; business, management, and marketing related; child care and support services management; computer and information sciences related; computer programming; data entry/microcomputer applications related; drafting and design technology; electrical and electronic engineering technologies related; engineering technology; general studies; graphic and printing equipment operation/ production; health professions related; heavy/industrial equipment maintenance technologies related; industrial mechanics and maintenance technology; legal assistant/paralegal; liberal arts and sciences and humanities related; liberal arts and sciences/liberal studies; machine shop technology; merchandising, sales, and marketing operations related (general); nursing (registered nurse training); precision production related; precision systems maintenance and repair technologies related; welding technology.
Academics *Calendar:* semesters. *Degree:* certificates and associate. *Special study options:* academic remediation for entering students, accelerated degree program, adult/continuing education programs, advanced placement credit, cooperative education, distance learning, double majors, English as a second language, honors programs, independent study, internships, part-time degree program, services for LD students, student-designed majors, summer session for credit.
Library Fred L. Mathews Library with 38,000 titles, 1,100 serial subscriptions, 1,750 audiovisual materials, an OPAC, a Web page.

Southwestern Michigan College (continued)

Computers on Campus 200 computers available on campus for general student use. A campuswide network can be accessed. Internet access, at least one staffed computer lab available.

Student Life *Housing:* college housing not available. *Activities and Organizations:* drama/theater group, student-run newspaper, choral group, Phi Theta Kappa. *Campus security:* 24-hour emergency response devices, evening police patrols.

Athletics *Intramural sports:* archery M/W, badminton M/W, basketball M/W, cross-country running M/W, football M/W, golf M/W, racquetball M/W, skiing (cross-country) M/W, skiing (downhill) M/W, soccer M/W, softball M/W, track and field M/W, volleyball M/W, weight lifting M/W.

Costs (2005–06) *Tuition:* area resident $2101 full-time; state resident $2659 full-time; nonresident $2868 full-time. Full-time tuition and fees vary according to course load. Part-time tuition and fees vary according to course load. *Required fees:* $465 full-time. *Payment plan:* installment. *Waivers:* senior citizens and employees or children of employees.

Financial Aid Of all full-time matriculated undergraduates who enrolled in 2004, 125 Federal Work-Study jobs (averaging $1000). 75 state and other part-time jobs (averaging $1000).

Applying *Options:* electronic application, deferred entrance. *Required:* high school transcript. *Required for some:* letters of recommendation, interview. *Application deadline:* rolling (freshmen), rolling (transfers). *Notification:* continuous until 9/10 (freshmen).

Freshmen Application Contact Dr. Margaret Hay, Dean of Students and Academic Support, Southwestern Michigan College, 58900 Cherry Grove Road, Dowagiac, MI 49047. *Phone:* 269-782-1000 Ext. 1306. *Toll-free phone:* 800-456-8675. *Fax:* 269-782-1331. *E-mail:* mhay@swmich.edu.

WASHTENAW COMMUNITY COLLEGE
Ann Arbor, Michigan　　　　　**www.wccnet.edu/**

Freshmen Application Contact Mr. Bradley D. Hoth, Admissions Representative, Washtenaw Community College, 4800 East Huron River Drive, PO Box D-1, Ann Arbor, MI 48106. *Phone:* 734-973-3676. *E-mail:* wccinfo@orchard.washtenaw.cc.mi.us.

WAYNE COUNTY COMMUNITY COLLEGE DISTRICT
Detroit, Michigan　　　　　**www.wcccd.edu/**

- **State and locally supported** 2-year, founded 1967
- **Urban** campus
- **Coed**

Undergraduates 2,912 full-time, 8,761 part-time.

Academics *Calendar:* semesters. *Degree:* certificates and associate. *Special study options:* academic remediation for entering students, adult/continuing education programs, cooperative education, English as a second language, honors programs, part-time degree program, summer session for credit.

Student Life *Campus security:* 24-hour emergency response devices.

Athletics Member NJCAA.

Standardized Tests *Required:* ACT ASSET (for placement).

Financial Aid Of all full-time matriculated undergraduates who enrolled in 2004, 239 Federal Work-Study jobs (averaging $2360). 147 state and other part-time jobs (averaging $1200).

Applying *Options:* common application, early admission, deferred entrance. *Application fee:* $10.

Freshmen Application Contact Office of Enrollment Management and Student Services, Wayne County Community College District, 801 West Fort Street, Detroit, MI 48226-2539. *Phone:* 313-496-2600. *E-mail:* caafjh@wccc.edu.

WEST SHORE COMMUNITY COLLEGE
Scottville, Michigan　　　　　**www.westshore.edu/**

Director of Admissions Mr. Tom Bell, Director of Admissions, West Shore Community College, PO Box 277, 3000 North Stiles Road, Scottville, MI 49454-0277. *Phone:* 231-845-6211 Ext. 3117. *E-mail:* admissions@westshore.cc.mi.us.

MICRONESIA

COLLEGE OF MICRONESIA–FSM
Kolonia Pohnpei, Federated States of Micronesia, Micronesia　　　　　**www.comfsm.fm/**

Director of Admissions Mr. Wilson J. Kalio, Coordinator of Admissions and Records, College of Micronesia–FSM, PO Box 159, Kolonia Pohnpei, FM 96941-0159, Micronesia. *Phone:* 691-320-2480 Ext. 6200.

MINNESOTA

ACADEMY COLLEGE
Minneapolis, Minnesota　　　　　**www.academycollege.edu/**

- **Proprietary** primarily 2-year
- **Urban** campus
- **Coed**

Undergraduates Students come from 5 states and territories.

Faculty *Student/faculty ratio:* 8:1.

Academics *Calendar:* quarters. *Degrees:* certificates, associate, and bachelor's. *Special study options:* academic remediation for entering students, accelerated degree program, adult/continuing education programs, advanced placement credit, cooperative education, distance learning, double majors, English as a second language, honors programs, internships, part-time degree program, services for LD students, summer session for credit.

Applying *Options:* common application, electronic application, early admission, deferred entrance. *Application fee:* $30. *Required:* high school transcript, interview.

Director of Admissions Mr. Paul Burhhartzmeyer, Director of Admissions, Academy College, 1101 East 78th Street, Suite 100, Minneapolis, MN 55420. *Phone:* 952-851-0066. *Toll-free phone:* 800-292-9149.

ALEXANDRIA TECHNICAL COLLEGE
Alexandria, Minnesota　　　　　**www.alextech.edu/**

- **State-supported** 2-year, founded 1961, part of Minnesota State Colleges and Universities System
- **Small-town** 40-acre campus
- **Coed,** 1,971 undergraduate students, 81% full-time, 45% women, 55% men

Undergraduates 1,591 full-time, 380 part-time. Students come from 14 states and territories, 4% are from out of state, 0.4% African American, 0.8% Asian American or Pacific Islander, 0.8% Hispanic American, 0.7% Native American. Freshmen *Admission:* 1,838 applied, 1,224 admitted.

Faculty *Total:* 89, 87% full-time, 42% with terminal degrees. *Student/faculty ratio:* 20:1.

Majors Accounting; administrative assistant and secretarial science; banking and financial support services; business administration and management; CAD/CADD drafting/design technology; carpentry; cartography; child care and support services management; child care provision; clinical/medical laboratory technology; commercial and advertising art; computer and information sciences; computer programming (specific applications); computer systems networking and telecommunications; computer technology/computer systems technology; criminal justice/police science; diesel mechanics technology; farm and ranch management; fashion merchandising; health and physical education; hospitality administration; hotel/motel administration; human services; hydraulics and fluid power technology; industrial technology; interior design; legal administrative assistant/secretary; legal assistant/paralegal; machine tool technology; marine maintenance and ship repair technology; marketing/marketing management;

masonry; mechanical drafting and CAD/CADD; medical administrative assistant and medical secretary; medical insurance coding; medical reception; medical transcription; nursing assistant/aide and patient care assistant; nursing (licensed practical/vocational nurse training); office management; office occupations and clerical services; operations management; phlebotomy; receptionist; selling skills and sales; small business administration; small engine mechanics and repair technology; truck and bus driver/commercial vehicle operation; web page, digital/multimedia and information resources design; welding technology.

Academics *Calendar:* semesters. *Degree:* certificates, diplomas, and associate. *Special study options:* academic remediation for entering students, advanced placement credit, distance learning, double majors, internships, part-time degree program, services for LD students.

Library Learning Resource Center with 16,636 titles, 346 serial subscriptions, 1,219 audiovisual materials, an OPAC, a Web page.

Computers on Campus 467 computers available on campus for general student use. A campuswide network can be accessed from off campus. Internet access, online (class) registration, at least one staffed computer lab available. Computer purchase or lease plan available.

Student Life *Housing:* college housing not available. *Activities and Organizations:* VICA (Vocational Industrial Clubs of America) Skills USA, BPA (Business Professionals of America), DECA (Delta Epsilon Club), Student Senate, Phi Theta Kappa. *Campus security:* late-night transport/escort service, security cameras inside and outside. *Student services:* personal/psychological counseling.

Athletics *Intercollegiate sports:* basketball M, volleyball W. *Intramural sports:* basketball M/W, football M/W, golf M/W, softball M/W, volleyball M/W.

Costs (2006–07) *Tuition:* state resident $4318 full-time, $127 per credit part-time; nonresident $8636 full-time, $254 per credit part-time. *Required fees:* $401 full-time, $12 per credit part-time.

Financial Aid Of all full-time matriculated undergraduates who enrolled in 2004, 94 Federal Work-Study jobs (averaging $1871).

Applying *Options:* common application, electronic application, early admission. *Application fee:* $20. *Required:* high school transcript, interview. *Application deadline:* rolling (freshmen), rolling (transfers).

Freshmen Application Contact Mr. Doug Tatge, Vice President of Academic and Student Affairs, Alexandria Technical College, 1601 Jefferson Street, Alexandria, MN 56308. *Phone:* 320-762-0221. *Toll-free phone:* 888-234-1222. *Fax:* 320-762-4603. *E-mail:* admissionsrep@alextech.edu.

ANOKA-RAMSEY COMMUNITY COLLEGE

Coon Rapids, Minnesota   www.anokaramsey.edu/

- **State-supported** 2-year, founded 1965, part of Minnesota State Colleges and Universities System
- **Suburban** 100-acre campus with easy access to Minneapolis–St. Paul
- **Coed**

Undergraduates 2,436 full-time, 3,170 part-time. 1% are from out of state, 4% African American, 3% Asian American or Pacific Islander, 0.7% Hispanic American, 0.7% Native American, 0.4% international.

Faculty *Student/faculty ratio:* 27:1.

Academics *Calendar:* semesters. *Degree:* certificates and associate. *Special study options:* academic remediation for entering students, accelerated degree program, advanced placement credit, cooperative education, distance learning, honors programs, independent study, internships, off-campus study, part-time degree program, services for LD students, study abroad, summer session for credit. *ROTC:* Air Force (c).

Student Life *Campus security:* 24-hour emergency response devices and patrols, late-night transport/escort service.

Athletics Member NJCAA.

Costs (2005–06) *Tuition:* state resident $3198 full-time, $107 per credit part-time; nonresident $6396 full-time, $213 per credit part-time. Full-time tuition and fees vary according to course load and reciprocity agreements. Part-time tuition and fees vary according to course load and reciprocity agreements. *Required fees:* $384 full-time, $13 per credit part-time.

Financial Aid Of all full-time matriculated undergraduates who enrolled in 2004, 88 Federal Work-Study jobs (averaging $4000). 106 state and other part-time jobs (averaging $4000).

Applying *Options:* early admission, deferred entrance. *Application fee:* $20. *Required for some:* high school transcript.

Freshmen Application Contact Mr. Tom Duval, Admissions Counselor, Anoka-Ramsey Community College, 11200 Mississippi Boulevard NW, Coon Rapids, MN 55433. *Phone:* 763-422-3458. *E-mail:* trallela@an.cc.mn.us.

ANOKA-RAMSEY COMMUNITY COLLEGE, CAMBRIDGE CAMPUS

Cambridge, Minnesota   www.anokaramsey.edu/

- **State-supported** 2-year, part of Minnesota State Colleges and Universities System
- **Small-town** campus
- **Coed**

Undergraduates 550 full-time, 1,227 part-time. 1% are from out of state, 1% African American, 0.8% Asian American or Pacific Islander, 2% Hispanic American, 0.9% Native American.

Faculty *Student/faculty ratio:* 25:1.

Academics *Calendar:* semesters. *Degree:* certificates and associate. *Special study options:* academic remediation for entering students, accelerated degree program, advanced placement credit, cooperative education, distance learning, honors programs, independent study, internships, off-campus study, part-time degree program, services for LD students, study abroad, summer session for credit. *ROTC:* Air Force (c).

Athletics Member NJCAA.

Applying *Options:* early admission, deferred entrance. *Application fee:* $20. *Required for some:* high school transcript.

Freshmen Application Contact Admissions/Records, Anoka-Ramsey Community College, Cambridge Campus, 300 Polk Street South, Cambridge, MN 55008. *Phone:* 763-689-7027.

ANOKA TECHNICAL COLLEGE

Anoka, Minnesota   www.ank.tec.mn.us/

Director of Admissions Mr. Robert Hoenie, Director of Admissions, Anoka Technical College, 1355 West Highway 10, Anoka, MN 55303. *Phone:* 763-576-4746.

ARGOSY UNIVERSITY/TWIN CITIES

Eagan, Minnesota   www.argosyu.edu/

- **Proprietary** university, founded 1961, part of Education Management Corporation, Pittsburgh, PA
- **Suburban** campus with easy access to Minneapolis–St. Paul, MN
- **Coed**, 1,100 undergraduate students

Undergraduates Students come from 20 states and territories, 1 other country, 10% are from out of state, 4% African American, 2% Asian American or Pacific Islander, 0.9% Hispanic American, 0.8% Native American.

Freshmen *Admission:* 570 applied, 492 admitted. *Test scores:* ACT scores over 18: 98%; ACT scores over 24: 38%; ACT scores over 30: 1%.

Faculty *Total:* 140, 38% full-time, 38% with terminal degrees. *Student/faculty ratio:* 12:1.

Majors Dental hygiene; diagnostic medical sonography and ultrasound technology; histologic technology/histotechnologist; medical/clinical assistant; medical laboratory technology; medical radiologic technology; veterinary technology.

Academics *Calendar:* semesters. *Degrees:* associate, bachelor's, master's, doctoral, post-master's, and first professional certificates. *Special study options:* academic remediation for entering students, accelerated degree program, double majors, independent study, internships, part-time degree program, services for LD students, study abroad, summer session for credit.

Library Argosy University/Twin Cities Library with 9,000 titles, 160 serial subscriptions, 800 audiovisual materials, an OPAC, a Web page.

Computers on Campus 50 computers available on campus for general student use. Internet access, online (class) registration, at least one staffed computer lab available.

Student Life *Housing:* college housing not available. *Campus security:* 24-hour emergency response devices, late-night transport/escort service.

Standardized Tests *Required:* SAT or ACT (for admission), Wonderlic Scholastic Level Exam (for admission). *Recommended:* SAT or ACT (for admission).

Financial Aid Of all full-time matriculated undergraduates who enrolled in 2004, 20 Federal Work-Study jobs (averaging $3000). 20 state and other part-time jobs (averaging $1500).

Applying *Options:* common application, electronic application, deferred entrance. *Application fee:* $50. *Required:* high school transcript, interview.

Argosy University / Twin Cities (continued)
Required for some: essay or personal statement, letters of recommendation. *Application deadline:* rolling (freshmen), rolling (out-of-state freshmen), rolling (transfers).
Director of Admissions Admissions Director, Argosy University/Twin Cities, 1515 Central Parkway, Eagan, MN 55121. *Phone:* 651-846-2882. *Toll-free phone:* 888-844-2004. *E-mail:* auadmissions@argosyu.edu.

▶ See page 474 for the College Close-Up.

BROWN COLLEGE
Mendota Heights, Minnesota   www.browncollege.edu/

- **Proprietary** primarily 2-year, founded 1946, part of Career Education Corporation
- **Suburban** 20-acre campus with easy access to Minneapolis–St. Paul
- **Endowment** $352,500
- **Coed,** 2,054 undergraduate students, 92% full-time, 35% women, 65% men

Undergraduates 1,891 full-time, 163 part-time. Students come from 15 states and territories, 21% are from out of state, 6% African American, 4% Asian American or Pacific Islander, 2% Hispanic American, 0.7% Native American. Freshmen *Admission:* 1,116 applied, 531 admitted, 531 enrolled.
Faculty *Total:* 122, 64% full-time, 0.8% with terminal degrees. *Student/faculty ratio:* 21:1.
Majors Animation, interactive technology, video graphics and special effects; business administration and management; cinematography and film/video production; communication and media related; computer software technology; computer systems networking and telecommunications; criminal justice/law enforcement administration; design and visual communications; electrical, electronic and communications engineering technology; information science/studies; information technology; interior design; photography; radio/television broadcasting technology.
Academics *Calendar:* quarters. *Degrees:* certificates, associate, and bachelor's. *Special study options:* academic remediation for entering students, internships, part-time degree program, summer session for credit.
Library Career Resource Center with 768 titles, 33 serial subscriptions.
Computers on Campus 60 computers available on campus for general student use.
Student Life *Housing:* college housing not available. *Activities and Organizations:* student-run radio station, Student Senate. *Campus security:* 24-hour emergency response devices, student patrols, late-night transport/escort service.
Financial Aid Of all full-time matriculated undergraduates who enrolled in 2004, 20 Federal Work-Study jobs (averaging $2000).
Applying *Options:* deferred entrance. *Application fee:* $50. *Required:* high school transcript, interview. *Required for some:* minimum 2.0 GPA. *Recommended:* letters of recommendation. *Application deadline:* rolling (freshmen), rolling (transfers).
Freshmen Application Contact Mr. Mark Fredrichs, Registrar, Brown College, 1440 Northland Drive, Mendota Heights, MN 55120. *Phone:* 651-905-3400. *Toll-free phone:* 800-6BROWN6. *Fax:* 651-905-3550.

CENTRAL LAKES COLLEGE
Brainerd, Minnesota   www.clcmn.edu/

- **State-supported** 2-year, founded 1938, part of Minnesota State Colleges and Universities System
- **Small-town** 1-acre campus
- **Coed,** 2,768 undergraduate students, 67% full-time, 57% women, 43% men

Undergraduates 1,848 full-time, 920 part-time. Students come from 10 states and territories, 1 other country, 0.3% are from out of state, 1% African American, 0.9% Asian American or Pacific Islander, 0.8% Hispanic American, 1% Native American.
Faculty *Total:* 162, 57% full-time. *Student/faculty ratio:* 17:1.
Majors Accounting; administrative assistant and secretarial science; business administration and management; developmental and child psychology; horticultural science; legal administrative assistant/secretary; liberal arts and sciences/liberal studies; marketing/marketing management; medical administrative assistant and medical secretary; nursing (registered nurse training).
Academics *Calendar:* semesters. *Degree:* certificates, diplomas, and associate. *Special study options:* academic remediation for entering students, advanced

placement credit, external degree program, off-campus study, part-time degree program, summer session for credit.
Library Learning Resource Center with 16,052 titles, 286 serial subscriptions, an OPAC.
Computers on Campus 100 computers available on campus for general student use. A campuswide network can be accessed. Internet access, at least one staffed computer lab available.
Student Life *Housing:* college housing not available. *Activities and Organizations:* drama/theater group, student-run newspaper, choral group. *Campus security:* late-night transport/escort service.
Athletics Member NJCAA. *Intercollegiate sports:* baseball M, basketball M/W, football M, golf M/W, soccer M/W, softball W, volleyball W. *Intramural sports:* basketball M/W, bowling M/W, football M, golf M/W, softball M/W, tennis M/W, volleyball M/W.
Costs (2006–07) *Tuition:* area resident $3940 full-time.
Applying *Options:* deferred entrance. *Application fee:* $20. *Required:* high school transcript. *Application deadline:* rolling (freshmen), rolling (transfers).
Freshmen Application Contact Ms. Charlotte Daniels, Director of Admissions, Central Lakes College, 501 West College Drive, Brainerd, MN 56401-3904. *Phone:* 218-828-2525. *Toll-free phone:* 800-933-0346 Ext. 2586. *Fax:* 218-855-8220. *E-mail:* cdaniels@clcmn.edu.

CENTURY COLLEGE
White Bear Lake, Minnesota   www.century.edu/

- **State-supported** 2-year, founded 1970, part of Minnesota State Colleges and Universities System
- **Suburban** 150-acre campus with easy access to Minneapolis–St. Paul
- **Endowment** $1.0 million
- **Coed,** 8,553 undergraduate students, 47% full-time, 58% women, 42% men

Undergraduates 4,042 full-time, 4,511 part-time. Students come from 28 states and territories, 60 other countries, 8% African American, 10% Asian American or Pacific Islander, 2% Hispanic American, 0.8% Native American, 1% international, 22% transferred in. *Retention:* 48% of 2003 full-time freshmen returned.
Freshmen *Admission:* 2,713 applied, 2,713 admitted, 1,491 enrolled.
Faculty *Total:* 366, 48% full-time. *Student/faculty ratio:* 23:1.
Majors Accounting; administrative assistant and secretarial science; autobody/collision and repair technology; automobile/automotive mechanics technology; business administration and management; computer engineering technology; cosmetology; criminal justice/police science; dental assisting; dental hygiene; dental laboratory technology; diesel mechanics technology; educational/instructional media design; emergency medical technology (EMT paramedic); environmental studies; fashion merchandising; general retailing/wholesaling; heating, air conditioning, ventilation and refrigeration maintenance technology; industrial technology; interior design; legal administrative assistant/secretary; liberal arts and sciences/liberal studies; machine tool technology; management information systems; medical administrative assistant and medical secretary; medical/clinical assistant; medical radiologic technology; music management and merchandising; nursing (registered nurse training); orthotics/prosthetics; pharmacy technician; quality control technology; selling skills and sales; small engine mechanics and repair technology; social work; substance abuse/addiction counseling.
Academics *Calendar:* semesters. *Degree:* certificates, diplomas, and associate. *Special study options:* academic remediation for entering students, adult/continuing education programs, advanced placement credit, distance learning, double majors, English as a second language, external degree program, honors programs, internships, part-time degree program, services for LD students, summer session for credit. *ROTC:* Air Force (c).
Library Century College Main Library plus 1 other with 56,867 titles, 486 serial subscriptions, 3,569 audiovisual materials, an OPAC, a Web page.
Computers on Campus 985 computers available on campus for general student use. A campuswide network can be accessed from off campus. Internet access, online (class) registration, at least one staffed computer lab available.
Student Life *Housing:* college housing not available. *Activities and Organizations:* drama/theater group, student-run newspaper, choral group, Student Senate, Phi Theta Kappa, Dental Assistants Club, Creative Arts Alliance, Christian Club. *Campus security:* late-night transport/escort service, day patrols. *Student services:* personal/psychological counseling, women's center.
Athletics *Intercollegiate sports:* golf M/W. *Intramural sports:* badminton M/W, basketball M/W, golf M/W, soccer M/W, softball M/W.
Costs (2006–07) *Tuition:* state resident $4233 full-time, $141 per credit part-time; nonresident $8043 full-time, $254 per credit part-time. *Required fees:* $423 full-time, $14 per credit part-time.

Financial Aid Of all full-time matriculated undergraduates who enrolled in 2004, 72 Federal Work-Study jobs (averaging $2544). 103 state and other part-time jobs (averaging $1360).

Applying *Application fee:* $20. *Required:* high school transcript. *Application deadline:* rolling (freshmen), rolling (transfers).

Freshmen Application Contact Ms. Christine Paulos, Admissions Director, Century College, 3300 Century Avenue North, White Bear Lake, MN 55110. *Phone:* 651-779-2619. *Toll-free phone:* 800-228-1978. *Fax:* 651-779-5810. *E-mail:* admissions@century.edu.

DAKOTA COUNTY TECHNICAL COLLEGE
Rosemount, Minnesota www.dctc.edu/

Director of Admissions Mr. Patrick Lair, Admissions Director, Dakota County Technical College, 1300 145th Street East, Rosemount, MN 55068. *Phone:* 651-423-8399. *Toll-free phone:* 877-YES-DCTC Ext. 302 (in-state); 877-YES-DCTC (out-of-state).

DULUTH BUSINESS UNIVERSITY
Duluth, Minnesota www.dbumn.edu/

Director of Admissions Mr. Mark Traux, Director of Admissions, Duluth Business University, 4724 Mike Colalillo Drive, Duluth, MN 55807. *Toll-free phone:* 800-777-8406.

DUNWOODY COLLEGE OF TECHNOLOGY
Minneapolis, Minnesota www.dunwoody.edu/

Freshmen Application Contact Ms. Yun-bok Christenson, Records Coordinator, Dunwoody College of Technology, 818 Dunwoody Boulevard, Minneapolis, MN 55403. *Phone:* 612-374-5800 Ext. 2019. *Toll-free phone:* 800-292-4625. *E-mail:* picann@dunwoody.tec.mn.us.

FOND DU LAC TRIBAL AND COMMUNITY COLLEGE
Cloquet, Minnesota www.fdltcc.edu/

Freshmen Application Contact Ms. Nancy Gordon, Admissions Representative, Fond du Lac Tribal and Community College, 2101 14th Street, Cloquet, MN 55720. *Phone:* 218-879-0808. *Toll-free phone:* 800-657-3712. *E-mail:* darla@asab.fdl.cc.mn.us.

GLOBE COLLEGE
Oakdale, Minnesota www.globecollege.com/

- **Private** primarily 2-year, founded 1885
- **Suburban** campus
- **Coed,** 845 undergraduate students, 63% full-time, 72% women, 28% men

Undergraduates 533 full-time, 312 part-time. Students come from 1 other country, 8% are from out of state.

Faculty *Student/faculty ratio:* 15:1.

Majors Accounting; animation, interactive technology, video graphics and special effects; business administration and management; business systems networking/ telecommunications; clinical laboratory science/medical technology; commercial and advertising art; computer graphics; computer systems networking and telecommunications; digital communication and media/multimedia; information technology; kinesiology and exercise science; massage therapy; medical administrative assistant; medical/clinical assistant; music related; nursing (registered nurse training); paralegal/legal assistant; taxation; veterinary technology.

Academics *Calendar:* quarters. *Degrees:* certificates, diplomas, associate, and bachelor's. *Special study options:* academic remediation for entering students,

accelerated degree program, adult/continuing education programs, cooperative education, distance learning, internships, part-time degree program, summer session for credit.

Library Globe College Library with 1,432 titles, 106 serial subscriptions, 13 audiovisual materials, an OPAC, a Web page.

Computers on Campus 180 computers available on campus for general student use. Internet access, online (class) registration, at least one staffed computer lab available.

Standardized Tests *Required:* CPAt (for admission).

Costs (2006–07) *Tuition:* $12,600 full-time, $350 per credit part-time. *Required fees:* $500 full-time.

Applying *Options:* common application, electronic application. *Application fee:* $50. *Required:* high school transcript, interview. *Required for some:* essay or personal statement. *Application deadline:* 10/5 (freshmen).

Freshmen Application Contact Ms. Christina Hilipipre, Globe College, 7166 10th Street North, Oakdale, MN 55128. *Phone:* 651-730-5100. *Fax:* 651-730-5151. *E-mail:* admissions@globecollege.edu.

HENNEPIN TECHNICAL COLLEGE
Brooklyn Park, Minnesota www.hennepintech.edu/

Director of Admissions Mrs. Joy Bodin, Director of Admissions, Hennepin Technical College, 9000 Brooklyn Boulevard, Brooklyn Park, MN 55445. *Phone:* 763-488-2415. *Fax:* 763-550-2113.

HERZING COLLEGE
Minneapolis, Minnesota www.herzing.edu/

- **Proprietary** primarily 2-year, part of Herzing College
- **Suburban** 1-acre campus
- **Coed, primarily women**

Undergraduates 205 full-time, 141 part-time. Students come from 3 states and territories, 1% are from out of state, 14% African American, 5% Asian American or Pacific Islander, 1% Hispanic American, 1% Native American.

Faculty *Student/faculty ratio:* 14:1.

Academics *Calendar:* semesters. *Degrees:* certificates, diplomas, associate, and bachelor's. *Special study options:* adult/continuing education programs, distance learning, internships, part-time degree program.

Student Life *Campus security:* 24-hour emergency response devices, late-night transport/escort service.

Standardized Tests *Required:* ACCUPLACER (for admission). *Recommended:* SAT and SAT Subject Tests or ACT (for admission).

Costs (2005–06) *Tuition:* $11,029 full-time, $367 per credit part-time. Full-time tuition and fees vary according to course load and program. Part-time tuition and fees vary according to course load and program. *Required fees:* $25 full-time.

Applying *Required:* high school transcript, interview.

Director of Admissions Mr. James Decker, Director of Admissions, Herzing College, 5700 West Broadway, Minneapolis, MN 55428. *Phone:* 763-231-3152. *Toll-free phone:* 800-878-DRAW. *Fax:* 763-535-9205.

HIBBING COMMUNITY COLLEGE
Hibbing, Minnesota www.hcc.mnscu.edu/

- **State-supported** 2-year, founded 1916, part of Minnesota State Colleges and Universities System
- **Small-town** 100-acre campus
- **Coed,** 1,176 undergraduate students

Undergraduates Students come from 20 states and territories, 5% African American, 0.9% Asian American or Pacific Islander, 1% Hispanic American, 2% Native American, 10% live on campus.

Freshmen *Admission:* 1,312 applied, 1,312 admitted.

Faculty *Total:* 86, 73% full-time, 2% with terminal degrees. *Student/faculty ratio:* 14:1.

Majors Administrative assistant and secretarial science; business administration and management; clinical/medical laboratory technology; computer and information sciences; computer installation and repair technology; computer systems networking and telecommunications; criminal justice/police science; culinary arts; dental assisting; drafting and design technology; educational/instructional media design; foodservice systems administration; legal adminis-

Hibbing Community College (continued)

trative assistant/secretary; liberal arts and sciences/liberal studies; medical administrative assistant and medical secretary; nursing (registered nurse training); pre-engineering; selling skills and sales; web page, digital/multimedia and information resources design.

Academics *Calendar:* semesters. *Degree:* certificates, diplomas, and associate. *Special study options:* academic remediation for entering students, adult/continuing education programs, advanced placement credit, cooperative education, distance learning, internships, off-campus study, part-time degree program, services for LD students, study abroad, summer session for credit.

Library Hibbing Community College Library with 19,536 titles, 190 serial subscriptions, a Web page.

Computers on Campus 150 computers available on campus for general student use. A campuswide network can be accessed from off campus. At least one staffed computer lab available.

Student Life *Activities and Organizations:* drama/theater group, choral group, marching band, Phi Theta Kappa, Performing Music Ensembles Club, Student Senate, Engineering Club, VICA. *Campus security:* late-night transport/escort service. *Student services:* personal/psychological counseling.

Athletics Member NJCAA. *Intercollegiate sports:* baseball M, basketball M/W, football M, golf M/W, softball W, volleyball W. *Intramural sports:* basketball M/W, bowling M/W, field hockey M/W, football W, golf M/W, skiing (cross-country) M/W, skiing (downhill) M/W, tennis M/W, volleyball M/W.

Costs (2005–06) *Tuition:* state resident $3950 full-time, $117 per credit part-time; nonresident $146 per credit part-time. Full-time tuition and fees vary according to course load and reciprocity agreements. Part-time tuition and fees vary according to course load and reciprocity agreements. *Required fees:* $459 full-time, $15 per credit part-time. *Room and board:* $4500; room only: $2900. *Payment plan:* installment. *Waivers:* senior citizens and employees or children of employees.

Applying *Options:* common application, early admission, deferred entrance. *Application fee:* $20. *Required:* high school transcript. *Application deadline:* rolling (freshmen), rolling (transfers). *Notification:* continuous (freshmen).

Freshmen Application Contact Ms. Shelly Corradi, Admissions, Hibbing Community College, 1515 East 25th Street, Hibbing, MN 55746. *Phone:* 218-262-7207. *Toll-free phone:* 800-224-4HCC. *Fax:* 218-262-6717. *E-mail:* admissions@hibbing.edu.

HIGH-TECH INSTITUTE
St. Louis Park, Minnesota

INVER HILLS COMMUNITY COLLEGE
Inver Grove Heights, Minnesota   www.inverhills.edu/

Freshmen Application Contact Ms. Susan Merkling, Admissions, Inver Hills Community College, 2500 East 80th Street, Inver Grove Heights, MN 55076-3224. *Phone:* 651-450-8501.

ITASCA COMMUNITY COLLEGE
Grand Rapids, Minnesota   www.itascacc.edu/

- **State-supported** 2-year, founded 1922, part of Minnesota State Colleges and Universities System
- **Rural** 24-acre campus
- **Endowment** $3.8 million
- **Coed,** 1,137 undergraduate students, 77% full-time, 48% women, 52% men

Undergraduates 876 full-time, 261 part-time. Students come from 10 states and territories, 2 other countries, 4% are from out of state, 2% African American, 1% Asian American or Pacific Islander, 0.4% Hispanic American, 4% Native American, 2% international. *Retention:* 54% of 2003 full-time freshmen returned. Freshmen *Admission:* 661 applied, 661 admitted. *Average high school GPA:* 2.78.

Faculty *Total:* 69, 61% full-time, 3% with terminal degrees. *Student/faculty ratio:* 16:1.

Majors Accounting; American Indian/Native American studies; business administration and management; chemical engineering; civil engineering; computer engineering; computer engineering related; education; education (K-12); engi-

neering; engineering related; engineering science; engineering technology; environmental studies; fish/game management; forestry; forestry technology; general studies; geography; human services; liberal arts and sciences/liberal studies; mechanical engineering; natural resources/conservation; natural resources management and policy; nuclear engineering; nursing (licensed practical/vocational nurse training); pre-engineering; psychology; special education (early childhood); wildlife and wildlands science and management.

Academics *Calendar:* semesters. *Degree:* certificates, diplomas, and associate. *Special study options:* academic remediation for entering students, adult/continuing education programs, advanced placement credit, cooperative education, double majors, independent study, internships, off-campus study, part-time degree program, services for LD students, study abroad, summer session for credit.

Library Itasca Community College Library with 28,790 titles, 280 serial subscriptions, 2,443 audiovisual materials, an OPAC, a Web page.

Computers on Campus 250 computers available on campus for general student use. A campuswide network can be accessed from student residence rooms and from off campus. Internet access, online (class) registration, at least one staffed computer lab available.

Student Life *Housing Options:* Campus housing is university owned. *Activities and Organizations:* student association, Circle K, Student Ambassadors, Minority Student Club, Psychology Club. *Campus security:* late-night transport/escort service, evening patrols by trained security personnel. *Student services:* legal services.

Athletics Member NJCAA. *Intercollegiate sports:* baseball M, basketball M/W, football M, softball W, volleyball W, wrestling M. *Intramural sports:* basketball M, bowling M/W, golf W, softball M/W, table tennis M/W, volleyball M/W.

Costs (2006–07) *Tuition:* state resident $4100 full-time, $128 per credit part-time; nonresident $5125 full-time, $160 per credit part-time. *Required fees:* $490 full-time, $15 per credit part-time. *Room and board:* $4190; room only: $3290.

Financial Aid Of all full-time matriculated undergraduates who enrolled in 2004, 63 Federal Work-Study jobs (averaging $1350). 155 state and other part-time jobs (averaging $910).

Applying *Options:* common application, electronic application. *Application fee:* $20. *Required:* high school transcript. *Required for some:* 3 letters of recommendation. *Application deadlines:* 9/6 (freshmen), 9/6 (transfers). *Notification:* continuous (freshmen).

Freshmen Application Contact Ms. Candace Perry, Director of Enrollment Services, Itasca Community College, 1851 East Highway 169, Grand Rapids, MN 55744. *Phone:* 218-327-4464. *Toll-free phone:* 800-996-6422 Ext. 4464. *Fax:* 218-327-4350. *E-mail:* iccinfo@itascacc.edu.

ITT TECHNICAL INSTITUTE
Eden Prairie, Minnesota   www.itt-tech.edu/

- **Proprietary** primarily 2-year, founded 2003
- **Coed**

Majors Animation, interactive technology, video graphics and special effects; CAD/CADD drafting/design technology; computer and information systems security; computer programming; computer software technology; electrical, electronic and communications engineering technology; system, networking, and LAN/WAN management; web page, digital/multimedia and information resources design.

Academics *Calendar:* quarters. *Degrees:* associate and bachelor's.

Standardized Tests *Required:* Wonderlic aptitude test (for admission).

Costs (2005–06) *Tuition:* Please see school catalog for specific information.

Applying *Application fee:* $100. *Required:* high school transcript, interview. *Recommended:* letters of recommendation. *Application deadline:* rolling (freshmen), rolling (transfers). *Notification:* continuous (freshmen).

Freshmen Application Contact Mr. Paul Rozeski, ITT Technical Institute, 8911 Columbine Road, Eden Prairie, MN 55347. *Phone:* 952-914-5300. *Toll-free phone:* 888-488-9646.

LAKE SUPERIOR COLLEGE
Duluth, Minnesota   www.lsc.edu/

- **State-supported** 2-year, founded 1995, part of Minnesota State Colleges and Universities System
- **Urban** 105-acre campus
- **Endowment** $148,576
- **Coed,** 4,200 undergraduate students, 58% full-time, 58% women, 42% men

Undergraduates 2,429 full-time, 1,771 part-time. 13% are from out of state, 2% African American, 1% Asian American or Pacific Islander, 0.7% Hispanic

American, 2% Native American.

Freshmen *Admission:* 789 admitted.

Faculty *Total:* 239, 41% full-time. *Student/faculty ratio:* 20:1.

Majors Accounting; airline pilot and flight crew; architectural drafting and CAD/CADD; automobile/automotive mechanics technology; business administration and management; carpentry; civil engineering technology; clinical/medical laboratory technology; computer programming (specific applications); computer technology/computer systems technology; dental hygiene; electrical, electronic and communications engineering technology; electrician; emergency medical technology (EMT paramedic); executive assistant/executive secretary; fire services administration; human resources management and services related; legal administrative assistant/secretary; legal assistant/paralegal; liberal arts and sciences and humanities related; liberal arts and sciences/liberal studies; machine tool technology; management information systems; mechanical drafting and CAD/CADD; medical administrative assistant and medical secretary; medical radiologic technology; nursing (registered nurse training); occupational therapist assistant; physical therapist assistant; respiratory care therapy; selling skills and sales; surgical technology.

Academics *Calendar:* semesters. *Degree:* certificates, diplomas, and associate. *Special study options:* academic remediation for entering students, advanced placement credit, distance learning, double majors, English as a second language, independent study, internships, part-time degree program, services for LD students, summer session for credit.

Library Harold P. Erickson Library with 2,869 titles, 100 serial subscriptions, 280 audiovisual materials, an OPAC, a Web page.

Computers on Campus 230 computers available on campus for general student use. A campuswide network can be accessed from off campus. Internet access, at least one staffed computer lab available.

Student Life *Housing:* college housing not available. *Activities and Organizations:* Business Professionals of America, Gus Gus Players, Art Club, All Nations, PTK Phi Theta Kappa. *Campus security:* late-night transport/escort service, 15-hour patrols by trained security personnel. *Student services:* health clinic, personal/psychological counseling, women's center.

Athletics *Intramural sports:* basketball M/W, softball M/W, volleyball M/W.

Costs (2006–07) *Tuition:* state resident $3450 full-time, $115 per credit part-time; nonresident $6900 full-time, $230 per credit part-time. *Required fees:* $477 full-time, $16 per credit part-time.

Financial Aid Of all full-time matriculated undergraduates who enrolled in 2004, 100 Federal Work-Study jobs (averaging $2380). 100 state and other part-time jobs (averaging $2380).

Applying *Options:* early admission, deferred entrance. *Application fee:* $20. *Required for some:* high school transcript. *Application deadline:* rolling (freshmen), rolling (transfers). *Notification:* continuous (freshmen).

Freshmen Application Contact Ms. Melissa Leno, Director of Admissions, Lake Superior College, 2101 Trinity Road, Duluth, MN 55811. *Phone:* 218-723-4895. *Toll-free phone:* 800-432-2884. *Fax:* 218-733-5945. *E-mail:* enroll@lsc.edu.

LEECH LAKE TRIBAL COLLEGE

Cass Lake, Minnesota   www.lltc.org/

Director of Admissions Admissions Director, Leech Lake Tribal College, PO Box 180, Cass Lake, MN 56633-0180. *Phone:* 218-335-4200. *Toll-free phone:* 888-829-4240 *Fax:* 218-335-4209. *E-mail:* chrisf@lltc.org.

MCNALLY SMITH COLLEGE OF MUSIC

Saint Paul, Minnesota   www.mcnallysmith.edu/

- **Proprietary** primarily 2-year, founded 1985
- **Urban** campus
- **Coed,** 471 undergraduate students, 80% full-time, 17% women, 83% men

Undergraduates 378 full-time, 93 part-time. Students come from 23 states and territories, 45% are from out of state, 6% African American, 1% Asian American or Pacific Islander, 3% Hispanic American, 1% Native American, 1% international, 7% transferred in.

Freshmen *Admission:* 160 applied, 135 admitted, 135 enrolled.

Faculty *Total:* 61, 54% full-time. *Student/faculty ratio:* 10:1.

Majors Engineering technologies related; music; music management and merchandising; music performance.

Academics *Calendar:* semesters. *Degrees:* certificates, diplomas, associate, and bachelor's. *Special study options:* adult/continuing education programs, advanced placement credit, independent study, internships, summer session for credit.

Library McNally Smith College Learning Center plus 1 other.

Computers on Campus 20 computers available on campus for general student use. Internet access, at least one staffed computer lab available.

Student Life *Housing:* college housing not available. *Activities and Organizations:* student-run newspaper, Student Advisory Board, Audio Engineering Society, Minnesota Songwriters Association. *Campus security:* 24-hour emergency response devices. *Student services:* personal/psychological counseling.

Standardized Tests *Recommended:* ACT (for admission).

Costs (2006–07) *Comprehensive fee:* $23,255 includes full-time tuition ($15,240), mandatory fees ($575). Part-time tuition: $635 per credit. *Required fees:* $75 per term part-time.

Applying *Application fee:* $75. *Required:* essay or personal statement, high school transcript, 2 letters of recommendation, interview. *Required for some:* audition. *Application deadline:* 8/1 (freshmen). *Notification:* 8/1 (freshmen).

Freshmen Application Contact Ms. Debbie Sandridge, Director of Admissions, McNally Smith College of Music, 19 Exchange Street East, St. Paul, MN 55101. *Phone:* 651-291-0177 Ext. 2382. *Toll-free phone:* 800-594-9500. *Fax:* 651-291-0366. *E-mail:* dsandridge@mcnallysmith.edu.

MESABI RANGE COMMUNITY AND TECHNICAL COLLEGE

Virginia, Minnesota   www.mr.mnscu.edu/

- **State-supported** 2-year, founded 1918, part of Minnesota State Colleges and Universities System
- **Small-town** 30-acre campus
- **Coed,** 1,371 undergraduate students, 100% full-time, 51% women, 49% men

Undergraduates 1,371 full-time. Students come from 6 states and territories, 5% African American, 0.9% Asian American or Pacific Islander, 0.3% Hispanic American, 1% Native American, 10% live on campus.

Faculty *Total:* 73, 60% full-time. *Student/faculty ratio:* 25:1.

Majors Administrative assistant and secretarial science; business/commerce; computer graphics; computer/information technology services administration related; computer programming related; computer programming (specific applications); computer software and media applications related; computer systems networking and telecommunications; electrical/electronics equipment installation and repair; human services; information technology; instrumentation technology; liberal arts and sciences/liberal studies; pre-engineering; substance abuse/addiction counseling; web page, digital/multimedia and information resources design.

Academics *Calendar:* semesters. *Degree:* certificates, diplomas, and associate. *Special study options:* academic remediation for entering students, adult/continuing education programs, advanced placement credit, cooperative education, internships, off-campus study, part-time degree program, services for LD students, student-designed majors, summer session for credit.

Library Mesabi Library with 23,000 titles, 167 serial subscriptions.

Computers on Campus 120 computers available on campus for general student use. At least one staffed computer lab available.

Student Life *Housing Options:* coed. Campus housing is provided by a third party. *Activities and Organizations:* drama/theater group, student-run newspaper, choral group, Student Senate, Human Services Club, Native American Club, Student Life Club, Black Awareness Club. *Campus security:* late-night transport/escort service. *Student services:* personal/psychological counseling.

Athletics Member NJCAA. *Intercollegiate sports:* baseball M, basketball M/W, football M, softball W, volleyball W. *Intramural sports:* badminton M/W, basketball M/W, bowling M/W, field hockey M/W, football M/W, golf M/W, ice hockey M/W, skiing (cross-country) M/W, skiing (downhill) M/W, tennis M/W, volleyball M/W.

Costs (2006–07) *Tuition:* state resident $4252 full-time; nonresident $5197 full-time. *Room and board:* room only: $3352.

Financial Aid Of all full-time matriculated undergraduates who enrolled in 2004, 117 Federal Work-Study jobs (averaging $1610). 77 state and other part-time jobs (averaging $1470).

Applying *Options:* common application, early admission, deferred entrance. *Application fee:* $20. *Application deadline:* rolling (freshmen), rolling (transfers). *Notification:* continuous (freshmen).

Freshmen Application Contact Ms. Brenda Kochevar, Enrollment Services Director, Mesabi Range Community and Technical College, 1001 Chestnut Street West, Virginia, MN 55792. *Phone:* 218-749-0314. *Toll-free phone:* 800-657-3860. *Fax:* 218-749-0318. *E-mail:* b.kochevar@mr.mnscu.edu.

MINNEAPOLIS BUSINESS COLLEGE
Roseville, Minnesota **www.minneapolisbusinesscollege.edu/**

- **Proprietary** 2-year, founded 1874, part of The Bradford School
- **Coed, primarily women,** 350 undergraduate students

Undergraduates Students come from 2 states and territories, 11% are from out of state.

Faculty *Total:* 18, 50% full-time. *Student/faculty ratio:* 30:1.

Majors Accounting; administrative assistant and secretarial science; allied health and medical assisting services related; computer programming; desktop publishing and digital imaging design; system, networking, and LAN/WAN management; tourism and travel services management.

Academics *Degree:* diplomas and associate.

Student Life *Housing Options:* Campus housing is leased by the school. *Campus security:* 24-hour emergency response devices.

Costs (2006–07) *Tuition:* $12,240 full-time. *Room only:* $6360.

Applying *Application fee:* $50. *Required:* high school transcript.

Freshmen Application Contact Mr. David Whitman, President, Minneapolis Business College, 1711 West County Road B, Roseville, MN 55113. *Phone:* 651-604-4118. *Toll-free phone:* 800-279-5200. *Fax:* 651-686-8185. *E-mail:* info@minneapolisbusinesscollege.edu.

MINNEAPOLIS COMMUNITY AND TECHNICAL COLLEGE
Minneapolis, Minnesota **www.mctc.mnscu.edu/**

- **State-supported** 2-year, founded 1965, part of Minnesota State Colleges and Universities System
- **Urban** 4-acre campus
- **Coed**

Undergraduates Students come from 45 states and territories, 81 other countries, 3% are from out of state, 25% African American, 5% Asian American or Pacific Islander, 3% Hispanic American, 2% Native American, 3% international. *Retention:* 51% of 2003 full-time freshmen returned.

Faculty *Student/faculty ratio:* 23:1.

Academics *Calendar:* semesters. *Degree:* certificates, diplomas, and associate. *Special study options:* academic remediation for entering students, adult/continuing education programs, advanced placement credit, distance learning, English as a second language, honors programs, independent study, internships, off-campus study, part-time degree program, services for LD students, student-designed majors, summer session for credit.

Student Life *Campus security:* 24-hour emergency response devices, late-night transport/escort service.

Athletics Member NJCAA.

Costs (2005–06) *Tuition:* state resident $4028 full-time, $134 per credit part-time; nonresident $7694 full-time, $256 per credit part-time. Full-time tuition and fees vary according to program and reciprocity agreements. Part-time tuition and fees vary according to program and reciprocity agreements.

Financial Aid Of all full-time matriculated undergraduates who enrolled in 2004, 188 Federal Work-Study jobs (averaging $5000). 190 state and other part-time jobs (averaging $5000).

Applying *Options:* early admission, deferred entrance. *Application fee:* $20. *Required:* high school transcript.

Freshmen Application Contact Dena Russell, Interim Director of Admissions, Minneapolis Community and Technical College, 1501 Hennepin Avenue, Minneapolis, MN 55403. *Phone:* 612-659-6206. *Toll-free phone:* 800-247-0911.

MINNESOTA SCHOOL OF BUSINESS– BROOKLYN CENTER
Brooklyn Center, Minnesota **www.msbcollege.edu/**

- **Proprietary** primarily 2-year, founded 1989
- **Suburban** campus
- **Coed,** 809 undergraduate students

Faculty *Student/faculty ratio:* 13:1.

Majors Accounting; administrative assistant and secretarial science; business administration and management; computer systems networking and telecommu-nications; information technology; intermedia/multimedia; legal administrative assistant/secretary; massage therapy; medical administrative assistant; music related; nursing science; paralegal/legal assistant; physician assistant; taxation; veterinary technology; web page, digital/multimedia and information resources design.

Academics *Calendar:* quarters. *Degrees:* certificates, diplomas, associate, bachelor's, and master's. *Special study options:* academic remediation for entering students, accelerated degree program, adult/continuing education programs, cooperative education, distance learning, internships, part-time degree program.

Library Minnesota School of Business – Brooklyn Center with 1,534 titles, 99 serial subscriptions, 53 audiovisual materials, an OPAC, a Web page.

Computers on Campus 179 computers available on campus for general student use. A campuswide network can be accessed. Internet access, at least one staffed computer lab available.

Student Life *Housing:* college housing not available.

Standardized Tests *Required:* CPAt (for admission).

Costs (2006–07) *Tuition:* $15,750 full-time, $350 per credit hour part-time.

Applying *Options:* common application, electronic application. *Application fee:* $50. *Required:* high school transcript, interview. *Required for some:* essay or personal statement. *Application deadline:* 10/6 (freshmen).

Freshmen Application Contact Ms. Kristen Swanson, Director of Admissions, Minnesota School of Business–Brooklyn Center, 5910 Shingle Creek Parkway, Brooklyn Center, MN 55430. *Phone:* 763-585-7777. *Fax:* 763-566-7030.

MINNESOTA SCHOOL OF BUSINESS– PLYMOUTH
Minneapolis, Minnesota **www.msbcollege.edu/**

- **Proprietary** primarily 2-year, founded 2002
- **Suburban** 3-acre campus
- **Coed,** 500 undergraduate students

Faculty *Student/faculty ratio:* 10:1.

Majors Accounting; administrative assistant and secretarial science; business administration and management; computer systems networking and telecommu-nications; information technology; intermedia/multimedia; massage therapy; medical administrative assistant; music related; nursing science; paralegal/legal assistant; physician assistant; taxation; veterinary technology; web page, digital/multimedia and information resources design.

Academics *Calendar:* quarters. *Degrees:* certificates, diplomas, associate, bachelor's, and master's. *Special study options:* academic remediation for entering students, accelerated degree program, adult/continuing education programs, cooperative education, distance learning, internships, part-time degree program, summer session for credit.

Library Minnesota School of Business-Plymouth with 1,189 titles, 106 serial subscriptions, 12 audiovisual materials, an OPAC, a Web page.

Computers on Campus 62 computers available on campus for general student use. A campuswide network can be accessed. Internet access, at least one staffed computer lab available.

Student Life *Housing:* college housing not available.

Standardized Tests *Required:* CPAt (for admission).

Costs (2006–07) *Tuition:* $15,750 full-time, $350 per credit part-time.

Applying *Options:* common application, electronic application. *Application fee:* $50. *Required:* high school transcript, interview. *Required for some:* essay or personal statement. *Application deadline:* 10/6 (freshmen).

Freshmen Application Contact Director of Admissions, Minnesota School of Business–Plymouth, 1455 County Road 101 North, Plymouth, MN 55447. *Phone:* 763-476-2000. *Fax:* 763-476-1000.

MINNESOTA SCHOOL OF BUSINESS– RICHFIELD
Richfield, Minnesota **www.msbcollege.edu/**

- **Proprietary** primarily 2-year, founded 1877
- **Urban** 3-acre campus with easy access to Minneapolis–St. Paul
- **Coed,** 944 undergraduate students

Undergraduates Students come from 5 states and territories.

Faculty *Student/faculty ratio:* 14:1.

Majors Accounting; administrative assistant and secretarial science; business administration and management; computer systems networking and telecommu-nications; information technology; intermedia/multimedia; legal assistant/

paralegal; massage therapy; medical/clinical assistant; medical office management; music related; nursing science; taxation; veterinary technology; web page, digital/multimedia and information resources design.

Academics *Calendar:* quarters. *Degrees:* certificates, diplomas, associate, bachelor's, and master's. *Special study options:* academic remediation for entering students, accelerated degree program, adult/continuing education programs, cooperative education, distance learning, internships, part-time degree program, summer session for credit.

Library Minnesota School of Business-Richfield with 2,420 titles, 93 serial subscriptions, 93 audiovisual materials, an OPAC, a Web page.

Computers on Campus 168 computers available on campus for general student use. A campuswide network can be accessed from off campus. Internet access, online (class) registration, at least one staffed computer lab available.

Student Life *Housing:* college housing not available.

Standardized Tests *Required:* CPAt (for admission).

Costs (2006–07) *Tuition:* $15,750 full-time, $350 per credit hour part-time.

Applying *Options:* common application, electronic application. *Application fee:* $50. *Required:* high school transcript, interview. *Required for some:* essay or personal statement. *Application deadline:* 10/6 (freshmen).

Freshmen Application Contact Ms. Patricia Murray, Director of Admissions, Minnesota School of Business–Richfield, 1401 West 76th Street, Richfield, MN 55430. *Phone:* 612-861-2000 Ext. 720. *Toll-free phone:* 800-752-4223. *Fax:* 612-861-5548. *E-mail:* pmurray@msbcollege.com.

MINNESOTA SCHOOL OF BUSINESS— ST. CLOUD

Waite Park, Minnesota   www.msbcollege.edu/

- **Proprietary** primarily 2-year
- **Coed,** 609 undergraduate students

Faculty *Student/faculty ratio:* 13:1.

Majors Accounting; administrative assistant and secretarial science; business administration and management; computer systems networking and telecommunications; information technology; intermedia/multimedia; massage therapy; medical administrative assistant; music related; nursing science; paralegal/legal assistant; physician assistant; taxation; veterinary technology; web page, digital/multimedia and information resources design.

Academics *Calendar:* quarters. *Degrees:* certificates, diplomas, associate, bachelor's, and master's. *Special study options:* academic remediation for entering students, accelerated degree program, adult/continuing education programs, cooperative education, distance learning, internships, part-time degree program, summer session for credit.

Library Minnesota School of Business-St. Cloud with 724 titles, 88 serial subscriptions, an OPAC, a Web page.

Computers on Campus 52 computers available on campus for general student use. A campuswide network can be accessed. Internet access available.

Student Life *Housing:* college housing not available.

Standardized Tests *Required:* CPAt (for admission).

Costs (2006–07) *Tuition:* $15,750 full-time, $350 per credit hour part-time.

Applying *Options:* common application, electronic application. *Application fee:* $50. *Required:* high school transcript, interview. *Required for some:* essay or personal statement. *Application deadline:* 10/6 (freshmen).

Freshmen Application Contact Mr. Jim Beck, Director of Admissions, Minnesota School of Business–St. Cloud, 1201 2nd Street S, Waite Park, MN 56387. *Phone:* 320-257-2000. *Toll-free phone:* 866-403-3333. *Fax:* 320-257-0131. *E-mail:* rkuhl@msbcollege.edu.

MINNESOTA SCHOOL OF BUSINESS— SHAKOPEE

Shakopee, Minnesota   www.msbcollege.edu/

- **Proprietary** primarily 2-year
- **Coed,** 360 undergraduate students

Faculty *Student/faculty ratio:* 12:1.

Majors Accounting; administrative assistant and secretarial science; business administration and management; computer systems networking and telecommunications; information technology; intermedia/multimedia; massage therapy; medical administrative assistant; music related; nursing science; paralegal/legal assistant; physician assistant; veterinary technology; web page, digital/multimedia and information resources design.

Academics *Calendar:* quarters. *Degrees:* certificates, diplomas, associate, bachelor's, and master's. *Special study options:* academic remediation for entering students, accelerated degree program, adult/continuing education programs, cooperative education, distance learning, internships, part-time degree program, summer session for credit.

Library Minnesota School of Business-Shakopee with 919 titles, 95 serial subscriptions, an OPAC, a Web page.

Computers on Campus 48 computers available on campus for general student use. A campuswide network can be accessed. At least one staffed computer lab available.

Student Life *Housing:* college housing not available.

Standardized Tests *Required:* CPAt (for admission).

Costs (2006–07) *Tuition:* $15,750 full-time, $350 per credit part-time.

Applying *Options:* common application, electronic application. *Application fee:* $50. *Required:* high school transcript, interview. *Required for some:* essay or personal statement. *Application deadline:* 10/6 (freshmen).

Freshmen Application Contact Ms. Gretchen Seifert, Director of Admissions, Minnesota School of Business–Shakopee, 1200 Shakopee Town Square, Shakopee, MN 55379. *Phone:* 952-516-7015. *Toll-free phone:* 866-766-1200. *Fax:* 952-345-1201.

MINNESOTA STATE COLLEGE— SOUTHEAST TECHNICAL

Winona, Minnesota   www.southeastmn.edu/

- **State-supported** 2-year, founded 1992, part of Minnesota State Colleges and Universities System
- **Small-town** campus with easy access to Minneapolis–St. Paul
- **Endowment** $110,000
- **Coed**

Undergraduates 1,060 full-time, 757 part-time. Students come from 20 states and territories, 2% African American, 1% Asian American or Pacific Islander, 0.6% Hispanic American, 1% Native American, 0.1% international.

Academics *Calendar:* semesters. *Degree:* certificates, diplomas, and associate. *Special study options:* academic remediation for entering students, English as a second language, internships, part-time degree program, services for LD students.

Student Life *Campus security:* 24-hour emergency response devices, late-night transport/escort service.

Costs (2005–06) *Tuition:* state resident $124 per credit part-time; nonresident $249 per credit part-time. Full-time tuition and fees vary according to reciprocity agreements. Part-time tuition and fees vary according to reciprocity agreements. *Required fees:* $12 per credit part-time.

Financial Aid Of all full-time matriculated undergraduates who enrolled in 2004, 65 Federal Work-Study jobs (averaging $2500). 65 state and other part-time jobs (averaging $2500).

Applying *Options:* common application, electronic application. *Application fee:* $20. *Required:* high school transcript.

Freshmen Application Contact Ms. Christine Humble, Director of Enrollment Services, Minnesota State College–Southeast Technical, PO Box 409, Winona, MN 55987. *Phone:* 507-453-2732. *Toll-free phone:* 800-372-8164. *E-mail:* chumble@win.tec.mn.us.

MINNESOTA STATE COMMUNITY AND TECHNICAL COLLEGE—FERGUS FALLS

Fergus Falls, Minnesota   www.minnesota.edu/

- **State-supported** 2-year, founded 1960, part of Minnesota State Colleges and Universities System
- **Rural** 146-acre campus
- **Endowment** $1.8 million
- **Coed,** 5,631 undergraduate students, 64% full-time, 59% women, 41% men

Undergraduates 3,587 full-time, 2,044 part-time. Students come from 12 states and territories, 2 other countries, 3% are from out of state, 2% African American, 1% Asian American or Pacific Islander, 1% Hispanic American, 3% Native American, 0.1% international, 1% transferred in, 22% live on campus. Freshmen *Admission:* 3,320 applied, 2,703 admitted, 1,545 enrolled.

Faculty *Total:* 352, 49% full-time. *Student/faculty ratio:* 18:1.

Majors Accounting; administrative assistant and secretarial science; architectural engineering technology; automotive engineering technology; biological and

Minnesota State Community and Technical College–Fergus Falls (continued)
physical sciences; business administration and management; clinical/medical laboratory assistant; clinical/medical laboratory technology; computer and information systems security; computer programming; computer systems networking and telecommunications; corrections; cosmetology; criminal justice/police science; dental hygiene; early childhood education; electrical and electronic engineering technologies related; electrical, electronic and communications engineering technology; financial planning and services; fire services administration; forensic science and technology; health information/medical records technology; heating, air conditioning and refrigeration technology; human resources management; industrial technology; legal administrative assistant; legal administrative assistant/secretary; liberal arts and sciences/liberal studies; manufacturing technology; marketing/marketing management; mechanical engineering/mechanical technology; medical administrative assistant and medical secretary; medical laboratory technology; merchandising, sales, and marketing operations related (general); nursing (licensed practical/vocational nurse training); nursing (registered nurse training); pharmacy technician; pre-engineering; radiologic technology/science; telecommunications technology; web page, digital/multimedia and information resources design.

Academics *Calendar:* semesters. *Degree:* certificates, diplomas, and associate. *Special study options:* academic remediation for entering students, advanced placement credit, English as a second language, independent study, off-campus study, part-time degree program, services for LD students, study abroad, summer session for credit.

Library Fergus Falls Community College Library with 30,000 titles, 173 serial subscriptions, an OPAC.

Computers on Campus 144 computers available on campus for general student use. A campuswide network can be accessed from off campus. Internet access, online (class) registration, at least one staffed computer lab available.

Student Life *Housing Options:* coed. Campus housing is university owned. *Activities and Organizations:* drama/theater group, student-run newspaper, choral group, Student Senate, Students In Free Enterprise, Phi Theta Kappa. *Campus security:* late-night transport/escort service, security for special events. *Student services:* personal/psychological counseling, women's center.

Athletics Member NJCAA. *Intercollegiate sports:* baseball M, basketball M/W, football M, golf M/W, softball W, volleyball W. *Intramural sports:* badminton M/W, basketball M, bowling M/W, football M/W, golf M/W, skiing (cross-country) M/W, skiing (downhill) M/W, softball M/W, table tennis M/W, tennis M/W, volleyball M/W, weight lifting M/W.

Standardized Tests *Recommended:* ACT (for admission).

Costs (2006–07) *Tuition:* state resident $3900 full-time, $133 per credit part-time; nonresident $3900 full-time, $133 per credit part-time. *Required fees:* $569 full-time, $18 per credit part-time. *Room and board:* room only: $3000.

Financial Aid Of all full-time matriculated undergraduates who enrolled in 2004, 80 Federal Work-Study jobs (averaging $1900). 80 state and other part-time jobs (averaging $1900).

Applying *Options:* common application, electronic application, early admission, deferred entrance. *Application fee:* $20. *Required:* high school transcript. *Application deadline:* rolling (freshmen), rolling (transfers). *Notification:* continuous (freshmen).

Freshmen Application Contact Ms. Carrie Brimhall, Director of Enrollment Management, Minnesota State Community and Technical College–Fergus Falls, 1414 College Way, Fergus Falls, MN 56537-1009. *Phone:* 218-736-1528. *Toll-free phone:* 888-MY-MSCTC. *Fax:* 218-736-1510. *E-mail:* carrie.brimhall@minnesota.edu.

MINNESOTA WEST COMMUNITY AND TECHNICAL COLLEGE

Pipestone, Minnesota　　　　　www.mnwest.edu/

- **State-supported** 2-year, founded 1967, part of Minnesota State Colleges and Universities System
- **Rural** 103-acre campus
- **Coed,** 2,783 undergraduate students, 52% full-time, 52% women, 48% men

Undergraduates 1,439 full-time, 1,344 part-time. Students come from 25 states and territories, 3 other countries, 11% are from out of state, 3% African American, 1% Asian American or Pacific Islander, 3% Hispanic American, 0.6% Native American, 5% transferred in. *Retention:* 63% of 2003 full-time freshmen returned.

Freshmen *Admission:* 2,160 applied, 1,751 admitted, 652 enrolled. *Average high school GPA:* 2.50.

Faculty *Total:* 252, 38% full-time. *Student/faculty ratio:* 13:1.

Majors Accounting; administrative assistant and secretarial science; clinical/medical laboratory technology; heating, air conditioning, ventilation and refrig-

eration maintenance technology; liberal arts and sciences/liberal studies; medical administrative assistant and medical secretary; medical/clinical assistant; plumbing technology.

Academics *Calendar:* semesters. *Degrees:* certificates, diplomas, and associate (profile contains information from Canby, Granite Falls, Jackson, and Worthington campuses). *Special study options:* academic remediation for entering students, advanced placement credit, cooperative education, distance learning, double majors, external degree program, honors programs, independent study, internships, part-time degree program, services for LD students, summer session for credit.

Library Minnesota West Library plus 4 others with 46,057 titles, 313 serial subscriptions, 4,632 audiovisual materials, an OPAC.

Computers on Campus A campuswide network can be accessed. Internet access, online (class) registration, at least one staffed computer lab available. Computer purchase or lease plan available.

Student Life *Housing:* college housing not available. *Student services:* personal/psychological counseling.

Athletics Member NJCAA. *Intercollegiate sports:* baseball M, basketball M/W, football M, golf M/W, softball W, volleyball W, wrestling M. *Intramural sports:* softball M/W, volleyball M/W.

Costs (2006–07) *Tuition:* state resident $4085 full-time, $136 per credit part-time; nonresident $8171 full-time, $272 per credit part-time. *Required fees:* $377 full-time, $13 per credit part-time.

Applying *Options:* common application, electronic application. *Application fee:* $20. *Required:* high school transcript. *Application deadline:* rolling (freshmen), rolling (transfers).

Freshmen Application Contact Mr. Gary Gillin, Dean of Communication and Enrollment, Minnesota West Community and Technical College, 1314 North Hiawatha Avenue, Pipestone, MN 56164. *Phone:* 507-825-6804. *Toll-free phone:* 800-658-2330. *Fax:* 507-825-4656. *E-mail:* garygillin@mnwest.edu.

NATIONAL AMERICAN UNIVERSITY
Bloomington, Minnesota

NATIONAL AMERICAN UNIVERSITY
Brooklyn Center, Minnesota

NORMANDALE COMMUNITY COLLEGE

Bloomington, Minnesota　　　　www.normandale.edu/

- **State-supported** 2-year, founded 1968, part of Minnesota State Colleges and Universities System
- **Suburban** 90-acre campus with easy access to Minneapolis–St. Paul
- **Endowment** $1.4 million
- **Coed,** 8,261 undergraduate students, 50% full-time, 58% women, 42% men

Undergraduates 4,139 full-time, 4,122 part-time. Students come from 22 states and territories, 2% are from out of state, 10% African American, 7% Asian American or Pacific Islander, 2% Hispanic American, 0.8% Native American, 1% international.

Freshmen *Admission:* 4,186 applied, 2,954 admitted.

Faculty *Total:* 230, 74% full-time, 18% with terminal degrees. *Student/faculty ratio:* 28:1.

Majors Accounting; architectural drafting and CAD/CADD; automobile/automotive mechanics technology; business administration and management; business automation/technology/data entry; child care and support services management; commercial photography; computer and information sciences; computer programming (specific applications); computer science; computer systems networking and telecommunications; criminal justice/police science; criminal justice/safety; dental assisting; dental hygiene; dietetics; electrical, electronic and communications engineering technology; general retailing/wholesaling; hospitality administration; hydraulics and fluid power technology; legal administrative assistant/secretary; liberal arts and sciences/liberal studies; management information systems; marketing/marketing management; mechanical drafting and CAD/CADD; mechanical engineering/mechanical technology;

medical administrative assistant and medical secretary; medical radiologic technology; nursing (registered nurse training).

Academics *Calendar:* semesters. *Degree:* certificates and associate. *Special study options:* academic remediation for entering students, accelerated degree program, adult/continuing education programs, advanced placement credit, cooperative education, distance learning, English as a second language, independent study, internships, off-campus study, part-time degree program, services for LD students, student-designed majors, study abroad, summer session for credit. *ROTC:* Army (c), Air Force (c).

Library Library plus 1 other with 98,141 titles, 623 serial subscriptions, 43,561 audiovisual materials, an OPAC.

Computers on Campus 450 computers available on campus for general student use. A campuswide network can be accessed from off campus. Internet access, online (class) registration, at least one staffed computer lab available.

Student Life *Housing:* college housing not available. *Activities and Organizations:* drama/theater group, student-run newspaper, choral group, Program Board (NPB), Student Senate, Phi Theta Kappa, Inter-Varsity Christian Fellowship Club, Spanish Club. *Campus security:* 24-hour emergency response devices, student patrols, late-night transport/escort service. *Student services:* personal/psychological counseling.

Athletics *Intramural sports:* archery M/W, badminton M/W, basketball M/W, bowling M/W, football M/W, ice hockey M/W, lacrosse M/W, racquetball M/W, soccer M/W, softball M/W, table tennis M/W, tennis M/W, volleyball M/W.

Costs (2005–06) *Tuition:* state resident $3614 full-time, $133 per credit part-time; nonresident $7227 full-time, $253 per credit part-time. *Required fee:* $362 full-time.

Financial Aid Of all full-time matriculated undergraduates who enrolled in 2004, 480 Federal Work-Study jobs (averaging $4000). 1,200 state and other part-time jobs (averaging $4000).

Applying *Options:* common application, early admission, deferred entrance. *Application fee:* $20. *Required for some:* high school transcript. *Application deadline:* rolling (freshmen), rolling (transfers). *Notification:* continuous (freshmen).

Freshmen Application Contact Information Center, Normandale Community College, 9700 France Avenue South, Bloomington, MN 55431. *Phone:* 952-487-8201. *Toll-free phone:* 866-880-8740. *Fax:* 952-487-8230. *E-mail:* information@normandale.edu.

NORTH HENNEPIN COMMUNITY COLLEGE

Brooklyn Park, Minnesota   **www.nhcc.edu/**

- **State-supported** 2-year, founded 1966, part of Minnesota State Colleges and Universities System
- **Suburban** 80-acre campus
- **Endowment** $838,054
- **Coed**, 6,382 undergraduate students

Undergraduates Students come from 4 states and territories, 96 other countries, 2% are from out of state, 15% African American, 8% Asian American or Pacific Islander, 1% Hispanic American, 0.5% Native American, 1% international. *Retention:* 99% of 2003 full-time freshmen returned. Freshmen *Admission:* 1,852 applied, 1,852 admitted.

Faculty *Total:* 215, 46% full-time. *Student/faculty ratio:* 29:1.

Majors Accounting; biology/biological sciences; chemistry; computer science; construction management; criminal justice/law enforcement administration; criminal justice/safety; finance; fine/studio arts; graphic design; histologic technology/histotechnologist; marketing/marketing management; medical laboratory technology; nursing (registered nurse training); paralegal/legal assistant; pre-engineering.

Academics *Calendar:* semesters. *Degree:* certificates and associate. *Special study options:* academic remediation for entering students, accelerated degree program, adult/continuing education programs, advanced placement credit, distance learning, English as a second language, honors programs, independent study, internships, off-campus study, part-time degree program, services for LD students, study abroad, summer session for credit.

Library Learning Resource Center with 69,375 titles, 2,500 serial subscriptions, 3,406 audiovisual materials, an OPAC, a Web page.

Computers on Campus 250 computers available on campus for general student use. A campuswide network can be accessed. Internet access, online (class) registration, at least one staffed computer lab available.

Student Life *Housing:* college housing not available. *Activities and Organizations:* drama/theater group, student-run newspaper, choral group. *Campus security:* 24-hour patrols, late-night transport/escort service. *Student services:* personal/psychological counseling.

Athletics Member NJCAA. *Intramural sports:* basketball M/W, bowling M/W, football M, golf M/W, soccer M, tennis M/W, volleyball M/W.

Costs (2006–07) *Tuition:* state resident $3158 full-time, $132 per credit part-time. *Required fees:* $309 full-time, $10 per credit part-time.

Applying *Options:* early admission, deferred entrance. *Application fee:* $20. *Recommended:* high school transcript. *Application deadline:* rolling (freshmen), rolling (transfers). *Notification:* continuous (freshmen).

Freshmen Application Contact Ms. Jeneifer Lambrecht, Director of Campus Outreach, North Hennepin Community College, 7411 85th Avenue North, Brooklyn Park, MN 55445-2231. *Phone:* 763-424-0702. *Fax:* 763-424-0929. *E-mail:* jlsummer@nhcc.edu.

NORTHLAND COMMUNITY AND TECHNICAL COLLEGE—EAST GRAND FORKS

East Grand Forks, Minnesota   **www.northlandcollege.edu/**

- **State-supported** 2-year, founded 1973
- **Coed**

Faculty *Student/faculty ratio:* 24:1.

Academics *Calendar:* semesters. *Degree:* certificates, diplomas, and associate.

Applying *Application fee:* $20.

Director of Admissions Ms. Rita Lealos, Enrollment Specialist, Northland Community and Technical College–East Grand Forks, 2022 Central Avenue, NW, East Grand Forks, MN 56721-2702. *Phone:* 218-773-4546. *Toll-free phone:* 800-451-3441. *Fax:* 218-773-4502.

NORTHLAND COMMUNITY AND TECHNICAL COLLEGE—THIEF RIVER FALLS

Thief River Falls, Minnesota   **www.northlandcollege.edu/**

- **State-supported** 2-year, founded 1965, part of Minnesota State Colleges and Universities System
- **Rural** campus
- **Coed**, 3,652 undergraduate students, 55% full-time, 58% women, 42% men

Undergraduates 2,017 full-time, 1,635 part-time. Students come from 27 states and territories, 3 other countries, 26% are from out of state, 3% African American, 0.8% Asian American or Pacific Islander, 2% Hispanic American, 4% Native American, 0.1% international. Freshmen *Admission:* 2,137 applied, 2,137 admitted.

Faculty *Total:* 91, 67% full-time, 10% with terminal degrees. *Student/faculty ratio:* 23:1.

Majors Accounting; administrative assistant and secretarial science; aeronautics/aviation/aerospace science and technology; architectural engineering technology; athletic training; automobile/automotive mechanics technology; aviation/airway management; avionics maintenance technology; broadcast journalism; business administration and management; child care provision; child development; computer and information sciences related; computer graphics; computer science; computer software and media applications related; computer systems networking and telecommunications; computer/technical support; consumer merchandising/retailing management; cosmetology; criminal justice/law enforcement administration; criminal justice/police science; criminology; data entry/microcomputer applications; data entry/microcomputer applications related; data modeling/warehousing and database administration; drafting and design technology; electrical, electronic and communications engineering technology; farm and ranch management; industrial electronics technology; information technology; international business/trade/commerce; legal administrative assistant/secretary; legal assistant/paralegal; legal studies; liberal arts and sciences/liberal studies; marketing/marketing management; mass communication/media; nursing (licensed practical/vocational nurse training); nursing (registered nurse training); radio and television; system administration; web/multimedia management and webmaster; web page, digital/multimedia and information resources design; welding technology; word processing.

Academics *Calendar:* semesters. *Degree:* certificates, diplomas, and associate. *Special study options:* academic remediation for entering students, adult/continuing education programs, advanced placement credit, distance learning, internships, off-campus study, part-time degree program, services for LD students, summer session for credit.

Library Northland College Library.

Northland Community and Technical College–Thief River Falls (continued)

Computers on Campus 567 computers available on campus for general student use. A campuswide network can be accessed from off campus. Internet access, online (class) registration, at least one staffed computer lab available. Computer purchase or lease plan available.

Student Life *Housing:* college housing not available. *Activities and Organizations:* drama/theater group, student-run newspaper, radio and television station, choral group, Law Enforcement Club, All-Nations Club, Environmental Club, PAMA, VICA. *Campus security:* student patrols, late-night transport/escort service. *Student services:* personal/psychological counseling, women's center.

Athletics Member NJCAA. *Intercollegiate sports:* baseball M, basketball M/W, football M, golf M(s)/W(s), softball W, volleyball W. *Intramural sports:* basketball M/W, bowling M/W, golf M/W, softball M/W, tennis M/W, volleyball M/W.

Costs (2006–07) *Tuition:* state resident $4170 full-time, $139 per credit part-time. *Required fees:* $490 full-time, $16 per credit part-time.

Financial Aid Of all full-time matriculated undergraduates who enrolled in 2004, 75 Federal Work-Study jobs (averaging $2500). 40 state and other part-time jobs (averaging $2500).

Applying *Options:* common application, electronic application, early admission, deferred entrance. *Application fee:* $20. *Required:* high school transcript. *Application deadlines:* 9/1 (freshmen), 9/1 (transfers). *Notification:* continuous (freshmen).

Freshmen Application Contact Mr. Eugene Klinke, Director of Enrollment Management, Northland Community and Technical College–Thief River Falls, 1101 Highway #1 East, Thief River Falls, MN 56701. *Phone:* 218-681-0862. *Toll-free phone:* 800-959-6282. *Fax:* 218-681-0774. *E-mail:* eugene.klinke@ northlandcollege.edu.

NORTHWEST TECHNICAL COLLEGE
Bemidji, Minnesota   bemidji.ntcmn.edu/

- **State-supported** 2-year, founded 1993, part of Minnesota State Colleges and Universities System
- **Small-town** campus
- **Coed**

Academics *Calendar:* semesters. *Degree:* certificates, diplomas, and associate. *Special study options:* cooperative education, distance learning, external degree program, independent study, internships, part-time degree program, services for LD students, summer session for credit.

Student Life *Campus security:* late-night transport/escort service.

Standardized Tests *Required:* ACCUPLACER (for placement).

Financial Aid Of all full-time matriculated undergraduates who enrolled in 2004, 20 Federal Work-Study jobs (averaging $1500). 10 state and other part-time jobs (averaging $1500).

Applying *Application fee:* $20.

Freshmen Application Contact Admissions Office, Northwest Technical College, 905 Grant Avenue, SE, Bemidji, MN 56601. *Phone:* 218-846-7444. *Toll-free phone:* 800-942-8324.

NORTHWEST TECHNICAL INSTITUTE
Eden Prairie, Minnesota   www.nti.edu/

Director of Admissions Mr. John Hartman, Director of Admissions, Northwest Technical Institute, 11995 Singletree Lane, Eden Prairie, MN 55344-5351. *Phone:* 952-944-0080 Ext. 103. *Toll-free phone:* 800-443-4223.

PINE TECHNICAL COLLEGE
Pine City, Minnesota   www.pinetech.edu/

Director of Admissions Mr. Phil Schroeder, Dean, Student Affairs, Pine Technical College, 900 Fourth Street, SE, Pine City, MN 55063. *Phone:* 320-629-5100. *Toll-free phone:* 800-521-7463.

RAINY RIVER COMMUNITY COLLEGE
International Falls, Minnesota   www.rrcc.mnscu.edu/

- **State-supported** 2-year, founded 1967, part of Minnesota State Colleges and Universities System
- **Small-town** 80-acre campus
- **Coed**

Undergraduates 265 full-time, 119 part-time. Students come from 8 states and territories, 18% African American, 0.5% Asian American or Pacific Islander, 1% Hispanic American, 3% Native American, 10% live on campus.

Academics *Calendar:* semesters. *Degree:* certificates, diplomas, and associate. *Special study options:* academic remediation for entering students, adult/ continuing education programs, advanced placement credit, cooperative education, English as a second language, honors programs, independent study, internships, part-time degree program, services for LD students, summer session for credit.

Student Life *Campus security:* 24-hour emergency response devices, late-night transport/escort service, controlled dormitory access.

Athletics Member NJCAA.

Standardized Tests *Required:* CPT (for placement). *Recommended:* ACT (for placement).

Financial Aid Of all full-time matriculated undergraduates who enrolled in 2004, 110 Federal Work-Study jobs (averaging $2000). 55 state and other part-time jobs (averaging $2000).

Applying *Options:* common application, early admission, deferred entrance. *Application fee:* $20. *Required:* high school transcript.

Director of Admissions Ms. Berta Hagen, Registrar, Rainy River Community College, 1501 Highway 71, International Falls, MN 56649. *Phone:* 218-285-2207. *Toll-free phone:* 800-456-3996. *E-mail:* admissions@rr.mn.us.

RASMUSSEN COLLEGE EAGAN
Eagan, Minnesota   www.rasmussen.edu/

Director of Admissions Ms. Jacinda Miller, Admissions Coordinator, Rasmussen College Eagan, 3500 Federal Drive, Eagan, MN 55122-1346. *Phone:* 651-687-9000. *Toll-free phone:* 651-687-0507 (in-state); 800-852-6367 (out-of-state).

RASMUSSEN COLLEGE EDEN PRARIE
Eden Prarie, Minnesota   www.rasmussen.edu/

- **Proprietary** 2-year, founded 1904, part of Rasmussen College System
- **Suburban** 2-acre campus with easy access to Minneapolis–St. Paul
- **Coed**, 363 undergraduate students, 58% full-time, 78% women, 22% men

Undergraduates 209 full-time, 154 part-time. Students come from 1 other state, 13% African American, 3% Asian American or Pacific Islander, 2% Hispanic American, 1% Native American.

Freshmen *Admission:* 75 enrolled. *Average high school GPA:* 3.10.

Faculty *Total:* 32, 47% full-time, 31% with terminal degrees. *Student/faculty ratio:* 11:1.

Majors Accounting; administrative assistant and secretarial science; business administration and management; child development; court reporting; legal administrative assistant/secretary; marketing/marketing management; medical administrative assistant and medical secretary.

Academics *Calendar:* quarters. *Degree:* certificates, diplomas, and associate. *Special study options:* academic remediation for entering students, internships, part-time degree program, summer session for credit.

Library 3,400 titles, 10 serial subscriptions.

Computers on Campus 300 computers available on campus for general student use. Internet access, at least one staffed computer lab available.

Student Life *Housing:* college housing not available. *Campus security:* late-night transport/escort service.

Standardized Tests *Required:* COMPASS (for admission).

Financial Aid Of all full-time matriculated undergraduates who enrolled in 2004, 3 state and other part-time jobs (averaging $4338).

Applying *Options:* early admission, deferred entrance. *Application fee:* $60. *Required:* high school transcript, interview. *Application deadline:* rolling (freshmen), rolling (transfers).

Freshmen Application Contact Mr. Jeff Hagy, Director of Admissions, Rasmussen College Eden Prarie, 7905 Golden Triangle Drive, Suite 100, Eden Prarie, MN 55344. *Phone:* 952-545-2000. *Toll-free phone:* 800-852-0929.

RASMUSSEN COLLEGE MANKATO
Mankato, Minnesota   www.rasmussen.edu/

- **Proprietary** 2-year, founded 1904, part of Rasmussen College System
- **Suburban** campus with easy access to Minneapolis–St. Paul
- **Coed, primarily women,** 463 undergraduate students, 100% full-time, 85% women, 15% men

Undergraduates 463 full-time. 1% African American, 1% Asian American or Pacific Islander, 4% Hispanic American.
Faculty *Total:* 42, 31% full-time. *Student/faculty ratio:* 18:1.
Majors Accounting; administrative assistant and secretarial science; banking and financial support services; business administration and management; child care and support services management; child care provision; child development; computer graphics; computer software and media applications related; computer systems networking and telecommunications; computer/technical support; computer typography and composition equipment operation; criminal justice/law enforcement administration; data entry/microcomputer applications; data entry/microcomputer applications related; data processing and data processing technology; health information/medical records administration; health unit coordinator/ward clerk; hospitality administration; hospitality and recreation marketing; hotel/motel administration; human resources development; legal administrative assistant/secretary; legal assistant/paralegal; legal studies; marketing/marketing management; medical administrative assistant and medical secretary; medical/clinical assistant; restaurant, culinary, and catering management; sales, distribution and marketing; system administration; tourism and travel services management; tourism and travel services marketing; tourism promotion; web page, digital/multimedia and information resources design; word processing.
Academics *Calendar:* quarters. *Degree:* certificates, diplomas, and associate. *Special study options:* academic remediation for entering students, advanced placement credit, cooperative education, internships, part-time degree program, services for LD students, summer session for credit.
Library Media Center with 1,000 titles, 3 serial subscriptions.
Computers on Campus 70 computers available on campus for general student use. Internet access, at least one staffed computer lab available.
Student Life *Housing:* college housing not available. *Activities and Organizations:* student-run newspaper, Student Senate, Student Ambassadors, Student Life Organization. *Campus security:* limited access to buildings after hours.
Standardized Tests *Required:* ACT COMPASS (for admission).
Costs (2006–07) *Tuition:* $295 per credit part-time.
Financial Aid Of all full-time matriculated undergraduates who enrolled in 2004, 5 Federal Work-Study jobs (averaging $4000). 3 state and other part-time jobs (averaging $4000).
Applying *Options:* common application, deferred entrance. *Application fee:* $60. *Required:* high school transcript, minimum 2.0 GPA, interview.
Freshmen Application Contact Ms. Kathy Clifford, Director of Admissions, Rasmussen College Mankato, 501 Holly Lane, Mankato, MN 56001-6803. *Phone:* 507-625-6556. *Toll-free phone:* 800-657-6767. *Fax:* 507-625-6557. *E-mail:* rascoll@ic.mankato.mn.us.

RASMUSSEN COLLEGE ST. CLOUD
St. Cloud, Minnesota   www.rasmussen.edu/

- **Proprietary** 2-year, founded 1904, part of Rasmussen College System
- **Urban** campus with easy access to Minneapolis–St. Paul
- **Coed, primarily women**

Undergraduates 252 full-time, 281 part-time. Students come from 3 states and territories, 1% are from out of state, 2% African American, 0.9% Asian American or Pacific Islander, 2% Hispanic American, 2% Native American.
Faculty *Student/faculty ratio:* 19:1.
Academics *Calendar:* quarters. *Degree:* certificates, diplomas, and associate. *Special study options:* academic remediation for entering students, adult/continuing education programs, distance learning, double majors, internships, part-time degree program, summer session for credit.
Standardized Tests *Required:* ACT COMPASS (for admission).
Financial Aid Of all full-time matriculated undergraduates who enrolled in 2004, 34 Federal Work-Study jobs (averaging $866). 51 state and other part-time jobs (averaging $700).
Applying *Options:* common application, electronic application, early admission, deferred entrance. *Application fee:* $60. *Required:* high school transcript, minimum 2.0 GPA, interview.
Director of Admissions Ms. Andrea Peters, Director of Admissions, Rasmussen College St. Cloud, 226 Park Avenue South, St. Cloud, MN 56301. *Phone:* 320-251-5600. *Toll-free phone:* 800-852-0460.

RIDGEWATER COLLEGE
Willmar, Minnesota   www.ridgewater.mnscu.edu/

Freshmen Application Contact Ms. Linda Barron, Admissions Assistant, Ridgewater College, PO Box 1097, Willmar, MN 56201-1097. *Phone:* 320-231-2906 Ext. 2906. *Toll-free phone:* 800-722-1151 Ext. 2906.

RIVERLAND COMMUNITY COLLEGE
Austin, Minnesota   www.riverland.edu/

- **State-supported** 2-year, founded 1940, part of Minnesota State Colleges and Universities System
- **Small-town** 187-acre campus with easy access to Minneapolis–St. Paul
- **Coed,** 3,600 undergraduate students

Undergraduates Students come from 5 states and territories, 3% are from out of state, 3% African American, 1% Asian American or Pacific Islander, 4% Hispanic American, 0.3% Native American, 2% live on campus.
Freshmen *Admission:* 2,400 admitted. *Average high school GPA:* 3.08.
Faculty *Total:* 158, 64% full-time. *Student/faculty ratio:* 18:1.
Majors Administrative assistant and secretarial science; autobody/collision and repair technology; business administration and management; computer and information systems security; computer installation and repair technology; computer programming (specific applications); computer programming (vendor/product certification); computer software and media applications related; computer systems networking and telecommunications; computer/technical support; corrections; criminal justice/police science; data entry/microcomputer applications; data entry/microcomputer applications related; diesel mechanics technology; electrical/electronics equipment installation and repair; health unit coordinator/ward clerk; human services; industrial mechanics and maintenance technology; legal administrative assistant/secretary; liberal arts and sciences/liberal studies; machine shop technology; medical administrative assistant and medical secretary; medical radiologic technology; nursing (registered nurse training); web/multimedia management and webmaster; web page, digital/multimedia and information resources design; word processing.
Academics *Calendar:* semesters. *Degree:* certificates, diplomas, and associate. *Special study options:* academic remediation for entering students, adult/continuing education programs, advanced placement credit, distance learning, double majors, English as a second language, independent study, internships, off-campus study, part-time degree program, services for LD students, study abroad, summer session for credit.
Library Riverland Community College Library plus 2 others with 33,500 titles, 278 serial subscriptions, an OPAC.
Computers on Campus 175 computers available on campus for general student use. A campuswide network can be accessed from student residence rooms. At least one staffed computer lab available.
Student Life *Housing Options:* Campus housing is provided by a third party. *Activities and Organizations:* drama/theater group, student-run newspaper, choral group, College Choir, student newspaper, Student Activities Board, Phi Theta Kappa, Theater Club. *Campus security:* late-night transport/escort service. *Student services:* personal/psychological counseling, women's center.
Athletics Member NJCAA. *Intercollegiate sports:* baseball M, basketball M/W, golf M/W, softball W, volleyball W. *Intramural sports:* basketball M.
Costs (2006–07) *Tuition:* state resident $3915 full-time, $131 per credit part-time; nonresident $3915 full-time, $131 per credit part-time. *Required fees:* $17 per credit part-time. *Room and board:* room only: $2600.
Applying *Options:* early admission. *Application fee:* $20. *Required:* high school transcript. *Application deadline:* rolling (freshmen), rolling (transfers).
Freshmen Application Contact Ms. Renee Njos, Admission Secretary, Riverland Community College, 1900 8th Avenue NW, Austin, MN 55912. *Phone:* 507-433-0820. *Toll-free phone:* 800-247-5039. *Fax:* 507-433-0515. *E-mail:* admissions@riverland.edu.

Rochester Community and Technical College

Rochester, Minnesota   www.roch.edu/

- **State-supported** primarily 2-year, founded 1915, part of Minnesota State Colleges and Universities System
- **Small-town** 460-acre campus
- **Endowment** $437,000
- **Coed**

Undergraduates Students come from 39 states and territories, 36 other countries, 10% are from out of state.

Academics *Calendar:* semesters. *Degrees:* certificates, diplomas, associate, and bachelor's (also offers 13 programs that lead to a bachelor's degree with Winona State University or University of Minnesota). *Special study options:* academic remediation for entering students, advanced placement credit, distance learning, English as a second language, honors programs, independent study, internships, off-campus study, part-time degree program, services for LD students, summer session for credit.

Student Life *Campus security:* student patrols, late-night transport/escort service.

Athletics Member NJCAA.

Financial Aid Of all full-time matriculated undergraduates who enrolled in 2004, 500 Federal Work-Study jobs (averaging $3000). 300 state and other part-time jobs (averaging $3000).

Applying *Options:* early admission. *Application fee:* $20. *Required:* high school transcript.

Director of Admissions Mr. Troy Tynsky, Director of Admissions, Rochester Community and Technical College, 851 30th Avenue, SE, Rochester, MN 55904-4999. *Phone:* 507-280-3509.

St. Cloud Technical College

St. Cloud, Minnesota   www.sctc.edu/

- **State-supported** 2-year, founded 1948, part of Minnesota State Colleges and Universities System
- **Urban** 35-acre campus with easy access to Minneapolis–St. Paul
- **Coed,** 3,348 undergraduate students, 65% full-time, 51% women, 49% men

Undergraduates 2,188 full-time, 1,160 part-time. Students come from 19 states and territories, 5 other countries, 2% are from out of state, 2% African American, 1% Asian American or Pacific Islander, 0.3% Hispanic American, 0.8% Native American, 0.2% international, 8% transferred in. Freshmen *Admission:* 2,653 applied, 1,649 admitted, 833 enrolled. *Average high school GPA:* 2.70.

Faculty *Total:* 252, 45% full-time, 3% with terminal degrees. *Student/faculty ratio:* 17:1.

Majors Accounting; accounting technology and bookkeeping; administrative assistant and secretarial science; advertising; architectural drafting and CAD/CADD; architectural engineering technology; autobody/collision and repair technology; automobile/automotive mechanics technology; banking and financial support services; business administration and management; cardiovascular technology; carpentry; child care and support services management; child development; civil engineering technology; computer/information technology services administration related; computer programming; computer programming related; computer programming (specific applications); computer systems networking and telecommunications; computer/technical support; construction engineering technology; consumer merchandising/retailing management; dental assisting; dental hygiene; diagnostic medical sonography and ultrasound technology; diesel mechanics technology; electrical and power transmission installation; electrical, electronic and communications engineering technology; electrocardiograph technology; emergency medical technology (EMT paramedic); finance; general retailing/wholesaling; heating, air conditioning and refrigeration technology; heating, air conditioning, ventilation and refrigeration maintenance technology; information technology; instrumentation technology; kindergarten/preschool education; legal administrative assistant/secretary; machine tool technology; marketing/marketing management; mechanical design technology; mechanical drafting and CAD/CADD; medical administrative assistant and medical secretary; medical office management; nursing (licensed practical/vocational nurse training); office management; pipefitting and sprinkler fitting; surgical technology; teacher assistant/aide; water quality and wastewater treatment management and recycling technology; welding technology.

Academics *Calendar:* semesters. *Degree:* certificates, diplomas, and associate. *Special study options:* academic remediation for entering students, adult/continuing education programs, advanced placement credit, cooperative education,

distance learning, English as a second language, internships, part-time degree program, services for LD students, summer session for credit.

Library Learning Resource Center plus 1 other with 10,000 titles, 600 serial subscriptions, an OPAC, a Web page.

Computers on Campus 500 computers available on campus for general student use. A campuswide network can be accessed. Internet access, online (class) registration, at least one staffed computer lab available. Computer purchase or lease plan available.

Student Life *Housing:* college housing not available. *Activities and Organizations:* student-run newspaper, Student Senate, Distributive Education Club of America, Business Professionals of America, Child and Adult Care Education, Central Minnesota Builders Association. *Campus security:* late-night transport/escort service. *Student services:* personal/psychological counseling, women's center.

Athletics Member NJCAA. *Intercollegiate sports:* baseball M, basketball M/W, softball W, volleyball W. *Intramural sports:* golf M/W, volleyball M/W.

Costs (2005–06) *Tuition:* state resident $3678 full-time, $123 per credit part-time; nonresident $7356 full-time, $145 per credit part-time. *Required fees:* $302 full-time, $10 per credit part-time.

Financial Aid Of all full-time matriculated undergraduates who enrolled in 2004, 38 Federal Work-Study jobs (averaging $4000). 38 state and other part-time jobs (averaging $4000).

Applying *Options:* electronic application, early admission, deferred entrance. *Application fee:* $20. *Required:* high school transcript. *Required for some:* interview. *Application deadline:* rolling (freshmen), rolling (transfers). *Notification:* continuous until 8/1 (freshmen).

Freshmen Application Contact Ms. Jodi Elness, Admissions Office, St. Cloud Technical College, 1540 Northway Drive, St. Cloud, MN 56303. *Phone:* 320-308-5089. *Toll-free phone:* 800-222-1009. *Fax:* 320-308-5981. *E-mail:* jelness@sctc.edu.

Saint Paul College—A Community & Technical College

St. Paul, Minnesota   www.saintpaul.edu/

- **State-related** 2-year, founded 1919, part of Minnesota State Colleges and Universities System
- **Urban** campus
- **Coed,** 5,169 undergraduate students, 30% full-time, 45% women, 55% men

Undergraduates 1,529 full-time, 3,640 part-time. 24% African American, 8% Asian American or Pacific Islander, 3% Hispanic American, 2% Native American, 0.2% international, 6% transferred in. Freshmen *Admission:* 3,379 applied, 3,011 admitted, 3,011 enrolled.

Faculty *Total:* 293, 37% full-time, 3% with terminal degrees. *Student/faculty ratio:* 16:1.

Majors Accounting; administrative assistant and secretarial science; child development; civil engineering technology; clinical/medical laboratory technology; computer programming; electrical, electronic and communications engineering technology; human resources management; industrial technology; international business/trade/commerce; medical administrative assistant and medical secretary; respiratory care therapy; sign language interpretation and translation.

Academics *Calendar:* semesters. *Degree:* certificates, diplomas, and associate. *Special study options:* academic remediation for entering students, adult/continuing education programs, distance learning, English as a second language, honors programs, internships, off-campus study.

Library Saint Paul College Library with 12,000 titles, 110 serial subscriptions, 260 audiovisual materials, an OPAC.

Computers on Campus A campuswide network can be accessed from off campus. Internet access, online (class) registration, at least one staffed computer lab available.

Student Life *Housing:* college housing not available. *Activities and Organizations:* Student Senate. *Campus security:* late-night transport/escort service. *Student services:* personal/psychological counseling, women's center.

Costs (2006–07) *Tuition:* state resident $3068 full-time, $128 per credit part-time; nonresident $6137 full-time, $256 per credit part-time. *Required fees:* $232 full-time, $9 per credit part-time.

Financial Aid Of all full-time matriculated undergraduates who enrolled in 2004, 48 Federal Work-Study jobs (averaging $2500). 94 state and other part-time jobs (averaging $2500).

Applying *Options:* electronic application, early admission. *Application fee:* $20. *Required for some:* high school transcript, interview. *Application deadline:* rolling (freshmen).

Freshmen Application Contact Mr. Thomas Matos, Dean of Student Development, Saint Paul College–A Community & Technical College, 235 Marshall

Avenue, Saint Paul, MN 55102. *Phone:* 651-846-1424. *Toll-free phone:* 800-227-6029. *Fax:* 665-221-1416. *E-mail:* admissions@saintpaul.edu.

SOUTH CENTRAL TECHNICAL COLLEGE
North Mankato, Minnesota   www.sctc.mnscu.edu/

- **State-supported** 2-year, founded 1946, part of Minnesota State Colleges and Universities System
- **Urban** campus
- **Coed**
- 100% of applicants were admitted

Undergraduates 2,350 full-time. Students come from 7 states and territories, 3 other counties, 1% African American, 1% Asian American or Pacific Islander, 1% Hispanic American, 0.2% Native American, 11% transferred in.
Faculty *Student/faculty ratio:* 18:1.
Academics *Calendar:* semesters. *Degree:* certificates, diplomas, and associate. *Special study options:* academic remediation for entering students, advanced placement credit, cooperative education, distance learning, independent study, part-time degree program, services for LD students.
Costs (2005–06) *Tuition:* $115 per credit part-time; state resident $3800 full-time. *Required fees:* $16 per credit part-time. *Payment plans:* installment, deferred payment.
Applying *Application fee:* $20. *Required:* high school transcript.
Director of Admissions Ms. Beverly Herda, Director of Admissions, South Central Technical College, 1920 Lee Boulevard, North Mankato, MN 56003. *Phone:* 507-389-7334. *Fax:* 507-388-9951.

VERMILION COMMUNITY COLLEGE
Ely, Minnesota   www.vcc.edu/

- **State-supported** 2-year, founded 1922, part of Minnesota State Colleges and Universities System
- **Rural** 5-acre campus
- **Coed,** 745 undergraduate students, 72% full-time, 34% women, 66% men

Undergraduates 533 full-time, 212 part-time. Students come from 42 states and territories, 3 other countries, 9% African American, 0.8% Asian American or Pacific Islander, 3% Hispanic American, 1% Native American, 50% live on campus.
Freshmen *Admission:* 595 applied, 341 admitted. *Average high school GPA:* 2.8.
Faculty *Total:* 85, 29% full-time. *Student/faculty ratio:* 13:1.
Majors Accounting; aeronautics/aviation/aerospace science and technology; agricultural business and management; agricultural economics; agricultural teacher education; agronomy and crop science; airline pilot and flight crew; architectural engineering technology; art; art history, criticism and conservation; art teacher education; aviation/airway management; biological and physical sciences; biology/biological sciences; business administration and management; business/managerial economics; chemistry; computer engineering technology; computer management; computer science; criminal justice/law enforcement administration; criminal justice/police science; criminal justice/safety; data processing and data processing technology; dramatic/theater arts; drawing; ecology; economics; education; elementary education; engineering; environmental education; environmental engineering technology; environmental studies; family and consumer sciences/human sciences; finance; fish/game management; forest/forest resources management; forestry; forestry technology; forest sciences and biology; geography; geology/earth science; health information/medical records administration; health teacher education; history; human ecology; hydrology and water resources science; industrial arts; industrial technology; interdisciplinary studies; kindergarten/preschool education; land use planning and management; liberal arts and sciences/liberal studies; mass communication/media; mathematics; medical administrative assistant and medical secretary; music; natural resources/conservation; natural resources management and policy; parks, recreation and leisure; parks, recreation and leisure facilities management; physical education teaching and coaching; physical sciences; physics; political science and government; pre-engineering; psychology; range science and management; science teacher education; sociology; soil conservation; special products marketing; speech and rhetoric; water quality and wastewater treatment management and recycling technology; wildlife and wildlands science and management; wildlife biology.
Academics *Calendar:* semesters. *Degree:* certificates, diplomas, and associate. *Special study options:* academic remediation for entering students, adult/continuing education programs, advanced placement credit, cooperative education, honors programs, internships, off-campus study, part-time degree program, services for LD students, summer session for credit.

Library Vermilion Community College Library with 19,500 titles, 100 serial subscriptions, an OPAC.
Computers on Campus 60 computers available on campus for general student use. A campuswide network can be accessed from student residence rooms and from off campus. At least one staffed computer lab available.
Student Life *Housing:* on-campus residence required for freshman year. *Options:* coed. Campus housing is university owned and leased by the school. *Activities and Organizations:* Student Life Committee, student government, Drama Club. *Campus security:* student patrols, late-night transport/escort service, controlled dormitory access. *Student services:* personal/psychological counseling, women's center.
Athletics Member NJCAA. *Intercollegiate sports:* baseball M, basketball M/W, football M, softball W, volleyball W. *Intramural sports:* basketball M/W, bowling M/W, cross-country running M/W, football M, golf M/W, ice hockey M, skiing (cross-country) M/W, skiing (downhill) M/W, softball M/W, tennis M/W, volleyball M/W, weight lifting M/W, wrestling M.
Costs (2006–07) *Tuition:* state resident $4190 full-time, $140 per credit part-time; nonresident $5120 full-time, $171 per credit part-time. *Room and board:* $4560; room only: $2900.
Financial Aid Of all full-time matriculated undergraduates who enrolled in 2004, 150 Federal Work-Study jobs (averaging $1000). 30 state and other part-time jobs (averaging $1000).
Applying *Options:* common application, electronic application, early admission, deferred entrance. *Application fee:* $20. *Required:* high school transcript. *Application deadline:* rolling (freshmen), rolling (transfers). *Notification:* continuous (freshmen).
Freshmen Application Contact Mr. Todd Heiman, Director of Enrollment Services, Vermilion Community College, 1900 East Camp Street, Ely, MN 55731-1996. *Phone:* 218-365-7224. *Toll-free phone:* 800-657-3608.

MISSISSIPPI

ANTONELLI COLLEGE
Hattiesburg, Mississippi   www.antonellic.com/
Director of Admissions Mrs. Karen Gautreau, Director, Antonelli College, 1500 North 31st Avenue, Hattiesburg, MS 39401. *Phone:* 601-583-4100. *Fax:* 601-583-0839.

ANTONELLI COLLEGE
Jackson, Mississippi   www.antonellic.com/
Director of Admissions Ms. Page McDaniel, Senior Admissions Officer, Antonelli College, 480 East Woodrow Wilson Drive, Jackson, MS 39216. *Phone:* 601-362-9991.

COAHOMA COMMUNITY COLLEGE
Clarksdale, Mississippi   www.ccc.cc.ms.us/

- **State and locally supported** 2-year, founded 1949, part of Mississippi State Board for Community and Junior Colleges
- **Small-town** 29-acre campus with easy access to Memphis
- **Coed,** 1,946 undergraduate students, 93% full-time, 71% women, 29% men

Undergraduates 1,801 full-time, 145 part-time. Students come from 8 states and territories, 3% are from out of state, 95% African American, 0.1% Hispanic American.
Freshmen *Admission:* 1,333 enrolled.
Faculty *Total:* 90, 81% full-time. *Student/faculty ratio:* 26:1.
Majors Accounting; administrative assistant and secretarial science; art; autobody/collision and repair technology; barbering; biology/biological sciences; business administration and management; business machine repair; carpentry; chemistry; clinical laboratory science/medical technology; computer installation and repair technology; computer science; cosmetology; criminal

Coahoma Community College (continued)

justice/law enforcement administration; elementary education; English; health teacher education; industrial mechanics and maintenance technology; kindergarten/ preschool education; liberal arts and sciences/liberal studies; nursing (licensed practical/vocational nurse training); radio and television; respiratory therapy technician; restaurant, culinary, and catering management; social work; sport and fitness administration/management; welding technology.

Academics *Calendar:* semesters. *Degree:* certificates and associate. *Special study options:* adult/continuing education programs, part-time degree program.

Library Dickerson-Johnson Library.

Computers on Campus 25 computers available on campus for general student use. A campuswide network can be accessed. Internet access available.

Student Life *Housing Options:* Campus housing is university owned. *Activities and Organizations:* drama/theater group, student-run newspaper, choral group, marching band, Student Government Association, VICA, Phi Theta Kappa Honor Society. *Campus security:* 24-hour patrols. *Student services:* health clinic, personal/psychological counseling.

Athletics Member NJCAA. *Intercollegiate sports:* baseball M, basketball M(s)/W(s), football M.

Costs (2006–07) *Tuition:* area resident $1600 full-time, $90 per semester hour part-time; nonresident $2900 full-time. *Required fees:* $140 full-time, $60 per term part-time. *Room and board:* $2914.

Financial Aid Of all full-time matriculated undergraduates who enrolled in 2004, 350 Federal Work-Study jobs (averaging $600). 45 state and other part-time jobs (averaging $1000).

Applying *Options:* common application. *Required:* high school transcript. *Required for some:* minimum X GPA, letters of recommendation, interview. *Application deadline:* rolling (freshmen), rolling (transfers). *Notification:* continuous (freshmen).

Freshmen Application Contact Mrs. Wanda Holmes, Director of Admissions and Records, Coahoma Community College, Route 1, PO Box 616, Clarksdale, MS 38614-9799. *Phone:* 662-621-4205. *Toll-free phone:* 800-844-1222.

COPIAH-LINCOLN COMMUNITY COLLEGE
Wesson, Mississippi
www.colin.edu/

- **State and locally supported** 2-year, founded 1928, part of Mississippi State Board for Community and Junior Colleges
- **Rural** 525-acre campus with easy access to Jackson
- **Coed**, 2,161 undergraduate students

Undergraduates Students come from 7 states and territories, 2 other countries, 2% are from out of state, 30% live on campus.

Faculty *Total:* 127, 65% full-time.

Majors Accounting; agribusiness; agricultural business and management; agricultural business and management related; agricultural business technology; agricultural economics; agricultural/farm supplies retailing and wholesaling; agriculture; architecture; art teacher education; biological and physical sciences; biology/biological sciences; business administration and management; chemistry; child development; civil engineering technology; clinical/medical laboratory technology; computer programming; cosmetology; criminal justice/police science; data processing and data processing technology; drafting and design technology; economics; education; electrical, electronic and communications engineering technology; elementary education; engineering; English; family and consumer sciences/home economics teacher education; farm and ranch management; food technology and processing; forestry; French; health teacher education; history; industrial radiologic technology; journalism; liberal arts and sciences/ liberal studies; library science; music teacher education; nursing (registered nurse training); physical education teaching and coaching; special products marketing; trade and industrial teacher education; wood science and wood products/pulp and paper technology.

Academics *Calendar:* semesters. *Degree:* certificates and associate. *Special study options:* academic remediation for entering students, adult/continuing education programs, advanced placement credit, honors programs, part-time degree program, student-designed majors, summer session for credit.

Library Oswalt Memorial Library with 38,900 titles, 255 serial subscriptions.

Computers on Campus 300 computers available on campus for general student use. At least one staffed computer lab available.

Student Life *Housing Options:* Campus housing is university owned. *Activities and Organizations:* drama/theater group, student-run newspaper, radio station, choral group, marching band. *Campus security:* 24-hour patrols. *Student services:* health clinic, personal/psychological counseling.

Athletics Member NJCAA. *Intercollegiate sports:* baseball M(s), basketball M(s)/W(s), football M(s), golf M/W, softball W, tennis M/W, track and field M. *Intramural sports:* basketball M/W, football M, golf M/W, tennis M/W, volleyball M/W.

Costs (2006–07) *Tuition:* state resident $1700 full-time; nonresident $1800 full-time. *Required fees:* $100 full-time.

Financial Aid Of all full-time matriculated undergraduates who enrolled in 2004, 125 Federal Work-Study jobs (averaging $1000).

Applying *Options:* early admission. *Required:* high school transcript. *Application deadline:* rolling (freshmen), rolling (transfers).

Freshmen Application Contact Laura Lofton, Director of Distance Learning, Copiah-Lincoln Community College, PO Box 371, Wesson, MS 39191-0457. *Phone:* 601-643-8307. *Fax:* 601-643-8222.

COPIAH-LINCOLN COMMUNITY COLLEGE—NATCHEZ CAMPUS
Natchez, Mississippi
www.colin.edu/

- **State and locally supported** 2-year, founded 1972, part of Mississippi State Board for Community and Junior Colleges
- **Small-town** 24-acre campus
- **Coed**

Undergraduates 554 full-time, 346 part-time. Students come from 4 states and territories, 53% African American, 0.3% Asian American or Pacific Islander, 0.3% Hispanic American.

Faculty *Student/faculty ratio:* 20:1.

Academics *Calendar:* semesters. *Degree:* certificates and associate. *Special study options:* academic remediation for entering students, adult/continuing education programs, advanced placement credit, distance learning, internships, part-time degree program, student-designed majors, summer session for credit.

Student Life *Campus security:* 24-hour patrols.

Athletics Member NJCAA.

Standardized Tests *Required for some:* ACT (for admission), TABE.

Costs (2005–06) *Tuition:* state resident $1600 full-time, $100 per semester hour part-time; nonresident $3400 full-time, $175 per semester hour part-time. *Required fees:* $100 full-time, $5 per semester hour part-time, $10 per year part-time. *Room and board:* $2600.

Financial Aid Of all full-time matriculated undergraduates who enrolled in 2004, 120 Federal Work-Study jobs (averaging $957). 15 state and other part-time jobs (averaging $1368).

Applying *Options:* early admission. *Required:* high school transcript.

Director of Admissions Mrs. Gwen S. McCalip, Director of Admissions and Records, Copiah-Lincoln Community College–Natchez Campus, 11 Co-Lin Circle, Natchez, MS 39120. *Phone:* 601-442-9111 Ext. 224.

EAST CENTRAL COMMUNITY COLLEGE
Decatur, Mississippi
www.eccc.cc.ms.us/

- **State and locally supported** 2-year, founded 1928, part of Mississippi State Board for Community and Junior Colleges
- **Rural** 200-acre campus
- **Coed**

Undergraduates Students come from 9 states and territories, 2% are from out of state, 27% live on campus.

Academics *Calendar:* semesters. *Degree:* certificates and associate. *Special study options:* academic remediation for entering students, adult/continuing education programs, advanced placement credit, honors programs, part-time degree program, services for LD students, summer session for credit.

Student Life *Campus security:* 24-hour patrols.

Athletics Member NJCAA.

Standardized Tests *Required:* ACT (for placement).

Financial Aid Of all full-time matriculated undergraduates who enrolled in 2004, 90 Federal Work-Study jobs (averaging $850). 38 state and other part-time jobs (averaging $1020).

Applying *Options:* common application, early admission. *Required:* high school transcript.

Director of Admissions Ms. Donna Luke, Director of Admissions, Records, and Research, East Central Community College, PO Box 129, Decatur, MS 39327-0129. *Phone:* 601-635-2111 Ext. 206. *Toll-free phone:* 877-462-3222.

EAST MISSISSIPPI COMMUNITY COLLEGE
Scooba, Mississippi
www.eastms.edu/

- **State and locally supported** 2-year, founded 1927, part of Mississippi State Board for Community and Junior Colleges
- **Rural** 25-acre campus
- **Endowment** $134,022
- **Coed**

Undergraduates 2,068 full-time, 1,349 part-time. Students come from 4 states and territories, 1% are from out of state, 51% African American, 0.4% Asian American or Pacific Islander, 0.5% Hispanic American, 0.1% Native American, 25% live on campus.

Faculty *Student/faculty ratio:* 22:1.

Academics *Calendar:* semesters. *Degree:* certificates and associate. *Special study options:* academic remediation for entering students, adult/continuing education programs, advanced placement credit, cooperative education, distance learning, double majors, honors programs, part-time degree program, services for LD students, summer session for credit.

Student Life *Campus security:* 24-hour emergency response devices and patrols.

Athletics Member NJCAA.

Standardized Tests *Required for some:* ACT (for placement).

Financial Aid Of all full-time matriculated undergraduates who enrolled in 2004, 200 Federal Work-Study jobs (averaging $1200).

Applying *Options:* common application, electronic application, deferred entrance. *Required:* high school transcript.

Director of Admissions Ms. Melinda Sciple, Admissions Officer, East Mississippi Community College, PO Box 158, Scooba, MS 39358-0158. *Phone:* 662-476-5041.

HINDS COMMUNITY COLLEGE
Raymond, Mississippi
www.hindscc.edu/

- **State and locally supported** 2-year, founded 1917, part of Mississippi State Board for Community and Junior Colleges
- **Small-town** 671-acre campus
- **Endowment** $948,556
- **Coed**

Undergraduates 7,145 full-time, 2,816 part-time. Students come from 16 states and territories, 1 other country, 3% are from out of state, 52% African American, 0.5% Asian American or Pacific Islander, 0.6% Hispanic American, 0.2% Native American, 15% live on campus.

Faculty *Student/faculty ratio:* 17:1.

Academics *Calendar:* semesters. *Degree:* certificates, diplomas, and associate. *Special study options:* academic remediation for entering students, accelerated degree program, adult/continuing education programs, advanced placement credit, cooperative education, distance learning, double majors, freshman honors college, honors programs, independent study, part-time degree program, services for LD students, summer session for credit. *ROTC:* Army (c).

Student Life *Campus security:* 24-hour emergency response devices and patrols, controlled dormitory access.

Athletics Member NJCAA.

Standardized Tests *Required for some:* SAT and SAT Subject Tests or ACT (for admission).

Financial Aid Of all full-time matriculated undergraduates who enrolled in 2004, 300 Federal Work-Study jobs (averaging $1250). 200 state and other part-time jobs (averaging $1000).

Applying *Options:* common application, early admission. *Required:* high school transcript.

Director of Admissions Mr. Jay Allen, Director of Admissions and Records, Hinds Community College, PO Box 1100, Raymond, MS 39154-1100. *Phone:* 601-857-3280. *Toll-free phone:* 800-HINDSCC.

HOLMES COMMUNITY COLLEGE
Goodman, Mississippi
www.holmescc.edu/

- **State and locally supported** 2-year, founded 1928, part of Mississippi State Board for Community and Junior Colleges
- **Small-town** 196-acre campus
- **Endowment** $2.4 million
- **Coed**

Undergraduates 3,251 full-time, 1,243 part-time. Students come from 11 states and territories, 1% are from out of state, 45% African American, 0.3% Hispanic American, 0.1% Native American, 12% live on campus. *Retention:* 55% of 2003 full-time freshmen returned.

Faculty *Student/faculty ratio:* 19:1.

Academics *Calendar:* semesters. *Degree:* certificates and associate. *Special study options:* academic remediation for entering students, adult/continuing education programs, advanced placement credit, cooperative education, distance learning, services for LD students, summer session for credit.

Student Life *Campus security:* 24-hour emergency response devices and patrols.

Athletics Member NJCAA.

Standardized Tests *Required:* ACT (for placement).

Costs (2005–06) *Tuition:* state resident $1100 full-time, $65 per semester hour part-time; nonresident $1750 full-time. Part-time tuition and fees vary according to course load. *Required fees:* $330 full-time, $10 per term part-time. *Room and board:* $3330. Room and board charges vary according to housing facility.

Financial Aid Of all full-time matriculated undergraduates who enrolled in 2004, 160 Federal Work-Study jobs (averaging $700).

Applying *Options:* early admission. *Required:* high school transcript.

Director of Admissions Dr. Lynn Wright, Dean of Admissions and Records, Holmes Community College, PO Box 369, Goodman, MS 39079-0369. *Phone:* 601-472-2312 Ext. 1023.

ITAWAMBA COMMUNITY COLLEGE
Fulton, Mississippi
www.icc.cc.ms.us/

- **State and locally supported** 2-year, founded 1947, part of Mississippi State Board for Community and Junior Colleges
- **Small-town** 300-acre campus
- **Coed**

Undergraduates Students come from 9 states and territories, 3 other countries.

Academics *Calendar:* semesters. *Degree:* associate. *Special study options:* academic remediation for entering students, adult/continuing education programs, honors programs, part-time degree program, services for LD students, summer session for credit. *ROTC:* Army (b).

Athletics Member NJCAA.

Standardized Tests *Required:* ACT (for placement).

Financial Aid Of all full-time matriculated undergraduates who enrolled in 2004, 250 Federal Work-Study jobs (averaging $2300). 30 state and other part-time jobs (averaging $2300).

Applying *Options:* early admission. *Required:* high school transcript.

Freshmen Application Contact Mr. Max Munn, Director of Recruiting, Itawamba Community College, 602 West Hill Street, Fulton, MS 38843. *Phone:* 601-862-8252.

JONES COUNTY JUNIOR COLLEGE
Ellisville, Mississippi
www.jcjc.edu/

Director of Admissions Mrs. Dianne Speed, Director of Admissions and Records, Jones County Junior College, 900 South Court Street, Ellisville, MS 39437. *Phone:* 601-477-4025.

MERIDIAN COMMUNITY COLLEGE

Meridian, Mississippi   www.meridiancc.edu

- **State and locally supported** 2-year, founded 1937, part of Mississippi State Board for Community and Junior Colleges
- **Small-town** 62-acre campus
- **Endowment** $4.8 million
- **Coed,** 3,572 undergraduate students, 74% full-time, 70% women, 30% men

Undergraduates 2,649 full-time, 923 part-time. Students come from 16 states and territories, 3% are from out of state, 39% African American, 0.4% Asian American or Pacific Islander, 0.8% Hispanic American, 2% Native American, 0.1% international, 12% live on campus.
Freshmen *Admission:* 882 admitted.

Faculty *Total:* 256, 56% full-time, 3% with terminal degrees.

Majors Administrative assistant and secretarial science; athletic training; broadcast journalism; clinical/medical laboratory technology; computer engineering technology; computer graphics; dental hygiene; drafting and design technology; electrical, electronic and communications engineering technology; emergency medical technology (EMT paramedic); fire science; health information/medical records administration; horticultural science; hotel/motel administration; machine tool technology; marketing/marketing management; medical radiologic technology; nursing (registered nurse training); physical therapy; respiratory care therapy; telecommunications.

Academics *Calendar:* semesters. *Degree:* certificates and associate. *Special study options:* academic remediation for entering students, adult/continuing education programs, advanced placement credit, cooperative education, distance learning, English as a second language, independent study, part-time degree program, services for LD students, summer session for credit.

Library L.O. Todd Library with 50,000 titles, 600 serial subscriptions.

Computers on Campus 123 computers available on campus for general student use. A campuswide network can be accessed from student residence rooms and from off campus. Internet access, online (class) registration, at least one staffed computer lab available.

Student Life *Housing Options:* coed, men-only, women-only. Campus housing is university owned and leased by the school. *Activities and Organizations:* drama/theater group, student-run newspaper, radio station, choral group, Phi Theta Kappa, Vocational Industrial Clubs of America, Health Occupations Students of America, Organization of Student Nurses, Distributive Education Clubs of America. *Campus security:* 24-hour patrols, student patrols. *Student services:* health clinic, personal/psychological counseling.

Athletics Member NJCAA. *Intercollegiate sports:* baseball M(s), basketball M(s)/W(s), cross-country running M(s)/W(s), golf M(s), soccer M(s), softball W(s), tennis M(s)/W(s), track and field M(s)/W(s). *Intramural sports:* basketball M/W, bowling M/W, cross-country running M/W, swimming and diving M/W, tennis M/W, volleyball M/W.

Standardized Tests *Required:* ACCUPLACER (for admission). *Recommended:* ACT (for admission).

Costs (2005–06) *Tuition:* state resident $1450 full-time, $80 per credit hour part-time; nonresident $2740 full-time, $137 per credit hour part-time. *Required fees:* $4 per credit hour part-time, $5 per term part-time. *Room and board:* $2600. Room and board charges vary according to board plan. *Payment plan:* installment. *Waivers:* employees or children of employees.

Financial Aid Of all full-time matriculated undergraduates who enrolled in 2004, 100 Federal Work-Study jobs (averaging $2100).

Applying *Options:* early admission. *Required:* high school transcript, minimum 2.0 GPA. *Required for some:* essay or personal statement. *Application deadline:* rolling (freshmen), rolling (transfers).

Freshmen Application Contact Ms. Dianne Walton, Director of Enrollment Services, Meridian Community College, 910 Highway 19 North, Meridian, MS 39307. *Phone:* 601-484-8895. *Toll-free phone:* 800-622-8731. *E-mail:* dwalton@mcc.cc.ms.us.

MISSISSIPPI DELTA COMMUNITY COLLEGE

Moorhead, Mississippi   www.msdelta.edu/

Director of Admissions Mr. Joseph F. Ray Jr., Vice President of Admissions, Mississippi Delta Community College, PO Box 668, Moorhead, MS 38761-0668. *Phone:* 662-246-6308.

MISSISSIPPI GULF COAST COMMUNITY COLLEGE

Perkinston, Mississippi   www.mgccc.edu/

- **District-supported** 2-year, founded 1911, part of Mississippi State Board for Community and Junior Colleges
- **Small-town** 600-acre campus with easy access to New Orleans
- **Endowment** $3.0 million
- **Coed,** 7,806 undergraduate students, 67% full-time, 62% women, 38% men

Undergraduates 5,209 full-time, 2,597 part-time. Students come from 15 states and territories, 4% are from out of state, 19% African American, 2% Asian American or Pacific Islander, 2% Hispanic American, 0.4% Native American, 7% live on campus. *Retention:* 62% of 2003 full-time freshmen returned.
Freshmen *Admission:* 2,363 applied, 2,363 admitted, 1,883 enrolled.

Faculty *Total:* 599, 56% full-time. *Student/faculty ratio:* 26:1.

Majors Accounting; administrative assistant and secretarial science; advertising; agricultural business and management; art; art teacher education; automobile/automotive mechanics technology; biological and physical sciences; business administration and management; business teacher education; chemical engineering; clinical/medical laboratory technology; computer and information sciences related; computer engineering technology; computer graphics; computer programming related; computer science; computer systems networking and telecommunications; court reporting; criminal justice/law enforcement administration; criminal justice/police science; data entry/microcomputer applications; data entry/microcomputer applications related; drafting and design technology; education; electrical, electronic and communications engineering technology; elementary education; emergency medical technology (EMT paramedic); fashion merchandising; finance; horticultural science; hotel/motel administration; human services; industrial radiologic technology; information technology; kindergarten/preschool education; legal assistant/paralegal; liberal arts and sciences/liberal studies; marketing/marketing management; nursing (registered nurse training); ornamental horticulture; postal management; pre-engineering; respiratory care therapy; welding technology; word processing.

Academics *Calendar:* semesters. *Degree:* certificates, diplomas, and associate. *Special study options:* academic remediation for entering students, adult/continuing education programs, advanced placement credit, cooperative education, distance learning, English as a second language, honors programs, internships, part-time degree program, services for LD students, summer session for credit.

Library Main Library plus 3 others with 100,472 titles, 933 serial subscriptions, an OPAC.

Computers on Campus 435 computers available on campus for general student use. A campuswide network can be accessed from student residence rooms. At least one staffed computer lab available.

Student Life *Housing Options:* men-only, women-only. Campus housing is university owned. *Activities and Organizations:* drama/theater group, student-run newspaper, choral group, marching band, VICA, SIFE, Student Government Association. *Campus security:* 24-hour emergency response devices and patrols. *Student services:* personal/psychological counseling, women's center.

Athletics Member NJCAA. *Intercollegiate sports:* baseball M(s), basketball M(s)/W(s), football M(s), golf M(s), soccer M(s)/W(s), softball W(s), tennis M(s)/W(s), track and field M(s). *Intramural sports:* basketball M/W, football M, soccer M/W, softball M/W, volleyball M/W.

Costs (2006–07) *Tuition:* area resident $1522 full-time, $75 per hour part-time; nonresident $3368 full-time, $152 per hour part-time. *Room and board:* $3800.

Applying *Options:* common application, electronic application, early admission. *Required:* high school transcript. *Application deadline:* rolling (freshmen), rolling (transfers). *Notification:* continuous (freshmen).

Freshmen Application Contact Ms. Michelle Sekul, Director of Admissions, Mississippi Gulf Coast Community College, PO Box 548, Perkinston, MS 39573. *Phone:* 601-928-6264. *Fax:* 601-928-6299. *E-mail:* michelle.sekul@mgccc.edu.

NORTHEAST MISSISSIPPI COMMUNITY COLLEGE

Booneville, Mississippi   www.nemcc.edu/

Freshmen Application Contact Office of Enrollment Services, Northeast Mississippi Community College, 101 Cunningham Boulevard, Booneville, MS 38829. *Phone:* 662-720-7239. *Toll-free phone:* 800-555-2154. *E-mail:* admitme@necc.cc.ms.us.

NORTHWEST MISSISSIPPI COMMUNITY COLLEGE
Senatobia, Mississippi www.northwestms.edu/
Director of Admissions Ms. Deanna Ferguson, Director of Admissions and Recruiting, Northwest Mississippi Community College, 4975 Highway 51 North, Senatobia, MS 38668-1701. *Phone:* 662-562-3222.

PEARL RIVER COMMUNITY COLLEGE
Poplarville, Mississippi www.prcc.edu/
Director of Admissions Mr. J. Dow Ford, Director of Admissions, Pearl River Community College, 101 Highway 11 North, Poplarville, MS 39470. *Phone:* 601-795-6801 Ext. 216. *E-mail:* dford@prcc.cc.ms.us.

SOUTHWEST MISSISSIPPI COMMUNITY COLLEGE
Summit, Mississippi www.smcc.cc.ms.us/
- **State and locally supported** 2-year, founded 1918, part of Mississippi State Board for Community and Junior Colleges
- **Rural** 701-acre campus
- **Coed,** 1,895 undergraduate students, 62% full-time, 65% women, 35% men

Undergraduates 1,176 full-time, 718 part-time. Students come from 6 states and territories, 10% are from out of state, 40% African American, 0.3% Asian American or Pacific Islander, 0.6% Native American, 35% live on campus. Freshmen *Test scores:* ACT scores over 18: 47%; ACT scores over 24: 6%.
Faculty *Total:* 94, 87% full-time, 6% with terminal degrees. *Student/faculty ratio:* 25:1.
Majors Accounting; administrative assistant and secretarial science; advertising; automobile/automotive mechanics technology; biological and physical sciences; biology/biological sciences; business administration and management; business teacher education; carpentry; chemistry; computer programming related; computer science; construction engineering technology; cosmetology; education; electrical, electronic and communications engineering technology; elementary education; emergency medical technology (EMT paramedic); engineering; English; fashion merchandising; finance; health science; history; humanities; information technology; legal administrative assistant/secretary; liberal arts and sciences/liberal studies; machine tool technology; marketing/marketing management; music; music teacher education; nursing (registered nurse training); physical education teaching and coaching; physical sciences; social sciences; system administration; welding technology.
Academics *Calendar:* semesters. *Degree:* certificates and associate. *Special study options:* academic remediation for entering students, adult/continuing education programs, distance learning, part-time degree program, summer session for credit.
Library Library Learning Resources Center (LLRC) with 34,000 titles, 150 serial subscriptions, an OPAC.
Computers on Campus 300 computers available on campus for general student use. A campuswide network can be accessed from off campus. Internet access, online (class) registration, at least one staffed computer lab available.
Student Life *Activities and Organizations:* student-run newspaper, choral group, marching band. *Campus security:* 24-hour patrols.
Athletics Member NJCAA. *Intercollegiate sports:* baseball M, basketball M(s)/W(s), football M(s), golf M, softball W, tennis M/W. *Intramural sports:* basketball M/W.
Costs (2006–07) *Tuition:* state resident $1700 full-time, $75 per hour part-time; nonresident $3900 full-time, $170 per hour part-time. *Required fees:* $100 full-time, $50 per term part-time. *Room and board:* $2180.
Financial Aid Of all full-time matriculated undergraduates who enrolled in 2004, 85 Federal Work-Study jobs (averaging $698). 6 state and other part-time jobs (averaging $550).
Applying *Required:* high school transcript. *Application deadlines:* 8/1 (freshmen), 8/1 (transfers).
Freshmen Application Contact Matthew Calhoun, Dean of Admissions, Southwest Mississippi Community College, College Drive, Summit, MS 39666. *Phone:* 601-276-2001. *Fax:* 601-276-3888. *E-mail:* mattc@smcc.edu.

VIRGINIA COLLEGE AT JACKSON
Jackson, Mississippi www.vc.edu/
Director of Admissions Mr. Bill Milstead, Vice President of Admissions, Virginia College at Jackson, Interstate 55 North, Jackson, MS 39211. *Phone:* 601-977-0960 Ext. 2704.

MISSOURI

ALLIED COLLEGE
Maryland Heights, Missouri www.hightechinstitute.edu/
Director of Admissions Mr. Larkin Hicks, President, Allied College, 13723 Riverport Drive, Suite 103, Maryland Heights, MO 63043. *Phone:* 314-739-4450. *Fax:* 314-739-5133.

AVIATION INSTITUTE OF MAINTENANCE—KANSAS CITY
Kansas City, Missouri www.aviationmaintenance.edu/aviation-kansascity.asp
- **Proprietary** 2-year

Faculty *Total:* 15.
Majors Airframe mechanics and aircraft maintenance technology.
Academics *Calendar:* quarters. *Degree:* certificates and associate.
Costs (2005–06) *Tuition:* Tuition and fees for Associates Degree, $34,560.
Applying *Required:* High School Diploma or GED.
Freshmen Application Contact Kansas City School Director, Aviation Institute of Maintenance–Kansas City, 3130 Terrace Street, Kansas City, MO 64111. *Phone:* 816-753-9920. *Toll-free phone:* 877-538-5627. *Fax:* 816-753-9941. *E-mail:* directoramk@tidetech.com.

BLUE RIVER COMMUNITY COLLEGE
Independence, Missouri www.mcckc.edu
- **State and locally supported** 2-year, part of Metropolitan Community Colleges System
- **Suburban** campus with easy access to Kansas City
- **Endowment** $2.4 million
- **Coed,** 2,662 undergraduate students, 40% full-time, 60% women, 40% men

Undergraduates 1,053 full-time, 1,609 part-time. Students come from 2 states and territories, 0.2% are from out of state, 2% African American, 0.7% Asian American or Pacific Islander, 2% Hispanic American, 0.8% Native American, 5% transferred in. *Retention:* 57% of 2003 full-time freshmen returned. Freshmen *Admission:* 487 applied, 487 admitted, 487 enrolled.
Faculty *Total:* 304, 10% full-time. *Student/faculty ratio:* 13:1.
Majors Accounting technology and bookkeeping; administrative assistant and secretarial science; business administration and management; computer and information sciences related; computer science; criminal justice/police science; fire science; information science/studies; liberal arts and sciences/liberal studies.
Academics *Calendar:* semesters. *Degree:* certificates and associate. *Special study options:* academic remediation for entering students, accelerated degree program, adult/continuing education programs, advanced placement credit, cooperative education, distance learning, English as a second language, honors programs, internships, off-campus study, part-time degree program, services for LD students, summer session for credit.
Library Blue River Community College Library with 10,312 titles, 66 serial subscriptions, 567 audiovisual materials, an OPAC, a Web page.

Blue River Community College (continued)

Computers on Campus 375 computers available on campus for general student use. A campuswide network can be accessed from off campus. Internet access, at least one staffed computer lab available.

Student Life *Housing:* college housing not available. *Activities and Organizations:* choral group. *Campus security:* 24-hour emergency response devices and patrols.

Costs (2006–07) *Tuition:* area resident $2190 full-time, $73 per hour part-time; state resident $3990 full-time, $133 per hour part-time; nonresident $5400 full-time, $180 per hour part-time. *Required fees:* $150 full-time, $5 per hour part-time.

Applying *Options:* early admission, deferred entrance. *Application deadline:* rolling (freshmen), rolling (transfers).

Freshmen Application Contact Mr. Jon Burke, Dean of Student Development, Blue River Community College, 20301 East 78 Highway, Independence, MO 64057. *Phone:* 816-655-6118. *Fax:* 816-655-6014.

CONCORDE CAREER INSTITUTE
Kansas City, Missouri

COTTEY COLLEGE
Nevada, Missouri www.cottey.edu/

- **Independent** 2-year, founded 1884
- **Small-town** 51-acre campus
- **Endowment** $78.4 million
- **Women only,** 308 undergraduate students

Undergraduates Students come from 42 states and territories, 15 other countries, 78% are from out of state, 3% African American, 2% Asian American or Pacific Islander, 6% Hispanic American, 0.3% Native American, 11% international, 98% live on campus. *Retention:* 75% of 2003 full-time freshmen returned.
Freshmen *Admission:* 507 applied, 185 admitted. *Average high school GPA:* 3.42. *Test scores:* SAT verbal scores over 500: 49%; SAT math scores over 500: 31%; ACT scores over 18: 92%; SAT verbal scores over 600: 13%; SAT math scores over 600: 9%; ACT scores over 24: 43%; ACT scores over 30: 2%.

Faculty *Total:* 37, 95% full-time. *Student/faculty ratio:* 10:1.

Majors Biological and physical sciences; liberal arts and sciences/liberal studies.

Academics *Calendar:* semesters. *Degree:* associate. *Special study options:* advanced placement credit, part-time degree program.

Library Blanche Skiff Ross Memorial Library with 54,200 titles, 246 serial subscriptions, an OPAC.

Computers on Campus 50 computers available on campus for general student use. A campuswide network can be accessed. Internet access, at least one staffed computer lab available.

Student Life *Housing:* on-campus residence required through sophomore year. *Options:* women-only. Campus housing is university owned. *Activities and Organizations:* drama/theater group, student-run newspaper, choral group, International Friendship Circle, Cottey Intramural Association, Ozarks Explorers Club, Inter-Varsity Club, Golden Keys. *Campus security:* 24-hour emergency response devices and patrols, late-night transport/escort service, controlled dormitory access. *Student services:* health clinic, personal/psychological counseling.

Athletics Member NAIA. *Intercollegiate sports:* basketball W, volleyball W. *Intramural sports:* badminton W, basketball W, fencing W, field hockey W, golf W, soccer W, softball W, swimming and diving W, tennis W, volleyball W, water polo W, weight lifting W.

Standardized Tests *Required:* SAT or ACT (for admission).

Costs (2005–06) *Comprehensive fee:* $17,510 includes full-time tuition ($11,600), mandatory fees ($710), and room and board ($5200).

Financial Aid Of all full-time matriculated undergraduates who enrolled in 2004, 26 Federal Work-Study jobs (averaging $1500). 131 state and other part-time jobs (averaging $1500).

Applying *Options:* electronic application, early admission, deferred entrance. *Application fee:* $20. *Required:* essay or personal statement, high school transcript, 1 letter of recommendation. *Recommended:* minimum 2.6 GPA, interview. *Application deadline:* rolling (freshmen), rolling (transfers).

Director of Admissions Ms. Marjorie J. Cooke, Dean of Enrollment Management, Cottey College, 1000 West Austin, Nevada, MO 64772. *Phone:* 417-667-8181. *Toll-free phone:* 888-526-8839. *Fax:* 417-667-8103. *E-mail:* enrollmgt@cottey.edu.

▶ **See page 538 for the College Close-Up.**

CROWDER COLLEGE
Neosho, Missouri www.crowder.edu/

- **State and locally supported** 2-year, founded 1963, part of Missouri Coordinating Board for Higher Education
- **Rural** 608-acre campus
- **Coed,** 2,615 undergraduate students, 50% full-time, 65% women, 35% men

Undergraduates 1,319 full-time, 1,296 part-time. Students come from 15 states and territories, 15 other countries, 4% are from out of state, 0.8% African American, 1% Asian American or Pacific Islander, 5% Hispanic American, 2% Native American, 0.5% international, 5% transferred in, 10% live on campus. Freshmen *Admission:* 1,253 applied, 1,253 admitted, 566 enrolled.

Faculty *Total:* 219, 29% full-time. *Student/faculty ratio:* 19:1.

Majors Administrative assistant and secretarial science; agribusiness; agriculture; art; biology/biological sciences; business administration and management; business automation/technology/data entry; computer systems networking and telecommunications; construction engineering technology; drafting and design technology; dramatic/theater arts; education; electrical, electronic and communications engineering technology; elementary education; environmental engineering technology; environmental health; executive assistant/executive secretary; farm and ranch management; fire science; general studies; industrial technology; legal administrative assistant/secretary; liberal arts and sciences/liberal studies; mass communication/media; mathematics; mathematics and computer science; medical administrative assistant and medical secretary; music; nursing (registered nurse training); physical education teaching and coaching; physical sciences; poultry science; pre-engineering; psychology; public relations/image management.

Academics *Calendar:* semesters. *Degree:* certificates and associate. *Special study options:* academic remediation for entering students, adult/continuing education programs, advanced placement credit, cooperative education, English as a second language, freshman honors college, honors programs, internships, part-time degree program, study abroad, summer session for credit.

Library Crowder College Learning Resources Center with 37,452 titles, 163 serial subscriptions, 3,632 audiovisual materials, an OPAC, a Web page.

Computers on Campus 515 computers available on campus for general student use. A campuswide network can be accessed. Internet access, at least one staffed computer lab available.

Student Life *Housing Options:* men-only, women-only. Campus housing is university owned. *Activities and Organizations:* drama/theater group, student-run newspaper, choral group, Phi Beta Lambda, Students in Free Enterprise, Baptist Student Union, Student Senate, Student Ambassadors. *Campus security:* 24-hour patrols. *Student services:* personal/psychological counseling.

Athletics Member NJCAA. *Intercollegiate sports:* baseball M(s), basketball W(s). *Intramural sports:* soccer M.

Costs (2006–07) *Tuition:* area resident $1860 full-time; state resident $2640 full-time; nonresident $3450 full-time. *Required fees:* $360 full-time. *Room and board:* $3870.

Financial Aid Of all full-time matriculated undergraduates who enrolled in 2004, 150 Federal Work-Study jobs (averaging $1000).

Applying *Application fee:* $25. *Required:* high school transcript. *Application deadline:* rolling (freshmen), rolling (transfers). *Notification:* continuous (freshmen).

Freshmen Application Contact Mr. Jim Riggs, Admissions Coordinator, Crowder College, 601 Laclede Avenue, Neosho, MO 64850. *Phone:* 417-451-3223 Ext. 5466. *Toll-free phone:* 866-238-7788. *Fax:* 417-455-5731.

EAST CENTRAL COLLEGE
Union, Missouri www.eastcentral.edu/

- **District-supported** 2-year, founded 1959, part of Missouri Coordinating Board for Higher Education
- **Rural** 207-acre campus with easy access to St. Louis
- **Endowment** $2.8 million
- **Coed,** 3,486 undergraduate students, 42% full-time, 62% women, 38% men

Undergraduates 1,447 full-time, 2,039 part-time. Students come from 4 states and territories, 0.6% African American, 0.8% Asian American or Pacific Islander,

1% Hispanic American, 0.4% Native American, 6% transferred in.
Freshmen *Admission:* 899 admitted, 899 enrolled. *Average high school GPA:* 2.50.

Faculty *Total:* 189, 29% full-time, 11% with terminal degrees. *Student/faculty ratio:* 21:1.

Majors Accounting; administrative assistant and secretarial science; automobile/automotive mechanics technology; biology/biological sciences; botany/plant biology; business administration and management; business operations support and secretarial services related; chemistry; commercial and advertising art; computer systems networking and telecommunications; construction engineering technology; construction trades; construction trades related; criminal justice/law enforcement administration; criminal justice/police science; culinary arts; design and visual communications; drafting and design technology; early childhood education; ecology; economics; education; electrical, electronic and communications engineering technology; emergency medical technology (EMT paramedic); engineering; English; family and consumer sciences/human sciences; fire science; fish/game management; forestry; general studies; geography; geology/earth science; heating, air conditioning, ventilation and refrigeration maintenance technology; history; horticultural science; hospitality administration; hotel/motel administration; industrial technology; interior design; journalism; legal administrative assistant/secretary; legal assistant/paralegal; library science; machine tool technology; management information systems; manufacturing technology; marketing/marketing management; mass communication/media; mathematics; medical administrative assistant and medical secretary; nursing (registered nurse training); parks, recreation and leisure; philosophy; physical education teaching and coaching; physics; political science and government; pre-engineering; psychology; radiologic technology/science; religious studies; respiratory therapy technician; sociology; special products marketing; speech and rhetoric; surgical technology; teacher assistant/aide; tourism and travel services management; welding technology; wildlife and wildlands science and management; zoology/animal biology.

Academics *Calendar:* semesters. *Degree:* certificates and associate. *Special study options:* academic remediation for entering students, adult/continuing education programs, advanced placement credit, distance learning, English as a second language, honors programs, independent study, internships, part-time degree program, services for LD students, study abroad, summer session for credit.

Library East Central College Library with 38,863 titles, 278 serial subscriptions, 1,420 audiovisual materials, an OPAC, a Web page.

Computers on Campus 372 computers available on campus for general student use. A campuswide network can be accessed from off campus. Internet access, online (class) registration, at least one staffed computer lab available.

Student Life *Housing:* college housing not available. *Activities and Organizations:* drama/theater group, student-run newspaper, choral group, student government, Phi Theta Kappa, Amnesty International, Multicultural Club. *Campus security:* 24-hour emergency response devices, late-night transport/escort service.

Athletics Member NJCAA. *Intercollegiate sports:* soccer M(s), softball W(s).

Costs (2006–07) *Tuition:* area resident $1464 full-time, $61 per credit hour part-time; state resident $2088 full-time, $87 per credit hour part-time; nonresident $3144 full-time, $131 per credit hour part-time. *Required fees:* $240 full-time, $10 per credit hour part-time.

Financial Aid Of all full-time matriculated undergraduates who enrolled in 2004, 35 Federal Work-Study jobs (averaging $1500). 35 state and other part-time jobs (averaging $1500).

Applying *Options:* common application, early admission, deferred entrance. *Required:* high school transcript. *Application deadline:* rolling (freshmen), rolling (transfers).

Director of Admissions Mrs. Karen Wieda, Registrar, East Central College, 1964 Prairie Dell Road, Union, MO 63084. *Phone:* 636-583-5195 Ext. 2220.

HERITAGE COLLEGE
Kansas City, Missouri

HICKEY COLLEGE
St. Louis, Missouri   www.hickeycollege.edu/

- **Proprietary** primarily 2-year, founded 1933
- **Suburban** campus
- **Coed,** 610 undergraduate students, 82% full-time, 78% women, 22% men

Founded in 1933, Hickey College offers diploma, associate, and bachelor's degree programs. Eight- to sixteen-month programs include accounting,

administrative assistant studies, computer programming, computer specialist studies, graphic design, legal administrative assistant studies, medical administrative assistant studies, network management, and paralegal studies. Tuition and fees vary by program. Financial assistance is available for those who qualify. Housing is offered. The College is an accredited member of ACICS. For more information, prospective students should call 314-434-2212 or 800-777-1544 (toll-free) or visit the College Web site at http://www.hickeycollege.edu.

Undergraduates 500 full-time, 110 part-time. 33% are from out of state.

Faculty *Total:* 18, 67% full-time. *Student/faculty ratio:* 38:1.

Majors Accounting; business administration and management; computer programming; executive assistant/executive secretary; graphic design; legal administrative assistant/secretary; legal assistant/paralegal; medical administrative assistant; system, networking, and LAN/WAN management.

Academics *Calendar:* semesters. *Degrees:* diplomas, associate, and bachelor's. *Special study options:* accelerated degree program.

Computers on Campus 109 computers available on campus for general student use.

Applying *Application fee:* $50. *Required:* high school transcript, interview. *Application deadline:* rolling (freshmen), rolling (transfers).

Freshmen Application Contact Ms. Michelle Hayes, Director of Admissions, Hickey College, 940 West Port Plaza Drive, St. Louis, MO 63146. *Phone:* 314-434-2212 Ext. 136. *Toll-free phone:* 800-777-1544. *Fax:* 314-434-1974. *E-mail:* admin@hickeycollege.edu.

HIGH-TECH INSTITUTE
Kansas City, Missouri

IHM HEALTH STUDIES CENTER
St. Louis, Missouri   www.ihmhealthstudies.com/

Director of Admissions Mr. Taz A. Meyer, Director of Education, IHM Health Studies Center, 2500 Abbott Place, St. Louis, MO 63143-2636. *Phone:* 314-768-1234 Ext. 1128. *E-mail:* meyer@abbottems.org.

ITT TECHNICAL INSTITUTE
Arnold, Missouri   www.itt-tech.edu/

- **Proprietary** primarily 2-year, part of ITT Educational Services, Inc
- **Coed**

Majors Accounting and business/management; animation, interactive technology, video graphics and special effects; business administration and management; CAD/CADD drafting/design technology; computer and information systems security; computer programming; computer software technology; computer systems networking and telecommunications; criminal justice/law enforcement administration; e-commerce; electrical, electronic and communications engineering technology; system, networking, and LAN/WAN management; web/multimedia management and webmaster; web page, digital/multimedia and information resources design.

Academics *Calendar:* quarters. *Degrees:* associate and bachelor's.

Library a Web page.

Computers on Campus Internet access, at least one staffed computer lab available.

Student Life *Housing:* college housing not available.

Standardized Tests *Required:* Wonderlic aptitude test (for admission).

Costs (2005–06) *Tuition:* Please see school catalog for specific information.

Applying *Options:* deferred entrance. *Application fee:* $100. *Required:* high school transcript, interview. *Recommended:* letters of recommendation. *Application deadline:* rolling (freshmen), rolling (transfers). *Notification:* continuous (freshmen).

Freshmen Application Contact Mr. James R. Rowe, Director of Recruitment, ITT Technical Institute, 1930 Meyer Drury Drive, Arnold, MO 63010. *Phone:* 636-464-6600. *Toll-free phone:* 888-488-1082.

ITT TECHNICAL INSTITUTE
Earth City, Missouri
www.itt-tech.edu/

- **Proprietary** primarily 2-year, founded 1936, part of ITT Educational Services, Inc
- **Suburban** 2-acre campus with easy access to St. Louis
- **Coed**

Majors Accounting and business/management; animation, interactive technology, video graphics and special effects; business administration and management; CAD/CADD drafting/design technology; computer and information systems security; computer programming; criminal justice/law enforcement administration; e-commerce; electrical, electronic and communications engineering technology; system, networking, and LAN/WAN management; web/multimedia management and webmaster; web page, digital/multimedia and information resources design.

Academics *Calendar:* quarters. *Degrees:* associate and bachelor's.

Library a Web page.

Computers on Campus Internet access, at least one staffed computer lab available.

Student Life *Housing:* college housing not available.

Standardized Tests *Required:* Wonderlic aptitude test (for admission).

Costs (2005–06) *Tuition:* Please see school catalog for specific information.

Applying *Options:* deferred entrance. *Application fee:* $100. *Required:* high school transcript, interview. *Recommended:* letters of recommendation. *Application deadline:* rolling (freshmen), rolling (transfers). *Notification:* continuous (freshmen).

Freshmen Application Contact Mr. Arlen K. Freeman, ITT Technical Institute, 13505 Lakefront Drive, Earth City, MO 63045. *Phone:* 314-298-7800. *Toll-free phone:* 800-235-5488.

ITT TECHNICAL INSTITUTE
Kansas City, Missouri
www.itt-tech.edu/

- primarily 2-year
- **Coed**

Majors Accounting and business/management; business administration and management; computer and information systems security; criminal justice/law enforcement administration; electrical, electronic and communications engineering technology; system, networking, and LAN/WAN management.

Academics *Calendar:* quarters. *Degrees:* associate and bachelor's.

Standardized Tests *Required:* Wonderlic aptitude test (for admission).

Costs (2005–06) *Tuition:* Please see school catalog for specific information.

Applying *Application fee:* $100. *Required:* high school transcript, interview. *Recommended:* letters of recommendation. *Application deadline:* rolling (freshmen), rolling (transfers). *Notification:* continuous (freshmen).

Freshmen Application Contact Mr. William Vinson, Director of Recruitment, ITT Technical Institute, 9150 East 41st Terrace, Kansas City, MO 64133. *Phone:* 816-276-1400. *Toll-free phone:* 877-488-1442.

JEFFERSON COLLEGE
Hillsboro, Missouri
www.jeffco.edu/

Director of Admissions Ms. Amy Martin-Small, Director of Admissions and Financial Aid, Jefferson College, 1000 Viking Drive, Hillsboro, MO 63050. *Phone:* 636-797-3000 Ext. 218.

LINN STATE TECHNICAL COLLEGE
Linn, Missouri
www.linnstate.edu/

- **State-supported** 2-year, founded 1961
- **Rural** 249-acre campus
- **Endowment** $48,357
- **Coed, primarily men,** 878 undergraduate students, 89% full-time, 10% women, 90% men

Undergraduates 785 full-time, 93 part-time. Students come from 11 states and territories, 2 other countries, 1% are from out of state, 1% African American, 0.3% Asian American or Pacific Islander, 0.8% Hispanic American, 0.3% Native American, 0.6% international, 9% transferred in, 15% live on campus. *Retention:* 58% of 2003 full-time freshmen returned.

Freshmen *Admission:* 976 applied, 599 admitted, 395 enrolled. *Average high school GPA:* 2.78. *Test scores:* ACT scores over 18: 63%; ACT scores over 24: 13%.

Faculty *Total:* 86, 87% full-time. *Student/faculty ratio:* 10:1.

Majors Aircraft powerplant technology; autobody/collision and repair technology; automobile/automotive mechanics technology; civil engineering technology; computer programming; computer systems analysis; drafting and design technology; electrical, electronic and communications engineering technology; electrician; heating, air conditioning, ventilation and refrigeration maintenance technology; heavy equipment maintenance technology; laser and optical technology; lineworker; machine tool technology; physical therapist assistant; turf and turfgrass management.

Academics *Calendar:* semesters. *Degree:* certificates and associate. *Special study options:* academic remediation for entering students, accelerated degree program, adult/continuing education programs, advanced placement credit, cooperative education, distance learning, double majors, English as a second language, independent study, internships, off-campus study, part-time degree program, services for LD students, summer session for credit. *ROTC:* Army (b).

Library Linn State Technical College Library plus 2 others with 13,774 titles, 132 serial subscriptions, 729 audiovisual materials, an OPAC, a Web page.

Computers on Campus 51 computers available on campus for general student use. A campuswide network can be accessed from student residence rooms. Internet access, at least one staffed computer lab available.

Student Life *Housing Options:* coed, men-only, women-only, disabled students. Campus housing is university owned. *Activities and Organizations:* Skills USA-VICA, Phi Theta Kappa, Student Government Association, Aviation Club, Electricity Club. *Campus security:* 24-hour emergency response devices, student patrols, controlled dormitory access, indoor and outdoor surveillance cameras. *Student services:* personal/psychological counseling.

Athletics *Intercollegiate sports:* archery M/W, basketball M/W, bowling M/W, softball M/W, table tennis M/W, volleyball M/W. *Intramural sports:* archery M/W, basketball M/W, bowling M/W, golf M/W, riflery M/W, softball M/W, table tennis M/W, volleyball M/W.

Standardized Tests *Required:* ACT ASSET, ACT COMPASS (for admission). *Required for some:* ACT (for admission), ACT (for placement), ACT ASSET, ACT COMPASS.

Costs (2006–07) *Tuition:* state resident $4080 full-time, $136 per credit part-time; nonresident $8160 full-time, $272 per credit part-time. *Required fees:* $630 full-time, $21 per credit part-time. *Room and board:* $1870; room only: $1445.

Financial Aid Of all full-time matriculated undergraduates who enrolled in 2004, 70 Federal Work-Study jobs (averaging $769).

Applying *Options:* common application, electronic application. *Required:* high school transcript. *Required for some:* essay or personal statement, letters of recommendation, interview, driving record, physical examination. *Notification:* continuous (freshmen).

Freshmen Application Contact Ms. Becky Dunn, Assistant Director of Admissions, Linn State Technical College, One Technology Drive, Linn, MO 65051. *Phone:* 573-897-5196. *Toll-free phone:* 800-743-TECH. *Fax:* 573-897-5026. *E-mail:* admissions@linnstate.edu.

LONGVIEW COMMUNITY COLLEGE
Lee's Summit, Missouri
www.mcckc.edu

- **State and locally supported** 2-year, founded 1969, part of Metropolitan Community Colleges System
- **Suburban** 147-acre campus with easy access to Kansas City
- **Endowment** $2.4 million
- **Coed,** 5,667 undergraduate students, 43% full-time, 58% women, 42% men

Undergraduates 2,419 full-time, 3,248 part-time. Students come from 6 states and territories, 1% are from out of state, 11% African American, 0.6% Asian American or Pacific Islander, 2% Hispanic American, 0.2% Native American, 5% transferred in. *Retention:* 55% of 2003 full-time freshmen returned.

Freshmen *Admission:* 963 applied, 963 admitted, 963 enrolled.

Faculty *Total:* 380, 22% full-time. *Student/faculty ratio:* 19:1.

Majors Accounting; administrative assistant and secretarial science; agricultural mechanization; automobile/automotive mechanics technology; biological and physical sciences; biology/biological sciences; business administration and management; chemistry; computer and information sciences related; computer programming; computer science; computer typography and composition equipment operation; corrections; criminal justice/law enforcement administration; criminal justice/police science; data processing and data processing technology; engineering; heavy equipment maintenance technology; human services; legal administrative assistant/secretary; liberal arts and sciences/liberal studies;

marketing/marketing management; medical administrative assistant and medical secretary; postal management; pre-engineering.

Academics *Calendar:* semesters. *Degree:* certificates and associate. *Special study options:* academic remediation for entering students, accelerated degree program, adult/continuing education programs, advanced placement credit, cooperative education, distance learning, English as a second language, honors programs, internships, off-campus study, part-time degree program, services for LD students, summer session for credit.

Library Longview Community College Library with 56,266 titles, 288 serial subscriptions, 806 audiovisual materials, an OPAC, a Web page.

Computers on Campus 650 computers available on campus for general student use. A campuswide network can be accessed from off campus. Internet access, at least one staffed computer lab available.

Student Life *Housing:* college housing not available. *Activities and Organizations:* drama/theater group, student-run newspaper, choral group, student newspaper, student government, Phi Theta Kappa, Longview Mighty Voices Choir, Longview Broadcasting Network, national fraternities. *Campus security:* 24-hour patrols. *Student services:* personal/psychological counseling.

Athletics Member NJCAA. *Intercollegiate sports:* baseball M(s), cross-country running W(s), volleyball W(s). *Intramural sports:* basketball M/W, swimming and diving M/W, volleyball M/W.

Costs (2006–07) *Tuition:* area resident $2190 full-time, $73 per hour part-time; state resident $3990 full-time, $133 per hour part-time; nonresident $5400 full-time, $180 per hour part-time. *Required fees:* $150 full-time.

Applying *Options:* early admission, deferred entrance. *Application deadline:* rolling (freshmen), rolling (transfers).

Freshmen Application Contact Ms. Janet Cline, Dean of Student Development, Longview Community College, 500 Southwest Longview Road, Lee's Summit, MO 64081-2105. *Phone:* 816-672-2249. *Fax:* 816-672-2040.

MAPLE WOODS COMMUNITY COLLEGE
Kansas City, Missouri   www.mcckc.edu

- **State and locally supported** 2-year, founded 1969, part of Metropolitan Community Colleges System
- **Suburban** 205-acre campus
- **Endowment** $2.4 million
- **Coed,** 4,442 undergraduate students, 41% full-time, 60% women, 40% men

Undergraduates 1,817 full-time, 2,625 part-time. Students come from 4 states and territories, 1% are from out of state, 3% African American, 1% Asian American or Pacific Islander, 2% Hispanic American, 0.3% Native American, 5% transferred in. *Retention:* 59% of 2003 full-time freshmen returned. Freshmen *Admission:* 856 applied, 856 admitted, 856 enrolled.

Faculty *Total:* 346, 15% full-time. *Student/faculty ratio:* 18:1.

Majors Accounting; administrative assistant and secretarial science; avionics maintenance technology; biological and physical sciences; biology/biological sciences; business administration and management; chemistry; computer and information sciences related; computer programming; computer science; criminal justice/law enforcement administration; criminal justice/police science; data processing and data processing technology; legal administrative assistant/secretary; liberal arts and sciences/liberal studies; marketing/marketing management; medical administrative assistant and medical secretary; pre-engineering; veterinary technology.

Academics *Calendar:* semesters. *Degree:* certificates and associate. *Special study options:* academic remediation for entering students, accelerated degree program, adult/continuing education programs, advanced placement credit, cooperative education, distance learning, English as a second language, honors programs, internships, off-campus study, part-time degree program, services for LD students, summer session for credit.

Library Maple Woods Community College Library with 32,906 titles, 250 serial subscriptions, 783 audiovisual materials, an OPAC.

Computers on Campus 400 computers available on campus for general student use. A campuswide network can be accessed from off campus. Internet access, at least one staffed computer lab available.

Student Life *Housing:* college housing not available. *Activities and Organizations:* drama/theater group, student-run newspaper, choral group, Student Activities Council, Art Club, Friends of All Cultures, Phi Theta Kappa, Engineering Club, national fraternities. *Campus security:* 24-hour patrols, late-night transport/escort service. *Student services:* personal/psychological counseling.

Athletics Member NJCAA. *Intercollegiate sports:* baseball M(s), softball W(s). *Intramural sports:* softball M/W, volleyball M/W.

Costs (2006–07) *Tuition:* area resident $2190 full-time, $73 per hour part-time; state resident $3990 full-time, $133 per hour part-time; nonresident $5400 full-time, $180 per hour part-time. *Required fees:* $150 full-time, $5 per hour part-time.

Applying *Options:* early admission, deferred entrance. *Application deadline:* rolling (freshmen), rolling (transfers). *Notification:* continuous (freshmen).

Freshmen Application Contact Ms. Marilyn Donatello, Dean of Student Services, Maple Woods Community College, 2601 Northeast Barry Road, Kansas City, MO 64156-1299. *Phone:* 816-437-3108. *Fax:* 816-437-3351.

METRO BUSINESS COLLEGE
Cape Girardeau, Missouri   www.metrobusinesscollege.edu/

Director of Admissions Ms. Kyla Evans, Admissions Director, Metro Business College, 1732 North Kingshighway, Cape Girardeau, MO 63701. *Phone:* 573-334-9181. *Fax:* 573-334-0617.

METRO BUSINESS COLLEGE
Jefferson City, Missouri   www.metrobusinesscollege.edu/

- **Proprietary** 2-year, founded 1979
- **Coed,** 155 undergraduate students, 90% full-time, 90% women, 10% men
- 75% of applicants were admitted

Undergraduates 140 full-time, 15 part-time. 1% are from out of state, 19% African American, 0.6% Hispanic American.
Freshmen *Admission:* 61 applied, 46 admitted, 46 enrolled.

Faculty *Total:* 11, 73% full-time, 9% with terminal degrees. *Student/faculty ratio:* 14:1.

Majors Computer and information sciences related; medical administrative assistant and medical secretary.

Academics *Calendar:* quarters. *Degree:* certificates, diplomas, and associate.

Student Life *Activities and Organizations:* student-run newspaper. *Student services:* personal/psychological counseling.

Standardized Tests *Required:* Wonderlic (for admission).

Costs (2006–07) *Tuition:* $8385 full-time. *Required fees:* $125 full-time.

Applying *Application fee:* $25. *Required:* essay or personal statement, high school transcript, interview. *Application deadline:* rolling (freshmen). *Notification:* continuous (freshmen).

Freshmen Application Contact Ms. Cheri Chockley, Campus Director, Metro Business College, 1407 Southwest Boulevard, Jefferson City, MO 65109. *Phone:* 573-635-6600. *Toll-free phone:* 800-467-0786. *Fax:* 573-635-6999. *E-mail:* cheri@metrobusinesscollege.edu.

METRO BUSINESS COLLEGE
Rolla, Missouri   www.metrobusinesscollege.edu/

Director of Admissions Ms. Cristie Barker, Director, Metro Business College, 1202 East State Route 72, Rolla, MO 65401. *Phone:* 314-364-8464. *Toll-free phone:* 800-467-0785. *Fax:* 314-364-8077. *E-mail:* cbarker@metrobusinesscollege.edu.

METROPOLITAN COMMUNITY COLLEGE-BUSINESS & TECHNOLOGY COLLEGE
Kansas City, Missouri   www.mcckc.edu

- **State and locally supported** 2-year, founded 1995, part of Metropolitan Community Colleges
- **Urban** 23-acre campus
- **Endowment** $2.4 million
- **Coed, primarily men,** 602 undergraduate students, 20% full-time, 10% women, 90% men
- 100% of applicants were admitted

Undergraduates 118 full-time, 484 part-time. Students come from 2 states and territories, 2 other countries, 2% are from out of state, 5% African American, 0.4% Asian American or Pacific Islander, 1% Hispanic American, 0.4% Native American, 2% transferred in. *Retention:* 26% of 2003 full-time freshmen returned. Freshmen *Admission:* 68 applied, 68 admitted, 68 enrolled.

Faculty *Total:* 47, 21% full-time. *Student/faculty ratio:* 13:1.

Metropolitan Community College-Business & Technology College (continued)

Majors Accounting; accounting technology and bookkeeping; artificial intelligence and robotics; building/construction site management; business administration and management; business/commerce; carpentry; computer and information sciences; computer and information sciences and support services related; computer and information sciences related; computer and information systems security; computer graphics; computer/information technology services administration related; computer programming; computer programming related; computer programming (specific applications); computer programming (vendor/product certification); computer science; computer software and media applications related; computer systems analysis; computer systems networking and telecommunications; data entry/microcomputer applications; data entry/microcomputer applications related; data modeling/warehousing and database administration; data processing and data processing technology; drafting and design technology; electrical, electronic and communications engineering technology; engineering; engineering-related technologies; environmental engineering technology; glazier; information science/studies; information technology; liberal arts and sciences/liberal studies; machine shop technology; management information systems and services related; masonry; quality control technology; system administration; system, networking, and LAN/WAN management; web/multimedia management and webmaster; web page, digital/multimedia and information resources design; word processing.

Academics *Calendar:* semesters. *Degree:* certificates and associate.

Library Learning Resource Center/Library with an OPAC.

Computers on Campus 355 computers available on campus for general student use.

Student Life *Housing:* college housing not available. *Campus security:* 24-hour patrols, late-night transport/escort service.

Costs (2006–07) *Tuition:* area resident $2190 full-time, $730 per hour part-time; state resident $3990 full-time, $133 per hour part-time; nonresident $5400 full-time, $180 per hour part-time. *Required fees:* $150 full-time, $5 per hour part-time.

Freshmen Application Contact Ms. Debbie Goodall, Dean of Student Development, Metropolitan Community College-Business & Technology College, 1775 Universal Avenue, Kansas City, MO 64120. *Toll-free phone:* 800-841-7158.

MIDWEST INSTITUTE
Earth City, Missouri

MIDWEST INSTITUTE
Kirkwood, Missouri

MINERAL AREA COLLEGE
Park Hills, Missouri   www.mineralarea.edu/

- **District-supported** 2-year, founded 1922, part of Missouri Coordinating Board for Higher Education
- **Rural** 240-acre campus with easy access to St. Louis
- **Endowment** $2.1 million
- **Coed**

Undergraduates 1,605 full-time, 1,215 part-time. Students come from 6 states and territories, 1% are from out of state, 2% African American, 0.3% Asian American or Pacific Islander, 0.5% Hispanic American, 0.6% Native American, 0.4% international, 3% transferred in.

Faculty *Student/faculty ratio:* 18:1.

Academics *Calendar:* semesters. *Degree:* certificates and associate. *Special study options:* academic remediation for entering students, advanced placement credit, distance learning, honors programs, internships, off-campus study, part-time degree program, services for LD students, summer session for credit.

Student Life *Campus security:* 24-hour patrols.

Athletics Member NJCAA.

Standardized Tests *Required for some:* ACT (for placement), ACT COMPASS.

Costs (2005–06) *Tuition:* area resident $2160 full-time, $72 per credit hour part-time; state resident $2880 full-time, $96 per credit hour part-time; nonresident $3540 full-time, $118 per credit hour part-time. *Room and board:* room only: $2475.

Financial Aid Of all full-time matriculated undergraduates who enrolled in 2004, 65 Federal Work-Study jobs (averaging $3708).

Applying *Options:* electronic application, early admission. *Application fee:* $15. *Required:* high school transcript.

Freshmen Application Contact Mrs. Linda Huffman, Registrar, Mineral Area College, PO Box 1000, Park Hills, MO 63601-1000. *Phone:* 573-518-2130. *E-mail:* lhuffman@mail.mac.cc.mo.us.

MISSOURI COLLEGE
St. Louis, Missouri   www.mocollege.com/

Director of Admissions Mr. Doug Brinker, Admissions Director, Missouri College, 10121 Manchester Road, St. Louis, MO 63122-1583. *Phone:* 314-821-7700. *Fax:* 314-821-0891.

MISSOURI STATE UNIVERSITY– WEST PLAINS
West Plains, Missouri   www.wp.missouristate.edu/

- **State-supported** 2-year, founded 1963, part of Missouri State University
- **Small-town** 11-acre campus
- **Coed**, 1,675 undergraduate students, 53% full-time, 65% women, 35% men

Undergraduates 886 full-time, 789 part-time. Students come from 15 states and territories, 6 other countries, 4% are from out of state, 1% African American, 0.5% Asian American or Pacific Islander, 1% Hispanic American, 0.7% Native American, 0.7% international, 3% transferred in, 6% live on campus. Freshmen *Admission:* 469 applied, 469 admitted, 391 enrolled.

Faculty *Total:* 117, 25% full-time. *Student/faculty ratio:* 17:1.

Majors Accounting; agriculture; business administration and management; business/commerce; computer and information sciences related; computer graphics; computer programming (specific applications); criminal justice/law enforcement administration; criminal justice/police science; engineering; entrepreneurship; fire science; general studies; industrial technology; information technology; legal assistant/paralegal; nursing (registered nurse training); respiratory therapy technician.

Academics *Calendar:* semesters. *Degree:* certificates and associate. *Special study options:* academic remediation for entering students, advanced placement credit, cooperative education, distance learning, honors programs, internships, part-time degree program, services for LD students, study abroad, summer session for credit.

Library Garnett Library with 21,210 titles, 189 serial subscriptions, 714 audiovisual materials, an OPAC, a Web page.

Computers on Campus 58 computers available on campus for general student use. A campuswide network can be accessed from student residence rooms and from off campus. At least one staffed computer lab available.

Student Life *Housing Options:* coed. Campus housing is university owned. *Activities and Organizations:* drama/theater group, choral group, Student Government Association, Chi Alpha, Adult Students in Higher Education, Lambda Lambda Lambda, Programming Board. *Campus security:* late-night transport/escort service, controlled dormitory access. *Student services:* personal/psychological counseling.

Athletics Member NJCAA. *Intercollegiate sports:* basketball M(s), volleyball W(s).

Costs (2006–07) *Tuition:* state resident $102 per credit hour part-time; nonresident $204 per credit hour part-time. *Required fees:* $77 per term part-time. *Room and board:* $4586.

Financial Aid Of all full-time matriculated undergraduates who enrolled in 2004, 63 Federal Work-Study jobs (averaging $2000).

Applying *Application fee:* $15. *Required for some:* high school transcript. *Application deadline:* rolling (freshmen), rolling (transfers).

Freshmen Application Contact Ms. Melissa Jett, Coordinator of Admission, Missouri State University–West Plains, 128 Garfield, West Plains, MO 65775. *Phone:* 417-255-7955. *Fax:* 417-255-7951. *E-mail:* melissajett@missouristate.edu.

MOBERLY AREA COMMUNITY COLLEGE
Moberly, Missouri   **www.macc.edu/**

- **State and locally supported** 2-year, founded 1927
- **Small-town** 32-acre campus
- **Coed,** 3,835 undergraduate students, 47% full-time, 62% women, 38% men

Undergraduates 1,818 full-time, 2,017 part-time. Students come from 17 states and territories, 12 other countries, 1% are from out of state, 6% African American, 1% Asian American or Pacific Islander, 1% Hispanic American, 0.4% Native American, 0.2% international, 4% transferred in, 1% live on campus. *Retention:* 57% of 2003 full-time freshmen returned.
Freshmen *Admission:* 906 admitted, 906 enrolled. *Average high school GPA:* 2.85. *Test scores:* ACT scores over 18: 68%; ACT scores over 24: 12%.
Faculty *Total:* 257, 26% full-time. *Student/faculty ratio:* 20:1.
Majors Accounting technology and bookkeeping; administrative assistant and secretarial science; child guidance; clinical/medical laboratory technology; computer and information sciences; criminal justice/police science; drafting and design technology; electrical, electronic and communications engineering technology; graphic and printing equipment operation/production; industrial technology; liberal arts and sciences/liberal studies; marketing/marketing management; nursing (registered nurse training); pre-engineering; welding technology.
Academics *Calendar:* semesters. *Degree:* certificates and associate. *Special study options:* academic remediation for entering students, adult/continuing education programs, advanced placement credit, cooperative education, distance learning, internships, part-time degree program, services for LD students, study abroad, summer session for credit.
Library Kate Stamper Wilhite Library with 23,027 titles, 88 serial subscriptions, 1,393 audiovisual materials, an OPAC, a Web page.
Computers on Campus 750 computers available on campus for general student use. A campuswide network can be accessed from off campus. Internet access, at least one staffed computer lab available.
Student Life *Housing Options:* men-only, women-only. Campus housing is university owned. *Activities and Organizations:* drama/theater group, student-run newspaper, choral group, Phi Theta Kappa, Student Nurses Association, Child Care Club, Delta Epsilon Chi, Brother Ox. *Campus security:* student patrols, extensive surveillance.
Athletics Member NJCAA. *Intercollegiate sports:* basketball M(s)/W(s), cheerleading M(s)/W(s). *Intramural sports:* basketball M/W, volleyball M/W.
Standardized Tests *Required for some:* ACT (for admission), ACT ASSET. *Recommended:* ACT (for admission), ACT ASSET.
Costs (2006–07) *Tuition:* area resident $1740 full-time, $58 per credit hour part-time; state resident $2550 full-time, $85 per credit hour part-time; nonresident S3960 full-time, $132 per credit hour part-time. *Required fees:* $300 full-time, $10 per credit hour part-time. *Room and board:* room only: $1800.
Financial Aid Of all full-time matriculated undergraduates who enrolled in 2004, 89 Federal Work-Study jobs (averaging $4193).
Applying *Options:* electronic application. *Required:* high school transcript. *Application deadline:* rolling (freshmen), rolling (transfers). *Notification:* continuous until 9/1 (freshmen).
Freshmen Application Contact Ms. Michele McCall, Dean of Off-Campus Programs and Instructional Technology, Moberly Area Community College, 101 College Avenue, Moberly, MO 65270-1304. *Phone:* 660-263-4110 Ext. 235. *Toll-free phone:* 800-622-2070 Ext. 270. *Fax:* 660-263-2406. *E-mail:* info@macc.edu.

NORTH CENTRAL MISSOURI COLLEGE
Trenton, Missouri   **www.ncmissouri.edu/**

- **District-supported** 2-year, founded 1925
- **Small-town** 2-acre campus
- **Endowment** $423,653
- **Coed,** 1,342 undergraduate students, 52% full-time, 71% women, 29% men

Undergraduates 702 full-time, 640 part-time. Students come from 7 states and territories, 1 other country, 1% are from out of state, 3% African American, 0.1% Asian American or Pacific Islander, 1% Hispanic American, 0.7% Native American, 0.4% international, 4% transferred in, 9% live on campus.
Freshmen *Admission:* 519 applied, 300 admitted, 282 enrolled.
Faculty *Total:* 108, 27% full-time, 6% with terminal degrees. *Student/faculty ratio:* 17:1.
Majors Accounting; administrative assistant and secretarial science; agricultural business and management; automobile/automotive mechanics technology; business administration and management; carpentry; computer engineering tech-

nology; construction engineering technology; criminal justice/law enforcement administration; data processing and data processing technology; drafting and design technology; early childhood education; e-commerce; electrical, electronic and communications engineering technology; emergency medical technology (EMT paramedic); farm and ranch management; human services; liberal arts and sciences/liberal studies; marketing/marketing management; medical/clinical assistant; nursing (registered nurse training).
Academics *Calendar:* semesters. *Degree:* certificates and associate. *Special study options:* academic remediation for entering students, accelerated degree program, adult/continuing education programs, advanced placement credit, cooperative education, distance learning, internships, part-time degree program, services for LD students, summer session for credit.
Library North Central Missouri College Library with 20,627 titles, 104 serial subscriptions.
Computers on Campus 159 computers available on campus for general student use. A campuswide network can be accessed. Internet access, at least one staffed computer lab available.
Student Life *Housing Options:* men-only, women-only. Campus housing is university owned. *Activities and Organizations:* drama/theater group. *Campus security:* controlled dormitory access. *Student services:* personal/psychological counseling.
Athletics Member NJCAA. *Intercollegiate sports:* baseball M(s), basketball M(s)/W(s), softball W(s).
Costs (2005–06) *Tuition:* area resident $1680 full-time, $56 per credit part-time; state resident $2550 full-time, $85 per credit part-time; nonresident $3570 full-time, $119 per credit part-time. Full-time tuition and fees vary according to course load and location. Part-time tuition and fees vary according to location. *Required fees:* $450 full-time, $15 per credit part-time. *Room and board:* $4149. Room and board charges vary according to board plan. *Payment plan:* installment. *Waivers:* senior citizens and employees or children of employees.
Financial Aid Of all full-time matriculated undergraduates who enrolled in 2004, 40 Federal Work-Study jobs (averaging $1500). 25 state and other part-time jobs (averaging $1200).
Applying *Required:* high school transcript. *Application deadline:* rolling (freshmen), rolling (transfers).
Freshmen Application Contact Ms. Susan Moffitt, Admissions Assistant, North Central Missouri College, 1301 Main Street, Trenton, MO 64683. *Phone:* 660-359-3948 Ext. 410. *Toll-free phone:* 800-880-6180 Ext. 401. *E-mail:* smoffitt@mail.ncmissouri.edu.

OZARKS TECHNICAL COMMUNITY COLLEGE
Springfield, Missouri   **www.otc.edu/**
Director of Admissions Mr. Jeff Jochems, Dean of Student Development, Ozarks Technical Community College, PO Box 5958, Springfield, MO 65801. *Phone:* 417-895-7136.

PATRICIA STEVENS COLLEGE
St. Louis, Missouri   **www.patriciastevenscollege.edu/**
Director of Admissions Mr. John Willmon, Director of Admissions, Patricia Stevens College, 330 North Fourth Street, Suite 306, St. Louis, MO 63102. *Phone:* 314-421-0949 Ext. 12. *Toll-free phone:* 800-871-0949.

PENN VALLEY COMMUNITY COLLEGE
Kansas City, Missouri   **www.mcckc.edu**

- **State and locally supported** 2-year, founded 1969, part of Metropolitan Community Colleges System
- **Urban** 25-acre campus
- **Endowment** $2.4 million
- **Coed,** 4,627 undergraduate students, 31% full-time, 72% women, 28% men

Undergraduates 1,457 full-time, 3,170 part-time. Students come from 6 states and territories, 5% are from out of state, 29% African American, 3% Asian American or Pacific Islander, 5% Hispanic American, 0.5% Native American, 5% transferred in. *Retention:* 52% of 2003 full-time freshmen returned.
Freshmen *Admission:* 785 applied, 785 admitted, 785 enrolled.

Penn Valley Community College (continued)

Faculty *Total:* 437, 23% full-time. *Student/faculty ratio:* 12:1.

Majors Accounting; administrative assistant and secretarial science; biological and physical sciences; biology/biological sciences; business administration and management; chemistry; child care provision; commercial and advertising art; computer and information sciences related; computer science; corrections; criminal justice/law enforcement administration; criminal justice/police science; data processing and data processing technology; emergency medical technology (EMT paramedic); engineering; family and consumer sciences/human sciences; fashion/apparel design; fashion merchandising; health information/medical records administration; kindergarten/preschool education; legal administrative assistant/secretary; legal assistant/paralegal; liberal arts and sciences/liberal studies; marketing/marketing management; medical administrative assistant and medical secretary; nursing (registered nurse training); occupational therapy; physical therapy; respiratory care therapy; special products marketing.

Academics *Calendar:* semesters. *Degree:* certificates and associate. *Special study options:* academic remediation for entering students, accelerated degree program, adult/continuing education programs, advanced placement credit, cooperative education, distance learning, English as a second language, honors programs, internships, off-campus study, part-time degree program, services for LD students, summer session for credit.

Library Penn Valley Community College Library with 91,428 titles, 89,242 serial subscriptions, 355 audiovisual materials, an OPAC.

Computers on Campus 1058 computers available on campus for general student use. A campuswide network can be accessed from off campus. Internet access, at least one staffed computer lab available.

Student Life *Housing:* college housing not available. *Activities and Organizations:* drama/theater group, student-run newspaper, choral group, Black Student Association, Los Americanos, Phi Theta Kappa, Fashion Club, national fraternities. *Campus security:* 24-hour patrols. *Student services:* personal/psychological counseling.

Athletics Member NJCAA. *Intercollegiate sports:* basketball M(s)/W(s).

Costs (2006–07) *Tuition:* area resident $2190 full-time, $73 per hour part-time; state resident $3990 full-time, $133 per hour part-time; nonresident $5400 full-time, $180 per hour part-time. *Required fees:* $150 full-time, $5 per hour part-time.

Applying *Options:* common application, early admission. *Required:* high school transcript. *Application deadline:* rolling (freshmen), rolling (transfers).

Freshmen Application Contact Ms. Lisa Minis, Dean of Student Services, Penn Valley Community College, 3201 Southwest Trafficway, Kansas City, MO 64111. *Phone:* 816-759-4101. *Fax:* 816-759-4478.

PINNACLE CAREER INSTITUTE

Kansas City, Missouri   www.pcitraining.edu/

Director of Admissions Ms. Ruth Matous, Director of Admissions, Pinnacle Career Institute, 15329 Kensington Avenue, Kansas City, MO 64147-1212. *Phone:* 816-331-5700 Ext. 212.

RANKEN TECHNICAL COLLEGE

St. Louis, Missouri   www.ranken.edu/

- **Independent** primarily 2-year, founded 1907
- **Urban** 10-acre campus
- **Endowment** $39.0 million
- **Coed, primarily men**

Undergraduates 743 full-time, 680 part-time. Students come from 3 states and territories, 40% are from out of state, 1% live on campus.

Faculty *Student/faculty ratio:* 15:1.

Academics *Calendar:* semesters. *Degrees:* certificates, associate, and bachelor's. *Special study options:* academic remediation for entering students, adult/continuing education programs, advanced placement credit, cooperative education, distance learning, independent study, internships, part-time degree program, services for LD students, summer session for credit.

Student Life *Campus security:* 24-hour emergency response devices and patrols.

Standardized Tests *Required:* SAT or ACT (for placement).

Costs (2005–06) *Tuition:* $10,000 full-time, $725 per term part-time. *Required fees:* $140 full-time, $95 per term part-time.

Financial Aid Of all full-time matriculated undergraduates who enrolled in 2004, 30 Federal Work-Study jobs (averaging $2000).

Applying *Options:* common application, electronic application. *Application fee:* $95. *Required:* essay or personal statement, high school transcript, interview.

Director of Admissions Ms. Elizabeth Keserauskis, Director of Admissions, Ranken Technical College, 4431 Finney Avenue, St. Louis, MO 63113. *Phone:* 314-371-0233 Ext. 4811. *Toll-free phone:* 866-4RANKEN.

SAINT CHARLES COMMUNITY COLLEGE

St. Peters, Missouri   www.stchas.edu/

- **State-supported** 2-year, founded 1986, part of Missouri Coordinating Board for Higher Education
- **Small-town** 234-acre campus with easy access to St. Louis
- **Endowment** $5.7 million
- **Coed,** 6,870 undergraduate students, 49% full-time, 61% women, 39% men

Undergraduates 3,378 full-time, 3,492 part-time. Students come from 4 states and territories, 6 other countries, 4% African American, 2% Asian American or Pacific Islander, 2% Hispanic American, 0.3% Native American, 0.3% international, 5% transferred in.

Freshmen *Admission:* 1,677 applied, 1,677 admitted, 1,428 enrolled.

Faculty *Total:* 429, 19% full-time. *Student/faculty ratio:* 21:1.

Majors Accounting; administrative assistant and secretarial science; business administration and management; child development; commercial and advertising art; computer programming related; computer programming (specific applications); computer science; computer systems networking and telecommunications; criminal justice/law enforcement administration; criminal justice/police science; drafting and design technology; health information/medical records administration; human services; liberal arts and sciences/liberal studies; marketing/marketing management; medical transcription; nursing (registered nurse training); occupational therapy; office management; pre-engineering; web/multimedia management and webmaster.

Academics *Calendar:* semesters. *Degree:* certificates and associate. *Special study options:* academic remediation for entering students, adult/continuing education programs, advanced placement credit, distance learning, double majors, English as a second language, independent study, internships, part-time degree program, services for LD students, summer session for credit.

Library Learning Resource Center with 54,110 titles, 8,282 serial subscriptions, 7,624 audiovisual materials, an OPAC, a Web page.

Computers on Campus 117 computers available on campus for general student use. A campuswide network can be accessed from off campus. Internet access, online (class) registration, at least one staffed computer lab available.

Student Life *Housing:* college housing not available. *Activities and Organizations:* drama/theater group, choral group, Phi Theta Kappa, SCCCC Roller Hockey Club, Student Senate, Criminal Justice Student Organization, Human Services Student Organization. *Campus security:* 24-hour emergency response devices and patrols, late-night transport/escort service. *Student services:* personal/psychological counseling.

Athletics Member NJCAA. *Intercollegiate sports:* baseball M(s), softball W(s). *Intramural sports:* basketball M/W, football M, soccer M/W, softball M/W, volleyball M/W.

Costs (2006–07) *Tuition:* area resident $2280 full-time; state resident $3360 full-time; nonresident $4980 full-time.

Financial Aid Of all full-time matriculated undergraduates who enrolled in 2004, 21 Federal Work-Study jobs (averaging $1848).

Applying *Options:* common application, early admission, deferred entrance. *Required for some:* high school transcript. *Recommended:* high school transcript. *Application deadline:* rolling (freshmen), rolling (transfers). *Notification:* continuous (freshmen).

Freshmen Application Contact Ms. Kathy Brockgreitens, Director of Admissions/Registrar/Financial/Assistance, Saint Charles Community College, 4601 Mid Rivers Mall Drive, St. Peters, MO 63376-0975. *Phone:* 636-922-8229. *Fax:* 636-922-8236. *E-mail:* regist@stchas.edu.

ST. LOUIS COLLEGE OF HEALTH CAREERS
St. Louis, Missouri

ST. LOUIS COMMUNITY COLLEGE AT FLORISSANT VALLEY
St. Louis, Missouri   www.stlcc.edu/

- **District-supported** 2-year, founded 1963, part of St. Louis Community College System
- **Suburban** 108-acre campus
- **Coed**

Undergraduates Students come from 31 other countries.

Majors Accounting; administrative assistant and secretarial science; art; broadcast journalism; business administration and management; chemical engineering; child development; cinematography and film/video production; civil engineering technology; commercial and advertising art; computer engineering technology; computer programming; computer science; construction engineering technology; corrections; criminal justice/law enforcement administration; criminal justice/police science; data processing and data processing technology; dietetics; dramatic/theater arts; electrical, electronic and communications engineering technology; elementary education; emergency medical technology (EMT paramedic); engineering; engineering science; engineering technology; fashion merchandising; finance; fire science; food science; food services technology; human services; information science/studies; journalism; legal studies; liberal arts and sciences/liberal studies; mass communication/media; mathematics; mechanical engineering/mechanical technology; music; nursing (registered nurse training); photography; pre-engineering; radio and television; real estate; sign language interpretation and translation; special products marketing; telecommunications.

Academics *Calendar:* semesters. *Degree:* certificates and associate. *Special study options:* academic remediation for entering students, adult/continuing education programs, advanced placement credit, cooperative education, English as a second language, honors programs, part-time degree program, services for LD students, study abroad, summer session for credit. *ROTC:* Army (c).

Library 90,021 titles, 655 serial subscriptions.

Computers on Campus 470 computers available on campus for general student use. A campuswide network can be accessed. At least one staffed computer lab available.

Student Life *Housing:* college housing not available. *Activities and Organizations:* drama/theater group, student-run newspaper, radio station, Phi Theta Kappa, Student Nurses Association, Women in New Goals, Florissant Valley Association of the Deaf, Student Government Association, national fraternities, national sororities. *Campus security:* 24-hour emergency response devices and patrols, late-night transport/escort service. *Student services:* health clinic, personal/psychological counseling.

Athletics Member NAIA, NJCAA. *Intercollegiate sports:* baseball M, basketball M(s)/W(s), cross-country running M(s)/W(s), soccer M(s)/W(s), softball W(s), track and field M(s)/W(s), volleyball W(s). *Intramural sports:* volleyball W.

Costs (2005–06) *Tuition:* $78 per credit hour part-time; state resident $103 per credit hour part-time; nonresident $138 per credit hour part-time.

Applying *Options:* electronic application, early admission. *Required:* high school transcript. *Application deadlines:* 8/19 (freshmen), 8/19 (transfers). *Notification:* continuous (freshmen).

Freshmen Application Contact Mr. Mitchell Egeston, Manager of Admissions and Registration, St. Louis Community College at Florissant Valley, 3400 Pershall Road, St. Louis, MO 63135-1499. *Phone:* 314-595-4245.

ST. LOUIS COMMUNITY COLLEGE AT FOREST PARK
St. Louis, Missouri   www.stlcc.edu/

- **District-supported** 2-year, founded 1962, part of St. Louis Community College System
- **Suburban** 34-acre campus
- **Coed**

Undergraduates Students come from 11 states and territories, 4% are from out of state, 43% African American, 4% Asian American or Pacific Islander, 1% Hispanic American, 0.4% Native American, 0.2% international.

Faculty *Student/faculty ratio:* 19:1.

Academics *Calendar:* semesters. *Degree:* associate. *Special study options:* academic remediation for entering students, adult/continuing education programs, distance learning, English as a second language, honors programs, part-time degree program, services for LD students, study abroad, summer session for credit.

Student Life *Campus security:* 24-hour patrols.

Athletics Member NJCAA.

Financial Aid Of all full-time matriculated undergraduates who enrolled in 2004, 165 Federal Work-Study jobs (averaging $3000).

Applying *Options:* electronic application, early admission. *Required:* high school transcript.

Freshmen Application Contact Mr. Glenn Marshall, Coordinator of Enrollment Services, St. Louis Community College at Forest Park, 5600 Oakland Avenue, St. Louis, MO 63110. *Phone:* 314-644-9125.

ST. LOUIS COMMUNITY COLLEGE AT MERAMEC
Kirkwood, Missouri   www.stlcc.edu/

- **District-supported** 2-year, founded 1963, part of St. Louis Community College System
- **Suburban** 80-acre campus with easy access to St. Louis
- **Coed**

Undergraduates Students come from 10 states and territories, 4% African American, 3% Asian American or Pacific Islander, 2% Hispanic American, 0.5% Native American.

Academics *Calendar:* semesters. *Degree:* certificates and associate. *Special study options:* academic remediation for entering students, adult/continuing education programs, advanced placement credit, English as a second language, freshman honors college, honors programs, internships, off-campus study, part-time degree program, services for LD students, study abroad, summer session for credit. *ROTC:* Army (c), Air Force (c).

Student Life *Campus security:* 24-hour emergency response devices and patrols.

Athletics Member NJCAA.

Standardized Tests *Required for some:* Michigan Test of English Language Proficiency.

Applying *Options:* early admission, deferred entrance. *Required for some:* high school transcript, interview.

Freshmen Application Contact Mr. Mike Cundiff, Coordinator of Admissions, St. Louis Community College at Meramec, 11333 Big Bend Boulevard, Kirkwood, MO 63122-5720. *Phone:* 314-984-7608.

SANFORD-BROWN COLLEGE
Fenton, Missouri   www.sanford-brown.edu/

Director of Admissions Ms. Judy Wilga, Director of Admissions, Sanford-Brown College, 1203 Smizer Mill Road, Fenton, MO 63026. *Phone:* 636-349-4900 Ext. 102. *Toll-free phone:* 800-456-7222. *Fax:* 636-349-9170.

SANFORD-BROWN COLLEGE
Hazelwood, Missouri   www.sanford-brown.edu/

Director of Admissions Sherri Bremer, Director of Admissions, Sanford-Brown College, 75 Village Square, Hazelwood, MO 63042. *Phone:* 314-731-5200 Ext. 201.

SANFORD-BROWN COLLEGE

North Kansas City, Missouri www.sanford-brown.edu/

Director of Admissions Mr. Edward A. Beauchamp, Director of Admissions, Sanford-Brown College, 520 East 19th Avenue, North Kansas City, MO 64116. *Phone:* 816-472-0275. *Toll-free phone:* 800-456-7222. *Fax:* 816-472-0888. *E-mail:* edward.beauchamp@wix.net.

SANFORD-BROWN COLLEGE

St. Charles, Missouri www.sanford-brown.edu/

Director of Admissions Karl J. Petersen, Executive Director, Sanford-Brown College, 3555 Franks Drive, St. Charles, MO 63301. *Phone:* 636-949-2620. *Toll-free phone:* 800-456-7222. *Fax:* 636-949-5081. *E-mail:* karl.peterson@wix.net.

SOUTHEAST MISSOURI HOSPITAL COLLEGE OF NURSING AND HEALTH SCIENCES

Cape Girardeau, Missouri www.southeastmissourihospital.com/college/

Director of Admissions Tonya L. Buttry, President, Southeast Missouri Hospital College of Nursing and Health Sciences, 1819 Broadway, Cape Girardeau, MO 63701. *Phone:* 534-334-6825. *E-mail:* tbuttry@sehosp.org.

SPRINGFIELD COLLEGE

Springfield, Missouri www.Springfield-college.com/

Director of Admissions Gerald F. Terrebrood, President, Springfield College, 1010 West Sunshine Street, Springfield, MO 65807. *Phone:* 417-864-7220. *Toll-free phone:* 800-864-5697 (in-state); 800-475-2669 (out-of-state). *Fax:* 417-864-5697. *E-mail:* gterrebr@cci.edu.

STATE FAIR COMMUNITY COLLEGE

Sedalia, Missouri www.sfcc.cc.mo.us/

Director of Admissions Mrs. Sharon Peacock, Registrar, State Fair Community College, 3201 West 16th, Sedalia, MO 65301. *Phone:* 660-530-5800 Ext. 293. *Toll-free phone:* 877-311-SFCC Ext. 217 (in-state); 877-311-SFCC (out-of-state).

THREE RIVERS COMMUNITY COLLEGE

Poplar Bluff, Missouri www.trcc.edu/

- **State and locally supported** 2-year, founded 1966, part of Missouri Coordinating Board for Higher Education
- **Rural** 70-acre campus
- **Endowment** $655,356
- **Coed,** 2,935 undergraduate students, 55% full-time, 66% women, 34% men

Undergraduates 1,622 full-time, 1,313 part-time. Students come from 11 states and territories, 2% are from out of state, 9% African American, 0.5% Asian American or Pacific Islander, 0.9% Hispanic American, 0.6% Native American, 1% transferred in, 10% live on campus.
Freshmen *Admission:* 619 applied, 619 admitted, 619 enrolled. *Test scores:* ACT scores over 18: 69%; ACT scores over 24: 16%; ACT scores over 30: 1%.
Faculty *Total:* 160, 36% full-time, 8% with terminal degrees. *Student/faculty ratio:* 22:1.
Majors Accounting; administrative assistant and secretarial science; agricultural business and management; agricultural mechanization; business administration and management; clinical/medical laboratory technology; computer and information sciences related; computer engineering technology; computer/technical support; construction engineering technology; criminal justice/law enforcement administration; criminal justice/police science; data entry/microcomputer applications; data entry/microcomputer applications related; education; elementary education; engineering technology; industrial technology; information technology; liberal arts and sciences/liberal studies; marketing/marketing management; music; nursing (registered nurse training); word processing.

Academics *Calendar:* semesters. *Degree:* certificates and associate. *Special study options:* academic remediation for entering students, accelerated degree program, adult/continuing education programs, advanced placement credit, distance learning, double majors, English as a second language, external degree program, honors programs, independent study, internships, part-time degree program, services for LD students, summer session for credit.
Library Rutland Library with 36,960 titles, 238 serial subscriptions, 1,027 audiovisual materials, an OPAC, a Web page.
Computers on Campus 200 computers available on campus for general student use. A campuswide network can be accessed from student residence rooms. Internet access, online (class) registration, at least one staffed computer lab available.
Student Life *Housing Options:* coed. Campus housing is university owned. *Activities and Organizations:* student government, PTK, PBL, Alpha Beta Gamma, Lambda Alpha Epsilon. *Campus security:* 24-hour patrols.
Athletics Member NJCAA. *Intercollegiate sports:* baseball M(s), basketball M(s)/W(s), cheerleading M(s)/W(s), softball W(s), volleyball W(s).
Costs (2006–07) *Tuition:* area resident $1830 full-time, $61 per credit hour part-time; state resident $2940 full-time, $98 per credit hour part-time; nonresident $3660 full-time, $122 per credit hour part-time. *Required fees:* $375 full-time, $9 per credit hour part-time. *Room and board:* room only: $3114.
Applying *Options:* early admission. *Application fee:* $20. *Required:* high school transcript.
Freshmen Application Contact Ms. Marcia Fields, Director of Admissions and Recruiting, Three Rivers Community College, 2080 Three Rivers Boulevard, Poplar Bluff, MO 63901. *Phone:* 573-840-9675. *Toll-free phone:* 877-TRY-TRCC Ext. 605 (in-state); 877-TRY-TRCC (out-of-state). *E-mail:* trytrcc@trcc.edu.

VATTEROTT COLLEGE

Kansas City, Missouri

VATTEROTT COLLEGE

O'Fallon, Missouri

VATTEROTT COLLEGE

St. Ann, Missouri www.vatterott-college.edu/

Director of Admissions Mrs. Shari H. Cobb, Director of Admissions, Vatterott College, 3925 Industrial Drive, St. Ann, MO 63074-1807. *Phone:* 314-428-5900 Ext. 215. *Toll-free phone:* 800-345-6018.

VATTEROTT COLLEGE

St. Joseph, Missouri www.vatterott-college.com/

- **Proprietary** 2-year
- **Urban** campus
- **Coed**

Academics *Calendar:* semesters. *Degree:* diplomas and associate.
Costs (2005–06) *Tuition:* No tuition increase for student's term of enrollment. Tuition varies by program.
Director of Admissions Ms. Sandra Wisdom, Director of Admissions, Vatterott College, 3131 Frederick Avenue, St. Joseph, MO 64506. *Phone:* 816-364-5399 Ext. 110. *Toll-free phone:* 800-282-5327.

VATTEROTT COLLEGE
Sunset Hills, Missouri   www.vatterott-college.edu/

Director of Admissions Ms. Michelle Tinsley, Director of Admission, Vatterott College, 12970 Maurer Industrial Drive, St. Louis, MO 63127. *Phone:* 314-843-4200.

VATTEROTT COLLEGE
Springfield, Missouri   www.vatterott-college.edu/

- **Proprietary** 2-year, part of Vatterott College
- **Urban** 2-acre campus
- **Coed**

Academics *Calendar:* quarters. *Degree:* diplomas and associate. *Special study options:* internships.
Student Life *Campus security:* alarm devices and personnel during open hours; security alarms during closed hours.
Costs (2005–06) *Tuition:* $8800 full-time. Full-time tuition and fees vary according to degree level and program. No tuition increase for student's term of enrollment. *Required fees:* $900 full-time. *Room only:* Room and board charges vary according to board plan.
Applying *Required:* high school transcript, interview.
Director of Admissions Ms. Jennifer Danzer, Co-Director, Vatterott College, 3850 South Campbell, Springfield, MO 65807. *Phone:* 417-831-8116 Ext. 223. *Toll-free phone:* 800-766-5829.

WENTWORTH MILITARY ACADEMY AND JUNIOR COLLEGE
Lexington, Missouri   www.wma1880.org/

- **Independent** 2-year, founded 1880
- **Small-town** 130-acre campus with easy access to Kansas City
- **Coed,** 561 undergraduate students, 42% full-time, 54% women, 46% men

Undergraduates 234 full-time, 327 part-time. Students come from 22 states and territories, 4 other countries, 18% are from out of state, 4% African American, 3% Asian American or Pacific Islander, 2% Hispanic American, 0.2% Native American, 0.4% international, 0.2% transferred in.
Freshmen *Admission:* 456 applied, 456 admitted, 393 enrolled. *Test scores:* SAT verbal scores over 500: 33%; SAT math scores over 500: 73%; SAT math scores over 600: 33%.
Faculty *Total:* 63, 30% full-time, 8% with terminal degrees. *Student/faculty ratio:* 10:1.
Majors Liberal arts and sciences/liberal studies.
Academics *Calendar:* semesters. *Degree:* associate. *Special study options:* academic remediation for entering students, adult/continuing education programs, advanced placement credit, English as a second language, part-time degree program, student-designed majors, summer session for credit. *ROTC:* Army (b).
Library Sellers-Coombs Library with 18,890 titles, 49 serial subscriptions, 919 audiovisual materials, a Web page.
Computers on Campus 35 computers available on campus for general student use. Internet access, at least one staffed computer lab available.
Student Life *Housing:* on-campus residence required through sophomore year. *Options:* men-only, women-only. Campus housing is university owned. *Activities and Organizations:* student-run newspaper, choral group, marching band. *Campus security:* 24-hour emergency response devices and patrols. *Student services:* health clinic, personal/psychological counseling.
Athletics Member NJCAA. *Intercollegiate sports:* cross-country running M, track and field M/W, wrestling M. *Intramural sports:* archery M/W, basketball M/W, racquetball M/W, riflery M/W, soccer W, swimming and diving M/W, table tennis M, tennis M/W, track and field M/W, volleyball M/W, weight lifting M/W.
Standardized Tests *Required for some:* SAT or ACT (for admission). *Recommended:* SAT or ACT (for admission).
Costs (2006–07) *One-time required fee:* $25. *Tuition:* $3480 full-time, $145 per hour part-time.
Applying *Options:* common application. *Application fee:* $100. *Required:* high school transcript. *Application deadline:* 9/11 (freshmen), rolling (transfers). *Notification:* 9/11 (freshmen).

Freshmen Application Contact Dr. Roger Hamilton, Vice President for Academic Affairs, Wentworth Military Academy and Junior College, 1880 Washington Avenue, Lexington, MO 64067. *Phone:* 660-259-2221. *Fax:* 660-259-2677. *E-mail:* admissions@wma1880.org.

MONTANA

BLACKFEET COMMUNITY COLLEGE
Browning, Montana   www.bfcc.org/

- **Independent** 2-year, founded 1974
- **Small-town** 5-acre campus
- **Endowment** $300,688
- **Coed**

Undergraduates 424 full-time, 79 part-time. Students come from 2 states and territories, 0.4% Hispanic American, 92% Native American, 6% transferred in.
Faculty *Student/faculty ratio:* 12:1.
Academics *Calendar:* semesters. *Degree:* certificates, diplomas, and associate. *Special study options:* academic remediation for entering students, adult/continuing education programs, off-campus study, part-time degree program.
Student Life *Campus security:* 16 hour patrols by security personnel.
Costs (2005–06) *One-time required fee:* $20. *Tuition:* state resident $1650 full-time, $69 per credit part-time; nonresident $1650 full-time, $69 per credit part-time. Full-time tuition and fees vary according to course load. Part-time tuition and fees vary according to course load. *Required fees:* $350 full-time, $80 per term part-time.
Financial Aid Of all full-time matriculated undergraduates who enrolled in 2004, 10 Federal Work-Study jobs (averaging $2316). *Financial aid deadline:* 6/30.
Applying *Options:* early admission. *Application fee:* $20. *Required:* high school transcript, immunization with 2nd MMR, certificate of Indian blood.
Director of Admissions Ms. Deana M. McNabb, Registrar and Admissions Officer, Blackfeet Community College, PO Box 819, Browning, MT 59417. *Phone:* 406-338-5421 Ext. 243. *Toll-free phone:* 800-549-7457.

CHIEF DULL KNIFE COLLEGE
Lame Deer, Montana   www.cdkc.edu/

Director of Admissions Mr. William L. Wertman, Registrar and Director of Admissions, Chief Dull Knife College, PO Box 98, Lame Deer, MT 59043-0098. *Phone:* 406-477-6215.

DAWSON COMMUNITY COLLEGE
Glendive, Montana   www.dawson.edu/

- **State and locally supported** 2-year, founded 1940, part of Montana University System
- **Rural** 300-acre campus
- **Endowment** $344,944
- **Coed**

Undergraduates 395 full-time, 144 part-time. Students come from 10 states and territories, 2 other countries, 2% African American, 1% Hispanic American, 3% Native American, 6% transferred in, 19% live on campus.
Faculty *Student/faculty ratio:* 16:1.
Academics *Calendar:* semesters. *Degree:* certificates and associate. *Special study options:* academic remediation for entering students, adult/continuing education programs, independent study, internships, part-time degree program, services for LD students, summer session for credit.
Student Life *Campus security:* 24-hour emergency response devices.
Athletics Member NJCAA.
Standardized Tests *Required for some:* ACT (for placement). *Recommended:* ACT (for placement).

Dawson Community College (continued)

Costs (2005–06) *Tuition:* area resident $1232 full-time, $44 per credit part-time; state resident $2103 full-time, $75 per credit part-time; nonresident $5762 full-time, $206 per credit part-time. Full-time tuition and fees vary according to reciprocity agreements. Part-time tuition and fees vary according to reciprocity agreements. *Required fees:* $1092 full-time, $39 per credit part-time. *Room and board:* room only: $1950.

Financial Aid Of all full-time matriculated undergraduates who enrolled in 2004, 45 Federal Work-Study jobs (averaging $1200). 17 state and other part-time jobs (averaging $1200).

Applying *Options:* deferred entrance. *Application fee:* $30. *Required:* high school transcript.

Director of Admissions Ms. Jolene Myers, Director of Admissions and Financial Aid, Dawson Community College, Box 421, Glendive, MT 59330-0421. *Phone:* 406-377-3396 Ext. 410. *Toll-free phone:* 800-821-8320.

FLATHEAD VALLEY COMMUNITY COLLEGE
Kalispell, Montana www.fvcc.edu/

- **State and locally supported** 2-year, founded 1967
- **Small-town** 40-acre campus
- **Endowment** $865,025
- **Coed**

Undergraduates 972 full-time, 1,128 part-time. Students come from 25 states and territories, 2 other countries, 2% are from out of state, 0.5% African American, 0.7% Asian American or Pacific Islander, 1% Hispanic American, 2% Native American, 0.5% international, 2% transferred in. *Retention:* 55% of 2003 full-time freshmen returned.

Faculty *Student/faculty ratio:* 15:1.

Academics *Calendar:* semesters. *Degree:* certificates and associate. *Special study options:* academic remediation for entering students, adult/continuing education programs, advanced placement credit, distance learning, double majors, independent study, internships, part-time degree program, services for LD students, summer session for credit.

Athletics Member NJCAA.

Costs (2005–06) *Tuition:* area resident $1739 full-time, $62 per credit part-time; state resident $2856 full-time, $102 per credit part-time; nonresident $7146 full-time, $255 per credit part-time. Part-time tuition and fees vary according to course load. *Required fees:* $26 per credit part-time, $610 per year part-time.

Financial Aid Of all full-time matriculated undergraduates who enrolled in 2004, 52 Federal Work-Study jobs (averaging $1000). 46 state and other part-time jobs (averaging $1020).

Applying *Options:* early admission, deferred entrance. *Application fee:* $15. *Required:* high school transcript.

Freshmen Application Contact Ms. Marlene C. Stoltz, Admissions/Graduation Coordinator, Flathead Valley Community College, 777 Grandview Avenue, Kalispell, MT 59901-2622. *Phone:* 406-756-3846. *Toll-free phone:* 800-313-3822. *E-mail:* mstoltz@fvcc.cc.mt.us.

FORT BELKNAP COLLEGE
Harlem, Montana www.fbcc.edu/

Director of Admissions Ms. Dixie Brockie, Registrar and Admissions Officer, Fort Belknap College, PO Box 159, Harlem, MT 59526-0159. *Phone:* 406-353-2607 Ext. 219. *Fax:* 406-353-2898.

FORT PECK COMMUNITY COLLEGE
Poplar, Montana www.fpcc.edu/

- **District-supported** 2-year, founded 1978
- **Small-town** campus
- **Coed**

Academics *Calendar:* semesters. *Degree:* certificates and associate. *Special study options:* off-campus study, part-time degree program, summer session for credit.

Standardized Tests *Required:* ACT ASSET (for placement).

Applying *Options:* electronic application, early admission. *Application fee:* $15.

Director of Admissions Mr. Robert McAnally, Vice President for Student Services, Fort Peck Community College, PO Box 398, Poplar, MT 59255-0398. *Phone:* 406-768-6329.

LITTLE BIG HORN COLLEGE
Crow Agency, Montana www.lbhc.cc.mt.us/

Freshmen Application Contact Ms. Ann Bullis, Dean of Student Services, Little Big Horn College, Box 370, Crow Agency, MT 59022-0370. *Phone:* 406-638-2228 Ext. 50.

MILES COMMUNITY COLLEGE
Miles City, Montana www.milescc.edu/

Director of Admissions Ms. Laura J. Pierce, Chief Student Services Officer, Miles Community College, 2715 Dickinson, Miles City, MT 59301-4799. *Phone:* 406-874-6159. *Toll-free phone:* 800-541-9281.

MONTANA STATE UNIVERSITY–GREAT FALLS COLLEGE OF TECHNOLOGY
Great Falls, Montana www.msugf.edu/

Director of Admissions Ms. Carol Schopfer, Registrar, Montana State University–Great Falls College of Technology, 2100 16th Avenue South, Great Falls, MT 59405. *Phone:* 406-771-4300. *Toll-free phone:* 800-446-2698. *Fax:* 406-771-4317. *E-mail:* zgf2001@maia.oscs.montana.edu.

SALISH KOOTENAI COLLEGE
Pablo, Montana www.skc.edu/

Director of Admissions Ms. Jackie Moran, Admissions Officer, Salish Kootenai College, PO 117, Highway 93, Pablo, MT 59855. *Phone:* 406-275-4866.

STONE CHILD COLLEGE
Box Elder, Montana www.montana.edu/wwwscc/

Director of Admissions Mr. Ted Whitford, Director of Admissions/Registrar, Stone Child College, RR1, Box 1082, Box Elder, MT 59521. *Phone:* 406-395-4313 Ext. 110. *E-mail:* uanet337@quest.ocsc.montana.edu.

THE UNIVERSITY OF MONTANA-HELENA COLLEGE OF TECHNOLOGY
Helena, Montana www.umhelena.edu/

Director of Admissions Ms. Vicki Cavanaugh, Director of Admissions, The University of Montana-Helena College of Technology, 1115 North Roberts Street, Helena, MT 59601. *Phone:* 406-444-6800. *Toll-free phone:* 800-241-4882.

NEBRASKA

CENTRAL COMMUNITY COLLEGE—COLUMBUS CAMPUS

Columbus, Nebraska   **www.cccneb.edu/**

- **State and locally supported** 2-year, founded 1968, part of Central Community College
- **Small-town** 90-acre campus
- **Coed,** 1,999 undergraduate students, 22% full-time, 62% women, 38% men

Undergraduates 445 full-time, 1,554 part-time. Students come from 21 states and territories, 4% are from out of state, 0.7% African American, 0.4% Asian American or Pacific Islander, 7% Hispanic American, 0.2% Native American, 2% transferred in, 17% live on campus.
Freshmen *Admission:* 250 enrolled.

Faculty *Total:* 89, 43% full-time, 6% with terminal degrees. *Student/faculty ratio:* 15:1.

Majors Accounting; administrative assistant and secretarial science; agricultural business and management; automobile/automotive mechanics technology; business administration and management; commercial and advertising art; computer and information sciences; computer programming (specific applications); drafting and design technology; electrical, electronic and communications engineering technology; electromechanical technology; family and consumer sciences/human sciences; industrial technology; information technology; liberal arts and sciences/liberal studies; machine tool technology; marketing/marketing management; nursing (licensed practical/vocational nurse training); quality control technology; system administration; web/multimedia management and webmaster; welding technology.

Academics *Calendar:* semesters plus six-week summer session. *Degree:* certificates, diplomas, and associate. *Special study options:* academic remediation for entering students, accelerated degree program, adult/continuing education programs, advanced placement credit, cooperative education, distance learning, English as a second language, external degree program, independent study, internships, off-campus study, part-time degree program, services for LD students, student-designed majors, summer session for credit.

Library Learning Resources Center with 22,000 titles, 118 serial subscriptions, 1,390 audiovisual materials, an OPAC.

Computers on Campus 100 computers available on campus for general student use. A campuswide network can be accessed from student residence rooms and from off campus. Internet access, online (class) registration, at least one staffed computer lab available.

Student Life *Housing Options:* coed. Campus housing is university owned. *Activities and Organizations:* choral group, Phi Theta Kappa, Drama Club, Art Club, Cantari, Chorale. *Campus security:* late-night transport/escort service, controlled dormitory access, night security. *Student services:* personal/psychological counseling, women's center.

Athletics Member NJCAA. *Intercollegiate sports:* basketball M(s), volleyball W(s). *Intramural sports:* basketball M/W, football M, softball M/W, table tennis M/W, volleyball M/W.

Costs (2006–07) *Tuition:* state resident $1860 full-time, $62 per credit part-time; nonresident $2790 full-time, $93 per credit part-time. *Required fees:* $120 full-time, $4 per credit part-time.

Applying *Options:* common application, electronic application, early admission. *Required:* high school transcript. *Required for some:* 3 letters of recommendation, interview. *Application deadline:* rolling (freshmen), rolling (transfers). *Notification:* continuous (freshmen).

Freshmen Application Contact Ms. Mary Young, Records Coordinator, Central Community College–Columbus Campus, PO Box 1027, Columbus, NE 68602-1027. *Phone:* 402-562-1296. *Toll-free phone:* 800-642-1083. *Fax:* 402-562-1201. *E-mail:* myoung@cccneb.edu.

CENTRAL COMMUNITY COLLEGE—GRAND ISLAND CAMPUS

Grand Island, Nebraska   **www.cccneb.edu/**

- **State and locally supported** 2-year, founded 1976, part of Central Community College
- **Small-town** 64-acre campus
- **Coed,** 2,916 undergraduate students, 14% full-time, 66% women, 34% men

Undergraduates 399 full-time, 2,517 part-time. Students come from 22 states and territories, 1 other country, 4% are from out of state, 0.9% African American, 1% Asian American or Pacific Islander, 9% Hispanic American, 0.3% Native American, 0.1% international, 2% transferred in, 10% live on campus.
Freshmen *Admission:* 322 enrolled.

Faculty *Total:* 112, 38% full-time, 4% with terminal degrees. *Student/faculty ratio:* 15:1.

Majors Accounting; administrative assistant and secretarial science; automobile/automotive mechanics technology; business administration and management; child development; clinical/medical social work; computer and information sciences; computer programming (specific applications); criminal justice/safety; data processing and data processing technology; drafting and design technology; electrical, electronic and communications engineering technology; heating, air conditioning, ventilation and refrigeration maintenance technology; industrial technology; information technology; legal assistant/paralegal; liberal arts and sciences/liberal studies; nursing (licensed practical/vocational nurse training); nursing (registered nurse training); system administration; web/multimedia management and webmaster; welding technology.

Academics *Calendar:* semesters plus six-week summer session. *Degree:* certificates, diplomas, and associate. *Special study options:* academic remediation for entering students, accelerated degree program, adult/continuing education programs, advanced placement credit, cooperative education, distance learning, English as a second language, external degree program, independent study, internships, off-campus study, part-time degree program, services for LD students, student-designed majors, summer session for credit.

Library Central Community College–Grand Island Campus Library with 5,700 titles, 94 serial subscriptions, 150 audiovisual materials, an OPAC, a Web page.

Computers on Campus 156 computers available on campus for general student use. A campuswide network can be accessed from off campus. Internet access, online (class) registration, at least one staffed computer lab available.

Student Life *Housing Options:* coed. Campus housing is provided by a third party. Freshman applicants given priority for college housing. *Activities and Organizations:* Mid-Nebraska Users of Computers, Student Activities Organization, intramurals. *Student services:* personal/psychological counseling.

Athletics *Intramural sports:* bowling M/W, table tennis M/W, volleyball M/W.

Costs (2006–07) *Tuition:* state resident $1860 full-time, $62 per credit part-time; nonresident $2790 full-time, $93 per credit part-time. *Required fees:* $120 full-time, $4 per credit part-time.

Financial Aid Of all full-time matriculated undergraduates who enrolled in 2004, 50 Federal Work-Study jobs (averaging $1000). 20 state and other part-time jobs (averaging $1000).

Applying *Options:* common application, electronic application, early admission. *Required:* high school transcript. *Required for some:* 3 letters of recommendation, interview. *Application deadline:* rolling (freshmen), rolling (transfers). *Notification:* continuous (freshmen).

Freshmen Application Contact Ms. Liz Kohout, Admissions Director, Central Community College–Grand Island Campus, PO Box 4903, Grand Island, NE 68802-4903. *Phone:* 308-398-7406 Ext. 406. *Toll-free phone:* 800-652-9177. *Fax:* 308-398-7398. *E-mail:* lkohout@cccneb.edu.

CENTRAL COMMUNITY COLLEGE—HASTINGS CAMPUS

Hastings, Nebraska   **www.cccneb.edu/**

- **State and locally supported** 2-year, founded 1966, part of Central Community College
- **Small-town** 600-acre campus
- **Coed,** 2,534 undergraduate students, 37% full-time, 57% women, 43% men

Undergraduates 933 full-time, 1,601 part-time. Students come from 36 states and territories, 4% are from out of state, 0.4% African American, 0.7% Asian American or Pacific Islander, 5% Hispanic American, 0.4% Native American, 3% transferred in, 26% live on campus.
Freshmen *Admission:* 497 enrolled.

Central Community College–Hastings Campus (continued)

Faculty *Total:* 90, 68% full-time, 4% with terminal degrees. *Student/faculty ratio:* 15:1.

Majors Accounting; administrative assistant and secretarial science; agricultural business and management; applied horticulture; autobody/collision and repair technology; automobile/automotive mechanics technology; business administration and management; child development; clinical/medical social work; commercial and advertising art; computer and information sciences; computer programming (specific applications); construction engineering technology; dental assisting; dental hygiene; diesel mechanics technology; drafting and design technology; electrical, electronic and communications engineering technology; graphic and printing equipment operation/production; health information/medical records technology; heating, air conditioning, ventilation and refrigeration maintenance technology; hospital and health care facilities administration; hospitality administration; hotel/motel administration; industrial technology; information technology; liberal arts and sciences/liberal studies; machine tool technology; mass communication/media; medical administrative assistant and medical secretary; medical/clinical assistant; radio and television broadcasting technology; system administration; vehicle/petroleum products marketing; web/multimedia management and webmaster; welding technology.

Academics *Calendar:* semesters plus six-week summer session. *Degree:* certificates, diplomas, and associate. *Special study options:* academic remediation for entering students, accelerated degree program, adult/continuing education programs, advanced placement credit, cooperative education, distance learning, English as a second language, external degree program, independent study, internships, off-campus study, part-time degree program, services for LD students, student-designed majors, summer session for credit.

Library Nuckolls Library with 4,025 titles, 52 serial subscriptions, 150 audiovisual materials, an OPAC.

Computers on Campus 190 computers available on campus for general student use. A campuswide network can be accessed from student residence rooms and from off campus. Internet access, online (class) registration, at least one staffed computer lab available.

Student Life *Housing Options:* coed. Campus housing is university owned. *Activities and Organizations:* student-run radio station, Student Senate, Central Dormitory Council, Judicial Board, Seeds and Soils, Young Farmers and Ranchers. *Campus security:* 24-hour patrols, controlled dormitory access. *Student services:* personal/psychological counseling, women's center.

Athletics *Intramural sports:* basketball M/W, bowling M/W, golf M/W, softball M/W, volleyball M/W, weight lifting M/W.

Costs (2006–07) *Tuition:* state resident $1860 full-time, $62 per credit part-time; nonresident $2790 full-time, $93 per credit part-time. *Required fees:* $120 full-time, $4 per credit part-time.

Financial Aid Of all full-time matriculated undergraduates who enrolled in 2004, 70 Federal Work-Study jobs (averaging $1200). 12 state and other part-time jobs (averaging $1250).

Applying *Options:* common application, electronic application, early admission. *Required:* high school transcript. *Required for some:* 3 letters of recommendation, interview. *Application deadline:* rolling (freshmen), rolling (transfers). *Notification:* continuous (freshmen).

Freshmen Application Contact Mr. Robert Glenn, Admissions and Recruiting Director, Central Community College–Hastings Campus, PO Box 1024, East Highway 6, Hastings, NE 68902-1024. *Phone:* 402-461-2428. *Toll-free phone:* 800-742-7872. *E-mail:* rglenn@ccneb.edu.

THE CREATIVE CENTER

Omaha, Nebraska　　　　www.thecreativecenter.com/

- **Proprietary** 2-year
- **Urban** campus
- **Coed**

Academics *Calendar:* semesters. *Degree:* associate.

Applying *Application fee:* $100. *Required:* essay or personal statement, high school transcript, 1 letter of recommendation, interview.

Freshmen Application Contact Admissions and Placement Coordinator, The Creative Center, 10850 Emmet Street, Omaha, NE 68164. *Phone:* 402-898-1000. *Toll-free phone:* 888-898-1789. *Fax:* 402-898-1301. *E-mail:* admission@creativecenter.edu.

HAMILTON COLLEGE-LINCOLN

Lincoln, Nebraska　　　　www.hamiltonlincoln.com/

Director of Admissions Mr. Andy Bossler, Director of Admissions, Hamilton College-Lincoln, 1821 K Street, Lincoln, NE 68508. *Phone:* 402-474-5315. *Toll-free phone:* 800-742-7738. *Fax:* 402-474-5302. *E-mail:* losc@ix.netcom.com.

HAMILTON COLLEGE-OMAHA

Omaha, Nebraska　　　　www.hamiltonomaha.edu/

Director of Admissions Mr. Mark Stoltenberger, Director of Admissions, Hamilton College-Omaha, 3350 North 90 Street, Omaha, NE 68134. *Phone:* 402-572-8500. *Toll-free phone:* 800-642-1456.

ITT TECHNICAL INSTITUTE

Omaha, Nebraska　　　　www.itt-tech.edu/

- **Proprietary** primarily 2-year, founded 1991, part of ITT Educational Services, Inc
- **Urban** 1-acre campus
- **Coed**

Majors Accounting and business/management; animation, interactive technology, video graphics and special effects; business administration and management; CAD/CADD drafting/design technology; computer and information systems security; computer programming; computer software technology; computer systems networking and telecommunications; criminal justice/law enforcement administration; e-commerce; electrical, electronic and communications engineering technology; system, networking, and LAN/WAN management; web/multimedia management and webmaster; web page, digital/multimedia and information resources design.

Academics *Calendar:* quarters. *Degrees:* associate and bachelor's.

Library a Web page.

Computers on Campus Internet access, at least one staffed computer lab available.

Student Life *Housing:* college housing not available.

Standardized Tests *Required:* Wonderlic aptitude test (for admission).

Costs (2005–06) *Tuition:* Please see school catalog for specific information.

Applying *Options:* deferred entrance. *Application fee:* $100. *Required:* high school transcript, interview. *Recommended:* letters of recommendation. *Application deadline:* rolling (freshmen), rolling (transfers). *Notification:* continuous (freshmen).

Freshmen Application Contact Schon Nielson, Director of Recruitment, ITT Technical Institute, 9814 M Street, Omaha, NE 68127. *Phone:* 402-331-2900. *Toll-free phone:* 800-677-9260.

LITTLE PRIEST TRIBAL COLLEGE

Winnebago, Nebraska　　　　www.lptc.bia.edu/

Director of Admissions Ms. Karen Kemling, Director of Admissions and Records, Little Priest Tribal College, PO Box 270, Winnebago, NE 68071. *Phone:* 402-878-2380.

METROPOLITAN COMMUNITY COLLEGE

Omaha, Nebraska　　　　www.mccneb.edu/

- **State and locally supported** 2-year, founded 1974, part of Nebraska Coordinating Commission for Postsecondary Education
- **Urban** 172-acre campus
- **Endowment** $1.4 million
- **Coed,** 12,461 undergraduate students, 39% full-time, 56% women, 44% men

Metropolitan Community College (MCC) is a full-service comprehensive, public institution that serves more than 46,000 students annually. Located in Omaha, Nebraska, MCC provides personalized services and high-quality programs in business administration, computer and office technologies, culinary arts, industrial and construction technologies, nursing and allied health, social sciences and services, and visual and electronic technologies as well as academic transfer programs at seven convenient locations. In addition, the College provides education that accommodates many schedules with on-campus, online, weekend, and evening classes. Prospective students should call MCC at 800-228-9553 (toll-free) or visit the College's Web site at http://www.mccneb.edu.

Undergraduates 4,798 full-time, 7,663 part-time. 3% are from out of state, 9% transferred in. *Retention:* 46% of 2003 full-time freshmen returned.

Freshmen *Admission:* 3,674 applied, 3,674 admitted, 1,413 enrolled.

Faculty *Total:* 718, 25% full-time. *Student/faculty ratio:* 13:1.

Majors Accounting; administrative assistant and secretarial science; architectural engineering technology; automobile/automotive mechanics technology; business administration and management; child development; civil engineering technology; commercial and advertising art; computer programming; construction engineering technology; criminal justice/police science; culinary arts; drafting and design technology; electrical, electronic and communications engineering technology; graphic and printing equipment operation/production; heating, air conditioning, ventilation and refrigeration maintenance technology; heavy equipment maintenance technology; human services; interior design; kindergarten/preschool education; legal administrative assistant/secretary; legal assistant/paralegal; legal studies; liberal arts and sciences/liberal studies; mental health/rehabilitation; nursing (licensed practical/vocational nurse training); nursing (registered nurse training); ornamental horticulture; photography; pre-engineering; respiratory care therapy; surgical technology; welding technology.

Academics *Calendar:* quarters. *Degree:* certificates, diplomas, and associate. *Special study options:* academic remediation for entering students, adult/continuing education programs, advanced placement credit, cooperative education, distance learning, English as a second language, independent study, internships, part-time degree program, services for LD students, summer session for credit. *ROTC:* Army (c).

Library Metropolitan Community College plus 2 others with 41,161 titles, 544 serial subscriptions, 10,702 audiovisual materials, an OPAC, a Web page.

Computers on Campus 1700 computers available on campus for general student use. A campuswide network can be accessed from off campus that provide access to online classes, e-mail. Internet access, online (class) registration, at least one staffed computer lab available.

Student Life *Housing:* college housing not available. *Campus security:* 24-hour emergency response devices and patrols, late-night transport/escort service, security on duty 9 pm to 6 am. *Student services:* personal/psychological counseling.

Costs (2005–06) *Tuition:* state resident $1733 full-time, $39 per credit hour part-time; nonresident $2610 full-time, $71 per credit hour part-time. *Required fees:* $135 full-time, $3 per credit hour part-time. *Payment plan:* deferred payment. *Waivers:* senior citizens and employees or children of employees.

Financial Aid Of all full-time matriculated undergraduates who enrolled in 2004, 180 Federal Work-Study jobs (averaging $1339).

Applying *Options:* early admission. *Recommended:* high school transcript. *Application deadline:* rolling (freshmen), rolling (transfers). *Notification:* continuous (freshmen).

Freshmen Application Contact Ms. Becky Nicks, Director of Admissions and Records, Metropolitan Community College, PO Box 3777, Omaha, NE 69103-0777. *Phone:* 402-457-2717. *Toll-free phone:* 800-228-9553. *Fax:* 402-457-2616. *E-mail:* bnicks@mccneb.edu.

MID-PLAINS COMMUNITY COLLEGE
North Platte, Nebraska www.mpcca.cc.ne.us/

Freshmen Application Contact Ms. Mary Schriefer, Advisor, Mid-Plains Community College, 1101 Halligan Drive, North Platte, NE 69101. *Phone:* 308-535-3710. *Toll-free phone:* 800-658-4308 (in-state); 800-658-4348 (out-of-state).

MYOTHERAPY INSTITUTE
Lincoln, Nebraska www.myotherapy.edu/

Director of Admissions Ms. Gerri Allen, Director of Admissions, Myotherapy Institute, 6020 South 58th Street, Lincoln, NE 68516. *Phone:* 402-421-7410. *Toll-free phone:* 800-896-3363. *E-mail:* admissions@myomassage.net.

NEBRASKA COLLEGE OF TECHNICAL AGRICULTURE
Curtis, Nebraska www.ncta.unl.edu/

Director of Admissions Mr. Gerald Sundquist, Director of Instruction, Nebraska College of Technical Agriculture, RR3, Box 23A, Curtis, NE 69025-9205. *Phone:* 308-367-4124 Ext. 205. *Toll-free phone:* 800-3CURTIS. *E-mail:* gsundquist1@unl.edu.

NEBRASKA INDIAN COMMUNITY COLLEGE
Macy, Nebraska www.thenicc.edu/

- **Federally supported** 2-year, founded 1979
- **Rural** 2-acre campus with easy access to Omaha, NE
- **Endowment** $68,020
- **Coed**

Undergraduates 97 full-time, 93 part-time. Students come from 2 states and territories, 13% are from out of state, 4% African American, 0.5% Hispanic American, 82% Native American.

Faculty *Student/faculty ratio:* 8:1.

Academics *Calendar:* semesters. *Degree:* certificates and associate. *Special study options:* academic remediation for entering students, adult/continuing education programs, double majors, part-time degree program, summer session for credit.

Applying *Options:* early admission, deferred entrance. *Application fee:* $10. *Required:* high school transcript, certificate of tribal enrollment if applicable.

Director of Admissions Mr. Ed Stevens, Admission Counselor, Nebraska Indian Community College, 2451 Saint Mary's Avenue, Omaha, NE 68105. *Phone:* 402-344-8428. *Toll-free phone:* 888-843-6432 Ext. 14.

NORTHEAST COMMUNITY COLLEGE
Norfolk, Nebraska www.northeastcollege.com/

- **State and locally supported** 2-year, founded 1973, part of Nebraska Coordinating Commission for Postsecondary Education
- **Small-town** 205-acre campus
- **Endowment** $1.5 million
- **Coed,** 5,101 undergraduate students, 42% full-time, 46% women, 54% men

Undergraduates 2,127 full-time, 2,974 part-time. Students come from 15 states and territories, 15 other countries, 4% are from out of state, 11% live on campus.

Freshmen *Admission:* 836 enrolled.

Faculty *Total:* 337, 30% full-time. *Student/faculty ratio:* 17:1.

Majors Accounting; administrative assistant and secretarial science; agricultural business and management; agricultural mechanization; agricultural production; agriculture; agronomy and crop science; animal sciences; applied horticulture; art; art teacher education; audio engineering; autobody/collision and repair technology; automobile/automotive mechanics technology; biological and physical sciences; biology/biological sciences; broadcast journalism; business administration and management; business teacher education; carpentry; chemistry; computer and information sciences; computer programming; computer programming (specific applications); computer science; corrections; criminal justice/law enforcement administration; criminal justice/police science; crop production; diesel mechanics technology; drafting and design technology; dramatic/theater arts; education; electrical, electronic and communications engineering technology; electrician; electromechanical technology; elementary education; emergency medical technology (EMT paramedic); engineering; English; entrepreneurship; farm and ranch management; general studies; health and physical education; heating, air conditioning, ventilation and refrigeration maintenance technology; horticultural science; journalism; legal administrative assistant/secretary; legal assistant/paralegal; liberal arts and sciences/liberal studies; lineworker; livestock management; marketing/marketing management; marketing related; mass communication/media; mathematics; medical administrative assistant and medical secretary; music; music management and merchandising; music performance; music teacher education; nursing (licensed practical/vocational nurse training); nursing (registered nurse training); physical education teaching and coaching; physical therapy; physics; pre-law studies; radio and television; real estate; retailing; social sciences; social work related; speech and rhetoric; surgical technology; veterinary technology; welding technology.

Academics *Calendar:* semesters. *Degree:* certificates, diplomas, and associate. *Special study options:* academic remediation for entering students, accelerated degree program, adult/continuing education programs, advanced placement credit, cooperative education, distance learning, English as a second language, independent study, internships, off-campus study, part-time degree program, services for LD students, summer session for credit.

Library Resource Center plus 1 other with 28,000 titles, 3,025 serial subscriptions, 1,298 audiovisual materials, an OPAC, a Web page.

Computers on Campus 300 computers available on campus for general student use. A campuswide network can be accessed. Internet access, online (class) registration, at least one staffed computer lab available.

Northeast Community College (continued)

Student Life *Housing Options:* coed, disabled students. Campus housing is university owned. *Activities and Organizations:* drama/theater group, student-run newspaper, radio and television station, choral group, Phi Theta Kappa, Campus Crusade for Christ, Diversified Ag Club, Electricians Club, Utility Line Club. *Campus security:* 24-hour patrols, controlled dormitory access. *Student services:* personal/psychological counseling.

Athletics Member NJCAA. *Intercollegiate sports:* basketball M(s)/W(s), cheerleading W(s). *Intramural sports:* basketball M/W, bowling M/W, football M/W, soccer M/W, softball M/W, table tennis M/W, volleyball M/W.

Costs (2006–07) *Tuition:* state resident $1770 full-time, $59 per credit hour part-time; nonresident $2213 full-time, $74 per credit hour part-time. *Required fees:* $315 full-time, $11 per credit hour part-time. *Room and board:* $4586.

Financial Aid Of all full-time matriculated undergraduates who enrolled in 2004, 90 Federal Work-Study jobs (averaging $1700).

Applying *Options:* electronic application, early admission. *Recommended:* high school transcript. *Application deadline:* rolling (freshmen), rolling (transfers). *Notification:* continuous (freshmen).

Freshmen Application Contact Ms. Maureen Baker, Dean of Enrollment Management, Northeast Community College, PO Box 469, Norfolk, NE 68702-0469. *Phone:* 402-844-7258. *Toll-free phone:* 800-348-9033 Ext. 7260. *Fax:* 402-844-7400. *E-mail:* admission@northeastcollege.com.

SOUTHEAST COMMUNITY COLLEGE, BEATRICE CAMPUS

Beatrice, Nebraska   **www.southeast.edu/**

Director of Admissions Ms. Mary Ann Harms, Admissions Technician, Southeast Community College, Beatrice Campus, 4771 W. Scott Road, Beatrice, NE 68310-7042. *Toll-free phone:* 800-233-5027 Ext. 214.

SOUTHEAST COMMUNITY COLLEGE, LINCOLN CAMPUS

Lincoln, Nebraska   **www.southeast.edu/**

- **District-supported** 2-year, founded 1973, part of Southeast Community College System
- **Suburban** 115-acre campus with easy access to Omaha
- **Coed**

Undergraduates 4,095 full-time, 3,822 part-time. Students come from 23 states and territories, 4% are from out of state, 3% African American, 2% Asian American or Pacific Islander, 3% Hispanic American, 0.5% Native American, 0.1% international.

Faculty *Student/faculty ratio:* 15:1.

Academics *Calendar:* quarters. *Degree:* certificates, diplomas, and associate. *Special study options:* academic remediation for entering students, adult/continuing education programs, advanced placement credit, cooperative education, distance learning, English as a second language, independent study, internships, off-campus study, part-time degree program, services for LD students, summer session for credit.

Student Life *Campus security:* late-night transport/escort service.

Standardized Tests *Recommended:* SAT or ACT (for placement).

Costs (2005–06) *Tuition:* state resident $1755 full-time, $39 per quarter hour part-time; nonresident $2138 full-time, $48 per quarter hour part-time. Full-time tuition and fees vary according to course load. Part-time tuition and fees vary according to course load. *Required fees:* $45 full-time, $1 per quarter hour part-time.

Applying *Options:* electronic application, early admission, deferred entrance. *Required:* high school transcript.

Freshmen Application Contact Ms. Pat Frakes, Admissions Representative, Southeast Community College, Lincoln Campus, 8800 "O" Street, Lincoln, NE 68520. *Phone:* 402-437-2600 Ext. 2600. *Toll-free phone:* 800-642-4075 Ext. 2600.

SOUTHEAST COMMUNITY COLLEGE, MILFORD CAMPUS

Milford, Nebraska   **www.southeast.edu/**

- **District-supported** 2-year, founded 1941, part of Southeast Community College System
- **Small-town** 50-acre campus with easy access to Omaha
- **Coed, primarily men**

Undergraduates 890 full-time, 32 part-time. 0.4% Asian American or Pacific Islander, 0.6% Hispanic American, 0.6% Native American, 33% live on campus.

Faculty *Student/faculty ratio:* 20:1.

Academics *Calendar:* quarters. *Degree:* diplomas and associate. *Special study options:* academic remediation for entering students, cooperative education, distance learning, internships, services for LD students.

Student Life *Campus security:* 24-hour patrols, late-night transport/escort service.

Standardized Tests *Recommended:* SAT (for admission), ACT (for admission).

Applying *Options:* common application. *Required:* high school transcript.

Director of Admissions Mr. Larry E. Meyer, Dean of Students, Southeast Community College, Milford Campus, 600 State Street, Milford, NE 68405. *Phone:* 402-761-2131 Ext. 8270. *Toll-free phone:* 800-933-7223 Ext. 8243.

VATTEROTT COLLEGE

Omaha, Nebraska   **www.vatterott-college.edu/**

Director of Admissions Dr. James G. Hadley, Campus Director, Vatterott College, 225 North 80th Street, Omaha, NE 68114. *Phone:* 402-392-1300 Ext. 207. *Toll-free phone:* 800-865-8628.

VATTEROTT COLLEGE

Omaha, Nebraska

WESTERN NEBRASKA COMMUNITY COLLEGE

Sidney, Nebraska   **www.wncc.net/**

Director of Admissions Mr. Troy Archuleta, Admissions and Recruitment Director, Western Nebraska Community College, 371 College Drive, Sidney, NE 69162. *Phone:* 308-635-6015. *Toll-free phone:* 800-222-9682 (in-state); 800-348-4435 (out-of-state). *E-mail:* rhovey@wncc.net.

NEVADA

CAREER COLLEGE OF NORTHERN NEVADA

Reno, Nevada   **www.ccnn.edu/**

- **Proprietary** 2-year, founded 1984
- **Urban** 1-acre campus
- **Coed,** 283 undergraduate students, 100% full-time, 79% women, 21% men

Undergraduates 283 full-time. Students come from 2 states and territories, 5% are from out of state, 8% African American, 6% Asian American or Pacific

Islander, 17% Hispanic American, 6% Native American.
Freshmen *Admission:* 419 applied, 419 admitted.
Faculty *Total:* 23, 48% full-time, 17% with terminal degrees. *Student/faculty ratio:* 20:1.
Majors Business administration and management; computer and information sciences; data processing and data processing technology; electrical, electronic and communications engineering technology; management information systems; medical/clinical assistant.
Academics *Calendar:* quarters six-week terms. *Degree:* diplomas and associate. *Special study options:* academic remediation for entering students, accelerated degree program, cooperative education, double majors, internships, summer session for credit.
Library 380 titles, 7 serial subscriptions.
Computers on Campus 120 computers available on campus for general student use. A campuswide network can be accessed. Internet access, at least one staffed computer lab available.
Student Life *Housing:* college housing not available. *Activities and Organizations:* student-run newspaper. *Campus security:* 24-hour emergency response devices.
Costs (2005–06) *Tuition:* $175 per credit hour part-time.
Financial Aid Of all full-time matriculated undergraduates who enrolled in 2004, 6 Federal Work-Study jobs (averaging $3000).
Applying *Application fee:* $25. *Required:* essay or personal statement, high school transcript, interview. *Application deadline:* rolling (freshmen), rolling (transfers). *Notification:* continuous (freshmen).
Freshmen Application Contact Ms. Laura Goldhammer, Director of Admissions, Career College of Northern Nevada, 1195-A Corporate Boulevard, Reno, NV 89502. *Phone:* 775-856-2266 Ext. 11. *Fax:* 775-856-0935. *E-mail:* lgoldhammer@ccnn4u.com.

COMMUNITY COLLEGE OF SOUTHERN NEVADA

North Las Vegas, Nevada   www.ccsn.nevada.edu/

- **State-supported** 2-year, founded 1971, part of University and Community College System of Nevada
- **Suburban** 89-acre campus with easy access to Las Vegas
- **Endowment** $2.6 million
- **Coed**

Undergraduates 7,850 full-time, 26,354 part-time. Students come from 55 states and territories, 13 other countries, 2% are from out of state, 0.8% transferred in.
Academics *Calendar:* semesters. *Degree:* certificates and associate. *Special study options:* academic remediation for entering students, accelerated degree program, adult/continuing education programs, advanced placement credit, cooperative education, distance learning, double majors, English as a second language, honors programs, independent study, internships, part-time degree program, services for LD students, summer session for credit. *ROTC:* Army (b).
Student Life *Campus security:* 24-hour emergency response devices and patrols.
Athletics Member NJCAA.
Costs (2005–06) *Tuition:* state resident $1523 full-time, $51 per credit part-time; nonresident $6557 full-time, $107 per credit part-time. *Required fees:* $120 full-time, $4 per credit part-time.
Financial Aid Of all full-time matriculated undergraduates who enrolled in 2004, 355 Federal Work-Study jobs (averaging $2000).
Applying *Options:* early admission. *Application fee:* $5. *Required:* student data form.
Director of Admissions Mr. Arlie J. Stops, Associate Vice President for Admissions and Records, Community College of Southern Nevada, 3200 East Cheyenne Avenue, North Las Vegas, NV 89030-4296. *Phone:* 702-651-4060. *Toll-free phone:* 800-492-5728. *E-mail:* stops@ccmail.ccsn.nevada.edu.

GREAT BASIN COLLEGE

Elko, Nevada   www.gbcnv.edu/

- **State-supported** primarily 2-year, founded 1967, part of University and Community College System of Nevada
- **Small-town** 45-acre campus
- **Endowment** $150,000
- **Coed,** 3,095 undergraduate students, 28% full-time, 61% women, 39% men

Undergraduates 853 full-time, 2,242 part-time. 1% are from out of state, 0.7% African American, 0.9% Asian American or Pacific Islander, 9% Hispanic American, 4% Native American.
Freshmen *Admission:* 377 enrolled.
Faculty *Total:* 231, 26% full-time. *Student/faculty ratio:* 13:1.
Majors Anthropology; art; business administration and management; business/commerce; chemistry; criminal justice/safety; data processing and data processing technology; diesel mechanics technology; electrical, electronic and communications engineering technology; elementary education; English; environmental studies; geology/earth science; history; industrial technology; interdisciplinary studies; kindergarten/preschool education; mathematics; nursing (registered nurse training); office management; operations management; physics; psychology; secondary education; social work; sociology; welding technology.
Academics *Calendar:* semesters. *Degrees:* certificates, associate, and bachelor's. *Special study options:* academic remediation for entering students, adult/continuing education programs, cooperative education, distance learning, English as a second language, external degree program, independent study, part-time degree program, services for LD students, summer session for credit.
Library Learning Resources Center with 27,521 titles, 250 serial subscriptions, an OPAC.
Computers on Campus 95 computers available on campus for general student use. A campuswide network can be accessed from off campus. Internet access, online (class) registration, at least one staffed computer lab available.
Student Life *Housing Options:* Campus housing is university owned. *Activities and Organizations:* drama/theater group, choral group. *Campus security:* evening patrols by trained security personnel. *Student services:* personal/psychological counseling.
Athletics *Intramural sports:* badminton M/W, basketball M/W, volleyball M/W, weight lifting M/W.
Costs (2006–07) *Tuition:* state resident $1575 full-time, $53 per credit part-time; nonresident $4962 full-time, $110 per credit part-time. *Room and board:* $4520; room only: $1900.
Financial Aid Of all full-time matriculated undergraduates who enrolled in 2004, 35 Federal Work-Study jobs (averaging $1000). 50 state and other part-time jobs (averaging $1800).
Applying *Options:* common application, electronic application, early admission, deferred entrance. *Application fee:* $5. *Required:* high school transcript. *Application deadline:* rolling (freshmen), rolling (transfers). *Notification:* continuous (freshmen).
Freshmen Application Contact Ms. Julie Byrnes, Director of Enrollment Management, Great Basin College, 1500 College Parkway, Elko, NV 89801-3348. *Phone:* 775-753-2271. *Fax:* 775-753-2311. *E-mail:* stdsvc@gbcnv.edu.

HERITAGE COLLEGE

Las Vegas, Nevada

HIGH-TECH INSTITUTE

Las Vegas, Nevada   www.high-techinstitute.com/

Director of Admissions Mr. Alvin J. Hollander, Director, High-Tech Institute, 2320 South Rancho Drive, Las Vegas, NV 89102. *Phone:* 702-385-6700. *Toll-free phone:* 800-987-0110. *Fax:* 702-388-4463. *E-mail:* ajhollander@hightechinstitute.com.

ITT TECHNICAL INSTITUTE
Henderson, Nevada   www.itt-tech.edu/

- **Proprietary** primarily 2-year, part of ITT Educational Services, Inc
- **Coed**

Majors Animation, interactive technology, video graphics and special effects; business administration and management; CAD/CADD drafting/design technology; computer and information systems security; computer programming; criminal justice/law enforcement administration; electrical, electronic and communications engineering technology; system, networking, and LAN/WAN management; web/multimedia management and webmaster; web page, digital/multimedia and information resources design.

Academics *Degrees:* associate and bachelor's.

Library a Web page.

Computers on Campus Internet access, at least one staffed computer lab available.

Student Life *Housing:* college housing not available.

Standardized Tests *Required:* Wonderlic aptitude test (for admission).

Costs (2005–06) *Tuition:* Please see school catalog for specific information.

Financial Aid Of all full-time matriculated undergraduates who enrolled in 2004, 6 Federal Work-Study jobs (averaging $5000).

Applying *Options:* deferred entrance. *Application fee:* $100. *Required:* high school transcript, interview. *Recommended:* letters of recommendation. *Application deadline:* rolling (freshmen), rolling (transfers). *Notification:* continuous (freshmen).

Freshmen Application Contact Ms. Anne Buzak, Director of Recruitment, ITT Technical Institute, 168 North Gibson Road, Henderson, NV 89014. *Phone:* 702-558-5404. *Toll-free phone:* 800-488-8459.

LAS VEGAS COLLEGE
Las Vegas, Nevada   www.lasvegas-college.com/

Director of Admissions Mr. Bill Hall, Director of Admissions, Las Vegas College, 4100 West Flamingo Road, Suite 2100, Las Vegas, NV 89103-3926. *Phone:* 702-368-6200. *Toll-free phone:* 800-903-3101.

LE CORDON BLEU COLLEGE OF CULINARY ARTS, LAS VEGAS
Las Vegas, Nevada

PIMA MEDICAL INSTITUTE
Las Vegas, Nevada   www.pmi.edu

- **Proprietary** 2-year, founded 2003, part of Vocational Training Institutes, Inc
- **Urban** campus
- **Coed**

Undergraduates 329 full-time. 10% are from out of state.

Faculty *Student/faculty ratio:* 20:1.

Academics *Calendar:* modular. *Degree:* certificates and associate. *Special study options:* advanced placement credit, internships.

Standardized Tests *Required:* Wonderlic Scholastic Level Exam (for admission).

Costs (2005–06) *Tuition:* Tuition varies depending on course.

Applying *Required:* interview. *Required for some:* essay or personal statement, high school transcript.

Freshmen Application Contact Admissions Office, Pima Medical Institute, Pima Medical Institute, 3333 East Flamingo Road, Las Vegas, NV 89121. *Phone:* 702-458-9650 Ext. 202. *Toll-free phone:* 800-477-PIMA.

TRUCKEE MEADOWS COMMUNITY COLLEGE
Reno, Nevada   www.tmcc.edu/

- **State-supported** 2-year, founded 1971, part of University and Community College System of Nevada
- **Suburban** 63-acre campus
- **Endowment** $5.6 million
- **Coed**

Undergraduates 1,963 full-time, 7,734 part-time. Students come from 12 states and territories, 3 other countries, 2% African American, 6% Asian American or Pacific Islander, 9% Hispanic American, 2% Native American, 2% international.

Faculty *Student/faculty ratio:* 31:1.

Academics *Calendar:* semesters. *Degree:* certificates and associate. *Special study options:* academic remediation for entering students, adult/continuing education programs, advanced placement credit, cooperative education, distance learning, English as a second language, internships, part-time degree program, services for LD students, summer session for credit. *ROTC:* Army (c).

Student Life *Campus security:* 24-hour emergency response devices and patrols, late-night transport/escort service.

Standardized Tests *Recommended:* SAT or ACT (for placement).

Costs (2005–06) *Tuition:* state resident $0 full-time; nonresident $4915 full-time, $56 per credit part-time. *Required fees:* $1314 full-time, $55 per credit part-time.

Financial Aid Of all full-time matriculated undergraduates who enrolled in 2004, 126 Federal Work-Study jobs (averaging $5000). 368 state and other part-time jobs (averaging $5000).

Applying *Options:* early admission, deferred entrance. *Application fee:* $10.

Director of Admissions Mr. Dave Harbeck, Director of Admissions and Records, Truckee Meadows Community College, Mail Station #15, 7000 Dandini Boulevard, MS RDMT 319, Reno, NV 89512-3901. *Phone:* 775-674-7623. *Fax:* 775-673-7028. *E-mail:* dharbeck@tmcc.edu.

WESTERN NEVADA COMMUNITY COLLEGE
Carson City, Nevada   www.wncc.edu/

- **State-supported** 2-year, founded 1971, part of University and Community College System of Nevada
- **Small-town** 200-acre campus
- **Endowment** $116,247
- **Coed**

Undergraduates 936 full-time, 3,961 part-time. 3% are from out of state.

Academics *Calendar:* semesters. *Degree:* certificates, diplomas, and associate. *Special study options:* academic remediation for entering students, adult/continuing education programs, advanced placement credit, cooperative education, distance learning, English as a second language, honors programs, independent study, internships, part-time degree program, services for LD students, summer session for credit.

Student Life *Campus security:* late-night transport/escort service.

Standardized Tests *Recommended:* SAT or ACT (for placement).

Costs (2005–06) *Tuition:* $51 per credit part-time; state resident $1523 full-time, $80 per credit part-time; nonresident $6588 full-time, $110 per credit part-time. Full-time tuition and fees vary according to course load and reciprocity agreements. Part-time tuition and fees vary according to course load and reciprocity agreements. *Required fees:* $120 full-time, $4 per credit part-time. *Payment plans:* installment, deferred payment.

Financial Aid Of all full-time matriculated undergraduates who enrolled in 2004, 24 Federal Work-Study jobs (averaging $4500). 48 state and other part-time jobs (averaging $4500).

Applying *Options:* early admission. *Application fee:* $15. *Required for some:* high school transcript.

Director of Admissions Ms. Dianne Hilliard, Director Admissions and Records, Western Nevada Community College, 2201 West College Parkway, Carson City, NV 89703-7399. *Phone:* 775-445-3271. *E-mail:* hull@wncc.edu.

HESSER COLLEGE
Manchester, New Hampshire   www.hesser.edu

- **Proprietary** primarily 2-year, founded 1900, part of Quest Education Corporation
- **Urban** 1-acre campus with easy access to Boston
- **Coed**

Undergraduates 2,104 full-time, 1,294 part-time. Students come from 12 states and territories, 50% live on campus.

Academics *Calendar:* semesters. *Degrees:* certificates, diplomas, associate, and bachelor's (also offers a graduate law program with Massachusetts School of Law at Andover). *Special study options:* accelerated degree program, adult/continuing education programs, advanced placement credit, cooperative education, double majors, internships, part-time degree program, student-designed majors, summer session for credit.

Student Life *Campus security:* 24-hour emergency response devices and patrols, student patrols, late-night transport/escort service, controlled dormitory access.

Standardized Tests *Recommended:* SAT (for admission).

Costs (2005–06) *Comprehensive fee:* $18,940 includes full-time tuition ($11,340), mandatory fees ($1000), and room and board ($6600). Part-time tuition: $410 per credit. *Room and board:* college room only: $3600.

Financial Aid Of all full-time matriculated undergraduates who enrolled in 2004, 700 Federal Work-Study jobs (averaging $1000).

Applying *Options:* common application, electronic application, deferred entrance. *Application fee:* $10. *Required:* high school transcript, interview. *Required for some:* essay or personal statement, letters of recommendation. *Recommended:* minimum 2.0 GPA.

Director of Admissions Ms. Julie English, Director of Admissions, Hesser College, 3 Sundial Avenue, Manchester, NH 03103. *Phone:* 603-668-6660 Ext. 2101. *Toll-free phone:* 800-526-9231 Ext. 2110.

▶ **See page 550 for the College Close-Up.**

MCINTOSH COLLEGE
Dover, New Hampshire   www.mcintoshcollege.edu/

- **Proprietary** 2-year, founded 1896
- **Small-town** 11-acre campus with easy access to Boston
- **Coed**

Undergraduates Students come from 20 states and territories, 10% are from out of state, 9% African American, 2% Asian American or Pacific Islander, 6% Hispanic American, 2% Native American, 1% international, 25% live on campus. *Retention:* 96% of 2003 full-time freshmen returned.

Faculty *Student/faculty ratio:* 25:1.

Academics *Calendar:* trimesters. *Degree:* certificates and associate. *Special study options:* accelerated degree program, adult/continuing education programs, advanced placement credit, cooperative education, double majors, internships, part-time degree program, services for LD students, summer session for credit.

Student Life *Campus security:* 24-hour emergency response devices and patrols, student patrols, controlled dormitory access.

Costs (2005–06) *Comprehensive fee:* $25,085 includes full-time tuition ($15,600), mandatory fees ($125), and room and board ($9360). Part-time tuition: $443 per credit. No tuition increase for student's term of enrollment. *Payment plans:* tuition prepayment, installment.

Applying *Options:* common application, electronic application, early admission, deferred entrance. *Application fee:* $15. *Required:* high school transcript. *Recommended:* interview.

Freshmen Application Contact Mrs. Jody LaBrie, Vice President of Admissions and Marketing, McIntosh College, 23 Cataract Avenue, Dover, NH 03820-3990. *Phone:* 603-742-1234. *Toll-free phone:* 800-McINTOSH. *Fax:* 603-743-0060. *E-mail:* admissions@mcintosh.edu.

▶ **See page 574 for the College Close-Up.**

NEW HAMPSHIRE COMMUNITY TECHNICAL COLLEGE, BERLIN/LACONIA
Berlin, New Hampshire   www.berlin.nhctc.edu/

Director of Admissions Ms. Martha P. Laflamme, Vice President of Student Affairs, New Hampshire Community Technical College, Berlin/Laconia, 2020 Riverside Drive, Berlin, NH 03570-3717. *Phone:* 603-752-1113 Ext. 1004. *Toll-free phone:* 800-445-4525.

NEW HAMPSHIRE COMMUNITY TECHNICAL COLLEGE, MANCHESTER/STRATHAM
Manchester, New Hampshire   www.manchester.nhctc.edu/

- **State-supported** 2-year, founded 1945, part of New Hampshire Community Technical College System
- **Urban** 60-acre campus with easy access to Boston
- **Coed**, 2,944 undergraduate students

Undergraduates Students come from 5 states and territories. *Freshmen Admission:* 2,800 applied, 2,525 admitted.

Faculty *Total:* 190, 25% full-time, 3% with terminal degrees. *Student/faculty ratio:* 14:1.

Majors Accounting; administrative assistant and secretarial science; athletic training; automobile/automotive mechanics technology; business administration and management; child development; commercial and advertising art; community organization and advocacy; construction engineering technology; drafting and design technology; heating, air conditioning, ventilation and refrigeration maintenance technology; human services; information science/studies; kindergarten/preschool education; kinesiology and exercise science; liberal arts and sciences/liberal studies; management information systems; marketing/marketing management; mechanical design technology; medical administrative assistant and medical secretary; nursing (registered nurse training); physical therapy; welding technology.

Academics *Calendar:* semesters. *Degree:* certificates, diplomas, and associate. *Special study options:* academic remediation for entering students, adult/continuing education programs, advanced placement credit, cooperative education, distance learning, English as a second language, external degree program, independent study, internships, part-time degree program, services for LD students, summer session for credit.

Library New Hampshire Community Technical College Library plus 1 other with 18,000 titles, 160 serial subscriptions, an OPAC.

Computers on Campus 210 computers available on campus for general student use. A campuswide network can be accessed. Internet access, online (class) registration, at least one staffed computer lab available.

Student Life *Housing:* college housing not available. *Activities and Organizations:* Student Senate, Phi Theta Kappa, American Society of Welders, Student Nurses Association. *Campus security:* trained security personnel. *Student services:* personal/psychological counseling.

Athletics *Intercollegiate sports:* baseball W, basketball M, skiing (downhill) M/W, soccer M/W, volleyball M/W. *Intramural sports:* basketball M/W, bowling M/W, ice hockey M, skiing (cross-country) M/W, skiing (downhill) M/W, volleyball M/W.

Costs (2006–07) *Tuition:* area resident $3936 full-time, $164 per credit part-time; state resident $5904 full-time, $246 per credit part-time; nonresident $9024 full-time, $376 per credit part-time. *Required fees:* $5 per credit part-time.

Applying *Options:* early admission, deferred entrance. *Application fee:* $10. *Required:* high school transcript, interview. *Recommended:* letters of recommendation. *Application deadline:* rolling (freshmen), rolling (transfers). *Notification:* continuous (freshmen).

Freshmen Application Contact Ms. Jacquie Poirier, Coordinator of Admissions, New Hampshire Community Technical College, Manchester/Stratham, 1066 Front Street, Manchester, NH 03102-8518. *Phone:* 603-668-6706 Ext. 283. *E-mail:* jpoirier@nhctc.edu.

NEW HAMPSHIRE COMMUNITY TECHNICAL COLLEGE, NASHUA/CLAREMONT

Nashua, New Hampshire **www.ncctc.edu/**

- **State-supported** 2-year, founded 1967, part of New Hampshire Community Technical College System
- **Urban** 66-acre campus with easy access to Boston
- **Coed,** 1,639 undergraduate students

Faculty *Total:* 108, 39% full-time. *Student/faculty ratio:* 9:1.

Majors Accounting; airframe mechanics and aircraft maintenance technology; artificial intelligence and robotics; autobody/collision and repair technology; automobile/automotive mechanics technology; avionics maintenance technology; business administration and management; child development; computer and information sciences; computer engineering technology; computer management; computer science; data processing and data processing technology; drafting and design technology; electrical, electronic and communications engineering technology; electromechanical technology; engineering technology; general studies; heavy equipment maintenance technology; human services; industrial technology; information science/studies; kindergarten/preschool education; legal assistant/paralegal; legal studies; liberal arts and sciences/liberal studies; machine tool technology; ophthalmic laboratory technology; quality control technology; social work; telecommunications.

Academics *Calendar:* semesters. *Degree:* certificates, diplomas, and associate. *Special study options:* academic remediation for entering students, adult/continuing education programs, cooperative education, distance learning, English as a second language, external degree program, internships, part-time degree program, services for LD students, student-designed majors, summer session for credit.

Library Walter B. Peterson Library and Media Center with 22,000 titles, 250 serial subscriptions, an OPAC.

Computers on Campus 150 computers available on campus for general student use. A campuswide network can be accessed. Internet access, at least one staffed computer lab available.

Student Life *Housing:* college housing not available. *Activities and Organizations:* drama/theater group, student-run newspaper, Student Senate, Phi Theta Kappa, AmeriCorp, Paralegal Club, Ski Club. *Campus security:* 24-hour emergency response devices. *Student services:* personal/psychological counseling.

Athletics *Intercollegiate sports:* soccer M/W. *Intramural sports:* skiing (cross-country) M/W, skiing (downhill) M/W, soccer M/W, weight lifting M/W.

Costs (2006–07) *Tuition:* state resident $5248 full-time, $164 per credit part-time; nonresident $12,032 full-time, $376 per credit part-time. *Required fees:* $512 full-time, $16 per credit part-time.

Financial Aid Of all full-time matriculated undergraduates who enrolled in 2004, 35 Federal Work-Study jobs (averaging $1000).

Applying *Options:* deferred entrance. *Application fee:* $10. *Required:* high school transcript, interview. *Required for some:* letters of recommendation, nursing exam. *Recommended:* letters of recommendation. *Application deadline:* rolling (freshmen), rolling (transfers). *Notification:* continuous (freshmen).

Freshmen Application Contact Ms. Patricia Goodman, Director of Student Services, New Hampshire Community Technical College, Nashua/Claremont, 505 Amherst Street, Nashua, NH 03063. *Phone:* 603-882-6923. *Fax:* 603-882-8690. *E-mail:* nashua@nhctc.edu.

NEW HAMPSHIRE TECHNICAL INSTITUTE

Concord, New Hampshire **www.nhti.edu/**

- **State-supported** 2-year, founded 1964, part of New Hampshire Community Technical College System
- **Small-town** 225-acre campus with easy access to Boston
- **Coed,** 3,650 undergraduate students, 42% full-time, 61% women, 39% men

Undergraduates 1,523 full-time, 2,127 part-time. Students come from 12 states and territories, 24 other countries, 2% are from out of state, 1% African American, 1% Asian American or Pacific Islander, 2% Hispanic American, 0.3% Native American, 23% live on campus.

Freshmen *Admission:* 1,919 applied, 1,408 admitted. *Average high school GPA:* 2.50.

Faculty *Total:* 146, 66% full-time, 8% with terminal degrees. *Student/faculty ratio:* 12:1.

Majors Accounting; animation, interactive technology, video graphics and special effects; architectural engineering technology; business administration and management; computer and information sciences; computer engineering technology; computer programming (specific applications); computer systems networking and telecommunications; criminal justice/law enforcement administration; dental assisting; dental hygiene; diagnostic medical sonography and ultrasound technology; electrical, electronic and communications engineering technology; emergency medical technology (EMT paramedic); engineering technology; general studies; hotel/motel administration; human resources management; human services; kindergarten/preschool education; legal assistant/paralegal; liberal arts and sciences/liberal studies; marketing/marketing management; mechanical engineering/mechanical technology; mental health/rehabilitation; nursing (registered nurse training); real estate; sport and fitness administration/management; substance abuse/addiction counseling; teacher assistant/aide; tourism and travel services management; visual and performing arts.

Academics *Calendar:* semesters. *Degree:* certificates, diplomas, and associate. *Special study options:* academic remediation for entering students, adult/continuing education programs, advanced placement credit, distance learning, double majors, English as a second language, external degree program, part-time degree program, services for LD students, summer session for credit.

Library Farnum Library plus 1 other with 32,000 titles, 500 serial subscriptions, 1,000 audiovisual materials, an OPAC, a Web page.

Computers on Campus 160 computers available on campus for general student use. Internet access, at least one staffed computer lab available.

Student Life *Housing Options:* coed. *Activities and Organizations:* drama/theater group, Phi Theta Kappa, Student Senate, Student Nurses Association, Criminal Justice Club, Outing Club. *Campus security:* 24-hour patrols, late-night transport/escort service, controlled dormitory access. *Student services:* health clinic, personal/psychological counseling.

Athletics Member NSCAA. *Intercollegiate sports:* baseball M, basketball M/W, soccer M/W, softball W, volleyball M/W. *Intramural sports:* softball W, volleyball M/W.

Standardized Tests *Required for some:* National League of Nursing Exam. *Recommended:* SAT or ACT (for admission).

Costs (2005–06) *Tuition:* state resident $4920 full-time, $164 per credit part-time; nonresident $11,280 full-time, $376 per credit part-time. *Required fees:* $480 full-time, $16 per credit part-time. *Room and board:* $6110; room only: $4150.

Financial Aid Of all full-time matriculated undergraduates who enrolled in 2004, 182 Federal Work-Study jobs (averaging $1000).

Applying *Options:* electronic application. *Application fee:* $10. *Required:* high school transcript. *Required for some:* essay or personal statement, letters of recommendation, interview. *Recommended:* minimum 2.0 GPA. *Application deadline:* rolling (freshmen), rolling (transfers). *Notification:* continuous (freshmen).

Director of Admissions Mr. Francis P. Meyer, Director of Admissions, New Hampshire Technical Institute, 11 Institute Drive, Concord, NH 03301-7412. *Phone:* 603-271-7131. *Toll-free phone:* 800-247-0179.

NEW JERSEY

ASSUMPTION COLLEGE FOR SISTERS

Mendham, New Jersey **www.acscollegeforsisters.org/**

- **Independent Roman Catholic** 2-year, founded 1953
- **Rural** 112-acre campus with easy access to New York City
- **Endowment** $86,392
- **Women only,** 37 undergraduate students, 81% full-time

Undergraduates 30 full-time, 7 part-time. Students come from 3 states and territories, 5 other countries, 60% are from out of state, 84% international.

Freshmen *Admission:* 16 applied, 16 admitted, 16 enrolled. *Test scores:* SAT verbal scores over 500: 50%.

Faculty *Total:* 17, 6% full-time, 12% with terminal degrees. *Student/faculty ratio:* 5:1.

Majors Liberal arts and sciences/liberal studies; theology.

Academics *Calendar:* semesters. *Degree:* certificates, diplomas, and associate. *Special study options:* academic remediation for entering students, advanced placement credit, English as a second language, part-time degree program, services for LD students, summer session for credit.

Library Assumption College for Sisters Library with 25,000 titles, 50 serial subscriptions, 3,000 audiovisual materials, an OPAC.

Computers on Campus 16 computers available on campus for general student use. A campuswide network can be accessed. Internet access, at least one staffed computer lab available.

Student Life *Housing:* college housing not available. *Options:* Campus housing is provided by a third party. *Activities and Organizations:* choral group. *Campus security:* 24-hour emergency response devices.

Costs (2006–07) *Tuition:* $3300 full-time, $100 per credit part-time. *Required fees:* $50 full-time.

Applying *Required:* high school transcript, 1 letter of recommendation, women religious or women in religious formation. *Required for some:* essay or personal statement, interview.

Freshmen Application Contact Sr. Gerardine Tantsits, Academic Dean/Registrar, Assumption College for Sisters, 350 Bernardsville Road, Mendham, NJ 07945-2923. *Phone:* 973-543-6528 Ext. 228. *Fax:* 973-543-1738.

ATLANTIC CAPE COMMUNITY COLLEGE
Mays Landing, New Jersey   www.atlantic.edu/

- **County-supported** 2-year, founded 1964
- **Small-town** 537-acre campus with easy access to Philadelphia
- **Endowment** $576,000
- **Coed**

Undergraduates 2,974 full-time, 3,541 part-time. Students come from 3 states and territories, 17 other countries, 1% are from out of state, 14% African American, 7% Asian American or Pacific Islander, 10% Hispanic American, 0.2% Native American, 4% transferred in.

Faculty *Student/faculty ratio:* 26:1.

Academics *Calendar:* semesters. *Degree:* certificates, diplomas, and associate. *Special study options:* academic remediation for entering students, adult/continuing education programs, advanced placement credit, cooperative education, distance learning, double majors, English as a second language, independent study, internships, part-time degree program, services for LD students, summer session for credit.

Student Life *Campus security:* 24-hour emergency response devices and patrols.

Athletics Member NJCAA.

Costs (2006–07) *Tuition:* area resident $2370 full-time, $79 per credit part-time; state resident $4740 full-time, $158 per credit part-time; nonresident $9480 full-time, $316 per credit part-time. *Required fees:* $550 full-time, $18 per credit part-time, $3 per term part-time.

Financial Aid Of all full-time matriculated undergraduates who enrolled in 2004, 90 Federal Work-Study jobs (averaging $2000). 1,800 state and other part-time jobs (averaging $1500).

Applying *Options:* common application, electronic application, early admission, deferred entrance. *Application fee:* $35. *Recommended:* high school transcript.

Freshmen Application Contact Mrs. Linda McLeod, Assistant Director, Admissions and College Recruitment, Atlantic Cape Community College, 5100 Black Horse Pike, Mays Landing, NJ 08330-2699. *Phone:* 609-343-5000 Ext. 5009. *Toll-free phone:* 800-645-CHIEF. *Fax:* 609-343-4921. *E-mail:* accadmit@atlantic.edu.

▶ **See page 484 for the College Close-Up.**

BERGEN COMMUNITY COLLEGE
Paramus, New Jersey   www.bergen.edu/

- **County-supported** 2-year, founded 1965
- **Suburban** 167-acre campus with easy access to New York City
- **Coed,** 14,812 undergraduate students, 51% full-time, 57% women, 43% men

Undergraduates 7,486 full-time, 7,326 part-time. Students come from 120 other countries, 7% African American, 11% Asian American or Pacific Islander, 23% Hispanic American, 0.2% Native American, 8% international. Freshmen *Admission:* 2,840 enrolled.

Faculty *Total:* 756, 39% full-time, 21% with terminal degrees. *Student/faculty ratio:* 22:1.

Majors Accounting; administrative assistant and secretarial science; automobile/automotive mechanics technology; biology/biological sciences; broadcast journalism; business administration and management; chemistry; clinical/medical laboratory technology; commercial and advertising art; computer engineering technology; computer programming; computer science; computer typography and composition equipment operation; consumer merchandising/retailing management; criminal justice/law enforcement administration; dance; dental hygiene; drafting and design technology; dramatic/theater arts; economics; education; electrical, electronic and communications engineering technology; engineering science; finance; health science; history; hotel/motel administration; industrial radiologic technology; industrial technology; kindergarten/preschool education; kinesiology and exercise science; legal administrative assistant/secretary; legal assistant/paralegal; liberal arts and sciences/liberal studies; literature; mass communication/media; mathematics; medical administrative assistant and medical secretary; medical/clinical assistant; music; nursing (registered nurse training); ornamental horticulture; parks, recreation and leisure; philosophy; photography; physics; political science and government; psychology; real estate; respiratory care therapy; sociology; special products marketing; tourism and travel services management; veterinary technology; women's studies.

Academics *Calendar:* semesters. *Degree:* certificates and associate. *Special study options:* academic remediation for entering students, adult/continuing education programs, cooperative education, distance learning, English as a second language, honors programs, internships, part-time degree program, services for LD students, study abroad, summer session for credit.

Library Sidney Silverman Library and Learning Resources Center plus 1 other with an OPAC.

Computers on Campus At least one staffed computer lab available.

Student Life *Housing:* college housing not available. *Activities and Organizations:* drama/theater group, student-run newspaper, choral group. *Campus security:* 24-hour patrols. *Student services:* health clinic, personal/psychological counseling.

Athletics Member NJCAA. *Intercollegiate sports:* baseball M, basketball M/W, cross-country running M/W, golf M, soccer M/W, softball W, tennis M/W, track and field M/W, volleyball W, wrestling M. *Intramural sports:* basketball M, soccer M, tennis M/W, volleyball M/W.

Costs (2006–07) *Tuition:* area resident $2249 full-time, $94 per credit part-time; state resident $4632 full-time, $193 per credit part-time; nonresident $4872 full-time, $203 per credit part-time. *Required fees:* $568 full-time, $23 per credit part-time, $8 per term part-time.

Financial Aid Of all full-time matriculated undergraduates who enrolled in 2004, 159 Federal Work-Study jobs (averaging $1575).

Applying *Notification:* continuous (freshmen).

Freshmen Application Contact Director of Admissions and Recruitment, Bergen Community College, 400 Paramus Road, Paramus, NJ 07652-1595. *Phone:* 201-447-7193. *Fax:* 201-670-7973. *E-mail:* admsoffice@bergen.edu.

BERKELEY COLLEGE
West Paterson, New Jersey   www.berkeleycollege.edu/

- **Proprietary** primarily 2-year, founded 1931
- **Suburban** 25-acre campus with easy access to New York City
- **Coed,** 2,422 undergraduate students, 84% full-time, 73% women, 27% men

Undergraduates 2,040 full-time, 382 part-time. Students come from 8 states and territories, 25 other countries, 4% are from out of state, 17% African American, 5% Asian American or Pacific Islander, 34% Hispanic American, 0.2% Native American, 2% international, 5% transferred in, 1% live on campus. *Retention:* 55% of 2003 full-time freshmen returned. Freshmen *Admission:* 1,955 applied, 1,645 admitted, 781 enrolled.

Faculty *Total:* 144, 35% full-time. *Student/faculty ratio:* 22:1.

Majors Accounting; business administration and management; business/commerce; computer management; fashion merchandising; interior design; international business/trade/commerce; legal assistant/paralegal; marketing/marketing management; system administration; web page, digital/multimedia and information resources design.

Academics *Calendar:* quarters. *Degrees:* certificates, associate, and bachelor's. *Special study options:* academic remediation for entering students, adult/continuing education programs, advanced placement credit, cooperative education, distance learning, English as a second language, internships, off-campus study, part-time degree program, study abroad, summer session for credit.

Library Walter A. Brower Library with 49,584 titles, 224 serial subscriptions, 2,659 audiovisual materials, an OPAC, a Web page.

Computers on Campus 300 computers available on campus for general student use. A campuswide network can be accessed from student residence rooms and from off campus. At least one staffed computer lab available.

Student Life *Housing Options:* coed. Campus housing is university owned. *Activities and Organizations:* student-run newspaper, Student Government Association, Athletics Club, Paralegal Student Association, International Club, Fashion and Marketing Club. *Campus security:* 24-hour emergency response devices, controlled dormitory access, security patrols. *Student services:* personal/psychological counseling.

Athletics *Intramural sports:* basketball M/W, football M/W, soccer M/W, softball M/W, volleyball M/W.

Berkeley College (continued)

Standardized Tests *Required:* SAT or ACT (for admission).

Costs (2006–07) *Comprehensive fee:* $26,700 includes full-time tuition ($16,950), mandatory fees ($750), and room and board ($9000).

Financial Aid Of all full-time matriculated undergraduates who enrolled in 2004, 150 Federal Work-Study jobs (averaging $1200).

Applying *Options:* electronic application, deferred entrance. *Application fee:* $50. *Required:* high school transcript. *Recommended:* interview. *Application deadline:* rolling (freshmen), rolling (transfers).

Freshmen Application Contact Mr. David Bertone, Director of High School Admissions, Berkeley College, 44 Rifle Camp Road, West Paterson, NJ 07424. *Phone:* 973-278-5400 Ext. 1210. *Toll-free phone:* 800-446-5400. *Fax:* 973-278-9141. *E-mail:* admissions@berkeley.org.

BROOKDALE COMMUNITY COLLEGE
Lincroft, New Jersey   www.brookdalecc.edu/

- **County-supported** 2-year, founded 1967, part of New Jersey Commission on Higher Education
- **Small-town** 221-acre campus with easy access to New York City
- **Coed**

Undergraduates 6,588 full-time, 6,136 part-time. Students come from 6 states and territories, 50 other countries, 0.1% are from out of state, 12% African American, 4% Asian American or Pacific Islander, 7% Hispanic American, 0.2% Native American, 1% international, 5% transferred in. *Retention:* 66% of 2003 full-time freshmen returned.

Faculty *Student/faculty ratio:* 22:1.

Academics *Calendar:* semesters plus 1 ten-week and 2 six-week summer terms. *Degree:* certificates and associate. *Special study options:* academic remediation for entering students, adult/continuing education programs, advanced placement credit, cooperative education, distance learning, English as a second language, honors programs, independent study, internships, part-time degree program, services for LD students, study abroad, summer session for credit. *ROTC:* Army (c), Air Force (c).

Student Life *Campus security:* 24-hour emergency response devices and patrols.

Athletics Member NJCAA.

Standardized Tests *Required for some:* ACCUPLACER.

Costs (2005–06) *Tuition:* area resident $2202 full-time, $92 per credit part-time; state resident $4404 full-time, $184 per credit part-time; nonresident $5400 full-time, $225 per credit part-time. *Required fees:* $462 full-time, $19 per credit part-time.

Applying *Options:* early admission, deferred entrance. *Application fee:* $25. *Required:* high school transcript.

Director of Admissions Ms. Kim Toomey, Registrar, Brookdale Community College, 765 Newman Springs Road, Lincroft, NJ 07738. *Phone:* 732-224-2268.

BURLINGTON COUNTY COLLEGE
Pemberton, New Jersey   www.bcc.edu/

Director of Admissions Ms. Elva DeJesus-Lopez, Admissions Coordinator, Burlington County College, 601 Pemberton-Browns Mills Road, Pemberton, NJ 08068-1599. *Phone:* 609-894-9311 Ext. 7282.

CAMDEN COUNTY COLLEGE
Blackwood, New Jersey   www.camdencc.edu/

Director of Admissions Jacqueline Baldwin, Enrollment Services, Camden County College, PO Box 200, College Drive, Blackwood, NJ 08012-0200. *Phone:* 856-227-7200 Ext. 4200. *Toll-free phone:* 888-228-2466.

COUNTY COLLEGE OF MORRIS
Randolph, New Jersey   www.ccm.edu/

Director of Admissions Ms. Jessica Chambers, Director of Admissions, County College of Morris, 214 Center Grove Road, Randolph, NJ 07869-2086. *Phone:* 973-328-5100. *Toll-free phone:* 888-226-8001. *E-mail:* admiss@ccm.edu.

CUMBERLAND COUNTY COLLEGE
Vineland, New Jersey   www.cccnj.edu/

- **State and locally supported** 2-year, founded 1963, part of New Jersey Commission on Higher Education
- **Small-town** 100-acre campus with easy access to Philadelphia
- **Coed**

Undergraduates 1,639 full-time, 1,537 part-time. Students come from 1 other state, 19% African American, 2% Asian American or Pacific Islander, 16% Hispanic American, 2% Native American. *Retention:* 64% of 2003 full-time freshmen returned.

Faculty *Student/faculty ratio:* 19:1.

Academics *Calendar:* semesters. *Degree:* certificates and associate. *Special study options:* academic remediation for entering students, adult/continuing education programs, advanced placement credit, cooperative education, distance learning, double majors, English as a second language, honors programs, part-time degree program, services for LD students, summer session for credit.

Student Life *Campus security:* 24-hour emergency response devices, late-night transport/escort service.

Athletics Member NJCAA.

Costs (2005–06) *Tuition:* area resident $1848 full-time, $77 per credit part-time; state resident $3696 full-time, $154 per credit part-time; nonresident $7392 full-time, $308 per credit part-time. *Required fees:* $600 full-time, $25 per credit part-time.

Financial Aid Of all full-time matriculated undergraduates who enrolled in 2004, 100 Federal Work-Study jobs (averaging $500). 100 state and other part-time jobs (averaging $600).

Applying *Options:* electronic application, early admission, deferred entrance. *Application fee:* $25. *Required:* high school transcript.

Director of Admissions Ms. Maud Fried-Goodnight, Executive Director of Enrollment Services, Cumberland County College, College Drive, Vineland, NJ 08362-1500. *Phone:* 856-691-8600 Ext. 228.

ESSEX COUNTY COLLEGE
Newark, New Jersey   www.essex.edu/

- **County-supported** 2-year, founded 1966, part of New Jersey Commission on Higher Education
- **Urban** 22-acre campus with easy access to New York City
- **Coed,** 10,435 undergraduate students, 54% full-time, 63% women, 37% men

Undergraduates 5,683 full-time, 4,752 part-time. Students come from 10 states and territories, 69 other countries, 2% are from out of state, 50% African American, 3% Asian American or Pacific Islander, 18% Hispanic American, 0.1% Native American, 8% international, 2% transferred in. *Retention:* 57% of 2003 full-time freshmen returned.

Freshmen *Admission:* 4,957 applied, 4,957 admitted, 2,314 enrolled.

Faculty *Total:* 592, 27% full-time. *Student/faculty ratio:* 28:1.

Majors Accounting; accounting technology and bookkeeping; administrative assistant and secretarial science; architectural engineering technology; art; biology/biological sciences; business administration and management; business teacher education; chemical technology; chemistry; civil engineering technology; communications technology; computer programming; computer programming (specific applications); computer science; criminal justice/law enforcement administration; criminal justice/police science; data processing and data processing technology; dental assisting; dental hygiene; electrical, electronic and communications engineering technology; elementary education; emergency medical technology (EMT paramedic); fire science; health/health care administration; health professions related; hotel/motel administration; human services; industrial production technologies related; information science/studies; kindergarten/preschool education; legal assistant/paralegal; legal professions and studies related; liberal arts and sciences/liberal studies; mathematics; medical administrative assistant and medical secretary; medical radiologic technology; music; nursing (registered nurse training); opticianry; physical education teaching and coaching; physical therapist assistant; physical therapy; pre-engineering; respiratory care therapy; secondary education; social sciences; social work.

Academics *Calendar:* semesters. *Degree:* certificates and associate. *Special study options:* academic remediation for entering students, accelerated degree program, adult/continuing education programs, advanced placement credit, cooperative education, distance learning, double majors, English as a second language, independent study, internships, off-campus study, part-time degree program, services for LD students, summer session for credit. *ROTC:* Army (c).

Library Martin Luther King, Jr. Library with 91,000 titles, 639 serial subscriptions, 3,618 audiovisual materials, an OPAC, a Web page.

Computers on Campus 700 computers available on campus for general student use. A campuswide network can be accessed from off campus. Internet access, at least one staffed computer lab available.

Student Life *Housing:* college housing not available. *Activities and Organizations:* drama/theater group, student-run newspaper, choral group, Fashion Entertainment Board, Phi Theta Kappa, Latin Student Union, DECA, Black Student Association. *Campus security:* 24-hour emergency response devices and patrols. *Student services:* health clinic, personal/psychological counseling, women's center.

Athletics Member NJCAA. *Intercollegiate sports:* basketball M(s)/W(s), cross-country running M(s)/W(s), soccer M, track and field M/W. *Intramural sports:* table tennis M, weight lifting M.

Costs (2005–06) *Tuition:* area resident $2318 full-time, $77 per credit hour part-time; state resident $4635 full-time, $155 per credit hour part-time. *Required fees:* $650 full-time, $26 per credit hour part-time. *Payment plan:* deferred payment.

Financial Aid Of all full-time matriculated undergraduates who enrolled in 2004, 250 Federal Work-Study jobs (averaging $2880).

Applying *Options:* deferred entrance. *Application fee:* $25. *Required:* high school transcript. *Application deadline:* 8/15 (freshmen), rolling (transfers). *Notification:* continuous (freshmen).

Freshmen Application Contact Ms. Marva Mack, Director of Admissions, Essex County College, 303 University Avenue, Newark, NJ 07102. *Phone:* 973-877-3119. *Fax:* 973-623-6449.

GIBBS COLLEGE
Livingston, New Jersey

GIBBS COLLEGE
Montclair, New Jersey   **www.njgibbscollege.net/**

Director of Admissions Mrs. Mary-Jo Greco, President, Gibbs College, 33 Plymouth Street, Montclair, NJ 07042-2699. *Phone:* 201-744-2010. *Fax:* 201-744-2298. *E-mail:* mgreco@njgibbscollege.net.

GLOUCESTER COUNTY COLLEGE
Sewell, New Jersey   **www.gccnj.edu/**

Freshmen Application Contact Ms. Carol L. Lange, Admissions and Recruitment Coordinator, Gloucester County College, 1400 Tanyard Road, Sewell, NJ 08080. *Phone:* 856-468-5000.

HUDSON COUNTY COMMUNITY COLLEGE
Jersey City, New Jersey   **www.hccc.edu/**

- **State and locally supported** 2-year, founded 1974, part of New Jersey Commission on Higher Education
- **Urban** campus with easy access to New York City
- **Endowment** $56,000
- **Coed**

Undergraduates 4,277 full-time, 2,212 part-time. 19% African American, 18% Asian American or Pacific Islander, 42% Hispanic American, 0.2% Native American, 3% international.

Academics *Calendar:* semesters. *Degree:* certificates, diplomas, and associate. *Special study options:* academic remediation for entering students, adult/continuing education programs, advanced placement credit, distance learning, double majors, English as a second language, honors programs, independent study, internships, part-time degree program, services for LD students, summer session for credit.

Student Life *Campus security:* 24-hour emergency response devices.

Standardized Tests *Required:* ACCUPLACER (for placement).

Financial Aid Of all full-time matriculated undergraduates who enrolled in 2004, 102 Federal Work-Study jobs (averaging $3000).

Applying *Application fee:* $15. *Required:* high school transcript.

Director of Admissions Mr. Robert Martin, Assistant Dean of Admissions, Hudson County Community College, 162 Sip Avenue, Jersey City, NJ 07306. *Phone:* 201-714-2115.

MERCER COUNTY COMMUNITY COLLEGE
Trenton, New Jersey   **www.mccc.edu/**

- **State and locally supported** 2-year, founded 1966
- **Suburban** 292-acre campus with easy access to New York City and Philadelphia
- **Coed,** 8,928 undergraduate students, 38% full-time, 57% women, 43% men

Undergraduates 3,404 full-time, 5,524 part-time. Students come from 5 states and territories, 7% are from out of state, 24% African American, 5% Asian American or Pacific Islander, 8% Hispanic American, 0.2% Native American, 5% international, 4% transferred in.

Freshmen *Admission:* 2,049 applied, 2,049 admitted, 2,049 enrolled.

Faculty *Total:* 529, 26% full-time. *Student/faculty ratio:* 20:1.

Majors Accounting; administrative assistant and secretarial science; airline flight attendant; airline pilot and flight crew; architectural engineering technology; art; art history, criticism and conservation; automotive engineering technology; aviation/airway management; biology/biological sciences; biology/biotechnology laboratory technician; business administration and management; ceramic arts and ceramics; chemistry; civil engineering technology; clinical/medical laboratory technology; commercial and advertising art; community organization and advocacy; computer graphics; computer science; computer systems networking and telecommunications; corrections; criminal justice/police science; culinary arts; dance; dramatic/theater arts; electrical, electronic and communications engineering technology; engineering science; fire science; funeral service and mortuary science; health science; heating, air conditioning and refrigeration technology; hotel/motel administration; humanities; legal assistant/paralegal; liberal arts and sciences/liberal studies; management information systems; mass communication/media; mathematics; medical radiologic technology; music; nursing (registered nurse training); ornamental horticulture; photography; physical therapist assistant; physics; plant sciences; radio and television broadcasting technology; respiratory care therapy; sculpture; teacher assistant/aide.

Academics *Calendar:* semesters. *Degree:* certificates and associate. *Special study options:* academic remediation for entering students, accelerated degree program, adult/continuing education programs, advanced placement credit, cooperative education, distance learning, double majors, English as a second language, external degree program, independent study, internships, part-time degree program, services for LD students, student-designed majors, summer session for credit. *ROTC:* Army (c), Air Force (c).

Library Mercer County Community College Library plus 1 other with 57,317 titles, 8,934 audiovisual materials, an OPAC, a Web page.

Computers on Campus A campuswide network can be accessed from off campus. At least one staffed computer lab available.

Student Life *Housing:* college housing not available. *Activities and Organizations:* drama/theater group, student-run newspaper, radio station, choral group, Student Government Association, student radio station, African-American Student Organization, Student Activities Board, Phi Theta Kappa. *Campus security:* 24-hour emergency response devices and patrols. *Student services:* personal/psychological counseling.

Athletics Member NJCAA. *Intercollegiate sports:* baseball M, basketball M(s)/W(s), golf M/W, soccer M(s)/W(s), softball W, tennis M/W, track and field M/W. *Intramural sports:* basketball M/W, skiing (downhill) M/W, softball M/W, volleyball M/W.

Costs (2006–07) *Tuition:* area resident $2940 full-time, $98 per credit part-time; state resident $3945 full-time, $132 per credit part-time; nonresident $6045 full-time, $202 per credit part-time. *Required fees:* $495 full-time, $17 per credit part-time.

Financial Aid Of all full-time matriculated undergraduates who enrolled in 2004, 100 Federal Work-Study jobs (averaging $1500). 12 state and other part-time jobs (averaging $1500).

Applying *Options:* common application, electronic application, deferred entrance. *Required:* high school transcript. *Recommended:* interview. *Application deadline:* rolling (freshmen), rolling (transfers). *Notification:* continuous (freshmen).

Freshmen Application Contact Dr. L. Campbell, Dean for Student and Academic Services, Mercer County Community College, 1200 Old Trenton Road, PO Box B, Trenton, NJ 08690-1004. *Phone:* 609-586-4800 Ext. 3222. *Toll-free phone:* 800-392-MCCC. *Fax:* 609-586-6944. *E-mail:* admiss@mccc.edu.

MIDDLESEX COUNTY COLLEGE

Edison, New Jersey   www.middlesexcc.edu/

- **County-supported** 2-year, founded 1964
- **Suburban** 200-acre campus with easy access to New York City
- **Coed,** 11,276 undergraduate students

Undergraduates   Students come from 4 states and territories.
Freshmen   *Admission:* 9,394 applied, 6,481 admitted.
Faculty   *Total:* 552, 37% full-time. *Student/faculty ratio:* 21:1.
Majors   Accounting; administrative assistant and secretarial science; advertising; applied art; art; automobile/automotive mechanics technology; biological and physical sciences; biology/biological sciences; biology/biotechnology laboratory technician; business administration and management; chemistry; child development; civil engineering technology; clinical/medical laboratory technology; commercial and advertising art; computer engineering technology; computer graphics; computer programming; computer science; computer systems networking and telecommunications; construction engineering technology; consumer merchandising/retailing management; corrections; criminal justice/law enforcement administration; criminal justice/police science; culinary arts; dance; dental hygiene; dietetics; drafting and design technology; dramatic/theater arts; education; electrical, electronic and communications engineering technology; engineering; engineering science; engineering technology; English; fashion/apparel design; fashion merchandising; fine/studio arts; fire science; general studies; history; hospitality administration; hotel/motel administration; information science/studies; journalism; kindergarten/preschool education; legal administrative assistant/secretary; legal assistant/paralegal; marketing/marketing management; mathematics; mechanical engineering/mechanical technology; modern languages; music; nursing (registered nurse training); photography; physical education teaching and coaching; physical sciences; physics; political science and government; psychology; radiologic technology/science; respiratory care therapy; social sciences; sociology; survey technology; teacher assistant/aide.
Academics   *Calendar:* semesters. *Degree:* certificates and associate. *Special study options:* academic remediation for entering students, adult/continuing education programs, advanced placement credit, cooperative education, distance learning, English as a second language, independent study, internships, off-campus study, part-time degree program, services for LD students, study abroad, summer session for credit. *ROTC:* Army (c).
Library   Middlesex County College Library plus 1 other with 85,160 titles, 599 serial subscriptions, 5,642 audiovisual materials, an OPAC, a Web page.
Computers on Campus   1290 computers available on campus for general student use. A campuswide network can be accessed from off campus. Internet access, at least one staffed computer lab available.
Student Life   *Housing:* college housing not available. *Activities and Organizations:* drama/theater group, student-run newspaper, radio station, choral group. *Campus security:* 24-hour emergency response devices and patrols. *Student services:* health clinic, personal/psychological counseling.
Athletics   Member NJCAA. *Intercollegiate sports:* baseball M, basketball M(s)/W(s), cross-country running M/W(s), field hockey W, golf M/W, soccer M/W, softball W, tennis M/W, track and field M/W, wrestling M.
Standardized Tests   *Required for some:* National League of Nursing Exam for most health-related programs.
Costs (2006–07)   *Tuition:* area resident $1957 full-time, $82 per credit part-time; state resident $4526 full-time, $189 per credit part-time. *Required fees:* $612 full-time, $26 per credit part-time.
Financial Aid   Of all full-time matriculated undergraduates who enrolled in 2004, 69 Federal Work-Study jobs (averaging $3350).
Applying   *Options:* early admission, deferred entrance. *Application fee:* $25. *Required:* high school transcript. *Application deadline:* rolling (freshmen), rolling (transfers). *Notification:* continuous (freshmen).
Director of Admissions   Mr. Peter W. Rice, Director of Admissions and Recruitment, Middlesex County College, 2600 Woodbridge Avenue, PO Box 3050, Edison, NJ 08818-3050. *Phone:* 732-906-4243.

▶ See page 578 for the College Close-Up.

OCEAN COUNTY COLLEGE

Toms River, New Jersey   www.ocean.edu/

- **County-supported** 2-year, founded 1964, part of New Jersey Commission on Higher Education
- **Small-town** 275-acre campus with easy access to Philadelphia
- **Coed,** 8,449 undergraduate students, 48% full-time, 59% women, 41% men

Undergraduates   4,023 full-time, 4,426 part-time. Students come from 6 other countries, 4% African American, 2% Asian American or Pacific Islander, 6%

Hispanic American, 0.3% Native American, 0.4% international.
Freshmen   *Admission:* 1,876 enrolled.
Faculty   *Total:* 410, 29% full-time.
Majors   Accounting; administrative assistant and secretarial science; business administration and management; business/commerce; child care and support services management; civil engineering technology; clinical/medical laboratory technology; commercial and advertising art; communications technology; computer and information sciences; computer programming; construction engineering technology; criminal justice/police science; electrical, electronic and communications engineering technology; engineering; fire protection and safety technology; general studies; health science; information science/studies; journalism; legal assistant/paralegal; liberal arts and sciences/liberal studies; medical/clinical assistant; nursing (registered nurse training); real estate; social work; teacher assistant/aide.
Academics   *Calendar:* semesters. *Degree:* certificates, diplomas, and associate. *Special study options:* academic remediation for entering students, accelerated degree program, adult/continuing education programs, advanced placement credit, cooperative education, distance learning, English as a second language, freshman honors college, honors programs, part-time degree program, services for LD students, study abroad, summer session for credit.
Library   Ocean County College Library with 74,215 titles, 428 serial subscriptions.
Computers on Campus   100 computers available on campus for general student use. Internet access, at least one staffed computer lab available.
Student Life   *Housing:* college housing not available. *Activities and Organizations:* drama/theater group, student-run newspaper, radio station, choral group. *Campus security:* 24-hour emergency response devices and patrols, late-night transport/escort service. *Student services:* health clinic, personal/psychological counseling.
Athletics   Member NJCAA. *Intercollegiate sports:* baseball M, basketball M/W, golf M/W, soccer M/W, softball W, swimming and diving M/W, tennis M/W. *Intramural sports:* basketball M/W, cross-country running M, tennis M/W, volleyball M/W.
Costs (2006–07)   *Tuition:* area resident $2460 full-time, $82 per credit part-time; state resident $3360 full-time, $112 per credit part-time; nonresident $5520 full-time, $184 per credit part-time. *Required fees:* $720 full-time, $24 per credit part-time.
Financial Aid   Of all full-time matriculated undergraduates who enrolled in 2004, 76 Federal Work-Study jobs (averaging $1300). 45 state and other part-time jobs (averaging $850).
Applying   *Options:* early admission, deferred entrance. *Application fee:* $15. *Required for some:* high school transcript. *Application deadline:* rolling (freshmen), rolling (transfers). *Notification:* continuous (freshmen).
Freshmen Application Contact   Ms. Mary Fennessy, Director of Admissions and Records, Ocean County College, College Drive, PO Box 2001, Toms River, NJ 08754-2001. *Phone:* 732-255-0304 Ext. 2423.

PASSAIC COUNTY COMMUNITY COLLEGE

Paterson, New Jersey   www.pccc.cc.nj.us/

Director of Admissions   Mr. Patrick Noonan, Director of Admissions, Passaic County Community College, One College Boulevard, Patterson, NJ 07505. *Phone:* 973-684-6304.

RARITAN VALLEY COMMUNITY COLLEGE

Somerville, New Jersey   www.raritanval.edu/

- **County-supported** 2-year, founded 1965
- **Small-town** 225-acre campus with easy access to New York City and Philadelphia
- **Coed,** 6,251 undergraduate students, 41% full-time, 58% women, 42% men

Undergraduates   2,575 full-time, 3,676 part-time. 7% are from out of state, 8% African American, 8% Asian American or Pacific Islander, 11% Hispanic American, 0.2% Native American, 3% international, 8% transferred in. *Retention:* 66% of 2003 full-time freshmen returned.
Freshmen   *Admission:* 2,433 applied, 1,646 admitted, 1,018 enrolled.
Faculty   *Total:* 401, 25% full-time, 23% with terminal degrees. *Student/faculty ratio:* 19:1.
Majors   Accounting; administrative assistant and secretarial science; aeronautics/aviation/aerospace science and technology; artificial intelligence and robotics; automobile/automotive mechanics technology; biology/biological sciences; busi-

ness administration and management; chemistry; commercial and advertising art; computer programming; computer science; construction engineering technology; consumer merchandising/retailing management; criminal justice/law enforcement administration; data processing and data processing technology; diesel mechanics technology; dramatic/theater arts; education; electrical, electronic and communications engineering technology; electromechanical technology; elementary education; engineering; environmental studies; heating, air conditioning, ventilation and refrigeration maintenance technology; hospitality and recreation marketing; hotel/motel administration; human services; industrial technology; information science/studies; intermedia/multimedia; international business/trade/commerce; kindergarten/preschool education; legal assistant/paralegal; liberal arts and sciences/liberal studies; management information systems; marketing/marketing management; mathematics; mechanical design technology; music; nursing (registered nurse training); ophthalmic laboratory technology; real estate; respiratory care therapy; social sciences; tourism and travel services management; visual and performing arts.

Academics *Calendar:* semesters. *Degree:* certificates and associate. *Special study options:* academic remediation for entering students, adult/continuing education programs, advanced placement credit, cooperative education, distance learning, English as a second language, honors programs, independent study, internships, off-campus study, part-time degree program, services for LD students, summer session for credit. *ROTC:* Army (c), Air Force (c).

Library Evelyn S. Field Learning Resources Center with 82,942 titles, 354 serial subscriptions, 1,140 audiovisual materials, an OPAC, a Web page.

Computers on Campus 844 computers available on campus for general student use. A campuswide network can be accessed from off campus that provide access to library services, degree audits, grades, class schedules. Internet access, online (class) registration, at least one staffed computer lab available.

Student Life *Housing:* college housing not available. *Activities and Organizations:* drama/theater group, student-run newspaper, choral group, International Club, The Latin Pride Club, Student Nurses Association, The Record (student newspaper), Christian Fellowship Club. *Campus security:* 24-hour emergency response devices and patrols, 24-hour outdoor surveillance cameras. *Student services:* personal/psychological counseling.

Athletics Member NJCAA. *Intercollegiate sports:* baseball M, basketball M, softball W. *Intramural sports:* golf M/W.

Costs (2006–07) *Tuition:* state resident $2430 full-time, $81 per credit part-time; nonresident $2430 full-time, $81 per credit part-time. *Required fees:* $850 full-time, $23 per credit part-time, $80 per term part-time.

Financial Aid Of all full-time matriculated undergraduates who enrolled in 2004, 12 Federal Work-Study jobs (averaging $2500).

Applying *Options:* electronic application, early admission. *Application fee:* $25. *Required:* high school transcript. *Application deadline:* rolling (freshmen), rolling (transfers).

Freshmen Application Contact Mr. Richard Cole, Registrar, Enrollment Services, Raritan Valley Community College, PO Box 3300, Somerville, NJ 08876-1265. *Phone:* 908-526-1200 Ext. 8206. *Fax:* 908-704-3442. *E-mail:* rcole@raritanval.edu.

SALEM COMMUNITY COLLEGE

Carneys Point, New Jersey   www.salemcc.org/

- **County-supported** 2-year, founded 1972, part of New Jersey Commission on Higher Education
- **Small-town** campus with easy access to Philadelphia
- **Coed,** 1,251 undergraduate students, 48% full-time, 64% women, 36% men

Undergraduates 598 full-time, 653 part-time. Students come from 6 states and territories, 15% are from out of state, 22% African American, 0.5% Asian American or Pacific Islander, 4% Hispanic American, 1% Native American, 5% international, 3% transferred in.
Freshmen *Admission:* 279 enrolled.
Faculty *Total:* 66, 33% full-time, 6% with terminal degrees. *Student/faculty ratio:* 19:1.
Majors Accounting; biological and physical sciences; biology/biological sciences; business administration and management; chemistry; computer and information sciences; computer systems networking and telecommunications; criminal justice/law enforcement administration; early childhood education; education; English; family and community services; health and physical education; history; humanities; human resources management; journalism; kinesiology and exercise science; liberal arts and sciences/liberal studies; management information systems; marketing/marketing management; mathematics; physics; political science and government; pre-engineering; psychology; public administration; social sciences; sociology; web/multimedia management and webmaster.
Academics *Calendar:* semesters. *Degree:* certificates and associate. *Special study options:* academic remediation for entering students, adult/continuing education programs, advanced placement credit, cooperative education, distance

learning, double majors, English as a second language, independent study, off-campus study, part-time degree program, services for LD students, summer session for credit.

Library Michael S. Cettei Memorial Library with 28,951 titles, 240 serial subscriptions, an OPAC.

Computers on Campus 200 computers available on campus for general student use. A campuswide network can be accessed from off campus. Internet access, online (class) registration, at least one staffed computer lab available.

Student Life *Housing:* college housing not available. *Activities and Organizations:* choral group, Drama Club, Science Club, Multicultural Exchange Club. *Campus security:* 24-hour emergency response devices and patrols, late-night transport/escort service. *Student services:* personal/psychological counseling, women's center.

Athletics Member NJCAA. *Intercollegiate sports:* baseball M(s), basketball M(s)/W(s), softball W(s), tennis M(s)/W(s).

Costs (2005–06) *Tuition:* area resident $2385 full-time, $80 per credit part-time; state resident $2685 full-time, $90 per credit part-time; nonresident $2685 full-time, $90 per credit part-time. Full-time tuition and fees vary according to course load. Part-time tuition and fees vary according to course load. *Required fees:* $920 full-time, $29 per credit part-time, $25 per term part-time. *Payment plans:* installment, deferred payment. *Waivers:* senior citizens and employees or children of employees.

Financial Aid Of all full-time matriculated undergraduates who enrolled in 2004, 63 Federal Work-Study jobs (averaging $1000).

Applying *Options:* early admission, deferred entrance. *Application fee:* $25. *Required:* essay or personal statement, high school transcript. *Application deadline:* rolling (freshmen), rolling (transfers). *Notification:* continuous (freshmen).

Freshmen Application Contact Dr. Reva Curry, Vice President of Student Services, Salem Community College, 460 Hollywood Avenue, Carney's Point, NJ 08069. *Phone:* 856-351-2707. *Fax:* 856-299-9193. *E-mail:* info@salemcc.edu.

SOMERSET CHRISTIAN COLLEGE

Zarephath, New Jersey   www.somerset.edu/

Director of Admissions Ms. Cheryl L. Burdick, Dean of Enrollment Management, Somerset Christian College, 10 Liberty Square, Zarephath, NJ 08890. *Phone:* 732-356-1595 Ext. 106. *Toll-free phone:* 800-234-9305. *Fax:* 732-356-4846.

SUSSEX COUNTY COMMUNITY COLLEGE

Newton, New Jersey   www.sussex.edu/

- **State and locally supported** 2-year, founded 1981, part of New Jersey Commission on Higher Education
- **Small-town** 160-acre campus with easy access to New York City
- **Endowment** $883,431
- **Coed,** 3,461 undergraduate students, 49% full-time, 60% women, 40% men

Undergraduates 1,706 full-time, 1,755 part-time. Students come from 3 states and territories, 12% are from out of state, 2% African American, 1% Asian American or Pacific Islander, 6% Hispanic American, 0.3% Native American, 0.6% international, 5% transferred in. *Retention:* 46% of 2003 full-time freshmen returned.
Freshmen *Admission:* 629 applied, 629 admitted, 629 enrolled.
Faculty *Total:* 233, 18% full-time, 15% with terminal degrees. *Student/faculty ratio:* 22:1.
Majors Accounting; administrative assistant and secretarial science; automotive engineering technology; biological and physical sciences; broadcast journalism; business administration and management; commercial and advertising art; computer and information sciences; consumer merchandising/retailing management; corrections and criminal justice related; English; environmental studies; fine/studio arts; fire protection related; health science; human services; journalism; legal assistant/paralegal; liberal arts and sciences/liberal studies; respiratory care therapy; veterinary/animal health technology.
Academics *Calendar:* semesters. *Degree:* certificates and associate. *Special study options:* academic remediation for entering students, advanced placement credit, distance learning, double majors, English as a second language, internships, part-time degree program, services for LD students, summer session for credit.
Library Sussex County Community College Library with 34,346 titles, 266 serial subscriptions, 602 audiovisual materials, an OPAC, a Web page.

Sussex County Community College (continued)

Computers on Campus 302 computers available on campus for general student use. A campuswide network can be accessed. Internet access, online (class) registration, at least one staffed computer lab available.

Student Life *Housing:* college housing not available. *Activities and Organizations:* drama/theater group, student-run newspaper, choral group, Student Government Association, "The College Hill" (newspaper), Human Services Club, Arts Club, Returning Adult Support Group. *Campus security:* late-night transport/escort service, trained security personnel. *Student services:* personal/psychological counseling, women's center.

Athletics Member NJCAA. *Intercollegiate sports:* baseball M, basketball M, soccer M/W, softball W. *Intramural sports:* football M/W, volleyball M/W.

Costs (2006–07) *Tuition:* area resident $2310 full-time, $77 per credit part-time; state resident $4620 full-time, $154 per credit part-time; nonresident $4620 full-time, $154 per credit part-time. *Required fees:* $510 full-time, $13 per credit part-time, $15 per term part-time.

Financial Aid Of all full-time matriculated undergraduates who enrolled in 2004, 29 Federal Work-Study jobs (averaging $1500).

Applying *Application fee:* $15. *Required:* high school transcript. *Application deadline:* rolling (freshmen), rolling (transfers). *Notification:* continuous (freshmen).

Freshmen Application Contact Mr. James Donohue, Director of Admissions and Registrar, Sussex County Community College, 1 College Hill, Newton, NJ 07860. *Phone:* 973-300-2219. *E-mail:* hdamato@sussex.cc.nj.us.

UNION COUNTY COLLEGE
Cranford, New Jersey   www.ucc.edu/

- **State and locally supported** 2-year, founded 1933, part of New Jersey Commission on Higher Education
- **Suburban** 48-acre campus with easy access to New York City
- **Endowment** $7.2 million
- **Coed,** 10,976 undergraduate students, 49% full-time, 65% women, 35% men

Undergraduates 5,327 full-time, 5,649 part-time. Students come from 8 states and territories, 82 other countries, 2% are from out of state, 24% African American, 6% Asian American or Pacific Islander, 25% Hispanic American, 0.4% Native American, 3% international, 9% transferred in. *Retention:* 77% of 2003 full-time freshmen returned.
Freshmen *Admission:* 6,593 applied, 6,473 admitted, 1,134 enrolled.

Faculty *Total:* 443, 42% full-time. *Student/faculty ratio:* 25:1.

Majors Accounting technology and bookkeeping; administrative assistant and secretarial science; allied health diagnostic, intervention, and treatment professions related; biology/biological sciences; business administration and management; business and personal/financial services marketing; business/commerce; chemistry; civil engineering technology; clinical/medical laboratory technology; communication/speech communication and rhetoric; criminal justice/police science; dental hygiene; electromechanical technology; engineering; fire protection and safety technology; gerontology; hotel/motel administration; industrial technology; information science/studies; language interpretation and translation; liberal arts and sciences/liberal studies; management information systems; mechanical engineering/mechanical technology; medical/clinical assistant; medical radiologic technology; nuclear medical technology; nursing (licensed practical/vocational nurse training); nursing (registered nurse training); occupational therapist assistant; physical sciences; physical therapist assistant; rehabilitation and therapeutic professions related; respiratory care therapy; sign language interpretation and translation.

Academics *Calendar:* semesters. *Degree:* certificates, diplomas, and associate. *Special study options:* academic remediation for entering students, accelerated degree program, adult/continuing education programs, advanced placement credit, distance learning, English as a second language, honors programs, independent study, internships, off-campus study, part-time degree program, services for LD students, student-designed majors, summer session for credit. *ROTC:* Air Force (c).

Library MacKay Library plus 2 others with 135,783 titles, 2,609 serial subscriptions, 3,455 audiovisual materials, an OPAC, a Web page.

Computers on Campus 881 computers available on campus for general student use. A campuswide network can be accessed from off campus. Internet access, at least one staffed computer lab available.

Student Life *Housing:* college housing not available. *Activities and Organizations:* drama/theater group, student-run newspaper, radio and television station, SIGN, Spanish Club, Black Students Heritage Organization, Student Government Organization, International Cultural Exchange Students. *Campus security:* 24-hour emergency response devices and patrols, late-night transport/escort service. *Student services:* personal/psychological counseling.

Athletics Member NJCAA. *Intercollegiate sports:* baseball M, basketball M/W(s), golf M/W, soccer M, volleyball W. *Intramural sports:* cheerleading W.

Costs (2006–07) *Tuition:* area resident $2460 full-time, $82 per credit part-time; state resident $4920 full-time, $164 per credit part-time. *Required fees:* $780 full-time.

Financial Aid Of all full-time matriculated undergraduates who enrolled in 2004, 150 Federal Work-Study jobs (averaging $1700).

Applying *Options:* electronic application, early admission, deferred entrance. *Application fee:* $30. *Required:* high school transcript. *Required for some:* interview. *Application deadline:* rolling (freshmen), rolling (transfers). *Notification:* continuous (freshmen).

Freshmen Application Contact Ms. Jo Ann Davis-Wayne, Director of Admissions, Records, and Registration, Union County College, 1033 Springfield Avenue, Cranford, NJ 07016. *Phone:* 908-709-7127. *Fax:* 908-709-7125.

WARREN COUNTY COMMUNITY COLLEGE
Washington, New Jersey   www.warren.edu/

Freshmen Application Contact Admissions Advisor, Warren County Community College, 475 Route 57 West, Washington, NJ 07882-9605. *Phone:* 908-835-2300.

NEW MEXICO

THE ART CENTER DESIGN COLLEGE
Albuquerque, New Mexico   www.theartcenter.edu/

Director of Admissions Ms. Colleen Gimbel-Froebe, Associate Director of Admissions and Placement, The Art Center Design College, 5000 Marble NE, Albuquerque, NM 87110. *Phone:* 520-325-0123. *Toll-free phone:* 800-825-8753.

CENTRAL NEW MEXICO COMMUNITY COLLEGE
Albuquerque, New Mexico   www.tvi.cc.nm.us/

- **State-supported** 2-year, founded 1965
- **Urban** 60-acre campus
- **Endowment** $1.2 million
- **Coed,** 23,107 undergraduate students, 30% full-time, 59% women, 41% men

Undergraduates 6,925 full-time, 16,182 part-time. 1% are from out of state, 3% African American, 2% Asian American or Pacific Islander, 42% Hispanic American, 8% Native American, 0.3% international, 8% transferred in.
Freshmen *Admission:* 4,388 applied, 4,388 admitted, 2,840 enrolled.

Faculty *Total:* 1,085, 31% full-time. *Student/faculty ratio:* 21:1.

Majors Accounting; administrative assistant and secretarial science; architectural drafting and CAD/CADD; banking and financial support services; biotechnology; building/construction finishing, management, and inspection related; business administration and management; child care and support services management; clinical/medical laboratory technology; computer systems analysis; construction trades related; cosmetology; court reporting; criminal justice/safety; culinary arts; data processing and data processing technology; diagnostic medical sonography and ultrasound technology; electrical, electronic and communications engineering technology; electrical/electronics drafting and CAD/CADD; elementary education; engineering; engineering technologies related; environmental/environmental health engineering; fire protection and safety technology; health information/medical records administration; hospitality administration; industrial technology; information science/studies; laser and optical technology; legal assistant/paralegal; liberal arts and sciences/liberal studies; nursing (registered nurse training); parks, recreation, and leisure related; respiratory care therapy; vehicle maintenance and repair technologies related.

Academics *Calendar:* trimesters. *Degree:* associate. *Special study options:* academic remediation for entering students, adult/continuing education programs, advanced placement credit, cooperative education, distance learning, double majors, English as a second language, internships, part-time degree program, services for LD students, summer session for credit. *ROTC:* Air Force (c).

Library Main Campus Library with an OPAC, a Web page.

Computers on Campus A campuswide network can be accessed. Internet access, at least one staffed computer lab available.

Student Life *Housing:* college housing not available. *Activities and Organizations:* student-run newspaper, Phi Theta Kappa, student government, Hispanic Club, TVI Times (student newspaper). *Campus security:* 24-hour emergency response devices and patrols, late-night transport/escort service. *Student services:* health clinic, personal/psychological counseling.

Costs (2006–07) *Tuition:* area resident $1490 full-time, $41 per credit hour part-time; state resident $1796 full-time, $50 per credit hour part-time; nonresident $7945 full-time, $221 per credit hour part-time. *Required fees:* $90 full-time, $30 per term part-time.

Financial Aid Of all full-time matriculated undergraduates who enrolled in 2004, 175 Federal Work-Study jobs (averaging $6000). 225 state and other part-time jobs (averaging $6000).

Applying *Options:* electronic application, early admission. *Recommended:* high school transcript. *Application deadline:* rolling (freshmen), rolling (transfers). *Notification:* continuous (freshmen).

Freshmen Application Contact Ms. Jane Campbell, Director, Enrollment Services, Central New Mexico Community College, 900 University, SE, Albuquerque, NM 87106-4096. *Phone:* 505-224-3160. *Fax:* 505-224-3237.

CLOVIS COMMUNITY COLLEGE

Clovis, New Mexico   **www.clovis.edu/**

- **State-supported** 2-year, founded 1990
- **Small-town** 25-acre campus
- **Endowment** $558,291
- **Coed,** 3,937 undergraduate students, 17% full-time, 65% women, 35% men

Undergraduates 688 full-time, 3,249 part-time. Students come from 47 states and territories, 29% are from out of state, 5% African American, 2% Asian American or Pacific Islander, 37% Hispanic American, 1% Native American, 5% transferred in. *Retention:* 55% of 2003 full-time freshmen returned. Freshmen *Admission:* 648 applied, 648 admitted, 241 enrolled.

Faculty *Total:* 184, 27% full-time, 11% with terminal degrees. *Student/faculty ratio:* 15:1.

Majors Accounting; administrative assistant and secretarial science; automobile/automotive mechanics technology; bilingual and multilingual education; business administration and management; business automation/technology/data entry; commercial and advertising art; computer and information sciences; computer typography and composition equipment operation; corrections; cosmetology; criminal justice/police science; electromechanical technology; executive assistant/executive secretary; finance; fine/studio arts; health and physical education; heating, air conditioning, ventilation and refrigeration maintenance technology; legal administrative assistant/secretary; legal assistant/paralegal; liberal arts and sciences/liberal studies; library assistant; management information systems; mathematics; medical administrative assistant and medical secretary; medical office assistant; medical radiologic technology; nail technician and manicurist; nursing (registered nurse training); physical sciences; psychology; sign language interpretation and translation; teacher assistant/aide; technical and business writing; web/multimedia management and webmaster; web page, digital/multimedia and information resources design.

Academics *Calendar:* semesters. *Degree:* certificates and associate. *Special study options:* academic remediation for entering students, advanced placement credit, cooperative education, distance learning, double majors, English as a second language, independent study, internships, part-time degree program, services for LD students, summer session for credit.

Library Clovis Community College Library and Learning Resources Center with 52,000 titles, 370 serial subscriptions, 2,900 audiovisual materials, an OPAC.

Computers on Campus 280 computers available on campus for general student use. A campuswide network can be accessed. Internet access, at least one staffed computer lab available.

Student Life *Housing:* college housing not available. *Activities and Organizations:* drama/theater group, choral group, Student Senate, Student Nursing Association, Black Advisory Council, Hispanic Advisory Council, student ambassadors. *Campus security:* student patrols, late-night transport/escort service. *Student services:* personal/psychological counseling.

Athletics *Intramural sports:* basketball M/W, cross-country running M/W, racquetball M/W, tennis M/W, volleyball M/W.

Costs (2006–07) *Tuition:* area resident $736 full-time, $29 per credit hour part-time; state resident $784 full-time, $31 per credit hour part-time; nonresident

$1480 full-time, $60 per credit hour part-time. *Required fees:* $36 full-time, $3 per credit part-time, $20 per term part-time.

Applying *Options:* common application. *Required:* high school transcript. *Required for some:* interview.

Freshmen Application Contact Ms. Rosie Corrie, Director of Admissions and Records/Registrar, Clovis Community College, 417 Schepps Boulevard, Clovis, NM 88101-8381. *Phone:* 505-769-4962. *Fax:* 505-769-4190. *E-mail:* admissions@clovis.edu.

CROWNPOINT INSTITUTE OF TECHNOLOGY

Crownpoint, New Mexico

DOÑA ANA BRANCH COMMUNITY COLLEGE

Las Cruces, New Mexico   **dabcc-www.nmsu.edu/**

- **State and locally supported** 2-year, founded 1973, part of New Mexico State University System
- **Urban** 15-acre campus with easy access to Ciudad Juárez and El Paso
- **Coed**

Undergraduates 3,596 full-time, 2,751 part-time. 2% African American, 0.8% Asian American or Pacific Islander, 63% Hispanic American, 2% Native American, 0.8% international, 3% transferred in. *Retention:* 80% of 2003 full-time freshmen returned.

Faculty *Student/faculty ratio:* 30:1.

Academics *Calendar:* semesters. *Degree:* certificates and associate. *Special study options:* academic remediation for entering students, adult/continuing education programs, advanced placement credit, cooperative education, English as a second language, freshman honors college, honors programs, internships, part-time degree program, services for LD students, summer session for credit. *ROTC:* Army (c), Air Force (c).

Student Life *Campus security:* 24-hour emergency response devices and patrols, late-night transport/escort service.

Standardized Tests *Recommended:* ACT, ACT ASSET, or ACT COMPASS.

Costs (2005–06) *Tuition:* area resident $1080 full-time, $45 per credit part-time; state resident $1320 full-time, $55 per credit part-time; nonresident $3240 full-time, $135 per credit part-time.

Financial Aid Of all full-time matriculated undergraduates who enrolled in 2004, 15 Federal Work-Study jobs (averaging $2800). 106 state and other part-time jobs (averaging $2800). *Financial aid deadline:* 6/30.

Applying *Options:* deferred entrance. *Application fee:* $15. *Required:* high school transcript. *Required for some:* letters of recommendation.

Freshmen Application Contact Admissions Counselor, Doña Ana Branch Community College, MSC-3DA, Box 30001, Las Cruces, NM 88003-8001. *Phone:* 505-527-7532. *Toll-free phone:* 800-903-7503.

EASTERN NEW MEXICO UNIVERSITY—ROSWELL

Roswell, New Mexico   **www.enmu.edu/**

Freshmen Application Contact Mr. James Mares, Assistant Director, Eastern New Mexico University–Roswell, PO Box 6000, Roswell, NM 88202-6000. *Phone:* 505-624-7149. *Toll-free phone:* 800-243-6687.

INSTITUTE OF AMERICAN INDIAN ARTS

Santa Fe, New Mexico   **www.iaia.edu/**

- **Federally supported** primarily 2-year, founded 1962
- **Urban** 120-acre campus
- **Endowment** $4.0 million
- **Coed**

Undergraduates 156 full-time, 27 part-time. Students come from 29 states and territories, 1% Asian American or Pacific Islander, 88% Native American. *Retention:* 46% of 2003 full-time freshmen returned.

Institute of American Indian Arts (continued)

Faculty *Student/faculty ratio:* 13:1.

Academics *Calendar:* semesters. *Degrees:* associate and bachelor's. *Special study options:* academic remediation for entering students, internships, off-campus study.

Student Life *Campus security:* 24-hour patrols, late-night transport/escort service.

Standardized Tests *Recommended:* ACT (for placement).

Costs (2005–06) *Tuition:* state resident $2400 full-time, $100 per credit hour part-time; nonresident $2400 full-time, $100 per credit hour part-time. *Required fees:* $200 full-time, $20 per term part-time. *Room and board:* $4648; room only: $2212. Room and board charges vary according to housing facility.

Applying *Options:* deferred entrance. *Required:* high school transcript, minimum 2.0 GPA, 3 letters of recommendation. *Recommended:* interview.

Director of Admissions Myra Garro, Manager of Enrollment and Admissions, Institute of American Indian Arts, 83 Avan Nu Po Road, Santa Fe, NM 87508. *Phone:* 505-424-2328.

INTERNATIONAL INSTITUTE OF THE AMERICAS

Albuquerque, New Mexico   **www.aibtonline.com/**

- **Independent** primarily 2-year
- **Urban** 1-acre campus
- **Coed,** 232 undergraduate students, 100% full-time, 80% women, 20% men

Undergraduates 232 full-time. 3% African American, 1% Asian American or Pacific Islander, 67% Hispanic American, 13% Native American. *Retention:* 100% of 2003 full-time freshmen returned.

Faculty *Total:* 19, 68% full-time, 21% with terminal degrees. *Student/faculty ratio:* 15:1.

Majors Accounting; business administration and management; criminal justice/law enforcement administration; health/health care administration; legal assistant/paralegal.

Academics *Calendar:* continuous. *Degrees:* diplomas, associate, and bachelor's.

Costs (2005–06) *One-time required fee:* $200. *Tuition:* $9850 full-time. *Required fees:* $350 full-time.

Applying *Required:* interview. *Application deadline:* rolling (freshmen), rolling (transfers). *Notification:* continuous (freshmen).

Freshmen Application Contact Mr. Ed Sigman, Campus Director, International Institute of the Americas, 4201 Central Avenue NW, Suite J, Albuquerque, NM 87105-1649. *Phone:* 505-880-2877. *Toll-free phone:* 888-660-2428. *Fax:* 505-352-0199. *E-mail:* esigman@iia.edu.

ITT TECHNICAL INSTITUTE

Albuquerque, New Mexico   **www.itt-tech.edu/**

- **Proprietary** primarily 2-year, founded 1989, part of ITT Educational Services, Inc
- **Coed**

Majors Animation, interactive technology, video graphics and special effects; business administration and management; computer and information systems security; computer programming; criminal justice/law enforcement administration; e-commerce; electrical, electronic and communications engineering technology; system, networking, and LAN/WAN management; web/multimedia management and webmaster; web page, digital/multimedia and information resources design.

Academics *Calendar:* quarters. *Degrees:* associate and bachelor's.

Library a Web page.

Computers on Campus Internet access, at least one staffed computer lab available.

Student Life *Housing:* college housing not available.

Standardized Tests *Required:* Wonderlic aptitude test (for admission).

Costs (2005–06) *Tuition:* Please see school catalog for specific information.

Applying *Options:* deferred entrance. *Application fee:* $100. *Required:* high school transcript, interview. *Recommended:* letters of recommendation. *Application deadline:* rolling (freshmen), rolling (transfers). *Notification:* continuous (freshmen).

Freshmen Application Contact Mr. John Crooks, Director of Recruitment, ITT Technical Institute, 5100 Masthead Street NE, Albuquerque, NM 87109. *Phone:* 505-828-1114. *Toll-free phone:* 800-636-1114.

LUNA COMMUNITY COLLEGE

Las Vegas, New Mexico   **www.luna.cc.nm.us/**

- **State-supported** 2-year
- **Rural** 25-acre campus
- **Endowment** $12,911
- **Coed**

Undergraduates 502 full-time, 1,539 part-time. 0.5% African American, 0.5% Asian American or Pacific Islander, 88% Hispanic American, 0.5% Native American.

Faculty *Student/faculty ratio:* 13:1.

Academics *Calendar:* semesters. *Degree:* certificates, diplomas, and associate. *Special study options:* academic remediation for entering students, cooperative education, distance learning, honors programs, independent study, part-time degree program.

Costs (2005–06) *Tuition:* area resident $600 full-time, $25 per credit hour part-time; state resident $888 full-time, $37 per credit hour part-time; nonresident $1824 full-time, $76 per credit hour part-time. Full-time tuition and fees vary according to course load, program, and reciprocity agreements. Part-time tuition and fees vary according to course load, program, and reciprocity agreements. *Required fees:* $44 full-time, $22 per term part-time. *Room and board:* Room and board charges vary according to housing facility.

Applying *Options:* common application, electronic application. *Required:* high school transcript.

Director of Admissions Ms. Henrietta Griego, Director of Admissions, Recruitment, and Retention, Luna Community College, 366 Luna Drive, Las Vegas, NM 87701. *Phone:* 505-454-2020 Ext. 1200. *Toll-free phone:* 800-588-7232 Ext. 1202. *E-mail:* hgriego@luna.cc.nm.us.

MESALANDS COMMUNITY COLLEGE

Tucumcari, New Mexico   **www.mesalands.edu/**

Director of Admissions Mr. Ken Brashear, Director of Enrollment Management, Mesalands Community College, 911 South Tenth Street, Tucumcari, NM 88401. *Phone:* 505-461-4413.

NATIONAL AMERICAN UNIVERSITY

Rio Rancho, New Mexico

NEW MEXICO JUNIOR COLLEGE

Hobbs, New Mexico   **www.nmjc.edu/**

Director of Admissions Mr. Robert Bensing, Dean of Enrollment Management, New Mexico Junior College, 5317 Lovington Highway, Hobbs, NM 88240-9123. *Phone:* 505-392-5092.

NEW MEXICO MILITARY INSTITUTE

Roswell, New Mexico   **www.nmmi.edu/**

- **State-supported** 2-year, founded 1891, part of New Mexico Commission on Higher Education
- **Small-town** 42-acre campus
- **Endowment** $298.5 million
- **Coed, primarily men,** 455 undergraduate students, 100% full-time, 16% women, 84% men

Excellence is a process achieved in stages, sustained through effort, accentuated by detail, and celebrated by all. At the New Mexico Military Institute (NMMI), excellence is a universal goal. For more than 100 years, NMMI has built a community and a world-class institute of higher learning based on shared values and disciplined behavior, which foster the highest standards of achievement in its cadets.

Undergraduates 455 full-time. Students come from 42 states and territories, 13 other countries, 55% are from out of state, 11% African American, 5% Asian American or Pacific Islander, 16% Hispanic American, 2% Native American, 3% international, 100% live on campus.

Freshmen *Admission:* 601 applied, 375 admitted. *Test scores:* ACT scores over 18: 89%; ACT scores over 24: 21%; ACT scores over 30: 1%.

Faculty *Total:* 69, 100% full-time. *Student/faculty ratio:* 7:1.

Majors Accounting; Army R.O.T.C./military science; art; biological and physical sciences; biology/biological sciences; business administration and management; chemistry; civil engineering technology; computer programming; computer science; criminal justice/law enforcement administration; criminal justice/police science; economics; engineering; English; finance; French; German; history; humanities; liberal arts and sciences/liberal studies; mathematics; physical education teaching and coaching; physics; pre-engineering; social sciences; Spanish; sport and fitness administration/management.

Academics *Calendar:* semesters. *Degree:* associate. *Special study options:* academic remediation for entering students, advanced placement credit, English as a second language, summer session for credit. *ROTC:* Army (b).

Library Paul Horgan Library plus 2 others with 65,000 titles, 200 serial subscriptions, an OPAC.

Computers on Campus 700 computers available on campus for general student use. A campuswide network can be accessed from student residence rooms and from off campus. Internet access, at least one staffed computer lab available. Computer purchase or lease plan available.

Student Life *Housing:* on-campus residence required through sophomore year. *Options:* coed. *Activities and Organizations:* drama/theater group, student-run newspaper, television station, choral group, marching band, band, chorus, drill teams, Officer's Club. *Campus security:* 24-hour emergency response devices and patrols, controlled dormitory access. *Student services:* health clinic, personal/psychological counseling.

Athletics Member NJCAA. *Intercollegiate sports:* baseball M(s), basketball M(s), fencing M/W, football M(s), golf M(s), riflery M/W, tennis M(s)/W(s), track and field M(s), volleyball W(s). *Intramural sports:* basketball M/W, bowling M/W, cross-country running M/W, fencing M/W, football M, golf M/W, racquetball M/W, riflery M/W, skiing (cross-country) M/W, skiing (downhill) M/W, soccer M/W, swimming and diving M/W, tennis M/W, track and field M/W, volleyball M/W, weight lifting M/W.

Standardized Tests *Required:* SAT or ACT (for admission).

Costs (2006–07) *Tuition:* state resident $1304 full-time; nonresident $4258 full-time. *Required fees:* $1558 full-time. *Room and board:* $3645.

Financial Aid Of all full-time matriculated undergraduates who enrolled in 2004, 15 Federal Work-Study jobs (averaging $181). 3 state and other part-time jobs (averaging $191).

Applying *Options:* early admission, deferred entrance. *Application fee:* $60. *Required:* high school transcript, minimum 2.0 GPA. *Application deadlines:* 8/1 (freshmen), 8/1 (transfers). *Notification:* continuous (freshmen).

Freshmen Application Contact Capt. Kerry Kiker, Associate Director of Admission, New Mexico Military Institute, 101 West College Boulevard, Roswell, NM 88201-5173. *Phone:* 505-624-8050. *Toll-free phone:* 800-421-5376. *Fax:* 505-624-8058. *E-mail:* admissions@nmmi.edu.

▶ **See page 584 for the College Close-Up.**

NEW MEXICO STATE UNIVERSITY– ALAMOGORDO

Alamogordo, New Mexico　　　　　**alamo.nmsu.edu/**

- **State-supported** 2-year, founded 1958, part of New Mexico State University System
- **Small-town** 540-acre campus
- **Coed,** 1,915 undergraduate students, 37% full-time, 66% women, 34% men

Undergraduates 714 full-time, 1,201 part-time. Students come from 5 other countries, 5% African American, 3% Asian American or Pacific Islander, 28% Hispanic American, 4% Native American, 1% international, 14% transferred in.

Freshmen *Admission:* 268 applied, 268 admitted, 268 enrolled.

Faculty *Total:* 98, 54% full-time. *Student/faculty ratio:* 14:1.

Majors Administrative assistant and secretarial science; business/commerce; clinical/medical laboratory technology; commercial and advertising art; criminal justice/safety; data processing and data processing technology; education; electrical, electronic and communications engineering technology; engineering; fire science; legal assistant/paralegal; liberal arts and sciences/liberal studies; nursing (registered nurse training); office occupations and clerical services; social work; teacher assistant/aide.

Academics *Calendar:* semesters. *Degree:* certificates and associate. *Special study options:* academic remediation for entering students, adult/continuing

education programs, advanced placement credit, distance learning, English as a second language, honors programs, internships, off-campus study, part-time degree program, services for LD students, student-designed majors, summer session for credit.

Library David H. Townsend Library with 39,000 titles, 350 serial subscriptions, an OPAC, a Web page.

Computers on Campus 200 computers available on campus for general student use. A campuswide network can be accessed from off campus. Internet access, online (class) registration, at least one staffed computer lab available.

Student Life *Housing:* college housing not available. *Activities and Organizations:* drama/theater group, choral group, Social Science Club, Phi Theta Kappa, Student/NEA, Christian Fellowship, Epsilon Tau Sigma. *Campus security:* 24-hour emergency response devices. *Student services:* personal/psychological counseling.

Athletics *Intramural sports:* basketball M/W, volleyball M/W.

Costs (2006–07) *Tuition:* area resident $1248 full-time, $52 per credit hour part-time; state resident $1416 full-time, $59 per credit hour part-time; nonresident $3960 full-time, $165 per credit hour part-time. *Required fees:* $48 full-time, $2 per credit hour part-time.

Financial Aid Of all full-time matriculated undergraduates who enrolled in 2004, 10 Federal Work-Study jobs (averaging $3300). 60 state and other part-time jobs (averaging $3300). *Financial aid deadline:* 5/1.

Applying *Options:* common application, electronic application, early admission, deferred entrance. *Application fee:* $15. *Required:* high school transcript, minimum 2.0 GPA. *Application deadline:* rolling (freshmen), rolling (transfers). *Notification:* continuous (freshmen).

Freshmen Application Contact Ms. Kathy Fuller, Coordinator of Admissions and Records, New Mexico State University–Alamogordo, 2400 North Scenic Drive, Alamogordo, NM 88311-0477. *Phone:* 505-439-3700. *E-mail:* advisor@nmsua.nmsu.edu.

NEW MEXICO STATE UNIVERSITY– CARLSBAD

Carlsbad, New Mexico　　　　　**www.cavern.nmsu.edu/**

Freshmen Application Contact Ms. Everal Shannon, Records Specialist, New Mexico State University–Carlsbad, 1500 University Drive, Carlsbad, NM 88220-3509. *Phone:* 505-234-9222.

NEW MEXICO STATE UNIVERSITY– GRANTS

Grants, New Mexico　　　　　**grants.nmsu.edu/**

Director of Admissions Ms. Irene Lutz, Campus Student Services Officer, New Mexico State University–Grants, 1500 3rd Street, Grants, NM 87020-2025. *Phone:* 505-287-7981.

NORTHERN NEW MEXICO COMMUNITY COLLEGE

Española, New Mexico　　　　　**www.nnmcc.edu/**

Director of Admissions Mr. Mike L. Costello, Registrar, Northern New Mexico Community College, 921 Paseo de Oñate, Española, NM 87532. *Phone:* 505-747-2193.

PIMA MEDICAL INSTITUTE

Albuquerque, New Mexico　　　　　**www.pmi.edu**

- **Proprietary** 2-year, founded 1985, part of Vocational Training Institutes, Inc
- **Urban** campus
- **Coed**

Undergraduates 576 full-time.

Faculty *Student/faculty ratio:* 20:1.

Pima Medical Institute (continued)

Academics *Calendar:* modular. *Degree:* certificates and associate. *Special study options:* academic remediation for entering students, cooperative education, internships, services for LD students.

Standardized Tests *Required:* Wonderlic Scholastic Level Exam (for admission).

Costs (2005–06) *Tuition:* Tuition varies depending on course.

Financial Aid Of all full-time matriculated undergraduates who enrolled in 2004, 6 Federal Work-Study jobs.

Applying *Options:* early admission. *Required:* interview. *Required for some:* high school transcript.

Freshmen Application Contact Admissions Office, Pima Medical Institute, 2201 San Pedro NE, Building 3, Suite 100, Albuquerque, NM 87110. *Phone:* 505-881-1234. *Toll-free phone:* 888-898-9048. *Fax:* 505-881-5329.

SAN JUAN COLLEGE

Farmington, New Mexico　　　　**www.sanjuancollege.edu/**

- **State-supported** 2-year, founded 1958, part of New Mexico Commission on Higher Education
- **Small-town** 698-acre campus
- **Endowment** $10.5 million
- **Coed,** 5,064 undergraduate students, 51% full-time, 60% women, 40% men

Undergraduates 2,606 full-time, 2,458 part-time. Students come from 18 states and territories, 7% are from out of state, 0.6% African American, 0.7% Asian American or Pacific Islander, 12% Hispanic American, 33% Native American, 0.3% international.

Freshmen *Admission:* 1,184 applied, 1,184 admitted, 838 enrolled.

Faculty *Total:* 320, 30% full-time. *Student/faculty ratio:* 19:1.

Majors Accounting technology and bookkeeping; administrative assistant and secretarial science; airline pilot and flight crew; anthropology; art; autobody/collision and repair technology; automobile/automotive mechanics technology; banking and financial support services; biology/biological sciences; business administration and management; carpentry; chemistry; commercial and advertising art; communication/speech communication and rhetoric; computer science; criminal justice/police science; criminal justice/safety; diesel mechanics technology; drafting and design technology; dramatic/theater arts; economics; education; engineering; English; fire protection and safety technology; foreign languages and literatures; general studies; geology/earth science; health information/medical records technology; history; human services; information science/studies; instrumentation technology; kindergarten/preschool education; legal assistant/paralegal; mathematics; music; nursing (registered nurse training); parks, recreation and leisure; philosophy; physical sciences; physical therapist assistant; physics; political science and government; pre-medical studies; psychology; public administration; real estate; social work; sociology; water quality and wastewater treatment management and recycling technology; welding technology.

Academics *Calendar:* semesters. *Degree:* certificates and associate. *Special study options:* academic remediation for entering students, adult/continuing education programs, advanced placement credit, cooperative education, distance learning, English as a second language, honors programs, independent study, internships, part-time degree program, services for LD students, summer session for credit.

Library San Juan College Library with 81,116 titles, 6,677 serial subscriptions, 1,779 audiovisual materials, an OPAC, a Web page.

Computers on Campus 900 computers available on campus for general student use. A campuswide network can be accessed from off campus. Internet access, online (class) registration, at least one staffed computer lab available.

Student Life *Housing:* college housing not available. *Activities and Organizations:* drama/theater group, student-run newspaper, radio station, choral group, national fraternities, national sororities. *Campus security:* 24-hour patrols, late-night transport/escort service. *Student services:* personal/psychological counseling.

Athletics *Intramural sports:* archery M/W, badminton M/W, basketball M/W, bowling M/W, cross-country running M/W, football M/W, golf M/W, racquetball M/W, rock climbing M/W, skiing (cross-country) M/W, skiing (downhill) M/W, soccer M/W, softball M/W, table tennis M/W, tennis M/W, volleyball M/W.

Costs (2006–07) *Tuition:* state resident $720 full-time, $30 per credit hour part-time; nonresident $960 full-time, $40 per credit hour part-time.

Financial Aid Of all full-time matriculated undergraduates who enrolled in 2004, 150 Federal Work-Study jobs (averaging $2500). 175 state and other part-time jobs (averaging $2500).

Applying *Options:* electronic application, early admission, deferred entrance. *Required:* high school transcript. *Application deadline:* rolling (freshmen), rolling (transfers). *Notification:* continuous (freshmen).

Freshmen Application Contact David Eppich, Vice President for Student Services, San Juan College, 4601 College Boulevard, Farmington, NM 87402. *Phone:* 505-566-3318.

SANTA FE COMMUNITY COLLEGE

Santa Fe, New Mexico　　　　**www.sfccnm.edu/**

Freshmen Application Contact Ms. Jennifer Nollette, Admissions Counselor, Santa Fe Community College, 6401 Richards Avenue, Santa Fe, NM 87505. *Phone:* 505-428-1410.

SOUTHWESTERN INDIAN POLYTECHNIC INSTITUTE

Albuquerque, New Mexico　　　　**www.sipi.bia.edu/**

Director of Admissions Ms. Myra Garro, Recruitment, Southwestern Indian Polytechnic Institute, PO Box 10146, Albuquerque, NM 87120-3103. *Phone:* 505-346-2362. *Toll-free phone:* 800-586-7474. *E-mail:* mgarro@sipi.bia.edu.

UNIVERSITY OF NEW MEXICO–GALLUP

Gallup, New Mexico　　　　**www.gallup.unm.edu/**

Director of Admissions Ms. Pearl A. Morris, Admissions Representative, University of New Mexico–Gallup, 200 College Road, Gallup, NM 87301-5603. *Phone:* 505-863-7576.

UNIVERSITY OF NEW MEXICO–LOS ALAMOS BRANCH

Los Alamos, New Mexico　　　　**www.la.unm.edu/**

Director of Admissions Ms. Anna Mae Apodaca, Associate Campus Director for Student Services, University of New Mexico–Los Alamos Branch, 4000 University Drive, Los Alamos, NM 87544-2233. *Phone:* 505-661-4692. *E-mail:* aapodaca@la.unm.edu.

UNIVERSITY OF NEW MEXICO–TAOS

Taos, New Mexico

UNIVERSITY OF NEW MEXICO–VALENCIA CAMPUS

Los Lunas, New Mexico　　　　**www.unm.edu/~unmvc/**

Director of Admissions Ms. Lucy Sanchez, Registrar, University of New Mexico–Valencia Campus, 280 La Entrada, Los Lunas, NM 87031-7633. *Phone:* 505-925-8580.

ADIRONDACK COMMUNITY COLLEGE

Queensbury, New York   www.sunyacc.edu/

- **State and locally supported** 2-year, founded 1960, part of State University of New York System
- **Small-town** 141-acre campus
- **Endowment** $1.0 million
- **Coed**

Undergraduates Students come from 5 states and territories, 5 other countries, 2% are from out of state.

Faculty *Student/faculty ratio:* 20:1.

Academics *Calendar:* semesters. *Degree:* certificates and associate. *Special study options:* academic remediation for entering students, accelerated degree program, adult/continuing education programs, advanced placement credit, cooperative education, double majors, external degree program, independent study, internships, part-time degree program, services for LD students, study abroad, summer session for credit.

Student Life *Campus security:* late-night transport/escort service, patrols by trained security personnel 8 a.m. to 10 p.m.

Athletics Member NJCAA.

Financial Aid Of all full-time matriculated undergraduates who enrolled in 2004, 98 Federal Work-Study jobs (averaging $462).

Applying *Options:* early admission, deferred entrance. *Application fee:* $30. *Required:* high school transcript. *Required for some:* minimum 2.0 GPA.

Freshmen Application Contact Office of Admissions, Adirondack Community College, 640 Bay Road, Queensbury, NY 12804. *Phone:* 518-743-2264. *Fax:* 518-743-2200.

AMERICAN ACADEMY MCALLISTER INSTITUTE OF FUNERAL SERVICE

New York, New York   www.a-a-m-i.org/

Freshmen Application Contact Mr. Norman Provost, Registrar, American Academy McAllister Institute of Funeral Service, 450 West 56th Street, New York, NY 10019-3602. *Phone:* 212-757-1190.

AMERICAN ACADEMY OF DRAMATIC ARTS

New York, New York   www.aada.org/

- **Independent** 2-year, founded 1884
- **Urban** campus
- **Endowment** $4.9 million
- **Coed,** 220 undergraduate students, 100% full-time, 63% women, 37% men

Undergraduates 220 full-time. Students come from 2 states and territories, 14 other countries, 84% are from out of state, 4% African American, 3% Asian American or Pacific Islander, 6% Hispanic American, 18% international. *Retention:* 61% of 2003 full-time freshmen returned.

Freshmen *Admission:* 349 applied, 132 admitted, 56 enrolled. *Average high school GPA:* 2.86.

Faculty *Total:* 26, 27% full-time, 12% with terminal degrees. *Student/faculty ratio:* 16:1.

Majors Dramatic/theater arts.

Academics *Calendar:* continuous. *Degree:* certificates and associate.

Library Academy/CBS Library with 7,467 titles, 24 serial subscriptions, 570 audiovisual materials.

Computers on Campus 2 computers available on campus for general student use. A campuswide network can be accessed. Internet access available.

Student Life *Housing:* college housing not available. *Campus security:* 24-hour emergency response devices, trained security guard during hours of operation.

Costs (2006–07) *Tuition:* $16,900 full-time. *Required fees:* $500 full-time.

Financial Aid Of all full-time matriculated undergraduates who enrolled in 2004, 40 Federal Work-Study jobs (averaging $3500). 10 state and other part-time jobs (averaging $2000). *Financial aid deadline:* 5/15.

Applying *Options:* deferred entrance. *Application fee:* $50. *Required:* essay or personal statement, high school transcript, minimum 2.00 GPA, 2 letters of recommendation, interview, audition. *Required for some:* high school transcript. *Recommended:* high school transcript. *Application deadline:* rolling (freshmen), rolling (transfers). *Notification:* continuous (freshmen).

Freshmen Application Contact Ms. Karen Higginbotham, Director of Admissions, American Academy of Dramatic Arts, 120 Madison Avenue, New York, NY 10016. *Toll-free phone:* 800-463-8990. *Fax:* 212-696-1284. *E-mail:* admissions-ny@aada.org.

► **See page 460 for the College Close-Up.**

THE ART INSTITUTE OF NEW YORK CITY

New York, New York   www.ainyc.aii.edu/

- **Proprietary** 2-year, founded 1980, part of Education Management Corporation
- **Urban** campus
- **Coed,** 1,477 undergraduate students

Undergraduates Students come from 3 states and territories, 25% are from out of state, 30% African American, 7% Asian American or Pacific Islander, 30% Hispanic American, 2% Native American.

Freshmen *Average high school GPA:* 2.5.

Faculty *Total:* 98, 81% full-time, 5% with terminal degrees. *Student/faculty ratio:* 16:1.

Majors Animation, interactive technology, video graphics and special effects; cinematography and film/video production; fashion/apparel design; graphic design; restaurant, culinary, and catering management.

Academics *Calendar:* quarters. *Degree:* certificates, diplomas, and associate. *Special study options:* academic remediation for entering students, advanced placement credit, cooperative education, internships, summer session for credit.

Library Metropolitan College of NYC.

Computers on Campus 20 computers available on campus for general student use. Internet access, at least one staffed computer lab available.

Student Life *Housing:* college housing not available.

Costs (2005–06) *Tuition:* $431 per credit part-time. Full-time tuition and fees vary according to course load and degree level. Part-time tuition and fees vary according to course load and degree level. No tuition increase for student's term of enrollment. Contact school directly as tuition and fees vary according to program. *Payment plans:* tuition prepayment, installment. *Waivers:* children of alumni and employees or children of employees.

Applying *Options:* common application. *Application fee:* $50. *Required:* essay or personal statement, high school transcript, interview. *Application deadline:* rolling (freshmen), rolling (transfers). *Notification:* continuous (freshmen).

Freshmen Application Contact The Art Institute of New York City, 75 Varick Street, 16th Floor, New York, NY 10013-1917. *Phone:* 212-226-5500. *Toll-free phone:* 800-654-2433. *Fax:* 212-966-0706.

► **See page 478 for the College Close-Up.**

ASA INSTITUTE, THE COLLEGE OF ADVANCED TECHNOLOGY

Brooklyn, New York   www.asa-institute.com/

Director of Admissions Ms. Alice Perez, Director of Admissions, ASA Institute, The College of Advanced Technology, 151 Lawrence Street, 2nd Floor, Brooklyn, NY 11201. *Phone:* 718-534-0773. *Fax:* 718-522-7251. *E-mail:* alice_perez@asa-institute.com.

BERKELEY COLLEGE-NEW YORK CITY CAMPUS

New York, New York　　　**www.berkeleycollege.edu/**

- **Proprietary** primarily 2-year, founded 1936
- **Urban** campus
- **Coed,** 2,321 undergraduate students, 92% full-time, 70% women, 30% men

Undergraduates 2,138 full-time, 183 part-time. Students come from 14 states and territories, 66 other countries, 9% are from out of state, 22% African American, 5% Asian American or Pacific Islander, 23% Hispanic American, 0.4% Native American, 15% international, 6% transferred in. *Retention:* 48% of 2003 full-time freshmen returned.
Freshmen *Admission:* 2,279 applied, 1,675 admitted, 680 enrolled.
Faculty *Total:* 140, 29% full-time. *Student/faculty ratio:* 26:1.
Majors Accounting; business administration and management; business/commerce; fashion merchandising; international business/trade/commerce; legal assistant/paralegal; marketing/marketing management; office management.
Academics *Calendar:* quarters. *Degrees:* certificates, associate, and bachelor's. *Special study options:* academic remediation for entering students, adult/continuing education programs, advanced placement credit, cooperative education, distance learning, English as a second language, internships, off-campus study, part-time degree program, study abroad, summer session for credit.
Library 13,164 titles, 138 serial subscriptions, 949 audiovisual materials, an OPAC, a Web page.
Computers on Campus 200 computers available on campus for general student use. A campuswide network can be accessed from off campus. Internet access, at least one staffed computer lab available.
Student Life *Housing:* college housing not available. *Activities and Organizations:* student-run newspaper, student government, International Club, Paralegal Club, Accounting Club. *Campus security:* 24-hour emergency response devices. *Student services:* personal/psychological counseling.
Standardized Tests *Required:* SAT or ACT (for admission).
Costs (2006–07) *Tuition:* $16,950 full-time. *Required fees:* $750 full-time.
Financial Aid Of all full-time matriculated undergraduates who enrolled in 2004, 120 Federal Work-Study jobs (averaging $1500).
Applying *Options:* electronic application, deferred entrance. *Application fee:* $50. *Required:* high school transcript. *Recommended:* interview. *Application deadline:* rolling (freshmen), rolling (transfers).
Freshmen Application Contact Mr. Stuart Siegman, Director, High School Admissions, Berkeley College-New York City Campus, 3 East 43rd Street, New York, NY 10017. *Phone:* 212-986-4343 Ext. 4117. *Toll-free phone:* 800-446-5400. *Fax:* 212-818-1079. *E-mail:* info@berkeleycollege.edu.

BERKELEY COLLEGE-WESTCHESTER CAMPUS

White Plains, New York　　　**www.berkeleycollege.edu/**

- **Proprietary** primarily 2-year, founded 1945
- **Suburban** 10-acre campus with easy access to New York City
- **Coed,** 610 undergraduate students, 92% full-time, 72% women, 28% men

Undergraduates 564 full-time, 46 part-time. Students come from 9 states and territories, 28 other countries, 15% are from out of state, 26% African American, 3% Asian American or Pacific Islander, 21% Hispanic American, 6% international, 14% transferred in, 10% live on campus. *Retention:* 55% of 2003 full-time freshmen returned.
Freshmen *Admission:* 156 enrolled.
Faculty *Total:* 42, 40% full-time. *Student/faculty ratio:* 22:1.
Majors Accounting; business administration and management; business/commerce; fashion merchandising; international business/trade/commerce; legal assistant/paralegal; marketing/marketing management; office management.
Academics *Calendar:* quarters. *Degrees:* certificates, associate, and bachelor's. *Special study options:* academic remediation for entering students, adult/continuing education programs, advanced placement credit, cooperative education, distance learning, English as a second language, internships, off-campus study, part-time degree program, services for LD students, study abroad, summer session for credit.
Library 9,526 titles, 66 serial subscriptions, 777 audiovisual materials, an OPAC, a Web page.
Computers on Campus 175 computers available on campus for general student use. A campuswide network can be accessed from off campus. Internet access, at least one staffed computer lab available.

Student Life *Housing Options:* coed. Campus housing is university owned. *Activities and Organizations:* student-run newspaper, student government, Paralegal Club, Fashion Club, Phi Theta Kappa. *Campus security:* monitored entrance with front desk security guard. *Student services:* personal/psychological counseling.
Standardized Tests *Required:* SAT or ACT (for admission).
Costs (2006–07) *Comprehensive fee:* $26,700 includes full-time tuition ($16,950), mandatory fees ($750), and room and board ($9000).
Financial Aid Of all full-time matriculated undergraduates who enrolled in 2004, 40 Federal Work-Study jobs (averaging $1100).
Applying *Options:* electronic application, deferred entrance. *Application fee:* $50. *Required:* high school transcript. *Recommended:* interview. *Application deadline:* rolling (freshmen), rolling (transfers).
Freshmen Application Contact Ms. Kimberly Satriale, Director of High School Admissions, Berkeley College-Westchester Campus, 99 Church Street, White Plains, NY 10601. *Phone:* 914-694-1122 Ext. 3150. *Toll-free phone:* 800-446-5400. *Fax:* 914-328-9469. *E-mail:* admissions@berkeley.org.

BOROUGH OF MANHATTAN COMMUNITY COLLEGE OF THE CITY UNIVERSITY OF NEW YORK

New York, New York　　　**www.bmcc.cuny.edu/**

- **State and locally supported** 2-year, founded 1963, part of City University of New York System
- **Urban** 5-acre campus
- **Endowment** $3.3 million
- **Coed,** 18,776 undergraduate students, 58% full-time, 63% women, 37% men

Undergraduates 10,809 full-time, 7,967 part-time. Students come from 3 states and territories, 100 other countries, 12% are from out of state, 36% African American, 10% Asian American or Pacific Islander, 29% Hispanic American, 0.1% Native American, 11% international, 10% transferred in.
Freshmen *Admission:* 6,446 applied, 5,718 admitted, 3,198 enrolled. *Average high school GPA:* 2.01. *Test scores:* SAT verbal scores over 500: 12%; SAT math scores over 500: 10%; SAT verbal scores over 600: 2%; SAT math scores over 600: 2%; SAT verbal scores over 700: 1%; SAT math scores over 700: 1%.
Faculty *Total:* 1,075, 35% full-time, 17% with terminal degrees. *Student/faculty ratio:* 22:1.
Majors Accounting; administrative assistant and secretarial science; biological and physical sciences; business administration and management; child development; computer programming; data processing and data processing technology; emergency medical technology (EMT paramedic); engineering science; health science; human services; kindergarten/preschool education; liberal arts and sciences/liberal studies; marketing/marketing management; mathematics; nursing (registered nurse training); respiratory care therapy.
Academics *Calendar:* semesters. *Degree:* certificates and associate. *Special study options:* academic remediation for entering students, adult/continuing education programs, advanced placement credit, cooperative education, distance learning, English as a second language, honors programs, independent study, internships, off-campus study, part-time degree program, services for LD students, study abroad, summer session for credit.
Library A. Philip Randolph Library with 101,869 titles, 8,594 serial subscriptions, 1,343 audiovisual materials, an OPAC, a Web page.
Computers on Campus Internet access, online (class) registration, at least one staffed computer lab available. Computer purchase or lease plan available.
Student Life *Housing:* college housing not available. *Activities and Organizations:* drama/theater group, student-run newspaper, choral group, Caribbean Students Association, Dominican Students Association, When One Voice is Not Enough (WOVINE), Students of Indian Descent Association, Asian Society. *Campus security:* 24-hour patrols. *Student services:* health clinic, personal/psychological counseling, women's center.
Athletics Member NJCAA. *Intercollegiate sports:* baseball M, basketball M/W, soccer M. *Intramural sports:* basketball M/W, soccer M, volleyball M/W.
Costs (2006–07) *Tuition:* state resident $2800 full-time, $120 per credit hour part-time; nonresident $4560 full-time, $190 per credit hour part-time. *Required fees:* $268 full-time.
Applying *Options:* electronic application, deferred entrance. *Application fee:* $65. *Required:* high school transcript. *Application deadline:* rolling (freshmen), rolling (transfers). *Notification:* continuous (freshmen).
Freshmen Application Contact Mr. Eugenio Barrios, Director of Admissions, Borough of Manhattan Community College of the City University of New York, 199 Chambers Street, Room S-300, New York, NY 10007. *Phone:* 212-220-1265. *Fax:* 212-220-2366. *E-mail:* admissions@bmcc.cuny.edu.

BRAMSON ORT COLLEGE

Forest Hills, New York   **www.bramsonort.edu/**

Freshmen Application Contact Admissions Office, Bramson ORT College, 69-30 Austin Street, Forest Hills, NY 11375-4239. *Phone:* 718-261-5800.

BRONX COMMUNITY COLLEGE OF THE CITY UNIVERSITY OF NEW YORK

Bronx, New York   **www.bcc.cuny.edu/**

- **State and locally supported** 2-year, founded 1959, part of City University of New York System
- **Urban** 50-acre campus
- **Coed,** 8,470 undergraduate students, 60% full-time, 64% women, 36% men

Undergraduates 5,088 full-time, 3,382 part-time. Students come from 16 states and territories, 100 other countries, 35% African American, 3% Asian American or Pacific Islander, 48% Hispanic American, 0.2% Native American, 11% international, 5% transferred in. *Retention:* 65% of 2003 full-time freshmen returned.
Freshmen *Admission:* 5,061 applied, 4,956 admitted, 1,457 enrolled.
Faculty *Total:* 547, 48% full-time. *Student/faculty ratio:* 15:1.
Majors Accounting; administrative assistant and secretarial science; African-American/Black studies; art; biology/biological sciences; business administration and management; business teacher education; chemistry; child development; clinical/medical laboratory technology; computer science; data processing and data processing technology; electrical, electronic and communications engineering technology; history; human services; international relations and affairs; legal assistant/paralegal; liberal arts and sciences/liberal studies; marketing/marketing management; mathematics; medical administrative assistant and medical secretary; music; nuclear medical technology; nursing (registered nurse training); ornamental horticulture; pre-engineering; psychology.
Academics *Calendar:* semesters. *Degree:* certificates and associate. *Special study options:* academic remediation for entering students, adult/continuing education programs, advanced placement credit, cooperative education, distance learning, English as a second language, honors programs, independent study, internships, part-time degree program, services for LD students, study abroad, summer session for credit.
Library 75,000 titles, 800 serial subscriptions.
Computers on Campus 300 computers available on campus for general student use.
Student Life *Housing:* college housing not available. *Activities and Organizations:* drama/theater group, student-run newspaper, television station, choral group, national fraternities, national sororities. *Campus security:* 24-hour patrols. *Student services:* health clinic, personal/psychological counseling.
Athletics Member NJCAA. *Intercollegiate sports:* basketball M/W, soccer M, tennis M/W, track and field M/W, volleyball W, wrestling M. *Intramural sports:* basketball M/W, soccer M, tennis M/W, track and field M/W, volleyball W, wrestling M.
Costs (2005–06) *Tuition:* state resident $2800 full-time, $120 per credit part-time; nonresident $4560 full-time, $190 per credit part-time. *Required fees:* $284 full-time, $90 per term part-time.
Applying *Application fee:* $65. *Required:* high school transcript. *Application deadlines:* 7/1 (freshmen), 7/1 (transfers). *Notification:* 8/15 (freshmen).
Freshmen Application Contact Ms. Alba N. Cancetty, Admissions Officer, Bronx Community College of the City University of New York, University Avenue and West 181st Street, Bronx, NY 10453. *Phone:* 718-289-5888. *E-mail:* admission@bcc.cuny.edu.

BROOME COMMUNITY COLLEGE

Binghamton, New York   **www.sunybroome.edu/**

- **State and locally supported** 2-year, founded 1946, part of State University of New York System
- **Suburban** 223-acre campus
- **Coed,** 6,231 undergraduate students, 63% full-time, 57% women, 43% men

Undergraduates 3,946 full-time, 2,285 part-time. Students come from 36 states and territories, 30 other countries, 4% are from out of state, 3% African American, 1% Asian American or Pacific Islander, 2% Hispanic American, 0.3% Native American, 2% international. *Retention:* 62% of 2003 full-time fresh-

men returned.
Freshmen *Admission:* 2,703 applied, 1,419 admitted, 1,391 enrolled.
Faculty *Total:* 399, 36% full-time. *Student/faculty ratio:* 21:1.
Majors Accounting technology and bookkeeping; business administration and management; child care and support services management; civil engineering technology; clinical/medical laboratory technology; communication/speech communication and rhetoric; communications systems installation and repair technology; computer and information sciences; computer engineering technology; corrections; criminal justice/police science; data processing and data processing technology; dental hygiene; electrical, electronic and communications engineering technology; emergency medical technology (EMT paramedic); engineering science; executive assistant/executive secretary; financial planning and services; fire science; health information/medical records technology; hotel/motel administration; industrial production technologies related; information science/studies; international finance; legal assistant/paralegal; liberal arts and sciences/liberal studies; mechanical engineering/mechanical technology; medical/clinical assistant; medical radiologic technology; mental and social health services and allied professions related; merchandising, sales, and marketing operations related (general); nursing (registered nurse training); physical therapist assistant; quality control technology; substance abuse/addiction counseling.
Academics *Calendar:* semesters. *Degree:* certificates and associate. *Special study options:* academic remediation for entering students, adult/continuing education programs, advanced placement credit, distance learning, English as a second language, external degree program, honors programs, independent study, internships, off-campus study, part-time degree program, services for LD students, student-designed majors, study abroad, summer session for credit.
Library Cecil C. Tyrrell Learning Resources Center plus 1 other with 60,518 titles, 301 serial subscriptions, 2,145 audiovisual materials, an OPAC, a Web page.
Computers on Campus 550 computers available on campus for general student use. A campuswide network can be accessed from off campus. Internet access, at least one staffed computer lab available.
Student Life *Housing:* college housing not available. *Activities and Organizations:* student-run newspaper, choral group, Broome Early Childhood Organization, Differentially Disabled Student Association, Ecology Club, Phi Theta Kappa, Criminal Justice Club. *Campus security:* 24-hour emergency response devices and patrols. *Student services:* health clinic, personal/psychological counseling.
Athletics Member NJCAA. *Intercollegiate sports:* baseball M, basketball M/W, cross-country running M/W, golf M, ice hockey M, lacrosse M, soccer M/W, softball W, tennis M/W, volleyball W. *Intramural sports:* basketball M/W, volleyball M/W.
Costs (2005–06) *One-time required fee:* $45. *Tuition:* state resident $2814 full-time, $118 per credit hour part-time; nonresident $5628 full-time, $236 per credit hour part-time. Full-time tuition and fees vary according to course load and location. Part-time tuition and fees vary according to course load and location. *Required fees:* $267 full-time, $5 per credit hour part-time, $29 per term part-time. *Waivers:* senior citizens and employees or children of employees.
Applying *Options:* electronic application, early admission. *Required:* high school transcript. *Required for some:* interview. *Application deadline:* rolling (freshmen), rolling (transfers). *Notification:* continuous (freshmen).
Freshmen Application Contact Mr. Anthony Fiorelli, Director of Admissions, Broome Community College, PO Box 1017, Upper Front Street, Binghamton, NY 13902. *Phone:* 607-778-5001. *Fax:* 607-778-5394. *E-mail:* admissions@sunybroome.edu.

BRYANT AND STRATTON COLLEGE

Albany, New York   **www.bryantstratton.edu/**

- **Proprietary** 2-year, founded 1857, part of Bryant and Stratton College, Inc
- **Suburban** campus
- **Coed,** 470 undergraduate students, 75% full-time, 78% women, 22% men

Undergraduates 354 full-time, 116 part-time. Students come from 1 other state, 48% African American, 2% Asian American or Pacific Islander, 7% Hispanic American, 1% Native American. *Retention:* 45% of 2003 full-time freshmen returned.
Freshmen *Admission:* 109 enrolled.
Faculty *Total:* 45, 27% full-time, 22% with terminal degrees.
Majors Accounting; administrative assistant and secretarial science; business/commerce; criminal justice/law enforcement administration; human resources management and services related; information technology; legal assistant/paralegal; medical administrative assistant and medical secretary; medical/clinical assistant.
Academics *Calendar:* semesters. *Degree:* associate. *Special study options:* academic remediation for entering students, distance learning, double majors,

Bryant and Stratton College (continued)

independent study, internships, part-time degree program, services for LD students, summer session for credit.

Library Library with 3,500 titles, 5 serial subscriptions, 136 audiovisual materials, an OPAC, a Web page.

Computers on Campus 110 computers available on campus for general student use. A campuswide network can be accessed. Internet access, at least one staffed computer lab available.

Student Life *Housing:* college housing not available. *Activities and Organizations:* student-run newspaper. *Campus security:* 24-hour emergency response devices.

Standardized Tests *Required:* CPAt, ACCUPLACER (for admission). *Recommended:* SAT or ACT (for admission).

Costs (2005–06) *Tuition:* $18,675 full-time, $415 per credit hour part-time. Full-time tuition and fees vary according to course load. Part-time tuition and fees vary according to course load. *Required fees:* $25 full-time. *Payment plan:* installment. *Waivers:* employees or children of employees.

Financial Aid Of all full-time matriculated undergraduates who enrolled in 2004, 10 Federal Work-Study jobs (averaging $800).

Applying *Options:* deferred entrance. *Required:* high school transcript, interview, entrance and placement evaluations. *Required for some:* letters of recommendation. *Application deadline:* rolling (freshmen), rolling (transfers).

Freshmen Application Contact Mr. Robert Ferrell, Director of Admissions, Bryant and Stratton College, 1259 Central Avenue, Albany, NY 12205. *Phone:* 518-437-1802 Ext. 205. *Fax:* 518-437-1048.

BRYANT AND STRATTON COLLEGE
Rochester, New York   **www.bryantstratton.edu/**

- **Proprietary** 2-year, founded 1985, part of Bryant and Stratton College
- **Suburban** 1-acre campus
- **Coed,** 297 undergraduate students, 80% full-time, 77% women, 23% men

Undergraduates 238 full-time, 59 part-time. Students come from 4 states and territories, 36% African American, 1% Asian American or Pacific Islander, 5% Hispanic American, 0.3% Native American, 6% transferred in.
Freshmen *Admission:* 97 enrolled.
Faculty *Total:* 59, 27% full-time, 2% with terminal degrees. *Student/faculty ratio:* 10:1.

Majors Accounting; administrative assistant and secretarial science; business administration and management; business/commerce; criminal justice/law enforcement administration; graphic design; human resources management and services related; information technology; legal assistant/paralegal; medical administrative assistant and medical secretary; medical/clinical assistant.

Academics *Calendar:* semesters. *Degree:* associate. *Special study options:* academic remediation for entering students, adult/continuing education programs, distance learning, double majors, independent study, internships, part-time degree program, services for LD students, summer session for credit.
Library Campus Library with 250 titles, 27 serial subscriptions.
Computers on Campus 195 computers available on campus for general student use. Internet access, at least one staffed computer lab available.
Student Life *Housing:* college housing not available. *Activities and Organizations:* student-run newspaper. *Campus security:* late-night transport/escort service.
Standardized Tests *Required:* CPAt (for admission). *Recommended:* SAT or ACT (for admission).
Costs (2005–06) *Tuition:* $18,675 full-time, $415 per credit hour part-time. *Required fees:* $25 full-time.
Financial Aid Of all full-time matriculated undergraduates who enrolled in 2004, 44 Federal Work-Study jobs (averaging $630).
Applying *Options:* electronic application, deferred entrance. *Required:* high school transcript, interview, entrance evaluation and placement evaluation. *Required for some:* letters of recommendation. *Recommended:* minimum 2.0 GPA. *Application deadline:* rolling (freshmen), rolling (transfers).
Freshmen Application Contact Ms. Maria Scalise, Market Director of Admissions, Bryant and Stratton College, 150 Bellwood Drive, Greece Campus, Rochester, NY 14606. *Phone:* 585-292-5627 Ext. 101. *Fax:* 716-292-6015.

BRYANT AND STRATTON COLLEGE
Rochester, New York   **www.bryantstratton.edu/**

- **Proprietary** 2-year, founded 1973, part of Bryant and Stratton College
- **Urban** campus
- **Coed,** 194 undergraduate students, 78% full-time, 86% women, 14% men

Undergraduates 152 full-time, 42 part-time. Students come from 4 states and territories, 26% African American, 12% Hispanic American, 0.5% Native American, 14% transferred in.
Freshmen *Admission:* 55 enrolled.
Faculty *Total:* 31, 6% full-time.

Majors Accounting; administrative assistant and secretarial science; business/commerce; human resources management and services related; information technology; medical administrative assistant and medical secretary; medical/clinical assistant.

Academics *Calendar:* semesters. *Degree:* associate. *Special study options:* academic remediation for entering students, adult/continuing education programs, distance learning, double majors, independent study, internships, part-time degree program, services for LD students, summer session for credit.
Library Campus Library with 250 titles, 27 serial subscriptions.
Computers on Campus 195 computers available on campus for general student use. Internet access, at least one staffed computer lab available.
Student Life *Housing:* college housing not available. *Activities and Organizations:* BASSA, SAMS Club. *Campus security:* 24-hour emergency response devices, late-night transport/escort service.
Athletics *Intramural sports:* bowling M/W, softball M/W, volleyball M/W.
Standardized Tests *Required:* CPAt (for admission). *Recommended:* SAT or ACT (for admission).
Costs (2005–06) *Tuition:* $18,675 full-time, $415 per credit hour part-time. *Required fees:* $25 full-time.
Financial Aid Of all full-time matriculated undergraduates who enrolled in 2004, 40 Federal Work-Study jobs (averaging $600).
Applying *Options:* electronic application, deferred entrance. *Required:* high school transcript, interview, entrance evaluation and placement evaluation. *Required for some:* letters of recommendation. *Application deadline:* rolling (freshmen), rolling (transfers).
Freshmen Application Contact Ms. Maria Scalise, Director of Admissions, Bryant and Stratton College, 1225 Jefferson Road, Henrietta Campus, Rochester, NY 14623. *Phone:* 585-720-0660 Ext. 201. *Fax:* 585-720-9226.

BRYANT AND STRATTON COLLEGE
Syracuse, New York   **www.bryantstratton.edu/**

- **Proprietary** 2-year, founded 1854, part of Bryant and Stratton Business Institute, Inc
- **Urban** campus
- **Coed,** 636 undergraduate students, 78% full-time, 77% women, 23% men

Undergraduates 494 full-time, 142 part-time. Students come from 1 other state, 2 other countries, 1% are from out of state, 47% African American, 0.6% Asian American or Pacific Islander, 5% Hispanic American, 2% Native American, 0.6% international, 3% transferred in, 26% live on campus.
Freshmen *Admission:* 252 enrolled.
Faculty *Total:* 51, 29% full-time.

Majors Accounting; administrative assistant and secretarial science; business/commerce; hotel and restaurant management; human resources management and services related; information technology; medical administrative assistant and medical secretary; medical/clinical assistant; tourism and travel services management.

Academics *Calendar:* semesters. *Degree:* associate. *Special study options:* academic remediation for entering students, distance learning, double majors, internships, part-time degree program, services for LD students, summer session for credit.
Library Bryant and Stratton, Syracuse Campus with 1,325 titles, 40 serial subscriptions, 40 audiovisual materials.
Computers on Campus 114 computers available on campus for general student use. At least one staffed computer lab available.
Student Life *Housing Options:* coed, disabled students. *Activities and Organizations:* student-run newspaper, Management Club, Travel Club, Medical Club, Computer Club. *Campus security:* 24-hour emergency response devices, controlled dormitory access.

Athletics Member NJCAA. *Intercollegiate sports:* soccer M(s)/W(s).
Standardized Tests *Required:* CPAt (for admission). *Recommended:* SAT or ACT (for admission).
Costs (2005–06) *Tuition:* $18,675 full-time, $415 per credit hour part-time. *Required fees:* $25 full-time.
Applying *Required:* high school transcript, interview, entrance, placement evaluations. *Required for some:* letters of recommendation. *Application deadline:* rolling (freshmen), rolling (transfers).
Freshmen Application Contact Ms. Dawn Rajkowski, Director of Admissions, Bryant and Stratton College, 953 James Street, Syracuse, NY 13203-2502. *Phone:* 315-472-6603 Ext. 248. *Fax:* 315-474-4383.

BRYANT AND STRATTON COLLEGE, AMHERST CAMPUS

Clarence, New York www.bryantstratton.edu/

- **Proprietary** primarily 2-year, founded 1977, part of Bryant and Stratton College
- **Suburban** 12-acre campus with easy access to Buffalo
- **Coed,** 403 undergraduate students, 60% full-time, 73% women, 27% men

Undergraduates 240 full-time, 163 part-time. 15% African American, 0.5% Asian American or Pacific Islander, 2% Hispanic American, 0.7% Native American, 17% transferred in.
Freshmen *Admission:* 73 applied, 58 admitted, 58 enrolled.
Faculty *Total:* 35, 23% full-time, 37% with terminal degrees.
Majors Accounting; administrative assistant and secretarial science; business administration, management and operations related; business/commerce; graphic design; human resources management and services related; information technology; legal assistant/paralegal.
Academics *Calendar:* trimesters. *Degrees:* associate and bachelor's. *Special study options:* academic remediation for entering students, advanced placement credit, cooperative education, distance learning, double majors, independent study, internships, part-time degree program, summer session for credit.
Library Library Resource Center with 4,500 titles, 25 serial subscriptions, 150 audiovisual materials, an OPAC, a Web page.
Computers on Campus 70 computers available on campus for general student use. Internet access, at least one staffed computer lab available.
Student Life *Housing:* college housing not available. *Activities and Organizations:* Phi Beta Lambda, Student Government Association, Information Technology Club, Ambassadors.
Standardized Tests *Required:* TABE, CPAt or ACCUPLACER (for admission). *Recommended:* SAT or ACT (for admission).
Costs (2005–06) *Tuition:* $18,675 full-time, $415 per credit hour part-time. Full-time tuition and fees vary according to class time and course load. Part-time tuition and fees vary according to class time and course load. *Required fees:* $25 full-time. *Payment plan:* installment. *Waivers:* employees or children of employees.
Applying *Options:* common application, deferred entrance. *Required:* high school transcript, interview, entrance evaluation and placement evaluation. *Required for some:* letters of recommendation. *Application deadline:* rolling (freshmen), rolling (transfers).
Freshmen Application Contact Ms. Mary Zachary, Associate Director of Admissions, Bryant and Stratton College, Amherst Campus, 40 Hazelwood Drive, Amherst, NY 14228. *Phone:* 716-691-0012. *Fax:* 716-691-6716. *E-mail:* mzachary@bryantstratton.edu.

BRYANT AND STRATTON COLLEGE, BUFFALO CAMPUS

Buffalo, New York www.bryantstratton.edu/

- **Proprietary** 2-year, founded 1854, part of Bryant and Stratton College
- **Urban** 2-acre campus
- **Coed,** 603 undergraduate students, 82% full-time, 75% women, 25% men

Undergraduates 495 full-time, 108 part-time. 65% African American, 0.2% Asian American or Pacific Islander, 5% Hispanic American, 0.7% Native American, 4% transferred in.
Freshmen *Admission:* 305 applied, 229 admitted, 229 enrolled.
Faculty *Total:* 52, 19% full-time, 29% with terminal degrees.

Majors Accounting; administrative assistant and secretarial science; business/commerce; criminal justice/law enforcement administration; human resources management and services related; information technology; medical administrative assistant and medical secretary; medical/clinical assistant.
Academics *Calendar:* trimesters. *Degree:* associate. *Special study options:* academic remediation for entering students, advanced placement credit, cooperative education, distance learning, double majors, independent study, internships, part-time degree program, summer session for credit.
Library Learning Center/Library with 30,000 titles, 28,217 serial subscriptions, 252 audiovisual materials, an OPAC.
Computers on Campus 125 computers available on campus for general student use. Internet access, at least one staffed computer lab available.
Student Life *Housing:* college housing not available. *Activities and Organizations:* Med-Assisting Club, Secretarial Club, Accounting/Business Club.
Standardized Tests *Required:* TABE, CPAt or ACCUPLACER (for admission). *Recommended:* SAT or ACT (for admission).
Costs (2005–06) *Tuition:* $18,675 full-time, $415 per credit hour part-time. Full-time tuition and fees vary according to class time and course load. Part-time tuition and fees vary according to course load. *Required fees:* $25 full-time. *Payment plan:* installment. *Waivers:* employees or children of employees.
Applying *Options:* common application, deferred entrance. *Required:* high school transcript, interview, entrance and placement evaluation. *Required for some:* letters of recommendation. *Application deadline:* rolling (freshmen), rolling (transfers).
Freshmen Application Contact Mr. Phil Strubel, Director of Admissions, Bryant and Stratton College, Buffalo Campus, 465 Main Street, Suite 400, Buffalo, NY 14203-1713. *Phone:* 716-884-9120. *Fax:* 716-884-0091.

BRYANT AND STRATTON COLLEGE, LACKAWANNA CAMPUS

Lackawanna, New York www.bryantstratton.edu/

- **Proprietary** 2-year, founded 1989, part of Bryant and Stratton College
- **Suburban** campus with easy access to Buffalo
- **Coed,** 269 undergraduate students, 70% full-time, 77% women, 23% men

Undergraduates 189 full-time, 80 part-time. 4% African American, 2% Hispanic American, 1% Native American.
Freshmen *Admission:* 98 applied, 72 admitted, 72 enrolled.
Faculty *Total:* 33, 21% full-time, 27% with terminal degrees.
Majors Accounting; administrative assistant and secretarial science; business/commerce; criminal justice/law enforcement administration; human resources management and services related; information technology; medical administrative assistant and medical secretary; medical/clinical assistant.
Academics *Calendar:* trimesters. *Degree:* associate. *Special study options:* academic remediation for entering students, advanced placement credit, cooperative education, distance learning, double majors, independent study, internships, part-time degree program, summer session for credit.
Library Southtowns Library with 1,402 titles, 42 serial subscriptions, 128 audiovisual materials, an OPAC, a Web page.
Computers on Campus 112 computers available on campus for general student use. Internet access, at least one staffed computer lab available.
Student Life *Housing:* college housing not available. *Activities and Organizations:* Accounting/Business Club, Administrative Professionals Club, Micro Club, Honor Society, student newsletter. *Campus security:* 24-hour emergency response devices, late-night transport/escort service. *Student services:* women's center.
Standardized Tests *Required:* TABE, CPAt or ACCUPLACER (for admission). *Recommended:* SAT or ACT (for admission).
Costs (2005–06) *Tuition:* $18,675 full-time, $415 per credit hour part-time. Full-time tuition and fees vary according to course load. Part-time tuition and fees vary according to course load. *Required fees:* $25 full-time. *Payment plan:* installment. *Waivers:* employees or children of employees.
Applying *Options:* common application, deferred entrance. *Required:* high school transcript, interview, entrance and placement evaluations. *Required for some:* letters of recommendation. *Application deadline:* rolling (freshmen), rolling (transfers).
Freshmen Application Contact Mr. Paul Kehr, WNY Market Admissions Director, Bryant and Stratton College, Lackawanna Campus, Sterling Park, 200 Redtail, Orchard Park, NY 14127. *Phone:* 716-677-9500. *Fax:* 716-677-9500. *E-mail:* jaweslowski@bryantstratton.edu.

BRYANT AND STRATTON COLLEGE, NORTH CAMPUS

Liverpool, New York www.bryantstratton.edu/

Freshmen Application Contact Ms. Heather Macnik, Director of Admissions, Bryant and Stratton College, North Campus, 8687 Carling Road, Liverpool, NY 13090-1315. *Phone:* 315-652-6500.

BUSINESS INFORMATICS CENTER, INC.

Valley Stream, New York

CAYUGA COUNTY COMMUNITY COLLEGE

Auburn, New York www.cayuga-cc.edu/

- **State and locally supported** 2-year, founded 1953, part of State University of New York System
- **Small-town** 50-acre campus with easy access to Rochester and Syracuse
- **Endowment** $6.5 million
- **Coed**

Undergraduates 2,220 full-time, 1,676 part-time. Students come from 9 states and territories, 3 other countries, 1% are from out of state, 3% African American, 0.7% Asian American or Pacific Islander, 1% Hispanic American, 1% Native American, 0.5% international, 4% transferred in.

Academics *Calendar:* semesters. *Degree:* certificates and associate. *Special study options:* academic remediation for entering students, accelerated degree program, adult/continuing education programs, advanced placement credit, distance learning, double majors, honors programs, independent study, internships, part-time degree program, services for LD students, study abroad, summer session for credit.

Student Life *Campus security:* security from 8 a.m. to 9 p.m.

Athletics Member NJCAA.

Standardized Tests *Required for some:* ACT ASSET, ACCUPLACER. *Recommended:* SAT or ACT (for placement).

Costs (2005–06) *Tuition:* state resident $2900 full-time, $105 per credit part-time; nonresident $5800 full-time, $210 per credit part-time. Full-time tuition and fees vary according to class time, course load, and program. Part-time tuition and fees vary according to class time, course load, and program. *Required fees:* $311 full-time, $12 per credit part-time, $2 per term part-time.

Financial Aid Of all full-time matriculated undergraduates who enrolled in 2004, 150 Federal Work-Study jobs (averaging $1800). 200 state and other part-time jobs (averaging $1000).

Applying *Options:* electronic application, deferred entrance. *Required:* high school transcript. *Required for some:* interview.

Director of Admissions Mr. Bruce M. Blodgett, Director of Admissions, Cayuga County Community College, 197 Franklin Street, Auburn, NY 13021-3099. *Phone:* 315-255-1743 Ext. 2244.

CLINTON COMMUNITY COLLEGE

Plattsburgh, New York clintoncc.suny.edu/

- **State and locally supported** 2-year, founded 1969, part of State University of New York System
- **Small-town** 100-acre campus
- **Endowment** $1.0 million
- **Coed**

Undergraduates 1,259 full-time, 933 part-time. Students come from 5 states and territories, 9 other countries, 1% are from out of state, 3% African American, 0.6% Asian American or Pacific Islander, 2% Hispanic American, 0.9% Native American, 2% international, 6% transferred in, 6% live on campus.

Faculty *Student/faculty ratio:* 18:1.

Academics *Calendar:* semesters. *Degree:* certificates and associate. *Special study options:* academic remediation for entering students, adult/continuing education programs, advanced placement credit, cooperative education, distance learning, English as a second language, external degree program, independent study, internships, off-campus study, part-time degree program, services for LD students, student-designed majors, summer session for credit.

Student Life *Campus security:* 24-hour emergency response devices, late-night transport/escort service, controlled dormitory access, security during class hours.

Athletics Member NJCAA.

Standardized Tests *Recommended:* SAT or ACT (for placement).

Costs (2005–06) *Tuition:* state resident $3020 full-time, $125 per credit hour part-time; nonresident $7550 full-time, $312 per credit hour part-time. *Required fees:* $166 full-time, $5 per credit hour part-time. *Room and board:* $6340; room only: $3800.

Financial Aid Of all full-time matriculated undergraduates who enrolled in 2004, 45 Federal Work-Study jobs (averaging $1260).

Applying *Options:* common application, electronic application, deferred entrance. *Required:* high school transcript. *Required for some:* essay or personal statement, minimum 2.5 GPA, 3 letters of recommendation, interview.

Director of Admissions Mrs. Karen L. Burnam, Director of Admissions and Financial Aid, Clinton Community College, 136 Clinton Point Drive, Plattsburgh, NY 12901. *Phone:* 518-562-4170. *Toll-free phone:* 800-552-1160.

COCHRAN SCHOOL OF NURSING

Yonkers, New York www.riversidehealth.org/

Director of Admissions Ms. Sandra Sclafani, Registrar, Cochran School of Nursing, 967 North Broadway, Yonkers, NY 10701. *Phone:* 914-964-4296.

THE COLLEGE OF WESTCHESTER

White Plains, New York www.cw.edu/

- **Proprietary** 2-year, founded 1915
- **Suburban** campus with easy access to New York City
- **Coed,** 1,039 undergraduate students, 80% full-time, 50% women, 50% men

Undergraduates 829 full-time, 210 part-time. Students come from 3 states and territories, 4 other countries, 8% are from out of state, 28% African American, 2% Asian American or Pacific Islander, 30% Hispanic American, 0.4% Native American, 7% transferred in.

Freshmen *Admission:* 253 enrolled.

Faculty *Total:* 82, 30% full-time, 7% with terminal degrees. *Student/faculty ratio:* 15:1.

Majors Accounting; administrative assistant and secretarial science; business administration and management; computer and information sciences related; computer graphics; computer/information technology services administration related; computer programming; computer programming related; computer programming (specific applications); computer programming (vendor/product certification); computer software and media applications related; computer systems networking and telecommunications; computer/technical support; computer typography and composition equipment operation; data entry/microcomputer applications; data entry/microcomputer applications related; data processing and data processing technology; information science/studies; information technology; management information systems; marketing/marketing management; medical administrative assistant and medical secretary; system administration; web/multimedia management and webmaster; web page, digital/multimedia and information resources design; word processing.

Academics *Calendar:* quarters for day division, semesters for evening and weekend divisions. *Degree:* certificates and associate. *Special study options:* academic remediation for entering students, accelerated degree program, adult/continuing education programs, cooperative education, double majors, honors programs, internships, part-time degree program, summer session for credit.

Library Westchester Business Institute Resource Center.

Computers on Campus 214 computers available on campus for general student use. A campuswide network can be accessed. Internet access, at least one staffed computer lab available.

Student Life *Housing:* college housing not available. *Activities and Organizations:* student-run newspaper. *Student services:* personal/psychological counseling.

Standardized Tests *Recommended:* SAT (for admission).

Costs (2006–07) *Tuition:* $18,315 full-time, $385 per credit part-time. *Required fees:* $795 full-time, $200 per term part-time.

Applying *Options:* common application, electronic application, deferred entrance. *Application fee:* $40. *Required:* high school transcript, interview.

Required for some: essay or personal statement. *Application deadline:* rolling (freshmen), rolling (transfers).

Freshmen Application Contact Mr. Dale T. Smith, Vice President, The College of Westchester, 325 Central Avenue, PO Box 710, White Plains, NY 10602. *Phone:* 914-948-4442 Ext. 311. *Toll-free phone:* 800-333-4924 Ext. 318. *Fax:* 914-948-5441. *E-mail:* admissions@cw.edu.

▶ **See page 530 for the College Close-Up.**

COLUMBIA-GREENE COMMUNITY COLLEGE
Hudson, New York
www.sunycgcc.edu/

- **State and locally supported** 2-year, founded 1969, part of State University of New York System
- **Rural** 143-acre campus
- **Endowment** $450,000
- **Coed**

Undergraduates 938 full-time, 777 part-time. Students come from 5 states and territories, 5 other countries, 1% are from out of state, 5% transferred in.
Faculty *Student/faculty ratio:* 18:1.
Academics *Calendar:* semesters. *Degree:* certificates and associate. *Special study options:* academic remediation for entering students, adult/continuing education programs, advanced placement credit, distance learning, honors programs, internships, part-time degree program, services for LD students, student-designed majors, summer session for credit.
Student Life *Campus security:* 24-hour patrols, late-night transport/escort service.
Athletics Member NJCAA.
Standardized Tests *Required:* College Qualifying Test (for placement). *Recommended:* SAT or ACT (for placement).
Applying *Options:* early admission, deferred entrance. *Application fee:* $30. *Required:* high school transcript. *Required for some:* interview.
Director of Admissions Mrs. Patricia Hallenbeck, Assistant Dean of Student Affairs, Columbia-Greene Community College, 4400 Route 23, Hudson, NY 12534-0327. *Phone:* 518-828-4181 Ext. 5513. *Fax:* 518-822-2015. *E-mail:* hallenbeck@sunycgcc.edu.

CORNING COMMUNITY COLLEGE
Corning, New York
www.corning-cc.edu/

- **State and locally supported** 2-year, founded 1956, part of State University of New York System
- **Rural** 275-acre campus
- **Endowment** $2.3 million
- **Coed,** 5,310 undergraduate students, 50% full-time, 57% women, 43% men

Undergraduates 2,638 full-time, 2,672 part-time. Students come from 13 states and territories, 5% are from out of state, 2% African American, 0.6% Asian American or Pacific Islander, 0.7% Hispanic American, 0.5% Native American, 0.1% international, 3% transferred in.
Freshmen *Admission:* 1,252 applied, 1,228 admitted, 1,077 enrolled.
Faculty *Total:* 258, 38% full-time, 9% with terminal degrees. *Student/faculty ratio:* 18:1.
Majors Accounting; administrative assistant and secretarial science; automobile/automotive mechanics technology; automotive engineering technology; biological and physical sciences; business administration and management; chemical technology; child care provision; computer and information sciences; computer and information sciences related; computer graphics; computer/information technology services administration related; computer programming; computer programming related; computer science; computer systems networking and telecommunications; computer technology/computer systems technology; corrections and criminal justice related; criminal justice/law enforcement administration; drafting and design technology; education related; electrical, electronic and communications engineering technology; elementary education; emergency medical technology (EMT paramedic); fire science; general studies; health and physical education; humanities; human services; industrial technology; information technology; legal assistant/paralegal; liberal arts and sciences/liberal studies; machine shop technology; machine tool technology; mathematics; mechanical engineering/mechanical technology; nursing (registered nurse training); optical sciences; pre-engineering; social sciences; substance abuse/addiction counseling; tourism and travel services management; word processing.

Academics *Calendar:* semesters. *Degree:* certificates and associate. *Special study options:* academic remediation for entering students, accelerated degree program, advanced placement credit, distance learning, double majors, honors programs, independent study, internships, part-time degree program, services for LD students, student-designed majors, summer session for credit. *ROTC:* Army (c), Navy (c), Air Force (c).
Library Arthur A. Houghton, Jr. Library with 71,233 titles, 2,500 serial subscriptions, 4,290 audiovisual materials, an OPAC, a Web page.
Computers on Campus 350 computers available on campus for general student use. A campuswide network can be accessed from off campus that provide access to e-mail, Internet courses. Internet access, at least one staffed computer lab available.
Student Life *Housing:* college housing not available. *Activities and Organizations:* drama/theater group, student-run newspaper, radio station, choral group, student association, WCEB, Two-Bit Players, Activities Programming Committee, Nursing Society. *Campus security:* 24-hour emergency response devices and patrols, late-night transport/escort service. *Student services:* health clinic, personal/psychological counseling.
Athletics Member NJCAA. *Intercollegiate sports:* basketball M/W, cheerleading W, soccer M/W, softball W, volleyball W. *Intramural sports:* archery M/W, badminton M/W, basketball M/W, bowling M/W, golf M/W, soccer M/W, softball M/W, table tennis M/W, volleyball M/W, weight lifting M/W.
Costs (2006–07) *Tuition:* state resident $3100 full-time, $128 per credit part-time; nonresident $6200 full-time, $258 per credit part-time.
Financial Aid Of all full-time matriculated undergraduates who enrolled in 2004, 264 Federal Work-Study jobs (averaging $1128).
Applying *Options:* electronic application, early admission. *Application fee:* $25. *Required:* high school transcript. *Required for some:* interview. *Application deadline:* rolling (freshmen), rolling (transfers). *Notification:* continuous (freshmen).
Freshmen Application Contact Ms. Karen McCarthy, Director of Admissions, Corning Community College, 1 Academic Drive, Corning, NY 14830. *Phone:* 607-962-9221. *Toll-free phone:* 800-358-7171 Ext. 220. *Fax:* 607-962-9520. *E-mail:* admissions@corning-cc.edu.

CROUSE HOSPITAL SCHOOL OF NURSING
Syracuse, New York
www.crouse.org/nursing/

- **Independent** 2-year, founded 1913
- **Urban** campus
- **Coed**

Undergraduates 140 full-time, 112 part-time. Students come from 4 states and territories, 2% are from out of state, 7% African American, 2% Asian American or Pacific Islander, 1% Hispanic American, 14% live on campus.
Faculty *Student/faculty ratio:* 9:1.
Academics *Calendar:* semesters. *Degree:* associate. *Special study options:* part-time degree program.
Student Life *Campus security:* 24-hour emergency response devices and patrols, late-night transport/escort service, controlled dormitory access.
Standardized Tests *Required for some:* SAT or ACT (for admission). *Recommended:* SAT or ACT (for admission).
Costs (2005–06) *Tuition:* $7352 full-time, $225 per credit hour part-time. *Required fees:* $360 full-time, $130 per term part-time. *Room only:* $1750.
Financial Aid Of all full-time matriculated undergraduates who enrolled in 2004, 18 Federal Work-Study jobs (averaging $880).
Applying *Options:* deferred entrance. *Application fee:* $30. *Required:* essay or personal statement, high school transcript, minimum 2.5 GPA, 3 letters of recommendation, interview.
Director of Admissions Ms. Karen Van Sise, Enrollment Management Supervisor, Crouse Hospital School of Nursing, 736 Irving Avenue, Syracuse, NY 13210. *Phone:* 315-470-7481.

DOROTHEA HOPFER SCHOOL OF NURSING AT THE MOUNT VERNON HOSPITAL
Mount Vernon, New York
www.ssmc.org/

Director of Admissions Office of Admissions, Dorothea Hopfer School of Nursing at The Mount Vernon Hospital, 53 Valentine Street, Mount Vernon, NY 10550. *Phone:* 914-664-8000 Ext. 3221.

DUTCHESS COMMUNITY COLLEGE
Poughkeepsie, New York　　　　**www.sunydutchess.edu/**

- **State and locally supported** 2-year, founded 1957, part of State University of New York System
- **Suburban** 130-acre campus with easy access to New York City
- **Coed**

Academics *Calendar:* semesters. *Degree:* certificates and associate. *Special study options:* academic remediation for entering students, adult/continuing education programs, advanced placement credit, English as a second language, freshman honors college, honors programs, internships, off-campus study, part-time degree program, summer session for credit.

Student Life *Campus security:* 24-hour emergency response devices and patrols, late-night transport/escort service.

Athletics Member NJCAA.

Costs (2005–06) *Tuition:* state resident $2600 full-time, $105 per credit part-time; nonresident $5200 full-time, $210 per credit part-time. *Required fees:* $387 full-time, $8 per credit part-time, $25 per term part-time.

Financial Aid Of all full-time matriculated undergraduates who enrolled in 2004, 500 Federal Work-Study jobs (averaging $1500).

Applying *Options:* early admission, deferred entrance. *Required:* high school transcript.

Director of Admissions Ms. Rita Banner, Director of Admissions, Dutchess Community College, 53 Pendell Road, Poughkeepsie, NY 12601. *Phone:* 845-431-8010. *Toll-free phone:* 800-763-3933. *E-mail:* banner@sunydutchess.edu.

ELLIS HOSPITAL SCHOOL OF NURSING
Schenectady, New York　　　　**www.ehson.org/**

Director of Admissions Mary Lee Pollard, Director of School, Ellis Hospital School of Nursing, 1101 Nott Street, Schenectady, NY 12308. *Phone:* 518-243-4471. *Fax:* 518-243-4470.

ELMIRA BUSINESS INSTITUTE
Elmira, New York　　　　**www.ebi-college.com/**

- **Private** 2-year, founded 1858
- **Coed, primarily women,** 361 undergraduate students, 78% full-time, 89% women, 11% men

Undergraduates 283 full-time, 78 part-time. Students come from 2 states and territories, 13% are from out of state, 7% African American, 0.3% Asian American or Pacific Islander, 0.8% Hispanic American, 0.6% transferred in. Freshmen *Admission:* 108 applied, 94 enrolled. *Average high school GPA:* 2.50.

Faculty *Total:* 34, 21% full-time.

Majors Accounting; administrative assistant and secretarial science; legal administrative assistant/secretary; medical administrative assistant and medical secretary; tourism and travel services management.

Academics *Calendar:* semesters. *Degree:* certificates and associate. *Special study options:* academic remediation for entering students, advanced placement credit, internships, part-time degree program.

Library Elmira Business Institute Library with 800 titles, 14 serial subscriptions, 15 audiovisual materials.

Computers on Campus 50 computers available on campus for general student use. Internet access available.

Student Life *Housing:* college housing not available.

Applying *Options:* common application, electronic application. *Required:* high school transcript, interview. *Application deadline:* rolling (freshmen).

Freshmen Application Contact Ms. Lisa Roan, Admissions Director, Elmira Business Institute, 303 North Main Street, Langdon Plaza, Elmira, NY 14901. *Toll-free phone:* 800-843-1812. *Fax:* 607-733-7178. *E-mail:* lroan@ebi-college.com.

ERIE COMMUNITY COLLEGE
Buffalo, New York　　　　**www.ecc.edu/**

- **State and locally supported** 2-year, founded 1971, part of State University of New York System
- **Urban** 1-acre campus
- **Coed,** 2,949 undergraduate students, 74% full-time, 63% women, 37% men

Undergraduates 2,188 full-time, 761 part-time. Students come from 12 states and territories, 3 other countries, 1% are from out of state, 42% African American, 2% Asian American or Pacific Islander, 8% Hispanic American, 1% Native American, 0.2% international, 5% transferred in. Freshmen *Admission:* 1,458 applied, 1,109 admitted, 632 enrolled. *Test scores:* SAT verbal scores over 500: 23%; SAT math scores over 500: 24%; SAT verbal scores over 600: 4%; SAT math scores over 600: 3%.

Faculty *Total:* 1,283, 27% full-time. *Student/faculty ratio:* 17:1.

Majors Administrative assistant and secretarial science; building/property maintenance and management; business administration and management; child care and support services management; community health services counseling; criminal justice/law enforcement administration; criminal justice/police science; culinary arts; humanities; industrial production technologies related; information science/studies; legal assistant/paralegal; liberal arts and sciences/liberal studies; medical radiologic technology; nursing (registered nurse training); office management; physical education teaching and coaching; public administration and social service professions related; substance abuse/addiction counseling.

Academics *Calendar:* semesters. *Degree:* certificates, diplomas, and associate. *Special study options:* academic remediation for entering students, adult/continuing education programs, advanced placement credit, cooperative education, distance learning, double majors, English as a second language, honors programs, independent study, internships, part-time degree program, services for LD students, student-designed majors, study abroad, summer session for credit. *ROTC:* Army (c).

Library Leon E. Butler Library with 24,927 titles, 208 serial subscriptions, 2,492 audiovisual materials, an OPAC, a Web page.

Computers on Campus 341 computers available on campus for general student use. A campuswide network can be accessed from off campus. Internet access, online (class) registration, at least one staffed computer lab available.

Student Life *Housing:* college housing not available. *Activities and Organizations:* drama/theater group, student-run newspaper, radio station, choral group, Alpha Beta Gamma, Anthropology Club, Black Student Union, Business Club, Campus Ministry Club. *Campus security:* 24-hour emergency response devices and patrols, late-night transport/escort service. *Student services:* health clinic, personal/psychological counseling, women's center.

Athletics Member NJCAA. *Intercollegiate sports:* baseball M, basketball M/W, bowling M/W, cheerleading W, cross-country running M/W, football M, golf M/W, ice hockey M, lacrosse W, soccer M/W, softball W, swimming and diving M/W, track and field M/W, volleyball W.

Costs (2005–06) *Tuition:* area resident $2900 full-time, $121 per credit hour part-time; state resident $5800 full-time, $242 per credit hour part-time; nonresident $5800 full-time, $242 per credit hour part-time. *Required fees:* $320 full-time, $5 per credit hour part-time, $30 per term part-time. *Payment plans:* installment, deferred payment. *Waivers:* senior citizens and employees or children of employees.

Financial Aid Of all full-time matriculated undergraduates who enrolled in 2004, 300 Federal Work-Study jobs (averaging $2000).

Applying *Options:* common application, electronic application. *Required:* high school transcript. *Required for some:* interview. *Application deadline:* rolling (freshmen), rolling (transfers). *Notification:* continuous (freshmen).

Freshmen Application Contact Ms. Petrina Hill-Cheatom, Director of Admissions, Erie Community College, 121 Ellicott Street, Buffalo, NY 14203-2698. *Phone:* 716-851-1588. *Fax:* 716-851-1129.

ERIE COMMUNITY COLLEGE, NORTH CAMPUS
Williamsville, New York　　　　**www.ecc.edu**

- **State and locally supported** 2-year, founded 1946, part of State University of New York System
- **Suburban** 20-acre campus with easy access to Buffalo
- **Coed,** 5,641 undergraduate students, 67% full-time, 51% women, 49% men

Undergraduates 3,779 full-time, 1,862 part-time. Students come from 17 states and territories, 24 other countries, 1% are from out of state, 12% African American, 2% Asian American or Pacific Islander, 2% Hispanic American, 0.6%

Native American, 0.9% international, 5% transferred in.
Freshmen *Admission:* 1,856 applied, 1,692 admitted, 1,150 enrolled. *Test scores:* SAT verbal scores over 500: 32%; SAT math scores over 500: 43%; SAT verbal scores over 600: 5%; SAT math scores over 600: 6%.
Faculty *Total:* 1,283, 27% full-time. *Student/faculty ratio:* 17:1.
Majors Business administration and management; civil engineering technology; clinical/medical laboratory technology; computer and information sciences; construction management; construction trades related; criminal justice/law enforcement administration; criminal justice/police science; culinary arts; dental hygiene; dietitian assistant; electrical, electronic and communications engineering technology; engineering; health information/medical records technology; humanities; information science/studies; liberal arts and sciences/liberal studies; mechanical engineering/mechanical technology; medical office management; nursing (registered nurse training); occupational therapist assistant; office management; opticianry; physical education teaching and coaching; respiratory care therapy; restaurant, culinary, and catering management.
Academics *Calendar:* semesters plus summer sessions. *Degree:* certificates, diplomas, and associate. *Special study options:* academic remediation for entering students, adult/continuing education programs, advanced placement credit, cooperative education, distance learning, double majors, English as a second language, honors programs, independent study, internships, part-time degree program, services for LD students, student-designed majors, study abroad, summer session for credit. *ROTC:* Army (c).
Library Richard R. Dry Memorial Library with 71,220 titles, 359 serial subscriptions, 8,084 audiovisual materials, an OPAC, a Web page.
Computers on Campus 457 computers available on campus for general student use. A campuswide network can be accessed from off campus. Internet access, online (class) registration, at least one staffed computer lab available.
Student Life *Housing:* college housing not available. *Activities and Organizations:* drama/theater group, student-run newspaper, radio station, choral group, APWA (American Public Works Association), Dental Hygiene Club, Environmental Awareness Club, Flame and Ice, Future Teachers. *Campus security:* 24-hour emergency response devices and patrols, late-night transport/escort service. *Student services:* health clinic, personal/psychological counseling, women's center.
Athletics Member NJCAA. *Intercollegiate sports:* baseball M, basketball M/W, bowling M/W, cheerleading W, cross-country running M/W, football M, golf M/W, ice hockey M, lacrosse W, soccer M/W, softball W, swimming and diving M/W, track and field M/W, volleyball W.
Costs (2005–06) *Tuition:* area resident $2900 full-time, $121 per credit hour part-time; state resident $5800 full-time, $242 per credit hour part-time; nonresident $5800 full-time, $242 per credit hour part-time. *Required fees:* $320 full-time, $5 per credit hour part-time, $30 per term part-time. *Payment plans:* installment, deferred payment. *Waivers:* senior citizens and employees or children of employees.
Financial Aid Of all full-time matriculated undergraduates who enrolled in 2004, 300 Federal Work-Study jobs (averaging $2000).
Applying *Options:* common application, electronic application. *Required:* high school transcript. *Required for some:* interview. *Application deadline:* rolling (freshmen), rolling (transfers). *Notification:* continuous (freshmen).
Freshmen Application Contact Ms. Petrina Hill-Cheatom, Director of Admissions, Erie Community College, North Campus, 6205 Main Street, Williamsville, NY 14221-7095. *Phone:* 716-851-1588. *Fax:* 716-851-1429.

ERIE COMMUNITY COLLEGE, SOUTH CAMPUS
Orchard Park, New York www.ecc.edu/

- **State and locally supported** 2-year, founded 1974, part of State University of New York System
- **Suburban** 20-acre campus with easy access to Buffalo
- **Coed,** 4,067 undergraduate students, 62% full-time, 44% women, 56% men

Undergraduates 2,521 full-time, 1,546 part-time. Students come from 19 states and territories, 4 other countries, 1% are from out of state, 5% African American, 0.6% Asian American or Pacific Islander, 3% Hispanic American, 1% Native American, 0.1% international, 5% transferred in.
Freshmen *Admission:* 1,377 applied, 1,232 admitted, 898 enrolled. *Test scores:* SAT verbal scores over 500: 31%; SAT math scores over 500: 37%; SAT verbal scores over 600: 4%; SAT math scores over 600: 6%.
Faculty *Total:* 1,283, 27% full-time. *Student/faculty ratio:* 17:1.
Majors Architectural engineering technology; autobody/collision and repair technology; automobile/automotive mechanics technology; biomedical technology; business administration and management; communication/speech communication and rhetoric; communications systems installation and repair technology; computer technology/computer systems technology; dental laboratory technol-

ogy; fire services administration; graphic and printing equipment operation/production; humanities; industrial technology; information science/studies; liberal arts and sciences/liberal studies; mechanical drafting and CAD/CADD; office management; parks, recreation and leisure facilities management; physical education teaching and coaching; public administration and social service professions related.
Academics *Calendar:* semesters plus summer sessions. *Degree:* certificates, diplomas, and associate. *Special study options:* academic remediation for entering students, adult/continuing education programs, advanced placement credit, cooperative education, distance learning, double majors, English as a second language, honors programs, independent study, internships, part-time degree program, services for LD students, student-designed majors, study abroad, summer session for credit. *ROTC:* Army (c).
Library 57,029 titles, 286 serial subscriptions, 5,401 audiovisual materials, an OPAC, a Web page.
Computers on Campus 434 computers available on campus for general student use. A campuswide network can be accessed from off campus. Internet access, online (class) registration, at least one staffed computer lab available.
Student Life *Housing:* college housing not available. *Activities and Organizations:* drama/theater group, student-run newspaper, radio station, Habitat for Humanity, Honors Society, Phi Theta Kappa, Photo Club, Recreation Leadership Club. *Campus security:* 24-hour emergency response devices and patrols, late-night transport/escort service. *Student services:* health clinic, personal/psychological counseling, women's center.
Athletics Member NJCAA. *Intercollegiate sports:* baseball M, basketball M/W, bowling M/W, cheerleading W, cross-country running M/W, football M, golf M/W, ice hockey M, lacrosse W, soccer M/W, softball W, swimming and diving M/W, track and field M/W, volleyball W.
Costs (2005–06) *Tuition:* area resident $2900 full-time, $121 per credit hour part-time; state resident $5800 full-time, $242 per credit hour part-time; nonresident $5800 full-time, $242 per credit hour part-time. *Required fees:* $320 full-time, $5 per credit hour part-time, $30 per term part-time. *Payment plans:* installment, deferred payment. *Waivers:* senior citizens and employees or children of employees.
Financial Aid Of all full-time matriculated undergraduates who enrolled in 2004, 300 Federal Work-Study jobs (averaging $2000).
Applying *Options:* common application, electronic application. *Required:* high school transcript. *Required for some:* interview. *Application deadline:* rolling (freshmen), rolling (transfers). *Notification:* continuous (freshmen).
Freshmen Application Contact Ms. Petrina Hill-Cheatom, Director of Admissions, Erie Community College, South Campus, 4041 Southwestern Boulevard, Orchard Park, NY 14127-2199. *Phone:* 716-851-1588. *Fax:* 716-851-1629.

EUGENIO MARÍA DE HOSTOS COMMUNITY COLLEGE OF THE CITY UNIVERSITY OF NEW YORK
Bronx, New York www.hostos.cuny.edu/

- **State and locally supported** 2-year, founded 1968, part of City University of New York System
- **Urban** 8-acre campus
- **Endowment** $211,655
- **Coed**

Undergraduates 2,917 full-time, 1,423 part-time. Students come from 4 states and territories, 91 other countries, 1% are from out of state, 29% African American, 2% Asian American or Pacific Islander, 58% Hispanic American, 0.1% Native American, 8% international, 12% transferred in.
Faculty *Student/faculty ratio:* 14:1.
Academics *Calendar:* semesters. *Degree:* certificates and associate. *Special study options:* academic remediation for entering students, adult/continuing education programs, distance learning, double majors, English as a second language, internships, part-time degree program, services for LD students, study abroad, summer session for credit.
Student Life *Campus security:* 24-hour emergency response devices and patrols, late-night transport/escort service.
Athletics Member NJCAA.
Standardized Tests *Required:* CUNY Skills Assessment Tests (for placement). *Required for some:* SAT (for placement), ACT (for placement), SAT Subject Tests (for placement).
Costs (2005–06) *Tuition:* state resident $2500 full-time, $105 per credit part-time; nonresident $3076 full-time, $130 per credit part-time. *Payment plans:* installment, deferred payment.
Financial Aid Of all full-time matriculated undergraduates who enrolled in 2004, 1,482 Federal Work-Study jobs (averaging $1600).

Eugenio María de Hostos Community College of the City University of New York (continued)

Applying *Options:* common application. *Application fee:* $65. *Required:* high school transcript.

Director of Admissions Mr. Roland Velez, Director of Admissions, Eugenio María de Hostos Community College of the City University of New York, 120 149th Street, Room D-210, Bronx, NY 10451. *Phone:* 718-518-4406.

FASHION INSTITUTE OF TECHNOLOGY
New York, New York
www.fitnyc.edu

- **State and locally supported** comprehensive, founded 1944, part of State University of New York System
- **Urban** 5-acre campus
- **Endowment** $18.5 million
- **Coed, primarily women,** 10,199 undergraduate students, 65% full-time, 84% women, 16% men

Undergraduates 6,661 full-time, 3,538 part-time. Students come from 51 states and territories, 60 other countries, 30% are from out of state, 7% African American, 10% Asian American or Pacific Islander, 10% Hispanic American, 0.3% Native American, 10% international, 8% transferred in, 16% live on campus. *Retention:* 84% of 2003 full-time freshmen returned. Freshmen *Admission:* 3,498 applied, 1,425 admitted, 1,028 enrolled. *Average high school GPA:* 3.13.

Faculty *Total:* 918, 23% full-time. *Student/faculty ratio:* 17:1.

Majors Advertising; apparel and textile manufacturing; apparel and textiles; art history, criticism and conservation; arts management; commercial and advertising art; commercial photography; digital communication and media/multimedia; fashion/apparel design; fashion merchandising; fashion modeling; fine/studio arts; graphic design; illustration; industrial design; interior design; international marketing; marketing related; marketing research; metal and jewelry arts; special products marketing.

Academics *Calendar:* 4-1-4. *Degrees:* certificates, associate, bachelor's, and master's. *Special study options:* academic remediation for entering students, adult/continuing education programs, advanced placement credit, cooperative education, distance learning, English as a second language, honors programs, internships, part-time degree program, services for LD students, study abroad, summer session for credit.

Library Gladys Marcus Library with 176,987 titles, 467 serial subscriptions, 177,801 audiovisual materials, an OPAC, a Web page.

Computers on Campus 300 computers available on campus for general student use. A campuswide network can be accessed from student residence rooms and from off campus. Internet access, online (class) registration, at least one staffed computer lab available.

Student Life *Housing Options:* coed, women-only. Campus housing is university owned and is provided by a third party. Freshman applicants given priority for college housing. *Activities and Organizations:* drama/theater group, student-run newspaper, radio station, choral group, Public Relations Student Society of America, Delta Epsilon Chi, Merchandising Society, Student Government. *Campus security:* 24-hour emergency response devices and patrols. *Student services:* health clinic, personal/psychological counseling.

Athletics Member NJCAA. *Intercollegiate sports:* basketball M/W, bowling M/W, tennis M/W, volleyball W. *Intramural sports:* basketball M/W, bowling M/W, table tennis M/W, tennis M/W, volleyball M/W.

Costs (2006–07) *Tuition:* state resident $4350 full-time, $181 per credit part-time; nonresident $10,610 full-time, $442 per credit part-time. *Required fees:* $420 full-time, $30 per term part-time. *Room and board:* $8409; room only: $7519.

Financial Aid Of all full-time matriculated undergraduates who enrolled in 2005, 4,317 applied for aid, 1,954 were judged to have need, 429 had their need fully met. 458 Federal Work-Study jobs (averaging $2048). In 2005, 95 non-need-based awards were made. *Average percent of need met:* 71%. *Average financial aid package:* $7555. *Average need-based loan:* $3664. *Average need-based gift aid:* $4138. *Average non-need-based aid:* $2208. *Average indebtedness upon graduation:* $12,869.

Applying *Options:* electronic application, early action, deferred entrance. *Application fee:* $40. *Required:* essay or personal statement, high school transcript, portfolio for art and design programs. *Application deadlines:* 2/15 (freshmen), 2/15 (transfers). *Notification:* continuous (freshmen), 1/31 (early action).

Freshmen Application Contact Ms. Dolores Lombardi, Director of Admissions, Fashion Institute of Technology, Seventh Avenue at 27th Street, New York, NY 10001-5992. *Phone:* 212-217-7675. *Toll-free phone:* 800-GOTOFIT. *Fax:* 212-217-7481. *E-mail:* fitinfo@fitnyc.edu.

▶ See page 542 for the College Close-Up.

FINGER LAKES COMMUNITY COLLEGE
Canandaigua, New York
www.flcc.edu/

- **State and locally supported** 2-year, founded 1965, part of State University of New York System
- **Small-town** 300-acre campus with easy access to Rochester
- **Coed,** 4,910 undergraduate students, 53% full-time, 57% women, 43% men

Undergraduates 2,599 full-time, 2,311 part-time. Students come from 6 states and territories, 3 other countries, 1% are from out of state, 4% African American, 0.7% Asian American or Pacific Islander, 2% Hispanic American, 0.6% Native American. Freshmen *Admission:* 4,023 applied, 991 enrolled.

Faculty *Total:* 280, 39% full-time. *Student/faculty ratio:* 20:1.

Majors Accounting; administrative assistant and secretarial science; architectural engineering technology; banking and financial support services; biological and physical sciences; biology/biological sciences; biology/biotechnology laboratory technician; broadcast journalism; business administration and management; chemistry; commercial and advertising art; computer and information sciences; computer science; consumer merchandising/retailing management; criminal justice/law enforcement administration; criminal justice/police science; data processing and data processing technology; drafting and design technology; dramatic/theater arts; engineering science; environmental studies; fine/studio arts; fish/game management; hotel/motel administration; humanities; human services; kindergarten/preschool education; legal assistant/paralegal; liberal arts and sciences/liberal studies; marketing/marketing management; mass communication/media; mathematics; mechanical engineering/mechanical technology; music; natural resources/conservation; natural resources management; natural resources management and policy; nursing (registered nurse training); ornamental horticulture; parks, recreation and leisure facilities management; physical education teaching and coaching; physics; political science and government; pre-engineering; psychology; social sciences; sociology; substance abuse/addiction counseling; tourism and travel services management.

Academics *Calendar:* semesters. *Degree:* certificates and associate. *Special study options:* academic remediation for entering students, advanced placement credit, distance learning, English as a second language, honors programs, internships, off-campus study, part-time degree program, services for LD students, summer session for credit. *ROTC:* Army (c).

Library Charles Meder Library with 73,305 titles, 464 serial subscriptions, an OPAC.

Computers on Campus 425 computers available on campus for general student use. A campuswide network can be accessed from off campus. Internet access, at least one staffed computer lab available.

Student Life *Housing:* college housing not available. *Options:* Campus housing is provided by a third party. *Activities and Organizations:* drama/theater group, student-run newspaper, radio station, choral group, national fraternities, national sororities. *Campus security:* 24-hour emergency response devices and patrols, late-night transport/escort service. *Student services:* health clinic, personal/psychological counseling, legal services.

Athletics Member NJCAA. *Intercollegiate sports:* baseball M, basketball M/W, cross-country running M/W, lacrosse M/W, soccer M/W, softball W. *Intramural sports:* basketball M/W, tennis M/W, volleyball M/W.

Costs (2005–06) *Tuition:* state resident $2900 full-time, $117 per credit hour part-time; nonresident $5800 full-time, $234 per credit hour part-time. *Required fees:* $260 full-time, $7 per credit hour part-time.

Financial Aid Of all full-time matriculated undergraduates who enrolled in 2004, 150 Federal Work-Study jobs (averaging $1800). 150 state and other part-time jobs (averaging $1800).

Applying *Options:* electronic application, early admission, deferred entrance. *Required:* high school transcript. *Recommended:* interview. *Application deadline:* rolling (freshmen), rolling (transfers). *Notification:* continuous until 8/31 (freshmen).

Freshmen Application Contact Ms. Bonnie Ritts, Director of Admissions, Finger Lakes Community College, 4355 Lake Shore Drive, Canandaigua, NY 14424-8395. *Phone:* 585-394-3500 Ext. 7278. *Fax:* 585-394-5005. *E-mail:* admissions@flcc.edu.

Fiorello H. LaGuardia Community College of the City University of New York

Long Island City, New York   www.lagcc.cuny.edu/

- **State and locally supported** 2-year, founded 1970, part of City University of New York System
- **Urban** 6-acre campus
- **Endowment** $351,000
- **Coed,** 13,489 undergraduate students, 55% full-time, 64% women, 36% men

Fiorello H. LaGuardia Community College of the City University of New York offers forty degree and certificate programs; day, evening, and weekend classes; a world-renowned internship program; an honors program; the Transfer Services Center; and strong support services to ensure student success. Recently named as one of two national winners of the Theodore M. Hesburgh Certificate of Excellence, LaGuardia also has the lowest college tuition in New York City. Based in western Queens, the College is 10 minutes from Manhattan and Brooklyn by subway or bus.

Undergraduates 7,453 full-time, 6,036 part-time. Students come from 9 states and territories, 135 other countries, 1% are from out of state, 17% African American, 14% Asian American or Pacific Islander, 31% Hispanic American, 0.2% Native American, 16% international, 7% transferred in.
Freshmen *Admission:* 3,606 applied, 3,606 admitted, 2,080 enrolled. *Average high school GPA:* 2.05.
Faculty *Total:* 773, 35% full-time, 27% with terminal degrees. *Student/faculty ratio:* 21:1.
Majors Accounting; administrative assistant and secretarial science; business administration and management; computer and information sciences related; computer engineering technology; computer programming; computer programming related; computer programming (specific applications); computer programming (vendor/product certification); computer science; computer systems networking and telecommunications; data entry/microcomputer applications; dietetics; education; emergency medical technology (EMT paramedic); fine/studio arts; funeral service and mortuary science; gerontology; human services; information science/studies; kindergarten/preschool education; legal administrative assistant/secretary; legal assistant/paralegal; liberal arts and sciences/liberal studies; mental health/rehabilitation; nursing (registered nurse training); occupational therapy; photography; physical therapy; special products marketing; system administration; tourism and travel services management; veterinary technology.
Academics *Calendar:* modified semester. *Degree:* certificates and associate. *Special study options:* academic remediation for entering students, adult/continuing education programs, advanced placement credit, cooperative education, double majors, English as a second language, honors programs, independent study, internships, off-campus study, part-time degree program, services for LD students, student-designed majors, study abroad.
Library Fiorello H. LaGuardia Community College Library Media Resources Center plus 1 other with 121,631 titles, 760 serial subscriptions, 5,529 audiovisual materials, an OPAC.
Computers on Campus 997 computers available on campus for general student use. A campuswide network can be accessed from off campus. At least one staffed computer lab available.
Student Life *Housing:* college housing not available. *Activities and Organizations:* drama/theater group, student-run newspaper, radio station, Latinos Unidos Club, Bangladesh Club, Dominican Club, Law Club. *Campus security:* 24-hour patrols. *Student services:* health clinic, personal/psychological counseling, women's center.
Athletics *Intramural sports:* basketball M/W, football M/W, golf M/W, soccer M/W, volleyball M/W, weight lifting M/W.
Costs (2005–06) *Tuition:* state resident $3072 full-time, $190 per credit hour part-time; nonresident $5700 full-time, $190 per credit hour part-time. *Required fees:* $272 full-time.
Financial Aid Of all full-time matriculated undergraduates who enrolled in 2004, 1,425 Federal Work-Study jobs (averaging $1194).
Applying *Options:* electronic application, early admission, deferred entrance. *Application fee:* $65. *Required:* high school transcript. *Application deadline:* rolling (freshmen), rolling (transfers). *Notification:* continuous (freshmen).
Freshmen Application Contact Ms. LaVora Desvigne, Director of Admissions, Fiorello H. LaGuardia Community College of the City University of New York, RM-147, 31-10 Thomson Avenue, Long Island City, NY 11101. *Phone:* 718-482-5114. *Fax:* 718-482-5112. *E-mail:* admissions@lagcc.cuny.edu.

Fulton-Montgomery Community College

Johnstown, New York   www.fmcc.suny.edu/

- **State and locally supported** 2-year, founded 1964, part of State University of New York System
- **Rural** 195-acre campus
- **Endowment** $1.5 million
- **Coed**

Undergraduates 1,404 full-time, 667 part-time. Students come from 2 states and territories, 20 other countries, 4% African American, 0.6% Asian American or Pacific Islander, 5% Hispanic American, 0.3% Native American, 7% international, 2% transferred in.
Faculty *Student/faculty ratio:* 21:1.
Academics *Calendar:* semesters plus winter session. *Degree:* certificates and associate. *Special study options:* academic remediation for entering students, accelerated degree program, adult/continuing education programs, advanced placement credit, cooperative education, distance learning, double majors, English as a second language, external degree program, honors programs, independent study, internships, off-campus study, part-time degree program, services for LD students, student-designed majors, study abroad, summer session for credit.
Student Life *Campus security:* weekend and night security.
Athletics Member NJCAA.
Costs (2005–06) *Tuition:* state resident $2925 full-time, $122 per credit hour part-time; nonresident $5850 full-time, $244 per credit hour part-time. Part-time tuition and fees vary according to course load. *Required fees:* $205 full-time, $2 per credit hour part-time, $38 per term part-time. *Payment plans:* installment, deferred payment.
Financial Aid Of all full-time matriculated undergraduates who enrolled in 2004, 87 Federal Work-Study jobs (averaging $1000).
Applying *Options:* common application, electronic application, early admission, deferred entrance. *Required:* high school transcript.
Director of Admissions Ms. Jane Kelley, Associate Dean for Enrollment Management, Fulton-Montgomery Community College, 2805 State Highway 67, Johnstown, NY 12095-3790. *Phone:* 518-762-4651 Ext. 8301. *E-mail:* jkelley@fmcc.suny.edu.

Gamla College
Brooklyn, New York

Genesee Community College

Batavia, New York   www.genesee.edu/

- **State and locally supported** 2-year, founded 1966, part of State University of New York System
- **Small-town** 256-acre campus with easy access to Buffalo
- **Endowment** $1.7 million
- **Coed,** 6,490 undergraduate students, 48% full-time, 65% women, 35% men

Undergraduates 3,113 full-time, 3,377 part-time. Students come from 13 states and territories, 26 other countries, 0.6% are from out of state, 4% African American, 0.5% Asian American or Pacific Islander, 1% Hispanic American, 0.9% Native American, 3% international, 5% transferred in.
Freshmen *Admission:* 2,547 applied, 2,547 admitted, 1,139 enrolled.
Faculty *Total:* 312, 24% full-time. *Student/faculty ratio:* 20:1.
Majors Accounting; administrative assistant and secretarial science; business administration and management; clinical/medical laboratory technology; commercial and advertising art; computer and information sciences related; computer engineering technology; computer graphics; computer software and media applications related; consumer merchandising/retailing management; criminal justice/law enforcement administration; drafting and design technology; dramatic/theater arts; education; electrical, electronic and communications engineering technology; elementary education; engineering science; fashion merchandising; gerontology; hotel/motel administration; human services; information science/studies; kindergarten/preschool education; legal assistant/paralegal; liberal arts and sciences/liberal studies; marketing/marketing management; mass communication/media; mathematics; nursing (registered nurse training); occupational therapy; physical education teaching and coaching; physical therapy; psychology; respi-

Genesee Community College (continued)

ratory care therapy; substance abuse/addiction counseling; system administration; tourism and travel services management.

Academics *Calendar:* semesters. *Degree:* certificates and associate. *Special study options:* academic remediation for entering students, adult/continuing education programs, advanced placement credit, cooperative education, distance learning, honors programs, independent study, internships, part-time degree program, services for LD students, summer session for credit. *ROTC:* Army (c).

Library Alfred C. O'Connell Library with 78,273 titles, 332 serial subscriptions, 4,729 audiovisual materials, an OPAC, a Web page.

Computers on Campus 408 computers available on campus for general student use. A campuswide network can be accessed from off campus that provide access to applications software. Internet access, at least one staffed computer lab available.

Student Life *Activities and Organizations:* drama/theater group, student-run newspaper, radio station, choral group, Student Government Association, Phi Theta Kappa, DECA, Student Activities Council, Forum Players. *Campus security:* 24-hour emergency response devices and patrols, late-night transport/escort service. *Student services:* health clinic, personal/psychological counseling.

Athletics Member NJCAA. *Intercollegiate sports:* baseball M, basketball M(s)/W(s), cross-country running M/W, soccer M/W(s), softball W, swimming and diving M/W, volleyball M/W(s). *Intramural sports:* badminton M/W, basketball M/W, football M/W, golf M/W, soccer M/W, softball M/W, swimming and diving M/W, table tennis M/W, tennis M/W, track and field M/W, volleyball M/W, water polo M/W, weight lifting M/W.

Costs (2006–07) *Tuition:* state resident $3200 full-time; nonresident $3600 full-time. *Required fees:* $290 full-time. *Room and board:* room only: $4250.

Financial Aid Of all full-time matriculated undergraduates who enrolled in 2004, 135 Federal Work-Study jobs (averaging $1450).

Applying *Options:* common application, electronic application. *Required:* high school transcript. *Required for some:* 1 letter of recommendation. *Application deadline:* rolling (freshmen), rolling (transfers). *Notification:* continuous (freshmen).

Freshmen Application Contact Mrs. Tanya Lane-Martin, Director of Admissions, Genesee Community College, 1 College Road, Batavia, NY 14020. *Phone:* 585-343-0055 Ext. 6413. *Toll-free phone:* 800-CALL GCC. *Fax:* 585-345-6892.

HELENE FULD COLLEGE OF NURSING OF NORTH GENERAL HOSPITAL

New York, New York www.helenefuld.edu/

Freshmen Application Contact Mrs. Gladys Pineda, Student Services, Helene Fuld College of Nursing of North General Hospital, 1879 Madison Avenue, New York, NY 10035. *Phone:* 212-423-2768.

HERKIMER COUNTY COMMUNITY COLLEGE

Herkimer, New York www.herkimer.edu

- **State and locally supported** 2-year, founded 1966, part of State University of New York System
- **Small-town** 500-acre campus with easy access to Syracuse
- **Endowment** $1.7 million
- **Coed**

Undergraduates Students come from 23 states and territories, 17 other countries, 2% are from out of state, 25% live on campus.

Faculty *Student/faculty ratio:* 22:1.

Academics *Calendar:* semesters. *Degree:* certificates and associate. *Special study options:* academic remediation for entering students, adult/continuing education programs, advanced placement credit, English as a second language, honors programs, internships, part-time degree program, services for LD students, summer session for credit.

Student Life *Campus security:* 24-hour emergency response devices and patrols.

Athletics Member NJCAA.

Standardized Tests *Recommended:* SAT or ACT (for placement).

Financial Aid Of all full-time matriculated undergraduates who enrolled in 2004, 150 Federal Work-Study jobs (averaging $700).

Applying *Options:* early admission. *Required:* high school transcript.

Director of Admissions Mr. Scott J. Hughes, Associate Dean for Enrollment Management, Herkimer County Community College, Herkimer, NY 13350. *Phone:* 315-866-0300 Ext. 278. *Toll-free phone:* 888-464-4222 Ext. 8278.

HUDSON VALLEY COMMUNITY COLLEGE

Troy, New York www.hvcc.edu/

- **State and locally supported** 2-year, founded 1953, part of State University of New York System
- **Suburban** 135-acre campus
- **Endowment** $3.7 million
- **Coed,** 12,205 undergraduate students

Undergraduates Students come from 21 states and territories, 18 other countries, 5% are from out of state, 8% African American, 2% Asian American or Pacific Islander, 3% Hispanic American, 0.3% Native American, 0.6% international. *Retention:* 60% of 2003 full-time freshmen returned.

Freshmen *Admission:* 8,000 applied, 7,200 admitted. *Average high school GPA:* 2.5.

Faculty *Total:* 574, 37% full-time. *Student/faculty ratio:* 19:1.

Majors Accounting; administrative assistant and secretarial science; automobile/automotive mechanics technology; biology/biotechnology laboratory technician; business administration and management; chemical technology; civil engineering technology; computer programming (specific applications); construction engineering technology; criminal justice/law enforcement administration; dental hygiene; early childhood education; e-commerce; electrical, electronic and communications engineering technology; electrical/electronics maintenance and repair technology related; emergency medical technology (EMT paramedic); engineering science; environmental studies; finance; fine/studio arts; forensic science and technology; funeral service and mortuary science; health and physical education related; health information/medical records technology; heating, air conditioning, ventilation and refrigeration maintenance technology; human services; industrial technology; information technology; interdisciplinary studies; liberal arts and sciences/liberal studies; marketing/marketing management; mechanical engineering/mechanical technology; nursing (registered nurse training); public administration; radiologic technology/science; radio/television broadcasting technology; respiratory care therapy; substance abuse/addiction counseling; system, networking, and LAN/WAN management; telecommunications technology; Web page, digital/multimedia and information resources design.

Academics *Calendar:* semesters. *Degree:* certificates and associate. *Special study options:* academic remediation for entering students, adult/continuing education programs, advanced placement credit, cooperative education, external degree program, internships, off-campus study, part-time degree program, services for LD students, student-designed majors, summer session for credit. *ROTC:* Army (b), Air Force (c).

Library Marvin Library with 148,189 titles, 691 serial subscriptions.

Computers on Campus 500 computers available on campus for general student use. A campuswide network can be accessed from off campus. Internet access, at least one staffed computer lab available.

Student Life *Housing:* college housing not available. *Activities and Organizations:* drama/theater group, student-run newspaper, radio station. *Campus security:* 24-hour emergency response devices and patrols, late-night transport/escort service. *Student services:* health clinic, personal/psychological counseling, women's center, legal services.

Athletics Member NJCAA. *Intercollegiate sports:* basketball M/W, bowling M/W, cross-country running M/W, football M, golf M/W, lacrosse M, soccer M, tennis M/W, track and field M/W, volleyball W. *Intramural sports:* archery M/W, badminton M/W, baseball M, basketball M/W, bowling M/W, football M, lacrosse M, racquetball M/W, softball W, table tennis M/W, tennis M/W, track and field M/W, volleyball M/W.

Costs (2006–07) *Tuition:* state resident $2700 full-time, $112 per credit hour part-time; nonresident $8100 full-time, $336 per credit hour part-time. *Required fees:* $480 full-time, $14 per credit hour part-time.

Financial Aid Of all full-time matriculated undergraduates who enrolled in 2004, 100 Federal Work-Study jobs (averaging $2000).

Applying *Options:* early admission, deferred entrance. *Application fee:* $30. *Required:* high school transcript. *Application deadline:* rolling (freshmen), rolling (transfers). *Notification:* continuous (freshmen).

Freshmen Application Contact Ms. MaryClaire Bauer, Director of Admissions, Hudson Valley Community College, 80 Vandenburgh Avenue, Troy, NY 12180-6096. *Phone:* 518-629-4603. *E-mail:* panzajul@hvcc.edu.

INSTITUTE OF DESIGN AND CONSTRUCTION

Brooklyn, New York   www.idcbrooklyn.org/

Director of Admissions Mr. Kevin Giannetti, Director of Admissions, Institute of Design and Construction, 141 Willoughby Street, Brooklyn, NY 11201-5317. *Phone:* 718-855-3661.

INTERBORO INSTITUTE

New York, New York   www.interboro.com/

Freshmen Application Contact Ms. Cheryl Ryan, Director of Admissions, Interboro Institute, 450 West 56th Street, New York, NY 10019. *Phone:* 212-399-0091 Ext. 6406. *E-mail:* ryan@interboro.com.

ISLAND DRAFTING AND TECHNICAL INSTITUTE

Amityville, New York   www.idti.edu/

- **Proprietary** 2-year, founded 1957
- **Suburban** campus
- **Coed, primarily men,** 185 undergraduate students, 100% full-time, 15% women, 85% men

Undergraduates 185 full-time. Students come from 1 other state, 14% African American, 1% Asian American or Pacific Islander, 18% Hispanic American, 2% Native American.
Freshmen *Admission:* 77 applied, 77 admitted, 66 enrolled. *Average high school GPA:* 3.50.
Faculty *Total:* 25, 20% full-time. *Student/faculty ratio:* 15:1.
Majors Architectural drafting and CAD/CADD; computer and information systems security; computer systems networking and telecommunications; computer/technical support; computer technology/computer systems technology; electrical, electronic and communications engineering technology; mechanical drafting and CAD/CADD; system administration.
Academics *Calendar:* semesters. *Degree:* certificates, diplomas, and associate. *Special study options:* accelerated degree program, adult/continuing education programs, summer session for credit.
Student Life *Housing:* college housing not available.
Costs (2006–07) *Tuition:* $11,850 full-time, $395 per credit part-time. *Required fees:* $350 full-time.
Applying *Options:* early admission. *Required:* interview. *Recommended:* high school transcript. *Notification:* continuous (freshmen).
Freshmen Application Contact Mr. Steven Rothenberg, Island Drafting and Technical Institute, 128 Broadway, Amityville, NY 11701. *Phone:* 631-691-8733. *Fax:* 631-691-8738. *E-mail:* info@idti.edu.

ITT TECHNICAL INSTITUTE

Albany, New York   www.itt-tech.edu/

- **Proprietary** 2-year, part of ITT Educational Services, Inc
- **Coed**

Majors Computer engineering technologies related; computer programming; computer programming (specific applications); electrical, electronic and communications engineering technology; system, networking, and LAN/WAN management; web/multimedia management and webmaster; web page, digital/multimedia and information resources design.
Academics *Calendar:* quarters. *Degree:* associate.
Library a Web page.
Computers on Campus Internet access, at least one staffed computer lab available.
Student Life *Housing:* college housing not available.
Standardized Tests *Required:* Wonderlic aptitude test (for admission).
Costs (2005–06) *Tuition:* Please see school catalog for specific information.
Applying *Options:* deferred entrance. *Application fee:* $100. *Required:* high school transcript, interview. *Recommended:* letters of recommendation. *Application deadline:* rolling (freshmen), rolling (transfers). *Notification:* continuous (freshmen).

Freshmen Application Contact Mr. John Henebry, Director of Recruitment, ITT Technical Institute, 13 Airline Drive, Albany, NY 12205. *Phone:* 518-452-9300. *Toll-free phone:* 800-489-1191.

ITT TECHNICAL INSTITUTE

Getzville, New York   www.itt-tech.edu/

- **Proprietary** 2-year, part of ITT Educational Services, Inc
- **Coed**

Majors CAD/CADD drafting/design technology; computer and information systems security; computer programming; electrical, electronic and communications engineering technology; system, networking, and LAN/WAN management; web page, digital/multimedia and information resources design.
Academics *Degree:* associate.
Library a Web page.
Computers on Campus Internet access, at least one staffed computer lab available.
Student Life *Housing:* college housing not available.
Standardized Tests *Required:* Wonderlic aptitude test (for admission).
Costs (2005–06) *Tuition:* Please see school catalog for specific information.
Applying *Options:* deferred entrance. *Application fee:* $100. *Required:* high school transcript, interview. *Recommended:* letters of recommendation. *Application deadline:* rolling (freshmen), rolling (transfers). *Notification:* continuous (freshmen).
Freshmen Application Contact Mr. Scott Jaskier, Director of Recruitment, ITT Technical Institute, 2295 Millersport Highway, PO Box 327, Getzville, NY 14068. *Phone:* 716-689-2200. *Toll-free phone:* 800-469-7593.

ITT TECHNICAL INSTITUTE

Liverpool, New York   www.itt-tech.edu/

- **Proprietary** 2-year, part of ITT Educational Services, Inc
- **Coed**

Majors Computer programming; system, networking, and LAN/WAN management; web/multimedia management and webmaster; web page, digital/multimedia and information resources design.
Academics *Calendar:* semesters. *Degree:* associate.
Library a Web page.
Computers on Campus Internet access, at least one staffed computer lab available.
Student Life *Housing:* college housing not available.
Standardized Tests *Required:* Wonderlic aptitude test (for admission).
Costs (2005–06) *Tuition:* Please see school catalog for specific information.
Applying *Options:* deferred entrance. *Application fee:* $100. *Required:* high school transcript, interview. *Recommended:* letters of recommendation. *Application deadline:* rolling (freshmen), rolling (transfers). *Notification:* continuous (freshmen).
Freshmen Application Contact Terry Riesel, Director of Recruitment, ITT Technical Institute, 235 Greenfield Parkway, Liverpool, NY 13088. *Phone:* 315-461-8000. *Toll-free phone:* 877-488-0011.

JAMESTOWN BUSINESS COLLEGE

Jamestown, New York   www.jbcny.org/

Director of Admissions Ms. Brenda Salemme, Director of Admissions and Placement, Jamestown Business College, 7 Fairmount Avenue, Jamestown, NY 14701. *Phone:* 716-664-5100. *E-mail:* jbc@epix.net.

JAMESTOWN COMMUNITY COLLEGE

Jamestown, New York   www.sunyjcc.edu/

- **State and locally supported** 2-year, founded 1950, part of State University of New York System
- **Small-town** 107-acre campus
- **Endowment** $274,625
- **Coed,** 3,672 undergraduate students, 67% full-time, 59% women, 41% men

Undergraduates 2,460 full-time, 1,212 part-time. Students come from 11 states and territories, 9% are from out of state, 3% African American, 0.7% Asian

Jamestown Community College (continued)
American or Pacific Islander, 2% Hispanic American, 0.9% Native American. Freshmen *Admission:* 1,668 applied, 1,372 admitted, 1,129 enrolled.

Faculty *Total:* 345, 24% full-time, 7% with terminal degrees. *Student/faculty ratio:* 18:1.

Majors Accounting; airline pilot and flight crew; business administration and management; clinical/medical laboratory technology; communication/speech communication and rhetoric; computer and information sciences; computer and information sciences related; computer and information systems security; computer engineering technology; computer science; criminal justice/police science; criminal justice/safety; electrical, electronic and communications engineering technology; electrical, electronics and communications engineering; engineering; fine/studio arts; humanities; human services; mechanical engineering/mechanical technology; nursing (registered nurse training); occupational therapist assistant; social sciences.

Academics *Calendar:* semesters. *Degree:* certificates and associate. *Special study options:* academic remediation for entering students, adult/continuing education programs, advanced placement credit, cooperative education, distance learning, double majors, honors programs, independent study, internships, off-campus study, part-time degree program, services for LD students, study abroad, summer session for credit.

Library Hultquist Library with 66,808 titles, 370 serial subscriptions, 4,605 audiovisual materials, an OPAC, a Web page.

Computers on Campus 400 computers available on campus for general student use. A campuswide network can be accessed from off campus that provide access to Angel course, management system. Internet access, online (class) registration, at least one staffed computer lab available.

Student Life *Housing:* college housing not available. *Activities and Organizations:* drama/theater group, student-run radio station, choral group, Nursing Club, Inter-Varsity Christian Fellowship, Earth Awareness, Adult Student Network, Student Senate. *Student services:* health clinic, personal/psychological counseling.

Athletics Member NJCAA. *Intercollegiate sports:* baseball M, basketball M/W, golf M, soccer M(s)/W, softball W, swimming and diving M/W, volleyball W, wrestling M. *Intramural sports:* basketball M/W, bowling M/W, table tennis M/W, volleyball M/W.

Costs (2005–06) *Tuition:* state resident $3150 full-time, $132 per credit hour part-time; nonresident $6300 full-time, $238 per credit hour part-time. Full-time tuition and fees vary according to program. *Required fees:* $530 full-time, $17 per credit hour part-time. *Payment plan:* installment. *Waivers:* senior citizens and employees or children of employees.

Financial Aid Of all full-time matriculated undergraduates who enrolled in 2004, 120 Federal Work-Study jobs (averaging $1000). 110 state and other part-time jobs (averaging $1000).

Applying *Options:* deferred entrance. *Application fee:* $40. *Required:* high school transcript. *Required for some:* standardized test scores. *Application deadline:* rolling (freshmen), rolling (transfers). *Notification:* continuous (freshmen).

Freshmen Application Contact Ms. Wendy Present, Director of Admissions and Recruitment, Jamestown Community College, 525 Falconer Street, PO Box 20, Jamestown, NY 14702-0020. *Phone:* 716-665-5220 Ext. 2240. *Toll-free phone:* 800-388-8557. *E-mail:* admissions@mail.sunyjcc.edu.

JEFFERSON COMMUNITY COLLEGE
Watertown, New York   **www.sunyjefferson.edu/**

- **State and locally supported** 2-year, founded 1961, part of State University of New York System
- **Small-town** 90-acre campus with easy access to Syracuse
- **Endowment** $2.1 million
- **Coed**, 3,545 undergraduate students, 51% full-time, 59% women, 41% men

Undergraduates 1,822 full-time, 1,723 part-time. Students come from 26 states and territories, 3 other countries, 1% are from out of state, 5% African American, 2% Asian American or Pacific Islander, 4% Hispanic American, 0.5% Native American, 0.2% international, 3% transferred in. Freshmen *Admission:* 714 enrolled.

Faculty *Total:* 188, 41% full-time, 6% with terminal degrees. *Student/faculty ratio:* 20:1.

Majors Accounting; administrative assistant and secretarial science; biology/biotechnology laboratory technician; business administration and management; chemical technology; computer science; computer systems networking and telecommunications; computer typography and composition equipment operation; consumer merchandising/retailing management; criminal justice/law enforcement administration; engineering science; forestry technology; hospitality administration; hotel/motel administration; humanities; human services; information science/studies; interdisciplinary studies; kindergarten/preschool educa-

tion; legal assistant/paralegal; liberal arts and sciences/liberal studies; marketing/marketing management; mathematics; medical administrative assistant and medical secretary; medical laboratory technology; natural sciences; nursing (registered nurse training); pre-engineering; tourism and travel services management.

Academics *Calendar:* semesters. *Degree:* certificates and associate. *Special study options:* academic remediation for entering students, advanced placement credit, cooperative education, distance learning, double majors, honors programs, independent study, internships, part-time degree program, services for LD students, student-designed majors, summer session for credit.

Library Melvil Dewey Library with 62,503 titles, 247 serial subscriptions, 4,097 audiovisual materials, an OPAC, a Web page.

Computers on Campus 354 computers available on campus for general student use. A campuswide network can be accessed. Internet access, at least one staffed computer lab available.

Student Life *Housing:* college housing not available. *Activities and Organizations:* drama/theater group, student-run newspaper, choral group, Student Nursing Association, newspaper, The Melting Pot, Paralegal Club, Criminal Justice Club. *Campus security:* 24-hour emergency response devices and patrols. *Student services:* health clinic, personal/psychological counseling.

Athletics Member NJCAA. *Intercollegiate sports:* baseball M, basketball M/W, golf M/W, lacrosse M/W, soccer M/W, softball W, tennis W, volleyball W. *Intramural sports:* badminton M/W, basketball M/W, soccer M/W, softball M/W, volleyball M/W.

Standardized Tests *Recommended:* SAT or ACT (for admission).

Costs (2005–06) *Tuition:* state resident $3294 full-time, $122 per credit hour part-time; nonresident $4724 full-time, $182 per credit hour part-time. *Required fees:* $366 full-time, $13 per credit hour part-time, $21 per semester part-time.

Financial Aid Of all full-time matriculated undergraduates who enrolled in 2004, 125 Federal Work-Study jobs (averaging $1200). 50 state and other part-time jobs (averaging $1000).

Applying *Options:* early admission, deferred entrance. *Required:* high school transcript. *Required for some:* letters of recommendation, interview. *Application deadline:* 9/6 (freshmen), rolling (transfers). *Notification:* continuous (freshmen).

Freshmen Application Contact Ms. Rosanne N. Weir, Director of Admissions, Jefferson Community College, 1220 Coffeen Street, Watertown, NY 13601. *Phone:* 315-786-2277. *Fax:* 315-786-2459. *E-mail:* admissions@sunyjefferson.edu.

KATHARINE GIBBS SCHOOL
Melville, New York   **www.gibbsmelville.com/**

Director of Admissions Ms. Cynthia Gamache, Director of Admissions, Katharine Gibbs School, 320 South Service Road, Melville, NY 11747-3785. *Phone:* 631-370-3307.

KATHARINE GIBBS SCHOOL
New York, New York   **www.katharinegibbs.com/**

Director of Admissions Ms. Pat Martin, Admissions Director, Katharine Gibbs School, 50 West 40th Street, New York, NY 10018. *Phone:* 212-867-9300.

KINGSBOROUGH COMMUNITY COLLEGE OF THE CITY UNIVERSITY OF NEW YORK
Brooklyn, New York   **www.kbcc.cuny.edu/**

- **State and locally supported** 2-year, founded 1963, part of City University of New York System
- **Urban** 72-acre campus with easy access to New York City
- **Coed**, 15,265 undergraduate students, 52% full-time, 58% women, 42% men

Undergraduates 7,968 full-time, 7,297 part-time. 2% are from out of state, 32% African American, 9% Asian American or Pacific Islander, 14% Hispanic American, 0.1% Native American, 10% international, 9% transferred in. Freshmen *Admission:* 1,970 enrolled. *Average high school GPA:* 2.70. *Test scores:* SAT verbal scores over 500: 8%; SAT math scores over 500: 12%; SAT verbal scores over 600: 1%; SAT math scores over 600: 2%.

Faculty *Total:* 671, 42% full-time, 44% with terminal degrees. *Student/faculty ratio:* 25:1.

Majors Accounting; administrative assistant and secretarial science; applied art; art; biology/biological sciences; broadcast journalism; business administration and management; chemistry; commercial and advertising art; community health services counseling; computer and information sciences; computer science; data processing and data processing technology; dramatic/theater arts; early childhood education; education; elementary education; engineering science; fashion merchandising; health and physical education related; human services; journalism; labor and industrial relations; liberal arts and sciences/liberal studies; marine technology; marketing/marketing management; mathematics; mental health/rehabilitation; music; nursing (registered nurse training); parks, recreation and leisure; physical therapist assistant; physical therapy; physics; psychiatric/mental health services technology; sport and fitness administration/management; teacher assistant/aide; tourism and travel services management.

Academics *Calendar:* semesters. *Degree:* associate. *Special study options:* academic remediation for entering students, adult/continuing education programs, advanced placement credit, English as a second language, honors programs, internships, off-campus study, part-time degree program, services for LD students, student-designed majors, summer session for credit.

Library Robert J. Kibbee Library with 185,912 titles, 458 serial subscriptions, 2,388 audiovisual materials, an OPAC.

Computers on Campus 900 computers available on campus for general student use. A campuswide network can be accessed. Internet access, at least one staffed computer lab available.

Student Life *Housing:* college housing not available. *Activities and Organizations:* drama/theater group, student-run newspaper, radio station, choral group, Peer Advisors, Caribbean Club, DECA. *Campus security:* 24-hour emergency response devices and patrols. *Student services:* health clinic, personal/psychological counseling, women's center.

Athletics Member NJCAA. *Intercollegiate sports:* baseball M, basketball M/W, soccer M, softball W, tennis M/W, track and field M/W, volleyball W. *Intramural sports:* baseball M, basketball M/W, soccer M, softball W, tennis M/W, track and field M/W, volleyball W.

Costs (2006–07) *Tuition:* state resident $2800 full-time, $120 per credit part-time; nonresident $4560 full-time, $190 per credit part-time. *Required fees:* $300 full-time, $80 per term part-time.

Applying *Options:* common application. *Application fee:* $60. *Required:* high school transcript. *Application deadline:* 8/23 (freshmen), rolling (transfers).

Freshmen Application Contact Mr. Robert Ingenito, Director of Admissions Information Center, Kingsborough Community College of the City University of New York, 2001 Oriental Boulevard, Brooklyn, NY 11235. *Phone:* 718-368-4600. *E-mail:* info@kbcc.cuny.edu.

LONG ISLAND BUSINESS INSTITUTE
Commack, New York　　　**www.libi.edu/commack/index.html**

- **Proprietary** 2-year, founded 1968
- **Suburban** campus with easy access to New York City
- **Coed, primarily women,** 890 undergraduate students, 76% full-time, 77% women, 23% men

Undergraduates 676 full-time, 214 part-time. Students come from 1 other state, 3% African American, 44% Asian American or Pacific Islander, 20% Hispanic American, 5% international.
Freshmen *Admission:* 325 applied, 325 admitted, 325 enrolled. *Average high school GPA:* 3.12.

Faculty *Total:* 97, 25% full-time, 1% with terminal degrees. *Student/faculty ratio:* 15:1.

Majors Accounting; administrative assistant and secretarial science; business administration and management; court reporting.

Academics *Calendar:* trimesters. *Degree:* certificates, diplomas, and associate. *Special study options:* academic remediation for entering students, adult/continuing education programs, advanced placement credit, independent study, internships, part-time degree program, summer session for credit.

Library Mendon W. Smith Memorial Library with 1,484 titles, 15 serial subscriptions, 184 audiovisual materials, an OPAC.

Computers on Campus 77 computers available on campus for general student use. Internet access, at least one staffed computer lab available.

Student Life *Housing:* college housing not available. *Campus security:* 24-hour emergency response devices.

Costs (2005–06) *Tuition:* $8500 full-time, $325 per credit part-time. Full-time tuition and fees vary according to course load and program. Part-time tuition and fees vary according to course load and program. *Required fees:* $400 full-time, $50 per year part-time. *Payment plans:* installment, deferred payment.

Applying *Application fee:* $50. *Required:* essay or personal statement, high school transcript, interview. *Application deadline:* rolling (freshmen), rolling (transfers).

Freshmen Application Contact Mr. Robert Nazar, Admissions Representative, Long Island Business Institute, 6500 Jericho Turnpike, Commack, NY 11725. *Phone:* 631-499-7100. *Fax:* 631-499-7114. *E-mail:* rnazar@libi.edu.

LONG ISLAND COLLEGE HOSPITAL SCHOOL OF NURSING
Brooklyn, New York　　　**www.futurenurselich.org/**

- **Independent** 2-year, founded 1883
- **Urban** campus
- **Coed, primarily women,** 147 undergraduate students, 50% full-time, 78% women, 22% men

Undergraduates 73 full-time, 74 part-time. Students come from 2 states and territories, 1% are from out of state, 45% African American, 14% Asian American or Pacific Islander, 7% Hispanic American, 32% transferred in.
Freshmen *Admission:* 65 applied, 2 admitted.

Faculty *Total:* 12, 50% full-time. *Student/faculty ratio:* 12:1.

Majors Nursing (registered nurse training).

Academics *Calendar:* semesters. *Degree:* associate. *Special study options:* advanced placement credit, cooperative education, independent study, internships, part-time degree program, summer session for credit.

Library E. King Morgan M.D. Health Sciences Library plus 1 other with 16,000 titles, 400 serial subscriptions.

Computers on Campus 14 computers available on campus for general student use. At least one staffed computer lab available.

Student Life *Housing:* college housing not available. *Activities and Organizations:* Student Government Association. *Campus security:* 24-hour emergency response devices, late-night transport/escort service. *Student services:* health clinic, personal/psychological counseling.

Costs (2006–07) *Tuition:* $23,025 full-time. *Required fees:* $370 full-time.

Financial Aid Of all full-time matriculated undergraduates who enrolled in 2004, 5 Federal Work-Study jobs. *Financial aid deadline:* 6/30.

Applying *Application fee:* $50. *Required:* essay or personal statement, high school transcript, minimum 2.0 GPA, 2 letters of recommendation, interview. *Recommended:* minimum 2.0 GPA. *Application deadlines:* 4/28 (freshmen), 4/28 (transfers). *Notification:* continuous (freshmen).

Freshmen Application Contact Ms. Barbara J. Evans, Admissions Assistant, Long Island College Hospital School of Nursing, 340 Court Street, Brooklyn, NY 11231. *Phone:* 718-780-1071.

MARIA COLLEGE
Albany, New York　　　**www.mariacollege.edu/**

- **Independent** 2-year, founded 1958
- **Urban** 9-acre campus
- **Coed,** 788 undergraduate students, 35% full-time, 87% women, 13% men

Maria College's clinical facilities for nursing and occupational therapy assistant studies majors are among the institutional leaders. The laboratory school for education majors is among the finest in the Capital District. Liberal arts, early childhood education, and business majors are highly transferable. Also offered are associate degrees in computer information systems, legal assistant studies, and research technologist studies. One-year certificate programs include legal assistant studies, bereavement studies, gerontology, and practical nursing.

Undergraduates 277 full-time, 511 part-time. Students come from 5 states and territories, 4 other countries, 2% are from out of state, 20% African American, 2% Asian American or Pacific Islander, 3% Hispanic American, 0.5% Native American, 0.5% international, 30% transferred in.
Freshmen *Admission:* 232 applied, 168 admitted, 84 enrolled. *Average high school GPA:* 2.53.

Faculty *Total:* 65, 45% full-time, 17% with terminal degrees. *Student/faculty ratio:* 10:1.

Majors Accounting; business administration and management; computer/information technology services administration related; kindergarten/preschool education; legal assistant/paralegal; legal studies; liberal arts and sciences/liberal studies; nursing (licensed practical/vocational nurse training); nursing (registered nurse training); occupational therapist assistant; physical therapist assistant; science technologies related.

Academics *Calendar:* semesters. *Degree:* certificates and associate. *Special study options:* academic remediation for entering students, adult/continuing

Maria College (continued)
education programs, advanced placement credit, independent study, off-campus study, part-time degree program, services for LD students, summer session for credit. *ROTC:* Air Force (c).

Library Maria College Library with 56,746 titles, 160 serial subscriptions, 375 audiovisual materials, an OPAC, a Web page.

Computers on Campus 78 computers available on campus for general student use. A campuswide network can be accessed. Internet access, online (class) registration, at least one staffed computer lab available.

Student Life *Housing:* college housing not available. *Campus security:* late-night transport/escort service. *Student services:* personal/psychological counseling.

Standardized Tests *Required:* SAT or ACT (for admission).

Costs (2006–07) *Tuition:* $7800 full-time, $285 per credit part-time. *Required fees:* $200 full-time.

Financial Aid Of all full-time matriculated undergraduates who enrolled in 2004, 25 Federal Work-Study jobs (averaging $1000).

Applying *Options:* early admission. *Application fee:* $35. *Required:* essay or personal statement, high school transcript, minimum 2.0 GPA, 1 letter of recommendation, interview. *Application deadlines:* 8/25 (freshmen), 8/25 (transfers).

Director of Admissions Ms. Laurie A. Gilmore, Director of Admissions, Maria College, 700 New Scotland Avenue, Albany, NY 12208. *Phone:* 518-438-3111 Ext. 217.

▶ See page 570 for the College Close-Up.

MEMORIAL HOSPITAL SCHOOL OF NURSING
Albany, New York

MILDRED ELLEY
Latham, New York www.mildred-elley.edu/

Director of Admissions Mr. Michael Cahalan, Enrollment Manager, Mildred Elley, 800 New Loudon Road, Suite 5120, Latham, NY 12110. *Phone:* 518-786-3171 Ext. 227. *Toll-free phone:* 800-622-6327.

MOHAWK VALLEY COMMUNITY COLLEGE
Utica, New York www.mvcc.edu/

- **State and locally supported** 2-year, founded 1946, part of State University of New York System
- **Suburban** 80-acre campus
- **Endowment** $3.1 million
- **Coed,** 5,984 undergraduate students, 63% full-time, 54% women, 46% men

Undergraduates 3,779 full-time, 2,205 part-time. Students come from 18 states and territories, 11 other countries, 2% are from out of state, 6% African American, 2% Asian American or Pacific Islander, 3% Hispanic American, 0.5% Native American, 0.4% international, 5% transferred in, 6% live on campus. *Retention:* 58% of 2003 full-time freshmen returned.
Freshmen *Admission:* 3,440 applied, 3,107 admitted, 1,434 enrolled.

Faculty *Total:* 296, 46% full-time. *Student/faculty ratio:* 24:1.

Majors Accounting technology and bookkeeping; administrative assistant and secretarial science; advertising; airframe mechanics and aircraft maintenance technology; appliance installation and repair technology; architectural drafting and CAD/CADD; art; avionics maintenance technology; banking and financial support services; building/property maintenance and management; business administration and management; business and personal services marketing related; carpentry; chemical technology; civil engineering technology; commercial and advertising art; commercial photography; communications systems installation and repair technology; community organization and advocacy; computer and information sciences; computer and information sciences and support services related; computer programming; criminal justice/law enforcement administration; culinary arts; design and applied arts related; drafting and design

technology; dramatic/theater arts; electrical and electronic engineering technologies related; electrical, electronic and communications engineering technology; electrical/electronics maintenance and repair technology related; elementary education; emergency medical technology (EMT paramedic); engineering; English language and literature related; entrepreneurship; food services technology; foodservice systems administration; forensic science and technology; general studies; health information/medical records technology; heating, air conditioning and refrigeration technology; heating, air conditioning, ventilation and refrigeration maintenance technology; heavy equipment maintenance technology; hotel/motel administration; humanities; human services; industrial production technologies related; liberal arts and sciences/liberal studies; machine shop technology; management information systems and services related; mechanical design technology; mechanical drafting and CAD/CADD; mechanical engineering/mechanical technology; medical/clinical assistant; medical laboratory technology; medical radiologic technology; mental health/rehabilitation; metallurgical technology; nursing (registered nurse training); nutrition sciences; office management; office occupations and clerical services; parks, recreation and leisure facilities management; photographic and film/video technology; physical education teaching and coaching; public administration; respiratory care therapy; restaurant, culinary, and catering management; secondary education; substance abuse/addiction counseling; surgical technology; survey technology; tool and die technology.

Academics *Calendar:* semesters. *Degree:* certificates and associate. *Special study options:* academic remediation for entering students, adult/continuing education programs, advanced placement credit, distance learning, double majors, English as a second language, honors programs, independent study, internships, off-campus study, part-time degree program, services for LD students, student-designed majors, study abroad, summer session for credit. *ROTC:* Army (c).

Library Mohawk Valley Community College Library plus 2 others with 91,000 titles, 925 serial subscriptions, an OPAC, a Web page.

Computers on Campus 380 computers available on campus for general student use. A campuswide network can be accessed from off campus. Internet access, online (class) registration, at least one staffed computer lab available.

Student Life *Housing Options:* coed. Freshman campus housing is guaranteed. *Activities and Organizations:* drama/theater group, student-run newspaper, radio station, choral group, Drama Club, Student Congress, Returning Adult Student Association, Black Student Union, Program Board. *Campus security:* 24-hour emergency response devices and patrols, late-night transport/escort service, controlled dormitory access. *Student services:* health clinic, personal/psychological counseling.

Athletics Member NJCAA. *Intercollegiate sports:* baseball M, basketball M/W, bowling M/W, cross-country running M/W, golf M/W, ice hockey M, lacrosse M, soccer M/W, softball W, tennis M/W, track and field M/W, volleyball W. *Intramural sports:* basketball M/W, cheerleading W, football M, racquetball M/W, softball M/W, table tennis M/W, tennis M/W, volleyball M/W, weight lifting M.

Costs (2005–06) *Tuition:* state resident $2950 full-time, $115 per credit hour part-time; nonresident $5900 full-time, $230 per credit hour part-time. *Required fees:* $344 full-time, $1 per credit hour part-time, $35 per term part-time. *Room and board:* $6260; room only: $3530.

Financial Aid Of all full-time matriculated undergraduates who enrolled in 2004, 229 Federal Work-Study jobs (averaging $1750).

Applying *Options:* electronic application, early admission, early decision, deferred entrance. *Required:* high school transcript. *Application deadline:* rolling (freshmen), rolling (transfers).

Freshmen Application Contact Mrs. Sandra Fiebiger, Electronic Data Processing Clerk, Admissions, Mohawk Valley Community College, 1101 Sherman Drive, Utica, NY 13501. *Phone:* 315-792-5640. *Toll-free phone:* 800-SEE-MVCC. *Fax:* 315-792-5527. *E-mail:* dkennelty@mvcc.edu.

▶ See page 580 for the College Close-Up.

MONROE COLLEGE
Bronx, New York

- **Proprietary** comprehensive, founded 1933
- **Urban** campus
- **Coed,** 4,285 undergraduate students, 85% full-time, 72% women, 28% men

Monroe College is a private, coeducational institution that offers associate and bachelor's (2+2) degrees, with New York City and Westchester County campuses. Programs encompass a variety of majors that help develop the students' careers. Monroe's dynamic faculty members and strong support services foster professional development opportunities for students. At Monroe, the focus is on each student's future.

Undergraduates 3,637 full-time, 648 part-time. Students come from 7 states and territories, 8 other countries, 1% are from out of state, 41% African American, 1% Asian American or Pacific Islander, 53% Hispanic American, 0.2% Native

American, 0.7% international, 7% transferred in, 1% live on campus. *Retention:* 71% of 2003 full-time freshmen returned.

Freshmen *Admission:* 1,508 applied, 916 admitted, 795 enrolled.

Faculty *Total:* 237, 24% full-time, 14% with terminal degrees. *Student/faculty ratio:* 21:1.

Majors Accounting; business administration and management; computer science; criminal justice/law enforcement administration; criminal justice/police science; hospitality administration; information science/studies; medical administrative assistant and medical secretary.

Academics *Calendar:* trimesters. *Degrees:* associate, bachelor's, and master's. *Special study options:* academic remediation for entering students, adult/continuing education programs, cooperative education, distance learning, English as a second language, internships, part-time degree program, summer session for credit.

Library Main Library plus 1 other with 28,000 titles, 301 serial subscriptions, an OPAC, a Web page.

Computers on Campus 541 computers available on campus for general student use. A campuswide network can be accessed. Internet access, at least one staffed computer lab available.

Student Life *Housing Options:* coed. Campus housing is university owned and leased by the school. Freshman applicants given priority for college housing. *Activities and Organizations:* drama/theater group, student-run newspaper. *Campus security:* late-night transport/escort service. *Student services:* personal/psychological counseling.

Athletics Member NJCAA. *Intercollegiate sports:* baseball M, basketball M/W, soccer M, softball W, volleyball W. *Intramural sports:* basketball M/W, bowling M/W, cheerleading W.

Costs (2005–06) *Comprehensive fee:* $16,660 includes full-time tuition ($9160), mandatory fees ($600), and room and board ($6900). Part-time tuition: $382 per credit hour. *Required fees:* $150 per term part-time.

Financial Aid Of all full-time matriculated undergraduates who enrolled in 2004, 3,436 applied for aid, 3,307 were judged to have need, 1,337 had their need fully met. 132 Federal Work-Study jobs (averaging $3100). *Average percent of need met:* 91%. *Average financial aid package:* $9832. *Average need-based loan:* $4100. *Average need-based gift aid:* $6237. *Average indebtedness upon graduation:* $5307.

Applying *Options:* early admission, deferred entrance. *Application fee:* $35. *Required:* high school transcript, interview. *Application deadlines:* 8/26 (freshmen), 8/26 (transfers). *Notification:* continuous until 9/3 (freshmen).

Freshmen Application Contact Mr. Brad Allison, Director of Admissions, Monroe College, Monroe College Way, 2501 Jerome Avenue, Bronx, NY 10468. *Phone:* 718-933-6700 Ext. 536. *Toll-free phone:* 800-55MONROE. *Fax:* 718-220-3032.

MONROE COMMUNITY COLLEGE
Rochester, New York www.monroecc.edu/

Director of Admissions Mr. Anthony Felicetti, Associate Vice President, Enrollment Management, Monroe Community College, 1000 East Henrietta Road, Rochester, NY 14623-5780. *Phone:* 585-292-2000 Ext. 2221.

NASSAU COMMUNITY COLLEGE
Garden City, New York www.ncc.edu/

- **State and locally supported** 2-year, founded 1959, part of State University of New York System
- **Suburban** 225-acre campus with easy access to New York City
- **Coed,** 20,979 undergraduate students, 64% full-time, 53% women, 47% men

Undergraduates 13,528 full-time, 7,451 part-time. 19% African American, 7% Asian American or Pacific Islander, 13% Hispanic American, 0.3% Native American, 5% international, 9% transferred in.

Freshmen *Admission:* 7,821 applied, 7,212 admitted, 5,094 enrolled.

Faculty *Total:* 1,571, 29% full-time, 72% with terminal degrees. *Student/faculty ratio:* 18:1.

Majors Accounting; accounting technology and bookkeeping; administrative assistant and secretarial science; African-American/Black studies; art; business administration and management; civil engineering technology; clinical/medical laboratory technology; commercial and advertising art; communication/speech communication and rhetoric; computer and information sciences; computer and information sciences related; computer graphics; computer science; computer systems networking and telecommunications; criminal justice/law enforcement administration; criminal justice/safety; dance; data processing and data processing technology; design and visual communications; dramatic/theater arts; engi-

neering; entrepreneurship; fashion/apparel design; fashion merchandising; funeral service and mortuary science; general retailing/wholesaling; general studies; health science; hotel/motel administration; instrumentation technology; insurance; interior design; kindergarten/preschool education; legal administrative assistant/secretary; legal assistant/paralegal; liberal arts and sciences/liberal studies; management information systems; marketing/marketing management; mass communication/media; mathematics; medical administrative assistant and medical secretary; medical radiologic technology; music performance; nursing (registered nurse training); photography; physical therapist assistant; real estate; rehabilitation therapy; respiratory care therapy; security and loss prevention; surgical technology; theater design and technology; transportation technology; visual and performing arts.

Academics *Calendar:* semesters. *Degree:* certificates and associate. *Special study options:* academic remediation for entering students, adult/continuing education programs, advanced placement credit, cooperative education, distance learning, English as a second language, honors programs, internships, off-campus study, part-time degree program, services for LD students, summer session for credit. *ROTC:* Army (c).

Library A. Holly Patterson Library with 171,938 titles, 753 serial subscriptions, 55,514 audiovisual materials, an OPAC, a Web page.

Computers on Campus 700 computers available on campus for general student use. A campuswide network can be accessed from off campus. At least one staffed computer lab available.

Student Life *Housing:* college housing not available. *Activities and Organizations:* drama/theater group, student-run newspaper, radio station, choral group, Student Organization of Latinos, Student Government Association, Programming Board, Caribbean Student Organization, NYPIRG. *Campus security:* 24-hour emergency response devices and patrols, late-night transport/escort service. *Student services:* health clinic, personal/psychological counseling, women's center.

Athletics Member NJCAA. *Intercollegiate sports:* baseball M, basketball M/W, bowling M/W, cheerleading W, cross-country running M/W, equestrian sports M/W, football M, golf M/W, lacrosse M, soccer M/W, softball W, tennis M/W, track and field M/W, volleyball M/W, wrestling M. *Intramural sports:* badminton M/W, basketball M/W, cross-country running M/W, football M, ice hockey M, lacrosse M/W, racquetball M/W, soccer M/W, softball M/W, table tennis M/W, tennis M/W, volleyball M/W.

Standardized Tests *Recommended:* SAT or ACT (for admission).

Costs (2006–07) *Tuition:* state resident $3310 full-time, $138 per credit part-time; nonresident $6620 full-time, $276 per credit part-time. *Required fees:* $242 full-time.

Financial Aid Of all full-time matriculated undergraduates who enrolled in 2004, 400 Federal Work-Study jobs (averaging $3000).

Applying *Options:* deferred entrance. *Application fee:* $30. *Required:* high school transcript. *Required for some:* minimum 3.0 GPA, interview. *Recommended:* minimum 2.0 GPA. *Application deadlines:* 8/1 (freshmen), 8/1 (transfers). *Notification:* continuous (freshmen).

Freshmen Application Contact Mr. Craig Wright, Vice President of Enrollment Management, Nassau Community College, One Education Drive, Garden City, NY 11530. *Phone:* 516-572-7345. *E-mail:* admissions@sunynassau.edu.

NEW YORK CAREER INSTITUTE
New York, New York www.nyci.com/

Director of Admissions Ms. Cindy McMahon, Enrollment Coordinator, New York Career Institute, 11 Park Place- 4th Floor, New York, NY 10007. *Phone:* 212-962-0002 Ext. 101. *Fax:* 212-680-8210. *E-mail:* cmcmahon@nyci.com.

NEW YORK CITY COLLEGE OF TECHNOLOGY OF THE CITY UNIVERSITY OF NEW YORK
Brooklyn, New York www.citytech.cuny.edu/

Director of Admissions Mr. Joseph Lento, Director of Admissions, New York City College of Technology of the City University of New York, 300 Jay Street, Brooklyn, NY 11201-2983. *Phone:* 718-260-5500.

NEW YORK COLLEGE OF HEALTH PROFESSIONS

Syosset, New York   www.nycollege.edu/

Director of Admissions Dr. Mary Rodas, Director of Admissions, New York College of Health Professions, 6801 Jericho Turnpike, Syosset, NY 11791. *Toll-free phone:* 800-922-7337 Ext. 351.

▶ **See page 586 for the College Close-Up.**

NIAGARA COUNTY COMMUNITY COLLEGE

Sanborn, New York   www.niagaracc.suny.edu/

- **State and locally supported** 2-year, founded 1962, part of State University of New York System
- **Rural** 287-acre campus with easy access to Buffalo
- **Endowment** $2.1 million
- **Coed,** 5,572 undergraduate students, 65% full-time, 60% women, 40% men

Undergraduates 3,605 full-time, 1,967 part-time. Students come from 15 states and territories, 1% are from out of state, 6% African American, 2% Asian American or Pacific Islander, 1% Hispanic American, 2% Native American, 1% international, 5% transferred in.
Freshmen *Admission:* 2,282 applied, 2,282 admitted, 1,159 enrolled. *Average high school GPA:* 2.48.

Faculty *Total:* 288, 44% full-time, 11% with terminal degrees. *Student/faculty ratio:* 17:1.

Majors Accounting; administrative assistant and secretarial science; animal sciences; biochemical technology; biological and physical sciences; business administration and management; computer science; consumer merchandising/retailing management; criminal justice/law enforcement administration; culinary arts; design and applied arts related; drafting and design technology; dramatic/theater arts; electrical, electronic and communications engineering technology; electroneurodiagnostic/electroencephalographic technology; fine/studio arts; general studies; hospitality administration; humanities; human services; information science/studies; liberal arts and sciences/liberal studies; mass communication/media; mathematics; mechanical design technology; medical/clinical assistant; music; natural resources/conservation; nursing (registered nurse training); occupational health and industrial hygiene; physical education teaching and coaching; physical therapist assistant; radiologic technology/science; social sciences; surgical technology; Web page, digital/multimedia and information resources design.

Academics *Calendar:* semesters. *Degree:* certificates and associate. *Special study options:* academic remediation for entering students, adult/continuing education programs, advanced placement credit, cooperative education, double majors, honors programs, independent study, internships, off-campus study, part-time degree program, services for LD students, student-designed majors, study abroad, summer session for credit. *ROTC:* Army (c).

Library Library Learning Center with 93,055 titles, 524 serial subscriptions, 20,207 audiovisual materials, an OPAC, a Web page.

Computers on Campus 414 computers available on campus for general student use. A campuswide network can be accessed. Internet access, at least one staffed computer lab available.

Student Life *Housing:* college housing not available. *Activities and Organizations:* drama/theater group, student-run newspaper, radio station, choral group, student radio station, Student Nurses Association, Phi Theta Kappa, Alpha Beta Gamma, Physical Education Club. *Campus security:* student patrols, late-night transport/escort service, emergency telephones. *Student services:* health clinic, personal/psychological counseling.

Athletics Member NJCAA. *Intercollegiate sports:* baseball M, basketball M(s)/W, golf M/W, soccer M/W, softball W, volleyball W, wrestling M(s). *Intramural sports:* basketball M/W, bowling M/W, cheerleading W, skiing (cross-country) M(c)/W(c), volleyball M/W.

Costs (2005–06) *Tuition:* state resident $3096 full-time, $129 per credit hour part-time; nonresident $4644 full-time, $194 per credit hour part-time. Full-time tuition and fees vary according to program. Part-time tuition and fees vary according to program. *Required fees:* $300 full-time, $62 per term part-time. *Payment plan:* installment. *Waivers:* senior citizens and employees or children of employees.

Financial Aid Of all full-time matriculated undergraduates who enrolled in 2004, 192 Federal Work-Study jobs (averaging $1925).

Applying *Options:* electronic application, early admission. *Required:* high school transcript. *Required for some:* minimum 2.0 GPA. *Notification:* continuous until 8/31 (freshmen).

Freshmen Application Contact Ms. Kathy Saunders, Director of Enrollment Services, Niagara County Community College, 3111 Saunders Settlement Road, Sanborn, NY 14132. *Phone:* 716-614-6200. *Fax:* 716-614-6820. *E-mail:* admissions@niagaracc.suny.edu.

NORTH COUNTRY COMMUNITY COLLEGE

Saranac Lake, New York   www.nccc.edu/

- **State and locally supported** 2-year, founded 1967, part of State University of New York System
- **Rural** 100-acre campus
- **Coed,** 1,605 undergraduate students, 62% full-time, 64% women, 36% men

Undergraduates 999 full-time, 606 part-time. Students come from 13 states and territories, 4 other countries, 3% are from out of state, 2% African American, 0.9% Asian American or Pacific Islander, 0.7% Hispanic American, 2% Native American, 1% international, 8% transferred in, 7% live on campus.
Freshmen *Admission:* 1,802 applied, 1,689 admitted, 339 enrolled. *Test scores:* SAT verbal scores over 500: 35%; SAT math scores over 500: 37%; ACT scores over 18: 57%; SAT verbal scores over 600: 3%; SAT math scores over 600: 2%; ACT scores over 24: 14%.

Faculty *Total:* 151, 30% full-time, 10% with terminal degrees. *Student/faculty ratio:* 17:1.

Majors Biological and physical sciences; business administration and management; computer graphics; consumer merchandising/retailing management; criminal justice/safety; interdisciplinary studies; kinesiology and exercise science; liberal arts and sciences/liberal studies; mathematics; medical radiologic technology; mental health/rehabilitation; nursing (registered nurse training); office occupations and clerical services; parks, recreation and leisure facilities management.

Academics *Calendar:* semesters. *Degree:* certificates and associate. *Special study options:* academic remediation for entering students, advanced placement credit, distance learning, double majors, internships, part-time degree program, services for LD students, student-designed majors, summer session for credit.

Library North Country Community College Library with 58,556 titles, 177 serial subscriptions, 1,217 audiovisual materials.

Computers on Campus 140 computers available on campus for general student use. Internet access, at least one staffed computer lab available.

Student Life *Housing Options:* coed. Campus housing is university owned. *Activities and Organizations:* drama/theater group, student-run newspaper, Student Government Association, Wilderness Recreation Club, Nursing Club, Radiology Club, Criminal Justice Club. *Student services:* personal/psychological counseling.

Athletics Member NJCAA. *Intercollegiate sports:* basketball M/W, ice hockey M, soccer M/W, softball W, volleyball W. *Intramural sports:* archery M/W, badminton M/W, basketball M/W, bowling M/W, football M/W, soccer M/W, softball M/W, swimming and diving M/W, tennis M/W, volleyball M/W, weight lifting M/W.

Standardized Tests *Recommended:* SAT or ACT (for admission).

Costs (2006–07) *Tuition:* state resident $3250 full-time, $160 per credit hour part-time; nonresident $8000 full-time, $375 per credit hour part-time. *Required fees:* $730 full-time, $38 per credit hour part-time, $225 per term part-time. *Room and board:* $8150; room only: $4750.

Financial Aid Of all full-time matriculated undergraduates who enrolled in 2004, 104 Federal Work-Study jobs (averaging $1164). 27 state and other part-time jobs (averaging $1600).

Applying *Options:* electronic application, early admission, early decision, deferred entrance. *Required:* high school transcript. *Recommended:* essay or personal statement, interview. *Application deadline:* rolling (freshmen), rolling (transfers). *Notification:* continuous (freshmen).

Freshmen Application Contact Enrollment Management Assistant, North Country Community College, 23 Santanoni Avenue, PO Box 89, Saranac Lake, NY 12983-0089. *Phone:* 518-891-2915 Ext. 686. *Toll-free phone:* 888-TRY-NCCC Ext. 233. *Fax:* 518-891-0898. *E-mail:* info@nccc.edu.

OLEAN BUSINESS INSTITUTE

Olean, New York   www.obi.edu/

Director of Admissions Ms. Lori Kincaid, Director of Admissions, Olean Business Institute, 301 North Union Street, Olean, NY 14760-2691. *Phone:* 716-372-7978.

ONONDAGA COMMUNITY COLLEGE

Syracuse, New York   **www.sunyocc.edu/**

Director of Admissions Mr. Monty R. Flynn, Director of Admissions, Onondaga Community College, 4941 Onondaga Road, Syracuse, NY 13215. *Phone:* 315-498-2201.

ORANGE COUNTY COMMUNITY COLLEGE

Middletown, New York   **www.orange.cc.ny.us/**

- **State and locally supported** 2-year, founded 1950, part of State University of New York System
- **Suburban** 37-acre campus with easy access to New York City
- **Coed,** 6,441 undergraduate students, 52% full-time, 61% women, 39% men

Undergraduates 3,344 full-time, 3,097 part-time. Students come from 22 states and territories, 20 other countries, 1% are from out of state, 10% African American, 2% Asian American or Pacific Islander, 13% Hispanic American, 0.4% Native American, 2% transferred in.
Freshmen *Admission:* 2,024 applied, 2,024 admitted, 1,654 enrolled. *Average high school GPA:* 2.25.
Faculty *Total:* 382, 36% full-time. *Student/faculty ratio:* 16:1.
Majors Accounting; administrative assistant and secretarial science; architectural engineering technology; biological and physical sciences; biology/biological sciences; business administration and management; child development; clinical/medical laboratory technology; computer and information sciences; computer and information sciences related; computer engineering related; computer engineering technology; computer programming; computer science; construction engineering technology; consumer merchandising/retailing management; criminal justice/law enforcement administration; criminal justice/police science; data entry/microcomputer applications; data processing and data processing technology; dental hygiene; drafting and design technology; electrical, electronic and communications engineering technology; elementary education; engineering science; finance; humanities; industrial radiologic technology; information science/studies; information technology; kinesiology and exercise science; liberal arts and sciences/liberal studies; marketing/marketing management; mental health/rehabilitation; nursing (registered nurse training); occupational therapy; parks, recreation and leisure; physical therapy; real estate; word processing.
Academics *Calendar:* semesters. *Degree:* certificates and associate. *Special study options:* academic remediation for entering students, accelerated degree program, adult/continuing education programs, English as a second language, external degree program, honors programs, internships, part-time degree program, services for LD students, summer session for credit.
Library Learning Resource Center with 101,342 titles, 345 serial subscriptions, 1,408 audiovisual materials, an OPAC, a Web page.
Computers on Campus 200 computers available on campus for general student use. A campuswide network can be accessed. Internet access, at least one staffed computer lab available.
Student Life *Housing:* college housing not available. *Activities and Organizations:* drama/theater group, student-run newspaper, radio station, choral group, Phi Theta Kappa, Masters of the Elements, Computer Club, Agassiz Society, Apprentice Players. *Campus security:* 24-hour emergency response devices, late-night transport/escort service. *Student services:* health clinic, personal/psychological counseling.
Athletics Member NJCAA. *Intercollegiate sports:* baseball M(s), basketball M(s)/W(s), golf M/W, soccer M(s)/W(s), softball W(s), tennis M(s)/W(s), volleyball W. *Intramural sports:* basketball M/W, field hockey M, football M, racquetball M/W, soccer M/W, tennis M/W, volleyball M/W.
Costs (2006–07) *Tuition:* state resident $3000 full-time, $125 per credit part-time; nonresident $6000 full-time, $250 per credit part-time. *Required fees:* $350 full-time.
Financial Aid Of all full-time matriculated undergraduates who enrolled in 2004, 70 Federal Work-Study jobs (averaging $2000). 25 state and other part-time jobs (averaging $2000).
Applying *Options:* common application, early admission, deferred entrance. *Application fee:* $30. *Required:* high school transcript. *Application deadlines:* 8/1 (freshmen), 8/1 (transfers). *Notification:* continuous (freshmen).
Freshmen Application Contact Ms. Margot St. Lawrence, Director of Admissions, Orange County Community College, 115 South Street, Middletown, NY 10940. *Phone:* 845-341-4030. *Fax:* 845-343-1228. *E-mail:* admssns@sunyorange.edu.

PHILLIPS BETH ISRAEL SCHOOL OF NURSING

New York, New York   **www.futurenursebi.org**

- **Independent** 2-year, founded 1904
- **Urban** campus
- **Endowment** $1.2 million
- **Coed, primarily women,** 200 undergraduate students

Undergraduates Students come from 8 states and territories, 5 other countries, 10% are from out of state, 15% African American, 22% Asian American or Pacific Islander, 14% Hispanic American, 4% international.
Freshmen *Admission:* 57 applied, 7 admitted. *Average high school GPA:* 2.90. *Test scores:* SAT verbal scores over 500: 100%; SAT math scores over 500: 100%.
Faculty *Total:* 18, 56% full-time, 44% with terminal degrees. *Student/faculty ratio:* 9:1.
Majors Health professions related; nursing (registered nurse training).
Academics *Calendar:* semesters. *Degree:* associate. *Special study options:* advanced placement credit, off-campus study, part-time degree program.
Library Phillips Health Science Library with 600 serial subscriptions, an OPAC.
Computers on Campus 15 computers available on campus for general student use. Internet access, at least one staffed computer lab available.
Student Life *Housing:* college housing not available. *Activities and Organizations:* student-run newspaper, choral group, Student Government Organization, National Student Nurses Association. *Campus security:* 24-hour emergency response devices. *Student services:* health clinic, personal/psychological counseling.
Standardized Tests *Required:* nursing exam (for admission). *Recommended:* SAT (for admission).
Costs (2006–07) *Tuition:* $12,300 full-time, $300 per credit part-time. *Required fees:* $2180 full-time.
Financial Aid *Financial aid deadline:* 6/1.
Applying *Options:* deferred entrance. *Application fee:* $50. *Required:* essay or personal statement, high school transcript, minimum 2.5 GPA, 2 letters of recommendation, interview. *Application deadlines:* 4/1 (freshmen), 4/1 (transfers). *Notification:* continuous (freshmen).
Director of Admissions Mrs. Bernice Pass-Stern, Assistant Dean, Phillips Beth Israel School of Nursing, 310 East 22nd Street, 9th Floor, New York, NY 10010-5702. *Phone:* 212-614-6176. *Fax:* 212-614-6109. *E-mail:* bstern@bethisraelny.org.

PLAZA COLLEGE

Jackson Heights, New York   **www.plazacollege.edu/**

Freshmen Application Contact Mr. Michael Talarico, Director of Admissions, Plaza College, 7409 37th Avenue, Jackson Heights, NY 11372-6300. *Phone:* 718-779-1430. *Toll-free phone:* 877-752-9233.

QUEENSBOROUGH COMMUNITY COLLEGE OF THE CITY UNIVERSITY OF NEW YORK

Bayside, New York   **www.qcc.cuny.edu/**

- **State and locally supported** 2-year, founded 1958, part of City University of New York System
- **Urban** 34-acre campus with easy access to New York City
- **Endowment** $1.0 million
- **Coed**

Undergraduates 6,195 full-time, 6,603 part-time. Students come from 2 states and territories, 132 other countries, 1% are from out of state, 27% African American, 20% Asian American or Pacific Islander, 22% Hispanic American, 0.2% Native American, 6% international, 5% transferred in.
Faculty *Student/faculty ratio:* 21:1.
Academics *Calendar:* semesters. *Degree:* certificates and associate. *Special study options:* academic remediation for entering students, adult/continuing education programs, advanced placement credit, cooperative education, English as a second language, honors programs, internships, part-time degree program, services for LD students, student-designed majors, summer session for credit. *ROTC:* Army (c).

Queensborough Community College of the City University of New York (continued)

Student Life *Campus security:* 24-hour patrols, late-night transport/escort service.

Athletics Member NJCAA.

Costs (2005–06) *Tuition:* area resident $2800 full-time; state resident $4560 full-time, $120 per credit part-time; nonresident $4560 full-time, $190 per credit part-time. Full-time tuition and fees vary according to course load. Part-time tuition and fees vary according to course load. *Required fees:* $266 full-time, $70 per term part-time.

Applying *Options:* electronic application, deferred entrance. *Application fee:* $40. *Required:* high school transcript.

Freshmen Application Contact Ms. Ann Tullio, Director of Registration, Queensborough Community College of the City University of New York, 222-05 56th Avenue, Bayside, NY 11364. *Phone:* 718-631-6307.

ROCHESTER BUSINESS INSTITUTE
Rochester, New York   www.rochester-institute.com/

Director of Admissions Ms. Deanna Pfluke, Director of Admissions, Rochester Business Institute, 1630 Portland Avenue, Rochester, NY 14621. *Phone:* 585-266-0430. *Fax:* 585-266-8243.

ROCKLAND COMMUNITY COLLEGE
Suffern, New York   www.sunyrockland.edu/

- **State and locally supported** 2-year, founded 1959, part of State University of New York System
- **Suburban** 150-acre campus with easy access to New York City
- **Coed**

Undergraduates 3,697 full-time, 2,852 part-time. Students come from 4 states and territories, 25 other countries, 4% are from out of state, 18% African American, 6% Asian American or Pacific Islander, 10% Hispanic American, 0.3% Native American, 5% international, 8% transferred in.

Faculty *Student/faculty ratio:* 17:1.

Academics *Calendar:* semesters. *Degree:* certificates and associate. *Special study options:* academic remediation for entering students, adult/continuing education programs, advanced placement credit, cooperative education, English as a second language, external degree program, honors programs, internships, part-time degree program, services for LD students, student-designed majors, study abroad, summer session for credit. *ROTC:* Navy (b), Air Force (c).

Student Life *Campus security:* 24-hour emergency response devices and patrols, student patrols, late-night transport/escort service.

Athletics Member NJCAA.

Standardized Tests *Recommended:* SAT or ACT (for placement).

Applying *Options:* early admission, deferred entrance. *Application fee:* $25. *Required:* high school transcript.

Freshmen Application Contact Ms. Lucy Hirsch, Admissions Office Secretary, Rockland Community College, 145 College Road, Suffern, NY 10901-3699. *Phone:* 845-574-4237. *Toll-free phone:* 800-722-7666.

ST. ELIZABETH COLLEGE OF NURSING
Utica, New York   www.stemc.org/

Director of Admissions Sr. Marianne Monahan, Dean, St. Elizabeth College of Nursing, 2215 Genesee Street, Utica, NY 13501. *Phone:* 315-798-8253. *E-mail:* mmonahan@stemc.org.

SAINT JOSEPH'S HOSPITAL HEALTH CENTER SCHOOL OF NURSING
Syracuse, New York   www.sjhsyr.org/nursing/

- **Independent** 2-year
- **Urban** campus
- **Coed, primarily women,** 293 undergraduate students

Undergraduates Students come from 2 states and territories, 3% African American, 1% Asian American or Pacific Islander, 2% Hispanic American, 2% Native American, 25% live on campus.

Freshmen *Admission:* 42 applied, 23 admitted. *Average high school GPA:* 3.0. *Test scores:* SAT verbal scores over 500: 56%; SAT math scores over 500: 50%; ACT scores over 18: 100%; ACT scores over 24: 1%.

Faculty *Total:* 29, 55% full-time. *Student/faculty ratio:* 9:1.

Majors Nursing (registered nurse training).

Academics *Calendar:* semesters. *Degree:* associate. *Special study options:* academic remediation for entering students, adult/continuing education programs, advanced placement credit, cooperative education, internships, part-time degree program, services for LD students.

Library St. Joseph's Hospital Health Center School of Nursing Library with 4,500 titles, 230 serial subscriptions, 500 audiovisual materials, an OPAC.

Computers on Campus 30 computers available on campus for general student use. Internet access, at least one staffed computer lab available.

Student Life *Housing Options:* coed. *Activities and Organizations:* New York State Student Nurse's Association, Syracuse Area Black Nurses Association, Student Body Organization. *Campus security:* 24-hour patrols. *Student services:* health clinic, personal/psychological counseling, legal services.

Standardized Tests *Required:* SAT or ACT (for admission).

Costs (2006–07) *Tuition:* $8735 full-time. *Required fees:* $1900 full-time. *Room only:* $3400.

Applying *Options:* deferred entrance. *Application fee:* $30. *Required:* essay or personal statement, high school transcript, minimum 3.0 GPA, 4 letters of recommendation, interview.

Freshmen Application Contact Ms. JoAnne Kiggins, Admissions and Recruitment Coordinator, Saint Joseph's Hospital Health Center School of Nursing, 206 Prospect Avenue, Syracuse, NY 13203. *Phone:* 315-448-5040. *Fax:* 315-448-5745.

SAINT VINCENT CATHOLIC MEDICAL CENTERS SCHOOL OF NURSING
Fresh Meadows, New York   www.svcmcny.org/

Director of Admissions Nancy Wolinski, Chairperson of Admissions, Saint Vincent Catholic Medical Centers School of Nursing, 175-05 Horace Harding Expressway, Fresh Meadows, NY 11365. *Phone:* 718-357-0500 Ext. 131.

SAMARITAN HOSPITAL SCHOOL OF NURSING
Troy, New York   www.nehealth.com/

Director of Admissions Ms. Jennifer DeBlois, Student Services Coordinator, Samaritan Hospital School of Nursing, 2215 Burdett Avenue, Troy, NY 12180. *Phone:* 518-271-3734. *Fax:* 518-271-3303. *E-mail:* deBlois@nehealth.com.

SCHENECTADY COUNTY COMMUNITY COLLEGE
Schenectady, New York   www.sunysccc.edu/

Director of Admissions Mr. David Sampson, Director of Admissions, Schenectady County Community College, 78 Washington Avenue, Schenectady, NY 12305. *Phone:* 518-381-1370.

SIMMONS INSTITUTE OF FUNERAL SERVICE
Syracuse, New York   www.simmonsinstitute.com/

Director of Admissions Ms. Vera Wightman, Director of Admissions, Simmons Institute of Funeral Service, 1828 South Avenue, Syracuse, NY 13207. *Phone:* 315-475-5142. *Toll-free phone:* 800-727-3536.

STATE UNIVERSITY OF NEW YORK COLLEGE OF AGRICULTURE AND TECHNOLOGY AT MORRISVILLE

Morrisville, New York   **www.morrisville.edu/**

Director of Admissions Mr. Timothy Williams, Dean of Enrollment Management, State University of New York College of Agriculture and Technology at Morrisville, Box 901, Morrisville, NY 13408. *Phone:* 315-684-6046. *Toll-free phone:* 800-258-0111.

STATE UNIVERSITY OF NEW YORK COLLEGE OF ENVIRONMENTAL SCIENCE & FORESTRY, RANGER SCHOOL

Wanakena, New York   **www.esf.edu/**

- **State-supported** 2-year, founded 1912, part of State University of New York System
- **Rural** 2800-acre campus
- **Endowment** $524,891
- **Coed, primarily men,** 43 undergraduate students, 100% full-time, 12% women, 88% men

Undergraduates 43 full-time. Students come from 4 states and territories, 6% are from out of state, 100% live on campus.
Freshmen *Admission:* 72 applied, 55 admitted.
Faculty *Total:* 5, 100% full-time, 20% with terminal degrees. *Student/faculty ratio:* 8:1.
Majors Forestry technology; survey technology.
Academics *Calendar:* semesters. *Degree:* associate. *Special study options:* advanced placement credit, distance learning.
Library Ranger School Library with 5,000 titles, 60 serial subscriptions, an OPAC.
Computers on Campus 20 computers available on campus for general student use. A campuswide network can be accessed from student residence rooms and from off campus. Internet access available.
Student Life *Housing Options:* coed. *Student services:* health clinic, personal/psychological counseling, legal services.
Athletics *Intramural sports:* basketball M/W, ice hockey M/W, skiing (cross-country) M/W, skiing (downhill) M/W, softball M/W, volleyball M/W, weight lifting M/W.
Standardized Tests *Required:* SAT or ACT (for admission).
Costs (2006–07) *Tuition:* state resident $4350 full-time, $181 per credit hour part-time; nonresident $10,610 full-time, $442 per credit hour part-time. *Required fees:* $527 per semester part-time. *Room and board:* $8400; room only: $2450.
Financial Aid Of all full-time matriculated undergraduates who enrolled in 2004, 300 Federal Work-Study jobs (averaging $1500). 150 state and other part-time jobs (averaging $1200).
Applying *Options:* electronic application, deferred entrance. *Application fee:* $40. *Required:* minimum 2.00 GPA. *Recommended:* essay or personal statement, high school transcript, minimum 2.50 GPA, interview. *Application deadline:* rolling (freshmen), rolling (transfers).
Freshmen Application Contact Ms. Susan Sanford, Director of Admissions, State University of New York College of Environmental Science & Forestry, Ranger School, Bray 106, Syracuse, NY 13210-2779. *Phone:* 315-470-6600. *Toll-free phone:* 800-777-7373. *Fax:* 315-470-6933. *E-mail:* esfinfo@esf.edu.

▶ See page 596 for the College Close-Up.

STATE UNIVERSITY OF NEW YORK COLLEGE OF TECHNOLOGY AT ALFRED

Alfred, New York   **www.alfredstate.edu/**

- **State-supported** primarily 2-year, founded 1908, part of State University of New York System
- **Rural** 175-acre campus
- **Endowment** $2.6 million
- **Coed,** 3,377 undergraduate students

Undergraduates Students come from 29 states and territories, 8% are from out of state, 3% African American, 1% Asian American or Pacific Islander, 3%

Hispanic American, 0.3% Native American, 70% live on campus. *Retention:* 96% of 2003 full-time freshmen returned.
Freshmen *Admission:* 4,463 applied, 2,889 admitted.
Faculty *Total:* 191, 77% full-time, 14% with terminal degrees. *Student/faculty ratio:* 20:1.
Majors Accounting; agricultural business and management; agriculture; animal sciences; architectural engineering technology; autobody/collision and repair technology; automobile/automotive mechanics technology; biological and physical sciences; biology/biotechnology laboratory technician; business administration and management; carpentry; civil engineering technology; computer and information sciences; computer engineering technology; computer graphics; computer hardware engineering; computer/information technology services administration related; computer installation and repair technology; computer science; computer/technical support; computer typography and composition equipment operation; construction engineering; construction engineering technology; court reporting; culinary arts; drafting and design technology; electrical, electronic and communications engineering technology; electrical/electronics equipment installation and repair; electromechanical technology; engineering science; environmental studies; finance; health information/medical records administration; heating, air conditioning and refrigeration technology; heating, air conditioning, ventilation and refrigeration maintenance technology; heavy equipment maintenance technology; humanities; human services; industrial electronics technology; landscaping and groundskeeping; liberal arts and sciences/liberal studies; machine tool technology; marketing/marketing management; masonry; mathematics; mechanical design technology; mechanical engineering/mechanical technology; nursing (registered nurse training); pipefitting and sprinkler fitting; restaurant, culinary, and catering management; sales, distribution and marketing; social sciences; sport and fitness administration/management; survey technology; system administration; veterinary sciences; welding technology.
Academics *Calendar:* semesters. *Degrees:* certificates, associate, and bachelor's. *Special study options:* academic remediation for entering students, adult/continuing education programs, advanced placement credit, cooperative education, distance learning, external degree program, honors programs, independent study, internships, off-campus study, part-time degree program, services for LD students, student-designed majors, study abroad, summer session for credit. *ROTC:* Army (c).
Library Walter C. Hinkle Memorial Library plus 1 other with 71,243 titles, 594 serial subscriptions, 8,148 audiovisual materials, an OPAC, a Web page.
Computers on Campus 1600 computers available on campus for general student use. A campuswide network can be accessed from student residence rooms and from off campus. Internet access, online (class) registration, at least one staffed computer lab available. Computer purchase or lease plan available.
Student Life *Housing Options:* coed, disabled students. Campus housing is university owned. Freshman campus housing is guaranteed. *Activities and Organizations:* drama/theater group, student-run newspaper, radio station, choral group, Outdoor Activity Club, BACCHUS, Sondai Society, Drama Club, choir. *Campus security:* 24-hour emergency response devices and patrols, late-night transport/escort service, residence hall entrance guards. *Student services:* health clinic, personal/psychological counseling.
Athletics Member NJCAA. *Intercollegiate sports:* baseball M, basketball M(s)/W(s), cheerleading M/W, cross-country running M(s)/W(s), football M(s), lacrosse M(s), soccer M(s)/W(s), softball W(s), swimming and diving M/W, track and field M(s)/W(s), volleyball W, wrestling M. *Intramural sports:* basketball M/W, bowling M/W, cross-country running M/W, football M, golf M/W, lacrosse M/W, racquetball M/W, rock climbing M/W, rugby M/W, skiing (cross-country) M/W, soccer M/W, softball M/W, table tennis M/W, tennis M/W, ultimate Frisbee M/W, volleyball M/W, water polo M/W.
Standardized Tests *Required for some:* SAT or ACT (for admission). *Recommended:* SAT or ACT (for admission).
Costs (2006–07) *Tuition:* state resident $4350 full-time; nonresident $7210 full-time. *Room and board:* $6700; room only: $3770.
Financial Aid Of all full-time matriculated undergraduates who enrolled in 2004, 350 Federal Work-Study jobs (averaging $1100).
Applying *Options:* common application, electronic application, deferred entrance. *Application fee:* $40. *Required:* high school transcript. *Required for some:* minimum 2.0 GPA. *Recommended:* essay or personal statement, letters of recommendation, interview. *Application deadline:* rolling (freshmen), rolling (transfers). *Notification:* continuous (freshmen).
Freshmen Application Contact Ms. Deborah Goodrich, Director of Admissions, State University of New York College of Technology at Alfred, Huntington Administration Building, 10 Upper College Drive, Alfred, NY 14802. *Phone:* 607-587-4215. *Toll-free phone:* 800-4-ALFRED. *Fax:* 607-587-4299. *E-mail:* admissions@alfredstate.edu.

STATE UNIVERSITY OF NEW YORK COLLEGE OF TECHNOLOGY AT CANTON

Canton, New York www.canton.edu/

- **State-supported** primarily 2-year, founded 1906, part of State University of New York System
- **Small-town** 555-acre campus
- **Endowment** $5.6 million
- **Coed**

Undergraduates 2,055 full-time, 463 part-time. Students come from 15 states and territories, 5 other countries, 3% are from out of state, 8% African American, 0.6% Asian American or Pacific Islander, 2% Hispanic American, 2% Native American, 0.5% international, 8% transferred in, 48% live on campus. *Retention:* 82% of 2003 full-time freshmen returned.

Faculty *Student/faculty ratio:* 23:1.

Academics *Calendar:* semesters. *Degrees:* certificates, associate, and bachelor's. *Special study options:* academic remediation for entering students, adult/continuing education programs, advanced placement credit, distance learning, independent study, internships, off-campus study, part-time degree program, services for LD students, student-designed majors, summer session for credit. *ROTC:* Army (c), Air Force (c).

Student Life *Campus security:* 24-hour emergency response devices and patrols, late-night transport/escort service, controlled dormitory access.

Athletics Member NJCAA.

Costs (2005–06) *One-time required fee:* $20. *Tuition:* state resident $4350 full-time, $181 per credit hour part-time; nonresident $10,610 full-time, $442 per credit hour part-time. Full-time tuition and fees vary according to degree level, location, and program. Part-time tuition and fees vary according to degree level, location, and program. *Required fees:* $1065 full-time, $39 per credit hour part-time, $5 per semester part-time. *Room and board:* $7350; room only: $4220. Room and board charges vary according to housing facility. *Payment plans:* installment, deferred payment.

Financial Aid Of all full-time matriculated undergraduates who enrolled in 2004, 200 Federal Work-Study jobs (averaging $1250). 10 state and other part-time jobs (averaging $1000).

Applying *Options:* electronic application, early admission, deferred entrance. *Application fee:* $40. *Required:* high school transcript. *Required for some:* interview. *Recommended:* minimum 2.0 GPA.

Director of Admissions Ms. Jodi L. Revill, Director of Admissions, State University of New York College of Technology at Canton, 34 Cornell Drive, Canton, NY 13617. *Phone:* 315-386-7123. *Toll-free phone:* 800-388-7123.

STATE UNIVERSITY OF NEW YORK COLLEGE OF TECHNOLOGY AT DELHI

Delhi, New York www.delhi.edu/

- **State-supported** primarily 2-year, founded 1913, part of State University of New York System
- **Rural** 405-acre campus
- **Endowment** $1.2 million
- **Coed,** 2,557 undergraduate students, 86% full-time, 45% women, 55% men

Undergraduates 2,206 full-time, 351 part-time. Students come from 7 states and territories, 3 other countries, 2% are from out of state, 12% African American, 2% Asian American or Pacific Islander, 6% Hispanic American, 0.2% Native American, 2% international, 61% live on campus.

Freshmen *Admission:* 3,650 applied, 2,236 admitted.

Faculty *Total:* 130, 75% full-time. *Student/faculty ratio:* 17:1.

Majors Accounting; architectural engineering technology; business administration and management; computer/information technology services administration related; construction engineering technology; construction management; culinary arts; electrical and power transmission installation; engineering science; engineering technology; general studies; health and physical education; heating, air conditioning and refrigeration technology; heating, air conditioning, ventilation and refrigeration maintenance technology; horticultural science; hospitality and recreation marketing; hotel/motel administration; humanities; landscape architecture; landscaping and groundskeeping; marketing/marketing management; mathematics; nursing (registered nurse training); parks, recreation and leisure; parks, recreation and leisure facilities management; pipefitting and sprinkler fitting; restaurant, culinary, and catering management; social sciences; tourism and travel services management; veterinary technology; web page, digital/multimedia and information resources design; welding technology; woodworking.

Academics *Calendar:* semesters. *Degrees:* certificates, associate, and bachelor's. *Special study options:* academic remediation for entering students, adult/continuing education programs, advanced placement credit, distance learning, English as a second language, honors programs, internships, part-time degree program, services for LD students, student-designed majors, summer session for credit.

Library Louis and Mildred Resnick Library with 47,909 titles, 384 serial subscriptions, an OPAC.

Computers on Campus 350 computers available on campus for general student use. A campuswide network can be accessed from off campus. Internet access, online (class) registration, at least one staffed computer lab available.

Student Life *Housing:* on-campus residence required through sophomore year. *Options:* coed. *Activities and Organizations:* drama/theater group, student-run newspaper, radio station, Latin American Student Organization, Hotel Sales Management Association, student radio station, Phi Theta Kappa, Student Programming Board, national fraternities. *Campus security:* 24-hour emergency response devices and patrols. *Student services:* health clinic, personal/psychological counseling, legal services.

Athletics Member NAIA, NJCAA. *Intercollegiate sports:* basketball M/W, cross-country running M/W, golf M/W, lacrosse M, soccer M/W, softball W, swimming and diving M/W, tennis M/W, track and field M/W, volleyball W, wrestling M. *Intramural sports:* basketball M/W, bowling M/W, cross-country running M/W, football M/W, golf M/W, racquetball M/W, skiing (cross-country) M/W, skiing (downhill) M/W, swimming and diving M/W, tennis M/W, volleyball M/W, weight lifting M/W.

Costs (2006–07) *Tuition:* state resident $4350 full-time, $181 per credit hour part-time; nonresident $7210 full-time, $300 per credit hour part-time. *Required fees:* $1248 full-time, $42 per credit hour part-time, $5 per term part-time. *Room and board:* $7880.

Financial Aid Of all full-time matriculated undergraduates who enrolled in 2004, 150 Federal Work-Study jobs (averaging $1050).

Applying *Options:* electronic application, early admission, deferred entrance. *Application fee:* $30. *Required:* high school transcript. *Required for some:* minimum 2.0 GPA. *Application deadline:* rolling (freshmen), rolling (transfers). *Notification:* continuous (freshmen).

Director of Admissions Mr. Larry Barrett, Dean of Enrollment, State University of New York College of Technology at Delhi, 2 Main Street, Delhi, NY 13753. *Phone:* 607-746-4000 Ext. 4856. *Toll-free phone:* 800-96-DELHI.

SUFFOLK COUNTY COMMUNITY COLLEGE

Selden, New York www.sunysuffolk.edu/

Director of Admissions Executive Director of Admissions and Enrollment Management, Suffolk County Community College, 533 College Road, Selden, NY 11784-2899. *Phone:* 631-451-4000.

SULLIVAN COUNTY COMMUNITY COLLEGE

Loch Sheldrake, New York www.sullivan.suny.edu/

- **State and locally supported** 2-year, founded 1962, part of State University of New York System
- **Rural** 405-acre campus
- **Endowment** $657,688
- **Coed,** 1,684 undergraduate students, 63% full-time, 60% women, 40% men

Undergraduates 1,067 full-time, 617 part-time. Students come from 6 states and territories, 9 other countries, 1% are from out of state, 18% African American, 1% Asian American or Pacific Islander, 10% Hispanic American, 0.4% Native American, 0.6% international, 6% transferred in.

Freshmen *Admission:* 2,573 applied, 1,824 admitted, 505 enrolled.

Faculty *Total:* 114, 43% full-time. *Student/faculty ratio:* 18:1.

Majors Accounting; administrative assistant and secretarial science; baking and pastry arts; business administration and management; commercial and advertising art; computer graphics; computer programming (specific applications); consumer merchandising/retailing management; corrections; culinary arts; data entry/microcomputer applications; electrical, electronic and communications engineering technology; elementary education; engineering science; environmental studies; hospitality administration; human services; information science/studies; kindergarten/preschool education; legal assistant/paralegal; liberal arts and sciences/liberal studies; marketing/marketing management; mathematics; nursing (registered nurse training); photography; radio and television;

sport and fitness administration/management; substance abuse/addiction counseling; survey technology; tourism and travel services management; web/multimedia management and webmaster.

Academics *Calendar:* 4-1-4. *Degree:* certificates and associate. *Special study options:* academic remediation for entering students, adult/continuing education programs, advanced placement credit, distance learning, double majors, honors programs, internships, part-time degree program, services for LD students, summer session for credit.

Library Hermann Memorial Library with 65,699 titles, 400 serial subscriptions, an OPAC, a Web page.

Computers on Campus 205 computers available on campus for general student use. A campuswide network can be accessed. Internet access, online (class) registration, at least one staffed computer lab available.

Student Life *Activities and Organizations:* student-run radio station, Science Alliance, Black Student Union, Drama Club, Baking Club, Honor Society. *Campus security:* 24-hour emergency response devices and patrols. *Student services:* health clinic, personal/psychological counseling, legal services.

Athletics Member NJCAA. *Intercollegiate sports:* basketball M/W, cheerleading W, cross-country running M/W, golf M, softball W, volleyball W. *Intramural sports:* basketball M/W, bowling M/W, cross-country running M/W, football M, golf M/W, racquetball M/W, skiing (downhill) M/W, soccer M/W, softball M/W, table tennis M/W, tennis M/W, volleyball M/W, weight lifting M/W.

Costs (2006–07) *Tuition:* state resident $3200 full-time, $125 per credit part-time; nonresident $6400 full-time, $160 per credit part-time. *Required fees:* $306 full-time, $12 per credit part-time. *Room and board:* $6500; room only: $4080.

Financial Aid Of all full-time matriculated undergraduates who enrolled in 2004, 105 Federal Work-Study jobs (averaging $800). 57 state and other part-time jobs (averaging $841).

Applying *Options:* common application, electronic application, early admission, deferred entrance. *Required:* high school transcript. *Application deadline:* rolling (freshmen), rolling (transfers). *Notification:* continuous (freshmen).

Freshmen Application Contact Ms. Sari Rosenheck, Director of Admissions and Registration Services, Sullivan County Community College, 112 College Road, Loch Sheldrake, NY 12759. *Phone:* 845-434-5750 Ext. 4200. *Toll-free phone:* 800-577-5243. *Fax:* 845-434-4806. *E-mail:* sarir@sullivan.suny.edu.

TAYLOR BUSINESS INSTITUTE
New York, New York

Freshmen Application Contact Mr. Orlando Mangual, Director of Admissions, Taylor Business Institute, 269 West 40th Street, New York, NY 10018. *Phone:* 212-302-4000.

TCI–THE COLLEGE OF TECHNOLOGY
New York, New York www.tciedu.com/

Director of Admissions Ms. Sandra Germer, Director of Admission, TCI–The College of Technology, 320 West 31st Street, New York, NY 10001-2705. *Phone:* 212-594-4000 Ext. 437. *E-mail:* admissions@tciedu.com.

TOMPKINS CORTLAND COMMUNITY COLLEGE
Dryden, New York www.sunytccc.edu/

- **State and locally supported** 2-year, founded 1968, part of State University of New York System
- **Rural** 250-acre campus with easy access to Syracuse
- **Endowment** $2.2 million
- **Coed,** 3,174 undergraduate students, 68% full-time, 60% women, 40% men

Undergraduates 2,146 full-time, 1,028 part-time. Students come from 22 states and territories, 43 other countries, 2% are from out of state, 6% African American, 2% Asian American or Pacific Islander, 3% Hispanic American, 0.3% Native American, 3% international, 10% transferred in, 4% live on campus. Freshmen *Admission:* 758 enrolled. *Average high school GPA:* 2.52. *Test scores:* SAT verbal scores over 500: 39%; SAT math scores over 500: 36%; ACT scores

over 18: 64%; SAT verbal scores over 600: 7%; SAT math scores over 600: 7%; ACT scores over 24: 7%; SAT math scores over 700: 1%; ACT scores over 30: 4%.

Faculty *Total:* 279, 25% full-time, 18% with terminal degrees. *Student/faculty ratio:* 18:1.

Majors Accounting; administrative assistant and secretarial science; aeronautics/aviation/aerospace science and technology; biological and physical sciences; business administration and management; child care provision; child development; commercial and advertising art; computer and information sciences related; computer and information systems security; computer graphics; computer hardware engineering; computer/information technology services administration related; computer programming related; computer science; computer software engineering; computer/technical support; construction engineering technology; criminal justice/law enforcement administration; data entry/microcomputer applications; electrical, electronic and communications engineering technology; engineering science; environmental studies; hotel/motel administration; humanities; human services; information science/studies; international business/trade/commerce; kindergarten/preschool education; legal assistant/paralegal; liberal arts and sciences/liberal studies; marketing/marketing management; mass communication/media; mathematics; nursing (registered nurse training); parks, recreation and leisure; radio and television; social sciences; sport and fitness administration/management; substance abuse/addiction counseling; system administration; tourism and travel services management; tourism and travel services marketing; web page, digital/multimedia and information resources design; women's studies.

Academics *Calendar:* semesters. *Degree:* certificates and associate. *Special study options:* academic remediation for entering students, adult/continuing education programs, advanced placement credit, cooperative education, English as a second language, honors programs, internships, off-campus study, part-time degree program, services for LD students, summer session for credit. *ROTC:* Army (c).

Library Gerald A. Barry Memorial Library with 50,630 titles, 489 serial subscriptions, an OPAC, a Web page.

Computers on Campus 350 computers available on campus for general student use. A campuswide network can be accessed from student residence rooms. Internet access, online (class) registration, at least one staffed computer lab available.

Student Life *Housing Options:* coed. Campus housing is provided by a third party. *Activities and Organizations:* drama/theater group, student-run newspaper, Art Works, Accounting Club, Nurse's Association. *Campus security:* 24-hour emergency response devices and patrols. *Student services:* personal/psychological counseling.

Athletics Member NJCAA. *Intercollegiate sports:* basketball M/W, cheerleading M/W, golf M/W, soccer M/W, softball W, volleyball W. *Intramural sports:* badminton M/W, basketball M/W, bowling M/W, football M/W, golf M/W, lacrosse M/W, racquetball M/W, skiing (cross-country) M/W, soccer M/W, softball M/W, swimming and diving M/W, table tennis M/W, tennis M/W, volleyball M/W, water polo M/W.

Costs (2006–07) *Tuition:* state resident $3200 full-time, $124 per credit part-time; nonresident $6700 full-time, $250 per credit part-time. *Required fees:* $553 full-time, $15 per credit part-time. *Room and board:* room only: $5400.

Financial Aid Of all full-time matriculated undergraduates who enrolled in 2004, 150 Federal Work-Study jobs (averaging $1000). 150 state and other part-time jobs (averaging $1000).

Applying *Options:* early admission, deferred entrance. *Application fee:* $15. *Required:* high school transcript. *Application deadline:* rolling (freshmen), rolling (transfers). *Notification:* continuous (freshmen).

Freshmen Application Contact Mr. Sandy Drumluk, Director of Admissions, Tompkins Cortland Community College, 170 North Street, PO Box 139, Dryden, NY 13053-0139. *Phone:* 607-844-8222. *Toll-free phone:* 888-567-8211. *Fax:* 607-844-6538. *E-mail:* admissions@tc3.edu.

TROCAIRE COLLEGE
Buffalo, New York www.trocaire.edu/

Freshmen Application Contact Mrs. Theresa Horner, Director of Records, Trocaire College, 360 Choate Avenue, Buffalo, NY 14220. *Phone:* 716-826-1200 Ext. 1259.

ULSTER COUNTY COMMUNITY COLLEGE
Stone Ridge, New York www.sunyulster.edu/

Freshmen Application Contact Admissions Office, Ulster County Community College, Cottekill Road, Stone Ridge, NY 12484. *Phone:* 914-687-5022. *Toll-free phone:* 800-724-0833.

UTICA SCHOOL OF COMMERCE
Utica, New York www.uscny.edu/

Director of Admissions Chris Tacea, Dean of Enrollment Management, Utica School of Commerce, 201 Bleecker Street, Utica, NY 13501. *Phone:* 315-733-2300. *Toll-free phone:* 800-321-4USC.

VILLA MARIA COLLEGE OF BUFFALO
Buffalo, New York www.villa.edu/

- **Independent** primarily 2-year, founded 1960, affiliated with Roman Catholic Church
- **Suburban** 9-acre campus
- **Endowment** $386,940
- **Coed,** 502 undergraduate students, 79% full-time, 74% women, 26% men

Undergraduates 396 full-time, 106 part-time. Students come from 3 states and territories, 5 other countries, 1% are from out of state, 30% African American, 1% Asian American or Pacific Islander, 1% Hispanic American, 0.8% Native American, 11% transferred in.
Freshmen *Admission:* 414 applied, 321 admitted, 132 enrolled. *Average high school GPA:* 2.5. *Test scores:* SAT verbal scores over 500: 20%; SAT math scores over 500: 17%; ACT scores over 18: 50%; SAT verbal scores over 600: 3%.
Faculty *Total:* 72, 36% full-time, 28% with terminal degrees. *Student/faculty ratio:* 11:1.
Majors Business administration and management; education; fine/studio arts; graphic design; health science; interior design; jazz; kindergarten/preschool education; liberal arts and sciences/liberal studies; music; music management and merchandising; physical therapist assistant.
Academics *Calendar:* semesters. *Degrees:* associate and bachelor's. *Special study options:* academic remediation for entering students, advanced placement credit, cooperative education, double majors, independent study, internships, off-campus study, part-time degree program, services for LD students, study abroad, summer session for credit.
Library Villa Maria College Library with 37,000 titles, 130 serial subscriptions, 3,500 audiovisual materials, an OPAC, a Web page.
Computers on Campus 127 computers available on campus for general student use. A campuswide network can be accessed. Internet access, at least one staffed computer lab available.
Student Life *Activities and Organizations:* student-run newspaper, choral group, Design and Beyond, Teachers Love Children, Multicultural Club, Phi Theta Kappa, Helping Adults New Dreams Succeed. *Campus security:* late-night transport/escort service. *Student services:* health clinic, personal/psychological counseling.
Costs (2006–07) *Tuition:* $11,280 full-time, $420 per credit hour part-time. *Required fees:* $430 full-time.
Financial Aid Of all full-time matriculated undergraduates who enrolled in 2004, 159 Federal Work-Study jobs (averaging $320).
Applying *Options:* electronic application, deferred entrance. *Required:* essay or personal statement, high school transcript, interview, writing sample. *Application deadline:* rolling (freshmen), rolling (transfers). *Notification:* continuous (freshmen).
Freshmen Application Contact Mr. Kevin Donovan, Director of Admissions, Villa Maria College of Buffalo, 240 Pine Ridge Road, Buffalo, NY 14225-3999. *Phone:* 716-896-0700 Ext. 1802. *Fax:* 716-896-0705. *E-mail:* admmissions@villa.edu.

WESTCHESTER COMMUNITY COLLEGE
Valhalla, New York www.sunywcc.edu/

- **State and locally supported** 2-year, founded 1946, part of State University of New York System
- **Suburban** 218-acre campus with easy access to New York City
- **Endowment** $8.5 million
- **Coed,** 11,564 undergraduate students

Undergraduates Students come from 14 states and territories, 70 other countries, 0.1% are from out of state, 19% African American, 5% Asian American or Pacific Islander, 18% Hispanic American, 1% Native American, 2% international.
Faculty *Total:* 156. *Student/faculty ratio:* 16:1.

Majors Accounting; administrative assistant and secretarial science; applied art; automobile/automotive mechanics technology; biological and physical sciences; business administration and management; chemical engineering; child care provision; child development; civil engineering technology; clinical laboratory science/medical technology; clinical/medical laboratory technology; computer and information sciences; computer and information sciences related; computer science; computer systems networking and telecommunications; consumer merchandising/retailing management; corrections; criminal justice/law enforcement administration; criminal justice/police science; culinary arts; dance; data processing and data processing technology; dietetics; electrical, electronic and communications engineering technology; emergency medical technology (EMT paramedic); engineering science; engineering technology; environmental engineering technology; finance; fine/studio arts; food services technology; hotel/motel administration; humanities; human services; industrial radiologic technology; information science/studies; international business/trade/commerce; legal administrative assistant/secretary; legal assistant/paralegal; liberal arts and sciences/liberal studies; marketing/marketing management; mass communication/media; mechanical engineering/mechanical technology; nursing (registered nurse training); public administration; respiratory care therapy; social sciences; special products marketing; substance abuse/addiction counseling; tourism and travel services management; tourism promotion.
Academics *Calendar:* semesters. *Degree:* certificates and associate. *Special study options:* academic remediation for entering students, adult/continuing education programs, cooperative education, distance learning, double majors, English as a second language, honors programs, independent study, internships, off-campus study, part-time degree program, services for LD students, student-designed majors, study abroad, summer session for credit.
Library Harold L. Drimmer Library with 96,419 titles, 531 serial subscriptions, 5,163 audiovisual materials, an OPAC, a Web page.
Computers on Campus 1200 computers available on campus for general student use. A campuswide network can be accessed. Internet access, online (class) registration, at least one staffed computer lab available.
Student Life *Housing:* college housing not available. *Activities and Organizations:* drama/theater group, student-run newspaper, radio station, choral group, Student Senate, African Culture Club, Italian Club, International Friendship Club, Alpha Beta Gamma. *Campus security:* 24-hour emergency response devices and patrols, late-night transport/escort service. *Student services:* health clinic, personal/psychological counseling, women's center.
Athletics Member NJCAA. *Intercollegiate sports:* baseball M, basketball M/W, bowling M/W, golf M, soccer M, softball W, volleyball W. *Intramural sports:* badminton M/W, basketball M/W, softball M/W, swimming and diving M/W, tennis M/W, volleyball M/W, weight lifting M/W.
Costs (2006–07) *Tuition:* state resident $3350 full-time, $140 per credit part-time; nonresident $8376 full-time, $350 per credit part-time.
Financial Aid Of all full-time matriculated undergraduates who enrolled in 2004, 200 Federal Work-Study jobs (averaging $1000).
Applying *Options:* electronic application, early admission. *Application fee:* $25. *Required:* high school transcript. *Recommended:* interview. *Application deadline:* rolling (freshmen), rolling (transfers). *Notification:* continuous until 2/2 (freshmen).
Freshmen Application Contact Ms. Terre Wisell, Director of Admissions, Westchester Community College, 75 Grasslands Road, Administration Building, Valhalla, NY 10595-1698. *Phone:* 914-606-6735. *E-mail:* admissions@sunywcc.edu.

WOOD TOBE—COBURN SCHOOL
New York, New York www.woodtobecoburn.com/

- **Proprietary** 2-year, founded 1879, part of Bradford Schools, Inc
- **Urban** campus
- **Coed, primarily women,** 269 undergraduate students, 100% full-time, 77% women, 23% men

Undergraduates 269 full-time. Students come from 3 states and territories, 5% are from out of state, 27% African American, 2% Asian American or Pacific Islander, 52% Hispanic American, 0.4% Native American, 2% international.
Freshmen *Admission:* 899 applied, 773 admitted, 201 enrolled.
Faculty *Total:* 21, 24% full-time, 10% with terminal degrees. *Student/faculty ratio:* 27:1.
Majors Accounting; fashion/apparel design; fashion merchandising; graphic design; marketing/marketing management; medical/clinical assistant; office management; system, networking, and LAN/WAN management; tourism/travel marketing.
Academics *Calendar:* semesters. *Degree:* diplomas and associate. *Special study options:* academic remediation for entering students, cooperative education, internships, summer session for credit.
Library WTC Learning Resources Center with 698 titles, 45 serial subscriptions, an OPAC.

Computers on Campus 134 computers available on campus for general student use. A campuswide network can be accessed. Internet access, at least one staffed computer lab available.

Student Life *Housing:* college housing not available. *Options:* Campus housing is provided by a third party. *Campus security:* 24-hour emergency response devices and patrols.

Costs (2006–07) *Tuition:* $14,400 full-time.

Applying *Application fee:* $50. *Required:* high school transcript, interview. *Application deadline:* rolling (freshmen), rolling (transfers).

Director of Admissions Ms. Sandra L. Andujar, Director of Admissions, Wood Tobe–Coburn School, 8 East 40th Street, New York, NY 10016. *Phone:* 212-686-9040 Ext. 103.

NORTH CAROLINA

ALAMANCE COMMUNITY COLLEGE
Graham, North Carolina www.alamance.cc.nc.us/

- **State-supported** 2-year, founded 1959, part of North Carolina Community College System
- **Small-town** 48-acre campus
- **Endowment** $2.9 million
- **Coed,** 4,285 undergraduate students, 41% full-time, 66% women, 34% men

Undergraduates 1,770 full-time, 2,515 part-time. Students come from 23 states and territories, 3 other countries, 1% are from out of state, 23% African American, 1% Asian American or Pacific Islander, 2% Hispanic American, 0.5% Native American, 2% international, 10% transferred in.
Freshmen *Admission:* 982 applied, 982 admitted, 599 enrolled. *Average high school GPA:* 2.00.

Faculty *Total:* 238, 42% full-time, 6% with terminal degrees. *Student/faculty ratio:* 16:1.

Majors Accounting technology and bookkeeping; animal sciences; applied horticulture; automobile/automotive mechanics technology; banking and financial support services; biotechnology; business administration and management; carpentry; clinical/medical laboratory technology; commercial and advertising art; computer programming; criminal justice/safety; culinary arts; electrical, electronic and communications engineering technology; electromechanical technology; executive assistant/executive secretary; general retailing/wholesaling; heating, air conditioning and refrigeration technology; information science/studies; kindergarten/preschool education; legal administrative assistant/secretary; liberal arts and sciences/liberal studies; machine tool technology; mechanical engineering/mechanical technology; medical administrative assistant and medical secretary; medical/clinical assistant; nursing (registered nurse training); office occupations and clerical services; operations management; real estate; social work; teacher assistant/aide; welding technology.

Academics *Calendar:* semesters. *Degree:* certificates, diplomas, and associate. *Special study options:* academic remediation for entering students, adult/continuing education programs, cooperative education, distance learning, double majors, English as a second language, independent study, off-campus study, part-time degree program, services for LD students, summer session for credit.

Library Learning Resources Center with 22,114 titles, 185 serial subscriptions, 3,033 audiovisual materials, an OPAC, a Web page.

Computers on Campus 56 computers available on campus for general student use. A campuswide network can be accessed. Internet access, at least one staffed computer lab available.

Student Life *Housing:* college housing not available. *Campus security:* 24-hour emergency response devices and patrols, student patrols, late-night transport/escort service. *Student services:* personal/psychological counseling.

Athletics *Intramural sports:* basketball M/W, bowling M/W, tennis M/W, volleyball M/W.

Costs (2005–06) *Tuition:* state resident $1264 full-time, $40 per credit hour part-time; nonresident $7024 full-time, $220 per credit hour part-time. *Required fees:* $30 full-time, $5 per term part-time.

Financial Aid Of all full-time matriculated undergraduates who enrolled in 2004, 185 Federal Work-Study jobs (averaging $3000).

Applying *Options:* common application, deferred entrance. *Required:* high school transcript. *Application deadline:* rolling (freshmen), rolling (transfers). *Notification:* continuous (freshmen).

Freshmen Application Contact Ms. Suzanne Lucier, Director for Enrollment Management, Alamance Community College, Jimmy Kerr Road, Graham, NC 27253-8000. *Phone:* 336-578-2002 Ext. 4138. *Fax:* 336-578-1987. *E-mail:* aacadmissions@alamance.cc.nc.us.

THE ART INSTITUTE OF CHARLOTTE
Charlotte, North Carolina www.aich.artinstitutes.edu/

- **Proprietary** primarily 2-year, founded 1973, part of Education Management Corporation
- **Suburban** campus
- **Coed,** 819 undergraduate students, 69% full-time, 69% women, 31% men

Undergraduates 564 full-time, 255 part-time. 26% are from out of state, 32% African American, 2% Asian American or Pacific Islander, 3% Hispanic American, 0.9% Native American, 26% live on campus.
Freshmen *Admission:* 697 applied, 202 enrolled. *Average high school GPA:* 2.62. *Test scores:* SAT verbal scores over 500: 22%; SAT math scores over 500: 14%; ACT scores over 18: 4%; SAT verbal scores over 600: 3%; SAT math scores over 600: 6%; ACT scores over 24: 2%; SAT verbal scores over 700: 1%.

Faculty *Total:* 52, 40% full-time, 13% with terminal degrees. *Student/faculty ratio:* 19:1.

Academics *Calendar:* quarters. *Degrees:* certificates, associate, and bachelor's. *Special study options:* academic remediation for entering students, accelerated degree program, advanced placement credit, distance learning, independent study, internships, part-time degree program, services for LD students, summer session for credit.

Library The Art Institute of Charlotte Library with 15,000 titles, 130 serial subscriptions, 825 audiovisual materials, an OPAC.

Computers on Campus 150 computers available on campus for general student use. A campuswide network can be accessed. Internet access, online (class) registration, at least one staffed computer lab available.

Student Life *Housing Options:* Campus housing is leased by the school. Freshman campus housing is guaranteed. *Student services:* personal/psychological counseling.

Standardized Tests *Required for some:* SAT or ACT (for admission). *Recommended:* SAT or ACT (for admission).

Costs (2006–07) *Tuition:* $23,232 full-time, $363 per credit part-time. *Required fees:* $200 full-time. *Room only:* $5580.

Applying *Options:* electronic application, deferred entrance. *Application fee:* $50. *Required:* essay or personal statement, high school transcript. *Required for some:* interview. *Application deadline:* rolling (freshmen), rolling (transfers). *Notification:* continuous (freshmen).

Director of Admissions Mr. Gil Cendejas, College President, The Art Institute of Charlotte, 2110 Water Ridge Parkway, Charlotte, NC 28217. *Phone:* 704-357-8020. *Fax:* 704-357-1133. *E-mail:* guinane@aii.edu.

▶ See page 476 for the College Close-Up.

ASHEVILLE-BUNCOMBE TECHNICAL COMMUNITY COLLEGE
Asheville, North Carolina www.abtech.edu/

- **State-supported** 2-year, founded 1959, part of North Carolina Community College System
- **Urban** 126-acre campus
- **Endowment** $98,442
- **Coed**

Undergraduates 2,042 full-time, 3,585 part-time. 2% are from out of state, 6% African American, 0.5% Asian American or Pacific Islander, 1% Hispanic American, 0.5% Native American, 0.6% international.

Faculty *Student/faculty ratio:* 17:1.

Academics *Calendar:* semesters. *Degree:* certificates, diplomas, and associate. *Special study options:* academic remediation for entering students, adult/continuing education programs, advanced placement credit, cooperative education, distance learning, double majors, independent study, internships, part-time degree program, services for LD students, summer session for credit.

Student Life *Campus security:* 24-hour emergency response devices and patrols.

Standardized Tests *Required:* CPT, SAT, or ACT (for placement).

Costs (2005–06) *Tuition:* state resident $1216 full-time, $38 per credit hour part-time; nonresident $6752 full-time, $211 per credit hour part-time. *Required fees:* $28 full-time, $11 per term part-time.

Asheville-Buncombe Technical Community College (continued)

Financial Aid Of all full-time matriculated undergraduates who enrolled in 2004, 55 Federal Work-Study jobs (averaging $2000).

Applying *Options:* deferred entrance. *Required:* high school transcript. *Required for some:* letters of recommendation, interview.

Director of Admissions Ms. Lisa Bush, Director, Admissions, Asheville-Buncombe Technical Community College, 340 Victoria Road, Asheville, NC 28801. *Phone:* 828-254-1921 Ext. 202. *E-mail:* lbush@abtech.edu.

BEAUFORT COUNTY COMMUNITY COLLEGE
Washington, North Carolina   www.beaufortccc.edu/

- **State-supported** 2-year, founded 1967, part of North Carolina Community College System
- **Rural** 67-acre campus
- **Coed,** 1,424 undergraduate students, 51% full-time, 67% women, 33% men

Undergraduates 733 full-time, 691 part-time. 1% are from out of state, 34% African American, 0.1% Asian American or Pacific Islander, 3% Hispanic American.

Faculty *Total:* 322, 49% full-time, 1% with terminal degrees.

Majors Accounting; administrative assistant and secretarial science; agricultural mechanization; automobile/automotive mechanics technology; business administration and management; clinical/medical laboratory technology; computer programming; computer systems networking and telecommunications; criminal justice/police science; drafting and design technology; electrical, electronic and communications engineering technology; heavy equipment maintenance technology; human resources management; information science/studies; kindergarten/preschool education; liberal arts and sciences/liberal studies; medical administrative assistant and medical secretary; medical office management; nursing (registered nurse training); social work; welding technology.

Academics *Calendar:* semesters. *Degree:* certificates, diplomas, and associate. *Special study options:* academic remediation for entering students, advanced placement credit, cooperative education, distance learning, part-time degree program, services for LD students, summer session for credit.

Library Beaufort Community College Library with 25,734 titles, 214 serial subscriptions, an OPAC, a Web page.

Computers on Campus 60 computers available on campus for general student use. A campuswide network can be accessed from off campus. Internet access, at least one staffed computer lab available.

Student Life *Housing:* college housing not available. *Activities and Organizations:* Student Government Association, Gama Beta Phi, Phi Beta Lambda, Hope Club. *Campus security:* 24-hour emergency response devices and patrols, late-night transport/escort service. *Student services:* personal/psychological counseling.

Standardized Tests *Required:* CPT (for admission). *Recommended:* SAT and SAT Subject Tests or ACT (for admission).

Costs (2005–06) *Tuition:* state resident $1264 full-time; nonresident $7024 full-time. Part-time tuition and fees vary according to course load. *Required fees:* $64 full-time. *Waivers:* senior citizens and employees or children of employees.

Financial Aid Of all full-time matriculated undergraduates who enrolled in 2004, 21 Federal Work-Study jobs (averaging $1600). *Financial aid deadline:* 7/15.

Applying *Options:* electronic application. *Required:* high school transcript. *Required for some:* essay or personal statement, letters of recommendation, interview. *Application deadline:* 8/18 (freshmen), rolling (transfers). *Notification:* continuous (freshmen).

Freshmen Application Contact Mr. Gary Burbage, Director of Admissions, Beaufort County Community College, PO Box 1069, 5337 US Highway 264 East, Washington, NC 27889-1069. *Phone:* 252-940-6233. *Fax:* 252-940-6393. *E-mail:* garyb@email.beaufort.cc.nc.us.

BLADEN COMMUNITY COLLEGE
Dublin, North Carolina   www.bladen.cc.nc.us/

- **State and locally supported** 2-year, founded 1967, part of North Carolina Community College System
- **Rural** 45-acre campus
- **Endowment** $72,151
- **Coed,** 1,407 undergraduate students, 60% full-time, 77% women, 23% men

Undergraduates 838 full-time, 569 part-time. Students come from 3 states and territories, 48% African American, 0.2% Asian American or Pacific Islander, 0.6% Hispanic American, 10% Native American. *Retention:* 35% of 2003 full-time freshmen returned.

Freshmen *Admission:* 267 enrolled. *Average high school GPA:* 2.6.

Faculty *Total:* 85, 38% full-time, 5% with terminal degrees.

Majors Administrative assistant and secretarial science; biotechnology; business administration and management; child care provision; computer programming; computer programming (specific applications); cosmetology; criminal justice/police science; electrical, electronic and communications engineering technology; general studies; industrial technology; information technology; liberal arts and sciences/liberal studies; nursing (registered nurse training); welding technology.

Academics *Calendar:* semesters. *Degree:* certificates, diplomas, and associate. *Special study options:* academic remediation for entering students, adult/continuing education programs, advanced placement credit, distance learning, double majors, independent study, part-time degree program, services for LD students, summer session for credit.

Library Learning Resource Center with 19,881 titles, 52 serial subscriptions, 2,364 audiovisual materials, an OPAC, a Web page.

Computers on Campus 150 computers available on campus for general student use. A campuswide network can be accessed from off campus. Internet access, at least one staffed computer lab available.

Student Life *Housing:* college housing not available. *Campus security:* 14-hour patrols. *Student services:* personal/psychological counseling.

Standardized Tests *Required:* ACT COMPASS (for admission).

Costs (2006–07) *Tuition:* state resident $1264 full-time, $40 per hour part-time; nonresident $7024 full-time, $220 per hour part-time. *Required fees:* $66 full-time, $26 per term part-time.

Financial Aid Of all full-time matriculated undergraduates who enrolled in 2004, 30 Federal Work-Study jobs (averaging $1200).

Applying *Options:* common application, electronic application, deferred entrance. *Required:* high school transcript. *Application deadlines:* 8/1 (freshmen), 8/1 (transfers). *Notification:* continuous until 8/15 (freshmen).

Freshmen Application Contact Ms. Yvonne Willoughby, Admissions Secretary, Bladen Community College, PO Box 266, Dublin, NC 28332. *Phone:* 910-879-5593. *Fax:* 910-879-5564. *E-mail:* ywilloughby@bladen.edu.

BLUE RIDGE COMMUNITY COLLEGE
Flat Rock, North Carolina   www.blueridge.edu/

- **State and locally supported** 2-year, founded 1969, part of North Carolina Community College System
- **Small-town** 109-acre campus
- **Endowment** $51,500
- **Coed**

Undergraduates 787 full-time, 1,172 part-time. Students come from 18 states and territories, 14 other countries, 5% African American, 0.6% Asian American or Pacific Islander, 2% Hispanic American, 0.2% Native American, 2% international, 6% transferred in.

Faculty *Student/faculty ratio:* 14:1.

Academics *Calendar:* semesters. *Degree:* certificates, diplomas, and associate. *Special study options:* academic remediation for entering students, adult/continuing education programs, advanced placement credit, cooperative education, distance learning, double majors, English as a second language, internships, part-time degree program, services for LD students, summer session for credit.

Student Life *Campus security:* sheriff's deputy during class hours.

Athletics Member NJCAA.

Financial Aid Of all full-time matriculated undergraduates who enrolled in 2004, 35 Federal Work-Study jobs (averaging $1920). 34 state and other part-time jobs (averaging $1920).

Applying *Options:* common application, early admission. *Required:* high school transcript.

Freshmen Application Contact Ms. Sarah Jones, Registrar, Blue Ridge Community College, 180 West Campus Drive, Flat Rock, NC 28731. *Phone:* 828-694-1810. *E-mail:* sarahj@blueridge.cc.nc.us.

BRUNSWICK COMMUNITY COLLEGE
Supply, North Carolina   www.brunswick.cc.nc.us/

- **State-supported** 2-year, founded 1979, part of North Carolina Community College System
- **Rural** 266-acre campus
- **Endowment** $1.3 million
- **Coed**

Undergraduates 493 full-time, 510 part-time. Students come from 5 states and territories, 1% are from out of state, 21% African American, 0.4% Asian American or Pacific Islander, 0.8% Hispanic American, 0.2% Native American, 4% transferred in.

Faculty *Student/faculty ratio:* 12:1.

Academics *Calendar:* semesters. *Degree:* certificates, diplomas, and associate. *Special study options:* academic remediation for entering students, advanced placement credit, cooperative education, distance learning, English as a second language, independent study, internships, part-time degree program, services for LD students, summer session for credit.

Student Life *Campus security:* late-night transport/escort service, campus police.

Athletics Member NJCAA.

Standardized Tests *Required:* ACT ASSET (for placement).

Costs (2005–06) *Tuition:* state resident $1185 full-time, $40 per semester hour part-time; nonresident $6585 full-time, $220 per semester hour part-time. Part-time tuition and fees vary according to course load. *Required fees:* $73 full-time, $37 per term part-time.

Applying *Options:* electronic application. *Required:* high school transcript. *Required for some:* letters of recommendation, interview.

Freshmen Application Contact Ms. Julie Olsen, Admissions Counselor, Brunswick Community College, PO Box 30, Supply, NC 28462. *Phone:* 910-755-7324. *Toll-free phone:* 800-754-1050 Ext. 324.

CALDWELL COMMUNITY COLLEGE AND TECHNICAL INSTITUTE
Hudson, North Carolina   www.cccti.edu/

- **State-supported** 2-year, founded 1964, part of North Carolina Community College System
- **Small-town** 50-acre campus
- **Coed,** 3,744 undergraduate students, 34% full-time, 56% women, 44% men

Undergraduates 1,281 full-time, 2,463 part-time. Students come from 24 states and territories, 5% African American, 1% Asian American or Pacific Islander, 1% Hispanic American, 0.3% Native American, 9% transferred in. Freshmen *Admission:* 763 applied, 763 admitted, 763 enrolled.

Faculty *Total:* 407, 29% full-time, 6% with terminal degrees.

Majors Accounting; aeronautics/aviation/aerospace science and technology; art; biological and physical sciences; biomedical technology; business administration and management; business systems networking/ telecommunications; cardiovascular technology; child care/guidance; computer programming (specific applications); cosmetology; diagnostic medical sonography and ultrasound technology; drafting and design technology; electrical, electronic and communications engineering technology; health/health care administration; information technology; landscaping and groundskeeping; legal assistant/paralegal; liberal arts and sciences/liberal studies; medical radiologic technology; music; nuclear medical technology; nursing (registered nurse training); physical therapy; pre-engineering.

Academics *Calendar:* semesters. *Degree:* certificates, diplomas, and associate. *Special study options:* academic remediation for entering students, adult/continuing education programs, advanced placement credit, cooperative education, distance learning, double majors, independent study, part-time degree program, services for LD students, summer session for credit.

Library Broyhill Center for Learning Resources with 50,770 titles, 251 serial subscriptions, 5,352 audiovisual materials, an OPAC, a Web page.

Computers on Campus 750 computers available on campus for general student use. A campuswide network can be accessed from off campus. Internet access, online (class) registration, at least one staffed computer lab available.

Student Life *Housing:* college housing not available. *Activities and Organizations:* drama/theater group, choral group. *Campus security:* trained security personnel during open hours.

Athletics Member NJCAA. *Intercollegiate sports:* basketball M/W, golf M, volleyball W. *Intramural sports:* basketball M/W, tennis M/W.

Costs (2005–06) *Tuition:* state resident $1185 full-time, $40 per credit hour part-time; nonresident $6585 full-time, $220 per credit hour part-time. *Required fees:* $4 per course part-time.

Financial Aid Of all full-time matriculated undergraduates who enrolled in 2004, 69 Federal Work-Study jobs (averaging $960).

Applying *Options:* early admission. *Required:* high school transcript. *Application deadline:* rolling (freshmen), rolling (transfers). *Notification:* continuous (freshmen).

Freshmen Application Contact Mrs. Carolyn Woodard, Director of Enrollment Management Services, Caldwell Community College and Technical Institute, 2855 Hickory Boulevard, Hudson, NC 28638. *Phone:* 828-726-2703. *Fax:* 828-726-2709. *E-mail:* cwoodard@cccti.edu.

CAPE FEAR COMMUNITY COLLEGE
Wilmington, North Carolina   www.cfcc.edu/

- **State-supported** 2-year, founded 1959, part of North Carolina Community College System
- **Urban** 150-acre campus
- **Endowment** $1.8 million
- **Coed,** 7,501 undergraduate students, 42% full-time, 55% women, 45% men

Undergraduates 3,160 full-time, 4,341 part-time. Students come from 29 states and territories, 2 other countries, 7% are from out of state, 14% African American, 0.6% Asian American or Pacific Islander, 2% Hispanic American, 0.6% Native American. Freshmen *Admission:* 1,028 admitted, 1,028 enrolled.

Faculty *Total:* 474, 47% full-time, 7% with terminal degrees. *Student/faculty ratio:* 13:1.

Majors Accounting technology and bookkeeping; architectural engineering technology; automobile/automotive mechanics technology; business administration and management; chemical technology; child care and support services management; computer systems analysis; computer systems networking and telecommunications; computer technology/computer systems technology; criminal justice/police science; dental hygiene; diagnostic medical sonography and ultrasound technology; electrical, electronic and communications engineering technology; electrical/electronics equipment installation and repair; engineering/industrial management; environmental studies; executive assistant/executive secretary; hotel/motel administration; industrial production technologies related; institutional food workers; instrumentation technology; interior design; landscaping and groundskeeping; liberal arts and sciences/liberal studies; machine shop technology; marine maintenance and ship repair technology; marine technology; mechanical engineering/mechanical technology; medical radiologic technology; nursing (registered nurse training); occupational therapist assistant.

Academics *Calendar:* semesters. *Degree:* certificates, diplomas, and associate. *Special study options:* academic remediation for entering students, adult/continuing education programs, cooperative education, distance learning, part-time degree program, services for LD students.

Library Cape Fear Community College Library with 47,761 titles, 936 serial subscriptions, 6,317 audiovisual materials, an OPAC, a Web page.

Computers on Campus 80 computers available on campus for general student use. A campuswide network can be accessed from off campus. At least one staffed computer lab available.

Student Life *Housing:* college housing not available. *Activities and Organizations:* student-run newspaper, choral group, Nursing Club, Dental Hygiene Club, Pineapple Guild. *Campus security:* 24-hour emergency response devices and patrols, late-night transport/escort service. *Student services:* personal/psychological counseling.

Athletics Member NJCAA. *Intercollegiate sports:* basketball M, cheerleading M/W, golf M, softball M/W, tennis M/W, volleyball M/W. *Intramural sports:* soccer M.

Costs (2005–06) *Tuition:* state resident $1264 full-time, $40 per credit part-time; nonresident $7024 full-time, $220 per credit part-time. Full-time tuition and fees vary according to course load. Part-time tuition and fees vary according to course load. *Required fees:* $70 full-time, $7 per credit part-time. *Payment plan:* deferred payment. *Waivers:* senior citizens and employees or children of employees.

Financial Aid Of all full-time matriculated undergraduates who enrolled in 2004, 50 Federal Work-Study jobs.

Applying *Options:* electronic application, early admission, deferred entrance. *Required:* high school transcript, placement testing. *Application deadline:* 8/19 (freshmen), rolling (transfers). *Notification:* continuous (freshmen).

Freshmen Application Contact Ms. Linda Kasyan, Director of Enrollment Management, Cape Fear Community College, 411 North Front Street, Wilmington, NC 28401-3993. *Phone:* 910-362-7054. *Toll-free phone:* 910-362-7557. *Fax:* 910-362-7080. *E-mail:* admissions@cfcc.edu.

CAROLINAS COLLEGE OF HEALTH SCIENCES

Charlotte, North Carolina   www.carolinascollege.edu/

- **Independent** 2-year, founded 1990, part of Carolinas Healthcare System
- **Urban** 3-acre campus
- **Endowment** $2.0 million
- **Coed, primarily women**

Undergraduates 146 full-time, 312 part-time. Students come from 3 states and territories, 6% are from out of state, 15% African American, 2% Asian American or Pacific Islander, 2% Hispanic American, 0.4% Native American, 5% live on campus.

Faculty *Student/faculty ratio:* 7:1.

Academics *Calendar:* semesters. *Degree:* certificates, diplomas, and associate. *Special study options:* advanced placement credit, distance learning, independent study, internships.

Student Life *Campus security:* 24-hour emergency response devices and patrols, student patrols, late-night transport/escort service.

Standardized Tests *Required for some:* SAT or ACT (for admission).

Costs (2005–06) *Tuition:* $6145 full-time, $175 per credit part-time. Full-time tuition and fees vary according to course load and program. Part-time tuition and fees vary according to course load and program. *Required fees:* $250 full-time.

Financial Aid Of all full-time matriculated undergraduates who enrolled in 2004, 12 Federal Work-Study jobs (averaging $1500).

Applying *Application fee:* $35. *Required:* high school transcript. *Required for some:* letters of recommendation, interview. *Recommended:* minimum 2.5 GPA.

Freshmen Application Contact Ms. Elizabeth West, Admissions Officer, Carolinas College of Health Sciences, PO Box 32861, Charlotte, NC 28232-2861. *Phone:* 704-355-5043.

CARTERET COMMUNITY COLLEGE

Morehead City, North Carolina   www.carteret.edu/

- **State-supported** 2-year, founded 1963, part of North Carolina Community College System
- **Small-town** 25-acre campus
- **Coed,** 1,659 undergraduate students, 39% full-time, 69% women, 31% men

Undergraduates 639 full-time, 1,020 part-time. Students come from 24 states and territories, 5% African American, 0.2% Asian American or Pacific Islander, 3% Hispanic American, 0.4% Native American.

Freshmen *Admission:* 331 enrolled.

Faculty *Total:* 115, 38% full-time.

Majors Administrative assistant and secretarial science; business administration and management; computer engineering technology; computer software and media applications related; computer systems networking and telecommunications; criminal justice/law enforcement administration; industrial radiologic technology; information technology; interior design; legal administrative assistant/secretary; legal assistant/paralegal; liberal arts and sciences/liberal studies; medical/clinical assistant; nursing (licensed practical/vocational nurse training); photography; respiratory care therapy; teacher assistant/aide; therapeutic recreation.

Academics *Calendar:* semesters. *Degree:* certificates, diplomas, and associate. *Special study options:* academic remediation for entering students, adult/continuing education programs, cooperative education, distance learning, double majors, internships, part-time degree program, services for LD students, summer session for credit.

Library Michael J. Smith Learning Resource Center with 22,000 titles, 168 serial subscriptions.

Computers on Campus 150 computers available on campus for general student use. A campuswide network can be accessed. Internet access, at least one staffed computer lab available.

Student Life *Housing:* college housing not available. *Activities and Organizations:* drama/theater group, student-run newspaper.

Athletics *Intercollegiate sports:* softball M/W, volleyball M/W.

Costs (2005–06) *Tuition:* state resident $1315 full-time, $56 per credit hour part-time; nonresident $7075 full-time, $236 per credit hour part-time. *Required fees:* $66 full-time, $15 per term part-time.

Financial Aid Of all full-time matriculated undergraduates who enrolled in 2004, 40 Federal Work-Study jobs (averaging $750).

Applying *Options:* common application, electronic application, early admission. *Required:* high school transcript. *Application deadline:* rolling (freshmen), rolling (transfers). *Notification:* continuous (freshmen).

Freshmen Application Contact Mr. Rick Hill, Director of Student Enrollment Resources, Carteret Community College, 3505 Arendell Street, Morehead City, NC 28557-2989. *Phone:* 252-222-6153 Ext. 6153. *Fax:* 252-222-6265. *E-mail:* mhw@carteret.edu.

CATAWBA VALLEY COMMUNITY COLLEGE

Hickory, North Carolina   www.cvcc.cc.nc.us/

- **State and locally supported** 2-year, founded 1960, part of North Carolina Community College System
- **Small-town** 50-acre campus with easy access to Charlotte
- **Endowment** $591,181
- **Coed**

Undergraduates 1,524 full-time, 2,419 part-time. Students come from 3 states and territories, 2 other countries, 1% are from out of state, 24% transferred in.

Faculty *Student/faculty ratio:* 11:1.

Academics *Calendar:* semesters. *Degree:* certificates, diplomas, and associate. *Special study options:* academic remediation for entering students, adult/continuing education programs, advanced placement credit, cooperative education, distance learning, double majors, English as a second language, independent study, part-time degree program, services for LD students, student-designed majors, summer session for credit.

Student Life *Campus security:* 24-hour patrols.

Athletics Member NJCAA.

Standardized Tests *Required:* ACT ASSET (for placement).

Applying *Options:* common application, early admission, deferred entrance. *Required:* high school transcript.

Director of Admissions Mrs. Caroline Farmer, Director of Admissions and Records, Catawba Valley Community College, 2550 Highway 70 SE, Hickory, NC 28602-9699. *Phone:* 828-327-7000 Ext. 4218.

CENTRAL CAROLINA COMMUNITY COLLEGE

Sanford, North Carolina   www.cccc.edu/

- **State and locally supported** 2-year, founded 1962, part of North Carolina Community College System
- **Small-town** 41-acre campus
- **Endowment** $1.0 million
- **Coed**

Undergraduates 1,845 full-time, 3,012 part-time. Students come from 36 states and territories, 5 other countries, 6% are from out of state, 25% African American, 1% Asian American or Pacific Islander, 4% Hispanic American, 0.8% Native American, 0.2% international, 20% transferred in.

Faculty *Student/faculty ratio:* 8:1.

Academics *Calendar:* semesters. *Degree:* certificates, diplomas, and associate. *Special study options:* academic remediation for entering students, adult/continuing education programs, advanced placement credit, distance learning, double majors, English as a second language, independent study, internships, part-time degree program, services for LD students, summer session for credit.

Student Life *Campus security:* patrols by trained security personnel during operating hours.

Athletics Member NJCAA.

Standardized Tests *Required:* CPT, ACCUPLACER, ACT COMPASS, ACT ASSET (for placement). *Recommended:* SAT or ACT (for placement).

Financial Aid Of all full-time matriculated undergraduates who enrolled in 2004, 70 Federal Work-Study jobs (averaging $1361). *Financial aid deadline:* 5/4.

Applying *Options:* electronic application, early admission, deferred entrance. *Required:* high school transcript.

Director of Admissions Mr. Ken R. Hoyle Jr., Dean of Student Services, Central Carolina Community College, 1105 Kelly Drive, Sanford, NC 27330. *Phone:* 919-775-5401. *Toll-free phone:* 800-682-8353 Ext. 7300.

CENTRAL PIEDMONT COMMUNITY COLLEGE

Charlotte, North Carolina
www.cpcc.edu/

- **State and locally supported** 2-year, founded 1963, part of North Carolina Community College System
- **Urban** 37-acre campus
- **Endowment** $16.1 million
- **Coed,** 16,631 undergraduate students, 37% full-time, 58% women, 42% men

Undergraduates 6,115 full-time, 10,516 part-time. Students come from 13 states and territories, 117 other countries, 3% are from out of state, 32% African American, 3% Asian American or Pacific Islander, 3% Hispanic American, 0.5% Native American, 9% international, 24% transferred in.
Freshmen *Admission:* 1,397 applied, 1,397 admitted, 1,397 enrolled.
Faculty *Total:* 2,034, 15% full-time. *Student/faculty ratio:* 16:1.
Majors Accounting; administrative assistant and secretarial science; advertising; applied art; architectural engineering technology; art; automobile/automotive mechanics technology; biology/biological sciences; business administration and management; business machine repair; child development; civil engineering technology; clinical laboratory science/medical technology; clinical/medical laboratory technology; commercial and advertising art; computer engineering technology; computer programming; computer programming (specific applications); computer science; consumer merchandising/retailing management; criminal justice/law enforcement administration; criminal justice/police science; culinary arts; dance; data processing and data processing technology; dental hygiene; drafting and design technology; electrical, electronic and communications engineering technology; electromechanical technology; engineering technology; environmental engineering technology; fashion merchandising; finance; fire science; food science; food services technology; graphic and printing equipment operation/production; health/health care administration; health information/medical records administration; horticultural science; hospitality administration; hotel/motel administration; human services; industrial technology; insurance; interior design; kindergarten/preschool education; legal administrative assistant/secretary; legal assistant/paralegal; liberal arts and sciences/liberal studies; machine tool technology; marketing/marketing management; mechanical engineering/mechanical technology; medical administrative assistant and medical secretary; medical/clinical assistant; music; nursing (licensed practical/vocational nurse training); nursing (registered nurse training); physical therapy; postal management; real estate; respiratory care therapy; sign language interpretation and translation; social work; special products marketing; survey technology; tourism and travel services management; transportation technology; welding technology.
Academics *Calendar:* semesters. *Degree:* certificates, diplomas, and associate. *Special study options:* academic remediation for entering students, accelerated degree program, advanced placement credit, cooperative education, distance learning, English as a second language, honors programs, off-campus study, part-time degree program, services for LD students, student-designed majors, summer session for credit.
Library Hagemeyer Learning Center plus 5 others with 102,649 titles, 750 serial subscriptions, 17,802 audiovisual materials, an OPAC, a Web page.
Computers on Campus A campuswide network can be accessed from off campus. Internet access, online (class) registration, at least one staffed computer lab available.
Student Life *Housing:* college housing not available. *Activities and Organizations:* drama/theater group, student-run newspaper, choral group, Phi Theta Kappa, Black Students Organization, Students for Environmental Sanity, Sierra Club, Nursing Club. *Campus security:* 24-hour emergency response devices and patrols. *Student services:* personal/psychological counseling, women's center.
Athletics Member NJCAA. *Intramural sports:* soccer M/W.
Costs (2005–06) *Tuition:* state resident $1264 full-time, $40 per semester hour part-time; nonresident $7024 full-time, $220 per semester hour part-time. *Required fees:* $170 full-time, $56 per term part-time. *Waivers:* senior citizens and employees or children of employees.
Financial Aid Of all full-time matriculated undergraduates who enrolled in 2004, 99 Federal Work-Study jobs (averaging $2988).
Applying *Options:* common application. *Required:* high school transcript. *Application deadline:* rolling (freshmen), rolling (out-of-state freshmen), rolling (transfers). *Notification:* continuous (freshmen), continuous (out-of-state freshmen).
Freshmen Application Contact Ms. Linda McComb, Associate Dean, Central Piedmont Community College, PO Box 35009, Charlotte, NC 28235-5009. *Phone:* 704-330-6784. *Fax:* 704-330-6136.

CLEVELAND COMMUNITY COLLEGE

Shelby, North Carolina www.clevelandcommunitycollege.edu/

- **State-supported** 2-year, founded 1965, part of North Carolina Community College System
- **Small-town** 43-acre campus with easy access to Charlotte
- **Endowment** $450,000
- **Coed,** 3,047 undergraduate students, 41% full-time, 67% women, 33% men

Undergraduates 1,241 full-time, 1,806 part-time. Students come from 3 states and territories, 1% are from out of state, 22% African American, 0.8% Asian American or Pacific Islander, 1% Hispanic American, 0.2% Native American, 0.8% transferred in.
Freshmen *Admission:* 279 applied, 279 admitted, 279 enrolled. *Average high school GPA:* 2.71.
Faculty *Total:* 243, 28% full-time, 2% with terminal degrees.
Majors Accounting; administrative assistant and secretarial science; biological and physical sciences; business administration and management; communications technology; computer engineering technology; computer programming (specific applications); criminal justice/law enforcement administration; criminal justice/safety; data entry/microcomputer applications; electrical, electronic and communications engineering technology; electrician; engineering technologies related; executive assistant/executive secretary; fashion merchandising; fire protection and safety technology; industrial radiologic technology; information science/studies; information technology; liberal arts and sciences and humanities related; liberal arts and sciences/liberal studies; management information systems and services related; mechanical engineering/mechanical technology; medical administrative assistant and medical secretary; medical radiologic technology; nursing (registered nurse training); operations management; Spanish; special education; system administration; teacher assistant/aide.
Academics *Calendar:* semesters. *Degree:* certificates, diplomas, and associate. *Special study options:* academic remediation for entering students, adult/continuing education programs, advanced placement credit, distance learning, double majors, English as a second language, independent study, off-campus study, part-time degree program, summer session for credit.
Library Cleveland Community College Library with 34,000 titles, 280 serial subscriptions, 3,619 audiovisual materials, an OPAC, a Web page.
Computers on Campus 325 computers available on campus for general student use. A campuswide network can be accessed. Internet access, at least one staffed computer lab available.
Student Life *Housing:* college housing not available. *Activities and Organizations:* drama/theater group, student-run television station, choral group, Gamma Beta Phi Honor Society, Student Government Association, Lamplighters, Mu Epsilon Delta, Black Awareness Club. *Campus security:* security personnel during open hours. *Student services:* personal/psychological counseling.
Costs (2005–06) *Tuition:* state resident $1264 full-time, $40 per credit hour part-time; nonresident $7024 full-time, $220 per credit hour part-time. Full-time tuition and fees vary according to course load. Part-time tuition and fees vary according to course load. *Required fees:* $38 full-time. *Waivers:* senior citizens.
Financial Aid Of all full-time matriculated undergraduates who enrolled in 2004, 20 Federal Work-Study jobs.
Applying *Options:* common application, electronic application, deferred entrance. *Required:* high school transcript. *Application deadline:* rolling (freshmen), rolling (transfers). *Notification:* continuous (freshmen).
Freshmen Application Contact Mr. Alan Price, Dean of Enrollment Management, Cleveland Community College, 137 South Post Road, Shelby, NC 28152. *Phone:* 704-484-4073. *Fax:* 704-484-5305. *E-mail:* price@cleveland.cc.nc.us.

COASTAL CAROLINA COMMUNITY COLLEGE

Jacksonville, North Carolina www.coastalcarolina.edu/

- **State and locally supported** 2-year, founded 1964, part of North Carolina Community College System
- **Small-town** 98-acre campus
- **Endowment** $1.9 million
- **Coed,** 4,111 undergraduate students, 50% full-time, 65% women, 35% men

Undergraduates 2,072 full-time, 2,039 part-time. Students come from 48 states and territories, 5 other countries, 31% are from out of state, 19% African American, 3% Asian American or Pacific Islander, 9% Hispanic American, 1% Native American, 0.7% international, 13% transferred in.
Freshmen *Admission:* 3,451 applied, 2,695 admitted, 832 enrolled.

Coastal Carolina Community College (continued)

Faculty *Total:* 261, 51% full-time, 11% with terminal degrees. *Student/faculty ratio:* 16:1.

Majors Accounting; architectural engineering technology; business administration and management; child care provision; clinical/medical laboratory technology; computer/information technology services administration related; computer programming (specific applications); computer systems analysis; computer systems networking and telecommunications; criminal justice/law enforcement administration; dental hygiene; emergency medical technology (EMT paramedic); executive assistant/executive secretary; fire science; legal assistant/paralegal; liberal arts and sciences/liberal studies; medical administrative assistant and medical secretary; nursing (registered nurse training); surgical technology.

Academics *Calendar:* semesters. *Degree:* certificates, diplomas, and associate. *Special study options:* academic remediation for entering students, adult/continuing education programs, advanced placement credit, distance learning, double majors, English as a second language, independent study, internships, part-time degree program, services for LD students, summer session for credit.

Library C. Louis Shields Learning Resources Center with 44,062 titles, 266 serial subscriptions, 10,460 audiovisual materials, an OPAC.

Computers on Campus 830 computers available on campus for general student use. A campuswide network can be accessed from off campus. Internet access, at least one staffed computer lab available.

Student Life *Housing:* college housing not available. *Activities and Organizations:* drama/theater group, SHELL (environmental group), SPYS (social sciences group), student government, Star of Life, Association of Nursing Students. *Campus security:* 24-hour emergency response devices and patrols, late-night transport/escort service. *Student services:* personal/psychological counseling.

Costs (2006–07) *Tuition:* state resident $1264 full-time, $40 per credit hour part-time; nonresident $7024 full-time, $220 per credit hour part-time. *Required fees:* $30 full-time, $5 per term part-time.

Applying *Options:* deferred entrance. *Required:* high school transcript. *Required for some:* 2 letters of recommendation, interview. *Application deadline:* rolling (freshmen), rolling (transfers). *Notification:* continuous (freshmen).

Freshmen Application Contact Mr. James B. Washington, Director of Admissions, Coastal Carolina Community College, 444 Western Boulevard, Jacksonville, NC 28546. *Phone:* 910-938-6246. *Fax:* 910-455-2767. *E-mail:* washingtonb@coastal.cc.nc.us.

COLLEGE OF THE ALBEMARLE
Elizabeth City, North Carolina   www.albemarle.edu/

- **State-supported** 2-year, founded 1960, part of North Carolina Community College System
- **Small-town** 40-acre campus
- **Coed,** 2,071 undergraduate students, 41% full-time, 66% women, 34% men

Undergraduates 854 full-time, 1,217 part-time. Students come from 17 states and territories, 4 other countries.

Freshmen *Admission:* 207 enrolled. *Test scores:* SAT verbal scores over 500: 8%; SAT math scores over 500: 20%; SAT verbal scores over 600: 1%; SAT math scores over 600: 5%.

Faculty *Total:* 122, 49% full-time.

Majors Administrative assistant and secretarial science; architectural engineering technology; art; biotechnology; business administration and management; computer engineering technology; computer programming; computer programming (specific applications); construction trades; crafts, folk art and artisanry; criminal justice/law enforcement administration; culinary arts; data entry/microcomputer applications; dramatic/theater arts; education; information science/studies; information technology; liberal arts and sciences/liberal studies; marine technology; mechanical design technology; medical administrative assistant and medical secretary; metal and jewelry arts; music; nursing (licensed practical/vocational nurse training); nursing (registered nurse training); teacher assistant/aide.

Academics *Calendar:* semesters. *Degree:* certificates, diplomas, and associate. *Special study options:* academic remediation for entering students, adult/continuing education programs, advanced placement credit, cooperative education, English as a second language, part-time degree program, services for LD students, summer session for credit.

Library Learning Resources Center with 48,400 titles, 280 serial subscriptions, an OPAC, a Web page.

Computers on Campus 85 computers available on campus for general student use. Internet access, at least one staffed computer lab available.

Student Life *Housing:* college housing not available. *Activities and Organizations:* drama/theater group, choral group, Phi Beta Lambda, Phi Theta Kappa. *Campus security:* 24-hour patrols. *Student services:* personal/psychological counseling.

Athletics *Intercollegiate sports:* soccer M. *Intramural sports:* archery M/W, badminton M/W, baseball M/W, basketball M/W, football M/W, golf M/W, gymnastics M/W, sailing M/W, soccer M(c), softball M/W, swimming and diving M/W, table tennis M/W, tennis M/W, volleyball M/W.

Costs (2005–06) *Tuition:* state resident $1264 full-time, $40 per credit hour part-time; nonresident $7024 full-time, $220 per credit hour part-time.

Financial Aid Of all full-time matriculated undergraduates who enrolled in 2004, 68 Federal Work-Study jobs (averaging $553).

Applying *Options:* early admission, deferred entrance. *Required:* high school transcript. *Application deadline:* rolling (freshmen), rolling (transfers). *Notification:* continuous (freshmen).

Director of Admissions Mr. Kenny Krentz, Director of Admissions and International Students, College of The Albemarle, PO Box 2327, 1208 North Road Street, Elizabeth City, NC 27909-2327. *Phone:* 252-335-0821 Ext. 2220.

CRAVEN COMMUNITY COLLEGE
New Bern, North Carolina   www.craven.cc.nc.us/

- **State-supported** 2-year, founded 1965, part of North Carolina Community College System
- **Suburban** 100-acre campus
- **Endowment** $576,211
- **Coed**

Undergraduates Students come from 25 states and territories, 2 other countries, 17% are from out of state, 26% African American, 2% Asian American or Pacific Islander, 3% Hispanic American, 1% Native American, 0.2% international.

Faculty *Student/faculty ratio:* 14:1.

Academics *Calendar:* semesters. *Degree:* certificates, diplomas, and associate. *Special study options:* academic remediation for entering students, adult/continuing education programs, advanced placement credit, cooperative education, distance learning, double majors, independent study, internships, part-time degree program, services for LD students, student-designed majors, summer session for credit.

Student Life *Campus security:* 24-hour patrols.

Athletics Member NJCAA.

Standardized Tests *Recommended:* SAT or ACT (for placement).

Financial Aid Of all full-time matriculated undergraduates who enrolled in 2004, 64 Federal Work-Study jobs (averaging $1446).

Applying *Required:* high school transcript, interview.

Freshmen Application Contact Ms. Millicent Fulford, Recruiter, Craven Community College, 800 College Court, New Bern, NC 28562-4984. *Phone:* 252-638-7232.

DAVIDSON COUNTY COMMUNITY COLLEGE
Lexington, North Carolina   www.davidson.cc.nc.us/

- **State and locally supported** 2-year, founded 1958, part of North Carolina Community College System
- **Rural** 83-acre campus
- **Endowment** $6.5 million
- **Coed**

Undergraduates 829 full-time, 1,474 part-time. Students come from 7 states and territories, 1% are from out of state, 13% African American, 1% Asian American or Pacific Islander, 1% Hispanic American, 0.4% Native American.

Faculty *Student/faculty ratio:* 11:1.

Academics *Calendar:* semesters. *Degree:* certificates, diplomas, and associate. *Special study options:* academic remediation for entering students, adult/continuing education programs, advanced placement credit, cooperative education, double majors, internships, off-campus study, part-time degree program, services for LD students, summer session for credit.

Student Life *Campus security:* late-night transport/escort service, security guards.

Standardized Tests *Required:* (for placement).

Costs (2005–06) *Tuition:* state resident $1140 full-time, $38 per credit hour part-time; nonresident $6330 full-time, $211 per credit hour part-time. *Required fees:* $1088 full-time, $27 per term part-time.

Financial Aid Of all full-time matriculated undergraduates who enrolled in 2004, 20 Federal Work-Study jobs (averaging $1800).

Applying *Options:* early admission, deferred entrance. *Required:* high school transcript. *Required for some:* interview.
Director of Admissions Mr. Rick Travis, Director, Career Services, Davidson County Community College, PO Box 1287, Lexington, NC 27293-1287. *Phone:* 336-249-8186 Ext. 224. *E-mail:* cottrell.judy@davidson.cc.nc.us.

DURHAM TECHNICAL COMMUNITY COLLEGE
Durham, North Carolina   www.durhamtech.edu/

- **State-supported** 2-year, founded 1961, part of North Carolina Community College System
- **Urban** campus
- **Coed**

Undergraduates 1,464 full-time, 4,178 part-time. Students come from 50 states and territories, 1% are from out of state, 41% African American, 3% Asian American or Pacific Islander, 2% Hispanic American, 0.2% Native American, 8% international, 59% transferred in.
Faculty *Student/faculty ratio:* 16:1.
Academics *Calendar:* semesters. *Degree:* certificates, diplomas, and associate. *Special study options:* academic remediation for entering students, accelerated degree program, adult/continuing education programs, advanced placement credit, cooperative education, distance learning, English as a second language, internships, off-campus study, part-time degree program, services for LD students, student-designed majors, summer session for credit.
Student Life *Campus security:* 24-hour patrols, late-night transport/escort service.
Standardized Tests *Required:* ACT ASSET or ACT COMPASS (for placement).
Financial Aid Of all full-time matriculated undergraduates who enrolled in 2004, 35 Federal Work-Study jobs (averaging $2000).
Applying *Options:* deferred entrance. *Required:* high school transcript. *Recommended:* interview.
Director of Admissions Ms. Penny Augustine, Director of Admissions and Testing, Durham Technical Community College, 1637 Lawson Street, Durham, NC 27703. *Phone:* 919-686-3619.

ECPI TECHNICAL COLLEGE
Raleigh, North Carolina   www.ecpi.net/

- **Proprietary** 2-year, founded 1990
- **Coed,** 550 undergraduate students

Undergraduates Students come from 1 other state, 60% African American, 2% Asian American or Pacific Islander, 2% Hispanic American, 0.8% Native American.
Faculty *Student/faculty ratio:* 13:1.
Majors Computer and information sciences; computer engineering technology; computer science; computer technology/computer systems technology; criminal justice/law enforcement administration; management information systems; medical/clinical assistant; nursing (licensed practical/vocational nurse training).
Academics *Calendar:* trimesters. *Degree:* diplomas and associate. *Special study options:* academic remediation for entering students, accelerated degree program, adult/continuing education programs, cooperative education, distance learning, independent study, internships, study abroad.
Computers on Campus 200 computers available on campus for general student use. A campuswide network can be accessed from off campus. Internet access, at least one staffed computer lab available.
Student Life *Housing:* college housing not available. *Activities and Organizations:* student-run newspaper, national fraternities, national sororities. *Student services:* personal/psychological counseling.
Standardized Tests *Recommended:* SAT (for admission), SAT or ACT (for admission), SAT Subject Tests (for admission).
Costs (2006–07) *Tuition:* $9750 full-time.
Applying *Options:* common application, electronic application. *Required:* high school transcript, interview. *Application deadline:* rolling (freshmen). *Notification:* continuous (freshmen).
Freshmen Application Contact Ms. Susan Wells, Campus President, ECPI Technical College, 4101 Doie Cope Road, Raleigh, NC 27613-7387. *Phone:* 919-571-0057. *Toll-free phone:* 800-986-1200. *Fax:* 919-571-0780. *E-mail:* swells@ecpi.edu.

EDGECOMBE COMMUNITY COLLEGE
Tarboro, North Carolina   www.edgecombe.edu/

- **State and locally supported** 2-year, founded 1968, part of North Carolina Community College System
- **Small-town** 90-acre campus
- **Endowment** $1.0 million
- **Coed**

Undergraduates 947 full-time, 1,606 part-time. Students come from 3 states and territories, 4 other countries, 1% are from out of state, 62% African American, 0.4% Asian American or Pacific Islander, 1% Hispanic American, 0.8% Native American, 0.1% international, 2% transferred in.
Faculty *Student/faculty ratio:* 16:1.
Academics *Calendar:* semesters. *Degree:* certificates, diplomas, and associate. *Special study options:* academic remediation for entering students, adult/continuing education programs, advanced placement credit, cooperative education, distance learning, double majors, English as a second language, independent study, off-campus study, part-time degree program, services for LD students, summer session for credit.
Standardized Tests *Recommended:* SAT or ACT (for placement), MAPS.
Costs (2005–06) *Tuition:* state resident $1264 full-time, $40 per credit part-time; nonresident $7024 full-time, $220 per credit part-time. *Required fees:* $72 full-time, $3 per credit part-time.
Financial Aid Of all full-time matriculated undergraduates who enrolled in 2004, 45 Federal Work-Study jobs (averaging $800).
Applying *Options:* common application, electronic application. *Required:* high school transcript, minimum 2.0 GPA. *Required for some:* letters of recommendation.
Freshmen Application Contact Ms. Jackie Heath, Admissions Officer, Edgecombe Community College, 2009 West Wilson Street, Tarboro, NC 27886. *Phone:* 252-823-5166 Ext. 254.

FAYETTEVILLE TECHNICAL COMMUNITY COLLEGE
Fayetteville, North Carolina   www.faytechcc.edu/

- **State-supported** 2-year, founded 1961, part of North Carolina Community College System
- **Suburban** 135-acre campus with easy access to Raleigh
- **Endowment** $39,050
- **Coed,** 9,950 undergraduate students, 31% full-time, 70% women, 30% men

Undergraduates 3,048 full-time, 6,902 part-time. Students come from 50 states and territories, 9 other countries, 10% are from out of state, 41% African American, 2% Asian American or Pacific Islander, 7% Hispanic American, 3% Native American, 21% transferred in.
Freshmen *Admission:* 4,471 applied, 4,471 admitted, 1,353 enrolled. *Average high school GPA:* 2.43.
Faculty *Total:* 863, 35% full-time. *Student/faculty ratio:* 29:1.
Majors Accounting; applied horticulture; architectural engineering technology; automobile/automotive mechanics technology; banking and financial support services; biology/biotechnology laboratory technician; building/construction finishing, management, and inspection related; business administration and management; business administration, management and operations related; civil engineering technology; commercial and advertising art; computer and information systems security; computer programming; corrections and criminal justice related; criminal justice/safety; culinary arts; dental hygiene; early childhood education; e-commerce; electrical, electronic and communications engineering technology; electrician; elementary education; emergency medical technology (EMT paramedic); fire protection and safety technology; fire protection related; forensic science and technology; funeral service and mortuary science; general studies; health information/medical records technology; heating, air conditioning, ventilation and refrigeration maintenance technology; hotel/motel administration; human resources management; information science/studies; information technology; language interpretation and translation; legal assistant/paralegal; liberal arts and sciences and humanities related; liberal arts and sciences/liberal studies; machine shop technology; medical office management; nuclear medical technology; nursing (registered nurse training); office management; operations management; physical therapist assistant; public administration; radiologic technology/science; respiratory care therapy; special education; speech-language pathology; surgical technology; survey technology; system, networking, and LAN/WAN management.
Academics *Calendar:* semesters. *Degree:* certificates, diplomas, and associate. *Special study options:* academic remediation for entering students, adult/

Fayetteville Technical Community College (continued)
continuing education programs, advanced placement credit, cooperative education, distance learning, double majors, English as a second language, independent study, internships, off-campus study, part-time degree program, services for LD students, student-designed majors, summer session for credit.

Library Paul H. Thompson Library with 61,580 titles, 398 serial subscriptions, 6,657 audiovisual materials, an OPAC, a Web page.

Computers on Campus 400 computers available on campus for general student use. A campuswide network can be accessed from off campus. Internet access, at least one staffed computer lab available.

Student Life *Housing:* college housing not available. *Activities and Organizations:* Criminal Justice Association, Early Childhood Club, Phi Beta Lambda, Student Nurses Club, Data Processing Management Association. *Campus security:* 24-hour emergency response devices and patrols, late-night transport/escort service. *Student services:* health clinic, personal/psychological counseling.

Athletics *Intramural sports:* basketball M/W, table tennis M/W, volleyball M/W.

Costs (2005–06) *Tuition:* state resident $1264 full-time, $40 per credit hour part-time; nonresident $7024 full-time, $220 per credit hour part-time. *Required fees:* $30 full-time, $30 per term part-time. *Waivers:* senior citizens and employees or children of employees.

Financial Aid Of all full-time matriculated undergraduates who enrolled in 2004, 75 Federal Work-Study jobs (averaging $2000). *Financial aid deadline:* 6/1.

Applying *Options:* electronic application, deferred entrance. *Required for some:* high school transcript. *Application deadline:* rolling (freshmen), rolling (transfers). *Notification:* continuous (freshmen).

Freshmen Application Contact Mr. James Kelley, Director of Admissions, Fayetteville Technical Community College, PO Box 35236, Fayetteville, NC 28303. *Phone:* 910-678-8274. *Fax:* 910-678-8407. *E-mail:* kelleyj@faytechcc.edu.

FORSYTH TECHNICAL COMMUNITY COLLEGE

Winston-Salem, North Carolina   www.forsythtech.edu/

- **State-supported** 2-year, founded 1964, part of North Carolina Community College System
- **Suburban** 38-acre campus
- **Endowment** $916,352
- **Coed,** 6,978 undergraduate students, 36% full-time, 64% women, 36% men

Undergraduates 2,509 full-time, 4,469 part-time. 23% African American, 1% Asian American or Pacific Islander, 2% Hispanic American, 0.6% Native American, 2% international.

Freshmen *Admission:* 932 applied, 932 admitted, 924 enrolled.

Faculty *Total:* 486, 36% full-time. *Student/faculty ratio:* 14:1.

Majors Accounting; administrative assistant and secretarial science; architectural engineering technology; automobile/automotive mechanics technology; business administration and management; carpentry; child development; commercial and advertising art; computer engineering technology; computer science; construction engineering technology; criminal justice/law enforcement administration; criminal justice/police science; data processing and data processing technology; drafting and design technology; electrical, electronic and communications engineering technology; electromechanical technology; engineering technology; finance; funeral service and mortuary science; graphic and printing equipment operation/production; heating, air conditioning, ventilation and refrigeration maintenance technology; horticultural science; industrial radiologic technology; industrial technology; kindergarten/preschool education; legal assistant/paralegal; machine tool technology; marketing/marketing management; mechanical design technology; medical/clinical assistant; nuclear medical technology; nursing (registered nurse training); ornamental horticulture; pipefitting and sprinkler fitting; real estate; respiratory care therapy; welding technology.

Academics *Calendar:* semesters. *Degree:* certificates, diplomas, and associate. *Special study options:* academic remediation for entering students, adult/continuing education programs, English as a second language, part-time degree program, services for LD students, summer session for credit.

Library Forsyth Technical Community College Library plus 1 other with 41,606 titles, 358 serial subscriptions.

Computers on Campus 450 computers available on campus for general student use. At least one staffed computer lab available.

Student Life *Housing:* college housing not available. *Activities and Organizations:* student-run newspaper. *Campus security:* 24-hour patrols. *Student services:* personal/psychological counseling, women's center.

Athletics *Intramural sports:* basketball M/W, bowling M/W, softball W, volleyball M/W.

Standardized Tests *Required for some:* SAT or ACT (for admission), TEAS, CPT, ASSET, COMPASS.

Costs (2006–07) *Tuition:* state resident $948 full-time, $40 per credit hour part-time; nonresident $5268 full-time, $220 per credit hour part-time. *Required fees:* $35 full-time, $24 per term part-time.

Financial Aid Of all full-time matriculated undergraduates who enrolled in 2004, 42 Federal Work-Study jobs (averaging $2083).

Applying *Required:* high school transcript. *Application deadlines:* 8/25 (freshmen), 9/1 (transfers). *Notification:* continuous until 8/25 (freshmen).

Freshmen Application Contact Ms. Patrice Mitchell, Dean of Enrollment Services, Forsyth Technical Community College, 2100 Silas Creek Parkway, Winston-Salem, NC 27103-5197. *Phone:* 336-734-7331. *Fax:* 336-761-2098. *E-mail:* admissions@forsythtech.edu.

GASTON COLLEGE

Dallas, North Carolina   www.gaston.edu/

- **State and locally supported** 2-year, founded 1963, part of North Carolina Community College System
- **Small-town** 166-acre campus with easy access to Charlotte
- **Endowment** $716,546
- **Coed,** 5,048 undergraduate students, 49% full-time, 68% women, 32% men

Undergraduates 2,449 full-time, 2,599 part-time. Students come from 10 states and territories, 15% African American, 1% Asian American or Pacific Islander, 3% Hispanic American, 0.4% Native American. *Retention:* 80% of 2003 full-time freshmen returned.

Freshmen *Admission:* 958 enrolled. *Average high school GPA:* 2.60.

Faculty *Total:* 357, 33% full-time. *Student/faculty ratio:* 18:1.

Majors Accounting; architectural engineering technology; art; automobile/automotive mechanics technology; business administration and management; civil engineering technology; computer programming; criminal justice/law enforcement administration; data processing and data processing technology; dietetics; electrical, electronic and communications engineering technology; fire science; information science/studies; kindergarten/preschool education; legal assistant/paralegal; mechanical drafting and CAD/CADD; mechanical engineering/mechanical technology; medical/clinical assistant; medical office management; nursing (registered nurse training); operations management; veterinary technology.

Academics *Calendar:* semesters. *Degree:* certificates, diplomas, and associate. *Special study options:* academic remediation for entering students, adult/continuing education programs, advanced placement credit, cooperative education, English as a second language, off-campus study, part-time degree program, services for LD students, summer session for credit.

Library Gaston College Library with 49,434 titles, 561 serial subscriptions, 3,343 audiovisual materials, an OPAC.

Computers on Campus A campuswide network can be accessed. Internet access, online (class) registration, at least one staffed computer lab available.

Student Life *Housing:* college housing not available. *Activities and Organizations:* student-run radio station, Student Government Association. *Campus security:* 24-hour patrols.

Costs (2005–06) *Tuition:* state resident $1264 full-time, $40 per credit hour part-time; nonresident $7024 full-time, $220 per credit hour part-time. *Required fees:* $80 full-time, $3 per credit hour part-time, $12 per term part-time.

Financial Aid Of all full-time matriculated undergraduates who enrolled in 2004, 50 Federal Work-Study jobs (averaging $1800). 30 state and other part-time jobs (averaging $1533).

Applying *Required for some:* high school transcript. *Application deadline:* rolling (freshmen), rolling (transfers). *Notification:* continuous (freshmen).

Freshmen Application Contact Ms. Alice D. Hopper, Admissions Specialist, Gaston College, 201 Highway 321 South, Dallas, NC 28034. *Phone:* 704-922-6214. *Fax:* 704-922-6443.

GUILFORD TECHNICAL COMMUNITY COLLEGE

Jamestown, North Carolina   www.gtcc.edu/

- **State and locally supported** 2-year, founded 1958, part of North Carolina Community College System
- **Suburban** 158-acre campus
- **Coed**

Undergraduates 2,930 full-time, 5,561 part-time. Students come from 21 states and territories, 34% African American, 3% Asian American or Pacific Islander, 2% Hispanic American, 0.5% Native American, 2% international.

Academics *Calendar:* semesters. *Degree:* certificates, diplomas, and associate. *Special study options:* academic remediation for entering students, adult/continuing education programs, advanced placement credit, cooperative education, distance learning, English as a second language, external degree program, independent study, internships, off-campus study, part-time degree program, services for LD students, student-designed majors, summer session for credit. *ROTC:* Army (c), Air Force (c).

Standardized Tests *Required:* ACT COMPASS (for placement).

Costs (2005–06) *Tuition:* state resident $1216 full-time; nonresident $6752 full-time. *Required fees:* $75 full-time.

Financial Aid Of all full-time matriculated undergraduates who enrolled in 2004, 84 Federal Work-Study jobs (averaging $3302).

Applying *Options:* early admission, deferred entrance. *Required:* high school transcript. *Required for some:* interview.

Freshmen Application Contact Ms. Jean Groome, Director of Admissions, Guilford Technical Community College, PO Box 309, Jamestown, NC 27282. *Phone:* 336-334-4822 Ext. 2396.

HALIFAX COMMUNITY COLLEGE
Weldon, North Carolina   www.hcc.cc.nc.us/

- **State and locally supported** 2-year, founded 1967, part of North Carolina Community College System
- **Rural** 109-acre campus
- **Coed**

Undergraduates Students come from 2 states and territories.

Academics *Calendar:* semesters. *Degree:* certificates, diplomas, and associate. *Special study options:* academic remediation for entering students, adult/continuing education programs, cooperative education, part-time degree program, summer session for credit.

Student Life *Campus security:* 12-hour patrols by trained security personnel.

Costs (2005–06) *Tuition:* state resident $1216 full-time, $38 per credit part-time; nonresident $6752 full-time, $211 per credit part-time. *Required fees:* $80 full-time, $5 per credit part-time.

Applying *Options:* deferred entrance. *Required:* high school transcript.

Director of Admissions Mrs. Scottie Dickens, Director of Admissions, Halifax Community College, PO Drawer 809, Weldon, NC 27890-0809. *Phone:* 252-536-7220.

HAYWOOD COMMUNITY COLLEGE
Clyde, North Carolina   www.haywood.edu/

- **State and locally supported** 2-year, founded 1964, part of North Carolina Community College System
- **Rural** 85-acre campus
- **Coed**

Undergraduates 876 full-time, 1,112 part-time. Students come from 7 states and territories, 1% are from out of state, 1% African American, 0.7% Asian American or Pacific Islander, 1% Hispanic American, 1% Native American, 13% transferred in.

Faculty *Student/faculty ratio:* 12:1.

Academics *Calendar:* semesters. *Degree:* certificates, diplomas, and associate. *Special study options:* academic remediation for entering students, adult/continuing education programs, advanced placement credit, cooperative education, distance learning, double majors, English as a second language, independent study, internships, part-time degree program, services for LD students.

Student Life *Campus security:* 24-hour patrols.

Costs (2005–06) *Tuition:* state resident $1216 full-time, $38 per credit hour part-time; nonresident $6752 full-time, $211 per credit hour part-time. *Required fees:* $49 full-time, $13 per term part-time.

Financial Aid Of all full-time matriculated undergraduates who enrolled in 2004, 59 Federal Work-Study jobs (averaging $907).

Applying *Required:* high school transcript. *Required for some:* interview.

Director of Admissions Ms. Debbie Rowland, Coordinator of Admissions, Haywood Community College, 185 Freedlander Drive, Clyde, NC 28721-9453. *Phone:* 828-627-4505.

ISOTHERMAL COMMUNITY COLLEGE
Spindale, North Carolina   www.isothermal.edu/

- **State-supported** 2-year, founded 1965, part of North Carolina Community College System
- **Rural** 120-acre campus
- **Coed**

Undergraduates 988 full-time, 1,017 part-time. Students come from 40 states and territories, 3 other countries, 16% African American, 0.3% Asian American or Pacific Islander, 0.9% Hispanic American, 0.3% Native American, 0.3% international. *Retention:* 33% of 2003 full-time freshmen returned.

Faculty *Student/faculty ratio:* 17:1.

Academics *Calendar:* semesters. *Degree:* certificates, diplomas, and associate. *Special study options:* academic remediation for entering students, adult/continuing education programs, advanced placement credit, cooperative education, English as a second language, external degree program, honors programs, part-time degree program, services for LD students, student-designed majors, summer session for credit.

Standardized Tests *Required:* ACT ASSET (for placement).

Financial Aid Of all full-time matriculated undergraduates who enrolled in 2004, 21 Federal Work-Study jobs (averaging $2365).

Applying *Options:* early admission, deferred entrance. *Required:* high school transcript.

Freshmen Application Contact Ms. Betty Gabriel, Director of Counseling, Isothermal Community College, PO Box 804, Spindale, NC 28160-0804. *Phone:* 828-286-3636 Ext. 243.

JAMES SPRUNT COMMUNITY COLLEGE
Kenansville, North Carolina   www.sprunt.com/

- **State-supported** 2-year, founded 1964, part of North Carolina Community College System
- **Rural** 51-acre campus
- **Endowment** $16,990
- **Coed,** 1,370 undergraduate students, 47% full-time, 71% women, 29% men

Undergraduates 643 full-time, 727 part-time. Students come from 2 states and territories, 1% are from out of state, 42% African American, 3% Hispanic American, 0.1% Native American, 0.2% international, 6% transferred in. Freshmen *Admission:* 247 applied, 205 admitted, 151 enrolled.

Faculty *Total:* 129, 47% full-time, 2% with terminal degrees. *Student/faculty ratio:* 21:1.

Majors Accounting; administrative assistant and secretarial science; agribusiness; animal sciences; business administration and management; commercial and advertising art; computer systems analysis; cosmetology; criminal justice/police science; kindergarten/preschool education; liberal arts and sciences/liberal studies; medical/clinical assistant; nursing (registered nurse training).

Academics *Calendar:* semesters. *Degree:* certificates, diplomas, and associate. *Special study options:* academic remediation for entering students, accelerated degree program, adult/continuing education programs, advanced placement credit, cooperative education, distance learning, double majors, English as a second language, external degree program, independent study, internships, part-time degree program, summer session for credit.

Library James Sprunt Community College Library with 23,497 titles, 235 serial subscriptions, 1,392 audiovisual materials, an OPAC.

Computers on Campus 100 computers available on campus for general student use. A campuswide network can be accessed from off campus. Internet access, at least one staffed computer lab available.

Student Life *Housing:* college housing not available. *Activities and Organizations:* student-run newspaper, Student Nurses Association, Art Club, Alumni Association, National Technical-Vocational Honor Society, Phi Theta Kappa. *Campus security:* trained security personnel. *Student services:* personal/psychological counseling.

Athletics *Intercollegiate sports:* softball W, volleyball M/W.

Costs (2005–06) *Tuition:* state resident $1264 full-time, $40 per semester hour part-time; nonresident $7024 full-time, $220 per semester hour part-time. *Required fees:* $70 full-time, $70 per term part-time. *Waivers:* senior citizens and employees or children of employees.

Financial Aid Of all full-time matriculated undergraduates who enrolled in 2004, 55 Federal Work-Study jobs (averaging $1387).

Applying *Options:* common application, electronic application, early admission, deferred entrance. *Required:* high school transcript. *Application deadline:* rolling (freshmen), rolling (transfers). *Notification:* continuous (freshmen).

James Sprunt Community College (continued)

Freshmen Application Contact Ms. Pat Norris, Admissions Specialist, James Sprunt Community College, Highway 11 South, 133 James Sprunt Drive, Kenansville, NC 28349. *Phone:* 910-296-2500. *Fax:* 910-296-1222. *E-mail:* pnorris@jscc.cc.nc.us.

JOHNSTON COMMUNITY COLLEGE

Smithfield, North Carolina   www.johnston.cc.nc.us/

- **State-supported** 2-year, founded 1969, part of North Carolina Community College System
- **Rural** 100-acre campus
- **Endowment** $2.2 million
- **Coed,** 4,095 undergraduate students, 40% full-time, 64% women, 36% men

Undergraduates 1,628 full-time, 2,467 part-time. Students come from 10 states and territories, 1 other country, 1% are from out of state, 20% African American, 0.5% Asian American or Pacific Islander, 4% Hispanic American, 0.5% Native American, 0.2% international. Freshmen *Admission:* 1,565 enrolled.

Faculty *Total:* 333, 37% full-time, 75% with terminal degrees. *Student/faculty ratio:* 18:1.

Majors Accounting technology and bookkeeping; administrative assistant and secretarial science; business administration and management; commercial and advertising art; computer programming; criminal justice/police science; diesel mechanics technology; electrical, electronic and communications engineering technology; heating, air conditioning, ventilation and refrigeration maintenance technology; kindergarten/preschool education; landscaping and groundskeeping; legal assistant/paralegal; liberal arts and sciences/liberal studies; machine tool technology; medical administrative assistant and medical secretary; medical/clinical assistant; medical radiologic technology; nursing (registered nurse training); operations management.

Academics *Calendar:* semesters. *Degree:* certificates, diplomas, and associate. *Special study options:* academic remediation for entering students, adult/continuing education programs, advanced placement credit, cooperative education, distance learning, double majors, honors programs, independent study, part-time degree program, services for LD students, summer session for credit.

Library Johnston Community College Library plus 1 other with 31,550 titles, 348 serial subscriptions, 4,445 audiovisual materials, an OPAC, a Web page.

Computers on Campus 186 computers available on campus for general student use. Internet access, at least one staffed computer lab available.

Student Life *Housing:* college housing not available. *Activities and Organizations:* choral group. *Campus security:* 24-hour patrols. *Student services:* personal/psychological counseling.

Athletics *Intercollegiate sports:* golf M/W, softball M/W, volleyball M/W. *Intramural sports:* basketball M/W.

Costs (2005–06) *Tuition:* state resident $1264 full-time, $40 per credit hour part-time; nonresident $7024 full-time, $220 per credit hour part-time. *Required fees:* $70 full-time, $1 per credit hour part-time, $15 per term part-time.

Financial Aid Of all full-time matriculated undergraduates who enrolled in 2004, 35 Federal Work-Study jobs (averaging $1853).

Applying *Options:* electronic application. *Required:* high school transcript, interview. *Application deadline:* rolling (freshmen), rolling (transfers). *Notification:* continuous (freshmen).

Freshmen Application Contact Dr. Pam Harrell, Dean of Student Services, Johnston Community College, PO Box 2350, Smithfield, NC 27577-2350. *Phone:* 919-209-2048. *Fax:* 919-989-7662. *E-mail:* harrellp@johnstoncc.edu.

KING'S COLLEGE

Charlotte, North Carolina   www.kingscollege.org/

Director of Admissions Ms. Barbara Rockecharlie, School Director, King's College, 322 Lamar Avenue, Charlotte, NC 28204-2436. *Phone:* 704-688-3613. *Toll-free phone:* 800-768-2255. *Fax:* 704-348-2029. *E-mail:* brockecharlie@kingscollege.org.

LENOIR COMMUNITY COLLEGE

Kinston, North Carolina   www.lenoircc.edu/

Director of Admissions Ms. Tammy Buck, Director of Enrollment Management, Lenoir Community College, PO Box 188, Kinston, NC 28502-0188. *Phone:* 252-527-6223 Ext. 309. *Fax:* 252-526-5112. *E-mail:* tsb706@email.lenoir.cc.nc.us.

LOUISBURG COLLEGE

Louisburg, North Carolina   www.louisburg.edu/

Director of Admissions Ms. Stephanie Buchanan, Director of Admissions, Louisburg College, 501 North Main Street, Louisburg, NC 27549-2399. *Phone:* 919-497-3228. *Toll-free phone:* 800-775-0208. *E-mail:* admissions@earthlink.net.

MARTIN COMMUNITY COLLEGE

Williamston, North Carolina   www.martin.cc.nc.us/

Director of Admissions Ms. Sonya C. Atkinson, Registrar and Admissions Officer, Martin Community College, 1161 Kehukee Park Road, Williamston, NC 27892. *Phone:* 252-792-1521 Ext. 243.

MAYLAND COMMUNITY COLLEGE

Spruce Pine, North Carolina   www.mayland.edu

- **State and locally supported** 2-year, founded 1971, part of North Carolina Community College System
- **Rural** 38-acre campus
- **Coed**

Undergraduates 487 full-time, 532 part-time. Students come from 3 states and territories, 5% African American, 0.5% Asian American or Pacific Islander, 1% Hispanic American, 1% Native American, 3% transferred in.

Faculty *Student/faculty ratio:* 10:1.

Academics *Calendar:* semesters. *Degree:* certificates, diplomas, and associate. *Special study options:* academic remediation for entering students, adult/continuing education programs, advanced placement credit, cooperative education, distance learning, double majors, independent study, internships, part-time degree program, services for LD students, summer session for credit.

Athletics Member NJCAA.

Standardized Tests *Required for some:* CPT required for all for placement, required for admission to nursing program.

Financial Aid Of all full-time matriculated undergraduates who enrolled in 2004, 20 Federal Work-Study jobs (averaging $1350).

Applying *Options:* common application, electronic application, deferred entrance. *Required:* high school transcript.

Director of Admissions Ms. Cathy Morrison, Director of Admissions, Mayland Community College, PO Box 547, Spruce Pine, NC 28777. *Phone:* 828-765-7351 Ext. 224.

MCDOWELL TECHNICAL COMMUNITY COLLEGE

Marion, North Carolina   www.mcdowelltech.cc.nc.us/

- **State-supported** 2-year, founded 1964, part of North Carolina Community College System
- **Rural** 31-acre campus
- **Coed**

Undergraduates Students come from 2 other countries.

Academics *Calendar:* semesters. *Degree:* certificates, diplomas, and associate. *Special study options:* academic remediation for entering students, accelerated degree program, adult/continuing education programs, cooperative education, distance learning, English as a second language, independent study, part-time degree program, services for LD students, summer session for credit.

Student Life *Campus security:* 24-hour emergency response devices.

Standardized Tests *Required for some:* CPT.

Financial Aid Of all full-time matriculated undergraduates who enrolled in 2004, 15 Federal Work-Study jobs (averaging $1900).

Applying *Options:* common application, early admission, deferred entrance. *Required for some:* high school transcript.

Director of Admissions Ms. Lisa D. Byrd, Admissions Officer, McDowell Technical Community College, Route 1, Box 170, Marion, NC 28752-9724. *Phone:* 828-652-6024. *Fax:* 828-652-1014. *E-mail:* lisab@mail.mcdowell.cc.nc.us.

MITCHELL COMMUNITY COLLEGE

Statesville, North Carolina   www.mitchell.cc.nc.us/

Freshmen Application Contact Mr. Doug Rhoney, Counselor, Mitchell Community College, 500 West Broad, Statesville, NC 28677-5293. *Phone:* 704-878-3280.

MONTGOMERY COMMUNITY COLLEGE

Troy, North Carolina   www.montgomery.edu/

- **State-supported** 2-year, founded 1967, part of North Carolina Community College System
- **Rural** 159-acre campus
- **Coed,** 850 undergraduate students, 46% full-time, 69% women, 31% men

Undergraduates 391 full-time, 459 part-time. Students come from 4 states and territories, 1% are from out of state, 24% African American, 2% Asian American or Pacific Islander, 4% Hispanic American, 0.7% Native American, 0.2% international, 14% transferred in.

Freshmen *Admission:* 152 applied, 152 admitted, 152 enrolled.

Faculty *Total:* 73, 42% full-time, 1% with terminal degrees.

Majors Accounting; administrative assistant and secretarial science; business administration and management; ceramic arts and ceramics; child care and support services management; criminal justice/police science; emergency medical technology (EMT paramedic); forestry technology; liberal arts and sciences/liberal studies; management information systems; medical/clinical assistant.

Academics *Calendar:* semesters. *Degree:* certificates, diplomas, and associate. *Special study options:* academic remediation for entering students, advanced placement credit, cooperative education, distance learning, double majors, English as a second language, part-time degree program, services for LD students, summer session for credit.

Library 14,859 titles, 99 serial subscriptions, 500 audiovisual materials, an OPAC.

Computers on Campus 80 computers available on campus for general student use. Internet access, at least one staffed computer lab available.

Student Life *Housing:* college housing not available. *Activities and Organizations:* Gunsmithing Club, Student Government Association, Literary Club, Forestry Club. *Student services:* personal/psychological counseling.

Costs (2005–06) *Tuition:* state resident $1264 full-time, $40 per semester hour part-time; nonresident $7024 full-time, $220 per semester hour part-time. Full-time tuition and fees vary according to course load. Part-time tuition and fees vary according to course load. *Required fees:* $57 full-time, $28 per term part-time. *Waivers:* senior citizens and employees or children of employees.

Financial Aid Of all full-time matriculated undergraduates who enrolled in 2004, 24 Federal Work-Study jobs (averaging $500).

Applying *Options:* early admission, deferred entrance. *Required:* high school transcript. *Application deadline:* rolling (freshmen), rolling (transfers). *Notification:* continuous (freshmen).

Freshmen Application Contact Ms. Karen Frye, Admissions Officer, Montgomery Community College, 1011 Page Street, Troy, NC 27371. *Phone:* 910-576-6222 Ext. 240. *Toll-free phone:* 800-839-6222. *E-mail:* fryek@montgomery.edu.

NASH COMMUNITY COLLEGE

Rocky Mount, North Carolina   www.nash.cc.nc.us/

Director of Admissions Ms. Mary Blount, Admissions Officer, Nash Community College, PO Box 7488, Rocky Mount, NC 27804-0488. *Phone:* 252-443-4011 Ext. 300.

PAMLICO COMMUNITY COLLEGE

Grantsboro, North Carolina   www.pamlico.cc.nc.us/

Director of Admissions Mr. Floyd H. Hardison, Admissions Counselor, Pamlico Community College, PO Box 185, Grantsboro, NC 28529-0185. *Phone:* 252-249-1851 Ext. 28.

PIEDMONT COMMUNITY COLLEGE

Roxboro, North Carolina   www.piedmont.cc.nc.us/

- **State-supported** 2-year, founded 1970, part of North Carolina Community College System
- **Small-town** 178-acre campus
- **Endowment** $1.8 million
- **Coed**

Undergraduates 826 full-time, 1,363 part-time. Students come from 10 states and territories, 2 other countries, 1% are from out of state, 42% African American, 0.4% Asian American or Pacific Islander, 0.6% Hispanic American, 0.8% Native American, 0.2% international.

Faculty *Student/faculty ratio:* 28:1.

Academics *Calendar:* semesters. *Degree:* certificates, diplomas, and associate. *Special study options:* academic remediation for entering students, adult/continuing education programs, advanced placement credit, cooperative education, English as a second language, off-campus study, part-time degree program, summer session for credit.

Student Life *Campus security:* security guard during certain evening and weekend hours.

Standardized Tests *Required:* ACT ASSET (for placement).

Financial Aid Of all full-time matriculated undergraduates who enrolled in 2004, 30 Federal Work-Study jobs (averaging $1500).

Applying *Options:* early admission, deferred entrance. *Required for some:* high school transcript.

Director of Admissions Ms. Sheila Williamson, Director of Admissions, Piedmont Community College, PO Box 1197, 1715 College Drive, Roxboro, NC 27573. *Phone:* 336-599-1181 Ext. 219.

PITT COMMUNITY COLLEGE

Greenville, North Carolina   www.pittcc.edu/

Freshmen Application Contact Ms. Mary Tate, Director of Counseling, Pitt Community College, PO Drawer 7007, 1986 Pitt Tech Road, Greenville, NC 27835-7007. *Phone:* 252-321-4217.

RANDOLPH COMMUNITY COLLEGE

Asheboro, North Carolina   www.randolph.edu/

- **State-supported** 2-year, founded 1962, part of North Carolina Community College System
- **Small-town** 27-acre campus
- **Endowment** $6.4 million
- **Coed**

Undergraduates Students come from 4 states and territories, 1 other country, 1% are from out of state, 8% African American, 0.8% Asian American or Pacific Islander, 2% Hispanic American, 0.9% Native American, 0.1% international.

Faculty *Student/faculty ratio:* 23:1.

Academics *Calendar:* semesters. *Degree:* certificates, diplomas, and associate. *Special study options:* academic remediation for entering students, adult/continuing education programs, advanced placement credit, cooperative education, distance learning, double majors, English as a second language, independent study, internships, off-campus study, part-time degree program, services for LD students, summer session for credit.

Student Life *Campus security:* security officer during open hours.

Standardized Tests *Required for some:* ACT ASSET or ACT COMPASS.

Applying *Options:* common application, deferred entrance. *Required:* high school transcript.

Freshmen Application Contact Mrs. Carol M. Elmore, Director of Admissions and Registrar, Randolph Community College, PO Box 1009, Asheboro, NC 27204-1009. *Phone:* 336-633-0213.

RICHMOND COMMUNITY COLLEGE
Hamlet, North Carolina   www.richmondcc.edu/

- **State-supported** 2-year, founded 1964, part of North Carolina Community College System
- **Rural** 163-acre campus
- **Endowment** $1.0 million
- **Coed,** 1,472 undergraduate students, 47% full-time, 73% women, 27% men

Undergraduates 691 full-time, 781 part-time. Students come from 3 states and territories, 0.5% are from out of state, 32% African American, 1% Asian American or Pacific Islander, 0.9% Hispanic American, 9% Native American, 7% transferred in.
Freshmen *Admission:* 123 enrolled.
Faculty *Total:* 60, 85% full-time, 5% with terminal degrees. *Student/faculty ratio:* 29:1.
Majors Accounting; administrative assistant and secretarial science; business administration and management; child care and support services management; computer engineering technology; computer systems analysis; criminal justice/law enforcement administration; electrical, electronic and communications engineering technology; human services; industrial production technologies related; liberal arts and sciences/liberal studies; machine tool technology; mechanical engineering/mechanical technology; medical/clinical assistant; nursing (registered nurse training); web page, digital/multimedia and information resources design.
Academics *Calendar:* semesters. *Degree:* diplomas and associate. *Special study options:* academic remediation for entering students, adult/continuing education programs, advanced placement credit, cooperative education, distance learning, double majors, English as a second language, independent study, internships, part-time degree program, student-designed majors, summer session for credit.
Library Richmond Community College Library with 26,381 titles, 192 serial subscriptions, 1,676 audiovisual materials, an OPAC.
Computers on Campus 600 computers available on campus for general student use. A campuswide network can be accessed from off campus. Internet access, at least one staffed computer lab available.
Student Life *Housing:* college housing not available. *Activities and Organizations:* Criminal Justice Club, Human Services Club, Native American Club. *Campus security:* 24-hour emergency response devices, security guard during evening hours. *Student services:* personal/psychological counseling.
Costs (2006–07) *Tuition:* state resident $40 per credit hour part-time; nonresident $220 per credit hour part-time. *Required fees:* $12 per term part-time.
Financial Aid Of all full-time matriculated undergraduates who enrolled in 2004, 35 Federal Work-Study jobs (averaging $2000).
Applying *Options:* deferred entrance. *Required:* high school transcript. *Application deadline:* rolling (freshmen), rolling (transfers). *Notification:* continuous until 8/1 (freshmen).
Freshmen Application Contact Ms. Wanda Watts, Director of Admissions/Registrar, Richmond Community College, PO Box 1189, Hamlet, NC 28345. *Phone:* 910-582-7113. *Fax:* 910-582-7102.

ROANOKE-CHOWAN COMMUNITY COLLEGE
Ahoskie, North Carolina   www.roanokechowan.edu/

- **State-supported** 2-year, founded 1967, part of North Carolina Community College System
- **Rural** 39-acre campus
- **Endowment** $125,000
- **Coed**

Undergraduates 491 full-time, 523 part-time. 67% African American, 0.4% Asian American or Pacific Islander, 0.4% Hispanic American, 0.9% Native American. *Retention:* 59% of 2003 full-time freshmen returned.
Faculty *Student/faculty ratio:* 11:1.
Academics *Calendar:* semesters. *Degree:* certificates, diplomas, and associate. *Special study options:* academic remediation for entering students, adult/continuing education programs, cooperative education, distance learning, part-time degree program, summer session for credit.
Standardized Tests *Required:* ACT ASSET (for placement).
Financial Aid Of all full-time matriculated undergraduates who enrolled in 2004, 50 Federal Work-Study jobs (averaging $1120).
Applying *Options:* early admission. *Required for some:* interview.
Director of Admissions Miss Sandra Copeland, Director, Counseling Services, Roanoke-Chowan Community College, 109 Community College Road, Ahoskie, NC 27910. *Phone:* 252-862-1225.

ROBESON COMMUNITY COLLEGE
Lumberton, North Carolina   www.robeson.cc.nc.us/

Director of Admissions Ms. Judy Revels, Director of Admissions, Robeson Community College, PO Box 1420, 5160 Fayetteville Road, Lumberton, NC 28359. *Phone:* 910-618-5680 Ext. 251.

ROCKINGHAM COMMUNITY COLLEGE
Wentworth, North Carolina   www.rcc.cc.nc.us/

- **State-supported** 2-year, founded 1964, part of North Carolina Community College System
- **Rural** 257-acre campus
- **Coed,** 2,036 undergraduate students, 30% full-time, 66% women, 34% men

Undergraduates 604 full-time, 1,432 part-time. Students come from 9 states and territories, 1 other country, 5% are from out of state, 21% African American, 0.6% Asian American or Pacific Islander, 1% Hispanic American, 0.5% Native American, 0.4% international.
Freshmen *Admission:* 421 enrolled.
Faculty *Total:* 111, 59% full-time, 5% with terminal degrees. *Student/faculty ratio:* 18:1.
Majors Accounting; administrative assistant and secretarial science; art; biological and physical sciences; business administration and management; business machine repair; carpentry; child development; construction engineering technology; consumer services and advocacy; cosmetology; criminal justice/law enforcement administration; criminal justice/police science; electromechanical technology; heating, air conditioning, ventilation and refrigeration maintenance technology; horticultural science; human resources management; industrial arts; information science/studies; labor and industrial relations; legal administrative assistant/secretary; legal assistant/paralegal; liberal arts and sciences/liberal studies; medical administrative assistant and medical secretary; medical/clinical assistant; nursing (licensed practical/vocational nurse training); nursing (registered nurse training); occupational therapist assistant; physical therapist assistant; respiratory care therapy; teacher assistant/aide; tourism and travel services management.
Academics *Calendar:* semesters. *Degree:* certificates, diplomas, and associate. *Special study options:* academic remediation for entering students, adult/continuing education programs, advanced placement credit, cooperative education, part-time degree program, student-designed majors, summer session for credit.
Library Gerald B. James Library with 43,044 titles, 374 serial subscriptions, 3,990 audiovisual materials, an OPAC, a Web page.
Computers on Campus 150 computers available on campus for general student use. A campuswide network can be accessed. Internet access, at least one staffed computer lab available.
Student Life *Housing:* college housing not available. *Activities and Organizations:* student-run newspaper, Phi Theta Kappa, Cultural Diversity Club, Paralegal Club. *Campus security:* late-night transport/escort service. *Student services:* personal/psychological counseling.
Athletics Member NJCAA. *Intercollegiate sports:* baseball M, basketball M/W, volleyball M/W. *Intramural sports:* archery M/W, badminton M/W, basketball M/W, cheerleading W, table tennis M/W, tennis M/W, volleyball M/W.
Costs (2005–06) *Tuition:* state resident $1264 full-time, $40 per credit hour part-time; nonresident $7061 full-time, $220 per credit hour part-time. *Required fees:* $52 full-time.
Financial Aid Of all full-time matriculated undergraduates who enrolled in 2004, 37 Federal Work-Study jobs (averaging $2300).
Applying *Options:* early admission, deferred entrance. *Application deadline:* rolling (freshmen), rolling (transfers). *Notification:* continuous (freshmen).
Freshmen Application Contact Mrs. Leigh Hawkins, Director of Enrollment Services, Rockingham Community College, PO Box 38, Wentworth, NC 27375-0038. *Phone:* 336-342-4261 Ext. 2333.

ROWAN-CABARRUS COMMUNITY COLLEGE
Salisbury, North Carolina   www.rccc.cc.nc.us/

- **State-supported** 2-year, founded 1963, part of North Carolina Community College System
- **Small-town** 100-acre campus
- **Coed**

Undergraduates 2,255 full-time, 2,945 part-time. Students come from 2 other countries, 20% African American, 1% Asian American or Pacific Islander, 2% Hispanic American, 0.4% Native American.
Academics *Calendar:* semesters. *Degree:* diplomas and associate. *Special study options:* academic remediation for entering students, adult/continuing education programs, advanced placement credit, cooperative education, distance learning, English as a second language, internships, part-time degree program, services for LD students, summer session for credit.
Student Life *Campus security:* on-campus security during operating hours.
Standardized Tests *Required:* ACT ASSET (for placement).
Applying *Required:* high school transcript.
Freshmen Application Contact Mr. Kenneth C. Hayes, Director of Admissions and Recruitment, Rowan-Cabarrus Community College, PO Box 1595, Salisbury, NC 28145. *Phone:* 704-637-0760 Ext. 212.

SAMPSON COMMUNITY COLLEGE
Clinton, North Carolina   www.sampsoncc.edu/
Director of Admissions Mr. William R. Jordan, Director of Admissions, Sampson Community College, PO Box 318, Clinton, NC 28329. *Phone:* 910-592-8084 Ext. 2022.

SANDHILLS COMMUNITY COLLEGE
Pinehurst, North Carolina   www.sandhills.edu/

- **State and locally supported** 2-year, founded 1963, part of North Carolina Community College System
- **Small-town** campus
- **Endowment** $4.1 million
- **Coed**

Undergraduates Students come from 42 states and territories, 23 other countries, 1% are from out of state, 28% African American, 0.6% Asian American or Pacific Islander, 1% Hispanic American, 6% Native American.
Faculty *Student/faculty ratio:* 18:1.
Academics *Calendar:* semesters. *Degree:* certificates, diplomas, and associate. *Special study options:* academic remediation for entering students, advanced placement credit, cooperative education, distance learning, double majors, honors programs, independent study, internships, part-time degree program, services for LD students, summer session for credit.
Student Life *Campus security:* 24-hour emergency response devices, security on duty until 12 a.m.
Standardized Tests *Required:* ACT ASSET or ACT COMPASS (for placement).
Financial Aid Of all full-time matriculated undergraduates who enrolled in 2004, 59 Federal Work-Study jobs (averaging $1750).
Applying *Options:* common application, deferred entrance. *Required:* high school transcript.
Freshmen Application Contact Ms. Rosa McAllister-McRae, Admissions Coordinator, Sandhills Community College, 3395 Airport Road, Pinehurst, NC 28374. *Phone:* 910-692-6185 Ext. 729. *Toll-free phone:* 800-338-3944. *E-mail:* offuttb@sandpiper.sandhills.cc.nc.us.

SCHOOL OF COMMUNICATION ARTS
Raleigh, North Carolina

SOUTH COLLEGE-ASHEVILLE
Asheville, North Carolina   www.southcollegenc.com/
Director of Admissions Mr. Michael Darnell, Director of Admissions, South College-Asheville, 1567 Patton Avenue, Asheville, NC 28806. *Phone:* 828-252-2486.

SOUTHEASTERN COMMUNITY COLLEGE
Whiteville, North Carolina   www.sccnc.edu/

- **State-supported** 2-year, founded 1964, part of North Carolina Community College System
- **Rural** 106-acre campus
- **Coed**, 1,825 undergraduate students, 92% full-time, 62% women, 38% men

Undergraduates 1,670 full-time, 155 part-time. Students come from 2 states and territories, 1% are from out of state, 26% African American, 4% Native American, 0.1% international.
Freshmen *Admission:* 845 applied, 845 admitted.
Faculty *Total:* 88, 82% full-time, 2% with terminal degrees. *Student/faculty ratio:* 20:1.
Majors Administrative assistant and secretarial science; art; biological and physical sciences; biotechnology; business administration and management; clinical/medical laboratory technology; computer engineering technology; cosmetology; criminal justice/law enforcement administration; electrical, electronic and communications engineering technology; environmental studies; forestry technology; industrial technology; kindergarten/preschool education; liberal arts and sciences/liberal studies; music; nursing (registered nurse training); parks, recreation and leisure; parks, recreation and leisure facilities management; teacher assistant/aide; welding technology.
Academics *Calendar:* semesters. *Degree:* certificates, diplomas, and associate. *Special study options:* academic remediation for entering students, adult/continuing education programs, advanced placement credit, cooperative education, distance learning, double majors, English as a second language, honors programs, independent study, internships, part-time degree program, services for LD students, summer session for credit.
Library Southeastern Community College Library with 50,297 titles, 192 serial subscriptions, an OPAC.
Computers on Campus 80 computers available on campus for general student use. A campuswide network can be accessed. Internet access, at least one staffed computer lab available.
Student Life *Housing:* college housing not available. *Activities and Organizations:* drama/theater group, choral group, Student Government Association, Forestry Club, Nursing Club, Environmental Club. *Campus security:* 24-hour emergency response devices. *Student services:* personal/psychological counseling.
Athletics Member NJCAA. *Intercollegiate sports:* baseball M(s), softball W, squash W, volleyball W(s).
Costs (2005–06) *Tuition:* state resident $948 full-time, $40 per credit part-time; nonresident $5268 full-time, $220 per credit part-time. *Required fees:* $64 full-time, $35 per term part-time.
Financial Aid Of all full-time matriculated undergraduates who enrolled in 2004, 80 Federal Work-Study jobs (averaging $1580).
Applying *Options:* common application, electronic application, early admission, deferred entrance. *Required:* high school transcript. *Application deadline:* rolling (freshmen), rolling (transfers).
Freshmen Application Contact Ms. Sylvia Tart, Registrar, Southeastern Community College, PO Box 151, Whiteville, NC 28472. *Phone:* 910-642-7141 Ext. 249. *Fax:* 910-642-5658. *E-mail:* start@sccnc.edu.

SOUTH PIEDMONT COMMUNITY COLLEGE
Polkton, North Carolina   **www.spcc.edu/**

Freshmen Application Contact Ms. Jeania Martin, Admissions Coordinator, South Piedmont Community College, PO Box 126, Polkton, NC 28135. *Phone:* 704-272-7635. *Toll-free phone:* 800-766-0319. *E-mail:* abaucom@vnet.net.

SOUTHWESTERN COMMUNITY COLLEGE
Sylva, North Carolina   **www.southwest.cc.nc.us/**

- **State-supported** 2-year, founded 1964, part of North Carolina Community College System
- **Small-town** 55-acre campus
- **Coed**

Undergraduates 899 full-time, 1,115 part-time. Students come from 6 states and territories, 1 other country, 1% are from out of state, 1% African American, 0.3% Asian American or Pacific Islander, 1% Hispanic American, 10% Native American, 0.3% international, 8% transferred in.
Faculty *Student/faculty ratio:* 12:1.
Academics *Calendar:* semesters. *Degree:* certificates, diplomas, and associate. *Special study options:* academic remediation for entering students, adult/continuing education programs, cooperative education, distance learning, double majors, English as a second language, independent study, off-campus study, part-time degree program, services for LD students, summer session for credit.
Student Life *Campus security:* security during hours college is open.
Standardized Tests *Recommended:* SAT or ACT (for admission).
Financial Aid Of all full-time matriculated undergraduates who enrolled in 2004, 55 Federal Work-Study jobs (averaging $900).
Applying *Options:* common application, early admission, deferred entrance. *Required:* high school transcript. *Required for some:* minimum 2.0 GPA, letters of recommendation, interview.
Director of Admissions Dr. Phil Weast, Director of Enrollment Management, Southwestern Community College, 447 College Drive, Sylva, NC 28779. *Phone:* 828-586-4091 Ext. 431. *Toll-free phone:* 800-447-4091. *E-mail:* pweast@southwest.cc.nc.us.

STANLY COMMUNITY COLLEGE
Albemarle, North Carolina   **www.stanly.edu/**

- **State-supported** 2-year, founded 1971, part of North Carolina Community College System
- **Small-town** 150-acre campus with easy access to Charlotte
- **Coed**

Undergraduates Students come from 13 states and territories, 3 other countries, 3% are from out of state.
Faculty *Student/faculty ratio:* 9:1.
Academics *Calendar:* semesters. *Degree:* certificates, diplomas, and associate. *Special study options:* academic remediation for entering students, adult/continuing education programs, advanced placement credit, cooperative education, distance learning, double majors, English as a second language, independent study, internships, part-time degree program, services for LD students, summer session for credit.
Standardized Tests *Required:* ACT ASSET (for placement). *Recommended:* SAT (for placement).
Financial Aid Of all full-time matriculated undergraduates who enrolled in 2004, 20 Federal Work-Study jobs (averaging $1800).
Applying *Options:* early admission, deferred entrance. *Required:* high school transcript.
Director of Admissions Mr. Ronnie Hinson, Director of Admissions, Stanly Community College, 141 College Drive, Albemarle, NC 28001. *Phone:* 704-982-0121 Ext. 233. *E-mail:* hinsonre@stanly.cc.nc.us.

SURRY COMMUNITY COLLEGE
Dobson, North Carolina   **www.surry.cc.nc.us/**

- **State-supported** 2-year, founded 1965, part of North Carolina Community College System
- **Rural** 100-acre campus
- **Coed**

Undergraduates Students come from 3 states and territories, 4% are from out of state, 5% African American, 0.3% Asian American or Pacific Islander, 2% Hispanic American, 0.3% Native American, 0.2% international.
Faculty *Student/faculty ratio:* 27:1.
Academics *Calendar:* semesters. *Degree:* certificates, diplomas, and associate. *Special study options:* academic remediation for entering students, adult/continuing education programs, advanced placement credit, cooperative education, distance learning, English as a second language, independent study, internships, off-campus study, part-time degree program, summer session for credit.
Student Life *Campus security:* security guard during day and evening hours.
Athletics Member NJCAA.
Standardized Tests *Required:* CPT (for placement).
Financial Aid Of all full-time matriculated undergraduates who enrolled in 2004, 35 Federal Work-Study jobs (averaging $2800).
Applying *Options:* electronic application, early admission, deferred entrance. *Required:* high school transcript.
Director of Admissions Mr. Michael McHone, Vice President of Student Services, Surry Community College, PO Box 304, Dobson, NC 27017-0304. *Phone:* 336-386-3238.

TRI-COUNTY COMMUNITY COLLEGE
Murphy, North Carolina   **www.tricountycc.edu**

- **State-supported** 2-year, founded 1964
- **Rural** 40-acre campus
- **Coed,** 1,155 undergraduate students, 44% full-time, 67% women, 33% men

Undergraduates 503 full-time, 652 part-time. Students come from 8 states and territories, 3% are from out of state, 0.9% African American, 1% Hispanic American, 2% Native American.
Freshmen *Admission:* 518 applied, 518 admitted. *Average high school GPA:* 2.9.
Faculty *Total:* 80, 58% full-time, 5% with terminal degrees. *Student/faculty ratio:* 21:1.
Majors Accounting; automobile/automotive mechanics technology; business administration and management; computer management; early childhood education; electrical, electronic and communications engineering technology; information technology; liberal arts and sciences/liberal studies; medical/clinical assistant; nursing (registered nurse training); welding technology.
Academics *Calendar:* semesters. *Degree:* certificates, diplomas, and associate. *Special study options:* academic remediation for entering students, adult/continuing education programs, distance learning, double majors, part-time degree program, services for LD students, summer session for credit.
Library 16,224 titles, 306 serial subscriptions.
Computers on Campus 33 computers available on campus for general student use. A campuswide network can be accessed. Internet access available.
Student Life *Housing:* college housing not available. *Student services:* personal/psychological counseling.
Costs (2005–06) *Tuition:* state resident $970 full-time, $38 per credit hour part-time; nonresident $5122 full-time, $211 per credit hour part-time. *Required fees:* $60 full-time, $29 per term part-time.
Financial Aid Of all full-time matriculated undergraduates who enrolled in 2004, 11 Federal Work-Study jobs.
Applying *Required:* high school transcript. *Application deadline:* rolling (freshmen), rolling (transfers). *Notification:* continuous (freshmen).
Freshmen Application Contact Mr. Jason Chambers, Director of Admissions, Tri-County Community College, 4600 East US 64, Murphy, NC 28906-7919. *Phone:* 828-837-6810 Ext. 4225. *Fax:* 828-837-3266.

VANCE-GRANVILLE COMMUNITY COLLEGE

Henderson, North Carolina www.vgcc.cc.nc.us/

- **State-supported** 2-year, founded 1969, part of North Carolina Community College System
- **Rural** 83-acre campus with easy access to Raleigh
- **Endowment** $3.0 million
- **Coed,** 4,057 undergraduate students, 42% full-time, 66% women, 34% men

Undergraduates 1,718 full-time, 2,339 part-time. Students come from 10 states and territories, 15 other countries, 2% are from out of state, 43% African American, 0.2% Asian American or Pacific Islander, 2% Hispanic American, 0.7% Native American, 1% international, 2% transferred in.
Freshmen *Admission:* 1,765 applied, 1,765 admitted, 495 enrolled. *Average high school GPA:* 2.50.
Faculty *Total:* 353, 40% full-time, 5% with terminal degrees. *Student/faculty ratio:* 9:1.
Majors Accounting; administrative assistant and secretarial science; automobile/automotive mechanics technology; business administration and management; carpentry; child development; computer engineering technology; construction engineering technology; corrections; cosmetology; criminal justice/law enforcement administration; criminal justice/police science; data processing and data processing technology; education; electrical, electronic and communications engineering technology; elementary education; heating, air conditioning, ventilation and refrigeration maintenance technology; human services; industrial radiologic technology; industrial technology; kindergarten/preschool education; legal administrative assistant/secretary; liberal arts and sciences/liberal studies; medical administrative assistant and medical secretary; medical/clinical assistant; nursing (licensed practical/vocational nurse training); nursing (registered nurse training); parks, recreation and leisure; teacher assistant/aide; welding technology.
Academics *Calendar:* semesters. *Degree:* certificates, diplomas, and associate. *Special study options:* academic remediation for entering students, accelerated degree program, adult/continuing education programs, advanced placement credit, cooperative education, distance learning, double majors, English as a second language, internships, part-time degree program, services for LD students, summer session for credit.
Library Vance-Granville Community College Learning Resource Center plus 1 other with 38,720 titles, 317 serial subscriptions, an OPAC, a Web page.
Computers on Campus 184 computers available on campus for general student use. A campuswide network can be accessed from off campus. Internet access, at least one staffed computer lab available.
Student Life *Housing:* college housing not available. *Activities and Organizations:* drama/theater group, Vocational Club, Phi Theta Kappa, Computer Club, Criminal Justice Club, Business Club. *Campus security:* 24-hour emergency response devices and patrols. *Student services:* personal/psychological counseling.
Athletics *Intramural sports:* basketball M/W, volleyball M/W.
Costs (2005–06) *Tuition:* state resident $948 full-time, $40 per credit hour part-time; nonresident $5592 full-time, $234 per credit hour part-time. *Required fees:* $38 full-time, $14 per term part-time.
Financial Aid Of all full-time matriculated undergraduates who enrolled in 2004, 38 Federal Work-Study jobs (averaging $1750).
Applying *Options:* common application, early admission, deferred entrance. *Required:* high school transcript. *Application deadline:* rolling (freshmen), rolling (transfers). *Notification:* continuous (freshmen).
Freshmen Application Contact Ms. Kathy Kutl, Admissions Officer, Vance-Granville Community College, PO Box 917, State Road 1126, Henderson, NC 27536. *Phone:* 252-492-2061 Ext. 3265. *Fax:* 252-430-0460.

WAKE TECHNICAL COMMUNITY COLLEGE

Raleigh, North Carolina www.waketech.edu/

- **State and locally supported** 2-year, founded 1958, part of North Carolina Community College System
- **Suburban** 79-acre campus
- **Coed**

Undergraduates 3,891 full-time, 7,481 part-time. Students come from 15 states and territories, 41 other countries, 15% transferred in.
Faculty *Student/faculty ratio:* 11:1.

Academics *Calendar:* semesters. *Degree:* certificates, diplomas, and associate. *Special study options:* academic remediation for entering students, adult/continuing education programs, advanced placement credit, cooperative education, double majors, English as a second language, part-time degree program, services for LD students, summer session for credit.
Student Life *Campus security:* 24-hour patrols.
Standardized Tests *Required:* ACT ASSET or ACT COMPASS (for placement). *Recommended:* SAT or ACT (for placement).
Costs (2005–06) *Tuition:* state resident $1264 full-time, $40 per credit hour part-time; nonresident $7024 full-time, $220 per credit hour part-time. *Required fees:* $52 full-time, $1 per credit hour part-time, $10 per term part-time.
Financial Aid Of all full-time matriculated undergraduates who enrolled in 2004, 35 Federal Work-Study jobs (averaging $2000). 15 state and other part-time jobs (averaging $2000).
Applying *Options:* common application, electronic application, early admission. *Required:* high school transcript.
Director of Admissions Ms. Susan Bloomfield, Director of Admissions, Wake Technical Community College, 9101 Fayetteville Road, Raleigh, NC 27603-5696. *Phone:* 919-662-3357.

WAYNE COMMUNITY COLLEGE

Goldsboro, North Carolina www.waynecc.edu/

Director of Admissions Ms. Susan Mooring Sasser, Director of Admissions and Records, Wayne Community College, PO Box 8002, Goldsboro, NC 27533-8002. *Phone:* 919-735-5151 Ext. 216. *E-mail:* msm@wayne.cc.nc.us.

WESTERN PIEDMONT COMMUNITY COLLEGE

Morganton, North Carolina www.wpcc.edu/

Director of Admissions Mrs. Susan Williams, Director of Admissions, Western Piedmont Community College, 1001 Burkemont Avenue, Morganton, NC 28655-4511. *Phone:* 828-438-6051. *Fax:* 828-438-6065. *E-mail:* swilliams@wpcc.edu.

WILKES COMMUNITY COLLEGE

Wilkesboro, North Carolina www.wilkescc.edu/

- **State-supported** 2-year, founded 1965, part of North Carolina Community College System
- **Small-town** 140-acre campus
- **Endowment** $2.7 million
- **Coed,** 2,617 undergraduate students, 51% full-time, 63% women, 37% men

Undergraduates 1,347 full-time, 1,270 part-time. Students come from 13 states and territories, 15 other countries, 1% are from out of state, 5% African American, 0.5% Asian American or Pacific Islander, 2% Hispanic American, 0.5% Native American, 3% transferred in.
Freshmen *Admission:* 1,215 applied, 1,215 admitted, 707 enrolled.
Faculty *Total:* 362, 20% full-time, 6% with terminal degrees. *Student/faculty ratio:* 10:1.
Majors Accounting technology and bookkeeping; applied horticulture; architectural engineering technology; automobile/automotive mechanics technology; building/construction finishing, management, and inspection related; business administration and management; child care and support services management; computer programming (specific applications); computer systems analysis; computer systems networking and telecommunications; criminal justice/police science; diesel mechanics technology; electrical, electronic and communications engineering technology; electromechanical technology; executive assistant/executive secretary; hotel/motel administration; institutional food workers; liberal arts and sciences/liberal studies; medical/clinical assistant; nursing (registered nurse training); psychiatric/mental health services technology; radio and television broadcasting technology; speech-language pathology.
Academics *Calendar:* semesters. *Degree:* certificates, diplomas, and associate. *Special study options:* academic remediation for entering students, accelerated degree program, adult/continuing education programs, advanced placement credit, cooperative education, distance learning, double majors, English as a second language, independent study, internships, part-time degree program, services for LD students, summer session for credit.

Wilkes Community College (continued)

Library Learning Resources Center with 56,142 titles, 127 serial subscriptions, 6,867 audiovisual materials, an OPAC, a Web page.

Computers on Campus 255 computers available on campus for general student use. A campuswide network can be accessed. Internet access, at least one staffed computer lab available.

Student Life *Housing:* college housing not available. *Activities and Organizations:* drama/theater group, student-run newspaper, radio station, choral group, Student Government Association, Phi Theta Kappa, Phi Beta Lambda, Rotaract, Baptist Student Union. *Campus security:* 24-hour emergency response devices, student patrols, late-night transport/escort service. *Student services:* personal/psychological counseling.

Athletics Member NJCAA. *Intercollegiate sports:* baseball M, basketball M/W, volleyball W. *Intramural sports:* basketball M/W, table tennis M/W.

Costs (2005–06) *Tuition:* state resident $1264 full-time, $40 per credit hour part-time; nonresident $7024 full-time, $220 per credit hour part-time. *Required fees:* $58 full-time, $2 per credit hour part-time, $11 per term part-time.

Financial Aid Of all full-time matriculated undergraduates who enrolled in 2004, 50 Federal Work-Study jobs (averaging $1800).

Applying *Options:* electronic application, deferred entrance. *Required:* high school transcript. *Application deadline:* rolling (freshmen), rolling (transfers). *Notification:* continuous (freshmen).

Freshmen Application Contact Mr. Mac Warren, Director of Admissions, Wilkes Community College, PO Box 120, Wilkesboro, NC 28697. *Phone:* 336-838-6141. *Fax:* 336-838-6547. *E-mail:* mac.warren@wilkescc.edu.

WILSON TECHNICAL COMMUNITY COLLEGE

Wilson, North Carolina　　　　**www.wilsontech.edu/**

- **State-supported** 2-year, founded 1958, part of North Carolina Community College System
- **Small-town** 35-acre campus
- **Endowment** $837,822
- **Coed,** 1,925 undergraduate students, 46% full-time, 73% women, 27% men

Undergraduates 883 full-time, 1,042 part-time. Students come from 4 states and territories, 4 other countries, 1% are from out of state, 48% African American, 0.3% Asian American or Pacific Islander, 2% Hispanic American, 0.3% Native American, 0.1% international, 16% transferred in.

Freshmen *Admission:* 507 applied, 491 admitted, 149 enrolled.

Faculty *Total:* 103, 52% full-time, 7% with terminal degrees. *Student/faculty ratio:* 19:1.

Majors Accounting; administrative assistant and secretarial science; business administration and management; computer programming; criminal justice/law enforcement administration; electrical, electronic and communications engineering technology; fire science; general studies; industrial technology; information science/studies; kindergarten/preschool education; language interpretation and translation; legal assistant/paralegal; liberal arts and sciences/liberal studies; mechanical engineering/mechanical technology; nursing (registered nurse training); sign language interpretation and translation; tool and die technology.

Academics *Calendar:* semesters. *Degree:* certificates, diplomas, and associate. *Special study options:* academic remediation for entering students, advanced placement credit, cooperative education, distance learning, double majors, English as a second language, independent study, internships, part-time degree program, services for LD students, summer session for credit.

Library 38,466 titles, 7,658 audiovisual materials, an OPAC.

Computers on Campus 33 computers available on campus for general student use. A campuswide network can be accessed. Internet access, at least one staffed computer lab available.

Student Life *Housing:* college housing not available. *Campus security:* 11-hour patrols by trained security personnel.

Costs (2005–06) *Tuition:* state resident $1264 full-time, $40 per credit hour part-time; nonresident $7024 full-time, $220 per credit hour part-time. *Required fees:* $38 full-time, $1 per credit hour part-time, $7 per semester part-time.

Financial Aid Of all full-time matriculated undergraduates who enrolled in 2004, 65 Federal Work-Study jobs (averaging $1500).

Applying *Options:* common application, electronic application, deferred entrance. *Required:* high school transcript. *Application deadline:* rolling (freshmen), rolling (transfers). *Notification:* continuous (freshmen).

Freshmen Application Contact Ms. Barbara Page, Admissions Technician, Wilson Technical Community College, PO Box 4305, Wilson, NC 27893-0305. *Phone:* 252-246-1275. *Fax:* 252-243-7148. *E-mail:* bpage@wilsontech.edu.

NORTH DAKOTA

AAKERS BUSINESS COLLEGE

Fargo, North Dakota　　　　**www.aakers-college.com/**

- **Proprietary** primarily 2-year, founded 1902
- **Coed,** 577 undergraduate students, 55% full-time, 79% women, 21% men

Undergraduates 320 full-time, 257 part-time. 24% are from out of state, 0.2% African American, 0.5% Asian American or Pacific Islander, 0.5% Hispanic American, 0.9% Native American.

Freshmen *Admission:* 262 enrolled.

Faculty *Total:* 26, 31% full-time. *Student/faculty ratio:* 13:1.

Majors Accounting; business administration and management; computer systems networking and telecommunications; criminal justice/law enforcement administration; health services/allied health/health sciences; human resources management and services related; legal studies.

Academics *Calendar:* quarters. *Degrees:* diplomas, associate, and bachelor's.

Costs (2006–07) *Tuition:* $2535 full-time, $845 per course part-time.

Applying *Application fee:* $60. *Required:* high school transcript. *Application deadlines:* 10/3 (freshmen), 10/3 (out-of-state freshmen), 10/3 (transfers).

Freshmen Application Contact Ms. Elizabeth Largent, Director, Aakers Business College, 4012 19th Avenue, SW, Fargo, ND 58103. *Phone:* 701-277-3889. *Toll-free phone:* 800-817-0009. *Fax:* 701-277-5604.

BISMARCK STATE COLLEGE

Bismarck, North Dakota　　　　**www.bismarckstate.edu/**

- **State-supported** 2-year, founded 1939, part of North Dakota University System
- **Suburban** 100-acre campus
- **Coed**

Undergraduates 2,329 full-time, 1,212 part-time. Students come from 18 states and territories, 11 other countries, 8% are from out of state, 0.9% African American, 0.4% Asian American or Pacific Islander, 0.8% Hispanic American, 3% Native American, 0.3% international, 11% transferred in, 8% live on campus.

Faculty *Student/faculty ratio:* 18:1.

Academics *Calendar:* semesters. *Degree:* certificates, diplomas, and associate. *Special study options:* academic remediation for entering students, adult/continuing education programs, advanced placement credit, cooperative education, distance learning, part-time degree program, services for LD students, summer session for credit. *ROTC:* Army (c), Air Force (c).

Student Life *Campus security:* 24-hour emergency response devices and patrols, controlled dormitory access.

Athletics Member NJCAA.

Standardized Tests *Required:* SAT or ACT (for admission).

Costs (2005–06) *Tuition:* state resident $3356 full-time, $93 per credit hour part-time; nonresident $8009 full-time, $248 per credit hour part-time. *Required fees:* $500 full-time, $22 per credit hour part-time. *Room and board:* $4288.

Financial Aid Of all full-time matriculated undergraduates who enrolled in 2004, 74 Federal Work-Study jobs (averaging $1012).

Applying *Options:* common application, electronic application. *Application fee:* $35. *Required:* high school transcript.

Freshmen Application Contact Ms. Karla Gabriel, Dean of Admissions and Enrollment Services, Bismarck State College, PO Box 5587, Bismarck, ND 58506-5587. *Phone:* 701-224-5426. *Toll-free phone:* 800-445-5073 Ext. 45429 (in-state); 800-445-5073 (out-of-state).

CANKDESKA CIKANA COMMUNITY COLLEGE

Fort Totten, North Dakota　　　　**www.littlehoop.edu/**

Director of Admissions Mr. Ermen Brown Jr., Registrar, Cankdeska Cikana Community College, PO Box 269, Fort Totten, ND 58335. *Phone:* 701-766-1342.

FORT BERTHOLD COMMUNITY COLLEGE

New Town, North Dakota   www.fbcc.bia.edu/

Director of Admissions Mr. Russell Mason Jr., President, Fort Berthold Community College, PO Box 490, New Town, ND 58763-0490. *Phone:* 701-627-3665. *Fax:* 701-627-3629.

LAKE REGION STATE COLLEGE

Devils Lake, North Dakota   www.lrsc.nodak.edu/

- **State-supported** 2-year, founded 1941, part of North Dakota University System
- **Small-town** 120-acre campus
- **Endowment** $2.2 million
- **Coed,** 1,471 undergraduate students, 28% full-time, 58% women, 42% men

Undergraduates 409 full-time, 1,062 part-time. Students come from 28 states and territories, 12 other countries, 10% are from out of state, 2% African American, 0.5% Asian American or Pacific Islander, 1% Hispanic American, 8% Native American, 2% international, 4% transferred in, 30% live on campus. Freshmen *Admission:* 164 applied, 164 admitted, 164 enrolled.

Faculty *Total:* 106, 28% full-time, 12% with terminal degrees. *Student/faculty ratio:* 15:1.

Majors Accounting; accounting technology and bookkeeping; administrative assistant and secretarial science; agricultural business and management; automobile/automotive mechanics technology; avionics maintenance technology; business administration and management; child care and support services management; child care provision; computer and information sciences; computer programming (specific applications); computer programming (vendor/product certification); computer science; computer systems networking and telecommunications; criminal justice/police science; diesel mechanics technology; electrical, electronics and communications engineering; electrical/electronics equipment installation and repair; executive assistant/executive secretary; fashion merchandising; information technology; legal administrative assistant/secretary; legal assistant/paralegal; liberal arts and sciences/liberal studies; management information systems; marketing research; medical administrative assistant and medical secretary; nursing assistant/aide and patient care assistant; nursing (licensed practical/vocational nurse training); office management; office occupations and clerical services; pathologist assistant; sales, distribution and marketing; sign language interpretation and translation; small business administration; teacher assistant/aide; technical teacher education.

Academics *Calendar:* semesters. *Degree:* certificates, diplomas, and associate. *Special study options:* academic remediation for entering students, adult/continuing education programs, cooperative education, distance learning, double majors, English as a second language, freshman honors college, honors programs, internships, part-time degree program, summer session for credit.

Library Paul Hoghaug Library plus 1 other with 42,000 titles, 200 serial subscriptions, 2,000 audiovisual materials, an OPAC.

Computers on Campus 275 computers available on campus for general student use. A campuswide network can be accessed from student residence rooms and from off campus. Internet access, online (class) registration, at least one staffed computer lab available. Computer purchase or lease plan available.

Student Life *Housing Options:* men-only, women-only. Campus housing is university owned. *Activities and Organizations:* drama/theater group, DECA, drama, SOTA (Students Other than Average), Student Senate, Computer Club. *Campus security:* 24-hour emergency response devices, controlled dormitory access. *Student services:* personal/psychological counseling.

Athletics Member NJCAA. *Intercollegiate sports:* basketball M(s)/W(s). *Intramural sports:* basketball M/W, bowling M, football M/W, golf M/W, ice hockey M/W, softball M/W, table tennis M/W, volleyball M/W.

Standardized Tests *Required:* SAT or ACT (for admission), COMPASS (for admission).

Costs (2006–07) *Tuition:* state resident $2550 full-time, $133 per credit part-time; nonresident $2550 full-time, $133 per credit part-time. *Required fees:* $783 full-time. *Room and board:* $3790.

Financial Aid Of all full-time matriculated undergraduates who enrolled in 2004, 40 Federal Work-Study jobs (averaging $1600).

Applying *Options:* electronic application. *Application fee:* $35. *Required:* high school transcript, immunizations. *Application deadline:* rolling (freshmen), rolling (transfers). *Notification:* continuous (freshmen).

Freshmen Application Contact Ms. Diane Knodel, Administrative Assistant, Lake Region State College, 1801 College Drive North, Devils Lake, ND 58301. *Phone:* 701-662-1514. *Toll-free phone:* 800-443-1313 Ext. 514. *Fax:* 701-662-1581. *E-mail:* diane.knodel@lrsc.nodak.edu.

MINOT STATE UNIVERSITY–BOTTINEAU CAMPUS

Bottineau, North Dakota   www.misu-b.nodak.edu/

Freshmen Application Contact Ms. Jody Klier, Admissions Counselor, Minot State University–Bottineau Campus, 105 Simrall Boulevard, Bottineau, ND 58318. *Phone:* 701-228-5426. *Toll-free phone:* 800-542-6866. *E-mail:* groszk@warp6.cs.misu.nodak.edu.

NORTH DAKOTA STATE COLLEGE OF SCIENCE

Wahpeton, North Dakota   www.ndscs.nodak.edu/

- **State-supported** 2-year, founded 1903, part of North Dakota University System
- **Rural** 125-acre campus
- **Endowment** $4000
- **Coed,** 2,468 undergraduate students, 79% full-time, 37% women, 63% men

Undergraduates 1,954 full-time, 514 part-time. Students come from 54 states and territories, 11 other countries, 27% are from out of state, 2% African American, 0.4% Asian American or Pacific Islander, 0.5% Hispanic American, 2% Native American, 0.9% international, 9% transferred in, 56% live on campus. Freshmen *Admission:* 2,468 admitted, 886 enrolled. *Average high school GPA:* 2.73. *Test scores:* ACT scores over 18: 58%; ACT scores over 24: 10%.

Faculty *Total:* 140, 91% full-time, 1% with terminal degrees. *Student/faculty ratio:* 15:1.

Majors Administrative assistant and secretarial science; agricultural business and management related; agricultural/farm supplies retailing and wholesaling; agricultural mechanization; agricultural production; architectural engineering technology; autobody/collision and repair technology; automobile/automotive mechanics technology; business/commerce; civil engineering technology; computer programming (specific applications); construction engineering technology; dental hygiene; diesel mechanics technology; electrical, electronic and communications engineering technology; foodservice systems administration; health information/medical records technology; heating, air conditioning and refrigeration technology; heating, air conditioning, ventilation and refrigeration maintenance technology; industrial electronics technology; industrial technology; liberal arts and sciences/liberal studies; machine shop technology; nursing (licensed practical/vocational nurse training); occupational therapist assistant; pharmacy technician; psychiatric/mental health services technology; small engine mechanics and repair technology; technical teacher education; vehicle maintenance and repair technologies related; welding technology.

Academics *Calendar:* semesters. *Degree:* certificates, diplomas, and associate. *Special study options:* academic remediation for entering students, adult/continuing education programs, cooperative education, distance learning, double majors, English as a second language, independent study, internships, part-time degree program, services for LD students, student-designed majors, summer session for credit.

Library Mildred Johnson Library with 124,508 titles, 852 serial subscriptions, 4,178 audiovisual materials, an OPAC, a Web page.

Computers on Campus 450 computers available on campus for general student use. A campuswide network can be accessed from student residence rooms and from off campus. Internet access, at least one staffed computer lab available. Computer purchase or lease plan available.

Student Life *Housing:* on-campus residence required for freshman year. *Options:* coed, men-only, women-only. Campus housing is university owned. *Activities and Organizations:* drama/theater group, choral group, marching band, Student Health Advisory Club, Drama Club, Inter-Varsity Christian Fellowship, Cultural Diversity, Habitat for Humanity. *Campus security:* 24-hour emergency response devices and patrols, student patrols, late-night transport/escort service, controlled dormitory access. *Student services:* health clinic, personal/psychological counseling, legal services.

Athletics Member NJCAA. *Intercollegiate sports:* basketball M(s)/W(s), football M(s), volleyball W(s). *Intramural sports:* baseball M, basketball M/W, cheerleading W, field hockey M/W, football M, racquetball M/W, softball M/W, volleyball M/W.

Costs (2006–07) *Tuition:* state resident $3757 full-time; nonresident $9197 full-time. *Room and board:* $4638.

Financial Aid Of all full-time matriculated undergraduates who enrolled in 2004, 90 Federal Work-Study jobs (averaging $1500).

Applying *Options:* common application, electronic application, early admission. *Application fee:* $35. *Required:* high school transcript. *Application deadline:* rolling (freshmen), rolling (transfers). *Notification:* continuous (freshmen).

North Dakota State College of Science (continued)
Freshmen Application Contact Ms. Karen Reilly, Director of Enrollment Services, North Dakota State College of Science, 800 North 6th Street, Wahpeton, ND 58076. *Phone:* 701-671-2189. *Toll-free phone:* 800-342-4325 Ext. 2202. *Fax:* 701-671-2332.

SITTING BULL COLLEGE

Fort Yates, North Dakota   **www.sittingbull.edu/**

Director of Admissions Ms. Melody Silk, Director of Registration and Admissions, Sitting Bull College, 1341 92nd Street, Fort Yates, ND 58538-9701. *Phone:* 701-854-3864. *Fax:* 701-854-3403. *E-mail:* melodys@sbcl.edu.

TURTLE MOUNTAIN COMMUNITY COLLEGE

Belcourt, North Dakota   **www.turtle-mountain.cc.nd.us/**

Director of Admissions Ms. Joni LaFontaine, Admissions/Records Officer, Turtle Mountain Community College, Box 340, Belcourt, ND 58316-0340. *Phone:* 701-477-5605 Ext. 217. *E-mail:* jlafontaine@tm.edu.

UNITED TRIBES TECHNICAL COLLEGE

Bismarck, North Dakota   **www.uttc.edu/**

- **Federally supported** 2-year, founded 1969
- **Small-town** 105-acre campus
- **Coed,** 885 undergraduate students, 72% full-time, 71% women, 29% men

Undergraduates 635 full-time, 250 part-time. 0.2% African American, 0.8% Asian American or Pacific Islander, 0.3% Hispanic American, 75% Native American.
Freshmen *Admission:* 179 applied, 151 admitted, 151 enrolled.
Faculty *Total:* 63, 78% full-time. *Student/faculty ratio:* 8:1.
Majors Administrative assistant and secretarial science; animation, interactive technology, video graphics and special effects; art; automobile/automotive mechanics technology; business administration and management; business automation/technology/data entry; child care provision; community health and preventive medicine; computer systems analysis; construction trades; criminal justice/law enforcement administration; early childhood education; education; entrepreneurship; environmental science; fine arts related; food/nutrition; health information/medical records technology; hospitality administration; medical administrative assistant and medical secretary; nursing (licensed practical/vocational nurse training); office occupations and clerical services.
Academics *Calendar:* semesters. *Degree:* certificates and associate. *Special study options:* academic remediation for entering students, cooperative education, honors programs, internships, part-time degree program, summer session for credit.
Library United Tribes Technical College Library plus 1 other with 6,000 titles, 86 serial subscriptions, an OPAC, a Web page.
Computers on Campus 210 computers available on campus for general student use. At least one staffed computer lab available.
Student Life *Housing Options:* men-only, women-only. *Activities and Organizations:* student-run newspaper. *Campus security:* 24-hour emergency response devices and patrols. *Student services:* personal/psychological counseling.
Athletics Member NJCAA. *Intercollegiate sports:* basketball M, cross-country running M/W. *Intramural sports:* basketball M, volleyball M/W.
Costs (2006–07) *One-time required fee:* $100. *Comprehensive fee:* $6580 includes full-time tuition ($2800), mandatory fees ($780), and room and board ($3000). Part-time tuition: $88 per credit.
Applying *Required:* high school transcript. *Application deadline:* rolling (freshmen), rolling (transfers).
Freshmen Application Contact Ms. Vivian Gillette, Director of Admissions, United Tribes Technical College, 3315 University Drive, Bismarck, ND 58504. *Phone:* 701-255-3285 Ext. 1334. *Fax:* 701-530-0640. *E-mail:* vgillette@uttc.edu.

WILLISTON STATE COLLEGE

Williston, North Dakota   **www.wsc.nodak.edu/**

- **State-supported** 2-year, founded 1957, part of North Dakota University System
- **Small-town** 80-acre campus
- **Endowment** $52,200
- **Coed,** 947 undergraduate students, 59% full-time, 73% women, 27% men

Undergraduates 557 full-time, 390 part-time. Students come from 9 states and territories, 3 other countries, 14% are from out of state, 1% African American, 0.3% Asian American or Pacific Islander, 2% Hispanic American, 5% Native American, 3% international, 84% transferred in, 13% live on campus.
Freshmen *Admission:* 540 applied, 529 admitted, 187 enrolled.
Faculty *Total:* 93, 28% full-time, 2% with terminal degrees. *Student/faculty ratio:* 14:1.
Majors Accounting technology and bookkeeping; administrative assistant and secretarial science; agriculture; automobile/automotive mechanics technology; computer and information sciences and support services related; data processing and data processing technology; diesel mechanics technology; entrepreneurial and small business related; health information/medical records technology; liberal arts and sciences/liberal studies; marketing/marketing management; medical transcription; multi-/interdisciplinary studies related; nursing (licensed practical/vocational nurse training); physical therapist assistant.
Academics *Calendar:* semesters. *Degree:* certificates, diplomas, and associate. *Special study options:* academic remediation for entering students, advanced placement credit, cooperative education, distance learning, honors programs, independent study, off-campus study, part-time degree program, services for LD students, student-designed majors, summer session for credit.
Library Williston State College Library with 16,218 titles, 214 serial subscriptions, 475 audiovisual materials, an OPAC, a Web page.
Computers on Campus 70 computers available on campus for general student use. A campuswide network can be accessed from student residence rooms and from off campus. Internet access, at least one staffed computer lab available. Computer purchase or lease plan available.
Student Life *Housing Options:* coed, men-only, women-only, cooperative. Campus housing is university owned. *Activities and Organizations:* drama/theater group, student-run newspaper, choral group, PTK, PBL, Student Senate, VICA, Student Nurses Association, national sororities. *Campus security:* controlled dormitory access. *Student services:* personal/psychological counseling.
Athletics Member NJCAA. *Intercollegiate sports:* baseball M(s), basketball M(s)/W(s), volleyball W(s). *Intramural sports:* basketball M/W, volleyball M/W.
Costs (2005–06) *Tuition:* state resident $2073 full-time, $80 per credit part-time; nonresident $3111 full-time, $120 per credit part-time. *Required fees:* $575 full-time, $22 per credit part-time. *Room and board:* $3500; room only: $1000. *Payment plan:* installment. *Waivers:* minority students and employees or children of employees.
Financial Aid Of all full-time matriculated undergraduates who enrolled in 2004, 30 Federal Work-Study jobs (averaging $1500). 15 state and other part-time jobs (averaging $1000).
Applying *Options:* common application, electronic application. *Application fee:* $35. *Required:* high school transcript. *Application deadline:* rolling (freshmen), rolling (transfers). *Notification:* continuous (freshmen).
Freshmen Application Contact Ms. Jan Solem, Director for Admission and Records, Williston State College, PO Box 1326, Williston, ND 58802-1326. *Phone:* 701-774-4554. *Toll-free phone:* 888-863-9455. *Fax:* 701-774-4211. *E-mail:* wsc.admission@wsc.nodak.edu.

NORTHERN MARIANA ISLANDS

NORTHERN MARIANAS COLLEGE

Saipan, Northern Mariana Islands   **www.nmcnet.edu/**

Director of Admissions Ms. Joyce Taro, Admission Specialist, Northern Marianas College, PO Box 501250, Saipan, MP 96950-1250. *Phone:* 670-234-3690 Ext. 1528.

ACADEMY OF COURT REPORTING
Cleveland, Ohio   www.acr.edu/

Director of Admissions Ms. Sheila Woods, Director of Admissions, Academy of Court Reporting, 2044 Euclid Avenue, Cleveland, OH 44115. *Phone:* 216-861-3222. *E-mail:* admissionaocr@hotmail.com.

ANTONELLI COLLEGE
Cincinnati, Ohio   www.antonellic.com/

Director of Admissions Ms. Connie D. Sharp, Director, Antonelli College, 124 East Seventh Street, Cincinnati, OH 45202. *Phone:* 513-241-4338. *Toll-free phone:* 800-505-4338.

THE ART INSTITUTE OF CINCINNATI
Cincinnati, Ohio   www.theartinstituteofcincinnati.com/

- **Proprietary** 2-year, part of Education Management Corporation
- **Coed**

Undergraduates 74 full-time. 1% are from out of state, 1% African American, 7% transferred in.
Faculty *Student/faculty ratio:* 9:1.
Academics *Degree:* associate.
Student Life *Campus security:* 24-hour emergency response devices.
Applying *Options:* common application. *Required:* high school transcript, letters of recommendation, interview, portfolio.
Director of Admissions Ms. Cyndi Mendell, Admissions, The Art Institute of Cincinnati, 1171 East Kemper Road, Cincinnati, OH 45246. *Phone:* 513-751-1206.

THE ART INSTITUTE OF OHIO– CINCINNATI
Cincinnati, Ohio   www.aiohc.aii.edu

- **Proprietary** 2-year, part of The Art Institutes
- **Coed,** 229 undergraduate students, 100% full-time, 62% women, 38% men

Undergraduates 229 full-time. Students come from 3 states and territories, 9% are from out of state, 32% African American, 2% Asian American or Pacific Islander, 0.4% Hispanic American, 0.4% Native American.
Faculty *Total:* 12, 17% full-time. *Student/faculty ratio:* 25:1.
Majors Graphic design; interior design.
Academics *Calendar:* continuous. *Degree:* associate. *Special study options:* accelerated degree program, cooperative education, distance learning, internships, part-time degree program, services for LD students.
Library Library with 7,018 titles, 75 serial subscriptions, 493 audiovisual materials, an OPAC.
Computers on Campus 229 computers available on campus for general student use. A campuswide network can be accessed. Internet access, at least one staffed computer lab available.
Applying *Options:* early admission, early decision, early action, deferred entrance. *Required:* high school transcript, interview. *Application deadline:* rolling (freshmen), rolling (transfers). *Notification:* continuous (freshmen).
Director of Admissions Mr. Maurice Lee, President, The Art Institute of Ohio–Cincinnati, 1011 Glendale-Milford Road, Cincinnati, OH 45215-1107. *Phone:* 513-771-2821. *Fax:* 877-477-8486. *E-mail:* mlee@aii.edu.

▶ **See page 480 for the College Close-Up.**

ATS INSTITUTE OF TECHNOLOGY
Highland Heights, Ohio

BELMONT TECHNICAL COLLEGE
St. Clairsville, Ohio   www.btc.edu/

- **State-supported** 2-year, founded 1971, part of Ohio Board of Regents
- **Rural** 55-acre campus
- **Coed**

Undergraduates 1,180 full-time, 560 part-time. Students come from 10 states and territories, 3% are from out of state, 3% African American, 0.2% Asian American or Pacific Islander, 0.1% Hispanic American, 0.5% Native American. *Retention:* 56% of 2003 full-time freshmen returned.
Academics *Calendar:* quarters. *Degree:* diplomas and associate. *Special study options:* academic remediation for entering students, distance learning, independent study, part-time degree program, summer session for credit.
Standardized Tests *Required:* ACT COMPASS (for placement).
Costs (2005–06) *Tuition:* state resident $2520 full-time, $56 per credit hour part-time; nonresident $5220 full-time, $116 per credit hour part-time. *Required fees:* $1050 full-time, $23 per credit hour part-time, $5 per term part-time.
Financial Aid Of all full-time matriculated undergraduates who enrolled in 2004, 15 Federal Work-Study jobs (averaging $4500).
Applying *Options:* early admission.
Director of Admissions Mr. Gregory A. Fehr, Executive Director of Marketing and Advancement, Belmont Technical College, 120 Fox Shannon Place, St. Clairsville, OH 43950-9735. *Phone:* 740-695-9500 Ext. 1018. *Toll-free phone:* 800-423-1188. *E-mail:* gfehr@btc.edu.

BOHECKER'S BUSINESS COLLEGE
Ravenna, Ohio

BOWLING GREEN STATE UNIVERSITY– FIRELANDS COLLEGE
Huron, Ohio   www.firelands.bgsu.edu/

- **State-supported** 2-year, founded 1968, part of Bowling Green State University System
- **Rural** 216-acre campus with easy access to Cleveland and Toledo
- **Endowment** $1.6 million
- **Coed**

Undergraduates 1,042 full-time, 876 part-time. Students come from 2 states and territories, 6% African American, 0.2% Asian American or Pacific Islander, 3% Hispanic American, 0.5% Native American, 22% transferred in. *Retention:* 42% of 2003 full-time freshmen returned.
Faculty *Student/faculty ratio:* 19:1.
Academics *Calendar:* semesters. *Degrees:* certificates and associate (also offers some upper-level and graduate courses). *Special study options:* academic remediation for entering students, adult/continuing education programs, advanced placement credit, distance learning, double majors, independent study, internships, part-time degree program, services for LD students, student-designed majors, summer session for credit. *ROTC:* Army (c), Air Force (c).
Student Life *Campus security:* 24-hour emergency response devices, late-night transport/escort service, patrols by trained security personnel.
Standardized Tests *Required for some:* SAT or ACT (for placement).
Applying *Options:* electronic application, early admission, deferred entrance. *Application fee:* $35. *Required:* high school transcript.
Director of Admissions Ms. Debralee Divers, Director of Admissions and Financial Aid, Bowling Green State University–Firelands College, One University Drive, Huron, OH 44839. *Phone:* 419-433-5560. *Toll-free phone:* 800-322-4787. *E-mail:* ahazlet@bgnet.bgsu.edu.

BRADFORD SCHOOL

Columbus, Ohio   **www.bradfordschoolcolumbus.edu/**

Director of Admissions Ms. Raeann Lee, Director of Admissions, Bradford School, 2469 Stelzer Road, Columbus, OH 43219. *Phone:* 614-416-6200. *Toll-free phone:* 800-678-7981.

BROWN MACKIE COLLEGE–AKRON

Akron, Ohio   **www.socaec.com/**

- **Proprietary** 2-year, founded 1968, administratively affiliated with Southern Ohio College
- **Suburban** 3-acre campus with easy access to Cleveland
- **Coed,** 521 undergraduate students, 100% full-time, 83% women, 17% men

Undergraduates 521 full-time. Students come from 1 other state, 1 other country, 44% African American, 0.4% Asian American or Pacific Islander, 0.8% Hispanic American, 0.8% Native American.
Faculty *Total:* 48, 15% full-time. *Student/faculty ratio:* 18:1.
Majors Accounting; business administration and management; computer software technology; computer systems networking and telecommunications; criminal justice/safety; health/health care administration; medical/clinical assistant; paralegal/legal assistant; pharmacy technician.
Academics *Calendar:* quarters. *Degree:* certificates, diplomas, and associate. *Special study options:* academic remediation for entering students, advanced placement credit, cooperative education, internships, summer session for credit.
Library 3,725 titles, 56 serial subscriptions.
Computers on Campus 51 computers available on campus for general student use. At least one staffed computer lab available.
Student Life *Housing:* college housing not available. *Activities and Organizations:* student-run newspaper, Phi Beta Lambda, Student Advisory Board, Collegiate Secretaries International. *Campus security:* late-night transport/escort service. *Student services:* personal/psychological counseling.
Costs (2006–07) *Tuition:* $179 per credit part-time. *Required fees:* $10 per credit part-time.
Applying *Options:* early admission, deferred entrance. *Recommended:* minimum 2.0 GPA. *Application deadline:* rolling (freshmen), rolling (transfers). *Notification:* continuous (freshmen).
Freshmen Application Contact Mrs. Tanya Foose, Director of Admissions, Brown Mackie College–Akron, 2791 Mogadore Road, Akron, OH 44312-1596. *Phone:* 330-733-8766. *Fax:* 330-733-5853. *E-mail:* tfoose@brownmackie.edu.

▶ **See page 496 for the College Close-Up.**

BROWN MACKIE COLLEGE–CINCINNATI

Cincinnati, Ohio

www.brownmackie.edu/locations.asp?locid=6

- **Proprietary** 2-year, founded 1927, part of American Education Centers, Inc
- **Suburban** 3-acre campus
- **Coed,** 971 undergraduate students

Undergraduates Students come from 3 states and territories, 1% are from out of state.
Faculty *Total:* 46, 26% full-time. *Student/faculty ratio:* 16:1.
Majors Accounting; administrative assistant and secretarial science; audio engineering; business administration and management; computer and information sciences related; computer graphics; computer science; laser and optical technology; medical administrative assistant and medical secretary; medical/clinical assistant.
Academics *Calendar:* quarters. *Degree:* certificates, diplomas, and associate. *Special study options:* academic remediation for entering students, adult/continuing education programs, advanced placement credit, internships, summer session for credit.
Library 8,747 titles, 80 serial subscriptions, 437 audiovisual materials.
Computers on Campus 125 computers available on campus for general student use.
Student Life *Housing:* college housing not available. *Campus security:* 24-hour emergency response devices, night security guard on-campus.
Costs (2005–06) *Tuition:* $6444 full-time. *Required fees:* $360 full-time.

Financial Aid Of all full-time matriculated undergraduates who enrolled in 2004, 4 Federal Work-Study jobs.
Applying *Options:* common application, early admission, deferred entrance. *Application fee:* $20. *Required:* high school transcript, interview. *Application deadline:* rolling (freshmen), rolling (transfers).
Director of Admissions Ms. Cherie McNeel, Director of Admissions, Brown Mackie College–Cincinnati, 1011 Glendale-Milford Road, Cincinnati, OH 45215. *Phone:* 513-771-2424.

▶ **See page 500 for the College Close-Up.**

BROWN MACKIE COLLEGE–FINDLAY

Findlay, Ohio   **www.brownmackie.edu**

- **Proprietary** 2-year, founded 1929, administratively affiliated with Education Management Corporation
- **Rural** 1-acre campus
- **Coed,** 632 undergraduate students, 73% full-time, 91% women, 9% men

Undergraduates 459 full-time, 173 part-time. Students come from 2 states and territories, 1% are from out of state, 32% African American, 0.6% Asian American or Pacific Islander, 6% Hispanic American, 0.6% Native American, 3% transferred in.
Freshmen *Admission:* 535 admitted, 535 enrolled.
Faculty *Total:* 57, 32% full-time, 7% with terminal degrees. *Student/faculty ratio:* 19:1.
Majors Accounting technology and bookkeeping; business administration and management; computer software technology; criminal justice/safety; health/health care administration; medical/clinical assistant; medical office management; paralegal/legal assistant; pharmacy technician.
Academics *Calendar:* continuous. *Degree:* diplomas and associate. *Special study options:* advanced placement credit, cooperative education, double majors, external degree program, independent study, internships.
Library 3,134 titles, 41 serial subscriptions, 26 audiovisual materials, an OPAC, a Web page.
Computers on Campus 74 computers available on campus for general student use. A campuswide network can be accessed. Internet access, at least one staffed computer lab available. Computer purchase or lease plan available.
Student Life *Housing:* college housing not available. *Campus security:* 24-hour emergency response devices.
Costs (2006–07) *Tuition:* $11,500 full-time, $250 per credit hour part-time. *Required fees:* $460 full-time, $10 per credit hour part-time.
Financial Aid Of all full-time matriculated undergraduates who enrolled in 2004, 14 Federal Work-Study jobs (averaging $1928).
Applying *Options:* common application. *Required:* high school transcript, interview. *Application deadline:* rolling (freshmen), rolling (transfers). *Notification:* continuous (freshmen).
Freshmen Application Contact Mr. Wayne Korpics, Brown Mackie College–Findlay, 1700 Fostoria Avenue, Suite 100, Findlay, OH 45840. *Phone:* 419-423-2211. *Toll-free phone:* 800-842-3687. *Fax:* 419-423-0725. *E-mail:* wkorpiccs@brownmackie.edu.

▶ **See page 502 for the College Close-Up.**

BROWN MACKIE COLLEGE–NORTH CANTON

North Canton, Ohio   **www.socaec.com/**

- **Proprietary** 2-year, founded 1929, part of Educational Management Corporation
- **Suburban** campus
- **Coed,** 1,131 undergraduate students, 100% full-time, 80% women, 20% men

Undergraduates 1,131 full-time. Students come from 1 other state, 25% African American, 1% Hispanic American, 0.4% transferred in.
Freshmen *Admission:* 631 applied, 621 admitted, 621 enrolled.
Faculty *Total:* 41, 29% full-time, 2% with terminal degrees. *Student/faculty ratio:* 21:1.
Majors Accounting technology and bookkeeping; business administration and management; CAD/CADD drafting/design technology; computer systems networking and telecommunications; criminal justice/safety; health/health care administration; industrial electronics technology; legal assistant/paralegal; medical/clinical assistant; pharmacy technician.

Academics *Calendar:* quarters. *Degree:* diplomas and associate. *Special study options:* adult/continuing education programs, advanced placement credit, independent study.

Computers on Campus 65 computers available on campus for general student use. Internet access available.

Student Life *Housing:* college housing not available. *Activities and Organizations:* student-run newspaper. *Student services:* personal/psychological counseling.

Standardized Tests *Required:* ASSET Evaluation (for admission).

Costs (2006–07) *Tuition:* $8592 full-time, $179 per credit part-time. *Required fees:* $480 full-time, $10 per credit part-time.

Applying *Options:* common application. *Required:* high school transcript, interview. *Required for some:* Transcript of GED record. *Application deadline:* rolling (freshmen), rolling (transfers). *Notification:* continuous (freshmen).

Freshmen Application Contact Ms. Crystal Bussell, Brown Mackie College–North Canton, 1320 West Maple Street, NW, North Canton, OH 44720-2854. *Phone:* 330-494-1214. *Fax:* 330-494-8112. *E-mail:* cbussell@brownmackie.edu.

▶ **See page 520 for the College Close-Up.**

BRYANT AND STRATTON COLLEGE
Parma, Ohio   www.bryantstratton.edu/

- **Proprietary** primarily 2-year, founded 1981, part of Bryant and Stratton Business Institute, Inc
- **Suburban** 4-acre campus with easy access to Cleveland
- **Coed,** 329 undergraduate students, 56% full-time, 74% women, 26% men

Undergraduates 183 full-time, 146 part-time. Students come from 1 other state, 25% African American, 0.3% Asian American or Pacific Islander, 13% Hispanic American, 2% transferred in. *Retention:* 33% of 2003 full-time freshmen returned.

Freshmen *Admission:* 83 applied, 135 enrolled.

Faculty *Total:* 35, 20% full-time.

Majors Accounting; administrative assistant and secretarial science; business administration and management; business/commerce; criminal justice/law enforcement administration; human resources management and services related; information technology; legal administrative assistant; medical administrative assistant and medical secretary; medical/clinical assistant; nursing (registered nurse training).

Academics *Calendar:* semesters. *Degrees:* associate and bachelor's. *Special study options:* academic remediation for entering students, cooperative education, distance learning, double majors, independent study, internships, part-time degree program, summer session for credit.

Library Main Library plus 1 other with 1,500 titles, 20 serial subscriptions, an OPAC.

Computers on Campus 96 computers available on campus for general student use. Internet access available.

Student Life *Housing:* college housing not available. *Activities and Organizations:* Business Professionals of America, Association for Computing Machinery, Baccus Gamma. *Campus security:* 24-hour emergency response devices.

Standardized Tests *Required:* CPAt (for admission). *Recommended:* SAT or ACT (for admission).

Costs (2005–06) *Tuition:* $18,675 full-time, $415 per credit hour part-time. *Required fees:* $25 full-time.

Applying *Options:* deferred entrance. *Required:* high school transcript, interview, entrance evaluation and placement evaluation. *Required for some:* letters of recommendation. *Application deadline:* rolling (freshmen), rolling (transfers).

Freshmen Application Contact Mr. F. Lee Nelly, Director of Admissions, Bryant and Stratton College, 12955 Snow Road, Parma, OH 44130. *Phone:* 216-265-3151 Ext. 229. *Toll-free phone:* 800-327-3151. *Fax:* 216-265-0325. *E-mail:* finelly@bryantstratton.edu.

BRYANT AND STRATTON COLLEGE
Willoughby Hills, Ohio   www.bryantstratton.edu/

Freshmen Application Contact Mr. James Pettit, Director of Admissions, Bryant and Stratton College, 27557 Chardon Road, Willoughby Hills, OH 44092. *Phone:* 440-944-6800.

CENTRAL OHIO TECHNICAL COLLEGE
Newark, Ohio   www.cotc.edu/

Freshmen Application Contact Admissions Representative, Central Ohio Technical College, 1179 University Drive, Newark, OH 43055-1767. *Phone:* 740-366-9222. *Toll-free phone:* 800-9NEWARK. *E-mail:* lnelson@bigvax.newark.ohio-state.edu.

CHATFIELD COLLEGE
St. Martin, Ohio   www.chatfield.edu/

- **Independent** 2-year, founded 1970, affiliated with Roman Catholic Church
- **Rural** 200-acre campus with easy access to Cincinnati and Dayton
- **Endowment** $700,000
- **Coed, primarily women,** 230 undergraduate students

Undergraduates Students come from 1 other state, 30% African American. Freshmen *Admission:* 129 applied, 129 admitted.

Faculty *Total:* 43, 7% full-time. *Student/faculty ratio:* 12:1.

Majors Business administration and management; human services; kindergarten/preschool education; liberal arts and sciences/liberal studies.

Academics *Calendar:* semesters. *Degree:* associate. *Special study options:* academic remediation for entering students, adult/continuing education programs, advanced placement credit, internships, off-campus study, part-time degree program, summer session for credit.

Library Chatfield College Library with 15,000 titles, 30 serial subscriptions, an OPAC.

Computers on Campus 16 computers available on campus for general student use. A campuswide network can be accessed from off campus. Internet access, at least one staffed computer lab available.

Student Life *Housing:* college housing not available. *Activities and Organizations:* drama/theater group, student-run newspaper, choral group. *Campus security:* 12-hour night patrols by security. *Student services:* personal/psychological counseling.

Costs (2006–07) *Tuition:* $3360 full-time, $280 per credit hour part-time. *Required fees:* $80 full-time.

Financial Aid Of all full-time matriculated undergraduates who enrolled in 2004, 10 Federal Work-Study jobs (averaging $800). 4 state and other part-time jobs (averaging $600). *Financial aid deadline:* 8/1.

Applying *Options:* common application, early admission, deferred entrance. *Application fee:* $10. *Required:* high school transcript. *Application deadline:* rolling (freshmen), rolling (transfers). *Notification:* continuous (freshmen).

Freshmen Application Contact Ms. Anna Jones, Director of Admissions, Chatfield College, St. Martin, OH 45118. *Phone:* 513-875-3344. *Fax:* 513-875-3912. *E-mail:* chatfield@chatfield.edu.

CINCINNATI COLLEGE OF MORTUARY SCIENCE
Cincinnati, Ohio   www.ccms.edu/

- **Independent** primarily 2-year, founded 1882
- **Urban** 10-acre campus
- **Coed,** 133 undergraduate students, 100% full-time, 46% women, 54% men

Undergraduates 133 full-time. Students come from 17 states and territories, 7% African American, 0.8% Hispanic American, 68% transferred in. Freshmen *Admission:* 12 applied, 12 admitted, 12 enrolled.

Faculty *Total:* 14, 64% full-time. *Student/faculty ratio:* 5:1.

Majors Funeral service and mortuary science.

Academics *Calendar:* quarters. *Degrees:* associate and bachelor's. *Special study options:* academic remediation for entering students, adult/continuing education programs, advanced placement credit, summer session for credit.

Library 5,000 titles, 30 serial subscriptions, a Web page.

Computers on Campus 16 computers available on campus for general student use. At least one staffed computer lab available.

Student Life *Housing:* college housing not available.

Athletics *Intramural sports:* basketball M/W, bowling M/W, football M/W, softball M/W.

Costs (2005–06) *Tuition:* $13,500 full-time, $180 per credit hour part-time.

Cincinnati College of Mortuary Science (continued)
Applying *Options:* deferred entrance. *Application fee:* $25. *Required:* high school transcript. *Recommended:* letters of recommendation. *Application deadline:* rolling (freshmen), rolling (transfers).
Freshmen Application Contact Ms. Pat Leon, Director of Financial Aid, Cincinnati College of Mortuary Science, 645 West North Bend Road, Cincinnati, OH 45224-1462. *Phone:* 513-761-2020.

CINCINNATI STATE TECHNICAL AND COMMUNITY COLLEGE
Cincinnati, Ohio   www.cincinnatistate.edu/

- **State-supported** 2-year, founded 1966, part of Ohio Board of Regents
- **Urban** 46-acre campus
- **Endowment** $1.4 million
- **Coed,** 8,470 undergraduate students, 41% full-time, 57% women, 43% men

Undergraduates 3,485 full-time, 4,985 part-time. Students come from 9 states and territories, 62 other countries, 11% are from out of state, 26% African American, 1% Asian American or Pacific Islander, 0.9% Hispanic American, 0.2% Native American, 3% international. *Retention:* 48% of 2003 full-time freshmen returned.
Freshmen *Admission:* 1,947 enrolled.
Faculty *Total:* 570, 32% full-time. *Student/faculty ratio:* 17:1.
Majors Accounting; administrative assistant and secretarial science; aeronautical/aerospace engineering technology; allied health and medical assisting services related; applied horticulture/horticultural business services related; architectural engineering technology; automotive engineering technology; biomedical technology; business administration and management; business, management, and marketing related; chemical technology; child care provision; cinematography and film/video production; civil engineering technology; clinical/medical laboratory technology; commercial and advertising art; computer and information sciences; computer engineering technology; computer programming; computer programming (specific applications); criminal justice/police science; culinary arts; diagnostic medical sonography and ultrasound technology; dietetics; electrical and electronic engineering technologies related; electrical, electronic and communications engineering technology; electromechanical technology; emergency medical technology (EMT paramedic); entrepreneurship; environmental engineering technology; executive assistant/executive secretary; fire science; general studies; health information/medical records technology; health professions related; heating, air conditioning and refrigeration technology; hotel/motel administration; information science/studies; international business/trade/commerce; landscaping and groundskeeping; laser and optical technology; liberal arts and sciences/liberal studies; management information systems; marketing/marketing management; mechanical engineering/mechanical technology; mechanic and repair technologies related; medical/clinical assistant; nursing (registered nurse training); nursing related; occupational therapist assistant; office management; parks, recreation, and leisure related; plastics engineering technology; purchasing, procurement/acquisitions and contracts management; real estate; respiratory care therapy; restaurant, culinary, and catering management; science technologies related; security and loss prevention; sign language interpretation and translation; surgical technology; survey technology; technical and business writing; telecommunications; turf and turfgrass management.
Academics *Calendar:* 5 ten-week terms. *Degree:* certificates and associate. *Special study options:* academic remediation for entering students, advanced placement credit, cooperative education, distance learning, double majors, English as a second language, honors programs, internships, off-campus study, part-time degree program, services for LD students, student-designed majors, summer session for credit.
Library Johnnie Mae Berry Library with 30,762 titles, 268 serial subscriptions, 3,428 audiovisual materials, an OPAC, a Web page.
Computers on Campus 150 computers available on campus for general student use. A campuswide network can be accessed from off campus. Internet access, online (class) registration, at least one staffed computer lab available.
Student Life *Housing:* college housing not available. *Activities and Organizations:* drama/theater group, student government, Nursing Student Association, Phi Theta Kappa, American Society of Civil Engineers, Students in Free Enterprise. *Campus security:* 24-hour emergency response devices and patrols, late-night transport/escort service. *Student services:* personal/psychological counseling.
Athletics Member NJCAA. *Intercollegiate sports:* basketball M/W, golf M/W, soccer M/W. *Intramural sports:* cheerleading W.
Costs (2006–07) *Tuition:* state resident $4411 full-time, $80 per credit hour part-time; nonresident $8822 full-time, $160 per credit hour part-time. *Required fees:* $344 full-time, $6 per credit hour part-time, $31 per term part-time.
Financial Aid Of all full-time matriculated undergraduates who enrolled in 2004, 100 Federal Work-Study jobs (averaging $3500).

Applying *Options:* electronic application. *Required:* high school transcript. *Application deadline:* rolling (freshmen), rolling (transfers). *Notification:* continuous (freshmen).
Freshmen Application Contact Ms. Gabriele Boeckermann, Director of Admission, Cincinnati State Technical and Community College, 3520 Central Parkway, Cincinnati, OH 45223-2690. *Phone:* 513-569-1550. *Fax:* 513-569-1562. *E-mail:* adm@cincinnatistate.edu.

CLARK STATE COMMUNITY COLLEGE
Springfield, Ohio   www.clarkstate.edu/

- **State-supported** 2-year, founded 1962, part of Ohio Board of Regents
- **Suburban** 60-acre campus with easy access to Columbus and Dayton
- **Coed,** 3,504 undergraduate students, 45% full-time, 69% women, 31% men

Undergraduates 1,583 full-time, 1,921 part-time. 14% African American, 0.7% Asian American or Pacific Islander, 0.7% Hispanic American, 0.4% Native American, 4% transferred in.
Freshmen *Admission:* 1,743 applied, 1,743 admitted, 694 enrolled.
Faculty *Total:* 289, 20% full-time. *Student/faculty ratio:* 16:1.
Majors Accounting; administrative assistant and secretarial science; agricultural business and management; agricultural mechanization; agriculture; business administration and management; civil engineering technology; clinical/medical laboratory technology; commercial and advertising art; computer programming; computer programming related; computer systems networking and telecommunications; computer/technical support; corrections; court reporting; criminal justice/law enforcement administration; criminal justice/police science; drafting and design technology; dramatic/theater arts; electrical, electronic and communications engineering technology; emergency medical technology (EMT paramedic); horticultural science; human services; industrial technology; information science/studies; information technology; kindergarten/preschool education; kinesiology and exercise science; landscaping and groundskeeping; legal assistant/paralegal; liberal arts and sciences/liberal studies; mechanical engineering/mechanical technology; medical administrative assistant and medical secretary; nursing (licensed practical/vocational nurse training); nursing (registered nurse training); physical therapy; social work.
Academics *Calendar:* quarters. *Degree:* certificates and associate. *Special study options:* academic remediation for entering students, adult/continuing education programs, advanced placement credit, cooperative education, distance learning, off-campus study, part-time degree program, services for LD students, summer session for credit. *ROTC:* Army (c).
Library Clark State Community College Library with 31,988 titles, 378 serial subscriptions, an OPAC, a Web page.
Computers on Campus 350 computers available on campus for general student use. A campuswide network can be accessed from off campus. Internet access, at least one staffed computer lab available.
Student Life *Housing:* college housing not available. *Activities and Organizations:* drama/theater group, student-run newspaper, choral group, Student Government Association, Minority Student Forum. *Campus security:* late-night transport/escort service. *Student services:* health clinic, personal/psychological counseling.
Athletics Member NJCAA. *Intercollegiate sports:* basketball M/W, softball W, volleyball W. *Intramural sports:* basketball M/W, tennis M/W, volleyball M/W.
Costs (2006–07) *Tuition:* state resident $3720 full-time, $78 per credit hour part-time; nonresident $7440 full-time, $155 per credit hour part-time. *Required fees:* $1500 full-time.
Applying *Options:* common application, electronic application, early admission, deferred entrance. *Application fee:* $15. *Required:* high school transcript. *Application deadline:* rolling (freshmen), rolling (transfers). *Notification:* continuous (freshmen).
Freshmen Application Contact Ms. Julie Schaid, Director, Enrollment and Precollege Program, Clark State Community College, PO Box 570, Springfield, OH 45501-0570. *Phone:* 937-328-6027. *Fax:* 937-328-3853. *E-mail:* admissions@clarkstate.edu.

CLEVELAND INSTITUTE OF ELECTRONICS
Cleveland, Ohio   www.cie-wc.edu/

- **Proprietary** 2-year, founded 1934
- **Coed, primarily men,** 2,602 undergraduate students

Undergraduates Students come from 52 states and territories, 70 other countries, 97% are from out of state.

Faculty *Total:* 6, 50% full-time.

Majors Electrical, electronic and communications engineering technology.

Academics *Calendar:* continuous. *Degrees:* associate (offers only external degree programs conducted through home study). *Special study options:* adult/continuing education programs, external degree program, part-time degree program.

Library 5,000 titles, 38 serial subscriptions.

Student Life *Housing:* college housing not available.

Costs (2005–06) *Tuition:* $1770 per term part-time.

Applying *Options:* common application, electronic application, early admission. *Required:* high school transcript. *Application deadline:* rolling (freshmen), rolling (transfers). *Notification:* continuous (freshmen).

Freshmen Application Contact Mr. Scott Katzenmeyer, Registrar, Cleveland Institute of Electronics, 1776 East 17th Street, Cleveland, OH 44114. *Phone:* 216-781-9400. *Toll-free phone:* 800-243-6446. *Fax:* 216-781-0331. *E-mail:* instruct@cie-wc.edu.

COLLEGE OF ART ADVERTISING

Cincinnati, Ohio   www.collegeofartadvertising.com/

Director of Admissions Ms. Janet Bussberg, Director of Admissions, College of Art Advertising, 4343 Bridgetown Road, Cincinnati, OH 45211-4427. *Phone:* 937-294-0592. *E-mail:* janet.bussberg@fuse.net.

COLUMBUS STATE COMMUNITY COLLEGE

Columbus, Ohio   www.cscc.edu/

- **State-supported** 2-year, founded 1963, part of Ohio Board of Regents
- **Urban** 75-acre campus
- **Coed**

Undergraduates 8,530 full-time, 13,342 part-time. Students come from 41 states and territories, 127 other countries, 1% are from out of state, 23% African American, 3% Asian American or Pacific Islander, 2% Hispanic American, 0.5% Native American, 0.8% international, 3% transferred in. *Retention:* 48% of 2003 full-time freshmen returned.

Faculty *Student/faculty ratio:* 19:1.

Academics *Calendar:* quarters. *Degree:* certificates and associate. *Special study options:* academic remediation for entering students, adult/continuing education programs, advanced placement credit, cooperative education, distance learning, English as a second language, honors programs, internships, off-campus study, part-time degree program, services for LD students, student-designed majors, summer session for credit. *ROTC:* Army (b), Air Force (c).

Student Life *Campus security:* 24-hour emergency response devices and patrols, late-night transport/escort service.

Athletics Member NJCAA.

Standardized Tests *Required:* ACT COMPASS (for placement).

Costs (2005–06) *One-time required fee:* $35. *Tuition:* state resident $2736 full-time, $76 per credit part-time; nonresident $6048 full-time, $168 per credit part-time.

Financial Aid Of all full-time matriculated undergraduates who enrolled in 2004, 133 Federal Work-Study jobs (averaging $1500).

Applying *Options:* common application, early admission, deferred entrance. *Application fee:* $10. *Recommended:* high school transcript.

Director of Admissions Mr. Kenneth Conner, Dean of Enrollment Services, Columbus State Community College, 550 East Spring Street, Madison Hall, Columbus, OH 43215. *Phone:* 614-287-2669 Ext. 3669. *Toll-free phone:* 800-621-6407 Ext. 2669. *Fax:* 614-287-6019. *E-mail:* kconner@cscc.edu.

CUYAHOGA COMMUNITY COLLEGE

Cleveland, Ohio   www.tri-c.edu/

- **State and locally supported** 2-year, founded 1963
- **Urban** campus
- **Coed,** 25,358 undergraduate students, 41% full-time, 63% women, 37% men

Undergraduates 10,326 full-time, 15,032 part-time. Students come from 21 states and territories, 63 other countries, 30% African American, 2% Asian

American or Pacific Islander, 4% Hispanic American, 0.6% Native American, 2% international, 3% transferred in.

Freshmen *Admission:* 8,438 applied, 8,438 admitted, 2,251 enrolled.

Faculty *Total:* 1,504, 20% full-time, 5% with terminal degrees. *Student/faculty ratio:* 18:1.

Majors Accounting; administrative assistant and secretarial science; automobile/automotive mechanics technology; avionics maintenance technology; business administration and management; clinical laboratory science/medical technology; commercial and advertising art; computer engineering technology; computer typography and composition equipment operation; court reporting; criminal justice/police science; engineering technology; finance; fire science; industrial radiologic technology; kindergarten/preschool education; legal assistant/paralegal; liberal arts and sciences/liberal studies; marketing/marketing management; merchandising; nursing (registered nurse training); opticianry; photography; physician assistant; real estate; respiratory care therapy; restaurant, culinary, and catering management; safety/security technology; sales, distribution and marketing; selling skills and sales; surgical technology; veterinary technology.

Academics *Calendar:* semesters. *Degree:* certificates and associate. *Special study options:* adult/continuing education programs, advanced placement credit, cooperative education, distance learning, English as a second language, external degree program, independent study, part-time degree program, services for LD students, summer session for credit.

Library 177,767 titles, 1,135 serial subscriptions, an OPAC, a Web page.

Computers on Campus 1275 computers available on campus for general student use. A campuswide network can be accessed from off campus. Internet access, at least one staffed computer lab available.

Student Life *Housing:* college housing not available. *Activities and Organizations:* drama/theater group, student-run newspaper, choral group, Student Senate, Student Nursing Organization, Business Focus, Phi Theta Kappa. *Campus security:* 24-hour emergency response devices and patrols, late-night transport/escort service. *Student services:* health clinic, personal/psychological counseling.

Athletics Member NJCAA. *Intercollegiate sports:* baseball M(s), basketball M(s), cross-country running M(s)/W(s), soccer M(s), softball W(s). *Intramural sports:* basketball M, tennis M/W, track and field M/W, volleyball M/W.

Costs (2005–06) *Tuition:* area resident $2416 full-time, $81 per credit hour part-time; state resident $3194 full-time, $106 per credit hour part-time; nonresident $6541 full-time, $218 per credit hour part-time.

Financial Aid Of all full-time matriculated undergraduates who enrolled in 2004, 802 Federal Work-Study jobs (averaging $3300).

Applying *Options:* early admission, deferred entrance. *Required for some:* high school transcript. *Application deadline:* rolling (freshmen), rolling (transfers). *Notification:* continuous (freshmen).

Freshmen Application Contact Mr. Kevin McDaniel, Director of Admissions and Records, Cuyahoga Community College, 2900 Community College Avenue, Cleveland, OH 44115. *Phone:* 216-987-4030. *Toll-free phone:* 800-954-8742. *Fax:* 216-696-2567.

DAVIS COLLEGE

Toledo, Ohio   daviscollege.edu/

- **Proprietary** 2-year, founded 1858
- **Urban** 1-acre campus with easy access to Detroit
- **Coed,** 451 undergraduate students, 50% full-time, 85% women, 15% men

Undergraduates 225 full-time, 226 part-time. Students come from 2 states and territories, 5% are from out of state, 29% African American, 2% Hispanic American, 0.5% Native American, 26% transferred in.

Freshmen *Admission:* 72 applied, 72 admitted, 72 enrolled.

Faculty *Total:* 23, 61% full-time, 4% with terminal degrees. *Student/faculty ratio:* 14:1.

Majors Accounting; administrative assistant and secretarial science; business administration and management; commercial and advertising art; computer systems networking and telecommunications; data processing and data processing technology; fashion merchandising; information technology; interior design; legal administrative assistant/secretary; medical administrative assistant and medical secretary; medical/clinical assistant; system administration; web page, digital/multimedia and information resources design.

Academics *Calendar:* quarters. *Degree:* diplomas and associate. *Special study options:* academic remediation for entering students, adult/continuing education programs, advanced placement credit, distance learning, internships, part-time degree program, summer session for credit.

Library Davis College Resource Center with 3,207 titles, 164 serial subscriptions, 341 audiovisual materials, an OPAC.

Computers on Campus 78 computers available on campus for general student use. Internet access, at least one staffed computer lab available.

Davis College (continued)

Student Life *Housing:* college housing not available. *Activities and Organizations:* Student Advisory Board. *Campus security:* 24-hour emergency response devices, security cameras for parking lot. *Student services:* personal/psychological counseling.

Standardized Tests *Required:* CPAt (for admission).

Costs (2006–07) *Tuition:* $8100 full-time, $225 per credit hour part-time. *Required fees:* $480 full-time.

Financial Aid Of all full-time matriculated undergraduates who enrolled in 2004, 10 Federal Work-Study jobs (averaging $3500).

Applying *Options:* common application, electronic application, early admission, deferred entrance. *Application fee:* $30. *Required:* high school transcript, interview. *Application deadline:* rolling (freshmen), rolling (transfers). *Notification:* continuous (freshmen).

Freshmen Application Contact Ms. Dana Stern, Davis College, 4747 Monroe Street, Toledo, OH 43623-4307. *Phone:* 419-473-2700. *Toll-free phone:* 800-477-7021. *Fax:* 419-473-2472. *E-mail:* dstern@daviscollege.edu.

EDISON STATE COMMUNITY COLLEGE

Piqua, Ohio www.edisonohio.edu/

- **State-supported** 2-year, founded 1973, part of Ohio Board of Regents
- **Small-town** 130-acre campus with easy access to Cincinnati and Dayton
- **Coed**

Undergraduates 1,028 full-time, 1,972 part-time. Students come from 5 states and territories, 2% African American, 0.7% Asian American or Pacific Islander, 0.5% Hispanic American, 0.3% Native American, 4% transferred in.

Faculty *Student/faculty ratio:* 19:1.

Academics *Calendar:* semesters. *Degree:* certificates and associate. *Special study options:* academic remediation for entering students, accelerated degree program, adult/continuing education programs, advanced placement credit, distance learning, double majors, independent study, internships, off-campus study, part-time degree program, services for LD students, student-designed majors, summer session for credit. *ROTC:* Army (c), Air Force (c).

Student Life *Campus security:* late-night transport/escort service, 18-hour patrols by trained security personnel.

Athletics Member NJCAA.

Standardized Tests *Required for some:* SAT or ACT (for placement), ACT ASSET, ACT COMPASS. *Recommended:* ACT ASSET, ACT COMPASS.

Financial Aid Of all full-time matriculated undergraduates who enrolled in 2004, 42 Federal Work-Study jobs (averaging $3000).

Applying *Options:* electronic application, early admission, deferred entrance. *Application fee:* $15. *Required:* high school transcript.

Director of Admissions Ms. Beth Iams Culbertson, Director of Admissions, Edison State Community College, 1973 Edison Drive, Piqua, OH 45356. *Phone:* 937-778-8600 Ext. 317. *Toll-free phone:* 800-922-3722. *Fax:* 937-778-4692. *E-mail:* info@edison.cc.oh.us.

ETI TECHNICAL COLLEGE OF NILES

Niles, Ohio www.eti-college.com/

Director of Admissions Ms. Diane Marstellar, Director of Admissions, ETI Technical College of Niles, 2076 Youngstown-Warren Road, Niles, OH 44446-4398. *Phone:* 330-652-9919.

GALLIPOLIS CAREER COLLEGE

Gallipolis, Ohio www.gallipoliscareercollege.com/

- **Independent** 2-year, founded 1962
- **Small-town** campus
- **Coed, primarily women,** 154 undergraduate students, 94% full-time, 83% women, 17% men

Undergraduates 145 full-time, 9 part-time. Students come from 2 states and territories, 13% are from out of state, 9% African American.

Freshmen *Admission:* 25 enrolled.

Faculty *Total:* 16, 13% full-time. *Student/faculty ratio:* 22:1.

Majors Accounting; administrative assistant and secretarial science; business administration and management; business/commerce; computer science; com-

puter software and media applications related; computer/technical support; data entry/microcomputer applications; medical administrative assistant and medical secretary.

Academics *Calendar:* quarters. *Degree:* certificates, diplomas, and associate. *Special study options:* academic remediation for entering students, adult/continuing education programs, double majors, independent study, internships, part-time degree program, summer session for credit.

Library Gallipolis Career College Library with 94 audiovisual materials.

Computers on Campus 28 computers available on campus for general student use. A campuswide network can be accessed. Internet access, at least one staffed computer lab available.

Student Life *Housing:* college housing not available.

Standardized Tests *Required:* Wonderlic aptitude test (for admission).

Costs (2005–06) *Tuition:* $8640 full-time, $180 per credit hour part-time. No tuition increase for student's term of enrollment. *Required fees:* $100 full-time. *Waivers:* employees or children of employees.

Applying *Application fee:* $50. *Required:* high school transcript, interview. *Application deadline:* rolling (freshmen), rolling (transfers).

Freshmen Application Contact Mr. Jack Henson, Director of Admissions, Gallipolis Career College, 1176 Jackson Pike, Suite 312, Gallipolis, OH 45631. *Phone:* 740-440-1124. *Toll-free phone:* 800-214-0452. *Fax:* 740-440-1124. *E-mail:* admissions@gallipaliscareercollege.com.

HOCKING COLLEGE

Nelsonville, Ohio www.hocking.edu/

Director of Admissions Ms. Lyn Hull, Director of Admissions, Hocking College, 3301 Hocking Parkway, Nelsonville, OH 45764-9588. *Phone:* 740-753-3591 Ext. 2803. *Toll-free phone:* 800-282-4163. *E-mail:* hull_lyn@hocking.edu.

HONDROS COLLEGE

Westerville, Ohio www.hondroscollege.com/

Director of Admissions Ms. Carol Thomas, Operations Manager, Hondros College, 4140 Executive Parkway, Westerville, OH 43081. *Phone:* 614-508-7244. *Toll-free phone:* 800-783-0095.

INTERNATIONAL COLLEGE OF BROADCASTING

Dayton, Ohio www.icbcollege.com/

- **Private** 2-year
- **Urban** 1-acre campus
- **Coed**
- **67% of applicants were admitted**

Undergraduates 87 full-time. 31% African American, 1% Hispanic American.

Faculty *Student/faculty ratio:* 10:1.

Academics *Calendar:* semesters. *Degree:* diplomas and associate.

Director of Admissions Mr. Aan McIntosh, Director of Admissions, International College of Broadcasting, 6 South Smithville Road, Dayton, OH 45431. *Phone:* 937-258-8251. *Fax:* 937-258-8714.

ITT TECHNICAL INSTITUTE

Dayton, Ohio www.itt-tech.edu/

- **Proprietary** 2-year, founded 1935, part of ITT Educational Services, Inc
- **Suburban** 7-acre campus
- **Coed**

Majors Accounting and business/management; business administration and management; CAD/CADD drafting/design technology; computer programming; criminal justice/law enforcement administration; electrical, electronic and communications engineering technology; system, networking, and LAN/WAN management; web/multimedia management and webmaster; web page, digital/multimedia and information resources design.

Academics *Calendar:* quarters. *Degree:* associate.
Library a Web page.
Computers on Campus Internet access, at least one staffed computer lab available.
Student Life *Housing:* college housing not available.
Standardized Tests *Required:* Wonderlic aptitude test (for admission).
Costs (2005–06) *Tuition:* Please see school catalog for specific information.
Applying *Options:* deferred entrance. *Application fee:* $100. *Required:* high school transcript, interview. *Recommended:* letters of recommendation. *Application deadline:* rolling (freshmen), rolling (transfers). *Notification:* continuous (freshmen).
Freshmen Application Contact Mr. Joe G. Graham, Director of Recruitment, ITT Technical Institute, 3325 Stop 8 Road, Dayton, OH 45414. *Phone:* 937-454-2267. *Toll-free phone:* 800-568-3241.

ITT TECHNICAL INSTITUTE
Hilliard, Ohio — www.itt-tech.edu/

- **Proprietary** 2-year, founded 2003
- **Coed**

Majors Accounting and business/management; business administration and management; CAD/CADD drafting/design technology; criminal justice/law enforcement administration; electrical, electronic and communications engineering technology; system, networking, and LAN/WAN management; web page, digital/multimedia and information resources design.
Academics *Calendar:* quarters. *Degree:* associate.
Standardized Tests *Required:* Wonderlic aptitude test (for admission).
Costs (2005–06) *Tuition:* Please see school catalog for specific information.
Applying *Application fee:* $100. *Required:* high school transcript, interview. *Recommended:* letters of recommendation. *Application deadline:* rolling (freshmen), rolling (transfers). *Notification:* continuous (freshmen).
Freshmen Application Contact Mr. Jim Tussing, Director of Recruitment, ITT Technical Institute, 3781 Park Mill Run Drive, Hilliard, OH 43026. *Phone:* 614-771-4888. *Toll-free phone:* 888-483-4888.

ITT TECHNICAL INSTITUTE
Norwood, Ohio — www.itt-tech.edu/

- **Proprietary** 2-year, part of ITT Educational Services, Inc
- **Coed**

Majors Accounting and business/management; business administration and management; CAD/CADD drafting/design technology; computer programming; criminal justice/law enforcement administration; electrical, electronic and communications engineering technology; system, networking, and LAN/WAN management; web/multimedia management and webmaster; web page, digital/multimedia and information resources design.
Academics *Calendar:* quarters. *Degree:* associate.
Library a Web page.
Computers on Campus Internet access, at least one staffed computer lab available.
Student Life *Housing:* college housing not available.
Standardized Tests *Required:* Wonderlic aptitude test (for admission).
Costs (2005–06) *Tuition:* Please see school catalog for specific information.
Applying *Options:* deferred entrance. *Application fee:* $100. *Required:* high school transcript, interview. *Recommended:* letters of recommendation. *Application deadline:* rolling (freshmen), rolling (transfers). *Notification:* continuous (freshmen).
Freshmen Application Contact Mr. Greg Hitt, Director of Recruitment, ITT Technical Institute, 4750 Wesley Avenue, Norwood, OH 45212. *Phone:* 513-531-8300. *Toll-free phone:* 800-314-8324.

ITT TECHNICAL INSTITUTE
Strongsville, Ohio — www.itt-tech.edu/

- **Proprietary** 2-year, part of ITT Educational Services, Inc
- **Coed**

Majors Accounting and business/management; business administration and management; CAD/CADD drafting/design technology; computer programming; criminal justice/law enforcement administration; electrical, electronic and communications engineering technology; system, networking, and LAN/WAN management; web/multimedia management and webmaster; web page, digital/multimedia and information resources design.
Academics *Calendar:* quarters. *Degree:* associate.
Library a Web page.
Computers on Campus Internet access, at least one staffed computer lab available.
Student Life *Housing:* college housing not available.
Standardized Tests *Required:* Wonderlic aptitude test (for admission).
Costs (2005–06) *Tuition:* Please see school catalog for specific information.
Applying *Options:* deferred entrance. *Application fee:* $100. *Required:* high school transcript, interview. *Recommended:* letters of recommendation. *Application deadline:* rolling (freshmen), rolling (transfers). *Notification:* continuous (freshmen).
Freshmen Application Contact Ms. Joanne M. Dyer, Director of Recruitment, ITT Technical Institute, 14955 Sprague Road, Strongsville, OH 44136. *Phone:* 440-234-9091. *Toll-free phone:* 800-331-1488.

ITT TECHNICAL INSTITUTE
Warrensville Heights, Ohio — www.itt-tech.edu/

- **2-year**
- **Coed**

Majors Business administration and management; CAD/CADD drafting/design technology; criminal justice/law enforcement administration; electrical, electronic and communications engineering technology; system, networking, and LAN/WAN management; web page, digital/multimedia and information resources design.
Academics *Calendar:* quarters. *Degree:* associate.
Standardized Tests *Required:* Wonderlic aptitude test (for admission).
Costs (2005–06) *Tuition:* Please see school catalog for specific information.
Applying *Application fee:* $100. *Required:* high school transcript, interview. *Recommended:* letters of recommendation. *Application deadline:* rolling (freshmen), rolling (transfers). *Notification:* continuous (freshmen).
Freshmen Application Contact Mr. Erik Andryszak, Director of Recruitment, ITT Technical Institute, 4700 Richmond Road, Warrensville Heights, OH 44128. *Phone:* 216-896-6500. *Toll-free phone:* 800-741-3494.

ITT TECHNICAL INSTITUTE
Youngstown, Ohio — www.itt-tech.edu/

- **Proprietary** 2-year, founded 1967, part of ITT Educational Services, Inc
- **Suburban** campus with easy access to Cleveland and Pittsburgh
- **Coed**

Majors CAD/CADD drafting/design technology; computer and information systems security; computer programming; system, networking, and LAN/WAN management; web/multimedia management and webmaster; web page, digital/multimedia and information resources design.
Academics *Calendar:* quarters. *Degree:* associate.
Library a Web page.
Computers on Campus Internet access, at least one staffed computer lab available.
Student Life *Housing:* college housing not available. *Activities and Organizations:* student-run newspaper.
Standardized Tests *Required:* Wonderlic aptitude test (for admission).
Costs (2005–06) *Tuition:* Please see school catalog for specific information.
Financial Aid Of all full-time matriculated undergraduates who enrolled in 2004, 5 Federal Work-Study jobs (averaging $3979).
Applying *Options:* deferred entrance. *Application fee:* $100. *Required:* high school transcript, interview. *Recommended:* letters of recommendation. *Application deadline:* rolling (freshmen), rolling (transfers). *Notification:* continuous (freshmen).
Freshmen Application Contact Mr. Mike Bishop, Director of Recruitment, ITT Technical Institute, 1030 North Meridian Road, Youngstown, OH 44509. *Phone:* 330-270-1600. *Toll-free phone:* 800-832-5001.

JAMES A. RHODES STATE COLLEGE

Lima, Ohio   www.rhodesstate.edu/

Freshmen Application Contact Mr. Scot Lingrell, Director, Student Advising and Development, James A. Rhodes State College, 4240 Campus Drive, Lima, OH 45804-3597. *Phone:* 419-995-8050. *E-mail:* peterl@ltc.tec.oh.us.

JEFFERSON COMMUNITY COLLEGE

Steubenville, Ohio   www.jcc.edu/

- **State and locally supported** 2-year, founded 1966, part of Ohio Board of Regents
- **Small-town** 83-acre campus with easy access to Pittsburgh
- **Endowment** $197,077
- **Coed,** 1,697 undergraduate students, 54% full-time, 62% women, 38% men

Undergraduates 911 full-time, 786 part-time. Students come from 23 states and territories, 16% are from out of state, 5% African American, 0.8% Asian American or Pacific Islander, 0.9% Hispanic American, 0.1% Native American, 28% transferred in.
Freshmen *Admission:* 879 applied, 879 admitted, 450 enrolled. *Average high school GPA:* 2.53.
Faculty *Total:* 124, 28% full-time, 6% with terminal degrees. *Student/faculty ratio:* 16:1.
Majors Accounting; administrative assistant and secretarial science; business administration and management; child care and support services management; computer engineering related; consumer merchandising/retailing management; corrections; criminal justice/police science; data processing and data processing technology; dental assisting; developmental and child psychology; drafting and design technology; electrical, electronic and communications engineering technology; emergency medical technology (EMT paramedic); finance; industrial radiologic technology; industrial technology; legal administrative assistant/secretary; mechanical engineering/mechanical technology; medical administrative assistant and medical secretary; medical/clinical assistant; nursing (licensed practical/vocational nurse training); real estate; respiratory care therapy; special products marketing.
Academics *Calendar:* semesters. *Degree:* certificates and associate. *Special study options:* academic remediation for entering students, adult/continuing education programs, internships, off-campus study, part-time degree program, services for LD students, summer session for credit.
Library Jefferson Community College Library with 12,500 titles, 180 serial subscriptions, 246 audiovisual materials, an OPAC.
Computers on Campus 325 computers available on campus for general student use. At least one staffed computer lab available.
Student Life *Housing:* college housing not available. *Activities and Organizations:* Student Senate, SADD, AITP (Association for Information Technology Professionals), American Drafting and Design Association, Writers Club. *Campus security:* student patrols.
Athletics *Intercollegiate sports:* basketball M/W. *Intramural sports:* basketball M/W, bowling M/W, football M/W, softball M/W, tennis M/W, volleyball M/W.
Standardized Tests *Required for some:* SAT or ACT (for admission).
Costs (2005–06) *Tuition:* area resident $2550 full-time, $85 per credit part-time; state resident $2730 full-time, $91 per credit part-time; nonresident $3450 full-time, $115 per credit part-time. Full-time tuition and fees vary according to reciprocity agreements. Part-time tuition and fees vary according to reciprocity agreements. *Required fees:* $600 full-time. *Payment plan:* deferred payment. *Waivers:* senior citizens and employees or children of employees.
Financial Aid Of all full-time matriculated undergraduates who enrolled in 2004, 30 Federal Work-Study jobs (averaging $1500).
Applying *Options:* early admission, deferred entrance. *Application fee:* $20. *Required for some:* high school transcript. *Application deadlines:* 8/20 (freshmen), 8/20 (transfers). *Notification:* continuous until 8/20 (freshmen).
Freshmen Application Contact Mr. Chuck Mascellino, Director of Admissions, Jefferson Community College, 4000 Sunset Boulevard, Steubenville, OH 43952. *Phone:* 740-264-5591 Ext. 142. *Toll-free phone:* 800-68-COLLEGE Ext. 142. *Fax:* 740-266-2944.

KENT STATE UNIVERSITY, ASHTABULA CAMPUS

Ashtabula, Ohio   www.ashtabula.kent.edu/

Director of Admissions Ms. Kelly Sanford, Director, Enrollment Management and Student Services, Kent State University, Ashtabula Campus, 3325 West 13th Street, Ashtabula, OH 44004-2299. *Phone:* 440-964-4217. *E-mail:* sanford@ashtabula.kent.edu.

KENT STATE UNIVERSITY, EAST LIVERPOOL CAMPUS

East Liverpool, Ohio   www.kenteliv.kent.edu/

Director of Admissions Mrs. Jamie Kenneally, Director of Enrollment Management and Student Services, Kent State University, East Liverpool Campus, 400 East Fourth Street, East Liverpool, OH 43920. *Phone:* 330-382-7414. *E-mail:* admissions@eliv.kent.edu.

KENT STATE UNIVERSITY, GEAUGA CAMPUS

Burton, Ohio   www.geauga.kent.edu/

- **State-supported** founded 1964, part of Kent State University System
- **Rural** 87-acre campus with easy access to Cleveland
- **Coed,** 918 undergraduate students, 34% full-time, 56% women, 44% men

Undergraduates 315 full-time, 603 part-time. Students come from 6 states and territories, 2 other countries, 1% are from out of state, 6% African American, 0.8% Asian American or Pacific Islander, 1% Hispanic American, 0.3% Native American, 0.4% international, 0.7% transferred in.
Freshmen *Admission:* 172 applied, 172 admitted, 126 enrolled. *Test scores:* SAT verbal scores over 500: 35%; SAT math scores over 500: 42%; ACT scores over 18: 67%; SAT verbal scores over 600: 8%; SAT math scores over 600: 4%; ACT scores over 24: 8%.
Faculty *Total:* 87, 15% full-time, 15% with terminal degrees. *Student/faculty ratio:* 14:1.
Majors Accounting technology and bookkeeping; applied horticulture; business administration and management; emergency medical technology (EMT paramedic); industrial technology; information technology; liberal arts and sciences/liberal studies; nursing science.
Academics *Calendar:* semesters. *Degrees:* certificates, diplomas, associate, and bachelor's. *Special study options:* academic remediation for entering students, adult/continuing education programs, advanced placement credit, distance learning, double majors, internships, part-time degree program, services for LD students, student-designed majors, summer session for credit. *ROTC:* Army (c), Air Force (c).
Library Kent State University Library with 8,300 titles, 6,600 serial subscriptions, an OPAC, a Web page.
Computers on Campus 50 computers available on campus for general student use. Internet access, at least one staffed computer lab available.
Student Life *Housing:* college housing not available. *Activities and Organizations:* student-run newspaper, Computer Club, Student Senate, Accounting Club, student newspaper. *Campus security:* 24-hour emergency response devices.
Athletics *Intramural sports:* basketball M/W, skiing (downhill) M/W, table tennis M/W, volleyball M/W.
Costs (2006–07) *Tuition:* $217 per credit hour part-time; state resident $4770 full-time, $217 per credit hour part-time; nonresident $12,202 full-time, $555 per credit hour part-time.
Financial Aid Of all full-time matriculated undergraduates who enrolled in 2004, 192 applied for aid, 165 were judged to have need, 11 had their need fully met. 11 Federal Work-Study jobs (averaging $1554). In 2004, 2 non-need-based awards were made. *Average percent of need met:* 51%. *Average financial aid package:* $5407. *Average need-based loan:* $3202. *Average need-based gift aid:* $3524. *Average non-need-based aid:* $1500. *Average indebtedness upon graduation:* $16,266.
Applying *Options:* early admission, deferred entrance. *Application fee:* $30. *Required:* high school transcript. *Application deadline:* rolling (freshmen), rolling (transfers).
Freshmen Application Contact Ms. Betty Landrus, Kent State University, Geauga Campus, 14111 Claridon-Troy Road, Burton, OH 44021. *Phone:* 440-834-4187. *Fax:* 440-834-8846. *E-mail:* blandrus@kent.edu.

KENT STATE UNIVERSITY, SALEM CAMPUS

Salem, Ohio   www.salem.kent.edu/

Freshmen Application Contact Mrs. Judy Heisler, Admissions Secretary, Kent State University, Salem Campus, 2491 State Route 45 South, Salem, OH 44460-9412. *Phone:* 330-332-0361 Ext. 74201. *E-mail:* ask-us@salem.kent.edu.

KENT STATE UNIVERSITY, STARK CAMPUS

Canton, Ohio   www.stark.kent.edu/

Freshmen Application Contact Ms. Deborah Ann Speck, Director of Admissions, Kent State University, Stark Campus, 6000 Frank Avenue NW, Canton, OH 44720-7599. *Phone:* 330-499-9600 Ext. 53259.

KENT STATE UNIVERSITY, TRUMBULL CAMPUS

Warren, Ohio   www.trumbull.kent.edu/

- **State-supported** primarily 2-year, founded 1954, part of Kent State University System
- **Suburban** 200-acre campus with easy access to Cleveland
- **Coed,** 2,036 undergraduate students, 44% full-time, 63% women, 37% men

Undergraduates 893 full-time, 1,143 part-time. Students come from 4 states and territories, 1% are from out of state, 12% African American, 0.4% Asian American or Pacific Islander, 1% Hispanic American, 0.3% Native American, 0.1% international. *Retention:* 58% of 2003 full-time freshmen returned.
Freshmen *Admission:* 432 applied, 432 admitted, 315 enrolled. *Average high school GPA:* 2.75. *Test scores:* SAT verbal scores over 500: 60%; SAT math scores over 500: 56%; ACT scores over 18: 83%; SAT verbal scores over 600: 17%; SAT math scores over 600: 18%; ACT scores over 24: 24%; SAT verbal scores over 700: 1%; SAT math scores over 700: 3%; ACT scores over 30: 2%.
Faculty *Total:* 124, 47% full-time, 35% with terminal degrees. *Student/faculty ratio:* 16:1.
Majors Automobile/automotive mechanics technology; business administration and management; computer engineering technology; criminal justice/law enforcement administration; electrical, electronic and communications engineering technology; English; environmental engineering technology; general studies; industrial technology; liberal arts and sciences/liberal studies; mechanical engineering/mechanical technology; nursing science.
Academics *Calendar:* semesters. *Degrees:* certificates, associate, and bachelor's (also offers some upper-level and graduate courses). *Special study options:* academic remediation for entering students, adult/continuing education programs, advanced placement credit, cooperative education, distance learning, freshman honors college, honors programs, independent study, internships, part-time degree program, services for LD students, student-designed majors, summer session for credit. *ROTC:* Army (c), Air Force (c).
Library Trumbull Campus Library with 65,951 titles, 759 serial subscriptions, an OPAC, a Web page.
Computers on Campus 300 computers available on campus for general student use. Internet access, at least one staffed computer lab available.
Student Life *Housing:* college housing not available. *Activities and Organizations:* drama/theater group, student-run newspaper, Student Senate, Trumbull Environmental Club, Union Activities Board, Gamemasters, Kent Christian Fellowship. *Campus security:* 24-hour emergency response devices, late-night transport/escort service, patrols by trained security personnel during open hours.
Athletics *Intramural sports:* basketball M/W, bowling M/W, skiing (downhill) M/W, volleyball M/W.
Costs (2006–07) *Tuition:* state resident $4770 full-time, $217 per credit hour part-time; nonresident $12,202 full-time, $555 per credit hour part-time.
Financial Aid Of all full-time matriculated undergraduates who enrolled in 2004, 31 Federal Work-Study jobs (averaging $2708).
Applying *Options:* early admission, deferred entrance. *Application fee:* $30. *Required:* high school transcript. *Application deadline:* 7/30 (freshmen), rolling (transfers). *Notification:* continuous until 8/30 (freshmen).

Freshmen Application Contact Ms. Patricia Davis, Clerical Specialist, Kent State University, Trumbull Campus, 4314 Mahoning Avenue, NW, Warren, OH 44483-1998. *Phone:* 330-847-0571 Ext. 2367. *Fax:* 330-847-6571. *E-mail:* info@trumbull.kent.edu.

KENT STATE UNIVERSITY, TUSCARAWAS CAMPUS

New Philadelphia, Ohio   www.tusc.kent.edu/

- **State-supported** primarily 2-year, founded 1962, part of Kent State University System
- **Small-town** 172-acre campus with easy access to Cleveland
- **Coed,** 1,905 undergraduate students, 49% full-time, 63% women, 37% men

Undergraduates 935 full-time, 970 part-time. 1% African American, 0.3% Asian American or Pacific Islander, 0.6% Hispanic American, 0.2% Native American, 0.2% international.
Freshmen *Admission:* 513 applied, 330 enrolled. *Test scores:* SAT verbal scores over 500: 29%; SAT math scores over 500: 43%; ACT scores over 18: 75%; SAT verbal scores over 600: 29%; ACT scores over 24: 20%; ACT scores over 30: 2%.
Faculty *Total:* 122, 39% full-time, 25% with terminal degrees. *Student/faculty ratio:* 18:1.
Majors Accounting; administrative assistant and secretarial science; animation, interactive technology, video graphics and special effects; business administration and management; communications technology; computer engineering technology; criminal justice/police science; early childhood education; electrical, electronic and communications engineering technology; engineering technology; environmental studies; industrial technology; liberal arts and sciences/liberal studies; mechanical engineering/mechanical technology; nursing (registered nurse training); plastics engineering technology.
Academics *Calendar:* semesters. *Degrees:* certificates, diplomas, associate, bachelor's, and master's (also offers some upper-level and graduate courses). *Special study options:* academic remediation for entering students, accelerated degree program, adult/continuing education programs, advanced placement credit, distance learning, double majors, freshman honors college, honors programs, internships, part-time degree program, services for LD students, student-designed majors, summer session for credit. *ROTC:* Army (c), Air Force (c).
Library Tuscarawas Campus Library with 62,783 titles, 250 serial subscriptions, 800 audiovisual materials, an OPAC, a Web page.
Computers on Campus 194 computers available on campus for general student use. A campuswide network can be accessed from off campus. Internet access, online (class) registration, at least one staffed computer lab available.
Student Life *Housing:* college housing not available. *Activities and Organizations:* choral group, Society of Mechanical Engineers, IEEE, Imagineers, Criminal Justice Club, Salt and Light.
Athletics *Intramural sports:* basketball M/W, volleyball M/W.
Standardized Tests *Required:* SAT and SAT Subject Tests or ACT (for admission).
Costs (2005–06) *Tuition:* state resident $2637 full-time; nonresident $6353 full-time.
Financial Aid Of all full-time matriculated undergraduates who enrolled in 2004, 26 Federal Work-Study jobs (averaging $2699).
Applying *Options:* common application, early admission, deferred entrance. *Application fee:* $30. *Required:* high school transcript. *Application deadlines:* 9/1 (freshmen), 9/1 (transfers). *Notification:* continuous (freshmen).
Freshmen Application Contact Ms. Denise Testa, Director of Admissions, Kent State University, Tuscarawas Campus, 330 University Drive NE, New Philadelphia, OH 44663-9403. *Phone:* 330-339-3391 Ext. 47425. *Fax:* 330-339-3321.

KETTERING COLLEGE OF MEDICAL ARTS

Kettering, Ohio   www.kcma.edu/

Director of Admissions Mr. David Lofthouse, Director of Enrollment Services, Kettering College of Medical Arts, 3737 Southern Boulevard, Kettering, OH 45429-1299. *Phone:* 937-296-7228. *Toll-free phone:* 800-433-5262.

LAKELAND COMMUNITY COLLEGE
Kirtland, Ohio   www.lakeland.cc.oh.us/

Director of Admissions Ms. Tracey Cooper, Director for Admissions/ Registrar, Lakeland Community College, 7700 Clocktower Drive, Kirtland, OH 44094. *Phone:* 440-525-7230. *Toll-free phone:* 800-589-8520.

LORAIN COUNTY COMMUNITY COLLEGE
Elyria, Ohio   www.lorainccc.edu/

Director of Admissions Ms. Dione Somervile, Director of Enrollment Services, Lorain County Community College, 1005 Abbe Road, North, Elyria, OH 44035. *Phone:* 440-366-7566. *Toll-free phone:* 800-995-5222 Ext. 4032. *Fax:* 440-366-4150.

MARION TECHNICAL COLLEGE
Marion, Ohio   www.mtc.edu/

Director of Admissions Mr. Joel O. Liles, Director of Admissions and Career Services, Marion Technical College, 1467 Mount Vernon Avenue, Marion, OH 43302. *Phone:* 740-389-4636 Ext. 249. *E-mail:* mtc@on-ramp.net.

MERCY COLLEGE OF NORTHWEST OHIO
Toledo, Ohio   www.mercycollege.edu/

- **Independent** primarily 2-year, founded 1993, affiliated with Roman Catholic Church
- **Urban** campus with easy access to Detroit
- **Endowment** $4.3 million
- **Coed, primarily women,** 756 undergraduate students, 53% full-time, 85% women, 15% men

Undergraduates 397 full-time, 359 part-time. Students come from 5 states and territories, 12% are from out of state, 7% African American, 0.5% Asian American or Pacific Islander, 4% Hispanic American, 0.7% Native American, 17% transferred in, 8% live on campus. *Retention:* 71% of 2003 full-time freshmen returned.
Freshmen *Admission:* 343 applied, 194 admitted, 89 enrolled. *Test scores:* ACT scores over 18: 87%; ACT scores over 24: 18%; ACT scores over 30: 1%.
Faculty *Total:* 76, 63% full-time, 20% with terminal degrees. *Student/faculty ratio:* 17:1.
Majors General studies; health/health care administration; health information/ medical records technology; massage therapy; medical radiologic technology; nursing (registered nurse training).
Academics *Calendar:* semesters. *Degrees:* certificates, associate, and bachelor's. *Special study options:* academic remediation for entering students, advanced placement credit, independent study, internships, part-time degree program, services for LD students, summer session for credit.
Library Mercy College of Northwest Ohio Library with 6,400 titles, 172 serial subscriptions, 351 audiovisual materials, an OPAC.
Computers on Campus 40 computers available on campus for general student use. A campuswide network can be accessed from student residence rooms and from off campus. Internet access, at least one staffed computer lab available.
Student Life *Housing Options:* coed. Campus housing is provided by a third party. *Activities and Organizations:* student-run newspaper, Campus Ministry, Student Senate, Mercy College Musical Ensemble, Student Nurses Association, Stress Busters. *Campus security:* 24-hour patrols, late-night transport/escort service, controlled dormitory access. *Student services:* personal/psychological counseling.
Standardized Tests *Required for some:* SAT or ACT (for admission). *Recommended:* SAT or ACT (for admission).
Costs (2006–07) *Tuition:* $8640 full-time, $299 per credit hour part-time. *Required fees:* $650 full-time, $5 per credit hour part-time, $650 per year part-time.
Financial Aid Of all full-time matriculated undergraduates who enrolled in 2004, 18 Federal Work-Study jobs.
Applying *Application fee:* $25. *Required:* high school transcript. *Application deadline:* rolling (freshmen), rolling (transfers). *Notification:* continuous (freshmen).

Freshmen Application Contact Ms. Erin Jones, Secretary, Mercy College of Northwest Ohio, 2221 Madison Avenue, Toledo, OH 43624-1197. *Phone:* 419-251-1313 Ext. 11723. *Toll-free phone:* 888-80-Mercy. *Fax:* 419-251-1462. *E-mail:* admissions@mercycollege.edu.

MIAMI–JACOBS COLLEGE
Dayton, Ohio   www.miamijacobs.edu/

Director of Admissions Mary Percell, Vice President of Information Services, Miami–Jacobs College, 110 North Patterson Street, PO Box 1433, Dayton, OH 45402. *Phone:* 937-461-5174 Ext. 118.

MIAMI UNIVERSITY HAMILTON
Hamilton, Ohio   www.ham.muohio.edu/

- **State-supported** founded 1968, part of Miami University System
- **Suburban** 78-acre campus with easy access to Cincinnati
- **Coed**

Undergraduates 2,432 full-time, 898 part-time. 6% African American, 2% Asian American or Pacific Islander, 1% Hispanic American, 0.2% Native American, 4% transferred in.
Faculty *Student/faculty ratio:* 21:1.
Academics *Calendar:* semesters plus summer sessions. *Degrees:* certificates, associate, bachelor's, and master's (degrees awarded by Miami University main campus). *Special study options:* academic remediation for entering students, adult/continuing education programs, advanced placement credit, cooperative education, double majors, English as a second language, honors programs, internships, part-time degree program, services for LD students, student-designed majors, study abroad, summer session for credit. *ROTC:* Navy (c), Air Force (c).
Student Life *Campus security:* 24-hour emergency response devices and patrols, late-night transport/escort service.
Costs (2005–06) *Tuition:* state resident $3714 full-time, $155 per credit part-time; nonresident $15,246 full-time, $650 per credit part-time. *Required fees:* $390 full-time, $15 per credit part-time, $18 per term part-time.
Applying *Options:* electronic application. *Application fee:* $25. *Required:* high school transcript.
Director of Admissions Mr. Archie Nelson, Director of Admission and Financial Aid, Miami University Hamilton, 1601 University Boulevard, Hamilton, OH 45011-3399. *Phone:* 513-785-3111. *E-mail:* nelsona3@muohio.edu.

MIAMI UNIVERSITY–MIDDLETOWN CAMPUS
Middletown, Ohio   www.mid.muohio.edu/

Director of Admissions Mrs. Mary Lou Flynn, Director of Enrollment Services, Miami University–Middletown Campus, 4200 East University Boulevard, Middletown, OH 45042. *Phone:* 513-727-3346. *Toll-free phone:* 800-622-2262. *E-mail:* flynnml@muohio.edu.

NATIONAL INSTITUTE OF TECHNOLOGY
Cuyahoga Falls, Ohio

NORTH CENTRAL STATE COLLEGE
Mansfield, Ohio   www.ncstatecollege.edu/

- **State-supported** 2-year, founded 1961, part of Ohio Board of Regents
- **Suburban** 600-acre campus with easy access to Cleveland and Columbus
- **Endowment** $624,998
- **Coed**

Undergraduates 969 full-time, 2,364 part-time. Students come from 1 other state, 5% African American, 0.7% Asian American or Pacific Islander, 1% Hispanic American, 0.4% Native American.

Academics *Calendar:* quarters. *Degree:* certificates and associate. *Special study options:* academic remediation for entering students, adult/continuing education programs, advanced placement credit, distance learning, independent study, internships, part-time degree program, services for LD students, student-designed majors, summer session for credit.

Student Life *Campus security:* 24-hour emergency response devices and patrols, late-night transport/escort service.

Standardized Tests *Required:* ACT COMPASS (for placement). *Required for some:* ACT (for placement).

Costs (2005–06) *Tuition:* state resident $3431 full-time, $76 per credit hour part-time; nonresident $6863 full-time, $153 per credit hour part-time. Full-time tuition and fees vary according to course load. Part-time tuition and fees vary according to course load. *Required fees:* $245 full-time, $12 per credit hour part-time.

Applying *Options:* early admission, deferred entrance. *Required for some:* high school transcript.

Director of Admissions Ms. Nikia L. Fletcher, Director of Admissions, North Central State College, PO Box 698, Mansfield, OH 44901-0698. *Phone:* 419-755-4813. *Toll-free phone:* 888-755-4899. *E-mail:* nfletcher@ncstatecollege.edu.

NORTHWEST STATE COMMUNITY COLLEGE

Archbold, Ohio　　　　　　**www.northweststate.edu**

- **State-supported** 2-year, founded 1968, part of Ohio Board of Regents
- **Rural** 80-acre campus with easy access to Toledo
- **Endowment** $529,395
- **Coed**

Undergraduates 1,088 full-time, 2,057 part-time. Students come from 6 states and territories, 2% are from out of state, 1% African American, 0.5% Asian American or Pacific Islander, 6% Hispanic American, 0.3% Native American, 0.1% international, 3% transferred in. *Retention:* 55% of 2003 full-time freshmen returned.

Faculty *Student/faculty ratio:* 18:1.

Academics *Calendar:* semesters. *Degree:* certificates and associate. *Special study options:* academic remediation for entering students, adult/continuing education programs, advanced placement credit, cooperative education, distance learning, double majors, external degree program, independent study, internships, off-campus study, part-time degree program, services for LD students, student-designed majors, summer session for credit.

Student Life *Campus security:* security patrols.

Costs (2005–06) *Tuition:* state resident $3660 full-time, $122 per credit part-time; nonresident $6750 full-time, $225 per credit part-time. Full-time tuition and fees vary according to course load. Part-time tuition and fees vary according to course load. *Required fees:* $180 full-time, $6 per credit part-time, $30 per term part-time.

Financial Aid Of all full-time matriculated undergraduates who enrolled in 2004, 43 Federal Work-Study jobs (averaging $1077).

Applying *Options:* electronic application, early admission, deferred entrance. *Application fee:* $20. *Required:* high school transcript.

Director of Admissions Mr. Jeffrey Ferezan, Dean of Student Success and Advocacy Center, Northwest State Community College, 22600 State Route 34, Archbold, OH 43502-9542. *Phone:* 419-267-1213.

OHIO BUSINESS COLLEGE

Lorain, Ohio　　　　　　**www.ohiobusinesscollege.com/**

Director of Admissions Mr. Jim Unger, Admissions Director, Ohio Business College, 1907 North Ridge Road, Lorain, OH 44055. *Toll-free phone:* 888-514-3126.

OHIO BUSINESS COLLEGE

Sandusky, Ohio　　　　　　**www.ohiobusinesscollege.com/**

- **Proprietary** 2-year, founded 1982
- **Suburban** 1-acre campus
- **Coed,** 192 undergraduate students, 82% full-time, 82% women, 18% men
- 100% of applicants were admitted

Undergraduates 157 full-time, 35 part-time.
Freshmen *Admission:* 38 applied, 38 admitted, 38 enrolled.

Faculty *Total:* 30. *Student/faculty ratio:* 10:1.

Majors Accounting; administrative assistant and secretarial science; business administration and management; computer programming; data entry/microcomputer applications; health/medical claims examination; legal administrative assistant/secretary; medical administrative assistant and medical secretary.

Academics *Calendar:* quarters. *Degree:* diplomas and associate.

Costs (2006–07) *Tuition:* $7380 full-time.

Applying *Application fee:* $25. *Required:* high school transcript.

Freshmen Application Contact Rohnda Pickering, Student Services Coordinator, Ohio Business College, 4020 Milan Road, Sandusky, OH 44870-5894. *Phone:* 419-627-8345. *Toll-free phone:* 888-627-8345. *Fax:* 419-627-1958. *E-mail:* Rpickering@ohiobusinesscollege.edu.

OHIO COLLEGE OF MASSOTHERAPY

Akron, Ohio　　　　　　**www.ocm.edu/**

Director of Admissions Mr. John Atkins, Director of Admissions and Marketing,, Ohio College of Massotherapy, 225 Heritage Woods Drive, Akron, OH 44321. *Phone:* 330-665-1084 Ext. 11. *E-mail:* johna@ocm.edu.

OHIO INSTITUTE OF PHOTOGRAPHY AND TECHNOLOGY

Dayton, Ohio　　　　　　**www.oipt.com/**

- **Proprietary** 2-year, founded 1971, part of Kaplan Higher Education
- **Urban** 2-acre campus with easy access to Cincinnati and Columbus
- **Coed,** 740 undergraduate students, 100% full-time, 78% women, 22% men

Undergraduates 740 full-time. Students come from 20 states and territories, 19% are from out of state, 26% African American, 0.1% Asian American or Pacific Islander, 0.5% Hispanic American, 0.3% Native American.
Freshmen *Admission:* 526 applied, 290 admitted, 155 enrolled.

Faculty *Total:* 46, 46% full-time. *Student/faculty ratio:* 25:1.

Majors Criminal justice/law enforcement administration; graphic design; medical office management; photography.

Academics *Calendar:* quarters. *Degree:* diplomas and associate. *Special study options:* cooperative education, internships, part-time degree program, student-designed majors, summer session for credit.

Library Main Library with 640 titles, 35 serial subscriptions.

Computers on Campus 90 computers available on campus for general student use. Internet access, at least one staffed computer lab available.

Student Life *Housing:* college housing not available. *Campus security:* 24-hour emergency response devices.

Costs (2006–07) *Tuition:* $17,641 full-time. *Required fees:* $1248 full-time.

Applying *Options:* common application, early admission, deferred entrance. *Application fee:* $100. *Required:* high school transcript, interview, entrance exam. *Application deadline:* rolling (freshmen), rolling (transfers). *Notification:* continuous (freshmen).

Freshmen Application Contact Ohio Institute of Photography and Technology, 2029 Edgefield Road, Dayton, OH 45439-1917. *Phone:* 937-294-6155. *Toll-free phone:* 800-932-9698. *Fax:* 937-294-2259. *E-mail:* info@oipt.com.

THE OHIO STATE UNIVERSITY AGRICULTURAL TECHNICAL INSTITUTE

Wooster, Ohio　　　　　　**www.ati.ohio-state.edu/**

- **State-supported** 2-year, founded 1971, part of Ohio State University
- **Small-town** campus with easy access to Cleveland and Columbus
- **Endowment** $2.1 million
- **Coed,** 821 undergraduate students, 88% full-time, 33% women, 67% men

Undergraduates 721 full-time, 100 part-time. Students come from 13 states and territories, 2 other countries, 2% are from out of state, 1% African American, 0.1% Asian American or Pacific Islander, 0.9% Hispanic American, 0.4% Native American, 0.2% international, 7% transferred in, 22% live on campus. *Retention:* 68% of 2003 full-time freshmen returned.

The Ohio State University Agricultural Technical Institute (continued)
Freshmen *Admission:* 554 applied, 525 admitted, 337 enrolled. *Test scores:* SAT verbal scores over 500: 22%; SAT math scores over 500: 22%; SAT verbal scores over 600: 11%.
Faculty *Total:* 70, 47% full-time, 33% with terminal degrees. *Student/faculty ratio:* 16:1.
Majors Agribusiness; agricultural business and management; agricultural business technology; agricultural communication/journalism; agricultural economics; agricultural mechanization; agricultural power machinery operation; agricultural teacher education; agronomy and crop science; animal/livestock husbandry and production; animal sciences; biology/biotechnology laboratory technician; building/construction site management; clinical/medical laboratory technology; construction engineering technology; construction management; crop production; dairy husbandry and production; dairy science; environmental science; equestrian studies; floriculture/floristry management; greenhouse management; heavy equipment maintenance technology; horse husbandry/equine science and management; horticultural science; hydraulics and fluid power technology; industrial technology; landscaping and groundskeeping; livestock management; medical laboratory technology; natural resources management; natural resources management and policy; plant nursery management; soil conservation; turf and turfgrass management.
Academics *Calendar:* quarters. *Degree:* certificates, diplomas, and associate. *Special study options:* academic remediation for entering students, accelerated degree program, adult/continuing education programs, advanced placement credit, cooperative education, honors programs, internships, part-time degree program, services for LD students, student-designed majors, summer session for credit. *ROTC:* Army (c), Navy (c), Air Force (c).
Library Agricultural Technical Institute Library with 19,009 titles, 595 serial subscriptions, an OPAC.
Computers on Campus 85 computers available on campus for general student use.
Student Life *Housing:* on-campus residence required for freshman year. *Options:* coed. Campus housing is university owned. *Activities and Organizations:* Hoof-n-Hide Club, Horticulture Club, Campus Crusade for Christ, Phi Theta Kappa, Artist de Fleur Club. *Campus security:* 24-hour emergency response devices and patrols, controlled dormitory access. *Student services:* health clinic, personal/psychological counseling.
Athletics *Intramural sports:* basketball M/W, football M/W, racquetball M/W, softball M/W, volleyball M/W.
Standardized Tests *Required for some:* SAT or ACT (for admission).
Costs (2005–06) *Tuition:* state resident $5478 full-time; nonresident $16,701 full-time. Full-time tuition and fees vary according to course load. Part-time tuition and fees vary according to course load. *Required fees:* $38 full-time. *Room and board:* $5475; room only: $4575. Room and board charges vary according to board plan. *Payment plan:* installment. *Waivers:* employees or children of employees.
Applying *Options:* early admission. *Application fee:* $40. *Required:* high school transcript. *Application deadlines:* 7/1 (freshmen), 7/1 (transfers). *Notification:* continuous until 9/15 (freshmen).
Freshmen Application Contact Coordinator of Admissions, The Ohio State University Agricultural Technical Institute, 1328 Dover Road, Wooster, OH 44691. *Phone:* 800-647-8283 Ext. 1327. *Toll-free phone:* 800-647-8283 Ext. 1327. *Fax:* 330-287-1333. *E-mail:* ati@osu.edu.

OHIO TECHNICAL COLLEGE
Cleveland, Ohio — www.ohiotechnicalcollege.com/
Director of Admissions Mr. Marc Brenner, President, Ohio Technical College, 1374 East 51st Street, Cleveland, OH 44103. *Phone:* 216-881-1700. *Toll-free phone:* 800-322-7000. *Fax:* 216-881-9145. *E-mail:* ohioauto@aol.com.

OHIO VALLEY COLLEGE OF TECHNOLOGY
East Liverpool, Ohio — www.ovct.edu/
Freshmen Application Contact Ms. Jessica M. Ewing, Program Information Coordinator, Ohio Valley College of Technology, PO Box 7000, East Liverpool, OH 43920. *Phone:* 330-385-1070. *Toll-free phone:* 877-777-8451.

OWENS COMMUNITY COLLEGE
Toledo, Ohio — www.owens.edu/
- **State-supported** 2-year, founded 1966
- **Small-town** 100-acre campus
- **Coed,** 20,244 undergraduate students, 37% full-time, 47% women, 53% men

Undergraduates 7,531 full-time, 12,713 part-time. Students come from 15 states and territories, 49 other countries, 3% are from out of state, 13% African American, 1% Asian American or Pacific Islander, 4% Hispanic American, 0.4% Native American, 0.6% international.
Freshmen *Admission:* 1,705 enrolled. *Average high school GPA:* 2.62.
Faculty *Total:* 1,218, 15% full-time. *Student/faculty ratio:* 22:1.
Majors Accounting technology and bookkeeping; agricultural business and management; automotive engineering technology; business/commerce; CAD/CADD drafting/design technology; commercial and advertising art; criminal justice/law enforcement administration; criminal justice/police science; early childhood education; electrical, electronic and communications engineering technology; fashion merchandising; fire protection and safety technology; food services technology; general studies; health information/medical records technology; management information systems; manufacturing technology; marketing/marketing management; mechanical design technology; mechanical engineering/mechanical technology; nursing (registered nurse training); occupational therapist assistant; physical therapist assistant; survey technology; telecommunications.
Academics *Calendar:* semesters. *Degree:* certificates and associate. *Special study options:* academic remediation for entering students, adult/continuing education programs, advanced placement credit, cooperative education, distance learning, double majors, English as a second language, external degree program, freshman honors college, honors programs, independent study, internships, part-time degree program, services for LD students, summer session for credit. *ROTC:* Army (c), Air Force (b).
Library Owens Community College Library with 78,344 titles, 6,230 serial subscriptions, 9,021 audiovisual materials, an OPAC, a Web page.
Computers on Campus 1000 computers available on campus for general student use. A campuswide network can be accessed from off campus. Internet access, online (class) registration, at least one staffed computer lab available.
Student Life *Housing:* college housing not available. *Activities and Organizations:* drama/theater group, student-run newspaper, choral group, intramurals, Alpha Beta Gamma, Drama Club, Student Association for Young Children, Phi Theta Kappa. *Campus security:* 24-hour emergency response devices and patrols, student patrols. *Student services:* health clinic, personal/psychological counseling.
Athletics Member NJCAA. *Intercollegiate sports:* baseball M, basketball M(s)/W(s), soccer M, softball W, volleyball W. *Intramural sports:* basketball M/W, bowling M/W, football M/W, golf M/W, softball M/W, table tennis M/W, tennis M/W, volleyball M/W, weight lifting M/W.
Costs (2006–07) *Tuition:* state resident $2784 full-time, $116 per credit part-time; nonresident $5208 full-time, $217 per credit part-time. *Required fees:* $400 full-time, $15 per credit part-time, $10 per term part-time.
Financial Aid Of all full-time matriculated undergraduates who enrolled in 2004, 200 Federal Work-Study jobs (averaging $4500).
Applying *Options:* common application, early admission. *Required for some:* minimum 2.0 GPA. *Recommended:* essay or personal statement, high school transcript, letters of recommendation. *Application deadline:* rolling (freshmen), rolling (transfers). *Notification:* continuous (freshmen).
Freshmen Application Contact Ms. Donna Gruber, Director, Enrollment Services, Owens Community College, PO Box 1000, Toledo, OH 43699. *Phone:* 567-661-7575. *Toll-free phone:* 800-GO-OWENS. *E-mail:* donna_gruber@owens.edu.

PROFESSIONAL SKILLS INSTITUTE
Toledo, Ohio — www.proskills.com/
Director of Admissions Ms. Hope Finch, Director of Marketing, Professional Skills Institute, 20 Arco Drive, Toledo, OH 43607. *Phone:* 419-531-9610.

REMINGTON COLLEGE—CLEVELAND CAMPUS

Cleveland, Ohio   www.remingtoncollege.edu/

- **Proprietary** 2-year
- **Urban** 2-acre campus
- **Coed**

Undergraduates 676 full-time.
Faculty *Student/faculty ratio:* 15:1.
Academics *Calendar:* continuous. *Degree:* diplomas and associate. *Special study options:* cooperative education.
Costs (2005–06) *Tuition:* $15,745 full-time. Full-time tuition and fees vary according to program.
Applying *Application fee:* $50. *Required:* essay or personal statement, high school transcript, interview.
Director of Admissions Mr. William Cassidy, Director of Recruitment, Remington College–Cleveland Campus, 14445 Broadway Avenue, Cleveland, OH 44125-1957. *Phone:* 216-475-7520.

REMINGTON COLLEGE—CLEVELAND WEST CAMPUS

North Olmstead, Ohio   www.remingtoncollege.edu/

- **Proprietary** 2-year, founded 2003
- **Coed,** 399 undergraduate students, 100% full-time, 83% women, 17% men

Undergraduates 399 full-time. 17% African American, 0.5% Asian American or Pacific Islander, 8% Hispanic American, 1% Native American.
Freshmen *Admission:* 57 admitted, 134 enrolled.
Faculty *Total:* 29, 38% full-time. *Student/faculty ratio:* 23:1.
Majors Business administration and management; computer systems networking and telecommunications; criminal justice/law enforcement administration.
Academics *Calendar:* quarters. *Degree:* diplomas and associate.
Applying *Required:* Wonderlic.
Freshmen Application Contact Mr. Gary Azotea, Campus President, Remington College–Cleveland West Campus, 26350 Brookpark Road, North Olmstead, OH 44070. *Phone:* 440-777-2560. *Fax:* 440-777-3238.

RETS TECH CENTER

Centerville, Ohio   www.retstechcenter.com/

- **Proprietary** 2-year, founded 1953
- **Suburban** 4-acre campus with easy access to Dayton
- **Coed**

Undergraduates 556 full-time. Students come from 2 states and territories, 1% are from out of state, 22% African American, 1% Hispanic American, 0.9% transferred in.
Academics *Calendar:* semesters. *Degree:* diplomas and associate. *Special study options:* advanced placement credit, internships, summer session for credit.
Student Life *Campus security:* 24-hour emergency response devices.
Standardized Tests *Required:* (for placement).
Applying *Options:* early admission, deferred entrance. *Required:* high school transcript, interview.
Freshmen Application Contact Mr. Rich Elkin, Director of Admissions, RETS Tech Center, 555 East Alex Bell Road, Centerville, OH 45459-2712. *Phone:* 937-433-3410. *Toll-free phone:* 800-837-7387.

ROSEDALE BIBLE COLLEGE

Irwin, Ohio   www.rosedalebible.org/

Director of Admissions Mr. John Showalter, Director of Enrollment Services, Rosedale Bible College, 2270 Rosedale Road, Irwin, OH 43029-9501. *Phone:* 740-857-1311. *Fax:* 740-857-1577. *E-mail:* pweber@rosedale.edu.

SCHOOL OF ADVERTISING ART

Kettering, Ohio   www.saacollege.com/

- **Proprietary** 2-year, founded 1983
- **Suburban** 5-acre campus with easy access to Dayton, Ohio; Cincinnati, Ohio
- **Coed,** 146 undergraduate students, 100% full-time, 51% women, 49% men

Undergraduates 146 full-time. Students come from 4 states and territories, 2% are from out of state, 5% African American, 1% Asian American or Pacific Islander, 3% Hispanic American, 0.7% Native American, 0.7% international. *Retention:* 75% of 2003 full-time freshmen returned.
Freshmen *Admission:* 96 enrolled. *Average high school GPA:* 2.75.
Faculty *Total:* 20, 45% full-time. *Student/faculty ratio:* 12:1.
Majors Commercial and advertising art.
Academics *Calendar:* trimesters. *Degree:* diplomas and associate.
Student Life *Housing:* college housing not available. *Student services:* personal/psychological counseling.
Costs (2006–07) *Tuition:* $17,775 full-time. *Required fees:* $210 full-time.
Applying *Required:* high school transcript, interview. *Required for some:* essay or personal statement, minimum 2.0 GPA, 1 letter of recommendation. *Recommended:* minimum 2.5 GPA. *Application deadlines:* 7/1 (freshmen), 7/1 (transfers). *Notification:* 7/1 (freshmen).
Freshman Application Contact Mr. Nathan Summers, Secretary, School of Advertising Art, 1725 East David Road, Kettering, OH 45440. *Phone:* 937-294-0592. *Toll-free phone:* 877-300-9866. *Fax:* 937-294-5869. *E-mail:* nathan@saacollege.com.

SINCLAIR COMMUNITY COLLEGE

Dayton, Ohio   www.sinclair.edu/

- **State and locally supported** 2-year, founded 1887, part of Ohio Board of Regents
- **Urban** 50-acre campus with easy access to Cincinnati
- **Endowment** $25.0 million
- **Coed,** 19,563 undergraduate students, 39% full-time, 57% women, 43% men

Undergraduates 7,550 full-time, 12,013 part-time. Students come from 31 states and territories, 4% are from out of state, 16% African American, 1% Asian American or Pacific Islander, 1% Hispanic American, 0.4% Native American, 0.7% international, 6% transferred in. *Retention:* 56% of 2003 full-time freshmen returned.
Freshmen *Admission:* 6,271 applied, 6,271 admitted, 2,235 enrolled.
Faculty *Total:* 1,117, 42% full-time, 61% with terminal degrees. *Student/faculty ratio:* 19:1.
Majors Accounting; administrative assistant and secretarial science; African studies; applied art; architectural engineering technology; art; artificial intelligence and robotics; automobile/automotive mechanics technology; aviation/airway management; biotechnology; business administration and management; child development; civil engineering technology; commercial and advertising art; computer and information sciences; computer and information sciences related; computer engineering related; computer graphics; computer hardware engineering; computer/information technology services administration related; computer programming related; computer programming (specific applications); computer programming (vendor/product certification); computer software engineering; computer systems networking and telecommunications; consumer merchandising/retailing management; corrections; criminal justice/law enforcement administration; criminal justice/police science; culinary arts; dance; data entry/microcomputer applications; data entry/microcomputer applications related; dental hygiene; dietetics; drafting and design technology; dramatic/theater arts; education; electrical, electronic and communications engineering technology; electromechanical technology; emergency medical technology (EMT paramedic); engineering; finance; fine/studio arts; fire science; foods, nutrition, and wellness; gerontology; graphic and printing equipment operation/production; health information/medical records administration; hotel/motel administration; human services; industrial radiologic technology; industrial technology; information science/studies; information technology; interior design; kindergarten/preschool education; labor and industrial relations; legal administrative assistant/secretary; legal assistant/paralegal; liberal arts and sciences/liberal studies; logistics and materials management; machine tool technology; marketing/marketing management; mass communication/media; mechanical engineering/mechanical technology; medical administrative assistant and medical secretary; medical/clinical assistant; mental health/rehabilitation; music; nursing (registered nurse training); occupational therapy; physical education teaching and coaching; physical therapy; plastics engineering technology; public administra-

Sinclair Community College (continued)

tion; quality control technology; radiologic technology/science; real estate; respiratory care therapy; sign language interpretation and translation; special products marketing; surgical technology; survey technology; system administration; tourism and travel services management; transportation technology; web/multimedia management and webmaster; word processing.

Academics *Calendar:* quarters. *Degree:* certificates and associate. *Special study options:* academic remediation for entering students, adult/continuing education programs, cooperative education, distance learning, English as a second language, external degree program, honors programs, independent study, internships, off-campus study, part-time degree program, services for LD students, student-designed majors, summer session for credit. *ROTC:* Army (c), Air Force (c).

Library Learning Resources Center with 147,613 titles, 576 serial subscriptions, 9,293 audiovisual materials, an OPAC, a Web page.

Computers on Campus 1800 computers available on campus for general student use. A campuswide network can be accessed from off campus that provide access to Portal. Internet access, at least one staffed computer lab available.

Student Life *Housing:* college housing not available. *Activities and Organizations:* drama/theater group, student-run newspaper, choral group, African-American Men of the Future, Ohio Fellows, Phi Theta Kappa, student government, student newspaper. *Campus security:* 24-hour emergency response devices and patrols, student patrols, late-night transport/escort service. *Student services:* personal/psychological counseling.

Athletics Member NJCAA. *Intercollegiate sports:* baseball M(s), basketball M(s)/W(s), golf M(s), tennis M(s)/W(s), volleyball W(s).

Costs (2005–06) *Tuition:* area resident $1910 full-time, $42 per credit hour part-time; state resident $3121 full-time, $69 per credit hour part-time; nonresident $5940 full-time, $132 per credit hour part-time. Full-time tuition and fees vary according to course load. Part-time tuition and fees vary according to course load.

Financial Aid Of all full-time matriculated undergraduates who enrolled in 2004, 50 Federal Work-Study jobs (averaging $800). *Financial aid deadline:* 8/15.

Applying *Options:* electronic application, early admission, deferred entrance. *Application fee:* $10. *Required for some:* high school transcript, interview. *Application deadline:* rolling (freshmen), rolling (transfers). *Notification:* continuous (freshmen).

Freshmen Application Contact Ms. Sara Smith, Director and Systems Manager, Outreach Services, Sinclair Community College, 444 West Third Street, Dayton, OH 45402-1460. *Phone:* 937-512-3060. *Toll-free phone:* 800-315-3000. *Fax:* 937-512-2393.

SOUTHEASTERN BUSINESS COLLEGE
Chillicothe, Ohio — www.careersohio.com/

Director of Admissions Ms. Elizabeth Scott, Admissions Representative, Southeastern Business College, 1855 Western Avenue, Chillicothe, OH 45601-1038. *Phone:* 740-774-6300.

SOUTHEASTERN BUSINESS COLLEGE
Jackson, Ohio — www.careersohio.com/

Director of Admissions Mr. Todd A. Riegel, Director of Education, Southeastern Business College, 504 McCarty Lane, Jackson, OH 45640. *Phone:* 740-286-1554. *Fax:* 740-286-4476. *E-mail:* todd_sbc@yahoo.com.

SOUTHEASTERN BUSINESS COLLEGE
Lancaster, Ohio — www.careersohio.com/

Director of Admissions Mr. Ray Predmore, Director, Southeastern Business College, 1522 Sheridan Drive, Lancaster, OH 43130-1303. *Phone:* 740-687-6126. *Fax:* 740-687-0431. *E-mail:* rp_sbc@yahoo.com.

SOUTHEASTERN BUSINESS COLLEGE
New Boston, Ohio

SOUTHERN STATE COMMUNITY COLLEGE
Hillsboro, Ohio — www.sscc.edu/

- **State-supported** 2-year, founded 1975
- **Rural** 60-acre campus
- **Endowment** $443,111
- **Coed,** 2,307 undergraduate students, 56% full-time, 74% women, 26% men

Undergraduates 1,297 full-time, 1,010 part-time. 1% African American, 0.5% Asian American or Pacific Islander, 0.3% Hispanic American, 0.4% Native American.
Freshmen *Admission:* 829 applied, 829 admitted.

Faculty *Total:* 134, 39% full-time, 7% with terminal degrees. *Student/faculty ratio:* 21:1.

Majors Accounting technology and bookkeeping; agricultural production; business/commerce; computer programming (specific applications); corrections; criminal justice/law enforcement administration; drafting and design technology; emergency medical technology (EMT paramedic); executive assistant/executive secretary; human services; kindergarten/preschool education; liberal arts and sciences/liberal studies; medical/clinical assistant; nursing (registered nurse training); real estate.

Academics *Calendar:* quarters. *Degree:* certificates and associate. *Special study options:* academic remediation for entering students, advanced placement credit, cooperative education, distance learning, double majors, independent study, internships, off-campus study, part-time degree program, services for LD students, student-designed majors, summer session for credit.

Library Learning Resources Center plus 3 others with 79,000 titles, 1,107 serial subscriptions, 7,428 audiovisual materials, an OPAC, a Web page.

Computers on Campus 300 computers available on campus for general student use. A campuswide network can be accessed from off campus. Internet access, online (class) registration, at least one staffed computer lab available.

Student Life *Housing:* college housing not available. *Activities and Organizations:* drama/theater group, choral group, Student Leadership, Student Nurses Association, Drama Club, Association of Medical Assistants, Phi Theta Kappa. *Student services:* personal/psychological counseling.

Athletics Member NJCAA. *Intercollegiate sports:* baseball M(c), basketball M(s)/W(s), soccer M(s), softball W(s), volleyball W(s).

Costs (2005–06) *Tuition:* state resident $3213 full-time; nonresident $6189 full-time. Full-time tuition and fees vary according to course load. Part-time tuition and fees vary according to course load. *Payment plan:* deferred payment. *Waivers:* senior citizens and employees or children of employees.

Applying *Options:* common application, early admission, deferred entrance. *Recommended:* high school transcript. *Application deadline:* rolling (freshmen), rolling (transfers). *Notification:* continuous (freshmen).

Freshmen Application Contact Ms. Wendy Johnson, Director of Admissions, Southern State Community College, 100 Hobart Drive, Hillsboro, OH 45133. *Phone:* 937-393-3431 Ext. 2720. *Toll-free phone:* 800-628-7722. *Fax:* 937-393-6682. *E-mail:* wjohnson@sscc.edu.

SOUTHWESTERN COLLEGE OF BUSINESS
Cincinnati, Ohio — www.swcollege.net/

Director of Admissions Mr. Greg Petree, Director of Admissions, Southwestern College of Business, 149 Northland Boulevard, Cincinnati, OH 45246-1122. *Phone:* 513-874-0432.

SOUTHWESTERN COLLEGE OF BUSINESS

Cincinnati, Ohio   www.swcollege.net/

Director of Admissions Ms. Betty Streber, Director of Admissions, Southwestern College of Business, 632 Vine Street, Suite 200, Cincinnati, OH 45202-4304. *Phone:* 513-421-3212.

SOUTHWESTERN COLLEGE OF BUSINESS

Dayton, Ohio   www.swcollege.net/

Director of Admissions Ms. Kathie Day, Director of Admissions, Southwestern College of Business, 111 West First Street, Dayton, OH 45402-3003. *Phone:* 937-224-0061 Ext. 17.

SOUTHWESTERN COLLEGE OF BUSINESS

Franklin, Ohio   www.swcollege.net/

Director of Admissions Ms. Susan Knodel, Director of Admissions, Southwestern College of Business, 201 East Second Street, Franklin, OH 45005. *Phone:* 937-746-6633. *Fax:* 937-746-6757.

STARK STATE COLLEGE OF TECHNOLOGY

North Canton, Ohio   www.starkstate.edu/

- **State and locally supported** 2-year, founded 1970, part of Ohio Board of Regents
- **Suburban** 34-acre campus with easy access to Cleveland
- **Endowment** $1.8 million
- **Coed,** 6,857 undergraduate students, 33% full-time, 58% women, 42% men

Undergraduates 2,297 full-time, 4,560 part-time. Students come from 4 states and territories, 0.7% are from out of state, 10% African American, 0.6% Asian American or Pacific Islander, 0.9% Hispanic American, 0.8% Native American, 0.2% international, 11% transferred in.
Freshmen *Admission:* 2,589 applied, 2,589 admitted, 1,531 enrolled.
Faculty *Total:* 603, 47% full-time. *Student/faculty ratio:* 19:1.
Majors Accounting; administrative assistant and secretarial science; architectural engineering technology; automobile/automotive mechanics technology; biomedical technology; business administration and management; child development; civil engineering technology; clinical/medical laboratory technology; computer and information sciences related; computer engineering related; computer hardware engineering; computer/information technology services administration related; computer programming; computer programming related; computer programming (specific applications); computer programming (vendor/product certification); computer software and media applications related; computer software engineering; computer systems networking and telecommunications; computer/technical support; consumer merchandising/retailing management; court reporting; data entry/microcomputer applications; data entry/microcomputer applications related; dental hygiene; drafting and design technology; environmental studies; finance; fire science; food services technology; health information/medical records administration; human services; industrial technology; information technology; international business/trade/commerce; legal administrative assistant/secretary; marketing/marketing management; mechanical engineering/mechanical technology; medical/clinical assistant; nursing (registered nurse training); occupational therapy; operations management; physical therapy; respiratory care therapy; survey technology; web/multimedia management and webmaster; web page, digital/multimedia and information resources design; word processing.
Academics *Calendar:* semesters. *Degree:* certificates and associate. *Special study options:* academic remediation for entering students, adult/continuing education programs, distance learning, external degree program, independent study, off-campus study, part-time degree program, services for LD students, student-designed majors, summer session for credit.

Library Learning Resource Center with 70,000 titles, 425 serial subscriptions, an OPAC.
Computers on Campus 500 computers available on campus for general student use. A campuswide network can be accessed from off campus. Internet access, online (class) registration, at least one staffed computer lab available.
Student Life *Housing:* college housing not available. *Activities and Organizations:* student-run newspaper. *Campus security:* 24-hour emergency response devices, late-night transport/escort service. *Student services:* personal/psychological counseling.
Costs (2006–07) *Tuition:* state resident $3810 full-time, $127 per credit hour part-time; nonresident $5610 full-time, $187 per credit hour part-time.
Financial Aid Of all full-time matriculated undergraduates who enrolled in 2004, 194 Federal Work-Study jobs (averaging $2383).
Applying *Options:* electronic application, early admission, deferred entrance. *Application fee:* $65. *Required:* high school transcript. *Application deadline:* rolling (freshmen), rolling (transfers).
Freshmen Application Contact Mr. Wallace Hoffer, Dean of Student Services, Stark State College of Technology, 6200 Frank Road, NW, Canton, OH 44720. *Phone:* 330-966-5450. *Toll-free phone:* 800-797-8275. *Fax:* 330-497-6313. *E-mail:* info@starkstate.edu.

STAUTZENBERGER COLLEGE

Toledo, Ohio   www.sctoday.com/

Director of Admissions Ms. Karen Fitzgerald, Director of Admissions and Marketing, Stautzenberger College, 5355 Southwyck Boulevard, Toledo, OH 43614. *Phone:* 419-866-0261. *Toll-free phone:* 800-552-5099. *Fax:* 419-867-9821. *E-mail:* klfitzgerald@stautzenberger.com.

TECHNOLOGY EDUCATION COLLEGE

Columbus, Ohio   www.teceducation.com/

Director of Admissions Michael Mongomery, Executive Director, Technology Education College, 288 South Hamilton Road, Columbus, OH 43213-2087. *Phone:* 614-456-4600. *Toll-free phone:* 800-838-3233. *Fax:* 614-456-4640. *E-mail:* mmontgomery@teceducation.com.

TERRA STATE COMMUNITY COLLEGE

Fremont, Ohio   www.terra.edu/

Freshmen Application Contact Mr. Dale Stearns, Associate Dean of Student Services, Terra State Community College, 2830 Napoleon Road, Fremont, OH 43420. *Phone:* 419-334-8400 Ext. 347. *Toll-free phone:* 800-334-3886. *E-mail:* dstearns@terra.edu.

TRUMBULL BUSINESS COLLEGE

Warren, Ohio   www.tbc-trumbullbusiness.com/

Director of Admissions Admissions Office, Trumbull Business College, 3200 Ridge Road, Warren, OH 44484. *Phone:* 330-369-3200.

THE UNIVERSITY OF AKRON—WAYNE COLLEGE

Orrville, Ohio   www.wayne.uakron.edu/

- **State-supported** 2-year, founded 1972, part of The University of Akron
- **Rural** 157-acre campus
- **Coed,** 1,737 undergraduate students, 53% full-time, 63% women, 37% men

Undergraduates 924 full-time, 813 part-time. Students come from 1 other state, 3% African American, 0.7% Asian American or Pacific Islander, 0.5% Hispanic American, 0.4% Native American, 5% transferred in.

The University of Akron–Wayne College (continued)

Freshmen *Admission:* 647 applied, 601 admitted, 320 enrolled. *Average high school GPA:* 2.93. *Test scores:* ACT scores over 18: 70%; ACT scores over 24: 15%; ACT scores over 30: 1%.

Faculty *Total:* 136, 20% full-time, 23% with terminal degrees. *Student/faculty ratio:* 17:1.

Majors Accounting; accounting technology and bookkeeping; administrative assistant and secretarial science; business administration and management; business automation/technology/data entry; computer science; computer systems networking and telecommunications; data processing and data processing technology; engineering; environmental health; executive assistant/executive secretary; general studies; interdisciplinary studies; legal administrative assistant/secretary; liberal arts and sciences/liberal studies; management information systems; medical administrative assistant and medical secretary; medical office management; occupational safety and health technology; social work.

Academics *Calendar:* semesters. *Degree:* certificates and associate. *Special study options:* academic remediation for entering students, adult/continuing education programs, advanced placement credit, cooperative education, distance learning, double majors, English as a second language, honors programs, independent study, internships, off-campus study, part-time degree program, services for LD students, summer session for credit. *ROTC:* Army (c), Air Force (c).

Library Wayne College Library with 23,450 titles, 219 serial subscriptions, 822 audiovisual materials, an OPAC.

Computers on Campus 240 computers available on campus for general student use. A campuswide network can be accessed from off campus. Internet access, online (class) registration, at least one staffed computer lab available. Computer purchase or lease plan available.

Student Life *Housing:* college housing not available. *Campus security:* late-night transport/escort service. *Student services:* personal/psychological counseling.

Athletics *Intercollegiate sports:* basketball M/W, cheerleading W, golf M, volleyball W. *Intramural sports:* basketball M/W, golf M, volleyball M/W.

Standardized Tests *Required for some:* SAT or ACT (for admission), ACT COMPASS. *Recommended:* SAT or ACT (for admission), ACT COMPASS.

Costs (2005–06) *Tuition:* state resident $4884 full-time, $203 per credit hour part-time; nonresident $13,202 full-time, $440 per credit hour part-time. *Required fees:* $146 full-time, $6 per credit hour part-time.

Financial Aid Of all full-time matriculated undergraduates who enrolled in 2004, 8 Federal Work-Study jobs (averaging $2200).

Applying *Options:* common application, electronic application, early admission, deferred entrance. *Application fee:* $30. *Required for some:* high school transcript. *Application deadlines:* 8/30 (freshmen), 8/30 (transfers). *Notification:* continuous until 8/30 (freshmen).

Freshmen Application Contact Ms. Alicia Broadus, Admissions Student Services Office, The University of Akron–Wayne College, 1901 Smucker Road, Orrville, OH 44667. *Phone:* 800-221-8308 Ext. 8901. *Toll-free phone:* 800-221-8308 Ext. 8900. *Fax:* 330-684-8989. *E-mail:* wayneadmissions@uakron.edu.

UNIVERSITY OF CINCINNATI CLERMONT COLLEGE

Batavia, Ohio   **www.clc.uc.edu/**

Freshmen Application Contact Ms. Tanya Bohart, Admissions Assistant, University of Cincinnati Clermont College, 4200 Clermont College Drive, Batavia, OH 45103-1785. *Phone:* 513-732-5202. *E-mail:* tanya.bohart@uc.edu.

UNIVERSITY OF CINCINNATI RAYMOND WALTERS COLLEGE

Cincinnati, Ohio   **www.rwc.uc.edu/**

- **State-supported** 2-year, founded 1967, part of University of Cincinnati System
- **Suburban** 120-acre campus
- **Endowment** $43,625
- **Coed**

Undergraduates 2,177 full-time, 2,244 part-time. Students come from 19 states and territories, 3% are from out of state, 15% African American, 2% Asian American or Pacific Islander, 2% Hispanic American, 0.3% Native American, 6% transferred in.

Faculty *Student/faculty ratio:* 25:1.

Academics *Calendar:* quarters. *Degrees:* certificates, associate, and post-bachelor's certificates. *Special study options:* academic remediation for entering students, accelerated degree program, adult/continuing education programs, advanced placement credit, cooperative education, distance learning, double majors, English as a second language, honors programs, internships, off-campus study, part-time degree program, services for LD students, student-designed majors, study abroad, summer session for credit. *ROTC:* Army (c), Air Force (c).

Student Life *Campus security:* 24-hour emergency response devices and patrols, student patrols, late-night transport/escort service.

Costs (2005–06) *Tuition:* state resident $4938 full-time, $142 per quarter hour part-time; nonresident $12,801 full-time, $336 per quarter hour part-time. *Required fees:* $222 full-time.

Financial Aid Of all full-time matriculated undergraduates who enrolled in 2004, 285 Federal Work-Study jobs (averaging $2903).

Applying *Options:* electronic application, deferred entrance. *Application fee:* $35. *Required:* high school transcript.

Freshmen Application Contact Ms. Angelica Kennedy, Admission Counselor, University of Cincinnati Raymond Walters College, 9555 Plainfield Road, Cincinnati, OH 45236-1007. *Phone:* 513-745-5700.

UNIVERSITY OF NORTHWESTERN OHIO
Lima, Ohio

- **Independent** primarily 2-year, founded 1920
- **Small-town** 35-acre campus with easy access to Dayton and Toledo
- **Coed,** 2,915 undergraduate students, 90% full-time, 21% women, 79% men

The University of Northwestern Ohio (UNOH) is a private, nonprofit university established in 1920. Located in Lima, Ohio, UNOH has a population of 3,200 students and offers associate degrees and diplomas in automotive, high performance, diesel, agriculture, alternative fuels, and HVAC/R. Associate degrees and diplomas are awarded in the College of Business for accounting, business, computers, and medical as well as various other majors.

Undergraduates 2,629 full-time, 286 part-time. Students come from 34 states and territories, 30% are from out of state, 0.5% African American, 0.1% Hispanic American, 2% transferred in, 45% live on campus. *Retention:* 70% of 2003 full-time freshmen returned.

Freshmen *Admission:* 3,758 applied, 3,699 admitted, 630 enrolled.

Faculty *Total:* 107, 75% full-time, 4% with terminal degrees. *Student/faculty ratio:* 20:1.

Majors Accounting; administrative assistant and secretarial science; agricultural business and management; automobile/automotive mechanics technology; business administration and management; computer programming; diesel mechanics technology; health/health care administration; heating, air conditioning, ventilation and refrigeration maintenance technology; legal administrative assistant/secretary; legal assistant/paralegal; marketing/marketing management; medical administrative assistant and medical secretary; medical/clinical assistant; pharmacy technician; tourism and travel services management.

Academics *Calendar:* quarters. *Degrees:* certificates, diplomas, associate, and bachelor's. *Special study options:* academic remediation for entering students, accelerated degree program, adult/continuing education programs, advanced placement credit, cooperative education, distance learning, double majors, part-time degree program, summer session for credit.

Library University of Northwestern Ohio Library with 4,553 titles, 95 serial subscriptions, an OPAC, a Web page.

Computers on Campus 149 computers available on campus for general student use. A campuswide network can be accessed from off campus. Internet access, at least one staffed computer lab available.

Student Life *Housing Options:* men-only, women-only, disabled students. Campus housing is university owned and leased by the school. Freshman campus housing is guaranteed. *Activities and Organizations:* student-run newspaper, Students in Free Enterprise. *Campus security:* 24-hour emergency response devices and patrols, late-night transport/escort service. *Student services:* personal/psychological counseling.

Athletics *Intramural sports:* basketball M, bowling M/W, volleyball M/W.

Costs (2005–06) *Tuition:* $11,400 full-time, $190 per credit hour part-time.

Financial Aid Of all full-time matriculated undergraduates who enrolled in 2004, 40 Federal Work-Study jobs (averaging $2000).

Applying *Options:* electronic application, early admission, deferred entrance. *Application fee:* $50. *Required:* high school transcript. *Application deadline:* rolling (freshmen), rolling (transfers).

Freshmen Application Contact Mr. Dan Klopp, Vice President for Enrollment Management, University of Northwestern Ohio, 1441 North Cable Road, Lima, OH 45805-1498. *Phone:* 419-227-3141. *Fax:* 419-229-6926. *E-mail:* info@nc.edu.

VATTEROTT COLLEGE

Broadview Heights, Ohio   www.vatterott-college.edu/

Director of Admissions Mr. Jack Chalk, Director of Admissions, Vatterott College, 5025 East Royalton Road, Broadview Heights, OH 44147. *Phone:* 440-526-1660. *Toll-free phone:* 800-864-5644.

VIRGINIA MARTI COLLEGE OF ART AND DESIGN

Lakewood, Ohio   www.vmcad.edu/

Director of Admissions Quinn Marti, Head of Admissions, Virginia Marti College of Art and Design, 11724 Detroit Avenue, PO Box 580, Lakewood, OH 44107-3002. *Phone:* 216-221-8584.

WASHINGTON STATE COMMUNITY COLLEGE

Marietta, Ohio   www.wscc.edu/

Director of Admissions Ms. Rebecca Peroni, Director of Admissions, Washington State Community College, 710 Colegate Drive, Marietta, OH 45750-9225. *Phone:* 740-374-8716.

WRIGHT STATE UNIVERSITY, LAKE CAMPUS

Celina, Ohio   www.wright.edu/lake/

Director of Admissions Mrs. B.J. Hobler, Student Services Officer, Wright State University, Lake Campus, 7600 State Route 703, Celina, OH 45822-2921. *Phone:* 419-586-0324. *Toll-free phone:* 800-237-1477.

ZANE STATE COLLEGE

Zanesville, Ohio   www.zanestate.edu/

Director of Admissions Mr. Paul Young, Director of Admissions, Zane State College, 1555 Newark Road, Zanesville, OH 43701-2626. *Phone:* 740-454-2501 Ext. 1225. *Toll-free phone:* 800-686-TECH Ext. 1225.

OKLAHOMA

CARL ALBERT STATE COLLEGE

Poteau, Oklahoma   www.carlalbert.edu/

- **State-supported** 2-year, founded 1934, part of Oklahoma State Regents for Higher Education
- **Small-town** 78-acre campus
- **Coed,** 2,501 undergraduate students, 59% full-time, 69% women, 31% men

Undergraduates 1,484 full-time, 1,017 part-time. 11% are from out of state, 3% African American, 0.9% Asian American or Pacific Islander, 2% Hispanic American, 27% Native American, 0.6% international, 18% live on campus. Freshmen *Admission:* 996 applied, 788 admitted, 720 enrolled.
Faculty *Total:* 154, 33% full-time, 1% with terminal degrees. *Student/faculty ratio:* 16:1.

Majors Accounting; administrative assistant and secretarial science; agricultural business and management; art teacher education; biology/biological sciences; business administration and management; business teacher education; computer science; elementary education; English; hotel/motel administration; industrial arts; journalism; kindergarten/preschool education; legal administrative assistant/secretary; mathematics; medical administrative assistant and medical secretary; music; nursing (registered nurse training); physical education teaching and coaching; physical sciences; physical therapist assistant; pre-engineering; psychology; social sciences; sociology; speech and rhetoric; zoology/animal biology.
Academics *Calendar:* semesters. *Degree:* certificates and associate. *Special study options:* academic remediation for entering students, adult/continuing education programs, cooperative education, part-time degree program.
Library Joe E. White Library with 27,200 titles, 1,350 serial subscriptions, an OPAC.
Computers on Campus 15 computers available on campus for general student use. A campuswide network can be accessed. At least one staffed computer lab available.
Student Life *Housing Options:* men-only, women-only. Campus housing is university owned. *Activities and Organizations:* drama/theater group, student-run newspaper, radio station, choral group, Student Government Association, Phi Theta Kappa, Baptist Student Union, BACCHUS, Student Physical Therapist Assistant Association. *Campus security:* security guards. *Student services:* health clinic, personal/psychological counseling.
Athletics Member NJCAA. *Intercollegiate sports:* baseball M, basketball M(s)/W(s), softball M. *Intramural sports:* tennis M/W, volleyball M/W, weight lifting M.
Costs (2005–06) *Tuition:* state resident $1632 full-time, $68 per credit hour part-time; nonresident $4004 full-time, $167 per credit hour part-time. *Required fees:* $4 full-time, $2 per term part-time. *Room and board:* $1520; room only: $1000.
Financial Aid Of all full-time matriculated undergraduates who enrolled in 2004, 125 Federal Work-Study jobs (averaging $1751).
Applying *Required:* high school transcript. *Application deadlines:* 8/13 (freshmen), 8/15 (transfers). *Notification:* continuous (freshmen).
Freshmen Application Contact Ms. Jennifer Williams, Admission Specialist, Carl Albert State College, 1507 South McKenna, Poteau, OK 74953-5208. *Phone:* 918-647-1300. *Fax:* 918-647-1306. *E-mail:* jwilliams@carlalbert.edu.

COMMUNITY CARE COLLEGE

Tulsa, Oklahoma   www.communitycarecollege.com/

- **Proprietary** 2-year, founded 1995, part of Dental Directions, Inc.
- **Coed,** 525 undergraduate students, 98% full-time, 90% women, 10% men

Undergraduates 512 full-time, 13 part-time. 4% are from out of state, 17% African American, 0.6% Asian American or Pacific Islander, 3% Hispanic American, 12% Native American.
Freshmen *Admission:* 438 enrolled.
Majors Business administration, management and operations related; dental assisting; health/health care administration; massage therapy; medical/clinical assistant; pharmacy technician; surgical technology; veterinary technology.
Academics *Calendar:* semesters. *Degree:* certificates, diplomas, and associate.
Student Life *Student services:* personal/psychological counseling.
Costs (2006–07) *Tuition:* $9000 full-time. *Required fees:* $850 full-time.
Applying *Application fee:* $15. *Required:* high school transcript, interview, Assessment.
Freshmen Application Contact Ms. Teresa Knox, Chief Executive Officer, Community Care College, 4242 South Sheridan, Tulsa, OK 74145. *Phone:* 918-610-0027. *Fax:* 918-610-0029. *E-mail:* tknox@communitycarecollege.com.

CONNORS STATE COLLEGE

Warner, Oklahoma   www.connorsstate.edu/

Director of Admissions Mr. John A. Turnbull, Director of Admissions/Registrar, Connors State College, Route 1 Box 1000 College Road, Warner, OK 74469. *Phone:* 918-463-6233 Ext. 6233. *Toll-free phone:* 918-463-2931 Ext. 6241.

EASTERN OKLAHOMA STATE COLLEGE
Wilburton, Oklahoma　　　www.eosc.edu/

Director of Admissions Ms. Leah Miller, Director of Admissions, Eastern Oklahoma State College, 1301 West Main, Wilburton, OK 74578-4999. *Phone:* 918-465-2361 Ext. 240. *E-mail:* lmiller@eosc.edu.

HERITAGE COLLEGE OF HAIR DESIGN
Oklahoma City, Oklahoma

ITT TECHNICAL INSTITUTE
Tulsa, Oklahoma　　　www.itt-tech.edu/

- primarily 2-year
- Coed

Majors Business administration and management; CAD/CADD drafting/design technology; computer and information systems security; criminal justice/law enforcement administration; electrical, electronic and communications engineering technology; system, networking, and LAN/WAN management; web page, digital/multimedia and information resources design.
Academics *Calendar:* quarters. *Degrees:* associate and bachelor's.
Standardized Tests *Required:* Wonderlic aptitude test (for admission).
Costs (2005–06) *Tuition:* Please see school catalog for specific information.
Applying *Application fee:* $100. *Required:* high school transcript, interview. *Recommended:* letters of recommendation. *Application deadline:* rolling (freshmen), rolling (transfers). *Notification:* continuous (freshmen).
Freshmen Application Contact Mr. James Dycus, Director of Recruitment, ITT Technical Institute, 4943 South 78th East Avenue, Tulsa, OK 74145. *Phone:* 918-619-8700.

MURRAY STATE COLLEGE
Tishomingo, Oklahoma　　　www.mscok.edu/

Director of Admissions Mrs. Ann Beck, Registrar and Director of Admissions, Murray State College, 1Murray Campus, Tishomingo, OK 73460. *Phone:* 580-371-2371 Ext. 171.

NORTHEASTERN OKLAHOMA AGRICULTURAL AND MECHANICAL COLLEGE
Miami, Oklahoma　　　www.neoam.cc.ok.us/

Director of Admissions Amy Ishmael, Dean of Enrollment Management, Northeastern Oklahoma Agricultural and Mechanical College, PO Box 3842, 200 I Street NE, Miami, OK 74354. *Phone:* 918-540-6212. *Toll-free phone:* 800-464-6636.

NORTHERN OKLAHOMA COLLEGE
Tonkawa, Oklahoma　　　www.north-ok.edu/

Freshmen Application Contact Ms. Sheri Snyder, Director of College Relations, Northern Oklahoma College, PO Box 310, Tonkawa, OK 74653. *Phone:* 580-628-6290. *Toll-free phone:* 800-429-5715.

OKLAHOMA CITY COMMUNITY COLLEGE
Oklahoma City, Oklahoma　　　www.okccc.edu/

Director of Admissions Ms. Gloria Cardenas-Barton, Dean of Admissions/Registrar, Oklahoma City Community College, 7777 South May Avenue, Oklahoma City, OK 73159. *Phone:* 405-682-7515.

OKLAHOMA STATE UNIVERSITY, OKLAHOMA CITY
Oklahoma City, Oklahoma　　　www.osuokc.edu/

Director of Admissions Ms. Jeanne Kubier, Director of Admissions and Registrar, Oklahoma State University, Oklahoma City, 900 North Portland Avenue, Oklahoma City, OK 73107. *Phone:* 405-945-3287.

OKLAHOMA STATE UNIVERSITY, OKMULGEE
Okmulgee, Oklahoma　　　www.osu-okmulgee.edu/

Director of Admissions Kelly Hildebrant, Director of Admissions, Oklahoma State University, Okmulgee, 1801 East Fourth Street, Okmulgee, OK 74447-3901. *Phone:* 918-293-5298. *Toll-free phone:* 800-722-4471.

PLATT COLLEGE
Oklahoma City, Oklahoma　　　www.plattcollege.org/

Director of Admissions Ms. Jane Nowlin, Director, Platt College, 309 South Ann Arbor Avenue, Oklahoma City, OK 73128. *Phone:* 405-946-7799. *Fax:* 405-943-2150. *E-mail:* janen@plattcollege.org.

PLATT COLLEGE
Tulsa, Oklahoma　　　www.plattcollege.org/

Director of Admissions Mrs. Susan Rone, Director, Platt College, 3801 South Sheridan Road, Tulsa, OK 74145-111. *Phone:* 918-663-9000. *Fax:* 918-622-1240. *E-mail:* susanr@plattcollege.org.

REDLANDS COMMUNITY COLLEGE
El Reno, Oklahoma　　　www.redlandscc.edu/

Director of Admissions Vice President for Student Services, Redlands Community College, El Reno, OK 73036. *Phone:* 405-262-2552 Ext. 1282.

ROSE STATE COLLEGE
Midwest City, Oklahoma　　　www.rose.edu/

Director of Admissions Ms. Evelyn K. Hutchings, Registrar and Director of Admissions, Rose State College, 6420 Southeast 15th Street, Midwest City, OK 73110-2799. *Phone:* 405-733-7673. *E-mail:* ekhutchings@ms.rose.cc.ok.us.

SEMINOLE STATE COLLEGE
Seminole, Oklahoma　　　www.ssc.cc.ok.us/

- **State-supported** 2-year, founded 1931, part of Oklahoma State Regents for Higher Education
- **Small-town** 40-acre campus with easy access to Oklahoma City
- **Coed,** 2,584 undergraduate students, 81% full-time, 70% women, 30% men

Undergraduates 2,096 full-time, 488 part-time. Students come from 13 states and territories, 5 other countries, 2% are from out of state, 6% African American,

0.3% Asian American or Pacific Islander, 2% Hispanic American, 23% Native American, 0.9% international, 43% transferred in, 8% live on campus. **Freshmen** *Admission:* 2,096 applied, 2,096 admitted, 1,668 enrolled. *Test scores:* ACT scores over 18: 56%; ACT scores over 24: 6%.

Faculty *Total:* 92, 52% full-time, 8% with terminal degrees.

Majors Accounting; administrative assistant and secretarial science; art; behavioral sciences; biology/biological sciences; business administration and management; clinical/medical laboratory technology; computer science; criminal justice/police science; elementary education; English; liberal arts and sciences/liberal studies; mathematics; nursing (registered nurse training); physical education teaching and coaching; physical sciences; pre-engineering; social sciences.

Academics *Calendar:* semesters. *Degree:* diplomas and associate. *Special study options:* academic remediation for entering students, accelerated degree program, adult/continuing education programs, advanced placement credit, cooperative education, distance learning, honors programs, independent study, off-campus study, part-time degree program, services for LD students, summer session for credit.

Library Boren Library with 27,507 titles, 200 serial subscriptions, an OPAC.

Computers on Campus 100 computers available on campus for general student use. A campuswide network can be accessed from off campus. Internet access, at least one staffed computer lab available.

Student Life *Housing Options:* coed. Campus housing is university owned. *Activities and Organizations:* student-run newspaper, choral group, Student Government Association, Native American Student Association, Psi Beta Honor Society, Student Nurses Association, Phi Theta Kappa. *Campus security:* 24-hour patrols. *Student services:* personal/psychological counseling.

Athletics Member NJCAA. *Intercollegiate sports:* baseball M(s), basketball M(s)/W(s), golf M(s)/W(s), softball W(s), volleyball W(s).

Costs (2006–07) *Tuition:* state resident $1116 full-time, $47 per credit hour part-time; nonresident $3589 full-time, $150 per credit hour part-time. *Required fees:* $719 full-time, $30 per credit hour part-time. *Room and board:* $2470.

Applying *Options:* common application, early admission, deferred entrance. *Application fee:* $15. *Required:* high school transcript. *Application deadline:* rolling (freshmen), rolling (transfers). *Notification:* continuous (freshmen).

Freshmen Application Contact Mr. Chris Lindley, Director of Enrollment Management, Seminole State College, PO Box 351, 2701 Boren Boulevard, Seminole, OK 74818-0351. *Phone:* 405-382-9272. *Fax:* 405-382-9524. *E-mail:* lindley_c@ssc.cc.ok.us.

SOUTHWESTERN OKLAHOMA STATE UNIVERSITY AT SAYRE

Sayre, Oklahoma   www.swosu.edu/sayre/

- **State and locally supported** 2-year, founded 1938, part of Southwestern Oklahoma State University
- **Rural** 6-acre campus
- **Coed,** 549 undergraduate students, 60% full-time, 73% women, 27% men

Undergraduates 328 full-time, 221 part-time. Students come from 2 states and territories, 3% are from out of state, 1% African American, 0.4% Asian American or Pacific Islander, 5% Hispanic American, 5% Native American.

Freshmen *Admission:* 107 applied, 107 admitted, 107 enrolled. *Test scores:* ACT scores over 18: 76%; ACT scores over 24: 13%.

Faculty *Total:* 19, 63% full-time. *Student/faculty ratio:* 18:1.

Majors Business administration and management; clinical/medical laboratory technology; computer science; corrections; criminal justice/safety; general studies; medical radiologic technology; nursing (registered nurse training); occupational therapist assistant; physical therapist assistant.

Academics *Calendar:* semesters. *Degree:* diplomas and associate. *Special study options:* academic remediation for entering students, adult/continuing education programs, advanced placement credit, cooperative education, distance learning, independent study, part-time degree program, services for LD students, summer session for credit.

Library Oscar McMahan Library with 9,975 titles, 45 serial subscriptions, an OPAC, a Web page.

Computers on Campus 100 computers available on campus for general student use. A campuswide network can be accessed. Internet access, online (class) registration, at least one staffed computer lab available.

Student Life *Housing:* college housing not available. *Activities and Organizations:* student-run newspaper.

Standardized Tests *Required for some:* ACT (for admission).

Costs (2005–06) *Tuition:* state resident $3456 full-time, $108 per credit hour part-time.

Applying *Options:* common application, early admission, deferred entrance. *Application fee:* $15. *Required:* high school transcript. *Application deadline:* rolling (freshmen), rolling (transfers).

Freshmen Application Contact Ms. Kim Seymour, Registrar, Southwestern Oklahoma State University at Sayre, 409 East Mississippi Street, Sayre, OK 73662-1236. *Phone:* 580-928-5533 Ext. 101. *Fax:* 580-928-1140.

SPARTAN COLLEGE OF AERONAUTICS AND TECHNOLOGY

Tulsa, Oklahoma   www.spartan.edu/

Freshmen Application Contact Mr. Mark Fowler, Vice President of Student Records and Finance, Spartan College of Aeronautics and Technology, 8820 East Pine Street, PO Box 582833, Tulsa, OK 74158-2833. *Phone:* 918-836-6886.

TULSA COMMUNITY COLLEGE

Tulsa, Oklahoma   www.tulsacc.edu/

- **State-supported** 2-year, founded 1968, part of Oklahoma State Regents for Higher Education
- **Urban** 160-acre campus
- **Coed,** 16,803 undergraduate students, 37% full-time, 63% women, 37% men

Undergraduates 6,162 full-time, 10,641 part-time. Students come from 16 states and territories, 1% are from out of state, 9% African American, 2% Asian American or Pacific Islander, 3% Hispanic American, 8% Native American, 18% transferred in.

Freshmen *Admission:* 15,911 applied, 15,911 admitted, 2,919 enrolled. *Average high school GPA:* 2.80.

Faculty *Total:* 1,285, 33% full-time. *Student/faculty ratio:* 20:1.

Majors Accounting; administrative assistant and secretarial science; advertising; aeronautics/aviation/aerospace science and technology; agriculture; airframe mechanics and aircraft maintenance technology; American studies; applied horticulture; architecture; art; artificial intelligence and robotics; astronomy; automobile/automotive mechanics technology; avionics maintenance technology; behavioral sciences; biology/biological sciences; biomedical technology; botany/plant biology; business administration and management; business and personal/financial services marketing; business teacher education; chemistry; child care and support services management; child development; child guidance; civil engineering technology; clinical/medical laboratory technology; computer and information sciences related; computer and information systems security; computer graphics; computer hardware engineering; computer/information technology services administration related; computer programming related; computer programming (specific applications); computer programming (vendor/product certification); computer science; computer software and media applications related; computer software engineering; computer systems networking and telecommunications; computer/technical support; construction engineering technology; corrections; creative writing; criminal justice/law enforcement administration; criminal justice/police science; data entry/microcomputer applications; data entry/microcomputer applications related; data modeling/warehousing and database administration; dental assisting; dental hygiene; desktop publishing and digital imaging design; drafting and design technology; dramatic/theater arts; ecology; economics; education; electrical, electronic and communications engineering technology; elementary and middle school administration/principalship; elementary education; emergency medical technology (EMT paramedic); engineering; English; environmental engineering technology; fashion/apparel design; fire protection and safety technology; fire science; forestry; French; geography; geology/earth science; German; health information/medical records administration; health science; health teacher education; heating, air conditioning, ventilation and refrigeration maintenance technology; history; horticultural science; hotel/motel administration; humanities; human resources management; human services; industrial radiologic technology; industrial technology; information science/studies; information technology; insurance; interior design; international business/trade/commerce; international relations and affairs; Italian; Japanese; journalism; kindergarten/preschool education; labor and industrial relations; landscape architecture; landscaping and groundskeeping; Latin; legal administrative assistant/secretary; legal assistant/paralegal; legal studies; liberal arts and sciences/liberal studies; library science; management science; marketing/marketing management; mass communication/media; materials science; mathematics; mechanical engineering/mechanical technology; medical administrative assistant and medical secretary; medical/clinical assistant; music; music teacher education; nursing (registered nurse training); occupational safety and health technology; occupational therapist assistant; occupational therapy; oceanography (chemical and physical); ornamental horticulture; petroleum technology; philosophy; physical education teaching and coaching; physical sciences; physical therapy; physician assistant; physics; plant protection and integrated pest management; political science and government; pre-dentistry studies; pre-engineering; pre-medical studies; pre-pharmacy studies; pre-veterinary studies; psychology;

Tulsa Community College (continued)

purchasing, procurement/acquisitions and contracts management; quality control technology; radio and television; radiologic technology/science; religious studies; respiratory care therapy; Russian; safety/security technology; sign language interpretation and translation; social sciences; social work; sociology; Spanish; speech and rhetoric; surgical technology; survey technology; system administration; telecommunications; therapeutic recreation; tourism and travel services management; veterinary technology; web/multimedia management and webmaster; web page, digital/multimedia and information resources design; word processing; zoology/animal biology.

Academics *Calendar:* semesters. *Degree:* certificates and associate. *Special study options:* academic remediation for entering students, accelerated degree program, adult/continuing education programs, advanced placement credit, cooperative education, distance learning, English as a second language, external degree program, freshman honors college, honors programs, internships, part-time degree program, services for LD students, summer session for credit.

Library Learning Resource Center plus 1 other with 110,000 titles, 987 serial subscriptions, a Web page.

Computers on Campus 1000 computers available on campus for general student use. A campuswide network can be accessed from off campus. Internet access, online (class) registration, at least one staffed computer lab available.

Student Life *Housing:* college housing not available. *Activities and Organizations:* drama/theater group, student-run newspaper. *Campus security:* 24-hour emergency response devices and patrols, student patrols, late-night transport/escort service. *Student services:* health clinic, personal/psychological counseling, women's center.

Athletics *Intramural sports:* basketball M/W, bowling M/W, cross-country running M/W, football M/W, golf M/W, racquetball M/W, soccer M/W, tennis M/W, track and field M/W, volleyball M/W.

Costs (2005–06) *Tuition:* state resident $48 per semester hour part-time; nonresident $172 per semester hour part-time. *Required fees:* $25 per semester hour part-time.

Financial Aid Of all full-time matriculated undergraduates who enrolled in 2004, 200 Federal Work-Study jobs (averaging $1500).

Applying *Options:* common application, early admission. *Application fee:* $20. *Required:* high school transcript. *Application deadline:* rolling (freshmen), rolling (transfers).

Freshmen Application Contact Ms. Leanne Brewer, Director of Admissions and Records, Tulsa Community College, 6111 East Skelly Drive, Tulsa, OK 74135. *Phone:* 918-595-7811. *Fax:* 918-595-7910. *E-mail:* lbrewer@tulsacc.edu.

TULSA WELDING SCHOOL

Tulsa, Oklahoma　　　　**www.weldingschool.com/**

- **Proprietary** 2-year, founded 1949, administratively affiliated with Tulsa Welding School, Jacksonville Branch
- **Urban** 5-acre campus
- **Coed, primarily men,** 362 undergraduate students, 100% full-time, 4% women, 96% men

Undergraduates 362 full-time. Students come from 21 states and territories, 41% are from out of state, 13% African American, 0.6% Asian American or Pacific Islander, 3% Hispanic American, 9% Native American.

Faculty *Total:* 17, 94% full-time. *Student/faculty ratio:* 16:1.

Majors Welding technology.

Academics *Calendar:* continuous (phased start every 3 weeks). *Degree:* diplomas and associate.

Library Technical Resource Center with 389 titles, 2 serial subscriptions, a Web page.

Computers on Campus 3 computers available on campus for general student use. A campuswide network can be accessed. Internet access available.

Student Life *Housing:* college housing not available. *Campus security:* 24-hour emergency response devices.

Costs (2006–07) *Tuition:* $11,090 full-time. *Required fees:* $1900 full-time.

Applying *Required:* high school diploma, GED, or ATB test.

Director of Admissions Mr. Mike Thurber, Director of Admissions, Tulsa Welding School, 2545 East 11th Street, Tulsa, OK 74104. *Phone:* 800-331-2934 Ext. 240. *Toll-free phone:* 800-WELD-PRO.

VATTEROTT COLLEGE

Oklahoma City, Oklahoma　　　**www.vatterott-college.edu/**

- **Proprietary** 2-year
- **Urban** campus
- **Coed**

Undergraduates 249 full-time. 36% African American, 2% Asian American or Pacific Islander, 5% Hispanic American, 7% Native American.

Faculty *Student/faculty ratio:* 12:1.

Academics *Calendar:* semesters. *Degrees:* diplomas, associate, and first professional.

Costs (2005–06) *Tuition:* $20,000 full-time. Full-time tuition and fees vary according to degree level and program. No tuition increase for student's term of enrollment. *Required fees:* $900 full-time. *Payment plans:* tuition prepayment, installment.

Applying *Required:* essay or personal statement, high school transcript, interview.

Director of Admissions Mark Hybers, Director of Admissions, Vatterott College, 4629 Northwest 23rd Street, Oklahoma City, OK 73127. *Phone:* 405-945-0088. *Toll-free phone:* 888-948-0088.

VATTEROTT COLLEGE

Tulsa, Oklahoma　　　　**www.vatterott-college.edu/**

- **Proprietary** 2-year
- **Urban** 3-acre campus
- **Coed, primarily women,** 226 undergraduate students, 100% full-time, 29% women, 71% men
- **78% of applicants were admitted**

Undergraduates 226 full-time. 28% African American, 4% Hispanic American, 11% Native American. *Retention:* 71% of 2003 full-time freshmen returned. Freshmen *Admission:* 117 applied, 91 admitted, 91 enrolled.

Faculty *Total:* 18, 100% full-time. *Student/faculty ratio:* 12:1.

Majors Computer programming; electrical, electronic and communications engineering technology; heating, air conditioning and refrigeration technology; medical administrative assistant and medical secretary.

Academics *Calendar:* semesters. *Degree:* diplomas and associate.

Freshmen Application Contact Mr. Tim Maloukis, Director of Admissions, Vatterott College, 555 South Memorial Drive, Tulsa, OK 74112. *Phone:* 918-836-6656. *Toll-free phone:* 888-857-4016. *Fax:* 918-836-9698. *E-mail:* tulsa@vatterott-college.edu.

WESTERN OKLAHOMA STATE COLLEGE

Altus, Oklahoma　　　　**www.wosc.edu/**

- **State-supported** 2-year, founded 1926, part of Oklahoma State Regents for Higher Education
- **Rural** 142-acre campus
- **Endowment** $2.5 million
- **Coed,** 2,061 undergraduate students, 42% full-time, 58% women, 42% men

Undergraduates 859 full-time, 1,202 part-time. Students come from 30 states and territories, 1 other country, 13% African American, 2% Asian American or Pacific Islander, 11% Hispanic American, 4% Native American. *Retention:* 50% of 2003 full-time freshmen returned. Freshmen *Admission:* 499 applied, 499 admitted, 499 enrolled.

Faculty *Total:* 100, 37% full-time, 3% with terminal degrees. *Student/faculty ratio:* 20:1.

Majors Accounting technology and bookkeeping; aviation/airway management; child development; computer/information technology services administration related; criminal justice/police science; emergency medical technology (EMT paramedic); fire protection related; general studies; liberal arts and sciences/liberal studies; mechanics and repair; medical radiologic technology; nursing (registered nurse training).

Academics *Calendar:* semesters. *Degree:* certificates and associate. *Special study options:* academic remediation for entering students, adult/continuing education programs, advanced placement credit, honors programs, off-campus study, part-time degree program, services for LD students, student-designed majors, summer session for credit.

Library Learning Resources Center with 33,000 titles, 1,000 serial subscriptions, an OPAC, a Web page.

Computers on Campus 50 computers available on campus for general student use. A campuswide network can be accessed from student residence rooms and from off campus. At least one staffed computer lab available.

Student Life *Housing Options:* coed. Campus housing is university owned. *Activities and Organizations:* drama/theater group, choral group, Baptist Student Union, Phi Theta Kappa, Student Senate, Behavioral Science Club, Aggie Club, national fraternities. *Campus security:* 24-hour emergency response devices. *Student services:* personal/psychological counseling.

Athletics Member NJCAA. *Intercollegiate sports:* baseball M(s), basketball M(s)/W(s), equestrian sports M/W, golf M/W, softball W(s). *Intramural sports:* basketball M/W, football M, golf M/W, tennis M/W, volleyball M/W.

Standardized Tests *Required for some:* ACT (for admission).

Costs (2006–07) *Tuition:* state resident $2213 full-time, $74 per semester hour part-time; nonresident $5348 full-time, $178 per semester hour part-time. *Room and board:* $4400.

Financial Aid Of all full-time matriculated undergraduates who enrolled in 2004, 85 Federal Work-Study jobs (averaging $1978).

Applying *Options:* electronic application, early admission. *Application fee:* $15. *Required:* high school transcript. *Application deadline:* rolling (freshmen), rolling (transfers). *Notification:* continuous (freshmen).

Freshmen Application Contact Dr. Larry W. Paxton, Director of Academic Services, Western Oklahoma State College, 2801 North Main Street, Altus, OK 73521-1397. *Phone:* 580-477-7720. *Fax:* 580-477-7723. *E-mail:* larry.paxton@wosc.edu.

OREGON

BLUE MOUNTAIN COMMUNITY COLLEGE
Pendleton, Oregon   www.bluecc.edu/

- **State and locally supported** 2-year, founded 1962
- **Rural** 170-acre campus
- **Endowment** $1.7 million
- **Coed**

Undergraduates 872 full-time, 1,006 part-time. Students come from 9 states and territories, 6 other countries, 2% are from out of state, 0.5% African American, 0.5% Asian American or Pacific Islander, 6% Hispanic American, 4% Native American, 0.6% international.

Faculty *Student/faculty ratio:* 25:1.

Academics *Calendar:* quarters. *Degree:* certificates and associate. *Special study options:* academic remediation for entering students, adult/continuing education programs, advanced placement credit, cooperative education, distance learning, English as a second language, part-time degree program, services for LD students, summer session for credit.

Athletics Member NJCAA.

Standardized Tests *Required:* ACT ASSET and ACT COMPASS (for placement).

Financial Aid Of all full-time matriculated undergraduates who enrolled in 2004, 60 Federal Work-Study jobs (averaging $1800). 100 state and other part-time jobs (averaging $1200).

Applying *Options:* electronic application. *Required:* high school transcript.

Director of Admissions Ms. Valerie Fouquette, Director, Admissions, Blue Mountain Community College, PO Box 100, Pendleton, OR 97801. *Phone:* 541-278-5774.

CENTRAL OREGON COMMUNITY COLLEGE
Bend, Oregon   www.cocc.edu/

- **District-supported** 2-year, founded 1949, part of Oregon Community College Association
- **Small-town** 193-acre campus
- **Endowment** $5.5 million
- **Coed,** 4,048 undergraduate students, 38% full-time, 58% women, 42% men

Located in Bend, Oregon, Central Oregon Community College (COCC) offers more than fifty certificate and degree options, affordable tuition, outstanding faculty members, small classes, and access to more than twenty bachelor's degree programs through Oregon State University's Cascades campus. COCC also features on-campus housing, intramural sports, and exceptional outdoor recreation opportunities.

Undergraduates 1,536 full-time, 2,512 part-time. Students come from 7 states and territories, 4% are from out of state, 0.2% African American, 1% Asian American or Pacific Islander, 4% Hispanic American, 3% Native American, 3% live on campus.

Freshmen *Admission:* 1,410 applied, 740 enrolled.

Faculty *Total:* 312, 28% full-time, 15% with terminal degrees. *Student/faculty ratio:* 23:1.

Majors Accounting; administrative assistant and secretarial science; art; automobile/automotive mechanics technology; biological and physical sciences; business administration and management; cartography; computer and information sciences related; computer science; criminal justice/law enforcement administration; culinary arts; dental assisting; early childhood education; education; emergency medical technology (EMT paramedic); fire science; fish/game management; forestry; forestry technology; health information/medical records technology; hospitality administration; hospitality and recreation marketing; hotel/motel administration; humanities; industrial technology; kinesiology and exercise science; liberal arts and sciences/liberal studies; marketing/marketing management; mathematics; medical/clinical assistant; nursing (licensed practical/vocational nurse training); nursing (registered nurse training); physical sciences; pre-engineering; social sciences; sport and fitness administration/management; tourism promotion; welding technology.

Academics *Calendar:* quarters. *Degree:* certificates and associate. *Special study options:* academic remediation for entering students, cooperative education, distance learning, double majors, English as a second language, independent study, internships, part-time degree program, student-designed majors, study abroad.

Library COCC Library plus 1 other with 76,421 titles, 329 serial subscriptions, 3,570 audiovisual materials, an OPAC, a Web page.

Computers on Campus 335 computers available on campus for general student use. A campuswide network can be accessed from student residence rooms and from off campus that provide access to e-mail. Internet access, online (class) registration, at least one staffed computer lab available.

Student Life *Housing Options:* coed. Campus housing is provided by a third party. *Activities and Organizations:* student-run newspaper, choral group, student government, club sports, Phi Theta Kappa, DEC, Science Learning Center. *Campus security:* 24-hour emergency response devices and patrols, late-night transport/escort service. *Student services:* health clinic, personal/psychological counseling.

Athletics *Intramural sports:* badminton M/W, baseball M/W, basketball M/W, cross-country running M/W, football M, soccer M/W, softball M/W, table tennis M/W, tennis M/W, track and field M/W, volleyball M/W, water polo M/W, weight lifting M/W.

Standardized Tests *Required:* (for placement).

Costs (2006–07) *Tuition:* area resident $2835 full-time, $63 per credit part-time; state resident $3870 full-time, $86 per credit part-time; nonresident $7920 full-time, $176 per credit part-time. *Required fees:* $114 full-time, $4 per credit part-time. *Room and board:* $6798.

Financial Aid Of all full-time matriculated undergraduates who enrolled in 2004, 400 Federal Work-Study jobs (averaging $1900).

Applying *Options:* electronic application. *Application fee:* $25. *Application deadline:* rolling (freshmen), rolling (transfers). *Notification:* continuous (freshmen).

Director of Admissions Ms. Alicia Moore, Director, Admissions, Central Oregon Community College, 2600 Northwest College Way, Bend, OR 97701-5998. *Phone:* 541-383-7211. *E-mail:* welcome@metolius.cocc.edu.

CHEMEKETA COMMUNITY COLLEGE

Salem, Oregon   www.chemeketa.edu/

- **State and locally supported** 2-year, founded 1955
- **Urban** 72-acre campus with easy access to Portland
- **Coed,** 15,000 undergraduate students

Undergraduates Students come from 5 states and territories, 1% are from out of state.

Majors Accounting; administrative assistant and secretarial science; agricultural teacher education; art teacher education; automobile/automotive mechanics technology; business administration and management; civil engineering technology; computer engineering technology; computer programming; computer science; construction engineering technology; criminal justice/law enforcement administration; dental hygiene; drafting and design technology; economics; education; electrical, electronic and communications engineering technology; emergency medical technology (EMT paramedic); engineering; English; finance; fire science; forestry; forestry technology; graphic and printing equipment operation/production; health/health care administration; health information/medical records administration; health teacher education; hospitality administration; hotel/motel administration; humanities; human services; industrial technology; kindergarten/preschool education; liberal arts and sciences/liberal studies; mathematics; mechanical design technology; medical administrative assistant and medical secretary; medical/clinical assistant; nursing (licensed practical/vocational nurse training); nursing (registered nurse training); physical education teaching and coaching; political science and government; real estate; science teacher education; social sciences; teacher assistant/aide; welding technology.

Academics *Calendar:* quarters. *Degree:* certificates, diplomas, and associate. *Special study options:* academic remediation for entering students, adult/continuing education programs, advanced placement credit, cooperative education, distance learning, double majors, English as a second language, independent study, internships, part-time degree program, services for LD students, summer session for credit.

Library Chemeketa Community College Library plus 1 other with 801 audiovisual materials, an OPAC, a Web page.

Computers on Campus A campuswide network can be accessed from off campus. Internet access, at least one staffed computer lab available.

Student Life *Housing:* college housing not available. *Activities and Organizations:* drama/theater group, student-run newspaper, choral group, Health Occupations Students of America, International Conference of Building Officials, Ski Club, Christian Fellowship. *Campus security:* 24-hour emergency response devices and patrols, late-night transport/escort service. *Student services:* personal/psychological counseling, women's center.

Athletics *Intercollegiate sports:* baseball M(s), basketball M(s)/W(s), cross-country running M(s)/W(s), track and field M(s)/W(s), volleyball W(s).

Costs (2005–06) *Tuition:* state resident $2610 full-time, $58 per quarter hour part-time; nonresident $8955 full-time, $199 per quarter hour part-time. *Required fees:* $180 full-time, $4 per quarter hour part-time.

Financial Aid Of all full-time matriculated undergraduates who enrolled in 2004, 316 Federal Work-Study jobs (averaging $1290).

Applying *Options:* deferred entrance. *Required for some:* high school transcript. *Application deadline:* rolling (freshmen), rolling (transfers). *Notification:* continuous (freshmen).

Freshmen Application Contact Enrollment Center, Chemeketa Community College, 4000 Lancaster Drive, NE, Salem, OR 97305-7070. *Phone:* 503-399-5001. *Fax:* 503-399-3918. *E-mail:* registrar@chemeketa.edu.

CLACKAMAS COMMUNITY COLLEGE

Oregon City, Oregon   www.clackamas.edu/

- **District-supported** 2-year, founded 1966
- **Suburban** 175-acre campus with easy access to Portland
- **Endowment** $5.6 million
- **Coed**

Undergraduates 2,852 full-time, 4,014 part-time. Students come from 38 states and territories, 16 other countries, 7% are from out of state, 1% African American, 4% Asian American or Pacific Islander, 4% Hispanic American, 1% Native American, 0.1% international, 31% transferred in.

Faculty *Student/faculty ratio:* 19:1.

Academics *Calendar:* quarters. *Degree:* certificates, diplomas, and associate. *Special study options:* academic remediation for entering students, accelerated degree program, adult/continuing education programs, advanced placement credit, cooperative education, distance learning, double majors, English as a second language, honors programs, independent study, internships, part-time degree program, services for LD students, study abroad, summer session for credit. *ROTC:* Air Force (c).

Student Life *Campus security:* 24-hour emergency response devices and patrols, student patrols, late-night transport/escort service.

Athletics Member NJCAA.

Standardized Tests *Required:* Assessment and Placement Services for Community Colleges (for placement). *Recommended:* SAT or ACT (for placement).

Financial Aid Of all full-time matriculated undergraduates who enrolled in 2004, 115 Federal Work-Study jobs (averaging $1330).

Applying *Options:* early admission. *Recommended:* high school transcript.

Director of Admissions Ms. Diane Drebin, Registrar, Clackamas Community College, 19600 South Molalla Avenue, Oregon City, OR 97045. *Phone:* 503-657-6958 Ext. 2742.

CLATSOP COMMUNITY COLLEGE

Astoria, Oregon   www.clatsopcc.edu/

- **County-supported** 2-year, founded 1958
- **Small-town** 20-acre campus
- **Endowment** $2.0 million
- **Coed,** 1,824 undergraduate students, 24% full-time, 48% women, 52% men

Undergraduates 445 full-time, 1,379 part-time. Students come from 28 states and territories, 1 other country, 15% are from out of state, 0.7% African American, 2% Asian American or Pacific Islander, 4% Hispanic American, 3% Native American, 0.9% international, 0.4% transferred in.

Freshmen *Admission:* 340 applied, 277 admitted, 205 enrolled.

Faculty *Total:* 198, 20% full-time, 3% with terminal degrees. *Student/faculty ratio:* 14:1.

Majors Accounting; administrative assistant and secretarial science; business administration and management; business automation/technology/data entry; computer engineering technology; computer systems networking and telecommunications; criminal justice/law enforcement administration; fire science; legal administrative assistant/secretary; liberal arts and sciences/liberal studies; medical administrative assistant and medical secretary; nursing (registered nurse training).

Academics *Calendar:* quarters. *Degree:* certificates and associate. *Special study options:* academic remediation for entering students, adult/continuing education programs, advanced placement credit, cooperative education, distance learning, English as a second language, external degree program, internships, part-time degree program, services for LD students, summer session for credit.

Library Dora Badollet Library plus 1 other with 48,517 titles, 180 serial subscriptions, 5,000 audiovisual materials, an OPAC, a Web page.

Computers on Campus 76 computers available on campus for general student use. A campuswide network can be accessed from off campus. Internet access, at least one staffed computer lab available.

Student Life *Housing:* college housing not available. *Activities and Organizations:* Lives in Transition, Phi Theta Kappa, Nursing Club, Spanish Club, Fine Arts Club. *Campus security:* 24-hour emergency response devices, late-night transport/escort service. *Student services:* personal/psychological counseling.

Costs (2005–06) *Tuition:* state resident $2700 full-time, $60 per credit part-time; nonresident $5400 full-time, $120 per credit part-time.

Financial Aid Of all full-time matriculated undergraduates who enrolled in 2004, 220 Federal Work-Study jobs (averaging $2175).

Applying *Options:* early admission. *Application fee:* $15. *Recommended:* high school transcript. *Application deadlines:* rolling (freshmen), 9/29 (transfers). *Notification:* continuous (freshmen).

Freshmen Application Contact Ms. Joanne Swenson, Admissions Coordinator, Clatsop Community College, 1653 Jerome, Astoria, OR 97103-3698. *Phone:* 503-338-2325. *Toll-free phone:* 866-252-8767. *Fax:* 503-325-5738. *E-mail:* admissions@clatsopcc.edu.

COLUMBIA GORGE COMMUNITY COLLEGE

The Dalles, Oregon   www.cgcc.cc.or.us/

- **State-supported** 2-year, founded 1977
- **Coed**

Academics *Calendar:* quarters. *Degree:* certificates, diplomas, and associate.

Director of Admissions Ms. Karen Carter, Dean of Student Services, Columbia Gorge Community College, 400 East Scenic Drive, The Dalles, OR 97058. *Phone:* 541-298-3110. *E-mail:* kcarter@cgcc.cc.or.us.

HEALD COLLEGE-PORTLAND

Portland, Oregon   www.heald.edu/

- **Independent** 2-year, founded 1863
- **Coed,** 206 undergraduate students, 72% full-time, 52% women, 48% men

Undergraduates 149 full-time, 57 part-time. 7% African American, 4% Asian American or Pacific Islander, 5% Hispanic American, 0.5% Native American. Freshmen *Admission:* 37 enrolled.
Faculty *Total:* 21, 71% full-time, 100% with terminal degrees. *Student/faculty ratio:* 10:1.
Majors Accounting; administrative assistant and secretarial science; business administration and management; information science/studies; medical administrative assistant and medical secretary.
Academics *Calendar:* quarters. *Degree:* certificates, diplomas, and associate. *Special study options:* academic remediation for entering students, advanced placement credit, internships, part-time degree program, summer session for credit.
Library Learning Resource Center with an OPAC.
Computers on Campus Internet access, at least one staffed computer lab available.
Standardized Tests *Required:* COMPASS (for admission).
Financial Aid Of all full-time matriculated undergraduates who enrolled in 2004, 15 Federal Work-Study jobs.
Applying *Options:* electronic application, early admission, deferred entrance. *Application fee:* $40. *Required:* high school transcript, interview. *Application deadline:* rolling (freshmen), rolling (transfers). *Notification:* continuous (freshmen).
Freshmen Application Contact Director of Admissions, Heald College-Portland, 625 Southwest Broadway, 4th Floor, Portland, OR 97205. *Phone:* 503-229-0492. *Toll-free phone:* 800-755-3550. *Fax:* 503-229-0498. *E-mail:* info@heald.edu.

ITT TECHNICAL INSTITUTE

Portland, Oregon   www.itt-tech.edu/

- **Proprietary** primarily 2-year, founded 1971, part of ITT Educational Services, Inc
- **Urban** 4-acre campus
- **Coed**

Majors Animation, interactive technology, video graphics and special effects; business administration and management; CAD/CADD drafting/design technology; computer and information systems security; computer programming; computer systems networking and telecommunications; criminal justice/law enforcement administration; e-commerce; electrical, electronic and communications engineering technology; robotics technology; system, networking, and LAN/WAN management; web/multimedia management and webmaster; web page, digital/multimedia and information resources design.
Academics *Calendar:* quarters. *Degrees:* associate and bachelor's.
Library a Web page.
Computers on Campus Internet access, at least one staffed computer lab available.
Student Life *Housing:* college housing not available. *Activities and Organizations:* student-run newspaper.
Standardized Tests *Required:* Wonderlic aptitude test (for admission).
Costs (2005–06) *Tuition:* Please see school catalog for specific information.
Financial Aid Of all full-time matriculated undergraduates who enrolled in 2004, 15 Federal Work-Study jobs (averaging $5000).
Applying *Options:* deferred entrance. *Application fee:* $100. *Required:* high school transcript, interview. *Recommended:* letters of recommendation. *Application deadline:* rolling (freshmen), rolling (transfers). *Notification:* continuous (freshmen).
Freshmen Application Contact Mr. Greg Lester, Director of Recruitment, ITT Technical Institute, 6035 Northeast 78th Court, Portland, OR 97218. *Phone:* 503-255-6500. *Toll-free phone:* 800-234-5488.

KLAMATH COMMUNITY COLLEGE

Klamath Falls, Oregon   www.kcc.cc.or.us/

Director of Admissions Mr. Greg Brown, Dean for Student Services, Klamath Community College, 7390 South 6th Street, Klamath Falls, OR 97603. *Phone:* 541-882-3521. *E-mail:* browng@kcc.cc.or.us.

LANE COMMUNITY COLLEGE

Eugene, Oregon   www.lanecc.edu/

- **State and locally supported** 2-year, founded 1964
- **Suburban** 240-acre campus
- **Endowment** $6.0 million
- **Coed**

Undergraduates 4,565 full-time, 7,269 part-time. Students come from 28 states and territories, 27 other countries, 1% African American, 2% Asian American or Pacific Islander, 4% Hispanic American, 2% Native American, 2% international. *Retention:* 62% of 2003 full-time freshmen returned.
Faculty *Student/faculty ratio:* 22:1.
Academics *Calendar:* quarters. *Degree:* certificates and associate. *Special study options:* academic remediation for entering students, adult/continuing education programs, advanced placement credit, English as a second language, internships, part-time degree program, services for LD students, summer session for credit.
Student Life *Campus security:* 24-hour emergency response devices and patrols, student patrols, late-night transport/escort service.
Financial Aid Of all full-time matriculated undergraduates who enrolled in 2004, 400 Federal Work-Study jobs (averaging $3600).
Applying *Options:* common application, early admission.
Director of Admissions Ms. Helen Garrett, Director of Admissions/Registrar, Lane Community College, 4000 East 30th Avenue, Eugene, OR 97405-0640. *Phone:* 541-747-4501 Ext. 2686.

LINN-BENTON COMMUNITY COLLEGE

Albany, Oregon   www.linnbenton.edu/

- **State and locally supported** 2-year, founded 1966
- **Small-town** 104-acre campus
- **Endowment** $2.1 million
- **Coed,** 5,289 undergraduate students, 54% full-time, 54% women, 46% men

Undergraduates 2,839 full-time, 2,450 part-time. Students come from 5 states and territories, 10 other countries.
Freshmen *Admission:* 2,896 applied, 2,896 admitted, 1,406 enrolled.
Faculty *Total:* 484, 32% full-time.
Majors Accounting; administrative assistant and secretarial science; agricultural business and management; agricultural teacher education; agriculture; animal sciences; art; automobile/automotive mechanics technology; biological and physical sciences; biology/biological sciences; business administration and management; chemistry; child care and support services management; civil engineering technology; commercial and advertising art; computer and information sciences; computer programming (specific applications); computer/technical support; criminal justice/police science; criminal justice/safety; culinary arts; culinary arts related; dairy husbandry and production; desktop publishing and digital imaging design; diesel mechanics technology; drafting and design technology; dramatic/theater arts; economics; education; elementary education; engineering; English; family and consumer sciences/human sciences; foreign languages and literatures; graphic communications related; horse husbandry/equine science and management; horticultural science; industrial technology; journalism; juvenile corrections; legal administrative assistant/secretary; liberal arts and sciences/liberal studies; machine tool technology; mathematics; medical administrative assistant and medical secretary; medical/clinical assistant; metallurgical technology; multi-/interdisciplinary studies related; nursing (registered nurse training); photography; physical education teaching and coaching; physical sciences; physics; pre-engineering; restaurant, culinary, and catering management; speech and rhetoric; system administration; teacher assistant/aide; technical and business writing; water quality and wastewater treatment management and recycling technology; welding technology.
Academics *Calendar:* quarters. *Degree:* certificates and associate. *Special study options:* academic remediation for entering students, adult/continuing education programs, advanced placement credit, cooperative education, distance learning, English as a second language, independent study, internships, part-time degree program, services for LD students, student-designed majors, summer session for credit. *ROTC:* Army (c), Air Force (c).
Library Linn-Benton Community College Library with 42,561 titles, 91 serial subscriptions, 8,758 audiovisual materials, an OPAC, a Web page.
Computers on Campus 500 computers available on campus for general student use. A campuswide network can be accessed from off campus. Internet access, online (class) registration, at least one staffed computer lab available.
Student Life *Housing:* college housing not available. *Activities and Organizations:* drama/theater group, student-run newspaper, choral group, EBOP Club,

Linn-Benton Community College (continued)
Multicultural Club, Campus Family Co-op, Horticulture Club, Collegiate Secretary Club. *Campus security:* 24-hour emergency response devices and patrols, student patrols, late-night transport/escort service. *Student services:* personal/psychological counseling.
Athletics *Intercollegiate sports:* baseball M(s), basketball M(s)/W(s), volleyball W(s). *Intramural sports:* basketball M/W, tennis M/W, ultimate Frisbee M/W, volleyball M/W.
Costs (2006–07) *Tuition:* state resident $2925 full-time; nonresident $7470 full-time.
Financial Aid Of all full-time matriculated undergraduates who enrolled in 2004, 290 Federal Work-Study jobs (averaging $1800).
Applying *Options:* deferred entrance. *Application fee:* $25. *Required for some:* high school transcript. *Application deadline:* rolling (freshmen), rolling (transfers).
Freshmen Application Contact Ms. Christine Baker, Outreach Coordinator, Linn-Benton Community College, 6500 Pacific Boulevard, SW, Albany, OR 97321. *Phone:* 541-917-4813. *Fax:* 541-917-4838. *E-mail:* admissions@linnbenton.edu.

MT. HOOD COMMUNITY COLLEGE
Gresham, Oregon www.mhcc.cc.or.us/

Director of Admissions Dr. Craig Kolins, Associate Vice President of Enrollment Services, Mt. Hood Community College, 26000 Southeast Stark Street, Gresham, OR 97030-3300. *Phone:* 503-491-7265.

OREGON COAST COMMUNITY COLLEGE
Newport, Oregon www.occc.cc.or.us

- **Public** 2-year
- **Coed,** 599 undergraduate students, 12% full-time, 64% women, 36% men

Undergraduates 73 full-time, 526 part-time. Students come from 5 states and territories, 1% are from out of state, 0.6% African American, 2% Asian American or Pacific Islander, 4% Hispanic American, 5% Native American, 43% transferred in.
Freshmen *Admission:* 86 applied, 86 admitted, 86 enrolled.
Faculty *Total:* 45, 7% full-time, 20% with terminal degrees. *Student/faculty ratio:* 14:1.
Majors General studies; liberal arts and sciences/liberal studies; marine biology and biological oceanography; nursing (registered nurse training).
Academics *Calendar:* quarters. *Degree:* certificates and associate. *Special study options:* academic remediation for entering students, cooperative education, distance learning, English as a second language, honors programs, internships, part-time degree program, services for LD students, summer session for credit.
Library Oregon Coast Community College Library with 8,652 titles, 51 serial subscriptions, 1,210 audiovisual materials, an OPAC, a Web page.
Computers on Campus 40 computers available on campus for general student use. A campuswide network can be accessed. Internet access, at least one staffed computer lab available.
Student Life *Housing:* college housing not available.
Costs (2006–07) *Tuition:* state resident $2790 full-time, $62 per credit part-time; nonresident $7740 full-time, $172 per credit part-time. *Required fees:* $210 full-time, $5 per credit part-time.
Applying *Options:* common application.
Freshmen Application Contact Student Services, Oregon Coast Community College, 332 SW Coast Highway, Newport, OR 97365. *Phone:* 541-574-7101. *Fax:* 541-574-7159. *E-mail:* webinfo@occc.cc.or.us.

PIONEER PACIFIC COLLEGE
Wilsonville, Oregon www.pioneerpacific.edu/

- **Proprietary** primarily 2-year, founded 1981
- **Suburban** campus with easy access to Portland
- **Coed,** 1,132 undergraduate students, 99% full-time, 77% women, 23% men

Undergraduates 1,126 full-time, 6 part-time. Students come from 2 states and territories, 1 other country, 6% are from out of state, 2% African American, 3%

Asian American or Pacific Islander, 5% Hispanic American, 0.4% Native American, 0.1% international, 17% transferred in.
Freshmen *Admission:* 752 applied, 631 admitted, 301 enrolled.
Faculty *Total:* 119, 41% full-time, 8% with terminal degrees. *Student/faculty ratio:* 15:1.
Majors Accounting; business administration and management; criminal justice/police science; health/health care administration; information science/studies; information technology; legal assistant/paralegal; medical/clinical assistant; sales, distribution and marketing; web/multimedia management and webmaster.
Academics *Calendar:* continuous. *Degrees:* diplomas, associate, and bachelor's. *Special study options:* accelerated degree program, honors programs, internships.
Library 2,500 titles.
Computers on Campus 300 computers available on campus for general student use. A campuswide network can be accessed. Internet access available. Computer purchase or lease plan available.
Student Life *Housing:* college housing not available. *Activities and Organizations:* Phi Beta Lambda.
Standardized Tests *Required:* CPAt (for admission).
Costs (2006–07) *Tuition:* $8280 full-time, $188 per credit hour part-time. *Required fees:* $150 full-time.
Applying *Application fee:* $50. *Required:* high school transcript, interview. *Application deadline:* rolling (freshmen).
Freshmen Application Contact Admissions, Pioneer Pacific College, 27501 Southwest Parkway Avenue, Wilsonville, OR 97070. *Phone:* 866-772-4636. *Toll-free phone:* 866-PPC-INFO. *Fax:* 503-682-1514. *E-mail:* inquiries@pioneerpacific.edu.

PORTLAND COMMUNITY COLLEGE
Portland, Oregon www.pcc.edu/

Director of Admissions Mr. Dennis Bailey-Fougnier, Director of Admissions, Portland Community College, PO Box 19000, Portland, OR 97280. *Phone:* 503-977-4519.

ROGUE COMMUNITY COLLEGE
Grants Pass, Oregon www.roguecc.edu/

- **State and locally supported** 2-year, founded 1970
- **Rural** 90-acre campus
- **Endowment** $6.1 million
- **Coed,** 4,224 undergraduate students, 32% full-time, 56% women, 44% men

Undergraduates 1,341 full-time, 2,883 part-time. Students come from 5 states and territories, 5 other countries, 0.2% are from out of state, 1% African American, 2% Asian American or Pacific Islander, 6% Hispanic American, 2% Native American, 0.2% international, 25% transferred in.
Freshmen *Admission:* 367 applied, 367 admitted, 367 enrolled.
Faculty *Total:* 499, 20% full-time. *Student/faculty ratio:* 11:1.
Majors Automobile/automotive mechanics technology; business administration and management; child development; computer science; construction management; criminal justice/law enforcement administration; education related; electrical, electronic and communications engineering technology; fire science; heavy equipment maintenance technology; humanities; human services; industrial technology; liberal arts and sciences/liberal studies; manufacturing technology; nursing (registered nurse training); social sciences; substance abuse/addiction counseling; welding technology.
Academics *Calendar:* quarters. *Degree:* certificates, diplomas, and associate. *Special study options:* academic remediation for entering students, adult/continuing education programs, advanced placement credit, cooperative education, distance learning, double majors, English as a second language, internships, part-time degree program, services for LD students, summer session for credit.
Library Rogue Community College Library with 33,000 titles, 275 serial subscriptions, an OPAC.
Computers on Campus 96 computers available on campus for general student use. A campuswide network can be accessed. Internet access, online (class) registration, at least one staffed computer lab available.
Student Life *Housing:* college housing not available. *Activities and Organizations:* drama/theater group, student-run newspaper, choral group. *Campus security:* 24-hour patrols, late-night transport/escort service. *Student services:* personal/psychological counseling, women's center.
Athletics *Intramural sports:* basketball M/W, soccer M/W, tennis M/W, volleyball M/W.

Costs (2006–07) *Tuition:* state resident $2304 full-time, $64 per credit hour part-time; nonresident $2772 full-time, $77 per credit hour part-time. *Required fees:* $294 full-time, $4 per credit hour part-time.

Financial Aid Of all full-time matriculated undergraduates who enrolled in 2004, 210 Federal Work-Study jobs (averaging $3200). 300 state and other part-time jobs (averaging $3000).

Applying *Options:* early admission. *Application deadline:* rolling (freshmen), rolling (transfers).

Freshmen Application Contact Ms. Claudia Sullivan, Director of Admissions, Rogue Community College, 3345 Redwood Highway, Grants Pass, OR 97527-9298. *Phone:* 541-956-7176. *Fax:* 541-471-3585. *E-mail:* csullivan@roguecc.edu.

SOUTHWESTERN OREGON COMMUNITY COLLEGE

Coos Bay, Oregon   www.socc.edu/

- **State and locally supported** 2-year, founded 1961
- **Small-town** 125-acre campus
- **Endowment** $769,894
- **Coed,** 1,980 undergraduate students, 49% full-time, 58% women, 42% men

Undergraduates 976 full-time, 1,004 part-time. Students come from 4 other countries, 15% are from out of state, 2% African American, 1% Asian American or Pacific Islander, 3% Hispanic American, 5% Native American, 1% international.
Freshmen *Admission:* 832 applied, 832 admitted, 458 enrolled. *Average high school GPA:* 3.40.

Faculty *Total:* 219, 30% full-time. *Student/faculty ratio:* 10:1.

Majors Accounting; adult development and aging; athletic training; business administration and management; child care provision; computer systems analysis; computer systems networking and telecommunications; corrections; criminal justice/police science; criminal justice/safety; engineering; environmental studies; fire science; forestry; health and physical education; industrial technology; liberal arts and sciences/liberal studies; machine tool technology; management information systems; marketing/marketing management; mathematics; medical/clinical assistant; natural sciences; nursing (registered nurse training); office management; restaurant, culinary, and catering management; social work; substance abuse/addiction counseling; turf and turfgrass management; welding technology.

Academics *Calendar:* quarters. *Degree:* certificates, diplomas, and associate. *Special study options:* academic remediation for entering students, adult/continuing education programs, advanced placement credit, cooperative education, distance learning, English as a second language, internships, part-time degree program, services for LD students, summer session for credit.

Library Southwestern Oregon Community College Library with 40,505 titles, 218 serial subscriptions, 3,673 audiovisual materials, an OPAC, a Web page.

Computers on Campus 65 computers available on campus for general student use. A campuswide network can be accessed. Internet access, online (class) registration, at least one staffed computer lab available.

Student Life *Housing:* on-campus residence required for freshman year. *Options:* coed. Campus housing is university owned. *Activities and Organizations:* drama/theater group, student-run newspaper, choral group. *Campus security:* controlled dormitory access.

Athletics Member NJCAA. *Intercollegiate sports:* baseball M(s), basketball M(s)/W(s), cheerleading M(s)/W(s), cross-country running M(s)/W(s), golf M(s)/W(s), soccer M(s)/W(s), softball W(s), track and field M(s)/W(s), volleyball W(s), wrestling M(s). *Intramural sports:* basketball M, volleyball M/W.

Costs (2006–07) *Tuition:* state resident $3330 full-time, $62 per credit part-time; nonresident $3330 full-time, $62 per credit part-time. *Required fees:* $330 full-time, $12 per credit part-time, $22 per course part-time. *Room and board:* $6160.

Financial Aid Of all full-time matriculated undergraduates who enrolled in 2004, 140 Federal Work-Study jobs (averaging $874). 42 state and other part-time jobs (averaging $545).

Applying *Options:* early admission. *Application fee:* $30. *Required for some:* high school transcript. *Application deadline:* rolling (freshmen), rolling (transfers). *Notification:* continuous (freshmen).

Freshmen Application Contact Miss Lela Wells, Southwestern Oregon Community College, Student First Stop, 1988 Newmark Avenue, Coos Bay, OR 97420. *Phone:* 541-888-7611. *Toll-free phone:* 800-962-2838. *E-mail:* lwells@socc.edu.

TILLAMOOK BAY COMMUNITY COLLEGE

Tillamook, Oregon   www.tbcc.cc.or.us/

- **District-supported** 2-year, founded 1984, administratively affiliated with Portland Community College
- **Coed,** 299 undergraduate students, 24% full-time, 68% women, 32% men
- **100% of applicants were admitted**

Undergraduates 73 full-time, 226 part-time. Students come from 2 states and territories, 1 other country, 2% are from out of state, 1% African American, 2% Asian American or Pacific Islander, 1% Hispanic American, 2% Native American, 4% transferred in.
Freshmen *Admission:* 90 applied, 90 admitted, 90 enrolled.

Faculty *Total:* 36, 17% full-time, 14% with terminal degrees. *Student/faculty ratio:* 8:1.

Majors Accounting; accounting technology and bookkeeping; administrative assistant and secretarial science; business automation/technology/data entry; criminal justice/law enforcement administration; early childhood education; emergency medical technology (EMT paramedic); general studies; liberal arts and sciences/liberal studies; management science; marketing related; nursing related; office management; substance abuse/addiction counseling.

Academics *Calendar:* quarters. *Degree:* certificates, diplomas, and associate.

Student Life *Housing:* college housing not available. *Campus security:* Evening security guard.

Costs (2006–07) *Tuition:* $62 per credit part-time; state resident $2976 full-time, $62 per credit part-time; nonresident $3936 full-time, $82 per credit part-time. *Required fees:* $530 full-time, $33 per course part-time.

Applying *Recommended:* high school transcript.

Freshmen Application Contact Lori Gates, Tillamook Bay Community College, 2510 First Street, Tillamook, OR 97141. *Phone:* 503-842-8222. *Fax:* 503-842-2214. *E-mail:* gates@tillamookbay.cc.

TREASURE VALLEY COMMUNITY COLLEGE

Ontario, Oregon   www.tvcc.cc.or.us/

- **State and locally supported** 2-year, founded 1962
- **Small-town** 95-acre campus
- **Coed,** 1,946 undergraduate students, 54% full-time, 62% women, 38% men

Undergraduates 1,056 full-time, 890 part-time. Students come from 8 states and territories, 64% are from out of state, 1% African American, 2% Asian American or Pacific Islander, 17% Hispanic American, 0.9% Native American, 0.1% international, 6% live on campus.
Freshmen *Admission:* 624 enrolled.

Faculty *Total:* 140, 34% full-time. *Student/faculty ratio:* 11:1.

Majors Administrative assistant and secretarial science; agricultural business and management; agricultural mechanization; agriculture; agronomy and crop science; biological and physical sciences; biology/biological sciences; business administration and management; chemistry; commercial and advertising art; computer science; criminal justice/law enforcement administration; criminal justice/police science; drafting and design technology; dramatic/theater arts; economics; education; engineering; English; forestry; forestry technology; history; humanities; legal administrative assistant/secretary; liberal arts and sciences/liberal studies; mass communication/media; mathematics; medical administrative assistant and medical secretary; music; music teacher education; natural resources management and policy; nursing (registered nurse training); physical education teaching and coaching; political science and government; range science and management; social sciences; sociology; survey technology; welding technology; wildlife and wildlands science and management.

Academics *Calendar:* quarters. *Degree:* certificates and associate. *Special study options:* academic remediation for entering students, accelerated degree program, adult/continuing education programs, advanced placement credit, cooperative education, distance learning, English as a second language, external degree program, honors programs, independent study, internships, part-time degree program, services for LD students, summer session for credit. *ROTC:* Army (c).

Library Treasure Valley Community College Library with 28,000 titles, 150 serial subscriptions, an OPAC.

Computers on Campus 70 computers available on campus for general student use. A campuswide network can be accessed from off campus. Internet access, at least one staffed computer lab available.

Treasure Valley Community College (continued)

Student Life *Activities and Organizations:* drama/theater group, choral group, marching band. *Campus security:* student patrols, controlled dormitory access. *Student services:* health clinic, personal/psychological counseling.

Athletics Member NJCAA. *Intercollegiate sports:* baseball M(s), basketball M(s)/W(s), volleyball W(s). *Intramural sports:* basketball M/W, golf M/W, soccer M/W, softball M/W, volleyball M/W.

Costs (2006–07) *Tuition:* state resident $2970 full-time, $66 per credit hour part-time; nonresident $3420 full-time, $76 per credit hour part-time. *Required fees:* $455 full-time, $10 per credit hour part-time. *Room and board:* $4470; room only: $1680.

Financial Aid Of all full-time matriculated undergraduates who enrolled in 2004, 90 Federal Work-Study jobs (averaging $1500).

Applying *Options:* common application, early admission, deferred entrance. *Application fee:* $10. *Application deadline:* rolling (freshmen), rolling (transfers). *Notification:* continuous (freshmen).

Freshmen Application Contact Ms. Candace Bell, Office of Admissions and Student Services, Treasure Valley Community College, 650 College Boulevard, Ontario, OR 97914. *Phone:* 541-881-8822 Ext. 239. *Fax:* 541-881-2721. *E-mail:* clbell@tvcc.cc.

UMPQUA COMMUNITY COLLEGE
Roseburg, Oregon   www.umpqua.edu/

- **State and locally supported** 2-year, founded 1964
- **Rural** 100-acre campus
- **Endowment** $2.9 million
- **Coed**

Undergraduates 987 full-time, 1,154 part-time. Students come from 5 states and territories, 1% are from out of state, 1% African American, 1% Asian American or Pacific Islander, 2% Hispanic American, 2% Native American.

Faculty *Student/faculty ratio:* 18:1.

Academics *Calendar:* quarters. *Degree:* certificates and associate. *Special study options:* academic remediation for entering students, accelerated degree program, adult/continuing education programs, advanced placement credit, cooperative education, distance learning, English as a second language, honors programs, part-time degree program, services for LD students, student-designed majors, summer session for credit.

Financial Aid Of all full-time matriculated undergraduates who enrolled in 2004, 120 Federal Work-Study jobs (averaging $3000).

Applying *Options:* early admission, deferred entrance. *Application fee:* $25. *Recommended:* high school transcript.

Freshmen Application Contact Lindsay Cameron, Recruiter/Admissions Officer, Umpqua Community College, PO Box 967, 1140 College Road, Roseburg, OR 97470. *Phone:* 541-440-4616.

WESTERN BUSINESS COLLEGE
Portland, Oregon

WESTERN CULINARY INSTITUTE
Portland, Oregon

PENNSYLVANIA

ACADEMY OF MEDICAL ARTS AND BUSINESS
Harrisburg, Pennsylvania   www.acadcampus.com/

Director of Admissions Mr. Gary Kay, Director of Admissions, Academy of Medical Arts and Business, 2301 Academy Drive, Harrisburg, PA 17112. *Phone:* 717-545-4747. *Toll-free phone:* 800-400-3322.

ALLIED MEDICAL AND TECHNICAL CAREERS
Forty Fort, Pennsylvania

ANTONELLI INSTITUTE
Erdenheim, Pennsylvania   www.antonelli.edu/

- **Proprietary** 2-year, founded 1938
- **Suburban** 15-acre campus with easy access to Philadelphia
- **Coed,** 189 undergraduate students, 97% full-time, 65% women, 35% men

Undergraduates 183 full-time, 6 part-time. Students come from 9 states and territories, 22% are from out of state, 5% African American, 3% Hispanic American, 40% live on campus. *Retention:* 100% of 2003 full-time freshmen returned.

Freshmen *Admission:* 182 applied, 119 admitted, 119 enrolled. *Average high school GPA:* 2.67.

Faculty *Total:* 16, 88% full-time, 13% with terminal degrees. *Student/faculty ratio:* 13:1.

Majors Commercial and advertising art; photography.

Academics *Calendar:* semesters. *Degree:* associate. *Special study options:* adult/continuing education programs, part-time degree program.

Library Antonelli Institute Library with 4,000 titles, 70 serial subscriptions, 50 audiovisual materials.

Computers on Campus 21 computers available on campus for general student use. A campuswide network can be accessed. Internet access, at least one staffed computer lab available. Computer purchase or lease plan available.

Student Life *Housing Options:* coed. Campus housing is leased by the school. Freshman applicants given priority for college housing. *Campus security:* 24-hour emergency response devices. *Student services:* personal/psychological counseling.

Costs (2006–07) *Tuition:* $16,300 full-time, $545 per credit part-time. *Required fees:* $25 full-time. *Room only:* $6200.

Financial Aid Of all full-time matriculated undergraduates who enrolled in 2004, 5 Federal Work-Study jobs (averaging $2000).

Applying *Options:* common application, deferred entrance. *Application fee:* $25. *Required:* high school transcript, interview. *Application deadlines:* 9/1 (freshmen), 9/1 (transfers).

Freshmen Application Contact Mr. Anthony Detore, Director of Admissions, Antonelli Institute, 300 Montgomery Avenue, Erdenheim, PA 19038. *Phone:* 215-836-2222. *Toll-free phone:* 800-722-7871. *Fax:* 215-836-2794.

THE ART INSTITUTE OF PHILADELPHIA
Philadelphia, Pennsylvania

- **Proprietary** primarily 2-year, founded 1966, part of Education Management Corporation
- **Urban** campus
- **Coed,** 3,374 undergraduate students, 72% full-time, 54% women, 46% men

Undergraduates 2,427 full-time, 947 part-time. Students come from 30 states and territories, 49% are from out of state, 20% African American, 4% Asian American or Pacific Islander, 5% Hispanic American, 0.4% Native American, 0.2% international, 1% transferred in, 27% live on campus.

Freshmen *Admission:* 3,214 applied, 2,764 admitted, 817 enrolled. *Average high school GPA:* 2.77. *Test scores:* SAT verbal scores over 500: 54%; SAT math scores over 500: 54%; SAT verbal scores over 600: 24%; SAT math scores over 600: 24%; SAT verbal scores over 700: 1%; SAT math scores over 700: 1%.

Faculty *Total:* 216, 37% full-time. *Student/faculty ratio:* 22:1.

Majors Animation, interactive technology, video graphics and special effects; cinematography and film/video production; culinary arts; desktop publishing and digital imaging design; fashion/apparel design; fashion merchandising; film/video and photographic arts related; graphic design; industrial design; interior design; intermedia/multimedia; photographic and film/video technology; photography.

Academics *Calendar:* quarters. *Degrees:* associate and bachelor's. *Special study options:* academic remediation for entering students, adult/continuing education programs, advanced placement credit, cooperative education, external degree program, independent study, internships, off-campus study, part-time degree program, services for LD students, summer session for credit.

Library The Art Institute of Philadelphia Library with 25,000 titles, 150 serial subscriptions, 2,000 audiovisual materials, an OPAC, a Web page.

Computers on Campus 368 computers available on campus for general student use. A campuswide network can be accessed. Internet access, online (class) registration, at least one staffed computer lab available. Computer purchase or lease plan available.

Student Life *Housing Options:* coed, disabled students. Campus housing is university owned. Freshman campus housing is guaranteed. *Campus security:* 24-hour patrols, controlled dormitory access. *Student services:* personal/psychological counseling.

Athletics *Intramural sports:* basketball M/W, softball M/W.

Costs (2006–07) *Tuition:* $401 per quarter hour part-time. *Room only:* $2334.

Financial Aid Of all full-time matriculated undergraduates who enrolled in 2004, 230 Federal Work-Study jobs (averaging $3500).

Applying *Options:* electronic application, early admission, early decision, deferred entrance. *Application fee:* $50. *Required:* essay or personal statement, high school transcript, interview. *Recommended:* minimum 2.5 GPA, letters of recommendation. *Application deadline:* rolling (freshmen), rolling (transfers). *Notification:* continuous (freshmen).

Freshmen Application Contact Admissions Office, The Art Institute of Philadelphia, 1622 Chestnut Street, Philadelphia, PA 19103. *Phone:* 800-567-7080. *Toll-free phone:* 800-275-2474. *Fax:* 215-405-6399. *E-mail:* aiphinfo@aii.edu.

BEREAN INSTITUTE
Philadelphia, Pennsylvania   **www.bereaninstitute.org/**

Director of Admissions Director of Recruitment, Berean Institute, 1901 West Girard Avenue, Philadelphia, PA 19130. *Phone:* 215-763-4833 Ext. 135.

BERKS TECHNICAL INSTITUTE
Wyomissing, Pennsylvania   **www.berkstech.com/**

- **Proprietary** 2-year, founded 1977, part of Fore Front Education, Inc
- **Small-town** 8-acre campus
- **Coed,** 650 undergraduate students

Undergraduates Students come from 1 other state, 6% African American, 0.8% Asian American or Pacific Islander, 10% Hispanic American, 0.2% Native American.

Freshmen *Admission:* 172 admitted.

Faculty *Total:* 53, 79% full-time. *Student/faculty ratio:* 12:1.

Majors Computer and information sciences related; computer graphics; computer programming; computer programming related; drafting and design technology; information technology; medical/clinical assistant; system administration.

Academics *Calendar:* semesters. *Degree:* diplomas and associate. *Special study options:* advanced placement credit, part-time degree program.

Library Learning Resource Center with 450 titles, 12 serial subscriptions.

Computers on Campus 8 computers available on campus for general student use. A campuswide network can be accessed. Internet access, online (class) registration, at least one staffed computer lab available.

Student Life *Housing:* college housing not available. *Campus security:* 24-hour emergency response devices.

Standardized Tests *Required for some:* SAT and SAT Subject Tests or ACT (for admission), CPat and COMPAS.

Costs (2006–07) *Tuition:* $23,405 full-time. *Required fees:* $300 full-time.

Applying *Options:* early admission. *Application fee:* $50. *Required:* high school transcript, letters of recommendation, interview.

Freshmen Application Contact Mr. Allan Brussolo, Academic Dean, Berks Technical Institute, 2205 Ridgewood Road, Wyomissing, PA 19610-1168. *Phone:* 610-372-1722. *Toll-free phone:* 800-284-4672 (in-state); 800-821-4662 (out-of-state). *Fax:* 610-376-4684. *E-mail:* abrussolo@berks.edu.

BIDWELL TRAINING CENTER
Pittsburgh, Pennsylvania

BRADFORD SCHOOL
Pittsburgh, Pennsylvania   **www.bradfordpittsburgh.edu/**

Director of Admissions Mr. Vincent S. Graziano, President, Bradford School, 707 Grant Street, Gulf Tower, Pittsburgh, PA 15219. *Phone:* 412-391-6710. *Fax:* 412-471-6714. *E-mail:* info@bradfordpittsburgh.edu.

BRADLEY ACADEMY FOR THE VISUAL ARTS
York, Pennsylvania   **www.bradleyacademy.net/**

- **Proprietary** 2-year, founded 1952, part of Education Management Corporation
- **Suburban** 7-acre campus with easy access to Baltimore
- **Endowment** $500,000
- **Coed,** 596 undergraduate students, 93% full-time, 60% women, 40% men

Undergraduates 552 full-time, 44 part-time. Students come from 9 states and territories, 16% are from out of state, 4% African American, 0.9% Asian American or Pacific Islander, 0.2% Native American, 5% transferred in.

Freshmen *Admission:* 302 applied, 197 admitted, 115 enrolled. *Average high school GPA:* 2.80. *Test scores:* SAT verbal scores over 500: 40%; SAT math scores over 500: 36%; SAT verbal scores over 600: 8%; SAT math scores over 600: 5%; SAT verbal scores over 700: 1%.

Faculty *Total:* 48, 31% full-time, 6% with terminal degrees. *Student/faculty ratio:* 15:1.

Majors Advertising; animation, interactive technology, video graphics and special effects; clothing/textiles; commercial and advertising art; computer graphics; design and visual communications; fashion merchandising; interior

Bradley Academy for the Visual Arts (continued)
design; web/multimedia management and webmaster; web page, digital/multimedia and information resources design.

Academics *Calendar:* quarters. *Degree:* associate. *Special study options:* academic remediation for entering students, adult/continuing education programs, internships, part-time degree program, summer session for credit.

Library Bradley Academy Library with 1,900 titles, 70 serial subscriptions, an OPAC, a Web page.

Computers on Campus 175 computers available on campus for general student use. A campuswide network can be accessed from off campus. Internet access, at least one staffed computer lab available. Computer purchase or lease plan available.

Student Life *Housing:* college housing not available. *Activities and Organizations:* student-run newspaper, ASID, Delta Epsilon Chi, AIGA. *Student services:* personal/psychological counseling.

Standardized Tests *Recommended:* SAT or ACT (for admission).

Costs (2006–07) *Tuition:* $15,840 full-time, $440 per credit part-time.

Financial Aid Of all full-time matriculated undergraduates who enrolled in 2004, 21 Federal Work-Study jobs (averaging $600).

Applying *Options:* deferred entrance. *Application fee:* $50. *Required:* essay or personal statement, high school transcript, interview. *Required for some:* minimum 2.5 GPA, portfolio. *Recommended:* minimum 2.5 GPA. *Application deadline:* rolling (freshmen), rolling (transfers). *Notification:* continuous (freshmen).

Freshmen Application Contact Mr. James Hannigan Jr., Director of Admissions, Bradley Academy for the Visual Arts, 1409 Williams Road, York, PA 17402. *Phone:* 717-755-2711. *Toll-free phone:* 800-864-7725. *Fax:* 717-840-1951. *E-mail:* info@bradleyacademy.net.

▶ See page 492 for the College Close-Up.

BUCKS COUNTY COMMUNITY COLLEGE

Newtown, Pennsylvania   **www.bucks.edu/**

- **County-supported** 2-year, founded 1964
- **Suburban** 200-acre campus with easy access to Philadelphia
- **Endowment** $2.4 million
- **Coed,** 9,596 undergraduate students, 42% full-time, 58% women, 42% men

Undergraduates 3,990 full-time, 5,603 part-time. Students come from 5 states and territories, 15 other countries, 1% are from out of state, 3% African American, 2% Asian American or Pacific Islander, 2% Hispanic American, 0.3% Native American, 6% international, 4% transferred in.
Freshmen *Admission:* 5,003 applied, 4,959 admitted, 2,672 enrolled.

Faculty *Total:* 574, 25% full-time. *Student/faculty ratio:* 23:1.

Majors Accounting; administrative assistant and secretarial science; American studies; art; biology/biological sciences; business administration and management; chemistry; cinematography and film/video production; commercial and advertising art; computer and information sciences; computer and information sciences related; computer engineering technology; computer/information technology services administration related; computer programming; computer programming related; computer programming (specific applications); computer science; consumer merchandising/retailing management; corrections; criminal justice/law enforcement administration; criminal justice/police science; culinary arts; data processing and data processing technology; dramatic/theater arts; education; engineering; entrepreneurship; environmental studies; health science; health teacher education; historic preservation and conservation; hospitality administration; hotel/motel administration; humanities; information science/studies; information technology; journalism; kindergarten/preschool education; legal assistant/paralegal; liberal arts and sciences/liberal studies; marketing/marketing management; mass communication/media; mathematics; medical/clinical assistant; music; nursing (registered nurse training); physical education teaching and coaching; psychology; radio and television; social sciences; social work; sport and fitness administration/management; teacher assistant/aide; visual and performing arts; woodworking.

Academics *Calendar:* semesters. *Degree:* certificates and associate. *Special study options:* academic remediation for entering students, adult/continuing education programs, advanced placement credit, cooperative education, distance learning, English as a second language, external degree program, independent study, internships, part-time degree program, services for LD students, student-designed majors, summer session for credit.

Library Bucks County Community College Library with 155,779 titles, 515 serial subscriptions, an OPAC, a Web page.

Computers on Campus 1600 computers available on campus for general student use. A campuswide network can be accessed from off campus that provide access to e-mail, online course work, WebCT. Internet access, online (class) registration, at least one staffed computer lab available.

Student Life *Housing:* college housing not available. *Activities and Organizations:* drama/theater group, student-run newspaper, television station, choral group, Phi Theta Kappa, Students in Free Enterprise, student council, The Centurion (student newspaper). *Campus security:* 24-hour emergency response devices and patrols, late-night transport/escort service. *Student services:* personal/psychological counseling, women's center.

Athletics Member NJCAA. *Intercollegiate sports:* baseball M, basketball M, equestrian sports M/W, golf M/W, soccer M/W, tennis M/W, volleyball W. *Intramural sports:* basketball M/W, soccer M/W, softball M/W, tennis M/W, volleyball W.

Costs (2006–07) *Tuition:* area resident $2760 full-time, $92 per credit part-time; state resident $5520 full-time, $184 per credit part-time; nonresident $8280 full-time, $276 per credit part-time. *Required fees:* $584 full-time.

Financial Aid Of all full-time matriculated undergraduates who enrolled in 2004, 200 Federal Work-Study jobs.

Applying *Options:* electronic application, early admission. *Application fee:* $30. *Required:* high school transcript. *Required for some:* essay or personal statement, interview.

Freshmen Application Contact Ms. Amy Wilson, Director of Admissions, Bucks County Community College, 275 Swamp Road, Newtown, PA 18940. *Phone:* 215-968-8119. *Fax:* 215-968-8110. *E-mail:* wilsona@bucks.edu.

BUSINESS INSTITUTE OF PENNSYLVANIA

Meadville, Pennsylvania   **www.biop.edu/**

- **Proprietary** 2-year, founded 1987
- **Coed, primarily women,** 68 undergraduate students, 100% full-time, 88% women, 12% men
- **82%** of applicants were admitted

Undergraduates 68 full-time. 6% African American.
Freshmen *Admission:* 38 applied, 31 admitted, 31 enrolled. *Average high school GPA:* 3.6.

Faculty *Total:* 6, 50% full-time, 100% with terminal degrees. *Student/faculty ratio:* 17:1.

Majors Business operations support and secretarial services related; data entry/microcomputer applications; executive assistant/executive secretary; health information/medical records technology; legal administrative assistant/secretary; medical administrative assistant; medical office assistant.

Academics *Calendar:* quarters. *Degree:* certificates, diplomas, and associate.

Student Life *Housing:* college housing not available.

Costs (2006–07) *Tuition:* $7500 full-time, $250 per credit part-time. *Required fees:* $650 full-time.

Applying *Application fee:* $50. *Required:* high school transcript, interview, CPAt.

Freshmen Application Contact Ms. Cheryl Mever, Admissions Officer, Business Institute of Pennsylvania, 628 Arch Street, Suite B105, Meadville, PA 16335. *Phone:* 814-724-0700. *Fax:* 814-724-2777. *E-mail:* info@biop.edu.

BUSINESS INSTITUTE OF PENNSYLVANIA

Sharon, Pennsylvania   **www.biop.edu/**

- **Proprietary** 2-year, founded 1926
- **Small-town** 2-acre campus
- **Coed, primarily women**
- **80%** of applicants were admitted

Undergraduates 98 full-time, 8 part-time. 5% African American.

Faculty *Student/faculty ratio:* 16:1.

Academics *Calendar:* quarters. *Degree:* certificates, diplomas, and associate.

Standardized Tests *Required:* ACT (for admission).

Costs (2005–06) *Tuition:* $7500 full-time, $250 per credit part-time. *Required fees:* $600 full-time.

Applying *Required:* high school transcript, interview.

Director of Admissions Ms. Shannon P. McNamara, President, Business Institute of Pennsylvania, 335 Boyd Drive, Sharon, PA 16146. *Phone:* 724-983-0700. *Toll-free phone:* 800-289-2069.

BUTLER COUNTY COMMUNITY COLLEGE

Butler, Pennsylvania www.bc3.edu/

- **County-supported** 2-year, founded 1965
- **Rural** 300-acre campus with easy access to Pittsburgh
- **Coed,** 3,809 undergraduate students, 52% full-time, 60% women, 40% men

Undergraduates 1,987 full-time, 1,822 part-time. Students come from 8 states and territories, 1 other country, 1% are from out of state, 2% African American, 0.7% Asian American or Pacific Islander, 0.8% Hispanic American, 0.1% Native American.
Freshmen *Admission:* 1,505 enrolled.
Faculty *Total:* 305, 21% full-time, 5% with terminal degrees. *Student/faculty ratio:* 20:1.
Majors Accounting; administrative assistant and secretarial science; architectural drafting and CAD/CADD; architectural engineering technology; biology/biological sciences; business administration and management; civil engineering technology; commercial and advertising art; computer and information sciences; computer programming; criminal justice/police science; criminology; dietetics; drafting and design technology; education; electrical, electronic and communications engineering technology; elementary education; emergency medical technology (EMT paramedic); English; executive assistant/executive secretary; food services technology; general studies; hospitality administration; humanities; instrumentation technology; kindergarten/preschool education; kinesiology and exercise science; legal administrative assistant/secretary; liberal arts and sciences/liberal studies; machine tool technology; marketing/marketing management; mass communication/media; mathematics; mechanical design technology; mechanical drafting and CAD/CADD; medical administrative assistant and medical secretary; medical/clinical assistant; nursing (registered nurse training); office occupations and clerical services; parks, recreation and leisure facilities management; physical education teaching and coaching; physical sciences; physical therapist assistant; pre-engineering; psychology; quality control technology; sport and fitness administration/management; therapeutic recreation; tourism and travel services management.
Academics *Calendar:* semesters. *Degree:* certificates, diplomas, and associate. *Special study options:* academic remediation for entering students, adult/continuing education programs, advanced placement credit, cooperative education, English as a second language, internships, part-time degree program, services for LD students, summer session for credit.
Library John A. Beck, Jr. Library with 70,000 titles, 305 serial subscriptions.
Computers on Campus 350 computers available on campus for general student use. Internet access, at least one staffed computer lab available.
Student Life *Housing:* college housing not available. *Activities and Organizations:* drama/theater group, student-run newspaper, choral group, student government, Ski Club, Drama Club, Outdoor Recreation Club. *Campus security:* 24-hour emergency response devices, late-night transport/escort service. *Student services:* personal/psychological counseling.
Athletics Member NJCAA. *Intercollegiate sports:* baseball M, basketball M, golf M/W, softball W, volleyball W. *Intramural sports:* badminton M/W, basketball M/W, racquetball M/W, soccer M/W, softball M, table tennis M/W, tennis M/W, volleyball M/W, weight lifting M/W.
Costs (2005–06) *Tuition:* area resident $2130 full-time, $71 per credit part-time; state resident $4260 full-time, $142 per credit part-time; nonresident $6390 full-time, $213 per credit part-time. *Required fees:* $510 full-time, $17 per credit part-time.
Financial Aid Of all full-time matriculated undergraduates who enrolled in 2004, 65 Federal Work-Study jobs (averaging $1545).
Applying *Options:* common application, early admission, deferred entrance. *Application fee:* $25. *Required:* high school transcript. *Required for some:* letters of recommendation, interview. *Application deadlines:* 8/15 (freshmen), 8/15 (transfers). *Notification:* continuous until 8/15 (freshmen).
Freshmen Application Contact Ms. Patricia Bajuszik, Director of Admissions, Butler County Community College, College Drive, PO Box 1203, Butler, PA 16003-1203. *Phone:* 724-287-8711 Ext. 344. *Toll-free phone:* 888-826-2829. *Fax:* 724-287-4961. *E-mail:* pattie.bajoszik@bc3.edu.

CAMBRIA-ROWE BUSINESS COLLEGE

Indiana, Pennsylvania www.crbc.net/

Freshmen Application Contact Laurie Price, Representative at Indiana Campus, Cambria-Rowe Business College, 422 South 13th Street, Indiana, PA 15701. *Phone:* 724-483-0222.

CAMBRIA-ROWE BUSINESS COLLEGE

Johnstown, Pennsylvania www.crbc.net/

- **Proprietary** 2-year, founded 1891
- **Small-town** campus with easy access to Pittsburgh
- **Coed, primarily women,** 230 undergraduate students, 100% full-time, 89% women, 11% men

Undergraduates 230 full-time. Students come from 1 other state, 3% African American, 4% transferred in.
Freshmen *Admission:* 125 enrolled.
Faculty *Total:* 11, 100% full-time. *Student/faculty ratio:* 20:1.
Majors Accounting; administrative assistant and secretarial science; business administration and management; legal administrative assistant/secretary; medical administrative assistant and medical secretary.
Academics *Calendar:* quarters. *Degree:* diplomas and associate. *Special study options:* accelerated degree program, adult/continuing education programs, advanced placement credit, part-time degree program, summer session for credit.
Computers on Campus 105 computers available on campus for general student use. Computer purchase or lease plan available.
Student Life *Housing:* college housing not available.
Costs (2006–07) *Tuition:* $15,600 full-time, $220 per credit part-time. *Required fees:* $1875 full-time, $300 per term part-time.
Financial Aid *Financial aid deadline:* 8/1.
Applying *Options:* common application, electronic application, early admission. *Application fee:* $15. *Required:* high school transcript, entrance exam. *Recommended:* interview. *Application deadline:* rolling (freshmen). *Notification:* continuous (freshmen).
Freshmen Application Contact Mrs. Amanda Artim, Director of Admissions, Cambria-Rowe Business College, 221 Central Avenue, Johnstown, PA 15902-2494. *Phone:* 814-536-5168. *Fax:* 814-536-5160. *E-mail:* admissions@crbc.net.

CAREER TRAINING ACADEMY

Monroeville, Pennsylvania

CAREER TRAINING ACADEMY

New Kensington, Pennsylvania www.careerta.com/

- **Proprietary** 2-year, founded 1986
- **Coed**
- 85% of applicants were admitted

Undergraduates 337 full-time. 12% African American, 0.3% Hispanic American, 0.6% Native American.
Freshmen *Admission:* 61 applied, 52 admitted.
Faculty *Total:* 22, 64% full-time, 18% with terminal degrees. *Student/faculty ratio:* 20:1.
Majors Massage therapy; medical/clinical assistant.
Academics *Calendar:* quarters. *Degrees:* diplomas and associate (profile includes branch campuses in Monroeville and Pittsburgh, PA).
Student Life *Student services:* personal/psychological counseling.
Costs (2006–07) *Comprehensive fee:* $8000 includes full-time tuition ($7000) and room and board ($1000). *Room and board:* college room only: $800.
Applying *Application fee:* $30. *Required:* essay or personal statement, high school transcript, minimum 1.5 GPA, interview. *Application deadline:* rolling (freshmen), rolling (transfers). *Notification:* continuous (freshmen).
Freshmen Application Contact Ms. Anna Bartolini, Career Training Academy, 950 Fifth Avenue, New Kensington, PA 15068-6301. *Phone:* 412-367-4000. *Fax:* 412-369-7223. *E-mail:* director3@caveerta.edu.

CAREER TRAINING ACADEMY
Pittsburgh, Pennsylvania

CENTER FOR ADVANCED MANUFACTURING & TECHNOLOGY
Erie, Pennsylvania   www.gocamtech.com/

Director of Admissions Ms. Lisa Peszel, Director of Admissions, Center for Advanced Manufacturing & Technology, 5451 Merwin Lane, Erie, PA 16510. *Phone:* 814-897-0391 Ext. 226. *Toll-free phone:* 888-834-4226. *E-mail:* lpeszel@gocamtech.com.

CHI INSTITUTE
Southampton, Pennsylvania   www.chitraining.com/

Director of Admissions Mr. Michael Herbert, Director of Admissions, CHI Institute, 520 Street Road, Southampton, PA 18966. *Phone:* 215-357-5100 Ext. 114. *Toll-free phone:* 800-336-7696.

CHI INSTITUTE, RETS CAMPUS
Broomall, Pennsylvania   www.chitraining.com/

Director of Admissions Mr. Stuart Kahn, Director of Admissions, CHI Institute, RETS Campus, Lawrence Park Shopping Center, Rt. 320 & Lawrence Road, Broomall, PA 19008. *Phone:* 610-353-7630.

COMMONWEALTH TECHNICAL INSTITUTE
Johnstown, Pennsylvania   www.hgac.org/

- **State-supported** 2-year
- **Coed,** 275 undergraduate students, 100% full-time, 35% women, 65% men

Undergraduates 275 full-time. 1% are from out of state, 11% African American, 0.7% Asian American or Pacific Islander, 1% Hispanic American, 0.7% Native American. *Retention:* 64% of 2003 full-time freshmen returned. Freshmen *Admission:* 113 applied, 101 admitted, 101 enrolled.
Faculty *Total:* 32, 100% full-time. *Student/faculty ratio:* 10:1.
Majors Accounting; architectural drafting and CAD/CADD; computer science; culinary arts; dental laboratory technology; mechanical drafting and CAD/CADD; medical office assistant.
Academics *Calendar:* trimesters. *Degree:* certificates, diplomas, and associate.
Library Commonwealth Technical Institute at the Hiram G. Andrews Center Library.
Student Life *Activities and Organizations:* choral group. *Campus security:* 24-hour patrols. *Student services:* health clinic, personal/psychological counseling.
Costs (2006–07) *Tuition:* state resident $16,836 full-time, $323 per credit part-time. *Required fees:* $75 full-time, $25 per term part-time. *Room and board:* $14,274.
Financial Aid Of all full-time matriculated undergraduates who enrolled in 2004, 20 Federal Work-Study jobs.
Applying *Required for some:* high school transcript. *Recommended:* high school transcript.
Freshmen Application Contact Ms. Rebecca Halza, Director of Admissions, Commonwealth Technical Institute, 727 Goucher Street, Johnstown, PA 15905-3092. *Phone:* 814-255-8200 Ext. 8372. *Toll-free phone:* 800-762-4211 Ext. 8237. *E-mail:* rhalza@state.pa.us.

COMMUNITY COLLEGE OF ALLEGHENY COUNTY
Pittsburgh, Pennsylvania   www.ccac.edu/

- **County-supported** 2-year, founded 1966
- **Urban** 242-acre campus
- **Coed,** 18,404 undergraduate students, 41% full-time, 57% women, 43% men

Undergraduates 7,580 full-time, 10,824 part-time. Students come from 17 states and territories, 79 other countries, 1% are from out of state, 16% African American, 1% Asian American or Pacific Islander, 0.6% Hispanic American, 0.7% Native American, 0.9% international, 11% transferred in.
Freshmen *Admission:* 7,333 applied, 6,211 admitted, 1,788 enrolled.
Faculty *Total:* 1,631, 16% full-time. *Student/faculty ratio:* 15:1.
Majors Accounting technology and bookkeeping; administrative assistant and secretarial science; airline pilot and flight crew; applied horticulture; architectural drafting and CAD/CADD; art; athletic training; automotive engineering technology; aviation/airway management; banking and financial support services; biology/biological sciences; building/property maintenance and management; business administration and management; business automation/technology/data entry; business machine repair; carpentry; chemical technology; chemistry; child care provision; child development; civil drafting and CAD/CADD; civil engineering technology; clinical/medical laboratory technology; commercial and advertising art; communications technologies and support services related; community health services counseling; computer engineering technology; computer systems networking and telecommunications; computer technology/computer systems technology; construction engineering technology; construction trades related; corrections; cosmetology and personal grooming arts related; court reporting; criminal justice/police science; culinary arts; diagnostic medical sonography and ultrasound technology; dietitian assistant; drafting and design technology; drafting/design engineering technologies related; dramatic/theater arts; education (specific levels and methods) related; education (specific subject areas) related; electrical, electronic and communications engineering technology; electroneurodiagnostic/electroencephalographic technology; energy management and systems technology; engineering technologies related; English; entrepreneurship; environmental engineering technology; fire protection and safety technology; foodservice systems administration; foreign languages and literatures; general studies; greenhouse management; health and physical education; health information/medical records technology; health professions related; health unit coordinator/ward clerk; heating, air conditioning, ventilation and refrigeration maintenance technology; hotel/motel administration; housing and human environments related; human development and family studies related; humanities; human resources management; industrial technology; insurance; journalism; landscaping and groundskeeping; legal administrative assistant/secretary; legal assistant/paralegal; liberal arts and sciences/liberal studies; machine shop technology; management information systems; marketing/marketing management; mathematics; mechanical design technology; mechanical drafting and CAD/CADD; medical administrative assistant and medical secretary; medical/clinical assistant; medical radiologic technology; music; nuclear medical technology; nursing assistant/aide and patient care assistant; nursing (licensed practical/vocational nurse training); nursing (registered nurse training); occupational therapist assistant; office management; ornamental horticulture; perioperative/operating room and surgical nursing; pharmacy technician; physical therapist assistant; physics; plant nursery management; psychiatric/mental health services technology; psychology; quality control technology; real estate; respiratory care therapy; restaurant, culinary, and catering management; retailing; robotics technology; science technologies related; sheet metal technology; sign language interpretation and translation; social sciences; social work; sociology; solar energy technology; substance abuse/addiction counseling; surgical technology; therapeutic recreation; tourism promotion; turf and turfgrass management; visual and performing arts related; welding technology.
Academics *Calendar:* semesters. *Degree:* certificates, diplomas, and associate. *Special study options:* academic remediation for entering students, advanced placement credit, distance learning, English as a second language, external degree program, honors programs, independent study, off-campus study, part-time degree program, services for LD students, study abroad, summer session for credit.
Library Community College of Allegheny County Library plus 4 others with 272,697 titles, 933 serial subscriptions, 13,165 audiovisual materials, an OPAC, a Web page.
Computers on Campus 3100 computers available on campus for general student use. A campuswide network can be accessed from off campus. Internet access, online (class) registration, at least one staffed computer lab available.
Student Life *Housing:* college housing not available. *Activities and Organizations:* drama/theater group, student-run newspaper, choral group, Phi Theta Kappa. *Campus security:* 24-hour emergency response devices and patrols, late-night transport/escort service. *Student services:* health clinic, personal/psychological counseling, women's center.

Athletics Member NJCAA. *Intercollegiate sports:* baseball M, basketball M/W, bowling M/W, golf M/W, ice hockey M, softball W, table tennis M/W, tennis M/W, volleyball W. *Intramural sports:* badminton M/W, basketball M/W, bowling M/W, cross-country running M/W, football M, golf M/W, lacrosse M, racquetball M/W, softball M/W, table tennis M/W, tennis M/W, volleyball M/W, weight lifting M/W.

Costs (2005–06) *Tuition:* area resident $2400 full-time, $80 per credit part-time; state resident $4800 full-time, $160 per credit part-time; nonresident $7200 full-time, $240 per credit part-time. *Required fees:* $295 full-time, $11 per credit part-time.

Applying *Options:* deferred entrance. *Recommended:* high school transcript. *Application deadline:* rolling (freshmen), rolling (transfers). *Notification:* continuous (freshmen).

Freshmen Application Contact Admissions, Community College of Allegheny County, 800 Allegheny Avenue, Pittsburgh, PA 15233.

▶ **See page 534 for the College Close-Up.**

COMMUNITY COLLEGE OF BEAVER COUNTY

Monaca, Pennsylvania   **www.ccbc.edu/**

- **State-supported** 2-year, founded 1966
- **Small-town** 75-acre campus with easy access to Pittsburgh
- **Coed**

Undergraduates Students come from 7 states and territories, 2 other countries, 3% are from out of state.

Academics *Calendar:* semesters. *Degree:* certificates, diplomas, and associate. *Special study options:* academic remediation for entering students, adult/continuing education programs, advanced placement credit, cooperative education, distance learning, double majors, independent study, internships, off-campus study, part-time degree program, services for LD students, summer session for credit.

Student Life *Campus security:* 24-hour emergency response devices and patrols, late-night transport/escort service.

Athletics Member NJCAA.

Standardized Tests *Required:* ACT ASSET, ACT, or nursing exam depending on program (for placement).

Costs (2005–06) *Tuition:* area resident $2400 full-time, $80 per credit part-time; state resident $4800 full-time, $160 per credit part-time; nonresident $7200 full-time, $240 per credit part-time. *Required fees:* $525 full-time, $18 per credit part-time.

Financial Aid Of all full-time matriculated undergraduates who enrolled in 2004, 50 Federal Work-Study jobs (averaging $1400).

Applying *Options:* early admission. *Application fee:* $25. *Recommended:* high school transcript, interview.

Director of Admissions Mr. Michael Macon, Vice President for Enrollment Management, Community College of Beaver County, One Campus Drive, Monaca, PA 15061-2588. *Phone:* 724-775-8561 Ext. 151. *Toll-free phone:* 800-335-0222. *E-mail:* mike.macon@ccbc.edu.

COMMUNITY COLLEGE OF PHILADELPHIA

Philadelphia, Pennsylvania   **www.ccp.edu/**

- **State and locally supported** 2-year, founded 1964
- **Urban** 14-acre campus
- **Coed**

Academics *Calendar:* semesters. *Degree:* certificates, diplomas, and associate. *Special study options:* academic remediation for entering students, accelerated degree program, adult/continuing education programs, English as a second language, honors programs, internships, part-time degree program, services for LD students, student-designed majors, summer session for credit.

Student Life *Campus security:* 24-hour emergency response devices and patrols.

Costs (2005–06) *Tuition:* $104 per credit hour part-time; state resident $208 per credit hour part-time; nonresident $312 per credit hour part-time.

Applying *Options:* early admission, deferred entrance. *Application fee:* $20. *Required for some:* high school transcript.

Director of Admissions Daivd Norris, Director of Admissions, Community College of Philadelphia, 1700 Spring Garden Street, Philadelphia, PA 19130-3991. *Phone:* 215-751-8199.

CONSOLIDATED SCHOOL OF BUSINESS

Lancaster, Pennsylvania   **www.csb.edu/**

- **Proprietary** 2-year, founded 1986
- **Suburban** campus with easy access to Philadelphia
- **Coed, primarily women,** 173 undergraduate students, 100% full-time, 80% women, 20% men

Undergraduates 173 full-time. 7% African American, 19% Hispanic American.

Freshmen *Average high school GPA:* 2.6.

Faculty *Total:* 20, 85% full-time. *Student/faculty ratio:* 15:1.

Majors Accounting; business administration and management; health/health care administration; legal administrative assistant/secretary; medical administrative assistant and medical secretary; office management; tourism and travel services management.

Academics *Calendar:* continuous. *Degree:* diplomas and associate. *Special study options:* accelerated degree program, honors programs, independent study, internships, part-time degree program, services for LD students, student-designed majors.

Computers on Campus 120 computers available on campus for general student use. Internet access, at least one staffed computer lab available.

Student Life *Housing:* college housing not available. *Activities and Organizations:* Community Service Club.

Costs (2006–07) *Tuition:* $3500 full-time.

Applying *Options:* common application. *Application fee:* $25. *Required:* high school transcript, interview. *Application deadline:* rolling (freshmen), rolling (transfers).

Freshmen Application Contact Mr. Jason McCue, Consolidated School of Business, 2124 Ambassador Circle, Lancaster, PA 17603. *Phone:* 717-764-9550. *Toll-free phone:* 800-541-8298. *Fax:* 717-394-6213. *E-mail:* jmccue@csb.edu.

CONSOLIDATED SCHOOL OF BUSINESS

York, Pennsylvania   **www.csb.edu/**

- **Proprietary** 2-year, founded 1981
- **Suburban** 6-acre campus with easy access to Baltimore
- **Coed, primarily women,** 176 undergraduate students, 100% full-time, 82% women, 18% men

Undergraduates 176 full-time.

Freshmen *Average high school GPA:* 2.8.

Faculty *Total:* 21, 86% full-time. *Student/faculty ratio:* 15:1.

Majors Accounting; business administration and management; health/health care administration; legal administrative assistant/secretary; medical administrative assistant and medical secretary; office management; tourism and travel services management.

Academics *Calendar:* continuous. *Degree:* diplomas and associate. *Special study options:* accelerated degree program, honors programs, independent study, internships, part-time degree program, services for LD students, student-designed majors.

Computers on Campus 120 computers available on campus for general student use. Internet access, at least one staffed computer lab available.

Student Life *Housing:* college housing not available. *Activities and Organizations:* Community Service Club.

Applying *Options:* common application. *Application fee:* $25. *Required:* high school transcript, interview. *Application deadline:* rolling (freshmen), rolling (transfers).

Freshmen Application Contact Mr. Aaron Hoffman, Admissions Representative, Consolidated School of Business, 1605 Clugston Road, York, PA 17404. *Phone:* 717-764-9550. *Toll-free phone:* 800-520-0691. *Fax:* 717-764-9469. *E-mail:* ahoffman@csb.edu.

DEAN INSTITUTE OF TECHNOLOGY

Pittsburgh, Pennsylvania   **home.earthlink.net/~deantech/**

Director of Admissions Mr. Richard D. Ali, Admissions Director, Dean Institute of Technology, 1501 West Liberty Avenue, Pittsburgh, PA 15226-1103. *Phone:* 412-531-4433.

DELAWARE COUNTY COMMUNITY COLLEGE

Media, Pennsylvania
www.dccc.edu/

- **State and locally supported** 2-year, founded 1967
- **Suburban** 123-acre campus with easy access to Philadelphia
- **Endowment** $676,410
- **Coed**

Undergraduates 4,263 full-time, 6,345 part-time. Students come from 13 states and territories, 46 other countries, 1% are from out of state, 15% African American, 4% Asian American or Pacific Islander, 2% Hispanic American, 0.2% Native American, 1% international.

Faculty *Student/faculty ratio:* 20:1.

Academics *Calendar:* semesters. *Degree:* certificates and associate. *Special study options:* academic remediation for entering students, adult/continuing education programs, advanced placement credit, cooperative education, distance learning, double majors, English as a second language, independent study, internships, part-time degree program, services for LD students, student-designed majors, summer session for credit.

Student Life *Campus security:* 24-hour emergency response devices and patrols, late-night transport/escort service.

Athletics Member NJCAA.

Costs (2005–06) *Tuition:* area resident $1968 full-time, $82 per credit part-time; state resident $3936 full-time, $164 per credit part-time; nonresident $5904 full-time, $246 per credit part-time. *Required fees:* $544 full-time, $21 per credit part-time, $20 per term part-time.

Financial Aid Of all full-time matriculated undergraduates who enrolled in 2004, 95 Federal Work-Study jobs (averaging $900).

Applying *Options:* early admission, deferred entrance. *Application fee:* $20. *Required:* high school transcript.

Director of Admissions Ms. Hope Lentine, Director of Admissions, Delaware County Community College, Admissions Office, 901 South Media Line Road, Media, PA 19063-1094. *Phone:* 610-359-5333. *Toll-free phone:* 800-872-1102 (in-state); 800-543-0146 (out-of-state). *E-mail:* admiss@dccc.edu.

DOUGLAS EDUCATION CENTER

Monessen, Pennsylvania
www.douglas-school.com/

Director of Admissions Ms. Linda Gambattista, Director of Admissions, Douglas Education Center, 130 Seventh Street, Monessen, PA 15062. *Phone:* 724-684-3684. *Fax:* 724-684-7463.

DUBOIS BUSINESS COLLEGE

DuBois, Pennsylvania
www.dbcollege.com/

Director of Admissions Ms. Lisa Stanford, Director of Admissions, DuBois Business College, 1 Beaver Drive, DuBois, PA 15801-2401. *Phone:* 814-371-6920. *Toll-free phone:* 800-692-6213. *Fax:* 814-371-3947. *E-mail:* stanfordlj@dbcollege.com.

DUFF'S BUSINESS INSTITUTE

Pittsburgh, Pennsylvania
www.duffs-institute.com/

Director of Admissions Ms. Lynn Fischer, Director of Admissions, Duff's Business Institute, 100 Forbes Avenue, Suite 1200, Pittsburgh, PA 15222. *Phone:* 412-261-4520 Ext. 212. *Toll-free phone:* 888-279-3314.

ERIE BUSINESS CENTER, MAIN

Erie, Pennsylvania
www.eriebc.edu/

- **Proprietary** 2-year, founded 1884
- **Urban** 1-acre campus with easy access to Cleveland and Buffalo
- **Coed**, 393 undergraduate students, 71% full-time, 72% women, 28% men

Undergraduates 279 full-time, 114 part-time. Students come from 3 states and territories, 2% are from out of state, 25% African American, 3% Hispanic American, 0.8% transferred in, 1% live on campus.

Freshmen *Admission:* 261 applied, 235 admitted, 122 enrolled. *Average high school GPA:* 3.20.

Faculty *Total:* 46, 26% full-time. *Student/faculty ratio:* 14:1.

Majors Accounting; administrative assistant and secretarial science; computer and information sciences; computer programming related; computer science; computer systems networking and telecommunications; information science/studies; legal administrative assistant/secretary; legal assistant/paralegal; marketing/marketing management; medical administrative assistant and medical secretary; medical/clinical assistant; medical transcription; tourism and travel services management; web page, digital/multimedia and information resources design.

Academics *Calendar:* trimesters. *Degree:* certificates, diplomas, and associate. *Special study options:* adult/continuing education programs, advanced placement credit, independent study, part-time degree program, summer session for credit.

Library EBC Blackmer Library with 3,035 titles, 84 serial subscriptions, an OPAC.

Computers on Campus 114 computers available on campus for general student use. A campuswide network can be accessed from off campus. Internet access, at least one staffed computer lab available.

Student Life *Housing Options:* coed. Campus housing is leased by the school. *Activities and Organizations:* drama/theater group, Student Ambassadors, Spring trip, Fall Festival, Holiday Dinner Dance, Flag football. *Campus security:* 24-hour emergency response devices, security guard.

Standardized Tests *Required:* Wonderlic aptitude test (for admission).

Costs (2006–07) *Tuition:* $7290 full-time, $243 per credit part-time. *Required fees:* $850 full-time, $25 per credit part-time, $25 per term part-time.

Financial Aid Of all full-time matriculated undergraduates who enrolled in 2004, 15 Federal Work-Study jobs (averaging $600).

Applying *Options:* common application, deferred entrance. *Application fee:* $25. *Required:* essay or personal statement, high school transcript, interview, Wonderlic aptitude test. *Application deadline:* rolling (freshmen), rolling (transfers). *Notification:* continuous (freshmen).

Freshmen Application Contact Ms. Rose Mello, Academic Administrator, Erie Business Center, Main, 220 West Ninth Street, Erie, PA 16501-1392. *Phone:* 814-456-7504 Ext. 102. *Toll-free phone:* 800-352-3743. *Fax:* 814-456-4882. *E-mail:* mellor@eriebc.com.

ERIE BUSINESS CENTER SOUTH

New Castle, Pennsylvania
www.eriebc.com/

- **Proprietary** 2-year, founded 1894
- **Small-town** 1-acre campus with easy access to Pittsburgh
- **Coed, primarily women**

Undergraduates 100 full-time. 8% African American. *Retention:* 80% of 2003 full-time freshmen returned.

Faculty *Student/faculty ratio:* 14:1.

Academics *Calendar:* quarters. *Degree:* diplomas and associate. *Special study options:* academic remediation for entering students, adult/continuing education programs, internships, part-time degree program.

Student Life *Campus security:* 24-hour patrols.

Standardized Tests *Recommended:* SAT and SAT Subject Tests or ACT (for admission).

Applying *Options:* common application, electronic application, deferred entrance. *Application fee:* $25. *Required:* high school transcript. *Recommended:* interview.

Freshmen Application Contact Mr. Nick DeSalvo, Administrative Representative, Erie Business Center South, 170 Cascade Galleria, New Castle, PA 16101-3950. *Phone:* 724-658-9066. *Toll-free phone:* 800-722-6227.

ERIE INSTITUTE OF TECHNOLOGY

Erie, Pennsylvania
www.erieit.org/

Director of Admissions Mr. Ken Haas, Admissions Representative, Erie Institute of Technology, 5539 Peach Street, Erie, PA 16509. *Phone:* 814-868-9900. *Toll-free phone:* 866-868-3743.

HARCUM COLLEGE

Bryn Mawr, Pennsylvania   www.harcum.edu/

- **Independent** 2-year, founded 1915
- **Suburban** 12-acre campus with easy access to Philadelphia
- **Endowment** $9.0 million
- **Coed, primarily women**

Undergraduates   385 full-time, 188 part-time. Students come from 8 states and territories, 6 other countries, 10% are from out of state, 20% African American, 3% Asian American or Pacific Islander, 3% Hispanic American, 0.3% Native American, 0.9% international, 21% transferred in, 23% live on campus. *Retention:* 90% of 2003 full-time freshmen returned.

Faculty   *Student/faculty ratio:* 9:1.

Academics   *Calendar:* semesters. *Degree:* certificates and associate. *Special study options:* academic remediation for entering students, adult/continuing education programs, advanced placement credit, distance learning, double majors, English as a second language, honors programs, independent study, internships, off-campus study, part-time degree program, services for LD students, summer session for credit.

Student Life   *Campus security:* 24-hour emergency response devices and patrols, controlled dormitory access.

Standardized Tests   *Required:* SAT or ACT (for admission).

Costs (2005–06)   *Comprehensive fee:* $21,522 includes full-time tuition ($14,322), mandatory fees ($300), and room and board ($6900). Part-time tuition: $478 per credit.

Financial Aid   Of all full-time matriculated undergraduates who enrolled in 2004, 161 Federal Work-Study jobs (averaging $1100).

Applying   *Options:* common application, electronic application, early admission, deferred entrance. *Application fee:* $25. *Required:* essay or personal statement, high school transcript, letters of recommendation. *Recommended:* interview.

Freshmen Application Contact   Office of Enrollment Management, Harcum College, 750 Montgomery Avenue, Melville Hall, Bryn Mawr, PA 19010-3476. *Phone:* 610-526-6050. *Toll-free phone:* 800-345-2600.

▶ **See page 548 for the College Close-Up.**

HARRISBURG AREA COMMUNITY COLLEGE

Harrisburg, Pennsylvania   www.hacc.edu/

- **State and locally supported** 2-year, founded 1964
- **Urban** 212-acre campus
- **Endowment** $31.9 million
- **Coed,** 16,899 undergraduate students, 39% full-time, 65% women, 35% men

Undergraduates   6,634 full-time, 10,265 part-time. Students come from 14 states and territories, 8 other countries, 1% are from out of state, 9% African American, 3% Asian American or Pacific Islander, 5% Hispanic American, 0.3% Native American, 1% international, 29% transferred in.
Freshmen *Admission:* 7,655 applied, 7,467 admitted, 1,756 enrolled.

Faculty   *Total:* 977, 27% full-time, 4% with terminal degrees. *Student/faculty ratio:* 20:1.

Majors   Accounting; actuarial science; administrative assistant and secretarial science; agricultural business and management; architectural engineering technology; architecture; art; automobile/automotive mechanics technology; automotive engineering technology; banking and financial support services; biology/biological sciences; business administration and management; business/commerce; business, management, and marketing related; business teacher education; cardiovascular technology; chemistry; civil engineering technology; clinical/medical laboratory assistant; clinical/medical laboratory technology; commercial and advertising art; computer and information sciences; computer and information sciences and support services related; computer installation and repair technology; computer systems networking and telecommunications; construction engineering technology; consumer merchandising/retailing management; criminal justice/law enforcement administration; criminal justice/police science; culinary arts; dental hygiene; design and visual communications; dietetics; dramatic/theater arts; education; electrical, electronic and communications engineering technology; elementary education; emergency medical technology (EMT paramedic); engineering; engineering technologies related; engineering technology; environmental studies; fire science; foods, nutrition, and wellness; general retailing/wholesaling; health information/medical records administration; heating, air conditioning and refrigeration technology; hospital and health care facilities administration; hotel/motel administration; human services; industrial

mechanics and maintenance technology; information technology; institutional food workers; international relations and affairs; journalism; kindergarten/preschool education; legal administrative assistant/secretary; legal assistant/paralegal; liberal arts and sciences/liberal studies; management information systems; management science; marketing/marketing management; mass communication/media; mathematics; mechanical engineering/mechanical technology; medical office assistant; medical radiologic technology; music; nuclear medical technology; nursing (registered nurse training); opticianry; pharmacy technician; photography; physical education teaching and coaching; physical sciences; psychology; real estate; respiratory care therapy; respiratory therapy technician; science teacher education; social sciences; social work; tourism and travel services management; tourism and travel services marketing; web/multimedia management and webmaster.

Academics   *Calendar:* semesters. *Degree:* certificates, diplomas, and associate. *Special study options:* academic remediation for entering students, adult/continuing education programs, advanced placement credit, distance learning, double majors, English as a second language, honors programs, independent study, internships, part-time degree program, services for LD students, student-designed majors, study abroad, summer session for credit. *ROTC:* Army (b).

Library   McCormick Library with 119,000 titles, 873 serial subscriptions, 12,733 audiovisual materials, an OPAC, a Web page.

Computers on Campus   974 computers available on campus for general student use. A campuswide network can be accessed from off campus. Internet access, online (class) registration, at least one staffed computer lab available.

Student Life   *Housing:* college housing not available. *Activities and Organizations:* drama/theater group, student-run newspaper, radio station, Student Government Association, Phi Theta Kappa, African American Student Association, Mosiaco Club, Fourth Estate. *Campus security:* 24-hour emergency response devices and patrols, late-night transport/escort service. *Student services:* personal/psychological counseling.

Athletics   *Intercollegiate sports:* basketball M/W, soccer M/W, swimming and diving M/W, tennis M/W, volleyball M/W. *Intramural sports:* basketball M/W, football M/W, golf M/W, racquetball M/W, skiing (downhill) M/W, soccer M, softball M/W, squash M/W, tennis M/W, volleyball W.

Costs (2005–06)   *Tuition:* area resident $2850 full-time, $95 per credit hour part-time; state resident $5250 full-time, $175 per credit hour part-time; nonresident $7650 full-time, $255 per credit hour part-time. *Required fees:* $510 full-time, $17 per credit hour part-time.

Applying   *Options:* electronic application, early admission. *Application fee:* $30. *Required:* high school transcript. *Application deadline:* rolling (freshmen), rolling (transfers).

Freshmen Application Contact   Mrs. Vanita L. Cowan, Administrative Clerk, Admissions, Harrisburg Area Community College, 1 HACC Drive, Harrisburg, PA 17110. *Phone:* 717-780-2406. *Toll-free phone:* 800-ABC-HACC. *Fax:* 717-231-7674. *E-mail:* admit@hacc.edu.

ICM SCHOOL OF BUSINESS & MEDICAL CAREERS

Pittsburgh, Pennsylvania   www.icmschool.com/

- **Proprietary** 2-year, founded 1963
- **Urban** campus
- **Coed**

Undergraduates   1,065 full-time, 30 part-time. Students come from 3 states and territories, 2% are from out of state, 48% African American, 0.3% Asian American or Pacific Islander, 0.7% Hispanic American, 0.5% Native American, 0.1% international.

Faculty   *Student/faculty ratio:* 18:1.

Academics   *Calendar:* continuous. *Degree:* diplomas and associate. *Special study options:* academic remediation for entering students, advanced placement credit, cooperative education, independent study, internships, part-time degree program, summer session for credit.

Student Life   *Campus security:* 24-hour emergency response devices, evening security personnel.

Standardized Tests   *Required:* Wonderlic aptitude test, CPAt (for admission). *Required for some:* SAT and SAT Subject Tests or ACT (for admission).

Costs (2005–06)   *Tuition:* $24,400 full-time. *Required fees:* $130 full-time.

Applying   *Options:* common application. *Application fee:* $30. *Required:* essay or personal statement, high school transcript, interview.

Director of Admissions   Mrs. Marcia Rosenberg, Director of Admissions, ICM School of Business & Medical Careers, 10 Wood Street, Pittsburgh, PA 15222. *Phone:* 412-261-2647 Ext. 229. *Toll-free phone:* 800-441-5222. *E-mail:* mrosenberg@icmschool.com.

INFORMATION COMPUTER SYSTEMS INSTITUTE

Allentown, Pennsylvania　　　www.icsinstitute.com/

Director of Admissions Bill Barber, Director, Information Computer Systems Institute, 2201 Hangar Place, Allentown, PA 18103-9504. *Phone:* 610-264-8029. *Fax:* 610-264-5579. *E-mail:* wbarber@ptd.net.

INTERNATIONAL ACADEMY OF DESIGN & TECHNOLOGY

Pittsburgh, Pennsylvania　　　www.iadtpitt.com/

Director of Admissions Ms. Debbie Love, Chief Admissions Officer, International Academy of Design & Technology, 555 Grant Street, Pittsburgh, PA 15219. *Phone:* 412-391-4197. *Toll-free phone:* 800-447-8324. *Fax:* 412-391-3912.

JNA INSTITUTE OF CULINARY ARTS

Philadelphia, Pennsylvania

JOHNSON COLLEGE

Scranton, Pennsylvania　　　www.johnson.edu/

Director of Admissions Ms. Melissa Turlip, Acting Director of Enrollment Management, Johnson College, 3427 North Main Avenue, Scranton, PA 18508. *Phone:* 570-342-6404 Ext. 122. *Toll-free phone:* 800-2-WE-WORK Ext. 125.

▶ **See page 556 for the College Close-Up.**

KATHARINE GIBBS SCHOOL

Norristown, Pennsylvania　　　www.pagibbs.com/

Director of Admissions Mr. Joseph Carretta, President, Katharine Gibbs School, 2501 Monroe Boulevard, Norristown, PA 19403. *Phone:* 610-676-0500. *Toll-free phone:* 866-PAGIBBS. *Fax:* 610-676-0539. *E-mail:* jcarretta@pagibbs.com.

KEYSTONE COLLEGE

La Plume, Pennsylvania　　　www.keystone.edu

- **Independent** primarily 2-year, founded 1868
- **Rural** 270-acre campus
- **Endowment** $8.9 million
- **Coed,** 1,638 undergraduate students, 75% full-time, 62% women, 38% men

Undergraduates 1,234 full-time, 404 part-time. Students come from 12 states and territories, 7 other countries, 18% are from out of state, 3% African American, 0.6% Asian American or Pacific Islander, 1% Hispanic American, 0.3% Native American, 1% international, 10% transferred in, 24% live on campus. *Retention:* 63% of 2003 full-time freshmen returned.

Freshmen *Admission:* 872 applied, 796 admitted, 361 enrolled. *Average high school GPA:* 2.30. *Test scores:* SAT verbal scores over 500: 21%; SAT math scores over 500: 16%; ACT scores over 18: 45%; SAT verbal scores over 600: 3%; SAT math scores over 600: 2%.

Faculty *Total:* 207, 30% full-time, 13% with terminal degrees. *Student/faculty ratio:* 12:1.

Majors Accounting; accounting and business/management; accounting related; art; art teacher education; biological and physical sciences; biology/biological sciences; business administration and management; business/commerce; communication and journalism related; communication and media related; communication/

speech communication and rhetoric; computer/information technology services administration related; computer programming; criminal justice/law enforcement administration; criminal justice/safety; culinary arts; culinary arts related; data processing and data processing technology; diagnostic medical sonography and ultrasound technology; drawing; early childhood education; education (K-12); elementary education; environmental biology; environmental science; environmental studies; family and community services; fine/studio arts; food preparation; forensic science and technology; forestry; forestry technology; graphic design; hotel/motel administration; human resources management; illustration; information technology; journalism; kindergarten/preschool education; landscape architecture; liberal arts and sciences/liberal studies; mathematics teacher education; medical radiologic technology; natural resources management; occupational therapy; painting; parks, recreation and leisure facilities management; photography; physical therapy; pre-nursing studies; printmaking; public relations, advertising, and applied communication related; radio and television; radiologic technology/science; radio, television, and digital communication related; restaurant, culinary, and catering management; restaurant/food services management; sculpture; social studies teacher education; sport and fitness administration/management; therapeutic recreation; water, wetlands, and marine resources management; wildlife and wildlands science and management; wildlife biology.

Academics *Calendar:* semesters. *Degrees:* certificates, associate, bachelor's, and postbachelor's certificates. *Special study options:* academic remediation for entering students, adult/continuing education programs, advanced placement credit, cooperative education, distance learning, external degree program, freshman honors college, honors programs, independent study, internships, part-time degree program, services for LD students, student-designed majors, summer session for credit. *ROTC:* Army (c), Air Force (c).

Library Miller Library with 65,000 titles, 309 serial subscriptions, 10,000 audiovisual materials, an OPAC, a Web page.

Computers on Campus 120 computers available on campus for general student use. A campuswide network can be accessed from student residence rooms and from off campus that provide access to wireless campus. Internet access, online (class) registration, at least one staffed computer lab available. Computer purchase or lease plan available.

Student Life *Housing Options:* coed, women-only, disabled students. Campus housing is university owned. Freshman campus housing is guaranteed. *Activities and Organizations:* drama/theater group, student-run newspaper, radio station, choral group, Campus Activity Board, Student Senate, Art Society, Inter-Hall Council, Commuter Council. *Campus security:* 24-hour emergency response devices and patrols, student patrols, late-night transport/escort service, controlled dormitory access. *Student services:* health clinic, personal/psychological counseling, women's center.

Athletics Member NCAA. *Intercollegiate sports:* baseball M, basketball M/W, cross-country running M/W, golf M, soccer M/W, softball W, tennis M/W, track and field M/W, volleyball W. *Intramural sports:* basketball M/W, cheerleading M(c)/W(c), equestrian sports M(c)/W(c), football M/W, lacrosse M/W, skiing (downhill) M(c)/W(c), soccer M/W, softball M/W, table tennis M/W, tennis M/W, volleyball M/W, weight lifting M/W.

Standardized Tests *Required for some:* SAT or ACT (for admission). *Recommended:* SAT or ACT (for admission).

Costs (2006–07) *Comprehensive fee:* $24,026 includes full-time tuition ($14,946), mandatory fees ($970), and room and board ($8110). Part-time tuition: $330 per credit. *Required fees:* $110 per term part-time. *Room and board:* college room only: $4300.

Financial Aid Of all full-time matriculated undergraduates who enrolled in 2004, 125 Federal Work-Study jobs (averaging $1000). 100 state and other part-time jobs (averaging $1000).

Applying *Options:* common application, electronic application, early admission, deferred entrance. *Application fee:* $25. *Required:* high school transcript, 1 letter of recommendation. *Required for some:* interview, art portfolio. *Recommended:* essay or personal statement, interview. *Application deadlines:* 7/1 (freshmen), 8/1 (transfers).

Freshmen Application Contact Ms. Sarah Keating, Director of Admissions, Keystone College, One College Green, La Plume, PA 18440-1099. *Phone:* 570-945-8112. *Toll-free phone:* 877-4COLLEGE Ext. 1. *Fax:* 570-945-7916. *E-mail:* admissions@keystone.edu.

▶ **See page 558 for the College Close-Up.**

LACKAWANNA COLLEGE

Scranton, Pennsylvania www.lackawanna.edu/

- **Independent** 2-year, founded 1894
- **Urban** 4-acre campus
- **Endowment** $1.2 million
- **Coed,** 1,197 undergraduate students, 63% full-time, 53% women, 47% men

Undergraduates 758 full-time, 439 part-time. Students come from 20 states and territories, 3% are from out of state, 11% African American, 0.5% Asian American or Pacific Islander, 2% Hispanic American, 0.3% Native American, 11% transferred in, 12% live on campus.
Freshmen *Admission:* 626 admitted, 362 enrolled.
Faculty *Total:* 56, 36% full-time, 11% with terminal degrees. *Student/faculty ratio:* 13:1.
Majors Accounting technology and bookkeeping; administrative assistant and secretarial science; banking and financial support services; biotechnology; business administration and management; business/commerce; communication/speech communication and rhetoric; communications technology; computer and information sciences; criminal justice/safety; diagnostic medical sonography and ultrasound technology; early childhood education; education; emergency medical technology (EMT paramedic); general studies; humanities; industrial technology; legal assistant/paralegal; liberal arts and sciences/liberal studies; management information systems; mass communication/media; medical administrative assistant and medical secretary; mental health/rehabilitation.
Academics *Calendar:* semesters. *Degree:* certificates, diplomas, and associate. *Special study options:* academic remediation for entering students, adult/continuing education programs, cooperative education, double majors, English as a second language, internships, part-time degree program, services for LD students, summer session for credit. *ROTC:* Army (c), Air Force (c).
Library Seeley Memorial Library with 15,276 titles, 58 serial subscriptions, 491 audiovisual materials, an OPAC, a Web page.
Computers on Campus 200 computers available on campus for general student use. A campuswide network can be accessed from student residence rooms and from off campus. Internet access, at least one staffed computer lab available.
Student Life *Housing:* on-campus residence required through sophomore year. *Options:* men-only. Campus housing is university owned. *Activities and Organizations:* drama/theater group, student-run newspaper, student government, Student/Alumni Association, Diversity Club, student newspaper, Phi Beta Lambda. *Campus security:* 24-hour emergency response devices, late-night transport/escort service, patrols by college liaison staff. *Student services:* personal/psychological counseling.
Athletics Member NJCAA. *Intercollegiate sports:* baseball M(s), basketball M(s)/W(s), football M(s), golf M(s)/W(s), softball W(s), volleyball W(s). *Intramural sports:* weight lifting M/W.
Standardized Tests *Recommended:* SAT (for admission), ACT (for admission), SAT or ACT (for admission).
Costs (2005–06) *Comprehensive fee:* $15,770 includes full-time tuition ($9400), mandatory fees ($70), and room and board ($6300). Full-time tuition and fees vary according to course load. Part-time tuition: $310 per credit. Part-time tuition and fees vary according to course load. *Required fees:* $35 per term part-time. *Room and board:* college room only: $4100. *Payment plan:* installment. *Waivers:* employees or children of employees.
Financial Aid Of all full-time matriculated undergraduates who enrolled in 2004, 101 Federal Work-Study jobs (averaging $1600).
Applying *Options:* electronic application, early admission, deferred entrance. *Application fee:* $30. *Required:* high school transcript, interview. *Application deadline:* rolling (freshmen), rolling (transfers).
Freshmen Application Contact Mr. Brian Costanzo, Director of Admissions, Lackawanna College, 501 Vine Street, Scranton, PA 18509. *Phone:* 570-961-7841. *Toll-free phone:* 877-346-3552. *Fax:* 570-961-7843. *E-mail:* constanzob@lackawanna.edu.

LANSDALE SCHOOL OF BUSINESS

North Wales, Pennsylvania www.lsbonline.com/

Director of Admissions Ms. Marianne H. Johnson, Director of Admissions, Lansdale School of Business, 201 Church Road, North Wales, PA 19454-4148. *Phone:* 215-699-5700 Ext. 112. *Fax:* 215-699-8770. *E-mail:* mjohnson@lsb.edu.

LAUREL BUSINESS INSTITUTE

Uniontown, Pennsylvania www.laurel.edu/

- **Proprietary** 2-year, founded 1985
- **Small-town** 10-acre campus with easy access to Pittsburgh
- **Coed,** 297 undergraduate students, 98% full-time, 79% women, 21% men

Undergraduates 292 full-time, 5 part-time. Students come from 2 states and territories, 1% are from out of state, 6% African American.
Freshmen *Admission:* 415 applied, 246 admitted. *Average high school GPA:* 2.75.
Faculty *Total:* 25, 64% full-time. *Student/faculty ratio:* 16:1.
Majors Accounting; administrative assistant and secretarial science; banking and financial support services; business administration and management; business automation/technology/data entry; child guidance; computer and information sciences related; computer and information systems security; computer/information technology services administration related; computer management; computer software and media applications related; computer systems networking and telecommunications; computer/technical support; consumer merchandising/retailing management; data entry/microcomputer applications; data entry/microcomputer applications related; executive assistant/executive secretary; home health aide/home attendant; information technology; insurance; legal administrative assistant/secretary; medical administrative assistant and medical secretary; medical/clinical assistant; medical transcription; office occupations and clerical services; system administration; web page, digital/multimedia and information resources design; word processing.
Academics *Calendar:* trimesters. *Degree:* certificates, diplomas, and associate. *Special study options:* academic remediation for entering students, adult/continuing education programs, advanced placement credit, cooperative education, double majors, freshman honors college, honors programs, internships, part-time degree program, services for LD students.
Computers on Campus 75 computers available on campus for general student use. A campuswide network can be accessed from off campus. Internet access, at least one staffed computer lab available.
Student Life *Housing:* college housing not available.
Standardized Tests *Required:* Wonderlic (for admission).
Costs (2006–07) *Tuition:* $10,125 full-time, $215 part-time. *Required fees:* $1828 full-time, $349 per term part-time.
Financial Aid Of all full-time matriculated undergraduates who enrolled in 2004, 60 Federal Work-Study jobs (averaging $710).
Applying *Options:* common application, electronic application, deferred entrance. *Application fee:* $55. *Required:* essay or personal statement, high school transcript, interview. *Application deadline:* rolling (freshmen), rolling (transfers). *Notification:* continuous (freshmen).
Freshmen Application Contact Mrs. Lisa Dolan, Laurel Business Institute, 11-15 Penn Street, PO Box 877, Uniontown, PA 15401. *Phone:* 724-439-4900 Ext. 158. *Fax:* 724-439-3607. *E-mail:* idolan@laurelbusiness.net.

LEHIGH CARBON COMMUNITY COLLEGE

Schnecksville, Pennsylvania www.lccc.edu/

- **State and locally supported** 2-year, founded 1967
- **Suburban** 153-acre campus with easy access to Philadelphia
- **Endowment** $841,000
- **Coed**

Undergraduates 2,607 full-time, 4,067 part-time. Students come from 19 states and territories, 9 other countries, 1% are from out of state, 5% African American, 2% Asian American or Pacific Islander, 8% Hispanic American, 0.1% Native American, 0.1% international, 33% transferred in.
Faculty *Student/faculty ratio:* 14:1.
Academics *Calendar:* semesters. *Degree:* certificates, diplomas, and associate. *Special study options:* academic remediation for entering students, adult/continuing education programs, advanced placement credit, cooperative education, distance learning, English as a second language, independent study, internships, part-time degree program, services for LD students, summer session for credit. *ROTC:* Army (c).
Student Life *Campus security:* 24-hour emergency response devices and patrols, student patrols, late-night transport/escort service.
Athletics Member NJCAA.
Standardized Tests *Required for some:* ACT or ACT COMPASS.
Costs (2005–06) *Tuition:* area resident $2700 full-time, $76 per credit part-time; state resident $5250 full-time, $152 per credit part-time; nonresident $7800 full-time, $228 per credit part-time. Full-time tuition and fees vary

Lehigh Carbon Community College (continued)
according to course load and reciprocity agreements. Part-time tuition and fees vary according to course load and reciprocity agreements. *Required fees:* $420 full-time, $14 per credit hour part-time.

Applying   *Application fee:* $25. *Required for some:* essay or personal statement, high school transcript, interview.

Director of Admissions   Mr. Jack Mosser, Associate Dean of Enrollment, Lehigh Carbon Community College, 4525 Education Park Drive, Schnecksville, PA 18078-2598. *Phone:* 610-799-1575. *Fax:* 610-799-1527. *E-mail:* tellme@ lccc.edu.

LEHIGH VALLEY COLLEGE

Center Valley, Pennsylvania   www.lehighvalley.edu/

- **Proprietary** 2-year, founded 1869, part of Career Education Corporation
- **Urban** 30-acre campus with easy access to Philadelphia
- **Endowment** $500,000
- **Coed,** 1,236 undergraduate students

Undergraduates   Students come from 3 states and territories, 1% are from out of state. *Retention:* 63% of 2003 full-time freshmen returned.

Freshmen   *Admission:* 707 applied, 176 admitted. *Average high school GPA:* 2.

Faculty   *Total:* 93, 43% full-time, 5% with terminal degrees. *Student/faculty ratio:* 26:1.

Majors   Accounting; business administration and management; computer and information sciences; computer programming; criminal justice/law enforcement administration; design and visual communications; hospitality administration related; information science/studies; legal assistant/paralegal; marketing/marketing management; massage therapy; medical administrative assistant and medical secretary; photography; tourism and travel services management.

Academics   *Calendar:* quarters. *Degree:* associate. *Special study options:* academic remediation for entering students, adult/continuing education programs, advanced placement credit, cooperative education, independent study, internships, services for LD students.

Library   Main Library plus 1 other.

Computers on Campus   100 computers available on campus for general student use. A campuswide network can be accessed. Internet access, at least one staffed computer lab available. Computer purchase or lease plan available.

Student Life   *Housing:* college housing not available. *Options:* Campus housing is provided by a third party. *Activities and Organizations:* Student Government, Travel Club. *Campus security:* evening security guard.

Standardized Tests   *Required:* ACCUPLACER (for admission).

Costs (2006–07)   *Tuition:* $325 per credit hour part-time. Varies by program.

Financial Aid   Of all full-time matriculated undergraduates who enrolled in 2004, 30 Federal Work-Study jobs (averaging $2500).

Applying   *Options:* common application, electronic application, deferred entrance. *Application fee:* $50. *Required:* high school transcript. *Recommended:* interview. *Application deadline:* rolling (freshmen), rolling (transfers). *Notification:* continuous (freshmen).

Freshmen Application Contact   Mr. Joshua Padron, Vice President of Marketing and Admissions, Lehigh Valley College, 2809 East Saucon Valley Road, Center Valley, PA 18034. *Phone:* 610-791-5100. *Toll-free phone:* 800-227-9109. *Fax:* 610-791-7810. *E-mail:* joshua.padron@lehighvalley.edu.

▶ See page 562 for the College Close-Up.

LINCOLN TECHNICAL INSTITUTE

Allentown, Pennsylvania   www.lincolntech.com/

Freshmen Application Contact   Admissions Office, Lincoln Technical Institute, 5151 Tilghman Street, Allentown, PA 18104-3298. *Phone:* 610-398-5301.

LINCOLN TECHNICAL INSTITUTE

Philadelphia, Pennsylvania   www.lincolntech.com/

Director of Admissions   Mr. James Kuntz, Executive Director, Lincoln Technical Institute, 9191 Torresdale Avenue, Philadelphia, PA 19136-1595. *Phone:* 215-335-0800. *Toll-free phone:* 800-238-8381. *Fax:* 215-335-1443. *E-mail:* jkuntz@lincolntech.com.

LUZERNE COUNTY COMMUNITY COLLEGE

Nanticoke, Pennsylvania   www.luzerne.edu/

- **County-supported** 2-year, founded 1966
- **Suburban** 122-acre campus with easy access to Philadelphia
- **Coed,** 6,170 undergraduate students, 48% full-time, 58% women, 42% men

Undergraduates   2,940 full-time, 3,230 part-time. Students come from 2 states and territories, 1 other country, 2% African American, 1% Asian American or Pacific Islander, 1% Hispanic American, 0.1% Native American, 0.1% international, 6% transferred in.

Freshmen   *Admission:* 2,337 applied, 1,574 admitted, 1,447 enrolled.

Faculty   *Total:* 475, 22% full-time. *Student/faculty ratio:* 19:1.

Majors   Accounting; administrative assistant and secretarial science; airline pilot and flight crew; architectural engineering; architectural engineering technology; automobile/automotive mechanics technology; aviation/airway management; baking and pastry arts; banking and financial support services; biological and physical sciences; building/property maintenance and management; business administration and management; child care provision; commercial and advertising art; commercial photography; computer and information sciences; computer and information sciences related; computer graphics; computer programming related; computer science; computer systems networking and telecommunications; computer technology/computer systems technology; court reporting; criminal justice/law enforcement administration; culinary arts; data entry/microcomputer applications; data processing and data processing technology; dental assisting; dental hygiene; drafting and design technology; drawing; early childhood education; education; electrical, electronic and communications engineering technology; electrician; emergency medical technology (EMT paramedic); engineering technology; executive assistant/executive secretary; fire science; food services technology; funeral service and mortuary science; general studies; graphic and printing equipment operation/production; graphic design; health and physical education; health/health care administration; heating, air conditioning, ventilation and refrigeration maintenance technology; horticultural science; hospitality and recreation marketing; hotel/motel administration; humanities; human services; industrial design; international business/trade/commerce; journalism; legal assistant/paralegal; liberal arts and sciences and humanities related; liberal arts and sciences/liberal studies; mathematics; mechanical design technology; medical administrative assistant and medical secretary; nursing (registered nurse training); ophthalmic/optometric services; painting; photography; physical education teaching and coaching; plumbing technology; pre-pharmacy studies; radio and television broadcasting technology; real estate; respiratory care therapy; social sciences; surgical technology; tourism and travel services management; tourism and travel services marketing.

Academics   *Calendar:* semesters. *Degree:* certificates, diplomas, and associate. *Special study options:* academic remediation for entering students, accelerated degree program, advanced placement credit, distance learning, external degree program, internships, part-time degree program, services for LD students, summer session for credit. *ROTC:* Air Force (c).

Library   Learning Resources Center plus 1 other with 60,000 titles, 744 serial subscriptions, 3,000 audiovisual materials, an OPAC, a Web page.

Computers on Campus   150 computers available on campus for general student use. A campuswide network can be accessed. Internet access, at least one staffed computer lab available.

Student Life   *Housing:* college housing not available. *Activities and Organizations:* student-run newspaper, radio and television station, student government, Circle K, Nursing Forum, Science Club, SADAH. *Campus security:* 24-hour patrols.

Athletics   Member NJCAA. *Intercollegiate sports:* baseball M, basketball M/W, cross-country running M/W, golf M/W, soccer M/W, softball W, volleyball W. *Intramural sports:* badminton M/W, basketball M/W, bowling M/W, softball M/W, tennis M/W, volleyball M/W.

Costs (2005–06)   *Tuition:* $76 per credit part-time; state resident $152 per credit part-time; nonresident $228 per credit part-time. *Required fees:* $16 per credit part-time.

Applying   *Options:* early admission, deferred entrance. *Application fee:* $40. *Recommended:* high school transcript. *Application deadline:* rolling (freshmen), rolling (transfers).

Freshmen Application Contact   Mr. Francis Curry, Director of Admissions, Luzerne County Community College, 1333 South Prospect Street, Nanticoke, PA 18634. *Phone:* 570-740-0200 Ext. 343. *Toll-free phone:* 800-377-5222 Ext. 337.

MANOR COLLEGE

Jenkintown, Pennsylvania   www.manor.edu/

- **Independent Byzantine Catholic** 2-year, founded 1947
- **Small-town** 35-acre campus with easy access to Philadelphia
- **Coed,** 865 undergraduate students, 50% full-time, 81% women, 19% men

Manor College, located in Jenkintown, a suburb of Philadelphia, offers associate degree and transfer programs in the allied health, business, and liberal arts fields. Areas of study include accounting, allied health, business administration, computer science, dental hygiene, early child care/elementary education, expanded functions dental assisting, human resource management, marketing, paralegal studies, psychology, and veterinary technology.

Undergraduates 433 full-time, 432 part-time. Students come from 5 states and territories, 8 other countries, 7% are from out of state, 27% transferred in. Freshmen *Admission:* 536 applied, 266 admitted, 192 enrolled. *Average high school GPA:* 2.85. *Test scores:* SAT verbal scores over 500: 20%; SAT math scores over 500: 20%; SAT verbal scores over 600: 4%; SAT math scores over 600: 4%.

Faculty *Total:* 111, 22% full-time. *Student/faculty ratio:* 14:1.

Majors Accounting; administrative assistant and secretarial science; animal sciences; biological and physical sciences; business administration and management; child development; clinical/medical laboratory technology; computer and information sciences related; computer science; computer/technical support; cytotechnology; dental hygiene; education; elementary education; health science; human services; international business/trade/commerce; kindergarten/preschool education; legal administrative assistant/secretary; legal assistant/paralegal; liberal arts and sciences/liberal studies; medical administrative assistant and medical secretary; occupational therapy; physical therapy; psychology; veterinary sciences; veterinary technology.

Academics *Calendar:* semesters. *Degrees:* certificates, diplomas, associate, and postbachelor's certificates. *Special study options:* academic remediation for entering students, adult/continuing education programs, advanced placement credit, distance learning, double majors, English as a second language, honors programs, independent study, internships, part-time degree program, summer session for credit.

Library Basileiad Library with 42,000 titles, 225 serial subscriptions, 300 audiovisual materials, an OPAC, a Web page.

Computers on Campus 35 computers available on campus for general student use. A campuswide network can be accessed from student residence rooms. Internet access, at least one staffed computer lab available.

Student Life *Housing Options:* coed. *Activities and Organizations:* choral group. *Campus security:* 24-hour emergency response devices and patrols. *Student services:* personal/psychological counseling.

Athletics *Intercollegiate sports:* basketball M(s)/W(s), soccer M(s)/W(s), volleyball W(s). *Intramural sports:* basketball M/W, soccer M/W, volleyball W.

Standardized Tests *Required:* SAT or ACT (for admission).

Costs (2006–07) *Comprehensive fee:* $16,514 includes full-time tuition ($10,868), mandatory fees ($350), and room and board ($5296). Part-time tuition: $235 per credit hour. *Required fees:* $25 per term part-time.

Financial Aid Of all full-time matriculated undergraduates who enrolled in 2004, 45 Federal Work-Study jobs (averaging $1000). 11 state and other part-time jobs (averaging $2260). *Financial aid deadline:* 9/30.

Applying *Options:* electronic application, deferred entrance. *Application fee:* $20. *Required:* high school transcript, interview. *Application deadline:* rolling (freshmen), rolling (transfers). *Notification:* continuous (freshmen).

Freshmen Application Contact I. Jerry Czentuch, Vice President of Enrollment Management, Manor College, 700 Fox Chase Road, Jenkintown, PA 19046. *Phone:* 215-884-2216. *E-mail:* ftadmiss@manor.edu.

▶ **See page 568 for the College Close-Up.**

McCann School of Business & Technology

Pottsville, Pennsylvania   www.mccannschool.com/

Director of Admissions Ms. Rachel M. Schoffstall, Director, Pottsville Campus, McCann School of Business & Technology, 2650 Woodglen Road, Pottsville, PA 17901. *Phone:* 570-622-7622. *Toll-free phone:* 888-622-2664.

Median School of Allied Health Careers

Pittsburgh, Pennsylvania   www.medianschool.edu/

Director of Admissions Ms. Kris Jackson, Admission Coordinator, Median School of Allied Health Careers, 125 7th Street, Pittsburgh, PA 15222-3400. *Toll-free phone:* 800-570-0693.

Metropolitan Career Center

Philadelphia, Pennsylvania   www.metropolitancareercenter.org/

Director of Admissions Mr. Ken Huselton, Director of Student Services, Metropolitan Career Center, 100 South Broad Street, Philadelphia, PA 19110. *Phone:* 215-843-6615. *Fax:* 215-843-7661. *E-mail:* khuselton@mcc-btc.org.

Montgomery County Community College

Blue Bell, Pennsylvania   www.mc3.edu

- **County-supported** 2-year, founded 1964
- **Suburban** 186-acre campus with easy access to Philadelphia
- **Coed,** 10,874 undergraduate students, 44% full-time, 59% women, 41% men

Undergraduates 4,761 full-time, 6,113 part-time. Students come from 10 states and territories, 41 other countries, 0.2% are from out of state, 9% African American, 6% Asian American or Pacific Islander, 3% Hispanic American, 0.2% Native American, 1% international. *Retention:* 61% of 2003 full-time freshmen returned.

Freshmen *Admission:* 4,184 applied, 4,184 admitted, 3,676 enrolled.

Faculty *Total:* 664, 25% full-time. *Student/faculty ratio:* 23:1.

Majors Accounting; accounting technology and bookkeeping; administrative assistant and secretarial science; architectural drafting and CAD/CADD; art; automotive engineering technology; baking and pastry arts; biology/biological sciences; biotechnology; business administration and management; business/commerce; business/corporate communications; child care and support services management; clinical/medical laboratory technology; commercial and advertising art; communication/speech communication and rhetoric; communications technologies and support services related; computer and information sciences; computer engineering technology; computer programming; computer systems networking and telecommunications; criminal justice/police science; culinary arts; dental hygiene; electrical, electronic and communications engineering technology; electromechanical technology; elementary education; engineering science; engineering technologies related; fire protection and safety technology; food sales operations; hospitality and recreation marketing; hotel/motel services marketing operations; humanities; information science/studies; liberal arts and sciences/liberal studies; management information systems and services related; mathematics; mechanical drafting and CAD/CADD; mechanical engineering/mechanical technology; medical radiologic technology; nursing (registered nurse training); physical education teaching and coaching; physical sciences; psychiatric/mental health services technology; radiologic technology/science; real estate; respiratory care therapy; sales, distribution and marketing; secondary education; social sciences; surgical technology; teacher assistant/aide.

Academics *Calendar:* semesters. *Degree:* certificates and associate. *Special study options:* academic remediation for entering students, adult/continuing education programs, advanced placement credit, distance learning, English as a second language, honors programs, independent study, internships, part-time degree program, services for LD students, student-designed majors, study abroad, summer session for credit.

Library The Brendlinger Library plus 1 other with 201,174 titles, 550 serial subscriptions, 19,450 audiovisual materials, an OPAC, a Web page.

Computers on Campus 800 computers available on campus for general student use. A campuswide network can be accessed from off campus. Internet access, online (class) registration, at least one staffed computer lab available.

Student Life *Housing:* college housing not available. *Activities and Organizations:* drama/theater group, student-run newspaper, radio and television station, choral group, student government, Meridians Non-traditional Age Club, student radio station. *Campus security:* 24-hour emergency response devices and patrols, late-night transport/escort service. *Student services:* health clinic, personal/psychological counseling.

Montgomery County Community College (continued)

Athletics *Intramural sports:* badminton M/W, basketball M/W, bowling M/W, cross-country running M/W, football M, racquetball M/W, soccer M/W, softball M/W, table tennis M/W, tennis M/W, volleyball M/W, weight lifting M/W.

Costs (2006–07) *Tuition:* area resident $2716 full-time, $83 per credit part-time; state resident $5348 full-time, $191 per credit part-time; nonresident $7980 full-time, $285 per credit part-time. *Required fees:* $14 per credit part-time.

Financial Aid Of all full-time matriculated undergraduates who enrolled in 2004, 60 Federal Work-Study jobs (averaging $2500).

Applying *Options:* electronic application, early admission, deferred entrance. *Application fee:* $25. *Required for some:* high school transcript, interview. *Application deadline:* 5/1 (freshmen), rolling (transfers). *Notification:* continuous (freshmen).

Freshmen Application Contact Ms. Penny Sawyer, Director of Admissions and Recruitment, Montgomery County Community College, Office of Admissions and Records, Blue Bell, PA 19422. *Phone:* 215-641-6551. *Fax:* 215-619-7188. *E-mail:* admrec@admin.mc3.edu.

NEW CASTLE SCHOOL OF TRADES
Pulaski, Pennsylvania   www.ncstrades.com/

Freshmen Application Contact Mr. James Catheline, Admissions Director, New Castle School of Trades, RD 1, Route 422, Pulaski, PA 16143. *Phone:* 724-964-8811. *Toll-free phone:* 800-837-8299 Ext. 12.

NEWPORT BUSINESS INSTITUTE
Lower Burrell, Pennsylvania   www.nbi.edu

- **Proprietary** 2-year, founded 1895
- **Small-town** 4-acre campus with easy access to Pittsburgh
- **Coed,** 79 undergraduate students, 100% full-time, 80% women, 20% men

Undergraduates 79 full-time. Students come from 1 other state, 3% African American, 4% transferred in.
Freshmen *Admission:* 32 applied, 32 admitted, 18 enrolled. *Average high school GPA:* 2.8.

Faculty *Total:* 6. *Student/faculty ratio:* 14:1.

Majors Accounting; business administration and management; computer programming; consumer merchandising/retailing management; data entry/microcomputer applications; data entry/microcomputer applications related; executive assistant/executive secretary; legal administrative assistant/secretary; medical administrative assistant and medical secretary; medical/clinical assistant; medical office management; tourism and travel services management; word processing.

Academics *Calendar:* quarters. *Degree:* certificates, diplomas, and associate. *Special study options:* advanced placement credit, double majors, internships, student-designed majors.

Library Jean H. Mullen Memorial Library with 962 titles, 18 serial subscriptions.

Computers on Campus 85 computers available on campus for general student use. Internet access, at least one staffed computer lab available.

Student Life *Housing:* college housing not available. *Activities and Organizations:* student-run newspaper, student services, Returning Adults Club, new student mentoring, peer liaison. *Campus security:* security system. *Student services:* personal/psychological counseling.

Costs (2006–07) *Tuition:* $7800 full-time, $655 per course part-time. *Required fees:* $1575 full-time.

Applying *Options:* common application, early admission. *Application fee:* $25. *Required:* high school transcript. *Recommended:* interview. *Application deadline:* rolling (freshmen), rolling (transfers). *Notification:* continuous (freshmen).

Freshmen Application Contact Ms. Melissa Beck, Admissions Coordinator, Newport Business Institute, Lower Burrell, PA 15068. *Phone:* 724-339-7542. *Toll-free phone:* 800-752-7695. *Fax:* 724-339-2950.

NEWPORT BUSINESS INSTITUTE
Williamsport, Pennsylvania   www.newportbusiness.com/

- **Proprietary** 2-year, founded 1955
- **Small-town** campus
- **Coed, primarily women,** 104 undergraduate students, 99% full-time, 86% women, 14% men

Undergraduates 103 full-time, 1 part-time. Students come from 1 other state, 7% African American, 1% Asian American or Pacific Islander, 15% transferred in.
Freshmen *Admission:* 35 applied, 35 admitted, 35 enrolled.

Faculty *Total:* 7, 86% full-time. *Student/faculty ratio:* 15:1.

Majors Administrative assistant and secretarial science; business administration and management; legal administrative assistant/secretary; medical administrative assistant and medical secretary.

Academics *Calendar:* quarters. *Degree:* associate. *Special study options:* internships, part-time degree program, summer session for credit.

Computers on Campus 64 computers available on campus for general student use. Internet access, at least one staffed computer lab available.

Student Life *Housing:* college housing not available. *Activities and Organizations:* Student Council.

Costs (2006–07) *Tuition:* $8850 full-time, $738 per course part-time. *Required fees:* $475 full-time.

Financial Aid *Financial aid deadline:* 8/1.

Applying *Options:* deferred entrance. *Application fee:* $25. *Required:* high school transcript, interview. *Application deadline:* rolling (freshmen), rolling (transfers).

Freshmen Application Contact Mr. David Andrus, Admissions Representative, Newport Business Institute, 941 West Third Street, Williamsport, PA 17701. *Phone:* 570-326-2869. *Toll-free phone:* 800-962-6971. *Fax:* 570-326-2136. *E-mail:* admissions_NBI@suscom.net.

NORTHAMPTON COUNTY AREA COMMUNITY COLLEGE
Bethlehem, Pennsylvania   www.northampton.edu/

- **State and locally supported** 2-year, founded 1967
- **Suburban** 165-acre campus with easy access to Philadelphia
- **Endowment** $14.7 million
- **Coed,** 8,754 undergraduate students, 42% full-time, 63% women, 37% men

Undergraduates 3,680 full-time, 5,074 part-time. Students come from 22 states and territories, 39 other countries, 3% are from out of state, 7% African American, 2% Asian American or Pacific Islander, 10% Hispanic American, 0.2% Native American, 1% international, 33% transferred in, 3% live on campus. *Retention:* 58% of 2003 full-time freshmen returned.
Freshmen *Admission:* 3,386 applied, 3,386 admitted, 2,714 enrolled.

Faculty *Total:* 542, 20% full-time, 22% with terminal degrees. *Student/faculty ratio:* 21:1.

Majors Accounting technology and bookkeeping; acting; administrative assistant and secretarial science; architectural engineering technology; automobile/automotive mechanics technology; biology/biological sciences; biotechnology; business administration and management; business/commerce; CAD/CADD drafting/design technology; chemical technology; chemistry; child care provision; communication disorders; communication/speech communication and rhetoric; computer and information systems security; computer installation and repair technology; computer programming; computer science; computer systems networking and telecommunications; criminal justice/safety; dental hygiene; diagnostic medical sonography and ultrasound technology; education; electrical, electronic and communications engineering technology; electrician; electromechanical technology; engineering; fine/studio arts; fire services administration; food preparation; funeral service and mortuary science; general studies; graphic design; heating, air conditioning, ventilation and refrigeration maintenance technology; hotel/motel administration; industrial electronics technology; interior design; journalism; legal administrative assistant/secretary; legal assistant/paralegal; liberal arts and sciences and humanities related; liberal arts and sciences/liberal studies; mathematics; medical administrative assistant and medical secretary; nursing (registered nurse training); physics; quality control technology; radio and television broadcasting technology; radiologic technology/science; restaurant/food services management; social work; sport and fitness administration/management; surgical technology; teacher assistant/aide; veterinary/animal health technology; web page, digital/multimedia and information resources design.

Academics *Calendar:* semesters. *Degree:* certificates, diplomas, and associate. *Special study options:* academic remediation for entering students, accelerated degree program, adult/continuing education programs, advanced placement credit, cooperative education, distance learning, double majors, English as a second language, internships, part-time degree program, services for LD students, student-designed majors, study abroad, summer session for credit.

Library Paul & Harriett Mack Library with 64,758 titles, 355 serial subscriptions, 9,169 audiovisual materials, an OPAC, a Web page.

Computers on Campus 1400 computers available on campus for general student use. A campuswide network can be accessed from student residence rooms and from off campus. Internet access, online (class) registration, at least one staffed computer lab available. Computer purchase or lease plan available.

Student Life *Housing Options:* coed. Campus housing is university owned. *Activities and Organizations:* drama/theater group, student-run newspaper, radio station, choral group, Phi Theta Kappa, Nursing Student Organization, NAVTA (Veterinary Technology Club), Student American Dental Hygiene Association, Video Waves. *Campus security:* 24-hour emergency response devices and patrols, controlled dormitory access. *Student services:* health clinic, personal/psychological counseling.

Athletics *Intercollegiate sports:* baseball M, basketball M/W, bowling M/W, golf M/W, ice hockey M/W, soccer M/W, softball W, tennis M/W, volleyball M/W, wrestling M(c). *Intramural sports:* basketball M/W, bowling M/W, football M/W, golf M/W, racquetball M/W, soccer M/W, volleyball M/W.

Costs (2005–06) *Tuition:* area resident $2100 full-time, $70 per credit hour part-time; state resident $4200 full-time, $140 per credit hour part-time; nonresident $6300 full-time, $210 per credit hour part-time. Full-time tuition and fees vary according to course load. Part-time tuition and fees vary according to course load. *Required fees:* $720 full-time, $24 per credit hour part-time. *Room and board:* $5944; room only: $3434. Room and board charges vary according to board plan and housing facility. *Payment plans:* installment, deferred payment. *Waivers:* senior citizens and employees or children of employees.

Financial Aid Of all full-time matriculated undergraduates who enrolled in 2004, 300 Federal Work-Study jobs (averaging $2400). 130 state and other part-time jobs (averaging $1500).

Applying *Options:* common application, electronic application, deferred entrance. *Application fee:* $25. *Required:* high school transcript. *Required for some:* minimum X GPA, interview, interview required for radiography, veterinary technician, and diagnostic medical sonography programs; portfolio required for fine art programs; audition required for theatre program. *Application deadline:* rolling (freshmen), rolling (transfers). *Notification:* continuous (freshmen).

Freshmen Application Contact Mr. James McCarthy, Director of Admissions, Northampton County Area Community College, 3835 Green Pond Road, Bethlehem, PA 18020-7599. *Phone:* 610-861-5506. *Fax:* 610-861-5551. *E-mail:* adminfo@northampton.edu.

NORTH CENTRAL INDUSTRIAL TECHNICAL EDUCATION CENTER
Ridgway, Pennsylvania

Director of Admissions Lugene Inzana, Director, North Central Industrial Technical Education Center, 651 Montmorenci Avenue, Ridgway, PA 15853. *Phone:* 814-772-1012. *Toll-free phone:* 800-242-5872. *Fax:* 814-772-1554. *E-mail:* linzana@ncentral.com.

OAKBRIDGE ACADEMY OF ARTS
Lower Burrell, Pennsylvania   www.akvalley.com/oakbridge/

- **Proprietary** 2-year, founded 1972
- **Small-town** 2-acre campus with easy access to Pittsburgh
- **Coed,** 66 undergraduate students, 100% full-time, 62% women, 38% men

Undergraduates 66 full-time. Students come from 4 states and territories, 9% transferred in.
Freshmen *Admission:* 32 enrolled. *Average high school GPA:* 2.30.

Faculty *Total:* 5, 60% full-time. *Student/faculty ratio:* 16:1.

Majors Commercial and advertising art; commercial photography; computer graphics.

Academics *Calendar:* quarters. *Degree:* associate. *Special study options:* academic remediation for entering students, advanced placement credit, internships.

Library Robert J. Mullen Memorial Library plus 1 other with 3,000 titles, 15 serial subscriptions, 80 audiovisual materials, a Web page.

Computers on Campus 40 computers available on campus for general student use. Internet access, at least one staffed computer lab available.

Student Life *Housing:* college housing not available. *Campus security:* 24-hour emergency response devices.

Costs (2006–07) *One-time required fee:* $30. *Tuition:* $22,400 full-time, $600 per course part-time. *Required fees:* $1750 full-time.

Financial Aid *Financial aid deadline:* 8/1.

Applying *Options:* common application, electronic application. *Application fee:* $50. *Required:* high school transcript, portfolio. *Application deadline:* 8/31 (freshmen).

Freshmen Application Contact Ms. Melissa Beck, Admissions Representative, Oakbridge Academy of Arts, 1250 Greensburg Road, Lower Burrell, PA 15068. *Phone:* 724-335-5336. *Toll-free phone:* 800-734-5601. *Fax:* 724-335-3367.

ORLEANS TECHNICAL INSTITUTE-CENTER CITY CAMPUS
Philadelphia, Pennsylvania   www.jevs.org/schools_svs.asp

- **Proprietary** 2-year
- **Urban** campus
- **Coed, primarily women**
- 76% of applicants were admitted

Undergraduates 87 full-time, 48 part-time. Students come from 3 states and territories, 1 other country, 60% are from out of state, 24% African American, 1% Asian American or Pacific Islander, 6% Hispanic American, 0.7% Native American, 6% transferred in.

Faculty *Student/faculty ratio:* 7:1.

Academics *Calendar:* trimesters. *Degree:* associate. *Special study options:* academic remediation for entering students, internships, part-time degree program, summer session for credit.

Standardized Tests *Required:* CPAt (for admission).

Costs (2005–06) *Tuition:* $10,500 full-time, $7350 per year part-time. Full-time tuition and fees vary according to program. Part-time tuition and fees vary according to program. *Required fees:* $150 full-time.

Financial Aid Of all full-time matriculated undergraduates who enrolled in 2004, 5 Federal Work-Study jobs (averaging $4800). *Financial aid deadline:* 8/1.

Applying *Application fee:* $150. *Required:* high school transcript, interview.

Director of Admissions Mr. Gary Bello, Admissions Representative, Orleans Technical Institute-Center City Campus, 1845 Walnut Street, 7th Floor, Philadelphia, PA 19103. *Phone:* 215-854-1853.

PACE INSTITUTE
Reading, Pennsylvania   www.paceinstitute.com/

Director of Admissions Mr. Ed Levandowski, Director of Enrollment Management, Pace Institute, 606 Court Street, Reading, PA 19601. *Phone:* 610-375-1212. *Fax:* 610-375-1924.

PENN COMMERCIAL BUSINESS AND TECHNICAL SCHOOL
Washington, Pennsylvania   www.penncommercial.net/

Director of Admissions Mr. Michael John Joyce, Director of Admissions, Penn Commercial Business and Technical School, 242 Oak Spring Road, Washington, PA 15301. *Phone:* 724-222-5330 Ext. 1. *E-mail:* mjoyce@penncommercial.com.

PENNCO TECH
Bristol, Pennsylvania   www.penncotech.com/

Director of Admissions Mr. Nate R. Aldsworth, Corporate Director of Admissions and Marketing, Pennco Tech, 3815 Otter Street, Bristol, PA 19007-3696. *Phone:* 215-824-3200. *Fax:* 215-785-1945. *E-mail:* admissions@penncotech.com.

PENN FOSTER CAREER SCHOOL

Scranton, Pennsylvania   **www.pennfoster.edu/**

- **Proprietary** 2-year, founded 1975
- **Coed,** 18,881 undergraduate students

Undergraduates Students come from 52 states and territories, 15 other countries.
Freshmen *Admission:* 18,941 applied, 18,811 admitted.

Faculty *Total:* 43, 40% full-time.

Majors Accounting technology and bookkeeping; business/commerce; child care and support services management; civil engineering technology; computer and information sciences and support services related; computer science; criminal justice/police science; electrical, electronic and communications engineering technology; health information/medical records technology; hotel/motel administration; industrial engineering; legal assistant/paralegal; mechanical engineering/mechanical technology; veterinary/animal health technology.

Academics *Calendar:* semesters. *Degrees:* associate (offers only external degree programs conducted through home study). *Special study options:* academic remediation for entering students, adult/continuing education programs, distance learning, external degree program, independent study, part-time degree program, summer session for credit.

Student Life *Housing:* college housing not available.

Standardized Tests *Required:* Math/Reading (for admission).

Costs (2006–07) *Tuition:* $900 per term part-time. *Required fees:* $60 per term part-time.

Applying *Required:* high school transcript. *Application deadline:* rolling (freshmen), rolling (transfers).

Freshmen Application Contact Ms. Connie Dempsey, Director of Compliance and Academic Affairs, Penn Foster Career School, 925 Oak Street, Scranton, PA 18515. *Phone:* 570-342-7701 Ext. 4692. *Toll-free phone:* 800-233-4191.

PENNSYLVANIA COLLEGE OF TECHNOLOGY

Williamsport, Pennsylvania   **www.pct.edu**

- **State-related** 4-year, founded 1965, administratively affiliated with Pennsylvania State University
- **Small-town** 958-acre campus
- **Endowment** $602,752
- **Coed,** 6,537 undergraduate students, 84% full-time, 35% women, 65% men

Undergraduates 5,515 full-time, 1,022 part-time. Students come from 32 states and territories, 19 other countries, 9% are from out of state, 3% African American, 1% Asian American or Pacific Islander, 1% Hispanic American, 0.5% Native American, 0.5% international, 3% transferred in, 23% live on campus. Freshmen *Admission:* 2,793 applied, 2,712 admitted, 1,671 enrolled.

Faculty *Total:* 491, 58% full-time. *Student/faculty ratio:* 19:1.

Majors Accounting; accounting technology and bookkeeping; administrative assistant and secretarial science; adult health nursing; aeronautical/aerospace engineering technology; aircraft powerplant technology; allied health diagnostic, intervention, and treatment professions related; applied horticulture/horticultural business services related; architectural engineering technology; autobody/collision and repair technology; automotive engineering technology; avionics maintenance technology; baking and pastry arts; banking and financial support services; biology/biological sciences; biomedical technology; broadcast journalism; business administration and management; business administration, management and operations related; business automation/technology/data entry; cabinetmaking and millwork; cardiovascular technology; carpentry; child care and support services management; child care provision; civil engineering technology; commercial and advertising art; computer and information sciences; computer and information sciences and support services related; computer/information technology services administration related; computer programming (specific applications); computer systems analysis; computer systems networking and telecommunications; computer technology/computer systems technology; construction engineering technology; culinary arts; dental hygiene; diesel mechanics technology; dietitian assistant; drafting and design technology; drafting/design engineering technologies related; education (specific subject areas) related; electrical and electronic engineering technologies related; electrical, electronic and communications engineering technology; electrician; emergency medical technology (EMT paramedic); engineering science; engineering technologies related; environmental control technologies related; environmental engineering technology; forestry technology; general studies; graphic and printing equipment operation/production; health and medical administrative services related; health and physical education related; health information/medical records administra-

tion; health professions related; heating, air conditioning and refrigeration technology; heavy equipment maintenance technology; heavy/industrial equipment maintenance technologies related; industrial electronics technology; industrial mechanics and maintenance technology; industrial production technologies related; industrial technology; information technology; institutional food workers; instrumentation technology; laser and optical technology; legal assistant/paralegal; legal professions and studies related; legal studies; liberal arts and sciences and humanities related; liberal arts and sciences/liberal studies; machine shop technology; management information systems; manufacturing technology; masonry; mass communication/media; mechanical drafting and CAD/CADD; mechanical engineering/mechanical technology; mechanic and repair technologies related; medical administrative assistant and medical secretary; medical radiologic technology; mental and social health services and allied professions related; multi-/interdisciplinary studies related; nursing (licensed practical/vocational nurse training); nursing (registered nurse training); occupational therapist assistant; office occupations and clerical services; ornamental horticulture; physical sciences; plant nursery management; plastics engineering technology; platemaking/imaging; plumbing technology; psychiatric/mental health services technology; quality control technology; solar energy technology; survey technology; technical and business writing; tool and die technology; tourism and travel services management; turf and turfgrass management; vehicle and vehicle parts and accessories marketing; vehicle maintenance and repair technologies related; web page, digital/multimedia and information resources design; welding technology; woodworking related.

Academics *Calendar:* semesters. *Degrees:* certificates, associate, and bachelor's. *Special study options:* academic remediation for entering students, advanced placement credit, cooperative education, distance learning, double majors, English as a second language, independent study, internships, off-campus study, part-time degree program, services for LD students, student-designed majors, summer session for credit. *ROTC:* Army (c).

Library Penn College Library plus 1 other with 96,281 titles, 9,118 serial subscriptions, 13,625 audiovisual materials, an OPAC, a Web page.

Computers on Campus 1400 computers available on campus for general student use. A campuswide network can be accessed from student residence rooms and from off campus. Internet access, online (class) registration, at least one staffed computer lab available. Computer purchase or lease plan available.

Student Life *Housing Options:* coed, disabled students. Campus housing is university owned. *Activities and Organizations:* student-run newspaper, radio station, Student Government Association, Resident Hall Association (RHA), Wildcats Event Board (WEB), Phi Beta Lambda, Early Educators. *Campus security:* 24-hour emergency response devices and patrols, late-night transport/escort service. *Student services:* personal/psychological counseling, women's center.

Athletics *Intercollegiate sports:* archery M/W, baseball M, basketball M/W, bowling M/W, cross-country running M/W, golf M/W, soccer M/W, softball W, tennis M/W, volleyball M/W. *Intramural sports:* archery M/W, badminton M/W, basketball M/W, bowling M/W, football M/W, golf M/W, lacrosse M/W, racquetball M/W, soccer M/W, softball M/W, table tennis M/W, tennis M/W, ultimate Frisbee M/W, volleyball M/W, weight lifting M/W, wrestling M.

Standardized Tests *Required for some:* SAT (for admission).

Costs (2005–06) *Tuition:* state resident $8580 full-time, $286 per credit part-time; nonresident $11,160 full-time, $372 per credit part-time. Full-time tuition and fees vary according to course load and program. Part-time tuition and fees vary according to course load and program. *Required fees:* $1500 full-time. *Room and board:* $6900; room only: $4200. Room and board charges vary according to board plan, housing facility, and location. *Payment plan:* deferred payment. *Waivers:* employees or children of employees.

Financial Aid Of all full-time matriculated undergraduates who enrolled in 2004, 308 Federal Work-Study jobs (averaging $1250). 294 state and other part-time jobs (averaging $1423).

Applying *Options:* electronic application, early admission, deferred entrance. *Application fee:* $50. *Required:* high school transcript. *Application deadline:* 7/1 (freshmen), rolling (transfers).

Freshmen Application Contact Mr. Chester Schuman, Director of Admissions, Pennsylvania College of Technology, One College Avenue, DIF #119, Williamsport, PA 17701. *Phone:* 570-327-4761. *Toll-free phone:* 800-367-9222. *Fax:* 570-321-5551. *E-mail:* cschuman@pct.edu.

▶ **See page 590 for the College Close-Up.**

PENNSYLVANIA CULINARY INSTITUTE

Pittsburgh, Pennsylvania   **www.paculinary.com/**

- **Proprietary** 2-year, founded 1986
- **Urban** campus
- **Coed**

Undergraduates 1,040 full-time. Students come from 31 states and territories, 10 other countries, 46% are from out of state, 11% African American, 1% Asian American or Pacific Islander, 2% Hispanic American, 0.2% Native American.

Faculty *Student/faculty ratio:* 18:1.

Academics *Calendar:* semesters. *Degree:* associate. *Special study options:* academic remediation for entering students, double majors, internships, services for LD students.

Costs (2005–06) *Comprehensive fee:* $25,570 includes full-time tuition ($18,550) and room and board ($7020). No tuition increase for student's term of enrollment. *Room and board:* college room only: $4450. Room and board charges vary according to board plan and housing facility. *Payment plans:* tuition prepayment, installment.

Applying *Options:* common application, electronic application. *Application fee:* $100. *Required:* high school transcript, interview. *Required for some:* entrance examination (qualifying score on either SAT or ACT will exempt applicant from examination). *Recommended:* essay or personal statement.

Director of Admissions Mr. Bob Cappel, Vice President of Admissions, Pennsylvania Culinary Institute, 717 Liberty Avenue, Pittsburgh, PA 15222-3500. *Phone:* 412-566-2433. *Toll-free phone:* 800-432-2433.

PENNSYLVANIA HIGHLAND COMMUNITY COLLEGE

Johnstown, Pennsylvania   www.pennhighlands.edu/

- **State and locally supported** 2-year
- **Small-town** campus
- **Coed**

Undergraduates 594 full-time, 733 part-time.

Faculty *Student/faculty ratio:* 14:1.

Academics *Calendar:* semesters. *Degree:* certificates, diplomas, and associate. *Special study options:* academic remediation for entering students, adult/continuing education programs, advanced placement credit, cooperative education, distance learning, honors programs, independent study, internships, part-time degree program, services for LD students.

Costs (2005–06) *Tuition:* area resident $1680 full-time, $70 per credit hour part-time; state resident $3360 full-time, $140 per credit hour part-time; nonresident $5040 full-time, $210 per credit hour part-time. *Required fees:* $390 full-time, $15 per credit hour part-time, $15 per term part-time.

Financial Aid Of all full-time matriculated undergraduates who enrolled in 2004, 25 Federal Work-Study jobs (averaging $2500).

Applying *Options:* common application. *Application fee:* $20. *Recommended:* high school transcript, interview.

Director of Admissions Mr. Jeff Maul, Admissions Officer, Pennsylvania Highland Community College, PO Box 68, Johnstown, PA 15907. *Phone:* 814-532-5327. *Fax:* 814-255-4977.

PENNSYLVANIA INSTITUTE OF TECHNOLOGY

Media, Pennsylvania   www.pit.edu/

- **Independent** 2-year, founded 1953
- **Small-town** 12-acre campus with easy access to Philadelphia
- **Coed,** 384 undergraduate students, 70% full-time, 51% women, 49% men

Undergraduates 270 full-time, 114 part-time. Students come from 3 states and territories, 3% are from out of state, 42% African American, 2% Asian American or Pacific Islander, 2% Hispanic American. *Retention:* 58% of 2003 full-time freshmen returned.

Freshmen *Admission:* 224 applied, 224 admitted, 205 enrolled.

Faculty *Total:* 47, 45% full-time. *Student/faculty ratio:* 10:1.

Majors Allied health and medical assisting services related; architectural engineering technology; business administration and management; electrical, electronic and communications engineering technology; engineering technology; mechanical engineering/mechanical technology; mechanical engineering technologies related; medical office management; office occupations and clerical services; web page, digital/multimedia and information resources design.

Academics *Calendar:* semesters. *Degree:* certificates and associate. *Special study options:* academic remediation for entering students, adult/continuing education programs, advanced placement credit, cooperative education, part-time degree program, summer session for credit.

Library Pennsylvania Institute of Technology Library/Learning Resource Center with 16,500 titles, 217 serial subscriptions, an OPAC, a Web page.

Computers on Campus 85 computers available on campus for general student use. At least one staffed computer lab available.

Student Life *Housing:* college housing not available. *Campus security:* 24-hour emergency response devices. *Student services:* personal/psychological counseling.

Athletics *Intramural sports:* basketball M/W, volleyball M/W.

Costs (2006–07) *Tuition:* $9000 full-time, $300 per credit part-time. *Required fees:* $330 full-time, $11 per credit part-time.

Financial Aid Of all full-time matriculated undergraduates who enrolled in 2004, 15 Federal Work-Study jobs (averaging $1025). *Financial aid deadline:* 8/1.

Applying *Options:* common application, electronic application, deferred entrance. *Application fee:* $25. *Required:* high school transcript, interview. *Required for some:* 2 letters of recommendation. *Recommended:* essay or personal statement. *Application deadlines:* 9/19 (freshmen), 9/19 (transfers). *Notification:* continuous until 9/19 (freshmen).

Freshmen Application Contact Ms. Angela Cassetta, Dean of Enrollment Management, Pennsylvania Institute of Technology, 800 Manchester Avenue, Media, PA 19063-4036. *Phone:* 610-892-1550 Ext. 1553. *Toll-free phone:* 800-422-0025. *Fax:* 610-892-1510. *E-mail:* info@pit.edu.

THE PENNSYLVANIA STATE UNIVERSITY BEAVER CAMPUS OF THE COMMONWEALTH COLLEGE

Monaca, Pennsylvania   www.br.psu.edu/

- **State-related** primarily 2-year, founded 1964, part of Pennsylvania State University
- **Small-town** 91-acre campus with easy access to Pittsburgh
- **Endowment** $1.2 billion
- **Coed,** 632 undergraduate students, 86% full-time, 41% women, 59% men

Undergraduates 546 full-time, 86 part-time. 4% are from out of state, 4% African American, 2% Asian American or Pacific Islander, 0.9% Hispanic American, 4% transferred in, 25% live on campus. *Retention:* 71% of 2003 full-time freshmen returned.

Freshmen *Admission:* 569 applied, 508 admitted, 203 enrolled. *Average high school GPA:* 2.97. *Test scores:* SAT verbal scores over 500: 47%; SAT math scores over 500: 52%; SAT verbal scores over 600: 9%; SAT math scores over 600: 18%; SAT verbal scores over 700: 1%; SAT math scores over 700: 1%.

Faculty *Total:* 55, 58% full-time, 38% with terminal degrees. *Student/faculty ratio:* 15:1.

Majors Accounting; acting; actuarial science; adult and continuing education administration; advertising; aerospace, aeronautical and astronautical engineering; African-American/Black studies; agribusiness; agricultural and extension education; agricultural/biological engineering and bioengineering; agricultural business and management related; agricultural mechanization; agriculture; agronomy and crop science; animal sciences; animal sciences related; anthropology; applied economics; archeology; architectural engineering; art; art history, criticism and conservation; art teacher education; Asian studies (East); astronomy; atmospheric sciences and meteorology; biochemistry; biological and biomedical sciences related; biological and physical sciences; biology/biological sciences; biology/biotechnology laboratory technician; biomedical/medical engineering; business administration and management; business/commerce; business/managerial economics; chemical engineering; chemistry; civil engineering; classics and languages, literatures and linguistics; communication and journalism related; communication disorders; communication/speech communication and rhetoric; comparative literature; computer and information sciences; computer engineering; criminal justice/law enforcement administration; economics; electrical, electronics and communications engineering; elementary education; engineering science; English; environmental/environmental health engineering; film/cinema studies; finance; food science; foreign language teacher education; forestry technology; forest sciences and biology; French; geography; geological and earth sciences/geosciences related; geology/earth science; German; graphic design; health/health care administration; history; horticultural science; hospitality administration related; human development and family studies; human nutrition; industrial engineering; information science/studies; international relations and affairs; Italian; Japanese; Jewish/Judaic studies; journalism; kinesiology and exercise science; labor and industrial relations; landscaping and groundskeeping; Latin American studies; liberal arts and sciences/liberal studies; logistics and materials management; management information systems; marketing/marketing management; materials science; mathematics; mechanical engineering; medical microbiology and bacteriology; medieval and Renaissance studies; mining and mineral engineering; music; natural resources and conservation related; natural resources/conservation; nuclear engineering; nursing (registered nurse training); organizational behavior; parks, recreation and leisure facilities management; petroleum engineering; philosophy; physics; political science and government; pre-medical studies; psychology; rehabilitation and therapeutic

The Pennsylvania State University Beaver Campus of the Commonwealth College (continued)

professions related; religious studies; Russian; secondary education; sociology; soil science and agronomy; Spanish; special education; statistics; theater design and technology; toxicology; turf and turfgrass management; visual and performing arts; women's studies.

Academics *Calendar:* semesters. *Degrees:* associate and bachelor's. *Special study options:* academic remediation for entering students, accelerated degree program, adult/continuing education programs, advanced placement credit, distance learning, double majors, English as a second language, honors programs, independent study, internships, services for LD students, study abroad, summer session for credit.

Library 39,861 titles, 222 serial subscriptions, 6,683 audiovisual materials.

Computers on Campus 106 computers available on campus for general student use. A campuswide network can be accessed from student residence rooms and from off campus. Internet access, online (class) registration, at least one staffed computer lab available. Computer purchase or lease plan available.

Student Life *Housing Options:* coed. Campus housing is university owned. Freshman campus housing is guaranteed. *Activities and Organizations:* drama/theater group, student-run newspaper, radio station. *Campus security:* 24-hour patrols, controlled dormitory access. *Student services:* health clinic, personal/psychological counseling.

Athletics Member NJCAA. *Intercollegiate sports:* baseball M, basketball M, softball M/W, volleyball W. *Intramural sports:* basketball M/W, cheerleading M(c)/W(c), cross-country running M/W, football M, golf M/W, soccer M/W, softball M/W, table tennis M/W.

Standardized Tests *Required:* SAT or ACT (for admission).

Costs (2005–06) *Tuition:* state resident $9722 full-time, $393 per credit hour part-time; nonresident $14,854 full-time, $619 per credit hour part-time. *Required fees:* $478 full-time. *Room and board:* $6530; room only: $3430. *Waivers:* senior citizens.

Financial Aid Of all full-time matriculated undergraduates who enrolled in 2004, 38 Federal Work-Study jobs (averaging $1495). 5 state and other part-time jobs (averaging $4655).

Applying *Options:* electronic application, early admission, deferred entrance. *Application fee:* $50. *Required:* high school transcript. *Required for some:* letters of recommendation, interview. *Recommended:* essay or personal statement. *Application deadline:* rolling (freshmen), rolling (transfers). *Notification:* continuous (freshmen).

Director of Admissions Mr. Randall C. Deike, Assistant Vice President for Enrollment Management, The Pennsylvania State University Beaver Campus of the Commonwealth College, 100 University Drive, Suite 113, Monaca, PA 15061-2799. *Phone:* 814-865-5471. *Toll-free phone:* 877-564-6778. *E-mail:* admissions@psu.edu.

THE PENNSYLVANIA STATE UNIVERSITY DELAWARE COUNTY CAMPUS OF THE COMMONWEALTH COLLEGE

Media, Pennsylvania   www.de.psu.edu/

- **State-related** primarily 2-year, founded 1966, part of Pennsylvania State University
- **Small-town** 87-acre campus with easy access to Philadelphia
- **Endowment** $1.2 billion
- **Coed,** 1,589 undergraduate students, 85% full-time, 43% women, 57% men

Undergraduates 1,356 full-time, 233 part-time. 3% are from out of state, 15% African American, 7% Asian American or Pacific Islander, 2% Hispanic American, 0.1% Native American, 0.4% international, 3% transferred in. *Retention:* 72% of 2003 full-time freshmen returned.

Freshmen *Admission:* 1,402 applied, 1,073 admitted, 394 enrolled. *Average high school GPA:* 2.82. *Test scores:* SAT verbal scores over 500: 35%; SAT math scores over 500: 38%; SAT verbal scores over 600: 9%; SAT math scores over 600: 12%; SAT math scores over 700: 1%.

Faculty *Total:* 125, 56% full-time, 39% with terminal degrees. *Student/faculty ratio:* 16:1.

Majors Accounting; acting; actuarial science; adult and continuing education administration; advertising; aerospace, aeronautical and astronautical engineering; African-American/Black studies; agribusiness; agricultural and extension education; agricultural/biological engineering and bioengineering; agricultural business and management related; agricultural mechanization; agriculture; agronomy and crop science; American studies; animal sciences; animal sciences related; anthropology; applied economics; archeology; architectural engineering; art; art history, criticism and conservation; art teacher education; Asian studies (East); astronomy; atmospheric sciences and meteorology; biochemistry; biologi-

cal and biomedical sciences related; biological and physical sciences; biology/biological sciences; biology/biotechnology laboratory technician; biomedical/medical engineering; business administration and management; business/commerce; business/managerial economics; chemical engineering; chemistry; civil engineering; classics and languages, literatures and linguistics; communication and journalism related; communication disorders; communication/speech communication and rhetoric; comparative literature; computer and information sciences; computer engineering; criminal justice/law enforcement administration; economics; electrical, electronic and communications engineering technology; electrical, electronics and communications engineering; elementary education; engineering science; English; environmental/environmental health engineering; film/cinema studies; finance; food science; foreign language teacher education; forestry technology; forest sciences and biology; French; geography; geological and earth sciences/geosciences related; geology/earth science; German; graphic design; health/health care administration; history; horticultural science; hospitality administration related; human development and family studies; human nutrition; industrial engineering; information science/studies; international relations and affairs; Italian; Japanese; Jewish/Judaic studies; journalism; kinesiology and exercise science; labor and industrial relations; landscape architecture; landscaping and groundskeeping; Latin American studies; liberal arts and sciences/liberal studies; logistics and materials management; management information systems; marketing/marketing management; materials science; mathematics; mechanical engineering; medical microbiology and bacteriology; medieval and Renaissance studies; mining and mineral engineering; music; natural resources and conservation related; natural resources/conservation; nuclear engineering; nursing (registered nurse training); organizational behavior; parks, recreation and leisure facilities management; petroleum engineering; philosophy; physics; political science and government; pre-medical studies; psychology; rehabilitation and therapeutic professions related; religious studies; Russian; secondary education; sociology; soil science and agronomy; Spanish; special education; statistics; theater design and technology; turf and turfgrass management; visual and performing arts; women's studies.

Academics *Calendar:* semesters. *Degrees:* associate and bachelor's. *Special study options:* academic remediation for entering students, adult/continuing education programs, advanced placement credit, distance learning, double majors, English as a second language, honors programs, independent study, internships, services for LD students, study abroad, summer session for credit. *ROTC:* Air Force (c).

Library 59,930 titles, 457 serial subscriptions, 3,987 audiovisual materials.

Computers on Campus 180 computers available on campus for general student use. A campuswide network can be accessed from off campus. Internet access, online (class) registration, at least one staffed computer lab available. Computer purchase or lease plan available.

Student Life *Housing:* college housing not available. *Activities and Organizations:* drama/theater group, student-run newspaper, choral group. *Campus security:* late-night transport/escort service, part-time trained security personnel. *Student services:* health clinic, personal/psychological counseling, women's center.

Athletics Member NJCAA. *Intercollegiate sports:* baseball M, basketball M/W, soccer M/W, tennis M/W, volleyball W. *Intramural sports:* basketball M/W, cheerleading M(c)/W(c), golf M/W, ice hockey M(c)/W(c), lacrosse M/W, soccer M/W, softball W(c), tennis M/W, volleyball M(c)/W.

Standardized Tests *Required:* SAT or ACT (for admission).

Costs (2005–06) *Tuition:* state resident $9722 full-time, $393 per credit hour part-time; nonresident $14,854 full-time, $619 per credit hour part-time. *Required fees:* $478 full-time.

Financial Aid Of all full-time matriculated undergraduates who enrolled in 2004, 58 Federal Work-Study jobs (averaging $1082).

Applying *Options:* electronic application, early admission, deferred entrance. *Application fee:* $50. *Required:* high school transcript. *Required for some:* letters of recommendation, interview. *Recommended:* essay or personal statement. *Application deadline:* rolling (freshmen), rolling (transfers). *Notification:* continuous (freshmen).

Director of Admissions Mr. Randall C. Deike, Assistant Vice President for Enrollment Management, The Pennsylvania State University Delaware County Campus of the Commonwealth College, 25 Yearsley Mill Road, Media, PA 19063-5596. *Phone:* 814-865-5471. *E-mail:* admissions@psu.edu.

THE PENNSYLVANIA STATE UNIVERSITY DUBOIS CAMPUS OF THE COMMONWEALTH COLLEGE

DuBois, Pennsylvania　　　　　　　**www.ds.psu.edu/**

- **State-related** primarily 2-year, founded 1935, part of Pennsylvania State University
- **Small-town** 20-acre campus
- **Endowment** $1.2 billion
- **Coed,** 804 undergraduate students, 74% full-time, 52% women, 48% men

Undergraduates 595 full-time, 209 part-time. 1% are from out of state, 0.8% African American, 0.5% Asian American or Pacific Islander, 0.3% Hispanic American, 0.3% Native American, 2% transferred in. *Retention:* 75% of 2003 full-time freshmen returned.
Freshmen *Admission:* 346 applied, 320 admitted, 174 enrolled. *Average high school GPA:* 2.89. *Test scores:* SAT verbal scores over 500: 48%; SAT math scores over 500: 55%; SAT verbal scores over 600: 17%; SAT math scores over 600: 18%; SAT math scores over 700: 3%.

Faculty *Total:* 82, 55% full-time, 46% with terminal degrees. *Student/faculty ratio:* 12:1.

Majors Accounting; acting; actuarial science; adult and continuing education administration; advertising; aerospace, aeronautical and astronautical engineering; African-American/Black studies; agribusiness; agricultural and extension education; agricultural/biological engineering and bioengineering; agricultural business and management related; agricultural mechanization; agriculture; agronomy and crop science; animal sciences; animal sciences related; anthropology; applied economics; archeology; architectural engineering; art; art history, criticism and conservation; art teacher education; Asian studies (East); astronomy; atmospheric sciences and meteorology; biochemistry; biological and biomedical sciences related; biological and physical sciences; biology/biological sciences; biology/biotechnology laboratory technician; biomedical/medical engineering; biomedical technology; business administration and management; business/commerce; business/managerial economics; chemical engineering; chemistry; civil engineering; classics and languages, literatures and linguistics; clinical/medical laboratory technology; communication and journalism related; communication disorders; communication/speech communication and rhetoric; comparative literature; computer and information sciences; computer engineering; criminal justice/law enforcement administration; economics; electrical, electronic and communications engineering technology; electrical, electronics and communications engineering; elementary education; engineering science; English; environmental/environmental health engineering; film/cinema studies; finance; food science; foreign language teacher education; forestry technology; forest sciences and biology; French; geography; geological and earth sciences/geosciences related; geology/earth science; German; graphic design; health/health care administration; history; horticultural science; hospitality administration related; human development and family studies; human nutrition; industrial engineering; information science/studies; international business/trade/commerce; international relations and affairs; Italian; Japanese; Jewish/Judaic studies; journalism; kinesiology and exercise science; labor and industrial relations; landscaping and groundskeeping; Latin American studies; liberal arts and sciences/liberal studies; management information systems; marketing/marketing management; materials science; mathematics; mechanical engineering; mechanical engineering/mechanical technology; medical microbiology and bacteriology; medieval and Renaissance studies; metallurgical technology; mining and mineral engineering; music; natural resources and conservation related; natural resources/conservation; nuclear engineering; nursing (registered nurse training); occupational therapist assistant; organizational behavior; parks, recreation and leisure facilities management; petroleum engineering; philosophy; physical therapist assistant; physics; political science and government; pre-medical studies; psychology; rehabilitation and therapeutic professions related; religious studies; Russian; secondary education; sociology; soil science and agronomy; Spanish; special education; statistics; telecommunications technology; theater design and technology; toxicology; turf and turfgrass management; visual and performing arts; wildlife and wildlands science and management; women's studies.

Academics *Calendar:* semesters. *Degrees:* associate and bachelor's. *Special study options:* academic remediation for entering students, accelerated degree program, adult/continuing education programs, advanced placement credit, distance learning, double majors, honors programs, independent study, internships, services for LD students, student-designed majors, study abroad, summer session for credit.

Library 43,710 titles, 224 serial subscriptions, 1,091 audiovisual materials.

Computers on Campus 126 computers available on campus for general student use. A campuswide network can be accessed from off campus. Internet access, online (class) registration, at least one staffed computer lab available. Computer purchase or lease plan available.

Student Life *Housing:* college housing not available. *Activities and Organizations:* drama/theater group, student-run newspaper, choral group. *Student services:* health clinic, personal/psychological counseling, women's center.

Athletics Member NJCAA. *Intercollegiate sports:* basketball M, cross-country running M/W, golf M/W, volleyball W. *Intramural sports:* basketball M/W, football M, soccer M/W, table tennis M/W, volleyball M/W.

Standardized Tests *Required:* SAT or ACT (for admission).

Costs (2005–06) *Tuition:* state resident $9722 full-time, $393 per credit hour part-time; nonresident $14,854 full-time, $619 per credit hour part-time. *Required fees:* $468 full-time.

Financial Aid Of all full-time matriculated undergraduates who enrolled in 2004, 94 Federal Work-Study jobs (averaging $1505). 4 state and other part-time jobs (averaging $1496).

Applying *Options:* electronic application, early admission, deferred entrance. *Application fee:* $50. *Required:* high school transcript. *Required for some:* letters of recommendation, interview. *Recommended:* essay or personal statement. *Application deadline:* rolling (freshmen), rolling (transfers). *Notification:* continuous (freshmen).

Director of Admissions Mr. Randall C. Deike, Assistant Vice President for Enrollment Management, The Pennsylvania State University DuBois Campus of the Commonwealth College, 101 Hiller Building, College Place, DuBois, PA 15801-3199. *Phone:* 814-865-5471. *Toll-free phone:* 800-346-7627. *E-mail:* admissions@psu.edu.

THE PENNSYLVANIA STATE UNIVERSITY FAYETTE CAMPUS OF THE COMMONWEALTH COLLEGE

Uniontown, Pennsylvania　　　　　　　**www.fe.psu.edu/**

- **State-related** primarily 2-year, founded 1934, part of Pennsylvania State University
- **Small-town** 92-acre campus
- **Endowment** $1.2 billion
- **Coed,** 995 undergraduate students, 73% full-time, 63% women, 37% men

Undergraduates 727 full-time, 268 part-time. 1% are from out of state, 7% African American, 0.7% Asian American or Pacific Islander, 0.5% Hispanic American, 3% transferred in. *Retention:* 67% of 2003 full-time freshmen returned.
Freshmen *Admission:* 382 applied, 329 admitted, 177 enrolled. *Average high school GPA:* 2.86. *Test scores:* SAT verbal scores over 500: 36%; SAT math scores over 500: 38%; SAT verbal scores over 600: 8%; SAT math scores over 600: 12%; SAT verbal scores over 700: 1%; SAT math scores over 700: 1%.

Faculty *Total:* 85, 59% full-time, 36% with terminal degrees. *Student/faculty ratio:* 13:1.

Majors Accounting; acting; actuarial science; adult and continuing education administration; advertising; aerospace, aeronautical and astronautical engineering; African-American/Black studies; agribusiness; agricultural and extension education; agricultural/biological engineering and bioengineering; agricultural business and management related; agricultural mechanization; agriculture; agronomy and crop science; animal sciences; animal sciences related; anthropology; applied economics; archeology; architectural engineering; architectural engineering technology; art; art history, criticism and conservation; art teacher education; Asian studies (East); astronomy; atmospheric sciences and meteorology; biochemistry; biological and biomedical sciences related; biological and physical sciences; biology/biological sciences; biology/biotechnology laboratory technician; biomedical/medical engineering; biomedical technology; business administration and management; business/commerce; business/managerial economics; chemical engineering; chemistry; civil engineering; classics and languages, literatures and linguistics; communication and journalism related; communication disorders; communication/speech communication and rhetoric; comparative literature; computer and information sciences; computer engineering; criminal justice/law enforcement administration; criminal justice/safety; economics; electrical, electronic and communications engineering technology; electrical, electronics and communications engineering; elementary education; engineering science; English; environmental/environmental health engineering; film/cinema studies; finance; food science; foreign language teacher education; forestry technology; forest sciences and biology; French; geography; geological and earth sciences/geosciences related; geology/earth science; German; graphic design; health/health care administration; history; horticultural science; hospitality administration related; human development and family studies; human nutrition; industrial engineering; information science/studies; international relations and affairs; Italian; Japanese; Jewish/Judaic studies; journalism; kinesiology and exercise science; labor and industrial relations; landscaping and groundskeeping; Latin American studies; liberal arts and sciences/liberal studies; logistics and materials management; management information systems; manufacturing engineering; marketing/marketing management; materials science;

The Pennsylvania State University Fayette Campus of the Commonwealth College (continued)

mathematics; mechanical engineering; medical microbiology and bacteriology; medieval and Renaissance studies; metallurgical technology; mining and mineral engineering; music; natural resources and conservation related; natural resources/conservation; nuclear engineering; nursing (registered nurse training); organizational behavior; parks, recreation and leisure facilities management; petroleum engineering; philosophy; physics; political science and government; pre-medical studies; psychology; rehabilitation and therapeutic professions related; religious studies; Russian; secondary education; sociology; soil science and agronomy; Spanish; special education; statistics; telecommunications technology; theater design and technology; toxicology; turf and turfgrass management; visual and performing arts; women's studies.

Academics *Calendar:* semesters. *Degrees:* associate and bachelor's. *Special study options:* academic remediation for entering students, accelerated degree program, adult/continuing education programs, advanced placement credit, distance learning, double majors, honors programs, independent study, internships, services for LD students, student-designed majors, study abroad, summer session for credit.

Library 54,610 titles, 187 serial subscriptions, 6,721 audiovisual materials.

Computers on Campus 103 computers available on campus for general student use. A campuswide network can be accessed from off campus. Internet access, online (class) registration, at least one staffed computer lab available. Computer purchase or lease plan available.

Student Life *Housing:* college housing not available. *Activities and Organizations:* drama/theater group, student-run newspaper, choral group. *Campus security:* student patrols, 8-hour patrols by trained security personnel. *Student services:* health clinic, personal/psychological counseling.

Athletics Member NJCAA. *Intercollegiate sports:* baseball M, basketball M, softball W, volleyball W. *Intramural sports:* badminton M/W, basketball M/W, cheerleading M(c)/W(c), equestrian sports M(c)/W(c), football M/W, golf M(c)/W(c), softball M/W, tennis M/W, volleyball M/W, weight lifting M/W.

Standardized Tests *Required:* SAT or ACT (for admission).

Costs (2005–06) *Tuition:* state resident $9722 full-time, $393 per credit hour part-time; nonresident $14,854 full-time, $619 per credit hour part-time. *Required fees:* $468 full-time.

Financial Aid Of all full-time matriculated undergraduates who enrolled in 2004, 76 Federal Work-Study jobs (averaging $1714).

Applying *Options:* electronic application, early admission, deferred entrance. *Application fee:* $50. *Required:* high school transcript. *Required for some:* letters of recommendation, interview. *Recommended:* essay or personal statement. *Application deadline:* rolling (freshmen), rolling (transfers). *Notification:* continuous (freshmen).

Director of Admissions Mr. Randall C. Deike, Assistant Vice President for Enrollment Management, The Pennsylvania State University Fayette Campus of the Commonwealth College, PO Box 519, Route 119 North, 108 Williams Building, Uniontown, PA 15401-0519. *Phone:* 814-865-5471. *Toll-free phone:* 877-568-4130. *E-mail:* admissions@psu.edu.

THE PENNSYLVANIA STATE UNIVERSITY HAZLETON CAMPUS OF THE COMMONWEALTH COLLEGE

Hazleton, Pennsylvania   **www.hn.psu.edu/**

- **State-related** primarily 2-year, founded 1934, part of Pennsylvania State University
- **Small-town** 98-acre campus
- **Endowment** $1.2 billion
- **Coed,** 1,065 undergraduate students, 95% full-time, 40% women, 60% men

Undergraduates 1,011 full-time, 54 part-time. 25% are from out of state, 7% African American, 6% Asian American or Pacific Islander, 7% Hispanic American, 0.2% Native American, 0.2% international, 3% transferred in, 43% live on campus. *Retention:* 80% of 2003 full-time freshmen returned.

Freshmen *Admission:* 1,084 applied, 983 admitted, 454 enrolled. *Average high school GPA:* 2.90. *Test scores:* SAT verbal scores over 500: 40%; SAT math scores over 500: 48%; SAT verbal scores over 600: 8%; SAT math scores over 600: 12%; SAT verbal scores over 700: 1%; SAT math scores over 700: 1%.

Faculty *Total:* 82, 65% full-time, 44% with terminal degrees. *Student/faculty ratio:* 16:1.

Majors Accounting; acting; actuarial science; adult and continuing education administration; advertising; aerospace, aeronautical and astronautical engineering; African-American/Black studies; agribusiness; agricultural and extension education; agricultural/biological engineering and bioengineering; agricultural business and management related; agricultural mechanization; agriculture;

agronomy and crop science; animal sciences; animal sciences related; anthropology; applied economics; archeology; architectural engineering; art; art history, criticism and conservation; art teacher education; Asian studies (East); astronomy; atmospheric sciences and meteorology; biochemistry; biological and biomedical sciences related; biological and physical sciences; biology/biological sciences; biology/biotechnology laboratory technician; biomedical/medical engineering; biomedical technology; business administration and management; business/commerce; business/managerial economics; chemical engineering; chemistry; civil engineering; classics and languages, literatures and linguistics; clinical/medical laboratory technology; communication and journalism related; communication disorders; communication/speech communication and rhetoric; comparative literature; computer and information sciences; computer engineering; criminal justice/law enforcement administration; economics; electrical, electronic and communications engineering technology; electrical, electronics and communications engineering; elementary education; engineering science; English; environmental/environmental health engineering; film/cinema studies; finance; food science; forestry technology; forest sciences and biology; French; geography; geological and earth sciences/geosciences related; geology/earth science; German; graphic design; health/health care administration; history; horticultural science; hospitality administration related; human development and family studies; human nutrition; industrial engineering; information science/studies; international relations and affairs; Italian; Japanese; Jewish/Judaic studies; journalism; kinesiology and exercise science; labor and industrial relations; landscaping and groundskeeping; Latin American studies; liberal arts and sciences/liberal studies; logistics and materials management; management information systems; manufacturing engineering; marketing/marketing management; materials science; mathematics; mechanical engineering; mechanical engineering/mechanical technology; medical microbiology and bacteriology; medieval and Renaissance studies; metallurgical technology; mining and mineral engineering; music; natural resources and conservation related; natural resources/conservation; nuclear engineering; nursing (registered nurse training); organizational behavior; parks, recreation and leisure facilities management; petroleum engineering; philosophy; physical therapist assistant; physics; political science and government; pre-medical studies; psychology; rehabilitation and therapeutic professions related; religious studies; Russian; secondary education; sociology; soil science and agronomy; Spanish; special education; statistics; telecommunications technology; theater design and technology; toxicology; turf and turfgrass management; visual and performing arts; women's studies.

Academics *Calendar:* semesters. *Degrees:* associate and bachelor's. *Special study options:* academic remediation for entering students, accelerated degree program, adult/continuing education programs, advanced placement credit, distance learning, double majors, English as a second language, honors programs, independent study, internships, services for LD students, student-designed majors, study abroad, summer session for credit. *ROTC:* Army (b), Air Force (c).

Library 83,266 titles, 996 serial subscriptions, 6,771 audiovisual materials.

Computers on Campus 131 computers available on campus for general student use. A campuswide network can be accessed from student residence rooms and from off campus. Internet access, online (class) registration, at least one staffed computer lab available. Computer purchase or lease plan available.

Student Life *Housing Options:* coed. Campus housing is university owned. Freshman campus housing is guaranteed. *Activities and Organizations:* drama/theater group, student-run newspaper, radio station, choral group. *Campus security:* 24-hour patrols, late-night transport/escort service, controlled dormitory access. *Student services:* health clinic, personal/psychological counseling, women's center, legal services.

Athletics Member NJCAA. *Intercollegiate sports:* baseball M, basketball M/W, cheerleading M/W, soccer M, softball W(s), tennis M/W, volleyball M/W. *Intramural sports:* basketball M/W, skiing (downhill) M(c)/W(c), soccer M/W, volleyball M/W.

Standardized Tests *Required:* SAT or ACT (for admission).

Costs (2005–06) *Tuition:* state resident $9722 full-time, $393 per credit hour part-time; nonresident $14,854 full-time, $619 per credit hour part-time. *Required fees:* $468 full-time. *Room and board:* $6530; room only: $3430.

Financial Aid Of all full-time matriculated undergraduates who enrolled in 2004, 67 Federal Work-Study jobs (averaging $1524). 12 state and other part-time jobs (averaging $5850).

Applying *Options:* electronic application, early admission, deferred entrance. *Application fee:* $50. *Required:* high school transcript. *Required for some:* letters of recommendation, interview. *Recommended:* essay or personal statement. *Application deadline:* rolling (freshmen), rolling (transfers). *Notification:* continuous (freshmen).

Director of Admissions Mr. Randall C. Deike, Assistant Vice President for Enrollment Management, The Pennsylvania State University Hazleton Campus of the Commonwealth College, 110 Administration Building, 76 University Drive, Hazleton, PA 18202-1291. *Phone:* 814-865-5471. *Toll-free phone:* 800-279-8495. *E-mail:* admissions@psu.edu.

THE PENNSYLVANIA STATE UNIVERSITY, LEHIGH VALLEY CAMPUS OF THE BERKS-LEHIGH VALLEY COLLEGE

Fogelsville, Pennsylvania   www.lv.psu.edu/

- **State-related** primarily 2-year, founded 1912, part of Pennsylvania State University
- **Small-town** 42-acre campus
- **Coed**

Undergraduates 491 full-time, 153 part-time. 2% are from out of state, 3% African American, 8% Asian American or Pacific Islander, 6% Hispanic American, 0.5% international, 5% transferred in. *Retention:* 82% of 2003 full-time freshmen returned.

Faculty *Student/faculty ratio:* 13:1.

Academics *Calendar:* semesters. *Degrees:* associate and bachelor's. *Special study options:* academic remediation for entering students, accelerated degree program, adult/continuing education programs, advanced placement credit, cooperative education, distance learning, honors programs, independent study, internships, services for LD students, study abroad, summer session for credit.

Athletics Member NJCAA.

Standardized Tests *Required:* SAT or ACT (for admission).

Costs (2005–06) *Tuition:* state resident $9722 full-time; nonresident $14,854 full-time. Full-time tuition and fees vary according to course level. Part-time tuition and fees vary according to course level and course load. *Required fees:* $478 full-time.

Financial Aid Of all full-time matriculated undergraduates who enrolled in 2003, 391 applied for aid, 301 were judged to have need, 21 had their need fully met. 23 Federal Work-Study jobs (averaging $1015). In 2003, 29. *Average percent of need met:* 67. *Average financial aid package:* $9068. *Average need-based loan:* $3196. *Average need-based gift aid:* $4017. *Average non-need-based aid:* $1379. *Average indebtedness upon graduation:* $18,600.

Applying *Options:* electronic application, early admission, deferred entrance. *Application fee:* $50. *Required:* high school transcript.

Director of Admissions Mr. Randall C. Deike, Assistant Vice President for Enrollment Management, The Pennsylvania State University, Lehigh Valley Campus of the Berks-Lehigh Valley College, 8380 Mohr Lane, Academic Building, Fogelsville, PA 18051-9999. *Phone:* 814-865-5471.

THE PENNSYLVANIA STATE UNIVERSITY MCKEESPORT CAMPUS OF THE COMMONWEALTH COLLEGE

McKeesport, Pennsylvania   www.mk.psu.edu/

- **State-related** primarily 2-year, founded 1947, part of Pennsylvania State University
- **Small-town** 40-acre campus with easy access to Pittsburgh
- **Endowment** $1.2 billion
- **Coed,** 682 undergraduate students, 87% full-time, 40% women, 60% men

Undergraduates 593 full-time, 89 part-time. 6% are from out of state, 14% African American, 3% Asian American or Pacific Islander, 1% Hispanic American, 0.2% international, 4% transferred in, 14% live on campus. *Retention:* 79% of 2003 full-time freshmen returned.

Freshmen *Admission:* 445 applied, 366 admitted, 170 enrolled. *Average high school GPA:* 2.90. *Test scores:* SAT verbal scores over 500: 49%; SAT math scores over 500: 60%; SAT verbal scores over 600: 10%; SAT math scores over 600: 17%; SAT verbal scores over 700: 1%; SAT math scores over 700: 2%.

Faculty *Total:* 72, 53% full-time, 40% with terminal degrees. *Student/faculty ratio:* 13:1.

Majors Accounting; acting; actuarial science; adult and continuing education administration; advertising; aerospace, aeronautical and astronautical engineering; African-American/Black studies; agribusiness; agricultural and extension education; agricultural/biological engineering and bioengineering; agricultural business and management related; agricultural mechanization; agriculture; agronomy and crop science; animal sciences; animal sciences related; anthropology; applied economics; archeology; architectural engineering; art; art history, criticism and conservation; art teacher education; Asian studies (East); astronomy; atmospheric sciences and meteorology; biochemistry; biological and biomedical sciences related; biological and physical sciences; biology/biological sciences; biology/biotechnology laboratory technician; biomedical/medical engineering;

business administration and management; business/commerce; business/managerial economics; chemical engineering; chemistry; civil engineering; classics and languages, literatures and linguistics; communication and journalism related; communication disorders; communication/speech communication and rhetoric; comparative literature; computer and information sciences; computer engineering; criminal justice/law enforcement administration; economics; electrical, electronics and communications engineering; elementary education; engineering science; English; environmental/environmental health engineering; film/cinema studies; finance; food science; foreign language teacher education; forestry technology; forest sciences and biology; French; geography; geological and earth sciences/geosciences related; geology/earth science; German; graphic design; health/health care administration; history; horticultural science; hospitality administration related; human development and family studies; human nutrition; industrial engineering; information science/studies; international relations and affairs; Italian; Japanese; Jewish/Judaic studies; journalism; kinesiology and exercise science; labor and industrial relations; landscaping and groundskeeping; Latin American studies; liberal arts and sciences/liberal studies; logistics and materials management; management information systems; manufacturing engineering; marketing/marketing management; materials science; mathematics; mechanical engineering; medical microbiology and bacteriology; medieval and Renaissance studies; mining and mineral engineering; music; natural resources and conservation related; natural resources/conservation; nuclear engineering; nursing (registered nurse training); organizational behavior; parks, recreation and leisure facilities management; petroleum engineering; philosophy; physics; political science and government; pre-medical studies; psychology; rehabilitation and therapeutic professions related; religious studies; Russian; secondary education; sociology; soil science and agronomy; Spanish; special education; statistics; theater design and technology; toxicology; turf and turfgrass management; visual and performing arts; women's studies.

Academics *Calendar:* semesters. *Degrees:* associate and bachelor's. *Special study options:* academic remediation for entering students, accelerated degree program, adult/continuing education programs, advanced placement credit, distance learning, double majors, honors programs, independent study, internships, services for LD students, study abroad, summer session for credit. *ROTC:* Air Force (c).

Library 40,851 titles, 300 serial subscriptions, 2,783 audiovisual materials.

Computers on Campus 167 computers available on campus for general student use. A campuswide network can be accessed from student residence rooms and from off campus. Internet access, online (class) registration, at least one staffed computer lab available. Computer purchase or lease plan available.

Student Life *Housing Options:* coed. Campus housing is university owned. Freshman campus housing is guaranteed. *Activities and Organizations:* drama/theater group, student-run newspaper, radio station, choral group. *Campus security:* 24-hour patrols, controlled dormitory access. *Student services:* health clinic, personal/psychological counseling, women's center.

Athletics Member NJCAA. *Intercollegiate sports:* baseball M, basketball M, softball W, volleyball W. *Intramural sports:* basketball M/W, cheerleading M(c)/W(c), football M/W, ice hockey M(c), racquetball M/W, skiing (cross-country) M(c)/W(c), skiing (downhill) M(c)/W(c), soccer M(c)/W(c), softball M/W, tennis M/W, volleyball M/W.

Standardized Tests *Required:* SAT or ACT (for admission).

Costs (2005–06) *Tuition:* state resident $9722 full-time, $393 per credit hour part-time; nonresident $14,854 full-time, $619 per credit hour part-time. *Required fees:* $458 full-time. *Room and board:* $6530; room only: $3430.

Financial Aid Of all full-time matriculated undergraduates who enrolled in 2004, 61 Federal Work-Study jobs (averaging $1321). 4 state and other part-time jobs (averaging $5929).

Applying *Options:* electronic application, early admission, deferred entrance. *Application fee:* $50. *Required:* high school transcript. *Required for some:* letters of recommendation, interview. *Recommended:* essay or personal statement. *Application deadline:* rolling (freshmen), rolling (transfers). *Notification:* continuous (freshmen).

Director of Admissions Mr. Randall C. Deike, Assistant Vice President for Enrollment Management, The Pennsylvania State University McKeesport Campus of the Commonwealth College, 101 Frable Building, 4000 University Drive, McKeesport, PA 15132-7698. *Phone:* 814-865-5471. *E-mail:* admissions@psu.edu.

THE PENNSYLVANIA STATE UNIVERSITY MONT ALTO CAMPUS OF THE COMMONWEALTH COLLEGE

Mont Alto, Pennsylvania   **www.ma.psu.edu/**

- **State-related** primarily 2-year, founded 1929, part of Pennsylvania State University
- **Small-town** 64-acre campus
- **Endowment** $1.2 billion
- **Coed,** 932 undergraduate students, 72% full-time, 57% women, 43% men

Undergraduates 674 full-time, 258 part-time. 12% are from out of state, 9% African American, 2% Asian American or Pacific Islander, 3% Hispanic American, 0.2% Native American, 0.4% international, 7% transferred in, 33% live on campus. *Retention:* 78% of 2003 full-time freshmen returned.
Freshmen *Admission:* 614 applied, 517 admitted, 274 enrolled. *Average high school GPA:* 2.82. *Test scores:* SAT verbal scores over 500: 43%; SAT math scores over 500: 47%; SAT verbal scores over 600: 8%; SAT math scores over 600: 12%; SAT math scores over 700: 1%.
Faculty *Total:* 91, 57% full-time, 32% with terminal degrees. *Student/faculty ratio:* 12:1.
Majors Accounting; acting; actuarial science; adult and continuing education administration; advertising; aerospace, aeronautical and astronautical engineering; African-American/Black studies; agribusiness; agricultural and extension education; agricultural/biological engineering and bioengineering; agricultural business and management related; agricultural mechanization; agriculture; agronomy and crop science; animal sciences; animal sciences related; anthropology; applied economics; archeology; architectural engineering; art; art history, criticism and conservation; art teacher education; Asian studies (East); astronomy; atmospheric sciences and meteorology; biochemistry; biological and biomedical sciences related; biological and physical sciences; biology/biological sciences; biology/biotechnology laboratory technician; biomedical/medical engineering; business administration and management; business/commerce; business/managerial economics; chemical engineering; chemistry; civil engineering; classics and languages, literatures and linguistics; communication and journalism related; communication disorders; communication/speech communication and rhetoric; comparative literature; computer and information sciences; computer engineering; criminal justice/law enforcement administration; economics; electrical, electronics and communications engineering; elementary education; engineering science; English; environmental/environmental health engineering; film/cinema studies; finance; food science; foreign language teacher education; forestry technology; forest sciences and biology; French; geography; geological and earth sciences/geosciences related; geology/earth science; German; graphic design; health/health care administration; history; horticultural science; hospitality administration related; human development and family studies; human nutrition; industrial engineering; information science/studies; international relations and affairs; Italian; Japanese; Jewish/Judaic studies; journalism; kinesiology and exercise science; labor and industrial relations; landscaping and groundskeeping; Latin American studies; liberal arts and sciences/liberal studies; management information systems; marketing/marketing management; materials science; mathematics; mechanical engineering; medical microbiology and bacteriology; medieval and Renaissance studies; mining and mineral engineering; music; natural resources and conservation related; natural resources/conservation; nuclear engineering; nursing (registered nurse training); occupational therapist assistant; occupational therapy; organizational behavior; parks, recreation and leisure facilities management; petroleum engineering; philosophy; physical therapist assistant; physics; political science and government; pre-medical studies; psychology; rehabilitation and therapeutic professions related; religious studies; Russian; secondary education; sociology; soil science and agronomy; Spanish; special education; statistics; theater design and technology; toxicology; turf and turfgrass management; visual and performing arts; women's studies.
Academics *Calendar:* semesters. *Degrees:* associate and bachelor's. *Special study options:* academic remediation for entering students, accelerated degree program, adult/continuing education programs, advanced placement credit, distance learning, double majors, honors programs, independent study, internships, services for LD students, study abroad, summer session for credit. *ROTC:* Army (c).
Library 38,962 titles, 273 serial subscriptions, 1,418 audiovisual materials.
Computers on Campus 182 computers available on campus for general student use. A campuswide network can be accessed from student residence rooms and from off campus. Internet access, online (class) registration, at least one staffed computer lab available. Computer purchase or lease plan available.
Student Life *Housing Options:* coed, disabled students. Campus housing is university owned. Freshman campus housing is guaranteed. *Activities and Organizations:* drama/theater group, student-run newspaper, radio station. *Campus security:* 24-hour patrols, controlled dormitory access. *Student services:* health clinic, women's center.

Athletics Member NJCAA. *Intercollegiate sports:* basketball M/W, cheerleading M/W, cross-country running M/W, golf M/W, soccer M/W, softball W, tennis M/W, volleyball W. *Intramural sports:* badminton M/W, basketball M/W, cheerleading M(c)/W(c), racquetball M/W, soccer M/W, softball W, volleyball M/W.
Standardized Tests *Required:* SAT or ACT (for admission).
Costs (2005–06) *Tuition:* state resident $9722 full-time, $393 per credit hour part-time; nonresident $14,854 full-time, $619 per credit hour part-time. *Required fees:* $478 full-time. *Room and board:* $6530; room only: $3430.
Financial Aid Of all full-time matriculated undergraduates who enrolled in 2004, 49 Federal Work-Study jobs (averaging $1165). 9 state and other part-time jobs (averaging $6156).
Applying *Options:* electronic application, early admission, deferred entrance. *Application fee:* $50. *Required:* high school transcript. *Required for some:* letters of recommendation, interview. *Recommended:* essay or personal statement. *Application deadline:* rolling (freshmen), rolling (transfers). *Notification:* continuous (freshmen).
Director of Admissions Mr. Randall C. Deike, Assistant Vice President for Enrollment Management, The Pennsylvania State University Mont Alto Campus of the Commonwealth College, 1 Campus Drive, Mont Alto, PA 17237-9703. *Phone:* 814-865-5471. *Toll-free phone:* 800-392-6173. *E-mail:* admissions@psu.edu.

THE PENNSYLVANIA STATE UNIVERSITY NEW KENSINGTON CAMPUS OF THE COMMONWEALTH COLLEGE

New Kensington, Pennsylvania   **www.nk.psu.edu/**

- **State-related** primarily 2-year, founded 1958, part of Pennsylvania State University
- **Small-town** 71-acre campus with easy access to Pittsburgh
- **Endowment** $1.2 billion
- **Coed,** 880 undergraduate students, 71% full-time, 44% women, 56% men

Undergraduates 628 full-time, 252 part-time. 2% are from out of state, 2% African American, 0.7% Asian American or Pacific Islander, 1% Hispanic American, 0.1% Native American, 5% transferred in. *Retention:* 77% of 2003 full-time freshmen returned.
Freshmen *Admission:* 376 applied, 323 admitted, 198 enrolled. *Average high school GPA:* 2.92. *Test scores:* SAT verbal scores over 500: 48%; SAT math scores over 500: 44%; SAT verbal scores over 600: 8%; SAT math scores over 600: 13%; SAT verbal scores over 700: 1%; SAT math scores over 700: 2%.
Faculty *Total:* 88, 50% full-time, 40% with terminal degrees. *Student/faculty ratio:* 12:1.
Majors Accounting; acting; actuarial science; adult and continuing education administration; advertising; aerospace, aeronautical and astronautical engineering; African-American/Black studies; agribusiness; agricultural and extension education; agricultural/biological engineering and bioengineering; agricultural business and management related; agricultural mechanization; agriculture; agronomy and crop science; animal sciences; animal sciences related; anthropology; applied economics; archeology; architectural engineering; art; art history, criticism and conservation; art teacher education; Asian studies (East); astronomy; atmospheric sciences and meteorology; biochemistry; biological and biomedical sciences related; biological and physical sciences; biology/biological sciences; biology/biotechnology laboratory technician; biomedical/medical engineering; biomedical technology; business administration and management; business/commerce; business/managerial economics; chemical engineering; chemistry; civil engineering; classics and languages, literatures and linguistics; communication and journalism related; communication disorders; communication/speech communication and rhetoric; comparative literature; computer and information sciences; computer engineering; computer engineering technology; criminal justice/law enforcement administration; economics; electrical, electronic and communications engineering technology; electrical, electronics and communications engineering; elementary education; engineering science; English; environmental/environmental health engineering; film/cinema studies; finance; food science; foreign language teacher education; forestry technology; forest sciences and biology; French; geography; geological and earth sciences/geosciences related; geology/earth science; German; graphic design; health/health care administration; history; horticultural science; hospitality administration related; human development and family studies; human nutrition; industrial engineering; information science/studies; international relations and affairs; Italian; Japanese; Jewish/Judaic studies; journalism; kinesiology and exercise science; labor and industrial relations; landscaping and groundskeeping; Latin American studies; liberal arts and sciences/liberal studies; logistics and materials management; management information systems; marketing/marketing management; materials science; mathematics; mechanical engineering; mechanical engineering/

mechanical technology; medical microbiology and bacteriology; medical radiologic technology; medieval and Renaissance studies; metallurgical technology; mining and mineral engineering; music; natural resources and conservation related; natural resources/conservation; nuclear engineering; nursing (registered nurse training); organizational behavior; parks, recreation and leisure facilities management; petroleum engineering; philosophy; physics; political science and government; pre-medical studies; psychology; rehabilitation and therapeutic professions related; religious studies; Russian; secondary education; sociology; soil science and agronomy; Spanish; special education; statistics; telecommunications technology; theater design and technology; toxicology; turf and turfgrass management; visual and performing arts; women's studies.

Academics *Calendar:* semesters. *Degrees:* associate and bachelor's. *Special study options:* academic remediation for entering students, accelerated degree program, adult/continuing education programs, advanced placement credit, distance learning, double majors, external degree program, honors programs, independent study, internships, services for LD students, summer session for credit.

Library 28,897 titles, 404 serial subscriptions, 4,294 audiovisual materials.

Computers on Campus 264 computers available on campus for general student use. A campuswide network can be accessed from off campus. Internet access, online (class) registration, at least one staffed computer lab available. Computer purchase or lease plan available.

Student Life *Housing:* college housing not available. *Activities and Organizations:* drama/theater group, student-run newspaper, choral group, marching band. *Campus security:* part-time trained security personnel. *Student services:* health clinic, women's center.

Athletics Member NJCAA. *Intercollegiate sports:* baseball M, basketball M/W, cheerleading M/W, golf M/W, softball W, volleyball W. *Intramural sports:* badminton M/W, basketball M/W, bowling M/W, cheerleading M(c)/W(c), football M/W, ice hockey M(c)/W(c), racquetball M/W, skiing (downhill) M(c)/W(c), soccer M/W, softball W, volleyball M/W.

Standardized Tests *Required:* SAT or ACT (for admission).

Costs (2005–06) *Tuition:* state resident $9722 full-time, $393 per credit hour part-time; nonresident $14,854 full-time, $619 per credit hour part-time. *Required fees:* $478 full-time.

Financial Aid Of all full-time matriculated undergraduates who enrolled in 2004, 40 Federal Work-Study jobs (averaging $1319). 1 state and other part-time job (averaging $1696).

Applying *Options:* electronic application, early admission, deferred entrance. *Application fee:* $50. *Required:* high school transcript. *Required for some:* letters of recommendation, interview. *Recommended:* essay or personal statement. *Application deadline:* rolling (freshmen), rolling (transfers). *Notification:* continuous (freshmen).

Director of Admissions Mr. Randall C. Deike, Assistant Vice President for Enrollment Management, The Pennsylvania State University New Kensington Campus of the Commonwealth College, 3550 7th Street Road, Route 780, Upper Burrell, PA 15068-1798. *Phone:* 814-865-5471. *Toll-free phone:* 888-968-7297. *E-mail:* admissions@psu.edu.

THE PENNSYLVANIA STATE UNIVERSITY SCHUYLKILL CAMPUS OF THE CAPITAL COLLEGE

Schuylkill Haven, Pennsylvania www.sl.psu.edu/

- **State-related** primarily 2-year, founded 1934, part of Pennsylvania State University
- **Small-town** 42-acre campus
- **Coed**

Undergraduates 773 full-time, 151 part-time. 15% are from out of state, 17% African American, 3% Asian American or Pacific Islander, 4% Hispanic American, 0.3% Native American, 0.5% international, 2% transferred in, 28% live on campus. *Retention:* 81% of 2003 full-time freshmen returned.

Faculty *Student/faculty ratio:* 14:1.

Academics *Calendar:* semesters. *Degrees:* associate and bachelor's (bachelor's degree programs completed at the Harrisburg campus). *Special study options:* academic remediation for entering students, accelerated degree program, adult/continuing education programs, advanced placement credit, cooperative education, distance learning, double majors, honors programs, independent study, internships, services for LD students, student-designed majors, study abroad, summer session for credit.

Student Life *Campus security:* 24-hour patrols, controlled dormitory access.

Athletics Member NJCAA.

Standardized Tests *Required:* SAT or ACT (for admission).

Costs (2005–06) *Tuition:* state resident $9722 full-time; nonresident $14,854 full-time. Full-time tuition and fees vary according to course level, location,

program, and student level. Part-time tuition and fees vary according to course level, course load, location, program, and student level. *Required fees:* $458 full-time. *Room and board:* $7110; room only: $3474. Room and board charges vary according to board plan and housing facility.

Financial Aid Of all full-time matriculated undergraduates who enrolled in 2003, 665 applied for aid, 563 were judged to have need, 39 had their need fully met. 86 Federal Work-Study jobs (averaging $1326). 7 state and other part-time jobs (averaging $3450). In 2003, 29. *Average percent of need met:* 68. *Average financial aid package:* $11,204. *Average need-based loan:* $3285. *Average need-based gift aid:* $4384. *Average non-need-based aid:* $2087. *Average indebtedness upon graduation:* $18,600.

Applying *Options:* electronic application, early admission, deferred entrance. *Application fee:* $50. *Required:* high school transcript.

Director of Admissions Mr. Randall C. Deike, Assistant Vice President for Enrollment Management, The Pennsylvania State University Schuylkill Campus of the Capital College, 200 University Drive, A102 Administration Building, Schuylkill Haven, PA 17972-2208. *Phone:* 814-865-5471. *E-mail:* admissions@psu.edu.

THE PENNSYLVANIA STATE UNIVERSITY SHENANGO CAMPUS OF THE COMMONWEALTH COLLEGE

Sharon, Pennsylvania www.shenango.psu.edu/

- **State-related** primarily 2-year, founded 1965, part of Pennsylvania State University
- **Small-town** 14-acre campus
- **Endowment** $1.2 billion
- **Coed,** 855 undergraduate students, 59% full-time, 66% women, 34% men

Undergraduates 508 full-time, 347 part-time. 11% are from out of state, 8% African American, 0.3% Asian American or Pacific Islander, 1% Hispanic American, 0.2% Native American, 4% transferred in. *Retention:* 74% of 2003 full-time freshmen returned.

Freshmen *Admission:* 211 applied, 190 admitted, 126 enrolled. *Average high school GPA:* 2.82. *Test scores:* SAT verbal scores over 500: 28%; SAT math scores over 500: 31%; SAT verbal scores over 600: 6%; SAT math scores over 600: 8%.

Faculty *Total:* 71, 41% full-time, 28% with terminal degrees. *Student/faculty ratio:* 14:1.

Majors Accounting; acting; actuarial science; adult and continuing education administration; advertising; aerospace, aeronautical and astronautical engineering; African-American/Black studies; agribusiness; agricultural and extension education; agricultural/biological engineering and bioengineering; agricultural business and management related; agricultural mechanization; agriculture; agronomy and crop science; animal sciences; animal sciences related; anthropology; applied economics; archeology; architectural engineering; art; art history, criticism and conservation; art teacher education; Asian studies (East); astronomy; atmospheric sciences and meteorology; biochemistry; biological and biomedical sciences related; biological and physical sciences; biology/biological sciences; biology/biotechnology laboratory technician; biomedical/medical engineering; biomedical technology; business administration and management; business/commerce; business/managerial economics; chemical engineering; chemistry; civil engineering; classics and languages, literatures and linguistics; communication and journalism related; communication disorders; communication/speech communication and rhetoric; comparative literature; computer and information sciences; computer engineering; criminal justice/law enforcement administration; economics; electrical, electronic and communications engineering technology; electrical, electronics and communications engineering; elementary education; engineering science; English; environmental/environmental health engineering; film/cinema studies; finance; food science; foreign language teacher education; forestry technology; forest sciences and biology; French; geography; geological and earth sciences/geosciences related; geology/earth science; German; graphic design; health/health care administration; history; horticultural science; hospitality administration related; human development and family studies; human nutrition; industrial engineering; information science/studies; international relations and affairs; Italian; Japanese; Jewish/Judaic studies; journalism; kinesiology and exercise science; labor and industrial relations; landscaping and groundskeeping; Latin American studies; liberal arts and sciences/liberal studies; logistics and materials management; management information systems; marketing/marketing management; materials science; mathematics; mechanical engineering; mechanical engineering/mechanical technology; medical microbiology and bacteriology; medieval and Renaissance studies; metallurgical technology; mining and mineral engineering; music; natural resources and conservation related; natural resources/conservation; nuclear engineering; nursing (registered nurse training); organizational behavior; parks, recreation and leisure facilities management; petroleum engineering; philosophy; physical therapist assistant; phys-

Pennsylvania

The Pennsylvania State University Shenango Campus of the Commonwealth College (continued)

ics; political science and government; pre-medical studies; psychology; rehabilitation and therapeutic professions related; religious studies; Russian; secondary education; sociology; soil science and agronomy; Spanish; special education; statistics; telecommunications technology; theater design and technology; toxicology; turf and turfgrass management; visual and performing arts; women's studies.

Academics *Calendar:* semesters. *Degrees:* associate and bachelor's. *Special study options:* academic remediation for entering students, accelerated degree program, adult/continuing education programs, advanced placement credit, distance learning, double majors, honors programs, independent study, internships, services for LD students, student-designed majors, study abroad, summer session for credit.

Library 25,273 titles, 346 serial subscriptions, 2,064 audiovisual materials.

Computers on Campus 102 computers available on campus for general student use. A campuswide network can be accessed from off campus. Internet access, online (class) registration, at least one staffed computer lab available. Computer purchase or lease plan available.

Student Life *Housing:* college housing not available. *Activities and Organizations:* drama/theater group. *Campus security:* part-time trained security personnel. *Student services:* health clinic, women's center.

Athletics *Intramural sports:* basketball M(c)/W, bowling M/W, football M(c), golf M/W, softball M/W, tennis M/W, volleyball M/W.

Standardized Tests *Required:* SAT or ACT (for admission).

Costs (2005–06) *Tuition:* state resident $9722 full-time, $393 per credit hour part-time; nonresident $14,854 full-time, $619 per credit hour part-time. *Required fees:* $478 full-time.

Financial Aid Of all full-time matriculated undergraduates who enrolled in 2004, 39 Federal Work-Study jobs (averaging $1790).

Applying *Options:* electronic application, early admission, deferred entrance. *Application fee:* $50. *Required:* high school transcript. *Required for some:* letters of recommendation, interview. *Recommended:* essay or personal statement. *Application deadline:* rolling (freshmen), rolling (transfers). *Notification:* continuous (freshmen).

Director of Admissions Mr. Randall C. Deike, Assistant Vice President for Enrollment Management, The Pennsylvania State University Shenango Campus of the Commonwealth College, 147 Shenango Avenue, Sharon, PA 16146-1597. *Phone:* 814-865-5471. *E-mail:* admissions@psu.edu.

THE PENNSYLVANIA STATE UNIVERSITY WILKES-BARRE CAMPUS OF THE COMMONWEALTH COLLEGE
Lehman, Pennsylvania   www.wb.psu.edu/

- **State-related** primarily 2-year, founded 1916, part of Pennsylvania State University
- **Rural** 156-acre campus
- **Endowment** $1.2 billion
- **Coed,** 666 undergraduate students, 80% full-time, 34% women, 66% men

Undergraduates 535 full-time, 131 part-time. 4% are from out of state, 2% African American, 0.9% Asian American or Pacific Islander, 2% Hispanic American, 6% transferred in. *Retention:* 79% of 2003 full-time freshmen returned. Freshmen *Admission:* 427 applied, 360 admitted, 163 enrolled. *Average high school GPA:* 2.92. *Test scores:* SAT verbal scores over 500: 56%; SAT math scores over 500: 55%; SAT verbal scores over 600: 15%; SAT math scores over 600: 14%; SAT verbal scores over 700: 1%.

Faculty *Total:* 67, 54% full-time, 39% with terminal degrees. *Student/faculty ratio:* 13:1.

Majors Accounting; acting; actuarial science; adult and continuing education administration; advertising; aerospace, aeronautical and astronautical engineering; African-American/Black studies; agribusiness; agricultural and extension education; agricultural/biological engineering and bioengineering; agricultural business and management related; agricultural mechanization; agriculture; agronomy and crop science; animal sciences; animal sciences related; anthropology; applied economics; archeology; architectural engineering; art; art history, criticism and conservation; art teacher education; astronomy; atmospheric sciences and meteorology; biochemistry; biological and biomedical sciences related; biological and physical sciences; biology/biological sciences; biology/biotechnology laboratory technician; biomedical/medical engineering; business administration and management; business/commerce; business/managerial economics; chemical engineering; chemistry; civil engineering; classics and languages, literatures and linguistics; communication and journalism related; communication disorders; communication/speech communication and rhetoric;

comparative literature; computer and information sciences; computer engineering; criminal justice/law enforcement administration; criminal justice/safety; economics; electrical, electronic and communications engineering technology; electrical, electronics and communications engineering; elementary education; engineering science; English; environmental/environmental health engineering; film/cinema studies; finance; food science; forestry technology; forest sciences and biology; French; geography; geological and earth sciences/geosciences related; geology/earth science; German; graphic design; health/health care administration; history; horticultural science; hospitality administration related; human development and family studies; human nutrition; industrial engineering; information science/studies; international relations and affairs; Italian; Japanese; Jewish/Judaic studies; journalism; kinesiology and exercise science; labor and industrial relations; landscape architecture; landscaping and groundskeeping; Latin American studies; liberal arts and sciences/liberal studies; management information systems; manufacturing engineering; marketing/marketing management; materials science; mathematics; mechanical engineering; medical microbiology and bacteriology; medieval and Renaissance studies; metallurgical technology; mining and mineral engineering; music; natural resources and conservation related; natural resources/conservation; nuclear engineering; nursing (registered nurse training); organizational behavior; parks, recreation and leisure facilities management; petroleum engineering; philosophy; physics; political science and government; pre-medical studies; psychology; rehabilitation and therapeutic professions related; religious studies; Russian; secondary education; sociology; soil science and agronomy; Spanish; special education; statistics; survey technology; telecommunications technology; theater design and technology; toxicology; turf and turfgrass management; visual and performing arts; women's studies.

Academics *Calendar:* semesters. *Degrees:* associate, bachelor's, and post-bachelor's certificates. *Special study options:* academic remediation for entering students, accelerated degree program, adult/continuing education programs, advanced placement credit, distance learning, double majors, honors programs, independent study, internships, services for LD students, student-designed majors, study abroad, summer session for credit. *ROTC:* Air Force (c).

Library 35,697 titles, 199 serial subscriptions, 394 audiovisual materials.

Computers on Campus 137 computers available on campus for general student use. A campuswide network can be accessed from off campus. Internet access, online (class) registration, at least one staffed computer lab available. Computer purchase or lease plan available.

Student Life *Housing:* college housing not available. *Activities and Organizations:* student-run newspaper, radio station. *Campus security:* part-time trained security personnel. *Student services:* health clinic, personal/psychological counseling.

Athletics Member NJCAA. *Intercollegiate sports:* baseball M, basketball M, cross-country running M/W, golf M/W, soccer M/W, volleyball W. *Intramural sports:* basketball M/W, bowling M(c)/W(c), cheerleading M(c)/W(c), football M, racquetball M/W, softball W, volleyball M/W.

Standardized Tests *Required:* SAT or ACT (for admission).

Costs (2005–06) *Tuition:* state resident $9722 full-time, $393 per credit hour part-time; nonresident $14,854 full-time, $619 per credit hour part-time. *Required fees:* $478 full-time.

Financial Aid Of all full-time matriculated undergraduates who enrolled in 2004, 30 Federal Work-Study jobs (averaging $1172).

Applying *Options:* electronic application, early admission, deferred entrance. *Application fee:* $50. *Required:* high school transcript. *Required for some:* letters of recommendation, interview. *Recommended:* essay or personal statement. *Application deadline:* rolling (freshmen), rolling (transfers). *Notification:* continuous (freshmen).

Director of Admissions Mr. Randall C. Deike, Assistant Vice President for Enrollment Management, The Pennsylvania State University Wilkes-Barre Campus of the Commonwealth College, PO Box PSU, Old Route 115, Lehman, PA 18627-9999. *Phone:* 814-865-5471. *Toll-free phone:* 800-966-6613. *E-mail:* admissions@psu.edu.

THE PENNSYLVANIA STATE UNIVERSITY WORTHINGTON SCRANTON CAMPUS OF THE COMMONWEALTH COLLEGE
Dunmore, Pennsylvania   www.sn.psu.edu/

- **State-related** primarily 2-year, founded 1923, part of Pennsylvania State University
- **Small-town** 43-acre campus
- **Endowment** $1.2 billion
- **Coed,** 1,241 undergraduate students, 77% full-time, 50% women, 50% men

Undergraduates 955 full-time, 286 part-time. 1% are from out of state, 2% African American, 0.9% Asian American or Pacific Islander, 2% Hispanic

American, 0.1% Native American, 0.3% international, 7% transferred in. *Retention:* 77% of 2003 full-time freshmen returned.

Freshmen *Admission:* 580 applied, 486 admitted, 253 enrolled. *Average high school GPA:* 2.83. *Test scores:* SAT verbal scores over 500: 41%; SAT math scores over 500: 47%; SAT verbal scores over 600: 10%; SAT math scores over 600: 12%.

Faculty *Total:* 104, 59% full-time, 38% with terminal degrees. *Student/faculty ratio:* 14:1.

Majors Accounting; acting; actuarial science; adult and continuing education administration; advertising; aerospace, aeronautical and astronautical engineering; African-American/Black studies; agribusiness; agricultural and extension education; agricultural/biological engineering and bioengineering; agricultural business and management related; agricultural mechanization; agriculture; agronomy and crop science; American studies; animal sciences; animal sciences related; anthropology; applied economics; archeology; architectural engineering; architectural engineering technology; art; art history, criticism and conservation; art teacher education; Asian studies (East); astronomy; atmospheric sciences and meteorology; biochemistry; biological and biomedical sciences related; biological and physical sciences; biology/biological sciences; biology/biotechnology laboratory technician; biomedical/medical engineering; business administration and management; business/commerce; business/managerial economics; chemical engineering; chemistry; civil engineering; classics and languages, literatures and linguistics; communication and journalism related; communication disorders; communication/speech communication and rhetoric; comparative literature; computer and information sciences; computer engineering; criminal justice/law enforcement administration; economics; electrical, electronic and communications engineering technology; electrical, electronics and communications engineering; elementary education; engineering science; English; environmental/environmental health engineering; film/cinema studies; finance; food science; foreign language teacher education; forestry technology; forest sciences and biology; French; geography; geological and earth sciences/geosciences related; geology/earth science; German; graphic design; health/health care administration; history; horticultural science; hospitality administration related; human development and family studies; human nutrition; industrial engineering; information science/studies; international relations and affairs; Italian; Japanese; Jewish/Judaic studies; journalism; kinesiology and exercise science; labor and industrial relations; landscaping and groundskeeping; Latin American studies; liberal arts and sciences/liberal studies; management information systems; marketing/marketing management; materials science; mathematics; mechanical engineering; medical microbiology and bacteriology; medieval and Renaissance studies; mining and mineral engineering; music; natural resources and conservation related; natural resources/conservation; nuclear engineering; nursing (registered nurse training); organizational behavior; parks, recreation and leisure facilities management; petroleum engineering; philosophy; physics; political science and government; pre-medical studies; psychology; rehabilitation and therapeutic professions related; religious studies; Russian; secondary education; sociology; soil science and agronomy; Spanish; special education; statistics; theater design and technology; turf and turfgrass management; visual and performing arts; women's studies.

Academics *Calendar:* semesters. *Degrees:* associate and bachelor's. *Special study options:* academic remediation for entering students, accelerated degree program, adult/continuing education programs, advanced placement credit, cooperative education, distance learning, double majors, honors programs, independent study, internships, services for LD students, study abroad, summer session for credit. *ROTC:* Air Force (c).

Library 53,572 titles, 102 serial subscriptions, 3,048 audiovisual materials.

Computers on Campus 104 computers available on campus for general student use. A campuswide network can be accessed from off campus. Internet access, online (class) registration, at least one staffed computer lab available. Computer purchase or lease plan available.

Student Life *Housing:* college housing not available. *Activities and Organizations:* drama/theater group, student-run newspaper, choral group. *Campus security:* part-time trained security personnel. *Student services:* health clinic, personal/psychological counseling, women's center.

Athletics Member NJCAA. *Intercollegiate sports:* baseball M, basketball M/W, cheerleading M/W, cross-country running M/W, soccer M, softball W, volleyball W. *Intramural sports:* basketball M/W, bowling M(c)/W(c), skiing (downhill) M(c)/W(c), soccer M/W, softball M/W, volleyball M/W(c), weight lifting M(c)/W(c).

Standardized Tests *Required:* SAT or ACT (for admission).

Costs (2005–06) *Tuition:* state resident $9722 full-time, $393 per credit hour part-time; nonresident $14,854 full-time, $619 per credit hour part-time. *Required fees:* $458 full-time.

Financial Aid Of all full-time matriculated undergraduates who enrolled in 2004, 28 Federal Work-Study jobs (averaging $1120).

Applying *Options:* electronic application, early admission, deferred entrance. *Application fee:* $50. *Required:* high school transcript. *Required for some:* letters of recommendation, interview. *Recommended:* essay or personal statement. *Application deadline:* rolling (freshmen), rolling (transfers). *Notification:* continuous (freshmen).

Director of Admissions Mr. Randall C. Deike, Assistant Vice President for Enrollment Management, The Pennsylvania State University Worthington Scranton

Campus of the Commonwealth College, 120 Ridge View Drive, Dunmore, PA 18512-1699. *Phone:* 814-865-5471. *E-mail:* admissions@psu.edu.

THE PENNSYLVANIA STATE UNIVERSITY YORK CAMPUS OF THE COMMONWEALTH COLLEGE

York, Pennsylvania   **www.yk.psu.edu/**

- **State-related** primarily 2-year, founded 1926, part of Pennsylvania State University
- **Suburban** 53-acre campus
- **Endowment** $1.2 billion
- **Coed,** 1,415 undergraduate students, 58% full-time, 44% women, 56% men

Undergraduates 822 full-time, 593 part-time. 2% are from out of state, 4% African American, 6% Asian American or Pacific Islander, 4% Hispanic American, 0.4% Native American, 0.2% international, 2% transferred in. *Retention:* 74% of 2003 full-time freshmen returned.

Freshmen *Admission:* 813 applied, 655 admitted, 269 enrolled. *Average high school GPA:* 2.77. *Test scores:* SAT verbal scores over 500: 56%; SAT math scores over 500: 58%; SAT verbal scores over 600: 17%; SAT math scores over 600: 25%; SAT verbal scores over 700: 1%; SAT math scores over 700: 3%.

Faculty *Total:* 123, 48% full-time, 40% with terminal degrees. *Student/faculty ratio:* 13:1.

Majors Accounting; acting; actuarial science; adult and continuing education administration; advertising; aerospace, aeronautical and astronautical engineering; African-American/Black studies; agribusiness; agricultural and extension education; agricultural/biological engineering and bioengineering; agricultural business and management related; agricultural mechanization; agriculture; agronomy and crop science; American studies; animal sciences; animal sciences related; anthropology; applied economics; archeology; architectural engineering; art; art history, criticism and conservation; art teacher education; Asian studies (East); astronomy; atmospheric sciences and meteorology; biochemistry; biological and biomedical sciences related; biological and physical sciences; biology/biological sciences; biology/biotechnology laboratory technician; biomedical/medical engineering; biomedical technology; business administration and management; business/commerce; business/managerial economics; chemical engineering; chemistry; civil engineering; classics and languages, literatures and linguistics; communication and journalism related; communication disorders; communication/speech communication and rhetoric; comparative literature; computer and information sciences; computer engineering; criminal justice/law enforcement administration; economics; electrical, electronic and communications engineering technology; electrical, electronics and communications engineering; elementary education; engineering science; English; environmental/environmental health engineering; film/cinema studies; finance; food science; foreign language teacher education; forestry technology; forest sciences and biology; French; geography; geological and earth sciences/geosciences related; geology/earth science; German; graphic design; health/health care administration; history; horticultural science; hospitality administration related; human development and family studies; human nutrition; industrial engineering; industrial technology; information science/studies; international relations and affairs; Italian; Japanese; Jewish/Judaic studies; journalism; kinesiology and exercise science; labor and industrial relations; landscaping and groundskeeping; Latin American studies; liberal arts and sciences/liberal studies; logistics and materials management; management information systems; manufacturing engineering; marketing/marketing management; materials science; mathematics; mechanical engineering; mechanical engineering/mechanical technology; medical microbiology and bacteriology; medieval and Renaissance studies; metallurgical technology; mining and mineral engineering; music; natural resources and conservation related; natural resources/conservation; nuclear engineering; nursing (registered nurse training); organizational behavior; parks, recreation and leisure facilities management; petroleum engineering; philosophy; physics; political science and government; pre-medical studies; psychology; rehabilitation and therapeutic professions related; religious studies; Russian; secondary education; sociology; soil science and agronomy; Spanish; special education; statistics; telecommunications technology; theater design and technology; toxicology; turf and turfgrass management; visual and performing arts; women's studies.

Academics *Calendar:* semesters. *Degrees:* associate and bachelor's (also offers up to 2 years of most bachelor's degree programs offered at University Park campus). *Special study options:* academic remediation for entering students, accelerated degree program, adult/continuing education programs, advanced placement credit, distance learning, double majors, English as a second language, honors programs, independent study, internships, services for LD students, student-designed majors, study abroad, summer session for credit.

Library 49,996 titles, 243 serial subscriptions, 3,567 audiovisual materials.

Computers on Campus 155 computers available on campus for general student use. A campuswide network can be accessed from off campus. Internet

*The Pennsylvania State University York Campus of the Commonwealth
College (continued)*

access, online (class) registration, at least one staffed computer lab available.
Computer purchase or lease plan available.

Student Life *Housing:* college housing not available. *Activities and Organizations:* student-run newspaper. *Campus security:* part-time trained security personnel. *Student services:* health clinic, personal/psychological counseling, women's center.

Athletics Member NJCAA. *Intercollegiate sports:* basketball M/W, cross-country running M/W, soccer M, tennis M/W, volleyball W. *Intramural sports:* badminton M/W, basketball M/W, cheerleading M(c)/W(c), football M, soccer M/W, softball M/W, tennis M/W, ultimate Frisbee M/W, volleyball M/W.

Standardized Tests *Required:* SAT or ACT (for admission).

Costs (2005–06) *Tuition:* state resident $9722 full-time, $393 per credit hour part-time; nonresident $14,854 full-time, $619 per credit hour part-time. *Required fees:* $458 full-time.

Financial Aid Of all full-time matriculated undergraduates who enrolled in 2004, 40 Federal Work-Study jobs (averaging $1033).

Applying *Options:* electronic application, early admission, deferred entrance. *Application fee:* $50. *Required:* high school transcript. *Required for some:* letters of recommendation, interview. *Recommended:* essay or personal statement. *Application deadline:* rolling (freshmen), rolling (transfers). *Notification:* continuous (freshmen).

Director of Admissions Mr. Randall C. Deike, Assistant Vice President for Enrollment Management, The Pennsylvania State University York Campus of the Commonwealth College, 1031 Edgecomb Avenue, York, PA 17403-3398. *Phone:* 814-865-5471. *Toll-free phone:* 800-778-6227. *E-mail:* admissions@psu.edu.

PITTSBURGH INSTITUTE OF AERONAUTICS
Pittsburgh, Pennsylvania   www.pia.edu/

Director of Admissions Ms. Michaelene F. Kalinowski, Director of Admissions, Pittsburgh Institute of Aeronautics, PO Box 10897, Pittsburgh, PA 15236. *Phone:* 412-346-2100 Ext. 2123. *Toll-free phone:* 800-444-1440. *E-mail:* admissions@piainfo.org.

PITTSBURGH INSTITUTE OF MORTUARY SCIENCE, INCORPORATED
Pittsburgh, Pennsylvania   www.pims.edu/

- **Independent** 2-year, founded 1939
- **Urban** campus
- **Coed,** 192 undergraduate students, 94% full-time, 43% women, 57% men

Undergraduates 181 full-time, 11 part-time. Students come from 10 states and territories, 23% are from out of state, 14% African American, 0.5% Hispanic American.

Freshmen *Admission:* 67 enrolled.

Faculty *Total:* 16, 25% full-time, 19% with terminal degrees. *Student/faculty ratio:* 13:1.

Majors Funeral service and mortuary science.

Academics *Calendar:* trimesters. *Degree:* diplomas and associate. *Special study options:* academic remediation for entering students, adult/continuing education programs, cooperative education, internships, part-time degree program, services for LD students.

Library William J. Musmanno Memorial Library with 2,167 titles, 48 serial subscriptions, an OPAC, a Web page.

Computers on Campus 10 computers available on campus for general student use. Internet access, at least one staffed computer lab available.

Student Life *Housing:* college housing not available. *Campus security:* 24-hour emergency response devices.

Costs (2006–07) *Tuition:* $8000 full-time, $240 per credit part-time. *Required fees:* $170 full-time.

Applying *Application fee:* $40. *Required:* high school transcript, 2 letters of recommendation, interview, immunizations. *Application deadline:* rolling (freshmen), rolling (transfers). *Notification:* continuous (freshmen).

Freshmen Application Contact Ms. Karen Rocco, Registrar, Pittsburgh Institute of Mortuary Science, Incorporated, 5808 Baum Boulevard, Pittsburgh, PA 15206-3706. *Phone:* 412-362-8500 Ext. 101. *Toll-free phone:* 800-933-5808. *Fax:* 412-362-1684. *E-mail:* pims5808@aol.com.

PITTSBURGH TECHNICAL INSTITUTE
Oakdale, Pennsylvania   www.pti.edu/

Director of Admissions Mary Lou Zook, Vice President of Admissions, Pittsburgh Technical Institute, 1111 McKee Road, Oakdale, PA 15071. *Phone:* 412-809-5100. *Toll-free phone:* 800-784-9675.

THE PJA SCHOOL
Upper Darby, Pennsylvania   www.pjaschool.com/

Director of Admissions Mr. David Hudiak, Director, The PJA School, 7900 West Chester Pike, Upper Darby, PA 19082-1926. *Phone:* 610-789-6700. *Toll-free phone:* 800-RING-PJA. *Fax:* 610-789-5208. *E-mail:* pjaschool@dvol.com.

READING AREA COMMUNITY COLLEGE
Reading, Pennsylvania   www.racc.edu/

Director of Admissions Mr. David J. Adams, Director of Admissions, Reading Area Community College, PO Box 1706, Reading, PA 19603-1706. *Phone:* 610-607-6224. *Toll-free phone:* 800-626-1665.

THE RESTAURANT SCHOOL AT WALNUT HILL COLLEGE
Philadelphia, Pennsylvania   www.walnuthillcollege.com

Director of Admissions Mr. Karl D. Becker, Director of Admissions, The Restaurant School at Walnut Hill College, 4207 Walnut Street, Philadelphia, PA 19104. *Phone:* 215-222-4200 Ext. 3011. *Toll-free phone:* 877-925-6884 Ext. 3011.

▶ **See page 592 for the College Close-Up.**

ROSEDALE TECHNICAL INSTITUTE
Pittsburgh, Pennsylvania   www.rosedaletech.org/

- **Independent** 2-year
- **Suburban** 6-acre campus
- **Coed, primarily men,** 200 undergraduate students, 100% full-time, 8% women, 93% men
- 65% of applicants were admitted

Undergraduates 200 full-time.

Freshmen *Admission:* 156 applied, 102 admitted.

Faculty *Total:* 18, 78% full-time, 33% with terminal degrees. *Student/faculty ratio:* 13:1.

Majors Automobile/automotive mechanics technology; diesel mechanics technology; electrician.

Academics *Calendar:* semesters. *Degree:* diplomas and associate.

Freshmen Application Contact Mr. Kevin Auld, Director, Rosedale Technical Institute, 215 Beecham Drive, Suite 2, Pittsburgh, PA 15205-9791. *Phone:* 412-521-6200. *Toll-free phone:* 800-521-6262. *Fax:* 412-521-2520. *E-mail:* admissions@rosedaletech.org.

SCHUYLKILL INSTITUTE OF BUSINESS AND TECHNOLOGY
Pottsville, Pennsylvania   www.sibt.edu/

- **Proprietary** 2-year, part of Fore Front Education, Inc
- **Rural** campus
- **Coed,** 136 undergraduate students, 100% full-time, 65% women, 35% men

Undergraduates 136 full-time. Students come from 1 other state, 0.7% African American, 0.7% Hispanic American, 0.7% Native American, 3% transferred in.

Freshmen *Admission:* 36 applied, 36 admitted, 36 enrolled. *Average high school GPA:* 3.0.

Faculty *Total:* 16, 94% full-time. *Student/faculty ratio:* 6:1.

Majors Administrative assistant and secretarial science; business administration and management; commercial and advertising art; computer and information sciences and support services related; drafting and design technology; electrical, electronic and communications engineering technology; legal assistant/paralegal; medical office management.

Academics *Calendar:* quarters. *Degree:* diplomas and associate. *Special study options:* academic remediation for entering students, advanced placement credit, cooperative education, independent study, internships, services for LD students.

Library Schuylkill Institute of Business and Technology Learning Resource Cent with 920 titles, 20 serial subscriptions, 300 audiovisual materials, an OPAC.

Computers on Campus 41 computers available on campus for general student use. A campuswide network can be accessed from off campus. Internet access, at least one staffed computer lab available.

Student Life *Housing:* college housing not available.

Costs (2005–06) *Tuition:* $10,000 full-time. Full-time tuition and fees vary according to degree level and program. No tuition increase for student's term of enrollment. *Required fees:* $450 full-time. *Payment plans:* installment, deferred payment. *Waivers:* employees or children of employees.

Applying *Options:* common application. *Application fee:* $50. *Required:* high school transcript, interview. *Application deadlines:* 10/25 (freshmen), 10/25 (transfers).

Freshmen Application Contact Stacy Seaman, Admissions Representative, Schuylkill Institute of Business and Technology, 171 Red Horse Road, Pottsville, PA 17901. *Phone:* 570-622-4835. *Fax:* 570-622-6563. *E-mail:* sseaman@sibt.edu.

SOUTH HILLS SCHOOL OF BUSINESS & TECHNOLOGY

Atloona, Pennsylvania www.southhills.edu/

Freshmen Application Contact Ms. Marianne M. Beyer, Director, South Hills School of Business & Technology, 508 58th Street, Altoona, PA 16602. *Phone:* 814-944-6134.

SOUTH HILLS SCHOOL OF BUSINESS & TECHNOLOGY

State College, Pennsylvania www.southhills.edu/

- **Proprietary** 2-year, founded 1970
- **Small-town** 6-acre campus
- **Coed,** 663 undergraduate students, 92% full-time, 69% women, 31% men

Undergraduates 611 full-time, 52 part-time. Students come from 1 other state, 1% are from out of state, 1% African American, 0.5% Asian American or Pacific Islander, 0.5% Hispanic American, 17% transferred in. *Retention:* 71% of 2003 full-time freshmen returned.

Freshmen *Admission:* 619 applied, 476 admitted, 342 enrolled. *Average high school GPA:* 2.75.

Faculty *Total:* 60, 62% full-time. *Student/faculty ratio:* 15:1.

Majors Accounting; administrative assistant and secretarial science; business administration and management; computer and information sciences; computer programming (specific applications); diagnostic medical sonography and ultrasound technology; engineering technology; health information/medical records technology; legal administrative assistant/secretary; marketing/marketing management; medical administrative assistant and medical secretary; office management.

Academics *Calendar:* quarters. *Degrees:* certificates, diplomas, and associate (also includes Altoona campus). *Special study options:* advanced placement credit, distance learning, double majors, independent study, internships, part-time degree program.

Library Main Library plus 1 other.

Computers on Campus 360 computers available on campus for general student use. Internet access available.

Student Life *Housing:* college housing not available. *Activities and Organizations:* student-run newspaper, Phi Beta Lambda, South Hills Executives, Student Forum, newspaper. *Campus security:* 24-hour emergency response devices.

Standardized Tests *Required:* CPAt (for admission). *Required for some:* CPAt.

Costs (2006–07) *Tuition:* $11,637 full-time, $323 per credit part-time. *Required fees:* $75 full-time, $25 per term part-time.

Applying *Options:* electronic application. *Application fee:* $25. *Required:* high school transcript, minimum 1.5 GPA, interview. *Required for some:* essay or personal statement, 2 letters of recommendation. *Recommended:* minimum 3.0 GPA. *Application deadline:* 9/2 (freshmen).

Freshmen Application Contact Ms. Diane M. Brown, Director of Admissions, South Hills School of Business & Technology, 480 Waupelani Drive, State College, PA 16801-4516. *Phone:* 814-234-7755 Ext. 2020. *Toll-free phone:* 888-282-7427 Ext. 2020. *Fax:* 814-234-0926. *E-mail:* admissions@southhills.edu.

THADDEUS STEVENS COLLEGE OF TECHNOLOGY

Lancaster, Pennsylvania www.stevenscollege.edu/

- **State-supported** 2-year, founded 1905
- **Urban** 33-acre campus with easy access to Philadelphia
- **Coed**

Undergraduates 660 full-time. Students come from 1 other state, 16% African American, 1% Asian American or Pacific Islander, 6% Hispanic American, 0.6% Native American, 48% live on campus. *Retention:* 60% of 2003 full-time freshmen returned.

Faculty *Student/faculty ratio:* 12:1.

Academics *Calendar:* semesters. *Degree:* associate. *Special study options:* academic remediation for entering students, internships, services for LD students.

Student Life *Campus security:* 24-hour emergency response devices.

Athletics Member NJCAA.

Standardized Tests *Required:* ACT ASSET (for admission).

Applying *Options:* common application, electronic application, deferred entrance. *Application fee:* $25. *Required:* essay or personal statement, high school transcript, minimum 2.0 GPA, letters of recommendation, ASSET Test. *Required for some:* interview.

Director of Admissions Ms. Erin Kate Nelsen, Director of Enrollment, Thaddeus Stevens College of Technology, Enrollment Services, 750 East King Street, Lancaster, PA 17602-3198. *Phone:* 717-299-7772. *Toll-free phone:* 800-842-3832.

THOMPSON INSTITUTE

Harrisburg, Pennsylvania www.thompson.edu/

- **Proprietary** primarily 2-year, founded 1918, part of Kaplan Higher Education Corporation
- **Suburban** 5-acre campus
- **Coed**

Undergraduates 485 full-time. Students come from 2 states and territories, 2% are from out of state, 14% African American, 1% Asian American or Pacific Islander, 5% Hispanic American.

Faculty *Student/faculty ratio:* 25:1.

Academics *Calendar:* quarters. *Degrees:* certificates, diplomas, associate, and bachelor's. *Special study options:* academic remediation for entering students, adult/continuing education programs, advanced placement credit, internships, services for LD students, summer session for credit.

Student Life *Campus security:* campus facilities manager.

Costs (2005–06) *Tuition:* $8600 full-time. *Room only:* $1600. *Payment plans:* installment, deferred payment.

Applying *Options:* common application, electronic application, deferred entrance. *Application fee:* $50. *Required:* high school transcript. *Recommended:* minimum 2.0 GPA.

Director of Admissions Mr. Charles Zimmerman, Admissions Director, Thompson Institute, 5650 Derry Street, Harrisburg, PA 17111. *Phone:* 717-564-4112. *Toll-free phone:* 800-272-4632.

TRIANGLE TECH, INC.—DUBOIS SCHOOL

DuBois, Pennsylvania   www.triangle-tech.edu/

- **Proprietary** 2-year, founded 1944, part of Triangle Tech, Inc
- **Small-town** 5-acre campus
- **Coed, primarily men,** 246 undergraduate students, 100% full-time, 9% women, 91% men

Undergraduates 246 full-time. Students come from 3 states and territories, 0.4% African American. *Retention:* 67% of 2003 full-time freshmen returned. Freshmen *Admission:* 142 applied, 137 admitted, 137 enrolled. *Average high school GPA:* 2.00.
Faculty *Total:* 22, 100% full-time. *Student/faculty ratio:* 11:1.
Majors Carpentry; drafting and design technology; electrical, electronic and communications engineering technology; welding technology.
Academics *Calendar:* semesters. *Degree:* diplomas and associate. *Special study options:* academic remediation for entering students, advanced placement credit, off-campus study.
Library 1,200 titles, 15 serial subscriptions.
Computers on Campus 40 computers available on campus for general student use. A campuswide network can be accessed from off campus. At least one staffed computer lab available.
Costs (2005–06) *Tuition:* $11,408 full-time.
Applying *Options:* deferred entrance. *Required:* high school transcript, minimum 2.0 GPA, interview. *Application deadline:* rolling (freshmen), rolling (transfers).
Freshmen Application Contact Mr. John Conway, Director of Admissions, Triangle Tech, Inc.–DuBois School, PO Box 551, DuBois, PA 15801. *Phone:* 412-359-1000. *Toll-free phone:* 800-874-8324. *Fax:* 814-371-9227. *E-mail:* info@triangle-tech.com.

TRIANGLE TECH, INC.—ERIE SCHOOL

Erie, Pennsylvania   www.triangle-tech.com/

Freshmen Application Contact Jennifer Provost, Admissions Representative, Triangle Tech, Inc.–Erie School, 2000 Liberty Street, Erie, PA 16502. *Phone:* 814-453-6016. *Toll-free phone:* 800-874-8324 (in-state); 800-TRI-TECH (out-of-state).

TRIANGLE TECH, INC.—GREENSBURG SCHOOL

Greensburg, Pennsylvania   www.triangle-tech.com/

- **Proprietary** 2-year, founded 1944, part of Triangle Tech, Inc
- **Small-town** 1-acre campus with easy access to Pittsburgh
- **Coed, primarily men,** 271 undergraduate students, 100% full-time, 1% women, 99% men

Undergraduates 271 full-time. Students come from 2 states and territories, 1% are from out of state, 0.7% African American, 0.4% Native American.
Freshmen *Admission:* 166 applied, 166 admitted, 113 enrolled.
Faculty *Total:* 26, 81% full-time. *Student/faculty ratio:* 12:1.
Majors Carpentry; construction trades; drafting and design technology; electrical/electronics equipment installation and repair; electrical/electronics maintenance and repair technology related; heating, air conditioning and refrigeration technology; heating, air conditioning, ventilation and refrigeration maintenance technology; mechanical drafting and CAD/CADD.
Academics *Calendar:* semesters. *Degree:* diplomas and associate. *Special study options:* academic remediation for entering students, adult/continuing education programs, advanced placement credit, summer session for credit.
Library Triangle Tech Library plus 2 others with 550 titles, 15 serial subscriptions.
Computers on Campus 100 computers available on campus for general student use. A campuswide network can be accessed from off campus. Internet access, at least one staffed computer lab available.
Student Life *Housing:* college housing not available. *Student services:* personal/psychological counseling.
Costs (2005–06) *Tuition:* $11,408 full-time. *Required fees:* $200 full-time.
Financial Aid Of all full-time matriculated undergraduates who enrolled in 2004, 5 Federal Work-Study jobs (averaging $2000).

Applying *Options:* common application, deferred entrance. *Application fee:* $75. *Required:* high school transcript. *Application deadline:* rolling (freshmen), rolling (transfers).
Freshmen Application Contact Mr. John Mazzarese, Vice President of Admissions, Triangle Tech, Inc.–Greensburg School, 222 East Pittsburgh Street, Greensburg, PA 15601. *Phone:* 412-359-1000. *Toll-free phone:* 800-874-8324.

TRIANGLE TECH, INC.—PITTSBURGH SCHOOL

Pittsburgh, Pennsylvania   www.triangle-tech.edu/

- **Proprietary** 2-year, founded 1944, part of Triangle Tech Group
- **Urban** 5-acre campus
- **Coed, primarily men**

Undergraduates 377 full-time. Students come from 3 states and territories, 6% are from out of state, 11% African American.
Faculty *Student/faculty ratio:* 10:1.
Academics *Calendar:* semesters. *Degree:* diplomas and associate. *Special study options:* academic remediation for entering students, advanced placement credit.
Student Life *Campus security:* 16-hour patrols by trained security personnel.
Costs (2005–06) *Tuition:* $302 per credit part-time.
Financial Aid Of all full-time matriculated undergraduates who enrolled in 2004, 16 Federal Work-Study jobs (averaging $1500). *Financial aid deadline:* 7/1.
Applying *Options:* early admission, deferred entrance. *Required:* high school transcript, minimum 2.0 GPA, interview.
Director of Admissions Mr. John A. Mazzarese, Vice President of Admissions, Triangle Tech, Inc.–Pittsburgh School, 1940 Perrysville Avenue, Pittsburgh, PA 15214. *Phone:* 412-359-1000 Ext. 7174. *Toll-free phone:* 800-874-8324.

TRIANGLE TECH, INC.—SUNBURY SCHOOL

Sunbury, Pennsylvania

TRI-STATE BUSINESS INSTITUTE

Erie, Pennsylvania   www.tsbi.org/

Director of Admissions Guy M. Euliano, President, Tri-State Business Institute, 5757 West 26th Street, Erie, PA 16506. *Phone:* 814-838-7673. *Fax:* 814-838-8642. *E-mail:* geuliano@tsbi.org.

UNIVERSITY OF PITTSBURGH AT TITUSVILLE

Titusville, Pennsylvania   www.upt.pitt.edu/

- **State-related** 2-year, founded 1963, part of University of Pittsburgh System
- **Small-town** 10-acre campus
- **Endowment** $825,000
- **Coed,** 547 undergraduate students, 76% full-time, 65% women, 35% men

Undergraduates 413 full-time, 134 part-time. Students come from 15 states and territories, 8% are from out of state, 16% African American, 2% Asian American or Pacific Islander, 1% Hispanic American, 6% transferred in, 48% live on campus.
Freshmen *Admission:* 281 applied, 243 admitted, 165 enrolled. *Average high school GPA:* 3.04. *Test scores:* SAT verbal scores over 500: 34%; SAT math scores over 500: 44%; ACT scores over 18: 31%; SAT verbal scores over 600: 9%; SAT math scores over 600: 13%; ACT scores over 24: 8%; SAT math scores over 700: 7%.

Faculty *Total:* 61, 34% full-time, 31% with terminal degrees. *Student/faculty ratio:* 12:1.

Majors Accounting; business/commerce; human services; liberal arts and sciences/liberal studies; management information systems; natural sciences; nursing (registered nurse training); physical therapist assistant.

Academics *Calendar:* semesters. *Degree:* certificates and associate. *Special study options:* academic remediation for entering students, advanced placement credit, distance learning, independent study, internships, part-time degree program, study abroad, summer session for credit.

Library Haskell Memorial Library with 49,256 titles, 126 serial subscriptions, 505 audiovisual materials, an OPAC.

Computers on Campus 62 computers available on campus for general student use. A campuswide network can be accessed from student residence rooms and from off campus. Internet access, at least one staffed computer lab available.

Student Life *Housing:* on-campus residence required through sophomore year. *Options:* coed, disabled students. Campus housing is university owned. Freshman campus housing is guaranteed. *Activities and Organizations:* drama/theater group, choral group, Phi Theta Kappa, Weight Club, SAB, SIFE, Diversity Club. *Campus security:* 24-hour emergency response devices and patrols, controlled dormitory access. *Student services:* health clinic, personal/psychological counseling.

Athletics Member NJCAA. *Intercollegiate sports:* basketball M(s)/W(s). *Intramural sports:* badminton M/W, basketball M/W, bowling M/W, football M/W, golf M/W, racquetball M/W, softball M/W, table tennis M/W, tennis M/W, volleyball M/W, weight lifting M/W.

Standardized Tests *Required:* SAT or ACT (for admission). *Recommended:* SAT (for admission).

Costs (2005–06) *Tuition:* state resident $8710 full-time, $335 per credit part-time; nonresident $17,610 full-time, $677 per credit part-time. Part-time tuition and fees vary according to student level. *Required fees:* $780 full-time, $93 per term part-time. *Room and board:* $7234. Room and board charges vary according to board plan. *Payment plan:* installment.

Applying *Options:* deferred entrance. *Application fee:* $35. *Required:* high school transcript, minimum 2.0 GPA. *Required for some:* essay or personal statement, 1 letter of recommendation. *Recommended:* interview. *Application deadline:* rolling (freshmen), rolling (transfers). *Notification:* continuous (freshmen).

Freshmen Application Contact Mr. John Mumford, Executive Director of Enrollment Management, University of Pittsburgh at Titusville, PO Box 287, Titusville, PA 16354. *Phone:* 814-827-4409. *Toll-free phone:* 888-878-0462. *Fax:* 814-827-4519. *E-mail:* uptadm@pitt.edu.

VALLEY FORGE MILITARY COLLEGE
Wayne, Pennsylvania   www.vfmac.edu/

- **Independent** 2-year, founded 1928
- **Suburban** 120-acre campus with easy access to Philadelphia
- **Endowment** $7.2 million
- **Coed,** 165 undergraduate students, 100% full-time, 100% men

The Valley Forge Military College's (VFMC) primary goal is to prepare young men and women to transfer to and succeed at the 4-year college or university of their choice. For more than 95 percent of the graduates, that goal is achieved through challenging academic programs, a structured environment that builds confidence and character and fosters academic success, and personal transfer counseling and transfer agreements with major universities. VFMC offers the only 2-year Army ROTC commissioning program in the Northeast U.S., with full-tuition scholarships for qualified applicants.

Undergraduates 165 full-time. Students come from 6 other countries, 85% are from out of state, 13% African American, 6% Asian American or Pacific Islander, 7% Hispanic American, 2% international, 73% transferred in, 100% live on campus.
Freshmen *Admission:* 256 applied, 228 admitted, 98 enrolled. *Average high school GPA:* 2.00. *Test scores:* SAT verbal scores over 500: 49%; SAT math scores over 500: 51%; ACT scores over 18: 71%; SAT verbal scores over 600: 23%; SAT math scores over 600: 30%; ACT scores over 24: 48%; SAT verbal scores over 700: 4%; SAT math scores over 700: 4%; ACT scores over 30: 7%.

Faculty *Total:* 26, 62% full-time, 42% with terminal degrees. *Student/faculty ratio:* 10:1.

Majors Biological and physical sciences; business administration and management; criminal justice/law enforcement administration; engineering; liberal arts and sciences/liberal studies.

Academics *Calendar:* 4-1-4. *Degree:* associate. *Special study options:* academic remediation for entering students, advanced placement credit, English as a second language. *ROTC:* Army (b), Air Force (c).

Library Baker Library with 75,830 titles, 189 serial subscriptions, 326 audiovisual materials, an OPAC.

Computers on Campus 44 computers available on campus for general student use. A campuswide network can be accessed from student residence rooms and from off campus. Internet access, at least one staffed computer lab available.

Student Life *Housing:* on-campus residence required through sophomore year. *Options:* men-only. *Activities and Organizations:* drama/theater group, student-run newspaper, choral group, marching band, Rotoract, Young Republicans, Phi Theta Kappa, Business Club, Criminal Justice Club, national fraternities. *Campus security:* 24-hour patrols, student patrols. *Student services:* health clinic, personal/psychological counseling.

Athletics *Intercollegiate sports:* basketball M(s), cross-country running M, equestrian sports M, football M(s), golf M, lacrosse M, riflery M, soccer M(s), tennis M, wrestling M. *Intramural sports:* basketball M, football M, rugby M, soccer M, volleyball M, water polo M, weight lifting M.

Standardized Tests *Required:* SAT or ACT (for admission).

Costs (2006–07) *Comprehensive fee:* $30,977 includes full-time tuition ($19,693) and room and board ($11,284).

Financial Aid Of all full-time matriculated undergraduates who enrolled in 2004, 20 Federal Work-Study jobs (averaging $1500).

Applying *Options:* common application, early admission, deferred entrance. *Application fee:* $25. *Required:* high school transcript, guidance counselor/teacher evaluation form. *Recommended:* minimum 2.0 GPA, interview. *Application deadline:* 8/2 (freshmen), rolling (transfers). *Notification:* continuous (freshmen).

Freshmen Application Contact Maj. Greg Potts, Dean of Enrollment Management, Valley Forge Military College, 1001 Eagle Road, Wayne, PA 19087-3695. *Phone:* 610-989-1300. *Toll-free phone:* 800-234-8362. *Fax:* 610-688-1545. *E-mail:* admissions@vfmac.edu.

▶ **See page 598 for the College Close-Up.**

WESTERN SCHOOL OF HEALTH AND BUSINESS CAREERS
Monroeville, Pennsylvania

WESTERN SCHOOL OF HEALTH AND BUSINESS CAREERS
Pittsburgh, Pennsylvania   www.westernschool.com/

Director of Admissions Mr. Bruce E. Jones, Director of Admission, Western School of Health and Business Careers, 421 Seventh Avenue, Pittsburgh, PA 15219. *Phone:* 412-281-7083 Ext. 114. *Toll-free phone:* 800-333-6607.

WESTMORELAND COUNTY COMMUNITY COLLEGE
Youngwood, Pennsylvania   www.wccc-pa.edu/

- **County-supported** 2-year, founded 1970
- **Rural** 85-acre campus with easy access to Pittsburgh
- **Coed,** 6,133 undergraduate students, 44% full-time, 64% women, 36% men

Undergraduates 2,670 full-time, 3,463 part-time. Students come from 5 states and territories, 9% are from out of state, 2% African American, 0.5% Asian American or Pacific Islander, 0.5% Hispanic American, 0.2% Native American. *Retention:* 58% of 2003 full-time freshmen returned.
Freshmen *Admission:* 3,539 applied, 3,539 admitted, 2,045 enrolled.

Faculty *Total:* 459, 17% full-time. *Student/faculty ratio:* 17:1.

Majors Accounting; administrative assistant and secretarial science; architectural engineering technology; artificial intelligence and robotics; business administration and management; child development; commercial and advertising art; computer and information sciences; computer engineering technology; computer graphics; computer science; consumer merchandising/retailing management; criminal justice/law enforcement administration; criminal justice/police science; culinary arts; data processing and data processing technology; dental hygiene; dietetics; drafting and design technology; electrical, electronic and communications engineering technology; engineering; environmental engineering technology; fashion/apparel design; fashion merchandising; finance; fire science; graphic and printing equipment operation/production; health information/medical records

Westmoreland County Community College (continued)
administration; health teacher education; heating, air conditioning, ventilation and refrigeration maintenance technology; horticultural science; hospitality administration; hotel/motel administration; human services; information science/studies; legal administrative assistant/secretary; legal assistant/paralegal; liberal arts and sciences/liberal studies; marketing/marketing management; mechanical design technology; mechanical engineering/mechanical technology; medical administrative assistant and medical secretary; nuclear/nuclear power technology; nursing (licensed practical/vocational nurse training); nursing (registered nurse training); ophthalmic laboratory technology; photography; public administration; publishing; real estate; special products marketing; tourism and travel services management; welding technology.
Academics *Calendar:* semesters. *Degree:* certificates, diplomas, and associate. *Special study options:* academic remediation for entering students, adult/continuing education programs, advanced placement credit, cooperative education, distance learning, double majors, English as a second language, honors programs, independent study, internships, off-campus study, part-time degree program, services for LD students, summer session for credit.
Library 34,522 titles, 643 serial subscriptions.
Computers on Campus 600 computers available on campus for general student use. A campuswide network can be accessed. Internet access, at least one staffed computer lab available.
Student Life *Housing:* college housing not available. *Activities and Organizations:* student-run newspaper, radio station, choral group. *Campus security:* 24-hour emergency response devices and patrols. *Student services:* personal/psychological counseling.
Athletics Member NJCAA. *Intercollegiate sports:* baseball M, golf M/W, softball W, tennis M/W, volleyball W. *Intramural sports:* basketball M/W, bowling M/W, football M/W, racquetball M/W, skiing (downhill) M/W, softball M/W, table tennis M/W, volleyball M/W, weight lifting M/W.
Costs (2006–07) *Tuition:* $68 per credit part-time; state resident $136 per credit part-time; nonresident $204 per credit part-time. *Required fees:* $7 per credit part-time.
Applying *Options:* electronic application, early admission. *Application fee:* $10. *Application deadline:* rolling (freshmen), rolling (transfers). *Notification:* continuous (freshmen).
Freshmen Application Contact Mr. Justin Tatar, Admissions Coordinator, Westmoreland County Community College, 400 Armbrust Road, Youngwood, PA 15697. *Phone:* 724-925-4064. *Toll-free phone:* 800-262-2103. *Fax:* 724-925-1150. *E-mail:* admission@wccc-pa.edu.

THE WILLIAMSON FREE SCHOOL OF MECHANICAL TRADES
Media, Pennsylvania   www.williamson.edu/

- **Independent** 2-year, founded 1888
- **Small-town** 240-acre campus with easy access to Philadelphia
- **Men only,** 251 undergraduate students, 100% full-time

Undergraduates 251 full-time. Students come from 5 states and territories, 13% African American, 2% Hispanic American, 100% live on campus. Freshmen *Admission:* 349 applied, 91 admitted, 91 enrolled. *Average high school GPA:* 2.3.
Faculty *Total:* 29. *Student/faculty ratio:* 14:1.
Majors Carpentry; construction engineering technology; electrical, electronic and communications engineering technology; energy management and systems technology; horticultural science; landscaping and groundskeeping; machine tool technology; turf and turfgrass management.
Academics *Calendar:* semesters. *Degree:* diplomas and associate. *Special study options:* academic remediation for entering students, internships, off-campus study.
Library Shrigley Library plus 3 others with 1,600 titles, 70 serial subscriptions.
Computers on Campus 20 computers available on campus for general student use. At least one staffed computer lab available.
Student Life *Activities and Organizations:* student-run newspaper, choral group, Campus Crusade for Christ, Vocational Industrial Clubs of America. *Campus security:* evening patrols, gate security. *Student services:* health clinic, personal/psychological counseling.
Athletics Member NJCAA. *Intercollegiate sports:* baseball M, basketball M, cross-country running M, football M, lacrosse M, soccer M, wrestling M. *Intramural sports:* archery M, badminton M, baseball M, basketball M, cross-country running M, football M, golf M, lacrosse M, racquetball M, soccer M, table tennis M, volleyball M, weight lifting M, wrestling M.
Standardized Tests *Required:* Armed Services Vocational Aptitude Battery (for admission).

Applying *Required:* essay or personal statement, high school transcript, minimum 2.0 GPA, interview. *Required for some:* 3 letters of recommendation. *Application deadline:* 3/15 (freshmen).
Freshmen Application Contact Mr. Edward D. Bailey, Director of Enrollments, The Williamson Free School of Mechanical Trades, 106 South New Middletown Road, Media, PA 19063. *Phone:* 610-566-1776 Ext. 235. *Fax:* 610-566-3854. *E-mail:* ebailey@williamson.edu.

WINNER INSTITUTE OF ARTS & SCIENCES
Transfer, Pennsylvania

WYOTECH
Blairsville, Pennsylvania   www.wyotech.com/

- **Proprietary** 2-year
- **Coed, primarily men**

Majors Autobody/collision and repair technology; automobile/automotive mechanics technology; diesel mechanics technology.
Academics *Calendar:* 9-month program. *Degree:* diplomas and associate.
Costs (2005–06) *Tuition:* $23,300 full-time.
Applying *Application fee:* $100. *Required:* high school transcript.
Freshmen Application Contact Mr. Tim Smyers, WyoTech, 500 Innovation Drive, Blairsville, PA 15717. *Phone:* 724-459-2311. *Toll-free phone:* 800-822-8253. *Fax:* 724-459-6499. *E-mail:* tsmyers@wyotech.edu.

YORK TECHNICAL INSTITUTE
York, Pennsylvania   www.yti.edu/

Freshmen Application Contact Ms. Sharon Mulligan, Associate Director of Admissions, York Technical Institute, 1405 Williams Road, York, PA 17402. *Phone:* 717-757-1100 Ext. 318. *Toll-free phone:* 800-229-9675 (in-state); 800-227-9675 (out-of-state).

YORKTOWNE BUSINESS INSTITUTE
York, Pennsylvania   www.ybi.edu/

Director of Admissions Ms. Bonnie Gillespie, Director of Admissions, Yorktowne Business Institute, West Seventh Avenue, York, PA 17404. *Phone:* 717-846-5000 Ext. 124. *Toll-free phone:* 800-840-1004.

PUERTO RICO

CENTRO DE ESTUDIOS MULTIDISCIPLINARIOS
San Juan, Puerto Rico   www.cempr.edu/

Director of Admissions Admissions Department, Centro de Estudios Multidisciplinarios, Calle 13 #1206, Ext. San Agustin, San Juan, PR 00926.

COLEGIO UNIVERSITARIO DE SAN JUAN
San Juan, Puerto Rico

COLUMBIA COLLEGE
Yauco, Puerto Rico   **www.columbiaco.edu/**
Director of Admissions Admissions Department, Columbia College, Box 3062, Yauco, PR 00698.

HUERTAS JUNIOR COLLEGE
Caguas, Puerto Rico   **www.huertasjrcollege.org/**
Director of Admissions Mrs. Barbara Hassim, Director of Admissions, Huertas Junior College, PO Box 8429, Caguas, PR 00726. *Phone:* 787-743-1242. *Fax:* 787-743-0203. *E-mail:* huertas@huertas.org.

HUMACAO COMMUNITY COLLEGE
Humacao, Puerto Rico
Director of Admissions Ms. Paula Serrano, Director of Admissions, Humacao Community College, PO Box 9139, Humacao, PR 00792. *Phone:* 787-852-2525.

ICPR JUNIOR COLLEGE—HATO REY CAMPUS
San Juan, Puerto Rico

INSTITUTO COMERCIAL DE PUERTO RICO JUNIOR COLLEGE
San Juan, Puerto Rico   **www.icprjc.edu/**
- **Proprietary** 2-year, founded 1946
- **Urban** 1-acre campus
- **Coed**

Undergraduates 1,086 full-time, 184 part-time. 1% are from out of state, 100% Hispanic American.
Faculty *Student/faculty ratio:* 17:1.
Academics *Calendar:* trimesters. *Degree:* certificates, diplomas, and associate. *Special study options:* adult/continuing education programs, double majors, English as a second language, independent study, part-time degree program. *ROTC:* Army (c).
Student Life *Campus security:* 24-hour emergency response devices.
Costs (2005–06) *Comprehensive fee:* $7716 includes full-time tuition ($4680), mandatory fees ($180), and room and board ($2856). Part-time tuition: $130 per credit. *Room and board:* college room only: $1142.
Applying *Options:* common application, early admission. *Application fee:* $25. *Required:* high school transcript, interview, proficiency in Spanish. *Recommended:* letters of recommendation.
Freshmen Application Contact Admissions Office, Instituto Comercial de Puerto Rico Junior College, PO Box 190304, San Juan, PR 00919-0304. *Phone:* 787-753-6335.

INTERNATIONAL JUNIOR COLLEGE
Santurce, Puerto Rico   **www.internationaljuniorcollege.com/**
Director of Admissions Admissions Department, International Junior College, 1254 Avenue Ponce de Leon, pda. 18½, Santurce, PR 00908.

NATIONAL COLLEGE
Bayamon, Puerto Rico   **www.nationalcollegepr.edu/**
Director of Admissions Mr. Ricardo Nieves, Vice President of Financial Aid and Compliance, National College, PO Box 2036, Bayamon, PR 00960. *Phone:* 787-780-5134 Ext. 4114. *Toll-free phone:* 800-780-5188. *E-mail:* desil@nationalcollegepr.edu.

PUERTO RICO TECHNICAL JUNIOR COLLEGE
Mayaguez, Puerto Rico
Director of Admissions Admissions Department, Puerto Rico Technical Junior College, Calle Santiago R. Palmer #15 Est, Mayaguez, PR 00680.

PUERTO RICO TECHNICAL JUNIOR COLLEGE
San Juan, Puerto Rico
Director of Admissions Admissions Department, Puerto Rico Technical Junior College, 703 Ponce De Leon Avenue, Hato Rey, San Juan, PR 00917.

RAMÍREZ COLLEGE OF BUSINESS AND TECHNOLOGY
San Juan, Puerto Rico
Director of Admissions Eliecer Ayala, Director of Admissions, Ramírez College of Business and Technology, Avenue Ponce de Leon #70, San Juan, PR 00918. *Phone:* 787-763-3120.

TECHNOLOGICAL COLLEGE OF SAN JUAN
San Juan, Puerto Rico
Freshmen Application Contact Mrs. Nilsa E. Rivera-Almenas, Director of Enrollment Management, Technological College of San Juan, 180 Jose R. Oliver Street, Tres Monjitas Industrial Park, San Juan, PR 00918. *Phone:* 787-250-7111 Ext. 2271.

UNIVERSIDAD CENTRAL DEL CARIBE
Bayamón, Puerto Rico   **www.uccaribe.edu/**
Director of Admissions Admissions Department, Universidad Central del Caribe, PO Box 60-327, Bayamón, PR 00960-6032.

UNIVERSITY COLLEGE OF CRIMINAL JUSTICE OF PUERTO RICO
Gurabo, Puerto Rico
Director of Admissions Admissions Department, University College of Criminal Justice of Puerto Rico, HC 02 Box 12000, Gurabo, PR 00778-9601.

UNIVERSITY OF PUERTO RICO AT CAROLINA

Carolina, Puerto Rico   uprc.edu/

Director of Admissions Ms. Celia Mendez, Admissions Officer, University of Puerto Rico at Carolina, PO Box 4800, Carolina, PR 00984-4800. *Phone:* 787-757-1485.

RHODE ISLAND

COMMUNITY COLLEGE OF RHODE ISLAND

Warwick, Rhode Island   www.ccri.edu/

- **State-supported** 2-year, founded 1964
- **Suburban** 205-acre campus with easy access to Boston
- **Endowment** $1.2 million
- **Coed**

Undergraduates 5,731 full-time, 10,562 part-time. Students come from 17 states and territories, 14 other countries, 7% African American, 3% Asian American or Pacific Islander, 10% Hispanic American, 0.6% Native American, 0.1% international, 3% transferred in.

Academics *Calendar:* semesters. *Degree:* certificates and associate. *Special study options:* academic remediation for entering students, adult/continuing education programs, advanced placement credit, cooperative education, distance learning, double majors, English as a second language, external degree program, honors programs, independent study, internships, off-campus study, part-time degree program, services for LD students, study abroad, summer session for credit. *ROTC:* Army (c).

Student Life *Campus security:* 24-hour emergency response devices and patrols.

Athletics Member NJCAA.

Costs (2005–06) *Tuition:* state resident $2180 full-time, $102 per credit hour part-time; nonresident $6410 full-time, $307 per credit hour part-time. Part-time tuition and fees vary according to course load. *Required fees:* $290 full-time, $8 per credit hour part-time, $32 per term part-time.

Financial Aid Of all full-time matriculated undergraduates who enrolled in 2004, 500 Federal Work-Study jobs (averaging $2500). 70 state and other part-time jobs (averaging $2000).

Applying *Options:* deferred entrance. *Application fee:* $20.

Freshmen Application Contact Dr. Heather C. Smith, Dean, Community College of Rhode Island, 400 East Avenue, Warwick, RI 02886. *Phone:* 401-333-7302.

NEW ENGLAND INSTITUTE OF TECHNOLOGY

Warwick, Rhode Island   www.neit.edu/

Director of Admissions Mr. Michael Kwiatkowski, Director of Admissions, New England Institute of Technology, 2500 Post Road, Warwick, RI 02886-2266. *Phone:* 401-739-5000. *E-mail:* neit@ids.net.

SOUTH CAROLINA

AIKEN TECHNICAL COLLEGE

Aiken, South Carolina   www.aik.tec.sc.us/

- **State and locally supported** 2-year, founded 1972, part of South Carolina State Board for Technical and Comprehensive Education
- **Rural** 88-acre campus
- **Coed,** 2,516 undergraduate students, 56% full-time, 65% women, 35% men

Undergraduates 1,397 full-time, 1,119 part-time. Students come from 6 states and territories, 2 other countries, 10% are from out of state, 2% African American, 88% Asian American or Pacific Islander, 4% Hispanic American, 3% Native American, 1% transferred in.

Freshmen *Admission:* 1,177 applied, 765 admitted, 586 enrolled.

Faculty *Total:* 164, 34% full-time.

Majors Accounting; administrative assistant and secretarial science; biological and physical sciences; business administration and management; computer engineering technology; electrical, electronic and communications engineering technology; electromechanical technology; engineering technology; human services; industrial technology; interdisciplinary studies; liberal arts and sciences/liberal studies; machine tool technology; marketing/marketing management; nuclear/nuclear power technology; social work.

Academics *Calendar:* semesters. *Degree:* certificates, diplomas, and associate. *Special study options:* academic remediation for entering students, adult/continuing education programs, advanced placement credit, cooperative education, internships, off-campus study, part-time degree program, services for LD students, summer session for credit.

Library Aiken Technical College Library with 32,118 titles, 425 serial subscriptions, an OPAC.

Computers on Campus 200 computers available on campus for general student use. A campuswide network can be accessed. Internet access, at least one staffed computer lab available.

Student Life *Housing:* college housing not available. *Activities and Organizations:* student-run newspaper, student government, Phi Theta Kappa, student newspaper. *Campus security:* 24-hour patrols, late-night transport/escort service. *Student services:* personal/psychological counseling.

Athletics Member NJCAA. *Intercollegiate sports:* basketball M. *Intramural sports:* softball M/W.

Costs (2005–06) *Tuition:* area resident $2816 full-time, $117 per credit hour part-time; state resident $3176 full-time, $132 per credit hour part-time; nonresident $8204 full-time, $337 per credit hour part-time. *Required fees:* $120 full-time, $4 per credit hour part-time, $60 per term part-time.

Financial Aid Of all full-time matriculated undergraduates who enrolled in 2004, 48 Federal Work-Study jobs (averaging $3000).

Applying *Options:* common application, deferred entrance. *Required:* high school transcript. *Required for some:* essay or personal statement. *Application deadline:* rolling (freshmen), rolling (transfers).

Freshmen Application Contact Ms. Evelyn Pride Patterson, Director of Admissions and Records, Aiken Technical College, PO Drawer 696, Aiken, SC 29802-0696. *Phone:* 803-593-9231. *E-mail:* pridepae@atc.edu.

CENTRAL CAROLINA TECHNICAL COLLEGE

Sumter, South Carolina   www.cctech.edu/

- **State-supported** 2-year, founded 1963, part of South Carolina State Board for Technical and Comprehensive Education
- **Small-town** 70-acre campus
- **Coed,** 3,244 undergraduate students, 29% full-time, 70% women, 30% men

Undergraduates 945 full-time, 2,299 part-time. Students come from 2 states and territories, 1% are from out of state, 49% African American, 1% Asian American or Pacific Islander, 1% Hispanic American, 0.5% Native American, 0.2% international, 13% transferred in.

Freshmen *Admission:* 567 enrolled.

Faculty *Total:* 180, 46% full-time, 9% with terminal degrees. *Student/faculty ratio:* 19:1.

Majors Accounting; administrative assistant and secretarial science; business administration and management; child care and support services management; civil engineering technology; criminal justice/safety; data processing and data processing technology; environmental control technologies related; industrial electronics technology; legal assistant/paralegal; liberal arts and sciences/liberal studies; mechanical drafting and CAD/CADD; multi-/interdisciplinary studies related; natural resources management and policy; nursing (registered nurse training); sales, distribution and marketing; surgical technology.

Academics *Calendar:* semesters. *Degree:* certificates, diplomas, and associate. *Special study options:* academic remediation for entering students, adult/continuing education programs, advanced placement credit, cooperative education, distance learning, external degree program, independent study, internships, part-time degree program, summer session for credit.

Library Central Carolina Technical College Library with 20,356 titles, 245 serial subscriptions, 1,317 audiovisual materials, an OPAC, a Web page.

Computers on Campus 556 computers available on campus for general student use. A campuswide network can be accessed from off campus that provide access to student account and grade information. Internet access, online (class) registration, at least one staffed computer lab available.

Student Life *Housing:* college housing not available. *Activities and Organizations:* Creative Arts Society, Phi Theta Kappa, Computer Club, National Student Nurses Association (local chapter), Natural Resources Management Club. *Campus security:* 24-hour emergency response devices. *Student services:* personal/psychological counseling.

Costs (2006–07) *Tuition:* area resident $2700 full-time, $113 per credit hour part-time; state resident $3168 full-time, $133 per credit hour part-time; nonresident $4800 full-time, $200 per credit hour part-time.

Applying *Options:* electronic application. *Application fee:* $25. *Required:* high school transcript. *Application deadline:* rolling (freshmen), rolling (transfers).

Freshmen Application Contact Ms. Lisa M. Bracken, Director of Admissions and Counseling, Central Carolina Technical College, 506 North Guignard Drive, Sumter, SC 29150. *Phone:* 803-778-6652. *Toll-free phone:* 800-221-8711 Ext. 455. *Fax:* 803-778-6696. *E-mail:* brackenlm@cctech.edu.

CLINTON JUNIOR COLLEGE

Rock Hill, South Carolina **www.clintonjuniorcollege.edu/**

Director of Admissions Dr. Janis Pen, President, Clinton Junior College, PO Box 968, 1029 Crawford Road, Rock Hill, SC 29730. *Phone:* 803-327-7402. *Fax:* 803-327-3261. *E-mail:* ecopeland@clintonjrcollege.org.

DENMARK TECHNICAL COLLEGE

Denmark, South Carolina **www.denmarktech.edu/**

- **State-supported** 2-year, founded 1948, part of South Carolina State Board for Technical and Comprehensive Education
- **Rural** 53-acre campus
- **Coed,** 1,408 undergraduate students, 69% full-time, 60% women, 40% men

Undergraduates 969 full-time, 439 part-time. Students come from 8 states and territories, 76% African American, 0.2% Native American.
Freshmen *Admission:* 876 applied, 876 admitted, 498 enrolled.

Faculty *Total:* 47, 64% full-time, 17% with terminal degrees. *Student/faculty ratio:* 19:1.

Majors Administrative assistant and secretarial science; automobile/automotive mechanics technology; business administration and management; computer and information sciences; criminal justice/law enforcement administration; early childhood education; engineering technology; human services.

Academics *Calendar:* semesters. *Degree:* certificates, diplomas, and associate. *Special study options:* academic remediation for entering students, adult/continuing education programs, advanced placement credit, cooperative education, internships, off-campus study, part-time degree program, summer session for credit. *ROTC:* Army (c).

Library Denmark Technical College Learning Resources Center with 15,437 titles, 200 serial subscriptions.

Computers on Campus 105 computers available on campus for general student use. At least one staffed computer lab available.

Student Life *Housing Options:* Campus housing is university owned. *Activities and Organizations:* student-run newspaper, choral group, Phi Beta Lambda, Gospel Choir, Drama Club, national fraternities, national sororities. *Campus security:* 24-hour patrols. *Student services:* health clinic, personal/psychological counseling.

Athletics *Intercollegiate sports:* baseball M, basketball M/W, softball W. *Intramural sports:* basketball M/W, tennis M/W, volleyball M/W.

Standardized Tests *Required:* ACT ASSET (for admission).

Costs (2006–07) *Tuition:* state resident $2088 full-time, $87 per credit hour part-time; nonresident $4176 full-time, $174 per credit hour part-time. *Required fees:* $190 full-time, $95 per term part-time. *Room and board:* $3096.

Financial Aid Of all full-time matriculated undergraduates who enrolled in 2004, 250 Federal Work-Study jobs (averaging $2000).

Applying *Options:* early admission, deferred entrance. *Application fee:* $10. *Required:* high school transcript. *Application deadline:* rolling (freshmen), rolling (transfers).

Freshmen Application Contact Mrs. Michelle McDowell, Director of Admissions and Records, Denmark Technical College, Solomon Blatt Boulevard, Box 327, Denmark, SC 29042-0327. *Phone:* 803-793-5176. *Fax:* 803-793-5942.

FLORENCE-DARLINGTON TECHNICAL COLLEGE

Florence, South Carolina **www.fdtc.edu/**

Director of Admissions Mr. Kevin Qualls, Director of Enrollment Services, Florence-Darlington Technical College, 2715 West Lucas Street, PO Box 100548, Florence, SC 29501-0548. *Phone:* 843-661-8153. *Toll-free phone:* 800-228-5745. *E-mail:* kirvenp@flo.tec.sc.us.

FORREST JUNIOR COLLEGE

Anderson, South Carolina **www.forrestcollege.com/**

- **Proprietary** 2-year, founded 1946
- **Small-town** 3-acre campus
- **Coed, primarily women**

Undergraduates 114 full-time, 51 part-time. Students come from 2 states and territories, 26% are from out of state, 47% African American.

Faculty *Student/faculty ratio:* 16:1.

Academics *Calendar:* quarters. *Degree:* certificates, diplomas, and associate. *Special study options:* accelerated degree program, advanced placement credit, cooperative education, distance learning, double majors, English as a second language, freshman honors college, internships, part-time degree program, summer session for credit.

Student Life *Campus security:* late-night transport/escort service.

Costs (2005–06) *Tuition:* $4950 full-time, $110 per quarter hour part-time. Full-time tuition and fees vary according to course load and program. Part-time tuition and fees vary according to course load and program. *Required fees:* $450 full-time, $150 per term part-time.

Financial Aid Of all full-time matriculated undergraduates who enrolled in 2004, 18 Federal Work-Study jobs (averaging $700).

Applying *Options:* deferred entrance. *Application fee:* $25. *Required:* essay or personal statement, high school transcript, letters of recommendation, interview.

Director of Admissions Ms. Janie Turmon, Admissions Representative, Forrest Junior College, 601 East River Street, Anderson, SC 29624. *Phone:* 864-225-7653 Ext. 206.

GREENVILLE TECHNICAL COLLEGE

Greenville, South Carolina **www.greenvilletech.com/**

Director of Admissions Ms. Martha S. White, Director of Admissions, Greenville Technical College, PO Box 5616, Greenville, SC 29606-5616. *Phone:* 864-250-8109. *Toll-free phone:* 800-922-1183 (in-state); 800-723-0673 (out-of-state).

HORRY-GEORGETOWN TECHNICAL COLLEGE

Conway, South Carolina www.hgtc.edu/

- **State and locally supported** 2-year, founded 1966, part of South Carolina State Board for Technical and Comprehensive Education
- **Small-town** campus
- **Coed,** 5,362 undergraduate students, 46% full-time, 66% women, 34% men

Undergraduates 2,446 full-time, 2,916 part-time. Students come from 10 states and territories, 22 other countries, 11% are from out of state, 24% African American, 0.8% Asian American or Pacific Islander, 1% Hispanic American, 0.6% Native American, 2% international. *Retention:* 51% of 2003 full-time freshmen returned.
Freshmen *Admission:* 1,037 enrolled. *Average high school GPA:* 2.50.
Faculty *Total:* 404, 32% full-time. *Student/faculty ratio:* 16:1.
Majors Administrative assistant and secretarial science; agriculture; business administration and management; civil engineering technology; computer engineering technology; computer/information technology services administration related; computer programming (specific applications); criminal justice/law enforcement administration; culinary arts; data entry/microcomputer applications; electrical, electronic and communications engineering technology; forestry technology; heating, air conditioning, ventilation and refrigeration maintenance technology; hotel/motel administration; industrial radiologic technology; landscaping and groundskeeping; legal assistant/paralegal; machine tool technology; nursing (licensed practical/vocational nurse training); nursing (registered nurse training); parks, recreation and leisure facilities management; pre-engineering; web/multimedia management and webmaster; web page, digital/multimedia and information resources design; word processing.
Academics *Calendar:* semesters. *Degree:* certificates, diplomas, and associate. *Special study options:* academic remediation for entering students, adult/continuing education programs, advanced placement credit, cooperative education, internships, part-time degree program, services for LD students, summer session for credit.
Library Conway Campus Learning Resource Center plus 2 others with a Web page.
Computers on Campus 300 computers available on campus for general student use. A campuswide network can be accessed from off campus. Internet access, at least one staffed computer lab available.
Student Life *Housing:* college housing not available. *Student services:* personal/psychological counseling.
Costs (2006–07) *Tuition:* area resident $2800 full-time, $117 per credit hour part-time; state resident $3544 full-time, $148 per credit hour part-time; nonresident $4264 full-time, $178 per credit hour part-time. *Required fees:* $144 full-time, $1 per credit hour part-time, $35 per term part-time.
Applying *Options:* early admission. *Application fee:* $25. *Required for some:* high school transcript. *Application deadline:* rolling (freshmen), rolling (out-of-state freshmen), rolling (transfers). *Notification:* continuous (freshmen), continuous (out-of-state freshmen).
Freshmen Application Contact Mr. George Swindoll, Vice President for Enrollment Development and Registration, Horry-Georgetown Technical College, 2050 Highway 501 East, PO Box 261966, Conway, SC 29528-6066. *Phone:* 84-349-5277. *Fax:* 843-349-7501. *E-mail:* george.swindoll@hgtc.edu.

ITT TECHNICAL INSTITUTE

Greenville, South Carolina www.itt-tech.edu/

- **Proprietary** primarily 2-year, founded 1992, part of ITT Educational Services, Inc
- **Coed**

Majors Animation, interactive technology, video graphics and special effects; CAD/CADD drafting/design technology; computer and information systems security; computer programming; e-commerce; electrical, electronic and communications engineering technology; system, networking, and LAN/WAN management; web/multimedia management and webmaster; web page, digital/multimedia and information resources design.
Academics *Calendar:* quarters. *Degrees:* associate and bachelor's.
Library a Web page.
Computers on Campus Internet access, at least one staffed computer lab available.
Student Life *Housing:* college housing not available.
Standardized Tests *Required:* Wonderlic aptitude test (for admission).
Costs (2005–06) *Tuition:* Please see school catalog for specific information.

Financial Aid Of all full-time matriculated undergraduates who enrolled in 2004, 3 Federal Work-Study jobs.
Applying *Options:* deferred entrance. *Application fee:* $100. *Required:* high school transcript, interview. *Recommended:* letters of recommendation. *Application deadline:* rolling (freshmen), rolling (transfers). *Notification:* continuous (freshmen).
Freshmen Application Contact Mr. Joseph F. Fisher, Director of Recruitment, ITT Technical Institute, Independence Corporate Park, Six Independence Point, Greenville, SC 29615. *Phone:* 864-288-0777. *Toll-free phone:* 800-932-4488.

MIDLANDS TECHNICAL COLLEGE

Columbia, South Carolina www.midlandstech.edu/

- **State and locally supported** 2-year, founded 1974, part of South Carolina State Board for Technical and Comprehensive Education
- **Suburban** 113-acre campus
- **Endowment** $2.5 million
- **Coed,** 10,779 undergraduate students, 44% full-time, 63% women, 37% men

Undergraduates 4,743 full-time, 6,036 part-time. Students come from 33 states and territories, 5% are from out of state, 37% African American, 2% Asian American or Pacific Islander, 2% Hispanic American, 0.8% Native American, 0.4% international.
Freshmen *Admission:* 4,409 applied, 3,045 admitted, 2,189 enrolled.
Faculty *Total:* 631, 35% full-time. *Student/faculty ratio:* 21:1.
Majors Accounting; administrative assistant and secretarial science; architectural engineering technology; automobile/automotive mechanics technology; business administration and management; business/commerce; cartography; chemical technology; child care provision; civil engineering technology; clinical/medical laboratory technology; commercial and advertising art; computer and information sciences and support services related; computer installation and repair technology; computer systems networking and telecommunications; construction engineering technology; court reporting; criminal justice/safety; data processing and data processing technology; dental assisting; dental hygiene; electrical, electronic and communications engineering technology; engineering technology; fashion merchandising; gerontology; graphic and printing equipment operation/production; health information/medical records technology; health professions related; heating, air conditioning, ventilation and refrigeration maintenance technology; industrial electronics technology; industrial mechanics and maintenance technology; legal assistant/paralegal; liberal arts and sciences/liberal studies; mechanical drafting and CAD/CADD; mechanical engineering/mechanical technology; medical/clinical assistant; medical radiologic technology; multi-/interdisciplinary studies related; nuclear medical technology; nursing (licensed practical/vocational nurse training); nursing (registered nurse training); occupational therapist assistant; pharmacy technician; physical therapist assistant; precision production related; precision production trades; respiratory care therapy; sales, distribution and marketing; surgical technology; youth services.
Academics *Calendar:* semesters. *Degree:* certificates, diplomas, and associate. *Special study options:* academic remediation for entering students, adult/continuing education programs, advanced placement credit, cooperative education, distance learning, double majors, English as a second language, internships, part-time degree program, services for LD students, student-designed majors, summer session for credit.
Library 89,618 titles, 551 serial subscriptions, 1,036 audiovisual materials, an OPAC, a Web page.
Computers on Campus 125 computers available on campus for general student use. A campuswide network can be accessed from off campus. Internet access, online (class) registration, at least one staffed computer lab available.
Student Life *Housing:* college housing not available. *Activities and Organizations:* student-run newspaper. *Campus security:* 24-hour emergency response devices and patrols.
Athletics *Intramural sports:* basketball M, football M, softball M/W, volleyball M/W.
Standardized Tests *Required:* ACT ASSET (for admission). *Recommended:* SAT or ACT (for admission).
Costs (2005–06) *Tuition:* area resident $2904 full-time, $121 per credit part-time; state resident $3676 full-time, $157 per credit part-time; nonresident $8612 full-time, $363 per credit part-time. Full-time tuition and fees vary according to class time. Part-time tuition and fees vary according to class time. *Required fees:* $100 full-time, $50 per term part-time. *Waivers:* senior citizens and employees or children of employees.
Financial Aid Of all full-time matriculated undergraduates who enrolled in 2004, 138 Federal Work-Study jobs (averaging $2496).
Applying *Options:* common application, electronic application, early admission, deferred entrance. *Recommended:* high school transcript. *Application deadline:* rolling (freshmen), rolling (transfers). *Notification:* continuous (freshmen).

Freshmen Application Contact Ms. Sylvia Littlejohn, Director of Admissions, Midlands Technical College, PO Box 2408, Columbia, SC 29202. *Phone:* 803-738-8324. *Fax:* 803-790-7524. *E-mail:* admissions@midlandstech.edu.

MILLER-MOTTE TECHNICAL COLLEGE
Charleston, South Carolina   www.miller-motte.com/

Director of Admissions Ms. Julie Corner, Campus President, Miller-Motte Technical College, 8085 Rivers Avenue, Suite E, Charleston, SC 29418. *Phone:* 843-574-0101. *Toll-free phone:* 877-617-4740. *Fax:* 843-266-3424. *E-mail:* juliasc@miller-mott.net.

NORTHEASTERN TECHNICAL COLLEGE
Cheraw, South Carolina   www.netc.edu/

- **State and locally supported** 2-year, founded 1967, part of South Carolina State Board for Technical and Comprehensive Education
- **Rural** 59-acre campus
- **Endowment** $27,621
- **Coed**

Undergraduates Students come from 2 states and territories, 1% are from out of state, 46% African American, 0.4% Asian American or Pacific Islander, 0.4% Hispanic American, 2% Native American.
Faculty *Student/faculty ratio:* 25:1.
Academics *Calendar:* semesters. *Degree:* certificates, diplomas, and associate. *Special study options:* academic remediation for entering students, adult/continuing education programs, advanced placement credit, part-time degree program, summer session for credit.
Student Life *Campus security:* 24-hour emergency response devices.
Standardized Tests *Required for some:* SAT (for admission).
Costs (2005–06) *Tuition:* area resident $2496 full-time, $104 per semester hour part-time; state resident $2688 full-time, $112 per semester hour part-time; nonresident $4080 full-time, $170 per semester hour part-time. *Required fees:* $30 full-time, $4 per semester hour part-time.
Financial Aid Of all full-time matriculated undergraduates who enrolled in 2004, 25 Federal Work-Study jobs (averaging $2700).
Applying *Options:* early admission. *Application fee:* $13. *Required:* high school transcript, interview.
Director of Admissions Mrs. Mary K. Newton, Dean of Students, Northeastern Technical College, PO Drawer 1007, Cheraw, SC 29520-1007. *Phone:* 843-921-6935. *E-mail:* mnewton@netc.edu.

ORANGEBURG-CALHOUN TECHNICAL COLLEGE
Orangeburg, South Carolina   www.octech.edu/

Freshmen Application Contact Dana Rickards, Director of Recruitment, Orangeburg-Calhoun Technical College, 3250 St. Matthews Road, Highway 601, Orangeburg, SC 29118. *Phone:* 803-535-1219. *Toll-free phone:* 800-813-6519.

PIEDMONT TECHNICAL COLLEGE
Greenwood, South Carolina   www.ptc.edu/

Director of Admissions Mr. Steve Coleman, Director of Admissions, Piedmont Technical College, PO Box 1467, Emerald Road, Greenwood, SC 29648. *Phone:* 864-941-8603. *Toll-free phone:* 800-868-5528.

SPARTANBURG METHODIST COLLEGE
Spartanburg, South Carolina   www.smcsc.edu/

- **Independent Methodist** 2-year, founded 1911
- **Urban** 111-acre campus with easy access to Charlotte, NC
- **Endowment** $14.3 million
- **Coed,** 779 undergraduate students, 92% full-time, 51% women, 49% men

Undergraduates 716 full-time, 63 part-time. Students come from 9 states and territories, 6 other countries, 6% are from out of state, 32% African American,

0.8% Asian American or Pacific Islander, 2% Hispanic American, 0.3% Native American, 2% international, 4% transferred in, 75% live on campus. *Retention:* 59% of 2003 full-time freshmen returned.
Freshmen *Admission:* 999 applied, 836 admitted, 426 enrolled. *Average high school GPA:* 3.0. *Test scores:* SAT verbal scores over 500: 100%; ACT scores over 18: 37%; SAT verbal scores over 600: 100%; ACT scores over 24: 3%.
Faculty *Total:* 46, 50% full-time, 26% with terminal degrees. *Student/faculty ratio:* 23:1.
Majors Administrative assistant and secretarial science; criminal justice/law enforcement administration; information technology; liberal arts and sciences/liberal studies.
Academics *Calendar:* semesters. *Degree:* certificates, diplomas, and associate. *Special study options:* academic remediation for entering students, advanced placement credit, English as a second language, honors programs, independent study, part-time degree program, services for LD students, summer session for credit. *ROTC:* Army (c).
Library Marie Blair Burgess Learning Resource Center with 75,000 titles, 5,000 serial subscriptions, 3,150 audiovisual materials, an OPAC, a Web page.
Computers on Campus 48 computers available on campus for general student use. A campuswide network can be accessed from student residence rooms and from off campus. Internet access, at least one staffed computer lab available.
Student Life *Housing:* on-campus residence required through sophomore year. *Options:* coed, men-only, women-only. Campus housing is university owned. *Activities and Organizations:* drama/theater group, student-run newspaper, choral group, College Christian Movement, Alpha Phi Omega, Campus Union, Fellowship of Christian Athletes, Kappa Sigma Alpha. *Campus security:* 24-hour emergency response devices and patrols, student patrols, late-night transport/escort service, controlled dormitory access. *Student services:* health clinic, personal/psychological counseling.
Athletics Member NJCAA. *Intercollegiate sports:* baseball M(s), basketball M(s)/W(s), cheerleading M(s)/W(s), cross-country running M(s)/W(s), golf M(s)/W(s), soccer M(s)/W(s), softball W(s), tennis M(s)/W(s), volleyball W(s), wrestling M(s). *Intramural sports:* basketball M/W, football M/W, golf M/W, racquetball M/W, soccer M/W, softball M/W, table tennis M/W, tennis M/W, volleyball M/W.
Standardized Tests *Required:* SAT or ACT (for admission).
Costs (2005–06) *Comprehensive fee:* $15,476 includes full-time tuition ($9816), mandatory fees ($150), and room and board ($5510). Part-time tuition: $260 per credit. Part-time tuition and fees vary according to course load. *Room and board:* college room only: $2784. Room and board charges vary according to housing facility. *Payment plan:* installment. *Waivers:* employees or children of employees.
Financial Aid Of all full-time matriculated undergraduates who enrolled in 2004, 80 Federal Work-Study jobs (averaging $1600). 90 state and other part-time jobs (averaging $1600). *Financial aid deadline:* 8/30.
Applying *Options:* common application, electronic application, deferred entrance. *Application fee:* $20. *Required:* essay or personal statement, high school transcript, minimum 2.0 GPA, rank in upper 75% of high school class. *Required for some:* letters of recommendation, interview. *Recommended:* interview. *Application deadline:* rolling (freshmen), rolling (transfers). *Notification:* continuous (freshmen).
Freshmen Application Contact Daniel L. Philbeck, Vice President for Enrollment Management, Spartanburg Methodist College, 1000 Powell Mill Road, Spartanburg, SC 29301-5899. *Phone:* 864-587-4223. *Toll-free phone:* 800-772-7286. *Fax:* 864-587-4355. *E-mail:* admiss@smcsc.edu.

SPARTANBURG TECHNICAL COLLEGE
Spartanburg, South Carolina   www.stcsc.edu/

- **State-supported** 2-year, founded 1961, part of South Carolina State Board for Technical and Comprehensive Education
- **Suburban** 104-acre campus
- **Coed,** 4,409 undergraduate students, 55% full-time, 67% women, 33% men

Undergraduates 2,435 full-time, 1,974 part-time. 2% are from out of state, 27% African American, 3% Asian American or Pacific Islander, 2% Hispanic American, 0.2% Native American.
Faculty *Total:* 100.
Majors Accounting; administrative assistant and secretarial science; architectural engineering technology; automobile/automotive mechanics technology; biological and physical sciences; business administration and management; civil engineering technology; clinical/medical laboratory technology; computer and information sciences; drafting and design technology; electrical, electronic and communications engineering technology; engineering technology; heating, air conditioning, ventilation and refrigeration maintenance technology; horticultural science; liberal arts and sciences/liberal studies; machine tool technology; marketing/marketing management; mechanical engineering/mechanical technol-

Spartanburg Technical College (continued)

ogy; medical administrative assistant and medical secretary; medical radiologic technology; respiratory care therapy; robotics technology; sign language interpretation and translation; trade and industrial teacher education.

Academics *Calendar:* semesters plus summer sessions. *Degree:* certificates, diplomas, and associate. *Special study options:* academic remediation for entering students, adult/continuing education programs, advanced placement credit, cooperative education, distance learning, part-time degree program, services for LD students, summer session for credit.

Library Spartanburg Technical College Library with 36,173 titles, 295 serial subscriptions, 3,534 audiovisual materials, an OPAC, a Web page.

Computers on Campus 360 computers available on campus for general student use. A campuswide network can be accessed from off campus. At least one staffed computer lab available.

Student Life *Housing:* college housing not available. *Activities and Organizations:* drama/theater group, student-run newspaper. *Campus security:* 24-hour patrols. *Student services:* personal/psychological counseling, women's center.

Costs (2006–07) *Tuition:* area resident $3094 full-time, $127 per hour part-time; state resident $3860 full-time, $159 per hour part-time; nonresident $5490 full-time, $228 per hour part-time. *Required fees:* $20 full-time.

Financial Aid Of all full-time matriculated undergraduates who enrolled in 2004, 75 Federal Work-Study jobs (averaging $2500).

Applying *Options:* early admission. *Required:* high school transcript. *Application deadline:* rolling (freshmen), rolling (transfers). *Notification:* continuous (freshmen).

Freshmen Application Contact Admissions Office, Spartanburg Technical College, PO Box 4386, Spartanburg, SC 29305. *Phone:* 864-592-4800. *Toll-free phone:* 866-591-3700. *Fax:* 864-592-4564. *E-mail:* admissions@stcsc.edu.

TECHNICAL COLLEGE OF THE LOWCOUNTRY

Beaufort, South Carolina　　　　**www.tclonline.org/**

- **State-supported** 2-year, founded 1972, part of South Carolina Technical and Comprehensive Education System
- **Small-town** 12-acre campus
- **Coed**

Academics *Calendar:* semesters. *Degree:* certificates, diplomas, and associate. *Special study options:* academic remediation for entering students, adult/continuing education programs, advanced placement credit, internships, part-time degree program, student-designed majors, summer session for credit.

Student Life *Campus security:* security during class hours.

Standardized Tests *Required:* ACT ASSET (for admission). *Recommended:* SAT and SAT Subject Tests or ACT (for admission).

Financial Aid Of all full-time matriculated undergraduates who enrolled in 2004, 56 Federal Work-Study jobs (averaging $1700).

Applying *Options:* early admission, deferred entrance. *Application fee:* $10.

Director of Admissions Mr. Les Brediger, Director of Admissions, Technical College of the Lowcountry, 921 Ribaut Road, PO Box 1288, Beaufort, SC 29901-1288. *Phone:* 843-525-8307. *E-mail:* lbrediger@tcl.edu.

TRI-COUNTY TECHNICAL COLLEGE

Pendleton, South Carolina　　　　**www.tctc.edu/**

- **State-supported** 2-year, founded 1962, part of South Carolina State Board for Technical and Comprehensive Education
- **Rural** 100-acre campus
- **Coed**

Undergraduates Students come from 3 states and territories, 7 other countries, 11% African American, 0.8% Asian American or Pacific Islander, 0.8% Hispanic American, 0.3% Native American, 2% international.

Faculty *Student/faculty ratio:* 25:1.

Academics *Calendar:* semesters. *Degree:* certificates, diplomas, and associate. *Special study options:* academic remediation for entering students, adult/continuing education programs, advanced placement credit, cooperative education, English as a second language, internships, part-time degree program, summer session for credit. *ROTC:* Army (c), Air Force (c).

Student Life *Campus security:* 24-hour emergency response devices and patrols.

Standardized Tests *Required for some:* SAT (for placement), National League of Nursing Exam.

Applying *Options:* early admission. *Application fee:* $20.

Director of Admissions Ms. Rachel Campbell, Director, Admission and Counseling, Tri-County Technical College, PO Box 587, Highway 76, Pendleton, SC 29670-0587. *Phone:* 864-646-1500. *E-mail:* admstaff@tricty.tricounty.tec.sc.us.

TRIDENT TECHNICAL COLLEGE

Charleston, South Carolina　　　　**www.tridenttech.edu/**

- **State and locally supported** 2-year, founded 1964, part of South Carolina State Board for Technical and Comprehensive Education
- **Urban** campus
- **Coed,** 11,795 undergraduate students, 45% full-time, 63% women, 37% men

Undergraduates 5,270 full-time, 6,525 part-time. 1% are from out of state, 28% African American, 2% Asian American or Pacific Islander, 2% Hispanic American, 0.5% Native American.

Freshmen *Admission:* 2,094 enrolled.

Faculty *Total:* 637, 41% full-time, 7% with terminal degrees. *Student/faculty ratio:* 18:1.

Majors Accounting; administrative assistant and secretarial science; airframe mechanics and aircraft maintenance technology; automobile/automotive mechanics technology; biological and physical sciences; broadcast journalism; business administration and management; child care provision; civil engineering technology; clinical/medical laboratory technology; commercial and advertising art; computer engineering technology; computer graphics; computer/information technology services administration related; computer programming (specific applications); computer systems networking and telecommunications; criminal justice/law enforcement administration; culinary arts; dental hygiene; electrical, electronic and communications engineering technology; engineering technology; horticultural science; hotel/motel administration; human services; industrial technology; legal assistant/paralegal; legal studies; liberal arts and sciences/liberal studies; machine tool technology; marketing/marketing management; mechanical engineering/mechanical technology; medical administrative assistant and medical secretary; nursing (registered nurse training); occupational therapy; physical therapy; respiratory care therapy; telecommunications; veterinary technology; web/multimedia management and webmaster; web page, digital/multimedia and information resources design.

Academics *Calendar:* semesters. *Degree:* certificates, diplomas, and associate. *Special study options:* academic remediation for entering students, advanced placement credit, cooperative education, English as a second language, part-time degree program, services for LD students, summer session for credit.

Library Learning Resources Center plus 3 others with 68,462 titles, 868 serial subscriptions.

Computers on Campus 500 computers available on campus for general student use. A campuswide network can be accessed. At least one staffed computer lab available. Computer purchase or lease plan available.

Student Life *Housing:* college housing not available. *Activities and Organizations:* student-run newspaper. *Campus security:* 24-hour emergency response devices and patrols, late-night transport/escort service. *Student services:* personal/psychological counseling.

Costs (2005–06) *Tuition:* area resident $2950 full-time, $120 per credit hour part-time; state resident $3276 full-time, $134 per credit hour part-time; nonresident $5586 full-time, $230 per credit hour part-time. *Required fees:* $50 full-time, $5 per credit hour part-time.

Financial Aid Of all full-time matriculated undergraduates who enrolled in 2004, 117 Federal Work-Study jobs (averaging $3000).

Applying *Options:* common application, early admission. *Application fee:* $25. *Required for some:* high school transcript. *Application deadlines:* 8/4 (freshmen), 8/4 (transfers). *Notification:* continuous (freshmen).

Freshmen Application Contact Ms. Clara Martin, Admissions Director (Interim), Trident Technical College, 7000 Rivers Avenue, Charleston, SC 29423-8067. *Phone:* 843-574-6483. *Fax:* 843-574-6109.

UNIVERSITY OF SOUTH CAROLINA LANCASTER

Lancaster, South Carolina　　　　**usclancaster.sc.edu/**

Director of Admissions Ms. Rebecca D. Parker, Director of Admissions, University of South Carolina Lancaster, PO Box 889, Lancaster, SC 29721-0889. *Phone:* 803-313-7000. *E-mail:* bparker@gwm.sc.edu.

UNIVERSITY OF SOUTH CAROLINA SALKEHATCHIE

Allendale, South Carolina   uscsalkehatchie.sc.edu/

Director of Admissions Ms. Jane T. Brewer, Associate Dean for Student Services, University of South Carolina Salkehatchie, PO Box 617, Allendale, SC 29810-0617. *Phone:* 803-584-3446. *Toll-free phone:* 800-922-5500.

UNIVERSITY OF SOUTH CAROLINA SUMTER

Sumter, South Carolina   www.uscsumter.edu/

- **State-supported** 2-year, founded 1966, part of University of South Carolina System
- **Urban** 50-acre campus
- **Endowment** $1.8 million
- **Coed,** 1,020 undergraduate students, 57% full-time, 61% women, 39% men

Undergraduates 580 full-time, 440 part-time. Students come from 2 states and territories, 4 other countries, 1% are from out of state, 26% African American, 3% Asian American or Pacific Islander, 2% Hispanic American, 1% Native American, 0.1% international, 11% transferred in. *Retention:* 56% of 2003 full-time freshmen returned.
Freshmen *Admission:* 453 applied, 281 admitted, 216 enrolled. *Average high school GPA:* 3.24. *Test scores:* SAT verbal scores over 500: 31%; SAT math scores over 500: 31%; ACT scores over 18: 61%; SAT verbal scores over 600: 6%; SAT math scores over 600: 6%; ACT scores over 24: 4%.
Faculty *Total:* 75, 53% full-time, 57% with terminal degrees. *Student/faculty ratio:* 19:1.
Majors Interdisciplinary studies; liberal arts and sciences/liberal studies.
Academics *Calendar:* semesters. *Degree:* associate. *Special study options:* adult/continuing education programs, advanced placement credit, distance learning, honors programs, independent study, part-time degree program, services for LD students, summer session for credit. *ROTC:* Army (c), Air Force (c).
Library University of South Carolina at Sumter Library with 81,114 titles, 1,114 serial subscriptions, 913 audiovisual materials, an OPAC, a Web page.
Computers on Campus 355 computers available on campus for general student use. A campuswide network can be accessed from off campus that provide access to online course evaluation, online student surveys. Internet access, online (class) registration, at least one staffed computer lab available.
Student Life *Housing:* college housing not available. *Activities and Organizations:* drama/theater group, choral group, Association of African-American Students, Baptist Student Union, Student Education Association, Gamecock Ambassadors, Environmental Club. *Campus security:* late-night transport/escort service. *Student services:* personal/psychological counseling.
Athletics Member NSCAA. *Intramural sports:* badminton M/W, basketball M/W, bowling M/W, gymnastics M/W, racquetball M/W, rock climbing M/W, soccer M, softball M/W, table tennis M/W, volleyball M/W.
Standardized Tests *Required:* SAT or ACT (for admission).
Costs (2005–06) *Tuition:* state resident $4064 full-time, $169 per semester hour part-time; nonresident $10,124 full-time, $422 per semester hour part-time. Full-time tuition and fees vary according to degree level. *Required fees:* $260 full-time. *Waivers:* senior citizens.
Financial Aid Of all full-time matriculated undergraduates who enrolled in 2004, 49 Federal Work-Study jobs (averaging $1428).
Applying *Options:* common application, electronic application. *Application fee:* $40. *Required:* high school transcript, minimum 2.0 GPA. *Application deadline:* 8/8 (freshmen), rolling (transfers).
Freshmen Application Contact Keith Britton, Director of Admissions, University of South Carolina Sumter, 200 Miller Road, Sumter, SC 29150-2498. *Phone:* 803-938-3882. *Fax:* 803-938-3901. *E-mail:* kbritton@usc.sumter.edu.

UNIVERSITY OF SOUTH CAROLINA UNION

Union, South Carolina   uscunion.sc.edu/

- **State-supported** 2-year, founded 1965, part of University of South Carolina System
- **Small-town** campus with easy access to Charlotte
- **Coed,** 321 undergraduate students, 50% full-time, 69% women, 31% men

Undergraduates 161 full-time, 160 part-time. Students come from 2 states and territories, 1% are from out of state, 27% African American, 0.6% Asian American or Pacific Islander, 0.6% Hispanic American, 0.3% Native American, 12% transferred in.
Freshmen *Admission:* 127 applied, 113 admitted, 72 enrolled. *Test scores:* SAT verbal scores over 500: 15%; SAT math scores over 500: 18%.
Faculty *Total:* 25, 48% full-time. *Student/faculty ratio:* 14:1.
Majors Biological and physical sciences; liberal arts and sciences/liberal studies.
Academics *Calendar:* semesters. *Degree:* associate. *Special study options:* part-time degree program.
Computers on Campus 30 computers available on campus for general student use. A campuswide network can be accessed from off campus.
Student Life *Housing:* college housing not available. *Activities and Organizations:* drama/theater group, student-run newspaper, choral group.
Standardized Tests *Required:* SAT or ACT (for admission).
Costs (2005–06) *Tuition:* state resident $4064 full-time, $169 per credit hour part-time; nonresident $10,124 full-time, $422 per credit hour part-time. *Required fees:* $100 full-time, $10 per hour part-time.
Financial Aid Of all full-time matriculated undergraduates who enrolled in 2004, 16 Federal Work-Study jobs (averaging $3400).
Applying *Application fee:* $40. *Required:* high school transcript. *Application deadline:* rolling (freshmen).
Freshmen Application Contact Mr. Terry Young, Director of Enrollment Services, University of South Carolina Union, PO Drawer 729, Union, SC 29379-0729. *Phone:* 864-429-8728.

WILLIAMSBURG TECHNICAL COLLEGE

Kingstree, South Carolina   www.wiltech.edu/

Freshmen Application Contact Ms. Elaine M. Hanna, Director of Admissions, Williamsburg Technical College, 601 Martin Luther King Jr Avenue, Kingstree, SC 29556-4197. *Phone:* 843-355-4110 Ext. 4162. *Toll-free phone:* 800-768-2021 Ext. 4162.

YORK TECHNICAL COLLEGE

Rock Hill, South Carolina   www.yorktech.com/

- **State-supported** 2-year, founded 1961, part of South Carolina State Board for Technical and Comprehensive Education
- **Small-town** 110-acre campus with easy access to Charlotte
- **Coed,** 4,153 undergraduate students, 49% full-time, 64% women, 36% men

Undergraduates 2,039 full-time, 2,114 part-time. 2% are from out of state, 24% African American, 1% Asian American or Pacific Islander, 1% Hispanic American, 2% Native American.
Freshmen *Admission:* 786 enrolled.
Faculty *Total:* 238, 48% full-time.
Majors Accounting; administrative assistant and secretarial science; automobile/automotive mechanics technology; business administration and management; business/commerce; child care and support services management; child care provision; clinical/medical laboratory technology; commercial and advertising art; computer and information sciences and support services related; computer engineering technology; data processing and data processing technology; dental assisting; dental hygiene; electrical and electronic engineering technologies related; electrical, electronic and communications engineering technology; electrical/electronics equipment installation and repair; heating, air conditioning, ventilation and refrigeration maintenance technology; industrial electronics technology; industrial mechanics and maintenance technology; legal administrative assistant/secretary; liberal arts and sciences/liberal studies; machine tool technology; mechanical drafting and CAD/CADD; mechanical engineering/mechanical

York Technical College (continued)

technology; medical administrative assistant and medical secretary; medical/clinical assistant; medical radiologic technology; multi-/interdisciplinary studies related; nursing (licensed practical/vocational nurse training); nursing (registered nurse training); office occupations and clerical services; radio and television broadcasting technology; surgical technology; welding technology.

Academics *Calendar:* semesters. *Degree:* certificates, diplomas, and associate. *Special study options:* academic remediation for entering students, adult/continuing education programs, advanced placement credit, cooperative education, distance learning, English as a second language, honors programs, internships, off-campus study, part-time degree program, services for LD students, summer session for credit.

Library Anne Springs Close Library with 26,947 titles, 475 serial subscriptions, 1,813 audiovisual materials, an OPAC, a Web page.

Computers on Campus 250 computers available on campus for general student use. A campuswide network can be accessed from off campus that provide access to grades, course search, account detail, placement test scores. Internet access, online (class) registration, at least one staffed computer lab available.

Student Life *Housing:* college housing not available. *Activities and Organizations:* Jacobin Society, Phi Theta Kappa, Student Government Association, Phi Beta Lambda, Student Activities Board. *Campus security:* 24-hour patrols.

Standardized Tests *Required for some:* SAT, ACT, or ACT ASSET, ACT COMPASS.

Costs (2005–06) *Tuition:* area resident $2900 full-time, $121 per credit hour part-time; state resident $3264 full-time, $136 per credit hour part-time; nonresident $6528 full-time, $272 per credit hour part-time. *Required fees:* $136 full-time, $4 per credit hour part-time, $68 per term part-time.

Financial Aid Of all full-time matriculated undergraduates who enrolled in 2004, 56 Federal Work-Study jobs (averaging $3500).

Applying *Options:* electronic application. *Required for some:* high school transcript. *Application deadline:* rolling (freshmen), rolling (transfers). *Notification:* continuous (freshmen).

Freshmen Application Contact Mr. Kenny Aldridge, Admissions Department Manager, York Technical College, 452 South Anderson Road, Rock Hill, SC 29730. *Phone:* 803-327-8008. *Toll-free phone:* 800-922-8324. *Fax:* 803-981-7237. *E-mail:* kaldridge@yorktech.com.

SOUTH DAKOTA

KILIAN COMMUNITY COLLEGE
Sioux Falls, South Dakota   www.kilian.edu/

- **Independent** 2-year, founded 1977
- **Urban** 2-acre campus
- **Coed,** 538 undergraduate students, 20% full-time, 76% women, 24% men
- **100% of applicants were admitted**

Undergraduates 108 full-time, 430 part-time. Students come from 3 states and territories, 4% are from out of state, 3% African American, 0.2% Asian American or Pacific Islander, 3% Hispanic American, 4% Native American, 6% transferred in.

Freshmen *Admission:* 195 applied, 195 admitted, 78 enrolled.

Faculty *Total:* 82, 9% full-time, 7% with terminal degrees. *Student/faculty ratio:* 8:1.

Majors Accounting; administrative assistant and secretarial science; business administration and management; computer science; computer software and media applications related; counseling psychology; criminal justice/law enforcement administration; information technology; liberal arts and sciences/liberal studies; medical insurance coding; medical office management; medical transcription; social work.

Academics *Calendar:* trimesters. *Degree:* certificates and associate. *Special study options:* academic remediation for entering students, cooperative education, double majors, independent study, internships, part-time degree program, services for LD students, summer session for credit.

Library University of Sioux Falls Mears Library with 78,000 titles, 395 serial subscriptions, an OPAC, a Web page.

Computers on Campus 37 computers available on campus for general student use. A campuswide network can be accessed. Internet access, at least one staffed computer lab available.

Student Life *Housing:* college housing not available. *Campus security:* late-night transport/escort service. *Student services:* personal/psychological counseling.

Costs (2005–06) *Tuition:* $7020 full-time, $195 per credit hour part-time. *Required fees:* $150 full-time, $50 per term part-time.

Financial Aid Of all full-time matriculated undergraduates who enrolled in 2004, 31 Federal Work-Study jobs (averaging $1200).

Applying *Options:* early admission, deferred entrance. *Application fee:* $25. *Required:* high school transcript. *Application deadline:* rolling (freshmen), rolling (transfers).

Freshmen Application Contact Ms. Amy Modrell, Director of Admissions, Kilian Community College, 224 North Phillips Avenue, Sioux Falls, SD 57104-6014. *Phone:* 605-221-3100. *Toll-free phone:* 800-888-1147. *Fax:* 605-336-2606. *E-mail:* info@killian.edu.

LAKE AREA TECHNICAL INSTITUTE
Watertown, South Dakota   www.lati.tec.sd.us/

Director of Admissions Ms. Debra Shephard, Assistant Director, Lake Area Technical Institute, 230 11th Street Northeast, Watertown, SD 57201. *Phone:* 605-882-5284. *Toll-free phone:* 800-657-4344. *E-mail:* latiinfo@lati.tec.sd.us.

MITCHELL TECHNICAL INSTITUTE
Mitchell, South Dakota   mti.tec.sd.us/

Freshmen Application Contact Mr. Clayton Deuter, Admissions Representative, Mitchell Technical Institute, 821 North Capital, Mitchell, SD 57301. *Phone:* 605-995-3025. *Toll-free phone:* 800-952-0042.

NATIONAL AMERICAN UNIVERSITY
Ellsworth AFB, South Dakota

SISSETON-WAHPETON COMMUNITY COLLEGE
Sisseton, South Dakota   www.swc.tc/

- **Federally supported** 2-year, founded 1979
- **Rural** 2-acre campus
- **Endowment** $253,820
- **Coed**

Undergraduates 147 full-time, 127 part-time. Students come from 3 states and territories, 82% Native American, 5% transferred in.

Faculty *Student/faculty ratio:* 10:1.

Academics *Calendar:* semesters. *Degree:* certificates and associate. *Special study options:* academic remediation for entering students, adult/continuing education programs, cooperative education, double majors, internships, off-campus study, part-time degree program, summer session for credit.

Student Life *Campus security:* 24-hour emergency response devices.

Standardized Tests *Required:* Assessment and Placement Services for Community Colleges (for placement).

Costs (2005–06) *Tuition:* state resident $2880 full-time. No tuition increase for student's term of enrollment. *Required fees:* $490 full-time.

Financial Aid Of all full-time matriculated undergraduates who enrolled in 2004, 5 Federal Work-Study jobs (averaging $1200).

Applying *Options:* common application, deferred entrance. *Required:* high school transcript. *Recommended:* minimum 2.0 GPA, letters of recommendation, interview.

Director of Admissions Ms. Darlene Redday, Director of Admissions, Sisseton-Wahpeton Community College, Old Agency Box 689, Sisseton, SD 57262. *Phone:* 605-698-3966 Ext. 1110.

SOUTHEAST TECHNICAL INSTITUTE
Sioux Falls, South Dakota www.southeasttech.com/

- **State-supported** 2-year, founded 1968
- **Urban** 169-acre campus
- **Endowment** $238,427
- **Coed,** 2,320 undergraduate students

Undergraduates Students come from 7 states and territories, 1 other country, 20% are from out of state, 0.5% African American, 0.5% Asian American or Pacific Islander, 0.2% Hispanic American, 0.5% Native American, 1% live on campus. *Retention:* 83% of 2003 full-time freshmen returned. Freshmen *Admission:* 2,685 applied, 1,240 admitted. *Average high school GPA:* 2.70.

Faculty *Total:* 157, 53% full-time, 4% with terminal degrees. *Student/faculty ratio:* 19:1.

Majors Accounting; architectural engineering technology; artificial intelligence and robotics; autobody/collision and repair technology; automobile/automotive mechanics technology; biomedical technology; business administration and management; cardiovascular technology; civil engineering technology; clinical/medical laboratory technology; commercial and advertising art; computer and information sciences related; computer graphics; computer/information technology services administration related; computer programming; computer programming related; computer programming (specific applications); computer programming (vendor/product certification); computer software and media applications related; computer software engineering; computer systems networking and telecommunications; computer/technical support; computer technology/computer systems technology; diesel mechanics technology; drafting and design technology; electrical, electronic and communications engineering technology; electromechanical technology; engineering technology; finance; graphic and printing equipment operation/production; health unit coordinator/ward clerk; heating, air conditioning, ventilation and refrigeration maintenance technology; horticultural science; industrial technology; information science/studies; information technology; laser and optical technology; machine tool technology; marketing/marketing management; mechanical engineering/mechanical technology; medical transcription; nuclear medical technology; nursing related; sign language interpretation and translation; surgical technology; survey technology; system administration; turf and turfgrass management; web/multimedia management and webmaster; web page, digital/multimedia and information resources design.

Academics *Calendar:* semesters. *Degree:* certificates, diplomas, and associate. *Special study options:* academic remediation for entering students, accelerated degree program, advanced placement credit, double majors, independent study, internships, part-time degree program, services for LD students, summer session for credit.

Library Southeast Library with 10,643 titles, 158 serial subscriptions, 182 audiovisual materials, an OPAC.

Computers on Campus 400 computers available on campus for general student use. A campuswide network can be accessed from off campus. Internet access, at least one staffed computer lab available. Computer purchase or lease plan available.

Student Life *Housing Options:* coed. Campus housing is provided by a third party. *Activities and Organizations:* VICA, ICON, PBL, American Landscape Contractors Association, Silent Tones. *Campus security:* 24-hour emergency response devices and patrols. *Student services:* personal/psychological counseling.

Athletics *Intramural sports:* basketball M/W, volleyball M/W.

Standardized Tests *Recommended:* ACT (for admission).

Costs (2006–07) *Tuition:* state resident $2112 full-time, $66 per credit part-time; nonresident $66 per credit part-time. *Required fees:* $1408 full-time, $44 per credit part-time. *Room and board:* room only: $4200.

Financial Aid Of all full-time matriculated undergraduates who enrolled in 2004, 35 Federal Work-Study jobs (averaging $2550).

Applying *Required:* high school transcript, minimum 2.2 GPA. *Required for some:* interview. *Application deadline:* rolling (freshmen), rolling (transfers). *Notification:* continuous (freshmen).

Freshmen Application Contact Mr. Scott Dorman, Recruiter, Southeast Technical Institute, 2320 North Career Avenue, Sioux Falls, SD 57107. *Phone:* 605-367-7624. *Toll-free phone:* 800-247-0789. *Fax:* 605-367-8305. *E-mail:* scott.dorman@southeasttech.com.

WESTERN DAKOTA TECHNICAL INSTITUTE
Rapid City, South Dakota www.westerndakotatech.org/

Freshmen Application Contact Janell Oberlander, Director of Admissions, Western Dakota Technical Institute, 800 Mickelson Drive, Rapid City, SD 57703. *Phone:* 605-394-4034 Ext. 111. *Toll-free phone:* 800-544-8765.

TENNESSEE

AMERICAN ACADEMY OF NUTRITION, COLLEGE OF NUTRITION
Knoxville, Tennessee www.nutritioneducation.com/

Director of Admissions Ms. Jennifer Green, Faculty, American Academy of Nutrition, College of Nutrition, 1204-D Kenesaw Avenue, Knoxville, TN 37919. *Phone:* 865-524-8079. *Toll-free phone:* 800-290-4226. *E-mail:* aantn@aol.com.

CHATTANOOGA STATE TECHNICAL COMMUNITY COLLEGE
Chattanooga, Tennessee www.chattanoogastate.edu/

- **State-supported** 2-year, founded 1965, part of Tennessee Board of Regents
- **Urban** 100-acre campus
- **Coed,** 7,836 undergraduate students, 45% full-time, 62% women, 38% men

Undergraduates 3,533 full-time, 4,303 part-time. Students come from 5 states and territories, 8% are from out of state, 19% African American, 2% Asian American or Pacific Islander, 2% Hispanic American, 0.4% Native American, 23% transferred in. Freshmen *Admission:* 1,341 applied, 1,341 admitted, 1,269 enrolled. *Average high school GPA:* 2.63. *Test scores:* ACT scores over 18: 56%; ACT scores over 24: 7%.

Faculty *Total:* 626, 32% full-time. *Student/faculty ratio:* 22:1.

Majors Accounting; administrative assistant and secretarial science; advertising; airline pilot and flight crew; applied art; artificial intelligence and robotics; automobile/automotive mechanics technology; aviation/airway management; avionics maintenance technology; biology/biological sciences; broadcast journalism; business administration and management; chemical engineering; chemistry; child development; civil engineering technology; commercial and advertising art; computer engineering technology; computer programming; computer science; consumer merchandising/retailing management; criminal justice/law enforcement administration; data processing and data processing technology; dental hygiene; drafting and design technology; electrical, electronic and communications engineering technology; emergency medical technology (EMT paramedic); energy management and systems technology; engineering related; environmental engineering technology; finance; fire science; fish/game management; food services technology; forestry; forestry technology; graphic and printing equipment operation/production; health information/medical records administration; heating, air conditioning, ventilation and refrigeration maintenance technology; hotel/motel administration; industrial radiologic technology; information science/studies; instrumentation technology; kindergarten/preschool education; legal administrative assistant/secretary; liberal arts and sciences/liberal studies; machine tool technology; mass communication/media; mechanical design technology; mechanical engineering/mechanical technology; medical administrative assistant and medical secretary; nuclear medical technology; nuclear/nuclear power technology; nursing (registered nurse training); occupational therapy; physical therapy; radio and television; respiratory care therapy; sign language interpretation and translation; survey technology; transportation technology; welding technology; wildlife and wildlands science and management.

Academics *Calendar:* semesters. *Degree:* certificates, diplomas, and associate. *Special study options:* academic remediation for entering students, acceler-

Chattanooga State Technical Community College (continued)
ated degree program, adult/continuing education programs, advanced placement credit, cooperative education, distance learning, English as a second language, honors programs, independent study, internships, part-time degree program, services for LD students, summer session for credit.
Library Augusta R. Kolwyck Library with 73,334 titles, 803 serial subscriptions, an OPAC, a Web page.
Computers on Campus 500 computers available on campus for general student use. A campuswide network can be accessed from off campus. Internet access, at least one staffed computer lab available.
Student Life *Housing:* college housing not available. *Activities and Organizations:* student-run newspaper, radio station, choral group, Black Student Association, Adult Connections, Human Services Specialists, Student Government Association, Student Nurses Association. *Campus security:* 24-hour emergency response devices and patrols, late-night transport/escort service. *Student services:* personal/psychological counseling, women's center.
Athletics Member NJCAA. *Intercollegiate sports:* baseball M(s), basketball M(s)/W(s), softball W(s). *Intramural sports:* softball W.
Costs (2005–06) *Tuition:* state resident $2142 full-time, $91 per semester hour part-time; nonresident $8556 full-time, $369 per semester hour part-time.
Financial Aid Of all full-time matriculated undergraduates who enrolled in 2004, 377 Federal Work-Study jobs (averaging $652).
Applying *Options:* early admission, deferred entrance. *Application fee:* $15. *Required:* high school transcript. *Application deadline:* rolling (freshmen), rolling (transfers). *Notification:* continuous (freshmen).
Freshmen Application Contact Ms. Diane Norris, Director of Admissions, Chattanooga State Technical Community College, 4501 Amnicola Highway, Chattanooga, TN 37406-1097. *Phone:* 423-697-4401 Ext. 3107. *Fax:* 423-697-4709. *E-mail:* admsis@chattanoogastate.edu.

CLEVELAND STATE COMMUNITY COLLEGE

Cleveland, Tennessee **www.clevelandstatecc.edu/**

- **State-supported** 2-year, founded 1967, part of Tennessee Board of Regents
- **Small-town** 105-acre campus
- **Endowment** $4.5 million
- **Coed,** 3,027 undergraduate students, 52% full-time, 61% women, 39% men

Undergraduates 1,586 full-time, 1,441 part-time. Students come from 9 states and territories, 1% are from out of state, 5% African American, 1% Asian American or Pacific Islander, 2% Hispanic American, 0.6% Native American, 5% transferred in.
Freshmen *Admission:* 920 applied, 558 admitted, 557 enrolled. *Average high school GPA:* 2.8.
Faculty *Total:* 190, 38% full-time, 16% with terminal degrees. *Student/faculty ratio:* 29:1.
Majors Administrative assistant and secretarial science; business administration and management; child development; community organization and advocacy; general studies; industrial arts; industrial technology; kindergarten/preschool education; liberal arts and sciences/liberal studies; nursing (registered nurse training); public administration and social service professions related.
Academics *Calendar:* semesters. *Degree:* certificates and associate. *Special study options:* academic remediation for entering students, adult/continuing education programs, advanced placement credit, cooperative education, distance learning, double majors, English as a second language, external degree program, honors programs, independent study, internships, off-campus study, part-time degree program, services for LD students, summer session for credit.
Library Cleveland State Community College Library with 65,347 titles, 368 serial subscriptions, 10,116 audiovisual materials, an OPAC, a Web page.
Computers on Campus 450 computers available on campus for general student use. A campuswide network can be accessed from off campus. Internet access, online (class) registration, at least one staffed computer lab available.
Student Life *Housing:* college housing not available. *Activities and Organizations:* student-run newspaper, choral group, Student Senate, International Association of Administration Professionals, Phi Theta Kappa, Student Nursing Association. *Campus security:* 24-hour emergency response devices and patrols, late-night transport/escort service. *Student services:* personal/psychological counseling.
Athletics Member NJCAA. *Intercollegiate sports:* baseball M(s), basketball M(s)/W(s), softball W(s). *Intramural sports:* archery M/W, badminton M/W, basketball M/W, bowling M/W, golf M/W, softball M/W, table tennis M/W, tennis M/W, volleyball M/W.
Costs (2005–06) *Tuition:* state resident $2142 full-time, $91 per credit hour part-time; nonresident $8556 full-time, $369 per credit hour part-time. Full-time

tuition and fees vary according to course load. *Required fees:* $263 full-time, $28 per credit hour part-time. *Payment plan:* deferred payment. *Waivers:* senior citizens and employees or children of employees.
Financial Aid Of all full-time matriculated undergraduates who enrolled in 2004, 52 Federal Work-Study jobs (averaging $1025).
Applying *Options:* early admission, deferred entrance. *Application fee:* $10. *Required:* high school transcript. *Application deadline:* rolling (freshmen), rolling (transfers). *Notification:* continuous (freshmen).
Freshmen Application Contact Ms. Midge Burnette, Director of Admissions and Recruitment, Cleveland State Community College, 3535 Adkisson Drive, Cleveland, TN 37320-3570. *Phone:* 423-478-6212. *Toll-free phone:* 800-604-2722. *Fax:* 423-478-6255. *E-mail:* mburnette@clevelandstatecc.edu.

COLUMBIA STATE COMMUNITY COLLEGE

Columbia, Tennessee **www.columbiastate.edu/**

- **State-supported** 2-year, founded 1966
- **Small-town** 179-acre campus with easy access to Nashville
- **Endowment** $707,627
- **Coed**

Undergraduates 2,423 full-time, 2,190 part-time. Students come from 6 states and territories, 2 other countries, 8% African American, 0.7% Asian American or Pacific Islander, 2% Hispanic American, 0.4% Native American, 0.1% international, 10% transferred in. *Retention:* 61% of 2003 full-time freshmen returned.
Academics *Calendar:* semesters. *Degree:* certificates and associate. *Special study options:* academic remediation for entering students, adult/continuing education programs, advanced placement credit, double majors, honors programs, part-time degree program, services for LD students, summer session for credit.
Student Life *Campus security:* 24-hour patrols.
Athletics Member NJCAA.
Standardized Tests *Required for some:* SAT or ACT (for placement).
Financial Aid Of all full-time matriculated undergraduates who enrolled in 2004, 50 Federal Work-Study jobs (averaging $1250).
Applying *Options:* early admission. *Application fee:* $10. *Required:* high school transcript.
Freshmen Application Contact Mr. Joey Scruggs, Coordinator of Recruitment, Columbia State Community College, PO Box 1315, Columbia, TN 38402-1315. *Phone:* 931-540-2540. *E-mail:* scruggs@coscc.cc.tn.us.

CONCORDE CAREER COLLEGE

Memphis, Tennessee

DRAUGHONS JUNIOR COLLEGE

Clarksville, Tennessee **www.draughons.edu/**
Director of Admissions Admissions Office, Draughons Junior College, 1860 Wilma Rudolph Boulevard, Clarksville, TN 37040.

DRAUGHONS JUNIOR COLLEGE

Nashville, Tennessee **www.draughons.edu/**
Director of Admissions Admissions Office, Draughons Junior College, 340 Plus Park, Nashville, TN 37217. *Phone:* 615-361-7555. *Fax:* 615-367-2736.

DYERSBURG STATE COMMUNITY COLLEGE

Dyersburg, Tennessee   **www.dscc.edu/**

- **State-supported** 2-year, founded 1969, part of Tennessee Board of Regents
- **Small-town** 100-acre campus with easy access to Memphis
- **Endowment** $3.2 million
- **Coed,** 2,457 undergraduate students, 58% full-time, 71% women, 29% men

Undergraduates 1,428 full-time, 1,029 part-time. Students come from 5 states and territories, 1% are from out of state, 20% African American, 0.5% Asian American or Pacific Islander, 1% Hispanic American, 0.5% Native American, 7% transferred in. *Retention:* 44% of 2003 full-time freshmen returned.
Freshmen *Admission:* 953 applied, 947 admitted, 585 enrolled. *Average high school GPA:* 2.58. *Test scores:* ACT scores over 18: 55%; ACT scores over 24: 5%.
Faculty *Total:* 205, 28% full-time, 13% with terminal degrees. *Student/faculty ratio:* 24:1.
Majors Business administration and management; child development; computer/information technology services administration related; criminal justice/police science; electrical, electronic and communications engineering technology; health information/medical records technology; liberal arts and sciences/liberal studies; nursing (registered nurse training).
Academics *Calendar:* semesters. *Degree:* certificates and associate. *Special study options:* academic remediation for entering students, adult/continuing education programs, advanced placement credit, distance learning, double majors, honors programs, independent study, part-time degree program, services for LD students, summer session for credit.
Library Learning Resource Center with 44,033 titles, 85 serial subscriptions, 2,231 audiovisual materials, an OPAC, a Web page.
Computers on Campus 501 computers available on campus for general student use. A campuswide network can be accessed from off campus. At least one staffed computer lab available.
Student Life *Housing:* college housing not available. *Activities and Organizations:* drama/theater group, choral group, student government, Phi Theta Kappa, Minority Association for Successful Students, Video Club, Psychology Club. *Campus security:* 24-hour patrols. *Student services:* personal/psychological counseling.
Athletics Member NJCAA. *Intercollegiate sports:* baseball M(s), basketball M(s)/W(s), cheerleading W(s), softball W(s).
Costs (2005–06) *Tuition:* state resident $2142 full-time, $91 per hour part-time; nonresident $8556 full-time, $369 per hour part-time. Part-time tuition and fees vary according to course load. *Required fees:* $251 full-time. *Payment plan:* deferred payment. *Waivers:* senior citizens and employees or children of employees.
Financial Aid Of all full-time matriculated undergraduates who enrolled in 2004, 84 Federal Work-Study jobs (averaging $997). 115 state and other part-time jobs (averaging $837).
Applying *Options:* common application, early admission. *Application fee:* $10. *Required:* high school transcript. *Application deadline:* rolling (freshmen), rolling (transfers). *Notification:* continuous (freshmen).
Freshmen Application Contact Mr. Dan Gullett, Assistant Vice President for Academic Affairs, Dyersburg State Community College, 1510 Lake Road, Dyersburg, TN 38024. *Phone:* 731-286-3327. *Fax:* 731-286-3325. *E-mail:* gulett@dscc.edu.

ELECTRONIC COMPUTER PROGRAMMING COLLEGE

Chattanooga, Tennessee   **www.ecpconline.com/**

Director of Admissions Toney McFadden, Admission Director, Electronic Computer Programming College, 3805 Brainerd Road, Chattanooga, TN 37411-3798. *Phone:* 423-624-0077. *Fax:* 423-624-1575.

FOUNTAINHEAD COLLEGE OF TECHNOLOGY

Knoxville, Tennessee   **www.fountainheadcollege.edu/**

- **Proprietary** primarily 2-year, founded 1947
- **Suburban** 1-acre campus
- **Coed,** 120 undergraduate students

Undergraduates Students come from 1 other state.
Faculty *Total:* 10, 90% full-time, 100% with terminal degrees. *Student/faculty ratio:* 13:1.
Majors Communications technology; computer and information systems security; computer engineering technology; electrical, electronic and communications engineering technology; industrial technology; information science/studies.
Academics *Calendar:* semesters. *Degrees:* associate and bachelor's. *Special study options:* summer session for credit.
Library 1,200 titles, 1,000 serial subscriptions, a Web page.
Computers on Campus 15 computers available on campus for general student use. A campuswide network can be accessed from off campus. Internet access, at least one staffed computer lab available.
Student Life *Housing:* college housing not available. *Campus security:* 24-hour emergency response devices.
Applying *Application fee:* $100. *Recommended:* high school transcript. *Application deadline:* rolling (freshmen), rolling (transfers). *Notification:* continuous (freshmen).
Freshmen Application Contact Mr. Todd Hill, Director of Administration, Fountainhead College of Technology, 3203 Tazewell Pike, Knoxville, TN 37918-2530. *Phone:* 865-688-9422. *Toll-free phone:* 888-218-7335. *Fax:* 865-688-2419.

HIGH-TECH INSTITUTE
Memphis, Tennessee

HIGH-TECH INSTITUTE

Nashville, Tennessee   **www.high-techinstitute.com/**

Director of Admissions Mr. David Martinez, College Director, High-Tech Institute, 2710 Old Lebanon Road, Suite 12, Nashville, TN 37214. *Phone:* 615-902-9705. *Toll-free phone:* 800-987-0110. *Fax:* 615-902-9766. *E-mail:* dmartinez@hightechschools.com.

ITT TECHNICAL INSTITUTE

Knoxville, Tennessee   **www.itt-tech.edu/**

- **Proprietary** primarily 2-year, founded 1988, part of ITT Educational Services, Inc
- **Suburban** 5-acre campus
- **Coed**

Majors Accounting and business/management; animation, interactive technology, video graphics and special effects; business administration and management; CAD/CADD drafting/design technology; computer and information systems security; computer programming; computer software technology; computer systems networking and telecommunications; criminal justice/law enforcement administration; e-commerce; electrical, electronic and communications engineering technology; system, networking, and LAN/WAN management; web/multimedia management and webmaster; web page, digital/multimedia and information resources design.
Academics *Calendar:* quarters. *Degrees:* associate and bachelor's.
Library a Web page.
Computers on Campus Internet access, at least one staffed computer lab available.
Student Life *Housing:* college housing not available.
Standardized Tests *Required:* Wonderlic aptitude test (for admission).
Costs (2005–06) *Tuition:* Please see school catalog for specific information.

ITT Technical Institute (continued)

Applying *Options:* deferred entrance. *Application fee:* $100. *Required:* high school transcript, interview. *Recommended:* letters of recommendation. *Application deadline:* rolling (freshmen), rolling (transfers). *Notification:* continuous (freshmen).

Freshmen Application Contact Ms. Holly L. Winters, Director of Recruitment, ITT Technical Institute, 10208 Technology Drive, Knoxville, TN 37932. *Phone:* 865-671-2800. *Toll-free phone:* 800-671-2801.

ITT TECHNICAL INSTITUTE

Memphis, Tennessee   www.itt-tech.edu/

- **Proprietary** primarily 2-year, founded 1994, part of ITT Educational Services, Inc
- **Suburban** 1-acre campus
- **Coed**

Majors Accounting and business/management; animation, interactive technology, video graphics and special effects; business administration and management; CAD/CADD drafting/design technology; computer and information systems security; computer programming; computer systems networking and telecommunications; criminal justice/law enforcement administration; e-commerce; electrical, electronic and communications engineering technology; system, networking, and LAN/WAN management; web page, digital/multimedia and information resources design.

Academics *Calendar:* quarters. *Degrees:* associate and bachelor's.

Library a Web page.

Computers on Campus Internet access, at least one staffed computer lab available.

Student Life *Housing:* college housing not available. *Activities and Organizations:* student-run newspaper.

Standardized Tests *Required:* Wonderlic aptitude test (for admission).

Costs (2005–06) *Tuition:* Please see school catalog for specific information.

Applying *Options:* deferred entrance. *Application fee:* $100. *Required:* high school transcript, interview. *Recommended:* letters of recommendation. *Application deadline:* rolling (freshmen), rolling (transfers). *Notification:* continuous (freshmen).

Freshmen Application Contact Mr. Mark Glennon, Director of Recruitment, ITT Technical Institute, 7260 Goodlett Farms Parkway, Cordova, TN 38016. *Phone:* 901-381-0200. *Toll-free phone:* 866-444-5141.

ITT TECHNICAL INSTITUTE

Nashville, Tennessee   www.itt-tech.edu/

- **Proprietary** primarily 2-year, founded 1984, part of ITT Educational Services, Inc
- **Urban** 21-acre campus
- **Coed**

Majors Accounting and business/management; animation, interactive technology, video graphics and special effects; business administration and management; CAD/CADD drafting/design technology; computer and information systems security; computer programming; computer software technology; computer systems networking and telecommunications; criminal justice/law enforcement administration; e-commerce; electrical, electronic and communications engineering technology; system, networking, and LAN/WAN management; web/multimedia management and webmaster; web page, digital/multimedia and information resources design.

Academics *Calendar:* quarters. *Degrees:* associate and bachelor's.

Library a Web page.

Computers on Campus Internet access, at least one staffed computer lab available.

Student Life *Housing:* college housing not available.

Standardized Tests *Required:* Wonderlic aptitude test (for admission).

Costs (2005–06) *Tuition:* Please see school catalog for specific information.

Applying *Options:* deferred entrance. *Application fee:* $100. *Required:* high school transcript, interview. *Recommended:* letters of recommendation. *Application deadline:* rolling (freshmen), rolling (transfers). *Notification:* continuous (freshmen).

Freshmen Application Contact Mr. Glenn Wallace, Director of Recruitment, ITT Technical Institute, 2845 Elm Hill Pike, Nashville, TN 37214. *Phone:* 615-889-8700. *Toll-free phone:* 800-331-8386.

JACKSON STATE COMMUNITY COLLEGE

Jackson, Tennessee   www.jscc.edu/

- **State-supported** 2-year, founded 1967, part of Tennessee Board of Regents
- **Small-town** 104-acre campus
- **Endowment** $672,925
- **Coed,** 3,866 undergraduate students, 53% full-time, 65% women, 35% men

Undergraduates 2,048 full-time, 1,818 part-time. Students come from 9 states and territories, 0.2% are from out of state, 18% African American, 0.4% Asian American or Pacific Islander, 1% Hispanic American, 0.2% Native American, 0.1% international, 18% transferred in. *Retention:* 56% of 2003 full-time freshmen returned.

Freshmen *Admission:* 1,273 applied, 1,069 admitted, 732 enrolled. *Average high school GPA:* 2.72.

Faculty *Total:* 216, 56% full-time, 10% with terminal degrees. *Student/faculty ratio:* 22:1.

Majors Agricultural business and management; business administration and management; child development; clinical/medical laboratory technology; commercial and advertising art; computer science; electromechanical technology; industrial technology; liberal arts and sciences/liberal studies; management information systems; medical radiologic technology; nursing (registered nurse training); physical therapist assistant; respiratory care therapy; tool and die technology.

Academics *Calendar:* semesters. *Degree:* certificates and associate. *Special study options:* academic remediation for entering students, adult/continuing education programs, advanced placement credit, cooperative education, distance learning, honors programs, internships, part-time degree program, summer session for credit.

Library Jackson State Community College Library with 63,620 titles, 225 serial subscriptions, 2,000 audiovisual materials, an OPAC, a Web page.

Computers on Campus 725 computers available on campus for general student use. A campuswide network can be accessed from off campus. Internet access, online (class) registration, at least one staffed computer lab available. Computer purchase or lease plan available.

Student Life *Housing:* college housing not available. *Activities and Organizations:* drama/theater group, choral group, Student Government Organization, Spanish Club, Biology Club, Art Club, Black Student Association. *Campus security:* 24-hour patrols. *Student services:* health clinic, personal/psychological counseling.

Athletics Member NJCAA. *Intercollegiate sports:* baseball M(s), basketball M(s)/W(s), cheerleading W(s), softball W(s). *Intramural sports:* basketball M/W, football M, golf M, tennis M/W, volleyball W.

Standardized Tests *Required:* ACT (for admission), COMPASS (for admission).

Costs (2005–06) *Tuition:* state resident $2142 full-time, $91 per credit hour part-time; nonresident $8556 full-time, $369 per credit hour part-time. *Required fees:* $253 full-time, $9 per credit hour part-time, $14 per term part-time.

Financial Aid Of all full-time matriculated undergraduates who enrolled in 2004, 60 Federal Work-Study jobs (averaging $3000). 10 state and other part-time jobs (averaging $3000).

Applying *Options:* electronic application, early admission, deferred entrance. *Application fee:* $10. *Required for some:* high school transcript. *Application deadline:* 8/29 (freshmen), rolling (transfers). *Notification:* continuous (freshmen).

Freshmen Application Contact Ms. Monica Ray, Director of Admissions and Records, Jackson State Community College, 2046 North Parkway, Jackson, TN 38301. *Phone:* 731-425-2644. *Toll-free phone:* 800-355-5722. *Fax:* 731-425-9559. *E-mail:* mray@jscc.edu.

JOHN A. GUPTON COLLEGE

Nashville, Tennessee   www.guptoncollege.edu/

Director of Admissions Ms. Lisa Bolin, Registrar, John A. Gupton College, 1616 Church Street, Nashville, TN 37203. *Phone:* 615-327-3927.

MEDVANCE INSTITUTE

Cookeville, Tennessee   www.medvance.org/

Director of Admissions Ms. Sharon Mellott, Director of Admissions, MedVance Institute, 1065 East 10th Street, Cookeville, TN 38501-1907. *Phone:* 931-526-3660. *Toll-free phone:* 800-259-3659 (in-state); 800-256-9085 (out-of-state).

MID-AMERICA BAPTIST THEOLOGICAL SEMINARY

Germantown, Tennessee   **www.mabts.edu/**

- **Independent Southern Baptist** founded 1972
- **Suburban** campus with easy access to Memphis
- **Endowment** $3.6 million
- **Coed, primarily men,** 62 undergraduate students, 60% full-time, 100% men

Undergraduates 37 full-time, 25 part-time. Students come from 26 states and territories, 5% African American.

Faculty *Total:* 27, 100% full-time. *Student/faculty ratio:* 15:1.

Majors Theology.

Academics *Calendar:* semesters. *Degrees:* associate, master's, doctoral, and first professional. *Special study options:* summer session for credit.

Library Ora Byram Allison Memorial Library with 119,000 titles, 931 serial subscriptions, an OPAC, a Web page.

Computers on Campus 10 computers available on campus for general student use. Internet access, at least one staffed computer lab available.

Student Life *Housing Options:* Campus housing is university owned. *Campus security:* 24-hour emergency response devices.

Costs (2006–07) *Tuition:* $3600 full-time.

Applying *Options:* common application. *Application fee:* $25. *Required:* 2 letters of recommendation. *Required for some:* high school transcript. *Application deadline:* 8/4 (freshmen).

Freshmen Application Contact Ms. Duffy Guyton, Admissions Counselor, Mid-America Baptist Theological Seminary, 2216 Germantown Road South, Germantown, TN 38138. *Phone:* 901-751-8453 Ext. 3066. *Fax:* 901-751-8454. *E-mail:* info@mabts.edu.

MILLER-MOTTE TECHNICAL COLLEGE

Clarksville, Tennessee   **www.miller-motte.com/**

Director of Admissions Ms. Lisa Teague, Director of Admissions, Miller-Motte Technical College, 1820 Business Park Drive, Clarksville, TN 37040. *Phone:* 800-558-0071. *E-mail:* lisateague@hotmail.com.

MOTLOW STATE COMMUNITY COLLEGE

Tullahoma, Tennessee   **www.mscc.cc.tn.us/**

- **State-supported** 2-year, founded 1969, part of Tennessee Board of Regents
- **Small-town** 187-acre campus with easy access to Nashville
- **Endowment** $3.2 million
- **Coed,** 3,407 undergraduate students, 59% full-time, 64% women, 36% men

Undergraduates 2,015 full-time, 1,392 part-time. Students come from 11 states and territories, 8 other countries, 1% are from out of state, 8% African American, 1% Asian American or Pacific Islander, 2% Hispanic American, 0.3% Native American, 0.4% international, 7% transferred in.

Freshmen *Admission:* 1,239 applied, 956 enrolled. *Average high school GPA:* 2.80. *Test scores:* SAT verbal scores over 500: 45%; SAT math scores over 500: 50%; ACT scores over 18: 64%; SAT verbal scores over 600: 5%; SAT math scores over 600: 15%; ACT scores over 24: 8%.

Faculty *Total:* 207, 36% full-time. *Student/faculty ratio:* 16:1.

Majors Business administration and management; liberal arts and sciences/liberal studies; nursing (registered nurse training); special education (early childhood).

Academics *Calendar:* semesters. *Degree:* certificates and associate. *Special study options:* academic remediation for entering students, adult/continuing education programs, advanced placement credit, cooperative education, distance learning, double majors, honors programs, independent study, part-time degree program, services for LD students, summer session for credit.

Library Crouch Library with 54,968 titles, 211 serial subscriptions, 4,464 audiovisual materials, an OPAC, a Web page.

Computers on Campus 600 computers available on campus for general student use. A campuswide network can be accessed from off campus that provide access to e-mail. Internet access, online (class) registration, at least one staffed computer lab available.

Student Life *Housing:* college housing not available. *Activities and Organizations:* drama/theater group, student-run newspaper, choral group, Photography Club, Psychology Club, Student Government Association, Outing Club, Baptist Student Union. *Campus security:* 24-hour patrols, late-night transport/escort service. *Student services:* health clinic, personal/psychological counseling.

Athletics Member NJCAA. *Intercollegiate sports:* baseball M(s), basketball M(s)/W(s), softball W(s). *Intramural sports:* archery M/W, badminton M/W, basketball M/W, bowling M/W, golf M/W, tennis M/W, volleyball M/W.

Costs (2005–06) *Tuition:* state resident $2142 full-time, $91 per credit part-time; nonresident $6414 full-time, $278 per credit part-time. Full-time tuition and fees vary according to program. Part-time tuition and fees vary according to course load and program. *Required fees:* $247 full-time, $40 per credit part-time. *Payment plans:* installment, deferred payment. *Waivers:* senior citizens and employees or children of employees.

Financial Aid Of all full-time matriculated undergraduates who enrolled in 2004, 66 Federal Work-Study jobs (averaging $1285).

Applying *Options:* electronic application, early admission, deferred entrance. *Application fee:* $10. *Required:* high school transcript. *Application deadlines:* 8/13 (freshmen), 8/13 (out-of-state freshmen), rolling (transfers). *Notification:* continuous (freshmen).

Freshmen Application Contact Laura Monks, Assistant Director of Student Services, Motlow State Community College, PO Box 8500, Lynchburg, TN 37352. *Phone:* 931-393-1764. *Toll-free phone:* 800-654-4877. *Fax:* 931-393-1681. *E-mail:* lmonks@mscc.edu.

NASHVILLE AUTO DIESEL COLLEGE

Nashville, Tennessee   **www.nadcedu.com/**

- **Proprietary** 2-year, founded 1919
- **Urban** 13-acre campus
- **Coed, primarily men,** 1,306 undergraduate students, 100% full-time, 0% women, 100% men

Undergraduates 1,306 full-time. Students come from 50 states and territories, 83% are from out of state, 30% African American, 0.8% Asian American or Pacific Islander, 0.8% Hispanic American, 1% Native American, 21% live on campus.

Freshmen *Admission:* 2,924 applied, 2,602 admitted, 95 enrolled. *Average high school GPA:* 2.3.

Faculty *Total:* 77, 95% full-time. *Student/faculty ratio:* 30:1.

Majors Autobody/collision and repair technology; automobile/automotive mechanics technology; diesel mechanics technology.

Academics *Calendar:* continuous. *Degree:* diplomas and associate. *Special study options:* advanced placement credit, cooperative education, honors programs.

Library NADC Library with 1,309 titles, 69 serial subscriptions.

Computers on Campus 40 computers available on campus for general student use. A campuswide network can be accessed. Internet access, at least one staffed computer lab available.

Student Life *Housing Options:* men-only. Campus housing is university owned. *Campus security:* 24-hour emergency response devices and patrols.

Standardized Tests *Recommended:* SAT or ACT (for admission).

Costs (2005–06) *Tuition:* $20,500 full-time. *Required fees:* $100 full-time.

Applying *Options:* deferred entrance. *Application fee:* $100. *Required:* high school transcript. *Required for some:* interview. *Application deadline:* rolling (freshmen).

Freshmen Application Contact Ms. Peggie Werrbach, Director of Admissions, Nashville Auto Diesel College, 1524 Gallatin Road, Nashville, TN 37206. *Phone:* 615-226-3990 Ext. 8465. *Toll-free phone:* 800-228-NADC. *Fax:* 615-262-8466. *E-mail:* wpruitt@nadcedu.com.

NASHVILLE STATE TECHNICAL COMMUNITY COLLEGE

Nashville, Tennessee   **www.nscc.edu/**

- **State-supported** 2-year, founded 1970, part of Tennessee Board of Regents
- **Urban** 85-acre campus
- **Coed**

Undergraduates 2,421 full-time, 4,600 part-time. Students come from 36 states and territories, 55 other countries, 2% are from out of state, 26% African American, 4% Asian American or Pacific Islander, 2% Hispanic American, 0.4% Native American, 3% international, 3% transferred in.

Nashville State Technical Community College (continued)

Academics *Calendar:* semesters. *Degree:* certificates and associate. *Special study options:* academic remediation for entering students, adult/continuing education programs, advanced placement credit, cooperative education, distance learning, English as a second language, off-campus study, part-time degree program, services for LD students, summer session for credit.

Student Life *Campus security:* 24-hour emergency response devices and patrols, late-night transport/escort service.

Standardized Tests *Required for some:* SAT or ACT (for placement).

Costs (2005–06) *Tuition:* state resident $2367 full-time, $91 per credit hour part-time; nonresident $8781 full-time, $369 per credit hour part-time. Part-time tuition and fees vary according to course load. *Required fees:* $235 full-time, $10 per credit hour part-time, $5 per term part-time.

Financial Aid Of all full-time matriculated undergraduates who enrolled in 2004, 66 Federal Work-Study jobs (averaging $806). 97 state and other part-time jobs (averaging $917).

Applying *Options:* electronic application, deferred entrance. *Application fee:* $5. *Required:* high school transcript.

Freshmen Application Contact Ms. Laura Potter, Coordinator of Recruitment, Nashville State Technical Community College, 120 White Bridge Road, Nashville, TN 37209. *Phone:* 615-353-3265. *Toll-free phone:* 800-272-7363.

NATIONAL COLLEGE OF BUSINESS & TECHNOLOGY

Bristol, Tennessee   www.ncbt.edu/

- **Proprietary** 2-year, founded 1992, part of National College of Business and Technology
- **Small-town** campus
- **Coed**

Faculty *Student/faculty ratio:* 12:1.

Academics *Calendar:* quarters. *Degree:* diplomas and associate. *Special study options:* advanced placement credit, double majors, honors programs, internships, part-time degree program, services for LD students, summer session for credit.

Costs (2005–06) *Tuition:* $6408 full-time, $178 per credit hour part-time. *Required fees:* $75 full-time, $15 per term part-time.

Financial Aid Of all full-time matriculated undergraduates who enrolled in 2004, 3 Federal Work-Study jobs.

Applying *Options:* electronic application. *Application fee:* $30. *Required:* high school transcript. *Recommended:* interview.

Director of Admissions Ms. Angela Carrier, Campus Director, National College of Business & Technology, 300 A Piedmont Avenue, Bristol, VA 24201. *Phone:* 423-878-4440. *E-mail:* adm@educorp.edu.

NATIONAL COLLEGE OF BUSINESS & TECHNOLOGY

Knoxville, Tennessee   www.ncbt.edu/

Director of Admissions Mr. Andy W. Wills, Director, National College of Business & Technology, 8415 Kingston Pike, Knoxville, TN 37919. *Phone:* 865-539-2011. *Toll-free phone:* 800-664-1886. *Fax:* 865-539-2049. *E-mail:* awills@ncbt.edu.

NATIONAL COLLEGE OF BUSINESS & TECHNOLOGY

Nashville, Tennessee   www.ncbt.edu/

- **Proprietary** 2-year, founded 1915, part of National College of Business and Technology
- **Urban** 1-acre campus
- **Coed**

Faculty *Student/faculty ratio:* 10:1.

Academics *Calendar:* quarters. *Degree:* diplomas and associate. *Special study options:* double majors, honors programs, part-time degree program, services for LD students, summer session for credit.

Costs (2005–06) *Tuition:* $6408 full-time, $178 per credit hour part-time. *Required fees:* $75 full-time, $15 per term part-time.

Financial Aid Of all full-time matriculated undergraduates who enrolled in 2004, 3 Federal Work-Study jobs.

Applying *Options:* electronic application. *Application fee:* $30. *Recommended:* interview.

Director of Admissions Mr. Robert Leonard, Campus Director, National College of Business & Technology, 3748 Nolensville Pike, Nashville, TN 37211. *Phone:* 615-333-3344. *Toll-free phone:* 800-664-1886.

NORTH CENTRAL INSTITUTE

Clarksville, Tennessee   www.nci.edu/

- **Proprietary** 2-year, founded 1988
- **Suburban** 14-acre campus
- **Coed, primarily men,** 130 undergraduate students, 40% full-time, 11% women, 89% men

Undergraduates 52 full-time, 78 part-time. Students come from 50 states and territories, 90% are from out of state, 24% African American, 3% Asian American or Pacific Islander, 10% Hispanic American, 7% Native American.

Freshmen *Admission:* 25 applied, 25 admitted, 25 enrolled. *Average high school GPA:* 3.1.

Faculty *Total:* 17, 35% full-time. *Student/faculty ratio:* 8:1.

Majors Aircraft powerplant technology; airframe mechanics and aircraft maintenance technology.

Academics *Calendar:* continuous. *Degree:* associate. *Special study options:* advanced placement credit, external degree program, independent study, part-time degree program, summer session for credit.

Library Media Resource Center plus 1 other with 200 titles, 12 serial subscriptions, 20 audiovisual materials.

Student Life *Housing:* college housing not available. *Activities and Organizations:* Alpha Eta Rho (aviation fraternity), national fraternities. *Campus security:* 24-hour emergency response devices.

Costs (2006–07) *Tuition:* $14,800 full-time, $60 per semester hour part-time. *Required fees:* $800 full-time.

Applying *Options:* common application, electronic application, early admission. *Application fee:* $35. *Required:* proof of high school. *Recommended:* high school transcript. *Application deadline:* rolling (freshmen). *Notification:* continuous (freshmen).

Freshmen Application Contact Mrs. Sheri Nash-Kutch, Dean of Student Services, North Central Institute, 168 Jack Miller Boulevard, Clarksville, TN 37042. *Phone:* 931-431-9700 Ext. 247. *Fax:* 931-431-9771. *E-mail:* admissions@nci.edu.

NORTHEAST STATE TECHNICAL COMMUNITY COLLEGE

Blountville, Tennessee   www.northeaststate.edu/

- **State-supported** 2-year, founded 1966, part of Tennessee Board of Regents
- **Small-town** 100-acre campus
- **Endowment** $3.5 million
- **Coed,** 4,860 undergraduate students, 54% full-time, 53% women, 47% men

Undergraduates 2,610 full-time, 2,250 part-time. Students come from 3 states and territories, 3% are from out of state, 3% African American, 0.8% Asian American or Pacific Islander, 1% Hispanic American, 0.3% Native American, 5% transferred in. *Retention:* 58% of 2003 full-time freshmen returned.

Freshmen *Admission:* 2,878 applied, 2,878 admitted, 921 enrolled. *Average high school GPA:* 2.51. *Test scores:* ACT scores over 18: 57%; ACT scores over 24: 8%; ACT scores over 30: 1%.

Faculty *Total:* 243, 41% full-time, 12% with terminal degrees. *Student/faculty ratio:* 22:1.

Majors Accounting; administrative assistant and secretarial science; automobile/automotive mechanics technology; business administration and management; cardiovascular technology; chemistry; computer programming; computer programming related; computer systems networking and telecommunications; data processing and data processing technology; drafting and design technology; early childhood education; electrical, electronic and communications engineering technology; emergency medical technology (EMT paramedic); engineering technology; general studies; industrial technology; information technology; instrumentation technology; kindergarten/preschool education; liberal arts and sciences/liberal studies; machine tool technology; medical/clinical assistant; surgical technology; welding technology.

Academics *Calendar:* semesters. *Degree:* certificates and associate. *Special study options:* academic remediation for entering students, advanced placement credit, cooperative education, distance learning, double majors, honors programs, part-time degree program, services for LD students, summer session for credit.

Library Wayne G. Basler Library plus 1 other with 44,997 titles, 438 serial subscriptions, 8,591 audiovisual materials, an OPAC, a Web page.

Computers on Campus 910 computers available on campus for general student use. A campuswide network can be accessed from off campus that provide access to WebCT, online transcripts. Internet access, online (class) registration, at least one staffed computer lab available.

Student Life *Housing:* college housing not available. *Activities and Organizations:* drama/theater group, student-run radio and television station, Phi Theta Kappa, Student Government Association, Student Tennessee Education Association, Students in Free Enterprise, Student Ambassadors. *Campus security:* 24-hour patrols, late-night transport/escort service. *Student services:* health clinic, personal/psychological counseling.

Athletics *Intramural sports:* basketball M/W, golf M/W, volleyball M/W.

Costs (2005–06) *Tuition:* state resident $2404 full-time, $91 per hour part-time; nonresident $6414 full-time, $278 per hour part-time. *Required fees:* $262 full-time, $12 per hour part-time, $18 per term part-time.

Financial Aid Of all full-time matriculated undergraduates who enrolled in 2004, 109 Federal Work-Study jobs (averaging $1318). 35 state and other part-time jobs.

Applying *Options:* electronic application. *Application fee:* $10. *Required:* high school transcript, minimum 2.0 GPA. *Application deadline:* rolling (freshmen), rolling (transfers). *Notification:* continuous (freshmen).

Freshmen Application Contact Dr. Jon P. Harr, Dean of Admissions and Records, Northeast State Technical Community College, PO Box 246, Blountville, TN 37617. *Phone:* 423-323-0231. *Toll-free phone:* 800-836-7822. *Fax:* 423-323-0215. *E-mail:* jpharr@nstcc.edu.

NOSSI COLLEGE OF ART

Goodlettsville, Tennessee www.nossi.com/

Freshmen Application Contact Ms. Mary Alexander, Admissions Director, Nossi College of Art, 907 Rivergate Parkway, Goodlettsville, TN 37072. *Phone:* 615-851-1088. *E-mail:* admissions@nossi.com.

PELLISSIPPI STATE TECHNICAL COMMUNITY COLLEGE

Knoxville, Tennessee www.pstcc.edu/

- **State-supported** 2-year, founded 1974, part of Tennessee Board of Regents
- **Suburban** 144-acre campus
- **Endowment** $2.8 million
- **Coed,** 7,686 undergraduate students, 51% full-time, 54% women, 46% men

Undergraduates 3,882 full-time, 3,804 part-time. Students come from 23 states and territories, 7% African American, 2% Asian American or Pacific Islander, 2% Hispanic American, 0.5% Native American, 0.6% international. Freshmen *Admission:* 1,388 enrolled. *Average high school GPA:* 2.50. *Test scores:* ACT scores over 18: 68%; ACT scores over 24: 13%; ACT scores over 30: 1%.

Faculty *Total:* 412, 41% full-time. *Student/faculty ratio:* 21:1.

Majors Accounting; accounting technology and bookkeeping; administrative assistant and secretarial science; automobile/automotive mechanics technology; business administration and management; business machine repair; chemical engineering; chemical technology; cinematography and film/video production; civil engineering technology; commercial and advertising art; computer and information sciences; computer and information sciences related; computer engineering technology; computer graphics; computer programming; computer science; computer software and media applications related; computer systems networking and telecommunications; construction engineering technology; data entry/microcomputer applications; data entry/microcomputer applications related; data processing and data processing technology; drafting and design technology; electrical, electronic and communications engineering technology; environmental engineering technology; finance; geography; hospitality administration; hotel/motel administration; industrial arts; industrial technology; interior design; legal administrative assistant/secretary; legal assistant/paralegal; liberal arts and

sciences/liberal studies; machine tool technology; marketing/marketing management; mechanical engineering/mechanical technology.

Academics *Calendar:* semesters. *Degree:* certificates and associate. *Special study options:* academic remediation for entering students, adult/continuing education programs, advanced placement credit, cooperative education, distance learning, double majors, English as a second language, freshman honors college, honors programs, internships, part-time degree program, services for LD students, student-designed majors, summer session for credit.

Library Educational Resources Center plus 1 other with 43,000 titles, 527 serial subscriptions, an OPAC, a Web page.

Computers on Campus 1200 computers available on campus for general student use. A campuswide network can be accessed from off campus. Internet access, online (class) registration, at least one staffed computer lab available.

Student Life *Housing:* college housing not available. *Activities and Organizations:* drama/theater group, student-run newspaper, choral group, Student Government Association, Active Black Students Association, Phi Theta Kappa, Baptist Student Union, Vision. *Campus security:* 24-hour patrols. *Student services:* personal/psychological counseling.

Athletics *Intramural sports:* basketball M/W, golf M/W, soccer M/W, softball M/W, tennis M/W, volleyball M/W.

Costs (2005–06) *Tuition:* $100 per credit hour part-time; state resident $1227 full-time; nonresident $4563 full-time, $397 per credit hour part-time. *Required fees:* $2500 full-time.

Applying *Options:* common application, electronic application, early admission, deferred entrance. *Application fee:* $5. *Required:* high school transcript. *Application deadline:* rolling (freshmen), rolling (transfers). *Notification:* continuous (freshmen).

Freshmen Application Contact Ms. Leigh Touzeau, Director of Admissions and Records, Pellissippi State Technical Community College, PO Box 22990, Knoxville, TN 37933-0990. *Phone:* 865-694-6681. *E-mail:* latouzeau@pstcc.cc.tn.us.

REMINGTON COLLEGE—MEMPHIS CAMPUS

Memphis, Tennessee www.remingtoncollege.edu/

Director of Admissions Dr. Lori May, Campus President, Remington College–Memphis Campus, 2731 Nonconnah Boulevard, Memphis, TN 38132-2131. *Phone:* 901-291-4225. *Fax:* 901-396-8310. *E-mail:* lori.may@remingtoncollege.edu.

REMINGTON COLLEGE—NASHVILLE CAMPUS

Nashville, Tennessee www.remingtoncollege.edu/

Director of Admissions Mr. Frank Vivelo, Campus President, Remington College–Nashville Campus, 441 Donnelson Pike, Suite 150, Nashville, TN 37214. *Phone:* 615-889-5520. *Fax:* 615-889-5528. *E-mail:* frank.vivelo@remingtoncollege.edu.

ROANE STATE COMMUNITY COLLEGE

Harriman, Tennessee www.roanestate.edu/

- **State-supported** 2-year, founded 1971, part of Tennessee Board of Regents
- **Rural** 104-acre campus with easy access to Knoxville
- **Endowment** $18,123
- **Coed,** 5,155 undergraduate students, 56% full-time, 68% women, 32% men

Undergraduates 2,873 full-time, 2,282 part-time. Students come from 6 states and territories, 5 other countries, 1% are from out of state, 2% African American, 1% Asian American or Pacific Islander, 0.6% Hispanic American, 0.3% Native American, 0.3% international, 5% transferred in. *Retention:* 57% of 2003 full-time freshmen returned.

Freshmen *Admission:* 2,240 applied, 2,240 admitted, 977 enrolled. *Average high school GPA:* 2.96. *Test scores:* ACT scores over 18: 70%; ACT scores over 24: 11%.

Faculty *Total:* 357, 36% full-time. *Student/faculty ratio:* 17:1.

Majors Accounting; administrative assistant and secretarial science; art; art teacher education; biology/biological sciences; business administration and man-

Roane State Community College (continued)

agement; business teacher education; chemistry; clinical/medical laboratory technology; computer engineering technology; computer science; corrections; criminal justice/law enforcement administration; criminal justice/police science; dental hygiene; early childhood education; education; elementary education; emergency medical technology (EMT paramedic); engineering; environmental health; general studies; health information/medical records administration; industrial radiologic technology; information technology; kindergarten/preschool education; laser and optical technology; legal administrative assistant/secretary; liberal arts and sciences/liberal studies; mathematics; medical administrative assistant and medical secretary; music teacher education; nursing (registered nurse training); occupational therapy; pharmacy technician; physical education teaching and coaching; physical sciences; physical therapy; pre-engineering; respiratory care therapy; social sciences; technology/industrial arts teacher education.

Academics *Calendar:* semesters. *Degree:* certificates and associate. *Special study options:* academic remediation for entering students, accelerated degree program, adult/continuing education programs, advanced placement credit, cooperative education, distance learning, double majors, external degree program, freshman honors college, honors programs, independent study, internships, off-campus study, part-time degree program, services for LD students, summer session for credit. *ROTC:* Army (c), Air Force (c).

Library Roane State Community College Library plus 1 other with 66,024 titles, 595 serial subscriptions, 8,808 audiovisual materials, an OPAC, a Web page.

Computers on Campus 750 computers available on campus for general student use. A campuswide network can be accessed. Internet access, online (class) registration, at least one staffed computer lab available.

Student Life *Housing:* college housing not available. *Activities and Organizations:* drama/theater group, student-run newspaper, choral group, Baptist Student Union, American Chemical Society, Physical Therapy Student Association, Student Artists At Roane State (S.T.A.R.S.), Phi Theta Kappa. *Campus security:* 24-hour patrols. *Student services:* health clinic, personal/psychological counseling.

Athletics Member NJCAA. *Intercollegiate sports:* baseball M(s), basketball M(s)/W(s), cheerleading W(s), softball W(s). *Intramural sports:* basketball M/W, football M, golf M, soccer M, softball M/W, volleyball M/W, weight lifting M.

Costs (2005–06) *Tuition:* state resident $1952 full-time, $83 per semester hour part-time; nonresident $7798 full-time, $346 per semester hour part-time. Full-time tuition and fees vary according to course load and program. Part-time tuition and fees vary according to program. *Required fees:* $265 full-time, $15 per semester hour part-time. *Payment plan:* deferred payment. *Waivers:* senior citizens and employees or children of employees.

Financial Aid Of all full-time matriculated undergraduates who enrolled in 2004, 150 Federal Work-Study jobs (averaging $3000).

Applying *Options:* common application, electronic application, early admission, deferred entrance. *Application fee:* $10. *Required:* high school transcript. *Application deadline:* rolling (freshmen), rolling (transfers). *Notification:* continuous (freshmen).

Freshmen Application Contact Ms. Brenda Rector, Director of Records and Registration, Roane State Community College, 276 Patton Lane, Harriman, TN 37748. *Phone:* 865-882-4526. *Toll-free phone:* 800-343-9104. *Fax:* 865-882-4562. *E-mail:* rectorbw@roanestate.edu.

SOUTH COLLEGE

Knoxville, Tennessee   www.southcollegetn.edu/

Director of Admissions Mr. Walter Hosea, Director of Admissions, South College, 720 North Fifth Avenue, Knoxville, TN 37917. *Phone:* 865-524-3043 Ext. 1825.

SOUTHEASTERN CAREER COLLEGE
Nashville, Tennessee

SOUTHWEST TENNESSEE COMMUNITY COLLEGE

Memphis, Tennessee   www.southwest.tn.edu/

- **State-supported** 2-year, part of Tennessee Board of Regents
- **Urban** 100-acre campus
- **Endowment** $641,526
- **Coed,** 11,556 undergraduate students, 49% full-time, 65% women, 35% men

Undergraduates 5,656 full-time, 5,900 part-time. Students come from 14 states and territories, 2% are from out of state, 59% African American, 1% Asian American or Pacific Islander, 2% Hispanic American, 0.7% Native American, 0.6% international, 4% transferred in.

Freshmen *Admission:* 1,901 applied, 1,901 admitted, 1,901 enrolled. *Average high school GPA:* 2.22. *Test scores:* ACT scores over 18: 38%; ACT scores over 24: 3%.

Faculty *Total:* 566, 45% full-time.

Majors Accounting; administrative assistant and secretarial science; applied horticulture/horticultural business services related; architectural engineering technology; automobile/automotive mechanics technology; biomedical technology; business administration and management; business/commerce; cartography; clinical/medical laboratory technology; commercial and advertising art; computer engineering technology; court reporting; criminal justice/safety; dietitian assistant; electrical, electronic and communications engineering technology; electrical/electronics equipment installation and repair; fire science; general studies; health professions related; heavy equipment maintenance technology; industrial arts; industrial technology; information technology; kindergarten/preschool education; legal assistant/paralegal; management information systems; mechanical engineering/mechanical technology; medical/clinical assistant; medical radiologic technology; nursing (registered nurse training); physical therapist assistant.

Academics *Calendar:* semesters. *Degree:* certificates and associate. *Special study options:* academic remediation for entering students, accelerated degree program, adult/continuing education programs, advanced placement credit, cooperative education, distance learning, double majors, English as a second language, internships, part-time degree program, services for LD students, student-designed majors, summer session for credit. *ROTC:* Army (c), Air Force (c).

Library Infonet Library plus 4 others with 87,280 titles, 522 serial subscriptions, 10,588 audiovisual materials, an OPAC, a Web page.

Computers on Campus 800 computers available on campus for general student use. A campuswide network can be accessed from off campus. Internet access, at least one staffed computer lab available.

Student Life *Housing:* college housing not available. *Activities and Organizations:* drama/theater group, student-run newspaper, choral group, Human Key Society, NAACP, Black Student Association, Honor Society, Collegiate Secretaries. *Campus security:* 24-hour emergency response devices and patrols, late-night transport/escort service. *Student services:* personal/psychological counseling.

Athletics Member NJCAA.

Costs (2005–06) *Tuition:* state resident $2184 full-time, $91 per credit hour part-time; nonresident $8856 full-time, $369 per credit hour part-time. *Required fees:* $213 full-time, $28 per credit hour part-time.

Financial Aid Of all full-time matriculated undergraduates who enrolled in 2004, 201 Federal Work-Study jobs (averaging $2600).

Applying *Options:* common application, early admission, deferred entrance. *Application fee:* $5. *Required:* high school transcript. *Application deadlines:* 9/1 (freshmen), 9/1 (transfers). *Notification:* continuous until 9/1 (freshmen).

Freshmen Application Contact Ms. Cindy Meziere, Assistant Director of Recruiting, Southwest Tennessee Community College, PO Box 780, Memphis, TN 38103-0780. *Phone:* 901-333-4195. *Toll-free phone:* 877-717-STCC. *Fax:* 901-333-4473. *E-mail:* cmeziere@southwest.tn.edu.

VATTEROTT COLLEGE
Memphis, Tennessee

VOLUNTEER STATE COMMUNITY COLLEGE
Gallatin, Tennessee   www.volstate.edu/

- **State-supported** 2-year, founded 1970, part of Tennessee Board of Regents
- **Small-town** 100-acre campus with easy access to Nashville
- **Coed,** 7,150 undergraduate students, 49% full-time, 63% women, 37% men

Undergraduates 3,503 full-time, 3,647 part-time. Students come from 8 states and territories, 24 other countries, 1% are from out of state, 10% African American, 2% Asian American or Pacific Islander, 2% Hispanic American, 0.3% Native American, 9% transferred in. *Retention:* 54% of 2003 full-time freshmen returned.
Freshmen *Admission:* 2,026 applied, 2,026 admitted, 1,215 enrolled. *Average high school GPA:* 2.76. *Test scores:* ACT scores over 18: 63%; ACT scores over 24: 9%; ACT scores over 30: 1%.
Faculty *Total:* 381, 38% full-time. *Student/faculty ratio:* 20:1.
Majors Business administration and management; fire science; health information/medical records technology; health professions related; industrial arts; legal assistant/paralegal; liberal arts and sciences/liberal studies; medical radiologic technology; ophthalmic technology; physical therapist assistant; respiratory care therapy.
Academics *Calendar:* semesters. *Degree:* certificates and associate. *Special study options:* academic remediation for entering students, accelerated degree program, adult/continuing education programs, advanced placement credit, distance learning, double majors, English as a second language, honors programs, independent study, part-time degree program, services for LD students, summer session for credit.
Library Thigpen Learning Resource Center with 52,571 titles, 274 serial subscriptions, 3,212 audiovisual materials, an OPAC, a Web page.
Computers on Campus 600 computers available on campus for general student use. A campuswide network can be accessed from off campus. Internet access, online (class) registration, at least one staffed computer lab available.
Student Life *Housing:* college housing not available. *Activities and Organizations:* drama/theater group, student-run newspaper, radio station, choral group, Gamma Beta Phi, Returning Women's Organization, Phi Theta Kappa, Student Government Association, The Settler. *Campus security:* 24-hour emergency response devices and patrols, late-night transport/escort service. *Student services:* health clinic, personal/psychological counseling.
Athletics Member NJCAA. *Intercollegiate sports:* baseball M(s), basketball M(s)/W(s), softball W(s). *Intramural sports:* basketball M/W.
Standardized Tests *Required for some:* SAT or ACT (for admission).
Costs (2005–06) *Tuition:* state resident $2142 full-time, $91 per credit hour part-time; nonresident $8556 full-time, $369 per credit hour part-time. Full-time tuition and fees vary according to course load. Part-time tuition and fees vary according to course load. *Required fees:* $241 full-time, $9 per credit hour part-time, $8 per term part-time. *Payment plan:* deferred payment. *Waivers:* senior citizens and employees or children of employees.
Financial Aid Of all full-time matriculated undergraduates who enrolled in 2004, 37 Federal Work-Study jobs (averaging $1900). 21 state and other part-time jobs (averaging $2000).
Applying *Options:* electronic application, early admission, deferred entrance. *Application fee:* $10. *Required:* high school transcript. *Required for some:* essay or personal statement, minimum 2.0 GPA. *Application deadlines:* 9/1 (freshmen), 9/1 (transfers). *Notification:* continuous (freshmen).
Freshmen Application Contact Mr. Tim Amyx, Director of Admissions and Records, Volunteer State Community College, 1480 Nashville Pike, Gallatin, TN 37066-3188. *Phone:* 615-452-8600 Ext. 3614. *Toll-free phone:* 888-335-8722. *Fax:* 615-230-3577.

WALTERS STATE COMMUNITY COLLEGE
Morristown, Tennessee   www.ws.edu/

- **State-supported** 2-year, founded 1970, part of Tennessee Board of Regents
- **Small-town** 100-acre campus
- **Endowment** $6.9 million
- **Coed**

Undergraduates 3,101 full-time, 2,863 part-time. Students come from 8 states and territories, 6 other countries, 1% are from out of state, 4% African American, 0.7% Asian American or Pacific Islander, 1% Hispanic American, 0.2% Native American, 0.1% international, 4% transferred in.
Faculty *Student/faculty ratio:* 22:1.
Academics *Calendar:* semesters. *Degree:* certificates and associate. *Special study options:* academic remediation for entering students, accelerated degree program, adult/continuing education programs, advanced placement credit, distance learning, freshman honors college, honors programs, part-time degree program, summer session for credit. *ROTC:* Army (c).
Student Life *Campus security:* 24-hour emergency response devices.
Athletics Member NJCAA.
Standardized Tests *Required:* SAT or ACT (for admission).
Costs (2005–06) *Tuition:* state resident $2142 full-time, $91 per hour part-time; nonresident $8556 full-time, $391 per hour part-time. *Required fees:* $239 full-time, $15 per hour part-time, $7 per term part-time.
Financial Aid Of all full-time matriculated undergraduates who enrolled in 2004, 60 Federal Work-Study jobs (averaging $2400).
Applying *Options:* early admission. *Application fee:* $10. *Required:* high school transcript.
Freshmen Application Contact Mr. Michael Campbell, Director of Admissions and Registration Services, Walters State Community College, 500 South Davy Crockett Parkway, Morristown, TN 37813-6899. *Phone:* 423-585-2682. *Toll-free phone:* 800-225-4770.

TEXAS

THE ACADEMY OF HEALTH CARE PROFESSIONS
Houston, Texas   www.academyofhealth.com/
Director of Admissions Ms. Wanda Federick, Director of Admissions, The Academy of Health Care Professions, 1900 North Loop West, Suite 100, Houston, TX 77018. *Phone:* 713-425-3111. *E-mail:* wfederick@academyofhealth.com.

ALVIN COMMUNITY COLLEGE
Alvin, Texas   www.alvincollege.edu/

- **State and locally supported** 2-year, founded 1949
- **Small-town** 114-acre campus with easy access to Houston
- **Coed**

Undergraduates 1,611 full-time, 2,321 part-time. Students come from 17 states and territories, 5 other countries, 0.8% are from out of state, 8% African American, 2% Asian American or Pacific Islander, 20% Hispanic American, 0.7% Native American, 0.3% international, 6% transferred in.
Faculty *Student/faculty ratio:* 15:1.
Academics *Calendar:* semesters. *Degree:* certificates, diplomas, and associate. *Special study options:* academic remediation for entering students, accelerated degree program, adult/continuing education programs, advanced placement credit, distance learning, double majors, English as a second language, honors programs, independent study, internships, part-time degree program, services for LD students, student-designed majors, study abroad, summer session for credit.
Student Life *Campus security:* 24-hour patrols, late-night transport/escort service.

Alvin Community College (continued)

Athletics Member NJCAA.

Standardized Tests *Required:* THEA, ACCUPLACER (for placement).

Financial Aid Of all full-time matriculated undergraduates who enrolled in 2004, 50 Federal Work-Study jobs (averaging $2200). 1 state and other part-time job (averaging $2500).

Applying *Required for some:* high school transcript.

Director of Admissions Ms. Stephanie Stockstill, Director of Admissions and Advising, Alvin Community College, 3110 Mustang Road, Alvin, TX 77511. *Phone:* 281-756-3531. *E-mail:* admiss.rec.acc@flipper.alvin.cc.tx.us.

AMARILLO COLLEGE

Amarillo, Texas   **www.actx.edu/**

- **State and locally supported** 2-year, founded 1929
- **Suburban** 58-acre campus
- **Endowment** $13.6 million
- **Coed**

Undergraduates 3,436 full-time, 6,760 part-time. Students come from 9 states and territories, 1% are from out of state, 3% African American, 3% Asian American or Pacific Islander, 22% Hispanic American, 0.9% Native American.

Faculty *Student/faculty ratio:* 17:1.

Academics *Calendar:* semesters. *Degree:* certificates and associate. *Special study options:* academic remediation for entering students, adult/continuing education programs, advanced placement credit, distance learning, English as a second language, honors programs, part-time degree program, services for LD students, summer session for credit.

Student Life *Campus security:* 24-hour patrols, late-night transport/escort service.

Standardized Tests *Required:* THEA, MAPS (for placement).

Costs (2005–06) *Tuition:* area resident $1278 full-time, $53 per credit part-time; state resident $1638 full-time, $68 per credit part-time; nonresident $5478 full-time, $228 per credit part-time.

Financial Aid Of all full-time matriculated undergraduates who enrolled in 2004, 100 Federal Work-Study jobs (averaging $3000).

Applying *Options:* early admission, deferred entrance. *Required:* high school transcript.

Director of Admissions Mr. Robert Austin, Associate Dean of Student Services, Amarillo College, PO Box 447, Amarillo, TX 79178-0001. *Phone:* 806-371-5024. *E-mail:* austin-rc@actx.edu.

ANGELINA COLLEGE

Lufkin, Texas   **www.angelina.cc.tx.us/**

Freshmen Application Contact Ms. Judith Cutting, Registrar/Enrollment Director, Angelina College, PO Box 1768, Lufkin, TX 75902-1768. *Phone:* 936-639-1301 Ext. 213.

ATI TECHNICAL TRAINING CENTER

Dallas, Texas   **www.aticareertraining.com/**

Director of Admissions Mr. Brian DeLozier, Director, ATI Technical Training Center, 6627 Maple Avenue, Dallas, TX 75235. *Phone:* 214-352-2222. *Fax:* 214-350-3951. *E-mail:* bdelozier@atienterprises.edu.

AUSTIN BUSINESS COLLEGE

Austin, Texas   **www.austinbusinesscollege.org/**

Director of Admissions Ms. Pam Binns, Director of Admissions, Austin Business College, 2101 Interstate Highway 35, Suite 300, Austin, TX 78741. *Phone:* 512-447-9415. *E-mail:* pambinns@austinbusinesscollege.org.

AUSTIN COMMUNITY COLLEGE

Austin, Texas   **www.austincc.edu/**

- **District-supported** 2-year, founded 1972
- **Urban** campus
- **Coed,** 31,908 undergraduate students, 28% full-time, 57% women, 43% men

Undergraduates 8,829 full-time, 23,079 part-time. Students come from 93 other countries, 2% are from out of state, 7% African American, 5% Asian American or Pacific Islander, 23% Hispanic American, 0.7% Native American, 2% international.

Freshmen *Admission:* 5,718 applied, 5,718 admitted, 5,718 enrolled.

Faculty *Total:* 1,601, 28% full-time. *Student/faculty ratio:* 20:1.

Majors Accounting; administrative assistant and secretarial science; art; astronomy; automobile/automotive mechanics technology; biology/biological sciences; business administration and management; chemistry; clinical/medical laboratory technology; commercial and advertising art; computer and information sciences related; computer programming; computer programming related; computer science; computer systems networking and telecommunications; construction engineering technology; consumer merchandising/retailing management; criminal justice/law enforcement administration; criminal justice/police science; data entry/microcomputer applications; developmental and child psychology; drafting and design technology; economics; electrical, electronic and communications engineering technology; emergency medical technology (EMT paramedic); English; fashion merchandising; finance; fire science; French; geology/earth science; German; graphic and printing equipment operation/production; heating, air conditioning, ventilation and refrigeration maintenance technology; history; hospitality and recreation marketing; hotel/motel administration; human services; industrial radiologic technology; industrial technology; information science/studies; information technology; insurance; Japanese; journalism; legal administrative assistant/secretary; legal assistant/paralegal; liberal arts and sciences/liberal studies; marketing/marketing management; mass communication/media; mathematics; medical/clinical assistant; music; nursing (registered nurse training); occupational therapy; photography; physical sciences; physics; political science and government; pre-engineering; psychology; quality control technology; radio and television; real estate; Russian; sign language interpretation and translation; social work; sociology; Spanish; speech and rhetoric; surgical technology; survey technology; system administration; technical and business writing; welding technology.

Academics *Calendar:* semesters. *Degree:* certificates and associate. *Special study options:* academic remediation for entering students, accelerated degree program, adult/continuing education programs, advanced placement credit, cooperative education, distance learning, English as a second language, external degree program, honors programs, independent study, internships, part-time degree program, services for LD students, summer session for credit. *ROTC:* Army (c), Air Force (c).

Library Main Library plus 6 others with 115,567 titles, 1,974 serial subscriptions, 14,044 audiovisual materials, an OPAC, a Web page.

Computers on Campus 225 computers available on campus for general student use. A campuswide network can be accessed from off campus. Internet access, at least one staffed computer lab available.

Student Life *Housing:* college housing not available. *Activities and Organizations:* drama/theater group, student-run newspaper. *Student services:* personal/psychological counseling.

Athletics *Intramural sports:* basketball M/W, football M, golf M, racquetball M/W, volleyball M/W, weight lifting M/W.

Costs (2006–07) *Tuition:* area resident $1170 full-time, $39 per credit hour part-time; state resident $3060 full-time, $102 per credit hour part-time; nonresident $5670 full-time, $189 per credit hour part-time. *Required fees:* $420 full-time, $14 per credit hour part-time.

Financial Aid Of all full-time matriculated undergraduates who enrolled in 2004, 296 Federal Work-Study jobs (averaging $2000). 12 state and other part-time jobs (averaging $2000).

Applying *Options:* electronic application. *Application deadline:* rolling (freshmen), rolling (transfers).

Freshmen Application Contact Ms. Linda Kluck, Director, Admissions and Records, Austin Community College, 5930 Middle Fiskville Road, Austin, TX 78752-4390. *Phone:* 512-223-7766. *Fax:* 512-223-7665. *E-mail:* outreach@austincc.edu.

BLINN COLLEGE

Brenham, Texas   **www.blinn.edu/**

Freshmen Application Contact Ms. Brandi Bothe, Coordinator, Recruitment and Admissions, Blinn College, 902 College Avenue, Brenham, TX 77833-4049. *Phone:* 979-830-4152.

BORDER INSTITUTE OF TECHNOLOGY
El Paso, Texas   bitelp.edu/

Director of Admissions Mr. Miguel Gamino, Admissions Director, Border Institute of Technology, 9611 Acer Avenue, El Paso, TX 79925-6744. *Phone:* 915-593-7328 Ext. 24.

BRAZOSPORT COLLEGE
Lake Jackson, Texas   www.brazosport.edu/

- **State and locally supported** 2-year, founded 1968
- **Small-town** 160-acre campus with easy access to Houston
- **Endowment** $3.3 million
- **Coed,** 3,503 undergraduate students, 48% full-time, 55% women, 45% men

Undergraduates 1,670 full-time, 1,833 part-time. Students come from 12 states and territories, 11 other countries, 1% are from out of state, 6% African American, 1% Asian American or Pacific Islander, 24% Hispanic American, 0.4% Native American, 0.5% international, 4% transferred in.

Faculty *Total:* 166, 43% full-time, 10% with terminal degrees. *Student/faculty ratio:* 18:1.

Majors Accounting; administrative assistant and secretarial science; agricultural business and management; architecture; art; automobile/automotive mechanics technology; biology/biological sciences; business administration and management; business/commerce; chemical technology; chemistry; child care and support services management; child development; computer and information sciences; computer hardware technology; computer programming; computer programming related; computer programming (specific applications); computer technology/computer systems technology; construction engineering technology; construction/heavy equipment/earthmoving equipment operation; corrections and criminal justice related; criminal justice/police science; data processing and data processing technology; drafting and design technology; dramatic/theater arts; economics; education; electrical, electronic and communications engineering technology; electrician; elementary education; emergency medical technology (EMT paramedic); engineering; English; environmental health; ethnic, cultural minority, and gender studies related; family and consumer sciences/human sciences; finance; fine/studio arts; foreign languages and literatures; general studies; geology/earth science; health and physical education; health professions related; heating, air conditioning, ventilation and refrigeration maintenance technology; history; information technology; instrumentation technology; journalism; legal assistant/paralegal; liberal arts and sciences/liberal studies; library science; machine tool technology; marketing/marketing management; mathematics; music; nursing (registered nurse training); occupational safety and health technology; physical education teaching and coaching; physics; pipefitting and sprinkler fitting; political science and government; pre-medical studies; psychology; public administration; purchasing, procurement/acquisitions and contracts management; quality control technology; secondary education; sheet metal technology; social sciences; sociology; speech and rhetoric; theology; vehicle/equipment operation; welding technology.

Academics *Calendar:* semesters. *Degree:* certificates and associate. *Special study options:* academic remediation for entering students, adult/continuing education programs, advanced placement credit, cooperative education, distance learning, honors programs, internships, part-time degree program, summer session for credit.

Library Brazosport College Library with 85,425 titles, 339 serial subscriptions, 397 audiovisual materials, an OPAC, a Web page.

Computers on Campus 420 computers available on campus for general student use. A campuswide network can be accessed from off campus. Internet access, online (class) registration, at least one staffed computer lab available.

Student Life *Housing:* college housing not available. *Activities and Organizations:* drama/theater group, student-run newspaper, choral group, Phi Theta Kappa, Baptist Student Ministry, Student Senate, Fencing Club. *Campus security:* 24-hour patrols.

Athletics *Intramural sports:* archery M/W, basketball M/W, bowling M/W, fencing M/W, football M/W, golf M/W, soccer M/W, softball M/W, table tennis M/W, tennis M/W, volleyball M/W.

Standardized Tests *Required for some:* THEA, ACT COMPASS.

Costs (2005–06) *Tuition:* area resident $840 full-time, $28 per hour part-time; state resident $1470 full-time, $49 per hour part-time; nonresident $2880 full-time, $96 per hour part-time. Full-time tuition and fees vary according to course load. Part-time tuition and fees vary according to course load. *Required fees:* $300 full-time, $9 per hour part-time, $15 per term part-time. *Payment plan:* installment. *Waivers:* employees or children of employees.

Applying *Options:* early admission, deferred entrance. *Required for some:* high school transcript. *Application deadlines:* 8/15 (freshmen), 8/15 (transfers).

Freshmen Application Contact Ms. Patricia S. Leyendecker, Director of Admissions/Registrar, Brazosport College, 500 College Drive, Lake Jackson, TX 77566. *Phone:* 979-230-3217. *Fax:* 979-230-3376. *E-mail:* pleyende@brazosport.edu.

BROOKHAVEN COLLEGE
Farmers Branch, Texas   www.brookhavencollege.edu/

Director of Admissions Thoa Vo, Registrar, Brookhaven College, 3939 Valley View Lane, Farmers Branch, TX 75244-4997. *Phone:* 972-860-4604.

BROWN MACKIE COLLEGE—DALLAS
Garland, Texas

BROWN MACKIE COLLEGE—FORT WORTH
Hurst, Texas

CEDAR VALLEY COLLEGE
Lancaster, Texas   www.cedarvalleycollege.edu/cvc.htm

- **State-supported** 2-year, founded 1977, part of Dallas County Community College District System
- **Suburban** 353-acre campus with easy access to Dallas–Fort Worth
- **Endowment** $17.2 million
- **Coed,** 4,290 undergraduate students, 34% full-time, 62% women, 38% men

Undergraduates 1,447 full-time, 2,843 part-time. Students come from 5 other countries, 2% are from out of state, 57% African American, 1% Asian American or Pacific Islander, 12% Hispanic American, 0.3% Native American, 0.3% international, 74% transferred in.

Freshmen *Admission:* 1,956 applied, 1,956 admitted, 547 enrolled.

Faculty *Total:* 174, 37% full-time. *Student/faculty ratio:* 26:1.

Majors Accounting; administrative assistant and secretarial science; automobile/automotive mechanics technology; business administration and management; computer programming; computer programming (specific applications); criminal justice/law enforcement administration; data processing and data processing technology; heating, air conditioning, ventilation and refrigeration maintenance technology; liberal arts and sciences/liberal studies; management information systems and services related; marketing/marketing management; music; radio and television broadcasting technology; real estate; veterinary/animal health technology.

Academics *Calendar:* semesters. *Degree:* certificates and associate. *Special study options:* academic remediation for entering students, advanced placement credit, cooperative education, distance learning, English as a second language, part-time degree program, services for LD students, summer session for credit. *ROTC:* Army (c).

Library Cedar Valley College Library with 43,788 titles, 217 serial subscriptions, 16,460 audiovisual materials, an OPAC, a Web page.

Computers on Campus 675 computers available on campus for general student use. A campuswide network can be accessed from off campus that provide access to video conferencing. Internet access, online (class) registration, at least one staffed computer lab available.

Student Life *Housing:* college housing not available. *Activities and Organizations:* drama/theater group, choral group, African-American Student Organization, Latin-American Student Organization, Veterinary Technology Club, Phi Theta Kappa, Police Academy Club. *Campus security:* 24-hour emergency response devices and patrols. *Student services:* health clinic, personal/psychological counseling.

Athletics Member NJCAA. *Intercollegiate sports:* baseball M, basketball M, soccer W, volleyball W. *Intramural sports:* cheerleading W.

Cedar Valley College (continued)

Standardized Tests *Required:* THEA (for admission). *Recommended:* SAT or ACT (for admission).

Costs (2006–07) *Tuition:* area resident $1080 full-time, $36 per credit part-time; state resident $1980 full-time, $66 per credit part-time; nonresident $3180 full-time, $200 per credit part-time.

Applying *Options:* electronic application, early admission. *Required for some:* letters of recommendation, interview. *Recommended:* high school transcript. *Application deadline:* rolling (freshmen), rolling (transfers). *Notification:* continuous (freshmen).

Freshmen Application Contact Ms. Carolyn Ward, Director of Admissions/Registrar, Cedar Valley College, 3030 North Dallas Avenue, Lancaster, TX 75134-3799. *Phone:* 972-860-8201. *E-mail:* cboswell-ward@dcccd.edu.

CENTER FOR ADVANCED LEGAL STUDIES
Houston, Texas

CENTRAL TEXAS COLLEGE
Killeen, Texas   **www.ctcd.edu/**

- **State and locally supported** 2-year, founded 1967
- **Suburban** 500-acre campus with easy access to Austin
- **Endowment** $1.5 million
- **Coed**

Undergraduates 2,986 full-time, 15,365 part-time. Students come from 48 states and territories, 19 other countries, 28% African American, 4% Asian American or Pacific Islander, 15% Hispanic American, 1% Native American, 0.2% international, 1% live on campus.

Faculty *Student/faculty ratio:* 40:1.

Academics *Calendar:* semesters. *Degree:* certificates and associate. *Special study options:* academic remediation for entering students, accelerated degree program, adult/continuing education programs, advanced placement credit, distance learning, English as a second language, external degree program, internships, part-time degree program, services for LD students, student-designed majors, summer session for credit. *ROTC:* Army (b).

Student Life *Campus security:* 24-hour emergency response devices and patrols.

Standardized Tests *Required:* THEA (for placement). *Recommended:* SAT or ACT (for placement), SAT Subject Tests (for placement).

Costs (2005–06) *Tuition:* area resident $912 full-time, $38 per hour part-time; state resident $1104 full-time, $46 per hour part-time; nonresident $2880 full-time, $60 per hour part-time. Full-time tuition and fees vary according to course load and location. Part-time tuition and fees vary according to course load and location. *Required fees:* $390 full-time, $8 per hour part-time. *Room and board:* $2990.

Financial Aid Of all full-time matriculated undergraduates who enrolled in 2004, 68 Federal Work-Study jobs.

Applying *Options:* electronic application, early admission, deferred entrance. *Required:* high school transcript, minimum 2.0 GPA.

Freshmen Application Contact Admissions Office, Central Texas College, PO Box 1800, Killeen, TX 76540-1800. *Phone:* 254-526-1696. *Toll-free phone:* 800-792-3348 Ext. 1696. *Fax:* 254-526-1545. *E-mail:* admrec@ctcd.edu.

CISCO JUNIOR COLLEGE
Cisco, Texas   **www.cisco.cc.tx.us/**

Director of Admissions Mr. Olin O. Odom III, Dean of Admission/Registrar, Cisco Junior College, 101 College Heights, Cisco, TX 76437-9321. *Phone:* 254-442-2567 Ext. 130.

CLARENDON COLLEGE
Clarendon, Texas   **www.clarendoncollege.edu/**

- **State and locally supported** 2-year, founded 1898
- **Rural** 88-acre campus
- **Endowment** $2.6 million
- **Coed**, 1,123 undergraduate students, 50% full-time, 46% women, 54% men

Undergraduates 557 full-time, 566 part-time. Students come from 14 states and territories, 3 other countries, 8% are from out of state, 12% African American, 1% Asian American or Pacific Islander, 17% Hispanic American, 0.5% Native American, 0.4% international.

Freshmen *Admission:* 586 applied, 586 admitted, 536 enrolled.

Faculty *Total:* 67, 45% full-time, 7% with terminal degrees. *Student/faculty ratio:* 17:1.

Majors Accounting; agribusiness; agricultural economics; agriculture; architecture; art; behavioral sciences; biology/biological sciences; business administration and management; chemistry; computer and information sciences; dramatic/theater arts; economics; education; elementary education; engineering; English; environmental science; farm and ranch management; finance; general studies; health services/allied health/health sciences; history; horse husbandry/equine science and management; kinesiology and exercise science; liberal arts and sciences/liberal studies; marketing/marketing management; mass communications; mathematics; music; nursing (registered nurse training); physical education teaching and coaching; physical therapy; pre-dentistry studies; pre-law studies; pre-medical studies; psychology; secondary education; social sciences; social work related; sociology; speech and rhetoric.

Academics *Calendar:* semesters. *Degree:* certificates and associate. *Special study options:* academic remediation for entering students, adult/continuing education programs, advanced placement credit, distance learning, double majors, independent study, part-time degree program, services for LD students, summer session for credit.

Library Vera Dial Dickey Library plus 1 other with 22,000 titles, 89 serial subscriptions, 350 audiovisual materials, an OPAC, a Web page.

Computers on Campus 57 computers available on campus for general student use. A campuswide network can be accessed from student residence rooms and from off campus. Internet access, online (class) registration, at least one staffed computer lab available. Computer purchase or lease plan available.

Student Life *Housing:* on-campus residence required through sophomore year. *Options:* Campus housing is university owned. *Activities and Organizations:* drama/theater group, choral group. *Campus security:* 8-hour patrols by trained security personnel.

Athletics Member NJCAA. *Intercollegiate sports:* baseball M(s), basketball M(s)/W(s), cheerleading M(s)/W(s), softball W(s), volleyball W(s). *Intramural sports:* basketball M/W, football M/W, volleyball M/W.

Costs (2006–07) *Tuition:* area resident $1140 full-time, $38 per credit hour part-time; state resident $1650 full-time, $55 per credit hour part-time; nonresident $2100 full-time, $70 per credit hour part-time. *Required fees:* $930 full-time, $24 per credit hour part-time, $72 per term part-time. *Room and board:* $3100; room only: $1000.

Financial Aid Of all full-time matriculated undergraduates who enrolled in 2004, 41 Federal Work-Study jobs (averaging $985). 9 state and other part-time jobs (averaging $860).

Applying *Options:* early admission, deferred entrance. *Required:* high school transcript. *Required for some:* letters of recommendation, interview. *Application deadline:* rolling (freshmen), rolling (transfers). *Notification:* continuous (freshmen).

Freshmen Application Contact Ms. Sharon Hannon, Admissions Director/Registrar, Clarendon College, PO Box 968, Clarendon, TX 79226-0968. *Phone:* 806-874-3571 Ext. 107. *Toll-free phone:* 800-687-9737. *Fax:* 806-874-3201.

COASTAL BEND COLLEGE
Beeville, Texas   **www.cbc.cc.tx.us/**

- **County-supported** 2-year, founded 1965
- **Rural** 100-acre campus
- **Endowment** $676,564
- **Coed**, 3,366 undergraduate students, 41% full-time, 61% women, 39% men

Undergraduates 1,380 full-time, 1,986 part-time. Students come from 15 states and territories, 3 other countries, 1% are from out of state, 3% African American, 0.6% Asian American or Pacific Islander, 64% Hispanic American, 0.4% Native American, 0.6% international, 65% transferred in, 5% live on campus. *Retention:* 62% of 2003 full-time freshmen returned.

Freshmen *Admission:* 1,193 applied, 1,193 admitted, 1,193 enrolled.
Faculty *Total:* 167, 57% full-time, 6% with terminal degrees. *Student/faculty ratio:* 17:1.
Majors Accounting; administrative assistant and secretarial science; agriculture; applied art; art; art teacher education; automobile/automotive mechanics technology; biological and physical sciences; biology/biological sciences; business administration and management; chemistry; child development; commercial and advertising art; computer and information sciences related; computer engineering technology; computer programming related; computer programming (specific applications); computer programming (vendor/product certification); computer science; computer systems networking and telecommunications; cosmetology; criminal justice/law enforcement administration; criminal justice/police science; data entry/microcomputer applications; data entry/microcomputer applications related; data processing and data processing technology; dental hygiene; developmental and child psychology; drafting and design technology; dramatic/theater arts; economics; education; elementary education; engineering; English; environmental engineering technology; finance; fine/studio arts; French; geology/earth science; German; health teacher education; history; information technology; journalism; legal administrative assistant/secretary; liberal arts and sciences/liberal studies; mathematics; music; music teacher education; nursing (licensed practical/vocational nurse training); nursing (registered nurse training); parks, recreation and leisure; petroleum technology; pharmacy; physical education teaching and coaching; physical sciences; physics; political science and government; psychology; public relations/image management; sociology; speech and rhetoric; system administration; voice and opera; welding technology; word processing.
Academics *Calendar:* semesters. *Degree:* certificates and associate. *Special study options:* academic remediation for entering students, adult/continuing education programs, advanced placement credit, cooperative education, distance learning, internships, part-time degree program, services for LD students, summer session for credit. *ROTC:* Army (c), Air Force (c).
Library Grady C. Hogue Learning Resource Center with 37,971 titles, 268 serial subscriptions, 2,974 audiovisual materials, an OPAC.
Computers on Campus 970 computers available on campus for general student use. A campuswide network can be accessed from off campus. Internet access, online (class) registration, at least one staffed computer lab available.
Student Life *Housing Options:* coed, men-only, women-only, disabled students. Campus housing is university owned. *Activities and Organizations:* student government, Computer Science Club, Creative Writing Club, Drama Club, Art Club. *Campus security:* 24-hour emergency response devices. *Student services:* personal/psychological counseling.
Athletics *Intramural sports:* archery M/W, badminton M/W, basketball M/W, bowling M/W, cross-country running M/W, golf M/W, soccer M/W, softball M/W, table tennis M/W, tennis M/W, track and field M/W, volleyball M/W, weight lifting M/W.
Costs (2006–07) *Room and board:* room only: $1560.
Financial Aid Of all full-time matriculated undergraduates who enrolled in 2004, 80 Federal Work-Study jobs (averaging $1484). 11 state and other part-time jobs (averaging $1159).
Applying *Options:* deferred entrance. *Required:* high school transcript. *Application deadline:* rolling (freshmen), rolling (transfers). *Notification:* continuous (freshmen).
Freshmen Application Contact Ms. Alicia Ulloa, Director of Admissions/Registrar, Coastal Bend College, 3800 Charco Road, Beeville, TX 78102-2197. *Phone:* 361-354-2245. *Fax:* 361-354-2254. *E-mail:* register@coastalbend.edu.

COLLEGE OF THE MAINLAND
Texas City, Texas
www.com.edu/

- **State and locally supported** 2-year, founded 1967
- **Suburban** 120-acre campus with easy access to Houston
- **Coed,** 3,999 undergraduate students, 35% full-time, 59% women, 41% men

Undergraduates 1,382 full-time, 2,617 part-time. Students come from 8 states and territories, 0.4% are from out of state, 16% African American, 2% Asian American or Pacific Islander, 20% Hispanic American, 0.7% Native American, 0.1% international, 8% transferred in. *Retention:* 48% of 2003 full-time freshmen returned.
Freshmen *Admission:* 517 admitted, 517 enrolled.
Faculty *Total:* 213, 43% full-time, 26% with terminal degrees. *Student/faculty ratio:* 17:1.
Majors Accounting technology and bookkeeping; administrative assistant and secretarial science; business administration and management; chemical technology; child development; computer programming; computer systems networking and telecommunications; criminal justice/law enforcement administration; criminal justice/safety; criminology; dramatic/theater arts; emergency medical tech-

nology (EMT paramedic); fine/studio arts; fire protection and safety technology; general studies; liberal arts and sciences/liberal studies; mathematics; music; natural sciences; nursing (registered nurse training); pre-engineering; public administration and social service professions related; social work; sociology; web page, digital/multimedia and information resources design.
Academics *Calendar:* semesters. *Degree:* certificates, diplomas, and associate. *Special study options:* academic remediation for entering students, adult/continuing education programs, cooperative education, distance learning, English as a second language, honors programs, part-time degree program, services for LD students, summer session for credit.
Library Com Library plus 1 other with 84,128 titles, 19,000 serial subscriptions, 492 audiovisual materials, an OPAC, a Web page.
Computers on Campus 307 computers available on campus for general student use. A campuswide network can be accessed from off campus that provide access to wireless access throughout campus to Com network and internet. Internet access, online (class) registration, at least one staffed computer lab available.
Student Life *Housing:* college housing not available. *Activities and Organizations:* drama/theater group, choral group, Student Activities Board, Student Government Association, COM Amigos, COM Soccer Club, Phi Theta Kappa. *Campus security:* 24-hour emergency response devices and patrols, student patrols. *Student services:* personal/psychological counseling, women's center.
Athletics *Intramural sports:* basketball M/W, football M/W, golf M/W, racquetball M/W, soccer M, softball M/W, swimming and diving M/W, table tennis M/W, tennis M/W, track and field M/W, volleyball M/W.
Costs (2006–07) *Tuition:* area resident $863 full-time, $26 per credit part-time; state resident $1655 full-time, $59 per credit part-time; nonresident $2423 full-time, $89 per credit part-time. *Required fees:* $167 full-time, $11 per credit part-time, $64 per term part-time.
Financial Aid Of all full-time matriculated undergraduates who enrolled in 2004, 204 Federal Work-Study jobs (averaging $789). 234 state and other part-time jobs (averaging $949).
Applying *Options:* electronic application, early admission, deferred entrance. *Required for some:* high school transcript. *Application deadline:* rolling (freshmen), rolling (transfers). *Notification:* continuous (freshmen).
Freshmen Application Contact Ms. Kelly Musick, Registrar/Director of Admissions, College of the Mainland, 1200 Amburn Road, Texas City, TX 77591. *Phone:* 409-938-1211 Ext. 469. *Toll-free phone:* 888-258-8859 Ext. 264. *Fax:* 409-938-3126. *E-mail:* sem@com.edu.

COLLIN COUNTY COMMUNITY COLLEGE DISTRICT
Plano, Texas
www.ccccd.edu/

- **State and locally supported** 2-year, founded 1985
- **Suburban** 333-acre campus with easy access to Dallas-Fort Worth
- **Endowment** $2.0 million
- **Coed,** 18,457 undergraduate students, 39% full-time, 56% women, 44% men

Undergraduates 7,226 full-time, 11,231 part-time. Students come from 44 states and territories, 86 other countries, 3% are from out of state, 8% African American, 8% Asian American or Pacific Islander, 10% Hispanic American, 0.6% Native American, 3% international, 10% transferred in. *Retention:* 55% of 2003 full-time freshmen returned.
Freshmen *Admission:* 3,676 admitted, 3,676 enrolled.
Faculty *Total:* 1,074, 23% full-time. *Student/faculty ratio:* 21:1.
Majors Biology/biotechnology laboratory technician; business administration and management; business automation/technology/data entry; commercial and advertising art; computer and information sciences; computer engineering technology; computer programming; computer systems networking and telecommunications; dental hygiene; drafting and design technology; educational/instructional media design; electrical, electronic and communications engineering technology; electrical/electronics drafting and CAD/CADD; electrical/electronics equipment installation and repair; emergency medical technology (EMT paramedic); environmental engineering technology; family and community services; fire protection and safety technology; hospitality administration; interior design; legal assistant/paralegal; liberal arts and sciences/liberal studies; music management and merchandising; nursing (registered nurse training); real estate; respiratory care therapy; sales, distribution and marketing; sign language interpretation and translation; telecommunications technology; water quality and wastewater treatment management and recycling technology; web page, digital/multimedia and information resources design.
Academics *Calendar:* semesters. *Degree:* certificates and associate. *Special study options:* academic remediation for entering students, adult/continuing education programs, advanced placement credit, cooperative education, distance

Texas

Collin County Community College District (continued)
learning, English as a second language, honors programs, internships, part-time degree program, services for LD students, study abroad, summer session for credit.

Library Main Library plus 3 others with 129,032 titles, 940 serial subscriptions, 17,342 audiovisual materials, an OPAC, a Web page.

Computers on Campus 1858 computers available on campus for general student use. A campuswide network can be accessed from student residence rooms. Internet access, online (class) registration, at least one staffed computer lab available. Computer purchase or lease plan available.

Student Life *Housing:* college housing not available. *Activities and Organizations:* drama/theater group, choral group, Phi Theta Kappa, LULAC/BSN, Baptist Student Ministry, Psi Beta, Collin Nursing Student Association. *Campus security:* 24-hour emergency response devices and patrols, late-night transport/escort service, controlled dormitory access. *Student services:* personal/psychological counseling.

Athletics Member NJCAA. *Intercollegiate sports:* basketball M(s)/W(s), tennis M(s)/W(s), volleyball W(s).

Standardized Tests *Required:* THEA (for admission).

Costs (2005–06) *Tuition:* area resident $810 full-time, $27 per credit hour part-time; state resident $1020 full-time, $33 per credit hour part-time; nonresident $2550 full-time, $80 per credit hour part-time. *Required fees:* $306 full-time, $10 per credit hour part-time, $2 per term part-time. *Payment plan:* installment. *Waivers:* senior citizens.

Financial Aid Of all full-time matriculated undergraduates who enrolled in 2004, 80 Federal Work-Study jobs (averaging $3490).

Applying *Options:* electronic application. *Application deadline:* rolling (freshmen). *Notification:* continuous (freshmen).

Freshmen Application Contact Ms. Stephanie Meinhardt, Registrar, Collin County Community College District, 2200 West University Drive, McKinney, TX 75070-8001. *Phone:* 972-881-5174. *Fax:* 972-881-5175. *E-mail:* smeinhardt@ccccd.edu.

COMMONWEALTH INSTITUTE OF FUNERAL SERVICE
Houston, Texas   www.commonwealthinst.org/

- **Independent** 2-year, founded 1988
- **Urban** campus
- **Coed**

Undergraduates 157 full-time, 7 part-time. Students come from 11 states and territories, 20% are from out of state, 30% African American, 0.6% Asian American or Pacific Islander, 17% Hispanic American, 7% transferred in.

Faculty *Student/faculty ratio:* 23:1.

Academics *Calendar:* quarters. *Degree:* certificates and associate. *Special study options:* adult/continuing education programs, external degree program.

Student Life *Campus security:* 24-hour emergency response devices.

Standardized Tests *Required for some:* Wonderlic aptitude test or THEA. *Recommended:* SAT or ACT (for admission).

Costs (2005–06) *Tuition:* $9400 full-time, $13 per contact hour part-time. Full-time tuition and fees vary according to course load and program. Part-time tuition and fees vary according to course load and program. *Required fees:* $100 full-time.

Applying *Options:* common application. *Application fee:* $50. *Required:* high school transcript.

Director of Admissions Mrs. Patricia Moreno, Registrar, Commonwealth Institute of Funeral Service, 415 Barren Springs Drive, Houston, TX 77090. *Phone:* 281-873-0262. *Toll-free phone:* 800-628-1580.

COMPUTER CAREER CENTER
El Paso, Texas   www.computercareercenter.com/

Director of Admissions Ms. Sarah Hernandez, Registrar, Computer Career Center, 6101 Montana Avenue, El Paso, TX 79925. *Phone:* 915-779-8031.

COURT REPORTING INSTITUTE OF DALLAS
Dallas, Texas   www.crid.com/

Director of Admissions Ms. Debra Smith-Armstrong, Director of Admissions, Court Reporting Institute of Dallas, 8585 North Stemmons, #200 North Tower, Dallas, TX 75247. *Phone:* 214-350-9722 Ext. 227. *Toll-free phone:* 800-880-9722.

COURT REPORTING INSTITUTE OF HOUSTON
Houston, Texas

CY-FAIR COLLEGE
Houston, Texas   www.cy-faircollege.com/

- **State and locally supported** 2-year, founded 2002, part of North Harris Montgomery Community Course District
- **Suburban** 200-acre campus
- **Coed**

Undergraduates 1,895 full-time, 6,645 part-time. Students come from 36 other countries, 9% African American, 8% Asian American or Pacific Islander, 21% Hispanic American, 0.4% Native American, 3% international.

Faculty *Student/faculty ratio:* 17:1.

Academics *Calendar:* semesters. *Degree:* certificates, diplomas, and associate. *Special study options:* academic remediation for entering students, adult/continuing education programs, advanced placement credit, cooperative education, distance learning, English as a second language, external degree program, honors programs, independent study, internships, part-time degree program, services for LD students.

Standardized Tests *Required for some:* SAT or ACT (for placement).

Costs (2005–06) *Tuition:* area resident $768 full-time, $32 per credit hour part-time; state resident $1728 full-time, $72 per credit hour part-time; nonresident $2088 full-time, $87 per credit hour part-time. *Required fees:* $216 full-time, $8 per credit hour part-time, $12 per term part-time.

Applying *Options:* electronic application.

Director of Admissions Dr. Earl Campa, Vice President of Student Success, Cy-Fair College, 9191 Barker Cypress Road, Cypress, TX 77433-1383. *Phone:* 281-290-3950.

DALLAS INSTITUTE OF FUNERAL SERVICE
Dallas, Texas   www.dallasinstitute.edu/

- **Independent** 2-year, founded 1945
- **Urban** 8-acre campus with easy access to Dallas/Ft. Worth
- **Coed,** 247 undergraduate students, 100% full-time, 48% women, 52% men

Undergraduates 247 full-time. Students come from 12 states and territories, 10% are from out of state, 26% African American, 0.8% Asian American or Pacific Islander, 9% Hispanic American, 0.4% Native American, 10% transferred in.

Freshmen *Admission:* 96 enrolled.

Faculty *Total:* 10, 60% full-time, 10% with terminal degrees. *Student/faculty ratio:* 32:1.

Majors Funeral service and mortuary science.

Academics *Calendar:* quarters. *Degree:* certificates and associate.

Student Life *Housing:* college housing not available. *Campus security:* 24-hour emergency response devices.

Costs (2006–07) *Tuition:* $10,000 full-time, $200 per hour part-time. *Required fees:* $50 full-time.

Applying *Application fee:* $50. *Required:* high school transcript.

Freshmen Application Contact Terry Parrish, Director of Admissions, Dallas Institute of Funeral Service, 3909 S. Buckner Boulevard, Dallas, TX 75227. *Phone:* 214-388-5466. *Toll-free phone:* 800-235-5444. *Fax:* 214-388-0316. *E-mail:* difs@dallasinstitute.edu.

DEL MAR COLLEGE

Corpus Christi, Texas

www.delmar.edu/

Director of Admissions Ms. Frances P. Jordan, Assistant Dean of Enrollment Services and Registrar, Del Mar College, 101 Baldwin Boulevard, Corpus Christi, TX 78404-3897. *Phone:* 361-698-1248. *Toll-free phone:* 800-652-3357.

EASTFIELD COLLEGE

Mesquite, Texas

www.efc.dcccd.edu/

- **State and locally supported** 2-year, founded 1970, part of Dallas County Community College District System
- **Suburban** 244-acre campus with easy access to Dallas–Fort Worth
- **Coed,** 12,111 undergraduate students, 19% full-time, 59% women, 41% men

Undergraduates 2,322 full-time, 9,789 part-time. Students come from 18 states and territories, 1% are from out of state, 21% African American, 4% Asian American or Pacific Islander, 23% Hispanic American, 0.6% Native American, 0.5% international, 3% transferred in. *Retention:* 39% of 2003 full-time freshmen returned.
Freshmen *Admission:* 1,466 applied, 1,466 admitted, 1,466 enrolled.
Faculty *Total:* 496, 19% full-time. *Student/faculty ratio:* 23:1.
Majors Accounting; autobody/collision and repair technology; automobile/automotive mechanics technology; business administration and management; child care and support services management; computer and information sciences related; computer engineering technology; computer hardware engineering; computer/information technology services administration related; computer programming; computer programming related; computer systems networking and telecommunications; criminal justice/safety; data entry/microcomputer applications; data processing and data processing technology; drafting and design technology; electrical, electronic and communications engineering technology; electrical/electronics drafting and CAD/CADD; executive assistant/executive secretary; graphic and printing equipment operation/production; heating, air conditioning, ventilation and refrigeration maintenance technology; legal administrative assistant/secretary; liberal arts and sciences/liberal studies; psychiatric/mental health services technology; sign language interpretation and translation; social work; substance abuse/addiction counseling; system administration; word processing.
Academics *Calendar:* semesters. *Degree:* certificates and associate. *Special study options:* academic remediation for entering students, adult/continuing education programs, advanced placement credit, cooperative education, distance learning, English as a second language, honors programs, part-time degree program, services for LD students, summer session for credit.
Library Eastfield College Learning Resource Center with 66,988 titles, 415 serial subscriptions, 2,620 audiovisual materials, an OPAC, a Web page.
Computers on Campus 50 computers available on campus for general student use. A campuswide network can be accessed from off campus. Internet access, at least one staffed computer lab available.
Student Life *Housing:* college housing not available. *Activities and Organizations:* drama/theater group, student-run newspaper, choral group, LULAC, Rodeo Club, PTK, Rising Star, Communications Club. *Campus security:* 24-hour emergency response devices and patrols. *Student services:* health clinic, personal/psychological counseling, women's center.
Athletics Member NJCAA. *Intercollegiate sports:* baseball M, basketball M, golf M, soccer W, tennis M/W, volleyball M/W. *Intramural sports:* basketball M, football M, softball M/W, volleyball M/W.
Costs (2006–07) *Tuition:* area resident $1080 full-time, $36 per credit part-time; state resident $1980 full-time, $66 per credit part-time; nonresident $3180 full-time, $106 per credit part-time.
Applying *Options:* early admission, deferred entrance. *Recommended:* high school transcript. *Application deadline:* rolling (freshmen), rolling (transfers). *Notification:* continuous (freshmen).
Freshmen Application Contact Ms. Linda Richardson, Director of Admissions/Registrar, Eastfield College, 3737 Motley Drive, Mesquite, TX 75150-2099. *Phone:* 972-860-7105. *Fax:* 912-860-8306. *E-mail:* efc@dcccd.edu.

EL CENTRO COLLEGE

Dallas, Texas

www.ecc.dcccd.edu/

- **County-supported** 2-year, founded 1966, part of Dallas County Community College District System
- **Urban** 2-acre campus
- **Coed,** 6,089 undergraduate students, 25% full-time, 69% women, 31% men

Undergraduates 1,546 full-time, 4,543 part-time. Students come from 20 states and territories, 40 other countries, 1% are from out of state, 36% African American, 5% Asian American or Pacific Islander, 25% Hispanic American, 0.5% Native American, 3% international, 16% transferred in.
Freshmen *Admission:* 1,253 applied, 1,253 admitted, 712 enrolled.
Faculty *Total:* 398, 28% full-time, 16% with terminal degrees. *Student/faculty ratio:* 16:1.
Majors Accounting; administrative assistant and secretarial science; baking and pastry arts; biotechnology research; business administration and management; business automation/technology/data entry; cardiovascular technology; clinical laboratory science/medical technology; clinical/medical laboratory technology; clothing/textiles; computer/information technology services administration related; computer programming; computer science; criminal justice/police science; criminal justice/safety; culinary arts; data processing and data processing technology; diagnostic medical sonography and ultrasound technology; drafting and design technology; emergency medical technology (EMT paramedic); fashion/apparel design; food science; food services technology; health information/medical records administration; hospitality administration; hotel/motel administration; information science/studies; information technology; interior design; legal administrative assistant/secretary; legal assistant/paralegal; legal studies; liberal arts and sciences/liberal studies; medical administrative assistant and medical secretary; medical/clinical assistant; medical radiologic technology; medical transcription; nursing (licensed practical/vocational nurse training); nursing (registered nurse training); office occupations and clerical services; radiologic technology/science; respiratory care therapy; special products marketing; surgical technology; teacher assistant/aide; web page, digital/multimedia and information resources design.
Academics *Calendar:* semesters. *Degree:* certificates and associate. *Special study options:* academic remediation for entering students, adult/continuing education programs, advanced placement credit, cooperative education, distance learning, double majors, English as a second language, freshman honors college, honors programs, internships, part-time degree program, services for LD students, summer session for credit. *ROTC:* Army (c).
Library El Centro College Library with 72,176 titles, 371 serial subscriptions, 5,463 audiovisual materials, an OPAC, a Web page.
Computers on Campus 832 computers available on campus for general student use. A campuswide network can be accessed from off campus. Internet access, online (class) registration, at least one staffed computer lab available.
Student Life *Housing:* college housing not available. *Activities and Organizations:* choral group, Phi Theta Kappa, Radiology Club, SPAR (Student Programs and Resources Office), Organization of Latin American Students. *Campus security:* 24-hour emergency response devices and patrols, late-night transport/escort service. *Student services:* health clinic, personal/psychological counseling.
Athletics *Intramural sports:* basketball M/W, table tennis M/W, volleyball M/W, weight lifting M/W.
Costs (2006–07) *Tuition:* $33 per credit part-time; state resident $60 per credit part-time; nonresident $96 per credit part-time.
Applying *Options:* electronic application, early admission. *Required for some:* high school transcript, 1 letter of recommendation. *Application deadline:* rolling (freshmen), rolling (transfers).
Freshmen Application Contact Ms. Stevie Stewart, Director of Admissions and Registrar, El Centro College, 801 Main Street, Dallas, TX 75202. *Phone:* 214-860-2618. *Fax:* 214-860-2233. *E-mail:* sgs5310@dcccd.edu.

EL PASO COMMUNITY COLLEGE

El Paso, Texas

www.epcc.edu/

- **County-supported** 2-year, founded 1969
- **Urban** campus
- **Endowment** $24,000
- **Coed**

Undergraduates Students come from 47 states and territories, 40 other countries, 5% are from out of state.
Academics *Calendar:* semesters. *Degree:* certificates and associate. *Special study options:* academic remediation for entering students, adult/continuing education programs, advanced placement credit, cooperative education, distance

El Paso Community College (continued)

learning, English as a second language, external degree program, honors programs, internships, off-campus study, part-time degree program, services for LD students, summer session for credit. *ROTC:* Army (c).

Student Life *Campus security:* 24-hour patrols, late-night transport/escort service.

Athletics Member NJCAA.

Standardized Tests *Required:* THEA (for placement).

Financial Aid Of all full-time matriculated undergraduates who enrolled in 2004, 750 Federal Work-Study jobs (averaging $1800). 50 state and other part-time jobs (averaging $1800).

Applying *Options:* early admission, deferred entrance. *Application fee:* $10.

Director of Admissions Daryle Hendry, Director of Admissions, El Paso Community College, PO Box 20500, El Paso, TX 79998-0500. *Phone:* 915-831-2580. *E-mail:* daryleh@epcc.edu.

EVEREST COLLEGE
Arlington, Texas

EVEREST COLLEGE
Dallas, Texas

EVEREST COLLEGE
Fort Worth, Texas

FRANK PHILLIPS COLLEGE
Borger, Texas　　　　　　www.fpc.cc.tx.us/

- **State and locally supported** 2-year, founded 1948
- **Small-town** 60-acre campus
- **Endowment** $402,582
- **Coed**

Undergraduates Students come from 11 states and territories, 12 other countries.

Academics *Calendar:* semesters. *Degree:* certificates and associate. *Special study options:* academic remediation for entering students, accelerated degree program, adult/continuing education programs, advanced placement credit, cooperative education, distance learning, honors programs, internships, part-time degree program, services for LD students, summer session for credit.

Student Life *Campus security:* 24-hour emergency response devices and patrols, controlled dormitory access.

Athletics Member NJCAA.

Standardized Tests *Required:* THEA (for placement).

Costs (2005–06) *Tuition:* area resident $720 full-time, $30 per semester hour part-time; state resident $1128 full-time, $47 per semester hour part-time; nonresident $1296 full-time, $54 per semester hour part-time. *Required fees:* $914 full-time, $36 per semester hour part-time, $50 per term part-time.

Financial Aid Of all full-time matriculated undergraduates who enrolled in 2004, 9 Federal Work-Study jobs (averaging $3000). 1 state and other part-time job (averaging $3000).

Applying *Options:* common application, early admission, deferred entrance. *Required:* high school transcript.

Director of Admissions Ms. Beth Raper, Director of Admissions, Frank Phillips College, Borger, TX 79008-5118. *Phone:* 806-457-4200 Ext. 741. *Toll-free phone:* 800-687-2056. *Fax:* 806-273-7642.

GALVESTON COLLEGE
Galveston, Texas　　　　　　www.gc.edu/

- **State and locally supported** 2-year, founded 1967
- **Urban** 11-acre campus with easy access to Houston
- **Coed,** 2,230 undergraduate students, 38% full-time, 65% women, 35% men

Undergraduates 851 full-time, 1,379 part-time. Students come from 29 states and territories, 19 other countries, 4% are from out of state, 19% African American, 3% Asian American or Pacific Islander, 24% Hispanic American, 0.3% Native American, 1% international, 14% transferred in.
Freshmen *Admission:* 300 applied, 300 admitted, 300 enrolled.

Faculty *Total:* 141, 38% full-time. *Student/faculty ratio:* 16:1.

Majors Administrative assistant and secretarial science; behavioral sciences; biological and physical sciences; business administration and management; computer and information sciences related; computer science; computer/technical support; criminal justice/police science; culinary arts; data entry/microcomputer applications; dramatic/theater arts; education; emergency medical technology (EMT paramedic); English; history; hotel/motel administration; humanities; information technology; liberal arts and sciences/liberal studies; mathematics; medical radiologic technology; modern languages; music; natural sciences; nuclear medical technology; nursing (licensed practical/vocational nurse training); nursing (registered nurse training); physical education teaching and coaching; social sciences; social work; web page, digital/multimedia and information resources design; word processing.

Academics *Calendar:* semesters. *Degree:* certificates and associate. *Special study options:* academic remediation for entering students, adult/continuing education programs, advanced placement credit, cooperative education, distance learning, English as a second language, internships, off-campus study, part-time degree program, services for LD students, summer session for credit.

Library David Glenn Hunt Memorial Library with 45,193 titles, 4,000 serial subscriptions, 1,500 audiovisual materials, an OPAC, a Web page.

Computers on Campus 173 computers available on campus for general student use. A campuswide network can be accessed. Internet access, at least one staffed computer lab available.

Student Life *Housing:* college housing not available. *Activities and Organizations:* drama/theater group, choral group, student government, Phi Theta Kappa, Student Nurses Association, ATTC, Hispanic Student Organization. *Campus security:* 24-hour emergency response devices, late-night transport/escort service. *Student services:* personal/psychological counseling.

Athletics Member NJCAA. *Intercollegiate sports:* baseball M(s), softball W(s), volleyball W(s). *Intramural sports:* basketball M/W, bowling M/W, volleyball M/W.

Costs (2005–06) *Tuition:* state resident $900 full-time, $30 per hour part-time; nonresident $1800 full-time, $60 per hour part-time. *Required fees:* $430 full-time, $12 per hour part-time, $30 per term part-time.

Financial Aid Of all full-time matriculated undergraduates who enrolled in 2004, 36 Federal Work-Study jobs (averaging $2000).

Applying *Options:* common application. *Required for some:* high school transcript. *Application deadline:* rolling (freshmen), rolling (transfers). *Notification:* continuous (freshmen).

Freshmen Application Contact MaEsther Francis, Dean of Enrollment Management and Student Success, Galveston College, 4015 Avenue Q, Galveston, TX 77550. *Phone:* 409-944-1340. *Fax:* 409-944-1501. *E-mail:* mfrancis@gc.edu.

GRAYSON COUNTY COLLEGE
Denison, Texas　　　　　　www.grayson.edu/

Director of Admissions Dr. David Petrash, Associate Vice President for Admissions, Records and Institutional Research, Grayson County College, 6101 Grayson Drive, Denison, TX 75020. *Phone:* 903-465-6030.

HALLMARK INSTITUTE OF AERONAUTICS
San Antonio, Texas

Director of Admissions Mr. David McSorley, Director, Hallmark Institute of Aeronautics, 8901 Wetmore Road, San Antonio, TX 78216. *Phone:* 210-690-9000. *Toll-free phone:* 800-683-3600.

HALLMARK INSTITUTE OF TECHNOLOGY

San Antonio, Texas   www.hallmarkinstitute.edu/

Director of Admissions Ms. Sonia Ross, Director of Admissions, Hallmark Institute of Technology, 10401 IH 10 West, San Antonio, TX 78230-1737. *Phone:* 210-690-9000 Ext. 212. *Toll-free phone:* 800-880-6600.

HIGH-TECH INSTITUTE

Irving, Texas   www.high-techinstitute.com/

Director of Admissions Ms. Cindy M. Lewellen, Director, High-Tech Institute, 4250 North Belt Line Road, Irving, TX 75038. *Phone:* 972-871-2824. *Toll-free phone:* 800-987-0110. *Fax:* 972-871-2860. *E-mail:* clewellen@hightechschools.com.

HILL COLLEGE OF THE HILL JUNIOR COLLEGE DISTRICT

Hillsboro, Texas   www.hillcollege.edu/

Freshmen Application Contact Ms. Diane Harvey, Director of Admissions/Registrar, Hill College of the Hill Junior College District, PO Box 619, Hillsboro, TX 76645-0619. *Phone:* 254-582-2555 Ext. 315.

HOUSTON COMMUNITY COLLEGE SYSTEM

Houston, Texas   www.hccs.edu/

- **State and locally supported** 2-year, founded 1971
- **Urban** campus
- **Coed,** 39,516 undergraduate students, 31% full-time, 58% women, 42% men

Undergraduates 12,198 full-time, 27,318 part-time. 25% African American, 12% Asian American or Pacific Islander, 27% Hispanic American, 0.2% Native American, 8% international.
Freshmen *Admission:* 6,379 enrolled.
Faculty *Total:* 3,205, 25% full-time, 12% with terminal degrees. *Student/faculty ratio:* 20:1.
Majors Accounting; administrative assistant and secretarial science; agriculture; automobile/automotive mechanics technology; business administration and management; business/corporate communications; cartography; child care and support services management; child development; civil engineering technology; clinical/medical laboratory technology; commercial and advertising art; commercial photography; computer and information sciences; computer engineering technology; computer science; construction engineering technology; court reporting; criminal justice/police science; drafting and design technology; dramatic/theater arts; electrical, electronic and communications engineering technology; emergency medical technology (EMT paramedic); engineering technology; family and consumer sciences/human sciences; fashion/apparel design; fashion merchandising; finance; fire science; graphic and printing equipment operation/production; health/health care administration; health information/medical records administration; health information/medical records technology; horticultural science; hotel/motel administration; human resources management; industrial radiologic technology; industrial technology; insurance; interior design; kinesiology and exercise science; legal assistant/paralegal; liberal arts and sciences/liberal studies; logistics and materials management; marketing/marketing management; mass communication/media; medical administrative assistant and medical secretary; medical radiologic technology; mental health/rehabilitation; music management and merchandising; music theory and composition; nuclear medical technology; nursing (registered nurse training); occupational safety and health technology; occupational therapist assistant; physical therapist assistant; psychiatric/mental health services technology; radio and television broadcasting technology; real estate; respiratory care therapy; sign language interpretation and translation; social sciences; technical and business writing; tourism and travel services management; transportation technology.
Academics *Calendar:* semesters. *Degree:* certificates and associate. *Special study options:* academic remediation for entering students, adult/continuing education programs, advanced placement credit, cooperative education, distance learning, English as a second language, honors programs, independent study,

internships, part-time degree program, services for LD students, study abroad, summer session for credit. *ROTC:* Army (c).
Library Main Library plus 19 others with 140,674 titles, 2,012 serial subscriptions, 16,334 audiovisual materials, an OPAC, a Web page.
Computers on Campus 3200 computers available on campus for general student use. A campuswide network can be accessed from off campus. At least one staffed computer lab available.
Student Life *Housing:* college housing not available. *Activities and Organizations:* drama/theater group, student-run newspaper, television station, Phi Theta Kappa, Eastwood Student Association, Eagle's Club, Society of Hispanic Professional Engineers, International Student Association. *Campus security:* 24-hour emergency response devices and patrols, late-night transport/escort service. *Student services:* personal/psychological counseling.
Costs (2005–06) *Tuition:* area resident $1176 full-time; state resident $2472 full-time; nonresident $2952 full-time.
Applying *Required for some:* high school transcript, interview. *Application deadline:* rolling (freshmen).
Freshmen Application Contact Ms. Mary Lemburg, Registrar, Houston Community College System, 3100 Main Street, PO Box 667517, Houston, TX 77266-7517. *Phone:* 713-718-8500. *Fax:* 713-718-2111.

HOWARD COLLEGE

Big Spring, Texas   www.howardcollege.edu/

- **State and locally supported** 2-year, founded 1945, part of Howard County Junior College District System
- **Small-town** 120-acre campus
- **Endowment** $1.2 million
- **Coed,** 2,725 undergraduate students, 43% full-time, 62% women, 38% men

Undergraduates 1,174 full-time, 1,551 part-time. Students come from 10 states and territories, 2 other countries, 2% are from out of state, 5% African American, 0.9% Asian American or Pacific Islander, 31% Hispanic American, 0.5% Native American, 0.2% international, 0.4% transferred in, 18% live on campus.
Freshmen *Admission:* 1,027 applied, 1,027 admitted, 1,027 enrolled.
Faculty *Total:* 188, 67% full-time, 4% with terminal degrees. *Student/faculty ratio:* 11:1.
Majors Accounting; agriculture; art; automobile/automotive mechanics technology; behavioral sciences; biology/biological sciences; business administration and management; chemistry; child development; computer and information sciences related; computer programming; computer science; cosmetology; criminal justice/police science; dental hygiene; drafting and design technology; dramatic/theater arts; English; finance; health information/medical records administration; industrial arts; mathematics; music teacher education; nursing (licensed practical/vocational nurse training); nursing (registered nurse training); ornamental horticulture; physical education teaching and coaching; respiratory care therapy; social sciences; speech and rhetoric; substance abuse/addiction counseling.
Academics *Calendar:* semesters. *Degree:* certificates and associate. *Special study options:* academic remediation for entering students, adult/continuing education programs, advanced placement credit, cooperative education, distance learning, English as a second language, independent study, internships, part-time degree program, services for LD students, summer session for credit.
Library Howard College Library with 30,921 titles, 16,006 serial subscriptions, 1,710 audiovisual materials, an OPAC, a Web page.
Computers on Campus 300 computers available on campus for general student use. A campuswide network can be accessed from student residence rooms. Internet access, at least one staffed computer lab available.
Student Life *Housing:* on-campus residence required for freshman year. *Options:* men-only, women-only. Campus housing is university owned. Freshman applicants given priority for college housing. *Activities and Organizations:* drama/theater group, choral group, Phi Theta Kappa, Student Government Association, Mexican-American Student Association, Baptist Student Ministries. *Campus security:* 24-hour patrols. *Student services:* personal/psychological counseling.
Athletics Member NJCAA. *Intercollegiate sports:* baseball M(s), basketball M(s)/W(s), cheerleading M(s)/W(s), softball W(s). *Intramural sports:* basketball M/W, bowling M/W, football M/W, racquetball M/W, softball W, volleyball M/W.
Costs (2005–06) *Tuition:* area resident $1140 full-time, $30 per credit hour part-time; state resident $1500 full-time, $40 per credit hour part-time; nonresident $2160 full-time, $60 per credit hour part-time. Full-time tuition and fees vary according to course load, location, and program. Part-time tuition and fees vary according to course load, location, and program. *Required fees:* $66 full-time, $50 per term part-time. *Room and board:* $3140. *Payment plan:* installment. *Waivers:* senior citizens.

Howard College (continued)

Applying *Options:* early admission. *Required:* high school transcript. *Application deadline:* rolling (freshmen), rolling (transfers). *Notification:* continuous until 8/31 (freshmen).

Freshmen Application Contact Ms. Dianah Collom, Outreach Coordinator, Howard College, 1001 Birdwell Lane, Big Spring, TX 79720-3702. *Phone:* 432-264-5105. *Toll-free phone:* 866-HC-HAWKS. *Fax:* 432-264-5082. *E-mail:* dcollom@howardcollege.edu.

ITT TECHNICAL INSTITUTE
Arlington, Texas www.itt-tech.edu/

- **Proprietary** 2-year, founded 1982, part of ITT Educational Services, Inc
- **Suburban** campus with easy access to Dallas–Fort Worth
- **Coed**

Majors CAD/CADD drafting/design technology; computer programming; electrical, electronic and communications engineering technology; system, networking, and LAN/WAN management; web/multimedia management and webmaster; web page, digital/multimedia and information resources design.

Academics *Calendar:* quarters. *Degree:* associate.

Library a Web page.

Computers on Campus Internet access, at least one staffed computer lab available.

Student Life *Housing:* college housing not available.

Standardized Tests *Required:* Wonderlic aptitude test (for admission).

Costs (2005–06) *Tuition:* Please see school catalog for specific information.

Applying *Options:* deferred entrance. *Application fee:* $100. *Required:* high school transcript, interview. *Recommended:* letters of recommendation. *Application deadline:* rolling (freshmen), rolling (transfers). *Notification:* continuous (freshmen).

Freshmen Application Contact Robert Perez Jr., Director of Recruitment, ITT Technical Institute, 551 Ryan Plaza Drive, Arlington, TX 76011. *Phone:* 817-794-5100. *Toll-free phone:* 888-288-4950. *Fax:* 817-275-8446.

ITT TECHNICAL INSTITUTE
Austin, Texas www.itt-tech.edu/

- **Proprietary** 2-year, founded 1985, part of ITT Educational Services, Inc
- **Urban** campus
- **Coed**

Majors CAD/CADD drafting/design technology; computer programming; electrical, electronic and communications engineering technology; system, networking, and LAN/WAN management; web/multimedia management and webmaster; web page, digital/multimedia and information resources design.

Academics *Calendar:* quarters. *Degree:* associate.

Library a Web page.

Computers on Campus Internet access, at least one staffed computer lab available.

Student Life *Housing:* college housing not available.

Standardized Tests *Required:* Wonderlic aptitude test (for admission).

Costs (2005–06) *Tuition:* Please see school catalog for specific information.

Financial Aid Of all full-time matriculated undergraduates who enrolled in 2004, 1 Federal Work-Study job.

Applying *Options:* deferred entrance. *Application fee:* $100. *Required:* high school transcript, interview. *Recommended:* letters of recommendation. *Application deadline:* rolling (freshmen), rolling (transfers). *Notification:* continuous (freshmen).

Freshmen Application Contact Mr. Jim Branham, Director of Recruitment, ITT Technical Institute, 6330 Highway 290 East, Suite 150, Austin, TX 78723. *Phone:* 512-467-6800. *Toll-free phone:* 800-431-0677. *Fax:* 512-467-6677.

ITT TECHNICAL INSTITUTE
Houston, Texas www.itt-tech.edu/

- **Proprietary** 2-year, founded 1985, part of ITT Educational Services, Inc
- **Suburban** 1-acre campus
- **Coed**

Majors CAD/CADD drafting/design technology; computer programming; electrical, electronic and communications engineering technology; system, networking, and LAN/WAN management; web/multimedia management and webmaster; web page, digital/multimedia and information resources design.

Academics *Calendar:* quarters. *Degree:* associate.

Library a Web page.

Computers on Campus At least one staffed computer lab available.

Student Life *Housing:* college housing not available.

Standardized Tests *Required:* Wonderlic aptitude test (for admission).

Costs (2005–06) *Tuition:* Please see school catalog for specific information.

Applying *Options:* deferred entrance. *Application fee:* $100. *Required:* high school transcript, interview. *Recommended:* letters of recommendation. *Application deadline:* rolling (freshmen), rolling (transfers). *Notification:* continuous (freshmen).

Freshmen Application Contact Mr. Benjamin Moore, Director of Recruitment, ITT Technical Institute, 15621 Blue Ash Drive, Suite 160, Houston, TX 77090. *Phone:* 281-873-0512. *Toll-free phone:* 800-879-6486.

ITT TECHNICAL INSTITUTE
Houston, Texas www.itt-tech.edu/

- **Proprietary** 2-year, founded 1995, part of ITT Educational Services, Inc
- **Coed**

Majors CAD/CADD drafting/design technology; computer programming; electrical, electronic and communications engineering technology; system, networking, and LAN/WAN management; web/multimedia management and webmaster; web page, digital/multimedia and information resources design.

Academics *Calendar:* quarters. *Degree:* associate.

Library a Web page.

Computers on Campus Internet access, at least one staffed computer lab available.

Student Life *Housing:* college housing not available.

Standardized Tests *Required:* Wonderlic aptitude test (for admission).

Costs (2005–06) *Tuition:* Please see school catalog for specific information.

Applying *Options:* deferred entrance. *Application fee:* $100. *Required:* high school transcript, interview. *Recommended:* letters of recommendation. *Application deadline:* rolling (freshmen), rolling (transfers). *Notification:* continuous (freshmen).

Freshmen Application Contact Claudio Cruz, Director of Recruitment, ITT Technical Institute, 2222 Bay Area Boulevard, Houston, TX 77058. *Phone:* 281-486-2630. *Toll-free phone:* 888-488-9347.

ITT TECHNICAL INSTITUTE
Houston, Texas www.itt-tech.edu/

- **Proprietary** 2-year, founded 1983, part of ITT Educational Services, Inc
- **Urban** 4-acre campus
- **Coed**, 585 undergraduate students

Majors CAD/CADD drafting/design technology; computer programming; electrical, electronic and communications engineering technology; system, networking, and LAN/WAN management; web/multimedia management and webmaster; web page, digital/multimedia and information resources design.

Academics *Calendar:* quarters. *Degree:* associate.

Library a Web page.

Computers on Campus Internet access, at least one staffed computer lab available.

Student Life *Housing:* college housing not available. *Activities and Organizations:* student-run newspaper.

Standardized Tests *Required:* Wonderlic aptitude test (for admission).

Costs (2005–06) *Tuition:* Please see school catalog for specific information.

Applying   *Options:* deferred entrance. *Application fee:* $100. *Required:* high school transcript, interview. *Recommended:* letters of recommendation. *Application deadline:* rolling (freshmen), rolling (transfers). *Notification:* continuous (freshmen).

Freshmen Application Contact   Ms. Jennifer Gomez, Director of Recruitment, ITT Technical Institute, 2950 South Gessner, Houston, TX 77063. *Phone:* 713-952-2294. *Toll-free phone:* 800-235-4787.

ITT TECHNICAL INSTITUTE
Richardson, Texas   www.itt-tech.edu/

- **Proprietary** 2-year, founded 1989, part of ITT Educational Services, Inc
- **Suburban** campus with easy access to Dallas–Fort Worth
- **Coed**

Majors   CAD/CADD drafting/design technology; computer programming; electrical, electronic and communications engineering technology; system, networking, and LAN/WAN management; web/multimedia management and webmaster; web page, digital/multimedia and information resources design.

Academics   *Calendar:* quarters. *Degree:* associate.

Library   a Web page.

Computers on Campus   Internet access, at least one staffed computer lab available.

Student Life   *Housing:* college housing not available.

Standardized Tests   *Required:* Wonderlic aptitude test (for admission).

Costs (2005–06)   *Tuition:* Please see school catalog for specific information.

Financial Aid   Of all full-time matriculated undergraduates who enrolled in 2004, 5 Federal Work-Study jobs (averaging $5000).

Applying   *Options:* deferred entrance. *Application fee:* $100. *Required:* high school transcript, interview. *Recommended:* letters of recommendation. *Application deadline:* rolling (freshmen), rolling (transfers). *Notification:* continuous (freshmen).

Freshmen Application Contact   Mr. Nate Wallace, Director of Recruitment, ITT Technical Institute, 2101 Waterview Parkway, Richardson, TX 75080. *Phone:* 972-690-9100. *Toll-free phone:* 888-488-5761.

ITT TECHNICAL INSTITUTE
San Antonio, Texas   www.itt-tech.edu/

- **Proprietary** 2-year, founded 1988, part of ITT Educational Services, Inc
- **Urban** campus
- **Coed**

Majors   CAD/CADD drafting/design technology; computer programming; electrical, electronic and communications engineering technology; system, networking, and LAN/WAN management; web/multimedia management and webmaster; web page, digital/multimedia and information resources design.

Academics   *Calendar:* quarters. *Degree:* associate.

Library   a Web page.

Computers on Campus   Internet access, at least one staffed computer lab available.

Student Life   *Housing:* college housing not available. *Activities and Organizations:* student-run newspaper.

Standardized Tests   *Required:* Wonderlic aptitude test (for admission).

Costs (2005–06)   *Tuition:* Please see school catalog for specific information.

Applying   *Options:* deferred entrance. *Application fee:* $100. *Required:* high school transcript, interview. *Recommended:* letters of recommendation. *Application deadline:* rolling (freshmen), rolling (transfers). *Notification:* continuous (freshmen).

Freshmen Application Contact   Mr. Michell Hoyt, Director of Recruitment, ITT Technical Institute, 5700 Northwest Parkway, San Antonio, TX 78249. *Phone:* 210-694-4612. *Toll-free phone:* 800-880-0570.

JACKSONVILLE COLLEGE
Jacksonville, Texas   www.jacksonville-college.edu/

- **Independent Baptist** 2-year, founded 1899
- **Small-town** 20-acre campus
- **Coed,** 300 undergraduate students, 73% full-time, 60% women, 40% men

Undergraduates   220 full-time, 80 part-time. Students come from 16 states and territories, 15 other countries, 3% are from out of state, 16% African American, 0.3% Asian American or Pacific Islander, 12% Hispanic American, 3% international, 39% live on campus.
Freshmen   *Admission:* 223 applied, 91 admitted, 91 enrolled.

Faculty   *Total:* 24, 42% full-time, 25% with terminal degrees. *Student/faculty ratio:* 16:1.

Majors   Biological and physical sciences; liberal arts and sciences/liberal studies.

Academics   *Calendar:* semesters. *Degree:* diplomas and associate. *Special study options:* academic remediation for entering students, adult/continuing education programs, advanced placement credit, part-time degree program, summer session for credit.

Library   Weatherby Memorial Building plus 1 other with 22,000 titles, 170 serial subscriptions.

Computers on Campus   20 computers available on campus for general student use. A campuswide network can be accessed. Internet access, at least one staffed computer lab available.

Student Life   *Housing:* on-campus residence required through sophomore year. *Activities and Organizations:* drama/theater group, choral group, Drama Club, Ministerial Alliance, Mission Band. *Campus security:* 24-hour emergency response devices, evening security personnel. *Student services:* health clinic, personal/psychological counseling.

Athletics   Member NJCAA. *Intercollegiate sports:* basketball M(s)/W, volleyball W(s). *Intramural sports:* basketball M/W, table tennis M/W, tennis M/W, volleyball M/W.

Standardized Tests   *Required for some:* SAT (for admission), ACT (for admission), THEA.

Costs (2006–07)   *Comprehensive fee:* $4480 includes full-time tuition ($2800), mandatory fees ($307), and room and board ($1373). Part-time tuition: $175 per credit hour.

Applying   *Options:* electronic application, early admission. *Application fee:* $15. *Application deadlines:* 8/15 (freshmen), 7/1 (transfers). *Notification:* continuous until 7/1 (freshmen).

Freshmen Application Contact   Ms. Melissa Walles, Director of Admissions, Jacksonville College, 105 B.J. Albritton Drive, Jacksonville, TX 75766. *Phone:* 903-586-2518 Ext. 7134. *Toll-free phone:* 800-256-8522. *Fax:* 903-586-0743. *E-mail:* admissions@jacksonville-college.org.

KD STUDIO
Dallas, Texas   www.kdstudio.com/

- **Proprietary** 2-year, founded 1979
- **Urban** campus
- **Coed,** 152 undergraduate students, 100% full-time, 51% women, 49% men

Undergraduates   152 full-time. Students come from 10 states and territories, 4% are from out of state, 36% African American, 13% Hispanic American.
Freshmen   *Admission:* 67 applied, 61 admitted, 61 enrolled.

Faculty   *Total:* 23, 100% full-time. *Student/faculty ratio:* 7:1.

Majors   Acting; music related.

Academics   *Calendar:* semesters. *Degree:* associate. *Special study options:* cooperative education.

Library   KD Studio Library with 800 titles, 15 serial subscriptions.

Computers on Campus   1 computer available on campus for general student use. . Internet access, at least one staffed computer lab available.

Student Life   *Housing:* college housing not available. *Activities and Organizations:* drama/theater group, Student Council. *Campus security:* 24-hour emergency response devices and patrols.

Applying   *Options:* common application, deferred entrance. *Application fee:* $100. *Required:* essay or personal statement, high school transcript, interview, audition. *Required for some:* letters of recommendation. *Application deadline:* rolling (freshmen), rolling (transfers).

Freshmen Application Contact   Mr. T. Taylor, Director of Education, KD Studio, 2600 Stemmons Freeway, #117, Dallas, TX 75207. *Phone:* 214-638-0484. *Fax:* 214-630-5140. *E-mail:* acting@onramp.net.

KILGORE COLLEGE

Kilgore, Texas   www.kilgore.edu/

- **State and locally supported** 2-year, founded 1935
- **Small-town** 35-acre campus with easy access to Dallas–Fort Worth
- **Endowment** $5.2 million
- **Coed**

Undergraduates 2,749 full-time, 2,208 part-time. Students come from 21 states and territories, 36 other countries, 1% are from out of state, 15% African American, 0.5% Asian American or Pacific Islander, 4% Hispanic American, 0.1% Native American, 2% international, 6% transferred in, 12% live on campus. *Retention:* 45% of 2003 full-time freshmen returned.

Faculty *Student/faculty ratio:* 19:1.

Academics *Calendar:* semesters. *Degree:* certificates and associate. *Special study options:* academic remediation for entering students, adult/continuing education programs, advanced placement credit, cooperative education, English as a second language, internships, part-time degree program, services for LD students, student-designed majors, summer session for credit. *ROTC:* Army (c).

Student Life *Campus security:* 24-hour emergency response devices and patrols.

Athletics Member NJCAA.

Standardized Tests *Required:* THEA (for placement). *Recommended:* SAT or ACT (for placement).

Costs (2005–06) *Tuition:* area resident $540 full-time, $18 per hour part-time; state resident $1680 full-time, $56 per hour part-time; nonresident $2520 full-time, $84 per hour part-time. *Required fees:* $510 full-time. *Room and board:* $3580; room only: $1580.

Financial Aid Of all full-time matriculated undergraduates who enrolled in 2004, 80 Federal Work-Study jobs (averaging $2500). *Financial aid deadline:* 6/1.

Applying *Options:* early admission. *Required:* high school transcript. *Required for some:* interview.

Freshmen Application Contact Ms. Jeanna Centers, Admissions Specialist, Kilgore College, 1100 Broadway, Kilgore, TX 75662. *Phone:* 903-983-8202.

KINGWOOD COLLEGE

Kingwood, Texas   kcweb.nhmccd.edu/

- **State and locally supported** 2-year, founded 1984, part of North Harris Montgomery Community College District
- **Suburban** 264-acre campus with easy access to Houston
- **Coed,** 6,842 undergraduate students, 19% full-time, 63% women, 37% men

Undergraduates 1,308 full-time, 5,534 part-time. Students come from 44 other countries, 0.6% are from out of state, 8% African American, 3% Asian American or Pacific Islander, 14% Hispanic American, 0.4% Native American, 2% international, 4% transferred in. **Freshmen** *Admission:* 3,898 applied, 3,898 admitted, 1,006 enrolled.

Faculty *Total:* 387, 26% full-time. *Student/faculty ratio:* 16:1.

Majors Accounting; biology/biological sciences; business administration and management; computer and information sciences; computer engineering technology; computer graphics; computer typography and composition equipment operation; education; English; foreign languages and literatures; information science/studies; mathematics; nursing (licensed practical/vocational nurse training); occupational therapy; psychology; social sciences; visual and performing arts.

Academics *Calendar:* semesters. *Degree:* certificates and associate. *Special study options:* academic remediation for entering students, accelerated degree program, advanced placement credit, cooperative education, distance learning, double majors, English as a second language, external degree program, honors programs, independent study, internships, part-time degree program, services for LD students, summer session for credit.

Library Kingwood College Library with 38,000 titles, 262 serial subscriptions, 3,177 audiovisual materials, an OPAC, a Web page.

Computers on Campus 540 computers available on campus for general student use. A campuswide network can be accessed from off campus. Internet access, online (class) registration, at least one staffed computer lab available.

Student Life *Housing:* college housing not available. *Activities and Organizations:* drama/theater group, student-run television station, choral group, Phi Theta Kappa, Office Administration Club, African American Student Association, Student Government Association, Delta Epsilon Chi. *Campus security:* 24-hour emergency response devices and patrols, late-night transport/escort service. *Student services:* personal/psychological counseling.

Athletics *Intramural sports:* baseball M.

Costs (2006–07) *Tuition:* area resident $984 full-time, $52 per credit part-time; state resident $1944 full-time, $92 per credit part-time; nonresident $2304 full-time, $220 per credit part-time.

Financial Aid Of all full-time matriculated undergraduates who enrolled in 2004, 13 Federal Work-Study jobs, 4 state and other part-time jobs. *Financial aid deadline:* 5/15.

Applying *Options:* common application, early admission. *Required:* high school transcript. *Required for some:* essay or personal statement. *Application deadline:* rolling (freshmen), rolling (transfers).

Freshmen Application Contact Dr. Ike Williams, Director of Enrollment Management, Kingwood College, 20000 Kingwood Drive, Kingwood, TX 77339. *Phone:* 281-312-1562. *Fax:* 281-312-1477. *E-mail:* ronald.shade@nhmccd.edu.

LAMAR INSTITUTE OF TECHNOLOGY

Beaumont, Texas   theinstitute.lamar.edu/

Director of Admissions Mr. James Rush, Director of Admissions, Lamar Institute of Technology, PO Box 10043, Beaumont, TX 77710. *Phone:* 409-880-8354. *Toll-free phone:* 800-950-8321. *Fax:* 409-880-8463. *E-mail:* rushjc@hal.lamar.edu.

LAMAR STATE COLLEGE–ORANGE

Orange, Texas   www.lsco.edu/

- **State-supported** 2-year, founded 1969, part of The Texas State University System
- **Small-town** 21-acre campus
- **Endowment** $5524
- **Coed,** 2,143 undergraduate students, 43% full-time, 72% women, 28% men

Undergraduates 920 full-time, 1,223 part-time. Students come from 1 other state, 10% are from out of state, 19% African American, 1% Asian American or Pacific Islander, 3% Hispanic American, 0.9% Native American, 6% transferred in. **Freshmen** *Admission:* 447 applied, 315 admitted, 315 enrolled.

Faculty *Total:* 98, 52% full-time, 13% with terminal degrees. *Student/faculty ratio:* 19:1.

Majors Accounting; administrative assistant and secretarial science; architectural engineering technology; business administration and management; clinical/medical laboratory technology; computer science; data processing and data processing technology; environmental studies; information science/studies; liberal arts and sciences/liberal studies; literature; mass communication/media; mathematics; nursing (registered nurse training); real estate; social sciences.

Academics *Calendar:* semesters. *Degree:* certificates and associate. *Special study options:* academic remediation for entering students, distance learning, double majors, internships, part-time degree program, summer session for credit.

Library Lamar State College-Orange Library plus 1 other with 71,092 titles, 1,306 serial subscriptions, 288 audiovisual materials, an OPAC.

Computers on Campus 70 computers available on campus for general student use. A campuswide network can be accessed from off campus. Internet access, at least one staffed computer lab available.

Student Life *Housing:* college housing not available. *Activities and Organizations:* student-run newspaper. *Campus security:* 24-hour emergency response devices, late-night transport/escort service.

Athletics *Intramural sports:* archery M, basketball M/W, volleyball M/W, weight lifting M/W.

Costs (2005–06) *Tuition:* state resident $1824 full-time; nonresident $8448 full-time. *Required fees:* $736 full-time.

Financial Aid Of all full-time matriculated undergraduates who enrolled in 2004, 20 Federal Work-Study jobs (averaging $3000). 2 state and other part-time jobs (averaging $2000).

Applying *Options:* common application, early admission, deferred entrance. *Required:* high school transcript. *Application deadline:* rolling (freshmen), rolling (transfers). *Notification:* continuous (freshmen).

Freshmen Application Contact Kerry Olson, Director of Admissions and Financial Aid, Lamar State College–Orange, 410 Front Street, Orange, TX 77632. *Phone:* 409-882-3362. *Fax:* 409-882-3374.

LAMAR STATE COLLEGE–PORT ARTHUR

Port Arthur, Texas   **www.lamarpa.edu/**

- **State-supported** 2-year, founded 1909, part of The Texas State University System
- **Suburban** 34-acre campus with easy access to Houston
- **Coed,** 2,530 undergraduate students, 39% full-time, 64% women, 36% men

Undergraduates 980 full-time, 1,550 part-time. 1% are from out of state, 28% African American, 6% Asian American or Pacific Islander, 12% Hispanic American, 0.4% Native American, 0.3% international, 9% transferred in. *Freshmen Admission:* 836 applied, 507 admitted, 453 enrolled.
Faculty *Total:* 125, 51% full-time, 18% with terminal degrees. *Student/faculty ratio:* 13:1.
Majors Accounting technology and bookkeeping; administrative assistant and secretarial science; automobile/automotive mechanics technology; business administration and management; business/commerce; child development; child guidance; computer systems networking and telecommunications; cosmetology; criminal justice/safety; data processing and data processing technology; electrical and electronic engineering technologies related; electrical, electronic and communications engineering technology; family and consumer sciences/human sciences; general studies; heating, air conditioning, ventilation and refrigeration maintenance technology; legal assistant/paralegal; liberal arts and sciences/liberal studies; medical administrative assistant and medical secretary; nursing (licensed practical/vocational nurse training); nursing (registered nurse training); occupational safety and health technology; social sciences; surgical technology.
Academics *Calendar:* semesters. *Degree:* certificates and associate. *Special study options:* academic remediation for entering students, accelerated degree program, adult/continuing education programs, advanced placement credit, cooperative education, distance learning, double majors, English as a second language, honors programs, independent study, internships, off-campus study, part-time degree program, services for LD students, summer session for credit. *ROTC:* Army (c).
Library Gates Memorial Library with 43,726 titles, 3,400 serial subscriptions, 1,493 audiovisual materials, an OPAC, a Web page.
Computers on Campus A campuswide network can be accessed from off campus. Internet access, online (class) registration, at least one staffed computer lab available.
Student Life *Housing:* college housing not available. *Activities and Organizations:* drama/theater group, choral group, Historical Society, Chi Alpha, tennis, Student Government Association, Baptist Student Ministry. *Campus security:* 24-hour emergency response devices, student patrols, late-night transport/escort service. *Student services:* personal/psychological counseling.
Costs (2006–07) *One-time required fee:* $10. *Tuition:* state resident $2340 full-time; nonresident $10,590 full-time. *Required fees:* $824 full-time.
Applying *Options:* common application, early admission, deferred entrance. *Required:* high school transcript. *Required for some:* interview. *Application deadline:* rolling (freshmen), rolling (transfers). *Notification:* continuous (freshmen).
Freshmen Application Contact Ms. Connie Nicholas, Registrar, Lamar State College–Port Arthur, PO Box 310, Port Arthur, TX 77641-0310. *Phone:* 409-984-6165. *Toll-free phone:* 800-477-5872. *Fax:* 409-984-6025. *E-mail:* connie.nicholas@lamarpa.edu.

LAREDO COMMUNITY COLLEGE

Laredo, Texas   **www.laredo.edu/**

- **State and locally supported** 2-year, founded 1946
- **Urban** 186-acre campus
- **Endowment** $1.9 million
- **Coed,** 8,298 undergraduate students, 39% full-time, 58% women, 42% men

Undergraduates 3,200 full-time, 5,098 part-time. Students come from 4 states and territories, 5 other countries, 0.1% are from out of state, 0.2% African American, 0.3% Asian American or Pacific Islander, 94% Hispanic American, 4% international. *Retention:* 83% of 2003 full-time freshmen returned. *Freshmen Admission:* 1,245 applied, 1,245 admitted, 1,195 enrolled.
Faculty *Total:* 370, 57% full-time, 12% with terminal degrees. *Student/faculty ratio:* 18:1.
Majors Administrative assistant and secretarial science; child development; clinical/medical laboratory technology; computer programming; computer programming related; computer software and media applications related; computer systems networking and telecommunications; construction engineering technology; criminal justice/police science; data entry/microcomputer applications; data

entry/microcomputer applications related; data processing and data processing technology; electrical, electronic and communications engineering technology; emergency medical technology (EMT paramedic); fashion merchandising; fire science; hotel/motel administration; industrial radiologic technology; information science/studies; information technology; international business/trade/commerce; liberal arts and sciences/liberal studies; marketing/marketing management; medical/clinical assistant; nursing (registered nurse training); physical therapy; radiologic technology/science; real estate; social sciences.
Academics *Calendar:* semesters. *Degree:* certificates and associate. *Special study options:* academic remediation for entering students, adult/continuing education programs, advanced placement credit, distance learning, double majors, English as a second language, freshman honors college, honors programs, independent study, internships, part-time degree program, services for LD students, summer session for credit.
Library Yeary Library with 88,006 titles, 555 serial subscriptions, an OPAC.
Student Life *Housing Options:* coed. Campus housing is university owned. *Activities and Organizations:* drama/theater group, student-run newspaper, choral group. *Campus security:* 24-hour emergency response devices and patrols, student patrols. *Student services:* personal/psychological counseling, women's center.
Athletics Member NJCAA. *Intercollegiate sports:* baseball M(s), tennis M(s)/W(s), volleyball W(s). *Intramural sports:* cross-country running M/W, gymnastics M/W, swimming and diving M/W, tennis M/W, track and field M/W, volleyball M/W.
Costs (2006–07) *Tuition:* area resident $840 full-time, $35 per credit hour part-time; state resident $1680 full-time, $70 per credit hour part-time; nonresident $2520 full-time, $105 per credit hour part-time. *Required fees:* $270 full-time, $24 per credit hour part-time, $28 per term part-time. *Room and board:* $4229.
Financial Aid Of all full-time matriculated undergraduates who enrolled in 2004, 282 Federal Work-Study jobs (averaging $1854). 127 state and other part-time jobs (averaging $1884).
Applying *Options:* common application, early admission, deferred entrance. *Required:* high school transcript. *Application deadline:* rolling (freshmen), rolling (transfers).
Freshmen Application Contact Ms. Josie Soliz, Admissions Records Supervisor, Laredo Community College, West End Washington Street, Laredo, TX 78040-4395. *Phone:* 956-721-5177. *Fax:* 956-721-5493.

LEE COLLEGE

Baytown, Texas   **www.lee.edu/**

Director of Admissions Ms. Becki Griffith, Registrar, Lee College, PO Box 818, Baytown, TX 77522-0818. *Phone:* 281-425-6399. *Toll-free phone:* 800-621-8724. *E-mail:* bgriffit@lee.edu.

LON MORRIS COLLEGE

Jacksonville, Texas   **www.lonmorris.edu/**

Director of Admissions Mr. Craig Lee, Director of Admissions, Lon Morris College, 800 College Avenue, Jacksonville, TX 75766-2923. *Phone:* 903-589-4000 Ext. 4063. *Toll-free phone:* 800-259-5753.

MCLENNAN COMMUNITY COLLEGE

Waco, Texas   **www.mclennan.edu/**

- **County-supported** 2-year, founded 1965
- **Urban** 200-acre campus
- **Coed**

Undergraduates 3,354 full-time, 4,208 part-time. Students come from 10 other countries, 17% African American, 1% Asian American or Pacific Islander, 15% Hispanic American, 0.3% Native American, 0.4% international.
Academics *Calendar:* semesters. *Degree:* certificates and associate. *Special study options:* academic remediation for entering students, adult/continuing education programs, advanced placement credit, cooperative education, distance learning, honors programs, internships, off-campus study, part-time degree program, services for LD students, student-designed majors, study abroad, summer session for credit. *ROTC:* Air Force (c).
Student Life *Campus security:* 24-hour emergency response devices and patrols.
Athletics Member NJCAA.

McLennan Community College (continued)
Standardized Tests *Required:* THEA (for placement).
Costs (2005–06) *Tuition:* area resident $1272 full-time; state resident $1560 full-time; nonresident $2712 full-time. *Required fees:* $216 full-time.
Financial Aid Of all full-time matriculated undergraduates who enrolled in 2004, 265 Federal Work-Study jobs (averaging $850). 35 state and other part-time jobs (averaging $1000).
Applying *Options:* early admission. *Required:* high school transcript.
Director of Admissions Ms. Vivian G. Jefferson, Director, Admissions and Recruitment, McLennan Community College, 1400 College Drive, Waco, TX 76708-1499. *Phone:* 254-299-8689. *E-mail:* vjefferson@mclennan.edu.

MIDLAND COLLEGE
Midland, Texas www.midland.edu/

- **State and locally supported** primarily 2-year, founded 1969
- **Suburban** 163-acre campus
- **Endowment** $3.3 million
- **Coed,** 5,531 undergraduate students, 37% full-time, 57% women, 43% men

Undergraduates 2,027 full-time, 3,504 part-time. Students come from 22 states and territories, 31 other countries, 2% are from out of state, 5% African American, 1% Asian American or Pacific Islander, 29% Hispanic American, 0.5% Native American, 1% international, 5% transferred in, 5% live on campus. Freshmen *Admission:* 2,457 applied, 2,457 admitted, 739 enrolled.
Faculty *Total:* 269, 48% full-time, 14% with terminal degrees. *Student/faculty ratio:* 18:1.
Majors Airline pilot and flight crew; anthropology; art; automobile/automotive mechanics technology; behavioral sciences; biology/biological sciences; business automation/technology/data entry; business/commerce; chemistry; child care provision; commercial and advertising art; computer management; computer programming (specific applications); criminal justice/police science; data modeling/warehousing and database administration; developmental and child psychology; drafting and design technology; drawing; economics; electrical, electronic and communications engineering technology; emergency medical technology (EMT paramedic); English; fine/studio arts; fire science; fire services administration; foreign languages and literatures; French; geology/earth science; German; health information/medical records technology; heating, air conditioning, ventilation and refrigeration maintenance technology; history; journalism; legal assistant/paralegal; liberal arts and sciences/liberal studies; literature; mass communication/media; mathematics; medical radiologic technology; modern languages; music; music teacher education; nursing (registered nurse training); physical education teaching and coaching; physics; political science and government; pre-engineering; psychology; radiologic technology/science; respiratory care therapy; sociology; Spanish; speech and rhetoric; substance abuse/addiction counseling; system administration; system, networking, and LAN/WAN management; veterinary/animal health technology; veterinary technology; welding technology.
Academics *Calendar:* semesters. *Degrees:* certificates, associate, and bachelor's. *Special study options:* academic remediation for entering students, adult/continuing education programs, advanced placement credit, distance learning, honors programs, services for LD students.
Library Murray Fasken Learning Resource Center plus 1 other with 65,760 titles, 285 serial subscriptions, 359 audiovisual materials, an OPAC, a Web page.
Computers on Campus 1200 computers available on campus for general student use. A campuswide network can be accessed from student residence rooms and from off campus. Internet access, online (class) registration, at least one staffed computer lab available.
Student Life *Housing Options:* coed, men-only, women-only. Campus housing is university owned. *Activities and Organizations:* drama/theater group, student-run newspaper, choral group, OIKOS, Midland College Latin American Student Society, Student Government Association, Student Nurses Association, Baptist Student Ministries. *Campus security:* 24-hour patrols. *Student services:* personal/psychological counseling.
Athletics Member NJCAA. *Intercollegiate sports:* baseball M(s), basketball M(s)/W(s), cheerleading M(s)/W(s), golf M(s), softball W(s), volleyball W(s). *Intramural sports:* football M/W, soccer M/W, table tennis M/W, tennis M/W, ultimate Frisbee M, volleyball M/W.
Costs (2006–07) *Tuition:* area resident $1204 full-time, $93 per credit hour part-time; state resident $1540 full-time, $105 per credit hour part-time; nonresident $2352 full-time, $470 per credit hour part-time. *Required fees:* $350 full-time. *Room and board:* $3600.
Financial Aid Of all full-time matriculated undergraduates who enrolled in 2004, 75 Federal Work-Study jobs (averaging $2000). 5 state and other part-time jobs (averaging $2000).

Applying *Options:* common application. *Required:* high school transcript. *Application deadline:* rolling (freshmen), rolling (transfers). *Notification:* continuous (freshmen).
Freshmen Application Contact Mr. Trey Wetendorf, Admissions Director, Midland College, 3600 North Garfield, Midland, TX 79705-6399. *Phone:* 432-685-5502. *Toll-free phone:* 432-685-5502. *Fax:* 432-685-6401. *E-mail:* twetendorf@midland.edu.

MONTGOMERY COLLEGE
Conroe, Texas www.woodstock.edu/

- **State and locally supported** 2-year, founded 1995, part of North Harris Montgomery Community College District
- **Suburban** 200-acre campus with easy access to Houston
- **Endowment** $500,000
- **Coed,** 8,306 undergraduate students, 36% full-time, 61% women, 39% men

Undergraduates 2,970 full-time, 5,336 part-time. 0.5% are from out of state, 6% African American, 2% Asian American or Pacific Islander, 12% Hispanic American, 0.5% Native American, 1% international, 4% transferred in. Freshmen *Admission:* 1,677 applied, 1,677 admitted, 1,614 enrolled.
Faculty *Total:* 466, 25% full-time. *Student/faculty ratio:* 20:1.
Majors Accounting and business/management; animation, interactive technology, video graphics and special effects; business administration and management; CAD/CADD drafting/design technology; computer and information systems security; computer programming; computer software technology; computer systems networking and telecommunications; criminal justice/law enforcement administration; drafting/design engineering technologies related; e-commerce; electrical, electronic and communications engineering technology; human services; information technology; robotics technology; system, networking, and LAN/WAN management; web/multimedia management and webmaster; web page, digital/multimedia and information resources design.
Academics *Calendar:* semesters. *Degree:* certificates and associate. *Special study options:* academic remediation for entering students, adult/continuing education programs, advanced placement credit, English as a second language, internships, part-time degree program, services for LD students, summer session for credit.
Library Library/Learning Resources Center with 4,000 titles, 375 serial subscriptions.
Computers on Campus 600 computers available on campus for general student use. A campuswide network can be accessed. At least one staffed computer lab available.
Student Life *Housing:* college housing not available. *Activities and Organizations:* drama/theater group, student-run newspaper, choral group, Campus Crusade for Christ, Criminal Justice Club, Phi Theta Kappa, Latino-American Student Association, African-American Cultural Awareness. *Campus security:* 24-hour emergency response devices and patrols, late-night transport/escort service. *Student services:* personal/psychological counseling.
Costs (2006–07) *Tuition:* area resident $984 full-time, $32 per credit hour part-time; state resident $1944 full-time, $72 per credit hour part-time; nonresident $2304 full-time, $87 per credit hour part-time. *Required fees:* $20 full-time, $8 per credit hour part-time, $12 per term part-time.
Financial Aid Of all full-time matriculated undergraduates who enrolled in 2004, 25 Federal Work-Study jobs (averaging $2500). 4 state and other part-time jobs.
Applying *Options:* common application, early admission. *Application deadline:* rolling (freshmen), rolling (transfers).
Freshmen Application Contact Ms. Cami Davey, Assistant Dean, Student Services, Montgomery College, 3200 College Park Drive, Conroe, TX 77384. *Phone:* 936-273-7236. *E-mail:* cami.davey@nhmccd.edu.

MOUNTAIN VIEW COLLEGE
Dallas, Texas www.mvc.dcccd.edu/

- **State and locally supported** 2-year, founded 1970, part of Dallas County Community College District System
- **Urban** 200-acre campus
- **Coed,** 6,496 undergraduate students, 100% full-time, 59% women, 41% men

Undergraduates 6,496 full-time. Students come from 9 states and territories, 36 other countries, 1% are from out of state, 29% African American, 3% Asian American or Pacific Islander, 44% Hispanic American, 0.6% Native American, 0.7% international.

Faculty *Total:* 310, 26% full-time.
Majors Accounting; artificial intelligence and robotics; aviation/airway management; avionics maintenance technology; computer programming; criminal justice/law enforcement administration; drafting and design technology; electrical, electronic and communications engineering technology; electromechanical technology; engineering technology; health information/medical records technology; information science/studies; legal administrative assistant/secretary; liberal arts and sciences/liberal studies; quality control technology; welding technology.
Academics *Calendar:* semesters. *Degree:* certificates and associate. *Special study options:* academic remediation for entering students, adult/continuing education programs, advanced placement credit, cooperative education, distance learning, double majors, English as a second language, external degree program, freshman honors college, honors programs, independent study, internships, part-time degree program, services for LD students, summer session for credit. *ROTC:* Army (c).
Computers on Campus 200 computers available on campus for general student use. Internet access, at least one staffed computer lab available.
Student Life *Housing:* college housing not available. *Activities and Organizations:* drama/theater group, choral group. *Campus security:* 24-hour patrols, late-night transport/escort service. *Student services:* personal/psychological counseling.
Athletics Member NJCAA. *Intramural sports:* basketball M, football M, golf M, tennis M/W.
Costs (2006–07) *Tuition:* area resident $1008 full-time; state resident $1848 full-time; nonresident $2968 full-time.
Financial Aid Of all full-time matriculated undergraduates who enrolled in 2004, 145 Federal Work-Study jobs (averaging $2700).
Applying *Options:* common application, electronic application, early admission, deferred entrance. *Required:* high school transcript. *Application deadline:* rolling (freshmen), rolling (transfers). *Notification:* continuous (freshmen).
Freshmen Application Contact Ms. Glenda Hall, Associate Dean of Student Support Services, Mountain View College, 4849 West Illinois Avenue, Dallas, TX 75211-6599. *Phone:* 214-860-8666. *Fax:* 214-860-8570. *E-mail:* ghall@dcccd.edu.

MTI COLLEGE OF BUSINESS AND TECHNOLOGY
Houston, Texas www.mti.edu/

- **Proprietary** 2-year, founded 1984
- **Suburban** 3-acre campus
- **Coed**

Undergraduates 217 full-time. 12% African American, 0.9% Asian American or Pacific Islander, 48% Hispanic American.
Faculty *Student/faculty ratio:* 20:1.
Academics *Calendar:* semesters. *Degree:* certificates, diplomas, and associate. *Special study options:* advanced placement credit, cooperative education, English as a second language.
Applying *Options:* electronic application. *Required:* high school transcript, interview.
Director of Admissions Mr. Derrell Beck, Admissions Manager, MTI College of Business and Technology, 1275 Space Park Drive, Houston, TX 77058. *Phone:* 281-333-3363. *Toll-free phone:* 888-532-7675. *E-mail:* derrell@mtitex.com.

MTI COLLEGE OF BUSINESS AND TECHNOLOGY
Houston, Texas www.mtitexas.com/

- **Proprietary** 2-year
- **Urban** 6-acre campus with easy access to Houston
- 718 undergraduate students, 100% full-time

Undergraduates 718 full-time. Students come from 1 other state.
Faculty *Student/faculty ratio:* 25:1.
Academics *Calendar:* semesters. *Degree:* certificates, diplomas, and associate.
Student Life *Campus security:* late-night transport/escort service.
Director of Admissions Mr. David Wood, Director of Admissions, MTI College of Business and Technology, 7277 Regency Square Boulevard, Houston, TX 77036-3163. *Phone:* 713-974-7181. *Toll-free phone:* 800-344-1990. *Fax:* 713-974-2090. *E-mail:* davidw@mti.edu.

NAVARRO COLLEGE
Corsicana, Texas www.nav.cc.tx.us/
Director of Admissions Judy Cutting, Registrar, Navarro College, 3200 West 7th Avenue, Corsicana, TX 75110-4899. *Phone:* 903-874-6501 Ext. 221. *Toll-free phone:* 800-NAVARRO (in-state); 800-628-2776 (out-of-state).

NORTH CENTRAL TEXAS COLLEGE
Gainesville, Texas www.nctc.cc.tx.us/
Director of Admissions Condoa Parrent, Director of Admissions/Registrar, North Central Texas College, 1525 West California Street, Gainesville, TX 76240-4699. *Phone:* 940-668-4222.

NORTHEAST TEXAS COMMUNITY COLLEGE
Mount Pleasant, Texas www.ntcc.edu/
Freshmen Application Contact Ms. Sherry Keys, Director of Admissions, Northeast Texas Community College, PO Box 1307, 1735 Farm to Market Road, Mount Pleasant, TX 75456-1307. *Phone:* 903-572-1911 Ext. 263.

NORTH HARRIS COLLEGE
Houston, Texas www.nhmccd.edu/
Freshmen Application Contact Mr. Michael Code, Assistant Dean, North Harris College, 2700 W.W. Thorne Drive, Houston, TX 77073. *Phone:* 281-618-5794.

NORTH LAKE COLLEGE
Irving, Texas www.northlakecollege.edu/

- **County-supported** 2-year, founded 1977, part of Dallas County Community College District System
- **Suburban** 250-acre campus with easy access to Dallas–Fort Worth
- **Coed**

Undergraduates 2,925 full-time, 5,854 part-time. Students come from 14 other countries, 16% African American, 13% Asian American or Pacific Islander, 20% Hispanic American, 0.6% Native American, 6% international.
Faculty *Student/faculty ratio:* 19:1.
Academics *Calendar:* semesters. *Degree:* certificates, diplomas, and associate. *Special study options:* academic remediation for entering students, advanced placement credit, cooperative education, distance learning, English as a second language, part-time degree program, services for LD students, summer session for credit.
Student Life *Campus security:* late-night transport/escort service.
Athletics Member NJCAA.
Applying *Options:* early admission. *Recommended:* high school transcript.
Director of Admissions Mr. Steve Twenge, Director of Admissions and Registration, North Lake College, 5001 North MacArthur Boulevard, Irving, TX 75038-3899. *Phone:* 972-273-3109.

NORTHWEST VISTA COLLEGE
San Antonio, Texas www.accd.edu/nvc/

- **State and locally supported** 2-year, founded 1995
- **Coed**, 8,463 undergraduate students

Undergraduates 6% African American, 3% Asian American or Pacific Islander, 44% Hispanic American, 0.5% Native American, 0.2% international.
Faculty *Total:* 497, 17% full-time, 87% with terminal degrees. *Student/faculty ratio:* 12:1.

Northwest Vista College (continued)

Majors Biology/biotechnology laboratory technician; business administration, management and operations related; community health and preventive medicine; computer and information sciences; computer and information systems security; computer/information technology services administration related; computer programming; computer science; computer/technical support; criminal justice/safety; international/global studies; liberal arts and sciences/liberal studies; pre-engineering; recording arts technology; water quality and wastewater treatment management and recycling technology; web page, digital/multimedia and information resources design.

Academics *Calendar:* semesters. *Degree:* associate.

Student Life *Activities and Organizations:* drama/theater group, student-run newspaper. *Student services:* health clinic, personal/psychological counseling.

Costs (2006–07) *Tuition:* area resident $1008 full-time; state resident $2016 full-time; nonresident $4032 full-time. *Required fees:* $288 full-time.

Freshmen Application Contact Dr. Elaine Lang, Interim Director of Enrollment Management, Northwest Vista College, 3535 North Ellison Drive, San Antonio, TX 78251. *Phone:* 210-348-2016. *E-mail:* elang@accd.edu.

ODESSA COLLEGE

Odessa, Texas www.odessa.edu/

- **State and locally supported** 2-year, founded 1946
- **Urban** 87-acre campus
- **Endowment** $2.5 million
- **Coed**

Undergraduates 1,799 full-time, 2,770 part-time. Students come from 32 states and territories, 1% are from out of state, 4% African American, 1% Asian American or Pacific Islander, 44% Hispanic American, 0.7% Native American, 0.2% international, 0.1% transferred in, 3% live on campus.

Faculty *Student/faculty ratio:* 15:1.

Academics *Calendar:* semesters. *Degree:* certificates and associate. *Special study options:* academic remediation for entering students, adult/continuing education programs, advanced placement credit, cooperative education, internships, part-time degree program, services for LD students, student-designed majors, summer session for credit.

Student Life *Campus security:* 24-hour emergency response devices and patrols, late-night transport/escort service.

Athletics Member NJCAA.

Costs (2005–06) *Tuition:* area resident $1110 full-time; state resident $1410 full-time; nonresident $1860 full-time. Full-time tuition and fees vary according to course load. Part-time tuition and fees vary according to course load. *Required fees:* $330 full-time. *Room and board:* $4948; room only: $3500. Room and board charges vary according to board plan and housing facility. *Payment plans:* installment, deferred payment.

Financial Aid Of all full-time matriculated undergraduates who enrolled in 2004, 105 Federal Work-Study jobs (averaging $1667). 11 state and other part-time jobs (averaging $2046).

Applying *Options:* common application, electronic application, early admission, deferred entrance.

Director of Admissions Ms. Norma Garcia, Director of Admissions, Odessa College, 201 West University Avenue, Odessa, TX 79764-7127. *Phone:* 432-335-6815. *E-mail:* regrs@odessa.edu.

PALO ALTO COLLEGE

San Antonio, Texas www.accd.edu/pac/htm/

- **State and locally supported** 2-year, founded 1987, part of Alamo Community College District System
- **Urban** campus
- **Coed,** 8,070 undergraduate students

Undergraduates Students come from 50 states and territories, 1% are from out of state, 2% African American, 0.9% Asian American or Pacific Islander, 64% Hispanic American, 0.3% Native American, 0.4% international.

Freshmen *Admission:* 1,044 applied, 1,044 admitted.

Faculty *Total:* 476, 40% full-time. *Student/faculty ratio:* 17:1.

Majors Agriculture; architectural engineering technology; art; aviation/airway management; avionics maintenance technology; biology/biological sciences; business administration and management; chemistry; computer and information sciences related; computer engineering technology; computer management; computer science; economics; education; engineering; English; finance; geology/earth science; health science; history; horticultural science; information science/studies; information technology; journalism; legal studies; liberal arts and

sciences/liberal studies; library science; mathematics; modern languages; music; philosophy; physical education teaching and coaching; physics; psychology; sociology; speech and rhetoric; trade and industrial teacher education; veterinary sciences.

Academics *Calendar:* semesters. *Degree:* certificates and associate. *Special study options:* academic remediation for entering students, adult/continuing education programs, cooperative education, English as a second language, part-time degree program, summer session for credit.

Library Ozuna Learning and Resource Center.

Computers on Campus 300 computers available on campus for general student use. A campuswide network can be accessed from off campus. Internet access, online (class) registration, at least one staffed computer lab available.

Student Life *Housing:* college housing not available. *Activities and Organizations:* drama/theater group, student-run newspaper, Catholic Campus Ministries, International Club, Veterinary Technician Association, Movimiento Estudiantil Chicano De Aztlan, Phi Theta Kappa. *Campus security:* 24-hour emergency response devices and patrols. *Student services:* health clinic, personal/psychological counseling.

Athletics Member NJCAA. *Intercollegiate sports:* cross-country running M/W, swimming and diving M/W, track and field M/W. *Intramural sports:* fencing M(c)/W(c).

Costs (2006–07) *Tuition:* area resident $1546 full-time, $252 per credit hour part-time; state resident $2806 full-time, $504 per credit hour part-time; nonresident $5318 full-time, $1008 per credit hour part-time. *Required fees:* $280 full-time, $1 per credit hour part-time, $138 per term part-time.

Financial Aid Of all full-time matriculated undergraduates who enrolled in 2004, 272 Federal Work-Study jobs (averaging $2000).

Applying *Options:* early admission. *Required:* high school transcript. *Application deadline:* rolling (freshmen).

Freshmen Application Contact Ms. Rachel Montejano, Director of Enrollment Management, Palo Alto College, 1400 West Villaret Boulevard, San Antonio, TX 78224. *Phone:* 210-921-5279. *Fax:* 210-921-5310. *E-mail:* pacar@accd.edu.

PANOLA COLLEGE

Carthage, Texas www.panola.edu/

- **State and locally supported** 2-year, founded 1947
- **Small-town** 35-acre campus
- **Endowment** $1.5 million
- **Coed,** 1,927 undergraduate students, 49% full-time, 66% women, 34% men

Undergraduates 946 full-time, 981 part-time. Students come from 15 states and territories, 5 other countries, 8% are from out of state, 17% African American, 0.7% Asian American or Pacific Islander, 4% Hispanic American, 0.6% Native American, 0.6% international, 12% live on campus. *Retention:* 42% of 2003 full-time freshmen returned.

Freshmen *Admission:* 360 applied, 360 admitted, 360 enrolled.

Faculty *Total:* 61, 100% full-time. *Student/faculty ratio:* 23:1.

Majors Business/commerce; health information/medical records technology; industrial technology; information science/studies; nursing (registered nurse training).

Academics *Calendar:* semesters. *Degree:* certificates and associate. *Special study options:* academic remediation for entering students, adult/continuing education programs, advanced placement credit, cooperative education, distance learning, English as a second language, part-time degree program, services for LD students, summer session for credit.

Library M. P. Baker Library with 88,897 titles, 347 serial subscriptions, 4,133 audiovisual materials, an OPAC, a Web page.

Computers on Campus 500 computers available on campus for general student use. A campuswide network can be accessed from off campus. Internet access, online (class) registration, at least one staffed computer lab available.

Student Life *Housing:* on-campus residence required through sophomore year. *Options:* coed, men-only, women-only. Campus housing is university owned. *Activities and Organizations:* drama/theater group, student-run newspaper, choral group, marching band, Student Senate, Excel Club, Baptist Student Union, Panola Pipers, Phi Theta Kappa. *Campus security:* controlled dormitory access.

Athletics Member NJCAA. *Intercollegiate sports:* baseball M(s), basketball M(s)/W(s), volleyball W(s). *Intramural sports:* basketball M/W, football M/W, racquetball M/W, table tennis M/W, volleyball M/W, weight lifting M/W.

Costs (2006–07) *Tuition:* area resident $630 full-time, $45 per semester hour part-time; state resident $1320 full-time, $68 per semester hour part-time; nonresident $1710 full-time, $81 per semester hour part-time. *Required fees:* $720 full-time. *Room and board:* $3300.

Financial Aid Of all full-time matriculated undergraduates who enrolled in 2004, 50 Federal Work-Study jobs (averaging $2472).

Applying *Options:* common application, electronic application, early admission. *Required for some:* high school transcript. *Recommended:* high school transcript. *Application deadline:* rolling (freshmen), rolling (out-of-state freshmen), rolling (transfers). *Notification:* continuous (freshmen), continuous (out-of-state freshmen).
Freshmen Application Contact Ms. Barbara Simpson, Registrar/Director of Admissions, Panola College, 1109 West Panola Street, Carthage, TX 75633-2397. *Phone:* 903-693-2009. *Fax:* 903-693-2031. *E-mail:* bsimpson@panola.edu.

PARIS JUNIOR COLLEGE
Paris, Texas www.parisjc.edu/

Director of Admissions Ms. Sheila Reece, Director of Admissions, Paris Junior College, 2400 Clarksville Street, Paris, TX 75460-6298. *Phone:* 903-782-0425. *Toll-free phone:* 800-232-5804.

RANGER COLLEGE
Ranger, Texas www.ranger.cc.tx.us/

Freshmen Application Contact Dr. Jim Davis, Dean of Students, Ranger College, College Circle, Ranger, TX 76470. *Phone:* 254-647-3234 Ext. 110.

REMINGTON COLLEGE–DALLAS CAMPUS
Garland, Texas www.remingtoncollege.edu/

Director of Admissions Mr. Skip Walls, Campus President, Remington College–Dallas Campus, 1800 East Gate Drive, Garland, TX 75041-5513. *Phone:* 972-686-7878. *Fax:* 972-686-5116. *E-mail:* skip.walls@remingtoncollege.edu.

REMINGTON COLLEGE–FORT WORTH CAMPUS
Fort Worth, Texas www.remingtoncollege.edu/

Director of Admissions Ms. Lynn Wey, Campus President, Remington College–Fort Worth Campus, 300 East Loop 820, Fort Worth, TX 76112. *Phone:* 817-451-0017. *Fax:* 817-496-1257. *E-mail:* lynn.wey@remingtoncollege.edu.

REMINGTON COLLEGE–HOUSTON CAMPUS
Houston, Texas www.remingtoncollege.edu/houston/

Director of Admissions Mr. Lance Stribling, Director of Recruitment, Remington College–Houston Campus, 3110 Hayes Road, Suite 380, Houston, TX 77082. *Phone:* 281-89-1240.

RICHLAND COLLEGE
Dallas, Texas www.rlc.dcccd.edu/

Freshmen Application Contact Ms. Carol McKinney, Department Assistant, Richland College, 12800 Abrams Road, Dallas, TX 75243-2199. *Phone:* 972-238-6100.

ST. PHILIP'S COLLEGE
San Antonio, Texas www.accd.edu/spc/

- **District-supported** 2-year, founded 1898, part of Alamo Community College District System
- **Urban** 16-acre campus
- **Coed,** 9,792 undergraduate students, 43% full-time, 58% women, 42% men

Undergraduates 4,209 full-time, 5,583 part-time. Students come from 35 states and territories, 8 other countries, 16% African American, 2% Asian American or Pacific Islander, 48% Hispanic American, 0.7% Native American, 0.2% international, 11% transferred in. Freshmen *Admission:* 1,915 enrolled.
Faculty *Total:* 587, 37% full-time, 7% with terminal degrees. *Student/faculty ratio:* 18:1.
Majors Accounting; administrative assistant and secretarial science; aircraft powerplant technology; airframe mechanics and aircraft maintenance technology; art; autobody/collision and repair technology; automobile/automotive mechanics technology; biology/biological sciences; biomedical technology; business administration and management; CAD/CADD drafting/design technology; chemistry; clinical/medical laboratory technology; communications technology; computer and information systems security; computer maintenance technology; computer systems networking and telecommunications; construction engineering technology; construction management; criminal justice/law enforcement administration; culinary arts; data entry/microcomputer applications; diesel mechanics technology; dramatic/theater arts; dramatic/theater arts and stagecraft related; early childhood education; e-commerce; economics; education; electrical/electronics equipment installation and repair; electromechanical technology; English; environmental science; geology/earth science; health information/medical records technology; heating, air conditioning, ventilation and refrigeration maintenance technology; history; home furnishings and equipment installation; hotel/motel administration; interior architecture; interior design; kinesiology and exercise science; leatherworking/upholstery; legal administrative assistant/secretary; liberal arts and sciences/liberal studies; mathematics; medical administrative assistant and medical secretary; medical radiologic technology; music; nursing (licensed practical/vocational nurse training); occupational therapist assistant; philosophy; physical therapist assistant; political science and government; pre-dentistry studies; pre-engineering; pre-law studies; pre-medical studies; pre-nursing studies; pre-pharmacy studies; psychology; respiratory care therapy; restaurant/food services management; social work; sociology; Spanish; speech and rhetoric; system, networking, and LAN/WAN management; teacher assistant/aide; tourism and travel services management; urban studies/affairs; web/multimedia management and webmaster; welding technology.
Academics *Calendar:* semesters. *Degree:* certificates, diplomas, and associate. *Special study options:* academic remediation for entering students, adult/continuing education programs, advanced placement credit, cooperative education, distance learning, double majors, English as a second language, honors programs, independent study, internships, off-campus study, part-time degree program, services for LD students, summer session for credit. *ROTC:* Army (c).
Library St. Philip's College Learning Resource Center plus 1 other with 112,197 titles, 577 serial subscriptions, 11,300 audiovisual materials, an OPAC, a Web page.
Computers on Campus 885 computers available on campus for general student use. A campuswide network can be accessed from off campus that provide access to e-mail. Internet access, online (class) registration, at least one staffed computer lab available.
Student Life *Housing:* college housing not available. *Activities and Organizations:* drama/theater group, student-run newspaper, choral group, student government, Delta Epsilon Chi, Radiography Club, Respiratory Therapy Club, Diagnostic Imaging Club. *Campus security:* 24-hour emergency response devices and patrols, late-night transport/escort service. *Student services:* health clinic, women's center.
Athletics *Intramural sports:* basketball M/W, cheerleading M/W, table tennis M/W, tennis M/W, volleyball M/W, weight lifting M/W.
Costs (2005–06) *Tuition:* area resident $1200 full-time, $40 per hour part-time; state resident $2400 full-time, $80 per hour part-time; nonresident $4800 full-time, $160 per hour part-time. *Required fees:* $272 full-time, $136 per term part-time.
Applying *Options:* common application, electronic application, early admission. *Required:* high school transcript. *Application deadline:* rolling (freshmen), rolling (transfers). *Notification:* continuous (freshmen).
Freshmen Application Contact Ms. Ana Lisa Garza, Recruiter, St. Philip's College, 1801 Martin Luther King Drive, San Antonio, TX 78203-2098. *Phone:* 210-531-4861. *Fax:* 210-531-4836. *E-mail:* angarza@accd.edu.

SAN ANTONIO COLLEGE
San Antonio, Texas   www.accd.edu/

- **State and locally supported** 2-year, founded 1925, part of Alamo Community College District System
- **Urban** 45-acre campus
- **Coed**

Undergraduates 8,587 full-time, 13,639 part-time. Students come from 54 states and territories, 112 other countries, 2% are from out of state, 5% African American, 2% Asian American or Pacific Islander, 49% Hispanic American, 0.5% Native American, 2% international, 8% transferred in.

Faculty *Student/faculty ratio:* 20:1.

Academics *Calendar:* semesters. *Degree:* certificates and associate. *Special study options:* academic remediation for entering students, adult/continuing education programs, advanced placement credit, cooperative education, distance learning, double majors, English as a second language, honors programs, independent study, internships, part-time degree program, services for LD students, summer session for credit. *ROTC:* Army (b), Air Force (c).

Student Life *Campus security:* 24-hour patrols, late-night transport/escort service.

Standardized Tests *Required for some:* ACT ASSET, THEA, ACCUPLACER. *Recommended:* SAT or ACT (for placement), ACT ASSET, THEA, ACCUPLACER.

Costs (2005–06) *Tuition:* area resident $960 full-time, $40 per semester hour part-time; state resident $1920 full-time, $80 per semester hour part-time; nonresident $3840 full-time, $160 per semester hour part-time. *Required fees:* $272 full-time, $136 per term part-time.

Financial Aid Of all full-time matriculated undergraduates who enrolled in 2004, 500 Federal Work-Study jobs (averaging $3000).

Applying *Options:* early admission. *Required:* minimum 2.0 GPA. *Required for some:* high school transcript. *Recommended:* high school transcript.

Director of Admissions Ms. Rosemarie Hoopes, Director of Admissions and Records, San Antonio College, 1300 San Pedro Avenue, San Antonio, TX 78212-4299. *Phone:* 210-733-2582. *Toll-free phone:* 800-944-7575.

SAN JACINTO COLLEGE DISTRICT
Pasadena, Texas

SOUTHEASTERN CAREER INSTITUTE
Dallas, Texas

SOUTH PLAINS COLLEGE
Levelland, Texas   www.southplainscollege.edu/

- **State and locally supported** 2-year, founded 1958
- **Small-town** 177-acre campus
- **Endowment** $3.0 million
- **Coed,** 9,273 undergraduate students, 51% full-time, 54% women, 46% men

Undergraduates 4,774 full-time, 4,499 part-time. Students come from 21 states and territories, 8 other countries, 4% are from out of state, 4% African American, 0.8% Asian American or Pacific Islander, 25% Hispanic American, 0.5% Native American, 0.8% international, 10% live on campus.

Freshmen *Admission:* 2,213 enrolled.

Faculty *Total:* 454, 60% full-time. *Student/faculty ratio:* 20:1.

Majors Accounting; administrative assistant and secretarial science; advertising; agricultural economics; agriculture; agronomy and crop science; art; audio engineering; automobile/automotive mechanics technology; biological and physical sciences; biology/biological sciences; business administration and management; carpentry; chemistry; child development; commercial and advertising art; computer engineering technology; computer programming; computer science; consumer merchandising/retailing management; cosmetology; criminal justice/law enforcement administration; criminal justice/police science; data processing

and data processing technology; developmental and child psychology; dietetics; drafting and design technology; education; electrical, electronic and communications engineering technology; engineering; fashion merchandising; fire science; health/health care administration; health information/medical records administration; heating, air conditioning, ventilation and refrigeration maintenance technology; industrial radiologic technology; journalism; legal administrative assistant/secretary; liberal arts and sciences/liberal studies; machine tool technology; marketing/marketing management; mass communication/media; medical administrative assistant and medical secretary; mental health/rehabilitation; music; nursing (licensed practical/vocational nurse training); nursing (registered nurse training); petroleum technology; physical education teaching and coaching; physical therapy; postal management; pre-engineering; real estate; respiratory care therapy; social work; special products marketing; surgical technology; telecommunications; welding technology.

Academics *Calendar:* semesters. *Degree:* certificates and associate. *Special study options:* academic remediation for entering students, accelerated degree program, adult/continuing education programs, advanced placement credit, distance learning, part-time degree program, services for LD students, student-designed majors, summer session for credit. *ROTC:* Army (c), Air Force (c).

Library 70,000 titles, 310 serial subscriptions, an OPAC.

Computers on Campus 130 computers available on campus for general student use. A campuswide network can be accessed. Internet access, at least one staffed computer lab available.

Student Life *Housing:* on-campus residence required through sophomore year. *Options:* men-only, women-only. Campus housing is university owned. *Activities and Organizations:* drama/theater group, student-run newspaper, television station, choral group, student government, Phi Beta Kappa, Bleacher Bums, Law Enforcement Association. *Campus security:* 24-hour emergency response devices and patrols. *Student services:* health clinic.

Athletics Member NJCAA. *Intercollegiate sports:* basketball M(s)/W(s), cross-country running M(s)/W(s), track and field M(s)/W(s). *Intramural sports:* basketball M/W, cross-country running M/W, football M/W, golf M/W, racquetball M/W, softball M/W, table tennis M/W, tennis M/W, volleyball M/W.

Standardized Tests *Recommended:* ACT (for admission), SAT Subject Tests (for admission).

Costs (2006–07) *Tuition:* area resident $1394 full-time, $26 per hour part-time; state resident $1922 full-time, $48 per hour part-time; nonresident $2306 full-time, $64 per hour part-time. *Room and board:* $3300.

Financial Aid Of all full-time matriculated undergraduates who enrolled in 2004, 80 Federal Work-Study jobs (averaging $2000). 22 state and other part-time jobs (averaging $2000).

Applying *Options:* early admission. *Required:* high school transcript. *Application deadline:* rolling (freshmen), rolling (transfers).

Freshmen Application Contact Mrs. Andrea Rangel, Dean of Admissions and Records, South Plains College, 1401 College Avenue, Levelland, TX 78336. *Phone:* 806-894-9611 Ext. 2370. *Fax:* 806-897-3167. *E-mail:* arangel@southplainscollege.edu.

SOUTH TEXAS COLLEGE
McAllen, Texas   www.southtexascollege.edu/

- **District-supported** primarily 2-year, founded 1993
- **Suburban** 20-acre campus
- **Endowment** $17,971
- **Coed,** 16,225 undergraduate students, 38% full-time, 59% women, 41% men

Undergraduates 6,194 full-time, 10,031 part-time. 0.2% African American, 1% Asian American or Pacific Islander, 95% Hispanic American, 0.4% international. *Retention:* 56% of 2003 full-time freshmen returned.

Freshmen *Admission:* 2,054 enrolled.

Faculty *Total:* 623, 57% full-time. *Student/faculty ratio:* 22:1.

Majors Accounting; automobile/automotive mechanics technology; behavioral sciences; business administration and management; clinical laboratory science/medical technology; computer science; computer typography and composition equipment operation; developmental and child psychology; education; emergency medical technology (EMT paramedic); heating, air conditioning, ventilation and refrigeration maintenance technology; heavy equipment maintenance technology; hospitality administration; hotel/motel administration; human services; industrial radiologic technology; industrial technology; information science/studies; interdisciplinary studies; legal administrative assistant/secretary; legal assistant/paralegal; liberal arts and sciences/liberal studies; machine tool technology; nursing (registered nurse training); occupational therapy; plastics engineering technology.

Academics *Calendar:* semesters. *Degrees:* certificates, associate, and bachelor's. *Special study options:* academic remediation for entering students, accelerated degree program, adult/continuing education programs, cooperative education, off-campus study, part-time degree program, services for LD students, summer session for credit. *ROTC:* Army (c).

Library Learning Resources Center with 12,611 titles, 177 serial subscriptions, an OPAC, a Web page.

Computers on Campus 240 computers available on campus for general student use. A campuswide network can be accessed from off campus. At least one staffed computer lab available.

Student Life *Housing:* college housing not available. *Activities and Organizations:* Beta Epsilon Mu Honor Society, Automotive Technology Club, Child Care and Development Association Club, Heating, Air Conditioning, and Ventilation Club, Writing in Literary Discussion Club. *Campus security:* 24-hour emergency response devices and patrols, late-night transport/escort service. *Student services:* personal/psychological counseling.

Athletics *Intramural sports:* badminton M/W, basketball M/W, bowling M/W, football M/W, golf M/W, racquetball M/W, soccer M/W, softball M/W, table tennis M/W, volleyball M/W.

Standardized Tests *Required for some:* SAT and SAT Subject Tests or ACT (for admission), THEA.

Costs (2005–06) *One-time required fee:* $75. *Tuition:* area resident $1416 full-time, $127 per credit hour part-time; state resident $1826 full-time, $165 per credit hour part-time; nonresident $4848 full-time, $202 per credit hour part-time. *Required fees:* $400 full-time, $6 per credit hour part-time, $85 per term part-time.

Applying *Options:* common application, early admission, deferred entrance. *Required:* high school transcript. *Application deadline:* rolling (freshmen), rolling (transfers).

Freshmen Application Contact Mr. Matthew Hebbard, Director of Enrollment Services and Registrar, South Texas College, 3201 West Pecan, McAllen, TX 78501. *Phone:* 956-872-2147. *Toll-free phone:* 800-742-7822. *E-mail:* mshebbar@southtexascollege.edu.

SOUTHWEST INSTITUTE OF TECHNOLOGY

Austin, Texas **www.swse.net/**

Director of Admissions Fredrico Garcia, Director of Admissions, Southwest Institute of Technology, 5424 Highway 290 West, Suite 200, Austin, TX 78735-8800. *Phone:* 512-892-2640.

SOUTHWEST TEXAS JUNIOR COLLEGE

Uvalde, Texas **www.swtjc.net/**

Director of Admissions Mr. Joe C. Barker, Dean of Admissions and Student Services, Southwest Texas Junior College, 2401 Garner Field Road, Uvalde, TX 78801. *Phone:* 830-278-4401 Ext. 7284.

TARRANT COUNTY COLLEGE DISTRICT

Fort Worth, Texas **web.tccd.net/**

- **County-supported** 2-year, founded 1967
- **Urban** 667-acre campus
- **Endowment** $1.5 million
- **Coed,** 34,892 undergraduate students, 35% full-time, 58% women, 42% men

Undergraduates 12,259 full-time, 22,633 part-time. Students come from 6 states and territories, 14% African American, 5% Asian American or Pacific Islander, 17% Hispanic American, 0.6% Native American, 1% international. Freshmen *Admission:* 7,181 applied, 7,181 admitted, 7,181 enrolled.

Faculty *Total:* 2,076, 25% full-time. *Student/faculty ratio:* 19:1.

Majors Accounting; administrative assistant and secretarial science; architectural engineering technology; automobile/automotive mechanics technology; avionics maintenance technology; business administration and management; clinical laboratory science/medical technology; clinical/medical laboratory technology; computer programming; computer science; construction engineering technology; consumer merchandising/retailing management; criminal justice/law enforcement administration; dental hygiene; developmental and child psychology; dietetics; drafting and design technology; educational/instructional media design; electrical, electronic and communications engineering technology; electromechanical technology; emergency medical technology (EMT paramedic); fashion merchandising; fire science; food services technology; graphic

and printing equipment operation/production; health information/medical records administration; heating, air conditioning, ventilation and refrigeration maintenance technology; horticultural science; industrial radiologic technology; legal assistant/paralegal; liberal arts and sciences/liberal studies; machine tool technology; marketing/marketing management; mechanical engineering/mechanical technology; mental health/rehabilitation; nursing (registered nurse training); physical therapy; postal management; quality control technology; respiratory care therapy; sign language interpretation and translation; surgical technology; welding technology.

Academics *Calendar:* semesters. *Degree:* certificates and associate. *Special study options:* academic remediation for entering students, adult/continuing education programs, advanced placement credit, distance learning, English as a second language, honors programs, part-time degree program, services for LD students, summer session for credit. *ROTC:* Army (c), Air Force (c).

Library 197,352 titles, 1,649 serial subscriptions, 18,833 audiovisual materials, an OPAC, a Web page.

Computers on Campus 2000 computers available on campus for general student use. Internet access, online (class) registration, at least one staffed computer lab available.

Student Life *Housing:* college housing not available. *Activities and Organizations:* drama/theater group, student-run newspaper, choral group. *Campus security:* 24-hour emergency response devices and patrols. *Student services:* health clinic, personal/psychological counseling.

Athletics *Intramural sports:* football M, golf M, sailing M/W, table tennis M, tennis M/W, volleyball M/W.

Costs (2006–07) *Tuition:* area resident $1200 full-time, $50 per credit hour part-time; state resident $1512 full-time, $63 per credit hour part-time; nonresident $3600 full-time, $150 per credit hour part-time.

Financial Aid Of all full-time matriculated undergraduates who enrolled in 2004, 372 Federal Work-Study jobs (averaging $1325). 39 state and other part-time jobs (averaging $927).

Applying *Options:* early admission. *Application deadline:* rolling (freshmen), rolling (transfers).

Freshmen Application Contact Dr. Cathie Jackson, Director of Admissions and Records, Tarrant County College District, 1500 Houston Street, Fort Worth, TX 76102-6599. *Phone:* 817-515-5291. *Fax:* 817-515-5295.

TEMPLE COLLEGE

Temple, Texas **www.templejc.edu/**

- **District-supported** 2-year, founded 1926
- **Suburban** 114-acre campus
- **Coed**

Undergraduates 1,533 full-time, 2,535 part-time. Students come from 20 states and territories, 8 other countries, 1% are from out of state, 14% African American, 2% Asian American or Pacific Islander, 15% Hispanic American, 0.6% Native American, 0.2% international, 7% transferred in, 1% live on campus. *Retention:* 51% of 2003 full-time freshmen returned.

Faculty *Student/faculty ratio:* 18:1.

Academics *Calendar:* semesters. *Degree:* certificates and associate. *Special study options:* academic remediation for entering students, adult/continuing education programs, distance learning, English as a second language, internships, off-campus study, part-time degree program, summer session for credit.

Student Life *Campus security:* 24-hour emergency response devices and patrols.

Athletics Member NJCAA.

Standardized Tests *Required:* THEA (for placement). *Recommended:* ACT (for placement).

Costs (2005–06) *Tuition:* area resident $1860 full-time, $62 per hour part-time; state resident $2850 full-time, $95 per hour part-time; nonresident $4500 full-time, $150 per hour part-time. *Required fees:* $65 full-time.

Financial Aid Of all full-time matriculated undergraduates who enrolled in 2004, 86 Federal Work-Study jobs (averaging $826). 7 state and other part-time jobs (averaging $951).

Applying *Options:* early admission. *Required for some:* high school transcript.

Director of Admissions Ms. Angela Balch, Director of Admissions and Records, Temple College, 2600 South First Street, Temple, TX 76504-7435. *Phone:* 254-298-8308. *Toll-free phone:* 800-460-4636.

TEXARKANA COLLEGE

Texarkana, Texas **www.texarkanacollege.edu/**

Director of Admissions Mr. Van Miller, Director of Admissions, Texarkana College, 2500 North Robison Road, Texarkana, TX 75599. *Phone:* 903-838-4541 Ext. 3358. *E-mail:* vmiller@texarkanacollege.edu.

TEXAS CULINARY ACADEMY

Austin, Texas   www.txca.com/

Director of Admissions Paula Paulette, Vice President of Marketing and Admissions, Texas Culinary Academy, 11400 Burnet Road, Austin, TX 78758. *Phone:* 512-837-2665. *Toll-free phone:* 888-553-2433. *E-mail:* ppaulette@txca.com.

TEXAS SOUTHMOST COLLEGE

Brownsville, Texas   www.utb.edu/

Director of Admissions Mr. Rene Villarreal, Director of Admissions, Texas Southmost College, 80 Fort Brown, Brownsville, TX 78520-4991. *Phone:* 956-544-8992. *E-mail:* rvillarreal@utb.edu.

TEXAS STATE TECHNICAL COLLEGE HARLINGEN

Harlingen, Texas   www.harlingen.tstc.edu/

Director of Admissions Mrs. Elva Short, Director of Admissions, Texas State Technical College Harlingen, 1902 North Loop 499, Harlingen, TX 78550-3697. *Phone:* 956-364-4100. *Toll-free phone:* 800-852-8784.

TEXAS STATE TECHNICAL COLLEGE— MARSHALL

Marshall, Texas

TEXAS STATE TECHNICAL COLLEGE WACO

Waco, Texas   waco.tstc.edu/

- **State-supported** 2-year, founded 1965, part of Texas State Technical College System
- **Suburban** 200-acre campus
- **Coed,** 4,452 undergraduate students, 67% full-time, 23% women, 77% men

Undergraduates 2,989 full-time, 1,463 part-time. Students come from 30 states and territories, 5 other countries, 2% are from out of state, 16% African American, 1% Asian American or Pacific Islander, 16% Hispanic American, 0.4% Native American, 2% international.

Freshmen *Admission:* 3,151 applied, 3,151 admitted, 1,319 enrolled.

Faculty *Total:* 278, 87% full-time. *Student/faculty ratio:* 16:1.

Majors Aeronautics/aviation/aerospace science and technology; agricultural and food products processing; aircraft powerplant technology; airframe mechanics and aircraft maintenance technology; airline pilot and flight crew; audio engineering; autobody/collision and repair technology; automobile/automotive mechanics technology; avionics maintenance technology; biomedical technology; chemical engineering; chemical technology; commercial and advertising art; computer and information sciences; computer and information systems security; computer engineering technology; computer programming; computer science; computer technology/computer systems technology; culinary arts; dental assisting; diesel mechanics technology; drafting and design technology; educational/instructional media design; electrical, electronic and communications engineering technology; electrical/electronics drafting and CAD/CADD; food services technology; graphic and printing equipment operation/production; heating, air conditioning and refrigeration technology; heating, air conditioning, ventilation and refrigeration maintenance technology; heavy equipment maintenance technology; industrial technology; information science/studies; institutional food workers; instrumentation technology; laser and optical technology; machine tool technology; mechanical engineering/mechanical technology; nuclear/nuclear power technology; occupational safety and health technology; ornamen-

tal horticulture; photographic and film/video technology; quality control technology; turf and turfgrass management; welding technology.

Academics *Calendar:* trimesters. *Degree:* certificates and associate. *Special study options:* academic remediation for entering students, adult/continuing education programs, cooperative education, distance learning, internships, part-time degree program, services for LD students, summer session for credit.

Library Texas State Technical College-Waco Campus Library with 60,000 titles, 400 serial subscriptions, 2,324 audiovisual materials, an OPAC, a Web page.

Computers on Campus 900 computers available on campus for general student use. A campuswide network can be accessed from student residence rooms that provide access to various software packages. At least one staffed computer lab available.

Student Life *Housing:* on-campus residence required for freshman year. *Options:* coed, men-only, women-only, disabled students. *Activities and Organizations:* student-run newspaper, Automotive VICA, Society of Mexican-American Engineers and Scientists, Texas Association of Black Persons In Higher Education, Phi Theta Kappa. *Campus security:* 24-hour emergency response devices and patrols, late-night transport/escort service, controlled dormitory access. *Student services:* health clinic, personal/psychological counseling, women's center.

Athletics *Intramural sports:* basketball M/W, football M, golf M/W, racquetball M/W, softball M/W, volleyball M/W, weight lifting M.

Standardized Tests *Required:* ACCUPLACER (for admission).

Costs (2006–07) *Tuition:* state resident $1950 full-time, $65 per credit hour part-time; nonresident $5460 full-time, $182 per credit hour part-time. *Required fees:* $2000 full-time, $21 per credit hour part-time. *Room and board:* $4100; room only: $1860.

Financial Aid Of all full-time matriculated undergraduates who enrolled in 2004, 125 Federal Work-Study jobs (averaging $2500). 150 state and other part-time jobs.

Applying *Options:* common application, electronic application, early admission. *Required:* high school transcript. *Required for some:* interview. *Application deadline:* rolling (freshmen), rolling (transfers). *Notification:* continuous (freshmen).

Freshmen Application Contact Mr. Marcus Balch, Director, Recruiting Services, Texas State Technical College Waco, 3801 Campus Drive, Waco, TX 76705. *Phone:* 254-867-2026. *Toll-free phone:* 800-792-8784 Ext. 2362. *Fax:* 254-867-3827. *E-mail:* mrcus.balch@tstc.edu.

TEXAS STATE TECHNICAL COLLEGE WEST TEXAS

Sweetwater, Texas   www.sweetwater.tstc.edu/

Freshmen Application Contact Ms. Maria Aguirre-Acuna, Coordinator of New Students, Texas State Technical College West Texas, 300 College Drive, Sweetwater, TX 79556-4108. *Phone:* 915-235-7349. *Toll-free phone:* 800-592-8784.

TOMBALL COLLEGE

Tomball, Texas   wwwtc.nhmccd.edu/

- **State and locally supported** 2-year, founded 1988, part of North Harris Montgomery Community College District
- **Suburban** 210-acre campus with easy access to Houston
- **Coed,** 7,647 undergraduate students, 19% full-time, 60% women, 40% men

Undergraduates 1,463 full-time, 6,184 part-time. 0.6% are from out of state, 7% African American, 5% Asian American or Pacific Islander, 13% Hispanic American, 0.4% Native American, 3% international, 6% transferred in.

Freshmen *Admission:* 1,142 enrolled.

Faculty *Total:* 358, 31% full-time. *Student/faculty ratio:* 8:1.

Majors Accounting; business administration and management; computer programming; electrical, electronic and communications engineering technology; human services; legal administrative assistant/secretary; medical administrative assistant and medical secretary; nursing (registered nurse training); occupational therapy; veterinary technology.

Academics *Calendar:* semesters. *Degree:* certificates and associate. *Special study options:* academic remediation for entering students, adult/continuing education programs, advanced placement credit, cooperative education, English as a second language, honors programs, internships, part-time degree program, services for LD students, summer session for credit.

Library Learning Resource Center with 24,063 titles, 385 serial subscriptions, an OPAC, a Web page.

Computers on Campus 92 computers available on campus for general student use. A campuswide network can be accessed from off campus. At least one staffed computer lab available.

Student Life *Housing:* college housing not available. *Activities and Organizations:* drama/theater group, student-run newspaper, Phi Theta Kappa, Culture Club, Veterinary Technicians Student Organization, Human Services Club, Student Nurses Association. *Campus security:* 24-hour emergency response devices, late-night transport/escort service, trained security personnel during open hours. *Student services:* personal/psychological counseling.

Standardized Tests *Recommended:* SAT or ACT (for admission), THEA, ACT COMPASS.

Costs (2006–07) *Tuition:* area resident $1080 full-time, $56 per credit hour part-time; state resident $2040 full-time, $96 per credit hour part-time; nonresident $2400 full-time, $220 per credit hour part-time.

Financial Aid Of all full-time matriculated undergraduates who enrolled in 2004, 34 Federal Work-Study jobs (averaging $3000).

Applying *Options:* common application, early admission.

Freshmen Application Contact Mr. Larry Rideaux, Dean of Enrollment Services, Tomball College, 30555 Tomball Parkway, Tomball, TX 77375-4036. *Phone:* 281-351-3334. *Fax:* 281-357-3773. *E-mail:* tc.advisors@nhmccd.edu.

TRINITY VALLEY COMMUNITY COLLEGE
Athens, Texas   www.tvcc.edu/

- **State and locally supported** 2-year, founded 1946
- **Small-town** 65-acre campus with easy access to Dallas–Fort Worth
- **Endowment** $1.9 million
- **Coed,** 5,821 undergraduate students, 42% full-time, 56% women, 44% men

Undergraduates 2,442 full-time, 3,379 part-time. Students come from 48 states and territories, 1% are from out of state, 13% African American, 0.3% Asian American or Pacific Islander, 6% Hispanic American, 0.3% Native American, 0.5% international. Freshmen *Admission:* 1,160 enrolled.

Faculty *Total:* 273, 45% full-time, 5% with terminal degrees. *Student/faculty ratio:* 20:1.

Majors Accounting; agricultural teacher education; animal sciences; art; automobile/automotive mechanics technology; biology/biological sciences; business administration and management; business teacher education; chemistry; child development; computer science; corrections; cosmetology; criminal justice/law enforcement administration; criminal justice/police science; dance; data processing and data processing technology; developmental and child psychology; drafting and design technology; dramatic/theater arts; education; elementary education; emergency medical technology (EMT paramedic); English; farm and ranch management; fashion merchandising; finance; geology/earth science; heating, air conditioning, ventilation and refrigeration maintenance technology; history; horticultural science; insurance; journalism; kindergarten/preschool education; legal administrative assistant/secretary; liberal arts and sciences/liberal studies; marketing/marketing management; mathematics; music; nursing (licensed practical/vocational nurse training); nursing (registered nurse training); physical education teaching and coaching; physical sciences; political science and government; pre-engineering; psychology; range science and management; real estate; religious studies; sociology; Spanish; speech and rhetoric; surgical technology; welding technology.

Academics *Calendar:* semesters. *Degree:* certificates, diplomas, and associate. *Special study options:* academic remediation for entering students, adult/continuing education programs, advanced placement credit, cooperative education, distance learning, honors programs, internships, part-time degree program, services for LD students, summer session for credit.

Library Ginger Murchison Learning Resource Center plus 3 others with 54,940 titles, 257 serial subscriptions, 1,954 audiovisual materials, an OPAC, a Web page.

Computers on Campus 66 computers available on campus for general student use. A campuswide network can be accessed. Internet access, at least one staffed computer lab available.

Student Life *Housing Options:* coed, men-only, women-only. Campus housing is university owned. *Activities and Organizations:* drama/theater group, student-run newspaper, choral group, marching band, Student Senate, Phi Theta Kappa, Delta Epsilon Chi. *Campus security:* 24-hour emergency response devices and patrols, controlled dormitory access. *Student services:* personal/psychological counseling.

Athletics Member NJCAA. *Intercollegiate sports:* basketball M(s)/W(s), cheerleading M(s)/W(s), football M(s). *Intramural sports:* baseball M/W, basketball M/W, football M, table tennis M/W, volleyball M/W.

Costs (2006–07) *Tuition:* state resident $1200 full-time, $20 per semester hour part-time; nonresident $3900 full-time, $65 per semester hour part-time. *Required fees:* $900 full-time, $15 per semester hour part-time. *Room and board:* $3470.

Financial Aid Of all full-time matriculated undergraduates who enrolled in 2004, 80 Federal Work-Study jobs (averaging $1544). 40 state and other part-time jobs (averaging $1544).

Applying *Options:* early admission. *Required:* high school transcript. *Application deadline:* rolling (freshmen), rolling (transfers). *Notification:* continuous (freshmen).

Freshmen Application Contact Dr. Colette Hilliard, Dean of Enrollment Management and Registrar, Trinity Valley Community College, 100 Cardinal Drive, Athens, TX 75751. *Phone:* 903-675-6209 Ext. 209.

TYLER JUNIOR COLLEGE
Tyler, Texas   www.tjc.edu/

Freshmen Application Contact Ms. Janna Chancey, Director of Enrollment Management, Tyler Junior College, PO Box 9020, Tyler, TX 75711. *Phone:* 903-510-2396. *Toll-free phone:* 800-687-5680.

UNIVERSAL TECHNICAL INSTITUTE
Houston, Texas   www.uticorp.com/

Director of Admissions Randy Whitman, Director of Admissions, Universal Technical Institute, 721 Lockhaven Drive, Houston, TX 77073-5598. *Phone:* 281-443-6262 Ext. 261. *Fax:* 281-443-0610.

VERNON COLLEGE
Vernon, Texas   www.vernoncollege.edu/

Director of Admissions Mr. Joe Hite, Dean of Admissions/Registrar, Vernon College, 4400 College Drive, Vernon, TX 76384-4092. *Phone:* 940-552-6291 Ext. 2204.

VICTORIA COLLEGE
Victoria, Texas   www.victoriacollege.edu/

Director of Admissions Lavern Dentler, Registrar, Victoria College, 2200 East Red River, Victoria, TX 77901-4494. *Phone:* 361-573-3291 Ext. 6407.

VIRGINIA COLLEGE AT AUSTIN
Austin, Texas

WADE COLLEGE
Dallas, Texas   www.wadecollege.edu/

Freshmen Application Contact Ms. Suzan Wade, Admissions Director, Wade College, International Apparel Mart at Dallas Market Center, 2350 Stemmons Expressway, Suite M5120, PO Box 586343, Dallas, TX 75258. *Phone:* 214-637-3530. *Toll-free phone:* 800-624-4850.

▶ See page 600 for the College Close-Up.

WEATHERFORD COLLEGE
Weatherford, Texas   www.wc.edu/

- **State and locally supported** 2-year, founded 1869
- **Small-town** 94-acre campus with easy access to Dallas–Fort Worth
- **Endowment** $42.5 million
- **Coed,** 4,552 undergraduate students, 50% full-time, 58% women, 42% men

Undergraduates 2,287 full-time, 2,265 part-time. 8% are from out of state, 2% African American, 0.5% Asian American or Pacific Islander, 8% Hispanic

Weatherford College (continued)

American, 1% Native American, 1% international, 7% live on campus. *Freshmen Admission:* 3,439 admitted.

Faculty *Total:* 220, 43% full-time. *Student/faculty ratio:* 22:1.

Majors Administrative assistant and secretarial science; biological and physical sciences; business administration and management; computer graphics; computer programming; corrections; cosmetology; criminal justice/law enforcement administration; emergency medical technology (EMT paramedic); fire science; information science/studies; liberal arts and sciences/liberal studies; nursing (registered nurse training); pharmacy technician; respiratory care therapy.

Academics *Calendar:* semesters. *Degree:* certificates, diplomas, and associate. *Special study options:* academic remediation for entering students, adult/continuing education programs, cooperative education, distance learning, freshman honors college, honors programs, internships, part-time degree program, services for LD students, student-designed majors, summer session for credit. *ROTC:* Air Force (c).

Library Weatherford College Library with 59,499 titles, 362 serial subscriptions, an OPAC, a Web page.

Computers on Campus 85 computers available on campus for general student use. A campuswide network can be accessed from off campus. Internet access, at least one staffed computer lab available.

Student Life *Housing Options:* coed. *Activities and Organizations:* drama/theater group, choral group, Black Awareness Student Organization, Criminal Justice Club, Phi Theta Kappa. *Campus security:* 24-hour emergency response devices and patrols, late-night transport/escort service. *Student services:* personal/psychological counseling.

Athletics Member NJCAA. *Intercollegiate sports:* baseball M(s), basketball M(s)/W(s), cheerleading W(s), tennis W(s).

Costs (2006–07) *Tuition:* area resident $1456 full-time, $52 per hour part-time; state resident $1960 full-time, $70 per hour part-time; nonresident $3164 full-time, $113 per hour part-time. *Room and board:* $6500.

Applying *Options:* early admission. *Application deadline:* rolling (freshmen), rolling (transfers). *Notification:* continuous (freshmen).

Freshmen Application Contact Mr. Ralph Willingham, Dean of Admissions, Weatherford College, 225 College Park Drive, Weatherford, TX 76086-5699. *Phone:* 817-598-6248. *Toll-free phone:* 800-287-5471 Ext. 248. *Fax:* 817-598-6205. *E-mail:* willingham@wc.edu.

WESTERN TECHNICAL COLLEGE
El Paso, Texas — www.wtc-ep.edu/

- **Private** 2-year
- **Coed,** 825 undergraduate students, 73% full-time, 15% women, 85% men

Undergraduates 600 full-time, 225 part-time. 3% African American, 85% Hispanic American.

Faculty *Total:* 130, 75% full-time. *Student/faculty ratio:* 18:1.

Majors Automobile/automotive mechanics technology; computer engineering technology; heating, air conditioning, ventilation and refrigeration maintenance technology.

Academics *Calendar:* continuous. *Degree:* certificates and associate.

Computers on Campus 25 computers available on campus for general student use. A campuswide network can be accessed from off campus. Internet access, at least one staffed computer lab available. Computer purchase or lease plan available.

Student Life *Housing:* college housing not available.

Applying *Options:* early admission, deferred entrance.

Freshmen Application Contact Mr. Bill Terrell, Chief Admissions Officer, Western Technical College, 1000 Texas Avenue, El Paso, TX 79901-1536. *Phone:* 915-532-3737 Ext. 117. *Fax:* 915-532-6946.

WESTERN TECHNICAL INSTITUTE
El Paso, Texas — www.wti-ep.com/

Director of Admissions Mr. Bill Terrell, Chief Admissions Officer, Western Technical Institute, 9451 Diana, El Paso, TX 79930-2610. *Phone:* 800-225-5984.

WESTERN TEXAS COLLEGE
Snyder, Texas — www.wtc.edu/

Director of Admissions Dr. Jim Clifton, Dean of Student Services, Western Texas College, 6200 College Avenue, Snyder, TX 79549-6105. *Phone:* 325-573-8511 Ext. 204. *Toll-free phone:* 888-GO-TO-WTC. *E-mail:* jclifton@wtc.cc.tx.us.

WESTWOOD COLLEGE—DALLAS
Dallas, Texas — www.westwood.edu/

Director of Admissions Eric Southwell, Director of Admissions, Westwood College–Dallas, Executive Plaza I, Suite 100, Dallas, TX 75243. *Phone:* 800-803-3140.

▶ **See page 622 for the College Close-Up.**

WESTWOOD COLLEGE—FORT WORTH
Euless, Texas — www.westwood.edu/

Director of Admissions Ms. Lisa Hecht, Director of Admissions, Westwood College–Fort Worth, 1331 Airport Freeway, Suite 402, Euless, TX 76040. *Phone:* 817-685-9994. *Toll-free phone:* 866-533-9997.

▶ **See page 628 for the College Close-Up.**

WESTWOOD COLLEGE—HOUSTON SOUTH CAMPUS
Houston, Texas — www.westwood.edu/

Director of Admissions Admissions, Westwood College–Houston South Campus, 7322 Southwest Freeway #1900, Houston, TX 77074. *Phone:* 713-777-4433.

▶ **See page 630 for the College Close-Up.**

WHARTON COUNTY JUNIOR COLLEGE
Wharton, Texas — www.wcjc.edu/

- **State and locally supported** 2-year, founded 1946
- **Rural** 90-acre campus with easy access to Houston
- **Coed,** 6,029 undergraduate students

Undergraduates Students come from 8 states and territories, 5 other countries, 9% African American, 4% Asian American or Pacific Islander, 24% Hispanic American, 0.2% Native American, 4% international, 5% live on campus.

Faculty *Total:* 257, 53% full-time. *Student/faculty ratio:* 22:1.

Majors Administrative assistant and secretarial science; agriculture; art; automobile/automotive mechanics technology; behavioral sciences; biology/biological sciences; business administration and management; chemistry; clinical/medical laboratory technology; computer science; criminal justice/law enforcement administration; data processing and data processing technology; dental hygiene; drafting and design technology; dramatic/theater arts; electrical, electronic and communications engineering technology; English; farm and ranch management; health information/medical records administration; industrial radiologic technology; mathematics; music; nursing (registered nurse training); ornamental horticulture; physical education teaching and coaching; physical therapy; pre-engineering; Spanish; speech and rhetoric.

Academics *Calendar:* semesters. *Degree:* certificates and associate. *Special study options:* academic remediation for entering students, adult/continuing education programs, advanced placement credit, part-time degree program, student-designed majors, summer session for credit.

Library J. M. Hodges Library with 51,478 titles, 536 serial subscriptions.

Computers on Campus 350 computers available on campus for general student use. At least one staffed computer lab available.

Student Life *Activities and Organizations:* drama/theater group. *Campus security:* 24-hour patrols. *Student services:* personal/psychological counseling.

Athletics Member NJCAA. *Intercollegiate sports:* baseball M(s), volleyball W(s).

Costs (2006–07) *Tuition:* area resident $1296 full-time, $54 per semester hour part-time; state resident $2160 full-time, $90 per semester hour part-time; nonresident $2928 full-time, $122 per semester hour part-time. *Room and board:* $2500; room only: $600.

Financial Aid Of all full-time matriculated undergraduates who enrolled in 2004, 65 Federal Work-Study jobs (averaging $3000). 8 state and other part-time jobs (averaging $2000).

Applying *Application fee:* $10. *Required:* high school transcript, minimum 2.0 GPA. *Application deadlines:* 8/14 (freshmen), 8/15 (transfers).

Freshmen Application Contact Mr. Albert Barnes, Dean of Admissions and Registration, Wharton County Junior College, 911 Boling Highway, Wharton, TX 77488-3298. *Phone:* 979-532-6381. *E-mail:* albertb@wcjc.edu.

UTAH

COLLEGE OF EASTERN UTAH
Price, Utah www.ceu.edu/

- **State-supported** 2-year, founded 1937, part of Utah System of Higher Education
- **Small-town** 15-acre campus
- **Coed,** 2,294 undergraduate students, 57% full-time, 55% women, 45% men

Undergraduates 1,317 full-time, 977 part-time. Students come from 21 states and territories, 9% are from out of state, 0.9% African American, 1% Asian American or Pacific Islander, 3% Hispanic American, 15% Native American, 0.7% international, 10% transferred in, 15% live on campus.
Freshmen *Admission:* 477 applied, 477 admitted, 477 enrolled. *Average high school GPA:* 3.15. *Test scores:* ACT scores over 18: 65%; ACT scores over 24: 16%.
Faculty *Total:* 189, 38% full-time, 12% with terminal degrees. *Student/faculty ratio:* 15:1.
Majors Administrative assistant and secretarial science; automobile/automotive mechanics technology; business administration and management; carpentry; child development; computer graphics; construction engineering technology; cosmetology; kindergarten/preschool education; liberal arts and sciences/liberal studies; machine tool technology; mining technology; nursing (registered nurse training); pre-engineering; welding technology.
Academics *Calendar:* semesters. *Degree:* certificates and associate. *Special study options:* academic remediation for entering students, adult/continuing education programs, advanced placement credit, cooperative education, distance learning, English as a second language, independent study, part-time degree program, services for LD students, summer session for credit.
Library College of Eastern Utah Library with 44,490 titles, 1,464 audiovisual materials, an OPAC, a Web page.
Computers on Campus 200 computers available on campus for general student use. A campuswide network can be accessed from student residence rooms and from off campus. Internet access, online (class) registration, at least one staffed computer lab available.
Student Life *Housing Options:* coed. Campus housing is university owned. *Activities and Organizations:* drama/theater group, student-run newspaper, choral group. *Campus security:* 24-hour emergency response devices and patrols, late-night transport/escort service. *Student services:* health clinic, personal/psychological counseling, women's center.
Athletics Member NJCAA. *Intercollegiate sports:* baseball M(s), basketball M(s)/W(s), golf M/W, volleyball W(s). *Intramural sports:* basketball M/W, racquetball M/W, soccer M, tennis M/W.
Standardized Tests *Recommended:* ACT (for admission).
Costs (2005–06) *Tuition:* state resident $2090 full-time, $88 per credit hour part-time; nonresident $7122 full-time, $339 per credit hour part-time. *Required fees:* $17 per credit hour part-time. *Room and board:* $3392.
Financial Aid Of all full-time matriculated undergraduates who enrolled in 2004, 66 Federal Work-Study jobs (averaging $1369). 27 state and other part-time jobs (averaging $773).
Applying *Options:* electronic application, early admission. *Application fee:* $25. *Recommended:* high school transcript. *Application deadline:* rolling (freshmen).

Freshmen Application Contact Mr. Todd Olsen, Director of Admissions, High School Relations, College of Eastern Utah, 451 East 400 North, Price, UT 84501. *Phone:* 435-613-5217. *Fax:* 435-613-5814. *E-mail:* todd.olsen@ceu.edu.

DIXIE STATE COLLEGE OF UTAH
St. George, Utah www.dixie.edu/

- **State-supported** primarily 2-year, founded 1911, part of Utah System of Higher Education
- **Small-town** 60-acre campus
- **Endowment** $9.9 million
- **Coed,** 8,992 undergraduate students, 38% full-time, 52% women, 48% men

Undergraduates 3,395 full-time, 5,597 part-time. Students come from 44 states and territories, 19 other countries, 13% are from out of state, 0.8% African American, 2% Asian American or Pacific Islander, 3% Hispanic American, 2% Native American, 0.8% international, 5% transferred in, 2% live on campus. *Retention:* 48% of 2003 full-time freshmen returned.
Freshmen *Admission:* 2,745 applied, 2,341 admitted, 1,477 enrolled. *Average high school GPA:* 3.3. *Test scores:* SAT verbal scores over 500: 41%; SAT math scores over 500: 34%; ACT scores over 18: 75%; SAT verbal scores over 600: 19%; SAT math scores over 600: 10%; ACT scores over 24: 20%; ACT scores over 30: 1%.
Faculty *Total:* 353, 27% full-time. *Student/faculty ratio:* 19:1.
Majors Accounting; administrative assistant and secretarial science; agriculture; airline pilot and flight crew; architectural drafting and CAD/CADD; art; art history, criticism and conservation; autobody/collision and repair technology; automobile/automotive mechanics technology; aviation/airway management; biology/biological sciences; biotechnology; botany/plant biology; broadcast journalism; business administration and management; cartography; ceramic arts and ceramics; chemistry; child care and support services management; commercial and advertising art; communication/speech communication and rhetoric; computer science; criminal justice/safety; dance; data processing and data processing technology; dental hygiene; diesel mechanics technology; dramatic/theater arts; drawing; ecology; economics; elementary education; emergency medical technology (EMT paramedic); engineering; English; environmental studies; foreign languages and literatures; forestry; general retailing/wholesaling; geology/earth science; health professions related; history; humanities; interior design; journalism; kindergarten/preschool education; liberal arts and sciences/liberal studies; marine biology and biological oceanography; mathematics; mechanical drafting and CAD/CADD; music; natural resources/conservation; natural resources management and policy; nursing (registered nurse training); painting; philosophy; photographic and film/video technology; photography; physical education teaching and coaching; physics; plant pathology/phytopathology; plant protection and integrated pest management; political science and government; pre-law studies; printmaking; psychology; radio and television; radio, television, and digital communication related; range science and management; sculpture; secondary education; social work; sociology; soil science and agronomy; tourism and travel services marketing; water resources engineering; web page, digital/multimedia and information resources design; wildlife and wildlands science and management; zoology/animal biology.
Academics *Calendar:* semesters. *Degrees:* certificates, diplomas, associate, and bachelor's. *Special study options:* academic remediation for entering students, adult/continuing education programs, advanced placement credit, cooperative education, distance learning, English as a second language, honors programs, off-campus study, part-time degree program, services for LD students, summer session for credit.
Library Val A. Browning Library with 94,747 titles, 263 serial subscriptions, 13,411 audiovisual materials, an OPAC, a Web page.
Computers on Campus A campuswide network can be accessed from student residence rooms. Internet access, online (class) registration, at least one staffed computer lab available.
Student Life *Housing Options:* coed, men-only, disabled students. Campus housing is university owned. *Activities and Organizations:* drama/theater group, student-run newspaper, radio and television station, choral group, Dixie Spirit, Outdoor Club, Association of Women Students. *Campus security:* 24-hour emergency response devices and patrols. *Student services:* health clinic, personal/psychological counseling.
Athletics Member NJCAA. *Intercollegiate sports:* baseball M(s), basketball M(s)/W(s), football M(s), golf M(s), soccer W(s), softball W(s), volleyball W(s). *Intramural sports:* basketball M/W, football M, golf M/W, soccer M/W, softball M/W, tennis M/W, ultimate Frisbee M/W, volleyball M/W.
Costs (2006–07) *Tuition:* state resident $2100 full-time, $88 per credit part-time; nonresident $8664 full-time, $361 per credit part-time. *Required fees:* $392 full-time.

Dixie State College of Utah (continued)

Financial Aid Of all full-time matriculated undergraduates who enrolled in 2004, 100 Federal Work-Study jobs (averaging $2700). 20 state and other part-time jobs (averaging $2700).

Applying *Options:* electronic application, early admission, deferred entrance. *Application fee:* $25. *Required:* high school transcript. *Application deadline:* rolling (freshmen).

Freshmen Application Contact Ms. Darla Rollins, Admissions Coordinator, Dixie State College of Utah, 225 South 700 East Street, St. George, UT 84770-3876. *Phone:* 435-652-7702. *Toll-free phone:* 888-GO2DIXIE. *Fax:* 435-656-4005. *E-mail:* rollins@dixie.edu.

ITT TECHNICAL INSTITUTE
Murray, Utah　　　　　　　　　**www.itt-tech.edu/**

- **Proprietary** primarily 2-year, founded 1984, part of ITT Educational Services, Inc
- **Suburban** 3-acre campus with easy access to Salt Lake City
- **Coed**

Majors Animation, interactive technology, video graphics and special effects; CAD/CADD drafting/design technology; computer and information systems security; computer programming; computer software technology; computer systems networking and telecommunications; criminal justice/law enforcement administration; e-commerce; electrical, electronic and communications engineering technology; system, networking, and LAN/WAN management; web/multimedia management and webmaster; web page, digital/multimedia and information resources design.

Academics *Calendar:* quarters. *Degrees:* associate and bachelor's.

Library a Web page.

Computers on Campus Internet access, at least one staffed computer lab available.

Student Life *Housing:* college housing not available.

Standardized Tests *Required:* Wonderlic aptitude test (for admission).

Costs (2005–06) *Tuition:* Please see school catalog for specific information.

Applying *Options:* deferred entrance. *Application fee:* $100. *Required:* high school transcript, interview. *Recommended:* letters of recommendation. *Application deadline:* rolling (freshmen), rolling (transfers). *Notification:* continuous (freshmen).

Freshmen Application Contact Mr. Gary Wood, Director of Recruitment, ITT Technical Institute, 920 West LeVoy Drive, Murray, UT 84123. *Phone:* 801-263-3313. *Toll-free phone:* 800-365-2136.

LDS BUSINESS COLLEGE
Salt Lake City, Utah　　　　　　　**www.ldsbc.edu/**

Freshmen Application Contact Mr. Matt D. Tittle, Assistant Dean of Students, LDS Business College, 411 East South Temple, Salt Lake City, UT 84111-1392. *Phone:* 801-524-8146. *Toll-free phone:* 800-999-5767.

MOUNTAIN WEST COLLEGE
West Valley City, Utah　　　　　**www.mwcollege.com/**

Director of Admissions Mr. Jason Peterson, Director of Admissions, Mountain West College, 3280 West 3500 South, West Valley City, UT 84119. *Phone:* 801-840-4800. *Toll-free phone:* 888-741-4271. *Fax:* 801-485-0057. *E-mail:* jasonp@cci.edu.

PROVO COLLEGE
Provo, Utah　　　　　　　　　**www.provocollege.com/**

Director of Admissions Mr. Gordon Peters, College Director, Provo College, 1450 West 820 North, Provo, UT 84601. *Phone:* 801-375-1861. *Toll-free phone:* 800-748-4834. *Fax:* 801-375-9728. *E-mail:* gordonp@provocollege.org.

SALT LAKE COMMUNITY COLLEGE
Salt Lake City, Utah　　　　　　　**www.slcc.edu/**

- **State-supported** 2-year, founded 1948, part of Utah System of Higher Education
- **Urban** 114-acre campus
- **Endowment** $5.8 million
- **Coed,** 24,111 undergraduate students, 34% full-time, 49% women, 51% men

Undergraduates 8,165 full-time, 15,946 part-time. 4% are from out of state, 1% African American, 4% Asian American or Pacific Islander, 7% Hispanic American, 1% Native American, 1% international, 6% transferred in. Freshmen *Admission:* 9,271 applied, 9,271 admitted, 3,694 enrolled.

Faculty *Total:* 1,283, 27% full-time. *Student/faculty ratio:* 18:1.

Majors Accounting; airline pilot and flight crew; architectural engineering technology; autobody/collision and repair technology; avionics maintenance technology; biology/biological sciences; biology/biotechnology laboratory technician; business administration and management; chemistry; clinical/medical laboratory technology; computer and information sciences; computer science; construction management; cosmetology; criminal justice/law enforcement administration; dental hygiene; diesel mechanics technology; drafting and design technology; economics; electrical, electronic and communications engineering technology; engineering; engineering technology; English; environmental engineering technology; finance and financial management services related; general studies; graphic design; health science; heating, air conditioning, ventilation and refrigeration maintenance technology; heavy equipment maintenance technology; history; human development and family studies; humanities; industrial radiologic technology; information science/studies; information technology; instrumentation technology; international/global studies; international relations and affairs; kinesiology and exercise science; legal assistant/paralegal; marketing/marketing management; mass communication/media; medical/clinical assistant; music; nursing (registered nurse training); occupational therapist assistant; photographic and film/video technology; physical sciences; physical therapist assistant; physics; political science and government; psychology; quality control technology; radiologic technology/science; radio/television broadcasting technology; sign language interpretation and translation; social work; sociology; survey technology; teacher assistant/aide; telecommunications technology; welding technology.

Academics *Calendar:* semesters. *Degree:* certificates, diplomas, and associate. *Special study options:* academic remediation for entering students, advanced placement credit, cooperative education, distance learning, double majors, English as a second language, internships, part-time degree program, services for LD students, student-designed majors, study abroad, summer session for credit. *ROTC:* Army (c), Air Force (c).

Library Markosian Library plus 2 others with 96,470 titles, 781 serial subscriptions, 29,810 audiovisual materials, an OPAC, a Web page.

Computers on Campus 2905 computers available on campus for general student use. A campuswide network can be accessed from off campus. Internet access, online (class) registration, at least one staffed computer lab available.

Student Life *Housing:* college housing not available. *Activities and Organizations:* drama/theater group, student-run newspaper, radio and television station, choral group, LDSSA, VICA, Phi Theta Kappa, PBL, Student Nurse Alliance. *Campus security:* 24-hour emergency response devices and patrols, late-night transport/escort service. *Student services:* health clinic, personal/psychological counseling.

Athletics Member NJCAA. *Intercollegiate sports:* baseball M(s), basketball M(s)/W(s), cheerleading M(s)/W(s), soccer M(c)/W(c), softball W(s), volleyball W(s).

Costs (2006–07) *Tuition:* state resident $2046 full-time; nonresident $7161 full-time. *Required fees:* $358 full-time.

Applying *Options:* electronic application, early admission, deferred entrance. *Application fee:* $35. *Application deadline:* rolling (freshmen), rolling (transfers).

Freshmen Application Contact Mr. Andy Young, Director of Student Orientation, Salt Lake Community College, Salt Lake City, UT 84130. *Phone:* 801-957-4433. *E-mail:* andy.young@slcc.edu.

SNOW COLLEGE
Ephraim, Utah
www.snow.edu/

- **State-supported** 2-year, founded 1888, part of Utah System of Higher Education
- **Rural** 50-acre campus
- **Endowment** $5.8 million
- **Coed,** 3,333 undergraduate students, 74% full-time, 53% women, 47% men

Undergraduates 2,463 full-time, 870 part-time. Students come from 34 states and territories, 15 other countries, 8% are from out of state, 0.4% African American, 2% Asian American or Pacific Islander, 2% Hispanic American, 1% Native American, 2% international, 1% transferred in, 10% live on campus. *Retention:* 92% of 2003 full-time freshmen returned.

Freshmen *Admission:* 1,764 applied, 1,317 admitted, 1,272 enrolled. *Average high school GPA:* 3.70. *Test scores:* ACT scores over 18: 81%; ACT scores over 24: 36%; ACT scores over 30: 6%.

Faculty *Total:* 253, 47% full-time, 8% with terminal degrees. *Student/faculty ratio:* 13:1.

Majors Accounting; administrative assistant and secretarial science; agricultural business and management; agricultural economics; agriculture; agronomy and crop science; animal physiology; animal sciences; art; automobile/automotive mechanics technology; biology/biological sciences; botany/plant biology; business administration and management; business teacher education; carpentry; chemistry; child development; computer science; construction engineering technology; construction management; criminal justice/law enforcement administration; dance; dramatic/theater arts; economics; education; electrical, electronic and communications engineering technology; elementary education; engineering; entomology; family and community services; family and consumer sciences/human sciences; farm and ranch management; foods, nutrition, and wellness; forestry; French; geography; geology/earth science; history; humanities; information science/studies; Japanese; kindergarten/preschool education; liberal arts and sciences/liberal studies; mass communication/media; mathematics; music; music history, literature, and theory; music teacher education; natural resources management and policy; natural sciences; philosophy; physical education teaching and coaching; physical sciences; physics; political science and government; pre-engineering; range science and management; science teacher education; sociology; soil conservation; Spanish; trade and industrial teacher education; veterinary sciences; voice and opera; wildlife and wildlands science and management; zoology/animal biology.

Academics *Calendar:* semesters. *Degree:* certificates, diplomas, and associate. *Special study options:* academic remediation for entering students, adult/continuing education programs, advanced placement credit, cooperative education, English as a second language, external degree program, honors programs, independent study, part-time degree program, services for LD students, summer session for credit.

Library Lucy Phillips Library with 31,911 titles, 1,870 audiovisual materials, an OPAC, a Web page.

Computers on Campus 220 computers available on campus for general student use. A campuswide network can be accessed from off campus. At least one staffed computer lab available.

Student Life *Housing Options:* coed. Campus housing is university owned. *Activities and Organizations:* drama/theater group, student-run newspaper, radio station, choral group, Drama Club, Latter-Day Saints Singers, Dead Cats Society, Associated Women Students, Associated Men Students. *Campus security:* student patrols. *Student services:* personal/psychological counseling.

Athletics Member NJCAA. *Intercollegiate sports:* baseball M, basketball M(s)/W(s), football M(s), golf M(s), softball W, volleyball W(s). *Intramural sports:* badminton M/W, basketball M/W, bowling M/W, football M/W, golf M/W, racquetball M/W, soccer M, softball M/W, tennis M/W, volleyball M/W, wrestling M.

Costs (2006–07) *Tuition:* state resident $1784 full-time, $60 per credit hour part-time; nonresident $7118 full-time, $237 per credit hour part-time. *Required fees:* $380 full-time, $380 per term part-time. *Room and board:* $4500.

Financial Aid Of all full-time matriculated undergraduates who enrolled in 2004, 127 Federal Work-Study jobs (averaging $1063).

Applying *Options:* early admission. *Application fee:* $30. *Required:* high school transcript. *Application deadlines:* 6/15 (freshmen), 6/1 (transfers). *Notification:* continuous (freshmen).

Freshmen Application Contact Mr. Brach Schleuter, Dean of Students, Snow College, 150 East College Avenue, Ephraim, UT 84627. *Phone:* 435-283-7151. *Fax:* 435-283-6879. *E-mail:* snowcollege@snow.edu.

STEVENS-HENAGER COLLEGE
Ogden, Utah
www.stevenshenager.edu/

Freshmen Application Contact Admissions Office, Stevens-Henager College, PO Box 9428, Ogden, UT 84409. *Phone:* 801-394-7791. *Toll-free phone:* 800-371-7791.

UTAH CAREER COLLEGE
West Jordan, Utah
www.utahcollege.edu/

- **Proprietary** 2-year
- **Suburban** 1-acre campus with easy access to Salt Lake City
- **Coed,** 570 undergraduate students, 27% full-time, 80% women, 20% men
- 100% of applicants were admitted

Undergraduates 152 full-time, 418 part-time. Students come from 2 states and territories, 1% are from out of state, 1% Asian American or Pacific Islander, 6% Hispanic American, 0.7% Native American.

Freshmen *Admission:* 95 applied, 95 admitted, 95 enrolled.

Faculty *Total:* 42, 21% full-time, 7% with terminal degrees. *Student/faculty ratio:* 12:1.

Majors Business administration and management; computer graphics; kinesiology and exercise science; massage therapy; medical/clinical assistant; nursing (registered nurse training); paralegal/legal assistant; pharmacy technician; veterinary/animal health technology.

Academics *Calendar:* quarters. *Degree:* certificates, diplomas, and associate.

Student Life *Housing:* college housing not available.

Costs (2006–07) *Tuition:* $12,060 full-time, $335 per credit part-time.

Applying *Required:* high school transcript, interview. *Application deadline:* 10/1 (freshmen).

Freshmen Application Contact Ms. Karma Cooper, Director of Admissions, Utah Career College, 1902 West 7800 South, West Jordan, UT 84088. *Phone:* 801-304-4224 Ext. 158. *Toll-free phone:* 866-304-4224. *Fax:* 801-304-4229. *E-mail:* kcooper@utahcollege.edu.

VERMONT

COMMUNITY COLLEGE OF VERMONT
Waterbury, Vermont
www.ccv.edu/

- **State-supported** 2-year, founded 1970, part of Vermont State Colleges System
- **Rural** campus
- **Coed**

Undergraduates Students come from 16 states and territories, 3% are from out of state, 2% African American, 1% Asian American or Pacific Islander, 1% Hispanic American, 0.8% Native American, 0.2% international.

Academics *Calendar:* semesters. *Degree:* certificates, diplomas, and associate. *Special study options:* academic remediation for entering students, accelerated degree program, adult/continuing education programs, cooperative education, distance learning, double majors, English as a second language, external degree program, independent study, internships, part-time degree program, services for LD students, student-designed majors, summer session for credit.

Standardized Tests *Required:* ACCUPLACER (for placement).

Costs (2005–06) *Tuition:* state resident $3912 full-time, $163 per credit part-time; nonresident $7824 full-time, $326 per credit part-time. *Required fees:* $100 full-time, $50 per term part-time.

Financial Aid Of all full-time matriculated undergraduates who enrolled in 2004, 35 Federal Work-Study jobs (averaging $2000).

Director of Admissions Ms. Susan Henry, Dean of Administration, Community College of Vermont, PO Box 120, Waterbury, VT 05676-0120. *Phone:* 802-865-4422.

LANDMARK COLLEGE
Putney, Vermont
www.landmark.edu/

- **Independent** 2-year, founded 1983
- **Rural** 125-acre campus
- **Endowment** $3.2 million
- **Coed,** 371 undergraduate students, 63% full-time, 25% women, 75% men

Undergraduates 233 full-time, 138 part-time. Students come from 37 states and territories, 11 other countries, 92% are from out of state, 5% African American, 3% Asian American or Pacific Islander, 2% Hispanic American, 3% international, 9% transferred in, 94% live on campus. *Retention:* 48% of 2003 full-time freshmen returned.
Freshmen *Admission:* 339 applied, 244 admitted, 120 enrolled.
Faculty *Total:* 97, 98% full-time, 10% with terminal degrees. *Student/faculty ratio:* 4:1.
Majors Liberal arts and sciences/liberal studies.
Academics *Calendar:* semesters. *Degree:* associate. *Special study options:* academic remediation for entering students, adult/continuing education programs, advanced placement credit, services for LD students, study abroad, summer session for credit.
Library Landmark College Library with 30,066 titles, 135 serial subscriptions, 1,555 audiovisual materials.
Computers on Campus 50 computers available on campus for general student use. A campuswide network can be accessed from student residence rooms and from off campus. Internet access, at least one staffed computer lab available. Computer purchase or lease plan available.
Student Life *Housing:* on-campus residence required for freshman year. *Options:* coed. Campus housing is university owned. Freshman campus housing is guaranteed. *Activities and Organizations:* drama/theater group, choral group, Student Government Association, Campus Activities Board, Phi Theta Kappa Honor Society, Jazz Band Club, Cultural Diversity Club. *Campus security:* 24-hour emergency response devices and patrols, controlled dormitory access. *Student services:* health clinic, personal/psychological counseling, women's center.
Athletics *Intercollegiate sports:* baseball M(c), basketball M(c)/W(c), cross-country running M(c)/W(c), rock climbing M(c)/W(c), soccer M(c)/W(c), softball W(c). *Intramural sports:* badminton M/W, fencing M/W, golf M/W, ice hockey M/W, skiing (cross-country) M/W, soccer M/W, softball W, tennis M/W, volleyball M/W.
Standardized Tests *Required:* Wechsler Adult Intelligence Scale III and Nelson Denny Reading Test (for admission).
Costs (2006–07) *One-time required fee:* $1850. *Comprehensive fee:* $46,470 includes full-time tuition ($38,500), mandatory fees ($770), and room and board ($7200). *Room and board:* college room only: $3600.
Financial Aid Of all full-time matriculated undergraduates who enrolled in 2004, 80 Federal Work-Study jobs (averaging $1200).
Applying *Options:* deferred entrance. *Application fee:* $75. *Required:* essay or personal statement, high school transcript, 2 letters of recommendation, interview, diagnosis of LD and/or AD/HD. *Application deadline:* rolling (freshmen), rolling (transfers). *Notification:* continuous (freshmen).
Freshmen Application Contact Admissions Main Desk, Landmark College, 1 River Road South, Putney, VT 05346. *Phone:* 802-387-6718. *Fax:* 802-387-6868. *E-mail:* admissions@landmark.edu.

▶ **See page 560 for the College Close-Up.**

NEW ENGLAND CULINARY INSTITUTE
Montpelier, Vermont
www.neci.edu/

Director of Admissions Ms. Dawn Hayward, Director of Admissions, New England Culinary Institute, 250 Main Street, Montpelier, VT 05602. *Toll-free phone:* 877-223-6324. *E-mail:* admissions@neci.edu.

NEW ENGLAND CULINARY INSTITUTE AT ESSEX
Essex Junction, Vermont
www.neci.edu/

- **Proprietary** primarily 2-year
- **Endowment** $336,943
- **Coed,** 501 undergraduate students, 100% full-time, 32% women, 68% men
- 78% of applicants were admitted

Undergraduates 501 full-time. 72% are from out of state, 2% African American, 3% Asian American or Pacific Islander, 2% Hispanic American, 0.6% Native American.
Freshmen *Admission:* 229 applied, 179 admitted, 61 enrolled.
Faculty *Total:* 76, 86% full-time.
Majors Baking and pastry arts; culinary arts; hotel and restaurant management.
Academics *Calendar:* quarters. *Degree:* certificates, diplomas, and bachelor's.
Student Life *Activities and Organizations:* student-run newspaper. *Student services:* personal/psychological counseling.
Costs (2006–07) *Comprehensive fee:* $33,830 includes full-time tuition ($23,835), mandatory fees ($3430), and room and board ($6565).
Applying *Required:* essay or personal statement, high school transcript, 1 letter of recommendation, interview, minimum TOEFL scores for foreign students. *Required for some:* 2 letters of recommendation.
Director of Admissions Sherri Gilmore, Associate Director of Admission, New England Culinary Institute at Essex, 48½ Park Street, Essex Junction, VT 05452. *Phone:* 802-223-6324. *Fax:* 802-225-3280. *E-mail:* sherrigilmore@neci.edu.

VIRGINIA

ACT COLLEGE
Arlington, Virginia

ADVANCED TECHNOLOGY INSTITUTE
Virginia Beach, Virginia

AVIATION INSTITUTE OF MAINTENANCE—MANASSAS
Manassas, Virginia
www.aviationmaintenance.edu/aviation-washington-dc.asp

- **Proprietary** 2-year

Faculty *Total:* 20.
Majors Airframe mechanics and aircraft maintenance technology.
Academics *Calendar:* quarters. *Degree:* certificates and associate.
Costs (2005–06) *Tuition:* Tuition and fees for Associates Degree, $34,560.
Applying *Application fee:* $25. *Required:* High School Diploma or GED.
Freshmen Application Contact Washington, D.C. School Director, Aviation Institute of Maintenance–Manassas, 9821 Godwin Drive, Manassas, VA 20110. *Phone:* 703-257-5515. *Toll-free phone:* 877-604-2121. *Fax:* 703-257-5523. *E-mail:* directoramm@tidetech.com.

AVIATION INSTITUTE OF MAINTENANCE—VIRGINIA BEACH
Virginia Beach, Virginia
www.aviationmaintenance.edu/aviation-norfolk.asp

- **Proprietary** 2-year

Faculty *Total:* 30.

Majors Airframe mechanics and aircraft maintenance technology.

Academics *Calendar:* quarters. *Degree:* certificates and associate.

Costs (2005–06) *Tuition:* $10,260 full-time, $220 per credit hour part-time.

Applying *Application fee:* $25. *Required:* High school diploma or GED.

Freshmen Application Contact Virginia Beach School Director, Aviation Institute of Maintenance–Virginia Beach, 1429 Miller Store Ro, Virginia Beach, VA 23455. *Phone:* 757-363-2121. *Toll-free phone:* 888-349-5387. *Fax:* 757-363-2044. *E-mail:* directoramn@tidetech.com.

BETA TECH
Richmond, Virginia

BLUE RIDGE COMMUNITY COLLEGE
Weyers Cave, Virginia
www.brcc.edu/

- **State-supported** 2-year, founded 1967, part of Virginia Community College System
- **Rural** 65-acre campus
- **Endowment** $2.1 million
- **Coed,** 3,804 undergraduate students, 40% full-time, 58% women, 42% men

Undergraduates 1,513 full-time, 2,291 part-time. Students come from 29 states and territories, 2 other countries, 2% are from out of state, 4% African American, 2% Asian American or Pacific Islander, 2% Hispanic American, 0.4% Native American, 42% transferred in. *Retention:* 41% of 2003 full-time freshmen returned.

Freshmen *Admission:* 681 applied, 681 admitted, 681 enrolled.

Faculty *Total:* 186, 32% full-time. *Student/faculty ratio:* 22:1.

Majors Accounting; administrative assistant and secretarial science; business administration and management; computer systems networking and telecommunications; electrical, electronic and communications engineering technology; information science/studies; information technology; mechanical design technology; nursing (registered nurse training); veterinary technology.

Academics *Calendar:* semesters. *Degree:* certificates, diplomas, and associate. *Special study options:* academic remediation for entering students, adult/continuing education programs, advanced placement credit, cooperative education, distance learning, double majors, English as a second language, honors programs, internships, off-campus study, part-time degree program, services for LD students, study abroad, summer session for credit.

Library Houff Library with 59,735 titles, 206 serial subscriptions, 1,646 audiovisual materials, an OPAC, a Web page.

Computers on Campus 285 computers available on campus for general student use. A campuswide network can be accessed. Internet access, at least one staffed computer lab available.

Student Life *Housing:* college housing not available. *Activities and Organizations:* Student Government Association, Phi Theta Kappa, Christian Fellowship, intramural athletics, special interest groups. *Campus security:* 24-hour emergency response devices and patrols, late-night transport/escort service. *Student services:* personal/psychological counseling, women's center.

Athletics *Intramural sports:* basketball M.

Costs (2006–07) *Tuition:* state resident $2040 full-time, $68 per credit hour part-time; nonresident $6420 full-time, $214 per credit hour part-time. *Required fees:* $146 full-time, $5 per credit hour part-time.

Financial Aid Of all full-time matriculated undergraduates who enrolled in 2004, 25 Federal Work-Study jobs (averaging $1582).

Applying *Options:* electronic application, early admission. *Required for some:* high school transcript, interview. *Application deadline:* rolling (freshmen), rolling (transfers). *Notification:* continuous (freshmen).

Freshmen Application Contact Ms. Mary Wayland, Dean of Admissions and Records, Blue Ridge Community College, PO Box 80, Weyers Cave, VA 24486-0080. *Phone:* 540-453-2332. *E-mail:* waylandm@brcc.edu.

BRYANT AND STRATTON COLLEGE, RICHMOND
Richmond, Virginia
www.bryantstratton.edu/

- **Proprietary** primarily 2-year, founded 1952, part of Bryant and Stratton Business Institute, Inc
- **Suburban** campus
- **Coed,** 421 undergraduate students, 33% full-time, 84% women, 16% men

Undergraduates 137 full-time, 284 part-time. Students come from 1 other state, 71% African American, 0.5% Asian American or Pacific Islander, 3% Hispanic American, 1% Native American.

Freshmen *Admission:* 149 admitted, 147 enrolled.

Faculty *Total:* 51, 20% full-time, 16% with terminal degrees. *Student/faculty ratio:* 10:1.

Majors Accounting; administrative assistant and secretarial science; business administration and management; business/commerce; criminal justice/law enforcement administration; human resources management and services related; information technology; legal administrative assistant/secretary; legal assistant/paralegal; medical administrative assistant and medical secretary; medical/clinical assistant.

Academics *Calendar:* semesters. *Degrees:* associate and bachelor's. *Special study options:* academic remediation for entering students, adult/continuing education programs, advanced placement credit, distance learning, double majors, independent study, internships, part-time degree program, summer session for credit.

Library Bryant and Stratton Library with 3,176 titles, 84 serial subscriptions.

Computers on Campus 50 computers available on campus for general student use. A campuswide network can be accessed. Internet access, at least one staffed computer lab available.

Student Life *Housing:* college housing not available. *Activities and Organizations:* Phi Beta Lambda, Alpha Beta Gamma, Student Council, Medical Assisting Club, Paralegal Club. *Campus security:* late-night transport/escort service.

Standardized Tests *Required:* TABE, CPAt (for admission). *Recommended:* SAT or ACT (for admission).

Costs (2005–06) *Tuition:* $18,675 full-time, $415 per credit hour part-time. *Required fees:* $25 full-time.

Applying *Options:* deferred entrance. *Required:* high school transcript, interview, entrance evaluation and placement evaluation. *Required for some:* letters of recommendation. *Application deadline:* rolling (freshmen), rolling (transfers).

Freshmen Application Contact Mr. Troy Lawson, Director of Admissions, Bryant and Stratton College, Richmond, 8141 Hull Street Road, Richmond, VA 23235-6411. *Phone:* 804-745-2444. *Fax:* 804-745-6884. *E-mail:* tlawson@bryantstratton.edu.

BRYANT AND STRATTON COLLEGE, VIRGINIA BEACH
Virginia Beach, Virginia
www.bryantstratton.edu/

Director of Admissions Mr. Greg Smith, Director of Admissions, Bryant and Stratton College, Virginia Beach, 301 Centre Pointe Drive, Virginia Beach, VA 23462-4417. *Phone:* 757-499-7900.

CENTRAL VIRGINIA COMMUNITY COLLEGE
Lynchburg, Virginia
www.cvcc.vccs.edu/

Director of Admissions Ms. Judy Wilhelm, Enrollment Services Coordinator, Central Virginia Community College, 3506 Wards Road, Lynchburg, VA 24502-2498. *Phone:* 434-832-7630. *Toll-free phone:* 800-562-3060.

DABNEY S. LANCASTER COMMUNITY COLLEGE

Clifton Forge, Virginia   **www.dl.vccs.edu/**

- **State-supported** 2-year, founded 1964, part of Virginia Community College System
- **Rural** 117-acre campus
- **Coed,** 1,453 undergraduate students

Undergraduates   Students come from 5 states and territories, 5% African American, 0.5% Asian American or Pacific Islander, 0.7% Hispanic American, 0.3% Native American.

Faculty   *Total:* 95, 22% full-time.

Majors   Administrative assistant and secretarial science; biological and physical sciences; business administration and management; computer programming; criminal justice/law enforcement administration; data processing and data processing technology; drafting and design technology; education; electrical, electronic and communications engineering technology; forestry technology; information science/studies; legal administrative assistant/secretary; liberal arts and sciences/liberal studies; mechanical design technology; medical administrative assistant and medical secretary; nursing (registered nurse training); wood science and wood products/pulp and paper technology.

Academics   *Calendar:* semesters. *Degree:* certificates, diplomas, and associate. *Special study options:* academic remediation for entering students, adult/continuing education programs, advanced placement credit, cooperative education, honors programs, internships, part-time degree program, services for LD students, summer session for credit.

Library   37,716 titles, 376 serial subscriptions.

Student Life   *Housing:* college housing not available. *Activities and Organizations:* drama/theater group. *Student services:* personal/psychological counseling.

Athletics   *Intercollegiate sports:* basketball M. *Intramural sports:* basketball M/W, bowling M/W, equestrian sports M/W, football M/W, golf M/W, skiing (downhill) M/W, soccer M/W, tennis M/W, volleyball M/W.

Costs (2006–07)   *Tuition:* state resident $1740 full-time, $73 per credit part-time; nonresident $5648 full-time, $235 per credit part-time. *Required fees:* $157 full-time, $7 per credit part-time.

Applying   *Options:* early admission, deferred entrance. *Application deadline:* rolling (freshmen), rolling (transfers). *Notification:* continuous (freshmen).

Freshmen Application Contact   Ms. Kathy Nicely, Registration Specialist, Dabney S. Lancaster Community College, 100 Dabney Drive, PO Box 1000, Clifton Forge, VA 24422. *Phone:* 540-863-2815. *E-mail:* knicely@dslcc.edu.

DANVILLE COMMUNITY COLLEGE

Danville, Virginia   **www.dcc.vccs.edu/**

- **State-supported** 2-year, founded 1967, part of Virginia Community College System
- **Urban** 76-acre campus
- **Coed**

Undergraduates   1,366 full-time, 2,723 part-time. Students come from 9 states and territories, 3 other countries, 2% are from out of state, 34% African American, 0.3% Asian American or Pacific Islander, 0.5% Hispanic American, 0.1% Native American. *Retention:* 100% of 2003 full-time freshmen returned.

Faculty   *Student/faculty ratio:* 19:1.

Academics   *Calendar:* semesters. *Degree:* certificates, diplomas, and associate. *Special study options:* academic remediation for entering students, adult/continuing education programs, advanced placement credit, cooperative education, distance learning, honors programs, part-time degree program, summer session for credit.

Student Life   *Campus security:* 24-hour patrols.

Standardized Tests   *Required for some:* ACT ASSET.

Costs (2005–06)   *Tuition:* state resident $2150 full-time, $72 per credit hour part-time; nonresident $6596 full-time, $220 per credit hour part-time. *Required fees:* $111 full-time, $4 per credit hour part-time.

Financial Aid   Of all full-time matriculated undergraduates who enrolled in 2004, 40 Federal Work-Study jobs (averaging $1700).

Applying   *Options:* early admission, deferred entrance. *Required:* high school transcript.

Director of Admissions   Mr. Peter Castiglione, Director of Student Development and Enrollment Management, Danville Community College, 1008 South Main Street, Danville, VA 24541-4088. *Phone:* 434-797-8490. *Toll-free phone:* 800-560-4291.

EASTERN SHORE COMMUNITY COLLEGE

Melfa, Virginia   **www.es.cc.va.us/**

- **State-supported** 2-year, founded 1971, part of Virginia Community College System
- **Rural** 117-acre campus
- **Coed**

Undergraduates   260 full-time, 547 part-time. 44% African American, 0.7% Asian American or Pacific Islander, 1% Hispanic American. *Retention:* 36% of 2003 full-time freshmen returned.

Faculty   *Student/faculty ratio:* 13:1.

Academics   *Calendar:* semesters. *Degree:* certificates and associate. *Special study options:* academic remediation for entering students, adult/continuing education programs, advanced placement credit, cooperative education, distance learning, English as a second language, off-campus study, part-time degree program, services for LD students, summer session for credit.

Student Life   *Campus security:* night security guard.

Costs (2005–06)   *Tuition:* state resident $2040 full-time, $68 per credit part-time; nonresident $6420 full-time, $214 per credit part-time. *Required fees:* $110 full-time, $4 per credit part-time.

Financial Aid   Of all full-time matriculated undergraduates who enrolled in 2004, 11 Federal Work-Study jobs.

Applying   *Required:* high school transcript.

Director of Admissions   Ms. Faye Wilson, Enrollment Services Assistant for Admissions, Eastern Shore Community College, 29300 Lankford Highway, Melfa, VA 23410. *Phone:* 757-789-1731. *Toll-free phone:* 877-871-8455. *E-mail:* eswilss@es.cc.va.us.

ECPI COLLEGE OF TECHNOLOGY

Newport News, Virginia   **www.ecpi.edu/**

- **Proprietary** primarily 2-year, founded 1966
- **Suburban** campus
- **Coed,** 556 undergraduate students, 100% full-time, 39% women, 61% men

Undergraduates   556 full-time. Students come from 34 states and territories, 2% are from out of state, 45% African American, 2% Asian American or Pacific Islander, 6% Hispanic American, 0.2% Native American, 77% transferred in. Freshmen *Admission:* 169 enrolled.

Faculty   *Total:* 130, 51% full-time, 2% with terminal degrees. *Student/faculty ratio:* 16:1.

Majors   Accounting; communications technology; computer and information sciences; computer engineering technology; computer management; computer science; computer typography and composition equipment operation; electrical, electronic and communications engineering technology; electromechanical technology; engineering technology; health/health care administration; health information/medical records administration; information science/studies; mechanical engineering/mechanical technology; medical administrative assistant and medical secretary; telecommunications; trade and industrial teacher education.

Academics   *Calendar:* trimesters. *Degrees:* certificates, diplomas, associate, and bachelor's. *Special study options:* adult/continuing education programs, advanced placement credit, freshman honors college, honors programs, internships, part-time degree program, summer session for credit.

Library   ECPI-Virginia Beach Library with 13,014 titles, 168 serial subscriptions, an OPAC, a Web page.

Computers on Campus   100 computers available on campus for general student use. A campuswide network can be accessed from off campus. Internet access, at least one staffed computer lab available.

Student Life   *Housing:* college housing not available. *Activities and Organizations:* SETA, IEEE, NVTHS, Accounting Society, CSI. *Campus security:* building and parking lot security. *Student services:* personal/psychological counseling.

Standardized Tests   *Recommended:* SAT (for admission), SAT or ACT (for admission), SAT Subject Tests (for admission).

Costs (2006–07)   *Tuition:* contact school for specific program expenses.

Financial Aid   Of all full-time matriculated undergraduates who enrolled in 2004, 30 Federal Work-Study jobs (averaging $2000).

Applying   *Options:* common application, deferred entrance. *Application fee:* $100. *Required:* high school transcript, minimum 2.0 GPA, interview. *Notification:* continuous (freshmen).

Freshmen Application Contact   Ms. Cheryl Lokey, Provost, ECPI College of Technology, 1001 Omni Boulevard, #100, Newport News, VA 23606. *Phone:* 757-838-9191. *Fax:* 757-829-5351.

ECPI College of Technology

Virginia Beach, Virginia www.ecpi.edu/

- **Proprietary** primarily 2-year, founded 1966
- **Suburban** 8-acre campus
- **Coed,** 4,391 undergraduate students, 98% full-time, 47% women, 53% men

Undergraduates 4,312 full-time, 79 part-time. Students come from 6 states and territories, 10% are from out of state, 43% African American, 3% Asian American or Pacific Islander, 4% Hispanic American, 0.4% Native American. Freshmen *Admission:* 1,433 applied, 982 admitted, 737 enrolled.

Faculty *Total:* 130, 51% full-time, 2% with terminal degrees.

Majors Accounting; biomedical technology; business machine repair; communications technology; computer and information sciences; computer engineering technology; computer management; computer programming; computer science; computer typography and composition equipment operation; data processing and data processing technology; electrical, electronic and communications engineering technology; electromechanical technology; engineering technology; health/health care administration; health information/medical records administration; information science/studies; mechanical engineering/mechanical technology; medical administrative assistant and medical secretary; telecommunications.

Academics *Calendar:* trimesters. *Degrees:* certificates, diplomas, associate, and bachelor's. *Special study options:* adult/continuing education programs, advanced placement credit, distance learning, freshman honors college, internships, part-time degree program, summer session for credit.

Library ECPI-Virginia Beach Library with an OPAC, a Web page.

Computers on Campus 600 computers available on campus for general student use. A campuswide network can be accessed from off campus. Internet access, at least one staffed computer lab available.

Student Life *Housing Options:* Campus housing is provided by a third party. *Activities and Organizations:* SETA, IEEE, NVTHS, ITE, Accounting Society, national fraternities, national sororities. *Campus security:* building and parking lot security. *Student services:* personal/psychological counseling.

Standardized Tests *Recommended:* SAT (for admission), SAT or ACT (for admission), SAT Subject Tests (for admission).

Costs (2006–07) *Tuition:* $9750 full-time.

Financial Aid Of all full-time matriculated undergraduates who enrolled in 2004, 80 Federal Work-Study jobs (averaging $2000).

Applying *Options:* common application, electronic application, deferred entrance. *Application fee:* $100. *Required:* high school transcript, interview. *Notification:* continuous (freshmen).

Freshmen Application Contact Mr. Ronald Ballance, Vice President, ECPI College of Technology, 5555 Greenwich Road, Suite 100, Virginia Beach, VA 23462. *Phone:* 757-671-7171. *Toll-free phone:* 800-986-1200. *Fax:* 757-671-8661. *E-mail:* rballance@ecpi.edu.

ECPI Technical College

Glen Allen, Virginia www.ecpitech.edu/

- **Proprietary** primarily 2-year
- **Urban** campus with easy access to Richmond
- **Coed,** 473 undergraduate students, 100% full-time, 38% women, 62% men

Undergraduates 473 full-time. Students come from 2 states and territories, 1% are from out of state, 36% African American, 4% Asian American or Pacific Islander, 2% Hispanic American, 0.6% Native American. Freshmen *Admission:* 148 applied, 121 admitted, 42 enrolled.

Faculty *Student/faculty ratio:* 15:1.

Majors Computer and information systems security; computer programming; computer technology/computer systems technology; data entry/microcomputer applications; telecommunications technology; web page, digital/multimedia and information resources design.

Academics *Calendar:* semesters. *Degrees:* certificates, diplomas, associate, and bachelor's.

Student Life *Housing:* college housing not available. *Activities and Organizations:* CSI, OPMA, SETA, NVTHS, ITE. *Campus security:* building and parking lot security.

Standardized Tests *Recommended:* SAT (for admission), SAT and SAT Subject Tests or ACT (for admission), SAT Subject Tests (for admission).

Costs (2006–07) *Tuition:* Contact college directly as tuition and fees vary by program.

Applying *Application fee:* $100. *Required:* high school transcript, interview. *Application deadline:* rolling (freshmen), rolling (transfers). *Notification:* continuous (freshmen).

Freshmen Application Contact Mr. Jacob Pope, Director, ECPI Technical College, 4305 Cox Road, Glen Allen, VA 23060. *Phone:* 804-934-0100. *Toll-free phone:* 800-986-1200. *Fax:* 804-934-0054. *E-mail:* jpope@ecpi.edu.

ECPI Technical College

Richmond, Virginia www.ecpitech.edu/

- **Proprietary** primarily 2-year, founded 1966
- **Urban** campus
- **Coed,** 400 undergraduate students

Undergraduates Students come from 2 states and territories, 1% are from out of state.

Freshmen *Admission:* 176 applied, 132 admitted.

Faculty *Student/faculty ratio:* 15:1.

Majors Accounting; business machine repair; communications technology; computer and information sciences; computer and information sciences related; computer and information systems security; computer management; computer programming; computer science; computer technology/computer systems technology; computer typography and composition equipment operation; data entry/microcomputer applications; data processing and data processing technology; electrical, electronic and communications engineering technology; electromechanical technology; engineering technology; health/health care administration; health information/medical records administration; information science/studies; mechanical engineering/mechanical technology; medical administrative assistant and medical secretary; telecommunications; telecommunications technology; trade and industrial teacher education; web page, digital/multimedia and information resources design.

Academics *Calendar:* semesters. *Degrees:* certificates, diplomas, associate, and bachelor's. *Special study options:* adult/continuing education programs, advanced placement credit, freshman honors college, honors programs, internships, part-time degree program, summer session for credit.

Library ECPI-Richmond Library with 3,165 titles, 81 serial subscriptions, an OPAC, a Web page.

Computers on Campus 190 computers available on campus for general student use. A campuswide network can be accessed from off campus. Internet access, at least one staffed computer lab available.

Student Life *Housing:* college housing not available. *Activities and Organizations:* Collegiate Secretaries International, Data Processing Management Association, Student Electronics Technicians Association, Future Office Assistants, National Vocational-Technical Honor Society. *Campus security:* building and parking lot security.

Standardized Tests *Recommended:* SAT (for admission), SAT and SAT Subject Tests or ACT (for admission), SAT Subject Tests (for admission).

Costs (2006–07) *Tuition:* $9750 full-time.

Financial Aid Of all full-time matriculated undergraduates who enrolled in 2004, 40 Federal Work-Study jobs (averaging $2000).

Applying *Options:* common application, deferred entrance. *Application fee:* $100. *Required:* high school transcript, interview. *Application deadline:* rolling (freshmen), rolling (transfers). *Notification:* continuous (freshmen).

Freshmen Application Contact Ms. Ada Gerard, Director, ECPI Technical College, 800 Moorefield Park Drive, Richmond, VA 23236. *Phone:* 804-330-5533. *Toll-free phone:* 800-986-1200. *Fax:* 804-330-5577. *E-mail:* agerard@ecpi.edu.

ECPI Technical College

Roanoke, Virginia www.ecpi.net/

- **Proprietary** primarily 2-year, founded 1966
- **Suburban** 3-acre campus
- **Coed,** 300 undergraduate students

Undergraduates Students come from 4 states and territories, 1% are from out of state.

Freshmen *Admission:* 159 applied, 103 admitted.

Faculty *Student/faculty ratio:* 15:1.

Majors Accounting; communications technology; computer and information sciences; computer and information sciences related; computer and information systems security; computer engineering technology; computer science; computer technology/computer systems technology; computer typography and composition equipment operation; data entry/microcomputer applications; electrical, electronic and communications engineering technology; electromechanical technology; engineering technology; health/health care administration; health information/medical records administration; information science/studies; mechani-

ECPI Technical College (continued)

cal engineering/mechanical technology; medical administrative assistant and medical secretary; medical/clinical assistant; telecommunications; telecommunications technology.

Academics *Calendar:* semesters. *Degrees:* certificates, diplomas, associate, and bachelor's. *Special study options:* accelerated degree program, adult/continuing education programs, advanced placement credit, distance learning, internships, part-time degree program, summer session for credit.

Library ECPI-Roanoke Library plus 1 other with 1,703 titles, 43 serial subscriptions, a Web page.

Computers on Campus 80 computers available on campus for general student use. A campuswide network can be accessed from off campus. Internet access, at least one staffed computer lab available.

Student Life *Housing:* college housing not available. *Activities and Organizations:* SETA, NVTHS, SAFA, FOAMA, ITE. *Campus security:* building and parking lot security.

Standardized Tests *Recommended:* SAT (for admission), SAT Subject Tests (for admission), SAT and SAT Subject Tests (for admission).

Costs (2006–07) *Tuition:* $9750 full-time.

Financial Aid Of all full-time matriculated undergraduates who enrolled in 2004, 20 Federal Work-Study jobs (averaging $2000).

Applying *Options:* common application, electronic application, deferred entrance. *Application fee:* $100. *Required:* high school transcript, interview. *Application deadline:* rolling (freshmen), rolling (transfers). *Notification:* continuous (freshmen).

Freshmen Application Contact Mr. Elmer Haas, Director, ECPI Technical College, 5234 Airport Road, Roanoke, VA 24012. *Phone:* 540-563-8080. *Toll-free phone:* 800-986-1200. *Fax:* 540-362-5400. *E-mail:* ehass@ecpi.edu.

GERMANNA COMMUNITY COLLEGE
Locust Grove, Virginia **www.gcc.vccs.edu/**

- **State-supported** 2-year, founded 1970, part of Virginia Community College System
- **Rural** 100-acre campus with easy access to Washington, DC
- **Coed,** 4,799 undergraduate students, 28% full-time, 66% women, 34% men

Undergraduates 1,359 full-time, 3,440 part-time. Students come from 5 states and territories, 1 other country, 13% African American, 3% Asian American or Pacific Islander, 3% Hispanic American, 0.5% Native American. Freshmen *Admission:* 838 applied, 838 admitted, 838 enrolled.

Faculty *Total:* 272, 18% full-time. *Student/faculty ratio:* 20:1.

Majors Biological and physical sciences; business administration and management; criminal justice/police science; dental hygiene; education; general studies; information technology; liberal arts and sciences/liberal studies; nursing (registered nurse training).

Academics *Calendar:* semesters. *Degree:* certificates and associate. *Special study options:* academic remediation for entering students, adult/continuing education programs, off-campus study, part-time degree program, summer session for credit.

Library 22,412 titles, 160 serial subscriptions.

Computers on Campus 55 computers available on campus for general student use. At least one staffed computer lab available.

Student Life *Housing:* college housing not available. *Activities and Organizations:* student-run newspaper, Student Nurses Association, Student Government Association, Phi Theta Kappa, Students Against Substance Abuse. *Campus security:* 24-hour patrols. *Student services:* personal/psychological counseling.

Athletics *Intramural sports:* archery M/W, basketball M/W, bowling M/W, football M/W, golf M/W, tennis M/W, volleyball M/W.

Costs (2005–06) *Tuition:* state resident $1632 full-time, $68 per credit part-time; nonresident $5136 full-time, $214 per credit part-time. Full-time tuition and fees vary according to course load. Part-time tuition and fees vary according to course load. *Required fees:* $118 full-time, $5 per credit part-time. *Payment plans:* installment, deferred payment. *Waivers:* senior citizens.

Financial Aid Of all full-time matriculated undergraduates who enrolled in 2004, 35 Federal Work-Study jobs (averaging $1212). 15 state and other part-time jobs (averaging $1667).

Applying *Options:* early admission. *Required for some:* high school transcript. *Application deadline:* rolling (freshmen), rolling (transfers). *Notification:* continuous (freshmen).

Freshmen Application Contact Ms. Rita Dunston, Registrar, Germanna Community College, 10000 Germanna Point Drive, Fredericksburg, VA 22408. *Phone:* 540-891-3016. *Fax:* 540-891-3092.

ITT TECHNICAL INSTITUTE
Chantilly, Virginia **www.itt-tech.edu/**

- **Proprietary** primarily 2-year, founded 2002, part of ITT Educational Services, Inc
- **Coed**

Majors Animation, interactive technology, video graphics and special effects; business administration and management; CAD/CADD drafting/design technology; computer and information systems security; computer programming; computer software technology; computer systems networking and telecommunications; criminal justice/law enforcement administration; electrical, electronic and communications engineering technology; web/multimedia management and webmaster; web page, digital/multimedia and information resources design.

Academics *Calendar:* quarters. *Degrees:* associate and bachelor's.

Library a Web page.

Computers on Campus Internet access, at least one staffed computer lab available.

Student Life *Housing:* college housing not available.

Standardized Tests *Required:* (for admission).

Costs (2005–06) *Tuition:* Please see school catalog for specific information.

Applying *Options:* deferred entrance. *Application fee:* $100. *Required:* high school transcript, interview. *Recommended:* letters of recommendation. *Application deadline:* rolling (freshmen), rolling (transfers). *Notification:* continuous (freshmen).

Freshmen Application Contact Foy Ann Roach, Director of Recruitment, ITT Technical Institute, 14420 Albemarle Point Place, Chantilly, VA 20151. *Phone:* 703-263-2541. *Toll-free phone:* 888-895-8324.

ITT TECHNICAL INSTITUTE
Norfolk, Virginia **www.itt-tech.edu/**

- **Proprietary** primarily 2-year, founded 1988, part of ITT Educational Services, Inc
- **Suburban** 2-acre campus
- **Coed**

Majors Accounting and business/management; animation, interactive technology, video graphics and special effects; business administration and management; CAD/CADD drafting/design technology; computer programming; criminal justice/law enforcement administration; e-commerce; electrical, electronic and communications engineering technology; information technology; robotics technology; system, networking, and LAN/WAN management; web/multimedia management and webmaster; web page, digital/multimedia and information resources design.

Academics *Calendar:* quarters. *Degrees:* associate and bachelor's.

Library a Web page.

Computers on Campus Internet access, at least one staffed computer lab available.

Student Life *Housing:* college housing not available. *Activities and Organizations:* student-run newspaper.

Standardized Tests *Required:* Wonderlic aptitude test (for admission).

Costs (2005–06) *Tuition:* Please see school catalog for specific information.

Financial Aid Of all full-time matriculated undergraduates who enrolled in 2004, 3 Federal Work-Study jobs (averaging $5000).

Applying *Options:* deferred entrance. *Application fee:* $100. *Required:* high school transcript, interview. *Recommended:* letters of recommendation. *Application deadline:* rolling (freshmen), rolling (transfers). *Notification:* continuous (freshmen).

Freshmen Application Contact Mr. Jack Keesee, Director of Recruitment, ITT Technical Institute, 863 Glenrock Road, Norfolk, VA 23502. *Phone:* 757-466-1260. *Toll-free phone:* 888-253-8324.

ITT TECHNICAL INSTITUTE
Richmond, Virginia **www.itt-tech.edu/**

- **Proprietary** primarily 2-year, part of ITT Educational Services, Inc
- **Coed**

Majors Animation, interactive technology, video graphics and special effects; business administration and management; CAD/CADD drafting/design technology; computer and information systems security; computer programming; criminal justice/law enforcement administration; electrical, electronic and communications engineering technology; system, networking, and LAN/WAN management; web/multimedia management and webmaster; web page, digital/multimedia and information resources design.

Academics *Calendar:* quarters. *Degrees:* associate and bachelor's.

Library a Web page.

Computers on Campus Internet access, at least one staffed computer lab available.

Student Life *Housing:* college housing not available.

Standardized Tests *Required:* Wonderlic aptitude test (for admission).

Costs (2005–06) *Tuition:* Please see school catalog for specific information.

Applying *Options:* deferred entrance. *Application fee:* $100. *Required:* high school transcript, interview. *Recommended:* letters of recommendation. *Application deadline:* rolling (freshmen), rolling (transfers). *Notification:* continuous (freshmen).

Freshmen Application Contact Ms. Arlene Harrington, Director of Recruitment, ITT Technical Institute, 300 Gateway Centre Parkway, Richmond, VA 23235. *Phone:* 804-330-4992. *Toll-free phone:* 888-330-4888.

ITT TECHNICAL INSTITUTE
Springfield, Virginia **www.itt-tech.edu/**

- **Proprietary** primarily 2-year, founded 2002, part of ITT Educational Services, Inc
- **Coed**

Majors Business administration and management; CAD/CADD drafting/design technology; computer and information systems security; computer programming; computer software technology; criminal justice/law enforcement administration; electrical, electronic and communications engineering technology; system, networking, and LAN/WAN management; web/multimedia management and webmaster; web page, digital/multimedia and information resources design.

Academics *Calendar:* quarters. *Degrees:* associate and bachelor's.

Library a Web page.

Computers on Campus Internet access, at least one staffed computer lab available.

Student Life *Housing:* college housing not available.

Standardized Tests *Required:* Wonderlic aptitude test (for admission).

Costs (2005–06) *Tuition:* Please see school catalog for specific information.

Applying *Options:* deferred entrance. *Application fee:* $100. *Required:* high school transcript, interview. *Recommended:* letters of recommendation. *Application deadline:* rolling (freshmen), rolling (transfers). *Notification:* continuous (freshmen).

Freshmen Application Contact Mr. Troy Richardson, Director of Recruitment, ITT Technical Institute, 7300 Boston Boulevard, Springfield, VA 22153. *Phone:* 703-440-9535. *Toll-free phone:* 866-817-8324.

JOHN TYLER COMMUNITY COLLEGE
Chester, Virginia **www.jtcc.edu/**

- **State-supported** 2-year, founded 1967, part of Virginia Community College System
- **Suburban** 160-acre campus with easy access to Richmond
- **Endowment** $399,044
- **Coed,** 6,314 undergraduate students, 25% full-time, 63% women, 37% men

Undergraduates 1,607 full-time, 4,707 part-time. Students come from 38 states and territories, 1% are from out of state, 25% African American, 3% Asian American or Pacific Islander, 3% Hispanic American, 0.5% Native American, 14% transferred in.

Freshmen *Admission:* 470 applied, 470 admitted, 470 enrolled.

Faculty *Total:* 420, 15% full-time, 4% with terminal degrees. *Student/faculty ratio:* 27:1.

Majors Administrative assistant and secretarial science; architectural engineering technology; biology/biotechnology laboratory technician; business/commerce; electrical, electronics and communications engineering; environmental engineering technology; funeral service and mortuary science; human services; liberal arts and sciences/liberal studies; management information systems; mechanical engineering/mechanical technology; nursing (registered nurse training); physical therapy; safety/security technology.

Academics *Calendar:* semesters. *Degree:* certificates and associate. *Special study options:* academic remediation for entering students, adult/continuing education programs, advanced placement credit, distance learning, external

degree program, honors programs, off-campus study, part-time degree program, services for LD students, study abroad, summer session for credit. *ROTC:* Army (c).

Library John Tyler Community College Learning Resource and Technology Center with 49,393 titles, 179 serial subscriptions, 1,544 audiovisual materials, an OPAC, a Web page.

Computers on Campus 465 computers available on campus for general student use. A campuswide network can be accessed from off campus. Internet access, at least one staffed computer lab available.

Student Life *Housing:* college housing not available. *Campus security:* 24-hour patrols.

Athletics *Intramural sports:* golf M/W, softball M/W, tennis M/W, volleyball M/W.

Costs (2005–06) *Tuition:* state resident $1708 full-time, $71 per credit part-time; nonresident $5264 full-time, $219 per credit part-time. *Required fees:* $50 full-time, $25 per term part-time.

Applying *Options:* common application, early admission, deferred entrance. *Recommended:* high school transcript. *Application deadline:* rolling (freshmen). *Notification:* continuous (freshmen).

Freshmen Application Contact Ms. Kristin Kelly, Instructional Technologist, John Tyler Community College, 13101 Jefferson Davis Highway, Chester, VA 23831. *Phone:* 804-796-4150. *Toll-free phone:* 800-552-3490. *Fax:* 804-796-4163.

J. SARGEANT REYNOLDS COMMUNITY COLLEGE
Richmond, Virginia **www.reynolds.edu**

- **State-supported** 2-year, founded 1972, part of Virginia Community College System
- **Suburban** 207-acre campus
- **Endowment** $2.3 million
- **Coed**

Undergraduates 2,871 full-time, 8,807 part-time. 36% African American, 3% Asian American or Pacific Islander, 2% Hispanic American, 0.6% Native American, 0.4% international.

Faculty *Student/faculty ratio:* 22:1.

Academics *Calendar:* semesters. *Degree:* certificates and associate. *Special study options:* academic remediation for entering students, adult/continuing education programs, advanced placement credit, distance learning, English as a second language, independent study, internships, off-campus study, part-time degree program, services for LD students, summer session for credit.

Student Life *Campus security:* security during open hours.

Costs (2005–06) *Tuition:* state resident $2282 full-time, $76 per credit hour part-time; nonresident $6728 full-time, $224 per credit hour part-time.

Financial Aid Of all full-time matriculated undergraduates who enrolled in 2004, 527 Federal Work-Study jobs (averaging $1711).

Applying *Options:* electronic application. *Required:* high school transcript. *Required for some:* interview.

Director of Admissions Ms. Karen Pettis-Walden, Acting Director of Admissions and Records, J. Sargeant Reynolds Community College, PO Box 85622, Richmond, VA 23285-5622. *Phone:* 804-371-3029. *E-mail:* srmarss@jsr.cc.va.us.

LORD FAIRFAX COMMUNITY COLLEGE
Middletown, Virginia **www.lfcc.edu/**

- **State-supported** 2-year, founded 1969, part of Virginia Community College System
- **Rural** 100-acre campus with easy access to Washington, DC
- **Coed,** 5,492 undergraduate students, 28% full-time, 62% women, 38% men

Undergraduates 1,535 full-time, 3,957 part-time. 2% are from out of state, 5% African American, 1% Asian American or Pacific Islander, 2% Hispanic American, 0.4% Native American. *Retention:* 52% of 2003 full-time freshmen returned.

Freshmen *Admission:* 687 enrolled.

Faculty *Total:* 309, 18% full-time.

Majors Accounting; administrative assistant and secretarial science; agricultural business and management; applied horticulture; biological and physical sciences; business administration and management; civil engineering technology; commercial and advertising art; communication/speech communication and rhetoric; computer and information sciences; computer programming; dental

Lord Fairfax Community College (continued)

hygiene; education; environmental engineering technology; information science/studies; liberal arts and sciences/liberal studies; mechanical engineering/mechanical technology; natural resources management and policy; nursing (registered nurse training); office management; philosophy.

Academics *Calendar:* semesters. *Degree:* certificates and associate. *Special study options:* academic remediation for entering students, adult/continuing education programs, advanced placement credit, cooperative education, distance learning, honors programs, part-time degree program, services for LD students, summer session for credit.

Library Learning Resources Center with 41,000 titles, 300 serial subscriptions, an OPAC.

Computers on Campus 450 computers available on campus for general student use. A campuswide network can be accessed from off campus. Internet access, at least one staffed computer lab available.

Student Life *Housing:* college housing not available. *Activities and Organizations:* drama/theater group, Phi Theta Kappa, Phi Beta Lambda, Performing Arts Club, Scientific Society, Ambassadors Club. *Campus security:* late-night transport/escort service. *Student services:* personal/psychological counseling, women's center.

Costs (2006–07) *Tuition:* state resident $1740 full-time, $73 per credit hour part-time; nonresident $5748 full-time, $235 per credit hour part-time. *Required fees:* $117 full-time, $4 per credit hour part-time.

Financial Aid Of all full-time matriculated undergraduates who enrolled in 2004, 28 Federal Work-Study jobs (averaging $1600).

Applying *Options:* early admission. *Recommended:* high school transcript. *Application deadline:* rolling (freshmen), rolling (transfers). *Notification:* continuous (freshmen).

Freshmen Application Contact Ms. Cynthia Bambara, Vice President of Student Success, Lord Fairfax Community College, 173 Skirmisher Lane, Middletown, VA 22645. *Phone:* 540-868-7105. *Toll-free phone:* 800-906-5322 Ext. 7107. *Fax:* 540-868-7005. *E-mail:* lfsmitt@lfcc.edu.

MEDICAL CAREERS INSTITUTE
Newport News, Virginia

MEDICAL CAREERS INSTITUTE
Richmond, Virginia   **www.medicalcareersinstitute.com/**

Director of Admissions David K. Mayle, Director of Admissions, Medical Careers Institute, 800 Moorefield Park Drive, Suite 302, Richmond, VA 23236-3659. *Phone:* 804-521-0400. *Fax:* 804-521-0406. *E-mail:* dmayle@medical.edu.

MEDICAL CAREERS INSTITUTE
Virginia Beach, Virginia

MOUNTAIN EMPIRE COMMUNITY COLLEGE
Big Stone Gap, Virginia   **www.me.vccs.edu/**

Director of Admissions Mr. Perry Carroll, Director of Enrollment Services, Mountain Empire Community College, 3441 Mountain Empire Road, Big Stone Gap, VA 24219. *Phone:* 276-523-2400 Ext. 219.

NATIONAL COLLEGE OF BUSINESS & TECHNOLOGY
Bluefield, Virginia   **www.ncbt.edu/**

- **Proprietary** 2-year, founded 1886, part of National College of Business and Technology
- **Small-town** campus
- **Coed**

Faculty *Student/faculty ratio:* 10:1.

Academics *Calendar:* quarters. *Degree:* diplomas and associate. *Special study options:* advanced placement credit, double majors, honors programs, internships, part-time degree program, services for LD students, summer session for credit.

Costs (2005–06) *Tuition:* $6408 full-time, $178 per credit hour part-time. Full-time tuition and fees vary according to course load. Part-time tuition and fees vary according to course load. *Required fees:* $75 full-time, $15 per term part-time. *Payment plans:* installment, deferred payment.

Financial Aid Of all full-time matriculated undergraduates who enrolled in 2004, 5 Federal Work-Study jobs.

Applying *Options:* electronic application. *Application fee:* $30. *Recommended:* interview.

Freshmen Application Contact Ms. Jennifer Hooper, Admissions Representative, National College of Business & Technology, 100 Logan Street, Bluefield, VA 24605. *Phone:* 540-326-6321. *Toll-free phone:* 800-664-1886.

NATIONAL COLLEGE OF BUSINESS & TECHNOLOGY
Charlottesville, Virginia   **www.ncbt.edu/**

- **Proprietary** 2-year, founded 1975, part of National College of Business and Technology
- **Small-town** campus with easy access to Richmond
- **Coed**

Faculty *Student/faculty ratio:* 12:1.

Academics *Calendar:* quarters. *Degree:* certificates, diplomas, and associate. *Special study options:* advanced placement credit, double majors, honors programs, internships, part-time degree program, services for LD students, summer session for credit.

Costs (2005–06) *Tuition:* $6408 full-time, $178 per credit hour part-time. Full-time tuition and fees vary according to course load. Part-time tuition and fees vary according to course load. *Required fees:* $75 full-time, $15 per term part-time. *Payment plans:* installment, deferred payment.

Financial Aid Of all full-time matriculated undergraduates who enrolled in 2004, 4 Federal Work-Study jobs.

Applying *Options:* electronic application. *Application fee:* $30. *Required for some:* high school transcript. *Recommended:* interview.

Director of Admissions Ms. Adrienne D. Granitz, Campus Director, National College of Business & Technology, 1819 Emmet Street, Charlottesville, VA 22903. *Phone:* 434-295-0136. *Toll-free phone:* 800-664-1886. *Fax:* 434-979-8061.

NATIONAL COLLEGE OF BUSINESS & TECHNOLOGY
Danville, Virginia   **www.ncbt.edu/**

Director of Admissions Ms. Amy Bracey, Campus Director, National College of Business & Technology, 734 Main Street, Danville, VA 24541. *Phone:* 434-793-6822. *Toll-free phone:* 800-664-1886.

NATIONAL COLLEGE OF BUSINESS & TECHNOLOGY
Harrisonburg, Virginia   **www.ncbt.edu/**

- **Proprietary** 2-year, founded 1988, part of National College of Business and Technology
- **Small-town** campus
- **Coed**

Faculty *Student/faculty ratio:* 12:1.

Academics *Calendar:* quarters. *Degree:* diplomas and associate. *Special study options:* advanced placement credit, double majors, honors programs, internships, part-time degree program, services for LD students, summer session for credit.

Costs (2005–06) *Tuition:* $6408 full-time, $178 per credit hour part-time. Full-time tuition and fees vary according to course load. Part-time tuition and fees vary according to course load. *Required fees:* $75 full-time, $15 per term part-time. *Payment plans:* installment, deferred payment.

Financial Aid Of all full-time matriculated undergraduates who enrolled in 2004, 2 Federal Work-Study jobs.

Applying *Options:* electronic application. *Application fee:* $30. *Required for some:* high school transcript. *Recommended:* interview.

Director of Admissions Jack Evey, Campus Director, National College of Business & Technology, 51 B Burgess Road, Harrisonburg, VA 22801. *Phone:* 540-432-0943. *Toll-free phone:* 800-664-1886.

NATIONAL COLLEGE OF BUSINESS & TECHNOLOGY
Lynchburg, Virginia   www.ncbt.edu/

- **Proprietary** 2-year, founded 1979, part of National College of Business and Technology
- **Small-town** 2-acre campus
- **Coed**

Undergraduates Students come from 15 other countries.

Faculty *Student/faculty ratio:* 12:1.

Academics *Calendar:* quarters. *Degree:* diplomas and associate. *Special study options:* advanced placement credit, double majors, honors programs, internships, part-time degree program, services for LD students, summer session for credit.

Costs (2005–06) *Tuition:* $6408 full-time, $178 per credit hour part-time. Full-time tuition and fees vary according to course load. Part-time tuition and fees vary according to course load. *Required fees:* $75 full-time, $15 per term part-time. *Payment plans:* installment, deferred payment.

Financial Aid Of all full-time matriculated undergraduates who enrolled in 2004, 3 Federal Work-Study jobs.

Applying *Options:* electronic application. *Application fee:* $30. *Required for some:* high school transcript. *Recommended:* interview.

Freshmen Application Contact Mr. George Wheelous, Admissions Representative, National College of Business & Technology, 104 Candlewood Court, Lynchburg, VA 24502. *Phone:* 804-239-3500. *Toll-free phone:* 800-664-1886.

NATIONAL COLLEGE OF BUSINESS & TECHNOLOGY
Martinsville, Virginia   www.ncbt.edu/

- **Proprietary** 2-year, founded 1975, part of National College of Business and Technology
- **Small-town** campus
- **Coed**

Faculty *Student/faculty ratio:* 12:1.

Academics *Calendar:* quarters. *Degree:* diplomas and associate. *Special study options:* advanced placement credit, double majors, honors programs, internships, part-time degree program, services for LD students, summer session for credit.

Costs (2005–06) *Tuition:* $6408 full-time, $178 per credit hour part-time. *Required fees:* $75 full-time, $15 per term part-time.

Financial Aid Of all full-time matriculated undergraduates who enrolled in 2004, 2 Federal Work-Study jobs.

Applying *Options:* electronic application. *Application fee:* $30. *Required for some:* high school transcript. *Recommended:* interview.

Director of Admissions Mr. John Scott, Campus Director, National College of Business & Technology, 10 Church Street, Martinsville, VA 24114. *Phone:* 276-632-5621. *Toll-free phone:* 800-664-1886 (in-state); 800-664-1866 (out-of-state).

NATIONAL COLLEGE OF BUSINESS & TECHNOLOGY
Salem, Virginia   www.ncbt.edu/

- **Proprietary** primarily 2-year, founded 1886, part of National College of Business and Technology
- **Urban** 3-acre campus
- **Coed**

Undergraduates Students come from 15 other countries, 24% are from out of state. *Retention:* 70% of 2003 full-time freshmen returned.

Faculty *Student/faculty ratio:* 12:1.

Academics *Calendar:* quarters. *Degrees:* certificates, diplomas, associate, bachelor's, and master's. *Special study options:* academic remediation for entering students, advanced placement credit, double majors, internships, part-time degree program, summer session for credit.

Costs (2005–06) *Tuition:* $6408 full-time, $178 per credit hour part-time. *Required fees:* $75 full-time, $15 per term part-time.

Financial Aid Of all full-time matriculated undergraduates who enrolled in 2004, 6 Federal Work-Study jobs.

Applying *Application fee:* $30. *Required:* high school transcript. *Recommended:* interview.

Freshmen Application Contact Ms. Bunnie Hancock, Admissions Representative, National College of Business & Technology, PO Box 6400, Roanoke, VA 24017. *Phone:* 540-986-1800. *Toll-free phone:* 800-664-1886.

NEW RIVER COMMUNITY COLLEGE
Dublin, Virginia   www.nr.cc.va.us/

Director of Admissions Ms. Margaret G. Taylor, Coordinator of Admissions and Records and Student Services, New River Community College, PO Box 1127, 5251 College Drive, Dublin, VA 24084. *Phone:* 540-674-3600 Ext. 4205. *E-mail:* nrchrim@vccscent.bitnet.

NORTHERN VIRGINIA COMMUNITY COLLEGE
Annandale, Virginia   www.nv.cc.va.us/

- **State-supported** 2-year, founded 1965, part of Virginia Community College System
- **Suburban** 435-acre campus with easy access to Washington, DC
- **Endowment** $1.1 million
- **Coed**

Undergraduates 2% are from out of state, 15% African American, 12% Asian American or Pacific Islander, 10% Hispanic American, 2% Native American, 4% international.

Academics *Calendar:* semesters. *Degree:* certificates and associate. *Special study options:* academic remediation for entering students, adult/continuing education programs, advanced placement credit, cooperative education, distance learning, double majors, English as a second language, external degree program, honors programs, part-time degree program, services for LD students, study abroad, summer session for credit.

Student Life *Campus security:* 24-hour emergency response devices, campus police.

Applying *Options:* common application, early admission, deferred entrance. *Required for some:* high school transcript.

Director of Admissions Dr. Max L. Bassett, Dean of Academic and Student Services, Northern Virginia Community College, 4001 Wakefield Chapel Road, Annandale, VA 22003-3796. *Phone:* 703-323-3195.

PARKS COLLEGE
Arlington, Virginia   www.parks-college.com/

Director of Admissions Lachelle Green, Director of Admissions, Parks College, 801 North Quincy Street, Arlington, VA 22203. *Phone:* 703-248-8887. *Fax:* 703-351-2202. *E-mail:* lgreen@cci.edu.

PATRICK HENRY COMMUNITY COLLEGE

Martinsville, Virginia   www.ph.vccs.edu/

- **State-supported** 2-year, founded 1962, part of Virginia Community College System
- **Rural** 137-acre campus
- **Coed**

Undergraduates Students come from 3 states and territories. *Retention:* 48% of 2003 full-time freshmen returned.

Academics *Calendar:* semesters. *Degree:* associate. *Special study options:* academic remediation for entering students, adult/continuing education programs, advanced placement credit, cooperative education, English as a second language, internships, part-time degree program, services for LD students, summer session for credit.

Student Life *Campus security:* 24-hour emergency response devices and patrols, late-night transport/escort service.

Standardized Tests *Required:* ACT ASSET (for placement).

Costs (2005–06) *Tuition:* state resident $1632 full-time, $68 per credit hour part-time; nonresident $5136 full-time, $214 per credit hour part-time. *Required fees:* $81 full-time, $3 per credit hour part-time, $5 per term part-time.

Financial Aid Of all full-time matriculated undergraduates who enrolled in 2004, 41 Federal Work-Study jobs (averaging $2000).

Applying *Options:* early admission, deferred entrance. *Required:* high school transcript.

Director of Admissions Dr. Nolan Browning, Vice President of Academic and Student Development, Patrick Henry Community College, PO Box 5311, 645 Patriot Avenue, Martinsville, VA 24115. *Phone:* 276-656-0315. *Toll-free phone:* 800-232-7997.

PAUL D. CAMP COMMUNITY COLLEGE

Franklin, Virginia   www.pc.vccs.edu/

Director of Admissions Ms. Monette Williams, Acting Director of Admissions and Records, Paul D. Camp Community College, PO Box 737, 100 North College Drive, Franklin, VA 23851-0737. *Phone:* 757-569-6725. *E-mail:* vccscent@pc.vccs.edu.

PIEDMONT VIRGINIA COMMUNITY COLLEGE

Charlottesville, Virginia   www.pvcc.edu/

- **State-supported** 2-year, founded 1972, part of Virginia Community College System
- **Suburban** 114-acre campus with easy access to Richmond
- **Coed,** 4,163 undergraduate students, 26% full-time, 59% women, 41% men

Undergraduates 1,079 full-time, 3,084 part-time. Students come from 12 states and territories, 1% are from out of state, 13% African American, 3% Asian American or Pacific Islander, 2% Hispanic American, 0.3% Native American, 0.4% international, 48% transferred in.

Freshmen *Admission:* 442 admitted, 442 enrolled.

Faculty *Total:* 212, 26% full-time, 11% with terminal degrees. *Student/faculty ratio:* 20:1.

Majors Accounting; administrative assistant and secretarial science; biological and physical sciences; biotechnology; business administration and management; carpentry; clinical/medical laboratory technology; computer engineering technology; computer programming; computer programming (specific applications); computer science; computer systems networking and telecommunications; computer/technical support; criminal justice/police science; data processing and data processing technology; education; electrician; emergency medical technology (EMT paramedic); engineering; general studies; heating, air conditioning and refrigeration technology; liberal arts and sciences/liberal studies; marketing/marketing management; masonry; mechanical drafting and CAD/CADD; nursing (registered nurse training); plumbing technology; respiratory care therapy; visual and performing arts; web/multimedia management and webmaster.

Academics *Calendar:* semesters. *Degree:* certificates and associate. *Special study options:* academic remediation for entering students, adult/continuing education programs, advanced placement credit, cooperative education, distance learning, English as a second language, honors programs, independent study, internships, part-time degree program, services for LD students, summer session for credit. *ROTC:* Army (c).

Library Jessup Library with 72,574 titles, 209 serial subscriptions, 10,254 audiovisual materials, an OPAC, a Web page.

Computers on Campus 60 computers available on campus for general student use. A campuswide network can be accessed from off campus that provide access to e-mail. Internet access, online (class) registration, at least one staffed computer lab available.

Student Life *Housing:* college housing not available. *Activities and Organizations:* drama/theater group, student-run newspaper, choral group, Phi Theta Kappa, Black Student Alliance, Science Club, Masquers, Christian Fellowship Club. *Campus security:* 24-hour patrols.

Athletics *Intramural sports:* basketball M/W, bowling M/W, football M/W, golf M/W, lacrosse M/W, skiing (cross-country) M/W, soccer M/W, softball M/W, tennis M/W, volleyball M/W, weight lifting M/W.

Costs (2006–07) *Tuition:* state resident $2175 full-time, $73 per credit hour part-time; nonresident $7126 full-time, $238 per credit hour part-time. *Required fees:* $159 full-time, $5 per credit hour part-time.

Financial Aid Of all full-time matriculated undergraduates who enrolled in 2004, 50 Federal Work-Study jobs.

Applying *Options:* common application, electronic application, early admission. *Required for some:* high school transcript, for nursing program: completion of any developmental studies; grade 'C' or better in high school or college developmental chemistry course; high school diploma/GED; and completion of nursing program application. *Application deadline:* rolling (freshmen), rolling (transfers). *Notification:* continuous (freshmen).

Freshmen Application Contact Ms. Mary Walsh, Director of Student Services, Piedmont Virginia Community College, 501 College Drive, Charlottesville, VA 22902-7589. *Phone:* 434-961-5400. *Fax:* 434-961-5425.

RAPPAHANNOCK COMMUNITY COLLEGE

Glenns, Virginia   www.rcc.vccs.edu/

Freshmen Application Contact Ms. Wilnet Willis, Admissions and Records Officer, Rappahannock Community College, Glenns Campus, 12745 College Drive, Glenns, VA 23149-2616. *Phone:* 804-758-6742.

RICHARD BLAND COLLEGE OF THE COLLEGE OF WILLIAM AND MARY

Petersburg, Virginia   www.rbc.edu/

- **State-supported** 2-year, founded 1961, part of College of William and Mary
- **Rural** 712-acre campus with easy access to Richmond
- **Coed,** 1,437 undergraduate students, 57% full-time, 66% women, 34% men

Undergraduates 814 full-time, 623 part-time. Students come from 8 states and territories, 1% are from out of state, 19% African American, 2% Asian American or Pacific Islander, 2% Hispanic American, 0.5% Native American, 7% transferred in. *Retention:* 61% of 2003 full-time freshmen returned.

Freshmen *Admission:* 528 applied, 464 admitted, 401 enrolled. *Average high school GPA:* 2.8. *Test scores:* SAT verbal scores over 500: 39%; SAT math scores over 500: 33%; SAT verbal scores over 600: 9%; SAT math scores over 600: 8%; SAT verbal scores over 700: 1%.

Faculty *Total:* 66, 48% full-time, 30% with terminal degrees. *Student/faculty ratio:* 23:1.

Majors Liberal arts and sciences/liberal studies.

Academics *Calendar:* semesters. *Degree:* associate. *Special study options:* academic remediation for entering students, accelerated degree program, advanced placement credit, part-time degree program, services for LD students, summer session for credit. *ROTC:* Army (c).

Library Richard Bland College Library with 91,000 titles, 9,000 serial subscriptions, 2,400 audiovisual materials, an OPAC, a Web page.

Computers on Campus 128 computers available on campus for general student use. A campuswide network can be accessed from off campus that provide access to e-mail, Blackboard. Internet access, at least one staffed computer lab available.

Student Life *Housing:* college housing not available. *Activities and Organizations:* drama/theater group, student-run newspaper, choral group, RBC Newspaper, Multicultural Alliance, student government, Spanish Club, Biology Club. *Campus security:* 24-hour patrols.

Athletics *Intramural sports:* basketball M/W, cheerleading M/W, golf M/W, tennis M/W, volleyball M/W.

Standardized Tests *Required:* ACT COMPASS (for admission). *Recommended:* SAT or ACT (for admission).

Costs (2005–06) *Tuition:* state resident $2350 full-time, $91 per credit hour part-time; nonresident $9608 full-time, $398 per credit hour part-time. Full-time tuition and fees vary according to course load and location. Part-time tuition and fees vary according to course load and location. *Required fees:* $170 full-time, $4 per credit hour part-time. *Waivers:* senior citizens.

Financial Aid Of all full-time matriculated undergraduates who enrolled in 2004, 10 Federal Work-Study jobs (averaging $2000).

Applying *Application fee:* $20. *Required:* essay or personal statement, high school transcript, minimum 2.0 GPA, In-State Residency Form. *Required for some:* letters of recommendation, interview. *Application deadline:* 8/15 (freshmen), rolling (transfers). *Notification:* continuous (freshmen).

Freshmen Application Contact Mr. Randy Dean, Director of Admissions and Student Services, Richard Bland College of The College of William and Mary, 11301 Johnson Road, Petersburg, VA 23805-7100. *Phone:* 804-862-6225. *Fax:* 804-862-6490. *E-mail:* admit@rbc.edu.

SOUTHSIDE VIRGINIA COMMUNITY COLLEGE

Alberta, Virginia www.sv.vccs.edu/

- **State-supported** 2-year, founded 1970, part of Virginia Community College System
- **Rural** 207-acre campus
- **Endowment** $527,455
- **Coed,** 4,686 undergraduate students, 29% full-time, 65% women, 35% men

Undergraduates 1,359 full-time, 3,327 part-time. Students come from 3 states and territories, 2 other countries, 1% are from out of state, 46% African American, 0.7% Asian American or Pacific Islander, 0.5% Hispanic American, 0.2% Native American.
Freshmen *Admission:* 380 enrolled.

Faculty *Total:* 295, 24% full-time, 6% with terminal degrees. *Student/faculty ratio:* 17:1.

Majors Administrative assistant and secretarial science; biological and physical sciences; business administration and management; criminal justice/law enforcement administration; drafting and design technology; education; electrical, electronic and communications engineering technology; general studies; human services; information science/studies; information technology; liberal arts and sciences/liberal studies; nursing (registered nurse training); respiratory care therapy.

Academics *Calendar:* semesters. *Degree:* certificates, diplomas, and associate. *Special study options:* academic remediation for entering students, advanced placement credit, distance learning, honors programs, off-campus study, part-time degree program, services for LD students, study abroad, summer session for credit. *ROTC:* Army (c).

Library Julian M. Howell Library plus 1 other with 27,691 titles, 164 serial subscriptions, 1,307 audiovisual materials, an OPAC, a Web page.

Computers on Campus 200 computers available on campus for general student use. A campuswide network can be accessed. Internet access, online (class) registration, at least one staffed computer lab available.

Student Life *Housing:* college housing not available. *Activities and Organizations:* choral group, Student Forum, Phi Theta Kappa, Phi Beta Lambda, Alpha Delta Omega.

Athletics *Intramural sports:* basketball M, softball M/W, table tennis M/W, tennis M/W, volleyball M/W.

Costs (2005–06) *Tuition:* state resident $2040 full-time, $68 per credit part-time; nonresident $6420 full-time, $214 per credit part-time. Full-time tuition and fees vary according to course load. Part-time tuition and fees vary according to course load. *Required fees:* $155 full-time, $5 per credit part-time. *Payment plan:* installment. *Waivers:* senior citizens.

Applying *Options:* common application, electronic application, deferred entrance. *Required:* high school transcript, interview. *Application deadline:* rolling (freshmen), rolling (transfers). *Notification:* continuous (freshmen).

Freshmen Application Contact Dr. Ronald Mattox, Dean of Admissions, Records, and Institutional Research, Southside Virginia Community College, 109 Campus Drive, Alberta, VA 23821. *Phone:* 434-949-1012. *Fax:* 434-949-7863. *E-mail:* rhina.jones@sv.vccs.edu.

SOUTHWEST VIRGINIA COMMUNITY COLLEGE

Richlands, Virginia www.sw.edu/

- **State-supported** 2-year, founded 1968, part of Virginia Community College System
- **Rural** 100-acre campus
- **Coed,** 3,666 undergraduate students, 41% full-time, 59% women, 41% men

Undergraduates 1,514 full-time, 2,152 part-time. Students come from 6 other countries, 2% African American, 0.4% Asian American or Pacific Islander, 0.2% Hispanic American, 0.1% Native American, 4% transferred in. *Retention:* 91% of 2003 full-time freshmen returned.
Freshmen *Admission:* 418 enrolled.

Faculty *Total:* 252, 28% full-time. *Student/faculty ratio:* 17:1.

Majors Accounting; administrative assistant and secretarial science; biological and physical sciences; business administration and management; criminal justice/police science; drafting and design technology; education; electrical, electronic and communications engineering technology; engineering; human services; industrial radiologic technology; information science/studies; land use planning and management; liberal arts and sciences/liberal studies; mining technology; music; nursing (registered nurse training); respiratory care therapy.

Academics *Calendar:* semesters. *Degree:* certificates, diplomas, and associate. *Special study options:* academic remediation for entering students, adult/continuing education programs, advanced placement credit, distance learning, double majors, honors programs, internships, part-time degree program, summer session for credit.

Library 58,000 titles, 225 serial subscriptions, an OPAC, a Web page.

Computers on Campus 150 computers available on campus for general student use. A campuswide network can be accessed from off campus. Internet access, at least one staffed computer lab available.

Student Life *Housing:* college housing not available. *Activities and Organizations:* drama/theater group, student-run newspaper, radio and television station, PTK, PBL, Intervoice, Black Student Union, Service Club. *Campus security:* 24-hour emergency response devices and patrols, student patrols. *Student services:* personal/psychological counseling, women's center.

Athletics *Intercollegiate sports:* baseball M, basketball M, golf M, rugby M. *Intramural sports:* basketball M/W, bowling M/W, football M, racquetball M/W, tennis M/W, volleyball M/W, weight lifting M/W.

Costs (2005–06) *Tuition:* state resident $1904 full-time, $68 per credit hour part-time; nonresident $5992 full-time, $214 per credit hour part-time. Full-time tuition and fees vary according to course load. Part-time tuition and fees vary according to course load. *Required fees:* $130 full-time, $5 per credit hour part-time. *Payment plan:* installment.

Financial Aid Of all full-time matriculated undergraduates who enrolled in 2004, 150 Federal Work-Study jobs (averaging $1140).

Applying *Options:* early admission, deferred entrance. *Required:* high school transcript, interview. *Application deadline:* rolling (freshmen), rolling (transfers).

Freshmen Application Contact Mr. Jim Farris, Director of Admissions, Records, and Counseling, Southwest Virginia Community College, Box SVCC, Richlands, VA 24641. *Phone:* 276-964-7300. *Toll-free phone:* 800-822-7822. *Fax:* 276-964-7716.

TESST COLLEGE OF TECHNOLOGY

Alexandria, Virginia www.tesst.com/

Director of Admissions Mr. Bob Somers, Director, TESST College of Technology, 6315 Bren Mar Drive, Alexandria, VA 22312-6342. *Phone:* 703-548-4800. *Toll-free phone:* 800-48-TESST. *Fax:* 703-683-2765. *E-mail:* tesstal@erols.com.

THOMAS NELSON COMMUNITY COLLEGE

Hampton, Virginia www.tncc.edu/

- **State-supported** 2-year, founded 1968, part of Virginia Community College System
- **Suburban** 85-acre campus with easy access to Virginia Beach
- **Coed,** 8,595 undergraduate students, 31% full-time, 59% women, 41% men

Undergraduates 2,658 full-time, 5,937 part-time. 34% African American, 4% Asian American or Pacific Islander, 4% Hispanic American, 0.6% Native

Thomas Nelson Community College (continued)
American.

Freshmen *Admission:* 1,211 enrolled.

Faculty *Total:* 433, 21% full-time.

Majors Accounting; administrative assistant and secretarial science; automobile/automotive mechanics technology; biological and physical sciences; business administration and management; clinical/medical laboratory technology; commercial and advertising art; computer science; criminal justice/police science; drafting and design technology; electrical, electronic and communications engineering technology; engineering; fire science; information science/studies; kindergarten/preschool education; liberal arts and sciences/liberal studies; mechanical engineering/mechanical technology; nursing (registered nurse training); ophthalmic laboratory technology; photography; public administration; social sciences.

Academics *Calendar:* semesters. *Degree:* certificates, diplomas, and associate. *Special study options:* academic remediation for entering students, adult/continuing education programs, advanced placement credit, cooperative education, English as a second language, external degree program, honors programs, internships, off-campus study, part-time degree program, services for LD students, summer session for credit.

Library Learning Resource Center with 66,281 titles, 467 serial subscriptions.

Computers on Campus 80 computers available on campus for general student use. A campuswide network can be accessed. At least one staffed computer lab available.

Student Life *Activities and Organizations:* student-run newspaper, choral group, Phi Theta Kappa, Future Nurses Association, Human Services Education Club, Student Government Association, Health Care Advocates. *Campus security:* 24-hour patrols. *Student services:* personal/psychological counseling.

Athletics *Intramural sports:* basketball M/W, sailing M/W, soccer M/W, tennis M/W, volleyball M/W.

Costs (2006–07) *Tuition:* state resident $2175 full-time, $73 per credit hour part-time; nonresident $7061 full-time, $235 per credit hour part-time. *Required fees:* $116 full-time, $3 per credit hour part-time, $11 per term part-time.

Financial Aid Of all full-time matriculated undergraduates who enrolled in 2004, 110 Federal Work-Study jobs (averaging $3000).

Applying *Options:* early admission, deferred entrance. *Required:* high school transcript. *Application deadline:* rolling (freshmen), rolling (transfers). *Notification:* continuous (freshmen).

Freshmen Application Contact Ms. Jerri Newson, Admissions Office Manager, Thomas Nelson Community College, PO Box 9407, 99 Thomas Nelson Drive, Hampton, VA 23670. *Phone:* 757-825-2800. *Fax:* 757-825-2763. *E-mail:* admissions@tncc.edu.

TIDEWATER COMMUNITY COLLEGE
Norfolk, Virginia   **www.tcc.edu/**

- **State-supported** 2-year, founded 1968, part of Virginia Community College System
- **Suburban** 520-acre campus
- **Coed,** 23,718 undergraduate students, 33% full-time, 61% women, 39% men

Undergraduates 7,850 full-time, 15,868 part-time. Students come from 53 states and territories, 12% are from out of state, 32% African American, 5% Asian American or Pacific Islander, 4% Hispanic American, 0.6% Native American.

Faculty *Total:* 1,322, 20% full-time. *Student/faculty ratio:* 15:1.

Majors Accounting; administrative assistant and secretarial science; advertising; automobile/automotive mechanics technology; biological and physical sciences; business administration and management; civil engineering; commercial and advertising art; computer programming; drafting and design technology; education; electrical, electronic and communications engineering technology; engineering; finance; fine/studio arts; graphic design; horticultural science; information technology; interior design; kindergarten/preschool education; liberal arts and sciences/liberal studies; marketing/marketing management; music; nursing (registered nurse training); paralegal/legal assistant; real estate.

Academics *Calendar:* semesters. *Degree:* certificates, diplomas, and associate. *Special study options:* academic remediation for entering students, accelerated degree program, adult/continuing education programs, advanced placement credit, cooperative education, distance learning, English as a second language, honors programs, independent study, internships, off-campus study, part-time degree program, services for LD students, summer session for credit.

Library 147,126 titles, 913 serial subscriptions.

Computers on Campus A campuswide network can be accessed from off campus. Internet access, online (class) registration, at least one staffed computer lab available.

Student Life *Housing:* college housing not available. *Activities and Organizations:* drama/theater group, student-run newspaper. *Campus security:* 24-hour patrols. *Student services:* personal/psychological counseling, women's center.

Athletics *Intramural sports:* basketball M/W, soccer M, softball W, tennis M/W, volleyball W.

Costs (2006–07) *Tuition:* state resident $1944 full-time, $73 per credit part-time; nonresident $5905 full-time, $246 per credit part-time. *Required fees:* $9 per credit part-time.

Financial Aid Of all full-time matriculated undergraduates who enrolled in 2004, 64 Federal Work-Study jobs (averaging $2000).

Applying *Options:* early admission, deferred entrance. *Application deadline:* rolling (freshmen), rolling (transfers). *Notification:* continuous (freshmen).

Freshmen Application Contact Ms. Tyjaun Lee, Associate Dean, Student Services, Tidewater Community College, 7000 College Drive, Portsmouth, VA 23703. *Phone:* 757-822-1068. *Fax:* 757-822-1060.

TIDEWATER TECH
Virginia Beach, Virginia

VIRGINIA HIGHLANDS COMMUNITY COLLEGE
Abingdon, Virginia   **www.vhcc.edu/**

Director of Admissions Mr. David N. Matlock, Director of Admissions, Records, and Financial Aid, Virginia Highlands Community College, PO Box 828, Abingdon, VA 24212-0828. *Phone:* 276-739-2414 Ext. 290. *Toll-free phone:* 877-207-6115.

VIRGINIA WESTERN COMMUNITY COLLEGE
Roanoke, Virginia   **www.virginiawestern.edu/**

Freshmen Application Contact Admissions Office, Virginia Western Community College, 3095 Colonial Avenue, Roanoke, VA 24038. *Phone:* 540-857-7231.

WESTWOOD COLLEGE—ANNANDALE CAMPUS
Annadale, Virginia   **westwood.edu**

▶ See page 606 for the College Close-Up.

WESTWOOD COLLEGE—ARLINGTON BALLSTON CAMPUS
Arlington, Virginia   **www.westwood.edu**

- **Proprietary** 4-year
- **Coed**

Academics *Degrees:* associate and bachelor's.

Student Life *Student services:* personal/psychological counseling.

Costs (2006–07) *Tuition:* $12,300 full-time, $467 per credit part-time.

Applying *Application fee:* $100. *Required:* interview, Accuplacer Test.

Freshmen Application Contact Shebony Corbin, Westwood College–Arlington Ballston Campus, 1901 North Ft. Myer Drive, Arlington, VA 22209. *Phone:* 877-268-5218. *Fax:* 703-243-3992. *E-mail:* scorbin@westwood.edu.

▶ See page 608 for the College Close-Up.

WYTHEVILLE COMMUNITY COLLEGE
Wytheville, Virginia   www.wcc.vccs.edu/

Director of Admissions Ms. Sherry K. Dix, Registrar, Wytheville Community College, 1000 East Main Street, Wytheville, VA 24382-3308. *Phone:* 276-223-4755. *Toll-free phone:* 800-468-1195. *E-mail:* wcdixxs@wcc.vccs.edu.

WASHINGTON

APOLLO COLLEGE
Spokane, Washington   www.apollocollege.com/

Director of Admissions Deanna Baker, Campus Director, Apollo College, 1101 North Francher Road, Spokane, WA 99212. *Phone:* 509-532-8888. *Fax:* 509-533-5983.

THE ART INSTITUTE OF SEATTLE
Seattle, Washington   www.ais.edu

- **Proprietary** 4-year, founded 1982, part of Education Management Corporation
- **Urban** campus
- **Coed,** 2,492 undergraduate students, 52% full-time, 49% women, 51% men

Undergraduates 1,298 full-time, 1,194 part-time. Students come from 49 states and territories, 21 other countries, 17% are from out of state, 3% African American, 8% Asian American or Pacific Islander, 3% Hispanic American, 1% Native American, 6% international, 2% transferred in. *Retention:* 66% of 2003 full-time freshmen returned.
Freshmen *Admission:* 693 applied, 466 admitted, 466 enrolled. *Average high school GPA:* 2.40.
Faculty *Total:* 174, 45% full-time, 18% with terminal degrees. *Student/faculty ratio:* 19:1.
Majors Animation, interactive technology, video graphics and special effects; audio engineering; cinematography and film/video production; culinary arts; fashion/apparel design; fashion merchandising; graphic design; industrial design; interior design; intermedia/multimedia; photography.
Academics *Calendar:* quarters. *Degrees:* diplomas, associate, and bachelor's. *Special study options:* academic remediation for entering students, adult/continuing education programs, honors programs, internships, off-campus study, part-time degree program, services for LD students, summer session for credit.
Library AIS Library plus 1 other with 17,164 titles, 303 serial subscriptions, 5,416 audiovisual materials, an OPAC, a Web page.
Computers on Campus 552 computers available on campus for general student use. A campuswide network can be accessed. Internet access, online (class) registration, at least one staffed computer lab available.
Student Life *Housing Options:* coed. Campus housing is leased by the school. Freshman campus housing is guaranteed. *Activities and Organizations:* Multicultural Affairs Organization, American Society of Interior Designers, DECA, Student Advisory Board. *Campus security:* 24-hour emergency response devices and patrols, controlled dormitory access, patrols by trained security personnel for 17 hours. *Student services:* personal/psychological counseling.
Athletics *Intramural sports:* soccer M/W.
Costs (2006–07) *Tuition:* $17,550 full-time, $390 per credit part-time. *Room only:* $6867.
Financial Aid Of all full-time matriculated undergraduates who enrolled in 2004, 18 Federal Work-Study jobs (averaging $1795).
Applying *Options:* electronic application, deferred entrance. *Application fee:* $50. *Required:* essay or personal statement, high school transcript, minimum 2.0 GPA, interview. *Required for some:* 2.5 GPA required for Bachelor degree applicants. *Recommended:* 3 letters of recommendation. *Application deadline:* rolling (freshmen), rolling (transfers). *Notification:* continuous (freshmen).
Freshmen Application Contact Mr. Mike Reese, Registrar, The Art Institute of Seattle, 2323 Elliott Avenue, Seattle, WA 98121-1622. *Phone:* 206-239-2284. *Toll-free phone:* 800-275-2471. *E-mail:* mreese@aii.edu.

▶ **See page 482 for the College Close-Up.**

BATES TECHNICAL COLLEGE
Tacoma, Washington   www.bates.ctc.edu/

Director of Admissions Ms. Gwen Sailer, Vice President for Student Services, Bates Technical College, 1101 South Yakima Avenue, Tacoma, WA 98405. *Phone:* 253-680-7000. *Toll-free phone:* 800-562-7099.

BELLEVUE COMMUNITY COLLEGE
Bellevue, Washington   www.bcc.ctc.edu/

Director of Admissions Ms. Tika Esler, Associate Dean of Enrollment Services, Bellevue Community College, 3000 Landerholm Circle SE, Bellerne, WA 98007. *Phone:* 425-564-2222.

BELLINGHAM TECHNICAL COLLEGE
Bellingham, Washington   www.btc.ctc.edu/

Director of Admissions Mr. David Klaffke, Vice President, Student Services, Bellingham Technical College, 3028 Lindbergh Avenue, Bellingham, WA 98225-1599. *Phone:* 360-738-3105 Ext. 440.

BIG BEND COMMUNITY COLLEGE
Moses Lake, Washington   www.bigbend.edu/

- **State-supported** 2-year, founded 1962
- **Small-town** 159-acre campus
- **Endowment** $1.1 million
- **Coed,** 1,800 undergraduate students, 66% full-time, 57% women, 43% men

Undergraduates 1,194 full-time, 606 part-time. Students come from 4 states and territories, 2 other countries, 5% are from out of state, 1% African American, 2% Asian American or Pacific Islander, 22% Hispanic American, 1% Native American, 0.3% international, 7% transferred in, 5% live on campus.
Freshmen *Admission:* 519 applied, 519 admitted, 245 enrolled.
Faculty *Total:* 132, 41% full-time, 3% with terminal degrees. *Student/faculty ratio:* 20:1.
Majors Accounting technology and bookkeeping; airline pilot and flight crew; automobile/automotive mechanics technology; avionics maintenance technology; civil engineering technology; heavy/industrial equipment maintenance technologies related; industrial electronics technology; information science/studies; liberal arts and sciences/liberal studies; nursing (licensed practical/vocational nurse training); nursing (registered nurse training); office management; teacher assistant/aide; welding technology.
Academics *Calendar:* quarters. *Degree:* certificates and associate. *Special study options:* academic remediation for entering students, advanced placement credit, cooperative education, distance learning, part-time degree program, services for LD students, summer session for credit.
Library Big Bend Community College Library with 41,900 titles, 3,700 serial subscriptions, 3,150 audiovisual materials, an OPAC, a Web page.
Computers on Campus 430 computers available on campus for general student use. A campuswide network can be accessed from off campus. Internet access, online (class) registration, at least one staffed computer lab available.
Student Life *Housing Options:* coed. Campus housing is university owned. *Activities and Organizations:* choral group. *Campus security:* 24-hour emergency response devices, student patrols. *Student services:* personal/psychological counseling.
Athletics *Intercollegiate sports:* baseball M(s), basketball M(s)/W(s), softball W(s), volleyball W(s).
Costs (2006–07) *Tuition:* state resident $2586 full-time, $77 per credit part-time; nonresident $2986 full-time, $91 per credit part-time. *Room and board:* $5200.
Financial Aid Of all full-time matriculated undergraduates who enrolled in 2004, 50 Federal Work-Study jobs (averaging $2700). 100 state and other part-time jobs (averaging $3240).
Applying *Options:* early admission, deferred entrance. *Application fee:* $30. *Required for some:* high school transcript. *Application deadline:* rolling (freshmen), rolling (transfers). *Notification:* continuous (freshmen).

Big Bend Community College (continued)
Freshmen Application Contact Ms. Candis Lacher, Dean of Enrollment Services, Big Bend Community College, 7662 Chanute Street, Moses Lake, WA 98837. *Phone:* 509-793-2061. *Fax:* 509-782-6243. *E-mail:* admissions@ bigbend.edu.

CASCADIA COMMUNITY COLLEGE
Bothell, Washington   **www.cascadia.ctc.edu/**

- **State-supported** 2-year, founded 1999
- **Suburban** 128-acre campus
- **Coed**

Undergraduates 952 full-time, 937 part-time. 2% African American, 6% Asian American or Pacific Islander, 4% Hispanic American, 0.2% Native American. *Retention:* 60% of 2003 full-time freshmen returned.
Faculty *Student/faculty ratio:* 26:1.
Academics *Calendar:* quarters. *Degree:* certificates and associate. *Special study options:* academic remediation for entering students, accelerated degree program, adult/continuing education programs, advanced placement credit, cooperative education, distance learning, English as a second language, external degree program, independent study, internships, off-campus study, part-time degree program, services for LD students, study abroad.
Student Life *Campus security:* 24-hour emergency response devices, late-night transport/escort service.
Costs (2005–06) *Tuition:* state resident $2230 full-time, $74 per credit part-time; nonresident $7738 full-time, $258 per credit part-time. *Required fees:* $75 full-time, $4 per credit part-time.
Director of Admissions Ms. Marla Coan, Dean for Student Success, Cascadia Community College, 18345 Campus Way, NE, Bothell, WA 98011. *Phone:* 425-352-8000.

CENTRALIA COLLEGE
Centralia, Washington   **www.centralia.ctc.edu/**

- **State-supported** 2-year, founded 1925, part of Washington State Board for Community and Technical Colleges
- **Small-town** 31-acre campus
- **Endowment** $4.0 million
- **Coed,** 3,827 undergraduate students, 49% full-time, 64% women, 36% men

Undergraduates 1,860 full-time, 1,967 part-time. Students come from 4 states and territories, 1% are from out of state, 0.8% African American, 2% Asian American or Pacific Islander, 10% Hispanic American, 2% Native American, 0.6% international. *Retention:* 72% of 2003 full-time freshmen returned.
Freshmen *Admission:* 2,428 applied, 2,327 admitted.
Faculty *Total:* 240, 24% full-time, 8% with terminal degrees. *Student/faculty ratio:* 24:1.
Majors Administrative assistant and secretarial science; applied art; art; biological and physical sciences; biology/biological sciences; botany/plant biology; broadcast journalism; business administration and management; business and personal/financial services marketing; business/commerce; chemistry; child care and support services management; child development; civil engineering technology; commercial and advertising art; computer and information sciences related; computer programming related; computer systems networking and telecommunications; consumer merchandising/retailing management; corrections; criminal justice/law enforcement administration; diesel mechanics technology; dramatic/theater arts; electrical, electronic and communications engineering technology; engineering; English; family living/parenthood; French; geology/earth science; German; heavy equipment maintenance technology; history; humanities; kindergarten/preschool education; legal administrative assistant/secretary; liberal arts and sciences/liberal studies; marketing/marketing management; mass communication/media; mathematics; medical administrative assistant and medical secretary; music; natural sciences; nursing (licensed practical/vocational nurse training); nursing (registered nurse training); parks, recreation and leisure; physical sciences; political science and government; pre-dentistry studies; pre-engineering; pre-law studies; pre-medical studies; pre-pharmacy studies; pre-veterinary studies; psychology; radio and television; receptionist; retailing; sales, distribution and marketing; social sciences; sociology; Spanish; survey technology; system administration; teacher assistant/aide; welding technology; zoology/animal biology.
Academics *Calendar:* quarters. *Degree:* certificates and associate. *Special study options:* academic remediation for entering students, adult/continuing education programs, advanced placement credit, cooperative education, distance learning, English as a second language, external degree program, freshman

honors college, honors programs, independent study, part-time degree program, services for LD students, study abroad, summer session for credit.
Library Kirk Library with 38,000 titles, 225 serial subscriptions, an OPAC, a Web page.
Computers on Campus 125 computers available on campus for general student use. A campuswide network can be accessed from off campus that provide access to online degree audits, transcripts. Internet access, online (class) registration, at least one staffed computer lab available. Computer purchase or lease plan available.
Student Life *Housing:* college housing not available. *Activities and Organizations:* drama/theater group, student-run newspaper, radio and television station, choral group, marching band, Phi Theta Kappa, Diesel Tech Club, Business Management Association, Student Activities/Admissions Team, International Club. *Campus security:* 24-hour patrols, late-night transport/escort service. *Student services:* personal/psychological counseling.
Athletics Member NJCAA. *Intercollegiate sports:* baseball M(s), basketball M(s)/W(s), golf W(s), softball W(s), volleyball W(s).
Costs (2006–07) *Tuition:* state resident $2586 full-time, $74 per credit part-time; nonresident $2946 full-time, $86 per credit part-time. *Required fees:* $274 full-time, $8 per credit part-time, $5 per term part-time.
Applying *Options:* electronic application. *Required:* high school transcript. *Application deadline:* rolling (freshmen), rolling (transfers). *Notification:* continuous until 9/15 (freshmen).
Freshmen Application Contact Mr. Scott Copeland, Director of Enrollment Services and College Registrar, Centralia College, 600 West Locust, Centralia, WA 98531. *Phone:* 360-736-9391 Ext. 682. *Fax:* 360-330-7503. *E-mail:* admissions@centralia.edu.

CLARK COLLEGE
Vancouver, Washington   **www.clark.edu/**

- **State-supported** 2-year, founded 1933, part of Washington State Board for Community and Technical Colleges
- **Urban** 80-acre campus with easy access to Portland
- **Endowment** $43.0 million
- **Coed,** 9,820 undergraduate students, 43% full-time, 60% women, 40% men

Undergraduates 4,255 full-time, 5,565 part-time. Students come from 6 states and territories, 16 other countries, 4% are from out of state, 9% transferred in. Freshmen *Admission:* 2,812 applied, 2,812 admitted, 1,114 enrolled.
Faculty *Total:* 576, 34% full-time, 10% with terminal degrees. *Student/faculty ratio:* 23:1.
Majors Accounting technology and bookkeeping; applied horticulture; automobile/automotive mechanics technology; baking and pastry arts; business administration and management; business automation/technology/data entry; computer programming; computer systems networking and telecommunications; construction engineering technology; culinary arts; data entry/microcomputer applications; dental hygiene; diesel mechanics technology; early childhood education; electrical, electronic and communications engineering technology; emergency medical technology (EMT paramedic); executive assistant/executive secretary; graphic communications; human resources management; landscaping and groundskeeping; legal assistant/paralegal; liberal arts and sciences/liberal studies; machine tool technology; manufacturing technology; medical administrative assistant and medical secretary; medical/clinical assistant; nursing (registered nurse training); retailing; retailing operations; selling skills and sales; sport and fitness administration/management; substance abuse/addiction counseling; telecommunications technology; web/multimedia management and webmaster; welding technology.
Academics *Calendar:* quarters. *Degree:* certificates, diplomas, and associate. *Special study options:* academic remediation for entering students, accelerated degree program, adult/continuing education programs, advanced placement credit, cooperative education, distance learning, English as a second language, independent study, internships, part-time degree program, services for LD students, study abroad, summer session for credit. *ROTC:* Army (c), Air Force (c).
Library Lewis D. Cannell Library with 63,525 titles, 417 serial subscriptions, 2,147 audiovisual materials, an OPAC, a Web page.
Computers on Campus 750 computers available on campus for general student use. A campuswide network can be accessed from off campus. Internet access, online (class) registration, at least one staffed computer lab available.
Student Life *Housing:* college housing not available. *Activities and Organizations:* drama/theater group, student-run newspaper, choral group, Phi Theta Kappa, Baptist Student Ministries, Multicultural Students United, Peace Project, Students for Political Activism Now (SPAN). *Campus security:* 24-hour patrols, late-night transport/escort service, security staff during hours of operation. *Student services:* health clinic, personal/psychological counseling, legal services.

Athletics *Intercollegiate sports:* basketball M(s)/W(s), cross-country running M(s)/W(s), fencing M(c)/W(c), soccer M(s)/W(s), softball W, track and field M(s)/W(s), volleyball W(s). *Intramural sports:* basketball M/W, fencing M/W, football M/W, soccer M/W, softball M/W, table tennis M/W, volleyball M/W.

Costs (2005–06) *Tuition:* state resident $2704 full-time, $78 per credit hour part-time; nonresident $3093 full-time, $91 per credit hour part-time. Full-time tuition and fees vary according to course load and reciprocity agreements. Part-time tuition and fees vary according to course load and reciprocity agreements. *Waivers:* senior citizens and employees or children of employees.

Financial Aid Of all full-time matriculated undergraduates who enrolled in 2004, 170 Federal Work-Study jobs (averaging $1900). 164 state and other part-time jobs (averaging $2150).

Applying *Options:* early admission, deferred entrance. *Required for some:* high school transcript, interview. *Application deadlines:* 8/3 (freshmen), 8/3 (transfers). *Notification:* continuous (freshmen).

Freshmen Application Contact Ms. Sheryl Anderson, Director of Admissions, Clark College, 1800 East McLoughlin Boulevard, Vancouver, WA 98663. *Phone:* 360-992-2308. *Toll-free phone:* 360-992-2107. *Fax:* 360-992-2867. *E-mail:* sanderson@clark.edu.

CLOVER PARK TECHNICAL COLLEGE
Lakewood, Washington　　　　　　**www.cptc.edu/**

- **State-supported** 2-year, founded 1942, part of Washington State Community and Technical College System
- **Coed**

Undergraduates 1,848 full-time, 6,640 part-time. Students come from 3 states and territories, 12% African American, 7% Asian American or Pacific Islander, 3% Hispanic American, 1% Native American, 1% international.

Faculty *Student/faculty ratio:* 22:1.

Academics *Degree:* certificates and associate. *Special study options:* academic remediation for entering students, accelerated degree program, cooperative education, distance learning, English as a second language, internships, part-time degree program, services for LD students.

Student Life *Campus security:* 24-hour patrols, late-night transport/escort service.

Standardized Tests *Required:* ACT COMPASS (for placement).

Costs (2005–06) *Tuition:* state resident $2529 full-time, $51 per credit hour part-time. *Required fees:* $579 full-time.

Applying *Options:* common application, electronic application. *Application fee:* $36. *Required for some:* high school transcript, interview.

Director of Admissions Ms. Judy Richardson, Registrar, Clover Park Technical College, 4500 Steilacoom Boulevard Southwest, Lakewood, WA 98499. *Phone:* 253-589-5570.

COLUMBIA BASIN COLLEGE
Pasco, Washington　　　　　　**www.columbiabasin.edu**

Freshmen Application Contact Ms. Donna Korstad, Program Support Supervisor, Enrollment Management, Columbia Basin College, 2600 North 20th Avenue, Pasco, WA 99301. *Phone:* 509-547-0511 Ext. 2250. *Toll-free phone:* 509-547-0511 Ext. 2250.

CROWN COLLEGE
Tacoma, Washington　　　　　　**www.crowncollege.edu/**

- **Proprietary** primarily 2-year, founded 1969, administratively affiliated with Killebrew Dalton, Inc
- **Urban** campus with easy access to Seattle
- **Coed,** 218 undergraduate students

Undergraduates Students come from 39 states and territories, 1 other country, 82% are from out of state.

Faculty *Total:* 23, 30% full-time. *Student/faculty ratio:* 20:1.

Majors Criminal justice/safety; legal administrative assistant/secretary; legal assistant/paralegal; public administration.

Academics *Calendar:* continuous. *Degrees:* associate and bachelor's (bachelor's degree in public administration only). *Special study options:* academic remediation for entering students, cooperative education, distance learning, double majors, honors programs, internships, off-campus study, study abroad.

Library Crown College Library plus 1 other with 9,500 titles, 37 serial subscriptions, 70 audiovisual materials, an OPAC, a Web page.

Computers on Campus 12 computers available on campus for general student use. A campuswide network can be accessed from student residence rooms and from off campus. Internet access, online (class) registration, at least one staffed computer lab available.

Student Life *Housing:* college housing not available. *Campus security:* 24-hour emergency response devices.

Costs (2006–07) *Tuition:* $7500 full-time. *Required fees:* $385 full-time.

Applying *Options:* common application, electronic application. *Application fee:* $135. *Required:* high school transcript, interview. *Required for some:* essay or personal statement. *Notification:* continuous (freshmen).

Freshmen Application Contact Mrs. Jesica McMullin, Crown College, 8739 South Hosmer, Tacoma, WA 98444. *Phone:* 253-531-3123. *Toll-free phone:* 800-755-9525 (in-state); 888-689-3688 (out-of-state). *Fax:* 253-531-3521. *E-mail:* admissions@crowncollege.edu.

DIGIPEN INSTITUTE OF TECHNOLOGY
Redmond, Washington　　　　　　**www.digipen.edu/**

- **Proprietary** primarily 2-year, founded 1988
- **Coed,** 657 undergraduate students, 94% full-time, 6% women, 94% men

Undergraduates 617 full-time, 40 part-time. 2% African American, 4% Asian American or Pacific Islander, 4% Hispanic American, 0.3% Native American, 3% international.

Freshmen *Admission:* 167 enrolled.

Faculty *Total:* 51. *Student/faculty ratio:* 13:1.

Majors Computer engineering related; intermedia/multimedia.

Academics *Calendar:* semesters. *Degrees:* certificates, associate, bachelor's, and master's.

Student Life *Student services:* personal/psychological counseling.

Standardized Tests *Required:* SAT or ACT (for admission).

Costs (2006–07) *One-time required fee:* $150. *Tuition:* $15,200 full-time, $380 per credit part-time. *Required fees:* $160 full-time, $80 per semester part-time.

Applying *Application fee:* $75. *Required:* essay or personal statement, high school transcript, minimum 2.5 GPA, 2 letters of recommendation. *Required for some:* SAT/ACT art portfolio. *Recommended:* SAT/ACT art portfolio.

Freshmen Application Contact Admissions and Outreach Manager, DigiPen Institute of Technology, 5001 150th Avenue, NE, Redmond, WA 98052. *Phone:* 425-895-4438. *Fax:* 425-558-0378. *E-mail:* akugler@digipen.edu.

EDMONDS COMMUNITY COLLEGE
Lynnwood, Washington　　　　　　**www.edcc.edu/**

- **State and locally supported** 2-year, founded 1967, part of Washington State Board for Community and Technical Colleges
- **Suburban** 115-acre campus with easy access to Seattle
- **Endowment** $2.7 million
- **Coed,** 7,581 undergraduate students, 45% full-time, 57% women, 43% men

Undergraduates 3,398 full-time, 4,183 part-time. Students come from 55 other countries, 2% are from out of state, 5% African American, 10% Asian American or Pacific Islander, 4% Hispanic American, 2% Native American, 11% international, 0.5% transferred in.

Freshmen *Admission:* 1,770 applied, 1,770 admitted, 767 enrolled.

Faculty *Total:* 428, 30% full-time, 5% with terminal degrees. *Student/faculty ratio:* 21:1.

Majors Accounting technology and bookkeeping; administrative assistant and secretarial science; applied horticulture; audiovisual communications technologies related; building/home/construction inspection; business administration and management; clinical/medical laboratory assistant; computer and information sciences and support services related; computer and information systems security; computer programming; computer programming (specific applications); computer programming (vendor/product certification); computer systems networking and telecommunications; computer technology/computer systems technology; construction engineering technology; culinary arts; data entry/microcomputer applications; data modeling/warehousing and database administration; data processing and data processing technology; desktop publishing and digital imaging design; early childhood education; e-commerce; electrical, electronic and communications engineering technology; electrocardiograph technology;

Edmonds Community College (continued)

entrepreneurship; fashion merchandising; fire services administration; health aide; health information/medical records technology; health professions related; human resources management; international business/trade/commerce; landscaping and groundskeeping; legal administrative assistant/secretary; legal assistant/paralegal; liberal arts and sciences/liberal studies; marketing/marketing management; medical administrative assistant and medical secretary; medical reception; mental and social health services and allied professions related; nursing assistant/aide and patient care assistant; office management; pharmacy technician; phlebotomy; plant nursery management; substance abuse/addiction counseling; system administration; travel services marketing operations; vocational rehabilitation counseling; web/multimedia management and webmaster; web page, digital/multimedia and information resources design.

Academics *Calendar:* quarters. *Degree:* certificates and associate. *Special study options:* academic remediation for entering students, adult/continuing education programs, advanced placement credit, cooperative education, distance learning, English as a second language, honors programs, internships, off-campus study, part-time degree program, services for LD students, student-designed majors, study abroad, summer session for credit.

Library Edmonds Community College Library with 47,947 titles, 312 serial subscriptions, 7,735 audiovisual materials, an OPAC, a Web page.

Computers on Campus 1129 computers available on campus for general student use. A campuswide network can be accessed from off campus. Internet access, online (class) registration, at least one staffed computer lab available.

Student Life *Housing:* college housing not available. *Activities and Organizations:* drama/theater group, student-run newspaper, choral group, Phi Theta Kappa, AITP, AAWCC, International Club, Pottery/Art Club. *Campus security:* 24-hour emergency response devices and patrols, student patrols, late-night transport/escort service. *Student services:* personal/psychological counseling, women's center.

Athletics *Intercollegiate sports:* baseball M(s), basketball M(s)/W(s), golf M(s)/W(s), soccer M(s)/W(s), softball W(s), volleyball W(s). *Intramural sports:* badminton M/W, baseball M, basketball M/W, bowling M/W, football M/W, golf M/W, soccer M, softball W, table tennis M/W, volleyball M/W.

Costs (2005–06) *Tuition:* state resident $2436 full-time, $72 per credit hour part-time; nonresident $7610 full-time, $251 per credit hour part-time. Full-time tuition and fees vary according to course load. Part-time tuition and fees vary according to course load. *Required fees:* $166 full-time, $4 per credit hour part-time. *Room and board:* room only: $4500.

Financial Aid Of all full-time matriculated undergraduates who enrolled in 2004, 125 Federal Work-Study jobs (averaging $7200). 100 state and other part-time jobs (averaging $7200).

Applying *Options:* common application, electronic application, early admission, deferred entrance. *Application fee:* $17. *Application deadline:* rolling (freshmen), rolling (transfers). *Notification:* continuous (freshmen).

Freshmen Application Contact Ms. Nancy Froemming, Enrollment Services Office Manager, Edmonds Community College, 20000 68th Avenue West, Lynnwood, WA 98036-5999. *Phone:* 425-640-1853. *Fax:* 425-640-1159. *E-mail:* nanci.froemming@edcc.edu.

EVERETT COMMUNITY COLLEGE

Everett, Washington　　　　　　**www.evcc.ctc.edu/**

- **State-supported** 2-year, founded 1941, part of Washington State Board for Community and Technical Colleges
- **Suburban** 25-acre campus with easy access to Seattle
- **Endowment** $1.5 million
- **Coed**

Undergraduates 3,262 full-time, 3,926 part-time. Students come from 17 states and territories, 13 other countries, 3% are from out of state, 2% African American, 5% Asian American or Pacific Islander, 4% Hispanic American, 2% Native American, 0.4% international, 3% transferred in. *Retention:* 59% of 2003 full-time freshmen returned.

Faculty *Student/faculty ratio:* 20:1.

Academics *Calendar:* quarters. *Degree:* certificates, diplomas, and associate. *Special study options:* academic remediation for entering students, adult/continuing education programs, advanced placement credit, cooperative education, distance learning, English as a second language, independent study, internships, part-time degree program, services for LD students, study abroad, summer session for credit.

Student Life *Campus security:* 24-hour emergency response devices and patrols, late-night transport/escort service.

Athletics Member NJCAA.

Standardized Tests *Recommended:* ACT ASSET, ACT COMPASS.

Costs (2005–06) *Tuition:* state resident $2313 full-time, $69 per credit part-time; nonresident $7521 full-time, $241 per credit part-time. Full-time tuition and fees vary according to course load. Part-time tuition and fees vary according to course load.

Financial Aid Of all full-time matriculated undergraduates who enrolled in 2004, 152 Federal Work-Study jobs (averaging $3000). 48 state and other part-time jobs (averaging $3000).

Applying *Options:* common application, electronic application, early admission, deferred entrance. *Recommended:* high school transcript.

Freshmen Application Contact Ms. Linda Baca, Admissions Manager, Everett Community College, 2000 Tower Street, Everett, WA 98201-1352. *Phone:* 425-388-9219.

GRAYS HARBOR COLLEGE

Aberdeen, Washington　　　　　　**www.ghc.ctc.edu/**

Freshmen Application Contact Ms. Brenda Dell, Admissions Officer, Grays Harbor College, 1620 Edward P. Smith Drive, Aberdeen, WA 98520-7599. *Phone:* 360-532-9020 Ext. 4026. *Toll-free phone:* 800-562-4830.

GREEN RIVER COMMUNITY COLLEGE

Auburn, Washington　　　　　　**www.greenriver.edu/**

- **State-supported** 2-year, founded 1965, part of Washington State Board for Community and Technical Colleges
- **Rural** 168-acre campus with easy access to Seattle
- **Coed**

Undergraduates 3,883 full-time, 2,738 part-time. Students come from 30 other countries, 1% are from out of state, 3% African American, 7% Asian American or Pacific Islander, 5% Hispanic American, 1% Native American, 4% international.

Faculty *Student/faculty ratio:* 22:1.

Academics *Calendar:* quarters. *Degree:* certificates, diplomas, and associate. *Special study options:* academic remediation for entering students, adult/continuing education programs, advanced placement credit, cooperative education, distance learning, English as a second language, internships, off-campus study, part-time degree program, services for LD students, summer session for credit.

Student Life *Campus security:* 24-hour emergency response devices and patrols, student patrols, late-night transport/escort service.

Athletics Member NJCAA.

Standardized Tests *Required:* ACT ASSET or ACT COMPASS (for placement).

Financial Aid Of all full-time matriculated undergraduates who enrolled in 2004, 113 Federal Work-Study jobs (averaging $2356). 174 state and other part-time jobs.

Applying *Options:* electronic application, early admission, deferred entrance. *Required for some:* high school transcript.

Freshmen Application Contact Ms. Peggy Morgan, Program Support Supervisor, Green River Community College, 12401 Southeast 320th Street, Auburn, WA 98092-3699. *Phone:* 253-833-9111 Ext. 2513.

HIGHLINE COMMUNITY COLLEGE

Des Moines, Washington　　　　　　**www.highline.edu/**

- **State-supported** 2-year, founded 1961, part of Washington State Board for Community and Technical Colleges
- **Suburban** 81-acre campus with easy access to Seattle
- **Coed,** 6,372 undergraduate students, 51% full-time, 64% women, 36% men

Highline Community College is one of the premier two-year schools in Washington State. The main 80-acre campus overlooks Puget Sound and the Olympic Mountains. Conveniently located between Seattle and Tacoma, Highline serves one of the most diverse student bodies in the region. Exceptional student services staff and faculty members, high-quality transfer and professional/technical programs, and affordable cost combine to make Highline a great choice for a promising future.

Undergraduates 3,229 full-time, 3,143 part-time. 11% African American, 17% Asian American or Pacific Islander, 5% Hispanic American, 1% Native

American, 0.2% international. *Retention:* 60% of 2003 full-time freshmen returned. Freshmen *Admission:* 3,933 applied, 3,933 admitted, 667 enrolled.

Faculty *Total:* 356, 39% full-time.

Majors Accounting; administrative assistant and secretarial science; art; behavioral sciences; biological and physical sciences; business administration and management; clinical/medical laboratory science and allied professions related; computer engineering technology; computer programming; computer systems networking and telecommunications; computer typography and composition equipment operation; criminal justice/law enforcement administration; criminal justice/police science; cultural studies; data entry/microcomputer applications related; dental hygiene; drafting and design technology; education; engineering; engineering technology; English; graphic and printing equipment operation/production; hotel/motel administration; humanities; human services; industrial technology; interior design; international business/trade/commerce; journalism; kindergarten/preschool education; legal administrative assistant/secretary; legal assistant/paralegal; library science; marine technology; mathematics; medical/clinical assistant; music; natural sciences; nursing (registered nurse training); plastics engineering technology; pre-engineering; psychology; respiratory care therapy; Romance languages; social sciences; tourism and travel services management; transportation technology; web page, digital/multimedia and information resources design.

Academics *Calendar:* quarters. *Degree:* certificates, diplomas, and associate. *Special study options:* academic remediation for entering students, advanced placement credit, cooperative education, English as a second language, freshman honors college, honors programs, internships, part-time degree program, services for LD students, student-designed majors, study abroad, summer session for credit. *ROTC:* Army (c), Air Force (c).

Library Highline Community College Library with 57,678 titles, 585 serial subscriptions, an OPAC.

Computers on Campus 300 computers available on campus for general student use. A campuswide network can be accessed. At least one staffed computer lab available.

Student Life *Housing:* college housing not available. *Activities and Organizations:* drama/theater group, student-run newspaper, choral group, Campus Crusade for Christ, Phi Theta Kappa, International Club, Respiratory Care. *Campus security:* 24-hour patrols. *Student services:* health clinic, personal/psychological counseling, women's center.

Athletics Member NJCAA. *Intercollegiate sports:* basketball M(s)/W(s), cross-country running M(s)/W(s), soccer M(s)/W(s), softball W(s), track and field M(s)/W(s), volleyball W(s), wrestling M(s).

Standardized Tests *Recommended:* ACT COMPASS.

Costs (2005–06) *Tuition:* state resident $2445 full-time, $72 per credit part-time; nonresident $2835 full-time, $85 per credit part-time. *Required fees:* $75 full-time, $3 per credit part-time.

Applying *Application fee:* $21. *Application deadline:* rolling (freshmen), rolling (transfers).

Director of Admissions Ms. Debbie Faison, Assistant Registrar, Highline Community College, PO Box 98000, 2400 South 240th Street, Des Moines, WA 98198-9800. *Phone:* 206-878-3710 Ext. 3363.

ITT TECHNICAL INSTITUTE
Bothell, Washington   www.itt-tech.edu/

- **Proprietary** primarily 2-year, founded 1993, part of ITT Educational Services, Inc
- **Coed**

Majors Animation, interactive technology, video graphics and special effects; business administration and management; CAD/CADD drafting/design technology; computer and information systems security; computer programming; computer systems networking and telecommunications; criminal justice/law enforcement administration; e-commerce; electrical, electronic and communications engineering technology; system, networking, and LAN/WAN management; web/multimedia management and webmaster; web page, digital/multimedia and information resources design.

Academics *Calendar:* quarters. *Degrees:* associate and bachelor's.

Library a Web page.

Computers on Campus Internet access, at least one staffed computer lab available.

Student Life *Housing:* college housing not available.

Standardized Tests *Required:* Wonderlic aptitude test (for admission).

Costs (2005–06) *Tuition:* Please see school catalog for specific information.

Applying *Options:* deferred entrance. *Application fee:* $100. *Required:* high school transcript, interview. *Recommended:* letters of recommendation. *Application deadline:* rolling (freshmen), rolling (transfers). *Notification:* continuous (freshmen).

Freshmen Application Contact Mr. Jon L. Scherrer, Director of Recruitment, ITT Technical Institute, 1615 75th Street SW, Everett, WA 98203. *Phone:* 425-583-0200. *Toll-free phone:* 800-272-3791.

ITT TECHNICAL INSTITUTE
Seattle, Washington   www.itt-tech.edu/

- **Proprietary** primarily 2-year, founded 1932, part of ITT Educational Services, Inc
- **Urban** campus
- **Coed**

Majors Animation, interactive technology, video graphics and special effects; business administration and management; CAD/CADD drafting/design technology; computer and information systems security; computer programming; criminal justice/law enforcement administration; electrical, electronic and communications engineering technology; system, networking, and LAN/WAN management; web/multimedia management and webmaster; web page, digital/multimedia and information resources design.

Academics *Calendar:* quarters. *Degrees:* associate and bachelor's.

Library a Web page.

Computers on Campus Internet access, at least one staffed computer lab available.

Student Life *Housing:* college housing not available.

Standardized Tests *Required:* Wonderlic aptitude test (for admission).

Costs (2005–06) *Tuition:* Please see school catalog for specific information.

Applying *Options:* deferred entrance. *Application fee:* $100. *Required:* high school transcript, interview. *Recommended:* letters of recommendation. *Application deadline:* rolling (freshmen), rolling (transfers). *Notification:* continuous (freshmen).

Freshmen Application Contact Mr. Jose Luis Saez Jr., Director of Recruitment, ITT Technical Institute, 12720 Gateway Drive, Seattle, WA 98168. *Phone:* 206-244-3300. *Toll-free phone:* 800-422-2029.

ITT TECHNICAL INSTITUTE
Spokane, Washington   www.itt-tech.edu/

- **Proprietary** primarily 2-year, founded 1985, part of ITT Educational Services, Inc
- **Suburban** 3-acre campus
- **Coed**

Majors Animation, interactive technology, video graphics and special effects; CAD/CADD drafting/design technology; computer and information systems security; computer programming; criminal justice/law enforcement administration; e-commerce; electrical, electronic and communications engineering technology; system, networking, and LAN/WAN management; web/multimedia management and webmaster; web page, digital/multimedia and information resources design.

Academics *Calendar:* quarters. *Degrees:* associate and bachelor's.

Library a Web page.

Computers on Campus Internet access, at least one staffed computer lab available.

Student Life *Housing:* college housing not available.

Standardized Tests *Required:* Wonderlic aptitude test (for admission).

Costs (2005–06) *Tuition:* Please see school catalog for specific information.

Financial Aid Of all full-time matriculated undergraduates who enrolled in 2004, 9 Federal Work-Study jobs (averaging $4000).

Applying *Options:* deferred entrance. *Application fee:* $100. *Required:* high school transcript, interview. *Recommended:* letters of recommendation. *Application deadline:* rolling (freshmen), rolling (transfers). *Notification:* continuous (freshmen).

Freshmen Application Contact Mr. Gregory L. Alexander, Director of Recruitment, ITT Technical Institute, 13518 East Indiana Avenue, Spokane Valley, WA 99216. *Phone:* 509-926-2900. *Toll-free phone:* 800-777-8324.

LAKE WASHINGTON TECHNICAL COLLEGE
Kirkland, Washington   www.lwtc.ctc.edu/

Director of Admissions Mr. Jim West, Director of Admissions and Registration, Lake Washington Technical College, 11605 132nd Avenue NE, Kirkland, WA 98034-8506. *Phone:* 425-739-8233.

LOWER COLUMBIA COLLEGE
Longview, Washington
www.lcc.ctc.edu/

- **State-supported** 2-year, founded 1934, part of Washington State Board for Community and Technical Colleges
- **Small-town** 30-acre campus with easy access to Portland
- **Endowment** $2.3 million
- **Coed,** 3,073 undergraduate students, 57% full-time, 64% women, 36% men

Undergraduates 1,755 full-time, 1,318 part-time. Students come from 5 states and territories, 9% are from out of state, 1% African American, 2% Asian American or Pacific Islander, 3% Hispanic American, 1% Native American, 0.1% international, 12% transferred in. *Retention:* 55% of 2003 full-time freshmen returned.
Freshmen *Admission:* 316 applied, 316 admitted, 277 enrolled.
Faculty *Total:* 155, 49% full-time. *Student/faculty ratio:* 21:1.
Majors Accounting; accounting technology and bookkeeping; administrative assistant and secretarial science; anthropology; art; automobile/automotive mechanics technology; biology/biological sciences; business administration and management; business/commerce; CAD/CADD drafting/design technology; computer and information sciences; computer engineering technology; computer programming; computer science; computer systems analysis; computer systems networking and telecommunications; computer technology/computer systems technology; corrections; criminal justice/law enforcement administration; criminal justice/police science; criminal justice/safety; data entry/microcomputer applications; data processing and data processing technology; diesel mechanics technology; dramatic/theater arts; early childhood education; economics; electrical, electronic and communications engineering technology; electrician; engineering; engineering technology; English; environmental studies; fire science; fire services administration; foreign languages and literatures; geography; geology/earth science; heavy equipment maintenance technology; history; industrial mechanics and maintenance technology; industrial technology; information science/studies; information technology; instrumentation technology; kindergarten/preschool education; legal administrative assistant/secretary; liberal arts and sciences/liberal studies; lineworker; machine tool technology; management information systems; mathematics; mechanical engineering/mechanical technology; medical administrative assistant and medical secretary; medical/clinical assistant; medical reception; medical transcription; music; nursing assistant/aide and patient care assistant; nursing (licensed practical/vocational nurse training); nursing (registered nurse training); office management; philosophy; photography; physical education teaching and coaching; physics; political science and government; pre-engineering; pre-law studies; psychology; receptionist; social sciences; sociology; speech and rhetoric; substance abuse/addiction counseling; teacher assistant/aide; welding technology; wood science and wood products/pulp and paper technology; word processing.
Academics *Calendar:* quarters. *Degree:* certificates, diplomas, and associate. *Special study options:* academic remediation for entering students, adult/continuing education programs, cooperative education, English as a second language, honors programs, part-time degree program, services for LD students, study abroad, summer session for credit.
Library Allan Thompson Library plus 1 other with 41,991 titles, 217 serial subscriptions, 3,376 audiovisual materials, an OPAC.
Computers on Campus 250 computers available on campus for general student use. A campuswide network can be accessed. At least one staffed computer lab available.
Student Life *Housing:* college housing not available. *Activities and Organizations:* drama/theater group, student-run newspaper, choral group, Campus Entertainment, Phi Theta Kappa, Services and Relations Club, Multicultural Students Club, Theater Club. *Campus security:* 24-hour emergency response devices and patrols. *Student services:* health clinic, personal/psychological counseling.
Athletics *Intercollegiate sports:* baseball M(s), basketball M(s)/W(s), soccer M(s)/W(s), softball W(s), volleyball W(s).
Costs (2005–06) *Tuition:* state resident $2465 full-time, $78 per credit part-time; nonresident $3161 full-time, $83 per credit part-time. *Required fees:* $6 per credit part-time.
Financial Aid Of all full-time matriculated undergraduates who enrolled in 2004, 440 Federal Work-Study jobs (averaging $708). 447 state and other part-time jobs (averaging $2415).
Applying *Options:* early admission, deferred entrance. *Application fee:* $13. *Recommended:* high school transcript. *Application deadline:* rolling (freshmen), rolling (transfers). *Notification:* continuous (freshmen).
Freshmen Application Contact Ms. Mary Harding, Vice President for Student Success, Lower Columbia College, 1600 Maple Street, Longview, WA 98632. *Phone:* 360-442-2300. *Fax:* 360-442-2379. *E-mail:* registration@lcc.ctc.edu.

NORTH SEATTLE COMMUNITY COLLEGE
Seattle, Washington
www.northseattle.edu/

- **State-supported** 2-year, founded 1970, part of Seattle Community College District System
- **Urban** 65-acre campus
- **Coed,** 5,959 undergraduate students, 48% full-time, 63% women, 37% men

Undergraduates 2,833 full-time, 3,126 part-time. Students come from 50 states and territories, 1% are from out of state, 8% African American, 16% Asian American or Pacific Islander, 6% Hispanic American, 2% Native American, 0.1% international, 39% transferred in.
Freshmen *Admission:* 5,726 applied, 5,726 admitted, 1,074 enrolled.
Faculty *Total:* 298, 34% full-time, 3% with terminal degrees. *Student/faculty ratio:* 23:1.
Majors Accounting technology and bookkeeping; administrative assistant and secretarial science; allied health and medical assisting services related; architectural drafting; art; biomedical technology; business/corporate communications; civil drafting and CAD/CADD; communications systems installation and repair technology; computer and information systems security; computer systems networking and telecommunications; early childhood education; electrical, electronic and communications engineering technology; electrical/electronics drafting and CAD/CADD; heating, air conditioning, ventilation and refrigeration maintenance technology; industrial technology; liberal arts and sciences/liberal studies; mechanical drafting and CAD/CADD; medical/clinical assistant; music; nursing (licensed practical/vocational nurse training); nursing (registered nurse training); pharmacy technician; real estate; telecommunications technology; watchmaking and jewelrymaking; web page, digital/multimedia and information resources design.
Academics *Calendar:* quarters. *Degree:* certificates, diplomas, and associate. *Special study options:* academic remediation for entering students, adult/continuing education programs, advanced placement credit, cooperative education, distance learning, English as a second language, external degree program, independent study, internships, part-time degree program, services for LD students, summer session for credit. *ROTC:* Army (c).
Library North Seattle Community College Library with 52,496 titles, 594 serial subscriptions, 2,957 audiovisual materials, an OPAC, a Web page.
Computers on Campus 1600 computers available on campus for general student use. A campuswide network can be accessed from off campus. Internet access, online (class) registration, at least one staffed computer lab available.
Student Life *Housing:* college housing not available. *Activities and Organizations:* drama/theater group, student-run newspaper, television station, choral group, Muslim Students Association, Indonesian Community Club, Literary Guild, Phi Theta Kappa, Vietnamese Student Association. *Campus security:* 24-hour emergency response devices and patrols, student patrols, late-night transport/escort service, patrols by security. *Student services:* personal/psychological counseling, women's center.
Athletics *Intercollegiate sports:* basketball M/W. *Intramural sports:* basketball M/W.
Costs (2005–06) *Tuition:* state resident $3213 full-time, $71 per credit part-time; nonresident $10,940 full-time, $243 per credit part-time. Full-time tuition and fees vary according to course load. Part-time tuition and fees vary according to course load. *Required fees:* $346 full-time, $115 per term part-time. *Waivers:* senior citizens and employees or children of employees.
Applying *Options:* common application, electronic application, early admission, deferred entrance. *Required:* high school transcript. *Required for some:* essay or personal statement. *Application deadline:* rolling (freshmen), rolling (transfers). *Notification:* continuous until 9/24 (freshmen).
Freshmen Application Contact Ms. Betsy Abts, Registrar, North Seattle Community College, 9600 College Way North, Seattle, WA 98103-3599. *Phone:* 206-527-3663. *Fax:* 206-527-3671. *E-mail:* babts@sccd.ctc.edu.

NORTHWEST AVIATION COLLEGE
Auburn, Washington
www.afsnac.com/

Director of Admissions Mr. Shawn Pratt, Assistant Director of Education, Northwest Aviation College, 506 23rd, NE, Auburn, WA 98002. *Phone:* 253-854-4960. *Toll-free phone:* 800-246-4960. *Fax:* 253-931-0768. *E-mail:* spratt@afsnac.com.

NORTHWEST INDIAN COLLEGE

Bellingham, Washington   **www.nwic.edu/**

- **Federally supported** 2-year, founded 1978
- **Rural** 5-acre campus
- **Endowment** $3.0 million
- **Coed,** 1,189 undergraduate students

Undergraduates Students come from 6 states and territories, 2 other countries, 1% African American, 0.9% Asian American or Pacific Islander, 1% Hispanic American, 78% Native American.
Freshmen *Average high school GPA:* 2.0.
Faculty *Total:* 63, 37% full-time.
Majors American Indian/Native American studies; biology/biological sciences; computer/technical support; construction engineering technology; education; general studies; human services; kindergarten/preschool education; substance abuse/addiction counseling.
Academics *Calendar:* quarters. *Degrees:* certificates and associate (also offers bachelor's degree in elementary education in conjunction with Washington State University). *Special study options:* academic remediation for entering students, adult/continuing education programs, cooperative education, external degree program, internships, part-time degree program, student-designed majors, study abroad, summer session for credit.
Computers on Campus 22 computers available on campus for general student use. Internet access available.
Student Life *Housing:* college housing not available. *Activities and Organizations:* drama/theater group, student-run newspaper, choral group. *Student services:* personal/psychological counseling.
Athletics *Intercollegiate sports:* basketball M/W. *Intramural sports:* baseball M/W, basketball M/W, volleyball M/W.
Costs (2005–06) *Tuition:* state resident $2646 full-time, $74 per credit part-time; nonresident $7182 full-time, $200 per credit part-time.
Applying *Application fee:* $25. *Required:* high school transcript. *Notification:* continuous (freshmen).
Freshmen Application Contact Admissions, Northwest Indian College, 2522 Kwina Road, Bellingham, WA 98226. *Phone:* 360-676-2772 Ext. 4269. *Toll-free phone:* 866-676-2772 Ext. 4264. *Fax:* 360-392-4333. *E-mail:* lignacio@nwic.edu.

NORTHWEST SCHOOL OF WOODEN BOATBUILDING

Port Townsend, Washington   **www.nwboatschool.org/**

Director of Admissions Ms. Gretchen Siegfried, Student Services Coordinator, Northwest School of Wooden Boatbuilding, 251 Otto Street, Port Townsend, WA 98368. *Phone:* 360-385-4948. *Fax:* 360-385-5089. *E-mail:* info@nwboatschool.org.

OLYMPIC COLLEGE

Bremerton, Washington   **www.oc.ctc.edu/~oc/**

- **State-supported** 2-year, founded 1946, part of Washington State Board for Community and Technical Colleges
- **Suburban** 32-acre campus with easy access to Seattle
- **Endowment** $3.3 million
- **Coed**

Undergraduates 3,253 full-time, 3,137 part-time. Students come from 50 states and territories, 4 other countries, 3% African American, 9% Asian American or Pacific Islander, 5% Hispanic American, 2% Native American, 0.1% international, 0.5% transferred in.
Faculty *Student/faculty ratio:* 25:1.
Academics *Calendar:* quarters. *Degree:* certificates, diplomas, and associate. *Special study options:* academic remediation for entering students, adult/continuing education programs, advanced placement credit, cooperative education, distance learning, English as a second language, honors programs, independent study, off-campus study, part-time degree program, services for LD students, summer session for credit.
Student Life *Campus security:* 24-hour emergency response devices and patrols, student patrols, late-night transport/escort service.
Standardized Tests *Required for some:* ACT ASSET.

Financial Aid Of all full-time matriculated undergraduates who enrolled in 2004, 105 Federal Work-Study jobs (averaging $2380). 31 state and other part-time jobs (averaging $2880).
Applying *Options:* early admission. *Required for some:* high school transcript.
Director of Admissions Ms. Gerry Stamm, Director of Admissions and Outreach, Olympic College, 1600 Chester Avenue, Bremerton, WA 98337-1699. *Phone:* 360-475-7126. *Toll-free phone:* 800-259-6718. *E-mail:* gstamm@ctc.edu.

PENINSULA COLLEGE

Port Angeles, Washington   **www.pc.ctc.edu/**

- **State-supported** 2-year, founded 1961
- **Small-town** 75-acre campus
- **Endowment** $1.1 million
- **Coed,** 4,256 undergraduate students, 33% full-time, 59% women, 41% men

Undergraduates 1,412 full-time, 2,844 part-time. Students come from 5 other countries, 1% are from out of state, 3% African American, 2% Asian American or Pacific Islander, 2% Hispanic American, 3% Native American, 0.5% international.
Freshmen *Admission:* 173 applied, 173 admitted, 173 enrolled.
Faculty *Total:* 191, 34% full-time, 10% with terminal degrees. *Student/faculty ratio:* 19:1.
Majors Accounting; automobile/automotive mechanics technology; biological and physical sciences; business administration and management; child care and support services management; child development; civil engineering technology; commercial fishing; computer programming (vendor/product certification); criminal justice/law enforcement administration; data entry/microcomputer applications related; diesel mechanics technology; electrical, electronic and communications engineering technology; engineering technology; fishing and fisheries sciences and management; nursing (registered nurse training); office management; substance abuse/addiction counseling; web page, digital/multimedia and information resources design.
Academics *Calendar:* quarters. *Degree:* certificates and associate. *Special study options:* academic remediation for entering students, adult/continuing education programs, advanced placement credit, distance learning, English as a second language, honors programs, internships, part-time degree program, services for LD students, summer session for credit.
Library 33,736 titles, 383 serial subscriptions.
Computers on Campus 38 computers available on campus for general student use. A campuswide network can be accessed from student residence rooms and from off campus. At least one staffed computer lab available.
Student Life *Housing Options:* coed. Campus housing is university owned. *Activities and Organizations:* drama/theater group, student-run newspaper, choral group, Phi Theta Kappa, SAGE (Students Advocating Global Environmentalism). *Campus security:* 8-hour patrols by trained security personnel. *Student services:* women's center.
Athletics *Intercollegiate sports:* basketball M/W, soccer M, softball W. *Intramural sports:* badminton M/W, basketball M/W, bowling M/W, football M, golf M, skiing (cross-country) M/W, soccer M/W, softball M/W, table tennis M/W, tennis M/W, volleyball M/W.
Costs (2006–07) *Tuition:* state resident $3325 full-time, $75 per credit part-time; nonresident $3715 full-time, $88 per credit part-time. *Required fees:* $135 full-time, $3 per credit part-time, $13 per term part-time.
Financial Aid Of all full-time matriculated undergraduates who enrolled in 2004, 30 Federal Work-Study jobs (averaging $3600). 25 state and other part-time jobs (averaging $3600).
Applying *Options:* common application, electronic application, deferred entrance. *Required for some:* high school transcript. *Application deadline:* rolling (freshmen), rolling (transfers). *Notification:* continuous (freshmen).
Freshmen Application Contact Vicki Sievert, Distance Learning Coordinator, Peninsula College, 1502 East Lauridsen Boulevard, Port Angeles, WA 98362-2779. *Phone:* 360-417-6272. *Fax:* 360-457-8100. *E-mail:* admissions@pcadmin.ctc.edu.

PIERCE COLLEGE

Puyallup, Washington   **www.pierce.ctc.edu/**

Director of Admissions Ms. Cindy Burbank, Director of Admissions, Pierce College, 1601 39th Avenue SE, Puyallup, WA 98374-2222. *Phone:* 253-964-6686.

PIMA MEDICAL INSTITUTE

Seattle, Washington   www.pmi.edu

- **Proprietary** 2-year, founded 1989, part of Vocational Training Institutes, Inc
- **Urban** campus
- **Coed**

Undergraduates 289 full-time.
Faculty *Student/faculty ratio:* 10:1.
Academics *Calendar:* modular. *Degree:* certificates and associate.
Standardized Tests *Required:* Wonderlic aptitude test (for admission).
Costs (2005–06) *Tuition:* Costs vary by program.
Applying *Required:* interview. *Required for some:* high school transcript.
Freshmen Application Contact Admissions Office, Pima Medical Institute, 1627 Eastlake Avenue East, Seattle, WA 98102. *Phone:* 206-322-6100. *Toll-free phone:* 888-898-9048.

RENTON TECHNICAL COLLEGE

Renton, Washington   www.rtc.edu/

Director of Admissions Mr. Jon Pozega, Vice President for Student Services, Renton Technical College, 3000 Fourth Street, NE, Renton, WA 98056. *Phone:* 425-235-2463.

SEATTLE CENTRAL COMMUNITY COLLEGE

Seattle, Washington   www.seattlecentral.edu/

- **State-supported** 2-year, founded 1966, part of Seattle Community College District System
- **Urban** 15-acre campus
- **Coed,** 9,418 undergraduate students

Undergraduates 10% African American, 14% Asian American or Pacific Islander, 5% Hispanic American, 0.9% Native American, 6% international.
Faculty *Total:* 438, 36% full-time.
Majors Accounting; administrative assistant and secretarial science; biological and physical sciences; biology/biotechnology laboratory technician; carpentry; cinematography and film/video production; commercial and advertising art; computer typography and composition equipment operation; cosmetology; culinary arts; drafting and design technology; fashion/apparel design; graphic and printing equipment operation/production; hospitality administration; hotel/motel administration; human services; kindergarten/preschool education; liberal arts and sciences/liberal studies; marine technology; nursing (registered nurse training); ophthalmic laboratory technology; photography; respiratory care therapy; sign language interpretation and translation; substance abuse/addiction counseling.
Academics *Calendar:* quarters. *Degree:* certificates and associate. *Special study options:* academic remediation for entering students, adult/continuing education programs, cooperative education, English as a second language, external degree program, internships, part-time degree program, services for LD students, summer session for credit. *ROTC:* Army (c), Navy (c), Air Force (c).
Library Main Library with 56,338 titles, 425 serial subscriptions.
Computers on Campus 366 computers available on campus for general student use. At least one staffed computer lab available.
Student Life *Housing:* college housing not available. *Activities and Organizations:* drama/theater group, student-run newspaper, choral group, Triangle Club, African Brothers of Unity, MECHA, Asian/Pacific Islander Student Union, Sea-King Club for the Deaf. *Campus security:* 24-hour emergency response devices. *Student services:* personal/psychological counseling, women's center.
Athletics *Intramural sports:* basketball M/W, softball M/W, tennis M/W, volleyball M/W, weight lifting M/W, wrestling M/W.
Applying *Application deadline:* rolling (freshmen), rolling (transfers).
Freshmen Application Contact Admissions Office, Seattle Central Community College, 1701 Broadway, Seattle, WA 98122-2400. *Phone:* 206-587-5450.

SHORELINE COMMUNITY COLLEGE

Shoreline, Washington   www.shore.ctc.edu/

- **State-supported** 2-year, founded 1964, part of Washington State Board for Community and Technical Colleges
- **Suburban** 80-acre campus
- **Coed**

Faculty *Student/faculty ratio:* 21:1.
Academics *Calendar:* quarters. *Degree:* certificates, diplomas, and associate. *Special study options:* academic remediation for entering students, adult/continuing education programs, advanced placement credit, cooperative education, English as a second language, internships, part-time degree program, services for LD students, study abroad, summer session for credit.
Student Life *Campus security:* 24-hour emergency response devices and patrols.
Standardized Tests *Required for some:* SAT or ACT (for placement), ACT ASSET or ACT COMPASS.
Applying *Options:* early admission. *Required:* high school transcript.
Director of Admissions Ms. Robin Young, Registrar, Shoreline Community College, 16101 Greenwood Avenue North, Seattle, WA 98133. *Phone:* 206-546-4581.

SKAGIT VALLEY COLLEGE

Mount Vernon, Washington   www.skagit.edu/

Freshmen Application Contact Ms. Karen Ackelson, Admissions and Recruitment Coordinator, Skagit Valley College, 2405 College Way, Mount Vernon, WA 98273-5899. *Phone:* 360-416-7620.

SOUTH PUGET SOUND COMMUNITY COLLEGE

Olympia, Washington   www.spscc.ctc.edu/

Director of Admissions Mr. Jerry Haynes, Dean of Enrollment Services, South Puget Sound Community College, 2011 Mottman Road, SW, Olympia, WA 98512. *Phone:* 360-754-7711 Ext. 5240.

SOUTH SEATTLE COMMUNITY COLLEGE

Seattle, Washington   www.sccd.ctc.edu/

Director of Admissions Ms. Kim Manderbach, Dean of Student Services/Registration, South Seattle Community College, 6000 16th Avenue, SW, Seattle, WA 98106-1499. *Phone:* 206-764-5378. *Fax:* 206-764-7947. *E-mail:* kimmanderb@sccd.ctc.edu.

SPOKANE COMMUNITY COLLEGE

Spokane, Washington   www.scc.spokane.edu/

- **State-supported** 2-year, founded 1963, part of Washington State Board for Community and Technical Colleges
- **Urban** 108-acre campus
- **Endowment** $33,508
- **Coed,** 6,152 undergraduate students, 85% full-time, 58% women, 42% men

Undergraduates 5,223 full-time, 929 part-time. Students come from 5 states and territories, 20 other countries, 17% are from out of state, 2% African American, 3% Asian American or Pacific Islander, 2% Hispanic American, 3% Native American, 0.1% international, 4% transferred in. *Retention:* 35% of 2003 full-time freshmen returned.
Freshmen *Admission:* 2,011 enrolled.
Faculty *Total:* 360, 53% full-time. *Student/faculty ratio:* 20:1.
Majors Accounting technology and bookkeeping; administrative assistant and secretarial science; agricultural business and management; agronomy and crop science; applied horticulture; architectural engineering technology; artificial intelligence and robotics; automobile/automotive mechanics technology; avion-

ics maintenance technology; biomedical technology; business administration and management; carpentry; civil engineering technology; computer programming; computer typography and composition equipment operation; construction engineering technology; corrections; cosmetology; criminal justice/police science; culinary arts; data processing and data processing technology; dental hygiene; dietetics; drafting and design technology; electrical, electronic and communications engineering technology; fire science; food services technology; forestry; health information/medical records administration; heating, air conditioning, ventilation and refrigeration maintenance technology; heavy equipment maintenance technology; hotel/motel administration; hydrology and water resources science; industrial technology; landscaping and groundskeeping; legal administrative assistant/secretary; legal assistant/paralegal; liberal arts and sciences/liberal studies; machine tool technology; marketing/marketing management; mechanical design technology; mechanical engineering/mechanical technology; medical administrative assistant and medical secretary; natural resources management and policy; nursing (licensed practical/vocational nurse training); nursing (registered nurse training); ophthalmic laboratory technology; ornamental horticulture; parks, recreation and leisure facilities management; respiratory care therapy; surgical technology; welding technology; wildlife and wildlands science and management.

Academics *Calendar:* quarters. *Degree:* certificates, diplomas, and associate. *Special study options:* academic remediation for entering students, adult/continuing education programs, advanced placement credit, cooperative education, distance learning, English as a second language, independent study, internships, part-time degree program, services for LD students, student-designed majors, summer session for credit. *ROTC:* Army (c).

Library Learning Resources Center plus 1 other with 38,967 titles, 466 serial subscriptions, an OPAC.

Computers on Campus 700 computers available on campus for general student use. A campuswide network can be accessed. Internet access, online (class) registration, at least one staffed computer lab available.

Student Life *Housing:* college housing not available. *Activities and Organizations:* drama/theater group, student-run newspaper, VICA, Delta Epsilon Chi, Intercultural Student Organization, Rho Beta Psi, Student Awareness League. *Campus security:* 24-hour emergency response devices and patrols, student patrols, late-night transport/escort service.

Athletics Member NJCAA. *Intercollegiate sports:* baseball M(s), basketball M(s)/W(s), cross-country running M(s)/W(s), soccer M(s)/W(s), softball W(s), tennis M(s)/W(s), track and field M(s)/W(s), volleyball W(s). *Intramural sports:* badminton M/W, basketball M/W, bowling M/W, softball M/W, table tennis M/W, tennis M/W, volleyball M/W, water polo M/W.

Costs (2005–06) *Tuition:* $72 per credit part-time.

Financial Aid Of all full-time matriculated undergraduates who enrolled in 2004, 291 Federal Work-Study jobs (averaging $3600). 250 state and other part-time jobs (averaging $3600).

Applying *Options:* early admission, deferred entrance. *Application fee:* $15. *Recommended:* high school transcript. *Application deadline:* rolling (freshmen), rolling (transfers). *Notification:* continuous (freshmen).

Freshmen Application Contact Mary Lee, Researcher District Institutional Research, Spokane Community College, North 1810 Greene Street, Spokane, WA 99217-5399. *Phone:* 509-434-5242. *Toll-free phone:* 800-248-5644. *Fax:* 509-434-5249. *E-mail:* mlee@ccs.spokane.edu.

SPOKANE FALLS COMMUNITY COLLEGE

Spokane, Washington   www.sfcc.spokane.cc.wa.us/

- **State-supported** 2-year, founded 1967, part of State Board for Washington Community and Technical Colleges
- **Urban** 125-acre campus
- **Endowment** $33,407
- **Coed,** 5,649 undergraduate students, 70% full-time, 57% women, 43% men

Undergraduates 3,934 full-time, 1,715 part-time. Students come from 6 states and territories, 14 other countries, 5% are from out of state, 2% African American, 4% Asian American or Pacific Islander, 0.4% Hispanic American, 2% Native American, 0.1% international. *Retention:* 29% of 2003 full-time freshmen returned.

Faculty *Total:* 592, 29% full-time. *Student/faculty ratio:* 22:1.

Majors Accounting technology and bookkeeping; administrative assistant and secretarial science; art; business administration and management; business and personal/financial services marketing; child care and support services management; commercial and advertising art; commercial photography; consumer merchandising/retailing management; fashion merchandising; gerontology; heavy equipment maintenance technology; information science/studies; interior design; international business/trade/commerce; leatherworking/upholstery; liberal arts and sciences/liberal studies; library assistant; marketing/marketing management; mass communication/media; music; office occupations and clerical services; orthotics/prosthetics; physical therapist assistant; real estate; sign language

interpretation and translation; social work; sport and fitness administration/management; substance abuse/addiction counseling; vocational rehabilitation counseling; welding technology.

Academics *Calendar:* quarters. *Degree:* certificates, diplomas, and associate. *Special study options:* academic remediation for entering students, adult/continuing education programs, advanced placement credit, cooperative education, English as a second language, internships, part-time degree program, services for LD students, student-designed majors, summer session for credit. *ROTC:* Army (c).

Library Learning Resources Center plus 1 other with 58,000 titles, 705 serial subscriptions, an OPAC.

Computers on Campus 400 computers available on campus for general student use. A campuswide network can be accessed. Internet access, online (class) registration, at least one staffed computer lab available.

Student Life *Housing:* college housing not available. *Activities and Organizations:* drama/theater group, student-run newspaper, radio station, choral group, DECA, Associated Men Students, Associated Women Students, chorale, Forensics Club. *Campus security:* late-night transport/escort service, 24-hour emergency dispatch. *Student services:* personal/psychological counseling, women's center.

Athletics Member NJCAA. *Intercollegiate sports:* baseball M(s), basketball M(s)/W(s), cross-country running M(s)/W(s), soccer M(s)/W(s), softball W(s), tennis M(s)/W(s), track and field M(s)/W(s), volleyball W(s). *Intramural sports:* badminton M/W, basketball M/W, bowling M/W, soccer M/W, softball M/W, table tennis M/W, tennis M/W, volleyball M/W.

Costs (2005–06) *Tuition:* area resident $813 full-time, $72 per credit part-time; nonresident $1392 full-time, $134 per credit part-time.

Financial Aid Of all full-time matriculated undergraduates who enrolled in 2004, 250 Federal Work-Study jobs (averaging $3600). 260 state and other part-time jobs (averaging $4500).

Applying *Options:* early admission, deferred entrance. *Application fee:* $15. *Recommended:* high school transcript. *Application deadline:* rolling (freshmen), rolling (transfers). *Notification:* continuous (freshmen).

Freshmen Application Contact Vice President of Student Services, Spokane Falls Community College, 3410 West Fort George Wright Drive, Spokane, WA 99224-5288. *Phone:* 509-533-3682. *Toll-free phone:* 888-509-7944. *Fax:* 509-533-3433.

TACOMA COMMUNITY COLLEGE

Tacoma, Washington   www.tacomacc.edu/

- **State-supported** 2-year, founded 1965, part of Washington State Board for Community and Technical Colleges
- **Urban** 150-acre campus with easy access to Seattle
- **Coed**

Undergraduates Students come from 20 other countries, 4% are from out of state, 12% African American, 10% Asian American or Pacific Islander, 7% Hispanic American, 2% Native American, 3% international.

Faculty *Student/faculty ratio:* 27:1.

Academics *Calendar:* quarters. *Degree:* certificates, diplomas, and associate. *Special study options:* academic remediation for entering students, accelerated degree program, adult/continuing education programs, advanced placement credit, distance learning, English as a second language, honors programs, independent study, internships, off-campus study, part-time degree program, services for LD students, student-designed majors, summer session for credit. *ROTC:* Army (c).

Student Life *Campus security:* Sonitrol electronic system.

Standardized Tests *Required:* ACCUPLACER (for placement).

Costs (2005–06) *Tuition:* state resident $2543 full-time; nonresident $2932 full-time. *Required fees:* $68 full-time.

Financial Aid Of all full-time matriculated undergraduates who enrolled in 2004, 81 Federal Work-Study jobs (averaging $2916). 146 state and other part-time jobs (averaging $2830). *Financial aid deadline:* 5/14.

Applying *Options:* early admission.

Freshmen Application Contact Ms. Annette Hayward, Admissions Officer, Tacoma Community College, 6501 South 19th Street, Tacoma, WA 98466. *Phone:* 253-566-5108. *E-mail:* ahayward@msmail.tacoma.ctc.edu.

Washington

WALLA WALLA COMMUNITY COLLEGE
Walla Walla, Washington   www.wwcc.edu/home/

- **State-supported** 2-year, founded 1967, part of Washington State Board for Community and Technical Colleges
- **Small-town** 125-acre campus
- **Endowment** $4.0 million
- **Coed**

Undergraduates 2,164 full-time, 2,276 part-time. Students come from 5 other countries, 12% are from out of state, 4% African American, 1% Asian American or Pacific Islander, 6% Hispanic American, 1% Native American, 0.2% international.
Faculty *Student/faculty ratio:* 21:1.
Academics *Calendar:* quarters. *Degree:* certificates, diplomas, and associate. *Special study options:* academic remediation for entering students, adult/continuing education programs, advanced placement credit, cooperative education, distance learning, double majors, English as a second language, external degree program, honors programs, independent study, internships, off-campus study, part-time degree program, services for LD students, summer session for credit.
Student Life *Campus security:* student patrols, late-night transport/escort service.
Athletics Member NJCAA.
Standardized Tests *Required:* ACT ASSET and ACT COMPASS (for placement).
Financial Aid Of all full-time matriculated undergraduates who enrolled in 2004, 95 Federal Work-Study jobs (averaging $1600). 20 state and other part-time jobs (averaging $2000).
Applying *Options:* common application, electronic application. *Application fee:* $40. *Required for some:* interview. *Recommended:* high school transcript.
Director of Admissions Ms. Sally Wagoner, Director of Admissions and Records, Walla Walla Community College, 500 Tausick Way, Walla Walla, WA 99362-9267. *Phone:* 509-527-4283. *Toll-free phone:* 877-992-9282 (in-state); 877-992-9292 (out-of-state). *E-mail:* admissions@mail.ww.cc.wa.us.

WENATCHEE VALLEY COLLEGE
Wenatchee, Washington   wvc.ctc.edu/

Freshmen Application Contact Ms. Marlene Sinko, Registrar/Admissions Coordinator, Wenatchee Valley College, 1300 Fifth Street, Wenatchee, WA 98801-1799. *Phone:* 509-664-2564.

WESTERN BUSINESS COLLEGE
Vancouver, Washington   www.western-college.com/

Director of Admissions Ms. Maryann Green, Director of Admission, Western Business College, 120 Northeast 136th Avenue, Suite 300, Vancouver, WA 98684. *Phone:* 360-254-3282.

WHATCOM COMMUNITY COLLEGE
Bellingham, Washington   www.whatcom.ctc.edu/

- **State-supported** 2-year, founded 1970, part of Washington State Board for Community and Technical Colleges
- **Small-town** 52-acre campus with easy access to Vancouver
- **Endowment** $2.0 million
- **Coed**

Undergraduates 5% are from out of state.
Academics *Calendar:* quarters. *Degree:* certificates, diplomas, and associate. *Special study options:* academic remediation for entering students, accelerated degree program, adult/continuing education programs, advanced placement credit, cooperative education, distance learning, English as a second language, external degree program, honors programs, independent study, internships, part-time degree program, services for LD students, student-designed majors, study abroad, summer session for credit.
Student Life *Campus security:* 24-hour emergency response devices.
Costs (2005–06) *Tuition:* state resident $2484 full-time, $73 per credit part-time; nonresident $7692 full-time, $245 per credit part-time. Full-time

tuition and fees vary according to course load and reciprocity agreements. Part-time tuition and fees vary according to course load and reciprocity agreements.
Financial Aid Of all full-time matriculated undergraduates who enrolled in 2004, 50 Federal Work-Study jobs (averaging $3500). 80 state and other part-time jobs (averaging $3690).
Applying *Options:* electronic application.
Freshmen Application Contact Entry and Advising Center, Whatcom Community College, 237 West Kellogg Road, Bellingham, WA 98226. *Phone:* 360-650-5358.

YAKIMA VALLEY COMMUNITY COLLEGE
Yakima, Washington   www.yvcc.edu/

- **State-supported** 2-year, founded 1928, part of Washington State Board for Community and Technical Colleges
- **Small-town** 20-acre campus
- **Endowment** $5.4 million
- **Coed,** 6,225 undergraduate students, 60% full-time, 66% women, 34% men

Undergraduates 3,755 full-time, 2,470 part-time. Students come from 10 other countries, 2% are from out of state, 1% African American, 2% Asian American or Pacific Islander, 37% Hispanic American, 3% Native American, 1% live on campus.
Freshmen *Admission:* 1,354 applied, 1,354 admitted.
Faculty *Total:* 299, 32% full-time, 11% with terminal degrees. *Student/faculty ratio:* 20:1.
Majors Accounting; administrative assistant and secretarial science; agricultural business and management; agricultural mechanization; agriculture; agronomy and crop science; animal sciences; automobile/automotive mechanics technology; broadcast journalism; business administration and management; child development; civil engineering technology; computer engineering technology; computer graphics; computer science; criminal justice/law enforcement administration; criminal justice/police science; dental hygiene; electrical, electronic and communications engineering technology; family and consumer economics related; fire science; hotel/motel administration; industrial radiologic technology; industrial technology; instrumentation technology; kindergarten/preschool education; legal administrative assistant/secretary; liberal arts and sciences/liberal studies; management information systems; marketing/marketing management; medical administrative assistant and medical secretary; nursing (registered nurse training); occupational therapy; pre-engineering; special products marketing; substance abuse/addiction counseling; tourism and travel services management; veterinary technology.
Academics *Calendar:* quarters. *Degree:* certificates and associate. *Special study options:* academic remediation for entering students, adult/continuing education programs, advanced placement credit, cooperative education, distance learning, English as a second language, internships, part-time degree program, services for LD students, summer session for credit.
Library Raymond Library with 31,716 titles, 860 serial subscriptions, an OPAC.
Computers on Campus 369 computers available on campus for general student use. A campuswide network can be accessed. Internet access, online (class) registration, at least one staffed computer lab available.
Student Life *Housing Options:* coed. Campus housing is university owned. *Activities and Organizations:* choral group, Veterans with Supporters, Business Management/Marketing Club, Image Makers, Agri-Business Club. *Campus security:* 24-hour emergency response devices, student patrols, late-night transport/escort service, controlled dormitory access. *Student services:* health clinic, personal/psychological counseling.
Athletics Member NJCAA. *Intercollegiate sports:* baseball M(s), basketball M(s)/W(s), soccer W, softball W(s), volleyball W(s), wrestling M(s). *Intramural sports:* basketball M/W, volleyball W, wrestling M.
Costs (2005–06) *Tuition:* state resident $2550 full-time, $72 per credit part-time; nonresident $2939 full-time. Full-time tuition and fees vary according to course load. Part-time tuition and fees vary according to course load. *Required fees:* $4 per credit part-time. *Room and board:* room only: $2400. *Payment plan:* installment. *Waivers:* senior citizens.
Financial Aid Of all full-time matriculated undergraduates who enrolled in 2004, 133 Federal Work-Study jobs (averaging $1164). 156 state and other part-time jobs (averaging $2083).
Applying *Options:* common application, electronic application, deferred entrance. *Application fee:* $20. *Required for some:* high school transcript, letters of recommendation, interview. *Recommended:* high school transcript. *Application deadlines:* 9/16 (freshmen), 9/16 (transfers). *Notification:* continuous until 9/16 (freshmen).
Freshmen Application Contact Tessa Southards, Admissions Assistant, Yakima Valley Community College, PO Box 22520, Yakima, WA 98907-2520. *Phone:* 509-574-4713. *Fax:* 509-574-6860. *E-mail:* admis@yvcc.edu.

COMMUNITY & TECHNICAL COLLEGE AT WEST VIRGINIA UNIVERSITY INSTITUTE OF TECHNOLOGY

Montgomery, West Virginia　　　　ctc.wvutech.edu/

- **County-supported** 2-year
- **Coed**

Academics *Degree:* certificates and associate.
Director of Admissions Ms. Lisa Graham, Director of Admissions, Community & Technical College at West Virginia University Institute of Technology, Box 10, Old Main, Montgomery, WV 25136. *Phone:* 304-442-3167. *Toll-free phone:* 888-554-8324.

COMMUNITY AND TECHNICAL COLLEGE OF SHEPHERD

Martinsburg, West Virginia　　www.shepherd.edu/ctcweb/

- **County-supported** 2-year
- **Coed,** 1,711 undergraduate students, 25% full-time, 60% women, 40% men

Undergraduates 427 full-time, 1,284 part-time. 40% are from out of state, 8% African American, 0.6% Asian American or Pacific Islander, 2% Hispanic American, 0.6% Native American, 0.2% international.
Freshmen *Admission:* 333 applied, 332 admitted, 205 enrolled. *Test scores:* SAT verbal scores over 500: 45%; SAT math scores over 500: 17%; ACT scores over 18: 34%; SAT verbal scores over 600: 10%; SAT math scores over 600: 6%; ACT scores over 24: 1%.
Faculty *Total:* 70, 19% full-time, 20% with terminal degrees. *Student/faculty ratio:* 29:1.
Majors Automobile/automotive mechanics technology; business, management, and marketing related; criminal justice/safety; culinary arts; design and visual communications; electromechanical technology; emergency medical technology (EMT paramedic); fashion merchandising; fire science; general studies; heating, air conditioning, ventilation and refrigeration maintenance technology; information technology; office occupations and clerical services; paralegal/legal assistant; safety/security technology.
Academics *Degree:* certificates and associate.
Student Life *Activities and Organizations:* national fraternities.
Standardized Tests *Recommended:* SAT and SAT Subject Tests or ACT (for admission).
Costs (2006–07) *Tuition:* state resident $2944 full-time, $123 per credit part-time; nonresident $8542 full-time, $355 per credit part-time.
Applying *Application fee:* $35. *Required:* high school transcript. *Required for some:* interview.
Freshmen Application Contact Leslie C. See, Director of Enrollment Management, Community and Technical College of Shepherd, 400 West Stephen Street, Martinsburg, WV 25401. *Phone:* 304-260-4380. *Fax:* 304-260-4376. *E-mail:* lseectc@shepherd.edu.

EASTERN WEST VIRGINIA COMMUNITY AND TECHNICAL COLLEGE

Moorefield, West Virginia　　www.eastern.wvnet.edu/

- **State-supported** 2-year, founded 1999
- **Rural** campus
- **Coed,** 882 undergraduate students, 8% full-time, 67% women, 33% men
- 100% of applicants were admitted

Undergraduates 68 full-time, 814 part-time. 3% African American, 0.4% Native American.
Freshmen *Admission:* 104 applied, 104 admitted, 75 enrolled.

Faculty *Total:* 41, 2% full-time, 5% with terminal degrees. *Student/faculty ratio:* 21:1.
Majors Administrative assistant and secretarial science; child care provision; general studies; heavy/industrial equipment maintenance technologies related; liberal arts and sciences and humanities related; liberal arts and sciences/liberal studies; multi-/interdisciplinary studies related; science technologies related.
Academics *Calendar:* semesters. *Degree:* certificates and associate.
Student Life *Housing:* college housing not available.
Costs (2006–07) *Tuition:* state resident $1704 full-time; nonresident $6822 full-time.
Freshmen Application Contact Ms. Sharon Bungard, Dean for Learner Support Services, Eastern West Virginia Community and Technical College, 1929 State Road 55, Moorefield, WV 26836. *Phone:* 304-434-8000. *Toll-free phone:* 877-982-2322. *Fax:* 304-434-7001.

FAIRMONT STATE COMMUNITY & TECHNICAL COLLEGE

Fairmont, West Virginia　　　　www.fscwv.edu/fsctc/

- **State-supported** 2-year, administratively affiliated with Fairmont State College
- **Small-town** 90-acre campus
- **Endowment** $91,000
- **Coed**

Undergraduates 1,878 full-time, 1,477 part-time. Students come from 11 states and territories, 5% African American, 1% Asian American or Pacific Islander, 0.6% Hispanic American, 0.5% Native American.
Academics *Calendar:* semesters. *Degree:* certificates and associate. *Special study options:* adult/continuing education programs, external degree program, part-time degree program, summer session for credit.
Athletics Member NCAA.
Standardized Tests *Required:* SAT or ACT (for admission). *Required for some:* ACT COMPASS.
Applying *Options:* common application, electronic application, deferred entrance. *Recommended:* high school transcript, minimum 2.25 GPA.
Director of Admissions Executive Director of Enrollment Services, Fairmont State Community & Technical College, 1201 Locust Avenue, Fairmont, WV 26554. *Phone:* 304-367-4062. *Toll-free phone:* 800-641-5678.

▶ **See page 540 for the College Close-Up.**

HUNTINGTON JUNIOR COLLEGE

Huntington, West Virginia www.huntingtonjuniorcollege.com/

Director of Admissions Mr. James Garrett, Educational Services Director, Huntington Junior College, 900 Fifth Avenue, Huntington, WV 25701-2004. *Phone:* 304-697-7550.

INTERNATIONAL ACADEMY OF DESIGN & TECHNOLOGY

Fairmont, West Virginia　　　　　　iadtwv.com/

Director of Admissions Mr. Dennis A. Hirsh, President, International Academy of Design & Technology, 2000 Green River Drive, Fairmont, WV 26554-9790. *Toll-free phone:* 888-406-8324. *Fax:* 304-534-5669. *E-mail:* dhirsh@iadtwv.com.

MARSHALL COMMUNITY AND TECHNICAL COLLEGE

Huntington, West Virginia　　　　www.marshall.edu/ctc/

- **County-supported** 2-year, part of Community and Technical College System of West Virginia, administratively affiliated with Marshall University
- **Endowment** $142,700
- **Coed,** 2,589 undergraduate students, 50% full-time, 38% women, 62% men

Undergraduates 1,305 full-time, 1,284 part-time. Students come from 24 states and territories, 3 other countries, 19% are from out of state, 6% African

Marshall Community and Technical College (continued)
American, 0.5% Asian American or Pacific Islander, 1% Hispanic American, 0.2% Native American, 0.1% international, 7% transferred in.
Freshmen *Admission:* 695 applied, 694 admitted, 467 enrolled. *Average high school GPA:* 2.64. *Test scores:* SAT verbal scores over 500: 27%; SAT math scores over 500: 27%; ACT scores over 18: 37%; SAT verbal scores over 600: 9%; ACT scores over 24: 7%; SAT verbal scores over 700: 9%.
Faculty *Total:* 123, 28% full-time, 10% with terminal degrees. *Student/faculty ratio:* 27:1.
Majors Accounting technology and bookkeeping; administrative assistant and secretarial science; business/commerce; computer engineering technology; criminal justice/police science; dental laboratory technology; electrical, electronic and communications engineering technology; emergency medical technology (EMT paramedic); finance; health information/medical records technology; hospitality administration; interior design; legal assistant/paralegal; liberal arts and sciences/liberal studies; manufacturing technology; medical/clinical assistant; medical radiologic technology; medical transcription; multi-/interdisciplinary studies related; physical science technologies related; physical therapist assistant; respiratory care therapy; science technologies related.
Academics *Calendar:* semesters. *Degree:* certificates and associate. *Special study options:* academic remediation for entering students, accelerated degree program, cooperative education, distance learning, double majors, English as a second language, independent study, internships, off-campus study, part-time degree program, services for LD students, summer session for credit. *ROTC:* Army (b).
Library John Deaver Drinko Library plus 2 others with 478,274 titles, 5,314 serial subscriptions, 24,759 audiovisual materials, an OPAC, a Web page.
Computers on Campus 1854 computers available on campus for general student use. A campuswide network can be accessed from student residence rooms and from off campus. Internet access, online (class) registration, at least one staffed computer lab available.
Student Life *Housing:* on-campus residence required for freshman year. *Options:* coed, men-only, women-only, disabled students. Campus housing is university owned. Freshman campus housing is guaranteed. *Activities and Organizations:* drama/theater group, student-run newspaper, radio and television station, choral group, marching band, national fraternities, national sororities. *Student services:* health clinic, personal/psychological counseling, women's center, legal services.
Standardized Tests *Recommended:* SAT (for admission), ACT (for admission).
Costs (2005–06) *Tuition:* state resident $2814 full-time, $118 per credit hour part-time; nonresident $8142 full-time, $340 per credit hour part-time. *Room and board:* $6272; room only: $3496.
Applying *Options:* common application, electronic application, early admission. *Application fee:* $25. *Required:* high school transcript, minimum 2.0 GPA. *Application deadline:* rolling (freshmen), rolling (transfers). *Notification:* continuous (freshmen).
Freshmen Application Contact Ms. Tammy Johnson, Admissions Director (Interim), Marshall Community and Technical College, 1 John Marshall Drive, Huntington, WV 25755. *Phone:* 304-696-3160. *Toll-free phone:* 800-642-3499. *Fax:* 304-696-3135. *E-mail:* admissions@marshall.edu.

MOUNTAIN STATE COLLEGE
Parkersburg, West Virginia   **www.mountainstate.org/**

- **Proprietary** 2-year, founded 1888
- **Small-town** campus
- **Coed, primarily women,** 166 undergraduate students, 100% full-time, 83% women, 17% men

Undergraduates 166 full-time. 1% African American, 0.6% Asian American or Pacific Islander, 0.6% Hispanic American. *Retention:* 70% of 2003 full-time freshmen returned.
Freshmen *Admission:* 27 enrolled.
Faculty *Total:* 11, 64% full-time, 36% with terminal degrees. *Student/faculty ratio:* 17:1.
Majors Accounting and business/management; administrative assistant and secretarial science; computer and information sciences; legal assistant/paralegal; medical/clinical assistant; medical transcription.
Academics *Calendar:* quarters. *Degree:* diplomas and associate.
Computers on Campus Internet access available.
Student Life *Housing:* college housing not available.
Standardized Tests *Required:* CPAt (for admission).
Costs (2006–07) *Tuition:* $7050 full-time. *Required fees:* $115 full-time.
Applying *Required:* interview.
Freshmen Application Contact Ms. Linda Craig, Director, Student Services, Mountain State College, 1508 Spring Street, Parkersburg, WV 26101-3993.

Phone: 304-485-5487. *Toll-free phone:* 800-841-0201. *Fax:* 304-485-3524. *E-mail:* adm@mountainstate.org.

NATIONAL INSTITUTE OF TECHNOLOGY
Cross Lanes, West Virginia   **www.nitschools.com/**
Director of Admissions Mrs. Karen Wilkinson, Director of Admissions, National Institute of Technology, 5514 Big Tyler Road, Cross Lanes, WV 25313. *Phone:* 304-776-6290. *Toll-free phone:* 888-741-4271.

NEW RIVER COMMUNITY AND TECHNICAL COLLEGE
Beckley, West Virginia   **www.nrctc.org/**

- **County-supported** 2-year
- **Coed**

Academics *Degree:* certificates and associate.
Director of Admissions Mr. Michael Palm, Director of Student Services, New River Community and Technical College, 101 Church Street, Lewisburg, WV 24901. *Phone:* 304-647-6564.

POTOMAC STATE COLLEGE OF WEST VIRGINIA UNIVERSITY
Keyser, West Virginia   **www.potomacstatecollege.edu/**
Director of Admissions Ms. Beth Little, Director of Enrollment Services, Potomac State College of West Virginia University, One Grand Central Business Center, Suite 2090, Keyser, WV 26726. *Phone:* 304-788-6820. *Toll-free phone:* 800-262-7332 Ext. 6820.

SOUTHERN WEST VIRGINIA COMMUNITY AND TECHNICAL COLLEGE
Mount Gay, West Virginia   **www.southern.wvnet.edu/**

- **State-supported** 2-year, founded 1971, part of State College System of West Virginia
- **Rural** 23-acre campus
- **Coed,** 1,982 undergraduate students, 63% full-time, 69% women, 31% men

Undergraduates 1,257 full-time, 725 part-time. Students come from 2 states and territories, 12% are from out of state, 2% African American, 0.3% Asian American or Pacific Islander, 0.2% Hispanic American, 0.2% Native American, 7% transferred in.
Freshmen *Admission:* 875 applied, 875 admitted, 431 enrolled. *Average high school GPA:* 2.77.
Faculty *Total:* 166, 40% full-time. *Student/faculty ratio:* 20:1.
Majors Accounting; administrative assistant and secretarial science; automobile/automotive mechanics technology; business administration and management; clinical/medical laboratory technology; communications technology; computer programming (specific applications); criminal justice/law enforcement administration; drafting and design technology; engineering technology; finance; industrial radiologic technology; information science/studies; liberal arts and sciences/liberal studies; nursing (registered nurse training); welding technology.
Academics *Calendar:* semesters. *Degree:* certificates and associate. *Special study options:* academic remediation for entering students, adult/continuing education programs, advanced placement credit, cooperative education, external degree program, part-time degree program, services for LD students, summer session for credit.
Library 70,576 titles, 233 serial subscriptions.
Computers on Campus 92 computers available on campus for general student use. A campuswide network can be accessed from off campus. Internet access, at least one staffed computer lab available.
Student Life *Housing:* college housing not available. *Activities and Organizations:* drama/theater group, student-run television station. *Student services:* personal/psychological counseling.

Costs (2006–07) *Tuition:* state resident $1634 full-time, $68 per credit hour part-time; nonresident $6486 full-time, $270 per credit hour part-time.
Financial Aid Of all full-time matriculated undergraduates who enrolled in 2004, 45 Federal Work-Study jobs (averaging $1500). *Financial aid deadline:* 3/1.
Applying *Options:* early admission, deferred entrance. *Required:* high school transcript. *Application deadline:* rolling (freshmen), rolling (transfers). *Notification:* continuous (freshmen).
Freshmen Application Contact Mr. Roy Simmons, Registrar, Southern West Virginia Community and Technical College, PO Box 2900, Mt. Gay, WV 25637. *Phone:* 304-792-7160 Ext. 120. *Fax:* 304-792-7096. *E-mail:* admissions@southern.wvnet.edu.

VALLEY COLLEGE
Martinsburg, West Virginia   www.valleycollege.com/

- **Proprietary** 2-year, founded 1983
- **Suburban** campus
- **Coed, primarily women,** 47 undergraduate students, 100% full-time, 94% women, 6% men

Undergraduates 47 full-time. 13% African American, 2% Hispanic American, 4% Native American.
Freshmen *Admission:* 40 enrolled.
Faculty *Total:* 6, 67% full-time. *Student/faculty ratio:* 14:1.
Majors Business administration and management.
Academics *Calendar:* continuous. *Degree:* certificates and associate.
Costs (2006–07) *Tuition:* $7200 full-time, $225 per credit part-time.
Applying *Required:* high school transcript, interview.
Freshmen Application Contact Ms. Gail Kennedy, Admissions Director, Valley College, 287 Aikens Center, Martinsburg, WV 25401. *Phone:* 304-263-0878. *Fax:* 304-263-2413. *E-mail:* gkennedy@vct.edu.

WEST VIRGINIA BUSINESS COLLEGE
Nutter Fort, West Virginia

WEST VIRGINIA BUSINESS COLLEGE
Wheeling, West Virginia   www.stratuswave.com/~wvbc/

- **Proprietary** 2-year, founded 1881
- **Urban** 5-acre campus
- **Coed, primarily women,** 78 undergraduate students
- 100% of applicants were admitted

Freshmen *Admission:* 12 applied, 12 admitted.
Faculty *Total:* 10, 100% with terminal degrees. *Student/faculty ratio:* 6:1.
Majors Accounting; administrative assistant and secretarial science; business administration and management; legal assistant/paralegal.
Academics *Calendar:* quarters. *Degree:* diplomas and associate.
Costs (2005–06) *Tuition:* $15,500 per degree program part-time.
Freshmen Application Contact Ms. Karen D. Shaw, Director, West Virginia Business College, 1052 Main Street, Wheeling, WV 26003. *Phone:* 304-232-0361. *Fax:* 304-232-0363. *E-mail:* wvbcwheeling@juno.com.

WEST VIRGINIA JUNIOR COLLEGE
Bridgeport, West Virginia   www.wvjc.com/

Freshmen Application Contact Ms. Cheryl Stickley, Executive Assistant, West Virginia Junior College, 176 Thompson Drive, Bridgeport, WV 26330. *Phone:* 304-363-8824.

WEST VIRGINIA JUNIOR COLLEGE
Charleston, West Virginia   www.wvjc.com/

Freshmen Application Contact Admission Department, West Virginia Junior College, 1000 Virginia Street East, Charleston, WV 25301-2817. *Phone:* 304-345-2820.

WEST VIRGINIA JUNIOR COLLEGE
Morgantown, West Virginia   www.wvjc.com/

Freshmen Application Contact Admissions Office, West Virginia Junior College, 148 Willey Street, Morgantown, WV 26505-5521. *Phone:* 304-296-8282.

WEST VIRGINIA NORTHERN COMMUNITY COLLEGE
Wheeling, West Virginia   www.northern.wvnet.edu/

- **State-supported** 2-year, founded 1972
- **Small-town** campus with easy access to Pittsburgh
- **Endowment** $700,706
- **Coed,** 2,842 undergraduate students, 50% full-time, 69% women, 31% men

Undergraduates 1,421 full-time, 1,421 part-time. Students come from 5 states and territories, 17% are from out of state, 3% African American, 0.4% Asian American or Pacific Islander, 0.3% Hispanic American, 0.2% Native American, 0.1% international, 8% transferred in. *Retention:* 51% of 2003 full-time freshmen returned.
Freshmen *Admission:* 788 applied, 418 admitted, 416 enrolled. *Average high school GPA:* 2.80. *Test scores:* SAT verbal scores over 500: 28%; SAT math scores over 500: 11%; ACT scores over 18: 60%; SAT verbal scores over 600: 6%; SAT math scores over 600: 6%; ACT scores over 24: 7%.
Faculty *Total:* 150, 37% full-time, 11% with terminal degrees. *Student/faculty ratio:* 19:1.
Majors Accounting technology and bookkeeping; administrative assistant and secretarial science; applied horticulture; banking and financial support services; business administration and management; computer programming; criminal justice/police science; electrical, electronic and communications engineering technology; health information/medical records technology; heating, air conditioning, ventilation and refrigeration maintenance technology; hospitality administration; industrial technology; information technology; institutional food workers; liberal arts and sciences/liberal studies; nursing (registered nurse training); social work; word processing.
Academics *Calendar:* semesters. *Degree:* certificates and associate. *Special study options:* academic remediation for entering students, accelerated degree program, adult/continuing education programs, advanced placement credit, distance learning, double majors, honors programs, internships, part-time degree program, student-designed majors, summer session for credit.
Library Wheeling B and O Campus Library plus 2 others with 36,650 titles, 188 serial subscriptions, 3,495 audiovisual materials, an OPAC, a Web page.
Computers on Campus 250 computers available on campus for general student use. A campuswide network can be accessed from off campus. Internet access, at least one staffed computer lab available.
Student Life *Housing:* college housing not available. *Activities and Organizations:* student-run newspaper. *Campus security:* security personnel during evening and night classes. *Student services:* personal/psychological counseling.
Athletics *Intramural sports:* basketball M/W, bowling M/W, softball M/W, volleyball M/W.
Costs (2005–06) *Tuition:* state resident $1752 full-time, $73 per credit part-time; nonresident $5592 full-time, $233 per credit part-time. Full-time tuition and fees vary according to course load and reciprocity agreements. Part-time tuition and fees vary according to course load and reciprocity agreements. *Payment plan:* installment. *Waivers:* employees or children of employees.
Financial Aid Of all full-time matriculated undergraduates who enrolled in 2004, 35 Federal Work-Study jobs (averaging $1650).
Applying *Options:* common application, electronic application, early admission, deferred entrance. *Required for some:* high school transcript. *Application deadline:* rolling (freshmen), rolling (transfers).
Freshmen Application Contact Ms. Janet Fike, Associate Dean of Enrollment Management, West Virginia Northern Community College, 1704 Market Street, Wheeling, WV 26003-3699. *Phone:* 304-233-5900 Ext. 4363. *Fax:* 304-233-5900.

WEST VIRGINIA STATE COMMUNITY AND TECHNICAL COLLEGE

Institute, West Virginia   **fozzy.wvsc.edu/ctc/index.html**

- **County-supported** 2-year
- **Coed**

Undergraduates 7% are from out of state.

Academics *Degree:* certificates and associate.

Costs (2005–06) *Tuition:* state resident $3222 full-time, $110 per credit hour part-time; nonresident $7400 full-time, $294 per credit hour part-time. Full-time tuition and fees vary according to class time, course level, and program. *Room and board:* $4720; room only: $2200. Room and board charges vary according to board plan and housing facility. *Payment plans:* installment, deferred payment.

Director of Admissions Mr. Tyreno N. Sowell Sr., Interim Director, Admissions and Recruitment Services, West Virginia State Community and Technical College, PO Box 1000, Institute, WV 25112-1000. *Phone:* 304-766-3033. *Toll-free phone:* 800-987-2112.

WEST VIRGINIA UNIVERSITY AT PARKERSBURG

Parkersburg, West Virginia   **www.wvup.edu/**

- **State-supported** primarily 2-year, founded 1961, administratively affiliated with West Virginia University
- **Small-town** 140-acre campus
- **Coed**

Undergraduates 2,148 full-time, 1,574 part-time. Students come from 5 states and territories, 2% are from out of state, 0.5% African American, 0.6% Asian American or Pacific Islander, 0.3% Hispanic American, 0.3% Native American, 5% transferred in. *Retention:* 56% of 2003 full-time freshmen returned.

Faculty *Student/faculty ratio:* 20:1.

Academics *Calendar:* semesters. *Degrees:* certificates, associate, and bachelor's. *Special study options:* academic remediation for entering students, adult/continuing education programs, advanced placement credit, cooperative education, distance learning, English as a second language, independent study, internships, part-time degree program, services for LD students, study abroad, summer session for credit. *ROTC:* Army (c).

Standardized Tests *Required:* ACT (for placement).

Costs (2005–06) *Tuition:* state resident $2280 full-time, $95 per credit hour part-time; nonresident $6024 full-time, $251 per credit hour part-time. Full-time tuition and fees vary according to degree level and reciprocity agreements. Part-time tuition and fees vary according to degree level and reciprocity agreements.

Applying *Options:* common application, electronic application, early admission, deferred entrance. *Required for some:* high school transcript.

Freshmen Application Contact Ms. Violet Mosser, Senior Admissions Counselor, West Virginia University at Parkersburg, 300 Campus Drive, Parkersburg, WV 26101. *Phone:* 304-424-8223 Ext. 223. *Toll-free phone:* 800-WVA-WVUP.

WISCONSIN

BLACKHAWK TECHNICAL COLLEGE

Janesville, Wisconsin   **www.blackhawk.edu/**

Director of Admissions Ms. Barbara Erlandson, Student Services Manager, Blackhawk Technical College, PO Box 5009, Janesville, WI 53547-5009. *Phone:* 608-757-7713. *Toll-free phone:* 800-472-0024.

BRYANT AND STRATTON COLLEGE

Milwaukee, Wisconsin   **www.bryantstratton.edu/**

- **Proprietary** primarily 2-year, founded 1863, part of Bryant and Stratton Business Institute, Inc
- **Urban** 2-acre campus
- **Coed,** 488 undergraduate students, 72% full-time, 87% women, 13% men

Undergraduates 351 full-time, 137 part-time. Students come from 1 other state, 84% African American, 0.6% Asian American or Pacific Islander, 4% Hispanic American, 0.2% Native American. *Retention:* 70% of 2003 full-time freshmen returned.

Freshmen *Admission:* 403 applied, 335 admitted.

Faculty *Total:* 102, 19% full-time. *Student/faculty ratio:* 10:1.

Majors Accounting; administrative assistant and secretarial science; business/commerce; criminal justice/law enforcement administration; human resources management and services related; information technology; medical administrative assistant and medical secretary; medical/clinical assistant.

Academics *Calendar:* semesters. *Degrees:* associate and bachelor's. *Special study options:* academic remediation for entering students, adult/continuing education programs, advanced placement credit, cooperative education, distance learning, double majors, independent study, internships, part-time degree program, summer session for credit.

Library Bryant and Stratton College Library with 120 serial subscriptions, 100 audiovisual materials.

Computers on Campus 130 computers available on campus for general student use. A campuswide network can be accessed. Internet access, at least one staffed computer lab available.

Student Life *Housing:* college housing not available. *Activities and Organizations:* student-run newspaper, Phi Beta Lambda, Association of Information Technology Professionals, Allied Health Association, Institute of Management Accountants, Student Advisory Board. *Campus security:* 24-hour emergency response devices and patrols.

Standardized Tests *Required:* TABE (for admission). *Recommended:* SAT or ACT (for admission).

Costs (2005–06) *Tuition:* $18,675 full-time, $415 per credit hour part-time. *Required fees:* $25 full-time.

Applying *Required:* high school transcript, interview, entrance and placement evaluations. *Required for some:* letters of recommendation. *Application deadline:* rolling (freshmen), rolling (transfers).

Freshmen Application Contact Ms. Kathryn Cotey, Director of Admissions, Bryant and Stratton College, 310 West Wisconsin Avenue, Milwaukee, WI 53203-2214. *Phone:* 414-276-5200.

CHIPPEWA VALLEY TECHNICAL COLLEGE

Eau Claire, Wisconsin   **www.cvtc.edu/**

Director of Admissions Mr. Timothy Shepardson, Director of Admissions, Chippewa Valley Technical College, 620 West Clairemont Avenue, Eau Claire, WI 54701-6162. *Phone:* 715-833-6245. *Toll-free phone:* 800-547-2882.

COLLEGE OF MENOMINEE NATION

Keshena, Wisconsin   **www.menominee.edu/**

Director of Admissions Ms. Cynthia Norton, Admissions Representative, College of Menominee Nation, PO Box 1179, Keshena, WI 54135. *Phone:* 715-799-5600 Ext. 3053.

FOX VALLEY TECHNICAL COLLEGE

Appleton, Wisconsin   **www.fvtc.edu/**

- **State and locally supported** 2-year, founded 1967, part of Wisconsin Technical College System
- **Suburban** 100-acre campus
- **Coed,** 7,855 undergraduate students, 21% full-time, 52% women, 48% men

Undergraduates 1,624 full-time, 6,231 part-time. Students come from 11 states and territories, 1% are from out of state, 1% African American, 3% Asian

American or Pacific Islander, 2% Hispanic American, 0.9% Native American. Freshmen *Admission:* 4,586 applied, 3,226 admitted, 1,003 enrolled.

Faculty *Total:* 983, 34% full-time. *Student/faculty ratio:* 18:1.

Majors Accounting; administrative assistant and secretarial science; agricultural business and management; airline pilot and flight crew; automobile/automotive mechanics technology; business administration and management; child development; commercial and advertising art; computer programming; computer typography and composition equipment operation; consumer merchandising/retailing management; criminal justice/law enforcement administration; criminal justice/police science; culinary arts; drafting and design technology; electrical, electronic and communications engineering technology; finance; fire science; fish/game management; forestry technology; graphic and printing equipment operation/production; hospitality administration; industrial technology; insurance; interior design; legal administrative assistant/secretary; marketing/marketing management; mechanical design technology; mechanical engineering/mechanical technology; natural resources/conservation; nursing (registered nurse training); occupational therapy; special products marketing; welding technology; wood science and wood products/pulp and paper technology.

Academics *Calendar:* semesters. *Degree:* certificates, diplomas, and associate. *Special study options:* academic remediation for entering students, accelerated degree program, adult/continuing education programs, advanced placement credit, cooperative education, distance learning, double majors, English as a second language, honors programs, independent study, internships, off-campus study, part-time degree program, services for LD students, student-designed majors, study abroad, summer session for credit.

Library William Sirek Educational Resource Center with 45,139 titles, 297 serial subscriptions, 7,953 audiovisual materials, an OPAC, a Web page.

Computers on Campus 300 computers available on campus for general student use. A campuswide network can be accessed from off campus that provide access to e-mail, personal web pages. Internet access, online (class) registration, at least one staffed computer lab available.

Student Life *Housing:* college housing not available. *Activities and Organizations:* student-run newspaper, Business Professionals of America, Delta Epsilon Chi, Vocational Industrial Clubs of America. *Campus security:* late-night transport/escort service, 16-hour patrols by trained security personnel. *Student services:* health clinic, personal/psychological counseling, women's center.

Athletics *Intramural sports:* archery M/W, basketball M/W, bowling M/W, skiing (downhill) M/W, tennis M/W, volleyball M/W, weight lifting M/W.

Costs (2006–07) *Tuition:* state resident $2610 full-time, $87 per credit part-time; nonresident $16,089 full-time, $536 per credit part-time. *Required fees:* $550 full-time.

Financial Aid Of all full-time matriculated undergraduates who enrolled in 2004, 165 Federal Work-Study jobs (averaging $2300).

Applying *Options:* common application, electronic application, early admission, deferred entrance. *Application fee:* $30. *Required:* high school transcript. *Application deadline:* rolling (freshmen), rolling (transfers).

Freshmen Application Contact Admissions Center, Fox Valley Technical College, 1825 North Bluemound Drive, PO Box 2277, Appleton, WI 54912-2277. *Phone:* 920-735-5643. *Toll-free phone:* 800-735-3882.

GATEWAY TECHNICAL COLLEGE
Kenosha, Wisconsin www.gtc.edu/

Director of Admissions Ms. Susan Roberts, Manager Admissions and Testing, Gateway Technical College, 3520 30th Avenue, Kenosha, WI 53144-1690. *Phone:* 262-564-3224.

HERZING COLLEGE
Madison, Wisconsin www.herzing.edu/madison

- **Proprietary** primarily 2-year, founded 1948, part of Herzing Institutes, Inc
- **Suburban** campus with easy access to Milwaukee
- **Coed, primarily men**

Undergraduates Students come from 5 states and territories, 2 other countries, 33% are from out of state.

Faculty *Student/faculty ratio:* 13:1.

Academics *Calendar:* semesters. *Degrees:* diplomas, associate, and bachelor's. *Special study options:* academic remediation for entering students, accelerated degree program, adult/continuing education programs, advanced placement credit, cooperative education, distance learning, double majors, honors programs, independent study, internships, part-time degree program, services for LD students.

Student Life *Campus security:* 24-hour emergency response devices.

Costs (2005–06) *Tuition:* $10,000 full-time, $290 per credit part-time. Full-time tuition and fees vary according to course load, location, and program. Part-time tuition and fees vary according to course load, location, and program. *Required fees:* $25 full-time.

Financial Aid *Financial aid deadline:* 6/30.

Applying *Options:* common application, electronic application, early admission. *Required:* high school transcript, interview, college entrance examination.

Director of Admissions Ms. Rebecca Abrams, Admissions Director, Herzing College, 5218 East Terrace Drive, Madison, WI 53718. *Phone:* 608-249-6611 Ext. 804. *Toll-free phone:* 800-582-1227. *E-mail:* info@msn.herzing.edu.

ITT TECHNICAL INSTITUTE
Green Bay, Wisconsin www.itt-tech.edu/

- **Proprietary** primarily 2-year, founded 2000, part of ITT Educational Services, Inc
- **Coed**

Majors Animation, interactive technology, video graphics and special effects; business administration and management; CAD/CADD drafting/design technology; computer and information systems security; computer programming; computer software technology; computer systems networking and telecommunications; criminal justice/law enforcement administration; e-commerce; electrical, electronic and communications engineering technology; system, networking, and LAN/WAN management; web/multimedia management and webmaster; web page, digital/multimedia and information resources design.

Academics *Calendar:* quarters. *Degrees:* associate and bachelor's.

Library a Web page.

Computers on Campus Internet access, at least one staffed computer lab available.

Student Life *Housing:* college housing not available.

Standardized Tests *Required:* Wonderlic aptitude test (for admission).

Costs (2005–06) *Tuition:* Please see school catalog for specific information.

Applying *Options:* deferred entrance. *Application fee:* $100. *Required:* high school transcript, interview. *Recommended:* letters of recommendation. *Application deadline:* rolling (freshmen), rolling (transfers). *Notification:* continuous (freshmen).

Freshmen Application Contact Mr. Jeffrey J. Murphy, ITT Technical Institute, 470 Security Boulevard, Green Bay, WI 54313. *Phone:* 920-662-9000. *Toll-free phone:* 888-884-3626. *Fax:* 920-662-9384.

ITT TECHNICAL INSTITUTE
Greenfield, Wisconsin www.itt-tech.edu/

- **Proprietary** primarily 2-year, founded 1968, part of ITT Educational Services, Inc
- **Suburban** campus with easy access to Milwaukee
- **Coed,** 548 undergraduate students

Majors Animation, interactive technology, video graphics and special effects; business administration and management; CAD/CADD drafting/design technology; computer and information systems security; computer programming; criminal justice/law enforcement administration; e-commerce; electrical, electronic and communications engineering technology; system, networking, and LAN/WAN management; web/multimedia management and webmaster; web page, digital/multimedia and information resources design.

Academics *Calendar:* quarters. *Degrees:* associate and bachelor's.

Library a Web page.

Computers on Campus Internet access, at least one staffed computer lab available.

Student Life *Housing:* college housing not available.

Standardized Tests *Required:* Wonderlic aptitude test (for admission).

Costs (2005–06) *Tuition:* Please see school catalog for specific information.

Applying *Options:* deferred entrance. *Application fee:* $100. *Required:* high school transcript, interview. *Recommended:* letters of recommendation. *Application deadline:* rolling (freshmen), rolling (transfers). *Notification:* continuous (freshmen).

Freshmen Application Contact Mr. Brian Guenther, Director of Recruitment, ITT Technical Institute, 6300 West Layton Avenue, Greenfield, WI 53220. *Phone:* 414-282-9494.

Lac Courte Oreilles Ojibwa Community College

Hayward, Wisconsin   www.lco-college.edu/

- **Federally supported** 2-year, founded 1982
- **Rural** 2-acre campus
- **Endowment** $950,616
- **Coed,** 505 undergraduate students, 58% full-time, 72% women, 28% men

Undergraduates   294 full-time, 211 part-time. Students come from 1 other state, 3% are from out of state, 0.6% African American, 0.6% Hispanic American, 77% Native American.
Freshmen *Admission:* 151 applied, 151 admitted, 151 enrolled.
Faculty *Total:* 75, 21% full-time, 1% with terminal degrees. *Student/faculty ratio:* 10:1.
Majors   Administrative assistant and secretarial science; American Indian/Native American studies; business administration and management; liberal arts and sciences/liberal studies; medical/clinical assistant; natural resources management and policy; nursing (registered nurse training); social work; substance abuse/addiction counseling.
Academics *Calendar:* semesters. *Degree:* certificates and associate. *Special study options:* academic remediation for entering students, adult/continuing education programs, distance learning, double majors, external degree program, honors programs, independent study, part-time degree program.
Library   Lac Courte Oreilles Ojibwa Community College Library with 13,800 titles, 100 serial subscriptions, an OPAC.
Computers on Campus   25 computers available on campus for general student use. A campuswide network can be accessed. Internet access, at least one staffed computer lab available.
Student Life *Housing:* college housing not available. *Activities and Organizations:* drama/theater group, student association. *Campus security:* 24-hour emergency response devices.
Athletics *Intramural sports:* basketball M, softball W, volleyball M/W, weight lifting M/W.
Standardized Tests *Required:* ACT COMPASS (for admission).
Costs (2006–07) *Tuition:* area resident $4050 full-time, $135 per credit part-time. *Required fees:* $25 full-time.
Financial Aid   Of all full-time matriculated undergraduates who enrolled in 2004, 15 Federal Work-Study jobs (averaging $1400).
Applying *Options:* common application, early admission. *Application fee:* $10. *Required:* high school transcript. *Application deadline:* rolling (freshmen), rolling (transfers).
Freshmen Application Contact   Ms. Annette Wiggins, Registrar, Lac Courte Oreilles Ojibwa Community College, 13466 West Trepania Road, Hayward, WI 54843-2181. *Phone:* 715-634-4790 Ext. 104. *Toll-free phone:* 888-526-6221.

Lakeshore Technical College

Cleveland, Wisconsin   www.gotoltc.com/

- **State and locally supported** 2-year, founded 1967, part of Wisconsin Technical College System
- **Rural** 160-acre campus with easy access to Milwaukee
- **Coed,** 2,939 undergraduate students, 26% full-time, 60% women, 40% men

Undergraduates   772 full-time, 2,167 part-time. Students come from 3 states and territories, 1% are from out of state, 0.4% African American, 2% Asian American or Pacific Islander, 2% Hispanic American, 0.4% Native American.
Freshmen *Admission:* 1,667 applied, 1,128 admitted, 537 enrolled.
Faculty *Total:* 215, 46% full-time. *Student/faculty ratio:* 14:1.
Majors   Accounting; administrative assistant and secretarial science; computer and information sciences related; computer management; computer programming; computer programming related; computer systems analysis; court reporting; criminal justice/police science; dental hygiene; electrical, electronic and communications engineering technology; electromechanical technology; finance; legal assistant/paralegal; management science; marketing/marketing management; mechanical design technology; medical administrative assistant and medical secretary; nursing (registered nurse training); quality control technology; radiologic technology/science.
Academics *Calendar:* semesters. *Degree:* certificates, diplomas, and associate. *Special study options:* academic remediation for entering students, accelerated degree program, adult/continuing education programs, advanced placement credit, cooperative education, distance learning, double majors, English as a

second language, external degree program, independent study, internships, part-time degree program, services for LD students, student-designed majors, summer session for credit.
Library   15,749 titles, 220 serial subscriptions, 9,931 audiovisual materials, an OPAC.
Computers on Campus   720 computers available on campus for general student use. A campuswide network can be accessed. Internet access, at least one staffed computer lab available.
Student Life *Housing:* college housing not available. *Activities and Organizations:* student government, Business Professionals of America, Police Science Club, Lakeshore Student Nurse Association, Dairy Herd Club. *Campus security:* 24-hour patrols. *Student services:* health clinic, personal/psychological counseling.
Standardized Tests *Recommended:* ACT (for admission), SAT or ACT (for admission), ACCUPLACER/ACT ASSET.
Costs (2006–07) *Tuition:* area resident $2610 full-time; state resident $16,089 full-time, $87 per credit part-time; nonresident $536 per credit part-time.
Financial Aid   Of all full-time matriculated undergraduates who enrolled in 2004, 37 Federal Work-Study jobs.
Applying *Options:* common application, electronic application, early admission, deferred entrance. *Application fee:* $30. *Required for some:* high school transcript, interview. *Application deadline:* rolling (freshmen), rolling (transfers). *Notification:* continuous (freshmen).
Freshmen Application Contact   Ms. Donna Gorzelitz, Enrollment Specialist, Lakeshore Technical College, 1290 North Avenue, Cleveland, WI 53015. *Phone:* 920-693-1339. *Toll-free phone:* 888-GO TO LTC. *Fax:* 920-693-3561. *E-mail:* enroll@ltc.tec.wi.us.

Madison Area Technical College

Madison, Wisconsin   www.matcmadison.edu/matc/

Director of Admissions   Ms. Maureen Menendez, Interim Admissions Administrator, Madison Area Technical College, 3550 Anderson Street, Madison, WI 53704-2599. *Phone:* 608-246-6212.

Madison Media Institute

Madison, Wisconsin   www.madisonmedia.com/

Director of Admissions   Mr. Chris K. Hutchings, President / Director, Madison Media Institute, 2702 Agriculture Drive, Suite 1, Madison, WI 53718. *Phone:* 608-663-2000. *Toll-free phone:* 800-236-4997. *Fax:* 608-442-0141. *E-mail:* chutch@madisonmedia.com.

Mid-State Technical College

Wisconsin Rapids, Wisconsin   www.mstc.edu/

Freshmen Application Contact   Ms. Carole Prochnow, Admissions Assistant, Mid-State Technical College, 500 32nd Street North, Wisconsin Rapids, WI 54494-5599. *Phone:* 715-422-5444. *Toll-free phone:* 888-575-6782.

Milwaukee Area Technical College

Milwaukee, Wisconsin   matc.edu

- **District-supported** 2-year, founded 1912, part of Wisconsin Technical College System
- **Urban** campus
- **Coed**

Faculty *Student/faculty ratio:* 16:1.
Academics *Calendar:* semesters. *Degree:* certificates, diplomas, and associate. *Special study options:* academic remediation for entering students, accelerated degree program, adult/continuing education programs, advanced placement credit, cooperative education, distance learning, double majors, English as a second language, external degree program, freshman honors college, honors programs, independent study, internships, off-campus study, part-time degree program, services for LD students, student-designed majors, summer session for credit.
Student Life *Campus security:* 24-hour emergency response devices and patrols, student patrols, late-night transport/escort service.

Athletics Member NJCAA.

Standardized Tests *Required:* ACCUPLACER (for admission).

Costs (2005–06) *Tuition:* state resident $2609 full-time; nonresident $15,503 full-time. Full-time tuition and fees vary according to course level and program. Part-time tuition and fees vary according to course level and program. *Required fees:* $262 full-time, $10 per credit part-time.

Financial Aid Of all full-time matriculated undergraduates who enrolled in 2004, 300 Federal Work-Study jobs (averaging $3900).

Applying *Options:* common application, electronic application. *Application fee:* $30. *Required:* high school transcript.

Director of Admissions Mr. Robert Bullock, Director, Admissions and Testing, Milwaukee Area Technical College, 700 West State Street, Milwaukee, WI 53233. *Phone:* 414-297-6274.

MORAINE PARK TECHNICAL COLLEGE

Fond du Lac, Wisconsin **www.morainepark.edu/**

- **State and locally supported** 2-year, founded 1967, part of Wisconsin Technical College System
- **Small-town** 40-acre campus with easy access to Milwaukee
- **Coed,** 7,509 undergraduate students, 16% full-time, 56% women, 44% men

Undergraduates 1,197 full-time, 6,312 part-time. Students come from 5 states and territories, 1% are from out of state, 4% African American, 1% Asian American or Pacific Islander, 2% Hispanic American, 0.8% Native American, 0.4% transferred in.

Freshmen *Admission:* 361 enrolled.

Faculty *Total:* 326, 43% full-time.

Majors Accounting; administrative assistant and secretarial science; automobile/automotive mechanics technology; business administration and management; business services marketing; business systems networking/ telecommunications; child care provider; chiropractic assistant; civil engineering technology; clinical/medical laboratory assistant; computer programming (specific applications); computer/technical support; construction trades; corrections and criminal justice related; cosmetology, barber/styling, and nail instruction; culinary arts; early childhood education; electrical and power transmission installation; electromechanical technology; engineering technology; graphic and printing equipment operation/production; health information/medical records technology; heating, air conditioning and refrigeration technology; legal administrative assistant; machine shop technology; marketing/marketing management; mechanical design technology; medical/clinical assistant; medical radiologic technology; medical transcription; nuclear medical technology; nursing assistant/aide and patient care assistant; nursing (licensed practical/vocational nurse training); nursing (registered nurse training); radiologic technology/science; respiratory care therapy; substance abuse/addiction counseling; surgical technology; tool and die technology; veterinary technology; water quality and wastewater treatment management and recycling technology; web page, digital/multimedia and information resources design; welding technology.

Academics *Calendar:* semesters. *Degree:* certificates, diplomas, and associate. *Special study options:* academic remediation for entering students, accelerated degree program, adult/continuing education programs, advanced placement credit, distance learning, English as a second language, external degree program, independent study, internships, part-time degree program, summer session for credit.

Library Moraine Park Technical College Library/Learning Resource Center with 32,166 titles, 630 serial subscriptions, 13,330 audiovisual materials, an OPAC, a Web page.

Computers on Campus A campuswide network can be accessed. Internet access, online (class) registration, at least one staffed computer lab available.

Student Life *Housing:* college housing not available. *Activities and Organizations:* Student Programming Board, student government, Corrections Club, HVAC Club, Food Service Executives. *Campus security:* 24-hour emergency response devices. *Student services:* personal/psychological counseling.

Standardized Tests *Required:* ACT ASSET, ACCUPLACER (for admission). *Required for some:* ACT (for admission).

Costs (2006–07) *Tuition:* state resident $2610 full-time, $87 per credit part-time; nonresident $16,089 full-time, $536 per credit part-time. *Required fees:* $251 full-time, $8 per credit part-time.

Applying *Options:* electronic application, deferred entrance. *Application fee:* $30. *Required:* interview. *Recommended:* high school transcript. *Application deadline:* rolling (freshmen), rolling (transfers). *Notification:* continuous (freshmen).

Freshmen Application Contact Ms. Karen Jarvis, Student Services, Moraine Park Technical College, 235 North National Ave, PO Box 1940, Fond du Lac, WI 54936-1940. *Phone:* 920-924-3200. *Toll-free phone:* 800-472-4554. *Fax:* 920-924-3421. *E-mail:* kjarvis@morainepark.edu.

NICOLET AREA TECHNICAL COLLEGE

Rhinelander, Wisconsin **www.nicoletcollege.edu/**

Freshmen Application Contact Ms. Susan Kordula, Director of Admissions and Marketing, Nicolet Area Technical College, Box 518, Rhinelander, WI 54501-0518. *Phone:* 715-365-4451. *Toll-free phone:* 800-544-3039 Ext. 4451. *E-mail:* inquire@nicolet.tec.wi.us.

NORTHCENTRAL TECHNICAL COLLEGE

Wausau, Wisconsin **www.ntc.edu/**

Director of Admissions Ms. Carolyn Michalski, Team Leader, Student Services, Northcentral Technical College, 1000 West Campus Drive, Wausau, WI 54401-1899. *Phone:* 715-675-3331 Ext. 4285.

NORTHEAST WISCONSIN TECHNICAL COLLEGE

Green Bay, Wisconsin **www.nwtc.edu/**

Freshmen Application Contact Ms. Heather Hill, Program Enrollment Team Supervisor, Northeast Wisconsin Technical College, 2740 West Mason Street, PO Box 19042, Green Bay, WI 54307-9042. *Phone:* 920-498-5612. *Toll-free phone:* 800-498-5444 (in-state); 800-422-6982 (out-of-state).

SOUTHWEST WISCONSIN TECHNICAL COLLEGE

Fennimore, Wisconsin **www.swtc.edu/**

- **State and locally supported** 2-year, founded 1967, part of Wisconsin Technical College System
- **Rural** 53-acre campus
- **Endowment** $935,000
- **Coed**

Undergraduates 778 full-time, 1,083 part-time. Students come from 4 states and territories, 1% are from out of state, 1% African American, 0.5% Asian American or Pacific Islander, 1% Hispanic American, 0.3% Native American, 3% live on campus.

Faculty *Student/faculty ratio:* 13:1.

Academics *Calendar:* semesters. *Degree:* certificates, diplomas, and associate. *Special study options:* academic remediation for entering students, adult/continuing education programs, advanced placement credit, distance learning, double majors, English as a second language, internships, part-time degree program, services for LD students, student-designed majors, summer session for credit.

Standardized Tests *Required:* TABE (for placement).

Applying *Options:* electronic application, early admission. *Application fee:* $30. *Required:* high school transcript, interview.

Freshmen Application Contact Ms. Kathy Kreul, Admissions, Southwest Wisconsin Technical College, 1800 Bronson Boulevard, Fennimore, WI 53813. *Phone:* 608-822-3262 Ext. 2355. *Toll-free phone:* 800-362-3322 Ext. 2355.

UNIVERSITY OF WISCONSIN–BARABOO/ SAUK COUNTY

Baraboo, Wisconsin **www.baraboo.uwc.edu/**

- **State-supported** 2-year, founded 1968, part of University of Wisconsin System
- **Small-town** 68-acre campus
- **Coed,** 548 undergraduate students, 63% full-time, 57% women, 43% men

Undergraduates 344 full-time, 204 part-time. Students come from 3 states and territories, 3 other countries, 1% are from out of state, 0.4% African American, 0.7% Asian American or Pacific Islander, 2% Hispanic American, 1% Native American.

University of Wisconsin–Baraboo/Sauk County (continued)

Faculty *Total:* 45, 38% full-time, 49% with terminal degrees. *Student/faculty ratio:* 16:1.

Majors Liberal arts and sciences/liberal studies.

Academics *Calendar:* semesters. *Degree:* certificates and associate. *Special study options:* academic remediation for entering students, advanced placement credit, distance learning, external degree program, honors programs, independent study, internships, off-campus study, part-time degree program, services for LD students, student-designed majors, study abroad, summer session for credit.

Library T. N. Savides Library with 45,000 titles, 300 serial subscriptions, 940 audiovisual materials, an OPAC.

Computers on Campus 50 computers available on campus for general student use. A campuswide network can be accessed from off campus that provide access to financial aid application. Internet access, online (class) registration, at least one staffed computer lab available.

Student Life *Housing:* college housing not available. *Activities and Organizations:* drama/theater group, student-run newspaper, choral group, Student Government Association, chorus and band, dance team, Gaming Club, Business Club. *Student services:* personal/psychological counseling.

Athletics Member NJCAA. *Intercollegiate sports:* basketball M(s), golf M(s)/W(s), soccer M(s)/W(s), tennis M/W, volleyball W(s). *Intramural sports:* racquetball M/W, softball M/W, table tennis M/W, volleyball M/W, weight lifting M/W.

Standardized Tests *Required:* SAT or ACT (for admission). *Recommended:* ACT (for admission).

Costs (2005–06) *Tuition:* state resident $4296 full-time, $181 per credit part-time; nonresident $12,992 full-time, $543 per credit part-time. Part-time tuition and fees vary according to course load. *Payment plans:* installment, deferred payment. *Waivers:* senior citizens.

Financial Aid Of all full-time matriculated undergraduates who enrolled in 2004, 650 Federal Work-Study jobs (averaging $2100).

Applying *Options:* electronic application, early admission, deferred entrance. *Application fee:* $35. *Required:* high school transcript. *Required for some:* interview. *Application deadline:* rolling (freshmen), rolling (transfers). *Notification:* continuous until 8/31 (freshmen).

Freshmen Application Contact Ms. Jan Gerlach, Assistant Director of Student Services, University of Wisconsin–Baraboo/Sauk County, 1006 Connie Road, Baraboo, WI 53913-1015. *Phone:* 608-355-5270. *E-mail:* booinfo@uwc.edu.

UNIVERSITY OF WISCONSIN–BARRON COUNTY

Rice Lake, Wisconsin

www.barron.uwc.edu/

- **State-supported** 2-year, founded 1966, part of University of Wisconsin System
- **Small-town** 142-acre campus
- **Coed**

Undergraduates 308 full-time, 308 part-time. Students come from 2 states and territories.

Academics *Calendar:* semesters. *Degree:* associate. *Special study options:* academic remediation for entering students, adult/continuing education programs, advanced placement credit, distance learning, independent study, internships, off-campus study, part-time degree program, services for LD students, study abroad, summer session for credit.

Athletics Member NJCAA.

Standardized Tests *Required:* ACT (for admission), SAT or ACT (for placement).

Costs (2005–06) *Tuition:* state resident $3996 full-time, $165 per credit part-time; nonresident $12,676 full-time, $528 per credit part-time. Full-time tuition and fees vary according to reciprocity agreements. Part-time tuition and fees vary according to reciprocity agreements. *Required fees:* $373 full-time, $16 per credit part-time.

Financial Aid Of all full-time matriculated undergraduates who enrolled in 2004, 650 Federal Work-Study jobs (averaging $2100).

Applying *Options:* electronic application, deferred entrance. *Application fee:* $35. *Required:* high school transcript. *Required for some:* essay or personal statement, 1 letter of recommendation.

Director of Admissions Mr. Dale Fenton, Assistant Dean for Student Services, University of Wisconsin–Barron County, 1800 College Drive, Rice Lake, WI 54868. *Phone:* 715-234-8024.

UNIVERSITY OF WISCONSIN–FOND DU LAC

Fond du Lac, Wisconsin

www.fdl.uwc.edu/

Director of Admissions Ms. Linda A. Reiss, Director of Student Services, University of Wisconsin–Fond du Lac, 400 University Drive, Fond du Lac, WI 54935-2950. *Phone:* 920-929-3606. *E-mail:* bstrande@uwcmail.uwc.edu.

UNIVERSITY OF WISCONSIN–FOX VALLEY

Menasha, Wisconsin

www.uwfoxvalley.uwc.edu/

Director of Admissions Ms. Rhonda Uschan, Director of Student Services, University of Wisconsin–Fox Valley, 1478 Midway Road, Menasha, WI 54952. *Phone:* 920-832-2620. *Toll-free phone:* 888-INFOUWC. *E-mail:* foxinfo@uwc.edu.

UNIVERSITY OF WISCONSIN–MANITOWOC

Manitowoc, Wisconsin

www.manitowoc.uwc.edu/

- **State-supported** 2-year, founded 1935, part of University of Wisconsin System
- **Small-town** 50-acre campus with easy access to Milwaukee
- **Coed,** 643 undergraduate students

Undergraduates Students come from 3 states and territories, 0.2% African American, 3% Asian American or Pacific Islander, 0.6% Hispanic American, 0.6% Native American, 0.6% international.

Freshmen *Admission:* 320 applied, 290 admitted.

Faculty *Total:* 40, 53% full-time, 55% with terminal degrees. *Student/faculty ratio:* 24:1.

Majors Liberal arts and sciences/liberal studies.

Academics *Calendar:* semesters. *Degree:* certificates and associate. *Special study options:* academic remediation for entering students, adult/continuing education programs, advanced placement credit, distance learning, off-campus study, part-time degree program, services for LD students, student-designed majors, summer session for credit.

Library 25,750 titles, 150 serial subscriptions, an OPAC.

Computers on Campus 50 computers available on campus for general student use. A campuswide network can be accessed from off campus. At least one staffed computer lab available.

Student Life *Housing:* college housing not available. *Activities and Organizations:* drama/theater group, student-run newspaper, choral group, Business Club, Drama Club, Music Club, Phi Kappa Theta, Environmental Awareness.

Athletics *Intercollegiate sports:* basketball M/W, golf M, tennis M/W, volleyball W. *Intramural sports:* rock climbing M/W.

Standardized Tests *Required:* SAT or ACT (for admission).

Costs (2005–06) *Tuition:* $166 per credit part-time; state resident $3977 full-time, $528 per credit part-time; nonresident $12,677 full-time, $528 per credit part-time. *Required fees:* $211 full-time, $9 per credit part-time, $9 per credit part-time.

Financial Aid Of all full-time matriculated undergraduates who enrolled in 2004, 650 Federal Work-Study jobs (averaging $2100).

Applying *Options:* electronic application, early admission. *Application fee:* $35. *Required:* high school transcript, minimum X GPA, ACT. *Required for some:* essay or personal statement, interview. *Notification:* continuous until 7/1 (freshmen), continuous until 7/1 (out-of-state freshmen).

Freshmen Application Contact Christopher Lewis, Assistant Campus Dean for Student Services, University of Wisconsin–Manitowoc, 705 Viebahn Street, Manitowoc, WI 54220-6699. *Phone:* 920-683-4708. *Fax:* 920-683-4776. *E-mail:* christopher.lewis@uwc.edu.

UNIVERSITY OF WISCONSIN– MARATHON COUNTY

Wausau, Wisconsin   www.uwmc.uwc.edu/

- **State-supported** 2-year, founded 1933, part of University of Wisconsin System
- **Small-town** 7-acre campus
- **Coed**

Undergraduates 883 full-time, 420 part-time. 0.7% African American, 7% Asian American or Pacific Islander, 0.8% Hispanic American, 0.5% Native American, 16% live on campus. *Retention:* 100% of 2003 full-time freshmen returned.

Faculty *Student/faculty ratio:* 24:1.

Academics *Calendar:* semesters. *Degree:* associate. *Special study options:* academic remediation for entering students, adult/continuing education programs, advanced placement credit, honors programs, off-campus study, part-time degree program, student-designed majors, study abroad, summer session for credit. *ROTC:* Army (c).

Student Life *Campus security:* 24-hour emergency response devices, controlled dormitory access.

Athletics Member NJCAA.

Standardized Tests *Required:* ACT (for admission).

Costs (2005–06) *Tuition:* state resident $4000 full-time, $175 per credit part-time; nonresident $13,000 full-time, $545 per credit part-time. *Room and board:* $3800. Room and board charges vary according to board plan.

Financial Aid Of all full-time matriculated undergraduates who enrolled in 2004, 650 Federal Work-Study jobs (averaging $2100).

Applying *Options:* common application, electronic application, early admission, deferred entrance. *Application fee:* $35. *Required for some:* interview. *Recommended:* minimum 2.0 GPA.

Director of Admissions Dr. Nolan Beck, Director of Student Services, University of Wisconsin–Marathon County, 518 South Seventh Avenue, Wausau, WI 54401-5396. *Phone:* 715-261-6238. *Toll-free phone:* 888-367-8962.

UNIVERSITY OF WISCONSIN– MARINETTE

Marinette, Wisconsin   www.uwc.edu/

- **State-supported** 2-year, founded 1965, part of University of Wisconsin System
- **Small-town** 36-acre campus
- **Endowment** $200,000
- **Coed**

Undergraduates 486 full-time. Students come from 2 states and territories, 16 other countries, 1% Asian American or Pacific Islander, 2% Hispanic American, 0.6% Native American, 6% international.

Faculty *Student/faculty ratio:* 21:1.

Academics *Calendar:* semesters. *Degree:* associate. *Special study options:* academic remediation for entering students, adult/continuing education programs, advanced placement credit, cooperative education, distance learning, English as a second language, independent study, internships, off-campus study, part-time degree program, services for LD students, summer session for credit.

Standardized Tests *Recommended:* SAT or ACT (for admission).

Financial Aid Of all full-time matriculated undergraduates who enrolled in 2004, 650 Federal Work-Study jobs (averaging $2100).

Applying *Options:* electronic application. *Application fee:* $35. *Required:* high school transcript.

Director of Admissions Ms. Cynthia M. Bailey, Director of Student Services, University of Wisconsin–Marinette, 750 West Bay Shore, Marinette, WI 54143-4299. *Phone:* 715-735-4301. *E-mail:* cbailey@uwc.edu.

UNIVERSITY OF WISCONSIN– MARSHFIELD/WOOD COUNTY

Marshfield, Wisconsin   marshfield.uwc.edu/

Director of Admissions Mr. Jeff Meece, Director of Student Services, University of Wisconsin–Marshfield/Wood County, 2000 West Fifth Street, Marshfield, WI 54449. *Phone:* 715-389-6500.

UNIVERSITY OF WISCONSIN–RICHLAND

Richland Center, Wisconsin   richland.uwc.edu/

- **State-supported** 2-year, founded 1967, part of University of Wisconsin System
- **Rural** 135-acre campus
- **Coed,** 464 undergraduate students, 67% full-time, 58% women, 42% men

Undergraduates 313 full-time, 151 part-time. Students come from 4 states and territories, 15 other countries, 1% are from out of state, 0.2% African American, 0.4% Asian American or Pacific Islander, 0.2% Hispanic American, 0.2% Native American, 4% international, 6% transferred in, 35% live on campus. *Retention:* 55% of 2003 full-time freshmen returned.

Freshmen *Admission:* 464 enrolled. *Test scores:* ACT scores over 18: 91%; ACT scores over 24: 19%.

Faculty *Total:* 26, 50% full-time, 35% with terminal degrees. *Student/faculty ratio:* 18:1.

Majors Biological and physical sciences; liberal arts and sciences/liberal studies.

Academics *Calendar:* semesters. *Degree:* associate. *Special study options:* academic remediation for entering students, adult/continuing education programs, advanced placement credit, distance learning, external degree program, independent study, off-campus study, part-time degree program, services for LD students, study abroad, summer session for credit.

Library Miller Memorial Library with 45,000 titles, 200 serial subscriptions, an OPAC, a Web page.

Computers on Campus 45 computers available on campus for general student use. A campuswide network can be accessed from off campus. Internet access, at least one staffed computer lab available.

Student Life *Housing Options:* coed. Campus housing is provided by a third party. *Activities and Organizations:* drama/theater group, student-run newspaper, choral group. *Student services:* personal/psychological counseling.

Athletics *Intercollegiate sports:* basketball M/W, volleyball W. *Intramural sports:* badminton M/W, basketball M/W, football M/W, golf M/W, racquetball M/W, swimming and diving M/W, table tennis M/W, tennis M/W, volleyball M/W.

Standardized Tests *Required:* SAT or ACT (for admission). *Recommended:* ACT (for admission).

Costs (2005–06) *Tuition:* state resident $4372 full-time, $182 per credit part-time; nonresident $13,072 full-time, $545 per credit part-time. *Required fees:* $395 full-time, $16 per credit part-time. *Room and board:* $4730; room only: $2990. Room and board charges vary according to board plan. *Payment plan:* installment. *Waivers:* senior citizens.

Financial Aid Of all full-time matriculated undergraduates who enrolled in 2004, 650 Federal Work-Study jobs (averaging $2100).

Applying *Options:* electronic application, early admission. *Application fee:* $35. *Required:* high school transcript. *Required for some:* letters of recommendation, interview. *Application deadlines:* rolling (freshmen), 9/1 (transfers). *Notification:* continuous until 9/1 (freshmen).

Freshmen Application Contact Mr. John Poole, Assistant Campus Dean, University of Wisconsin–Richland, 1200 Highway 14 West, Richland Center, WI 53581. *Phone:* 608-647-8422 Ext. 223. *Fax:* 608-647-6225. *E-mail:* jpoole@uwc.edu.

UNIVERSITY OF WISCONSIN– ROCK COUNTY

Janesville, Wisconsin   rock.uwc.edu/

- **State-supported** 2-year, founded 1966, part of University of Wisconsin System
- **Suburban** 50-acre campus with easy access to Milwaukee
- **Coed**

Undergraduates 751 full-time, 129 part-time. Students come from 10 states and territories, 4 other countries, 1% are from out of state, 11% transferred in.

Faculty *Student/faculty ratio:* 16:1.

Academics *Calendar:* semesters. *Degree:* certificates and associate. *Special study options:* academic remediation for entering students, adult/continuing education programs, advanced placement credit, distance learning, off-campus study, part-time degree program, services for LD students, summer session for credit.

Standardized Tests *Required:* ACT (for admission).

Financial Aid Of all full-time matriculated undergraduates who enrolled in 2004, 650 Federal Work-Study jobs (averaging $2100).

University of Wisconsin–Rock County (continued)

Applying *Options:* electronic application, deferred entrance. *Application fee:* $35. *Required:* high school transcript.

Freshmen Application Contact Ms. Donna Johnson, Program Manager, University of Wisconsin–Rock County, 2909 Kellogg Avenue, Janesville, WI 53456. *Phone:* 608-758-6523. *Toll-free phone:* 888-INFO-UWC.

UNIVERSITY OF WISCONSIN–SHEBOYGAN

Sheboygan, Wisconsin　　　　**www.sheboygan.uwc.edu/**

- **State-supported** 2-year, founded 1933, part of University of Wisconsin System
- **Small-town** 75-acre campus with easy access to Milwaukee
- **Coed**

Undergraduates Students come from 5 other countries, 1% African American, 6% Asian American or Pacific Islander, 3% Hispanic American, 0.5% Native American, 0.1% international.

Faculty *Student/faculty ratio:* 15:1.

Academics *Calendar:* semesters. *Degree:* associate. *Special study options:* academic remediation for entering students, adult/continuing education programs, advanced placement credit, distance learning, English as a second language, independent study, off-campus study, part-time degree program, services for LD students, summer session for credit.

Student Life *Campus security:* 24-hour patrols by city police.

Athletics Member NJCAA.

Standardized Tests *Required:* ACT (for placement).

Financial Aid Of all full-time matriculated undergraduates who enrolled in 2004, 650 Federal Work-Study jobs (averaging $2100).

Applying *Options:* common application, electronic application. *Application fee:* $35. *Required:* high school transcript. *Required for some:* interview.

Director of Admissions Beth Raffaelli, Assistant Campus Dean for Student Services, University of Wisconsin–Sheboygan, One University Drive, Sheboygan, WI 53081-4789. *Phone:* 920-459-6633.

UNIVERSITY OF WISCONSIN–WASHINGTON COUNTY

West Bend, Wisconsin　　　　**www.washington.uwc.edu/**

- **State-supported** 2-year, founded 1968, part of University of Wisconsin System
- **Small-town** 87-acre campus with easy access to Milwaukee
- **Coed,** 951 undergraduate students, 70% full-time, 56% women, 44% men

Undergraduates 663 full-time, 288 part-time. Students come from 2 states and territories, 2 other countries, 1% are from out of state, 0.2% African American, 1% Hispanic American, 0.6% Native American, 7% transferred in.

Freshmen *Admission:* 708 applied, 477 admitted, 477 enrolled. *Test scores:* ACT scores over 18: 65%; ACT scores over 24: 26%; ACT scores over 30: 6%.

Faculty *Total:* 52, 56% full-time, 63% with terminal degrees. *Student/faculty ratio:* 21:1.

Majors Liberal arts and sciences/liberal studies.

Academics *Calendar:* semesters. *Degree:* associate. *Special study options:* academic remediation for entering students, advanced placement credit, distance learning, double majors, honors programs, independent study, off-campus study, part-time degree program, services for LD students, summer session for credit.

Library University of Wisconsin-Washington County Library with 46,429 titles, 247 serial subscriptions, 4,998 audiovisual materials, an OPAC, a Web page.

Computers on Campus 78 computers available on campus for general student use. A campuswide network can be accessed from off campus. Internet access, at least one staffed computer lab available.

Student Life *Housing:* college housing not available. *Activities and Organizations:* drama/theater group, student-run newspaper, choral group, Student Government Association, Business Club, Phi Theta Kappa, Writers' Guild, Student Impact. *Student services:* personal/psychological counseling.

Athletics Member NAIA. *Intercollegiate sports:* basketball M/W, golf M/W, soccer M/W, tennis M/W, volleyball W. *Intramural sports:* basketball M/W, football M/W, softball M/W, volleyball M/W.

Standardized Tests *Required:* SAT and SAT Subject Tests or ACT (for admission). *Recommended:* ACT (for admission).

Costs (2006–07) *Tuition:* state resident $4520 full-time, $190 per credit part-time; nonresident $11,700 full-time, $488 per credit part-time. *Required fees:* $268 full-time, $11 per credit part-time, $132 per term part-time.

Financial Aid Of all full-time matriculated undergraduates who enrolled in 2004, 650 Federal Work-Study jobs (averaging $2100).

Applying *Options:* electronic application, deferred entrance. *Application fee:* $35. *Required:* high school transcript. *Required for some:* essay or personal statement, letters of recommendation, interview. *Application deadline:* rolling (freshmen), rolling (transfers).

Freshmen Application Contact Mr. Dan Cebrario, Associate Director of Student Services, University of Wisconsin–Washington County, Student Services Office, 400 University Drive, West Bend, WI 53095. *Phone:* 262-335-5201. *Fax:* 262-335-5220. *E-mail:* dan.cibrario@uwc.edu.

UNIVERSITY OF WISCONSIN–WAUKESHA

Waukesha, Wisconsin　　　　**www.waukesha.uwc.edu/**

- **State-supported** 2-year, founded 1966, part of University of Wisconsin System
- **Suburban** 86-acre campus with easy access to Milwaukee
- **Coed,** 2,064 undergraduate students, 61% full-time, 50% women, 50% men

Undergraduates 1,258 full-time, 806 part-time. Students come from 5 states and territories, 1% are from out of state, 2% African American, 3% Asian American or Pacific Islander, 4% Hispanic American, 0.6% Native American, 0.1% international.

Freshmen *Admission:* 1,886 applied, 1,254 admitted.

Faculty *Total:* 93, 40% full-time, 55% with terminal degrees.

Majors Liberal arts and sciences/liberal studies.

Academics *Calendar:* semesters. *Degree:* associate. *Special study options:* academic remediation for entering students, adult/continuing education programs, advanced placement credit, honors programs, off-campus study, part-time degree program, services for LD students, student-designed majors, summer session for credit.

Library University of Wisconsin-Waukesha Library plus 1 other with 41,000 titles, 300 serial subscriptions.

Computers on Campus 90 computers available on campus for general student use. A campuswide network can be accessed. Internet access, at least one staffed computer lab available.

Student Life *Housing:* college housing not available. *Activities and Organizations:* drama/theater group, student-run newspaper, radio station, choral group, student government, Student Activities Committee, Campus Crusade, Phi Theta Kappa, Circle K. *Campus security:* late-night transport/escort service, part-time patrols by trained security personnel.

Athletics Member NJCAA. *Intercollegiate sports:* basketball M/W, golf M/W, soccer M/W, tennis M/W, volleyball W. *Intramural sports:* basketball M, bowling M/W, football M/W, skiing (downhill) M/W, table tennis M/W, volleyball M(c).

Standardized Tests *Required:* SAT or ACT (for admission). *Required for some:* SAT (for admission).

Costs (2005–06) *Tuition:* state resident $4210 full-time, $177 per credit part-time; nonresident $12,910 full-time, $540 per credit part-time.

Financial Aid Of all full-time matriculated undergraduates who enrolled in 2004, 650 Federal Work-Study jobs (averaging $2100).

Applying *Options:* early admission, deferred entrance. *Application fee:* $35. *Required:* high school transcript. *Required for some:* letters of recommendation. *Recommended:* interview. *Application deadline:* rolling (freshmen). *Notification:* continuous (freshmen).

Freshmen Application Contact Admissions, University of Wisconsin–Waukesha, 1500 North University Drive, Waukesha, WI 53188. *Phone:* 262-521-5200. *Fax:* 262-521-5491.

WAUKESHA COUNTY TECHNICAL COLLEGE

Pewaukee, Wisconsin　　　　**www.wctc.edu/**

- **State and locally supported** 2-year, founded 1923, part of Wisconsin Technical College System
- **Small-town** 137-acre campus with easy access to Milwaukee
- **Coed,** 6,386 undergraduate students, 25% full-time, 54% women, 46% men

Undergraduates 1,614 full-time, 4,772 part-time. Students come from 4 other countries, 4% African American, 2% Asian American or Pacific Islander, 4%

Hispanic American, 0.4% Native American.
Freshmen *Admission:* 746 enrolled.
Faculty *Total:* 837, 21% full-time. *Student/faculty ratio:* 8:1.
Majors Accounting; administrative assistant and secretarial science; architectural drafting and CAD/CADD; autobody/collision and repair technology; automobile/automotive mechanics technology; computer and information sciences and support services related; computer installation and repair technology; computer programming; computer systems analysis; computer systems networking and telecommunications; criminal justice/police science; dental hygiene; early childhood education; electrical, electronic and communications engineering technology; electrical/electronics drafting and CAD/CADD; electromechanical and instrumentation and maintenance technologies related; financial planning and services; fire protection and safety technology; graphic communications; graphic design; hospitality administration; interior design; manufacturing technology; marketing/marketing management; mechanical drafting and CAD/CADD; mental and social health services and allied professions related; multi-/interdisciplinary studies related; nursing (registered nurse training); operations management; restaurant, culinary, and catering management; retailing; surgical technology; teacher assistant/aide; telecommunications technology.
Academics *Calendar:* semesters. *Degree:* certificates, diplomas, and associate. *Special study options:* academic remediation for entering students, adult/continuing education programs, advanced placement credit, cooperative education, English as a second language, external degree program, part-time degree program, services for LD students, summer session for credit.
Computers on Campus 50 computers available on campus for general student use.
Student Life *Housing:* college housing not available. *Campus security:* patrols by police officers 8 a.m. to 10 p.m. *Student services:* health clinic.
Athletics Member NJCAA. *Intramural sports:* basketball M, bowling M/W, fencing W, football M, soccer M, tennis M/W(c), volleyball M.
Costs (2006–07) *Tuition:* state resident $2610 full-time, $87 per credit part-time; nonresident $16,089 full-time, $536 per credit part-time.
Financial Aid Of all full-time matriculated undergraduates who enrolled in 2004, 67 Federal Work-Study jobs (averaging $4000).
Applying *Options:* early admission. *Application fee:* $30. *Required:* high school transcript. *Required for some:* interview, varies. *Application deadline:* rolling (freshmen), rolling (transfers).
Freshmen Application Contact Lesley Frederick, Admission Recruitment and Enrollment Services Manager, Waukesha County Technical College, 800 Main Street, Pewaukee, WI 53072-4601. *Phone:* 262-691-5464. *Toll-free phone:* 888-892-WCTC. *Fax:* 262-695-3464. *E-mail:* lfrederick@wctc.edu.

WESTERN TECHNICAL COLLEGE
La Crosse, Wisconsin   www.wwtc.edu/

- **District-supported** 2-year, founded 1911, part of Wisconsin Technical College System
- **Urban** 10-acre campus
- **Coed,** 4,765 undergraduate students, 40% full-time, 57% women, 43% men

Undergraduates 1,910 full-time, 2,855 part-time. Students come from 4 states and territories, 7% are from out of state, 2% African American, 3% Asian American or Pacific Islander, 1% Hispanic American, 1% Native American, 2% live on campus.
Freshmen *Admission:* 3,443 applied, 1,221 admitted.
Faculty *Total:* 888, 23% full-time. *Student/faculty ratio:* 7:1.
Majors Accounting; administrative assistant and secretarial science; agricultural mechanization; architectural engineering technology; automobile/automotive mechanics technology; business administration and management; business administration, management and operations related; child care provision; child development; clinical/medical laboratory technology; commercial and advertising art; communications technologies and support services related; computer programming; consumer merchandising/retailing management; criminal justice/police science; data processing and data processing technology; dental hygiene; electrical, electronic and communications engineering technology; electromechanical technology; electroneurodiagnostic/electroencephalographic technology; fashion merchandising; finance; fire protection and safety technology; food services technology; health information/medical records technology; heating, air conditioning, ventilation and refrigeration maintenance technology; hospital and health care facilities administration; human resources management; interior design; legal assistant/paralegal; marketing/marketing management; mass communication/media; mechanical design technology; medical administrative assistant and medical secretary; nursing (registered nurse training); occupational therapy; office management; physical therapist assistant; precision production related; public health related; radiologic technology/science; respiratory care therapy; retailing; sales, distribution and marketing; surgical technology; system administration.

Academics *Calendar:* semesters. *Degree:* certificates, diplomas, and associate. *Special study options:* academic remediation for entering students, accelerated degree program, adult/continuing education programs, advanced placement credit, cooperative education, distance learning, English as a second language, external degree program, internships, off-campus study, part-time degree program, services for LD students, student-designed majors, summer session for credit.
Library Western Wisconsin Technical College Library plus 1 other with 31,243 titles, 313 serial subscriptions, 3,750 audiovisual materials, an OPAC.
Computers on Campus 800 computers available on campus for general student use. A campuswide network can be accessed from student residence rooms and from off campus. Internet access, online (class) registration, at least one staffed computer lab available.
Student Life *Housing Options:* coed. *Activities and Organizations:* student-run newspaper, Wisconsin Marketing Management Association (WMMA), Air Conditioning, Refrigeration Organization (ACRO), Multicultural Club, Business Professionals of America (BPA), Advertising Club. *Campus security:* 24-hour emergency response devices and patrols, student patrols, late-night transport/escort service, controlled dormitory access. *Student services:* personal/psychological counseling.
Athletics Member NJCAA. *Intercollegiate sports:* baseball M, basketball M/W, volleyball W. *Intramural sports:* basketball M/W, volleyball M/W.
Standardized Tests *Required for some:* ACT ASSET. *Recommended:* ACT (for admission).
Costs (2006–07) *Tuition:* state resident $2610 full-time, $87 per credit part-time; nonresident $16,089 full-time, $536 per credit part-time. *Required fees:* $185 full-time, $185 per term part-time. *Room and board:* room only: $2312.
Financial Aid Of all full-time matriculated undergraduates who enrolled in 2004, 102 Federal Work-Study jobs (averaging $1444).
Applying *Options:* common application, electronic application, early admission. *Application fee:* $30. *Required:* high school transcript. *Recommended:* interview. *Application deadline:* rolling (freshmen), rolling (transfers).
Freshmen Application Contact Ms. Jane Wells, Manager of Admissions, Registration and Records, Western Technical College, PO Box 908, La Crosse, WI 54602-0908. *Phone:* 608-785-9158. *Toll-free phone:* 800-322-9982 (in-state); 800-248-9982 (out-of-state). *Fax:* 608-785-9094. *E-mail:* mildes@wwtc.edu.

WISCONSIN INDIANHEAD TECHNICAL COLLEGE
Shell Lake, Wisconsin   www.witc.edu/

- **District-supported** 2-year, founded 1912, part of Wisconsin Technical College System
- **Urban** 113-acre campus
- **Endowment** $1.8 million
- **Coed,** 3,533 undergraduate students, 44% full-time, 61% women, 39% men

Undergraduates 1,561 full-time, 1,972 part-time. 0.3% African American, 0.8% Asian American or Pacific Islander, 0.6% Hispanic American, 3% Native American.
Freshmen *Admission:* 1,041 enrolled.
Faculty *Total:* 336, 43% full-time. *Student/faculty ratio:* 6:1.
Majors Accounting; administrative assistant and secretarial science; agricultural/farm supplies retailing and wholesaling; architectural engineering technology; business and personal/financial services marketing; business operations support and secretarial services related; child care and support services management; communications systems installation and repair technology; computer programming (specific applications); computer systems networking and telecommunications; corrections and criminal justice related; court reporting; criminal justice/police science; electromechanical technology; emergency medical technology (EMT paramedic); engineering technologies related; finance; heating, air conditioning and refrigeration technology; information technology; management information systems and services related; mechanical engineering/mechanical technology; medical administrative assistant and medical secretary; merchandising, sales, and marketing operations related (general); occupational therapy; quality control technology; retailing.
Academics *Calendar:* semesters. *Degree:* certificates, diplomas, and associate.
Applying *Application fee:* $35. *Application deadline:* rolling (freshmen).
Freshmen Application Contact Ms. Mimi Crandall, Dean, Student Services, Wisconsin Indianhead Technical College, 505 Pine Ridge Drive, Shell Lake, WI 54871. *Phone:* 715-468-2815 Ext. 2208. *Toll-free phone:* 800-243-9482. *Fax:* 719-468-2819. *E-mail:* mcrandal@witc.edu.

WYOMING

CASPER COLLEGE
Casper, Wyoming　　　　　　**www.caspercollege.edu/**

- **District-supported** 2-year, founded 1945, part of Wyoming Community College Commission
- **Small-town** 125-acre campus
- **Coed,** 4,285 undergraduate students, 44% full-time, 60% women, 40% men

Undergraduates 1,896 full-time, 2,389 part-time. Students come from 40 states and territories, 15 other countries, 8% are from out of state, 0.8% African American, 0.4% Asian American or Pacific Islander, 3% Hispanic American, 1% Native American, 0.9% international, 6% transferred in, 15% live on campus. *Retention:* 61% of 2003 full-time freshmen returned.
Freshmen *Admission:* 1,046 applied, 1,046 admitted, 664 enrolled. *Average high school GPA:* 3. *Test scores:* SAT verbal scores over 500: 50%; SAT math scores over 500: 40%; ACT scores over 18: 74%; SAT verbal scores over 600: 20%; ACT scores over 24: 20%; ACT scores over 30: 1%.
Faculty *Total:* 252, 61% full-time, 15% with terminal degrees. *Student/faculty ratio:* 14:1.
Majors Accounting; administrative assistant and secretarial science; agricultural business and management; agricultural mechanization; agriculture; airline pilot and flight crew; animal sciences; anthropology; applied art; art; automobile/automotive mechanics technology; biology/biological sciences; business administration and management; carpentry; ceramic arts and ceramics; chemistry; clinical laboratory science/medical technology; commercial and advertising art; computer programming; computer science; construction engineering technology; consumer merchandising/retailing management; corrections; criminal justice/law enforcement administration; criminal justice/police science; dance; data processing and data processing technology; drafting and design technology; dramatic/theater arts; economics; education; electrical, electronic and communications engineering technology; elementary education; emergency medical technology (EMT paramedic); engineering; English; fire science; French; geology/earth science; German; history; hospitality administration; industrial arts; Italian; journalism; kindergarten/preschool education; legal assistant/paralegal; liberal arts and sciences/liberal studies; machine tool technology; marketing/marketing management; mass communication/media; mathematics; music; music teacher education; nursing (registered nurse training); nutrition sciences; occupational therapy; pharmacy technician; photography; physical education teaching and coaching; physical sciences; physics; political science and government; psychology; respiratory care therapy; social sciences; social work; sociology; Spanish; speech and rhetoric; welding technology; wildlife and wildlands science and management; women's studies.
Academics *Calendar:* semesters. *Degree:* certificates and associate. *Special study options:* academic remediation for entering students, accelerated degree program, adult/continuing education programs, advanced placement credit, cooperative education, distance learning, English as a second language, independent study, internships, off-campus study, part-time degree program, services for LD students, summer session for credit. *ROTC:* Army (c).
Library Goodstein Library with 118,000 titles, 500 serial subscriptions, an OPAC, a Web page.
Computers on Campus 130 computers available on campus for general student use. A campuswide network can be accessed from student residence rooms. Internet access, online (class) registration, at least one staffed computer lab available.
Student Life *Housing Options:* coed. Campus housing is university owned. *Activities and Organizations:* drama/theater group, student-run newspaper, choral group, Student Senate, Student Activities Board, Agriculture Club, Theater Club, Phi Theta Kappa. *Campus security:* 24-hour patrols, late-night transport/escort service. *Student services:* health clinic, personal/psychological counseling, women's center.
Athletics Member NJCAA. *Intercollegiate sports:* basketball M(s)/W(s), cheerleading M/W, equestrian sports M/W, volleyball W(s). *Intramural sports:* badminton M/W, basketball M/W, bowling M/W, football M/W, golf M/W, racquetball M/W, soccer M/W, softball M/W, tennis M/W.
Costs (2006–07) *Tuition:* state resident $1416 full-time, $59 per credit part-time; nonresident $4272 full-time, $178 per credit part-time. *Required fees:* $168 full-time, $7 per credit part-time. *Room and board:* $3590.
Financial Aid Of all full-time matriculated undergraduates who enrolled in 2004, 104 Federal Work-Study jobs (averaging $1410).
Applying *Options:* electronic application, early admission. *Required:* high school transcript. *Application deadlines:* 8/15 (freshmen), 8/15 (transfers). *Notification:* continuous until 8/15 (freshmen).

Freshmen Application Contact Ms. Donna Hoffman, Admission Specialist, Casper College, 125 College Drive, Casper, WY 82601. *Phone:* 307-268-2458. *Toll-free phone:* 800-442-2963. *Fax:* 307-268-2611. *E-mail:* dhoffman@caspercollege.edu.

CENTRAL WYOMING COLLEGE
Riverton, Wyoming　　　　　　**www.cwc.edu/**

- **State and locally supported** 2-year, founded 1966, part of Wyoming Community College Commission
- **Small-town** 200-acre campus
- **Endowment** $3.9 million
- **Coed,** 1,637 undergraduate students, 43% full-time, 65% women, 35% men

Undergraduates 696 full-time, 941 part-time. Students come from 39 states and territories, 6 other countries, 4% are from out of state, 0.5% African American, 0.2% Asian American or Pacific Islander, 4% Hispanic American, 19% Native American, 2% international, 12% transferred in, 9% live on campus. *Retention:* 51% of 2003 full-time freshmen returned.
Freshmen *Admission:* 346 applied, 346 admitted, 242 enrolled. *Average high school GPA:* 3.10. *Test scores:* SAT verbal scores over 500: 55%; SAT math scores over 500: 67%; ACT scores over 18: 79%; SAT verbal scores over 600: 22%; SAT math scores over 600: 17%; ACT scores over 24: 24%; ACT scores over 30: 2%.
Faculty *Total:* 164, 25% full-time, 48% with terminal degrees. *Student/faculty ratio:* 14:1.
Majors Accounting; accounting technology and bookkeeping; acting; agribusiness; agricultural business and management; agriculture; American Indian/Native American studies; art; automobile/automotive mechanics technology; biology/biological sciences; business administration and management; business automation/technology/data entry; child care and support services management; computer science; computer systems networking and telecommunications; computer technology/computer systems technology; criminal justice/law enforcement administration; digital communication and media/multimedia; dramatic/theater arts; elementary education; English; environmental science; equestrian studies; general studies; horse husbandry/equine science and management; human services; management information systems; music; nursing (registered nurse training); parts, warehousing, and inventory management; physical sciences; pre-law studies; psychology; radio and television broadcasting technology; range science and management; secondary education; social sciences; surgical technology; theater design and technology; web page, digital/multimedia and information resources design; welding technology.
Academics *Calendar:* semesters. *Degree:* certificates and associate. *Special study options:* academic remediation for entering students, adult/continuing education programs, advanced placement credit, cooperative education, distance learning, English as a second language, honors programs, independent study, off-campus study, part-time degree program, services for LD students, student-designed majors, summer session for credit.
Library Central Wyoming College Library with 78,167 titles, 183 serial subscriptions, 1,256 audiovisual materials, an OPAC, a Web page.
Computers on Campus 323 computers available on campus for general student use. A campuswide network can be accessed from student residence rooms and from off campus. Internet access, online (class) registration, at least one staffed computer lab available.
Student Life *Housing Options:* coed. Campus housing is university owned. *Activities and Organizations:* drama/theater group, student-run newspaper, radio and television station, choral group, Multi-Cultural Club, La Vida Nueva Club, Fellowship of College Christians, Quality Leaders, Science Club. *Campus security:* 24-hour patrols. *Student services:* personal/psychological counseling.
Athletics *Intercollegiate sports:* equestrian sports M(s)/W(s). *Intramural sports:* badminton M/W, basketball M/W, football M/W, skiing (downhill) M/W, soccer M/W, softball M/W, swimming and diving M/W, table tennis M/W, tennis M/W, volleyball M/W, weight lifting M/W.
Costs (2006–07) *Tuition:* state resident $1416 full-time, $59 per credit part-time; nonresident $4272 full-time, $178 per credit part-time. *Required fees:* $528 full-time, $22 per credit part-time. *Room and board:* $3060; room only: $1460.
Financial Aid Of all full-time matriculated undergraduates who enrolled in 2004, 46 Federal Work-Study jobs (averaging $1337). *Financial aid deadline:* 6/30.
Applying *Options:* early admission, deferred entrance. *Recommended:* high school transcript. *Application deadline:* rolling (freshmen), rolling (transfers).
Freshmen Application Contact Mrs. Tami Shultz, Admissions Officer, Central Wyoming College, 2660 Peck Avenue, Riverton, WY 82501-2273. *Phone:* 307-855-2119. *Toll-free phone:* 800-735-8418 Ext. 2119. *Fax:* 307-855-2065. *E-mail:* admit@cwc.edu.

EASTERN WYOMING COLLEGE
Torrington, Wyoming
www.ewc.wy.edu/

- **State and locally supported** 2-year, founded 1948, part of Wyoming Community College Commission
- **Rural** 40-acre campus
- **Coed,** 1,346 undergraduate students, 39% full-time, 67% women, 33% men

Undergraduates 522 full-time, 824 part-time. Students come from 23 states and territories, 3 other countries, 26% are from out of state, 1% African American, 7% Hispanic American, 0.8% Native American, 0.8% international, 4% transferred in, 26% live on campus.
Freshmen *Admission:* 168 enrolled. *Average high school GPA:* 2.93.
Faculty *Total:* 105, 36% full-time, 11% with terminal degrees. *Student/faculty ratio:* 13:1.
Majors Accounting; administrative assistant and secretarial science; agribusiness; agricultural economics; agricultural teacher education; agriculture; animal sciences; art; biology/biological sciences; business administration and management; business teacher education; communication/speech communication and rhetoric; cosmetology; criminal justice/police science; criminal justice/safety; economics; elementary education; English; environmental biology; farm and ranch management; foreign languages and literatures; general studies; health/medical preparatory programs related; history; liberal arts and sciences/liberal studies; management information systems; mathematics; mathematics teacher education; music; music teacher education; office management; physical education teaching and coaching; political science and government; pre-dentistry studies; pre-medical studies; pre-pharmacy studies; pre-veterinary studies; psychology; range science and management; secondary education; sociology; statistics; veterinary/animal health technology; welding technology; wildlife and wildlands science and management.
Academics *Calendar:* semesters. *Degree:* certificates, diplomas, and associate. *Special study options:* academic remediation for entering students, accelerated degree program, adult/continuing education programs, advanced placement credit, cooperative education, distance learning, English as a second language, independent study, internships, part-time degree program, services for LD students, student-designed majors, summer session for credit.
Library Eastern Wyoming College Library with an OPAC, a Web page.
Computers on Campus 124 computers available on campus for general student use. A campuswide network can be accessed. Internet access, at least one staffed computer lab available.
Student Life *Housing Options:* coed, men-only, women-only. Campus housing is university owned. *Activities and Organizations:* drama/theater group, student-run newspaper, choral group, Criminal Justice Club, Veterinary Technology Club, Student Senate, Music Club, Rodeo Club. *Campus security:* 24-hour emergency response devices, controlled dormitory access. *Student services:* personal/psychological counseling.
Athletics Member NJCAA. *Intercollegiate sports:* basketball M(s), cheerleading M(s)/W(s), equestrian sports M(s)/W(s), golf M(s), volleyball W(s). *Intramural sports:* badminton M/W, basketball M/W, bowling M/W, football M, racquetball M/W, softball M/W, table tennis M/W, tennis M/W, volleyball M/W.
Costs (2006–07) *Tuition:* state resident $1416 full-time, $59 per credit hour part-time; nonresident $4272 full-time, $178 per credit hour part-time. *Required fees:* $384 full-time, $16 per credit hour part-time. *Room and board:* $3220; room only: $1364.
Financial Aid Of all full-time matriculated undergraduates who enrolled in 2004, 100 Federal Work-Study jobs (averaging $700). 60 state and other part-time jobs (averaging $700).
Applying *Options:* electronic application, early admission. *Recommended:* high school transcript. *Application deadline:* rolling (freshmen), rolling (transfers).
Freshmen Application Contact Mrs. Marilyn Cotant, Dean of Students, Eastern Wyoming College, 3200 West C Street, Torrington, WY 82240. *Phone:* 307-532-8257. *Toll-free phone:* 800-658-3195. *Fax:* 307-532-8222. *E-mail:* mcotant@ewc.wy.edu.

LARAMIE COUNTY COMMUNITY COLLEGE
Cheyenne, Wyoming
www.lccc.wy.edu/

- **State-supported** 2-year, founded 1968, part of Wyoming Community College Commission
- **Small-town** 270-acre campus
- **Endowment** $5.8 million
- **Coed,** 4,603 undergraduate students, 37% full-time, 61% women, 39% men

Undergraduates 1,704 full-time, 2,899 part-time. Students come from 40 states and territories, 14 other countries, 7% are from out of state, 2% African American, 1% Asian American or Pacific Islander, 7% Hispanic American, 0.6% Native American, 0.4% international, 4% transferred in, 2% live on campus.
Freshmen *Admission:* 1,561 applied, 1,561 admitted, 340 enrolled.
Faculty *Total:* 277, 32% full-time. *Student/faculty ratio:* 18:1.
Majors Accounting; agribusiness; agricultural business technology; agricultural production; agriculture; anthropology; art; autobody/collision and repair technology; automobile/automotive mechanics technology; biological and physical sciences; biology/biological sciences; business administration and management; business/commerce; business operations support and secretarial services related; carpentry; chemistry; civil engineering technology; communication/speech communication and rhetoric; computer and information sciences; computer and information sciences and support services related; computer hardware technology; computer programming; computer science; computer systems analysis; construction engineering technology; construction trades; construction trades related; corrections; criminal justice/law enforcement administration; customer service support/call center/teleservice operation; data modeling/warehousing and database administration; dental assisting; dental hygiene; diagnostic medical sonography and ultrasound technology; diesel mechanics technology; digital communication and media/multimedia; dramatic/theater arts; early childhood education; economics; education; education (specific levels and methods) related; engineering; engineering technology; English; entrepreneurship; equestrian studies; health/medical preparatory programs related; history; humanities; industrial radiologic technology; information technology; journalism; mass communication/media; mathematics; multi-/interdisciplinary studies related; music; nursing assistant/aide and patient care assistant; nursing (registered nurse training); philosophy; physical education teaching and coaching; political science and government; pre-dentistry studies; pre-engineering; pre-law studies; pre-medical studies; pre-pharmacy studies; pre-veterinary studies; psychology; public administration; radiologic technology/science; religious studies; social sciences; sociology; Spanish; visual and performing arts; web/multimedia management and webmaster; web page, digital/multimedia and information resources design; wildlife and wildlands science and management.
Academics *Calendar:* semesters. *Degree:* certificates and associate. *Special study options:* academic remediation for entering students, adult/continuing education programs, advanced placement credit, cooperative education, distance learning, double majors, English as a second language, honors programs, independent study, internships, off-campus study, part-time degree program, services for LD students, summer session for credit. *ROTC:* Air Force (c).
Library Laramie County Community College Library with 51,872 titles, 323 serial subscriptions, 31,514 audiovisual materials, an OPAC, a Web page.
Computers on Campus 720 computers available on campus for general student use. A campuswide network can be accessed from off campus. Internet access, online (class) registration, at least one staffed computer lab available.
Student Life *Housing Options:* coed. Campus housing is university owned. *Activities and Organizations:* drama/theater group, student-run newspaper, choral group, Block and Bridle Club, Phi Theta Kappa, music, Student Nurses Association, STAR Club. *Campus security:* 24-hour patrols, controlled dormitory access. *Student services:* personal/psychological counseling.
Athletics Member NJCAA. *Intercollegiate sports:* basketball M(s), cheerleading M(s)/W(s), soccer M(s)/W(s), volleyball W(s). *Intramural sports:* basketball M/W, golf M/W, racquetball M/W, rock climbing M/W, skiing (cross-country) M/W, soccer M/W, table tennis M/W, ultimate Frisbee M/W, volleyball M/W.
Costs (2006–07) *Tuition:* state resident $2004 full-time, $84 per credit hour part-time; nonresident $4860 full-time, $203 per credit hour part-time. *Required fees:* $25 per credit hour part-time. *Room and board:* $5024.
Applying *Options:* electronic application, early admission. *Application fee:* $20. *Required:* high school transcript. *Required for some:* interview. *Application deadline:* rolling (freshmen), rolling (transfers). *Notification:* continuous until 8/31 (freshmen).
Freshmen Application Contact Ms. Jenny Hargett, Assistant Director of Enrollment Management, Laramie County Community College, 1400 East College Drive, Cheyenne, WY 82007. *Phone:* 307-778-5222 Ext. 1117. *Toll-free phone:* 800-522-2993 Ext. 1357. *Fax:* 307-778-1360. *E-mail:* learnmore@lccc.wy.edu.

NORTHWEST COLLEGE

Powell, Wyoming www.northwestcollege.edu/

Freshmen Application Contact Assistant Director of Admissions, Northwest College, 231 West Sixth Street, Powell, WY 82435. *Phone:* 307-754-6043. *Toll-free phone:* 800-560-4692.

SHERIDAN COLLEGE–GILLETTE CAMPUS

Gillette, Wyoming

SHERIDAN COLLEGE–SHERIDAN AND GILLETTE

Sheridan, Wyoming www.sheridan.edu/

- **State and locally supported** 2-year, founded 1948, part of Wyoming Community College Commission
- **Small-town** 124-acre campus
- **Coed,** 2,895 undergraduate students, 36% full-time, 57% women, 43% men

Undergraduates 1,047 full-time, 1,848 part-time. Students come from 31 states and territories, 3 other countries, 9% are from out of state, 0.8% African American, 0.6% Asian American or Pacific Islander, 2% Hispanic American, 2% Native American, 0.5% international, 3% transferred in, 20% live on campus. Freshmen *Admission:* 329 admitted, 329 enrolled.

Faculty *Total:* 169, 45% full-time, 9% with terminal degrees. *Student/faculty ratio:* 14:1.

Majors Administrative assistant and secretarial science; agricultural business and management; agriculture; art; biological and physical sciences; biology/biological sciences; business administration and management; business/commerce; computer programming (specific applications); computer software and media applications related; computer systems networking and telecommunications; criminal justice/law enforcement administration; criminal justice/police science; data entry/microcomputer applications; dental hygiene; diesel mechanics technology; drafting and design technology; education; elementary education; engineering; engineering technology; English; foreign languages and literatures; general studies; health and physical education; heavy equipment maintenance technology; history; hospitality administration; humanities; information science/studies; liberal arts and sciences/liberal studies; machine tool technology; mathematics; music; nursing (registered nurse training); respiratory care therapy; sign language interpretation and translation; social sciences; system administration; web/multimedia management and webmaster; web page, digital/multimedia and information resources design; welding technology.

Academics *Calendar:* semesters. *Degree:* certificates and associate. *Special study options:* academic remediation for entering students, adult/continuing education programs, advanced placement credit, cooperative education, distance learning, double majors, English as a second language, independent study, internships, off-campus study, part-time degree program, services for LD students, student-designed majors, summer session for credit.

Library Griffith Memorial Library plus 1 other with 46,589 titles, 545 serial subscriptions, 17,122 audiovisual materials, an OPAC, a Web page.

Computers on Campus 200 computers available on campus for general student use. A campuswide network can be accessed from student residence rooms and from off campus. Internet access, at least one staffed computer lab available.

Student Life *Housing Options:* coed, women-only, disabled students. Campus housing is university owned. *Activities and Organizations:* drama/theater group, choral group, student government, Phi Theta Kappa, Art Club, Nursing Club, Police Science Club. *Campus security:* 24-hour emergency response devices, student patrols, controlled dormitory access, night patrols by certified officers. *Student services:* personal/psychological counseling.

Athletics Member NJCAA. *Intercollegiate sports:* basketball M(s)/W(s), volleyball W(s). *Intramural sports:* basketball M/W, bowling M/W, soccer M/W, softball M/W, table tennis M/W, tennis M/W, ultimate Frisbee M/W, volleyball M/W.

Costs (2006–07) *Tuition:* state resident $1416 full-time, $59 per credit hour part-time; nonresident $4248 full-time, $177 per credit hour part-time. *Required fees:* $480 full-time, $20 per credit hour part-time. *Room and board:* $3920.

Financial Aid Of all full-time matriculated undergraduates who enrolled in 2004, 59 Federal Work-Study jobs (averaging $912).

Applying *Options:* electronic application, early admission, deferred entrance. *Required for some:* high school transcript. *Recommended:* high school transcript. *Application deadline:* rolling (freshmen), rolling (transfers). *Notification:* continuous (freshmen).

Freshmen Application Contact Mr. Zane Garstad, Director of Admissions, Sheridan College–Sheridan and Gillette, PO Box 1500, Sheridan, WY 82801-1500. *Phone:* 307-674-6446 Ext. 2002. *Toll-free phone:* 800-913-9139 Ext. 2002. *Fax:* 307-674-7205. *E-mail:* admissions@sheridan.edu.

WESTERN WYOMING COMMUNITY COLLEGE

Rock Springs, Wyoming www.wwcc.wy.edu

- **State and locally supported** 2-year, founded 1959
- **Small-town** 10-acre campus
- **Endowment** $6.0 million
- **Coed**

Undergraduates 1,099 full-time, 1,555 part-time. Students come from 12 states and territories, 17 other countries, 7% are from out of state, 0.6% African American, 0.5% Asian American or Pacific Islander, 7% Hispanic American, 0.8% Native American, 3% international, 3% transferred in, 13% live on campus. *Retention:* 47% of 2003 full-time freshmen returned.

Faculty *Student/faculty ratio:* 17:1.

Academics *Calendar:* semesters. *Degree:* certificates, diplomas, and associate. *Special study options:* academic remediation for entering students, adult/continuing education programs, advanced placement credit, cooperative education, distance learning, English as a second language, freshman honors college, honors programs, independent study, internships, part-time degree program, services for LD students, summer session for credit.

Student Life *Campus security:* 24-hour emergency response devices, late-night transport/escort service, controlled dormitory access, patrols by trained security personnel from 4 p.m. to 8 a.m., 24-hour patrols on weekends and holidays.

Athletics Member NJCAA.

Standardized Tests *Required:* ACT COMPASS (for placement). *Recommended:* SAT or ACT (for placement).

Costs (2005–06) *Tuition:* state resident $1658 full-time, $70 per credit hour part-time; nonresident $4418 full-time, $185 per credit hour part-time. Full-time tuition and fees vary according to reciprocity agreements. Part-time tuition and fees vary according to course load and reciprocity agreements. *Room and board:* $3033; room only: $1474. Room and board charges vary according to board plan and housing facility.

Financial Aid Of all full-time matriculated undergraduates who enrolled in 2004, 20 Federal Work-Study jobs (averaging $1500).

Applying *Options:* common application, electronic application, early admission, deferred entrance. *Required:* high school transcript.

Director of Admissions Ms. Laurie Watkins, Director of Admissions, Western Wyoming Community College, PO Box 428, 2500 College Drive, Rock Springs, WY 82902-0428. *Phone:* 307-382-1647. *Toll-free phone:* 800-226-1181. *E-mail:* lwatkins@wwcc.cc.wy.us.

WYOTECH

Laramie, Wyoming www.wyotech.com/

Director of Admissions Mr. Troy Chaney, Director of Admissions, WyoTech, 4373 North Third Street, Laramie, WY 82072-9519. *Phone:* 307-742-3776. *Toll-free phone:* 800-521-7158.

INTERNATIONAL

MARSHALL ISLANDS

COLLEGE OF THE MARSHALL ISLANDS
Majuro, Marshall Islands

MEXICO

WESTHILL UNIVERSITY
Sante Fe, Mexico

PALAU

PALAU COMMUNITY COLLEGE
Koror, Palau

- **Territory-supported** 2-year, founded 1969
- **Small-town** 30-acre campus
- **Endowment** $849,401
- **Coed,** 651 undergraduate students, 66% full-time, 57% women, 43% men

Undergraduates 431 full-time, 220 part-time. Students come from 1 other state, 100% Asian American or Pacific Islander, 20% live on campus.
Freshmen *Admission:* 228 applied, 156 admitted, 104 enrolled. *Average high school GPA:* 2.62.

Faculty *Total:* 45, 53% full-time, 2% with terminal degrees. *Student/faculty ratio:* 16:1.
Majors Accounting; administrative assistant and secretarial science; agriculture; automobile/automotive mechanics technology; business teacher education; carpentry; construction engineering technology; criminal justice/police science; education; electrical, electronic and communications engineering technology; hotel/motel administration; liberal arts and sciences/liberal studies; natural resources and conservation related; nursing (registered nurse training).
Academics *Calendar:* semesters. *Degree:* certificates and associate. *Special study options:* academic remediation for entering students, cooperative education, distance learning, double majors, English as a second language, internships, part-time degree program, summer session for credit.
Library Palau Community College Library with 15,101 titles, 666 serial subscriptions, 247 audiovisual materials, an OPAC.
Computers on Campus 52 computers available on campus for general student use.
Student Life *Housing:* on-campus residence required through sophomore year. *Options:* coed, men-only. *Activities and Organizations:* Yapese Student Organization, Chuukes Student Organization, Palauans Student Organization, Environmental Club, Writing Club. *Campus security:* late-night transport/escort service, evening patrols by trained security personnel. *Student services:* health clinic, personal/psychological counseling, legal services.
Athletics *Intramural sports:* baseball M, basketball M, softball M/W, table tennis M/W, volleyball M/W, weight lifting M, wrestling M.
Costs (2006–07) *Tuition:* area resident $1680 full-time; state resident $70 per credit part-time. *Required fees:* $460 full-time. *Room and board:* $2352; room only: $588.
Financial Aid Of all full-time matriculated undergraduates who enrolled in 2004, 200 Federal Work-Study jobs (averaging $200). *Financial aid deadline:* 6/30.
Applying *Options:* early admission, deferred entrance. *Application fee:* $10. *Required:* high school transcript, minimum 2.00 GPA. *Application deadlines:* 8/15 (freshmen), 8/1 (out-of-state freshmen), 8/15 (transfers). *Notification:* continuous (freshmen), continuous (out-of-state freshmen).
Freshmen Application Contact Ms. Dahlia Katosang, Director of Admissions and Financial Aid, Palau Community College, PO Box 9, Koror, PW 96940-0009, Palau. *Phone:* 680-488-2471 Ext. 233. *Fax:* 680-488-4468. *E-mail:* dahliapcc@palaunet.com.

SWITZERLAND

SCHILLER INTERNATIONAL UNIVERSITY
Engelberg, Switzerland   www.schiller-university.ch/

Freshmen Application Contact Ms. Annelies Muff, Administrative Assistant, Schiller International University, Hotel Europe, Dorfstrasse 40, Engelberg 6390, Switzerland. *Phone:* 41-41-639 74 74.

College
CLOSE-UPS

AMERICAN ACADEMY OF DRAMATIC ARTS
NEW YORK, NEW YORK, AND LOS ANGELES, CALIFORNIA

The American Academy of Dramatic Arts

The College and Its Mission

Founded in New York in 1884, the American Academy of Dramatic Arts (AADA) was the first school in the United States to provide a professional education for actors. Since 1974, the Academy has operated an additional campus in the Los Angeles area, making AADA the only degree granting conservatory for actors offering programs in both of the major centers of theatrical activity in the country. Now in its second century, the Academy remains dedicated to a single purpose: training actors. The love of acting, as an art and as an occupation, is the spirit that impels the school. For the serious, well-motivated student ready to make a commitment to acting and to concentrated professional training, the Academy offers more than a century of success; a well-balanced, carefully structured curriculum; and a vital, dedicated, and caring faculty. Academy training involves the student intellectually, physically, and emotionally. Designed for the individual, it stresses self-discovery and self-discipline. Underlying the training are the beliefs that an actor prepared to work on the stage has the best foundation for acting in any medium and that classroom learning must be put to the test in the practical arena of a theater. The soundness of this approach is reflected in the achievements of the alumni, a diverse body of professionals unmatched by the alumni of any other institution. (Performances by Academy alumni have received nominations for 72 Oscars, 58 Tonys, 205 Emmys, and 5 Kennedy Center Honorees.) The time spent at the Academy can be an important period of development for those who become professional actors as well as for those who eventually choose other paths. All students are expected to make a commitment to professionalism, excellence, and discipline while enrolled at the Academy. The American Academy of Dramatic Arts is a nonprofit educational institution, chartered in New York by the Board of Regents of the University of the State of New York. In New York the Academy is accredited by the Middle States Association of Colleges and Schools and in California by the Western Association of Schools and Colleges. Both schools are accredited by the National Association of Schools of Theatre.

Academic Programs

The Professional Training Program requires two years to complete. Students who meet the requirements of the program receive an associate degree. A third-year performance program is offered to selected graduates. Students who successfully complete this program earn the Certificate of Advanced Studies in Actor training.

The first year consists of two 12-week terms and one 6-week term, providing a total of 30 transferable college credits. Classes include acting, movement, voice and speech, vocal production, acting styles, and theater history. The primary goals of the first-year program are to achieve relaxed, free, and truthful use of oneself in imaginary circumstances; to gain awareness of the body in terms of alignment, flexibility, and strength; to develop an open, well-placed, and well-supported vocal tone; to acquire clearly articulated standard American speech; and to increase understanding of the historical and stylistic backgrounds of drama. Students may enter the first year in mid-September or late January for the course in Los Angeles; late October or early February for New York. Admission to the second year is by invitation. Selection is made on the basis of progress, potential, and readiness to benefit from advanced training, as evidenced by the quality of first-year classwork and examination play performances. The second year begins with advanced classwork designed to reinforce and build upon the learning experiences of the first year. Emphasis is gradually shifted to performance opportunities. Additional courses are given in fencing and stage makeup. The second-year course provides 30 transferable undergraduate credits. Workshops to deal with specific acting problems are set up as needed, and, toward the end of the second

year, seminars are scheduled to familiarize students with basic procedures for attaining professional employment. Upon completion of the second year, students graduate from the Professional Training Program with associate degrees. Admission to the third-year program, which emphasizes performance, is also by invitation. Students who undertake a third year of study become members of the Academy Company, the school's performance ensemble. Selection is based on the individual's potential and the overall concept of a balanced acting company. The practical development of the actor is continued through study, rehearsal, and performance of fully-produced plays in Academy theaters over a thirty-week period from late summer to late winter. Agents, casting directors, and other professional personnel are invited to see Academy Company productions, and counseling is offered to assist third-year students in launching professional careers. Students completing the third-year program earn an additional 30 college credits and are awarded a certificate. Guest speakers, including Academy alumni, from the professional world are regularly invited to the Academy to share insights with the students at special assemblies.

The Academy also offers a six-week summer conservatory for those who would like to begin to study, to refresh basic skills, or to test interest and ability in an environment of professional training. Classes begin shortly after the Fourth of July and are open to anyone of high school age or older. Teaching standards are identical to those of the Academy's degree and certificate programs.

Costs

In 2006–07, the cost of the full-time program is $16,900 for tuition and $500 for the general fee. (The general fee covers the cost of accident insurance, costume and production costs, use of the library, and student identification.) Students need to budget an additional $600 for purchasing books and scripts, dance attire for movement class, a makeup kit, and other expenses related to the training. The cost of housing varies. On the average, housing, food, transportation, and personal expenses can amount to approximately $11,000 to $13,000.

Financial Aid

The Academy makes every effort to assist students in need of financial aid. The Academy participates in various financial aid programs, including government administered grants, loans, and college work-study. Grant awards are determined by financial need. (Only United States citizens and permanent residents are eligible for government-sponsored aid programs.) Payment plans (for those eligible) assist students by extending the payment of tuition over a period of time. Scholarships, awarded on the basis of both need and merit, are available to qualified students, including a limited number of Trustee Awards to first-year students. New York City and Los Angeles offer numerous job opportunities for students desiring part-time employment, including on-campus employment (work-study).

Faculty

To achieve its objectives, the Academy requires that its faculty members be well trained in the various performing arts disciplines; seasoned by professional experience; mature, objective, and sympathetic in their relations with students; and exemplars of the commitment to excellence that the Academy hopes to instill in its students. In their own training, the Academy's faculty members represent all of the master teachers and significant systems and philosophies of the performing arts of the past half-century. Their professional experience is diversified, encompassing a variety of positions in film, television, and theater. In selecting faculty members to support its specialized programs, the Academy places more importance on an instructor's professional training and experience and teaching ability than on traditional academic credentials. The student-faculty ratio ranges from 16:1 in classroom instruction, to 4:1 or 3:1 in some performance situations.

Student Body Profile

Academy students reflect a wide diversity of backgrounds and geographical origin; they come from every region of the United States, from Canada, and from many other countries. Enrollment in 2005 was 310 in California and 302 in New York, with a combined average of 20 percent members of minority groups and 20 percent international students. Forty percent of the students are men. The average age of an entering Academy student is 22. Less than half of all first-year students come directly after high school; others enroll after a range of experiences, including college, military service, or other careers.

Student Activities

Students at the American Academy of Dramatic Arts are bonded by their love of acting. A common interest and the collaborative nature of the training contribute to genial social relations among the student body, and, accordingly, school-arranged activities are usually related to the performing arts. Academy students are frequently invited to attend all types of theatrical events for free or given the opportunity to purchase reduced-priced tickets. Every effort is made by the school to facilitate the cultural enrichment of the students.

Facilities and Resources

The Academy in New York is housed in a six-story building that is a registered New York City landmark. It includes classrooms, rehearsal studios, dance studios, a video studio, a student lounge, locker areas, and dressing rooms. A library, made possible by a grant from CBS, is a handsome facility, organized to serve the special research and study needs of the actor. Three theaters—a 160-seat proscenium theater, an intimate 160-seat thrust-stage theater, and a semiarena theater that seats 103—are used for classes, rehearsals, and productions. Production facilities include a prop department, a costume department, a scene shop, and a sound room.

After housing its West Coast operation in leased space in Pasadena for more than twenty-five years, the Academy purchased a campus in the heart of Hollywood and took residence in 2000. Situated on 2.25 acres adjacent to the historic Charlie Chaplin Studios, the new campus includes a theater, ample parking, a library, and spacious classrooms and studios.

In place of on-campus housing, AADA offers a variety of attractive off-campus options through special arrangements with local housing resources.

Location

Located in midtown Manhattan, the New York home of the Academy is within walking distance of the Grand Central and Pennsylvania train stations, the Port Authority bus terminal, and Broadway and off-Broadway theaters.

AADA Los Angeles is located in the center of the motion picture and television production capital of the world. The new campus is a short walk from Hollywood Boulevard and is surrounded by film and television production companies. The California Freeway system affords access to beaches, deserts, and mountains.

At each location, the training at the Academy is enhanced by the exciting variety of nearby cultural and recreational opportunities afforded by New York and Los Angeles.

Admission Requirements

AADA seeks talented and highly motivated applicants. An audition/interview is the cornerstone of the admission process. The overall policy is to admit individuals who seem both artistically and academically qualified to undertake a rigorous conservatory program of professional training. Readiness to benefit fully from such training is assessed in the audition/interview. Auditions, whether for entrance into the program in New York City or Los Angeles, may be held at either school. In addition, regional auditions are held annually in major cities in the United States, Canada, and London. The audition requires the performance of two contrasting,

memorized speeches (one comedic and one dramatic) from published plays (one period and one contemporary), the total performance time to be no more than 4 minutes. The audition appointment includes an interview. In the audition/interview, special attention is given to the quality of the applicant's instinctive emotional connection to the audition material. Since good listening is so fundamental to good acting, the auditioner notes how well the applicant listens in the "real world" context of the interview. Other criteria include sensitivity, sense of language, sense of humor, vitality, presence, vocal quality, cultural interests, a realistic sense of self, and the challenge involved in pursuing an acting career.

All entering students must hold a diploma from an accredited secondary school or its equivalent. Transcripts of all previous academic work must be submitted; previous college credits may not be transferred. High school seniors should submit SAT or ACT scores. Two letters of recommendation are required before an audition is scheduled. International students who are fluent in English are welcome to apply. AADA is approved for the training of veterans.

Application and Information

The Academy operates on a rolling admission basis, but early application is encouraged. There is a nonrefundable application fee of $50. Admission decisions are made within four weeks of the audition. Further information may be obtained from:

For AADA New York:
Karen Higginbotham
Director of Admissions
American Academy of Dramatic Arts
120 Madison Avenue
New York, New York 10016
Telephone: 212-686-0620
　　　　　　800-463-8990 (toll-free)
E-mail: admissions-ny@aada.org

For AADA Los Angeles:
Dan Justin
Director of Admissions
American Academy of Dramatic Arts
1336 North La Brea Avenue
Hollywood, California 90028
Telephone: 800-222-2867 (toll-free)
E-mail: admissions-ca@aada.org
World Wide Web: http://www.aada.org (both campuses)

Robert Redford presents fellow AADA alumnus Jason Robards with the Alumni Achievement Award at the Centennial Gala.

ANDREW COLLEGE
CUTHBERT, GEORGIA

The College and Its Mission

Founded in 1854, Andrew College is a small, two-year, residential college related to the United Methodist Church. Its mission is to provide an academically challenging liberal arts curriculum within a nurturing community. As a two-year, senior college–parallel, church-related college, Andrew exists to provide students with a better beginning to their college careers. Andrew specializes in the education of freshmen and sophomores.

For a quarter of a century, the Andrew College chapter of Phi Theta Kappa, the international honor society for two-year colleges, has won national recognition and was the number one chapter during five of those years. There are more than 1,000 chapters of Phi Theta Kappa, and no other chapter, in public or private institutions, has established a more impressive record. Andrew College seeks to achieve its goals by providing several advantages, many of which are unique to a small campus with a church-related environment: the opportunity for intellectual, social, and spiritual development; a professionally competent faculty that is dedicated to teaching; individual attention to students at all levels of operation within the College; a two-year curriculum that parallels that of four-year colleges and universities; a cultural enrichment program that encourages students to appreciate the arts; the opportunity to learn leisure-time skills that lead to the development of a healthy body; remediation in the basic skills; orientation experiences for successful adjustment to college life; academic advising; a student community committed to the earning of a college education; and cultural and academic resources for the community and churches in the area.

Andrew College is accredited by the Commission on Colleges of the Southern Association of Colleges and Schools (1866 Southern Lane, Decatur, Georgia 30033-4097; telephone: 404-679-4501) to award associate degrees. Andrew College is listed by the University Senate of the United Methodist Church.

Academic Programs

The academic program at Andrew College is specifically designed for freshman and sophomore students. The faculty members serve at Andrew because they enjoy teaching freshmen and sophomores. This attitude and expertise contribute significantly to the quality of education that students receive.

Andrew College offers programs that lead to advanced degrees in the arts and sciences. The College offers the Associate of Arts degree, the Associate of Science degree, and the Associate of Music degree. To be eligible for graduation, a student must have earned at least a 2.0 cumulative grade point average on the work attempted at Andrew College. All associate degrees have a core curriculum of liberal studies, including a required curriculum of essential skills, humanities/ fine arts, science/mathematics/technology, social science, and physical education. Each student must satisfactorily complete a course in religion or philosophy and satisfy Cultural Enrichment Program requirements. All students who graduate from Andrew College must demonstrate proficiency in computer and oral communication skills.

All students entering Andrew College are assigned a faculty adviser who assists students in all matters relating to their academic progress. Andrew College schedules free tutoring during each term for students who need extra help with their studies. Some students, including students on academic probation and those admitted on a conditional basis, are assigned to mandatory study and tutoring sessions. Enrichment seminars are offered in areas beyond those covered in regular class study. These courses provide students with a challenge to do in-depth study and carry institutional credit only. Andrew College offers a number of programs that assist students in reaching their educational potential. For a variety of reasons, some applicants to Andrew College may need to improve their academic skills in order to be successful in a full-time schedule of college-level courses. The Strategic Studies Program serves students who need to improve their academic skills before embarking on a full-time schedule of college-level courses. The program contains a selected schedule of college-level course work as well as other specially designed courses that provide intensive study and individual guidance at a pace that is compatible with the students' abilities. Tutorial assistance is provided.

Andrew College has established an intensive level of academic support services designed for and limited to specifically identified and accepted students with documented learning disabilities and/or attention deficit disorders. While the Focus Program supplements and complements the tutorial and advising services available to all students, it provides an additional level of professional assistance and monitoring to enhance the students' probability for success.

Andrew College offers an English as a Second Language (ESL) Program for students whose native language is not English and gives them a choice in the selection of the instructional program.

Through the Cultural Enrichment Program (CEP), Andrew College recognizes the fact that exposure to the cultural arts is an essential part of a liberal arts education. As a graduation requirement, all degree-seeking students must attend designated programs relating to the cultural arts during their enrollment.

Costs

Although Andrew College is a private college, an Andrew education is affordable. Tuition and fees for the 2006–07 academic year are $9814. Room and board are $6166 for the academic year. Books and supplies average $600 to $700 per academic year. Approximately $2300 per year should be allowed for other costs, including transportation and personal expenses.

Financial Aid

Approximately 90 percent of Andrew College students receive some type of federal or institutional aid. Students from Georgia are eligible for the Georgia Tuition Equalization Grant and may be eligible for the HOPE Scholarship. Scholarships are given for academic excellence, community service, intercollegiate sports, spiritual life, and programs such as chorus, art, drama, piano, photography, yearbook, and newspaper.

Every year, the Office of Admission holds a Scholarship Day program, where students who have a 3.0 GPA or above and at least a 1000 on the SAT I are invited to compete for academic scholarships. Up to four Margaret A. Pitts Scholarships (full tuition, room, and board scholarships) are awarded at the competition, along with other academic awards. Scholarships or loans may be awarded to students who are members of the United Methodist Church. Other churches, religious and community organizations, and fraternal or business groups may also sponsor financial awards. Government programs at the federal and state levels provide a variety of grants, low-interest educational loans, and work-study employment opportunities for students. Eligibility for many of these programs is based on need.

Faculty

The faculty at Andrew College is committed to the education of freshmen and sophomores. The success of the students at the next level and beyond is the focus of the faculty and the academic program at Andrew.

The College employs 29 full-time and 5 part-time faculty members. The student-faculty ratio varies each year but is maintained at or below 15:1, resulting in lively discussions, teacher-student interaction, and individual attention. The student-faculty ratio for 2003–04 was 13:1. Eight members of the full-time faculty hold doctoral degrees, two have terminal degrees in their field, and the remainder hold master's degrees in their area of specialty.

Student Body Profile

Andrew College has a diverse population of students from all over the world. Approximately 3 percent of the College population is international students from countries such as Japan, Nigeria, Trinidad, Mexico, Guatemala, and Korea. Based on figures from fall 2003, 80 percent of students were from Georgia, 10 percent were from Florida, 5 percent were from Alabama, and 2 percent were from other states.

The total student population in fall 2003 was 320 students. Ninety percent of Andrew College students live in a College residence hall. While most students transfer to schools in Georgia, graduates have chosen to transfer to schools as far away as New England or California.

Student Activities

The student life program at Andrew College is designed to promote activities and programs that are supportive of the College's aims and purposes. The first two years of college are critical for academic success; therefore, programs that support and enhance students' lives are very important.

Andrew College is committed to the idea that total education involves more than academic pursuit. Activities, including intramural recreation, student activities, religious activities, career and transfer services, student government, and residential and commuter student programs, are among the many programs offered. All freshman students are required to complete a student orientation program.

Informal recreation opportunities available to students include basketball, indoor and outdoor volleyball, racquetball, walleyball, weight training, and tennis. Formalized recreational opportunities exist under the umbrella of intramurals and include team and individual sports and exercise programs. Off-campus recreational opportunities are promoted throughout the year. A wide variety of student activities take place at Andrew. Many organizations and various offices of the College provide a diversity of programs. The Student Events and Activities (SEA) Board is the chief programming committee in the student life area and sponsors events such as Homecoming, major dances, movies, coffeehouse performers, speakers, and comedy acts. Student organizations at Andrew College offer many leadership opportunities and operate under the jurisdiction of the Student Development Committee. Such organizations include the Student Government Association, International Student Association, Phi Theta Kappa Honor Society, AndrewServes, and the Residence Hall Association.

Sports Andrew College maintains membership in the National Junior College Athletic Association and the Georgia Junior College Athletic Association. Andrew offers scholarships in all intercollegiate sports in which the College participates. Andrew participates competitively in baseball, cross-country, golf, and soccer for men and basketball, cross-country, fast-pitch softball, golf, and soccer for women.

Facilities and Resources

Pitts Library subscribes to more than 100 periodicals, five daily newspapers, and three weekly newspapers. These publications supplement the library's holdings and provide reading and sources for the students and faculty members. Library computers provide students with access to holdings at other libraries and access to the World Wide Web through the Internet. A substantial collection of audiovisual and microfilm materials is maintained. An attractive main reading room provides areas for individual study, and a special reference section supplies ample space for research work.

The Andrew College Interactive Distance Learning Center is located adjacent to the main reading room and contains videoconferencing and Web-based instructional program development facilities.

In 1999, the College completed construction of an athletic complex, which contains baseball, soccer, and softball fields. The Fort Residence Building was completed and ready for occupancy by 142 students in fall 2000. The Phyllis and Jack Jones Chapel was completed in September 2001.

Location

Andrew College is located in southwest Georgia in the town of Cuthbert. Cuthbert is the county seat of Randolph County, which has a total population of 8,000 people. The Cuthbert area is a safe, friendly community located 40 miles east of Albany, Georgia; 161 miles southwest of Atlanta; 60 miles south of Columbus, Georgia; and 30 miles east of Eufaula, Alabama. The weather year-round is ideally suited to the many recreational opportunities in the region. A championship state park golf course is located 20 minutes from the campus of Andrew College. Lake George is also 20 minutes away and provides an ideal place for fishing, boating, and waterskiing. Large cities and shopping malls are within 1 hour's drive. Providence Canyon, for hiking, picnicking, and nature watching, is only a 20-minute drive from the campus.

Admission Requirements

Andrew College admits applicants who demonstrate abilities that are necessary for successful completion of the program. Admission decisions are based on the applicant's previous academic record, test scores, recommendations, and, in some cases, a personal interview. Equal educational opportunities are offered to students regardless of race, color, religion, disability, gender, age, creed, or national origin.

Applicants may be admitted for any term. In order to ensure proper processing, all credentials should be on file in the Office of Admission approximately thirty days prior to semester registration. All applicants must submit the following materials: a completed application for admission, a $20 application fee, transcripts of high school (or GED) and/or college course work attempted, and scores from either the SAT or ACT. Transfer students who have successfully completed college-level courses in English and math need not submit SAT/ACT scores. In addition, applicants whose native language is not English must submit scores from the Test of English as a Foreign Language (TOEFL) or an acceptable score on an equivalent English language examination.

Admission to Andrew College is gained through an individual selection process. Minimum academic requirements for nonconditional acceptance include a high school diploma, graduation from an accredited high school, an evaluated high school GPA of 2.0 or better on a 4.0 scale, and SAT I scores of at least 460 on verbal and 430 on math or the ACT equivalent. Students not meeting the minimum academic requirements for nonconditional acceptance may be conditionally accepted but are required to take placement examinations prior to registering for their first semester.

Application and Information

A new student may enter Andrew College at the beginning of the fall, spring, and summer semesters. There is an application deadline set at two weeks prior to the registration date for each term.

For an application and further information about Andrew College, students should contact:

Office of Admission and Financial Aid
Andrew College
413 College Street
Cuthbert, Georgia 39840

Telephone: 800-664-9250 (toll-free)
Fax: 229-732-2176
E-mail: admissions@andrewcollege.edu
World Wide Web: http://www.andrewcollege.edu

APOLLO COLLEGE
TUCSON, ARIZONA

The College and Its Mission

Apollo College's mission is to educate individuals to become professionals competent to serve the needs of their communities, provide programs and courses for the development of a broad range of knowledge and skills needed for careers where trained employees are in demand, provide students with a foundation for lifelong learning in and out of their chosen field, and accommodate student needs with programs, locations, guidance, didactic instruction, hands-on training, and other opportunities to develop professional skills, understanding, and values.

The College opened its doors in 1976; today, 4,000 students are enrolled in sixteen programs in allied health. Apollo has developed partnerships with employers, and the Graduate Placement Department is recognized for high placement rates. The College carefully monitors trends and can move quickly to offer cutting-edge curriculum to meet the demand of employers.

Specially designed degree and diploma programs are based on class sizes of 15 to 24 students. The small classes and individual attention from first-rate instructors encourage lively interaction and allow students to get excellent, practical, hands-on experience. As the demand for better-educated workers continues to grow, so does Apollo College. Course offerings and campus sites are expanded to meet the needs of both students and employers across the United States.

In addition to Tucson, the College has campuses in Albuquerque, Boise, Mesa, Phoenix, Portland, and Spokane. Apollo College–Tucson and its programs are accredited or approved by the Accrediting Bureau of Health Education Schools, the U.S. Department of Education, the American Association of Medical Assistants (medical assistant program), and the Arizona State Board of Private Postsecondary Education.

Academic Programs

Each program prepares students for entry-level positions in the health and medical fields. Students must complete 24–36 academic credits, depending on the chosen program of study. Students may choose from the following programs: dental assistant, massage therapy, medical administrative assistant, medical assistant, medical billing and coding, medical laboratory technician, pharmacy technician, physical therapy technician, and veterinary assistant.

Financial Aid

Financial aid is available for those who qualify. The U.S. Department of Education has approved Apollo College as an eligible institution to provide access to the federal student aid programs. Students who are eligible for financial aid can apply for all federal grants and loans. State financial aid is also available. Once the student has selected a course of study, a financial aid officer reviews that student's individual financial situation and dependency status. Some aid can be used as additional funding for tuition, books, and tools.

Student Activities

The Tucson campus takes an active role in community service. Students participate in a variety of health-related activities, such as Alzheimer's screening exams, health fairs, wellness checks, AIDS walks, and, in the case of the veterinary assistant program, work with the Pima Animal Control Center. Internally, the campus student council coordinates a variety of events that raise funds for causes such as Katrina relief and aid to the needy.

Academic Facilities

The Tucson campus has high-tech equipment to support the training of each medical program, including specialized medical equipment, microscopes, electrocardiograph machines, autoclaves, anatomical charts, and an array of other laboratory and multifunctional equipment. A variety of audiovisual equipment as well as modem computers are available for instructional purposes. Administrative offices include the Admissions Department, the Financial Aid Department, the Placement Office, the Office of the Registrar, and the Director's Office.

Location

Tucson is one of the oldest towns in the United States, and it also blends the progress and innovation of a metropolitan community and the friendly, caring atmosphere of a small town. The city's rich cultural heritage centers around a unique blend of Native American, Spanish, Mexican, and Anglo American influences, and its natural beauty comes from the Sonoran Desert, the Santa Catalina Mountains, and 360 sunny days a year. Some of its more prolific industries include electronics and missile production and leisure and hospitality, and its unemployment rate falls below the national average.

Admission Requirements

The requirements to enroll include an interview with an admissions representative, the program director, and/or an instructional staff member; completion of an application for enrollment; evidence of meeting the program's educational requirements; an evaluation to determine eligibility for some programs; entrance exams; payment of a registration fee; acceptance of the application by the campus director, based on academic and personal qualifications; and official high school or college transcripts.

Application and Information

For more information, prospective students should contact:

Admissions Office
Apollo College
3550 North Oracle Road
Tucson, Arizona 85705
Telephone: 520-888-5885
Fax: 520-887-3005
World Wide Web: http://www.apollocollege.com

ARGOSY UNIVERSITY/DENVER

DENVER, COLORADO

The University and Its Mission

Argosy University is a private institution of higher education dedicated to providing high-quality professional education programs at doctoral, master's, baccalaureate, and associate degree levels, as well as continuing education to individuals who seek to advance their professional and personal lives. The University emphasizes programs in the behavioral sciences, business, education, and the health-care professions. A limited number of preprofessional programs and general education offerings are provided to permit students to prepare for entry into these professional fields. The programs of Argosy University are designed to instill the knowledge, skills, and ethical values of professional practice and to foster values of social responsibility in a supportive, learning-centered environment of mutual respect and professional excellence.

As one of thirteen Argosy University campuses and six extension sites nationwide, Argosy University/Denver provides students with a network of resources found at larger universities, including a career resources office, an academic resources center, and extensive information access for research. The Argosy University/Denver campus offers an educational environment that meets the needs of busy individuals, with convenient, flexible class schedules that enable students to earn a degree while fulfilling other responsibilities.

Argosy University is accredited by the Higher Learning Commission and is a member of the North Central Association (NCA) (30 North LaSalle Street, Suite 2400, Chicago, Illinois 60602; telephone: 800-621-7440; http://www.ncahlc.org).

Academic Programs

Argosy University/Denver offers associate degree programs in business management, criminal justice, medical assisting, and paralegal studies. Typically, associate degree programs are completed in one to two years.

The Associate of Applied Science in Business Management Degree Program equips graduates with skills and knowledge necessary to enter the contemporary world of business management. The curriculum reaches this objective through course work in management principles, technical business procedures, computer operations, and general education. The program prepares the graduate to fill any of a variety of entry-level management positions.

The Associate of Applied Science in Criminal Justice Degree Program is designed to prepare graduates for admission to law enforcement academies or for entry-level employment in law enforcement, corrections, investigations, or juvenile administration.

The Associate of Applied Science in Medical Assisting Degree Program prepares students to work in a health-care environment as part of a professional team dedicated to providing top-quality medical care. In support of this, the Argosy University faculty and staff members provide an educational environment in which the students develop their personal and technical skills to become dedicated, knowledgeable, and ethical caregivers demonstrating utmost respect and concern for the well being of the patients and families they serve. Medical assistants are trained to be multiskilled allied health-care professionals. Their responsibilities include patient care, laboratory testing, limited X ray, office management, and assisting the physician. Their versatility keeps them in high demand in clinics and doctors' offices.

The Associate of Applied Science in Paralegal Studies Degree Program is designed to prepare the student to work directly under the supervision of an attorney and perform general background work for a legal firm. The objective of the program is to train students in the many phases of paralegal responsibilities. Legal courses are supplemented with business, computer applications, and general education courses that ensure the student's versatility and productivity in the business environment.

Costs

Tuition information can be obtained from Argosy University/ Denver.

Financial Aid

A wide range of financial aid options is available to students who qualify. Argosy University/Denver offers access to federal aid programs, work-study, and merit-based awards. As a first step, students should complete the Free Application for Federal Student Aid (FAFSA). Prospective students can apply electronically at http://fafsa.ed.gov or at the campus. To receive consideration for the maximum amount of aid and ensure timely receipt of funds, it is best for students to submit their application promptly.

Faculty

The most outstanding aspect of the institution is the dedication of the faculty members and their ability to cultivate a supportive learning environment. From them, students learn to integrate formal knowledge with professional practice. Argosy University/ Denver faculty members believe that their primary roles are those of mentor, teacher, and co-learner. They are dedicated to training students to assume leadership roles within various health science fields. Students have access to faculty members and counseling with regard to course and program matters.

Student Activities

Argosy University/Denver offers a number of activities designed to involve students in experiences not normally available through academic courses. A student organization group meets with faculty and administration members regularly to discuss issues pertinent to the campus.

Facilities and Resources

Argosy University libraries provide such curriculum support and educational resources as current text materials, diagnostic training documents, reference materials and databases, journals and dissertations, and major and current titles in program areas. Argosy University provides an online public-access catalog encompassing library resources throughout the Argosy University system. Students have full remote access to their campus library's database, enabling them to study and conduct research at home. The available academic databases offer dissertation abstracts, academic journals, and professional periodicals. All library computers are Internet accessible. Software applications include Word, Excel, PowerPoint, SPSS, and various test-scoring programs. All electronic resources are Web based and therefore accessible from the library or home.

Location

Argosy University/Denver is conveniently located at 1200 Lincoln Street in Denver, Colorado. The 10-story downtown facility includes classrooms, computer labs, resource center with Internet access, student lounge, staff and faculty offices, and other amenities.

Admission Requirements

Students who have successfully completed a program of secondary education or the equivalent (GED) are eligible for admission to the health sciences programs. Entrance requirements include either an ACT composite score of 18 or above, a combined math and verbal SAT score of 850 or above, or a passing score on the Argosy University entrance exam. In addition, a minimum TOEFL score of 173 (computer version) or 500 (paper version) is required for applicants whose native language is not English or who have not graduated from an institution in which English is the language of instruction. All applicants must include a completed application form, the application fee, proof of high school graduation or successful completion of the GED test, official postsecondary transcripts, and SAT, ACT, or Argosy University exam scores. Additional materials are required prior to matriculation. Some programs have additional application requirements. An admissions representative can provide further detailed information.

Application and Information

Argosy University/Denver accepts students on a rolling admissions basis year-round, depending on availability of required courses. Applications for admission are available online or by contacting the campus, using the information listed in this description.

Argosy University/Denver
1200 Lincoln Street
Denver, Colorado 80203
Telephone: 303-248-2700
         866-431-5981 (toll-free)
E-mail: auadmissions@argosyu.edu
World Wide Web: http://www.argosyu.edu/pg

ARGOSY UNIVERSITY/ORANGE COUNTY

SANTA ANA, CALIFORNIA

The University and Its Mission

Argosy University is a private institution of higher education dedicated to providing high-quality professional education programs at doctoral, master's, baccalaureate, and associate degree levels, as well as continuing education to individuals who seek to advance their professional and personal lives. The University emphasizes programs in the behavioral sciences, business, education, and the health-care professions. A limited number of preprofessional programs and general education offerings are provided to permit students to prepare for entry into these professional fields. The programs of Argosy University are designed to instill the knowledge, skills, and ethical values of professional practice and to foster values of social responsibility in a supportive, learning-centered environment of mutual respect and professional excellence.

As one of thirteen Argosy University campuses and six extension sites nationwide, Argosy University/Orange County provides students with a network of resources found at larger universities, including a career resources office, an academic resources center, and extensive information access for research. The Argosy University/Orange County campus offers an educational environment that meets the needs of busy individuals, with convenient, flexible class schedules that enable students to earn a degree while fulfilling other responsibilities.

Argosy University is accredited by the Higher Learning Commission and is a member of the North Central Association (NCA) (30 North LaSalle Street, Suite 2400, Chicago, Illinois 60602; telephone: 800-621-7440; http://www.ncahlc.org).

Academic Programs

Argosy University/Orange County offers associate degree programs in business management, criminal justice, medical assisting, and paralegal studies. Typically, associate degree programs are completed in one to two years.

The Associate of Applied Science in Business Management Degree Program equips graduates with skills and knowledge necessary to enter the contemporary world of business management. The curriculum reaches this objective through course work in management principles, technical business procedures, computer operations, and general education. The program prepares the graduate to fill any of a variety of entry-level management positions.

The Associate of Applied Science in Criminal Justice Degree Program is designed to prepare graduates for admission to law enforcement academies or for entry-level employment in law enforcement, corrections, investigations, or juvenile administration.

The Associate of Applied Science in Medical Assisting Degree Program prepares students to work in a health-care environment as part of a professional team dedicated to providing top-quality medical care. In support of this, the Argosy University faculty and staff members provide an educational environment in which the students develop their personal and technical skills to become dedicated, knowledgeable, and ethical caregivers demonstrating utmost respect and concern for the well being of the patients and families they serve. Medical assistants are trained to be multiskilled allied health-care professionals. Their responsibilities include patient care, laboratory testing, limited X ray, office management, and assisting the physician. Their versatility keeps them in high demand in clinics and doctors' offices.

The Associate of Applied Science in Paralegal Degree Program is designed to prepare the student to work directly under the supervision of an attorney and perform general background work for a legal firm. The objective of the program is to train students in the many phases of paralegal responsibilities. Legal courses are supplemented with business, computer applications, and general education courses that ensure the student's versatility and productivity in the business environment.

Costs

Tuition information can be obtained from Argosy University/Orange County.

Financial Aid

A wide range of financial aid options is available to students who qualify. Argosy University/Orange County offers access to federal aid programs, work-study, and merit-based awards. As a first step, students should complete the Free Application for Federal Student Aid (FAFSA). Prospective students can apply electronically at http://fafsa.ed.gov or at the campus. To receive consideration for the maximum amount of aid and ensure timely receipt of funds, it is best for students to submit their application promptly.

Faculty

The most outstanding aspect of the institution is the dedication of the faculty members and their ability to cultivate a supportive learning environment. From them, students learn to integrate formal knowledge with professional practice. Argosy University/Orange County faculty members believe that their primary roles are those of mentor, teacher, and co-learner. They are dedicated to training students to assume leadership roles within various health science fields. Students have access to faculty members and counseling with regard to course and program matters.

Student Activities

Argosy University/Orange County offers a number of activities designed to involve students in experiences not normally available through academic courses. A student organization group meets with faculty and administration members regularly to discuss issues pertinent to the campus.

Facilities and Resources

Argosy University libraries provide such curriculum support and educational resources as current text materials, diagnostic training documents, reference materials and databases, journals and dissertations, and major and current titles in program areas. Argosy University provides an online public-access catalog encompassing library resources throughout the Argosy University system. Students have full remote access to their campus library's database, enabling them to study and conduct research at home. The available academic databases offer dissertation abstracts, academic journals, and professional periodicals. All library computers are Internet accessible.

Software applications include Word, Excel, PowerPoint, SPSS, and various test-scoring programs. All electronic resources are Web based and therefore accessible from the library or home.

Location

Argosy University/Orange County is located approximately 30 miles south of downtown Los Angeles and 90 miles north of San Diego. Centered in the heart of Orange County, Argosy University/Orange County attracts students from southern California as well as from around the country and the world.

Argosy University/Orange County is the home of beautiful southern California weather and is located just a few miles from Disneyland. Whether it's ultra-chic Newport Beach, artsy Laguna Beach, or unspoiled Catalina Island, Orange County's oceanside personalities are as varied as the people who visit there. Regional parks and preserved lands provide visitors with hiking, biking, riding, and other recreational activities.

Admission Requirements

Students who have successfully completed a program of secondary education or the equivalent (GED) are eligible for admission to the health sciences programs. Entrance requirements include either an ACT composite score of 18 or above, a combined math and verbal SAT score of 850 or above, or a passing score on the Argosy University entrance exam. In addition, a minimum TOEFL score of 173 (computer version) or 500 (paper version) is required for applicants whose native language is not English or who have not graduated from an institution in which English is the language of instruction. All applicants must include a completed application form, the application fee, proof of high school graduation or successful completion of the GED test, official postsecondary transcripts, and SAT, ACT, or Argosy University exam scores. Additional materials are required prior to matriculation. Some programs have additional application requirements. An admissions representative can provide further detailed information.

Application and Information

Argosy University/Orange County accepts students on a rolling admissions basis year-round, depending on availability of required courses. Applications for admission are available online or by contacting the campus, using the information listed in this description.

Argosy University/Orange County
3501 West Sunflower Avenue, Suite 110
Santa Ana, California 92704
Telephone: 714-338-6200
800-716-9598 (toll-free)
E-mail: auadmissions@argosyu.edu
World Wide Web: http://www.argosyu.edu/pg

ARGOSY UNIVERSITY/SAN DIEGO

SAN DIEGO, CALIFORNIA

The University and Its Mission

Argosy University is a private institution of higher education dedicated to providing high-quality professional education programs at doctoral, master's, baccalaureate, and associate degree levels, as well as continuing education to individuals who seek to advance their professional and personal lives. The University emphasizes programs in the behavioral sciences, business, education, and the health-care professions. A limited number of preprofessional programs and general education offerings are provided to permit students to prepare for entry into these professional fields. The programs of Argosy University are designed to instill the knowledge, skills, and ethical values of professional practice and to foster values of social responsibility in a supportive, learning-centered environment of mutual respect and professional excellence.

As one of thirteen Argosy University campuses and six extension sites nationwide, Argosy University/San Diego provides students with a network of resources found at larger universities, including a career resources office, an academic resources center, and extensive information access for research. The Argosy University/San Diego campus offers an educational environment that meets the needs of busy individuals, with convenient, flexible class schedules that enable students to earn a degree while fulfilling other responsibilities.

Argosy University is accredited by the Higher Learning Commission and is a member of the North Central Association (NCA) (30 North LaSalle Street, Suite 2400, Chicago, Illinois 60602; telephone: 800-621-7440; http://www.ncahlc.org).

Academic Programs

Argosy University/San Diego offers associate degree programs in business management, criminal justice, medical assisting, and paralegal studies. Typically, associate degree programs are completed in one to two years.

The Associate of Applied Science in Business Management Degree Program equips graduates with skills and knowledge necessary to enter the contemporary world of business management. The curriculum reaches this objective through course work in management principles, technical business procedures, computer operations, and general education. The program prepares the graduate to fill any of a variety of entry-level management positions.

The Associate of Applied Science in Criminal Justice Degree Program is designed to prepare graduates for admission to law enforcement academies or for entry-level employment in law enforcement, corrections, investigations, or juvenile administration.

The Associate of Applied Science in Medical Assisting Degree Program prepares students to work in a health-care environment as part of a professional team dedicated to providing top-quality medical care. In support of this, the Argosy University faculty and staff members provide an educational environment in which the students develop their personal and technical skills to become dedicated, knowledgeable, and ethical caregivers demonstrating utmost respect and concern for the well being of the patients and families they serve. Medical assistants are trained to be multiskilled allied health-care professionals. Their responsibilities include patient care, laboratory testing, limited X ray, office management, and assisting the physician. Their versatility keeps them in high demand in clinics and doctors' offices.

The Associate of Applied Science in Paralegal Studies Degree Program is designed to prepare the student to work directly under the supervision of an attorney and perform general background work for a legal firm. The objective of the program is to train students in the many phases of paralegal responsibilities. Legal courses are supplemented with business, computer applications, and general education courses that ensure the student's versatility and productivity in the business environment.

Costs

Tuition information can be obtained from Argosy University/San Diego.

Financial Aid

A wide range of financial aid options is available to students who qualify. Argosy University/San Diego offers access to federal aid programs, work-study, and merit-based awards. As a first step, students should complete the Free Application for Federal Student Aid (FAFSA). Prospective students can apply electronically at http://fafsa.ed.gov or at the campus. To receive consideration for the maximum amount of aid and ensure timely receipt of funds, it is best for students to submit their application promptly.

Faculty

The most outstanding aspect of the institution is the dedication of the faculty members and their ability to cultivate a supportive learning environment. From them, students learn to integrate formal knowledge with professional practice. Argosy University/San Diego faculty members believe that their primary roles are those of mentor, teacher, and co-learner. They are dedicated to training students to assume leadership roles within various health science fields. Students have access to faculty members and counseling with regard to course and program matters.

Student Activities

Argosy University/San Diego offers a number of activities designed to involve students in experiences not normally available through academic courses. A student organization group meets with faculty and administration members regularly to discuss issues pertinent to the campus.

Facilities and Resources

Argosy University libraries provide such curriculum support and educational resources as current text materials, diagnostic training documents, reference materials and databases, journals and dissertations, and major and current titles in program areas. Argosy University provides an online public-access catalog encompassing library resources throughout the Argosy University system. Students have full remote access to their campus library's database, enabling them to study and conduct research at home. The available academic databases offer dissertation abstracts, academic journals, and professional periodicals. All library computers are Internet accessible. Software applications include Word, Excel, PowerPoint, SPSS, and various test-scoring programs. All electronic resources are Web based and therefore accessible from the library or home.

Location

Argosy University/San Diego is conveniently located at 7650 Mission Valley Road in San Diego California. The facility includes classrooms, a library resource center, student lounge, staff and faculty offices, and other amenities.

Argosy University/San Diego is the home of beautiful southern California weather and is located just a few miles from Disneyland. Whether it's ultra-chic Newport Beach, artsy Laguna Beach, or unspoiled Catalina Island, San Diego's oceanside personalities are as varied as the people who visit there. Regional parks and preserved lands provide visitors with hiking, biking, riding, and other recreational activities.

Admission Requirements

Students who have successfully completed a program of secondary education or the equivalent (GED) are eligible for admission to the health sciences programs. Entrance requirements include either an ACT composite score of 18 or above, a combined math and verbal SAT score of 850 or above, or a passing score on the Argosy University entrance exam. In addition, a minimum TOEFL score of 173 (computer version) or 500 (paper version) is required for applicants whose native language is not English or who have not graduated from an institution in which English is the language of instruction. All applicants must include a completed application form, the application fee, proof of high school graduation or successful completion of the GED test, official postsecondary transcripts, and SAT, ACT, or Argosy University exam scores. Additional materials are required prior to matriculation. Some programs have additional application requirements. An admissions representative can provide further detailed information.

Application and Information

Argosy University/San Diego accepts students on a rolling admissions basis year-round, depending on availability of required courses. Applications for admission are available online or by contacting the campus, using the information listed in this description.

Argosy University/San Diego
7650 Mission Valley Road
San Diego, California 92108
Telephone: 858-598-1900
          866-505-0333 (toll-free)
E-mail: auadmissions@argosyu.edu
World Wide Web: http://www.argosyu.edu/pg

ARGOSY UNIVERSITY/SANTA MONICA
SANTA MONICA, CALIFORNIA

The University and Its Mission

Argosy University is a private institution of higher education dedicated to providing high-quality professional education programs at doctoral, master's, baccalaureate, and associate degree levels, as well as continuing education to individuals who seek to advance their professional and personal lives. The University emphasizes programs in the behavioral sciences, business, education, and the health-care professions. A limited number of preprofessional programs and general education offerings are provided to permit students to prepare for entry into these professional fields. The programs of Argosy University are designed to instill the knowledge, skills, and ethical values of professional practice and to foster values of social responsibility in a supportive, learning-centered environment of mutual respect and professional excellence.

As one of thirteen Argosy University campuses and six extension sites nationwide, Argosy University/Santa Monica provides students with a network of resources found at larger universities, including a career resources office, an academic resources center, and extensive information access for research. The Argosy University/Santa Monica campus offers an educational environment that meets the needs of busy individuals, with convenient, flexible class schedules that enable students to earn a degree while fulfilling other responsibilities.

Argosy University is accredited by the Higher Learning Commission and is a member of the North Central Association (NCA) (30 North LaSalle Street, Suite 2400, Chicago, Illinois 60602; telephone: 800-621-7440; http://www.ncahlc.org).

Academic Programs

Argosy University/Santa Monica offers associate degree programs in business management, criminal justice, medical assisting, and paralegal studies. Typically, associate degree programs are completed in one to two years.

The Associate of Applied Science in Business Management Degree Program equips graduates with skills and knowledge necessary to enter the contemporary world of business management. The curriculum reaches this objective through course work in management principles, technical business procedures, computer operations, and general education. The program prepares the graduate to fill any of a variety of entry-level management positions.

The Associate of Applied Science in Criminal Justice Degree Program is designed to prepare graduates for admission to law enforcement academies or for entry-level employment in law enforcement, corrections, investigations, or juvenile administration.

The Associate of Applied Science in Medical Assisting Degree Program prepares students to work in a health-care environment as part of a professional team dedicated to providing top-quality medical care. In support of this, the Argosy University faculty and staff members provide an educational environment in which the students develop their personal and technical skills to become dedicated, knowledgeable, and ethical caregivers demonstrating utmost respect and concern for the well being of the patients and families they serve. Medical assistants are trained to be multiskilled allied health-care professionals. Their responsibilities include patient care, laboratory testing, limited X ray, office management, and assisting the physician. Their versatility keeps them in high demand in clinics and doctors' offices.

The Associate of Applied Science in Paralegal Studies Degree Program is designed to prepare the student to work directly under the supervision of an attorney and perform general background work for a legal firm. The objective of the program is to train students in the many phases of paralegal responsibilities. Legal courses are supplemented with business, computer applications, and general education courses that ensure the student's versatility and productivity in the business environment.

Costs

Tuition information can be obtained from Argosy University/Santa Monica.

Financial Aid

A wide range of financial aid options is available to students who qualify. Argosy University/Santa Monica offers access to federal aid programs, work-study, and merit-based awards. As a first step, students should complete the Free Application for Federal Student Aid (FAFSA). Prospective students can apply electronically at http://fafsa.ed.gov or at the campus. To receive consideration for the maximum amount of aid and ensure timely receipt of funds, it is best for students to submit their application promptly.

Faculty

The most outstanding aspect of the institution is the dedication of the faculty members and their ability to cultivate a supportive learning environment. From them, students learn to integrate formal knowledge with professional practice. Argosy University/Santa Monica faculty members believe that their primary roles are those of mentor, teacher, and co-learner. They are dedicated to training students to assume leadership roles within various health science fields. Students have access to faculty members and counseling with regard to course and program matters.

Student Activities

Argosy University/Santa Monica offers a number of activities designed to involve students in experiences not normally available through academic courses. A student organization group meets with faculty and administration members regularly to discuss issues pertinent to the campus.

Facilities and Resources

Argosy University libraries provide such curriculum support and educational resources as current text materials, diagnostic training documents, reference materials and databases, journals and dissertations, and major and current titles in program areas. Argosy University provides an online public-access catalog encompassing library resources throughout the Argosy University system. Students have full remote access to their campus library's database, enabling them to study and conduct research at home. The available academic databases offer dissertation abstracts, academic journals, and professional periodicals. All library computers are Internet accessible. Software applications include Word, Excel, PowerPoint, SPSS, and various test-scoring programs. All electronic resources are Web based and therefore accessible from the library or home.

Location

Argosy University/Santa Monica is conveniently located at 2900 31st Street in Santa Monica, California. The main facility covers approximately 107,000 square feet and houses classrooms, laboratories, offices, a student lounge, and a library.

Admission Requirements

Students who have successfully completed a program of secondary education or the equivalent (GED) are eligible for admission to the health sciences programs. Entrance requirements include either an ACT composite score of 18 or above, a combined math and verbal SAT score of 850 or above, or a passing score on the Argosy University entrance exam. In addition, a minimum TOEFL score of 173 (computer version) or 500 (paper version) is required for applicants whose native language is not English or who have not graduated from an institution in which English is the language of instruction. All applicants must include a completed application form, the application fee, proof of high school graduation or successful completion of the GED test, official postsecondary transcripts, and SAT, ACT, or Argosy University exam scores. Additional materials are required prior to matriculation. Some programs have additional application requirements. An admissions representative can provide further detailed information.

Application and Information

Argosy University/Santa Monica accepts students on a rolling admissions basis year-round, depending on availability of required courses. Applications for admission are available online or by contacting the campus, using the information listed in this description.

Argosy University/Santa Monica
2900 31st Street
Santa Monica, California 90405

Telephone: 310-866-4000
866-505-0332 (toll-free)
Fax: 310-399-1804
E-mail: auadmissions@argosyu.edu
World Wide Web: http://www.argosyu.edu/pg

ARGOSY UNIVERSITY/TWIN CITIES
College of Health Sciences
EAGAN, MINNESOTA

The University and Its Mission

Argosy University is a private institution of higher education dedicated to providing high-quality professional education programs at doctoral, master's, baccalaureate, and associate degree levels, as well as continuing education to individuals who seek to advance their professional and personal lives. The University emphasizes programs in the behavioral sciences, business, education, and the health-care professions. A limited number of preprofessional programs and general education offerings are provided to permit students to prepare for entry into these professional fields. The programs of Argosy University are designed to instill the knowledge, skills, and ethical values of professional practice and to foster values of social responsibility in a supportive, learning-centered environment of mutual respect and professional excellence.

As one of thirteen Argosy University campuses and six extension sites nationwide, Argosy University/Twin Cities provides students with a network of resources found at larger universities, including a career resources office, an academic resources center, and extensive information access for research. The Argosy University/Twin Cities campus offers an educational environment that meets the needs of busy individuals, with convenient, flexible class schedules that enable students to earn a degree while fulfilling other responsibilities.

Argosy University is accredited by the Higher Learning Commission of the North Central Association (NCA) (30 North LaSalle Street, Suite 2400, Chicago, Illinois 60602; telephone: 800-621-7440 (toll-free); Web site: http://www.ncahlc.org).

The Associate of Applied Science in Diagnostic Medical Sonography Degree Program is accredited by the Commission on Accreditation of Allied Health Education Programs on recommendation of the Joint Review Committee on Education in Diagnostic Medical Sonography (35 East Wacker Drive, Suite 1970, Chicago, Illinois 60601-2208; telephone: 312-553-9355).

The Associate of Applied Science in Histotechnology and the Associate of Science in Medical Laboratory Technology Degree Programs are accredited by the National Accrediting Agency for Clinical Laboratory Sciences (8410 West Bryn Mawr, Suite 670, Chicago, Illinois 60631; telephone: 773-714-8880).

The Associate of Applied Science in Medical Assisting Degree Program is accredited by the Commission on Accreditation of Allied Health Education Programs on recommendation of the Committee on Accreditation for Medical Assistant Education (35 East Wacker Drive, Suite 1970, Chicago, Illinois 60601-2208; telephone: 312-553-9355).

The Associate of Applied Science in Radiologic Technology and the Associate of Science in Radiation Therapy Degree Programs are accredited by the Joint Review Committee on Education in Radiologic Technology (20 North Wacker Drive, Suite 900, Chicago, Illinois 60606; telephone: 312-704-5300).

The Associate of Applied Science in Veterinary Technology Degree Program is accredited through the Council on Education of the American Veterinary Medical Association (1931 North Meachum Road, Suite 100, Schaumburg, Illinois 60173; telephone: 847-925-8070).

The Associate of Science in Dental Hygiene Degree Program is accredited by the Commission on Dental Accreditation (211 East Chicago Avenue, Chicago, Illinois 60611; telephone: 312-440-4653.) The commission is a specialized accrediting body recognized by the United States Department of Education.

The Associate of Science in Medical Laboratory Technology Degree Program is accredited by the National Accrediting Agency for Clinical Laboratory Sciences (8410 West Bryn Mawr, Suite 670, Chicago, Illinois 60631; telephone: 773-714-8880).

The Associate of Science in Radiation Therapy Degree Program is accredited by the Joint Review Committee on Education in Radiologic Technology (20 North Wacker Drive, Suite 900, Chicago, Illinois 60606, telephone: 312-704-5300).

Academic Programs

Argosy University/Twin Cities College of Health Sciences offers associate degree programs in dental hygiene, diagnostic medical sonography, histotechnology, medical assisting, medical laboratory technology, radiation therapy, radiologic technology, and veterinary technology. Typically, associate degree programs are completed in one to two years.

Costs

Tuition information can be obtained from Argosy University/ Twin Cities.

Financial Aid

A wide range of financial aid options is available to students who qualify. Argosy University/Twin Cities offers access to federal aid programs, work-study, and merit-based awards. As a first step, students should complete the Free Application for Federal Student Aid (FAFSA). Prospective students can apply electronically at http://fafsa.ed.gov or at the campus. To receive consideration for the maximum amount of aid and ensure timely receipt of funds, it is best for students to submit their application promptly.

Faculty

The most outstanding aspect of the institution is the dedication of the faculty members and their ability to cultivate a supportive learning environment. From them, students learn to integrate formal knowledge with professional practice. Argosy University/ Twin Cities faculty members believe that their primary roles are those of mentor, teacher, and co-learner. They are dedicated to training students to assume leadership roles within various health science fields. Students have access to faculty members and counseling with regard to course and program matters.

Student Activities

Argosy University/Twin Cities offers a number of activities designed to involve students in experiences not normally available through academic courses. A student organization group meets with faculty and administration members regularly to discuss issues pertinent to the campus.

Facilities and Resources

Argosy University libraries provide such curriculum support and educational resources as current text materials, diagnostic training documents, reference materials and databases, journals and dissertations, and major and current titles in program areas. Argosy University provides an online public-access catalog encompassing library resources throughout the Argosy University system. Students have full remote access to their campus library's database, enabling them to study and conduct research at home. The available academic databases offer dissertation abstracts, academic journals, and professional periodicals. All library computers are Internet accessible. Software applications include Word, Excel, PowerPoint, SPSS, and various test-scoring programs. All electronic resources are Web based and therefore accessible from the library or home.

Location

The new Argosy University/Twin Cities campus is in a convenient location, with easy freeway access and within 10 miles of the airport and the Mall of America. Located in a very pleasant suburban area that has many shops and restaurants and nearby housing, the new campus is in a parklike setting next to the new Eagan Community Center, which offers numerous amenities, including walking paths, a fitness center, meeting rooms, and an outdoor amphitheater.

The Twin Cities of Minneapolis and St. Paul have been rated as one of the most livable in the country. With a population of 2.5 million, the area offers an abundance of recreational opportunities. Year-round outdoor activities, nationally acclaimed theater and arts, music venues, and professional sports teams attract and inspire residents and visitors alike.

Admission Requirements

Students who have successfully completed a program of secondary education or the equivalent (GED) are eligible for admission to the health sciences programs. Entrance requirements include either an ACT composite score of 18 or above, a combined math and verbal SAT score of 850 or above, or a passing score on the Argosy University entrance exam. In addition, a minimum TOEFL score of 173 (computer version) or 500 (paper version) is required for applicants whose native language is not English or who have not graduated from an institution in which English is the language of instruction. All applicants must include a completed application form, the application fee, proof of high school graduation or successful completion of the GED test, official postsecondary transcripts, and SAT, ACT, or Argosy University exam scores. Additional materials are required prior to matriculation. Some programs have additional application requirements. An admissions representative can provide further detailed information.

Application and Information

Argosy University/Twin Cities accepts students on a rolling admissions basis year-round, depending on availability of required courses. Applications for admission are available online or by contacting the campus, using the information listed in this description.

Argosy University/Twin Cities
1515 Central Parkway
Eagan, Minnesota 55121
Telephone: 651-846-2882
          888-844-2004 (toll-free)
E-mail: auadmissions@argosyu.edu
World Wide Web: http://www.argosyu.edu/pg

THE ART INSTITUTE OF CHARLOTTE

CHARLOTTE, NORTH CAROLINA

The Institute and Its Mission

The Art Institute of Charlotte prepares students for entry-level employment in the creative arts. Students learn through programs of study that reflect the needs of a changing job market. Courses are taught by faculty members who have professional experience in their fields of expertise. The school offers five bachelor's degree programs and five associate degree programs.

Of all 2004 Art Institute of Charlotte graduates available for employment, 92.2 percent were working in a field related to their program of study within six months of graduation and earning an average salary of $26,782.

Student housing options include apartments that comfortably accommodate 4 students in two-bedroom, two-bath units complete with living room, dining area, and full kitchen. Students submit a roommate preference form and are assigned to apartments by the housing staff. The apartments are located close to The Art Institute of Charlotte and shopping, dining, and entertainment venues.

Services are available to assist students with resume writing, networking, and keeping aware of what employers are looking for in job applicants.

The school is accredited by the Accrediting Council for Independent Colleges and Schools (ACICS) and is licensed by the North Carolina Department of Community Colleges and the University of North Carolina Board of Governors.

Academic Programs

Bachelor's degree programs are available in culinary arts management, fashion marketing and management, graphic design, interactive media design, and interior design. Associate degree programs are available in culinary arts, fashion marketing, graphic design, interactive media design, and interior design. The school also offers certificate programs.

Costs

Tuition for the academic year 2006–07 is $23,232. Housing is $5580. Students are required to purchase a starting kit during their first year of study. Cost varies depending on the program.

Financial Aid

Financial aid is available to those who qualify. Financial aid programs are designed to supplement, rather than replace, a student's resources. Most financial aid is based on individual economic circumstances and is determined by analyzing the financial information provided by the student on the Free Application for Federal Student Aid (FAFSA) form.

Faculty

Faculty members at The Art Institute of Charlotte are experienced instructors, many of whom have professional experience outside of the classroom. There are 56 full-time and part-time faculty members. The student-faculty ratio is approximately 19:1.

Student Body Profile

There are more than 800 students attending the school. Students come to The Art Institute of Charlotte from throughout the southeastern United States and abroad. The student population includes recent high school graduates, transfer students, and those who have left a previous employment situation to study and train for a new career. Students are creative, competitive, and open to new ideas. They place great value on an education that prepares them for an exciting entry-level position in the arts.

Student Activities

Students enrolled in The Art Institute of Charlotte can get involved in student-led activities through the Student Affairs Department. Activities stimulate cultural awareness, creativity, and social and professional development. Students enrolled in the Interior Design program may join the Interior Design Student Association. In addition, academic departments regularly organize trips to the International Home Furnishing Market in High Point, North Carolina, as well as to local museums and galleries.

Facilities and Resources

The Art Institute of Charlotte facility has computer labs for student use. Additional computers are available in the library. Studios, classrooms, and meetings rooms are available for students and faculty members.

Location

Charlotte mixes the characteristics of a large urban center with the charm of suburban life. With a mild climate and central location, Charlotte residents are only 2 hours from the Blue Ridge Mountains and 3 hours from the Atlantic coast. Charlotte is known for its arts community, sports, shopping, and restaurants. More than 300 Fortune 500 companies have offices in Charlotte, the nation's second-largest banking center. The city is the nation's fifth-largest urban region, with 6.3 million people living within a 100-mile radius.

Admission Requirements

Applicants must be high school graduates or have a General Educational Development (GED) certificate. A 150-word written essay is required, as are high school transcripts and any records from other academic institu-

tions attended. All interested students are interviewed in person or over the phone. Following this interview, prospective students complete an application for admission and an enrollment fee. Applicants who have taken the SAT or ACT are encouraged to submit their scores to the Admissions Office for evaluation. There is a $50 application fee.

Application and Information

To obtain an application or make arrangements for an interview or tour of the school, prospective students should contact:

The Art Institute of Charlotte
Three LakePointe Plaza
2110 Water Ridge Parkway
Charlotte, North Carolina 28217-4536

Telephone: 704-357-8020
    800-872-4417 (toll-free)
Fax: 704-357-1133
E-mail: aichadm@aii.edu
World Wide Web: http://www.aich.artinstitutes.edu

The Art Institute of Atlanta®, GA; The Art Institute of California^{SM}–Inland Empire*; The Art Institute of California^{SM}–Los Angeles; The Art Institute of California^{SM}–Orange County; The Art Institute of California^{SM}–San Diego; The Art Institute of California^{SM}–San Francisco; The Art Institute of Charlotte®, NC; The Art Institute of Colorado® (Denver); The Art Institute of Dallas®, TX; The Art Institute of Fort Lauderdale®, FL; The Art Institute of Houston®, TX; The Art Institute of Indianapolis^{SM}, IN**; The Art Institute of Las Vegas®, NV; The Art Institute of New York City®, NY; The Art Institute of Ohio^{SM}–Cincinnati***; The Art Institute of Philadelphia®, PA; The Art Institute of Phoenix®, AZ; The Art Institute of Pittsburgh®, PA; The Art Institute of Portland®, OR; The Art Institute of Seattle®, WA; The Art Institute of Tampa^{SM}, FL, A branch of Miami International University of Art & Design; The Art Institute of Toronto^{SM}, ON; The Art Institute of Vancouver^{SM}, BC (Burnaby location, Downtown location, Dubrulle Culinary Arts location); The Art Institute of Washington® (Arlington, VA), A branch of The Art Institute of Atlanta, GA; The Art Institute Online^{SM}, A division of The Art Institute of Pittsburgh, PA; The Art Institutes International Minnesota^{SM} (Minneapolis); Bradley Academy for the Visual Arts^{SM} (York, PA); California Design College^{SM} (Wilshire Boulevard, Los Angeles); The Illinois Institute of Art®–Chicago; The Illinois Institute of Art®–Schaumburg; Miami International University of Art & Design^{SM}, FL; The New England Institute of Art^{SM} (Boston, MA).
*This institution has received temporary approval to operate from the Bureau for Private Postsecondary and Vocational Education (400 R Street, Suite 5000, Sacramento, CA 95814-6200, 916-445-3427, www.bppve.ca.gov) in order to enable the Bureau to conduct a quality inspection of the institution.
**The Art Institute of Indianapolis is licensed by the Indiana Commission on Proprietary Education, 302 West Washington Street, Room E201, Indianapolis, IN 46204, AC-0080.
***The Art Institute of Ohio–Cincinnati, 1011 Glendale-Milford Road, Cincinnati, OH 45215-1107, Reg. #04-01-1698B.

THE ART INSTITUTE OF NEW YORK CITY

NEW YORK, NEW YORK

The Institute and Its Mission

The Art Institute of New York City prepares students for entry-level employment in the creative arts. Students learn through programs of study that reflect the needs of a changing job market. Courses are taught by faculty members who have knowledge and experience in their fields of expertise.

Of all 2004 Art Institute of New York City graduates available for employment, 89.3 percent were working in a field related to their program of study within six months and earning an average salary of $24,407. In addition, assistance is available to help students with resume writing, networking, and keeping aware of what employers are looking for in job candidates.

The Art Institute of New York City is accredited by the Accrediting Council for Independent Colleges and Schools (ACICS).

Academic Programs

The Art Institute of New York City offers associate degree programs in culinary arts and restaurant management, fashion design, graphic design, interactive media design, interior design, and video production. Certificates are available in culinary arts, pastry arts, and restaurant management. Each academic program is offered on a year-round basis, allowing students to continue to work uninterrupted toward their degrees.

Costs

Tuition since November 2005 has been $441 per credit hour. There are additional supply costs that vary by program.

Financial Aid

Financial aid is available to those who qualify. The Art Institute of New York City participates in federal, state, and other financial aid programs. Financial aid is divided into grants, loans, and work-study. Students may be eligible for several loans, including the Federal Stafford Student Loan,

the Federal PLUS Program loan (parents), and the Creative Education Loan. Application deadlines and eligibility requirements vary.

Faculty

Faculty members at the The Art Institute of New York City are professionals, many of whom have experience in their respective fields. There are 98 full-time and part-time faculty members at the school. The student-faculty ratio is 16:1.

Student Body Profile

There are more than 1,470 students at the school. Students come to The Art Institute of New York City from throughout the United States and abroad. The student population includes recent high school graduates, transfer students, and those who have left a previous employment situation to study and train for a new career. Students are creative, competitive, and open to new ideas. They place great value on an education that prepares them for an exciting entry-level position in the arts.

Student Activities

There are several events for students throughout the year that celebrate culture, health, and holidays. The Student Activities Office also provides shape-up and wellness programs for students, along with The Art Institute of New York City Celebrates Women program. Students are offered many opportunities to volunteer throughout the year. Culinary students work at various events throughout the city as well as open-house programs at the school.

Facilities and Resources

The Art Institute of New York City occupies approximately 42,000 square feet of space at 75 Varick Street and 33,000 square feet at 11 Beach Street in the SoHo/Tribeca district of New York City.

Students study culinary techniques at the Varick Street location in nine kitchens that include ovens, broilers, food slicers, mixers, charcoal grills, stove tops, convection ovens, dishwashers, and refrigerators. The Art Institute of New York City restaurant, One Hudson Place, provides students with the opportunity to cook and serve in a professional setting. The Education Department is situated at the Varick Street location, as are library resources, facilities, and services that are shared with Metropolitan College.

The school's Beach Street location houses the Graphic Design, Interactive Media Design, Video Production, Interior Design, Advertising, and Fashion Design Departments. There are thirteen classrooms, four computer labs (two Macintosh computers and two PCs), two drawing studios (one for life drawing), and a dining room for wine seminars and service management classes. A large bookstore and an art gallery are located on the first floor. All lecture classes are housed at the Beach Street site, many in classrooms equipped with TV monitors, VCRs, and overhead projectors.

Location

The Art Institute of New York City is located in downtown Manhattan's SoHo/Tribeca area, a hub of contemporary style. SoHo is a focal point for individuals who appreciate and possess creative talents. West Broadway is the district's main thoroughfare, lined with avant-garde boutiques and trendsetting galleries, including a branch of the Guggenheim Museum, which exhibits both contemporary collec-

tions and selections from the museum's permanent collection. The New Museum of Contemporary Art is a major venue for innovative shows.

Admission Requirements

Applicants must complete an application form and complete a 150-word essay to apply for admission to The Art Institute of New York City. A personal interview with an admissions representative is required. Applicants must provide official high school transcripts, proof of successful completion of the General Educational Development (GED) test, or transcripts from any college previously attended. There is a $50 application fee.

Application and Information

To obtain an application or make arrangements for an interview or tour of the school, prospective students should contact:

The Art Institute of New York City
75 Varick Street, 16th Floor
New York, New York 10013-1917
Telephone: 212-226-5500
              800-654-2433 (toll-free)
Fax: 212-966-0706
World Wide Web: http://www.ainyc.artinstitutes.edu

The Art Institute of Atlanta®, GA; The Art Institute of California^{SM}–Inland Empire*; The Art Institute of California^{SM}–Los Angeles; The Art Institute of California^{SM}–Orange County; The Art Institute of California^{SM}–San Diego; The Art Institute of California^{SM}–San Francisco; The Art Institute of Charlotte®, NC; The Art Institute of Colorado® (Denver); The Art Institute of Dallas®, TX; The Art Institute of Fort Lauderdale®, FL; The Art Institute of Houston®, TX; The Art Institute of Indianapolis^{SM}, IN**; The Art Institute of Las Vegas®, NV; The Art Institute of New York City®, NY; The Art Institute of Ohio^{SM}–Cincinnati***; The Art Institute of Philadelphia®, PA; The Art Institute of Phoenix®, AZ; The Art Institute of Pittsburgh®, PA; The Art Institute of Portland®, OR; The Art Institute of Seattle®, WA; The Art Institute of Tampa^{SM}, FL, A branch of Miami International University of Art & Design; The Art Institute of Toronto^{SM}, ON; The Art Institute of Vancouver^{SM}, BC (Burnaby location, Downtown location, Dubrulle Culinary Arts location); The Art Institute of Washington® (Arlington, VA), A branch of The Art Institute of Atlanta, GA; The Art Institute Online^{SM}, A division of The Art Institute of Pittsburgh, PA; The Art Institutes International Minnesota^{SM} (Minneapolis); Bradley Academy for the Visual Arts^{SM} (York, PA); California Design College^{SM} (Wilshire Boulevard, Los Angeles); The Illinois Institute of Art®–Chicago; The Illinois Institute of Art®–Schaumburg; Miami International University of Art & Design^{SM}, FL; The New England Institute of Art^{SM} (Boston, MA).

*This institution has received temporary approval to operate from the Bureau for Private Postsecondary and Vocational Education (400 R Street, Suite 5000, Sacramento, CA 95814-6200, 916-445-3427, www.bppve.ca.gov) in order to enable the Bureau to conduct a quality inspection of the institution.
**The Art Institute of Indianapolis is licensed by the Indiana Commission on Proprietary Education, 302 West Washington Street, Room E201, Indianapolis, IN 46204, AC-0080.
***The Art Institute of Ohio–Cincinnati, 1011 Glendale-Milford Road, Cincinnati, OH 45215-1107, Reg. #04-01-1698B.

THE ART INSTITUTE OF OHIO–CINCINNATI

CINCINNATI, OHIO

The Art Institute of Ohio™-Cincinnati
One of The Art Institutes, America's Leader in Creative Education

The Institute and Its Mission

The Art Institute of Ohio–Cincinnati prepares students for entry-level employment in the creative arts. The school offers four associate degree programs.

The Art Institute of Ohio–Cincinnati includes more than 57,000 square feet of classroom, laboratory, and office space designed according to the school's specifications for its design programs. The school shares facility space with Brown Mackie College–Cincinnati campus.

The Art Institute of Ohio–Cincinnati provides students with convenient living accommodations. Students who choose school-sponsored housing share their living space with other students. The school is accessible by public transportation and provides ample student parking. Assistance is available to help students with resume writing, networking, and keeping aware of what employers are looking for in job candidates.

The Art Institute of Ohio–Cincinnati is accredited by the Accrediting Council for Independent Colleges and Schools (ACICS) to award the associate degree. ACICS is listed as a nationally recognized accrediting agency by the United States Department of Education (USDE). Its accreditation of degree-granting institutions also is recognized by the Council for Higher Education Accreditation (CHEA). The school is a branch of Brown Mackie College in Findlay, and the campus is approved under Chapter 3332 of the Ohio Revised Code for the offering of all programs by the State Board of Career Colleges and Schools. The Art Institute of Ohio–Cincinnati is a member of the Ohio Council of Private Colleges and Schools.

Academic Programs

Students attending The Art Institute of Ohio–Cincinnati may pursue an Associate of Applied Science degree in fashion marketing, graphic design, interactive media design, or interior design. Each program requires the successful completion of 96 credits.

Costs

Tuition costs vary by program. Prospective students should contact the school for current tuition costs. Other charges include a starting kit for all first-quarter students. Kits vary in price depending on the program of study.

Financial Aid

Financial aid is available for those who qualify. The Art Institute of Ohio–Cincinnati offers student financial planning. The goal of which is to structure affordable monthly payment plans so that students may concentrate on fulfilling their educational and career aspirations.

Available resources include federal and state aid, student loans from private lenders, and Federal Work-Study Program (FWS) opportunities, both on and off campus. Students seeking financial aid must complete the Free Application for Federal Student Aid (FAFSA). Application deadlines and eligibility requirements vary.

Faculty

The Art Institute of Ohio–Cincinnati's faculty members have experience in their fields and are committed to the academic and technical preparation of their students.

Student Body Profile

Students come to The Art Institute of Ohio–Cincinnati from throughout the United States. The student population includes recent high school graduates, transfer students, and those who have left a previous employment situation to study and train for a new career. Students are creative, competitive, and open to new ideas. They place great value on an education that prepares them for an exciting entry-level position in the arts.

Student Activities

Student life is an integral part of The Art Institute of Ohio–Cincinnati experience. The Office of Student Affairs sponsors a variety of events, including intramural sports, dances, parties, lunch-and-learn sessions, and off-campus trips.

Facilities and Resources

The Art Institute of Ohio–Cincinnati provides easy access to the technology, tools, and facilities needed to complete projects in all disciplines. Students may produce work in an environment that is appropriate for their chosen creative endeavors. The facilities include media presentation rooms for special instructional needs, libraries that provide instructional resources, and academic support for both faculty members and students.

Location

Cincinnati is home to major-league sporting events, concerts, a professional symphony, theater, Paramount's Kings Island, award-winning restaurants, and downtown entertainment districts that offer exciting nightlife.

The city is known for its great beauty with steep hills, wooded suburbs, a picturesque downtown riverfront, and four distinct seasons. Cincinnati is an affordable city in which to live and has been designated by *Fortune* magazine as one of the top ten places to live and work in the United States.

Admission Requirements

Applicants to The Art Institute of Ohio–Cincinnati must demonstrate proof of high school graduation or its equivalent. An official copy of the high school transcript or General Educational Development (GED) certificate is required. Candidates are interviewed and must write an essay on how an education at The Art Institute of Ohio–Cincinnati can help them reach their career goals.

Each applicant's academic transcript and completed essay is evaluated by the Admissions Acceptance Committee. A separate application and enrollment form must be completed and signed by the applicant and then submitted to The Art Institute of Ohio–Cincinnati. There is an application fee of $50.

Application and Information

To obtain an application or make arrangements for an interview or tour of the school, prospective students should contact:

The Art Institute of Ohio–Cincinnati
1011 Glendale-Milford Road
Cincinnati, Ohio 45215-1107
Telephone: 513-771-2821
               866-613-5184 (toll-free)
Fax: 877-477-8486 (toll-free)
World Wide Web: http://www.aioc.artinstitutes.edu

The Art Institute of Atlanta®, GA; The Art Institute of California^SM–Inland Empire*; The Art Institute of California^SM–Los Angeles; The Art Institute of California^SM–Orange County; The Art Institute of California^SM–San Diego; The Art Institute of California^SM–San Francisco; The Art Institute of Charlotte®, NC; The Art Institute of Colorado® (Denver); The Art Institute of Dallas®, TX; The Art Institute of Fort Lauderdale®, FL; The Art Institute of Houston®, TX; The Art Institute of Indianapolis^SM, IN**; The Art Institute of Las Vegas®, NV; The Art Institute of New York City®, NY; The Art Institute of Ohio^SM–Cincinnati***; The Art Institute of Philadelphia®, PA; The Art Institute of Phoenix®, AZ; The Art Institute of Pittsburgh®, PA; The Art Institute of Portland®, OR; The Art Institute of Seattle®, WA; The Art Institute of Tampa^SM, FL, A branch of Miami International University of Art & Design; The Art Institute of Toronto^SM, ON; The Art Institute of Vancouver^SM, BC (Burnaby location, Downtown location, Dubrulle Culinary Arts location); The Art Institute of Washington® (Arlington, VA), A branch of The Art Institute of Atlanta, GA; The Art Institute Online^SM, A division of The Art Institute of Pittsburgh, PA; The Art Institutes International Minnesota^SM (Minneapolis); Bradley Academy for the Visual Arts^SM (York, PA); California Design College^SM (Wilshire Boulevard, Los Angeles); The Illinois Institute of Art®–Chicago; The Illinois Institute of Art®–Schaumburg; Miami International University of Art & Design^SM, FL; The New England Institute of Art^SM (Boston, MA).
*This institution has received temporary approval to operate from the Bureau for Private Postsecondary and Vocational Education (400 R Street, Suite 5000, Sacramento, CA 95814-6200, 916-445-3427, www.bppve.ca.gov) in order to enable the Bureau to conduct a quality inspection of the institution.
**The Art Institute of Indianapolis is licensed by the Indiana Commission on Proprietary Education, 302 West Washington Street, Room E201, Indianapolis, IN 46204, AC-0080.
***The Art Institute of Ohio–Cincinnati, 1011 Glendale-Milford Road, Cincinnati, OH 45215-1107, Reg. #04-01-1698B.

THE ART INSTITUTE OF SEATTLE
SEATTLE, WASHINGTON

The Institute and Its Mission

The Art Institute of Seattle provides programs that prepare graduates for entry-level employment in the creative arts. Programs are developed with and taught by experienced educators. The Art Institute of Seattle has a proud history both as a part of the Seattle community and as a contributor to the Northwest's creative industries.

The school offers three bachelor's degree programs and eleven associate degree programs.

The Career Services Department works with students to refine their presentations to potential employers. The department also helps provide student advisers with insight into each student's specialized skills and interests. Specific career advising occurs during the last two quarters of a student's education. Interviewing techniques and resume-writing skills are developed, and students receive portfolio advising from faculty members. Of all 2004 Art Institute of Seattle graduates available for employment, 89 percent were working in a field related to their program of study within six months of graduation and earning an average salary of $27,303.

The Student Affairs Department offers a variety of services to students to help them make the most of their educational experience. These services include both school-sponsored and independent housing options.

The Art Institute of Seattle is accredited by the Northwest Commission on Colleges and Universities (NWCCU) and is licensed by the Washington Workforce Training and Education Coordinating Board. The Art Institute of Seattle is approved for the training of veterans and eligible veterans' dependents and is authorized to enroll nonimmigrant international students.

Academic Programs

The Art Institute of Seattle operates on a year-round, quarterly basis. Each quarter totals eleven weeks. Bachelor's degree programs are available in graphic design, interior design, and media arts and animation. Associate degrees are offered in animation art and design, audio production, culinary arts, fashion design, fashion marketing, graphic design, industrial design technology, interactive media design, interior design, photography, and video production. Diploma programs are available in the art of cooking, baking and pastry, digital design, and residential design.

Bachelor's degree programs are twelve quarters in length. Associate degree programs vary between six and nine quarters in length, and diploma programs require four quarters for completion.

Costs

Tuition costs vary by program. Prospective students should contact the school for current tuition costs. Other charges include a starting kit for all first-quarter students. Kits vary in price depending on the program of study.

Financial Aid

Financial aid is available for those who qualify. The school's student financial aid officers take a holistic approach to developing a financial plan to assist the student in meeting projected education costs.

Eligible students may apply for financial assistance under the various federal and state programs, including Federal Pell Grant, Federal Supplemental Educational Opportunity Grant (FSEOG), Federal Perkins Loan, Federal Stafford Student Loan (subsidized and unsubsidized), Federal Work-Study Program (FWS), Alaska State Student Loan, Federal PLUS Program (for parents), Washington State Need Grant, Vocational Rehabilitation Assistance, Veterans Administration benefits, and Bureau of Indian Affairs awards. Awards are based on individual need, the availability of funds, and the individual student's eligibility.

The Art Institute of Seattle offers scholarships based on merit, motivation, and financial need. Scholarships include the Advantage Grant Program award, The Art Institute of Seattle Excellence Award, The Art Institute of Seattle Scholarship Competition award, The Art Institute of Seattle Culinary Scholarship Competition award, the National Art Honor Society Scholarship, the Evelyn Keedy Memorial Scholarship, the VICA Skills USA Championship award, the Scholastic Arts Competition award, the HERO award, the IACP Foundation award, the C-Cap award, the ProStart award, the Technology Student Association Competition award, and the New York City Public Schools Scholarship Competition award. Application deadlines and eligibility requirements vary.

Faculty

Faculty members at The Art Institute of Seattle are experienced professionals, many of whom bring real-world knowledge into the classroom. There are 162 full-time and part-time faculty members. The student-faculty ratio is 19:1.

Student Body Profile

There are nearly 2,500 students at The Art Institute of Seattle. Students come to The Art Institute of Seattle from throughout the United States and abroad. The student population includes recent high school graduates, transfer students, and those who have left a previous employment situation to study and train for a new career. Students are creative, competitive, and open to new ideas. They place great value on an education that prepares them for an exciting entry-level position in the arts.

Student Activities

The Art Institute of Seattle places high importance on student life, both inside and outside the classroom. The school provides an environment that encourages involvement in a wide variety of activities, including clubs and organizations, community service opportunities, and various committees designed to enhance the quality of student life. Numerous all-school programs and events are planned throughout the year to meet students' needs.

Facilities and Resources

The Art Institute of Seattle is an urban campus that comprises three facilities. The school houses classrooms, audio and video studios, a student store, student lounges, copy centers, a gallery, a woodshop, a sculpture room, fashion display windows, a resource center, a technology center, and culinary facilities. The Art Institute of Seattle is also home to a public restaurant.

Location

The Art Institute of Seattle is located in the city's Belltown district. Founded by Native Americans and traders, the city has retained respect for its different cultures and customs. People from all over the world come to study, work, and live in this city, known for its friendly people and beautiful natural surroundings.

World-class companies, such as Microsoft, Boeing, Starbucks, Amazon.com, and Nordstrom, make their global headquarters in Seattle. As a gateway to the Pacific Rim, Seattle is a crossroads where creativity, technology, and business meet.

Admission Requirements

A student seeking admission to The Art Institute of Seattle is required to interview with an admissions representative (in person or over the phone). Applicants are required to have a high school diploma or a General Educational Development (GED) certificate and to submit an admissions application and an essay describing how an education at The Art Institute of Seattle may help the student to achieve creative goals. For advanced placement, additional information, including college transcripts, letters of recommendation, or portfolio work, may be required. Students may apply for admission online.

The Art Institute of Seattle follows a rolling admissions schedule. Students are encouraged to apply for their chosen quarter early so that they may take advantage of orientation activities. Students may apply up until the actual start date for any given quarter, depending on space availability. There is a $50 application fee.

Application and Information

To obtain an application or make arrangements for an interview or tour of the school, prospective students should contact:

The Art Institute of Seattle
2323 Elliott Avenue
Seattle, Washington 98121-1622
Telephone: 206-448-6600
　　　　　　800-275-2471 (toll-free)
Fax: 206-269-0275
World Wide Web: http://www.ais.edu

The Art Institute of Seattle's faculty members bring their professional experience into the classroom to create a collaborative, real-world learning environment.

The Art Institute of Atlanta®, GA; The Art Institute of California℠–Inland Empire*; The Art Institute of California℠–Los Angeles; The Art Institute of California℠–Orange County; The Art Institute of California℠–San Diego; The Art Institute of California℠–San Francisco; The Art Institute of Charlotte®, NC; The Art Institute of Colorado® (Denver); The Art Institute of Dallas®, TX; The Art Institute of Fort Lauderdale®, FL; The Art Institute of Houston®, TX; The Art Institute of Indianapolis℠, IN**; The Art Institute of Las Vegas®, NV; The Art Institute of New York City®, NY; The Art Institute of Ohio℠–Cincinnati***; The Art Institute of Philadelphia®, PA; The Art Institute of Phoenix®, AZ; The Art Institute of Pittsburgh®, PA; The Art Institute of Portland®, OR; The Art Institute of Seattle®, WA; The Art Institute of Tampa℠, FL, A branch of Miami International University of Art & Design; The Art Institute of Toronto℠, ON; The Art Institute of Vancouver℠, BC (Burnaby location, Downtown location, Dubrulle Culinary Arts location); The Art Institute of Washington® (Arlington, VA), A branch of The Art Institute of Atlanta, GA; The Art Institute Online℠, A division of The Art Institute of Pittsburgh, PA; The Art Institutes International Minnesota℠ (Minneapolis); Bradley Academy for the Visual Arts℠ (York, PA); California Design College℠ (Wilshire Boulevard, Los Angeles); The Illinois Institute of Art®–Chicago; The Illinois Institute of Art®–Schaumburg; Miami International University of Art & Design℠, FL; The New England Institute of Art℠ (Boston, MA).
*This institution has received temporary approval to operate from the Bureau for Private Postsecondary and Vocational Education (400 R Street, Suite 5000, Sacramento, CA 95814-6200, 916-445-3427, www.bppve.ca.gov) in order to enable the Bureau to conduct a quality inspection of the institution.
**The Art Institute of Indianapolis is licensed by the Indiana Commission on Proprietary Education, 302 West Washington Street, Room E201, Indianapolis, IN 46204, AC-0080.
***The Art Institute of Ohio–Cincinnati, 1011 Glendale-Milford Road, Cincinnati, OH 45215-1107, Reg. #04-01-1698B.

ATLANTIC CAPE COMMUNITY COLLEGE

MAYS LANDING, ATLANTIC CITY, AND CAPE MAY COUNTY, NEW JERSEY

The College and Its Mission

Founded in 1964, Atlantic Cape Community College (ACCC) held its first classes in fall 1966 in rented facilities in Atlantic City, New Jersey. In February 1968, the College moved to its present main campus location in Mays Landing, the Atlantic County seat. ACCC was the second community college organized in the state.

ACCC is a comprehensive, two-year public institution serving the residents of Atlantic and Cape May counties, enrolling more than 6,800 credit students. The College operates nationally recognized casino career and culinary arts programs and is a leader in online education. In addition to the College's main campus in Mays Landing, ACCC operates an extension center in Atlantic City and a full-service branch campus in Cape May County.

The Casino Career Institute (CCI), located at the Charles D. Worthington Atlantic City Center, was the first casino gaming school in the nation affiliated with a community college and the only licensed slot training school in New Jersey. Opened in 1978, CCI has trained more than 50,000 people for careers in the casino industry. It has provided training for members of several federal agencies and many state police forces as other jurisdictions prepare themselves for legalized gaming.

In 1981, as another extension of its role to train workers for the southern New Jersey hospitality industry, ACCC opened the Academy of Culinary Arts, a chefs training program that has graduated more than 2,500 students. The Academy of Culinary Arts has a full-time enrollment of nearly 300 students.

Academic Programs

ACCC offers nineteen transfer and career degree programs with twenty-five options and thirty-three professional series programs as well as noncredit professional development and customized training services. ACCC requires a minimum of 64 credits for its associate degrees.

Associate Degree Programs Associate in Arts degree programs are designed for students who wish to continue their education at a four-year college or university and pursue studies in the liberal arts, humanities, or social sciences. The A.A. degree requires a minimum of 45 credits in general education. One basic program of study in liberal arts is available, with options in business administration, child development/child care, communication, cultural studies, education, history, humanities, literature, performing arts, philosophy, psychology, social science, sociology, or studio art.

Associate in Science degrees are awarded to students who successfully complete programs that emphasize mathematics, the biological or physical sciences, and business programs intended as prebaccalaureate work. The A.S. degree requires a minimum of 30 credits in general education. Degree programs are available in business administration (with an option in economics), computer information systems, criminal justice (with an option in corrections), general studies, health sciences, paralegal studies, science and mathematics (with options in biology, chemistry, and mathematics), and social work.

Associate in Applied Science degree programs emphasize preparation for careers, typically at the technical or semiprofessional level. The A.A.S. degree requires a minimum of 20 credits in general education. Degree programs are available in accounting (with an option in accounting information systems), baking and pastry, business administration, computer programming, computer systems support (with options in microcomputer technologies and Web technologies), culinary arts, food service management, hospitality management, (with an option in travel and tourism), nursing, office systems technology, paralegal studies, and respiratory therapy.

In addition, ACCC offers a number of certificate programs to meet the short-term training needs of the local workforce.

The largest cooking school in New Jersey, the Academy of Culinary Arts, was founded in 1981 to meet the growing need for highly skilled chefs and food service professionals for the Atlantic City hospitality industry. Facilities include eight teaching kitchens with overhead mirrors, a bake shop, classrooms, computer lab, banquet room, pastry/baking retail store, and gourmet public restaurant.

The culinary arts program, including the option in baking and pastry, features hands-on and academic training and an externship program. Classes meet 5 hours a day, Monday through Friday, in a morning or afternoon session from January through May and August/September through December. Part-time evening courses are also available. As part of their training, students operate a gourmet restaurant on the College's campus. Specialized certificate programs are available in catering, food service management, hot foods, and baking and pastry.

The food service management program combines liberal arts classes, hands-on culinary training, and management-related courses in the specifics of the hospitality industry. The combination of front-of-the-house and back-of-the-house courses provides students with the broad-based knowledge of the industry that is key to succeeding in the field.

Off-Campus Programs

Cooperative education is an academic program that allows students to receive college credits for working in jobs related to their major while pursuing their studies at ACCC. A cooperative education component is required for the culinary arts program and is optional for office systems technology, criminal justice, and paralegal studies students.

ACCC, a leader in educational technology, now offers eleven associate degrees and several professional series programs online through distance education. The degree programs available through distance education are business administration (A.A.S. and A.S.), computer information systems (A.S.), general studies (A.S.), liberal arts (A.A., with options in business administration, history, humanities, literature, psychology, and social science), and office systems technology (A.A.S.). ACCC offers more than 150 online courses and has trained faculty members from colleges across New Jersey to use the technology for instruction. It hosts the New Jersey Virtual Community College Consortium (NJVCCC).

Costs

In 2006–07, full-time tuition and fees for Atlantic and Cape May County residents or out-of-county New Jersey residents with a chargeback is approximately $2400 per year. Part-time tuition is $79 per credit. Out-of-county New Jersey residents without a chargeback pay $158 per credit. Out-of-state and out-of-country residents pay $316 per credit.

The 2006–07 full-time tuition and fees for in-county and out-of-county students with a chargeback for the Academy of Culinary Arts are approximately $5600 per semester. Part-time culinary tuition is $237 per credit for Atlantic and Cape May County residents. Out-of-county New Jersey residents without a chargeback pay $316 per credit; out-of-state and out-of-country residents pay $434.55 per credit.

All on-campus students also pay required fees of $18 per credit. Culinary students pay an additional program fee of $230 per credit for applicable culinary courses only.

There are also mandatory accident, liability, and health insurance fees. Some classes require special lab or material costs or other fees.

Tuition for online courses is $96 per credit.

Financial Aid

About 65 percent of ACCC students who apply receive some form of financial aid, including scholarships, grants, loans, and work-study assistance. Funds are available from federal, state, and private sources for those with a demonstrated need or who meet eligibility requirements. All applicants for aid must complete the Free Application for Federal Student Aid (FAFSA), available online or from ACCC's financial aid office or most high school guidance offices.

Faculty

ACCC has 84 full-time and 242 part-time faculty members. Full-time faculty members hold master's degrees, and many also have doctoral degrees in their field of study. Most faculty members also serve as academic advisers. ACCC's student-faculty ratio is 26:1.

Student Body Profile

In fall 2005, there were 6,804 students at Atlantic Cape Community College. Atlantic County residents accounted for 73 percent of the student body; Cape May County residents accounted for 20 percent. Members of minority groups were as follows: Hispanic, 9.8 percent; Asian, 8.4 percent; Native American, 0.3 percent; and African American, 13.7 percent. International students made up 0.7 percent of the total. The average age of students was 27.

Student Activities

Every ACCC student is a member of the Student Government Association (SGA). The main policy-making body of the SGA is the Student Senate, which charters student clubs and organizations, approves budgets, determines student policy, and works with the faculty and administration to improve the College. There are numerous special interest clubs and organizations open to all students, including the *Atlantic Cape Review* (student newspaper), Art Club, Black Student Alliance, Computer Club, Criminal Justice Club, Cross-Cultural Student Association, Culinary Student Association, Future Teachers of America Club, International Club, Jewish Student Association, Latino Experience Club, Performing Arts Club, Phi Theta Kappa International Honor Society, *Rewrites* literary magazine, Shakespeare Club, Student Nurses Club, and WACC, Campus Radio.

ACCC sports include intercollegiate men's basketball, coed archery, and coed cheerleading; men's intramural soccer; and women's intramural baseball, basketball, and softball.

Facilities and Resources

ACCC's main campus is built around a quadrangle of lawn. The buildings, designed of split-face brick, natural cedar shakes, and tinted glass, are joined by a system of walkways. A central loop connects buildings and parking areas with the Black Horse Pike (Route 322). ACCC's indoor athletic facilities include a gymnasium with a seating capacity of 800 and a weight room with lockers and showers. Outdoor facilities include baseball, softball, and soccer fields; two basketball courts; a nature trail; and an archery range. ACCC's housing program assists culinary students who are not Atlantic or Cape May County residents in obtaining quality living arrangements in an off-campus setting. There is no on-campus housing available.

The College's cultural events are staged in a 460-seat theater located in Walter E. Edge Hall. The resources and facilities of the William Spangler Library are available to the College community and to the residents of Atlantic and Cape May counties. The library owns more than 89,000 books, audiocassettes, videocassettes, music CD's and art reproductions, as well as subscriptions to more than 300 periodicals. More than 200 videos are accessible from the College's video server. Twelve computer workstations and sixteen wireless laptops are available for student and faculty use in the library. Students have access to Science Direct, Dialog, EBSCO Host, Literature Resource Center, and LexisNexis (1,000 full-text journals); and the World Wide Web.

Location

Located on 541 acres in the picturesque New Jersey Pinelands, Atlantic Cape Community College is in Atlantic County, New Jersey, 17 miles west of Atlantic City's boardwalk, 45 miles from Philadelphia, and 115 miles from New York City. It operates an extension center in Atlantic City and a full-service branch campus in Cape May Court House, Cape May County.

Admission Requirements

Admission is available to all applicants who are 18 years of age and older, those who have graduated from an accredited secondary or preparatory school, and those with a state equivalency certificate. Applicants under 18 years of age not currently enrolled in a high school or not having a high school diploma or GED certificate may qualify for admission through special programs.

Admission to specific programs, such as culinary arts or nursing, is dependent upon students meeting the necessary program requirements and completing course prerequisites. A high school diploma is required for admission to these programs.

Application and Information

Applications are reviewed on a continuous basis. The preferred deadline for fall admission is July 1; for spring admission, November 1. There is a $35 application fee, which includes the cost of administering the placement test. Culinary applicants must pay an additional, nonrefundable $300 deposit. The deposit reserves a seat for a maximum of two semesters and is applied toward the semester tuition bill when the student registers. Seats are assigned on a first-come, first-served basis according to the completion of the steps toward admission.

For an application or additional information, students should contact:

Admissions Office
Atlantic Cape Community College
5100 Black Horse Pike
Mays Landing, New Jersey 08330-2699
Telephone: 609-343-5000
               800-645-CHEF (toll-free)
E-mail: accadmit@atlantic.edu
World Wide Web: http://www.atlantic.edu

The Academy of Culinary Arts, housed at Atlantic Cape Community College, is New Jersey's largest cooking school, with nearly 300 students.

BALTIMORE INTERNATIONAL COLLEGE
BALTIMORE, MARYLAND; VIRGINIA, COUNTY CAVAN, IRELAND

The College and Its Mission

The Baltimore International College, a regionally accredited, independent college, was founded in 1972 to provide students with the education and experience they need to pursue progressive careers within the international hospitality industry. The College is committed to providing students with the knowledge and ability necessary for employment and success in the hospitality industry.

In 1985, the College was authorized by the state of Maryland to grant associate degrees. In 1987, the Virginia Park Campus in Ireland was founded, enabling students to study under European chefs and hoteliers in a European environment. In 1996, the College was granted accreditation by the Commission on Higher Education of the Middle States Association of College and Schools. In 1998, the College was authorized by the state of Maryland to grant four-year baccalaureate degrees. In addition to classrooms, offices, and dorms, the College's campus in Baltimore includes a campus bookstore, a student union, a hotel, an inn, a restaurant, parking, student dining facilities, a Career Development Center, and a Learning Resource Center comprising a library, two academic computer labs, and an art gallery.

Freshman students who are single, under 21, and live farther than 50 miles from campus are required to live in student housing.

Academic Programs

The College provides a comprehensive curriculum, which includes an honors study abroad program at the Baltimore International College Virginia Park Campus near Dublin, Ireland.

The College's professional cooking program and the combined programs in professional cooking and baking and baking and pastry operate throughout the calendar year; new classes begin in the spring, summer, and fall. The College's business and management programs accept freshmen in the fall and spring semesters. The culinary arts certificate, which combines cooking and baking, and the certificate in professional marketing are available through evening classes and begin in the fall and spring semesters.

Associate Degree Programs Baltimore International College awards the associate degree in the following programs: professional baking and pastry, professional cooking, and professional cooking and baking. The associate degree is offered separately and as part of the 2+2 program at Baltimore International College. In the 2+2 program, students receive their two-year associate degree and then continue two additional years to complete the four-year bachelor's degree. Bachelor's degree programs require 125 to 133 credits.

To earn an associate degree in professional cooking, professional baking and pastry, or professional cooking and baking, the student must complete 62–66 credits. Certificate candidates must complete 54 credits. The certificate program concentrates on technical courses and is intended for students who already have a strong academic background. The associate degree program combines technical hands-on courses with general education courses such as nutrition, sanitation, psychology, English, and mathematics, as well as an internship or externship.

Off-Campus Programs

The honors program has been developed for qualified culinary arts and business and management majors. The honors program

is taught at the College's historic, 100-acre Virginia Park campus in County Cavan, Ireland. Culinary students who are selected for the honors program further enhance their skills in and knowledge of European cuisine, baking and pastry, and a la carte service. Business and management students selected for the honors program have the opportunity to learn the day-to-day operation of a hotel and restaurant, from reception to housekeeping and from restaurant management to accounting. Students fully enjoy the cross-cultural experience of living in an English-speaking foreign country.

Costs

Tuition for 2005–06 was $7375. Student housing costs ranged from $3255 to $5456 per semester for dormitory-style housing (includes meal plan).

Financial Aid

Students receive financial aid from federal, state, institutional, and private sources and may be employed during their attendance as full-time students. The forms of financial aid available at the College through federal sources include the Federal Pell Grant, the Federal Supplemental Educational Opportunity Grant, the Federal Work-Study Program, the Federal Subsidized and Unsubsidized Stafford Student Loans, FPLUS loans, and veterans' educational benefits. Students are encouraged to investigate the scholarship programs in their home state and apply for state scholarships if the grants can be used in Maryland. The College also offers its own series of scholarships and payment options. In 2003–04, College-funded scholarships averaged $3300 per academic year. Students can request a financial aid application from the Student Financial Planning Office. The College employs the Federal Methodology of Need Analysis, approved by the U.S. Department of Education, as a fair and equitable means of determining the family's ability to contribute to the student's educational expenses, as well as eligibility for other financial aid programs.

Faculty

Baltimore International College faculty members include 29 chefs and academic instructors of high academic distinction. The student-faculty ratio averages 16:1 in culinary labs and 25:1 in academic classes. Each student is assigned a faculty adviser who oversees the student's progress and answers questions about academic and career concerns. Students are encouraged to discuss program-related issues with the Director of Student Counseling.

Student Body Profile

Current enrollment is 750 annually, with 52 percent men and 48 percent women. Approximately 17 percent of students are from out-of-state, representing twenty-four states and several other countries. Students can join the Greater Baltimore Chapter of the American Culinary Federation and can participate in a variety of other activities through Student Affairs.

Student Activities

The College offers general academic counseling for all students, peer tutoring on request, and a variety of referrals for support services. In addition, student services provide many recreation and leisure activities, including the student union, a series of activities sponsored by the College, and information about cultural programs around the city. Student services also provides ongoing support to the College's alumni through surveys, mailings about the College's growth, and involvement in College-sponsored events such as open houses, resume referrals, and career fairs.

Facilities and Resources

The Baltimore campus includes the Culinary Arts Center, kitchens, storerooms, cooking demonstration theaters, academic classrooms, multipurpose rooms, a library, computer labs, a student union, and auxiliary services. Public operations that function as in-house training for students include the Mount Vernon Hotel, the Bay Atlantic Club Restaurant, and the Hopkins Inn.

The Virginia Park Campus is located on 100 acres, 50 miles from Dublin student housing, with laboratory kitchens and lecture facilities. The complex also includes the Park Hotel, with public operations that function as in-house training for students, including the Marquis Dining Room and the Marchioness Ballroom. The Park Hotel has thirty-six guest rooms. All students enjoy unlimited golf and fishing as well as hiking trails.

Career Planning/Placement Offices The College's Career Development Center offers students access to information about careers in food service and hospitality management. The College's career development services are located in the Career Information Center where coordinators organize on-campus recruiting and offer workshops and assistance in resume writing and interviewing skills.

Library and Audiovisual Services The College's Learning Resource Center is a member of an interlibrary loan network that enables users to borrow from public, academic, and private libraries throughout Maryland. The library's current core collection has approximately 13,000 volumes, 200 periodicals, and almost 800 audiovisual selections. The library offers students access to the Internet, a worldwide network of electronic information. In-house services include two academic computer labs, electronic databases for research, and a photocopier.

The College's art gallery is part of the Learning Resource Center and features a permanent display of edible art. Student participation in all exhibits is encouraged.

Location

The College's main campus, located in downtown Baltimore, is just two blocks from the city's famous Inner Harbor, a location that puts the College in the midst of numerous hotels and restaurants. The city offers year-round cultural and entertainment opportunities, such as theater, opera, the Baltimore Symphony Orchestra, museums, sporting events, and festivals. Other attractions in Baltimore, within walking distance of the College, are the National Aquarium, Harborplace, Oriole Park at Camden Yards, Ravens Stadium, Maryland Science Center, and many historic sites, including Fort McHenry, Mount Vernon, and the Walters Art Museum. Baltimore also has parks and miles of waterfront for those who enjoy outdoor recreation. Washington, D.C., the nation's capital, is just 30 miles from downtown Baltimore. The city of Baltimore is easily accessed by major highways and bus, rail, and air service. Baltimore/Washington International Airport is a short drive from the campus.

Admission Requirements

Creativity and skill of students must be matched by dedication. The College seeks candidates who desire a professional career in the hospitality industry.

Individuals seeking admission to the College must have earned a high school diploma or have passed the GED. Applicants must either pass the College's Admissions Test, take developmental courses during their first semester, or have one of the following: minimum SAT I scores of 430 verbal and 420 math, a minimum composite ACT score of 16, minimum CLEP scores in the 50th percentile in math and English composition with essay, a secondary degree, or 16 credit hours at the postsecondary level with a minimum average of C in math and English. Transfer students must submit an official college transcript as well as catalog course descriptions for credits they wish to transfer.

The College affords equally to all students the rights, privileges, programs, activities, scholarships and loan programs, and other programs administered by the College without regard to race, color, creed, sex, age, handicap, or national or ethnic origin.

Application and Information

Applicants are required to submit an application form along with a $35 nonrefundable fee. Requests by the College for additional information must be handled in a timely manner. An admission decision is made as soon as a file is complete. Upon acceptance, applicants are asked to submit a $100 tuition deposit.

For additional information, students should contact:

Office of Admissions
Commerce Exchange
Baltimore International College
17 Commerce Street
Baltimore, Maryland 21202-3230
Telephone: 410-752-4710 Ext. 120
       800-624-9926 Ext. 120 (toll-free)
E-mail: admissions@bic.edu
World Wide Web: http://www.bic.edu

Small classes at Baltimore International College enable students to receive individual instruction that helps them perfect their skills.

BAY STATE COLLEGE
BOSTON, MASSACHUSETTS

The College and Its Mission

Bay State College, a private, two-year, independent, coeducational institution, is located in Boston's historic Back Bay. Since 1946, Bay State College has been preparing young men and women with the skills necessary to attain outstanding careers in the business and allied health disciplines.

The College's goal is to prepare and educate students for successful and rewarding professional opportunities. Bay State College accomplishes this by providing the best possible education, which enables students to go out into the working world equipped with all the skills needed to succeed professionally or to transfer to a four-year college of choice. Bay State College assists, encourages, supports, and educates students in all their academic, professional, and personal goals and aspirations.

Bay State College is accredited by the New England Association of Schools and Colleges, is authorized to award the Associate in Science and Associate in Applied Science degrees by the Commonwealth of Massachusetts, and is a member of several professional educational associations.

Bay State College's allied health programs are accredited by the Accrediting Bureau of Health Education Schools (ABHES). The Physical Therapist Assistant Program is accredited by the Commission on Accreditation in Physical Therapy Education (CAPTE) of the American Physical Therapy Association (APTA).

Academic Programs

Bay State College offers unique courses preparing students for careers in accounting, business, criminal justice, early childhood education, entertainment management, fashion design, fashion merchandising, general studies, medical assisting studies, and physical therapist assistant studies. In addition, students are exceptionally prepared to transfer to four-year colleges and universities.

The College's current programs include accounting (A.A.S.), business administration (A.A.S.), early childhood education (A.S.), entertainment management (A.A.S.), fashion design (A.S.), fashion merchandising (A.A.S.), general studies (A.S.), medical assisting studies (A.S.), physical therapist assistant studies (A.S.), retail business management (A.A.S.), and travel and hospitality management (A.A.S.).

In addition, Bay State is now offering three baccalaureate degrees in entertainment management, fashion merchandising, and management.

Bay State College's Day and Continuing Education Divisions offer day and evening classes. Two satellite campuses for continuing education are located in Gloucester and Middleboro, Massachusetts.

Off-Campus Programs

The internship program, available in all major areas of study, provides practical field experience so that the students gain the skills and experience with the technologies used in the business and medical settings.

Students from Bay State College are among the 250 students participating in the Walt Disney World College Program. During their stay at Walt Disney World, students receive on-the-job training and classroom experience. This is just one of the many internship possibilities for students each year at Bay State College.

Costs

For the 2006–07 academic year, the College's Day Division charges a comprehensive fee of $25,725, which includes full-time tuition ($15,900) and room and board ($9825). There is an allied health lab fee of $475 per year (medical assisting studies and physical therapist assistant studies only). Textbooks are estimated at $700 per year. Bay State College's Continuing Education Division, the Boston, Middleboro, and Gloucester campuses, charge $383 per credit. Tuition, dormitory charges, and fees are subject to change.

Financial Aid

Personal financial planning and counseling is completed with all students and families. Approximately 85 percent of students receive some form of financial assistance. Bay State College requires a completed Free Application for Federal Student Aid (FAFSA) form and signed federal tax forms. The College's institutional financial aid priority deadline is March 1. Financial aid is granted on a rolling basis.

Faculty

There are 50 faculty members, with 53 percent holding advanced degrees and 6 percent holding doctoral degrees. The student-faculty ratio is 15:1.

Student Body Profile

There are 638 students in terminal programs. The average age is 18. The student body is ethnically and culturally diverse; 90 percent are state residents, 9 percent are transfer students, 4 percent are international students, 75 percent are women, 18 percent are African American, 11 percent are Hispanic, and 5 percent are Asian American. In the past year, 33 percent of Bay State College's graduating class continued on to a four-year college.

Bay State College's residence halls are located on Commonwealth Avenue. There are 230 college housing spaces available. Each residence hall is designed to accommodate from 1 to 5 students per room. Housing is guaranteed to freshmen who complete and submit a dorm contract by May 1.

Each hall is staffed by professional live-in directors and a paraprofessional staff of resident assistants. The staff members strive to foster a living and learning environment that complements the academic mission. All residents have the opportunity to experience a wide variety of programs such as in-house educational, cultural, and awareness seminars; study breaks; discounts to area movies and theater productions; and holiday celebrations. Twenty-four-hour quiet hours are in effect during midterm and final periods. Students are also provided with wireless Internet access in every room. A campus dining facility is available, as are microwaves, laundry facilities, cable-ready outlets, and computer labs.

Student Activities

Students participate in a multitude of activities offered by the College through student groups. These include the Business Club, Travel Club, Fashion Club, Early Childhood Education Club, Accounting Club, Student Leader Organization, Medical Assisting Society, Physical Therapist Assistant Club, a talent show, a student-produced fashion show, a literary magazine, literary readings, and access to a gym.

Facilities and Resources

Advisement/Counseling Trained staff members assist students in selecting courses and programs of study to satisfy their educational objectives. A counseling center is available to provide mental and physical health referrals to all Bay State students in need of such services. Referral networks are extensive, within a wide range of geographic areas, and provide access to a variety of public and private health agencies.

Specialized Services The Learning Center has been renamed the Center for Learning and Academic Support (CLAS). A learning center serves as a supplementary learning tool for those individuals wishing to improve their skills through self-paced individualized instruction. The center offers assistance through the use of peer and faculty tutors, individualized learning packets, and audio, visual, and other self-study resources. Introductory studies courses are designed for a diverse population of students, including workers returning to school, recent high school graduates seeking academic reinforcement, and ESL students. Their individual needs are met so they can be successful in the traditional course of study leading to an associate degree.

Career Planning/Placement Of the number of students seeking assistance from the Career Services Office, there was a 95 percent job placement rate. The primary purpose of the Career Services Office at Bay State College is to see that every graduating senior secures the best possible position in his or her chosen career. The Career Services Office, offering lifelong service to all alumni, continually posts job openings for current students and graduates. An average of 10,000 job openings are posted every year. The Career Services Office, under the guidance of Kristin Pedicone, Assistant Director of Student Career Services (telephone: 617-217-9230), assists each student through one-on-one career counseling. Services include career fairs on campus, with more than seventy attending companies; resume preparation; career counseling; the career library; and a professional dynamics course.

Library and Audiovisual Services The library has a combined book collection of approximately 5,300 books. In addition, Bay State College has 100 periodicals and 200 audiovisual titles. The College's sixty computers have access to the Internet and several databases for magazine and journal articles, including ProQuest, LexisNexis Academic, and Westlaw legal database.

Location

The location of Bay State College makes it the perfect place to attend to get a complete education. While the academics are great, students are also within a mile of major-league sports, free concerts, museums, the Freedom Trail, Boston Symphony Hall, the Boston Public Library, the Boston Public Garden, and much more. The city is known for its college atmosphere. Tree-lined streets are mirrored in the skyscrapers of the Back Bay. Major shopping, cultural, and sporting events make College life an experience that students will always remember. The College's location is accessible by public transportation and in proximity to Boston Logan International Airport.

Admission Requirements

Students must be in pursuit of a high school diploma or GED certificate in order to apply and must receive it before the start of classes at Bay State College. A personal interview is strongly recommended for all students. Transcripts are requested once a student has applied. A decision is made by the Admissions Office upon completion and receipt of all documents. International students must complete an International Student Application and provide a transcript, a TOEFL score, and final documents in order to be considered for admission.

Application and Information

Bay State College accepts applications on a rolling basis, so students may apply at any time. A $40 fee is required at the time of application, but application fee waivers are available upon request.

Applications should be submitted to:

Admissions Office
Bay State College
122 Commonwealth Avenue
Boston, Massachusetts 02116
Telephone: 800-81-LEARN (toll-free)
Fax: 617-217-9195
World Wide Web: http://www.baystate.edu

BENJAMIN FRANKLIN INSTITUTE OF TECHNOLOGY

BOSTON, MASSACHUSETTS

The Institute and Its Mission

Benjamin Franklin Institute of Technology (BFIT) is a small technical college offering a variety of instructional programs based on science, engineering, and technology. Programs of one, two, three, and four years' duration are provided for various levels of interest, abilities, and objectives. The aim of the Franklin Institute is to prepare the students in each program for immediate employment upon graduation in a chosen career field and at the same time to give students a technical education upon which they can continue to build. Because of the Institute's student-teacher ratio of 11:1, students receive a great deal of individual attention with a hands-on approach to learning.

The objectives of the Franklin Institute are threefold: to provide educational opportunities in science and technology for men and women in order that they may better themselves both economically and socially, to provide a sound educational foundation upon which the graduates of the Institute's programs may continue to grow both in personal terms as well as professional and educational terms, and to assess the present and future needs of industry and technology in order to anticipate and respond to those needs through curriculum revisions and the addition of new programs.

Academic Programs

Bachelor's Degree Programs Franklin Institute is one of the few colleges in the nation to offer a **Bachelor of Science** degree in automotive technology. The program follows completion of all requirements at the Franklin associate level. Its primary objective is to prepare students for middle management positions in the automotive industry and raise the standards for education industry-wide in an increasingly complex and technical profession. The curriculum is a combination of technical and business management courses. A total of eight semesters and 134 credit hours must be successfully completed for graduation.

Associate Degree Programs Franklin Institute grants the **Associate in Science** degree in automotive technology. The **Associate in Engineering** degree is awarded in architectural technology, computer engineering technology, computer technology, electrical engineering technology, electronic engineering technology, mechanical engineering technology, and medical electronics engineering technology.

The engineering technology associate degree programs require four semesters for completion, with a total of 74 semester hours of credit. Half of the total curriculum in each engineering technology program is devoted to the technical specialty. One fourth of the total curriculum is devoted to physical science and mathematics, courses in college algebra and trigonometry, analytic geometry, calculus, and college physics. The remaining fourth of the curriculum includes English, humanities, and social studies. Most of the graduates of the engineering technology associate degree programs are employed by industry in various capacities in engineering and scientific fields. A high percentage of graduates continue their education at other colleges and universities.

The computer engineering technology program includes both fundamental and advanced courses in digital computer circuits, systems and languages, and electronic devices and circuit theory.

The electrical engineering technology program includes basic and advanced courses in the design and construction of electrical distribution systems for modern commercial and industrial buildings, commercial lighting design, and electrical estimating.

The electronic engineering technology program includes basic and advanced courses in electric and electronic circuit theory, semiconductor devices, principles and design of electrical and electronic equipment, and measurement techniques up to and including microwave frequencies.

The mechanical engineering technology program includes fundamental and advanced courses in applied mechanics, mechanics of materials, thermodynamics, heat transfer, machine design, fluid power, and instrumentation.

The medical electronics engineering technology curriculum incorporates basic and advanced courses in minicomputers and microcomputers, electronic devices, electric and electronic circuit theory, medical instrumentation, human physiology, medical instrument safety and grounding techniques, semiconductor circuitry, and principles and design of medical electronic instruments.

The industrial technology associate degree programs require four semesters for completion, with a total of 70 semester hours of credit. More than half of the total curriculum in each industrial technology program is devoted to the technical specialty. About one fourth of the total curriculum is devoted to basic science and mathematics, including algebra, trigonometry, and precalculus mathematics. The remainder of the curriculum includes English, humanities, and social studies.

More than half of the automotive technology two-year program is devoted to automotive technical specialties, including actual work on vehicles in the student instructional garage. About one third of the program is devoted to basic mathematics, physics, humanities, and social sciences, and the remaining time is devoted to basic mechanical technology studies.

The computer technology program prepares students to meet the rapidly growing demand for technicians who can install, maintain, and repair computer equipment and digital electronic systems.

The architectural technology program is designed to enable its graduates to become skilled and knowledgeable architectural draftspersons, capable of making important contributions to the architectural and/or engineering team that produces the complete working drawings from which buildings, residences, and other structures are erected.

Transfer Arrangements Transfer credit received for courses completed at Franklin Institute is dependent on the policies of the transferring institution. Many graduates receive a full two years' credit toward a baccalaureate degree.

Certificate Programs The BFIT certificate programs require two to three semesters for completion, with a total of 18 to 36 semester hours of credit. Instruction is concentrated in the student's main area of interest. The Institute currently offers certificate programs in digital photography and imaging technology (DPIT), marine technology, pharmacy technology, and practical electricity.

Costs

For the 2004–05 academic year, tuition was $12,500 per year. Books and supplies average $600. While the Institute does not maintain its own residence halls, various housing options exist.

Financial Aid

Franklin Institute offers financial assistance to students on the basis of demonstrated financial need and satisfactory academic progress. All students are encouraged to file the Free Application for Federal Student Aid (FAFSA). The Institute participates in the Federal Pell Grant, Federal Supplemental Educational Opportunity Grant, Federal Direct Loan, and Federal Work-Study programs and offers Franklin Institute grants and academic scholarships. State scholarships, VA assistance, rehabilitation funding, and payment plans are available for eligible students.

Faculty

The faculty at Franklin Institute consists of instructors with practical experience in their field of expertise and many years of instruction. Instructors meet annually with the Industrial Advisory Board for each program to review and update the curricula. There are 32 full-time and 9 part-time faculty members.

Student Body Profile

Ninety-two percent of students are state residents, 8 percent are transfer students, and 3 percent are international students. Fourteen percent of the student body are 25 years of age or older, and 14 percent are women. The student body is ethnically and culturally diverse: 30 percent are African American, 15 percent are Hispanic, and 14 percent are Asian American. Thirty-five percent of students work full-time.

Student Activities

All students are encouraged to participate in the campus environment. Activities include student government, Women's Support Group, engineering week competitions, yearbook, professional honor societies, and athletics.

Sports Franklin Institute offers outdoor recreation programs, including basketball and soccer. Indoor activities include table tennis.

Facilities and Resources

The Union building houses the library, which holds 10,000 bound volumes, 160 periodical subscriptions, eighty-five computer terminals, and a word processing lab for student use. Other labs associated with individual programs include digital and analog electronics, electrical wiring, computer systems, materials testing, machine tool, CAD, automotive engines, transmissions, drivability, and electrical as well as a full-service garage.

Location

The land on which the Institute stands, at the corner of Berkeley and Appleton Streets in the South End of Boston, was provided by the city in 1906. The Institute complex consists of three buildings, a plaza, a landscaped mall connecting the buildings on Berkeley and Appleton Streets, and a modern underground automotive technology shop. The facilities of the Kendall Administration Building and the Dunham Building are handicapped accessible. The Institute is readily accessible by public transportation and is within close walking distance of many cultural, social, and recreational activities offered in the city of Boston. Franklin Institute students have the opportunity to meet other college students from around the world, as there are more than seventy postsecondary institutions in the greater Boston area.

Admission Requirements

All applicants must possess a high school diploma or its equivalent and must have completed four full-year courses in high school English. For associate degrees in engineering technology, satisfactory completion of the following courses in mathematics and science is also required: algebra I, algebra II, and a laboratory science, preferably physics, although courses in chemistry or biology are acceptable. Additional courses in mathematics, such as trigonometry, math analysis, or precalculus, are helpful but not required.

Admission requirements for associate degree in industrial technology programs include a minimum of two high school courses in mathematics, including the study of elementary algebra, and one course in science.

Admission requirements for the Certificate of Proficiency include a minimum of two high school courses in mathematics and one course in science. The study of elementary algebra is recommended and in some cases required.

Application and Information

All applicants should complete a Franklin Institute Application for Admission and submit it with the required $25 processing fee to the Office of Admission. Official transcripts of high school records, including first-term senior-year grades, should be requested by the student and sent directly from the high school to the Office of Admission. Because applications are processed on a rolling basis, applicants are notified of their admission status shortly after all required documents have been received. International applicants are also required to demonstrate English language proficiency and provide a financial statement showing proof of ability to pay the first year's costs.

State and institutional financial aid resources can be exhausted early in the application process. For financial aid priority consideration, applicants should apply for admission and financial aid no later than April 15.

Requests for additional information and application forms should be addressed to:

Office of Admission
Benjamin Franklin Institute of Technology
41 Berkeley Street
Boston, Massachusetts 02116
Telephone: 617-423-4630
Fax: 617-482-3706
E-mail: admissions@bfit.edu
World Wide Web: http://www.bfit.edu

BRADLEY ACADEMY
FOR THE VISUAL ARTS

YORK, PENNSYLVANIA

The Academy and Its Mission

Bradley Academy for the Visual Arts provides students with an educational environment and dedicated faculty members who are committed to preparing students for entry-level positions in the creative arts. Professional academic courses encourage the achievement of self-knowledge and the development of critical thinking. Under the guidance of industry professionals, students learn by doing the types of tasks they are likely to encounter in the workplace. In addition, assistance is available to help students with resume writing, networking, and keeping aware of what employers are looking for in job candidates.

Whenever possible and appropriate, courses are taught in a studio or lab setting. While at the school, students can access the wireless network to check mail, hand in assignments, and work on a project, anywhere on campus.

Of all 2004 Bradley Academy for the Visual Arts students available for employment, 90.6 percent were working in a field related to their program of study within six months of graduation and earning an average salary of $23,188.

Bradley Academy for the Visual Arts is accredited by the Accrediting Commission of Career Schools and Colleges of Technology (ACCSCT), which is listed by the U.S. Department of Education as a nationally recognized accrediting agency. Bradley Academy for the Visual Arts is also licensed by the State Board of Private Licensed Schools (Pennsylvania Department of Education).

Academic Programs

Bradley Academy for the Visual Arts operates on a year-round, four-quarter system. Associate degrees are offered in animation, digital arts, fashion marketing, graphic design, interior design, and Web design.

Costs

Tuition costs vary by program. Prospective students should contact the school for current tuition costs. Other charges include a starting kit for all first-quarter students. Kits vary in price depending on the program of study.

Financial Aid

Financial aid is available to those who qualify. Eligible students may apply for federal and state financial aid, including student loans, grants, and scholarships. Work-study programs are also available for qualifying students. Bradley Academy for the Visual Arts participates in the Imagine America Scholarship Program, which is sponsored by the Career Training Foundation. These scholarships are matched by the school and are awarded to qualifying high school seniors through the guidance offices at their high schools. Bradley Academy for the Visual Arts has committed to matching most Dollars for Scholars awards up to a

maximum of $1000 per student, provided the student has demonstrated financial need. Application deadlines and eligibility requirements vary.

Faculty

Faculty members at Bradley Academy for the Visual Arts are professionals, many of whom have experience in their fields of expertise. The school has nearly 50 full-time and part-time faculty members who provide their students with a unique, relevant educational experience. The student-faculty ratio is 15:1.

Student Body Profile

There are approximately 550 students attending Bradley Academy for the Visual Arts. Many of the school's students come from the York, Harrisburg, and Philadelphia, Pennsylvania, areas. There are also students enrolled in short-term enrichment and self-improvement courses, which usually meet in the evening or on Saturdays.

The student population includes recent high school graduates, transfer students, and those who have left a previous employment situation to study and train for a new career. Students are creative, competitive, and open to new ideas. They place great value on an education that prepares them for an exciting entry-level position in the arts.

Student Activities

In addition to a traditional student government association, many professional organizations exist on campus, including the American Society of Interior Designers (ASID), the National Kitchen and Bath Association (NKBA), the Baltimore chapter of the American Institute of Graphic Arts (AIGA), and DECA/Delta Epsilon Chi. Students maintaining a GPA of 3.5 or higher at the end of the fifth term are considered for induction into Alpha Beta Kappa, a national honor society. There is also a student-run newspaper.

Facilities and Resources

Bradley Academy for the Visual Arts is housed within a 38,000-square-foot building in suburban York, Pennsylvania. The new facility contains classrooms and studios, a student computer commons, a gallery, an art store, and a library.

Computer labs contain both Macintosh computers and PCs. All labs are equipped with color scanners and have access to more than 200 gigabytes of network storage. Each lab is supported by desktop and high-resolution printers. The school also has a graphics lab, display windows, and vignette space to allow students to apply skills learned in the classroom.

In association with the York Martin Memorial Library, Bradley Academy houses a 1,000-square-foot library on the first floor of the school. In addition to general reference books, the library houses titles specifically related to programs offered at the school. Eight Windows NT workstations with direct access to the Internet and to Martin Library's catalog are available for students. Open every weekday, the library features full-time staffing, interlibrary loan, CD-ROM–based reference materials, and PC business software for use by students and the public.

Location

Bradley Academy for the Visual Arts is located in York, a suburban area in south central Pennsylvania. Surrounded by sprawling hills and Amish farmlands, York offers visitors an abundance of shopping areas and museums and three centuries of American history, including the battle sites of the Revolutionary and Civil Wars. York is a 30-minute drive from Hershey and Harrisburg, Pennsylvania; approximately a 90-minute drive from Philadelphia; and a 1-hour drive from Baltimore, Maryland.

Admission Requirements

Bradley Academy for the Visual Arts encourages interested students to apply early. To apply, students must possess a high school diploma or General Educational Development (GED) certificate and a minimum SAT score of 800 (at least 400 math and 400 verbal) or a minimum ACT score of 16. A portfolio review is required for students majoring in graphic design and animation and is welcomed from students pursuing a degree in digital arts, interior design, or Web design. There is a $50 application fee.

Application and Information

To obtain an application or make arrangements for an interview or tour of the school, prospective students should contact:

Bradley Academy for the Visual Arts
1409 Williams Road
York, Pennsylvania 17402-9012

Telephone: 717-755-2300
  800-864-7725 (toll-free)
Fax: 717-840-1951
World Wide Web: http://www.bradleyacademy.edu

The Art Institute of Atlanta®, GA; The Art Institute of California^SM–Inland Empire*; The Art Institute of California^SM–Los Angeles; The Art Institute of California^SM–Orange County; The Art Institute of California^SM–San Diego; The Art Institute of California^SM–San Francisco; The Art Institute of Charlotte®, NC; The Art Institute of Colorado® (Denver); The Art Institute of Dallas®, TX; The Art Institute of Fort Lauderdale®, FL; The Art Institute of Houston®, TX; The Art Institute of Indianapolis^SM, IN**; The Art Institute of Las Vegas®, NV; The Art Institute of New York City®, NY; The Art Institute of Ohio^SM–Cincinnati***; The Art Institute of Philadelphia®, PA; The Art Institute of Phoenix®, AZ; The Art Institute of Pittsburgh®, PA; The Art Institute of Portland®, OR; The Art Institute of Seattle®, WA; The Art Institute of Tampa^SM, FL, A branch of Miami International University of Art & Design; The Art Institute of Toronto^SM, ON; The Art Institute of Vancouver^SM, BC (Burnaby location, Downtown location, Dubrulle Culinary Arts location); The Art Institute of Washington® (Arlington, VA), A branch of The Art Institute of Atlanta, GA; The Art Institute Online^SM, A division of The Art Institute of Pittsburgh, PA; The Art Institutes International Minnesota^SM (Minneapolis); Bradley Academy for the Visual Arts^SM (York, PA); California Design College^SM (Wilshire Boulevard, Los Angeles); The Illinois Institute of Art®–Chicago; The Illinois Institute of Art®–Schaumburg; Miami International University of Art & Design^SM, FL; The New England Institute of Art^SM (Boston, MA).
*This institution has received temporary approval to operate from the Bureau for Private Postsecondary and Vocational Education (400 R Street, Suite 5000, Sacramento, CA 95814-6200, 916-445-3427, www.bppve.ca.gov) in order to enable the Bureau to conduct a quality inspection of the institution.
**The Art Institute of Indianapolis is licensed by the Indiana Commission on Proprietary Education, 302 West Washington Street, Room E201, Indianapolis, IN 46204, AC-0080.
***The Art Institute of Ohio–Cincinnati, 1011 Glendale-Milford Road, Cincinnati, OH 45215-1107, Reg. #04-01-1698B.

BRIARWOOD COLLEGE
SOUTHINGTON, CONNECTICUT

The College and Its Mission

Briarwood College is a coed, two-year and four-year private college whose mission is to develop students' critical-thinking, self-discipline, and communication skills within the context of career and technical programs. An emphasis on small classes, comprehensive academic support services, and programs closely connected to opportunities in the employment market account for more than 85 percent of Briarwood's graduates being placed in jobs in their field within six months of graduation.

The College offers full- and part-time opportunities, evening classes, an accelerated option on Saturdays that is designed for working adults, and a variety of continuing education offerings through the Division of Lifelong Learning. In addition, alumni of the College receive a unique benefit, *Education for Life*®, which allows them to return for further course work tuition-free for the rest of their lives.

Academic Programs

Briarwood College offers a variety of career-oriented programs, both full- and part-time, leading to a certificate, diploma, or associate degree. In general, an associate degree program requires two years of study and a certificate program, one year. Diploma programs may take up to one year.

Associate Degree Programs Briarwood College offers associate degrees in twenty-seven majors. The **Associate in Arts** (A.A.) degree is offered in general studies, with concentrations in ballet, biotechnology, computer information systems, English, environmental technology, fine arts, history, mathematics, psychology, and science. The **Associate in Applied Science** (A.A.S.) degree is offered in accounting, administrative technology (with concentrations in executive, legal, and management), child development, communication, computer information systems, criminal justice, dental administrative assistant studies, dietetic technician studies, executive medical assistant studies, fashion merchandising, fitness technician studies, health information technology, hospitality (with concentrations in hotel and restaurant management and travel and tourism management), marketing, medical office management, mortuary science, occupational therapy assistant studies, and paralegal studies.

Certificate Programs The following programs lead to a certificate after one year: administrative legal professional studies, administrative medical professional studies, child development assistant studies, dental chairside assistant studies, health information coding, health information processing, medical assistant studies, medical transcription, pharmacy technician studies, and word processing. Most of these programs may be applied toward an associate degree program. The College also offers noncredit certificate programs in acupuncture and court reporting.

Diploma Programs Briarwood also offers diploma courses in computer information systems, leading to certification in Microsoft certified systems engineer, Microsoft certified system administrator, certified Novell administrator, and Computer Technology Industry Association: A+ certification for hardware repair.

Saturday College Saturday College is an accelerated degree program for mature adults who want to complete their studies while continuing to work full-time. Students complete two courses every eight weeks, enabling them to complete an associate degree in twenty months.

Education for Life® is a unique benefit offered to graduates of Briarwood College who complete associate degrees after at least three full-time semesters of study. Graduates are able to return to Briarwood for additional credit or noncredit courses tuition-free for the rest of their lives.

Costs

For the 2006–07 academic year, costs are as follows: tuition is $15,800 for resident and commuter students; part-time students pay $525 per credit. Resident students are also charged a $3320 residency fee. The nonrefundable registration fee for resident and commuter students is $95; part-time students pay $95 per semester.

Financial Aid

The following types of financial aid are available individually or in combination with other resources: presidential scholarships, state scholarships, and the Capitol Scholarship Program. Briarwood College, in conjunction with outside professional associations, also awards several scholarships in the business, health, and office administration fields. As other scholarships become available in specific program fields, they are announced in Briarwood College publications and posted outside the Financial Aid Office. A number of scholarships are awarded annually to students by local civic groups, churches, and fraternal and union organizations. Students are encouraged to explore all outside possibilities, utilizing the assistance of high school guidance officers or the Briarwood College Financial Aid Office. Recipients are selected on the basis of their academic achievement, extracurricular activities, recommendation letters, and personal essays. Eligible students are encouraged to seek, and are assisted in obtaining, educational benefits from the Veterans Administration, G.I. Bill, and state agencies. There are also grants and loans available, including Connecticut Independent College Student Grants (CICS), Federal Pell Grants, Federal Stafford Student Loans, Federal PLUS loans, Federal Supplemental Educational Opportunity Grants, and Federal Perkins Loans. For more information, students should contact the Financial Aid Office at 860-628-4751 or 800-952-2444 (toll-free).

Faculty

The teaching experience among the faculty members at Briarwood College is distinct in its variety of professional, business, and years of teaching experience. There are several faculty members who remain active in their line of work. For example, the Allied Health Division has on its staff several faculty members who are currently active in their vocation who bring expertise to their students. The faculty members in this category include the Program Director of the Pharmacy Technician Program, who is a practicing pharmacist; the Program Director of Travel and Tourism, who has more than twenty years of experience in the travel industry and is still active in the field; and adjunct faculty members in the Mortuary Science Program, who are presently working in the funeral service business.

Student Body Profile

There were 637 full- and part-time students enrolled in fall 2004. Students come from eight states and two other countries. Approximately 33 percent (218 students) live on campus.

Student Activities

The Dean of Student Life and her staff coordinate a variety of recreational opportunities, including clubs, fitness activities, student organizations, volunteer opportunities, and special events. Popular events include an annual fashion show, international night, a formal dinner/dance, award ceremonies, trips, picnics, and noon-hour programs on a variety of topics.

Briarwood students participate in a number of community volunteer activities, including America Reads, food and toy drives, a soup kitchen, and a blood drive.

The College Culture Committee coordinates cultural and educational events with various academic departments. Recent events have included presentations by visiting authors, films, and panel discussions.

Sports Briarwood College is a member of the National Junior College Athletic Association and competes with other colleges in Region 21. The College currently offers men's basketball and women's soccer at the varsity level. Students may also become involved in a wide variety of outdoor/indoor recreational activities, such as softball, volleyball, and golf. Skiing is available locally at Mount Southington, only 1 mile from the College. Annual trips to area ski resorts are also planned.

Briarwood has an affiliation with a local gym, enabling students to use the facilities for a nominal fee. The gym is a 24,000-square-foot facility with large cardiovascular and free-weight areas, as well as areas for yoga, group cycling, pilates, and group exercise. Briarwood also has an affiliation with the Southington YMCA that allows students to use this facility during the academic year for a greatly reduced rate. This facility includes a gym and a pool as well as a complete line of cardiovascular and strength-training equipment.

Facilities and Resources

There are two residential facilities on campus: Eder Hall, with its town house–style apartments, and Palmisano Hall. All units have furnished bedrooms, kitchens, and living rooms as well as laundry facilities. The residence halls also have Internet and cable access. A student center provides recreation space, pool tables, lounge chairs, and a large-screen television. A softball/soccer field is located adjacent to the residence halls.

Career Services The Career Service Office at Briarwood College provides a comprehensive career development program designed to assist students in making appropriate career choices and in developing plans to achieve their goals. Both individual and group sessions are offered to assist students with resume writing, interviewing, and job search skills.

Counseling Services Students who experience academic, personal, learning, or study problems are urged to seek help as soon as the problem is recognized. Counselors provide academic intervention activities designed to assist students who are experiencing academic difficulties. These activities include Early Alert notices, midterm intervention sessions, and individual assistance. A counselor is available to assist students who are having academic difficulties by working with them individually or by referring them to the services of the College Learning Center.

College counselors are available to aid students in resolving many types of problems, including social, emotional, vocational, and personal concerns. All information is handled in a confidential setting. Services of the Counseling Center include short-term personal counseling, crisis intervention, career development, and administering and interpreting self-assessment inventories.

In some cases, a counselor determines that the needs of a student would be best met through a community agency off campus. Referrals are made when the student is in crisis; has a long-term, ongoing problem; or can otherwise benefit from the resources of an outside agency. Counselors assist students in obtaining such services when appropriate.

Disability Services The Disability Services Office is responsible for all disability-related concerns of Briarwood College students. Briarwood College encourages qualified students with disabilities to take advantage of its educational programs. The College is responsible for ensuring that courses, programs, services, activities, and facilities are available and usable in the most integrated and appropriate settings. Students with disabilities seeking accommodations must identify themselves as individuals with disabilities, request needed accommodations, and provide documentation from the appropriate professional as to how the disabilities limit their participation in courses, programs, activities, and use of facilities. Upon receipt of documentation of a disability, it is the responsibility of the Disability Services Office to explore and facilitate reasonable accommodations, academic adjustments, and/or auxiliary aids and services for individuals with disabilities in courses, programs, services, activities, and facilities. Students

anticipating the need for accommodations, both before and after enrollment, are encouraged to contact the Dean of Student Services, whose office is located in the lower level of Eder Hall Center.

Health and Wellness Services The Health Office provides basic first aid and health education information to Briarwood College students. In some cases, a nurse determines that the needs of a student would be best met through an off-campus community facility. All students are required by federal law to provide their medical history and documentation of illnesses and immunizations prior to matriculation at Briarwood College. This information is used by the nurse in providing routine and emergency care.

Library and Audiovisual Services The Dr. Anthony A. Pupillo Library, staffed by a professional librarian and knowledgeable library assistants, plays an integral part in the education process of the students. The library is committed to providing support for the various courses and programs of study offered by Briarwood College. Although the library's resources are richest in the curricula taught at the College, a wide variety of works for individual interest and personal growth are also offered. The library offers a wide variety of electronic resources to facilitate student research. Novice users quickly learn to utilize the capabilities of the library's computer technology. The library offers research-only computers for student use and one-on-one sessions with students to familiarize them with its resources. Interlibrary loan is available to the students.

Location

Briarwood College is located in Southington, Connecticut, only 2 hours from Boston and New York. Students find skiing and Connecticut beaches readily accessible, and the school is minutes from the Hartford and New Haven metropolitan areas. The picturesque 42-acre campus is nestled at the base of Mount Southington, next to an 18-hole golf course and close to Lake Compounce Amusement Park, the Mount Southington ski area, and ESPN. Hartford, Connecticut's capital city, is just 15 minutes from the campus and offers numerous restaurants, indoor and outdoor concert venues, theaters, museums, parks, and shopping centers. The greater Hartford area is also home to seven colleges and universities.

Admission Requirements

The College requires applicants for full-time study to submit a completed application form, a $25 application fee, and official high school transcripts or GED scores. A personal statement and one letter of recommendation should be submitted for scholarship opportunities. SAT scores are not required, but are also recommended for scholarship opportunities. International students for whom English is not the first language are required to show proof of English competency. Part-time and transfer applicants are ordinarily not required to submit a personal statement and recommendation letter. Transfer applicants are also required to submit transcripts from all colleges or universities previously attended. Interviews with the program directors are also required for applicants to the dental assisting and occupational therapy assisting programs. Applications are reviewed on a rolling basis and acceptances are mailed, usually within one week of receipt of all required documents. Applicants for fall semester are encouraged to apply by March 30 for priority scholarship consideration.

Application and Information

For more information, students should contact:

Admissions Department
Briarwood College
2279 Mt. Vernon Road
Southington, Connecticut 06489
Telephone: 860-628-4751
            800-952-2444 (toll-free)
E-mail: admis@briarwood.edu
World Wide Web: http://www.briarwood.edu

BROWN MACKIE COLLEGE–AKRON

AKRON, OHIO

The College and Its Mission

Brown Mackie College–Akron is dedicated to providing education programs that prepare students for entry-level positions in a competitive, rapidly changing workplace. The College provides associate degree and diploma programs in the areas of business and accounting, allied health sciences, legal studies, and computer-technology fields to approximately 595 students.

The College was founded in Cincinnati, Ohio, in February 1927, as a traditional business college. In March 1980, the College added a branch location in Akron, Ohio. This facility was extensively renovated, and a new classroom wing was added in the spring of 1986.

Brown Mackie College–Akron is accredited by the Accrediting Council for Independent Colleges and Schools (ACICS) to award associate degrees and diplomas. ACICS is listed as a nationally recognized accrediting agency by the United States Department of Education. Its accreditation of degree-granting institutions also is recognized by the Council for Higher Education Accreditation. ACICS can be contacted at 750 First Street NE, Suite 980, Washington, D.C. 20002-4241; 202-336-6780. The College is licensed by the Ohio State Board of Career Colleges and Schools, 35 East Gay Street, Suite 403, Columbus, Ohio 43215.

The Medical Assisting degree program is accredited by the Commission on Accreditation of Allied Health Education Programs (CAAHEP), 35 East Wacker Drive, Suite 1970, Chicago, Illinois 60601-2208; 312-553-2208, on recommendation of the Curriculum Review Board of the American Association of Medical Assistants Endowment (AAMAE).

The College is a nonresidential, smoke-free institution and is owned and operated by Education Management Corporation (EDMC), 210 Sixth Avenue, 33rd floor, Pittsburgh, Pennsylvania 15222-2603; 800-275-2440 (toll-free); http://www.edmc.edu.

Academic Programs

Brown Mackie College–Akron provides higher education to traditional and nontraditional students through associate degree and diploma programs that assist them in enhancing their career opportunities, broadening their perspectives through appropriate general education courses, thinking independently and critically, and improving problem-solving abilities.

Each College quarter comprises twelve weeks. Associate degree programs require a minimum of eight quarters to complete. Programs are offered on a year-round basis, providing students with the ability to work uninterrupted toward their degree.

Associate Degree Programs The Associate of Applied Business degree (96 credits) is awarded in accounting technology, business management, computer networking and applications, computer programming and applications, computer software technology, criminal justice, and paralegal studies. The Associate of Applied Science degree (96 credits) is awarded in computer-aided design and drafting technology, electronics, health-care administration, medical assisting, and pharmacy technology.

Diploma Programs The College also offers diploma programs (48 credits) in accounting, business, computer applications, computer software applications, criminal justice, medical assistant studies, and paralegal assistant studies.

Costs

Tuition for the 2005–06 academic year was $179 per credit hour. The cost of textbooks and other instructional materials varies by program.

Financial Aid

The College maintains a full-time staff of financial aid professionals to assist qualified students in obtaining the financial assistance they require to meet their educational expenses. The College participates in several student aid programs. Forms of financial aid available through federal resources include the Federal Pell Grant Program, Federal Supplemental Educational Opportunity Grant (FSEOG) Program, Federal Work-Study Program, Federal Perkins Loan Program, Federal Stafford Student Loan Program (subsidized and unsubsidized), and the Federal PLUS Loan Program. Through the Ohio Instructional Grant (OIG) program, Ohio residents enrolled in a degree program may receive an award to apply to their tuition costs. The amount of the award varies according to family income and other determining factors. Eligible students may also apply for veterans' educational benefits. Students with physical or mental disabilities that are a handicap to employment may be eligible for training services through the state Agency for Vocational Rehabilitation. For further information, students should contact the College Student Financial Services Office.

Each year, the College makes available scholarships of $1000 each to qualifying seniors from area high schools. Only one scholarship is awarded per high school. In order to qualify, a senior must be graduating from a participating high school, maintain a cumulative grade point average of at least 2.0, and submit a brief essay. The student's extracurricular activities and community service are also considered. The President's Scholarship is available only to students enrolling in one of the College's degree programs. Students awarded the scholarship must enroll at Brown Mackie College–Akron between June and September immediately following their high school graduation. Applications for these scholarships can be obtained from the guidance departments of participating high schools. These applications must be completed and returned to the College by March 31. Those who are awarded scholarships are notified by April 30.

Faculty

There are 8 full-time and 20 part-time faculty members. The student-faculty ratio is 20:1.

Facilities and Resources

Brown Mackie College–Akron provides media presentation rooms for special instructional needs, libraries that provide instructional resources and academic support for both faculty members and students, and qualified and experienced faculty members who are committed to the academic and technical preparation of their students. The College is nonresidential; students who are unable to commute daily from their homes may request assistance from the Office of Admissions in locating off-campus housing. The College is accessible by public transportation and provides ample free parking.

Location

The College is located at 2791 Mogadore Road in Akron, Ohio.

Admission Requirements

Each applicant for admission is assigned an Assistant Director of Admissions who directs the applicant through the steps of the admissions process, providing information on curriculum, policies, procedures, and services and assisting the applicant in setting necessary appointments and interviews.

To qualify for admission, each applicant must provide documentation of graduation from an accredited high school or from a state-approved secondary education curriculum or provide official documentation of high school graduation equivalency. All transcripts become the property of the College. Admission to the College is based upon the applicant's meeting the above requirements, a review of the applicant's previous education records, and a review of the applicant's career interests. If previous academic records indicate that the College's education and training would not benefit the applicant, the College reserves the right to advise the applicant not to enroll. Special requirements for enrollment into certain programs are discussed in the descriptions of those programs.

Application and Information

Applicants must complete and submit an application form along with documentation of graduation from an accredited high school or state-approved secondary education curriculum, or applicants must provide official documentation of high school graduation equivalency. For additional information, prospective students should contact:

Director of Admissions
Brown Mackie College–Akron
2791 Mogadore Road
Akron, Ohio 44312
Telephone: 330-733-8766
Fax: 330-733-5853
E-mail: bmcakadm@amedcts.com
World Wide Web: http://www.brownmackie.edu

BROWN MACKIE COLLEGE–ATLANTA
ATLANTA, GEORGIA

The College and Its Mission

Brown Mackie College–Atlanta is dedicated to providing education programs that prepare students for entry-level positions in a competitive, rapidly changing workplace. The College provides associate degree and diploma programs in the areas of business and accounting, allied health sciences, legal studies, and computer technology to approximately 140 students.

Brown Mackie College–Atlanta is accredited by the Accrediting Council for Independent Colleges and Schools (ACICS) to award associate degrees, diplomas, and certificates. The Accrediting Council for Independent Colleges and Schools is listed as a nationally recognized accrediting agency by the United States Department of Education. Its accreditation of degree-granting institutions also is recognized by the Council for Higher Education Accreditation. The Accrediting Council can be contacted at 750 First Street, NE, Suite 980, Washington, D.C. 20002-4241; 202-336-6780. The College is a nonresidential, smoke-free institution and is owned and operated by Education Management Corporation (EDMC), 210 Sixth Avenue, 33rd floor, Pittsburgh, Pennsylvania 15222-2603; 800-275-2440 (toll-free); http://www.edmc.edu.

Academic Programs

Brown Mackie College–Atlanta provides higher education to traditional and nontraditional students through associate degree and diploma programs that assist them in enhancing their career opportunities, broadening their perspectives through appropriate general education courses, thinking independently and critically, and improving problem-solving abilities. The College strives to develop within its students the desire for lifelong and continued education.

Each College quarter comprises twelve weeks. Associate degree programs require a minimum of eight quarters to complete. Programs are offered on a year-round basis, providing students with the ability to work uninterrupted toward their degrees.

Associate Degree Programs The Associate of Applied Business degree (96 credits) is awarded in accounting technology, business management, computer programming and applications, computer software technology, criminal justice, and paralegal studies. The Associate of Applied Science degree (96 credits) is awarded in computer-aided design and drafting technology, electronics, and medical assisting.

Diploma Programs The College also offers diploma programs (48 credits) in accounting, business, computer-aided design and drafting technician studies, computer applications, computer software applications, criminal justice, medical assistant studies, and paralegal assistant studies.

Costs

Tuition for the 2005–06 academic year was $179 per credit hour. Textbook fees were estimated at $425 per quarter.

Financial Aid

The College maintains a full-time staff of financial aid professionals to assist qualified students in obtaining the financial assistance they require to meet their educational expenses. The College participates in several student aid programs. Forms of financial aid available through federal resources include the Federal Pell Grant Program, Federal Supplemental Educational Opportunity Grant (FSEOG) Program, Federal Work-Study Program, Federal Perkins Loan Program, Federal Stafford Student Loan Program (subsidized and unsubsidized), and the Federal PLUS Loan Program. Eligible students may also apply for state awards and veterans' educational benefits. Students with physical or mental disabilities that are a handicap to employment may be eligible for training services through the state Agency for Vocational Rehabilitation. For further information, students should contact the College Student Financial Services Office.

Each year, the College makes available scholarships of $1000 each to qualifying seniors from area high schools. Only one scholarship is awarded per high school. In order to qualify, a senior must be graduating from a participating high school, maintain a cumulative grade point average of at least 2.0, and submit a brief essay. The student's extracurricular activities and community service are also considered. The President's Scholarship is available only to students enrolling in one of the College's degree programs. Students awarded the scholarship must enroll at Brown Mackie College–Atlanta between June and September immediately following their high school graduation. Applications for these scholarships can be obtained from the guidance departments of participating high schools. These applications must be completed and returned to the College by March 31. Those who are awarded scholarships are notified by April 30.

Faculty

There are 5 full-time and 3 part-time faculty members. The average student-faculty ratio is 17:1. Each student has a faculty and student adviser.

Facilities and Resources

The College comprises administrative offices, faculty and student lounges, a reception area, and spacious classrooms and laboratories. Instructional equipment includes personal computers, LANs, printers, and transcribers. The library provides support for the academic programs through volumes covering a broad range of subjects, as well as through Internet access. Vehicle parking is provided for both students and staff members.

Location

Brown Mackie College–Atlanta is located at 6600 Peachtree Dunwoody Road, 600 Embassy Row, Suite 130, in Atlanta, Georgia, and is easily accessible from interstate highway I-285 and the MARTA Sandy Springs rail station.

Admission Requirements

Each applicant for admission is assigned an Assistant Director of Admissions who directs the applicant through the steps of the admissions process, providing information on curriculum, policies, procedures, and services and assisting the applicant in setting necessary appointments and interviews.

To qualify for admission, each applicant must provide documentation of graduation from an accredited high school or from a state-approved secondary education curriculum or provide official documentation of high school graduation equivalency. All transcripts become the property of the College. Admission to the College is based upon the applicant's meeting the above requirements, a review of the applicant's previous education records, and a review of the applicant's career interests. If previous academic records indicate that the College's education and training would not benefit the applicant, the College reserves the right to advise the applicant not to enroll. Special requirements for enrollment into certain programs are discussed in the descriptions of those programs.

Application and Information

Applicants must complete and submit an application form along with documentation of graduation from an accredited high school or state-approved secondary education curriculum, or applicants must provide official documentation of high school graduation equivalency. For additional information, prospective students should contact:

Director of Admissions
Brown Mackie College–Atlanta
6600 Peachtree Dunwoody Road NE
600 Embassy Row
Suite 130
Atlanta, Georgia 30328
Telephone: 770-638-0121
Fax: 770-638-0479
E-mail: bmcatadm@amedcts.com
World Wide Web: http://www.brownmackie.edu

BROWN MACKIE COLLEGE–CINCINNATI

CINCINNATI, OHIO

The College and Its Mission

Brown Mackie College–Cincinnati is dedicated to providing education programs that prepare students for entry-level positions in a competitive, rapidly changing workplace. The College provides associate degree, diploma, and certificate programs in the areas of business and accounting, allied health sciences, legal studies, computer technology, and electronics fields to approximately 1,400 students.

The College was founded in February 1927 as Southern Ohio Business College. In 1978, the College's main location was relocated from downtown Cincinnati to the Bond Hill–Roselawn area and in 1995 to its current location at 1011 Glendale-Milford Road in the community of Woodlawn.

Brown Mackie College–Cincinnati is accredited by the Accrediting Council for Independent Colleges and Schools (ACICS) to award associate degrees, diplomas, and certificates. The Accrediting Council for Independent Colleges and Schools is listed as a nationally recognized accrediting agency by the United States Department of Education. Its accreditation of degree-granting institutions is also recognized by the Council for Higher Education Accreditation. The Accrediting Council's address is 750 First Street, NE, Suite 980, Washington, D.C. 20002-4241; 202-336-6780. The medical assisting program is accredited by the Commission on Accreditation of Allied Health Education Programs (CAAHEP), on recommendation of the Committee on Accreditation for Medical Assistant Education. The College is licensed by the Ohio State Board of Career Colleges and Schools, 35 East Gay Street, Suite 403, Columbus, Ohio 43215.

The College is a nonresidential, smoke-free institution and is owned and operated by Education Management Corporation, 210 Sixth Avenue, 33rd Floor, Pittsburgh, Pennsylvania 15222-2603; http://www.edmc.edu.

Academic Programs

Brown Mackie College–Cincinnati provides higher education to traditional and nontraditional students through associate degree, diploma, and certificate programs that assist them in enhancing their career opportunities, broadening their perspectives through appropriate general education courses, thinking independently and critically, and improving problem-solving abilities. The College strives to develop within its students the desire for lifelong and continued education.

Each College quarter comprises twelve weeks. Associate degree programs require a minimum of eight quarters to complete. Programs are offered on a year-round basis, providing students with the ability to work uninterrupted toward their degrees.

Associate Degree Programs The Associate of Applied Business degree (96 credits) is awarded in accounting technology, business management, computer networking and applications, computer programming and applications, computer software technology, criminal justice, and paralegal studies. The Associate

of Applied Science degree (96 credits) is awarded in audio/video production, computer-aided design and drafting technology, electronics, gerontology, health-care administration, medical assisting, and pharmacy technology.

Diploma Programs The College offers diploma programs (48 credits) in accounting, audio/video technician studies, business, computer-aided design and drafting technician studies, computer applications, computer software applications, criminal justice, medical assistant studies, paralegal assistant studies, and practical nursing studies (76 credits).

Certificate Program The College offers a certificate program (24 credits) in computer networking.

Costs

Tuition for the 2005–06 academic year was $179 per credit hour, with the exception of the practical nursing program at $250 per credit hour and Microsoft Certified Systems Engineer (MCSE) courses at $300 per credit hour. Textbook expenses were approximately $425 per quarter.

Financial Aid

The College maintains a full-time staff of financial aid professionals to assist qualified students in obtaining the financial assistance they require to meet their educational expenses. The College participates in several student aid programs. Forms of financial aid available through federal resources include the Federal Pell Grant Program, Federal Supplemental Educational Opportunity Grant (FSEOG) Program, Federal Work-Study Program, Federal Perkins Loan Program, Federal Stafford Student Loan Program (subsidized and unsubsidized), and the Federal PLUS Loan Program. Eligible students may apply for state awards, such as the Ohio Instructional Grant (OIG), and veterans' educational benefits. Students with physical or mental disabilities that are a handicap to employment may be eligible for training services through the state Agency for Vocational Rehabilitation. For further information, students should contact the College Student Financial Services Office.

Each year, the College makes available President's Scholarships of $1000 each to qualifying seniors from area high schools. No more than one scholarship is awarded per high school. In order to qualify, a senior must be graduating from a participating high school, must be maintaining a cumulative grade point average of at least 2.0, and must submit a brief essay. The student's extracurricular activities and community service are also considered. The President's Scholarship is available only to students enrolling in one of the College's degree programs. Students awarded the scholarship must enroll at Brown Mackie College–Cincinnati between June and September immediately following their high school graduation. Applications for these scholarships can be obtained from the guidance departments of participating high schools. These applications must be completed and returned to the College by March 31. Those awarded scholarships are notified by April 30.

Faculty

There are 27 full-time and 46 part-time faculty members. The average student-faculty ratio is 20:1. Each student has a faculty and student adviser.

Academic Facilities

Completely renovated in December 2003, Brown Mackie College–Cincinnati consists of more than 57,000 square feet of classroom, laboratory, and office space designed to specifications of the College for its business, medical, and technical programs.

Location

Brown Mackie College–Cincinnati is located in the Woodlawn section of Cincinnati, Ohio. The College is accessible by public transportation and provides ample free parking. It shares its facility space with The Art Institute of Ohio–Cincinnati.

Admission Requirements

Each applicant for admission is assigned an Assistant Director of Admissions, who directs the applicant through the steps of the admissions process, providing information on curriculum, policies, procedures, and services and assisting the applicant in setting necessary appointments and interviews. To qualify for admission, each applicant must provide documentation of graduation from an accredited high school or from a state-approved secondary education curriculum or provide official documentation of high school graduation equivalency. All transcripts become the property of the College. Admission to the College is based on the applicant's meeting the above requirements, a review of the applicant's previous educational records, and a review of the applicant's career interests. If previous academic records indicate that the College's education and training would not benefit the applicant, the College reserves the right to advise the applicant not to enroll. Special requirements for enrollment into certain programs are discussed in the descriptions of those programs.

Application and Information

Applicants must complete and submit an application form, along with documentation of graduation from an accredited high school or state-approved secondary education curriculum or official documentation of high school graduation equivalency.

For additional information, prospective students should contact:

Director of Admissions
Brown Mackie College–Cincinnati
1011 Glendale-Milford Road
Cincinnati, Ohio 45215
Telephone: 512-771-2424
               800-888-1445 (toll-free)
Fax: 513-771-3413
E-mail: bmcciadm@amedcts.com
World Wide Web: http://www.brownmackie.edu

BROWN MACKIE COLLEGE–FINDLAY

FINDLAY, OHIO

The College and Its Mission

Brown Mackie College–Findlay is dedicated to providing education programs that prepare students for entry-level positions in a competitive, rapidly changing workplace. The College provides associate degree and diploma programs in business and accounting, the allied health sciences, legal studies, electronics, and computer technology to approximately 615 students.

Brown Mackie College–Findlay was founded in 1926 by William H. Stautzenberger to provide solid business education at a reasonable cost. In 1960, the College was acquired by George R. Hawes, who served as its president until 1969. The College changed its name from Southern Ohio College–Findlay in 2001 to AEC Southern Ohio College; it was acquired by Education Management Corporation (EDMC) on September 2, 2003, and changed to Brown Mackie College–Findlay in November 2004.

Brown Mackie College–Findlay is accredited by the Accrediting Council for Independent Colleges and Schools (ACICS) to award associate degrees and diplomas. The Accrediting Council for Independent Colleges and Schools is listed as a nationally recognized accrediting agency by the United States Department of Education. Its accreditation of degree-granting institutions also is recognized by the Council for Higher Education Accreditation. The Accrediting Council's address is 750 First Street, NE, Suite 980, Washington, D.C. 20002-4241; 202-336-6780. The practical nursing program is approved by the Ohio Board of Nursing, 17 South High Street, Suite 400, Columbus, Ohio 43215-3413; 614-466-3947.

Brown Mackie College–Findlay is a nonresidential, smoke-free institution and is owned and operated by Education Management Corporation, 210 Sixth Avenue, 33rd Floor, Pittsburgh, Pennsylvania 15222-2603; http://www.edmc.edu. Although the College does not offer residential housing, students who are unable to commute daily from their homes may request assistance from the Admissions Office in locating housing. Ample parking is available at no additional cost.

Academic Programs

Brown Mackie College–Findlay provides higher education to traditional and nontraditional students through associate degree and diploma programs that assist them in enhancing their career opportunities, broadening their perspectives through appropriate general education courses, thinking independently and critically, and improving problem-solving abilities. The College strives to develop within its students the desire for lifelong and continued education.

Each College quarter comprises twelve weeks. Associate degree programs require a minimum of eight quarters to complete. Programs are offered on a year-round basis, providing students with the ability to work uninterrupted toward completion of their programs.

Associate Degree Programs The Associate of Applied Business degree (96 credits) is awarded in accounting technology, business management, computer software technology, criminal justice, and paralegal studies. The Associate of Applied Science degree (96 credits) is awarded in gerontology, health-care administration, medical assisting, and pharmacy technology.

Diploma Programs In addition to the associate degree programs, the College offers diploma programs (76 credits) in business, computer software applications, medical assistant studies, and practical nursing.

Costs

Tuition for programs in the 2005–06 academic year was $179 per credit hour, with the exception of the practical nursing diploma program, which was $250 per credit hour. The length of the program determines total cost. Textbooks per quarter for traditional programs were approximately $380; for the practical nursing program, they were approximately $435.

Financial Aid

The College maintains a full-time staff of financial aid professionals to assist qualified students in obtaining the financial assistance they require to meet their educational expenses. The College participates in several student aid programs. Forms of financial aid available through federal resources include the Federal Pell Grant Program, Federal Supplemental Educational Opportunity Grant (FSEOG) Program, Federal Work-Study Program, Federal Perkins Loan Program, Federal Stafford Student Loan Program (subsidized and unsubsidized), and the Federal PLUS Loan Program. Eligible students may apply for state awards, such as the Ohio Instructional Grant (OIG), and veterans' educational benefits. Students with physical or mental disabilities that are a handicap to employment may be eligible for training services through the state Agency for Vocational Rehabilitation. For further information, students should contact the College Student Financial Services Office.

Each year, the College makes available President's Scholarships of $1000 each to qualifying seniors from area high schools. No more than one scholarship is awarded per high school. In order to qualify, a senior must be graduating from a participating high school, must be maintaining a cumulative grade point average of at least 2.0, and must submit a brief essay. The student's extracurricular activities and community service are also considered. The President's Scholarship is available only to students enrolling in one of the College's degree programs. Students awarded the scholarship must enroll at Brown Mackie College–Findlay between June and September immediately following their high school graduation. Applications for these scholarships can be obtained from the guidance departments of participating high schools. These applications must be completed and returned to the College by March 31. Those awarded scholarships are notified by April 30.

Faculty

There are 14 full-time and 37 part-time instructors at the College. The average student-faculty ratio is 16:1. Each student is assigned a faculty adviser.

Academic Facilities

The College has 22,000 square feet of academic classrooms, laboratories, and offices.

Location

Located at 1700 Fostoria Avenue, Suite 100, in Findlay, Ohio, the College is easily accessible from Interstate 75.

Admission Requirements

Each applicant for admission is assigned an Assistant Director of Admissions, who directs the applicant through the steps of the admissions process, providing information on curriculum, policies, procedures, and services and assisting the applicant in setting necessary appointments and interviews. To qualify for admission, each applicant must provide documentation of graduation from an accredited high school or from a state-approved secondary education curriculum or provide official documentation of high school graduation equivalency. All transcripts become the property of the College. Admission to the College is based upon the applicant's meeting the above requirements, a review of the applicant's previous educational records, and a review of the applicant's career interests. If previous academic records indicate that the College's education and training would not benefit the applicant, the College reserves the right to advise the applicant not to enroll. Special requirements for enrollment into certain programs are discussed in the descriptions of those programs. For further information, students should contact the College Admissions Office.

Application and Information

Applicants must complete and submit an application form, along with documentation of graduation from an accredited high school or state-approved secondary education curriculum or official documentation of high school graduation equivalency.

For additional information, prospective students should contact:

Director of Admissions
Brown Mackie College–Findlay
1700 Fostoria Avenue, Suite 100
Findlay, Ohio 45840
Telephone: 419-423-2211
          800-842-3687 (toll-free)
Fax: 419-423-0725
E-mail: bmcfiadm@amedcts.com
World Wide Web: http://www.brownmackie.edu

BROWN MACKIE COLLEGE–FORT WAYNE

FORT WAYNE, INDIANA

The College and Its Mission

Brown Mackie College–Fort Wayne is dedicated to providing educational programs that prepare students for entry-level positions in a competitive, rapidly changing workplace. The College provides associate degree, diploma, and certificate programs in the areas of business and accounting, allied health sciences, legal studies, computer technology, and electronics to approximately 700 students.

Brown Mackie College–Fort Wayne is one of the oldest institutions of its kind in the country and the oldest in the state of Indiana. Established in 1882 as the South Bend Commercial College, the school later changed its name to Michiana College. In 1930, the College was incorporated under the laws of the state of Indiana and was authorized to confer associate degrees and certificates in business. In 1992, the College in South Bend added a branch location in Fort Wayne, Indiana. In 2004, Michiana College changed its name to Brown Mackie College–Fort Wayne.

Brown Mackie College–Fort Wayne is accredited by the Accrediting Council for Independent Colleges and Schools (ACICS) to award associate degrees, diplomas, and certificates. The Accrediting Council for Independent Colleges and Schools is listed as a nationally recognized accrediting agency by the United States Department of Education. Its accreditation of degree-granting institutions also is recognized by the Council for Higher Education Accreditation. The Accrediting Council's address is 750 First Street, NE, Suite 980, Washington, D.C. 20002-4241; 202-336-6780. Brown Mackie College–Fort Wayne is owned and operated by Education Management Corporation, 210 Sixth Avenue, 33rd Floor, Pittsburgh, Pennsylvania 15222-2603 (http://www.edmc.edu), a publicly held corporation engaged in providing career education and training.

The College's medical assisting degree program is accredited by the Commission on Accreditation of Allied Health Education Programs (CAAHEP), on recommendation of the Curriculum Review Board of the American Association of Medical Assistants Endowment (AAMAE). The commission's address is 35 East Wacker Drive, Chicago, Illinois 60601; 312-553-9355. The College is licensed and regulated by the Indiana Commission on Proprietary Education, 302 West Washington Street, Indianapolis, Indiana 46204; 317-232-1320 or 800-227-5695 (toll-free). The College's occupational therapy assistant studies program is accredited by the Accreditation Council for Occupational Therapy Education (ACOTE) of the American Occupational Therapy Association (AOTA), 4720 Montgomery Lane, P.O. Box 31220, Bethesda, Maryland 20824-1220; 301-652-2682. The College's practical nursing program is accredited by the Indiana State Board of Nursing, 402 West Washington Street, Room W066, Indianapolis, Indiana 46204; 317-234-2043.

Brown Mackie College–Fort Wayne is a smoke-free institution.

Academic Programs

Brown Mackie College–Fort Wayne provides higher education to traditional and nontraditional students through associate degree, diploma, and certificate programs that assist them in enhancing their career opportunities, broadening their perspectives through appropriate general education courses, thinking independently and critically, and improving problem solving abilities. The College strives to develop within its students the desire for lifelong and continued education.

Each College quarter comprises twelve weeks. Associate degree programs require a minimum of eight quarters to complete. Programs are offered on a year-round basis, providing students with the ability to work uninterrupted toward their degrees.

Associate Degree Programs The Associate of Science degree (96 credits) is awarded in accounting technology, business management, computer software technology, criminal justice, medical assisting, and paralegal studies. The Associate of Applied Science degree (96 credits) is awarded in occupational therapy assistant studies.

Diploma Program A diploma (76 credits) is awarded in practical nursing.

Certificate Programs Certificates (48 credits) are awarded in accounting, business, computer software applications, criminal justice, medical assistant studies, and paralegal assistant studies.

Costs

Tuition in the 2005–06 academic year for all programs except practical nursing and occupational therapy assistant studies was $179 per credit hour; fees were $10 per credit hour. Textbook expenses were estimated at $372 per quarter. For the practical nursing program, tuition was $250 per credit hour; fees were $10 per credit hour. Textbook expenses were estimated at $400 for the first term, $600 for the second term, and $100 for the third, fourth, and fifth terms. For the occupational therapy assistant studies program, tuition was $179 per credit hour for general education courses and $300 per credit hour for occupational therapy courses; fees were $10 per credit hour. Textbook expenses were estimated at $372 per quarter for the first six terms and $458 for the seventh term.

Financial Aid

The College maintains a full-time staff of financial aid professionals to assist qualified students in obtaining the financial assistance they require to meet their educational expenses. The College participates in several student aid programs. Forms of financial aid available through federal resources include the Federal Pell Grant Program, Federal Supplemental Educational Opportunity Grant (FSEOG) Program, Federal Work-Study Program, Federal Perkins Loan Program, Federal Stafford Student Loan Program (subsidized and unsubsidized), and the Federal PLUS Loan Program. Eligible students may apply for Indiana state awards, such as the Frank O'Bannon Grant Program (formerly the Indiana State Grant Program), the Higher Education Award, and Twenty-First Century Scholarships for high school students; for the Core 40 awards; and for veterans' educational benefits. Students with physical or mental disabilities that are a handicap to employment may be eligible for training services through the state Agency for Vocational Rehabilitation. For further information, students should contact the College Student Financial Services Office.

Each year, the College makes available President's Scholarships of $1000 each to qualifying seniors from area high schools. No more than one scholarship is awarded per high school. In order to qualify, a senior must be graduating from a participating high school, must be maintaining a cumulative grade point average of at least 2.0, and must submit a brief essay. The student's extracurricular activities and community service are also considered. The President's Scholarship is available only to students enrolling in one of the College's degree programs. Students awarded the scholarship must enroll at Brown Mackie College–Fort Wayne between June and September immediately following their high school graduation. Applications for these scholarships can be obtained from the guidance departments of participating high schools. These applications must be completed and returned to the College by March 31. Those awarded scholarships are notified by April 30.

Faculty

The College has 21 full-time and 39 part-time instructors, with a student-faculty ratio of 12:1. Each student is assigned a faculty adviser.

Academic Facilities

Brown Mackie College–Fort Wayne consists of 32,000 square feet of classrooms; medical, nursing, computer, and occupational therapy labs; a library; a bookstore; and office space.

Location

Brown Mackie College–Fort Wayne is located at 3000 East Coliseum Boulevard in Fort Wayne, Indiana. The College facility is accessible by public transportation. Ample parking is provided at no additional charge.

Admission Requirements

Each applicant for admission is assigned an Assistant Director of Admissions, who directs the applicant through the steps of the admissions process, providing information on curriculum, policies, procedures, and services and assisting the applicant in setting necessary appointments and interviews. To qualify for admission, each applicant must provide documentation of graduation from an accredited high school or from a state-approved secondary education curriculum or provide official documentation of high school graduation equivalency. All transcripts become the property of the College. Admission to the College is based upon the applicant's meeting the above requirements, a review of the applicant's previous educational records, and a review of the applicant's career interests. If previous academic records indicate that the College's education and training would not benefit the applicant, the College reserves the right to advise the applicant not to enroll. Special requirements for enrollment into certain programs are discussed in the descriptions of those programs.

As part of the admissions process, students are given an assessment of academic skills. Though the results of this assessment do not determine eligibility for admission, they provide the College with a means of determining the need for academic support, as well as a means by which the College can evaluate the effectiveness of its educational programs. All new students are required to complete this assessment, which is readministered at the end of the student's program so that results may be compared with those of the initial administration.

In addition to the College's general admission requirements, applicants enrolling in the practical nursing program must document the following, which must be completed and a record of proof must appear in the student's file prior to the start of the Nursing Fundamentals course. No student will be admitted to a clinical agency unless all paperwork is completed. The paperwork is a requirement of all contracted agencies. This paperwork includes records of (1) a complete physical, current to within six months of admission; (2) a two-step Mantoux test that is kept current throughout schooling; (3) a hepatitis B vaccination or signed refusal; (4) up-to-date immunizations, including tetanus and rubella; (5) a record of current CPR certification that is maintained throughout the student's clinical experience; and (6) hospitalization insurance or a signed waiver.

Application and Information

Applicants must complete and submit an application form, along with documentation of graduation from an accredited high school or state-approved secondary education curriculum or official documentation of high school graduation equivalency.

For additional information, prospective students should contact:

Director of Admissions
Brown Mackie College–Fort Wayne
3000 East Coliseum Boulevard
Fort Wayne, Indiana 46805
Telephone: 260-484-4400
        866-433-2289 (toll-free)
Fax: 260-484-2678
E-mail: bmcfwaadm@amedcts.com
World Wide Web: http://www.brownmackie.edu

BROWN MACKIE COLLEGE–HOPKINSVILLE

HOPKINSVILLE, KENTUCKY

The College and Its Mission

Brown Mackie College–Hopkinsville is dedicated to providing education programs that prepare students for entry-level positions in a competitive, rapidly changing workplace. The College provides associate degree and diploma programs in the areas of business and accounting, allied health sciences, legal studies, and computer technology to approximately 150 students.

Brown Mackie College–Hopkinsville is accredited by the Accrediting Council for Independent Colleges and Schools (ACICS) to award associate degrees and diplomas. ACICS is listed as a nationally recognized accrediting agency by the United States Department of Education. Its accreditation of degree-granting institutions also is recognized by the Council for Higher Education Accreditation. ACICS may be contacted at 750 First Street, NE, Suite 980, Washington, D.C. 20002-4241; phone: 202-336-6780. The College is a nonresidential, smoke-free institution and is owned and operated by Education Management Corporation (EDMC), 210 Sixth Avenue, 33rd Floor, Pittsburgh, Pennsylvania 15222-2603; phone: 800-275-2440 (toll-free); Web site: http://www.edmc.edu.

Academic Programs

Brown Mackie College–Hopkinsville provides higher education to traditional and nontraditional students through associate degree and diploma programs that assist them in enhancing their career opportunities, broadening their perspectives through appropriate general education courses, thinking independently and critically, and improving problem-solving abilities. Each College quarter comprises ten to twelve weeks.

Associate Degree Programs Associate degree programs require a minimum of eight quarters to complete. Programs are offered on a year-round basis, providing students with the ability to work uninterrupted toward their degrees. The Associate of Applied Business degree (96 credits) is awarded in accounting technology, business management, computer programming and applications, computer software technology, criminal justice, and paralegal studies. The Associate of Applied Science degree (96 credits) is awarded in medical assisting.

Diploma Programs The College also offers diploma programs (48 credits) in accounting, business, computer software applications, criminal justice, medical assistant studies, and paralegal assistant studies.

Costs

Tuition is $169 per credit hour. A general fee of $10 per credit hour is charged and applied to the cost of institutional activities and services. The cost of textbooks and other instructional materials varies by program.

Financial Aid

The College maintains a full-time staff of financial aid professionals to assist qualified students in obtaining the financial assistance they require to meet their educational expenses. The College participates in several student aid programs. Forms of financial aid available through federal resources include Federal Pell Grants, Federal Supplemental Educational Opportunity Grants (FSEOG), the Federal Work-Study Program, Federal Perkins Loans, Federal Stafford Student Loans (subsidized and unsubsidized), and the Federal PLUS Program. Students may apply for the College Access Program (CAP) Grant Program and the Kentucky Education Excellence Award (KEES), a scholarship program based on their final high school grade point average. Eligible students may also apply for veterans' educational benefits. Students with physical or mental disabilities that are a handicap to employment may be eligible for training services through the State Vocational Rehabilitation Agency. For further information, students should contact the College Student Financial Services Office.

Each year, the College makes available President's Scholarships of $1000 each to qualifying seniors from area high schools. No more than one scholarship is awarded per high school. In order to qualify, a senior must be graduating from a participating high school, maintain a cumulative grade point average of at least 2.0, and submit a brief essay. The student's extracurricular activities and community service are also considered. The President's Scholarship is available only to students enrolling in one of the College's degree programs. Students awarded the scholarship must enroll at Brown Mackie College–Hopkinsville between June and September immediately following their high school graduation. Applications for these scholarships can be obtained from the guidance departments of participating high schools. These applications must be completed and returned to the College by March 31. Those awarded scholarships are notified by April 30.

Faculty

There are 3 full-time and 8 part-time faculty members. The student-faculty ratio is 12:1.

Facilities and Resources

Brown Mackie College–Hopkinsville occupies a spacious building that has been specifically designed to provide a comfortable and effective environment for learning. The facility comprises approximately 11,250 square feet, including six classrooms, a medical laboratory, an electronics laboratory, three computer laboratories, an academic resource center, administrative and faculty offices, a bookstore, and a student lounge. Computer equipment for hands-on learning includes three networked laboratories. Medical equipment includes monocular and binocular microscopes, electrocardiograph, autoclave, centrifuge, and other equipment appropriate to hands-on laboratory and clinical instruction. Convenient parking is available to all students.

Location

The College is located at 4001 Fort Campbell Boulevard in Hopkinsville, Kentucky.

Admission Requirements

Each applicant for admission is assigned an Assistant Director of Admissions who directs the applicant through the steps of the admissions process, providing information on curriculum, policies, procedures, and services and assisting the applicant in setting necessary appointments and interviews. To qualify for admission, each applicant must provide documentation of graduation from an accredited high school or from a state-approved secondary education curriculum or provide official documentation of high school graduation equivalency. All transcripts become the property of the College. Admission to the College is based upon the applicant's meeting the above requirements, a review of the applicant's previous education records, and a review of the applicant's career interests. If previous academic records indicate that the College's education and training would not benefit the applicant, the College reserves the right to advise the applicant not to enroll. Special requirements for enrollment into certain programs are discussed in the descriptions of those programs.

Application and Information

Applicants must complete and submit an application form, along with documentation of graduation from an accredited high school or state-approved secondary education curriculum or provide official documentation of high school graduation equivalency. For additional information, prospective students should contact:

Director of Admissions
Brown Mackie College–Hopkinsville
4001 Fort Campbell Boulevard
Hopkinsville, Kentucky 42240
Telephone: 270-886-1302
          800-359-4753 (toll-free)
E-mail: bmchoadm@amedcts.com
World Wide Web: http://www.brownmackie.edu

BROWN MACKIE COLLEGE–KANSAS CITY

LENEXA, KANSAS

The College and Its Mission

Brown Mackie College–Kansas City is dedicated to providing education programs that prepare students for entry-level positions in a competitive, rapidly changing workplace. The College provides associate degree, diploma, and certificate programs in the areas of business and accounting, allied health sciences, legal studies, and computer technology to approximately 350 students.

The College was originally founded in Salina, Kansas, in July 1892 as the Kansas Wesleyan School of Business. In 1938, the College was incorporated as the Brown Mackie School of Business under the ownership of former Kansas Wesleyan instructors Perry E. Brown and A. B. Mackie. It became Brown Mackie College in January 1975.

Brown Mackie College–Kansas City is accredited as a branch of Brown Mackie College–Salina, Kansas, by the Higher Learning Commission of the North Central Association of Colleges and Schools, 30 North LaSalle Street, Suite 2400, Chicago, Illinois 60602; phone: 800-621-7440 (toll-free). The College, which is operating in Salina and Lenexa, Kansas, is approved and authorized to grant the Associate of Applied Science degree by the Kansas Board of Regents, 1000 Southwest Jackson Street, Suite 520, Topeka, Kansas 66612-1368. The College is a nonresidential, smoke-free institution and is a subsidiary of Brown Mackie Holding Company of Education Management Corporation (EDMC), 210 Sixth Avenue, 33rd Floor, Pittsburgh, Pennsylvania 15222-2603; phone: 800-275-2440 (toll-free); Web site: http://www.edmc.edu.

Academic Programs

Brown Mackie College–Kansas City provides higher education to traditional and nontraditional students through associate degree, diploma, and certificate programs that assist them in enhancing their career opportunities, broadening their perspectives through appropriate general education courses, thinking independently and critically, and improving problem-solving abilities. The College strives to develop within its students the desire for lifelong and continued education. Each College quarter comprises twelve weeks.

Associate Degree Programs Associate degree programs require a minimum of ten quarters to complete. Programs are offered on a year-round basis, providing students with the ability to work uninterrupted toward their degrees. The Associate of Applied Science degree (96 credits) is awarded in accounting technology, business management, computer-aided design and drafting technology, computer networking and applications, computer software technology, criminal justice, medical assisting, medical office management, paralegal studies, and sales and marketing.

Diploma Programs The College also offers diploma programs (48 credits) in accounting, advertising, business, computer-aided design and drafting technician studies, computer applications, computer software applications, criminal justice, medical assistant studies, medical coding and billing, and paralegal assistant studies.

Certificate Program A certificate program (24 credits) is offered in computer networking.

Costs

Tuition is $189 per credit hour. Textbook fees are estimated at $360 per quarter.

Financial Aid

The College maintains a full-time staff of financial aid professionals to assist qualified students in obtaining the financial assistance they require to meet their educational expenses. The College participates in several student aid programs. Forms of financial aid available through federal resources include Federal Pell Grants, Federal Supplemental Educational Opportunity Grants (FSEOG), the Federal Work-Study Program, Federal Perkins Loans, Federal Stafford Student Loans (subsidized and unsubsidized), and the Federal PLUS Program. Eligible students may apply for veterans' educational benefits. Students with physical or mental disabilities that are a handicap to employment may be eligible for training services through the state Vocational Rehabilitation Agency. For further information, students should contact the College Student Financial Services Office.

Scholarship applications are reviewed by the College President, who is solely responsible for award decisions. Awards are disbursed to recipients in monthly increments over the academic year for which the scholarship has been awarded. All scholarship recipients must maintain full-time status and a minimum cumulative grade point average, or they must forfeit their awards. The total value of all college scholarships awarded to any one student shall not exceed the cost of one academic year (36 credits) of tuition.

Faculty

There are 7 full-time faculty members. The average classroom size is 14:1, with a student-faculty ratio of 50:1.

Facilities and Resources

In addition to classrooms and computer labs, the College maintains a library of curriculum-related resources, technical and general education materials, academic and professional periodicals, and audiovisual resources. Internet access also is available for research. The College has a bookstore that stocks texts, courseware, and other educational supplies required for courses and a variety of personal, recreational, and gift items, including apparel, supplies, and general merchandise incorporating the College logo. Hours are posted at the bookstore entrance.

Location

Brown Mackie College–Kansas City is located at 9705 Lenexa Drive in Lenexa, Kansas, just off the I-435 loop at 95th Street in Johnson County.

Admission Requirements

Each applicant for admission is assigned an Assistant Director of Admissions, who directs the applicant through the steps of the admissions process, providing information on curriculum, policies, procedures, and services and assisting the applicant in setting necessary appointments and interviews. To qualify for admission, each applicant must provide documentation of graduation from an accredited high school or from a state-approved secondary education curriculum or provide official documentation of high school graduation equivalency. All transcripts become the property of the College. Admission to the College is based upon the applicant's meeting the above requirements, a review of the applicant's previous education records, and a review of the applicant's career interests. If previous academic records indicate that the College's education and training would not benefit the applicant, the College reserves the right to advise the applicant not to enroll. Special requirements for enrollment into certain programs are discussed in the descriptions of those programs.

Application and Information

Applicants must complete and submit an application form, along with documentation of graduation from an accredited high school or state-approved secondary education curriculum or official documentation of high school graduation equivalency. For additional information, prospective students should contact:

Director of Admissions
Brown Mackie College–Kansas City
9705 Lenexa Drive
Lenexa, Kansas 66215
Telephone: 913-768-1900
Fax: 800-635-9101 (toll-free)
E-mail: bmckcadm@amedcts.com
World Wide Web: http://www.brownmackie.edu

BROWN MACKIE COLLEGE–LOUISVILLE
LOUISVILLE, KENTUCKY

The College and Its Mission

Brown Mackie College–Louisville is dedicated to providing education programs that prepare students for entry-level positions in a competitive, rapidly changing workplace. The College provides associate degree and diploma programs in the areas of business and accounting, the allied health sciences, legal studies, computer technology, graphic design, and electronics to approximately 300 students.

Brown Mackie College–Louisville opened in 1972 as RETS Institute of Technology. The first RETS school was founded in 1935 in Detroit in response to the rapid growth of radio broadcasting and the need for qualified radio technicians. The RETS Institute changed its name to Brown Mackie College–Louisville in 2004.

Brown Mackie College–Louisville is accredited by the Accrediting Council for Independent Colleges and Schools (ACICS) to award associate degrees and diplomas. ACICS is listed as a nationally recognized accrediting agency by the U.S. Department of Education. Its accreditation of degree-granting institutions is recognized by the Council for Higher Education Accreditation. ACICS can be reached at 750 First Street NE, Suite 980, Washington, D.C. 20002-4241; 202-336-6780.

The College is a nonresidential, smoke-free institution and a subsidiary of Education Management Corporation (EDMC), 210 Sixth Avenue, 33rd floor, Pittsburgh, Pennsylvania 15222-2603; http://www.edmc.edu.

Academic Programs

Brown Mackie College–Louisville provides higher education to traditional and nontraditional students through associate degree and diploma programs that assist them in enhancing their career opportunities, broadening their perspectives through appropriate general education courses, thinking independently and critically, and improving problem-solving abilities.

Each College quarter comprises ten to twelve weeks. Associate degree programs require a minimum of eight quarters to complete. Programs are offered on a year-round basis, providing students with the ability to work uninterrupted toward their degrees.

Associate Degree Programs The Associate of Applied Business degree (96 credits) is awarded in accounting technology, business management, computer networking and applications, criminal justice, graphic design, and paralegal studies. The Associate of Applied Science degree (96 credits) is awarded in electronics, gerontology, health-care administration, medical assisting, and pharmacy technology.

Diploma Programs The College offers diploma programs (48 credits) in electronics, medical assistant studies, and paralegal assistant studies.

Costs

Tuition is $179 per credit hour. Textbook fees vary according to program.

Financial Aid

The College maintains a full-time staff of financial aid professionals to assist qualified students in obtaining the financial assistance they require to meet their educational expenses. The College participates in several student aid programs. Forms of financial aid available through federal resources include the Federal Pell Grant Program, Federal Supplemental Educational Opportunity Grant (FSEOG) Program, Federal Work-Study Program, Federal Perkins Loan Program, Federal Stafford Student Loan Program (subsidized and unsubsidized), and the Federal PLUS Loan Program. Students may apply for state-based award programs, such as the College Access Program (CAP) Grant Program and the Kentucky Educational Excellence Award (KEES). Eligible students may also apply for veterans' benefits. Students with physical or mental disabilities that are a handicap to employment may be eligible for training services through the state Agency for Vocational Rehabilitation. For further information, students should contact the College Student Financial Services Office.

Each year, the College makes available scholarships of $1000 each to qualifying seniors from area high schools. No more than one scholarship is awarded per high school. In order to qualify, a senior must be graduating from a participating high school, must be maintaining a cumulative grade point average of at least 2.0, and must submit a brief essay. The student's extracurricular activities and community service are also considered. The President's Scholarship is available only to students enrolling in one of the College's degree programs. Students awarded the scholarship must enroll at Brown Mackie College–Louisville between June and September immediately following their high school graduation. Applications for these scholarships can be obtained from the guidance departments of participating high schools. These applications must be completed and returned to the College by March 31. Those awarded scholarships are notified by April 30.

Faculty

There are 7 full-time and 7 part-time faculty members at the College. The average student-faculty ratio is 13:1

Facilities and Resources

Brown Mackie College–Louisville has more than 23,000 square feet of multipurpose classrooms, including networked computer laboratories, electronics laboratories, a resource center, and offices for administrative personnel as well as for student services such as admissions, student financial services, and career-services assistance.

Location

The College is located at 300 High Rise Drive, Louisville, Kentucky, adjacent to Interstate 65 and south of the Louisville International Airport.

Admission Requirements

Each applicant for admission is assigned an Assistant Director of Admissions who directs the applicant through the steps of the admissions process, providing information on curriculum, policies, procedures, and services and assisting the applicant in setting necessary appointments and interviews. To qualify for admission, each applicant must provide documentation of graduation from an accredited high school or completion of a state-approved secondary education curriculum or provide official documentation of high school graduation equivalency. All transcripts become the property of the College. Admission to the College is based on the applicant's meeting the above requirements, a review of the applicant's previous educational records, and a review of the applicant's career interests. If previous academic records indicate that the College's education and training would not benefit the applicant, the College reserves the right to advise the applicant not to enroll. Special requirements for enrollment into certain programs are discussed in the descriptions of those programs.

Application and Information

Applicants must complete and submit an application form along with documentation of graduation from an accredited high school or completion of state-approved secondary education curriculum or provide official documentation of high school graduation equivalency. For additional information, prospective students should contact:

Director of Admissions
Brown Mackie College–Louisville
300 High Rise Drive
Louisville, Kentucky 40213
Telephone: 502-968-7191
    800-999-7387 (toll-free)
Fax: 501-357-9956
E-mail: bmcloadm@amedcts.com
World Wide Web: http://www.brownmackie.edu

BROWN MACKIE COLLEGE–MERRILLVILLE

MERRILLVILLE, INDIANA

The College and Its Mission

Brown Mackie College–Merrillville is dedicated to providing educational programs that prepare students for entry-level positions in a competitive, rapidly changing workplace. The College provides associate degree, diploma, and certificate programs in business and accounting, allied health sciences, legal studies, computer technology, and electronics to approximately 615 students.

Founded in 1890 by A. N. Hirons as LaPorte Business College in LaPorte, Indiana, the institution later became known as Commonwealth Business College. In 1919, ownership was transferred to Grace and J. J. Moore, who successfully operated the College under the name of Reese School of Business for several decades. In 1975, the College came under the ownership of Steven C. Smith as Commonwealth Business College. A second location, now known as Brown Mackie College–Merrillville, was opened in 1984, in Merrillville, Indiana. The College changed ownership again in September 2003 when it was acquired by Education Management Corporation, and the College name was changed to Brown Mackie College–Merrillville in November 2004.

Brown Mackie College–Merrillville is accredited by the Accrediting Council for Independent Colleges and Schools (ACICS) to award associate degrees and certificates. ACICS is listed as a nationally recognized accrediting agency by the U.S. Department of Education. Its accreditation of degree-granting institutions also is recognized by the Council for Higher Education Accreditation. ACICS can be contacted at 750 First Street, NE, Suite 980, Washington, D.C. 20002-4241; 202-336-6780. Brown Mackie College–Merrillville has two branches: Brown Mackie College–Michigan City and Brown Mackie College–Moline.

The College's Medical Assisting degree program is accredited by the Accrediting Bureau of Health Education Schools (ABHES), 7777 Leesburg Pike, Suite 314N, Falls Church, Virginia 22403; 703-917-9503. The College's diploma program in practical nursing is accredited by the Health Professions Bureau (Attn: Indiana State Board of Nursing) 402 West Washington Street, Room W066, Indianapolis, Indiana 46204; 317-234-2043.

The College is a nonresidential, smoke-free institution and a subsidiary of Education Management Corporation (EDMC), 210 Sixth Avenue, 33rd floor, Pittsburgh, Pennsylvania 15222-2603; http://www.edmc.edu.

Academic Programs

Brown Mackie College–Merrillville provides higher education to traditional and nontraditional students through associate degree, diploma, and certificate programs that assist them in enhancing their career opportunities, broadening their perspectives through appropriate general education courses, thinking independently and critically, and improving problem-solving abilities. The College strives to develop within its students the desire for lifelong and continued education.

Each College quarter comprises ten to twelve weeks. Associate degree programs require a minimum of eight quarters to complete. Programs are offered on a year-round basis, providing students with the ability to work uninterrupted toward completion of their programs.

Associate Degree Programs The Associate of Science degree (96 credits) is awarded in accounting technology, administration in gerontology, business management, computer programming and applications, computer software technology, criminal justice, electronics, medical assisting, medical office management, surgical technology, and paralegal studies.

Diploma Programs A diploma program (76 credits) in practical nursing is offered.

Certificate Programs The College offers certificate programs (48 credits) in accounting, business, computer software applications, criminal justice, medical assistant studies, and paralegal assistant studies.

Costs

Tuition for programs in the 2005–06 academic year was $179 per credit hour with the exception of the Practical Nursing Diploma program, which was $250 per credit hour. The length of the program determines total cost. Textbook fees vary according to program.

Financial Aid

The College maintains a full-time staff of financial aid professionals to assist qualified students in obtaining the financial assistance they require to meet their educational expenses. The College participates in several student aid programs. Forms of financial aid available through federal resources include the Federal Pell Grant Program, Federal Supplemental Educational Opportunity Grant (FSEOG) Program, Federal Work-Study Program, Federal Perkins Loan Program, Federal Stafford Student Loan Program (subsidized and unsubsidized), and the Federal PLUS Loan Program. Eligible students may apply for Indiana state awards such as the Higher Education Award and Twenty-First Century Scholarships for high school students, the Core 40 awards, and veterans' educational benefits. Students with physical or mental disabilities that are a handicap to employment may be eligible for training services through the state Agency for Vocational Rehabilitation.

For further information, students should contact the College Student Financial Services Office.

Each year, the College makes available scholarships of $1000 each to qualifying seniors from area high schools. No more than one scholarship is awarded per high school. In order to qualify, a senior must be graduating from a participating high school, must be maintaining a cumulative grade point average of at least 2.0, and must submit a brief essay. The student's extracurricular activities and community service are also considered. The President's Scholarship is available only to students enrolling in one of the College's degree programs. Students awarded the scholarship must enroll at Brown Mackie College–Merrillville between June and September immediately following their high school graduation. Applications for these scholarships can be obtained from the guidance departments of participating high schools. These applications must be completed and returned to the College by March 31. Those awarded scholarships are notified by April 30.

Faculty

There are 11 full-time and 29 part-time faculty members at the College who are practitioners in their fields of expertise. The average student-faculty ratio is 17:1.

Facilities and Resources

Occupying 18,000 square feet, Brown Mackie College–Merrillville was opened to students in October 1998 in the Twin Towers complex of Merrillville and comprises several instructional rooms, including five computer labs with networked computers and four medical laboratories. The administrative offices, college library, and student lounge are all easily accessible to students. The college bookstore stocks texts, courseware, and other educational supplies required for courses at the College. Students also find a variety of personal, recreational, and gift items, including apparel, supplies, and general merchandise incorporating the College logo. Hours are posted at the bookstore entrance. A spacious parking lot provides ample parking at no additional charge.

Location

Brown Mackie College–Merrillville is located in northwest Indiana, in the Twin Towers business complex of Merrillville just west of the intersection of U.S. Route 30 and Interstate 65.

Admission Requirements

Each applicant for admission is assigned an Assistant Director of Admissions who directs the applicant through the steps of the admissions process, providing information on curriculum, policies, procedures, and services, and assisting the applicant in setting necessary appointments and interviews. To qualify for admission, each applicant must provide documentation of graduation from an accredited high school or completion of a state-approved secondary education curriculum or provide official documentation of high school graduation equivalency. All transcripts become the property of the College. Admission to the College is based upon the applicant's meeting the above requirements, a review of the applicant's previous educational records, and a review of the applicant's career interests. If previous academic records indicate that the College's education and training would not benefit the applicant, the College reserves the right to advise the applicant not to enroll. Special requirements for enrollment into certain programs are discussed in the descriptions of those programs.

Application and Information

Applicants must complete and submit an application form along with documentation of graduation from an accredited high school or completion of state-approved secondary education curriculum or provide official documentation of high school graduation equivalency. For additional information, prospective students should contact:

Director of Admissions
Brown Mackie College–Merrillville
1000 East 80th Place, Suite 101N
Merrillville, Indiana 46410
Telephone: 219-769-3321
            800-258-3321 (toll-free)
Fax: 219-738-1076
E-mail: bmcmeadm@amedcts.com
World Wide Web: http://www.brownmackie.edu

BROWN MACKIE COLLEGE–MIAMI

MIAMI, FLORIDA

The College and Its Mission

Brown Mackie College–Miami is dedicated to providing education programs that prepare students for entry-level positions in a competitive, rapidly changing workplace. The College provides associate degree and diploma programs in the areas of business and accounting, allied health sciences, legal studies, and computer technology to approximately 160 students.

Brown Mackie College–Miami was established as a branch of Brown Mackie College–Cincinnati in 2004. Brown Mackie College–Cincinnati was founded in Cincinnati, Ohio, in February 1927 as a traditional business college. In 1964, the College was granted accreditation as a business school by the Association of Independent Colleges and Schools (AICS) and as a junior college of business by the Accrediting Council of Independent Colleges and Schools (ACICS) in 1972. The school is accredited by ACICS to award associate degrees and diplomas. ACICS is listed as a nationally recognized accrediting agency by the United States Department of Education. ACICS is located at 750 First Street, NE, Suite 980, Washington, D.C. 20002-4241; 202-336-6780. Brown Mackie College–Miami's accreditation of degree-granting institutions is also recognized by the Council for Higher Education Accreditation.

The College is a nonresidential, smoke-free institution and a subsidiary of Education Management Corporation (EDMC), 210 Sixth Avenue, 33rd Floor, Pittsburgh, Pennsylvania 15222-2603; http://www.edmc.edu. Students who are unable to commute daily from their homes may request housing assistance from the Housing Department.

Academic Programs

Brown Mackie College–Miami provides higher education to traditional and nontraditional students through associate degree and diploma programs that assist them in enhancing their career opportunities, broadening their perspectives through appropriate general education courses, thinking independently and critically, and improving problem-solving abilities. The College strives to develop within its students the desire for lifelong and continued education.

Each College quarter comprises twelve weeks. Associate degree programs require a minimum of eight quarters to complete. Programs are offered on a year-round basis, providing students with the ability to work uninterrupted toward their degree.

Associate Degree Programs   The Associate of Science degree (96 credits) is awarded in accounting technology, business management, computer software technology, criminal justice, medical assisting, and paralegal studies.

Diploma Programs   The College also offers diploma programs (48 credits) in accounting, criminal justice, medical assistant studies, and paralegal assistant studies.

Costs

Tuition is $229 per credit hour. Textbook fees vary according to the program.

Financial Aid

The College maintains a full-time staff of financial aid professionals to assist qualified students in obtaining the financial assistance they require to meet their educational expenses. The College participates in several student aid programs. Forms of financial aid available through federal resources include the Federal Pell Grant Program, Federal Supplemental Educational Opportunity Grant (FSEOG) Program, Federal Work-Study Program, Federal Perkins Loan Program, Federal Stafford Student Loan Program (subsidized and unsubsidized), and the Federal PLUS Loan Program. Eligible students may apply for veterans' educational benefits. Students with physical or mental disabilities that are a handicap to employment may be eligible for training services through the state Agency for Vocational Rehabilitation. For further information, students should contact the College Student Financial Services Office.

Faculty

There are 8 adjunct faculty members at the College. The average student-faculty ratio is 20:1.

Academic Facilities

Brown Mackie College–Miami co-locates with the Miami International University of Art & Design in 80,000 square feet of shared and dedicated space that includes computer labs, medical labs, lecture rooms, administrative offices, and a student lounge. The College facilities comprise media presentation rooms for special instructional needs and a library with more than 19,750 volumes, including books and visual aids and subscriptions to more than 200 periodicals specific to the academic programs offered. The College bookstore stocks texts, courseware, and other educational supplies required for courses at the College. Students also find a variety of personal, recreational, and gift items, including apparel, supplies, and general merchandise incorporating the College logo. Hours are posted at the bookstore entrance.

Location

Brown Mackie College–Miami occupies space within the newly renovated OMNI building at 1501 Biscayne Boulevard in Miami, Florida. It is conveniently located adjacent to the OMNI Metro Mover and bus stop, with access to Metro Rail and Florida's regional Tri-Rail system. Ample parking is also available.

Admission Requirements

Each applicant for admission is assigned an Assistant Director of Admissions, who directs the applicant through the steps of the admissions process, providing information on curriculum, policies, procedures, and services and assisting the applicant in setting necessary appointments and interviews. To qualify for admission, each applicant must provide documentation of graduation from an accredited high school or from a state-approved secondary education curriculum or provide official documentation of high school graduation equivalency. All transcripts become the property of the College. Admission to the College is based on the applicant's meeting the above requirements, a review of the applicant's previous educational records, and a review of the applicant's career interests. If previous academic records indicate that the College's education and training would not benefit the applicant, the College reserves the right to advise the applicant not to enroll. Special requirements for enrollment into certain programs are discussed in the descriptions of those programs.

Application and Information

Applicants must complete and submit an application form, along with documentation of graduation from an accredited high school or state-approved secondary education curriculum or official documentation of high school graduation equivalency.

For additional information, prospective students should contact:

Director of Admissions
Brown Mackie College–Miami
1501 Biscayne Boulevard
Miami, Florida 33132-1418
Telephone: 305-341-6600
             866-505-0335 (toll-free)
Fax: 305-373-8814
E-mail: bmmiadm@edmc.edu
World Wide Web: http://www.brownmackie.edu

BROWN MACKIE COLLEGE– MICHIGAN CITY
MICHIGAN CITY, INDIANA

The College and Its Mission

Brown Mackie College–Michigan City is dedicated to providing education programs that prepare students for entry-level positions in a competitive, rapidly changing workplace. The College provides associate degree and certificate programs in the areas of business and accounting, the allied health sciences, legal studies, electronics, and computer technology to approximately 280 students.

Founded in 1890 by A. N. Hirons as LaPorte Business College in LaPorte, Indiana, the institution later became known as Commonwealth Business College. In 1919, ownership was transferred to Grace and J. J. Moore, who successfully operated the College under the name of Reese School of Business for several decades. In 1975, the College came under the ownership of Steven C. Smith as Commonwealth Business College. In 1997, the College site relocated to its present site in Michigan City, Indiana. The College was acquired by Education Management Corporation on September 2, 2003 and changed its name to Brown Mackie College–Michigan City in November 2004.

Brown Mackie College–Michigan City is accredited by the Accrediting Council for Independent Colleges and Schools (ACICS) to award associate degrees and certificates. ACICS is listed as a nationally recognized accrediting agency by the U.S. Department of Education. Its accreditation of degree-granting institutions is recognized by the Council for Higher Education Accreditation. ACICS can be reached at 750 First Street NE, Suite 980, Washington, D.C. 20002-4241; 202-336-6780.

The College's Medical Assisting degree program is accredited by the Accrediting Bureau of Health Education Schools (ABHES), 803 West Broad Street, Suite 730, Falls Church, Virginia 22046; 703-533-2082.

The College is a nonresidential, smoke-free institution and a subsidiary of Education Management Corporation (EDMC), 210 Sixth Avenue, 33rd floor, Pittsburgh, Pennsylvania 15222-2603; http://www.edmc.edu.

Academic Programs

Brown Mackie College–Michigan City provides higher education to traditional and nontraditional students through associate degree and certificate programs that assist them in enhancing their career opportunities, broadening their perspectives through appropriate general education courses, thinking independently and critically, and improving problem-solving abilities. The College strives to develop within its students the desire for lifelong and continued education.

Each College quarter comprises twelve weeks. Associate degree programs require a minimum of eight quarters to complete. Programs are offered on a year-round basis, providing students with the ability to work uninterrupted toward their degrees.

Associate Degree Programs The Associate of Science degree (96 credits) is awarded in accounting technology, business management, computer-aided design and drafting technology, computer programming and applications, computer software technology, criminal justice, medical assisting, medical office management, paralegal studies, and surgical technology.

Certificate Programs The College offers certificate programs (48 credits) in accounting, business, computer software applications, criminal justice, medical assistant studies, and paralegal assistant studies.

Costs

Tuition is $189 per credit hour. Textbook fees vary according to program.

Financial Aid

The College maintains a full-time staff of financial aid professionals to assist qualified students in obtaining the financial assistance they require to meet their educational expenses. The College participates in several student aid programs. Forms of financial aid available through federal resources include the Federal Pell Grant Program, Federal Supplemental Educational Opportunity Grant (FSEOG) Program, Federal Work-Study Program, Federal Stafford Student Loan Program (subsidized and unsubsidized), and the Federal PLUS Loan Program. Eligible students may apply for Indiana state awards such as the Higher Education Award and Twenty-First Century Scholarships for high school students, the Core 40 awards, and veterans' educational benefits. Students with physical or mental disabilities that are a handicap to employment may be eligible for training services through the state Agency for Vocational Rehabilitation. For further information, students should contact the College Student Financial Services Office.

Faculty

There are 3 full-time and 15 part-time faculty members at the College. Each student is assigned a faculty adviser.

Facilities and Resources

In 2002, the College underwent a major renovation and completed the addition of 3,360 square feet for a total of 10,338 square feet of occupancy. An additional medical laboratory, a larger library, new classrooms, and a bookstore were added. All classrooms and the library are equipped with new technology to include multimedia projectors, surround-sound audio systems, VCRs, and DVD players. Five of the ten new classrooms are equipped with networked computer systems. The two medical laboratories contain newly acquired medical equipment and instructional tools and supplies. Administrative offices are easily accessible to students. Additional parking spaces were added in 2002, providing students and employees with ample parking at no additional charge.

Location

Brown Mackie College–Michigan City is located in northwest Indiana, one mile north of Interstate 94, near the intersection of routes 20 and 421.

Admission Requirements

Each applicant for admission is assigned an Assistant Director of Admissions who directs the applicant through the steps of the admissions process, providing information on curriculum, policies, procedures, and services and assisting the applicant in setting necessary appointments and interviews. To qualify for admission, each applicant must provide documentation of graduation from an accredited high school or completion of a state-approved secondary education curriculum or provide official documentation of high school graduation equivalency. All transcripts become the property of the College. Admission to the College is based on the applicant's meeting the above requirements, a review of the applicant's previous educational records, and a review of the applicant's career interests. If previous academic records indicate that the College's education and training would not benefit the applicant, the College reserves the right to advise the applicant not to enroll. Special requirements for enrollment into certain programs are discussed in the descriptions of those programs.

Application and Information

Applicants must complete and submit an application form along with documentation of graduation from an accredited high school or completion of state-approved secondary education curriculum or provide official documentation of high school graduation equivalency. For additional information, prospective students should contact:

Director of Admissions
Brown Mackie College–Michigan City
325 East U.S. Highway 20
Michigan City, Indiana 46360
Telephone: 219-877-3100
          800-519-2416 (toll-free)
Fax: 219-877-3110
E-mail: bmcmcadm@amedcts.com
World Wide Web: http://www.brownmackie.edu

BROWN MACKIE COLLEGE–MOLINE

MOLINE, ILLINOIS

The College and Its Mission

Brown Mackie College–Moline is dedicated to providing education programs that prepare students for entry-level positions in a competitive, rapidly changing workplace. The College provides diploma programs in business, health sciences, legal studies, information technology, and electronic fields to approximately 130 students.

Founded in 1890 by A. N. Hirons as LaPorte Business College in LaPorte, Indiana, the institution later became known as Commonwealth Business College. In 1919, ownership was transferred to Grace and J. J. Moore, who successfully operated the College for almost thirty years. Following World War II, Harley and Stephanie Reese operated the College under the name of Reese School of Business for several decades.

In 1975, the College came under the ownership of Steven C. Smith as Commonwealth Business College. A second location, now known as Brown Mackie College–Merrillville, was opened in 1984 in Merrillville, Indiana, and a third location was opened a year later in Davenport, Iowa. In 1987, the Davenport location relocated to its present site in Moline, Illinois. In September 2003, the College changed ownership again when it was acquired by Education Management Corporation, and the College's name was changed to Brown Mackie College–Moline in November 2004.

Brown Mackie College–Moline is accredited by the Accrediting Council for Independent Colleges and Schools (ACICS) to award diplomas and certificates. The Accrediting Council for Independent Colleges and Schools is listed as a nationally recognized accrediting agency by the United States Department of Education. Its accreditation of degree-granting institutions also is recognized by the Council for Higher Education Accreditation. The Accrediting Council can be contacted at 750 First Street NE, Suite 980, Washington, D.C. 20002-4241; 202-336-6780. The College is a nonresidential, smoke-free institution and is a subsidiary of Education Management Corporation (EDMC), 210 Sixth Avenue, 33rd floor, Pittsburgh, Pennsylvania 15222-2603; 800-275-2440 (toll-free); http://www.edmc.edu.

Academic Programs

Brown Mackie College–Moline provides higher education to traditional and nontraditional students through diploma programs that assist them in enhancing their career opportunities, broadening their perspectives through appropriate general education courses, thinking independently and critically, and improving problem-solving abilities. The College strives to develop within its students the desire for lifelong and continued education.

Each College quarter comprises twelve weeks. Programs are offered on a year-round basis, providing students with the ability to work uninterrupted toward the completion of their programs.

Diploma Programs The College offers diploma programs (48 credits) in accounting, business, computer applications, computer software applications, medical office management, and paralegal assistant studies as well as a diploma program (56 credits) in medical assistant studies.

Costs

Tuition for the 2005–06 academic year was $179 per credit hour; fees were $10 per credit hour. Textbook costs vary by program.

Financial Aid

The College maintains a full-time staff of financial aid professionals to assist qualified students in obtaining the financial assistance they require to meet their educational expenses. The College participates in several student aid programs. Forms of financial aid available through federal resources include the Federal Pell Grant Program, Federal Supplemental Educational Opportunity Grant (FSEOG) Program, Federal Work-Study Program, Federal Perkins Loan Program, Federal Stafford Student Loan Program (subsidized and unsubsidized), and the Federal PLUS Loan Program. Eligible students may apply for veterans' educational benefits. Students with physical or mental disabilities that are a handicap to employment may be eligible for training services through the state Agency for Vocational Rehabilitation. For further information, students should contact the College Student Financial Services Office.

Each year, the College makes available scholarships of $1000 each to qualifying seniors from area high schools. Only one scholarship is awarded per high school. In order to qualify, a senior must be graduating from a participating high school, maintain a cumulative grade point average of at least 2.0, and submit a brief essay. The student's extracurricular activities and community service are also considered. The President's Scholarship is available only to students enrolling in one of the College's diploma programs. Students awarded the scholarship must enroll at Brown Mackie College–Moline between June and September immediately following their high school graduation. Applications for these scholarships can be obtained from the guidance departments of participating high schools. These applications must be completed and returned to the College by March 31. Those who are awarded scholarships are notified by April 30.

Faculty

Brown Mackie College–Moline has 12 full- and part-time faculty members, with an average student-faculty ratio of 12:1.

Facilities and Resources

The College maintains a library of curriculum-related resources. Technical and general education materials, academic and professional periodicals, and audiovisual resources are available to both students and faculty members. Students have borrowing privileges at several local libraries. Internet access is available for research.

Location

Brown Mackie College–Moline is located at 1527 47th Avenue in Moline, Illinois. The College is easily accessible by public transportation, and ample parking is available at no charge.

Admission Requirements

Each applicant for admission is assigned an Assistant Director of Admissions who directs the applicant through the steps of the admissions process, providing information on curriculum, policies, procedures, and services and assisting the applicant in setting necessary appointments and interviews.

To qualify for admission, each applicant must provide documentation of graduation from an accredited high school or from a state-approved secondary education curriculum or provide official documentation of high school graduation equivalency. All transcripts become the property of the College. Admission to the College is based on the applicant's meeting the above requirements, a review of the applicant's previous education records, and a review of the applicant's career interests. If previous academic records indicate that the College's education and training would not benefit the applicant, the College reserves the right to advise the applicant not to enroll. Special requirements for enrollment into certain programs are discussed in the descriptions of those programs.

Application and Information

Applicants must complete and submit an application form along with documentation of graduation from an accredited high school or state-approved secondary education curriculum, or applicants must provide official documentation of high school graduation equivalency. For further information, prospective students should contact:

Director of Admissions
Brown Mackie College–Moline
1527 47th Avenue
Moline, Illinois 61265
Telephone: 309-762-2100
Fax: 309-762-2374
E-mail: bmcmoadm@amedcts.com
World Wide Web: http://www.brownmackie.edu

BROWN MACKIE COLLEGE–NORTH CANTON

NORTH CANTON, OHIO

The College and Its Mission

Brown Mackie College–North Canton is dedicated to providing educational programs that prepare students for entry-level positions in a competitive, rapidly changing workplace. The College provides associate degree and diploma programs in business and accounting, allied health sciences, legal studies, computer technology and electronics to approximately 930 students.

Brown Mackie College–North Canton opened its classroom doors in January 1984 as National Electronics Institute (NEI). In July 1985, the school was purchased by Electronics Technology Institute of Cleveland and became a branch facility, accredited by the Accrediting Commission of the National Association of Trade and Technical Schools (NATTS). The name was changed to Electronic Technology Institute. In June 2002, the College came under the ownership of Southern Ohio College LLC, and the College's name then changed to AEC Southern Ohio College. In September 2003, the College came under the ownership of Education Management Corporation (EDMC), and the name of the College was subsequently changed to Brown Mackie College in November 2004.

Brown Mackie College–North Canton is accredited by the Accrediting Council for Independent Colleges and Schools (ACICS) to award associate degrees and diplomas. ACICS is listed as a nationally recognized accrediting agency by the U.S. Department of Education. Its accreditation of degree-granting institutions also is recognized by the Council for Higher Education Accreditation. ACICS may be contacted at 750 First Street, NE, Suite 980, Washington, D.C. 20002-4241; phone: 202-336-6780.

The College is a nonresidential, smoke-free institution and is owned and operated by Education Management Corporation, 210 Sixth Avenue, 33rd Floor, Pittsburgh, Pennsylvania 15222-2603; Web site: http://www.edmc.edu.

Academic Programs

Brown Mackie College–North Canton provides higher education to traditional and nontraditional students through associate degree and diploma programs that assist them in enhancing their career opportunities, broadening their perspectives through appropriate general education courses, thinking independently and critically, and improving problem-solving abilities. The College strives to develop within its students the desire for lifelong and continued education. Each College quarter comprises twelve weeks.

Associate Degree Programs Associate degree programs require a minimum of eight quarters to complete. Programs are offered on a year-round basis, providing students with the ability to work uninterrupted toward completion of their programs. The Associate of Applied Business degree (96 credits) is awarded in accounting technology, business management, computer programming and applications, computer software technology, criminal justice, and paralegal studies. The Associate of Applied Science degree is awarded in computer-aided design and drafting technology, computer networking and applications, electronics, health-care assisting, and pharmacy technology.

Diploma Programs The College offers diploma programs (48 credits) in accounting, business, computer-aided design and drafting technician studies, computer applications, computer software applications, criminal justice, electronics, medical assistant studies, and paralegal assistant studies.

Costs

Tuition for programs in the 2005–06 academic year was $179 per credit hour. Textbook fees were approximately $425 per quarter.

Financial Aid

The College maintains a full-time staff of financial aid professionals to assist qualified students in obtaining the financial assistance they require to meet their educational expenses. The College participates in several student aid programs. Forms of financial aid available through federal resources include Federal Pell Grants, Federal Supplemental Educational Opportunity Grants (FSEOG), Federal Work-Study Program awards, Federal Perkins Loans, Federal Stafford Student Loans (subsidized and unsubsidized), and Federal PLUS loans. Eligible students may apply for state awards such as the Ohio Instructional Grant (OIG) and veterans' educational benefits. Students with physical or mental disabilities that are a handicap to employment may be eligible for training services through the state Vocational Rehabilitation Agency. For further information, students should contact the College Student Financial Services Office.

Each year, the College makes available President's Scholarships of $1000 each to qualifying seniors from area high schools. No more than one scholarship is awarded per high school. In order to qualify, a senior must be graduating from a participating high school, maintain a cumulative grade point average of at least 2.0, and submit a brief essay. The student's extracurricular activities and community service are also considered. The President's Scholarship is available only to students enrolling in one of the College's degree programs. Students who receive the scholarship must enroll at Brown Mackie College–North Canton between June and September immediately following their high school graduation. Applications for these scholarships can be obtained from the guidance departments of participating high schools. These applications must be completed and returned to the College by March 31. Those awarded scholarships are notified by April 30.

Faculty

There are 8 full-time and 21 part-time faculty members. The average student-faculty ratio is 21:1. Each student has an adviser.

Facilities and Resources

In addition to classrooms and computer labs, the College maintains a library of curriculum-related resources, technical and general education materials, academic and professional periodicals, and audiovisual resources. Internet access also is available for research.

Location

Brown Mackie College–North Canton is located at 1320 West Maple Avenue in North Canton, Ohio.

Admission Requirements

Each applicant for admission is assigned an Assistant Director of Admissions, who directs the applicant through the steps of the admissions process, providing information on curriculum, policies, procedures, and services and assisting the applicant in setting necessary appointments and interviews. To qualify for admission, each applicant must provide documentation of graduation from an accredited high school or from a state-approved secondary education curriculum or provide official documentation of high school graduation equivalency. All transcripts become the property of the College. Admission to the College is based upon the applicant's meeting the above requirements, a review of the applicant's previous educational records, and a review of the applicant's career interests. If previous academic records indicate that the College's education and training would not benefit the applicant, the College reserves the right to advise the applicant not to enroll. Special requirements for enrollment into certain programs are discussed in the descriptions of those programs.

Application and Information

Applicants must complete and submit an application form, along with documentation of graduation from an accredited high school or state-approved secondary education curriculum or official documentation of high school graduation equivalency. For further information, prospective students should contact:

Director of Admissions
Brown Mackie College–North Canton
1320 West Maple Street
North Canton, Ohio 44720
Telephone: 330-494-1214
Fax: 330-494-8112
E-mail: bmcncadm@amedcts.com
World Wide Web: http://www.brownmackie.edu

BROWN MACKIE COLLEGE–NORTHERN KENTUCKY

FORT MITCHELL, KENTUCKY

The College and Its Mission

Brown Mackie College–Northern Kentucky is dedicated to providing education programs that prepare students for entry-level positions in a competitive, rapidly changing workplace. The College provides associate degree and diploma programs in the areas of business and accounting, allied health sciences, legal studies, and computer technology to approximately 480 students.

The College was founded in Cincinnati, Ohio, in February 1927 as a traditional business college. In 1964, the College was granted accreditation as a business school by the Association of Independent Colleges and Schools (ACICS); it was accredited as a junior college of business by ACICS in 1972. In May 1981, the College opened a branch location in northern Kentucky, which moved in 1986 to its current location in Fort Mitchell. ACICS is listed as a nationally recognized accrediting agency by the U.S. Department of Education. Its accreditation of degree-granting institutions also is recognized by the Council for Higher Education Accreditation. ACICS may be contacted at 750 First Street, NE, Suite 980, Washington, D.C. 20002-4241; phone: 202-336-6780.

The College is a nonresidential, smoke-free institution and a subsidiary of Education Management Corporation (EDMC), 210 Sixth Avenue, 33rd Floor, Pittsburgh, Pennsylvania 15222-2603; phone: 800-275-2440 (toll-free); Web site: http://www.edmc.edu.

Academic Programs

Brown Mackie College–Northern Kentucky provides higher education to traditional and nontraditional students through associate degree and diploma programs that assist them in enhancing their career opportunities, broadening their perspectives through appropriate general education courses, thinking independently and critically, and improving problem-solving abilities. Each College quarter comprises ten to twelve weeks.

Associate Degree Programs Associate degree programs require a minimum of eight quarters to complete. Programs are offered on a year-round basis, providing students with the ability to work uninterrupted toward their degrees. The Associate of Applied Business degree (96 credits) is awarded in accounting technology, business management, computer networking and applications, computer software technology, criminal justice, and paralegal studies. The Associate of Applied Science degree (96 credits) is awarded in computer-aided design and drafting technology, medical assisting, and pharmacy technology.

Diploma Programs The College also offers diploma programs (48 credits) in accounting, business, computer applications, computer software applications, medical assistant studies, and practical nursing (76 credits).

Costs

Tuition for all programs, except practical nursing, is $179 per credit hour. Tuition for the practical nursing program is $250 per credit hour. Textbooks and other instructional materials vary by program.

Financial Aid

The College maintains a full-time staff of financial aid professionals to assist qualified students in obtaining the financial assistance they require to meet their educational expenses. The College participates in several student aid programs. Forms of financial aid available through federal resources include Federal Pell Grants, Federal Supplemental Educational Opportunity Grants (FSEOG), Federal Work-Study Program awards, Federal Perkins Loans, Federal Stafford Student Loans (subsidized and unsubsidized), and Federal PLUS loans. Eligible students may apply for veterans' educational benefits. Students with physical or mental disabilities that are a handicap to employment may be eligible for training services through the state Vocational Rehabilitation Agency. For further information, students should contact the College Student Financial Services Office.

Each year, the College makes available President's Scholarships of $1000 each to qualifying seniors from area high schools. No more than one scholarship is awarded per high school. In order to qualify, a senior must be graduating from a participating high school, maintain a cumulative grade point average of at least 2.0, and submit a brief essay. The student's extracurricular activities and community service are also considered. The President's Scholarship is available only to students enrolling in one of the College's degree programs. Students who receive the scholarship must enroll at Brown Mackie College–Northern Kentucky between June and September immediately following their high school graduation. Applications for these scholarships can be obtained from the guidance departments of participating high schools. These applications must be completed and returned to the College by March 31. Those awarded scholarships are notified by April 30.

Faculty

There are 4 full-time and 18 part-time faculty members. The student-faculty ratio is 14:1.

Facilities and Resources

Brown Mackie College–Northern Kentucky provides media presentation rooms for special instructional needs and a library that provides instructional resources and academic support for both faculty members and students. The College is nonresidential; students who are unable to commute daily from their homes may request assistance from the Office of Admissions in locating off-site housing. The College is accessible by public transportation and provides ample free parking.

Location

The College is located at 309 Buttermilk Pike in Fort Mitchell, Kentucky.

Admission Requirements

Each applicant for admission is assigned an Assistant Director of Admissions, who directs the applicant through the steps of the admissions process, providing information on curriculum, policies, procedures, and services and assisting the applicant in setting necessary appointments and interviews. To qualify for admission, each applicant must provide documentation of graduation from an accredited high school or from a state-approved secondary education curriculum or provide official documentation of high school graduation equivalency. All transcripts become the property of the College. Admission to the College is based upon the applicant's meeting the above requirements, a review of the applicant's previous education records, and a review of the applicant's career interests. If previous academic records indicate that the College's education and training would not benefit the applicant, the College reserves the right to advise the applicant not to enroll. Special requirements for enrollment into certain programs are discussed in the descriptions of those programs.

Application and Information

Applicants must complete and submit an application form, along with documentation of graduation from an accredited high school or state-approved secondary education curriculum or official documentation of high school graduation equivalency. For additional information, prospective students should contact:

Director of Admissions
Brown Mackie College–Northern Kentucky
309 Buttermilk Pike
Fort Mitchell, Kentucky 41017
Telephone: 859-341-5627
            800-888-1445 (toll-free)
Fax: 859-341-6483
E-mail: bmcnkadm@amedcts.com
World Wide Web: http://www.brownmackie.edu

BROWN MACKIE COLLEGE–SALINA

SALINA, KANSAS

The College and Its Mission

Brown Mackie College–Salina is dedicated to providing education programs that prepare students for entry-level positions in a competitive, rapidly changing workplace. The College provides associate degree, diploma, and certificate programs in the areas of business and accounting, allied health sciences, legal studies, and computer technology to approximately 400 students.

The College was originally founded in July 1892 as the Kansas Wesleyan School of Business. In 1938, the College was incorporated as the Brown Mackie School of Business under the ownership of former Kansas Wesleyan instructors Perry E. Brown and A. B. Mackie; it became Brown Mackie College in January 1975.

Brown Mackie College is accredited by the Higher Learning Commission of the North Central Association of Colleges and Schools, 30 North LaSalle Street, Suite 2400, Chicago, Illinois 60602; phone: 800-621-7440 (toll-free). The College, which operates in Salina and Lenexa, Kansas, is approved and authorized to grant the Associate of Applied Science degree by the Kansas Board of Regents, 1000 Southwest Jackson Street, Suite 520, Topeka, Kansas 66612. The College is a nonresidential, smoke-free institution and is a subsidiary of Education Management Corporation (EDMC), 210 Sixth Avenue, 33rd Floor, Pittsburgh, Pennsylvania 15222-2603; phone: 800-275-2440 (toll-free); Web site: http://www.edmc.edu.

Academic Programs

Brown Mackie College–Salina provides higher education to traditional and nontraditional students through associate degree, diploma, and certificate programs that assist them in enhancing their career opportunities, broadening their perspectives through appropriate general education courses, thinking independently and critically, and improving problem-solving abilities. The College strives to develop within its students the desire for lifelong and continued education.

In most programs, students can complete classes part-time or full-time, day or evening. Classes begin every month and programs are offered on a year-round basis, providing students with the ability to work uninterrupted toward their degrees. Students focus on and complete a single class every month.

Associate Degree Programs The Associate of Applied Science degree (96 credits) is awarded in accounting technology, business management, computer-aided design and drafting technology, computer networking and applications, computer software technology, criminal justice, medical assisting, medical office management, paralegal studies, and sales and marketing.

Diploma Programs The College also offers diploma programs (48 credits) in accounting, advertising, business, computer-aided design and drafting technician studies, computer software applications, criminal justice, medical assistant studies, medical coding and billing, and paralegal assistant studies.

Certificate Programs Certificate programs (24 credits) are offered in computer networking, medical coding and billing for health-care professionals, and practical nursing.

Costs

The cost of tuition for all programs, except computer networking and practical nursing, is $189 per quarter credit hour. Courses in the practical nursing program are $250 per quarter credit hour. Computer networking courses are $300 per quarter credit hour. Textbook fees for all programs are estimated at $360 per quarter.

Financial Aid

The College maintains a full-time staff of financial aid professionals to assist qualified students in obtaining the financial assistance they require to meet their educational expenses. The College participates in several student aid programs. Forms of financial aid that are available through federal resources include Federal Pell Grants, Federal Supplemental Educational Opportunity Grants (FSEOG), Federal Work-Study Program awards, Federal Perkins Loans, Federal Stafford Student Loans (subsidized and unsubsidized), and Federal PLUS loans. Eligible students may apply for veterans' educational benefits. Students with physical or mental disabilities that are a handicap to employment may be eligible for training services through the state Vocational Rehabilitation Agency. For further information, students should contact the College Student Financial Services Office.

The Merit Scholarship is a College-sponsored scholarship that may be awarded to students who demonstrate exceptional academic ability. To qualify for a Merit Scholarship, an applicant or student must have scored 21 or higher on the ACT or 900 or higher on the SAT. The maximum amount awarded by this scholarship to any student is $500.

Athletic scholarships may be awarded to students who participate in athletic programs that are sponsored by the College. Current sports are men's baseball, men's and women's basketball, and women's fast-pitch softball. Maximum awards for any applicant or student are determined by the College President. Further information is available from the Athletic Office. Recipients of athletic scholarships must achieve a cumulative grade point average of at least 2.0 by their graduation. Recipients who fail to maintain full-time status or the required grade point average forfeit their awards.

Faculty

There are 7 full-time faculty members. The average classroom size is 14 students, with a student-faculty ratio of 35:1.

Facilities and Resources

In addition to classrooms and computer labs, the College maintains a library of curriculum-related resources, technical and general education materials, academic and professional periodicals, and audiovisual resources. Internet access is also available for research. The College has a bookstore that stocks texts, courseware, and other educational supplies that are required for courses and a variety of personal, recreational, and gift items, including apparel, supplies, and general merchandise incorporating the College logo. Hours are posted at the bookstore entrance.

Location

Brown Mackie College–Salina is located at 2106 South Ninth Street in Salina, Kansas.

Admission Requirements

Each applicant for admission is assigned an Assistant Director of Admissions, who directs the applicant through the steps of the admissions process, providing information on curriculum, policies, procedures, and services and assisting the applicant in setting necessary appointments and interviews. To qualify for admission, each applicant must provide documentation of graduation from an accredited high school or from a state-approved secondary education curriculum or provide official documentation of high school graduation equivalency. All transcripts become the property of the College. Admission to the College is based upon the applicant's meeting the above requirements, a review of the applicant's previous education records, and a review of the applicant's career interests. If previous academic records indicate that the College's education and training would not benefit the applicant, the College reserves the right to advise the applicant not to enroll. Special requirements for enrollment into certain programs are discussed in the descriptions of those programs.

Application and Information

Applicants must complete and submit an application form, along with documentation of graduation from an accredited high school or state-approved secondary education curriculum or official documentation of high school graduation equivalency. For additional information, prospective students should contact:

Director of Admissions
Brown Mackie College–Salina
2106 South Ninth Street
Salina, Kansas 67401
Telephone: 785-825-5422
          800-365-0433 (toll-free)
Fax: 785-827-7623
E-mail: bmcsaadm@amedcts.com
World Wide Web: http://www.brownmackie.edu

BROWN MACKIE COLLEGE–SOUTH BEND

SOUTH BEND, INDIANA

The College and Its Mission

Brown Mackie College–South Bend is dedicated to providing education programs that prepare students for entry-level positions in a competitive, rapidly changing workplace. The College provides associate degree, diploma, and certificate programs in business and accounting, allied health sciences, legal studies, computer technology, and electronics to approximately 600 students.

The College is one of the oldest institutions of its kind in the country and the oldest in the state of Indiana. Established in 1882 as the South Bend Commercial College, the school later changed its name to Michiana College. In 1930, the school was incorporated under the laws of the state of Indiana and was authorized to confer associate degrees and certificates in business. The College relocated to its current location on East Jefferson Boulevard in 1987. Five years later it added a branch location in Fort Wayne, Indiana, now known as Brown Mackie College–Fort Wayne.

Brown Mackie College–South Bend is accredited by the Accrediting Council for Independent Colleges and Schools (ACICS) to award associate degrees, diplomas, and certificates. The Accrediting Council for Independent Colleges and Schools is listed as a nationally recognized accrediting agency by the United States Department of Education. Its accreditation of degree-granting institutions is also recognized by the Council for Higher Education Accreditation. The Accrediting Council's address is 750 First Street, NE, Suite 980, Washington, D.C. 20002-4241; 202-336-6780.

The medical assisting program is accredited by the Commission on Accreditation of Allied Health Education Programs (CAAHEP), on recommendation of the Curriculum Review Board. The Commission's address is 35 East Wacker Drive, Chicago, Illinois 60601; 312-553-9355.

The occupational therapy assistant program is accredited by the Accreditation Council for Occupational Therapy Education (ACOTE) of the American Occupational Therapy Association (AOTA), 4720 Montgomery Lane, P.O. Box 31220, Bethesda, Maryland 20824-1220; 301-652-2682.

The physical therapist assistant program is accredited by the Commission on Accreditation in Physical Therapy Education (CAPTE) of the American Physical Therapy Association (APTA), 1111 North Fairfax Street, Alexandria, Virginia 22314; 703-706-3241.

The practical nursing program is accredited by the Indiana State Board of Nursing, 402 West Washington Street, Room W066, Indianapolis, Indiana 46204; 317-234-2043.

The College is a nonresidential, smoke-free institution and is owned and operated by Education Management Corporation, 210 Sixth Avenue, 33rd Floor, Pittsburgh, Pennsylvania 15222-2603; 800-275-2440 (toll-free); http://www.edmc.edu.

Academic Programs

Brown Mackie College–South Bend provides higher education to traditional and nontraditional students through associate degree, diploma, and certificate programs that assist them in enhancing their career opportunities, broadening their perspectives through appropriate general education courses, thinking independently and critically, and improving problem-solving abilities.

Each College quarter comprises twelve weeks. Associate degree programs require a minimum of eight quarters to complete. Programs are offered on a year-round basis, providing students with the ability to work uninterrupted toward completion of their programs.

Associate Degree Programs The Associate of Science degree (96 credits) is awarded in accounting technology, business management, computer-aided design and drafting technology, computer networking and applications, computer programming and applications, computer software technology, criminal justice, electronics, medical assisting, and paralegal studies. The Associate of Applied Science degree (96 credits) is awarded in occupational therapy assistant studies and physical therapist assistant studies.

Diploma Program The College offers a diploma program (76 credits) in practical nursing.

Certificate Programs The College offers the following certificate programs (48 credits): accounting, business, computer applications, computer software applications, criminal justice, medical assistant studies, and paralegal assistant studies.

Costs

Tuition for programs in the 2005–06 academic year was $179 per credit hour, with a $10 per-credit-hour general fee applied to instructional costs for activities and services. Textbooks and other instructional materials varied by program. Tuition for all courses in the practical nursing program was $250 per credit hour. Tuition for the physical therapist assistant program was $300 per credit hour. Tuition for the occupational therapy assistant program was $300 per credit hour.

Financial Aid

The College maintains a full-time staff of financial aid professionals to assist qualified students in obtaining the financial assistance they require to meet their educational expenses. The College participates in several student aid programs. Forms of financial aid available through federal resources include the Federal Pell Grant Program, Federal Supplemental Educational Opportunity Grant (FSEOG) Program, Federal Work-Study Program, Federal Perkins Loan Program, Federal Stafford Student Loan Program (subsidized and unsubsidized), and the Federal PLUS Loan Program. Eligible students may apply for Indiana state awards such as the Frank O'Bannon Grant Program (formerly the Indiana Higher Education

Grant) and Twenty-First Century Scholars Program for high school students, the Core 40 awards, and veterans' educational benefits. Students with physical or mental disabilities that are a handicap to employment may be eligible for training services through the state Agency for Vocational Rehabilitation. For further information, students should contact the College Student Financial Services Office.

Each year, the College makes available President's Scholarships of $1000 each to qualifying seniors from area high schools. No more than one scholarship is awarded per high school. In order to qualify, a senior must be graduating from a participating high school, must be maintaining a cumulative grade point average of at least 2.0, and must submit a brief essay. The student's extracurricular activities and community service are also considered. The President's Scholarship is available only to students enrolling in one of the College's degree programs. Students awarded the scholarship must enroll at Brown Mackie College–South Bend between June and September immediately following their high school graduation. Applications for these scholarships can be obtained from the guidance departments of participating high schools. These applications must be completed and returned to the College by March 31. Those awarded scholarships are notified by April 30.

Faculty

There are 15 full-time and 33 part-time faculty members at the College. The average student-faculty ratio is 12:1. Each student is assigned a program director as an adviser.

Academic Facilities

Brown Mackie College–South Bend comprises 31,000 square feet of classrooms; medical, computer, occupational, and physical therapy laboratories; and a library, a bookstore, and office space.

Location

Brown Mackie College–South Bend is located in the Woodlawn section of Cincinnati, Ohio. The College is easily accessible by public transportation and provides ample parking at no charge.

Admission Requirements

Each applicant for admission is assigned an Assistant Director of Admissions, who directs the applicant through the steps of the admissions process, providing information on curriculum, policies, procedures, and services and assisting the applicant in setting necessary appointments and interviews. To qualify for admission, each applicant must provide documentation of graduation from an accredited high school or from a state-approved secondary education curriculum or provide official documentation of high school graduation equivalency. All transcripts become the property of the College. Admission to the College is based on the applicant's meeting the above requirements, a review of the applicant's previous educational records, and a review of the applicant's career interests. If previous academic records indicate that the College's education and training would not benefit the applicant, the College reserves the right to advise the applicant not to enroll. Special requirements for enrollment into certain programs are discussed in the descriptions of those programs.

In addition to the College's general admission requirements, applicants enrolling in the occupational therapy assistant or physical therapist assistant programs must document one of the following: a high school cumulative grade point average of at least 2.5, a score on the GED examination of at least 57 (557 if taken on or after January 15, 2002), or completion of 12 quarter-credit hours or 8 semester-credit hours of collegiate course work with a grade point average of at least 2.5. Credit hours may not include Professional Development (CF 1100), the Brown Mackie College–South Bend course. Students entering either program must also have completed a biology course with a grade of at least a C (or an average of at least 2.0 on a 4.0 scale).

In addition to the College's general admission requirements, applicants enrolling in the practical nursing program must document the following: fulfillment of Brown Mackie College–South Bend general requirements; complete physical (must be current to within six months of admission); two-step Mantoux TB skin test (must be current throughout schooling); hepatitis B vaccination or signed refusal; up-to-date immunizations, including tetanus and rubella; record of current CPR certification (certification must be current throughout the clinical experience through health-care provider certification or the American Heart Association); and hospitalization insurance or a signed waiver.

Application and Information

Applicants must complete and submit an application form, along with documentation of graduation from an accredited high school or state-approved secondary education curriculum or official documentation of high school graduation equivalency.

For additional information, prospective students should contact:

Director of Admissions
Brown Mackie College–South Bend
1030 East Jefferson Boulevard
South Bend, Indiana 46617
Telephone: 574-237-0774
        800-743-2447 (toll-free)
Fax: 574-237-3585
E-mail: bmcsbadm@amedcts.com
World Wide Web: http://www.brownmackie.edu

BUNKER HILL COMMUNITY COLLEGE
BOSTON, MASSACHUSETTS

The College and Its Mission

A public institution of higher education, Bunker Hill Community College (BHCC) offers wide-ranging workforce education curricula interwoven throughout comprehensive programs and courses of study, including nursing and allied health, an extensive information technology program, criminal justice, hospitality and culinary arts, business, and early childhood development. Accredited by the Commission on Institutions of Higher Education of the New England Association of Schools and Colleges, BHCC supports open access to postsecondary education by providing a strong liberal arts foundation and a range of educational opportunities that include distance learning, self-directed learning, an honors program, and, for nonnative English-speaking students, a variety of levels of English as a second language (ESL) instruction. BHCC graduates have gone on to continue their education at many four-year institutions, including Bentley College, Boston University, Cambridge College, Northeastern University, Salem State College, Smith College, Suffolk University, Tufts University, Wellesley College, and the University of Massachusetts. BHCC seeks to enhance its position as a primary educational and economic asset for the commonwealth through cooperative planning and program implementation involving neighboring institutions of higher education, the public schools, community organizations, and area businesses and industries.

Academic Programs

BHCC offers numerous programs of study. They include Associate in Arts (A.A.) degrees, Associate in Science (A.S.) degrees, and certificate programs. Associate in Arts concentrations are designed to permit the student to transfer smoothly to four-year colleges and universities. Although extreme care has been taken in fashioning these transfer-focused degrees, students are advised to consult the institution to which they wish to transfer to ensure the wisest choice of courses at BHCC. These students should also work with the BHCC transfer counselor and academic advisers in planning both the curriculum at BHCC and the transfer process.

Associate in Science programs are designed to develop the knowledge and skills required for employment at the conclusion of the associate degree. In addition to employment preparation, many Associate in Science programs have transfer options. To ensure smooth transfer to four-year programs, students are advised to consult the institution to which they wish to transfer.

A wide variety of certificate programs provide skills training and job-upgrade opportunities for students who successfully complete these programs.

The honors program offers students the opportunity to study and learn in an academically challenging and enriching learning environment.

Associate Degree Programs

Associate in Arts degrees are available in biological science, business, chemical science, communication, computer information systems, computer science, education, English, fine arts, foreign language, general concentration, history and government, mathematics, music, physics/engineering, psychology, sociology, and theater. Students enrolling in any A.A. degree program can earn world-studies emphasis certification simultaneously.

Associate in Science degrees are offered in business administration (accounting, finance, international business, management), computer information technology (computer support specialist studies, database programming and administration, network technology and administration), criminal justice, culinary arts, early childhood development, fire protection and safety, graphic arts and visual communication, hotel/restaurant/travel (hotel/restaurant management, travel and tourism management), human services, media technology, medical imaging (cardiac sonography, general sonography, medical radiography, medical radiography–part-time evening), nursing (day, evening, or weekend), office and information management (administrative information management, medical information management), and pharmacy technology.

Certificate Programs

Certificates are available in allied health (medical assistant studies, medical lab assistant studies, patient-care assistant studies, phlebotomy technician studies), business administration (accounting, e-commerce marketing management, international business, paralegal studies), computer information technology (computer support specialist studies, database programming and administration, network technology and administration, object-oriented computer programming and design), culinary arts, early childhood development, human services, law enforcement, medical coding, office and information management (information management specialist studies, medical information management assistant studies), surgical technology (central processing (sterile processing and distribution management), surgical technology), and travel and tourism management.

Off-Campus Programs

Bunker Hill Community College offers home study and online distance learning courses as a convenient alternative to the traditional classroom. These courses are designed for self-directed, motivated learners. The courses are equivalent in content and academic rigor to traditional classroom courses but offer students the flexibility and convenience of learning virtually anytime and anywhere. The College also offers hybrid courses. These courses incorporate both traditional classroom and online components. Hybrid courses generally meet on-site for 50 percent of the instructional time, with the remaining instruction conducted online.

BHCC offers a range of educational opportunities at its five satellite campuses, each intended to serve the distinct needs and interests of the host communities—Cambridge, Chinatown, Revere, Somerville, and Boston's South End. The curricula available at the satellites allow students to prepare for workforce advancement while earning credits toward an associate degree or certificate in several of the wide variety of fields offered by the College. Programs include foundation courses that fulfill general education requirements as well as courses in response to community interest, such as offerings in computer technology, business management, and hospitality.

Bunker Hill Community College has a comprehensive study-abroad program that allows students to experience different cultures. Each year, approximately twenty scholarships are awarded to further assist BHCC students in realizing their dream of studying abroad. Faculty, staff, and interested community members are also invited to take part in the programs, although scholarships are available only to qualified BHCC students.

Credit for Nontraditional Learning Experiences

The Prior Learning Assessment Program provides an opportunity to students to condense their time of study by granting credits for college-level knowledge and skills. This program assists students in examining their outside learning experiences and identifying those that might be considered for college credits. Common sources for this kind of learning are jobs, volunteer work, skills training, workshops or study groups, and community involvement.

Students can earn college credits in four ways: portfolio evaluation, the College-Level Examination Program (CLEP), military evaluation, and departmental challenge exams.

Costs

Tuition for Massachusetts residents is $100 per credit; for non-Massachusetts residents, it is $306 per credit. The New England Regional Student Program costs $112 per credit. The health course fee is $35 per credit (for health program courses only).

Financial Aid

The Financial Aid Office at Bunker Hill Community College assists students and their families in meeting the costs of a college education. Bunker Hill Community College participates in a wide variety of federal, state, and private financial aid programs. Students should be aware that all institutions, including Bunker Hill Community College, are subject to adjustments in funding allocations from both the commonwealth of Massachusetts and the United States Department of Education.

In order to be eligible for financial aid, an applicant must be a United States citizen or an eligible noncitizen enrolled or accepted for enrollment in an eligible program. In addition, the applicant must maintain satisfactory academic progress, comply with Federal Selective Service Law, and not be in default on any educational loans or owe a refund on any federal grants or loans to any institution. Students who have obtained a previous bachelor's degree at any U.S. or international institution are not eligible for financial aid.

Financial aid awards are subject to change if any of the factors used to calculate eligibility from the Free Application for Federal Student Aid (FAFSA) change after the date of original application. Other examples of factors that impact eligibility include increases in income and changes in family size and/or in the number of family members enrolled in college. Students are strongly advised to consult with the Financial Aid Office if they are contemplating a change in enrollment status.

Faculty

There are 123 full-time faculty members and 325 adjunct faculty members at BHCC. The average class size is 19.

Student Body Profile

The student body reflects the diversity of the urban community, and an essential part of the College's mission is to encourage this diversity. The average student age is 28. Nearly 60 percent of the students are women, more than half are people of color, and most are employed while attending school.

Student Activities

Bunker Hill Community College has an active student life program. The activities coordinated through the Student Activities and Athletics Office provide students with the opportunity to have fun, meet people, and make a difference in campus life at the College. BHCC celebrates cultural diversity and encourages cultural interaction.

There are more than twenty-five student organizations and athletic teams at Bunker Hill Community College, which provide the campus with social, cultural, and educational programs as well as competitive sports, intramural/recreational programs, and leisure-time activities. New members are always welcome.

Athletic programs provide opportunities for students to participate in competitive or recreational activities on the intercollegiate and intramural levels. The Intercollegiate Athletic Program consists of men's baseball, basketball, and soccer; women's basketball, soccer, and softball; and coed golf. The Intramural Athletic Program includes basketball, table tennis, and tennis.

Student clubs and organizations include African-American Cultural Society; Alpha Kappa Mu Honor Society; Amnesty International; Arab Students Association; Asian Students Association; Brazilian Cultural Club; Business Club; Campus Activities Board; Cape Verdean Club; Criminal Justice Society; Debating Society; Evening Student Association; Gay, Lesbian, and Bisexual Student Union; Gospel Choir; Haitian Club; Hillel Club; Hospitality Club; Islamic Students Association; Italian-American Society; Latinos Unidos Club; Multicultural Club; Nurse Mentor Club; Real Life Club; Stage and Screen Club; Student Government Association; Upsidedown Club; Veterans of All Nations Club; and WBCC radio station.

Facilities and Resources

Facilities available at BHCC include the library and information center, advising and counseling center, center for self-directed learning, tutoring and academic support center, career center, international center, and technology support services center.

Location

All Bunker Hill Community College sites are located in urban communities within 5 miles of downtown Boston. The main campus is located in the historic Charlestown neighborhood of Boston. An annex campus is located in Bellingham Square in Chelsea. The satellites are in Cambridge, Chinatown, Revere, Somerville, and the South End. All locations are easily accessible via public transportation. A subway stop is located steps from the Charlestown Campus.

Admission Requirements

Bunker Hill Community College is committed to an open admission policy. This policy offers the opportunity to enroll to those who have earned a high school diploma, a GED certificate, or an associate degree or higher and who express a desire to pursue a college education. All students admitted to degree or certificate programs are required to take computerized placement tests (CPTs) in English, reading, and mathematics. Students whose first language is not English, and who have not earned a high school diploma or GED in the United States, must take the English Placement Test (EPT). International students must take the Levels of English Proficiency (LOEP) assessment if they have not scored at least 423 on the TOEFL paper test or 113 on the computerized version. The purpose of these tests is to determine the levels at which students begin their study. Based upon test results, the College may prescribe developmental courses or limit a student's enrollment, in an effort to enhance that student's ability to succeed. Applicants to health careers and technical programs must comply with program entrance requirements and application deadlines.

Application and Information

Although the College has a rolling admissions process, students should contact the Admissions and Transfer Counseling Office for program-specific application deadlines.

Admissions and Transfer Counseling
Charlestown Campus, Room B130
Bunker Hill Community College
250 New Rutherford Avenue
Boston, Massachusetts 02129
Telephone: 617-228-2019
Fax: 617-228-3336
E-mail: admissions@bhcc.mass.edu
World Wide Web: http://www.bhcc.mass.edu

THE COLLEGE OF WESTCHESTER
WHITE PLAINS, NEW YORK

The College and Its Mission

Founded in 1915, the College of Westchester (CW) has a rich history of providing the community with affordable, private education at the collegiate level. The beautiful, state-of-the-art campus in White Plains offers an environment that is conducive to learning. Programs are designed for college-bound students with an interest in a career-focused education leading to long-term security and financial success.

The College's mission is to offer high-quality, career-oriented programs that challenge both the traditional and returning student to advanced levels of intellectual and personal development. This commitment to educational excellence is reflected in a carefully constructed and distinctive curriculum that is designed to provide students with sophisticated, marketable skills and to promote in students those attributes that contribute to personal and career success and a desire for lifelong learning. In order to maximize student success, the College maintains a student-centered environment.

CW is accredited by the Commission on Higher Education (CHE) of the Middle States Association of Colleges and Schools (3624 Market Street, Philadelphia, Pennsylvania 19104; telephone: 215-662-5606). The CHE is an institutional accrediting agency recognized by the U.S. Department of Education and the Council for Higher Education Accreditation.

Academic Programs

The Associate in Applied Science (A.A.S.) degree or the Associate in Occupational Studies (A.O.S.) degree is awarded upon successful completion of a two-year program. The requirements include courses in basic college skills, courses pertaining to the student's major, and, for those students pursuing an A.A.S. degree, courses in general education.

The Business Administration–Management/Marketing program provides students with an opportunity to concentrate in either e-commerce marketing, entrepreneurial management, or information systems. Three new concentrations have been added to the day program: entertainment, music, and sports management; fashion/retail merchandising; and hotel and resort management. Graduates pursue management training, Internet marketing, and sales positions. The program also affords self-employment opportunities through an appropriate educational background.

The Computer Network Administration program provides students with a leading-edge career education for today's technical world. Students study administration, design, support, and maintenance of local area networks through lectures and by using Microsoft Windows 2000 systems and software. The program includes additional nontechnical courses to enhance the student's career opportunities.

The Multimedia Development and Management program provides students with the tools to design and develop multimedia applications for the general media, business, education, the Internet, and entertainment markets. The program utilizes the most current multimedia technologies that enable students to create portfolios of their work.

The Computer Applications Management program prepares students for various professional-level employment opportunities in the rapidly expanding information processing and office technology fields. Graduates of this program are qualified to seek office technology and information processing positions that require expert computer applications skills and knowledge of technical office procedures.

The Office Administration program prepares students for various professional-level employment opportunities. Graduates of the program are qualified to seek office administration, executive administrative assistant, executive assistant, or office management positions.

The Medical Office Systems Management program prepares students for entry-level employment in such administrative positions as medical billers, coders, collectors, and office managers in organizations ranging from small medical practices to large health-care institutions.

Students in nondegree programs receive a certificate from CW if all courses are successfully completed. Credits may be transferred to the associate degree programs, providing a 2.0 or better cumulative grade point average has been achieved in addition to the successful completion of all required courses.

In a short certificate program, students can obtain specialized job skills to launch or upgrade their career. These programs are popular among students who already have some advanced skills or education as well as those who want to be employable and promotable in the shortest possible time.

Certificate programs include Computer Applications Specialist, Computer Networking Specialist, Intensive Accounting/Computer Applications, Multimedia Technology, and Word Processing Specialist.

Costs

The cost of tuition and fees varies, depending on the student's program. Current costs are available from the CW admissions office.

Financial Aid

All students at CW are encouraged to apply for financial assistance and meet with a financial assistance counselor who conducts a confidential analysis detailing the funds available to finance their education. In addition to federal- and state-funded programs, the College offers a variety of institutional scholarships, grants, and payment plans each year.

Faculty

CW instructors are highly qualified, dedicated, and respected educators who are committed to excellence in teaching and service to students. Most faculty members have advanced degrees and all have extensive business experience. A comprehensive faculty development program ensures that all instructors remain current in their field of expertise and utilizes state-of-the-art technology and teaching methodologies.

Student Body Profile

Students come to CW from throughout the New York metropolitan area. The present student body represents 117 high schools, five states, and six countries. The breadth of racial, ethnic, and socioeconomic backgrounds represented in the student body creates a genuinely diverse institution. There are nearly equal numbers of women and men enrolled and a sizable population of mature, nontraditional students who primarily attend convenient evening and weekend classes.

Student Activities

CW offers an array of student activities and support services designed to help students achieve their fullest potential for growth. Activities include Student Government Association, Alpha Beta Kappa honor society, business- and technology-related clubs, field trips to businesses and corporations, and social events.

Academic Facilities

The College of Westchester is located in a beautiful five-story, 50,000-square-foot building. The College's academic facilities include nineteen classrooms; a library; a student life center that houses all student organizations and clubs; an academic advancement center, an open computer lab that also serves as a tutoring and study center; a student lounge; and faculty offices. The facility also includes the Admissions Office; the Academic Center, where the academic administrators, including academic advisers, are housed; the Financial Services Center; and Career Placement Services.

CW's Career Placement Services specializes in finding part-time work for currently enrolled students and full-time, career-related positions for graduates. The staff members work with students to secure internships, co-op opportunities, and work-study positions while they are attending the College and also carefully guide students through the many facets of planning and preparing for job searches. This may include guidance in areas such as properly completing resumes, writing letters of application, securing job interviews, researching companies, and conducting interviews.

At CW, leading-edge technology defines the teaching and learning environment. The computer classrooms feature Pentium-based personal computers, outfitted with an extensive selection of current software applications. The recent addition of a G5 Macintosh lab has enabled CW students to learn applications on both Macintosh and PC platforms.

Location

CW is located in White Plains, the county seat and hub of Westchester County. Many of the College's graduates work for area corporations, including IBM, Verizon, Kraft General Foods USA, the Bank of New York, PepsiCo, AT&T, the Reader's Digest Association, Philip Morris, MasterCard, Citibank, Con Ed, CIBA, Texaco, MCI, Bayer Corporation, MBIA, Lillian Vernon, Fuji Film USA, Sunburst Communications, Hitachi America, Ltd., MetLife Corporation, MTA, Nine West, Avon Products, Carolee Designs, Online Design, Pitney Bowes, American Express, Coca Cola Corporation, Dannon Corporation, Doral Arrowwood, FedEx, International Paper, *The Journal News*, KPMG Peat Marwick, Lincoln Center for the Performing Arts, MCS Cannon,

Manulife Wood Logan, Marsh & McLennan, the United Way, Xerox, and Zurich Reinsurance.

The New York Metro North Railroad Station and the transportation center are both a short walk from CW.

Admission Requirements

To properly assist applicants in selecting the program that is best suited to their needs, a personal interview is conducted with an admissions associate. Prospective students should call the Admissions Office for an appointment. In addition to the interview, all applicants must be graduates of an accredited high school or its equivalent or have received a high school equivalency diploma (GED). In some cases, mature, non–high school graduates who have demonstrated an ability to benefit based upon an interview, counseling, and testing may be admitted. These individuals may qualify for a high school equivalency diploma through CW from the New York State Education Department by successfully completing 36 quarter hours of academic work with a minimum of a 2.0 GPA in one of the College programs.

Application and Information

CW has a rolling admissions policy. Students may apply at any time up to the beginning of the quarter; although, students are strongly encouraged to apply as early as possible. To be considered for admission, the following must be submitted: an application for admission, a $40 nonrefundable application fee, and an official high school transcript, its equivalent, or a GED equivalency diploma. If transferring credits from a prior college, students must submit an official college transcript. Students seeking to transfer credits from another institution of higher education should request that an official transcript be mailed to Transfer Credits, Office of Admissions. Students who have attended another accredited college or university may obtain credit toward graduation for courses taken at that institution. Credit is transferable for comparable courses in the student's selected curriculum in which the applicant has obtained a grade of C (2.0) or higher. A maximum of 50 percent of the credits required for program completion may be transferred. Official documentation of successful completion of high school or the equivalent must be received prior to the completion of the first quarter at the College.

For application materials and additional information, prospective students should contact:

Office of Admissions
The College of Westchester
325 Central Park Avenue
White Plains, New York 10606

Telephone: 800-333-4924
E-mail: admissions@cw.edu
World Wide Web: http://www.cw.edu

COLORADO MOUNTAIN COLLEGE
GLENWOOD SPRINGS, COLORADO

The College and Its Mission

There is a different view of the Rocky Mountains at each Colorado Mountain College campus. Learning is personal; classes are small; faculty members are friendly. Colorado Mountain College is a multicampus community college with three residential campuses and eight commuter locations. This coeducational public institution began operation in 1967. Colorado Mountain College operates on a semester system with a limited summer session and is accredited by the North Central Association of Colleges and Secondary Schools.

The three residential campuses include Alpine Campus in Steamboat Springs, Spring Valley Campus outside of Glenwood Springs, and Timberline Campus in Leadville. At these locations, students find a traditional college experience, including residence halls, cafeterias, extensive libraries, laboratories, and many opportunities to participate in residence life. The commuter campuses serve primarily local residents, and classes are scheduled for the convenience of working adults. Commuter sites are located in Aspen, Breckenridge, Buena Vista, Carbondale, Dillon, Edwards, Glenwood Springs, and Rifle.

Colorado Mountain College offers academic programs for transfer and for occupational training in several specialty areas. Students can begin their four-year degree because the State Guaranteed Transfer courses are guaranteed to satisfy general education requirements at all Colorado public higher-education institutions.

Students may also choose to start a career with occupational training programs. In one or two years, students can learn the skills for employment in some unique and exciting programs. The mountain environment gives students many opportunities to learn outside the classroom.

Academic Programs

Colorado Mountain College offers both occupational and transfer programs. Degrees awarded include the **Associate in Arts** degree, **Associate in Science** degree, **Associate in General Studies** degree, **Associate in Applied Science** degree, and a one-year Occupational Proficiency certificate. The Associate in Arts degree is available at all Colorado Mountain College campuses.

Degrees and programs vary by campus, with the residential campuses offering the fullest range of degrees and certificates. Alpine Campus offerings include the Associate in Arts (areas of specialization are business, fine arts, liberal arts, and wilderness studies), the Associate in Science (areas of specialization are biology, chemistry, geology, and mathematics), and the Associate in Applied Science and Certificates of Occupational Proficiency (offerings include accounting, business, resort management, and ski and snowboard business). Spring Valley Campus offerings include the Associate in Arts (areas of specialization are business, liberal arts, outdoor education, and theater), Associate in Science (areas of specialization are biology, chemistry, geology, mathematics, and nursing), and Associate in Applied Science and Certificates of Occupational Proficiency (offerings include accounting, business, graphic design, law enforcement, microcomputer support specialist studies, photography, practical nursing, and veterinary technology). Timberline Campus offerings include the Associate in Arts (areas of specialization are business, liberal arts, and Outdoor Semester in the Rockies), the Associate in General Studies degree in outdoor recreational leadership, the Associate in Science (areas of specialization are biology, chemistry, geology, and mathematics), and the Associate in Applied Science and Certificates of Occupational Proficiency (offerings include accounting, business, microcomputer support specialist studies,

natural resources management, natural resources recreation management, and ski area operations).

Off-Campus Programs

One of the most popular off-campus programs is the Outdoor Semester in the Rockies. This program blends outdoor adventure with the disciplines of college classes such as science, history, and philosophy. Colorado Mountain College encourages students to take advantage of several study-abroad class tours. The College also offers exciting distance education opportunities to district and residential campus students through telecourses, an interactive video system, and some Internet courses.

Credit for Nontraditional Learning Experiences

Colorado Mountain College awards credit through national standardized exams, challenge exams, and credit for life experience. To be awarded credit, testing options are used if possible, and students must be enrolled in a degree or certificate program. Credits posted to a student's academic record through one of these nontraditional methods are noted, indicating the method by which they were awarded.

Costs

Colorado Mountain College's tuition for the academic year 2006–07 is $43 per credit hour for in-district students, $72 per credit hour for in-state students, and $231 per credit hour for out-of-state students. Residential campuses had student activity fees of $180 per academic year. Room and board costs average $6600 per year, and the housing reservation deposit is $300. Books average $650 per academic year.

Financial Aid

Colorado Mountain College is approved for participation in all major federal and state financial aid programs, including Federal Pell Grant, loan programs, and work-study. Financial assistance is awarded through a central district office for all Colorado Mountain College campuses and education centers. The application for financial assistance is the Free Application for Federal Student Aid (FAFSA). First priority is given to those students applying on or before March 31. Applications received after this date are processed pending availability of funds. Questions may be addressed to Student Financial Assistance, District Office, 831 Grand Avenue, Glenwood Springs, Colorado 81602. The College's financial aid code is 004506.

Faculty

Colorado Mountain College faculty members are accessible to students. They are at Colorado Mountain College because they believe in teaching and learning. There are 72 full-time faculty members and 144 part-time faculty members at the three residential campuses. The faculty members pride themselves on the high-quality education students receive in the classroom, with classes averaging 15 students. The student-faculty ratio is 12:1. Many faculty members have taught at colleges and universities and have chosen to teach at Colorado Mountain College.

Student Body Profile

Colorado Mountain College students are from the local area, forty-eight states, and six other countries. Undergraduate students at the residential campuses number approximately 500 full-time students at Alpine as well as Spring Valley, and Timberline has about 300 full-time students. The Alpine Campus can house about 236 students on campus, the Spring Valley Campus about 226 students, and the Timberline Campus about 136 students.

Student Activities

Each residential campus has active student government organizations. Each student government determines the student activity fee and how the funds are utilized on each campus. Student government helps to sponsor student activities, clubs and organizations, and guest speakers. Colorado Mountain College's Alpine ski team holds six national titles. Men's and women's varsity soccer teams are offered at the Spring Valley Campus, and there is a Nordic ski team at the Timberline campus. Every season brings new activities and celebrations to the mountain resort towns.

Facilities and Resources

The residential campuses offer a full college experience with residence halls, cafeterias, libraries, academic classrooms, learning labs, laboratories, and student center facilities.

The Alpine Campus offers residence halls and classroom buildings. At the Spring Valley Campus, students can enjoy the hot springs pool in Glenwood Springs, the charm of Carbondale, and the culture of Aspen. Spring Valley offers residence halls, a cafeteria, a gymnasium and climbing wall, a student center, a bookstore, classrooms, a working farm, laboratories, and an extensive library. A new academic building opened in fall 1998. This building houses a theater, photography labs and studio, a graphic design computer lab, a student computer center, and classrooms. The faculty offices surround the classrooms so students can easily access their instructors and professors. At the Timberline Campus, many students combine their environmental interests and their college education. Colorado's highest mountain peak is in the backyard, cross-country skiing begins at the edge of campus, and many of Colorado's big name slopes are no more than an hour away. The campus offers classroom facilities, a library and learning lab, a computer lab, and a bookstore. In fall 1999, a new academic building opened at the Timberline Campus. It houses classrooms, a computer center, laboratories, student services, and faculty offices. Students enjoy a relaxing student center and cafeteria and have access to Leadville's modern recreation complex.

Location

Like the Rockies that surround it, Colorado Mountain College is wide open and full of possibilities. There are miles of spruce and aspen, wildflowers, backroads, whitewater and bareback ranchland, three national forests, six wilderness areas, and most of Colorado's major ski resorts. There is a spirit among the teachers and students, an atmosphere of encouragement, and an attitude of confidence. **Alpine Campus** is situated above the downtown area on the west end of Steamboat Springs. In Leadville, **Timberline Campus** is less than an hour's drive from Vail and is surrounded by Colorado's highest peaks and the legends of a town built by silver. High above the Roaring Fork River, **Spring Valley Campus** is located 10 miles south of Glenwood Springs and within 40 miles of Aspen. All Colorado Mountain College locations are resort or mountain communities accessible by air, rail, or bus, and provide excellent outdoor opportunities.

Admission Requirements

Colorado Mountain College seeks, encourages, and assists all interested students beyond high-school age who demonstrate a desire to learn. With a few exceptions, admission follows an open-door policy. Even though Colorado Mountain College has open admission, certain occupational programs have selective admission. Programs with selection or testing requirements and admission deadlines include culinary arts, nursing, outdoor recreation leadership, paramedicine, professional photography, and veterinary technology.

To apply for admission, students must complete and return the Colorado Mountain College admissions application and official high school and/or college transcripts. There is no application fee. All entering students should submit ACT or SAT scores for scholarship, advising, and placement purposes. Some programs require testing for admission.

Transfer students are welcome and should have attained a cumulative grade point average of at least 2.0 on any college work attempted. Nongraduates may take the General Educational Development test (GED) to meet graduation equivalence. International students may be considered for admission to the residential campuses. International admission packets are available and must be completed and returned to apply for admission, and a minimum TOEFL score of 500 on the paper exam or a minimum score of 173 on the computerized exam is required for admission.

Students are encouraged to apply as soon as possible to secure on-campus housing. After applying for admission to a residential campus, students receive housing reservation information.

Application and Information

For more information, students should contact:

Central Admissions
Colorado Mountain College
831 Grand Avenue
Glenwood Springs, Colorado 81602
Telephone: 970-945-8691
        800-621-8559 (toll-free)
Fax: 970-947-8324
E-mail: joinus@coloradomtn.edu
World Wide Web: http://www.coloradomtn.edu

The Colorado Rockies are a classroom for Colorado Mountain College students.

COMMUNITY COLLEGE OF ALLEGHENY COUNTY

PITTSBURGH, MC CANDLESS, MONROEVILLE, AND WEST MIFFLIN, PENNSYLVANIA

The College and Its Mission

The Community College of Allegheny County (CCAC) has been helping students realize their futures for nearly forty years. CCAC's educational influence extends far beyond the 350 acres that compose its four campuses. The College reaches deep into the communities. Classes are offered at **Allegheny Campus** on Pittsburgh's North Shore, **Boyce Campus** in Monroeville, **South Campus** in West Mifflin, and **North Campus** in McCandless. Classes are also offered at more than 400 other locations in Allegheny County. CCAC is one of the largest community colleges in Pennsylvania. While its size is a great advantage in terms of the depth and breadth of academic opportunities, the College also specializes in offering individualized attention to students to help them meet their academic goals. High school graduates beginning their college studies find themselves supported and inspired by faculty members who have made a commitment to teaching. Nontraditional students who are returning to school and have family responsibilities can find a wide range of course offerings scheduled at convenient times and locations. CCAC is fully accredited by the Middle States Association of Colleges and Schools.

Academic Programs

CCAC offers academic, career, and technical programs that prepare students for the workforce or to transfer into baccalaureate degree programs at other colleges or universities. The College offers both full- and part-time programs leading to certificates or associate degrees. Program requirements vary; in general, an associate degree program requires two years of study, and a certificate program requires one year or less.

Associate Degree Programs The associate degrees offered by CCAC can be grouped into several different areas. University parallel and transfer programs offer associate degrees in accounting, Africana and ethnic studies, art, biology, business, chemistry, computer information science, criminal justice and criminology, engineering science, engineering technology, foreign language, humanities, journalism, liberal arts and sciences, manufacturing engineering, mathematics, music, physics, pre-athletic training, pre-health professions, psychology, social sciences, sociology/anthropology, teacher education, and theater.

Career programs in business offer associate degrees in accounting specialist studies, aviation management, aviation technology, business management, cosmetology management, court reporter studies, culinary arts, hotel-restaurant management, marketing management, paralegal studies, personnel management, public administration, and tourism management.

Career programs in computer information technology offer associate degrees in application software development, e-commerce development, network administration, and user support.

Career programs in health include biotechnology, diagnostic medical sonographer studies, dietetic technician studies, health information technology, massage therapy, medical assistant studies, medical laboratory technician studies, nuclear medicine technology, nursing, occupational therapy assistant studies, pharmacy technician studies, physical therapy assistant studies, radiation therapy, radiologic technologist studies, respiratory therapy, and surgical technologist studies.

Career programs in social service include child and family studies, criminal justice and criminology, fire science and administration, mental health/mental retardation specialist studies, social work technician studies and teacher's assistant studies.

Career programs in applied arts technologies include graphics communications, horticulture technology (floriculture), horticulture

technology (landscape design), horticulture technology (landscape and turfgrass management), industrial design and art, and multimedia communications.

Career programs in applied service and trade technologies offer associate degrees in automotive service, automotive technology, building construction estimating, building construction supervision, building construction technology, building maintenance technology, electrical distribution technology, heating and air-conditioning technology, mechanical electronics technology, mechanical maintenance technology, motor winding technology, and welding technology.

Career programs in engineering and science technologies offer associate degrees in architectural drafting and design technology, civil engineering technology, computer-aided drafting and design, electronic engineering technology, laboratory technology, mechanical drafting and design technology, microcomputer electronics technology, robotics and automated systems technology, and science and engineering technology.

Certificate Programs CCAC offers the following certificate programs: accounting, Africana and ethnic studies, American Sign Language, automotive technology, basic CAD, basic preparation cook studies, biotechnology, building construction, building maintenance technology, business management, carpentry, CAT scanning, central services technology, child and family studies, CIT application software development, CIT computer programming, CIT e-commerce development, CIT network administration, CIT survivability and information assurance, CIT user support, CIT Web designer studies, computer numerical control programming, construction estimating, court reporting, diagnostic medical sonography, dietary manager studies, digital graphic design, drafting and/or surveying, electronics (basic or digital), floriculture, foreman and superintendent training, health unit coordinator studies, heating and air conditioning, hotel management, human resources management, ironworking, landscape design, landscape maintenance, machine studies (basic), massage therapy, mechanical electronic technology, mechanical maintenance technology, medical insurance specialist studies, medical transcription, motor winding technology, MRI scanning, nanofabrication, network cable technology, nuclear medicine technology, operating room nursing, paralegal studies, pharmacy technician studies, phlebotomist studies, plumbing, private pilot, radiation therapy, rehabilitation aide studies, restaurant management, sheet-metal studies, social work specialist (family intervention or geriatrics), surgical technology, teacher's assistant studies, turfgrass maintenance, and welding.

Diploma Programs CCAC offers diploma programs in child care, child development, children with special needs, drug and alcohol, floral and art design, global studies, landscape horticulture, medical assistant, practical nursing, social work specialist, and technical theater.

Costs

For residents of Allegheny County, CCAC's tuition was $80 per credit. Residents of other Pennsylvania counties that do not have a community college paid $94 per credit. Residents of Pennsylvania counties with community colleges paid $160 per credit. Students living out of state paid $240 per credit. A College fee of $50.40 per semester was charged to students taking classes at each campus location. Some courses offered by CCAC require special course or lab fees in addition to the tuition and College fee. All of these costs were estimated for the 2005–06 academic year. CCAC reserves the right to change the tuition and fees at any time and without prior notice.

Financial Aid

Financial aid programs at CCAC are designed to assist students whose family circumstances limit their ability to contribute toward educational costs. Under federal guidelines, students are expected to seek assistance first from funds that are available through their own personal resources and then from the government. Most awards are need-based, which means that a determination of the expected family contribution is made through a formula established by the U.S. Department of Education. Financial aid consists of scholarships, grants, loans, and employment. Aid may be offered in some combination of these sources, depending on the student's financial need and the requirements for each program. Awards are based on the enrollment of the student, the expected family contribution of the student, and the availability of funding at the time the application for aid is received. Students who have taken out student loans in the past and who are in default on those loans are not eligible for any type of federal, state, or institutional financial aid. Students must complete the Free Application for Federal Student Aid (FAFSA) to be considered for financial aid. Other supporting documents may be required by the Financial Aid Office. Students are notified as to which forms are required once the FAFSA results are received.

Faculty

CCAC has 270 full-time professors and more than 1,100 part-time educators who are experienced, knowledgeable, and committed to teaching. While most faculty members continue their studies and research to remain current in their respective fields, their first commitment is to the students. The average class size is 20.

Student Body Profile

There 18,925 students enrolled as full- and part-time credit students in fall 2005. The average age of this student population is 24. In a typical fall semester, the CCAC minority group enrollment is approximately 19 percent.

Student Activities

CCAC student activities include the opportunity to acquire leadership experience as part of student government or to participate in creative endeavors, including student publications, drama productions, and art programs. Many cultural clubs and organizations exist as well. Students may also enrich themselves in their chosen field of studies as a member of an academically related club or organization. For those who prefer the competitive edge, athletic programs for both men and women are available at designated CCAC campuses. Basketball, baseball, golf, tennis, bowling, softball, volleyball, cross-country, racquetball, and weightlifting are just some of the intramural and intercollegiate athletic programs available.

Academic Facilities

A multicampus institution, the Community College of Allegheny County provides access to modern facilities and comprehensive services to enhance the educational experience. Facilities at CCAC are designed to accommodate students with physical disabilities. Paved walkways, accessible building entrances, and elevator systems provide easy access to classrooms and laboratories. In addition, interpreters for the deaf, Braille materials, note-taking, scanning, voice output, and use of technology are available for students with documented disabilities. The College maintains excellent computer facilities at each of its four campuses. Students receive hands-on experience on state-of-the-art computers and instructional equipment. Campus and center computer labs offer convenient day and evening hours.

CCAC's four campus libraries house more than 200,000 volumes and subscribe to 847 periodicals. Quiet reading and study areas are available, as are knowledgeable librarians to provide the research assistance students may need. Tutoring services and workshops in test taking, study techniques, and basic academic skills are provided at no cost to students through CCAC's Learning Assistance Centers.

In support of classroom instruction, audiovisual instructional and technical support services are provided to faculty members.

For students who are also parents, each of the four CCAC campuses provides a child development center, staffed by professionals who not only care for each child's physical needs but also provide a stimulating learning environment. CCAC adult reentry services provide educational and emotional support for students returning to an academic environment after a long absence. Services offered include career and educational planning, basic skills instruction, and confidence building.

CCAC provides valuable job search assistance for its students and graduates through its Career Services department. These offices host the Pennsylvania CareerLink program, which maintains a database containing more than 5,000 annual job listings.

Location

The College has four campuses and seven college centers located strategically throughout Allegheny County. The city of Pittsburgh, located in Allegheny County, is one of the largest sites of corporate headquarters in the United States and has an abundance of cultural activities.

Admission Requirements

As an open-door institution, CCAC provides learning opportunities for all students regardless of prior educational background. CCAC can help applicants with a high school diploma or a General Educational Development (GED) certificate or those who are 18 years of age or older with reasonably equivalent experience to achieve their academic goals. The college placement tests may be given to first-time college students. These tests are intended to assist students in selecting courses that are most appropriate for their current academic skill level; they are not admissions tests. Students who have completed college-level course work at another school or have ACT or SAT scores may be exempt from testing. Students should check with the registration and advisement offices for exemption criteria.

Students should request an admission application form from the admission office on any CCAC campus and should return the completed application to the admission office. Students can also apply online at CCAC's Web site (http://www.ccac.edu). There is no application fee.

Application and Information

Application forms and additional information are available at the following CCAC campus locations:

Allegheny Campus (North Shore)
Community College of Allegheny County
808 Ridge Avenue
Pittsburgh, Pennsylvania 15212
Telephone: 412-237-2511

North Campus (McCandless)
Community College of Allegheny County
8701 Perry Highway
Pittsburgh, Pennsylvania 15237
Telephone: 412-369-3600

Boyce Campus (Monroeville)
Community College of Allegheny County
595 Beatty Road
Monroeville, Pennsylvania 15146
Telephone: 724-325-6614

South Campus (West Mifflin)
Community College of Allegheny County
1750 Clairton Road
West Mifflin, Pennsylvania 15122
Telephone: 412-469-4301
World Wide Web: http://www.ccac.edu

COOKING AND HOSPITALITY INSTITUTE OF CHICAGO

CHICAGO, ILLINOIS

The Cooking and Hospitality
Institute of Chicago
Le Cordon Bleu Program

The Institute and Its Mission

The Cooking and Hospitality Institute of Chicago is a Le Cordon Bleu Program. Le Cordon Bleu is the famous cooking school founded in Paris in 1895. Thousands of graduates have become professional cooks, bakers, and chefs now staffing some of the most prestigious hospitality establishments in Chicago, the nation, and the world. The Institute is the only school in the Great Lakes Region offering the Le Cordon Bleu Program. The Institute awards Associate of Applied Science degrees as well as the Le Cordon Bleu Diplôme in culinary arts and pâtisserie and baking. By combining classical French cooking methods with modern American techniques, graduates are eagerly embraced by the hospitality industry.

The mission of the Cooking and Hospitality Institute of Chicago is to prepare students to fulfill their career aspirations and meet the needs of the food-service industry through high-quality culinary, pastry arts, hospitality, and general education curriculums of higher education.

The Cooking and Hospitality Institute of Chicago was established in 1983 to provide culinary education using the traditional European hands-on approach. As soon as the first students completed the Professional Cooking Program, most were employed at major hotels and restaurants. In 1989, the school undertook a major expansion into its present facility, and in 1991, it received degree-granting authority from the Illinois Board of Higher Education and began offering an Associate of Applied Science (AAS) degree in culinary arts. In June 2000, it became affiliated with Le Cordon Bleu. Le Cordon Bleu chefs evaluated the facilities and modified the curriculum to include exposure to an array of culinary proficiencies—skills taught in culinary arts programs. Le Cordon Bleu continues to monitor and train school faculty members to ensure not only that the curriculum is being delivered but also that the spirit of Le Cordon Bleu is communicated to the students. Through affiliation with Le Cordon Bleu, the school has been able to expand program offerings with the addition of an Associate of Applied Science in Pâtisserie and Baking degree.

In 2003, the Cooking and Hospitality Institute became a member of the North Central Association of Colleges and Schools and was accredited by the Higher Learning Commission. In 2004, due to demand for the Le Cordon Bleu Program, additional kitchen space was required. Five industry-current kitchens were built in a 20,000-square-foot space across the street from the main campus. The new campus also includes two classrooms and a modern computer lounge. By anticipating the dynamic changes in the food-service industry, the Cooking and Hospitality Institute of Chicago has developed an evolutionary set of programs that continually adapts to these needs.

Academic Programs

The Cooking and Hospitality Institute of Chicago offers accredited Associate of Applied Science (A.A.S.) degrees in Le Cordon Bleu Culinary Arts and Le Cordon Bleu Patisserie and Baking. The Cooking and Hospitality Institute of Chicago is devoted to fostering a lifelong love of learning and holding students to high academic standards. The Institute's premier Le Cordon Bleu A.A.S. program combines course work in three areas: culinary, baking and pastry, and restaurant management. Students at the Institute can complete the program in as little as fifteen months. There are currently eight start dates available per year. Morning, midmorning, and evening courses are offered to accommodate most students' schedules. Students enrolled in the Le Cordon Bleu programs show commitment to those programs as well as to the culinary profession by completing their education in a timely manner.

Associate Degree Programs The Cooking and Hospitality Institute of Chicago offers an Associate of Applied Science degree in Le Cordon Bleu Pâtisserie and Baking. This program teaches the principles and techniques of professional pastry and baking production and is intended for students who have an interest in large-quantity baking or who want to work for establishments that have in-house baking and pastry operations.

The Cooking and Hospitality Institute of Chicago also offers an Associate of Applied Science degree in Le Cordon Bleu culinary arts. The program includes professional cooking skills, baking and pastry skills, restaurant management skills, nutrition sciences, and general education. This well-rounded program is designed to give students the technical skills and theoretical expertise necessary for a career in the food service industry. Graduates can expect employment in entry-level to midlevel positions as well as rapid advancement into management and sous chef positions and further. Students with or without prior experience find that this program offers everything they need to begin a fast-track career in the fastest-growing industry in the United States.

Transfer Arrangements The Cooking and Hospitality Institute of Chicago may accept transfer credits from accredited colleges, provided that the credits are in courses comparable to the courses required under the student's program of study at the Institute. The school registrar determines if credits are transferable.

Off-Campus Programs

The Cooking and Hospitality Institute of Chicago has entered into cooperative agreements with three area colleges that allow students to transfer credits from the Institute toward a bachelor's degree. At Dominican University in River Forest, Illinois, students can continue on for a Bachelor of General Studies (B.G.S.) in culinary arts and management or a Bachelor of Science (B.S.) in nutrition and dietetics, food science management, or food science and nutrition. Students may opt to include in these programs elective courses for nursing home administrator licensure in Illinois. Students may also continue their studies at Robert Morris College, which has campuses in Chicago, Orland Park, Naperville, and Springfield, Illinois, to pursue a Bachelor of Business Administration (B.B.A.). Graduates of the Institute who transfer to Robert Morris with a GPA of at least 3.0 may also receive a tuition scholarship of up to $4800. Students also have the opportunity to continue their studies at Roosevelt University, which accepts 39 credits from the Cooking and Hospitality Institute of Chicago toward their B.S. in hospitality and tourism.

Credit for Nontraditional Learning Experiences

The Institute awards credit to students who have demonstrated proficiency through the Advanced Placement (AP) program and the College-Level Examination Program (CLEP).

Costs

As of January 2005, tuition for the entire culinary program was $39,950. The current tuition for the entire patisserie and baking program is $38,500. In addition, students can expect a one-time purchase of a supply kit. Books, uniforms, activity fees, application fee, and supplies can cost up to approximately $3600 for the full program (start through graduation).

Financial Aid

Tuition planning is provided free of charge to all applicants. The Institute participates in Federal Title IV assistance programs, such as Federal Stafford Student Loans, Federal PLUS loans, Federal Pell Grants, Federal Supplemental Educational Opportunity Grants, and the Federal Work-Study Program. Students may also receive funding from a variety of institutional and industry-related scholarships, which include the Nancy Abrams Academic Excellence Scholarship, the Educational Foundation's ProMgmt. Scholarship, and the Career College Association's Imagine America Scholarships for high school seniors as well as scholarships from the James Beard Foundation, the International Association of Culinary Professionals, the Illinois Restaurant Association, and the National Restaurant Association. Scholarships range from $500 to $10,000.

Nongovernmental loans are available through Sallie Mae. These loans may be used to supplement federal financial aid and in cases where students do not qualify for federal aid. The loan terms are similar to federal student loans, but the application procedure is greatly simplified.

Faculty

The best ingredient at the Institute is the faculty. Faculty members are selected for their professional backgrounds and academic experience. Students work closely with talented chefs and learn from their combined 400 years of industry experience.

Student Body Profile

The Cooking and Hospitality Institute of Chicago is both ethnically and culturally diverse, with international students representing more than fifteen different countries. Students range in age from 17 to 70. Twenty percent of the students are recent high school graduates, while more than half are career changers whose average age is about 30. In addition, 20 percent of the students are from out of state and have relocated to Chicago in order to participate in the Le Cordon Bleu programs.

Student Activities

The Cooking and Hospitality Institute of Chicago supports many student organizations that provide students with interesting networking and experiential opportunities. Under the advisement of the Dean of Education and faculty advisers, these organizations are the Student Recipe Development Association, the Alpha Beta Kappa Society, the Student Board, the Cellar Club, the Pastry Display Club, the Bread Guild, the Culinary Competition Team, and many more. The Culinary Competition Team has won medals and certificates throughout the country.

Facilities and Resources

The Cooking and Hospitality Institute occupies more than 85,000 square feet of space. The North Campus is located at 361 West Chestnut in a two-story red brick building, with easy access to both public transportation, the major expressways, and two international airports. The new South Campus is just across the parking lot at 820 North Orleans. All thirteen air-conditioned kitchens feature industry-current technology with complete cooking lines, automatic dishwashers, and several preparation areas. The Institute features multiple walk-in refrigerators, freezers, dry storage, and cleaning-supply areas. There are fourteen classrooms on campus as well as a library, computer lab, student lounge, tutoring center, and café. The café features a formal dining room with seating for up to 80 guests. The café is operated by students and is open to the public for breakfast, lunch, and dinner.

Student Housing A student housing program is available to students through a real estate firm. Apartments (shared housing) are competitively priced and accessible to the campus via public transportation.

Learning Resource Center Students and faculty members have full access to a collection of more than 5,000 volumes, forty related periodicals and newsletters, and reference materials in hospitality-related areas, as well as CD-ROMs and numerous online resources. Online services include a reference catalog, Internet access, ProQuest, and Infotrac. In addition to the current holdings, the library has cooperative arrangements with various local libraries and professional associations. Interlibrary loan service is available through Illinet (Illinois Library and Information Network). The LRC also maintains a staffed computer laboratory for student use, with access to the Internet, various hospitality and purchasing software, word processing, and scanners.

Career Planning/Placement Offices Whether a current student or alumni, Career Services is the first stop for career and employment information and guidance. The Cooking and Hospitality Institute of Chicago encourages current students to participate in networking opportunities available through Career Services for exposure to a variety of professionals in the culinary and hospitality industries. In addition, the Career Services Department offers workshops, tutoring, and personal career coaching. Students and alumni wishing to meet with a representative of the office to discuss career planning or to gain access to current job openings should contact the Career Services Office.

Career Services recognizes that many students may require employment during their tenure at the Cooking and Hospitality Institute of Chicago, so it provides assistance to these students in their search for part-time employment. In order to maximize the benefits of this program, Career Services recommends that students work a maximum of 25 hours a week. The Cooking and Hospitality Institute of Chicago has formed partnerships with employers so students may gain practical experience in the culinary/hospitality industry both during and after their attendance at the Institute. The student captures the opportunity to apply classroom theory to real-world practice and develops speed, efficiency, and food-production skills. Career Services is committed to the success of the students and works hard to assist with employment for all interested students; however, the Institute cannot guarantee employment placement. Career Services provides information on the student portal on temporary, part-time, and full-time positions; volunteer opportunities; and upcoming site visits.

Location

The Institute is located in the River North area of Chicago, within walking distance of some of the finest restaurants and art galleries in the city. It is eight blocks west of Chicago's famed shopping district, the Magnificent Mile, and only a few blocks north of Chicago's business district, the Loop. It is easily accessible by public transportation, two major expressways, and two international airports.

Admission Requirements

All applicants must be beyond compulsory school age and must furnish documentation of at least a high school diploma or a GED diploma. In addition, applicants must demonstrate their math and English abilities by providing high school or college transcripts or ACT or SAT scores, or they may take the Institute's math and/or English placement exams. International students may submit TOEFL scores for initial acceptance and issuance of an I-20 visa, but they must take the Institute's placement tests upon arrival for course determination.

Application and Information

Applications are accepted on an ongoing basis. Prospective students should contact:

Director of Admissions
Cooking and Hospitality Institute of Chicago
361 West Chestnut
Chicago, Illinois 60610
Telephone: 312-944-0882
          877-828-7772 (toll-free)
Fax: 312-944-8557
E-mail: chic@chicnet.org
World Wide Web: http://www.chic.edu

Students receive personalized, hands-on instruction from Le Cordon Bleu instructors.

COTTEY COLLEGE

NEVADA, MISSOURI

The College and Its Mission

Cottey College is a two-year independent, residential, liberal arts and sciences college for women. Virginia Alice Cottey founded the College in 1884 with the firm belief that women deserved the same quality of education as men. When the founder became a member of the P.E.O. Sisterhood—a philanthropic educational organization of more than 250,000 members dedicated to providing educational opportunities for women—she realized the organization paralleled her own goals and ideas about higher education for women. The P.E.O. Sisterhood accepted the College as a gift from the founder in 1927, which made it the only nonsectarian college owned and supported by women.

Cottey College concentrates on what it does best—providing two years of very focused and rigorous academics to move students closer to earning a four-year degree. A Cottey education emphasizes high academic standards with unique opportunities for personal growth through residential, cultural, and intellectual experiences. Cottey College educates qualified women in the arts and sciences to prepare them to transfer to programs beyond the associate degree by enhancing their intellectual ability, their store of knowledge, their personal skills, and, thereby, their capacity for contribution to society and their chosen fields.

Cottey is a member of the Missouri American Council on Education (ACE) Network for the Office of Women in Higher Education (OWHE) and hosts the state Web site on its server.

Academic Programs

The academic tradition at Cottey College is firmly established in the liberal arts. Because its mission is, in part, "to educate qualified women in arts and sciences to prepare them for transfer to programs beyond the associate degree," Cottey emphasizes general education. Fields of study are, in effect, prospective majors for Cottey students, allowing them to focus on specialized personal interests growing out of a general education in the liberal arts and sciences. A Cottey education in a chosen field of study permits students to start learning and working toward careers that interest them and prepares them to enter a major or preprofessional program when they transfer to another institution to complete their bachelor's degree.

Cottey College grants the Associate in Arts (A.A.) and the Associate in Science (A.S.) degrees. Both associate degrees require the completion of 62 credit hours with a cumulative grade point average (GPA) of 2.0 or higher. Thirty-two credit hours must be completed at Cottey College. All students must complete a 24-credit common core curriculum. The core includes 11 credits in basic skills, such as English composition (writing), mathematics, and physical activities. The other 13 credits are distribution requirements in the fine arts, humanities, natural sciences, and social sciences. Depending on their interests and prospective majors, Cottey graduates earn either the A.A. or A.S. degree by meeting additional degree requirements beyond the core curriculum. The A.A. degree requires 12 additional credits focusing on the humanities, foreign languages, and fine arts. The A.S. degree requires 11 additional credits focusing on the sciences and mathematics.

More than 95 percent of graduates transfer to four-year institutions, including such top schools as MIT, Smith, Grinnell, Pepperdine, and the University of Washington, to name a few. As a two-year college, Cottey does not pressure students to declare a major, but they are prepared to declare one at their next college or university.

Off-Campus Programs

In March 2000, for the first time in the College's history, second-year Cottey students spent the first week of the spring break in London, England. The Cottey College Board of Trustees approved a three-year pilot program that sends students to a European city during the spring break of their second year. The program continues to receive approval from the Board and in the last six years, the College has traveled to London, Paris, and Madrid. In 2006, the second-year class is scheduled to return to London for the first time since 2001. There are no additional costs in terms of tuition increases or program or transportation fees placed upon students to participate in this program. Members of the Cottey faculty and staff are involved in the planning of this program and integrate on-campus instruction and activities with the trip preparations. Professors selected for the international trip create educational modules related to their disciplines or interests that they present during two days of the trip. Students have ample time for individual sight-seeing and group-touring opportunities, and all participants attend a farewell dinner at a first-class restaurant.

Costs

In the 2005–06 academic year, the total cost was $17,510. This included tuition, room and board, and all fees.

Financial Aid

Approximately 97 percent of the students receive some form of need- or merit-based aid. Assistance programs include P.E.O. and Cottey scholarships, grants, campus employment, and loans. Amounts depend on financial need, talents, high school GPA, and ACT and/or SAT scores. More information can be obtained from the financial aid office.

Faculty

There are 35 full-time faculty members, of whom more than 94 percent hold doctoral degrees or the terminal degrees in their fields. Twenty-two hold a Ph.D. degree. The student-faculty ratio is 10:1, and the average class size is 13 students. The faculty members are first and foremost teachers. Their subject areas are obvious and inspiring, and their primary interest is in teaching and mentoring young women of promise. All classes are taught by Cottey professors, not teaching assistants. Students know their professors, and this access to faculty members allows students to ask questions and get the answers they need. Many faculty members accept calls at home, and some are known to regularly visit campus study groups on nights or weekends for last-minute tutoring sessions before a test.

Student Body Profile

Cottey students come from everywhere. Generally, no more than 10 percent of students come from any one state, and approximately 10 percent come from outside the United States.

Cottey's residential student population of 350 women typically represents forty states, Canada, and ten to fourteen countries.

Student Activities

Many outstanding cultural events, performances, lectures, workshops, and recreational activities are offered without charge to students. More than thirty-five clubs and organizations at Cottey represent varying student interests in academics, culture, recreation, social concerns, religion, and volunteerism. The clubs and organizations also offer many leadership positions for students each year, enabling women to gain valuable leadership experiences that can help shape their future, their education, and their career paths. Many students become involved in the programs at Cottey's Helen and George Washburn Center for Women's Leadership (CWL), which was established to build girls' and women's lives through enrichment, education, and leadership development. The CWL offers special guest lecturers and notable speakers, and Cottey students can obtain leadership certification through its Leadership, Education, Opportunities (LEO) program, which provides student leaders with an opportunity to document and receive recognition for their experiences inside and outside the classroom and to further develop leadership skills. The LEO program offers four levels of certification.

Cottey's regular slate of national and international guests and performers makes Nevada seem like a larger city. The CLASS series brings to campus such artists, experts, and entertainers as the National Theatre for the Deaf, a Japanese storyteller, the Preservation Hall Jazz Band, Alvin Ailey II Dance Company, Tibetan monks performing sacred music and dance, the Kansas City Symphony, State Ballet, and folk singer Karla Bonhoff. Cottey students take the lead in celebrating International Focus Week, during which they share the food, stories, artifacts, and artistry of their native or ancestral cultures.

Cottey College offers volleyball and basketball in its intercollegiate sports program. Cottey is a member of the National Junior College Athletic Association (NJCAA) Division II, Region XVI. The NJCAA is the athletic association for all two-year colleges. Division II is a mix of small and large two-year colleges. Region XVI is the state of Missouri. There are six colleges that are Division II in Missouri, and those colleges compete in the Regional Tournament.

Facilities and Resources

Completed in 1963, the Blanche Skiff Ross Memorial Library was named in honor of Mrs. Frank Ross of Oak Park, Illinois, niece of Alice Virginia Coffin, one of the 7 founders of the P.E.O. Sisterhood. Browsing the shelves of more than 50,000 volumes of books, videos, DVDs, CDs, slides, maps, and music scores can lead to exploring a broad range of subjects, viewpoints, and cultures. More than 180 current periodical subscriptions reflect the variety of today's interests; some titles extend to 150 years of history. On campus, the library Web site links to databases with full texts of more than 2,000 periodicals as well as news services, government documents, and scholarly databases. The library is a member of the Missouri Bibliographic Information User System (MOBIUS), a group of more than fifty libraries in Missouri, as well as SouthWest Academic Libraries (SWAN), which is a regional branch of the MOBIUS system. MOBIUS and SWAN allow a Cottey student to request a book from libraries within this system. Items requested from MOBIUS and SWAN are delivered to Cottey's library usually within three to four days. This gives students access to resources and information beyond what Cottey can offer.

Location

A community of about 9,000 people, Nevada, Missouri, is approximately 100 miles south of Kansas City. The campus occupies fourteen buildings on eleven city blocks and a 33-acre wooded recreational area with a lodge. Nevada is a fairly self-sufficient town, with grocery stores, restaurants, local shops, and a Wal-Mart. In addition, there are several large cities and recreational areas within a 90-minute drive of the Cottey campus.

Admission Requirements

All applicants for admission to Cottey College should take a college preparatory sequence. The minimum required high school curriculum includes 4 years of study in English composition and literature, 3 years of math (algebra I and II and geometry), 2 years of history and government, 2 years of a laboratory science, and 2 years of the same foreign language. Acceptance to Cottey is based on prior performance, academic aptitude, and the student's likelihood for success.

Students can apply online or by mail. If applying by mail, there is a $20 nonrefundable application fee. Along with a completed application, students must submit an evaluation form completed by a high school teacher or guidance counselor, an official copy of the high school transcript (showing the completion of at least six semesters of course work), and official ACT or SAT scores. All international students must complete the international application for admission, even if they are currently living in the United States.

Application and Information

The application for admission should be on file with the Office of Enrollment Management as early as possible. The College accepts students for admission only until it reaches its capacity of 350 residential students. If a student has a high school GPA of at least 2.6 and standardized test results that meet the current eligibility requirements (ACT composite of 21 or better or an SAT total of 970 or better on the critical thinking and math sections), she is notified of an admission decision within two to four weeks after completing the application process. Cottey College does not require the Writing section of the SAT at this time.

Office of Enrollment Management
Cottey College
1000 West Austin Boulevard
Nevada, Missouri 64772
Telephone: 417-667-8181
            888-5-COTTEY (toll-free)
Fax: 417-667-8103
E-mail: enrollmgt@cottey.edu
World Wide Web: http://www.cottey.edu

FAIRMONT STATE COMMUNITY & TECHNICAL COLLEGE
FAIRMONT, WEST VIRGINIA

The College and Its Mission

Fairmont State Community & Technical College (FSC&TC) has an enrollment of approximately 3,500 students. Founded in 1974, the College is located in Fairmont, West Virginia.

FSC&TC enhances the quality of life for the people of north-central West Virginia through accessible, affordable, comprehensive, responsive, workforce-related training and high-quality higher education opportunities.

FSC&TC offers a variety of courses at more than twenty-five sites each semester in its thirteen-county service area through its Off-Campus Programs and provides job training for the region through its Center for Workforce Education in downtown Fairmont. The Weekend College program allows adults the opportunity to earn degrees by attending classes on Saturdays on the main campus in Fairmont and at the Gaston Caperton Center in Clarksburg, West Virginia. The Televised Classes Program offers adult students the opportunity to earn College credits from home. The Community Education Program has been developed to meet the needs of the community by offering noncredit classes as an introduction to lifelong learning.

Academic Programs

FSC&TC offers more than fifty associate degrees, certificates, skill-set certificates, and occupational development classes. A complete list of majors and programs offered is available on the College's Web site at http://www.fairmontstate.edu.

Associate degree programs offered include accounting, airframe and aerospace electronics maintenance, aviation maintenance technology, business technology, criminal justice, culinary arts, emergency medical services, fashion design, graphics, health information technology, homeland security, information systems, interior design, interpreter training program, medical laboratory technology, nursing, paralegal studies, physical therapist assistant studies, radiologic technology, resort and hotel management, and veterinary technology.

Certificates are available in emergency medical technician–paramedic studies, laboratory assistant studies, paraprofessional education studies, and sign language communications. Skill-set certificates include accounting, administrative assistant studies, ballroom dancing, classroom teacher's aide and assistant studies, computer-aided design, computer forensics, early childhood teaching aide and assistant studies, intelligence research and analysis, office technician studies, ProMgmt®, and ServSafe®.

Occupational-development classes are offered for those in certain trades. These work-based programs include building and construction trades, correctional officer, early childhood practitioner, EMS specialist, food service specialist, highway technician, water and wastewater treatment, and wood production technology.

Costs

During the 2005–06 academic year, per-semester charges for Fairmont State students from West Virginia were $1639 for tuition and fees, $3310 for room and board, and $600 for books and supplies, for a total of $5549. Out-of-state students paid $3649 for tuition and fees, $3310 for room and board, and $600 for books and supplies each semester, for a total of $7559.

Financial Aid

About 86 percent of Fairmont State students receive some form of aid. Guidelines and forms for West Virginia and out-of-state residents are available from high school guidance counselors or the Fairmont State Financial Aid Office. Fairmont State awards more than $36 million in financial assistance each year.

Faculty

FSC&TC employs 50 full-time faculty members, ensuring a low student-teacher ratio. Dedicated academic advisers and faculty members work one-on-one with students to meet their individual needs.

Student Activities

Fairmont State is a member of the NCAA Division II and the West Virginia Intercollegiate Athletic Conference. Varsity programs for men are offered in baseball, basketball, cross-country, football, golf, swimming, and tennis. Intercollegiate athletic programs for women include basketball, cross-country, golf, softball, swimming, tennis, and volleyball.

Fairmont State offers more than eighty clubs, organizations, student publications, honoraries, sororities, and fraternities as well as a wide range of intramural sports. Many fine arts performances and exhibits are planned each semester. Nationally prominent speakers are invited to the campus.

Student Government actively seeks to supplement the academic atmosphere with intellectual, cultural, and social activities. Student Government members are involved in all aspects of life on campus and work cooperatively with the administration.

The new student activity center, the Falcon Center, features 7,000 square feet of fitness equipment; five versatile courts for indoor sports; space for fitness classes; a four-lane pool with a whirlpool, sauna, and outdoor sunning deck; a four-lane cushioned jogging/walking track; game rooms; dining facilities; and more.

Academic Facilities

The Ruth Ann Musick Library has a collection of more than 200,000 books and more than 15,000 bound periodicals, microfilms, and other materials, including a large collection of audiotapes and videotapes. The library also has sites at the Caperton Center and the National Aerospace Education Center.

Fairmont State's state-of-the-art technology infrastructure includes thirty computer labs and high-speed network connections that are accessible from the library, classrooms, and every residence hall room, as well as the most up-to-date teaching software.

Location

Fairmont, a city of more than 19,000 in north-central West Virginia, is the county seat of Marion County. Located along Interstate 79 approximately 90 miles south of Pittsburgh, the city and the College are easily accessible to all travelers. Shopping malls, restaurants, cultural entertainment, and nightlife are easily found throughout the area.

West Virginia's natural treasures—mountains, rivers, waterfalls, wildlife, wildflowers, clean air, and vast tracts of national forest—are all close at hand. In and near Fairmont are popular trails for hiking and biking; rivers for white-water rafting; excellent spots for rock and mountain climbing, camping, and fishing; and some of the best skiing in the East.

FSC&TC shares a main campus with Fairmont State University. The campus features fifteen buildings on more than 90 acres. From the historic administration building, Hardway Hall, to the brand-new residence hall, Bryant Place, the facilities are a blend of tradition and technology. Facilities also include the Robert C. Byrd National Aerospace Education Center in Bridgeport, West Virginia, and the Gaston Caperton Center in Clarksburg, West Virginia.

Admission Requirements

First-time freshmen who are applying to Fairmont State Community & Technical College must submit the following: 1) application for admission; 2) an official high school transcript from an accredited high school (partial or complete) or a GED certificate (for home-schooled students or for students who do not have a high school diploma) or placement test results (administered by the College to all students without ACT or SAT scores; ACT or SAT scores are required for admission into most health career, selective, and competitive programs); 3) immunization records (for students born after January 1, 1957); and 4) statement of activities (for students out of high school six months or longer).

Transfer students must submit an application for admission, college transcripts from accredited institutions (ACT, SAT, or COMPASS scores are also required if there are fewer than 15 earned credit hours), a statement of activities, and immunization records. Transient students (those enrolled at another school who are returning to that institution) must submit an application for admission and a course approval form (from the Registrar's office). Non-degree-seeking students (those with fewer than 15 hours who are not seeking a degree) must submit an application. Current high school students must submit an application for admission, have completed their junior year of high school with a GPA of at least 3.0, and submit a letter of recommendation from their high school principal.

Application and Information

On a Saturday each fall, Fairmont State schedules a Campus Visitation Day so potential students and their family members and friends can visit the campus and attend information sessions on admissions, financial aid, and living on campus. An Academic Fair is also scheduled so students can meet with faculty members about the academic schools and departments.

Campus tours through the Office of Admissions are available Mondays through Fridays. To set up a tour, students should call 800-641-5678 Ext. 2 (toll-free) or 304-367-4855. Tours can also be scheduled online at Fairmont State's Web site at http://www.fairmontstate.edu.

Office of Admissions
Fairmont State Community & Technical College
1201 Locust Avenue
Fairmont, West Virginia 26554
Telephone: 304-367-4892
         800-641-5678 (toll-free)
         304-367-4213 (financial aid)
         304-367-4216 (residence life)
         304-367-4000 (campus operator)
         304-367-4026 (Gaston Caperton Center)
         304-842-8300 (Robert C. Byrd National
            Aerospace Education Center)
         304-367-4200 (TDD)
Fax: 304-367-4789
E-mail: admit@fairmontstate.edu
World Wide Web: http://www.fairmontstate.edu

Fairmont State Community & Technical College students explore airframe and aerospace electronics, aviation maintenance, and more at the Robert C. Byrd National Aerospace Education Center in Bridgeport, West Virginia.

FASHION INSTITUTE OF TECHNOLOGY

NEW YORK, NEW YORK

The Institute and Its Mission

Known worldwide as the premier institution of fashion education, the Fashion Institute of Technology (FIT) offers more than thirty majors leading to the Associate in Applied Science (A.A.S.), Bachelor of Fine Arts (B.F.A.), Bachelor of Science (B.S.), Master of Arts (M.A.), and Master of Professional Studies (M.P.S.) degrees—all based on a solid liberal arts foundation. The programs span a variety of business and design professions, including interior design, fashion merchandising management, and advertising and marketing communications. As a State University of New York college of art and design, business, and technology, FIT's tuition is affordable for both in- and out-of-state students.

FIT is rooted in industry and the world of work. Although the college is now associated with many professions, FIT's commitment to career education is still its hallmark and a source of pride to an institution whose industry connection is an integral part of its history. FIT counts among its alumni such luminaries as Calvin Klein and Nanette Lepore, as well as successful and talented professionals in advertising, packaging, television, the design fields, merchandising, manufacturing, public relations, retailing, and more. This growing network does more than just provide employment opportunities for FIT's graduates. Through departmental industry advisory boards, regular guest lectures from leaders in their field, degree-related internships, and a faculty that includes successful business and design professionals, FIT's programs and schools evolve and adapt apace with industry.

For the A.A.S. degree, FIT offers eleven majors through the School of Art and Design and five majors through the Jay and Patty Baker School of Business and Technology. For those interested in continuing their education, FIT has twenty-three baccalaureate programs, and its School of Graduate Studies offers six programs leading to either an M.A. or M.P.S. degree. FIT is an accredited institutional member of the Middle States Association of Colleges and Schools, the National Association of Schools of Art and Design, and the Foundation for Interior Design Education Research. With a job placement rate of nearly 90 percent, FIT graduates are well-prepared to meet employers' needs. Placement counselors help students generate job opportunities for full-time, part-time, freelance, and summer employment.

The nine-building campus includes classrooms, studios, and labs that reflect the most advanced education and industry practices. FIT serves more than 6,500 full-time and 4,000 part-time students who come not only from within commuting distances but also from around the nation and all over the world. Three residence halls serve approximately 1,250 students and offer a variety of accommodations, and a fourth hall is scheduled to open in fall 2006.

Academic Programs

FIT offers sixteen 2-year programs leading to the A.A.S. degree. Majors offered in the School of Art and Design are accessories design, communication design, display and exhibit design, fashion design, fine arts (with a career-exploration component), illustration, interior design, jewelry design, menswear, photography, and textile/surface design. Majors offered in the Jay and Patty Baker School of Business and Technology are advertising and marketing communications, fashion merchandising management, patternmaking technology, production management: fashion and related industries, and textile development and marketing. There are eight 1-year A.A.S. options available for students who hold a four-year degree from an accredited college or university or for students who have completed at least 30 transferable credits at an accredited college, with 24 credits equivalent to FIT's liberal arts requirements, plus a minimum of one semester of physical education. These one-year options are accessories design, advertising and marketing communications, communication design, fashion design, fashion merchandising management, jewelry design, textile development and marketing, and textile/surface design.

Programs are designed to prepare students for creative and/or business careers in the fashion and related professions and industries and to provide them with the necessary prerequisite studies so that they may go on to bachelor's degree programs, either at FIT or

elsewhere. To qualify for the A.A.S. degree, a student must be in degree status, satisfactorily complete the credit hours prescribed for a given major with approximately one third of all required credits in the liberal arts, achieve a minimum GPA of 2.0, and receive the recommendation of the faculty.

To qualify for the B.S. or B.F.A., a student must be in degree status, satisfactorily complete the credit and course requirements prescribed by the major, and receive the recommendation of the faculty. A minimum of 60 approved credits is required; at least half of the credits required in the major area must be earned in residence at the upper-division level. If the student has an appropriate FIT associate degree, a minimum of 30 approved credits must be earned in residence at the upper-division level.

Precollege programs (Saturday/Summer Live) are available during the fall, spring, and summer. More than forty-five classes offer students in high school and middle school the chance to learn in a range of creative environments, develop their portfolios, explore the business and technological sides of the fashion industry, and discover their natural talents and abilities.

Off-Campus Programs

Through its Office of International Programs, FIT provides select students, chosen on a competitive basis, the opportunity to study abroad for a year, a semester, or in the summer or winter sessions. Fashion design and fashion merchandising management majors may apply to the international program in their field, which includes a year spent studying in Florence, Italy. Winter and summer programs in countries, such as Costa Rica, France, England, and Mexico are also available to A.A.S. students.

Credit for Nontraditional Learning Experiences

FIT student internships provide firsthand learning experience in industry and ease the transition from the classroom to the workplace. In many majors, internships are a required part of the students' course of study, earning them academic credit that is applied toward their degree. In other programs, students may take internships on a supplemental-credit or noncredit basis. In the 2005–06 academic year, FIT's Internship Center provided more than 1,400 associate, bachelor's, and master's degree students with a credit-bearing internship in one of more than 2,500 organizations. Sponsor organizations include American Eagle, Bloomingdale's, Calvin Klein, Estée Lauder, Fairchild Publications, MTV, Polo Ralph Lauren, and WPI Advertising.

Costs

As a State University of New York, FIT offers an affordable tuition rate to both New York and out-of-state residents. The 2005–06 associate-level tuition per semester was $1537 for in-state residents and $4611 for nonresidents. Baccalaureate-level tuition per semester was $2175 for state residents, $5375 for out-of-state students. Residence hall and meal plan fees were $4204.50 per semester. Textbook costs and other nominal fees, such as locker rental or laboratory use, vary per program of study. All costs are subject to change.

Financial Aid

FIT attempts to remove financial barriers to college entrance by providing scholarships, grants, loans, and work-study employment for students in financial need. Sixty-five percent of full-time, undergraduate, degree-seeking students who applied for financial aid in fall 2005 received some type of assistance. The college directly administers its own institutional grants and scholarships, which are provided by the Educational Foundation for the Fashion Industries. College-administered federal funding includes Federal Pell Grants, Federal Supplemental Educational Opportunity Grants, Federal Perkins Loans, Federal Work-Study Program awards, and the Federal Family Educational Loan Program, which includes student and parent loans. New York state residents who meet state guidelines for eligibility may also receive Tuition Assistance Program (TAP) and/or Educational Opportunity Program (EOP) grants. The college tries to meet students' needs by awarding a financial aid package from institutional scholarships and federal grants, loans, and Federal Work-Study Program awards. Financial aid applicants must file the Free Application for Federal Student Aid (FAFSA), on which they apply for the Federal Pell Grant, and should also apply to all available outside sources of aid. Other documentation must be requested from the Financial Aid Office. Applications for financial aid should be completed prior to February 15 for fall admission or prior to November 1 for spring.

Faculty

Those who do, teach at FIT. The faculty includes both full-time academics and working professionals at the forefront of their respective fields and industries, offering a collegiate experience rich in both real world experience and the traditions of a liberal arts education.

Student Body Profile

The fall 2005 undergraduate enrollment was 10,199, of which 7,540 were degree-seeking students. Fifty-two percent of the degree-seeking students are enrolled in the School of Art and Design; 48 percent are in the Jay and Patty Baker School of Business and Technology. The average student age is 23. Seventy percent of FIT's students are New York State residents; 30 percent are out-of-state or international students. The college's residence halls house 17 percent of the undergraduate population. The ethnic/racial makeup of the student body is approximately 13 percent Asian/Pacific Islander; 8 percent black, non-Hispanic; 10 percent Hispanic; and 43 percent white, non-Hispanic. Eighteen percent chose not to identify with any of the listed groups. There are more than 700 international students from over seventy different countries.

Student Activities

Participation in campus life is encouraged for both residential and commuter students through more than sixty campus clubs, numerous organizations, and several athletic teams. Each club is open to all full- and part-time students who have paid their student activity fee. All students who wish to participate in athletics or hold leadership positions in student organizations must maintain a minimum GPA of 2.0; Student Association and Programming Board members must maintain a minimum GPA of 2.3. The Student Council, the governing body of the Student Association, gives all students the privileges and responsibilities of citizens in a self-governing college community. Many faculty committees include student representatives, and the president of the student government sits on FIT's Board of Trustees.

Dances, concerts, flea markets, films, field trips, and other special and social events are planned by the Student Association and Programming Board and the various FIT clubs throughout the year. On selected Tuesdays, from 1–2 p.m., all students and faculty members are welcome to attend and participate in events arranged by the Entertainment Hour Committee. Student-run publications include a campus newspaper, a literary and art magazine, and the annual FIT yearbook.

FIT has intercollegiate teams in basketball, bowling, cross-country track, dance, table tennis, tennis, and volleyball. In addition, the Athletic and Recreation Department sponsors group fitness classes each semester, available at no extra cost to students. Classes include body toning, boxing, dance, soccer, tennis, and yoga. Intramural activities allow students to participate in team and individual sports.

Facilities and Resources

A modern campus with outstanding facilities, FIT comprises an entire city block in Manhattan's Chelsea neighborhood. The Fred P. Pomerantz Art and Design Center offers up-to-date facilities for design studies, including photography studios; drawing, painting, and sculpture studios; a printmaking room; a graphics laboratory; display and exhibit design rooms; and a model-making workshop.

The Shirley Goodman Resource Center houses the Gladys Marcus Library, which contains specialized reference works for history, sociology, technology, art, and literature; international journals and periodicals; sketchbooks and records donated by designers, manufacturers, and merchants; slides, tapes, and periodicals; a voluminous clipping file; and more than 290,000 volumes, including books, periodicals, and nonprint materials. The Museum at FIT is the repository for one of the world's most important collections of fashion and textiles, with an emphasis on twentieth-century apparel, and it is used by students, designers, and historians alike for research and inspiration. The museum's galleries provide a showcase for a wide spectrum of exhibitions relevant to fashion and its satellite industries, and the new permanent gallery of fashion and textile history serves as an overview of fashion's past, present, and future. The Student Space

gallery regularly exhibits the work of FIT's art and design students; student work is also displayed throughout the campus.

FIT also has many computer labs, both Mac and PC, for both independent student use and class sessions. The Instructional Media Services Department provides audiovisual and television support and a complete in-house broadcast studio. The Design/Research Lighting Laboratory, an educational and professional development facility for interior design and other academic disciplines, features more than 400 commercially available lighting fixtures, controlled by computer. The Peter G. Scotese Computer-Aided Design and Communications Facility provides art and design students with the opportunity to explore the latest advancements in technology and their integration in the design of textiles, toys, interiors, fashion, and advertising, as well as photography and computer graphics. A state-of-the-art language lab is equipped with twenty-seven individual booths that are capable of playing and/or recording a variety of audiovisual media, including CDs, DVDs, and video- and audiocassettes.

The eight-story David Dubinsky Student Center houses lounges, a game room, a student radio station, the Style Shop (the FIT student-run boutique), student government and club offices, a comprehensive health center, two gyms, a dance studio, a weight room, and a counseling center. Also on campus are three venues—the Katie Murphy Amphitheatre, the Morris W. and Fannie B. Haft Auditorium, and the John E. Reeves Great Hall—that are used for student presentations, industry panels, conferences, and special events.

Three residence halls house approximately 1,250 students in double-, triple-, and quad-occupancy rooms. A fourth residence hall on West 31st Street, scheduled to open in fall 2006, should double FIT's housing capacity. All rooms are furnished and equipped with phone and data jacks and access to a cable jack. Each residence hall has centrally located lounges and laundry facilities. Counselors and student staff members also live in the halls and can help students adjust to college life and living in New York City. As housing is limited, priority is given to first-time, fully matriculated students who have paid their tuition deposit and submitted their housing application before June 15 and live outside a 35-mile radius of the city.

Location

FIT's urban campus is situated amidst the activity and excitement of New York City, world capital of fashion, media, business, and the arts. FIT's location—where midtown Manhattan, the fashion district, and the art galleries of Chelsea converge—permits an exceptional two-way flow between the college and the industries and professions it serves. Students are encouraged to participate in the cultural richness of New York, where premier music, dance, theater, and visual arts are readily accessible. In addition, all of FIT's programs and departments take full advantage of the city's special offerings through frequent guest lectures, field trips, and internship opportunities.

Admission Requirements

Applicants for admission must be either candidates for or recipients of a high school diploma or the General Educational Development (GED) certificate. Candidates are judged on class rank, grades in college-preparatory course work, and the student essay. Letters of recommendation from teachers and counselors are accepted and considered but are not required. A portfolio evaluation is required for art and design majors only. Specific portfolio requirements are explained on FIT's Web site.

Transfer students from regionally accredited colleges must submit official transcripts for credit evaluation. Students may qualify for the one-year A.A.S. option if they hold a baccalaureate degree or if they have a minimum of 30 transferable credits from an accredited college, including a minimum of 24 credits that are equivalent to FIT's liberal arts requirements.

Application and Information

Candidates who have graduated from a New York state high school should obtain applications from their high school guidance offices. Candidates from out-of-state high schools should obtain applications from FIT's Web site or by contacting:

Office of Admissions
Fashion Institute of Technology
Seventh Avenue at 27th Street
New York, New York 10001-5992

Telephone: 212-217-7675
           800-GO-TO-FIT (toll-free)
E-mail: fitinfo@fitnyc.edu
World Wide Web: http://www.fitnyc.edu

FIDM/THE FASHION INSTITUTE OF DESIGN & MERCHANDISING

LOS ANGELES, CALIFORNIA

The Institute and Its Mission

FIDM/The Fashion Institute of Design and Merchandising provides a dynamic and exciting community of learning in the fashion, graphics, interior design, digital media, and entertainment industries. The purpose of the Institute is to provide an educational environment designed to combine student goals with industry needs.

FIDM has a reputation for graduating professionally competent and confident men and women capable of creative thought. It has graduated more than 30,000 students in its thirty-five-year history.

In addition to its associate degree programs, FIDM is currently offering a Bachelor of Science degree in business management (candidacy status WASC-ACSCU).

FIDM is accredited by the Accrediting Commission for Community and Junior Colleges of the Western Association of Schools and Colleges (WASC) and the National Association of Schools of Art and Design (NASAD).

Academic Programs

FIDM operates on a four-quarter academic calendar. New students may begin their studies any quarter throughout the year. The requirement for a two-year Associate of Arts degree is the completion of 90 units.

Associate Degree Programs FIDM offers Associate of Arts degrees in apparel manufacturing management, beauty industry merchandising and marketing, digital media, fashion design, footwear design, graphic design, interior design, international manufacturing and product development, merchandise marketing (fashion merchandising or product development), textile design, theater costume design, TV and film costume design, and visual communication. All of these programs offer the highly specialized curriculum of a specific major combined with a core general education/liberal arts foundation.

Transfer Arrangements FIDM accepts course work from other accredited colleges if there is an equivalent course at FIDM and the grade is a C or better. FIDM courses at the 100, 200, and 300 levels are certified by FIDM to be baccalaureate level. FIDM maintains articulation agreements with selected colleges with the intent of enhancing a student's transfer opportunities. Academic counselors will provide assistance to students interested in transferring to other institutions to attain a four-year degree.

Internship and Co-op Programs Internships are available within each of the various majors. Paid and volunteer positions provide work experience for students to gain practical application of classroom skills.

Special Programs and Services FIDM offers Associate of Arts professional designation degrees for individuals with substantial academic and professional experience who wish to add a new field of specialization. These are nine- or twelve-month programs of intensive study in one of the Institute's specialized majors. Students from other regionally accredited programs have the opportunity to complement their previous education by enrolling in a professional designation program. Requirements for completion range from 45 to 66 units, depending on the field

of study. FIDM also offers Associate of Arts Advanced Study Programs that develop specialized expertise in the student's unique area of study. These programs are open to students who possess extensive prior academic and professional experience within the discipline area. These areas include fashion design–advanced study, interior design–advanced study, theater costume–advanced study, and international manufacturing and product development. Completion requirements for these programs are 45 units. Some classes are offered online.

In response to student needs, FIDM has established an evening program in addition to the regular daytime courses. The program has been designed to accommodate the time requirements of working students. The entire evening program for the Associate in Arts degree can be completed in 2½ years.

FIDM offers English as a second language (ESL) for students requiring English development to complete their major field of study. The program is concurrent and within FIDM's existing college-level course work. These classes focus on the special needs of students in the areas of oral communication, reading comprehension, and English composition.

Community Programs Community service programs are offered both independently and in cooperation with various community groups. General studies course credit may be awarded to participating students. Each FIDM campus identifies community projects that allow students to support local service agencies.

Off-Campus Programs

FIDM provides the opportunity for students to participate in academic study tours in Europe, Asia, and New York. These tours are specifically designed to broaden and enhance the specialized education offered at the Institute. Study tour participants may earn academic credit under faculty-supervised directed studies. Exchange programs are also available with Esmod, Paris; Instituto Artictico dell' Abbigliamento Marangoni, Milan; Accademia Internazionale d'Alta Mode e d'Arte del Costume Koefia, Rome; St. Martins School of Art, London; College of Distributive Trades, London; and Janette Klein Design School, Mexico City.

Credit for Nontraditional Learning Experiences

The Institute may give credit for demonstrated proficiency in areas related to college-level courses. Sources used to determine proficiency are the College-Level Examination Program (CLEP) and Credit for Academically Relevant Experience (CARE), an Institute-sponsored program.

Costs

For the 2006–07 academic year, tuition starts at $18,285, depending on the major selected by the student. Textbooks and supplies start at $1900 per year, depending on the major. Yearly fees are $525. First-year application fees start at $225 for California residents and range up to $525 for international students.

Financial Aid

There are several sources of financial funding available to the student, including federal financial aid and education loan programs, California state aid programs, institutional loan programs, and FIDM awards and scholarships.

Faculty

FIDM faculty members are selected as specialists in their fields. Many are actively employed in their respective fields of expertise. They bring daily exposure to their industry into the classroom for the benefit of the students. In pursuit of the best faculty members, consideration is given to both academic excellence as well as practical experience. FIDM has a 16:1 student-instructor ratio.

Student Body Profile

FIDM's ethnically and culturally diverse student body is one of the attractions to the Institute. Fifteen percent of the current student body are international students from more than thirty different countries. Twenty percent of the students are more than 25 years of age. More than 90 percent find career positions within one year of graduation.

Student Activities

The Student Activities Committee plans and coordinates social activities, cultural events, and community projects, including the ASID Student Chapter, International Club, Delta Epsilon Chi (DEX), Association of Manufacturing Students, Honor Society, and the Alumni Association. The students also produce their own trend newsletter, *The Mode*.

Facilities and Resources

Advisement/Counseling Department Chairs and other trained staff members provide assistance to students in selecting the correct sequence of courses to allow each student to complete degree requirements. The counseling department provides personal guidance and referral to outside counseling services as well as matching peer tutors to specific students' needs. Individual Development and Education Assistance (IDEA) centers at each campus provide students with additional educational assistance to supplement classroom instruction. Services are available in the areas of writing, mathematics, computer competency, study skills, research skills, and reading comprehension.

Career Planning/Placement Offices Career planning and job placement are among the most important services offered by the Institute. Career assistance includes job search techniques, preparation for employment interviews, resume preparation, and job adjustment assistance. Services provided by the center include undergraduate placement, graduate placement, alumni placement, internships, and industry work/study programs.

Library and Audiovisual Services FIDM's library goes beyond the traditional sources of information. In addition to more than 12,000 books and reference materials, FIDM also features an international video library, subscriptions to major predictive services, international and domestic periodicals, interior design workrooms, textile samples, a trimmings/findings collection, and access to the Internet. FIDM's Costume Museum houses more than 4,500 garments from the seventeenth century to present day. The collection includes items from the California Historical Society (First Families), the Hollywood Collection, and the Rudi Gernreich Collection.

State-of-the-art computer labs support and enhance the educational programs of the Institute. Specialized labs offer computerized cutting and marking, graphic and textile design, word processing, and database management.

Location

Established in 1969, FIDM is a private college that is proud to enroll more than 5,500 students a year. The main campus is in the heart of downtown Los Angeles near the famed California Mart and Garment District. This campus is adjacent to the beautiful Grand Hope Park. There are additional California branch campuses located in San Francisco, San Diego, and Orange County.

Admission Requirements

The Institute provides educational opportunities to high school graduates or applicants that meet the Institute's Ability to Benefit (ATB) criteria to pursue a two-year Associate of Arts degree. Qualifications for professional designation programs include students that meet the general education core requirements or who have a U.S. accredited degree. All applicants must have an initial interview with an admissions representative. In addition, students must submit references and specific portfolio projects if applicable to the chosen major. The Institute is on the approved list of the U.S. Department of Justice for nonimmigrant students and is authorized to issue Certificates of Eligibility (Form I-20).

Application and Information

Applications are accepted on an ongoing basis. All prospective students should contact:

Director of Admissions
FIDM/The Fashion Institute of Design & Merchandising,
    Los Angeles Campus
919 South Grand Avenue
Los Angeles, California 90015

Telephone: 800-624-1200 (toll-free)
Fax: 213-624-4799
World Wide Web: http://www.fidm.edu/

Debut. Student designer: Kim Yen Cao.

FULL SAIL REAL WORLD EDUCATION

WINTER PARK, FLORIDA

The College and Its Mission

Established in 1979, Full Sail Real World Education is a private, coeducational college offering extensive training and education in the entertainment media production industry and entertainment technology. Hands-on experience and solid practical knowledge combine to provide an education where learning meets the real world. Students receive an introduction to many job opportunities in each career field and an overview of what each position requires. Full Sail's campus facilities include recording consoles, digital video editing workstations, cameras, concert sound systems, computerized moving lights, and computer/graphic workstations that are used to create Web sites, animation sequences, 3-D graphics, computer generated models, characters, visual effects, and interactive games. Full Sail provides extensive instruction in all of these areas and more, offering a unique style of training that puts students hands-on and right in the middle of the entertainment and media production industry while in school.

Traditional learning techniques have their place at Full Sail, but the technology-intensive field of creative media demands a more rigorous pace than that offered by books, lectures, and seminars. As helpful as those are, their effectiveness is severely limited without practical, hands-on experience inside the school environment. Full Sail takes students' education beyond the confines of the classroom into real-world situations and puts them to work on the same kind of equipment encountered in media production facilities throughout the world.

Instructors and guest lecturers are professionals in their fields, and the low student-faculty ratio in labs allows students to interact with their mentors. Students come to Full Sail from around the world, and musicians, artists, and technicians come for the training and business savvy needed to further their careers.

The school is fully accredited by the Accrediting Commission of Career Schools and Colleges of Technology (ACCSCT).

Academic Programs

Full Sail offers Associate of Science degrees in recording arts and show production and touring. Bachelor of Science degrees are also offered in computer animation, digital arts and design, film, game development, and entertainment business.

Full Sail runs on a modular schedule, with new classes beginning every month. Schedules vary depending on the degree programs. Once enrolled, students attend classes and labs five to six days, 35 to 40 hours each week. By doing so, students typically earn a bachelor's degree in less than twenty-one months. Lectures are scheduled during daytime hours, but some labs occur during evening and early morning hours. Full Sail recently won a Florida statewide award for the school with the "Most Innovative Program," due in part to this type of scheduling. It benefits students by ensuring a low student-teacher ratio and by representing the realistic demands of the entertainment and media production industry.

Full Sail's Recording Arts Program is an intensive audio education that covers every facet of music and audio production—from tracking and overdubs to mixing and mastering—in a college environment unlike any other. Full Sail's professional recording studios allow students to record bands using the same microphones, mixing boards, and digital audio workstations used in studios all over the world. Students learn from the best: Full Sail's instructors are studio professionals, and they bring years of audio engineering experience into the classroom as they show how to run a professional recording session. In addition, students explore techniques for the growing world of audio for video games and dive headfirst into the challenges of audio postproduction for movies and television shows.

Full Sail's Show Production and Touring Program covers everything from the rigors of life on the road to lighting design for live production, all in the space of only thirteen months. Students learn the ropes at Full Sail Live, a custom-designed theater environment outfitted with the same gear that is installed in live-sound venues and that travels the world with top touring acts. Students learn every aspect of live-event production from experienced instructors who have spent much of their lives on tour. At the time of graduation, students are ready to start careers in event production.

The entertainment business curriculum may be taken in addition to either the Show Production and Touring Program or the Recording Arts Program to receive a Bachelor of Science in entertainment business.

Costs

Tuition costs vary depending on program. Tuition ranges from $40,005 to $61,775 per degree program. At Full Sail, these tuition costs include books, lab fees, course materials, career-development assistance, and lifetime auditing.

Financial Aid

Everyone's financial aid package is unique to them. The type of package that works best is determined by the important decisions made during this process as well as specific needs. Financial advisers work to ensure that students have all the information needed to make financial aid decisions that allow them the opportunity to attend Full Sail. Full Sail wants to assist every financial aid applicant in obtaining the financial aid assistance they are legally entitled to receive. The student's eligibility, the school's packaging criteria, and the amount and types of financial aid available determine this. Since Full Sail is an accredited school, the Financial Aid Department has a number of packages consisting of grants and loans available to those who qualify. These packages are tailored to each student's financial need.

Faculty

Full Sail has 482 full-time instructors, and the student-faculty ratio is 10:1. The typical Full Sail teacher has spent years working in the entertainment and media production industry doing the type of work that he/she now teaches at Full Sail. Instructors have earned hundreds of movie, record, game, television show, and Web credits, including GRAMMY® and EMMY awards. These dedicated professionals come to Full Sail because of the school's reputation in the industry as one of the best colleges in entertainment media education. The majority of the instructors continue to be active in their professional field, which allows them to bring current product knowledge and examples to their students.

Student Body Profile

Full Sail is home to more than 5,000 students representing fifty states and thirty-five countries worldwide. The student body is primarily men (89 percent). Approximately 70 percent of the student population is white (non-Hispanic), 10 percent black, 10 percent Hispanic, and 2 percent Asian or Pacific Islander.

Academic Facilities

The 91-acre Full Sail campus houses more than 100 studios, production suites, soundstages, and computer labs as well as more than fifty advanced college classrooms. Full Sail is a production facility that rivals any professional multimedia studio in the world.

Student advisers are available to assist students with questions about academics and referrals, and the Student Services Desk is open 24 hours a day for emergencies. Full Sail students and alumni can also utilize the school's Career Development Center. This center assists students with finding internships and entry-level employment, educates students on how to successfully market themselves, and promotes networking and professional relationships among students, alumni, and industry professionals.

Full Sail does not feature on-campus living arrangements, but does employ a Housing Manager who is dedicated to providing information about affordable accommodations in the many apartment complexes near the school. The Housing Manager can also help with information about roommates (other incoming Full Sail students), power, phones, furniture, and helpful community programs in the central Florida area.

Location

Full Sail's college campus is situated in a beautiful area of central Florida in Winter Park, a town that plays host to residential communities and light commerce. Thanks to tourism being Central Florida's primary business, entertainment, restaurants, and shopping are plentiful. The school is 20 minutes from downtown Orlando, 35 minutes from Disney and Universal Studios, 1 hour from Cape Canaveral and the Atlantic beaches, and 2 hours from the Gulf of Mexico.

Admission Requirements

There are only two things necessary for applicants to be ready to attend school at Full Sail—a sincere passion for a career in the entertainment and media production industry and a high school diploma or GED.

Application and Information

For details concerning applications and deadlines, students should contact a Full Sail Admissions Representative.

Full Sail Real World Education
3300 University Boulevard
Winter Park, Florida 39792-7429
800-226-7625 (toll-free)
Fax: 407-678-0070
E-mail: admissions@fullsail.com
World Wide Web: http://www.fullsail.com

Entrance to Full Sail Real World Education.

HARCUM COLLEGE
BRYN MAWR, PENNSYLVANIA

The College and Its Mission

Harcum College seeks to provide men and women with outstanding career preparation that meets or exceeds the standards of their chosen professions. At Harcum, self-realization and preparation for participative citizenship are also of great importance. Intent upon remaining among the foremost independent two-year colleges in America, Harcum aims to provide every student with the opportunity not only for a rewarding career but also for a fulfilling life.

Academic Programs

Harcum's academic programs are diverse and fall under four centers: the Center for Allied Health, the Center for Business and Professional Studies, the Center for Legal Studies, and the Center for Liberal Studies and Education. In addition, there are the School of Continuing and Professional Studies, which includes an evening/weekend college, and the Center for International Studies, which includes the English Language Academy. The four centers offer associate degrees and certificates.

Transfer Arrangements The Career and Transfer Services staff assists students in preparing for transfer to a four-year institution. Harcum students have been accepted by more than 200 colleges and universities nationwide and abroad. Harcum has close relationships with many colleges. The College has a number of articulation agreements with four-year colleges, whereby credit is seamlessly transferred to the four-year institution.

Internship and Co-op Programs All of Harcum's programs require an internship as part of the curriculum. Students spend a period of time gaining valuable work experience in a workplace appropriate to their program, where they apply the knowledge they have acquired in the classroom. Many students subsequently receive job offers from their internship sponsors.

Special Programs and Services The College offers a number of special programs to assist students in succeeding at college. Summer Advance is a five-week summer program that gives students an opportunity to adjust to college life while strengthening their academic preparation in reading, writing, math, and other areas. Achieving Individual Motivation for Success (A.I.M.) develops academic and personal skills, cultural awareness, career plans, and lifelong learning tools for students who have disabilities, are economically disadvantaged, or are first-generation college attendees. The English Language Academy offers full- and part-time instruction in English as a second language. The Developmental Program provides courses to strengthen skills in English, math, and reading. Independent study is offered for students who want to study a topic that deeply interests them. A qualified, conscientious instructor guides students in their study, independent of regular classroom attendance. Periodic meetings and discussion seminars are held. The Center for Student Development and Counseling offers personal and individualized career and academic counseling.

Continuing Education Programs The College's School of Continuing and Professional Studies offers programs year-round. Courses are offered for professional development and personal enrichment. Continuing Education Units (CEUs) may be earned in the dental and veterinary fields and in many other fields related to the College's degree programs. Other popular programs include the pharmacy technician training course and the phlebotomy technician training course. For adult students looking to further their education in the evenings and on weekends, Harcum College offers flexible scheduling, a large selection of Internet courses, and an accelerated core curriculum to make the associate degree attainable. The College also offers a full schedule of evening and weekend classes for credit at a reduced tuition that is approximately one half the regular undergraduate studies rate.

Credit for Nontraditional Learning Experiences

The College awards credit for knowledge acquired outside the usual educational setting by accepting College-Level Examination Program (CLEP) scores for credit toward a degree. The College accepts general and subject examination CLEP scores based on the American Council on Education's recommended cut scores. Students working toward an associate degree may earn a total of 30 credits through CLEP, challenge exams, portfolio-assisted assessment, or traditional transfer.

Costs

The 2006–07 annual tuition for full-time students is $7625 per semester. Tuition for part-time students is $508 per credit. There are additional miscellaneous fees and deposits. Annual room and board charges are $3623 per semester. All fees and tuition are subject to change. In addition, tuition for classes in the evening/weekend college is $192 per credit.

Financial Aid

More than 90 percent of students at Harcum receive some form of financial aid. Available aid includes Harcum grants-in-aid, scholarships, Federal Pell Grants, Federal Supplemental Educational Opportunity Grants, state grants, Federal Perkins Loans, and Federal Work-Study Program awards. The priority deadline for financial aid applications is May 1 for fall enrollment.

Faculty

All of Harcum's programs are led by full-time directors and have full-time professors. Their expertise is augmented by part-time adjunct instructors who usually are practicing professionals in their fields. There are 26 full-time faculty members. Eighty percent of full-time faculty members have advanced degrees, including 13 percent who hold doctorates. The student-faculty ratio is 9:1.

Student Body Profile

The student body is 80 percent women. The largest age group is between 18 and 26, but nearly as many are between 26 and 39 years of age. Seventy percent of the students are white, 16 percent are African American, and 3 percent are Asian. Full-time students make up 68 percent of the total. Commuters account for 83 percent. Eighty-nine percent of the students are from Pennsylvania, primarily from the five-county Philadelphia region. The next-largest group (4 percent) is from New Jersey. International students make up 2 percent. Sixty percent of those accepted to Harcum College enroll. Of those who enroll, 60 percent graduate.

Student Activities

It is easy to get involved on campus. Harcum has clubs and organizations for students with many different interests. Students make their mark on campus by joining one of more than twenty clubs, such as the student newspaper, the yearbook, the

Organization for Animal Technician Students, or the Student American Dental Hygienists Association. The College has a chapter of Phi Theta Kappa, the national honor society for two-year colleges, and Chi Alpha Epsilon, a national honor society for A.I.M. students. The College also organizes many community service activities and events. Students participate in volunteer projects on and off campus, such as peer tutoring, clothing drives, and Earth Day.

Facilities and Resources

Harcum gives students full support throughout their time at the College and after graduation. At the Center for Student Development and Counseling, counselors give a hand with everything from advice on balancing a schedule to resolving a personal problem. The College also has academic tutors to help students with course work.

Students at Harcum have the option of living on campus in the residence halls, which is a great way to make friends and be in the middle of everything that is happening on campus. The residence hall staff plans programs and events, including seminars and discussion groups on topics ranging from study skills to current events, and stress-buster pizza parties.

Students feel at home at Harcum College. Even the students who commute say they do not feel like outsiders. Harcum is a small community, and students quickly find that they recognize friendly faces all over the campus.

Library and Audiovisual Services The library collection has 39,000 volumes, 300 periodicals, and more than 1,000 audiovisual items. It is a member of the Tri-State College Library Cooperative, a forty-two-college consortium, which provides access to more than 6 million volumes. Harcum's library also provides connections to the Internet and FirstSearch, an online database, and it is networked with 20 CD-ROM databases.

Location

Harcum is located in Bryn Mawr, Pennsylvania, 12 miles west of Philadelphia, in the heart of the Main Line, a string of attractive, safe, friendly suburban communities. The College is in the midst of one of the largest concentrations of educational institutions in the country. There are fifty-five colleges and universities in the Philadelphia area. The campus is on a parklike 12-acre site next to a commuter railroad station, which makes travel to Philadelphia and throughout the area easy. Available in Philadelphia are the world-renowned Philadelphia Orchestra, the Pennsylvania Ballet, the Opera Company of Philadelphia, and the world-famous Philadelphia Museum of Art. The city has major-league teams in baseball, football, ice hockey, and basketball. There are numerous historic sites in and around Philadelphia to visit, including Independence Hall, the Liberty Bell, and Valley Forge National Park.

Admission Requirements

All applicants are required to submit official academic transcripts, results of any standardized tests taken, a written essay, and a letter of recommendation. An interview is recommended. The dental hygiene application deadline is February 15. All other programs follow a rolling admission policy. Prospective students should consult the enrollment office for additional requirements specific to each program.

Application and Information

For more information, students should contact:

Office of Enrollment Management
Harcum College
750 Montgomery Avenue
Bryn Mawr, Pennsylvania 19010-3476
Telephone: 610-526-6050
          800-345-2600 (toll-free)
Fax: 610-526-6147
E-mail: enroll@harcum.edu
World Wide Web: http://www.harcum.edu

Library and Academic Center.

HESSER COLLEGE
MANCHESTER, NEW HAMPSHIRE

The College and Its Mission

The primary purpose of Hesser College is to provide a high-quality education that is personalized and employment oriented. Hesser College's innovative approach to higher education provides students with increased flexibility. After two years of college, students can earn an associate degree and are prepared to enter the workplace, or, if they prefer, students can continue on in one of Hesser College's bachelor's degree programs.

Hesser College was established in 1900 as Hesser Business College, a private, nonsectarian college. Since 1972, Hesser College has expanded and enriched its curriculum in keeping with its tradition of providing an affordable career education of high quality.

Hesser College is accredited by the New England Association of Schools and Colleges. Students who choose Hesser College receive a high-quality education.

Academic Programs

The primary goal of the curricula is to prepare students for success in specific career areas. The general education requirements are designed to provide the skills necessary for career growth and lifelong learning. Internships, practicums, and opportunities for part-time work experience are available in all majors. An education from Hesser College provides a solid career foundation. The College's goal is quite simple: to prepare people for careers and career advancement.

Many of the Hesser College programs are for the career-minded student who wants to concentrate on the skills required to be successful in the workplace. Seventy-five percent of the courses that students take are directly related to their career choices. Upon completion of the associate degree program, a student may pursue a four-year degree by enrolling in one of Hesser's bachelor's degree programs.

Associate Degree Programs Hesser offers a wide range of programs that prepare students for high-demand careers. They include accounting, business administration, business computer applications, communications and public relations, criminal justice, early childhood education, graphic design, interior design, liberal studies, medical assistant studies, paralegal studies, physical therapist assistant studies, psychology, radio and video production and broadcasting, and sports management.

Bachelor's Degree Programs Hesser College offers bachelor's degree programs in accounting, business administration, criminal justice, and psychology.

Off-Campus Programs

The College offers opportunities for cooperative education and internships in most of its academic programs. The early childhood education program includes practicums and supervised fieldwork in the freshman and senior years, utilizing a variety of child-care facilities. In addition, the curricula of several programs incorporate short-term study trips to such places as Walt Disney World and Washington, D.C.

Costs

Costs vary by program. Interested students should contact Hesser College for more information.

Financial Aid

Hesser College offers financial assistance to students who qualify. Many students receive some form of aid. Scholarships are awarded each year to students based on academic and financial standing. Hesser College also offers loans and grants.

Faculty

The faculty members of Hesser College consistently receive high student evaluations for their interest in each student's success and for the high quality of their teaching. The majority of the faculty members have completed programs of advanced study, many hold doctoral degrees, and all have practical experience in business or other career fields.

Student Body Profile

Most students work in the afternoons, evenings, or weekends while attending Hesser. The men and women currently enrolled represent several states and more than fifteen countries. A large part of the student population is from the New England region.

Student Activities

Hesser College offers intercollegiate sports teams in men's and women's basketball, soccer, and volleyball; men's baseball; and women's softball. The basketball and volleyball teams have consistently been a major power in the Northern New England Small College Conference. Students also participate in a number of intramural sports programs. Extracurricular activities are varied and include social activities, clubs, trips, and programs in the residence halls.

Facilities and Resources

The College includes dormitories for many students. A wide range of resources are located on campus. Academic advising is coordinated through department chairpersons and the Center for Teaching, Learning, and Assessment. The size of the College allows for individual attention to the financial and career counseling needs of each student.

The academic facilities include five computer labs, a Mac-based graphic design lab, medical assistant labs, a physical therapist assistant lab, and a radio/video production lab. Hesser College's library contains more than 30,000 titles. The Center for Teaching, Learning, and Assessment provides special tutoring and programs in study skills, reading, writing, math, and computer skills.

Hesser College has also developed a number of learning assistance programs to help students succeed in their studies. Tutoring and special classes are provided by the faculty throughout each semester. In addition, several departments offer honor programs and special opportunities for independent study. The College also sponsors an active chapter of the national honor society Phi Theta Kappa, which promotes scholarship and service to the College and the community.

Location

Hesser College is located in Manchester, New Hampshire. With a population of more than 100,000, Manchester is a medium-sized city that offers many cultural, historical, and social events. Hesser College's central location provides easy access to entertainment, shopping, and a variety of part-time jobs and academic work experiences.

Manchester was recently named by *Money* magazine as the number one small city in the northeast United States. In addition, Manchester was recently named as one of the best cities in the United States for business. According to *U.S. News & World Report*, Manchester is "at the hub of things" in the fast-growing, high-technology, financial, and information-oriented businesses of southern New Hampshire. Manchester has been called the "Gateway to Northern New England," and several major carriers serve the Manchester Airport.

Manchester is within 1 hour of Boston, and the mountains and major ski resorts are within 1–2 hours of Hesser's campus.

Admission Requirements

Hesser College has a rolling admissions policy. Students may apply for admission at any time.

Advisers are available to talk with students about their education and career goals, and interested students should contact Hesser College for more information.

Application and Information

Applicants must submit an application form with a $10 nonrefundable fee. Applications are reviewed on a first-come, first-served basis and normally take seven to fourteen days to be fully reviewed upon receipt of all required information.

Requests for additional information and application forms should be addressed to:

Director of Admissions
Hesser College
3 Sundial Avenue
Manchester, New Hampshire 03103
Telephone: 603-668-6660 Ext. 2110
          800-526-9231 Ext. 2110 (toll-free)
Fax: 603-666-4722
E-mail: admissions@hesser.edu
World Wide Web: http://www.hesser.edu

Students at Hesser College's main campus.

INDIANA BUSINESS COLLEGE
INDIANAPOLIS, INDIANA

INDIANA BUSINESS COLLEGE
WE CHANGE LIVES, ONE STUDENT AT A TIME©

The College and Its Mission

Indiana Business College was founded in 1902 to serve the specific education and career needs and interests of students planning to enter the business community. Indiana Business College consists of eleven campuses at convenient locations across the state. Full- and part-time programs, online classes, and day and evening classes are available at all locations. The philosophy behind the curriculum at the College is one of individual attention, allowing for flexibility and higher achievement in the classroom. The career-oriented emphasis enables course work to be highly specialized. Indiana Business College has a commitment to providing career-related education; students are trained by practical application and hands-on experience. This commitment, coupled with a reputation for offering a high-quality education, contributes to the employment opportunities for graduates. The College offers lifetime career assistance to its graduates and is continually updating the curriculum to meet the demands of today's business world. Indiana Business College is accredited by the Accrediting Council for Independent Colleges and Schools and is regulated by the Indiana Commission on Proprietary Education. The medical assisting programs at the Evansville, Fort Wayne, Medical (Indianapolis), and Terre Haute campuses are accredited by the Commission on Accreditation of Allied Health Education Programs on the recommendation of the Committee on Accreditation for Medical Assistant Education.

Academic Programs

Indiana Business College offers Associate of Applied Science degrees in accounting, administrative assistant studies, business administration, business administration/network technology, business and information technology, Cisco Network Associate studies, criminal justice, fashion merchandising, home technology integrator, health claims examiner studies, human resources, medical assisting, medical coding technology, organizational management, and therapeutic massage and bodyworks.

Indiana Business College also offers diplomas in the areas of accounting assistant studies, medical office assistant studies, medical transcription, and office assistant studies.

Certificates are available in computer network technician studies and therapeutic massage practitioner studies.

Indiana Business College operates throughout the calendar year; classes begin quarterly in January, April, June, and September. To be awarded a degree, diploma, or certificate, students must maintain a minimum cumulative GPA of 2.0 (on a 4.0 scale).

The computer programs at Indiana Business College include courses in Cisco network administration, A+ computer technology, and Network+. The College has some of the state's top information technology programs available, including MCSE and MCSA. IBC is an associate member of CompTIA, offering A+ and Network+ certifications. The College is also a Microsoft IT Academy and one of the only Transcender Training partners in Indianapolis offering on-site testing for all IT certification programs.

The Associate degree program for home technology integrator provides training in the automation of technology that is related to homes and businesses. The prospective student is involved in wiring, networking, lighting, HVAC, water, security, audiovideo, and integration of services.

The organizational management degree is designed to prepare individuals for careers in project management, where sound business principles and state-of-the-art computer skills are essential for success in today's high-speed, high-technology marketplace. Topics include project integration, human and material resource allocation, risk analysis, cost engineering, procurement management, information technology topics, and e-business. Project managers are employed in every aspect of the business community.

The accounting programs offered at Indiana Business College include courses in intermediate and cost accounting, income tax, and payroll. Both diploma and Associate of Applied Science degree accounting programs incorporate the courses necessary to prepare students for excellent positions in private business, public accounting, and departments within the government.

The Associate of Applied Science degree program in business administration includes courses in the areas of computers, accounting, marketing, management, and sales. This program helps students to develop the creativity and the supervisory skills needed for managerial positions.

Indiana Business College's administrative support programs include administrative assistant studies and office assistant studies. These programs provide students with the necessary foundation in keyboarding, information processing, and computer technology.

The Associate of Applied Science degree program in criminal justice provides students with a broad spectrum of course work in corrections, law enforcement, private security, and investigation. This program is designed to prepare students for a variety of careers in the criminal justice field in both the public and private sector.

The Associate of Applied Science degree program in fashion merchandising prepares the graduate for a career in the fashion industry. Combining business classes with fashion studies prepares the student to succeed in this competitive field. Included in this curriculum are courses such as textiles, display and design, marketing, and apparel merchandising.

The Associate of Applied Science degree program in human resources trains individuals to maintain the personnel records of an organization's employees, assist with internal and external notification of position openings, assist in the hiring process, answer employee question, prepare reports for managers, administer aptitude tests, and screen applicants.

Indiana Business College's medical programs include health claims examiner studies, medical assistant studies, medical coding technology, medical office assistant studies, medical transcription, surgical technology, and therapeutic massage studies. The medical assistant studies degree program provides the student with skills to be competent in both front and back office procedures. The medical assistant may assist the physician in minor surgery, perform laboratory tests, assess vital signs, administer medication, operate an EKG machine, or perform other therapeutic modalities prescribed by the physician. The Associate of Applied Science degree program in surgical technology is designed to provide students with an academic and clinical background in the field of surgical technology. Students in this program develop the skills necessary to be a knowledgeable, professional, and responsible member of the surgical team. Programs in medical coding technology provide training to analyze medical records, to assign codes to index diagnoses and procedures, and to provide information for reimbursement purposes. Courses in medical science, medical terminology, medical office administration, and medical insurance processing are offered to help students meet the needs of the industry. The therapeutic massage and bodyworks studies program at Indiana Business College allows graduates to possess the necessary skills for applications and treatment goals of muscular and general relaxation, stress reduction, pain management, recovery from injury, health promotion, education, and body awareness. The successful practitioner must therefore be proficient at more than a simple massage; he or she must understand the body and its functions, master a variety of techniques, and hone such skills as client assessment, communication, and self-evaluation.

Costs

For 2004–05 the cost per credit hour ranged from $154 to $220. Tuition varies according to the program chosen and does not include books or fees.

Financial Aid

Many Indiana Business College students qualify for some form of financial aid. The College participates in the Federal Pell Grant, Federal Supplemental Educational Opportunity Grant, Federal Stafford Student Loan, Federal PLUS programs, the Federal Work-Study Program, the Twenty-first Century Scholars Program, and state grants. Students' eligibility to participate in these programs is contingent upon demonstration of financial need. In addition, the College offers scholarships to both graduating high school seniors and nontraditional students.

Financial planning and financial aid personnel are available to assist the student in the application process.

Students are also encouraged to investigate possibilities for private scholarships.

Faculty

The faculty at Indiana Business College is composed of dedicated professionals who are committed to giving personal attention to every student. The selection of instructors is based not only on their academic credentials, professional training, and business experience, but also on their capacity to develop students' abilities in preparation for the world of work.

Student Body Profile

The student body consists of approximately 3,500 students.

Student Activities

Students may join independent student groups and student councils. Coordinating activities with an executive director or department head, student groups organize a variety of on-campus and off-campus events. Professional organizations are also available for student participation. Intramural sports and group functions vary by campus.

Facilities and Resources

Indiana Business College offers resource centers and computer labs for its students. These facilities provide access to up-to-date information and programs.

Career Planning/Placement Offices The Career Services Department at Indiana Business College assists graduates in securing employment. The Career Services Department offers lifetime career assistance to all alumni and posts job openings for current students and graduates. Students are assisted in all aspects of the job search through career development classes focusing on goal setting, resumes, interviewing, and networking.

Location

Indiana Business College has three convenient Indianapolis locations (northwest, downtown, and southeast) as well as eight other statewide locations. Situated in the heart of Indianapolis, the downtown campus of Indiana Business College houses the Corporate Office for all branches of the College. The excitement of urban living, combined with the cultural and historical sites, makes Indiana Business College's locations ideal. Indianapolis' Children's Museum, Indiana Repertory Theater, and White River Park Zoo provide a variety of educational and recreational activities. The College is within walking distance of downtown shopping centers and major sports centers, such as Circle Centre Mall, Conseco Field House, and the RCA Dome. It is also readily accessible from many different transportation systems.

In addition to the three Indianapolis locations, Indiana Business College has campuses in Anderson, Columbus, Evansville, Fort Wayne, Lafayette, Marion, Muncie, and Terre Haute.

Students may earn credits toward the completion of a program at more than one location. The convenience of having eleven locations and online classes significantly lessens the cost of an education by eliminating additional housing and transportation expenses.

Admission Requirements

Applicants must be high school graduates or have obtained a General Educational Development (GED) certificate to be considered for admission to Indiana Business College. The College reviews each application for admission and bases the admission decision on a personal interview and scores from the Wonderlic Scholastic Level Exam.

The College is open to men and women of any race, faith, or national origin. All students are given equal opportunity to pursue their educational and career goals through the programs offered at Indiana Business College.

Application and Information

All applications must be accompanied by a $50 application fee. High school transcripts are requested directly from the student's school by Indiana Business College. Applicants are notified within two weeks of the completion of all application requirements.

All inquiries should be directed to:

Admissions Office
Indiana Business College
550 East Washington Street
Indianapolis, Indiana 46204
Telephone: 800-IBC-GRAD (toll-free)
Fax: 317-264-5650
World Wide Web: http://www.ibcschools.edu

INTERNATIONAL COLLEGE OF HOSPITALITY MANAGEMENT

SUFFIELD, CONNECTICUT

The College and Its Mission

The International College of Hospitality Management (ICHM), located in the town of Suffield in northwest Connecticut, is the only Swiss college of hospitality management in the U.S. The mission of ICHM is to prepare students for successful careers in the hospitality industry by combining the renowned Swiss art of hotel management with American business techniques.

With a maximum of 120 students on a 56-acre residential campus set among woods and rolling lawns, the College occupies a former seminary, St. Alphonsus College. Hospitality faculty members have extensive professional experience and instruct alongside liberal studies teachers of the highest caliber. Students receive intensive course training over four 11-week terms. This training is reinforced by a paid internship in prestigious hotels of the U.S.

The internship is an essential component in the program at ICHM. The resulting combination of professional, academic, and practical training provides graduates with a firm base for managing their careers. The internship also supplies ICHM students with a competitive edge in finding employment when they leave the College. The College's Director of Internships and Placements helps guide students in their career development. In addition, the College organizes career fairs twice each year. The College has a 100 percent placement rate, a record of which it is very proud.

ICHM students are encouraged to actively participate in the social and recreational life of the College, in much the same way that they assume significant responsibilities in managing their academic progress and professional comportment. Because students are very involved in many aspects of College life, a great sense of community has developed at ICHM.

Academic Programs

Associate of Science Degree in Hospitality Management The first year of the program consists of two 11-week terms, followed by a six-month (810-hour) internship. The first two terms of study are very hands-on, with courses based in practical skills and hotel industry norms. The internship that follows is carefully structured and supervised and enhances the concepts previously introduced in the classroom.

In their second academic year, students develop skills in business planning and strategy, and learn about control procedures and staff management. The second academic year is followed by an optional 810-hour internship, with an option to prolong the internship contract by six or twelve months.

Certificate in Hospitality Management Candidates holding a bachelor's degree in a different discipline or those with professional hospitality experience may choose to enroll in the certificate program in hospitality management. This one-year program consists of two 11-week terms followed by an internship of at least 810 hours. It is designed to provide graduates with the skills and experience necessary to enter the hospitality industry with confidence.

Special Program Services Career fairs are held twice each year, wherein students and alumni are selected for 810-hour paid internships and positions of longer duration. The fairs are attended by recruiters from approximately thirty leading hotel and resort properties, typically five-star hospitality establishments. Many students receive multiple internship offers. In addition, individual hotel and resort properties often recruit directly on campus.

Transfer Arrangements Course-credit transfers must be comparable to ICHM courses and must have been awarded by an accredited institution. The student must have earned a minimum C grade (2.0 GPA) for transfer credits to be considered. This information must be provided on official sealed transcripts mailed directly to ICHM's Office of Admissions.

Credit for Nontraditional Learning Experiences

Credit may be awarded for prior professional experience in the hospitality industry. For details, applicants should consult the Registrar.

Costs

Expenses for the 2006–07 academic year include tuition of $15,900 and room and board of $4978. Each student is required to purchase books, uniforms, and supplies.

Financial Aid

To help eligible students meet their educational expense, the College offers financial assistance programs such as scholarships, grants, low-interest loans, and part-time employment opportunities. The College's Financial Aid Officer is happy to work with families on an individual basis to help them plan the cost of education.

Faculty

The student-faculty ratio at the College is 15:1. All full-time faculty members have student advising responsibilities and are involved in the administration of the College. The faculty members have a wide range of international hospitality experience, a diversity that supports the College's mission of offering students an intellectually challenging education in a multicultural environment.

Student Body Profile

The College attracts students from the United States and nearly thirty different countries each year, representing many different cultures. Most students are in their early twenties and, for many, English is a second language. Some are seeking a change of career, others have already obtained advanced qualifications in a different discipline, and all are drawn to the dynamics of international hospitality.

Student Activities

The Student Committee organizes sports, activities, theme nights, and excursions and serves as a representative of all students. Officers of the Student Committee are elected by a democratic vote and arrange meetings and activities with the Coordinator of Student Services. In addition, within the College is a voluntary organization called the Ritz Guild. Its members plan and coordinate events to benefit the local community, often with the help of civic organizations such as the Lions Club and the House of Bread. Each year, Ritz Guild members are given official recognition for their contributions. The College maintains several vans for student activities around the region.

Facilities and Resources

In 2003, the College moved from rural Washington, Connecticut, to a larger, more convenient campus in Suffield, Connecticut. The new location offers an array of activities and amenities to ICHM students.

The meal plan is provided by ICHM's sister school, the Connecticut Culinary Institute, with which it shares a campus. Students can enjoy an excellent regulation-size gymnasium and a modern exercise facility. There are also sports fields and hiking trails on campus. The area has many fine theaters, music venues, restaurants, clubs, and dancing. There are also many well-regarded museums and historic sites within a short distance.

ICHM's spacious library offers more than 10,000 volumes plus numerous industry periodicals and videotapes. The College's computer labs are all connected to broadband Internet services, and the entire building is a wireless broadband environment as well.

Location

The College is situated on 56 wooded acres in Suffield, Connecticut, a charming New England town. Next door to the campus is Six Flags New England Amusement Park, with a new $140-million water park. The 135,000-square-foot building is located minutes from Springfield, Massachusetts, and Hartford, Connecticut. It is a short drive to Boston and New York City and only 10 minutes from Bradley International Airport.

Admission Requirements

The College requires U.S. applicants to submit a completed application form, $100 application fee, official high school transcripts or GED scores, and two letters of recommendation. SAT scores are not required but are highly recommended. Students for whom English is not the first language are required to show proof of English competency. The College seeks applications from both U.S. and international citizens and welcomes motivated students who have a desire to succeed in international hospitality management. The cultural mix of ICHM benefits students as they move towards their chosen profession. Because of the unique nature of the College and its program, applicants are strongly encouraged to schedule an on-campus interview. Prospective students may take advantage of the Visitor Information Program (VIP), wherein they can stay on campus for up to two nights and participate in classes and campus activities. Applicants should contact the Office of Admissions for details.

Application and Information

The College accepts applications throughout the year for its August, November, February, and May starting dates. Applicants are notified of their admission status shortly after their forms are received, usually within two weeks. For application materials and additional information, students should contact:

Office of Admissions
International College of Hospitality Management
1760 Mapleton Avenue
Suffield, Connecticut 06078

Telephone: 860-668-3515
Fax: 860-668-7369
E-mail: admissions@ichm.edu
World Wide Web: http://www.ichm.edu

The elegant grounds of the International College of Hospitality Management.

JOHNSON COLLEGE
SCRANTON, PENNSYLVANIA

The College and Its Mission

Johnson College, a two-year technical college, was founded by Orlando S. Johnson, a wealthy coal baron in the Scranton area who died in 1912. Mr. Johnson left the bulk of his estate to establish and maintain a trade school, and his purpose became the mission of the College as an institution "where young men and women can be taught useful arts and trades that may enable them to make an honorable living and become contributing members of society."

A board of directors was created and a 65-acre tract in Scranton known as the William H. Richmond estate was selected as the site for the new enterprise. Opening in 1918, the school admitted young men and women who had completed a minimum of eight years of school and were at least 14 years old.

In 1964, the school became a postsecondary institution, requiring applicants to be high school graduates or to have equivalency certificates. The name of the institution changed from the Johnson Trade School to the Johnson School of Technology in 1966. The school was incorporated as a nonprofit corporation in 1967, and in 1968, it was licensed by the Commonwealth of Pennsylvania Bureau of Private Trade Schools. Approval to award an Associate in Specialized Technology degree came in 1974, with accreditation by the National Association of Trade and Technical Schools (NATTS) following in 1979.

In 1985, the name of the school was changed to Johnson Technical Institute, and the three-year Associate in Specialized Technology degree programs were changed to two-year programs in 1987.

Responding to the continuing technological changes in society, students along with members of the board, administration, faculty, and staff conducted an intense two-year self-study, beginning in 1994, to assess the institution's strengths and weaknesses. The study led to a formal application to the Commission on Higher Education for status as a two-year college. The Pennsylvania Department of Education approved the application of Johnson Technical Institute as a two-year college in 1997; the change of name to Johnson College was instituted in 2001.

The graduating class of 1998 was the first class to receive either an Associate in Applied Science (A.A.S.) degree or an Associate in Science (A.S.) degree.

Continuing the expansion of the technology programs, a Veterinary Technology program was introduced in 1994. Clinical classes were held off campus until the completion of a 6,500-square-foot Science Center on campus. The program received full accreditation from the American Veterinary Medical Association (AVMA) for the fall semester of 2000. In January 2004, the College opened the Animal Care Center as a teaching facility to enhance the Veterinary Technology educational experience. In 1995, Electrical Construction and Maintenance Technology was added to the curriculum, and the Bureau of Private Licensed Schools approved the Diesel Truck Technology program in November 1996.

A Computer Information Technology program that specializes in enterprise computer networking, was approved by the Commission on Higher Education in 2000, and a curriculum in Radiologic Technology received the Commission's approval for the fall 2002 semester. The Radiologic Technology program received accreditation by the Joint Review Committee on Education in Radiologic Technology (JRCERT) in May 2005.

Today, approximately 400 students pursue careers in eleven different trade, technical, and clinical programs. The College's eight buildings include a library, a bookstore, a gymnasium, a physical fitness center, classrooms, shops, laboratories, administrative offices, and a student apartment complex for on-campus living.

Over the years, the College has served the region by providing technical education programs, and it continually evaluates its programs to meet the technology needs of society. This evaluation process is assisted by the Program Advisory Committees of each program area, consisting of regional business and community leaders who meet several times during the year to advise the College on curriculum content, length of programs, and current materials and equipment. They also review placement and retention statistics. The College has maintained the initial intent of Mr. Johnson with a professional and dedicated staff to ensure up-to-date training that prepares graduates to readily step into entry-level positions in business and industry.

The current student count is composed of approximately 74 percent men and 26 percent women. The students spend 60 percent of their time in technology courses and the remainder in general education classes. The College has an extensive program of internships, cooperative education, and practicums with a variety of businesses and professional organizations. One of the important success factors of Johnson College is a consistently high employment rate of students within a short time after graduation.

Today, Johnson College is a valuable resource for society's changing technological needs. The mission of Johnson College is to provide a foundation of education and skills necessary for specialized employment, career advancement, and lifelong learning.

Academic Programs

Johnson College offers eleven technical and clinical programs, awarding Associate in Applied Science and Associate in Science degrees.

The technology programs include Architectural Drafting and Design Technology, Automotive Technology, Biomedical Equipment Technology, Carpentry and Cabinetmaking Technology, Diesel Truck Technology, Electrical Construction and Maintenance Technology, Electronic Technology, and Precision Machining Technology.

The science programs include Computer Information Technology, Radiologic Technology, and Veterinary Technology.

Johnson College is accredited by the Accrediting Commission of Career Schools and Colleges of Technology (ACCSCT), and the Veterinary Science Technology program is accredited by the American Veterinary Medical Association (AVMA). The Radiologic Technology program is accredited by the Joint Review Committee on Education in Radiologic Technology. The Pennsylvania

Department of Education and the State Board of Education have approved Johnson College as a two-year college.

Transfer Arrangements The College maintains articulation agreements with the State University of New York Institute of Technology at Utica/Rome for the following programs: Architectural Drafting and Design Technology, Biomedical Equipment Technology, and Electronic Technology. Johnson College also has an articulation agreement with Marywood University in Scranton for the Veterinary Technology program.

Costs

The tuition for full-time attendance for 2005–06 (12 to 21 credit hours) was $5831.50 per semester for all programs. Books and supplies were approximately $1500 per school year; however, this amount varied by program. Program fees vary by department. On-campus housing is available in double-occupancy apartments at a rate of $350 per month per student. Students should consult the current College catalog for additional and recent financial information.

Financial Aid

Johnson College provides financial support through the Financial Aid Office, with several programs and opportunities available for students from all income categories. Scholarships are available and are awarded on the basis of merit, academic performance, and extracurricular involvement. The College also participates in the following federally sponsored programs: Federal Pell Grants, Federal Supplemental Educational Opportunity Grants (FSEOG), Federal PLUS loans, and Federal Stafford Student Loans. Other opportunities include employment programs and alternative loans at the College and state and College grants. For consideration for any financial assistance program, students must complete the Free Application for Federal Student Aid (FAFSA). In addition, the College offers $30,000 in merit scholarships for those who are eligible.

Faculty

There are 26 faculty members at the College, and the student-faculty ratio is 17:1. Counseling is available for academic, personal, and vocational issues. The College maintains strong interpersonal relationships among its students and faculty and staff members.

Student Activities

There are a variety of activities available for students on campus, including a Student Government Association, which consists of a student from each technical, trade, and clinical program. The Social Force Club, funded by Act 101, is a community service organization that involves students in on- and off-campus activities, including field trips. Students participate in an active intramural sports program, social functions, holiday parties, talent shows, clubs, and other events and functions.

Facilities and Resources

The Library Resource Center at the College is a technology-based library and is a participating member of the Northeastern Pennsylvania Library Network Consortium. Located in the Moffat Building, the collection consists of more than 4,000 volumes of books and more than 100 current periodical subscriptions. The library complements the curriculum of the academic and technical, trade, and clinical programs. This unique collection offers students the resources necessary to research issues that pertain to their fields of study and for which students should keep abreast of new technological developments. The library also offers online computer services and CD-ROM searching. A professionally staffed cafeteria is available for breakfast, lunch, and snacks. The Moffat Building contains two fitness centers that offer a variety of exercise equipment. A campus bookstore is available for student supplies, clothing items, and a variety of other items. Limited on-campus housing is available in fully furnished two-story apartment-style units.

Location

Johnson College is conveniently located in Scranton, Pennsylvania, at Exit 190 on Interstate 81. Highway exit ramps clearly indicate the location of the campus. The College is just under 2 hours from New York City and Philadelphia. The campus is minutes from great skiing and other recreational activities, along with a variety of sports, arts, music, cultural, and historical events at places like Lackawanna County Stadium (home of the Triple-A Red Barons baseball team), Montage Amphitheater, and the Steamtown National Park and Mall.

Admission Requirements

Johnson College accepts qualified students regardless of race, religion, handicap, or national origin, and admissions are on a rolling basis. Applicants should be secondary school seniors, secondary school graduates, or recipients of a secondary school equivalency certificate. Successful completion of one year of algebra is required for all programs. Veterinary Technology applicants must have successfully completed 1 unit of biology and chemistry; Radiologic Technology applicants must have either 1 unit of biology or chemistry (a grade of C or better is considered successful completion). To complete the Radiologic Technology program in two years, including summers, entering students are required to have successfully completed one unit of chemistry or biology with a grade of C or better and a minimum of one year of algebra. Each applicant is encouraged to arrange for a campus visit and a personal interview with an admissions representative, and appointments may be made for meeting with appropriate faculty members and current students.

Application and Information

Applications may be submitted in person, by mail, or online at the http://www.johnson.edu. Accompanying information must include an official secondary school or equivalency transcript, satisfactory SAT or ACT test scores, one letter of recommendation, and a $30 nonrefundable processing fee. The deadline date for applicants for the Veterinary Technology and Radiologic Technology programs is February 15. Students applying to the Veterinary Technology program are required to submit a questionnaire and observation hours as part of the application process.

Additional information may be obtained by contacting:

Office of Admissions
Johnson College
3427 North Main Avenue
Scranton, Pennsylvania 18508
Telephone: 800-293-9675 (toll-free)
World Wide Web: http://www.johnson.edu

KEYSTONE COLLEGE
LA PLUME, PENNSYLVANIA

The College and Its Mission

Keystone College was founded in 1868 as Keystone Academy in La Plume, Pennsylvania. Initially opened as the only high school between Binghamton, New York, and Scranton, Pennsylvania, Keystone flourished as a secondary school for more than sixty-five years. Rechartered as Scranton-Keystone Junior College in 1934 and then Keystone Junior College in 1944, the College served as one of the premier two-year institutions in the Northeast until 1995. In this year the school was again renamed, as Keystone College, and began its tenure as an "ideal" four-year degree-granting college. Keystone College has a current enrollment of 1,600, including students from fourteen states and seven other countries. Students can choose from sixteen different four-year majors and more than twenty-five different two-year degree and certificate programs.

Academic Programs

Associate Degree Programs   Associate of Applied Science degrees are offered in accounting, culinary arts, hotel and restaurant management, and information technology. The Associate in Fine Arts is offered in art. The Associate in Arts is offered in communications, forest/resource management, landscape architecture, liberal studies, liberal studies–education emphasis, and wildlife biology. The Associate in Science is offered in biology; business; criminal justice; early childhood education; health sciences with emphasis in medical technology, nursing/cytotechnology, occupational therapy/respiratory care, and radiotherapy/medical imaging/cardiac perfusion; and sport and recreation management. In addition, there are one-year programs in Cisco, forestry technology, Microsoft Certified Systems Administrator, Microsoft Certified Systems Engineer, and pre–major studies (undeclared major).

Bachelor's Degree Programs   The Bachelor of Arts degree is offered in communications and visual arts. The Bachelor of Science degree is offered in accounting, biology with tracks in the medical professions, business, criminal justice with a track in prelaw, early childhood education, elementary education, environmental biology, forensic biology, information technology, sport and recreation management, teaching–art education, teaching–child and society, teaching–special education, and water resource management.

Postbaccalaureate certification is available in elementary education, early childhood education, and teaching–art education (K–12).

The College runs on a two-semester schedule (fall and spring) and has night and weekend classes available. The number of credit hours required to earn a degree is dependent on the field of study chosen, and students must have attained a minimum cumulative GPA of 2.0. Every student must complete a set of general core curriculum requirements as well as the courses specific to his or her major course of study. All students are required to complete one internship or co-op before graduation, depending on the course of study.

Students have the opportunity to participate in both the Army and Navy ROTC programs in conjunction with other local participating institutions. There are opportunities for double majors as well as minors in various fields of study.

Off-Campus Programs

The College maintains articulation agreements with Thomas Jefferson University, College Misericordia, and SUNY Upstate Medical for students enrolling in the health science curriculums. Students enrolled in the environmental programs may opt to pursue Keystone's articulation with State University of New York College of Environmental Science and Forestry (SUNY-ESF) in Syracuse. Other transfer opportunities exist with Marywood University, University of Scranton, Bloomsburg University, Wilkes University, Temple University, University of the Arts, Parson's School of Design, Penn State University, and many others.

Costs

Tuition and fees for Keystone College for 2005–06 were $14,945 per year, while room and board costs were $7790 per year. Books and general supplies averaged $500 per semester and varied according to major.

Financial Aid

The Financial Aid Office provides adequate funds and resources to meet the financial needs of students from all income categories. Scholarships are awarded based on merit, academic performance, and extracurricular involvement. Keystone College also participates in the following federally sponsored programs: Federal Perkins Loan, Federal Pell Grant, Federal Supplemental Educational Opportunity Grant (FSEOG), Federal PLUS Loan, and Federal Stafford Student Loan. The College also offers college employment programs to students and alternative loans as well as state grants and Keystone grants. In order to be considered for financial aid, students must complete the Free Application for Federal Student Aid (FAFSA).

Faculty

The student-faculty ratio is 12:1, and the average class size is 22 students. Counseling is available for academic, personal, and vocational issues. Keystone College is supported by strong interpersonal relationships among its students and faculty and staff members. All faculty members post regular office hours and are generally available outside of these hours.

Student Activities

Student Senate is the central governing body of all student government organizations on the campus. It serves as the liaison between the student body and the College administration. Members of Student Senate are chosen by their peers and are responsible for improving and maintaining student life both on and off campus. Students may choose from more than twenty-five different clubs and organizations, including those with academic, service-oriented, and social interests.

Facilities and Resources

The Harry K. Miller Library is available on campus to all students. This facility offers standard print and online research opportunities. The Hibbard Campus Center is the setting for the student cafeteria, a full-service restaurant, and The Chef's Table (a student-run restaurant), as well as a U.S. post office, a print shop, a student-run radio station, and reception halls. The campus also includes an art gallery, a celestial observatory, and the Poinsard Greenhouse. Keystone College also serves as the home for the Urban Forestry Center, Willary Water Discovery Center, and the Countryside Conservancy.

There are more than 120 computers available on campus for general student use, and both the Internet and campus network can be accessed from all residence halls and most buildings on campus.

Location

Located at the foot of the Endless Mountains in northeastern Pennsylvania, the 270-acre campus is both scenic and historic, with buildings dating back to 1870. Located 13 miles from Scranton, Pennsylvania, the campus offers easy access to major East Coast cities, including New York, Philadelphia, and Baltimore.

Admission Requirements

Keystone accepts qualified students regardless of race, religion, handicap, or national origin, and admissions are on a rolling basis. Admission is based on prior academic performance and the ability of the applicant to profit from and contribute to the academic, interpersonal, and extracurricular life of the College. Keystone considers applicants who meet the following criteria: graduation from an approved secondary school or the equivalent (with official transcripts), satisfactory scores on the SAT or ACT, one letter of recommendation, and evidence of potential for successful college achievement. All students are strongly encouraged to visit the campus for a personal interview with the admissions staff and a member of the faculty from the student's area of interest. Students applying to the art and teaching–art education programs are required to participate in a portfolio interview.

Transfer students in good academic and financial standing at their current institution are also encouraged to apply to Keystone. Transfer students should contact the Office of Admissions and may be required to submit either high school transcripts or transcripts from each college attended, or both.

Admissions decisions are made within two weeks from the day all required materials are received in the Office of Admissions.

Application and Information

Students wishing to be considered for admission must submit an application and a $25 processing fee, along with official high school transcripts, college transcripts (if applicable), a letter of recommendation from someone other than a friend or relative, and scores from either the SAT or ACT (submitted directly to the Office of Admissions; Keystone's CEEB code numbers are 2351 for the SAT, 2602 for the ACT).

Applications and any additional information about Keystone College may be obtained by contacting:

Office of Admissions
Keystone College
One College Green
La Plume, Pennsylvania 18440
Telephone: 570-945-8111
          800-824-2764 Option 1 (toll-free)
E-mail: admissions@keystone.edu
World Wide Web: http://www.keystone.edu

Students on the campus of Keystone College.

LANDMARK COLLEGE
PUTNEY, VERMONT

The College and Its Mission

Landmark College is one of only two accredited colleges in the country designed exclusively for students of average to superior intellectual potential with LD or AD/HD or other specific learning disabilities. Life-changing experiences are commonplace at Landmark College.

Landmark's beautiful campus offers all the resources students expect at a high-quality higher education institution, including a new athletics center, a student center, a dining facility, a café, residence halls, and a Center for Academic Support. The College has also invested substantially in technology and offers a wireless network in all of its classrooms, along with LAN, telephone, and cable connections in all the residence rooms. Notebook computers are required and are used in nearly every class session. The College's programs extensively integrate assistive technologies, such as Dragon Naturally Speaking, Kurzweil text-to-speech software, and Inspiration.

Landmark's faculty and staff members make it unique. The College's more than 100 full-time faculty members are all highly experienced in serving students with learning disabilities and attention deficit disorders. More than 100 staff members provide an array of support services that are unusually comprehensive for a student population of slightly more than 420 students.

Academic Programs

Students can earn an associate degree in either general studies or business studies. Landmark College builds strong literacy, organizational, study, and other skills—positioning students to successfully pursue a baccalaureate or advanced degree and to be successful in their professional careers. More than 90 percent of Landmark College graduates go on to a four-year college or university.

With more than 100 faculty members and slightly more than 420 students, Landmark College's small classes and personalized instruction provide a uniquely challenging, yet supportive, academic program. At Landmark College, students learn how to learn.

The College's diverse curriculum includes English, communications, the humanities, math, science, foreign language, theater, video, music, art, physical education, and other classes taught in a multimodal, multimedia environment that is highly interactive. There is no "back of the room" in a Landmark College classroom, and all students participate in class discussions while building strong academic skills.

Landmark College has articulation agreements with a number of other colleges. These colleges have agreed to admit Landmark College graduates as juniors and transfer all of their credits if they attain a specific grade point average on graduation from Landmark.

Through a carefully sequenced, integrated curriculum, students develop the confidence and independence needed to meet the demands of college work. When students graduate with an associate degree from Landmark College, they are ready to succeed in a four-year college, a technical or professional program, or the workforce.

Off-Campus Programs

The Landmark Study Abroad Program has developed programs with students' diverse learning styles in mind. Landmark College's faculty members design and teach experiential courses in their specific disciplines that fulfill Landmark core requirements while helping students gain confidence and independence in new academic structures. College faculty members accompany students abroad, providing them with the Landmark College academic experience in an international setting. The College offers summer credit programs in England, Greece, Ireland, Italy, and Spain; in January, a two-week program in Costa Rica is offered.

Costs

Landmark College's tuition for the 2005–06 academic year was $37,000. Room and board costs were $6800. Single rooms or suites are available at an added cost of between $1000 and $1500. A damage deposit of $300 is required.

Since admission to Landmark College requires a medical diagnosis of a learning disability or attention deficit disorder, in most cases, the entire cost of a Landmark College education may be tax deductible as a medical expense. For more information, parents are advised to consult a tax attorney.

Financial Aid

Landmark College participates in all major federal and state financial aid programs, including the Federal Pell Grant, Federal Family Education Loans, and work-study. Institutional scholarships are available. To apply for financial assistance, students should submit the Free Application for Federal Student Aid (FAFSA), the Landmark College Financial Aid Application, and federal tax returns.

Faculty

With the College's low student-faculty ratio, Landmark College faculty members are unusually accessible to students. There are more than 100 full-time faculty members, who provide classroom teaching, professional advising, and office hours to students. In addition, faculty members provide individualized instruction throughout the day and into the evening at one of three Centers for Academic Support. Landmark College does not typically employ adjunct faculty members or student teaching assistants. Regular faculty members deliver all instruction. Their depth of experience in serving students with learning differences ensures that students receive the individualized education that is most appropriate to their learning style.

Student Body Profile

Landmark College students come from thirty-three states, two U.S. territories, and five other countries. Approximately two thirds of the student body are men. Ninety percent of all students are residential students living on campus in one of twelve residence facilities. Representatives of multicultural groups make up approximately 12 percent of Landmark College students.

Student Activities

Landmark College closely integrates academics and student life. Academic deans, advisers, and faculty members work closely with student life deans and directors to provide a comprehensive program that serves the whole student. The goal is not simply to support academic success but also to guide and challenge students in their personal and social development. Each student has access to a comprehensive support team, including an academic adviser, classroom instructors, a resident dean, an extensive program of athletics, adventure education, and activities, and a highly trained and experienced counseling department.

For a college its size, Landmark College has an extraordinary range of student-development resources, providing general educational, social, and recreational opportunities. Clubs at Landmark are active. In the past, they have included the Running Club, Monday Night Art, the Multicultural Awareness Club, the Gay/Lesbian/Bisexual/Transgender Alliance, the Mountain Biking Club, the Jazz Ensemble, *Impressions Literary Magazine,* the Coffee House Writers Group, the International Club, the Small Business Management Club, Choral Singing, the Weight Lifting Group, and the Spirituality Group.

Landmark College outdoor programs provide students with a diverse range of outdoor and experiential learning opportunities, including wilderness first-aid training, a ropes course, rock-climbing instruction, an indoor climbing wall, and a full inventory of camping equipment, cross-country skis, snowshoes, and mountain bikes. The College has an active intercollegiate and intramural athletics program that is supported by a well-equipped athletics center that opened in 2001.

Facilities and Resources

Landmark College's residence halls, academic buildings, athletics center, and student center provide a rich array of resources and educational, recreational, and social opportunities. The traditional brick campus, which was designed by noted architect Edward Durell Stone in the 1960s and entirely renovated beginning in the mid-1980s, includes such amenities as a 400-seat theater, an NCAA regulation basketball court, an exercise pool, three fitness centers, a tennis court, science laboratories, an infirmary, a Center for Academic Support, a bookstore, learning centers, a café, a game room, an indoor climbing wall, and a ropes course.

Location

Located in scenic southeastern Vermont, Landmark College overlooks the Connecticut River Valley, with sweeping views of the mountains and valleys of southern Vermont and northern Massachusetts. Wilderness areas, national forests, ski areas, lakes and streams, and other natural attractions abound. Nearby Brattleboro, Vermont, and the five-college region in the Amherst, Massachusetts, area offer opportunities for culture, the arts, fine dining, and more. Putney is a picturesque Vermont village with several shops, stores, restaurants, a bakery/coffeehouse, a bookstore, and other resources.

The College is located just off Exit 4 on Interstate 91. The most convenient airport is Bradley International Airport in Hartford, Connecticut, which is about 1½ hours away by car. Metropolitan areas within a 4-hour driving radius include Boston, New York, and Providence.

Admission Requirements

Applicants to Landmark College must have a diagnosis of dyslexia, attention deficit disorder, or other specific learning disability. Diagnostic testing within the last three years is required, along with a diagnosis of a learning disability or AD/HD. One of the Wechsler Scales (WAIS-III or WISC-III) administered within three years of application is required. Scores and subtest scores and their analysis are required to be submitted as well. Alternately, the Woodcock Johnson Cognitive Assessment may be substituted if administered within three years of application. Other criteria for admission include average to superior intellectual potential and high motivation to undertake the program.

The College offers rolling admission and enrolls academic semester students for fall and spring semesters. Students may begin in August (for the fall semester) or January (for the spring semester). The College offers credit-bearing courses each summer in addition to programs for students from other colleges, high school students, and students entering other colleges in the fall.

Application and Information

For more information, students should contact:

Office of Admissions
Landmark College
River Road South
Putney, Vermont 05346-0820
Telephone: 802-387-6718
Fax: 802-387-6868
E-mail: admissions@landmark.edu
World Wide Web: http://www.landmark.edu

Twenty years serving students with learning disabilities and AD/HD.

LEHIGH VALLEY COLLEGE
CENTER VALLEY, PENNSYLVANIA

The College and Its Mission

Located in the Lehigh Valley for more than 134 years, Lehigh Valley College (LVC) is steeped in a tradition of educational excellence. LVC is dedicated to developing people for career positions using hands-on teaching methods, industry-current technology, and externships. The vast majority of graduates are either employed or continuing their education within one year of graduation. Because LVC is a private college, it can put students first and promote an atmosphere in which students can learn, grow, and meet or even exceed their expectations of achievement. Lehigh Valley College is accredited by the Accrediting Council for Independent Colleges and Schools.

Academic Programs

LVC provides career training leading to a diploma or an Associate in Specialized Business or Technology degree. All programs follow the quarterly schedule. These programs are eighteen to twenty-four months long. Associate degree programs consist of prescribed subjects that are divided into periods of instruction approximately twelve weeks in length and offered every twelve weeks.

Associate Degree Programs Accounting: eighteen months (day), 1,568 clock hours, 95 credits. Graduates are qualified for such positions as junior accountant, accounts receivable/payable clerk, bookkeeper, and payroll clerk upon completion of the course.

Computer Programming: eighteen months (day), 1,568 clock hours, 91 credits. The program prepares students for careers in the field of application development and system design. The program enhances the basic philosophies with a detailed study of modern programming languages. Programming skills are applicable to the PC market, the mainframe market, or the emerging Internet programming market. Graduates are awarded the Associate in Specialized Technology degree.

Criminal Justice: eighteen months (day), twenty-four months (evening), 1,638 clock hours, 92 credits. This program prepares students for positions as corrections officers; local, county, and state police officers; campus police; investigators; detectives; child case workers; juvenile service officers; drug task officers; customs inspectors; loss prevention managers; and U.S. marshals.

Hospitality and Tourism Management: eighteen months (day), 1,638 clock hours, 93 credits. After completing their internship, students are prepared for positions in the hospitality industry and tourism field.

Medical Assisting and Office Administration: eighteen months (day), twenty-four months (evening), 1,638 clock hours, 90.5 credits. After an internship is completed in the health-care field, graduates take positions in hospitals, doctors' offices, clinics, and insurance agencies.

Management/Marketing: eighteen months (day), twenty-four months (evening), 1,568 clock hours, 98 credits. Graduates of this program are qualified for entry-level positions in business, banking, insurance, finance, and government.

Personal Computers and Network Technology: eighteen months (day), twenty-four months (evening), 1,568 clock hours, 93 credits. Students are provided with the latest technology, software, and core business subjects to perform entry-level tasks in PC and LAN setups, diagnoses, upgrades, configurations, and repairs.

Visual Communications: eighteen months (day), twenty-four months (evening), 1,568 clock hours, 90 credits. Graduates of this program find employment as entry-level production artists, layout artists, illustrators, and freelance graphic designers. Employment opportunities are in advertising agencies, design studios, art departments, printing companies, and newspaper/magazine publishers.

E-Business Management: eighteen months (day), 1,680 clock hours, 96 credits. The high level of instruction and variety of courses in this program help students gain successful employment by providing skills to design, launch, and manage Web sites for businesses.

Paralegal Studies: eighteen months (day), 1,750 clock hours, 96 credits. This program prepares students for a career in the legal field, doing work with closings, hearings, trials, and corporate meetings; in the business field, helping with contracts; and in the government field, analyzing legal material, doing research, collecting evidence, and writing memoranda.

Diploma Programs Massage Therapy: eighteen months (day), twenty-four months (evening), 1,582 clock hours, 90 credits. This program prepares students for a career in the massage field working is such places as chiropractic offices, clinics, hospitals, health and beauty spas, fitness centers and health clubs, resorts, hotels, and physical therapy centers. Graduates may work from home, an office, or onsite at public events.

Early Childhood Education: eighteen months (day), twenty-four months (evening), 1,540 clock hours, 90 credits. This program instructs students on how to effectively stimulate the emotional, physical, intellectual, and social growth of children in their care. They are also prepared to manage employees, learn about operating budgets, and establish relationships with parents and the community.

Costs

The following costs are estimates and subject to change. Costs for diploma programs include Massage Therapy: $25,200 (estimated cost of books and supplies, $2200; laptop, $2500) and Early Childhood Education: $25,200 (estimated cost of books and supplies, $2200; laptop, $2500). Business associate degree programs are estimated at $26,520 (estimated cost of books and supplies, $2200; laptop, $2500); Other associate degree program costs include E-Business Management: $29,520 (estimated cost of books/supplies, $2400; laptop, $2500); Personal Computer and Network Technology: $29,520 (estimated cost of books and supplies, $3500; laptop, $2500); and the Visual Communications program: $29,520 (estimated cost of books and supplies, $4625; laptop, $2800). All books, supplies, and laptop costs are estimates. All costs are for the entire program. Additional fees include a registration fee of $20 and a graduation fee of $150.

The Education Department evaluates any previous education and training that may be applicable to an educational program. If the education and/or training meets the standards for transfer of credit, the program may be shortened and the tuition reduced accordingly. Students who request credit for previous education or training are required to provide the Registrar's Office with an official transcript from the educational institution.

Financial Aid

The Financial Aid Department devotes personal attention to every student by individually mapping out financial options. In addition to more than $100,000 in scholarships, grants and loans available to those who qualify include Federal Pell Grant, Federal Stafford Student Loan, Federal Supplemental Educational Opportunity Grant, Federal Parent Loan for Undergraduate Students, Federal Work-Study Program, and alternative funding. Scholarships from Lehigh Valley College and Future Business Leaders of America for graduating high school seniors are also available.

Faculty

Lehigh Valley College has more than 100 full- and part-time instructors with bachelor's, master's, or doctoral degrees in addition to occupational qualifications.

Student Body Profile

There are currently more than 1,500 students enrolled at the College. The students who attend Lehigh Valley College come from a number of areas within a 50-mile radius. All students reside off campus; however, LVC assists with housing when necessary.

Student Activities

LVC has a number of activities and organizations for the students to participate in, such as SIFE, Student Government Association, and various organizations in the program specialties. The students are also encouraged to participate in community events and help raise money for worthy causes.

Throughout the academic year, activities that encourage college spirit and develop student leadership may be offered. The College believes that participation in these activities is an important part of the educational process, and student involvement is encouraged.

Facilities and Resources

Students are provided with facilities that have the latest industry-standard equipment. LVC's new facility houses a variety of teaching and resource tools, including a library, a bookstore, and student lounges. The building also houses six PC labs, three Mac labs, two art studios, and a photography studio. The wireless environment allows students to work freely throughout the campus with access to the network at all times.

Career Planning Lehigh Valley College provides career planning services to all students and graduates. While at LVC, students may take advantage of job fairs and part-time job postings. As students prepare for graduation, career planning representatives assist them with resume writing, interviewing skills, and all other job search techniques to help maximize employment opportunities. Through relationships developed and maintained with employers, the career planning department stays informed about current hiring and industry trends to better serve students and graduates.

Lehigh Valley College assists students in finding part-time employment while they attend college. Assistance includes advice in preparing for an interview, aid with securing an interview, and offering a list of available jobs.

The College encourages students to maintain satisfactory attendance, conduct, and academic progress so they may be viewed favorably by prospective employers. While LVC cannot guarantee employment, it has been successful in placing the majority of its graduates in their field of training. All graduating students participate in the following career planning activities: preparation of resumes and letters of introduction, an important step in a well-planned job search; interviewing techniques, where students acquire effective interviewing skills through practice exercises; job referral, as the Career Planning Services Department compiles job openings from employers in the area; and on-campus interviews, in which companies visit the College to interview graduates for employment opportunities.

All students are expected to participate in the career-planning program, and failure to do so may jeopardize these privileges.

Alumni may continue to utilize the College's career-planning program at no additional cost.

Location

Lehigh Valley College is located at 2809 East Saucon Valley Road, Center Valley, Pennsylvania. Its new 97,000-square foot building is easily accessible from I-78 and the Pennsylvania Turnpike. It is on a local bus route and within a short driving distance of the Poconos, Philadelphia, and New York. Nearby are Blue Mountain Ski Area, Doe Mountain Ski Area, Dorney Park and Wildwater Kingdom, and the Lehigh County Velodrome. Year-round activities include Musikfest, the Celtic Classic, the Great Allentown Fair, Mayfair, and the Pennsylvania Shakespeare Festival.

Admission Requirements

Students are required to have a personal interview to be accepted into the College. This can be done by meeting with an admissions representative in person. This is also a time to tour the facilities and ask any questions that the student, spouse, or parents may have. Personal interviews enable the College representative to determine whether an applicant is likely to benefit from enrollment into the program. The following items must be included at the time of application: a high school transcript or General Educational Development (GED) test scores, an enrollment agreement (if the applicant is under 18 years of age, it must be signed by the parent or guardian), financial aid forms (if the applicant wishes to apply for financial aid), and the registration fee of $20.

The College reserves the right to reject students if the requirements listed above are not successfully completed.

Prior to beginning at LVC or upon receipt of the student's records, diagnostic testing is used to assess basic learning skills and the student's ability to benefit from enrolling in the College. The diagnostic tests used are the Test of English as a Foreign Language (TOEFL) and the Accuplacer Assessment Exam.

Students who graduate from a high school outside of the United States must have successfully completed the TOEFL with a minimum score of 450.

Application and Information

Lehigh Valley College follows an open enrollment system; applications to the College are accepted at all times. Students should apply for admission as early as possible in order to be officially accepted for a specific program and starting date. To apply, students should call to set up an interview with one of the admissions representatives. To meet with one of the representatives and tour the College or to get additional information, interested students should contact the Admissions Department.

Admissions Department
Lehigh Valley College
2809 East Saucon Valley Road
Center Valley, Pennsylvania 18034
Telephone: 610-791-5100
Fax: 610-791-7810
World Wide Web: http://www.lehighvalley.edu

LINCOLN COLLEGE
LINCOLN, ILLINOIS

The College and Its Mission

The mission of Lincoln College is to assist each student in the development and achievement of personal and educational goals and to ensure that its degree recipients are liberally educated and personally and academically prepared to succeed in four-year colleges. Lincoln College is an excellent beginning for those students with a 15–21 ACT score who desire a residential experience in a supportive atmosphere. Lincoln College has a solid reputation for a high percentage/retention of students who transfer to four-year institutions and is the only two-year residential institution in Illinois.

Academic Programs

Associate Degree Programs The majority of students graduate with an **Associate in Arts** degree. This is designed to provide the student with a liberal grounding in the fundamental areas of human knowledge and allow elective selection of courses of general interest or pre-major preparation. This degree is transfer-oriented and fulfills the general education requirements of most four-year colleges and universities nationwide.

A variety of courses and scholarships exist in the performing arts arena. Subjects include broadcasting, creative writing, dance, graphic arts, music-instrumental, music-vocal, photography, speech, technical theater, theater, and visual arts.

Costs

Costs for the 2005–06 academic year included tuition ($15,000), room and board ($5600), and fees ($570). Textbooks and supplies were estimated at $240.

Financial Aid

Financial assistance is generally determined by the need of the applicant, along with the availability of funds from federal, state, institutional, and private sources. Lincoln College considers the needs of each individual applicant in creating the financial package. Scholarships are awarded for academic, fine arts, and athletic excellence. Approximately 90 percent of Lincoln College students receive financial aid.

Faculty

The majority of Lincoln College faculty members are full-time. They are directly involved in instruction, advising, and counseling. Of full-time faculty members, 100 percent hold advanced degrees. The student-faculty ratio is 13:1, and the average class size is 16.

Student Body Profile

Fourteen different states and six other countries are represented through the Lincoln campus student body. Approximately 650 students attend Lincoln College, and 90 percent are classified as residential. The average age is 18.5. Approximately 89 percent of Lincoln College graduates enter immediately into four-year institutions.

Student Activities

Students may participate in a variety of fine arts activities, including music-vocal, music-instrumental, theater, technical theater, dance, photography, ceramics, visual art, and speech.

Sports Varsity sports for women include athletic training/management, basketball, cheerleading, cross-country, golf, soccer, softball, swimming/diving, track, and volleyball. Varsity sports for men include athletic training/management, baseball, basketball, cheerleading, cross-country, golf, soccer, swimming/diving, track, and wrestling.

Facilities and Resources

Lincoln College was established in 1865 and since that time has grown into a 60-acre campus with ten instructional buildings, a library, a swimming pool, a gymnasium, a performing arts center, a student center, two modern computer centers, an art gallery and studio, the Lincoln Museum and Museum of Presidents, administrative offices, a dance studio, a radio station, seven residential halls, a bookstore, a post office, softball and baseball diamonds, a soccer field, several intramural fields, a weight training center, tennis courts, and several supporting physical plant structures.

The original structure of Lincoln College, University Hall, has been in continuous use since 1866. For both its historic ties to Abraham Lincoln and its Italianate Victorian style of architecture, University Hall is listed on the National Registry of Historical Sites and Places.

Lincoln College is well established in its commitment to a supportive environment. Many programs are designed to assist the student both academically and socially. A very personal approach to education includes the residential component, outstanding faculty members and advising, tutorial services, enriched classes, detailed orientation, academic tracking, and a campus-wide commitment to student achievement.

Location

The city of Lincoln (population 16,000) is located in the geographic center of Illinois. The city is the hub of six major urban areas: Springfield, Decatur, Bloomington-Normal, Champaign-Urbana, Pekin, and Peoria. There are two airports within an hour's drive, and daily Amtrak service to Chicago and St. Louis is available. The College is located directly off of Interstate 55.

Admission Requirements

For freshman students, acceptance to Lincoln College is based on high school record, standardized test scores, a personal interview, and letters of recommendation. Students with an ACT composite score of 16 or better may be admitted without restriction. Those with an ACT composite score of 15 or lower may be admitted on provisional status. The admissions committee also considers high school transcript data, and high school counselor recommendations are given a high priority. Students entering Lincoln College provisionally are required to attend and successfully complete the Academic Development Seminar, which occurs one week prior to the fall semester. Students who are transferring to Lincoln College from another college or university may enter the College at the beginning of any semester. Students who were on probation at their previous institution and/or maintained less than a 2.0 GPA (on a 4.0 scale) may be admitted to Lincoln College on provisional status as well. Students for whom English is a second language must take the TOEFL examination and have their scores sent to Lincoln College. International students who score at least 480 on the Test of English as a Foreign Language (TOEFL) are granted admission to Lincoln College. Students whose scores are below 480 may be granted conditional acceptance if space is available.

Application and Information

Applications are accepted contingent on the availability of housing. Freshmen are encouraged to apply before July 1. Individuals interested in Lincoln College should contact:

Lincoln College Admissions
Lincoln College
300 Keokuk
Lincoln, Illinois 62656
Telephone: 217-732-3155
        800-569-0556 (toll-free)
Fax: 217-732-7715
E-mail: tschilling@lincolncollege.com
World Wide Web: http://www.lincolncollege.edu

Lincoln College is well established in its commitment to a supportive environment.

LINCOLN COLLEGE–NORMAL
NORMAL, ILLINOIS

The College and Its Mission

Lincoln College, a private two-year residential college, has been offering students the opportunity to study and succeed in a highly supportive environment since 1865. Accredited by the North Central Association of Colleges and Schools, Lincoln offers Associate in Arts, Associate in Science, Associate in Applied Science, Bachelor of Arts, and Bachelor of Science degrees.

The mission of Lincoln College is to assist each student in the development and achievement of personal and educational goals and to ensure that degree recipients are liberally educated and personally and academically prepared to succeed in four-year colleges and/or careers. The College is an excellent beginning for those students with a 15–21 ACT score who desire a residential experience in a supportive atmosphere.

Lincoln College has a national reputation for academic achievement, and the College's associate degree graduates have continued their studies at more than 200 different four-year colleges and universities in the last decade. Small class sizes, outstanding faculty advisement, free professional tutoring, and a residential experience result in approximately 89 percent of Lincoln College graduates entering immediately into four-year institutions. In addition, the College offers bachelor's degree programs in liberal arts and business management for students who may want to stay all four years with Lincoln College.

Lincoln College at Normal opened in 1979 as an extension of Lincoln College in Lincoln, Illinois. Today, Lincoln College at Normal has two modern academic facilities on campus, which house classrooms, laboratories, and administrative offices. In addition, five student residential units are available on campus, offering apartment/suite-style living with private bedrooms and shared kitchens and living rooms. Students may also enjoy the Student Activity Center on campus. Coexisting in the Bloomington-Normal area with a major state university as well as a private four-year college, Lincoln College at Normal offers students the excitement and diversity of a large university community while still preserving the benefits of a small-college atmosphere.

Academic Programs

The College is on a two-semester schedule, with fall and spring components. A limited number of classes are also offered in the summer.

Bachelor's Degree Programs In the fall of 2001, Lincoln College at Normal established two new bachelor's degree programs: a Bachelor of Arts in liberal arts and a Bachelor of Science in business management. These programs are organized in a "2+2" structure, where students must first complete an Associate in Arts or an Associate in Science degree (or the equivalent) before being accepted to the bachelor's degree program.

Associate Degree Programs The Associate in Arts degree is designed to provide the student with a liberal grounding in the fundamental areas of human knowledge and allow a variety of elective selection of courses of general interest or premajor preparation. This degree is transfer-oriented and fulfills the general education requirements of most four-year colleges and universities nationwide. Typical premajor interests include American studies, art, biology, business administration, chemistry/physics, criminal justice, education, English/literature, environmental science, history/political science, law enforcement, mathematics, media/journalism, music, philosophy and religion, physical education, prenursing, psychology, sociology, speech, and theater. The College also offers an Associate in Science degree, where more emphasis is placed upon math and science, as well as Associate in Applied Science degrees in cosmetology and travel/tourism.

Certificate and Diploma Programs These programs are typically completed in one year and include cosmetology and travel/tourism.

Costs

Costs for the 2006–07 academic year include tuition, $15,000; room and board, $5000; and fees, $570. Textbook rentals and supplies are estimated at $300.

Financial Aid

Approximately 95 percent of students at Lincoln College at Normal benefit from some type of financial aid each year. Financial assistance is generally determined by the need of the applicant (from the Free Application for Federal Student Aid) along with the availability of funds from federal, state, institutional, and private sources. Lincoln College considers the needs of each individual applicant in creating the financial aid package. Scholarships are also awarded for academic, fine arts, and athletic excellence.

Faculty

The majority of Lincoln College faculty members are full-time. Their direct involvement with students includes instruction, advisement, and counseling. Of the full-time faculty, 100 percent hold advanced degrees. The student-faculty ratio is 14:1, and the average class size is 16.

Student Body Profile

Six different states and three other countries are represented through the approximately 500 students enrolled at Lincoln College at Normal. Approximately 65 percent of students are full-time and 36 percent of the full-time students reside on campus. The average age of the student body is 21. Typically, 72 percent of students graduate on time with a two-year degree, with 89 percent of those students transferring successfully either to the bachelor's degree program on campus or to a four-year university the following semester.

Student Activities

Student Activities The Student Activities Committee works to get the student body involved both in the College and in the various extracurricular activities. Student activities include intramural sports, outdoor activities (camping, canoeing, etc.), volunteering and community service events, music concerts, shopping trips, and athletic events.

Fine Arts Students may participate in a variety of fine arts activities, including the areas of visual arts, theater, and music.

Sports Opportunities in intramural athletics are available on campus as well as through the intramural programs offered at neighboring Illinois State University. Students also have access to the Student Recreation Complex at Illinois State University for exercise and workout needs. Opportunities in varsity athletics are available through the campus in Lincoln, Illinois.

Facilities and Resources

Lincoln College at Normal consists of two modern academic facilities with classrooms, laboratories, an art center, a lecture hall, and administrative offices. In addition, five student residential buildings are located on campus, offering apartment/suite-style living with private bedrooms and shared kitchens and living rooms. This represents the primary housing option for students, with private off-campus apartment housing also available in the community for juniors and seniors. In addition, Student Activity Center features workout facilities, a multimedia room, a game room, and meeting spaces.

Advisement/Counseling Trained full-time faculty members assist students in selecting courses and programs of study to satisfy their educational objectives. The Learning Resource Center provides free professional tutoring to all students in any subject. This takes the form of one-on-one sessions as well as online tutorial programs. Students can also make up assignments and do extra credit projects under the direction of the Learning Resource Center personnel.

Recreation/Career Counseling/Placement Services Students enjoy full access and privileges to each of these facilities and offices at Illinois State University as part of their enrollment at Lincoln College at Normal.

Health Services Lincoln College students at the campus in Normal may also elect to take advantage of the student health center at Illinois State University in Normal. This offering is available on an à la carte basis and can be arranged with the assistance of Lincoln College personnel.

Library and Audiovisual Services Lincoln College students at the campus in Normal have library privileges for the Illinois State University library in Normal, with a combined book collection of 1,659,983 volumes. CD-ROM and online databases are also available for student use. The College offers two state-of-the-art computer labs for classroom, homework, and project use. These labs have more than forty computers for the students' use, all with Internet access. In addition, the student housing on campus features high-speed Internet access in every bedroom, and additional computers are also available in the Student Activity Center.

Location

Lincoln College at Normal is located in the city of Normal near the geographic center of Illinois, and with the adjoining city of Bloomington, has a population of more than 100,000. The College is situated on 10 acres of land approximately two blocks west of Route 51 (North Main Street) in north Normal, just off Interstate 55. The Bloomington/Normal area is served by three interstate highways, I-55, I-74, and I-39. It also features an airport, bus service, and Amtrak service. Driving time from Chicago and St. Louis is 2½ hours.

Admission Requirements

Associate Degree Program Acceptance to the associate degree program at Lincoln College at Normal is based on a student's high school record, standardized test scores, a personal interview, and letters of recommendation. Students with a minimum ACT composite score of 17 may be admitted without restriction. Those with an ACT composite score of 16 or less may be admitted on provisional status, based on the decision of the Admissions Committee. Students who are transferring to Lincoln College at Normal from another college or university may enter the College at the beginning of any semester. If they have been on academic probation at the previous institution and/or have maintained less than a 2.0 GPA (on a 4.0 scale), they may be admitted to the College on provisional status as well. Students for whom English is a second language must take the TOEFL examination and have their scores sent to the College. Any international student with a minimum score of 157 (computer-based) on the TOEFL may be granted admission to Lincoln College. Students whose scores are below 157 may be granted conditional acceptance if space is available.

Bachelor's Degree Program Students who are applying to the bachelor's degree program are required to have earned an Associate in Arts or Associate in Science degree or the equivalent at an accredited institution in order to be admitted without restriction. Students who have not yet met this requirement may be admitted on a conditional basis, based on the decision of the Admissions Committee.

Application and Information

Applications are accepted on a rolling basis and housing on campus is contingent on availability. All students are encouraged to apply before June 1 for the fall semester. Individuals interested in Lincoln College at Normal should contact:

Lincoln College Admissions
Lincoln College at Normal
715 West Raab Road
Normal, Illinois 61761
Telephone: 309-452-0500
            800-569-0558 (toll-free)
Fax: 309-862-3352
E-mail: ncadmissioninfo@lincolncollege.edu
World Wide Web: http://www.lincolncollege.edu/normal

Students enjoy various activities on campus at Lincoln College at Normal.

MANOR COLLEGE
JENKINTOWN, PENNSYLVANIA

The College and Its Mission

Manor College is a private, coed Catholic college founded in 1947 by the Ukrainian Sisters of Saint Basil the Great. The College is characterized by its dedication to the education, growth, and self-actualization of the whole person through its personalized and nurturing atmosphere. Upon graduation, 40 percent of Manor's students are employed in their chosen fields; the remaining 60 percent of students transfer to four-year institutions to earn baccalaureate degrees. There are approximately 800 full- and part-time students enrolled at Manor. Extracurricular activities include honor societies and men's and women's intercollegiate soccer and basketball as well as the yearbook and special interest and cultural clubs. Manor provides free counseling and tutoring services through an on-campus learning center. Trained counselors are available to assist students on an individual and confidential basis for academic, career, and personal concerns. Upon entering Manor, students are assigned an academic adviser, who provides guidance and support throughout their Manor experience. Transfer counseling is available for students interested in pursuing a four-year degree. The College's 35-acre campus includes a modern three-story dormitory, a library/administration building, and an academic building that also houses the bookstore, dining hall, an auditorium/gymnasium, and a student lounge. The Ukrainian Heritage Studies Center and the Manor Dental Health Center are also located on the campus grounds. Manor is accredited by the Middle States Association of Colleges and Schools.

Academic Programs

Manor offers career-oriented, two-year associate degrees, as well as transfer programs for the purpose of pursuing a bachelor's degree. Internships provide theory with practice, enhancing employment opportunities. The liberal arts core ensures a common breadth of knowledge along with mobility and future advancement. Manor offers ten programs with twenty majors/concentrations leading to associate degrees and transfer programs through its three divisions: Liberal Arts, Allied Health/Science/Mathematics, and Business.

The Liberal Arts Division offers **Associate in Arts** degrees in early childhood education, psychology, and liberal arts. In addition, the Liberal Arts Division provides a liberal arts transfer major as well as an elementary education transfer major, an early child-care major, a three-year English as a second language (ESL) concentration, a concentration in catechetical education, and a concentration in communications. The Allied Health/Science/Mathematics Division offers **Associate in Science** degrees in dental hygiene, expanded functions dental assisting, and veterinary technology. This division also includes allied health and science transfer programs for students who seek preprofessional programs in biotechnology, chiropractic, cytotechnology, general sciences, medical technology, nursing, occupational therapy, pharmacy, physical therapy, radiologic science, and veterinary animal science. The Business Division offers **Associate in Science** degrees in accounting, business administration, business administration/computer science, business administration/human resource management, business administration/international business, business administration/management, business administration/marketing, and paralegal studies. There are four certificate programs. There are a PC technician/computer support specialist studies certificate and a certificate program in paralegal studies for students who have a bachelor's degree, as well as a legal nurse consultant certificate. A certificate program in catechist/educator development is offered for both Roman and Byzantine rites. Manor also offers selected courses through two modes of distance learning: online Web-based learning and teleconferencing.

The Office of Continuing Education serves adult learners by providing educational options for those who want to attend college on a part-time basis. The office also supports the needs of the community and business and industry by offering noncredit classes and workshops, as well as on- and off-site corporate training programs, throughout the year. Approved as an authorized provider by the International Association for Continuing Education and Training, the office also grants continuing education units (CEUs) for selected professional development courses each semester.

Off-Campus Programs

Externships are incorporated into the academic studies programs. Students earn credits as they gain practical experience under the supervision of professionals in a specific field of study. Externships are offered in the career-oriented programs of study and in some transfer programs. Manor's affiliation with several area hospitals, as well as Manor College's on-campus Dental Health Center, enables the allied health program student to fulfill clinical requirements at these sites. Students in other programs serve externships in law offices, courtrooms, day-care centers, businesses, health-care organizations, and veterinary facilities. Manor has dual admissions, 2+2, and 2+3 articulation agreements with major allied health universities, hospitals, and local universities.

Credit for Nontraditional Learning Experiences

Manor College awards credit by examination for college-level learning through the College-Level Examination Program (CLEP). Manor administers exemption tests for courses not available through CLEP. Adults may also receive college credit for military experience and education through the Army/American Council on Education Registry Transcript System (AARTS), by submitting a transcript to Manor for evaluation of credits, and by requesting assessment of previous life and job experiences through nontraditional means.

Costs

Tuition for the 2005–06 academic year was $10,450 for full-time studies. Part-time study was $229 per credit hour. Students in certain allied health programs paid an additional $510 per year for full-time study or an additional $96 per credit hour for part-time study. On-campus room and board are available for men and women and cost $5096 per year. There is an additional $800 fee for a private room. Other fees included a $350 general fee per year and a $100 graduation fee.

Financial Aid

Manor College offers need-based financial aid to eligible applicants in the form of grants, loans, and campus employment. Scholarships are awarded on the basis of academic promise. Approximately 85 percent of Manor's students receive some form of financial aid. Federally funded sources include the Federal Pell Grant, Federal Supplemental Educational Opportunity Grant, Federal Perkins Loan, Federal Stafford Student Loan, Federal PLUS loan, and Federal Work-Study Program. State-funded programs offered are the PHEAA State Grant and State Work-Study programs. The institutionally funded sources are the Manor Grant and the Resident Grant. Scholarships available for attendance at Manor include the following: Manor Presidential Scholarship; Joseph and Rose Wawriw Scholarships; Henry Lewandowski Memorial Scholarship; Elizabeth A. Stahlecker Memorial Scholarship; Mary Wolchonsky Scholarship; John Woloschuk Memorial Scholarship; Lorraine Osinski Keating Memorial Scholarship; Yuri and Jaroslava Rybak Scholarship; Dr. and Mrs. Volodymyr and Lydia Bazarko Scholarship; Heritage Foundation Scholarship of First Securities Federal Savings Bank; Father Chlystun Scholarship; Sesok Family Memorial Scholarship; Eileen Freedman Memorial Scholarship; Manor Allied Health,

Science, and Math Division Scholarship; Business Division Scholarship; Liberal Arts Division Scholarship; Basilian Scholarships; Scholar Athlete Award; St. Basil Academy Scholarship; Wasyl and Jozefa Soroka Scholarships; and International Scholarships. Scholarship eligibility requirements vary; details are available from the Admissions Office.

Faculty

There are 24 full-time and 98 part-time faculty members at Manor. Forty-seven percent of the faculty members have master's degrees and 32 percent possess doctorates in their field. Faculty members spend three fourths of their time teaching and the remainder counseling and advising students. The overall faculty-student ratio is 1:13. Small class size allows for personal attention in an environment conducive to learning.

Student Body Profile

Of the approximately 800 full- and part-time students enrolled at Manor, 207 entered the College as full-time freshman students in fall 2002. Twenty percent of that freshman class lived in the on-campus residence hall. Seventeen percent of the recent freshman class were members of minority groups, and 9 percent were international students from Albania, Brazil, India, Jamaica, Japan, Korea, Liberia, Nigeria, Poland, Sierra Leone, Ukraine, and Uzbekistan.

Student Activities

Manor encourages students to develop leadership skills through active participation in all aspects of College life. A variety of options for extracurricular participation fall under the umbrella of Manor's student life department, including the Student Senate, athletic teams, and clubs. The Student Senate forms an important part of the College community. The Senate, representing the student population, responds to student interests and concerns and acts as a liaison between the administration and the student body. Other extracurricular activities include intercollegiate men's and women's basketball and soccer. Manor's sports teams compete in the Eastern Pennsylvania Collegiate Conference. Additional extracurricular activities include the honor societies, intramural sports, the yearbook, and various special interest and cultural clubs. Student services is also responsible for the campus ministry, the counseling center, the residence hall, and the on-campus security force.

Facilities and Resources

The Academic Building (also called Mother of Perpetual Help Hall) includes classrooms, lecture rooms, laboratories, the chapel, and the Offices of Student Services, Campus Ministry, and Counseling. The Academic Building is equipped with up-to-date facilities, including biology, chemistry, and clinical laboratories, as well as modern IBM-compatible microsystems network labs. The Learning Center provides professional and student tutors in all College subjects and conducts workshops in study and research skills. Courses in English as a second language are also offered at the center.

The Basileiad Library has the capacity for 60,000 books, journals, multimedia materials, and periodicals. The library offers study areas, a multimedia room, a special collections and rare book archive, and computer access. The current library collection contains 50,000 volumes, including a special law collection and a Ukrainian Language collection. An on-campus community Manor Dental Health Center was established in 1979 as an adjunct to the Expanded Functions Dental Assisting (EFDA) Program. Located on the lower level of St. Josaphat Hall, the center provides students enrolled in the EFDA Program or the Dental Hygiene Program at Manor with training under the direct supervision of faculty dentists. Currently, more than 2,000 patients receive care, including the following services: general dentistry, oral hygiene, orthodontics, prosthodontics, endodontics, and cosmetic dentistry. Because Manor Dental Health Center is a teaching facility, the fees charged for services are lower than those charged by private practitioners. Community residents are welcome as patients. The Ukrainian Heritage Studies Center, located on the campus, preserves and promotes Ukrainian heritage, arts, and culture through four areas: academic programs, a museum collection, a library, and archives. Special events, exhibits, workshops, and seminars are offered throughout the year. The center is open to the public for tours and educational presentations by appointment.

Location

Manor is located in Jenkintown, Pennsylvania, 15 miles north of Center City Philadelphia. Manor is accessible via public transportation and is located near the Pennsylvania Turnpike, Route 611, U.S. 1, and Route 232. Centers of cultural and historic interest are found in nearby Philadelphia, Valley Forge, and beautiful Bucks County. Manor's suburban campus is within walking distance of a large shopping mall, medical offices, and a township park.

Admission Requirements

Manor is open to qualified applicants of all races, creeds, and national origins. Candidates are required to have a high school diploma or its equivalent. Admission is based on the applicant's scholastic record, test scores, and interviews. The application procedure involves submission of a completed application form, a high school transcript, SAT or ACT scores (required for students less than 21 years old), an interview, and Manor's entrance/ placement test (waived for candidates who hold the baccalaureate degree). Transfer students must submit transcripts of all college work completed. International students must also submit results of the Test of English as a Foreign Language (TOEFL) or, for the Liberal Arts/ESL program, must have completed two years of English language study at the high school or college level in their native country.

Application and Information

Manor has a rolling admission policy. Students may apply for admission in either the fall or the spring semester. Interested students are invited to visit the campus and meet with admissions staff, faculty members, program directors, and students. Open houses, career days and nights, and classroom visits are scheduled throughout the year. The Admissions Office is open Monday through Friday, 8:30 a.m. to 6 p.m. (Saturday hours are by appointment). Admissions staff members can schedule visits and answer questions concerning admission, careers, programs, special features, and student life. For application forms, program-of-study bulletins, and catalogs, students should write to:

I. Jerry Czenstuch
Vice President of Enrollment Management
Manor College
700 Fox Chase Road
Jenkintown, Pennsylvania 19046

Telephone: 215-884-2216
E-mail: ftadmiss@manor.edu
World Wide Web: http://www.manor.edu

Manor College students relax between classes on the steps outside Mother of Perpetual Help Hall.

MARIA COLLEGE
ALBANY, NEW YORK

The College and Its Mission

Maria College was established in 1958 by the Religious Sisters of Mercy as an independent two-year, degree-granting institution. The College is career oriented and admits both men and women. The current enrollment is 723; about 90 percent are women. It is accredited by the Middle States Association of Colleges and Schools.

Located in a quiet corner of New York State's capital, Albany, Maria College concentrates on preparing its students for productive careers in health, education, and business. Nursing graduates are prepared for the state examination for licensure as registered nurses. The occupational therapy assistant studies program leads to certification by the state of New York upon graduation. In addition, following an examination, occupational therapy assistants are certified by the American Occupational Therapy Association.

The College's Career Planning and Placement Office is responsible for counseling students and alumni on career development, helping students obtain employment upon graduation, and assisting students in the process of transferring to other institutions. With the cooperation of program chairpersons, this office conducts seminars on resume preparation, interviewing techniques, and the job search. Individual counseling is available. Placement Office records show nearly 100 percent employment and/or transfer to four-year schools for Maria College graduates over the past fifteen years.

Academic Programs

Associate Degree Programs Maria College offers the Associate in Applied Science (A.A.S.) degree in allied health (nursing and occupational therapy assistant studies), business sciences (accounting, legal assistant studies, and management), computer information systems, and early childhood education. The **Associate in Arts (A.A.)** degree is offered in liberal arts. The **Associate in Science (A.S.)** degree is offered in general studies and research technologist studies. Degrees are conferred on students who have completed at least 64 college credits through courses taken at Maria, transfer credit, credit earned through approved proficiency examinations, or life experience credit. Graduates also must complete the College's requirements of 6 credit hours in religious studies/philosophy and 6 credit hours in English. The required liberal arts core consists of 48 credit hours for an A.A., 32 credit hours for an A.S., and 22 credit hours for an A.A.S. An overall quality point average of at least 2.0 (on a 4.0 scale) is also required.

In addition to traditional day classes, Maria College's Evening Division offers degree programs in accounting, computer information systems, general studies, liberal arts, management, and nursing.

The first Weekend College to be established in northeastern New York is conducted at Maria. This innovative, degree-granting option allows students to complete degree programs in business, computer information systems, general studies, legal assistant studies, and liberal arts by attending classes every other weekend for two years. The occupational therapy assistant studies program takes three years to complete.

Students who wish to continue studies toward a baccalaureate degree may complete the first two years of study at Maria and then transfer to a senior institution for the next two years. To facilitate such a transfer, Maria College has articulation agreements with a wide range of senior colleges. For nursing students, for example, articulation agreements exist with the baccalaureate nursing programs at Russell Sage College in Troy, New York, the College of Health Related Professions of the State University of New York Health Science Center at Syracuse, and Drexel University in Philadelphia, Pennsylvania.

Certificate Programs Certificate programs are available in bereavement studies, gerontology, legal assistant studies, and practical nursing. The legal assistant studies certificate is available only for those with associate or bachelor's degrees. The practical nursing program has three unique tracks and can be completed solely on the weekends. Completion of this program allows graduates to transition into the senior year of the associate degree program in nursing.

Off-Campus Programs

Clinical experiences for nursing students are provided at Albany Medical Center, Our Lady of Mercy Life Center, and St. Peter's Hospital. Students in the occupational therapy assistant studies program complete field work experience in hospitals, developmental centers, nursing homes, and rehabilitation centers in New York State and at selected sites out-of-state. Senior students in the early childhood education program are trained in a variety of outside agencies, which may include day-care centers, Head Start, and centers providing programs for infants and toddlers or for children with special needs.

Credit for Nontraditional Learning Experiences

Maria College recognizes college-level courses taken by students while they are still attending high school. Advanced Placement scores of 5, 4, and 3 normally earn college credit. Maria College grants credit for Excelsior College Examinations and the College-Level Examination Program (CLEP) when these examinations cover comparable material. Proficiency credits are treated as transfer credits.

Maria College recognizes that certain adult students may have gained valuable knowledge in their lives from diverse experiences. Some of this learning may qualify as college-level course work. Students requesting credit are required to substantiate this learning experience. Total credit obtained through life experience is limited to a maximum of 16 nonduplicative transfer credits applied toward a degree, 25 percent of the required 64 credits.

The Nursing Program offers advanced placement for licensed practical nurses in two unique ways. The Challenge Program is a series of classes held twice a year to assist licensed practical nurses in meeting the requirements to gain credit for the first semester of nursing. Each candidate for advanced placement must be successful in both a written and a skill examination. Maria College also participates in the LPN–RN Transition Course, which allows credit for up to fifteen credits in the freshman year of nursing. Maria Colleges offers the LPN–RN Transition Course each summer term.

Costs

Tuition for the 2006–07 academic year is $7800 for full-time study and $285 per credit hour for part-time study. Fees were $200 per academic year (higher for those in the allied health programs). The College does not provide housing, but arrangements for off-campus housing may be made through the Admissions Office.

Financial Aid

Tuition Assistance Program (TAP) awards are available to New York State residents only. Financial aid is available to students through Federal Stafford Student Loans, Federal PLUS loans, Federal Perkins Loans, Federal Nursing Loans, Federal Pell Grants, Federal Supplemental Educational Opportunity Grants, Federal Work-Study Program awards, and Veterans Administration educational benefits. Approximately 78 percent of the College's students receive aid. To apply for aid, students must submit both the Free Application for Federal Student Aid (FAFSA) and the NYS TAP form.

Faculty

Maria College has full- and part-time faculty members. Every freshman is assigned to a faculty adviser, who encourages communication and a strong working relationship. The student-faculty ratio is 14:1.

Student Body Profile

For the entering fall 2005 class, 52 percent were first-time freshmen. Approximately 85 percent of all students were from a radius of 50 miles from the College. Nonresident aliens made up less than 1 percent of the student body, and approximately 30 percent of full-time enrollees belonged to a minority group. Fifty-three percent of students were older than 25. Maria College is a commuter-based institution; less than 5 percent of students seek housing through the Admissions Office.

Student Activities

Student government is handled on a departmental basis; each department operates independently of all other departments.

Facilities and Resources

Maria's facilities are located in three buildings. The Administration Building's modern facilities include offices, technology-equipped classrooms, computerized science laboratories, a computer center, a working library of 60,000 volumes, a multimedia center, and a multimedia large lecture hall. Marian Hall, Maria's allied health facility, has been renovated through grants from the Helene Fuld Foundation and gifts from the College's alumni and friends. It includes the Helene Fuld Audio-Visual Laboratory for nursing students, the Bearldean B. Burke Occupational Therapy Teaching Center, the Activities of Daily Living Suite, a multimedia auditorium, classrooms, offices, and nursing labs. The Campus School is a fully equipped teaching facility that provides preschool and full-day kindergarten classes and serves as a laboratory school for students majoring in early childhood education.

Location

Maria's urban location makes the many attractions of the capital district readily accessible. City buses provide convenient transportation to the area's sister cities of Schenectady and Troy, to many fine shopping centers, and to the impressive Nelson A. Rockefeller Empire State Plaza, which has the State Museum, indoor and outdoor entertainment areas, and performing arts facilities. Access to the Adirondack Northway—leading to the Saratoga Performing Arts Center and Canada—is minutes away. Amtrak trains are available from Schenectady and Rensselaer. Opportunities for outdoor activities in the area are numerous. The Catskills, the Helderbergs, the Adirondacks, and their many lakes provide four seasons of outdoor enjoyment.

Admission Requirements

Admission to Maria College is based on a review of the applicant's high school and (when applicable) college performance, SAT or ACT scores and other objective test data, letters of recommendation, and the applicant's interests, maturity, and objectives. Interviews are required. An early admission program is offered for qualified high school students. Part-time study is also available.

Application and Information

It is recommended that application be made early in the first semester of the last year of high school. Applicants must submit an application form and a nonrefundable $35 fee, offer evidence of completion or anticipated completion of a high school program or its equivalent and arrange for transcripts and SAT or ACT scores to be sent to Maria College. Students whose SAT or ACT scores fall below a particular level are required to take placement tests in the basic skills of reading, writing, and mathematics. Inquiries regarding academic programs or admission to Maria College may be directed to:

Director of Admissions
Maria College
700 New Scotland Avenue
Albany, New York 12208

Telephone: 518-438-3111
Fax: 518-453-1366
E-mail: admissions@mariacollege.edu
World Wide Web: http://www.mariacollege.edu

Students wait in the College courtyard for exam doors to open.

MASSACHUSETTS BAY COMMUNITY COLLEGE

WELLESLEY HILLS, FRAMINGHAM, AND ASHLAND, MASSACHUSETTS

The College and Its Mission

Massachusetts Bay Community College (MassBay) provides a student-centered learning environment in which a diverse student body explores, develops, and achieves educational goals. MassBay is committed to academic excellence and student success. The College is a comprehensive, two-year public institution offering career programs for immediate employability and programs paralleling the first two years of a bachelor's degree. MassBay emphasizes technology and health-care programs and has strong transfer programs in the liberal arts and business. While the majority of the students hail from the Metro West and Boston areas, its reputation has attracted students from throughout the United States and worldwide. It has been serving the academic needs of the community since it was founded in 1961.

The student body at MassBay comprises a diverse group of individuals, all with various goals and educational needs. Some may be working toward an associate degree or certificate program by taking day or evening classes. Others may have plans to transfer to a four-year college or university to continue their education. Still others may have some college experience but want to broaden their professional skills. MassBay's programs are geared to meet the needs of this diverse population, ensuring access to education and flexibility to students by offering a variety of instructional delivery systems, including day and night schedules and online courses.

Each of MassBay's programs of study belongs to one of its specialized Centers of Excellence—the Business, Engineering, Science and Technology Institute (BEST), the Health, Human Services, and Education Institute (HHSEI), and the Liberal Arts Institute (LAI). Whether a student's level of study is undergraduate, professional training, or continuing education, the goal of the Centers of Excellence is to provide students with a seamless learning and training experience. In addition, the Centers of Excellence enable students to easily plan their education to meet their career goals and at a pace that fits their lifestyle. For example, they can decide to complete a degree or certificate program to obtain an entry-level position and then return to the Center for more advanced training as they prepare for the next step of their career ladder. Because MassBay is committed to the success of its students, the Centers of Excellence are designed to provide open and enriching dialogue among faculty members and fellow students in similar programs of study. This allows for students to share experiences, compare similarities in career fields, or mentor each other in a particular project. Through the Centers of Excellence, students experience an innovative way of learning that provides a rewarding college experience and prepares them to excel in meeting the ever-changing demands of today's workforce.

MassBay students perform better than the state average on the registered nurse licensing exam (NCLEX-RN) and the practical nurse licensing exam (NCLEX-PN). All of MassBay's automotive-technician training programs have received Automotive Service Excellence (ASE) MASTER certification, the highest level of achievement recognized by the National Institute for Automotive Service Excellence. MassBay students have received the prestigious and world-recognized Barry M. Goldwater Scholarship Award for mathematics, natural science, or engineering excellence. MassBay students regularly receive several Elizabeth Davis Scholarships from Wellesley College. MassBay's athletic teams routinely contend for state, regional, and national honors and championships.

MassBay is accredited by the New England Association of Schools and Colleges (NEASC), the Council for Accreditation of Allied Health Education Programs (NEASC), the Council for Accreditation for Allied Health Education Programs (CAAHEP), the Joint Review Committee on Education in Radiologic Technology (JRCERT), the National League for Nursing (NLN), Commission on Accreditation in Physical Therapy Education (CAPTE), and the National Automotive Technician Educational Foundation (NATEF).

Academic Programs

MassBay Community College offers two-year professional and liberal arts programs and certificate programs. From automotive technology, business, education, engineering, health, information systems and computer technology, liberal arts, and physical sciences, MassBay students have a wide range of choices. Many of the College's professional programs give students the opportunity to learn not only in the classroom but also in the field, with hands-on experience and state-of-the-art labs simulating the real experiences faced on the job. MassBay's liberal arts program provides the foundation for further learning and career advancement. Certificates can help students enter a new field or advance their current one. MassBay recommends that students work with an adviser in designing their specific course of study and planning for further college study or employment.

Students who complete a MassBay degree program may receive an Associate of Arts or an Associate of Science degree and are fully prepared for further study at four-year institutions for a baccalaureate degree. Students may be eligible for transfer status as a junior to many colleges and universities. Many of these programs also qualify students for immediate employment in their chosen field.

MassBay also participates in the Joint Admissions Program for students to transfer from MassBay to one of the four University of Massachusetts campuses or seven state colleges. The program is open to students who receive an associate degree in an approved major with a 2.5 or higher grade point average. In addition, the Tuition Advantage Plan may help transferring graduates lower their tuition costs.

The associate degree programs offered are accounting, automotive technology, biotechnology, business administration, communication, computer information systems, computer science, criminal justice, early childhood education, electrical and computer engineering, electronics technology, engineering, engineering design, environmental science and occupational safety, forensic science, general business, general studies, hospitality management, human services, information systems technology and management, liberal arts, liberal arts: early childhood education, liberal arts: elementary education, liberal arts: global studies, life sciences, mechanical engineering, nursing, paralegal studies, physical therapist assistant, psychology/sociology/anthropology, and radiologic technology.

The certificate programs offered are accounting, automotive technology, central processing technology, central services and material management, communication, computer-aided design (CAD), CAD with Web option, early childhood education, early childhood education: infant-toddler teacher, emergency medical technician, hospitality management, human services, information technology, interior design, liberal arts, management, medical coding, medical interpreter, medical office administrative assistant, paralegal studies, paramedicine, personal fitness trainer, phlebotomy, practical nursing, surgical technology, and therapeutic massage.

Internships, clinicals, and co-ops play a critical role in the MassBay learning experience. Counselors in the Office of Career Development can assist students in finding internship opportunities that fit into their career paths. Internships are valuable experiences that allow students to gain experience in the field of their interest and develop professional contacts.

Costs

For January 2006, the cost per credit hour for Massachusetts residents was $119. For out-of-state/nonresidents, the cost was $325 per credit hour. Fees for health insurance, student parking, lab, or material costs may be added. Continuing education is $136 per credit hour for Massachusetts residents. For out-of-state/ nonresidents, the cost per credit hour is $325. All evening AD nursing courses are $283 per credit hour plus additional fees. All evening practical nursing courses (CE, PN) are $245 per credit hour plus additional fees. Under the New England Regional Student Program, some New England students may attend MassBay for 150 percent of the in-state tuition rate, which is less than the out-of-state tuition rate.

Financial Aid

Financial assistance is available to all qualified students. Such aid is designed to help students meet basic college expenses. Financial assistance may be in the form of a grant, a scholarship, a loan, work-study employment, or any combination of these. MassBay's resources are obtained from federal, state, local, or private sources. Applicant eligibility and program guidelines are defined by the funding source. Grants and scholarships generally do not need to be paid back to MassBay or the sponsor. Loans can be made to the student or a student's parent and must be paid back. Loans can be need-based or non-need-based depending upon the individual circumstances of the student. A monthly payment plan through Academic Management Services (AMS) is also available.

Faculty

The faculty members at MassBay totaled 336, with 73 full-time and 257 part-time as of November 2005. Many members of the faculty are affiliated with other colleges and universities in the state, providing MassBay students with a valuable resource.

Student Body Profile

The student body at MassBay comprises a diverse group of individuals, all with various goals and educational needs. There are more than 5,000 students enrolled at MassBay. While the majority of students hail from the Metro West and the Boston vicinity, there are many international students as well, representing countries such as Brazil, Haiti, India, Russia, and Uganda. Fifty percent of MassBay students are between 17 and 22 years of age.

Student Activities

The College supports intercollegiate athletic programs, including men's baseball; women's softball; and men's and women's basketball, cross-country, golf, soccer, tennis, and volleyball.

Some other student clubs and organizations offered by MassBay are the Student Senate and Student Government; honor societies, such as Alpha Beta Gamma, the National Business Honor Society, Alpha Kappa Lamda, Psi Beta, Sigma Delta Mus, and Silver Key; the student-run theater group, the MassBay Players; concert/ lecture series; the International and Multicultural Student Development program; and the student newspaper, *The Beacon.*

For students interested in a healthy lifestyle, the Recreation Center, built in 2003, offers a variety of activities, such as exercising, weight training, and pickup basketball.

Facilities and Resources

MassBay provides the College community with resources and facilities that support the academic programs and courses offered, including a Student Development Office; Advising Center, where students can speak with an academic adviser; an Academic Achievement Center that supplements classroom instruction with one-on-one support while accommodating MassBay students' diverse learning styles; the Reading and Writing Centers, which offer one-on-one help in completing a reading or writing assignment for any college course; smart classrooms, used by faculty members and students to enhance the classroom learning experience; a library with more than 49,000 volumes; wireless technologies; and computer labs with more than 400 computers for student use.

Location

MassBay serves students from three convenient locations. The Wellesley Hills Campus is located on Route 9 approximately 10 miles west of Boston. The Framingham Campus is near Routes 9 and 126. The Technology Center in Ashland is approximately 4 miles south of the Framingham Campus off Route 126.

Admission Requirements

MassBay maintains an open-door admissions policy, and there is no application deadline. If students have proof of a GED, high school graduation, or an associate degree or higher, they will be admitted to MassBay on a first-come, first-served basis, provided there is a vacancy in the program to which they have applied.

Application and Information

MassBay enrollment is open to Massachusetts residents at the in-state tuition rate. A Massachusetts resident is currently defined as a U.S. citizen or permanent resident having a minimum of six consecutive months of verifiable domicile in the Commonwealth. Others may attend MassBay at the out-of-state tuition rate.

All applicants must include a non-refundable application fee of $20 with their application. Credit card payment is accepted for the online application. For an application and information, students should contact the Office of Admissions.

Office of Admissions
Massachusetts Bay Community College
50 Oakland Street
Wellesley Hills, Massachusetts 02481
Telephone: 781-239-2500
World Wide Web: http://www.massbay.edu

The MassBay Wellesley Hills campus.

McINTOSH COLLEGE
DOVER, NEW HAMPSHIRE

The College and Its Mission

For the residential or commuting student seeking the intimate personal experience of a small college and the technical training in practical skills needed to compete in today's computer-oriented job market, McIntosh College is the answer. For more than 100 years, McIntosh has provided an exciting variety of business and professional opportunities to recent high school graduates and adults seeking career changes or re-entry into the job market. McIntosh is a two-year degree-granting institution accredited by the New England Association of Schools and Colleges. The College currently enrolls more than 1,000 students at its campus in Dover, New Hampshire.

The mission of the College combines a clearly defined educational philosophy with a profound understanding of the College's role in providing effective business-oriented associate degree and certificate programs in a fully equipped learning facility. This integration allows the College to enhance the quality of personal and professional life of the business and academic communities that it serves.

McIntosh is a career-oriented institution dedicated to the personal, intellectual, and professional growth of its students. The College has a century-long tradition of providing academic programs that integrate the acquisition of job-related skills with the development of clear, critical thinking and effective reasoning. While McIntosh recognizes its obligation to provide the specific skills necessary for the student to function in a contemporary work environment, it operates under the philosophy that a college is more than a training facility. Students must leave the college experience with a sense of competence in their chosen fields, a belief in themselves as individuals, and an enhanced critical awareness of the world around them.

Academic Programs

McIntosh College offers a unique blend of courses and programs of study designed to prepare students for careers in business, hospitality and tourism management, the computer industry, public service, allied health, paralegal studies, and criminal justice. All programs of study provide students with academic credit, which allows them to continue their studies at four-year institutions.

Associate Degree Programs McIntosh College is authorized by the Postsecondary Education Commission of the state of New Hampshire to offer associate degree programs with major areas of concentration in accounting, business management, criminal justice, culinary arts, fashion merchandising, graphic design, medical assisting, medical lab technician, paralegal studies, and professional photography as well as a certificate program in massage therapy.

Honors Programs The McIntosh College Beta Gamma Gamma Chapter of the Phi Theta Kappa Honor Society supports a number of scholarship opportunities and activities for honor students.

Transfer Arrangements McIntosh students can earn an associate degree and an articulated bachelor's degree in one continuous program of study through the uniquely structured McIntosh/Southern New Hampshire University (formerly New

Hampshire College) 2+2 Program or the recent agreement with American Intercontinental University (AIU) located across the world. Academic counseling is available and full support is provided for students wishing to continue their education at other institutions of higher learning.

Internship and Co-op Programs All academic departments supporting degree programs support for-credit internship opportunities for qualified students. The Office of Career Services assists students in finding appropriate internships in accounting, business management, criminal justice, culinary arts, fashion merchandising, graphic design, massage therapy, medical assisting, medical lab technician, paralegal studies, and professional photography.

Credit for Nontraditional Learning Experiences

The College grants credit to students who have passed authorized advanced placement courses in high school with grades of B or better or who present evidence of having received scores of 460 or better on CLEP examinations in subject areas that directly correspond to the content of individual McIntosh courses.

Costs

The 2005–06 annual tuition for a full-time degree candidate was $15,600. Tuition and costs are subject to change.

Financial Aid

The Office of Student Finance provides information and personal counseling with respect to the various federal grant and loan programs and institutional scholarships available to students attending McIntosh College. McIntosh College believes that every student should have access to the financial resources needed to pursue academic or career interests. Pell Grants, Supplemental Educational Opportunity Grants, Federal Work-Study, Stafford Student Loans, Plus Loans, State Incentive Programs, direct loans, scholarships, and family discounts are all available to students attending McIntosh College.

Faculty

There are 48 full-time faculty members at McIntosh College. Of these, 70 percent hold advanced degrees and specialized certifications.

Student Body Profile

McIntosh College attracts students from a wide age spectrum. Because the College offers parallel day and evening programs, there is a substantial mix of recent high school graduates and adult students returning to school. The average age of a McIntosh student is 24, slightly higher at night and slightly lower during the day program. Students are generally career oriented. More than 50 percent of graduates continue their studies at the bachelor's-degree level.

Student Activities

The College supports a variety of social clubs, organizations, and other extracurricular activities designed to enhance and enrich the student's educational experience at McIntosh. The Student Activities Committee provides a forum for students interested in planning and implementing social and cultural events at the College. There is a chapter of Delta Epsilon Chi on campus. Departmental associations include the McIntosh Paralegal Association and the Criminal Justice Association.

Facilities and Resources

In recent years, McIntosh has anticipated changes in the business environment and the need for a newly oriented work force by establishing a superior computer facility consisting of four computer labs housing more than 100 individual and networked stations. An integrated curriculum provides specific computer instruction related to each major field of study. In addition, McIntosh students can roam the Internet, explore online services such as WestLaw, or browse through an extensive CD-ROM collection in the McIntosh academic and paralegal library facilities. A fully equipped medical lab and a real-world operative teaching kitchen provide hands-on working environments for medical assisting and culinary arts majors. At McIntosh, emphasis is placed on the practical aspects of career development. Internships are available in all departments.

On-campus student housing facilities at McIntosh College have been carefully designed to provide a warm, supportive living and learning environment that serves to nurture students' personal development and to enhance their opportunities for academic and professional success. The residential facility includes spacious furnished living units that are cable-ready and have air-conditioning, a full bath, and access to a computer lab. Residential students may choose from a variety of meal plans. Initial inquiries about eligibility requirements and the availability of on-campus housing should be directed to the Office of Admissions. Room assignments are made on a first-come, first-served basis, depending on eligibility.

Advisement/Counseling The faculty and administration of the College are committed to the principle that students should be given every possible opportunity to achieve academic and professional success. For this reason, the College offers extensive academic and career counseling to its students. Free study skills workshops are regularly available. In addition, the College provides free tutorial assistance in accounting, computer applications, English, and math.

Office of Career Services The College provides free career counseling and placement referral services to its students and graduates through the Office of Career Services. Workshops on resume writing are frequently offered to currently enrolled students.

Location

McIntosh College consists of several separate facilities situated next to the Spaulding Turnpike in Dover, New Hampshire. Dover is a city of about 26,000, located in the Seacoast area of New Hampshire about one hour north of Boston. The College is conveniently located just a short drive from coastal beaches and world-class skiing. The academic center is located on a 13-acre tract of land on Cataract Avenue.

Admission Requirements

A high school diploma or its equivalent (GED) is required of all students accepted for admission at McIntosh College with matriculated student status. Students can apply and can be admitted at any time during the year. A student attending a full-time degree program can expect to graduate in eighteen or twenty-four months.

Application and Information

Applications for admission are accepted on an ongoing basis. Most students may begin classes at the start of any term scheduled throughout the year. For application materials, students should contact:

Office of Admissions
McIntosh College
23 Cataract Avenue
Dover, New Hampshire 03820

Telephone: 800-262-1111 (toll-free)
Fax: 603-742-0060
E-mail: admissions@mcintoshcollege.com
World Wide Web: http://www.mcintoshcollege.edu

McIntosh has small-school charm with students' careers in mind.

MIAMI DADE COLLEGE

MIAMI, FLORIDA

The College and Its Mission

Miami Dade College (MDC) is recognized as one of the most outstanding community colleges in the nation. With more than 163,000 students, it is also the largest institution of higher learning in America. At Miami Dade, student success is the priority. The mission of the College is to provide accessible, affordable, high-quality education that keeps the learner's needs at the center of the decision-making process. The College is accredited by the Southern Association of Colleges and Schools and offers undergraduate study in more than 200 areas and professions.

Academic Programs

The College offers more than 200 undergraduate areas of study. An Associate in Arts (A.A.) prepares students to transfer to upper-division colleges and universities. An Associate in Science (A.S.) degree is designed for students seeking immediate job placement after graduation. In addition, the College offers bachelor's degree programs leading to teacher certification in exceptional student education (K–12), secondary mathematics (6–12), and secondary science (6–12). As of fall 2006, the College plans to offer a Bachelor of Applied Science degree in public safety management, to be housed at the School of Justice; the program provides ten areas of specialization, including the option to obtain law enforcement certification.

The A.A. degree, offered for students planning to transfer to a university, can be earned in 60 credits, including 36 credits of required general education and 24 credits of electives. The state of Florida has developed a set of common program prerequisites for each program to facilitate student transfer. A variety of A.S. and Associate in Applied Science (A.A.S.) degrees, college credit certificate programs, vocational credit certificate programs, and supplemental courses are offered to prepare students to enter the job market or upgrade skills. These programs vary in length. The A.S. degree includes 15 credits of general education requirements. Several A.S. and A.A.S. degree programs include courses that have matriculation agreements for transfer to one or more universities; others offer advanced certificate training. The Medical Center Campus offers a wide range of allied health and nursing programs, with clinicals in major local hospitals and health-care centers. Courses are offered year-round in two major terms of sixteen weeks each and summer terms consisting of two 6-week terms or one 12-week term.

The following A.S. degree programs, which prepare students for employment and may transfer to a four-year institution, are available: accounting technology; air-conditioning, refrigeration, and heating; architectural design and construction technology; automotive service management technology; aviation administration; aviation maintenance management; biomedical engineering technology; building construction technology; business administration; civil engineering technology; computer engineering technology; computer information technology; computer programming and analysis; court reporting technology; criminal justice technology; dietetic technician studies; drafting and design technology; electronics engineering technology; environmental science technology; film production technology; financial services; fire science technology; funeral services; graphic arts technology; graphic design technology; graphic Internet technology; hospitality and tourism management; human services; industrial management technology; interior design technology; Internet services technology; landscape technology; legal assisting; marketing management; music business; networking services technology; office systems technology; photographic technology; professional pilot technology; radio and television broadcast programming; sign language interpretation; telecommunications engineering; theater and entertainment technology; translation/interpretation: English/Spanish track; and travel industry management.

Allied health A.S. degree programs offered at the Medical Center Campus include dental hygiene, diagnostic medical sonography technology, emergency medical services, health information management, histologic technology, medical laboratory technology, midwifery, nuclear medicine technology, nursing-RN, opticianry,

physical therapist assistant and physician assistant studies, radiation therapy technology, respiratory care, and veterinary technology. In addition, an A.A.S. degree is offered in radiography.

College credit certificates are offered in accounting applications, air cargo agent, airline reservation and ticketing agent studies, airline/aviation management, business management, Cisco network associate studies, computer specialist studies, computer programming, computer-aided design assistant or operator studies, embalming, emergency medical technician studies, information technology support, interpretation studies: English/Spanish, marketing operations, microcomputer repairer/installer studies, Microsoft database administrator studies, Microsoft solutions developer studies, mortgage finance, network systems developer studies, nuclear medicine technology specialist studies, office systems specialist studies, Oracle database administrator or database developer studies, passenger service agent studies, paramedic studies, translation studies: English/Spanish, and Web development specialist studies. An Applied Technology Diploma is offered in emergency medical technician studies.

Distance Education Through the Virtual College, high-quality online academic and vocational programs are offered to meet the needs of nontraditional and out-of-area students as well as students who find it difficult to attend classes during scheduled hours and at specific locations. The array of instructional activities in the Web courses is designed to engage students in interactive and collaborative learning and cover the established competencies.

The Honors College Miami Dade's Honors College provides a rigorous and comprehensive curriculum, seminars, and enrichment activities in a scholarly and supportive environment where goal-oriented, academically gifted students explore new ideas and engage in inspired creativity and intellectual collaborations with experienced faculty members. Honors College graduates continue their studies at some of the nation's finest schools, including Columbia, Georgetown, Harvard, Smith, Yale, and the Universities of Indiana, Michigan, Texas, and Wisconsin.

Transfer Arrangements A statewide matriculation agreement among all Florida institutions of higher education facilitates transfers and ensures that a student who is awarded the Associate in Arts degree at Miami Dade College has met general education requirements for admission to the upper division in public and private colleges and universities. In all, MDC has established matriculation agreements with fifty-eight prestigious colleges and universities.

Certificate Programs Vocational credit certificates are offered in academy of international marketing, accounting operations, administrative assistant studies, architectural drafting, bail bonding, business computer programming, business supervision and management, commercial art technology, community service officer/police service aide studies, correctional officer and correctional probation officer studies, customer assistance, early childhood education, electronic technology, fire fighting, insurance marketing, law enforcement officer studies, legal secretary studies, massage therapy, mechanical drafting, medical assisting, medical coder/biller studies, medical record transcribing, medical secretary studies, network support services, PC support services, pharmacy technician studies, phlebotomy, practical nursing, private security officer studies, public safety telecommunications, real estate marketing, television production, teller operations, and travel and tourism. Applied Technology Diplomas are offered in medical coder/biller and medical record transcribing.

Internship and Co-op Programs These programs provide an opportunity for students to obtain career-related work experience (paid or voluntary) while earning academic credit.

Special Programs and Services New World School of the Arts (NWSA) is a unique educational partnership of Miami-Dade County Public Schools, Miami Dade College, and the University of Florida. Through its sponsoring institutions, NWSA awards high school diplomas, A.A. degrees, and Bachelor of Music and Bachelor of Fine

Arts degrees. Students are admitted through audition or portfolio presentation. Other special programs include academic remediation for entering students, English as a second language, services for disabled students (including learning disabled), study abroad, and advanced placement.

The College is a leader in working proactively to assist students with disabilities. Each campus has a ground floor ACCESS office to provide the guidance and technological accommodations required. Computers equipped with voice synthesizer programs are available, as are note-takers to help the physically challenged students.

Continuing Education Unit Certificate Programs Miami Dade College provides students the opportunity to obtain Continuing Education Units (CEUs) for certain courses. Transcripts designating CEUs are provided.

Personal Enrichment/Noncredit Courses A wide array of noncredit courses and programs are offered both on and off campus.

Off-Campus Programs

Study-abroad programs, both short-term and full semester, are available in many countries. Internships and clinicals may be scheduled off campus.

Credit for Nontraditional Learning Experiences

The College may award credit for demonstrated proficiency in areas related to college-level courses. Sources used to determine such proficiency are the College-Level Examination Program, the Advanced Placement Program, the Proficiency Examination Program, the International Baccalaureate Program, Dual Enrollment, Tech Prep Matriculation, the Defense Activity for Nontraditional Education Support, the United States Armed Forces Institute, the Institutional Credit by Exam, and the internal MDC procedures for awarding credit related to specific programs for approval licensures.

Costs

For the 2005–06 academic year, tuition was $64.05 per college credit for Florida residents; it was $219.95 per college credit for nonresidents. Textbooks and supplies for full-time students were estimated at $1500. Although housing is not available on campus, there are numerous housing options near the College at varying costs.

Financial Aid

Financial aid that a student receives is determined through federal, state, and institutional guidelines and is offered to students in packages that may consist of grants, loans, employment, and scholarships. It is based upon financial need. The College also offers merit-based aid to qualified students as funds are available. Assistance includes Federal Pell Grants, Federal Supplemental Educational Opportunity Grants, the Florida Student Assistance Grant, the Florida Bright Futures Scholarship, the Federal Work-Study Program, the Florida Work Experience Program (FWEP), Federal Perkins Loans, Federal Family Education Loan Programs, and Federal PLUS Loans. The College also offers Foundation and Institutional Grants, scholarships, short-term tuition loans, and employment to students as well as funding for the purchase of special equipment for disabled students. About 45 percent of the student body receives some form of financial aid. In 2005, 36,000 students received Pell Grants.

Faculty

There are 722 full-time faculty members and 1,976 part-time faculty members. Of the full-time faculty members, 93 percent hold advanced degrees.

Student Body Profile

Of the 163,000 credit and noncredit students enrolled at Miami Dade College, almost 1,800 are international students. Seventy-three percent of students with an A.A. degree continue their education at a four-year college. Of the upper-division students in the Florida State University System, 15 percent started college at MDC. The average age of students is 27, although about 30 percent of MDC-credit students are the "traditional" college age of 18–20 years old. Almost 66 percent attend on a part-time basis, and 62 percent are women. The student body is ethnically and culturally diverse. MDC enrolls and graduates more Hispanic students than any other college or university and is second in African-American enrollment in the United States.

Student Activities

More than 100 organizations offer opportunities to participate in student government, student publications, music ensembles, drama productions (in English and Spanish), religious activities, service and political clubs, national and local fraternities and sororities, professional organizations, and honor societies.

Intercollegiate and intramural athletics play an important role at Miami Dade College, which is a member of NJCAA and competes at the Division I level. Intercollegiate teams include women's basketball, softball, and volleyball and men's baseball and basketball. Sports facilities include racquetball, tennis, and handball courts; wellness centers; swimming pools; and a track.

Facilities and Resources

Career Planning/Placement Offices Trained staff members assist students in selecting courses and programs of study to satisfy their educational objectives. Each campus has a career center where students may obtain career counseling and vocational interest testing. The campus Job Placement Centers provide part-time or full-time job referral services to actively enrolled students or graduates. The centers also prepare students for resume writing and successful job search. Career Fairs bring employers to the campuses.

Library and Audiovisual Services The campus libraries have a combined book collection of more than 342,000 titles and more than 17,000 periodicals. There are approximately 25,000 audiovisual materials, and online databases are available. Computers for student use are available in computer labs, learning resource centers, labs, classrooms, and the library.

Location

Blessed with a sunny, subtropical climate, beautiful beaches, and an international flavor, Miami offers a rich variety of exciting cultural, sporting, and intellectual activities. Opportunities abound to explore unique settings, such as the historic Art Deco District of Miami Beach and Miami's colorful Little Havana or the nearby Everglades National Park. Eight campuses and numerous outreach centers are located throughout the Greater Miami area. **North Campus** is located on a 245-acre, fully landscaped site, and its buildings are clustered around a beautiful lake. **Kendall Campus** is situated 23 miles southwest of the North Campus on a 185-acre site. Focal points of the campus' award-winning landscape designs are the lakes and lush tropical growth. **Wolfson Campus** is located in the heart of downtown Miami's business community and has two award-winning buildings. **Medical Center Campus** is located in Miami's medical/civic center complex. **Homestead Campus** is located on an 8-acre site in the historic business district of Homestead. **InterAmerican Campus** is located in the heart of Little Havana. **Hialeah Campus** is centrally located in the growing city of Hialeah. **West Campus** is located in the western suburb of Doral. Off-campus commuter sites are located in the major suburbs.

Admission Requirements

Miami Dade has an open-door admission policy. The College provides educational opportunities to all high school graduates, including those who have a state high school equivalency diploma, and to transfer students from other colleges and universities. In addition to the College's application and the $20 application fee, students must have official transcripts from high school, college, university, or other postsecondary educational institutions sent directly to the Office of Admissions from the institutions. High school equivalency diploma or certificate holders must provide the original document and score report (which are returned) or an exact copy of the documents. Florida residents must complete a Florida residency statement. SAT, ACT, or TOEFL test scores should be sent directly to the Office of Admissions by the testing board. Students not presenting test scores are tested for placement purposes upon acceptance.

Application and Information

Applications are accepted on an ongoing basis. All prospective students should contact:

District Office of Admissions and Registration Services
Miami Dade College
300 N.E. Second Avenue
Miami, Florida 33132
Telephone: 305-237-8888
Fax: 305-237-2964
World Wide Web: http://www.mdc.edu

MIDDLESEX COUNTY COLLEGE

EDISON, NEW JERSEY

The College and Its Mission

More students are choosing community colleges for their educational needs than ever before. Middlesex County College, with its diverse programs and specialized services, is the college of choice for more than 13,000 students in 2005–06. More students than ever are enrolled in full-time degree programs and are preparing to transfer as juniors to four-year colleges and universities.

Middlesex County College is one of the largest and among the oldest county colleges in New Jersey. The College, a two-year publicly supported coeducational institution, is committed to serving all those who can benefit from postsecondary learning, and the student body reflects this belief. More than 550 courses are offered during the day, evening, and on weekends. Students have the opportunity to prepare academically and through cooperative work placements, clinical experience, and laboratory work for careers in business, health, social science, and science technologies.

Middlesex County College offers modern, well-equipped facilities located on a beautiful 200-acre campus, together with excellent learning resources and dedicated faculty members. Most students commute to the College from Middlesex County. Each year, more and more students from outside the United States enroll as international students. All students have the opportunity to add to their collegiate experience through participation in a variety of student activities and clubs. The College has a recreational facility with a 25-meter pool, dance studio, wrestling and weight rooms, and racquetball courts. The College philosophy is directed toward assisting each individual in reaching his or her maximum potential, and counselors work with students to ensure this goal.

Academic Programs

More than seventy different degree and certificate programs, either transfer or career oriented, may be taken full-time or part-time during the day, evening, and on weekends. Courses are offered during the fall and spring semesters, a January winter session, and summer sessions. The College offers **Associate in Arts (A.A.)** and **Associate in Science (A.S.)** degree programs designed specifically to transfer to four-year colleges and universities in the fields of arts, business education, engineering, and sciences. Students interested in preparing for careers in medicine or law begin their studies at Middlesex County College with courses in science and liberal arts.

Middlesex offers formal credit articulation transfer agreements and/or dual-degree admissions programs with more than 50 four-year institutions, including Rutgers, Montclair State, Kean, and NYU. It has always been the largest "feeder" school to the New Jersey Institute of Technology (NJIT), where its graduates are continually recognized for their outstanding academic achievements.

Students who complete the requirements of a transfer curriculum earn an associate degree and are accepted into the receiving college or university as members of the junior class. Working closely with their faculty and advisers assures this seamless transition, and students find that the cost of their undergraduate education is substantially lower because of their work at Middlesex.

Many challenging programs and options designed to prepare students for entry into the job market are available in business education, engineering technologies, health technologies, and science. Graduates of career programs receive an **Associate in Applied Science (A.A.S.)** degree. Many graduates holding the A.A.S. degree transfer to four-year colleges, which may accept all or part of the credits earned at Middlesex. Certificate programs are also available.

In addition to associate degree and certificate curricula, the College offers students the opportunity to enroll in a plan of study through the Open College Program. Open College serves students who want to try out an individualized academic program prior to formally enrolling in a specific degree or certificate program. The College offers Project Connections, a nationally recognized program for students with learning disabilities. Students interested in military education may participate in the Army or Air Force ROTC program through cross-registration at Rutgers University.

Degree and certificate programs are offered in accounting, biology transfer program, biotechnology, business administration, business software applications, chemical technology, chemistry transfer program, civil construction engineering technology, computer-aided drafting, computer and information systems, computer programming, computer science transfer program, criminal justice, culinary arts certificate, dental hygiene, dietetic technology, education practitioner, electronic and computer engineering technology, energy utility technology, engineering science, English as a second language, environmental technology, fashion merchandising, fine arts (options in art, music, and theater), fire science technology, graphics for digital media, health science, help desk administration, hotel restaurant and institution management, information systems security, land surveying technology, liberal arts (options in business, communications, dance, English, general, health and physical education, history, journalism, media arts and design, modern languages, music, political science, psychology, sociology, social rehabilitation services, social science, theater, visual arts, and writing), management, marketing, mathematics transfer program, mechanical manufacturing technology, medical laboratory technology, nursing, paralegal studies, pharmacy assistant, physics transfer program, psychosocial rehabilitation and treatment, radiography education, respiratory care, small business management, and teacher aide.

Off-Campus Programs

In addition to the main campus in Edison, Middlesex offers outreach centers in New Brunswick and Perth Amboy. Both centers offer credit-level classes as well as classes in English as a second language. Credit and noncredit courses are also offered at selected locations throughout the county.

Credit for Nontraditional Learning Experiences

There are several programs at the College through which applicants may earn credit for knowledge learned in nontraditional ways. Both Credit by Examination and the College-Level Examination Program (CLEP) are available.

Costs

Tuition for the summer 2006 semester is $81.55 per credit for a Middlesex County resident and $163.10 per credit for an out-of-county resident. There is a $13.50-per-credit general service fee, a $3.50-per-credit student service fee and an $8.50-per-credit technology fee for Middlesex residents. The fees for out-of-county residents are $27 per credit for general service, $7 per credit for student service and $17 per credit for technology. There are also mandatory accident and health insurance fees. Some classes require special laboratory, material, or other fees.

Financial Aid

Through its financial aid programs, Middlesex County College makes every effort to overcome economic barriers. Funds from federal, state, and private sources are available to those who have need and meet the eligibility requirements. To be considered for financial aid, a student must complete the Free Application for Federal Student Aid (FAFSA) and the Middlesex County College Financial Aid Form. The priority deadline for the fall semester is April 1 and November 1 for the spring semester. Before a financial aid application can be reviewed, the student must be accepted to a degree program and be matriculated for a minimum of 6 credits.

Students who graduate from a New Jersey high school and finish in the top 20 percent of their graduating class may qualify for the NJSTARS free tuition program. Students must also apply for federal financial aid, be a U.S. citizen or permanent resident, be admitted to a degree program, and register for at least 12 college-level credits to be eligible for the program. NJSTARS II allows NJSTARS students who maintain eligibility and graduate with an associate degree and a minimum 3.0 grade point average to attend a public New Jersey college or university with tuition and fees covered.

Faculty

There are 200 full-time and 500 part-time members of the faculty. The student-faculty ratio is 21:1. Of the full-time faculty members, nearly 90 percent are teaching faculty members and serve as academic advisers. Middlesex faculty members have impressive resumes, outstanding accomplishments, and degrees from some of the country's finest colleges and universities. Many bring to the classroom years of workplace experience in their field. However, most important is the faculty's commitment to help students reach their potential and gain the confidence to achieve their life goals.

Student Body Profile

There are about 13,000 students on campus, about half are full-time. The campus population is diverse, with students from more than sixty countries in attendance. Approximately half of the students come directly from high school, with an average age of 24 for the entire student body.

Student Activities

There are more than sixty chartered clubs and organizations, a College Center Program Board, College Assembly, national honor societies, special minority student activities, and a College newspaper, radio station, and literary magazine. The College offers intercollegiate competition through membership in Region XIX of the National Junior College Athletic Association and the Garden State Athletic Conference.

Facilities and Resources

The campus features twenty-five buildings, including a state-of-the-art Technical Services Center, a fully equipped Recreation Center, and a 440-seat Performing Arts Center. The Counseling and Career Services Center provides students with assistance in making decisions about career choices, education programs, college transfer, job placement, and other personal concerns. Bilingual counseling is available to Spanish-speaking students.

Location

The College is located just 15 minutes from New Brunswick, New Jersey. The College is conveniently located near numerous restaurants and shopping centers. The New Jersey shore is less than 30 minutes away. Mass transit to the College is available from many surrounding areas.

Admission Requirements

The admission policy is based on the premise that the College should provide an opportunity for further education to all citizens of the community. Enrollment is open to anyone who holds a high school diploma or any non–high school graduates 18 years of age or older who can demonstrate an ability to benefit from a college education. SAT scores are optional. Applicants to most programs are not required to submit any standardized test scores.

Admission to programs that specify additional selective criteria may require a review of prior educational performance, standardized test scores, the completion of an appropriate developmental program, or, when suitable, an assessment of an applicant's aptitude and interest, as determined during an admission counseling interview.

Application and Information

Completed applications are reviewed on a continuous basis, with the exception of the limited-seat programs in dental hygiene, medical laboratory technology, nursing, psychosocial rehabilitation, radiography education, and respiratory care. Automotive technology is offered every other year. A completed application form, a required $25 nonrefundable application fee, and all supporting materials should be sent to the Office of Admissions.

For further information or to schedule a campus visit, students should contact:

Office of Admissions
Middlesex County College
2600 Woodbridge Avenue, P.O. Box 3050
Edison, New Jersey 08818-3050
Telephone: 732-906-4243
    888-YOU-4MCC (toll-free)
Fax: 732-906-7728
E-mail: admissions@middlesexcc.edu
World Wide Web: http://www.middlesexcc.edu

MOHAWK VALLEY COMMUNITY COLLEGE

UTICA AND ROME, NEW YORK

The College and Its Mission

Mohawk Valley Community College (MVCC) offers choice, opportunity, and hope by providing accessible and affordable higher education, training, and services that emphasize academic excellence, diversity, and a global view.

Mohawk Valley Community College strives to be a college of choice through innovative educational leadership, programs, and services that address the current and future needs of rapidly changing local, regional, and global communities.

The College was founded in 1946 as the New York State Institute of Applied Arts and Sciences at Utica. One of five postsecondary institutions established on an experimental basis after World War II, the public institute offered programs leading to technical and semiprofessional employment in business and industry. After name changes in the 1950s, redefining its mission, the College moved to its current 80-acre campus location in Utica in 1960. In 1961, the College was renamed Mohawk Valley Community College. Today, the College offers a full range of academic programs.

The College is accredited by the Middle States Association of Colleges and Schools. Individual program accreditations are as follows: civil, electrical, and mechanical engineering technology and surveying technology by the Commission for Technology Accreditation of the Accreditation Board for Engineering and Technology, Inc. (ABET); nursing by the National League for Nursing Accrediting Commission (NLNAC); and respiratory care and health information technology–medical records by the Commission on Accreditation of Allied Health Education Programs, in cooperation with the Committee on Accreditation for Respiratory Care and the American Health Information Management Association's Council on Accreditation, respectively.

Academic Programs

The College has been authorized to offer the following degrees and certificates: Associate in Arts (A.A.) degree, Associate in Science (A.S.) degree, Associate in Applied Science (A.A.S.) degree, Associate in Occupational Studies (A.O.S.) degree, and the MVCC Certificate.

The structure and goals of academic programming at MVCC have two main purposes. Certificate, A.O.S., and A.A.S. programs emphasize the development of employable skills through a combination of classroom and laboratory instruction. Some programs also include internship experiences. A.A. and A.S. programs provide students with the liberal arts, science, mathematics, business, engineering, or computer course work necessary for transfer into the junior year of a preprofessional program at a four-year public or private college or university upon the completion of their associate degree.

The minimum number of credits needed to earn an associate degree is 62. The maximum credits required for a degree differ by program and degree type.

Opportunities for specialization include the honors program, independent study, internships, study abroad, and ROTC (Army).

The College operates on a semester calendar. Fall classes begin before Labor Day and end before Christmas. Spring classes begin in mid-January and end in mid-May.

Career and transfer programs are available. Majors offered include accounting (A.A.S.); air conditioning technology (A.O.S.); building management and maintenance (A.A.S.); business administration (A.S.); business management (A.A.S.); chemical dependency practitioner studies (A.A.S.); civil engineering technology (A.A.S.); computer-aided drafting (A.O.S.); computer information systems (A.A.S.); computer science (A.S.); criminal justice (A.A.S.); culinary arts management (A.O.S.), also with baking and pastry emphasis; digital animation (A.A.S.); electrical engineering technology (A.A.S.); electrical service technician studies (A.O.S.), with options in electrical maintenance, fiber optics, and robotics; emergency medical services/paramedic studies (A.A.S.); engineering science (A.S.); environmental analysis–chemical technology (A.A.S.); financial services management (A.A.S.); fine arts (A.S.); general studies (A.S.); general studies–childhood education (A.S., joint admission with the State University of New York (SUNY) College at Oneonta); graphic arts technology (A.A.S.); graphic design (A.A.S.); health information technology–medical records (A.A.S.); hotel technology–meeting services (A.A.S.); human services (A.A.S.); illustration (A.A.S.); individual studies (A.A., A.A.S., A.S., and A.O.S.); international studies (A.A.); liberal arts–adolescence education (teacher transfer) (A.S.); liberal arts–childhood education (teacher transfer) (A.S.); liberal arts–humanities and social science (A.A.); liberal arts–psychology (A.S.); liberal arts–public policy (A.S.); liberal arts–theater (A.A.); manufacturing technology (A.O.S.); mathematics (A.S.); mechanical engineering technology (A.A.S.); mechanical technology–aircraft maintenance (A.A.S.); media marketing and management (A.A.S.); medical assisting (A.A.S.); nursing (A.A.S.); nutrition and dietetics (A.S.); office technologies (A.A.S.); photography (A.A.S.); pre–environmental science (A.S.); programming and systems (A.A.S.); radiologic technology (A.S.); recreation and leisure services (A.A.S.); respiratory care (A.A.S.); restaurant management (A.A.S.); science (A.S.), with emphasis areas in biology, chemistry, physical education, physics, and sports medicine; semiconductor manufacturing technology (A.A.S.); surveying technology (A.A.S.); telecommunications technology (A.A.S.); Web site design and management (A.A.S.); and welding technology (A.O.S.).

Certificate programs include appliance repair, refrigeration, and air conditioning; architectural drafting; carpentry and masonry; chef training; clinical lab assistant studies; CNC machinist technology; coaching; electronic technician studies; engineering drawing; English as a second language; finance; forensic photography; graphic communication; heating and air conditioning; individual studies: business and industry; industrial and commercial electricity; industrial engineering technician studies; insurance; machinist technology; managerial accounting; mechanical drafting; media marketing and management; medical assistant studies; metallurgy lab technician studies; office practices; phlebotomy; photography; production planning; refrigeration; small-business management; supervisory management; surveying; tool design; transportation management; Web site design and management; and welding.

A jointly registered degree program with SUNY College at Oneonta offers applicants the opportunity to complete a bachelor's degree in childhood education (grades 1–6) at MVCC.

Credit for Nontraditional Learning Experiences

MVCC offers adult students the opportunity to earn credits through the CLEP examination, MVCC-administered examinations, life experience, and course work completed in a noncollegiate setting. The accumulated credit earned cannot exceed 75 percent of the student's degree program.

Costs

Tuition for New York State residents is $1475 per semester for full-time students and $115 per credit hour for part-time students; for out-of-state and international students, it is $2950 per semester for full-time students and $250 per credit hour for part-time students. Student fees are $65 per semester for full-time students and $1 per credit hour for part-time students. Books and supplies range from $300 to $500 per semester, depending on the student's major. Residence hall occupants must purchase one of the available room and board packages each semester. Costs are approximately $3300 per semester, depending on type of accommodations and number of meals chosen. The residence hall technology fee is $100 per semester for Internet and phone access. The residence hall social fee is $10 per semester. The residence hall orientation fee is $40 and covers new-resident orientation programming and meals.

Financial Aid

One of MVCC's major objectives is to make college affordable for all. Approximately 90 percent of MVCC students receive some form of state or federal financial aid. The College offers a comprehensive financial assistance program of scholarships, loans, and grants. Most of the financial assistance received by MVCC students is need based. Non-need-based scholarships include the Presidential Scholarship Program for the top 10 percent of Oneida County (the College's sponsoring county) graduates, two similar Exceptional Student Scholarships for those not from Oneida County, and the Sodexho/MVCC Meal Plan Scholarships, which consider exceptional citizenship. Students eligible for non-need-based scholarships are expected to apply for state and federal financial assistance as applicable.

Faculty

The full-time faculty numbers 149, and the part-time faculty numbers 130. Approximately 8 percent of all faculty members have doctoral degrees. The student-faculty ratio is approximately 21:1.

Student Body Profile

MVCC enrolls approximately 5,300 students each year. Enrollment is divided between the main campus in Utica, New York, and the branch campus in Rome, New York, with approximately 80 percent of the student population enrolled on the main campus.

The College is designed to be predominantly commuter based; 85 percent of the students live within 60 miles of the campus in central New York State. For fall 2005, the College plans to add a fifth residence hall on the main campus in Utica, increasing housing capacity to 500 students. The residence life staff provides listings of off-campus apartment-style housing options.

The international student population is currently 90 students. Nineteen different countries are represented on campus.

The average age of students is about 22, with approximately 35 percent of the population being over the age of 25. Approximately 52 percent of the enrolled students are women. The racial/ethnic makeup of the campus is currently 80 percent white, non-Hispanic; 7 percent black, non-Hispanic; 1 percent American Indian/Alaskan native; 1 percent Asian/Pacific Islander; and 3 percent Hispanic. Of the total student body, 8 percent chose not to identify with any of the listed groups.

Enrolling students typically exhibit an 80 percent grade average in high school and a rank in the top 50 percent of their high school class.

Student Activities

The Student Activities program offers a wide variety of experiences for students through clubs, Student Congress, and other activities. On each campus, the staff assists students with the planning of events and programs. There are seventeen professional, curriculum-related clubs. In addition, there are thirty service/interest clubs that provide students with the opportunity to participate in a wide range of social, cultural, theatrical, athletic, and international activities to broaden their experiences.

MVCC participates in Division III of the National Junior College Athletic Association. Men's teams include baseball, basketball, bowling, cross-country, golf, ice hockey, indoor track, lacrosse, tennis, track and field, and soccer. Women's teams include basketball, bowling, cross-country, golf, indoor track, softball, soccer, tennis, track and field, and volleyball. In 2005–06, MVCC's women's cross-country team was crowned National Champions in Division III of the NJCAA. In addition, the College's men's cross-country and women's basketball programs achieved National Runner-up status.

Facilities and Resources

MVCC has completed renovations as part of a $21-million campus master plan. The renovations have included practice lab facilities for nursing and respiratory-care students, cadaver labs for anatomy and physiology, and a student service center in Payne Hall that includes admissions, financial aid, the registrar, counseling, the business office, an advisement center, and a help desk. Renovations to the Alumni College Center provided an expanded bookstore and a student health center. In fall 2005, a new 155-bed residence hall was opened for student occupancy.

The 65,000-square-foot information technology and performing arts conference center, the central feature of the renovations, houses computer labs, conferencing facilities, a state-of-the-art theater, and additional instructional computer support laboratories. It is a focal point of campus activities.

The campus collection includes 94,500 books and more than 727 periodical titles. CDs, audiotapes, DVDs, and videotapes are available for loan. Each campus library has a bestseller collection for recreational reading. The main campus library in Utica maintains a Career Center for job-search assistance. Each library provides a number of electronic resources, including Internet access.

Academic tutoring is available at no cost to students in the Learning Centers on both campuses. The centers offer instructional support in mathematics, writing, reading, study skills, life sciences, and computer and social sciences.

Location

The main campus is in Utica, New York, a small city of 50,000 people. The branch campus in Rome, New York, is located in a community of 30,000 people. The small-city atmosphere, coupled with a wide range of cultural activities, museums, access to the Adirondack Mountains, good public transportation, and sports venues, provides an excellent location for student growth and development.

Admission Requirements

The College is an open-admission, full-opportunity college. The College does not require applicants to complete standardized admissions tests such as the ACT or SAT.

Application and Information

Students can apply in a variety of ways. MVCC provides its own admission application; no processing fee is required. It is available from the Admissions Office or high schools in New York State, or it can be printed out from the College's Web site. MVCC also participates in the SUNY application process. Students can use the SUNY application, which costs $40 per college choice, as well.

For further information, interested students should contact:

Admissions Office
Mohawk Valley Community College
1101 Sherman Drive
Utica, New York 13501
Telephone: 315-792-5354
Fax: 315-792-5527
E-mail: admissions@mvcc.edu (U.S.)
        international_admissions@mvcc.edu (international)
World Wide Web: http://www.mvcc.edu

MORRISON INSTITUTE OF TECHNOLOGY

MORRISON, ILLINOIS

The Institute and Its Mission

Morrison Institute of Technology is an independent, coeducational, not-for-profit, two-year college specializing in engineering technology. Founded in 1973, the college provides a cost-effective educational program that leads to a professional career in engineering technology. While many graduates go directly into industry, some transfer to four-year colleges offering a continuation of studies in the engineering technology fields.

All classes are day classes offered at the campus in Morrison, Illinois. Courses are offered on a semester basis, with semesters starting in January and August.

Morrison has an open admissions policy. Anyone with a valid high school diploma or equivalent may enroll. It has been found from experience that some students who have had an otherwise undistinguished high school career often thrive and blossom when challenged by a college program that specializes in the area in which they are interested. Many students who have found their niche at Morrison have gone on to earn advanced technical degrees and some have even founded thriving technical businesses.

The college is authorized to operate and grant degrees in the state of Illinois under the applicable state statutes administered by the Illinois Board of Higher Education. The Engineering Technology program is accredited by the Technology Accreditation Commission (TAC) of the Accreditation Board for Engineering and Technology (ABET), 111 Market Place, Suite 1050, Baltimore, Maryland 21201; telephone: 410-347-7700. In addition, the drafting design program at Morrison Institute of Technology is certified by the American Drafting Design Association, P.O. Box 11937, Columbia, South Carolina 29211 (telephone: 803-771-0008), at the design/drafter level. The college is also fully accredited by the Council on Occupational Education, 41 Perimeter Center, NE Suite 640, Atlanta, Georgia 30346; telephone: 800-917-2081 (toll-free). The state of Illinois, Department of Veterans Affairs, State Approving Agency, has approved Morrison Institute of Technology for veteran's training under Chapter 36 of Title #38, U.S. Code. The Division of Rehabilitation Services (DORS) and the Job Training Partnership Act (JTPA) both refer clients to the college for training. The college is listed in the Educational Directory, U.S. Department of Education, as a legally authorized institution of higher learning, allowing qualified students to participate in a number of federally funded student financial aid and grant programs. The college is also a member of the Service Members Opportunity Colleges (SOC), thus extending educational opportunities to service personnel while on active duty. The college is also a member of the Better Business Bureau.

Student housing facilities are available on campus in Odey Residence Hall. This facility has been designed to provide housing for students in an efficiency apartment arrangement. The residence hall is coeducational, but individual rooms are not coeducational and accommodations for married couples are not available.

Academic Programs

The engineering technology program has been developed and is kept current in accordance with suggested guidelines provided by nationally recognized technical education groups, accrediting organizations, and the college Industrial Advisory Board.

The curriculum for the engineering technology program has been designed with an appropriate balance of study in the areas of engineering and construction technology and manual drafting. In addition, to ensure that a student is prepared to assume a productive and contributing role as a citizen locally, nationally, and worldwide, a core of general education courses, including basic sciences, humanities, written and oral communications, mathematics, and computer literacy, are required to provide that academic foundation which the student must acquire to continue a lifelong learning process on a formal or informal basis. Extensive exposure to computer usage in computer-aided drafting (CAD) is also provided to all students.

The program has a very open architecture to permit students to concentrate their technical electives in the construction area or the design drafting area. A student may also elect to choose technical electives from both concentrations, if he or she desires a more general background. The minimum total number of technical elective credit hours required is 21 in order to meet the minimum total number of credit hours required to receive the Associate in Applied Science (A.A.S.) degree in engineering technology.

The college also has an associate degree program in systems and network administration. This program gives students hands-on learning experiences in computer hardware and network wiring and equipment. It provides the student with the fundamentals required to gain industry-recognized certifications such as Microsoft MCP, Microsoft MCP + Internet, CompTIA A+, Microsoft MCSE, and CCNP.

Costs

The tuition for 2005–06 was $5775 per semester, based upon taking a typical academic load of 12 to 19 semester credit hours. The computer account fee was $100 per semester. Campus housing costs were $1200 per semester (not required if the student lives off campus). An additional $100 housing security deposit is required for first-time residents. The housing cost figure does not include food, laundry, or general living expenses. Parking fees were $25 per semester (not required if the student does not park a car on campus). The recreation center/activity fee was $30 per semester, and the technology fee was $150.

Financial Aid

The curricula offered at Morrison Institute of Technology have been accredited by a nationally recognized accrediting agency. Qualified students, therefore, may take advantage of a number of federally funded student financial aid programs.

Grant programs at Morrison include the Federal Pell Grant, the Illinois Student Assistance Commission Monetary Award Program Grant, the Federal Supplemental Educational Opportunity Grant (FSEOG), the Federal Work-Study Program (FWS), tutorial and lab supervisors, the Department of Rehabilitation Services, the Job Training Partnership Act and the Veterans Educational Program.

Morrison Institute of Technology has available a limited number of scholarships for students now attending high school or the associated area vocational technical school, who wish to pursue engineering technology studies at Morrison Institute of Technology. These scholarships are independent of, and in addition to, any other financial aid a student may obtain. There are three areas in which a student can qualify for a Morrison Institute of Technology sponsored scholarship: the Morrison Institute of Technology Academic Scholarships, the Morrison Institute of Technology Performance Scholarships, or the Morrison Institute of Technology Parent Scholarships.

Loan programs at Morrison include the Subsidized Federal Family Education Loan Program (student loan), the Unsubsidized Federal Family Education Loan Program (student loan), and the Federal PLUS loan.

All prospective students are encouraged to complete the Free Application for Federal Student Aid (FAFSA). Applications may be obtained from student's high school or the college Federal Aid Office or by downloading the FAFSA Express Software from the Web at http://www.ed.gov/offices/OPE/express.html.

Faculty

Morrison's faculty members are full-time employees. The student-faculty ratio is about 15:1, which means that students at Morrison receive a lot of personal attention. The faculty members are experienced in the areas they teach, and many are sought out by businesses to provide private consultative services; therefore, students learn what the profession is all about from persons who actually do the work. Approximately 30 percent of the faculty members are licensed professional engineers or surveyors. Approximately 23 percent have earned graduate-level degrees.

Student Body Profile

Morrison is a small college. The total full-time enrollment is about 200 students. The majority of the students attending are from the Midwest, mostly Illinois, Iowa, Wisconsin, and Indiana, with a few from the Eastern and Western states. Approximately 8–12 percent of the student enrollment is female, Hispanics make up 2–6 percent, African Americans number 6–10 percent, and Asians compose 1–2 percent. Approximately 75 percent of the students receive financial aid of some kind. About 60 percent are enrolled in the construction option while the remaining 40 percent are enrolled in the design drafting CAD option.

Student Activities

A student recreation center is provided for all students. The recreation center provides a place for students to relax; play pool, video games, Ping-Pong, card games, or chess; or watch TV. The facility also has a fitness room and Laundromat. Vending machines are also available in the recreation center. Morrison Institute of Technology sponsors a student chapter of the Society of Manufacturing Engineers (SME). Activities associated with SME include attending regional meetings, field trips, and SME-sponsored exhibitions and seminars.

Facilities and Resources

The college has two main educational facilities, the A. E. Rambo Center, which also houses the administrative offices and student learning center, and the Technical Center, which houses mainly the computer laboratories, survey, soils laboratory, and multimedia lecture halls. The college also has the student recreation center complex and Odey Residence Hall.

Location

The campus is located on 17 acres on the south side of Morrison, Illinois. Morrison is about 45 minutes by car from the Quad-Cities area and about 2¼ hours by car from Chicago. Morrison is a picturesque small town with a population of 4,300. It is a neat, clean, and friendly town with tree-lined streets, neighborhood churches, and a small but busy business district. The college took its mascot emblem, "The Thoroughbreds," because there are many horse ranches in the area. The town is considered very safe: children play on the streets after dark here, and many people don't bother to lock their doors. Nearby is Rockwood State Park, several wildlife sanctuaries along the Mississippi River, and several park areas featuring Native American pre-Columbian settlements.

Admission Requirements

Admission to Morrison Institute of Technology is considered if the applicant has graduated from high school or has completed GED testing with scores that can be accepted as meeting high school requirements. It is recommended, but not required, that an applicant's educational background include at least one semester each of high school algebra and geometry. ACT or SAT test scores are not required but, if available, are used for academic counseling. Those students not having either test score are administered an institutional placement test to assist in academic placement.

All applicants are encouraged to schedule a tour of the campus. Tours are conducted during any of the formal open houses held by the college. If an applicant is unable to attend an open house, tours can be arranged on an individual basis by appointment. To complete the application process the following items are to be mailed to the college: a completed application for enrollment; the appropriate fees; an official high school transcript; if transfer analysis is requested, an official transcript from the institution granting the credit, mailed directly from the institution to Morrison Institute of Technology; a copy of the applicant's immunization record; and ACT, SAT, or placement test scores.

Application and Information

Students who wish to attend Morrison Institute of Technology may obtain the required admission application material and additional information by contacting:

Admissions Office
Morrison Institute of Technology
701 Portland Avenue
Morrison, Illinois 61270

Telephone: 815-772-7218
Fax: 815-772-7584
E-mail: admissions@morrison.tec.il.us
World Wide Web: http://www.morrison.tec.il.us

NEW MEXICO MILITARY INSTITUTE

ROSWELL, NEW MEXICO

The Institute and Its Mission

New Mexico Military Institute (NMMI) was established in 1891 and became a State (Territorial) School in 1893. Its purpose then and now was "for the education and training of the youth of this country with a mandate by law to be of as high a standard as like institutions in other states and territories of the United States." New Mexico Military Institute is primarily an academic institution operating within the framework of a military environment. NMMI is accredited by the North Central Association of Colleges and Schools, by the State of New Mexico Department of Education, and by the Department of the Army as a Military Junior college offering Junior and Senior ROTC. The Department of the Army has annually rated NMMI as an Honor School with Distinction or its equivalent since 1909.

Academic Programs

New Mexico Military Institute provides a comprehensive liberal arts curriculum including such disciplines as criminal justice, English, foreign language (Arabic, German, Spanish), history, sociology, philosophy, political science, psychology, business administration, economics, computer science, chemistry, physics, biology, math through college calculus, geology, art, music, and physical education.

Associate Degree Programs The school awards an **Associate in Arts** degree, which requires 68 hours (6 in English, 6 to 8 in the humanities, 9 in social science/history, 8 in laboratory science, 6 to 12 in military science, 3 in mathematics, 2 in physical education, with the balance in electives). A normal load is 17 hours per semester. A cadet may choose to concentrate in a particular area while pursuing the Associate in Arts degree.

Many cadets are interested in pursuing a military career through the ROTC Leader's Training Course (LTC) approach. In order to qualify for the two-year commissioning program, a student must successfully complete a four-week training program conducted by the U.S. Army. This course occurs the summer before cadets enter their freshman (second class) year at New Mexico Military Institute. In special cases, students who have three or more years of high school ROTC or prior military service may apply for advanced placement credit. If accepted, they need not attend the LTC. All eligible camp cadets can compete for a two-year scholarship that is awarded upon completion of the LTC. The PMS has numerous Army ROTC two-year scholarships to award each year. Two years of advanced military science (MS III and MS IV), are required during the freshman and sophomore years, respectively. An advanced ROTC camp, Leader's Development Assessment Course (LDAC), is required during the summer between MS III and MS IV. This camp is five weeks long. Upon successful completion of all phases, two years of college, LTC, MS III, Advanced LDAC, and MS IV, the cadet is commissioned as a second lieutenant in the United States Army Reserve.

Costs

For the academic year 2006–07, in-state tuition is $1273, out-of-state tuition is $4017, room is $1291, board is $2265, and the matriculation fee is $5. Accident insurance costs $200. Other fixed fees are $1320. Uniforms and supplies cost $1700. This includes all uniform purchases. Additional funds are necessary

for personal expenses and text books. The amount needed varies depending on a cadet's spending habits. New Mexico Military Institute offers a deferred payment plan requiring an initial deposit of $2200. All costs are subject to change.

Financial Aid

Federal financial aid is available to all eligible college students. New Mexico Military Institute participates in the Federal Pell Grant, Federal Supplemental Educational Opportunity Grant, Federal Perkins Loan, Federal Work Study program, Stafford Loan, Parent Loan for Undergraduate Students program and specialized programs for New Mexico residents. New Mexico Military Institute offers a varied scholarship program for merit-based and need-based considerations. The New Mexico Legislator Scholarship Program is available only to New Mexico residents. Scholarships are renewable based on the continued eligibility of the recipient. In 2003–04, more than 76 percent of the college student body received either federal or scholarship assistance amounting to more than $1.3 million. Currently, 410 college students receive $1,368,295 in assistance, ranging from $500 scholarships to $7000 in federal financial aid. A full-time financial aid staff is available.

Faculty

NMMI has 63 full-time faculty members, many with terminal degrees, and all are required to have at least a master's degree. The student-faculty ratio is 18:1.

Student Body Profile

The junior college population of 450 to 500 at New Mexico Military Institute generally includes cadets from more than forty-four different states and twelve other countries. Typically, the ethnic breakdown includes 17 percent Hispanic, 8 percent African American, 6 percent Asian, and 2 percent Native American students. In 2005–06, there were 76 cadets representing thirteen different nations. Twenty percent of the Corps of Cadets were female. More than one third of college students are pursuing an Army commission. College cadets entering the Corps of Cadets for the first time are new cadets for one semester. New cadets receive yearling status at the completion of one semester and old cadet status with the completion of one year. The new cadet environment is stressful, formal, strict, and just. All cadets are held strictly accountable for their actions. NMMI operates with a Cadet Honor Code that states, "A cadet will not lie, cheat, or steal, or tolerate those who do. Every cadet is obligated to support and enforce the honor system." NMMI maintains a strict policy regarding the possession, use, or sale of alcoholic beverages and illegal drugs. All cadets live on campus.

Student Activities

Students enjoy video games, pool, bowling, and the snack bar during their free time. Movies on Saturday nights also contribute to weekend activities. Informal dances are held about twice a month. Recorded music is provided by students and professional disc jockeys. Two formal balls are held each year, the Homecoming Ball in the fall and the Final Ball in the spring. Escorts from all over the country attend. NMMI students can participate in outdoor activities at the nearby ski resort area of Ruidoso and the Mescalero Apache Indian Reservation. Other attractions include Carlsbad Caverns, Lincoln National Forest, Bottomless Lakes, Living Desert State Park, and the historical town of Lincoln, famous for the exploits of Billy the Kid, Pat Garrett, and John Chisum. Rounding out the Institute's extracurricular activities, students enjoy marching and concert bands, soccer, judo and karate clubs, color guards, and rifle and drill teams. Students may also participate in swimming, drama, and academic honorary societies. Student publications include *The Maverick* and the Bronco yearbook.

Facilities and Resources

NMMI's campus encompasses more than 40 acres and has some of the finest academic facilities in the country. The yellow brick buildings reflect a military style traditional to the campus since 1909. The Toles Learning Center houses the library and its 68,000-volume collection, TV/communication studio, academic computer center, 200-seat lecture hall, classrooms, and the Student Assistance Center. Available to cadets is an online catalog. Also located in the Toles Learning Center are the Computer Services Center and the Career Lab, housed in the Student Assistance Center. College faculty academic advisers are available to provide students with assistance in college exploration and selection. A computerized college scholarship search program is available in the center for cadet use. NMMI is a regional test center for the ACT, SAT, and GRE. College-Level Examination Program (CLEP) exams are available to those cadets wishing to challenge a course. A liaison officer is available whose duties include working with and assisting students interested in attending the national service academies. The Student Assistance Center provides professional advisers who offer academic and career counseling. Transfer guidance on colleges and service academy admission is also available. Approximately $15 million in cadet room renovations have allowed each cadet access to a state-of-the-art computer network, cable TV, and telephones. New Mexico Military Institute has excellent athletic facilities and athletic playing fields. They include a physical education building with four regulation basketball courts, four handball/racquetball courts, an Olympic-size swimming pool with sunning decks, Nautilus exercise equipment and Universal exercise machines. A separate building houses the varsity team locker and weight rooms and a gymnasium for varsity basketball games. The playing fields include twelve tennis courts, a baseball diamond, running tracks (quarter-mile and half-mile), football and soccer fields, and an eighteen-hole golf course.

Location

New Mexico Military Institute is located in the city of Roswell in the southeastern part of New Mexico. It is within 70 miles of skiing in the mountains of Ruidoso and within 200 miles of El Paso to the south and Albuquerque and Santa Fe to the north. The nearest regional airports are Albuquerque International Airport and Lubbock International Airport.

Admission Requirements

The minimum standards for normal admission to the college are graduation from high school with a 2.0 GPA (on a 4.0 scale) or the equivalent and a composite score of 18 on the ACT, or a combined verbal/mathematics score of 870 on the recentered SAT I, or a minimum 2.5 GPA for all high school core courses and graduating in the top 50 percent of the high school class. Prospective students for the Army Commissioning program need a composite score of 19 on the ACT, or a combined verbal/mathematics score of 920 on the recentered SAT I. Applicants and members of the Corps of Cadets must have never been married, have no dependent children, be in good physical condition, and be able to participate in athletic and leadership development activities. In addition, they cannot be more than the age of 21 at the time of matriculation. The admissions policy of New Mexico Military Institute is nondiscriminatory with respect to race, color, creed, or national or ethnic origin and is in compliance with federal laws with respect to sex and the handicapped. Priority of admission is given to New Mexico residents.

Application and Information

An initial inquiry is welcome at any time. Campus tours are conducted weekdays, Monday through Friday at 8 a.m. and Monday through Thursday at 1 p.m. Interested students should call to schedule an appointment at any time except for school holidays. There is an annual open house every March. Applications are accepted through July into all classes. Notification of acceptance is made on a rolling admissions basis.

For more information, students should contact:

Director of Admissions
New Mexico Military Institute
101 West College Boulevard
Roswell, New Mexico 88201-5173
Telephone: 505-624-8050
          800-421-5376 (toll-free)
Fax: 505-624-8058
E-mail: admissions@nmmi.edu
World Wide Web: http://www.nmmi.edu

Cadets find time to study in the New Mexico sunshine.

NEW YORK COLLEGE OF HEALTH PROFESSIONS
School of Massage Therapy
SYOSSET, NEW YORK

The College and Its Mission

New York College of Health Professions, a private nonprofit institution, is one of the nation's premier centers of holistic medicine. The College educates students, treats patients, and conducts research. Founded in 1981, New York College has been a leader in holistic education and care for more than twenty-five years. It is firmly rooted in the principles of blending Western and Eastern practices, or Integrative medicine.

New York College offers approved degree programs in the field of complementary medicine. Undergraduate programs include an associate degree in massage therapy and a bachelor's degree in advanced Asian bodywork. Graduate programs include combined bachelor's and master's degrees in acupuncture or Oriental medicine (the combined study of acupuncture and Chinese herbology). All programs lead to New York State licensing and/or national certification.

The College also offers a 495-clock-hour continuing education program in holistic nursing for RNs and a selection of other continuing education courses and workshops for both health-care professionals and the general public. New York College was awarded a grant from New York State to train all the RNs at Bellevue Hospital in New York City in an Introduction to Holistic Nursing course and receives grants from SEIU 1199, the health-care workers' union, for RNs from Flushing Hospital and Beth Israel Hospital Center to also participate in the College's holistic nursing programs.

New York College is chartered by the Board of Regents of the University of the State of New York, and all programs are registered by the New York State Education Department. The Acupuncture and Oriental Medicine programs are accredited by the Accrediting Commission for Acupuncture and Oriental Medicine (ACAOM). The Oriental Medicine program is also approved by the California Acupuncture Board. The College is approved as a provider of Continuing Education by the New York State Nurses Association Council on Continuing Education and the National Certification Board for Therapeutic Massage and Bodywork. The College is a member of numerous professional organizations related to the fields of oriental medicine and massage therapy.

Academic Programs

The Massage Therapy program at New York College began in 1981 and was the School's first educational program. It has since become nationally recognized and was cited for academic excellence in 1997 by the National Certification Board for Therapeutic Massage and Bodywork. In 1996, New York College became the first college in the United States to award an associate degree in massage therapy. The program exceeds national certification and state licensing requirements. First-time candidates from New York College rank competitively in pass rates on the New York State Massage Therapy Licensing Examination for all first-time takers.

The benefits of massage therapy have become widely recognized. Documentation on the effects of massage shows that it improves circulation and lymph drainage and can help treat sports injuries and alleviate stress, headaches, and other aches and pains. When practiced in conjunction with Western medical treatment, massage can also be used to treat arthritis, hypertension, diabetes, asthma, bronchitis, and neuromuscular diseases, among others. Massage therapy most commonly falls into two categories: Western (Swedish), which focuses on the musculoskeletal system and is based on standard Western anatomy and physiology, and Eastern, or Oriental, which is based on the movement of energy through various channels in the body. At New York College, students learn both of these modalities as well as the specific techniques for sports massage, chair massage, shiatsu, hot stone massage, reflexology,

and more. Career opportunities in the field of massage therapy continue to grow and range from owning one's own business to working in spas, health clubs, resorts, Wellness Centers, hospitals, or doctors' offices or with sports teams.

New York College's Massage Therapy program is a 72-credit program. Upon completion, graduates receive an Associate of Occupational Studies (A.O.S.) degree in massage therapy. They are eligible to sit for the New York State Licensing Exam in Massage Therapy, the National Certification Exam for Therapeutic Massage and Bodywork, and the NCCAOM National Certification Exam for Oriental Bodywork Therapy. Course work for the Massage Therapy program includes in-depth study of both Western and Eastern health sciences, Western and Oriental bodywork techniques, and tai chi chuan, qi gong, or yoga. Courses are also offered in ethics, professional development, and business practice. The culmination of the program is the intensive clinical internship that students undergo in the College's on-site teaching clinic.

New York College operates on a fifteen-week trimester system. New students are admitted to the College for the September, January, and May trimesters. Ten-week, second-cycle trimester admissions may be added when there is sufficient demand. The program can be completed in twenty months, twenty-four months, or thirty-six months on a part-time basis.

Off-Campus Programs

New York College offers travel/life-experience trips abroad to its Luo Yang Medical Center facility in the People's Republic of China. Programs are three-week immersion trips to China that include visits to hospitals as well as attendance at lectures and demonstrations at medical centers and visits to historic sites throughout the country.

Costs

Tuition is based on a per-credit charge of $275 and is paid each trimester. The application fee is $85. Students should expect to incur an additional $2000 in expenses for texts and supplies throughout their course of study.

Financial Aid

New York College is an eligible institution approved by the United States Department of Education and the New York State Education Department to participate in the following programs: Federal Pell Grant, Federal Supplemental Educational Opportunity Grant (FSEOG), Tuition Assistance Program (TAP), Aid for Part-Time Study, Federal Work-Study Program, Veterans Administration, Vocational Rehabilitation, Federal Stafford Student Loan, Federal PLUS loan, and alternative financing. For additional information, students should contact the College's Financial Aid Office (800-922-7337 Ext. 244).

Faculty

New York College has a total of 98 faculty members, 17 of whom are full-time. The faculty-student ratio is 1:16 for technique classes, 1:40 for didactic classes, and up to 1:6 for clinical internships.

Student Body Profile

Total current enrollment at New York College is about 900 students, most of whom are enrolled in the Massage Therapy program. New York College does not have student housing; therefore, the majority of students are from the local area, with the largest group coming from Long Island, Brooklyn, and Queens. However, the College attracts a percentage of both international and out-of-state students.

Facilities and Resources

The main Syosset, Long Island, campus occupies 70,000 square feet in a modern facility on three levels. Within the facility are the administrative offices, classrooms for all College educational programs, a physical arts deck, the Integrative Health Center, Academic Health Care Teaching Clinics, the Herbal Dispensary, the James and Lenore Jacobson Library, the café, the bookstore, and student lounges. Classrooms are designed and used specifically for lecture or technique work and contain the most recent instructional materials. The physical arts deck for the practice of tai chi, hatha yoga, and qi gong is specifically designed with space, light, and quiet.

The James and Lenore Jacobson Library contains the most extensive collection of materials about complementary and alternative medicine available on Long Island. The library houses a collection of books and journals specializing in Oriental medicine, complementary and alternative therapies, acupuncture, herbs, massage therapy, and holistic nursing. The library belongs to a consortium of special and medical libraries that provide interloans of additional books and journal articles. Several networked workstations provide access to the computerized book collection catalog and magazine subject index, various software and CD-ROM programs, the Internet, and various online professional databases

The Academic Health Care Teaching Clinics are an integral part of a student's educational experience through this internship. The clinics provide affordable holistic health care to members of the community, treating more than 17,000 patients annually. Supervised student treatments include Swedish massage, Amma massage, acupuncture, herbal consultations, and holistic nursing.

The Integrative Health Center is the professional clinic of the College and offers the skills and services of licensed holistic practitioners to patients of all ages. For more than twenty-five years, this fully integrated clinic has provided patients with minimally invasive therapies, including acupuncture; herbal medicine; many modalities of massage therapy, such as Swedish, sports, Amma, shiatsu, reflexology, and pregnancy massage; and holistic nursing. Special patient programs exist for smoking cessation, weight loss, and cancer support.

The Dean of Student Services is responsible for special-needs students, academic progress advisement, the organization of study groups, and tutoring services. New York College's Career Services Office offers graduates assistance with job placement. Currently, the College lists more than 300 employment and rental opportunities for its licensed graduates. Sponsorship opportunities for graduates waiting to sit for licensure are also available.

Location

Long Island The main campus of New York College is located in Syosset, on the North Shore of Long Island, approximately 30 miles from Manhattan. Its proximity to all major parkways and railroad service provides easy access to one of the world's most exciting cities, while capturing the serenity, beauty, and open space of the suburbs. Long Island stretches for 110 miles and is a wealth of natural, cultural, and historic treasures. Some of the world's most beautiful sandy beaches surround the island—from the popular Jones Beach to the chic Hamptons and the barrier isle of Fire Island with its pristine beaches and absence of automobiles. The island's fifteen state parks also offer an abundance of recreational opportunities and even include a polo field. There are nearly 100 museums on the island.

China New York College owns the Luo Yang Medical Center in the People's Republic of China. Situated in the ancient capital of China, the 35-acre site is surrounded by historic and important attractions. Modern buildings are fully equipped with Western fixtures.

Admission Requirements

New York College is deeply committed to recruiting the highest qualified and motivated candidates for admission. The College is particularly proud of its diverse population, comprising individuals from a variety of cultural backgrounds and with many unique strengths. New York College students contribute to the friendly and supportive atmosphere at the College.

Applicants who have graduated from high school must have achieved a minimum GPA of 2.0 or have equivalent qualifications. Students may earn their GED certificate while enrolled in a massage therapy degree program by successfully completing 24 credits of specified credit courses in six subject areas. Candidates must be at least 17 years of age and, in accordance with New York State guidelines, must hold U.S. citizenship, be an alien lawfully admitted for permanent residence in the U.S., or hold a valid visa. The College is authorized under federal law to enroll nonimmigrant alien students.

Candidates must complete and submit an application along with an $85 application fee and arrange for the submission of an official high school transcript (or proof of equivalency) and official transcripts from all previously attended higher educational institutions. Candidates are notified promptly of the receipt of their application and advised which, if any, of the required documents have not been received by the Admissions Office. An admissions interview is required. The College offers on-the-spot enrollment: a student can be interviewed and conditionally admitted and enrolled in one visit.

Application and Information

New students are admitted to New York College for the September, January, and May trimesters. Additional second-cycle trimesters in October, February, and June may be added if there is sufficient demand. It is recommended that applications be submitted three to four months prior to the desired entrance date.

Admissions Office
New York College of Health Professions
6801 Jericho Turnpike
Syosset, New York 11791

Telephone: 800-9-CAREER Ext. 351 (toll-free)
Fax: 516-364-0989
E-mail: admissions@nycollege.edu
World Wide Web: http://www.nycollege.edu

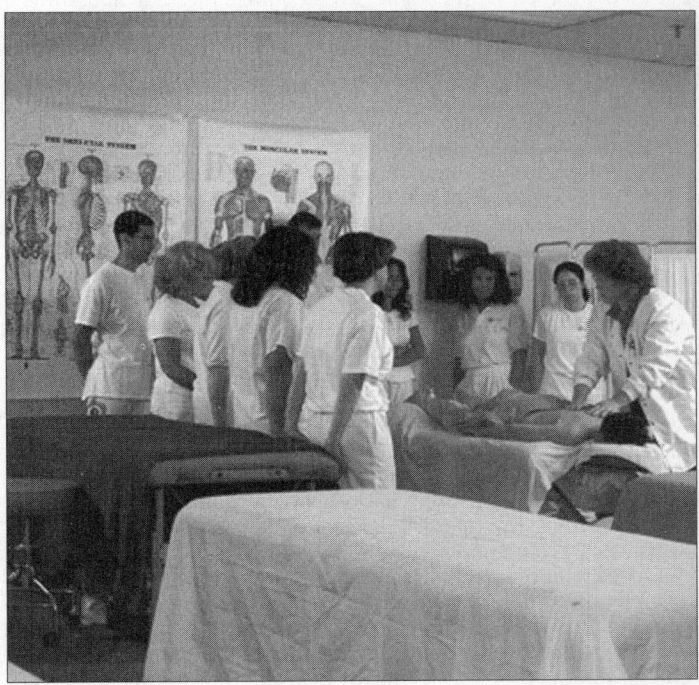

The Academic Health Care Teaching Clinics are an integral part of a student's education.

NORTHWESTERN BUSINESS COLLEGE

CHICAGO, ILLINOIS

The College and Its Mission

Northwestern Business College (NBC) was established in 1902 as Chicago's first private business college, and for more than a century it has been helping ambitious students get started on the path to success. As business needs have changed over the years, so have the College's programs of study. Students find that today's NBC is much different from the traditional "business college" of years past. Just like its students, NBC is diversified, career-oriented, and right in step with the times. More than 2,200 students attend classes at the College's three easily accessible campuses: one in Jefferson Park, just northwest of the Chicago Loop; another in suburban Bridgeview; and the third, in Naperville on Mill Street and Diehl Road.

The College believes in its mission: "The professionals of Northwestern Business College, an institution of higher education, empower students to realize their career potential and individual goals. Our quality educational programs combined with our commitment, integrity, and personal attention provide a vital human resource to the community." These educational programs provide hands-on knowledge and training in many of today's most-sought-after professions. A highly focused curriculum and career-relevant courses make it possible for students to earn an Associate in Applied Science degree in only eighteen months or complete a certificate in less than a year.

Northwestern Business College is accredited by the Higher Learning Commission of the North Central Association of Colleges and Schools (30 North LaSalle Street, Suite 2400, Chicago, Illinois 60602-2504; telephone: 312-263-0456; Web site: http://www. ncahigherlearningcommission.org). The medical assisting program is accredited by the Commission on Accreditation of Allied Health Education Programs (CAAHEP) on the recommendation of the Committee on Accreditation for Medical Assistant Education, also known as the Curriculum Review Board of the American Association of Medical Assistants' Endowment (AAMAE; 35 East Wacker Drive, Suite 1970, Chicago, Illinois 60601; telephone: 312-553-9355). Graduates of the medical assisting program are eligible to sit for the national Certified Medical Assistant (CMA) exam. The health information technology program is accredited by the Commission on Accreditation of Allied Health Education Programs (CAAHEP), in cooperation with the Council on Accreditation of the American Health Information Management Association (AHIMA). Graduates of accredited programs are eligible to take the national qualifying examination for certification as an accredited record technician (ART). The business administration, executive accounting, computer, and administrative assisting programs are accredited by the Association of Collegiate Business Schools and Programs (ACBSP; 7007 College Boulevard, Suite 420, Overland Park, Kansas 66211; telephone: 913-339-9356). The paralegal and legal nurse consultant programs are approved by the American Bar Association (ABA). The College is also approved for veterans' training under the G.I. bill for veterans' educational assistance, as well as by the United States Department of Justice Immigration and Naturalization Service as an institution of higher education for training international students. It is approved by the Board of Higher Education of the State of Illinois and authorized by the board to award the Associate in Applied Science degree.

Academic Programs

The academic calendar year is divided into four quarters: fall, winter, spring, and summer. Each term is approximately twelve weeks in length. The fall, winter, and spring terms constitute a traditional academic year. The summer quarter is ten weeks, and students who wish to graduate early attend all four quarters.

Northwestern Business College is committed to providing students with both a foundation and the essential tools necessary for continued personal and intellectual growth. To that end, the College requires that a minimum of 34 percent of a student's course work be in general education. This general education core requirement includes courses in communications, humanities, social and behavioral sciences, mathematics, and life skills and is intended to help students build a foundation for learning through study and exploration.

Associate Degree Programs The College offers Associate in Applied Science degrees in administrative assisting, business administration, business computer programming, business information systems, computer technical support, criminal justice, cyber security, executive accounting, health information technology, hospitality tourism management, massage therapy, medical assisting, and paralegal studies. In order to graduate with an Associate in Applied Science degree, each student must successfully complete a minimum of 100 quarter hours of credit, with a cumulative GPA of at least 2.0.

Certificate Programs Certificates are offered in accounting, business, EKG technician studies, health-care billing specialist studies, health-care coding specialist studies, legal nurse consultant studies, massage therapy, and phlebotomy.

Externship and Co-op Programs Many programs require students to complete an externship, which puts students on-site with one of the area's major employers. Students work in their fields of study, earn college credit, and gain valuable business skills at the same time, while also opening doors to potential full-time employment. Externship participants are not paid and assume the costs of transportation, lunch, appropriate wardrobe, and other related expenses.

Credit for Nontraditional Learning Experiences

The College evaluates life experience credits through written examination. Northwestern Business College offers two types of proficiency examinations to determine a student's prior knowledge of a subject. Advanced Status Examinations are given to determine advanced class placement but do not provide college credit. Credit by Examination (CBE) is a comprehensive exam that relates specifically to the subject matter for which credit is sought, and students who pass the CBE receive credit for that course. Students should contact the Student Services Department for the list of classes for which proficiency examinations may be taken.

Costs

For the 2005–06 academic year, tuition was $315 per credit hour for lecture classes and $390 per credit hour for laboratory and computer classes.

Financial Aid

Northwestern Business College recognizes that many students need financial assistance. The College's Financial Aid Office is available to assist those students and families requiring financial assistance in addition to their own contributions to cover the cost of their NBC education. Financial assistance is available to eligible students who are enrolled for 6 or more credit hours. Available assistance includes Federal Work-Study, Pell Grants, Supplemental Educational Opportunity Grants, Federal PLUS Program, TERI Loans, and Federal Stafford Student Loans, as well as veterans' benefits and state of Illinois MAP and IIA grants.

In addition, the College offers institutional scholarships and a payment plan. All students applying for financial aid must complete and submit the FAFSA as well as any other required forms, depending upon the type of aid sought.

Faculty

Because NBC's faculty comprises working professionals who have built successful careers in the same fields in which they teach, they are able to share insights and perspectives that give meaning to the "real world" outside of the classroom. The more than 130 faculty members at Northwestern Business College include practicing lawyers, certified public accountants, travel agents, computer programmers, and medical personnel. Small class size (the College has an average student-faculty ratio of 18:1) and a comfortable atmosphere allow faculty members and students to work together on a more personal level.

Student Body Profile

The caliber of NBC's faculty members is matched by the quality of the students who enroll. The commitment, creativity, and seriousness of the student body is one of the school's greatest strengths. NBC's enrollment includes approximately 2,200 students. Seventy percent reside within Chicago city limits; others travel from neighboring suburbs, and some come from as far away as Indiana. Several hundred of these students attend classes part-time.

Nearly twenty countries are represented in the student body. NBC's international students come from diverse ethnic heritages and pride themselves on their bilingual expertise. The College encourages and welcomes economic, racial, ethnic, and religious diversity in its student body.

Student Activities

NBC believes that college is about more than simply attending classes. It is also about participating in activities, sharing interests, helping others succeed, and building lasting friendships. The College's numerous organizations encourage students to explore their career interests outside of the classroom. NBC also sponsors a chapter of Alpha Beta Gamma, a national business society established in 1970 to recognize and encourage scholarship among college students in business curricula. In addition, the College sponsors Student Ambassadors, a service organization of students responsible for representing NBC at special community and college events; the NBC Paralegal Association, a professional association for paralegal students; and Students Helping Students, a peer-tutoring program.

Facilities and Resources

Advisement/Counseling All new students are assigned a faculty adviser, who is available throughout the school year to provide advice and assistance with scheduling classes and other academic matters. The College provides personal counseling to help students with school-related problems and/or to provide referral assistance to appropriate outside agencies.

Career Development and Alumni Relations Offices Because the majority of NBC students are interested in gaining work experience while attending college, job placement assistance is available after their first quarter. The NBC Office of Career Development and Alumni Relations also serves as an active liaison between employers and graduates and has a 95 percent placement rate when helping NBC graduates to find employment in their field of choice. The College offers a lifetime placement assistance program that NBC graduates may use at any time. In addition to on-campus recruitment and career fairs, NBC offers guidance in resume writing, interviewing, and job-search techniques, which build the confidence of students and enhance their professional images.

Library Services Each campus has a library equipped with current books, periodicals, and reference material for student use

in classroom research. Students also have access to the Internet as well as Westlaw, LexisNexis, and ProQuest; videotapes and audiotapes are available as well.

Location

Chicago The Chicago campus, located on Milwaukee Avenue and Lawrence Avenue, is 7 miles northwest of Chicago's Loop, in a residential/commercial area. It is easily accessible by bus, rapid transit, commuter train, and car and is convenient to both the Kennedy and Edens Expressways.

Bridgeview Located at 79th and Harlem, the Bridgeview campus is especially convenient for Chicagoans from the south and southwest sides as well as those who live and work in the southwest suburbs. This totally renovated facility offers 88,000 square feet of space and educational opportunity—more than three times that of the former campus in Hickory Hills, which the Bridgeview campus replaced in fall 2003.

Naperville NBC's Naperville location was opened in 2002 on the corner of Mill Street and Diehl Road in an office complex near Interstate 88 and Naperville Road. This location serves DuPage, Kane, Will, and Cook Counties.

Admission Requirements

Northwestern Business College seeks students who have the desire for practical career preparation in their chosen fields and have the ability to achieve academic success. To be admitted to the College, a prospective student must be a high school graduate or hold a General Educational Development (GED) certificate and also complete the NBC placement exam that is administered on campus.

Northwestern Business College may accept credit for a course taken at another accredited college or university if the grade earned is a C or better and the course is college level, credit bearing, and equivalent to one taught at NBC in the student's major. Fifty percent of the entire program and 67 percent of the major program must be completed at NBC. If a student changes majors, his or her transferred credits are reevaluated.

International applicants are expected to meet the same admissions requirements as all other students. In addition, applicants whose native language is not English are requested to take the Test of English as a Foreign Language (TOEFL) and must achieve a minimum score of 500; or they may use the placement exam administered on campus in lieu of the TOEFL.

Application and Information

Applications are accepted on an ongoing basis. All prospective students should contact the Admissions Department to schedule an interview with an Admissions Representative and visit Northwestern Business College's Web site at http://www.northwesternbc.edu.

Chicago Campus
Northwestern Business College
4839 North Milwaukee Avenue
Chicago, Illinois 60630
Telephone: 800-396-5613 (toll-free)

Bridgeview Campus
Northwestern Business College
7725 South Harlem Avenue
Bridgeview, Illinois 60455
Telephone: 800-682-9113 (toll-free)

Naperville Campus
Northwestern Business College
1805 F Mill Street
Naperville, Illinois 60563
Telephone: 866-622-6785 (toll-free)

PENNSYLVANIA COLLEGE OF TECHNOLOGY
An Affiliate of The Pennsylvania State University
WILLIAMSPORT, PENNSYLVANIA

Pennsylvania
College of
Technology

PENNSTATE

The College and Its Mission

Pennsylvania College of Technology (Penn College) is a special mission affiliate of Penn State, committed to applied technology education. The College has a national reputation for the high quality and diversity of its "degrees that work" in traditional and advanced technology majors. Partnerships with industry leaders, including Honda, Toyota, Ford, Mack Trucks, and Caterpillar, provide students unique opportunities to advance their careers. Excellent placement rates exceed 90 percent annually (100 percent in some majors). Among the keys to graduate success are Penn College's emphasis on small classes, personal attention, and hands-on experience using the latest technology. Student projects reflect real working situations. A number of campus buildings were designed and constructed by students—including a conference center, a Victorian guest house, an athletic field house, and a rustic retreat used for professional gatherings—and are maintained by students. The facilities stand as testimony to the quality of a Penn College education. State-of-the-art classrooms and laboratories on the ultramodern campus located in Williamsport, Pennsylvania, reflect the expectations of the modern workforce.

Academic Programs

Associate Degree Majors Associate degrees (A.A.S., A.A.A., or A.A.) are offered in accounting; advertising art; architectural technology; automated manufacturing technology; automotive service sales and marketing; automotive technology (including Ford, Ford ASSET, Honda, and Toyota industry-sponsored majors); aviation technology; baking and pastry arts; building construction technology; building construction technology/masonry; business management; civil engineering technology; collision repair technology; computer-aided drafting technology; culinary arts technology; dental hygiene; diesel technology (including a Mack Trucks industry-sponsored major); early childhood education; electric power generation technology; electrical technology; electromechanical maintenance technology; electronics and computer engineering technology (emphases in Cisco systems, communications and fiber optics, nanofabrication technology, robotics and automation); emergency medical services; environmental technology; forest technology; general studies; graphic communications technology; health arts; health information technology; heating, ventilation, and air conditioning (HVAC) technology; heavy construction equipment technology (emphases in Caterpillar industry-sponsored, operator, or technician); hospitality management; human services; individual studies; information technology (emphases in Cisco technology, information technology technician studies, network technology, technical support technology, and Web and applications technology); landscape/nursery technology (turfgrass management emphasis); legal assistant/paralegal studies; mass media communication; nursing; occupational therapy assistant studies; office information technology (medical office information and specialized office information emphases); physical fitness specialist studies; plastics and polymer technology; radiography; studio arts; surgical technology; surveying technology; toolmaking technology; transmission and distribution technology; and welding technology.

Bachelor's Degree Majors Many associate degree graduates choose to continue their education with unique **Bachelor of Science (B.S.) degrees** that focus on applied technology in traditional and emerging career fields. Majors include accounting; applied health studies; applied human services; automotive technology management; aviation maintenance technology; building automation technology; business administration (concentrations in banking and finance, human resources management, management, management information systems, marketing, and small business and entrepreneurship); civil engineering technology; computer-

aided product design; construction management; culinary arts and systems; dental hygiene (concentrations in health policy and administration and special-population care); electronics and computer engineering technology; environmental technology management; graphic communications management; graphic design; heating, ventilation, and air conditioning (HVAC) technology; information technology (concentrations in IT security specialist, network specialist, and Web and applications development); legal assistant/paralegal studies; manufacturing engineering technology; nursing; physician assistant studies; plastics and polymer engineering technology; residential construction technology and management; technology management; and welding and fabrication engineering technology.

Certificate Majors Certificates are offered in automotive service technician studies, aviation maintenance technician studies, cabinetmaking and millwork, collision repair technician studies, construction carpentry, diesel technician studies, electrical occupations, machinist general, nurse/health-care, paralegal studies, paramedic technician studies, plumbing, practical nursing, and welding.

Off-Campus Programs

Cooperative education and internships give students the opportunity to gain workforce experience. Penn College students have worked throughout Pennsylvania, the United States, and around the world.

Costs

Tuition and related fees are based on a per-credit-hour charge. Pennsylvania residents attending Penn College in 2005–06 paid approximately $16,680 per year, and out-of-state students paid approximately $19,260 per year. These estimated costs were based on tuition and fees for an average 15 credits per semester, plus estimated expenses for housing, meals, books, and supplies. Rates vary according to specific choices for classes, housing, and meal plans.

All on-campus housing is apartment-style (kitchen, living room, bedrooms, and bathroom). On-campus housing is alcohol-free, drug-free, noise-controlled, and secure. Resident and nonresident students may purchase meal plans, which are accepted in the College's dining facilities, including the main dining hall, an all-you-can-eat buffet, a gourmet restaurant, a convenience store, snack areas, and on-campus pizza delivery.

Financial Aid

Approximately 4 out of 5 Penn College students receive some form of financial assistance. Types of aid available include Federal Pell Grants, Pennsylvania Higher Education Assistance Agency grants, Federal Supplemental Educational Opportunity Grants, Federal Work-Study Program awards, Federal Stafford Student Loans, Federal PLUS loans, veterans' benefits, and Bureau of Vocational Rehabilitation benefits. A deferred-payment plan allows students to spread their tuition cost over two payments each semester. Penn College offers academic, need-based, and technical scholarships to qualified students. For detailed information on scholarships, students should contact the Financial Aid Office or visit the Web at http://www.pct.edu/scholarships.

Faculty

Penn College's faculty members (294 full-time and 223 part-time) provide individual attention that students need to be successful in the classroom and the workplace. Faculty members are experienced in their fields. Each year, Penn College recognizes excellence among the faculty members through distinguished faculty award programs. Small class sizes (fewer than 20 students in most classes) promote student success. Advisory committees of faculty members and business and industry leaders work together to ensure that programs meet current workplace needs.

Student Body Profile

More than 6,000 students attend Penn College. More than 2,000 additional men and women take part in noncredit classes, including customized business and industry courses offered through Workforce Development and Continuing Education.

Student Activities

Penn College is a place where future technicians and designers mingle easily with chefs, health-care personnel, and business students. It is a place where students actually construct campus buildings, cater important campus functions, compute strategies for engineering technology problems, and care for children in an on-campus day-care center and kindergarten program. The magnificent Campus Center provides an opportunity to eat, shop, work out, and spend time with friends. A modern fitness center, College Store, convenience store, art gallery, TV lounge, Internet lounge, video rental and game room, and an all-you-can-eat restaurant are among the features of the Campus Center. Impressive cultural activities are available both on the main campus and at Penn College's Community Arts Center, a restored 1920s-era theater in downtown Williamsport. Student ticket rates are available for performances that include Broadway shows, opera, ballet, symphony orchestras, and popular entertainers.

Student Government Association (SGA) and Wildcat Events Board (WEB) represent the student body in matters related to College policy and activities. Participation offers students the opportunity to develop leadership skills while contributing to the well-being of the College and the student body. In addition, more than forty student organizations, including the Residence Hall Association that represents all on-campus student residents, offer opportunities for organized campus activity and leadership experiences.

The Penn College Wildcats compete in Penn State's Commonwealth Campus Athletics Conferences. Varsity sports include archery, baseball, basketball, bowling, cross-country, golf, soccer, softball, team tennis, and volleyball. Penn College's men's compound-bow archery team is a former two-time national champion in the National Archery Association (NAA).

Facilities and Resources

The hands-on experience offered at Penn College creates a need for a variety of special academic facilities. Campus computers are very accessible. Wireless zones and networked on-campus residences make study across the campus very convenient. Besides extensive, accessible computer labs, the main campus has an automated manufacturing center, plastics manufacturing center, printing and publishing facility, dental hygiene clinic, automotive repair center, machine shop, welding shop, building trades center, architectural studio, computer-aided drafting labs, broadcast studio, modern science laboratories, fine-dining restaurant, campus guest house, aviation and avionics instructional facility located at the regional airport, greenhouses, working sawmill, diesel center, and heavy-equipment training site.

Library Services The library on the main campus is open every day during the academic semesters and offers an impressive selection of print and electronic resources. Services available include a professional reference staff, a well-developed instructional program, reciprocal borrowing at twenty-two regional libraries, interlibrary loans, and paper and electronic reserves.

Location

Penn College is located in north-central Pennsylvania. The main campus is in Williamsport, a city known around the world as the home of the Little League Baseball World Series. Penn College also offers classes at three other locations: the Advanced Automotive Technology Center at Wahoo Drive Industrial Park in Williamsport, the Aviation Center at the Williamsport Regional Airport in Montoursville, and the Earth Science Center, 10 miles south of Williamsport near Allenwood. Noncredit classes are offered from locations in Williamsport and Wellsboro.

Admission Requirements

Penn College offers educational opportunities to anyone who has the interest, desire, and ability to pursue advanced study. Due to the wide variety of majors, admission criteria vary according to the major. At a minimum, applicants must have a high school diploma or its equivalent. Some majors are restricted to persons who meet certain academic skill levels and prerequisites, have attained certain levels of academic achievement, and have earned an acceptable score on the SAT or ACT. Questions regarding the admission standards for specific majors should be directed to the Office of Admissions. To ensure that applicants have the entry-level skills needed for success in college majors, all students are required to take placement examinations, which are used to assess skills in math, English, and reading. The College provides opportunities for students to develop the basic skills necessary for enrollment in associate degree and certificate majors when the placement tests indicate that such help is needed. International students whose native language is not English are required to take the TOEFL, submit an affidavit of support, and comply with test regulations of the Immigration and Naturalization Service, along with meeting all other admission requirements. The College offers equal opportunity for admission without regard to age, race, color, creed, sex, national origin, disability, veteran status, or political affiliation.

Penn College offers opportunities for students to transfer the following course credits: credit earned at other institutions, college credit earned before high school graduation, service credit, DANTES credit, and credit earned through the College-Level Examination Program (CLEP).

Application and Information

College catalogs, viewbooks, financial aid information, and other informative brochures, along with applications for admission, are available from the Office of Admissions. Prospective students and their families should contact the Office of Admissions to arrange a personal interview or campus tour. Fall and spring visitation events are held annually.

All inquiries should be addressed to:

Office of Admissions
Pennsylvania College of Technology
One College Avenue
Williamsport, Pennsylvania 17701-5799
Telephone: 570-327-4761
          800-367-9222 (toll-free)
E-mail: admissions@pct.edu
World Wide Web: http://www.pct.edu/peter2

Banners representing each of the eight academic schools at Penn College adorn lampposts leading from the new main entrance to the heart of the campus.

THE RESTAURANT SCHOOL AT WALNUT HILL COLLEGE

PHILADELPHIA, PENNSYLVANIA

The College and Its Mission

The Restaurant School at Walnut Hill College, *Philadelphia's Home of Hospitality Excellence*, was established in 1974 and is dedicated to inspiring the future of the restaurant and hotel industry through training that is dynamic, timely, and insightful, with a commitment of service to its students. The Restaurant School at Walnut Hill College combines both intensive classroom training and practical experience; students use their knowledge while they learn. Within eighteen months, graduates are working in the field, earning an income, building a resume, and gaining practical and professional experience.

A student's education is cultivated by the College's philosophy that hands-on training is an essential part of education. This approach has multiple benefits—it enhances learning abilities, creates marketable skills and experience for a resume, brings education to life, and, most importantly, puts the student at the center of it all.

The Restaurant School at Walnut Hill College is licensed by the Pennsylvania Department of Education State Board of Private License Schools, is a member of the Pennsylvania Association of Private School Administrators, is accredited by the Accrediting Commission of Career Schools and Colleges of Technology, is certified for veteran's training by the Veterans Administration, is approved by the United States Department of Justice to grant student visas, and is recognized as a Professional Management Development Partner of the Educational Foundation of the National Restaurant Association.

Academic Programs

Associate and Bachelor's Degree Programs There are four majors at the Restaurant School at Walnut Hill College: hotel management, restaurant management, culinary arts, and pastry arts. Each major provides the student with a broad-based knowledge of the overall workings of a fine restaurant or hotel. Beyond that, the programs prepare the student with the day-to-day skills and specific knowledge that are required as he or she develops a career as a restaurant manager, chef, pastry chef, hotel manager, or restaurateur. In partnership with the Educational Foundation of the National Restaurant Association, the College's curriculum includes up to twelve nationally recognized food service and hospitality management courses. Upon successful completion of the courses and the certification exam, students receive national certification.

All students must successfully complete four 15-week semesters to be awarded an Associate of Science degree or eight 15-week semesters to be awarded a Bachelor of Science degree.

Off-Campus Programs

The Restaurant School at Walnut Hill College was one of the first schools in the country to offer a travel experience as part of a curriculum. Culinary and pastry students participate in an eight-day tour of France, while hotel and restaurant management students participate in an eight-day Orlando resort and cruise tour. This travel experience enhances both training and resumes.

A study-abroad program to France and England is currently being formulated. Students may contact the College for detailed information.

Costs

Tuition for the two-year program for students who start September 2006, is $28,800 ($14,400 per academic year for the two-year Associate of Science degree program) or $57,600 ($14,400 per academic year for the four-year Bachelor of Science degree program). Equipment, books, activity fees, culinary whites, and management dining room attire cost approximately $1200. Students may contact the College for information on on-campus housing.

Financial Aid

Financial aid programs are available to those who qualify. It is recommended that students apply early. The College participates in the Federal Pell Grant, the Pennsylvania PHEAA State Grant, the Subsidized Federal Stafford Student Loan, the Unsubsidized Federal Stafford Student Loan, and the parents' Federal PLUS loan programs. The financial aid officers assist students and their families with the creation of a personal plan that outlines expenses and identifies financial resources that are available to students. Scholarships and grants are available to incoming students; for more specific information, students may contact the College.

Faculty

Learning comes to life under the guiding hands and encouragement of the highly trained, technically skilled faculty; the Restaurant School at Walnut Hill College has on staff 1 of only 20 Certified Master Pastry Chefs in the country. The faculty members are seasoned professionals, having logged many years of experience in restaurants and food service. Through their instruction, students gain professional insight, which gives them a competitive edge upon entering the hospitality field. The chefs and instructors are committed to helping students achieve success. As professionals, they continuously keep pace with current trends in the hospitality industry and convey their professional dedication and work ethic to their students.

Student Body Profile

There is a diverse population at the Restaurant School at Walnut Hill College, with students coming from throughout the United States and abroad and ranging in age from the high school graduate to the adult who wants to change careers.

Student Activities

Whether it is a celebrity chef's cooking demonstration, dinner and a tour at a notable restaurant or hotel, or a winery tour and tasting, students at the Restaurant School at Walnut Hill College are exposed to the very best Philadelphia has to offer. There are activities and weekly special events that are sponsored by student clubs. The Student Culinary Team has been the winner of several major competitions in recent years—both nationally and internationally. Activities are both educational and fun, combining opportunities to learn and to establish camaraderie and professional development. Events are listed in the student newsletter and monthly calendar.

Facilities and Resources

Recently completing a yearlong renovation, the Restaurant School at Walnut Hill College is poised to offer one of the most dynamic hands-on learning opportunities in the country. The dining experience, situated in the breathtakingly restored 1853 Allison Mansion, turns into a dining event with the addition of three theme restaurants, including Terraza di Italia, a casual Italian trattoria that features classic pasta presentations set amidst an Italian terrace. Guests are invited to sit inside the restaurant, where they can enjoy homemade pasta or dine amongst the twinkling lights in the European Courtyard.

American cuisine is presented in an innovative new style in the American Heartland. Depicting a country farm with a painted blue sky and cornfields, this restaurant allows students to explore some of America's best cooking while guests enjoy the comfort of a country dining or veranda setting.

Most notable is the elegant Great Chefs of Philadelphia restaurant. Amidst glittering crystal chandeliers and a rich tapestry motif, guests enjoy wonderful cuisine and service designed by some of Philadelphia's and America's top chefs.

Also in the mansion is the student resource center, featuring state-of-the-art computer lab stations as well as the Alumni Library, which encompasses thousands of books, magazines, and videotapes on cooking, management, and wines. The building also houses a student conference room and a wines and bartending training salon.

The Pastry Shop and Café is filled each morning with buttery croissants, crisp French baguettes, and glistening pastries that are prepared by the pastry arts students. Also available is a selection of pastas, salads, soups, and entrées for an informal café lunch, prepared by the culinary arts students.

The education building is the focal point of a student's training. It houses four modern classroom kitchens, two lecture halls, and the College's purchasing center.

Hunter Hall is a turn-of-the-century masterpiece that features magnificent carved mahogany, marble, and fireplaces. The College's Office of Admissions, Financial Aid, and Independent Student Housing is located in this building.

Career Development and Job Placement Assistance at the Restaurant School at Walnut Hill College begins on the first day of school with training that is thorough and realistic. In the classroom, students learn how to develop effective resumes and portfolios as well as various interviewing techniques. Career development never ends—graduates can always contact the College for assistance with employment possibilities and resume updates. The College regularly invites personnel directors and proprietors of successful restaurants, hotels, and other food businesses to visit the College. Placement of Restaurant School at Walnut Hill College graduates averages at approximately 97 percent.

Location

Philadelphia is a great place to live and learn. As the fourth-largest city in the United States, Philadelphia has much to offer and is a city of firsts—the first public library, the first college, the first zoo—all in a first-class city.

The Restaurant School at Walnut Hill College is located in the University City section of Philadelphia, neighboring both the University of Pennsylvania and Drexel University. Located just across the Schuylkill River from Center City, University City has a wonderful college-town ambiance. Restaurants, museums, shops, and theaters abound, with local merchants offering discounts to students. The Amtrak train station is within walking distance of the campus, and the airport is 20 minutes away by car.

Center City is located just minutes from campus. Here, students find a bustling shopping and business district, complete with award-winning restaurant row, luxury hotels, and exclusive boutiques.

Ethnic diversity abounds in this city of neighborhoods, including Chinatown, complete with exotic restaurants and shops; South Philadelphia, with its famed Italian Market; and the ever-eclectic South Street, with blocks of restaurants, galleries, shops, and entertainment. There are also the historic district, which was the birthplace of the nation, and a waterfront that features exciting nightlife.

Philadelphia is rich in culture and heritage. Students find world-class art and science museums, theaters that feature major Broadway shows and renowned regional productions, and music, including everything from jazz to pop to the internationally acclaimed Philadelphia Orchestra.

Admission Requirements

Typically, the admissions procedure begins with a visit to the College. At that time, prospective students and their families tour the College, watch hands-on classes in action, and get a feel for campus life. Application for admission to the College is available to any individual with a high school diploma or its equivalent and an interest in developing a career or ownership options in fine restaurants, food service, or hospitality. Applicants are evaluated on their educational background and demonstrated or stated interest in their chosen field. Two references are required, as are high school transcripts.

Students may contact the College for information on the early decision program for high school juniors and seniors.

Application and Information

The Restaurant School at Walnut Hill College practices rolling admission; qualified applicants are accepted at any time. Applications for admission are submitted with a $50 application fee and a $150 registration fee. Prospective students should contact:

Office of Admissions
The Restaurant School at Walnut Hill College
4207 Walnut Street
Philadelphia, Pennsylvania 19104
Telephone: 215-222-4200 Ext. 3011
                   877-925-6884 Ext. 3011 (toll-free)
Fax: 215-222-4219
E-mail: info@walnuthillcollege.com
World Wide Web: http://www.walnuthillcollege.com

The Restaurant School at Walnut Hill College.

SANTA MONICA COLLEGE
SANTA MONICA, CALIFORNIA

The College and Its Mission

Santa Monica College is a two-year community college, founded in 1929. The College is supported by the state of California and is accredited by the Western Association of Schools and Colleges. It has an enrollment of 27,700 students, including 2,628 students from 105 other countries.

Santa Monica College welcomes students from all countries in the world and provides special assistance to them through the International Student Center. New incoming students are given an orientation that includes an introduction to the College and its services. In addition, information on immigration issues, housing, and registration are also covered in these sessions.

Santa Monica College ranks first among the 109 community colleges in California in transferring students to the University of California. The College also has articulation agreements with the California State Universities as well as with outstanding private universities, including the University of Southern California and Pepperdine and Loyola Marymount Universities.

To a great extent, the reputation of Santa Monica as one of the leading community colleges in America is based on the quality of its teaching faculty. Unlike some universities that place more emphasis on research, Santa Monica College chooses its professors for their ability to teach as well as their expertise in their fields.

A high priority is placed on individual interaction between instructors and students. Smaller classes give students the opportunity to receive more personal attention than they would in introductory courses at large universities.

The College radio station, KCRW, is the leading public radio station in southern California, providing both local and national news and entertainment programs. The Santa Monica Associates, a community-based foundation, enables the College to bring some of the world's outstanding scientists, writers, and artists to the campus for lectures and interaction with students. Santa Monica College students also present symphony concerts, plays, and operas.

Academic Programs

Graduation from Santa Monica College with the **Associate in Arts** degree is granted upon successful completion of a program of studies that includes the mastery of minimum skill requirements in English and mathematics; a selection of courses from the natural sciences, social sciences, and humanities; and prescribed courses in the major field. Graduating students are required to complete a minimum of 60 units with at least a C (2.0) average. A unit is based on the number of hours of classroom instruction. Most courses offer 3 units of credit for classes that meet 3 hours a week for a semester. Full-time students take a minimum of 12 units per semester.

Santa Monica College offers programs of courses that parallel the lower division, or the first two years, of four-year universities and colleges. Students wishing to transfer must complete a minimum of 56 transfer-level units in fields including English, mathematics, humanities, the physical sciences, and the social sciences. Requirements vary among universities, and it is to the student's advantage to choose the university to which he or she plans to transfer as soon as possible.

All nine campuses of the University of California, including UCLA and Berkeley, give preference to California's community college students over all other applicants for third-year transfer; however, students must complete the required courses with at least a 2.8 grade point average. In some majors, such as engineering and economics, a higher grade point average may be necessary for acceptance at high-demand campuses such as UCLA.

The twenty-three campuses of the California State University also give preference to community college students who have completed a prescribed program of lower-division courses with 56 transfer-level units and a minimum grade point average of 2.5. Campuses and majors in high demand by students may require higher grade point averages.

Associate Degree Programs Santa Monica College offers courses in sixty academic major fields of study, including accounting, anatomy, anthropology, art, astronomy, bilingual education, biological sciences, botany, broadcasting, business administration, chemistry, child development, Chinese, cinema, communication, computer information systems, economics, electronics, engineering, English, fashion merchandising, French, geography, geology, German, graphic design, history, interior design, Italian, Japanese, journalism, management, mathematics, merchandising, philosophy, photography, physical education, physics, physiology, political science, respiratory therapy, Russian, sociology, Spanish, speech, theater arts, and zoology. Courses for preprofessional study in such fields as chiropractic studies, medicine, optometry, pharmacy, physical therapy, and veterinary science are also offered.

Students who complete their first two years of undergraduate requirements may receive an Associate in Arts degree before transferring to a four-year university to complete their bachelor's degree. Occupational certificates are also granted in certain two-year programs including accounting, automotive technology, child development, computer information systems, cosmetology, electronics, fashion design, management, office information systems, photography, printing, real estate, recreational leadership, and supervision.

Credit for Nontraditional Learning Experiences

The cooperative work experience program at Santa Monica College makes it possible for students to earn College credit for work experience in technical, business, or professional settings. The program is a joint effort of the College and the community to combine on-the-job training with classroom instruction, enabling the student to acquire knowledge, skills, and attitudes necessary to enter into or progress in a chosen occupation.

Costs

For the 2006–07 academic year, California residents pay an enrollment fee of $26 per unit. Nonresidents paid an enrollment fee of $26 per unit plus $180 per unit in tuition. It is estimated that room and board in a homestay or apartment for this period cost $9832. Other costs include mandatory health insurance for F-1 international students ($684 per year) and textbooks and supplies ($1500). International students should have a minimum of $17,000 available to them to cover all of their costs for the year.

Financial Aid

U.S. students receive government support in the form of grants and loans based on their financial need. International students do not qualify for government support, but they are eligible to compete for 200 non-need scholarships (averaging $500) given by private donors.

Faculty

Santa Monica has 321 full-time faculty members and 581 part-time faculty members. All hold the equivalent of a master's degree or higher and are certified by the state of California. Although faculty members are chosen on the basis of their teaching ability, many of the professors hold doctoral degrees, particularly in the sciences. The student-faculty ratio is 40:1, although some classes are larger or smaller than 40, depending on the subject. Many faculty members maintain office hours to advise students on an individual basis. In addition, counselors on the faculty help students plan their schedules and provide special assistance for personal learning problems.

Student Body Profile

Santa Monica College has a total enrollment of 27,700 students, of whom 44 percent are men and 56 percent are women. The average age is 29. The racial breakdown of the student group includes Asian, 23 percent; African American, 9 percent; Hispanic, 24 percent; Native American, 1 percent; Pacific Islander, 1 percent; other (nonwhites), 2 percent; and white (non-Hispanic), 40 percent. Of the full-time students enrolled, 65 percent plan to transfer to a four-year college or university, 13 percent are undecided, 6 percent are taking classes for personal interest, 4 percent enroll for professional development, 3 percent enroll for a vocational certificate or an associate degree, and 9 percent enroll for other reasons. The international student population numbers 2,628.

Student Activities

All students are encouraged to join a variety of clubs supported by the Associated Students. The clubs are organized by students with special interests such as ecology, geology, biology, skiing, karate, dance, music, and drama. There is also an international club and clubs organized by students from Hong Kong, Indonesia, and India. The clubs normally meet once a week and conduct activities on and off campus throughout the year.

Sports Sports facilities at the College include off-site tennis courts, a gymnasium, an Olympic-size swimming pool, and the track built for the 1984 Olympics in Los Angeles. The College competes on the varsity level in men's football and men's and women's basketball, tennis, track, and volleyball. All students have access to the sports facilities for classes and individual training.

Facilities and Resources

Santa Monica College has excellent teaching facilities, including laboratories for science, electronics, computers, and nursing. It also has a new state-of the-art library with 103,392 bound volumes, and a learning resources center provides media-assisted individual instruction and free tutoring. There are 160 terminals/PCs available for student use at various locations throughout the campus. Other facilities include an amphitheater, a music room and auditorium, a little theater, an art gallery, a planetarium, a media center, and a student activities building.

The Associated Student Center provides study areas and a computer laboratory with free use of Macintosh computers to all students. The Student Center also includes a cafeteria, conference center, and bookstore.

The Santa Monica College Transfer Center assists students who are seeking to continue their studies at a four-year college or university. Its services include workshops on the application process, opportunities to meet with representatives from the four-year institutions, and tours of the campuses throughout California.

A Mentor Program in the arts gives exceptionally talented students in the performing and applied arts an opportunity to further develop their abilities through individual instruction. Mentor programs exist in architecture, art, dance, fashion design, music, photography, and theater arts. Students wishing to be part of the Mentor Program must demonstrate exceptional abilities and commitment. The program of study is tailored to the goals of the individual and often results in a 1-person show of the student's work or a public performance.

Location

Santa Monica College is located on the beautiful coast of Southern California in the city of Santa Monica. Because of the nearness to the ocean, Santa Monica has clean air and a mild climate throughout the year. It is just to the west of Los Angeles, one of the most cosmopolitan cities in the world. The campus provides easy access to outstanding theater, music, and museum facilities in Los Angeles as well as to Universal Studios and other centers of the entertainment industry. Santa Monica College is less than 10 miles from UCLA, USC, Pepperdine University, Loyola Marymount University, and other fine institutions of higher education in the Los Angeles area.

Admission Requirements

Santa Monica College has an open admission policy. Math and English tests are given upon entry in order to counsel students and place them at the proper course levels. International students who are below the university level in English are able to take preuniversity courses in ESL while they are taking university transfer-level courses, such as mathematics, that are not as dependent on English skills. International students are required to have an English level equivalent to a TOEFL score of 450 (133 CBT/45–46 iBT) in order to enroll in academic courses. Students who do not have the required English proficiency (TOEFL score) can enroll in the Intensive ESL Program at Santa Monica College.

Application and Information

Applications are accepted on an ongoing basis prior to the beginning of each semester. For the 2006–07 academic year, the fall semester begins August 28, the winter session begins January 2, the spring semester begins February 12, and the summer session begins June 18. All students should apply two months prior to the beginning of each semester or session in order to have the best selection of classes. International students must submit the documents required by the U.S. government for issuing I-20 student visas two months in advance. These documents include transcripts from high school and other colleges or universities attended, verification of financial support, and a certification of the minimum English level. International student applications are processed within one week, and notification of acceptance can be made by fax or express mail when necessary.

For more information, students should contact:

Teresita Rodriguez
Dean of Admissions
Santa Monica College
1900 Pico Boulevard
Santa Monica, California 90405-1628
Telephone: 310-434-4380

International students should contact:

Dr. Elena M. Garate
Dean, International Education
International Student Center
Santa Monica College
1900 Pico Boulevard
Santa Monica, California 90405-1628
Telephone: 310-434-4217
Fax: 310-434-3651

STATE UNIVERSITY OF NEW YORK COLLEGE OF ENVIRONMENTAL SCIENCE AND FORESTRY, RANGER SCHOOL

WANAKENA, NEW YORK

The College and Its Mission

The forest technology and land surveying technology programs are offered through the State University of New York College of Environmental Science and Forestry (ESF) at the Ranger School campus. Throughout its history, the College has focused on the environmental issues of the time in each of its three mission areas: instruction, research, and public service. The College is dedicated to educating future scientists and managers who, through specialized skills, will be able to use a holistic approach to solving the environmental and resource problems facing society.

More than 3,200 students have graduated from the program over the past ninety-three years, including more than 180 women since 1974. Established in 1912 with the gift of 1,800 acres of land in the Adirondack Mountains, the ESF forest technology program is the oldest in the nation. The Ranger School's managed forest includes both hardwood and coniferous trees and is bounded on two sides by the New York State Forest Preserve. It is also adjacent to several acres of virgin timber in the Adirondack Forest preserve.

The main campus building houses the central academic, dining, and recreational facilities. Dormitory wings are located on either side of the main campus building. Dorm rooms are designed to accommodate 1 or 2 people. All second-year students live on campus, with the exception of married students accompanied by their families. These students should arrange for rental accommodations well before the start of the academic year.

A $5-million renovation and expansion of the Ranger school was just completed. This project included renovations and an addition to the main campus building, a new dining hall, distance learning classrooms, additional residence hall facilities, and a new student recreational area.

Academic Programs

Associate Degree Programs Students who complete the program earn an **Associate in Applied Science (A.A.S.)** degree in forest technology or land surveying technology.

Both degree programs at the Ranger School are 1+1 programs, meaning they require 30 credit hours of course work in general studies to fulfill the program's freshman liberal arts requirements. Students who are considering later transfer to a four-year program should follow the suggestions for freshman-year selections outlined in the ESF catalog. The 30 credits taken in the freshman year may be taken at the college's Syracuse campus or any other accredited college a student chooses to attend. These are followed by an additional 48 credit hours at the Wanakena campus in the second year of the program. The sophomore year takes place at the Ranger School, where time is equally divided between classroom and laboratory work, and experience in the field. Fieldwork is a large component of the curriculum. Students take several short field trips during the second year of study, at no additional expense to them. These

trips enhance courses in dendrology, silviculture, forest management, recreation, wildlife, ecology, and surveying. On weekends and evenings, students will devote much of their time to studying, but there is time for recreation as well, when student can take advantage of the college's beautiful setting in the Adirondacks.

Transfer Arrangements Counseling is available for students interested in pursuing a four-year degree on the main campus in Syracuse. Students should contact the ESF admissions office.

Costs

The cost of the first year varies according to the institution attended. Estimated tuition and fees for the 2005–06 academic year at the Wanakena campus total $5325 for residents of New York State and $11,585 for out-of-state residents. Room and board at the Wanakena campus are $8050 and the estimated cost of books, personal expenses, and travel is $3050. (Books and supplies are sold on campus.)

Financial Aid

More than 80 percent of Ranger School students receive some form of financial aid, including grants and scholarships, low-interest loans, and student employment. All students are encouraged to apply for financial aid by completing the Free Application for Federal Student Aid.

Faculty

Five full-time faculty members and 1 part-time instructor teach at the Wanakena campus. The student-faculty ratio is approximately 10:1. Students have ready access to faculty members for consultations. Faculty members are housed on campus, and faculty offices are located near student living quarters. There is close contact between students and faculty members in the classroom and at fieldwork sites.

Student Body Profile

Ninety percent of all students complete the forest technology or land surveying technology program. About 50 percent go on to careers as forest technicians or aides with private companies or government agencies; some 30 percent become surveyors. Many graduates of the forest technology program or land surveying technology program go on to receive Bachelor of Science and even graduate-level degrees at ESF's main campus in Syracuse or at other colleges and universities.

Student Activities

Students have a variety of activities available to them at the Wanakena campus. Many recreational activities are readily available, including hiking, camping, canoeing, cross-country skiing, and ice-skating. Students are assigned a canoe for their use during the year. Each class forms a student government, which plans a number of class activities. A new recreational facility is available for student use. Students at the Ranger

School follow the ESF code of student conduct and follow the house rules of the Wanakena campus.

Location

The 2,800-acre campus is situated on the banks of the Oswegatchie River near the Adirondack Mountain hamlet of Wanakena, approximately 65 miles east of Watertown, New York, and 35 miles west of Tupper Lake on New York State's Route 3. At the Wanakena campus, social and recreational activities utilize the area's year-round opportunities for outdoor enjoyment. An excellent hospital, located in Star Lake, New York, serves the community.

Admission Requirements

Students may apply to ESF for admission to the Ranger School's programs during their senior year in high school for guaranteed transfer admission or during their freshman year of college for transfer admission. Prospective students should consult the current catalog for specific information concerning the application process. ESF cooperates with more than fifty colleges in cooperative transfer programs. Acceptance to the Ranger School is contingent upon satisfactory completion of first-year courses. While in high school, applicants should successfully complete a college-preparatory program with an emphasis in mathematics and science. Electives in such areas as computer applications and mechanical drawing are recommended. Transfer students are considered on the basis of college course work and interest in the program. In addition to academic requirements, applicants must be able to meet the physical requirements of the Ranger School program and must submit a full medical report. Parents of applicants under 18 years old should be aware of the field nature of the program and its rigorous study-work regimen.

Application and Information

The Ranger School accepts students for fall admission only. Fall admission decisions are made beginning around the middle of January and continue on a rolling basis until the class is filled. Application forms for New York State residents are available at all high schools in the state and at all colleges in the state university system. Out-of-state students should request application forms from the Office of Undergraduate Admissions at the address below. Prospective students who wish to visit the 2,800-acre campus can do so by contacting the Director, New York State Ranger School, Wanakena, New York 13695-0106 (telephone: 315-848-2566 or fax: 315-848-3249).

The Admissions office at the Syracuse campus also serves as the Admissions Office for the Ranger School. Students may request an application or information about course or college selection for the freshman year from the address listed below.

Office of Undergraduate Admissions
106 Bray Hall
State University of New York College of Environmental
    Science and Forestry
1 Forestry Drive
Syracuse, New York 13210-2779
Telephone: 315-470-6600
                800-777-7373 (toll-free)
Fax: 315-470-6933
E-mail: esfinfo@esf.edu
World Wide Web: http://rangerschool.esf.edu

VALLEY FORGE MILITARY COLLEGE
WAYNE, PENNSYLVANIA

The College and Its Mission

Valley Forge Military College (VFMC) is a private, coeducational residential college that offers the freshman and sophomore years of college. The primary mission of the College is to prepare students for transfer to competitive four-year colleges and universities. Established in 1935, the College has a long tradition of fostering personal growth through a comprehensive system built on the five cornerstones that make Valley Forge unique: academic excellence, character development, personal motivation, physical development, and leadership to all students regardless of race, creed, or national origin. The diverse student body represents more than nineteen states and four countries. The College has an excellent transfer record, with 95 percent of cadets accepted to their first- or second-choice schools. More than 63 percent were admitted to the top-tier schools in the country.

Valley Forge Military College is the only college in the northeastern United States that offers qualified freshmen the opportunity to participate in an Early Commissioning Program, leading to a commission as a second lieutenant in the U.S. Army Reserves or Army National Guard at the end of their sophomore year. The U.S. Air Force Academy, the U.S. Military Academy, the U.S. Coast Guard Academy, and the U.S. Naval Academy have all sponsored cadets through their Foundation Scholarship Programs and other programs to attend Valley Forge Military College.

The College is accredited by the Middle States Association of Colleges and Schools and is approved by the Pennsylvania State Council of Education and the Commission on Higher Education of the Pennsylvania State Department of Education. The College is a member of the National Association of Independent Colleges and Universities, the Association of Independent Colleges/Universities of Pennsylvania, the Pennsylvania Association of Two-Year Colleges, and the Association of Military Colleges and Schools in the United States.

Academic Programs

All students are required to complete an academic program of 60 credits, including a core program of approximately 45 credits that is designed to establish the essential competencies that are necessary for continued intellectual development and to facilitate the transfer process. Included in the core program are two semesters of English, one semester of literature, one semester of Western civilization, two semesters of mathematics, one semester of science, and one semester of computer science. Qualified cadets must also complete a minimum of two semesters of military science. To satisfy the requirement for the associate degree, cadets must complete at least 15 additional credits in courses related to their selected area of concentration. Associate degrees are awarded upon satisfactory completion of the degree requirements with a quality point average of 2.0 or higher.

Associate Degree Programs Valley Forge Military College offers concentrations in the liberal arts, business, criminal justice, leadership, and general studies, leading to an Associate of Arts degree, as well as concentrations in pre-engineering, physical sciences, life sciences, and general studies, leading to an Associate of Science degree.

Transfer Arrangements Transfer of academic credits and completion of the baccalaureate degree is facilitated by established relationships with a number of outstanding colleges and universities, including articulation agreements with the neighboring institutions of Eastern University, Cabrini College, and Rosemont College.

Credit for Nontraditional Learning Experiences

Valley Forge Military College may give credit for demonstrated proficiency in areas related to college-level courses. Sources used to determine such proficiency are the College-Level Examination Program (CLEP), Advanced Placement (AP) examinations, Defense Activity for Nontraditional Education Support (DANTES), and the Office of Education Credit and Credentials of the American Council on Education (ACE). All such requests must be approved by the Office of the Dean.

Costs

The annual charge for 2005–06 was $28,550. This charge included tuition, room and board, uniforms, maintenance, haircuts, and other fees. Optional expenses may include fee-based courses, such as scuba, aviation, and driver's education, or membership in the cavalry troop or artillery battery. A fee is charged for Health Center confinement over 24 hours' duration. For information on the payment plan, students should contact the Business Office.

Financial Aid

The College offers a combination of merit- and need-based scholarships and grants as well as endowed scholarships based on donor specifications to help VFMC cadets finance their education. The academic scholarships reward incoming and returning cadets for demonstrated academic excellence. Performance scholarships are awarded to eligible cadets who participate in the athletic teams, band, or choir. To qualify for federal, state, and VFMC grants, students must file the Free Application for Federal Student Aid (FAFSA) by the published priority deadlines. In addition, qualified cadets in the advanced ROTC commissioning program are eligible for two-year, full-tuition scholarships. These scholarships are supplemented by assistance for room and board provided by the College. The FAFSA is also required for ROTC scholarship applications.

Valley Forge Military College offers federal student aid to eligible cadets in the form of Federal Pell Grants, Federal Supplemental Educational Opportunity Grants (FSEOG), Federal Work-Study (FWS) Program positions, Federal Stafford Student Loans, and Parent Loans for Undergraduate Students (PLUS) through the Federal Family Education Loan Program. Applicants must file the FAFSA and the VFMC financial aid application for consideration for all student aid.

Faculty

There are 12 full-time and 11 part-time faculty members holding the academic rank of professor, associate professor, assistant professor, or instructor. These faculty members are selected for their professional ability and strong personal leadership qualities; 50 percent of the full-time staff members hold doctorates in their field. Faculty members perform additional duties as athletic coaches and advisers of extracurricular activities. The Military Science Department has 5 active-duty Army officers and 4 noncommissioned officers assigned as full-time faculty members for the ROTC program. The faculty-student ratio is approximately 1:14. Classes are small, and the classroom atmosphere contributes to a harmonious relationship between faculty members and the students.

Student Body Profile

The military structure of Valley Forge provides extraordinary opportunities for cadets to develop and exercise leadership abilities. The Corps of Cadets is a self-administering body organized in nine company units along military lines, with a cadet officer and noncommissioned officer organization for cadet control and administration. The College's cadets are appointed to major command positions in the Corps. The First Captain is generally a sophomore in the College. Cadet leadership and positive peer pressure within this structured setting result in a unique camaraderie among cadets. Cadets, through their student representatives, cooperate with the administration in enforcing regulations regarding student conduct. A Student Advisory Council represents the cadets in the school administration. The Dean's Council meets regularly to discuss aspects of academic life.

Student Activities

The proximity to many colleges and universities ensures a full schedule of local college-oriented events in addition to Valley Forge's own activities. Cadets are encouraged to become involved in community-service activities. The scholarship-supported Regimental Band has performed for U.S. presidents, royalty, and countless military and social events. The Regimental Chorus has performed at the Capitol Building in Washington, D.C.; the Philadelphia Academy of Music; and New York's Carnegie Hall. In addition, eligible students can participate in VFMC honor societies: Phi Theta Kappa, Lambda Alpha Epsilon, or Alpha Beta Gamma. Other available activities include business and political clubs, French Club, Black Student Union, Rotoract, flight training, and participation in the local Radnor Fire Company.

Sports Athletics and physical well-being are important elements in a Valley Forge education. The aim of the program is to develop all-around fitness, alertness, character, esprit de corps, leadership, courage, competitive spirit, and genuine desire for physical and mental achievement. For students aspiring to compete at the Division I-A or Division I-AA level, Valley Forge's residential college football and basketball programs offer a distinctive opportunity that combines such a strong academic transfer program with a highly successful athletic program that has habitually placed players at the national level. Continuing a legacy that began with its high school program, in only eight years, the College has placed 40 players on national-level teams in basketball and football. In the last seven years, the Valley Forge wrestling program has also produced 3 National Champions and 7 All-Americans in the National Collegiate Wrestling Association. Students may also compete at the collegiate level in cross-country, lacrosse, soccer, and tennis. Club and interscholastic teams are available in golf, polo, and riflery. The Valley Forge polo team is consistently among the top-ranked polo teams in the nation, regularly competing against nationally ranked teams.

Facilities and Resources

Campus buildings are equipped to meet student needs. A fiber-optic, Internet-capable computer network connects all classrooms, laboratories, library, and dormitory rooms on the campus. All rooms are computer accessible and provide access to CadetNET, the institutional local area network. This network provides access to the library and the Internet. College classrooms are located in two buildings and contain chemistry, biology, and physics laboratories. A computer laboratory supports the computer science curriculum and student requirements through a local area network.

Library and Audiovisual Services The May H. Baker Memorial Library is a learning resource center for independent study and research. The library has more than 100,000 volumes and audiovisual materials, microfilm, and periodicals and houses the newly created Cadet Achievement Center. It provides online database access, membership in the Tri-State Library Consortium, and computer links to ACCESS Pennsylvania and other databases to support the College requirements.

Location

Valley Forge Military College is situated on a beautifully landscaped 120-acre campus in the Main Line community of Wayne, 15 miles west of Philadelphia and close to Valley Forge National Historic Park. Ample opportunities exist for cadets to enjoy cultural and entertainment resources and activities in the Philadelphia area.

Admission Requirements

Admission to the College is based upon review of an applicant's SAT or ACT scores, high school transcript, recommendations from a guidance counselor, and personal interview. Students may be accepted for midyear admission. Minimum requirements for admission on a nonprobation status are a high school diploma or equivalency diploma with a minimum 2.0 average, rank in the upper half of the class, and minimum combined SAT score of 850 or ACT score of 17. The College reviews the new SAT standards and scores on a case-by-case basis. An international student for whom English is a second language must have a minimum score of 550 on the Test of English as a Foreign Language (TOEFL). Up to 20 percent of an entering class may be admitted on a conditional or probationary status, and individual entrance requirements may be waived by the Dean of the College for students who display a sincere commitment to pursuing a college degree.

Application and Information

Valley Forge Military College follows a program of rolling admissions. Applicants are notified of the admission decision as soon as their files are complete. A nonrefundable registration fee of $25 is required of all applicants.

For application forms and further information, students should contact:

College Admissions Officer
Valley Forge Military College
1001 Eagle Road
Wayne, Pennsylvania 19087

Telephone: 800-234-VFMC (toll-free)
E-mail: admissions@vfmac.edu
World Wide Web: http://www.vfmac.edu

A Valley Forge Military College cadet rappels down the Rappel Tower.

WADE COLLEGE
DALLAS, TEXAS

The College and Its Mission

Wade College is a small private college offering an associate degree program in merchandising and design. The College is a teaching institution that emphasizes professional study and the liberal arts.

Wade College exists and operates to provide its students with the skills and knowledge that are needed to be productive members of society. It further seeks to provide them with an enriching cultural, moral, economic, and social experience. The College is committed to serving the changing requirements of the merchandising, fashion design, computer graphic design, and interior design fields.

The purpose of Wade College is to offer programs of instruction that are designed to allow students to develop the competencies necessary for immediate employment and career advancement in their chosen fields; continue and complete a formal education in upper-level and graduate colleges and universities, if so desired; develop intellectual, humanitarian, and leadership skills that will advance their potential for success; and engage in continual self-improvement.

Wade College emphasizes individual student attention. To facilitate this, class sizes are usually small.

Academic Programs

The educational program emphasizes the importance of both general education and specialized study. The values of the former are deemed important to the development of responsible citizens in a free society; the experience of the latter is regarded as indispensable to students preparing for active careers. General education is versatile and helps students to better adapt to change so that they may advance in their careers. Specialized study helps them develop the professional skills that are required in their career fields.

Through the integration of diverse disciplines in art, design, business, computers, and the liberal arts, the Associate of Arts degree program reaches beyond specialized professional skills to a broader spectrum of knowledge. The curriculum promotes a well-rounded perspective of the world in general and the field of merchandising and design in particular.

For more than forty years, Wade College has specialized in academic programs leading to careers in the fields of merchandising and design. The Associate of Arts degree is a balanced program with dual majors in merchandising and design. Concentrations are offered in fashion design, interior design, computer graphic design, merchandise marketing, fashion merchandising, and interior merchandising. A minimum of 63 semester credit hours is required for degree completion. The associate degree is normally completed in four consecutive trimesters of full-time study. Each trimester is fifteen weeks in length and is equivalent to a traditional semester. Full-time students are expected to graduate sixteen months after entering the program. Individual degree plans can be developed for students with special needs.

Costs

In 2006–07, tuition for the academic year is $9050. Optional student housing is $3360 per academic year. There are additional fees and deposits. Textbooks, supplies, and course fees are estimated at $1480 per academic year. All tuition and fee costs are subject to change. Wade College has a guaranteed tuition rate for the four trimesters of the student's program.

Financial Aid

Wade College offers financial aid counseling and assistance in applying for a variety of federal financial aid programs. The U.S. Department of Education offers several financial aid programs to help students meet educational expenses. Students at Wade College are eligible to apply for financial assistance under the following federal student aid programs: the Federal Pell Grant Program, Federal Supplemental Educational Opportunity Grants, Federal Work-Study Program, Federal Perkins Loan, William D. Ford Federal Direct Loan Program, and the Federal Parent Loan for Undergraduate Students (PLUS) program. Private lending programs are also available.

The College is committed to helping every student plan for educational expenses. An individual Student Financial Plan is prepared for each registered student prior to the start of classes. Various payment options are also available.

Faculty

Each educational area is headed by a full-time faculty member. Other full-time and part-time instructors are also available. Usually, instructors have advanced degrees and are also practicing professionals in their fields. Approximately 80 percent of the faculty members have advanced degrees.

Student Body Profile

The student body is approximately 90 percent female and 10 percent male. The majority of students are from Texas. The average age is 20.5 years old. Most students are between the ages of 18 and 24, but there are students over 30. The ethnic composition of the student body is similar to that of the North Texas area. Approximately 45 percent are white, 35 percent are African American, 15 percent are Hispanic, and 5 percent are Asian.

Student Activities

Numerous campus organizations and activities are available for student participation. The College has a chapter of Phi Theta Kappa, the national honor society for two-year colleges. Many students participate in the seasonal apparel and furniture wholesale markets held at the Dallas Market Center. They are assisted through the College's Career Planning and Placement Office.

Comprehensive student services are offered in the areas of housing, financial aid, part-time employment, counseling, and graduate placement. Student needs are given a high priority. Career planning and placement for students of Wade College is offered through the offices of the Executive Director and the Director of Student Services. Career development and professional job search assistance is provided to students and alumni though individual career counseling and exploration of various career opportunities. The office also provides instruction in writing resumes and cover letters, portfolio presentations and self-promotion, interviewing skills, and networking techniques to prepare students for the job market.

Facilities and Resources

Wade College offers students the opportunity to learn in the heart of the merchandising and design industries. The College is part of the Dallas Market Center, the world's largest wholesale merchandising and design complex. Wade College occupies approximately 14,000 square feet on the second floor of the INFOMART building and another 1,000 square feet on the first floor of the World Trade Center of the Dallas Market Center. Student-to-instructor ratio is approximately 18:1, and the student-to-computer ratio is about 4:1. Wade College uses state-of-the-art equipment, including multimedia-equipped classrooms, a fashion design studio, an interior design studio, an art studio, and two computer labs, including one dedicated to graphic design. Various other equipment and support material is available for the art, fashion, design, and interior design studio courses.

The student residence apartments are located in the dynamic environment of North Dallas, 12 miles from downtown.

Wade College Library is located on the campus of Wade College. The library provides access to a specialty collection of materials reflecting the College's curriculum. The library's collection contains approximately 5,000 bound volumes, 125 periodical subscriptions, and 400 audiovisual items, including films, microfilms, videos, slides, and machine-readable units. The library is a member of AMIGOS library service, a regional network for resource sharing and technology, has access to film and video lending through the Northeast Texas Library System (NETLS), and has electronic access to numerous indexes, databases, and full-text periodical sources. The library also provides access to the Internet.

Location

Dallas, Texas is an international business, technology, and retail center. Dallas is known for its shopping, restaurants, and entertainment. Dallas is also home to the Cowboys, the Mavericks, the Rangers, and the Stars—major professional sports teams in the NFL, NBA, MLB, and NHL, respectively. The city and surrounding areas have a population of well over 2 million. The area is served by public transportation, including bus and light rail. Situated on a major interstate highway, the campus is easily accessible by car. Fort Worth, another major urban center, is within easy driving distance. The climate of Dallas is relatively mild in winter, warm in spring and fall, and hot in the summer.

Admission Requirements

Wade College adheres to a policy of open admissions for high school graduates or those students who have passed the GED test. This policy precludes admitting students on the basis of qualitative selection procedures. The philosophy of admission is that an educationally motivated individual is entitled to an opportunity for improved professional and personal success. The College provides a supportive educational environment so that individuals with a sincere interest have the opportunity to meet the educational rigors placed on them and successfully progress through course requirements.

Prospective students may apply for admission as early as one year in advance of the desired class starting date. Since annual enrollment is limited, interested students are encouraged to submit their applications as early as possible. Wade College does not have an application fee. All applicants are required to interview with a representative from the Admissions Office prior to the start of classes. It is highly recommended that this interview take place at the College; however, in circumstances where the applicant's home is a great distance from the College, the interview may be conducted on the telephone or via the Internet.

Applicants are expected to register within thirty days of their acceptance by paying a nonrefundable $125 enrollment fee. Prior to entry, accepted applicants must verify their high school graduation or their possession of a General Educational Development (GED) credential on their Application for Admission. If applicable, they must also submit the Free Application for Federal Student Aid (FAFSA).

Application and Information

For more information, prospective students should contact:

Admissions Office
Wade College
Dallas Market Center
2050 Stemmons Freeway, Suite 158
P.O. Box 421149
Dallas, Texas 75342
Telephone: 214-637-3530
          800-624-4850 (toll-free)
Fax: 214-637-0827
E-mail: admissions@wadecollege.edu
World Wide Web: http://www.wadecollege.edu

WESTERN CAREER COLLEGE
School of Health Professionals
PLEASANT HILL, CALIFORNIA

The College and Its Mission

Western Career College (WCC) was founded in 1967 in Sacramento, California. In 1983, the College was purchased by the Education Corporation of America (EdCOA); in 2003, U.S. Education Corporation acquired EdCOA.

Western Career College has campuses in the following locations: Antioch, Citrus Heights, Emeryville, Fremont, Pleasant Hill, Sacramento, San Jose, San Leandro, and Stockton, California.

The mission of Western Career College is to provide education in the majors and disciplines of the health, legal, and technical fields of study that lead to an Associate in Science degree and/or a Certificate of Achievement. Western Career College is committed to a skills-based approach to education and strives to identify and support the achievement of student learning outcomes throughout its institution and learning community.

The Western Career College philosophy is centered on outcomes-based learning. The College's focus on retention, placement, and job performance results in graduates who are highly qualified and motivated employees. The communities served by the College benefit from this focus on outcomes-based learning and the College's ability to adapt to their changing needs.

In addition to their academic preparation and skills training, students learn how to think critically, make decisions, gain independence, organize work, take initiative, supervise others, and be responsible employees. In degree programs, a broad base of general education course offerings provides students with communication, critical-thinking, mathematical, and computer skills as well as perspectives from the sciences, humanities, and social sciences.

Western Career College encourages students to work to achieve their highest potential while attaining their career goals. The College strives for excellence and quality in everything it does and instills in its students the same aspirations.

Academic Programs

The College offers Associate in Science degrees and Certificates of Achievement in the following areas: biotech-

nology, criminal justice, dental assisting, dental hygiene, design drafting, graphic design, health-care administration, health information technology, massage therapy, medical assisting, medical billing, pharmacy technology, registered nursing, surgical technology, veterinary technology, and vocational nursing. Not all programs are offered at all campus locations.

Off-Campus Programs

All Western Career College programs are taught on campus; however, most programs require an externship, clinical rotation, and/or fieldwork experience in a physician's office, hospital, clinic, or other appropriate work location.

Credit for Nontraditional Learning Experiences

Students should discuss credit transfer options with the campus admissions department.

Costs

Tuition varies by program. Students should contact the admissions department to determine program tuition.

Financial Aid

The College participates in a number of state and federal financial aid programs. Available loan programs include the Federal Perkins Loan, Federal Stafford Student Loan, and Federal PLUS loan. Students may also be eligible for a Federal Pell Grant, Federal Supplemental Educational Opportunity Grant, or Cal Grant, and scholarships may be available. In addition, the College participates in the Federal Work-Study Program.

Academic Facilities

The campus classrooms and laboratories contain the latest in equipment, administrative offices, computer labs, and attractively decorated and comfortably appointed student unions. In addition, a campus library is equipped with furnishings that provide a comfortable setting in which students can do research and/or study as well as computers that provide Internet access to a wide variety of educational resources. Current library holdings have been chosen to support the programs that are taught at the College and include program-specific materials as well as other support materials.

Location

Pleasant Hill is located in Contra Costa County, in the East Bay area of San Francisco. The campus is conveniently located at 380 Civic Drive, just down the street from the Pleasant Hill police department and the YMCA, off the Willow Pass Road exit on Interstate 680, about a mile past the Sun Valley Mall.

Admission Requirements

All applicants must be at least 16 years of age. The College admits students who have graduated from high school or those who are beyond the age of compulsory school attendance and who have a General Educational Develop-

ment (GED) certificate or Proficiency Certificate as an equivalency to high school graduation. Students who are admitted to the College without a high school diploma or a recognized equivalency must pass an Ability-to-Benefit (ATB) evaluation. Not all programs accept ATB students. All applicants must take an entrance test administered by Western Career College or meet specific programmatic requirements, as listed in the catalog.

The admissions procedure consists of an exchange of information between the applicant and the College. The College maintains a staff of Admissions Representatives who are responsible for this discussion.

Application and Information

Western Career College
380 Civic Drive, Suite 300
Pleasant Hill, California 94523
Telephone: 925-609-6650
Fax: 925-609-6666
World Wide Web: http://www.westerncollege.com/?ad=
petersons

WESTWOOD COLLEGE–ANAHEIM

ANAHEIM, CALIFORNIA

The College and Its Mission

Today, the variables that define career success are ever changing. In order to get ahead and stay ahead, students need the right kind of preparation. To prepare them for the working world, students need a career-focused education program that teaches the skills employers demand and offers hands-on practical experience with real-world applications and the right kind of job-placement assistance to help them get started in their new careers.

Students also need a fast-track learning program that shortens the time from education to career, with an academic schedule that fits their lifestyle. They need a high level of student services to help them reach their goals and the right financial package to make it all possible.

All of these are the focus at Westwood College, which operates twenty campuses, with locations in California, Colorado, Georgia, Illinois, Texas, and Virginia. The seventeen campuses of Westwood College offer degree programs in high-technology fields, while the three aviation campuses (Redstone College of Aviation Technology–Denver, Redstone College of Aviation Technology–Los Angeles, and Redstone Aviation Institute–Houston) offer aviation maintenance training.

Such fields as computer networking, graphic design, computer-aided design, and e-business are featured at the Westwood College campuses located in Anaheim, Inland Empire (Upland), Long Beach, and Los Angeles, California; Atlanta, Georgia; DuPage, O'Hare Airport, River Oaks, and Chicago–Loop, Illinois; Denver–North and Denver–South, Colorado; Dallas, Fort Worth, and Houston, Texas; and the Washington, D.C., area. The Redstone College of Aviation Technology offers the aviation curriculum at the Denver, Colorado and Los Angeles, California, campuses, while Redstone Aviation Institute offers the aviation curriculum in Houston.

The Anaheim campus is accredited by the Accrediting Commission of Career Schools and Colleges of Technology (ACCSCT).

Westwood College–Anaheim is a branch of Westwood College–Denver North.

Academic Programs

The Anaheim campus focuses on computer-based technology programs that prepare graduates to take advantage of southern California's unique, high-tech career opportunities. Bachelor's degree programs are offered in computer network management, criminal justice, e-business management, game art and design, information systems security, interior design, visual communications, and Web design and multimedia. Associate degree programs are offered in computer-aided design/architectural drafting, computer network engineering, and graphic design and multimedia.

The programs, which feature hands-on learning experience, are designed to prepare students for entry-level positions in their chosen careers.

Costs

Standard program costs can be found in the Westwood College academic catalog.

Financial Aid

Tuition assistance is available for those who qualify. Scholarships include the Westwood High School Scholarship Program, which offers two scholarships to every high school in the United States; the Colorado Undergraduate Merit State Scholarships for Colorado residents; and several loan programs.

Student Body Profile

Student enrollment at the Anaheim campus totals 780, of whom approximately 25 percent are women.

Student Activities

In addition to on-campus activities, the Anaheim area offers many cultural and recreational opportunities for students.

Facilities and Resources

The campus includes a primary building with approximately 25,000 square feet dedicated to classrooms, labs, and administrative offices. A nearby campus annex houses additional classroom space.

Location

The Anaheim campus is in Orange County, minutes from attractions such as Disneyland, Knott's Berry Farm, and Edison International Park. The area offers students an active lifestyle and is rich in career opportunities. Located directly across the street from Anaheim's arena, the Arrowhead Pond, the campus is easily accessible from I-5 at Katella.

Admission Requirements

Applicants must have either a diploma from an accredited high school or a GED certificate and passing scores on the College entrance exam (or qualifying ACT/SAT scores).

Application and Information

Director of Admissions
Westwood College–Anaheim
1551 South Douglas Road
Anaheim, California 92801

Telephone: 714-704-2721
           877-650-6050 (toll-free)
Fax: 714-456-9971
E-mail: info@westwood.edu
World Wide Web: http://www.westwood.edu

Westwood College–Anaheim campus.

WESTWOOD COLLEGE–ANNANDALE

ANNANDALE, VIRGINIA

The College and Its Mission

Today, the variables that define career success are ever changing. In order to get ahead and stay ahead, students need the right kind of preparation. To prepare for the working world, they need a career-focused education program that teaches the skills employers demand and offers hands-on, practical experience with real-world applications and the right kind of job-placement assistance to help students get started in their new careers.

Students also need a fast-track learning program that shortens the time from education to career, with an academic schedule that fits their lifestyle. They need a high level of student services to help them reach their goals and the right financial package to make it all possible.

All of these are the focus at Westwood, which operates eighteen campuses, with locations in California, Colorado, Illinois, Georgia, Texas, and Virginia. The seventeen campuses of Westwood College offer degree programs in high-technology fields, while the three aviation campuses (Redstone College of Aviation Technology–Denver, Redstone College of Aviation Technology–Los Angeles, and Redstone Aviation Institute–Houston) offer aviation maintenance training.

Such fields as computer networking, graphic design, computer-aided design (CAD), and e-business are featured at the Westwood College campuses located in Anaheim, Inland Empire (Upland), Long Beach, and Los Angeles, California; Atlanta, Georgia; DuPage, O'Hare Airport, River Oaks, and Chicago Loop, Illinois; Denver North and Denver South, Colorado; and Dallas, Fort Worth, and Houston, Texas. The Redstone College of Aviation Technology offers the aviation curriculum at the Denver, Colorado, and Los Angeles, California, campuses, while Redstone Aviation Institute offers the aviation curriculum in Houston.

The Annandale campus, a satellite campus of Westwood College–Arlington Ballston, is accredited by the Accrediting Commission of Career Schools and Colleges of Technology (ACCSCT).

Academic Programs

Associate degree programs are in computer-aided design/architectural drafting and in graphic design and multimedia. The computer-aided design/architectural drafting program equips students with the skills necessary to become a candidate for many careers available to the skilled CAD operator. Students receive training on recent releases of AutoCAD, a popular CAD application that provides experience in developing technical drawings related to the field of architecture. Students learn to use CAD combined with theory and lab environment, where they are exposed to the ideas and principles in a lecture setting, and then immediately put that instruction to use in practical lab projects. This hands-on learning environment, coupled with an industry-experienced faculty, ensures that graduates are well prepared for the workforce.

The graphic design and multimedia program prepares students for entry-level jobs in the graphic design and multimedia industry. Students learn to create effective designs that communicate visually in both print and multimedia environments. The combination of technical and general education courses helps students develop skills in critical thinking, logic, communication, and problem solving. The program prepares graduates for positions as graphic designers, production artists, Web page designers, and multimedia designers within a diverse industry.

Bachelor's degrees are available in criminal justice and in design, with concentrations in animation or interior design. The criminal justice program equips students academically and professionally by developing a knowledge base, social awareness, and technological skills for an entry-level position in today's criminal justice environment. The curriculum provides an understanding of criminal justice methods, techniques, technologies, and required skills and abilities, with topics such as introduction to criminal justice, criminology, criminal procedure, criminal investigation, and juvenile justice as well as critical courses in interpersonal communication, victimology, and ethics in criminal justice.

The Bachelor of Science in animation covers topics such as the laws of human motion, physics, psychology as applied to 2-D or 3-D characters, life drawing and rendering techniques, and the application of audio and video to an animation project. In addition, the combination of management and general education courses in the program helps students apply skills in general management, critical thinking, logic, communication, and problem solving to workplace challenges. The program includes critical business courses that cover such topics as project management, determining client need, working within a team environment, and working within a deadline. The degree program prepares students for entry-level positions, including graphic artist and assistant animator for Web-based or computer-based team projects.

The interior design program offers students a well-rounded foundation that nurtures the technical, creative, and human factors of interior design necessary to enter the field. Students build on a foundation of drawing, drafting, color, and basic design principles while learning about human factors, space planning, interior construction and detailing, safety and building codes, and CAD. In addition, students are equipped with a historical perspective of interior design, an understanding of interior design business practices, collaboration techniques for working with related professionals, and, finally, an awareness of professional responsibilities and ethics for personal practice. The B.S. in interior design prepares students for entry-level positions in the industry, including in-house design assistant for both large and small commercial and residential design and architectural firms.

Costs

Standard program costs can be found in the Westwood College academic catalog.

Financial Aid

Tuition assistance is available for those who qualify. Scholarships include the Westwood High School Scholarship Program, in which two scholarships are offered to every high school in the United States. In addition, several loan programs are available.

Faculty

Westwood has 528 faculty members in all. Half are employed on a full-time basis. Forty percent hold master's degrees, and 5 percent have doctorates.

Student Body Profile

Westwood College recruits recent high school graduates, young adults, and working adults who want to acquire new skills to take advantage of growing opportunities in the professional workplace. Students come to Westwood from all across the United States and from many countries around the world. Westwood's students are highly motivated, hardworking, and committed to preparing for rewarding careers.

Student Activities

In addition to on-campus activities, the northern Virginia–Washington, D.C., area offers many cultural and recreational opportunities for students.

Facilities and Resources

Westwood offers a variety of information and research resources, including on-campus Resource Centers, links to Internet-based information services, and a bookstore at each campus. The Campus Resource Centers offer a library of program-specific materials that have been carefully selected to aid that school's career-focused educational mission. The Education Department at each campus collaborates closely with the campus' Resource Center staff to ensure that materials support the school's hands-on curriculum. Typical learning aids include books, periodicals, and Internet access. A virtual library, providing remote access to several selected databases, is also offered. Staff members are available to assist students during regular library hours and can provide instruction on how to conduct research in the library and online.

Location

The region offers an array of sporting and cultural events, famous exhibits and museums, and a variety of outdoor activities to keep students busy when not in class.

Admission Requirements

A diploma from an accredited high school or a GED certificate and passing scores on the college entrance exam (or qualifying ACT/SAT scores) are required. In addition, international students must submit TOEFL, IELTS, or MELAB scores. To apply, students must first contact the campus to schedule a personal career assessment.

Application and Information

Director of Admissions
Westwood College–Annandale Campus
7611 Little River Turnpike, 3rd floor
Annandale, Virginia 22003
Telephone: 703-642-3770
Fax: 703-642-3772
E-mail: info@westwood.edu
World Wide Web: http://www.westwood.edu/locations/
virginia-colleges/annandale-college.asp

WESTWOOD COLLEGE–ARLINGTON BALLSTON

ARLINGTON, VIRGINIA

The College and Its Mission

Today, the variables that define career success are ever changing. In order to get ahead and stay ahead, students need the right kind of preparation. To prepare for the working world, they need a career-focused education program that teaches the skills employers demand and offers hands-on, practical experience with real-world applications and the right kind of job-placement assistance to help students get started in their new careers.

Students also need a fast-track learning program that shortens the time from education to career, with an academic schedule that fits their lifestyle. They need a high level of student services to help them reach their goals and the right financial package to make it all possible.

All of these are the focus at Westwood, which operates eighteen campuses, with locations in California, Colorado, Illinois, Georgia, Texas, and Virginia. The seventeen campuses of Westwood College offer degree programs in high-technology fields, while the three aviation campuses (Redstone College of Aviation Technology–Denver, Redstone College of Aviation Technology–Los Angeles, and Redstone Aviation Institute–Houston) offer aviation maintenance training.

Such fields as computer networking, graphic design, computer-aided design (CAD), and e-business are featured at the Westwood College campuses located in Anaheim, Inland Empire (Upland), Long Beach, and Los Angeles, California; Atlanta, Georgia; DuPage, O'Hare Airport, River Oaks, and Chicago Loop, Illinois; Denver North and Denver South, Colorado; and Dallas, Fort Worth, and Houston, Texas. The Redstone College of Aviation Technology offers the aviation curriculum at the Denver, Colorado, and Los Angeles, California, campuses, while Redstone Aviation Institute offers the aviation curriculum in Houston.

The Arlington Ballston campus is accredited by the Accrediting Commission of Career Schools and Colleges of Technology (ACCSCT).

Academic Programs

Associate degree programs are in computer-aided design/architectural drafting and in graphic design and multimedia. The computer-aided design/architectural drafting program equips students with the skills necessary to become a candidate for many careers available to the skilled CAD operator. Students receive training on recent releases of AutoCAD, a popular CAD application that provides experience in developing technical drawings related to the field of architecture. Students learn to use CAD combined with theory and lab environment, where they are exposed to the ideas and principles in a lecture setting, and then immediately put that instruction to use in practical lab projects. This hands-on learning environment, coupled with an industry-experienced faculty, ensures that graduates are well prepared for the workforce.

The graphic design and multimedia program prepares students for entry-level jobs in the graphic design and multimedia industry. Students learn to create effective designs that communicate visually in both print and multimedia environments. The combination of technical and general education courses helps students develop skills in critical thinking, logic, communication, and problem solving. The program prepares graduates for positions as graphic designers, production artists, Web page designers, and multimedia designers within a diverse industry.

Bachelor's degrees are available in criminal justice and in design, with concentrations in animation or interior design. The criminal justice program equips students academically and professionally by developing a knowledge base, social awareness, and technological skills for an entry-level position in today's criminal justice environment. The curriculum provides an understanding of criminal justice methods, techniques, technologies, and required skills and abilities, with topics such as introduction to criminal justice, criminology, criminal procedure, criminal investigation, and juvenile justice as well as critical courses in interpersonal communication, victimology, and ethics in criminal justice.

The Bachelor of Science in animation covers topics such as the laws of human motion, physics, psychology as applied to 2-D or 3-D characters, life drawing and rendering techniques, and the application of audio and video to an animation project. In addition, the combination of management and general education courses in the program helps students apply skills in general management, critical thinking, logic, communication, and problem solving to workplace challenges. The program includes critical business courses that cover such topics as project management, determining client need, working within a team environment, and working within a deadline. The degree program prepares students for entry-level positions, including graphic artist and assistant animator for Web-based or computer-based team projects.

The interior design program offers students a well-rounded foundation that nurtures the technical, creative, and human factors of interior design necessary to enter the field. Students build on a foundation of drawing, drafting, color, and basic design principles while learning about human factors, space planning, interior construction and detailing, safety and building codes, and CAD. In addition, students are equipped with a historical perspective of interior design, an understanding of interior design business practices, collaboration techniques for working with related professionals, and, finally, an awareness of professional responsibilities and ethics for personal practice. The B.S. in interior design prepares students for entry-level positions in the industry, including in-house design assistant for both large and small commercial and residential design and architectural firms.

Costs

Standard program costs can be found in the Westwood College academic catalog.

Financial Aid

Tuition assistance is available for those who qualify. Scholarships include the Westwood High School Scholarship Program, in which two scholarships are offered to every high school in the United States. In addition, several loan programs are available.

Faculty

Westwood has 528 faculty members in all. Half are employed on a full-time basis. Forty percent hold master's degrees, and 5 percent have doctorates.

Student Body Profile

Westwood College recruits recent high school graduates, young adults, and working adults who want to acquire new skills to take advantage of growing opportunities in the professional workplace. Students come to Westwood from all across the United States and from many countries around the world. Westwood's students are highly motivated, hardworking, and committed to preparing for rewarding careers.

Student Activities

In addition to on-campus activities, the northern Virginia–Washington, D.C., area offers many cultural and recreational opportunities for students.

Facilities and Resources

Westwood offers a variety of information and research resources, including on-campus Resource Centers, links to Internet-based information services, and a bookstore at each campus. The Campus Resource Centers offer a library of program-specific materials that have been carefully selected to aid that school's career-focused educational mission. The Education Department at each campus collaborates closely with the campus' Resource Center staff to ensure that materials support the school's hands-on curriculum. Typical learning aids include books, periodicals, and Internet access. A virtual library, providing remote access to several selected databases, is also offered. Staff members are available to assist students during regular library hours and can provide instruction on how to conduct research in the library and online.

Location

The region offers an array of sporting and cultural events, famous exhibits and museums, and a variety of outdoor activities to keep students busy when not in class.

Admission Requirements

A diploma from an accredited high school or a GED certificate and passing scores on the college entrance exam (or qualifying ACT/SAT scores) are required. In addition, international students must submit TOEFL, IELTS, or MELAB scores. To apply, students must first contact the campus to schedule a personal career assessment.

Application and Information

Director of Admissions
Westwood College–Arlington Ballston Campus
1901 North Fort Myer Drive
Arlington, Virginia 22209
Telephone: 703-243-3900
Fax: 703-243-3992
E-mail: info@westwood.edu
World Wide Web: http://www.westwood.edu

WESTWOOD COLLEGE–ATLANTA MIDTOWN

ATLANTA, GEORGIA

WESTWOOD COLLEGE

The College and Its Mission

Today, the variables that define career success are ever changing. In order to get ahead and stay ahead, students need the right kind of preparation. To prepare for the working world, they need a career-focused education program that teaches the skills employers demand and offers hands-on, practical experience with real-world applications and the right kind of job-placement assistance to help students get started in their new careers.

Students also need a fast-track learning program that shortens the time from education to career, with an academic schedule that fits their lifestyle. They need a high level of student services to help them reach their goals and the right financial package to make it all possible.

All of these are the focus at Westwood College, which operates twenty campuses, with locations in California, Colorado, Illinois, Georgia, Texas, and Virginia. The seventeen campuses of Westwood College offer degree programs in high-technology fields, while the three aviation campuses (Redstone College of Aviation Technology–Denver, Redstone College of Aviation Technology–Los Angeles, and Redstone Aviation Institute–Houston) offer aviation maintenance training.

Such fields as computer networking, graphic design, computer-aided design, and e-business are featured at the Westwood College campuses located in Anaheim, Inland Empire (Upland), Long Beach, and Los Angeles, California; Atlanta, Georgia; DuPage, O'Hare Airport, River Oaks, and Chicago–Loop, Illinois; Denver–North and Denver–South, Colorado; Dallas, Fort Worth, and Houston, Texas; and the Washington, D.C., area. The Redstone College of Aviation Technology offers the aviation curriculum at the Denver, Colorado and Los Angeles, California, campuses, while Redstone Aviation Institute offers the aviation curriculum in Houston.

The Atlanta Midtown campus is a branch of Westwood College–DuPage and is accredited by the Accrediting Council for Independent Colleges and Schools (ACICS).

Academic Programs

The Atlanta Midtown campus offers bachelor's degree programs in game art and design, information systems security, interior design, and visual communications. Associate degree programs include computer-aided design/architectural drafting, computer network engineering, and graphic design and multimedia.

Costs

Standard program costs can be found in the Westwood College academic catalog.

Financial Aid

Tuition assistance is available for those who qualify. Scholarships include the Westwood High School Scholarship Program, in which two scholarships are offered to every high school in the United States. In addition, several loan programs are available.

Student Body Profile

Student enrollment at the Atlanta Midtown campus totals 130, of whom approximately 40 percent are women.

Student Activities

In addition to on-campus activities, many cultural and recreational activities are available in the greater Atlanta area.

Facilities and Resources

Westwood offers a variety of information and research resources, including on-campus Resource Centers, links to Internet-based information services, and a bookstore at each campus. The Campus Resource Centers offer a library of program-specific materials that have been carefully selected to aid that school's career-focused educational mission. The Education Department at each campus collaborates closely with the campus' Resource Center staff to ensure that materials support the school's hands-on curriculum. Typical learning aids include books, periodicals, and Internet access. A virtual library, providing remote access to several selected databases, is also offered. Staff members are available to assist students during regular library hours and can provide instruction on how to conduct research in the library and online.

Location

Westwood College–Atlanta Midtown's convenient campus location just off I-85 and north of I-20 in midtown Atlanta is in the cultural heart of the city. Metropolitan Atlanta's population is more than 4 million, and the community offers all the entertainment advantages of a large city, including scores of galleries and alternative spaces that exhibit a broad variety of artwork; a ballet and opera; numerous movie houses showing new releases and foreign and classic films; a growing number of theater companies; and many opportunities for rock, jazz, avant-garde music, and outdoor performances. In addition, Atlanta has myriad natural areas and parks, restaurants and coffee houses of every description, and four professional sports teams. The Arts Center Station of MARTA, Atlanta's clean, safe, and efficient rapid transit system, is located just around the corner and offers easy access to many points of interest. The Georgia Institute of Technology and the Atlanta College of Design are only blocks away. Atlanta is a city full of life with a job market that values career-ready individuals such as Westwood College graduates.

Admission Requirements

A diploma from an accredited high school or a GED certificate and passing scores on the college entrance exam (or qualifying ACT/SAT scores) are required.

Application and Information

Director of Admissions
Westwood College–Atlanta Midtown
1100 Spring Street NW
Atlanta, Georgia 30309

Telephone: 404-745-9862
Fax: 404-892-7253
E-mail: info@westwood.edu
World Wide Web: http://www.westwood.edu

WESTWOOD COLLEGE–ATLANTA NORTHLAKE
ATLANTA, GEORGIA

The College and Its Mission

Today, the variables that define career success are ever changing. In order to get ahead and stay ahead, students need the right kind of preparation. To prepare for the working world, they need a career-focused education program that teaches the skills employers demand and offers hands-on, practical experience with real-world applications and the right kind of job-placement assistance to help students get started in their new careers.

Students also need a fast-track learning program that shortens the time from education to career, with an academic schedule that fits their lifestyle. They need a high level of student services to help them reach their goals and the right financial package to make it all possible.

All of these are the focus at Westwood College, which operates twenty campuses, with locations in California, Colorado, Illinois, Georgia, Texas, and Virginia. The seventeen campuses of Westwood College offer degree programs in high-technology fields, while the three aviation campuses (Redstone College of Aviation Technology–Denver, Redstone College of Aviation Technology–Los Angeles, and Redstone Aviation Institute–Houston) offer aviation maintenance training.

Such fields as computer networking, graphic design, computer-aided design, and e-business are featured at the Westwood College campuses located in Anaheim, Inland Empire (Upland), Long Beach, and Los Angeles, California; Atlanta, Georgia; DuPage, O'Hare Airport, River Oaks, and Chicago–Loop, Illinois; Denver–North and Denver–South, Colorado; Dallas, Fort Worth, and Houston, Texas; and the Washington, D.C., area. The Redstone College of Aviation Technology offers the aviation curriculum at the Denver, Colorado and Los Angeles, California, campuses, while Redstone Aviation Institute offers the aviation curriculum in Houston.

The Atlanta Northlake campus is a branch of Westwood College–O'Hare Airport and is accredited by the Accrediting Council for Independent Colleges and Schools (ACICS).

Academic Programs

The Atlanta Northlake campus offers bachelor's degree programs in computer network engineering, game art design, information systems security, interior design, and visual communications. Associate degree programs include computer-aided design/architectural drafting, computer network engineering, and graphic design and multimedia.

Costs

Standard program costs can be found in the Westwood College academic catalog.

Financial Aid

Tuition assistance is available for those who qualify. Scholarships include the Westwood High School Scholarship Program, in which two scholarships are offered to every high school in the United States. In addition, several loan programs are available.

Student Body Profile

Student enrollment at the newly opened Atlanta Northlake campus totals about 100, of whom approximately 40 percent are women.

Student Activities

In addition to on-campus activities, many cultural and recreational activities are available in the greater Atlanta area.

Facilities and Resources

Westwood offers a variety of information and research resources, including on-campus Resource Centers, links to Internet-based information services, and a bookstore at each campus. The Campus Resource Centers offer a library of program-specific materials that have been carefully selected to aid that school's career-focused educational mission. The Education Department at each campus collaborates closely with the campus' Resource Center staff to ensure that materials support the school's hands-on curriculum. Typical learning aids include books, periodicals, and Internet access. A virtual library, providing remote access to several selected databases, is also offered. Staff members are available to assist students during regular library hours and can provide instruction on how to conduct research in the library and online.

Location

Westwood College–Atlanta Northlake's convenient campus location is just off I-285 northeast of downtown Atlanta. Metropolitan Atlanta's population is more than 4 million, and the community offers all the entertainment advantages of a large city, including scores of galleries and alternative spaces that exhibit a broad variety of artwork; a ballet and opera; numerous movie houses showing new releases and foreign and classic films; a growing number of theater companies; and many opportunities for rock, jazz, avant-garde music, and outdoor performances. In addition, Atlanta has myriad natural areas and parks, restaurants and coffee houses of every description, and four professional sports teams. The Arts Center Station of MARTA, Atlanta's clean, safe, and efficient rapid transit system, is located just around the corner and offers easy access to many points of interest. The Georgia Institute of Technology and the Atlanta College of Design are only blocks away. Atlanta is a city full of life with a job market that values career-ready individuals such as Westwood College graduates.

Admission Requirements

A diploma from an accredited high school or a GED certificate and passing scores on the college entrance exam (or qualifying ACT/SAT scores) are required.

Application and Information

Director of Admissions
Westwood College–Atlanta Northlake
2309 Parklake Drive NE
Atlanta, Georgia 30345
Telephone: 404-962-2998
Fax: 770-934-9539
E-mail: info@westwood.edu
World Wide Web: http://www.westwood.edu

WESTWOOD COLLEGE–CHICAGO DUPAGE

WOODRIDGE, ILLINOIS

The College and Its Mission

Today, the variables that define career success are ever changing. In order to get ahead and stay ahead, students need the right kind of preparation. To prepare for the working world, they need a career-focused education program that teaches the skills employers demand and offers hands-on, practical experience with real-world applications and the right kind of job-placement assistance to help students get started in their new careers.

Students also need a fast-track learning program that shortens the time from education to career, with an academic schedule that fits their lifestyle. They need a high level of student services to help them reach their goals and the right financial package to make it all possible.

All of these are the focus at Westwood College, which operates twenty campuses, with locations in California, Colorado, Illinois, Georgia, Texas, and Virginia. The seventeen campuses of Westwood College offer degree programs in high-technology fields, while the three aviation campuses (Redstone College of Aviation Technology–Denver, Redstone College of Aviation Technology–Los Angeles, and Redstone Aviation Institute–Houston) offer aviation maintenance training.

Such fields as computer networking, graphic design, computer-aided design, and e-business are featured at the Westwood College campuses located in Anaheim, Inland Empire (Upland), Long Beach, and Los Angeles, California; Atlanta, Georgia; DuPage, O'Hare Airport, River Oaks, and Chicago–Loop, Illinois; Denver–North and Denver–South, Colorado; Dallas, Fort Worth, and Houston, Texas; and the Washington, D.C., area. The Redstone College of Aviation Technology offers the aviation curriculum at the Denver, Colorado and Los Angeles, California, campuses, while Redstone Aviation Institute offers the aviation curriculum in Houston.

The DuPage campus is accredited by the Accrediting Council for Independent Colleges and Schools (ACICS) for Associate of Applied Science and Bachelor degrees.

Academic Programs

The DuPage campus focuses on computer-based technology programs that prepare graduates to take advantage of high-technology career opportunities. Both the faculty and campus have been designed specifically to meet the unique needs of Westwood's students. Associate degree programs in computer-assisted design (CAD), computer network engineering, and graphic design and multimedia are offered in addition to bachelor's degree programs in game software development, information systems security, visual communications, and Web design and multimedia.

Costs

Standard program costs can be found in the Westwood College academic catalog.

Financial Aid

Tuition assistance is available for those who qualify. Scholarships include the Westwood High School Scholarship Program, in which two scholarships are offered to every high school in the United States, and the Colorado Undergraduate Merit State Scholarships for Colorado residents. In addition, several loan programs are available.

Student Body Profile

Student enrollment at the DuPage campus totals 550, of whom approximately 30 percent are women.

Student Activities

The greater Chicago area offers many cultural and recreational activities.

Facilities and Resources

The campus occupies 25,000 square feet of classroom, lab, and administrative space.

Location

One of three Westwood campuses in the greater Chicago area, the DuPage campus is located an hour's drive southwest of Chicago in Woodridge, Illinois.

Admission Requirements

A diploma from an accredited four-year high school or a GED certificate is required.

Application and Information

Director of Admissions
Westwood College–Chicago DuPage
7155 Janes Avenue
Woodridge, Illinois 60517-2321

Telephone: 630-434-8244
              888-721-7646 (toll-free)
Fax: 630-434-8255
E-mail: info@westwood.edu
World Wide Web: http://www.westwood.edu

Westwood College–Chicago DuPage campus.

WESTWOOD COLLEGE–
CHICAGO LOOP

CHICAGO, ILLINOIS

The College and Its Mission

Today, the variables that define career success are ever changing. In order to get ahead and stay ahead, students need the right kind of preparation. To prepare for the working world, they need a career-focused education program that teaches the skills employers demand. The curriculum should include hands-on, practical experience and real-world applications to help graduates get started in their new careers.

Students also need a fast-track learning program that shortens the time from education to career, with an academic schedule that fits their lifestyle. They need a high level of student services to help them reach their goals and the right financial package to make it all possible.

All of these are the focus at Westwood College, which operates twenty campuses, with locations in California, Colorado, Illinois, Georgia, Texas, and Virginia. The seventeen campuses of Westwood College offer degree programs in high-technology fields, while the three aviation campuses (Redstone College of Aviation Technology–Denver, Redstone College of Aviation Technology–Los Angeles, and Redstone Aviation Institute–Houston) offer aviation maintenance training.

Such fields as computer networking, graphic design, computer-aided design, and e-business are featured at the Westwood College campuses located in Anaheim, Inland Empire (Upland), Long Beach, and Los Angeles, California; Atlanta, Georgia; DuPage, O'Hare Airport, River Oaks, and Chicago–Loop, Illinois; Denver–North and Denver–South, Colorado; Dallas, Fort Worth, and Houston, Texas; and the Washington, D.C., area. The Redstone College of Aviation Technology offers the aviation curriculum at the Denver, Colorado and Los Angeles, California, campuses, while Redstone Aviation Institute offers the aviation curriculum in Houston.

Westwood College–Chicago Loop is a branch of Westwood College–Los Angeles and is accredited by the Accrediting Council for Independent Colleges and Schools (ACICS).

Academic Programs

At the Westwood College–Chicago Loop campus, students may obtain a bachelor's degree in thirty-six months or an associate degree in twenty months through day and evening classes. The programs are designed to help adults move quickly into the high-technology world of work. Classes provide hands-on skills and career-focused training. Skilled technology workers with fine-tuned critical-thinking skills graduate from Westwood ready to succeed. Westwood College's career development services match students with employers to get graduates started on the right career path.

The Chicago Loop campus offers such programs as bachelor's degree programs in animation, computer network management, criminal justice, information systems security, interior design, and visual communications. The College offers associate degree programs in computer-aided design/architectural drafting, computer network engineering, and graphic design and multimedia.

Costs

Standard program costs can be found in the Westwood College academic catalog.

Financial Aid

Tuition assistance is available for those who qualify. Scholarships include the Westwood High School Scholarship Program, in which two scholarships are offered to every high school in the United States. In addition, several loan programs are available.

Student Body Profile

Westwood College recruits recent high school graduates, young adults, and working adults who want to acquire new skills to take advantage of growing opportunities in the professional workplace. Students come to Westwood from all across the U.S. and many other countries. Currently, the Loop campus has more than 300 students, of whom 30 percent are women.

Student Activities

In addition to the many on-campus activities available at Westwood College, the greater Chicago area abounds in cultural and recreational opportunities.

Facilities and Resources

Campus Resource Centers located on each Westwood campus contain a library of program-specific materials, books, and periodicals and Internet access. A virtual library provides remote access to several selected databases and links to Internet-based information that is specific to technology study. The Resource Center also contains the campus bookstore. Resource Center staff members can assist students in navigating all the research materials that are available.

Location

Westwood College's Chicago Loop campus is located on North State Street, in the heart of downtown Chicago, one of the nation's major urban hubs. Students find plenty of diversity and activity in Chicago's Loop area, the hub of central Chicago's shopping, dining, and commerce district. Arts and theater, nightlife, and city activities abound—all within easy access by foot, trolley, or public transit.

Chicago is situated on Lake Michigan, providing plenty of outdoor recreational choices as well.

Admission Requirements

Admission requirements include a diploma from an accredited four-year high school or a GED certificate and passing scores on the College placement exam or qualifying SAT/ACT scores.

Application and Information

Director of Admissions
Westwood College–Chicago Loop
17 North State Street, 15th floor
Chicago, Illinois 60602
Telephone: 312-739-0850
           800-693-5415 (toll-free)
Fax: 312-739-1004
E-mail: info@westwood.edu
World Wide Web: http://www.westwood.edu

WESTWOOD COLLEGE–CHICAGO O'HARE AIRPORT

SCHILLER PARK, ILLINOIS

WESTWOOD COLLEGE

The College and Its Mission

Today, the variables that define career success are ever changing. In order to get ahead and stay ahead, students need the right kind of preparation. To prepare for the working world, students need a programmed, career-focused education that teaches the skills employers demand—that is, hands-on, practical experience with real-world applications and the right kind of job-placement assistance to help them get started in their new career.

Students also need a fast-track learning program that shortens the time from education to career, with an academic schedule that fits their lifestyle. Students need a high level of student services to help them reach their goals and the right financial package to make it all possible.

All of these are the focus at Westwood College, which operates twenty campuses, with locations in California, Colorado, Illinois, Georgia, Texas, and Virginia. The seventeen campuses of Westwood College offer degree programs in high-technology fields, while the three aviation campuses (Redstone College of Aviation Technology–Denver, Redstone College of Aviation Technology–Los Angeles, and Redstone Aviation Institute–Houston) offer aviation maintenance training.

Such fields as computer networking, graphic design, computer-aided design, and e-business are featured at the Westwood College campuses located in Anaheim, Inland Empire (Upland), Long Beach, and Los Angeles, California; Atlanta, Georgia; DuPage, O'Hare Airport, River Oaks, and Chicago–Loop, Illinois; Denver–North and Denver–South, Colorado; Dallas, Fort Worth, and Houston, Texas; and the Washington, D.C., area. The Redstone College of Aviation Technology offers the aviation curriculum at the Denver, Colorado, and Los Angeles, California, campuses, while Redstone Aviation Institute offers the aviation curriculum in Houston.

The Westwood–O'Hare Airport campus is accredited by the Accrediting Council for Independent Colleges and Schools (ACICS).

Academic Programs

The Westwood College–O'Hare Airport campus focuses on computer-based technology programs that prepare graduates to take advantage of their high-technology career opportunities. Associate degree programs are offered in computer-aided design/architectural drafting (CAD), computer network engineering, and graphic design and multimedia. Bachelor's degree programs are offered in animation, computer network management, criminal justice, game software development, and information systems security.

Costs

Standard program costs can be found in the Westwood College academic catalog.

Financial Aid

Tuition assistance is available for those who qualify. Scholarships include the Westwood High School Scholarship Program, in which two scholarships are offered to every high school in the United States. In addition, several loan programs are available.

Student Body Profile

A total of 500 students are enrolled at the O'Hare Airport campus, of whom approximately 75 percent are men and 25 percent are women.

Student Activities

In addition to on-campus activities, the greater Chicago area offers many cultural and recreational opportunities.

Facilities and Resources

The campus includes 27,000 square feet of classrooms, labs, and administrative offices. In addition to an on-campus Resource Center, students benefit through cooperation with the suburban Inter-Library Loan Consortium and Illinet.

Location

The campus is located in Schiller Park, close to major highways and O'Hare International Airport.

Admission Requirements

A diploma from an accredited high school or GED certificate is required, as are passing scores on the college entrance exam (or qualifying ACT/SAT scores).

Application and Information

Director of Admissions
Westwood College–Chicago O'Hare Airport
4825 North Scott Street, Suite 100
Schiller Park, Illinois 60176-1209
Telephone: 847-928-0200
         877-877-8857 (toll-free)
Fax: 847-928-2120
E-mail: info@westwood.edu
World Wide Web: http://www.westwood.edu

Westwood College–Chicago O'Hare Airport campus.

WESTWOOD COLLEGE–CHICAGO RIVER OAKS
CALUMET CITY, ILLINOIS

The College and Its Mission

Today, the variables that define career success are ever changing. In order to get ahead and stay ahead, students need the right kind of preparation. To prepare for the working world, students need a career-focused education program that teaches the skills employers demand and offers hands-on, practical experience with real-world applications and the right kind of job-placement assistance to help them get started in their new careers.

Students also need a fast-track learning program that shortens the time from education to career, with an academic schedule that fits their lifestyle. They need a high level of student services to help them reach their goals and the right financial package to make it all possible.

All of these are the focus at Westwood College, which operates twenty campuses, with locations in California, Colorado, Illinois, Georgia, Texas, and Virginia. The seventeen campuses of Westwood College offer degree programs in high-technology fields, while the three aviation campuses (Redstone College of Aviation Technology–Denver, Redstone College of Aviation Technology–Los Angeles, and Redstone Aviation Institute–Houston) offer aviation maintenance training.

Such fields as computer networking, graphic design, computer-aided design, and e-business are featured at the Westwood College campuses located in Anaheim, Inland Empire (Up-land), Long Beach, and Los Angeles, California; Atlanta, Georgia; DuPage, O'Hare Airport, River Oaks, and Chicago–Loop, Illinois; Denver–North and Denver–South, Colorado; Dallas, Fort Worth, and Houston, Texas; and the Washington, D.C., area. The Redstone College of Aviation Technology offers the aviation curriculum at the Denver, Colorado and Los Angeles, California, campuses, while Redstone Aviation Institute offers the aviation curriculum in Houston.

The River Oaks campus is accredited by the Accrediting Council for Independent Colleges and Schools (ACICS).

Westwood College–River Oaks is a branch of Westwood College–Los Angeles.

Academic Programs

The River Oaks Campus focuses on computer-based technology programs that prepare students to take advantage of high-tech careers. Associate degree programs in computer-aided design/architectural drafting (CAD), computer network engineering and graphic design and multimedia are offered. Bachelor's degree programs are offered in animation, business administration, computer network management, e-business management, and visual communications.

Costs

Standard program costs can be found in the Westwood College academic catalog.

Financial Aid

Tuition assistance is available for those who qualify. Scholarships include the Westwood High School Scholarship Program, through which two scholarships are offered to every high school in the United States; the Colorado Undergraduate Merit State Scholarships for Colorado residents; and several loan programs.

Student Body Profile

There are 640 students enrolled at this campus, of whom 25 percent are women.

Student Activities

In addition to on-campus activities, many cultural and recreational opportunities are available in the Greater Chicago area.

Facilities and Resources

The campus includes 25,000 square feet of classrooms, labs, and administrative offices. In addition to an on-campus resource center, students benefit from cooperation with the suburban Inter-Library Loan Consortium and Illinet.

Location

The campus is located an hour south of Chicago at 80 River Oaks Center in Calumet City. It is easily reached by several major freeways.

Admission Requirements

A diploma from an accredited high school or a GED certificate and passing scores on the college entrance exam (or qualifying ACT/SAT scores) are required.

Application and Information

Director of Admissions
Westwood College–Chicago River Oaks
80 River Oaks Drive, Suite D-49
Calumet City, Illinois 60409-5802

Telephone: 708-832-1988
            888-549-6873 (toll-free)
Fax: 708-832-9617
E-mail: info@westwood.edu
World Wide Web: http://www.westwood.edu

Westwood College–Chicago River Oaks campus.

WESTWOOD COLLEGE– DALLAS

DALLAS, TEXAS

The College and Its Mission

Today, the variables that define career success are ever changing. In order to get ahead and stay ahead, students need the right kind of preparation. To prepare for the working world, they need a career-focused education program that teaches the skills employers demand. The curriculum should include hands-on, practical experience and real-world applications to help graduates get started in their new career.

Students also need a fast-track learning program that shortens the time from education to career, with an academic schedule that fits their lifestyle. They need a high level of student services to help them reach their goals and the right financial package to make it all possible.

All of these are the focus at Westwood College, which operates twenty campuses, with locations in California, Colorado, Illinois, Georgia, Texas, and Virginia. The seventeen campuses of Westwood College offer degree programs in high-technology fields, while the three aviation campuses (Redstone College of Aviation Technology–Denver, Redstone College of Aviation Technology–Los Angeles, and Redstone Aviation Institute–Houston) offer aviation maintenance training.

Such fields as computer networking, graphic design, computer-aided design, and e-business are featured at the Westwood College campuses located in Anaheim, Inland Empire (Upland), Long Beach, and Los Angeles, California; Atlanta, Georgia; DuPage, O'Hare Airport, River Oaks, and Chicago–Loop, Illinois; Denver–North and Denver–South, Colorado; Dallas, Fort Worth, and Houston, Texas; and the Washington, D.C., area. The Redstone College of Aviation Technology offers the aviation curriculum at the Denver, Colorado and Los Angeles, California, campuses, while Redstone Aviation Institute offers the aviation curriculum in Houston.

Westwood College–Dallas is a branch of Westwood College–O'Hare Airport and is accredited by the Accrediting Council for Independent Colleges and Schools (ACICS).

Academic Programs

At the Westwood College–Dallas campus, students may obtain an associate degree in twenty months through day and evening classes. The programs are designed to help adults move into the high-tech world of work quickly. Classes provide hands-on skills and career-focused training. Skilled technology workers with fine-tuned critical-thinking skills graduate from Westwood ready to succeed. Westwood College's career development services work to match students with employers to get graduates started on the right career path.

The Dallas campus offers associate degree programs in computer-aided design, with a concentration in architectural drafting, and computer network engineering.

The Dallas campus also offers a diploma in medical assisting and medical insurance coding and billing.

Costs

Standard program costs can be found in the Westwood College academic catalog.

Financial Aid

Tuition assistance is available for those who qualify. Scholarships include the Westwood High School Scholarship Program, in which two scholarships are offered to every high school in the United States. In addition, several loan programs are available.

Student Body Profile

Westwood College recruits recent high school graduates, young adults, and working adults who want to acquire new skills to take advantage of growing opportunities in the professional workplace. Students come to Westwood from all across the U.S. and many other countries. Students enrolled at the Dallas campus total more than 500, of whom 30 percent are women.

Student Activities

In addition to the on-campus activities available at the College, the greater Dallas area offers unlimited recreational opportunities for students.

Facilities and Resources

Campus Resource Centers located on each Westwood campus contain a library of program-specific materials, books, and periodicals and Internet access. A virtual library provides remote access to several selected databases and links to Internet-based information that is specific to technology study. The Resource Center also contains the campus bookstore. Resource Center staff members can assist students in navigating all the research materials that are available.

Location

Westwood's Dallas campus is located on LBJ Freeway in the heart of Dallas, Texas. One of the largest cities in the southern United States, Dallas offers a wide range of cultural and recreational activities in an urban setting. A 60-acre arts district is home to theater, dance, music, sculpture, and museums. The city maintains more than 20,000 acres of lake and park space within its borders.

Admission Requirements

Admission requirements include a diploma from an accredited four-year high school or a GED certificate and passing scores on the College placement exam or qualifying SAT or ACT scores.

Application and Information

Admissions Office
Westwood College–Dallas
Executive Center I, Suite 100
8390 LBJ Freeway
Dallas, Texas 75243
Telephone: 214-570-9100
         800-803-3140 (toll-free)
Fax: 214-570-8502
E-mail: info@westwood.edu
World Wide Web: http://www.westwood.edu

Westwood College–Dallas campus.

WESTWOOD COLLEGE–DENVER NORTH

DENVER, COLORADO

The College and Its Mission

Today, the variables that define career success are ever changing. In order to get ahead and stay ahead, students need the right kind of preparation. To prepare for the working world, they need a career-focused education program that teaches the skills employers demand and offers hands-on, practical experience with real-world applications and the right kind of job-placement assistance to help students get started in their new careers.

Students also need a fast-track learning program that shortens the time from education to career, with an academic schedule that fits their lifestyle. They need a high level of student services to help them reach their goals and the right financial package to make it all possible.

All of these are the focus at Westwood College, which operates twenty campuses, with locations in California, Colorado, Illinois, Georgia, Texas, and Virginia. The seventeen campuses of Westwood College offer degree programs in high-technology fields, while the three aviation campuses (Redstone College of Aviation Technology–Denver, Redstone College of Aviation Technology–Los Angeles, and Redstone Aviation Institute–Houston) offer aviation maintenance training.

Such fields as computer networking, graphic design, computer-aided design, and e-business are featured at the Westwood College campuses located in Anaheim, Inland Empire (Upland), Long Beach, and Los Angeles, California; Atlanta, Georgia; DuPage, O'Hare Airport, River Oaks, and Chicago–Loop, Illinois; Denver–North and Denver–South, Colorado; Dallas, Fort Worth, and Houston, Texas; and the Washington, D.C., area. The Redstone College of Aviation Technology offers the aviation curriculum at the Denver, Colorado and Los Angeles, California, campuses, while Redstone Aviation Institute offers the aviation curriculum in Houston.

The Denver North campus is accredited by the Accrediting Commission of Career Schools and Colleges of Technology (ACCSCT).

Academic Programs

Denver North offers the largest variety of Westwood's bachelor's and associate degree programs. The campus, in addition to featuring high-technology opportunities, offers programs in high-demand industrial and medical fields. Bachelor's degree programs in animation, computer network management, criminal justice, e-business management, electronic engineering technology, game art and design, game software development, information systems security, interior design, visual communications, and Web design and multimedia are offered. Associate degree programs in technology are offered in computer-aided design/architectural drafting, computer-aided design/mechanical drafting, computer network engineering, electronic engineering technology, graphic design and multimedia, and software engineering. Associate degree programs in service and industrial fields are offered in automotive technology; heating, ventilation, air conditioning, and refrigeration; hotel and restaurant management; and surveying.

Westwood College welcomes students to the exciting world of fashion with the introduction of a new bachelor's degree program in fashion merchandising. The Westwood College fashion merchandising degree program gives students exposure to all of the important areas in fashion, with courses that include Apparel Analysis, Trend Forecasting, Consumer Behavior, Retail Management, Retail Buying, Visual Merchandising, and Fashion Product Development. This new program explores all aspects of the clothing industry, such as product buying, retailing, visual merchandising, and promotion. The program is available only at the Denver campuses.

Off-Campus Programs

Many of the College's degree programs are also available online. This offers students the chance to obtain a degree at any time and location through a virtual campus. Students should call 800-992-5050 Ext. 244 for information.

Costs

Standard program costs can be found in the Westwood College academic catalog.

Financial Aid

Tuition assistance is available for those who qualify. Scholarships include the Westwood High School Scholarship Program, through which two scholarships are offered to every high school in the United States; the Colorado Undergraduate Merit State Scholarships for Colorado residents; and several loan programs.

Student Body Profile

There are 1,100 students enrolled at the Denver North campus, of whom 25 percent are women.

Student Activities

With a diverse population of nearly 2 million and proximity to the Rocky Mountains, Denver offers students a unique opportunity to combine advanced learning with a healthy, active lifestyle. Skiing, snowboarding, mountain climbing, and other outdoor, recreational, and cultural activities abound.

Facilities and Resources

The Denver North campus is the largest of Westwood's campuses and recently underwent a $4-million renovation. The campus provides industry-standard classrooms and labs, which provides a completely functional learning environment that complements Westwood's mission.

Location

The campus is located at 7350 North Broadway in Denver, near the intersection of Interstate 25 and the Boulder Turnpike. Students have easy access to the downtown business districts, LoDo cultural activities, and the I-36 High-Tech Corridor.

Admission Requirements

A diploma from an accredited high school or a GED certificate and passing scores on the college placement exam (or qualifying SAT/ACT scores) are required.

Application and Information

Ben Simms, Director of Admissions
Westwood College–Denver North
7350 North Broadway
Denver, Colorado 80221-3653
Telephone: 303-650-5050
          800-992-5050 (toll-free)
Fax: 303-487-0214
E-mail: info@westwood.edu
World Wide Web: http://www.westwood.edu

Westwood College–Denver North campus.

WESTWOOD COLLEGE–DENVER SOUTH

DENVER, COLORADO

The College and Its Mission

Today, the variables that define career success are ever changing. In order to get ahead and stay ahead, students need the right kind of preparation. To prepare for the working world, they need a program of career-focused education that teaches the skills employers demand and offers hands-on, practical experience with real-world applications and the right kind of job-placement assistance to help students get started in their new careers.

Students also need a fast-track learning program that shortens the time from education to career, with an academic schedule that fits their lifestyle. They need a high level of student services to help reach their goals and the right financial package to make it all possible.

All of these are the focus at Westwood College, which operates twenty campuses, with locations in California, Colorado, Illinois, Georgia, Texas, and Virginia. The seventeen campuses of Westwood College offer degree programs in high-technology fields, while the three aviation campuses (Redstone College of Aviation Technology–Denver, Redstone College of Aviation Technology–Los Angeles, and Redstone Aviation Institute–Houston) offer aviation maintenance training.

Such fields as computer networking, graphic design, computer-aided design, and e-business are featured at the Westwood College campuses located in Anaheim, Inland Empire (Upland), Long Beach, and Los Angeles, California; Atlanta, Georgia; DuPage, O'Hare Airport, River Oaks, and Chicago–Loop, Illinois; Denver–North and Denver–South, Colorado; Dallas, Fort Worth, and Houston, Texas; and the Washington, D.C., area. The Redstone College of Aviation Technology offers the aviation curriculum at the Denver, Colorado and Los Angeles, California, campuses, while Redstone Aviation Institute offers the aviation curriculum in Houston.

The Denver South Campus is accredited by the Accrediting Commission of Career Schools and Colleges of Technology (ACCSCT).

Academic Programs

Denver South concentrates on computer-based high-technology bachelor's and associate degree programs. It offers daytime, evening, and weekend class schedules in order to serve as many students as possible. Bachelor's programs in animation, criminal justice, e-business management, game art and design, information systems security, interior design, and visual communications are offered. Associate degree programs in computer-aided design/architectural drafting (CAD), computer network engineering, graphic design and multimedia, and medical assisting are available.

Costs

Standard program costs can be found in the Westwood College academic catalog.

Financial Aid

Tuition assistance is available for those who qualify. Scholarships include the Westwood High School Scholarship Program, through which two scholarships are offered to every high school in the United States; the Colorado Undergraduate Merit State Scholarships for Colorado residents; and several loan programs.

Student Body Profile

There are 350 students enrolled at Denver South, of whom 75 percent are men and 25 percent women.

Student Activities

With a diverse population of nearly 2 million and proximity to the Rocky Mountains, students have a unique opportunity to combine advanced learning with a healthy, active lifestyle. Skiing, snowboarding, mountain climbing, and other outdoor, recreational, and cultural activities abound.

Facilities and Resources

The campus includes two dedicated buildings totaling more than 30,000 square feet of classrooms, labs, and administrative offices. There is also an annex containing classroom space.

Location

The campus is located at 3150 South Sheridan Boulevard in Denver, at the intersection of South Sheridan Boulevard and Hampden Avenue (Highway 285). It is easily accessible from Lakewood, Englewood, Littleton, and Denver's entire southwest metro area.

Admission Requirements

A diploma from an accredited high school or a GED certificate and passing scores on the college entrance exam (or qualifying ACT/SAT scores) are required.

Application and Information

Director of Admissions
Westwood College–Denver South
3150 South Sheridan Boulevard
Denver, Colorado 80227-5548
Telephone: 303-934-2790
Fax: 303-934-2583
E-mail: info@westwood.edu

Westwood College–Denver South campus.

WESTWOOD COLLEGE–FORT WORTH

EULESS, TEXAS

The College and Its Mission

Today, the variables that define career success are ever changing. In order to get ahead and stay ahead, students need the right kind of preparation. To prepare for the working world, students need a programmed, career-focused education that teaches the skills employers demand, that is, hands-on practical experience with real-world applications and the right kind of job-placement assistance to help them get started in their new career.

Students also need a fast-track leaning program that shortens the time from education to career, with an academic schedule that fits their lifestyle. Students need a high level of student services to help them reach their goals, and the right financial package to make it all possible.

All of these are the focus at Westwood College, which operates twenty campuses, with locations in California, Colorado, Illinois, Georgia, Texas, and Virginia. The seventeen campuses of Westwood College offer degree programs in high-technology fields, while the three aviation campuses (Redstone College of Aviation Technology–Denver, Redstone College of Aviation Technology–Los Angeles, and Redstone Aviation Institute–Houston) offer aviation maintenance training.

Such fields as computer networking, graphic design, computer-aided design, and e-business are featured at the Westwood College campuses located in Anaheim, Inland Empire (Upland), Long Beach, and Los Angeles, California; Atlanta, Georgia; DuPage, O'Hare Airport, River Oaks, and Chicago–Loop, Illinois; Denver–North and Denver–South, Colorado; Dallas, Fort Worth, and Houston, Texas; and the Washington, D.C., area. The Redstone College of Aviation Technology offers the aviation curriculum at the Denver, Colorado and Los Angeles, California, campuses, while Redstone Aviation Institute offers the aviation curriculum in Houston.

The Fort Worth campus is accredited by the Accrediting Council for Independent Colleges and Schools (ACICS).

Westwood College–Fort Worth (Euless, Texas) is a branch of Westwood College–DuPage (Woodridge, Illinois).

Academic Programs

The Fort Worth campus focuses on computer-based technology programs that prepare graduates to take advantage of the high-technology career opportunities that exist in the Dallas–Fort Worth metroplex. Associate degree programs are offered in computer-aided design/architectural drafting, computer network engineering, and graphic design and multimedia. The Fort Worth campus also offers diploma programs in medical assisting and medical insurance coding and billing.

Costs

Standard program costs can be found in the Westwood College academic catalog.

Financial Aid

Tuition assistance is available for those who qualify. Scholarships include the Westwood High School Scholarship Program, in which two scholarships are offered to every high school in the United States. In addition, several loan programs are available.

Student Body Profile

Students enrolled at the Forth Worth campus total 415, of whom 30 percent are women.

Student Activities

In addition to on-campus activities, students can take advantage of a vast array of recreational and cultural activities in this dynamic area with a Southwestern flavor.

Facilities and Resources

Westwood College–Fort Worth currently occupies 12,000 square feet of administrative and instructional space. Also available is a Resource Center, with occupation-related reference materials and a number of resources that link students to library assets nationwide.

Location

The Fort Worth campus is located in Euless, Texas, between Dallas and Fort Worth.

Admission Requirements

A diploma from an accredited high school or GED certificate and passing scores on the college entrance exam (or qualifying ACT/SAT scores) are required.

Application and Information

Director of Admissions
Westwood College–Fort Worth
1331 Airport Freeway, Suite 402
Euless, Texas 76040

Telephone: 817-685-9994
            866-533-9997 (toll-free)
Fax: 817-685-8929
E-mail: info@westwood.edu
World Wide Web: http://www.westwood.edu

Westwood college–Fort Worth campus.

WESTWOOD COLLEGE–HOUSTON SOUTH

HOUSTON, TEXAS

The College and Its Mission

Today, the variables that define career success are ever changing. In order to get ahead and stay ahead, students need the right kind of preparation. To prepare for the working world, they need a career-focused education program that teaches the skills employers demand. The curriculum should include hands-on, practical experience and real-world applications to help graduates get started in their new careers.

Students also need a fast-track learning program that shortens the time from education to career, with an academic schedule that fits their lifestyle. They need a high level of student services to help them reach their goals and the right financial package to make it all possible.

All of these are the focus at Westwood College, which operates twenty campuses, with locations in California, Colorado, Georgia, Illinois, Texas, and Virginia. The seventeen campuses of Westwood College offer degree programs in high-technology fields, while the three aviation campuses (Redstone College of Aviation Technology–Denver, Redstone College of Aviation Technology–Los Angeles, and Redstone Aviation Institute–Houston) offer aviation maintenance training.

Such fields as computer networking, graphic design, computer-aided design, and e-business are featured at the Westwood College campuses located in Anaheim, Inland Empire (Upland), Long Beach, and Los Angeles, California; Atlanta, Georgia; DuPage, O'Hare Airport, River Oaks, and Chicago Loop, Illinois; Denver North and Denver South, Colorado; Dallas, Fort Worth, and Houston South, Texas; and the Washington, D.C., area. The Redstone College of Aviation Technology offers the aviation curriculum at the Denver, Colorado, and Los Angeles, California, campuses, while Redstone Aviation Institute offers the aviation curriculum in Houston.

Westwood College–Houston South is accredited by the Accrediting Commission of Career Schools and Colleges of Technology (ACCSCT) and is a branch of Westwood College–Denver North.

Academic Programs

At the Westwood College–Houston South campus, students may obtain an associate degree in twenty months through day and evening classes. The programs are designed to help adults move into the high-technology world of work quickly. Classes provide hands-on skills and career-focused training. Skilled technology workers with fine-tuned critical-thinking skills graduate from Westwood ready to succeed. Westwood College's career development services work to match students with employers to get graduates started on the right career path.

The Houston South campus focuses on computer-based programs that prepare graduates to take advantage of the high-technology career opportunities available in Houston. Associate degree programs are offered in computer-aided design/architectural drafting (CAD), computer network engineering, and graphic design and multimedia. Houston South also offers diploma programs in medical assisting and medical insurance coding and billing.

Costs

Standard program costs can be found in the Westwood College academic catalog.

Financial Aid

Tuition assistance is available for those who qualify. Scholarships include the Westwood High School Scholarship Program, in which two scholarships are offered to every high school in the United States. In addition, several loan programs are available.

Student Body Profile

Student enrollment at the Houston South campus totals 160 students, 30 percent of whom are women.

Student Activities

In addition to on-campus activities, students can take advantage of the many cultural and recreational activities of the city and surrounding communities.

Facilities and Resources

The Campus Resource Center offers a library of program-specific materials that have been carefully selected to aid that school's career-focused educational mission. Typical learning aids include books, periodicals, and Internet access. A virtual library provides remote access to several selected databases, and staff members are available to assist with research and provide instruction on how to conduct research. Westwood offers tutoring at no charge, and specialized Student Success Workshops help students improve skills in areas such as test taking, time management, resume preparation, and general study skills.

Location

With the campus located in the nation's fourth-largest city, cultural and recreational opportunities abound for students. A cosmopolitan city of many cultures and world-class theater, music, museums, architecture, dance, art, sports, and shopping, Houston also offers nearby beaches, rivers, and outdoor activities.

Admission Requirements

Admission requirements include a diploma from an accredited high school or a GED certificate and passing scores on the College placement exam or qualifying SAT/ACT scores.

Application and Information

Westwood College–Houston South
One Arena Place
7322 Southwest Freeway #1900
Houston, Texas 77074
Telephone: 713-777-4433
E-mail: info@westwood.edu
World Wide Web: http://www.westwood.edu

WESTWOOD COLLEGE–INLAND EMPIRE

UPLAND, CALIFORNIA

The College and Its Mission

Today, the variables that define career success are ever changing. In order to get ahead and stay ahead, students needs the right kind of preparation. To prepare for the working world, students need a career-focused education program that teaches the skills employers demand and offers hands-on, practical experience with real-world applications and the right kind of job-placement assistance to help them get started in their new careers.

Students also need a fast-track learning program that shortens the time from education to career, with an academic schedule that fits their lifestyle. They need a high level of student services to help them reach their goals and the right financial package to make it all possible.

All of these are the focus at Westwood College, which operates twenty campuses, with locations in California, Colorado, Georgia, Illinois, Texas, and Virginia. The seventeen campuses of Westwood College offer degree programs in high-technology fields, while the three aviation campuses (Redstone College of Aviation Technology–Denver, Redstone College of Aviation Technology–Los Angeles, and Redstone Aviation Institute–Houston) offer aviation maintenance training.

Such fields as computer networking, graphic design, computer-aided design, and e-business are featured at the Westwood College campuses located in Anaheim, Inland Empire (Upland), Long Beach, and Los Angeles, California; Atlanta, Georgia; DuPage, O'Hare Airport, River Oaks, and Chicago Loop, Illinois; Denver North and Denver South, Colorado; Dallas, Fort Worth, and Houston South, Texas; and the Washington, D.C., area. The Redstone College of Aviation Technology offers the aviation curriculum at the Denver, Colorado, and Los Angeles, California, campuses, while Redstone Aviation Institute offers the aviation curriculum in Houston.

The Inland Empire campus is accredited by the Accrediting Commission of Career Schools and Colleges of Technology (ACCSCT).

Westwood College–Inland Empire is a branch of Westwood College–Denver North.

Academic Programs

The Inland Empire campus focuses on computer-based programs that prepare graduates to take advantage of Southern California's high-tech career opportunities. Bachelor's degree programs are offered in computer network management, criminal justice, e-business management, game art and design, game software development, information systems security, interior design, and visual communications. Associate degree programs are offered in computer-aided design/architectural drafting (CAD), computer network engineering, and graphic design and multimedia.

Costs

Standard program costs can be found in the Westwood College academic catalog.

Financial Aid

Tuition assistance is available to those students who qualify. Scholarships include the Westwood High School Scholarship Program, which offers two scholarships to every high school in the United States; the Colorado Undergraduate Merit State Scholarships for Colorado residents; and several loan programs.

Student Body Profile

Student enrollment at the Inland Empire campus totals more than 1,000 students, 30 percent of whom are women.

Student Activities

In addition to on-campus activities, students can take advantage of many outdoor recreational activities. Several minor-league baseball teams play in the area. Many cultural opportunities are available as well.

Facilities and Resources

The campus features an all-new facility that was designed and built specifically for Westwood College. The design, layout, and features of the facility are the product of an extensive research project that evaluated the unique requirements of Westwood's students, faculty, and staff.

Location

The campus is located on the western edge of Southern California's Inland Empire, just minutes from the Ontario International Airport. It is easily reached by Interstate 10 and Interstate 15 from surrounding communities such as Ontario, Pomona, Rancho Cucamonga, Covina, Redlands, and San Bernardino.

Admission Requirements

A diploma from an accredited high school or a GED certificate and passing scores on the college entrance exam (or qualifying ACT/SAT scores) are required.

Application and Information

Director of Admissions
Westwood College–Inland Empire
20 West 7th Street
Upland, California 91786-7148

Telephone: 909-931-7550
             866-288-9488 (toll-free)
Fax: 909-931-9195
E-mail: info@westwood.edu
World Wide Web: http://www.westwood.edu

Westwood College–Inland Empire campus.

WESTWOOD COLLEGE–LONG BEACH

LONG BEACH, CALIFORNIA

The College and Its Mission

Today, the variables that define career success are ever changing. In order to get ahead and stay ahead, students need the right kind of preparation. To prepare for the working world, they need a career-focused education program that teaches the skills employers demand. The curriculum should include hands-on, practical experience and real-world applications to help graduates get started in their new careers.

Students also need a fast-track learning program that shortens the time from education to career, with an academic schedule that fits their lifestyle. They need a high level of student services to help them reach their goals and the right financial package to make it all possible.

All of these are the focus at Westwood College, which operates twenty campuses, with locations in California, Colorado, Illinois, Georgia, Texas, and Virginia. The seventeen campuses of Westwood College offer degree programs in high-technology fields, while the three aviation campuses (Redstone College of Aviation Technology–Denver, Redstone College of Aviation Technology–Los Angeles, and Redstone Aviation Institute–Houston) offer aviation maintenance training.

Such fields as computer networking, graphic design, computer-aided design, and e-business are featured at the Westwood College campuses located in Anaheim, Inland Empire (Upland), Long Beach, and Los Angeles, California; Atlanta, Georgia; DuPage, O'Hare Airport, River Oaks, and Chicago–Loop, Illinois; Denver–North and Denver–South, Colorado; Dallas, Fort Worth, and Houston, Texas; and the Washington, D.C., area. The Redstone College of Aviation Technology offers the aviation curriculum at the Denver, Colorado, and Los Angeles, California, campuses, and Redstone Aviation Institute offers the aviation curriculum in Houston.

Westwood College–Long Beach is accredited by the Accrediting Commission of Career Schools and Colleges of Technology (ACCSCT) and has received temporary approval from the Bureau for Private Postsecondary and Vocational Education.

Academic Programs

At the Westwood College–Long Beach campus, students may obtain a bachelor's degree in thirty-six months or an associate degree in twenty months through day and evening classes. The programs are designed to help adults move into the high-tech world of work quickly. Classes provide hands-on skills and career-focused training. Skilled technology workers with fine-tuned critical-thinking skills graduate from Westwood ready to succeed. Westwood College's career development services match students with employers to get graduates started on the right career path.

The Long Beach campus offers such bachelor's degree programs as animation, computer network management, criminal justice, information systems security, and visual communications. The College offers associate degree programs in computer-aided design/architectural drafting, computer network engineering, and graphic design and multimedia.

Costs

Standard program costs can be found in the Westwood College academic catalog.

Financial Aid

Tuition assistance is available for those who qualify. Scholarships include the Westwood High School Scholarship Program, in which two scholarships are offered to every high school in the United States. In addition, several loan programs are available.

Student Body Profile

Westwood College recruits recent high school graduates, young adults, and working adults who want to acquire new skills to take advantage of growing opportunities in the professional workplace. Students come to Westwood from all across the U.S. and many other countries. Currently, there are more than 250 students enrolled on the Westwood College–Long Beach campus, of whom 30 percent are women.

Student Activities

In addition to the many on-campus activities available at Westwood College, the greater Long Beach area abounds in cultural and recreational opportunities.

Facilities and Resources

Campus Resource Centers located on each Westwood campus contain a library of program-specific materials, books, and periodicals and Internet access. A virtual library provides remote access to several selected databases and links to Internet-based information that is specific to technology study. The Resource Center also contains the campus bookstore. Resource Center staff members can assist students in navigating all the research materials that are available.

Location

Long Beach is located in southern California, on the Pacific coast. Outstanding cultural arts and music festivals, plus a short boat ride to Catalina Island and gorgeous weather year-round, make Long Beach a paradise. Shopping, dining, sporting events, endless beaches, and an array of cultural diversity and nightlife make Long Beach a terrific place to begin a visitor's California adventure. Nearby Los Angeles as well as the many diverse towns and cities along the edge of the Pacific Ocean supply visitors with limitless opportunities for recreation, culture, and arts.

Admission Requirements

Admission requirements include a diploma from an accredited four-year high school or a GED certificate and passing scores on the College placement exam or qualifying SAT or ACT scores.

Application and Information

Westwood College–Long Beach Campus
19700 South Vermont Avenue #100
Torrance, California 90502
Telephone: 310-965-0888
Fax: 310-965-0881
E-mail: info@westwood.edu
World Wide Web: http://www.westwood.edu

Westwood College–Long Beach campus.

WESTWOOD COLLEGE–
LOS ANGELES

LOS ANGELES, CALIFORNIA

The College and Its Mission

Today, the variables that define career success are ever changing. In order to get ahead and stay ahead, students need the right kind of preparation. To prepare for the working world, they need a career-focused education program that teaches the skills employers demand and offers hands-on, practical experience with real-world applications and the right kind of job-placement assistance to help students get started in their new careers.

Students also need a fast-track learning program that shortens the time from education to career, with an academic schedule that fits their lifestyle. They need a high level of student services to help them reach their goals and the right financial package to make it all possible.

All of these are the focus at Westwood College, which operates twenty campuses, with locations in California, Colorado, Illinois, Georgia, Texas, and Virginia. The seventeen campuses of Westwood College offer degree programs in high-technology fields, while the three aviation campuses (Redstone College of Aviation Technology–Denver, Redstone College of Aviation Technology–Los Angeles, and Redstone Aviation Institute–Houston) offer aviation maintenance training.

Such fields as computer networking, graphic design, computer-aided design, and e-business are featured at the Westwood College campuses located in Anaheim, Inland Empire (Upland), Long Beach, and Los Angeles, California; Atlanta, Georgia; DuPage, O'Hare Airport, River Oaks, and Chicago–Loop, Illinois; Denver–North and Denver–South, Colorado; Dallas, Fort Worth, and Houston, Texas; and the Washington, D.C., area. The Redstone College of Aviation Technology offers the aviation curriculum at the Denver, Colorado and Los Angeles, California, campuses, while Redstone Aviation Institute offers the aviation curriculum in Houston.

The Los Angeles campus is accredited by the Accrediting Council for Independent Colleges and Schools (ACICS).

Academic Programs

The Los Angeles campus focuses on computer-based technologies that prepare graduates to take advantage of southern California's unique career opportunities. Associate degree programs are offered in computer network engineering and graphic design and multimedia. Bachelor's degree programs are offered in animation, computer network management, criminal justice, e-business management, game art and design, information systems security, visual communications, and Web design and multimedia.

Costs

Standard program costs can be found in the Westwood College academic catalog.

Financial Aid

Tuition assistance is available for those who qualify. Scholarships include the Westwood High School Scholarship Program, through which two scholarships are offered to every high school in the United States; the Colorado Undergraduate Merit State Scholarships for Colorado residents; and several loan programs.

Student Body Profile

The campus has an enrollment of 800, of whom 75 percent are men and 25 percent are women.

Student Activities

The Los Angeles area, given its climate and recreational and cultural diversity, offers unlimited opportunities for students.

Facilities and Resources

The campus includes computer labs, featuring both PC and Macintosh machines running the most popular software applications used throughout industry to give students the hands-on experience that employers demand. The campus offers both day and evening classes.

Location

The campus is located at 3460 Wilshire Boulevard, Suite 700, in the Central Plaza Complex, just minutes from downtown Los Angeles in an urban environment.

Admission Requirements

A diploma from an accredited high school or a GED certificate as well as passing scores on the college's entrance exam (or qualifying ACT/SAT scores) are required.

Application and Information

Director of Admissions
Westwood College–Los Angeles
3460 Wilshire Boulevard, Suite 700
Los Angeles, California 90010-2210

Telephone: 213-739-9999
         877-377-4600 (toll-free)
Fax: 213-382-2468
E-mail: info@westwood.edu
World Wide Web: http://www.westwood.edu

Westwood College–Los Angeles campus.

Appendix

2005–06 Changes in Institutions

Following is an alphabetical listing of institutions that have recently closed, merged with other institutions, or changed their name or status. In the case of a name change, the former name appears first, followed by the new name.

Albuquerque Technical Vocational Institute (Albuquerque, NM): name changed to Central New Mexico Community College.

Allentown Business School (Center Valley, PA): name changed to Lehigh Valley College.

Brown Mackie College (North Canton, OH): name changed to Brown Mackie College–North Canton.

The Brown Mackie College (Salina, KS): name changed to Brown Mackie College–Salina.

Brown Mackie College, Akron Campus (Akron, OH): name changed to Brown Mackie College–Akron.

The Brown Mackie College–Cincinnati Campus (Cincinnati, OH): name changed to Brown Mackie College–Cincinnati.

Brown Mackie College, Findlay Campus (Findlay, OH): name changed to Brown Mackie College–Findlay.

The Brown Mackie College–Lenexa Campus (Lenexa, KS): name changed to Brown Mackie College–Kansas City.

Brown Mackie College, Northern Kentucky Campus (Fort Mitchell, KY): name changed to Brown Mackie College–Northern Kentucky.

The Brown Mackie College–South Bend Campus (South Bend, IN): name changed to Brown Mackie College–South Bend.

Bryman College (San Bernardino, CA): closed.

Butler County Community College (El Dorado, KS): name changed to Butler Community College.

Colorado Mountain College, Spring Valley Campus (Glenwood Springs, CO): name changed to Colorado Mountain College.

Commonwealth Business College (Michigan City, IN): name changed to Brown Mackie College–Michigan City.

Commonwealth Business College (Merrillville, IN): name changed to Brown Mackie College–Merrillville.

Crestmont College (Rancho Palos Verdes, CA): name changed to The Salvation Army College for Officer Training at Crestmont.

Education Direct Center for Degree Studies (Scranton, PA): name changed to Penn Foster Career School.

Fashion Careers of California College (San Diego, CA): name changed to Fashion Careers College.

Floyd College (Rome, GA): name changed to Georgia Highlands College.

International College of Hospitality Management, *César Ritz* (Suffield, CT): name changed to International College of Hospitality Management.

Ivy Tech State College–Central Indiana (Indianapolis, IN): name changed to Ivy Tech Community College–Central Indiana.

Ivy Tech State College–Columbus (Columbus, IN): name changed to Ivy Tech Community College–Columbus.

Ivy Tech State College–Eastcentral (Muncie, IN): name changed to Ivy Tech Community College–East Central.

Ivy Tech State College–Kokomo (Kokomo, IN): name changed to Ivy Tech Community College–Kokomo.

Ivy Tech State College–Lafayette (Lafayette, IN): name changed to Ivy Tech Community College–Lafayette.

Ivy Tech State College–North Central (South Bend, IN): name changed to Ivy Tech Community College–North Central.

Ivy Tech State College–Northeast (Fort Wayne, IN): name changed to Ivy Tech Community College–Northeast.

Ivy Tech State College–Northwest (Gary, IN): name changed to Ivy Tech Community College–Northwest.

Ivy Tech State College–Southcentral (Sellersburg, IN): name changed to Ivy Tech Community College–Southern Indiana.

Ivy Tech State College–Southeast (Madison, IN): name changed to Ivy Tech Community College–Southeast.

Ivy Tech State College–Southwest (Evansville, IN): name changed to Ivy Tech Community College–Southwest.

Ivy Tech State College–Wabash Valley (Terre Haute, IN): name changed to Ivy Tech Community College–Wabash Valley.

Ivy Tech State College–Whitewater (Richmond, IN): name changed to Ivy Tech Community College–Whitewater.

Jefferson Community College (Louisville, KY): name changed to Jefferson Community and Technical College.

Kaplan College (Davenport, IA): name changed to Kaplan University.

Lincoln College (Normal, IL): name changed to Lincoln College–Normal.

National College of Business & Technology (Bayamon, PR): name changed to National College.

Plaza Institute (Jackson Heights, NY): name changed to Plaza College.

Rasmussen College Minnetonka (Minnetonka, MN): name changed to Rasmussen College Eden Prarie.

RETS Institute of Technology (Louisville, KY): name changed to Brown Mackie College–Louisville.

RETS Medical and Business Institute (Hopkinsville, KY): name changed to Brown Mackie College–Hopkinsville.

Riverside Community College (Riverside, CA): name changed to Riverside Community College District.

Sheridan College (Sheridan, WY): name changed to Sheridan College–Sheridan and Gillette.

Silicon Valley College (Fremont, CA): name changed to Western Career College.

South Texas Community College (McAllen, TX): name changed to South Texas College.

Southwest Missouri State University–West Plains (West Plains, MO): name changed to Missouri State University–West Plains.

Summit Institute (West Palm Beach, FL): closed.

Vista Community College (Berkeley, CA): name changed to Berkeley City College.

Western Technical Institute (El Paso, TX): name changed to Western Technical College.

Western Wisconsin Technical College (La Crosse, WI): name changed to Western Technical College.

Westwood College–Denver (Broomfield, CO): name changed to Redstone College–Denver.

Westwood College–Los Angeles (Inglewood, CA): name changed to Redstone College–Los Angeles.

Indexes

Associate Degree Programs at Two-Year Colleges

Accounting

Aakers Business Coll (ND)
Abraham Baldwin Ag Coll (GA)
Aiken Tech Coll (SC)
Albany Tech Coll (GA)
Alexandria Tech Coll (MN)
Allan Hancock Coll (CA)
Allen County Comm Coll (KS)
Appalachian Tech Coll (GA)
Asnuntuck Comm Coll (CT)
Athens Tech Coll (GA)
Atlanta Tech Coll (GA)
Augusta Tech Coll (GA)
Austin Comm Coll (TX)
Bainbridge Coll (GA)
Barton County Comm Coll (KS)
Bay State Coll (MA)
Beal Coll (ME)
Beaufort County Comm Coll (NC)
Bergen Comm Coll (NJ)
Berkeley City Coll (CA)
Berkeley Coll (NJ)
Berkeley Coll–New York City Campus (NY)
Berkeley Coll–Westchester Campus (NY)
Blue Ridge Comm Coll (VA)
Borough of Manhattan Comm Coll of the City U of New York (NY)
Brazosport Coll (TX)
Brevard Comm Coll (FL)
Briarwood Coll (CT)
Bristol Comm Coll (MA)
Bronx Comm Coll of the City U of New York (NY)
Broward Comm Coll (FL)
Brown Mackie Coll–Akron (OH)
Brown Mackie Coll–Cincinnati (OH)
Brown Mackie Coll–Kansas City (KS)
Brown Mackie Coll–Salina (KS)
Bryant and Stratton Coll, Albany (NY)
Bryant and Stratton Coll, Rochester (NY)
Bryant and Stratton Coll, Rochester (NY)
Bryant and Stratton Coll, Syracuse (NY)
Bryant and Stratton Coll, Parma (OH)
Bryant and Stratton Coll (WI)
Bryant and Stratton Coll, Amherst Campus (NY)
Bryant and Stratton Coll, Buffalo Campus (NY)
Bryant and Stratton Coll, Lackawanna Campus (NY)
Bryant and Stratton Coll, Richmond (VA)
Bucks County Comm Coll (PA)
Bunker Hill Comm Coll (MA)
Butler Comm Coll (KS)
Butler County Comm Coll (PA)

Caldwell Comm Coll and Tech Inst (NC)
Cambria-Rowe Business Coll, Johnstown (PA)
Capital Comm Coll (CT)
Carl Albert State Coll (OK)
Carroll Comm Coll (MD)
Casper Coll (WY)
Cecil Comm Coll (MD)
Cedar Valley Coll (TX)
Central Arizona Coll (AZ)
Central Carolina Tech Coll (SC)
Central Comm Coll–Columbus Campus (NE)
Central Comm Coll–Grand Island Campus (NE)
Central Comm Coll–Hastings Campus (NE)
Central Georgia Tech Coll (GA)
Central Lakes Coll (MN)
Central New Mexico Comm Coll (NM)
Central Oregon Comm Coll (OR)
Central Piedmont Comm Coll (NC)
Central Wyoming Coll (WY)
Century Coll (MN)
Chattahoochee Tech Coll (GA)
Chattanooga State Tech Comm Coll (TN)
Chemeketa Comm Coll (OR)
Cincinnati State Tech and Comm Coll (OH)
City Colls of Chicago, Wilbur Wright College (IL)
Clarendon Coll (TX)
Clark State Comm Coll (OH)
Clatsop Comm Coll (OR)
Cleveland Comm Coll (NC)
Clovis Comm Coll (NM)
Coahoma Comm Coll (MS)
Coastal Bend Coll (TX)
Coastal Carolina Comm Coll (NC)
Colby Comm Coll (KS)
Coll of Business and Technology (FL)
Coll of DuPage (IL)
Coll of Southern Maryland (MD)
Coll of the Canyons (CA)
Coll of the Siskiyous (CA)
The Coll of Westchester (NY)
Colorado Mountain Coll (CO)
Colorado Mountain Coll, Alpine Campus (CO)
Colorado Mountain Coll, Timberline Campus (CO)
Columbus Tech Coll (GA)
Commonwealth Tech Inst (PA)
Comm Coll of Denver (CO)
Consolidated School of Business, Lancaster (PA)
Consolidated School of Business, York (PA)
Coosa Valley Tech Coll (GA)
Copiah-Lincoln Comm Coll (MS)

Corning Comm Coll (NY)
Cowley County Comm Coll and Area Vocational–Tech School (KS)
Cuyahoga Comm Coll (OH)
Davis Coll (OH)
DeKalb Tech Coll (GA)
Delaware Tech & Comm Coll, Jack F. Owens Campus (DE)
Delaware Tech & Comm Coll, Stanton/Wilmington Campus (DE)
Delaware Tech & Comm Coll, Terry Campus (DE)
Delgado Comm Coll (LA)
Delta Coll (MI)
Dixie State Coll of Utah (UT)
East Central Coll (MO)
Eastern Idaho Tech Coll (ID)
Eastern Wyoming Coll (WY)
Eastfield Coll (TX)
ECPI Coll of Technology, Newport News (VA)
ECPI Coll of Technology, Virginia Beach (VA)
ECPI Tech Coll (VA)
ECPI Tech Coll, Richmond (VA)
El Centro Coll (TX)
Elmira Business Inst (NY)
Erie Business Center, Main (PA)
Essex County Coll (NJ)
Everest Coll (AZ)
Evergreen Valley Coll (CA)
Fayetteville Tech Comm Coll (NC)
Finger Lakes Comm Coll (NY)
Fiorello H. LaGuardia Comm Coll of the City U of New York (NY)
Fisher Coll (MA)
Flint River Tech Coll (GA)
Florida Comm Coll at Jacksonville (FL)
Florida National Coll (FL)
Foothill Coll (CA)
Forsyth Tech Comm Coll (NC)
Fox Valley Tech Coll (WI)
Frederick Comm Coll (MD)
Front Range Comm Coll (CO)
Gallipolis Career Coll (OH)
Gaston Coll (NC)
GateWay Comm Coll (AZ)
Gateway Comm Coll (CT)
Gavilan Coll (CA)
Genesee Comm Coll (NY)
George C. Wallace Comm Coll (AL)
Georgia Highlands Coll (GA)
Globe Coll (MN)
Greenfield Comm Coll (MA)
Griffin Tech Coll (GA)
Guam Comm Coll (GU)
Gwinnett Tech Coll (GA)
Hagerstown Business Coll (MD)
Hamilton Coll, Cedar Falls (IA)
Hamilton Coll, Cedar Rapids (IA)

Harrisburg Area Comm Coll (PA)
Hawkeye Comm Coll (IA)
Heald Coll-Fresno (CA)
Heald Coll-Hayward (CA)
Heald Coll-Honolulu (HI)
Heald Coll-Portland (OR)
Heald Coll-Rancho Cordova (CA)
Heald Coll-Salinas (CA)
Heald Coll-San Francisco (CA)
Heald Coll-San Jose (CA)
Heald Coll-Stockton (CA)
Hickey Coll (MO)
Highland Comm Coll (IL)
Highline Comm Coll (WA)
Holyoke Comm Coll (MA)
Houston Comm Coll System (TX)
Howard Coll (TX)
Howard Comm Coll (MD)
Hudson Valley Comm Coll (NY)
Illinois Central Coll (IL)
Illinois Eastern Comm Colls, Olney Central College (IL)
Illinois Valley Comm Coll (IL)
Independence Comm Coll (KS)
Indiana Business Coll, Anderson (IN)
Indiana Business Coll, Columbus (IN)
Indiana Business Coll, Evansville (IN)
Indiana Business Coll, Fort Wayne (IN)
Indiana Business Coll, Indianapolis (IN)
Indiana Business Coll, Indianapolis (IN)
Indiana Business Coll, Lafayette (IN)
Indiana Business Coll, Marion (IN)
Indiana Business Coll, Muncie (IN)
Indiana Business Coll, Terre Haute (IN)
International Inst of the Americas, Mesa (AZ)
International Inst of the Americas, Phoenix (AZ)
International Inst of the Americas, Phoenix (AZ)
International Inst of the Americas, Tucson (AZ)
International Inst of the Americas (NM)
Itasca Comm Coll (MN)
Ivy Tech Comm Coll–Lafayette (IN)
James Sprunt Comm Coll (NC)
Jamestown Comm Coll (NY)
Jefferson Comm and Tech Coll (KY)
Jefferson Comm Coll (NY)
Jefferson Comm Coll (OH)
J. F. Drake State Tech Coll (AL)
John Wood Comm Coll (IL)
Joliet Jr Coll (IL)

Kapiolani Comm Coll (HI)
Kauai Comm Coll (HI)
Kellogg Comm Coll (MI)
Kennebec Valley Comm Coll (ME)
Kent State U, Tuscarawas Campus (OH)
Keystone Coll (PA)
Kilian Comm Coll (SD)
Kingsborough Comm Coll of the City U of New York (NY)
Kingwood Coll (TX)
Lake Region State Coll (ND)
Lakeshore Tech Coll (WI)
Lake Superior Coll (MN)
Lamar State Coll–Orange (TX)
Lanier Tech Coll (GA)
Lansing Comm Coll (MI)
Laramie County Comm Coll (WY)
Laurel Business Inst (PA)
Lawson State Comm Coll (AL)
Lehigh Valley Coll (PA)
Lincoln Coll (IL)
Lincoln Coll–Normal (IL)
Linn-Benton Comm Coll (OR)
Long Beach City Coll (CA)
Long Island Business Inst (NY)
Longview Comm Coll (MO)
Lord Fairfax Comm Coll (VA)
Lower Columbia Coll (WA)
Luzerne County Comm Coll (PA)
Macomb Comm Coll (MI)
Manatee Comm Coll (FL)
Manchester Comm Coll (CT)
Manor Coll (PA)
Maple Woods Comm Coll (MO)
Maria Coll (NY)
Massachusetts Bay Comm Coll (MA)
Mercer County Comm Coll (NJ)
Metropolitan Comm Coll (NE)
Metropolitan Comm Coll-Business & Technology College (MO)
Middle Georgia Tech Coll (GA)
Middlesex Comm Coll (CT)
Middlesex County Coll (NJ)
Midlands Tech Coll (SC)
Minneapolis Business Coll (MN)
Minnesota School of Business–Brooklyn Center (MN)
Minnesota School of Business–Plymouth (MN)
Minnesota School of Business–Richfield (MN)
Minnesota School of Business–St. Cloud (MN)
Minnesota School of Business–Shakopee (MN)

Minnesota State Comm and Tech Coll–Fergus Falls (MN)
Minnesota West Comm and Tech Coll (MN)
MiraCosta Coll (CA)
Mississippi Gulf Coast Comm Coll (MS)
Missouri State U–West Plains (MO)
Modesto Jr Coll (CA)
Montgomery Comm Coll (NC)
Montgomery County Comm Coll (PA)
Moraine Park Tech Coll (WI)
Moultrie Tech Coll (GA)
Mountain View Coll (TX)
Mt. San Antonio Coll (CA)
Mount Wachusett Comm Coll (MA)
MTI Coll of Business and Technology (CA)
Nassau Comm Coll (NY)
Naugatuck Valley Comm Coll (CT)
New England Coll of Finance (MA)
New Hampshire Comm Tech Coll, Manchester/Stratham (NH)
New Hampshire Comm Tech Coll, Nashua/Claremont (NH)
New Hampshire Tech Inst (NH)
New Mexico Military Inst (NM)
Newport Business Inst, Lower Burrell (PA)
Niagara County Comm Coll (NY)
Normandale Comm Coll (MN)
North Central Missouri Coll (MO)
Northeast Comm Coll (NE)
Northeast Iowa Comm Coll (IA)
Northeast State Tech Comm Coll (TN)
Northern Essex Comm Coll (MA)
Northern Maine Comm Coll (ME)
North Hennepin Comm Coll (MN)
North Iowa Area Comm Coll (IA)
Northland Comm and Tech Coll–Thief River Falls (MN)
North Metro Tech Coll (GA)
North Shore Comm Coll (MA)
Northwestern Connecticut Comm Coll (CT)
Northwestern Tech Coll (GA)
Northwest-Shoals Comm Coll (AL)
Norwalk Comm Coll (CT)
Oakland Comm Coll (MI)
Ocean County Coll (NJ)
Ogeechee Tech Coll (GA)

Ohio Business Coll, Sandusky (OH)
Okaloosa-Walton Coll (FL)
Orange Coast Coll (CA)
Orange County Comm Coll (NY)
Ouachita Tech Coll (AR)
Palau Comm CollPalau)
Palm Beach Comm Coll (FL)
Palo Verde Coll (CA)
Pasadena City Coll (CA)
Pellissippi State Tech Comm Coll (TN)
Peninsula Coll (WA)
Penn Valley Comm Coll (MO)
Phoenix Coll (AZ)
Piedmont Virginia Comm Coll (VA)
Pima Comm Coll (AZ)
Pioneer Pacific Coll (OR)
Pratt Comm Coll (KS)
Quinebaug Valley Comm Coll (CT)
Quinsigamond Comm Coll (MA)
Raritan Valley Comm Coll (NJ)
Rasmussen Coll Eden Prarie (MN)
Rasmussen Coll Mankato (MN)
Richland Comm Coll (IL)
Richmond Comm Coll (NC)
Roane State Comm Coll (TN)
Rockingham Comm Coll (NC)
Rock Valley Coll (IL)
Saddleback Coll (CA)
Saint Charles Comm Coll (MO)
St. Cloud Tech Coll (MN)
St. Louis Comm Coll at Florissant Valley (MO)
Saint Paul Coll—A Comm & Tech College (MN)
St. Philip's Coll (TX)
Salem Comm Coll (NJ)
Salt Lake Comm Coll (UT)
Sandersville Tech Coll (GA)
San Diego City Coll (CA)
San Diego Mesa Coll (CA)
San Joaquin Delta Coll (CA)
Santa Barbara City Coll (CA)
Sauk Valley Comm Coll (IL)
Savannah Tech Coll (GA)
Scottsdale Comm Coll (AZ)
Seattle Central Comm Coll (WA)
Seminole Comm Coll (FL)
Seminole State Coll (OK)
Sinclair Comm Coll (OH)
Skyline Coll (CA)
Snow Coll (UT)
Southeastern Tech Coll (GA)
Southeast Tech Inst (SD)
Southern West Virginia Comm and Tech Coll (WV)
South Georgia Tech Coll (GA)
South Hills School of Business & Technology, State College (PA)
South Plains Coll (TX)
South Texas Coll (TX)
South U, West Palm Beach (FL)
Southwestern Illinois Coll (IL)
Southwestern Oregon Comm Coll (OR)
Southwest Florida Coll, Fort Myers (FL)
Southwest Georgia Tech Coll (GA)
Southwest Mississippi Comm Coll (MS)
Southwest Tennessee Comm Coll (TN)
Southwest Virginia Comm Coll (VA)
Spartanburg Tech Coll (SC)
Spoon River Coll (IL)
Springfield Tech Comm Coll (MA)
Stark State Coll of Technology (OH)
State U of New York Coll of Technology at Alfred (NY)

State U of New York Coll of Technology at Delhi (NY)
Sullivan County Comm Coll (NY)
Sussex County Comm Coll (NJ)
Swainsboro Tech Coll (GA)
Tarrant County Coll District (TX)
Thomas Nelson Comm Coll (VA)
Three Rivers Comm Coll (MO)
Tidewater Comm Coll (VA)
Tillamook Bay Comm Coll (OR)
Tomball Coll (TX)
Tompkins Cortland Comm Coll (NY)
Tri-County Comm Coll (NC)
Trident Tech Coll (SC)
Trinidad State Jr Coll (CO)
Trinity Valley Comm Coll (TX)
Triton Coll (IL)
Tulsa Comm Coll (OK)
Tunxis Comm Coll (CT)
The U of Akron—Wayne Coll (OH)
U of Alaska Anchorage, Matanuska-Susitna Coll (AK)
U of Northwestern Ohio (OH)
U of Pittsburgh at Titusville (PA)
Valdosta Tech Coll (GA)
Valencia Comm Coll (FL)
Vance-Granville Comm Coll (NC)
Ventura Coll (CA)
Vermilion Comm Coll (MN)
Waukesha County Tech Coll (WI)
West Central Tech Coll (GA)
Westchester Comm Coll (NY)
Western Tech Coll (WI)
West Georgia Tech Coll (GA)
Westmoreland County Comm Coll (PA)
West Virginia Business Coll, Wheeling (WV)
William Rainey Harper Coll (IL)
Wilson Tech Comm Coll (NC)
Wisconsin Indianhead Tech Coll (WI)
Wood Tobe—Coburn School (NY)
Yakima Valley Comm Coll (WA)
Yavapai Coll (AZ)
York Tech Coll (SC)
Yuba Coll (CA)

Accounting and Business/ Management
ITT Tech Inst, Dayton (OH)
ITT Tech Inst, Hilliard (OH)
ITT Tech Inst, Norwood (OH)
ITT Tech Inst, Strongsville (OH)
Montgomery Coll (TX)
Mountain State Coll (WV)

Accounting and Finance
Jackson Comm Coll (MI)

Accounting Technology and Bookkeeping
Alamance Comm Coll (NC)
Allegany Coll of Maryland (MD)
Big Bend Comm Coll (WA)
Bishop State Comm Coll (AL)
Blue River Comm Coll (MO)
Broome Comm Coll (NY)
Brown Mackie Coll—Atlanta (GA)
Brown Mackie Coll—Findlay (OH)
Brown Mackie Coll—Fort Wayne (IN)
Brown Mackie Coll—Hopkinsville (KY)
Brown Mackie Coll—Louisville (KY)
Brown Mackie Coll—Merrillville (IN)

Brown Mackie Coll—Miami (FL)
Brown Mackie Coll—Michigan City (IN)
Brown Mackie Coll—North Canton (OH)
Brown Mackie Coll—Northern Kentucky (KY)
Cape Fear Comm Coll (NC)
Central Florida Comm Coll (FL)
Central Wyoming Coll (WY)
Clark Coll (WA)
Coll of Lake County (IL)
Coll of the Mainland (TX)
Comm Coll of Allegheny County (PA)
Edmonds Comm Coll (WA)
Essex County Coll (NJ)
Glendale Comm Coll (AZ)
Goodwin Coll (CT)
Hagerstown Comm Coll (MD)
H. Councill Trenholm State Tech Coll (AL)
Ilisagvik Coll (AK)
International Business Coll, Indianapolis (IN)
Ivy Tech Comm Coll—Bloomington (IN)
Ivy Tech Comm Coll—Central Indiana (IN)
Ivy Tech Comm Coll—Columbus (IN)
Ivy Tech Comm Coll—East Central (IN)
Ivy Tech Comm Coll—Kokomo (IN)
Ivy Tech Comm Coll—Lafayette (IN)
Ivy Tech Comm Coll—North Central (IN)
Ivy Tech Comm Coll—Northeast (IN)
Ivy Tech Comm Coll—Northwest (IN)
Ivy Tech Comm Coll—Southeast (IN)
Ivy Tech Comm Coll—Southern Indiana (IN)
Ivy Tech Comm Coll—Southwest (IN)
Ivy Tech Comm Coll—Wabash Valley (IN)
Ivy Tech Comm Coll—Whitewater (IN)
Jefferson State Comm Coll (AL)
Johnston Comm Coll (NC)
John Wood Comm Coll (IL)
Kellogg Comm Coll (MI)
Kent State U, Geauga Campus (OH)
Lackawanna Coll (PA)
Lake Land Coll (IL)
Lake Michigan Coll (MI)
Lake Region State Coll (ND)
Lamar State Coll—Port Arthur (TX)
Louisiana Tech Coll (LA)
Lower Columbia Coll (WA)
Marshall Comm and Tech Coll (WV)
Metropolitan Comm Coll-Business & Technology College (MO)
Miami Dade Coll (FL)
Moberly Area Comm Coll (MO)
Mohawk Valley Comm Coll (NY)
Montgomery County Comm Coll (PA)
Mott Comm Coll (MI)
Nassau Comm Coll (NY)
Northampton County Area Comm Coll (PA)
North Iowa Area Comm Coll (IA)
North Seattle Comm Coll (WA)
Owens Comm Coll, Toledo (OH)
Parkland Coll (IL)
Pellissippi State Tech Comm Coll (TN)
Penn Foster Career School (PA)
Polk Comm Coll (FL)
St. Cloud Tech Coll (MN)

St. Petersburg Coll (FL)
San Juan Coll (NM)
Southern State Comm Coll (OH)
Southwestern Michigan Coll (MI)
Spokane Comm Coll (WA)
Spokane Falls Comm Coll (WA)
Tillamook Bay Comm Coll (OR)
Union County Coll (NJ)
The U of Akron—Wayne Coll (OH)
Waubonsee Comm Coll (IL)
Western Oklahoma State Coll (OK)
West Virginia Northern Comm Coll (WV)
Wilkes Comm Coll (NC)
Williston State Coll (ND)
Wor-Wic Comm Coll (MD)

Acting
Central Wyoming Coll (WY)
KD Studio (TX)
Northampton County Area Comm Coll (PA)
Santa Barbara City Coll (CA)

Actuarial Science
Harrisburg Area Comm Coll (PA)

Administrative Assistant and Secretarial Science
Abraham Baldwin Ag Coll (GA)
Aiken Tech Coll (SC)
Alexandria Tech Coll (MN)
Allan Hancock Coll (CA)
Allegany Coll of Maryland (MD)
Allen County Comm Coll (KS)
Altamaha Tech Coll (GA)
Appalachian Tech Coll (GA)
Arapahoe Comm Coll (CO)
Arizona Western Coll (AZ)
Asnuntuck Comm Coll (CT)
Athens Tech Coll (GA)
Augusta Tech Coll (GA)
Austin Comm Coll (TX)
Bainbridge Coll (GA)
Barton County Comm Coll (KS)
Bay State Coll (MA)
Beal Coll (ME)
Beaufort County Comm Coll (NC)
Bergen Comm Coll (NJ)
Bishop State Comm Coll (AL)
Bladen Comm Coll (NC)
Blue Ridge Comm Coll (VA)
Blue River Comm Coll (MO)
Borough of Manhattan Comm Coll of the City U of New York (NY)
Brazosport Coll (TX)
Briarwood Coll (CT)
Bristol Comm Coll (MA)
Bronx Comm Coll of the City U of New York (NY)
Broward Comm Coll (FL)
Brown Mackie Coll—Cincinnati (OH)
Bryant and Stratton Coll, Albany (NY)
Bryant and Stratton Coll, Rochester (NY)
Bryant and Stratton Coll, Rochester (NY)
Bryant and Stratton Coll, Syracuse (NY)
Bryant and Stratton Coll, Parma (OH)
Bryant and Stratton Coll (WI)
Bryant and Stratton Coll, Amherst Campus (NY)
Bryant and Stratton Coll, Buffalo Campus (NY)
Bryant and Stratton Coll, Lackawanna Campus (NY)
Bryant and Stratton Coll, Richmond (VA)
Bucks County Comm Coll (PA)
Butler Comm Coll (KS)
Butler County Comm Coll (PA)

Cambria-Rowe Business Coll, Johnstown (PA)
Capital Comm Coll (CT)
Carl Albert State Coll (OK)
Carteret Comm Coll (NC)
Casper Coll (WY)
Cecil Comm Coll (MD)
Cedar Valley Coll (TX)
Central Arizona Coll (AZ)
Central Carolina Tech Coll (SC)
Central Comm Coll—Columbus Campus (NE)
Central Comm Coll—Grand Island Campus (NE)
Central Comm Coll—Hastings Campus (NE)
Central Georgia Tech Coll (GA)
Centralia Coll (WA)
Central Lakes Coll (MN)
Central New Mexico Comm Coll (NM)
Central Oregon Comm Coll (OR)
Central Piedmont Comm Coll (NC)
Century Coll (MN)
Chattahoochee Tech Coll (GA)
Chattahoochee Valley Comm Coll (AL)
Chattanooga State Tech Comm Coll (TN)
Chemeketa Comm Coll (OR)
Cincinnati State Tech and Comm Coll (OH)
Citrus Coll (CA)
Clark State Comm Coll (OH)
Clatsop Comm Coll (OR)
Cleveland Comm Coll (NC)
Cleveland State Comm Coll (TN)
Clovis Comm Coll (NM)
Coahoma Comm Coll (MS)
Coastal Bend Coll (TX)
Cochise Coll, Douglas (AZ)
Coll of DuPage (IL)
Coll of Eastern Utah (UT)
Coll of Lake County (IL)
Coll of The Albemarle (NC)
Coll of the Canyons (CA)
Coll of the Mainland (TX)
The Coll of Westchester (NY)
Columbia Coll (CA)
Columbus Tech Coll (GA)
Comm Coll of Allegheny County (PA)
Comm Coll of Denver (CO)
Corning Comm Coll (NY)
Cowley County Comm Coll and Area Vocational—Tech School (KS)
Crowder Coll (MO)
Cuyahoga Comm Coll (OH)
Dabney S. Lancaster Comm Coll (VA)
Davis Coll (OH)
DeKalb Tech Coll (GA)
Delaware Tech & Comm Coll, Jack F. Owens Campus (DE)
Delaware Tech & Comm Coll, Stanton/Wilmington Campus (DE)
Delaware Tech & Comm Coll, Terry Campus (DE)
Delgado Comm Coll (LA)
Delta Coll (MI)
Denmark Tech Coll (SC)
Diné Coll (AZ)
Dixie State Coll of Utah (UT)
East Central Coll (MO)
East Central Tech Coll (GA)
Eastern Idaho Tech Coll (ID)
Eastern West Virginia Comm and Tech Coll (WV)
Eastern Wyoming Coll (WY)
Edmonds Comm Coll (WA)
El Centro Coll (TX)
Elmira Business Inst (NY)
Erie Business Center, Main (PA)
Erie Comm Coll (NY)
Essex County Coll (NJ)
Feather River Coll (CA)
Finger Lakes Comm Coll (NY)

Fiorello H. LaGuardia Comm Coll of the City U of New York (NY)
Flint River Tech Coll (GA)
Florida Comm Coll at Jacksonville (FL)
Florida National Coll (FL)
Forsyth Tech Comm Coll (NC)
Fox Valley Tech Coll (WI)
Gadsden State Comm Coll (AL)
Gallipolis Career Coll (OH)
Galveston Coll (TX)
Gavilan Coll (CA)
Genesee Comm Coll (NY)
George C. Wallace Comm Coll (AL)
Glendale Comm Coll (AZ)
Grand Rapids Comm Coll (MI)
Greenfield Comm Coll (MA)
Griffin Tech Coll (GA)
Guam Comm Coll (GU)
Gwinnett Tech Coll (GA)
Hagerstown Business Coll (MD)
Hamilton Coll, Cedar Rapids (IA)
Harrisburg Area Comm Coll (PA)
Hawkeye Comm Coll (IA)
H. Councill Trenholm State Tech Coll (AL)
Heald Coll-Fresno (CA)
Heald Coll-Hayward (CA)
Heald Coll-Honolulu (HI)
Heald Coll-Portland (OR)
Heald Coll-Rancho Cordova (CA)
Heald Coll-San Francisco (CA)
Heartland Comm Coll (IL)
Hibbing Comm Coll (MN)
Highland Comm Coll (IL)
Highline Comm Coll (WA)
Holyoke Comm Coll (MA)
Horry-Georgetown Tech Coll (SC)
Houston Comm Coll System (TX)
Howard Comm Coll (MD)
Hudson Valley Comm Coll (NY)
Hutchinson Comm Coll and Area Vocational School (KS)
Illinois Central Coll (IL)
Illinois Eastern Comm Colls, Frontier Community College (IL)
Illinois Eastern Comm Colls, Olney Central College (IL)
Illinois Eastern Comm Colls, Wabash Valley College (IL)
Illinois Valley Comm Coll (IL)
Independence Comm Coll (KS)
Indiana Business Coll, Anderson (IN)
Indiana Business Coll, Columbus (IN)
Indiana Business Coll, Evansville (IN)
Indiana Business Coll, Fort Wayne (IN)
Indiana Business Coll, Indianapolis (IN)
Indiana Business Coll, Indianapolis (IN)
Indiana Business Coll, Lafayette (IN)
Indiana Business Coll, Marion (IN)
Indiana Business Coll, Muncie (IN)
Indiana Business Coll, Terre Haute (IN)
International Business Coll, Indianapolis (IN)
Jackson Comm Coll (MI)
James H. Faulkner State Comm Coll (AL)
James Sprunt Comm Coll (NC)
Jefferson Comm Coll (NY)
Jefferson Comm Coll (OH)
Jefferson State Comm Coll (AL)

J. F. Drake State Tech Coll (AL)
Johnston Comm Coll (NC)
John Tyler Comm Coll (VA)
John Wood Comm Coll (IL)
Joliet Jr Coll (IL)
Kansas City Kansas Comm Coll (KS)
Kauai Comm Coll (HI)
Kellogg Comm Coll (MI)
Kennebec Valley Comm Coll (ME)
Kent State U, Tuscarawas Campus (OH)
Kilian Comm Coll (SD)
Kingsborough Comm Coll of the City U of New York (NY)
Lac Courte Oreilles Ojibwa Comm Coll (WI)
Lackawanna Coll (PA)
Lake City Comm Coll (FL)
Lake Land Coll (IL)
Lake Michigan Coll (MI)
Lake Region State Coll (ND)
Lakeshore Tech Coll (WI)
Lamar State Coll–Orange (TX)
Lamar State Coll–Port Arthur (TX)
Lanier Tech Coll (GA)
Lansing Comm Coll (MI)
Laredo Comm Coll (TX)
Laurel Business Inst (PA)
Lawson State Comm Coll (AL)
Lincoln Land Comm Coll (IL)
Linn-Benton Comm Coll (OR)
Long Beach City Coll (CA)
Long Island Business Inst (NY)
Longview Comm Coll (MO)
Lord Fairfax Comm Coll (VA)
Louisiana Tech Coll (LA)
Lower Columbia Coll (WA)
Luzerne County Comm Coll (PA)
Macomb Comm Coll (MI)
Manatee Comm Coll (FL)
Manchester Comm Coll (CT)
Manor Coll (PA)
Maple Woods Comm Coll (MO)
Marshall Comm and Tech Coll (WV)
Mercer County Comm Coll (NJ)
Meridian Comm Coll (MS)
Mesabi Range Comm and Tech Coll (MN)
Metropolitan Comm Coll (NE)
Miami Dade Coll (FL)
Middle Georgia Tech Coll (GA)
Middlesex Comm Coll (CT)
Middlesex County Coll (NJ)
Midlands Tech Coll (SC)
Minneapolis Business Coll (MN)
Minnesota School of Business–Brooklyn Center (MN)
Minnesota School of Business–Plymouth (MN)
Minnesota School of Business–Richfield (MN)
Minnesota School of Business–St. Cloud (MN)
Minnesota State Comm and Tech Coll–Fergus Falls (MN)
Minnesota West Comm and Tech Coll (MN)
MiraCosta Coll (CA)
Mississippi Gulf Coast Comm Coll (MS)
Moberly Area Comm Coll (MO)
Modesto Jr Coll (CA)
Mohawk Valley Comm Coll (NY)
Montgomery Comm Coll (NC)
Montgomery County Comm Coll (PA)
Moraine Park Tech Coll (WI)
Moraine Valley Comm Coll (IL)

Mott Comm Coll (MI)
Moultrie Tech Coll (GA)
Mountain State Coll (WV)
Mt. San Antonio Coll (CA)
Nassau Comm Coll (NY)
Naugatuck Valley Comm Coll (CT)
New Hampshire Comm Tech Coll, Manchester/Stratham (NH)
New Mexico State U–Alamogordo (NM)
Newport Business Inst, Williamsport (PA)
Niagara County Comm Coll (NY)
Northampton County Area Comm Coll (PA)
North Arkansas Coll (AR)
North Central Missouri Coll (MO)
North Dakota State Coll of Science (ND)
Northeast Comm Coll (NE)
Northeast State Tech Comm Coll (TN)
Northern Essex Comm Coll (MA)
Northern Maine Comm Coll (ME)
North Georgia Tech Coll (GA)
North Idaho Coll (ID)
North Iowa Area Comm Coll (IA)
Northland Comm and Tech Coll–Thief River Falls (MN)
North Metro Tech Coll (GA)
North Seattle Comm Coll (WA)
North Shore Comm Coll (MA)
Northwestern Connecticut Comm Coll (CT)
Northwestern Tech Coll (GA)
Northwest-Shoals Comm Coll (AL)
Norwalk Comm Coll (CT)
Ocean County Coll (NJ)
Ogeechee Tech Coll (GA)
Ohio Business Coll, Sandusky (OH)
Okaloosa-Walton Coll (FL)
Okefenokee Tech Coll (GA)
Orange Coast Coll (CA)
Orange County Comm Coll (NY)
Otero Jr Coll (CO)
Ouachita Tech Coll (AR)
Palau Comm CollPalau)
Palm Beach Comm Coll (FL)
Palo Verde Coll (CA)
Parkland Coll (IL)
Pasadena City Coll (CA)
Pellissippi State Tech Comm Coll (TN)
Penn Valley Comm Coll (MO)
Phoenix Coll (AZ)
Piedmont Virginia Comm Coll (VA)
Pima Comm Coll (AZ)
Pratt Comm Coll (KS)
Pulaski Tech Coll (AR)
Quinebaug Valley Comm Coll (CT)
Quinsigamond Comm Coll (MA)
Raritan Valley Comm Coll (NJ)
Rasmussen Coll Eden Prarie (MN)
Rasmussen Coll Mankato (MN)
Richland Comm Coll (IL)
Richmond Comm Coll (NC)
Riverland Comm Coll (MN)
Roane State Comm Coll (TN)
Rockingham Comm Coll (NC)
Saddleback Coll (CA)
Saint Charles Comm Coll (MO)
St. Cloud Tech Coll (MN)
St. Louis Comm Coll at Florissant Valley (MO)
Saint Paul Coll–A Comm & Tech College (MN)
St. Philip's Coll (TX)

Sandersville Tech Coll (GA)
San Diego City Coll (CA)
San Diego Mesa Coll (CA)
San Juan Coll (NM)
Santa Barbara City Coll (CA)
Sauk Valley Comm Coll (IL)
Savannah Tech Coll (GA)
Schuylkill Inst of Business and Technology (PA)
Scottsdale Comm Coll (AZ)
Seattle Central Comm Coll (WA)
Seminole Comm Coll (FL)
Seminole State Coll (OK)
Shelton State Comm Coll (AL)
Sheridan Coll–Sheridan and Gillette (WY)
Sinclair Comm Coll (OH)
Skyline Coll (CA)
Snow Coll (UT)
South Arkansas Comm Coll (AR)
Southeastern Comm Coll (NC)
Southeastern Tech Coll (GA)
Southern West Virginia Comm and Tech Coll (WV)
South Georgia Tech Coll (GA)
South Hills School of Business & Technology, State College (PA)
South Plains Coll (TX)
Southside Virginia Comm Coll (VA)
South U, West Palm Beach (FL)
Southwestern Illinois Coll (IL)
Southwestern Michigan Coll (MI)
Southwest Florida Coll, Fort Myers (FL)
Southwest Georgia Tech Coll (GA)
Southwest Mississippi Comm Coll (MS)
Southwest Tennessee Comm Coll (TN)
Southwest Virginia Comm Coll (VA)
Spartanburg Methodist Coll (SC)
Spartanburg Tech Coll (SC)
Spokane Comm Coll (WA)
Spokane Falls Comm Coll (WA)
Spoon River Coll (IL)
Springfield Tech Comm Coll (MA)
Stark State Coll of Technology (OH)
Sullivan County Comm Coll (NY)
Sussex County Comm Coll (NJ)
Swainsboro Tech Coll (GA)
Tarrant County Coll District (TX)
Thomas Nelson Comm Coll (VA)
Three Rivers Comm Coll (MO)
Tidewater Comm Coll (VA)
Tillamook Bay Comm Coll (OR)
Tompkins Cortland Comm Coll (NY)
Treasure Valley Comm Coll (OR)
Trident Tech Coll (SC)
Trinidad State Jr Coll (CO)
Triton Coll (IL)
Tulsa Comm Coll (OK)
Tunxis Comm Coll (CT)
Union County Coll (NJ)
United Tribes Tech Coll (ND)
The U of Akron–Wayne Coll (OH)
U of Alaska Anchorage, Matanuska-Susitna Coll (AK)
U of Northwestern Ohio (OH)
Valdosta Tech Coll (GA)
Valencia Comm Coll (FL)
Vance-Granville Comm Coll (NC)
Waubonsee Comm Coll (IL)
Waukesha County Tech Coll (WI)

Weatherford Coll (TX)
West Central Tech Coll (GA)
Westchester Comm Coll (NY)
Western Tech Coll (WI)
West Georgia Tech Coll (GA)
Westmoreland County Comm Coll (PA)
West Virginia Business Coll, Wheeling (WV)
West Virginia Northern Comm Coll (WV)
Wharton County Jr Coll (TX)
William Rainey Harper Coll (IL)
Williston State Coll (ND)
Wilson Tech Comm Coll (NC)
Wisconsin Indianhead Tech Coll (WI)
Wor-Wic Comm Coll (MD)
Yakima Valley Comm Coll (WA)
Yavapai Coll (AZ)
York Tech Coll (SC)
Yuba Coll (CA)

Adult Development and Aging
Southwestern Oregon Comm Coll (OR)

Advertising
Bradley Academy for the Visual Arts (PA)
Central Piedmont Comm Coll (NC)
Chattanooga State Tech Comm Coll (TN)
Long Beach City Coll (CA)
Manatee Comm Coll (FL)
Middlesex County Coll (NJ)
Mississippi Gulf Coast Comm Coll (MS)
Mohawk Valley Comm Coll (NY)
Mt. San Antonio Coll (CA)
Parkland Coll (IL)
Pasadena City Coll (CA)
St. Cloud Tech Coll (MN)
Santa Rosa Jr Coll (CA)
South Plains Coll (TX)
Southwest Mississippi Comm Coll (MS)
Tidewater Comm Coll (VA)
Tulsa Comm Coll (OK)
Yuba Coll (CA)

Aeronautical/Aerospace Engineering Technology
Cincinnati State Tech and Comm Coll (OH)
GateWay Comm Coll (AZ)
Santa Rosa Jr Coll (CA)

Aeronautics/Aviation/Aerospace Science and Technology
Caldwell Comm Coll and Tech Inst (NC)
Comm Coll of the Air Force (AL)
Delaware Tech & Comm Coll, Terry Campus (DE)
Hesston Coll (KS)
Miami Dade Coll (FL)
Northland Comm and Tech Coll–Thief River Falls (MN)
Orange Coast Coll (CA)
Raritan Valley Comm Coll (NJ)
Texas State Tech Coll Waco (TX)
Tompkins Cortland Comm Coll (NY)
Tulsa Comm Coll (OK)
Vermilion Comm Coll (MN)

Aerospace, Aeronautical and Astronautical Engineering
Allan Hancock Coll (CA)

African-American/Black Studies
Atlanta Metropolitan Coll (GA)
Bronx Comm Coll of the City U of New York (NY)
Manatee Comm Coll (FL)
Nassau Comm Coll (NY)
Pasadena City Coll (CA)
San Diego City Coll (CA)
San Diego Mesa Coll (CA)

Santa Barbara City Coll (CA)
Yuba Coll (CA)

African Studies
MiraCosta Coll (CA)
Pasadena City Coll (CA)
Sinclair Comm Coll (OH)

Agribusiness
Allan Hancock Coll (CA)
Central Wyoming Coll (WY)
Clarendon Coll (TX)
Coll of Southern Maryland (MD)
Copiah-Lincoln Comm Coll (MS)
Crowder Coll (MO)
Eastern Arizona Coll (AZ)
Eastern Wyoming Coll (WY)
Glendale Comm Coll (AZ)
James Sprunt Comm Coll (NC)
Laramie County Comm Coll (WY)
Ogeechee Tech Coll (GA)
The Ohio State U Ag Tech Inst (OH)
Yavapai Coll (AZ)

Agricultural and Food Products Processing
Texas State Tech Coll Waco (TX)

Agricultural Business and Management
Abraham Baldwin Ag Coll (GA)
Arizona Western Coll (AZ)
Barton County Comm Coll (KS)
Brazosport Coll (TX)
Butler Comm Coll (KS)
Carl Albert State Coll (OK)
Casper Coll (WY)
Central Comm Coll–Columbus Campus (NE)
Central Comm Coll–Hastings Campus (NE)
Central Wyoming Coll (WY)
Clark State Comm Coll (OH)
Coastal Georgia Comm Coll (GA)
Cochise Coll, Douglas (AZ)
Colby Comm Coll (KS)
Copiah-Lincoln Comm Coll (MS)
Delaware Tech & Comm Coll, Jack F. Owens Campus (DE)
Fox Valley Tech Coll (WI)
Harrisburg Area Comm Coll (PA)
Hawkeye Comm Coll (IA)
Highland Comm Coll (IL)
Illinois Central Coll (IL)
Illinois Eastern Comm Colls, Wabash Valley College (IL)
Illinois Valley Comm Coll (IL)
Jackson State Comm Coll (TN)
Jefferson State Comm Coll (AL)
John Wood Comm Coll (IL)
Joliet Jr Coll (IL)
Kaskaskia Coll (IL)
Lake Land Coll (IL)
Lake Region State Coll (ND)
Linn-Benton Comm Coll (OR)
Lord Fairfax Comm Coll (VA)
Mississippi Gulf Coast Comm Coll (MS)
Modesto Jr Coll (CA)
Mt. San Antonio Coll (CA)
North Arkansas Coll (AR)
North Central Missouri Coll (MO)
Northeast Comm Coll (NE)
Northeast Iowa Comm Coll (IA)
The Ohio State U Ag Tech Inst (OH)
Otero Jr Coll (CO)
Owens Comm Coll, Toledo (OH)
Parkland Coll (IL)
Pratt Comm Coll (KS)
Richland Comm Coll (IL)
San Joaquin Delta Coll (CA)
Santa Rosa Jr Coll (CA)

Sheridan Coll–Sheridan and Gillette (WY)
Snow Coll (UT)
Spokane Comm Coll (WA)
State U of New York Coll of Technology at Alfred (NY)
Three Rivers Comm Coll (MO)
Treasure Valley Comm Coll (OR)
U of Northwestern Ohio (OH)
Vermilion Comm Coll (MN)
Yakima Valley Comm Coll (WA)
Yavapai Coll (AZ)
Yuba Coll (CA)

Agricultural Business and Management Related
Copiah-Lincoln Comm Coll (MS)
North Dakota State Coll of Science (ND)
The Pennsylvania State U Beaver Campus of the Commonwealth Coll (PA)
The Pennsylvania State U Delaware County Campus of the Commonwealth Coll (PA)
The Pennsylvania State U DuBois Campus of the Commonwealth Coll (PA)
The Pennsylvania State U Fayette Campus of the Commonwealth Coll (PA)
The Pennsylvania State U Hazleton Campus of the Commonwealth Coll (PA)
The Pennsylvania State U McKeesport Campus of the Commonwealth Coll (PA)
The Pennsylvania State U Mont Alto Campus of the Commonwealth Coll (PA)
The Pennsylvania State U New Kensington Campus of the Commonwealth Coll (PA)
The Pennsylvania State U Shenango Campus of the Commonwealth Coll (PA)
The Pennsylvania State U Wilkes-Barre Campus of the Commonwealth Coll (PA)
The Pennsylvania State U Worthington Scranton Campus of the Commonwealth Coll (PA)
The Pennsylvania State U York Campus of the Commonwealth Coll (PA)

Agricultural Business Technology
Copiah-Lincoln Comm Coll (MS)
Laramie County Comm Coll (WY)
North Iowa Area Comm Coll (IA)
The Ohio State U Ag Tech Inst (OH)

Agricultural Communication/Journalism
The Ohio State U Ag Tech Inst (OH)

Agricultural Economics
Abraham Baldwin Ag Coll (GA)
Clarendon Coll (TX)
Colby Comm Coll (KS)
Copiah-Lincoln Comm Coll (MS)
Eastern Wyoming Coll (WY)
James H. Faulkner State Comm Coll (AL)
North Iowa Area Comm Coll (IA)
The Ohio State U Ag Tech Inst (OH)
Pratt Comm Coll (KS)
Snow Coll (UT)
South Plains Coll (TX)
Vermilion Comm Coll (MN)

Agricultural/Farm Supplies Retailing and Wholesaling
Copiah-Lincoln Comm Coll (MS)
North Dakota State Coll of Science (ND)
Western Iowa Tech Comm Coll (IA)
Wisconsin Indianhead Tech Coll (WI)

Agricultural Mechanization
Abraham Baldwin Ag Coll (GA)
Beaufort County Comm Coll (NC)
Casper Coll (WY)
Clark State Comm Coll (OH)
Cowley County Comm Coll and Area Vocational–Tech School (KS)
Hawkeye Comm Coll (IA)
Highland Comm Coll (IL)
Hutchinson Comm Coll and Area Vocational School (KS)
Illinois Central Coll (IL)
Lake Land Coll (IL)
Longview Comm Coll (MO)
Modesto Jr Coll (CA)
Mt. San Antonio Coll (CA)
North Dakota State Coll of Science (ND)
Northeast Comm Coll (NE)
The Ohio State U Ag Tech Inst (OH)
Parkland Coll (IL)
Pratt Comm Coll (KS)
San Joaquin Delta Coll (CA)
Santa Rosa Jr Coll (CA)
Southwest Georgia Tech Coll (GA)
Spoon River Coll (IL)
Three Rivers Comm Coll (MO)
Treasure Valley Comm Coll (OR)
Western Tech Coll (WI)
Yakima Valley Comm Coll (WA)
Yuba Coll (CA)

Agricultural Power Machinery Operation
The Ohio State U Ag Tech Inst (OH)

Agricultural Production
Allen County Comm Coll (KS)
Illinois Eastern Comm Colls, Wabash Valley College (IL)
John Wood Comm Coll (IL)
Lake Land Coll (IL)
Laramie County Comm Coll (WY)
Lincoln Land Comm Coll (IL)
Modesto Jr Coll (CA)
North Dakota State Coll of Science (ND)
Northeast Comm Coll (NE)
North Iowa Area Comm Coll (IA)
Southern State Comm Coll (OH)

Agricultural Teacher Education
Chemeketa Comm Coll (OR)
Colby Comm Coll (KS)
Eastern Wyoming Coll (WY)
Linn-Benton Comm Coll (OR)
Northwest-Shoals Comm Coll (AL)
The Ohio State U Ag Tech Inst (OH)
Pratt Comm Coll (KS)
Spoon River Coll (IL)
Trinity Valley Comm Coll (TX)
Vermilion Comm Coll (MN)

Agriculture
Abraham Baldwin Ag Coll (GA)
Arizona Western Coll (AZ)
Arkansas Northeastern Coll (AR)
Arkansas State U–Beebe (AR)
Bainbridge Coll (GA)

Barton County Comm Coll (KS)
Casper Coll (WY)
Central Arizona Coll (AZ)
Central Wyoming Coll (WY)
Chattahoochee Valley Comm Coll (AL)
Clarendon Coll (TX)
Clark State Comm Coll (OH)
Coastal Bend Coll (TX)
Colby Comm Coll (KS)
Copiah-Lincoln Comm Coll (MS)
Cowley County Comm Coll and Area Vocational–Tech School (KS)
Crowder Coll (MO)
Dixie State Coll of Utah (UT)
Eastern Arizona Coll (AZ)
Eastern Wyoming Coll (WY)
Georgia Highlands Coll (GA)
Horry-Georgetown Tech Coll (SC)
Houston Comm Coll System (TX)
Howard Coll (TX)
Hutchinson Comm Coll and Area Vocational School (KS)
Illinois Valley Comm Coll (IL)
Laramie County Comm Coll (WY)
Linn-Benton Comm Coll (OR)
Macomb Comm Coll (MI)
Miami Dade Coll (FL)
Missouri State U–West Plains (MO)
Modesto Jr Coll (CA)
Mt. San Antonio Coll (CA)
North Arkansas Coll (AR)
Northeast Comm Coll (NE)
North Idaho Coll (ID)
Palau Comm CollPalau)
Palo Alto Coll (TX)
Palo Verde Coll (CA)
Pratt Comm Coll (KS)
San Joaquin Delta Coll (CA)
Santa Rosa Jr Coll (CA)
Sheridan Coll–Sheridan and Gillette (WY)
Snow Coll (UT)
South Plains Coll (TX)
State U of New York Coll of Technology at Alfred (NY)
Treasure Valley Comm Coll (OR)
Tulsa Comm Coll (OK)
Ventura Coll (CA)
Wharton County Jr Coll (TX)
Williston State Coll (ND)
Yakima Valley Comm Coll (WA)
Yavapai Coll (AZ)
Young Harris Coll (GA)
Yuba Coll (CA)

Agronomy and Crop Science
Colby Comm Coll (KS)
Cowley County Comm Coll and Area Vocational–Tech School (KS)
Hawkeye Comm Coll (IA)
Modesto Jr Coll (CA)
Mt. San Antonio Coll (CA)
Northeast Comm Coll (NE)
The Ohio State U Ag Tech Inst (OH)
Snow Coll (UT)
South Plains Coll (TX)
Spokane Comm Coll (WA)
Treasure Valley Comm Coll (OR)
Vermilion Comm Coll (MN)
Yakima Valley Comm Coll (WA)
Yuba Coll (CA)

Aircraft Powerplant Technology
Florida Comm Coll at Jacksonville (FL)
Linn State Tech Coll (MO)
Louisiana Tech Coll (LA)
North Central Inst (TN)
Pima Comm Coll (AZ)
St. Philip's Coll (TX)
San Joaquin Valley Coll (CA)
Texas State Tech Coll Waco (TX)

Airframe Mechanics and Aircraft Maintenance Technology
Aviation Inst of Maintenance–Kansas City (MO)
Aviation Inst of Maintenance–Manassas (VA)
Aviation Inst of Maintenance–Virginia Beach (VA)
Cochise Coll, Douglas (AZ)
Comm Coll of the Air Force (AL)
Cowley County Comm Coll and Area Vocational–Tech School (KS)
Florida Comm Coll at Jacksonville (FL)
Ivy Tech Comm Coll–Wabash Valley (IN)
Middle Georgia Tech Coll (GA)
Mohawk Valley Comm Coll (NY)
Mt. San Antonio Coll (CA)
New Hampshire Comm Tech Coll, Nashua/Claremont (NH)
North Central Inst (TN)
St. Philip's Coll (TX)
San Joaquin Valley Coll (CA)
Southern Arkansas U Tech (AR)
Southwestern Illinois Coll (IL)
Southwestern Michigan Coll (MI)
Texas State Tech Coll Waco (TX)
Trident Tech Coll (SC)
Tulsa Comm Coll (OK)

Airline Flight Attendant
Mercer County Comm Coll (NJ)

Airline Pilot and Flight Crew
Big Bend Comm Coll (WA)
Broward Comm Coll (FL)
Casper Coll (WY)
Chattanooga State Tech Comm Coll (TN)
Cochise Coll, Douglas (AZ)
Comm Coll of Allegheny County (PA)
Dixie State Coll of Utah (UT)
Florida Comm Coll at Jacksonville (FL)
Fox Valley Tech Coll (WI)
Georgia Aviation & Tech Coll (GA)
Jackson Comm Coll (MI)
Jamestown Comm Coll (NY)
Lake Superior Coll (MN)
Lansing Comm Coll (MI)
Long Beach City Coll (CA)
Luzerne County Comm Coll (PA)
Mercer County Comm Coll (NJ)
Miami Dade Coll (FL)
Midland Coll (TX)
Mt. San Antonio Coll (CA)
North Shore Comm Coll (MA)
Orange Coast Coll (CA)
Palm Beach Comm Coll (FL)
Pasadena City Coll (CA)
Salt Lake Comm Coll (UT)
San Juan Coll (NM)
Texas State Tech Coll Waco (TX)
Vermilion Comm Coll (MN)

Air Traffic Control
Cecil Comm Coll (MD)
Comm Coll of the Air Force (AL)
Georgia Aviation & Tech Coll (GA)
Miami Dade Coll (FL)
Mt. San Antonio Coll (CA)

Allied Health and Medical Assisting Services Related
Cincinnati State Tech and Comm Coll (OH)
Florida National Coll (FL)
Minneapolis Business Coll (MN)

North Seattle Comm Coll (WA)
Pennsylvania Inst of Technology (PA)

Allied Health Diagnostic, Intervention, and Treatment Professions Related
Ivy Tech Comm Coll–Wabash Valley (IN)
Oakland Comm Coll (MI)
Union County Coll (NJ)

American Government and Politics
Manatee Comm Coll (FL)

American Indian/Native American Studies
Central Wyoming Coll (WY)
Diné Coll (AZ)
Itasca Comm Coll (MN)
Lac Courte Oreilles Ojibwa Comm Coll (WI)
North Idaho Coll (ID)
Northwest Indian Coll (WA)
Pima Comm Coll (AZ)
Saginaw Chippewa Tribal Coll (MI)
Santa Barbara City Coll (CA)

American Studies
Bucks County Comm Coll (PA)
Foothill Coll (CA)
Greenfield Comm Coll (MA)
Holyoke Comm Coll (MA)
Manatee Comm Coll (FL)
Miami Dade Coll (FL)
Naugatuck Valley Comm Coll (CT)
Saddleback Coll (CA)
Tulsa Comm Coll (OK)

Animal Health
Santa Rosa Jr Coll (CA)

Animal/Livestock Husbandry and Production
Feather River Coll (CA)
John Wood Comm Coll (IL)
The Ohio State U Ag Tech Inst (OH)
Pratt Comm Coll (KS)

Animal Physiology
Joliet Jr Coll (IL)
Santa Rosa Jr Coll (CA)
Snow Coll (UT)

Animal Sciences
Abraham Baldwin Ag Coll (GA)
Alamance Comm Coll (NC)
Arkansas State U–Beebe (AR)
Casper Coll (WY)
Colby Comm Coll (KS)
Eastern Wyoming Coll (WY)
Hawkeye Comm Coll (IA)
James Sprunt Comm Coll (NC)
Linn-Benton Comm Coll (OR)
Manor Coll (PA)
Modesto Jr Coll (CA)
Mt. San Antonio Coll (CA)
Niagara County Comm Coll (NY)
Northeast Comm Coll (NE)
The Ohio State U Ag Tech Inst (OH)
Pratt Comm Coll (KS)
San Joaquin Delta Coll (CA)
Santa Rosa Jr Coll (CA)
Snow Coll (UT)
State U of New York Coll of Technology at Alfred (NY)
Trinity Valley Comm Coll (TX)
Yakima Valley Comm Coll (WA)
Yuba Coll (CA)

Animation, Interactive Technology, Video Graphics and Special Effects
The Art Inst of New York City (NY)
The Art Inst of Philadelphia (PA)
Bradley Academy for the Visual Arts (PA)

Brooks Coll, Long Beach (CA)
Delaware Coll of Art and Design (DE)
Globe Coll (MN)
Hagerstown Comm Coll (MD)
Kent State U, Tuscarawas Campus (OH)
Montgomery Coll (TX)
New Hampshire Tech Inst (NH)
Platt Coll San Diego (CA)
United Tribes Tech Coll (ND)

Anthropology
Barton County Comm Coll (KS)
Casper Coll (WY)
Cochise Coll, Douglas (AZ)
Columbia Coll (CA)
Eastern Arizona Coll (AZ)
Foothill Coll (CA)
Gainesville Coll (GA)
Great Basin Coll (NV)
Kellogg Comm Coll (MI)
Laramie County Comm Coll (WY)
Lower Columbia Coll (WA)
Miami Dade Coll (FL)
Midland Coll (TX)
North Idaho Coll (ID)
Orange Coast Coll (CA)
Pasadena City Coll (CA)
Pima Comm Coll (AZ)
Saddleback Coll (CA)
San Diego City Coll (CA)
San Joaquin Delta Coll (CA)
San Juan Coll (NM)
Santa Barbara City Coll (CA)
Santa Rosa Jr Coll (CA)
Skyline Coll (CA)

Apparel and Accessories Marketing
FIDM/The Fashion Inst of Design & Merchandising, Los Angeles Campus (CA)
FIDM/The Fashion Inst of Design & Merchandising, San Diego Campus (CA)
FIDM/The Fashion Inst of Design & Merchandising, San Francisco Campus (CA)

Apparel and Textile Marketing Management
Comm Coll of the Air Force (AL)
Delta Coll (MI)

Apparel and Textiles
FIDM/The Fashion Inst of Design & Merchandising, Los Angeles Campus (CA)
FIDM/The Fashion Inst of Design & Merchandising, San Francisco Campus (CA)
Modesto Jr Coll (CA)
Mt. San Antonio Coll (CA)

Appliance Installation and Repair Technology
Mohawk Valley Comm Coll (NY)

Applied Art
Allan Hancock Coll (CA)
Casper Coll (WY)
Centralia Coll (WA)
Central Piedmont Comm Coll (NC)
Chattanooga State Tech Comm Coll (TN)
Coastal Bend Coll (TX)
Evergreen Valley Coll (CA)
Howard Comm Coll (MD)
Kingsborough Comm Coll of the City U of New York (NY)
Lincoln Coll (IL)
Lincoln Coll–Normal (IL)
Middlesex County Coll (NJ)
Pratt Comm Coll (KS)
Sinclair Comm Coll (OH)
Skyline Coll (CA)
Tunxis Comm Coll (CT)
Westchester Comm Coll (NY)

Applied Horticulture
Alamance Comm Coll (NC)
Arkansas Northeastern Coll (AR)
Central Comm Coll–Hastings Campus (NE)
Clark Coll (WA)
Comm Coll of Allegheny County (PA)
Delgado Comm Coll (LA)
Edmonds Comm Coll (WA)
Fayetteville Tech Comm Coll (NC)
Glendale Comm Coll (AZ)
John Wood Comm Coll (IL)
Kaskaskia Coll (IL)
Kent State U, Geauga Campus (OH)
Lord Fairfax Comm Coll (VA)
Northeast Comm Coll (NE)
North Shore Comm Coll (MA)
Oakland Comm Coll (MI)
Santa Barbara City Coll (CA)
Spokane Comm Coll (WA)
Tulsa Comm Coll (OK)
West Virginia Northern Comm Coll (WV)
Wilkes Comm Coll (NC)

Applied Horticulture/Horticultural Business Services Related
Cincinnati State Tech and Comm Coll (OH)
Southwest Tennessee Comm Coll (TN)

Applied Mathematics
Lincoln Coll (IL)

Aquaculture
Trinidad State Jr Coll (CO)
Yavapai Coll (AZ)

Architectural Drafting
Coll of Lake County (IL)
IntelliTec Coll, Grand Junction (CO)
North Seattle Comm Coll (WA)

Architectural Drafting and Cad/Cadd
Butler County Comm Coll (PA)
Central New Mexico Comm Coll (NM)
Commonwealth Tech Inst (PA)
Comm Coll of Allegheny County (PA)
Dixie State Coll of Utah (UT)
Florida Comm Coll at Jacksonville (FL)
Glendale Comm Coll (AZ)
Island Drafting and Tech Inst (NY)
Kaskaskia Coll (IL)
Lake Superior Coll (MN)
Lincoln Land Comm Coll (IL)
Macomb Comm Coll (MI)
Miami Dade Coll (FL)
Mohawk Valley Comm Coll (NY)
Montgomery County Comm Coll (PA)
Normandale Comm Coll (MN)
Pima Comm Coll (AZ)
St. Cloud Tech Coll (MN)
Waukesha County Tech Coll (WI)
Yavapai Coll (AZ)

Architectural Engineering
Luzerne County Comm Coll (PA)

Architectural Engineering Technology
Allan Hancock Coll (CA)
Arapahoe Comm Coll (CO)
Benjamin Franklin Inst of Technology (MA)
Broward Comm Coll (FL)
Butler County Comm Coll (PA)
Cape Fear Comm Coll (NC)
Central Piedmont Comm Coll (NC)
Cincinnati State Tech and Comm Coll (OH)

City Colls of Chicago, Wilbur Wright College (IL)
Coastal Carolina Comm Coll (NC)
Coll of The Albemarle (NC)
Delaware Tech & Comm Coll, Jack F. Owens Campus (DE)
Delaware Tech & Comm Coll, Stanton/Wilmington Campus (DE)
Delaware Tech & Comm Coll, Terry Campus (DE)
Delgado Comm Coll (LA)
Delta Coll (MI)
Erie Comm Coll, South Campus (NY)
Essex County Coll (NJ)
Fayetteville Tech Comm Coll (NC)
Finger Lakes Comm Coll (NY)
Florida Comm Coll at Jacksonville (FL)
Forsyth Tech Comm Coll (NC)
Front Range Comm Coll (CO)
Gaston Coll (NC)
Grand Rapids Comm Coll (MI)
Guam Comm Coll (GU)
Harrisburg Area Comm Coll (PA)
Hawkeye Comm Coll (IA)
Illinois Central Coll (IL)
John Tyler Comm Coll (VA)
Lake Land Coll (IL)
Lamar State Coll–Orange (TX)
Lansing Comm Coll (MI)
Long Beach City Coll (CA)
Luzerne County Comm Coll (PA)
Mercer County Comm Coll (NJ)
Metropolitan Comm Coll (NE)
Miami Dade Coll (FL)
Midlands Tech Coll (SC)
Minnesota State Comm and Tech Coll–Fergus Falls (MN)
MiraCosta Coll (CA)
Modesto Jr Coll (CA)
Mott Comm Coll (MI)
Mt. San Antonio Coll (CA)
New Hampshire Tech Inst (NH)
Northampton County Area Comm Coll (PA)
North Dakota State Coll of Science (ND)
Northland Comm and Tech Coll–Thief River Falls (MN)
Norwalk Comm Coll (CT)
Oakland Comm Coll (MI)
Orange Coast Coll (CA)
Orange County Comm Coll (NY)
Palo Alto Coll (TX)
Pasadena City Coll (CA)
Pennsylvania Inst of Technology (PA)
The Pennsylvania State U Fayette Campus of the Commonwealth Coll (PA)
The Pennsylvania State U Worthington Scranton Campus of the Commonwealth Coll (PA)
Phoenix Coll (AZ)
Saddleback Coll (CA)
St. Cloud Tech Coll (MN)
St. Petersburg Coll (FL)
Salt Lake Comm Coll (UT)
San Diego Mesa Coll (CA)
Seminole Comm Coll (FL)
Sinclair Comm Coll (OH)
Southeast Tech Inst (SD)
Southwest Tennessee Comm Coll (TN)
Spartanburg Tech Coll (SC)
Spokane Comm Coll (WA)
Springfield Tech Comm Coll (MA)
Stark State Coll of Technology (OH)
State U of New York Coll of Technology at Alfred (NY)

State U of New York Coll of Technology at Delhi (NY)
Tarrant County Coll District (TX)
Triton Coll (IL)
Vermilion Comm Coll (MN)
Western Iowa Tech Comm Coll (IA)
Western Tech Coll (WI)
Westmoreland County Comm Coll (PA)
Wilkes Comm Coll (NC)
William Rainey Harper Coll (IL)
Wisconsin Indianhead Tech Coll (WI)

Architectural Technology
City Colls of Chicago, Wilbur Wright College (IL)

Architecture
Allen County Comm Coll (KS)
Barton County Comm Coll (KS)
Brazosport Coll (TX)
Clarendon Coll (TX)
Copiah-Lincoln Comm Coll (MS)
Harrisburg Area Comm Coll (PA)
Howard Comm Coll (MD)
Oakland Comm Coll (MI)
San Diego Mesa Coll (CA)
Sauk Valley Comm Coll (IL)
Tulsa Comm Coll (OK)

Army R.O.T.C./Military Science
New Mexico Military Inst (NM)

Art
Abraham Baldwin Ag Coll (GA)
Allan Hancock Coll (CA)
Allen County Comm Coll (KS)
Ancilla Coll (IN)
Arizona Western Coll (AZ)
Atlanta Metropolitan Coll (GA)
Austin Comm Coll (TX)
Bainbridge Coll (GA)
Barton County Comm Coll (KS)
Berkeley City Coll (CA)
Brazosport Coll (TX)
Bronx Comm Coll of the City U of New York (NY)
Bucks County Comm Coll (PA)
Bunker Hill Comm Coll (MA)
Butler Comm Coll (KS)
Caldwell Comm Coll and Tech Inst (NC)
Casper Coll (WY)
Cecil Comm Coll (MD)
Centralia Coll (WA)
Central Oregon Comm Coll (OR)
Central Piedmont Comm Coll (NC)
Central Wyoming Coll (WY)
Citrus Coll (CA)
City Colls of Chicago, Wilbur Wright College (IL)
Clarendon Coll (TX)
Coahoma Comm Coll (MS)
Coastal Bend Coll (TX)
Coastal Georgia Comm Coll (GA)
Cochise Coll, Douglas (AZ)
Coll of Lake County (IL)
Coll of Southern Maryland (MD)
Coll of The Albemarle (NC)
Coll of the Canyons (CA)
Columbia Coll (CA)
Comm Coll of Allegheny County (PA)
Cowley County Comm Coll and Area Vocational–Tech School (KS)
Crowder Coll (MO)
Delta Coll (MI)
Diné Coll (AZ)
Dixie State Coll of Utah (UT)
Eastern Arizona Coll (AZ)
Eastern Wyoming Coll (WY)
Essex County Coll (NJ)

Foothill Coll (CA)
Frederick Comm Coll (MD)
Gaston Coll (NC)
Gavilan Coll (CA)
Georgia Highlands Coll (GA)
Grand Rapids Comm Coll (MI)
Great Basin Coll (NV)
Greenfield Comm Coll (MA)
Harrisburg Area Comm Coll (PA)
Highland Comm Coll (IL)
Highline Comm Coll (WA)
Howard Coll (TX)
Howard Comm Coll (MD)
Joliet Jr Coll (IL)
Kellogg Comm Coll (MI)
Keystone Coll (PA)
Kingsborough Comm Coll of the City U of New York (NY)
Lansing Comm Coll (MI)
Laramie County Comm Coll (WY)
Lawson State Comm Coll (AL)
Lincoln Land Comm Coll (IL)
Linn-Benton Comm Coll (OR)
Long Beach City Coll (CA)
Lower Columbia Coll (WA)
Manatee Comm Coll (FL)
Mercer County Comm Coll (NJ)
Miami Dade Coll (FL)
Middlesex County Coll (NJ)
Midland Coll (TX)
MiraCosta Coll (CA)
Mississippi Gulf Coast Comm Coll (MS)
Modesto Jr Coll (CA)
Mohawk Valley Comm Coll (NY)
Montgomery County Comm Coll (PA)
Mount Wachusett Comm Coll (MA)
Nassau Comm Coll (NY)
New Mexico Military Inst (NM)
Northeast Comm Coll (NE)
North Idaho Coll (ID)
North Seattle Comm Coll (WA)
Northwestern Connecticut Comm Coll (CT)
Northwest-Shoals Comm Coll (AL)
Norwalk Comm Coll (CT)
Okaloosa-Walton Comm Coll (FL)
Orange Coast Coll (CA)
Palm Beach Comm Coll (FL)
Palo Alto Coll (TX)
Parkland Coll (IL)
Pasadena City Coll (CA)
Phoenix Coll (AZ)
Pratt Comm Coll (KS)
Quinebaug Valley Comm Coll (CT)
Quinsigamond Comm Coll (MA)
Roane State Comm Coll (TN)
Rockingham Comm Coll (NC)
Saddleback Coll (CA)
St. Louis Comm Coll at Florissant Valley (MO)
St. Philip's Coll (TX)
San Diego City Coll (CA)
San Diego Mesa Coll (CA)
San Joaquin Delta Coll (CA)
San Juan Coll (NM)
Santa Rosa Jr Coll (CA)
Sauk Valley Comm Coll (IL)
Seminole State Coll (OK)
Sheridan Coll–Sheridan and Gillette (WY)
Sinclair Comm Coll (OH)
Skyline Coll (CA)
Snow Coll (UT)
Southeastern Comm Coll (NC)
South Plains Coll (TX)
Spokane Falls Comm Coll (WA)
Spoon River Coll (IL)
Springfield Coll in Illinois (IL)
Trinity Valley Comm Coll (TX)

Triton Coll (IL)
Tulsa Comm Coll (OK)
Tunxis Comm Coll (CT)
United Tribes Tech Coll (ND)
Vermilion Comm Coll (MN)
Waubonsee Comm Coll (IL)
Wharton County Jr Coll (TX)
William Rainey Harper Coll (IL)
Young Harris Coll (GA)
Yuba Coll (CA)

Art History, Criticism and Conservation
Dixie State Coll of Utah (UT)
Foothill Coll (CA)
Lincoln Coll (IL)
Manatee Comm Coll (FL)
Mercer County Comm Coll (NJ)
Palm Beach Comm Coll (FL)
Pasadena City Coll (CA)
Santa Barbara City Coll (CA)
Skyline Coll (CA)
Vermilion Comm Coll (MN)

Artificial Intelligence and Robotics
Cecil Comm Coll (MD)
Chattanooga State Tech Comm Coll (TN)
Illinois Central Coll (IL)
Metropolitan Comm Coll-Business & Technology College (MO)
Mountain View Coll (TX)
New Hampshire Comm Tech Coll, Nashua/Claremont (NH)
Raritan Valley Comm Coll (NJ)
San Diego City Coll (CA)
Sinclair Comm Coll (OH)
Southeast Tech Inst (SD)
Spokane Comm Coll (WA)
Tulsa Comm Coll (OK)
Westmoreland County Comm Coll (PA)

Art Teacher Education
Ancilla Coll (IN)
Carl Albert State Coll (OK)
Chemeketa Comm Coll (OR)
Coastal Bend Coll (TX)
Copiah-Lincoln Comm Coll (MS)
Eastern Arizona Coll (AZ)
Independence Comm Coll (KS)
Kellogg Comm Coll (MI)
Lincoln Coll (IL)
Lincoln Coll–Normal (IL)
Mississippi Gulf Coast Comm Coll (MS)
Northeast Comm Coll (NE)
Parkland Coll (IL)
Pratt Comm Coll (KS)
Roane State Comm Coll (TN)
Trinidad State Jr Coll (CO)
Vermilion Comm Coll (MN)
Waubonsee Comm Coll (IL)
Young Harris Coll (GA)

Asian Studies
Manatee Comm Coll (FL)
Miami Dade Coll (FL)

Astronomy
Austin Comm Coll (TX)
Manatee Comm Coll (FL)
North Idaho Coll (ID)
Pasadena City Coll (CA)
Saddleback Coll (CA)
Santa Rosa Jr Coll (CA)
Tulsa Comm Coll (OK)

Athletic Training
Allen County Comm Coll (KS)
Barton County Comm Coll (KS)
Comm Coll of Allegheny County (PA)
Dean Coll (MA)
Foothill Coll (CA)
Independence Comm Coll (KS)
Meridian Comm Coll (MS)
New Hampshire Comm Tech Coll, Manchester/Stratham (NH)
North Idaho Coll (ID)

Northland Comm and Tech Coll–Thief River Falls (MN)
Orange Coast Coll (CA)
Pratt Comm Coll (KS)
Santa Barbara City Coll (CA)
Santa Rosa Jr Coll (CA)
Sauk Valley Comm Coll (IL)
Southwestern Oregon Comm Coll (OR)

Atmospheric Sciences and Meteorology
Comm Coll of the Air Force (AL)
Okaloosa-Walton Coll (FL)
Santa Rosa Jr Coll (CA)

Audio Engineering
Brown Mackie Coll–Cincinnati (OH)
Northeast Comm Coll (NE)
South Plains Coll (TX)
Texas State Tech Coll Waco (TX)

Audiology and Hearing Sciences
Arkansas State U–Mountain Home (AR)
Bristol Comm Coll (MA)

Audiology and Speech-Language Pathology
Miami Dade Coll (FL)

Audiovisual Communications Technologies Related
Edmonds Comm Coll (WA)

Autobody/Collision and Repair Technology
Central Comm Coll–Hastings Campus (NE)
Century Coll (MN)
Coahoma Comm Coll (MS)
Dixie State Coll of Utah (UT)
Eastfield Coll (TX)
Erie Comm Coll, South Campus (NY)
Florida Comm Coll at Jacksonville (FL)
Hawkeye Comm Coll (IA)
Hutchinson Comm Coll and Area Vocational School (KS)
Illinois Eastern Comm Colls, Olney Central College (IL)
Kaskaskia Coll (IL)
Kauai Comm Coll (HI)
Laramie County Comm Coll (WY)
Linn State Tech Coll (MO)
Manhattan Area Tech Coll (KS)
Modesto Jr Coll (CA)
Mott Comm Coll (MI)
Nashville Auto Diesel Coll (TN)
New Hampshire Comm Tech Coll, Nashua/Claremont (NH)
North Dakota State Coll of Science (ND)
Northeast Comm Coll (NE)
Parkland Coll (IL)
Prairie State Coll (IL)
Riverland Comm Coll (MN)
Riverside Comm Coll District (CA)
St. Cloud Tech Coll (MN)
St. Philip's Coll (TX)
Salt Lake Comm Coll (UT)
San Juan Coll (NM)
Southeast Tech Inst (SD)
Southwestern Illinois Coll (IL)
State U of New York Coll of Technology at Alfred (NY)
Texas State Tech Coll Waco (TX)
Waubonsee Comm Coll (IL)
Waukesha County Tech Coll (WI)
Western Iowa Tech Comm Coll (IA)

Automobile/Automotive Mechanics Technology
Alamance Comm Coll (NC)
Allan Hancock Coll (CA)
Allegany Coll of Maryland (MD)

Arapahoe Comm Coll (CO)
Arizona Western Coll (AZ)
Austin Comm Coll (TX)
Bainbridge Coll (GA)
Barton County Comm Coll (KS)
Beaufort County Comm Coll (NC)
Benjamin Franklin Inst of Technology (MA)
Bergen Comm Coll (NJ)
Big Bend Comm Coll (WA)
Brazosport Coll (TX)
Broward Comm Coll (FL)
Butler Comm Coll (KS)
Cape Fear Comm Coll (NC)
Casper Coll (WY)
Cedar Valley Coll (TX)
Central Arizona Coll (AZ)
Central Comm Coll–Columbus Campus (NE)
Central Comm Coll–Grand Island Campus (NE)
Central Comm Coll–Hastings Campus (NE)
Central Florida Comm Coll (FL)
Central Oregon Comm Coll (OR)
Central Piedmont Comm Coll (NC)
Central Wyoming Coll (WY)
Century Coll (MN)
Chattahoochee Tech Coll (GA)
Chattanooga State Tech Comm Coll (TN)
Chemeketa Comm Coll (OR)
Citrus Coll (CA)
Clark Coll (WA)
Clovis Comm Coll (NM)
Coastal Bend Coll (TX)
Coll of DuPage (IL)
Coll of Eastern Utah (UT)
Coll of Lake County (IL)
Columbia Coll (CA)
Columbus Tech Coll (GA)
Comm and Tech Coll of Shepherd (WV)
Comm Coll of the Air Force (AL)
Corning Comm Coll (NY)
Cossatot Comm Coll of the U of Arkansas (AR)
Cowley County Comm Coll and Area Vocational–Tech School (KS)
Cuyahoga Comm Coll (OH)
DeKalb Tech Coll (GA)
Delaware Tech & Comm Coll, Jack F. Owens Campus (DE)
Delgado Comm Coll (LA)
Delta Coll (MI)
Denmark Tech Coll (SC)
Dixie State Coll of Utah (UT)
East Central Coll (MO)
Eastern Arizona Coll (AZ)
Eastern Idaho Tech Coll (ID)
Eastfield Coll (TX)
Erie Comm Coll, South Campus (NY)
Evergreen Valley Coll (CA)
Fayetteville Tech Comm Coll (NC)
Florida Comm Coll at Jacksonville (FL)
Forsyth Tech Comm Coll (NC)
Fox Valley Tech Coll (WI)
Gaston Coll (NC)
GateWay Comm Coll (AZ)
Gateway Comm Coll (CT)
George C. Wallace Comm Coll (AL)
Georgia Highlands Coll (GA)
Glendale Comm Coll (AZ)
Grand Rapids Comm Coll (MI)
Griffin Tech Coll (GA)
Guam Comm Coll (GU)
Gwinnett Tech Coll (GA)
Harrisburg Area Comm Coll (PA)
Hawkeye Comm Coll (IA)
H. Councill Trenholm State Tech Coll (AL)
Highland Comm Coll (IL)
Houston Comm Coll System (TX)

Howard Coll (TX)
Hudson Valley Comm Coll (NY)
Hutchinson Comm Coll and Area Vocational School (KS)
Illinois Central Coll (IL)
Illinois Eastern Comm Colls, Olney Central College (IL)
Illinois Valley Comm Coll (IL)
Ivy Tech Comm Coll–Central Indiana (IN)
Ivy Tech Comm Coll–Columbus (IN)
Ivy Tech Comm Coll–East Central (IN)
Ivy Tech Comm Coll–Kokomo (IN)
Ivy Tech Comm Coll–Lafayette (IN)
Ivy Tech Comm Coll–North Central (IN)
Ivy Tech Comm Coll–Northeast (IN)
Ivy Tech Comm Coll–Northwest (IN)
Ivy Tech Comm Coll–Southern Indiana (IN)
Ivy Tech Comm Coll–Southwest (IN)
Ivy Tech Comm Coll–Wabash Valley (IN)
Ivy Tech Comm Coll–Whitewater (IN)
Jackson Comm Coll (MI)
Joliet Jr Coll (IL)
Kaskaskia Coll (IL)
Kauai Comm Coll (HI)
Kent State U, Trumbull Campus (OH)
Lake Land Coll (IL)
Lake Region State Coll (ND)
Lake Superior Coll (MN)
Lamar State Coll–Port Arthur (TX)
Lansing Comm Coll (MI)
Laramie County Comm Coll (WY)
Lincoln Land Comm Coll (IL)
Linn-Benton Comm Coll (OR)
Linn State Tech Coll (MO)
Long Beach City Coll (CA)
Longview Comm Coll (MO)
Louisiana Tech Coll (LA)
Lower Columbia Coll (WA)
Luzerne County Comm Coll (PA)
Macomb Comm Coll (MI)
Manhattan Area Tech Coll (KS)
Metropolitan Comm Coll (NE)
Middlesex County Coll (NJ)
Midland Coll (TX)
Midlands Tech Coll (SC)
MiraCosta Coll (CA)
Mississippi Gulf Coast Comm Coll (MS)
Modesto Jr Coll (CA)
Moraine Park Tech Coll (WI)
Moraine Valley Comm Coll (IL)
Mott Comm Coll (MI)
Mount Wachusett Comm Coll (MA)
Nashville Auto Diesel Coll (TN)
Naugatuck Valley Comm Coll (CT)
New Hampshire Comm Tech Coll, Manchester/Stratham (NH)
New Hampshire Comm Tech Coll, Nashua/Claremont (NH)
Normandale Comm Coll (MN)
Northampton County Area Comm Coll (PA)
North Arkansas Coll (AR)
North Central Missouri Coll (MO)
North Dakota State Coll of Science (ND)
Northeast Comm Coll (NE)
Northeast State Tech Comm Coll (TN)
Northern Maine Comm Coll (ME)

North Idaho Coll (ID)
North Iowa Area Comm Coll (IA)
Northland Comm and Tech Coll–Thief River Falls (MN)
Northwestern Tech Coll (GA)
Oakland Comm Coll (MI)
Ogeechee Tech Coll (GA)
Okaloosa-Walton Coll (FL)
Otero Jr Coll (CO)
Ouachita Tech Coll (AR)
Palau Comm CollPalau)
Palo Verde Coll (CA)
Parkland Coll (IL)
Pasadena City Coll (CA)
Pellissippi State Tech Comm Coll (TN)
Peninsula Coll (WA)
Pima Comm Coll (AZ)
Prairie State Coll (IL)
Pratt Comm Coll (KS)
Quinsigamond Comm Coll (MA)
Raritan Valley Comm Coll (NJ)
Richland Comm Coll (IL)
Riverside Comm Coll District (CA)
Rock Valley Coll (IL)
Rogue Comm Coll (OR)
Rosedale Tech Inst (PA)
Saddleback Coll (CA)
St. Cloud Tech Coll (MN)
St. Philip's Coll (TX)
San Diego City Coll (CA)
San Joaquin Delta Coll (CA)
San Juan Coll (NM)
Santa Barbara City Coll (CA)
Savannah Tech Coll (GA)
Seminole Comm Coll (FL)
Sinclair Comm Coll (OH)
Skyline Coll (CA)
Snow Coll (UT)
Southeast Tech Inst (SD)
Southern West Virginia Comm and Tech Coll (WV)
South Plains Coll (TX)
South Texas Coll (TX)
Southwestern Michigan Coll (MI)
Southwest Mississippi Comm Coll (MS)
Southwest Tennessee Comm Coll (TN)
Spartanburg Tech Coll (SC)
Spokane Comm Coll (WA)
Spoon River Coll (IL)
Stark State Coll of Technology (OH)
State U of New York Coll of Technology at Alfred (NY)
Tarrant County Coll District (TX)
Texas State Tech Coll Waco (TX)
Thomas Nelson Comm Coll (VA)
Tidewater Comm Coll (VA)
Tri-County Comm Coll (NC)
Trident Tech Coll (SC)
Trinidad State Jr Coll (CO)
Trinity Valley Comm Coll (TX)
Triton Coll (IL)
Tulsa Comm Coll (OK)
United Tribes Tech Coll (ND)
U of Northwestern Ohio (OH)
Vance-Granville Comm Coll (NC)
Ventura Coll (CA)
Waubonsee Comm Coll (IL)
Waukesha County Tech Coll (WI)
Westchester Comm Coll (NY)
Western Iowa Tech Comm Coll (IA)
Western Tech Coll (TX)
Western Tech Coll (WI)
West Georgia Tech Coll (GA)
Wharton County Jr Coll (TX)
Wichita Area Tech Coll (KS)
Wilkes Comm Coll (NC)
Williston State Coll (ND)
WyoTech, Fremont (CA)
Yakima Valley Comm Coll (WA)
Yavapai Coll (AZ)
York Tech Coll (SC)
Yuba Coll (CA)

Automotive Engineering Technology

Benjamin Franklin Inst of Technology (MA)
Cincinnati State Tech and Comm Coll (OH)
Comm Coll of Allegheny County (PA)
Corning Comm Coll (NY)
Front Range Comm Coll (CO)
Harrisburg Area Comm Coll (PA)
H. Councill Trenholm State Tech Coll (AL)
Macomb Comm Coll (MI)
Massachusetts Bay Comm Coll (MA)
Mercer County Comm Coll (NJ)
Minnesota State Comm and Tech Coll–Fergus Falls (MN)
Montgomery County Comm Coll (PA)
Owens Comm Coll, Toledo (OH)
Springfield Tech Comm Coll (MA)
Sussex County Comm Coll (NJ)
WyoTech, Fremont (CA)

Aviation/Airway Management

Broward Comm Coll (FL)
Chattanooga State Tech Comm Coll (TN)
Comm Coll of Allegheny County (PA)
Delaware Tech & Comm Coll, Terry Campus (DE)
Dixie State Coll of Utah (UT)
Florida Comm Coll at Jacksonville (FL)
Georgia Aviation & Tech Coll (GA)
Long Beach City Coll (CA)
Luzerne County Comm Coll (PA)
Mercer County Comm Coll (NJ)
Miami Dade Coll (FL)
Mountain View Coll (TX)
Northland Comm and Tech Coll–Thief River Falls (MN)
Oakland Comm Coll (MI)
Palo Alto Coll (TX)
Pasadena City Coll (CA)
St. Petersburg Coll (FL)
Sinclair Comm Coll (OH)
Vermilion Comm Coll (MN)
Western Oklahoma State Coll (OK)

Avionics Maintenance Technology

Big Bend Comm Coll (WA)
Broward Comm Coll (FL)
Chattanooga State Tech Comm Coll (TN)
Cochise Coll, Douglas (AZ)
Comm Coll of the Air Force (AL)
Cuyahoga Comm Coll (OH)
Delaware Tech & Comm Coll, Terry Campus (DE)
Delta Coll (MI)
Foothill Coll (CA)
Gateway Comm Coll (CT)
Gavilan Coll (CA)
Hawkeye Comm Coll (IA)
Lake Region State Coll (ND)
Lansing Comm Coll (MI)
Long Beach City Coll (CA)
Maple Woods Comm Coll (MO)
Mohawk Valley Comm Coll (NY)
Mountain View Coll (TX)
Mt. San Antonio Coll (CA)
New Hampshire Comm Tech Coll, Nashua/Claremont (NH)
Northland Comm and Tech Coll–Thief River Falls (MN)
Okaloosa-Walton Coll (FL)
Orange Coast Coll (CA)
Palo Alto Coll (TX)
Pasadena City Coll (CA)

Quinebaug Valley Comm Coll (CT)
Rock Valley Coll (IL)
Salt Lake Comm Coll (UT)
Southwestern Illinois Coll (IL)
Spokane Comm Coll (WA)
Tarrant County Coll District (TX)
Texas State Tech Coll Waco (TX)
Tulsa Comm Coll (OK)

Baking and Pastry Arts

Baltimore International Coll (MD)
Clark Coll (WA)
Coll of DuPage (IL)
El Centro Coll (TX)
Luzerne County Comm Coll (PA)
Montgomery County Comm Coll (PA)
New England Culinary Inst at Essex (VT)
Sullivan County Comm Coll (NY)
Triton Coll (IL)

Banking and Financial Support Services

Alamance Comm Coll (NC)
Alexandria Tech Coll (MN)
Allen County Comm Coll (KS)
Asnuntuck Comm Coll (CT)
Barton County Comm Coll (KS)
Berkshire Comm Coll (MA)
Central Georgia Tech Coll (GA)
Central New Mexico Comm Coll (NM)
Comm Coll of Allegheny County (PA)
Delaware Tech & Comm Coll, Stanton/Wilmington Campus (DE)
Fayetteville Tech Comm Coll (NC)
Finger Lakes Comm Coll (NY)
Florida Comm Coll at Jacksonville (FL)
Harrisburg Area Comm Coll (PA)
Jefferson State Comm Coll (AL)
Lackawanna Coll (PA)
Lanier Tech Coll (GA)
Laurel Business Inst (PA)
Luzerne County Comm Coll (PA)
Modesto Jr Coll (CA)
Mohawk Valley Comm Coll (NY)
Ogeechee Tech Coll (GA)
St. Cloud Tech Coll (MN)
San Juan Coll (NM)
Seminole Comm Coll (FL)
Southwestern Illinois Coll (IL)
Valdosta Tech Coll (GA)
Waubonsee Comm Coll (IL)
West Virginia Northern Comm Coll (WV)

Barbering

Coahoma Comm Coll (MS)

Behavioral Sciences

Ancilla Coll (IN)
Citrus Coll (CA)
Clarendon Coll (TX)
Colby Comm Coll (KS)
Colorado Mountain Coll (CO)
Colorado Mountain Coll, Alpine Campus (CO)
Galveston Coll (TX)
Greenfield Comm Coll (MA)
Highline Comm Coll (WA)
Howard Coll (TX)
Lincoln Coll (IL)
Lincoln Coll–Normal (IL)
Louisiana State U at Alexandria (LA)
Miami Dade Coll (FL)
Midland Coll (TX)
MiraCosta Coll (CA)
Modesto Jr Coll (CA)
Northwestern Connecticut Comm Coll (CT)
Orange Coast Coll (CA)
Palo Verde Coll (CA)

Phoenix Coll (AZ)
San Diego City Coll (CA)
San Joaquin Delta Coll (CA)
Santa Rosa Jr Coll (CA)
Seminole Coll (OK)
South Texas Coll (TX)
Tulsa Comm Coll (OK)
Wharton County Jr Coll (TX)

Biblical Studies

Hesston Coll (KS)

Bilingual and Multilingual Education

Clovis Comm Coll (NM)

Biochemical Technology

Niagara County Comm Coll (NY)

Biological and Physical Sciences

Abraham Baldwin Ag Coll (GA)
Aiken Tech Coll (SC)
Ancilla Coll (IN)
Arapahoe Comm Coll (CO)
Arizona Western Coll (AZ)
Borough of Manhattan Comm Coll of the City U of New York (NY)
Caldwell Comm Coll and Tech Inst (NC)
Centralia Coll (WA)
Central Oregon Comm Coll (OR)
City Colls of Chicago, Wilbur Wright College (IL)
Cleveland Comm Coll (NC)
Coastal Bend Coll (TX)
Colby Comm Coll (KS)
Coll of DuPage (IL)
Coll of Lake County (IL)
Coll of the Canyons (CA)
Colorado Mountain Coll (CO)
Colorado Mountain Coll, Alpine Campus (CO)
Copiah-Lincoln Comm Coll (MS)
Corning Comm Coll (NY)
Cottey Coll (MO)
Dabney S. Lancaster Comm Coll (VA)
Delgado Comm Coll (LA)
Finger Lakes Comm Coll (NY)
Galveston Coll (TX)
Gavilan Coll (CA)
Georgia Highlands Coll (GA)
Germanna Comm Coll (VA)
Greenfield Comm Coll (MA)
Heartland Comm Coll (IL)
Highland Comm Coll (IL)
Highline Comm Coll (WA)
Howard Comm Coll (MD)
Illinois Central Coll (IL)
Illinois Eastern Comm Colls, Frontier Community College (IL)
Illinois Eastern Comm Colls, Lincoln Trail College (IL)
Illinois Eastern Comm Colls, Olney Central College (IL)
Illinois Eastern Comm Colls, Wabash Valley College (IL)
Independence Comm Coll (KS)
Jacksonville Coll (TX)
John Wood Comm Coll (IL)
Kaskaskia Coll (IL)
Lake Land Coll (IL)
Lansing Comm Coll (MI)
Laramie County Comm Coll (WY)
Lincoln Coll (IL)
Lincoln Land Comm Coll (IL)
Linn-Benton Comm Coll (OR)
Longview Comm Coll (MO)
Lord Fairfax Comm Coll (VA)
Luzerne County Comm Coll (PA)
Manor Coll (PA)
Maple Woods Comm Coll (MO)
Massachusetts Bay Comm Coll (MA)
Middlesex Comm Coll (CT)
Middlesex County Coll (NJ)
Minnesota State Comm and Tech Coll–Fergus Falls (MN)

Mississippi Gulf Coast Comm Coll (MS)
Moraine Valley Comm Coll (IL)
Naugatuck Valley Comm Coll (CT)
New Mexico Military Inst (NM)
Niagara County Comm Coll (NY)
North Country Comm Coll (NY)
Northeast Comm Coll (NE)
Northern Essex Comm Coll (MA)
North Idaho Coll (ID)
Okaloosa-Walton Coll (FL)
Orange County Comm Coll (NY)
Otero Jr Coll (CO)
Parkland Coll (IL)
Pasadena City Coll (CA)
Peninsula Coll (WA)
The Pennsylvania State U Beaver Campus of the Commonwealth Coll (PA)
The Pennsylvania State U DuBois Campus of the Commonwealth Coll (PA)
The Pennsylvania State U Fayette Campus of the Commonwealth Coll (PA)
The Pennsylvania State U McKeesport Campus of the Commonwealth Coll (PA)
The Pennsylvania State U New Kensington Campus of the Commonwealth Coll (PA)
The Pennsylvania State U Shenango Campus of the Commonwealth Coll (PA)
Penn Valley Comm Coll (MO)
Piedmont Virginia Comm Coll (VA)
Pratt Comm Coll (KS)
Richland Comm Coll (IL)
Rockingham Comm Coll (NC)
Salem Comm Coll (NJ)
Seattle Central Comm Coll (WA)
Sheridan Coll–Sheridan and Gillette (WY)
Skyline Coll (CA)
Southeastern Comm Coll (NC)
South Plains Coll (TX)
Southside Virginia Comm Coll (VA)
Southwest Mississippi Comm Coll (MS)
Southwest Virginia Comm Coll (VA)
Spartanburg Tech Coll (SC)
Spoon River Coll (IL)
State U of New York Coll of Technology at Alfred (NY)
Sussex County Comm Coll (NJ)
Thomas Nelson Comm Coll (VA)
Tidewater Comm Coll (VA)
Tompkins Cortland Comm Coll (NY)
Treasure Valley Comm Coll (OR)
Trident Tech Coll (SC)
Trinidad State Jr Coll (CO)
U of South Carolina Union (SC)
U of Wisconsin–Richland (WI)
Valley Forge Military Coll (PA)
Vermilion Comm Coll (MN)
Waubonsee Comm Coll (IL)
Weatherford Coll (TX)
Westchester Comm Coll (NY)
William Rainey Harper Coll (IL)
Young Harris Coll (GA)
Yuba Coll (CA)

Biology/Biological Sciences

Abraham Baldwin Ag Coll (GA)
Allan Hancock Coll (CA)

Allen County Comm Coll (KS)
Ancilla Coll (IN)
Arizona Western Coll (AZ)
Atlanta Metropolitan Coll (GA)
Austin Comm Coll (TX)
Bainbridge Coll (GA)
Barton County Comm Coll (KS)
Bergen Comm Coll (NJ)
Berkshire Comm Coll (MA)
Brazosport Coll (TX)
Bronx Comm Coll of the City U of New York (NY)
Bucks County Comm Coll (PA)
Butler Comm Coll (KS)
Butler County Comm Coll (PA)
Carl Albert State Coll (OK)
Casper Coll (WY)
Cecil Comm Coll (MD)
Centralia Coll (WA)
Central Piedmont Comm Coll (NC)
Central Wyoming Coll (WY)
Chattahoochee Valley Comm Coll (AL)
Chattanooga State Tech Comm Coll (TN)
Citrus Coll (CA)
Clarendon Coll (TX)
Coahoma Comm Coll (MS)
Coastal Bend Coll (TX)
Coastal Georgia Comm Coll (GA)
Cochise Coll, Douglas (AZ)
Colby Comm Coll (KS)
Coll of Southern Maryland (MD)
Coll of the Canyons (CA)
Coll of the Siskiyous (CA)
Colorado Mountain Coll (CO)
Colorado Mountain Coll, Alpine Campus (CO)
Columbia Coll (CA)
Comm Coll of Allegheny County (PA)
Copiah-Lincoln Comm Coll (MS)
Crowder Coll (MO)
Dixie State Coll of Utah (UT)
East Central Coll (MO)
Eastern Arizona Coll (AZ)
Eastern Wyoming Coll (WY)
Essex County Coll (NJ)
Evergreen Valley Coll (CA)
Feather River Coll (CA)
Finger Lakes Comm Coll (NY)
Foothill Coll (CA)
Frederick Comm Coll (MD)
Gainesville Coll (GA)
Gavilan Coll (CA)
Harrisburg Area Comm Coll (PA)
Hawkeye Comm Coll (IA)
Holyoke Comm Coll (MA)
Howard Coll (TX)
Hutchinson Comm Coll and Area Vocational School (KS)
Independence Comm Coll (KS)
Joliet Jr Coll (IL)
Kellogg Comm Coll (MI)
Kennebec Valley Comm Coll (ME)
Keystone Coll (PA)
Kingsborough Comm Coll of the City U of New York (NY)
Kingwood Coll (TX)
Lansing Comm Coll (MI)
Laramie County Comm Coll (WY)
Lawson State Comm Coll (AL)
Lincoln Coll (IL)
Linn-Benton Comm Coll (OR)
Long Beach City Coll (CA)
Longview Comm Coll (MO)
Louisiana State U at Alexandria (LA)
Lower Columbia Coll (WA)
Macomb Comm Coll (MI)
Manatee Comm Coll (FL)

Maple Woods Comm Coll (MO)
Mercer County Comm Coll (NJ)
Miami Dade Coll (FL)
Middlesex County Coll (NJ)
Midland Coll (TX)
MiraCosta Coll (CA)
Modesto Jr Coll (CA)
Montgomery County Comm Coll (PA)
New Mexico Military Inst (NM)
Northampton County Area Comm Coll (PA)
Northeast Comm Coll (NE)
North Hennepin Comm Coll (MN)
North Idaho Coll (ID)
Northwestern Connecticut Comm Coll (CT)
Northwest Indian Coll (WA)
Okaloosa-Walton Coll (FL)
Orange Coast Coll (CA)
Orange County Comm Coll (NY)
Otero Jr Coll (CO)
Palm Beach Comm Coll (FL)
Palo Alto Coll (TX)
Palo Verde Coll (CA)
Pasadena City Coll (CA)
Penn Valley Comm Coll (MO)
Pratt Comm Coll (KS)
Raritan Valley Comm Coll (NJ)
Roane State Comm Coll (TN)
Saddleback Coll (CA)
St. Philip's Coll (TX)
Salem Comm Coll (NJ)
Salt Lake Comm Coll (UT)
San Diego City Coll (CA)
San Diego Mesa Coll (CA)
San Joaquin Delta Coll (CA)
San Juan Coll (NM)
Santa Barbara City Coll (CA)
Santa Rosa Jr Coll (CA)
Sauk Valley Comm Coll (IL)
Seminole State Coll (OK)
Sheridan Coll—Sheridan and Gillette (WY)
Skyline Coll (CA)
Snow Coll (UT)
South Plains Coll (TX)
Southwest Mississippi Comm Coll (MS)
Spoon River Coll (IL)
Springfield Tech Comm Coll (MA)
Treasure Valley Comm Coll (OR)
Trinidad State Jr Coll (CO)
Trinity Valley Comm Coll (TX)
Tulsa Comm Coll (OK)
Union County Coll (NJ)
Ventura Coll (CA)
Vermilion Comm Coll (MN)
Wharton County Jr Coll (TX)
William Rainey Harper Coll (IL)
Young Harris Coll (GA)
Yuba Coll (CA)

Biology/Biotechnology Laboratory Technician
Athens Tech Coll (GA)
Berkeley City Coll (CA)
Collin County Comm Coll District (TX)
Fayetteville Tech Comm Coll (NC)
Finger Lakes Comm Coll (NY)
Foothill Coll (CA)
Hudson Valley Comm Coll (NY)
Jefferson Comm Coll (NY)
John Tyler Comm Coll (VA)
Lansing Comm Coll (MI)
Massachusetts Bay Comm Coll (MA)
Mercer County Comm Coll (NJ)
Middlesex Comm Coll (CT)
Middlesex County Coll (NJ)
North Shore Comm Coll (MA)
Northwest Vista Coll (TX)

The Ohio State U Ag Tech Inst (OH)
Salt Lake Comm Coll (UT)
Seattle Central Comm Coll (WA)
State U of New York Coll of Technology at Alfred (NY)

Biology Teacher Education
Ancilla Coll (IN)
Coll of the Siskiyous (CA)
Manatee Comm Coll (FL)

Biomedical Technology
Caldwell Comm Coll and Tech Inst (NC)
Chattahoochee Tech Coll (GA)
Cincinnati State Tech and Comm Coll (OH)
Comm Coll of the Air Force (AL)
Delaware Tech & Comm Coll, Stanton/Wilmington Campus (DE)
Delgado Comm Coll (LA)
ECPI Coll of Technology, Virginia Beach (VA)
Erie Comm Coll, South Campus (NY)
Florida Comm Coll at Jacksonville (FL)
Gateway Comm Coll (CT)
Howard Comm Coll (MD)
Jefferson State Comm Coll (AL)
Miami Dade Coll (FL)
North Arkansas Coll (AR)
North Seattle Comm Coll (WA)
Parkland Coll (IL)
The Pennsylvania State U DuBois Campus of the Commonwealth Coll (PA)
The Pennsylvania State U Fayette Campus of the Commonwealth Coll (PA)
The Pennsylvania State U Hazleton Campus of the Commonwealth Coll (PA)
The Pennsylvania State U New Kensington Campus of the Commonwealth Coll (PA)
The Pennsylvania State U Shenango Campus of the Commonwealth Coll (PA)
The Pennsylvania State U York Campus of the Commonwealth Coll (PA)
St. Philip's Coll (TX)
Santa Barbara City Coll (CA)
Southeast Tech Inst (SD)
Southwest Tennessee Comm Coll (TN)
Spokane Comm Coll (WA)
Stark State Coll of Technology (OH)
Texas State Tech Coll Waco (TX)
Tulsa Comm Coll (OK)
Western Iowa Tech Comm Coll (IA)

Biotechnology
Alamance Comm Coll (NC)
Augusta Tech Coll (GA)
Bladen Comm Coll (NC)
Briarwood Coll (CT)
Central New Mexico Comm Coll (NM)
Coll of Southern Maryland (MD)
Coll of The Albemarle (NC)
Dixie State Coll of Utah (UT)
Howard Comm Coll (MD)
Ivy Tech Comm Coll—Central Indiana (IN)
Ivy Tech Comm Coll—Lafayette (IN)
Ivy Tech Comm Coll—North Central (IN)
Lackawanna Coll (PA)
Montgomery County Comm Coll (PA)
Northampton County Area Comm Coll (PA)
Piedmont Virginia Comm Coll (VA)
Santa Barbara City Coll (CA)
Sinclair Comm Coll (OH)

Southeastern Comm Coll (NC)
Springfield Tech Comm Coll (MA)

Biotechnology Research
El Centro Coll (TX)

Boilermaking
Ivy Tech Comm Coll—Southwest (IN)

Botany/Plant Biology
Centralia Coll (WA)
Dixie State Coll of Utah (UT)
East Central Coll (MO)
Lincoln Coll (IL)
North Idaho Coll (ID)
Palm Beach Comm Coll (FL)
San Joaquin Delta Coll (CA)
Santa Rosa Jr Coll (CA)
Snow Coll (UT)
Spoon River Coll (IL)
Tulsa Comm Coll (OK)
William Rainey Harper Coll (IL)

Broadcast Journalism
Arizona Western Coll (AZ)
Bergen Comm Coll (NJ)
Centralia Coll (WA)
Chattanooga State Tech Comm Coll (TN)
Colby Comm Coll (KS)
Dixie State Coll of Utah (UT)
Finger Lakes Comm Coll (NY)
Kingsborough Comm Coll of the City U of New York (NY)
Lansing Comm Coll (MI)
Lincoln Coll (IL)
Meridian Comm Coll (MS)
Middlesex Comm Coll (CT)
Northeast Comm Coll (NE)
Northland Comm and Tech Coll—Thief River Falls (MN)
Pasadena City Coll (CA)
Pratt Comm Coll (KS)
St. Louis Comm Coll at Florissant Valley (MO)
San Joaquin Delta Coll (CA)
Sussex County Comm Coll (NJ)
Trident Tech Coll (SC)
Yakima Valley Comm Coll (WA)

Building/Construction Finishing, Management, and Inspection Related
Central New Mexico Comm Coll (NM)
Fayetteville Tech Comm Coll (NC)
Ivy Tech Comm Coll—Northwest (IN)
Manhattan Area Tech Coll (KS)
Pima Comm Coll (AZ)
Wilkes Comm Coll (NC)

Building/Construction Site Management
Metropolitan Comm Coll-Business & Technology College (MO)
The Ohio State U Ag Tech Inst (OH)

Building/Home/Construction Inspection
Arapahoe Comm Coll (CO)
Edmonds Comm Coll (WA)
Modesto Jr Coll (CA)
Orange Coast Coll (CA)

Building/Property Maintenance and Management
Coll of DuPage (IL)
Comm Coll of Allegheny County (PA)
Delgado Comm Coll (LA)
Erie Comm Coll (NY)
Illinois Eastern Comm Colls, Lincoln Trail College (IL)
Ivy Tech Comm Coll—Bloomington (IN)
Ivy Tech Comm Coll—Central Indiana (IN)
Ivy Tech Comm Coll—Columbus (IN)

Ivy Tech Comm Coll—East Central (IN)
Ivy Tech Comm Coll—Kokomo (IN)
Ivy Tech Comm Coll—Lafayette (IN)
Ivy Tech Comm Coll—North Central (IN)
Ivy Tech Comm Coll—Northeast (IN)
Ivy Tech Comm Coll—Northwest (IN)
Ivy Tech Comm Coll—Southern Indiana (IN)
Ivy Tech Comm Coll—Southwest (IN)
Ivy Tech Comm Coll—Wabash Valley (IN)
Ivy Tech Comm Coll—Whitewater (IN)
Luzerne County Comm Coll (PA)
Mohawk Valley Comm Coll (NY)
Pima Comm Coll (AZ)

Business Administration and Management
Aakers Business Coll (ND)
Abraham Baldwin Ag Coll (GA)
Aiken Tech Coll (SC)
Alamance Comm Coll (NC)
Alexandria Tech Coll (MN)
Allan Hancock Coll (CA)
Allegany Coll of Maryland (MD)
Allen County Comm Coll (KS)
Ancilla Coll (IN)
Appalachian Tech Coll (GA)
Arapahoe Comm Coll (CO)
Arizona Western Coll (AZ)
Arkansas State U—Beebe (AR)
Asnuntuck Comm Coll (CT)
Atlanta Metropolitan Coll (GA)
Augusta Tech Coll (GA)
Austin Comm Coll (TX)
Bainbridge Coll (GA)
Barton County Comm Coll (KS)
Bay State Coll (MA)
Beal Coll (ME)
Beaufort County Comm Coll (NC)
Bergen Comm Coll (NJ)
Berkeley City Coll (CA)
Berkeley Coll (NJ)
Berkeley Coll-New York City Campus (NY)
Berkeley Coll-Westchester Campus (NY)
Berkshire Comm Coll (MA)
Bladen Comm Coll (NC)
Blue Ridge Comm Coll (VA)
Blue River Comm Coll (MO)
Borough of Manhattan Comm Coll of the City U of New York (NY)
Brazosport Coll (TX)
Brevard Comm Coll (FL)
Briarwood Coll (CT)
Bristol Comm Coll (MA)
Bronx Comm Coll of the City U of New York (NY)
Broome Comm Coll (NY)
Broward Comm Coll (FL)
Brown Mackie Coll—Akron (OH)
Brown Mackie Coll—Atlanta (GA)
Brown Mackie Coll—Cincinnati (OH)
Brown Mackie Coll—Findlay (OH)
Brown Mackie Coll—Fort Wayne (IN)
Brown Mackie Coll—Hopkinsville (KY)
Brown Mackie Coll—Kansas City (KS)
Brown Mackie Coll—Louisville (KY)
Brown Mackie Coll—Merrillville (IN)
Brown Mackie Coll—Miami (FL)

Brown Mackie Coll—Michigan City (IN)
Brown Mackie Coll—North Canton (OH)
Brown Mackie Coll—Northern Kentucky (KY)
Brown Mackie Coll—Salina (KS)
Brown Mackie Coll—South Bend (IN)
Bryant and Stratton Coll, Rochester (NY)
Bucks County Comm Coll (PA)
Bunker Hill Comm Coll (MA)
Butler Comm Coll (KS)
Butler County Comm Coll (PA)
Caldwell Comm Coll and Tech Inst (NC)
Cambria-Rowe Business Coll, Johnstown (PA)
Cape Fear Comm Coll (NC)
Capital Comm Coll (CT)
Career Coll of Northern Nevada (NV)
Carl Albert State Coll (OK)
Carroll Comm Coll (MD)
Carteret Comm Coll (NC)
Casper Coll (WY)
Cecil Comm Coll (MD)
Cedar Valley Coll (TX)
Central Arizona Coll (AZ)
Central Carolina Tech Coll (SC)
Central Comm Coll—Columbus Campus (NE)
Central Comm Coll—Grand Island Campus (NE)
Central Comm Coll—Hastings Campus (NE)
Central Georgia Tech Coll (GA)
Centralia Coll (WA)
Central Lakes Coll (MN)
Central New Mexico Comm Coll (NM)
Central Oregon Comm Coll (OR)
Central Piedmont Comm Coll (NC)
Central Wyoming Coll (WY)
Century Coll (MN)
Chatfield Coll (OH)
Chattahoochee Tech Coll (GA)
Chattahoochee Valley Comm Coll (AL)
Chattanooga State Tech Comm Coll (TN)
Chemeketa Comm Coll (OR)
Cincinnati State Tech and Comm Coll (OH)
Citrus Coll (CA)
City Colls of Chicago, Wilbur Wright College (IL)
Clarendon Coll (TX)
Clark Coll (WA)
Clark State Comm Coll (OH)
Clatsop Comm Coll (OR)
Cleveland Comm Coll (NC)
Cleveland State Comm Coll (TN)
Clovis Comm Coll (NM)
Coahoma Comm Coll (MS)
Coastal Bend Coll (TX)
Coastal Carolina Comm Coll (NC)
Coastal Georgia Comm Coll (GA)
Cochise Coll, Douglas (AZ)
Colby Comm Coll (KS)
Coll of Business and Technology (FL)
Coll of DuPage (IL)
Coll of Eastern Utah (UT)
Coll of Lake County (IL)
Coll of Southern Maryland (MD)
Coll of The Albemarle (NC)
Coll of the Canyons (CA)
Coll of the Mainland (TX)
Coll of the Siskiyous (CA)
The Coll of Westchester (NY)
Collin County Comm Coll District (TX)
Colorado Mountain Coll (CO)
Colorado Mountain Coll, Alpine Campus (CO)
Columbia Coll (CA)

Comm Coll of Allegheny County (PA)
Comm Coll of Denver (CO)
Consolidated School of Business, Lancaster (PA)
Consolidated School of Business, York (PA)
Copiah-Lincoln Comm Coll (MS)
Corning Comm Coll (NY)
Cossatot Comm Coll of the U of Arkansas (AR)
Cowley County Comm Coll and Area Vocational–Tech School (KS)
Crowder Coll (MO)
Cuyahoga Comm Coll (OH)
Dabney S. Lancaster Comm Coll (VA)
Davis Coll (OH)
Dean Coll (MA)
Delaware Tech & Comm Coll, Jack F. Owens Campus (DE)
Delaware Tech & Comm Coll, Stanton/Wilmington Campus (DE)
Delaware Tech & Comm Coll, Terry Campus (DE)
Delgado Comm Coll (LA)
Delta Coll (MI)
Denmark Tech Coll (SC)
Diné Coll (AZ)
Dixie State Coll of Utah (UT)
Dyersburg State Comm Coll (TN)
East Arkansas Comm Coll (AR)
East Central Coll (MO)
Eastern Arizona Coll (AZ)
Eastern Wyoming Coll (WY)
Eastfield Coll (TX)
Edmonds Comm Coll (WA)
El Centro Coll (TX)
Erie Comm Coll (NY)
Erie Comm Coll, North Campus (NY)
Erie Comm Coll, South Campus (NY)
Essex County Coll (NJ)
Evergreen Valley Coll (CA)
Fayetteville Tech Comm Coll (NC)
Finger Lakes Comm Coll (NY)
Fiorello H. LaGuardia Comm Coll of the City U of New York (NY)
Fisher Coll (MA)
Florida Comm Coll at Jacksonville (FL)
Florida National Coll (FL)
Foothill Coll (CA)
Forsyth Tech Comm Coll (NC)
Fox Valley Tech Coll (WI)
Frederick Comm Coll (MD)
Front Range Comm Coll (CO)
Gainesville Coll (GA)
Gallipolis Career Coll (OH)
Galveston Coll (TX)
Gaston Coll (NC)
Gateway Comm Coll (CT)
Gavilan Coll (CA)
Genesee Comm Coll (NY)
George C. Wallace Comm Coll (AL)
Georgia Highlands Coll (GA)
Germanna Comm Coll (VA)
Glendale Comm Coll (AZ)
Globe Coll (MN)
Goodwin Coll (CT)
Grand Rapids Comm Coll (MI)
Great Basin Coll (NV)
Greenfield Comm Coll (MA)
Griffin Tech Coll (GA)
Guam Comm Coll (GU)
Gwinnett Tech Coll (GA)
Hagerstown Business Coll (MD)
Hagerstown Comm Coll (MD)
Hamilton Coll, Cedar Rapids (IA)
Harrisburg Area Comm Coll (PA)
Hawkeye Comm Coll (IA)
Heald Coll-Fresno (CA)

Heald Coll-Honolulu (HI)
Heald Coll-Portland (OR)
Heald Coll-Rancho Cordova (CA)
Heald Coll-Roseville (CA)
Heald Coll-Salinas (CA)
Heartland Comm Coll (IL)
Herzing Coll (GA)
Hesston Coll (KS)
Hibbing Comm Coll (MN)
Highland Comm Coll (IL)
Highline Comm Coll (WA)
Holyoke Comm Coll (MA)
Horry-Georgetown Tech Coll (SC)
Houston Comm Coll System (TX)
Howard Coll (TX)
Howard Comm Coll (MD)
Hudson Valley Comm Coll (NY)
Illinois Central Coll (IL)
Illinois Eastern Comm Colls, Wabash Valley College (IL)
Illinois Valley Comm Coll (IL)
Independence Comm Coll (KS)
Indiana Business Coll, Anderson (IN)
Indiana Business Coll, Columbus (IN)
Indiana Business Coll, Evansville (IN)
Indiana Business Coll, Fort Wayne (IN)
Indiana Business Coll, Indianapolis (IN)
Indiana Business Coll, Indianapolis (IN)
Indiana Business Coll, Lafayette (IN)
Indiana Business Coll, Marion (IN)
Indiana Business Coll, Muncie (IN)
Indiana Business Coll, Terre Haute (IN)
International Inst of the Americas, Mesa (AZ)
International Inst of the Americas, Phoenix (AZ)
International Inst of the Americas, Phoenix (AZ)
International Inst of the Americas, Tucson (AZ)
International Inst of the Americas (NM)
Itasca Comm Coll (MN)
ITT Tech Inst, Canton (MI)
ITT Tech Inst, Grand Rapids (MI)
ITT Tech Inst, Troy (MI)
ITT Tech Inst, Dayton (OH)
ITT Tech Inst, Hilliard (OH)
ITT Tech Inst, Norwood (OH)
ITT Tech Inst, Strongsville (OH)
ITT Tech Inst, Warrensville Heights (OH)
Ivy Tech Comm Coll– Bloomington (IN)
Ivy Tech Comm Coll–Central Indiana (IN)
Ivy Tech Comm Coll– Columbus (IN)
Ivy Tech Comm Coll–East Central (IN)
Ivy Tech Comm Coll– Kokomo (IN)
Ivy Tech Comm Coll– Lafayette (IN)
Ivy Tech Comm Coll–North Central (IN)
Ivy Tech Comm Coll– Northeast (IN)
Ivy Tech Comm Coll– Northwest (IN)
Ivy Tech Comm Coll– Southeast (IN)
Ivy Tech Comm Coll– Southern Indiana (IN)
Ivy Tech Comm Coll– Southwest (IN)
Ivy Tech Comm Coll– Wabash Valley (IN)
Ivy Tech Comm Coll– Whitewater (IN)
Jackson Comm Coll (MI)
Jackson State Comm Coll (TN)

James H. Faulkner State Comm Coll (AL)
James Sprunt Comm Coll (NC)
Jamestown Comm Coll (NY)
Jefferson Comm and Tech Coll (KY)
Jefferson Comm Coll (NY)
Jefferson Comm Coll (OH)
Johnston Comm Coll (NC)
John Wood Comm Coll (IL)
Joliet Jr Coll (IL)
Kansas City Kansas Comm Coll (KS)
Kaskaskia Coll (IL)
Keiser Coll, Miami (FL)
Kellogg Comm Coll (MI)
Kennebec Valley Comm Coll (ME)
Kent State U, Geauga Campus (OH)
Kent State U, Trumbull Campus (OH)
Kent State U, Tuscarawas Campus (OH)
Keystone Coll (PA)
Kilian Comm Coll (SD)
Kingsborough Comm Coll of the City U of New York (NY)
Kingwood Coll (TX)
Lac Courte Oreilles Ojibwa Comm Coll (WI)
Lackawanna Coll (PA)
Lake City Comm Coll (FL)
Lake Land Coll (IL)
Lake Michigan Coll (MI)
Lake Region State Coll (ND)
Lake-Sumter Comm Coll (FL)
Lake Superior Coll (MN)
Lamar State Coll–Orange (TX)
Lamar State Coll–Port Arthur (TX)
Lansing Comm Coll (MI)
Laramie County Comm Coll (WY)
Laurel Business Inst (PA)
Lawson State Comm Coll (AL)
Lehigh Valley Coll (PA)
Lincoln Coll (IL)
Lincoln Coll–Normal (IL)
Lincoln Land Comm Coll (IL)
Linn-Benton Comm Coll (OR)
Long Beach City Coll (CA)
Long Island Business Inst (NY)
Longview Comm Coll (MO)
Lord Fairfax Comm Coll (VA)
Louisiana State U at Alexandria (LA)
Lower Columbia Coll (WA)
Luzerne County Comm Coll (PA)
Macomb Comm Coll (MI)
Manatee Comm Coll (FL)
Manchester Comm Coll (CT)
Manor Coll (PA)
Maple Woods Comm Coll (MO)
Maria Coll (NY)
Massachusetts Bay Comm Coll (MA)
Mercer County Comm Coll (NJ)
Metropolitan Comm Coll (NE)
Metropolitan Comm Coll-Business & Technology College (MO)
Miami Dade Coll (FL)
Middle Georgia Coll (GA)
Middlesex Comm Coll (CT)
Middlesex County Coll (NJ)
Midlands Tech Coll (SC)
Minnesota School of Business–Brooklyn Center (MN)
Minnesota School of Business–Plymouth (MN)
Minnesota School of Business–Richfield (MN)
Minnesota School of Business–St. Cloud (MN)
Minnesota School of Business–Shakopee (MN)

Minnesota State Comm and Tech Coll–Fergus Falls (MN)
MiraCosta Coll (CA)
Mississippi Gulf Coast Comm Coll (MS)
Missouri State U–West Plains (MO)
Modesto Jr Coll (CA)
Mohawk Valley Comm Coll (NY)
Montgomery Coll (TX)
Montgomery Comm Coll (NC)
Montgomery County Comm Coll (PA)
Moraine Valley Comm Coll (IL)
Motlow State Comm Coll (TN)
Mott Comm Coll (MI)
Mt. San Antonio Coll (CA)
Mount Wachusett Comm Coll (MA)
MTI Coll of Business and Technology (CA)
Nassau Comm Coll (NY)
Naugatuck Valley Comm Coll (CT)
New England Coll of Finance (MA)
New Hampshire Comm Tech Coll, Manchester/Stratham (NH)
New Hampshire Comm Tech Coll, Nashua/Claremont (NH)
New Hampshire Tech Inst (NH)
New Mexico Military Inst (NM)
Newport Business Inst, Lower Burrell (PA)
Newport Business Inst, Williamsport (PA)
Niagara County Comm Coll (NY)
Normandale Comm Coll (MN)
Northampton County Area Comm Coll (PA)
North Central Missouri Coll (MO)
North Country Comm Coll (NY)
Northeast Comm Coll (NE)
Northeast State Tech Comm Coll (TN)
Northern Essex Comm Coll (MA)
Northern Maine Comm Coll (ME)
North Idaho Coll (ID)
North Iowa Area Comm Coll (IA)
Northland Comm and Tech Coll–Thief River Falls (MN)
North Shore Comm Coll (MA)
Northwestern Connecticut Comm Coll (CT)
Northwest-Shoals Comm Coll (AL)
Norwalk Comm Coll (CT)
Oakland Comm Coll (MI)
Ocean County Coll (NJ)
Ohio Business Coll, Sandusky (OH)
Okaloosa-Walton Coll (FL)
Orange Coast Coll (CA)
Orange County Comm Coll (NY)
Otero Jr Coll (CO)
Ouachita Tech Coll (AR)
Palm Beach Comm Coll (FL)
Palo Alto Coll (TX)
Palo Verde Coll (CA)
Parkland Coll (IL)
Pasadena City Coll (CA)
Pasco-Hernando Comm Coll (FL)
Pellissippi State Tech Comm Coll (TN)
Peninsula Coll (WA)
Pennsylvania Inst of Technology (PA)
Penn Valley Comm Coll (MO)
Phoenix Coll (AZ)

Piedmont Virginia Comm Coll (VA)
Pima Comm Coll (AZ)
Pioneer Pacific Coll (OR)
Polk Comm Coll (FL)
Pratt Comm Coll (KS)
Quinebaug Valley Comm Coll (CT)
Quinsigamond Comm Coll (MA)
Raritan Valley Comm Coll (NJ)
Rasmussen Coll Eden Prarie (MN)
Rasmussen Coll Mankato (MN)
Remington Coll–Cleveland West Campus (OH)
Remington Coll–Lafayette Campus (LA)
Remington Coll–Tampa Campus (FL)
Richland Comm Coll (IL)
Richmond Comm Coll (NC)
Riverland Comm Coll (MN)
Riverside Comm Coll District (CA)
Roane State Comm Coll (TN)
Rockingham Comm Coll (NC)
Rock Valley Coll (IL)
Rogue Comm Coll (OR)
Saddleback Coll (CA)
Saint Charles Comm Coll (MO)
St. Cloud Tech Coll (MN)
St. Louis Comm Coll at Florissant Valley (MO)
St. Petersburg Coll (FL)
St. Philip's Coll (TX)
Salem Comm Coll (NJ)
Salt Lake Comm Coll (UT)
San Diego City Coll (CA)
San Diego Mesa Coll (CA)
San Joaquin Delta Coll (CA)
San Juan Coll (NM)
Santa Barbara City Coll (CA)
Santa Rosa Jr Coll (CA)
Sauk Valley Comm Coll (IL)
Schuylkill Inst of Business and Technology (PA)
Scottsdale Comm Coll (AZ)
Seminole Comm Coll (FL)
Seminole State Coll (OK)
Sheridan Coll–Sheridan and Gillette (WY)
Sinclair Comm Coll (OH)
Skyline Coll (CA)
Snead State Comm Coll (AL)
Snow Coll (UT)
Southeastern Comm Coll (NC)
Southeast Tech Inst (SD)
Southern Arkansas U Tech (AR)
Southern West Virginia Comm and Tech Coll (WV)
South Hills School of Business & Technology, State College (PA)
South Plains Coll (TX)
Southside Virginia Comm Coll (VA)
South Texas Coll (TX)
South U, West Palm Beach (FL)
Southwestern Illinois Coll (IL)
Southwestern Michigan Coll (MI)
Southwestern Oklahoma State U at Sayre (OK)
Southwestern Oregon Comm Coll (OR)
Southwest Florida Coll, Fort Myers (FL)
Southwest Mississippi Comm Coll (MS)
Southwest Tennessee Comm Coll (TN)
Southwest Virginia Comm Coll (VA)
Spartanburg Tech Coll (SC)
Spokane Comm Coll (WA)
Spokane Falls Comm Coll (WA)
Spoon River Coll (IL)
Springfield Coll in Illinois (IL)
Springfield Tech Comm Coll (MA)

Stark State Coll of Technology (OH)
State U of New York Coll of Technology at Alfred (NY)
State U of New York Coll of Technology at Delhi (NY)
Sullivan County Comm Coll (NY)
Sussex County Comm Coll (NJ)
Tarrant County Coll District (TX)
Thomas Nelson Comm Coll (VA)
Three Rivers Comm Coll (MO)
Tidewater Comm Coll (VA)
Tomball Coll (TX)
Tompkins Cortland Comm Coll (NY)
Treasure Valley Comm Coll (OR)
Tri-County Comm Coll (NC)
Trident Tech Coll (SC)
Trinidad State Jr Coll (CO)
Trinity Valley Comm Coll (TX)
Triton Coll (IL)
Tulsa Comm Coll (OK)
Tunxis Comm Coll (CT)
Union County Coll (NJ)
United Tribes Tech Coll (ND)
The U of Akron–Wayne Coll (OH)
U of Alaska Anchorage, Matanuska-Susitna Coll (AK)
U of Northwestern Ohio (OH)
Utah Career Coll (UT)
Valencia Comm Coll (FL)
Valley Coll (WV)
Valley Forge Military Coll (PA)
Vance-Granville Comm Coll (NC)
Ventura Coll (CA)
Vermilion Comm Coll (MN)
Villa Maria Coll of Buffalo (NY)
Volunteer State Comm Coll (TN)
Waubonsee Comm Coll (IL)
Weatherford Coll (TX)
West Central Tech Coll (GA)
Westchester Comm Coll (NY)
Western Iowa Tech Comm Coll (IA)
Western Tech Coll (WI)
Westmoreland County Comm Coll (PA)
West Virginia Business Coll, Wheeling (WV)
West Virginia Northern Comm Coll (WV)
Wharton County Jr Coll (TX)
Wilkes Comm Coll (NC)
William Rainey Harper Coll (IL)
Wilson Tech Comm Coll (NC)
Wor-Wic Comm Coll (MD)
Yakima Valley Comm Coll (WA)
Yavapai Coll (AZ)
York Tech Coll (SC)
Young Harris Coll (GA)
Yuba Coll (CA)

Business Administration, Management and Operations Related

Argosy U/Denver (CO)
Argosy U/Orange County (CA)
Argosy U/San Diego (CA)
Comm Care Coll (OK)
Fayetteville Tech Comm Coll (NC)
Indiana Business Coll, Anderson (IN)
Indiana Business Coll, Columbus (IN)
Indiana Business Coll, Indianapolis (IN)
Indiana Business Coll, Lafayette (IN)
Indiana Business Coll, Muncie (IN)
Indiana Business Coll, Terre Haute (IN)

Northwest Vista Coll (TX)
Western Tech Coll (WI)

Business and Personal/ Financial Services Marketing
Centralia Coll (WA)
Heartland Comm Coll (IL)
Hutchinson Comm Coll and Area Vocational School (KS)
Spokane Falls Comm Coll (WA)
Tulsa Comm Coll (OK)
Union County Coll (NJ)
Wisconsin Indianhead Tech Coll (WI)

Business and Personal Services Marketing Related
Mohawk Valley Comm Coll (NY)

Business Automation/ Technology/Data Entry
Arkansas State U–Mountain Home (AR)
Asnuntuck Comm Coll (CT)
Berkshire Comm Coll (MA)
Bristol Comm Coll (MA)
Central Wyoming Coll (WY)
Clark Coll (WA)
Clatsop Comm Coll (OR)
Clovis Comm Coll (NM)
Coll of Lake County (IL)
Collin County Comm Coll District (TX)
Comm Coll of Allegheny County (PA)
Crowder Coll (MO)
El Centro Coll (TX)
Front Range Comm Coll (CO)
Illinois Eastern Comm Colls, Frontier Community College (IL)
Illinois Eastern Comm Colls, Lincoln Trail College (IL)
Illinois Eastern Comm Colls, Olney Central College (IL)
Illinois Eastern Comm Colls, Wabash Valley College (IL)
Ivy Tech Comm Coll–East Central (IN)
Ivy Tech Comm Coll–Kokomo (IN)
Ivy Tech Comm Coll–North Central (IN)
Ivy Tech Comm Coll–Northeast (IN)
Ivy Tech Comm Coll–Southern Indiana (IN)
Joliet Jr Coll (IL)
Kaskaskia Coll (IL)
Laurel Business Inst (PA)
Lincoln Land Comm Coll (IL)
Macomb Comm Coll (MI)
Midland Coll (TX)
Normandale Comm Coll (MN)
Oakland Comm Coll (MI)
Parkland Coll (IL)
Tillamook Bay Comm Coll (OR)
United Tribes Tech Coll (ND)
The U of Akron–Wayne Coll (OH)
Waubonsee Comm Coll (IL)

Business/Commerce
Allen County Comm Coll (KS)
Ancilla Coll (IN)
Arkansas Northeastern Coll (AR)
Berkeley City Coll (CA)
Berkeley Coll (NJ)
Berkshire Comm Coll (MA)
Brazosport Coll (TX)
Bryant and Stratton Coll, Albany (NY)
Bryant and Stratton Coll, Rochester (NY)
Bryant and Stratton Coll, Rochester (NY)
Bryant and Stratton Coll, Syracuse (NY)
Bryant and Stratton Coll, Parma (OH)
Bryant and Stratton Coll (WI)
Bryant and Stratton Coll, Amherst Campus (NY)

Bryant and Stratton Coll, Buffalo Campus (NY)
Bryant and Stratton Coll, Lackawanna Campus (NY)
Bryant and Stratton Coll, Richmond (VA)
Central Florida Comm Coll (FL)
Centralia Coll (WA)
Colorado Mountain Coll, Timberline Campus (CO)
DeKalb Tech Coll (GA)
Everest Coll (AZ)
Evergreen Valley Coll (CA)
Feather River Coll (CA)
Gallipolis Career Coll (OH)
GateWay Comm Coll (AZ)
Glendale Comm Coll (AZ)
Goodwin Coll (CT)
Great Basin Coll (NV)
Hagerstown Comm Coll (MD)
Harrisburg Area Comm Coll (PA)
Hawkeye Comm Coll (IA)
Hutchinson Comm Coll and Area Vocational School (KS)
Ilisagvik Coll (AK)
Jefferson State Comm Coll (AL)
John Tyler Comm Coll (VA)
John Wood Comm Coll (IL)
Keystone Coll (PA)
Lackawanna Coll (PA)
Lamar State Coll–Port Arthur (TX)
Laramie County Comm Coll (WY)
Lower Columbia Coll (WA)
Macomb Comm Coll (MI)
Manatee Comm Coll (FL)
Marshall Comm and Tech Coll (WV)
Massachusetts Bay Comm Coll (MA)
Mesabi Range Comm and Tech Coll (MN)
Metropolitan Comm Coll-Business & Technology College (MO)
Midland Coll (TX)
Midlands Tech Coll (SC)
Missouri State U–West Plains (MO)
Montgomery County Comm Coll (PA)
Moraine Valley Comm Coll (IL)
Mott Comm Coll (MI)
New Mexico State U–Alamogordo (NM)
Northampton County Area Comm Coll (PA)
North Arkansas Coll (AR)
North Dakota State Coll of Science (ND)
Ocean County Coll (NJ)
Owens Comm Coll, Toledo (OH)
Panola Coll (TX)
Penn Foster Career School (PA)
The Pennsylvania State U Beaver Campus of the Commonwealth Coll (PA)
The Pennsylvania State U Delaware County Campus of the Commonwealth Coll (PA)
The Pennsylvania State U DuBois Campus of the Commonwealth Coll (PA)
The Pennsylvania State U Fayette Campus of the Commonwealth Coll (PA)
The Pennsylvania State U Hazleton Campus of the Commonwealth Coll (PA)
The Pennsylvania State U McKeesport Campus of the Commonwealth Coll (PA)
The Pennsylvania State U Mont Alto Campus of the Commonwealth Coll (PA)
The Pennsylvania State U New Kensington Campus of the Commonwealth Coll (PA)

The Pennsylvania State U Shenango Campus of the Commonwealth Coll (PA)
The Pennsylvania State U Wilkes-Barre Campus of the Commonwealth Coll (PA)
The Pennsylvania State U Worthington Scranton Campus of the Commonwealth Coll (PA)
The Pennsylvania State U York Campus of the Commonwealth Coll (PA)
Saginaw Chippewa Tribal Coll (MI)
San Joaquin Valley Coll (CA)
Sheridan Coll–Sheridan and Gillette (WY)
South Arkansas Comm Coll (AR)
Southern State Comm Coll (OH)
Southwest Tennessee Comm Coll (TN)
Springfield Tech Comm Coll (MA)
Truett-McConnell Coll (GA)
Union County Coll (NJ)
U of Pittsburgh at Titusville (PA)
Wor-Wic Comm Coll (MD)
York Tech Coll (SC)

Business Computer Programming
Barton County Comm Coll (KS)
Coll of Lake County (IL)

Business/Corporate Communications
Houston Comm Coll System (TX)
Montgomery County Comm Coll (PA)
North Seattle Comm Coll (WA)

Business Machine Repair
Central Piedmont Comm Coll (NC)
Coahoma Comm Coll (MS)
Comm Coll of Allegheny County (PA)
ECPI Coll of Technology, Virginia Beach (VA)
ECPI Tech Coll, Richmond (VA)
Pellissippi State Tech Comm Coll (TN)
Rockingham Comm Coll (NC)

Business, Management, and Marketing Related
Cincinnati State Tech and Comm Coll (OH)
Comm and Tech Coll of Shepherd (WV)
Eastern Arizona Coll (AZ)
Hamilton Coll, Cedar Falls (IA)
Harrisburg Area Comm Coll (PA)
Heart of Georgia Tech Coll (GA)
Southwestern Michigan Coll (MI)

Business/Managerial Economics
Colby Comm Coll (KS)
Joliet Jr Coll (IL)
Lincoln Coll (IL)
Manatee Comm Coll (FL)
San Joaquin Delta Coll (CA)
Vermilion Comm Coll (MN)

Business Operations Support and Secretarial Services Related
Ancilla Coll (IN)
Business Inst of Pennsylvania, Meadville (PA)
East Central Coll (MO)
Eastern Arizona Coll (AZ)
Laramie County Comm Coll (WY)
Wisconsin Indianhead Tech Coll (WI)

Business Services Marketing
Moraine Park Tech Coll (WI)

Business Systems Networking/ Telecommunications
Caldwell Comm Coll and Tech Inst (NC)
Coll of Business and Technology (FL)
Coll of Lake County (IL)
Globe Coll (MN)
Hamilton Coll, Cedar Falls (IA)
Moraine Park Tech Coll (WI)

Business Teacher Education
Allen County Comm Coll (KS)
Bainbridge Coll (GA)
Bronx Comm Coll of the City U of New York (NY)
Carl Albert State Coll (OK)
Colby Comm Coll (KS)
Eastern Arizona Coll (AZ)
Eastern Wyoming Coll (WY)
Essex County Coll (NJ)
Harrisburg Area Comm Coll (PA)
Holyoke Comm Coll (MA)
Independence Comm Coll (KS)
Lawson State Comm Coll (AL)
Lincoln Coll (IL)
Lincoln Coll–Normal (IL)
Mississippi Gulf Coast Comm Coll (MS)
Mt. San Antonio Coll (CA)
Northeast Comm Coll (NE)
Northern Essex Comm Coll (MA)
North Idaho Coll (ID)
Palau Comm CollPalau)
Pasadena City Coll (CA)
Pratt Comm Coll (KS)
Roane State Comm Coll (TN)
Snow Coll (UT)
Southwest Mississippi Comm Coll (MS)
Spoon River Coll (IL)
Trinity Valley Comm Coll (TX)
Tulsa Comm Coll (OK)

Cabinetmaking and Millwork
Central Georgia Tech Coll (GA)
Illinois Eastern Comm Colls, Olney Central College (IL)
Ivy Tech Comm Coll–Bloomington (IN)
Ivy Tech Comm Coll–Central Indiana (IN)
Ivy Tech Comm Coll–Columbus (IN)
Ivy Tech Comm Coll–East Central (IN)
Ivy Tech Comm Coll–Kokomo (IN)
Ivy Tech Comm Coll–Lafayette (IN)
Ivy Tech Comm Coll–North Central (IN)
Ivy Tech Comm Coll–Northeast (IN)
Ivy Tech Comm Coll–Northwest (IN)
Ivy Tech Comm Coll–Southern Indiana (IN)
Ivy Tech Comm Coll–Southwest (IN)
Ivy Tech Comm Coll–Wabash Valley (IN)
Ivy Tech Comm Coll–Whitewater (IN)
Macomb Comm Coll (MI)
Oakland Comm Coll (MI)

Cad/Cadd Drafting/Design Technology
Alexandria Tech Coll (MN)
Brown Mackie Coll–North Canton (OH)
Brown Mackie Coll–Northern Kentucky (KY)
Florida Tech Coll, DeLand (FL)
ITT Tech Inst, Tucson (AZ)
ITT Tech Inst (AR)

ITT Tech Inst, Anaheim (CA)
ITT Tech Inst, Lathrop (CA)
ITT Tech Inst, Oxnard (CA)
ITT Tech Inst, Rancho Cordova (CA)
ITT Tech Inst, San Bernardino (CA)
ITT Tech Inst, San Diego (CA)
ITT Tech Inst, Sylmar (CA)
ITT Tech Inst, Torrance (CA)
ITT Tech Inst, West Covina (CA)
ITT Tech Inst (CO)
ITT Tech Inst, Fort Lauderdale (FL)
ITT Tech Inst, Jacksonville (FL)
ITT Tech Inst, Lake Mary (FL)
ITT Tech Inst, Tampa (FL)
ITT Tech Inst, Duluth (GA)
ITT Tech Inst, Kennesaw (GA)
ITT Tech Inst (ID)
ITT Tech Inst, Matteson (IL)
ITT Tech Inst, Mount Prospect (IL)
ITT Tech Inst, Fort Wayne (IN)
ITT Tech Inst, Indianapolis (IN)
ITT Tech Inst, Newburgh (IN)
ITT Tech Inst, Louisville (KY)
ITT Tech Inst (LA)
ITT Tech Inst (MD)
ITT Tech Inst, Norwood (MA)
ITT Tech Inst, Woburn (MA)
ITT Tech Inst, Canton (MI)
ITT Tech Inst, Grand Rapids (MI)
ITT Tech Inst, Troy (MI)
ITT Tech Inst (MN)
ITT Tech Inst, Arnold (MO)
ITT Tech Inst, Earth City (MO)
ITT Tech Inst (NE)
ITT Tech Inst (NV)
ITT Tech Inst, Getzville (NY)
ITT Tech Inst, Dayton (OH)
ITT Tech Inst, Hilliard (OH)
ITT Tech Inst, Norwood (OH)
ITT Tech Inst, Strongsville (OH)
ITT Tech Inst, Warrensville Heights (OH)
ITT Tech Inst, Youngstown (OH)
ITT Tech Inst (OK)
ITT Tech Inst (OR)
ITT Tech Inst (SC)
ITT Tech Inst, Knoxville (TN)
ITT Tech Inst, Memphis (TN)
ITT Tech Inst, Nashville (TN)
ITT Tech Inst, Arlington (TX)
ITT Tech Inst, Austin (TX)
ITT Tech Inst, Houston (TX)
ITT Tech Inst, Houston (TX)
ITT Tech Inst, Houston (TX)
ITT Tech Inst, Richardson (TX)
ITT Tech Inst, San Antonio (TX)
ITT Tech Inst (UT)
ITT Tech Inst, Chantilly (VA)
ITT Tech Inst, Norfolk (VA)
ITT Tech Inst, Richmond (VA)
ITT Tech Inst, Springfield (VA)
ITT Tech Inst, Bothell (WA)
ITT Tech Inst, Seattle (WA)
ITT Tech Inst, Spokane (WA)
ITT Tech Inst, Green Bay (WI)
ITT Tech Inst, Greenfield (WI)
Lower Columbia Coll (WA)
Montgomery Coll (TX)
Morrison Inst of Technology (IL)
Northampton County Area Comm Coll (PA)
Owens Comm Coll, Toledo (OH)
St. Philip's Coll (TX)
Springfield Tech Comm Coll (MA)
TESST Coll of Technology, Towson (MD)
Vatterott Coll (IA)

Waubonsee Comm Coll (IL)

Cardiovascular Technology
Augusta Tech Coll (GA)
Bunker Hill Comm Coll (MA)
Caldwell Comm Coll and Tech Inst (NC)
Central Georgia Tech Coll (GA)
Comm Coll of the Air Force (AL)
El Centro Coll (TX)
Harrisburg Area Comm Coll (PA)
Howard Comm Coll (MD)
Northeast State Tech Comm Coll (TN)
Northwestern Tech Coll (GA)
Orange Coast Coll (CA)
St. Cloud Tech Coll (MN)
Southeast Tech Inst (SD)
Valencia Comm Coll (FL)

Carpentry
Alamance Comm Coll (NC)
Alexandria Tech Coll (MN)
Casper Coll (WY)
Cecil Comm Coll (MD)
Central Georgia Tech Coll (GA)
Coahoma Comm Coll (MS)
Coll of Eastern Utah (UT)
Comm Coll of Allegheny County (PA)
Cossatot Comm Coll of the U of Arkansas (AR)
Delaware Tech & Comm Coll, Jack F. Owens Campus (DE)
Delta Coll (MI)
Forsyth Tech Comm Coll (NC)
GateWay Comm Coll (AZ)
George C. Wallace Comm Coll (AL)
H. Councill Trenholm State Tech Coll (AL)
Hutchinson Comm Coll and Area Vocational School (KS)
Illinois Valley Comm Coll (IL)
Ivy Tech Comm Coll–Central Indiana (IN)
Ivy Tech Comm Coll–East Central (IN)
Ivy Tech Comm Coll–Lafayette (IN)
Ivy Tech Comm Coll–North Central (IN)
Ivy Tech Comm Coll–Northwest (IN)
Ivy Tech Comm Coll–Southern Indiana (IN)
Ivy Tech Comm Coll–Southwest (IN)
Ivy Tech Comm Coll–Wabash Valley (IN)
Kaskaskia Coll (IL)
Kauai Comm Coll (HI)
Lake Superior Coll (MN)
Lansing Comm Coll (MI)
Laramie County Comm Coll (WY)
Lawson State Comm Coll (AL)
Long Beach City Coll (CA)
Metropolitan Comm Coll-Business & Technology College (MO)
Mohawk Valley Comm Col (NY)
North Central Missouri Coll (MO)
Northeast Comm Coll (NE)
Northern Maine Comm Coll (ME)
North Idaho Coll (ID)
North Iowa Area Comm Coll (IA)
Oakland Comm Coll (MI)
Palau Comm CollPalau)
Pasadena City Coll (CA)
Piedmont Virginia Comm Coll (VA)
Rockingham Comm Coll (NC)
Saddleback Coll (CA)
St. Cloud Tech Coll (MN)
San Diego City Coll (CA)
San Joaquin Delta Coll (CA)
San Juan Coll (NM)

Seattle Central Comm Coll (WA)
Snow Coll (UT)
South Plains Coll (TX)
Southwestern Illinois Coll (IL)
Southwest Mississippi Comm Coll (MS)
Spokane Comm Coll (WA)
State U of New York Coll of Technology at Alfred (NY)
Triangle Tech, Inc.–DuBois School (PA)
Triangle Tech, Inc.– Greensburg School (PA)
Trinidad State Jr Coll (CO)
Vance-Granville Comm Coll (NC)
The Williamson Free School of Mecha Trades (PA)

Cartography
Alexandria Tech Coll (MN)
Central Oregon Comm Coll (OR)
Dixie State Coll of Utah (UT)
Houston Comm Coll System (TX)
Midlands Tech Coll (SC)
Southwest Tennessee Comm Coll (TN)

Ceramic Arts and Ceramics
Casper Coll (WY)
Dixie State Coll of Utah (UT)
Lincoln Coll (IL)
Mercer County Comm Coll (NJ)
Montgomery Comm Coll (NC)
Oakland Comm Coll (MI)
Palm Beach Comm Coll (FL)
Pasadena City Coll (CA)
Ventura Coll (CA)

Ceramic Sciences and Engineering
Pasadena City Coll (CA)

Chemical Engineering
Brevard Comm Coll (FL)
Chattanooga State Tech Comm Coll (TN)
Delaware Tech & Comm Coll, Jack F. Owens Campus (DE)
Delaware Tech & Comm Coll, Stanton/Wilmington Campus (DE)
Itasca Comm Coll (MN)
Lansing Comm Coll (MI)
Mississippi Gulf Coast Comm Coll (MS)
Naugatuck Valley Comm Coll (CT)
Pellissippi State Tech Comm Coll (TN)
Saddleback Coll (CA)
St. Louis Comm Coll at Florissant Valley (MO)
Texas State Tech Coll Waco (TX)
Westchester Comm Coll (NY)

Chemical Engineering Technology
Delta Coll (MI)

Chemical Technology
Brazosport Coll (TX)
Cape Fear Comm Coll (NC)
Cincinnati State Tech and Comm Coll (OH)
Coll of Lake County (IL)
Coll of the Mainland (TX)
Comm Coll of Allegheny County (PA)
Corning Comm Coll (NY)
Essex County Coll (NJ)
Hudson Valley Comm Coll (NY)
Jefferson Comm Coll (NY)
Kellogg Comm Coll (MI)
Massachusetts Bay Comm Coll (MA)
Midlands Tech Coll (SC)
Mohawk Valley Comm Coll (NY)
Northampton County Area Comm Coll (PA)
Pellissippi State Tech Comm Coll (TN)

Texas State Tech Coll Waco (TX)

Chemistry
Abraham Baldwin Ag Coll (GA)
Allan Hancock Coll (CA)
Allen County Comm Coll (KS)
Ancilla Coll (IN)
Arizona Western Coll (AZ)
Atlanta Metropolitan Coll (GA)
Austin Comm Coll (TX)
Bainbridge Coll (GA)
Barton County Comm Coll (KS)
Bergen Comm Coll (NJ)
Brazosport Coll (TX)
Bronx Comm Coll of the City U of New York (NY)
Bucks County Comm Coll (PA)
Bunker Hill Comm Coll (MA)
Butler Comm Coll (KS)
Casper Coll (WY)
Centralia Coll (WA)
Chattahoochee Valley Comm Coll (AL)
Chattanooga State Tech Comm Coll (TN)
Clarendon Coll (TX)
Coahoma Comm Coll (MS)
Coastal Bend Coll (TX)
Coastal Georgia Comm Coll (GA)
Cochise Coll, Douglas (AZ)
Colby Comm Coll (KS)
Coll of the Canyons (CA)
Coll of the Siskiyous (CA)
Columbia Coll (CA)
Comm Coll of Allegheny County (PA)
Copiah-Lincoln Comm Coll (MS)
Cowley County Comm Coll and Area Vocational–Tech School (KS)
Dixie State Coll of Utah (UT)
East Central Coll (MO)
Eastern Arizona Coll (AZ)
Essex County Coll (NJ)
Finger Lakes Comm Coll (NY)
Foothill Coll (CA)
Frederick Comm Coll (MD)
Gainesville Coll (GA)
Gavilan Coll (CA)
Great Basin Coll (NV)
Harrisburg Area Comm Coll (PA)
Highland Comm Coll (IL)
Holyoke Comm Coll (MA)
Howard Coll (TX)
Independence Comm Coll (KS)
Joliet Jr Coll (IL)
Kellogg Comm Coll (MI)
Kingsborough Comm Coll of the City U of New York (NY)
Lansing Comm Coll (MI)
Laramie County Comm Coll (WY)
Lawson State Comm Coll (AL)
Lincoln Coll (IL)
Linn-Benton Comm Coll (OR)
Longview Comm Coll (MO)
Macomb Comm Coll (MI)
Manatee Comm Coll (FL)
Maple Woods Comm Coll (MO)
Mercer County Comm Coll (NJ)
Miami Dade Coll (FL)
Middlesex County Coll (NJ)
Midland Coll (TX)
MiraCosta Coll (CA)
New Mexico Military Inst (NM)
Northampton County Area Comm Coll (PA)
Northeast Comm Coll (NE)
Northeast State Tech Comm Coll (TN)
North Hennepin Comm Coll (MN)
North Idaho Coll (ID)

Okaloosa-Walton Coll (FL)
Orange Coast Coll (CA)
Palm Beach Comm Coll (FL)
Palo Alto Coll (TX)
Pasadena City Coll (CA)
Penn Valley Comm Coll (MO)
Pratt Comm Coll (KS)
Raritan Valley Comm Coll (NJ)
Roane State Comm Coll (TN)
Saddleback Coll (CA)
St. Philip's Coll (TX)
Salem Comm Coll (NJ)
Salt Lake Comm Coll (UT)
San Diego Mesa Coll (CA)
San Joaquin Delta Coll (CA)
San Juan Coll (NM)
Santa Barbara City Coll (CA)
Santa Rosa Jr Coll (CA)
Sauk Valley Comm Coll (IL)
Skyline Coll (CA)
Snow Coll (UT)
South Plains Coll (TX)
Southwest Mississippi Comm Coll (MS)
Spoon River Coll (IL)
Springfield Tech Comm Coll (MA)
Treasure Valley Comm Coll (OR)
Trinidad State Jr Coll (CO)
Trinity Valley Comm Coll (TX)
Tulsa Comm Coll (OK)
Union County Coll (NJ)
Vermilion Comm Coll (MN)
Wharton County Jr Coll (TX)
Young Harris Coll (GA)
Yuba Coll (CA)

Chemistry Teacher Education
Ancilla Coll (IN)
Coll of the Siskiyous (CA)
Manatee Comm Coll (FL)

Child Care and Guidance Related
Albany Tech Coll (GA)

Child Care and Support Services Management
Alexandria Tech Coll (MN)
Arapahoe Comm Coll (CO)
Barton County Comm Coll (KS)
Brazosport Coll (TX)
Broome Comm Coll (NY)
Cape Fear Comm Coll (NC)
Central Carolina Tech Coll (SC)
Central Georgia Tech Coll (GA)
Centralia Coll (WA)
Central New Mexico Comm Coll (NM)
Central Wyoming Coll (WY)
Coll of DuPage (IL)
Dixie State Coll of Utah (UT)
Eastfield Coll (TX)
Erie Comm Coll (NY)
Feather River Coll (CA)
Florida Comm Coll at Jacksonville (FL)
Gadsden State Comm Coll (AL)
Hagerstown Comm Coll (MD)
H. Councill Trenholm State Tech Coll (AL)
Highland Comm Coll (IL)
Houston Comm Coll System (TX)
Hutchinson Comm Coll and Area Vocational School (KS)
Ivy Tech Comm Coll–Bloomington (IN)
Ivy Tech Comm Coll–Central Indiana (IN)
Ivy Tech Comm Coll–Columbus (IN)
Ivy Tech Comm Coll–East Central (IN)
Ivy Tech Comm Coll–Kokomo (IN)
Ivy Tech Comm Coll–Lafayette (IN)

Ivy Tech Comm Coll–North Central (IN)
Ivy Tech Comm Coll–Northeast (IN)
Ivy Tech Comm Coll–Northwest (IN)
Ivy Tech Comm Coll–Southeast (IN)
Ivy Tech Comm Coll–Southern Indiana (IN)
Ivy Tech Comm Coll–Southwest (IN)
Ivy Tech Comm Coll–Wabash Valley (IN)
Ivy Tech Comm Coll–Whitewater (IN)
Jefferson Comm Coll (OH)
Jefferson State Comm Coll (AL)
Kansas City Kansas Comm Coll (KS)
Kennebec Valley Comm Coll (ME)
Lake Land Coll (IL)
Lake Region State Coll (ND)
Linn-Benton Comm Coll (OR)
Macomb Comm Coll (MI)
Massachusetts Bay Comm Coll (MA)
MiraCosta Coll (CA)
Modesto Jr Coll (CA)
Montgomery Comm Coll (NC)
Montgomery County Comm Coll (PA)
Normandale Comm Coll (MN)
Oakland Comm Coll (MI)
Ocean County Coll (NJ)
Orange Coast Coll (CA)
Ouachita Tech Coll (AR)
Peninsula Coll (WA)
Penn Foster Career School (PA)
Pima Comm Coll (AZ)
Rasmussen Coll Mankato (MN)
Richmond Comm Coll (NC)
St. Cloud Tech Coll (MN)
Santa Barbara City Coll (CA)
Snead State Comm Coll (AL)
Southwestern Michigan Coll (MI)
Spokane Falls Comm Coll (WA)
Tulsa Comm Coll (OK)
Western Iowa Tech Comm Coll (IA)
Wilkes Comm Coll (NC)
Wisconsin Indianhead Tech Coll (WI)
Wor-Wic Comm Coll (MD)
York Tech Coll (SC)

Child Care/Guidance
Bristol Comm Coll (MA)
Caldwell Comm Coll and Tech Inst (NC)
Feather River Coll (CA)

Child Care Provider
Moraine Park Tech Coll (WI)

Child Care Provision
Alexandria Tech Coll (MN)
Arapahoe Comm Coll (CO)
Bladen Comm Coll (NC)
Cincinnati State Tech and Comm Coll (OH)
Coastal Carolina Comm Coll (NC)
Coll of DuPage (IL)
Coll of Lake County (IL)
Comm Coll of Allegheny County (PA)
Corning Comm Coll (NY)
Eastern Arizona Coll (AZ)
Eastern West Virginia Comm and Tech Coll (WV)
Florida Comm Coll at Jacksonville (FL)
Heartland Comm Coll (IL)
Highland Comm Coll (IL)
Kennebec Valley Comm Coll (ME)
Lake Region State Coll (ND)
Lincoln Land Comm Coll (IL)
Louisiana Tech Coll (LA)
Luzerne County Comm Coll (PA)

Midland Coll (TX)
Midlands Tech Coll (SC)
Modesto Jr Coll (CA)
Moraine Valley Comm Coll (IL)
Northampton County Area Comm Coll (PA)
Northland Comm and Tech Coll–Thief River Falls (MN)
Orange Coast Coll (CA)
Parkland Coll (IL)
Penn Valley Comm Coll (MO)
Pima Comm Coll (AZ)
Rasmussen Coll Mankato (MN)
San Diego Mesa Coll (CA)
Southwestern Oregon Comm Coll (OR)
Tompkins Cortland Comm Coll (NY)
Trident Tech Coll (SC)
Triton Coll (IL)
United Tribes Tech Coll (ND)
Waubonsee Comm Coll (IL)
Westchester Comm Coll (NY)
Western Tech Coll (WI)
York Tech Coll (SC)

Child Development
Abraham Baldwin Ag Coll (GA)
Albany Tech Coll (GA)
Allen County Comm Coll (KS)
Altamaha Tech Coll (GA)
Appalachian Tech Coll (GA)
Athens Tech Coll (GA)
Atlanta Metropolitan Coll (GA)
Atlanta Tech Coll (GA)
Augusta Tech Coll (GA)
Borough of Manhattan Comm Coll of the City U of New York (NY)
Brazosport Coll (TX)
Briarwood Coll (CT)
Bronx Comm Coll of the City U of New York (NY)
Broward Comm Coll (FL)
Butler Comm Coll (KS)
Central Arizona Coll (AZ)
Central Comm Coll–Grand Island Campus (NE)
Central Comm Coll–Hastings Campus (NE)
Central Georgia Tech Coll (GA)
Centralia Coll (WA)
Central Piedmont Comm Coll (NC)
Chattahoochee Tech Coll (GA)
Chattanooga State Tech Comm Coll (TN)
Cleveland State Comm Coll (TN)
Coastal Bend Coll (TX)
Colby Comm Coll (KS)
Coll of DuPage (IL)
Coll of Eastern Utah (UT)
Coll of the Canyons (CA)
Coll of the Mainland (TX)
Columbus Tech Coll (GA)
Comm Coll of Allegheny County (PA)
Coosa Valley Tech Coll (GA)
Copiah-Lincoln Comm Coll (MS)
Cowley County Comm Coll and Area Vocational–Tech School (KS)
Delaware Tech & Comm Coll, Jack F. Owens Campus (DE)
Delta Coll (MI)
Dyersburg State Comm Coll (TN)
East Central Tech Coll (GA)
Flint River Tech Coll (GA)
Foothill Coll (CA)
Forsyth Tech Comm Coll (NC)
Fox Valley Tech Coll (WI)
Frederick Comm Coll (MD)
Gavilan Coll (CA)
Griffin Tech Coll (GA)
Guam Comm Coll (GU)
Hawkeye Comm Coll (IA)

Heartland Comm Coll (IL)
Heart of Georgia Tech Coll (GA)
Highland Comm Coll (IL)
Houston Comm Coll System (TX)
Howard Coll (TX)
Howard Comm Coll (MD)
Illinois Eastern Comm Colls, Wabash Valley College (IL)
Illinois Valley Comm Coll (IL)
Independence Comm Coll (KS)
Jackson State Comm Coll (TN)
Jefferson Comm and Tech Coll (KY)
Lamar State Coll–Port Arthur (TX)
Lanier Tech Coll (GA)
Lansing Comm Coll (MI)
Laredo Comm Coll (TX)
Manor Coll (PA)
Metropolitan Comm Coll (NE)
Miami Dade Coll (FL)
Middle Georgia Tech Coll (GA)
Middlesex County Coll (NJ)
Modesto Jr Coll (CA)
Moultrie Tech Coll (GA)
Mt. San Antonio Coll (CA)
Mount Wachusett Comm Coll (MA)
New Hampshire Comm Tech Coll, Manchester/Stratham (NH)
New Hampshire Comm Tech Coll, Nashua/Claremont (NH)
Northland Comm and Tech Coll–Thief River Falls (MN)
North Metro Tech Coll (GA)
North Shore Comm Coll (MA)
Northwestern Connecticut Comm Coll (CT)
Northwestern Tech Coll (GA)
Northwest-Shoals Comm Coll (AL)
Ogeechee Tech Coll (GA)
Okaloosa-Walton Coll (FL)
Okefenokee Tech Coll (GA)
Orange County Comm Coll (NY)
Otero Jr Coll (CO)
Peninsula Coll (WA)
Polk Comm Coll (FL)
Pratt Comm Coll (KS)
Rasmussen Coll Eden Prarie (MN)
Rasmussen Coll Mankato (MN)
Richland Comm Coll (IL)
Rockingham Comm Coll (NC)
Rock Valley Coll (IL)
Rogue Comm Coll (OR)
Saddleback Coll (CA)
Saint Charles Comm Coll (MO)
St. Cloud Tech Coll (MN)
St. Louis Comm Coll at Florissant Valley (MO)
Saint Paul Coll–A Comm & Tech College (MN)
Sandersville Tech Coll (GA)
San Joaquin Delta Coll (CA)
Savannah Tech Coll (GA)
Seminole Comm Coll (FL)
Sinclair Comm Coll (OH)
Snow Coll (UT)
Southeastern Tech Coll (GA)
South Georgia Tech Coll (GA)
South Plains Coll (TX)
Southwestern Illinois Coll (IL)
Southwest Georgia Tech Coll (GA)
Spoon River Coll (IL)
Stark State Coll of Technology (OH)
Swainsboro Tech Coll (GA)
Tompkins Cortland Comm Coll (NY)
Trinity Valley Comm Coll (TX)
Tulsa Comm Coll (OK)
Valdosta Tech Coll (GA)

Vance-Granville Comm Coll (NC)
West Central Tech Coll (GA)
Westchester Comm Coll (NY)
Western Oklahoma State Coll (OK)
Western Tech Coll (WI)
West Georgia Tech Coll (GA)
Westmoreland County Comm Coll (PA)
William Rainey Harper Coll (IL)
Yakima Valley Comm Coll (WA)
Yuba Coll (CA)

Child Guidance
Delta Coll (MI)
Ivy Tech Comm Coll–Central Indiana (IN)
John Wood Comm Coll (IL)
Lamar State Coll–Port Arthur (TX)
Laurel Business Inst (PA)
Lincoln Land Comm Coll (IL)
Manatee Comm Coll (FL)
Moberly Area Comm Coll (MO)
Palo Verde Coll (CA)
Prairie State Coll (IL)
Santa Rosa Jr Coll (CA)
Tulsa Comm Coll (OK)

Chiropractic Assistant
Barton County Comm Coll (KS)
Moraine Park Tech Coll (WI)
Sauk Valley Comm Coll (IL)

Christian Studies
Truett-McConnell Coll (GA)

Cinematography and Film/Video Production
The Art Inst of New York City (NY)
The Art Inst of Philadelphia (PA)
Brown Coll (MN)
Bucks County Comm Coll (PA)
Cincinnati State Tech and Comm Coll (OH)
Coll of DuPage (IL)
Coll of the Canyons (CA)
Glendale Comm Coll (AZ)
Holyoke Comm Coll (MA)
Lansing Comm Coll (MI)
Miami Dade Coll (FL)
Orange Coast Coll (CA)
Pellissippi State Tech Comm Coll (TN)
Riverside Comm Coll District (CA)
Saddleback Coll (CA)
St. Louis Comm Coll at Florissant Valley (MO)
Seattle Central Comm Coll (WA)
Valencia Comm Coll (FL)

Civil Drafting and Cad/Cadd
Comm Coll of Allegheny County (PA)
North Seattle Comm Coll (WA)

Civil Engineering
Itasca Comm Coll (MN)
Santa Rosa Jr Coll (CA)
Tidewater Comm Coll (VA)

Civil Engineering Related
Bristol Comm Coll (MA)

Civil Engineering Technology
Allan Hancock Coll (CA)
Big Bend Comm Coll (WA)
Bishop State Comm Coll (AL)
Bristol Comm Coll (MA)
Broome Comm Coll (NY)
Broward Comm Coll (FL)
Butler County Comm Coll (PA)
Central Arizona Coll (AZ)
Central Carolina Tech Coll (SC)
Centralia Coll (WA)
Central Piedmont Comm Coll (NC)

Chattahoochee Tech Coll (GA)
Chattanooga State Tech Comm Coll (TN)
Chemeketa Comm Coll (OR)
Cincinnati State Tech and Comm Coll (OH)
Clark State Comm Coll (OH)
Coll of Lake County (IL)
Comm Coll of Allegheny County (PA)
Copiah-Lincoln Comm Coll (MS)
Delaware Tech & Comm Coll, Jack F. Owens Campus (DE)
Delaware Tech & Comm Coll, Stanton/Wilmington Campus (DE)
Delaware Tech & Comm Coll, Terry Campus (DE)
Delgado Comm Coll (LA)
Eastern Arizona Coll (AZ)
Erie Comm Coll, North Campus (NY)
Essex County Coll (NJ)
Fayetteville Tech Comm Coll (NC)
Florida Comm Coll at Jacksonville (FL)
Gadsden State Comm Coll (AL)
Gaston Coll (NC)
Guam Comm Coll (GU)
Harrisburg Area Comm Coll (PA)
Hawkeye Comm Coll (IA)
Horry-Georgetown Tech Coll (SC)
Houston Comm Coll System (TX)
Hudson Valley Comm Coll (NY)
Independence Comm Coll (KS)
Lake Land Coll (IL)
Lake Superior Coll (MN)
Lansing Comm Coll (MI)
Laramie County Comm Coll (WY)
Linn-Benton Comm Coll (OR)
Linn State Tech Coll (MO)
Lord Fairfax Comm Coll (VA)
Macomb Comm Coll (MI)
Manatee Comm Coll (FL)
Mercer County Comm Coll (NJ)
Metropolitan Comm Coll (NE)
Miami Dade Coll (FL)
Middlesex County Coll (NJ)
Midlands Tech Coll (SC)
Mohawk Valley Comm Coll (NY)
Moraine Park Tech Coll (WI)
Moultrie Tech Coll (GA)
Mt. San Antonio Coll (CA)
Nassau Comm Coll (NY)
New Mexico Military Inst (NM)
North Dakota State Coll of Science (ND)
Northern Essex Comm Coll (MA)
Ocean County Coll (NJ)
Pasadena City Coll (CA)
Pellissippi State Tech Comm Coll (TN)
Peninsula Coll (WA)
Penn Foster Career School (PA)
Phoenix Coll (AZ)
St. Cloud Tech Coll (MN)
St. Louis Comm Coll at Florissant Valley (MO)
Saint Paul Coll–A Comm & Tech College (MN)
San Joaquin Delta Coll (CA)
Seminole Comm Coll (FL)
Sinclair Comm Coll (OH)
Southeast Tech Inst (SD)
Spartanburg Tech Coll (SC)
Spokane Comm Coll (WA)
Springfield Tech Comm Coll (MA)
Stark State Coll of Technology (OH)
State U of New York Coll of Technology at Alfred (NY)

Trident Tech Coll (SC)
Trinidad State Jr Coll (CO)
Tulsa Comm Coll (OK)
Union County Coll (NJ)
Valencia Comm Coll (FL)
Westchester Comm Coll (NY)
Yakima Valley Comm Coll (WA)

Classics and Languages, Literatures And Linguistics
Foothill Coll (CA)

Clinical Laboratory Science/ Medical Technology
Arapahoe Comm Coll (CO)
Athens Tech Coll (GA)
Broward Comm Coll (FL)
Casper Coll (WY)
Central Piedmont Comm Coll (NC)
Chattahoochee Valley Comm Coll (AL)
Coahoma Comm Coll (MS)
Cuyahoga Comm Coll (OH)
El Centro Coll (TX)
Georgia Highlands Coll (GA)
Globe Coll (MN)
Holyoke Comm Coll (MA)
Howard Comm Coll (MD)
Joliet Jr Coll (IL)
Lansing Comm Coll (MI)
Lawson State Comm Coll (AL)
Louisiana State U at Alexandria (LA)
North Idaho Coll (ID)
Northwest-Shoals Comm Coll (AL)
Okaloosa-Walton Coll (FL)
Orange Coast Coll (CA)
Phoenix Coll (AZ)
South Texas Coll (TX)
Tarrant County Coll District (TX)
Westchester Comm Coll (NY)
Young Harris Coll (GA)

Clinical/Medical Laboratory Assistant
Allegany Coll of Maryland (MD)
Edmonds Comm Coll (WA)
Harrisburg Area Comm Coll (PA)
IntelliTec Coll, Grand Junction (CO)
Louisiana Tech Coll (LA)
Minnesota State Comm and Tech Coll–Fergus Falls (MN)
Moraine Park Tech Coll (WI)
North Arkansas Coll (AR)

Clinical/Medical Laboratory Science and Allied Professions Related
Highline Comm Coll (WA)
Oakland Comm Coll (MI)

Clinical/Medical Laboratory Technology
Alamance Comm Coll (NC)
Alexandria Tech Coll (MN)
Allegany Coll of Maryland (MD)
Arapahoe Comm Coll (CO)
Arkansas State U–Beebe (AR)
Austin Comm Coll (TX)
Barton County Comm Coll (KS)
Beaufort County Comm Coll (NC)
Bergen Comm Coll (NJ)
Brevard Comm Coll (FL)
Bristol Comm Coll (MA)
Bronx Comm Coll of the City U of New York (NY)
Broome Comm Coll (NY)
Broward Comm Coll (FL)
Central Georgia Tech Coll (GA)
Central New Mexico Comm Coll (NM)
Central Piedmont Comm Coll (NC)
Cincinnati State Tech and Comm Coll (OH)
Clark State Comm Coll (OH)

Coastal Carolina Comm Coll (NC)
Coastal Georgia Comm Coll (GA)
Comm Coll of Allegheny County (PA)
Comm Coll of the Air Force (AL)
Copiah-Lincoln Comm Coll (MS)
DeKalb Tech Coll (GA)
Delaware Tech & Comm Coll, Jack F. Owens Campus (DE)
Delgado Comm Coll (LA)
El Centro Coll (TX)
Erie Comm Coll, North Campus (NY)
Gadsden State Comm Coll (AL)
Genesee Comm Coll (NY)
George C. Wallace Comm Coll (AL)
Harrisburg Area Comm Coll (PA)
Hawkeye Comm Coll (IA)
Hibbing Comm Coll (MN)
Houston Comm Coll System (TX)
Illinois Central Coll (IL)
Indiana Business Coll-Medical (IN)
Ivy Tech Comm Coll–North Central (IN)
Ivy Tech Comm Coll– Wabash Valley (IN)
Jackson State Comm Coll (TN)
Jamestown Comm Coll (NY)
Jefferson State Comm Coll (AL)
John Wood Comm Coll (IL)
Kapiolani Comm Coll (HI)
Kellogg Comm Coll (MI)
Lake City Comm Coll (FL)
Lake Superior Coll (MN)
Lamar State Coll–Orange (TX)
Laredo Comm Coll (TX)
Manchester Comm Coll (CT)
Manor Coll (PA)
Mercer County Comm Coll (NJ)
Meridian Comm Coll (MS)
Miami Dade Coll (FL)
Middlesex County Coll (NJ)
Midlands Tech Coll (SC)
Minnesota State Comm and Tech Coll–Fergus Falls (MN)
Minnesota West Comm and Tech Coll (MN)
Mississippi Gulf Coast Comm Coll (MS)
Moberly Area Comm Coll (MO)
Montgomery County Comm Coll (PA)
Nassau Comm Coll (NY)
New Mexico State U– Alamogordo (NM)
North Arkansas Coll (AR)
Northeast Iowa Comm Coll (IA)
North Iowa Area Comm Coll (IA)
Ocean County Coll (NJ)
The Ohio State U Ag Tech Inst (OH)
Okefenokee Tech Coll (GA)
Orange County Comm Coll (NY)
The Pennsylvania State U Hazleton Campus of the Commonwealth Coll (PA)
Phoenix Coll (AZ)
Piedmont Virginia Comm Coll (VA)
Roane State Comm Coll (TN)
Saint Paul Coll–A Comm & Tech College (MN)
St. Petersburg Coll (FL)
St. Philip's Coll (TX)
Salt Lake Comm Coll (UT)
San Diego Mesa Coll (CA)
Seminole State Coll (OK)
South Arkansas Comm Coll (AR)

Southeastern Comm Coll (NC)
Southeast Tech Inst (SD)
Southern West Virginia Comm and Tech Coll (WV)
Southwestern Illinois Coll (IL)
Southwestern Oklahoma State U at Sayre (OK)
Southwest Tennessee Comm Coll (TN)
Spartanburg Tech Coll (SC)
Springfield Tech Comm Coll (MA)
Stark State Coll of Technology (OH)
Tarrant County Coll District (TX)
Thomas Nelson Comm Coll (VA)
Three Rivers Comm Coll (MO)
Trident Tech Coll (SC)
Tulsa Comm Coll (OK)
Union County Coll (NJ)
Westchester Comm Coll (NY)
Western Iowa Tech Comm Coll (IA)
Western Tech Coll (WI)
Wharton County Jr Coll (TX)
Wichita Area Tech Coll (KS)
York Tech Coll (SC)

Clinical/Medical Social Work
Central Comm Coll–Grand Island Campus (NE)
Central Comm Coll–Hastings Campus (NE)

Clothing/Textiles
Bradley Academy for the Visual Arts (PA)
Brooks Coll, Long Beach (CA)
El Centro Coll (TX)
H. Councill Trenholm State Tech Coll (AL)
Lawson State Comm Coll (AL)
Palm Beach Comm Coll (FL)

Commercial and Advertising Art
Alamance Comm Coll (NC)
Alexandria Tech Coll (MN)
Allan Hancock Coll (CA)
Antonelli Inst (PA)
Arapahoe Comm Coll (CO)
Austin Comm Coll (TX)
Bergen Comm Coll (NJ)
Bradley Academy for the Visual Arts (PA)
Brooks Coll, Long Beach (CA)
Bucks County Comm Coll (PA)
Butler County Comm Coll (PA)
Casper Coll (WY)
Central Comm Coll– Columbus Campus (NE)
Central Comm Coll–Hastings Campus (NE)
Centralia Coll (WA)
Central Piedmont Comm Coll (NC)
Chattanooga State Tech Comm Coll (TN)
Cincinnati State Tech and Comm Coll (OH)
Clark State Comm Coll (OH)
Clovis Comm Coll (NM)
Coastal Bend Coll (TX)
Colby Comm Coll (KS)
Coll of DuPage (IL)
Collin County Comm Coll District (TX)
Colorado Mountain Coll (CO)
Comm Coll of Allegheny County (PA)
Comm Coll of the Air Force (AL)
Cuyahoga Comm Coll (OH)
Davis Coll (OH)
Delgado Comm Coll (LA)
Dixie State Coll of Utah (UT)
East Central Coll (MO)
Eastern Arizona Coll (AZ)
Fayetteville Tech Comm Coll (NC)

FIDM/The Fashion Inst of Design & Merchandising, Los Angeles Campus (CA)
FIDM/The Fashion Inst of Design & Merchandising, San Diego Campus (CA)
FIDM/The Fashion Inst of Design & Merchandising, San Francisco Campus (CA)
Finger Lakes Comm Coll (NY)
Florida Comm Coll at Jacksonville (FL)
Forsyth Tech Comm Coll (NC)
Fox Valley Tech Coll (WI)
Genesee Comm Coll (NY)
George C. Wallace Comm Coll (AL)
Glendale Comm Coll (AZ)
Globe Coll (MN)
Greenfield Comm Coll (MA)
Hagerstown Comm Coll (MD)
Harrisburg Area Comm Coll (PA)
Hawkeye Comm Coll (IA)
Highland Comm Coll (IL)
Holyoke Comm Coll (MA)
Houston Comm Coll System (TX)
Illinois Central Coll (IL)
Jackson State Comm Coll (TN)
James H. Faulkner State Comm Coll (AL)
James Sprunt Comm Coll (NC)
Jefferson Comm and Tech Coll (KY)
J. F. Drake State Tech Coll (AL)
Johnston Comm Coll (NC)
Kellogg Comm Coll (MI)
Kingsborough Comm Coll of the City U of New York (NY)
Lake-Sumter Comm Coll (FL)
Lansing Comm Coll (MI)
Lincoln Coll (IL)
Lincoln Coll–Normal (IL)
Linn-Benton Comm Coll (OR)
Lord Fairfax Comm Coll (VA)
Luzerne County Comm Coll (PA)
Macomb Comm Coll (MI)
Manatee Comm Coll (FL)
Manchester Comm Coll (CT)
Mercer County Comm Coll (NJ)
Metropolitan Comm Coll (NE)
Miami Dade Coll (FL)
Middlesex Comm Coll (CT)
Middlesex County Coll (NJ)
Midland Coll (TX)
Midlands Tech Coll (SC)
Modesto Jr Coll (CA)
Mohawk Valley Comm Coll (NY)
Montgomery County Comm Coll (PA)
Mt. San Antonio Coll (CA)
Nassau Comm Coll (NY)
New Hampshire Comm Tech Coll, Manchester/Stratham (NH)
New Mexico State U– Alamogordo (NM)
Northern Essex Comm Coll (MA)
North Idaho Coll (ID)
Northwestern Connecticut Comm Coll (CT)
Norwalk Comm Coll (CT)
Oakbridge Academy of Arts (PA)
Ocean County Coll (NJ)
Okaloosa-Walton Coll (FL)
Orange Coast Coll (CA)
Owens Comm Coll, Toledo (OH)
Palm Beach Comm Coll (FL)
Pellissippi State Tech Comm Coll (TN)
Penn Valley Comm Coll (MO)

Platt Coll San Diego (CA)
Pratt Comm Coll (KS)
Quinsigamond Comm Coll (MA)
Raritan Valley Comm Coll (NJ)
Saddleback Coll (CA)
Saint Charles Comm Coll (MO)
St. Louis Comm Coll at Florissant Valley (MO)
St. Petersburg Coll (FL)
San Diego City Coll (CA)
San Joaquin Delta Coll (CA)
San Juan Coll (NM)
Santa Barbara City Coll (CA)
School of Advertising Art (OH)
Schuylkill Inst of Business and Technology (PA)
Seattle Central Comm Coll (WA)
Sinclair Comm Coll (OH)
Southeast Tech Inst (SD)
South Plains Coll (TX)
Southwest Tennessee Comm Coll (TN)
Spokane Falls Comm Coll (WA)
Springfield Tech Comm Coll (MA)
Sullivan County Comm Coll (NY)
Sussex County Comm Coll (NJ)
Texas State Tech Coll Waco (TX)
Thomas Nelson Comm Coll (VA)
Tidewater Comm Coll (VA)
Tompkins Cortland Comm Coll (NY)
Treasure Valley Comm Coll (OR)
Trident Tech Coll (SC)
Trinidad State Jr Coll (CO)
Triton Coll (IL)
Tunxis Comm Coll (CT)
Valencia Comm Coll (FL)
Ventura Coll (CA)
Western Tech Coll (WI)
Westmoreland County Comm Coll (PA)
Yavapai Coll (AZ)
York Tech Coll (SC)

Commercial Fishing
Peninsula Coll (WA)

Commercial Photography
Houston Comm Coll System (TX)
Luzerne County Comm Coll (PA)
Mohawk Valley Comm Coll (NY)
Normandale Comm Coll (MN)
Oakbridge Academy of Arts (PA)
Spokane Falls Comm Coll (WA)

Communication and Journalism Related
Delgado Comm Coll (LA)
Keystone Coll (PA)

Communication and Media Related
Asnuntuck Comm Coll (CT)
Keystone Coll (PA)

Communication Disorders
Northampton County Area Comm Coll (PA)

Communication/Speech Communication and Rhetoric
Atlanta Metropolitan Coll (GA)
Barton County Comm Coll (KS)
Briarwood Coll (CT)
Bristol Comm Coll (MA)
Broome Comm Coll (NY)
Bunker Hill Comm Coll (MA)
Cochise Coll, Douglas (AZ)
Coll of Southern Maryland (MD)
Dean Coll (MA)
Dixie State Coll of Utah (UT)

Eastern Wyoming Coll (WY)
Erie Comm Coll, South Campus (NY)
Hutchinson Comm Coll and Area Vocational School (KS)
Jamestown Comm Coll (NY)
Kellogg Comm Coll (MI)
Keystone Coll (PA)
Lackawanna Coll (PA)
Laramie County Comm Coll (WY)
Lord Fairfax Comm Coll (VA)
Macomb Comm Coll (MI)
Manchester Comm Coll (CT)
Massachusetts Bay Comm Coll (MA)
Montgomery County Comm Coll (PA)
Nassau Comm Coll (NY)
Northampton County Area Comm Coll (PA)
San Juan Coll (NM)
Santa Barbara City Coll (CA)
Santa Rosa Jr Coll (CA)
Sauk Valley Comm Coll (IL)
Union County Coll (NJ)
Waubonsee Comm Coll (IL)
Yuba Coll (CA)

Communications Systems Installation and Repair Technology
Arapahoe Comm Coll (CO)
Broome Comm Coll (NY)
Coll of DuPage (IL)
Erie Comm Coll, South Campus (NY)
Kennebec Valley Comm Coll (ME)
Louisiana Tech Coll (LA)
Modesto Jr Coll (CA)
Mohawk Valley Comm Coll (NY)
North Seattle Comm Coll (WA)
Wisconsin Indianhead Tech Coll (WI)

Communications Technologies and Support Services Related
Comm Coll of Allegheny County (PA)
Montgomery County Comm Coll (PA)
Springfield Tech Comm Coll (MA)
Western Tech Coll (WI)

Communications Technology
Allegany Coll of Maryland (MD)
Arapahoe Comm Coll (CO)
Athens Tech Coll (GA)
Cleveland Comm Coll (NC)
Coll of DuPage (IL)
Comm Coll of the Air Force (AL)
ECPI Coll of Technology, Newport News (VA)
ECPI Coll of Technology, Virginia Beach (VA)
ECPI Tech Coll (VA)
ECPI Tech Coll, Richmond (VA)
Essex County Coll (NJ)
Fountainhead Coll of Technology (TN)
Hutchinson Comm Coll and Area Vocational School (KS)
Kent State U, Tuscarawas Campus (OH)
Lackawanna Coll (PA)
Mott Comm Coll (MI)
Northwestern Connecticut Comm Coll (CT)
Ocean County Coll (NJ)
Orange Coast Coll (CA)
Pasadena City Coll (CA)
St. Philip's Coll (TX)
Southern West Virginia Comm and Tech Coll (WV)

Community Health and Preventive Medicine
Northwest Vista Coll (TX)
United Tribes Tech Coll (ND)

Community Health Services Counseling
Comm Coll of Allegheny County (PA)
Erie Comm Coll (NY)
Kingsborough Comm Coll of the City U of New York (NY)
Manatee Comm Coll (FL)
Mott Comm Coll (MI)

Community Organization and Advocacy
Cleveland State Comm Coll (TN)
Mercer County Comm Coll (NJ)
Mohawk Valley Comm Coll (NY)
New Hampshire Comm Tech Coll, Manchester/Stratham (NH)

Computer and Information Sciences
Albany Tech Coll (GA)
Alexandria Tech Coll (MN)
Asnuntuck Comm Coll (CT)
Atlanta Metropolitan Coll (GA)
Beal Coll (ME)
Berkeley City Coll (CA)
Berkshire Comm Coll (MA)
Bishop State Comm Coll (AL)
Brazosport Coll (TX)
Bristol Comm Coll (MA)
Broome Comm Coll (NY)
Brown Mackie Coll–Salina (KS)
Bucks County Comm Coll (PA)
Butler Comm Coll (KS)
Butler County Comm Coll (PA)
Capital Comm Coll (CT)
Career Coll of Northern Nevada (NV)
Carroll Comm Coll (MD)
Central Arizona Coll (AZ)
Central Comm Coll– Columbus Campus (NE)
Central Comm Coll–Grand Island Campus (NE)
Central Comm Coll–Hastings Campus (NE)
Cincinnati State Tech and Comm Coll (OH)
City Colls of Chicago, Wilbur Wright College (IL)
Clarendon Coll (TX)
Clovis Comm Coll (NM)
Collin County Comm Coll District (TX)
Comm Coll of Denver (CO)
Corning Comm Coll (NY)
Denmark Tech Coll (SC)
ECPI Coll of Technology, Newport News (VA)
ECPI Coll of Technology, Virginia Beach (VA)
ECPI Tech Coll (VA)
ECPI Tech Coll (NC)
ECPI Tech Coll, Richmond (VA)
Erie Business Center, Main (PA)
Erie Comm Coll, North Campus (NY)
Evergreen Valley Coll (CA)
Finger Lakes Comm Coll (NY)
Florida Comm Coll at Jacksonville (FL)
Front Range Comm Coll (CO)
Gadsden State Comm Coll (AL)
GateWay Comm Coll (AZ)
Goodwin Coll (CT)
Hagerstown Comm Coll (MD)
Harrisburg Area Comm Coll (PA)
H. Councill Trenholm State Tech Coll (AL)
Heartland Comm Coll (IL)
Herzing Coll (GA)
Hibbing Comm Coll (MN)
Houston Comm Coll System (TX)

Hutchinson Comm Coll and Area Vocational School (KS)
Indiana Business Coll, Indianapolis (IN)
IntelliTec Coll, Grand Junction (CO)
Ivy Tech Comm Coll– Bloomington (IN)
Ivy Tech Comm Coll–Central Indiana (IN)
Ivy Tech Comm Coll– Columbus (IN)
Ivy Tech Comm Coll–East Central (IN)
Ivy Tech Comm Coll– Kokomo (IN)
Ivy Tech Comm Coll– Lafayette (IN)
Ivy Tech Comm Coll–North Central (IN)
Ivy Tech Comm Coll– Northeast (IN)
Ivy Tech Comm Coll– Northwest (IN)
Ivy Tech Comm Coll– Southeast (IN)
Ivy Tech Comm Coll– Southern Indiana (IN)
Ivy Tech Comm Coll– Southwest (IN)
Ivy Tech Comm Coll– Wabash Valley (IN)
Ivy Tech Comm Coll– Whitewater (IN)
James H. Faulkner State Comm Coll (AL)
Jamestown Comm Coll (NY)
Jefferson State Comm Coll (AL)
Joliet Jr Coll (IL)
Kingsborough Comm Coll of the City U of New York (NY)
Kingwood Coll (TX)
Lackawanna Coll (PA)
Lake Michigan Coll (MI)
Lake Region State Coll (ND)
Laramie County Comm Coll (WY)
Lehigh Valley Coll (PA)
Linn-Benton Comm Coll (OR)
Lord Fairfax Comm Coll (VA)
Lower Columbia Coll (WA)
Luzerne County Comm Coll (PA)
Manatee Comm Coll (FL)
Massachusetts Bay Comm Coll (MA)
Metropolitan Comm Coll-Business & Technology College (MO)
Mid-South Comm Coll (AR)
Moberly Area Comm Coll (MO)
Mohawk Valley Comm Coll (NY)
Montgomery County Comm Coll (PA)
Mountain State Coll (WV)
Nassau Comm Coll (NY)
New Hampshire Comm Tech Coll, Nashua/Claremont (NH)
New Hampshire Tech Inst (NH)
Normandale Comm Coll (MN)
North Arkansas Coll (AR)
Northeast Comm Coll (NE)
Northern Essex Comm Coll (MA)
North Iowa Area Comm Coll (IA)
Northwest-Shoals Comm Coll (AL)
Northwest Vista Coll (TX)
Oakland Comm Coll (MI)
Ocean County Coll (NJ)
Orange County Comm Coll (NY)
Ouachita Tech Coll (AR)
Palo Verde Coll (CA)
Parkland Coll (IL)
Pellissippi State Tech Comm Coll (TN)
Phoenix Coll (AZ)
Pima Comm Coll (AZ)
Prairie State Coll (IL)

Remington Coll–Mobile Campus (AL)
Saddleback Coll (CA)
Salem Comm Coll (NJ)
Salt Lake Comm Coll (UT)
San Diego Mesa Coll (CA)
Sinclair Comm Coll (OH)
Snead State Comm Coll (AL)
Southern Arkansas U Tech (AR)
South Hills School of Business & Technology, State College (PA)
Spartanburg Tech Coll (SC)
State U of New York Coll of Technology at Alfred (NY)
Sussex County Comm Coll (NJ)
Texas State Tech Coll Waco (TX)
Ventura Coll (CA)
Waubonsee Comm Coll (IL)
Westchester Comm Coll (NY)
Westmoreland County Comm Coll (PA)
William Rainey Harper Coll (IL)
Wor-Wic Comm Coll (MD)

Computer and Information Sciences And Support Services Related
Bunker Hill Comm Coll (MA)
Edmonds Comm Coll (WA)
Harrisburg Area Comm Coll (PA)
Indiana Business Coll, Indianapolis (IN)
Indiana Business Coll, Lafayette (IN)
Indiana Business Coll, Muncie (IN)
Jackson Comm Coll (MI)
Laramie County Comm Coll (WY)
Metropolitan Comm Coll-Business & Technology College (MO)
Midlands Tech Coll (SC)
Mohawk Valley Comm Coll (NY)
Mott Comm Coll (MI)
Penn Foster Career School (PA)
Schuylkill Inst of Business and Technology (PA)
Southern Arkansas U Tech (AR)
Springfield Tech Comm Coll (MA)
Waukesha County Tech Coll (WI)
Williston State Coll (ND)
York Tech Coll (SC)

Computer and Information Sciences Related
Austin Comm Coll (TX)
Berkeley City Coll (CA)
Berks Tech Inst (PA)
Blue River Comm Coll (MO)
Bristol Comm Coll (MA)
Brown Mackie Coll– Cincinnati (OH)
Bucks County Comm Coll (PA)
Capital Comm Coll (CT)
Centralia Coll (WA)
Central Oregon Comm Coll (OR)
Citrus Coll (CA)
Coastal Bend Coll (TX)
Colby Comm Coll (KS)
Coll of the Canyons (CA)
The Coll of Westchester (NY)
Corning Comm Coll (NY)
Eastfield Coll (TX)
ECPI Tech Coll (VA)
ECPI Tech Coll, Richmond (VA)
Fiorello H. LaGuardia Comm Coll of the City U of New York (NY)
Florida Comm Coll at Jacksonville (FL)
Galveston Coll (TX)
GateWay Comm Coll (AZ)
Gateway Comm Coll (CT)
Gavilan Coll (CA)
Genesee Comm Coll (NY)

Heald Coll-Hayward (CA)
Heartland Comm Coll (IL)
Highland Comm Coll (IL)
Howard Coll (TX)
Howard Comm Coll (MD)
Jamestown Comm Coll (NY)
Lakeshore Tech Coll (WI)
Lake-Sumter Comm Coll (FL)
Laurel Business Inst (PA)
Lawson State Comm Coll (AL)
Longview Comm Coll (MO)
Luzerne County Comm Coll (PA)
Manatee Comm Coll (FL)
Manor Coll (PA)
Maple Woods Comm Coll (MO)
Metro Business Coll, Jefferson City (MO)
Metropolitan Comm Coll-Business & Technology College (MO)
Middle Georgia Coll (GA)
Mississippi Gulf Coast Comm Coll (MS)
Missouri State U–West Plains (MO)
Nassau Comm Coll (NY)
North Idaho Coll (ID)
Northland Comm and Tech Coll–Thief River Falls (MN)
North Shore Comm Coll (MA)
Norwalk Comm Coll (CT)
Orange County Comm Coll (NY)
Palo Alto Coll (TX)
Pellissippi State Tech Comm Coll (TN)
Penn Valley Comm Coll (MO)
Quinebaug Valley Comm Coll (CT)
Richland Comm Coll (IL)
Sauk Valley Comm Coll (IL)
Seminole Comm Coll (FL)
Sinclair Comm Coll (OH)
Southeast Tech Inst (SD)
Southwestern Michigan Coll (MI)
Stark State Coll of Technology (OH)
Three Rivers Comm Coll (MO)
Tompkins Cortland Comm Coll (NY)
Trinidad State Jr Coll (CO)
Tulsa Comm Coll (OK)
Waubonsee Comm Coll (IL)
West Central Tech Coll (GA)
Westchester Comm Coll (NY)
Yuba Coll (CA)

Computer and Information Systems Security
Berkeley City Coll (CA)
Chattahoochee Tech Coll (GA)
City Colls of Chicago, Wilbur Wright College (IL)
Cochise Coll, Douglas (AZ)
Delta Coll (MI)
ECPI Tech Coll (VA)
ECPI Tech Coll, Glen Allen (VA)
ECPI Tech Coll, Richmond (VA)
Edmonds Comm Coll (WA)
Fayetteville Tech Comm Coll (NC)
Flint River Tech Coll (GA)
Florida Comm Coll at Jacksonville (FL)
Florida National Coll (FL)
Griffin Tech Coll (GA)
Hagerstown Business Coll (MD)
Island Drafting and Tech Inst (NY)
ITT Tech Inst, Getzville (NY)
ITT Tech Inst, Youngstown (OH)
ITT Tech Inst (UT)
ITT Tech Inst, Chantilly (VA)
Jamestown Comm Coll (NY)
Lanier Tech Coll (GA)
Laurel Business Inst (PA)

Metropolitan Comm Coll-Business & Technology College (MO)
Minnesota State Comm and Tech Coll–Fergus Falls (MN)
Montgomery Coll (TX)
Northampton County Area Comm Coll (PA)
North Seattle Comm Coll (WA)
Northwest Vista Coll (TX)
Riverland Comm Coll (MN)
St. Philip's Coll (TX)
Seminole Comm Coll (FL)
Tompkins Cortland Comm Coll (NY)
Triton Coll (IL)
Tulsa Comm Coll (OK)
Valdosta Tech Coll (GA)

Computer Engineering
Itasca Comm Coll (MN)
Santa Barbara City Coll (CA)

Computer Engineering Related
Coll of the Canyons (CA)
Columbus Tech Coll (GA)
Gateway Comm Coll (CT)
Itasca Comm Coll (MN)
Jefferson Comm Coll (OH)
Middle Georgia Coll (GA)
Okaloosa-Walton Coll (FL)
Orange County Comm Coll (NY)
Seminole Comm Coll (FL)
Sinclair Comm Coll (OH)
Stark State Coll of Technology (OH)

Computer Engineering Technologies Related
ITT Tech Inst, Albany (NY)

Computer Engineering Technology
Abraham Baldwin Ag Coll (GA)
Aiken Tech Coll (SC)
Allan Hancock Coll (CA)
Allegany Coll of Maryland (MD)
Benjamin Franklin Inst of Technology (MA)
Bergen Comm Coll (NJ)
Brevard Comm Coll (FL)
Broome Comm Coll (NY)
Broward Comm Coll (FL)
Bucks County Comm Coll (PA)
Capital Comm Coll (CT)
Carteret Comm Coll (NC)
Cecil Comm Coll (MD)
Central Piedmont Comm Coll (NC)
Century Coll (MN)
Chattanooga State Tech Comm Coll (TN)
Chemeketa Comm Coll (OR)
Cincinnati State Tech and Comm Coll (OH)
Clatsop Comm Coll (OR)
Cleveland Comm Coll (NC)
Coastal Bend Coll (TX)
Coll of The Albemarle (NC)
Collin County Comm Coll District (TX)
Colorado Mountain Coll (CO)
Colorado Mountain Coll, Alpine Campus (CO)
Comm Coll of Allegheny County (PA)
Cuyahoga Comm Coll (OH)
DeKalb Tech Coll (GA)
Delaware Tech & Comm Coll, Terry Campus (DE)
Delgado Comm Coll (LA)
East Arkansas Comm Coll (AR)
Eastfield Coll (TX)
ECPI Coll of Technology, Newport News (VA)
ECPI Coll of Technology, Virginia Beach (VA)
ECPI Tech Coll (VA)
ECPI Tech Coll (NC)
Fiorello H. LaGuardia Comm Coll of the City U of New York (NY)
Florida Comm Coll at Jacksonville (FL)

Forsyth Tech Comm Coll (NC)
Fountainhead Coll of Technology (TN)
Frederick Comm Coll (MD)
Gateway Comm Coll (CT)
Genesee Comm Coll (NY)
Grand Rapids Comm Coll (MI)
Hawkeye Comm Coll (IA)
Heald Coll-Concord (CA)
Heald Coll-Fresno (CA)
Heald Coll-Roseville (CA)
Heald Coll-San Francisco (CA)
Heald Coll-San Jose (CA)
Heartland Comm Coll (IL)
Highline Comm Coll (WA)
Horry-Georgetown Tech Coll (SC)
Houston Comm Coll System (TX)
Jamestown Comm Coll (NY)
Kansas City Kansas Comm Coll (KS)
Kellogg Comm Coll (MI)
Kent State U, Trumbull Campus (OH)
Kent State U, Tuscarawas Campus (OH)
Kingwood Coll (TX)
Lansing Comm Coll (MI)
Lower Columbia Coll (WA)
Manatee Comm Coll (FL)
Marshall Comm and Tech Coll (WV)
Massachusetts Bay Comm Coll (MA)
Meridian Comm Coll (MS)
Miami Dade Coll (FL)
Middlesex County Coll (NJ)
MiraCosta Coll (CA)
Mississippi Gulf Coast Comm Coll (MS)
Montgomery County Comm Coll (PA)
Mt. San Antonio Coll (CA)
New Hampshire Comm Tech Coll, Nashua/Claremont (NH)
New Hampshire Tech Inst (NH)
North Central Missouri Coll (MO)
Northeast Iowa Comm Coll (IA)
Northern Essex Comm Coll (MA)
Northern Maine Comm Coll (ME)
North Shore Comm Coll (MA)
Northwestern Connecticut Comm Coll (CT)
Northwest-Shoals Comm Coll (AL)
Orange Coast Coll (CA)
Orange County Comm Coll (NY)
Palo Alto Coll (TX)
Pasadena City Coll (CA)
Pellissippi State Tech Comm Coll (TN)
The Pennsylvania State U New Kensington Campus of the Commonwealth Coll (PA)
Piedmont Virginia Comm Coll (VA)
Pima Comm Coll (AZ)
Pulaski Tech Coll (AR)
Remington Coll–Mobile Campus (AL)
Richmond Comm Coll (NC)
Roane State Comm Coll (TN)
Rock Valley Coll (IL)
St. Louis Comm Coll at Florissant Valley (MO)
St. Petersburg Coll (FL)
San Diego City Coll (CA)
San Joaquin Delta Coll (CA)
Seminole Comm Coll (FL)
Southeastern Comm Coll (NC)
South Plains Coll (TX)
Southwest Tennessee Comm Coll (TN)
Springfield Tech Comm Coll (MA)

State U of New York Coll of Technology at Alfred (NY)
Texas State Tech Coll Waco (TX)
Three Rivers Comm Coll (MO)
Trident Tech Coll (SC)
Triton Coll (IL)
Vance-Granville Comm Coll (NC)
Vermilion Comm Coll (MN)
Western Tech Coll (TX)
Westmoreland County Comm Coll (PA)
William Rainey Harper Coll (IL)
Yakima Valley Comm Coll (WA)
York Tech Coll (SC)

Computer Graphics
Arapahoe Comm Coll (CO)
Berkeley City Coll (CA)
Berks Tech Inst (PA)
Bradley Academy for the Visual Arts (PA)
Brown Mackie Coll–Cincinnati (OH)
Carroll Comm Coll (MD)
Cecil Comm Coll (MD)
Coll of Business and Technology (FL)
Coll of Eastern Utah (UT)
Coll of the Siskiyous (CA)
The Coll of Westchester (NY)
Corning Comm Coll (NY)
Cowley County Comm Coll and Area Vocational–Tech School (KS)
Evergreen Valley Coll (CA)
Florida Comm Coll at Jacksonville (FL)
Florida National Coll (FL)
Gateway Comm Coll (CT)
Gavilan Coll (CA)
Genesee Comm Coll (NY)
Globe Coll (MN)
Howard Comm Coll (MD)
Kellogg Comm Coll (MI)
Kingwood Coll (TX)
Lansing Comm Coll (MI)
Lincoln Coll–Normal (IL)
Luzerne County Comm Coll (PA)
Manatee Comm Coll (FL)
Mercer County Comm Coll (NJ)
Meridian Comm Coll (MS)
Mesabi Range Comm and Tech Coll (MN)
Metropolitan Comm Coll-Business & Technology College (MO)
Miami Dade Coll (FL)
Middlesex County Coll (NJ)
Mississippi Gulf Coast Comm Coll (MS)
Missouri State U–West Plains (MO)
Modesto Jr Coll (CA)
Mt. San Antonio Coll (CA)
Mount Wachusett Comm Coll (MA)
Nassau Comm Coll (NY)
North Country Comm Coll (NY)
Northern Essex Comm Coll (MA)
Northland Comm and Tech Coll–Thief River Falls (MN)
North Shore Comm Coll (MA)
Northwestern Connecticut Comm Coll (CT)
Oakbridge Academy of Arts (PA)
Orange Coast Coll (CA)
Parkland Coll (IL)
Pellissippi State Tech Comm Coll (TN)
Phoenix Coll (AZ)
Platt Coll San Diego (CA)
Prairie State Coll (IL)
Quinebaug Valley Comm Coll (CT)
Rasmussen Coll Mankato (MN)
Richland Comm Coll (IL)
Seminole Comm Coll (FL)
Sinclair Comm Coll (OH)

Southeast Tech Inst (SD)
State U of New York Coll of Technology at Alfred (NY)
Sullivan County Comm Coll (NY)
Tompkins Cortland Comm Coll (NY)
Trident Tech Coll (SC)
Triton Coll (IL)
Tulsa Comm Coll (OK)
Utah Career Coll (UT)
Weatherford Coll (TX)
Westmoreland County Comm Coll (PA)
Yakima Valley Comm Coll (WA)

Computer Hardware Engineering
Eastfield Coll (TX)
Florida Comm Coll at Jacksonville (FL)
Lake City Comm Coll (FL)
Seminole Comm Coll (FL)
Sinclair Comm Coll (OH)
Stark State Coll of Technology (OH)
Tompkins Cortland Comm Coll (NY)
Tulsa Comm Coll (OK)

Computer Hardware Technology
Brazosport Coll (TX)
Laramie County Comm Coll (WY)

Computer/Information Technology Services Administration Related
Arapahoe Comm Coll (CO)
Atlanta Metropolitan Coll (GA)
Barton County Comm Coll (KS)
Brevard Comm Coll (FL)
Bucks County Comm Coll (PA)
Coastal Carolina Comm Coll (NC)
The Coll of Westchester (NY)
Corning Comm Coll (NY)
Dyersburg State Comm Coll (TN)
Eastfield Coll (TX)
El Centro Coll (TX)
Florida Comm Coll at Jacksonville (FL)
Hawkeye Comm Coll (IA)
Heald Coll-Hayward (CA)
Hesston Coll (KS)
Horry-Georgetown Tech Coll (SC)
Howard Comm Coll (MD)
Kennebec Valley Comm Coll (ME)
Keystone Coll (PA)
Laurel Business Inst (PA)
Maria Coll (NY)
Mesabi Range Comm and Tech Coll (MN)
Metropolitan Comm Coll-Business & Technology College (MO)
Middle Georgia Coll (GA)
Modesto Jr Coll (CA)
Naugatuck Valley Comm Coll (CT)
Northwest Vista Coll (TX)
Parkland Coll (IL)
St. Cloud Tech Coll (MN)
St. Petersburg Coll (FL)
Seminole Comm Coll (FL)
Sinclair Comm Coll (OH)
Southeast Tech Inst (SD)
Stark State Coll of Technology (OH)
Tompkins Cortland Comm Coll (NY)
Trident Tech Coll (SC)
Tulsa Comm Coll (OK)
Western Oklahoma State Coll (OK)

Computer Installation and Repair Technology
Coahoma Comm Coll (MS)
Coll of DuPage (IL)
Coll of Lake County (IL)
Delgado Comm Coll (LA)
Harrisburg Area Comm Coll (PA)

Hibbing Comm Coll (MN)
Kennebec Valley Comm Coll (ME)
Louisiana Tech Coll (LA)
Midlands Tech Coll (SC)
Modesto Jr Coll (CA)
Northampton County Area Comm Coll (PA)
Riverland Comm Coll (MN)
State U of New York Coll of Technology at Alfred (NY)
Waukesha County Tech Coll (WI)

Computer Maintenance Technology
St. Philip's Coll (TX)
TESST Coll of Technology, Towson (MD)

Computer Management
Berkeley Coll (NJ)
Cossatot Comm Coll of the U of Arkansas (AR)
ECPI Coll of Technology, Newport News (VA)
ECPI Coll of Technology, Virginia Beach (VA)
ECPI Tech Coll, Richmond (VA)
Heald Coll-Hayward (CA)
Heald Coll-Stockton (CA)
Kennebec Valley Comm Coll (ME)
Lakeshore Tech Coll (WI)
Lansing Comm Coll (MI)
Laurel Business Inst (PA)
Lincoln Coll–Normal (IL)
New Hampshire Comm Tech Coll, Nashua/Claremont (NH)
Otero Jr Coll (CO)
Palo Alto Coll (TX)
Tri-County Comm Coll (NC)
Vermilion Comm Coll (MN)
William Rainey Harper Coll (IL)

Computer Programming
Abraham Baldwin Ag Coll (GA)
Alamance Comm Coll (NC)
Altamaha Tech Coll (GA)
Ancilla Coll (IN)
Arapahoe Comm Coll (CO)
Athens Tech Coll (GA)
Atlanta Tech Coll (GA)
Augusta Tech Coll (GA)
Austin Comm Coll (TX)
Beaufort County Comm Coll (NC)
Bergen Comm Coll (NJ)
Berks Tech Inst (PA)
Bladen Comm Coll (NC)
Borough of Manhattan Comm Coll of the City U of New York (NY)
Brazosport Coll (TX)
Brevard Comm Coll (FL)
Bristol Comm Coll (MA)
Broward Comm Coll (FL)
Brown Mackie Coll–Hopkinsville (KY)
Bucks County Comm Coll (PA)
Bunker Hill Comm Coll (MA)
Butler County Comm Coll (PA)
Casper Coll (WY)
Cecil Comm Coll (MD)
Cedar Valley Coll (TX)
Central Georgia Tech Coll (GA)
Central Piedmont Comm Coll (NC)
Chattahoochee Tech Coll (GA)
Chattanooga State Tech Comm Coll (TN)
Chemeketa Comm Coll (OR)
Cincinnati State Tech and Comm Coll (OH)
Clark Coll (WA)
Clark State Comm Coll (OH)
Cochise Coll, Douglas (AZ)
Coll of Southern Maryland (MD)
Coll of The Albemarle (NC)
Coll of the Mainland (TX)
Coll of the Siskiyous (CA)
The Coll of Westchester (NY)

Collin County Comm Coll District (TX)
Coosa Valley Tech Coll (GA)
Copiah-Lincoln Comm Coll (MS)
Corning Comm Coll (NY)
Dabney S. Lancaster Comm Coll (VA)
DeKalb Tech Coll (GA)
Delaware Tech & Comm Coll, Jack F. Owens Campus (DE)
Delaware Tech & Comm Coll, Terry Campus (DE)
Eastfield Coll (TX)
ECPI Coll of Technology, Virginia Beach (VA)
ECPI Tech Coll, Glen Allen (VA)
ECPI Tech Coll, Richmond (VA)
Edmonds Comm Coll (WA)
El Centro Coll (TX)
Essex County Coll (NJ)
Fayetteville Tech Comm Ccll (NC)
Fiorello H. LaGuardia Comm Coll of the City U of New York (NY)
Florida Comm Coll at Jacksonville (FL)
Florida National Coll (FL)
Fox Valley Tech Coll (WI)
Gaston Coll (NC)
Gavilan Coll (CA)
Georgia Highlands Coll (GA)
Grand Rapids Comm Coll (MI)
Greenfield Comm Coll (MA)
Griffin Tech Coll (GA)
Gwinnett Tech Coll (GA)
Hamilton Coll, Cedar Falls (IA)
Heartland Comm Coll (IL)
Hickey Coll (MO)
Highline Comm Coll (WA)
Howard Coll (TX)
Illinois Valley Comm Coll (IL)
Indiana Business Coll, Indianapolis (IN)
International Business Coll, Indianapolis (IN)
ITT Tech Inst, Tucson (AZ)
ITT Tech Inst (AR)
ITT Tech Inst, Lathrop (CA)
ITT Tech Inst, Rancho Cordova (CA)
ITT Tech Inst, San Bernardino (CA)
ITT Tech Inst, San Diego (CA)
ITT Tech Inst, Sylmar (CA)
ITT Tech Inst (CO)
ITT Tech Inst, Fort Lauderdale (FL)
ITT Tech Inst, Jacksonville (FL)
ITT Tech Inst, Lake Mary (FL)
ITT Tech Inst, Miami (FL)
ITT Tech Inst, Tampa (FL)
ITT Tech Inst (ID)
ITT Tech Inst, Burr Ridge (IL)
ITT Tech Inst, Matteson (IL)
ITT Tech Inst, Mount Prospect (IL)
ITT Tech Inst, Fort Wayne (IN)
ITT Tech Inst, Indianapolis (IN)
ITT Tech Inst, Newburgh (IN)
ITT Tech Inst, Louisville (KY)
ITT Tech Inst (LA)
ITT Tech Inst (MD)
ITT Tech Inst, Norwood (MA)
ITT Tech Inst, Woburn (MA)
ITT Tech Inst, Canton (MI)
ITT Tech Inst, Grand Rapids (MI)
ITT Tech Inst, Troy (MI)
ITT Tech Inst (MN)
ITT Tech Inst, Arnold (MO)
ITT Tech Inst, Earth City (MO)
ITT Tech Inst (NE)
ITT Tech Inst (NV)
ITT Tech Inst (NM)
ITT Tech Inst, Albany (NY)
ITT Tech Inst, Getzville (NY)
ITT Tech Inst, Liverpool (NY)

ITT Tech Inst, Dayton (OH)
ITT Tech Inst, Norwood (OH)
ITT Tech Inst, Strongsville (OH)
ITT Tech Inst, Youngstown (OH)
ITT Tech Inst (OR)
ITT Tech Inst (SC)
ITT Tech Inst, Knoxville (TN)
ITT Tech Inst, Memphis (TN)
ITT Tech Inst, Nashville (TN)
ITT Tech Inst, Arlington (TX)
ITT Tech Inst, Austin (TX)
ITT Tech Inst, Houston (TX)
ITT Tech Inst, Houston (TX)
ITT Tech Inst, Houston (TX)
ITT Tech Inst, Richardson (TX)
ITT Tech Inst, San Antonio (TX)
ITT Tech Inst (UT)
ITT Tech Inst, Chantilly (VA)
ITT Tech Inst, Norfolk (VA)
ITT Tech Inst, Richmond (VA)
ITT Tech Inst, Springfield (VA)
ITT Tech Inst, Bothell (WA)
ITT Tech Inst, Seattle (WA)
ITT Tech Inst, Spokane (WA)
ITT Tech Inst, Green Bay (WI)
ITT Tech Inst, Greenfield (WI)
Johnston Comm Coll (NC)
Joliet Jr Coll (IL)
Kellogg Comm Coll (MI)
Keystone Coll (PA)
Lake City Comm Coll (FL)
Lakeshore Tech Coll (WI)
Lanier Tech Coll (GA)
Lansing Comm Coll (MI)
Laramie County Comm Coll (WY)
Laredo Comm Coll (TX)
Lehigh Valley Coll (PA)
Lincoln Coll (IL)
Lincoln Coll–Normal (IL)
Linn State Tech Coll (MO)
Long Beach City Coll (CA)
Longview Comm Coll (MO)
Lord Fairfax Comm Coll (VA)
Lower Columbia Coll (WA)
Macomb Comm Coll (MI)
Manatee Comm Coll (FL)
Maple Woods Comm Coll (MO)
Metropolitan Comm Coll (NE)
Metropolitan Comm Coll–Business & Technology College (MO)
Miami Dade Coll (FL)
Middlesex Comm Coll (CT)
Middlesex County Coll (NJ)
Minneapolis Business Coll (MN)
Minnesota State Comm and Tech Coll–Fergus Falls (MN)
Mohawk Valley Comm Coll (NY)
Montgomery Coll (TX)
Montgomery County Comm Coll (PA)
Mountain View Coll (TX)
Naugatuck Valley Comm Coll (CT)
New Mexico Military Inst (NM)
Newport Business Inst, Lower Burrell (PA)
Northampton County Area Comm Coll (PA)
Northeast Comm Coll (NE)
Northeast State Tech Comm Coll (TN)
Northern Essex Comm Coll (MA)
Northern Maine Comm Coll (ME)
North Idaho Coll (ID)
North Shore Comm Coll (MA)
Northwestern Connecticut Comm Coll (CT)
Northwest-Shoals Comm Coll (AL)
Northwest Vista Coll (TX)
Oakland Comm Coll (MI)
Ocean County Coll (NJ)

Ohio Business Coll, Sandusky (OH)
Okaloosa-Walton Coll (FL)
Orange Coast Coll (CA)
Orange County Comm Coll (NY)
Palm Beach Comm Coll (FL)
Parkland Coll (IL)
Pasadena City Coll (CA)
Pellissippi State Tech Comm Coll (TN)
Piedmont Virginia Comm Coll (VA)
Quinsigamond Comm Coll (MA)
Raritan Valley Comm Coll (NJ)
Remington Coll–Lafayette Campus (LA)
Riverside Comm Coll District (CA)
Saddleback Coll (CA)
St. Cloud Tech Coll (MN)
St. Louis Comm Coll at Florissant Valley (MO)
Saint Paul Coll–A Comm & Tech College (MN)
San Joaquin Delta Coll (CA)
Seminole Comm Coll (FL)
Skyline Coll (CA)
Southeast Tech Inst (SD)
South Plains Coll (TX)
Southwestern Michigan Coll (MI)
Spokane Comm Coll (WA)
Stark State Coll of Technology (OH)
Tarrant County Coll District (TX)
Texas State Tech Coll Waco (TX)
Tidewater Comm Coll (VA)
Tomball Coll (TX)
U of Northwestern Ohio (OH)
Valdosta Tech Coll (GA)
Valencia Comm Coll (FL)
Vatterott Coll, Tulsa (OK)
Waukesha County Tech Coll (WI)
Weatherford Coll (TX)
Western Tech Coll (WI)
West Virginia Northern Comm Coll (WV)
William Rainey Harper Coll (IL)
Wilson Tech Comm Coll (NC)

Computer Programming Related
Arapahoe Comm Coll (CO)
Austin Comm Coll (TX)
Berks Tech Inst (PA)
Brazosport Coll (TX)
Brown Mackie Coll–Kansas City (KS)
Bucks County Comm Coll (PA)
Centralia Coll (WA)
Clark State Comm Coll (OH)
Coastal Bend Coll (TX)
The Coll of Westchester (NY)
Corning Comm Coll (NY)
Eastfield Coll (TX)
Erie Business Center, Main (PA)
Fiorello H. LaGuardia Comm Coll of the City U of New York (NY)
Florida Comm Coll at Jacksonville (FL)
Florida National Coll (FL)
Kennebec Valley Comm Coll (ME)
Lakeshore Tech Coll (WI)
Laredo Comm Coll (TX)
Luzerne County Comm Coll (PA)
Manatee Comm Coll (FL)
Mesabi Range Comm and Tech Coll (MN)
Metropolitan Comm Coll–Business & Technology College (MO)
Mississippi Gulf Coast Comm Coll (MS)
Northeast State Tech Comm Coll (TN)
Northern Essex Comm Coll (MA)
Norwalk Comm Coll (CT)

Pasco-Hernando Comm Coll (FL)
Remington Coll–Lafayette Campus (LA)
Riverside Comm Coll District (CA)
Saint Charles Comm Coll (MO)
St. Cloud Tech Coll (MN)
San Diego Mesa Coll (CA)
Seminole Comm Coll (FL)
Sinclair Comm Coll (OH)
Southeast Tech Inst (SD)
Southwest Mississippi Comm Coll (MS)
Stark State Coll of Technology (OH)
Tompkins Cortland Comm Coll (NY)
Triton Coll (IL)
Tulsa Comm Coll (OK)
Valencia Comm Coll (FL)

Computer Programming (Specific Applications)
Alexandria Tech Coll (MN)
Arapahoe Comm Coll (CO)
Bladen Comm Coll (NC)
Brazosport Coll (TX)
Brevard Comm Coll (FL)
Brown Mackie Coll–Hopkinsville (KY)
Brown Mackie Coll–Northern Kentucky (KY)
Bucks County Comm Coll (PA)
Bunker Hill Comm Coll (MA)
Caldwell Comm Coll and Tech Inst (NC)
Cedar Valley Coll (TX)
Central Comm Coll–Columbus Campus (NE)
Central Comm Coll–Grand Island Campus (NE)
Central Comm Coll–Hastings Campus (NE)
Central Piedmont Comm Coll (NC)
Cincinnati State Tech and Comm Coll (OH)
Cleveland Comm Coll (NC)
Coastal Bend Coll (TX)
Coastal Carolina Comm Coll (NC)
Coll of DuPage (IL)
Coll of The Albemarle (NC)
The Coll of Westchester (NY)
Edmonds Comm Coll (WA)
Essex County Coll (NJ)
Fiorello H. LaGuardia Comm Coll of the City U of New York (NY)
Florida Comm Coll at Jacksonville (FL)
Florida National Coll (FL)
GateWay Comm Coll (AZ)
Heartland Comm Coll (IL)
Highland Comm Coll (IL)
Horry-Georgetown Tech Coll (SC)
Hudson Valley Comm Coll (NY)
Indiana Business Coll, Indianapolis (IN)
Indiana Business Coll, Muncie (IN)
ITT Tech Inst, Albany (NY)
John Wood Comm Coll (IL)
Joliet Jr Coll (IL)
Kaskaskia Coll (IL)
Kellogg Comm Coll (MI)
Lake City Comm Coll (FL)
Lake Land Coll (IL)
Lake Region State Coll (ND)
Lake Superior Coll (MN)
Lincoln Land Comm Coll (IL)
Linn-Benton Comm Coll (OR)
Louisiana Tech Coll (LA)
Macomb Comm Coll (MI)
Mesabi Range Comm and Tech Coll (MN)
Metropolitan Comm Coll–Business & Technology College (MO)
Midland Coll (TX)
Missouri State U–West Plains (MO)
Moraine Park Tech Coll (WI)

Moraine Valley Comm Coll (IL)
Naugatuck Valley Comm Coll (CT)
New Hampshire Tech Inst (NH)
North Dakota State Coll of Science (ND)
Northeast Comm Coll (NE)
Northern Essex Comm Coll (MA)
North Shore Comm Coll (MA)
Okaloosa-Walton Coll (FL)
Orange Coast Coll (CA)
Palm Beach Comm Coll (FL)
Parkland Coll (IL)
Pasco-Hernando Comm Coll (FL)
Piedmont Virginia Comm Coll (VA)
Richland Comm Coll (IL)
Riverland Comm Coll (MN)
Saint Charles Comm Coll (MO)
St. Cloud Tech Coll (MN)
San Diego Mesa Coll (CA)
Seminole Comm Coll (FL)
Sheridan Coll–Sheridan and Gillette (WY)
Sinclair Comm Coll (OH)
Southeast Tech Inst (SD)
Southern State Comm Coll (OH)
Southern West Virginia Comm and Tech Coll (WV)
South Hills School of Business & Technology, State College (PA)
Stark State Coll of Technology (OH)
Sullivan County Comm Coll (NY)
Trident Tech Coll (SC)
Tulsa Comm Coll (OK)
Valencia Comm Coll (FL)
Waubonsee Comm Coll (IL)
West Central Tech Coll (GA)
Western Iowa Tech Comm Coll (IA)
Wilkes Comm Coll (NC)
Wisconsin Indianhead Tech Coll (WI)

Computer Programming (Vendor/Product Certification)
Arkansas State U–Beebe (AR)
Coastal Bend Coll (TX)
The Coll of Westchester (NY)
Edmonds Comm Coll (WA)
Fiorello H. LaGuardia Comm Coll of the City U of New York (NY)
Florida Comm Coll at Jacksonville (FL)
GateWay Comm Coll (AZ)
Guam Comm Coll (GU)
Heald Coll–Hayward (CA)
Heartland Comm Coll (IL)
Lake City Comm Coll (FL)
Lake Region State Coll (ND)
Metropolitan Comm Coll–Business & Technology College (MO)
Parkland Coll (IL)
Peninsula Coll (WA)
Riverland Comm Coll (MN)
Seminole Comm Coll (FL)
Sinclair Comm Coll (OH)
Southeast Tech Inst (SD)
Stark State Coll of Technology (OH)
Tulsa Comm Coll (OK)

Computer Science
Abraham Baldwin Ag Coll (GA)
Allan Hancock Coll (CA)
Allen County Comm Coll (KS)
Arapahoe Comm Coll (CO)
Arizona Western Coll (AZ)
Atlanta Metropolitan Coll (GA)
Austin Comm Coll (TX)
Barton County Comm Coll (KS)
Benjamin Franklin Inst of Technology (MA)

Bergen Comm Coll (NJ)
Blue River Comm Coll (MO)
Bristol Comm Coll (MA)
Bronx Comm Coll of the City U of New York (NY)
Broward Comm Coll (FL)
Brown Mackie Coll–Cincinnati (OH)
Bucks County Comm Coll (PA)
Bunker Hill Comm Coll (MA)
Butler Comm Coll (KS)
Carl Albert State Coll (OK)
Casper Coll (WY)
Central Arizona Coll (AZ)
Central Oregon Comm Coll (OR)
Central Piedmont Comm Coll (NC)
Central Wyoming Coll (WY)
Chattanooga State Tech Comm Coll (TN)
Chemeketa Comm Coll (OR)
Citrus Coll (CA)
Coahoma Comm Coll (MS)
Coastal Bend Coll (TX)
Coastal Georgia Comm Coll (GA)
Cochise Coll, Douglas (AZ)
Colby Comm Coll (KS)
Coll of the Canyons (CA)
Coll of the Siskiyous (CA)
Columbia Coll (CA)
Commonwealth Tech Inst (PA)
Corning Comm Coll (NY)
Delta Coll (MI)
Diné Coll (AZ)
Dixie State Coll of Utah (UT)
ECPI Coll of Technology, Newport News (VA)
ECPI Coll of Technology, Virginia Beach (VA)
ECPI Tech Coll (VA)
ECPI Tech Coll (NC)
ECPI Tech Coll, Richmond (VA)
El Centro Coll (TX)
Erie Business Center, Main (PA)
Essex County Coll (NJ)
Finger Lakes Comm Coll (NY)
Fiorello H. LaGuardia Comm Coll of the City U of New York (NY)
Florida National Coll (FL)
Florida Tech Coll, DeLand (FL)
Forsyth Tech Comm Coll (NC)
Frederick Comm Coll (MD)
Gainesville Coll (GA)
Gallipolis Career Coll (OH)
Galveston Coll (TX)
Gavilan Coll (CA)
George C. Wallace Comm Coll (AL)
Grand Rapids Comm Coll (MI)
Guam Comm Coll (GU)
Gwinnett Tech Coll (GA)
Heald Coll–Hayward (CA)
Heald Coll-San Jose (CA)
Heartland Comm Coll (IL)
Highland Comm Coll (IL)
Houston Comm Coll System (TX)
Howard Coll (TX)
Howard Comm Coll (MD)
Jackson State Comm Coll (TN)
Jamestown Comm Coll (NY)
Jefferson Comm Coll (NY)
Kilian Comm Coll (SD)
Kingsborough Comm Coll of the City U of New York (NY)
Lake Region State Coll (ND)
Lake-Sumter Comm Coll (FL)
Lamar State Coll–Orange (TX)
Lanier Tech Coll (GA)
Laramie County Comm Coll (WY)
Lincoln Coll (IL)
Lincoln Coll–Normal (IL)
Longview Comm Coll (MO)
Lower Columbia Coll (WA)

Luzerne County Comm Coll (PA)
Manor Coll (PA)
Maple Woods Comm Coll (MO)
Massachusetts Bay Comm Coll (MA)
Mercer County Comm Coll (NJ)
Metropolitan Comm Coll–Business & Technology College (MO)
Miami Dade Coll (FL)
Middle Georgia Coll (GA)
Middlesex County Coll (NJ)
Mississippi Gulf Coast Comm Coll (MS)
Modesto Jr Coll (CA)
Mt. San Antonio Coll (CA)
Nassau Comm Coll (NY)
New England Coll of Finance (MA)
New Hampshire Comm Tech Coll, Nashua/Claremont (NH)
New Mexico Military Inst (NM)
Niagara County Comm Coll (NY)
Normandale Comm Coll (MN)
Northampton County Area Comm Coll (PA)
Northeast Comm Coll (NE)
Northern Essex Comm Coll (MA)
North Hennepin Comm Coll (MN)
North Idaho Coll (ID)
Northland Comm and Tech Coll–Thief River Falls (MN)
North Shore Comm Coll (MA)
Northwestern Connecticut Comm Coll (CT)
Northwest-Shoals Comm Coll (AL)
Northwest Vista Coll (TX)
Okaloosa-Walton Coll (FL)
Orange County Comm Coll (NY)
Palm Beach Comm Coll (FL)
Palo Alto Coll (TX)
Parkland Coll (IL)
Pasadena City Coll (CA)
Pellissippi State Tech Comm Coll (TN)
Penn Foster Career School (PA)
Penn Valley Comm Coll (MO)
Piedmont Virginia Comm Coll (VA)
Raritan Valley Comm Coll (NJ)
Roane State Comm Coll (TN)
Rock Valley Coll (IL)
Rogue Comm Coll (OR)
Saddleback Coll (CA)
Saint Charles Comm Coll (MO)
St. Louis Comm Coll at Florissant Valley (MO)
Salt Lake Comm Coll (UT)
San Diego Mesa Coll (CA)
San Joaquin Delta Coll (CA)
San Juan Coll (NM)
Santa Barbara City Coll (CA)
Santa Rosa Jr Coll (CA)
Seminole State Coll (OK)
Skyline Coll (CA)
Snow Coll (UT)
South Plains Coll (TX)
South Texas Coll (TX)
Southwestern Oklahoma State U at Sayre (OK)
Southwest Mississippi Comm Coll (MS)
Springfield Coll in Illinois (IL)
Springfield Tech Comm Coll (MA)
State U of New York Coll of Technology at Alfred (NY)
Tarrant County Coll District (TX)
Texas State Tech Coll Waco (TX)
Thomas Nelson Comm Coll (VA)

Tompkins Cortland Comm Coll (NY)
Treasure Valley Comm Coll (OR)
Trinidad State Jr Coll (CO)
Trinity Valley Comm Coll (TX)
Triton Coll (IL)
Tulsa Comm Coll (OK)
The U of Akron–Wayne Coll (OH)
Vermilion Comm Coll (MN)
Westchester Comm Coll (NY)
Westmoreland County Comm Coll (PA)
Wharton County Jr Coll (TX)
William Rainey Harper Coll (IL)
Yakima Valley Comm Coll (WA)
Young Harris Coll (GA)
Yuba Coll (CA)

Computer Software and Media Applications Related
Ancilla Coll (IN)
Arapahoe Comm Coll (CO)
Berkeley City Coll (CA)
Brevard Comm Coll (FL)
Carteret Comm Coll (NC)
The Coll of Westchester (NY)
Florida Comm Coll at Jacksonville (FL)
Gallipolis Career Coll (OH)
Genesee Comm Coll (NY)
Kellogg Comm Coll (MI)
Kennebec Valley Comm Coll (ME)
Kilian Comm Coll (SD)
Laredo Comm Coll (TX)
Laurel Business Inst (PA)
Mesabi Range Comm and Tech Coll (MN)
Metropolitan Comm Coll–Business & Technology College (MO)
Northland Comm and Tech Coll–Thief River Falls (MN)
Parkland Coll (IL)
Pellissippi State Tech Comm Coll (TN)
Platt Coll San Diego (CA)
Rasmussen Coll Mankato (MN)
Riverland Comm Coll (MN)
San Diego Mesa Coll (CA)
Seminole Comm Coll (FL)
Sheridan Coll–Sheridan and Gillette (WY)
Southeast Tech Inst (SD)
Stark State Coll of Technology (OH)
Triton Coll (IL)
Tulsa Comm Coll (OK)

Computer Software Engineering
Florida Comm Coll at Jacksonville (FL)
Lake City Comm Coll (FL)
Seminole Comm Coll (FL)
Sinclair Comm Coll (OH)
Southeast Tech Inst (SD)
Stark State Coll of Technology (OH)
Tompkins Cortland Comm Coll (NY)
Tulsa Comm Coll (OK)

Computer Software Technology
Brown Coll (MN)
Brown Mackie Coll–Akron (OH)
Brown Mackie Coll–Atlanta (GA)
Brown Mackie Coll–Findlay (OH)
Brown Mackie Coll–Fort Wayne (IN)
Brown Mackie Coll–Hopkinsville (KY)
Brown Mackie Coll–Merrillville (IN)
Brown Mackie Coll–Miami (FL)
Brown Mackie Coll–Michigan City (IN)
Brown Mackie Coll–Northern Kentucky (KY)

ITT Tech Inst, Lathrop (CA)
Miami Dade Coll (FL)
Montgomery Coll (TX)

Computer Systems Analysis
Brevard Comm Coll (FL)
Cape Fear Comm Coll (NC)
Central New Mexico Comm Coll (NM)
Coastal Carolina Comm Coll (NC)
Florida Comm Coll at Jacksonville (FL)
Heald Coll–Stockton (CA)
James Sprunt Comm Coll (NC)
Lakeshore Tech Coll (WI)
Laramie County Comm Coll (WY)
Linn State Tech Coll (MO)
Louisiana Tech Coll (LA)
Lower Columbia Coll (WA)
Metropolitan Comm Coll–Business & Technology College (MO)
Pima Comm Coll (AZ)
Remington Coll–Lafayette Campus (LA)
Richmond Comm Coll (NC)
Southwestern Oregon Comm Coll (OR)
United Tribes Tech Coll (ND)
Waukesha County Tech Coll (WI)
Wilkes Comm Coll (NC)
Wor-Wic Comm Coll (MD)

Computer Systems Networking and Telecommunications
Aakers Business Coll (ND)
Alexandria Tech Coll (MN)
Allen County Comm Coll (KS)
Altamaha Tech Coll (GA)
Ancilla Coll (IN)
Appalachian Tech Coll (GA)
Arapahoe Comm Coll (CO)
Arkansas State U–Beebe (AR)
Athens Tech Coll (GA)
Augusta Tech Coll (GA)
Austin Comm Coll (TX)
Barton County Comm Coll (KS)
Beaufort County Comm Coll (NC)
Blue Ridge Comm Coll (VA)
Brevard Comm Coll (FL)
Brown Coll (MN)
Brown Mackie Coll–Akron (OH)
Brown Mackie Coll–Louisville (KY)
Brown Mackie Coll–North Canton (OH)
Bunker Hill Comm Coll (MA)
Cape Fear Comm Coll (NC)
Carteret Comm Coll (NC)
Central Georgia Tech Coll (GA)
Centralia Coll (WA)
Central Wyoming Coll (WY)
Chattahoochee Tech Coll (GA)
Clark Coll (WA)
Clark State Comm Coll (OH)
Clatsop Comm Coll (OR)
Coastal Bend Coll (TX)
Coastal Carolina Comm Coll (NC)
Cochise Coll, Douglas (AZ)
Coll of the Mainland (TX)
The Coll of Westchester (NY)
Collin County Comm Coll District (TX)
Colorado Mountain Coll (CO)
Columbus Tech Coll (GA)
Comm Coll of Allegheny County (PA)
Corning Comm Coll (NY)
Crowder Coll (MO)
Davis Coll (OH)
DeKalb Tech Coll (GA)
East Central Coll (MO)
East Central Tech Coll (GA)
Eastern Idaho Tech Coll (ID)
Eastfield Coll (TX)
Edmonds Comm Coll (WA)
Erie Business Center, Main (PA)

Fiorello H. LaGuardia Comm Coll of the City U of New York (NY)
Flint River Tech Coll (GA)
Florida Comm Coll at Jacksonville (FL)
Florida National Coll (FL)
Glendale Comm Coll (AZ)
Globe Coll (MN)
Griffin Tech Coll (GA)
Gwinnett Tech Coll (GA)
Hamilton Coll, Cedar Falls (IA)
Harrisburg Area Comm Coll (PA)
Hawkeye Comm Coll (IA)
Heald Coll–San Francisco (CA)
Heartland Comm Coll (IL)
Hibbing Comm Coll (MN)
Highline Comm Coll (WA)
Howard Comm Coll (MD)
Illinois Valley Comm Coll (IL)
IntelliTec Coll, Grand Junction (CO)
Island Drafting and Tech Inst (NY)
Jefferson Comm Coll (NY)
Joliet Jr Coll (IL)
Keiser Coll, Miami (FL)
Kennebec Valley Comm Coll (ME)
Lake Land Coll (IL)
Lake Region State Coll (ND)
Lamar State Coll–Port Arthur (TX)
Lanier Tech Coll (GA)
Laredo Comm Coll (TX)
Laurel Business Inst (PA)
Lincoln Land Comm Coll (IL)
Louisiana Tech Coll (LA)
Lower Columbia Coll (WA)
Luzerne County Comm Coll (PA)
Manhattan Area Tech Coll (KS)
Mercer County Comm Coll (NJ)
Mesabi Range Comm and Tech Coll (MN)
Metropolitan Comm Coll–Business & Technology College (MO)
Middle Georgia Tech Coll (GA)
Middlesex County Coll (NJ)
Midlands Tech Coll (SC)
Minnesota School of Business–Brooklyn Center (MN)
Minnesota School of Business–Plymouth (MN)
Minnesota School of Business–Richfield (MN)
Minnesota School of Business–St. Cloud (MN)
Minnesota School of Business–Shakopee (MN)
Minnesota State Comm and Tech Coll–Fergus Falls (MN)
Mississippi Gulf Coast Comm Coll (MS)
Montgomery Coll (TX)
Montgomery County Comm Coll (PA)
Moraine Valley Comm Coll (IL)
Mott Comm Coll (MI)
Moultrie Tech Coll (GA)
Nassau Comm Coll (NY)
New Hampshire Tech Inst (NH)
Normandale Comm Coll (MN)
Northampton County Area Comm Coll (PA)
Northeast State Tech Comm Coll (TN)
Northern Essex Comm Coll (MA)
North Georgia Tech Coll (GA)
Northland Comm and Tech Coll–Thief River Falls (MN)
North Metro Tech Coll (GA)
North Seattle Comm Coll (WA)
Northwestern Tech Coll (GA)
Ogeechee Tech Coll (GA)

Okaloosa-Walton Coll (FL)
Okefenokee Tech Coll (GA)
Parkland Coll (IL)
Pasco-Hernando Comm Coll (FL)
Pellissippi State Tech Comm Coll (TN)
Piedmont Virginia Comm Coll (VA)
Pima Comm Coll (AZ)
Pratt Comm Coll (KS)
Quinebaug Valley Comm Coll (CT)
Rasmussen Coll Mankato (MN)
Remington Coll–Cleveland West Campus (OH)
Remington Coll–Lafayette Campus (LA)
Remington Coll–Mobile Campus (AL)
Riverland Comm Coll (MN)
Saint Charles Comm Coll (MO)
St. Cloud Tech Coll (MN)
St. Petersburg Coll (FL)
St. Philip's Coll (TX)
Salem Comm Coll (NJ)
Sandersville Tech Coll (GA)
San Joaquin Valley Coll (CA)
Savannah Tech Coll (GA)
Seminole Comm Coll (FL)
Sheridan Coll–Sheridan and Gillette (WY)
Sinclair Comm Coll (OH)
Southeastern Tech Coll (GA)
Southeast Tech Inst (SD)
South Georgia Tech Coll (GA)
Southwestern Oregon Comm Coll (OR)
Southwest Georgia Tech Coll (GA)
Stark State Coll of Technology (OH)
Swainsboro Tech Coll (GA)
TESST Coll of Technology, Towson (MD)
Trident Tech Coll (SC)
Trinidad State Jr Coll (CO)
Triton Coll (IL)
Tulsa Comm Coll (OK)
The U of Akron–Wayne Coll (OH)
Valdosta Tech Coll (GA)
Waukesha County Tech Coll (WI)
West Central Tech Coll (GA)
Westchester Comm Coll (NY)
West Georgia Tech Coll (GA)
Wilkes Comm Coll (NC)
Wisconsin Indianhead Tech Coll (WI)

Computer/Technical Support
Arapahoe Comm Coll (CO)
Brown Mackie Coll–Kansas City (KS)
Clark State Comm Coll (OH)
Coll of the Siskiyous (CA)
The Coll of Westchester (NY)
Colorado Mountain Coll (CO)
Florida Comm Coll at Jacksonville (FL)
Florida National Coll (FL)
Gallipolis Career Coll (OH)
Galveston Coll (TX)
Hawkeye Comm Coll (IA)
Heartland Comm Coll (IL)
Highland Comm Coll (IL)
Ilisagvik Coll (AK)
International Business Coll, Indianapolis (IN)
Island Drafting and Tech Inst (NY)
Joliet Jr Coll (IL)
Laurel Business Inst (PA)
Linn-Benton Comm Coll (OR)
Manor Coll (PA)
Moraine Park Tech Coll (WI)
North Idaho Coll (ID)
Northland Comm and Tech Coll–Thief River Falls (MN)
Northwest Indian Coll (WA)
Northwest Vista Coll (TX)
Palm Beach Comm Coll (FL)
Parkland Coll (IL)

Piedmont Virginia Comm Coll (VA)
Pratt Comm Coll (KS)
Rasmussen Coll Mankato (MN)
Remington Coll–Lafayette Campus (LA)
Riverland Comm Coll (MN)
St. Cloud Tech Coll (MN)
San Joaquin Valley Coll (CA)
Seminole Comm Coll (FL)
Southeast Tech Inst (SD)
Stark State Coll of Technology (OH)
Three Rivers Comm Coll (MO)
Tompkins Cortland Comm Coll (NY)
Triton Coll (IL)
Tulsa Comm Coll (OK)

Computer Technology/Computer Systems Technology
Alexandria Tech Coll (MN)
Arkansas State U–Beebe (AR)
Brazosport Coll (TX)
Cape Fear Comm Coll (NC)
Central Wyoming Coll (WY)
Comm Coll of Allegheny County (PA)
Corning Comm Coll (NY)
ECPI Tech Coll (VA)
ECPI Tech Coll (NC)
ECPI Tech Coll, Glen Allen (VA)
ECPI Tech Coll, Richmond (VA)
Edmonds Comm Coll (WA)
Erie Comm Coll, South Campus (NY)
Island Drafting and Tech Inst (NY)
ITI Tech Coll (LA)
Lake Superior Coll (MN)
Lower Columbia Coll (WA)
Luzerne County Comm Coll (PA)
Manhattan Area Tech Coll (KS)
Miami Dade Coll (FL)
Mount Wachusett Comm Coll (MA)
MTI Coll of Business and Technology (CA)
Oakland Comm Coll (MI)
Okefenokee Tech Coll (GA)
Pasco-Hernando Comm Coll (FL)
Pima Comm Coll (AZ)
Quinsigamond Comm Coll (MA)
Remington Coll–Tampa Campus (FL)
Southeast Tech Inst (SD)
Texas State Tech Coll Waco (TX)
Vatterott Coll (IA)

Computer Typography and Composition Equipment Operation
Abraham Baldwin Ag Coll (GA)
Bergen Comm Coll (NJ)
Brown Mackie Coll–Kansas City (KS)
Clovis Comm Coll (NM)
Coll of DuPage (IL)
The Coll of Westchester (NY)
Cuyahoga Comm Coll (OH)
ECPI Coll of Technology, Newport News (VA)
ECPI Coll of Technology, Virginia Beach (VA)
ECPI Tech Coll (VA)
ECPI Tech Coll, Richmond (VA)
Fox Valley Tech Coll (WI)
Gateway Comm Coll (CT)
Highline Comm Coll (WA)
Holyoke Comm Coll (MA)
Jefferson Comm Coll (NY)
Kingwood Coll (TX)
Lansing Comm Coll (MI)
Lincoln Coll (IL)
Lincoln Coll–Normal (IL)
Long Beach City Coll (CA)
Longview Comm Coll (MO)

Northern Essex Comm Coll (MA)
Northwest-Shoals Comm Coll (AL)
Orange Coast Coll (CA)
Pasadena City Coll (CA)
Pratt Comm Coll (KS)
Rasmussen Coll Mankato (MN)
Saddleback Coll (CA)
Seattle Central Comm Coll (WA)
South Texas Coll (TX)
Spokane Comm Coll (WA)
State U of New York Coll of Technology at Alfred (NY)
Triton Coll (IL)
Western Iowa Tech Comm Coll (IA)
William Rainey Harper Coll (IL)

Construction Engineering
State U of New York Coll of Technology at Alfred (NY)

Construction Engineering Technology
Austin Comm Coll (TX)
Brazosport Coll (TX)
Casper Coll (WY)
Cecil Comm Coll (MD)
Central Comm Coll–Hastings Campus (NE)
Chemeketa Comm Coll (OR)
Clark Coll (WA)
Coll of Eastern Utah (UT)
Coll of Lake County (IL)
Comm Coll of Allegheny County (PA)
Comm Coll of the Air Force (AL)
Crowder Coll (MO)
Delaware Tech & Comm Coll, Terry Campus (DE)
Delta Coll (MI)
East Central Coll (MO)
Edmonds Comm Coll (WA)
Feather River Coll (CA)
Florida Comm Coll at Jacksonville (FL)
Forsyth Tech Comm Coll (NC)
GateWay Comm Coll (AZ)
Harrisburg Area Comm Coll (PA)
H. Councill Trenholm State Tech Coll (AL)
Houston Comm Coll System (TX)
Hudson Valley Comm Coll (NY)
Jefferson State Comm Coll (AL)
Joliet Jr Coll (IL)
Lansing Comm Coll (MI)
Laramie County Comm Coll (WY)
Laredo Comm Coll (TX)
Macomb Comm Coll (MI)
Manatee Comm Coll (FL)
Metropolitan Comm Coll (NE)
Miami Dade Coll (FL)
Middlesex County Coll (NJ)
Midlands Tech Coll (SC)
Morrison Inst of Technology (IL)
New Hampshire Comm Tech Coll, Manchester/Stratham (NH)
North Central Missouri Coll (MO)
North Dakota State Coll of Science (ND)
Northeast Iowa Comm Coll (IA)
Northwest Indian Coll (WA)
Norwalk Comm Coll (CT)
Ocean County Coll (NJ)
The Ohio State U Ag Tech Inst (OH)
Okaloosa-Walton Coll (FL)
Orange Coast Coll (CA)
Orange County Comm Coll (NY)
Palau Comm Coll Palau)
Pasadena City Coll (CA)
Pellissippi State Tech Comm Coll (TN)
Phoenix Coll (AZ)

Pima Comm Coll (AZ)
Raritan Valley Comm Coll
  (NJ)
Richland Comm Coll (IL)
Riverside Comm Coll District
  (CA)
Rockingham Comm Coll
  (NC)
Rock Valley Coll (IL)
Saddleback Coll (CA)
St. Cloud Tech Coll (MN)
St. Louis Comm Coll at
  Florissant Valley (MO)
St. Petersburg Coll (FL)
St. Philip's Coll (TX)
San Diego Mesa Coll (CA)
San Joaquin Delta Coll (CA)
Seminole Comm Coll (FL)
Snow Coll (UT)
Southwestern Illinois Coll (IL)
Southwest Mississippi
  Comm Coll (MS)
Spokane Comm Coll (WA)
State U of New York Coll of
  Technology at Alfred (NY)
State U of New York Coll of
  Technology at Delhi (NY)
Tarrant County Coll District
  (TX)
Three Rivers Comm Coll
  (MO)
Tompkins Cortland Comm
  Coll (NY)
Trinidad State Jr Coll (CO)
Triton Coll (IL)
Tulsa Comm Coll (OK)
Valencia Comm Coll (FL)
Vance-Granville Comm Coll
  (NC)
Ventura Coll (CA)
The Williamson Free School
  of Mecha Trades (PA)
Yavapai Coll (AZ)

**Construction/Heavy
Equipment/Earthmoving
Equipment Operation**
Brazosport Coll (TX)
Ivy Tech Comm Coll–
  Southwest (IN)
Ivy Tech Comm Coll–
  Wabash Valley (IN)

Construction Management
Arapahoe Comm Coll (CO)
Broward Comm Coll (FL)
Delaware Tech & Comm
  Coll, Jack F. Owens
  Campus (DE)
Delaware Tech & Comm
  Coll, Terry Campus (DE)
Delgado Comm Coll (LA)
Delta Coll (MI)
Erie Comm Coll, North
  Campus (NY)
Frederick Comm Coll (MD)
Gwinnett Tech Coll (GA)
Modesto Jr Coll (CA)
Mt. San Antonio Coll (CA)
North Hennepin Comm Coll
  (MN)
Oakland Comm Coll (MI)
The Ohio State U Ag Tech
  Inst (OH)
Palm Beach Comm Coll (FL)
Parkland Coll (IL)
Rogue Comm Coll (OR)
St. Philip's Coll (TX)
Salt Lake Comm Coll (UT)
San Joaquin Valley Coll (CA)
Santa Rosa Jr Coll (CA)
Seminole Comm Coll (FL)
Snow Coll (UT)
Southwestern Illinois Coll (IL)
State U of New York Coll of
  Technology at Delhi (NY)
Triton Coll (IL)

Construction Trades
Coll of The Albemarle (NC)
Delta Coll (MI)
East Central Coll (MO)
Front Range Comm Coll
  (CO)
Ilisagvik Coll (AK)
Ivy Tech Comm Coll–East
  Central (IN)
Ivy Tech Comm Coll–
  Northeast (IN)
Ivy Tech Comm Coll–
  Northwest (IN)

Ivy Tech Comm Coll–
  Whitewater (IN)
Laramie County Comm Coll
  (WY)
Moraine Park Tech Coll (WI)
Ogeechee Tech Coll (GA)
Triangle Tech, Inc.–
  Greensburg School (PA)
United Tribes Tech Coll (ND)

Construction Trades Related
Central New Mexico Comm
  Coll (NM)
Comm Coll of Allegheny
  County (PA)
East Central Coll (MO)
Erie Comm Coll, North
  Campus (NY)
Ivy Tech Comm Coll–East
  Central (IN)
Ivy Tech Comm Coll–
  Kokomo (IN)
Ivy Tech Comm Coll–
  Northeast (IN)
Ivy Tech Comm Coll–
  Whitewater (IN)
Jackson Comm Coll (MI)
Laramie County Comm Coll
  (WY)
Palo Verde Coll (CA)

**Consumer/Homemaking
Education**
MiraCosta Coll (CA)

**Consumer Merchandising/
Retailing Management**
Arapahoe Comm Coll (CO)
Austin Comm Coll (TX)
Bay State Coll (MA)
Bergen Comm Coll (NJ)
Bucks County Comm Coll
  (PA)
Casper Coll (WY)
Centralia Coll (WA)
Central Piedmont Comm Coll
  (NC)
Chattanooga State Tech
  Comm Coll (TN)
Colorado Mountain Coll,
  Alpine Campus (CO)
Cowley County Comm Coll
  and Area Vocational–Tech
  School (KS)
Delaware Tech & Comm
  Coll, Jack F. Owens
  Campus (DE)
Delta Coll (MI)
FIDM/The Fashion Inst of
  Design & Merchandising,
  Los Angeles Campus (CA)
FIDM/The Fashion Inst of
  Design & Merchandising,
  San Diego Campus (CA)
FIDM/The Fashion Inst of
  Design & Merchandising,
  San Francisco Campus
  (CA)
Finger Lakes Comm Coll
  (NY)
Fox Valley Tech Coll (WI)
Gateway Comm Coll (CT)
Genesee Comm Coll (NY)
Glendale Comm Coll (AZ)
Harrisburg Area Comm Coll
  (PA)
Holyoke Comm Coll (MA)
Howard Comm Coll (MD)
Jefferson Comm Coll (NY)
Jefferson Comm Coll (OH)
Lansing Comm Coll (MI)
Laurel Business Inst (PA)
Long Beach City Coll (CA)
Middlesex County Coll (NJ)
Newport Business Inst,
  Lower Burrell (PA)
Niagara County Comm Coll
  (NY)
North Country Comm Coll
  (NY)
Northland Comm and Tech
  Coll–Thief River Falls (MN)
Oakland Comm Coll (MI)
Orange County Comm Coll
  (NY)
Parkland Coll (IL)
Quinsigamond Comm Coll
  (MA)
Raritan Valley Comm Coll
  (NJ)
Saddleback Coll (CA)

St. Cloud Tech Coll (MN)
Sinclair Comm Coll (OH)
South Plains Coll (TX)
Spokane Falls Comm Coll
  (WA)
Stark State Coll of
  Technology (OH)
Sullivan County Comm Coll
  (NY)
Sussex County Comm Coll
  (NJ)
Tarrant County Coll District
  (TX)
Triton Coll (IL)
Westchester Comm Coll
  (NY)
Western Tech Coll (WI)
Westmoreland County
  Comm Coll (PA)

**Consumer Services and
Advocacy**
Rockingham Comm Coll
  (NC)
Saddleback Coll (CA)
San Diego City Coll (CA)

Corrections
Brevard Comm Coll (FL)
Broome Comm Coll (NY)
Broward Comm Coll (FL)
Bucks County Comm Coll
  (PA)
Casper Coll (WY)
Central Arizona Coll (AZ)
Centralia Coll (WA)
Clark State Comm Coll (OH)
Clovis Comm Coll (NM)
Coll of DuPage (IL)
Colorado Mountain Coll,
  Timberline Campus (CO)
Comm Coll of Allegheny
  County (PA)
Cowley County Comm Coll
  and Area Vocational–Tech
  School (KS)
Delaware Tech & Comm
  Coll, Stanton/Wilmington
  Campus (DE)
Delaware Tech & Comm
  Coll, Terry Campus (DE)
Delta Coll (MI)
Eastern Arizona Coll (AZ)
Gavilan Coll (CA)
Grand Rapids Comm Coll
  (MI)
Guam Comm Coll (GU)
Hawkeye Comm Coll (IA)
Heartland Comm Coll (IL)
Illinois Eastern Comm Colls,
  Frontier Community
  College (IL)
Illinois Eastern Comm Colls,
  Lincoln Trail College (IL)
Illinois Eastern Comm Colls,
  Olney Central College (IL)
Illinois Eastern Comm Colls,
  Wabash Valley College (IL)
Jackson Comm Coll (MI)
Jefferson Comm Coll (OH)
Joliet Jr Coll (IL)
Kellogg Comm Coll (MI)
Lake Land Coll (IL)
Lansing Comm Coll (MI)
Laramie County Comm Coll
  (WY)
Lincoln Coll (IL)
Lincoln Coll–Normal (IL)
Longview Comm Coll (MO)
Lower Columbia Coll (WA)
Mercer County Comm Coll
  (NJ)
Middlesex County Coll (NJ)
Minnesota State Comm and
  Tech Coll–Fergus Falls
  (MN)
Modesto Jr Coll (CA)
Moraine Valley Comm Coll
  (IL)
Mt. San Antonio Coll (CA)
Northeast Comm Coll (NE)
Penn Valley Comm Coll
  (MO)
Phoenix Coll (AZ)
Polk Comm Coll (FL)
Riverland Comm Coll (MN)
Roane State Comm Coll
  (TN)
St. Louis Comm Coll at
  Florissant Valley (MO)
St. Petersburg Coll (FL)

San Joaquin Delta Coll (CA)
San Joaquin Valley Coll (CA)
Sauk Valley Comm Coll (IL)
Sinclair Comm Coll (OH)
Southern State Comm Coll
  (OH)
Southwestern Oklahoma
  State U at Sayre (OK)
Southwestern Oregon Comm
  Coll (OR)
Spokane Comm Coll (WA)
Sullivan County Comm Coll
  (NY)
Trinidad State Jr Coll (CO)
Trinity Valley Comm Coll
  (TX)
Tulsa Comm Coll (OK)
Tunxis Comm Coll (CT)
Vance-Granville Comm Coll
  (NC)
Weatherford Coll (TX)
Westchester Comm Coll
  (NY)
Yuba Coll (CA)

Corrections Administration
St. Petersburg Coll (FL)

**Corrections and Criminal
Justice Related**
Albany Tech Coll (GA)
Brazosport Coll (TX)
Corning Comm Coll (NY)
Fayetteville Tech Comm Coll
  (NC)
Moraine Park Tech Coll (WI)
Oakland Comm Coll (MI)
Wisconsin Indianhead Tech
  Coll (WI)

Cosmetology
Allan Hancock Coll (CA)
Bladen Comm Coll (NC)
Caldwell Comm Coll and
  Tech Inst (NC)
Central New Mexico Comm
  Coll (NM)
Century Coll (MN)
Citrus Coll (CA)
Clovis Comm Coll (NM)
Coahoma Comm Coll (MS)
Coastal Bend Coll (TX)
Coll of Eastern Utah (UT)
Copiah-Lincoln Comm Coll
  (MS)
Cowley County Comm Coll
  and Area Vocational–Tech
  School (KS)
Delta Coll (MI)
Eastern Wyoming Coll (WY)
Gavilan Coll (CA)
H. Councill Trenholm State
  Tech Coll (AL)
Howard Coll (TX)
Independence Comm Coll
  (KS)
James Sprunt Comm Coll
  (NC)
Lamar State Coll–Port Arthur
  (TX)
Lawson State Comm Coll
  (AL)
Lincoln Coll (IL)
Minnesota State Comm and
  Tech Coll–Fergus Falls
  (MN)
MiraCosta Coll (CA)
Northland Comm and Tech
  Coll–Thief River Falls (MN)
Oakland Comm Coll (MI)
Pasadena City Coll (CA)
Riverside Comm Coll District
  (CA)
Rockingham Comm Coll
  (NC)
Saddleback Coll (CA)
Salt Lake Comm Coll (UT)
San Diego City Coll (CA)
Santa Barbara City Coll (CA)
Seattle Central Comm Coll
  (WA)
Skyline Coll (CA)
Southeastern Comm Coll
  (NC)
South Plains Coll (TX)
Southwest Mississippi
  Comm Coll (MS)
Spokane Comm Coll (WA)
Springfield Tech Comm Coll
  (MA)
Trinidad State Jr Coll (CO)

Trinity Valley Comm Coll
  (TX)
Vance-Granville Comm Coll
  (NC)
Weatherford Coll (TX)
Yuba Coll (CA)

**Cosmetology and Personal
Grooming Arts Related**
Allegany Coll of Maryland
  (MD)
Comm Coll of Allegheny
  County (PA)

**Cosmetology, Barber/
Styling, and Nail Instruction**
Moraine Park Tech Coll (WI)

Counseling Psychology
Kilian Comm Coll (SD)

**Counselor Education/
School Counseling and
Guidance**
Pratt Comm Coll (KS)

Court Reporting
Central New Mexico Comm
  Coll (NM)
Clark State Comm Coll (OH)
Comm Coll of Allegheny
  County (PA)
Cuyahoga Comm Coll (OH)
Gadsden State Comm Coll
  (AL)
GateWay Comm Coll (AZ)
Houston Comm Coll System
  (TX)
Illinois Central Coll (IL)
Illinois Eastern Comm Colls,
  Wabash Valley College (IL)
Lakeshore Tech Coll (WI)
Lansing Comm Coll (MI)
Long Island Business Inst
  (NY)
Luzerne County Comm Coll
  (PA)
Miami Dade Coll (FL)
Midlands Tech Coll (SC)
Mississippi Gulf Coast
  Comm Coll (MS)
Oakland Comm Coll (MI)
Prince Inst of Professional
  Studies (AL)
Rasmussen Coll Eden Prarie
  (MN)
San Diego City Coll (CA)
Southwest Florida Coll, Fort
  Myers (FL)
Southwest Tennessee
  Comm Coll (TN)
Stark State Coll of
  Technology (OH)
State U of New York Coll of
  Technology at Alfred (NY)
Triton Coll (IL)
Wisconsin Indianhead Tech
  Coll (WI)

**Crafts, Folk Art and
Artisanry**
Coll of The Albemarle (NC)
Lawson State Comm Coll
  (AL)

Creative Writing
Berkeley City Coll (CA)
Foothill Coll (CA)
Lincoln Coll (IL)
Tulsa Comm Coll (OK)

**Criminalistics and Criminal
Science**
St. Petersburg Coll (FL)

**Criminal Justice/Law
Enforcement Administration**
Aakers Business Coll (ND)
Abraham Baldwin Ag Coll
  (GA)
Allen County Comm Coll
  (KS)
Ancilla Coll (IN)
Arapahoe Comm Coll (CO)
Argosy U/Denver (CO)
Argosy U/Orange County
  (CA)
Argosy U/San Diego (CA)
Arizona Western Coll (AZ)
Arkansas State U–Mountain
  Home (AR)
Athens Tech Coll (GA)
Atlanta Metropolitan Coll
  (GA)

Austin Comm Coll (TX)
Bainbridge Coll (GA)
Bay State Coll (MA)
Beal Coll (ME)
Bergen Comm Coll (NJ)
Brevard Comm Coll (FL)
Briarwood Coll (CT)
Broward Comm Coll (FL)
Brown Coll (MN)
Brown Mackie Coll–Northern
  Kentucky (KY)
Brown Mackie Coll–Salina
  (KS)
Bryant and Stratton Coll,
  Albany (NY)
Bryant and Stratton Coll,
  Rochester (NY)
Bryant and Stratton Coll,
  Parma (OH)
Bryant and Stratton Coll (WI)
Bryant and Stratton Coll,
  Buffalo Campus (NY)
Bryant and Stratton Coll,
  Lackawanna Campus (NY)
Bryant and Stratton Coll,
  Richmond (VA)
Bucks County Comm Coll
  (PA)
Bunker Hill Comm Coll (MA)
Carteret Comm Coll (NC)
Casper Coll (WY)
Cecil Comm Coll (MD)
Cedar Valley Coll (TX)
Central Arizona Coll (AZ)
Centralia Coll (WA)
Central Oregon Comm Coll
  (OR)
Central Piedmont Comm Coll
  (NC)
Central Wyoming Coll (WY)
Chattahoochee Valley Comm
  Coll (AL)
Chattanooga State Tech
  Comm Coll (TN)
Chemeketa Comm Coll (OR)
Citrus Coll (CA)
Clark State Comm Coll (OH)
Clatsop Comm Coll (OR)
Cleveland Comm Coll (NC)
Coahoma Comm Coll (MS)
Coastal Bend Coll (TX)
Coastal Carolina Comm Coll
  (NC)
Coastal Georgia Comm Coll
  (GA)
Colby Comm Coll (KS)
Coll of DuPage (IL)
Coll of The Albemarle (NC)
Coll of the Canyons (CA)
Coll of the Mainland (TX)
Coll of the Siskiyous (CA)
Colorado Mountain Coll (CO)
Colorado Mountain Coll,
  Timberline Campus (CO)
Comm Coll of the Air Force
  (AL)
Corning Comm Coll (NY)
Cowley County Comm Coll
  and Area Vocational–Tech
  School (KS)
Dabney S. Lancaster Comm
  Coll (VA)
Dean Coll (MA)
Delaware Tech & Comm
  Coll, Jack F. Owens
  Campus (DE)
Delaware Tech & Comm
  Coll, Stanton/Wilmington
  Campus (DE)
Delaware Tech & Comm
  Coll, Terry Campus (DE)
Delta Coll (MI)
Denmark Tech Coll (SC)
East Arkansas Comm Coll
  (AR)
East Central Coll (MO)
Eastern Arizona Coll (AZ)
ECPI Tech Coll (NC)
Erie Comm Coll (NY)
Erie Comm Coll, North
  Campus (NY)
Essex County Coll (NJ)
Evergreen Valley Coll (CA)
Feather River Coll (CA)
Finger Lakes Comm Coll
  (NY)
Florida Comm Coll at
  Jacksonville (FL)
Forsyth Tech Comm Coll
  (NC)

Fox Valley Tech Coll (WI)
Frederick Comm Coll (MD)
Gainesville Coll (GA)
Gaston Coll (NC)
Gavilan Coll (CA)
Genesee Comm Coll (NY)
Glendale Comm Coll (AZ)
Grand Rapids Comm Coll (MI)
Greenfield Comm Coll (MA)
Guam Comm Coll (GU)
Hagerstown Business Coll (MD)
Hamilton Coll, Cedar Rapids (IA)
Harrisburg Area Comm Coll (PA)
Hawkeye Comm Coll (IA)
Highline Comm Coll (WA)
Horry-Georgetown Tech Coll (SC)
Howard Comm Coll (MD)
Hudson Valley Comm Coll (NY)
Illinois Valley Comm Coll (IL)
International Inst of the Americas, Mesa (AZ)
International Inst of the Americas, Phoenix (AZ)
International Inst of the Americas, Tucson (AZ)
International Inst of the Americas (NM)
ITT Tech Inst, Fort Lauderdale (FL)
ITT Tech Inst, Jacksonville (FL)
ITT Tech Inst, Lake Mary (FL)
ITT Tech Inst, Tampa (FL)
ITT Tech Inst, Canton (MI)
ITT Tech Inst, Grand Rapids (MI)
ITT Tech Inst, Troy (MI)
ITT Tech Inst (NE)
ITT Tech Inst, Dayton (OH)
ITT Tech Inst, Hilliard (OH)
ITT Tech Inst, Norwood (OH)
ITT Tech Inst, Strongsville (OH)
ITT Tech Inst, Warrensville Heights (OH)
Jackson Comm Coll (MI)
James H. Faulkner State Comm Coll (AL)
Jefferson Comm Coll (NY)
Joliet Jr Coll (IL)
Keiser Coll, Miami (FL)
Kent State U, Trumbull Campus (OH)
Kilian Comm Coll (SD)
Lake City Comm Coll (FL)
Lake-Sumter Comm Coll (FL)
Lansing Comm Coll (MI)
Laramie County Comm Coll (WY)
Lawson State Comm Coll (AL)
Lehigh Valley Coll (PA)
Lincoln Coll (IL)
Long Beach City Coll (CA)
Longview Comm Coll (MO)
Lower Columbia Coll (WA)
Luzerne County Comm Coll (PA)
Macomb Comm Coll (MI)
Manchester Comm Coll (CT)
Maple Woods Comm Coll (MO)
Massachusetts Bay Comm Coll (MA)
Miami Dade Coll (FL)
Middlesex County Coll (NJ)
MiraCosta Coll (CA)
Mississippi Gulf Coast Comm Coll (MS)
Missouri State U–West Plains (MO)
Modesto Jr Coll (CA)
Mohawk Valley Comm Coll (NY)
Montgomery Coll (TX)
Mountain View Coll (TX)
Mount Wachusett Comm Coll (MA)
Nassau Comm Coll (NY)
Naugatuck Valley Comm Coll (CT)

New Hampshire Tech Inst (NH)
New Mexico Military Inst (NM)
Niagara County Comm Coll (NY)
North Arkansas Coll (AR)
North Central Missouri Coll (MO)
Northeast Comm Coll (NE)
Northern Essex Comm Coll (MA)
North Hennepin Comm Coll (MN)
North Idaho Coll (ID)
Northland Comm and Tech Coll–Thief River Falls (MN)
North Shore Comm Coll (MA)
Northwestern Connecticut Comm Coll (CT)
Northwest-Shoals Comm Coll (AL)
Norwalk Comm Coll (CT)
Oakland Comm Coll (MI)
Ohio Inst of Photography and Technology (OH)
Okaloosa-Walton Coll (FL)
Orange County Comm Coll (NY)
Owens Comm Coll, Toledo (OH)
Palm Beach Comm Coll (FL)
Palo Verde Coll (CA)
The Paralegal Inst, Inc. (AZ)
Pasadena City Coll (CA)
Pasco-Hernando Comm Coll (FL)
Peninsula Coll (WA)
Penn Valley Comm Coll (MO)
Polk Comm Coll (FL)
Prairie State Coll (IL)
Quinsigamond Comm Coll (MA)
Raritan Valley Comm Coll (NJ)
Remington Coll–Cleveland West Campus (OH)
Richmond Comm Coll (NC)
Riverside Comm Coll District (CA)
Roane State Comm Coll (TN)
Rockingham Comm Coll (NC)
Rock Valley Coll (IL)
Rogue Comm Coll (OR)
Saint Charles Comm Coll (MO)
St. Louis Comm Coll at Florissant Valley (MO)
St. Petersburg Coll (FL)
St. Philip's Coll (TX)
Salem Comm Coll (NJ)
Salt Lake Comm Coll (UT)
Santa Barbara City Coll (CA)
Santa Rosa Jr Coll (CA)
Sauk Valley Comm Coll (IL)
Scottsdale Comm Coll (AZ)
Seminole Comm Coll (FL)
Sheridan Coll–Sheridan and Gillette (WY)
Sinclair Comm Coll (OH)
Skyline Coll (CA)
Snow Coll (UT)
Southeastern Comm Coll (NC)
Southern State Comm Coll (OH)
Southern West Virginia Comm and Tech Coll (WV)
South Plains Coll (TX)
Southside Virginia Comm Coll (VA)
Southwestern Illinois Coll (IL)
Spartanburg Methodist Coll (SC)
Spoon River Coll (IL)
Tarrant County Coll District (TX)
Three Rivers Comm Coll (MO)
Tillamook Bay Comm Coll (OR)
Tompkins Cortland Comm Coll (NY)
Treasure Valley Comm Coll (OR)
Trident Tech Coll (SC)

Trinity Valley Comm Coll (TX)
Triton Coll (IL)
Tulsa Comm Coll (OK)
Tunxis Comm Coll (CT)
United Tribes Tech Coll (ND)
Valencia Comm Coll (FL)
Valley Forge Military Coll (PA)
Vance-Granville Comm Coll (NC)
Ventura Coll (CA)
Vermilion Comm Coll (MN)
Weatherford Coll (TX)
Westchester Comm Coll (NY)
Western Iowa Tech Comm Coll (IA)
Westmoreland County Comm Coll (PA)
Wharton County Jr Coll (TX)
William Rainey Harper Coll (IL)
Wilson Tech Comm Coll (NC)
Yakima Valley Comm Coll (WA)
Young Harris Coll (GA)
Yuba Coll (CA)

Criminal Justice/Police Science
Abraham Baldwin Ag Coll (GA)
Alexandria Tech Coll (MN)
Allan Hancock Coll (CA)
Allegany Coll of Maryland (MD)
Arapahoe Comm Coll (CO)
Arizona Western Coll (AZ)
Arkansas Northeastern Coll (AR)
Austin Comm Coll (TX)
Barton County Comm Coll (KS)
Beaufort County Comm Coll (NC)
Bladen Comm Coll (NC)
Blue River Comm Coll (MO)
Brazosport Coll (TX)
Brevard Comm Coll (FL)
Broome Comm Coll (NY)
Broward Comm Coll (FL)
Brown Mackie Coll–Fort Wayne (IN)
Bucks County Comm Coll (PA)
Butler Comm Coll (KS)
Butler County Comm Coll (PA)
Cape Fear Comm Coll (NC)
Casper Coll (WY)
Central Piedmont Comm Coll (NC)
Century Coll (MN)
Cincinnati State Tech and Comm Coll (OH)
Citrus Coll (CA)
City Colls of Chicago, Wilbur Wright College (IL)
Clark State Comm Coll (OH)
Clovis Comm Coll (NM)
Coastal Bend Coll (TX)
Cochise Coll, Douglas (AZ)
Coll of DuPage (IL)
Coll of Lake County (IL)
Coll of the Canyons (CA)
Comm Coll of Allegheny County (PA)
Copiah-Lincoln Comm Coll (MS)
Cowley County Comm Coll and Area Vocational–Tech School (KS)
Cuyahoga Comm Coll (OH)
Dean Coll (MA)
Delaware Tech & Comm Coll, Stanton/Wilmington Campus (DE)
Delgado Comm Coll (LA)
Delta Coll (MI)
Dyersburg State Comm Coll (TN)
East Arkansas Comm Coll (AR)
East Central Coll (MO)
Eastern Arizona Coll (AZ)
Eastern Wyoming Coll (WY)
El Centro Coll (TX)
Erie Comm Coll (NY)

Erie Comm Coll, North Campus (NY)
Essex County Coll (NJ)
Everest Coll (AZ)
Finger Lakes Comm Coll (NY)
Florida Comm Coll at Jacksonville (FL)
Forsyth Tech Comm Coll (NC)
Fox Valley Tech Coll (WI)
Gadsden State Comm Coll (AL)
Galveston Coll (TX)
Gavilan Coll (CA)
George C. Wallace Comm Coll (AL)
Georgia Highlands Coll (GA)
Germanna Comm Coll (VA)
Glendale Comm Coll (AZ)
Grand Rapids Comm Coll (MI)
Guam Comm Coll (GU)
Hagerstown Comm Coll (MD)
Harrisburg Area Comm Coll (PA)
Hawkeye Comm Coll (IA)
Hibbing Comm Coll (MN)
Highline Comm Coll (WA)
Holyoke Comm Coll (MA)
Houston Comm Coll System (TX)
Howard Coll (TX)
Hutchinson Comm Coll and Area Vocational School (KS)
Illinois Central Coll (IL)
Illinois Eastern Comm Colls, Olney Central College (IL)
Illinois Valley Comm Coll (IL)
James Sprunt Comm Coll (NC)
Jamestown Comm Coll (NY)
Jefferson Comm Coll (OH)
Jefferson State Comm Coll (AL)
Johnston Comm Coll (NC)
John Wood Comm Coll (IL)
Joliet Jr Coll (IL)
Kansas City Kansas Comm Coll (KS)
Kaskaskia Coll (IL)
Kellogg Comm Coll (MI)
Kent State U, Tuscarawas Campus (OH)
Lake Land Coll (IL)
Lake Michigan Coll (MI)
Lake Region State Coll (ND)
Lakeshore Tech Coll (WI)
Lansing Comm Coll (MI)
Laredo Comm Coll (TX)
Lawson State Comm Coll (AL)
Lincoln Coll (IL)
Lincoln Land Comm Coll (IL)
Linn-Benton Comm Coll (OR)
Longview Comm Coll (MO)
Louisiana State U at Alexandria (LA)
Lower Columbia Coll (WA)
Macomb Comm Coll (MI)
Maple Woods Comm Coll (MO)
Marshall Comm and Tech Coll (WV)
Mercer County Comm Coll (NJ)
Metropolitan Comm Coll (NE)
Miami Dade Coll (FL)
Middle Georgia Coll (GA)
Middlesex County Comm Coll (NJ)
Midland Coll (TX)
Minnesota State Comm and Tech Coll–Fergus Falls (MN)
MiraCosta Coll (CA)
Mississippi Gulf Coast Comm Coll (MS)
Missouri State U–West Plains (MO)
Moberly Area Comm Coll (MO)
Modesto Jr Coll (CA)
Montgomery Comm Coll (NC)
Montgomery County Comm Coll (PA)

Moraine Valley Comm Coll (IL)
Mott Comm Coll (MI)
Mt. San Antonio Coll (CA)
New Mexico Military Inst (NM)
Normandale Comm Coll (MN)
North Arkansas Coll (AR)
Northeast Comm Coll (NE)
North Idaho Coll (ID)
North Iowa Area Comm Coll (IA)
Northland Comm and Tech Coll–Thief River Falls (MN)
Northwestern Connecticut Comm Coll (CT)
Northwest-Shoals Comm Coll (AL)
Oakland Comm Coll (MI)
Ocean County Coll (NJ)
Okaloosa-Walton Coll (FL)
Okefenokee Tech Coll (GA)
Orange County Comm Coll (NY)
Owens Comm Coll, Toledo (OH)
Palau Comm CollPalau (Palau)
Palm Beach Comm Coll (FL)
Palo Verde Coll (CA)
Penn Foster Career School (PA)
Penn Valley Comm Coll (MO)
Phoenix Coll (AZ)
Piedmont Virginia Comm Coll (VA)
Pima Comm Coll (AZ)
Pioneer Pacific Coll (OR)
Richland Comm Coll (IL)
Riverland Comm Coll (MN)
Roane State Comm Coll (TN)
Rockingham Comm Coll (NC)
Saint Charles Comm Coll (MO)
St. Louis Comm Coll at Florissant Valley (MO)
St. Petersburg Coll (FL)
San Joaquin Delta Coll (CA)
San Juan Coll (NM)
Sauk Valley Comm Coll (IL)
Seminole State Coll (OK)
Sheridan Coll–Sheridan and Gillette (WY)
Sinclair Comm Coll (OH)
Skyline Coll (CA)
South Arkansas Comm Coll (AR)
South Plains Coll (TX)
Southwestern Oregon Comm Coll (OR)
Southwest Virginia Comm Coll (VA)
Spokane Comm Coll (WA)
Spoon River Coll (IL)
Springfield Tech Comm Coll (MA)
Thomas Nelson Comm Coll (VA)
Three Rivers Comm Coll (MO)
Treasure Valley Comm Coll (OR)
Trinidad State Jr Coll (CO)
Trinity Valley Comm Coll (TX)
Triton Coll (IL)
Tulsa Comm Coll (OK)
Union County Coll (NJ)
Vance-Granville Comm Coll (NC)
Vermilion Comm Coll (MN)
Waubonsee Comm Coll (IL)
Waukesha County Tech Coll (WI)
Westchester Comm Coll (NY)
Western Oklahoma State Coll (OK)
Western Tech Coll (WI)
Westmoreland County Comm Coll (PA)
West Virginia Northern Comm Coll (WV)
Wilkes Comm Coll (NC)
William Rainey Harper Coll (IL)

Wisconsin Indianhead Tech Coll (WI)
Wor-Wic Comm Coll (MD)
Yakima Valley Comm Coll (WA)
Yavapai Coll (AZ)
Yuba Coll (CA)

Criminal Justice/Safety
Alamance Comm Coll (NC)
Altamaha Tech Coll (GA)
Ancilla Coll (IN)
Appalachian Tech Coll (GA)
Arkansas State U–Mountain Home (AR)
Asnuntuck Comm Coll (CT)
Augusta Tech Coll (GA)
Berkshire Comm Coll (MA)
Bristol Comm Coll (MA)
Brown Mackie Coll–Akron (OH)
Brown Mackie Coll–Atlanta (GA)
Brown Mackie Coll–Findlay (OH)
Brown Mackie Coll–Hopkinsville (KY)
Brown Mackie Coll–Louisville (KY)
Brown Mackie Coll–Merrillville (IN)
Brown Mackie Coll–Miami (FL)
Brown Mackie Coll–Michigan City (IN)
Brown Mackie Coll–North Canton (OH)
Central Carolina Tech Coll (SC)
Central Comm Coll–Grand Island Campus (NE)
Central Georgia Tech Coll (GA)
Central New Mexico Comm Coll (NM)
Chattahoochee Tech Coll (GA)
Cleveland Comm Coll (NC)
Coll of the Mainland (TX)
Comm and Tech Coll of Shepherd (WV)
Coosa Valley Tech Coll (GA)
Crown Coll (WA)
DeKalb Tech Coll (GA)
Dixie State Coll of Utah (UT)
East Central Tech Coll (GA)
Eastern Wyoming Coll (WY)
Eastfield Coll (TX)
El Centro Coll (TX)
Fayetteville Tech Comm Coll (NC)
Flint River Tech Coll (GA)
Florida Tech Coll, DeLand (FL)
Georgia Highlands Coll (GA)
Great Basin Coll (NV)
Griffin Tech Coll (GA)
Hamilton Coll, Cedar Falls (IA)
Heart of Georgia Tech Coll (GA)
Indiana Business Coll, Anderson (IN)
Indiana Business Coll, Columbus (IN)
Indiana Business Coll, Muncie (IN)
Indiana Business Coll, Terre Haute (IN)
Ivy Tech Comm Coll–Bloomington (IN)
Ivy Tech Comm Coll–Central Indiana (IN)
Ivy Tech Comm Coll–East Central (IN)
Ivy Tech Comm Coll–Kokomo (IN)
Ivy Tech Comm Coll–North Central (IN)
Ivy Tech Comm Coll–Northwest (IN)
Ivy Tech Comm Coll–Southwest (IN)
Ivy Tech Comm Coll–Wabash Valley (IN)
Jamestown Comm Coll (NY)
Kellogg Comm Coll (MI)
Keystone Coll (PA)
Lackawanna Coll (PA)

Lamar State Coll–Port Arthur (TX)
Lanier Tech Coll (GA)
Linn-Benton Comm Coll (OR)
Louisiana Tech Coll (LA)
Lower Columbia Coll (WA)
Manatee Comm Coll (FL)
Midlands Tech Coll (SC)
Moultrie Tech Coll (GA)
Nassau Comm Coll (NY)
New Mexico State U–Alamogordo (NM)
Normandale Comm Coll (MN)
Northampton County Area Comm Coll (PA)
North Country Comm Coll (NY)
North Georgia Tech Coll (GA)
North Hennepin Comm Coll (MN)
Northwestern Tech Coll (GA)
Northwest Vista Coll (TX)
Parkland Coll (IL)
Phoenix Coll (AZ)
Pima Comm Coll (AZ)
Remington Coll–Tampa Campus (FL)
San Juan Coll (NM)
Savannah Tech Coll (GA)
Southeastern Tech Coll (GA)
South Georgia Tech Coll (GA)
Southwestern Oklahoma State U at Sayre (OK)
Southwestern Oregon Comm Coll (OR)
Southwest Georgia Tech Coll (GA)
Southwest Tennessee Comm Coll (TN)
Swainsboro Tech Coll (GA)
TESST Coll of Technology, Towson (MD)
Valdosta Tech Coll (GA)
Vermilion Comm Coll (MN)
West Central Tech Coll (GA)
West Georgia Tech Coll (GA)

Criminology
Butler County Comm Coll (PA)
Coll of the Mainland (TX)
Lincoln Coll (IL)
Northland Comm and Tech Coll–Thief River Falls (MN)

Crop Production
Barton County Comm Coll (KS)
Northeast Comm Coll (NE)
The Ohio State U Ag Tech Inst (OH)

Culinary Arts
Alamance Comm Coll (NC)
Albany Tech Coll (GA)
Allegany Coll of Maryland (MD)
The Art Inst of Philadelphia (PA)
Atlanta Tech Coll (GA)
Augusta Tech Coll (GA)
Baltimore International Coll (MD)
Brevard Comm Coll (FL)
Bristol Comm Coll (MA)
Bucks County Comm Coll (PA)
Bunker Hill Comm Coll (MA)
Central New Mexico Comm Coll (NM)
Central Oregon Comm Coll (OR)
Central Piedmont Comm Coll (NC)
Chattahoochee Tech Coll (GA)
Cincinnati State Tech and Comm Coll (OH)
Clark Coll (WA)
Cochise Coll, Douglas (AZ)
Coll of DuPage (IL)
Coll of The Albemarle (NC)
Columbia Coll (CA)
Commonwealth Tech Inst (PA)
Comm and Tech Coll of Shepherd (WV)

Comm Coll of Allegheny County (PA)
Delaware Tech & Comm Coll, Stanton/Wilmington Campus (DE)
East Central Coll (MO)
Edmonds Comm Coll (WA)
El Centro Coll (TX)
Erie Comm Coll (NY)
Erie Comm Coll, North Campus (NY)
Fayetteville Tech Comm Coll (NC)
Florida Comm Coll at Jacksonville (FL)
Fox Valley Tech Coll (WI)
Galveston Coll (TX)
Grand Rapids Comm Coll (MI)
Harrisburg Area Comm Coll (PA)
H. Councill Trenholm State Tech Coll (AL)
Hibbing Comm Coll (MN)
Horry-Georgetown Tech Coll (SC)
Illinois Eastern Comm Colls, Lincoln Trail College (IL)
International Coll of Hospitality Management (CT)
Jefferson Comm and Tech Coll (KY)
Joliet Jr Coll (IL)
Kapiolani Comm Coll (HI)
Kaskaskia Coll (IL)
Kauai Comm Coll (HI)
Keystone Coll (PA)
Linn-Benton Comm Coll (OR)
Long Beach City Coll (CA)
Louisiana Tech Coll (LA)
Luzerne County Comm Coll (PA)
Macomb Comm Coll (MI)
Mercer County Comm Coll (NJ)
Metropolitan Comm Coll (NE)
Middlesex County Coll (NJ)
Mohawk Valley Comm Coll (NY)
Montgomery County Comm Coll (PA)
Moraine Park Tech Coll (WI)
Mott Comm Coll (MI)
New England Culinary Inst at Essex (VT)
Niagara County Comm Coll (NY)
North Georgia Tech Coll (GA)
North Idaho Coll (ID)
North Shore Comm Coll (MA)
Oakland Comm Coll (MI)
Ogeechee Tech Coll (GA)
Orange Coast Coll (CA)
Riverside Comm Coll District (CA)
St. Philip's Coll (TX)
San Joaquin Delta Coll (CA)
Santa Rosa Jr Coll (CA)
Savannah Tech Coll (GA)
Scottsdale Comm Coll (AZ)
Seattle Central Comm Coll (WA)
Shelton State Comm Coll (AL)
Sinclair Comm Coll (OH)
South Georgia Tech Coll (GA)
Spokane Comm Coll (WA)
State U of New York Coll of Technology at Alfred (NY)
State U of New York Coll of Technology at Delhi (NY)
Sullivan County Comm Coll (NY)
Texas State Tech Coll Waco (TX)
Trident Tech Coll (SC)
Triton Coll (IL)
Valencia Comm Coll (FL)
Westchester Comm Coll (NY)
Westmoreland County Comm Coll (PA)
William Rainey Harper Coll (IL)

Culinary Arts Related
Keystone Coll (PA)
Linn-Benton Comm Coll (OR)
Santa Barbara City Coll (CA)

Cultural Studies
Foothill Coll (CA)
Highline Comm Coll (WA)
Orange Coast Coll (CA)
Pasadena City Coll (CA)
Santa Barbara City Coll (CA)
Santa Rosa Jr Coll (CA)
Yuba Coll (CA)

Customer Service Support/ Call Center/Teleservice Operation
Laramie County Comm Coll (WY)

Cytotechnology
Barton County Comm Coll (KS)
Manor Coll (PA)

Dairy Husbandry and Production
Linn-Benton Comm Coll (OR)
The Ohio State U Ag Tech Inst (OH)

Dairy Science
Modesto Jr Coll (CA)
Mt. San Antonio Coll (CA)
Northeast Iowa Comm Coll (IA)
The Ohio State U Ag Tech Inst (OH)

Dance
Allan Hancock Coll (CA)
Barton County Comm Coll (KS)
Bergen Comm Coll (NJ)
Casper Coll (WY)
Central Piedmont Comm Coll (NC)
Citrus Coll (CA)
Dean Coll (MA)
Dixie State Coll of Utah (UT)
Lansing Comm Coll (MI)
Lincoln Coll (IL)
Long Beach City Coll (CA)
Mercer County Comm Coll (NJ)
Miami Dade Coll (FL)
Middlesex County Coll (NJ)
MiraCosta Coll (CA)
Nassau Comm Coll (NY)
Northern Essex Comm Coll (MA)
Orange Coast Coll (CA)
San Joaquin Delta Coll (CA)
Santa Rosa Jr Coll (CA)
Sinclair Comm Coll (OH)
Snow Coll (UT)
Trinity Valley Comm Coll (TX)
Westchester Comm Coll (NY)

Data Entry/Microcomputer Applications
Austin Comm Coll (TX)
Brown Mackie Coll–Kansas City (KS)
Bunker Hill Comm Coll (MA)
Business Inst of Pennsylvania, Meadville (PA)
Clark Coll (WA)
Cleveland Comm Coll (NC)
Coastal Bend Coll (TX)
Coll of The Albemarle (NC)
The Coll of Westchester (NY)
Eastern Arizona Coll (AZ)
Eastfield Coll (TX)
ECPI Tech Coll (VA)
ECPI Tech Coll, Glen Allen (VA)
ECPI Tech Coll, Richmond (VA)
Edmonds Comm Coll (WA)
Fiorello H. LaGuardia Comm Coll of the City U of New York (NY)
Florida Comm Coll at Jacksonville (FL)
Florida National Coll (FL)
Gallipolis Career Coll (OH)
Galveston Coll (TX)

Gateway Comm Coll (CT)
Heartland Comm Coll (IL)
Horry-Georgetown Tech Coll (SC)
Howard Comm Coll (MD)
IntelliTec Coll, Grand Junction (CO)
Laredo Comm Coll (TX)
Laurel Business Inst (PA)
Lower Columbia Coll (WA)
Luzerne County Comm Coll (PA)
Metropolitan Comm Coll-Business & Technology College (MO)
Mississippi Gulf Coast Comm Coll (MS)
Modesto Jr Coll (CA)
Newport Business Inst, Lower Burrell (PA)
Northland Comm and Tech Coll–Thief River Falls (MN)
North Shore Comm Coll (MA)
Ohio Business Coll, Sandusky (OH)
Okaloosa-Walton Coll (FL)
Orange County Comm Coll (NY)
Parkland Coll (IL)
Pellissippi State Tech Comm Coll (TN)
Pratt Comm Coll (KS)
Quinebaug Valley Comm Coll (CT)
Rasmussen Coll Mankato (MN)
Richland Comm Coll (IL)
Riverland Comm Coll (MN)
St. Philip's Coll (TX)
Seminole Comm Coll (FL)
Sheridan Coll–Sheridan and Gillette (WY)
Sinclair Comm Coll (OH)
Stark State Coll of Technology (OH)
Sullivan County Comm Coll (NY)
TESST Coll of Technology, Towson (MD)
Three Rivers Comm Coll (MO)
Tompkins Cortland Comm Coll (NY)
Tulsa Comm Coll (OK)
Valencia Comm Coll (FL)
West Central Tech Coll (GA)

Data Entry/Microcomputer Applications Related
Berkeley City Coll (CA)
Brown Mackie Coll–Kansas City (KS)
Capital Comm Coll (CT)
Coastal Bend Coll (TX)
Coll of DuPage (IL)
The Coll of Westchester (NY)
Colorado Mountain Coll (CO)
Colorado Mountain Coll, Alpine Campus (CO)
Florida Comm Coll at Jacksonville (FL)
Florida National Coll (FL)
Hawkeye Comm Coll (IA)
Heartland Comm Coll (IL)
Highline Comm Coll (WA)
Kellogg Comm Coll (MI)
Laredo Comm Coll (TX)
Laurel Business Inst (PA)
Metropolitan Comm Coll-Business & Technology College (MO)
Mississippi Gulf Coast Comm Coll (MS)
Newport Business Inst, Lower Burrell (PA)
Northland Comm and Tech Coll–Thief River Falls (MN)
Orange Coast Coll (CA)
Pellissippi State Tech Comm Coll (TN)
Peninsula Coll (WA)
Pratt Comm Coll (KS)
Rasmussen Coll Mankato (MN)
Remington Coll–Lafayette Campus (LA)
Richland Comm Coll (IL)
Riverland Comm Coll (MN)
San Diego Mesa Coll (CA)

Seminole Comm Coll (FL)
Sinclair Comm Coll (OH)
Southwestern Michigan Coll (MI)
Stark State Coll of Technology (OH)
Three Rivers Comm Coll (MO)
Tulsa Comm Coll (OK)

Data Modeling/Warehousing and Database Administration
Arapahoe Comm Coll (CO)
Edmonds Comm Coll (WA)
Florida Comm Coll at Jacksonville (FL)
Kennebec Valley Comm Coll (ME)
Laramie County Comm Coll (WY)
Metropolitan Comm Coll-Business & Technology College (MO)
Midland Coll (TX)
Northland Comm and Tech Coll–Thief River Falls (MN)
St. Petersburg Coll (FL)
Seminole Comm Coll (FL)
Tulsa Comm Coll (OK)

Data Processing and Data Processing Technology
Abraham Baldwin Ag Coll (GA)
Allen County Comm Coll (KS)
Bainbridge Coll (GA)
Borough of Manhattan Comm Coll of the City U of New York (NY)
Brazosport Coll (TX)
Bristol Comm Coll (MA)
Bronx Comm Coll of the City U of New York (NY)
Broome Comm Coll (NY)
Broward Comm Coll (FL)
Bucks County Comm Coll (PA)
Butler Comm Coll (KS)
Career Coll of Northern Nevada (NV)
Carroll Comm Coll (MD)
Casper Coll (WY)
Cecil Comm Coll (MD)
Cedar Valley Coll (TX)
Central Carolina Tech Coll (SC)
Central Comm Coll–Grand Island Campus (NE)
Central New Mexico Comm Coll (NM)
Central Piedmont Comm Coll (NC)
Chattahoochee Valley Comm Coll (AL)
Chattanooga State Tech Comm Coll (TN)
Citrus Coll (CA)
City Colls of Chicago, Wilbur Wright College (IL)
Coastal Bend Coll (TX)
Cochise Coll, Douglas (AZ)
The Coll of Westchester (NY)
Copiah-Lincoln Comm Coll (MS)
Dabney S. Lancaster Comm Coll (VA)
Davis Coll (OH)
Delaware Tech & Comm Coll, Jack F. Owens Campus (DE)
Delaware Tech & Comm Coll, Stanton/Wilmington Campus (DE)
Delaware Tech & Comm Coll, Terry Campus (DE)
Delgado Comm Coll (LA)
Dixie State Coll of Utah (UT)
Eastfield Coll (TX)
ECPI Coll of Technology, Virginia Beach (VA)
ECPI Tech Coll, Richmond (VA)
Edmonds Comm Coll (WA)
El Centro Coll (TX)
Essex County Coll (NJ)
Evergreen Valley Coll (CA)
Finger Lakes Comm Coll (NY)
Florida National Coll (FL)

Seminole Comm Coll (FL)
Sinclair Comm Coll (OH)
Southwestern Michigan Coll (MI)
Stark State Coll of Technology (OH)
Three Rivers Comm Coll (MO)
Tulsa Comm Coll (OK)

Forsyth Tech Comm Coll (NC)
Frederick Comm Coll (MD)
Gaston Coll (NC)
Gateway Comm Coll (CT)
George C. Wallace Comm Coll (AL)
Great Basin Coll (NV)
Hagerstown Business Coll (MD)
Heald Coll-Stockton (CA)
Highland Comm Coll (IL)
Illinois Central Coll (IL)
Illinois Valley Comm Coll (IL)
Independence Comm Coll (KS)
Jackson Comm Coll (MI)
Jefferson Comm and Tech Coll (KY)
Jefferson Comm Coll (OH)
Kansas City Kansas Comm Coll (KS)
Kapiolani Comm Coll (HI)
Keystone Coll (PA)
Kingsborough Comm Coll of the City U of New York (NY)
Lake Michigan Coll (MI)
Lamar State Coll–Orange (TX)
Lamar State Coll–Port Arthur (TX)
Laredo Comm Coll (TX)
Lincoln Coll (IL)
Lincoln Coll–Normal (IL)
Long Beach City Coll (CA)
Longview Comm Coll (MO)
Louisiana Tech Coll (LA)
Lower Columbia Coll (WA)
Luzerne County Comm Coll (PA)
Maple Woods Comm Coll (MO)
Metropolitan Comm Coll-Business & Technology College (MO)
Miami Dade Coll (FL)
Middle Georgia Coll (GA)
Midlands Tech Coll (SC)
Mt. San Antonio Coll (CA)
Nassau Comm Coll (NY)
New Hampshire Comm Tech Coll, Nashua/Claremont (NH)
New Mexico State U–Alamogordo (NM)
North Central Missouri Coll (MO)
Northeast State Tech Comm Coll (TN)
Northern Essex Comm Coll (MA)
Northern Maine Comm Coll (ME)
Norwalk Comm Coll (CT)
Orange Coast Coll (CA)
Orange County Comm Coll (NY)
Otero Jr Coll (CO)
Palm Beach Comm Coll (FL)
Pasadena City Coll (CA)
Pellissippi State Tech Comm Coll (TN)
Penn Valley Comm Coll (MO)
Phoenix Coll (AZ)
Piedmont Virginia Comm Coll (VA)
Polk Comm Coll (FL)
Quinsigamond Comm Coll (MA)
Raritan Valley Comm Coll (NJ)
Rasmussen Coll Mankato (MN)
St. Louis Comm Coll at Florissant Valley (MO)
San Diego City Coll (CA)
Seminole Comm Coll (FL)
Skyline Coll (CA)
Snead State Comm Coll (AL)
South Plains Coll (TX)
Southwestern Illinois Coll (IL)
Spokane Comm Coll (WA)
Trinidad State Jr Coll (CO)
Trinity Valley Comm Coll (TX)
Triton Coll (IL)
Tunxis Comm Coll (CT)

The U of Akron–Wayne Coll (OH)
Vance-Granville Comm Coll (NC)
Vermilion Comm Coll (MN)
Westchester Comm Coll (NY)
Western Tech Coll (WI)
Westmoreland County Comm Coll (PA)
Wharton County Jr Coll (TX)
William Rainey Harper Coll (IL)
Williston State Coll (ND)
York Tech Coll (SC)

Dental Assisting
Allan Hancock Coll (CA)
Athens Tech Coll (GA)
Briarwood Coll (CT)
Central Comm Coll–Hastings Campus (NE)
Central Oregon Comm Coll (OR)
Century Coll (MN)
Citrus Coll (CA)
Comm Care Coll (OK)
Comm Coll of the Air Force (AL)
Delta Coll (MI)
Essex County Coll (NJ)
Foothill Coll (CA)
H. Councill Trenholm State Tech Coll (AL)
Hibbing Comm Coll (MN)
James H. Faulkner State Comm Coll (AL)
Jefferson Comm Coll (OH)
Lake Michigan Coll (MI)
Laramie County Comm Coll (WY)
Luzerne County Comm Coll (PA)
Midlands Tech Coll (SC)
Modesto Jr Coll (CA)
Mott Comm Coll (MI)
New Hampshire Tech Inst (NH)
Normandale Comm Coll (MN)
Northern Essex Comm Coll (MA)
St. Cloud Tech Coll (MN)
San Diego Mesa Coll (CA)
San Joaquin Valley Coll (CA)
Texas State Tech Coll Waco (TX)
Tulsa Comm Coll (OK)
Vatterott Coll (IA)
York Tech Coll (SC)

Dental Hygiene
Allegany Coll of Maryland (MD)
Athens Tech Coll (GA)
Atlanta Tech Coll (GA)
Barton County Comm Coll (KS)
Bergen Comm Coll (NJ)
Brevard Comm Coll (FL)
Bristol Comm Coll (MA)
Broome Comm Coll (NY)
Broward Comm Coll (FL)
Brown Mackie Coll–Kansas City (KS)
Cape Fear Comm Coll (NC)
Central Comm Coll–Hastings Campus (NE)
Central Georgia Tech Coll (GA)
Central Piedmont Comm Coll (NC)
Century Coll (MN)
Chattanooga State Tech Comm Coll (TN)
Chemeketa Comm Coll (OR)
Clark Coll (WA)
Coastal Bend Coll (TX)
Coastal Carolina Comm Coll (NC)
Coastal Georgia Comm Coll (GA)
Colby Comm Coll (KS)
Coll of DuPage (IL)
Coll of Lake County (IL)
Collin County Comm Coll District (TX)
Columbus Tech Coll (GA)
Comm Coll of Denver (CO)

Delaware Tech & Comm Coll, Stanton/Wilmington Campus (DE)
Delgado Comm Coll (LA)
Delta Coll (MI)
Dixie State Coll of Utah (UT)
Erie Comm Coll, North Campus (NY)
Essex County Coll (NJ)
Fayetteville Tech Comm Coll (NC)
Florida Comm Coll at Jacksonville (FL)
Florida National Coll (FL)
Foothill Coll (CA)
Georgia Highlands Coll (GA)
Germanna Comm Coll (VA)
Grand Rapids Comm Coll (MI)
Harrisburg Area Comm Coll (PA)
Hawkeye Comm Coll (IA)
Highline Comm Coll (WA)
Howard Coll (TX)
Hudson Valley Comm Coll (NY)
Illinois Central Coll (IL)
Kellogg Comm Coll (MI)
Lake Land Coll (IL)
Lakeshore Tech Coll (WI)
Lake Superior Coll (MN)
Lansing Comm Coll (MI)
Laramie County Comm Coll (WY)
Lord Fairfax Comm Coll (VA)
Luzerne County Comm Coll (PA)
Manor Coll (PA)
Meridian Comm Coll (MS)
Miami Dade Coll (FL)
Middle Georgia Tech Coll (GA)
Middlesex County Coll (NJ)
Midlands Tech Coll (SC)
Minnesota State Comm and Tech Coll–Fergus Falls (MN)
Montgomery County Comm Coll (PA)
Mott Comm Coll (MI)
Mount Wachusett Comm Coll (MA)
New Hampshire Tech Inst (NH)
Normandale Comm Coll (MN)
Northampton County Area Comm Coll (PA)
North Dakota State Coll of Science (ND)
Oakland Comm Coll (MI)
Ogeechee Tech Coll (GA)
Orange Coast Coll (CA)
Orange County Comm Coll (NY)
Palm Beach Comm Coll (FL)
Parkland Coll (IL)
Pasadena City Coll (CA)
Pasco-Hernando Comm Coll (FL)
Phoenix Coll (AZ)
Pima Comm Coll (AZ)
Prairie State Coll (IL)
Quinsigamond Comm Coll (MA)
Roane State Comm Coll (TN)
St. Cloud Tech Coll (MN)
St. Petersburg Coll (FL)
Salt Lake Comm Coll (UT)
San Joaquin Valley Coll (CA)
Santa Rosa Jr Coll (CA)
Sheridan Coll–Sheridan and Gillette (WY)
Sinclair Comm Coll (OH)
Southeastern Tech Coll (GA)
Spokane Comm Coll (WA)
Springfield Tech Comm Coll (MA)
Stark State Coll of Technology (OH)
Tarrant County Coll District (TX)
Trident Tech Coll (SC)
Tulsa Comm Coll (OK)
Tunxis Comm Coll (CT)
Union County Coll (NJ)
Valencia Comm Coll (FL)
Waukesha County Tech Coll (WI)

West Central Tech Coll (GA)
Western Tech Coll (WI)
Westmoreland County Comm Coll (PA)
Wharton County Jr Coll (TX)
William Rainey Harper Coll (IL)
Yakima Valley Comm Coll (WA)
York Tech Coll (SC)

Dental Laboratory Technology
Century Coll (MN)
Commonwealth Tech Inst (PA)
Comm Coll of the Air Force (AL)
Delgado Comm Coll (LA)
Erie Comm Coll, South Campus (NY)
H. Councill Trenholm State Tech Coll (AL)
Marshall Comm and Tech Coll (WV)
Pima Comm Coll (AZ)

Design and Applied Arts Related
Mohawk Valley Comm Coll (NY)
Niagara County Comm Coll (NY)

Design and Visual Communications
Bradley Academy for the Visual Arts (PA)
Brown Coll (MN)
Bunker Hill Comm Coll (MA)
Coll of DuPage (IL)
Comm and Tech Coll of Shepherd (WV)
East Central Coll (MO)
FIDM/The Fashion Inst of Design & Merchandising, Los Angeles Campus (CA)
FIDM/The Fashion Inst of Design & Merchandising, San Diego Campus (CA)
FIDM/The Fashion Inst of Design & Merchandising, San Francisco Campus (CA)
Florida Comm Coll at Jacksonville (FL)
Harrisburg Area Comm Coll (PA)
Ivy Tech Comm Coll–Central Indiana (IN)
Ivy Tech Comm Coll–Columbus (IN)
Ivy Tech Comm Coll–North Central (IN)
Ivy Tech Comm Coll–Southern Indiana (IN)
Ivy Tech Comm Coll–Southwest (IN)
Ivy Tech Comm Coll–Wabash Valley (IN)
Lehigh Valley Coll (PA)
Moraine Valley Comm Coll (IL)
Nassau Comm Coll (NY)
North Metro Tech Coll (GA)
Parkland Coll (IL)
Pima Comm Coll (AZ)
Southeastern Tech Coll (GA)
Trinidad State Jr Coll (CO)
Waubonsee Comm Coll (IL)

Desktop Publishing and Digital Imaging Design
The Art Inst of Philadelphia (PA)
Coll of DuPage (IL)
Eastern Idaho Tech Coll (ID)
Edmonds Comm Coll (WA)
Evergreen Valley Coll (CA)
Lake Land Coll (IL)
Linn-Benton Comm Coll (OR)
Louisiana Tech Coll (LA)
Minneapolis Business Coll (MN)
Southwestern Illinois Coll (IL)
Springfield Tech Comm Coll (MA)
Tulsa Comm Coll (OK)

Developmental and Child Psychology
Arizona Western Coll (AZ)
Austin Comm Coll (TX)
Central Lakes Coll (MN)
Coastal Bend Coll (TX)
Coll of the Canyons (CA)
Columbia Coll (CA)
Gavilan Coll (CA)
Illinois Central Coll (IL)
Jefferson Comm Coll (OH)
Lansing Comm Coll (MI)
Lincoln Coll (IL)
Long Beach City Coll (CA)
Midland Coll (TX)
MiraCosta Coll (CA)
North Idaho Coll (ID)
Palo Verde Coll (CA)
Pasadena City Coll (CA)
Saddleback Coll (CA)
San Diego City Coll (CA)
San Joaquin Delta Coll (CA)
South Plains Coll (TX)
South Texas Coll (TX)
Tarrant County Coll District (TX)
Trinity Valley Comm Coll (TX)

Diagnostic Medical Sonography and Ultrasound Technology
Athens Tech Coll (GA)
Caldwell Comm Coll and Tech Inst (NC)
Cape Fear Comm Coll (NC)
Central New Mexico Comm Coll (NM)
Cincinnati State Tech and Comm Coll (OH)
Columbus Tech Coll (GA)
Comm Coll of Allegheny County (PA)
Delaware Tech & Comm Coll, Stanton/Wilmington Campus (DE)
Delta Coll (MI)
El Centro Coll (TX)
Florida Comm Coll at Jacksonville (FL)
Florida National Coll (FL)
Foothill Coll (CA)
GateWay Comm Coll (AZ)
Jackson Comm Coll (MI)
Keystone Coll (PA)
Lackawanna Coll (PA)
Lansing Comm Coll (MI)
Laramie County Comm Coll (WY)
Miami Dade Coll (FL)
New Hampshire Tech Inst (NH)
Northampton County Area Comm Coll (PA)
Oakland Comm Coll (MI)
St. Cloud Tech Coll (MN)
South Hills School of Business & Technology, State College (PA)
Springfield Tech Comm Coll (MA)
Valencia Comm Coll (FL)

Diesel Mechanics Technology
Alexandria Tech Coll (MN)
Central Comm Coll–Hastings Campus (NE)
Centralia Coll (WA)
Century Coll (MN)
Clark Coll (WA)
Dixie State Coll of Utah (UT)
Eastern Idaho Tech Coll (ID)
Great Basin Coll (NV)
Illinois Eastern Comm Colls, Wabash Valley College (IL)
Johnston Comm Coll (NC)
Lake Region State Coll (ND)
Laramie County Comm Coll (WY)
Linn-Benton Comm Coll (OR)
Louisiana Tech Coll (LA)
Lower Columbia Coll (WA)
Nashville Auto Diesel Coll (TN)
North Dakota State Coll of Science (ND)
Northeast Comm Coll (NE)
Peninsula Coll (WA)

Raritan Valley Comm Coll (NJ)
Riverland Comm Coll (MN)
Rosedale Tech Inst (PA)
St. Cloud Tech Coll (MN)
St. Philip's Coll (TX)
Salt Lake Comm Coll (UT)
San Juan Coll (NM)
Shelton State Comm Coll (AL)
Sheridan Coll–Sheridan and Gillette (WY)
Southeast Tech Inst (SD)
Texas State Tech Coll Waco (TX)
U of Northwestern Ohio (OH)
Western Iowa Tech Comm Coll (IA)
Wilkes Comm Coll (NC)
Williston State Coll (ND)

Dietetics
Allan Hancock Coll (CA)
Briarwood Coll (CT)
Butler County Comm Coll (PA)
Central Arizona Coll (AZ)
Cincinnati State Tech and Comm Coll (OH)
Comm Coll of the Air Force (AL)
Delgado Comm Coll (LA)
Fiorello H. LaGuardia Comm Coll of the City U of New York (NY)
Florida Comm Coll at Jacksonville (FL)
Gaston Coll (NC)
Gateway Comm Coll (CT)
Harrisburg Area Comm Coll (PA)
Lawson State Comm Coll (AL)
Long Beach City Coll (CA)
Manatee Comm Coll (FL)
Miami Dade Coll (FL)
Middlesex County Coll (NJ)
Normandale Comm Coll (MN)
Okaloosa-Walton Coll (FL)
Orange Coast Coll (CA)
St. Louis Comm Coll at Florissant Valley (MO)
Santa Rosa Jr Coll (CA)
Sinclair Comm Coll (OH)
South Plains Coll (TX)
Spokane Comm Coll (WA)
Tarrant County Coll District (TX)
Westchester Comm Coll (NY)
Westmoreland County Comm Coll (PA)
William Rainey Harper Coll (IL)

Dietetic Technician
Front Range Comm Coll (CO)
Miami Dade Coll (FL)

Dietitian Assistant
Barton County Comm Coll (KS)
Comm Coll of Allegheny County (PA)
Erie Comm Coll, North Campus (NY)
Florida Comm Coll at Jacksonville (FL)
Southwest Tennessee Comm Coll (TN)

Digital Communication and Media/Multimedia
Brevard Comm Coll (FL)
Central Wyoming Coll (WY)
Gavilan Coll (CA)
Globe Coll (MN)
Laramie County Comm Coll (WY)
Platt Coll San Diego (CA)
Trinidad State Jr Coll (CO)

Divinity/Ministry
Okaloosa-Walton Coll (FL)
The Salvation Army Coll for Officer Training at Crestmont (CA)

Drafting
Comm Coll of Denver (CO)

Drafting and Design Technology
Albany Tech Coll (GA)
Allen County Comm Coll (KS)
Arapahoe Comm Coll (CO)
Arizona Western Coll (AZ)
Arkansas State U–Beebe (AR)
Austin Comm Coll (TX)
Bainbridge Coll (GA)
Beaufort County Comm Coll (NC)
Benjamin Franklin Inst of Technology (MA)
Bergen Comm Coll (NJ)
Berks Tech Inst (PA)
Bishop State Comm Coll (AL)
Brazosport Coll (TX)
Brevard Comm Coll (FL)
Butler Comm Coll (KS)
Butler County Comm Coll (PA)
Caldwell Comm Coll and Tech Inst (NC)
Casper Coll (WY)
Central Comm Coll–Columbus Campus (NE)
Central Comm Coll–Grand Island Campus (NE)
Central Comm Coll–Hastings Campus (NE)
Central Florida Comm Coll (FL)
Central Georgia Tech Coll (GA)
Central Piedmont Comm Coll (NC)
Chattahoochee Tech Coll (GA)
Chattanooga State Tech Comm Coll (TN)
Chemeketa Comm Coll (OR)
Citrus Coll (CA)
Clark State Comm Coll (OH)
Coastal Bend Coll (TX)
Coll of DuPage (IL)
Coll of the Canyons (CA)
Collin County Comm Coll District (TX)
Columbus Tech Coll (GA)
Comm Coll of Allegheny County (PA)
Copiah-Lincoln Comm Coll (MS)
Corning Comm Coll (NY)
Cowley County Comm Coll and Area Vocational–Tech School (KS)
Crowder Coll (MO)
Dabney S. Lancaster Comm Coll (VA)
DeKalb Tech Coll (GA)
Delaware Tech & Comm Coll, Jack F. Owens Campus (DE)
Delaware Tech & Comm Coll, Stanton/Wilmington Campus (DE)
Delaware Tech & Comm Coll, Terry Campus (DE)
Delgado Comm Coll (LA)
Delta Coll (MI)
East Arkansas Comm Coll (AR)
East Central Coll (MO)
Eastern Arizona Coll (AZ)
Eastfield Coll (TX)
El Centro Coll (TX)
Evergreen Valley Coll (CA)
Finger Lakes Comm Coll (NY)
Florida Comm Coll at Jacksonville (FL)
Forsyth Tech Comm Coll (NC)
Fox Valley Tech Coll (WI)
Frederick Comm Coll (MD)
Gavilan Coll (CA)
Genesee Comm Coll (NY)
George C. Wallace Comm Coll (AL)
Grand Rapids Comm Coll (MI)
Griffin Tech Coll (GA)
Gwinnett Tech Coll (GA)
Hawkeye Comm Coll (IA)
H. Councill Trenholm State Tech Coll (AL)

Heartland Comm Coll (IL)
Hibbing Comm Coll (MN)
Highland Comm Coll (IL)
Highline Comm Coll (WA)
Houston Comm Coll System (TX)
Howard Coll (TX)
Hutchinson Comm Coll and Area Vocational School (KS)
Illinois Valley Comm Coll (IL)
Independence Comm Coll (KS)
ITI Tech Coll (LA)
Ivy Tech Comm Coll–Central Indiana (IN)
Ivy Tech Comm Coll–Columbus (IN)
Ivy Tech Comm Coll–Kokomo (IN)
Ivy Tech Comm Coll–Lafayette (IN)
Ivy Tech Comm Coll–Northeast (IN)
Ivy Tech Comm Coll–Northwest (IN)
Jefferson Comm Coll (OH)
J. F. Drake State Tech Coll (AL)
Kansas City Kansas Comm Coll (KS)
Kellogg Comm Coll (MI)
Kennebec Valley Comm Coll (ME)
Lake Land Coll (IL)
Lake Michigan Coll (MI)
Lanier Tech Coll (GA)
Lansing Comm Coll (MI)
Lawson State Comm Coll (AL)
Linn-Benton Comm Coll (OR)
Linn State Tech Coll (MO)
Long Beach City Coll (CA)
Louisiana Tech Coll (LA)
Luzerne County Comm Coll (PA)
Macomb Comm Coll (MI)
Manatee Comm Coll (FL)
Manhattan Area Tech Coll (KS)
Massachusetts Bay Comm Coll (MA)
Meridian Comm Coll (MS)
Metropolitan Comm Coll (NE)
Metropolitan Comm Coll–Business & Technology College (MO)
Miami Dade Coll (FL)
Middle Georgia Tech Coll (GA)
Middlesex County Coll (NJ)
Midland Coll (TX)
MiraCosta Coll (CA)
Mississippi Gulf Coast Comm Coll (MS)
Moberly Area Comm Coll (MO)
Modesto Jr Coll (CA)
Mohawk Valley Comm Coll (NY)
Morrison Inst of Technology (IL)
Mott Comm Coll (MI)
Mountain View Coll (TX)
Mt. San Antonio Coll (CA)
Naugatuck Valley Comm Coll (CT)
New Hampshire Comm Tech Coll, Manchester/Stratham (NH)
New Hampshire Comm Tech Coll, Nashua/Claremont (NH)
Niagara County Comm Coll (NY)
North Central Missouri Coll (MO)
Northeast Comm Coll (NE)
Northeast State Tech Comm Coll (TN)
Northern Maine Comm Coll (ME)
North Idaho Coll (ID)
Northland Comm and Tech Coll–Thief River Falls (MN)
Northwestern Tech Coll (GA)
Northwest-Shoals Comm Coll (AL)

Okaloosa-Walton Coll (FL)
Orange Coast Coll (CA)
Orange County Comm Coll (NY)
Palm Beach Comm Coll (FL)
Pasadena City Coll (CA)
Pasco-Hernando Comm Coll (FL)
Pellissippi State Tech Comm Coll (TN)
Phoenix Coll (AZ)
Pulaski Tech Coll (AR)
Remington Coll–Mobile Campus (AL)
Richland Comm Coll (IL)
Saddleback Coll (CA)
Saint Charles Comm Coll (MO)
St. Petersburg Coll (FL)
Salt Lake Comm Coll (UT)
San Diego City Coll (CA)
San Joaquin Delta Coll (CA)
San Juan Coll (NM)
Santa Barbara City Coll (CA)
Schuylkill Inst of Business and Technology (PA)
Seattle Central Comm Coll (WA)
Seminole Comm Coll (FL)
Shelton State Comm Coll (AL)
Sheridan Coll–Sheridan and Gillette (WY)
Sinclair Comm Coll (OH)
Southeast Tech Inst (SD)
Southern State Comm Coll (OH)
Southern West Virginia Comm and Tech Coll (WV)
South Georgia Tech Coll (GA)
South Plains Coll (TX)
Southside Virginia Comm Coll (VA)
Southwestern Illinois Coll (IL)
Southwestern Michigan Coll (MI)
Southwest Virginia Comm Coll (VA)
Spartanburg Tech Coll (SC)
Spokane Comm Coll (WA)
Stark State Coll of Technology (OH)
State U of New York Coll of Technology at Alfred (NY)
Swainsboro Tech Coll (GA)
Tarrant County Coll District (TX)
Texas State Tech Coll Waco (TX)
Thomas Nelson Comm Coll (VA)
Tidewater Comm Coll (VA)
Treasure Valley Comm Coll (OR)
Triangle Tech, Inc.–DuBois School (PA)
Triangle Tech, Inc.–Greensburg School (PA)
Trinidad State Jr Coll (CO)
Trinity Valley Comm Coll (TX)
Triton Coll (IL)
Tulsa Comm Coll (OK)
Valdosta Tech Coll (GA)
Valencia Comm Coll (FL)
Westmoreland County Comm Coll (PA)
Wharton County Jr Coll (TX)
William Rainey Harper Coll (IL)

Drafting/Design Engineering Technologies Related
Comm Coll of Allegheny County (PA)
Front Range Comm Coll (CO)
Montgomery Coll (TX)

Drafting/Design Technology
North Arkansas Coll (AR)

Dramatic/Theater Arts
Allen County Comm Coll (KS)
American Academy of Dramatic Arts (NY)
Arizona Western Coll (AZ)
Bainbridge Coll (GA)

Barton County Comm Coll (KS)
Bergen Comm Coll (NJ)
Berkshire Comm Coll (MA)
Brazosport Coll (TX)
Bucks County Comm Coll (PA)
Bunker Hill Comm Coll (MA)
Butler Comm Coll (KS)
Casper Coll (WY)
Centralia Coll (WA)
Central Wyoming Coll (WY)
Chattahoochee Valley Comm Coll (AL)
Citrus Coll (CA)
Clarendon Coll (TX)
Clark State Comm Coll (OH)
Coastal Bend Coll (TX)
Colby Comm Coll (KS)
Coll of Southern Maryland (MD)
Coll of The Albemarle (NC)
Coll of the Mainland (TX)
Colorado Mountain Coll (CO)
Columbia Coll (CA)
Comm Coll of Allegheny County (PA)
Cowley County Comm Coll and Area Vocational–Tech School (KS)
Crowder Coll (MO)
Dean Coll (MA)
Dixie State Coll of Utah (UT)
Eastern Arizona Coll (AZ)
Finger Lakes Comm Coll (NY)
Gainesville Coll (GA)
Galveston Coll (TX)
Genesee Comm Coll (NY)
Harrisburg Area Comm Coll (PA)
Highland Comm Coll (IL)
Holyoke Comm Coll (MA)
Houston Comm Coll System (TX)
Howard Coll (TX)
Howard Comm Coll (MD)
Kellogg Comm Coll (MI)
Kingsborough Comm Coll of the City U of New York (NY)
Lansing Comm Coll (MI)
Laramie County Comm Coll (WY)
Lincoln Coll (IL)
Linn-Benton Comm Coll (OR)
Long Beach City Coll (CA)
Lower Columbia Coll (WA)
Manatee Comm Coll (FL)
Manchester Comm Coll (CT)
Mercer County Comm Coll (NJ)
Miami Dade Coll (FL)
Middlesex County Coll (NJ)
MiraCosta Coll (CA)
Modesto Jr Coll (CA)
Mohawk Valley Comm Coll (NY)
Nassau Comm Coll (NY)
Niagara County Comm Coll (NY)
Northeast Comm Coll (NE)
Northern Essex Comm Coll (MA)
North Idaho Coll (ID)
Orange Coast Coll (CA)
Otero Jr Coll (CO)
Palm Beach Comm Coll (FL)
Pasadena City Coll (CA)
Pima Comm Coll (AZ)
Raritan Valley Comm Coll (NJ)
Saddleback Coll (CA)
St. Louis Comm Coll at Florissant Valley (MO)
St. Philip's Coll (TX)
San Diego City Coll (CA)
San Joaquin Delta Coll (CA)
San Juan Coll (NM)
Santa Barbara City Coll (CA)
Santa Rosa Jr Coll (CA)
Sauk Valley Comm Coll (IL)
Scottsdale Comm Coll (AZ)
Sinclair Comm Coll (OH)
Snow Coll (UT)
Spoon River Coll (IL)
Treasure Valley Comm Coll (OR)
Trinidad State Jr Coll (CO)

Trinity Valley Comm Coll (TX)
Triton Coll (IL)
Tulsa Comm Coll (OK)
Valencia Comm Coll (FL)
Ventura Coll (CA)
Vermilion Comm Coll (MN)
Wharton County Jr Coll (TX)
Young Harris Coll (GA)
Yuba Coll (CA)

Dramatic/Theater Arts and Stagecraft Related
Bristol Comm Coll (MA)
Full Sail Real World Education (FL)
St. Philip's Coll (TX)

Drawing
Dixie State Coll of Utah (UT)
Keystone Coll (PA)
Lincoln Coll (IL)
Lincoln Coll–Normal (IL)
Luzerne County Comm Coll (PA)
Midland Coll (TX)
Pasadena City Coll (CA)
San Joaquin Delta Coll (CA)
Vermilion Comm Coll (MN)

Early Childhood Education
Ancilla Coll (IN)
Asnuntuck Comm Coll (CT)
Barton County Comm Coll (KS)
Bay State Coll (MA)
Beal Coll (ME)
Berkshire Comm Coll (MA)
Brevard Comm Coll (FL)
Bristol Comm Coll (MA)
Bunker Hill Comm Coll (MA)
Central Florida Comm Coll (FL)
Central Oregon Comm Coll (OR)
Clark Coll (WA)
Cochise Coll, Douglas (AZ)
Coll of Southern Maryland (MD)
Colorado Mountain Coll, Timberline Campus (CO)
Dean Coll (MA)
Denmark Tech Coll (SC)
East Central Coll (MO)
Edmonds Comm Coll (WA)
Fayetteville Tech Comm Coll (NC)
Front Range Comm Coll (CO)
Gainesville Coll (GA)
Goodwin Coll (CT)
Hagerstown Comm Coll (MD)
Hudson Valley Comm Coll (NY)
Ivy Tech Comm Coll–East Central (IN)
Ivy Tech Comm Coll–Kokomo (IN)
Ivy Tech Comm Coll–North Central (IN)
Ivy Tech Comm Coll–Northeast (IN)
Jackson Comm Coll (MI)
John Wood Comm Coll (IL)
Kent State U, Tuscarawas Campus (OH)
Keystone Coll (PA)
Kingsborough Comm Coll of the City U of New York (NY)
Lackawanna Coll (PA)
Lake Michigan Coll (MI)
Laramie County Comm Coll (WY)
Louisiana State U at Alexandria (LA)
Lower Columbia Coll (WA)
Luzerne County Comm Coll (PA)
Minnesota State Comm and Tech Coll–Fergus Falls (MN)
Moraine Park Tech Coll (WI)
Mott Comm Coll (MI)
North Central Missouri Coll (MO)
North Seattle Comm Coll (WA)
Owens Comm Coll, Toledo (OH)

Parkland Coll (IL)
St. Petersburg Coll (FL)
St. Philip's Coll (TX)
Salem Comm Coll (NJ)
Sauk Valley Comm Coll (IL)
Tillamook Bay Comm Coll (OR)
Tri-County Comm Coll (NC)
United Tribes Tech Coll (ND)
Waukesha County Tech Coll (WI)

Ecology
Abraham Baldwin Ag Coll (GA)
Dixie State Coll of Utah (UT)
East Central Coll (MO)
Joliet Jr Coll (IL)
Tulsa Comm Coll (OK)
Vermilion Comm Coll (MN)

E-Commerce
Augusta Tech Coll (GA)
Central Georgia Tech Coll (GA)
Edmonds Comm Coll (WA)
Fayetteville Tech Comm Coll (NC)
Hudson Valley Comm Coll (NY)
Montgomery Coll (TX)
North Central Missouri Coll (MO)
Pasco-Hernando Comm Coll (FL)
St. Philip's Coll (TX)
Valdosta Tech Coll (GA)

Economics
Allen County Comm Coll (KS)
Austin Comm Coll (TX)
Barton County Comm Coll (KS)
Bergen Comm Coll (NJ)
Brazosport Coll (TX)
Casper Coll (WY)
Chemeketa Comm Coll (OR)
Clarendon Coll (TX)
Coastal Bend Coll (TX)
Cochise Coll, Douglas (AZ)
Copiah-Lincoln Comm Coll (MS)
Dixie State Coll of Utah (UT)
East Central Coll (MO)
Eastern Wyoming Coll (WY)
Foothill Coll (CA)
GateWay Comm Coll (AZ)
Georgia Highlands Coll (GA)
Laramie County Comm Coll (WY)
Lincoln Coll (IL)
Lincoln Coll–Normal (IL)
Linn-Benton Comm Coll (OR)
Lower Columbia Coll (WA)
Manatee Comm Coll (FL)
Miami Dade Coll (FL)
Midland Coll (TX)
MiraCosta Coll (CA)
New Mexico Military Inst (NM)
Orange Coast Coll (CA)
Palm Beach Comm Coll (FL)
Palo Alto Coll (TX)
Palo Verde Coll (CA)
Pasadena City Coll (CA)
Saddleback Coll (CA)
St. Philip's Coll (TX)
Salt Lake Comm Coll (UT)
San Joaquin Delta Coll (CA)
San Juan Coll (NM)
Santa Barbara City Coll (CA)
Santa Rosa Jr Coll (CA)
Sauk Valley Comm Coll (IL)
Skyline Coll (CA)
Snow Coll (UT)
Treasure Valley Comm Coll (OR)
Tulsa Comm Coll (OK)
Vermilion Comm Coll (MN)

Education
Abraham Baldwin Ag Coll (GA)
Arizona Western Coll (AZ)
Bainbridge Coll (GA)
Bergen Comm Coll (NJ)
Brazosport Coll (TX)
Bucks County Comm Coll (PA)
Bunker Hill Comm Coll (MA)

Butler County Comm Coll (PA)
Casper Coll (WY)
Cecil Comm Coll (MD)
Central Oregon Comm Coll (OR)
Chemeketa Comm Coll (OR)
Clarendon Coll (TX)
Coastal Bend Coll (TX)
Cochise Coll, Douglas (AZ)
Colby Comm Coll (KS)
Coll of Southern Maryland (MD)
Coll of The Albemarle (NC)
Copiah-Lincoln Comm Coll (MS)
Cowley County Comm Coll and Area Vocational–Tech School (KS)
Crowder Coll (MO)
Dabney S. Lancaster Comm Coll (VA)
East Central Coll (MO)
Fiorello H. LaGuardia Comm Coll of the City U of New York (NY)
Florida National Coll (FL)
Frederick Comm Coll (MD)
Galveston Coll (TX)
GateWay Comm Coll (AZ)
Genesee Comm Coll (NY)
Germanna Comm Coll (VA)
Greenfield Comm Coll (MA)
Guam Comm Coll (GU)
Hagerstown Comm Coll (MD)
Harrisburg Area Comm Coll (PA)
Hawkeye Comm Coll (IA)
Highland Comm Coll (IL)
Highline Comm Coll (WA)
Hutchinson Comm Coll and Area Vocational School (KS)
Illinois Valley Comm Coll (IL)
Itasca Comm Coll (MN)
Joliet Jr Coll (IL)
Kennebec Valley Comm Coll (ME)
Kingsborough Comm Coll of the City U of New York (NY)
Kingwood Coll (TX)
Lackawanna Coll (PA)
Lansing Comm Coll (MI)
Laramie County Comm Coll (WY)
Lawson State Comm Coll (AL)
Lincoln Coll (IL)
Lincoln Coll–Normal (IL)
Linn-Benton Comm Coll (OR)
Lord Fairfax Comm Coll (VA)
Luzerne County Comm Coll (PA)
Manor Coll (PA)
Miami Dade Coll (FL)
Middlesex County Coll (NJ)
Mississippi Gulf Coast Comm Coll (MS)
New Mexico State U–Alamogordo (NM)
Northampton County Area Comm Coll (PA)
Northeast Comm Coll (NE)
Northern Essex Comm Coll (MA)
North Idaho Coll (ID)
Northwest Indian Coll (WA)
Northwest-Shoals Comm Coll (AL)
Okaloosa-Walton Coll (FL)
Palau Comm CollPalau)
Palm Beach Comm Coll (FL)
Palo Alto Coll (TX)
Palo Verde Coll (CA)
Piedmont Virginia Comm Coll (VA)
Raritan Valley Comm Coll (NJ)
Roane State Comm Coll (TN)
St. Philip's Coll (TX)
Salem Comm Coll (NJ)
San Juan Coll (NM)
Santa Rosa Jr Coll (CA)
Sauk Valley Comm Coll (IL)
Sheridan Coll–Sheridan and Gillette (WY)

Sinclair Comm Coll (OH)
Snow Coll (UT)
South Plains Coll (TX)
Southside Virginia Comm Coll (VA)
South Texas Coll (TX)
Southwest Mississippi Comm Coll (MS)
Southwest Virginia Comm Coll (VA)
Spoon River Coll (IL)
Springfield Coll in Illinois (IL)
Three Rivers Comm Coll (MO)
Tidewater Comm Coll (VA)
Treasure Valley Comm Coll (OR)
Trinidad State Jr Coll (CO)
Trinity Valley Comm Coll (TX)
Truett-McConnell Coll (GA)
Tulsa Comm Coll (OK)
United Tribes Tech Coll (ND)
Vance-Granville Comm Coll (NC)
Vermilion Comm Coll (MN)
Villa Maria Coll of Buffalo (NY)
Young Harris Coll (GA)
Yuba Coll (CA)

Educational/Instructional Media Design
Century Coll (MN)
Collin County Comm Coll District (TX)
Comm Coll of the Air Force (AL)
Hibbing Comm Coll (MN)
Hutchinson Comm Coll and Area Vocational School (KS)
Ivy Tech Comm Coll–North Central (IN)
Tarrant County Coll District (TX)
Texas State Tech Coll Waco (TX)

Educational Leadership and Administration
Comm Coll of the Air Force (AL)

Education (K-12)
Cecil Comm Coll (MD)
Itasca Comm Coll (MN)
Keystone Coll (PA)
Pratt Comm Coll (KS)

Education (Multiple Levels)
Atlanta Metropolitan Coll (GA)
Carroll Comm Coll (MD)
Coastal Georgia Comm Coll (GA)

Education Related
Corning Comm Coll (NY)
Rogue Comm Coll (OR)
Yavapai Coll (AZ)

Education (Specific Levels and Methods) Related
Comm Coll of Allegheny County (PA)
Laramie County Comm Coll (WY)

Education (Specific Subject Areas) Related
Comm Coll of Allegheny County (PA)

Electrical and Electronic Engineering Technologies Related
Albany Tech Coll (GA)
Cincinnati State Tech and Comm Coll (OH)
Lamar State Coll–Port Arthur (TX)
Miami Dade Coll (FL)
Minnesota State Comm and Tech Coll–Fergus Falls (MN)
Mohawk Valley Comm Coll (NY)
Southwestern Michigan Coll (MI)
Springfield Tech Comm Coll (MA)
York Tech Coll (SC)

Electrical and Power Transmission Installation
Benjamin Franklin Inst of Technology (MA)
Ivy Tech Comm Coll–Columbus (IN)
Moraine Park Tech Coll (WI)
Orange Coast Coll (CA)
St. Cloud Tech Coll (MN)
State U of New York Coll of Technology at Delhi (NY)

Electrical and Power Transmission Installation Related
Manhattan Area Tech Coll (KS)

Electrical, Electronic and Communications Engineering Technology
Aiken Tech Coll (SC)
Alamance Comm Coll (NC)
Allan Hancock Coll (CA)
Allen County Comm Coll (KS)
Arapahoe Comm Coll (CO)
Arizona Western Coll (AZ)
Arkansas State U–Beebe (AR)
Athens Tech Coll (GA)
Augusta Tech Coll (GA)
Austin Comm Coll (TX)
Bainbridge Coll (GA)
Beaufort County Comm Coll (NC)
Benjamin Franklin Inst of Technology (MA)
Bergen Comm Coll (NJ)
Berkshire Comm Coll (MA)
Bishop State Comm Coll (AL)
Bladen Comm Coll (NC)
Blue Ridge Comm Coll (VA)
Brazosport Coll (TX)
Brevard Comm Coll (FL)
Bristol Comm Coll (MA)
Bronx Comm Coll of the City U of New York (NY)
Broome Comm Coll (NY)
Broward Comm Coll (FL)
Brown Coll (MN)
Butler Comm Coll (KS)
Butler County Comm Coll (PA)
Caldwell Comm Coll and Tech Inst (NC)
Cape Fear Comm Coll (NC)
Capital Comm Coll (CT)
Career Coll of Northern Nevada (NV)
Casper Coll (WY)
Cecil Comm Coll (MD)
Central Comm Coll–Columbus Campus (NE)
Central Comm Coll–Grand Island Campus (NE)
Central Comm Coll–Hastings Campus (NE)
Central Georgia Tech Coll (GA)
Centralia Coll (WA)
Central New Mexico Comm Coll (NM)
Central Piedmont Comm Coll (NC)
Chattahoochee Tech Coll (GA)
Chattanooga State Tech Comm Coll (TN)
Chemeketa Comm Coll (OR)
Cincinnati State Tech and Comm Coll (OH)
Citrus Coll (CA)
Clark Coll (WA)
Clark State Comm Coll (OH)
Cleveland Comm Coll (NC)
Cochise Coll, Douglas (AZ)
Coll of DuPage (IL)
Coll of Lake County (IL)
Coll of Southern Maryland (MD)
Coll of the Canyons (CA)
Collin County Comm Coll District (TX)
Columbus Tech Coll (GA)
Comm Coll of Allegheny County (PA)
Comm Coll of the Air Force (AL)
Copiah-Lincoln Comm Coll (MS)
Corning Comm Coll (NY)
Crowder Coll (MO)
Dabney S. Lancaster Comm Coll (VA)
DeKalb Tech Coll (GA)
Delaware Tech & Comm Coll, Jack F. Owens Campus (DE)
Delaware Tech & Comm Coll, Stanton/Wilmington Campus (DE)
Delaware Tech & Comm Coll, Terry Campus (DE)
Delgado Comm Coll (LA)
Dyersburg State Comm Coll (TN)
East Central Coll (MO)
Eastern Idaho Tech Coll (ID)
Eastfield Coll (TX)
ECPI Coll of Technology, Newport News (VA)
ECPI Coll of Technology, Virginia Beach (VA)
ECPI Tech Coll (VA)
ECPI Tech Coll, Richmond (VA)
Edmonds Comm Coll (WA)
Erie Comm Coll, North Campus (NY)
Essex County Coll (NJ)
Evergreen Valley Coll (CA)
Fayetteville Tech Comm Coll (NC)
Flint River Tech Coll (GA)
Florida Comm Coll at Jacksonville (FL)
Foothill Coll (CA)
Forsyth Tech Comm Coll (NC)
Fountainhead Coll of Technology (TN)
Fox Valley Tech Coll (WI)
Frederick Comm Coll (MD)
Gaston Coll (NC)
Gateway Comm Coll (CT)
Genesee Comm Coll (NY)
George C. Wallace Comm Coll (AL)
Georgia Highlands Coll (GA)
Glendale Comm Coll (AZ)
Grand Rapids Comm Coll (MI)
Great Basin Coll (NV)
Griffin Tech Coll (GA)
Guam Comm Coll (GU)
Gwinnett Tech Coll (GA)
Harrisburg Area Comm Coll (PA)
H. Councill Trenholm State Tech Coll (AL)
Heald Coll-Concord (CA)
Heald Coll-Fresno (CA)
Heald Coll-Honolulu (HI)
Heald Coll-Roseville (CA)
Heald Coll-San Francisco (CA)
Heald Coll-San Jose (CA)
Heartland Comm Coll (IL)
Heart of Georgia Tech Coll (GA)
Herzing Coll (GA)
Highland Comm Coll (IL)
Horry-Georgetown Tech Coll (SC)
Houston Comm Coll System (TX)
Howard Comm Coll (MD)
Hudson Valley Comm Coll (NY)
Illinois Central Coll (IL)
Illinois Eastern Comm Colls, Wabash Valley College (IL)
Illinois Valley Comm Coll (IL)
Independence Comm Coll (KS)
IntelliTec Coll, Grand Junction (CO)
Island Drafting and Tech Inst (NY)
ITI Tech Coll (LA)
ITT Tech Inst, Tucson (AZ)
ITT Tech Inst (AR)
ITT Tech Inst, Anaheim (CA)
ITT Tech Inst, Lathrop (CA)
ITT Tech Inst, Oxnard (CA)
ITT Tech Inst, Rancho Cordova (CA)
ITT Tech Inst, San Bernardino (CA)
ITT Tech Inst, San Diego (CA)
ITT Tech Inst, Sylmar (CA)
ITT Tech Inst, Torrance (CA)
ITT Tech Inst, West Covina (CA)
ITT Tech Inst (CO)
ITT Tech Inst, Fort Lauderdale (FL)
ITT Tech Inst, Jacksonville (FL)
ITT Tech Inst, Lake Mary (FL)
ITT Tech Inst, Miami (FL)
ITT Tech Inst, Tampa (FL)
ITT Tech Inst, Duluth (GA)
ITT Tech Inst, Kennesaw (GA)
ITT Tech Inst (ID)
ITT Tech Inst, Burr Ridge (IL)
ITT Tech Inst, Matteson (IL)
ITT Tech Inst, Mount Prospect (IL)
ITT Tech Inst, Fort Wayne (IN)
ITT Tech Inst, Indianapolis (IN)
ITT Tech Inst, Newburgh (IN)
ITT Tech Inst, Louisville (KY)
ITT Tech Inst (LA)
ITT Tech Inst (MD)
ITT Tech Inst, Norwood (MA)
ITT Tech Inst, Woburn (MA)
ITT Tech Inst, Canton (MI)
ITT Tech Inst, Grand Rapids (MI)
ITT Tech Inst, Troy (MI)
ITT Tech Inst (MN)
ITT Tech Inst, Arnold (MO)
ITT Tech Inst, Earth City (MO)
ITT Tech Inst, Kansas City (MO)
ITT Tech Inst (NE)
ITT Tech Inst (NV)
ITT Tech Inst (NM)
ITT Tech Inst, Albany (NY)
ITT Tech Inst, Getzville (NY)
ITT Tech Inst, Dayton (OH)
ITT Tech Inst, Hilliard (OH)
ITT Tech Inst, Norwood (OH)
ITT Tech Inst, Strongsville (OH)
ITT Tech Inst, Warrensville Heights (OH)
ITT Tech Inst (OK)
ITT Tech Inst (OR)
ITT Tech Inst (SC)
ITT Tech Inst, Knoxville (TN)
ITT Tech Inst, Memphis (TN)
ITT Tech Inst, Nashville (TN)
ITT Tech Inst, Arlington (TX)
ITT Tech Inst, Austin (TX)
ITT Tech Inst, Houston (TX)
ITT Tech Inst, Houston (TX)
ITT Tech Inst, Houston (TX)
ITT Tech Inst, Richardson (TX)
ITT Tech Inst, San Antonio (TX)
ITT Tech Inst (UT)
ITT Tech Inst, Chantilly (VA)
ITT Tech Inst, Norfolk (VA)
ITT Tech Inst, Richmond (VA)
ITT Tech Inst, Springfield (VA)
ITT Tech Inst, Bothell (WA)
ITT Tech Inst, Seattle (WA)
ITT Tech Inst, Spokane (WA)
ITT Tech Inst, Green Bay (WI)
ITT Tech Inst, Greenfield (WI)
Ivy Tech Comm Coll–Bloomington (IN)
Ivy Tech Comm Coll–Central Indiana (IN)
Ivy Tech Comm Coll–Columbus (IN)
Ivy Tech Comm Coll–East Central (IN)
Ivy Tech Comm Coll–Kokomo (IN)
Ivy Tech Comm Coll–Lafayette (IN)
Ivy Tech Comm Coll–North Central (IN)
Ivy Tech Comm Coll–Northeast (IN)
Ivy Tech Comm Coll–Northwest (IN)
Ivy Tech Comm Coll–Southeast (IN)
Ivy Tech Comm Coll–Southern Indiana (IN)
Ivy Tech Comm Coll–Southwest (IN)
Ivy Tech Comm Coll–Wabash Valley (IN)
Ivy Tech Comm Coll–Whitewater (IN)
Jackson Comm Coll (MI)
Jamestown Comm Coll (NY)
Jefferson Comm and Tech Coll (KY)
Jefferson Comm Coll (OH)
J. F. Drake State Tech Coll (AL)
Johnston Comm Coll (NC)
John Wood Comm Coll (IL)
Joliet Jr Coll (IL)
Kaskaskia Coll (IL)
Kauai Comm Coll (HI)
Kent State U, Trumbull Campus (OH)
Kent State U, Tuscarawas Campus (OH)
Lake City Comm Coll (FL)
Lake Land Coll (IL)
Lake Michigan Coll (MI)
Lakeshore Tech Coll (WI)
Lake Superior Coll (MN)
Lamar State Coll–Port Arthur (TX)
Lanier Tech Coll (GA)
Lansing Comm Coll (MI)
Laredo Comm Coll (TX)
Lawson State Comm Coll (AL)
Lincoln Land Comm Coll (IL)
Linn State Tech Coll (MO)
Long Beach City Coll (CA)
Lower Columbia Coll (WA)
Luzerne County Comm Coll (PA)
Macomb Comm Coll (MI)
Manatee Comm Coll (FL)
Marshall Comm and Tech Coll (WV)
Mercer County Comm Coll (NJ)
Meridian Comm Coll (MS)
Metropolitan Comm Coll (NE)
Metropolitan Comm Coll-Business & Technology College (MO)
Miami Dade Coll (FL)
Middlesex County Coll (NJ)
Midland Coll (TX)
Midlands Tech Coll (SC)
Minnesota State Comm and Tech Coll–Fergus Falls (MN)
Mississippi Gulf Coast Comm Coll (MS)
Moberly Area Comm Coll (MO)
Modesto Jr Coll (CA)
Mohawk Valley Comm Coll (NY)
Montgomery Coll (TX)
Montgomery County Comm Coll (PA)
Mott Comm Coll (MI)
Moultrie Tech Coll (GA)
Mountain View Coll (TX)
Mt. San Antonio Coll (CA)
Mount Wachusett Comm Coll (MA)
Naugatuck Valley Comm Coll (CT)
New Hampshire Comm Tech Coll, Nashua/Claremont (NH)
New Hampshire Tech Inst (NH)
New Mexico State U–Alamogordo (NM)
Niagara County Comm Coll (NY)
Normandale Comm Coll (MN)
Northampton County Area Comm Coll (PA)
North Arkansas Coll (AR)
North Central Missouri Coll (MO)
North Dakota State Coll of Science (ND)
Northeast Comm Coll (NE)
Northeast Iowa Comm Coll (IA)
Northeast State Tech Comm Coll (TN)
Northern Essex Comm Coll (MA)
Northern Maine Comm Coll (ME)
North Idaho Coll (ID)
North Iowa Area Comm Coll (IA)
Northland Comm and Tech Coll–Thief River Falls (MN)
North Metro Tech Coll (GA)
North Seattle Comm Coll (WA)
Northwestern Connecticut Comm Coll (CT)
Northwestern Tech Coll (GA)
Northwest-Shoals Comm Coll (AL)
Norwalk Comm Coll (CT)
Oakland Comm Coll (MI)
Ocean County Coll (NJ)
Okaloosa-Walton Coll (FL)
Orange Coast Coll (CA)
Orange County Comm Coll (NY)
Owens Comm Coll, Toledo (OH)
Palau Comm CollPalau)
Palm Beach Comm Coll (FL)
Pasadena City Coll (CA)
Pellissippi State Tech Comm Coll (TN)
Peninsula Coll (WA)
Penn Foster Career School (PA)
Pennsylvania Inst of Technology (PA)
The Pennsylvania State U Delaware County Campus of the Commonwealth Coll (PA)
The Pennsylvania State U DuBois Campus of the Commonwealth Coll (PA)
The Pennsylvania State U Fayette Campus of the Commonwealth Coll (PA)
The Pennsylvania State U Hazleton Campus of the Commonwealth Coll (PA)
The Pennsylvania State U New Kensington Campus of the Commonwealth Coll (PA)
The Pennsylvania State U Shenango Campus of the Commonwealth Coll (PA)
The Pennsylvania State U Wilkes-Barre Campus of the Commonwealth Coll (PA)
The Pennsylvania State U Worthington Scranton Campus of the Commonwealth Coll (PA)
The Pennsylvania State U York Campus of the Commonwealth Coll (PA)
Pima Comm Coll (AZ)
Prairie State Coll (IL)
Quinsigamond Comm Coll (MA)
Raritan Valley Comm Coll (NJ)
Remington Coll–Lafayette Campus (LA)
Remington Coll–Tampa Campus (FL)
Richland Comm Coll (IL)
Richmond Comm Coll (NC)
Rock Valley Coll (IL)
Rogue Comm Coll (OR)
Saddleback Coll (CA)
St. Cloud Tech Coll (MN)
St. Louis Comm Coll at Florissant Valley (MO)
Saint Paul Coll–A Comm & Tech College (MN)
St. Petersburg Coll (FL)
Salt Lake Comm Coll (UT)
San Diego City Coll (CA)
San Joaquin Delta Coll (CA)

Santa Barbara City Coll (CA)
Santa Rosa Jr Coll (CA)
Sauk Valley Comm Coll (IL)
Savannah Tech Coll (GA)
Schuylkill Inst of Business and Technology (PA)
Scottsdale Comm Coll (AZ)
Seminole Comm Coll (FL)
Shelton State Comm Coll (AL)
Sinclair Comm Coll (OH)
Snow Coll (UT)
Southeastern Comm Coll (NC)
Southeastern Tech Coll (GA)
Southeast Tech Inst (SD)
South Georgia Tech Coll (GA)
South Plains Coll (TX)
Southside Virginia Comm Coll (VA)
Southwestern Illinois Coll (IL)
Southwest Mississippi Comm Coll (MS)
Southwest Tennessee Comm Coll (TN)
Southwest Virginia Comm Coll (VA)
Spartanburg Tech Coll (SC)
Spokane Comm Coll (WA)
Spoon River Coll (IL)
Springfield Tech Comm Coll (MA)
State U of New York Coll of Technology at Alfred (NY)
Sullivan County Comm Coll (NY)
Swainsboro Tech Coll (GA)
Tarrant County Coll District (TX)
Texas State Tech Coll Waco (TX)
Thomas Nelson Comm Coll (VA)
Tidewater Comm Coll (VA)
Tomball Coll (TX)
Tompkins Cortland Comm Coll (NY)
Triangle Tech, Inc.–DuBois School (PA)
Tri-County Comm Coll (NC)
Trident Tech Coll (SC)
Triton Coll (IL)
Tulsa Comm Coll (OK)
U of Alaska Anchorage, Matanuska-Susitna Coll (AK)
Valencia Comm Coll (FL)
Vance-Granville Comm Coll (NC)
Vatterott Coll, Tulsa (OK)
Waubonsee Comm Coll (IL)
Waukesha County Tech Coll (WI)
West Central Tech Coll (GA)
Westchester Comm Coll (NY)
Western Iowa Tech Comm Coll (IA)
Western Tech Coll (WI)
West Georgia Tech Coll (GA)
Westmoreland County Comm Coll (PA)
West Virginia Northern Comm Coll (WV)
Wharton County Jr Coll (TX)
Wilkes Comm Coll (NC)
William Rainey Harper Coll (IL)
The Williamson Free School of Mecha Trades (PA)
Wilson Tech Comm Coll (NC)
Wor-Wic Comm Coll (MD)
Yakima Valley Comm Coll (WA)
York Tech Coll (SC)
Yuba Coll (CA)

Electrical, Electronics and Communications Engineering
Allen County Comm Coll (KS)
Jamestown Comm Coll (NY)
John Tyler Comm Coll (VA)
Lake Region State Coll (ND)

Electrical/Electronics Drafting and Cad/Cadd
Brevard Comm Coll (FL)

Central New Mexico Comm Coll (NM)
Collin County Comm Coll District (TX)
Eastfield Coll (TX)
Joliet Jr Coll (IL)
North Seattle Comm Coll (WA)
Texas State Tech Coll Waco (TX)
Waukesha County Tech Coll (WI)

Electrical/Electronics Equipment Installation and Repair
Cape Fear Comm Coll (NC)
Coll of DuPage (IL)
Collin County Comm Coll District (TX)
Delgado Comm Coll (LA)
Hutchinson Comm Coll and Area Vocational School (KS)
Kennebec Valley Comm Coll (ME)
Lake Region State Coll (ND)
Macomb Comm Coll (MI)
Mesabi Range Comm and Tech Coll (MN)
Modesto Jr Coll (CA)
Orange Coast Coll (CA)
Riverland Comm Coll (MN)
St. Philip's Coll (TX)
Santa Barbara City Coll (CA)
Southwest Tennessee Comm Coll (TN)
State U of New York Coll of Technology at Alfred (NY)
Triangle Tech, Inc.– Greensburg School (PA)
York Tech Coll (SC)

Electrical/Electronics Maintenance and Repair Technology Related
Bunker Hill Comm Coll (MA)
Front Range Comm Coll (CO)
Hudson Valley Comm Coll (NY)
Mohawk Valley Comm Coll (NY)
Triangle Tech, Inc.– Greensburg School (PA)

Electrician
Brazosport Coll (TX)
Cleveland Comm Coll (NC)
Coll of Lake County (IL)
Delta Coll (MI)
Fayetteville Tech Comm Coll (NC)
H. Councill Trenholm State Tech Coll (AL)
Ivy Tech Comm Coll– Bloomington (IN)
Ivy Tech Comm Coll–Central Indiana (IN)
Ivy Tech Comm Coll–East Central (IN)
Ivy Tech Comm Coll– Kokomo (IN)
Ivy Tech Comm Coll– Lafayette (IN)
Ivy Tech Comm Coll–North Central (IN)
Ivy Tech Comm Coll– Northeast (IN)
Ivy Tech Comm Coll– Northwest (IN)
Ivy Tech Comm Coll– Southern Indiana (IN)
Ivy Tech Comm Coll– Southwest (IN)
Ivy Tech Comm Coll– Wabash Valley (IN)
Ivy Tech Comm Coll– Whitewater (IN)
John Wood Comm Coll (IL)
Lake Superior Coll (MN)
Linn State Tech Coll (MO)
Lower Columbia Coll (WA)
Luzerne County Comm Coll (PA)
Northampton County Area Comm Coll (PA)
Northeast Comm Coll (NE)
Piedmont Virginia Comm Coll (VA)
Rosedale Tech Inst (PA)

TESST Coll of Technology, Towson (MD)

Electrocardiograph Technology
Edmonds Comm Coll (WA)
St. Cloud Tech Coll (MN)

Electromechanical and Instrumentation And Maintenance Technologies Related
North Arkansas Coll (AR)
St. Petersburg Coll (FL)
Waukesha County Tech Coll (WI)

Electromechanical Technology
Aiken Tech Coll (SC)
Alamance Comm Coll (NC)
Central Comm Coll– Columbus Campus (NE)
Central Piedmont Comm Coll (NC)
Cincinnati State Tech and Comm Coll (OH)
Clovis Comm Coll (NM)
Coll of DuPage (IL)
Comm and Tech Coll of Shepherd (WV)
DeKalb Tech Coll (GA)
Delaware Tech & Comm Coll, Terry Campus (DE)
ECPI Coll of Technology, Newport News (VA)
ECPI Coll of Technology, Virginia Beach (VA)
ECPI Tech Coll (VA)
ECPI Tech Coll, Richmond (VA)
Forsyth Tech Comm Coll (NC)
GateWay Comm Coll (AZ)
Hagerstown Comm Coll (MD)
Jackson State Comm Coll (TN)
Lake Land Coll (IL)
Lake Michigan Coll (MI)
Lakeshore Tech Coll (WI)
Lansing Comm Coll (MI)
Macomb Comm Coll (MI)
Montgomery County Comm Coll (PA)
Moraine Park Tech Coll (WI)
Mountain View Coll (TX)
New Hampshire Comm Tech Coll, Nashua/Claremont (NH)
Northampton County Area Comm Coll (PA)
North Arkansas Coll (AR)
Northeast Comm Coll (NE)
Oakland Comm Coll (MI)
Pulaski Tech Coll (AR)
Raritan Valley Comm Coll (NJ)
Rockingham Comm Coll (NC)
St. Philip's Coll (TX)
Sinclair Comm Coll (OH)
Southeast Tech Inst (SD)
Springfield Tech Comm Coll (MA)
State U of New York Coll of Technology at Alfred (NY)
Tarrant County Coll District (TX)
Union County Coll (NJ)
Western Tech Coll (WI)
Wilkes Comm Coll (NC)
Wisconsin Indianhead Tech Coll (WI)

Electroneurodiagnostic/ Electroencephalographic Technology
Comm Coll of Allegheny County (PA)
Comm Coll of Denver (CO)
Niagara County Comm Coll (NY)
Oakland Comm Coll (MI)
Parkland Coll (IL)
Western Tech Coll (WI)

Elementary and Middle School Administration/ Principalship
Tulsa Comm Coll (OK)

Elementary Education
Abraham Baldwin Ag Coll (GA)
Allen County Comm Coll (KS)
Ancilla Coll (IN)
Bainbridge Coll (GA)
Barton County Comm Coll (KS)
Brazosport Coll (TX)
Bristol Comm Coll (MA)
Broward Comm Coll (FL)
Butler County Comm Coll (PA)
Carl Albert State Coll (OK)
Casper Coll (WY)
Cecil Comm Coll (MD)
Central New Mexico Comm Coll (NM)
Central Wyoming Coll (WY)
Chattahoochee Valley Comm Coll (AL)
City Colls of Chicago, Wilbur Wright College (IL)
Clarendon Coll (TX)
Coahoma Comm Coll (MS)
Coastal Bend Coll (TX)
Coll of Southern Maryland (MD)
Copiah-Lincoln Comm Coll (MS)
Corning Comm Coll (NY)
Cowley County Comm Coll and Area Vocational–Tech School (KS)
Crowder Coll (MO)
Diné Coll (AZ)
Dixie State Coll of Utah (UT)
Eastern Arizona Coll (AZ)
Eastern Wyoming Coll (WY)
Essex County Coll (NJ)
Fayetteville Tech Comm Coll (NC)
Frederick Comm Coll (MD)
Gainesville Coll (GA)
Genesee Comm Coll (NY)
Great Basin Coll (NV)
Hagerstown Comm Coll (MD)
Harrisburg Area Comm Coll (PA)
Holyoke Comm Coll (MA)
Howard Comm Coll (MD)
Illinois Valley Comm Coll (IL)
Independence Comm Coll (KS)
Kellogg Comm Coll (MI)
Kingsborough Comm Coll of the City U of New York (NY)
Lansing Comm Coll (MI)
Lincoln Coll (IL)
Linn-Benton Comm Coll (OR)
Manor Coll (PA)
Miami Dade Coll (FL)
Mississippi Gulf Coast Comm Coll (MS)
Mohawk Valley Comm Coll (NY)
Montgomery County Comm Coll (PA)
Northeast Comm Coll (NE)
Northern Essex Comm Coll (MA)
North Idaho Coll (ID)
Northwest-Shoals Comm Coll (AL)
Okaloosa-Walton Coll (FL)
Orange County Comm Coll (NY)
Otero Jr Coll (CO)
Palm Beach Comm Coll (FL)
Parkland Coll (IL)
Pima Comm Coll (AZ)
Pratt Comm Coll (KS)
Raritan Valley Comm Coll (NJ)
Roane State Comm Coll (TN)
St. Louis Comm Coll at Florissant Valley (MO)
Sauk Valley Comm Coll (IL)
Seminole State Coll (OK)
Sheridan Coll–Sheridan and Gillette (WY)
Snow Coll (UT)
Southwestern Illinois Coll (IL)
Southwest Mississippi Comm Coll (MS)

Springfield Tech Comm Coll (MA)
Sullivan County Comm Coll (NY)
Three Rivers Comm Coll (MO)
Trinity Valley Comm Coll (TX)
Tulsa Comm Coll (OK)
Vance-Granville Comm Coll (NC)
Vermilion Comm Coll (MN)
Wor-Wic Comm Coll (MD)
Yuba Coll (CA)

Emergency Medical Technology (EMT Paramedic)
Allen County Comm Coll (KS)
Arapahoe Comm Coll (CO)
Arkansas State U–Mountain Home (AR)
Athens Tech Coll (GA)
Augusta Tech Coll (GA)
Austin Comm Coll (TX)
Barton County Comm Coll (KS)
Borough of Manhattan Comm Coll of the City U of New York (NY)
Brazosport Coll (TX)
Brevard Comm Coll (FL)
Broome Comm Coll (NY)
Broward Comm Coll (FL)
Butler County Comm Coll (PA)
Capital Comm Coll (CT)
Casper Coll (WY)
Central Arizona Coll (AZ)
Central Florida Comm Coll (FL)
Central Oregon Comm Coll (OR)
Century Coll (MN)
Chattanooga State Tech Comm Coll (TN)
Chemeketa Comm Coll (OR)
Cincinnati State Tech and Comm Coll (OH)
Clark Coll (WA)
Clark State Comm Coll (OH)
Coastal Carolina Comm Coll (NC)
Cochise Coll, Douglas (AZ)
Coll of DuPage (IL)
Coll of Southern Maryland (MD)
Coll of the Mainland (TX)
Collin County Comm Coll District (TX)
Columbus Tech Coll (GA)
Comm and Tech Coll of Shepherd (WV)
Corning Comm Coll (NY)
Cossatot Comm Coll of the U of Arkansas (AR)
Cowley County Comm Coll and Area Vocational–Tech School (KS)
Delaware Tech & Comm Coll, Jack F. Owens Campus (DE)
Delaware Tech & Comm Coll, Stanton/Wilmington Campus (DE)
Delgado Comm Coll (LA)
Delta Coll (MI)
Dixie State Coll of Utah (UT)
East Central Coll (MO)
Eastern Arizona Coll (AZ)
El Centro Coll (TX)
Essex County Coll (NJ)
Fayetteville Tech Comm Coll (NC)
Fiorello H. LaGuardia Comm Coll of the City U of New York (NY)
Florida Comm Coll at Jacksonville (FL)
Foothill Coll (CA)
Frederick Comm Coll (MD)
Gadsden State Comm Coll (AL)
Galveston Coll (TX)
George C. Wallace Comm Coll (AL)
Georgia Highlands Coll (GA)
Glendale Comm Coll (AZ)
Goodwin Coll (CT)

Griffin Tech Coll (GA)
Gwinnett Tech Coll (GA)
Hagerstown Comm Coll (MD)
Harrisburg Area Comm Coll (PA)
H. Councill Trenholm State Tech Coll (AL)
Houston Comm Coll System (TX)
Howard Comm Coll (MD)
Hudson Valley Comm Coll (NY)
Hutchinson Comm Coll and Area Vocational School (KS)
Independence Comm Coll (KS)
Ivy Tech Comm Coll– Bloomington (IN)
Ivy Tech Comm Coll– Kokomo (IN)
Ivy Tech Comm Coll–North Central (IN)
Ivy Tech Comm Coll– Southwest (IN)
Ivy Tech Comm Coll– Wabash Valley (IN)
Jackson Comm Coll (MI)
Jefferson Comm Coll (OH)
John Wood Comm Coll (IL)
Joliet Jr Coll (IL)
Kansas City Kansas Comm Coll (KS)
Kellogg Comm Coll (MI)
Kennebec Valley Comm Coll (ME)
Kent State U, Geauga Campus (OH)
Lackawanna Coll (PA)
Lake City Comm Coll (FL)
Lake-Sumter Comm Coll (FL)
Lake Superior Coll (MN)
Lansing Comm Coll (MI)
Laredo Comm Coll (TX)
Luzerne County Comm Coll (PA)
Macomb Comm Coll (MI)
Marshall Comm and Tech Coll (WV)
Meridian Comm Coll (MS)
Miami Dade Coll (FL)
Midland Coll (TX)
Mississippi Gulf Coast Comm Coll (MS)
Modesto Jr Coll (CA)
Mohawk Valley Comm Coll (NY)
Montgomery Comm Coll (NC)
Mott Comm Coll (MI)
Mt. San Antonio Coll (CA)
New Hampshire Tech Inst (NH)
North Arkansas Coll (AR)
North Central Missouri Coll (MO)
Northeast Comm Coll (NE)
Northeast State Tech Comm Coll (TN)
Northern Maine Comm Coll (ME)
North Iowa Area Comm Coll (IA)
Oakland Comm Coll (MI)
Orange Coast Coll (CA)
Pasco-Hernando Comm Coll (FL)
Penn Valley Comm Coll (MO)
Phoenix Coll (AZ)
Piedmont Virginia Comm Coll (VA)
Pima Comm Coll (AZ)
Polk Comm Coll (FL)
Quinsigamond Comm Coll (MA)
Roane State Comm Coll (TN)
Saddleback Coll (CA)
St. Cloud Tech Coll (MN)
St. Louis Comm Coll at Florissant Valley (MO)
St. Petersburg Coll (FL)
San Diego City Coll (CA)
San Joaquin Delta Coll (CA)
Santa Rosa Jr Coll (CA)
Scottsdale Comm Coll (AZ)
Seminole Comm Coll (FL)

Shelton State Comm Coll (AL)
Sinclair Comm Coll (OH)
Skyline Coll (CA)
South Arkansas Comm Coll (AR)
Southern Arkansas U Tech (AR)
Southern State Comm Coll (OH)
South Texas Coll (TX)
Southwest Mississippi Comm Coll (MS)
Tarrant County Coll District (TX)
Tillamook Bay Comm Coll (OR)
Trinity Valley Comm Coll (TX)
Tulsa Comm Coll (OK)
Valencia Comm Coll (FL)
Weatherford Coll (TX)
Westchester Comm Coll (NY)
Western Iowa Tech Comm Coll (IA)
Western Oklahoma State Coll (OK)
Wisconsin Indianhead Tech Coll (WI)
Wor-Wic Comm Coll (MD)

Energy Management and Systems Technology
Chattanooga State Tech Comm Coll (TN)
Comm Coll of Allegheny County (PA)
Macomb Comm Coll (MI)
Pratt Comm Coll (KS)
The Williamson Free School of Mecha Trades (PA)

Engineering
Allan Hancock Coll (CA)
Allen County Comm Coll (KS)
Berkshire Comm Coll (MA)
Brazosport Coll (TX)
Bucks County Comm Coll (PA)
Casper Coll (WY)
Central Arizona Coll (AZ)
Centralia Coll (WA)
Central New Mexico Comm Coll (NM)
Chemeketa Comm Coll (OR)
Citrus Coll (CA)
City Colls of Chicago, Wilbur Wright College (IL)
Clarendon Coll (TX)
Coastal Bend Coll (TX)
Coll of DuPage (IL)
Coll of Lake County (IL)
Copiah-Lincoln Comm Coll (MS)
Delaware Tech & Comm Coll, Jack F. Owens Campus (DE)
Delaware Tech & Comm Coll, Stanton/Wilmington Campus (DE)
Dixie State Coll of Utah (UT)
East Central Coll (MO)
Erie Comm Coll, North Campus (NY)
Evergreen Valley Coll (CA)
Frederick Comm Coll (MD)
Hagerstown Comm Coll (MD)
Harrisburg Area Comm Coll (PA)
Heartland Comm Coll (IL)
Highland Comm Coll (IL)
Highline Comm Coll (WA)
Howard Comm Coll (MD)
Hutchinson Comm Coll and Area Vocational School (KS)
Independence Comm Coll (KS)
Itasca Comm Coll (MN)
Jamestown Comm Coll (NY)
Kellogg Comm Coll (MI)
Lansing Comm Coll (MI)
Laramie County Comm Coll (WY)
Linn-Benton Comm Coll (OR)
Long Beach City Coll (CA)
Longview Comm Coll (MO)

Lower Columbia Coll (WA)
Manatee Comm Coll (FL)
Metropolitan Comm Coll-Business & Technology College (MO)
Miami Dade Coll (FL)
Middlesex County Coll (NJ)
Missouri State U–West Plains (MO)
Modesto Jr Coll (CA)
Mohawk Valley Comm Coll (NY)
Nassau Comm Coll (NY)
New Mexico Military Inst (NM)
New Mexico State U–Alamogordo (NM)
Northampton County Area Comm Coll (PA)
Northeast Comm Coll (NE)
North Idaho Coll (ID)
Northwestern Connecticut Comm Coll (CT)
Oakland Comm Coll (MI)
Ocean County Coll (NJ)
Okaloosa-Walton Coll (FL)
Orange Coast Coll (CA)
Palo Alto Coll (TX)
Pasadena City Coll (CA)
Penn Valley Comm Coll (MO)
Piedmont Virginia Comm Coll (VA)
Raritan Valley Comm Coll (NJ)
Roane State Comm Coll (TN)
Saddleback Coll (CA)
St. Louis Comm Coll at Florissant Valley (MO)
Salt Lake Comm Coll (UT)
San Diego Mesa Coll (CA)
San Joaquin Delta Coll (CA)
San Juan Coll (NM)
Santa Barbara City Coll (CA)
Santa Rosa Jr Coll (CA)
Sheridan Coll–Sheridan and Gillette (WY)
Sinclair Comm Coll (OH)
Snow Coll (UT)
South Plains Coll (TX)
Southwestern Oregon Comm Coll (OR)
Southwest Mississippi Comm Coll (MS)
Southwest Virginia Comm Coll (VA)
Springfield Tech Comm Coll (MA)
Thomas Nelson Comm Coll (VA)
Tidewater Comm Coll (VA)
Treasure Valley Comm Coll (OR)
Trinidad State Jr Coll (CO)
Tulsa Comm Coll (OK)
Tunxis Comm Coll (CT)
Union County Coll (NJ)
The U of Akron–Wayne Coll (OH)
Valley Forge Military Coll (PA)
Ventura Coll (CA)
Vermilion Comm Coll (MN)
Waubonsee Comm Coll (IL)
Westmoreland County Comm Coll (PA)
William Rainey Harper Coll (IL)

Engineering/Industrial Management
Cape Fear Comm Coll (NC)
St. Petersburg Coll (FL)

Engineering Related
Bristol Comm Coll (MA)
Chattanooga State Tech Comm Coll (TN)
Itasca Comm Coll (MN)
Macomb Comm Coll (MI)
Miami Dade Coll (FL)
San Joaquin Delta Coll (CA)

Engineering-Related Technologies
Metropolitan Comm Coll-Business & Technology College (MO)

Engineering Science
Asnuntuck Comm Coll (CT)
Bergen Comm Coll (NJ)
Borough of Manhattan Comm Coll of the City U of New York (NY)
Bristol Comm Coll (MA)
Broome Comm Coll (NY)
Broward Comm Coll (FL)
Finger Lakes Comm Coll (NY)
Genesee Comm Coll (NY)
Greenfield Comm Coll (MA)
Highland Comm Coll (IL)
Holyoke Comm Coll (MA)
Hudson Valley Comm Coll (NY)
Itasca Comm Coll (MN)
Jefferson Comm Coll (NY)
Kingsborough Comm Coll of the City U of New York (NY)
Manchester Comm Coll (CT)
Mercer County Comm Coll (NJ)
Middlesex Comm Coll (CT)
Middlesex County Coll (NJ)
Montgomery County Comm Coll (PA)
Northern Essex Comm Coll (MA)
North Shore Comm Coll (MA)
Norwalk Comm Coll (CT)
Orange County Comm Coll (NY)
Parkland Coll (IL)
St. Louis Comm Coll at Florissant Valley (MO)
State U of New York Coll of Technology at Alfred (NY)
State U of New York Coll of Technology at Delhi (NY)
Sullivan County Comm Coll (NY)
Tompkins Cortland Comm Coll (NY)
Westchester Comm Coll (NY)

Engineering Technologies Related
Bristol Comm Coll (MA)
Central New Mexico Comm Coll (NM)
Cleveland Comm Coll (NC)
Comm Coll of Allegheny County (PA)
Harrisburg Area Comm Coll (PA)
McNally Smith Coll of Music (MN)
Montgomery County Comm Coll (PA)
Mott Comm Coll (MI)
Southern Arkansas U Tech (AR)
Wisconsin Indianhead Tech Coll (WI)
Wor-Wic Comm Coll (MD)

Engineering Technology
Aiken Tech Coll (SC)
Allan Hancock Coll (CA)
Allen County Comm Coll (KS)
Arizona Western Coll (AZ)
Atlanta Metropolitan Coll (GA)
Atlanta Metropolitan Coll (GA)
Barton County Comm Coll (KS)
Benjamin Franklin Inst of Technology (MA)
Berkshire Comm Coll (MA)
Bishop State Comm Coll (AL)
Central Piedmont Comm Coll (NC)
Citrus Coll (CA)
Cowley County Comm Coll and Area Vocational–Tech School (KS)
Cuyahoga Comm Coll (OH)
DeKalb Tech Coll (GA)
Delaware Tech & Comm Coll, Jack F. Owens Campus (DE)
Delaware Tech & Comm Coll, Terry Campus (DE)

Delta Coll (MI)
Denmark Tech Coll (SC)
ECPI Coll of Technology, Newport News (VA)
ECPI Coll of Technology, Virginia Beach (VA)
ECPI Tech Coll (VA)
ECPI Tech Coll, Richmond (VA)
Florida Comm Coll at Jacksonville (FL)
Forsyth Tech Comm Coll (NC)
Gainesville Coll (GA)
Gateway Comm Coll (CT)
Glendale Comm Coll (AZ)
Harrisburg Area Comm Coll (PA)
Hawkeye Comm Coll (IA)
Highland Comm Coll (IL)
Highline Comm Coll (WA)
Houston Comm Coll System (TX)
Illinois Central Coll (IL)
Independence Comm Coll (KS)
Itasca Comm Coll (MN)
Kent State U, Tuscarawas Campus (OH)
Lansing Comm Coll (MI)
Laramie County Comm Coll (WY)
Lower Columbia Coll (WA)
Luzerne County Comm Coll (PA)
Massachusetts Bay Comm Coll (MA)
Miami Dade Coll (FL)
Middlesex Comm Coll (CT)
Middlesex County Coll (NJ)
Midlands Tech Coll (SC)
Moraine Park Tech Coll (WI)
Morrison Inst of Technology (IL)
Mountain View Coll (TX)
Mt. San Antonio Coll (CA)
Naugatuck Valley Comm Coll (CT)
New Hampshire Comm Tech Coll, Nashua/Claremont (NH)
New Hampshire Tech Inst (NH)
Northeast State Tech Comm Coll (TN)
Norwalk Comm Coll (CT)
Pasadena City Coll (CA)
Peninsula Coll (WA)
Pennsylvania Inst of Technology (PA)
Quinebaug Valley Comm Coll (CT)
St. Louis Comm Coll at Florissant Valley (MO)
Salt Lake Comm Coll (UT)
San Diego City Coll (CA)
San Joaquin Delta Coll (CA)
Santa Barbara City Coll (CA)
Santa Rosa Jr Coll (CA)
Sheridan Coll–Sheridan and Gillette (WY)
Snead State Comm Coll (AL)
Southeast Tech Inst (SD)
Southern West Virginia Comm and Tech Coll (WV)
South Hills School of Business & Technology, State College (PA)
Southwestern Illinois Coll (IL)
Southwestern Michigan Coll (MI)
Spartanburg Tech Coll (SC)
State U of New York Coll of Technology at Delhi (NY)
Three Rivers Comm Coll (MO)
Trident Tech Coll (SC)
Triton Coll (IL)
Tunxis Comm Coll (CT)
Westchester Comm Coll (NY)

English
Abraham Baldwin Ag Coll (GA)
Allan Hancock Coll (CA)
Ancilla Coll (IN)
Arizona Western Coll (AZ)
Atlanta Metropolitan Coll (GA)

Austin Comm Coll (TX)
Bainbridge Coll (GA)
Barton County Comm Coll (KS)
Berkeley City Coll (CA)
Brazosport Coll (TX)
Bunker Hill Comm Coll (MA)
Butler Comm Coll (KS)
Butler County Comm Coll (PA)
Carl Albert State Coll (OK)
Casper Coll (WY)
Centralia Coll (WA)
Central Wyoming Coll (WY)
Chemeketa Comm Coll (OR)
Citrus Coll (CA)
City Colls of Chicago, Wilbur Wright College (IL)
Clarendon Coll (TX)
Coahoma Comm Coll (MS)
Coastal Bend Coll (TX)
Coastal Georgia Comm Coll (GA)
Cochise Coll, Douglas (AZ)
Colby Comm Coll (KS)
Coll of Southern Maryland (MD)
Coll of the Canyons (CA)
Coll of the Siskiyous (CA)
Colorado Mountain Coll (CO)
Colorado Mountain Coll, Alpine Campus (CO)
Columbia Coll (CA)
Comm Coll of Allegheny County (PA)
Copiah-Lincoln Comm Coll (MS)
Dixie State Coll of Utah (UT)
East Central Coll (MO)
Eastern Arizona Coll (AZ)
Eastern Wyoming Coll (WY)
Evergreen Valley Coll (CA)
Feather River Coll (CA)
Foothill Coll (CA)
Frederick Comm Coll (MD)
Gainesville Coll (GA)
Galveston Coll (TX)
Gavilan Coll (CA)
Georgia Highlands Coll (GA)
Great Basin Coll (NV)
Highline Comm Coll (WA)
Howard Coll (TX)
Hutchinson Comm Coll and Area Vocational School (KS)
Illinois Valley Comm Coll (IL)
Independence Comm Coll (KS)
Kellogg Comm Coll (MI)
Kingwood Coll (TX)
Lansing Comm Coll (MI)
Laramie County Comm Coll (WY)
Lawson State Comm Coll (AL)
Lincoln Coll (IL)
Linn-Benton Comm Coll (OR)
Long Beach City Coll (CA)
Lower Columbia Coll (WA)
Manatee Comm Coll (FL)
Miami Dade Coll (FL)
Middlesex County Coll (NJ)
Midland Coll (TX)
MiraCosta Coll (CA)
Modesto Jr Coll (CA)
New Mexico Military Inst (NM)
Northeast Comm Coll (NE)
North Idaho Coll (ID)
Northwestern Connecticut Comm Coll (CT)
Orange Coast Coll (CA)
Palm Beach Comm Coll (FL)
Palo Alto Coll (TX)
Palo Verde Coll (CA)
Parkland Coll (IL)
Pasadena City Coll (CA)
Pratt Comm Coll (KS)
St. Philip's Coll (TX)
Salem Comm Coll (NJ)
Salt Lake Comm Coll (UT)
San Diego City Coll (CA)
San Diego Mesa Coll (CA)
San Joaquin Delta Coll (CA)
San Juan Coll (NM)
Santa Barbara City Coll (CA)
Santa Rosa Jr Coll (CA)
Sauk Valley Comm Coll (IL)
Seminole State Coll (OK)

Sheridan Coll–Sheridan and Gillette (WY)
Skyline Coll (CA)
Southwest Mississippi Comm Coll (MS)
Spoon River Coll (IL)
Sussex County Comm Coll (NJ)
Treasure Valley Comm Coll (OR)
Trinidad State Jr Coll (CO)
Trinity Valley Comm Coll (TX)
Tulsa Comm Coll (OK)
Wharton County Jr Coll (TX)
Young Harris Coll (GA)
Yuba Coll (CA)

English Composition
Allen County Comm Coll (KS)
Berkeley City Coll (CA)

English Language and Literature Related
Coll of the Siskiyous (CA)
Mohawk Valley Comm Coll (NY)

English/Language Arts Teacher Education
Ancilla Coll (IN)
Coll of the Siskiyous (CA)
Manatee Comm Coll (FL)

Entomology
Snow Coll (UT)

Entrepreneurial and Small Business Related
Williston State Coll (ND)

Entrepreneurship
Bucks County Comm Coll (PA)
Cincinnati State Tech and Comm Coll (OH)
Comm Coll of Allegheny County (PA)
Delta Coll (MI)
Eastern Arizona Coll (AZ)
Edmonds Comm Coll (WA)
Goodwin Coll (CT)
Laramie County Comm Coll (WY)
Missouri State U–West Plains (MO)
Mohawk Valley Comm Coll (NY)
Moraine Valley Comm Coll (IL)
Mott Comm Coll (MI)
Mount Wachusett Comm Coll (MA)
Nassau Comm Coll (NY)
Northeast Comm Coll (NE)
North Iowa Area Comm Coll (IA)
Oakland Comm Coll (MI)
Palo Verde Coll (CA)
Springfield Tech Comm Coll (MA)
United Tribes Tech Coll (ND)
Waubonsee Comm Coll (IL)

Environmental Biology
Eastern Wyoming Coll (WY)
Northwest-Shoals Comm Coll (AL)

Environmental Control Technologies Related
Central Carolina Tech Coll (SC)
Oakland Comm Coll (MI)

Environmental Design/Architecture
Abraham Baldwin Ag Coll (GA)
Scottsdale Comm Coll (AZ)

Environmental Education
Vermilion Comm Coll (MN)

Environmental Engineering Technology
Allan Hancock Coll (CA)
Arapahoe Comm Coll (CO)
Bristol Comm Coll (MA)
Broward Comm Coll (FL)
Central Piedmont Comm Coll (NC)
Chattanooga State Tech Comm Coll (TN)

Cincinnati State Tech and Comm Coll (OH)
City Colls of Chicago, Wilbur Wright College (IL)
Coastal Bend Coll (TX)
Collin County Comm Coll District (TX)
Comm Coll of Allegheny County (PA)
Coosa Valley Tech Coll (GA)
Crowder Coll (MO)
Delaware Tech & Comm Coll, Jack F. Owens Campus (DE)
Delta Coll (MI)
James H. Faulkner State Comm Coll (AL)
John Tyler Comm Coll (VA)
Kent State U, Trumbull Campus (OH)
Lord Fairfax Ccmm Coll (VA)
Massachusetts Bay Comm Coll (MA)
Metropolitan Comm Coll-Business & Technology College (MO)
Miami Dade Ccll (FL)
Pellissippi State Tech Comm Coll (TN)
Pima Comm Coll (AZ)
Salt Lake Comm Coll (UT)
San Diego City Coll (CA)
Southern Arkansas U Tech (AR)
Tulsa Comm Coll (OK)
Valencia Comm Coll (FL)
Vermilion Comm Coll (MN)
Westchester Comm Coll (NY)
Westmoreland County Comm Coll (PA)

Environmental/Environmental Health Engineering
Bristol Comm Coll (MA)
Central New Mexico Comm Coll (NM)
Santa Barbara City Coll (CA)

Environmental Health
Brazosport Coll (TX)
Comm Coll of the Air Force (AL)
Crowder Coll (MO)
North Idaho Coll (ID)
Roane State Comm Coll (TN)
The U of Akron–Wayne Coll (OH)

Environmental Science
Berkshire Comm Coll (MA)
Bristol Comm Coll (MA)
Central Wyoming Coll (WY)
City Colls of Chicago, Wilbur Wright College (IL)
Clarendon Coll (TX)
Northwest-Shoals Comm Coll (AL)
The Ohio State U Ag Tech Inst (OH)
St. Philip's Coll (TX)
Santa Rosa Jr Coll (CA)
United Tribes Tech Coll (ND)

Environmental Studies
Arizona Western Coll (AZ)
Bucks County Comm Coll (PA)
Cape Fear Comm Coll (NC)
Century Coll (MN)
Colorado Mountain Coll, Timberline Campus (CO)
Columbia Coll (CA)
Comm Coll of the Air Force (AL)
Cossatot Comm Coll of the U of Arkansas (AR)
Dixie State Coll of Utah (UT)
Finger Lakes Comm Coll (NY)
Great Basin Coll (NV)
Harrisburg Area Comm Coll (PA)
Holyoke Comm Coll (MA)
Howard Comm Coll (MD)
Hudson Valley Comm Coll (NY)
Itasca Comm Coll (MN)
Kent State U, Tuscarawas Campus (OH)

Keystone Coll (PA)
Lamar State Coll–Orange (TX)
Lower Columbia Coll (WA)
Middlesex Comm Coll (CT)
Mount Wachusett Comm Coll (MA)
Naugatuck Valley Comm Coll (CT)
Raritan Valley Comm Coll (NJ)
Saddleback Coll (CA)
Santa Barbara City Coll (CA)
Santa Rosa Jr Coll (CA)
Southeastern Comm Coll (NC)
Southwestern Oregon Comm Coll (OR)
Stark State Coll of Technology (OH)
State U of New York Coll of Technology at Alfred (NY)
Sullivan County Comm Coll (NY)
Sussex County Comm Coll (NJ)
Tompkins Cortland Comm Coll (NY)
Vermilion Comm Coll (MN)

Equestrian Studies
Allen County Comm Coll (KS)
Central Wyoming Coll (WY)
Laramie County Comm Coll (WY)
The Ohio State U Ag Tech Inst (OH)
Scottsdale Comm Coll (AZ)
Yavapai Coll (AZ)

Ethnic, Cultural Minority, and Gender Studies Related
Brazosport Coll (TX)
Santa Rosa Jr Coll (CA)

European Studies (Central and Eastern)
Manatee Comm Coll (FL)

Executive Assistant/Executive Secretary
Alamance Comm Coll (NC)
Broome Comm Coll (NY)
Business Inst of Pennsylvania, Meadville (PA)
Butler County Comm Coll (PA)
Cape Fear Comm Coll (NC)
Cincinnati State Tech and Comm Coll (OH)
Clark Coll (WA)
Cleveland Comm Coll (NC)
Clovis Comm Coll (NM)
Coastal Carolina Comm Coll (NC)
Crowder Coll (MO)
Delta Coll (MI)
Eastfield Coll (TX)
Hamilton Coll, Cedar Falls (IA)
Hickey Coll (MO)
Ivy Tech Comm Coll–Bloomington (IN)
Ivy Tech Comm Coll–Central Indiana (IN)
Ivy Tech Comm Coll–Columbus (IN)
Ivy Tech Comm Coll–East Central (IN)
Ivy Tech Comm Coll–Kokomo (IN)
Ivy Tech Comm Coll–Lafayette (IN)
Ivy Tech Comm Coll–North Central (IN)
Ivy Tech Comm Coll–Northeast (IN)
Ivy Tech Comm Coll–Northwest (IN)
Ivy Tech Comm Coll–Southeast (IN)
Ivy Tech Comm Coll–Southern Indiana (IN)
Ivy Tech Comm Coll–Southwest (IN)
Ivy Tech Comm Coll–Wabash Valley (IN)
Ivy Tech Comm Coll–Whitewater (IN)
Jackson Comm Coll (MI)

John Wood Comm Coll (IL)
Kaskaskia Coll (IL)
Kellogg Comm Coll (MI)
Kennebec Valley Comm Coll (ME)
Lake Land Coll (IL)
Lake Region State Coll (ND)
Lake Superior Coll (MN)
Laurel Business Inst (PA)
Luzerne County Comm Coll (PA)
Newport Business Inst, Lower Burrell (PA)
Prairie State Coll (IL)
Southern State Comm Coll (OH)
The U of Akron–Wayne Coll (OH)
Waubonsee Comm Coll (IL)
Western Iowa Tech Comm Coll (IA)
Wilkes Comm Coll (NC)

Family and Community Services
Collin County Comm Coll District (TX)
Saddleback Coll (CA)
Salem Comm Coll (NJ)
Snow Coll (UT)

Family and Consumer Economics Related
Allan Hancock Coll (CA)
Arizona Western Coll (AZ)
Cowley County Comm Coll and Area Vocational–Tech School (KS)
Evergreen Valley Coll (CA)
Long Beach City Coll (CA)
Modesto Jr Coll (CA)
Orange Coast Coll (CA)
Yakima Valley Comm Coll (WA)
Yuba Coll (CA)

Family and Consumer Sciences/Home Economics Teacher Education
Copiah-Lincoln Comm Coll (MS)
Manatee Comm Coll (FL)
Okaloosa-Walton Coll (FL)

Family and Consumer Sciences/Human Sciences
Abraham Baldwin Ag Coll (GA)
Allen County Comm Coll (KS)
Bainbridge Coll (GA)
Brazosport Coll (TX)
Central Comm Coll–Columbus Campus (NE)
Colby Comm Coll (KS)
Delta Coll (MI)
East Central Comm Coll (MO)
Holyoke Comm Coll (MA)
Houston Comm Coll System (TX)
Hutchinson Comm Coll and Area Vocational School (KS)
Lamar State Coll–Port Arthur (TX)
Linn-Benton Comm Coll (OR)
Long Beach City Coll (CA)
Mt. San Antonio Coll (CA)
Orange Coast Coll (CA)
Palm Beach Comm Coll (FL)
Penn Valley Comm Coll (MO)
Phoenix Coll (AZ)
Pratt Comm Coll (KS)
Saddleback Coll (CA)
San Joaquin Delta Coll (CA)
Santa Rosa Jr Coll (CA)
Skyline Coll (CA)
Snow Coll (UT)
Vermilion Comm Coll (MN)
Yuba Coll (CA)

Family Living/Parenthood
Centralia Coll (WA)

Family Psychology
Cochise Coll, Douglas (AZ)

Farm and Ranch Management
Abraham Baldwin Ag Coll (GA)

Alexandria Tech Coll (MN)
Allen County Comm Coll (KS)
Butler Comm Coll (KS)
Clarendon Coll (TX)
Colby Comm Coll (KS)
Copiah-Lincoln Comm Coll (MS)
Cowley County Comm Coll and Area Vocational–Tech School (KS)
Crowder Coll (MO)
Eastern Wyoming Coll (WY)
Hawkeye Comm Coll (IA)
Hutchinson Comm Coll and Area Vocational School (KS)
North Central Missouri Coll (MO)
Northeast Comm Coll (NE)
Northland Comm and Tech Coll–Thief River Falls (MN)
Pratt Comm Coll (KS)
Snow Coll (UT)
Trinidad State Jr Coll (CO)
Trinity Valley Comm Coll (TX)
Wharton County Jr Coll (TX)

Fashion and Fabric Consulting
Coll of DuPage (IL)

Fashion/Apparel Design
Allan Hancock Coll (CA)
The Art Inst of New York City (NY)
The Art Inst of Philadelphia (PA)
Bay State Coll (MA)
Brooks Coll, Long Beach (CA)
Coll of DuPage (IL)
El Centro Coll (TX)
Fashion Careers Coll (CA)
FIDM/The Fashion Inst of Design & Merchandising, Los Angeles Campus (CA)
FIDM/The Fashion Inst of Design & Merchandising, San Diego Campus (CA)
FIDM/The Fashion Inst of Design & Merchandising, San Francisco Campus (CA)
Fisher Coll (MA)
Houston Comm Coll System (TX)
Long Beach City Coll (CA)
Middlesex County Coll (NJ)
Nassau Comm Coll (NY)
Palm Beach Comm Coll (FL)
Penn Valley Comm Coll (MO)
Phoenix Coll (AZ)
Saddleback Coll (CA)
San Diego Mesa Coll (CA)
Seattle Central Comm Coll (WA)
Tulsa Comm Coll (OK)
Ventura Coll (CA)
Westmoreland County Comm Coll (PA)
William Rainey Harper Coll (IL)
Wood Tobe–Coburn School (NY)

Fashion Merchandising
Abraham Baldwin Ag Coll (GA)
Alexandria Tech Coll (MN)
The Art Inst of Philadelphia (PA)
Austin Comm Coll (TX)
Bay State Coll (MA)
Berkeley Coll (NJ)
Berkeley Coll-New York City Campus (NY)
Berkeley Coll-Westchester Campus (NY)
Bradley Academy for the Visual Arts (PA)
Briarwood Coll (CT)
Brooks Coll, Long Beach (CA)
Central Piedmont Comm Coll (NC)
Century Coll (MN)
Cleveland Comm Coll (NC)
Coll of DuPage (IL)

Comm and Tech Coll of Shepherd (WV)
Davis Coll (OH)
Edmonds Comm Coll (WA)
Evergreen Valley Coll (CA)
Fashion Careers Coll (CA)
FIDM/The Fashion Inst of Design & Merchandising, Los Angeles Campus (CA)
FIDM/The Fashion Inst of Design & Merchandising, San Diego Campus (CA)
FIDM/The Fashion Inst of Design & Merchandising, San Francisco Campus (CA)
Fisher Coll (MA)
Florida Comm Coll at Jacksonville (FL)
Gateway Comm Coll (CT)
Genesee Comm Coll (NY)
Grand Rapids Comm Coll (MI)
Houston Comm Coll System (TX)
Howard Comm Coll (MD)
Indiana Business Coll, Indianapolis (IN)
Joliet Jr Coll (IL)
Kingsborough Comm Coll of the City U of New York (NY)
Lake Region State Coll (ND)
Laredo Comm Coll (TX)
Long Beach City Coll (CA)
Middle Georgia Coll (GA)
Middlesex County Coll (NJ)
Midlands Tech Coll (SC)
Mississippi Gulf Coast Comm Coll (MS)
Modesto Jr Coll (CA)
Mt. San Antonio Coll (CA)
Nassau Comm Coll (NY)
Oakland Comm Coll (MI)
Okaloosa-Walton Coll (FL)
Orange Coast Coll (CA)
Owens Comm Coll, Toledo (OH)
Palm Beach Comm Coll (FL)
Pasadena City Coll (CA)
Penn Valley Comm Coll (MO)
Saddleback Coll (CA)
St. Louis Comm Coll at Florissant Valley (MO)
San Diego City Coll (CA)
San Diego Mesa Coll (CA)
San Joaquin Delta Coll (CA)
Scottsdale Comm Coll (AZ)
Skyline Coll (CA)
South Plains Coll (TX)
Southwest Mississippi Comm Coll (MS)
Spokane Falls Comm Coll (WA)
Tarrant County Coll District (TX)
Trinity Valley Comm Coll (TX)
Triton Coll (IL)
Tunxis Comm Coll (CT)
Western Tech Coll (WI)
Westmoreland County Comm Coll (PA)
William Rainey Harper Coll (IL)
Wood Tobe–Coburn School (NY)

Fiber, Textile and Weaving Arts
Pasadena City Coll (CA)

Film/Cinema Studies
Allan Hancock Coll (CA)
Lansing Comm Coll (MI)
Long Beach City Coll (CA)
Orange Coast Coll (CA)
Santa Barbara City Coll (CA)
Santa Rosa Jr Coll (CA)
Yavapai Coll (AZ)

Finance
Arapahoe Comm Coll (CO)
Austin Comm Coll (TX)
Bergen Comm Coll (NJ)
Brazosport Coll (TX)
Broward Comm Coll (FL)
Bunker Hill Comm Coll (MA)
Central Piedmont Comm Coll (NC)

Chattanooga State Tech Comm Coll (TN)
Chemeketa Comm Coll (OR)
Clarendon Coll (TX)
Clovis Comm Coll (NM)
Coastal Bend Coll (TX)
Comm Coll of the Air Force (AL)
Cuyahoga Comm Coll (OH)
Forsyth Tech Comm Coll (NC)
Fox Valley Tech Coll (WI)
Frederick Comm Coll (MD)
GateWay Comm Coll (AZ)
Houston Comm Coll System (TX)
Howard Coll (TX)
Hudson Valley Comm Coll (NY)
Illinois Central Coll (IL)
Independence Comm Coll (KS)
Jefferson Comm Coll (OH)
Lakeshore Tech Coll (WI)
Lansing Comm Coll (MI)
Macomb Comm Coll (MI)
Manatee Comm Coll (FL)
Marshall Comm and Tech Coll (WV)
Miami Dade Coll (FL)
Mississippi Gulf Coast Comm Coll (MS)
Modesto Jr Coll (CA)
Mt. San Antonio Coll (CA)
Naugatuck Valley Comm Coll (CT)
New England Coll of Finance (MA)
New Mexico Military Inst (NM)
Northern Essex Comm Coll (MA)
North Hennepin Comm Coll (MN)
Norwalk Comm Coll (CT)
Okaloosa-Walton Coll (FL)
Orange County Comm Coll (NY)
Palm Beach Comm Coll (FL)
Palo Alto Coll (TX)
Pasadena City Coll (CA)
Pellissippi State Tech Comm Coll (TN)
Phoenix Coll (AZ)
Polk Comm Coll (FL)
Prairie State Coll (IL)
St. Cloud Tech Coll (MN)
St. Louis Comm Coll at Florissant Valley (MO)
San Diego City Coll (CA)
Santa Barbara City Coll (CA)
Scottsdale Comm Coll (AZ)
Seminole Comm Coll (FL)
Sinclair Comm Coll (OH)
Skyline Coll (CA)
Southeast Tech Inst (SD)
Southern West Virginia Comm and Tech Coll (WV)
Southwest Mississippi Comm Coll (MS)
Spoon River Coll (IL)
Springfield Tech Comm Coll (MA)
Stark State Coll of Technology (OH)
State U of New York Coll of Technology at Alfred (NY)
Tidewater Comm Coll (VA)
Trinity Valley Comm Coll (TX)
Vermilion Comm Coll (MN)
Westchester Comm Coll (NY)
Western Tech Coll (WI)
Westmoreland County Comm Coll (PA)
William Rainey Harper Coll (IL)
Wisconsin Indianhead Tech Coll (WI)

Finance and Financial Management Services Related
Bristol Comm Coll (MA)
Salt Lake Comm Coll (UT)

Financial Planning and Services
Broome Comm Coll (NY)
Howard Comm Coll (MD)

Minnesota State Comm and Tech Coll–Fergus Falls (MN)

Waukesha County Tech Coll (WI)

Fine Arts Related
Ancilla Coll (IN)
Oakland Comm Coll (MI)
United Tribes Tech Coll (ND)
Yavapai Coll (AZ)

Fine/Studio Arts
Ancilla Coll (IN)
Asnuntuck Comm Coll (CT)
Berkeley City Coll (CA)
Brazosport Coll (TX)
Bristol Comm Coll (MA)
Clovis Comm Coll (NM)
Coastal Bend Coll (TX)
Coll of the Mainland (TX)
Colorado Mountain Coll, Alpine Campus (CO)
Delaware Coll of Art and Design (DE)
Delgado Comm Coll (LA)
Finger Lakes Comm Coll (NY)
Fiorello H. LaGuardia Comm Coll of the City U of New York (NY)
Foothill Coll (CA)
Holyoke Comm Coll (MA)
Hudson Valley Comm Coll (NY)
Jamestown Comm Coll (NY)
Lansing Comm Coll (MI)
Lincoln Coll (IL)
Manatee Comm Coll (FL)
Manchester Comm Coll (CT)
Middlesex Comm Coll (CT)
Middlesex County Comm Coll (NJ)
Midland Coll (TX)
Mount Wachusett Comm Coll (MA)
Niagara County Comm Coll (NY)
Northampton County Area Comm Coll (PA)
North Hennepin Comm Coll (MN)
Norwalk Comm Coll (CT)
Pratt Comm Coll (KS)
Santa Barbara City Coll (CA)
Sinclair Comm Coll (OH)
Skyline Coll (CA)
Southwestern Illinois Coll (IL)
Springfield Tech Comm Coll (MA)
Sussex County Comm Coll (NJ)
Tidewater Comm Coll (VA)
Ventura Coll (CA)
Villa Maria Coll of Buffalo (NY)
Westchester Comm Coll (NY)

Fire Protection and Safety Technology
Bunker Hill Comm Coll (MA)
Capital Comm Coll (CT)
Central New Mexico Comm Coll (NM)
Cleveland Comm Coll (NC)
Coll of Lake County (IL)
Coll of Southern Maryland (MD)
Coll of the Mainland (TX)
Collin County Comm Coll District (TX)
Comm Coll of Allegheny County (PA)
Delgado Comm Coll (LA)
Fayetteville Tech Comm Coll (NC)
Florida Comm Coll at Jacksonville (FL)
John Wood Comm Coll (IL)
Kellogg Comm Coll (MI)
Lincoln Land Comm Coll (IL)
Macomb Comm Coll (MI)
Montgomery County Comm Coll (PA)
Moraine Valley Comm Coll (IL)
Mott Comm Coll (MI)
Ocean County Coll (NJ)
Owens Comm Coll, Toledo (OH)
St. Petersburg Coll (FL)

San Juan Coll (NM)
Tulsa Comm Coll (OK)
Union County Coll (NJ)
Waubonsee Comm Coll (IL)
Waukesha County Tech Coll (WI)
Western Tech Coll (WI)

Fire Protection Related
Fayetteville Tech Comm Coll (NC)
Sussex County Comm Coll (NJ)
Western Oklahoma State Coll (OK)

Fire Science
Allan Hancock Coll (CA)
Arizona Western Coll (AZ)
Augusta Tech Coll (GA)
Austin Comm Coll (TX)
Barton County Comm Coll (KS)
Berkshire Comm Coll (MA)
Blue River Comm Coll (MO)
Brevard Comm Coll (FL)
Bristol Comm Coll (MA)
Broome Comm Coll (NY)
Broward Comm Coll (FL)
Butler Comm Coll (KS)
Casper Coll (WY)
Central Florida Comm Coll (FL)
Central Oregon Comm Coll (OR)
Central Piedmont Comm Coll (NC)
Chattahoochee Tech Coll (GA)
Chattahoochee Valley Comm Coll (AL)
Chattanooga State Tech Comm Coll (TN)
Chemeketa Comm Coll (OR)
Cincinnati State Tech and Comm Coll (OH)
Clatsop Comm Coll (OR)
Coastal Carolina Comm Coll (NC)
Cochise Coll, Douglas (AZ)
Coll of DuPage (IL)
Coll of the Siskiyous (CA)
Columbia Coll (CA)
Comm and Tech Coll of Shepherd (WV)
Comm Coll of the Air Force (AL)
Coosa Valley Tech Coll (GA)
Corning Comm Coll (NY)
Crowder Coll (MO)
Cuyahoga Comm Coll (OH)
Delaware Tech & Comm Coll, Stanton/Wilmington Campus (DE)
Delta Coll (MI)
East Central Coll (MO)
Essex County Coll (NJ)
Florida Comm Coll at Jacksonville (FL)
Fox Valley Tech Coll (WI)
Frederick Comm Coll (MD)
Gaston Coll (NC)
Gateway Comm Coll (CT)
Glendale Comm Coll (AZ)
Greenfield Comm Coll (MA)
Guam Comm Coll (GU)
Harrisburg Area Comm Coll (PA)
Hawkeye Comm Coll (IA)
Houston Comm Coll System (TX)
Hutchinson Comm Coll and Area Vocational School (KS)
Illinois Central Coll (IL)
Joliet Jr Coll (IL)
Kansas City Kansas Comm Coll (KS)
Lake-Sumter Comm Coll (FL)
Lanier Tech Coll (GA)
Lansing Comm Coll (MI)
Laredo Comm Coll (TX)
Lawson State Comm Coll (AL)
Long Beach City Coll (CA)
Lower Columbia Coll (WA)
Luzerne County Comm Coll (PA)
Manatee Comm Coll (FL)

Mercer County Comm Coll (NJ)
Meridian Comm Coll (MS)
Miami Dade Coll (FL)
Middlesex County Comm Coll (NJ)
Midland Coll (TX)
Missouri State U–West Plains (MO)
Modesto Jr Coll (CA)
Mt. San Antonio Coll (CA)
Mount Wachusett Comm Coll (MA)
Naugatuck Valley Comm Coll (CT)
New Mexico State U–Alamogordo (NM)
North Shore Comm Coll (MA)
Northwest-Shoals Comm Coll (AL)
Norwalk Comm Coll (CT)
Oakland Comm Coll (MI)
Palm Beach Comm Coll (FL)
Pasadena City Coll (CA)
Phoenix (AZ)
Pima Comm Coll (AZ)
Polk Comm Coll (FL)
Prairie State Coll (IL)
Quinsigamond Comm Coll (MA)
Richland Comm Coll (IL)
Riverside Comm Coll District (CA)
Rock Valley Coll (IL)
Rogue Comm Coll (OR)
St. Louis Comm Coll at Florissant Valley (MO)
St. Petersburg Coll (FL)
San Joaquin Delta Coll (CA)
Santa Rosa Jr Coll (CA)
Savannah Tech Coll (GA)
Scottsdale Comm Coll (AZ)
Seminole Comm Coll (FL)
Sinclair Comm Coll (OH)
Southern Arkansas U Tech (AR)
South Plains Coll (TX)
Southwestern Illinois Coll (IL)
Southwestern Oregon Comm Coll (OR)
Southwest Tennessee Comm Coll (TN)
Spokane Comm Coll (WA)
Springfield Tech Comm Coll (MA)
Stark State Coll of Technology (OH)
Tarrant County Coll District (TX)
Thomas Nelson Comm Coll (VA)
Triton Coll (IL)
Tulsa Comm Coll (OK)
U of Alaska Anchorage, Matanuska-Susitna Coll (AK)
Valdosta Tech Coll (GA)
Valencia Comm Coll (FL)
Volunteer State Comm Coll (TN)
Weatherford Coll (TX)
West Georgia Tech Coll (GA)
Westmoreland County Comm Coll (PA)
William Rainey Harper Coll (IL)
Wilson Tech Comm Coll (NC)
Yakima Valley Comm Coll (WA)
Yavapai Coll (AZ)
Yuba Coll (CA)

Fire Services Administration
Capital Comm Coll (CT)
Edmonds Comm Coll (WA)
Erie Comm Coll, South Campus (NY)
Jefferson State Comm Coll (AL)
Lake Superior Coll (MN)
Lower Columbia Coll (WA)
Midland Coll (TX)
Minnesota State Comm and Tech Coll–Fergus Falls (MN)
Northampton County Area Comm Coll (PA)
North Iowa Area Comm Coll (IA)

Fish/Game Management
Abraham Baldwin Ag Coll (GA)
Central Oregon Comm Coll (OR)
Chattanooga State Tech Comm Coll (TN)
East Central Coll (MO)
Finger Lakes Comm Coll (NY)
Fox Valley Tech Coll (WI)
Itasca Comm Coll (MN)
North Idaho Coll (ID)
Pratt Comm Coll (KS)
Swainsboro Tech Coll (GA)
Vermilion Comm Coll (MN)

Fishing and Fisheries Sciences And Management
Peninsula Coll (WA)
Santa Rosa Jr Coll (CA)

Floriculture/Floristry Management
The Ohio State U Ag Tech Inst (OH)
Santa Rosa Jr Coll (CA)

Food/Nutrition
United Tribes Tech Coll (ND)

Food Preparation
Keystone Coll (PA)
Northampton County Area Comm Coll (PA)

Food Sales Operations
Montgomery County Comm Coll (PA)

Foods and Nutrition Related
San Diego Mesa Coll (CA)

Food Science
Central Piedmont Comm Coll (NC)
El Centro Coll (TX)
Greenfield Comm Coll (MA)
Hawkeye Comm Coll (IA)
Miami Dade Coll (FL)
Modesto Jr Coll (CA)
Orange Coast Coll (CA)
Saddleback Coll (CA)
St. Louis Comm Coll at Florissant Valley (MO)

Food Services Technology
Arapahoe Comm Coll (CO)
Butler County Comm Coll (PA)
Central Piedmont Comm Coll (NC)
Chattanooga State Tech Comm Coll (TN)
Columbia Coll (CA)
Delaware Tech & Comm Coll, Stanton/Wilmington Campus (DE)
El Centro Coll (TX)
Long Beach City Coll (CA)
Luzerne County Comm Coll (PA)
Modesto Jr Coll (CA)
Mohawk Valley Comm Coll (NY)
Orange Coast Coll (CA)
Owens Comm Coll, Toledo (OH)
Richland Comm Coll (IL)
Saddleback Coll (CA)
St. Louis Comm Coll at Florissant Valley (MO)
San Joaquin Delta Coll (CA)
Spokane Comm Coll (WA)
Stark State Coll of Technology (OH)
Tarrant County Coll District (TX)
Texas State Tech Coll Waco (TX)
Westchester Comm Coll (NY)
Western Tech Coll (WI)

Foodservice Systems Administration
Comm Coll of Allegheny County (PA)
Florida Comm Coll at Jacksonville (FL)
Hibbing Comm Coll (MN)
Mohawk Valley Comm Coll (NY)
Mott Comm Coll (MI)

North Dakota State Coll of Science (ND)
Oakland Comm Coll (MI)
Santa Barbara City Coll (CA)

Foods, Nutrition, and Wellness
Colby Comm Coll (KS)
Harrisburg Area Comm Coll (PA)
Holyoke Comm Coll (MA)
Lincoln Coll (IL)
North Shore Comm Coll (MA)
Okaloosa-Walton Coll (FL)
Orange Coast Coll (CA)
Palm Beach Comm Coll (FL)
Saddleback Coll (CA)
San Diego Mesa Coll (CA)
Sinclair Comm Coll (OH)
Snow Coll (UT)

Food Technology and Processing
Copiah-Lincoln Comm Coll (MS)

Foreign Languages and Literatures
Atlanta Metropolitan Coll (GA)
Brazosport Coll (TX)
Coastal Georgia Comm Coll (GA)
Cochise Coll, Douglas (AZ)
Comm Coll of Allegheny County (PA)
Dixie State Coll of Utah (UT)
Eastern Arizona Coll (AZ)
Eastern Wyoming Coll (WY)
Gainesville Coll (GA)
Georgia Highlands Coll (GA)
Hutchinson Comm Coll and Area Vocational School (KS)
Kingwood Coll (TX)
Linn-Benton Comm Coll (OR)
Lower Columbia Coll (WA)
Midland Coll (TX)
Modesto Jr Coll (CA)
San Juan Coll (NM)
Sheridan Coll–Sheridan and Gillette (WY)

Foreign Language Teacher Education
Manatee Comm Coll (FL)

Forensic Science and Technology
Appalachian Tech Coll (GA)
Arkansas State U–Mountain Home (AR)
Fayetteville Tech Comm Coll (NC)
Hudson Valley Comm Coll (NY)
Macomb Comm Coll (MI)
Massachusetts Bay Comm Coll (MA)
Minnesota State Comm and Tech Coll–Fergus Falls (MN)
Mohawk Valley Comm Coll (NY)
North Arkansas Coll (AR)
Oakland Comm Coll (MI)
Springfield Coll in Illinois (IL)
Tunxis Comm Coll (CT)

Forest/Forest Resources Management
Allegany Coll of Maryland (MD)
Lake City Comm Coll (FL)
Vermilion Comm Coll (MN)

Forestry
Abraham Baldwin Ag Coll (GA)
Allen County Comm Coll (KS)
Bainbridge Coll (GA)
Barton County Comm Coll (KS)
Central Oregon Comm Coll (OR)
Chattahoochee Valley Comm Coll (AL)
Chattanooga State Tech Comm Coll (TN)
Chemeketa Comm Coll (OR)

Coastal Georgia Comm Coll (GA)
Colby Comm Coll (KS)
Copiah-Lincoln Comm Coll (MS)
Dixie State Coll of Utah (UT)
East Central Coll (MO)
Eastern Arizona Coll (AZ)
Feather River Coll (CA)
Gainesville Coll (GA)
Georgia Highlands Coll (GA)
Grand Rapids Comm Coll (MI)
Itasca Comm Coll (MN)
Keystone Coll (PA)
Miami Dade Coll (FL)
Modesto Jr Coll (CA)
North Idaho Coll (ID)
North Shore Comm Coll (MA)
Northwest-Shoals Comm Coll (AL)
Palo Verde Coll (CA)
Snow Coll (UT)
Southwestern Oregon Comm Coll (OR)
Spokane Comm Coll (WA)
Treasure Valley Comm Coll (OR)
Trinidad State Jr Coll (CO)
Tulsa Comm Coll (OK)
Vermilion Comm Coll (MN)

Forestry Technology
Abraham Baldwin Ag Coll (GA)
Albany Tech Coll (GA)
Central Oregon Comm Coll (OR)
Chattanooga State Tech Comm Coll (TN)
Chemeketa Comm Coll (OR)
Columbia Coll (CA)
Dabney S. Lancaster Comm Coll (VA)
Fox Valley Tech Coll (WI)
Horry-Georgetown Tech Coll (SC)
Itasca Comm Coll (MN)
Jefferson Comm Coll (NY)
Keystone Coll (PA)
Lake City Comm Coll (FL)
Louisiana Tech Coll (LA)
Modesto Jr Coll (CA)
Montgomery Comm Coll (NC)
Mt. San Antonio Coll (CA)
Ogeechee Tech Coll (GA)
Okefenokee Tech Coll (GA)
Pasadena City Coll (CA)
The Pennsylvania State U Mont Alto Campus of the Commonwealth Coll (PA)
Southeastern Comm Coll (NC)
State U of New York Coll of Environmental Science & Forestry, Ranger School (NY)
Swainsboro Tech Coll (GA)
Treasure Valley Comm Coll (OR)
Vermilion Comm Coll (MN)

Forest Sciences and Biology
Vermilion Comm Coll (MN)

French
Austin Comm Coll (TX)
Casper Coll (WY)
Centralia Coll (WA)
Citrus Coll (CA)
Coastal Bend Coll (TX)
Coll of the Canyons (CA)
Copiah-Lincoln Comm Coll (MS)
Independence Comm Coll (KS)
Long Beach City Coll (CA)
Manatee Comm Coll (FL)
Miami Dade Coll (FL)
Midland Coll (TX)
MiraCosta Coll (CA)
New Mexico Military Inst (NM)
North Idaho Coll (ID)
Orange Coast Coll (CA)
Pasadena City Coll (CA)
San Diego Mesa Coll (CA)
San Joaquin Delta Coll (CA)

Santa Barbara City Coll (CA)
Sauk Valley Comm Coll (IL)
Skyline Coll (CA)
Snow Coll (UT)
Tulsa Comm Coll (OK)
Young Harris Coll (GA)

Funeral Service and Mortuary Science
Allen County Comm Coll (KS)
Arapahoe Comm Coll (CO)
Arkansas State U–Mountain Home (AR)
Barton County Comm Coll (KS)
Bishop State Comm Coll (AL)
Briarwood Coll (CT)
Cincinnati Coll of Mortuary Science (OH)
Dallas Inst of Funeral Service (TX)
Delgado Comm Coll (LA)
Fayetteville Tech Comm Coll (NC)
Fiorello H. LaGuardia Comm Coll of the City U of New York (NY)
Forsyth Tech Comm Coll (NC)
Hudson Valley Comm Coll (NY)
Ivy Tech Comm Coll–Northwest (IN)
Jefferson State Comm Coll (AL)
John Tyler Comm Coll (VA)
Kansas City Kansas Comm Coll (KS)
Luzerne County Comm Coll (PA)
Mercer County Comm Coll (NJ)
Miami Dade Coll (FL)
Nassau Comm Coll (NY)
Northampton County Area Comm Coll (PA)
Ogeechee Tech Coll (GA)
Pittsburgh Inst of Mortuary Science, Incorporated (PA)
St. Petersburg Coll (FL)

General Retailing/ Wholesaling
Alamance Comm Coll (NC)
Century Coll (MN)
Dixie State Coll of Utah (UT)
Gadsden State Comm Coll (AL)
Harrisburg Area Comm Coll (PA)
Nassau Comm Coll (NY)
Normandale Comm Coll (MN)
Orange Coast Coll (CA)
St. Cloud Tech Coll (MN)

General Studies
Allen County Comm Coll (KS)
Arkansas Northeastern Coll (AR)
Arkansas State U–Beebe (AR)
Asnuntuck Comm Coll (CT)
Atlanta Metropolitan Coll (GA)
Barton County Comm Coll (KS)
Bay State Coll (MA)
Berkeley City Coll (CA)
Bishop State Comm Coll (AL)
Bladen Comm Coll (NC)
Brazosport Coll (TX)
Briarwood Coll (CT)
Bristol Comm Coll (MA)
Bunker Hill Comm Coll (MA)
Butler County Comm Coll (PA)
Carroll Comm Coll (MD)
Cecil Comm Coll (MD)
Central Wyoming Coll (WY)
Cincinnati State Tech and Comm Coll (OH)
City Colls of Chicago, Wilbur Wright College (IL)
Clarendon Coll (TX)
Cleveland State Comm Coll (TN)

Cochise Coll, Douglas (AZ)
Coll of the Mainland (TX)
Colorado Mountain Coll, Timberline Campus (CO)
Comm and Tech Coll of Shepherd (WV)
Comm Coll of Allegheny County (PA)
Comm Coll of Denver (CO)
Corning Comm Coll (NY)
Crowder Coll (MO)
Delgado Comm Coll (LA)
East Central Coll (MO)
Eastern West Virginia Comm and Tech Coll (WV)
Eastern Wyoming Coll (WY)
Evergreen Valley Coll (CA)
Fayetteville Tech Comm Coll (NC)
Frederick Comm Coll (MD)
Front Range Comm Coll (CO)
Gadsden State Comm Coll (AL)
Gainesville Coll (GA)
GateWay Comm Coll (AZ)
Germanna Comm Coll (VA)
Hamilton Coll, Cedar Rapids (IA)
Howard Comm Coll (MD)
Ilisagvik Coll (AK)
Illinois Eastern Comm Colls, Frontier Community College (IL)
Illinois Eastern Comm Colls, Lincoln Trail College (IL)
Illinois Eastern Comm Colls, Olney Central College (IL)
Illinois Eastern Comm Colls, Wabash Valley College (IL)
Itasca Comm Coll (MN)
Ivy Tech Comm Coll–East Central (IN)
Ivy Tech Comm Coll–Kokomo (IN)
Ivy Tech Comm Coll–North Central (IN)
Ivy Tech Comm Coll–Northeast (IN)
Ivy Tech Comm Coll–Northwest (IN)
Jackson Comm Coll (MI)
James H. Faulkner State Comm Coll (AL)
Jefferson State Comm Coll (AL)
John Wood Comm Coll (IL)
Kaskaskia Coll (IL)
Kellogg Comm Coll (MI)
Kennebec Valley Comm Coll (ME)
Lackawanna Coll (PA)
Lake Land Coll (IL)
Lamar State Coll–Port Arthur (TX)
Lincoln Land Comm Coll (IL)
Luzerne County Comm Coll (PA)
Macomb Comm Coll (MI)
Manchester Comm Coll (CT)
Massachusetts Bay Comm Coll (MA)
Mercy Coll of Northwest Ohio (OH)
Miami Dade Coll (FL)
Middlesex County Coll (NJ)
MiraCosta Coll (CA)
Missouri State U–West Plains (MO)
Modesto Jr Coll (CA)
Mohawk Valley Comm Coll (NY)
Mott Comm Coll (MI)
Mount Wachusett Comm Coll (MA)
Nassau Comm Coll (NY)
New Hampshire Comm Tech Coll, Nashua/Claremont (NH)
New Hampshire Tech Inst (NH)
Niagara County Comm Coll (NY)
Northampton County Area Comm Coll (PA)
Northeast Comm Coll (NE)
Northern Essex Comm Coll (MA)
Northwest Indian Coll (WA)

Northwest-Shoals Comm Coll (AL)
Norwalk Comm Coll (CT)
Oakland Comm Coll (MI)
Ocean County Coll (NJ)
Oregon Coast Comm Coll (OR)
Owens Comm Coll, Toledo (OH)
Palo Verde Coll (CA)
Parkland Coll (IL)
Piedmont Virginia Comm Coll (VA)
Pima Comm Coll (AZ)
Quinsigamond Comm Coll (MA)
Salt Lake Comm Coll (UT)
San Juan Coll (NM)
Sheridan Coll–Sheridan and Gillette (WY)
Snead State Comm Coll (AL)
South Arkansas Comm Coll (AR)
Southern Arkansas U Tech (AR)
Southside Virginia Comm Coll (VA)
Southwestern Michigan Coll (MI)
Southwestern Oklahoma State U at Sayre (OK)
Southwest Tennessee Comm Coll (TN)
Springfield Coll in Illinois (IL)
Springfield Tech Comm Coll (MA)
State U of New York Coll of Technology at Delhi (NY)
Tillamook Bay Comm Coll (OR)
Truett-McConnell Coll (GA)
The U of Akron–Wayne Coll (OH)
Waubonsee Comm Coll (IL)
Western Oklahoma State Coll (OK)
Wilson Tech Comm Coll (NC)

Geography
Allen County Comm Coll (KS)
Coll of the Canyons (CA)
East Central Coll (MO)
Gainesville Coll (GA)
Itasca Comm Coll (MN)
Joliet Jr Coll (IL)
Lansing Comm Coll (MI)
Lincoln Coll (IL)
Lower Columbia Coll (WA)
Orange Coast Coll (CA)
Pasadena City Coll (CA)
Pellissippi State Tech Comm Coll (TN)
Saddleback Coll (CA)
San Diego Mesa Coll (CA)
Santa Barbara City Coll (CA)
Santa Rosa Jr Coll (CA)
Snow Coll (UT)
Tulsa Comm Coll (OK)
Vermilion Comm Coll (MN)

Geology/Earth Science
Arizona Western Coll (AZ)
Austin Comm Coll (TX)
Barton County Comm Coll (KS)
Brazosport Coll (TX)
Casper Coll (WY)
Centralia Coll (WA)
Coastal Bend Coll (TX)
Coastal Georgia Comm Coll (GA)
Colby Comm Coll (KS)
Coll of the Canyons (CA)
Coll of the Siskiyous (CA)
Colorado Mountain Coll, Alpine Campus (CO)
Columbia Coll (CA)
Diné Coll (AZ)
Dixie State Coll of Utah (UT)
East Central Coll (MO)
Eastern Arizona Coll (AZ)
Gainesville Coll (GA)
Georgia Highlands Coll (GA)
Grand Rapids Comm Coll (MI)
Great Basin Coll (NV)
Highland Comm Coll (IL)
Lansing Comm Coll (MI)
Lincoln Coll (IL)
Lower Columbia Coll (WA)

Miami Dade Coll (FL)
Midland Coll (TX)
North Idaho Coll (ID)
Orange Coast Coll (CA)
Palo Alto Coll (TX)
Pasadena City Coll (CA)
Saddleback Coll (CA)
St. Philip's Coll (TX)
San Joaquin Delta Coll (CA)
San Juan Coll (NM)
Santa Barbara City Coll (CA)
Santa Rosa Jr Coll (CA)
Snow Coll (UT)
Trinity Valley Comm Coll (TX)
Tulsa Comm Coll (OK)
Vermilion Comm Coll (MN)
Young Harris Coll (GA)

German
Austin Comm Coll (TX)
Casper Coll (WY)
Centralia Coll (WA)
Citrus Coll (CA)
Coastal Bend Coll (TX)
Coll of the Canyons (CA)
Long Beach City Coll (CA)
Manatee Comm Coll (FL)
Miami Dade Coll (FL)
Midland Coll (TX)
New Mexico Military Inst (NM)
North Idaho Coll (ID)
Orange Coast Coll (CA)
Pasadena City Coll (CA)
San Joaquin Delta Coll (CA)
Tulsa Comm Coll (OK)

Gerontological Services
Albany Tech Coll (GA)
Central Georgia Tech Coll (GA)
Santa Rosa Jr Coll (CA)

Gerontology
Brown Mackie Coll–Louisville (KY)
Brown Mackie Coll–Merrillville (IN)
City Colls of Chicago, Wilbur Wright College (IL)
Delaware Tech & Comm Coll, Stanton/Wilmington Campus (DE)
Fiorello H. LaGuardia Comm Coll of the City U of New York (NY)
Gateway Comm Coll (CT)
Genesee Comm Coll (NY)
Lansing Comm Coll (MI)
Midlands Tech Coll (SC)
Naugatuck Valley Comm Coll (CT)
North Shore Comm Coll (MA)
Oakland Comm Coll (MI)
Saddleback Coll (CA)
Sinclair Comm Coll (OH)
Spokane Falls Comm Coll (WA)
Union County Coll (NJ)

Glazier
Metropolitan Comm Coll-Business & Technology College (MO)

Graphic and Printing Equipment Operation/ Production
Austin Comm Coll (TX)
Bishop State Comm Coll (AL)
Central Comm Coll–Hastings Campus (NE)
Central Piedmont Comm Coll (NC)
Chattanooga State Tech Comm Coll (TN)
Chemeketa Comm Coll (OR)
Coll of DuPage (IL)
Eastfield Coll (TX)
Erie Comm Coll, South Campus (NY)
Forsyth Tech Comm Coll (NC)
Fox Valley Tech Coll (WI)
H. Councill Trenholm State Tech Coll (AL)
Highline Comm Coll (WA)
Houston Comm Coll System (TX)

Lake Land Coll (IL)
Luzerne County Comm Coll (PA)
Macomb Comm Coll (MI)
Metropolitan Comm Coll (NE)
Midlands Tech Coll (SC)
Moberly Area Comm Coll (MO)
Modesto Jr Coll (CA)
Moraine Park Tech Coll (WI)
Riverside Comm Coll District (CA)
San Diego City Coll (CA)
San Joaquin Delta Coll (CA)
Seattle Central Comm Coll (WA)
Sinclair Comm Coll (OH)
Southeast Tech Inst (SD)
Southwestern Michigan Coll (MI)
Tarrant County Coll District (TX)
Texas State Tech Coll Waco (TX)
Triton Coll (IL)
Westmoreland County Comm Coll (PA)

Graphic Communications
Clark Coll (WA)
Waukesha County Tech Coll (WI)

Graphic Communications Related
H. Councill Trenholm State Tech Coll (AL)
Linn-Benton Comm Coll (OR)

Graphic Design
Ancilla Coll (IN)
The Art Inst of New York City (NY)
The Art Inst of Ohio–Cincinnati (OH)
The Art Inst of Philadelphia (PA)
Barton County Comm Coll (KS)
Bristol Comm Coll (MA)
Brown Mackie Coll–Louisville (KY)
Bryant and Stratton Coll, Rochester (NY)
Bryant and Stratton Coll, Amherst Campus (NY)
Comm Coll of Denver (CO)
Delaware Coll of Art and Design (DE)
Hickey Coll (MO)
International Business Coll, Indianapolis (IN)
Ivy Tech Comm Coll–Southwest (IN)
Jackson Comm Coll (MI)
Keystone Coll (PA)
Lake Michigan Coll (MI)
Luzerne County Comm Coll (PA)
Mott Comm Coll (MI)
Northampton County Area Comm Coll (PA)
North Hennepin Comm Coll (MN)
Oakland Comm Coll (MI)
Ohio Inst of Photography and Technology (OH)
Parkland Coll (IL)
Platt Coll San Diego (CA)
St. Petersburg Coll (FL)
Salt Lake Comm Coll (UT)
Santa Rosa Jr Coll (CA)
Springfield Tech Comm Coll (MA)
TESST Coll of Technology, Towson (MD)
Tidewater Comm Coll (VA)
Villa Maria Coll of Buffalo (NY)
Waubonsee Comm Coll (IL)
Waukesha County Tech Coll (WI)
Wood Tobe–Coburn School (NY)
Yavapai Coll (AZ)

Greenhouse Management
Comm Coll of Allegheny County (PA)
Joliet Jr Coll (IL)

The Ohio State U Ag Tech Inst (OH)

Gunsmithing
Colorado School of Trades (CO)
Trinidad State Jr Coll (CO)
Yavapai Coll (AZ)

Hazardous Materials Management and Waste Technology
Barton County Comm Coll (KS)
Kansas City Kansas Comm Coll (KS)

Health Aide
Allen County Comm Coll (KS)
Central Arizona Coll (AZ)
Edmonds Comm Coll (WA)
Springfield Tech Comm Coll (MA)

Health and Medical Administrative Services Related
Keiser Coll, Miami (FL)

Health and Physical Education
Alexandria Tech Coll (MN)
Allen County Comm Coll (KS)
Atlanta Metropolitan Coll (GA)
Brazosport Coll (TX)
Citrus Coll (CA)
Clovis Comm Coll (NM)
Coastal Georgia Comm Coll (GA)
Cochise Coll, Douglas (AZ)
Comm Coll of Allegheny County (PA)
Corning Comm Coll (NY)
Eastern Arizona Coll (AZ)
John Wood Comm Coll (IL)
Lawson State Comm Coll (AL)
Luzerne County Comm Coll (PA)
Northeast Comm Coll (NE)
Salem Comm Coll (NJ)
Sheridan Coll–Sheridan and Gillette (WY)
Southwestern Oregon Comm Coll (OR)
State U of New York Coll of Technology at Delhi (NY)

Health and Physical Education Related
Hudson Valley Comm Coll (NY)
Kingsborough Comm Coll of the City U of New York (NY)
Oakland Comm Coll (MI)
Santa Rosa Jr Coll (CA)

Health/Health Care Administration
Brown Mackie Coll–Akron (OH)
Brown Mackie Coll–Findlay (OH)
Brown Mackie Coll–Louisville (KY)
Brown Mackie Coll–North Canton (OH)
Caldwell Comm Coll and Tech Inst (NC)
Central Piedmont Comm Coll (NC)
Chemeketa Comm Coll (OR)
Coll of DuPage (IL)
Comm Care Coll (OK)
Comm Coll of the Air Force (AL)
Consolidated School of Business, Lancaster (PA)
Consolidated School of Business, York (PA)
ECPI Coll of Technology, Newport News (VA)
ECPI Coll of Technology, Virginia Beach (VA)
ECPI Tech Coll (VA)
ECPI Tech Coll, Richmond (VA)
Essex County Coll (NJ)
GateWay Comm Coll (AZ)

Houston Comm Coll System (TX)
Illinois Central Coll (IL)
International Inst of the Americas, Mesa (AZ)
International Inst of the Americas, Phoenix (AZ)
International Inst of the Americas, Phoenix (AZ)
International Inst of the Americas, Tucson (AZ)
International Inst of the Americas (NM)
Luzerne County Comm Coll (PA)
Manatee Comm Coll (FL)
North Idaho Coll (ID)
Oakland Comm Coll (MI)
Pioneer Pacific Coll (OR)
St. Petersburg Coll (FL)
South Plains Coll (TX)

Health Information/Medical Records Administration
Arapahoe Comm Coll (CO)
Barton County Comm Coll (KS)
Briarwood Coll (CT)
Brown Mackie Coll–Kansas City (KS)
Bunker Hill Comm Coll (MA)
Butler Comm Coll (KS)
Central New Mexico Comm Coll (NM)
Central Piedmont Comm Coll (NC)
Chattanooga State Tech Comm Coll (TN)
Chemeketa Comm Coll (OR)
Coll of DuPage (IL)
ECPI Coll of Technology, Newport News (VA)
ECPI Coll of Technology, Virginia Beach (VA)
ECPI Tech Coll (VA)
ECPI Tech Coll, Richmond (VA)
El Centro Coll (TX)
Florida Comm Coll at Jacksonville (FL)
Hagerstown Business Coll (MD)
Hagerstown Comm Coll (MD)
Harrisburg Area Comm Coll (PA)
Holyoke Comm Coll (MA)
Houston Comm Coll System (TX)
Howard Coll (TX)
Illinois Central Coll (IL)
Kennebec Valley Comm Coll (ME)
Lake-Sumter Comm Coll (FL)
Meridian Comm Coll (MS)
Miami Dade Coll (FL)
Northeast Iowa Comm Coll (IA)
Northern Essex Comm Coll (MA)
Penn Valley Comm Coll (MO)
Phoenix Coll (AZ)
Polk Comm Coll (FL)
Rasmussen Coll Mankato (MN)
Roane State Comm Coll (TN)
Saint Charles Comm Coll (MO)
St. Petersburg Coll (FL)
San Diego Mesa Coll (CA)
Sinclair Comm Coll (OH)
South Plains Coll (TX)
Southwestern Illinois Coll (IL)
Spokane Comm Coll (WA)
Stark State Coll of Technology (OH)
State U of New York Coll of Technology at Alfred (NY)
Tarrant County Coll District (TX)
Tulsa Comm Coll (OK)
Vermilion Comm Coll (MN)
Westmoreland County Comm Coll (PA)
Wharton County Jr Coll (TX)

Health Information/Medical Records Technology
Atlanta Tech Coll (GA)
Bishop State Comm Coll (AL)
Bristol Comm Coll (MA)
Broome Comm Coll (NY)
Business Inst of Pennsylvania, Meadville (PA)
Central Comm Coll–Hastings Campus (NE)
Central Florida Comm Coll (FL)
Central Oregon Comm Coll (OR)
Cincinnati State Tech and Comm Coll (OH)
Coll of DuPage (IL)
Columbus Tech Coll (GA)
Comm Coll of Allegheny County (PA)
Delgado Comm Coll (LA)
Dyersburg State Comm Coll (TN)
Edmonds Comm Coll (WA)
Erie Comm Coll, North Campus (NY)
Fayetteville Tech Comm Coll (NC)
Heart of Georgia Tech Coll (GA)
Houston Comm Coll System (TX)
Hudson Valley Comm Coll (NY)
Hutchinson Comm Coll and Area Vocational School (KS)
Indiana Business Coll, Anderson (IN)
Indiana Business Coll, Muncie (IN)
Jefferson Comm and Tech Coll (KY)
Marshall Comm and Tech Coll (WV)
Mercy Coll of Northwest Ohio (OH)
Midland Coll (TX)
Midlands Tech Coll (SC)
Mohawk Valley Comm Coll (NY)
Moraine Park Tech Coll (WI)
Moraine Valley Comm Coll (IL)
Mountain View Coll (TX)
North Dakota State Coll of Science (ND)
Northwestern Tech Coll (GA)
Ogeechee Tech Coll (GA)
Owens Comm Coll, Toledo (OH)
Panola Coll (TX)
St. Philip's Coll (TX)
San Juan Coll (NM)
Santa Barbara City Coll (CA)
South Hills School of Business & Technology, State College (PA)
United Tribes Tech Coll (ND)
Volunteer State Comm Coll (TN)
West Georgia Tech Coll (GA)
West Virginia Northern Comm Coll (WV)
Williston State Coll (ND)

Health/Medical Claims Examination
Ohio Business Coll, Sandusky (OH)

Health/Medical Preparatory Programs Related
Ancilla Coll (IN)
Arkansas State U–Beebe (AR)
Eastern Arizona Coll (AZ)
Eastern Wyoming Coll (WY)
Laramie County Comm Coll (WY)
Miami Dade Coll (FL)

Health Professions Related
Allegany Coll of Maryland (MD)
Berkshire Comm Coll (MA)
Brazosport Coll (TX)
Cincinnati State Tech and Comm Coll (OH)

Comm Coll of Allegheny County (PA)
Dixie State Coll of Utah (UT)
Edmonds Comm Coll (WA)
Essex County Coll (NJ)
Lanier Tech Coll (GA)
Miami Dade Coll (FL)
Midlands Tech Coll (SC)
Oakland Comm Coll (MI)
Phillips Beth Israel School of Nursing (NY)
Southwestern Michigan Coll (MI)
Southwest Tennessee Comm Coll (TN)
Volunteer State Comm Coll (TN)

Health Science
Arizona Western Coll (AZ)
Bergen Comm Coll (NJ)
Borough of Manhattan Comm Coll of the City U of New York (NY)
Bucks County Comm Coll (PA)
Carroll Comm Coll (MD)
Coll of the Canyons (CA)
Diné Coll (AZ)
Fisher Coll (MA)
Manor Coll (PA)
Mercer County Comm Coll (NJ)
Nassau Comm Coll (NY)
North Shore Comm Coll (MA)
Northwestern Connecticut Comm Coll (CT)
Ocean County Coll (NJ)
Orange Coast Coll (CA)
Palo Alto Coll (TX)
Palo Verde Coll (CA)
Salt Lake Comm Coll (UT)
San Joaquin Delta Coll (CA)
Southwest Mississippi Comm Coll (MS)
Spoon River Coll (IL)
Sussex County Comm Coll (NJ)
Tulsa Comm Coll (OK)
Villa Maria Coll of Buffalo (NY)

Health Services/Allied Health/Health Sciences
Aakers Business Coll (ND)
Ancilla Coll (IN)
Atlanta Metropolitan Coll (GA)
Clarendon Coll (TX)
Cochise Coll, Douglas (AZ)
Florida National Coll (FL)
Keiser Coll, Miami (FL)
Louisiana State U at Alexandria (LA)
South U, West Palm Beach (FL)

Health Teacher Education
Bainbridge Coll (GA)
Bucks County Comm Coll (PA)
Chemeketa Comm Coll (OR)
Coahoma Comm Coll (MS)
Coastal Bend Coll (TX)
Columbia Coll (CA)
Copiah-Lincoln Comm Coll (MS)
Howard Comm Coll (MD)
Manatee Comm Coll (FL)
Palm Beach Comm Coll (FL)
Pratt Comm Coll (KS)
Tulsa Comm Coll (OK)
Vermilion Comm Coll (MN)
Westmoreland County Comm Coll (PA)
William Rainey Harper Coll (IL)
Young Harris Coll (GA)
Yuba Coll (CA)

Health Unit Coordinator/Ward Clerk
Brown Mackie Coll–Kansas City (KS)
Comm Coll of Allegheny County (PA)
Rasmussen Coll Mankato (MN)
Riverland Comm Coll (MN)
Southeast Tech Inst (SD)

Health Unit Management/Ward Supervision
Brown Mackie Coll–Kansas City (KS)

Heating, Air Conditioning and Refrigeration Technology
Alamance Comm Coll (NC)
Benjamin Franklin Inst of Technology (MA)
Cincinnati State Tech and Comm Coll (OH)
DeKalb Tech Coll (GA)
Delta Coll (MI)
Front Range Comm Coll (CO)
Gadsden State Comm Coll (AL)
GateWay Comm Coll (AZ)
Griffin Tech Coll (GA)
Harrisburg Area Comm Coll (PA)
Jackson Comm Coll (MI)
Macomb Comm Coll (MI)
Manhattan Area Tech Coll (KS)
Mercer County Comm Coll (NJ)
Miami Dade Coll (FL)
Minnesota State Comm and Tech Coll–Fergus Falls (MN)
Mohawk Valley Comm Coll (NY)
Moraine Park Tech Coll (WI)
Mott Comm Coll (MI)
North Dakota State Coll of Science (ND)
North Georgia Tech Coll (GA)
Oakland Comm Coll (MI)
Piedmont Virginia Comm Coll (VA)
Riverside Comm Coll District (CA)
St. Cloud Tech Coll (MN)
Savannah Tech Coll (GA)
South Georgia Tech Coll (GA)
Springfield Tech Comm Coll (MA)
State U of New York Coll of Technology at Alfred (NY)
State U of New York Coll of Technology at Delhi (NY)
TESST Coll of Technology, Towson (MD)
Texas State Tech Coll Waco (TX)
Triangle Tech, Inc.– Greensburg School (PA)
Vatterott Coll, Tulsa (OK)
Wisconsin Indianhead Tech Coll (WI)

Heating, Air Conditioning, Ventilation and Refrigeration Maintenance Technology
Arizona Western Coll (AZ)
Austin Comm Coll (TX)
Brazosport Coll (TX)
Cedar Valley Coll (TX)
Central Comm Coll–Grand Island Campus (NE)
Central Comm Coll–Hastings Campus (NE)
Century Coll (MN)
Chattanooga State Tech Comm Coll (TN)
Clovis Comm Coll (NM)
Coll of Business and Technology (FL)
Coll of DuPage (IL)
Coll of Lake County (IL)
Comm and Tech Coll of Shepherd (WV)
Comm Coll of Allegheny County (PA)
Delta Coll (MI)
East Central Coll (MO)
Eastfield Coll (TX)
Fayetteville Tech Comm Coll (NC)
Forsyth Tech Comm Coll (NC)
GateWay Comm Coll (AZ)
George C. Wallace Comm Coll (AL)

Grand Rapids Comm Coll (MI)
H. Councill Trenholm State Tech Coll (AL)
Heartland Comm Coll (IL)
Horry-Georgetown Tech Coll (SC)
Hudson Valley Comm Coll (NY)
Illinois Eastern Comm Colls, Lincoln Trail College (IL)
IntelliTec Coll, Grand Junction (CO)
Ivy Tech Comm Coll–Bloomington (IN)
Ivy Tech Comm Coll–Central Indiana (IN)
Ivy Tech Comm Coll–Columbus (IN)
Ivy Tech Comm Coll–East Central (IN)
Ivy Tech Comm Coll–Kokomo (IN)
Ivy Tech Comm Coll–Lafayette (IN)
Ivy Tech Comm Coll–North Central (IN)
Ivy Tech Comm Coll–Northeast (IN)
Ivy Tech Comm Coll–Northwest (IN)
Ivy Tech Comm Coll–Southern Indiana (IN)
Ivy Tech Comm Coll–Southwest (IN)
Ivy Tech Comm Coll–Wabash Valley (IN)
Ivy Tech Comm Coll–Whitewater (IN)
Johnston Comm Coll (NC)
Kellogg Comm Coll (MI)
Lamar State Coll–Port Arthur (TX)
Lansing Comm Coll (MI)
Linn State Tech Coll (MO)
Long Beach City Coll (CA)
Luzerne County Comm Coll (PA)
Macomb Comm Coll (MI)
Metropolitan Comm Coll (NE)
Miami Dade Coll (FL)
Midland Coll (TX)
Midlands Tech Coll (SC)
Minnesota West Comm and Tech Coll (MN)
Modesto Jr Coll (CA)
Mohawk Valley Comm Coll (NY)
Mt. San Antonio Coll (CA)
New Hampshire Comm Tech Coll, Manchester/Stratham (NH)
Northampton County Area Comm Coll (PA)
North Dakota State Coll of Science (ND)
Northeast Comm Coll (NE)
Northern Maine Comm Coll (ME)
North Idaho Coll (ID)
North Iowa Area Comm Coll (IA)
North Seattle Comm Coll (WA)
Okaloosa-Walton Coll (FL)
Orange Coast Coll (CA)
Raritan Valley Comm Coll (NJ)
Rockingham Comm Coll (NC)
St. Cloud Tech Coll (MN)
St. Philip's Coll (TX)
Salt Lake Comm Coll (UT)
San Joaquin Delta Coll (CA)
San Joaquin Valley Coll (CA)
Sauk Valley Comm Coll (IL)
Shelton State Comm Coll (AL)
Southeast Tech Inst (SD)
South Plains Coll (TX)
South Texas Coll (TX)
Southwestern Illinois Coll (IL)
Spartanburg Tech Coll (SC)
Spokane Comm Coll (WA)
State U of New York Coll of Technology at Alfred (NY)
State U of New York Coll of Technology at Delhi (NY)

Tarrant County Coll District (TX)
Texas State Tech Coll Waco (TX)
Triangle Tech, Inc.– Greensburg School (PA)
Trinity Valley Comm Coll (TX)
Triton Coll (IL)
Tulsa Comm Coll (OK)
U of Alaska Anchorage, Matanuska-Susitna Coll (AK)
U of Northwestern Ohio (OH)
Vance-Granville Comm Coll (NC)
Waubonsee Comm Coll (IL)
Western Iowa Tech Comm Coll (IA)
Western Tech Coll (TX)
Western Tech Coll (WI)
Westmoreland County Comm Coll (PA)
West Virginia Northern Comm Coll (WV)
William Rainey Harper Coll (IL)
WyoTech, Fremont (CA)
York Tech Coll (SC)

Heavy Equipment Maintenance Technology
Allan Hancock Coll (CA)
Beaufort County Comm Coll (NC)
Centralia Coll (WA)
Delaware Tech & Comm Coll, Jack F. Owens Campus (DE)
Hawkeye Comm Coll (IA)
H. Councill Trenholm State Tech Coll (AL)
Illinois Eastern Comm Colls, Olney Central College (IL)
Lansing Comm Coll (MI)
Lawson State Comm Coll (AL)
Linn State Tech Coll (MO)
Long Beach City Coll (CA)
Longview Comm Coll (MO)
Lower Columbia Coll (WA)
Metropolitan Comm Coll (NE)
Mohawk Valley Comm Coll (NY)
New Hampshire Comm Tech Coll, Nashua/Claremont (NH)
Northern Maine Comm Coll (ME)
North Idaho Coll (ID)
The Ohio State U Ag Tech Inst (OH)
Rogue Comm Coll (OR)
Salt Lake Comm Coll (UT)
Sheridan Coll–Sheridan and Gillette (WY)
South Texas Coll (TX)
Southwest Tennessee Comm Coll (TN)
Spokane Comm Coll (WA)
Spokane Falls Comm Coll (WA)
State U of New York Coll of Technology at Alfred (NY)
Texas State Tech Coll Waco (TX)
Trinidad State Jr Coll (CO)
West Central Tech Coll (GA)

Heavy/Industrial Equipment Maintenance Technologies Related
Big Bend Comm Coll (WA)
Eastern West Virginia Comm and Tech Coll (WV)
Southwestern Michigan Coll (MI)

Hematology Technology
Comm Coll of the Air Force (AL)

Hispanic-American, Puerto Rican, and Mexican-American/Chicano Studies
City Colls of Chicago, Wilbur Wright College (IL)
Pasadena City Coll (CA)
San Diego City Coll (CA)
San Diego Mesa Coll (CA)

Santa Barbara City Coll (CA)
Yuba Coll (CA)

Histologic Technician
Goodwin Coll (CT)
Miami Dade Coll (FL)
Mott Comm Coll (MI)
Oakland Comm Coll (MI)

**Histologic Technology/
Histotechnologist**
North Hennepin Comm Coll
(MN)

**Historic Preservation and
Conservation**
Bucks County Comm Coll
(PA)
Colorado Mountain Coll,
Timberline Campus (CO)

History
Abraham Baldwin Ag Coll
(GA)
Allen County Comm Coll
(KS)
Ancilla Coll (IN)
Atlanta Metropolitan Coll
(GA)
Austin Comm Coll (TX)
Bainbridge Coll (GA)
Barton County Comm Coll
(KS)
Bergen Comm Coll (NJ)
Brazosport Coll (TX)
Bronx Comm Coll of the City
U of New York (NY)
Bunker Hill Comm Coll (MA)
Butler Comm Coll (KS)
Casper Coll (WY)
Centralia Coll (WA)
Clarendon Coll (TX)
Coastal Bend Coll (TX)
Coastal Georgia Comm Coll
(GA)
Cochise Coll, Douglas (AZ)
Colby Comm Coll (KS)
Coll of Southern Maryland
(MD)
Coll of the Canyons (CA)
Coll of the Siskiyous (CA)
Columbia Coll (CA)
Copiah-Lincoln Comm Coll
(MS)
Dixie State Coll of Utah (UT)
East Central Coll (MO)
Eastern Arizona Coll (AZ)
Eastern Wyoming Coll (WY)
Feather River Coll (CA)
Foothill Coll (CA)
Gainesville Coll (GA)
Galveston Coll (TX)
Gavilan Coll (CA)
Georgia Highlands Coll (GA)
Great Basin Coll (NV)
Highland Comm Coll (IL)
Independence Comm Coll
(KS)
Kellogg Comm Coll (MI)
Laramie County Comm Coll
(WY)
Lawson State Comm Coll
(AL)
Lincoln Coll (IL)
Lower Columbia Coll (WA)
Manatee Comm Coll (FL)
Miami Dade Coll (FL)
Middlesex County Coll (NJ)
Midland Coll (TX)
MiraCosta Coll (CA)
Naugatuck Valley Comm Coll
(CT)
New Mexico Military Inst
(NM)
Northern Essex Comm Coll
(MA)
North Idaho Coll (ID)
Orange Coast Coll (CA)
Otero Jr Coll (CO)
Palm Beach Comm Coll (FL)
Palo Alto Coll (TX)
Palo Verde Coll (CA)
Parkland Coll (IL)
Pasadena City Coll (CA)
Pratt Comm Coll (KS)
Saddleback Coll (CA)
St. Philip's Coll (TX)
Salem Comm Coll (NJ)
Salt Lake Comm Coll (UT)
San Joaquin Delta Coll (CA)
San Juan Coll (NM)
Santa Barbara City Coll (CA)

Santa Rosa Jr Coll (CA)
Sauk Valley Comm Coll (IL)
Sheridan Coll–Sheridan and
Gillette (WY)
Skyline Coll (CA)
Snow Coll (UT)
Southwest Mississippi
Comm Coll (MS)
Spoon River Coll (IL)
Treasure Valley Comm Coll
(OR)
Trinity Valley Comm Coll
(TX)
Tulsa Comm Coll (OK)
Vermilion Comm Coll (MN)
Young Harris Coll (GA)
Yuba Coll (CA)

History Related
Coll of the Siskiyous (CA)

History Teacher Education
Ancilla Coll (IN)

**Home Furnishings and
Equipment Installation**
Jefferson State Comm Coll
(AL)
St. Philip's Coll (TX)

Home Health Aide
Barton County Comm Coll
(KS)

**Home Health Aide/Home
Attendant**
Allen County Comm Coll
(KS)
Laurel Business Inst (PA)

**Horse Husbandry/Equine
Science and Management**
Central Wyoming Coll (WY)
Clarendon Coll (TX)
Linn-Benton Comm Coll
(OR)
The Ohio State U Ag Tech
Inst (OH)
Santa Rosa Jr Coll (CA)
Yavapai Coll (AZ)

Horticultural Science
Abraham Baldwin Ag Coll
(GA)
Central Lakes Coll (MN)
Central Piedmont Comm Coll
(NC)
Chattahoochee Tech Coll
(GA)
Clark State Comm Coll (OH)
Columbus Tech Coll (GA)
East Central Coll (MO)
Forsyth Tech Comm Coll
(NC)
Georgia Highlands Coll (GA)
Griffin Tech Coll (GA)
Gwinnett Tech Coll (GA)
Hawkeye Comm Coll (IA)
Houston Comm Coll System
(TX)
Illinois Central Coll (IL)
Joliet Jr Coll (IL)
Lansing Comm Coll (MI)
Linn-Benton Comm Coll
(OR)
Long Beach City Coll (CA)
Luzerne County Comm Coll
(PA)
Meridian Comm Coll (MS)
Miami Dade Coll (FL)
MiraCosta Coll (CA)
Mississippi Gulf Coast
Comm Coll (MS)
Mt. San Antonio Coll (CA)
Naugatuck Valley Comm Coll
(CT)
Northeast Comm Coll (NE)
North Georgia Tech Coll
(GA)
North Metro Tech Coll (GA)
The Ohio State U Ag Tech
Inst (OH)
Orange Coast Coll (CA)
Palo Alto Coll (TX)
Rockingham Comm Coll
(NC)
Saddleback Coll (CA)
Southeast Tech Inst (SD)
South Georgia Tech Coll
(GA)
Southwestern Illinois Coll (IL)
Spartanburg Tech Coll (SC)

State U of New York Coll of
Technology at Delhi (NY)
Tarrant County Coll District
(TX)
Tidewater Comm Coll (VA)
Trident Tech Coll (SC)
Trinity Valley Comm Coll
(TX)
Tulsa Comm Coll (OK)
Westmoreland County
Comm Coll (PA)
William Rainey Harper Coll
(IL)
The Williamson Free School
of Mecha Trades (PA)

**Hospital and Health Care
Facilities Administration**
Allen County Comm Coll
(KS)
Central Comm Coll–Hastings
Campus (NE)
Coll of DuPage (IL)
Harrisburg Area Comm Coll
(PA)
Manatee Comm Coll (FL)
Western Tech Coll (WI)

Hospitality Administration
Abraham Baldwin Ag Coll
(GA)
Alexandria Tech Coll (MN)
Allegany Coll of Maryland
(MD)
Arizona Western Coll (AZ)
Baltimore International Coll
(MD)
Bay State Coll (MA)
Berkshire Comm Coll (MA)
Bucks County Comm Coll
(PA)
Bunker Hill Comm Coll (MA)
Butler County Comm Coll
(PA)
Casper Coll (WY)
Central Comm Coll–Hastings
Campus (NE)
Central New Mexico Comm
Coll (NM)
Central Oregon Comm Coll
(OR)
Central Piedmont Comm Coll
(NC)
Chemeketa Comm Coll (OR)
Cochise Coll, Douglas (AZ)
Coll of DuPage (IL)
Collin County Comm Coll
District (TX)
Colorado Mountain Coll,
Alpine Campus (CO)
Delaware Tech & Comm
Coll, Jack F. Owens
Campus (DE)
Delgado Comm Coll (LA)
East Central Coll (MO)
El Centro Coll (TX)
Fisher Coll (MA)
Florida Comm Coll at
Jacksonville (FL)
Florida National Coll (FL)
Fox Valley Tech Coll (WI)
Guam Comm Coll (GU)
Heald Coll-Salinas (CA)
Heald Coll-San Francisco
(CA)
Holyoke Comm Coll (MA)
International Coll of
Hospitality Management
(CT)
Ivy Tech Comm Coll–East
Central (IN)
Ivy Tech Comm Coll–North
Central (IN)
Ivy Tech Comm Coll–
Northeast (IN)
Ivy Tech Comm Coll–
Northwest (IN)
James H. Faulkner State
Comm Coll (AL)
Jefferson Comm Coll (NY)
Jefferson State Comm Coll
(AL)
Joliet Jr Coll (IL)
Kauai Comm Coll (HI)
Lake Michigan Coll (MI)
Lansing Comm Coll (MI)
Marshall Comm and Tech
Coll (WV)
Massachusetts Bay Comm
Coll (MA)
Miami Dade Coll (FL)

Middlesex County Coll (NJ)
Naugatuck Valley Comm Coll
(CT)
Niagara County Comm Coll
(NY)
Normandale Comm Coll
(MN)
North Idaho Coll (ID)
North Shore Comm Coll
(MA)
Pellissippi State Tech Comm
Coll (TN)
Pima Comm Coll (AZ)
Rasmussen Coll Mankato
(MN)
St. Petersburg Coll (FL)
San Diego City Coll (CA)
Scottsdale Comm Coll (AZ)
Seattle Central Comm Coll
(WA)
Sheridan Coll–Sheridan and
Gillette (WY)
South Texas Coll (TX)
Southwestern Illinois Coll (IL)
Sullivan County Comm Coll
(NY)
Triton Coll (IL)
United Tribes Tech Coll (ND)
Valencia Comm Coll (FL)
Waukesha County Tech Coll
(WI)
Westmoreland County
Comm Coll (PA)
West Virginia Northern
Comm Coll (WV)
William Rainey Harper Coll
(IL)
Wor-Wic Comm Coll (MD)
Young Harris Coll (GA)

**Hospitality Administration
Related**
Arizona Western Coll (AZ)
Ivy Tech Comm Coll–Central
Indiana (IN)
Ivy Tech Comm Coll–East
Central (IN)
Ivy Tech Comm Coll–
Northeast (IN)
Lehigh Valley Coll (PA)
The Pennsylvania State U
Beaver Campus of the
Commonwealth Coll (PA)

**Hospitality and Recreation
Marketing**
Austin Comm Coll (TX)
Central Oregon Comm Coll
(OR)
Florida Comm Coll at
Jacksonville (FL)
Guam Comm Coll (GU)
Luzerne County Comm Coll
(PA)
Montgomery County Comm
Coll (PA)
Raritan Valley Comm Coll
(NJ)
Rasmussen Coll Mankato
(MN)
San Diego Mesa Coll (CA)
State U of New York Coll of
Technology at Delhi (NY)

**Hotel and Restaurant
Management**
Albany Tech Coll (GA)
Athens Tech Coll (GA)
Atlanta Tech Coll (GA)
Bryant and Stratton Coll,
Syracuse (NY)
Central Georgia Tech Coll
(GA)
New England Culinary Inst at
Essex (VT)
Ogeechee Tech Coll (GA)
Savannah Tech Coll (GA)

Hotel/Motel Administration
Alexandria Tech Coll (MN)
Austin Comm Coll (TX)
Bergen Comm Coll (NJ)
Briarwood Coll (CT)
Broome Comm Coll (NY)
Broward Comm Coll (FL)
Bucks County Comm Coll
(PA)
Bunker Hill Comm Coll (MA)
Butler Comm Coll (KS)
Cape Fear Comm Coll (NC)
Carl Albert State Coll (OK)
Central Arizona Coll (AZ)

Central Comm Coll–Hastings
Campus (NE)
Central Oregon Comm Coll
(OR)
Central Piedmont Comm Coll
(NC)
Chattanooga State Tech
Comm Coll (TN)
Chemeketa Comm Coll (OR)
Cincinnati State Tech and
Comm Coll (OH)
Coll of DuPage (IL)
Coll of the Canyons (CA)
Colorado Mountain Coll,
Alpine Campus (CO)
Columbia Coll (CA)
Comm Coll of Allegheny
County (PA)
Comm Coll of the Air Force
(AL)
Cowley County Comm Coll
and Area Vocational–Tech
School (KS)
Delaware Tech & Comm
Coll, Jack F. Owens
Campus (DE)
Delaware Tech & Comm
Coll, Stanton/Wilmington
Campus (DE)
East Central Coll (MO)
El Centro Coll (TX)
Essex County Coll (NJ)
Fayetteville Tech Comm Coll
(NC)
Finger Lakes Comm Coll
(NY)
Florida Comm Coll at
Jacksonville (FL)
Galveston Coll (TX)
Gateway Comm Coll (CT)
Genesee Comm Coll (NY)
Georgia Highlands Coll (GA)
Guam Comm Coll (GU)
Gwinnett Tech Coll (GA)
Harrisburg Area Comm Coll
(PA)
Highline Comm Coll (WA)
Holyoke Comm Coll (MA)
Horry-Georgetown Tech Coll
(SC)
Houston Comm Coll System
(TX)
Jefferson Comm Coll (NY)
John Wood Comm Coll (IL)
Kapiolani Comm Coll (HI)
Keystone Coll (PA)
Lansing Comm Coll (MI)
Laredo Comm Coll (TX)
Lincoln Land Comm Coll (IL)
Long Beach City Coll (CA)
Louisiana Tech Coll (LA)
Luzerne County Comm Coll
(PA)
Manchester Comm Coll (CT)
Mercer County Comm Coll
(NJ)
Meridian Comm Coll (MS)
Middlesex County Coll (NJ)
MiraCosta Coll (CA)
Mississippi Gulf Coast
Comm Coll (MS)
Mohawk Valley Comm Coll
(NY)
Mt. San Antonio Coll (CA)
Nassau Comm Coll (NY)
Naugatuck Valley Comm Coll
(CT)
New Hampshire Tech Inst
(NH)
Northampton County Area
Comm Coll (PA)
Northern Essex Comm Coll
(MA)
Norwalk Comm Coll (CT)
Oakland Comm Coll (MI)
Okaloosa-Walton Coll (FL)
Orange Coast Coll (CA)
Palau Comm CollPalau)
Palm Beach Comm Coll (FL)
Pellissippi State Tech Comm
Coll (TN)
Penn Foster Career School
(PA)
Quinsigamond Comm Coll
(MA)
Raritan Valley Comm Coll
(NJ)
Rasmussen Coll Mankato
(MN)
St. Philip's Coll (TX)

San Diego Mesa Coll (CA)
Santa Barbara City Coll (CA)
Santa Rosa Jr Coll (CA)
Scottsdale Comm Coll (AZ)
Seattle Central Comm Coll
(WA)
Sinclair Comm Coll (OH)
Skyline Coll (CA)
South Texas Coll (TX)
Spokane Comm Coll (WA)
State U of New York Coll of
Technology at Delhi (NY)
Tompkins Cortland Comm
Coll (NY)
Trident Tech Coll (SC)
Triton Coll (IL)
Tulsa Comm Coll (OK)
Union County Coll (NJ)
Westchester Comm Coll
(NY)
Westmoreland County
Comm Coll (PA)
Wilkes Comm Coll (NC)
William Rainey Harper Coll
(IL)
Yakima Valley Comm Coll
(WA)

**Hotel/Motel Services
Marketing Operations**
Montgomery County Comm
Coll (PA)

**Housing and Human
Environments**
Modesto Jr Coll (CA)
Orange Coast Coll (CA)

**Housing and Human
Environments Related**
Comm Coll of Allegheny
County (PA)

**Human Development and
Family Studies**
Lincoln Coll (IL)
Orange Coast Coll (CA)
The Pennsylvania State U
Delaware County Campus
of the Commonwealth Coll
(PA)
The Pennsylvania State U
DuBois Campus of the
Commonwealth Coll (PA)
The Pennsylvania State U
Fayette Campus of the
Commonwealth Coll (PA)
The Pennsylvania State U
Mont Alto Campus of the
Commonwealth Coll (PA)
The Pennsylvania State U
New Kensington Campus
of the Commonwealth Coll
(PA)
The Pennsylvania State U
Shenango Campus of the
Commonwealth Coll (PA)
The Pennsylvania State U
Worthington Scranton
Campus of the
Commonwealth Coll (PA)
The Pennsylvania State U
York Campus of the
Commonwealth Coll (PA)
Saddleback Coll (CA)
Salt Lake Comm Coll (UT)

**Human Development and
Family Studies Related**
Comm Coll of Allegheny
County (PA)

Human Ecology
Greenfield Comm Coll (MA)
Vermilion Comm Coll (MN)

Humanities
Abraham Baldwin Ag Coll
(GA)
Allen County Comm Coll
(KS)
Ancilla Coll (IN)
Bristol Comm Coll (MA)
Bucks County Comm Coll
(PA)
Butler County Comm Coll
(PA)
Centralia Coll (WA)
Central Oregon Comm Coll
(OR)
Chemeketa Comm Coll (OR)
Cochise Coll, Douglas (AZ)
Colby Comm Coll (KS)

Coll of the Canyons (CA)
Colorado Mountain Coll (CO)
Colorado Mountain Coll, Alpine Campus (CO)
Columbia Coll (CA)
Comm Coll of Allegheny County (PA)
Corning Comm Coll (NY)
Dixie State Coll of Utah (UT)
Erie Comm Coll (NY)
Erie Comm Coll, North Campus (NY)
Erie Comm Coll, South Campus (NY)
Finger Lakes Comm Coll (NY)
Fisher Coll (MA)
Galveston Coll (TX)
Greenfield Comm Coll (MA)
Highline Comm Coll (WA)
Independence Comm Coll (KS)
Jamestown Comm Coll (NY)
Jefferson Comm Coll (NY)
Lackawanna Coll (PA)
Laramie County Comm Coll (WY)
Lincoln Coll (IL)
Lincoln Coll–Normal (IL)
Luzerne County Comm Coll (PA)
Manatee Comm Coll (FL)
Mercer County Comm Coll (NJ)
Miami Dade Coll (FL)
MiraCosta Coll (CA)
Modesto Jr Coll (CA)
Mohawk Valley Comm Coll (NY)
Montgomery County Comm Coll (PA)
New Mexico Military Inst (NM)
Niagara County Comm Coll (NY)
Okaloosa-Walton Coll (FL)
Orange Coast Coll (CA)
Orange County Comm Coll (NY)
Otero Jr Coll (CO)
Pratt Comm Coll (KS)
Rogue Comm Coll (OR)
Saddleback Coll (CA)
Salem Comm Coll (NJ)
Salt Lake Comm Coll (UT)
San Joaquin Delta Coll (CA)
Sheridan Coll–Sheridan and Gillette (WY)
Snow Coll (UT)
Southwest Mississippi Comm Coll (MS)
State U of New York Coll of Technology at Alfred (NY)
State U of New York Coll of Technology at Delhi (NY)
Tompkins Cortland Comm Coll (NY)
Treasure Valley Comm Coll (OR)
Tulsa Comm Coll (OK)
Westchester Comm Coll (NY)
William Rainey Harper Coll (IL)

Human Resources Management
Beaufort County Comm Coll (NC)
Clark Coll (WA)
Comm Coll of Allegheny County (PA)
Comm Coll of the Air Force (AL)
Edmonds Comm Coll (WA)
Fayetteville Tech Comm Coll (NC)
Houston Comm Coll System (TX)
Indiana Business Coll, Anderson (IN)
Indiana Business Coll, Columbus (IN)
Indiana Business Coll, Indianapolis (IN)
Indiana Business Coll, Terre Haute (IN)
Keystone Coll (PA)
Lansing Comm Coll (MI)

Minnesota State Comm and Tech Coll–Fergus Falls (MN)
Moraine Valley Comm Coll (IL)
New Hampshire Tech Inst (NH)
Okaloosa-Walton Coll (FL)
Prairie State Coll (IL)
Rockingham Comm Coll (NC)
Saint Paul Coll–A Comm & Tech College (MN)
Salem Comm Coll (NJ)
Tulsa Comm Coll (OK)
Valencia Comm Coll (FL)
Western Tech Coll (WI)
William Rainey Harper Coll (IL)

Human Resources Management and Services Related
Aakers Business Coll (ND)
Barton County Comm Coll (KS)
Bryant and Stratton Coll, Albany (NY)
Bryant and Stratton Coll, Rochester (NY)
Bryant and Stratton Coll, Rochester (NY)
Bryant and Stratton Coll, Syracuse (NY)
Bryant and Stratton Coll, Parma (OH)
Bryant and Stratton Coll (WI)
Bryant and Stratton Coll, Amherst Campus (NY)
Bryant and Stratton Coll, Buffalo Campus (NY)
Bryant and Stratton Coll, Lackawanna Campus (NY)
Bryant and Stratton Coll, Richmond (VA)
Lake Superior Coll (MN)

Human Services
Aiken Tech Coll (SC)
Alexandria Tech Coll (MN)
Allan Hancock Coll (CA)
Arizona Western Coll (AZ)
Asnuntuck Comm Coll (CT)
Atlanta Metropolitan Coll (GA)
Austin Comm Coll (TX)
Berkshire Comm Coll (MA)
Borough of Manhattan Comm Coll of the City U of New York (NY)
Bristol Comm Coll (MA)
Bristol Comm Coll (MA)
Bronx Comm Coll of the City U of New York (NY)
Bunker Hill Comm Coll (MA)
Bunker Hill Comm Coll (MA)
Carroll Comm Coll (MD)
Central Florida Comm Coll (FL)
Central Piedmont Comm Coll (NC)
Central Wyoming Coll (WY)
Chatfield Coll (OH)
Chemeketa Comm Coll (OR)
Clark State Comm Coll (OH)
Cochise Coll, Douglas (AZ)
Coll of DuPage (IL)
Coll of DuPage (IL)
Coll of Southern Maryland (MD)
Comm Coll of Denver (CO)
Corning Comm Coll (NY)
Delaware Tech & Comm Coll, Jack F. Owens Campus (DE)
Delaware Tech & Comm Coll, Stanton/Wilmington Campus (DE)
Delaware Tech & Comm Coll, Terry Campus (DE)
Denmark Tech Coll (SC)
Essex County Coll (NJ)
Finger Lakes Comm Coll (NY)
Fiorello H. LaGuardia Comm Coll of the City U of New York (NY)
Florida Comm Coll at Jacksonville (FL)
Frederick Comm Coll (MD)
Gateway Comm Coll (CT)

Genesee Comm Coll (NY)
Georgia Highlands Coll (GA)
Glendale Comm Coll (AZ)
Goodwin Coll (CT)
Greenfield Comm Coll (MA)
Harrisburg Area Comm Coll (PA)
Harrisburg Area Comm Coll (PA)
Highland Comm Coll (IL)
Highline Comm Coll (WA)
Holyoke Comm Coll (MA)
Hudson Valley Comm Coll (NY)
Itasca Comm Coll (MN)
Ivy Tech Comm Coll–East Central (IN)
Ivy Tech Comm Coll–Kokomo (IN)
Ivy Tech Comm Coll–North Central (IN)
Ivy Tech Comm Coll–Northeast (IN)
Jamestown Comm Coll (NY)
Jefferson Comm Coll (NY)
John Tyler Comm Coll (VA)
Kellogg Comm Coll (MI)
Kingsborough Comm Coll of the City U of New York (NY)
Lake Land Coll (IL)
Lansing Comm Coll (MI)
Long Beach City Coll (CA)
Longview Comm Coll (MO)
Luzerne County Comm Coll (PA)
Manchester Comm Coll (CT)
Manor Coll (PA)
Massachusetts Bay Comm Coll (MA)
Mesabi Range Comm and Tech Coll (MN)
Metropolitan Comm Coll (NE)
Miami Dade Coll (FL)
Middlesex Comm Coll (CT)
Mississippi Gulf Coast Comm Coll (MS)
Modesto Jr Coll (CA)
Mohawk Valley Comm Coll (NY)
Montgomery Coll (TX)
Mount Wachusett Comm Coll (MA)
Naugatuck Valley Comm Coll (CT)
New Hampshire Comm Tech Coll, Manchester/Stratham (NH)
New Hampshire Comm Tech Coll, Nashua/Claremont (NH)
New Hampshire Tech Inst (NH)
Niagara County Comm Coll (NY)
North Central Missouri Coll (MO)
Northern Essex Comm Coll (MA)
North Idaho Coll (ID)
Northwestern Connecticut Comm Coll (CT)
Northwest Indian Coll (WA)
Norwalk Comm Coll (CT)
Parkland Coll (IL)
Pasadena City Coll (CA)
Pasco-Hernando Comm Coll (FL)
Pratt Comm Coll (KS)
Quinebaug Valley Comm Coll (CT)
Quinsigamond Comm Coll (MA)
Raritan Valley Comm Coll (NJ)
Richmond Comm Coll (NC)
Riverland Comm Coll (MN)
Rock Valley Coll (IL)
Rogue Comm Coll (OR)
Saddleback Coll (CA)
Saint Charles Comm Coll (MO)
St. Louis Comm Coll at Florissant Valley (MO)
St. Petersburg Coll (FL)
San Juan Coll (NM)
Santa Rosa Jr Coll (CA)
Sauk Valley Comm Coll (IL)

Seattle Central Comm Coll (WA)
Sinclair Comm Coll (OH)
Southern State Comm Coll (OH)
Southside Virginia Comm Coll (VA)
South Texas Coll (TX)
Southwest Virginia Comm Coll (VA)
Stark State Coll of Technology (OH)
State U of New York Coll of Technology at Alfred (NY)
Sullivan County Comm Coll (NY)
Sussex County Comm Coll (NJ)
Tomball Coll (TX)
Tompkins Cortland Comm Coll (NY)
Trident Tech Coll (SC)
Tulsa Comm Coll (OK)
Tunxis Comm Coll (CT)
U of Alaska Anchorage, Matanuska-Susitna Coll (AK)
U of Pittsburgh at Titusville (PA)
Vance-Granville Comm Coll (NC)
Westchester Comm Coll (NY)
Westmoreland County Comm Coll (PA)
Yuba Coll (CA)

Hydraulics and Fluid Power Technology
Alexandria Tech Coll (MN)
Normandale Comm Coll (MN)
The Ohio State U Ag Tech Inst (OH)

Hydrology and Water Resources Science
Cecil Comm Coll (MD)
Citrus Coll (CA)
Coll of the Canyons (CA)
Lawson State Comm Coll (AL)
St. Petersburg Coll (FL)
Spokane Comm Coll (WA)
Ventura Coll (CA)
Vermilion Comm Coll (MN)

Illustration
Delaware Coll of Art and Design (DE)
Keystone Coll (PA)

Industrial Arts
Allen County Comm Coll (KS)
Carl Albert State Coll (OK)
Casper Coll (WY)
Cleveland State Comm Coll (TN)
Cowley County Comm Coll and Area Vocational–Tech School (KS)
Delta Coll (MI)
Howard Coll (TX)
Long Beach City Coll (CA)
Modesto Jr Coll (CA)
Mt. San Antonio Coll (CA)
Northern Maine Comm Coll (ME)
Ouachita Tech Coll (AR)
Pellissippi State Tech Comm Coll (TN)
Pratt Comm Coll (KS)
Rockingham Comm Coll (NC)
Saddleback Coll (CA)
San Diego City Coll (CA)
Southwest Tennessee Comm Coll (TN)
Vermilion Comm Coll (MN)
Volunteer State Comm Coll (TN)

Industrial Design
Luzerne County Comm Coll (PA)
Mt. San Antonio Coll (CA)
Orange Coast Coll (CA)
Rock Valley Coll (IL)
Santa Rosa Jr Coll (CA)

Industrial Electronics Technology
Big Bend Comm Coll (WA)
Brown Mackie Coll–Louisville (KY)
Brown Mackie Coll–North Canton (OH)
Central Carolina Tech Coll (SC)
Coll of DuPage (IL)
H. Councill Trenholm State Tech Coll (AL)
John Wood Comm Coll (IL)
Kennebec Valley Comm Coll (ME)
Louisiana Tech Coll (LA)
Midlands Tech Coll (SC)
Modesto Jr Coll (CA)
Northampton County Area Comm Coll (PA)
North Dakota State Coll of Science (ND)
North Iowa Area Comm Coll (IA)
Northland Comm and Tech Coll–Thief River Falls (MN)
Northwest-Shoals Comm Coll (AL)
Oakland Comm Coll (MI)
Shelton State Comm Coll (AL)
State U of New York Coll of Technology at Alfred (NY)
York Tech Coll (SC)

Industrial Engineering
Manchester Comm Coll (CT)
Mount Wachusett Comm Coll (MA)
Penn Foster Career School (PA)
Santa Barbara City Coll (CA)

Industrial Mechanics and Maintenance Technology
Arkansas Northeastern Coll (AR)
Arkansas State U–Beebe (AR)
Coahoma Comm Coll (MS)
Coll of Lake County (IL)
George C. Wallace Comm Coll (AL)
Harrisburg Area Comm Coll (PA)
H. Councill Trenholm State Tech Coll (AL)
Heartland Comm Coll (IL)
Illinois Eastern Comm Colls, Olney Central College (IL)
Ivy Tech Comm Coll–East Central (IN)
John Wood Comm Coll (IL)
Kaskaskia Coll (IL)
Kennebec Valley Comm Coll (ME)
Lower Columbia Coll (WA)
Macomb Comm Coll (MI)
Midlands Tech Coll (SC)
Northwest-Shoals Comm Coll (AL)
Riverland Comm Coll (MN)
San Joaquin Valley Coll (CA)
Southern Arkansas U Tech (AR)
Southwestern Michigan Coll (MI)
Waubonsee Comm Coll (IL)
York Tech Coll (SC)

Industrial Production Technologies Related
Arkansas Northeastern Coll (AR)
Broome Comm Coll (NY)
Cape Fear Comm Coll (NC)
Erie Comm Coll (NY)
Essex County Coll (NJ)
Ivy Tech Comm Coll–Central Indiana (IN)
Ivy Tech Comm Coll–East Central (IN)
Ivy Tech Comm Coll–Lafayette (IN)
Ivy Tech Comm Coll–North Central (IN)
Ivy Tech Comm Coll–Northeast (IN)
Ivy Tech Comm Coll–Southwest (IN)

Ivy Tech Comm Coll–Wabash Valley (IN)
Ivy Tech Comm Coll–Whitewater (IN)
Louisiana Tech Coll (LA)
Mohawk Valley Comm Coll (NY)
Richmond Comm Coll (NC)

Industrial Radiologic Technology
Austin Comm Coll (TX)
Bergen Comm Coll (NJ)
Broward Comm Coll (FL)
Carteret Comm Coll (NC)
Chattahoochee Valley Comm Coll (AL)
Chattanooga State Tech Comm Coll (TN)
Cleveland Comm Coll (NC)
Copiah-Lincoln Comm Coll (MS)
Cowley County Comm Coll and Area Vocational–Tech School (KS)
Cuyahoga Comm Coll (OH)
Delaware Tech & Comm Coll, Stanton/Wilmington Campus (DE)
Delta Coll (MI)
Forsyth Tech Comm Coll (NC)
Gateway Comm Coll (CT)
Horry-Georgetown Tech Coll (SC)
Houston Comm Coll System (TX)
Illinois Central Coll (IL)
Jefferson Comm Coll (OH)
Kapiolani Comm Coll (HI)
Laramie County Comm Coll (WY)
Laredo Comm Coll (TX)
Long Beach City Coll (CA)
Middlesex Comm Coll (CT)
Mississippi Gulf Coast Comm Coll (MS)
Mt. San Antonio Coll (CA)
Naugatuck Valley Comm Coll (CT)
Northern Essex Comm Coll (MA)
Orange Coast Coll (CA)
Orange County Comm Coll (NY)
Palm Beach Comm Coll (FL)
Pasadena City Coll (CA)
Roane State Comm Coll (TN)
St. Petersburg Coll (FL)
Salt Lake Comm Coll (UT)
San Diego Mesa Coll (CA)
San Joaquin Delta Coll (CA)
Sauk Valley Comm Coll (IL)
Sinclair Comm Coll (OH)
Southern West Virginia Comm and Tech Coll (WV)
South Plains Coll (TX)
South Texas Coll (TX)
Southwestern Illinois Coll (IL)
Southwest Virginia Comm Coll (VA)
Tarrant County Coll District (TX)
Tulsa Comm Coll (OK)
Vance-Granville Comm Coll (NC)
West Central Tech Coll (GA)
Westchester Comm Coll (NY)
Wharton County Jr Coll (TX)
Yakima Valley Comm Coll (WA)
Yuba Coll (CA)

Industrial Technology
Aiken Tech Coll (SC)
Albany Tech Coll (GA)
Alexandria Tech Coll (MN)
Allen County Comm Coll (KS)
Arkansas Northeastern Coll (AR)
Asnuntuck Comm Coll (CT)
Austin Comm Coll (TX)
Bergen Comm Coll (NJ)
Bladen Comm Coll (NC)
Central Arizona Coll (AZ)
Central Comm Coll–Columbus Campus (NE)

Central Comm Coll–Grand Island Campus (NE)
Central Comm Coll–Hastings Campus (NE)
Central Georgia Tech Coll (GA)
Central New Mexico Comm Coll (NM)
Central Oregon Comm Coll (OR)
Central Piedmont Comm Coll (NC)
Century Coll (MN)
Chemeketa Comm Coll (OR)
Clark State Comm Coll (OH)
Cleveland State Comm Coll (TN)
Coll of DuPage (IL)
Columbus Tech Coll (GA)
Comm Coll of Allegheny County (PA)
Comm Coll of the Air Force (AL)
Corning Comm Coll (NY)
Cossatot Comm Coll of the U of Arkansas (AR)
Crowder Coll (MO)
DeKalb Tech Coll (GA)
Delaware Tech & Comm Coll, Stanton/Wilmington Campus (DE)
Delaware Tech & Comm Coll, Terry Campus (DE)
East Central Coll (MO)
Erie Comm Coll, South Campus (NY)
Evergreen Valley Coll (CA)
Forsyth Tech Comm Coll (NC)
Fountainhead Coll of Technology (TN)
Fox Valley Tech Coll (WI)
GateWay Comm Coll (AZ)
Gateway Comm Coll (CT)
Glendale Comm Coll (AZ)
Grand Rapids Comm Coll (MI)
Great Basin Coll (NV)
Greenfield Comm Coll (MA)
Griffin Tech Coll (GA)
Hagerstown Comm Coll (MD)
Heartland Comm Coll (IL)
Highline Comm Coll (WA)
Houston Comm Coll System (TX)
Hudson Valley Comm Coll (NY)
Illinois Central Coll (IL)
Illinois Eastern Comm Colls, Wabash Valley College (IL)
Illinois Eastern Comm Colls, Wabash Valley College (IL)
Illinois Valley Comm Coll (IL)
Ivy Tech Comm Coll–Bloomington (IN)
Ivy Tech Comm Coll–Central Indiana (IN)
Ivy Tech Comm Coll–Columbus (IN)
Ivy Tech Comm Coll–East Central (IN)
Ivy Tech Comm Coll–Kokomo (IN)
Ivy Tech Comm Coll–Lafayette (IN)
Ivy Tech Comm Coll–North Central (IN)
Ivy Tech Comm Coll–Northeast (IN)
Ivy Tech Comm Coll–Northwest (IN)
Ivy Tech Comm Coll–Southeast (IN)
Ivy Tech Comm Coll–Southern Indiana (IN)
Ivy Tech Comm Coll–Southwest (IN)
Ivy Tech Comm Coll–Wabash Valley (IN)
Ivy Tech Comm Coll–Whitewater (IN)
Jackson State Comm Coll (TN)
Jefferson Comm Coll (OH)
Joliet Jr Coll (IL)
Kellogg Comm Coll (MI)
Kent State U, Geauga Campus (OH)

Kent State U, Trumbull Campus (OH)
Kent State U, Tuscarawas Campus (OH)
Lackawanna Coll (PA)
Lake Land Coll (IL)
Lake Michigan Coll (MI)
Lanier Tech Coll (GA)
Lansing Comm Coll (MI)
Linn-Benton Comm Coll (OR)
Long Beach City Coll (CA)
Lower Columbia Coll (WA)
Macomb Comm Coll (MI)
Manchester Comm Coll (CT)
Miami Dade Coll (FL)
Minnesota State Comm and Tech Coll–Fergus Falls (MN)
MiraCosta Coll (CA)
Missouri State U–West Plains (MO)
Moberly Area Comm Coll (MO)
Mount Wachusett Comm Coll (MA)
Naugatuck Valley Comm Coll (CT)
New Hampshire Comm Tech Coll, Nashua/Claremont (NH)
North Arkansas Coll (AR)
North Dakota State Coll of Science (ND)
Northeast State Tech Comm Coll (TN)
North Georgia Tech Coll (GA)
North Seattle Comm Coll (WA)
Oakland Comm Coll (MI)
The Ohio State U Ag Tech Inst (OH)
Ouachita Tech Coll (AR)
Panola Coll (TX)
Parkland Coll (IL)
Pellissippi State Tech Comm Coll (TN)
The Pennsylvania State U York Campus of the Commonwealth Coll (PA)
Prairie State Coll (IL)
Pulaski Tech Coll (AR)
Raritan Valley Comm Coll (NJ)
Richland Comm Coll (IL)
Rock Valley Coll (IL)
Rogue Comm Coll (OR)
Saint Paul Coll–A Comm & Tech College (MN)
St. Petersburg Coll (FL)
San Diego City Coll (CA)
Santa Barbara City Coll (CA)
Savannah Tech Coll (GA)
Seminole Comm Coll (FL)
Sinclair Comm Coll (OH)
South Arkansas Comm Coll (AR)
Southeastern Comm Coll (NC)
Southeast Tech Inst (SD)
Southern Arkansas U Tech (AR)
South Georgia Tech Coll (GA)
South Texas Coll (TX)
Southwestern Oregon Comm Coll (OR)
Southwest Tennessee Comm Coll (TN)
Spokane Comm Coll (WA)
Spoon River Coll (IL)
Stark State Coll of Technology (OH)
Texas State Tech Coll Waco (TX)
Three Rivers Comm Coll (MO)
Trident Tech Coll (SC)
Trinidad State Jr Coll (CO)
Triton Coll (IL)
Tulsa Comm Coll (OK)
Union County Coll (NJ)
Valencia Comm Coll (FL)
Vance-Granville Comm Coll (NC)
Vermilion Comm Coll (MN)
Waubonsee Comm Coll (IL)
West Georgia Tech Coll (GA)

West Virginia Northern Comm Coll (WV)
William Rainey Harper Coll (IL)
Wilson Tech Comm Coll (NC)
Yakima Valley Comm Coll (WA)
Yuba Coll (CA)

Information Resources Management
Mott Comm Coll (MI)

Information Science/Studies
Alamance Comm Coll (NC)
Allan Hancock Coll (CA)
Allen County Comm Coll (KS)
Altamaha Tech Coll (GA)
Appalachian Tech Coll (GA)
Arapahoe Comm Coll (CO)
Arizona Western Coll (AZ)
Arkansas State U–Mountain Home (AR)
Athens Tech Coll (GA)
Atlanta Metropolitan Coll (GA)
Augusta Tech Coll (GA)
Austin Comm Coll (TX)
Bainbridge Coll (GA)
Barton County Comm Coll (KS)
Beaufort County Comm Coll (NC)
Big Bend Comm Coll (WA)
Blue Ridge Comm Coll (VA)
Blue River Comm Coll (MO)
Bristol Comm Coll (MA)
Broome Comm Coll (NY)
Broward Comm Coll (FL)
Brown Coll (MN)
Bucks County Comm Coll (PA)
Cecil Comm Coll (MD)
Central Georgia Tech Coll (GA)
Central New Mexico Comm Coll (NM)
Chattahoochee Tech Coll (GA)
Chattahoochee Valley Comm Coll (AL)
Chattanooga State Tech Comm Coll (TN)
Cincinnati State Tech and Comm Coll (OH)
Clark State Comm Coll (OH)
Cleveland Comm Coll (NC)
Cochise Coll, Douglas (AZ)
Coll of Southern Maryland (MD)
Coll of The Albemarle (NC)
Coll of the Canyons (CA)
The Coll of Westchester (NY)
Columbus Tech Coll (GA)
Coosa Valley Tech Coll (GA)
Dabney S. Lancaster Comm Coll (VA)
DeKalb Tech Coll (GA)
Delaware Tech & Comm Coll, Stanton/Wilmington Campus (DE)
Diné Coll (AZ)
East Central Tech Coll (GA)
Eastern Arizona Coll (AZ)
ECPI Coll of Technology, Newport News (VA)
ECPI Coll of Technology, Virginia Beach (VA)
ECPI Tech Coll (VA)
ECPI Tech Coll, Richmond (VA)
El Centro Coll (TX)
Erie Business Center, Main (PA)
Erie Comm Coll (NY)
Erie Comm Coll, North Campus (NY)
Erie Comm Coll, South Campus (NY)
Essex County Coll (NJ)
Evergreen Valley Coll (CA)
Fayetteville Tech Comm Coll (NC)
Fiorello H. LaGuardia Comm Coll of the City U of New York (NY)
Flint River Tech Coll (GA)
Florida Comm Coll at Jacksonville (FL)

Fountainhead Coll of Technology (TN)
Gaston Coll (NC)
Gavilan Coll (CA)
Genesee Comm Coll (NY)
Georgia Highlands Coll (GA)
Greenfield Comm Coll (MA)
Gwinnett Tech Coll (GA)
Hagerstown Business Coll (MD)
H. Councill Trenholm State Tech Coll (AL)
Heald Coll–Fresno (CA)
Heald Coll–Honolulu (HI)
Heald Coll–Portland (OR)
Heartland Comm Coll (IL)
Herzing Coll (GA)
Holyoke Comm Coll (MA)
Howard Comm Coll (MD)
Jefferson Comm Coll (NY)
J. F. Drake State Tech Coll (AL)
Kingwood Coll (TX)
Lamar State Coll–Orange (TX)
Lanier Tech Coll (GA)
Lansing Comm Coll (MI)
Laredo Comm Coll (TX)
Lawson State Comm Coll (AL)
Lehigh Valley Coll (PA)
Lincoln Coll–Normal (IL)
Lord Fairfax Comm Coll (VA)
Lower Columbia Coll (WA)
Manatee Comm Coll (FL)
Manchester Comm Coll (CT)
Massachusetts Bay Comm Coll (MA)
Metropolitan Comm Coll–Business & Technology College (MO)
Miami Dade Coll (FL)
Middle Georgia Coll (GA)
Middle Georgia Tech Coll (GA)
Middlesex County Coll (NJ)
MiraCosta Coll (CA)
Montgomery County Comm Coll (PA)
Moultrie Tech Coll (GA)
Mountain View Coll (TX)
Mount Wachusett Comm Coll (MA)
Naugatuck Valley Comm Coll (CT)
New Hampshire Comm Tech Coll, Manchester/Stratham (NH)
New Hampshire Comm Tech Coll, Nashua/Claremont (NH)
Niagara County Comm Coll (NY)
North Shore Comm Coll (MA)
Northwestern Connecticut Comm Coll (CT)
Northwestern Tech Coll (GA)
Northwest-Shoals Comm Coll (AL)
Norwalk Comm Coll (CT)
Ocean County Coll (NJ)
Ogeechee Tech Coll (GA)
Okefenokee Tech Coll (GA)
Orange Coast Coll (CA)
Orange County Comm Coll (NY)
Palo Alto Coll (TX)
Panola Coll (TX)
Parkland Coll (IL)
Pasadena City Coll (CA)
The Pennsylvania State U DuBois Campus of the Commonwealth Coll (PA)
The Pennsylvania State U Hazleton Campus of the Commonwealth Coll (PA)
The Pennsylvania State U New Kensington Campus of the Commonwealth Coll (PA)
Phoenix Coll (AZ)
Pioneer Pacific Coll (OR)
Polk Comm Coll (FL)
Pulaski Tech Coll (AR)
Quinsigamond Comm Coll (MA)
Raritan Valley Comm Coll (NJ)

Remington Coll–Mobile Campus (AL)
Remington Coll–Tampa Campus (FL)
Richland Comm Coll (IL)
Rockingham Comm Coll (NC)
Saddleback Coll (CA)
St. Louis Comm Coll at Florissant Valley (MO)
Salt Lake Comm Coll (UT)
Sandersville Tech Coll (GA)
San Juan Coll (NM)
Santa Barbara City Coll (CA)
Scottsdale Comm Coll (AZ)
Seminole Comm Coll (FL)
Sheridan Coll–Sheridan and Gillette (WY)
Sinclair Comm Coll (OH)
Snow Coll (UT)
Southeastern Tech Coll (GA)
Southeast Tech Inst (SD)
Southern West Virginia Comm and Tech Coll (WV)
South Georgia Tech Coll (GA)
Southside Virginia Comm Coll (VA)
South Texas Coll (TX)
South U, West Palm Beach (FL)
Southwestern Illinois Coll (IL)
Southwest Florida Coll, Fort Myers (FL)
Southwest Georgia Tech Coll (GA)
Southwest Virginia Comm Coll (VA)
Spokane Falls Comm Coll (WA)
Spoon River Coll (IL)
Sullivan County Comm Coll (NY)
Swainsboro Tech Coll (GA)
Texas State Tech Coll Waco (TX)
Thomas Nelson Comm Coll (VA)
Tompkins Cortland Comm Coll (NY)
Trinidad State Jr Coll (CO)
Triton Coll (IL)
Tulsa Comm Coll (OK)
Tunxis Comm Coll (CT)
Union County Coll (NJ)
Weatherford Coll (TX)
West Central Tech Coll (GA)
Westchester Comm Coll (NY)
West Georgia Tech Coll (GA)
Westmoreland County Comm Coll (PA)
William Rainey Harper Coll (IL)
Wilson Tech Comm Coll (NC)
Yavapai Coll (AZ)

Information Technology
Arkansas State U–Beebe (AR)
Atlanta Metropolitan Coll (GA)
Atlanta Tech Coll (GA)
Austin Comm Coll (TX)
Berks Tech Inst (PA)
Bladen Comm Coll (NC)
Blue Ridge Comm Coll (VA)
Brazosport Coll (TX)
Bristol Comm Coll (MA)
Brown Mackie Coll–Kansas City (KS)
Bryant and Stratton Coll, Albany (NY)
Bryant and Stratton Coll, Rochester (NY)
Bryant and Stratton Coll, Rochester (NY)
Bryant and Stratton Coll, Syracuse (NY)
Bryant and Stratton Coll, Parma (OH)
Bryant and Stratton Coll (WI)
Bryant and Stratton Coll, Amherst Campus (NY)
Bryant and Stratton Coll, Buffalo Campus (NY)
Bryant and Stratton Coll, Lackawanna Campus (NY)
Bryant and Stratton Coll, Richmond (VA)

Bucks County Comm Coll (PA)
Caldwell Comm Coll and Tech Inst (NC)
Capital Comm Coll (CT)
Carteret Comm Coll (NC)
Cecil Comm Coll (MD)
Central Comm Coll–Columbus Campus (NE)
Central Comm Coll–Grand Island Campus (NE)
Central Comm Coll–Hastings Campus (NE)
Central Florida Comm Coll (FL)
Clark State Comm Coll (OH)
Cleveland Comm Coll (NC)
Coastal Bend Coll (TX)
Coll of The Albemarle (NC)
Coll of the Siskiyous (CA)
The Coll of Westchester (NY)
Comm and Tech Coll of Shepherd (WV)
Corning Comm Coll (NY)
Davis Coll (OH)
Delta Coll (MI)
El Centro Coll (TX)
Fayetteville Tech Comm Coll (NC)
Florida Comm Coll at Jacksonville (FL)
Frederick Comm Coll (MD)
Galveston Coll (TX)
GateWay Comm Coll (AZ)
Germanna Comm Coll (VA)
Harrisburg Area Comm Coll (PA)
Hawkeye Comm Coll (IA)
Heartland Comm Coll (IL)
Howard Comm Coll (MD)
Hudson Valley Comm Coll (NY)
Indiana Business Coll, Evansville (IN)
Indiana Business Coll, Indianapolis (IN)
Indiana Business Coll, Lafayette (IN)
Indiana Business Coll, Muncie (IN)
ITI Tech Coll (LA)
Kent State U, Geauga Campus (OH)
Keystone Coll (PA)
Kilian Comm Coll (SD)
Lake Land Coll (IL)
Lake Region State Coll (ND)
Laramie County Comm Coll (WY)
Laredo Comm Coll (TX)
Laurel Business Inst (PA)
Louisiana State U at Alexandria (LA)
Lower Columbia Coll (WA)
Mesabi Range Comm and Tech Coll (MN)
Metropolitan Comm Coll–Business & Technology College (MO)
Minnesota School of Business–Brooklyn Center (MN)
Minnesota School of Business–Plymouth (MN)
Minnesota School of Business–Richfield (MN)
Minnesota School of Business–St. Cloud (MN)
Minnesota School of Business–Shakopee (MN)
Mississippi Gulf Coast Comm Coll (MS)
Missouri State U–West Plains (MO)
Montgomery Coll (TX)
Naugatuck Valley Comm Coll (CT)
Northland Comm and Tech Coll–Thief River Falls (MN)
Okaloosa-Walton Coll (FL)
Orange County Comm Coll (NY)
Palo Alto Coll (TX)
Pasco-Hernando Comm Coll (FL)
St. Cloud Tech Coll (MN)
St. Petersburg Coll (FL)
Salt Lake Comm Coll (UT)
Santa Barbara City Coll (CA)
Savannah Tech Coll (GA)

Seminole Comm Coll (FL)
Sinclair Comm Coll (OH)
Southeast Tech Inst (SD)
Southside Virginia Comm Coll (VA)
South U, West Palm Beach (FL)
Southwest Mississippi Comm Coll (MS)
Spartanburg Methodist Coll (SC)
Stark State Coll of Technology (OH)
Three Rivers Comm Coll (MO)
Tidewater Comm Coll (VA)
Tri-County Comm Coll (NC)
Trinidad State Jr Coll (CO)
Tulsa Comm Coll (OK)
Valencia Comm Coll (FL)
West Virginia Northern Comm Coll (WV)

Institutional Food Workers
Cape Fear Comm Coll (NC)
Delgado Comm Coll (LA)
Harrisburg Area Comm Coll (PA)
MiraCosta Coll (CA)
North Arkansas Coll (AR)
Santa Barbara City Coll (CA)
Texas State Tech Coll Waco (TX)
West Virginia Northern Comm Coll (WV)
Wilkes Comm Coll (NC)

Instrumentation Technology
Bishop State Comm Coll (AL)
Brazosport Coll (TX)
Butler County Comm Coll (PA)
Cape Fear Comm Coll (NC)
Chattanooga State Tech Comm Coll (TN)
DeKalb Tech Coll (GA)
Delaware Tech & Comm Coll, Stanton/Wilmington Campus (DE)
Florida Comm Coll at Jacksonville (FL)
H. Councill Trenholm State Tech Coll (AL)
ITI Tech Coll (LA)
Louisiana Tech Coll (LA)
Lower Columbia Coll (WA)
Mesabi Range Comm and Tech Coll (MN)
Moraine Valley Comm Coll (IL)
Nassau Comm Coll (NY)
Northeast State Tech Comm Coll (TN)
Northern Maine Comm Coll (ME)
St. Cloud Tech Coll (MN)
Salt Lake Comm Coll (UT)
San Juan Coll (NM)
Southwestern Illinois Coll (IL)
Texas State Tech Coll Waco (TX)
Yakima Valley Comm Coll (WA)

Insurance
Austin Comm Coll (TX)
Broward Comm Coll (FL)
Central Piedmont Comm Coll (NC)
Comm Coll of Allegheny County (PA)
Florida Comm Coll at Jacksonville (FL)
Fox Valley Tech Coll (WI)
Houston Comm Coll System (TX)
Laurel Business Inst (PA)
Nassau Comm Coll (NY)
Richland Comm Coll (IL)
San Diego City Coll (CA)
Trinity Valley Comm Coll (TX)
Tulsa Comm Coll (OK)
William Rainey Harper Coll (IL)

Interdisciplinary Studies
Aiken Tech Coll (SC)
Evergreen Valley Coll (CA)
Great Basin Coll (NV)
Hawkeye Comm Coll (IA)

Hudson Valley Comm Coll (NY)
Jefferson Comm Coll (NY)
North Country Comm Coll (NY)
North Shore Comm Coll (MA)
Pasadena City Coll (CA)
South Texas Coll (TX)
Triton Coll (IL)
The U of Akron–Wayne Coll (OH)
U of South Carolina Sumter (SC)
Vermilion Comm Coll (MN)

Interior Architecture
Delgado Comm Coll (LA)
St. Philip's Coll (TX)

Interior Design
Alexandria Tech Coll (MN)
Allan Hancock Coll (CA)
The Art Inst of Ohio–Cincinnati (OH)
The Art Inst of Philadelphia (PA)
Berkeley Coll (NJ)
Bradley Academy for the Visual Arts (PA)
Brooks Coll, Long Beach (CA)
Broward Comm Coll (FL)
Cape Fear Comm Coll (NC)
Carteret Comm Coll (NC)
Central Piedmont Comm Coll (NC)
Century Coll (MN)
Coll of DuPage (IL)
Coll of the Canyons (CA)
Collin County Comm Coll District (TX)
Davis Coll (OH)
Delaware Coll of Art and Design (DE)
Delta Coll (MI)
Dixie State Coll of Utah (UT)
East Central Coll (MO)
El Centro Coll (TX)
FIDM/The Fashion Inst of Design & Merchandising, Los Angeles Campus (CA)
FIDM/The Fashion Inst of Design & Merchandising, San Diego Campus (CA)
FIDM/The Fashion Inst of Design & Merchandising, San Francisco Campus (CA)
Florida Comm Coll at Jacksonville (FL)
Fox Valley Tech Coll (WI)
Gwinnett Tech Coll (GA)
Hawkeye Comm Coll (IA)
Highline Comm Coll (WA)
Houston Comm Coll System (TX)
Illinois Central Coll (IL)
Ivy Tech Comm Coll–North Central (IN)
Ivy Tech Comm Coll–Southwest (IN)
Joliet Jr Coll (IL)
Lanier Tech Coll (GA)
Long Beach City Coll (CA)
Marshall Comm and Tech Coll (WV)
Metropolitan Comm Coll (NE)
Miami Dade Coll (FL)
Modesto Jr Coll (CA)
Mt. San Antonio Coll (CA)
Nassau Comm Coll (NY)
Northampton County Area Comm Coll (PA)
Oakland Comm Coll (MI)
Ogeechee Tech Coll (GA)
Okaloosa-Walton Coll (FL)
Orange Coast Coll (CA)
Palm Beach Comm Coll (FL)
Palo Verde Coll (CA)
Pasadena City Coll (CA)
Pellissippi State Tech Comm Coll (TN)
Phoenix Coll (AZ)
Prairie State Coll (IL)
Saddleback Coll (CA)
St. Philip's Coll (TX)
San Diego City Coll (CA)
San Diego Mesa Coll (CA)
San Joaquin Delta Coll (CA)

Santa Barbara City Coll (CA)
Santa Rosa Jr Coll (CA)
Scottsdale Comm Coll (AZ)
Seminole Comm Coll (FL)
Sinclair Comm Coll (OH)
Spokane Falls Comm Coll (WA)
Tidewater Comm Coll (VA)
Triton Coll (IL)
Tulsa Comm Coll (OK)
Villa Maria Coll of Buffalo (NY)
Waukesha County Tech Coll (WI)
Western Tech Coll (WI)
Wichita Area Tech Coll (KS)
William Rainey Harper Coll (IL)

Intermedia/Multimedia
The Art Inst of Philadelphia (PA)
Coll of the Siskiyous (CA)
DigiPen Inst of Technology (WA)
Front Range Comm Coll (CO)
Middlesex Comm Coll (CT)
Minnesota School of Business–Brooklyn Center (MN)
Minnesota School of Business–Plymouth (MN)
Minnesota School of Business–Richfield (MN)
Minnesota School of Business–St. Cloud (MN)
Minnesota School of Business–Shakopee (MN)
Platt Coll San Diego (CA)
Raritan Valley Comm Coll (NJ)
San Diego Mesa Coll (CA)

International Business/Trade/Commerce
Berkeley Coll (NJ)
Berkeley Coll–New York City Campus (NY)
Berkeley Coll–Westchester Campus (NY)
Brevard Comm Coll (FL)
Bunker Hill Comm Coll (MA)
Cincinnati State Tech and Comm Coll (OH)
Edmonds Comm Coll (WA)
Foothill Coll (CA)
Frederick Comm Coll (MD)
GateWay Comm Coll (AZ)
Highline Comm Coll (WA)
Kansas City Kansas Comm Coll (KS)
Lansing Comm Coll (MI)
Laredo Comm Coll (TX)
Long Beach City Coll (CA)
Luzerne County Comm Coll (PA)
Manor Coll (PA)
Mott Comm Coll (MI)
Northland Comm and Tech Coll–Thief River Falls (MN)
Oakland Comm Coll (MI)
Pima Comm Coll (AZ)
Raritan Valley Comm Coll (NJ)
Saint Paul Coll–A Comm & Tech College (MN)
Spokane Falls Comm Coll (WA)
Stark State Coll of Technology (OH)
Tompkins Cortland Comm Coll (NY)
Triton Coll (IL)
Tulsa Comm Coll (OK)
Westchester Comm Coll (NY)
William Rainey Harper Coll (IL)
Young Harris Coll (GA)

International Finance
Broome Comm Coll (NY)

International/Global Studies
Berkshire Comm Coll (MA)
Macomb Comm Coll (MI)
Northwest Vista Coll (TX)
Salt Lake Comm Coll (UT)

International Relations and Affairs
Allan Hancock Coll (CA)
Bronx Comm Coll of the City U of New York (NY)
Harrisburg Area Comm Coll (PA)
Kellogg Comm Coll (MI)
Massachusetts Bay Comm Coll (MA)
Miami Dade Coll (FL)
Naugatuck Valley Comm Coll (CT)
Northern Essex Comm Coll (MA)
Salt Lake Comm Coll (UT)
Santa Barbara City Coll (CA)
Tulsa Comm Coll (OK)

Ironworking
Ivy Tech Comm Coll–Lafayette (IN)
Ivy Tech Comm Coll–North Central (IN)
Ivy Tech Comm Coll–Northeast (IN)
Ivy Tech Comm Coll–Northwest (IN)
Ivy Tech Comm Coll–Southwest (IN)
Ivy Tech Comm Coll–Wabash Valley (IN)

Italian
Casper Coll (WY)
Miami Dade Coll (FL)
San Joaquin Delta Coll (CA)
Tulsa Comm Coll (OK)

Japanese
Austin Comm Coll (TX)
Citrus Coll (CA)
Hawaii Tokai International Coll (HI)
MiraCosta Coll (CA)
San Joaquin Delta Coll (CA)
Snow Coll (UT)
Tulsa Comm Coll (OK)

Japanese Studies
Hawaii Tokai International Coll (HI)

Jazz
Villa Maria Coll of Buffalo (NY)

Jazz/Jazz Studies
Lincoln Coll (IL)
Manatee Comm Coll (FL)

Jewish/Judaic Studies
Manatee Comm Coll (FL)

Journalism
Abraham Baldwin Ag Coll (GA)
Allen County Comm Coll (KS)
Austin Comm Coll (TX)
Bainbridge Coll (GA)
Barton County Comm Coll (KS)
Brazosport Coll (TX)
Bucks County Comm Coll (PA)
Butler Comm Coll (KS)
Carl Albert State Coll (OK)
Casper Coll (WY)
Citrus Coll (CA)
City Colls of Chicago, Wilbur Wright College (IL)
Coastal Bend Coll (TX)
Cochise Coll, Douglas (AZ)
Colby Comm Coll (KS)
Coll of Southern Maryland (MD)
Coll of the Canyons (CA)
Comm Coll of Allegheny County (PA)
Copiah-Lincoln Comm Coll (MS)
Cowley County Comm Coll and Area Vocational–Tech School (KS)
Delaware Tech & Comm Coll, Jack F. Owens Campus (DE)
Dixie State Coll of Utah (UT)
East Central Coll (MO)
Gainesville Coll (GA)
Gavilan Coll (CA)
Georgia Highlands Coll (GA)

Harrisburg Area Comm Coll (PA)
Highline Comm Coll (WA)
Illinois Valley Comm Coll (IL)
Kellogg Comm Coll (MI)
Keystone Coll (PA)
Kingsborough Comm Coll of the City U of New York (NY)
Lansing Comm Coll (MI)
Laramie County Comm Coll (WY)
Lincoln Coll (IL)
Linn-Benton Comm Coll (OR)
Long Beach City Coll (CA)
Luzerne County Comm Coll (PA)
Manatee Comm Coll (FL)
Manchester Comm Coll (CT)
Miami Dade Coll (FL)
Middlesex County Coll (NJ)
Midland Coll (TX)
MiraCosta Coll (CA)
Mt. San Antonio Coll (CA)
Northampton County Area Comm Coll (PA)
Northeast Comm Coll (NE)
Northern Essex Comm Coll (MA)
North Idaho Coll (ID)
Ocean County Coll (NJ)
Orange Coast Coll (CA)
Palm Beach Comm Coll (FL)
Palo Alto Coll (TX)
Pasadena City Coll (CA)
Saddleback Coll (CA)
St. Louis Comm Coll at Florissant Valley (MO)
Salem Comm Coll (NJ)
San Diego City Coll (CA)
San Joaquin Delta Coll (CA)
Santa Rosa Jr Coll (CA)
Skyline Coll (CA)
South Plains Coll (TX)
Sussex County Comm Coll (NJ)
Trinity Valley Comm Coll (TX)
Tulsa Comm Coll (OK)
Ventura Coll (CA)
William Rainey Harper Coll (IL)
Young Harris Coll (GA)

Juvenile Corrections
Linn-Benton Comm Coll (OR)

Kindergarten/Preschool Education
Abraham Baldwin Ag Coll (GA)
Alamance Comm Coll (NC)
Allan Hancock Coll (CA)
Bainbridge Coll (GA)
Beaufort County Comm Coll (NC)
Bergen Comm Coll (NJ)
Borough of Manhattan Comm Coll of the City U of New York (NY)
Broward Comm Coll (FL)
Bucks County Comm Coll (PA)
Butler Comm Coll (KS)
Butler County Comm Coll (PA)
Capital Comm Coll (CT)
Carl Albert State Coll (OK)
Carroll Comm Coll (MD)
Casper Coll (WY)
Cecil Comm Coll (MD)
Central Arizona Coll (AZ)
Centralia Coll (WA)
Central Piedmont Comm Coll (NC)
Chatfield Coll (OH)
Chattanooga State Tech Comm Coll (TN)
Chemeketa Comm Coll (OR)
Clark State Comm Coll (OH)
Cleveland State Comm Coll (TN)
Coahoma Comm Coll (MS)
Colby Comm Coll (KS)
Coll of Eastern Utah (UT)
Coll of the Canyons (CA)
Coll of the Siskiyous (CA)
Cuyahoga Comm Coll (OH)

Delaware Tech & Comm Coll, Stanton/Wilmington Campus (DE)
Delaware Tech & Comm Coll, Terry Campus (DE)
Delgado Comm Coll (LA)
Dixie State Coll of Utah (UT)
Essex County Coll (NJ)
Finger Lakes Comm Coll (NY)
Fiorello H. LaGuardia Comm Coll of the City U of New York (NY)
Fisher Coll (MA)
Forsyth Tech Comm Coll (NC)
Frederick Comm Coll (MD)
Gaston Coll (NC)
Gateway Comm Coll (CT)
Gavilan Coll (CA)
Genesee Comm Coll (NY)
Georgia Highlands Coll (GA)
Glendale Comm Coll (AZ)
Great Basin Coll (NV)
Greenfield Comm Coll (MA)
Guam Comm Coll (GU)
Harrisburg Area Comm Coll (PA)
Heartland Comm Coll (IL)
Hesston Coll (KS)
Highland Comm Coll (IL)
Highline Comm Coll (WA)
Holyoke Comm Coll (MA)
Howard Comm Coll (MD)
Independence Comm Coll (KS)
James Sprunt Comm Coll (NC)
Jefferson Comm Coll (NY)
Johnston Comm Coll (NC)
Kauai Comm Coll (HI)
Kellogg Comm Coll (MI)
Keystone Coll (PA)
Lansing Comm Coll (MI)
Lincoln Coll (IL)
Long Beach City Coll (CA)
Lower Columbia Coll (WA)
Manatee Comm Coll (FL)
Manchester Comm Coll (CT)
Manor Coll (PA)
Maria Coll (NY)
Metropolitan Comm Coll (NE)
Miami Dade Coll (FL)
Middlesex County Coll (NJ)
MiraCosta Coll (CA)
Mississippi Gulf Coast Comm Coll (MS)
Modesto Jr Coll (CA)
Mt. San Antonio Coll (CA)
Nassau Comm Coll (NY)
Naugatuck Valley Comm Coll (CT)
New Hampshire Comm Tech Coll, Manchester/Stratham (NH)
New Hampshire Comm Tech Coll, Nashua/Claremont (NH)
New Hampshire Tech Inst (NH)
Northeast State Tech Comm Coll (TN)
Northern Essex Comm Coll (MA)
Northern Maine Comm Coll (ME)
North Shore Comm Coll (MA)
Northwestern Connecticut Comm Coll (CT)
Northwest Indian Coll (WA)
Norwalk Comm Coll (CT)
Okaloosa-Walton Coll (FL)
Orange Coast Coll (CA)
Otero Jr Coll (CO)
Palm Beach Comm Coll (FL)
Palo Verde Coll (CA)
Pasadena City Coll (CA)
Penn Valley Comm Coll (MO)
Pratt Comm Coll (KS)
Quinsigamond Comm Coll (MA)
Raritan Valley Comm Coll (NJ)
Roane State Comm Coll (TN)
Saddleback Coll (CA)
St. Cloud Tech Coll (MN)

St. Petersburg Coll (FL)
San Joaquin Delta Coll (CA)
San Juan Coll (NM)
Santa Barbara City Coll (CA)
Scottsdale Comm Coll (AZ)
Seattle Central Comm Coll (WA)
Sinclair Comm Coll (OH)
Snow Coll (UT)
Southeastern Comm Coll (NC)
Southern State Comm Coll (OH)
Southwest Tennessee Comm Coll (TN)
Spoon River Coll (IL)
Springfield Tech Comm Coll (MA)
Sullivan County Comm Coll (NY)
Thomas Nelson Comm Coll (VA)
Tidewater Comm Coll (VA)
Tompkins Cortland Comm Coll (NY)
Trinidad State Jr Coll (CO)
Trinity Valley Comm Coll (TX)
Triton Coll (IL)
Tulsa Comm Coll (OK)
Tunxis Comm Coll (CT)
Vance-Granville Comm Coll (NC)
Vermilion Comm Coll (MN)
Villa Maria Coll of Buffalo (NY)
Waubonsee Comm Coll (IL)
William Rainey Harper Coll (IL)
Wilson Tech Comm Coll (NC)
Yakima Valley Comm Coll (WA)
Yuba Coll (CA)

Kinesiology and Exercise Science
Barton County Comm Coll (KS)
Bergen Comm Coll (NJ)
Butler County Comm Coll (PA)
Central Oregon Comm Coll (OR)
Clarendon Coll (TX)
Clark State Comm Coll (OH)
Delaware Tech & Comm Coll, Stanton/Wilmington Campus (DE)
Diné Coll (AZ)
Gainesville Coll (GA)
Globe Coll (MN)
Houston Comm Coll System (TX)
Mount Wachusett Comm Coll (MA)
Naugatuck Valley Comm Coll (CT)
New Hampshire Comm Tech Coll, Manchester/Stratham (NH)
North Country Comm Coll (NY)
Oakland Comm Coll (MI)
Orange Coast Coll (CA)
Orange County Comm Coll (NY)
St. Philip's Coll (TX)
Salem Comm Coll (NJ)
Salt Lake Comm Coll (UT)
Santa Barbara City Coll (CA)
Utah Career Coll (UT)
William Rainey Harper Coll (IL)

Labor and Industrial Relations
Kingsborough Comm Coll of the City U of New York (NY)
Lansing Comm Coll (MI)
Rockingham Comm Coll (NC)
San Diego City Coll (CA)
Sinclair Comm Coll (OH)
Tulsa Comm Coll (OK)

Landscape Architecture
Foothill Coll (CA)
Keystone Coll (PA)
Lansing Comm Coll (MI)
Modesto Jr Coll (CA)

Mt. San Antonio Coll (CA)
Oakland Comm Coll (MI)
Pasadena City Coll (CA)
Saddleback Coll (CA)
San Diego Mesa Coll (CA)
Santa Rosa Jr Coll (CA)
State U of New York Coll of Technology at Delhi (NY)
Triton Coll (IL)
Tulsa Comm Coll (OK)
William Rainey Harper Coll (IL)

Landscaping and Groundskeeping
Abraham Baldwin Ag Coll (GA)
Caldwell Comm Coll and Tech Inst (NC)
Cape Fear Comm Coll (NC)
Central Florida Comm Coll (FL)
Cincinnati State Tech and Comm Coll (OH)
Clark Coll (WA)
Clark State Comm Coll (OH)
Coll of DuPage (IL)
Coll of Lake County (IL)
Comm Coll of Allegheny County (PA)
Edmonds Comm Coll (WA)
Front Range Comm Coll (CO)
Glendale Comm Coll (AZ)
Horry-Georgetown Tech Coll (SC)
James H. Faulkner State Comm Coll (AL)
Johnston Comm Coll (NC)
Joliet Jr Coll (IL)
Lake City Comm Coll (FL)
Lincoln Land Comm Coll (IL)
Miami Dade Coll (FL)
MiraCosta Coll (CA)
North Shore Comm Coll (MA)
Oakland Comm Coll (MI)
The Ohio State U Ag Tech Inst (OH)
Parkland Coll (IL)
Santa Barbara City Coll (CA)
Spokane Comm Coll (WA)
Springfield Tech Comm Coll (MA)
State U of New York Coll of Technology at Alfred (NY)
State U of New York Coll of Technology at Delhi (NY)
Triton Coll (IL)
Tulsa Comm Coll (OK)
William Rainey Harper Coll (IL)
The Williamson Free School of Mecha Trades (PA)

Land Use Planning and Management
Colorado Mountain Coll, Timberline Campus (CO)
Southwest Virginia Comm Coll (VA)
Vermilion Comm Coll (MN)

Language Interpretation and Translation
Allen County Comm Coll (KS)
Cochise Coll, Douglas (AZ)
Fayetteville Tech Comm Coll (NC)
Front Range Comm Coll (CO)
Union County Coll (NJ)
Wilson Tech Comm Coll (NC)

Laser and Optical Technology
Brown Mackie Coll–Cincinnati (OH)
Central New Mexico Comm Coll (NM)
Cincinnati State Tech and Comm Coll (OH)
George C. Wallace Comm Coll (AL)
Linn State Tech Coll (MO)
Roane State Comm Coll (TN)
Southeast Tech Inst (SD)
Springfield Tech Comm Coll (MA)

Texas State Tech Coll Waco (TX)

Latin
Tulsa Comm Coll (OK)

Latin American Studies
Manatee Comm Coll (FL)
Miami Dade Coll (FL)
Pasadena City Coll (CA)
San Diego City Coll (CA)
Santa Rosa Jr Coll (CA)

Leatherworking/Upholstery
St. Philip's Coll (TX)
Spokane Falls Comm Coll (WA)

Legal Administrative Assistant
Asnuntuck Comm Coll (CT)
Bryant and Stratton Coll, Parma (OH)
International Business Coll, Indianapolis (IN)
Minnesota State Comm and Tech Coll–Fergus Falls (MN)
Moraine Park Tech Coll (WI)

Legal Administrative Assistant/Secretary
Alamance Comm Coll (NC)
Alexandria Tech Coll (MN)
Allan Hancock Coll (CA)
Arapahoe Comm Coll (CO)
Austin Comm Coll (TX)
Bay State Coll (MA)
Beal Coll (ME)
Bergen Comm Coll (NJ)
Briarwood Coll (CT)
Bristol Comm Coll (MA)
Broward Comm Coll (FL)
Brown Mackie Coll–Michigan City (IN)
Bryant and Stratton Coll, Richmond (VA)
Business Inst of Pennsylvania, Meadville (PA)
Butler County Comm Coll (PA)
Cambria-Rowe Business Coll, Johnstown (PA)
Carl Albert State Coll (OK)
Carteret Comm Coll (NC)
Central Arizona Coll (AZ)
Centralia Coll (WA)
Central Lakes Coll (MN)
Central Piedmont Comm Coll (NC)
Century Coll (MN)
Chattahoochee Valley Comm Coll (AL)
Chattanooga State Tech Comm Coll (TN)
Clatsop Comm Coll (OR)
Clovis Comm Coll (NM)
Coastal Bend Coll (TX)
Coll of DuPage (IL)
Comm Coll of Allegheny County (PA)
Consolidated School of Business, Lancaster (PA)
Consolidated School of Business, York (PA)
Crowder Coll (MO)
Crown Coll (WA)
Dabney S. Lancaster Comm Coll (VA)
Davis Coll (OH)
DeKalb Tech Coll (GA)
Delaware Tech & Comm Coll, Jack F. Owens Campus (DE)
Delta Coll (MI)
East Central Coll (MO)
Eastfield Coll (TX)
Edmonds Comm Coll (WA)
El Centro Coll (TX)
Elmira Business Inst (NY)
Erie Business Center, Main (PA)
Fiorello H. LaGuardia Comm Coll of the City U of New York (NY)
Florida National Coll (FL)
Fox Valley Tech Coll (WI)
Frederick Comm Coll (MD)
Gateway Comm Coll (CT)
Grand Rapids Comm Coll (MI)

Hagerstown Business Coll (MD)
Harrisburg Area Comm Coll (PA)
Heald Coll-Fresno (CA)
Heald Coll-Hayward (CA)
Heald Coll-Honolulu (HI)
Heald Coll-Rancho Cordova (CA)
Heald Coll-Salinas (CA)
Heald Coll-San Francisco (CA)
Heald Coll-San Jose (CA)
Hibbing Comm Coll (MN)
Hickey Coll (MO)
Highline Comm Coll (WA)
Holyoke Comm Coll (MA)
Howard Comm Coll (MD)
Indiana Business Coll, Indianapolis (IN)
Jefferson Comm Coll (OH)
John Wood Comm Coll (IL)
Kapiolani Comm Coll (HI)
Kellogg Comm Coll (MI)
Kennebec Valley Comm Coll (ME)
Lake Land Coll (IL)
Lake Michigan Coll (MI)
Lake Region State Coll (ND)
Lake Superior Coll (MN)
Lansing Comm Coll (MI)
Laurel Business Inst (PA)
Lawson State Comm Coll (AL)
Lincoln Coll–Normal (IL)
Lincoln Land Comm Coll (IL)
Linn-Benton Comm Coll (OR)
Long Beach City Coll (CA)
Longview Comm Coll (MO)
Lower Columbia Coll (WA)
Manchester Comm Coll (CT)
Manor Coll (PA)
Maple Woods Comm Coll (MO)
Metropolitan Comm Coll (NE)
Miami Dade Coll (FL)
Middlesex Comm Coll (CT)
Middlesex County Coll (NJ)
Minnesota School of Business–Brooklyn Center (MN)
Minnesota State Comm and Tech Coll–Fergus Falls (MN)
Mott Comm Coll (MI)
Mountain View Coll (TX)
Mt. San Antonio Coll (CA)
MTI Coll of Business and Technology (CA)
Nassau Comm Coll (NY)
Naugatuck Valley Comm Coll (CT)
Newport Business Inst, Lower Burrell (PA)
Newport Business Inst, Williamsport (PA)
Normandale Comm Coll (MN)
Northampton County Area Comm Coll (PA)
Northeast Comm Coll (NE)
Northern Maine Comm Coll (ME)
North Idaho Coll (ID)
Northland Comm and Tech Coll–Thief River Falls (MN)
North Shore Comm Coll (MA)
Ohio Business Coll, Sandusky (OH)
Orange Coast Coll (CA)
Otero Jr Coll (CO)
Ouachita Tech Coll (AR)
Palm Beach Comm Coll (FL)
Pasadena City Coll (CA)
Pellissippi State Tech Comm Coll (TN)
Penn Valley Comm Coll (MO)
Phoenix Coll (AZ)
Polk Comm Coll (FL)
Rasmussen Coll Eden Prarie (MN)
Rasmussen Coll Mankato (MN)
Richland Comm Coll (IL)
Riverland Comm Coll (MN)

Roane State Comm Coll (TN)
Rockingham Comm Coll (NC)
Saddleback Coll (CA)
St. Cloud Tech Coll (MN)
St. Petersburg Coll (FL)
St. Philip's Coll (TX)
San Diego City Coll (CA)
San Diego Mesa Coll (CA)
Sauk Valley Comm Coll (IL)
Sinclair Comm Coll (OH)
Skyline Coll (CA)
South Hills School of Business & Technology, State College (PA)
South Plains Coll (TX)
South Texas Coll (TX)
Southwestern Illinois Coll (IL)
Southwest Mississippi Comm Coll (MS)
Spokane Comm Coll (WA)
Spoon River Coll (IL)
Stark State Coll of Technology (OH)
Tomball Coll (TX)
Treasure Valley Comm Coll (OR)
Trinity Valley Comm Coll (TX)
Triton Coll (IL)
Tulsa Comm Coll (OK)
Tunxis Comm Coll (CT)
The U of Akron–Wayne Coll (OH)
U of Northwestern Ohio (OH)
Valencia Comm Coll (FL)
Vance-Granville Comm Coll (NC)
Westchester Comm Coll (NY)
Western Iowa Tech Comm Coll (IA)
Westmoreland County Comm Coll (PA)
William Rainey Harper Coll (IL)
Yakima Valley Comm Coll (WA)
Yavapai Coll (AZ)
York Tech Coll (SC)

Legal Assistant/Paralegal
Alexandria Tech Coll (MN)
Allegany Coll of Maryland (MD)
Arapahoe Comm Coll (CO)
Athens Tech Coll (GA)
Austin Comm Coll (TX)
Bergen Comm Coll (NJ)
Berkeley Coll (NJ)
Berkeley Coll-New York City Campus (NY)
Berkeley Coll-Westchester Campus (NY)
Brazosport Coll (TX)
Brevard Comm Coll (FL)
Briarwood Coll (CT)
Bronx Comm Coll of the City U of New York (NY)
Broome Comm Coll (NY)
Broward Comm Coll (FL)
Brown Mackie Coll–Fort Wayne (IN)
Brown Mackie Coll–Kansas City (KS)
Brown Mackie Coll–Merrillville (IN)
Brown Mackie Coll–North Canton (OH)
Brown Mackie Coll–Salina (KS)
Brown Mackie Coll–South Bend (IN)
Bryant and Stratton Coll, Albany (NY)
Bryant and Stratton Coll, Rochester (NY)
Bryant and Stratton Coll, Amherst Campus (NY)
Bryant and Stratton Coll, Richmond (VA)
Bucks County Comm Coll (PA)
Caldwell Comm Coll and Tech Inst (NC)
Carteret Comm Coll (NC)
Casper Coll (WY)
Central Carolina Tech Coll (SC)

Central Comm Coll–Grand Island Campus (NE)
Central New Mexico Comm Coll (NM)
Central Piedmont Comm Coll (NC)
Clark Coll (WA)
Clark State Comm Coll (OH)
Clovis Comm Coll (NM)
Coastal Carolina Comm Coll (NC)
Coll of Southern Maryland (MD)
Coll of the Siskiyous (CA)
Collin County Comm Coll District (TX)
Comm Coll of Allegheny County (PA)
Comm Coll of the Air Force (AL)
Corning Comm Coll (NY)
Crown Coll (WA)
Cuyahoga Comm Coll (OH)
Delta Coll (MI)
East Central Coll (MO)
Eastern Idaho Tech Coll (ID)
Edmonds Comm Coll (WA)
El Centro Coll (TX)
Erie Business Center, Main (PA)
Erie Comm Coll (NY)
Essex County Coll (NJ)
Everest Coll (AZ)
Evergreen Valley Coll (CA)
Fayetteville Tech Comm Coll (NC)
Finger Lakes Comm Coll (NY)
Fiorello H. LaGuardia Comm Coll of the City U of New York (NY)
Florida Comm Coll at Jacksonville (FL)
Florida National Coll (FL)
Forsyth Tech Comm Coll (NC)
Frederick Comm Coll (MD)
Gadsden State Comm Coll (AL)
Gaston Coll (NC)
Genesee Comm Coll (NY)
Georgia Highlands Coll (GA)
Hagerstown Business Coll (MD)
Hamilton Coll, Cedar Falls (IA)
Harrisburg Area Comm Coll (PA)
Hickey Coll (MO)
Highline Comm Coll (WA)
Horry-Georgetown Tech Coll (SC)
Houston Comm Coll System (TX)
Hutchinson Comm Coll and Area Vocational School (KS)
Illinois Central Coll (IL)
International Inst of the Americas, Mesa (AZ)
International Inst of the Americas, Phoenix (AZ)
International Inst of the Americas, Phoenix (AZ)
International Inst of the Americas, Tucson (AZ)
Ivy Tech Comm Coll–Bloomington (IN)
Ivy Tech Comm Coll–Central Indiana (IN)
Ivy Tech Comm Coll–Columbus (IN)
Ivy Tech Comm Coll–East Central (IN)
Ivy Tech Comm Coll–Kokomo (IN)
Ivy Tech Comm Coll–Lafayette (IN)
Ivy Tech Comm Coll–North Central (IN)
Ivy Tech Comm Coll–Northeast (IN)
Ivy Tech Comm Coll–Northwest (IN)
Ivy Tech Comm Coll–Southeast (IN)
Ivy Tech Comm Coll–Southern Indiana (IN)
Ivy Tech Comm Coll–Southwest (IN)

Ivy Tech Comm Coll–
  Wabash Valley (IN)
Ivy Tech Comm Coll–
  Whitewater (IN)
James H. Faulkner State
  Comm Coll (AL)
Jefferson Comm Coll (NY)
Johnston Comm Coll (NC)
Kansas City Kansas Comm
  Coll (KS)
Kapiolani Comm Coll (HI)
Keiser Coll, Miami (FL)
Kellogg Comm Coll (MI)
Lackawanna Coll (PA)
Lake Region State Coll (ND)
Lakeshore Tech Coll (WI)
Lake-Sumter Comm Coll
  (FL)
Lake Superior Coll (MN)
Lamar State Coll–Port Arthur
  (TX)
Lansing Comm Coll (MI)
Lehigh Valley Coll (PA)
Lincoln Coll–Normal (IL)
Luzerne County Comm Coll
  (PA)
Macomb Comm Coll (MI)
Manatee Comm Coll (FL)
Manchester Comm Coll (CT)
Manor Coll (PA)
Maria Coll (NY)
Marshall Comm and Tech
  Coll (WV)
Massachusetts Bay Comm
  Coll (MA)
Mercer County Comm Coll
  (NJ)
Metropolitan Comm Coll
  (NE)
Miami Dade Coll (FL)
Middlesex County Coll (NJ)
Midland Coll (TX)
Midlands Tech Coll (SC)
Minnesota School of
  Business–Richfield (MN)
Mississippi Gulf Coast
  Comm Coll (MS)
Missouri State U–West
  Plains (MO)
Mountain State Coll (WV)
Mt. San Antonio Coll (CA)
Mount Wachusett Comm Coll
  (MA)
Nassau Comm Coll (NY)
Naugatuck Valley Comm Coll
  (CT)
New Hampshire Comm Tech
  Coll, Nashua/Claremont
  (NH)
New Hampshire Tech Inst
  (NH)
New Mexico State U–
  Alamogordo (NM)
Northampton County Area
  Comm Coll (PA)
Northeast Comm Coll (NE)
Northern Essex Comm Coll
  (MA)
North Idaho Coll (ID)
Northland Comm and Tech
  Coll–Thief River Falls (MN)
North Shore Comm Coll
  (MA)
Northwestern Connecticut
  Comm Coll (CT)
Norwalk Comm Coll (CT)
Oakland Comm Coll (MI)
Ocean County Coll (NJ)
Okaloosa-Walton Coll (FL)
Ouachita Tech Coll (AR)
The Paralegal Inst, Inc. (AZ)
Pasco-Hernando Comm Coll
  (FL)
Pellissippi State Tech Comm
  Coll (TN)
Penn Foster Career School
  (PA)
Penn Valley Comm Coll
  (MO)
Phoenix Coll (AZ)
Pima Comm Coll (AZ)
Pioneer Pacific Coll (OR)
Raritan Valley Comm Coll
  (NJ)
Rasmussen Coll Mankato
  (MN)
Remington Coll–Lafayette
  Campus (LA)
Rockingham Comm Coll
  (NC)

Saddleback Coll (CA)
St. Petersburg Coll (FL)
Salt Lake Comm Coll (UT)
San Diego City Coll (CA)
San Juan Coll (NM)
Schuylkill Inst of Business
  and Technology (PA)
Seminole Comm Coll (FL)
Sinclair Comm Coll (OH)
Skyline Coll (CA)
South Texas Coll (TX)
South U, West Palm Beach
  (FL)
Southwestern Illinois Coll (IL)
Southwestern Michigan Coll
  (MI)
Southwest Florida Coll, Fort
  Myers (FL)
Southwest Tennessee
  Comm Coll (TN)
Spokane Comm Coll (WA)
Sullivan County Comm Coll
  (NY)
Sussex County Comm Coll
  (NJ)
Tarrant County Coll District
  (TX)
Tompkins Cortland Comm
  Coll (NY)
Trident Tech Coll (SC)
Tulsa Comm Coll (OK)
U of Northwestern Ohio (OH)
Valencia Comm Coll (FL)
Volunteer State Comm Coll
  (TN)
Westchester Comm Coll
  (NY)
Western Tech Coll (WI)
Westmoreland County
  Comm Coll (PA)
West Virginia Business Coll,
  Wheeling (WV)
William Rainey Harper Coll
  (IL)
Wilson Tech Comm Coll (NC)
Yavapai Coll (AZ)

Legal Professions and Studies Related
Essex County Coll (NJ)
Florida National Coll (FL)

Legal Studies
Aakers Business Coll (ND)
Coll of the Siskiyous (CA)
El Centro Coll (TX)
Florida National Coll (FL)
Foothill Coll (CA)
Macomb Comm Coll (MI)
Maria Coll (NY)
Metropolitan Comm Coll
  (NE)
New Hampshire Comm Tech
  Coll, Nashua/Claremont
  (NH)
Northland Comm and Tech
  Coll–Thief River Falls (MN)
Okaloosa-Walton Coll (FL)
Palo Alto Coll (TX)
Pasadena City Coll (CA)
Rasmussen Coll Mankato
  (MN)
Saddleback Coll (CA)
St. Louis Comm Coll at
  Florissant Valley (MO)
Santa Barbara City Coll (CA)
Trident Tech Coll (SC)
Tulsa Comm Coll (OK)

Liberal Arts and Sciences And Humanities Related
Cleveland Comm Coll (NC)
Eastern West Virginia Comm
  and Tech Coll (WV)
Fayetteville Tech Comm Coll
  (NC)
Hagerstown Comm Coll
  (MD)
Kansas City Kansas Comm
  Coll (KS)
Lake Superior Coll (MN)
Luzerne County Comm Coll
  (PA)
Northampton County Area
  Comm Coll (PA)
Oakland Comm Coll (MI)
Southwestern Michigan Coll
  (MI)
Wor-Wic Comm Coll (MD)

Liberal Arts and Sciences/ Liberal Studies
Abraham Baldwin Ag Coll
  (GA)
Aiken Tech Coll (SC)
Alamance Comm Coll (NC)
Allan Hancock Coll (CA)
Allegany Coll of Maryland
  (MD)
Ancilla Coll (IN)
Arapahoe Comm Coll (CO)
Arkansas State U–Beebe
  (AR)
Arkansas State U–Mountain
  Home (AR)
Asnuntuck Comm Coll (CT)
Assumption Coll for Sisters
  (NJ)
Austin Comm Coll (TX)
Bainbridge Coll (GA)
Barton County Comm Coll
  (KS)
Bay State Coll (MA)
Beaufort County Comm Coll
  (NC)
Bergen Comm Coll (NJ)
Berkeley City Coll (CA)
Berkshire Comm Coll (MA)
Big Bend Comm Coll (WA)
Bishop State Comm Coll
  (AL)
Bladen Comm Coll (NC)
Blue River Comm Coll (MO)
Borough of Manhattan
  Comm Coll of the City U of
  New York (NY)
Brazosport Coll (TX)
Brevard Comm Coll (FL)
Bristol Comm Coll (MA)
Bronx Comm Coll of the City
  U of New York (NY)
Broome Comm Coll (NY)
Broward Comm Coll (FL)
Bucks County Comm Coll
  (PA)
Butler Comm Coll (KS)
Butler County Comm Coll
  (PA)
Caldwell Comm Coll and
  Tech Inst (NC)
Cape Fear Comm Coll (NC)
Capital Comm Coll (CT)
Carroll Comm Coll (MD)
Carteret Comm Coll (NC)
Casper Coll (WY)
Cecil Comm Coll (MD)
Cedar Valley Coll (TX)
Central Arizona Coll (AZ)
Central Carolina Tech Coll
  (SC)
Central Comm Coll–
  Columbus Campus (NE)
Central Comm Coll–Grand
  Island Campus (NE)
Central Comm Coll–Hastings
  Campus (NE)
Central Florida Comm Coll
  (FL)
Centralia Coll (WA)
Central Lakes Coll (MN)
Central New Mexico Comm
  Coll (NM)
Central Oregon Comm Coll
  (OR)
Central Piedmont Comm Coll
  (NC)
Century Coll (MN)
Chatfield Coll (OH)
Chattahoochee Valley Comm
  Coll (AL)
Chattanooga State Tech
  Comm Coll (TN)
Chemeketa Comm Coll (OR)
Cincinnati State Tech and
  Comm Coll (OH)
Citrus Coll (CA)
City Colls of Chicago, Wilbur
  Wright College (IL)
Clarendon Coll (TX)
Clark Coll (WA)
Clark State Comm Coll (OH)
Clatsop Comm Coll (OR)
Cleveland Comm Coll (NC)
Cleveland State Comm Coll
  (TN)
Clovis Comm Coll (NM)
Coahoma Comm Coll (MS)
Coastal Bend Coll (TX)
Coastal Carolina Comm Coll
  (NC)

Coastal Georgia Comm Coll
  (GA)
Cochise Coll, Douglas (AZ)
Colby Comm Coll (KS)
Coll of DuPage (IL)
Coll of Eastern Utah (UT)
Coll of Lake County (IL)
Coll of Southern Maryland
  (MD)
Coll of The Albemarle (NC)
Coll of the Canyons (CA)
Coll of the Mainland (TX)
Collin County Comm Coll
  District (TX)
Colorado Mountain Coll (CO)
Colorado Mountain Coll,
  Alpine Campus (CO)
Colorado Mountain Coll,
  Timberline Campus (CO)
Columbia Coll (CA)
Comm Coll of Allegheny
  County (PA)
Copiah-Lincoln Comm Coll
  (MS)
Corning Comm Coll (NY)
Cossatot Comm Coll of the U
  of Arkansas (AR)
Cottey Coll (MO)
Cowley County Comm Coll
  and Area Vocational–Tech
  School (KS)
Crowder Coll (MO)
Cuyahoga Comm Coll (OH)
Dabney S. Lancaster Comm
  Coll (VA)
Dean Coll (MA)
Deep Springs Coll (CA)
Delta Coll (MI)
Diablo Valley Coll (CA)
Diné Coll (AZ)
Dixie State Coll of Utah (UT)
Dyersburg State Comm Coll
  (TN)
East Arkansas Comm Coll
  (AR)
Eastern Arizona Coll (AZ)
Eastern West Virginia Comm
  and Tech Coll (WV)
Eastern Wyoming Coll (WY)
Eastfield Coll (TX)
Edmonds Comm Coll (WA)
El Centro Coll (TX)
Erie Comm Coll (NY)
Erie Comm Coll, North
  Campus (NY)
Erie Comm Coll, South
  Campus (NY)
Essex County Coll (NJ)
Evergreen Valley Coll (CA)
Fayetteville Tech Comm Coll
  (NC)
Feather River Coll (CA)
Finger Lakes Comm Coll
  (NY)
Fiorello H. LaGuardia Comm
  Coll of the City U of New
  York (NY)
Fisher Coll (MA)
Florida Comm Coll at
  Jacksonville (FL)
Florida National Coll (FL)
Frederick Comm Coll (MD)
Front Range Comm Coll
  (CO)
Gadsden State Comm Coll
  (AL)
Galveston Coll (TX)
GateWay Comm Coll (AZ)
Gateway Comm Coll (CT)
Gavilan Coll (CA)
Genesee Comm Coll (NY)
George C. Wallace Comm
  Coll (AL)
Georgia Highlands Coll (GA)
Germanna Comm Coll (VA)
Glendale Comm Coll (AZ)
Grand Rapids Comm Coll
  (MI)
Greenfield Comm Coll (MA)
Hagerstown Comm Coll
  (MD)
Harrisburg Area Comm Coll
  (PA)
Hawkeye Comm Coll (IA)
Heartland Comm Coll (IL)
Hesston Coll (KS)
Hibbing Comm Coll (MN)
Highland Comm Coll (IL)
Holy Cross Coll (IN)
Holyoke Comm Coll (MA)

Houston Comm Coll System
  (TX)
Howard Comm Coll (MD)
Hudson Valley Comm Coll
  (NY)
Hutchinson Comm Coll and
  Area Vocational School
  (KS)
Illinois Central Coll (IL)
Illinois Eastern Comm Colls,
  Frontier Community
  College (IL)
Illinois Eastern Comm Colls,
  Lincoln Trail College (IL)
Illinois Eastern Comm Colls,
  Olney Central College (IL)
Illinois Eastern Comm Colls,
  Wabash Valley College (IL)
Illinois Valley Comm Coll (IL)
Independence Comm Coll
  (KS)
Itasca Comm Coll (MN)
Ivy Tech Comm Coll–
  Bloomington (IN)
Ivy Tech Comm Coll–Central
  Indiana (IN)
Ivy Tech Comm Coll–
  Columbus (IN)
Ivy Tech Comm Coll–East
  Central (IN)
Ivy Tech Comm Coll–
  Kokomo (IN)
Ivy Tech Comm Coll–
  Lafayette (IN)
Ivy Tech Comm Coll–North
  Central (IN)
Ivy Tech Comm Coll–
  Northeast (IN)
Ivy Tech Comm Coll–
  Northwest (IN)
Ivy Tech Comm Coll–
  Southeast (IN)
Ivy Tech Comm Coll–
  Southern Indiana (IN)
Ivy Tech Comm Coll–
  Southwest (IN)
Ivy Tech Comm Coll–
  Wabash Valley (IN)
Ivy Tech Comm Coll–
  Whitewater (IN)
Jackson Comm Coll (MI)
Jackson State Comm Coll
  (TN)
Jacksonville Coll (TX)
James H. Faulkner State
  Comm Coll (AL)
James Sprunt Comm Coll
  (NC)
Jefferson Comm and Tech
  Coll (KY)
Jefferson Comm Coll (NY)
Jefferson State Comm Coll
  (AL)
Johnston Comm Coll (NC)
John Tyler Comm Coll (VA)
John Wood Comm Coll (IL)
Kansas City Kansas Comm
  Coll (KS)
Kapiolani Comm Coll (HI)
Kaskaskia Coll (IL)
Kauai Comm Coll (HI)
Kellogg Comm Coll (MI)
Kennebec Valley Comm Coll
  (ME)
Kent State U, Geauga
  Campus (OH)
Kent State U, Trumbull
  Campus (OH)
Kent State U, Tuscarawas
  Campus (OH)
Keystone Coll (PA)
Kilian Comm Coll (SD)
Kingsborough Comm Coll of
  the City U of New York
  (NY)
Lac Courte Oreilles Ojibwa
  Comm Coll (WI)
Lackawanna Coll (PA)
Lake City Comm Coll (FL)
Lake Land Coll (IL)
Lake Michigan Coll (MI)
Lake Region State Coll (ND)
Lake-Sumter Comm Coll
  (FL)
Lake Superior Coll (MN)
Lamar State Coll–Orange
  (TX)
Lamar State Coll–Port Arthur
  (TX)
Landmark Coll (VT)

Lansing Comm Coll (MI)
Laredo Comm Coll (TX)
Lawson State Comm Coll
  (AL)
Lincoln Coll (IL)
Lincoln Coll–Normal (IL)
Lincoln Land Comm Coll (IL)
Linn-Benton Comm Coll
  (OR)
Long Beach City Coll (CA)
Longview Comm Coll (MO)
Lord Fairfax Comm Coll (VA)
Louisiana State U at
  Alexandria (LA)
Lower Columbia Coll (WA)
Luzerne County Comm Coll
  (PA)
Macomb Comm Coll (MI)
Manatee Comm Coll (FL)
Manchester Comm Coll (CT)
Manor Coll (PA)
Maple Woods Comm Coll
  (MO)
Maria Coll (NY)
Marshall Comm and Tech
  Coll (WV)
Massachusetts Bay Comm
  Coll (MA)
Mercer County Comm Coll
  (NJ)
Mesabi Range Comm and
  Tech Coll (MN)
Metropolitan Comm Coll
  (NE)
Metropolitan Comm
  Coll-Business &
  Technology College (MO)
Middle Georgia Coll (GA)
Middlesex Comm Coll (CT)
Midland Coll (TX)
Midlands Tech Coll (SC)
Mid-South Comm Coll (AR)
Minnesota State Comm and
  Tech Coll–Fergus Falls
  (MN)
Minnesota West Comm and
  Tech Coll (MN)
MiraCosta Coll (CA)
Mississippi Gulf Coast
  Comm Coll (MS)
Moberly Area Comm Coll
  (MO)
Mohawk Valley Comm Coll
  (NY)
Montgomery Comm Coll
  (NC)
Montgomery County Comm
  Coll (PA)
Moraine Valley Comm Coll
  (IL)
Motlow State Comm Coll
  (TN)
Mott Comm Coll (MI)
Mountain View Coll (TX)
Mt. San Antonio Coll (CA)
Mount Wachusett Comm Coll
  (MA)
Nassau Comm Coll (NY)
Naugatuck Valley Comm Coll
  (CT)
New Hampshire Comm Tech
  Coll, Manchester/Stratham
  (NH)
New Hampshire Comm Tech
  Coll, Nashua/Claremont
  (NH)
New Hampshire Tech Inst
  (NH)
New Mexico Military Inst
  (NM)
New Mexico State U–
  Alamogordo (NM)
Niagara County Comm Coll
  (NY)
Normandale Comm Coll
  (MN)
Northampton County Area
  Comm Coll (PA)
North Arkansas Coll (AR)
North Central Missouri Coll
  (MO)
North Country Comm Coll
  (NY)
North Dakota State Coll of
  Science (ND)
Northeast Comm Coll (NE)
Northeast Iowa Comm Coll
  (IA)
Northeast State Tech Comm
  Coll (TN)

Northern Essex Comm Coll (MA)
North Idaho Coll (ID)
North Iowa Area Comm Coll (IA)
Northland Comm and Tech Coll–Thief River Falls (MN)
North Seattle Comm Coll (WA)
North Shore Comm Coll (MA)
Northwestern Connecticut Comm Coll (CT)
Northwest-Shoals Comm Coll (AL)
Northwest Vista Coll (TX)
Norwalk Comm Coll (CT)
Oakland Comm Coll (MI)
Ocean County Coll (NJ)
Okaloosa-Walton Coll (FL)
Orange Coast Coll (CA)
Orange County Comm Coll (NY)
Oregon Coast Comm Coll (OR)
Otero Jr Coll (CO)
Ouachita Tech Coll (AR)
Palau Comm CollPalau)
Palm Beach Comm Coll (FL)
Palo Alto Coll (TX)
Palo Verde Coll (CA)
Parkland Coll (IL)
Pasadena City Coll (CA)
Pasco-Hernando Comm Coll (FL)
Pellissippi State Tech Comm Coll (TN)
The Pennsylvania State U Beaver Campus of the Commonwealth Coll (PA)
The Pennsylvania State U Delaware County Campus of the Commonwealth Coll (PA)
The Pennsylvania State U DuBois Campus of the Commonwealth Coll (PA)
The Pennsylvania State U Fayette Campus of the Commonwealth Coll (PA)
The Pennsylvania State U Hazleton Campus of the Commonwealth Coll (PA)
The Pennsylvania State U McKeesport Campus of the Commonwealth Coll (PA)
The Pennsylvania State U Mont Alto Campus of the Commonwealth Coll (PA)
The Pennsylvania State U New Kensington Campus of the Commonwealth Coll (PA)
The Pennsylvania State U Shenango Campus of the Commonwealth Coll (PA)
The Pennsylvania State U Wilkes-Barre Campus of the Commonwealth Coll (PA)
The Pennsylvania State U Worthington Scranton Campus of the Commonwealth Coll (PA)
The Pennsylvania State U York Campus of the Commonwealth Coll (PA)
Penn Valley Comm Coll (MO)
Phoenix Coll (AZ)
Piedmont Virginia Comm Coll (VA)
Pima Comm Coll (AZ)
Polk Comm Coll (FL)
Prairie State Coll (IL)
Pratt Comm Coll (KS)
Quinebaug Valley Comm Coll (CT)
Quinsigamond Comm Coll (MA)
Raritan Valley Comm Coll (NJ)
Richard Bland Coll of The College of William and Mary (VA)
Richland Comm Coll (IL)
Richmond Comm Coll (NC)
Riverland Comm Coll (MN)
Riverside Comm Coll District (CA)

Roane State Comm Coll (TN)
Rockingham Comm Coll (NC)
Rock Valley Coll (IL)
Rogue Comm Coll (OR)
Saddleback Coll (CA)
Saginaw Chippewa Tribal Coll (MI)
Saint Charles Comm Coll (MO)
St. Louis Comm Coll at Florissant Valley (MO)
St. Petersburg Coll (FL)
St. Philip's Coll (TX)
Salem Comm Coll (NJ)
San Diego City Coll (CA)
San Diego Mesa Coll (CA)
San Joaquin Delta Coll (CA)
Santa Barbara City Coll (CA)
Santa Rosa Jr Coll (CA)
Sauk Valley Comm Coll (IL)
Seattle Central Comm Coll (WA)
Seminole Comm Coll (FL)
Seminole State Coll (OK)
Shelton State Comm Coll (AL)
Sheridan Coll–Sheridan and Gillette (WY)
Sinclair Comm Coll (OH)
Skyline Coll (CA)
Snead State Comm Coll (AL)
Snow Coll (UT)
Southeastern Comm Coll (NC)
Southern State Comm Coll (OH)
Southern West Virginia Comm and Tech Coll (WV)
South Plains Coll (TX)
Southside Virginia Comm Coll (VA)
South Texas Coll (TX)
Southwestern Illinois Coll (IL)
Southwestern Michigan Coll (MI)
Southwestern Oregon Comm Coll (OR)
Southwest Mississippi Comm Coll (MS)
Southwest Virginia Comm Coll (VA)
Spartanburg Methodist Coll (SC)
Spartanburg Tech Coll (SC)
Spokane Comm Coll (WA)
Spokane Falls Comm Coll (WA)
Spoon River Coll (IL)
Springfield Coll in Illinois (IL)
Springfield Tech Comm Coll (MA)
State U of New York Coll of Technology at Alfred (NY)
Sullivan County Comm Coll (NY)
Sussex County Comm Coll (NJ)
Tarrant County Coll District (TX)
Thomas Nelson Comm Coll (VA)
Three Rivers Comm Coll (MO)
Tidewater Comm Coll (VA)
Tillamook Bay Comm Coll (OR)
Tompkins Cortland Comm Coll (NY)
TransPacific Hawaii Coll (HI)
Treasure Valley Comm Coll (OR)
Tri-County Comm Coll (NC)
Trident Tech Coll (SC)
Trinidad State Jr Coll (CO)
Trinity Valley Comm Coll (TX)
Triton Coll (IL)
Truett-McConnell Coll (GA)
Tulsa Comm Coll (OK)
Tunxis Comm Coll (CT)
Union County Coll (NJ)
The U of Akron–Wayne Coll (OH)
U of Alaska Anchorage, Matanuska-Susitna Coll (AK)
U of Pittsburgh at Titusville (PA)

U of South Carolina Sumter (SC)
U of South Carolina Union (SC)
U of Wisconsin–Baraboo/Sauk County (WI)
U of Wisconsin–Manitowoc (WI)
U of Wisconsin–Richland (WI)
U of Wisconsin–Washington County (WI)
U of Wisconsin–Waukesha (WI)
Valencia Comm Coll (FL)
Valley Forge Military Coll (PA)
Vance-Granville Comm Coll (NC)
Ventura Coll (CA)
Vermilion Comm Coll (MN)
Villa Maria Coll of Buffalo (NY)
Volunteer State Comm Coll (TN)
Waubonsee Comm Coll (IL)
Weatherford Coll (TX)
Wentworth Military Academy and Jr Coll (MO)
Westchester Comm Coll (NY)
Western Iowa Tech Comm Coll (IA)
Western Oklahoma State Coll (OK)
Westmoreland County Comm Coll (PA)
West Virginia Northern Comm Coll (WV)
Wilkes Comm Coll (NC)
William Rainey Harper Coll (IL)
Williston State Coll (ND)
Wilson Tech Comm Coll (NC)
Yakima Valley Comm Coll (WA)
Yavapai Coll (AZ)
York Tech Coll (SC)
Young Harris Coll (GA)

Library Assistant
Citrus Coll (CA)
Clovis Comm Coll (NM)
Coll of DuPage (IL)
Ivy Tech Comm Coll–Bloomington (IN)
Ivy Tech Comm Coll–Columbus (IN)
Ivy Tech Comm Coll–East Central (IN)
Ivy Tech Comm Coll–Kokomo (IN)
Ivy Tech Comm Coll–North Central (IN)
Ivy Tech Comm Coll–Northeast (IN)
Ivy Tech Comm Coll–Northwest (IN)
Ivy Tech Comm Coll–Southeast (IN)
Ivy Tech Comm Coll–Southern Indiana (IN)
Ivy Tech Comm Coll–Southwest (IN)
Ivy Tech Comm Coll–Wabash Valley (IN)
Ivy Tech Comm Coll–Whitewater (IN)
Oakland Comm Coll (MI)
Spokane Falls Comm Coll (WA)

Library Science
Allen County Comm Coll (KS)
Brazosport Coll (TX)
Citrus Coll (CA)
City Colls of Chicago, Wilbur Wright College (IL)
Colby Comm Coll (KS)
Coll of DuPage (IL)
Copiah-Lincoln Comm Coll (MS)
East Central Coll (MO)
Highline Comm Coll (WA)
Illinois Central Coll (IL)
Lawson State Comm Coll (AL)
Palo Alto Coll (TX)
Pasadena City Coll (CA)
Tulsa Comm Coll (OK)

Lineworker
Ivy Tech Comm Coll–Lafayette (IN)
Linn State Tech Coll (MO)
Lower Columbia Coll (WA)
Northeast Comm Coll (NE)

Linguistics
Foothill Coll (CA)

Literature
Bergen Comm Coll (NJ)
Foothill Coll (CA)
Lamar State Coll–Orange (TX)
Lincoln Land Comm Coll (IL)
Miami Dade Coll (FL)
Midland Coll (TX)
Otero Jr Coll (CO)
Palm Beach Comm Coll (FL)
Pratt Comm Coll (KS)
Saddleback Coll (CA)
San Joaquin Delta Coll (CA)
Skyline Coll (CA)

Livestock Management
Barton County Comm Coll (KS)
Northeast Comm Coll (NE)
The Ohio State U Ag Tech Inst (OH)

Logistics and Materials Management
Athens Tech Coll (GA)
Chattahoochee Tech Coll (GA)
Comm Coll of the Air Force (AL)
Houston Comm Coll System (TX)
Prairie State Coll (IL)
Sinclair Comm Coll (OH)
Springfield Tech Comm Coll (MA)
Waubonsee Comm Coll (IL)

Machine Shop Technology
Cape Fear Comm Coll (NC)
Coll of Lake County (IL)
Comm Coll of Allegheny County (PA)
Corning Comm Coll (NY)
Delgado Comm Coll (LA)
Eastern Arizona Coll (AZ)
Fayetteville Tech Comm Coll (NC)
Florida Comm Coll at Jacksonville (FL)
Illinois Eastern Comm Colls, Wabash Valley College (IL)
Ivy Tech Comm Coll–Central Indiana (IN)
Metropolitan Comm Coll–Business & Technology College (MO)
Modesto Jr Coll (CA)
Mohawk Valley Comm Coll (NY)
Moraine Park Tech Coll (WI)
North Dakota State Coll of Science (ND)
North Iowa Area Comm Coll (IA)
Orange Coast Coll (CA)
Pima Comm Coll (AZ)
Riverland Comm Coll (MN)
Southwestern Michigan Coll (MI)

Machine Tool Technology
Aiken Tech Coll (SC)
Alamance Comm Coll (NC)
Alexandria Tech Coll (MN)
Allan Hancock Coll (CA)
Altamaha Tech Coll (GA)
Asnuntuck Comm Coll (CT)
Brazosport Coll (TX)
Butler County Comm Coll (PA)
Casper Coll (WY)
Central Comm Coll–Columbus Campus (NE)
Central Comm Coll–Hastings Campus (NE)
Central Piedmont Comm Coll (NC)
Century Coll (MN)
Chattanooga State Tech Comm Coll (TN)
City Colls of Chicago, Wilbur Wright College (IL)
Clark Coll (WA)

Coll of DuPage (IL)
Coll of Eastern Utah (UT)
Columbus Tech Coll (GA)
Corning Comm Coll (NY)
Cowley County Comm Coll and Area Vocational–Tech School (KS)
DeKalb Tech Coll (GA)
Delgado Comm Coll (LA)
Delta Coll (MI)
East Central Coll (MO)
Forsyth Tech Comm Coll (NC)
Front Range Comm Coll (CO)
George C. Wallace Comm Coll (AL)
Gwinnett Tech Coll (GA)
Hawkeye Comm Coll (IA)
H. Councill Trenholm State Tech Coll (AL)
Heartland Comm Coll (IL)
Heart of Georgia Tech Coll (GA)
Horry-Georgetown Tech Coll (SC)
Hutchinson Comm Coll and Area Vocational School (KS)
Ivy Tech Comm Coll–Bloomington (IN)
Ivy Tech Comm Coll–Central Indiana (IN)
Ivy Tech Comm Coll–Columbus (IN)
Ivy Tech Comm Coll–East Central (IN)
Ivy Tech Comm Coll–Kokomo (IN)
Ivy Tech Comm Coll–Lafayette (IN)
Ivy Tech Comm Coll–North Central (IN)
Ivy Tech Comm Coll–Northeast (IN)
Ivy Tech Comm Coll–Northwest (IN)
Ivy Tech Comm Coll–Southern Indiana (IN)
Ivy Tech Comm Coll–Southwest (IN)
Ivy Tech Comm Coll–Wabash Valley (IN)
Ivy Tech Comm Coll–Whitewater (IN)
J. F. Drake State Tech Coll (AL)
Johnston Comm Coll (NC)
Kellogg Comm Coll (MI)
Kennebec Valley Comm Coll (ME)
Lake Michigan Coll (MI)
Lake Superior Coll (MN)
Lansing Comm Coll (MI)
Linn-Benton Comm Coll (OR)
Linn State Tech Coll (MO)
Long Beach City Coll (CA)
Lower Columbia Coll (WA)
Macomb Comm Coll (MI)
Meridian Comm Coll (MS)
MiraCosta Coll (CA)
Modesto Jr Coll (CA)
Mt. San Antonio Coll (CA)
New Hampshire Comm Tech Coll, Nashua/Claremont (NH)
Northeast State Tech Comm Coll (TN)
Northern Essex Comm Coll (MA)
North Idaho Coll (ID)
North Iowa Area Comm Coll (IA)
Oakland Comm Coll (MI)
Orange Coast Coll (CA)
Ouachita Tech Coll (AR)
Pasadena City Coll (CA)
Pellissippi State Tech Comm Coll (TN)
Richmond Comm Coll (NC)
St. Cloud Tech Coll (MN)
San Diego City Coll (CA)
San Joaquin Delta Coll (CA)
Shelton State Comm Coll (AL)
Sheridan Coll–Sheridan and Gillette (WY)
Sinclair Comm Coll (OH)
Southeast Tech Inst (SD)

South Plains Coll (TX)
South Texas Coll (TX)
Southwestern Illinois Coll (IL)
Southwestern Oregon Comm Coll (OR)
Southwest Mississippi Comm Coll (MS)
Spartanburg Tech Coll (SC)
Spokane Comm Coll (WA)
State U of New York Coll of Technology at Alfred (NY)
Tarrant County Coll District (TX)
Texas State Tech Coll Waco (TX)
Trident Tech Coll (SC)
Triton Coll (IL)
Valdosta Tech Coll (GA)
Ventura Coll (CA)
Waubonsee Comm Coll (IL)
Western Iowa Tech Comm Coll (IA)
William Rainey Harper Coll (IL)
The Williamson Free School of Mecha Trades (PA)
York Tech Coll (SC)
Yuba Coll (CA)

Management Information Systems
Allegany Coll of Maryland (MD)
Arapahoe Comm Coll (CO)
Bristol Comm Coll (MA)
Career Coll of Northern Nevada (NV)
Central Wyoming Coll (WY)
Century Coll (MN)
Cincinnati State Tech and Comm Coll (OH)
Clovis Comm Coll (NM)
The Coll of Westchester (NY)
Comm Coll of Allegheny County (PA)
Comm Coll of the Air Force (AL)
Delaware Tech & Comm Coll, Stanton/Wilmington Campus (DE)
East Central Coll (MO)
Eastern Wyoming Coll (WY)
ECPI Tech Coll (NC)
Evergreen Valley Coll (CA)
Glendale Comm Coll (AZ)
Gwinnett Tech Coll (GA)
Hagerstown Comm Coll (MD)
Hamilton Coll, Cedar Rapids (IA)
Harrisburg Area Comm Coll (PA)
Heartland Comm Coll (IL)
Hutchinson Comm Coll and Area Vocational School (KS)
Jackson State Comm Coll (TN)
John Tyler Comm Coll (VA)
Lackawanna Coll (PA)
Lake Region State Coll (ND)
Lake Superior Coll (MN)
Lansing Comm Coll (MI)
Lower Columbia Coll (WA)
Manchester Comm Coll (CT)
Manhattan Area Tech Coll (KS)
Mercer County Comm Coll (NJ)
Miami Dade Coll (FL)
Modesto Jr Coll (CA)
Montgomery Comm Coll (NC)
Mott Comm Coll (MI)
Mount Wachusett Comm Coll (MA)
Nassau Comm Coll (NY)
New England Coll of Finance (MA)
New Hampshire Comm Tech Coll, Manchester/Stratham (NH)
Normandale Comm Coll (MN)
Ouachita Tech Coll (AR)
Owens Comm Coll, Toledo (OH)
Raritan Valley Comm Coll (NJ)
Salem Comm Coll (NJ)

South Arkansas Comm Coll (AR)
Southwestern Oregon Comm Coll (OR)
Southwest Tennessee Comm Coll (TN)
Trinidad State Jr Coll (CO)
Triton Coll (IL)
Union County Coll (NJ)
The U of Akron–Wayne Coll (OH)
U of Pittsburgh at Titusville (PA)
William Rainey Harper Coll (IL)
Yakima Valley Comm Coll (WA)

Management Information Systems and Services Related
Cedar Valley Coll (TX)
Cleveland Comm Coll (NC)
Eastern Arizona Coll (AZ)
Indiana Business Coll, Indianapolis (IN)
Indiana Business Coll, Muncie (IN)
Metropolitan Comm Coll-Business & Technology College (MO)
Mid-South Comm Coll (AR)
Mohawk Valley Comm Coll (NY)
Montgomery County Comm Coll (PA)
Oakland Comm Coll (MI)
Wisconsin Indianhead Tech Coll (WI)

Management Science
GateWay Comm Coll (AZ)
Harrisburg Area Comm Coll (PA)
Lakeshore Tech Coll (WI)
Oakland Comm Coll (MI)
Phoenix Coll (AZ)
Prairie State Coll (IL)
Tillamook Bay Comm Coll (OR)
Tulsa Comm Coll (OK)

Manufacturing Engineering
Cochise Coll, Douglas (AZ)
The Pennsylvania State U Fayette Campus of the Commonwealth Coll (PA)
The Pennsylvania State U Hazleton Campus of the Commonwealth Coll (PA)
The Pennsylvania State U McKeesport Campus of the Commonwealth Coll (PA)
The Pennsylvania State U Wilkes-Barre Campus of the Commonwealth Coll (PA)
The Pennsylvania State U York Campus of the Commonwealth Coll (PA)

Manufacturing Technology
Albany Tech Coll (GA)
Altamaha Tech Coll (GA)
Brevard Comm Coll (FL)
Clark Coll (WA)
Coll of DuPage (IL)
East Central Coll (MO)
Flint River Tech Coll (GA)
Griffin Tech Coll (GA)
Hutchinson Comm Coll and Area Vocational School (KS)
Illinois Eastern Comm Colls, Wabash Valley College (IL)
Macomb Comm Coll (MI)
Marshall Comm and Tech Coll (WV)
Minnesota State Comm and Tech Coll–Fergus Falls (MN)
Mott Comm Coll (MI)
Mount Wachusett Comm Coll (MA)
Oakland Comm Coll (MI)
Owens Comm Coll, Toledo (OH)
Rogue Comm Coll (OR)
St. Petersburg Coll (FL)
South Georgia Tech Coll (GA)

Waukesha County Tech Coll (WI)
West Central Tech Coll (GA)

Marine Biology and Biological Oceanography
Dixie State Coll of Utah (UT)
Lincoln Coll (IL)
Oregon Coast Comm Coll (OR)

Marine Maintenance and Ship Repair Technology
Alexandria Tech Coll (MN)
Cape Fear Comm Coll (NC)

Marine Science/Merchant Marine Officer
Saddleback Coll (CA)

Marine Technology
Cape Fear Comm Coll (NC)
Coll of The Albemarle (NC)
Highline Comm Coll (WA)
Kingsborough Comm Coll of the City U of New York (NY)
North Idaho Coll (ID)
Orange Coast Coll (CA)
Saddleback Coll (CA)
Santa Barbara City Coll (CA)
Seattle Central Comm Coll (WA)

Marketing/Marketing Management
Abraham Baldwin Ag Coll (GA)
Aiken Tech Coll (SC)
Albany Tech Coll (GA)
Alexandria Tech Coll (MN)
Allegany Coll of Maryland (MD)
Altamaha Tech Coll (GA)
Arapahoe Comm Coll (CO)
Arizona Western Coll (AZ)
Arkansas Northeastern Coll (AR)
Athens Tech Coll (GA)
Atlanta Tech Coll (GA)
Augusta Tech Coll (GA)
Austin Comm Coll (TX)
Bainbridge Coll (GA)
Barton County Comm Coll (KS)
Berkeley Coll (NJ)
Berkeley Coll-New York City Campus (NY)
Berkeley Coll-Westchester Campus (NY)
Borough of Manhattan Comm Coll of the City U of New York (NY)
Brazosport Coll (TX)
Bristol Comm Coll (MA)
Bronx Comm Coll of the City U of New York (NY)
Broward Comm Coll (FL)
Bucks County Comm Coll (PA)
Butler Comm Coll (KS)
Butler County Comm Coll (PA)
Casper Coll (WY)
Cecil Comm Coll (MD)
Cedar Valley Coll (TX)
Central Arizona Coll (AZ)
Central Comm Coll–Columbus Campus (NE)
Central Florida Comm Coll (FL)
Central Georgia Tech Coll (GA)
Centralia Coll (WA)
Central Lakes Coll (MN)
Central Oregon Comm Coll (OR)
Central Piedmont Comm Coll (NC)
Chattahoochee Tech Coll (GA)
Cincinnati State Tech and Comm Coll (OH)
City Colls of Chicago, Wilbur Wright College (IL)
Clarendon Coll (TX)
Colby Comm Coll (KS)
Coll of DuPage (IL)
The Coll of Westchester (NY)
Colorado Mountain Coll, Alpine Campus (CO)

Comm Coll of Allegheny County (PA)
Coosa Valley Tech Coll (GA)
Cowley County Comm Coll and Area Vocational–Tech School (KS)
Cuyahoga Comm Coll (OH)
DeKalb Tech Coll (GA)
Delaware Tech & Comm Coll, Jack F. Owens Campus (DE)
Delaware Tech & Comm Coll, Stanton/Wilmington Campus (DE)
Delta Coll (MI)
East Central Coll (MO)
Eastern Idaho Tech Coll (ID)
Edmonds Comm Coll (WA)
Erie Business Center, Main (PA)
Finger Lakes Comm Coll (NY)
Florida Comm Coll at Jacksonville (FL)
Forsyth Tech Comm Coll (NC)
Fox Valley Tech Coll (WI)
Frederick Comm Coll (MD)
Genesee Comm Coll (NY)
Georgia Highlands Coll (GA)
Greenfield Comm Coll (MA)
Griffin Tech Coll (GA)
Guam Comm Coll (GU)
Gwinnett Tech Coll (GA)
Hagerstown Business Coll (MD)
Harrisburg Area Comm Coll (PA)
Hawkeye Comm Coll (IA)
Heart of Georgia Tech Coll (GA)
Highland Comm Coll (IL)
Houston Comm Coll System (TX)
Hudson Valley Comm Coll (NY)
Illinois Central Coll (IL)
Illinois Valley Comm Coll (IL)
Jackson Comm Coll (MI)
Jefferson Comm Coll (NY)
Joliet Jr Coll (IL)
Kapiolani Comm Coll (HI)
Kennebec Valley Comm Coll (ME)
Kingsborough Comm Coll of the City U of New York (NY)
Lake Land Coll (IL)
Lake Michigan Coll (MI)
Lakeshore Tech Coll (WI)
Lanier Tech Coll (GA)
Lansing Comm Coll (MI)
Laredo Comm Coll (TX)
Lehigh Valley Coll (PA)
Lincoln Coll (IL)
Lincoln Coll–Normal (IL)
Long Beach City Coll (CA)
Longview Comm Coll (MO)
Macomb Comm Coll (MI)
Manchester Comm Coll (CT)
Maple Woods Comm Coll (MO)
Meridian Comm Coll (MS)
Miami Dade Coll (FL)
Middle Georgia Tech Coll (GA)
Middlesex Comm Coll (CT)
Middlesex County Coll (NJ)
Minnesota State Comm and Tech Coll–Fergus Falls (MN)
MiraCosta Coll (CA)
Mississippi Gulf Coast Comm Coll (MS)
Moberly Area Comm Coll (MO)
Modesto Jr Coll (CA)
Moraine Park Tech Coll (WI)
Mott Comm Coll (MI)
Moultrie Tech Coll (GA)
Mt. San Antonio Coll (CA)
Nassau Comm Coll (NY)
Naugatuck Valley Comm Coll (CT)
New England Coll of Finance (MA)
New Hampshire Comm Tech Coll, Manchester/Stratham (NH)

New Hampshire Tech Inst (NH)
Normandale Comm Coll (MN)
North Central Missouri Coll (MO)
Northeast Comm Coll (NE)
Northeast Iowa Comm Coll (IA)
Northern Essex Comm Coll (MA)
North Hennepin Comm Coll (MN)
Northland Comm and Tech Coll–Thief River Falls (MN)
North Metro Tech Coll (GA)
North Shore Comm Coll (MA)
Norwalk Comm Coll (CT)
Ogeechee Tech Coll (GA)
Orange Coast Coll (CA)
Orange County Comm Coll (NY)
Ouachita Tech Coll (AR)
Owens Comm Coll, Toledo (OH)
Palm Beach Comm Coll (FL)
Palo Verde Coll (CA)
Pasadena City Coll (CA)
Pasco-Hernando Comm Coll (FL)
Pellissippi State Tech Comm Coll (TN)
Penn Valley Comm Coll (MO)
Phoenix Coll (AZ)
Piedmont Virginia Comm Coll (VA)
Polk Comm Coll (FL)
Pratt Comm Coll (KS)
Raritan Valley Comm Coll (NJ)
Rasmussen Coll Eden Prarie (MN)
Rasmussen Coll Mankato (MN)
Rock Valley Coll (IL)
Saint Charles Comm Coll (MO)
St. Cloud Tech Coll (MN)
St. Petersburg Coll (FL)
Salem Comm Coll (NJ)
Salt Lake Comm Coll (UT)
San Diego City Coll (CA)
San Diego Mesa Coll (CA)
San Joaquin Delta Coll (CA)
Santa Barbara City Coll (CA)
Sauk Valley Comm Coll (IL)
Savannah Tech Coll (GA)
Seminole Comm Coll (FL)
Sinclair Comm Coll (OH)
Southeastern Tech Coll (GA)
Southeast Tech Inst (SD)
South Georgia Tech Coll (GA)
South Hills School of Business & Technology, State College (PA)
South Plains Coll (TX)
Southwestern Illinois Coll (IL)
Southwestern Oregon Comm Coll (OR)
Southwest Mississippi Comm Coll (MS)
Spartanburg Tech Coll (SC)
Spokane Comm Coll (WA)
Spokane Falls Comm Coll (WA)
Springfield Tech Comm Coll (MA)
Stark State Coll of Technology (OH)
State U of New York Coll of Technology at Alfred (NY)
State U of New York Coll of Technology at Delhi (NY)
Sullivan County Comm Coll (NY)
Tarrant County Coll District (TX)
Three Rivers Comm Coll (MO)
Tidewater Comm Coll (VA)
Tompkins Cortland Comm Coll (NY)
Trident Tech Coll (SC)
Trinity Valley Comm Coll (TX)
Triton Coll (IL)
Tulsa Comm Coll (OK)

Tunxis Comm Coll (CT)
U of Northwestern Ohio (OH)
Valdosta Tech Coll (GA)
Valencia Comm Coll (FL)
Waukesha County Tech Coll (WI)
West Central Tech Coll (GA)
Westchester Comm Coll (NY)
Western Tech Coll (WI)
West Georgia Tech Coll (GA)
Westmoreland County Comm Coll (PA)
William Rainey Harper Coll (IL)
Williston State Coll (ND)
Wood Tobe–Coburn School (NY)
Yakima Valley Comm Coll (WA)

Marketing Related
Northeast Comm Coll (NE)
Oakland Comm Coll (MI)
Tillamook Bay Comm Coll (OR)

Marketing Research
Guam Comm Coll (GU)
Lake Region State Coll (ND)
San Diego Mesa Coll (CA)

Masonry
Alexandria Tech Coll (MN)
Florida Comm Coll at Jacksonville (FL)
Ivy Tech Comm Coll–Central Indiana (IN)
Ivy Tech Comm Coll–Columbus (IN)
Ivy Tech Comm Coll–East Central (IN)
Ivy Tech Comm Coll–Lafayette (IN)
Ivy Tech Comm Coll–North Central (IN)
Ivy Tech Comm Coll–Northeast (IN)
Ivy Tech Comm Coll–Northwest (IN)
Ivy Tech Comm Coll–Southern Indiana (IN)
Ivy Tech Comm Coll–Southwest (IN)
Ivy Tech Comm Coll–Wabash Valley (IN)
Metropolitan Comm Coll-Business & Technology College (MO)
Piedmont Virginia Comm Coll (VA)
State U of New York Coll of Technology at Alfred (NY)

Massage Therapy
Arizona Western Coll (AZ)
Career Training Academy, New Kensington (PA)
Coll of DuPage (IL)
Coll of Southern Maryland (MD)
Colorado School of Healing Arts (CO)
Comm Care Coll (OK)
Globe Coll (MN)
H. Councill Trenholm State Tech Coll (AL)
Indiana Business Coll, Indianapolis (IN)
Indiana Business Coll-Medical (IN)
IntelliTec Coll, Grand Junction (CO)
Ivy Tech Comm Coll–Northeast (IN)
Joliet Jr Coll (IL)
Lehigh Valley Coll (PA)
Mercy Coll of Northwest Ohio (OH)
Minnesota School of Business–Brooklyn Center (MN)
Minnesota School of Business–Plymouth (MN)
Minnesota School of Business–Richfield (MN)
Minnesota School of Business–St. Cloud (MN)
Minnesota School of Business–Shakopee (MN)
Mount Wachusett Comm Coll (MA)

Oakland Comm Coll (MI)
Springfield Tech Comm Coll (MA)
Utah Career Coll (UT)
Waubonsee Comm Coll (IL)

Mass Communication/Media
Asnuntuck Comm Coll (CT)
Austin Comm Coll (TX)
Bergen Comm Coll (NJ)
Bucks County Comm Coll (PA)
Bunker Hill Comm Coll (MA)
Butler Comm Coll (KS)
Butler County Comm Coll (PA)
Casper Coll (WY)
Central Comm Coll–Hastings Campus (NE)
Centralia Coll (WA)
Chattanooga State Tech Comm Coll (TN)
Colby Comm Coll (KS)
Crowder Coll (MO)
East Central Coll (MO)
Finger Lakes Comm Coll (NY)
Frederick Comm Coll (MD)
Gainesville Coll (GA)
Genesee Comm Coll (NY)
Grand Rapids Comm Coll (MI)
Greenfield Comm Coll (MA)
Harrisburg Area Comm Coll (PA)
Holyoke Comm Coll (MA)
Houston Comm Coll System (TX)
Lackawanna Coll (PA)
Lamar State Coll–Orange (TX)
Lansing Comm Coll (MI)
Laramie County Comm Coll (WY)
Lincoln Coll (IL)
Manatee Comm Coll (FL)
Mercer County Comm Coll (NJ)
Miami Dade Coll (FL)
Middlesex Comm Coll (CT)
Midland Coll (TX)
Modesto Jr Coll (CA)
Nassau Comm Coll (NY)
Niagara County Comm Coll (NY)
Northeast Comm Coll (NE)
North Idaho Coll (ID)
Northland Comm and Tech Coll–Thief River Falls (MN)
Norwalk Comm Coll (CT)
Orange Coast Coll (CA)
Palm Beach Comm Coll (FL)
Parkland Coll (IL)
Pasadena City Coll (CA)
Phoenix Coll (AZ)
Pratt Comm Coll (KS)
St. Louis Comm Coll at Florissant Valley (MO)
Salt Lake Comm Coll (UT)
Sinclair Comm Coll (OH)
Snow Coll (UT)
South Plains Coll (TX)
Spokane Falls Comm Coll (WA)
Spoon River Coll (IL)
Springfield Coll in Illinois (IL)
Tompkins Cortland Comm Coll (NY)
Treasure Valley Comm Coll (OR)
Tulsa Comm Coll (OK)
Vermilion Comm Coll (MN)
Waubonsee Comm Coll (IL)
Westchester Comm Coll (NY)
Western Tech Coll (WI)
Yuba Coll (CA)

Mass Communications
Clarendon Coll (TX)
James H. Faulkner State Comm Coll (AL)

Materials Science
Central Arizona Coll (AZ)
GateWay Comm Coll (AZ)
Mt. San Antonio Coll (CA)
Northern Essex Comm Coll (MA)
Tulsa Comm Coll (OK)

William Rainey Harper Coll (IL)

Mathematics

Abraham Baldwin Ag Coll (GA)
Allen County Comm Coll (KS)
Ancilla Coll (IN)
Arizona Western Coll (AZ)
Atlanta Metropolitan Coll (GA)
Austin Comm Coll (TX)
Bainbridge Coll (GA)
Barton County Comm Coll (KS)
Bergen Comm Coll (NJ)
Borough of Manhattan Comm Coll of the City U of New York (NY)
Brazosport Coll (TX)
Bronx Comm Coll of the City U of New York (NY)
Bucks County Comm Coll (PA)
Bunker Hill Comm Coll (MA)
Butler Comm Coll (KS)
Butler County Comm Coll (PA)
Carl Albert State Coll (OK)
Casper Coll (WY)
Cecil Comm Coll (MD)
Centralia Coll (WA)
Central Oregon Comm Coll (OR)
Chattahoochee Valley Comm Coll (AL)
Chemeketa Comm Coll (OR)
Citrus Coll (CA)
Clarendon Coll (TX)
Clovis Comm Coll (NM)
Coastal Bend Coll (TX)
Coastal Georgia Comm Coll (GA)
Cochise Coll, Douglas (AZ)
Colby Comm Coll (KS)
Coll of the Canyons (CA)
Coll of the Mainland (TX)
Coll of the Siskiyous (CA)
Colorado Mountain Coll (CO)
Colorado Mountain Coll, Alpine Campus (CO)
Columbia Coll (CA)
Comm Coll of Allegheny County (PA)
Corning Comm Coll (NY)
Crowder Coll (MO)
Dixie State Coll of Utah (UT)
East Central Coll (MO)
Eastern Arizona Coll (AZ)
Eastern Wyoming Coll (WY)
Essex County Coll (NJ)
Feather River Coll (CA)
Finger Lakes Comm Coll (NY)
Foothill Coll (CA)
Frederick Comm Coll (MD)
Gainesville Coll (GA)
Galveston Coll (TX)
Gavilan Coll (CA)
Genesee Comm Coll (NY)
Great Basin Coll (NV)
Greenfield Comm Coll (MA)
Harrisburg Area Comm Coll (PA)
Highland Comm Coll (IL)
Highline Comm Coll (WA)
Howard Coll (TX)
Hutchinson Comm Coll and Area Vocational School (KS)
Independence Comm Coll (KS)
Jefferson Comm Coll (NY)
Joliet Jr Coll (IL)
Kellogg Comm Coll (MI)
Kingsborough Comm Coll of the City U of New York (NY)
Kingwood Coll (TX)
Lamar State Coll–Orange (TX)
Lansing Comm Coll (MI)
Laramie County Comm Coll (WY)
Lawson State Comm Coll (AL)
Lincoln Coll (IL)
Linn-Benton Comm Coll (OR)

Long Beach City Coll (CA)
Louisiana State U at Alexandria (LA)
Lower Columbia Coll (WA)
Luzerne County Comm Coll (PA)
Macomb Comm Coll (MI)
Mercer County Comm Coll (NJ)
Miami Dade Coll (FL)
Middlesex County Coll (NJ)
Midland Coll (TX)
MiraCosta Coll (CA)
Modesto Jr Coll (CA)
Montgomery County Comm Coll (PA)
Nassau Comm Coll (NY)
Naugatuck Valley Comm Coll (CT)
New Mexico Military Inst (NM)
Niagara County Comm Coll (NY)
Northampton County Area Comm Coll (PA)
North Country Comm Coll (NY)
Northeast Comm Coll (NE)
North Idaho Coll (ID)
Northwestern Connecticut Comm Coll (CT)
Okaloosa-Walton Coll (FL)
Orange Coast Coll (CA)
Otero Jr Coll (CO)
Palm Beach Comm Coll (FL)
Palo Alto Coll (TX)
Pasadena City Coll (CA)
Pratt Comm Coll (KS)
Raritan Valley Comm Coll (NJ)
Roane State Comm Coll (TN)
Saddleback Coll (CA)
St. Louis Comm Coll at Florissant Valley (MO)
St. Philip's Coll (TX)
Salem Comm Coll (NJ)
San Diego City Coll (CA)
San Diego Mesa Coll (CA)
San Joaquin Delta Coll (CA)
San Juan Coll (NM)
Santa Barbara City Coll (CA)
Santa Rosa Jr Coll (CA)
Sauk Valley Comm Coll (IL)
Scottsdale Comm Coll (AZ)
Seminole State Coll (OK)
Sheridan Coll–Sheridan and Gillette (WY)
Skyline Coll (CA)
Snow Coll (UT)
Southwestern Oregon Comm Coll (OR)
Spoon River Coll (IL)
Springfield Coll in Illinois (IL)
Springfield Tech Comm Coll (MA)
State U of New York Coll of Technology at Alfred (NY)
State U of New York Coll of Technology at Delhi (NY)
Sullivan County Comm Coll (NY)
Tompkins Cortland Comm Coll (NY)
Treasure Valley Comm Coll (OR)
Trinity Valley Comm Coll (TX)
Tulsa Comm Coll (OK)
Vermilion Comm Coll (MN)
Wharton County Jr Coll (TX)
William Rainey Harper Coll (IL)
Young Harris Coll (GA)
Yuba Coll (CA)

Mathematics and Computer Science

Crowder Coll (MO)
Dean Coll (MA)

Mathematics Teacher Education

Ancilla Coll (IN)
Eastern Wyoming Coll (WY)
Frederick Comm Coll (MD)
Manatee Comm Coll (FL)

Mechanical Design Technology

Arapahoe Comm Coll (CO)
Blue Ridge Comm Coll (VA)
Butler County Comm Coll (PA)
Carroll Comm Coll (MD)
Chattanooga State Tech Comm Coll (TN)
Chemeketa Comm Coll (OR)
Coll of DuPage (IL)
Coll of The Albemarle (NC)
Comm Coll of Allegheny County (PA)
Dabney S. Lancaster Comm Coll (VA)
Delta Coll (MI)
Forsyth Tech Comm Coll (NC)
Fox Valley Tech Coll (WI)
Hawkeye Comm Coll (IA)
Heartland Comm Coll (IL)
Illinois Central Coll (IL)
Illinois Valley Comm Coll (IL)
Joliet Jr Coll (IL)
Lakeshore Tech Coll (WI)
Lansing Comm Coll (MI)
Luzerne County Comm Coll (PA)
Macomb Comm Coll (MI)
Mohawk Valley Comm Coll (NY)
Moraine Park Tech Coll (WI)
Mt. San Antonio Coll (CA)
New Hampshire Comm Tech Coll, Manchester/Stratham (NH)
Niagara County Comm Coll (NY)
Northeast Iowa Comm Coll (IA)
Owens Comm Coll, Toledo (OH)
Phoenix Coll (AZ)
Prairie State Coll (IL)
Raritan Valley Comm Coll (NJ)
Rock Valley Coll (IL)
St. Cloud Tech Coll (MN)
Spokane Comm Coll (WA)
State U of New York Coll of Technology at Alfred (NY)
Western Tech Coll (WI)
Westmoreland County Comm Coll (PA)
William Rainey Harper Coll (IL)

Mechanical Drafting

IntelliTec Coll, Grand Junction (CO)

Mechanical Drafting and Cad/Cadd

Alexandria Tech Coll (MN)
Butler County Comm Coll (PA)
Central Carolina Tech Coll (SC)
Commonwealth Tech Inst (PA)
Comm Coll of Allegheny County (PA)
Dixie State Coll of Utah (UT)
Erie Comm Coll, South Campus (NY)
Gaston Coll (NC)
Island Drafting and Tech Inst (NY)
John Wood Comm Coll (IL)
Lake Superior Coll (MN)
Macomb Comm Coll (MI)
Midlands Tech Coll (SC)
Mohawk Valley Comm Coll (NY)
Montgomery County Comm Coll (PA)
Morrison Inst of Technology (IL)
Mott Comm Coll (MI)
Normandale Comm Coll (MN)
North Seattle Comm Coll (WA)
Oakland Comm Coll (MI)
Piedmont Virginia Comm Coll (VA)
St. Cloud Tech Coll (MN)
Triangle Tech, Inc.– Greensburg School (PA)

Waukesha County Tech Coll (WI)
York Tech Coll (SC)

Mechanical Engineering

Itasca Comm Coll (MN)

Mechanical Engineering/ Mechanical Technology

Alamance Comm Coll (NC)
Augusta Tech Coll (GA)
Benjamin Franklin Inst of Technology (MA)
Broome Comm Coll (NY)
Broward Comm Coll (FL)
Cape Fear Comm Coll (NC)
Central Piedmont Comm Coll (NC)
Chattanooga State Tech Comm Coll (TN)
Cincinnati State Tech and Comm Coll (OH)
Citrus Coll (CA)
Clark State Comm Coll (OH)
Cleveland Comm Coll (NC)
Coll of Lake County (IL)
Columbus Tech Coll (GA)
Corning Comm Coll (NY)
Delaware Tech & Comm Coll, Stanton/Wilmington Campus (DE)
Delta Coll (MI)
ECPI Coll of Technology, Newport News (VA)
ECPI Coll of Technology, Virginia Beach (VA)
ECPI Tech Coll (VA)
ECPI Tech Coll, Richmond (VA)
Erie Comm Coll, North Campus (NY)
Finger Lakes Comm Coll (NY)
Fox Valley Tech Coll (WI)
Gadsden State Comm Coll (AL)
Gaston Coll (NC)
Gateway Comm Coll (CT)
Hagerstown Comm Coll (MD)
Harrisburg Area Comm Coll (PA)
Hawkeye Comm Coll (IA)
Highland Comm Coll (IL)
Hudson Valley Comm Coll (NY)
Illinois Eastern Comm Colls, Lincoln Trail College (IL)
Illinois Valley Comm Coll (IL)
Jamestown Comm Coll (NY)
Jefferson Comm and Tech Coll (KY)
Jefferson Comm Coll (OH)
John Tyler Comm Coll (VA)
Kent State U, Trumbull Campus (OH)
Kent State U, Tuscarawas Campus (OH)
Lansing Comm Coll (MI)
Lord Fairfax Comm Coll (VA)
Lower Columbia Coll (WA)
Macomb Comm Coll (MI)
Massachusetts Bay Comm Coll (MA)
Middlesex County Coll (NJ)
Midlands Tech Coll (SC)
Minnesota State Comm and Tech Coll–Fergus Falls (MN)
Mohawk Valley Comm Coll (NY)
Montgomery County Comm Coll (PA)
Moraine Valley Comm Coll (IL)
Mott Comm Coll (MI)
Naugatuck Valley Comm Coll (CT)
New Hampshire Tech Inst (NH)
Normandale Comm Coll (MN)
Owens Comm Coll, Toledo (OH)
Pasadena City Coll (CA)
Pellissippi State Tech Comm Coll (TN)
Penn Foster Career School (PA)
Pennsylvania Inst of Technology (PA)

The Pennsylvania State U DuBois Campus of the Commonwealth Coll (PA)
The Pennsylvania State U Hazleton Campus of the Commonwealth Coll (PA)
The Pennsylvania State U New Kensington Campus of the Commonwealth Coll (PA)
The Pennsylvania State U Shenango Campus of the Commonwealth Coll (PA)
The Pennsylvania State U York Campus of the Commonwealth Coll (PA)
Richmond Comm Coll (NC)
St. Louis Comm Coll at Florissant Valley (MO)
San Joaquin Delta Coll (CA)
Sauk Valley Comm Coll (IL)
Sinclair Comm Coll (OH)
Southeast Tech Inst (SD)
Southwest Tennessee Comm Coll (TN)
Spartanburg Tech Coll (SC)
Spokane Comm Coll (WA)
Springfield Tech Comm Coll (MA)
Stark State Coll of Technology (OH)
State U of New York Coll of Technology at Alfred (NY)
Tarrant County Coll District (TX)
Texas State Tech Coll Waco (TX)
Thomas Nelson Comm Coll (VA)
Trident Tech Coll (SC)
Tulsa Comm Coll (OK)
Union County Coll (NJ)
Westchester Comm Coll (NY)
Westmoreland County Comm Coll (PA)
Wichita Area Tech Coll (KS)
William Rainey Harper Coll (IL)
Wilson Tech Comm Coll (NC)
Wisconsin Indianhead Tech Coll (WI)
York Tech Coll (SC)

Mechanical Engineering Technologies Related

Pennsylvania Inst of Technology (PA)

Mechanic and Repair Technologies Related

Cincinnati State Tech and Comm Coll (OH)
Delta Coll (MI)
Ivy Tech Comm Coll– Bloomington (IN)
Ivy Tech Comm Coll– Columbus (IN)
Ivy Tech Comm Coll– Kokomo (IN)
Ivy Tech Comm Coll– Lafayette (IN)
Ivy Tech Comm Coll–North Central (IN)
Ivy Tech Comm Coll– Southwest (IN)
Macomb Comm Coll (MI)

Mechanics and Repair

Ivy Tech Comm Coll– Bloomington (IN)
Ivy Tech Comm Coll–Central Indiana (IN)
Ivy Tech Comm Coll– Columbus (IN)
Ivy Tech Comm Coll– Kokomo (IN)
Ivy Tech Comm Coll– Lafayette (IN)
Ivy Tech Comm Coll–North Central (IN)
Ivy Tech Comm Coll– Northeast (IN)
Ivy Tech Comm Coll– Northwest (IN)
Ivy Tech Comm Coll– Southern Indiana (IN)
Ivy Tech Comm Coll– Southwest (IN)
Ivy Tech Comm Coll– Wabash Valley (IN)

Ivy Tech Comm Coll– Whitewater (IN)
Santa Rosa Jr Coll (CA)
Western Oklahoma State Coll (OK)

Medical Administrative Assistant

Business Inst of Pennsylvania, Meadville (PA)
Globe Coll (MN)
Hickey Coll (MO)
Minnesota School of Business–Brooklyn Center (MN)
Minnesota School of Business–Plymouth (MN)
Minnesota School of Business–St. Cloud (MN)

Medical Administrative Assistant and Medical Secretary

Alamance Comm Coll (NC)
Alexandria Tech Coll (MN)
Barton County Comm Coll (KS)
Bay State Coll (MA)
Beal Coll (ME)
Beaufort County Comm Coll (NC)
Bergen Comm Coll (NJ)
Berkeley City Coll (CA)
Brevard Comm Coll (FL)
Briarwood Coll (CT)
Bristol Comm Coll (MA)
Bronx Comm Coll of the City U of New York (NY)
Broward Comm Coll (FL)
Brown Mackie Coll– Cincinnati (OH)
Brown Mackie Coll–Kansas City (KS)
Brown Mackie Coll–Michigan City (IN)
Bryant and Stratton Coll, Albany (NY)
Bryant and Stratton Coll, Rochester (NY)
Bryant and Stratton Coll, Rochester (NY)
Bryant and Stratton Coll, Syracuse (NY)
Bryant and Stratton Coll, Parma (OH)
Bryant and Stratton Coll (WI)
Bryant and Stratton Coll, Buffalo Campus (NY)
Bryant and Stratton Coll, Lackawanna Campus (NY)
Bryant and Stratton Coll, Richmond (VA)
Butler Comm Coll (KS)
Butler County Comm Coll (PA)
Cambria-Rowe Business Coll, Johnstown (PA)
Carl Albert State Coll (OK)
Central Arizona Coll (AZ)
Central Comm Coll–Hastings Campus (NE)
Centralia Coll (WA)
Central Lakes Coll (MN)
Central Piedmont Comm Coll (NC)
Century Coll (MN)
Chattanooga State Tech Comm Coll (TN)
Chemeketa Comm Coll (OR)
Clark Coll (WA)
Clark State Comm Coll (OH)
Clatsop Comm Coll (OR)
Cleveland Comm Coll (NC)
Clovis Comm Coll (NM)
Coastal Carolina Comm Coll (NC)
Coll of The Albemarle (NC)
The Coll of Westchester (NY)
Comm Coll of Allegheny County (PA)
Consolidated School of Business, Lancaster (PA)
Consolidated School of Business, York (PA)
Crowder Coll (MO)
Dabney S. Lancaster Comm Coll (VA)
Davis Coll (OH)

Delaware Tech & Comm Coll, Jack F. Owens Campus (DE)
Delaware Tech & Comm Coll, Stanton/Wilmington Campus (DE)
Delta Coll (MI)
East Central Coll (MO)
ECPI Coll of Technology, Newport News (VA)
ECPI Coll of Technology, Virginia Beach (VA)
ECPI Tech Coll (VA)
ECPI Tech Coll, Richmond (VA)
Edmonds Comm Coll (WA)
El Centro Coll (TX)
Elmira Business Inst (NY)
Erie Business Center, Main (PA)
Essex County Coll (NJ)
Florida National Coll (FL)
Florida Tech Coll, DeLand (FL)
Frederick Comm Coll (MD)
Gallipolis Career Coll (OH)
Gateway Comm Coll (CT)
George C. Wallace Comm Coll (AL)
Goodwin Coll (CT)
Grand Rapids Comm Coll (MI)
Hagerstown Business Coll (MD)
Hawkeye Comm Coll (IA)
Heald Coll–Fresno (CA)
Heald Coll–Hayward (CA)
Heald Coll–Honolulu (HI)
Heald Coll–Portland (OR)
Heald Coll–Rancho Cordova (CA)
Heald Coll–Salinas (CA)
Heald Coll–San Francisco (CA)
Hibbing Comm Coll (MN)
Houston Comm Coll System (TX)
Howard Comm Coll (MD)
Illinois Eastern Comm Colls, Olney Central College (IL)
IntelliTec Coll, Grand Junction (CO)
Jefferson Comm Coll (NY)
Jefferson Comm Coll (OH)
Johnston Comm Coll (NC)
John Wood Comm Coll (IL)
Joliet Jr Coll (IL)
Kellogg Comm Coll (MI)
Lackawanna Coll (PA)
Lake Land Coll (IL)
Lake Michigan Coll (MI)
Lake Region State Coll (ND)
Lakeshore Tech Coll (WI)
Lake Superior Coll (MN)
Lamar State Coll–Port Arthur (TX)
Laurel Business Inst (PA)
Lehigh Valley Coll (PA)
Lincoln Coll–Normal (IL)
Linn-Benton Comm Coll (OR)
Long Beach City Coll (CA)
Longview Comm Coll (MO)
Lower Columbia Coll (WA)
Luzerne County Comm Coll (PA)
Manchester Comm Coll (CT)
Manor Coll (PA)
Maple Woods Comm Coll (MO)
Metro Business Coll, Jefferson City (MO)
Middlesex Comm Coll (CT)
Minnesota State Comm and Tech Coll–Fergus Falls (MN)
Minnesota West Comm and Tech Coll (MN)
Mott Comm Coll (MI)
Mt. San Antonio Coll (CA)
Nassau Comm Coll (NY)
Naugatuck Valley Comm Coll (CT)
New Hampshire Comm Tech Coll, Manchester/Stratham (NH)
Newport Business Inst, Lower Burrell (PA)
Newport Business Inst, Williamsport (PA)

Normandale Comm Coll (MN)
Northampton County Area Comm Coll (PA)
Northeast Comm Coll (NE)
Northern Essex Comm Coll (MA)
Northern Maine Comm Coll (ME)
North Idaho Coll (ID)
North Shore Comm Coll (MA)
Ohio Business Coll, Sandusky (OH)
Orange Coast Coll (CA)
Otero Jr Coll (CO)
Ouachita Tech Coll (AR)
Penn Valley Comm Coll (MO)
Phoenix Coll (AZ)
Polk Comm Coll (FL)
Rasmussen Coll Eden Prarie (MN)
Rasmussen Coll Mankato (MN)
Richland Comm Coll (IL)
Riverland Comm Coll (MN)
Roane State Comm Coll (TN)
Rockingham Comm Coll (NC)
St. Cloud Tech Coll (MN)
Saint Paul Coll–A Comm & Tech College (MN)
St. Philip's Coll (TX)
San Joaquin Valley Coll (CA)
Scottsdale Comm Coll (AZ)
Shelton State Comm Coll (AL)
Sinclair Comm Coll (OH)
South Hills School of Business & Technology, State College (PA)
South Plains Coll (TX)
Southwestern Illinois Coll (IL)
Spartanburg Tech Coll (SC)
Spokane Comm Coll (WA)
Spoon River Coll (IL)
Springfield Tech Comm Coll (MA)
Tomball Coll (TX)
Treasure Valley Comm Coll (OR)
Trident Tech Coll (SC)
Tulsa Comm Coll (OK)
Tunxis Comm Coll (CT)
United Tribes Tech Coll (ND)
The U of Akron–Wayne Coll (OH)
U of Northwestern Ohio (OH)
Valencia Comm Coll (FL)
Vance-Granville Comm Coll (NC)
Vatterott Coll, Tulsa (OK)
Vermilion Comm Coll (MN)
Western Iowa Tech Comm Coll (IA)
Western Tech Coll (WI)
Westmoreland County Comm Coll (PA)
William Rainey Harper Coll (IL)
Wisconsin Indianhead Tech Coll (WI)
Yakima Valley Comm Coll (WA)
York Tech Coll (SC)

Medical/Clinical Assistant
Alamance Comm Coll (NC)
Allan Hancock Coll (CA)
Arapahoe Comm Coll (CO)
Argosy U/Denver (CO)
Argosy U/Orange County (CA)
Argosy U/San Diego (CA)
Austin Comm Coll (TX)
Barton County Comm Coll (KS)
Bay State Coll (MA)
Beal Coll (ME)
Bergen Comm Coll (NJ)
Berks Tech Inst (PA)
Brevard Comm Coll (FL)
Briarwood Coll (CT)
Broome Comm Coll (NY)
Broward Comm Coll (FL)
Brown Mackie Coll–Akron (OH)

Brown Mackie Coll–Cincinnati (OH)
Brown Mackie Coll–Findlay (OH)
Brown Mackie Coll–Fort Wayne (IN)
Brown Mackie Coll–Hopkinsville (KY)
Brown Mackie Coll–Kansas City (KS)
Brown Mackie Coll–Louisville (KY)
Brown Mackie Coll–Merrillville (IN)
Brown Mackie Coll–Miami (FL)
Brown Mackie Coll–Michigan City (IN)
Brown Mackie Coll–North Canton (OH)
Brown Mackie Coll–Northern Kentucky (KY)
Brown Mackie Coll–South Bend (IN)
Bryant and Stratton Coll, Albany (NY)
Bryant and Stratton Coll, Rochester (NY)
Bryant and Stratton Coll, Rochester (NY)
Bryant and Stratton Coll, Syracuse (NY)
Bryant and Stratton Coll, Parma (OH)
Bryant and Stratton Coll (WI)
Bryant and Stratton Coll, Buffalo Campus (NY)
Bryant and Stratton Coll, Lackawanna Campus (NY)
Bryant and Stratton Coll, Richmond (VA)
Bucks County Comm Coll (PA)
Butler County Comm Coll (PA)
Capital Comm Coll (CT)
Career Coll of Northern Nevada (NV)
Career Training Academy, New Kensington (PA)
Carteret Comm Coll (NC)
Central Comm Coll–Hastings Campus (NE)
Central Oregon Comm Coll (OR)
Central Piedmont Comm Coll (NC)
Century Coll (MN)
Chemeketa Comm Coll (OR)
Cincinnati State Tech and Comm Coll (OH)
Clark Coll (WA)
Coll of Business and Technology (FL)
Comm Care Coll (OK)
Comm Coll of Allegheny County (PA)
Cossatot Comm Coll of the U of Arkansas (AR)
Davis Coll (OH)
DeKalb Tech Coll (GA)
Delaware Tech & Comm Coll, Jack F. Owens Campus (DE)
Delta Coll (MI)
Eastern Idaho Tech Coll (ID)
ECPI Tech Coll (VA)
ECPI Tech Coll (NC)
El Centro Coll (TX)
Erie Business Center, Main (PA)
Everest Coll (AZ)
Florida National Coll (FL)
Florida Tech Coll, DeLand (FL)
Forsyth Tech Comm Coll (NC)
Gaston Coll (NC)
George C. Wallace Comm Coll (AL)
Globe Coll (MN)
Goodwin Coll (CT)
Guam Comm Coll (GU)
Gwinnett Tech Coll (GA)
Hagerstown Business Coll (MD)
Hamilton Coll, Cedar Falls (IA)
Hamilton Coll, Cedar Rapids (IA)

H. Councill Trenholm State Tech Coll (AL)
Highline Comm Coll (WA)
Indiana Business Coll, Anderson (IN)
Indiana Business Coll, Columbus (IN)
Indiana Business Coll, Evansville (IN)
Indiana Business Coll, Fort Wayne (IN)
Indiana Business Coll, Indianapolis (IN)
Indiana Business Coll, Indianapolis (IN)
Indiana Business Coll, Indianapolis (IN)
Indiana Business Coll, Lafayette (IN)
Indiana Business Coll, Marion (IN)
Indiana Business Coll, Terre Haute (IN)
Indiana Business Coll-Medical (IN)
International Business Coll, Indianapolis (IN)
Ivy Tech Comm Coll–Central Indiana (IN)
Ivy Tech Comm Coll–Columbus (IN)
Ivy Tech Comm Coll–East Central (IN)
Ivy Tech Comm Coll–Kokomo (IN)
Ivy Tech Comm Coll–Lafayette (IN)
Ivy Tech Comm Coll–North Central (IN)
Ivy Tech Comm Coll–Northeast (IN)
Ivy Tech Comm Coll–Northwest (IN)
Ivy Tech Comm Coll–Southeast (IN)
Ivy Tech Comm Coll–Southern Indiana (IN)
Ivy Tech Comm Coll–Southwest (IN)
Ivy Tech Comm Coll–Wabash Valley (IN)
Ivy Tech Comm Coll–Whitewater (IN)
Jackson Comm Coll (MI)
James Sprunt Comm Coll (NC)
Jefferson Comm Coll (OH)
Johnston Comm Coll (NC)
Kapiolani Comm Coll (HI)
Kennebec Valley Comm Coll (ME)
Lac Courte Oreilles Ojibwa Comm Coll (WI)
Lansing Comm Coll (MI)
Laredo Comm Coll (TX)
Laurel Business Inst (PA)
Linn-Benton Comm Coll (OR)
Long Beach City Coll (CA)
Lower Columbia Coll (WA)
Macomb Comm Coll (MI)
Marshall Comm and Tech Coll (WV)
Miami Dade Coll (FL)
Midlands Tech Coll (SC)
Minnesota School of Business–Richfield (MN)
Minnesota West Comm and Tech Coll (MN)
Modesto Jr Coll (CA)
Mohawk Valley Comm Coll (NY)
Montgomery Comm Coll (NC)
Moraine Park Tech Coll (WI)
Mountain State Coll (WV)
Mount Wachusett Comm Coll (MA)
Newport Business Inst, Lower Burrell (PA)
Niagara County Comm Coll (NY)
North Central Missouri Coll (MO)
Northeast State Tech Comm Coll (TN)
North Iowa Area Comm Coll (IA)
North Seattle Comm Coll (WA)

Northwestern Connecticut Comm Coll (CT)
Oakland Comm Coll (MI)
Ocean County Coll (NJ)
Orange Coast Coll (CA)
Pasadena City Coll (CA)
Phoenix Coll (AZ)
Pioneer Pacific Coll (OR)
Quinebaug Valley Comm Coll (CT)
Rasmussen Coll Mankato (MN)
Remington Coll–Lafayette Campus (LA)
Richmond Comm Coll (NC)
Rockingham Comm Coll (NC)
Saddleback Coll (CA)
Salt Lake Comm Coll (UT)
San Diego Mesa Coll (CA)
San Joaquin Valley Coll (CA)
Sinclair Comm Coll (OH)
Southern State Comm Coll (OH)
South U, West Palm Beach (FL)
Southwestern Illinois Coll (IL)
Southwestern Oregon Comm Coll (OR)
Southwest Florida Coll, Fort Myers (FL)
Southwest Tennessee Comm Coll (TN)
Springfield Tech Comm Coll (MA)
Stark State Coll of Technology (OH)
TESST Coll of Technology, Towson (MD)
Tri-County Comm Coll (NC)
Tulsa Comm Coll (OK)
Union County Coll (NJ)
U of Northwestern Ohio (OH)
Utah Career Coll (UT)
Vance-Granville Comm Coll (NC)
Vatterott Coll (IA)
Ventura Coll (CA)
Waubonsee Comm Coll (IL)
Wilkes Comm Coll (NC)
William Rainey Harper Coll (IL)
Wood Tobe–Coburn School (NY)
York Tech Coll (SC)

Medical Insurance Coding
Alexandria Tech Coll (MN)
Goodwin Coll (CT)
Indiana Business Coll, Evansville (IN)
Indiana Business Coll, Indianapolis (IN)
Indiana Business Coll, Indianapolis (IN)
Indiana Business Coll, Lafayette (IN)
Indiana Business Coll, Marion (IN)
Indiana Business Coll-Medical (IN)
Kilian Comm Coll (SD)
Springfield Tech Comm Coll (MA)

Medical Insurance/Medical Billing
Goodwin Coll (CT)
Indiana Business Coll, Anderson (IN)
Indiana Business Coll, Columbus (IN)
Indiana Business Coll, Evansville (IN)
Indiana Business Coll, Fort Wayne (IN)
Indiana Business Coll, Indianapolis (IN)
Indiana Business Coll, Indianapolis (IN)
Indiana Business Coll, Lafayette (IN)
Indiana Business Coll, Terre Haute (IN)
Indiana Business Coll-Medical (IN)
Jackson Comm Coll (MI)
San Joaquin Valley Coll (CA)

Medical Laboratory Technology
Athens Tech Coll (GA)
Cecil Comm Coll (MD)
Central Georgia Tech Coll (GA)
Chattahoochee Tech Coll (GA)
DeKalb Tech Coll (GA)
Delaware Tech & Comm Coll, Jack F. Owens Campus (DE)
Flint River Tech Coll (GA)
Florida Comm Coll at Jacksonville (FL)
Frederick Comm Coll (MD)
Indiana Business Coll, Indianapolis (IN)
Jefferson Comm Coll (NY)
Lanier Tech Coll (GA)
Minnesota State Comm and Tech Coll–Fergus Falls (MN)
Mohawk Valley Comm Coll (NY)
North Georgia Tech Coll (GA)
North Hennepin Comm Coll (MN)
Northwest-Shoals Comm Coll (AL)
The Ohio State U Ag Tech Inst (OH)
Phoenix Coll (AZ)
Southeastern Tech Coll (GA)
Southwest Georgia Tech Coll (GA)
Valdosta Tech Coll (GA)
West Central Tech Coll (GA)

Medical Office Assistant
Asnuntuck Comm Coll (CT)
Business Inst of Pennsylvania, Meadville (PA)
Clovis Comm Coll (NM)
Commonwealth Tech Inst (PA)
Harrisburg Area Comm Coll (PA)
Indiana Business Coll, Muncie (IN)
Keiser Coll, Miami (FL)
Lake Michigan Coll (MI)
Sauk Valley Comm Coll (IL)

Medical Office Management
Beaufort County Comm Coll (NC)
Briarwood Coll (CT)
Brown Mackie Coll–Findlay (OH)
Brown Mackie Coll–Merrillville (IN)
Brown Mackie Coll–Salina (KS)
Coll of Lake County (IL)
Columbus Tech Coll (GA)
Coosa Valley Tech Coll (GA)
Erie Comm Coll, North Campus (NY)
Fayetteville Tech Comm Coll (NC)
Florida Comm Coll at Jacksonville (FL)
Gaston Coll (NC)
Kilian Comm Coll (SD)
Minnesota School of Business–Richfield (MN)
MTI Coll of Business and Technology (CA)
Newport Business Inst, Lower Burrell (PA)
Ohio Inst of Photography and Technology (OH)
Pennsylvania Inst of Technology (PA)
St. Cloud Tech Coll (MN)
San Joaquin Valley Coll (CA)
Schuylkill Inst of Business and Technology (PA)
The U of Akron–Wayne Coll (OH)
Vatterott Coll (IA)

Medical Physiology
Comm Coll of the Air Force (AL)

Medical Radiologic Technology
Albany Tech Coll (GA)

Allegany Coll of Maryland (MD)
Athens Tech Coll (GA)
Augusta Tech Coll (GA)
Broome Comm Coll (NY)
Bunker Hill Comm Coll (MA)
Caldwell Comm Coll and Tech Inst (NC)
Cape Fear Comm Coll (NC)
Capital Comm Coll (CT)
Central Georgia Tech Coll (GA)
Century Coll (MN)
Chattahoochee Tech Coll (GA)
City Colls of Chicago, Wilbur Wright College (IL)
Cleveland Comm Coll (NC)
Clovis Comm Coll (NM)
Coastal Georgia Comm Coll (GA)
Coll of DuPage (IL)
Coll of Lake County (IL)
Columbus Tech Coll (GA)
Comm Coll of Allegheny County (PA)
Comm Coll of the Air Force (AL)
Delgado Comm Coll (LA)
El Centro Coll (TX)
Erie Comm Coll (NY)
Essex County Coll (NJ)
Florida Comm Coll at Jacksonville (FL)
Foothill Coll (CA)
Gadsden State Comm Coll (AL)
Galveston Coll (TX)
GateWay Comm Coll (AZ)
Griffin Tech Coll (GA)
Gwinnett Tech Coll (GA)
Hagerstown Comm Coll (MD)
Harrisburg Area Comm Coll (PA)
Heart of Georgia Tech Coll (GA)
Houston Comm Coll System (TX)
Hutchinson Comm Coll and Area Vocational School (KS)
Illinois Eastern Comm Colls, Olney Central College (IL)
Ivy Tech Comm Coll–Central Indiana (IN)
Ivy Tech Comm Coll–Columbus (IN)
Ivy Tech Comm Coll–East Central (IN)
Ivy Tech Comm Coll–Wabash Valley (IN)
Jackson Comm Coll (MI)
Jackson State Comm Coll (TN)
Jefferson Comm and Tech Coll (KY)
Jefferson State Comm Coll (AL)
Johnston Comm Coll (NC)
John Wood Comm Coll (IL)
Kaskaskia Coll (IL)
Kellogg Comm Coll (MI)
Keystone Coll (PA)
Lake Michigan Coll (MI)
Lake Superior Coll (MN)
Lanier Tech Coll (GA)
Lansing Comm Coll (MI)
Lincoln Land Comm Coll (IL)
Louisiana State U at Alexandria (LA)
Manatee Comm Coll (FL)
Marshall Comm and Tech Coll (WV)
Massachusetts Bay Comm Coll (MA)
Mercer County Comm Coll (NJ)
Mercy Coll of Northwest Ohio (OH)
Meridian Comm Coll (MS)
Middle Georgia Tech Coll (GA)
Midland Coll (TX)
Midlands Tech Coll (SC)
Mohawk Valley Comm Coll (NY)
Montgomery County Comm Coll (PA)
Moraine Park Tech Coll (WI)

Moraine Valley Comm Coll (IL)
Mott Comm Coll (MI)
Nassau Comm Coll (NY)
Normandale Comm Coll (MN)
North Arkansas Coll (AR)
North Country Comm Coll (NY)
North Metro Tech Coll (GA)
North Shore Comm Coll (MA)
Oakland Comm Coll (MI)
Parkland Coll (IL)
The Pennsylvania State U New Kensington Campus of the Commonwealth Coll (PA)
Pima Comm Coll (AZ)
Quinsigamond Comm Coll (MA)
Riverland Comm Coll (MN)
St. Philip's Coll (TX)
Santa Barbara City Coll (CA)
South Arkansas Comm Coll (AR)
Southeastern Tech Coll (GA)
Southwestern Oklahoma State U at Sayre (OK)
Southwest Georgia Tech Coll (GA)
Southwest Tennessee Comm Coll (TN)
Spartanburg Tech Coll (SC)
Springfield Tech Comm Coll (MA)
Union County Coll (NJ)
Valdosta Tech Coll (GA)
Valencia Comm Coll (FL)
Volunteer State Comm Coll (TN)
West Central Tech Coll (GA)
Western Oklahoma State Coll (OK)
West Georgia Tech Coll (GA)
Wor-Wic Comm Coll (MD)
York Tech Coll (SC)

Medical Reception
Alexandria Tech Coll (MN)
Edmonds Comm Coll (WA)
Lower Columbia Coll (WA)

Medical Staff Services Technology
Front Range Comm Coll (CO)

Medical Transcription
Alexandria Tech Coll (MN)
Brown Mackie Coll–Salina (KS)
Central Arizona Coll (AZ)
El Centro Coll (TX)
Erie Business Center, Main (PA)
Jackson Comm Coll (MI)
Kilian Comm Coll (SD)
Laurel Business Inst (PA)
Lower Columbia Coll (WA)
Marshall Comm and Tech Coll (WV)
Moraine Park Tech Coll (WI)
Mountain State Coll (WV)
Northern Essex Comm Coll (MA)
Oakland Comm Coll (MI)
Saint Charles Comm Coll (MO)
Southeast Tech Inst (SD)
Ventura Coll (CA)
Williston State Coll (ND)

Mental and Social Health Services And Allied Professions Related
Broome Comm Coll (NY)
Edmonds Comm Coll (WA)
Oakland Comm Coll (MI)
Waukesha County Tech Coll (WI)

Mental Health/Rehabilitation
Comm Coll of the Air Force (AL)
Evergreen Valley Coll (CA)
Fiorello H. LaGuardia Comm Coll of the City U of New York (NY)
Gateway Comm Coll (CT)
Houston Comm Coll System (TX)

Kingsborough Comm Coll of the City U of New York (NY)
Lackawanna Coll (PA)
Macomb Comm Coll (MI)
Metropolitan Comm Coll (NE)
Middlesex Comm Coll (CT)
Mohawk Valley Comm Coll (NY)
Mt. San Antonio Coll (CA)
Naugatuck Valley Comm Coll (CT)
New Hampshire Tech Inst (NH)
North Country Comm Coll (NY)
Northern Essex Comm Coll (MA)
North Shore Comm Coll (MA)
Orange County Comm Coll (NY)
Prairie State Coll (IL)
Sinclair Comm Coll (OH)
South Plains Coll (TX)
Tarrant County Coll District (TX)

Merchandising
Coll of DuPage (IL)
Cuyahoga Comm Coll (OH)
Delta Coll (MI)

Merchandising, Sales, and Marketing Operations Related (General)
Broome Comm Coll (NY)
Minnesota State Comm and Tech Coll–Fergus Falls (MN)
Southwestern Michigan Coll (MI)
Wisconsin Indianhead Tech Coll (WI)

Metal and Jewelry Arts
Coll of The Albemarle (NC)
Pasadena City Coll (CA)

Metallurgical Technology
Arkansas Northeastern Coll (AR)
Comm Coll of the Air Force (AL)
Linn-Benton Comm Coll (OR)
Macomb Comm Coll (MI)
Mohawk Valley Comm Coll (NY)
The Pennsylvania State U DuBois Campus of the Commonwealth Coll (PA)
The Pennsylvania State U Fayette Campus of the Commonwealth Coll (PA)
The Pennsylvania State U Hazleton Campus of the Commonwealth Coll (PA)
The Pennsylvania State U New Kensington Campus of the Commonwealth Coll (PA)
The Pennsylvania State U Shenango Campus of the Commonwealth Coll (PA)
The Pennsylvania State U Wilkes-Barre Campus of the Commonwealth Coll (PA)
The Pennsylvania State U York Campus of the Commonwealth Coll (PA)
Southwestern Illinois Coll (IL)

Mexican-American Studies
Pasadena City Coll (CA)

Middle School Education
Arkansas Northeastern Coll (AR)
Arkansas State U–Mountain Home (AR)
Gainesville Coll (GA)
Lincoln Coll (IL)
Miami Dade Coll (FL)
North Arkansas Coll (AR)

Military Studies
Barton County Comm Coll (KS)

Military Technologies
Cochise Coll, Douglas (AZ)

Comm Coll of the Air Force (AL)

Mining Technology
Coll of Eastern Utah (UT)
Eastern Arizona Coll (AZ)
Illinois Eastern Comm Colls, Wabash Valley College (IL)
Southwest Virginia Comm Coll (VA)

Modern Languages
Barton County Comm Coll (KS)
Citrus Coll (CA)
City Colls of Chicago, Wilbur Wright College (IL)
Galveston Coll (TX)
Independence Comm Coll (KS)
Middlesex County Coll (NJ)
Midland Coll (TX)
Okaloosa-Walton Coll (FL)
Otero Jr Coll (CO)
Palo Alto Coll (TX)
Pasadena City Coll (CA)
San Diego City Coll (CA)

Multi-/Interdisciplinary Studies Related
Central Carolina Tech Coll (SC)
Eastern West Virginia Comm and Tech Coll (WV)
Hamilton Coll, Cedar Falls (IA)
Laramie County Comm Coll (WY)
Linn-Benton Comm Coll (OR)
Marshall Comm and Tech Coll (WV)
Midlands Tech Coll (SC)
Mid-South Comm Coll (AR)
Northwest-Shoals Comm Coll (AL)
Waukesha County Tech Coll (WI)
Williston State Coll (ND)
York Tech Coll (SC)

Music
Abraham Baldwin Ag Coll (GA)
Allan Hancock Coll (CA)
Allen County Comm Coll (KS)
Arizona Western Coll (AZ)
Atlanta Metropolitan Coll (GA)
Austin Comm Coll (TX)
Barton County Comm Coll (KS)
Bergen Comm Coll (NJ)
Berkshire Comm Coll (MA)
Brazosport Coll (TX)
Bronx Comm Coll of the City U of New York (NY)
Bucks County Comm Coll (PA)
Butler Comm Coll (KS)
Caldwell Comm Coll and Tech Inst (NC)
Carl Albert State Coll (OK)
Carroll Comm Coll (MD)
Casper Coll (WY)
Cedar Valley Coll (TX)
Centralia Coll (WA)
Central Piedmont Comm Coll (NC)
Central Wyoming Coll (WY)
Chattahoochee Valley Comm Coll (AL)
Citrus Coll (CA)
City Colls of Chicago, Wilbur Wright College (IL)
Clarendon Coll (TX)
Coastal Bend Coll (TX)
Colby Comm Coll (KS)
Coll of Lake County (IL)
Coll of Southern Maryland (MD)
Coll of The Albemarle (NC)
Coll of the Mainland (TX)
Columbia Coll (CA)
Comm Coll of Allegheny County (PA)
Cowley County Comm Coll and Area Vocational–Tech School (KS)
Crowder Coll (MO)
Delgado Comm Coll (LA)

Dixie State Coll of Utah (UT)
Eastern Arizona Coll (AZ)
Eastern Wyoming Coll (WY)
Essex County Coll (NJ)
Finger Lakes Comm Coll (NY)
Foothill Coll (CA)
Gainesville Coll (GA)
Galveston Coll (TX)
Gavilan Coll (CA)
Grand Rapids Comm Coll (MI)
Harrisburg Area Comm Coll (PA)
Highline Comm Coll (WA)
Holyoke Comm Coll (MA)
Howard Comm Coll (MD)
Illinois Eastern Comm Colls, Lincoln Trail College (IL)
Illinois Eastern Comm Colls, Olney Central College (IL)
Independence Comm Coll (KS)
Kellogg Comm Coll (MI)
Kingsborough Comm Coll of the City U of New York (NY)
Lansing Comm Coll (MI)
Laramie County Comm Coll (WY)
Lawson State Comm Coll (AL)
Lincoln Coll (IL)
Lincoln Land Comm Coll (IL)
Long Beach City Coll (CA)
Lower Columbia Coll (WA)
Manatee Comm Coll (FL)
Manchester Comm Coll (CT)
McNally Smith Coll of Music (MN)
Mercer County Comm Coll (NJ)
Miami Dade Coll (FL)
Middlesex County Coll (NJ)
Midland Coll (TX)
MiraCosta Coll (CA)
Modesto Jr Coll (CA)
Naugatuck Valley Comm Coll (CT)
Niagara County Comm Coll (NY)
Northeast Comm Coll (NE)
Northern Essex Comm Coll (MA)
North Idaho Coll (ID)
North Seattle Comm Coll (WA)
Okaloosa-Walton Coll (FL)
Orange Coast Coll (CA)
Palm Beach Comm Coll (FL)
Palo Alto Coll (TX)
Pasadena City Coll (CA)
Pima Comm Coll (AZ)
Pratt Comm Coll (KS)
Raritan Valley Comm Coll (NJ)
Saddleback Coll (CA)
St. Louis Comm Coll at Florissant Valley (MO)
St. Philip's Coll (TX)
Salt Lake Comm Coll (UT)
San Diego City Coll (CA)
San Diego Mesa Coll (CA)
San Joaquin Delta Coll (CA)
San Juan Coll (NM)
Santa Barbara City Coll (CA)
Santa Rosa Jr Coll (CA)
Sauk Valley Comm Coll (IL)
Sheridan Coll–Sheridan and Gillette (WY)
Sinclair Comm Coll (OH)
Skyline Coll (CA)
Snow Coll (UT)
Southeastern Comm Coll (NC)
South Plains Coll (TX)
Southwest Mississippi Comm Coll (MS)
Southwest Virginia Comm Coll (VA)
Spokane Falls Comm Coll (WA)
Three Rivers Comm Coll (MO)
Tidewater Comm Coll (VA)
Treasure Valley Comm Coll (OR)
Trinidad State Jr Coll (CO)
Trinity Valley Comm Coll (TX)

Triton Coll (IL)
Truett-McConnell Coll (GA)
Tulsa Comm Coll (OK)
Ventura Coll (CA)
Vermilion Comm Coll (MN)
Villa Maria Coll of Buffalo (NY)
Waubonsee Comm Coll (IL)
Wharton County Jr Coll (TX)
William Rainey Harper Coll (IL)
Young Harris Coll (GA)
Yuba Coll (CA)

Musical Instrument Fabrication and Repair
Orange Coast Coll (CA)

Music History, Literature, and Theory
Lincoln Coll (IL)
Snow Coll (UT)

Music Management and Merchandising
Century Coll (MN)
Collin County Comm Coll District (TX)
Houston Comm Coll System (TX)
Independence Comm Coll (KS)
Lincoln Coll (IL)
McNally Smith Coll of Music (MN)
Northeast Comm Coll (NE)
Orange Coast Coll (CA)
Villa Maria Coll of Buffalo (NY)

Music Performance
Butler Comm Coll (KS)
Comm Coll of the Air Force (AL)
Macomb Comm Coll (MI)
Manatee Comm Coll (FL)
McNally Smith Coll of Music (MN)
Miami Dade Coll (FL)
Nassau Comm Coll (NY)
Northeast Comm Coll (NE)
Parkland Coll (IL)

Music Related
Globe Coll (MN)
KD Studio (TX)
Minnesota School of Business–Brooklyn Center (MN)
Minnesota School of Business–Plymouth (MN)
Minnesota School of Business–Richfield (MN)
Minnesota School of Business–St. Cloud (MN)
Minnesota School of Business–Shakopee (MN)
Young Harris Coll (GA)

Music Teacher Education
Casper Coll (WY)
Chattahoochee Valley Comm Coll (AL)
Coastal Bend Coll (TX)
Colby Comm Coll (KS)
Coll of Lake County (IL)
Copiah-Lincoln Comm Coll (MS)
Eastern Wyoming Coll (WY)
Frederick Comm Coll (MD)
Highland Comm Coll (IL)
Howard Coll (TX)
Illinois Eastern Comm Colls, Lincoln Trail College (IL)
Illinois Eastern Comm Colls, Olney Central College (IL)
Independence Comm Coll (KS)
Manatee Comm Coll (FL)
Miami Dade Coll (FL)
Midland Coll (TX)
Northeast Comm Coll (NE)
North Idaho Coll (ID)
Parkland Coll (IL)
Roane State Comm Coll (TN)
Snow Coll (UT)
Southwest Mississippi Comm Coll (MS)
Treasure Valley Comm Coll (OR)
Tulsa Comm Coll (OK)
Waubonsee Comm Coll (IL)

Young Harris Coll (GA)

Music Theory and Composition
Houston Comm Coll System (TX)
Manatee Comm Coll (FL)

Music Therapy
Pasadena City Coll (CA)

Nail Technician and Manicurist
Clovis Comm Coll (NM)

Natural Resources and Conservation Related
Palau Comm CollPalau)

Natural Resources/ Conservation
Dixie State Coll of Utah (UT)
Finger Lakes Comm Coll (NY)
Fox Valley Tech Coll (WI)
Itasca Comm Coll (MN)
Niagara County Comm Coll (NY)
Santa Rosa Jr Coll (CA)
Vermilion Comm Coll (MN)

Natural Resources Management
Feather River Coll (CA)
Finger Lakes Comm Coll (NY)
The Ohio State U Ag Tech Inst (OH)

Natural Resources Management and Policy
Central Carolina Tech Coll (SC)
Coll of Lake County (IL)
Columbia Coll (CA)
Dixie State Coll of Utah (UT)
Finger Lakes Comm Coll (NY)
Greenfield Comm Coll (MA)
Hawkeye Comm Coll (IA)
Itasca Comm Coll (MN)
Lac Courte Oreilles Ojibwa Comm Coll (WI)
Lord Fairfax Comm Coll (VA)
The Ohio State U Ag Tech Inst (OH)
San Joaquin Delta Coll (CA)
Santa Rosa Jr Coll (CA)
Snow Coll (UT)
Spokane Comm Coll (WA)
Treasure Valley Comm Coll (OR)
Trinidad State Jr Coll (CO)
Ventura Coll (CA)
Vermilion Comm Coll (MN)

Natural Sciences
Centralia Coll (WA)
Citrus Coll (CA)
Coll of the Canyons (CA)
Coll of the Mainland (TX)
Colorado Mountain Coll (CO)
Galveston Coll (TX)
Gavilan Coll (CA)
Highline Comm Coll (WA)
Independence Comm Coll (KS)
Jefferson Comm Coll (NY)
Miami Dade Coll (FL)
Naugatuck Valley Comm Coll (CT)
Orange Coast Coll (CA)
Saddleback Coll (CA)
San Joaquin Delta Coll (CA)
Snow Coll (UT)
Southwestern Oregon Comm Coll (OR)
U of Pittsburgh at Titusville (PA)
Young Harris Coll (GA)

Non-Profit Management
Miami Dade Coll (FL)

Nuclear Engineering
Itasca Comm Coll (MN)

Nuclear Medical Technology
Bronx Comm Coll of the City U of New York (NY)
Broward Comm Coll (FL)
Caldwell Comm Coll and Tech Inst (NC)
Chattanooga State Tech Comm Coll (TN)

Coll of DuPage (IL)
Comm Coll of Allegheny County (PA)
Comm Coll of the Air Force (AL)
Delaware Tech & Comm Coll, Stanton/Wilmington Campus (DE)
Fayetteville Tech Comm Coll (NC)
Forsyth Tech Comm Coll (NC)
Frederick Comm Coll (MD)
Galveston Coll (TX)
GateWay Comm Coll (AZ)
Gateway Comm Coll (CT)
Harrisburg Area Comm Coll (PA)
Houston Comm Coll System (TX)
Howard Comm Coll (MD)
Jefferson Comm and Tech Coll (KY)
Miami Dade Coll (FL)
Midlands Tech Coll (SC)
Moraine Park Tech Coll (WI)
Oakland Comm Coll (MI)
Orange Coast Coll (CA)
Southeast Tech Inst (SD)
Springfield Tech Comm Coll (MA)
Triton Coll (IL)
Union County Coll (NJ)

Nuclear/Nuclear Power Technology
Aiken Tech Coll (SC)
Allen County Comm Coll (KS)
Chattanooga State Tech Comm Coll (TN)
Florida Comm Coll at Jacksonville (FL)
Joliet Jr Coll (IL)
Lake Michigan Coll (MI)
Texas State Tech Coll Waco (TX)
Westmoreland County Comm Coll (PA)

Nursing Assistant/Aide and Patient Care Assistant
Alexandria Tech Coll (MN)
Allen County Comm Coll (KS)
Comm Coll of Allegheny County (PA)
Edmonds Comm Coll (WA)
Front Range Comm Coll (CO)
Glendale Comm Coll (AZ)
Lake Region State Coll (ND)
Laramie County Comm Coll (WY)
Lower Columbia Coll (WA)
Modesto Jr Coll (CA)
Moraine Park Tech Coll (WI)
North Iowa Area Comm Coll (IA)
Trinidad State Jr Coll (CO)
Waubonsee Comm Coll (IL)
Western Iowa Tech Comm Coll (IA)

Nursing (Licensed Practical/ Vocational Nurse Training)
Alexandria Tech Coll (MN)
Allan Hancock Coll (CA)
Arizona Western Coll (AZ)
Athens Tech Coll (GA)
Atlanta Metropolitan Coll (GA)
Bainbridge Coll (GA)
Big Bend Comm Coll (WA)
Carteret Comm Coll (NC)
Central Arizona Coll (AZ)
Central Comm Coll– Columbus Campus (NE)
Central Comm Coll–Grand Island Campus (NE)
Centralia Coll (WA)
Central Oregon Comm Coll (OR)
Central Piedmont Comm Coll (NC)
Chattahoochee Valley Comm Coll (AL)
Chemeketa Comm Coll (OR)
Citrus Coll (CA)
Clark State Comm Coll (OH)
Coahoma Comm Coll (MS)

Coastal Bend Coll (TX)
Colby Comm Coll (KS)
Coll of Southern Maryland (MD)
Coll of The Albemarle (NC)
Coll of the Canyons (CA)
Colorado Mountain Coll (CO)
Comm Coll of Allegheny County (PA)
Comm Coll of Denver (CO)
Delaware Tech & Comm Coll, Jack F. Owens Campus (DE)
Delaware Tech & Comm Coll, Terry Campus (DE)
Delta Coll (MI)
East Arkansas Comm Coll (AR)
ECPI Tech Coll (NC)
El Centro Coll (TX)
Feather River Coll (CA)
Galveston Coll (TX)
Gavilan Coll (CA)
George C. Wallace Comm Coll (AL)
Grand Rapids Comm Coll (MI)
Heartland Comm Coll (IL)
Horry-Georgetown Tech Coll (SC)
Howard Coll (TX)
Howard Comm Coll (MD)
Illinois Eastern Comm Colls, Olney Central College (IL)
Itasca Comm Coll (MN)
Ivy Tech Comm Coll– Southeast (IN)
Jackson Comm Coll (MI)
James H. Faulkner State Comm Coll (AL)
Jefferson Comm Coll (OH)
Kellogg Comm Coll (MI)
Kingwood Coll (TX)
Lake Region State Coll (ND)
Lamar State Coll–Port Arthur (TX)
Lansing Comm Coll (MI)
Lincoln Coll (IL)
Lincoln Coll–Normal (IL)
Lower Columbia Coll (WA)
Manhattan Area Tech Coll (KS)
Maria Coll (NY)
Metropolitan Comm Coll (NE)
Midlands Tech Coll (SC)
Minnesota State Comm and Tech Coll–Fergus Falls (MN)
MiraCosta Coll (CA)
Moraine Park Tech Coll (WI)
Mount Wachusett Comm Coll (MA)
North Dakota State Coll of Science (ND)
Northeast Comm Coll (NE)
North Idaho Coll (ID)
North Iowa Area Comm Coll (IA)
Northland Comm and Tech Coll–Thief River Falls (MN)
North Seattle Comm Coll (WA)
Northwest-Shoals Comm Coll (AL)
Oakland Comm Coll (MI)
Ouachita Tech Coll (AR)
Pasadena City Coll (CA)
Riverside Comm Coll District (CA)
Rockingham Comm Coll (NC)
St. Cloud Tech Coll (MN)
St. Philip's Coll (TX)
San Diego City Coll (CA)
San Joaquin Delta Coll (CA)
San Joaquin Valley Coll (CA)
Santa Barbara City Coll (CA)
South Plains Coll (TX)
Spokane Comm Coll (WA)
Trinidad State Jr Coll (CO)
Trinity Valley Comm Coll (TX)
Triton Coll (IL)
Union County Coll (NJ)
United Tribes Tech Coll (ND)
Vance-Granville Comm Coll (NC)
Westmoreland County Comm Coll (PA)

William Rainey Harper Coll (IL)
Williston State Coll (ND)
York Tech Coll (SC)
Yuba Coll (CA)

Nursing (Registered Nurse Training)
Abraham Baldwin Ag Coll (GA)
Alamance Comm Coll (NC)
Allan Hancock Coll (CA)
Allegany Coll of Maryland (MD)
Ancilla Coll (IN)
Arapahoe Comm Coll (CO)
Arizona Western Coll (AZ)
Arkansas Northeastern Coll (AR)
Arkansas State U–Beebe (AR)
Athens Tech Coll (GA)
Austin Comm Coll (TX)
Bainbridge Coll (GA)
Barton County Comm Coll (KS)
Beaufort County Comm Coll (NC)
Bergen Comm Coll (NJ)
Berkshire Comm Coll (MA)
Big Bend Comm Coll (WA)
Bishop State Comm Coll (AL)
Bladen Comm Coll (NC)
Blue Ridge Comm Coll (VA)
Borough of Manhattan Comm Coll of the City U of New York (NY)
Brazosport Coll (TX)
Brevard Comm Coll (FL)
Bristol Comm Coll (MA)
Bronx Comm Coll of the City U of New York (NY)
Broome Comm Coll (NY)
Broward Comm Coll (FL)
Bryant and Stratton Coll, Parma (OH)
Bucks County Comm Coll (PA)
Bunker Hill Comm Coll (MA)
Butler Comm Coll (KS)
Butler County Comm Coll (PA)
Caldwell Comm Coll and Tech Inst (NC)
Cape Fear Comm Coll (NC)
Capital Comm Coll (CT)
Carl Albert State Coll (OK)
Carroll Comm Coll (MD)
Casper Coll (WY)
Cecil Comm Coll (MD)
Central Arizona Coll (AZ)
Central Carolina Tech Coll (SC)
Central Comm Coll–Grand Island Campus (NE)
Central Florida Comm Coll (FL)
Centralia Coll (WA)
Central Lakes Coll (MN)
Central New Mexico Comm Coll (NM)
Central Oregon Comm Coll (OR)
Central Piedmont Comm Coll (NC)
Central Wyoming Coll (WY)
Century Coll (MN)
Chattahoochee Valley Comm Coll (AL)
Chattanooga State Tech Comm Coll (TN)
Chemeketa Comm Coll (OR)
Cincinnati State Tech and Comm Coll (OH)
Clarendon Coll (TX)
Clark Coll (WA)
Clark State Comm Coll (OH)
Clatsop Comm Coll (OR)
Cleveland Comm Coll (NC)
Cleveland State Comm Coll (TN)
Clovis Comm Coll (NM)
Coastal Bend Coll (TX)
Coastal Carolina Comm Coll (NC)
Coastal Georgia Comm Coll (GA)
Cochise Coll, Douglas (AZ)
Colby Comm Coll (KS)

Coll of DuPage (IL)
Coll of Eastern Utah (UT)
Coll of Lake County (IL)
Coll of Southern Maryland (MD)
Coll of The Albemarle (NC)
Coll of the Canyons (CA)
Coll of the Mainland (TX)
Collin County Comm Coll District (TX)
Colorado Mountain Coll (CO)
Columbus Tech Coll (GA)
Comm Coll of Allegheny County (PA)
Comm Coll of Denver (CO)
Copiah-Lincoln Comm Coll (MS)
Corning Comm Coll (NY)
Crowder Coll (MO)
Cuyahoga Comm Coll (OH)
Dabney S. Lancaster Comm Coll (VA)
Delaware Tech & Comm Coll, Jack F. Owens Campus (DE)
Delaware Tech & Comm Coll, Stanton/Wilmington Campus (DE)
Delaware Tech & Comm Coll, Terry Campus (DE)
Delgado Comm Coll (LA)
Delta Coll (MI)
Dixie State Coll of Utah (UT)
Dyersburg State Comm Coll (TN)
East Central Coll (MO)
Eastern Arizona Coll (AZ)
El Centro Coll (TX)
Erie Comm Coll (NY)
Erie Comm Coll, North Campus (NY)
Essex County Coll (NJ)
Evergreen Valley Coll (CA)
Fayetteville Tech Comm Coll (NC)
Finger Lakes Comm Coll (NY)
Fiorello H. LaGuardia Comm Coll of the City U of New York (NY)
Florida Comm Coll at Jacksonville (FL)
Forsyth Tech Comm Coll (NC)
Fox Valley Tech Coll (WI)
Frederick Comm Coll (MD)
Front Range Comm Coll (CO)
Gadsden State Comm Coll (AL)
Galveston Coll (TX)
Gaston Coll (NC)
GateWay Comm Coll (AZ)
Gavilan Coll (CA)
Genesee Comm Coll (NY)
George C. Wallace Comm Coll (AL)
Georgia Highlands Coll (GA)
Germanna Comm Coll (VA)
Glendale Comm Coll (AZ)
Goodwin Coll (CT)
Grand Rapids Comm Coll (MI)
Great Basin Coll (NV)
Greenfield Comm Coll (MA)
Hagerstown Comm Coll (MD)
Harrisburg Area Comm Coll (PA)
Hawkeye Comm Coll (IA)
Heartland Comm Coll (IL)
Hesston Coll (KS)
Hibbing Comm Coll (MN)
Highland Comm Coll (IL)
Highline Comm Coll (WA)
Holyoke Comm Coll (MA)
Horry-Georgetown Tech Coll (SC)
Houston Comm Coll System (TX)
Howard Coll (TX)
Howard Comm Coll (MD)
Hudson Valley Comm Coll (NY)
Hutchinson Comm Coll and Area Vocational School (KS)
Illinois Central Coll (IL)

Illinois Eastern Comm Colls, Frontier Community College (IL)
Illinois Eastern Comm Colls, Olney Central College (IL)
Illinois Valley Comm Coll (IL)
International Inst of the Americas, Phoenix (AZ)
Ivy Tech Comm Coll– Bloomington (IN)
Ivy Tech Comm Coll–Central Indiana (IN)
Ivy Tech Comm Coll–East Central (IN)
Ivy Tech Comm Coll– Lafayette (IN)
Ivy Tech Comm Coll–North Central (IN)
Ivy Tech Comm Coll– Northwest (IN)
Ivy Tech Comm Coll– Southeast (IN)
Ivy Tech Comm Coll– Southern Indiana (IN)
Ivy Tech Comm Coll– Southwest (IN)
Ivy Tech Comm Coll– Wabash Valley (IN)
Ivy Tech Comm Coll– Whitewater (IN)
Jackson Comm Coll (MI)
Jackson State Comm Coll (TN)
James H. Faulkner State Comm Coll (AL)
James Sprunt Comm Coll (NC)
Jamestown Comm Coll (NY)
Jefferson Comm and Tech Coll (KY)
Jefferson Comm Coll (NY)
Jefferson State Comm Coll (AL)
Johnston Comm Coll (NC)
John Tyler Comm Coll (VA)
John Wood Comm Coll (IL)
Joliet Jr Coll (IL)
Kansas City Kansas Comm Coll (KS)
Kapiolani Comm Coll (HI)
Kaskaskia Coll (IL)
Kauai Comm Coll (HI)
Keiser Coll, Miami (FL)
Kellogg Comm Coll (MI)
Kennebec Valley Comm Coll (ME)
Kent State U, Tuscarawas Campus (OH)
Kingsborough Comm Coll of the City U of New York (NY)
Lac Courte Oreilles Ojibwa Comm Coll (WI)
Lake City Comm Coll (FL)
Lake Land Coll (IL)
Lake Michigan Coll (MI)
Lakeshore Tech Coll (WI)
Lake-Sumter Comm Coll (FL)
Lake Superior Coll (MN)
Lamar State Coll–Orange (TX)
Lamar State Coll–Port Arthur (TX)
Lansing Comm Coll (MI)
Laramie County Comm Coll (WY)
Laredo Comm Coll (TX)
Lawson State Comm Coll (AL)
Lincoln Coll (IL)
Lincoln Coll–Normal (IL)
Lincoln Land Comm Coll (IL)
Linn-Benton Comm Coll (OR)
Long Beach City Coll (CA)
Long Island Coll Hospital School of Nursing (NY)
Lord Fairfax Comm Coll (VA)
Louisiana State U at Alexandria (LA)
Lower Columbia Coll (WA)
Luzerne County Comm Coll (PA)
Macomb Comm Coll (MI)
Manatee Comm Coll (FL)
Manhattan Area Tech Coll (KS)
Maria Coll (NY)

Massachusetts Bay Comm Coll (MA)
Mercer County Comm Coll (NJ)
Mercy Coll of Northwest Ohio (OH)
Meridian Comm Coll (MS)
Metropolitan Comm Coll (NE)
Miami Dade Coll (FL)
Middle Georgia Coll (GA)
Middlesex County Coll (NJ)
Midland Coll (TX)
Midlands Tech Coll (SC)
Minnesota State Comm and Tech Coll–Fergus Falls (MN)
Mississippi Gulf Coast Comm Coll (MS)
Missouri State U–West Plains (MO)
Moberly Area Comm Coll (MO)
Modesto Jr Coll (CA)
Mohawk Valley Comm Coll (NY)
Montgomery County Comm Coll (PA)
Moraine Park Tech Coll (WI)
Moraine Valley Comm Coll (IL)
Motlow State Comm Coll (TN)
Mott Comm Coll (MI)
Mt. San Antonio Coll (CA)
Mount Wachusett Comm Coll (MA)
Nassau Comm Coll (NY)
Naugatuck Valley Comm Coll (CT)
New Hampshire Comm Tech Coll, Manchester/Stratham (NH)
New Hampshire Tech Inst (NH)
New Mexico State U–Alamogordo (NM)
Niagara County Comm Coll (NY)
Normandale Comm Coll (MN)
Northampton County Area Comm Coll (PA)
North Arkansas Coll (AR)
North Central Missouri Coll (MO)
North Country Comm Coll (NY)
Northeast Comm Coll (NE)
Northeast Iowa Comm Coll (IA)
Northern Essex Comm Coll (MA)
Northern Maine Comm Coll (ME)
North Hennepin Comm Coll (MN)
North Idaho Coll (ID)
North Iowa Area Comm Coll (IA)
Northland Comm and Tech Coll–Thief River Falls (MN)
North Seattle Comm Coll (WA)
North Shore Comm Coll (MA)
Northwestern Tech Coll (GA)
Northwest-Shoals Comm Coll (AL)
Norwalk Comm Coll (CT)
Oakland Comm Coll (MI)
Ocean County Coll (NJ)
Okaloosa-Walton Coll (FL)
Orange County Comm Coll (NY)
Oregon Coast Comm Coll (OR)
Otero Jr Coll (CO)
Owens Comm Coll, Toledo (OH)
Palau Comm CollPalau)
Palm Beach Comm Coll (FL)
Panola Coll (TX)
Parkland Coll (IL)
Pasadena City Coll (CA)
Pasco-Hernando Comm Coll (FL)
Peninsula Coll (WA)

The Pennsylvania State U Fayette Campus of the Commonwealth Coll (PA)
The Pennsylvania State U Mont Alto Campus of the Commonwealth Coll (PA)
The Pennsylvania State U Worthington Scranton Campus of the Commonwealth Coll (PA)
Penn Valley Comm Coll (MO)
Phillips Beth Israel School of Nursing (NY)
Phoenix Coll (AZ)
Piedmont Virginia Comm Coll (VA)
Pima Comm Coll (AZ)
Polk Comm Coll (FL)
Prairie State Coll (IL)
Pratt Comm Coll (KS)
Quinsigamond Comm Coll (MA)
Raritan Valley Comm Coll (NJ)
Richland Comm Coll (IL)
Richmond Comm Coll (NC)
Riverland Comm Coll (MN)
Riverside Comm Coll District (CA)
Roane State Comm Coll (TN)
Rockingham Comm Coll (NC)
Rock Valley Coll (IL)
Rogue Comm Coll (OR)
Saddleback Coll (CA)
Saint Charles Comm Coll (MO)
Saint Joseph's Hospital Health Center School of Nursing (NY)
St. Louis Comm Coll at Florissant Valley (MO)
St. Luke's Coll (IA)
St. Petersburg Coll (FL)
Salt Lake Comm Coll (UT)
San Diego City Coll (CA)
San Joaquin Delta Coll (CA)
San Joaquin Valley Coll (CA)
San Juan Coll (NM)
Santa Barbara City Coll (CA)
Santa Rosa Jr Coll (CA)
Sauk Valley Comm Coll (IL)
Scottsdale Comm Coll (AZ)
Seattle Central Comm Coll (WA)
Seminole Comm Coll (FL)
Seminole State Coll (OK)
Shelton State Comm Coll (AL)
Sheridan Coll–Sheridan and Gillette (WY)
Sinclair Comm Coll (OH)
Southeastern Comm Coll (NC)
Southern State Comm Coll (OH)
Southern West Virginia Comm and Tech Coll (WV)
South Plains Coll (TX)
Southside Virginia Comm Coll (VA)
South Texas Coll (TX)
Southwestern Illinois Coll (IL)
Southwestern Michigan Coll (MI)
Southwestern Oklahoma State U at Sayre (OK)
Southwestern Oregon Comm Coll (OR)
Southwest Georgia Tech Coll (GA)
Southwest Mississippi Comm Coll (MS)
Southwest Tennessee Comm Coll (TN)
Southwest Virginia Comm Coll (VA)
Spokane Comm Coll (WA)
Spoon River Coll (IL)
Springfield Tech Comm Coll (MA)
Stark State Coll of Technology (OH)
State U of New York Coll of Technology at Alfred (NY)
State U of New York Coll of Technology at Delhi (NY)

Sullivan County Comm Coll (NY)
Tarrant County Coll District (TX)
Thomas Nelson Comm Coll (VA)
Three Rivers Comm Coll (MO)
Tidewater Comm Coll (VA)
Tomball Coll (TX)
Tompkins Cortland Comm Coll (NY)
Treasure Valley Comm Coll (OR)
Tri-County Comm Coll (NC)
Trident Tech Coll (SC)
Trinidad State Jr Coll (CO)
Trinity Valley Comm Coll (TX)
Triton Coll (IL)
Tulsa Comm Coll (OK)
Union County Coll (NJ)
U of Pittsburgh at Titusville (PA)
Utah Career Coll (UT)
Valencia Comm Coll (FL)
Vance-Granville Comm Coll (NC)
Ventura Coll (CA)
Waubonsee Comm Coll (IL)
Waukesha County Tech Coll (WI)
Weatherford Coll (TX)
West Central Tech Coll (GA)
Westchester Comm Coll (NY)
Western Iowa Tech Comm Coll (IA)
Western Oklahoma State Coll (OK)
Western Tech Coll (WI)
Westmoreland County Comm Coll (PA)
West Virginia Northern Comm Coll (WV)
Wharton County Jr Coll (TX)
Wilkes Comm Coll (NC)
William Rainey Harper Coll (IL)
Wilson Tech Comm Coll (NC)
Wor-Wic Comm Coll (MD)
Yakima Valley Comm Coll (WA)
Yavapai Coll (AZ)
York Tech Coll (SC)
Young Harris Coll (GA)
Yuba Coll (CA)

Nursing Related

Cincinnati State Tech and Comm Coll (OH)
Southeast Tech Inst (SD)
Tillamook Bay Comm Coll (OR)

Nutrition Sciences

Casper Coll (WY)
Mohawk Valley Comm Coll (NY)

Occupational Health and Industrial Hygiene

Niagara County Comm Coll (NY)

Occupational Safety and Health Technology

Brazosport Coll (TX)
Comm Coll of the Air Force (AL)
Cossatot Comm Coll of the U of Arkansas (AR)
Delaware Tech & Comm Coll, Stanton/Wilmington Campus (DE)
Delgado Comm Coll (LA)
GateWay Comm Coll (AZ)
Houston Comm Coll System (TX)
Ivy Tech Comm Coll–Central Indiana (IN)
Ivy Tech Comm Coll–Northeast (IN)
Ivy Tech Comm Coll–Northwest (IN)
Ivy Tech Comm Coll–Wabash Valley (IN)
Lamar State Coll–Port Arthur (TX)
Lanier Tech Coll (GA)
Mt. San Antonio Coll (CA)
Okefenokee Tech Coll (GA)

San Diego City Coll (CA)
Texas State Tech Coll Waco (TX)
Trinidad State Jr Coll (CO)
Tulsa Comm Coll (OK)
The U of Akron–Wayne Coll (OH)

Occupational Therapist Assistant

Allegany Coll of Maryland (MD)
Augusta Tech Coll (GA)
Briarwood Coll (CT)
Bristol Comm Coll (MA)
Brown Mackie Coll–Fort Wayne (IN)
Brown Mackie Coll–South Bend (IN)
Cape Fear Comm Coll (NC)
Cincinnati State Tech and Comm Coll (OH)
Coll of DuPage (IL)
Comm Coll of Allegheny County (PA)
Delaware Tech & Comm Coll, Stanton/Wilmington Campus (DE)
Delgado Comm Coll (LA)
Erie Comm Coll, North Campus (NY)
Houston Comm Coll System (TX)
Ivy Tech Comm Coll–Central Indiana (IN)
Jamestown Comm Coll (NY)
Kennebec Valley Comm Coll (ME)
Lake Superior Coll (MN)
Lincoln Land Comm Coll (IL)
Macomb Comm Coll (MI)
Manatee Comm Coll (FL)
Manchester Comm Coll (CT)
Maria Coll (NY)
Middle Georgia Coll (GA)
Midlands Tech Coll (SC)
Mott Comm Coll (MI)
North Dakota State Coll of Science (ND)
Northwestern Tech Coll (GA)
Owens Comm Coll, Toledo (OH)
Parkland Coll (IL)
The Pennsylvania State U DuBois Campus of the Commonwealth Coll (PA)
The Pennsylvania State U Mont Alto Campus of the Commonwealth Coll (PA)
Polk Comm Coll (FL)
Pulaski Tech Coll (AR)
Quinsigamond Comm Coll (MA)
Rockingham Comm Coll (NC)
St. Philip's Coll (TX)
Salt Lake Comm Coll (UT)
Southwestern Oklahoma State U at Sayre (OK)
Springfield Tech Comm Coll (MA)
Tulsa Comm Coll (OK)
Union County Coll (NJ)
Western Iowa Tech Comm Coll (IA)

Occupational Therapy

Allegany Coll of Maryland (MD)
Austin Comm Coll (TX)
Barton County Comm Coll (KS)
Casper Coll (WY)
Chattanooga State Tech Comm Coll (TN)
City Colls of Chicago, Wilbur Wright College (IL)
Coastal Georgia Comm Coll (GA)
Coll of DuPage (IL)
Fiorello H. LaGuardia Comm Coll of the City U of New York (NY)
Fox Valley Tech Coll (WI)
Genesee Comm Coll (NY)
Georgia Highlands Coll (GA)
Illinois Central Coll (IL)
Kapiolani Comm Coll (HI)
Keystone Coll (PA)
Kingwood Coll (TX)
Manatee Comm Coll (FL)

Manor Coll (PA)
North Shore Comm Coll (MA)
Orange County Comm Coll (NY)
Palm Beach Comm Coll (FL)
Pasadena City Coll (CA)
Penn Valley Comm Coll (MO)
Quinsigamond Comm Coll (MA)
Roane State Comm Coll (TN)
Saint Charles Comm Coll (MO)
Sauk Valley Comm Coll (IL)
Sinclair Comm Coll (OH)
South Texas Coll (TX)
Stark State Coll of Technology (OH)
Tomball Coll (TX)
Trident Tech Coll (SC)
Tulsa Comm Coll (OK)
Western Tech Coll (WI)
Wisconsin Indianhead Tech Coll (WI)
Yakima Valley Comm Coll (WA)

Oceanography (Chemical and Physical)

Santa Rosa Jr Coll (CA)
Tulsa Comm Coll (OK)

Office Management

Alexandria Tech Coll (MN)
Berkeley City Coll (CA)
Berkeley Coll-New York City Campus (NY)
Berkeley Coll-Westchester Campus (NY)
Big Bend Comm Coll (WA)
Central Florida Comm Coll (FL)
Cincinnati State Tech and Comm Coll (OH)
Coll of DuPage (IL)
Comm Coll of Allegheny County (PA)
Comm Coll of Denver (CO)
Comm Coll of the Air Force (AL)
Consolidated School of Business, Lancaster (PA)
Consolidated School of Business, York (PA)
Delta Coll (MI)
Eastern Wyoming Coll (WY)
Edmonds Comm Coll (WA)
Erie Comm Coll (NY)
Erie Comm Coll, North Campus (NY)
Erie Comm Coll, South Campus (NY)
Fayetteville Tech Comm Coll (NC)
Florida Comm Coll at Jacksonville (FL)
Great Basin Coll (NV)
Howard Comm Coll (MD)
Lake Land Coll (IL)
Lake Region State Coll (ND)
Lake-Sumter Comm Coll (FL)
Lord Fairfax Comm Coll (VA)
Lower Columbia Coll (WA)
Modesto Jr Coll (CA)
Mohawk Valley Comm Coll (NY)
Mott Comm Coll (MI)
Oakland Comm Coll (MI)
Peninsula Coll (WA)
Riverside Comm Coll District (CA)
Saint Charles Comm Coll (MO)
St. Cloud Tech Coll (MN)
Southern Arkansas U Tech (AR)
South Hills School of Business & Technology, State College (PA)
Southwestern Oregon Comm Coll (OR)
Tillamook Bay Comm Coll (OR)
Valencia Comm Coll (FL)
Western Tech Coll (WI)
Wood Tobe–Coburn School (NY)

Office Occupations and Clerical Services

Alamance Comm Coll (NC)
Alexandria Tech Coll (MN)
Butler County Comm Coll (PA)
Comm and Tech Coll of Shepherd (WV)
Delta Coll (MI)
El Centro Coll (TX)
Florida Comm Coll at Jacksonville (FL)
GateWay Comm Coll (AZ)
ITI Tech Coll (LA)
Lake Region State Coll (ND)
Laurel Business Inst (PA)
Modesto Jr Coll (CA)
Mohawk Valley Comm Coll (NY)
New Mexico State U–Alamogordo (NM)
North Country Comm Coll (NY)
Pennsylvania Inst of Technology (PA)
Spokane Falls Comm Coll (WA)
United Tribes Tech Coll (ND)
York Tech Coll (SC)

Operations Management

Alamance Comm Coll (NC)
Alexandria Tech Coll (MN)
Atlanta Metropolitan Coll (GA)
Bunker Hill Comm Coll (MA)
Cleveland Comm Coll (NC)
DeKalb Tech Coll (GA)
Fayetteville Tech Comm Coll (NC)
Gaston Coll (NC)
Great Basin Coll (NV)
Guam Comm Coll (GU)
Johnston Comm Coll (NC)
Macomb Comm Coll (MI)
Oakland Comm Coll (MI)
Remington Coll–Mobile Campus (AL)
Stark State Coll of Technology (OH)
Waubonsee Comm Coll (IL)
Waukesha County Tech Coll (WI)

Ophthalmic Laboratory Technology

Comm Coll of the Air Force (AL)
DeKalb Tech Coll (GA)
Middlesex Comm Coll (CT)
New Hampshire Comm Tech Coll, Nashua/Claremont (NH)
Raritan Valley Comm Coll (NJ)
Santa Rosa Jr Coll (CA)
Seattle Central Comm Coll (WA)
Spokane Comm Coll (WA)
Thomas Nelson Comm Coll (VA)
Triton Coll (IL)
Westmoreland County Comm Coll (PA)

Ophthalmic/Optometric Services

Howard Comm Coll (MD)
Luzerne County Comm Coll (PA)

Ophthalmic Technology

Miami Dade Coll (FL)
Triton Coll (IL)
Volunteer State Comm Coll (TN)

Optical Sciences

Corning Comm Coll (NY)

Opticianry

Arkansas State U–Mountain Home (AR)
Cuyahoga Comm Coll (OH)
DeKalb Tech Coll (GA)
Erie Comm Coll, North Campus (NY)
Essex County Coll (NJ)
Harrisburg Area Comm Coll (PA)
Ogeechee Tech Coll (GA)
Triton Coll (IL)

Optometric Technician
Barton County Comm Coll (KS)
Sauk Valley Comm Coll (IL)

Ornamental Horticulture
Abraham Baldwin Ag Coll (GA)
Bergen Comm Coll (NJ)
Bronx Comm Coll of the City U of New York (NY)
Coll of DuPage (IL)
Coll of Lake County (IL)
Comm Coll of Allegheny County (PA)
Finger Lakes Comm Coll (NY)
Foothill Coll (CA)
Forsyth Tech Comm Coll (NC)
Gwinnett Tech Coll (GA)
Hawkeye Comm Coll (IA)
Howard Coll (TX)
Long Beach City Coll (CA)
Mercer County Comm Coll (NJ)
Metropolitan Comm Coll (NE)
Miami Dade Coll (FL)
MiraCosta Coll (CA)
Mississippi Gulf Coast Comm Coll (MS)
Modesto Jr Coll (CA)
Mt. San Antonio Coll (CA)
Oakland Comm Coll (MI)
Orange Coast Coll (CA)
Saddleback Coll (CA)
San Joaquin Delta Coll (CA)
Santa Barbara City Coll (CA)
Spokane Comm Coll (WA)
Texas State Tech Coll Waco (TX)
Triton Coll (IL)
Tulsa Comm Coll (OK)
Valencia Comm Coll (FL)
Wharton County Jr Coll (TX)

Orthotics/Prosthetics
Century Coll (MN)
Spokane Falls Comm Coll (WA)

Painting
Dixie State Coll of Utah (UT)
Keystone Coll (PA)
Lincoln Coll (IL)
Luzerne County Comm Coll (PA)

Painting and Wall Covering
Ivy Tech Comm Coll–Central Indiana (IN)
Ivy Tech Comm Coll–East Central (IN)
Ivy Tech Comm Coll–Lafayette (IN)
Ivy Tech Comm Coll–North Central (IN)
Ivy Tech Comm Coll–Northeast (IN)
Ivy Tech Comm Coll–Northwest (IN)
Ivy Tech Comm Coll–Southwest (IN)
Ivy Tech Comm Coll–Wabash Valley (IN)

Paralegal/Legal Assistant
Appalachian Tech Coll (GA)
Argosy U/Denver (CO)
Argosy U/Orange County (CA)
Argosy U/San Diego (CA)
Atlanta Tech Coll (GA)
Brown Mackie Coll–Akron (OH)
Brown Mackie Coll–Atlanta (GA)
Brown Mackie Coll–Findlay (OH)
Brown Mackie Coll–Hopkinsville (KY)
Brown Mackie Coll–Louisville (KY)
Brown Mackie Coll–Miami (FL)
Brown Mackie Coll–Northern Kentucky (KY)
Central Georgia Tech Coll (GA)
Comm and Tech Coll of Shepherd (WV)

Comm Coll of Denver (CO)
Coosa Valley Tech Coll (GA)
DeKalb Tech Coll (GA)
Florida Tech Coll, DeLand (FL)
Front Range Comm Coll (CO)
Globe Coll (MN)
Griffin Tech Coll (GA)
International Business Coll, Indianapolis (IN)
Minnesota School of Business–Brooklyn Center (MN)
Minnesota School of Business–Plymouth (MN)
Minnesota School of Business–St. Cloud (MN)
Minnesota School of Business–Shakopee (MN)
North Hennepin Comm Coll (MN)
Ogeechee Tech Coll (GA)
Riverside Comm Coll District (CA)
South Georgia Tech Coll (GA)
Tidewater Comm Coll (VA)
Utah Career Coll (UT)

Parks, Recreation and Leisure
Allan Hancock Coll (CA)
Bergen Comm Coll (NJ)
Central Florida Comm Coll (FL)
Centralia Coll (WA)
Coastal Bend Coll (TX)
Colorado Mountain Coll, Timberline Campus (CO)
Comm Coll of the Air Force (AL)
Cowley County Comm Coll and Area Vocational–Tech School (KS)
East Central Coll (MO)
Greenfield Comm Coll (MA)
Kingsborough Comm Coll of the City U of New York (NY)
Lawson State Comm Coll (AL)
Miami Dade Coll (FL)
Mt. San Antonio Coll (CA)
Northern Essex Comm Coll (MA)
Northwestern Connecticut Comm Coll (CT)
Norwalk Comm Coll (CT)
Orange County Comm Coll (NY)
Pasadena City Coll (CA)
San Diego City Coll (CA)
San Juan Coll (NM)
Santa Barbara City Coll (CA)
Skyline Coll (CA)
Southeastern Comm Coll (NC)
State U of New York Coll of Technology at Delhi (NY)
Tompkins Cortland Comm Coll (NY)
Vance-Granville Comm Coll (NC)
Ventura Coll (CA)
Vermilion Comm Coll (MN)
Young Harris Coll (GA)

Parks, Recreation and Leisure Facilities Management
Abraham Baldwin Ag Coll (GA)
Allen County Comm Coll (KS)
Augusta Tech Coll (GA)
Butler County Comm Coll (PA)
Chattahoochee Tech Coll (GA)
Coastal Georgia Comm Coll (GA)
Colorado Mountain Coll, Alpine Campus (CO)
Colorado Mountain Coll, Timberline Campus (CO)
Erie Comm Coll, South Campus (NY)
Feather River Coll (CA)
Finger Lakes Comm Coll (NY)

Hawkeye Comm Coll (IA)
Horry-Georgetown Tech Coll (SC)
James H. Faulkner State Comm Coll (AL)
Keystone Coll (PA)
Modesto Jr Coll (CA)
Mohawk Valley Comm Coll (NY)
Moraine Valley Comm Coll (IL)
Mt. San Antonio Coll (CA)
North Country Comm Coll (NY)
North Georgia Tech Coll (GA)
Northwestern Connecticut Comm Coll (CT)
Southeastern Comm Coll (NC)
Spokane Comm Coll (WA)
State U of New York Coll of Technology at Delhi (NY)
Vermilion Comm Coll (MN)
William Rainey Harper Coll (IL)

Parks, Recreation, and Leisure Related
Central New Mexico Comm Coll (NM)
Cincinnati State Tech and Comm Coll (OH)
Feather River Coll (CA)

Parts, Warehousing, and Inventory Management
Central Wyoming Coll (WY)

Pastoral Studies/Counseling
Hesston Coll (KS)

Peace Studies and Conflict Resolution
Berkshire Comm Coll (MA)

Perioperative/Operating Room and Surgical Nursing
Comm Coll of Allegheny County (PA)

Petroleum Technology
Coastal Bend Coll (TX)
South Plains Coll (TX)
Tulsa Comm Coll (OK)

Pharmacy
Barton County Comm Coll (KS)
Coastal Bend Coll (TX)
Colby Comm Coll (KS)
Pasadena City Coll (CA)

Pharmacy Technician
Abraham Baldwin Ag Coll (GA)
Albany Tech Coll (GA)
Augusta Tech Coll (GA)
Brown Mackie Coll–Akron (OH)
Brown Mackie Coll–Findlay (OH)
Brown Mackie Coll–Louisville (KY)
Brown Mackie Coll–North Canton (OH)
Brown Mackie Coll–Northern Kentucky (KY)
Casper Coll (WY)
Century Coll (MN)
Columbus Tech Coll (GA)
Comm Care Coll (OK)
Comm Coll of Allegheny County (PA)
Comm Coll of the Air Force (AL)
Edmonds Comm Coll (WA)
Griffin Tech Coll (GA)
Harrisburg Area Comm Coll (PA)
Midlands Tech Coll (SC)
Minnesota State Comm and Tech Coll–Fergus Falls (MN)
North Dakota State Coll of Science (ND)
North Seattle Comm Coll (WA)
Northwestern Tech Coll (GA)
Oakland Comm Coll (MI)
Pima Comm Coll (AZ)
Roane State Comm Coll (TN)
San Joaquin Valley Coll (CA)

TESST Coll of Technology, Towson (MD)
U of Northwestern Ohio (OH)
Utah Career Coll (UT)
Weatherford Coll (TX)
West Georgia Tech Coll (GA)

Philosophy
Allen County Comm Coll (KS)
Barton County Comm Coll (KS)
Bergen Comm Coll (NJ)
Coastal Georgia Comm Coll (GA)
Coll of the Siskiyous (CA)
Dixie State Coll of Utah (UT)
East Central Coll (MO)
Foothill Coll (CA)
Georgia Highlands Coll (GA)
Kellogg Comm Coll (MI)
Lansing Comm Coll (MI)
Laramie County Comm Coll (WY)
Lincoln Coll (IL)
Lincoln Coll–Normal (IL)
Lord Fairfax Comm Coll (VA)
Lower Columbia Coll (WA)
Manatee Comm Coll (FL)
Miami Dade Coll (FL)
MiraCosta Coll (CA)
Orange Coast Coll (CA)
Palm Beach Comm Coll (FL)
Palo Alto Coll (TX)
Pasadena City Coll (CA)
Saddleback Coll (CA)
St. Philip's Coll (TX)
San Joaquin Delta Coll (CA)
San Juan Coll (NM)
Santa Barbara City Coll (CA)
Santa Rosa Jr Coll (CA)
Skyline Coll (CA)
Snow Coll (UT)
Tulsa Comm Coll (OK)
Yuba Coll (CA)

Phlebotomy
Alexandria Tech Coll (MN)
Edmonds Comm Coll (WA)

Photographic and Film/Video Technology
The Art Inst of Philadelphia (PA)
Dixie State Coll of Utah (UT)
Miami Dade Coll (FL)
Mohawk Valley Comm Coll (NY)
Salt Lake Comm Coll (UT)
Texas State Tech Coll Waco (TX)

Photography
Allan Hancock Coll (CA)
Antonelli Inst (PA)
The Art Inst of Philadelphia (PA)
Austin Comm Coll (TX)
Bergen Comm Coll (NJ)
Carteret Comm Coll (NC)
Casper Coll (WY)
Cecil Comm Coll (MD)
Citrus Coll (CA)
Coll of DuPage (IL)
Colorado Mountain Coll (CO)
Columbia Coll (CA)
Cuyahoga Comm Coll (OH)
Delaware Coll of Art and Design (DE)
Dixie State Coll of Utah (UT)
Fiorello H. LaGuardia Comm Coll of the City U of New York (NY)
Foothill Coll (CA)
Greenfield Comm Coll (MA)
Gwinnett Tech Coll (GA)
Harrisburg Area Comm Coll (PA)
Hawkeye Comm Coll (IA)
Holyoke Comm Coll (MA)
Howard Comm Coll (MD)
Keystone Coll (PA)
Lansing Comm Coll (MI)
Lehigh Valley Coll (PA)
Lincoln Coll (IL)
Linn-Benton Comm Coll (OR)
Long Beach City Coll (CA)
Lower Columbia Coll (WA)
Luzerne County Comm Coll (PA)

Mercer County Comm Coll (NJ)
Metropolitan Comm Coll (NE)
Miami Dade Coll (FL)
Middlesex County Coll (NJ)
Modesto Jr Coll (CA)
Mott Comm Coll (MI)
Mt. San Antonio Coll (CA)
Nassau Comm Coll (NY)
Oakland Comm Coll (MI)
Ohio Inst of Photography and Technology (OH)
Orange Coast Coll (CA)
Palm Beach Comm Coll (FL)
Pasadena City Coll (CA)
Prairie State Coll (IL)
Riverside Comm Coll District (CA)
Saddleback Coll (CA)
St. Louis Comm Coll at Florissant Valley (MO)
San Diego City Coll (CA)
San Joaquin Delta Coll (CA)
Scottsdale Comm Coll (AZ)
Seattle Central Comm Coll (WA)
Sullivan County Comm Coll (NY)
Thomas Nelson Comm Coll (VA)
Westmoreland County Comm Coll (PA)
Yuba Coll (CA)

Physical Education Teaching and Coaching
Abraham Baldwin Ag Coll (GA)
Allan Hancock Coll (CA)
Arizona Western Coll (AZ)
Barton County Comm Coll (KS)
Brazosport Coll (TX)
Bucks County Comm Coll (PA)
Butler Comm Coll (KS)
Butler County Comm Coll (PA)
Carl Albert State Coll (OK)
Casper Coll (WY)
Chattahoochee Valley Comm Coll (AL)
Chemeketa Comm Coll (OR)
Citrus Coll (CA)
Clarendon Coll (TX)
Coastal Bend Coll (TX)
Cochise Coll, Douglas (AZ)
Colby Comm Coll (KS)
Coll of the Canyons (CA)
Columbia Coll (CA)
Copiah-Lincoln Comm Coll (MS)
Cowley County Comm Coll and Area Vocational–Tech School (KS)
Crowder Coll (MO)
Dean Coll (MA)
Dixie State Coll of Utah (UT)
East Central Coll (MO)
Eastern Wyoming Coll (WY)
Erie Comm Coll (NY)
Erie Comm Coll, North Campus (NY)
Erie Comm Coll, South Campus (NY)
Essex County Coll (NJ)
Finger Lakes Comm Coll (NY)
Foothill Coll (CA)
Frederick Comm Coll (MD)
Gadsden State Comm Coll (AL)
Galveston Coll (TX)
Gavilan Coll (CA)
Genesee Comm Coll (NY)
Harrisburg Area Comm Coll (PA)
Howard Coll (TX)
Independence Comm Coll (KS)
Kellogg Comm Coll (MI)
Lansing Comm Coll (MI)
Laramie County Comm Coll (WY)
Lincoln Coll (IL)
Lincoln Coll–Normal (IL)
Linn-Benton Comm Coll (OR)
Long Beach City Coll (CA)

Lower Columbia Coll (WA)
Luzerne County Comm Coll (PA)
Manatee Comm Coll (FL)
Miami Dade Coll (FL)
Middlesex County Coll (NJ)
Midland Coll (TX)
Modesto Jr Coll (CA)
Mohawk Valley Comm Coll (NY)
Montgomery County Comm Coll (PA)
New Mexico Military Inst (NM)
Niagara County Comm Coll (NY)
Northeast Comm Coll (NE)
Northern Essex Comm Coll (MA)
Okaloosa-Walton Coll (FL)
Orange Coast Coll (CA)
Palm Beach Comm Coll (FL)
Palo Alto Coll (TX)
Pasadena City Coll (CA)
Pratt Comm Coll (KS)
Roane State Comm Coll (TN)
Saddleback Coll (CA)
San Diego City Coll (CA)
San Diego Mesa Coll (CA)
San Joaquin Delta Coll (CA)
Santa Barbara City Coll (CA)
Santa Rosa Jr Coll (CA)
Sauk Valley Comm Coll (IL)
Seminole State Coll (OK)
Sinclair Comm Coll (OH)
Skyline Coll (CA)
Snow Coll (UT)
South Plains Coll (TX)
Southwestern Illinois Coll (IL)
Southwest Mississippi Comm Coll (MS)
Spoon River Coll (IL)
Treasure Valley Comm Coll (OR)
Trinidad State Jr Coll (CO)
Trinity Valley Comm Coll (TX)
Tulsa Comm Coll (OK)
Valencia Comm Coll (FL)
Vermilion Comm Coll (MN)
Wharton County Jr Coll (TX)
William Rainey Harper Coll (IL)
Yuba Coll (CA)

Physical Sciences
Abraham Baldwin Ag Coll (GA)
Austin Comm Coll (TX)
Barton County Comm Coll (KS)
Butler County Comm Coll (PA)
Carl Albert State Coll (OK)
Casper Coll (WY)
Cecil Comm Coll (MD)
Centralia Coll (WA)
Central Oregon Comm Coll (OR)
Central Wyoming Coll (WY)
Citrus Coll (CA)
City Colls of Chicago, Wilbur Wright College (IL)
Clovis Comm Coll (NM)
Coastal Bend Coll (TX)
Coll of the Canyons (CA)
Coll of the Siskiyous (CA)
Colorado Mountain Coll, Alpine Campus (CO)
Columbia Coll (CA)
Crowder Coll (MO)
Feather River Coll (CA)
Frederick Comm Coll (MD)
Harrisburg Area Comm Coll (PA)
Highland Comm Coll (IL)
Howard Comm Coll (MD)
Hutchinson Comm Coll and Area Vocational School (KS)
Independence Comm Coll (KS)
Lawson State Comm Coll (AL)
Lincoln Coll (IL)
Linn-Benton Comm Coll (OR)
Long Beach City Coll (CA)
Miami Dade Coll (FL)

Middlesex County Coll (NJ)
MiraCosta Coll (CA)
Montgomery County Comm Coll (PA)
Naugatuck Valley Comm Coll (CT)
North Idaho Coll (ID)
Northwestern Connecticut Comm Coll (CT)
Palm Beach Comm Coll (FL)
Pasadena City Coll (CA)
Roane State Comm Coll (TN)
Saddleback Coll (CA)
Salt Lake Comm Coll (UT)
San Diego City Coll (CA)
San Diego Mesa Coll (CA)
San Joaquin Delta Coll (CA)
San Juan Coll (NM)
Santa Rosa Jr Coll (CA)
Seminole State Coll (OK)
Snow Coll (UT)
Southwest Mississippi Comm Coll (MS)
Spoon River Coll (IL)
Trinity Valley Comm Coll (TX)
Tulsa Comm Coll (OK)
Union County Coll (NJ)
Ventura Coll (CA)
Vermilion Comm Coll (MN)
William Rainey Harper Coll (IL)

Physical Sciences Related
Mt. San Antonio Coll (CA)

Physical Science Technologies Related
Marshall Comm and Tech Coll (WV)

Physical Therapist Assistant
Allegany Coll of Maryland (MD)
Barton County Comm Coll (KS)
Berkshire Comm Coll (MA)
Bishop State Comm Coll (AL)
Broome Comm Coll (NY)
Brown Mackie Coll–South Bend (IN)
Butler County Comm Coll (PA)
Capital Comm Coll (CT)
Carl Albert State Coll (OK)
Carroll Comm Coll (MD)
Central Florida Comm Coll (FL)
Colby Comm Coll (KS)
Coll of DuPage (IL)
Coll of Southern Maryland (MD)
Comm Coll of Allegheny County (PA)
Comm Coll of the Air Force (AL)
Delaware Tech & Comm Coll, Stanton/Wilmington Campus (DE)
Delgado Comm Coll (LA)
Delta Coll (MI)
Essex County Coll (NJ)
Fayetteville Tech Comm Coll (NC)
Florida Comm Coll at Jacksonville (FL)
GateWay Comm Coll (AZ)
George C. Wallace Comm Coll (AL)
Georgia Highlands Coll (GA)
Gwinnett Tech Coll (GA)
Houston Comm Coll System (TX)
Ivy Tech Comm Coll–East Central (IN)
Jackson State Comm Coll (TN)
Jefferson State Comm Coll (AL)
Kansas City Kansas Comm Coll (KS)
Kaskaskia Coll (IL)
Kellogg Comm Coll (MI)
Kennebec Valley Comm Coll (ME)
Kingsborough Comm Coll of the City U of New York (NY)
Lake City Comm Coll (FL)

Lake Land Coll (IL)
Lake Superior Coll (MN)
Lincoln Land Comm Coll (IL)
Linn State Tech Coll (MO)
Macomb Comm Coll (MI)
Manatee Comm Coll (FL)
Manchester Comm Coll (CT)
Maria Coll (NY)
Marshall Comm and Tech Coll (WV)
Massachusetts Bay Comm Coll (MA)
Mercer County Comm Coll (NJ)
Miami Dade Coll (FL)
Middle Georgia Coll (GA)
Midlands Tech Coll (SC)
Mott Comm Coll (MI)
Nassau Comm Coll (NY)
Naugatuck Valley Comm Coll (CT)
Niagara County Comm Coll (NY)
North Iowa Area Comm Coll (IA)
North Shore Comm Coll (MA)
Owens Comm Coll, Toledo (OH)
Pasco-Hernando Comm Coll (FL)
The Pennsylvania State U DuBois Campus of the Commonwealth Coll (PA)
The Pennsylvania State U Hazleton Campus of the Commonwealth Coll (PA)
The Pennsylvania State U Mont Alto Campus of the Commonwealth Coll (PA)
The Pennsylvania State U Shenango Campus of the Commonwealth Coll (PA)
Polk Comm Coll (FL)
Rockingham Comm Coll (NC)
St. Petersburg Coll (FL)
St. Philip's Coll (TX)
Salt Lake Comm Coll (UT)
San Diego Mesa Coll (CA)
San Juan Coll (NM)
South Arkansas Comm Coll (AR)
South U, West Palm Beach (FL)
Southwestern Illinois Coll (IL)
Southwestern Oklahoma State U at Sayre (OK)
Southwest Tennessee Comm Coll (TN)
Spokane Falls Comm Coll (WA)
Springfield Tech Comm Coll (MA)
Union County Coll (NJ)
U of Pittsburgh at Titusville (PA)
Villa Maria Coll of Buffalo (NY)
Volunteer State Comm Coll (TN)
Western Iowa Tech Comm Coll (IA)
Western Tech Coll (WI)
Williston State Coll (ND)

Physical Therapy
Allan Hancock Coll (CA)
Allen County Comm Coll (KS)
Arapahoe Comm Coll (CO)
Athens Tech Coll (GA)
Barton County Comm Coll (KS)
Bay State Coll (MA)
Broward Comm Coll (FL)
Butler Comm Coll (KS)
Caldwell Comm Coll and Tech Inst (NC)
Central Piedmont Comm Coll (NC)
Chattanooga State Tech Comm Coll (TN)
Clarendon Coll (TX)
Clark State Comm Coll (OH)
Coastal Georgia Comm Coll (GA)
Colby Comm Coll (KS)

Cowley County Comm Coll and Area Vocational–Tech School (KS)
Essex County Coll (NJ)
Fiorello H. LaGuardia Comm Coll of the City U of New York (NY)
Genesee Comm Coll (NY)
Georgia Highlands Coll (GA)
Gwinnett Tech Coll (GA)
Illinois Central Coll (IL)
Jefferson Comm and Tech Coll (KY)
John Tyler Comm Coll (VA)
Kapiolani Comm Coll (HI)
Kingsborough Comm Coll of the City U of New York (NY)
Laredo Comm Coll (TX)
Lawson State Comm Coll (AL)
Manatee Comm Coll (FL)
Manor Coll (PA)
Meridian Comm Coll (MS)
Mount Wachusett Comm Coll (MA)
New Hampshire Comm Tech Coll, Manchester/Stratham (NH)
Northeast Comm Coll (NE)
Orange County Comm Coll (NY)
Palm Beach Comm Coll (FL)
Penn Valley Comm Coll (MO)
Roane State Comm Coll (TN)
Sauk Valley Comm Coll (IL)
Seminole Comm Coll (FL)
Sinclair Comm Coll (OH)
South Plains Coll (TX)
Stark State Coll of Technology (OH)
Tarrant County Coll District (TX)
Trident Tech Coll (SC)
Tulsa Comm Coll (OK)
Tunxis Comm Coll (CT)
Wharton County Jr Coll (TX)
Young Harris Coll (GA)

Physician Assistant
Barton County Comm Coll (KS)
Coastal Georgia Comm Coll (GA)
Cuyahoga Comm Coll (OH)
Delta Coll (MI)
Foothill Coll (CA)
Georgia Highlands Coll (GA)
Manatee Comm Coll (FL)
Minnesota School of Business–Brooklyn Center (MN)
Minnesota School of Business–Plymouth (MN)
Minnesota School of Business–St. Cloud (MN)
Minnesota School of Business–Shakopee (MN)
Santa Rosa Jr Coll (CA)
Tulsa Comm Coll (OK)

Physics
Allan Hancock Coll (CA)
Allen County Comm Coll (KS)
Arizona Western Coll (AZ)
Atlanta Metropolitan Coll (GA)
Austin Comm Coll (TX)
Barton County Comm Coll (KS)
Bergen Comm Coll (NJ)
Brazosport Coll (TX)
Bunker Hill Comm Coll (MA)
Butler Comm Coll (KS)
Casper Coll (WY)
Cecil Comm Coll (MD)
Chattahoochee Valley Comm Coll (AL)
Coastal Bend Coll (TX)
Coastal Georgia Comm Coll (GA)
Coll of the Siskiyous (CA)
Columbia Coll (CA)
Comm Coll of Allegheny County (PA)
Dixie State Coll of Utah (UT)
East Central Coll (MO)
Eastern Arizona Coll (AZ)

Finger Lakes Comm Coll (NY)
Foothill Coll (CA)
Gainesville Coll (GA)
Great Basin Coll (NV)
Highland Comm Coll (IL)
Holyoke Comm Coll (MA)
Kellogg Comm Coll (MI)
Kingsborough Comm Coll of the City U of New York (NY)
Linn-Benton Comm Coll (OR)
Lower Columbia Coll (WA)
Manatee Comm Coll (FL)
Mercer County Comm Coll (NJ)
Miami Dade Coll (FL)
Middlesex County Coll (NJ)
Midland Coll (TX)
MiraCosta Coll (CA)
New Mexico Military Inst (NM)
Northampton County Area Comm Coll (PA)
Northeast Comm Coll (NE)
North Idaho Coll (ID)
Okaloosa-Walton Coll (FL)
Orange Coast Coll (CA)
Palo Alto Coll (TX)
Pasadena City Coll (CA)
Saddleback Coll (CA)
Salem Comm Coll (NJ)
Salt Lake Comm Coll (UT)
San Diego Mesa Coll (CA)
San Juan Coll (NM)
Santa Barbara City Coll (CA)
Santa Rosa Jr Coll (CA)
Sauk Valley Comm Coll (IL)
Skyline Coll (CA)
Snow Coll (UT)
Spoon River Coll (IL)
Tulsa Comm Coll (OK)
Vermilion Comm Coll (MN)
Young Harris Coll (GA)

Physics Teacher Education
Coll of the Siskiyous (CA)
Manatee Comm Coll (FL)

Piano and Organ
Ancilla Coll (IN)
Lincoln Coll (IL)

Pipefitting and Sprinkler Fitting
Brazosport Coll (TX)
Cecil Comm Coll (MD)
Delta Coll (MI)
Forsyth Tech Comm Coll (NC)
GateWay Comm Coll (AZ)
H. Councill Trenholm State Tech Coll (AL)
Ivy Tech Comm Coll–Bloomington (IN)
Ivy Tech Comm Coll–Central Indiana (IN)
Ivy Tech Comm Coll–Columbus (IN)
Ivy Tech Comm Coll–East Central (IN)
Ivy Tech Comm Coll–Kokomo (IN)
Ivy Tech Comm Coll–Lafayette (IN)
Ivy Tech Comm Coll–North Central (IN)
Ivy Tech Comm Coll–Northeast (IN)
Ivy Tech Comm Coll–Northwest (IN)
Ivy Tech Comm Coll–Southern Indiana (IN)
Ivy Tech Comm Coll–Southwest (IN)
Ivy Tech Comm Coll–Wabash Valley (IN)
Ivy Tech Comm Coll–Whitewater (IN)
Kellogg Comm Coll (MI)
Northern Maine Comm Coll (ME)
St. Cloud Tech Coll (MN)
State U of New York Coll of Technology at Alfred (NY)
State U of New York Coll of Technology at Delhi (NY)

Plant Nursery Management
Comm Coll of Allegheny County (PA)

Edmonds Comm Coll (WA)
Foothill Coll (CA)
Joliet Jr Coll (IL)
Miami Dade Coll (FL)
Modesto Jr Coll (CA)
The Ohio State U Ag Tech Inst (OH)

Plant Pathology/ Phytopathology
Dixie State Coll of Utah (UT)

Plant Protection and Integrated Pest Management
Dixie State Coll of Utah (UT)
Tulsa Comm Coll (OK)

Plant Sciences
Mercer County Comm Coll (NJ)
Ventura Coll (CA)

Plastics Engineering Technology
Cincinnati State Tech and Comm Coll (OH)
Coll of DuPage (IL)
Grand Rapids Comm Coll (MI)
Highline Comm Coll (WA)
Kellogg Comm Coll (MI)
Kent State U, Tuscarawas Campus (OH)
Lake Michigan Coll (MI)
Macomb Comm Coll (MI)
Mount Wachusett Comm Coll (MA)
Quinebaug Valley Comm Coll (CT)
St. Petersburg Coll (FL)
Sinclair Comm Coll (OH)
South Texas Coll (TX)
West Georgia Tech Coll (GA)

Plumbing Technology
Luzerne County Comm Coll (PA)
Macomb Comm Coll (MI)
Minnesota West Comm and Tech Coll (MN)
Piedmont Virginia Comm Coll (VA)

Political Science and Government
Abraham Baldwin Ag Coll (GA)
Allen County Comm Coll (KS)
Atlanta Metropolitan Coll (GA)
Austin Comm Coll (TX)
Bainbridge Coll (GA)
Barton County Comm Coll (KS)
Bergen Comm Coll (NJ)
Brazosport Coll (TX)
Butler Comm Coll (KS)
Casper Coll (WY)
Centralia Coll (WA)
Chemeketa Comm Coll (OR)
Coastal Bend Coll (TX)
Coastal Georgia Comm Coll (GA)
Cochise Coll, Douglas (AZ)
Colby Comm Coll (KS)
Coll of the Canyons (CA)
Dixie State Coll of Utah (UT)
East Central Coll (MO)
Eastern Arizona Coll (AZ)
Eastern Wyoming Coll (WY)
Finger Lakes Comm Coll (NY)
Foothill Coll (CA)
Frederick Comm Coll (MD)
Gainesville Coll (GA)
Gavilan Coll (CA)
Georgia Highlands Coll (GA)
Highland Comm Coll (IL)
Independence Comm Coll (KS)
Kellogg Comm Coll (MI)
Laramie County Comm Coll (WY)
Lawson State Comm Coll (AL)
Lincoln Coll (IL)
Lower Columbia Coll (WA)
Miami Dade Coll (FL)
Middlesex County Coll (NJ)
Midland Coll (TX)
MiraCosta Coll (CA)

Northern Essex Comm Coll (MA)
North Idaho Coll (ID)
Orange Coast Coll (CA)
Otero Jr Coll (CO)
Palm Beach Comm Coll (FL)
Palo Verde Coll (CA)
Pasadena City Coll (CA)
Pima Comm Coll (AZ)
Saddleback Coll (CA)
St. Philip's Coll (TX)
Salem Comm Coll (NJ)
Salt Lake Comm Coll (UT)
San Diego City Coll (CA)
San Joaquin Delta Coll (CA)
San Juan Coll (NM)
Santa Barbara City Coll (CA)
Santa Rosa Jr Coll (CA)
Sauk Valley Comm Coll (IL)
Skyline Coll (CA)
Snow Coll (UT)
Spoon River Coll (IL)
Treasure Valley Comm Coll (OR)
Trinity Valley Comm Coll (TX)
Tulsa Comm Coll (OK)
Vermilion Comm Coll (MN)
Young Harris Coll (GA)

Portuguese
Miami Dade Coll (FL)

Postal Management
Allen County Comm Coll (KS)
Central Piedmont Comm Coll (NC)
Longview Comm Coll (MO)
Mississippi Gulf Coast Comm Coll (MS)
San Diego City Coll (CA)
South Plains Coll (TX)
Tarrant County Coll District (TX)

Poultry Science
Abraham Baldwin Ag Coll (GA)
Crowder Coll (MO)
Modesto Jr Coll (CA)

Precision Metal Working Related
Oakland Comm Coll (MI)

Precision Production Related
Midlands Tech Coll (SC)
Mott Comm Coll (MI)
Southwestern Michigan Coll (MI)
Western Tech Coll (WI)

Precision Production Trades
Coll of DuPage (IL)
Lake Michigan Coll (MI)
Santa Rosa Jr Coll (CA)

Precision Systems Maintenance and Repair Technologies Related
Louisiana Tech Coll (LA)
Southwestern Michigan Coll (MI)

Pre-Dentistry Studies
Allen County Comm Coll (KS)
Barton County Comm Coll (KS)
Centralia Coll (WA)
Clarendon Coll (TX)
Coastal Georgia Comm Coll (GA)
Eastern Wyoming Coll (WY)
Howard Comm Coll (MD)
Laramie County Comm Coll (WY)
Northwest-Shoals Comm Coll (AL)
St. Philip's Coll (TX)
Sauk Valley Comm Coll (IL)
Springfield Coll in Illinois (IL)
Tulsa Comm Coll (OK)

Pre-Engineering
Abraham Baldwin Ag Coll (GA)
Austin Comm Coll (TX)
Barton County Comm Coll (KS)
Bristol Comm Coll (MA)

Bronx Comm Coll of the City
  U of New York (NY)
Broward Comm Coll (FL)
Butler Comm Coll (KS)
Butler County Comm Coll
  (PA)
Caldwell Comm Coll and
  Tech Inst (NC)
Carl Albert State Coll (OK)
Centralia Coll (WA)
Central Oregon Comm Coll
  (OR)
Chattahoochee Valley Comm
  Coll (AL)
City Colls of Chicago, Wilbur
  Wright College (IL)
Coastal Georgia Comm Coll
  (GA)
Colby Comm Coll (KS)
Coll of Eastern Utah (UT)
Coll of the Canyons (CA)
Coll of the Mainland (TX)
Colorado Mountain Coll,
  Alpine Campus (CO)
Corning Comm Coll (NY)
Cowley County Comm Coll
  and Area Vocational–Tech
  School (KS)
Crowder Coll (MO)
Diné Coll (AZ)
East Central Coll (MO)
Essex County Coll (NJ)
Evergreen Valley Coll (CA)
Finger Lakes Comm Coll
  (NY)
Gavilan Coll (CA)
Greenfield Comm Coll (MA)
Hibbing Comm Coll (MN)
Highland Comm Coll (IL)
Highline Comm Coll (WA)
Holyoke Comm Coll (MA)
Horry-Georgetown Tech Coll
  (SC)
Illinois Valley Comm Coll (IL)
Independence Comm Coll
  (KS)
Itasca Comm Coll (MN)
Jefferson Comm Coll (NY)
Lansing Comm Coll (MI)
Laramie County Comm Coll
  (WY)
Lawson State Comm Coll
  (AL)
Lincoln Land Comm Coll (IL)
Linn-Benton Comm Coll
  (OR)
Long Beach City Coll (CA)
Longview Comm Coll (MO)
Lower Columbia Coll (WA)
Macomb Comm Coll (MI)
Maple Woods Comm Coll
  (MO)
Mesabi Range Comm and
  Tech Coll (MN)
Metropolitan Comm Coll
  (NE)
Miami Dade Coll (FL)
Middlesex Comm Coll (CT)
Midland Coll (TX)
Minnesota State Comm and
  Tech Coll–Fergus Falls
  (MN)
Mississippi Gulf Coast
  Comm Coll (MS)
Moberly Area Comm Coll
  (MO)
Mt. San Antonio Coll (CA)
Naugatuck Valley Comm Coll
  (CT)
New Mexico Military Inst
  (NM)
North Hennepin Comm Coll
  (MN)
North Shore Comm Coll
  (MA)
Northwestern Connecticut
  Comm Coll (CT)
Northwest-Shoals Comm
  Coll (AL)
Northwest Vista Coll (TX)
Oakland Comm Coll (MI)
Otero Jr Coll (CO)
Palm Beach Comm Coll (FL)
Palo Verde Coll (CA)
Polk Comm Coll (FL)
Pratt Comm Coll (KS)
Quinebaug Valley Comm
  Coll (CT)
Richland Comm Coll (IL)

Roane State Comm Coll
  (TN)
Rock Valley Coll (IL)
Saddleback Coll (CA)
Saint Charles Comm Coll
  (MO)
St. Louis Comm Coll at
  Florissant Valley (MO)
St. Philip's Coll (TX)
Salem Comm Coll (NJ)
San Diego City Coll (CA)
Seminole State Coll (OK)
Snow Coll (UT)
South Plains Coll (TX)
Spoon River Coll (IL)
Trinidad State Jr Coll (CO)
Trinity Valley Comm Coll
  (TX)
Tulsa Comm Coll (OK)
Valencia Comm Coll (FL)
Vermilion Comm Coll (MN)
Wharton County Jr Coll (TX)
William Rainey Harper Coll
  (IL)
Yakima Valley Comm Coll
  (WA)
Young Harris Coll (GA)
Yuba Coll (CA)

Pre-Law Studies
Allen County Comm Coll
  (KS)
Barton County Comm Coll
  (KS)
Centralia Coll (WA)
Central Wyoming Coll (WY)
Clarendon Coll (TX)
Dixie State Coll of Utah (UT)
Eastern Arizona Coll (AZ)
Kellogg Comm Coll (MI)
Laramie County Comm Coll
  (WY)
Lawson State Comm Coll
  (AL)
Lower Columbia Coll (WA)
Northeast Comm Coll (NE)
Northwest-Shoals Comm
  Coll (AL)
St. Philip's Coll (TX)
Springfield Coll in Illinois (IL)

Pre-Medical Studies
Allen County Comm Coll
  (KS)
Barton County Comm Coll
  (KS)
Brazosport Coll (TX)
Centralia Coll (WA)
Clarendon Coll (TX)
Coastal Georgia Comm Coll
  (GA)
Eastern Arizona Coll (AZ)
Eastern Wyoming Coll (WY)
Gainesville Coll (GA)
Howard Comm Coll (MD)
Kellogg Comm Coll (MI)
Laramie County Comm Coll
  (WY)
St. Philip's Coll (TX)
San Juan Coll (NM)
Sauk Valley Comm Coll (IL)
Springfield Coll in Illinois (IL)
Tulsa Comm Coll (OK)

Pre-Nursing Studies
Cochise Coll, Douglas (AZ)
Gainesville Coll (GA)
Keystone Coll (PA)
Northwest-Shoals Comm
  Coll (AL)
St. Philip's Coll (TX)
South U, West Palm Beach
  (FL)
Springfield Coll in Illinois (IL)

Pre-Pharmacy Studies
Allen County Comm Coll
  (KS)
Centralia Coll (WA)
Coastal Georgia Comm Coll
  (GA)
Eastern Arizona Coll (AZ)
Eastern Wyoming Coll (WY)
Gainesville Coll (GA)
Howard Comm Coll (MD)
Kellogg Comm Coll (MI)
Laramie County Comm Coll
  (WY)
Luzerne County Comm Coll
  (PA)
Manatee Comm Coll (FL)

Northwest-Shoals Comm
  Coll (AL)
St. Philip's Coll (TX)
Santa Rosa Jr Coll (CA)
Sauk Valley Comm Coll (IL)
Southwestern Illinois Coll (IL)
Springfield Coll in Illinois (IL)
Tulsa Comm Coll (OK)

Pre-Theology/Pre-Ministerial Studies
Kellogg Comm Coll (MI)

Pre-Veterinary Studies
Allen County Comm Coll
  (KS)
Barton County Comm Coll
  (KS)
Centralia Coll (WA)
Coastal Georgia Comm Coll
  (GA)
Eastern Wyoming Coll (WY)
Howard Comm Coll (MD)
Kellogg Comm Coll (MI)
Laramie County Comm Coll
  (WY)
Northwest-Shoals Comm
  Coll (AL)
Sauk Valley Comm Coll (IL)
Springfield Coll in Illinois (IL)
Tulsa Comm Coll (OK)

Printing Press Operation
Lake Land Coll (IL)
Louisiana Tech Coll (LA)

Printmaking
Dixie State Coll of Utah (UT)
Florida Comm Coll at
  Jacksonville (FL)
Keystone Coll (PA)

Professional Studies
Pratt Comm Coll (KS)

Psychiatric/Mental Health Services Technology
Allegany Coll of Maryland
  (MD)
Comm Coll of Allegheny
  County (PA)
Eastfield Coll (TX)
Hagerstown Comm Coll
  (MD)
Houston Comm Coll System
  (TX)
Ivy Tech Comm Coll–
  Bloomington (IN)
Ivy Tech Comm Coll–Central
  Indiana (IN)
Ivy Tech Comm Coll–
  Columbus (IN)
Ivy Tech Comm Coll–East
  Central (IN)
Ivy Tech Comm Coll–
  Kokomo (IN)
Ivy Tech Comm Coll–
  Lafayette (IN)
Ivy Tech Comm Coll–
  Northeast (IN)
Ivy Tech Comm Coll–
  Northwest (IN)
Ivy Tech Comm Coll–
  Southeast (IN)
Ivy Tech Comm Coll–
  Southern Indiana (IN)
Ivy Tech Comm Coll–
  Southwest (IN)
Ivy Tech Comm Coll–
  Wabash Valley (IN)
Ivy Tech Comm Coll–
  Whitewater (IN)
Kingsborough Comm Coll of
  the City U of New York
  (NY)
Montgomery County Comm
  Coll (PA)
North Dakota State Coll of
  Science (ND)
San Joaquin Delta Coll (CA)
Wilkes Comm Coll (NC)
Yuba Coll (CA)

Psychology
Abraham Baldwin Ag Coll
  (GA)
Allen County Comm Coll
  (KS)
Atlanta Metropolitan Coll
  (GA)
Austin Comm Coll (TX)
Bainbridge Coll (GA)

Barton County Comm Coll
  (KS)
Bergen Comm Coll (NJ)
Brazosport Coll (TX)
Bronx Comm Coll of the City
  U of New York (NY)
Bucks County Comm Coll
  (PA)
Bunker Hill Comm Coll (MA)
Butler Comm Coll (KS)
Butler County Comm Coll
  (PA)
Carl Albert State Coll (OK)
Casper Coll (WY)
Centralia Coll (WA)
Central Wyoming Coll (WY)
Clarendon Coll (TX)
Clovis Comm Coll (NM)
Coastal Bend Coll (TX)
Coastal Georgia Comm Coll
  (GA)
Cochise Coll, Douglas (AZ)
Colby Comm Coll (KS)
Coll of the Canyons (CA)
Colorado Mountain Coll (CO)
Columbia Coll (CA)
Comm Coll of Allegheny
  County (PA)
Crowder Coll (MO)
Delta Coll (MI)
Dixie State Coll of Utah (UT)
East Central Coll (MO)
Eastern Arizona Coll (AZ)
Eastern Wyoming Coll (WY)
Finger Lakes Comm Coll
  (NY)
Fisher Coll (MA)
Foothill Coll (CA)
Frederick Comm Coll (MD)
Gainesville Coll (GA)
GateWay Comm Coll (AZ)
Gavilan Coll (CA)
Genesee Comm Coll (NY)
Georgia Highlands Coll (GA)
Great Basin Coll (NV)
Harrisburg Area Comm Coll
  (PA)
Highland Comm Coll (IL)
Highline Comm Coll (WA)
Howard Comm Coll (MD)
Hutchinson Comm Coll and
  Area Vocational School
  (KS)
Independence Comm Coll
  (KS)
Itasca Comm Coll (MN)
John Wood Comm Coll (IL)
Kellogg Comm Coll (MI)
Kingwood Coll (TX)
Laramie County Comm Coll
  (WY)
Lawson State Comm Coll
  (AL)
Lincoln Coll (IL)
Lincoln Coll–Normal (IL)
Lower Columbia Coll (WA)
Manatee Comm Coll (FL)
Manor Coll (PA)
Miami Dade Coll (FL)
Middlesex County Coll (NJ)
Midland Coll (TX)
MiraCosta Coll (CA)
North Idaho Coll (ID)
Otero Jr Coll (CO)
Palm Beach Comm Coll (FL)
Palo Alto Coll (TX)
Palo Verde Coll (CA)
Pasadena City Coll (CA)
Pratt Comm Coll (KS)
Saddleback Coll (CA)
St. Philip's Coll (TX)
Salem Comm Coll (NJ)
Salt Lake Comm Coll (UT)
San Diego City Coll (CA)
San Diego Mesa Coll (CA)
San Joaquin Delta Coll (CA)
San Juan Coll (NM)
Santa Barbara City Coll (CA)
Santa Rosa Jr Coll (CA)
Sauk Valley Comm Coll (IL)
Skyline Coll (CA)
Spoon River Coll (IL)
Trinidad State Jr Coll (CO)
Trinity Valley Comm Coll
  (TX)
Tulsa Comm Coll (OK)
Vermilion Comm Coll (MN)
Young Harris Coll (GA)
Yuba Coll (CA)

Public Administration
Barton County Comm Coll
  (KS)
Brazosport Coll (TX)
Citrus Coll (CA)
Fayetteville Tech Comm Coll
  (NC)
Hudson Valley Comm Coll
  (NY)
Lansing Comm Coll (MI)
Laramie County Comm Coll
  (WY)
Manatee Comm Coll (FL)
Miami Dade Coll (FL)
Middle Georgia Coll (GA)
Mohawk Valley Comm Coll
  (NY)
Salem Comm Coll (NJ)
San Joaquin Delta Coll (CA)
San Juan Coll (NM)
Scottsdale Comm Coll (AZ)
Sinclair Comm Coll (OH)
Thomas Nelson Comm Coll
  (VA)
Westchester Comm Coll
  (NY)
Westmoreland County
  Comm Coll (PA)

Public Administration and Social Service Professions Related
Cleveland State Comm Coll
  (TN)
Coll of the Mainland (TX)
Erie Comm Coll (NY)
Erie Comm Coll, South
  Campus (NY)
Sauk Valley Comm Coll (IL)

Public Health Education and Promotion
Delta Coll (MI)

Public Health Related
Western Tech Coll (WI)

Public Relations, Advertising, and Applied Communication Related
Keystone Coll (PA)

Public Relations/Image Management
Coastal Bend Coll (TX)
Comm Coll of the Air Force
  (AL)
Crowder Coll (MO)
Glendale Comm Coll (AZ)
Kellogg Comm Coll (MI)
Lansing Comm Coll (MI)

Publishing
Westmoreland County
  Comm Coll (PA)

Purchasing, Procurement/Acquisitions and Contracts Management
Brazosport Coll (TX)
Cincinnati State Tech and
  Comm Coll (OH)
Comm Coll of the Air Force
  (AL)
Tulsa Comm Coll (OK)
William Rainey Harper Coll
  (IL)

Quality Control and Safety Technologies Related
Ivy Tech Comm Coll–
  Lafayette (IN)
Ivy Tech Comm Coll–
  Wabash Valley (IN)

Quality Control Technology
Arkansas State U–Beebe
  (AR)
Austin Comm Coll (TX)
Brazosport Coll (TX)
Broome Comm Coll (NY)
Butler County Comm Coll
  (PA)
Central Comm Coll–
  Columbus Campus (NE)
Century Coll (MN)
Coll of the Canyons (CA)
Comm Coll of Allegheny
  County (PA)
Grand Rapids Comm Coll
  (MI)
Heartland Comm Coll (IL)

Illinois Eastern Comm Colls,
  Frontier Community
  College (IL)
Illinois Eastern Comm Colls,
  Lincoln Trail College (IL)
Ivy Tech Comm Coll–
  Lafayette (IN)
Lakeshore Tech Coll (WI)
Lansing Comm Coll (MI)
Macomb Comm Coll (MI)
Metropolitan Comm
  Coll–Business &
  Technology College (MO)
Mott Comm Coll (MI)
Mountain View Coll (TX)
Mt. San Antonio Coll (CA)
Naugatuck Valley Comm Coll
  (CT)
New Hampshire Comm Tech
  Coll, Nashua/Claremont
  (NH)
Northampton County Area
  Comm Coll (PA)
Rock Valley Coll (IL)
St. Petersburg Coll (FL)
Salt Lake Comm Coll (UT)
Sinclair Comm Coll (OH)
Springfield Tech Comm Coll
  (MA)
Tarrant County Coll District
  (TX)
Texas State Tech Coll Waco
  (TX)
Tulsa Comm Coll (OK)
Waubonsee Comm Coll (IL)
William Rainey Harper Coll
  (IL)
Wisconsin Indianhead Tech
  Coll (WI)

Radio and Television
Asnuntuck Comm Coll (CT)
Austin Comm Coll (TX)
Brevard Comm Coll (FL)
Bucks County Comm Coll
  (PA)
Centralia Coll (WA)
Chattanooga State Tech
  Comm Coll (TN)
Coahoma Comm Coll (MS)
Colby Comm Coll (KS)
Dixie State Coll of Utah (UT)
Foothill Coll (CA)
Illinois Eastern Comm Colls,
  Wabash Valley College (IL)
Keystone Coll (PA)
Lake Land Coll (IL)
Lansing Comm Coll (MI)
Lawson State Comm Coll
  (AL)
Lincoln Coll (IL)
Long Beach City Coll (CA)
Manatee Comm Coll (FL)
Miami Dade Coll (FL)
Middlesex Comm Coll (CT)
Modesto Jr Coll (CA)
Mt. San Antonio Coll (CA)
Northeast Comm Coll (NE)
Northland Comm and Tech
  Coll–Thief River Falls (MN)
Parkland Coll (IL)
Pasadena City Coll (CA)
Saddleback Coll (CA)
St. Louis Comm Coll at
  Florissant Valley (MO)
San Diego City Coll (CA)
Sullivan County Comm Coll
  (NY)
Tompkins Cortland Comm
  Coll (NY)
Tulsa Comm Coll (OK)

Radio and Television Broadcasting Technology
Briarwood Coll (CT)
Cedar Valley Coll (TX)
Central Comm Coll–Hastings
  Campus (NE)
Central Wyoming Coll (WY)
Gadsden State Comm Coll
  (AL)
Houston Comm Coll System
  (TX)
Jefferson State Comm Coll
  (AL)
Kellogg Comm Coll (MI)
Luzerne County Comm Coll
  (PA)
Manatee Comm Coll (FL)
Mercer County Comm Coll
  (NJ)

Miami Dade Coll (FL)
Northampton County Area Comm Coll (PA)
Oakland Comm Coll (MI)
Parkland Coll (IL)
Wilkes Comm Coll (NC)
York Tech Coll (SC)

Radiologic Technology/ Science
Arizona Western Coll (AZ)
Barton County Comm Coll (KS)
Brevard Comm Coll (FL)
Comm Coll of Denver (CO)
Delta Coll (MI)
East Central Coll (MO)
El Centro Coll (TX)
Fayetteville Tech Comm Coll (NC)
Florida National Coll (FL)
Foothill Coll (CA)
George C. Wallace Comm Coll (AL)
Georgia Highlands Coll (GA)
Holyoke Comm Coll (MA)
Hudson Valley Comm Coll (NY)
Keiser Coll, Miami (FL)
Keystone Coll (PA)
Lakeshore Tech Coll (WI)
Laramie County Comm Coll (WY)
Laredo Comm Coll (TX)
Louisiana State U at Alexandria (LA)
Manatee Comm Coll (FL)
Miami Dade Coll (FL)
Middlesex County Coll (NJ)
Midland Coll (TX)
Minnesota State Comm and Tech Coll–Fergus Falls (MN)
Montgomery County Comm Coll (PA)
Moraine Park Tech Coll (WI)
Niagara County Comm Coll (NY)
Northampton County Area Comm Coll (PA)
Northern Essex Comm Coll (MA)
Pasco-Hernando Comm Coll (FL)
Polk Comm Coll (FL)
St. Luke's Coll (IA)
St. Petersburg Coll (FL)
Salt Lake Comm Coll (UT)
Sinclair Comm Coll (OH)
Triton Coll (IL)
Tulsa Comm Coll (OK)
Western Tech Coll (WI)

Radio, Television, and Digital Communication Related
Keystone Coll (PA)

Radio/Television Broadcasting Technology
Brown Coll (MN)
Delta Coll (MI)
Hudson Valley Comm Coll (NY)
Mount Wachusett Comm Coll (MA)
Salt Lake Comm Coll (UT)

Range Science and Management
Central Wyoming Coll (WY)
Colby Comm Coll (KS)
Dixie State Coll of Utah (UT)
Eastern Wyoming Coll (WY)
Snow Coll (UT)
Treasure Valley Comm Coll (OR)
Trinity Valley Comm Coll (TX)
Vermilion Comm Coll (MN)

Real Estate
Alamance Comm Coll (NC)
Austin Comm Coll (TX)
Bergen Comm Coll (NJ)
Cedar Valley Coll (TX)
Central Piedmont Comm Coll (NC)
Chemeketa Comm Coll (OR)
Cincinnati State Tech and Comm Coll (OH)
Citrus Coll (CA)

Coll of DuPage (IL)
Coll of the Canyons (CA)
Collin County Comm Coll District (TX)
Comm Coll of Allegheny County (PA)
Cuyahoga Comm Coll (OH)
Florida Comm Coll at Jacksonville (FL)
Foothill Coll (CA)
Forsyth Tech Comm Coll (NC)
GateWay Comm Coll (AZ)
Glendale Comm Coll (AZ)
Harrisburg Area Comm Coll (PA)
Houston Comm Coll System (TX)
Illinois Central Coll (IL)
Jefferson Comm and Tech Coll (KY)
Jefferson Comm Coll (OH)
Joliet Jr Coll (IL)
Lamar State Coll–Orange (TX)
Lansing Comm Coll (MI)
Laredo Comm Coll (TX)
Long Beach City Coll (CA)
Luzerne County Comm Coll (PA)
MiraCosta Coll (CA)
Modesto Jr Coll (CA)
Montgomery County Comm Coll (PA)
Mt. San Antonio Coll (CA)
Nassau Comm Coll (NY)
New Hampshire Tech Inst (NH)
Northeast Comm Coll (NE)
Northern Essex Comm Coll (MA)
North Seattle Comm Coll (WA)
Ocean County Coll (NJ)
Okaloosa-Walton Coll (FL)
Orange County Comm Coll (NY)
Pasadena City Coll (CA)
Phoenix Coll (AZ)
Pima Comm Coll (AZ)
Raritan Valley Comm Coll (NJ)
Saddleback Coll (CA)
St. Louis Comm Coll at Florissant Valley (MO)
San Diego City Coll (CA)
San Diego Mesa Coll (CA)
San Juan Coll (NM)
Santa Barbara City Coll (CA)
Scottsdale Comm Coll (AZ)
Sinclair Comm Coll (OH)
Southern State Comm Coll (OH)
South Plains Coll (TX)
Southwestern Illinois Coll (IL)
Spokane Falls Comm Coll (WA)
Tidewater Comm Coll (VA)
Trinity Valley Comm Coll (TX)
Triton Coll (IL)
Ventura Coll (CA)
Westmoreland County Comm Coll (PA)
William Rainey Harper Coll (IL)

Receptionist
Alexandria Tech Coll (MN)
Centralia Coll (WA)
Lower Columbia Coll (WA)

Recording Arts Technology
Bay State Coll (MA)
Full Sail Real World Education (FL)
Kansas City Kansas Comm Coll (KS)
Miami Dade Coll (FL)
Northwest Vista Coll (TX)

Rehabilitation and Therapeutic Professions Related
Springfield Tech Comm Coll (MA)
Union County Coll (NJ)

Rehabilitation Therapy
Nassau Comm Coll (NY)
William Rainey Harper Coll (IL)

Religious Education
Lincoln Coll (IL)

Religious Studies
Allen County Comm Coll (KS)
Barton County Comm Coll (KS)
Cowley County Comm Coll and Area Vocational–Tech School (KS)
East Central Coll (MO)
Lansing Comm Coll (MI)
Laramie County Comm Coll (WY)
Manatee Comm Coll (FL)
Orange Coast Coll (CA)
Palm Beach Comm Coll (FL)
Pasadena City Coll (CA)
San Joaquin Delta Coll (CA)
Trinity Valley Comm Coll (TX)
Tulsa Comm Coll (OK)
Young Harris Coll (GA)

Respiratory Care Therapy
Allegany Coll of Maryland (MD)
Athens Tech Coll (GA)
Augusta Tech Coll (GA)
Barton County Comm Coll (KS)
Bergen Comm Coll (NJ)
Berkshire Comm Coll (MA)
Borough of Manhattan Comm Coll of the City U of New York (NY)
Broward Comm Coll (FL)
Carteret Comm Coll (NC)
Casper Coll (WY)
Central New Mexico Comm Coll (NM)
Central Piedmont Comm Coll (NC)
Chattanooga State Tech Comm Coll (TN)
Cincinnati State Tech and Comm Coll (OH)
Coastal Georgia Comm Coll (GA)
Coll of DuPage (IL)
Collin County Comm Coll District (TX)
Comm Coll of Allegheny County (PA)
Cuyahoga Comm Coll (OH)
Delaware Tech & Comm Coll, Stanton/Wilmington Campus (DE)
Delgado Comm Coll (LA)
Delta Coll (MI)
El Centro Coll (TX)
Erie Comm Coll, North Campus (NY)
Essex County Coll (NJ)
Fayetteville Tech Comm Coll (NC)
Florida Comm Coll at Jacksonville (FL)
Foothill Coll (CA)
Forsyth Tech Comm Coll (NC)
Frederick Comm Coll (MD)
GateWay Comm Coll (AZ)
Genesee Comm Coll (NY)
George C. Wallace Comm Coll (AL)
Georgia Highlands Coll (GA)
Goodwin Coll (CT)
Gwinnett Tech Coll (GA)
Harrisburg Area Comm Coll (PA)
Hawkeye Comm Coll (IA)
Highline Comm Coll (WA)
Houston Comm Coll System (TX)
Howard Coll (TX)
Hudson Valley Comm Coll (NY)
Illinois Central Coll (IL)
Ivy Tech Comm Coll–Central Indiana (IN)
Ivy Tech Comm Coll–Lafayette (IN)
Ivy Tech Comm Coll–Northeast (IN)
Ivy Tech Comm Coll–Northwest (IN)
Ivy Tech Comm Coll–Southern Indiana (IN)

Jackson State Comm Coll (TN)
Jefferson Comm and Tech Coll (KY)
Jefferson Comm Coll (OH)
Kansas City Kansas Comm Coll (KS)
Kapiolani Comm Coll (HI)
Kaskaskia Coll (IL)
Kennebec Valley Comm Coll (ME)
Lake Superior Coll (MN)
Lansing Comm Coll (MI)
Lincoln Land Comm Coll (IL)
Luzerne County Comm Coll (PA)
Macomb Comm Coll (MI)
Manatee Comm Coll (FL)
Manchester Comm Coll (CT)
Marshall Comm and Tech Coll (WV)
Massachusetts Bay Comm Coll (MA)
Mercer County Comm Coll (NJ)
Meridian Comm Coll (MS)
Metropolitan Comm Coll (NE)
Miami Dade Coll (FL)
Middlesex County Coll (NJ)
Midland Coll (TX)
Midlands Tech Coll (SC)
Mississippi Gulf Coast Comm Coll (MS)
Modesto Jr Coll (CA)
Mohawk Valley Comm Coll (NY)
Montgomery County Comm Coll (PA)
Moraine Park Tech Coll (WI)
Moraine Valley Comm Coll (IL)
Mott Comm Coll (MI)
Mt. San Antonio Coll (CA)
Nassau Comm Coll (NY)
Northern Essex Comm Coll (MA)
North Shore Comm Coll (MA)
Norwalk Comm Coll (CT)
Oakland Comm Coll (MI)
Orange Coast Coll (CA)
Parkland Coll (IL)
Penn Valley Comm Coll (MO)
Piedmont Virginia Comm Coll (VA)
Pima Comm Coll (AZ)
Polk Comm Coll (FL)
Pulaski Tech Coll (AR)
Quinsigamond Comm Coll (MA)
Raritan Valley Comm Coll (NJ)
Roane State Comm Coll (TN)
Rockingham Comm Coll (NC)
Rock Valley Coll (IL)
St. Luke's Coll (IA)
Saint Paul Coll–A Comm & Tech College (MN)
St. Petersburg Coll (FL)
St. Philip's Coll (TX)
San Joaquin Valley Coll (CA)
Seattle Central Comm Coll (WA)
Seminole Comm Coll (FL)
Shelton State Comm Coll (AL)
Sheridan Coll–Sheridan and Gillette (WY)
Sinclair Comm Coll (OH)
Skyline Coll (CA)
South Plains Coll (TX)
Southside Virginia Comm Coll (VA)
Southwest Georgia Tech Coll (GA)
Southwest Virginia Comm Coll (VA)
Spartanburg Tech Coll (SC)
Spokane Comm Coll (WA)
Springfield Tech Comm Coll (MA)
Stark State Coll of Technology (OH)
Sussex County Comm Coll (NJ)

Tarrant County Coll District (TX)
Trident Tech Coll (SC)
Triton Coll (IL)
Tulsa Comm Coll (OK)
Union County Coll (NJ)
Valencia Comm Coll (FL)
Volunteer State Comm Coll (TN)
Weatherford Coll (TX)
Westchester Comm Coll (NY)
Western Tech Coll (WI)

Respiratory Therapy Technician
Augusta Tech Coll (GA)
Coahoma Comm Coll (MS)
Columbus Tech Coll (GA)
Coosa Valley Tech Coll (GA)
East Central Coll (MO)
Griffin Tech Coll (GA)
Harrisburg Area Comm Coll (PA)
Heart of Georgia Tech Coll (GA)
Kansas City Kansas Comm Coll (KS)
Louisiana Tech Coll (LA)
Miami Dade Coll (FL)
Missouri State U–West Plains (MO)
Northern Essex Comm Coll (MA)
Okefenokee Tech Coll (GA)
Southeastern Tech Coll (GA)

Restaurant, Culinary, and Catering Management
The Art Inst of New York City (NY)
Central Florida Comm Coll (FL)
Cincinnati State Tech and Comm Coll (OH)
Coahoma Comm Coll (MS)
Coll of DuPage (IL)
Coll of Lake County (IL)
Comm Coll of Allegheny County (PA)
Cuyahoga Comm Coll (OH)
Erie Comm Coll, North Campus (NY)
John Wood Comm Coll (IL)
Keystone Coll (PA)
Linn-Benton Comm Coll (OR)
Mohawk Valley Comm Coll (NY)
Moraine Valley Comm Coll (IL)
Orange Coast Coll (CA)
Pima Comm Coll (AZ)
Rasmussen Coll Mankato (MN)
Southwestern Oregon Comm Coll (OR)
State U of New York Coll of Technology at Alfred (NY)
State U of New York Coll of Technology at Delhi (NY)
Waukesha County Tech Coll (WI)

Restaurant/Food Services Management
Front Range Comm Coll (CO)
Keystone Coll (PA)
Northampton County Area Comm Coll (PA)
Oakland Comm Coll (MI)
St. Philip's Coll (TX)

Retailing
Centralia Coll (WA)
Clark Coll (WA)
Coll of DuPage (IL)
Comm Coll of Allegheny County (PA)
Florida Comm Coll at Jacksonville (FL)
Hutchinson Comm Coll and Area Vocational School (KS)
Moraine Valley Comm Coll (IL)
Northeast Comm Coll (NE)
Orange Coast Coll (CA)
Waubonsee Comm Coll (IL)
Waukesha County Tech Coll (WI)

Western Tech Coll (WI)
Wisconsin Indianhead Tech Coll (WI)

Retailing Operations
Clark Coll (WA)

Retail Management
Bristol Comm Coll (MA)
Delta Coll (MI)
Riverside Comm Coll District (CA)

Robotics Technology
Coll of DuPage (IL)
Comm Coll of Allegheny County (PA)
Ivy Tech Comm Coll–Columbus (IN)
Ivy Tech Comm Coll–Lafayette (IN)
Ivy Tech Comm Coll–North Central (IN)
Ivy Tech Comm Coll–Northeast (IN)
Ivy Tech Comm Coll–Southwest (IN)
Ivy Tech Comm Coll–Wabash Valley (IN)
Ivy Tech Comm Coll–Whitewater (IN)
Jefferson State Comm Coll (AL)
Kellogg Comm Coll (MI)
Macomb Comm Coll (MI)
Montgomery Coll (TX)
Oakland Comm Coll (MI)
Spartanburg Tech Coll (SC)
Waubonsee Comm Coll (IL)
Yuba Coll (CA)

Romance Languages
Highline Comm Coll (WA)

Russian
Austin Comm Coll (TX)
Tulsa Comm Coll (OK)

Russian Studies
Manatee Comm Coll (FL)

Safety/Security Technology
Comm and Tech Coll of Shepherd (WV)
Comm Coll of Denver (CO)
Cuyahoga Comm Coll (OH)
Guam Comm Coll (GU)
John Tyler Comm Coll (VA)
Macomb Comm Coll (MI)
Tulsa Comm Coll (OK)

Sales and Marketing/ Marketing And Distribution Teacher Education
Parkland Coll (IL)

Sales, Distribution and Marketing
Central Carolina Tech Coll (SC)
Centralia Coll (WA)
Coll of DuPage (IL)
Collin County Comm Coll District (TX)
Cuyahoga Comm Coll (OH)
John Wood Comm Coll (IL)
Kennebec Valley Comm Coll (ME)
Lake Region State Coll (ND)
Midlands Tech Coll (SC)
Montgomery County Comm Coll (PA)
Norwalk Comm Coll (CT)
Pioneer Pacific Coll (OR)
Santa Barbara City Coll (CA)
State U of New York Coll of Technology at Alfred (NY)
Western Tech Coll (WI)

Sales Operations
Coll of Lake County (IL)

Salon/Beauty Salon Management
Mott Comm Coll (MI)
Oakland Comm Coll (MI)

Science Teacher Education
Chemeketa Comm Coll (OR)
Colby Comm Coll (KS)
Harrisburg Area Comm Coll (PA)
Independence Comm Coll (KS)
Manatee Comm Coll (FL)
Miami Dade Coll (FL)

Snow Coll (UT)
Vermilion Comm Coll (MN)

Science Technologies Related
Cincinnati State Tech and Comm Coll (OH)
Comm Coll of Allegheny County (PA)
Eastern West Virginia Comm and Tech Coll (WV)
Maria Coll (NY)
Marshall Comm and Tech Coll (WV)

Sculpture
Dixie State Coll of Utah (UT)
Keystone Coll (PA)
Mercer County Comm Coll (NJ)

Secondary Education
Allen County Comm Coll (KS)
Barton County Comm Coll (KS)
Brazosport Coll (TX)
Central Wyoming Coll (WY)
Clarendon Coll (TX)
Dixie State Coll of Utah (UT)
Eastern Arizona Coll (AZ)
Eastern Wyoming Coll (WY)
Essex County Coll (NJ)
Gainesville Coll (GA)
Georgia Highlands Coll (GA)
Howard Comm Coll (MD)
Kellogg Comm Coll (MI)
Mohawk Valley Comm Coll (NY)
Montgomery County Comm Coll (PA)
Northwest-Shoals Comm Coll (AL)
Parkland Coll (IL)
Sauk Valley Comm Coll (IL)

Securities Services Administration
Herzing Coll (GA)

Security and Loss Prevention
Cincinnati State Tech and Comm Coll (OH)
Comm Coll of the Air Force (AL)
Delta Coll (MI)
Nassau Comm Coll (NY)
St. Petersburg Coll (FL)
San Joaquin Valley Coll (CA)

Security and Protective Services Related
Goodwin Coll (CT)
Pima Comm Coll (AZ)
St. Petersburg Coll (FL)

Selling Skills and Sales
Alexandria Tech Coll (MN)
Century Coll (MN)
Clark Coll (WA)
Coll of DuPage (IL)
Cuyahoga Comm Coll (OH)
Hibbing Comm Coll (MN)
Lake Superior Coll (MN)
Lincoln Land Comm Coll (IL)
Moraine Valley Comm Coll (IL)
Orange Coast Coll (CA)
Santa Barbara City Coll (CA)

Sheet Metal Technology
Brazosport Coll (TX)
Comm Coll of Allegheny County (PA)
Ivy Tech Comm Coll–Central Indiana (IN)
Ivy Tech Comm Coll–Lafayette (IN)
Ivy Tech Comm Coll–North Central (IN)
Ivy Tech Comm Coll–Northeast (IN)
Ivy Tech Comm Coll–Northwest (IN)
Ivy Tech Comm Coll–Southern Indiana (IN)
Ivy Tech Comm Coll–Southwest (IN)
Ivy Tech Comm Coll–Wabash Valley (IN)
Kellogg Comm Coll (MI)
Macomb Comm Coll (MI)

Sign Language Interpretation and Translation
Austin Comm Coll (TX)
Central Piedmont Comm Coll (NC)
Chattanooga State Tech Comm Coll (TN)
Cincinnati State Tech and Comm Coll (OH)
Clovis Comm Coll (NM)
Collin County Comm Coll District (TX)
Comm Coll of Allegheny County (PA)
Cowley County Comm Coll and Area Vocational–Tech School (KS)
Delaware Tech & Comm Coll, Stanton/Wilmington Campus (DE)
Delgado Comm Coll (LA)
Eastfield Coll (TX)
Florida Comm Coll at Jacksonville (FL)
Guam Comm Coll (GU)
Houston Comm Coll System (TX)
Lake Region State Coll (ND)
Lansing Comm Coll (MI)
Miami Dade Coll (FL)
Mott Comm Coll (MI)
Mt. San Antonio Coll (CA)
Mount Wachusett Comm Coll (MA)
Northern Essex Comm Coll (MA)
Northwestern Connecticut Comm Coll (CT)
Pasadena City Coll (CA)
Pima Comm Coll (AZ)
Riverside Comm Coll District (CA)
St. Louis Comm Coll at Florissant Valley (MO)
Saint Paul Coll–A Comm & Tech College (MN)
St. Petersburg Coll (FL)
Salt Lake Comm Coll (UT)
Seattle Central Comm Coll (WA)
Sheridan Coll–Sheridan and Gillette (WY)
Sinclair Comm Coll (OH)
Southeast Tech Inst (SD)
Southwestern Illinois Coll (IL)
Spartanburg Tech Coll (SC)
Spokane Falls Comm Coll (WA)
Tarrant County Coll District (TX)
Tulsa Comm Coll (OK)
Union County Coll (NJ)
Waubonsee Comm Coll (IL)
William Rainey Harper Coll (IL)
Wilson Tech Comm Coll (NC)

Small Business Administration
Alexandria Tech Coll (MN)
Lake Region State Coll (ND)

Small Engine Mechanics and Repair Technology
Alexandria Tech Coll (MN)
Century Coll (MN)
North Dakota State Coll of Science (ND)

Social Psychology
Macomb Comm Coll (MI)
Manatee Comm Coll (FL)

Social Sciences
Abraham Baldwin Ag Coll (GA)
Allan Hancock Coll (CA)
Ancilla Coll (IN)
Arizona Western Coll (AZ)
Brazosport Coll (TX)
Bucks County Comm Coll (PA)
Carl Albert State Coll (OK)
Casper Coll (WY)
Centralia Coll (WA)
Central Oregon Comm Coll (OR)
Central Wyoming Coll (WY)
Chemeketa Comm Coll (OR)
Citrus Coll (CA)
Clarendon Coll (TX)

Coll of Southern Maryland (MD)
Coll of the Canyons (CA)
Colorado Mountain Coll (CO)
Colorado Mountain Coll, Alpine Campus (CO)
Comm Coll of Allegheny County (PA)
Corning Comm Coll (NY)
Diné Coll (AZ)
Essex County Coll (NJ)
Feather River Coll (CA)
Finger Lakes Comm Coll (NY)
Foothill Coll (CA)
Galveston Coll (TX)
Gavilan Coll (CA)
Harrisburg Area Comm Coll (PA)
Highline Comm Coll (WA)
Houston Comm Coll System (TX)
Howard Coll (TX)
Howard Comm Coll (MD)
Hutchinson Comm Coll and Area Vocational School (KS)
Jamestown Comm Coll (NY)
Kingwood Coll (TX)
Lamar State Coll–Orange (TX)
Lamar State Coll–Port Arthur (TX)
Laramie County Comm Coll (WY)
Laredo Comm Coll (TX)
Lawson State Comm Coll (AL)
Lincoln Coll–Normal (IL)
Long Beach City Coll (CA)
Lower Columbia Coll (WA)
Luzerne County Comm Coll (PA)
Manatee Comm Coll (FL)
Massachusetts Bay Comm Coll (MA)
Miami Dade Coll (FL)
Middlesex County Coll (NJ)
MiraCosta Coll (CA)
Modesto Jr Coll (CA)
Montgomery County Comm Coll (PA)
New Mexico Military Inst (NM)
Niagara County Comm Coll (NY)
Northeast Comm Coll (NE)
North Idaho Coll (ID)
Northwestern Connecticut Comm Coll (CT)
Okaloosa-Walton Coll (FL)
Orange Coast Coll (CA)
Otero Jr Coll (CO)
Palm Beach Comm Coll (FL)
Pasadena City Coll (CA)
Pratt Comm Coll (KS)
Raritan Valley Comm Coll (NJ)
Roane State Comm Coll (TN)
Rogue Comm Coll (OR)
Saddleback Coll (CA)
Salem Comm Coll (NJ)
San Diego City Coll (CA)
San Diego Mesa Coll (CA)
San Joaquin Delta Coll (CA)
Santa Rosa Jr Coll (CA)
Seminole State Coll (OK)
Sheridan Coll–Sheridan and Gillette (WY)
Skyline Coll (CA)
Southwest Mississippi Comm Coll (MS)
Spoon River Coll (IL)
State U of New York Coll of Technology at Alfred (NY)
State U of New York Coll of Technology at Delhi (NY)
Thomas Nelson Comm Coll (VA)
Tompkins Cortland Comm Coll (NY)
Treasure Valley Comm Coll (OR)
Tulsa Comm Coll (OK)
Westchester Comm Coll (NY)
William Rainey Harper Coll (IL)
Yuba Coll (CA)

Social Studies Teacher Education
Manatee Comm Coll (FL)

Social Work
Abraham Baldwin Ag Coll (GA)
Aiken Tech Coll (SC)
Alamance Comm Coll (NC)
Allen County Comm Coll (KS)
Atlanta Metropolitan Coll (GA)
Austin Comm Coll (TX)
Barton County Comm Coll (KS)
Beaufort County Comm Coll (NC)
Berkshire Comm Coll (MA)
Bucks County Comm Coll (PA)
Capital Comm Coll (CT)
Casper Coll (WY)
Central Piedmont Comm Coll (NC)
Century Coll (MN)
Clark State Comm Coll (OH)
Coahoma Comm Coll (MS)
Cochise Coll, Douglas (AZ)
Colby Comm Coll (KS)
Coll of Lake County (IL)
Coll of the Mainland (TX)
Comm Coll of Allegheny County (PA)
Comm Coll of the Air Force (AL)
Cowley County Comm Coll and Area Vocational–Tech School (KS)
Diné Coll (AZ)
Dixie State Coll of Utah (UT)
Eastfield Coll (TX)
Essex County Coll (NJ)
Gainesville Coll (GA)
Galveston Coll (TX)
GateWay Comm Coll (AZ)
Harrisburg Area Comm Coll (PA)
Illinois Eastern Comm Colls, Wabash Valley College (IL)
Jefferson Comm and Tech Coll (KY)
Kellogg Comm Coll (MI)
Kilian Comm Coll (SD)
Lac Courte Oreilles Ojibwa Comm Coll (WI)
Lake Land Coll (IL)
Lansing Comm Coll (MI)
Lawson State Comm Coll (AL)
Manatee Comm Coll (FL)
Manchester Comm Coll (CT)
Miami Dade Coll (FL)
Naugatuck Valley Comm Coll (CT)
New Hampshire Comm Tech Coll, Nashua/Claremont (NH)
New Mexico State U–Alamogordo (NM)
Northampton County Area Comm Coll (PA)
Northwestern Tech Coll (GA)
Ocean County Coll (NJ)
Okaloosa-Walton Coll (FL)
Palm Beach Comm Coll (FL)
Pratt Comm Coll (KS)
St. Philip's Coll (TX)
Salt Lake Comm Coll (UT)
San Diego City Coll (CA)
San Juan Coll (NM)
Sauk Valley Comm Coll (IL)
South Plains Coll (TX)
Southwestern Oregon Comm Coll (OR)
Spokane Falls Comm Coll (WA)
Springfield Coll in Illinois (IL)
Tulsa Comm Coll (OK)
The U of Akron–Wayne Coll (OH)
Waubonsee Comm Coll (IL)
West Georgia Tech Coll (GA)
West Virginia Northern Comm Coll (WV)

Social Work Related
Clarendon Coll (TX)
Northeast Comm Coll (NE)

Sociology
Abraham Baldwin Ag Coll (GA)
Allen County Comm Coll (KS)
Austin Comm Coll (TX)
Bainbridge Coll (GA)
Barton County Comm Coll (KS)
Bergen Comm Coll (NJ)
Brazosport Coll (TX)
Bunker Hill Comm Coll (MA)
Butler Comm Coll (KS)
Casper Coll (WY)
Centralia Coll (WA)
Clarendon Coll (TX)
Coastal Bend Coll (TX)
Coastal Georgia Comm Coll (GA)
Cochise Coll, Douglas (AZ)
Colby Comm Coll (KS)
Coll of the Mainland (TX)
Columbia Coll (CA)
Comm Coll of Allegheny County (PA)
Dixie State Coll of Utah (UT)
East Central Coll (MO)
Eastern Arizona Coll (AZ)
Eastern Wyoming Coll (WY)
Finger Lakes Comm Coll (NY)
Foothill Coll (CA)
Gainesville Coll (GA)
Gavilan Coll (CA)
Georgia Highlands Coll (GA)
Great Basin Coll (NV)
Highland Comm Coll (IL)
Independence Comm Coll (KS)
John Wood Comm Coll (IL)
Kellogg Comm Coll (MI)
Laramie County Comm Coll (WY)
Lawson State Comm Coll (AL)
Lincoln Coll (IL)
Lower Columbia Coll (WA)
Miami Dade Coll (FL)
Middlesex County Coll (NJ)
Midland Coll (TX)
MiraCosta Coll (CA)
North Idaho Coll (ID)
Orange Coast Coll (CA)
Palo Alto Coll (TX)
Palo Verde Coll (CA)
Pasadena City Coll (CA)
Pima Comm Coll (AZ)
Pratt Comm Coll (KS)
Saddleback Coll (CA)
St. Philip's Coll (TX)
Salem Comm Coll (NJ)
Salt Lake Comm Coll (UT)
San Diego City Coll (CA)
San Diego Mesa Coll (CA)
San Joaquin Delta Coll (CA)
San Juan Coll (NM)
Santa Barbara City Coll (CA)
Santa Rosa Jr Coll (CA)
Sauk Valley Comm Coll (IL)
Skyline Coll (CA)
Snow Coll (UT)
Spoon River Coll (IL)
Treasure Valley Comm Coll (OR)
Trinity Valley Comm Coll (TX)
Tulsa Comm Coll (OK)
Vermilion Comm Coll (MN)
Young Harris Coll (GA)

Soil Conservation
The Ohio State U Ag Tech Inst (OH)
Snow Coll (UT)
Vermilion Comm Coll (MN)

Soil Science and Agronomy
Dixie State Coll of Utah (UT)

Solar Energy Technology
Comm Coll of Allegheny County (PA)

Spanish
Allan Hancock Coll (CA)
Arizona Western Coll (AZ)
Austin Comm Coll (TX)
Berkeley City Coll (CA)
Casper Coll (WY)
Centralia Coll (WA)
Citrus Coll (CA)
Cleveland Comm Coll (NC)

Coll of the Canyons (CA)
Foothill Coll (CA)
Gavilan Coll (CA)
Independence Comm Coll (KS)
Laramie County Comm Coll (WY)
Lincoln Coll (IL)
Long Beach City Coll (CA)
Manatee Comm Coll (FL)
Miami Dade Coll (FL)
Midland Coll (TX)
MiraCosta Coll (CA)
New Mexico Military Inst (NM)
North Idaho Coll (ID)
Orange Coast Coll (CA)
Pasadena City Coll (CA)
St. Philip's Coll (TX)
San Diego Mesa Coll (CA)
San Joaquin Delta Coll (CA)
Santa Barbara City Coll (CA)
Sauk Valley Comm Coll (IL)
Skyline Coll (CA)
Snow Coll (UT)
Trinity Valley Comm Coll (TX)
Tulsa Comm Coll (OK)
Wharton County Jr Coll (TX)
Young Harris Coll (GA)

Spanish Language Teacher Education
Frederick Comm Coll (MD)

Special Education
Cleveland Comm Coll (NC)
Fayetteville Tech Comm Coll (NC)
Kellogg Comm Coll (MI)
Sauk Valley Comm Coll (IL)

Special Education (Early Childhood)
Itasca Comm Coll (MN)
Motlow State Comm Coll (TN)

Special Education (Hearing Impaired)
Bishop State Comm Coll (AL)

Special Products Marketing
Asnuntuck Comm Coll (CT)
Bergen Comm Coll (NJ)
Broward Comm Coll (FL)
Central Piedmont Comm Coll (NC)
Columbia Coll (CA)
Copiah-Lincoln Comm Coll (MS)
East Central Coll (MO)
El Centro Coll (TX)
Fiorello H. LaGuardia Comm Coll of the City U of New York (NY)
Fox Valley Tech Coll (WI)
Gateway Comm Coll (CT)
Jefferson Comm Coll (OH)
Joliet Jr Coll (IL)
Kapiolani Comm Coll (HI)
Lansing Comm Coll (MI)
Long Beach City Coll (CA)
Modesto Jr Coll (CA)
Naugatuck Valley Comm Coll (CT)
Orange Coast Coll (CA)
Palm Beach Comm Coll (FL)
Penn Valley Comm Coll (MO)
Phoenix Coll (AZ)
Saddleback Coll (CA)
St. Louis Comm Coll at Florissant Valley (MO)
San Diego City Coll (CA)
San Joaquin Delta Coll (CA)
Scottsdale Comm Coll (AZ)
Sinclair Comm Coll (OH)
South Plains Coll (TX)
Vermilion Comm Coll (MN)
Westchester Comm Coll (NY)
Westmoreland County Comm Coll (PA)
Yakima Valley Comm Coll (WA)

Speech and Rhetoric
Abraham Baldwin Ag Coll (GA)
Allen County Comm Coll (KS)

Atlanta Metropolitan Coll (GA)
Austin Comm Coll (TX)
Bainbridge Coll (GA)
Brazosport Coll (TX)
Carl Albert State Coll (OK)
Casper Coll (WY)
City Colls of Chicago, Wilbur Wright College (IL)
Clarendon Coll (TX)
Coastal Bend Coll (TX)
East Central Coll (MO)
Foothill Coll (CA)
Howard Coll (TX)
Lansing Comm Coll (MI)
Linn-Benton Comm Coll (OR)
Long Beach City Coll (CA)
Lower Columbia Coll (WA)
Manatee Comm Coll (FL)
Midland Coll (TX)
MiraCosta Coll (CA)
Modesto Jr Coll (CA)
Northeast Comm Coll (NE)
Palo Alto Coll (TX)
Pasadena City Coll (CA)
Pratt Comm Coll (KS)
Saddleback Coll (CA)
St. Philip's Coll (TX)
San Diego City Coll (CA)
San Diego Mesa Coll (CA)
San Joaquin Delta Coll (CA)
Sauk Valley Comm Coll (IL)
Skyline Coll (CA)
Spoon River Coll (IL)
Trinity Valley Comm Coll (TX)
Tulsa Comm Coll (OK)
Vermilion Comm Coll (MN)
Wharton County Jr Coll (TX)

Speech-Language Pathology
Coll of DuPage (IL)
Fayetteville Tech Comm Coll (NC)
Parkland Coll (IL)
Santa Rosa Jr Coll (CA)
Wilkes Comm Coll (NC)

Speech/Theater Education
Highland Comm Coll (IL)
Pratt Comm Coll (KS)

Speech Therapy
Mount Wachusett Comm Coll (MA)

Sport and Fitness Administration/Management
Barton County Comm Coll (KS)
Bucks County Comm Coll (PA)
Butler County Comm Coll (PA)
Central Oregon Comm Coll (OR)
Clark Coll (WA)
Coahoma Comm Coll (MS)
Dean Coll (MA)
Gainesville Coll (GA)
Holyoke Comm Coll (MA)
Howard Comm Coll (MD)
Keystone Coll (PA)
Kingsborough Comm Coll of the City U of New York (NY)
Lake-Sumter Comm Coll (FL)
New Hampshire Tech Inst (NH)
New Mexico Military Inst (NM)
Northampton County Area Comm Coll (PA)
North Iowa Area Comm Coll (IA)
Oakland Comm Coll (MI)
Spokane Falls Comm Coll (WA)
State U of New York Coll of Technology at Alfred (NY)
Sullivan County Comm Coll (NY)
Tompkins Cortland Comm Coll (NY)

Stationary Energy Sources Installation
Ivy Tech Comm Coll–Northwest (IN)

Statistics
Eastern Wyoming Coll (WY)
Lincoln Coll (IL)
Manatee Comm Coll (FL)
Pasadena City Coll (CA)

Substance Abuse/Addiction Counseling
Broome Comm Coll (NY)
Butler Comm Coll (KS)
Century Coll (MN)
Clark Coll (WA)
Coll of DuPage (IL)
Coll of Lake County (IL)
Comm Coll of Allegheny County (PA)
Corning Comm Coll (NY)
Delaware Tech & Comm Coll, Stanton/Wilmington Campus (DE)
Eastfield Coll (TX)
Edmonds Comm Coll (WA)
Erie Comm Coll (NY)
Finger Lakes Comm Coll (NY)
Florida Comm Coll at Jacksonville (FL)
Gadsden State Comm Coll (AL)
Gateway Comm Coll (CT)
Genesee Comm Coll (NY)
Howard Coll (TX)
Howard Comm Coll (MD)
Hudson Valley Comm Coll (NY)
Kansas City Kansas Comm Coll (KS)
Lac Courte Oreilles Ojibwa Comm Coll (WI)
Lower Columbia Coll (WA)
Mesabi Range Comm and Tech Coll (MN)
Miami Dade Coll (FL)
Middlesex Comm Coll (CT)
Midland Coll (TX)
Mohawk Valley Comm Coll (NY)
Moraine Park Tech Coll (WI)
Naugatuck Valley Comm Coll (CT)
New Hampshire Tech Inst (NH)
North Shore Comm Coll (MA)
Northwestern Connecticut Comm Coll (CT)
Northwest Indian Coll (WA)
Norwalk Comm Coll (CT)
Peninsula Coll (WA)
Prairie State Coll (IL)
Quinebaug Valley Comm Coll (CT)
Rogue Comm Coll (OR)
Saddleback Coll (CA)
St. Petersburg Coll (FL)
Seattle Central Comm Coll (WA)
Southwestern Oregon Comm Coll (OR)
Spokane Falls Comm Coll (WA)
Sullivan County Comm Coll (NY)
Tillamook Bay Comm Coll (OR)
Tompkins Cortland Comm Coll (NY)
Triton Coll (IL)
Tunxis Comm Coll (CT)
Westchester Comm Coll (NY)
Wor-Wic Comm Coll (MD)
Yakima Valley Comm Coll (WA)
Yuba Coll (CA)

Surgical Technology
Athens Tech Coll (GA)
Augusta Tech Coll (GA)
Austin Comm Coll (TX)
Berkshire Comm Coll (MA)
Brevard Comm Coll (FL)
Brown Mackie Coll–Merrillville (IN)
Central Carolina Tech Coll (SC)
Central Wyoming Coll (WY)
Cincinnati State Tech and Comm Coll (OH)
Coastal Carolina Comm Coll (NC)

Coll of DuPage (IL)
Columbus Tech Coll (GA)
Comm Care Coll (OK)
Comm Coll of Allegheny County (PA)
Comm Coll of the Air Force (AL)
Coosa Valley Tech Coll (GA)
Cuyahoga Comm Coll (OH)
DeKalb Tech Coll (GA)
Delta Coll (MI)
East Central Coll (MO)
Eastern Idaho Tech Coll (ID)
El Centro Coll (TX)
Fayetteville Tech Comm Coll (NC)
Frederick Comm Coll (MD)
GateWay Comm Coll (AZ)
Griffin Tech Coll (GA)
Indiana Business Coll, Fort Wayne (IN)
Indiana Business Coll, Indianapolis (IN)
Indiana Business Coll, Indianapolis (IN)
Indiana Business Coll-Medical (IN)
Ivy Tech Comm Coll–Central Indiana (IN)
Ivy Tech Comm Coll–Columbus (IN)
Ivy Tech Comm Coll–East Central (IN)
Ivy Tech Comm Coll–Kokomo (IN)
Ivy Tech Comm Coll–Lafayette (IN)
Ivy Tech Comm Coll–Northwest (IN)
Ivy Tech Comm Coll–Southwest (IN)
Ivy Tech Comm Coll–Wabash Valley (IN)
James H. Faulkner State Comm Coll (AL)
Lake Superior Coll (MN)
Lamar State Coll–Port Arthur (TX)
Lanier Tech Coll (GA)
Lansing Comm Coll (MI)
Louisiana Tech Coll (LA)
Luzerne County Comm Coll (PA)
Macomb Comm Coll (MI)
Manchester Comm Coll (CT)
Metropolitan Comm Coll (NE)
Midlands Tech Coll (SC)
Mohawk Valley Comm Coll (NY)
Montgomery County Comm Coll (PA)
Moraine Park Tech Coll (WI)
Nassau Comm Coll (NY)
Niagara County Comm Coll (NY)
Northampton County Area Comm Coll (PA)
North Arkansas Coll (AR)
Northeast Comm Coll (NE)
Northeast State Tech Comm Coll (TN)
Northwestern Tech Coll (GA)
Oakland Comm Coll (MI)
Okefenokee Tech Coll (GA)
Parkland Coll (IL)
St. Cloud Tech Coll (MN)
San Joaquin Valley Coll (CA)
Savannah Tech Coll (GA)
Sinclair Comm Coll (OH)
Skyline Coll (CA)
Southeast Tech Inst (SD)
South Plains Coll (TX)
Southwest Georgia Tech Coll (GA)
Spokane Comm Coll (WA)
Springfield Tech Comm Coll (MA)
Tarrant County Coll District (TX)
Trinity Valley Comm Coll (TX)
Tulsa Comm Coll (OK)
Waukesha County Tech Coll (WI)
Western Tech Coll (WI)
York Tech Coll (SC)

Surveying Engineering
Santa Rosa Jr Coll (CA)

Survey Technology
Austin Comm Coll (TX)
Centralia Coll (WA)
Central Piedmont Comm Coll (NC)
Chattanooga State Tech Comm Coll (TN)
Cincinnati State Tech and Comm Coll (OH)
Delaware Tech & Comm Coll, Terry Campus (DE)
Fayetteville Tech Comm Coll (NC)
Hawkeye Comm Coll (IA)
Lansing Comm Coll (MI)
Louisiana Tech Coll (LA)
Macomb Comm Coll (MI)
Middle Georgia Coll (GA)
Middlesex County Coll (NJ)
Mohawk Valley Comm Coll (NY)
Morrison Inst of Technology (IL)
Mott Comm Coll (MI)
Mt. San Antonio Coll (CA)
Owens Comm Coll, Toledo (OH)
Palm Beach Comm Coll (FL)
The Pennsylvania State U Wilkes-Barre Campus of the Commonwealth Coll (PA)
Salt Lake Comm Coll (UT)
Sinclair Comm Coll (OH)
Southeast Tech Inst (SD)
Stark State Coll of Technology (OH)
State U of New York Coll of Environmental Science & Forestry, Ranger School (NY)
State U of New York Coll of Technology at Alfred (NY)
Sullivan County Comm Coll (NY)
Treasure Valley Comm Coll (OR)
Tulsa Comm Coll (OK)
Valencia Comm Coll (FL)

System Administration
Austin Comm Coll (TX)
Berkeley Coll (NJ)
Berks Tech Inst (PA)
Brevard Comm Coll (FL)
Brown Mackie Coll–Kansas City (KS)
Central Comm Coll–Columbus Campus (NE)
Central Comm Coll–Grand Island Campus (NE)
Central Comm Coll–Hastings Campus (NE)
Centralia Coll (WA)
Cleveland Comm Coll (NC)
Coastal Bend Coll (TX)
The Coll of Westchester (NY)
Davis Coll (OH)
Eastfield Coll (TX)
Edmonds Comm Coll (WA)
Fiorello H. LaGuardia Comm Coll of the City U of New York (NY)
Florida Comm Coll at Jacksonville (FL)
Florida National Coll (FL)
GateWay Comm Coll (AZ)
Genesee Comm Coll (NY)
Hawkeye Comm Coll (IA)
Heartland Comm Coll (IL)
IntelliTec Coll, Grand Junction (CO)
Island Drafting and Tech Inst (NY)
Laurel Business Inst (PA)
Linn-Benton Comm Coll (OR)
Louisiana Tech Coll (LA)
Metropolitan Comm Coll-Business & Technology College (MO)
Midland Coll (TX)
Naugatuck Valley Comm Coll (CT)
Northland Comm and Tech Coll–Thief River Falls (MN)
Palm Beach Comm Coll (FL)
Parkland Coll (IL)
Quinebaug Valley Comm Coll (CT)

Rasmussen Coll Mankato (MN)
Santa Barbara City Coll (CA)
Seminole Comm Coll (FL)
Sheridan Coll–Sheridan and Gillette (WY)
Sinclair Comm Coll (OH)
Southeast Tech Inst (SD)
Southwest Mississippi Comm Coll (MS)
Tompkins Cortland Comm Coll (NY)
Triton Coll (IL)
Tulsa Comm Coll (OK)
Western Tech Coll (WI)

System, Networking, and Lan/Wan Management
Berkshire Comm Coll (MA)
Brevard Comm Coll (FL)
Brown Mackie Coll–Northern Kentucky (KY)
Coll of Business and Technology (FL)
Fayetteville Tech Comm Coll (NC)
Herzing Coll (GA)
Hickey Coll (MO)
Hudson Valley Comm Coll (NY)
International Business Coll, Indianapolis (IN)
ITT Tech Inst, Tucson (AZ)
ITT Tech Inst (AR)
ITT Tech Inst, Anaheim (CA)
ITT Tech Inst, Lathrop (CA)
ITT Tech Inst, Oxnard (CA)
ITT Tech Inst, Rancho Cordova (CA)
ITT Tech Inst, San Bernardino (CA)
ITT Tech Inst, San Diego (CA)
ITT Tech Inst, Sylmar (CA)
ITT Tech Inst, Torrance (CA)
ITT Tech Inst, West Covina (CA)
ITT Tech Inst (CO)
ITT Tech Inst, Fort Lauderdale (FL)
ITT Tech Inst, Jacksonville (FL)
ITT Tech Inst, Lake Mary (FL)
ITT Tech Inst, Miami (FL)
ITT Tech Inst, Tampa (FL)
ITT Tech Inst, Duluth (GA)
ITT Tech Inst, Kennesaw (GA)
ITT Tech Inst (ID)
ITT Tech Inst, Burr Ridge (IL)
ITT Tech Inst, Matteson (IL)
ITT Tech Inst, Mount Prospect (IL)
ITT Tech Inst, Fort Wayne (IN)
ITT Tech Inst, Indianapolis (IN)
ITT Tech Inst, Newburgh (IN)
ITT Tech Inst, Louisville (KY)
ITT Tech Inst (LA)
ITT Tech Inst (MD)
ITT Tech Inst, Norwood (MA)
ITT Tech Inst, Woburn (MA)
ITT Tech Inst, Canton (MI)
ITT Tech Inst, Grand Rapids (MI)
ITT Tech Inst, Troy (MI)
ITT Tech Inst (MN)
ITT Tech Inst, Arnold (MO)
ITT Tech Inst, Earth City (MO)
ITT Tech Inst, Kansas City (MO)
ITT Tech Inst (NE)
ITT Tech Inst (NV)
ITT Tech Inst (NM)
ITT Tech Inst, Albany (NY)
ITT Tech Inst, Getzville (NY)
ITT Tech Inst, Liverpool (NY)
ITT Tech Inst, Dayton (OH)
ITT Tech Inst, Hilliard (OH)
ITT Tech Inst, Norwood (OH)
ITT Tech Inst, Strongsville (OH)
ITT Tech Inst, Warrensville Heights (OH)
ITT Tech Inst, Youngstown (OH)
ITT Tech Inst (OK)

ITT Tech Inst (OR)
ITT Tech Inst (SC)
ITT Tech Inst, Knoxville (TN)
ITT Tech Inst, Memphis (TN)
ITT Tech Inst, Nashville (TN)
ITT Tech Inst, Arlington (TX)
ITT Tech Inst, Austin (TX)
ITT Tech Inst, Houston (TX)
ITT Tech Inst, Houston (TX)
ITT Tech Inst, Houston (TX)
ITT Tech Inst, Richardson (TX)
ITT Tech Inst, San Antonio (TX)
ITT Tech Inst (UT)
ITT Tech Inst, Norfolk (VA)
ITT Tech Inst, Richmond (VA)
ITT Tech Inst, Springfield (VA)
ITT Tech Inst, Bothell (WA)
ITT Tech Inst, Seattle (WA)
ITT Tech Inst, Spokane (WA)
ITT Tech Inst, Green Bay (WI)
ITT Tech Inst, Greenfield (WI)
Metropolitan Comm Coll-Business & Technology College (MO)
Midland Coll (TX)
Minneapolis Business Coll (MN)
Montgomery Coll (TX)
St. Philip's Coll (TX)
Wood Tobe–Coburn School (NY)

Taxation
Globe Coll (MN)
Minnesota School of Business–Brooklyn Center (MN)
Minnesota School of Business–Plymouth (MN)
Minnesota School of Business–Richfield (MN)
Minnesota School of Business–St. Cloud (MN)

Teacher Assistant/Aide
Alamance Comm Coll (NC)
Big Bend Comm Coll (WA)
Bucks County Comm Coll (PA)
Carteret Comm Coll (NC)
Centralia Coll (WA)
Chemeketa Comm Coll (OR)
Cleveland Comm Coll (NC)
Clovis Comm Coll (NM)
Coll of The Albemarle (NC)
Comm Coll of Denver (CO)
East Central Coll (MO)
El Centro Coll (TX)
Goodwin Coll (CT)
Illinois Eastern Comm Colls, Lincoln Trail College (IL)
Joliet Jr Coll (IL)
Kingsborough Comm Coll of the City U of New York (NY)
Lansing Comm Coll (MI)
Linn-Benton Comm Coll (OR)
Lower Columbia Coll (WA)
Manchester Comm Coll (CT)
Mercer County Comm Coll (NJ)
Miami Dade Coll (FL)
Middlesex County Coll (NJ)
MiraCosta Coll (CA)
Montgomery County Comm Coll (PA)
Mott Comm Coll (MI)
New Hampshire Tech Inst (NH)
New Mexico State U–Alamogordo (NM)
Northampton County Area Comm Coll (PA)
Ocean County Coll (NJ)
Pasadena City Coll (CA)
Prairie State Coll (IL)
Rockingham Comm Coll (NC)
Saddleback Coll (CA)
St. Cloud Tech Coll (MN)
St. Philip's Coll (TX)
Salt Lake Comm Coll (UT)
San Diego City Coll (CA)
Southeastern Comm Coll (NC)

Vance-Granville Comm Coll (NC)
Waukesha County Tech Coll (WI)

Teaching Assistants/Aides Related
Southern Arkansas U Tech (AR)

Technical and Business Writing
Austin Comm Coll (TX)
Cincinnati State Tech and Comm Coll (OH)
Clovis Comm Coll (NM)
Coll of Lake County (IL)
Florida National Coll (FL)
Houston Comm Coll System (TX)
Linn-Benton Comm Coll (OR)

Technical Teacher Education
Lake Region State Coll (ND)
Louisiana Tech Coll (LA)
North Dakota State Coll of Science (ND)

Technology/Industrial Arts Teacher Education
Allen County Comm Coll (KS)
Cowley County Comm Coll and Area Vocational–Tech School (KS)
Eastern Arizona Coll (AZ)
Kellogg Comm Coll (MI)
Manatee Comm Coll (FL)
Roane State Comm Coll (TN)

Telecommunications
Cincinnati State Tech and Comm Coll (OH)
DeKalb Tech Coll (GA)
ECPI Coll of Technology, Newport News (VA)
ECPI Coll of Technology, Virginia Beach (VA)
ECPI Tech Coll (VA)
ECPI Tech Coll, Richmond (VA)
Gadsden State Comm Coll (AL)
Heald Coll-San Jose (CA)
Howard Comm Coll (MD)
Illinois Eastern Comm Colls, Lincoln Trail College (IL)
Lake Land Coll (IL)
Lansing Comm Coll (MI)
Meridian Comm Coll (MS)
Mount Wachusett Comm Coll (MA)
New Hampshire Comm Tech Coll, Nashua/Claremont (NH)
Owens Comm Coll, Toledo (OH)
Pasadena City Coll (CA)
St. Louis Comm Coll at Florissant Valley (MO)
San Diego City Coll (CA)
Seminole Comm Coll (FL)
Skyline Coll (CA)
South Plains Coll (TX)
Trident Tech Coll (SC)
Tulsa Comm Coll (OK)

Telecommunications Technology
Brooks Coll, Long Beach (CA)
Clark Coll (WA)
Collin County Comm Coll District (TX)
ECPI Tech Coll (VA)
ECPI Tech Coll, Glen Allen (VA)
ECPI Tech Coll, Richmond (VA)
Hudson Valley Comm Coll (NY)
Ivy Tech Comm Coll–North Central (IN)
Ivy Tech Comm Coll–Northwest (IN)
Miami Dade Coll (FL)
Minnesota State Comm and Tech Coll–Fergus Falls (MN)

Northern Essex Comm Coll (MA)
North Seattle Comm Coll (WA)
The Pennsylvania State U DuBois Campus of the Commonwealth Coll (PA)
The Pennsylvania State U Fayette Campus of the Commonwealth Coll (PA)
The Pennsylvania State U Hazleton Campus of the Commonwealth Coll (PA)
The Pennsylvania State U New Kensington Campus of the Commonwealth Coll (PA)
The Pennsylvania State U Shenango Campus of the Commonwealth Coll (PA)
The Pennsylvania State U Wilkes-Barre Campus of the Commonwealth Coll (PA)
The Pennsylvania State U York Campus of the Commonwealth Coll (PA)
St. Petersburg Coll (FL)
Salt Lake Comm Coll (UT)
TESST Coll of Technology, Towson (MD)
Waukesha County Tech Coll (WI)

Theater Design and Technology
Central Wyoming Coll (WY)
Florida Comm Coll at Jacksonville (FL)
Howard Comm Coll (MD)
Lake-Sumter Comm Coll (FL)
Nassau Comm Coll (NY)
Santa Barbara City Coll (CA)

Theater/Theater Arts Management
Parkland Coll (IL)

Theology
Assumption Coll for Sisters (NJ)
Brazosport Coll (TX)
Mid-America Baptist Theological Seminary (TN)

Therapeutic Recreation
Butler County Comm Coll (PA)
Carteret Comm Coll (NC)
Colorado Mountain Coll (CO)
Comm Coll of Allegheny County (PA)
Keystone Coll (PA)
Moraine Valley Comm Coll (IL)
Northwestern Connecticut Comm Coll (CT)
Norwalk Comm Coll (CT)
Santa Barbara City Coll (CA)
Tulsa Comm Coll (OK)

Tool and Die Technology
Delta Coll (MI)
Gadsden State Comm Coll (AL)
Hawkeye Comm Coll (IA)
H. Councill Trenholm State Tech Coll (AL)
Ivy Tech Comm Coll–Bloomington (IN)
Ivy Tech Comm Coll–Central Indiana (IN)
Ivy Tech Comm Coll–Columbus (IN)
Ivy Tech Comm Coll–East Central (IN)
Ivy Tech Comm Coll–Kokomo (IN)
Ivy Tech Comm Coll–Lafayette (IN)
Ivy Tech Comm Coll–North Central (IN)
Ivy Tech Comm Coll–Northeast (IN)
Ivy Tech Comm Coll–Northwest (IN)
Ivy Tech Comm Coll–Southern Indiana (IN)
Ivy Tech Comm Coll–Southwest (IN)

Ivy Tech Comm Coll–Wabash Valley (IN)
Ivy Tech Comm Coll–Whitewater (IN)
Jackson State Comm Coll (TN)
Macomb Comm Coll (MI)
Mohawk Valley Comm Coll (NY)
Moraine Park Tech Coll (WI)
North Iowa Area Comm Coll (IA)
Oakland Comm Coll (MI)
Prairie State Coll (IL)
Ventura Coll (CA)
Western Iowa Tech Comm Coll (IA)
Wilson Tech Comm Coll (NC)

Tourism and Travel Services Management
Albany Tech Coll (GA)
Arapahoe Comm Coll (CO)
Athens Tech Coll (GA)
Atlanta Tech Coll (GA)
Bay State Coll (MA)
Beal Coll (ME)
Bergen Comm Coll (NJ)
Briarwood Coll (CT)
Broward Comm Coll (FL)
Bryant and Stratton Coll, Syracuse (NY)
Bunker Hill Comm Coll (MA)
Butler County Comm Coll (PA)
Central Georgia Tech Coll (GA)
Central Piedmont Comm Coll (NC)
Coll of DuPage (IL)
Consolidated School of Business, Lancaster (PA)
Consolidated School of Business, York (PA)
Corning Comm Coll (NY)
East Central Coll (MO)
Elmira Business Inst (NY)
Erie Business Center, Main (PA)
Finger Lakes Comm Coll (NY)
Fiorello H. LaGuardia Comm Coll of the City U of New York (NY)
Fisher Coll (MA)
Florida National Coll (FL)
Foothill Coll (CA)
Genesee Comm Coll (NY)
Guam Comm Coll (GU)
Gwinnett Tech Coll (GA)
Hamilton Coll, Cedar Rapids (IA)
Harrisburg Area Comm Coll (PA)
Heald Coll-Honolulu (HI)
Highline Comm Coll (WA)
Holyoke Comm Coll (MA)
Houston Comm Coll System (TX)
Jefferson Comm Coll (NY)
Kapiolani Comm Coll (HI)
Kingsborough Comm Coll of the City U of New York (NY)
Lansing Comm Coll (MI)
Lehigh Valley Coll (PA)
Lincoln Coll (IL)
Lincoln Coll–Normal (IL)
Long Beach City Coll (CA)
Luzerne County Comm Coll (PA)
Miami Dade Coll (FL)
Minneapolis Business Coll (MN)
MiraCosta Coll (CA)
New Hampshire Tech Inst (NH)
Newport Business Inst, Lower Burrell (PA)
Northern Essex Comm Coll (MA)
North Shore Comm Coll (MA)
Ogeechee Tech Coll (GA)
Pasadena City Coll (CA)
Phoenix Coll (AZ)
Quinsigamond Comm Coll (MA)
Raritan Valley Comm Coll (NJ)

Rasmussen Coll Mankato (MN)
Rockingham Comm Coll (NC)
Saddleback Coll (CA)
St. Petersburg Coll (FL)
St. Philip's Coll (TX)
San Diego City Coll (CA)
San Diego Mesa Coll (CA)
Savannah Tech Coll (GA)
Sinclair Comm Coll (OH)
State U of New York Coll of Technology at Delhi (NY)
Sullivan County Comm Coll (NY)
Tompkins Cortland Comm Coll (NY)
Tulsa Comm Coll (OK)
U of Northwestern Ohio (OH)
Valencia Comm Coll (FL)
Westchester Comm Coll (NY)
Westmoreland County Comm Coll (PA)
Yakima Valley Comm Coll (WA)

Tourism and Travel Services Marketing
Coll of DuPage (IL)
Dixie State Coll of Utah (UT)
Florida Comm Coll at Jacksonville (FL)
Guam Comm Coll (GU)
Hamilton Coll, Cedar Falls (IA)
Harrisburg Area Comm Coll (PA)
Luzerne County Comm Coll (PA)
Moraine Valley Comm Coll (IL)
Rasmussen Coll Mankato (MN)
San Diego Mesa Coll (CA)
Tompkins Cortland Comm Coll (NY)
Waubonsee Comm Coll (IL)

Tourism Promotion
Central Oregon Comm Coll (OR)
Coll of DuPage (IL)
Comm Coll of Allegheny County (PA)
Florida National Coll (FL)
Guam Comm Coll (GU)
Rasmussen Coll Mankato (MN)
Westchester Comm Coll (NY)

Tourism/Travel Marketing
International Business Coll, Indianapolis (IN)
Wood Tobe–Coburn School (NY)

Trade and Industrial Teacher Education
Copiah-Lincoln Comm Coll (MS)
ECPI Coll of Technology, Newport News (VA)
ECPI Tech Coll, Richmond (VA)
Manatee Comm Coll (FL)
Northeast Iowa Comm Coll (IA)
Palo Alto Coll (TX)
Pratt Comm Coll (KS)
Snow Coll (UT)
Spartanburg Tech Coll (SC)

Transportation and Materials Moving Related
Cecil Comm Coll (MD)
Palo Verde Coll (CA)

Transportation Technology
Central Piedmont Comm Coll (NC)
Chattanooga State Tech Comm Coll (TN)
Coll of DuPage (IL)
Delaware Tech & Comm Coll, Stanton/Wilmington Campus (DE)
Highline Comm Coll (WA)
Houston Comm Coll System (TX)
Mt. San Antonio Coll (CA)
Nassau Comm Coll (NY)

San Diego City Coll (CA)
Sinclair Comm Coll (OH)
Triton Coll (IL)

Travel Services Marketing Operations
Edmonds Comm Coll (WA)

Truck and Bus Driver/Commercial Vehicle Operation
Alexandria Tech Coll (MN)

Turf and Turfgrass Management
Cincinnati State Tech and Comm Coll (OH)
Coll of Lake County (IL)
Comm Coll of Allegheny County (PA)
Joliet Jr Coll (IL)
Lake City Comm Coll (FL)
Linn State Tech Coll (MO)
North Georgia Tech Coll (GA)
The Ohio State U Ag Tech Inst (OH)
Southeast Tech Inst (SD)
Southwestern Oregon Comm Coll (OR)
Texas State Tech Coll Waco (TX)
Western Iowa Tech Comm Coll (IA)
The Williamson Free School of Mecha Trades (PA)

Urban Studies/Affairs
Lawson State Comm Coll (AL)
St. Philip's Coll (TX)

Vehicle and Vehicle Parts And Accessories Marketing
Guam Comm Coll (GU)

Vehicle/Equipment Operation
Brazosport Coll (TX)
Comm Coll of the Air Force (AL)

Vehicle Maintenance and Repair Technologies Related
Arkansas State U–Beebe (AR)
Central New Mexico Comm Coll (NM)
North Dakota State Coll of Science (ND)

Vehicle/Petroleum Products Marketing
Central Comm Coll–Hastings Campus (NE)

Veterinary/Animal Health Technology
Cedar Valley Coll (TX)
Central Florida Comm Coll (FL)
Eastern Wyoming Coll (WY)
Gwinnett Tech Coll (GA)
Joliet Jr Coll (IL)
Macomb Comm Coll (MI)
Midland Coll (TX)
Northampton County Area Comm Coll (PA)
Parkland Coll (IL)
Penn Foster Career School (PA)
Pima Comm Coll (AZ)
St. Petersburg Coll (FL)
Sussex County Comm Coll (NJ)
Utah Career Coll (UT)

Veterinary Sciences
Colby Comm Coll (KS)
Holyoke Comm Coll (MA)
Macomb Comm Coll (MI)
Manor Coll (PA)
Northwest-Shoals Comm Coll (AL)
Palo Alto Coll (TX)
Pasadena City Coll (CA)
Snow Coll (UT)
State U of New York Coll of Technology at Alfred (NY)

Veterinary Technology
Athens Tech Coll (GA)
Bergen Comm Coll (NJ)
Blue Ridge Comm Coll (VA)

Brevard Comm Coll (FL)
Central Georgia Tech Coll (GA)
Colby Comm Coll (KS)
Colorado Mountain Coll (CO)
Comm Care Coll (OK)
Comm Coll of Denver (CO)
Cuyahoga Comm Coll (OH)
Delaware Tech & Comm Coll, Jack F. Owens Campus (DE)
Fiorello H. LaGuardia Comm Coll of the City U of New York (NY)
Foothill Coll (CA)
Front Range Comm Coll (CO)
Gaston Coll (NC)
Globe Coll (MN)
Holyoke Comm Coll (MA)
Jefferson State Comm Coll (AL)
Lansing Comm Coll (MI)
Manor Coll (PA)
Maple Woods Comm Coll (MO)
Midland Coll (TX)
Minnesota School of Business–Brooklyn Center (MN)
Minnesota School of Business–Plymouth (MN)
Minnesota School of Business–Richfield (MN)
Minnesota School of Business–St. Cloud (MN)
Minnesota School of Business–Shakopee (MN)
Northeast Comm Coll (NE)
North Shore Comm Coll (MA)
Northwestern Connecticut Comm Coll (CT)
Ogeechee Tech Coll (GA)
St. Petersburg Coll (FL)
San Diego Mesa Coll (CA)
San Joaquin Valley Coll (CA)
State U of New York Coll of Technology at Delhi (NY)
Tomball Coll (TX)
Trident Tech Coll (SC)
Tulsa Comm Coll (OK)
Yakima Valley Comm Coll (WA)
Yuba Coll (CA)

Visual and Performing Arts
Berkshire Comm Coll (MA)
Bucks County Comm Coll (PA)
Citrus Coll (CA)
Holyoke Comm Coll (MA)
Hutchinson Comm Coll and Area Vocational School (KS)
Kingwood Coll (TX)
Laramie County Comm Coll (WY)
Moraine Valley Comm Coll (IL)
Nassau Comm Coll (NY)
New Hampshire Tech Inst (NH)
Piedmont Virginia Comm Coll (VA)
Raritan Valley Comm Coll (NJ)

Visual and Performing Arts Related
Comm Coll of Allegheny County (PA)
Florida Comm Coll at Jacksonville (FL)

Vocational Rehabilitation Counseling
Edmonds Comm Coll (WA)
Manatee Comm Coll (FL)
Spokane Falls Comm Coll (WA)

Voice and Opera
Coastal Bend Coll (TX)
Lansing Comm Coll (MI)
Lincoln Coll (IL)
Snow Coll (UT)

Watchmaking and Jewelrymaking
North Seattle Comm Coll (WA)

Water Quality and Wastewater Treatment Management And Recycling Technology
Arizona Western Coll (AZ)
Collin County Comm Coll District (TX)
Delta Coll (MI)
Florida Comm Coll at Jacksonville (FL)
Linn-Benton Comm Coll (OR)
Northwest-Shoals Comm Coll (AL)
Northwest Vista Coll (TX)
Ogeechee Tech Coll (GA)
St. Cloud Tech Coll (MN)
San Juan Coll (NM)
Vermilion Comm Coll (MN)

Water Resources Engineering
Dixie State Coll of Utah (UT)

Water, Wetlands, and Marine Resources Management
Keystone Coll (PA)

Web/Multimedia Management and Webmaster
Bradley Academy for the Visual Arts (PA)
Bristol Comm Coll (MA)
Central Comm Coll–Columbus Campus (NE)
Central Comm Coll–Grand Island Campus (NE)
Central Comm Coll–Hastings Campus (NE)
Clark Coll (WA)
Clovis Comm Coll (NM)
Coll of the Siskiyous (CA)
The Coll of Westchester (NY)
Delta Coll (MI)
Edmonds Comm Coll (WA)
Florida Comm Coll at Jacksonville (FL)
Harrisburg Area Comm Coll (PA)
Hawkeye Comm Coll (IA)
Horry-Georgetown Tech Coll (SC)
ITT Tech Inst, Tucson (AZ)
ITT Tech Inst (AR)
ITT Tech Inst, Rancho Cordova (CA)
ITT Tech Inst (CO)
ITT Tech Inst, Fort Lauderdale (FL)
ITT Tech Inst, Jacksonville (FL)
ITT Tech Inst, Lake Mary (FL)
ITT Tech Inst, Miami (FL)
ITT Tech Inst, Tampa (FL)
ITT Tech Inst (ID)
ITT Tech Inst, Burr Ridge (IL)
ITT Tech Inst, Matteson (IL)
ITT Tech Inst, Indianapolis (IN)
ITT Tech Inst, Newburgh (IN)
ITT Tech Inst (LA)
ITT Tech Inst (MD)
ITT Tech Inst, Norwood (MA)
ITT Tech Inst, Woburn (MA)
ITT Tech Inst, Canton (MI)
ITT Tech Inst, Grand Rapids (MI)
ITT Tech Inst, Troy (MI)
ITT Tech Inst, Arnold (MO)
ITT Tech Inst, Earth City (MO)
ITT Tech Inst (NE)
ITT Tech Inst (NV)
ITT Tech Inst (NM)
ITT Tech Inst, Albany (NY)
ITT Tech Inst, Liverpool (NY)
ITT Tech Inst, Dayton (OH)
ITT Tech Inst, Norwood (OH)
ITT Tech Inst, Strongsville (OH)
ITT Tech Inst, Youngstown (OH)
ITT Tech Inst (OR)
ITT Tech Inst (SC)
ITT Tech Inst, Knoxville (TN)
ITT Tech Inst, Nashville (TN)
ITT Tech Inst, Arlington (TX)
ITT Tech Inst, Austin (TX)
ITT Tech Inst, Houston (TX)
ITT Tech Inst, Houston (TX)
ITT Tech Inst, Houston (TX)
ITT Tech Inst, Richardson (TX)
ITT Tech Inst, San Antonio (TX)
ITT Tech Inst (UT)
ITT Tech Inst, Chantilly (VA)
ITT Tech Inst, Norfolk (VA)
ITT Tech Inst, Richmond (VA)
ITT Tech Inst, Bothell (WA)
ITT Tech Inst, Seattle (WA)
ITT Tech Inst, Spokane (WA)
ITT Tech Inst, Green Bay (WI)
ITT Tech Inst, Greenfield (WI)
Kennebec Valley Comm Coll (ME)
Laramie County Comm Coll (WY)
Metropolitan Comm Coll-Business & Technology College (MO)
Mid-South Comm Coll (AR)
Montgomery Coll (TX)
Northern Essex Comm Coll (MA)
Northland Comm and Tech Coll–Thief River Falls (MN)
Piedmont Virginia Comm Coll (VA)
Pioneer Pacific Coll (OR)
Platt Coll San Diego (CA)
Remington Coll–Mobile Campus (AL)
Riverland Comm Coll (MN)
Saint Charles Comm Coll (MO)
St. Petersburg Coll (FL)
St. Philip's Coll (TX)
Salem Comm Coll (NJ)
Seminole Comm Coll (FL)
Sheridan Coll–Sheridan and Gillette (WY)
Sinclair Comm Coll (OH)
Southeast Tech Inst (SD)
Southern Arkansas U Tech (AR)
Springfield Tech Comm Coll (MA)
Stark State Coll of Technology (OH)
Sullivan County Comm Coll (NY)
Trident Tech Coll (SC)
Triton Coll (IL)
Tulsa Comm Coll (OK)

Web Page, Digital/Multimedia and Information Resources Design
Alexandria Tech Coll (MN)
Arapahoe Comm Coll (CO)
Berkeley City Coll (CA)
Berkeley Coll (NJ)
Bradley Academy for the Visual Arts (PA)
Brevard Comm Coll (FL)
Bunker Hill Comm Coll (MA)
Capital Comm Coll (CT)
Central Georgia Tech Coll (GA)
Central Wyoming Coll (WY)
Chattahoochee Tech Coll (GA)
Clovis Comm Coll (NM)
Coll of the Mainland (TX)
Coll of the Siskiyous (CA)
The Coll of Westchester (NY)
Collin County Comm Coll District (TX)
Columbus Tech Coll (GA)
Coosa Valley Tech Coll (GA)
Davis Coll (OH)
Delta Coll (MI)
Dixie State Coll of Utah (UT)
ECPI Tech Coll, Glen Allen (VA)
ECPI Tech Coll, Richmond (VA)
Edmonds Comm Coll (WA)
El Centro Coll (TX)
Erie Business Center, Main (PA)
Flint River Tech Coll (GA)
Florida Comm Coll at Jacksonville (FL)
Florida National Coll (FL)
Florida Tech Coll, DeLand (FL)
Galveston Coll (TX)
Griffin Tech Coll (GA)
Hagerstown Comm Coll (MD)
Hawkeye Comm Coll (IA)
Heartland Comm Coll (IL)
Hibbing Comm Coll (MN)
Highland Comm Coll (IL)
Highline Comm Coll (WA)
Horry-Georgetown Tech Coll (SC)
Hudson Valley Comm Coll (NY)
ITT Tech Inst, Tucson (AZ)
ITT Tech Inst (AR)
ITT Tech Inst, Anaheim (CA)
ITT Tech Inst, Lathrop (CA)
ITT Tech Inst, Oxnard (CA)
ITT Tech Inst, Rancho Cordova (CA)
ITT Tech Inst, San Bernardino (CA)
ITT Tech Inst, San Diego (CA)
ITT Tech Inst, Sylmar (CA)
ITT Tech Inst, Torrance (CA)
ITT Tech Inst, West Covina (CA)
ITT Tech Inst (CO)
ITT Tech Inst, Fort Lauderdale (FL)
ITT Tech Inst, Jacksonville (FL)
ITT Tech Inst, Lake Mary (FL)
ITT Tech Inst, Miami (FL)
ITT Tech Inst, Tampa (FL)
ITT Tech Inst, Duluth (GA)
ITT Tech Inst, Kennesaw (GA)
ITT Tech Inst (ID)
ITT Tech Inst, Burr Ridge (IL)
ITT Tech Inst, Matteson (IL)
ITT Tech Inst, Mount Prospect (IL)
ITT Tech Inst, Fort Wayne (IN)
ITT Tech Inst, Indianapolis (IN)
ITT Tech Inst, Newburgh (IN)
ITT Tech Inst, Louisville (KY)
ITT Tech Inst (LA)
ITT Tech Inst (MD)
ITT Tech Inst, Norwood (MA)
ITT Tech Inst, Woburn (MA)
ITT Tech Inst, Canton (MI)
ITT Tech Inst, Grand Rapids (MI)
ITT Tech Inst, Troy (MI)
ITT Tech Inst (MN)
ITT Tech Inst, Arnold (MO)
ITT Tech Inst, Earth City (MO)
ITT Tech Inst (NE)
ITT Tech Inst (NV)
ITT Tech Inst (NM)
ITT Tech Inst, Albany (NY)
ITT Tech Inst, Getzville (NY)
ITT Tech Inst, Liverpool (NY)
ITT Tech Inst, Dayton (OH)
ITT Tech Inst, Hilliard (OH)
ITT Tech Inst, Norwood (OH)
ITT Tech Inst, Strongsville (OH)
ITT Tech Inst, Warrensville Heights (OH)
ITT Tech Inst, Youngstown (OH)
ITT Tech Inst (OK)
ITT Tech Inst (OR)
ITT Tech Inst (SC)
ITT Tech Inst, Knoxville (TN)
ITT Tech Inst, Memphis (TN)
ITT Tech Inst, Nashville (TN)
ITT Tech Inst, Arlington (TX)
ITT Tech Inst, Austin (TX)
ITT Tech Inst, Houston (TX)
ITT Tech Inst, Houston (TX)
ITT Tech Inst, Houston (TX)
ITT Tech Inst, Richardson (TX)
ITT Tech Inst, San Antonio (TX)
ITT Tech Inst (UT)
ITT Tech Inst, Chantilly (VA)
ITT Tech Inst, Norfolk (VA)
ITT Tech Inst, Richmond (VA)
ITT Tech Inst, Springfield (VA)
ITT Tech Inst, Bothell (WA)
ITT Tech Inst, Seattle (WA)
ITT Tech Inst, Spokane (WA)
ITT Tech Inst, Green Bay (WI)
ITT Tech Inst, Greenfield (WI)
Joliet Jr Coll (IL)
Kansas City Kansas Comm Coll (KS)
Kennebec Valley Comm Coll (ME)
Lake City Comm Coll (FL)
Lanier Tech Coll (GA)
Laramie County Comm Coll (WY)
Laurel Business Inst (PA)
Mesabi Range Comm and Tech Coll (MN)
Metropolitan Comm Coll-Business & Technology College (MO)
Middle Georgia Tech Coll (GA)
Minnesota School of Business–Brooklyn Center (MN)
Minnesota School of Business–Plymouth (MN)
Minnesota School of Business–Richfield (MN)
Minnesota School of Business–St. Cloud (MN)
Minnesota School of Business–Shakopee (MN)
Minnesota State Comm and Tech Coll–Fergus Falls (MN)
Montgomery Coll (TX)
Moraine Park Tech Coll (WI)
Moultrie Tech Coll (GA)
Mount Wachusett Comm Coll (MA)
Niagara County Comm Coll (NY)
Northampton County Area Comm Coll (PA)
Northern Essex Comm Coll (MA)
North Georgia Tech Coll (GA)
Northland Comm and Tech Coll–Thief River Falls (MN)
North Metro Tech Coll (GA)
North Seattle Comm Coll (WA)
Northwestern Tech Coll (GA)
Northwest Vista Coll (TX)
Palm Beach Comm Coll (FL)
Parkland Coll (IL)
Pasco-Hernando Comm Coll (FL)
Peninsula Coll (WA)
Pennsylvania Inst of Technology (PA)
Platt Coll San Diego (CA)
Rasmussen Coll Mankato (MN)
Remington Coll–Lafayette Campus (LA)
Richmond Comm Coll (NC)
Riverland Comm Coll (MN)
St. Petersburg Coll (FL)
Seminole Comm Coll (FL)
Sheridan Coll–Sheridan and Gillette (WY)
Southeastern Tech Coll (GA)
Southeast Tech Inst (SD)
Southern Arkansas U Tech (AR)
Stark State Coll of Technology (OH)
Tompkins Cortland Comm Coll (NY)
Trident Tech Coll (SC)
Triton Coll (IL)
Tulsa Comm Coll (OK)
Valdosta Tech Coll (GA)
West Central Tech Coll (GA)
West Georgia Tech Coll (GA)

Welding Technology
Alamance Comm Coll (NC)
Alexandria Tech Coll (MN)
Allan Hancock Coll (CA)
Arizona Western Coll (AZ)
Austin Comm Coll (TX)
Bainbridge Coll (GA)
Beaufort County Comm Coll (NC)
Big Bend Comm Coll (WA)
Bladen Comm Coll (NC)
Brazosport Coll (TX)
Butler Comm Coll (KS)
Casper Coll (WY)
Cecil Comm Coll (MD)
Central Comm Coll–Columbus Campus (NE)
Central Comm Coll–Grand Island Campus (NE)
Central Comm Coll–Hastings Campus (NE)
Centralia Coll (WA)
Central Oregon Comm Coll (OR)
Central Piedmont Comm Coll (NC)
Central Wyoming Coll (WY)
Chattanooga State Tech Comm Coll (TN)
Chemeketa Comm Coll (OR)
Clark Coll (WA)
Coahoma Comm Coll (MS)
Coastal Bend Coll (TX)
Cochise Coll, Douglas (AZ)
Coll of DuPage (IL)
Coll of Eastern Utah (UT)
Coll of the Canyons (CA)
Comm Coll of Allegheny County (PA)
Comm Coll of Denver (CO)
Cossatot Comm Coll of the U of Arkansas (AR)
Cowley County Comm Coll and Area Vocational–Tech School (KS)
Delaware Tech & Comm Coll, Jack F. Owens Campus (DE)
Delta Coll (MI)
East Central Coll (MO)
Eastern Arizona Coll (AZ)
Eastern Idaho Tech Coll (ID)
Eastern Wyoming Coll (WY)
Forsyth Tech Comm Coll (NC)
Fox Valley Tech Coll (WI)
Front Range Comm Coll (CO)
George C. Wallace Comm Coll (AL)
Grand Rapids Comm Coll (MI)
Great Basin Coll (NV)
H. Councill Trenholm State Tech Coll (AL)
Heartland Comm Coll (IL)
Hutchinson Comm Coll and Area Vocational School (KS)
Illinois Central Coll (IL)
Jefferson Comm and Tech Coll (KY)
Joliet Jr Coll (IL)
Kellogg Comm Coll (MI)
Lansing Comm Coll (MI)
Linn-Benton Comm Coll (OR)
Long Beach City Coll (CA)
Lower Columbia Coll (WA)
Macomb Comm Coll (MI)
Manhattan Area Tech Coll (KS)
Metropolitan Comm Coll (NE)
Midland Coll (TX)
Mississippi Gulf Coast Comm Coll (MS)
Moberly Area Comm Coll (MO)
Modesto Jr Coll (CA)
Moraine Park Tech Coll (WI)
Mountain View Coll (TX)
Mt. San Antonio Coll (CA)
New Hampshire Comm Tech Coll, Manchester/Stratham (NH)
North Dakota State Coll of Science (ND)
Northeast Comm Coll (NE)
Northeast State Tech Comm Coll (TN)
North Idaho Coll (ID)
North Iowa Area Comm Coll (IA)
Northland Comm and Tech Coll–Thief River Falls (MN)
Northwest-Shoals Comm Coll (AL)
Oakland Comm Coll (MI)
Okaloosa-Walton Coll (FL)
Orange Coast Coll (CA)
Pasadena City Coll (CA)
Pima Comm Coll (AZ)
Pratt Comm Coll (KS)
Riverside Comm Coll District (CA)
Rock Valley Coll (IL)
Rogue Comm Coll (OR)
St. Cloud Tech Coll (MN)
St. Philip's Coll (TX)
Salt Lake Comm Coll (UT)
San Diego City Coll (CA)
San Juan Coll (NM)
Shelton State Comm Coll (AL)
Sheridan Coll–Sheridan and Gillette (WY)
Southeastern Comm Coll (NC)
Southern West Virginia Comm and Tech Coll (WV)
South Plains Coll (TX)
Southwestern Illinois Coll (IL)
Southwestern Michigan Coll (MI)
Southwestern Oregon Comm Coll (OR)
Southwest Mississippi Comm Coll (MS)
Spokane Comm Coll (WA)
Spokane Falls Comm Coll (WA)
State U of New York Coll of Technology at Alfred (NY)
State U of New York Coll of Technology at Delhi (NY)
Tarrant County Coll District (TX)
Texas State Tech Coll Waco (TX)
Treasure Valley Comm Coll (OR)
Triangle Tech, Inc.–DuBois School (PA)
Tri-County Comm Coll (NC)
Trinity Valley Comm Coll (TX)
Triton Coll (IL)
Tulsa Welding School (OK)
Vance-Granville Comm Coll (NC)
Ventura Coll (CA)
Westmoreland County Comm Coll (PA)
York Tech Coll (SC)
Yuba Coll (CA)

Western Civilization
Lincoln Coll (IL)

Wildlife and Wildlands Science And Management
Abraham Baldwin Ag Coll (GA)
Barton County Comm Coll (KS)
Casper Coll (WY)
Chattanooga State Tech Comm Coll (TN)
Dixie State Coll of Utah (UT)
East Central Coll (MO)
Eastern Wyoming Coll (WY)
Itasca Comm Coll (MN)
Keystone Coll (PA)
Laramie County Comm Coll (WY)
Mt. San Antonio Coll (CA)
North Idaho Coll (ID)
Ogeechee Tech Coll (GA)
The Pennsylvania State U DuBois Campus of the Commonwealth Coll (PA)
Pratt Comm Coll (KS)
Santa Rosa Jr Coll (CA)
Snow Coll (UT)
Spokane Comm Coll (WA)
Treasure Valley Comm Coll (OR)
Vermilion Comm Coll (MN)

Wildlife Biology
Colby Comm Coll (KS)
Eastern Arizona Coll (AZ)
Keystone Coll (PA)
North Idaho Coll (ID)
Pratt Comm Coll (KS)
Vermilion Comm Coll (MN)

Women'S Studies
Bergen Comm Coll (NJ)
Casper Coll (WY)
Foothill Coll (CA)
Manatee Comm Coll (FL)
Northern Essex Comm Coll (MA)
Saddleback Coll (CA)
Santa Rosa Jr Coll (CA)
Tompkins Cortland Comm Coll (NY)
Yuba Coll (CA)

Wood Science and Wood Products/Pulp And Paper Technology
Allen County Comm Coll (KS)

Copiah-Lincoln Comm Coll (MS)
Cossatot Comm Coll of the U of Arkansas (AR)
Dabney S. Lancaster Comm Coll (VA)
Fox Valley Tech Coll (WI)
Kennebec Valley Comm Coll (ME)
Lower Columbia Coll (WA)
Ogeechee Tech Coll (GA)

Woodworking
Bucks County Comm Coll (PA)
State U of New York Coll of Technology at Delhi (NY)

Woodworking Related
Oakland Comm Coll (MI)

Word Processing
Coastal Bend Coll (TX)
The Coll of Westchester (NY)
Corning Comm Coll (NY)
Eastfield Coll (TX)
Florida Comm Coll at Jacksonville (FL)
Florida National Coll (FL)
Galveston Coll (TX)
Gateway Comm Coll (CT)
Hawkeye Comm Coll (IA)
Horry-Georgetown Tech Coll (SC)
Kellogg Comm Coll (MI)
Laurel Business Inst (PA)
Lower Columbia Coll (WA)

Metropolitan Comm Coll-Business & Technology College (MO)
Mississippi Gulf Coast Comm Coll (MS)
Modesto Jr Coll (CA)
Naugatuck Valley Comm Coll (CT)
Newport Business Inst, Lower Burrell (PA)
Northern Essex Comm Coll (MA)
Northland Comm and Tech Coll–Thief River Falls (MN)
Okaloosa-Walton Coll (FL)
Orange Coast Coll (CA)
Orange County Comm Coll (NY)

Palm Beach Comm Coll (FL)
Pratt Comm Coll (KS)
Quinebaug Valley Comm Coll (CT)
Rasmussen Coll Mankato (MN)
Richland Comm Coll (IL)
Riverland Comm Coll (MN)
Seminole Comm Coll (FL)
Sinclair Comm Coll (OH)
Stark State Coll of Technology (OH)
Three Rivers Comm Coll (MO)
Tulsa Comm Coll (OK)
Valencia Comm Coll (FL)
West Central Tech Coll (GA)

West Virginia Northern Comm Coll (WV)
Yuba Coll (CA)

Youth Services
Midlands Tech Coll (SC)

Zoology/Animal Biology
Carl Albert State Coll (OK)
Centralia Coll (WA)
Colby Comm Coll (KS)
Dixie State Coll of Utah (UT)
East Central Coll (MO)
Lincoln Coll (IL)
North Idaho Coll (ID)
Palm Beach Comm Coll (FL)
Snow Coll (UT)
Spoon River Coll (IL)
Tulsa Comm Coll (OK)

Associate Degree Programs at Four-Year Colleges

Accounting
Aivernia Coll (PA)
Baker Coll of Allen Park (MI)
Baker Coll of Auburn Hills (MI)
Baker Coll of Cadillac (MI)
Baker Coll of Clinton Township (MI)
Baker Coll of Flint (MI)
Baker Coll of Jackson (MI)
Baker Coll of Muskegon (MI)
Baker Coll of Owosso (MI)
Baker Coll of Port Huron (MI)
Bluefield State Coll (WV)
Briarcliffe Coll (NY)
California U of Pennsylvania (PA)
Calumet Coll of Saint Joseph (IN)
Central Pennsylvania Coll (PA)
Champlain Coll (VT)
Chestnut Hill Coll (PA)
Clayton State U (GA)
Coll of Mount St. Joseph (OH)
Coll of St. Joseph (VT)
Coll of Saint Mary (NE)
Columbia Union Coll (MD)
Davenport U, Dearborn (MI)
Evangel U (MO)
Fairmont State U (WV)
Faulkner U (AL)
Ferris State U (MI)
Florida Metropolitan U–Brandon Campus (FL)
Franciscan U of Steubenville (OH)
Gwynedd-Mercy Coll (PA)
Hawai'i Pacific U (HI)
Husson Coll (ME)
Immaculata U (PA)
Indiana Tech (IN)
Inter American U of Puerto Rico, Aguadilla Campus (PR)
Inter American U of Puerto Rico, Barranquitas Campus (PR)
Inter American U of Puerto Rico, Bayamón Campus (PR)
Inter American U of Puerto Rico, Ponce Campus (PR)
Inter American U of Puerto Rico, San Germán Campus (PR)
Johnson & Wales U (CO)
Johnson & Wales U (FL)
Johnson & Wales U (NC)
Johnson & Wales U (RI)
Johnson State Coll (VT)
Jones Coll, Jacksonville (FL)
Lake Superior State U (MI)
Lebanon Valley Coll (PA)
Macon State Coll (GA)
Manchester Coll (IN)
Marygrove Coll (MI)
Midland Lutheran Coll (NE)
Minnesota School of Business (MN)
Missouri Southern State U (MO)
Mitchell Coll (CT)
Monroe Coll, Bronx (NY)
Monroe Coll, New Rochelle (NY)
Mount Aloysius Coll (PA)
Mount Marty Coll (SD)
Mount Olive Coll (NC)
National American U, Rapid City (SD)
Newbury Coll (MA)
Northwood U (MI)
Northwood U, Florida Campus (FL)
Northwood U, Texas Campus (TX)
Oakland City U (IN)
Oakwood Coll (AL)
Peirce Coll (PA)
Point Park U (PA)
Post U (CT)
Potomac Coll (DC)
Purdue U North Central (IN)
Sacred Heart U (CT)
Saint Francis U (PA)
St. John's U (NY)
Saint Joseph's U (PA)
Shawnee State U (OH)
Southern Adventist U (TN)
Southern New Hampshire U (NH)
South U (AL)
South U (GA)
South U (SC)
Southwest Baptist U (MO)
State U of New York Coll of Agriculture and Technology at Cobleskill (NY)
Sullivan U (KY)
Thiel Coll (PA)
Thomas Coll (ME)
Thomas More Coll (KY)
Tiffin U (OH)
Tri-State U (IN)
Union Coll (NE)
U of Charleston (WV)
U of Cincinnati (OH)
U of Dubuque (IA)
The U of Findlay (OH)
U of Mary (ND)
U of Minnesota, Crookston (MN)
U of Rio Grande (OH)
U of the District of Columbia (DC)
U of the Virgin Islands (VI)
Urbana U (OH)
Utah Valley State Coll (UT)
Villa Julie Coll (MD)
Walsh U (OH)
Webber International U (FL)
West Virginia State U (WV)
Wilson Coll (PA)
Youngstown State U (OH)

Accounting and Business/Management
Central Christian Coll of Kansas (KS)
Chestnut Hill Coll (PA)
Davis & Elkins Coll (WV)
Mount Aloysius Coll (PA)
Peirce Coll (PA)

Accounting Related
Central Pennsylvania Coll (PA)
Montana State U–Billings (MT)
Park U (MO)
Peirce Coll (PA)

Accounting Technology and Bookkeeping
Baker Coll of Flint (MI)
Cleary U (MI)
Gannon U (PA)
Georgia Southwestern State U (GA)
Lewis-Clark State Coll (ID)
Montana State U–Billings (MT)
New York Inst of Technology (NY)
Ohio U (OH)
Peirce Coll (PA)
Pennsylvania Coll of Technology (PA)
Robert Morris Coll (IL)
The U of Akron (OH)
U of Alaska Fairbanks (AK)
The U of Montana–Missoula (MT)
U of Rio Grande (OH)
Wright State U (OH)

Acting
Central Christian Coll of Kansas (KS)
New World School of the Arts (FL)

Administrative Assistant and Secretarial Science
Alabama State U (AL)
Arkansas State U (AR)
Arkansas Tech U (AR)
Baker Coll of Auburn Hills (MI)
Baker Coll of Cadillac (MI)
Baker Coll of Clinton Township (MI)
Baker Coll of Flint (MI)
Baker Coll of Jackson (MI)
Baker Coll of Muskegon (MI)
Baker Coll of Owosso (MI)
Baker Coll of Port Huron (MI)
Ball State U (IN)
Baptist Bible Coll of Pennsylvania (PA)
Bluefield State Coll (WV)
Briarcliffe Coll (NY)
Bryant and Stratton Coll, Cleveland (OH)
Campbellsville U (KY)
Central Missouri State U (MO)
Clayton State U (GA)
Clearwater Christian Coll (FL)
Columbia Coll, Caguas (PR)
Concordia Coll (NY)
Davenport U, Dearborn (MI)
Dickinson State U (ND)
Dordt Coll (IA)
Eastern Kentucky U (KY)
Eastern Oregon U (OR)
Evangel U (MO)
Fairmont State U (WV)
Faith Baptist Bible Coll and Theological Seminary (IA)
Faulkner U (AL)
Fort Valley State U (GA)
Free Will Baptist Bible Coll (TN)
Georgia Southwestern State U (GA)
God's Bible School and Coll (OH)
Grace Coll (IN)
Henderson State U (AR)
Hobe Sound Bible Coll (FL)
Idaho State U (ID)
Inter American U of Puerto Rico, Aguadilla Campus (PR)
Inter American U of Puerto Rico, Barranquitas Campus (PR)
Inter American U of Puerto Rico, Bayamón Campus (PR)
Inter American U of Puerto Rico, Ponce Campus (PR)
Inter American U of Puerto Rico, San Germán Campus (PR)
Jones Coll, Jacksonville (FL)
Kuyper Coll (MI)
Lamar U (TX)
Lancaster Bible Coll (PA)
Lewis-Clark State Coll (ID)
Lincoln Christian Coll (IL)
Macon State Coll (GA)
Mayville State U (ND)
Mercyhurst Coll (PA)
Mesa State Coll (CO)
Minnesota School of Business (MN)
Montana State U–Billings (MT)
Montana Tech of The U of Montana (MT)
Mountain State U (WV)
Murray State U (KY)
New York Inst of Technology (NY)
Northern State U (SD)
Northwestern State U of Louisiana (LA)
Oakland City U (IN)
Oakwood Coll (AL)
Ohio U (OH)
Pennsylvania Coll of Technology (PA)
Pontifical Catholic U of Puerto Rico (PR)
Robert Morris Coll (IL)
Southeastern Baptist Coll (MS)
Southeastern Louisiana U (LA)
Sullivan U (KY)
Tennessee State U (TN)
Trinity Baptist Coll (FL)
Universidad Adventista de las Antillas (PR)
The U of Akron (OH)
U of Alaska Fairbanks (AK)
U of Alaska Southeast (AK)
U of Arkansas at Fort Smith (AR)
U of Cincinnati (OH)
The U of Findlay (OH)
The U of Montana–Western (MT)
U of Rio Grande (OH)
U of Sioux Falls (SD)
U of the District of Columbia (DC)
U of the Virgin Islands (VI)
Utah State U (UT)
Washburn U (KS)
Weber State U (UT)
West Virginia State U (WV)
Wright State U (OH)

Adult Development and Aging
Madonna U (MI)
Saint Mary-of-the-Woods Coll (IN)

Advertising
Academy of Art U (CA)
The Art Inst of California–San Diego (CA)
Fashion Inst of Technology (NY)
Hussian School of Art (PA)
Johnson & Wales U (CO)
Johnson & Wales U (FL)
Johnson & Wales U (RI)
New England School of Communications (ME)
Northwood U (MI)
Northwood U, Florida Campus (FL)
Northwood U, Texas Campus (TX)
U of the District of Columbia (DC)
West Virginia State U (WV)
Xavier U (OH)

Aeronautical/Aerospace Engineering Technology
Pennsylvania Coll of Technology (PA)
Purdue U (IN)

Aeronautics/Aviation/Aerospace Science and Technology
Embry-Riddle Aeronautical U, Extended Campus (FL)
Indiana State U (IN)
Purdue U (IN)
Vaughn Coll of Aeronautics and Technology (NY)

Agribusiness
Morehead State U (KY)
Vermont Tech Coll (VT)

Agricultural and Domestic Animals Services Related
Sterling Coll (VT)

Agricultural and Food Products Processing
North Carolina State U (NC)

Agricultural and Horticultural Plant Breeding
Sterling Coll (VT)

Agricultural Animal Breeding
Sterling Coll (VT)

Agricultural/Biological Engineering and Bioengineering
State U of New York Coll of Agriculture and Technology at Cobleskill (NY)

Agricultural Business and Management
Andrews U (MI)
Central Christian Coll of Kansas (KS)
Clayton State U (GA)

Agricultural Business and Management Related
The Pennsylvania State U Abington Coll (PA)
The Pennsylvania State U Altoona Coll (PA)
The Pennsylvania State U at Erie, The Behrend Coll (PA)
The Pennsylvania State U Berks Campus of the Berks–Lehigh Valley Coll (PA)
The Pennsylvania State U University Park Campus (PA)

Agricultural Economics
The U of British Columbia (BC, Canada)

Agricultural Mechanization
Andrews U (MI)
Clayton State U (GA)
State U of New York Coll of Agriculture and Technology at Cobleskill (NY)

Agricultural Production
Western Kentucky U (KY)

Agricultural Production Related
Sterling Coll (VT)

Agricultural Public Services Related
Sterling Coll (VT)

Agriculture
Andrews U (MI)
Clayton State U (GA)
Dalton State Coll (GA)
Fort Lewis Coll (CO)
Lubbock Christian U (TX)
Macon State Coll (GA)
Murray State U (KY)
North Carolina State U (NC)
Oklahoma Panhandle State U (OK)
Purdue U (IN)
South Dakota State U (SD)
Southern Utah U (UT)
State U of New York Coll of Agriculture and Technology at Cobleskill (NY)
Sterling Coll (VT)
U of Delaware (DE)
U of Minnesota, Crookston (MN)

Agriculture and Agriculture Operations Related
Eastern Kentucky U (KY)
Sterling Coll (VT)

Agronomy and Crop Science
Andrews U (MI)

Dickinson State U (ND)
Dordt Coll (IA)
North Carolina State U (NC)
State U of New York Coll of Agriculture and Technology at Cobleskill (NY)
U of Minnesota, Crookston (MN)
U of New Hampshire (NH)

State U of New York Coll of
Agriculture and Technology
at Cobleskill (NY)
U of Minnesota, Crookston
(MN)

**Aircraft Powerplant
Technology**
Embry-Riddle Aeronautical
U, Extended Campus (FL)
Georgia Southwestern State
U (GA)
Idaho State U (ID)
Pennsylvania Coll of
Technology (PA)

**Airframe Mechanics and
Aircraft Maintenance
Technology**
Clayton State U (GA)
Georgia Southwestern State
U (GA)
Kansas State U (KS)
Lewis U (IL)
U of Alaska Fairbanks (AK)
Utah State U (UT)
Vaughn Coll of Aeronautics
and Technology (NY)
Wentworth Inst of
Technology (MA)

Airline Flight Attendant
The U of Akron (OH)

Airline Pilot and Flight Crew
Andrews U (MI)
Baker Coll of Flint (MI)
Baker Coll of Muskegon (MI)
Central Christian Coll of
Kansas (KS)
Kansas State U (KS)
Southern Illinois U
Carbondale (IL)
U of Dubuque (IA)
Utah Valley State Coll (UT)
Vaughn Coll of Aeronautics
and Technology (NY)

**Allied Health and Medical
Assisting Services Related**
Bloomsburg U of
Pennsylvania (PA)
Washburn U (KS)

**Allied Health Diagnostic,
Intervention, and Treatment
Professions Related**
Cameron U (OK)
Gwynedd-Mercy Coll (PA)
Pennsylvania Coll of
Technology (PA)
The U of Akron (OH)

**American Native/Native
American Languages**
Idaho State U (ID)

**American Sign Language
(Asl)**
Bethel Coll (IN)
Idaho State U (ID)
Madonna U (MI)
Rochester Inst of Technology
(NY)

Anesthesiologist Assistant
Thompson Rivers U (BC,
Canada)

Animal Health
Sterling Coll (VT)

**Animal/Livestock
Husbandry and Production**
Saint Mary-of-the-Woods
Coll (IN)
Sterling Coll (VT)
Thompson Rivers U (BC,
Canada)
U of Connecticut (CT)
U of New Hampshire (NH)

Animal Nutrition
Sterling Coll (VT)

Animal Sciences
State U of New York Coll of
Agriculture and Technology
at Cobleskill (NY)
Sterling Coll (VT)
U of Connecticut (CT)
U of Minnesota, Crookston
(MN)
U of New Hampshire (NH)

Animal Sciences Related
Sterling Coll (VT)

**Animation, Interactive
Technology, Video Graphics
and Special Effects**
Academy of Art U (CA)
The Art Inst of Dallas (TX)
The Art Inst of Houston (TX)
The Art Inst of Seattle (WA)
The Art Inst of Tampa (FL)
Champlain Coll (VT)
The Illinois Inst of Art–
Chicago (IL)
National U (CA)
New England School of
Communications (ME)

Anthropology
Kwantlen U Coll (BC,
Canada)
Université Laval (QC,
Canada)

**Apparel and Accessories
Marketing**
Clayton State U (GA)
The U of Montana–Missoula
(MT)

**Apparel and Textile
Manufacturing**
Fashion Inst of Technology
(NY)

Apparel and Textiles
Academy of Art U (CA)
Fashion Inst of Technology
(NY)
The Illinois Inst of Art–
Chicago (IL)

Applied Art
Academy of Art U (CA)
New World School of the Arts
(FL)
Rochester Inst of Technology
(NY)
U of Maine at Presque Isle
(ME)
The U of Montana–Western
(MT)
Villa Julie Coll (MD)

Applied Horticulture
Bob Jones U (SC)
Georgia Southwestern State
U (GA)
Oakland City U (IN)
Sterling Coll (VT)
Temple U (PA)
U of Connecticut (CT)
The U of Maine at Augusta
(ME)

**Applied Horticulture/
Horticultural Business
Services Related**
Pennsylvania Coll of
Technology (PA)
U of Massachusetts Amherst
(MA)

Applied Mathematics
Hawai'i Pacific U (HI)
Rochester Inst of Technology
(NY)

Archeology
Weber State U (UT)

**Architectural Drafting and
Cad/Cadd**
Baker Coll of Flint (MI)
Baker Coll of Muskegon (MI)
Indiana State U (IN)
Indiana U–Purdue University
Indianapolis (IN)
Montana Tech of The U of
Montana (MT)
Western Kentucky U (KY)
Westwood Coll–Atlanta
Northlake (GA)

**Architectural Engineering
Technology**
Baker Coll of Cadillac (MI)
Baker Coll of Clinton
Township (MI)
Baker Coll of Owosso (MI)
Baker Coll of Port Huron (MI)
Bluefield State Coll (WV)
Clayton State U (GA)
Ferris State U (MI)
Indiana U–Purdue University
Fort Wayne (IN)
Norfolk State U (VA)
Northern Kentucky U (KY)

Pennsylvania Coll of
Technology (PA)
Purdue U (IN)
Purdue U Calumet (IN)
Purdue U North Central (IN)
U of Cincinnati (OH)
U of the District of Columbia
(DC)
Vermont Tech Coll (VT)
Wentworth Inst of
Technology (MA)
West Virginia State U (WV)

Architectural Technology
The U of Maine at Augusta
(ME)

Architecture
Central Christian Coll of
Kansas (KS)
Coll of Staten Island of the
City U of New York (NY)
New York Inst of Technology
(NY)

Architecture Related
Abilene Christian U (TX)

Art
The Art Inst of Colorado (CO)
Ashland U (OH)
Carroll Coll (MT)
Central Christian Coll of
Kansas (KS)
Clayton State U (GA)
Coll of Mount St. Joseph
(OH)
Defiance Coll (OH)
Eastern New Mexico U (NM)
Felician Coll (NJ)
Idaho State U (ID)
Lindsey Wilson Coll (KY)
Macon State Coll (GA)
Madonna U (MI)
Manchester Coll (IN)
Mesa State Coll (CO)
Miami International U of Art &
Design (FL)
Mount Olive Coll (NC)
Parsons The New School for
Design (NY)
Pontifical Catholic U of
Puerto Rico (PR)
Rivier Coll (NH)
Rochester Inst of Technology
(NY)
St. Gregory's U (OK)
Shawnee State U (OH)
State U of New York Empire
State Coll (NY)
Suffolk U (MA)
Union Coll (NE)
U of Rio Grande (OH)
U of Wisconsin–Green Bay
(WI)
Villa Julie Coll (MD)
West Virginia State U (WV)

**Art History, Criticism and
Conservation**
John Cabot Ultaly)
Thomas More Coll (KY)
Université Laval (QC,
Canada)

**Artificial Intelligence and
Robotics**
Clayton State U (GA)
Lamar U (TX)
U of Cincinnati (OH)

Art Teacher Education
Central Christian Coll of
Kansas (KS)
Clayton State U (GA)

Athletic Training
Central Christian Coll of
Kansas (KS)
Mitchell Coll (CT)

**Athletic Training/Sports
Medicine**
Southern Nazarene U (OK)

Audio Engineering
The Art Inst of Seattle (WA)
Five Towns Coll (NY)
New England School of
Communications (ME)

**Audiology and Hearing
Sciences**
Ohio U (OH)

**Autobody/Collision and
Repair Technology**
Georgia Southwestern State
U (GA)
Idaho State U (ID)
Lewis-Clark State Coll (ID)
Montana State U–Billings
(MT)
Montana Tech of The U of
Montana (MT)
Pennsylvania Coll of
Technology (PA)
Utah Valley State Coll (UT)
Weber State U (UT)

**Automobile/Automotive
Mechanics Technology**
Arkansas State U (AR)
Baker Coll of Flint (MI)
Boise State U (ID)
Ferris State U (MI)
Georgia Southwestern State
U (GA)
Idaho State U (ID)
Lamar U (TX)
Lewis-Clark State Coll (ID)
Mesa State Coll (CO)
Montana State U–Billings
(MT)
Montana Tech of The U of
Montana (MT)
Northern Michigan U (MI)
Oakland City U (IN)
Pittsburg State U (KS)
Southern Adventist U (TN)
Southern Utah U (UT)
Utah Valley State Coll (UT)
Walla Walla Coll (WA)
Weber State U (UT)

**Automotive Engineering
Technology**
Farmingdale State U of New
York (NY)
Pennsylvania Coll of
Technology (PA)
The U of Akron (OH)
Vermont Tech Coll (VT)

**Aviation/Airway
Management**
Clayton State U (GA)
Fairmont State U (WV)
Mountain State U (WV)
Northern Kentucky U (KY)
Park U (MO)
The U of Akron (OH)
U of Alaska Fairbanks (AK)
U of Dubuque (IA)
U of Minnesota, Crookston
(MN)
U of the District of Columbia
(DC)

**Avionics Maintenance
Technology**
Andrews U (MI)
Baker Coll of Flint (MI)
Clayton State U (GA)
Excelsior Coll (NY)
Fairmont State U (WV)
Georgia Southwestern State
U (GA)
Hampton U (VA)
Lewis U (IL)
Northern Michigan U (MI)
Pennsylvania Coll of
Technology (PA)
U of Minnesota, Crookston
(MN)
U of the District of Columbia
(DC)
Vaughn Coll of Aeronautics
and Technology (NY)
Walla Walla Coll (WA)
Wentworth Inst of
Technology (MA)

Baking and Pastry Arts
The Art Inst of California–
San Diego (CA)
The Art Inst of Houston (TX)
The Culinary Inst of America
(NY)
Johnson & Wales U (CO)
Johnson & Wales U (FL)
Johnson & Wales U (NC)
Johnson & Wales U (RI)
Kendall Coll (IL)
Pennsylvania Coll of
Technology (PA)

Southern New Hampshire U
(NH)

**Banking and Financial
Support Services**
Globe Inst of Technology
(NY)
Hilbert Coll (NY)
Mercy Coll (NY)
Mountain State U (WV)
Northwood U (MI)
Northwood U, Florida
Campus (FL)
Northwood U, Texas Campus
(TX)
Pennsylvania Coll of
Technology (PA)
The U of Akron (OH)
U of Indianapolis (IN)
Utah Valley State Coll (UT)
Washburn U (KS)

Behavioral Sciences
Felician Coll (NJ)
Lewis-Clark State Coll (ID)
Mount Aloysius Coll (PA)
Utah Valley State Coll (UT)

Biblical Studies
Alaska Bible Coll (AK)
American Baptist Coll of
American Baptist
Theological Seminary (TN)
Barclay Coll (KS)
Bethel Coll (IN)
Boston Baptist Coll (MA)
Calvary Bible Coll and
Theological Seminary (MO)
Central Christian Coll of the
Bible (MO)
Columbia International U
(SC)
Corban Coll (OR)
Covenant Coll (GA)
Crown Coll (MN)
Dallas Baptist U (TX)
Davis Coll (NY)
Eastern Mennonite U (VA)
Faith Baptist Bible Coll and
Theological Seminary (IA)
Faulkner U (AL)
Fresno Pacific U (CA)
God's Bible School and Coll
(OH)
Grace Coll (IN)
Hobe Sound Bible Coll (FL)
Houghton Coll (NY)
International Baptist Coll
(AZ)
John Brown U (AR)
Kuyper Coll (MI)
Lancaster Bible Coll (PA)
Life Pacific Coll (CA)
Lincoln Christian Coll (IL)
Nazarene Bible Coll (CO)
Oak Hills Christian Coll (MN)
Oakwood Coll (AL)
Ohio Valley U (WV)
Ouachita Baptist U (AR)
Pacific Union Coll (CA)
Roanoke Bible Coll (NC)
Simpson U (CA)
Southeastern Baptist Coll
(MS)
Southeastern Bible Coll (AL)
Universidad Adventista de
las Antillas (PR)
Valley Forge Christian Coll
(PA)
Warner Pacific Coll (OR)

Biochemistry
Saint Joseph's Coll (IN)

**Biological and Biomedical
Sciences Related**
Gwynedd-Mercy Coll (PA)

**Biological and Physical
Sciences**
Bluefield State Coll (WV)
Central Christian Coll of
Kansas (KS)
Clayton State U (GA)
Crown Coll (MN)
Dalton State Coll (GA)
Heritage U (WA)
Indiana U East (IN)
Madonna U (MI)
Medgar Evers Coll of the City
U of New York (NY)
Mitchell Coll (CT)

Montana Tech of The U of
Montana (MT)
Mount Olive Coll (NC)
Ohio U (OH)
Ohio U–Zanesville (OH)
The Pennsylvania State U
Altoona Coll (PA)
Sacred Heart U (CT)
State U of New York Coll of
Agriculture and Technology
at Cobleskill (NY)
State U of New York Empire
State Coll (NY)
Sterling Coll (VT)
Tri-State U (IN)
U of Cincinnati (OH)
Valparaiso U (IN)
Villa Julie Coll (MD)

Biology/Biological Sciences
Brewton-Parker Coll (GA)
Canadian Mennonite U (MB,
Canada)
Chestnut Hill Coll (PA)
Cleveland Chiropractic
Coll-Los Angeles Campus
(CA)
Crown Coll (MN)
Cumberland U (TN)
Dalton State Coll (GA)
Felician Coll (NJ)
Fresno Pacific U (CA)
Idaho State U (ID)
Indiana U–Purdue University
Fort Wayne (IN)
Indiana U South Bend (IN)
Inter American U of Puerto
Rico, Barranquitas
Campus (PR)
Macon State Coll (GA)
Mesa State Coll (CO)
Montana Tech of The U of
Montana (MT)
Mount Olive Coll (NC)
Pennsylvania Coll of
Technology (PA)
Pine Manor Coll (MA)
Presentation Coll (SD)
Rochester Inst of Technology
(NY)
Sacred Heart U (CT)
Saint Joseph's U (PA)
Shawnee State U (OH)
Thomas More Coll (KY)
U of Dubuque (IA)
The U of Maine at Augusta
(ME)
U of New Hampshire at
Manchester (NH)
U of Rio Grande (OH)
The U of Tampa (FL)
U of Wisconsin–Green Bay
(WI)
Utah Valley State Coll (UT)
Villa Julie Coll (MD)
Wright State U (OH)
York Coll of Pennsylvania
(PA)

**Biology/Biotechnology
Laboratory Technician**
Ferris State U (MI)
State U of New York Coll of
Agriculture and Technology
at Cobleskill (NY)
U of the District of Columbia
(DC)
Villa Julie Coll (MD)
Weber State U (UT)

Biology Teacher Education
Central Christian Coll of
Kansas (KS)

Biomedical Technology
Baker Coll of Flint (MI)
DeVry U (NJ)
Faulkner U (AL)
Indiana U–Purdue University
Indianapolis (IN)
Pennsylvania Coll of
Technology (PA)
The Pennsylvania State U
Altoona Coll (PA)
The Pennsylvania State U at
Erie, The Behrend Coll
(PA)
The Pennsylvania State U
Berks Campus of the
Berks–Lehigh Valley Coll
(PA)

Wentworth Inst of
Technology (MA)

Broadcast Journalism
Cornerstone U (MI)
Evangel U (MO)
Five Towns Coll (NY)
John Brown U (AR)
Manchester Coll (IN)
New England School of
Communications (ME)
Ohio U–Zanesville (OH)
Pennsylvania Coll of
Technology (PA)
Trevecca Nazarene U (TN)

Buddhist Studies
Heritage Bible Coll (NC)

Building/Home/Construction Inspection
Utah Valley State Coll (UT)

Building/Property Maintenance and Management
Park U (MO)

Business Administration and Management
Alabama State U (AL)
Alaska Pacific U (AK)
Alderson-Broaddus Coll (WV)
Alvernia Coll (PA)
American InterContinental U (TX)
American International Coll (MA)
The American U in DubaiUnited Arab Emirates)
The American U of RomeItaly)
Andrews U (MI)
Anna Maria Coll (MA)
Austin Peay State U (TN)
Averett U (VA)
Baker Coll of Allen Park (MI)
Baker Coll of Auburn Hills (MI)
Baker Coll of Cadillac (MI)
Baker Coll of Clinton Township (MI)
Baker Coll of Flint (MI)
Baker Coll of Jackson (MI)
Baker Coll of Muskegon (MI)
Baker Coll of Owosso (MI)
Baker Coll of Port Huron (MI)
Ball State U (IN)
Benedictine U (IL)
Bentley Coll (MA)
Bethel Coll (IN)
Briarcliffe Coll (NY)
Bryan Coll (TN)
California U of Pennsylvania (PA)
Calumet Coll of Saint Joseph (IN)
Cameron U (OK)
Campbellsville U (KY)
Carroll Coll (MT)
Cazenovia Coll (NY)
Central Baptist Coll (AR)
Central Christian Coll of Kansas (KS)
Central Pennsylvania Coll (PA)
Chaminade U of Honolulu (HI)
Champlain Coll (VT)
Charleston Southern U (SC)
Chestnut Hill Coll (PA)
Clarion U of Pennsylvania (PA)
Clayton State U (GA)
Cleary U (MI)
Coll of Mount St. Joseph (OH)
Coll of Mount Saint Vincent (NY)
Coll of St. Joseph (VT)
Coll of Saint Mary (NE)
Coll of Santa Fe (NM)
Columbia Coll (MO)
Columbia Coll, Caguas (PR)
Concordia Coll (NY)
Concordia U (OR)
Concord U (WV)
Corban Coll (OR)
Covenant Coll (GA)
Crown Coll (MN)

Dakota State U (SD)
Dakota Wesleyan U (SD)
Dallas Baptist U (TX)
Dalton State Coll (GA)
Davenport U, Dearborn (MI)
Defiance Coll (OH)
DeVry U (NJ)
Edinboro U of Pennsylvania (PA)
Emmanuel Coll (GA)
Excelsior Coll (NY)
Fairmont State U (WV)
Farmingdale State U of New York (NY)
Faulkner U (AL)
Felician Coll (NJ)
Five Towns Coll (NY)
Florida Metropolitan U–Brandon Campus (FL)
Franciscan U of Steubenville (OH)
Free Will Baptist Bible Coll (TN)
Fresno Pacific U (CA)
Globe Inst of Technology (NY)
Grace Bible Coll (MI)
Grantham U (MO)
Gwynedd-Mercy Coll (PA)
Hawai'i Pacific U (HI)
Heritage U (WA)
Hilbert Coll (NY)
Husson Coll (ME)
Immaculata U (PA)
Indiana Tech (IN)
Indiana U Northwest (IN)
Indiana U of Pennsylvania (PA)
Indiana U–Purdue University Fort Wayne (IN)
Inter American U of Puerto Rico, Aguadilla Campus (PR)
Inter American U of Puerto Rico, Barranquitas Campus (PR)
Inter American U of Puerto Rico, Bayamón Campus (PR)
Inter American U of Puerto Rico, Ponce Campus (PR)
Inter American U of Puerto Rico, San Germán Campus (PR)
John Cabot UItaly)
Johnson & Wales U (CO)
Johnson & Wales U (FL)
Johnson & Wales U (NC)
Johnson & Wales U (RI)
Johnson State Coll (VT)
Jones Coll, Jacksonville (FL)
Kent State U (OH)
King's Coll (PA)
Lake Superior State U (MI)
Lebanon Valley Coll (PA)
Limestone Coll (SC)
Lincoln Memorial U (TN)
Lindsey Wilson Coll (KY)
Long Island U, Brooklyn Campus (NY)
Lyndon State Coll (VT)
MacMurray Coll (IL)
Macon State Coll (GA)
Madonna U (MI)
Manchester Coll (IN)
Marietta Coll (OH)
Mayville State U (ND)
Medaille Coll (NY)
Medgar Evers Coll of the City U of New York (NY)
Mercy Coll (NY)
Mercyhurst Coll (PA)
Merrimack Coll (MA)
Mesa State Coll (CO)
MidAmerica Nazarene U (KS)
Midway Coll (KY)
Minnesota School of Business (MN)
Missouri Baptist U (MO)
Missouri Western State U (MO)
Mitchell Coll (CT)
Monroe Coll, Bronx (NY)
Monroe Coll, New Rochelle (NY)
Montana State U–Billings (MT)
Mount Aloysius Coll (PA)

Mount Marty Coll (SD)
Mount Olive Coll (NC)
Mount St. Mary's Coll (CA)
National American U, Rapid City (SD)
Newbury Coll (MA)
Newman U (KS)
New Mexico Inst of Mining and Technology (NM)
New York Inst of Technology (NY)
Niagara U (NY)
Northern Kentucky U (KY)
Northern Michigan U (MI)
Northern State U (SD)
Northwestern State U of Louisiana (LA)
Northwood U (MI)
Northwood U, Florida Campus (FL)
Northwood U, Texas Campus (TX)
Nyack Coll (NY)
Oakland City U (IN)
Ohio Dominican U (OH)
Ohio U (OH)
Oklahoma Panhandle State U (OK)
Park U (MO)
Paul Smith's Coll of Arts and Sciences (NY)
Peirce Coll (PA)
Pennsylvania Coll of Technology (PA)
Pikeville Coll (KY)
Pine Manor Coll (MA)
Point Park U (PA)
Pontifical Catholic U of Puerto Rico (PR)
Post U (CT)
Presentation Coll (SD)
Purdue U North Central (IN)
Reinhardt Coll (GA)
Rider U (NJ)
Rivier Coll (NH)
Robert Morris Coll (IL)
Rochester Inst of Technology (NY)
Roger Williams U (RI)
Rust Coll (MS)
Sacred Heart U (CT)
Sage Coll of Albany (NY)
St. Francis Coll (NY)
Saint Francis U (PA)
St. Gregory's U (OK)
Saint Joseph's U (PA)
Salve Regina U (RI)
Schiller International UFrance)
Schiller International USpain)
Shawnee State U (OH)
Shaw U (NC)
Southeastern Baptist Coll (MS)
Southern New Hampshire U (NH)
Southern Vermont Coll (VT)
Southern Wesleyan U (SC)
South U (AL)
South U (GA)
South U (SC)
Spalding U (KY)
Spring Hill Coll (AL)
State U of New York Coll of Agriculture and Technology at Cobleskill (NY)
State U of New York Empire State Coll (NY)
Stratford U (VA)
Sullivan U (KY)
Taylor U (IN)
Thomas Coll (ME)
Tiffin U (OH)
Tri-State U (IN)
Tulane U (LA)
Union Coll (NE)
Universidad Adventista de las Antillas (PR)
U of Alaska Fairbanks (AK)
U of Alaska Southeast (AK)
U of Arkansas at Fort Smith (AR)
U of Bridgeport (CT)
U of Charleston (WV)
U of Cincinnati (OH)
U of Dubuque (IA)
The U of Findlay (OH)
U of Indianapolis (IN)
The U of Maine at Augusta (ME)

U of Management and Technology (VA)
U of Mary (ND)
U of Minnesota, Crookston (MN)
The U of Montana–Western (MT)
U of New Hampshire (NH)
U of New Hampshire at Manchester (NH)
U of Regina (SK, Canada)
U of Rio Grande (OH)
U of Saint Francis (IN)
The U of Scranton (PA)
U of Sioux Falls (SD)
U of the Virgin Islands (VI)
U of Wisconsin–Green Bay (WI)
Urbana U (OH)
Utah Valley State Coll (UT)
Vermont Tech Coll (VT)
Villa Julie Coll (MD)
Walla Walla Coll (WA)
Walsh U (OH)
Wayland Baptist U (TX)
Waynesburg Coll (PA)
Webber International U (FL)
Wentworth Inst of Technology (MA)
Western Kentucky U (KY)
West Virginia State U (WV)
Wilson Coll (PA)
Xavier U (OH)
York Coll of Pennsylvania (PA)
Youngstown State U (OH)

Business Administration, Management and Operations Related
Argosy U/Santa Monica (CA)
Briarcliffe Coll (NY)
DeVry U (NJ)
Embry-Riddle Aeronautical U, Extended Campus (FL)
Peirce Coll (PA)
U of Management and Technology (VA)

Business and Personal/Financial Services Marketing
Southern New Hampshire U (NH)

Business Automation/Technology/Data Entry
Austin Peay State U (TN)
Baker Coll of Clinton Township (MI)
Central Christian Coll of Kansas (KS)
Montana State U–Billings (MT)
Montana Tech of The U of Montana (MT)
Pennsylvania Coll of Technology (PA)
The U of Akron (OH)
The U of Montana–Western (MT)
U of Rio Grande (OH)
Utah Valley State Coll (UT)

Business/Commerce
Anderson U (IN)
Andrew Jackson U (AL)
Baker Coll of Flint (MI)
Bluefield State Coll (WV)
Bryant and Stratton Coll, Cleveland (OH)
Bryant and Stratton Coll, Wauwatosa Campus (WI)
California U of Pennsylvania (PA)
Castleton State Coll (VT)
Champlain Coll (VT)
Coll of Staten Island of the City U of New York (NY)
Crown Coll (MN)
Cumberland U (TN)
Dalton State Coll (GA)
Delaware Valley Coll (PA)
Gannon U (PA)
Glenville State Coll (WV)
God's Bible School and Coll (OH)
Idaho State U (ID)
Indiana U East (IN)
Indiana U Kokomo (IN)
Indiana U South Bend (IN)
Indiana U Southeast (IN)

Limestone Coll (SC)
Macon State Coll (GA)
Marygrove Coll (MI)
Metropolitan Coll of New York (NY)
Montana State U–Billings (MT)
Mountain State U (WV)
Mount Vernon Nazarene U (OH)
New Mexico State U (NM)
Nicholls State U (LA)
Northern Kentucky U (KY)
Northern Michigan U (MI)
Peirce Coll (PA)
The Pennsylvania State U Abington Coll (PA)
The Pennsylvania State U Altoona Coll (PA)
The Pennsylvania State U at Erie, The Behrend Coll (PA)
The Pennsylvania State U Berks Campus of the Berks–Lehigh Valley Coll (PA)
The Pennsylvania State U Harrisburg Campus (PA)
The Pennsylvania State U University Park Campus (PA)
Southern Nazarene U (OK)
Southern Wesleyan U (SC)
Southwest Baptist U (MO)
Spalding U (KY)
Thomas More Coll (KY)
Thomas U (GA)
Troy U (AL)
Tulane U (LA)
U of Management and Technology (VA)
The U of Montana–Western (MT)
Utah Valley State Coll (UT)
Webber International U (FL)
Youngstown State U (OH)

Business/Corporate Communications
Central Christian Coll of Kansas (KS)
Chestnut Hill Coll (PA)

Business Machine Repair
Boise State U (ID)
Idaho State U (ID)
Lamar U (TX)

Business, Management, and Marketing Related
Taylor U Fort Wayne (IN)
The U of Akron (OH)
U of Southern Indiana (IN)

Business/Managerial Economics
Central Christian Coll of Kansas (KS)
Hawai'i Pacific U (HI)
Northwood U (MI)
Urbana U (OH)

Business Operations Support and Secretarial Services Related
The U of Akron (OH)

Business Teacher Education
Central Christian Coll of Kansas (KS)
Clayton State U (GA)
Faulkner U (AL)
Macon State Coll (GA)
U of the District of Columbia (DC)

Cabinetmaking and Millwork
Pennsylvania Coll of Technology (PA)
Utah Valley State Coll (UT)

Cad/Cadd Drafting/Design Technology
The Art Inst of Las Vegas (NV)
ITT Tech Inst, Tempe (AZ)
ITT Tech Inst, Lexington (KY)
Johnson & Wales U (RI)
Shawnee State U (OH)

Cardiopulmonary Technology
Nicholls State U (LA)

Cardiovascular Technology
Gwynedd-Mercy Coll (PA)
Molloy Coll (NY)
Nebraska Methodist Coll (NE)
Thompson Rivers U (BC, Canada)

Carpentry
Bob Jones U (SC)
Idaho State U (ID)
Pennsylvania Coll of Technology (PA)
Southern Utah U (UT)
Thompson Rivers U (BC, Canada)

Celtic Languages
Sacred Heart U (CT)

Ceramic Arts and Ceramics
Rochester Inst of Technology (NY)

Chemical Engineering
Ball State U (IN)
Excelsior Coll (NY)
Ferris State U (MI)
U of New Haven (CT)
U of the District of Columbia (DC)
West Virginia State U (WV)

Chemical Technology
Indiana U–Purdue University Fort Wayne (IN)
Lawrence Technological U (MI)
Millersville U of Pennsylvania (PA)
Nicholls State U (LA)
State U of New York Coll of Agriculture and Technology at Cobleskill (NY)
The U of Akron (OH)
Weber State U (UT)

Chemistry
Bethel Coll (IN)
Castleton State Coll (VT)
Chestnut Hill Coll (PA)
Clayton State U (GA)
Dalton State Coll (GA)
Hannibal-LaGrange Coll (MO)
Idaho State U (ID)
Indiana U South Bend (IN)
Keene State Coll (NH)
Lake Superior State U (MI)
Lindsey Wilson Coll (KY)
Macon State Coll (GA)
Madonna U (MI)
Ohio Dominican U (OH)
Presentation Coll (SD)
Rochester Inst of Technology (NY)
Sacred Heart U (CT)
Saint Joseph's U (PA)
Thomas More Coll (KY)
U of Indianapolis (IN)
U of Rio Grande (OH)
The U of Tampa (FL)
U of Wisconsin–Green Bay (WI)
Utah Valley State Coll (UT)
Villa Julie Coll (MD)
Wright State U (OH)
York Coll of Pennsylvania (PA)

Chemistry Related
U of the Incarnate Word (TX)

Chemistry Teacher Education
Central Christian Coll of Kansas (KS)

Child Care and Support Services Management
The Baptist Coll of Florida (FL)
Bob Jones U (SC)
Cameron U (OK)
Chestnut Hill Coll (PA)
Eastern New Mexico U (NM)
Georgia Southwestern State U (GA)
Henderson State U (AR)
Idaho State U (ID)
Mount Aloysius Coll (PA)
Mount Vernon Nazarene U (OH)
Nicholls State U (LA)

Pennsylvania Coll of Technology (PA)
Post U (CT)
Southeast Missouri State U (MO)
Thompson Rivers U (BC, Canada)
U of Central Arkansas (AR)
Weber State U (UT)
Youngstown State U (OH)

Child Care/Guidance
Eastern Kentucky U (KY)

Child Care Provision
Eastern Kentucky U (KY)
Mayville State U (ND)
Murray State U (KY)
Pacific Union Coll (CA)
Pennsylvania Coll of Technology (PA)
Saint Mary-of-the-Woods Coll (IN)
U of Alaska Fairbanks (AK)

Child Care Services Management
Cameron U (OK)
U of Louisiana at Monroe (LA)

Child Development
Alabama State U (AL)
Arkansas Tech U (AR)
Boise State U (ID)
Central Pennsylvania Coll (PA)
Eastern Kentucky U (KY)
Evangel U (MO)
Fairmont State U (WV)
Franciscan U of Steubenville (OH)
Kuyper Coll (MI)
Lamar U (TX)
Lewis-Clark State Coll (ID)
Madonna U (MI)
Mitchell Coll (CT)
Northern Michigan U (MI)
Ohio U (OH)
Purdue U Calumet (IN)
Southern Utah U (UT)
Southern Vermont Coll (VT)
Trevecca Nazarene U (TN)
U of Arkansas at Fort Smith (AR)
U of Cincinnati (OH)
U of the District of Columbia (DC)
Villa Julie Coll (MD)
Weber State U (UT)
Youngstown State U (OH)

Christian Studies
God's Bible School and Coll (OH)
Heritage Bible Coll (NC)
Wayland Baptist U (TX)

Cinematography and Film/Video Production
Academy of Art U (CA)
The Art Inst of California–Los Angeles (CA)
The Art Inst of Colorado (CO)
The Art Inst of Dallas (TX)
The Art Inst of Seattle (WA)
Collins Coll: A School of Design and Technology (AZ)
Five Towns Coll (NY)
New England School of Communications (ME)
Rochester Inst of Technology (NY)
Southern Adventist U (TN)

City/Urban, Community and Regional Planning
U of the District of Columbia (DC)

Civil Drafting and Cad/Cadd
Montana Tech of The U of Montana (MT)

Civil Engineering
Macon State Coll (GA)

Civil Engineering Technology
Bluefield State Coll (WV)
Fairmont State U (WV)
Ferris State U (MI)
Idaho State U (ID)

Indiana U–Purdue University Fort Wayne (IN)
Indiana U–Purdue University Indianapolis (IN)
Michigan Technological U (MI)
Missouri Western State U (MO)
Murray State U (KY)
Pennsylvania Coll of Technology (PA)
Point Park U (PA)
Purdue U Calumet (IN)
Purdue U North Central (IN)
U of Cincinnati (OH)
U of Massachusetts Lowell (MA)
U of New Hampshire (NH)
U of the District of Columbia (DC)
Vermont Tech Coll (VT)
Wentworth Inst of Technology (MA)
Youngstown State U (OH)

Clinical Laboratory Science/Medical Technology
Arkansas State U (AR)
Clayton State U (GA)
Dalton State Coll (GA)
Faulkner U (AL)
Indiana U East (IN)
Villa Julie Coll (MD)
Weber State U (UT)

Clinical/Medical Laboratory Assistant
Northern Michigan U (MI)
The U of Maine at Augusta (ME)

Clinical/Medical Laboratory Science and Allied Professions Related
The U of Akron (OH)

Clinical/Medical Laboratory Technology
Baker Coll of Owosso (MI)
Clayton State U (GA)
Coll of Staten Island of the City U of New York (NY)
Dalton State Coll (GA)
Eastern Kentucky U (KY)
Fairmont State U (WV)
Farmingdale State U of New York (NY)
Faulkner U (AL)
Felician Coll (NJ)
Ferris State U (MI)
The George Washington U (DC)
Indiana U Northwest (IN)
Macon State Coll (GA)
Madonna U (MI)
Marshall U (WV)
Presentation Coll (SD)
Shawnee State U (OH)
State U of New York Coll of Agriculture and Technology at Cobleskill (NY)
U of Cincinnati (OH)
U of Maine at Presque Isle (ME)
U of Rio Grande (OH)
U of the District of Columbia (DC)
Villa Julie Coll (MD)
Weber State U (UT)
Youngstown State U (OH)

Clothing/Textiles
Indiana U Bloomington (IN)

Commercial and Advertising Art
Academy of Art U (CA)
American InterContinental U (TX)
Andrews U (MI)
The Art Center Design Coll (AZ)
The Art Inst of California–San Diego (CA)
The Art Inst of Colorado (CO)
The Art Inst of Washington (VA)
The Art Insts International Minnesota (MN)
Baker Coll of Auburn Hills (MI)
Baker Coll of Clinton Township (MI)

Baker Coll of Flint (MI)
Baker Coll of Muskegon (MI)
Baker Coll of Owosso (MI)
Baker Coll of Port Huron (MI)
Briarcliffe Coll (NY)
Champlain Coll (VT)
Collins Coll: A School of Design and Technology (AZ)
Fairmont State U (WV)
Fashion Inst of Technology (NY)
Felician Coll (NJ)
Ferris State U (MI)
Hussian School of Art (PA)
The Illinois Inst of Art–Chicago (IL)
Indiana U–Purdue University Fort Wayne (IN)
International Academy of Design & Technology (FL)
International Academy of Design & Technology (IL)
Mercy Coll (NY)
Mesa State Coll (CO)
Miami International U of Art & Design (FL)
Mitchell Coll (CT)
Newbury Coll (MA)
Northern Michigan U (MI)
Northern State U (SD)
Oakwood Coll (AL)
Pace U (NY)
Parsons The New School for Design (NY)
Pennsylvania Coll of Technology (PA)
Pratt Inst (NY)
Robert Morris Coll (IL)
Sacred Heart U (CT)
Silver Lake Coll (WI)
Suffolk U (MA)
U of New Haven (CT)
U of Saint Francis (IN)
U of the District of Columbia (DC)
Utah Valley State Coll (UT)
Villa Julie Coll (MD)
Virginia Intermont Coll (VA)
Walla Walla Coll (WA)

Commercial Photography
Fashion Inst of Technology (NY)
Harrington Coll of Design (IL)
Paier Coll of Art, Inc. (CT)
The U of Akron (OH)

Communication and Journalism Related
Champlain Coll (VT)
New England School of Communications (ME)
Tulane U (LA)

Communication and Media Related
Champlain Coll (VT)

Communication/Speech Communication and Rhetoric
Andrew Jackson U (AL)
Baker Coll of Jackson (MI)
Cameron U (OK)
Central Christian Coll of Kansas (KS)
Coll of Mount St. Joseph (OH)
Idaho State U (ID)
Lyndon State Coll (VT)
The New England Inst of Art (MA)
Presentation Coll (SD)
Southern Nazarene U (OK)
Thomas More Coll (KY)
Tri-State U (IN)
Tulane U (LA)
U of New Haven (CT)
U of Rio Grande (OH)
Utah Valley State Coll (UT)
West Virginia State U (WV)
Wright State U (OH)

Communications Systems Installation and Repair Technology
Idaho State U (ID)
Thompson Rivers U (BC, Canada)

Communications Technologies and Support Services Related
New England School of Communications (ME)

Communications Technology
Bluefield State Coll (WV)
East Stroudsburg U of Pennsylvania (PA)
Ferris State U (MI)

Community Health and Preventive Medicine
Utah Valley State Coll (UT)

Community Organization and Advocacy
Alabama State U (AL)
Fairmont State U (WV)
Midland Lutheran Coll (NE)
Samford U (AL)
State U of New York Empire State Coll (NY)
The U of Akron (OH)
The U of Findlay (OH)
U of New Hampshire (NH)
U of New Mexico (NM)

Community Psychology
Kwantlen U Coll (BC, Canada)

Computer and Information Sciences
Baker Coll of Allen Park (MI)
Bluefield State Coll (WV)
Chaminade U of Honolulu (HI)
Champlain Coll (VT)
Columbia Coll (MO)
Dalton State Coll (GA)
Davenport U, Dearborn (MI)
Delaware Valley Coll (PA)
Edinboro U of Pennsylvania (PA)
Florida Metropolitan U–Brandon Campus (FL)
Globe Inst of Technology (NY)
Inter American U of Puerto Rico, Barranquitas Campus (PR)
Keene State Coll (NH)
Kentucky State U (KY)
King's Coll (PA)
Lewis-Clark State Coll (ID)
Lyndon State Coll (VT)
Madonna U (MI)
Midway Coll (KY)
Millersville U of Pennsylvania (PA)
Montana State U–Billings (MT)
Oklahoma Panhandle State U (OK)
Pennsylvania Coll of Technology (PA)
Sacred Heart U (CT)
Sage Coll of Albany (NY)
Spring Hill Coll (AL)
Thomas Coll (ME)
Thomas More Coll (KY)
Tri-State U (IN)
Troy U (AL)
Tulane U (LA)
U of Charleston (WV)
U of Cincinnati (OH)
The U of Maine at Augusta (ME)
The U of Montana–Western (MT)
Utah Valley State Coll (UT)
Villa Julie Coll (MD)
Weber State U (UT)

Computer and Information Sciences And Support Services Related
Cleary U (MI)
Florida Metropolitan U–Brandon Campus (FL)
Montana State U–Billings (MT)
Pennsylvania Coll of Technology (PA)
U of Arkansas at Fort Smith (AR)

Computer and Information Sciences Related
Lindsey Wilson Coll (KY)
Madonna U (MI)
Washburn U (KS)

Computer and Information Systems Security
Champlain Coll (VT)
ITT Tech Inst, Tempe (AZ)

Computer Engineering
Missouri Western State U (MO)
The U of Scranton (PA)

Computer Engineering Related
Thompson Rivers U (BC, Canada)

Computer Engineering Technology
Andrews U (MI)
Baker Coll of Owosso (MI)
Clayton State U (GA)
Dalton State Coll (GA)
DeVry U, Pomona (CA)
DeVry U, Fort Washington (PA)
Eastern Kentucky U (KY)
Excelsior Coll (NY)
Grantham U (MO)
Johnson & Wales U (RI)
Lake Superior State U (MI)
Madonna U (MI)
National American U, Rapid City (SD)
Oakland City U (IN)
Peirce Coll (PA)
Purdue U Calumet (IN)
Purdue U North Central (IN)
U of Cincinnati (OH)
U of Hartford (CT)
U of the District of Columbia (DC)
Vermont Tech Coll (VT)
Weber State U (UT)
Wentworth Inst of Technology (MA)

Computer Graphics
Academy of Art U (CA)
The Art Inst of California–Orange County (CA)
The Art Inst of Colorado (CO)
The Art Inst of Dallas (TX)
The Art Inst of Washington (VA)
Baker Coll of Cadillac (MI)
Champlain Coll (VT)
International Academy of Design & Technology (FL)
International Academy of Design & Technology (IL)
Johnson & Wales U (RI)
Miami International U of Art & Design (FL)
New England School of Communications (ME)
Thompson Rivers U (BC, Canada)
Vaughn Coll of Aeronautics and Technology (NY)
Villa Julie Coll (MD)

Computer Hardware Technology
Inter American U of Puerto Rico, Aguadilla Campus (PR)

Computer/Information Technology Services Administration Related
Champlain Coll (VT)
Dalton State Coll (GA)
Johnson & Wales U (RI)
Medgar Evers Coll of the City U of New York (NY)
Mercy Coll (NY)
Pennsylvania Coll of Technology (PA)
The U of Akron (OH)

Computer Installation and Repair Technology
Dalton State Coll (GA)
Inter American U of Puerto Rico, Bayamón Campus (PR)
Thompson Rivers U (BC, Canada)

Computer Maintenance Technology
Eastern Kentucky U (KY)

Computer Management
Champlain Coll (VT)
Faulkner U (AL)
Five Towns Coll (NY)
Life U (GA)
Northwood U (MI)
Northwood U, Florida Campus (FL)
Oakland City U (IN)
Thomas Coll (ME)

Computer Programming
Baker Coll of Flint (MI)
Baker Coll of Muskegon (MI)
Baker Coll of Owosso (MI)
Baker Coll of Port Huron (MI)
Briarcliffe Coll (NY)
California U of Pennsylvania (PA)
Castleton State Coll (VT)
Charleston Southern U (SC)
Coll of Staten Island of the City U of New York (NY)
Dakota State U (SD)
Delaware Valley Coll (PA)
Farmingdale State U of New York (NY)
Gwynedd-Mercy Coll (PA)
Indiana U East (IN)
ITT Tech Inst, Tempe (AZ)
Johnson & Wales U (RI)
Kent State U (OH)
Limestone Coll (SC)
Lindsey Wilson Coll (KY)
Macon State Coll (GA)
Midland Lutheran Coll (NE)
National American U, Rapid City (SD)
Newbury Coll (MA)
New York U (NY)
Oakland City U (IN)
Pontifical Catholic U of Puerto Rico (PR)
Purdue U Calumet (IN)
Purdue U North Central (IN)
Saint Francis U (PA)
State U of New York Coll of Agriculture and Technology at Cobleskill (NY)
Stratford U (VA)
Tiffin U (OH)
U of Cincinnati (OH)
Villa Julie Coll (MD)
Walla Walla Coll (WA)
West Virginia State U (WV)
Youngstown State U (OH)

Computer Programming Related
Central Pennsylvania Coll (PA)
Inter American U of Puerto Rico, Barranquitas Campus (PR)
Stratford U (VA)

Computer Programming (Specific Applications)
Georgia Southwestern State U (GA)
Idaho State U (ID)
Kent State U (OH)
Macon State Coll (GA)
Peirce Coll (PA)
Pennsylvania Coll of Technology (PA)
Robert Morris Coll (IL)

Computer Science
Alderson-Broaddus Coll (WV)
Baker Coll of Allen Park (MI)
Baker Coll of Owosso (MI)
Bethel Coll (IN)
Calumet Coll of Saint Joseph (IN)
Carroll Coll (MT)
Central Christian Coll of Kansas (KS)
Clayton State U (GA)
Columbia Union Coll (MD)
Columbus State U (GA)
Creighton U (NE)
Dalton State Coll (GA)
Defiance Coll (OH)
Excelsior Coll (NY)
Farmingdale State U of New York (NY)

Felician Coll (NJ)
Grantham U (MO)
Heritage U (WA)
Indiana U–Purdue University Fort Wayne (IN)
Indiana U South Bend (IN)
Indiana U Southeast (IN)
Inter American U of Puerto Rico, Aguadilla Campus (PR)
Inter American U of Puerto Rico, Barranquitas Campus (PR)
Inter American U of Puerto Rico, Bayamón Campus (PR)
Inter American U of Puerto Rico, Ponce Campus (PR)
John Cabot U(Italy)
Keene State Coll (NH)
Limestone Coll (SC)
Lincoln U (MO)
Lyndon State Coll (VT)
Macon State Coll (GA)
Madonna U (MI)
Manchester Coll (IN)
Medgar Evers Coll of the City U of New York (NY)
Merrimack Coll (MA)
Mesa State Coll (CO)
Millersville U of Pennsylvania (PA)
Missouri Southern State U (MO)
Monroe Coll, Bronx (NY)
Monroe Coll, New Rochelle (NY)
Montana Tech of The U of Montana (MT)
Mountain State U (WV)
Mount Aloysius Coll (PA)
Newbury Coll (MA)
Oakland City U (IN)
Park U (MO)
Rivier Coll (NH)
Rochester Inst of Technology (NY)
Sacred Heart U (CT)
Sage Coll of Albany (NY)
Saint Joseph's U (PA)
Southern Adventist U (TN)
Southwest Baptist U (MO)
State U of New York Coll of Agriculture and Technology at Cobleskill (NY)
Sullivan U (KY)
Universidad Adventista de las Antillas (PR)
U of Dubuque (IA)
The U of Findlay (OH)
U of New Haven (CT)
U of Rio Grande (OH)
U of the Virgin Islands (VI)
Utah Valley State Coll (UT)
Weber State U (UT)
Wentworth Inst of Technology (MA)
West Virginia State U (WV)

Computer Software and Media Applications Related
Indiana U–Purdue University Fort Wayne (IN)
New England School of Communications (ME)

Computer Software Engineering
Grantham U (MO)
Vermont Tech Coll (VT)

Computer Software Technology
U of New Hampshire (NH)

Computer Systems Analysis
Baker Coll of Flint (MI)
Davenport U, Dearborn (MI)
The U of Akron (OH)

Computer Systems Networking and Telecommunications
Baker Coll of Allen Park (MI)
Baker Coll of Flint (MI)
Champlain Coll (VT)
DeVry Inst of Technology (NY)
DeVry U, Fremont (CA)
DeVry U, Long Beach (CA)
DeVry U, Pomona (CA)
DeVry U, West Hills (CA)

DeVry U, Colorado Springs (CO)
DeVry U, Westminster (CO)
DeVry U, Miramar (FL)
DeVry U, Orlando (FL)
DeVry U, Alpharetta (GA)
DeVry U, Decatur (GA)
DeVry U, Addison (IL)
DeVry U, Chicago (IL)
DeVry U, Tinley Park (IL)
DeVry U (NJ)
DeVry U, Columbus (OH)
DeVry U, Irving (TX)
DeVry U, Arlington (VA)
DeVry U, Federal Way (WA)
Minnesota School of Business (MN)
Pennsylvania Coll of Technology (PA)
Robert Morris Coll (IL)
Stratford U (VA)
Westwood Coll–Atlanta Northlake (GA)

Computer Teacher Education
Baker Coll of Flint (MI)
Central Christian Coll of Kansas (KS)

Computer/Technical Support
Davenport U, Dearborn (MI)

Computer Technology/ Computer Systems Technology
Collins Coll: A School of Design and Technology (AZ)
Dalton State Coll (GA)
DeVry U, Westminster (CO)
DeVry U (NV)
Eastern Kentucky U (KY)
Peirce Coll (PA)
Pennsylvania Coll of Technology (PA)
Southeast Missouri State U (MO)
State U of New York Coll of Agriculture and Technology at Cobleskill (NY)
Thompson Rivers U (BC, Canada)

Computer Typography and Composition Equipment Operation
Baker Coll of Auburn Hills (MI)
Baker Coll of Cadillac (MI)
Baker Coll of Clinton Township (MI)
Baker Coll of Flint (MI)
Baker Coll of Jackson (MI)
Calumet Coll of Saint Joseph (IN)
Faulkner U (AL)

Construction Engineering Technology
Baker Coll of Owosso (MI)
Coll of Staten Island of the City U of New York (NY)
Fairmont State U (WV)
Ferris State U (MI)
Lake Superior State U (MI)
Lawrence Technological U (MI)
Pennsylvania Coll of Technology (PA)
Purdue U Calumet (IN)
Purdue U North Central (IN)
The U of Akron (OH)
U of Cincinnati (OH)
U of New Hampshire (NH)
Vermont Tech Coll (VT)
Wentworth Inst of Technology (MA)
Wright State U (OH)

Construction Management
Baker Coll of Flint (MI)
John Brown U (AR)
Pratt Inst (NY)
U of New Hampshire (NH)
Vermont Tech Coll (VT)
Wentworth Inst of Technology (MA)

Construction Trades
Northern Michigan U (MI)
U of Alaska Southeast (AK)

Utah Valley State Coll (UT)

Consumer Economics
U of Alaska Southeast (AK)

Consumer Merchandising/ Retailing Management
Baker Coll of Owosso (MI)
Central Pennsylvania Coll (PA)
Fairmont State U (WV)
Johnson & Wales U (RI)
Madonna U (MI)
Newbury Coll (MA)
Sullivan U (KY)

Cooking and Related Culinary Arts
The Art Inst of California–Los Angeles (CA)
The Art Inst of California–Orange County (CA)
The Art Inst of California–San Diego (CA)
Kendall Coll (IL)
Lexington Coll (IL)

Corrections
Baker Coll of Muskegon (MI)
Bluefield State Coll (WV)
Eastern Kentucky U (KY)
Lake Superior State U (MI)
Lamar U (TX)
Macon State Coll (GA)
Marygrove Coll (MI)
Northern Michigan U (MI)
U of Indianapolis (IN)
U of the District of Columbia (DC)
Washburn U (KS)
Weber State U (UT)
Xavier U (OH)

Corrections and Criminal Justice Related
Monroe Coll, New Rochelle (NY)

Cosmetology
Bob Jones U (SC)
Georgia Southwestern State U (GA)
Lamar U (TX)

Court Reporting
U of Cincinnati (OH)
Villa Julie Coll (MD)

Creative Writing
Bethel Coll (IN)
Manchester Coll (IN)
U of Maine at Presque Isle (ME)
The U of Tampa (FL)

Criminal Justice/Law Enforcement Administration
Anderson U (IN)
Argosy U/Santa Monica (CA)
Arkansas State U (AR)
Ashland U (OH)
Ball State U (IN)
Bemidji State U (MN)
Boise State U (ID)
Bryant and Stratton Coll, Cleveland (OH)
Bryant and Stratton Coll, Wauwatosa Campus (WI)
Calumet Coll of Saint Joseph (IN)
Campbellsville U (KY)
Castleton State Coll (VT)
Central Christian Coll of Kansas (KS)
Central Pennsylvania Coll (PA)
Champlain Coll (VT)
Chestnut Hill Coll (PA)
Clayton State U (GA)
Columbia Coll (MO)
Columbus State U (GA)
Dakota Wesleyan U (SD)
Dalton State Coll (GA)
Defiance Coll (OH)
Eastern Kentucky U (KY)
Farmingdale State U of New York (NY)
Faulkner U (AL)
Finlandia U (MI)
Fort Valley State U (GA)
Georgia Southwestern State U (GA)
Glenville State Coll (WV)
Grantham U (MO)

Hannibal-LaGrange Coll (MO)
Hilbert Coll (NY)
Indiana Tech (IN)
Indiana U Northwest (IN)
Indiana U South Bend (IN)
Johnson & Wales U (CO)
Johnson & Wales U (FL)
Johnson & Wales U (RI)
Lake Superior State U (MI)
Lincoln U (MO)
MacMurray Coll (IL)
Macon State Coll (GA)
Mansfield U of Pennsylvania (PA)
Mercyhurst Coll (PA)
Mesa State Coll (CO)
Mitchell Coll (CT)
Monroe Coll, Bronx (NY)
Newbury Coll (MA)
Northern Michigan U (MI)
Park U (MO)
Roger Williams U (RI)
St. John's U (NY)
Saint Joseph's U (PA)
Southern Utah U (UT)
Southern Vermont Coll (VT)
Suffolk U (MA)
Thomas More Coll (KY)
Thomas U (GA)
Tri-State U (IN)
U of Arkansas at Fort Smith (AR)
U of Cincinnati (OH)
The U of Findlay (OH)
U of Indianapolis (IN)
U of Maine at Presque Isle (ME)
U of the District of Columbia (DC)
Urbana U (OH)
Utah Valley State Coll (UT)
Washburn U (KS)
West Virginia State U (WV)

Criminal Justice/Police Science
Arkansas State U (AR)
Armstrong Atlantic State U (GA)
Bluefield State Coll (WV)
Cameron U (OK)
Dalton State Coll (GA)
Davis & Elkins Coll (WV)
Defiance Coll (OH)
Eastern Kentucky U (KY)
Edinboro U of Pennsylvania (PA)
Fairmont State U (WV)
Grantham U (MO)
Husson Coll (ME)
Idaho State U (ID)
Lake Superior State U (MI)
MacMurray Coll (IL)
Macon State Coll (GA)
Mercyhurst Coll (PA)
Middle Tennessee State U (TN)
Missouri Southern State U (MO)
Monroe Coll, Bronx (NY)
Nicholls State U (LA)
Northern Kentucky U (KY)
Northern Michigan U (MI)
Northwestern State U of Louisiana (LA)
Ohio U (OH)
Southeastern Louisiana U (LA)
Southern U and A&M Coll (LA)
Tiffin U (OH)
The U of Akron (OH)
U of Cincinnati (OH)
U of Louisiana at Monroe (LA)
U of New Haven (CT)
U of the District of Columbia (DC)
U of the Virgin Islands (VI)
Washburn U (KS)
Weber State U (UT)
York Coll of Pennsylvania (PA)

Criminal Justice/Safety
Andrew Jackson U (AL)
Arkansas Tech U (AR)
Augusta State U (GA)
Bethel Coll (IN)
Cazenovia Coll (NY)

Central Christian Coll of Kansas (KS)
Champlain Coll (VT)
Florida Metropolitan U–Brandon Campus (FL)
Gannon U (PA)
Georgia Southwestern State U (GA)
Grantham U (MO)
Husson Coll (ME)
Idaho State U (ID)
Indiana U East (IN)
Indiana U Kokomo (IN)
Indiana U–Purdue University Fort Wayne (IN)
Indiana U–Purdue University Indianapolis (IN)
King's Coll (PA)
Madonna U (MI)
Manchester Coll (IN)
Missouri Western State U (MO)
Mountain State U (WV)
Mount Aloysius Coll (PA)
Murray State U (KY)
New Mexico State U (NM)
The Pennsylvania State U Altoona Coll (PA)
Pikeville Coll (KY)
St. Francis Coll (NY)
St. Gregory's U (OK)
Shaw U (NC)
Sullivan U (KY)
The U of Maine at Augusta (ME)
The U of Scranton (PA)
Weber State U (UT)
Xavier U (OH)
Youngstown State U (OH)

Criminology
Ball State U (IN)
Chaminade U of Honolulu (HI)
Dalton State Coll (GA)
Faulkner U (AL)
Indiana State U (IN)
Indiana U of Pennsylvania (PA)
Kwantlen U Coll (BC, Canada)
Marquette U (WI)
U of the District of Columbia (DC)

Crop Production
Sterling Coll (VT)
U of Massachusetts Amherst (MA)

Culinary Arts
The Art Inst of California–San Diego (CA)
The Art Inst of Colorado (CO)
The Art Inst of Dallas (TX)
The Art Inst of Houston (TX)
The Art Inst of Phoenix (AZ)
The Art Inst of Seattle (WA)
The Art Inst of Tampa (FL)
The Art Inst of Washington (VA)
The Art Insts International Minnesota (MN)
Baker Coll of Muskegon (MI)
Boise State U (ID)
The Culinary Inst of America (NY)
Georgia Southwestern State U (GA)
Idaho State U (ID)
The Illinois Inst of Art–Chicago (IL)
Johnson & Wales U (CO)
Johnson & Wales U (FL)
Johnson & Wales U (NC)
Johnson & Wales U (RI)
Kendall Coll (IL)
Lexington Coll (IL)
Mercyhurst Coll (PA)
Mesa State Coll (CO)
Mountain State U (WV)
Newbury Coll (MA)
Nicholls State U (LA)
Oakland City U (IN)
Paul Smith's Coll of Arts and Sciences (NY)
Pennsylvania Coll of Technology (PA)
Purdue U Calumet (IN)
Robert Morris Coll (IL)
Saint Francis U (PA)

Southern New Hampshire U (NH)
State U of New York Coll of Agriculture and Technology at Cobleskill (NY)
Stratford U (VA)
Sullivan U (KY)
The U of Akron (OH)
U of Alaska Fairbanks (AK)
The U of Montana–Missoula (MT)
U of New Hampshire (NH)
Utah Valley State Coll (UT)
Virginia Intermont Coll (VA)

Culinary Arts Related
Delaware Valley Coll (PA)
Lexington Coll (IL)
New York Inst of Technology (NY)

Cultural Studies
Baptist U of the Americas (TX)

Cytotechnology
Indiana U–Purdue University Indianapolis (IN)
Indiana U Southeast (IN)

Dairy Husbandry and Production
Sterling Coll (VT)

Dairy Science
State U of New York Coll of Agriculture and Technology at Cobleskill (NY)
U of New Hampshire (NH)
Vermont Tech Coll (VT)

Dance
New World School of the Arts (FL)
Utah Valley State Coll (UT)

Data Entry/Microcomputer Applications
Baker Coll of Allen Park (MI)

Data Entry/Microcomputer Applications Related
Baker Coll of Allen Park (MI)

Data Processing and Data Processing Technology
Austin Peay State U (TN)
Baker Coll of Auburn Hills (MI)
Baker Coll of Cadillac (MI)
Baker Coll of Clinton Township (MI)
Baker Coll of Flint (MI)
Baker Coll of Jackson (MI)
Baker Coll of Muskegon (MI)
Baker Coll of Owosso (MI)
Baker Coll of Port Huron (MI)
Campbellsville U (KY)
Clayton State U (GA)
Dordt Coll (IA)
Farmingdale State U of New York (NY)
Five Towns Coll (NY)
Hawai'i Pacific U (HI)
Lamar U (TX)
Macon State Coll (GA)
Missouri Southern State U (MO)
Montana State U–Billings (MT)
Montana Tech of The U of Montana (MT)
New York Inst of Technology (NY)
Northern State U (SD)
Sacred Heart U (CT)
St. Francis Coll (NY)
Saint Francis U (PA)
St. John's U (NY)
State U of New York Coll of Agriculture and Technology at Cobleskill (NY)
Thomas More Coll (KY)
The U of Akron (OH)
U of Cincinnati (OH)
The U of Montana–Western (MT)
U of the Virgin Islands (VI)
Utah Valley State Coll (UT)
Western Kentucky U (KY)
Wright State U (OH)
Youngstown State U (OH)

Dental Assisting
Georgia Southwestern State U (GA)
Robert Morris Coll (IL)
The U of Maine at Augusta (ME)
U of Southern Indiana (IN)

Dental Hygiene
Argosy U/Twin Cities (MN)
Armstrong Atlantic State U (GA)
Baker Coll of Port Huron (MI)
Clayton State U (GA)
Dalton State Coll (GA)
Farmingdale State U of New York (NY)
Ferris State U (MI)
Indiana U Northwest (IN)
Indiana U–Purdue University Fort Wayne (IN)
Indiana U–Purdue University Indianapolis (IN)
Indiana U South Bend (IN)
Lamar U (TX)
Minnesota State U Mankato (MN)
Missouri Southern State U (MO)
Montana State U–Billings (MT)
New York U (NY)
Pennsylvania Coll of Technology (PA)
Shawnee State U (OH)
Southern Adventist U (TN)
Tennessee State U (TN)
U of Arkansas at Fort Smith (AR)
U of Bridgeport (CT)
U of Louisville (KY)
The U of Maine at Augusta (ME)
U of New England (ME)
U of New Haven (CT)
U of New Mexico (NM)
The U of South Dakota (SD)
U of Southern Indiana (IN)
Utah Valley State Coll (UT)
Vermont Tech Coll (VT)
Weber State U (UT)
Western Kentucky U (KY)
West Liberty State Coll (WV)
Wichita State U (KS)
Youngstown State U (OH)

Dental Laboratory Technology
Idaho State U (ID)
Indiana U–Purdue University Fort Wayne (IN)
Southern Illinois U Carbondale (IL)

Design and Visual Communications
The American U in DubaiUnited Arab Emirates)
Champlain Coll (VT)
Collins Coll: A School of Design and Technology (AZ)
International Academy of Design & Technology (FL)
Pace U (NY)
Wilmington Coll (DE)

Desktop Publishing and Digital Imaging Design
Davenport U, Dearborn (MI)
Thompson Rivers U (BC, Canada)

Developmental and Child Psychology
Fresno Pacific U (CA)
Mitchell Coll (CT)
U of Sioux Falls (SD)
Villa Julie Coll (MD)

Diagnostic Medical Sonography and Ultrasound Technology
Argosy U/Twin Cities (MN)
Baker Coll of Auburn Hills (MI)
Baker Coll of Owosso (MI)
Baker Coll of Port Huron (MI)
Coll of St. Catherine (MN)
Ferris State U (MI)
Mountain State U (WV)

Diesel Mechanics Technology
Georgia Southwestern State U (GA)
Idaho State U (ID)
Lewis-Clark State Coll (ID)
Montana State U–Billings (MT)
Pennsylvania Coll of Technology (PA)
Utah Valley State Coll (UT)
Weber State U (UT)

Dietetics
Ball State U (IN)
Faulkner U (AL)
Loma Linda U (CA)
Oakwood Coll (AL)
Rochester Inst of Technology (NY)
U of Minnesota, Crookston (MN)
U of New Hampshire (NH)
U of Ottawa (ON, Canada)
Youngstown State U (OH)

Dietetic Technician
U of New Hampshire (NH)

Dietician Assistant
Eastern Kentucky U (KY)

Dietitian Assistant
Pennsylvania Coll of Technology (PA)
The Pennsylvania State U University Park Campus (PA)
Youngstown State U (OH)

Digital Communication and Media/Multimedia
Academy of Art U (CA)
The Art Insts International Minnesota (MN)
Cameron U (OK)
Champlain Coll (VT)
Corcoran Coll of Art and Design (DC)
Utah Valley State Coll (UT)

Divinity/Ministry
Carson-Newman Coll (TN)
Faith Baptist Bible Coll and Theological Seminary (IA)
Faulkner U (AL)
Mount Olive Coll (NC)
Warner Pacific Coll (OR)
Warner Southern Coll (FL)

Drafting
Eastern Kentucky U (KY)

Drafting and Design Technology
Baker Coll of Auburn Hills (MI)
Baker Coll of Cadillac (MI)
Baker Coll of Clinton Township (MI)
Baker Coll of Flint (MI)
Baker Coll of Muskegon (MI)
Baker Coll of Owosso (MI)
Baker Coll of Port Huron (MI)
Boise State U (ID)
California U of Pennsylvania (PA)
Central Missouri State U (MO)
Clayton State U (GA)
Dalton State Coll (GA)
Eastern Kentucky U (KY)
Fairmont State U (WV)
Ferris State U (MI)
Georgia Southwestern State U (GA)
Idaho State U (ID)
Keene State Coll (NH)
Kentucky State U (KY)
Lamar U (TX)
LeTourneau U (TX)
Lewis-Clark State Coll (ID)
Lincoln U (MO)
Missouri Southern State U (MO)
Montana State U–Billings (MT)
Montana Tech of The U of Montana (MT)
Murray State U (KY)

Northern Michigan U (MI)
Pennsylvania Coll of Technology (PA)
Robert Morris Coll (IL)
Saint Francis U (PA)
Southern Utah U (UT)
Thompson Rivers U (BC, Canada)
Tri-State U (IN)
The U of Akron (OH)
U of Cincinnati (OH)
U of Rio Grande (OH)
Utah State U (UT)
Utah Valley State Coll (UT)
Washburn U (KS)
Weber State U (UT)
West Virginia State U (WV)
Wright State U (OH)
Youngstown State U (OH)

Drafting/Design Engineering Technologies Related
Idaho State U (ID)
Pennsylvania Coll of Technology (PA)
The U of Akron (OH)

Drafting/Design Technology
U of Arkansas at Fort Smith (AR)

Drama and Dance Teacher Education
Central Christian Coll of Kansas (KS)

Dramatic/Theater Arts
Clayton State U (GA)
Five Towns Coll (NY)
Indiana U Bloomington (IN)
Macon State Coll (GA)
Mesa State Coll (CO)
New World School of the Arts (FL)
Thomas More Coll (KY)
Université Laval (QC, Canada)
U of Sioux Falls (SD)
U of Wisconsin–Green Bay (WI)
Utah Valley State Coll (UT)
Villa Julie Coll (MD)

Drawing
Academy of Art U (CA)
New World School of the Arts (FL)
Parsons The New School for Design (NY)
Pratt Inst (NY)
Sacred Heart U (CT)

Early Childhood Education
Baker Coll of Allen Park (MI)
Baker Coll of Jackson (MI)
Bethel Coll (IN)
Champlain Coll (VT)
Coll of Saint Mary (NE)
Columbia Union Coll (MD)
Crown Coll (MN)
Gannon U (PA)
Indiana U–Purdue University Fort Wayne (IN)
Keene State Coll (NH)
Lake Superior State U (MI)
Lancaster Bible Coll (PA)
Lincoln U (MO)
Lindsey Wilson Coll (KY)
Mercyhurst Coll (PA)
Oakland City U (IN)
Point Park U (PA)
Rust Coll (MS)
Taylor U Fort Wayne (IN)
Thompson Rivers U (BC, Canada)
U of Great Falls (MT)
Utah Valley State Coll (UT)
Washburn U (KS)
Wheelock Coll (MA)
Wilmington Coll (DE)

Ecology
Paul Smith's Coll of Arts and Sciences (NY)
Sterling Coll (VT)

E-Commerce
Champlain Coll (VT)

Economics
Central Christian Coll of Kansas (KS)
Clayton State U (GA)
Dalton State Coll (GA)

John Cabot UItaly)
Macon State Coll (GA)
Sacred Heart U (CT)
State U of New York Empire State Coll (NY)
Thomas More Coll (KY)
U of Sioux Falls (SD)
The U of Tampa (FL)
U of Wisconsin–Green Bay (WI)

Education
Alabama State U (AL)
Baker Coll of Auburn Hills (MI)
Baker Coll of Cadillac (MI)
Central Baptist Coll (AR)
Clayton State U (GA)
Dalton State Coll (GA)
Evangel U (MO)
Inter American U of Puerto Rico, Barranquitas Campus (PR)
Kent State U (OH)
Lamar U (TX)
Macon State Coll (GA)
Medgar Evers Coll of the City U of New York (NY)
Montana State U–Billings (MT)
National U (CA)
Pontifical Catholic U of Puerto Rico (PR)
Reinhardt Coll (GA)
Saint Francis U (PA)
Spring Hill Coll (AL)
State U of New York Empire State Coll (NY)
U of Southern Indiana (IN)

Education Related
The U of Akron (OH)
Wayland Baptist U (TX)

Education (Specific Subject Areas) Related
Pennsylvania Coll of Technology (PA)

Electrical and Electronic Engineering Technologies Related
Boise State U (ID)
Lawrence Technological U (MI)
New York Inst of Technology (NY)
Pennsylvania Coll of Technology (PA)

Electrical, Electronic and Communications Engineering Technology
Andrews U (MI)
Arkansas State U (AR)
Baker Coll of Cadillac (MI)
Baker Coll of Muskegon (MI)
Baker Coll of Owosso (MI)
Bluefield State Coll (WV)
Boise State U (ID)
Briarcliffe Coll (NY)
Bryant and Stratton Coll, Cleveland (OH)
Cameron U (OK)
Clayton State U (GA)
Columbia Coll, Caguas (PR)
Dalton State Coll (GA)
Davenport U, Dearborn (MI)
DeVry Inst of Technology (NY)
DeVry U, Phoenix (AZ)
DeVry U, Fremont (CA)
DeVry U, Long Beach (CA)
DeVry U, Pomona (CA)
DeVry U, West Hills (CA)
DeVry U, Colorado Springs (CO)
DeVry U, Westminster (CO)
DeVry U, Miramar (FL)
DeVry U, Orlando (FL)
DeVry U, Alpharetta (GA)
DeVry U, Decatur (GA)
DeVry U, Addison (IL)
DeVry U, Chicago (IL)
DeVry U, Tinley Park (IL)
DeVry U, Indianapolis (IN)
DeVry U, Kansas City (MO)
DeVry U (NV)
DeVry U (NJ)
DeVry U, Columbus (OH)
DeVry U, Houston (TX)

DeVry U, Irving (TX)
DeVry U, Arlington (VA)
DeVry U, Federal Way (WA)
Eastern Kentucky U (KY)
Excelsior Coll (NY)
Fairmont State U (WV)
Fort Valley State U (GA)
Grantham U (MO)
Idaho State U (ID)
Indiana State U (IN)
Indiana U–Purdue University Fort Wayne (IN)
Indiana U–Purdue University Indianapolis (IN)
ITT Tech Inst, Tempe (AZ)
ITT Tech Inst, Lexington (KY)
Johnson & Wales U (RI)
Keene State Coll (NH)
Kentucky State U (KY)
Lake Superior State U (MI)
Lamar U (TX)
Lawrence Technological U (MI)
Merrimack Coll (MA)
Mesa State Coll (CO)
Michigan Technological U (MI)
Missouri Western State U (MO)
Northern Michigan U (MI)
Northern State U (SD)
Northwestern State U of Louisiana (LA)
Ohio U (OH)
Pennsylvania Coll of Technology (PA)
The Pennsylvania State U Abington Coll (PA)
The Pennsylvania State U Altoona Coll (PA)
The Pennsylvania State U at Erie, The Behrend Coll (PA)
The Pennsylvania State U Berks Campus of the Berks–Lehigh Valley Coll (PA)
Pittsburg State U (KS)
Point Park U (PA)
Purdue U (IN)
Purdue U Calumet (IN)
Purdue U North Central (IN)
Rochester Inst of Technology (NY)
Southern Utah U (UT)
The U of Akron (OH)
U of Cincinnati (OH)
U of Hartford (CT)
U of Massachusetts Lowell (MA)
The U of Montana–Missoula (MT)
U of the District of Columbia (DC)
Utah Valley State Coll (UT)
Vermont Tech Coll (VT)
Weber State U (UT)
Wentworth Inst of Technology (MA)
West Virginia State U (WV)
Wright State U (OH)
Youngstown State U (OH)

Electrical, Electronics and Communications Engineering
Fairfield U (CT)
Macon State Coll (GA)
Thompson Rivers U (BC, Canada)

Electrical/Electronics Equipment Installation and Repair
Georgia Southwestern State U (GA)
Idaho State U (ID)
Lewis-Clark State Coll (ID)
Thompson Rivers U (BC, Canada)
U of Arkansas at Fort Smith (AR)

Electrician
Georgia Southwestern State U (GA)
Pennsylvania Coll of Technology (PA)
Thompson Rivers U (BC, Canada)

Electromechanical and Instrumentation And Maintenance Technologies Related
Georgia Southwestern State U (GA)

Electromechanical Technology
Clayton State U (GA)
Excelsior Coll (NY)
Idaho State U (ID)
Michigan Technological U (MI)
Northern Michigan U (MI)
Shawnee State U (OH)
The U of Akron (OH)
U of the District of Columbia (DC)
Utah Valley State Coll (UT)
Walla Walla Coll (WA)
Wright State U (OH)

Elementary and Middle School Administration/ Principalship
Inter American U of Puerto Rico, Barranquitas Campus (PR)

Elementary Education
Alaska Pacific U (AK)
Central Christian Coll of Kansas (KS)
Clayton State U (GA)
Dalton State Coll (GA)
God's Bible School and Coll (OH)
Inter American U of Puerto Rico, Barranquitas Campus (PR)
Macon State Coll (GA)
Mountain State U (WV)
New Mexico Highlands U (NM)
Villa Julie Coll (MD)
Wilson Coll (PA)

Emergency Medical Technology (EMT Paramedic)
Arkansas State U (AR)
Baker Coll of Cadillac (MI)
Baker Coll of Clinton Township (MI)
Baker Coll of Muskegon (MI)
Ball State U (IN)
Clayton State U (GA)
Creighton U (NE)
Eastern Kentucky U (KY)
Faulkner U (AL)
Hannibal-LaGrange Coll (MO)
Idaho State U (ID)
Indiana U–Purdue University Indianapolis (IN)
Missouri Western State U (MO)
Montana State U–Billings (MT)
Mountain State U (WV)
Nebraska Methodist Coll (NE)
Nicholls State U (LA)
Pennsylvania Coll of Technology (PA)
Saint Francis U (PA)
Shawnee State U (OH)
Southwest Baptist U (MO)
Spalding U (KY)
U of Pittsburgh at Johnstown (PA)
U of Saint Francis (IN)
U of the District of Columbia (DC)
Weber State U (UT)
Western Kentucky U (KY)
Youngstown State U (OH)

Energy Management and Systems Technology
Baker Coll of Flint (MI)
U of Cincinnati (OH)
U of Rio Grande (OH)

Engineering
Campbell U (NC)
Central Christian Coll of Kansas (KS)
Clayton State U (GA)
Coll of Staten Island of the City U of New York (NY)

Columbia Union Coll (MD)
Columbus State U (GA)
Lake Superior State U (MI)
Macon State Coll (GA)
Mesa State Coll (CO)
Mitchell Coll (CT)
Montana Tech of The U of Montana (MT)
Mountain State U (WV)
Palm Beach Atlantic U (FL)
Southern Adventist U (TN)
Thompson Rivers U (BC, Canada)
Union Coll (NE)
York Coll of Pennsylvania (PA)

Engineering/Industrial Management
Grantham U (MO)

Engineering Related
Eastern Kentucky U (KY)
Montana State U–Billings (MT)

Engineering-Related Technologies
U of Alaska Southeast (AK)

Engineering Science
Merrimack Coll (MA)
Pennsylvania Coll of Technology (PA)
Rochester Inst of Technology (NY)
U of Cincinnati (OH)

Engineering Technologies Related
Cameron U (OK)
Keene State Coll (NH)
The U of Akron (OH)
Western Kentucky U (KY)

Engineering Technology
Andrews U (MI)
Arkansas State U (AR)
Clayton State U (GA)
Fairmont State U (WV)
John Brown U (AR)
Lake Superior State U (MI)
Macon State Coll (GA)
Michigan Technological U (MI)
Montana Tech of The U of Montana (MT)
New Mexico State U (NM)
Pacific Union Coll (CA)
Rochester Inst of Technology (NY)
State U of New York Coll of Agriculture and Technology at Cobleskill (NY)
Tri-State U (IN)
U of the District of Columbia (DC)
Vaughn Coll of Aeronautics and Technology (NY)
Wentworth Inst of Technology (MA)
Youngstown State U (OH)

English
Calumet Coll of Saint Joseph (IN)
Carroll Coll (MT)
Clayton State U (GA)
Coll of Santa Fe (NM)
Dalton State Coll (GA)
Felician Coll (NJ)
Fresno Pacific U (CA)
Hannibal-LaGrange Coll (MO)
Idaho State U (ID)
Indiana U–Purdue University Fort Wayne (IN)
Kwantlen U Coll (BC, Canada)
Macon State Coll (GA)
Madonna U (MI)
Manchester Coll (IN)
Mesa State Coll (CO)
Pine Manor Coll (MA)
Presentation Coll (SD)
Sacred Heart U (CT)
Thomas More Coll (KY)
Université Laval (QC, Canada)
U of Dubuque (IA)
U of Rio Grande (OH)
The U of Tampa (FL)

U of the District of Columbia (DC)
U of Wisconsin–Green Bay (WI)
Utah Valley State Coll (UT)
Xavier U (OH)

English Composition
Kwantlen U Coll (BC, Canada)

English/Language Arts Teacher Education
Lyndon State Coll (VT)

Entrepreneurship
Baker Coll of Flint (MI)
Davenport U, Dearborn (MI)
Johnson & Wales U (CO)
Lyndon State Coll (VT)
Mountain State U (WV)
Northwood U (MI)
The U of Akron (OH)
U of the District of Columbia (DC)

Environmental Control Technologies Related
Pennsylvania Coll of Technology (PA)

Environmental Engineering Technology
Baker Coll of Flint (MI)
Baker Coll of Owosso (MI)
Baker Coll of Port Huron (MI)
Mesa State Coll (CO)
New York Inst of Technology (NY)
Ohio U (OH)
Pennsylvania Coll of Technology (PA)
U of Cincinnati (OH)
U of the District of Columbia (DC)
Utah Valley State Coll (UT)
Wentworth Inst of Technology (MA)

Environmental/ Environmental Health Engineering
Ohio U (OH)

Environmental Health
The U of Akron (OH)

Environmental Science
U of Wisconsin–Green Bay (WI)

Environmental Studies
Central Christian Coll of Kansas (KS)
Defiance Coll (OH)
Dickinson State U (ND)
Macon State Coll (GA)
Mountain State U (WV)
Paul Smith's Coll of Arts and Sciences (NY)
Samford U (AL)
Southern Vermont Coll (VT)
State U of New York Coll of Agriculture and Technology at Cobleskill (NY)
Sterling Coll (VT)
U of Cincinnati (OH)
U of Dubuque (IA)
The U of Findlay (OH)
U of Ottawa (ON, Canada)
U of Wisconsin–Green Bay (WI)

Equestrian Studies
Centenary Coll (NJ)
Johnson & Wales U (RI)
Midway Coll (KY)
National American U, Rapid City (SD)
Ohio U (OH)
Post U (CT)
Saint Mary-of-the-Woods Coll (IN)
State U of New York Coll of Agriculture and Technology at Cobleskill (NY)
The U of Findlay (OH)
U of Massachusetts Amherst (MA)
U of Minnesota, Crookston (MN)
The U of Montana–Western (MT)
U of New Hampshire (NH)

U of the District of Columbia (DC)
U of Wisconsin–Green Bay (WI)
Utah Valley State Coll (UT)
Xavier U (OH)

European Studies
Sacred Heart U (CT)

Executive Assistant/ Executive Secretary
Baker Coll of Allen Park (MI)
Baker Coll of Flint (MI)
Central Pennsylvania Coll (PA)
Kentucky State U (KY)
Montana Tech of The U of Montana (MT)
Murray State U (KY)
Robert Morris Coll (IL)
Thompson Rivers U (BC, Canada)
The U of Akron (OH)
The U of Montana–Missoula (MT)
Utah Valley State Coll (UT)
Western Kentucky U (KY)

Family and Community Services
Baker Coll of Flint (MI)
Central Christian Coll of Kansas (KS)
State U of New York Coll of Agriculture and Technology at Cobleskill (NY)

Family and Consumer Economics Related
Dalton State Coll (GA)
Fairmont State U (WV)

Family and Consumer Sciences/Human Sciences
Clayton State U (GA)
Mount Vernon Nazarene U (OH)

Family and Consumer Sciences/Human Sciences Related
Morehead State U (KY)

Farm and Ranch Management
Idaho State U (ID)
Johnson & Wales U (RI)
Oklahoma Panhandle State U (OK)

Fashion/Apparel Design
Academy of Art U (CA)
The Art Inst of Dallas (TX)
The Art Inst of Portland (OR)
The Art Inst of Seattle (WA)
Fashion Inst of Technology (NY)
Indiana U Bloomington (IN)
International Academy of Design & Technology (FL)
International Academy of Design & Technology (IL)
Miami International U of Art & Design (FL)
Parsons The New School for Design (NY)
U of the Incarnate Word (TX)

Fashion Merchandising
Academy of Art U (CA)
The Art Inst of Seattle (WA)
Clayton State U (GA)
Fairmont State U (WV)
Fashion Inst of Technology (NY)
International Academy of Design & Technology (IL)
Johnson & Wales U (CO)
Johnson & Wales U (FL)
Johnson & Wales U (NC)
Johnson & Wales U (RI)
Laboratory Inst of Merchandising (NY)
Lynn U (FL)
Miami International U of Art & Design (FL)
Newbury Coll (MA)
Northwood U (MI)
Northwood U, Texas Campus (TX)
Parsons The New School for Design (NY)
Southern New Hampshire U (NH)
The U of Akron (OH)
U of Bridgeport (CT)
U of the District of Columbia (DC)
U of the Incarnate Word (TX)
Weber State U (UT)

West Virginia State U (WV)

Fashion Modeling
Fashion Inst of Technology (NY)

Fiber, Textile and Weaving Arts
Academy of Art U (CA)

Film/Cinema Studies
Academy of Art U (CA)
Indiana U South Bend (IN)

Film/Video and Photographic Arts Related
New England School of Communications (ME)

Finance
Central Christian Coll of Kansas (KS)
Central Pennsylvania Coll (PA)
Clayton State U (GA)
Davenport U, Dearborn (MI)
Fairmont State U (WV)
Hawai'i Pacific U (HI)
Indiana U South Bend (IN)
Newbury Coll (MA)
Sacred Heart U (CT)
Saint Joseph's U (PA)
U of Cincinnati (OH)
Walsh U (OH)
Webber International U (FL)
West Virginia State U (WV)
Youngstown State U (OH)

Financial Planning and Services
The U of Maine at Augusta (ME)

Fine Arts Related
Saint Francis U (PA)
York Coll of Pennsylvania (PA)

Fine/Studio Arts
Academy of Art U (CA)
Corcoran Coll of Art and Design (DC)
Fashion Inst of Technology (NY)
Manchester Coll (IN)
Pace U (NY)
Pine Manor Coll (MA)
Pratt Inst (NY)
Rochester Inst of Technology (NY)
Sage Coll of Albany (NY)
St. Gregory's U (OK)
Thomas More Coll (KY)
The U of Maine at Augusta (ME)
U of New Hampshire at Manchester (NH)

Fire Protection and Safety Technology
Eastern Kentucky U (KY)
Montana State U–Billings (MT)
The U of Akron (OH)
U of Nebraska–Lincoln (NE)
U of New Haven (CT)

Fire Science
Idaho State U (ID)
Lake Superior State U (MI)
Lamar U (TX)
Lewis-Clark State Coll (ID)
Madonna U (MI)
Mountain State U (WV)
U of Alaska Fairbanks (AK)
U of Cincinnati (OH)
U of the District of Columbia (DC)
Utah Valley State Coll (UT)

Fish/Game Management
State U of New York Coll of Agriculture and Technology at Cobleskill (NY)

Fishing and Fisheries Sciences And Management
Sterling Coll (VT)

Floriculture/Floristry Management
Inter American U of Puerto Rico, Barranquitas Campus (PR)

Folklore
Université Laval (QC, Canada)

Food Preparation
Lexington Coll (IL)

Food Science
Lamar U (TX)
Macon State Coll (GA)

Food Service and Dining Room Management
Johnson & Wales U (FL)
Johnson & Wales U (NC)
Lexington Coll (IL)

Food Services Technology
Purdue U Calumet (IN)
State U of New York Coll of Agriculture and Technology at Cobleskill (NY)
U of the District of Columbia (DC)
Washburn U (KS)

Foodservice Systems Administration
Murray State U (KY)
U of New Haven (CT)

Foods, Nutrition, and Wellness
Eastern Kentucky U (KY)
Madonna U (MI)
Southern Adventist U (TN)
U of Maine at Presque Isle (ME)
U of New Hampshire (NH)
U of Ottawa (ON, Canada)

Foreign Languages and Literatures
Dalton State Coll (GA)

Foreign Languages Related
U of Alaska Fairbanks (AK)

Forensic Science and Technology
Arkansas State U (AR)
U of Arkansas at Fort Smith (AR)

Forest Engineering
Columbus State U (GA)

Forest/Forest Resources Management
Sterling Coll (VT)

Forest Products Technology
Pittsburg State U (KS)

Forest Resources Production and Management
Sterling Coll (VT)

Forestry
Clayton State U (GA)
Columbus State U (GA)
Dalton State Coll (GA)
Paul Smith's Coll of Arts and Sciences (NY)
Sterling Coll (VT)

Forestry Related
Sterling Coll (VT)

Forestry Technology
Georgia Southwestern State U (GA)
Glenville State Coll (WV)
Michigan Technological U (MI)
Paul Smith's Coll of Arts and Sciences (NY)
Pennsylvania Coll of Technology (PA)
U of New Hampshire (NH)

Forest Sciences and Biology
Sterling Coll (VT)

French
Chestnut Hill Coll (PA)
Clayton State U (GA)
Idaho State U (ID)
Indiana U–Purdue University Fort Wayne (IN)
Université Laval (QC, Canada)
U of Wisconsin–Green Bay (WI)
Xavier U (OH)

Funeral Service and Mortuary Science
Lynn U (FL)
Point Park U (PA)

Furniture Design and Manufacturing
Rochester Inst of Technology (NY)

General Studies
Alderson-Broaddus Coll (WV)
American Public U System (WV)
Anderson U (IN)
Arkansas State U (AR)
Arkansas Tech U (AR)
Averett U (VA)
Avila U (MO)
Barclay Coll (KS)
Brewton-Parker Coll (GA)
Calumet Coll of Saint Joseph (IN)
Castleton State Coll (VT)
Central Baptist Coll (AR)
Chaminade U of Honolulu (HI)
City U (WA)
Clearwater Christian Coll (FL)
Coll of Saint Mary (NE)
Columbia Union Coll (MD)
Concordia U (MI)
Concordia U at Austin (TX)
Concordia U, St. Paul (MN)
Crown Coll (MN)
Dakota State U (SD)
Dalton State Coll (GA)
Eastern Connecticut State U (CT)
Eastern Mennonite U (VA)
Eastern New Mexico U (NM)
Finlandia U (MI)
Franciscan U of Steubenville (OH)
Grantham U (MO)
Hope International U (CA)
Idaho State U (ID)
Indiana U Bloomington (IN)
Indiana U East (IN)
Indiana U Kokomo (IN)
Indiana U Northwest (IN)
Indiana U of Pennsylvania (PA)
Indiana U–Purdue University Fort Wayne (IN)
Indiana U–Purdue University Indianapolis (IN)
Indiana U South Bend (IN)
Indiana U Southeast (IN)
Johnson State Coll (VT)
Lawrence Technological U (MI)
Lebanon Valley Coll (PA)
Liberty U (VA)
Macon State Coll (GA)
Monmouth U (NJ)
Montana State U–Billings (MT)
Morehead State U (KY)
Mount Aloysius Coll (PA)
Mount Marty Coll (SD)
Mount Vernon Nazarene U (OH)
New Mexico Inst of Mining and Technology (NM)
New York U (NY)
Nicholls State U (LA)
Northern Michigan U (MI)
Northwestern State U of Louisiana (LA)
Northwest U (WA)
Nyack Coll (NY)
Oak Hills Christian Coll (MN)
Oakland City U (IN)
Ohio Dominican U (OH)
Oklahoma Panhandle State U (OK)
Palm Beach Atlantic U (FL)
Pennsylvania Coll of Technology (PA)
Presentation Coll (SD)
Rider U (NJ)
Rochester Inst of Technology (NY)
Shawnee State U (OH)
Silver Lake Coll (WI)
Simpson U (CA)

South Dakota School of
    Mines and Technology
    (SD)
Southeastern Louisiana U
    (LA)
Southern Adventist U (TN)
Southwest Baptist U (MO)
Taylor U Fort Wayne (IN)
Temple U (PA)
Toccoa Falls Coll (GA)
Trevecca Nazarene U (TN)
U of Alaska Southeast (AK)
U of Arkansas at Fort Smith
    (AR)
U of Central Arkansas (AR)
U of Hartford (CT)
U of Louisiana at Monroe
    (LA)
U of Mobile (AL)
U of New Hampshire (NH)
U of New Haven (CT)
U of North Florida (FL)
U of Phoenix–Hawaii
    Campus (HI)
U of Phoenix–Louisiana
    Campus (LA)
U of Phoenix–Phoenix
    Campus (AZ)
U of Rio Grande (OH)
The U of South Dakota (SD)
U of Wisconsin–Superior
    (WI)
Utah State U (UT)
Utah Valley State Coll (UT)
Virginia Intermont Coll (VA)
Warner Southern Coll (FL)
Western Kentucky U (KY)
Wilmington Coll (DE)

Geography
Dalton State Coll (GA)
Kwantlen U Coll (BC,
    Canada)
Université Laval (QC,
    Canada)
The U of Tampa (FL)
Wright State U (OH)

**Geological and Earth
Sciences/Geosciences
Related**
Kwantlen U Coll (BC,
    Canada)

Geology/Earth Science
Clayton State U (GA)
Dalton State Coll (GA)
Idaho State U (ID)
Indiana U East (IN)
Mesa State Coll (CO)
U of Wisconsin–Green Bay
    (WI)
Utah Valley State Coll (UT)

Geophysics and Seismology
U of Ottawa (ON, Canada)

German
Idaho State U (ID)
Indiana U–Purdue University
    Fort Wayne (IN)
Xavier U (OH)

Germanic Languages
U of Wisconsin–Green Bay
    (WI)

Gerontology
Madonna U (MI)
Manchester Coll (IN)
Millersville U of Pennsylvania
    (PA)
Ohio Dominican U (OH)
Pontifical Catholic U of
    Puerto Rico (PR)
Thomas More Coll (KY)
Washburn U (KS)
West Virginia State U (WV)

**Graphic and Printing
Equipment Operation/
Production**
Ball State U (IN)
Fairmont State U (WV)
Georgia Southwestern State
    U (GA)
Idaho State U (ID)
Lewis-Clark State Coll (ID)
Pennsylvania Coll of
    Technology (PA)
U of the District of Columbia
    (DC)

Graphic Communications
Academy of Art U (CA)
Indiana Tech (IN)
New England School of
    Communications (ME)
Robert Morris Coll (IL)

**Graphic Communications
Related**
The Art Insts International
    Minnesota (MN)

Graphic Design
Academy of Art U (CA)
Art Academy of Cincinnati
    (OH)
The Art Inst of California–
    Inland Empire (CA)
The Art Inst of California–Los
    Angeles (CA)
The Art Inst of California–
    Orange County (CA)
The Art Inst of California–
    San Diego (CA)
The Art Inst of Dallas (TX)
The Art Inst of Houston (TX)
The Art Inst of Phoenix (AZ)
The Art Inst of Portland (OR)
The Art Inst of Seattle (WA)
The Art Inst of Tampa (FL)
The Art Insts International
    Minnesota (MN)
Bryant and Stratton Coll,
    Wauwatosa Campus (WI)
Champlain Coll (VT)
Coll of Mount St. Joseph
    (OH)
Corcoran Coll of Art and
    Design (DC)
New World School of the Arts
    (FL)
Pratt Inst (NY)
Rochester Inst of Technology
    (NY)
Sage Coll of Albany (NY)
Thompson Rivers U (BC,
    Canada)
Union Coll (NE)
U of Arkansas at Fort Smith
    (AR)
Westwood Coll–Atlanta
    Northlake (GA)

Graphic/Printing Equipment
Eastern Kentucky U (KY)

Greenhouse Management
Sterling Coll (VT)

**Hazardous Materials
Information Systems
Technology**
Ohio U (OH)

**Hazardous Materials
Management and Waste
Technology**
Ohio U (OH)

**Health and Medical
Administrative Services
Related**
Kent State U (OH)
The U of Akron (OH)

**Health and Physical
Education**
Bethel Coll (IN)
Central Christian Coll of
    Kansas (KS)
Mount Vernon Nazarene U
    (OH)
Robert Morris Coll (IL)
Utah Valley State Coll (UT)

**Health and Physical
Education Related**
Pennsylvania Coll of
    Technology (PA)
Utah Valley State Coll (UT)

**Health/Health Care
Administration**
Baker Coll of Auburn Hills
    (MI)
Baker Coll of Flint (MI)
Baker Coll of Muskegon (MI)
Cabarrus Coll of Health
    Sciences (NC)
Chestnut Hill Coll (PA)
Madonna U (MI)
New York U (NY)
Point Park U (PA)
Saint Joseph's U (PA)
The U of Scranton (PA)

**Health Information/Medical
Records Administration**
Baker Coll of Auburn Hills
    (MI)
Baker Coll of Cadillac (MI)
Baker Coll of Clinton
    Township (MI)
Baker Coll of Flint (MI)
Baker Coll of Jackson (MI)
Baker Coll of Port Huron (MI)
Boise State U (ID)
Charles R. Drew U of
    Medicine and Science (CA)
Clayton State U (GA)
Coll of Saint Mary (NE)
Dalton State Coll (GA)
Eastern Kentucky U (KY)
Fairmont State U (WV)
Faulkner U (AL)
Ferris State U (MI)
Gwynedd-Mercy Coll (PA)
Indiana U Northwest (IN)
Inter American U of Puerto
    Rico, San Germán
    Campus (PR)
Montana State U–Billings
    (MT)
Northern Michigan U (MI)
Park U (MO)
Pennsylvania Coll of
    Technology (PA)
Universidad Adventista de
    las Antillas (PR)

**Health Information/Medical
Records Technology**
Baker Coll of Flint (MI)
Baker Coll of Jackson (MI)
Charles R. Drew U of
    Medicine and Science (CA)
Coll of St. Catherine (MN)
Dakota State U (SD)
Davenport U, Dearborn (MI)
DeVry U, Fremont (CA)
DeVry U, Long Beach (CA)
DeVry U, Pomona (CA)
DeVry U, West Hills (CA)
DeVry U, Westminster (CO)
DeVry U, Miramar (FL)
DeVry U, Orlando (FL)
DeVry U, Alpharetta (GA)
DeVry U, Decatur (GA)
DeVry U, Chicago (IL)
DeVry U (NJ)
DeVry U, Columbus (OH)
DeVry U, Fort Washington
    (PA)
DeVry U, Houston (TX)
DeVry U, Irving (TX)
Eastern Kentucky U (KY)
Gwynedd-Mercy Coll (PA)
Idaho State U (ID)
Macon State Coll (GA)
Missouri Western State U
    (MO)
Molloy Coll (NY)
New York U (NY)
Robert Morris Coll (IL)
Washburn U (KS)
Weber State U (UT)
Western Kentucky U (KY)

**Health/Medical Preparatory
Programs Related**
Emmanuel Coll (GA)
Union Coll (NE)

Health Professions Related
East Tennessee State U (TN)
Lock Haven U of
    Pennsylvania (PA)
U of Alaska Southeast (AK)

Health Science
Covenant Coll (GA)
Macon State Coll (GA)
National U (CA)
Newman U (KS)
Northwest U (WA)
South U (AL)
Union Coll (NE)
U of Hartford (CT)

**Health Services/Allied
Health/Health Sciences**
Immaculata U (PA)
Lindsey Wilson Coll (KY)

Health Teacher Education
Central Christian Coll of
    Kansas (KS)
Clayton State U (GA)

**Heating, Air Conditioning
and Refrigeration
Technology**
Oakland City U (IN)
Pennsylvania Coll of
    Technology (PA)

**Heating, Air Conditioning,
Ventilation and Refrigeration
Maintenance Technology**
Boise State U (ID)
Ferris State U (MI)
Lamar U (TX)
Lewis-Clark State Coll (ID)
Montana State U–Billings
    (MT)
Northern Michigan U (MI)
Oakland City U (IN)
U of Cincinnati (OH)
Utah Valley State Coll (UT)

**Heavy Equipment
Maintenance Technology**
Ferris State U (MI)
Georgia Southwestern State
    U (GA)
Mesa State Coll (CO)
Pennsylvania Coll of
    Technology (PA)
The U of Montana–Missoula
    (MT)

**Heavy/Industrial Equipment
Maintenance Technologies
Related**
Pennsylvania Coll of
    Technology (PA)

**Histologic Technology/
Histotechnologist**
Argosy U/Twin Cities (MN)
Tarleton State U (TX)

History
Central Christian Coll of
    Kansas (KS)
Dalton State Coll (GA)
Felician Coll (NJ)
Fresno Pacific U (CA)
Idaho State U (ID)
Indiana U East (IN)
Indiana U–Purdue University
    Fort Wayne (IN)
Kwantlen U Coll (BC,
    Canada)
Lindsey Wilson Coll (KY)
Macon State Coll (GA)
Millersville U of Pennsylvania
    (PA)
Pine Manor Coll (MA)
Sacred Heart U (CT)
State U of New York Empire
    State Coll (NY)
Thomas More Coll (KY)
U of Rio Grande (OH)
The U of Tampa (FL)
U of the District of Columbia
    (DC)
U of Wisconsin–Green Bay
    (WI)
Villa Julie Coll (MD)
Wright State U (OH)
Xavier U (OH)

History Teacher Education
Central Christian Coll of
    Kansas (KS)

Home Furnishings
Eastern Kentucky U (KY)

**Home Furnishings and
Equipment Installation**
Eastern Kentucky U (KY)

Horticultural Science
Andrews U (MI)
Boise State U (ID)
Eastern Kentucky U (KY)
State U of New York Coll of
    Agriculture and Technology
    at Cobleskill (NY)
U of Connecticut (CT)
U of Minnesota, Crookston
    (MN)
U of New Hampshire (NH)

Hospitality Administration
Baker Coll of Flint (MI)
Baker Coll of Owosso (MI)
Bob Jones U (SC)
Champlain Coll (VT)
Davis & Elkins Coll (WV)
Indiana U–Purdue University
    Fort Wayne (IN)

Johnson & Wales U (FL)
Kendall Coll (IL)
Lewis-Clark State Coll (ID)
Lexington Coll (IL)
Monroe Coll, Bronx (NY)
Monroe Coll, New Rochelle
    (NY)
Mountain State U (WV)
Paul Smith's Coll of Arts and
    Sciences (NY)
The U of Akron (OH)
U of Minnesota, Crookston
    (MN)
U of the District of Columbia
    (DC)
Utah Valley State Coll (UT)
Youngstown State U (OH)

**Hospitality Administration
Related**
Champlain Coll (VT)
Lexington Coll (IL)
Mountain State U (WV)
The Pennsylvania State U
    Berks Campus of the
    Berks–Lehigh Valley Coll
    (PA)
The Pennsylvania State U
    University Park Campus
    (PA)
Purdue U (IN)

**Hospitality and Recreation
Marketing**
Champlain Coll (VT)
Johnson & Wales U (RI)
Thompson Rivers U (BC,
    Canada)
The U of Akron (OH)

**Hotel and Restaurant
Management**
Georgia Southwestern State
    U (GA)
Johnson & Wales U (NC)

Hotel/Motel Administration
Baker Coll of Muskegon (MI)
Baker Coll of Owosso (MI)
Baker Coll of Port Huron (MI)
Bluefield State Coll (WV)
Central Pennsylvania Coll
    (PA)
Champlain Coll (VT)
Indiana U–Purdue University
    Indianapolis (IN)
Johnson & Wales U (FL)
Johnson & Wales U (RI)
Kendall Coll (IL)
Lexington Coll (IL)
Mercyhurst Coll (PA)
Mesa State Coll (CO)
Newbury Coll (MA)
Northwood U (MI)
Northwood U, Florida
    Campus (FL)
Northwood U, Texas Campus
    (TX)
Paul Smith's Coll of Arts and
    Sciences (NY)
Purdue U Calumet (IN)
Rochester Inst of Technology
    (NY)
State U of New York Coll of
    Agriculture and Technology
    at Cobleskill (NY)
Stratford U (VA)
Sullivan U (KY)
Thompson Rivers U (BC,
    Canada)
The U of Akron (OH)
U of Minnesota, Crookston
    (MN)
U of the Virgin Islands (VI)
Webber International U (FL)
West Virginia State U (WV)

**Human Development and
Family Studies**
Mitchell Coll (CT)
The Pennsylvania State U
    Altoona Coll (PA)
The Pennsylvania State U
    University Park Campus
    (PA)
State U of New York Empire
    State Coll (NY)

**Human Development and
Family Studies Related**
Utah State U (UT)

Human Ecology
Sterling Coll (VT)

Humanities
Faulkner U (AL)
Felician Coll (NJ)
John Cabot U(Italy)
Macon State Coll (GA)
Mesa State Coll (CO)
Michigan Technological U
    (MI)
Newbury Coll (MA)
Ohio U (OH)
Rider U (NJ)
Sage Coll of Albany (NY)
St. Gregory's U (OK)
Shawnee State U (OH)
State U of New York Empire
    State Coll (NY)
Taylor U Fort Wayne (IN)
U of Alaska Southeast (AK)
U of Cincinnati (OH)
The U of Findlay (OH)
U of Sioux Falls (SD)
U of Wisconsin–Green Bay
    (WI)
Utah Valley State Coll (UT)
Washburn U (KS)

**Human Resources
Development**
Georgia Southwestern State
    U (GA)

**Human Resources
Management**
Baker Coll of Owosso (MI)
Central Christian Coll of
    Kansas (KS)
Chestnut Hill Coll (PA)
King's Coll (PA)
Montana State U–Billings
    (MT)
Montana Tech of The U of
    Montana (MT)
The U of Findlay (OH)
The U of Montana–Western
    (MT)
U of Richmond (VA)
U of Saint Francis (IN)
Urbana U (OH)

**Human Resources
Management and Services
Related**
Bryant and Stratton Coll,
    Cleveland (OH)
Bryant and Stratton Coll,
    Wauwatosa Campus (WI)

Human Services
Baker Coll of Clinton
    Township (MI)
Baker Coll of Flint (MI)
Baker Coll of Muskegon (MI)
Beacon Coll (FL)
Cazenovia Coll (NY)
Champlain Coll (VT)
Chestnut Hill Coll (PA)
Hilbert Coll (NY)
Indiana U East (IN)
Indiana U–Purdue University
    Fort Wayne (IN)
Kendall Coll (IL)
Mercy Coll (NY)
Merrimack Coll (MA)
Metropolitan Coll of New
    York (NY)
Mitchell Coll (CT)
Mount Vernon Nazarene U
    (OH)
New York U (NY)
Northern Kentucky U (KY)
Ohio U (OH)
Southern Vermont Coll (VT)
State U of New York Empire
    State Coll (NY)
U of Cincinnati (OH)
U of Great Falls (MT)
The U of Maine at Augusta
    (ME)
U of Saint Francis (IN)
The U of Scranton (PA)
Walsh U (OH)
Washburn U (KS)

**Hydrology and Water
Resources Science**
Lake Superior State U (MI)
U of the District of Columbia
    (DC)

Illustration
Academy of Art U (CA)
Fashion Inst of Technology (NY)
Pratt Inst (NY)

Industrial Arts
Austin Peay State U (TN)
Dalton State Coll (GA)
Eastern Kentucky U (KY)
U of Cincinnati (OH)
The U of Montana–Missoula (MT)
Weber State U (UT)

Industrial Design
Academy of Art U (CA)
The Art Inst of Seattle (WA)
Ferris State U (MI)
Oakland City U (IN)
Rochester Inst of Technology (NY)
Wentworth Inst of Technology (MA)

Industrial Electronics Technology
Dalton State Coll (GA)
Lewis-Clark State Coll (ID)
Pennsylvania Coll of Technology (PA)
Thompson Rivers U (BC, Canada)

Industrial Mechanics and Maintenance Technology
Arkansas Tech U (AR)
Dalton State Coll (GA)
Pennsylvania Coll of Technology (PA)

Industrial Production Technologies Related
Ferris State U (MI)
Pennsylvania Coll of Technology (PA)
U of Nebraska–Lincoln (NE)

Industrial Radiologic Technology
Baker Coll of Owosso (MI)
Ball State U (IN)
Boise State U (ID)
Faulkner U (AL)
Ferris State U (MI)
The George Washington U (DC)
Inter American U of Puerto Rico, San Germán Campus (PR)
Lamar U (TX)
Mesa State Coll (CO)
Northern Kentucky U (KY)
U of Cincinnati (OH)
U of the District of Columbia (DC)
Widener U (PA)

Industrial Technology
Baker Coll of Muskegon (MI)
Ball State U (IN)
Cameron U (OK)
Central Missouri State U (MO)
Dalton State Coll (GA)
Eastern Kentucky U (KY)
Edinboro U of Pennsylvania (PA)
Excelsior Coll (NY)
Fairmont State U (WV)
Ferris State U (MI)
Indiana U–Purdue University Fort Wayne (IN)
Keene State Coll (NH)
Kent State U (OH)
Mesa State Coll (CO)
Millersville U of Pennsylvania (PA)
Morehead State U (KY)
Murray State U (KY)
Oklahoma Panhandle State U (OK)
Pennsylvania Coll of Technology (PA)
Purdue U Calumet (IN)
Purdue U North Central (IN)
Southeastern Louisiana U (LA)
Tri-State U (IN)
The U of Akron (OH)
U of Alaska Fairbanks (AK)
U of Cincinnati (OH)
U of Rio Grande (OH)

Washburn U (KS)
Weber State U (UT)
Wentworth Inst of Technology (MA)
Wright State U (OH)

Information Science/Studies
Albertus Magnus Coll (CT)
Alvernia Coll (PA)
Arkansas Tech U (AR)
Baker Coll of Cadillac (MI)
Baker Coll of Clinton Township (MI)
Baker Coll of Flint (MI)
Baker Coll of Jackson (MI)
Baker Coll of Muskegon (MI)
Baker Coll of Owosso (MI)
Baker Coll of Port Huron (MI)
Ball State U (IN)
Beacon Coll (FL)
Briarcliffe Coll (NY)
Calumet Coll of Saint Joseph (IN)
Campbellsville U (KY)
Central Pennsylvania Coll (PA)
Champlain Coll (VT)
Clayton State U (GA)
Coll of St. Joseph (VT)
Dakota State U (SD)
Dalton State Coll (GA)
DeVry U, Colorado Springs (CO)
DeVry U (NJ)
Fairmont State U (WV)
Farmingdale State U of New York (NY)
Faulkner U (AL)
Husson Coll (ME)
Immaculata U (PA)
Indiana Tech (IN)
Johnson State Coll (VT)
Jones Coll, Jacksonville (FL)
Limestone Coll (SC)
Macon State Coll (GA)
Mansfield U of Pennsylvania (PA)
Missouri Southern State U (MO)
Monroe Coll, Bronx (NY)
Monroe Coll, New Rochelle (NY)
Mountain State U (WV)
Mount Olive Coll (NC)
Murray State U (KY)
National American U, Rapid City (SD)
Newman U (KS)
Oakland City U (IN)
Oakwood Coll (AL)
Oklahoma Panhandle State U (OK)
Pacific Union Coll (CA)
The Pennsylvania State U Altoona Coll (PA)
The Pennsylvania State U Berks Campus of the Berks–Lehigh Valley Coll (PA)
Purdue U North Central (IN)
Rivier Coll (NH)
Sage Coll of Albany (NY)
Southern Utah U (UT)
South U (AL)
State U of New York Coll of Agriculture and Technology at Cobleskill (NY)
Trevecca Nazarene U (TN)
Tulane U (LA)
Union Coll (NE)
U of Cincinnati (OH)
U of Minnesota, Crookston (MN)
The U of Montana–Western (MT)
U of Pittsburgh at Bradford (PA)
The U of Scranton (PA)
The U of Tampa (FL)
U of Wisconsin–Green Bay (WI)
Villa Julie Coll (MD)
Weber State U (UT)

Information Technology
Bryant and Stratton Coll, Cleveland (OH)
Davenport U, Dearborn (MI)
Grantham U (MO)
Indiana Tech (IN)

International Academy of Design & Technology (IL)
Minnesota School of Business (MN)
Mountain State U (WV)
Pennsylvania Coll of Technology (PA)
Point Park U (PA)
Southern New Hampshire U (NH)
South U (GA)
South U (SC)
U of Massachusetts Lowell (MA)
Utah Valley State Coll (UT)

Institutional Food Workers
Fairmont State U (WV)
Kendall Coll (IL)
Lexington Coll (IL)
Pennsylvania Coll of Technology (PA)
State U of New York Coll of Agriculture and Technology at Cobleskill (NY)

Instrumentation Technology
Clayton State U (GA)
Excelsior Coll (NY)
Idaho State U (ID)
Pennsylvania Coll of Technology (PA)

Insurance
Mercyhurst Coll (PA)
Université Laval (QC, Canada)
U of Cincinnati (OH)

Intercultural/Multicultural and Diversity Studies
Immaculata U (PA)

Interdisciplinary Studies
Bluefield State Coll (WV)
Coll of Mount Saint Vincent (NY)
Grantham U (MO)
Heritage U (WA)
Kansas State U (KS)
Lesley U (MA)
Mountain State U (WV)
Ohio Dominican U (OH)
State U of New York Empire State Coll (NY)
Suffolk U (MA)
The U of Akron (OH)
U of Sioux Falls (SD)
U of Wisconsin–Green Bay (WI)
Villa Julie Coll (MD)

Interior Architecture
U of New Haven (CT)

Interior Design
Academy of Art U (CA)
The American U in DubaiUnited Arab Emirates)
The Art Center Design Coll (AZ)
The Art Inst of Dallas (TX)
The Art Inst of Las Vegas (NV)
The Art Inst of Portland (OR)
The Art Inst of Seattle (WA)
The Art Insts International Minnesota (MN)
Baker Coll of Allen Park (MI)
Baker Coll of Auburn Hills (MI)
Baker Coll of Clinton Township (MI)
Baker Coll of Flint (MI)
Baker Coll of Muskegon (MI)
Baker Coll of Owosso (MI)
Baker Coll of Port Huron (MI)
Chaminade U of Honolulu (HI)
Coll of Mount St. Joseph (OH)
Eastern Kentucky U (KY)
Fairmont State U (WV)
Fashion Inst of Technology (NY)
Harrington Coll of Design (IL)
The Illinois Inst of Art–Chicago (IL)
Indiana U–Purdue University Fort Wayne (IN)
International Academy of Design & Technology (FL)

International Academy of Design & Technology (IL)
Miami International U of Art & Design (FL)
Newbury Coll (MA)
New York School of Interior Design (NY)
Parsons The New School for Design (NY)
Robert Morris Coll (IL)
Rochester Inst of Technology (NY)
Sage Coll of Albany (NY)
Southern Utah U (UT)
U of the Incarnate Word (TX)
Watkins Coll of Art and Design (TN)
Weber State U (UT)
Wentworth Inst of Technology (MA)

Intermedia/Multimedia
The Art Inst of Colorado (CO)
The Art Inst of Portland (OR)
The Art Inst of Seattle (WA)
The Art Inst of Washington (VA)
The Art Insts International Minnesota (MN)
Champlain Coll (VT)
International Academy of Design & Technology (FL)
International Academy of Design & Technology (IL)
Minnesota School of Business (MN)
New England School of Communications (ME)
New World School of the Arts (FL)
Robert Morris Coll (IL)

International Business/Trade/Commerce
The American U of Romeltaly)
Bob Jones U (SC)
Champlain Coll (VT)
Northwood U (MI)
Northwood U, Florida Campus (FL)
Potomac Coll (DC)
Schiller International U (FL)
Schiller International UFrance)
Schiller International UGermany)
Schiller International USpain)
Schiller International UUnited Kingdom)
Southern New Hampshire U (NH)
State U of New York Coll of Agriculture and Technology at Cobleskill (NY)
Webber International U (FL)

International Relations and Affairs
John Cabot Ultaly)
Thomas More Coll (KY)

Italian Studies
John Cabot Ultaly)

Jazz/Jazz Studies
Five Towns Coll (NY)
Indiana U South Bend (IN)
Southern U and A&M Coll (LA)
Université Laval (QC, Canada)

Journalism
Ball State U (IN)
Bethel Coll (IN)
Clayton State U (GA)
Dalton State Coll (GA)
Evangel U (MO)
Indiana U Southeast (IN)
John Brown U (AR)
Macon State Coll (GA)
Madonna U (MI)
Manchester Coll (IN)
Villa Julie Coll (MD)

Kindergarten/Preschool Education
Baker Coll of Clinton Township (MI)
Baker Coll of Muskegon (MI)
Baker Coll of Owosso (MI)
Bethany U (CA)

California U of Pennsylvania (PA)
Central Christian Coll of Kansas (KS)
Champlain Coll (VT)
Clayton State U (GA)
Coll of Mount St. Joseph (OH)
Crown Coll (MN)
Edinboro U of Pennsylvania (PA)
Heritage U (WA)
Hope International U (CA)
Indiana U–Purdue University Indianapolis (IN)
Indiana U South Bend (IN)
Keene State Coll (NH)
Kendall Coll (IL)
Lynn U (FL)
Manchester Coll (IN)
Marygrove Coll (MI)
Mesa State Coll (CO)
Midland Lutheran Coll (NE)
Mitchell Coll (CT)
Mount Aloysius Coll (PA)
Mount St. Mary's Coll (CA)
Nova Southeastern U (FL)
Pacific Union Coll (CA)
Purdue U Calumet (IN)
Rivier Coll (NH)
State U of New York Coll of Agriculture and Technology at Cobleskill (NY)
Taylor U (IN)
Tennessee State U (TN)
U of Alaska Fairbanks (AK)
U of Great Falls (MT)
The U of Montana–Western (MT)
U of Rio Grande (OH)
U of Sioux Falls (SD)
Valley Forge Christian Coll (PA)
Villa Julie Coll (MD)
Western Kentucky U (KY)
Wilmington Coll (DE)

Kinesiology and Exercise Science
Manchester Coll (IN)
Thomas More Coll (KY)

Labor and Industrial Relations
Indiana U Bloomington (IN)
Indiana U Kokomo (IN)
Indiana U Northwest (IN)
Indiana U–Purdue University Indianapolis (IN)
Indiana U South Bend (IN)
Indiana U Southeast (IN)
State U of New York Empire State Coll (NY)
Université Laval (QC, Canada)
The U of Akron (OH)
Youngstown State U (OH)

Labor Studies
Indiana U–Purdue University Fort Wayne (IN)

Landscape Architecture
Eastern Kentucky U (KY)
State U of New York Coll of Agriculture and Technology at Cobleskill (NY)
U of New Hampshire (NH)

Landscaping and Groundskeeping
Farmingdale State U of New York (NY)
North Carolina State U (NC)
State U of New York Coll of Agriculture and Technology at Cobleskill (NY)
U of Massachusetts Amherst (MA)
U of New Hampshire (NH)
Vermont Tech Coll (VT)

Laser and Optical Technology
Excelsior Coll (NY)
Idaho State U (ID)
Indiana U Bloomington (IN)
Pennsylvania Coll of Technology (PA)

Latin
Idaho State U (ID)

Legal Administrative Assistant
Bryant and Stratton Coll, Cleveland (OH)

Legal Administrative Assistant/Secretary
Baker Coll of Auburn Hills (MI)
Baker Coll of Clinton Township (MI)
Baker Coll of Flint (MI)
Baker Coll of Jackson (MI)
Baker Coll of Muskegon (MI)
Baker Coll of Owosso (MI)
Baker Coll of Port Huron (MI)
Ball State U (IN)
Central Pennsylvania Coll (PA)
Clarion U of Pennsylvania (PA)
Clayton State U (GA)
Dordt Coll (IA)
Ferris State U (MI)
Lamar U (TX)
Lewis-Clark State Coll (ID)
Mesa State Coll (CO)
Midland Lutheran Coll (NE)
Minnesota School of Business (MN)
Montana State U–Billings (MT)
Montana Tech of The U of Montana (MT)
Pacific Union Coll (CA)
Peirce Coll (PA)
Robert Morris Coll (IL)
Shawnee State U (OH)
Sullivan U (KY)
The U of Akron (OH)
U of Cincinnati (OH)
The U of Montana–Missoula (MT)
U of Richmond (VA)
U of Rio Grande (OH)
U of the District of Columbia (DC)
Washburn U (KS)
Wright State U (OH)
Youngstown State U (OH)

Legal Assistant/Paralegal
Anna Maria Coll (MA)
Ball State U (IN)
Bluefield State Coll (WV)
Boise State U (ID)
Briarcliffe Coll (NY)
Central Pennsylvania Coll (PA)
Champlain Coll (VT)
Clayton State U (GA)
Coll of Mount St. Joseph (OH)
Coll of Saint Mary (NE)
Eastern Kentucky U (KY)
Faulkner U (AL)
Ferris State U (MI)
Florida Metropolitan U–Brandon Campus (FL)
Gannon U (PA)
Hilbert Coll (NY)
Husson Coll (ME)
Indiana U South Bend (IN)
Johnson & Wales U (RI)
Jones Coll, Jacksonville (FL)
Lake Superior State U (MI)
Lewis-Clark State Coll (ID)
Madonna U (MI)
Merrimack Coll (MA)
Missouri Western State U (MO)
Mountain State U (WV)
Mount Aloysius Coll (PA)
National American U, Rapid City (SD)
Newbury Coll (MA)
Nicholls State U (LA)
Peirce Coll (PA)
Pennsylvania Coll of Technology (PA)
Post U (CT)
Robert Morris Coll (IL)
St. John's U (NY)
Saint Mary-of-the-Woods Coll (IN)
Shawnee State U (OH)
South U (AL)
South U (GA)
South U (SC)
Suffolk U (MA)
Sullivan U (KY)

Tulane U (LA)
The U of Akron (OH)
U of Alaska Fairbanks (AK)
U of Arkansas at Fort Smith (AR)
U of Cincinnati (OH)
U of Great Falls (MT)
U of Louisville (KY)
The U of Montana–Missoula (MT)
Utah Valley State Coll (UT)
Villa Julie Coll (MD)
Western Kentucky U (KY)
Widener U (PA)
William Woods U (MO)

Legal Professions and Studies Related
Peirce Coll (PA)

Legal Studies
Central Christian Coll of Kansas (KS)
Clayton State U (GA)
Hilbert Coll (NY)
Lake Superior State U (MI)
Mountain State U (WV)
Ohio Dominican U (OH)
Sage Coll of Albany (NY)
U of Alaska Southeast (AK)
U of Hartford (CT)
The U of Montana–Missoula (MT)
U of New Haven (CT)

Liberal Arts and Sciences And Humanities Related
Beacon Coll (FL)
Pennsylvania Coll of Technology (PA)
The U of Akron (OH)

Liberal Arts and Sciences/ Liberal Studies
Adams State Coll (CO)
Adelphi U (NY)
Alabama State U (AL)
Albertus Magnus Coll (CT)
Alvernia Coll (PA)
Alverno Coll (WI)
American International Coll (MA)
The American U of Rome Italy)
Anderson U (SC)
Andrews U (MI)
Aquinas Coll (TN)
Armstrong Atlantic State U (GA)
Ashland U (OH)
Augusta State U (GA)
Austin Peay State U (TN)
Averett U (VA)
Ball State U (IN)
Beacon Coll (FL)
Bemidji State U (MN)
Bethany Lutheran Coll (MN)
Bethany U (CA)
Bethel Coll (IN)
Bethel U (MN)
Bluefield State Coll (WV)
Briar Cliff U (IA)
Bryan Coll (TN)
Bryn Athyn Coll of the New Church (PA)
Butler U (IN)
Calumet Coll of Saint Joseph (IN)
Campbell U (NC)
Cazenovia Coll (NY)
Centenary Coll (NJ)
Champlain Coll (VT)
Charleston Southern U (SC)
Charter Oak State Coll (CT)
Christendom Coll (VA)
Clarion U of Pennsylvania (PA)
Clarke Coll (IA)
Colby-Sawyer Coll (NH)
Coll of St. Catherine (MN)
Coll of St. Joseph (VT)
The Coll of Saint Thomas More (TX)
Coll of Staten Island of the City U of New York (NY)
Colorado Christian U (CO)
Columbia Coll (MO)
Columbus State U (GA)
Concordia Coll (NY)
Concordia U (OR)
Concordia U at Austin (TX)
Crossroads Coll (MN)

Crown Coll (MN)
Cumberland U (TN)
Dakota Wesleyan U (SD)
Dallas Baptist U (TX)
Dickinson State U (ND)
Dominican Coll (NY)
East Texas Baptist U (TX)
Edgewood Coll (WI)
Edinboro U of Pennsylvania (PA)
Emmanuel Coll (GA)
Emory U (GA)
Endicott Coll (MA)
Excelsior Coll (NY)
Fairleigh Dickinson U, Metropolitan Campus (NJ)
Fairmont State U (WV)
Farmingdale State U of New York (NY)
Faulkner U (AL)
Felician Coll (NJ)
Ferris State U (MI)
Five Towns Coll (NY)
Florida Atlantic U (FL)
Florida Coll (FL)
Florida State U (FL)
Franklin Coll Switzerland Switzerland)
Fresno Pacific U (CA)
Gannon U (PA)
Glenville State Coll (WV)
Grace Bible Coll (MI)
Grand View Coll (IA)
Gwynedd-Mercy Coll (PA)
Heritage U (WA)
Hilbert Coll (NY)
Houghton Coll (NY)
Indiana State U (IN)
John Brown U (AR)
Johnson State Coll (VT)
John Wesley Coll (NC)
Keene State Coll (NH)
Kent State U (OH)
Kentucky State U (KY)
Kuyper Coll (MI)
LaGrange Coll (GA)
Lake Superior State U (MI)
La Salle U (PA)
Lebanon Valley Coll (PA)
Lewis-Clark State Coll (ID)
Limestone Coll (SC)
Long Island U, Brooklyn Campus (NY)
Loras Coll (IA)
Lyndon State Coll (VT)
Macon State Coll (GA)
Marietta Coll (OH)
Marygrove Coll (MI)
Marymount U (VA)
Medaille Coll (NY)
Medgar Evers Coll of the City U of New York (NY)
Mercy Coll (NY)
Mercyhurst Coll (PA)
Merrimack Coll (MA)
Mesa State Coll (CO)
MidAmerica Nazarene U (KS)
Midwestern State U (TX)
Millersville U of Pennsylvania (PA)
Minnesota State U Mankato (MN)
Minnesota State U Moorhead (MN)
Mitchell Coll (CT)
Molloy Coll (NY)
Montana State U–Billings (MT)
Montana Tech of The U of Montana (MT)
Mountain State U (WV)
Mount Aloysius Coll (PA)
Mount Marty Coll (SD)
Mount Olive Coll (NC)
Mount St. Mary's Coll (CA)
Murray State U (KY)
National American U, Rapid City (SD)
Neumann Coll (PA)
New England Coll (NH)
Newman U (KS)
New York U (NY)
Niagara U (NY)
Nicholls State U (LA)
Northern Michigan U (MI)
Northern State U (SD)
Northwestern Coll (MN)
Nyack Coll (NY)
Oakland City U (IN)

The Ohio State U at Lima (OH)
The Ohio State U at Marion (OH)
The Ohio State U–Mansfield Campus (OH)
The Ohio State U–Newark Campus (OH)
Ohio U (OH)
Ohio U–Zanesville (OH)
Ohio Valley U (WV)
Pace U (NY)
Park U (MO)
Paul Smith's Coll of Arts and Sciences (NY)
Peace Coll (NC)
Pennsylvania Coll of Technology (PA)
The Pennsylvania State U Abington Coll (PA)
The Pennsylvania State U Altoona Coll (PA)
The Pennsylvania State U at Erie, The Behrend Coll (PA)
The Pennsylvania State U Berks Campus of the Berks–Lehigh Valley Coll (PA)
The Pennsylvania State U Harrisburg Campus (PA)
The Pennsylvania State U University Park Campus (PA)
Pine Manor Coll (MA)
Post U (CT)
Reinhardt Coll (GA)
Rider U (NJ)
Rivier Coll (NH)
Rochester Coll (MI)
Rocky Mountain Coll (MT)
Roger Williams U (RI)
Sacred Heart U (CT)
Sage Coll of Albany (NY)
St. Cloud State U (MN)
St. Francis Coll (NY)
St. Gregory's U (OK)
St. John's U (NY)
Saint Joseph's U (PA)
Saint Leo U (FL)
Saint Mary-of-the-Woods Coll (IN)
Salve Regina U (RI)
Schiller International U (FL)
Schiller International U France)
Schiller International U Germany)
Schiller International U Spain)
Schiller International U United Kingdom)
Schiller International U, American Coll of Switzerland Switzerland)
Simon's Rock Coll of Bard (MA)
Southern Connecticut State U (CT)
Southern New Hampshire U (NH)
Southern Polytechnic State U (GA)
Southern Vermont Coll (VT)
Spring Arbor U (MI)
State U of New York Coll of Agriculture and Technology at Cobleskill (NY)
Stephens Coll (MO)
Sterling Coll (VT)
Taylor U Fort Wayne (IN)
Thiel Coll (PA)
Thomas Coll (ME)
Thomas More Coll (KY)
Thomas U (GA)
Tri-State U (IN)
Troy U (AL)
The U of Akron (OH)
U of Alaska Fairbanks (AK)
U of Alaska Southeast (AK)
U of Arkansas at Fort Smith (AR)
U of Bridgeport (CT)
U of Central Florida (FL)
U of Cincinnati (OH)
U of Delaware (DE)
U of Hartford (CT)
U of Indianapolis (IN)
U of La Verne (CA)
The U of Maine at Augusta (ME)

U of Maine at Presque Isle (ME)
U of New Hampshire (NH)
U of New Hampshire at Manchester (NH)
U of Pittsburgh at Bradford (PA)
U of Saint Francis (IN)
U of Saint Mary (KS)
U of South Carolina Beaufort (SC)
U of South Florida (FL)
U of West Florida (FL)
U of Wisconsin–Eau Claire (WI)
U of Wisconsin–Oshkosh (WI)
U of Wisconsin–Platteville (WI)
U of Wisconsin–Stevens Point (WI)
U of Wisconsin–Whitewater (WI)
Urbana U (OH)
Valdosta State U (GA)
Villa Julie Coll (MD)
Villanova U (PA)
Virginia Intermont Coll (VA)
Walsh U (OH)
Washburn U (KS)
Waynesburg Coll (PA)
Weber State U (UT)
Western Connecticut State U (CT)
Western New England Coll (MA)
Western Oregon U (OR)
West Virginia State U (WV)
Wichita State U (KS)
Wilson Coll (PA)
Xavier U (OH)
York Coll (NE)
York Coll of Pennsylvania (PA)
Youngstown State U (OH)

Library Assistant
Ohio Dominican U (OH)
The U of Maine at Augusta (ME)

Library Science
Mountain State U (WV)
U of the District of Columbia (DC)

Lineworker
Utah Valley State Coll (UT)

Literature
John Cabot U Italy)
Manchester Coll (IN)
Sacred Heart U (CT)
Université Laval (QC, Canada)

Livestock Management
Sterling Coll (VT)

Logistics and Materials Management
Park U (MO)
The U of Akron (OH)

Machine Shop Technology
Dalton State Coll (GA)
Georgia Southwestern State U (GA)
Pennsylvania Coll of Technology (PA)

Machine Tool Technology
Boise State U (ID)
Ferris State U (MI)
Georgia Southwestern State U (GA)
Idaho State U (ID)
Lamar U (TX)
Mesa State Coll (CO)
Missouri Southern State U (MO)
Utah Valley State Coll (UT)
Vaughn Coll of Aeronautics and Technology (NY)
Weber State U (UT)

Management Information Systems
Arkansas State U (AR)
Cameron U (OK)
Colorado Christian U (CO)
Columbia Coll, Caguas (PR)
Davenport U, Dearborn (MI)

Georgia Southwestern State U (GA)
Globe Inst of Technology (NY)
Hilbert Coll (NY)
Husson Coll (ME)
Inter American U of Puerto Rico, Bayamón Campus (PR)
Johnson State Coll (VT)
Lake Superior State U (MI)
Lindsey Wilson Coll (KY)
Lock Haven U of Pennsylvania (PA)
Morehead State U (KY)
Northern Michigan U (MI)
Northwood U (MI)
Northwood U, Texas Campus (TX)
Peirce Coll (PA)
Potomac Coll (DC)
Robert Morris Coll (IL)
Saint Joseph's Coll (IN)
Saint Joseph's U (PA)
Shawnee State U (OH)
Taylor U (IN)
Thiel Coll (PA)
U of Management and Technology (VA)
Weber State U (UT)
Wilson Coll (PA)
Wright State U (OH)

Management Information Systems and Services Related
Coll of Mount St. Joseph (OH)
Davis & Elkins Coll (WV)
Purdue U (IN)
U of Southern Indiana (IN)

Management Science
Mountain State U (WV)

Manufacturing Technology
Excelsior Coll (NY)
Lawrence Technological U (MI)
Lewis-Clark State Coll (ID)
Missouri Western State U (MO)
Pennsylvania Coll of Technology (PA)
The Pennsylvania State U at Erie, The Behrend Coll (PA)
Thompson Rivers U (BC, Canada)
Utah Valley State Coll (UT)

Marine Biology and Biological Oceanography
Mitchell Coll (CT)

Marine Science/Merchant Marine Officer
State U of New York Maritime Coll (NY)
U of the District of Columbia (DC)

Marketing/Marketing Management
Baker Coll of Allen Park (MI)
Baker Coll of Auburn Hills (MI)
Baker Coll of Cadillac (MI)
Baker Coll of Clinton Township (MI)
Baker Coll of Flint (MI)
Baker Coll of Jackson (MI)
Baker Coll of Muskegon (MI)
Baker Coll of Owosso (MI)
Baker Coll of Port Huron (MI)
Ball State U (IN)
Bluefield State Coll (WV)
Boise State U (ID)
Central Christian Coll of Kansas (KS)
Central Pennsylvania Coll (PA)
Champlain Coll (VT)
Chestnut Hill Coll (PA)
Clayton State U (GA)
Dalton State Coll (GA)
Davenport U, Dearborn (MI)
Five Towns Coll (NY)
Florida Metropolitan U–Brandon Campus (FL)
Georgia Southwestern State U (GA)
Hawai'i Pacific U (HI)

Georgia Southwestern State U (GA)
Globe Inst of Technology (NY)
Hilbert Coll (NY)
Husson Coll (ME)
Idaho State U (ID)
Johnson & Wales U (CO)
Johnson & Wales U (FL)
Johnson & Wales U (RI)
Mountain State U (WV)
Newbury Coll (MA)
New England School of Communications (ME)
Peirce Coll (PA)
Post U (CT)
Purdue U North Central (IN)
Sage Coll of Albany (NY)
Saint Joseph's U (PA)
Southern New Hampshire U (NH)
Sullivan U (KY)
Tulane U (LA)
U of Bridgeport (CT)
U of Cincinnati (OH)
U of Management and Technology (VA)
U of Sioux Falls (SD)
U of the District of Columbia (DC)
Urbana U (OH)
Walsh U (OH)
Webber International U (FL)
Weber State U (UT)
West Virginia State U (WV)
Wright State U (UT)
Youngstown State U (OH)

Marketing Related
Fashion Inst of Technology (NY)

Masonry
Pennsylvania Coll of Technology (PA)

Massage Therapy
Minnesota School of Business (MN)

Mass Communication/Media
Central Pennsylvania Coll (PA)
Champlain Coll (VT)
Clayton State U (GA)
Cornerstone U (MI)
Evangel U (MO)
Five Towns Coll (NY)
Fresno Pacific U (CA)
Inter American U of Puerto Rico, Bayamón Campus (PR)
Macon State Coll (GA)
Madonna U (MI)
Newbury Coll (MA)
Pennsylvania Coll of Technology (PA)
Sacred Heart U (CT)
Sage Coll of Albany (NY)
U of Dubuque (IA)
U of Rio Grande (OH)
Villa Julie Coll (MD)
Wilson Coll (PA)

Mass Communications
John Cabot U Italy)

Materials Science
U of New Hampshire (NH)

Mathematics
Central Christian Coll of Kansas (KS)
Clayton State U (GA)
Creighton U (NE)
Dalton State Coll (GA)
Felician Coll (NJ)
Fresno Pacific U (CA)
Heritage U (WA)
Idaho State U (ID)
Indiana U East (IN)
Indiana U–Purdue University Fort Wayne (IN)
Lindsey Wilson Coll (KY)
Macon State Coll (GA)
Mesa State Coll (CO)
Sacred Heart U (CT)
State U of New York Empire State Coll (NY)
Thomas More Coll (KY)
Thomas U (GA)
Tri-State U (IN)
U of Great Falls (MT)
U of Rio Grande (OH)
The U of Tampa (FL)
U of Wisconsin–Green Bay (WI)
Utah Valley State Coll (UT)

York Coll of Pennsylvania
(PA)

Mathematics and Computer Science
Immaculata U (PA)

Mathematics Teacher Education
Central Christian Coll of Kansas (KS)

Mechanical Design Technology
Clayton State U (GA)
Ferris State U (MI)

Mechanical Drafting
Cameron U (OK)

Mechanical Drafting and Cad/Cadd
Baker Coll of Flint (MI)
Cameron U (OK)
Indiana U–Purdue University Indianapolis (IN)
Montana Tech of The U of Montana (MT)
Purdue U (IN)

Mechanical Engineering
Fairfield U (CT)
Macon State Coll (GA)

Mechanical Engineering/ Mechanical Technology
Andrews U (MI)
Baker Coll of Flint (MI)
Bluefield State Coll (WV)
Fairmont State U (WV)
Farmingdale State U of New York (NY)
Ferris State U (MI)
Indiana U–Purdue University Fort Wayne (IN)
Indiana U–Purdue University Indianapolis (IN)
Lake Superior State U (MI)
Lawrence Technological U (MI)
Michigan Technological U (MI)
Murray State U (KY)
New York Inst of Technology (NY)
The Pennsylvania State U Altoona Coll (PA)
The Pennsylvania State U at Erie, The Behrend Coll (PA)
The Pennsylvania State U Berks Campus of the Berks–Lehigh Valley Coll (PA)
Point Park U (PA)
Purdue U Calumet (IN)
Purdue U North Central (IN)
Rochester Inst of Technology (NY)
The U of Akron (OH)
U of Cincinnati (OH)
U of Massachusetts Lowell (MA)
U of Rio Grande (OH)
U of the District of Columbia (DC)
Vermont Tech Coll (VT)
Weber State U (UT)
Wentworth Inst of Technology (MA)
Youngstown State U (OH)

Mechanical Engineering Technologies Related
Purdue U (IN)

Mechanic and Repair Technologies Related
Bob Jones U (SC)
Pennsylvania Coll of Technology (PA)

Mechanics and Repair
Idaho State U (ID)
Lewis-Clark State Coll (ID)

Medical Administrative Assistant
Minnesota School of Business (MN)

Medical Administrative Assistant and Medical Secretary
Baker Coll of Auburn Hills (MI)

Baker Coll of Cadillac (MI)
Baker Coll of Clinton Township (MI)
Baker Coll of Flint (MI)
Baker Coll of Jackson (MI)
Baker Coll of Muskegon (MI)
Baker Coll of Owosso (MI)
Baker Coll of Port Huron (MI)
Boise State U (ID)
Central Pennsylvania Coll (PA)
Dickinson State U (ND)
Hannibal-LaGrange Coll (MO)
Lamar U (TX)
Mesa State Coll (CO)
Midland Lutheran Coll (NE)
Monroe Coll, Bronx (NY)
Monroe Coll, New Rochelle (NY)
Montana State U–Billings (MT)
Montana Tech of The U of Montana (MT)
Pacific Union Coll (CA)
Pennsylvania Coll of Technology (PA)
Sullivan U (KY)
Universidad Adventista de las Antillas (PR)
The U of Akron (OH)
U of Cincinnati (OH)
The U of Montana–Missoula (MT)
U of Rio Grande (OH)
Wright State U (OH)

Medical/Clinical Assistant
Argosy U/Santa Monica (CA)
Argosy U/Twin Cities (MN)
Arkansas Tech U (AR)
Baker Coll of Allen Park (MI)
Baker Coll of Auburn Hills (MI)
Baker Coll of Cadillac (MI)
Baker Coll of Clinton Township (MI)
Baker Coll of Flint (MI)
Baker Coll of Jackson (MI)
Baker Coll of Muskegon (MI)
Baker Coll of Owosso (MI)
Baker Coll of Port Huron (MI)
Bluefield State Coll (WV)
Cabarrus Coll of Health Sciences (NC)
Central Pennsylvania Coll (PA)
Clayton State U (GA)
Davenport U, Dearborn (MI)
Eastern Kentucky U (KY)
Faulkner U (AL)
Florida Metropolitan U– Brandon Campus (FL)
Georgia Southwestern State U (GA)
Idaho State U (ID)
Jones Coll, Jacksonville (FL)
Montana State U–Billings (MT)
Mountain State U (WV)
Mount Aloysius Coll (PA)
Ohio U (OH)
Palmer Coll of Chiropractic (IA)
Presentation Coll (SD)
Robert Morris Coll (IL)
South U (AL)
South U (GA)
South U (SC)
The U of Akron (OH)
U of Alaska Fairbanks (AK)
West Virginia State U (WV)
Youngstown State U (OH)

Medical/Health Management and Clinical Assistant
Lewis-Clark State Coll (ID)

Medical Illustration
Clayton State U (GA)

Medical Insurance Coding
Baker Coll of Allen Park (MI)

Medical Insurance/Medical Billing
Baker Coll of Allen Park (MI)

Medical Laboratory Technology
Argosy U/Twin Cities (MN)
Evangel U (MO)
Villa Julie Coll (MD)

Medical Office Assistant
Bryant and Stratton Coll, Wauwatosa Campus (WI)
Lewis-Clark State Coll (ID)

Medical Office Computer Specialist
Baker Coll of Allen Park (MI)

Medical Office Management
Dalton State Coll (GA)
The U of Akron (OH)

Medical Radiologic Technology
Argosy U/Twin Cities (MN)
Arkansas State U (AR)
Bluefield State Coll (WV)
Charles R. Drew U of Medicine and Science (CA)
Coll of St. Catherine (MN)
Fairleigh Dickinson U, Coll at Florham (NJ)
Fairleigh Dickinson U, Metropolitan Campus (NJ)
Gannon U (PA)
Georgia Southwestern State U (GA)
Idaho State U (ID)
Indiana U Northwest (IN)
Indiana U–Purdue University Indianapolis (IN)
Indiana U South Bend (IN)
La Roche Coll (PA)
Loma Linda U (CA)
Missouri Southern State U (MO)
Morehead State U (KY)
Mountain State U (WV)
Northern Kentucky U (KY)
Pennsylvania Coll of Technology (PA)
Presentation Coll (SD)
Shawnee State U (OH)
The U of Akron (OH)
U of New Mexico (NM)
U of Saint Francis (IN)
U of Southern Indiana (IN)
Weber State U (UT)

Medical Transcription
Baker Coll of Flint (MI)
Baker Coll of Jackson (MI)
Dalton State Coll (GA)
Presentation Coll (SD)

Mental and Social Health Services And Allied Professions Related
U of Alaska Fairbanks (AK)
The U of Maine at Augusta (ME)

Mental Health Counseling
Washburn U (KS)

Mental Health/Rehabilitation
Evangel U (MO)
Felician Coll (NJ)
Lake Superior State U (MI)

Merchandising
Clayton State U (GA)
The U of Akron (OH)

Merchandising, Sales, and Marketing Operations Related (General)
Clayton State U (GA)

Merchandising, Sales, and Marketing Operations Related (Specialized)
Clayton State U (GA)

Metal and Jewelry Arts
Academy of Art U (CA)
Fashion Inst of Technology (NY)
Miami International U of Art & Design (FL)
Rochester Inst of Technology (NY)

Metallurgical Technology
The Pennsylvania State U Altoona Coll (PA)
The Pennsylvania State U at Erie, The Behrend Coll (PA)
The Pennsylvania State U Berks Campus of the Berks–Lehigh Valley Coll (PA)
Purdue U Calumet (IN)

Microbiology
Canadian Mennonite U (MB, Canada)
Inter American U of Puerto Rico, Barranquitas Campus (PR)

Middle School Education
Dalton State Coll (GA)
U of Arkansas at Fort Smith (AR)

Military Studies
Hawai'i Pacific U (HI)

Military Technologies
Murray State U (KY)

Missionary Studies and Missiology
Bob Jones U (SC)
Central Christian Coll of Kansas (KS)
Faith Baptist Bible Coll and Theological Seminary (IA)
God's Bible School and Coll (OH)
Hobe Sound Bible Coll (FL)
Hope International U (CA)

Modern Languages
Macon State Coll (GA)
Sacred Heart U (CT)

Molecular Biochemistry
Sacred Heart U (CT)

Mortuary Science and Embalming
Ferris State U (MI)

Multi-/Interdisciplinary Studies Related
Arkansas Tech U (AR)
Ohio U (OH)
Pennsylvania Coll of Technology (PA)
Sterling Coll (VT)
The U of Akron (OH)
U of Alaska Fairbanks (AK)
U of Arkansas at Fort Smith (AR)

Music
Alverno Coll (WI)
Bethel Coll (IN)
Central Baptist Coll (AR)
Clayton State U (GA)
Crown Coll (MN)
Dallas Baptist U (TX)
Five Towns Coll (NY)
Fresno Pacific U (CA)
John Brown U (AR)
Kwantlen U Coll (BC, Canada)
Macon State Coll (GA)
Mesa State Coll (CO)
Mount Olive Coll (NC)
Mount Vernon Nazarene U (OH)
Peace Coll (NC)
Sacred Heart U (CT)
Shawnee State U (OH)
Thomas More Coll (KY)
The U of Maine at Augusta (ME)
U of Rio Grande (OH)
The U of Tampa (FL)
U of the District of Columbia (DC)
Utah Valley State Coll (UT)
York Coll of Pennsylvania (PA)

Musical Instrument Fabrication and Repair
Indiana U Bloomington (IN)

Music History, Literature, and Theory
Central Christian Coll of Kansas (KS)

Music Management and Merchandising
Five Towns Coll (NY)
The New England Inst of Art (MA)

Music Performance
Central Christian Coll of Kansas (KS)
New World School of the Arts (FL)
Northwestern Coll (MN)

Music Related
Minnesota School of Business (MN)

Music Teacher Education
Central Christian Coll of Kansas (KS)
Union Coll (NE)

Music Theory and Composition
Kwantlen U Coll (BC, Canada)
New World School of the Arts (FL)

Natural Resources and Conservation Related
Sterling Coll (VT)

Natural Resources/ Conservation
Sterling Coll (VT)
U of Alaska Southeast (AK)
U of Minnesota, Crookston (MN)

Natural Resources/ Conservation Related
Sterling Coll (VT)

Natural Resources Management
Sterling Coll (VT)

Natural Resources Management and Policy
Heritage U (WA)
Lake Superior State U (MI)
Sterling Coll (VT)
U of Alaska Fairbanks (AK)
U of Minnesota, Crookston (MN)

Natural Sciences
Alderson-Broaddus Coll (WV)
Charleston Southern U (SC)
Felician Coll (NJ)
Fresno Pacific U (CA)
Madonna U (MI)
Medgar Evers Coll of the City U of New York (NY)
Roberts Wesleyan Coll (NY)
Shawnee State U (OH)
Sterling Coll (VT)
U of Cincinnati (OH)
Utah Valley State Coll (UT)
Villanova U (PA)
Washburn U (KS)

Naval Architecture and Marine Engineering
Maine Maritime Academy (ME)

Nuclear Engineering Technology
Arkansas Tech U (AR)
Excelsior Coll (NY)

Nuclear Medical Technology
Ball State U (IN)
Dalton State Coll (GA)
Ferris State U (MI)
The George Washington U (DC)
Molloy Coll (NY)
The U of Findlay (OH)
West Virginia State U (WV)

Nursing Assistant/Aide and Patient Care Assistant
Cabarrus Coll of Health Sciences (NC)
Central Christian Coll of Kansas (KS)
Montana Tech of The U of Montana (MT)

Nursing (Licensed Practical/ Vocational Nurse Training)
Central Christian Coll of Kansas (KS)
Dickinson State U (ND)
Georgia Southwestern State U (GA)
Lamar U (TX)
Lewis-Clark State Coll (ID)
Medgar Evers Coll of the City U of New York (NY)
Montana State U–Billings (MT)
Pennsylvania Coll of Technology (PA)

Thompson Rivers U (BC, Canada)
The U of Montana–Missoula (MT)
U of the District of Columbia (DC)
Vermont Tech Coll (VT)
Virginia State U (VA)

Nursing (Registered Nurse Training)
Alcorn State U (MS)
Alvernia Coll (PA)
Angelo State U (TX)
Aquinas Coll (TN)
Arkansas State U (AR)
Augusta State U (GA)
Baker Coll of Clinton Township (MI)
Baker Coll of Flint (MI)
Baker Coll of Muskegon (MI)
Baker Coll of Owosso (MI)
Ball State U (IN)
Bethel Coll (IN)
Bluefield State Coll (WV)
Boise State U (ID)
Bryant and Stratton Coll, Wauwatosa Campus (WI)
Cabarrus Coll of Health Sciences (NC)
Castleton State Coll (VT)
Central Christian Coll of Kansas (KS)
Clarion U of Pennsylvania (PA)
Coll of Saint Mary (NE)
Coll of Staten Island of the City U of New York (NY)
Columbia Coll (MO)
Columbia Coll, Caguas (PR)
Covenant Coll (GA)
Cox Coll of Nursing and Health Sciences (MO)
Dakota Wesleyan U (SD)
Dalton State Coll (GA)
Davenport U, Dearborn (MI)
Davis & Elkins Coll (WV)
Eastern Kentucky U (KY)
Excelsior Coll (NY)
Fairmont State U (WV)
Farmingdale State U of New York (NY)
Felician Coll (NJ)
Ferris State U (MI)
Gardner-Webb U (NC)
Gwynedd-Mercy Coll (PA)
Hannibal-LaGrange Coll (MO)
Heritage U (WA)
Houston Baptist U (TX)
Indiana U East (IN)
Indiana U Kokomo (IN)
Indiana U Northwest (IN)
Indiana U–Purdue University Fort Wayne (IN)
Indiana U–Purdue University Indianapolis (IN)
Indiana U South Bend (IN)
Inter American U of Puerto Rico, Barranquitas Campus (PR)
Inter American U of Puerto Rico, Ponce Campus (PR)
Kent State U (OH)
Kentucky State U (KY)
Lamar U (TX)
Lincoln Memorial U (TN)
Lincoln U (MO)
Lock Haven U of Pennsylvania (PA)
Loma Linda U (CA)
Macon State Coll (GA)
Marshall U (WV)
Mercyhurst Coll (PA)
Mesa State Coll (CO)
Midway Coll (KY)
Montana Tech of The U of Montana (MT)
Morehead State U (KY)
Mount Aloysius Coll (PA)
Mount St. Mary's Coll (CA)
Nebraska Methodist Coll (NE)
Nicholls State U (LA)
Norfolk State U (VA)
Northern Kentucky U (KY)
North Georgia Coll & State U (GA)
Northwestern State U of Louisiana (LA)

Oakwood Coll (AL)
Ohio U–Zanesville (OH)
Oklahoma Panhandle State U (OK)
Pacific Union Coll (CA)
Park U (MO)
Pennsylvania Coll of Technology (PA)
The Pennsylvania State U Altoona Coll (PA)
Pikeville Coll (KY)
Presentation Coll (SD)
Purdue U Calumet (IN)
Purdue U North Central (IN)
Regis Coll (MA)
Reinhardt Coll (GA)
Rivier Coll (NH)
Shawnee State U (OH)
Southern Adventist U (TN)
Southern Vermont Coll (VT)
Southwest Baptist U (MO)
Tennessee State U (TN)
Thomas U (GA)
Troy U (AL)
Universidad Adventista de las Antillas (PR)
U of Arkansas at Fort Smith (AR)
U of Charleston (WV)
U of Cincinnati (OH)
U of Indianapolis (IN)
The U of Maine at Augusta (ME)
U of Mobile (AL)
U of New England (ME)
U of Pittsburgh at Bradford (PA)
U of Rio Grande (OH)
U of Saint Francis (IN)
U of South Carolina Upstate (SC)
The U of South Dakota (SD)
U of Southern Indiana (IN)
U of the District of Columbia (DC)
U of the Virgin Islands (VI)
Utah Valley State Coll (UT)
Vermont Tech Coll (VT)
Walsh U (OH)
Warner Pacific Coll (OR)
Weber State U (UT)
Western Kentucky U (KY)

Nursing Related
Inter American U of Puerto Rico, Aguadilla Campus (PR)
Madonna U (MI)

Nursing Science
Davenport U, Dearborn (MI)
La Roche Coll (PA)
National U (CA)

Occupational Safety and Health Technology
Ferris State U (MI)
Indiana U Bloomington (IN)
Lamar U (TX)
Montana Tech of The U of Montana (MT)
Southwest Baptist U (MO)
U of Cincinnati (OH)
U of New Haven (CT)
Wright State U (OH)

Occupational Therapist Assistant
Baker Coll of Muskegon (MI)
Cabarrus Coll of Health Sciences (NC)
California U of Pennsylvania (PA)
Clarion U of Pennsylvania (PA)
Coll of St. Catherine (MN)
Idaho State U (ID)
Loma Linda U (CA)
Mercy Coll (NY)
Mountain State U (WV)
Mount Aloysius Coll (PA)
Mount St. Mary's Coll (CA)
Pennsylvania Coll of Technology (PA)
U of Louisiana at Monroe (LA)
U of Saint Francis (IN)
U of Southern Indiana (IN)

Occupational Therapy
Clayton State U (GA)
Dalton State Coll (GA)

Faulkner U (AL)
Oakwood Coll (AL)
Shawnee State U (OH)
Southern Adventist U (TN)

Office Management
Baker Coll of Flint (MI)
Baker Coll of Jackson (MI)
Dakota State U (SD)
Dalton State Coll (GA)
Emmanuel Coll (GA)
God's Bible School and Coll (OH)
Lake Superior State U (MI)
Mercyhurst Coll (PA)
Mountain State U (WV)
Park U (MO)
Peirce Coll (PA)
Shawnee State U (OH)
Thompson Rivers U (BC, Canada)
Washburn U (KS)

Office Occupations and Clerical Services
Bob Jones U (SC)
Georgia Southwestern State U (GA)
Pennsylvania Coll of Technology (PA)
U of Alaska Fairbanks (AK)
Wright State U (OH)

Operations Management
Baker Coll of Flint (MI)
Indiana U–Purdue University Fort Wayne (IN)
Indiana U–Purdue University Indianapolis (IN)
Northern Kentucky U (KY)
Purdue U (IN)

Ophthalmic Laboratory Technology
Central Pennsylvania Coll (PA)
Indiana U Bloomington (IN)
Rochester Inst of Technology (NY)

Opticianry
Ferris State U (MI)
The U of Akron (OH)

Optometric Technician
Indiana U Bloomington (IN)

Organizational Communication
Creighton U (NE)

Ornamental Horticulture
Farmingdale State U of New York (NY)
Ferris State U (MI)
Pennsylvania Coll of Technology (PA)
State U of New York Coll of Agriculture and Technology at Cobleskill (NY)
U of Massachusetts Amherst (MA)
Utah State U (UT)

Orthotics/Prosthetics
Baker Coll of Flint (MI)

Painting
Academy of Art U (CA)
New World School of the Arts (FL)
Pratt Inst (NY)

Paralegal/Legal Assistant
Argosy U/Santa Monica (CA)
Bryant and Stratton Coll, Cleveland (OH)
Bryant and Stratton Coll, Wauwatosa Campus (WI)
Davenport U, Dearborn (MI)
Elms Coll (MA)
Minnesota School of Business (MN)
Newman U (KS)
Utah Valley State Coll (UT)

Parks, Recreation and Leisure
Central Christian Coll of Kansas (KS)
Clayton State U (GA)
Johnson & Wales U (NC)
Johnson & Wales U (RI)
Mitchell Coll (CT)
Mount Olive Coll (NC)

Oklahoma Panhandle State U (OK)
U of Maine at Presque Isle (ME)
U of the District of Columbia (DC)
Utah Valley State Coll (UT)

Parks, Recreation and Leisure Facilities Management
Eastern Kentucky U (KY)
Indiana Tech (IN)
Johnson & Wales U (NC)
Johnson & Wales U (RI)
Paul Smith's Coll of Arts and Sciences (NY)
State U of New York Coll of Agriculture and Technology at Cobleskill (NY)

Pastoral Studies/Counseling
Oakwood Coll (AL)

Perfusion Technology
Boise State U (ID)
Thompson Rivers U (BC, Canada)

Personal and Culinary Services Related
Lexington Coll (IL)

Petroleum Technology
Montana State U–Billings (MT)
Montana Tech of The U of Montana (MT)
Nicholls State U (LA)

Pharmacy
Clayton State U (GA)

Pharmacy Technician
Baker Coll of Flint (MI)
Baker Coll of Jackson (MI)
Baker Coll of Muskegon (MI)
Charles R. Drew U of Medicine and Science (CA)
Florida Metropolitan U–Brandon Campus (FL)
Idaho State U (ID)
Inter American U of Puerto Rico, Aguadilla Campus (PR)
Mount Aloysius Coll (PA)

Philosophy
Clayton State U (GA)
Dalton State Coll (GA)
Felician Coll (NJ)
Kwantlen U Coll (BC, Canada)
Sacred Heart U (CT)
Thomas More Coll (KY)
Université Laval (QC, Canada)
The U of Tampa (FL)
U of the District of Columbia (DC)
U of Wisconsin–Green Bay (WI)
Utah Valley State Coll (UT)
York Coll of Pennsylvania (PA)

Photographic and Film/Video Technology
New England School of Communications (ME)

Photography
Academy of Art U (CA)
Andrews U (MI)
The Art Inst of Colorado (CO)
The Art Inst of Seattle (WA)
Central Christian Coll of Kansas (KS)
Corcoran Coll of Art and Design (DC)
New World School of the Arts (FL)
Pacific Union Coll (CA)
Rochester Inst of Technology (NY)
Sage Coll of Albany (NY)
The U of Maine at Augusta (ME)
Villa Julie Coll (MD)

Physical Education Teaching and Coaching
Central Christian Coll of Kansas (KS)
Clayton State U (GA)

Fresno Pacific U (CA)
Macon State Coll (GA)
Mitchell Coll (CT)
U of Rio Grande (OH)

Physical Sciences
Faulkner U (AL)
Mitchell Coll (CT)
Pennsylvania Coll of Technology (PA)
Roberts Wesleyan Coll (NY)
U of the District of Columbia (DC)
Utah Valley State Coll (UT)
Villa Julie Coll (MD)

Physical Science Technologies Related
The U of Akron (OH)
Western Kentucky U (KY)

Physical Therapist Assistant
Arkansas State U (AR)
Baker Coll of Flint (MI)
Baker Coll of Muskegon (MI)
Central Pennsylvania Coll (PA)
Coll of St. Catherine (MN)
Finlandia U (MI)
Idaho State U (ID)
Loma Linda U (CA)
Missouri Western State U (MO)
Mountain State U (WV)
Mount Aloysius Coll (PA)
Mount St. Mary's Coll (CA)
New York U (NY)
Southern Illinois U Carbondale (IL)
South U (AL)
South U (GA)
U of Central Arkansas (AR)
U of Evansville (IN)
U of Indianapolis (IN)
U of Saint Francis (IN)
Washburn U (KS)

Physical Therapy
Alvernia Coll (PA)
Clayton State U (GA)
Dalton State Coll (GA)
Fairmont State U (WV)
Faulkner U (AL)
Lynn U (FL)
Macon State Coll (GA)
Mercyhurst Coll (PA)
Oakwood Coll (AL)
Shawnee State U (OH)
Southern Adventist U (TN)
U of Central Arkansas (AR)
U of Cincinnati (OH)

Physician Assistant
Bryant and Stratton Coll, Wauwatosa Campus (WI)
Central Christian Coll of Kansas (KS)
Dalton State Coll (GA)
Minnesota School of Business (MN)
Southern Adventist U (TN)

Physics
Clayton State U (GA)
Dalton State Coll (GA)
Idaho State U (ID)
Macon State Coll (GA)
Mesa State Coll (CO)
Rochester Inst of Technology (NY)
Thomas More Coll (KY)
U of the Virgin Islands (VI)
Utah Valley State Coll (UT)
York Coll of Pennsylvania (PA)

Piano and Organ
Kwantlen U Coll (BC, Canada)
New World School of the Arts (FL)

Pipefitting and Sprinkler Fitting
Thompson Rivers U (BC, Canada)

Plant Nursery Management
Inter American U of Puerto Rico, Barranquitas Campus (PR)
Pennsylvania Coll of Technology (PA)

State U of New York Coll of Agriculture and Technology at Cobleskill (NY)

Plant Protection and Integrated Pest Management
North Carolina State U (NC)
Sterling Coll (VT)

Plant Sciences
State U of New York Coll of Agriculture and Technology at Cobleskill (NY)

Plant Sciences Related
Sterling Coll (VT)

Plastics Engineering Technology
Ferris State U (MI)
Pennsylvania Coll of Technology (PA)
The Pennsylvania State U at Erie, The Behrend Coll (PA)
Shawnee State U (OH)

Platemaking/Imaging
Pennsylvania Coll of Technology (PA)

Plumbing Technology
Pennsylvania Coll of Technology (PA)
Thompson Rivers U (BC, Canada)

Political Science and Government
Clayton State U (GA)
Dalton State Coll (GA)
Fresno Pacific U (CA)
Idaho State U (ID)
Indiana U–Purdue University Fort Wayne (IN)
John Cabot U Italy)
Kwantlen U Coll (BC, Canada)
Macon State Coll (GA)
Sacred Heart U (CT)
Thomas More Coll (KY)
Université Laval (QC, Canada)
The U of Scranton (PA)
The U of Tampa (FL)
U of Wisconsin–Green Bay (WI)
Villa Julie Coll (MD)
Xavier U (OH)
York Coll of Pennsylvania (PA)

Postal Management
Macon State Coll (GA)

Pre-Dentistry Studies
Concordia U Wisconsin (WI)

Pre-Engineering
Anderson U (IN)
Boise State U (ID)
Campbell U (NC)
Charleston Southern U (SC)
Clayton State U (GA)
Columbus State U (GA)
Covenant Coll (GA)
Eastern Kentucky U (KY)
Edgewood Coll (WI)
Faulkner U (AL)
Ferris State U (MI)
Fort Valley State U (GA)
Hannibal-LaGrange Coll (MO)
Keene State Coll (NH)
LaGrange Coll (GA)
Lincoln U (MO)
Macon State Coll (GA)
Medgar Evers Coll of the City U of New York (NY)
Mesa State Coll (CO)
Minnesota State U Mankato (MN)
Missouri Southern State U (MO)
Montana State U–Billings (MT)
Newman U (KS)
Niagara U (NY)
Northern State U (SD)
Purdue U North Central (IN)
St. Gregory's U (OK)
Shawnee State U (OH)
Southern Utah U (UT)
U of New Hampshire (NH)
U of Sioux Falls (SD)

Utah Valley State Coll (UT)
Vaughn Coll of Aeronautics and Technology (NY)
West Virginia State U (WV)

Pre-Law Studies
Calumet Coll of Saint Joseph (IN)
Ferris State U (MI)
Immaculata U (PA)
Peirce Coll (PA)
Thomas More Coll (KY)

Pre-Medical Studies
Concordia U Wisconsin (WI)
Schiller International USpain)
Schiller International UUnited Kingdom)
State U of New York Coll of Agriculture and Technology at Cobleskill (NY)
U of Ottawa (ON, Canada)

Pre-Nursing Studies
Concordia U Wisconsin (WI)
Trinity International U (IL)

Pre-Pharmacy Studies
Dalton State Coll (GA)
Emmanuel Coll (GA)
Ferris State U (MI)
Macon State Coll (GA)
Thompson Rivers U (BC, Canada)

Pre-Theology/Pre-Ministerial Studies
Manchester Coll (IN)
Nazarene Bible Coll (CO)
St. Gregory's U (OK)

Pre-Veterinary Studies
Schiller International USpain)
Schiller International UUnited Kingdom)
Shawnee State U (OH)

Printmaking
Academy of Art U (CA)
New World School of the Arts (FL)

Professional Studies
Ohio Valley U (WV)

Psychiatric/Mental Health Services Technology
Lake Superior State U (MI)
Northern Kentucky U (KY)
Pennsylvania Coll of Technology (PA)

Psychology
Bluefield State Coll (WV)
Chestnut Hill Coll (PA)
Crown Coll (MN)
Dalton State Coll (GA)
Eastern New Mexico U (NM)
Felician Coll (NJ)
Fresno Pacific U (CA)
Heritage U (WA)
Indiana U–Purdue University Fort Wayne (IN)
Kwantlen U Coll (BC, Canada)
Macon State Coll (GA)
Mitchell Coll (CT)
Montana State U–Billings (MT)
Mount Olive Coll (NC)
Newbury Coll (MA)
Sacred Heart U (CT)
Thomas More Coll (KY)
U of Rio Grande (OH)
The U of Tampa (FL)
U of Wisconsin–Green Bay (WI)
Villa Julie Coll (MD)
Wright State U (OH)
Xavier U (OH)

Psychology Teacher Education
Central Christian Coll of Kansas (KS)

Public Administration
Indiana U Bloomington (IN)
Indiana U Northwest (IN)
Indiana U–Purdue University Fort Wayne (IN)
Indiana U–Purdue University Indianapolis (IN)
Indiana U South Bend (IN)
Macon State Coll (GA)

Medgar Evers Coll of the City
U of New York (NY)
Point Park U (PA)
The U of Maine at Augusta
(ME)
U of Regina (SK, Canada)
U of the District of Columbia
(DC)

**Public Administration and
Social Service Professions
Related**
Indiana U–Purdue University
Fort Wayne (IN)
The U of Akron (OH)
U of Saint Francis (IN)

Public Health
U of Alaska Fairbanks (AK)

Public Policy Analysis
Indiana U Bloomington (IN)

**Public Relations,
Advertising, and Applied
Communication Related**
Champlain Coll (VT)
John Brown U (AR)
Madonna U (MI)

**Public Relations/Image
Management**
Champlain Coll (VT)
John Brown U (AR)
Johnson & Wales U (NC)
Madonna U (MI)
New England School of
Communications (ME)
Xavier U (OH)

**Purchasing, Procurement/
Acquisitions and Contracts
Management**
Mercyhurst Coll (PA)
Saint Joseph's U (PA)
U of Management and
Technology (VA)
Washburn U (KS)

**Quality Control and Safety
Technologies Related**
Madonna U (MI)

Quality Control Technology
Baker Coll of Cadillac (MI)
Baker Coll of Flint (MI)
Baker Coll of Muskegon (MI)
Eastern Kentucky U (KY)
Pennsylvania Coll of
Technology (PA)
U of Cincinnati (OH)

Rabbinical Studies
Université Laval (QC,
Canada)

Radiation Biology
Inter American U of Puerto
Rico, Barranquitas
Campus (PR)

Radio and Television
Academy of Art U (CA)
Ashland U (OH)
Lawrence Technological U
(MI)
Newbury Coll (MA)
New England School of
Communications (ME)
Northwestern Coll (MN)
Ohio U (OH)
Ohio U–Zanesville (OH)
Xavier U (OH)
York Coll of Pennsylvania
(PA)

**Radio and Television
Broadcasting Technology**
Lyndon State Coll (VT)
The New England Inst of Art
(MA)
New England School of
Communications (ME)
New York Inst of Technology
(NY)
Southern Adventist U (TN)

**Radiologic Technology/
Science**
Allen Coll (IA)
Baker Coll of Clinton
Township (MI)
Baker Coll of Muskegon (MI)
Boise State U (ID)
Champlain Coll (VT)
Clayton State U (GA)

Dalton State Coll (GA)
Indiana U Northwest (IN)
Indiana U–Purdue University
Fort Wayne (IN)
Lewis-Clark State Coll (ID)
Mansfield U of Pennsylvania
(PA)
Mesa State Coll (CO)
Midwestern State U (TX)
Mountain State U (WV)
Mount Aloysius Coll (PA)
Nebraska Methodist Coll
(NE)
Newman U (KS)
U of Arkansas at Fort Smith
(AR)
The U of Montana–Missoula
(MT)
U of Rio Grande (OH)
Washburn U (KS)

**Range Science and
Management**
Sterling Coll (VT)

Real Estate
Fairmont State U (WV)
Ferris State U (MI)
Lamar U (TX)
Saint Francis U (PA)
U of Cincinnati (OH)

Receptionist
Baker Coll of Allen Park (MI)
The U of Montana–Missoula
(MT)

Recording Arts Technology
New England School of
Communications (ME)

Religious Education
Apex School of Theology
(NC)
The Baptist Coll of Florida
(FL)
Calvary Bible Coll and
Theological Seminary (MO)
Cornerstone U (MI)
Dallas Baptist U (TX)
Houghton Coll (NY)
Kuyper Coll (MI)
Mercyhurst Coll (PA)
Nazarene Bible Coll (CO)
Warner Pacific Coll (OR)

Religious/Sacred Music
Aquinas Coll (MI)
The Baptist Coll of Florida
(FL)
Immaculata U (PA)
MidAmerica Nazarene U
(KS)
Mount Vernon Nazarene U
(OH)
Nazarene Bible Coll (CO)
Southeastern Baptist Coll
(MS)

Religious Studies
Brewton-Parker Coll (GA)
Calumet Coll of Saint Joseph
(IN)
Central Christian Coll of
Kansas (KS)
Felician Coll (NJ)
Global U of the Assemblies
of God (MO)
Grace Bible Coll (MI)
Holy Apostles Coll and
Seminary (CT)
Kentucky Mountain Bible
Coll (KY)
Liberty U (VA)
Madonna U (MI)
Manchester Coll (IN)
Missouri Baptist U (MO)
Mount Marty Coll (SD)
Mount Olive Coll (NC)
Oakwood Coll (AL)
Pacific Islands Bible Coll
(GU)
Presentation Coll (SD)
Sacred Heart U (CT)
Shaw U (NC)
Thomas More Coll (KY)
The U of Findlay (OH)
U of Sioux Falls (SD)

Religious Studies Related
Lindsey Wilson Coll (KY)

Resort Management
Rochester Inst of Technology
(NY)
Thompson Rivers U (BC,
Canada)

Respiratory Care Therapy
Ball State U (IN)
Cameron U (OK)
Columbia Union Coll (MD)
Dakota State U (SD)
Dalton State Coll (GA)
Faulkner U (AL)
Ferris State U (MI)
Gannon U (PA)
Gwynedd-Mercy Coll (PA)
Indiana U Northwest (IN)
Indiana U–Purdue University
Indianapolis (IN)
Lamar U (TX)
Loma Linda U (CA)
Macon State Coll (GA)
Mansfield U of Pennsylvania
(PA)
Midland Lutheran Coll (NE)
Missouri Southern State U
(MO)
Molloy Coll (NY)
Morehead State U (KY)
Mountain State U (WV)
Nebraska Methodist Coll
(NE)
Newman U (KS)
Northern Kentucky U (KY)
Point Park U (PA)
Shawnee State U (OH)
Shenandoah U (VA)
Southern Adventist U (TN)
Southern Illinois U
Carbondale (IL)
Universidad Adventista de
las Antillas (PR)
The U of Akron (OH)
U of Arkansas at Fort Smith
(AR)
The U of Montana–Missoula
(MT)
U of Pittsburgh at Johnstown
(PA)
U of Southern Indiana (IN)
U of the District of Columbia
(DC)
Vermont Tech Coll (VT)
Washburn U (KS)
Weber State U (UT)
Western Kentucky U (KY)
York Coll of Pennsylvania
(PA)

**Respiratory Therapy
Technician**
Thompson Rivers U (BC,
Canada)

**Restaurant, Culinary, and
Catering Management**
The Art Inst of Dallas (TX)
The Art Inst of Houston (TX)
Bob Jones U (SC)
Ferris State U (MI)
Johnson & Wales U (FL)
Johnson & Wales U (NC)
Johnson & Wales U (RI)
Lexington Coll (IL)
The U of Akron (OH)
U of New Hampshire (NH)

**Restaurant/Food Services
Management**
Ferris State U (MI)
Johnson & Wales U (CO)
Lexington Coll (IL)
Rochester Inst of Technology
(NY)
U of New Hampshire (NH)

Retailing
Johnson & Wales U (RI)

Robotics Technology
Indiana U–Purdue University
Indianapolis (IN)
Purdue U (IN)
U of Rio Grande (OH)

Safety/Security Technology
Keene State Coll (NH)
Lamar U (TX)
Madonna U (MI)
Ohio U (OH)
U of Cincinnati (OH)

**Sales and Marketing/
Marketing And Distribution
Teacher Education**
Central Christian Coll of
Kansas (KS)

**Sales, Distribution and
Marketing**
Baker Coll of Flint (MI)
Baker Coll of Jackson (MI)
Central Pennsylvania Coll
(PA)
Champlain Coll (VT)
Dalton State Coll (GA)
Johnson & Wales U (NC)
Johnson & Wales U (RI)
Purdue U North Central (IN)
Thompson Rivers U (BC,
Canada)
The U of Findlay (OH)

Science Teacher Education
Central Christian Coll of
Kansas (KS)
U of Cincinnati (OH)

**Science Technologies
Related**
Madonna U (MI)
Ohio Valley U (WV)

**Science, Technology and
Society**
Samford U (AL)

Sculpture
Academy of Art U (CA)
New World School of the Arts
(FL)

Secondary Education
Central Christian Coll of
Kansas (KS)
Dalton State Coll (GA)
Mountain State U (WV)

**Security and Loss
Prevention**
Potomac Coll (DC)

**Security and Protective
Services Related**
Ohio U (OH)

Selling Skills and Sales
The U of Akron (OH)

Sheet Metal Technology
Montana State U–Billings
(MT)

**Sign Language
Interpretation and
Translation**
Bethel Coll (IN)
Coll of St. Catherine (MN)
Fairmont State U (WV)
Mount Aloysius Coll (PA)
Rochester Inst of Technology
(NY)
U of Louisville (KY)

Slavic Languages
U of Ottawa (ON, Canada)

**Small Business
Administration**
Central Christian Coll of
Kansas (KS)
Lewis-Clark State Coll (ID)

**Small Engine Mechanics
and Repair Technology**
The U of Montana–Missoula
(MT)

Social Psychology
Central Christian Coll of
Kansas (KS)
Kwantlen U Coll (BC,
Canada)
Park U (MO)

Social Sciences
Campbellsville U (KY)
Clayton State U (GA)
Crown Coll (MN)
Evangel U (MO)
Faulkner U (AL)
Felician Coll (NJ)
Heritage U (WA)
Kwantlen U Coll (BC,
Canada)
Lindsey Wilson Coll (KY)
Long Island U, Brooklyn
Campus (NY)
Marymount Manhattan Coll
(NY)

Mesa State Coll (CO)
Newbury Coll (MA)
Ohio U (OH)
Ohio U–Zanesville (OH)
Sage Coll of Albany (NY)
Samford U (AL)
Shawnee State U (OH)
State U of New York Empire
State Coll (NY)
Tri-State U (IN)
U of Cincinnati (OH)
The U of Findlay (OH)
The U of Maine at Augusta
(ME)
U of Sioux Falls (SD)
U of Southern Indiana (IN)
Valparaiso U (IN)
Villa Julie Coll (MD)
Warner Pacific Coll (OR)
Wayland Baptist U (TX)

Social Sciences Related
Concordia U at Austin (TX)

**Social Science Teacher
Education**
Central Christian Coll of
Kansas (KS)

**Social Studies Teacher
Education**
Central Christian Coll of
Kansas (KS)

Social Work
Central Christian Coll of
Kansas (KS)
Champlain Coll (VT)
Dalton State Coll (GA)
Edinboro U of Pennsylvania
(PA)
Indiana U East (IN)
Northern State U (SD)
Suffolk U (MA)
U of Cincinnati (OH)
U of Rio Grande (OH)
U of Wisconsin–Green Bay
(WI)
Wright State U (OH)

Sociology
Central Christian Coll of
Kansas (KS)
Clayton State U (GA)
Dalton State Coll (GA)
Felician Coll (NJ)
Fresno Pacific U (CA)
Grand View Coll (IA)
Kwantlen U Coll (BC,
Canada)
Macon State Coll (GA)
Montana State U–Billings
(MT)
Newbury Coll (MA)
The Pennsylvania State U
University Park Campus
(PA)
Sacred Heart U (CT)
Thomas More Coll (KY)
U of Dubuque (IA)
U of Rio Grande (OH)
The U of Scranton (PA)
The U of Tampa (FL)
Villa Julie Coll (MD)
Wright State U (OH)
Xavier U (OH)

Soil Conservation
U of Minnesota, Crookston
(MN)

Soil Science and Agronomy
Sterling Coll (VT)

Soil Sciences Related
Sterling Coll (VT)

Solar Energy Technology
Pennsylvania Coll of
Technology (PA)

Spanish
Chestnut Hill Coll (PA)
Clayton State U (GA)
Fresno Pacific U (CA)
Idaho State U (ID)
Indiana U–Purdue University
Fort Wayne (IN)
Sacred Heart U (CT)
Thomas More Coll (KY)
The U of Tampa (FL)
U of Wisconsin–Green Bay
(WI)
Xavier U (OH)

Special Education
Edinboro U of Pennsylvania
(PA)
Montana State U–Billings
(MT)

**Special Education (Multiply
Disabled)**
Inter American U of Puerto
Rico, Barranquitas
Campus (PR)

Special Education Related
Minot State U (ND)

**Special Education (Speech
Or Language Impaired)**
U of Nebraska at Omaha
(NE)

Special Products Marketing
Ball State U (IN)
Ferris State U (MI)
Johnson & Wales U (FL)
Johnson & Wales U (RI)
Lamar U (TX)
Newbury Coll (MA)
U of Minnesota, Crookston
(MN)

Speech and Rhetoric
Clayton State U (GA)
Dalton State Coll (GA)
Ferris State U (MI)
Macon State Coll (GA)
Madonna U (MI)

**Speech-Language
Pathology**
Baker Coll of Muskegon (MI)
Elms Coll (MA)
Southern Adventist U (TN)

Speech Teacher Education
Central Christian Coll of
Kansas (KS)

**Sport and Fitness
Administration/Management**
Lake Superior State U (MI)
Mitchell Coll (CT)
Northwood U (MI)
Northwood U, Florida
Campus (FL)
Northwood U, Texas Campus
(TX)
Thompson Rivers U (BC,
Canada)
Webber International U (FL)

**Substance Abuse/Addiction
Counseling**
Charles R. Drew U of
Medicine and Science (CA)
Keene State Coll (NH)
Newman U (KS)
The U of Akron (OH)
U of Great Falls (MT)
Washburn U (KS)

Surgical Technology
Baker Coll of Clinton
Township (MI)
Baker Coll of Flint (MI)
Baker Coll of Jackson (MI)
Baker Coll of Muskegon (MI)
Boise State U (ID)
Cabarrus Coll of Health
Sciences (NC)
Florida Metropolitan U–
Brandon Campus (FL)
Georgia Southwestern State
U (GA)
Loma Linda U (CA)
Montana State U–Billings
(MT)
Mount Aloysius Coll (PA)
Presentation Coll (SD)
Robert Morris Coll (IL)
The U of Akron (OH)
U of Arkansas at Fort Smith
(AR)
The U of Montana–Missoula
(MT)
U of Pittsburgh at Johnstown
(PA)
U of Saint Francis (IN)

Survey Technology
Ferris State U (MI)
Glenville State Coll (WV)
Paul Smith's Coll of Arts and
Sciences (NY)
Pennsylvania Coll of
Technology (PA)

The U of Akron (OH)
U of New Hampshire (NH)

System Administration
Sage Coll of Albany (NY)
Thompson Rivers U (BC, Canada)

System, Networking, and Lan/Wan Management
Baker Coll of Auburn Hills (MI)
Champlain Coll (VT)
DeVry U (MN)
DeVry U, Kansas City (MO)
DeVry U, Fort Washington (PA)
ITT Tech Inst, Tempe (AZ)
ITT Tech Inst, Lexington (KY)
Peirce Coll (PA)
Thompson Rivers U (BC, Canada)

Taxation
Minnesota School of Business (MN)

Teacher Assistant/Aide
Alabama State U (AL)
Alverno Coll (WI)
Boise State U (ID)
Dordt Coll (IA)
Lamar U (TX)
New Mexico Highlands U (NM)
New Mexico State U (NM)
The U of Akron (OH)
U of New Mexico (NM)

Technical and Business Writing
Ferris State U (MI)
Murray State U (KY)

Technical Teacher Education
Eastern Kentucky U (KY)
New York Inst of Technology (NY)
Northern Kentucky U (KY)
Western Kentucky U (KY)

Technology/Industrial Arts Teacher Education
Arkansas State U (AR)

Telecommunications
Briarcliffe Coll (NY)
Champlain Coll (VT)
Clayton State U (GA)
Inter American U of Puerto Rico, Bayamón Campus (PR)

State U of New York Coll of Agriculture and Technology at Cobleskill (NY)

Telecommunications Technology
The Pennsylvania State U Altoona Coll (PA)
The Pennsylvania State U at Erie, The Behrend Coll (PA)
The Pennsylvania State U Berks Campus of the Berks–Lehigh Valley Coll (PA)

Theater Design and Technology
Indiana U Bloomington (IN)
Johnson State Coll (VT)
U of Rio Grande (OH)

Theological and Ministerial Studies Related
Bob Jones U (SC)
U of Saint Francis (IN)

Theology
The Baptist Coll of Florida (FL)
Briar Cliff U (IA)
Central Christian Coll of Kansas (KS)
Creighton U (NE)
Franciscan U of Steubenville (OH)
Heritage Bible Coll (NC)
Ohio Dominican U (OH)
Sacred Heart Major Seminary (MI)
Université Laval (QC, Canada)
William Jessup U (CA)
Xavier U (OH)

Therapeutic Recreation
Indiana Tech (IN)
Mitchell Coll (CT)
U of Southern Maine (ME)

Tool and Die Technology
Pennsylvania Coll of Technology (PA)

Tourism and Travel Services Management
Baker Coll of Flint (MI)
Baker Coll of Muskegon (MI)
Central Pennsylvania Coll (PA)
Champlain Coll (VT)
Inter American U of Puerto Rico, Ponce Campus (PR)
Johnson & Wales U (FL)

Johnson & Wales U (RI)
Mesa State Coll (CO)
Midland Lutheran Coll (NE)
Mountain State U (WV)
Newbury Coll (MA)
Ohio U (OH)
Paul Smith's Coll of Arts and Sciences (NY)
Pennsylvania Coll of Technology (PA)
Robert Morris Coll (IL)
Rochester Inst of Technology (NY)
Schiller International U (FL)
Sullivan U (KY)
The U of Akron (OH)
The U of Montana–Western (MT)
Webber International U (FL)

Tourism and Travel Services Marketing
Champlain Coll (VT)
Johnson & Wales U (RI)
Ohio U (OH)
Pontifical Catholic U of Puerto Rico (PR)
State U of New York Coll of Agriculture and Technology at Cobleskill (NY)
The U of Montana–Western (MT)

Tourism Promotion
Champlain Coll (VT)
Thompson Rivers U (BC, Canada)

Tourism/Travel Marketing
Mountain State U (WV)

Trade and Industrial Teacher Education
Indiana State U (IN)
Murray State U (KY)
Purdue U (IN)

Transportation Technology
Baker Coll of Flint (MI)
Maine Maritime Academy (ME)
U of Cincinnati (OH)

Turf and Turfgrass Management
North Carolina State U (NC)
Pennsylvania Coll of Technology (PA)
State U of New York Coll of Agriculture and Technology at Cobleskill (NY)
U of Massachusetts Amherst (MA)

Urban Studies/Affairs
Clayton State U (GA)
Mount St. Mary's Coll (CA)
U of the District of Columbia (DC)
U of Wisconsin–Green Bay (WI)

Vehicle and Vehicle Parts And Accessories Marketing
Northwood U (MI)
Northwood U, Florida Campus (FL)
Northwood U, Texas Campus (TX)
Pennsylvania Coll of Technology (PA)

Vehicle/Equipment Operation
Baker Coll of Flint (MI)
The U of Montana–Missoula (MT)

Vehicle Maintenance and Repair Technologies Related
Pennsylvania Coll of Technology (PA)
U of Alaska Fairbanks (AK)

Veterinary/Animal Health Technology
Baker Coll of Cadillac (MI)
Baker Coll of Jackson (MI)
Baker Coll of Muskegon (MI)
Medaille Coll (NY)
Morehead State U (KY)
Northwestern State U of Louisiana (LA)
Purdue U (IN)
Thompson Rivers U (BC, Canada)
The U of Maine at Augusta (ME)

Veterinary Sciences
Clayton State U (GA)
Fort Valley State U (GA)

Veterinary Technology
Argosy U/Twin Cities (MN)
Fairmont State U (WV)
Fort Valley State U (GA)
Lincoln Memorial U (TN)
Medaille Coll (NY)
Minnesota School of Business (MN)
National American U, Rapid City (SD)
Vermont Tech Coll (VT)

Violin, Viola, Guitar and Other Stringed Instruments
Five Towns Coll (NY)
Kwantlen U Coll (BC, Canada)
New World School of the Arts (FL)

Visual and Performing Arts
Briarcliffe Coll (NY)
Indiana U East (IN)
Miami International U of Art & Design (FL)
Thomas More Coll (KY)
U of Arkansas at Fort Smith (AR)

Voice and Opera
Five Towns Coll (NY)
Kwantlen U Coll (BC, Canada)
New World School of the Arts (FL)

Water Quality and Wastewater Treatment Management And Recycling Technology
Lake Superior State U (MI)
Murray State U (KY)
U of the District of Columbia (DC)
Wright State U (OH)

Web/Multimedia Management and Webmaster
Academy of Art U (CA)
Central Pennsylvania Coll (PA)
Champlain Coll (VT)
ITT Tech Inst, Tempe (AZ)
Lewis-Clark State Coll (ID)
Limestone Coll (SC)
New England School of Communications (ME)

Web Page, Digital/ Multimedia and Information Resources Design
The Art Inst of California–Los Angeles (CA)
The Art Inst of Dallas (TX)
The Art Inst of Houston (TX)
The Art Inst of Portland (OR)
The Art Insts International Minnesota (MN)
Baker Coll of Allen Park (MI)
Champlain Coll (VT)
Indiana Tech (IN)
ITT Tech Inst, Tempe (AZ)
ITT Tech Inst, Lexington (KY)

Minnesota School of Business (MN)
Mountain State U (WV)
New England School of Communications (ME)
Pennsylvania Coll of Technology (PA)
Robert Morris Coll (IL)
Thomas More Coll (KY)
Thompson Rivers U (BC, Canada)

Welding Technology
Boise State U (ID)
Excelsior Coll (NY)
Ferris State U (MI)
Georgia Southwestern State U (GA)
Idaho State U (ID)
Lamar U (TX)
Lewis-Clark State Coll (ID)
Mesa State Coll (CO)
Oakland City U (IN)
Pennsylvania Coll of Technology (PA)
The U of Montana–Missoula (MT)
Utah Valley State Coll (UT)

Wildlife and Wildlands Science And Management
State U of New York Coll of Agriculture and Technology at Cobleskill (NY)
Sterling Coll (VT)
U of Minnesota, Crookston (MN)
Winona State U (MN)

Wildlife Biology
Central Christian Coll of Kansas (KS)

Wind/Percussion Instruments
Five Towns Coll (NY)
New World School of the Arts (FL)

Women'S Studies
Indiana U–Purdue University Fort Wayne (IN)
Nazarene Bible Coll (CO)

Woodworking Related
Pennsylvania Coll of Technology (PA)

Word Processing
Baker Coll of Allen Park (MI)

Zoology/Animal Biology
Central Christian Coll of Kansas (KS)

Alphabetical Listing of Two-Year Colleges

In this index, the page locations of profiles are printed in regular type, **Special Messages** in *italics*, and **Close-Ups** in **bold type**. When there is more than one number in **bold type**, it indicates that the institution has more than one **Close-Up**; in most such cases, the first of the series is a general institutional description.

Thomson Peterson's
Book Satisfaction Survey

Give Us Your Feedback

Thank you for choosing Thomson Peterson's as your source for personalized solutions for your education and career achievement. Please take a few minutes to answer the following questions. Your answers will go a long way in helping us to produce the most user-friendly and comprehensive resources to meet your individual needs.

When completed, please tear out this page and mail it to us at:

> Publishing Department
> Thomson Peterson's
> 2000 Lenox Drive
> Lawrenceville, NJ 08648

You can also complete this survey online at **www.petersons.com/booksurvey.**

1. **What is the ISBN of the book you have purchased? (The ISBN can be found on the book's back cover in the lower right-hand corner.)** _____

2. **Where did you purchase this book?**
   - ❑ Retailer, such as Barnes & Noble
   - ❑ Online reseller, such as Amazon.com
   - ❑ Petersons.com or Thomson Learning Bookstore
   - ❑ Other (please specify) _____

3. **If you purchased this book on Petersons.com or through the Thomson Learning Bookstore, please rate the following aspects of your online purchasing experience on a scale of 4 to 1 (4 = Excellent and 1 = Poor).**

	4	3	2	1
Comprehensiveness of Peterson's Online Bookstore page	❑	❑	❑	❑
Overall online customer experience	❑	❑	❑	❑

4. **Which category best describes you?**
   - ❑ High school student
   - ❑ Parent of high school student
   - ❑ College student
   - ❑ Graduate/professional student
   - ❑ Returning adult student
   - ❑ Teacher
   - ❑ Counselor
   - ❑ Working professional/military
   - ❑ Other (please specify) _____

5. **Rate your overall satisfaction with this book.**

Extremely Satisfied	Satisfied	Not Satisfied
❑	❑	❑

6. Rate each of the following aspects of this book on a scale of 4 to 1 (4 = Excellent and 1 = Poor).

	4	3	2	1
Comprehensiveness of the information	❏	❏	❏	❏
Accuracy of the information	❏	❏	❏	❏
Usability	❏	❏	❏	❏
Cover design	❏	❏	❏	❏
Book layout	❏	❏	❏	❏
Special features *(e.g., CD, flashcards, charts, etc.)*	❏	❏	❏	❏
Value for the money	❏	❏	❏	❏

7. This book was recommended by:
- ❏ Guidance counselor
- ❏ Parent/guardian
- ❏ Family member/relative
- ❏ Friend
- ❏ Teacher
- ❏ Not recommended by anyone—I found the book on my own
- ❏ Other (please specify) _____

8. Would you recommend this book to others?

Yes	Not Sure	No
❏	❏	❏

9. Please provide any additional comments.

_____

_____

_____

_____

_____

Remember, you can tear out this page and mail it to us at:

Publishing Department
Thomson Peterson's
2000 Lenox Drive
Lawrenceville, NJ 08648

or you can complete the survey online at **www.petersons.com/booksurvey.**

Your feedback is important to us at Thomson Peterson's, and we thank you for your time!

If you would like us to keep in touch with you about new products and services, please include your e-mail here: _____